Australia

THE ROUGH GUIDE

WITHDRAW

There are more than one hundred and fifty Rough Guide titles
covering destinations from Amsterdam to Zimbabwe

Forthcoming titles include
Dominican Republic • Las Vegas • Sardinia • Switzerland

Rough Guide Reference Series
Classical Music • Drum 'n' Bass • European Football • House
The Internet • Jazz • Opera • Reggae • Rock Music • World Music

Rough Guide Phrasebooks
Czech • Dutch • European • French • German • Greek • Hindi & Urdu
Hungarian • Indonesian • Italian • Japanese • Mandarin Chinese
Mexican Spanish • Polish • Portuguese • Russian • Spanish
Thai • Turkish • Vietnamese

Rough Guides on the Internet
www.roughguides.com

ROUGH GUIDE CREDITS

Text editors: Kieran Falconer and Harriet Sharkey
Series editor: Mark Ellingham
Editorial: Martin Dunford, Jonathan Buckley, Jo Mead, Kate Berens, Amanda Tomlin, Ann-Marie Shaw, Paul Gray, Helena Smith, Judith Bamber, Orla Duane, Olivia Eccleshall, Ruth Blackmore, Sophie Martin, Geoff Howard, Claire Saunders, Gavin Thomas, Alexander Mark Rogers, Polly Thomas, Joe Staines, Lisa Nellis, Andrew Tomicić (UK); Andrew Rosenberg, Mary Beth Maioli (US)
Production: Susanne Hillen, Andy Hilliard, Link Hall, Helen Ostick, Julia Bovis, Michelle Draycott, Anna Wray, Katie Pringle

Cartography: Melissa Baker, Maxine Burke, Nichola Goodliffe, Ed Wright
Picture research: Louise Boulton
Online editors: Alan Spicer, Kate Hands (UK); Kelly Cross (US)
Finance: John Fisher, Katy Miesiaczek, Gary Singh, Ed Downey, Catherine Robertson
Marketing & Publicity: Richard Trillo, Simon Carloss, Niki Smith, David Wearn Jemima Broadbridge(UK); Jean-Marie Kelly, Myra Campolo (US)
Administration: Tania Hummel, Charlotte Marriott, Demelza Dallow

ACKNOWLEDGEMENTS

The authors: would like to give a huge thank-you to Kieran Falconer and Harriet Sharkey for tireless editing around the clock, Jo Mead for overseeing the project and the fabulous cartographer Nichola Goodliffe; thanks also to Demelza Dallow for endless checking and Camille Obering. Particular thanks go to the updaters, Alan Bradshaw (and Frans Zuijderwijh and his family who rescued him), Cameron Wilson (and Sara Wilson for supporting him), Silke Kerwick and Niah Thomson for updating Basics. Thanks also to the proofreader Russell Walton for his Oz insights.

Margo: A big thank you to Kendell Airlines and Tony Duboudin; David Beard at Access Rent a Car in Adelaide; and Judith Mayer at Greyhound Coaches; YHA NSW; Rosanna Arcuili for the Leichhardt home; Brad Miller and Kate Daly for the study and the sojourn in Melbourne, Sha Sha Kwa and Caleb Gardner in Hobart; Janine Daly and Michael Schofield for on the road adventures in Tasmania;

Paul Andrew of the ALSO Foundation and Pamela Gibbs of Newcastle Tourism; Justine Scott McCarthy for refuge in London; Bettina Daly, Hervé Bethuel and the girls in Paris; Matthew Buchanan, a girl's best friend; Beth Yahp; Michael and Brigitte Daly for a reintroduction to Pearl Beach; Mary Daly, Gabe Kessler and Ella Rose for the Hunter Valley road-trip, and as always Margaret and Tony Daly.

Anne. Thank you to Chris White of Tourism Victoria and the helpful staff at various tourist information centres in Victoria. A very special thanks to everybody who gave me love, support and encouragement in stressful times, in particular Harry and, as always, Katharina.

David: For Narrell. In gratitude for 24-hour technical assistance, advice on housebreaking, and introducing me to the delights of eating native species, thanks to Barry and Linda, and Peter and Brigitte.

Chris: The people at Wittenoom.

PUBLISHING INFORMATION

This fourth edition published August 1999 by Rough Guides Ltd, 62–70 Shorts Gardens, London WC2H 9AB.
Distributed by the Penguin Group:
Penguin Books Ltd, 27 Wrights Lane, London W8 5TZ
Penguin Books USA Inc., 375 Hudson Street, New York 10014, USA
Penguin Books Australia Ltd, 487 Maroondah Highway, PO Box 257, Ringwood, Victoria 3134, Australia
Penguin Books Canada Ltd, 10 Alcorn Avenue, Toronto, Ontario, Canada M4V 1E4
Penguin Books (NZ) Ltd, 182–190 Wairau Road, Auckland 10, New Zealand
Typeset in Linotron Univers and Century Old Style to an original design by Andrew Oliver.
Printed in England by Clays Ltd, St Ives PLC
Illustrations in Part One and Part Three by Edward Briant.

Illustrations on p.1 & p.989 by Henry Iles
© Margo Daly, Anne Dehne, David Leffman and Chris Scott 1999
No part of this book may be reproduced in any form without permission from the publisher except for the quotation of brief passages in reviews.
1088pp – Includes index
A catalogue record for this book is available from the British Library
ISBN 1-85828-461-9

The publishers and authors have done their best to ensure the accuracy and currency of all the information in *The Rough Guide to Australia*, however, they can accept no responsibility for any loss, injury, or inconvenience sustained by any traveller as a result of information or advice contained in the guide.

Australia

THE ROUGH GUIDE

written and researched by

Margo Daly, Anne Dehne,
David Leffman and Chris Scott

with additional contributions by
Alan Bradshaw, Silke Kerwick
and Cameron Wilson

THE ROUGH GUIDES

THE ROUGH GUIDES

TRAVEL GUIDES • PHRASEBOOKS • MUSIC AND REFERENCE GUIDES

 We set out to do something different when the first Rough Guide was published in 1982. Mark Ellingham, just out of university, was travelling in Greece. He brought along the popular guides of the day, but found they were all lacking in some way. They were either strong on ruins and museums but went on for pages without mentioning a beach or taverna. Or they were so conscious of the need to save money that they lost sight of Greece's cultural and historical significance. Also, none of the books told him anything about Greece's contemporary life – its politics, its culture, its people, and how they lived.

So with no job in prospect, Mark decided to write his own guidebook, one which aimed to provide practical information that was second to none, detailing the best beaches and the hottest clubs and restaurants, while also giving hard-hitting accounts of every sight, both famous and obscure, and providing up-to-the-minute information on contemporary culture. It was a guide that encouraged independent travellers to find the best of Greece, and was a great success, getting shortlisted for the Thomas Cook travel guide award,

and encouraging Mark, along with three friends, to expand the series.

The Rough Guide list grew rapidly and the letters flooded in, indicating a much broader readership than had been anticipated, but one which uniformly appreciated the Rough Guide mix of practical detail and humour, irreverence and enthusiasm. Things haven't changed. The same four friends who began the series are still the caretakers of the Rough Guide mission today: to provide the most reliable, up-to-date and entertaining information to independent-minded travellers of all ages, on all budgets.

We now publish more than 100 titles and have offices in London and New York. The travel guides are written and researched by a dedicated team of more than 100 authors, based in Britain, Europe, the USA and Australia. We have also created a unique series of phrasebooks to accompany the travel series, along with an acclaimed series of music guides, and a best-selling pocket guide to the Internet and World Wide Web. We also publish comprehensive travel information on our Web site:

www.roughguides.com

THE AUTHORS

Margo Daly was born in Sydney where she studied Communications at the University of Technology; she has an MA in Writing from Sheffield Hallam University. She is the co-author of *The Rough Guide to Australia* and has contributed to Rough Guides to France, Paris, Thailand, Europe and More Women Travel. She is the co-editor, with Jill Dawson, of the Sceptre fiction anthology *Wild Ways: New Stories of Women on the Road*.

Anne Dehne arrived in Australia in 1988. Originally from Berlin, she lived in Singapore for a few years before deciding to move to Melbourne. Apart from researching and writing part of this book, she has written titles for other travel publishers, mainly on Australia.

David Leffman is an established Rough Guide author and inveterate traveller. When not on the road, he spends much of his time scuba diving near his home in Queensland.

Chris Scott has contributed to various Rough Guides, including England, Poland, France and West Africa. He has also written about his visits to northwest Africa in *Desert Travels* (Travellers' Bookshop), *The Adventure Motorcycling Handbook* and *Sahara Overland* (Trailblazer) as well as their related Web sites.

READERS' LETTERS

Our thanks to everyone who has contributed letters, comments, accounts and suggestions over the years, and especially to this 1999 edition. In particular:
Jim Cowie, R.A.R Cockitt, Jeremy Morris, Jill McCarthy, Andre Bellisle, David and Cynthia Whetfield, Matthew Brooks, Peter J. Smith, Gillian Long, David Dickenson, Melanie Oley, Pauline Kaye, Peter Field, Heide Baumüller, Andrea Intelligenza, Lina Morgera, Pam Snaddon, Therase Hill, Clare Everard, Sunil Gogna, Kerry Parkin, Neal Brown, Treacle, Richard Williams, Doris Flood, Tim Searle, Debbie Wilson, Tania King, Jolene Billwiller, Pamela Farries, Anne Fitcher, Tracy Dickson, Lisa Simpson, T. Godfrey, Pat Rolburo, Noriko Abe, Philip Beeson, Siye Wu, Silvano Negrini, Joe Griffen, Karen Smith, Giles Hemmings, Eric, I J Pedder, Phil Davies, Julie Cameron, Tomasz Cienkus, Maria Tardini, Simon Lesser, Jaroslaw Stachiw, Jenny Rankine, Alan Weiley, Michael D Moore, Eva Okholm, Tony Howe, Jonathan Yates, Philip Harle, Tony Carne, Paula Bayford, Zane Katsikis, R J Banks, Philip Lisamer, Helen Wilson, Frank Willemse, Moira McBride, Joe Pateman, Alison Horsfeld, Angie Gaunt, William Huntingdon, L J Prins, Suzanne Lee, Denise Hughes, Andrew Pichett, Roz Jeaseily, Julia Aline.

CONTENTS

PART THREE CONTEXTS 989

LIST OF MAPS

MAP SYMBOLS

═══	Main road		⌒	Cave
═══	Minor road		⌂	Conservation hut
▬▬▬	Pedestrianised street (town maps)		♦	Museum
┄┄┄	Tunnel		⸙	Lighthouse
╌╌╌	Path		⚑	Golf course
━━━	Track		★	Bus stop
▬●▬	Railway		ⓘ	Tourist information
── ──	Ferry route		⊠	Post office
⋯⋯⋯	River		◉	Hotel
▬▬ ▪	Provincial boundary		▣	Restaurant
━ ━ ━	Chapter division boundary		▬	Building
▲	Mountain peak		⊞	Church/cathedral
⌃⌃	Mountain range		▨	Built up area
ᔕᔕ	Gorge		▨	Aboriginal land
⬇	Viewpoint		░	Beach
𝍠	Waterfall		⊡	Cemetery
ⱳⱳ	Reef		▭	Marsh land
♦	Point of interest		▨	National Park
✈	Airport		░	Park

INTRODUCTION

A ustralia is massive, and very sparsely peopled: in size it rivals the USA, yet its population is just over eighteen million – little more than that of the Netherlands. This is an ancient land, and often looks it: in places, it's the most eroded, denuded and driest of continents, with much of central and western Australia – the bulk of the country – overwhelmingly arid and flat. In contrast, its cities – most of which were founded as recently as the mid-nineteenth century – express a youthful energy. The most memorable scenery is in the Outback, the vast desert in the centre of the country west of the Great Dividing Range. Here, vivid blue skies, cinnamon-red earth, deserted gorges and other striking geological features as well as bizarre wildlife comprise a unique ecology – one that has played host to the oldest surviving human culture for at least fifty thousand years.

The harshness of the interior has forced modern Australia to become a coastal country. Most of the population lives within 20km of the ocean, occupying a suburban, southeastern arc extending from southern Queensland to Adelaide. These urban Australians celebrate the typical New World values of material self-improvement through hard work and hard play, with an easy-going vitality that visitors, especially Europeans, often find refreshingly hedonistic. A sunny climate also contributes to this exuberance, with an outdoor life in which a thriving beach culture and the congenial backyard "barbie" are central.

While visitors might eventually find this *Home and Away* lifestyle rather prosaic, there are opportunities – particularly in the Northern Territory – to gain some experience of Australia's indigenous peoples and their culture, through visiting ancient art sites, taking tours and, less easily, making personal contact. Many Aboriginal people – especially in central Australia – have managed to maintain their traditional way of life (albeit with some modern accoutrements), speaking their own languages and living according to their law (the tjukurpa). Conversely, most Aboriginal people you'll come across in country towns and cities are victims of what is scathingly referred to as "welfare colonialism" – a disempowering system in which, supported by dole cheques and other subsidies, they often fall prey to a destructive cycle of poverty, ill health and alcoholism. There's still a long way to go before black and white people in Australia can exist on genuinely equal terms.

For visitors, deciding where to go can mean juggling with distance, money and time. You could spend months driving around the Outback, exploring the national parks, or just hanging out at beaches; or you could take an all-in two-week "Reef, Rock and Harbour" package, encompassing Australia's outstanding trinity of "must sees".

Both options provide thoroughly Australian experiences, but neither will leave you with a feeling of having more than scraped the surface of this vast country. The two big natural attractions are the two-thousand-kilometre-long Great Barrier Reef in far north Queensland, with its complex of islands and underwater splendour, and the brooding monolith of Uluru (Ayers Rock), in the Northern Territory's Red Centre. You should certainly try to see them, but exploration of other parts of the country will bring you into contact with more subtle but equally rewarding sights and opportunities.

The cities are surprisingly cosmopolitan: waves of postwar immigrants from southern Europe and, more recently, Southeast Asia have done much to erode Australia's Anglocentrism. Each Australian state has a capital stamped with its own personality, and nowhere is this more apparent than in New South Wales where glamorous Sydney has the iconic landmarks of the Opera House and Harbour Bridge. Elsewhere, the sophisticated café society of Melbourne (Victoria) contrasts with the vitality of Brisbane (Queensland). Adelaide, in South Australia, has a human-scale and old-fash-

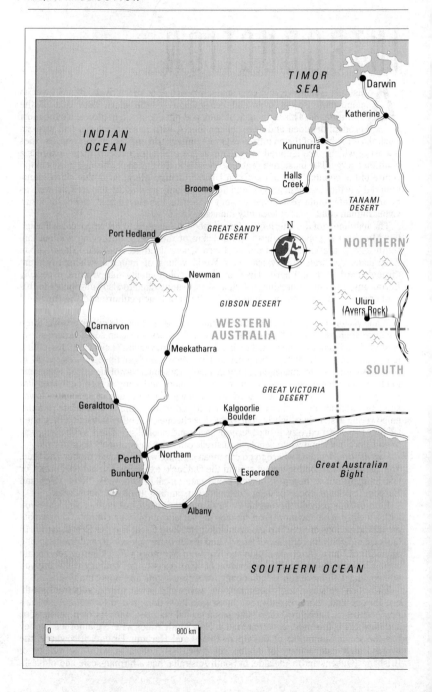

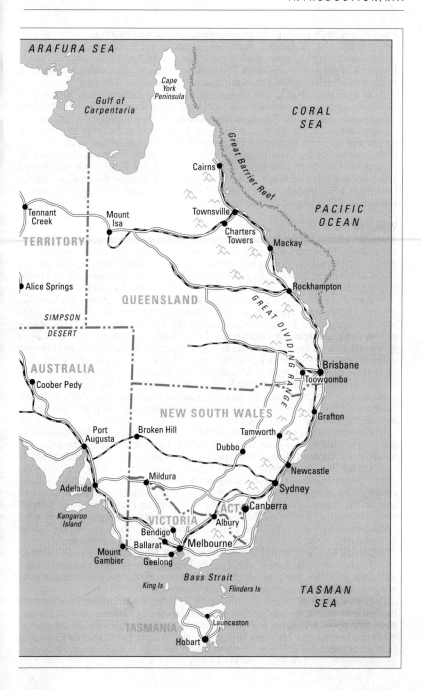

ioned charm, while Perth, in Western Australia, camouflages its isolation with a leisure-oriented urbanity. In Hobart, capital of Tasmania, you'll encounter fine heritage streetscapes and get a distinct maritime feel. The purpose-built administrative centre of Canberra, in the Australian Capital Territory, often fails to grip visitors, but Darwin's long overdue revival enlivens an exploration of the distinctive "Territory".

Away from the suburbs, with their satellite shopping malls and quarter-acre residential blocks, is the transitional "bush", and beyond that the wilderness of the Outback – the quintessential Australian experience. Protected from the drier interior, the east coast has the pick of the country's greenery and scenery, from the north's tropical rainforests and the Great Barrier Reef to the surf-lined beaches further south. The east coast is backed by the Great Dividing Range, which steadily decreases in elevation as it extends from Mount Kosciuszko (2228m) in New South Wales north into tropical Queensland. If you have time to spare, a trip to often-overlooked Tasmania, across the Bass Strait, is worthwhile: you'll be rewarded with vast tracts of wilderness as well as landscapes almost English in their bucolic qualities.

When to go

Australia's climate has become less predictable in recent times, although like the rest of the planet the country has rarely had stable weather patterns over the last few thousand years. Recently observed phenomena, such as an extended drought in the eastern Outback, the cyclic El Niño effect, and even the hole in the ozone layer – which is disturbingly close to the country – are probably part of a long-term pattern.

Visitors from the northern hemisphere should remember that, as early colonials observed, in Australia "Nature is horribly reversed", when it's winter or summer in the northern hemisphere, the opposite season prevails Down Under. Although this is easy to remember, the principle becomes harder to apply to the transitional seasons of spring and autumn. To confuse things further, the four seasons only really exist outside of the tropics in the southern half of the country. Here, you'll find reliably warm summers at the coast with regular, but thankfully brief, heatwaves in excess of 40°C. Head inland, and the temperatures rise further. Winters, on the other hand, can be miserable, particularly in Victoria, where the short days add to the gloom. Tasmania's highlands make for unpredictable weather all year round, although summer is the best time to explore the island's outdoor attractions.

In the coastal tropics, weather basically falls into two seasons. The best time to visit is during the hot and cloudless Dry (from April to November), with moderate coastal humidity maintaining a pleasant temperature day and night and cooler nights inland. In contrast, the Wet – particularly the "Build Up" in November or December before the rains – is very uncomfortable and is marked by stifling, near-total humidity. As storm clouds gather, rising temperatures, humidity and tension can provoke irrational behaviour in the psychologically unacclimatized – something known as "going troppo". Nevertheless, the mid-Wet's daily downpours and enervating mugginess can be quite intoxicating, compelling a hyper-relaxed inactivity for which these regions are known; furthermore, the countryside – if you can reach it – looks its best at this time.

Australia's interior is an arid semi-desert with very little rain, high summer temperatures and occasionally freezing winter nights. Unless you're properly equipped to cope with these extremes, you'd be better off coming here during the transitional seasons between April and June, and or October and November.

In general, the best time to visit the south is during the Australian summer, from December to March, though long summer holidays from Christmas through January mean that prices are higher and beaches more crowded at this time. In the tropical north the best months are from May to October, while in the Centre they are from October to November and from March to May. If you want to tour extensively, keep to the southern coasts in summer and head north for the winter.

AVERAGE TEMPERATURE (°C)

	Jan	Feb	Mar	Apr	May	June	July	Aug	Sept	Oct	Nov	Dec
Sydney	25	25	24	23	20	17	16	17	19	22	23	24
Canberra	27	25	23	20	15	13	12	13	15	18	22	25
Brisbane	27	27	26	25	23	21	23	22	24	25	26	27
Cairns	31	31	30	29	28	25	25	27	27	28	30	31
Darwin	31	30	31	32	31	30	30	31	32	32	33	32
Alice	36	35	32	27	22	21	19	21	25	30	32	35
Perth	30	30	28	25	22	20	19	19	20	22	25	28
Adelaide	28	27	25	22	18	16	14	15	17	21	22	25
Melbourne	26	26	24	21	16	15	14	15	17	19	21	20
Hobart	21	21	20	17	14	12	11	12	15	18	19	20

AVERAGE RAINFALL (MM)

	Jan	Feb	Mar	Apr	May	June	July	Aug	Sept	Oct	Nov	Dec
Sydney	100	105	125	130	125	130	110	75	60	75	70	75
Canberra	55	50	50	45	50	30	30	50	50	70	65	65
Brisbane	160	160	150	80	70	60	55	50	50	75	100	140
Cairns	400	440	450	180	100	50	30	25	35	35	90	160
Darwin	400	430	435	75	50	10	5	10	15	70	110	310
Alice	35	40	25	20	25	25	20	20	10	25	30	35
Perth	10	15	25	50	125	185	175	145	80	75	25	20
Adelaide	20	20	25	45	65	70	65	60	55	40	25	20
Melbourne	45	50	55	60	55	50	50	50	55	65	55	55
Hobart	50	45	50	55	50	45	50	50	55	55	50	50

PART ONE

THE

BASICS

GETTING THERE FROM BRITAIN AND IRELAND

The market for flights between Britain and Australia is one of the most competitive in the world, and in real terms prices have never been lower. Modern aircraft can now reach the north Australian coast from London in just fifteen hours' flying time, though in practice the journey to Sydney or the other eastern cities takes a minimum of 21 hours by the time you've stopped and refuelled. If you take a bit longer – breaking the journey in Southeast Asia or North America – it need not be the tedious, seat-bound slog you may have imagined. There are no direct flights from Ireland.

A word of warning: don't actually buy your ticket until you're sure that you've been granted a visa (see p.16 for more details).

Before booking, you need to decide where you want to fly to in Australia, where you would like to stop en route (or on the way back) and whether you want to use flights to get around once you're there. Sydney and Melbourne are served by the greatest number of airlines, and carriers such as Qantas offer the same price to fly to any east coast city between Cairns and Adelaide; flights to Darwin and Perth are around £100 cheaper, but you need to consider the expense of the overland journey from here. An **open-jaw ticket** (flying into one city and out from another) usually costs no more than an ordinary return.

All direct **scheduled flights** to Australia depart from London's two main airports, Gatwick

and Heathrow, although Singapore Airlines has five flights a week from Manchester to Singapore which connect with onward flights to Sydney.

The advent of **charter flights** to Australia hasn't made a huge difference to the flight scene, except perhaps to make prices even more keen. The two charter companies, Britannia and Airtours, fly from London Gatwick (Airtours also flies from Manchester), but their flights are bound with restrictions which can make them a less attractive option. In most cases you must stay for a minimum of two weeks but no longer than eight weeks, and no stopovers are allowed; however, new long-stay fares allow you to arrive in February or March and depart in November.

FARES

You'll see eye-catching low fares in the masses of small ads in newspapers (the quality Sunday papers are the best place to start your search), or, in London, in the listings magazine *Time Out* or the free travellers' magazine *TNT*, but in practice these are often unavailable by the time you call. **Booking ahead** as far as possible is the best way to secure the most reasonable prices: it is almost invariably cheaper to buy tickets through **agents**, but we've also listed a selection of airlines along with the variety of routes available (see box on pp.4–5). We've also included **airline Web sites** where available – it's worth checking out these sites for last-minute cheap deals, though prices are often quoted in the airways national currency. For example, Lauda Air's site has a "special offers" area while KLM has an "On-line specials" section. South African Airways has a "seat auctions" button on its site; typically, there are no set times for **auctions** – the latest way to sell seats on the Internet – you can register as a bidder at any time and you will be forwarded your log-in ID and password via email and then be notified when an auction is taking place.

In the end, you'll find the available flights at much the same price everywhere, the main difference being between the plusher airlines such as Qantas, British Airways (BA) and Singapore Airlines – which offer more leg room, better-quality inflight entertainment, service and meals and more drinks – and Garuda Indonesia Airlines or

AIRLINES

Aerolineas Argentinas, 54 Conduit St, London W1R 9FD (☎0171/494 1001). London Heathrow to Madrid, changing planes to Buenos Aires, changing again to Sydney via Auckland.

Air New Zealand, Travel Centre, ground floor, New Zealand House, 80 Haymarket, London SW1Y 4TE (☎0181/741 2299; www.airnz.co.nz). Daily scheduled flights from London Heathrow to all major Australian airports via Los Angeles. Their popular Pacific routing enables a choice of stopovers in Honolulu, Fiji, Western Samoa, the Cook Islands, Tahiti, Tonga and New Zealand. Discounts on Ansett G'day Passes.

Airtours, Wavell House, Holcombe Rd, Hemshore, Rossendale, Lancashire (☎01706/260 0000). Charter flights from London Gatwick or Manchester to Sydney, November–April only; package holidays, too – see box on p.8.

Alitalia, 4 Portman Square, London W1H 9PS (☎0171/602 7111; www.alitalia.it). Three flights weekly from Heathrow changing planes in Milan, then onto Bangkok and Sydney.

All Nippon Airways (ANA), ANA House, 6–8 Old Bond St, London W1X 3TA (☎0171/355 1155; www.ana.co.jp). From London Heathrow to Osaka, with connecting flights four times weekly to Sydney and Brisbane (Tues & Fri–Sun).

Britannia Airways, London Luton Airport, Luton, Bedfordshire LU2 9ND (via Austravel ☎0171/734 775). Charter flights from London

Gatwick to Adelaide, Brisbane, Melbourne and Perth; November–April only. Austravel deals with all charter bookings (see box on pp.6–7).

British Airways, 156 Regent St, London W1R 5TA; 101–102 Cheapside, London EC2V 6DT; Victoria Place, Victoria Station, London SW1W 9SJ (☎0171/828 4895); 146 New St, Birmingham B2 4HN; 41–43 Deansgate, Manchester M3 2AY; 6 New Broadmead, Union St, Bristol BS1 2DL; 66 Gordon St, Glasgow G1 3RS; 30–32 Frederick St, Edinburgh EH2 2JR; 209 Union St, Aberdeen AB1 2BA (all enquiries ☎0345/222111; www.british-airways.com). Daily scheduled flights from London Heathrow to all major Australian airports via Bangkok, Kuala Lumpur, Singapore or Hong Kong. Discounts on Qantas Boomerang Passes.

Emirates Airlines, 95 Cromwell Rd, London SW7 4DL (☎0171/808 0808; www.emirates.com). Daily from Gatwick and Manchester with connecting flights from Dubai to Melbourne thrice weekly.

Garuda Indonesia, 35 Duke St, London W1M JDF (☎0171/486 3011); International House, 2nd floor, 82 Deansgate, Manchester M3 2ER (☎0161/834 3747; www.garuda.co.id).Three flights weekly from London Gatwick via Bali and Bangkok flying into Sydney, Melbourne, Brisbane, Adelaide, Perth, Darwin and Cairns. The airline no longer flies via the Middle East.

Lauda Air, 1 2 Colonnade Walk, 123 Buckingham Palace Rd, London SW1W 9SH

Royal Brunei (to Brisbane, Darwin and Perth only), which are generally the least expensive.

Tourists and those on one-year working visas (see p.16 for the lowdown on visas) are generally required by Australian immigration to arrive with a ticket out of the country, so one-way tickets are really only viable for Australian and New Zealand residents. If you've purchased a return ticket and find you want to stay longer or head off on a totally different route, it's sometimes possible to cash in the return half of your ticket (though you'll make a loss on the deal) at the travel agent where you bought it: either post it back to them or arrange for someone in the UK to do it on your behalf.

With any international ticket, you can buy a Qantas Boomerang Pass or an Ansett G'Day Pass,

both of which entitle you to cheap internal flights, but these must be purchased before you leave the UK (see p.30). You will get further discounts on these if you buy your international ticket from Qantas or British Airways for a Boomerang Pass, and Air New Zealand or Singapore Airlines for a G'day Pass.

The cheapest **scheduled fare** you're likely to find is around £580 return, available during the **low-season** months of April to June though special offers can go as low as £495; if you insist on flying with Qantas, BA or Singapore Airlines, expect to pay from around £720 for a flight in this off-peak period with special offers sometimes taking prices down to £620. The most expensive time to fly is in the two weeks before **Christmas**, when you'd be lucky to find anything for less than

(☎0171/630 5924; *www.laudaair.com*). Four flights weekly from Heathrow via Vienna and Kuala Lumpur to Sydney and two flights weekly from Gatwick with the same routing.

Japan Airlines, 5 Hanover Court, Hanover Square, London W1R 0DR (☎0345/747700 or 0171/408 1000; *www.jal.co.jp*). From London Heathrow, daily non-stop flights to Tokyo and five times weekly to Osaka, with connecting flights to Sydney from both airports. Connecting flights to Brisbane and Cairns daily from Tokyo, three times weekly from Osaka.

KLM Royal Dutch Airlines (reservations ☎0990/750900; *www.klm.nl*). Daily flights to Amsterdam from just about every British airport except Gatwick and Luton but including London Heathrow, London City, Edinburgh, Manchester, Glasgow and Bristol with three connecting flights to Sydney per week (Mon, Tues & Fri). Ticket office at Terminal 4, Heathrow and at London City airport.

Malaysian Airlines, 61 Piccadilly, London W1V 9HL(☎0171/3412020;*www.malaysiaairlines.co.my*). Daily flights from London Heathrow to Kuala Lumpur connecting daily to Sydney and Perth, four times weekly to Melbourne, five times weekly to Brisbane and twice weekly to Darwin and Cairns.

Olympic Airways, 11 Conduit St, W1R 0LP (☎0171/409 3400). Twice daily flights from London Heathrow to Athens with twice weekly connecting flights to Sydney and Melbourne.

Qantas, 182 Strand, London WC2R 1ET, 395 King St, London W6 9NJ (☎0345/747767; *www.qantas.com.au*). Twice-daily flights from London Heathrow to all the mainland Australian state capitals and Cairns, via Singapore, Kuala Lumpur or Bangkok. Discounted Boomerang Passes for internal flights.

Royal Brunei Airlines, 49 Cromwell Rd, London SW7 2ED (☎0171/584 6660, fax 581 9279). London Heathrow to Perth, Darwin or Brisbane – all via Brunei.

Singapore Airlines, 143–147 Regent St, London W1R 7LB (☎0181/747 0007); 37 King St, Manchester M2 7AT (☎0161/830 8888; *www.singaporeair.com*). Twice-daily flights from London Heathrow, and five times weekly from Manchester to Singapore, with connections to Adelaide, Brisbane, Darwin, Melbourne, Perth and Sydney. Discounts on Ansett G'day Passes.

South African Airways, St George's House, 61 Conduit St, London W1R ONE (☎0171/312 5000; *www.saa.co.za*). Daily flights to Johannesburg, with connecting flights three times weekly to Perth and Sydney.

Thai Airways, 41 Albemarle St, London W1X 4LE (☎0171/499 9113; *www.thaiair.com*). Daily flights to Bangkok from London Heathrow, with connections to Sydney, Melbourne, Brisbane and Perth.

United Airlines, 7–8 Conduit St, London W1R 9TG (☎0845/844 4777; *www.ual.com*). Daily flights from London Heathrow to Los Angeles or San Francisco with a six hour wait for connections to Sydney and Melbourne.

£1000 return: to stand a chance of getting one of the cheaper tickets, aim to book at least six months in advance. Prices also go up from mid-June or the beginning of July to the middle of August coinciding with the peak European holiday times. In between times (the **shoulder seasons** of mid-Aug to Nov and mid-Jan to March) you should expect to pay £650–750 (around £870 with one of the prestige airlines). The lowest **charter fares** start at £499 return, rising through £609–779, up to £909 in the peak Christmas period. Lauda Air has good-value deals – check their Web site for "Special Offers" usually from Vienna – as do Alitalia and Malaysian Airlines. The prestige airlines, in particular Qantas, also often have great special deals which include discounted or free flights; Qantas and British Airways often offer two extra stopovers if you book before a certain date.

With Qantas you can fly from **regional airports** at Aberdeen, Belfast, Edinburgh, Glasgow, Manchester or Newcastle to connect with your international flight at Heathrow for a supplement of £25 each way. However, if you fly from these airports via Frankfurt, Rome or Paris and thence to Australia via Singapore, Bangkok or Kuala Lumpur, discounts are available.

United Kingdom departure tax of £20 and an Australian departure tax of £13 is normally included in the ticket price.

STOPOVERS AND RTW TICKETS

An excellent alternative to a long direct flight is a **multi-stopover ticket**, which can cost the same

DISCOUNT TRAVEL AGENTS

Austravel, 50–51 Conduit St, London W1R 9FB (☎0171/734 7755); 152 Brompton Rd, London SW3 1HX (☎0171/838 1011); 17 Blomfield St, London E2M 7AJ (☎0171/588 1516); 45 Colston St, Bristol BS1 5AX (☎0117/927 7425); 3 Barton Arcade, Deansgate, Manchester M3 2BB (☎0161/832 2445); 16–18 County Arcade, Victoria Quarter, Leeds LS1 6BN (☎0113/244 8880); 107 Old Christchurch Rd, Bournemouth BH1 1EP (☎01202/311488). Specialists for flights and tours to Australia and appointed agents for Britannia Airways charter flights. Austravel also lays on audiovisual presentations all over the UK to help you make up your mind, aimed at independent travellers heading round the world via Australia. Issues ETA's and traditional visas for an administration fee of £16. *www.austravel.net*

Bridge the World, 47 Chalk Farm Rd, London NW1 8AN (☎0171/734 7447). Specialists in RTW tickets, many with Australian components, with good deals aimed at the backpacker market.

Campus Travel, 52 Grosvenor Gardens, London SW1W 0AG (☎0171/730 8111); 541 Bristol Rd, Selly Oak, Birmingham B29 6AU (☎0121/414 1848); 61 Ditchling Rd, Brighton BN1 4SD (☎01273/570226); 37–39 Queen's Rd, Clifton, Bristol BS8 1QE (☎0117/929 2494); 5 Emmanuel St, Cambridge CB1 1NE (☎01223/324283); 53 Forest Rd, Edinburgh EH1 2QP (☎0131/225 6111); 122 George St, Glasgow G1 1RS (☎0141/553 1818); 166 Deansgate, Manchester M3 3FE (☎0161/833 2046); 105–106 St Aldates, Oxford OX1 1DD (☎01865/242067). Student/youth travel specialists, with further branches in YHA shops and on university campuses all over Britain. *www.campustravel.co.uk*

Flightbookers, 177–178 Tottenham Court Rd, London W1P 0LX (☎0171/757 2468; open daily); Gatwick Airport, South Terminal, RH6 0LP (☎01293/568300; daily 7am–10pm). Offers low fares on an extensive range of scheduled flights. There's also the *Travel Café* in Oxford, at 1–5 Broad St, Oxford (☎01865/727737) which can do online bookings. *www.flightbookers.net*

The London Flight Centre, 131 Earls Court Rd, London SW5 9RH (☎0171/244 6411); 47 Notting Hill Gate, London W11 3JS (☎0171/727 4290); Shop 33, The Broadway Centre at Hammersmith Underground station, London W6 9YF (☎0181/748 6777). Long-established agent dealing in discount flights; vaccinations and Australian visas arranged at the Earls Court office.

North South Travel, Moulsham Mill Centre, Parkway, Chelmsford, Essex CM2 7PX (☎01245/492882, fax 356612). Friendly, competitive travel agency, offering discounted fares

or just a little more than the price of an ordinary return; check out the routing of the airlines detailed in the box on p.8 for some ideas. Unusual routes are inevitably more expensive, but it's possible to fly **via South America** with Aerolineas Argentinas, which offers stops in Buenos Aires and Auckland – at least £925 return – or **via Africa** with South African Airways, which offers return fares via Johannesburg to Perth and Sydney from close to £900, with the added bonus of discounted internal flights to Harare (Botswana), Victoria Falls, Nairobi and many other African destinations. You can also often get good deals via **Japan** on All Nippon Airlines and Japan Airlines.

More expensive, but still good value, **round-the-world** (RTW) tickets incorporating Australia provide a chance to see the world on your way to and from down under. RTW flights come prepackaged in a tantalizing variety of permutations, with stopovers chiefly in Asia, the Pacific and North America, but you can pretty much devise your fantasy itinerary and get it priced. A good agent should be able to piece together sector fares from various airlines: prices range from around £750 for a simple London–Bangkok–Sydney–LA–London deal to well over £1000. It's also possible to incorporate substantial overland segments for variety. A sample itinerary Manchester–Bombay–overland to Kathmandu–Singapore–Ho Chi Minh City–Perth–Ayers Rock–Sydney–Christchurch–Wellington–Auckland–Fiji–Honolulu–LA–London costs from £1000.

PACKAGES AND ORGANIZED TOURS

There are relatively few traditional **package holidays** available – nobody's going to fly all the way to Australia just to spend a couple of weeks on the beach – but if your time is short and you're reasonably sure of what you want to do, it may not be a bad idea to pre-book some of your accommodation, worldwide – profits are used to support projects in the developing world, especially the promotion of sustainable tourism.

Quest Worldwide, 10 Richmond Rd, Kingston, Surrey KT2 5HL (☎0181/547 3322). Specialists in RTW and Australian discount fares.

STA Travel, London offices: 86 Old Brompton Rd, SW7 3LH; 117 Euston Rd, NW1 2SX; 38 Store St, WC1E 7BZ (all ☎0171/361 6262). Rest of Britain: 38 North St, Brighton (☎01273/728282); 25 Queen's Rd, Bristol BS8 1QE (☎0117/929 4399); 38 Sidney St, Cambridge CB2 3HX (☎01223/366966); 88 Vicar Lane, Leeds LS1 7JH (☎0113/244 9212); 75 Deansgate, Manchester M3 2BW (☎0161/834 0668); 9 St Mary's Place, Newcastle-upon-Tyne NE1 7PG (☎0191/233 2111); 36 George St, Oxford OX1 2OJ (☎01865/792800); 184 Byres Rd, Glasgow G1 1JH (☎0141/338 6000), and branches on university campuses in London, Aberdeen, Birmingham, Brighton, Bristol, Cambridge, Canterbury, Cardiff, Coventry, Durham, Glasgow, Leicestershire, Leeds, Loughborough, Nottingham, Manchester, Oxford, Sheffield and Warwick. Worldwide specialists in low-cost flights and tours for students and under-26s, though other customers welcome. Also has offices in Australia. *www.statravel.co.uk*

Trailfinders, 42–50 Earls Court Rd, London W8 6FT (☎0171/938 3366); 194 Kensington High St, London W8 7RG (☎0171/938 3939); 22–24 The Priory, Queensway, Birmingham B4 6BS (☎0121/236 1234); 48 Corn St, Bristol BS1 1HU (☎0117/929 9000); 58 Deansgate, Manchester M3 2FF (☎0161/839 6969); 7–9 Ridley Place, Newcastle-upon-Tyne NE1 8JQ (☎0191/261 2345); 254–284 Sauchiehall St, Glasgow G2 3EH (☎0141/353 2224). Excellent for multistop and RTW tickets, including some unusual routings via South Africa, the Pacific and the US. Well-informed and efficient – visa service available at the Kensington High St branch. Convenient opening hours – all branches open daily. Also has branches in Brisbane, Cairns and Sydney.

Travel Bag, 52 Regent St, London W1R 6DX (☎0171/287 5556); 373–375 Strand, London WC2R 0JF (☎0171/497 0515),12 High St, Alton, Hants GU34 1BN (☎0171/287 5556). Well established long-haul travel agent with a good reputation for Australian coverage. Direct and RTW flights on all the best airlines like Qantas, British Airways and Singapore plus packages (see p.8).

The Travel Bug, 125A Gloucester Rd, London SW7 4SF (☎0171/835 2000); 597 Cheetham Hill Rd, Manchester M8 5EJ (☎0161/721 4000). Large range of discounted tickets. *www.travel-bug.co.uk*

Travelmood, 246 Edgware Rd, London W2 1DS (☎0171/258 0280); 61 Reform St, Dundee DD1 (☎01382/322713). Direct and RTW flights.

tours and vehicle rental. Many companies offer minimal packages, consisting of a flight with some accommodation and a couple of tours. Full "see-it-all" packages can work out quite expensive and the pace can be rather tiring, but they aren't bad value, considering what you'd be spending anyway. The ultimate package must be the **sea trip** to Australia from Southampton in England or Los Angeles in the US on either P&O or Cunard Line (see box on p.8).

Many of the Australian specialists also offer such things as **bus and train passes** (see pp.31-32), discounted hotel vouchers and the like – all of which are worth considering.

FLIGHTS FROM IRELAND

Flying from Ireland, prices are rather higher, but since you can't fly direct anyway, the choice of routes and airlines is if anything even wider.

Although most of the cheaper routings involve a stopover in London and transfer to one of the airlines listed on pp.4–5, there are often good deals on Olympic (☎01/608 0090) from Dublin via Greece. Singapore Airlines (☎01/671 0722) has flights ticketed through from Dublin, Shannon or Cork via London to Singapore and Sydney, while Malaysian Airlines (☎01/676 1561) also goes from all three Irish airports via Kuala Lumpur. The three airports are also served by the affiliated British Airways and Qantas (both ☎01/874 7747); all their flights to Australia have a Dublin–London add-on included in the price. Malaysian Airlines fares start from around IR£780 for an open one-year return in low season, up to IR£1480 in the Christmas period, while a Singapore Airlines' ticket would cost around IR£920 in the shoulder season. There are good deals ticketed through from Belfast with Malaysian Airlines with a low season ticket from IR£652 and a high season ticket from

PACKAGE TOURS AND SPECIALIST OPERATORS

Some discount flight agents also arrange tours and accommodation –
check out Austravel and Trailfinders, among others – see box on pp.6-7.

Airtours (☎01706/830130). Long-haul package holiday operator with its own airline offers charter-flights packages from London Gatwick or Manchester. A 14-night package over the Xmas period, staying at the *Gazebo Hotel* in Sydney is £1149.

Contiki (☎0181/225 4200; *www.contiki.com*). Big group, countrywide bus tours for 18- to 35-year-olds "thriving on good times and loads of fun". All transport (excluding flights to Australia) and most meals covered; plenty of additional excursions (hot-air ballooning, diving, etc) at extra cost. From £599 for a 15-day Sydney to Cairns trip; 29-day Sydney to Darwin via the east coast from £1290 and a 16-day Western Australia trip is £815.

Cunard Line (☎01703/716605, fax 225843). Their annual four-month "World Cruise" on the flagship *QE2* takes in Australia in February visiting Sydney, Melbourne, Perth and Fremantle. Cruising from LA to Sydney costs from £5300 per person which includes the flight London to LA and Sydney to London.

Explore Worldwide (☎01252/319448; *www.explore.co.uk*). Bus and 4WD tours through Western Australia and the Northern Territory, ranging from a 15-day trip from Perth to Broome (£1160) to the full whack of the 38 day "Western Half Explorer" (£2200): all the way up the coast from Perth to Darwin and Kakadu then down to Alice Springs; all including flights from the UK.

Jetabout (☎0181/741 3111, fax 748 7505). Qantas' holiday arm, specializing in tailor-made itineraries, as well as vehicle rentals and a couple of see-it-all deals.

Newmans Holidays (☎0181/879 1999; *www.newmans.com*). New Zealand-based company offering self-drive tours of Australia; the smallest 2-berth motor home starts from £28 to £58 per day.

P&O (☎0171/800 2222). Once-yearly cruises to Sydney westbound on the *Oriana* (via Rio de Janeiro) or eastbound on the *Arcadia* (via LA) for £3995 (20 percent discount for early booking).

P&O's own price is £5436 on the *Oriana* and £4156 on the *Arcadia* but you can get a cheaper price from a travel agent.

Qantas Holidays (☎0990/673464). Quality packages from undoubted Australian experts. Car and campervan rental, accommodation and sightseeing passes, rail holidays, cruises, coach transport, city packages and tours can all be priced in.

Travel Bag (☎0171/497 0515; *freequote1@travelbag.co.uk*). Everything from flights to car and campervan rental, farmstays and coach and 4WD tours all over the country, including a six-day "Tropical North" tour for £251 including airport transfers, 5 nights accommodation, breakfast and Barrier Reef cruise. Several action and eco-oriented trips including Barrier Reef diving packages. Flights extra.

Travel Marvel (☎0181/879 3003). Offers major bus tours Australia-wide, from 8 days in Tasmania (£740) through to the 21-day "Best of Australia" tour (£2425). Accommodation and meals included; flights extra.

Travelmood (London ☎0171/258 1234; Dundee ☎01382/322713). Flights, quality accommodation, car and campervan rental; tailor-made itineraries and, and bus passes and tickets and package tours.

Wildlife Worldwide (☎0181/667 9158; *www.wildlife-ww.co.uk*). Tailor-made trips for wildlife and wilderness enthusiasts: includes a 7-day "Jabiru Safari" ex-Darwin for £850, 10-day Kimberley Wildlife £1095 ex-Broome and a 14-day London to London "Wilderness Queensland" trip for £1695.

World Expeditions (☎0181/870 2600 *www.worldexpeditions.com.au*). Australian-owned adventure company; small-group active wilderness holidays; cycling, canoeing, rafting, 4WD excursions, walking and camping. All expeditions are graded by difficulty, and over-50s adventurers are well catered for.

IR£932. British Airways from Belfast may have tickets from as low as IR£661 return. For youth and student discount fares, the best first stop is USIT (see box opposite for address).

When it comes to **packages**, you're best off contacting one of the UK-based companies listed above, or booking through one of the agents in the box above.

IRISH OPERATORS

Australia Travel Centre, 43 Middle Abbey St, Dublin 1 (☎01/874 7747). In the same offices as Qantas; specialist travel agent.

Thomas Cook, 118 Grafton St, Dublin (☎01/677 1721, fax 677 1258); 11 Donegall Place Belfast (☎01232/550232). Mainstream package-holiday and flight agent, with occasional discount offers.

Trailfinders, 4–5 Dawson St, Dublin 2 (☎01/677 7888). Excellent for multistop and RTW tickets.

Unijet, 2nd floor, Albany House, Great Victoria St, Belfast BT2 (☎01232/314656). Discount scheduled fares to major Australian cities; the best agent to contact for Malaysian Airline ticket deals.

USIT, branches at: 19–21 Aston Quay, O'Connell Bridge, Dublin 2 (☎01/602 1700, fax 671 2408); 10–11 Market Parade, Patrick St, Cork (☎021/270900); Fountain Centre, College St, Belfast BT1 6ET (☎01232/324073, fax 238845); 33 Ferryquay St, Derry (☎01504/371888); Victoria Place, Eyre Square, Galway (☎091/565177); Central Buildings, O'Connell St, Limerick (☎061/415064); 36–37 Georges St, Waterford (☎051/872601). Also branches in Athlone, Coleraine, Jordanstown and Maynooth. Student and youth specialist. *www.usit.ie*

GETTING THERE FROM SOUTHEAST ASIA

A satisfying way of reaching Australia and really getting some impression of the distance you've come is to travel overland through Southeast Asia. Plenty of people make this journey, especially Australian backpackers heading in the other direction at the start of their trip. Southeast Asia isn't as straightforward or relaxing as Australia (and you'll need to take appropriate health precautions), but it's a fascinating region

and is unlikely to make a big dent in your budget.

Bangkok, in Thailand, is a popular starting point, with return flights available from around £400 in the UK and US$600 in the US. From Bangkok an inexpensive bus service leaves twice daily for the 2000km ride to **Singapore**, though it's a gruelling 48-hour trip unless you make a stop or two along the way; a more comfortable option is the daily train to Singapore via Padang Besar (28hr, £60/US$90) – book a day or two in advance to be sure of a seat.

From Singapore, you can cross to the **Indonesian islands** of Sumatra or Kalimantan (Indonesian Borneo) and from there island-hop via local buses and ferries southeast through to Java, Bali, and the Lesser Sunda islands to Kupang in East Timor, from where there's a weekly Merpati flight to Darwin (A$350). Allow at least a month from Bangkok to Kupang, and count on minimum living expenses of £7/US$10 a day, not including flights. With more money and less time – or if you've simply had enough at any stage – you can also catch direct flights to various cities across Australia from Singapore, Jakarta (in Java) or Denpasar (Bali).

GETTING THERE FROM NEW ZEALAND

New Zealand–Australia routes are busy and competition is fierce, resulting in an ever-changing range of deals and special offers; your best bet is to check the latest with a specialist travel agent (see box below). It's a relatively short hop across the Tasman Sea: flying time from Auckland to Sydney is around three and a half hours.

All the fares quoted below are for travel during low or shoulder seasons; flying at peak times (primarily December to mid-January) can add substantially to these prices. Ultimately, the price you pay for your flight will depend on how much flexibility you want; many of the cheapest deals are hedged with restrictions – typically a maximum stay of thirty days and an advance-purchase requirement. The cheapest return **fares from Auckland** are to Sydney with Thai (NZ$470 for a maximum stay of thirty days; NZ$570 for a ticket valid for six months), and to Brisbane with Malaysian Airlines (starting at NZ$680), but these tend to be heavily booked. Qantas and Air New Zealand each have daily direct flights to Sydney, Brisbane (both NZ$680), Cairns and Perth (both NZ$800). Flying from **Wellington** or **Christchurch** adds an extra NZ$150-200. Outside peak season, when the airlines often have surplus capacity, they may offer **promotional fares**, which can bring down prices to as low

---

AIRLINES

Air New Zealand, 139 Queen St, Auckland (☎09/357 3000).

Ansett Australia, 2/50 Grafton Rd, Auckland (☎09/796 409; *www.ansett.com.au/*).

Ansett New Zealand, 75 Queen St, Auckland (☎09/302 2146), and branches throughout New Zealand.

Malaysian Airlines, 12/12 Swanson St, Auckland (☎09/373 2741).

Qantas, Qantas House, 154 Queen St, Auckland (☎09/357 8900).

Thai Airways, Kensington Swan Building, 22 Fanshawe St, Auckland (☎1300/651 960).

United Airlines, 7 City Rd, Auckland (☎09/379 3800).

SPECIALIST TRAVEL AGENTS

Budget Travel, 16 Fort St, Auckland, plus other branches around the city (☎09/366 0061, free call ☎0800/808 040).

Destinations Unlimited, 3 Milford Rd, Milford, Auckland (☎09/373 4033).

Flight Centres, National Bank Towers, 205–225 Queen St, Auckland (☎09/309 6171); Shop 1M, National Mutual Arcade, 152 Hereford St, Christchurch (☎03/379 7145); 50–52 Willis St, Wellington (☎04/472 8101); and other branches countrywide.

STA Travel, Travellers' Centre, 10 High St, Auckland (☎09/309 0458; fastfare telesales ☎09/366 6673); 233 Cuba St, Wellington (☎04/385 0561); 90 Cashel St, Christchurch (☎03/379 9098); other offices in Dunedin, Palmerston North, Hamilton and major universities.

Thomas Cook, 96–98 Anzac Ave, Auckland (☎09/379 3920).

as NZ$660 for a thirty-day return from Auckland to Cairns.

Open-jaw tickets – which let you fly into one city and out of another, making your own way between – can save a lot of backtracking and don't add hugely to the total fare. For example, flying into Cairns and out of Sydney, or vice versa, with Qantas or Air New Zealand costs from NZ$740. There are also various **internal** flight deals available to buy with your main ticket (see "Getting Around", p.30, for details).

RTW TICKETS

If you're taking in Australia at the beginning (or end) of your grand tour, you can usually add one or two Australian stops at negligible extra cost, since many airlines go via Australian gateway airports anyway. There's a vast range of RTW routes and your choice will largely depend on where you plan to travel after the Antipodes: sample routes from Auckland might take in Sydney–Bangkok–London–Johannesburg–Perth, and back to Auckland (from NZ$2999); or Los Angeles–Rome–London–Bangkok–Melbourne, returning to Auckland (from NZ$2599).

PACKAGES AND TOURS

There's a huge variety of holidays and tours to Australia available in New Zealand; call any of the travel agents listed in the box opposite. The holiday subsidiaries of airlines such as Air New Zealand, Ansett and Qantas package short **city-breaks** (flight and accommodation) and **fly-drive** deals for little more than the cost of the regular airfare. On the other hand, if romping around the Outback is a high priority, check out any available **adventure tours** as they can be a good way of covering a lot of ground in a short time and getting you to remote places that would otherwise be inaccessible without your own transport. Itineraries range from 14 to 39 days and concentrate on exploring remoter regions, as well as classic rainforest-and-reef trips; prices (not including airfare from New Zealand) start at NZ$1500 and go up to NZ$4000 for extended journeys. A more economical option is offered by backpacker-oriented companies based in Australia, such as Oz Experience and Wayward Bus (see "Getting Around", p.34), whose tours can be booked through STA offices in New Zealand if you want to plan ahead.

GETTING THERE FROM THE US AND CANADA

From Los Angeles it's possible to fly nonstop to Sydney in fourteen and a half hours. Qantas, United, Canadian Airlines and Air New Zealand all operate direct to the east coast of Australia. Flying on an Asian airline will most likely involve a stop in their capital city (Singapore, Tokyo, Hong Kong, etc) and if you're travelling from the West Coast of North America to the East Coast of Australia you'll probably find their fares on the Pacific route somewhat higher than their American or Australian competitors. However, if you're travelling from the East Coast with Perth, say, as you're destination, a carrier such as Singapore Airlines or Malaysian Airlines with a trans-Atlantic routing may offer the best value. Flights leave the US West Coast in the evening, and there are good connections from most North American cities.

Many of the major airlines offer deals whereby you can make stopovers either at **Pacific Rim** destinations such as Tokyo, Honolulu or Kuala Lumpur or at a number of exotic South Pacific locations. Either there will be a flat surcharge on your ticket ($60 per stop, in the case of Singapore

AIRLINES

Air New Zealand (US ☎1-800/262-1234; Canada ☎1-800/563-5494; *www.airnz.com*). Daily non-stop flights from Los Angeles to Sydney plus sporadic service from Vancouver.

Canadian Airlines (Canada ☎1-800/665-1177; US ☎1-800/426-7000; *www.cdnair.ca*). Daily flights to Sydney from Vancouver and Toronto via Honolulu and from Montréal, via Toronto and Honolulu.

Cathay Pacific (☎1-800/233-2742; *www.cathayusa.com*). Daily flights to Sydney via Hong Kong from Los Angeles, San Francisco and Vancouver; from New York via Vancouver and Hong Kong; from Toronto via Anchorage and Hong Kong.

Japan Airlines (☎1-800/525-3663; *www.jal.co.jp*). Daily flights via Tokyo to Sydney, Melbourne or Cairns from New York, Chicago, Los Angeles, San Francisco and Vancouver plus a few flights a week from Dallas and Las Vegas.

Malaysia Airlines (☎1-800/552-9264; *www.malaysiaairlines.com*). Pacific and Atlantic route flights from Los Angeles and New York to Sydney or Perth. All via Kuala Lumpur.

Qantas (☎1-800/227-4500; *www.qantas.com.au*). Non-stop flights twice daily (3 flights Wednesday, Friday and Sunday) from Los Angeles with connections available from other major cities. Special fares and Boomerang Passes available for travel within Australia.

Singapore Airlines (☎1-800/742-3333; *www.singaporeair.com*). Daily flights via Singapore to Sydney and Perth from Los Angeles, San Francisco (both Pacific routes) and New York (via the Atlantic).

United Airlines (☎1-800/538-2929; *www.ual.com*). Daily non-stop flights to Sydney from Los Angeles and San Francisco with connections from many other cities.

Airlines, with a maximum of four stops) or they may offer you a higher priced ticket allowing you to make as many stops as you like, within certain perameters, over a fixed period of time. But the best deal, if you don't mind planning your itinerary in advance, will most likely be a Circle Pacific or a **Round-the-world** (RTW) ticket from a discount (see box opposite) outfit like High Adventure Travel, Inc.

FARES

Fares vary significantly according to **season** – most airlines regard December through February as the high season, April to August as the low season, and other times as shoulder. These boundaries are by no means fixed and can differ radically from airline to airline, so if you want to make sure you're getting the best deal available, always double check. However, you can be sure that fares will be at their highest over Christmas and New Year, when seats are at a premium and booking as far in advance as possible is highly recommended. Note also that midweek fares tend to be cheaper ($60–100) than weekend departures.

Sample lowest standard **scheduled fares** for low/high seasons are approximately as follows: to **Sydney** or Melbourne from Chicago or New York ($1325/$1880); Los Angeles or San Francisco ($1000/$1500); Montréal or Toronto (CDN$1965/

$2465); Vancouver (CDN$1670/$2170); to **Perth** from New York, Los Angeles or San Francisco ($1450/$1950); Vancouver, Toronto or Montréal (CDN$2450/$3245). If your destination is on the west coast you might also want to check out Qantas' "Boomerang Pass" which offers coast to coast return flights in Australia for $440 ($220 one-way). The price of an **open-jaw ticket** (flying into one city and returning from another) should be approximately the average of the return fares to the two cities. Be sure to ask if there are any special limited promotional fares on offer when you call the airlines. At the time of writing, Qantas, Air New Zealand, and United, for instance, have a return LA–Sydney fare of $874.

Charter flights to Australia, a recent arrival on the scene, are offered by companies such as Jetset (who will only take bookings through a travel agent). Fares may slightly undercut those on scheduled flights, but this is offset by more restrictions to contend with, so check conditions carefully. A further possibility is to see if you can arrange a **courier flight**, although the hit-or-miss nature of these makes them most suitable for the single traveller who travels light and has a very flexible schedule. In return for shepherding a parcel through customs and possibly giving up your baggage allowance, you can expect to get a deeply discounted ticket. You'll probably also be restricted in the duration of your stay. Courier flights are generally available to Sydney, Brisbane, Melbourne and Cairns.

SHOPPING FOR TICKETS

A specialist flight agent is generally the best starting point – either a **consolidator**, who buys up blocks of tickets from the airlines and sells them at a discount, or a **discount agent**, who wheels and deals in blocks of tickets offloaded by the airlines, and often offers special student and youth fares and a range of other travel-related services such as travel insurance, bus and train passes, car rentals, tours and the like. Bear in mind, though, that penalties for changing your plans can be stiff. Remember, too, that these companies make their money by dealing in bulk – don't expect them to answer lots of questions.

If you travel a lot, **discount travel clubs** are another option – the annual membership fee may be worth it for benefits such as cut-price air tickets and car rental. Many airlines offer youth or student fares to **under-26s**; a passport or driving licence is sufficient proof of age, though these tickets are subject to availability and can have eccentric booking conditions.

Don't automatically assume that tickets purchased through a travel specialist will be cheapest – once you get a quote, check with the airlines and you may turn up an even better deal. Be advised also that the pool of travel companies is swimming with sharks – exercise caution and never deal with a company that demands cash up front or refuses to accept payment by credit card.

DISCOUNT FLIGHT AGENTS, TRAVEL CLUBS, COURIER BROKERS AND CONSOLIDATORS

Air Brokers International, 150 Post St, Suite 620, San Francisco, CA 94108 (☎1-800/883-3273 or 415/397-1383; www.airbrokers.com). Consolidator.

Air Courier Association, 15000 W sixth Ave, Suite 203, Golden, CO 80206 (☎1-800/282-1202 or 303/215-0900; www.aircourier.org). Courier flight broker.

Airtech, 588 Broadway, Suite 204, New York, NY 10017 (☎1-800/575-8324 or 212/219-7000; www.airtech.com). Courier flight broker.

Austravel, 51 E 42nd St, Suite 616, New York, NY 10017 (☎1-800/633-3404, fax 212/983-8376; australia-online.com/austravel). Full-service agency offering flights and customized tours. Other locations in Chicago, Houston and San Francisco.

Council Travel, 205 E 42nd St, New York, NY 10017 (☎1-800/226-8624,1-888/COUNCIL or 212/822-2700; www.ciee.com). Other branches San Francisco, Los Angeles, Boston, Chicago, Washington DC, etc. Nationwide specialists in student travel.

Educational Travel Center, 438 N Frances St, Madison, WI 53703 (☎1-800/747-5551 or 608/256 -5551; www.edtrav.com). Student/youth and consolidator fares.

High Adventure Travel, 442 Post St, 4th floor, San Francisco, CA 94102 (☎1-800/350-0612 or 415/912-5600; www.highadv.com). Round-the-World and Circle Pacific tickets. Web site features interactive database that lets you build and price your own RTW itinerary.

Moment's Notice, 7301 New Utrecht Ave, Brooklyn, NY 11204 (☎718/234-6295; www.moments-notice.com). Discount travel club.

Now Voyager, 74 Varick St, Suite 307, New York, NY 10013 (☎212/431-1616; www.nowvoyagertravel.com). Courier flight broker and consolidator.

Pacific Experience,181 Spring St, Newport, RI 02840 (☎1-800/233-4255). Good deals on flights made in conjunction with land bookings.

STA Travel, 10 Downing St, New York, NY 10014 (☎1-800/777-0112 or 212/627-3111; www. statravel.com). Other branches in Los Angeles, Chicago, San Francisco, Philadelphia, Boston, etc. Worldwide discount travel firm specializing in student/youth fares; also student IDs, travel insurance, car rental, train passes, etc.

Travel Avenue, 10 S Riverside, Suite 1404, Chicago, IL 60606 (☎1-800/333 - 3335 or 312/876 - 6866; www.travelavenue.com). Discount travel company.

Travel Cuts, 187 College St, Toronto, ON M5T 1P7 (☎1-800/667-2887 or 416/979-2406; www.travelcuts.com). Branches in Montréal, Vancouver, Calgary, Winnipeg. Canadian discount travel organization.

Traveler's Advantage, 3033 S Parker Rd, Suite 900, Aurora, CO 80014 (☎1-800/548-1116; www.travelersadvantage.com). Discount travel club.

TOUR OPERATORS

All prices quoted below are subject to availability and change. Accommodation is based on single person/double occupancy. Unless stated otherwise, return fares are from Los Angeles.

AAT King's (☎1-800/353-4525; *www.world.net/travel/australia/austtour*). Offers a wide selection of escorted, independent tours, city stopovers, etc.

Abercrombie and Kent International Inc (☎1-800/323-7308 or 630/954-2944, fax 954-3324; *www.abercrombiekent.com*). Offers twelve- to twenty-day tours, ranging from basic tours (Sydney; Melbourne; Great Barrier Reef, etc) to more extensive ones, including Kangaroo Island tours and Outback tours. Also specializes in family tours and customized itineraries. Extensions available to Papua New Guinea, New Zealand and Fiji (US$2990–5390, land only).

Adventure Center (☎1-800/227-8747 or 510/654-1879 fax 654-4200; *www.adventure-center.com*). Customized tour service, 4WD safaris, nature and wildlife tours, Aboriginal culture tours, Harley Davidson tours, 18 to 35 group tours, car rentals, hotel passes, camel safaris and rainforest lodges.

Adventures Abroad (☎1-800/665-3998, fax 604/303-1076; *www.adventures-abroad.com*). Small group cultural/historical/nature interest tours. A choice of multi-country South Pacific and Australia specific tours. Two and a half weeks in Australia from US$3894 (land/air).

Asian Pacific Adventures (☎1-800/825-1680 or 213/935-3156). Specialists in arts/cultural tours

including the Laura Festival of Aboriginal art.

Asia Transpacific Journeys (☎1-800/642-2742, fax 303/443-7078; *www.southeastasia.com*). Wide range of customized itineraries and group tours including nature, adventure, Aboriginal rock art.

ATS Tours (☎1-800/423-2880, fax 310/643-0032). Huge Australian and New Zealand specialist; diving deals, fly-drives, city stopovers, rail/bus passes, motel vouchers and other add-ons.

Australian Pacific Tours (☎1-800/290-8687, fax 416/234-8385). General interest escorted tours (eg 15-day "Classic South Pacific" from US$4750 land/air) and safaris; specializes in coach tours (US$1500–4000 land only) and fully independent travel.

Austravel (☎1-800/633-3404, fax 212/983-8376; *australia-online.com/austravel*). Escorted tours and customized itineraries to Australia, New Zealand and the South Pacific.

Brendan Tours (☎1-800/421-8446; *www.brendantours.com*). Fully escorted tours, city stopovers, fly-drives and custom-designed itineraries.

Destination World (☎1-800/426-3644, fax 805/569-3795; *www.destinationworld.com*). Offers a wide variety of tours, from budget to expensive. Off-the-beaten-track tours – including a pub-crawl on horseback and motorcycle tours.

As mentioned above, you might also want to consider buying a Round-the-World (RTW) or Circle Pacific ticket. Here are some sample itineraries. **RTW**: Los Angeles–Sydney–Bangkok–Delhi–Bombay–London–Los Angeles ($1920); New York–Tokyo–Hong Kong–Bangkok–Singapore–Jakarta–Yogyakarta–Denpasar (Bali) –Darwin, overland on your own through Australia, Sydney–Kuala Lumpur–Amsterdam– New York ($2700). **Circle Pacific**: Los Angeles–Tokyo–Kuala Lumpur–Singapore–Perth–Sydney–Los Angeles ($1880); New York–Hong Kong–Bangkok–Bandar Seri Begawan (Brunei)–Perth, overland on your own through Australia, Sydney–Kuala Lumpur–Tokyo–Los Angeles/New York ($2090).

There are also deals on Qantas involving free or low-price flights within Australia (see "Getting Around", p.30, for more on these and internal air passes).

PACKAGE TOURS

Organized **tours** of Australia are usually tailored for those short on time and long on funds; that said, even independent travellers may want to build their stay around one or two planned activities arranged through a tour company. Several of the operators listed in the box above offer so-called **city stopovers/city modules**, providing, for instance, three nights' accommodation, and perhaps a day tour, starting at around $225–375 depending on the location (Gold Coast $225;

Also offers a wheelchair-accessible bus for disabled groups.

Down Under Answers (☎1-800/788-6685, fax 425/895-8929; *www.adventours.com*). Offering "Boomerang Bicycle" tours, hiking, kayaking and white - water rafting trips.

Down Under Direct/Swain Australia Tours (☎1-800/642-6224 or 22-SWAIN, fax 610/896-9592; *www.swaintours.com*). Customized tours to meet individual travel needs and budgets.

Earthwatch (☎1-800/776-0188 or 617/926-8200, fax 926-8532; *www.earthwatch.org*). Arranges placements for paying volunteers in scientific projects around the country.

Esplanade Tours (☎1-800/426-5492, fax 617/262-9829). Customized itineraries from Sydney to the Outback, Qantas air deals and much more.

Goway Travel (☎1-800/387-8850, fax 665 4432; *www.goway.com*). Airfare deals, independent land bookings, fully escorted tours, over-50s vacations, bus tours, hostel passes, camping safaris, cruises, rail, fly-drives and group arrangements.

International Gay and Lesbian Travel Association (☎1-800/448-8550; *www.iglta.org*). Trade group with lists of gay-owned or gay-friendly travel agents, accommodations and other travel businesses.

Maupintour (☎1-800/255-4266, fax 785/331-1057; *www.maupintour.com*). Variety of South Pacific tours, including 15 days in Australia (US$4525–5125 land/air).

Nature Expeditions International (☎1-800/869-0639, fax 520/721-6719; (*www.naturexp.com*). Sixteen-day educational/nature-focused tour including Sydney, Brisbane, Blue Mountains National Park, the Outback, Heron Island and the Great Barrier Reef, led by professional guides (US$3390, land only).

Newmans Vacations (☎1-800/468-2665, fax 310/648-7066; *www.newmans.com*). New Zealand-based company that also offers city modules and tours in Australia.

Qantas Vacations (☎1-800/641-8772, fax 310/535-1057; *www.qantasvacations.com*). Offers a variety of special travel deals to cities (Sydney/Melbourne), the Great Barrier Reef, the Outback, and Fiji or New Zealand extensions.

Saga Holidays (☎1-800/343-0273) Specialists in group travel for seniors. Their "Australian Adventure" 19-night escorted coach and rail tour is available from US$4299 land/air.

Tauck Tours (☎1-800/468-2825, fax 203/221-6828; *www.tauck.com*). Upmarket guided group tours of varying duration, with optional extensions to Fiji.

Tropical Adventures (☎1-800/247-3483 or 348-9778, fax 206/441-5431; *www.divetropical.com*). Independent diving excursions to Australia and neighbouring islands.

United Vacations (☎1-800/351-4200). Varied assortment of individual tours, city break packages, and multi-city excursions.

Sydney/Perth $325; Alice Springs & Ayers Rock $365. Though **fly-drive** deals don't always make sense in sprawling Australia, they're worth considering if you plan to explore just one part of the country closely. Typical prices for the smallest class of car work out at about $65 a day. And even if a package tour is the furthest thing from your mind, before you leave home you may want to check out tour or specialist operators for **rail** or **bus passes** (see pp.31-32 for some of the options).

VISAS AND RED TAPE

All visitors to Australia, except New Zealanders, require a visa or Electronic Travel Authority (ETA) to enter the country; if you're heading overland, you'll obviously need to check visa requirements for countries en route. You can get visa application forms from the Australian High Commissions, embassies or consulates listed opposite or citizens of the US can get visa application forms from the Washington, Los Angeles and Ottawa offices listed opposite and from the embassy Internet sites.

Three-month tourist visas (valid for multiple entry over one year) are issued free and processed over the counter, providing all your documentation and other details are in order, or are returned in three weeks by mail. However, a new computerized system, Electronic Travel Authority (ETA) is speeding things up and doing away with all the bother of filling in forms, queueing or sending off passports for visits of up to three months: customers give their details to airline or travel agents who transmit them to Australia, with confirmation taking only a few minutes. The ETA replaces the visa label in your passport. The system, begun in early 1997, is only available to nationals of the UK, Ireland, US, Canada, Malaysia, Singapore, Japan and several European and Scandinavian countries; you must also be flying on a major airline. In Britain, travel agents charge about £14–16 to process the visas, but to avoid this you can apply in the old way. Visits from three to six months incur a fee (in the UK, £18; in the US, $33); if you

think you might stay more than three months, it's best to get the longer visa before departure, because once you get to Australia extensions cost A$145. Once issued, a visa usually allows multiple entries within twelve months so long as your passport is valid.

An important condition for all holiday visa applications is that you have **adequate funds** both to support yourself during your stay – at least A$1000 a month – and eventually to get yourself home again.

If you're visiting immediate family who live in Australia – parent, spouse, child, brother or sister – you can apply for a **Close Family Visa**, which has fewer restrictions.

Twelve-month **working holiday visas** are easily available to British, Irish, Canadian, Dutch, Japanese and Korean single people aged 18–25, though exceptions are made for people up to 30 and young married couples without children. It is not normally a chance to further your career, since the stress is on casual employment: you are meant to work for no more than three months at any one job. You must arrange the visa before you arrive in Australia, and several months in advance to avoid disappointment as numbers are sometimes capped. The working visas are £60 in the UK and CDN$150 in Canada; some travel agents such as Trailfinders in the UK (see p.7) can arrange them for you.

Having a visa is not an absolute guarantee that you'll be allowed into Australia – immigration officials may well check again that you have enough money to cover you during your stay, and that you have a return or onward ticket. In extreme cases they may refuse entry, or more likely restrict your visit to a shorter period.

CUSTOMS

Australia has strict **quarantine** laws that apply to fruit, vegetables, fresh and packaged food, seed and some animal products, among other things; there are also strict laws prohibiting drugs, steroids, firearms, protected wildlife and associated products. Those over 18 can take advantage of a **duty-free allowance** on entry of 1 litre of alcohol and 250 cigarettes or 250g of tobacco.

AUSTRALIAN EMBASSIES AND CONSULATES ABROAD

UK

London Australian High Commission, Australia House, Strand, London WC2B 4LA (☎0171/379 4334, fax 240 5333).

Manchester Australian Consulate, Chatsworth House, Lever St, Manchester M1 2DL (☎0161/228 1344, fax 236 4074).

US

Atlanta Australian Consulate-General, Suite 2920, 1 Peachtree Center, 303 Peachtree St NE, Atlanta, GA 30308 (☎404/880-1700, fax 880-1701).

Honolulu Australian Consulate-General, 1000 Bishop St, Honolulu, HI 96813 (☎808/524-5050, fax 531-5142).

Los Angeles Australian Consulate-General, Century Plaza Towers, 19th floor, 2049 Century Park E, Los Angeles, CA 90067 (☎310/229-4800, fax 277-2258).

New York Australian Consulate-General, International Building,150 East 42nd St, 34th floor, New York, NY 10117-5612 (☎212/351-6500, fax 351-6501).

San Francisco Australian Consulate-General, 1 Bush St, 7th floor, San Francisco, CA 94104-4413 (☎415/362-6160, fax 986-5440).

Washington Australian Embassy, 1601 Massachusetts Ave NW, Washington, DC 20036 (☎202/797-3000, fax 797-3168).

CANADA

Ottawa Australian High Commission, Suite 710, 50 O'Connor St, Ottawa, Ontario K1P 6L2 (☎613/236-0841, fax 236-4376).

Toronto Australian Consulate-General, Suite 316, 175 Bloor St E, Toronto, Ontario M4W 3R8 (☎416/323-1155, fax 323-3910).

Vancouver Australian Consulate, World Trade Centre Complex, Suite 602–999 Canada Place, Vancouver, BC V6C 3E1 (☎604/684 - 1177, fax 684 - 1856).

INDONESIA

Bali Australian Consulate, Jalan Prof Moh Yamin 51, Renon, Denpasar, Bali (☎0361/23 5092, fax 23 1990).

Jakarta Australian Embassy, Jalan HR Rasuna Said Kav C15–16, Jakarta Selatan 12940 (☎021/522 7111, fax 522 7101).

IRELAND

Dublin Australian Embassy, Fitzwilton House, Wilton Terrace, Dublin 2 (☎01/676 1517, fax 678 5185).

MALAYSIA

Kuala Lumpur Australian High Commission, 6 Jalan Yap Kwan Seng, Kuala Lumpur 50450 (☎246 5555, fax 241 5773).

NEW ZEALAND

Auckland Australian Consulate-General, 8th floor, Union House, 32–38 Quay St, Auckland 1 (☎09/303 2429, fax 377 0798).

Wellington Australian High Commission, 72–78 Hobson St, Thorndon, Wellington (☎04/473 6411, fax 498 7135).

SINGAPORE

Singapore Australian High Commission, 25 Napier Rd, Singapore 258507 (☎065/737 9311, fax 737 5481).

THAILAND

Bangkok Australian Embassy, 37 S Sathorn Rd, Bangkok 10120 (☎02/287 2680, fax 287 2029).

INSURANCE

UK TRAVEL INSURANCE COMPANIES

Columbus Travel Insurance, 17 Devonshire Square, London EC2M 4SQ (☎0171/375 0011).

Endsleigh Insurance, Cranfield House, 97–107 Southampton Row, London WC1B 4AG (☎0171/436 4451).

Marcus Hearne & Co Ltd, 65–66 Shoreditch High St, London E1 6JL (☎0171/739 3444).

Worldwide, The Business Centre, 1–7 Commercial Rd, Tonbridge, Kent TN12 6YT (☎01892/833338).

Note: Good-value policies are also available through **Campus Travel**, **STA** and **Travel Bug** (see pp.6-7 for addresses).

If you're entitled to free emergency health-care from Medicare (see p.25 for details of reciprocal arrangements), you may feel that the need for the health element of travel insurance is reduced, but check carefully what is included (ambulance trips, among other things, will not be reimbursed). In any case, some form of travel insurance can help plug the gaps and will cover you in the event of losing your baggage, missing a plane and the like. Most policies only cover up to £200 in lost cash and £250 for the value of any one item, though £1250 might be the full cover. Check, also, what cover you already have: some home policies cover your possessions abroad, for example, and if you pay for your trip with a credit card, some limited cover may well be provided by the credit card company (check the small print on this, though, as it may not be of much use).

Note that very few insurers will arrange on-the-spot payments in the event of a major expense or loss; you will usually be reimbursed only after returning home. In all cases of loss or theft of goods, it is essential to contact the local police to have a report made out so that your insurer can process the claim. If you plan to participate in any **"high-risk" activities** – and, depending on the insurer, this can extend to water sports (especially diving), skiing or even just hiking – you'll probably have to pay an extra premium; check carefully that any policy you are considering will cover you in case of an accident.

BRITISH, IRISH AND NEW ZEALAND TRAVELLERS

In **Britain and Ireland**, travel insurance schemes are sold by almost every travel agent and bank, and by specialist insurance companies (see box above). Decent single-trip policies start at around £38 a month, though most people are going to Australia for longer periods: 3 months costs from £94. If you are going on a working holiday, a year of full cover can cost around £279 but Columbus Travel Insurance (see above) offer an extended "backpacker" cover for one year for £199 with more basic cover. In **New Zealand**, travel agents are the best people to see for specific travel packages; comprehensive three-month coverage will cost around NZ$275, and six-month coverage NZ$400.

US AND CANADIAN TRAVELLERS

Before buying an insurance policy, check that you're not already covered. **Canadian** provincial health plans typically provide some overseas medical coverage, although they are unlikely to pick up the full tab in the event of a mishap. Holders of official **student/teacher/youth cards** are entitled to accident coverage and hospital inpatient benefits – the annual membership is far less than the cost of comparable insurance. **Students** may also find that their student health coverage extends during the vacations and for one term beyond the date of last enrolment. Bank and credit cards (particularly American Express) often provide certain levels of medical or other insurance, and travel insurance may also be included if you use a major credit or charge card to pay for your trip. **Homeowners' or renters'** insurance often covers theft or loss of documents, money and valuables while overseas.

After exhausting the possibilities above, you might want to contact a specialist **travel insur-ance** company; your travel agent can usually recommend one, or see the box .

Travel insurance policies vary: some are comprehensive while others cover only certain risks (accidents, illnesses, delayed or lost luggage or cancelled flights). In particular, ask whether the policy pays medical costs up front or reimburses you later, and whether it provides for medical evacuation to your home country. For policies that include lost or stolen luggage, check exactly what is and isn't covered, and make sure the per-article limit will cover your most valuable possession. The best premiums are usually to be had through student/youth travel agencies – the current rates for STA policies, for example, are US$35 (for up to 7 days); US$55 (8–15 days); US$115 (1 month); US$180 (2 months); US $55 (for each extra month). If you're planning to do any "dangerous sports" (eg skiing, mountaineering), be sure to ask whether these activities are covered: some companies levy a surcharge.

Most North American travel policies apply only to items lost, stolen or damaged while in the custody of an identifiable, responsible third party – hotel porter, airline, luggage consignment, etc. Even in these cases you will have to contact the local police within a certain time limit to have a complete report made out so that your insurer can process the claim.

TRAVELLERS WITH DISABILITIES

The vast distances between Australia's cities and popular tourist resorts present visitors with mobility difficulties with a unique challenge, but, overall, travel in Australia for people with disabilities is rather easier than it would be in the UK and Europe.

The federal government provides information and various nationwide services through the **National Information Communication Awareness Network** (NICAN) and the **Australian Council for the Rehabilitation of the Disabled** (ACROD) – see box on p.22 for contact details. The **Australian Tourist Commission** offices provide a helpline service and publish a factsheet, *Travelling in Australia for People with Disabilities*, available from its offices worldwide (see p.27 for addresses and phone numbers).

Disability needn't interfere with your sightseeing: the attitude of the management at Australia's major tourist attractions is excellent, and they will provide assistance where they can. For example, you'll find you can view the rock art at Kakadu National Park, do a tour around the base of Uluru (Ayers Rock), snorkel unhindered on the Great Barrier Reef (contact Great Adventures at Cairns, freecall ☎1800/079 080 or Quicksilver at Port Douglas, ☎07/4031 4299), go on a cruise around Sydney Harbour, and see the penguins at Phillip Island.

PLANNING A HOLIDAY

There are **organized tours and holidays** specifically for people with disabilities (including mobility, hearing, vision and intellectual restrictions). Some arrange travel only, some organize travel and accommodation, and others provide a complete package – travel, accommodation, meals and carer support. This last type, as well as catering fully for special needs, provides company for the trip. The contacts in the box opposite will be able to put you in touch with any specialists for trips to Australia; several are listed in the Australian Tourist Commission factsheet. If you want to be more independent, it's important to become an authority on where you must be self-reliant and where you may expect help, especially regarding transport and accommodation. It is also vital to be honest – with travel agencies, insurance companies and travel companions. Know your limitations and make sure others know them. If you do not use a wheelchair all the time but your walking capabilities are limited, remember that you are likely to need to cover greater distances while travelling (often over rougher terrain and in hotter temperatures) than you are used to. If you use a wheelchair, have it serviced before you go and carry a repair kit.

Read your **travel insurance** small print carefully to make sure that people with a pre-existing medical condition are not excluded. And use your travel agent to make your journey simpler. Airline or bus companies can cope better if they are expecting you, with a wheelchair provided at airports and staff primed to help. A **medical certificate** of your fitness to travel (provided by your doctor) is also extremely useful; some airlines or insurance companies may insist on it. Make sure that you have extra supplies of medication carried with you if you fly – and a prescription including the generic name in case of emergency.

There are several **books** which give a good overview of accessible travel in Australia, and you may want to consult one or more of these before you leave: *Smooth Ride Guides: Australia and New Zealand, Freewheeling Made Easy* (FT Publishing), which lists support organizations, airports and transport, specialist tour operators and places to visit and stay; *Easy Access Australia* (Easy Access Australia Publishing), which has information on all the states, with maps, and a separate section with floor plans of hotel rooms; and *A Wheelie's Handbook of Australia* (Program Print).

ACCOMMODATION

Much of Australia's tourist accommodation is well set up for people with disabilities, because buildings tend to be built outwards rather than upwards. New buildings in Australia must comply with a legal minimum **accessibility standard**, requiring that bathrooms contain toilets at the appropriate height, proper circulation and transfer space, wheel-in showers (sometimes with fold-down seat, but if this is lacking, proprietors will provide a plastic chair), grab rails, adequate doorways, and space next to toilets and beds for transfer. There are, of course, many older hotels which may have no wheelchair access at all or perhaps just one or two rooms with full wheelchair access. Most hotels also have refrigerators for medication which needs to be kept cool.

The best place to start looking for accommodation is the *A–Z Australian Accommodation Guide* published by the Australian Automobile Association (AAA) – the umbrella organization for state- and territory-based motoring associations that rate accommodation. They also offer some specialized services, a centralized **booking service** and a repair service for motorized wheelchairs, with reciprocal rights if you are a member of an affiliated overseas motoring organization. The guide is available from any of the state organizations. NICAN also has access to their database via computer, so you can choose your accommodation over the phone. Many travel shops and bookshops have accommodation guides which detail places that have wheelchair access.

The greatest range of accessible accommodation is found in the more densely populated areas of Australia – especially the east coast. In the **cities**, the big chain hotels have rooms with wheelchair access. Some of the smaller hotels do provide accessible accommodation, and a large proportion of suburban motels will have one or two suitable rooms. In the **country** there are fewer specially equipped hotels, but many motels have accessible units; this is particularly true of those that belong to a chain such as Flag – consult their directories for locations. The newest YHA **hostels** are all accessible, and there has been an effort to improve facilities throughout; accessible hostels are detailed in the *YHA Handbook*, or contact them direct (see box on p.42). **Caravan parks** are also worth considering, since some have accessible cabins. Others may have accessible toilets and washing facilities.

There are also a few **resorts** which are fully designed and equipped for wheelchair travellers. Two of these excellent facilities – both of which have a pool and spa with hoist, and fully accessible cooking facilities – are the *Wheel Resort*, 39–51 Broken Head Rd, Byron Bay, NSW 2481 (☎02/6685 6139, fax 6685 8754), which was developed by and for wheelchair users; and *Clark Bay Farm*, Riverview Drive, Narooma, NSW 2546 (☎02/4476 1640). These are both reasonably priced family holiday venues, set in quiet, private and pleasant surroundings. Another well-equipped facility is the *YAL Tropicana Lodge*, 158c Martyn St, Cairns, QLD (☎07/4051 1727), which has seven accessible rooms.

In all cases, it's sensible to check what facilities are available when booking.

TRANSPORT

Interstate buses and trains are generally not an option, although in Victoria, V/Line operates "Sprinter" trains and buses with wheelchair access on country routes and to Adelaide; and in New South Wales, Countrylink runs "XPT" and "Xplorer" trains between Sydney and Melbourne, and it also provides access to some country areas. Information about both services is available on ☎13 2232. However, the most convenient ways of getting around are by **plane** and car. Both Qantas and Ansett have special services to help people with disabilities, and will do their best to minimize discomfort and difficulty. Qantas staff undergo special disability-awareness training and on international flights their aircraft carry the sky chair and are equipped with a larger toilet cubicle.

Of the major car rental agencies, Hertz and Avis offer **vehicles with hand controls** at no extra cost, but advance notice is required. Reserved **parking** is available for vehicles displaying the wheelchair symbol (available from local council offices) in all major centres. There is no formal acceptance of overseas parking permits, but states will generally accept most home-country permits as sufficient evidence to obtain a temporary country-wide permit in Australia. Parking charges and designated spaces differ from state to state (call NICAN for further information). A specially adapted **taxi service** operates from all the major national airports, booked in advance on free call ☎1800/043 187; in addition every capital city has wheelchair-accessible taxis. Some **suburban rail services** can be used with a wheelchair: Melbourne's MET leads the way – call Disability Services (☎03/9619 2355).

USEFUL ORGANIZATIONS

UK

Holiday Care Service, 2nd floor, Imperial Building, Victoria Rd, Horley, Surrey RH6 7PZ (☎01293/774535). Information on all aspects of travel.

Mobility International, 228 Borough High St, London SE1 1JX (☎0171/403 5688). Information, access guides, tours and exchange programmes.

RADAR (Royal Association for Disability and Rehabilitation), 12 City Forum, 250 City Rd, London EC1V 8AF (☎0171/250 3222). A good source of advice on holidays and travel abroad.

US

Directions Unlimited, 720 N Bedford Rd, Bedford Hills, NY 10507 (☎1 800/533-5343). Tour operator specializing in custom tours for people with disabilities.

Mobility International US, PO Box 10767, Eugene, OR 97440 (voice and TDD: ☎503/343-1284). Information and referral services, access guides, tours and exchange programmes. Annual membership $25 (including a quarterly newsletter).

Society for the Advancement of Travel for the Handicapped (SATH), 347 Fifth Ave, New York, NY 10016 (☎212/447-7284). Non-profit travel-industry referral service; allow plenty of time for a response.

Travel Information Service, Moss Rehabilitation Hospital, 1200 W Tabor Rd, Philadelphia, PA 19141 (☎215/456-9600). Telephone information and referral service.

Twin Peaks Press, Box 129, Vancouver, WA 98666 ☎206/694-2462 or 1 800/637-2256). Publisher of the *Directory of Travel Agencies for the Disabled* ($19.95), listing more than 370 agencies worldwide; *Travel for the Disabled* ($19.95); the *Directory of Accessible Van Rentals* ($9.95); and *Wheelchair Vagabond* ($14.95), loaded with personal tips.

CANADA

Jewish Rehabilitation Hospital, 3205 Place Alton Goldbloom, Montréal, PQ H7V 1R2 (☎514/688-9550 ext 226). Guidebooks and travel information.

USEFUL CONTACTS IN AUSTRALIA

ACROD (Australian Council for the Rehabilitation of the Disabled), PO Box 60, Curtin, ACT 2605 (☎02/6282 4333, fax 6281 3488). Regional offices provide lists of state-based help organizations, accommodation, travel agencies and tour operators.

Aged and Disability Care Information Service, "Westella", 181 Elizabeth St, Hobart, TAS 7000 (☎03/6234 7448).

Barrier-Free Travel, 36 Wheatley St, North Bellingen, NSW 2454 (☎02/6655 1733). Fee-based travel access information service.

DIRC (Disability Information Resource Centre), 195 Gilles St, Adelaide, SA 5000 (☎08/8223 7522).

Disability Services and Liaison, PO Box 721, Alice Springs, NT 0871 (☎08/8951 5177).

IDEAS (Information on Disability, Equipment, Access and Services), PO Box 479, Tumut, NSW 2720 (☎02/6947 3377).

NICAN (National Information Communication Awareness Network), PO Box 407, Curtin, ACT 2605 (☎02/6285 3713, fax 6285 3714, free call

☎1800/806 769; *nican@spirit.com.au*). A national, non-profit, free information service on recreation, sport, tourism, the arts, and much more, for people with disabilities. Has a database of 4500 organizations – such as wheelchair-accessible tourist accommodation venues, sports and recreation organizations, and rental companies who have accessible buses and vans.

Paraplegic and Quadriplegic Association of NSW, 33–35 Burlington Rd, Homebush, NSW 2140 (☎02/9764 4166). Serves the interests of the spinally injured; offices also in each state capital (see "Listings" sections of city accounts).

Travellers Aid Support Centre, 2nd floor, 169 Swanston St, Melbourne, VIC 3000 (☎03/9654 7690).

Western Australia Disability Services Commission, 53 Ord St, West Perth, WA 6005 (☎08/9426 9200).

YHA Travel & Membership, 205 King St, Melbourne, VIC 3000 (☎03/9670 7991).

Note: see the "Listings" sections throughout the guide for regional contacts.

Minibuses in some cities have either a hoist or a ramp for rental (call NICAN for further information).

All capital cities and most regional centres produce **mobility maps** showing accessible paths, car parking, toilets, etc, which can be obtained from local councils. Other cities have gone further and their tourist authorities produce comprehensive books such as *Access Brisbane* and *Darwin City without Steps*, while ACROD in New South Wales publishes *Accessing Sydney* (available from them at 55 Ryde St, Ryde, NSW 2112). *Easy Access Australia – A Travel Guide to Australia* is a comprehensive guide written by wheelchair-users for anyone with a mobility difficulty and is available for £11.95 in the UK from the following address: c/o Prawles Oast, Ewhurst Green, near Robertsbridge, E. Sussex TN32 5RG.

COSTS, MONEY AND BANKS

If you've travelled down from Southeast Asia you'll find Australia expensive on a day-to-day basis, but fresh from Europe or the US you'll find prices comparable or cheaper. Australia is well set up for independent travellers, and with a student, YHA, or one of the various backpackers' cards (see box on p.42) you can get discounts on a wide range of travel and entertainment.

Australia's currency is the Australian dollar, or "buck", divided into 100 cents. Plastic notes with forgery-proof clear windows come in $100, $50, $20, $10 and $5 denominations, along with $2, $1, 50¢, 20¢, 10¢ and 5¢ coins.

Exchange rates fluctuate around an over-the-counter rate of A$2.54 for £1; A$1.58 for US$1; A$1.05 for CDN$1.

SOME BASIC COSTS

If you're prepared to camp you might get by on as little as $35 a day, but you should count on around $55 a day for food, board and transport if you stay in hostels, travel on buses and eat and drink carefully. Stay in motels and B&Bs, and eat out regularly, and you'll need to budget $70–90: extras such as scuba-diving courses, clubbing, car rental and tours will all add to your costs.

Hostel **accommodation** will set you back $15–20 a person, while a double room in an inexpensive motel costs between $35 and $50 – most, though, are in the $50–70 bracket. **Food**, on the whole, is good value: counter meals in hotels rarely cost more than $10; restaurants cost upwards of $20 for a reasonable three-course

feed, and many let you BYO (Bring Your Own) wine or beer. Buying your own ingredients is not always the cheapest way to eat in the bigger cities, where there's sure to be a range of budget diners and food halls, but overall you'll save; meat and fresh seasonal produce are generally inexpensive. For a nation of sociable boozers, **drinking** out is surprisingly costly – around $2.50 or more for a beer – compared with buying in bulk from a bottle shop.

Given the size of the country, **transport** can make a major dent in your budget and is perhaps the area in which you're most likely to overspend. **Pre-planning** helps – an open-jaw plane ticket, for example, saves you having to get back to where you started; or pay a little extra for an international flight that gives you some discounted internal fares. There are also a huge variety of **bus and train passes** available overseas (see "Getting Around", pp.31-32, for more on the options available). **Driving** yourself may not always save money, but it does give you a great deal more flexibility. Finding passengers willing to share costs is one way to minimize expenses and is usually not too difficult – try the notice boards at hostels and other meeting places. Buying a used car will, realistically, set you back $4000 or more for a mechanically sound vehicle with a reasonable resale value (see p.36 for more advice), but even $1000 should buy something that will get you around – if not in the greatest of style. Renting a car starts at $25 a day for local rental to at least $65 a day for longer distances. **Fuel** averages 70¢ a litre, but with substantial local variations.

TRAVELLERS' CHEQUES, CREDIT AND CASH CARDS

Travellers' cheques are the best way to bring your funds into Australia, as they can be replaced if lost or stolen (remember to keep a list of the serial numbers separate from the cheques). Australian dollar travellers' cheques are ideal as theoretically they're valid as cash, though smaller businesses may be unwilling to take them. Cheques in US dollars and pounds sterling are also widely accepted, and banks should be able to handle all major currencies. It's worth checking both the rate and the commission when you change your cheques (as well as when you buy them), as these can vary quite widely – many places charge a set amount for every cheque, in which case you're better off changing relatively large denominations.

Credit cards can come in very handy as a backup source of funds, and they can even save on exchange-rate commissions. They can also be used to leave a deposit – for example, for a rental car or a hotel booking – even if you settle the final bill with cash. MasterCard and Visa are the most widely recognized; you can also use Amex, Bankcard and Diners Club. Supermarkets tend not to take credit cards at all. In addition, with an **international debit card** you may be able to pay for goods via EFTPOS (see below) and gain direct access to your home funds via ATM machines displaying the Cirrus-Maestro symbol. As a flat rate is charged for these transactions, this can work out to be cheaper than travellers' cheques for large sums – check with your bank before leaving.

BANKS AND EXCHANGE

You'll find a branch of one of the main **banks** in every town of any size, and in smaller places there will be a local **agency** which handles bank business, usually based at the general store or roadhouse. The major banks, with branches countrywide, are Westpac, ANZ and the Commonwealth and National banks.

Banking hours are Monday to Thursday 9.30am to 4pm, Friday 9.30am to 5pm, though in country areas some agencies will be open later, and some big-city branches might also have extended hours; **autotellers** or **ATM**s are generally open 24 hours. **Bureaux de change** are only found in major tourist centres and airports, so

make sure you exchange your currency during banking hours. All **post offices** act as Commonwealth Bank agents, which means there's a fair chance of changing money even in the smallest Outback settlements – withdrawals at these places are often limited by a lack of ready cash, however, though less remote post offices may even have EFTPOS facilities (see below).

If you're spending some time in Australia – say a month or more – and plan to work or move around, it makes life a great deal easier if you open a **bank account**. To do this you'll need to take along every piece of ID documentation you own (a passport may not be enough), though it's otherwise a fairly straightforward process. The Commonwealth Bank and Westpac are the most widespread options, and their **passbook accounts** are easy enough to obtain; if you can, however, opt for a **keycard account** as a keycard gives you access not only to ATM machines but also anywhere that offers **EFTPOS** facilities (Electronic Funds Transfer at Point of Sale). This includes many Outback service stations and supermarkets, where you can use your card to pay directly for goods; some of them will also give you cash.

International money transfers can be made from any bank in Australia to a nominated bank abroad and cost approximately A\$25. Transfers can take anywhere from a few days to several months. For **moneygrams**, you can make arrangements with either American Express Moneygram (within Sydney ☎02/9886 0666; elsewhere free call ☎1800/230 100) or Western Union (within Brisbane ☎07/3229 8610).

HEALTH

Australia has high standards of hygiene, and there are few exceptional health hazards – at least in terms of disease. No vaccination certificates are required unless you've come from a yellow-fever zone within the past week. Standards in Australia's hospitals are also very high, and medical costs are reasonable by world standards.

The national healthcare scheme, Medicare, offers a reciprocal arrangement – free essential healthcare – for citizens of the UK, New Zealand, Italy, Malta, Finland, the Netherlands and Sweden. This free treatment is limited to public hospitals and casualty departments (though the ambulance ride to get you there isn't covered), at GPs you pay up front (about $40 minimum) with two-thirds of your fee reimbursed by Medicare.

The whole process is made easier by the production of a Medicare Card, available from any Medicare Centre. Anyone eligible who's staying in Australia for a while – particularly those on extended working holidays – is advised to obtain one. Dental treatment is not included: if you find yourself in need of dental treatment in one of the larger cities, try the dental hospital, where dental students may treat you cheaply or for free.

THE SUN

Australia's biggest health problem for fair-skinned visitors is also one of its chief attractions: sunshine. A sunny day in London, Toronto, or even Miami, is not the same as a cloudless day in Cairns, and the intensity of the Australian sun's damaging ultraviolet rays is far greater. Whether this is because of Australia's proximity to the reputed ozone hole is a matter of debate, but there's absolutely no doubt that the southern sun burns more fiercely than anything in the northern hemisphere, and you need to take extra care.

Australians of European origin, especially those of Anglo-Saxon or Celtic decent, could not be less suited to Australia's fierce sun, which – together with an outdoor lifestyle – is why two out of three Australians are statistically likely to develop skin cancer in their lifetime, the world's worst record. About five percent of these will develop potentially fatal melanomas, and about a thousand die each year. Looking at the ravaged complexions of some older Australians (who had prolonged exposure to the sun in the days before there was an awareness of the great dangers of skin cancer) should be enough to make you want to cover yourself with lashings of the highest factor (SPF 15+) sunblock, widely used and sold just about everywhere. Don't bring along those tubes you took on holiday to the Aegean last year either: it has recently been proven that sunscreen loses its effectiveness with age. Sunscreen should not be used on babies less than six months old: instead, keep them out of direct sunlight. What looks like war paint on the noses of surfers and small children is actually zinc cream; the thick, sticky waterproof cream, which comes in fun colours, provides a total blockout and is particularly useful when applied to protruding parts of the body, such as noses and shoulders.

These days, Australians are fully aware of the sun's dangers, and you're constantly reminded to "Slip, Slop, Slap", the government-approved catch phrase reminding you to slip on a T-shirt, slop on some sun block and slap on a hat – sound advice. Pay attention to any moles on your body: if you notice any changes, either during or after your trip, see a doctor; cancerous melanomas are generally easily removed if caught early. To prevent headaches and – in the long term – cataracts, it's a good idea to wear sunglasses; look for "UV block" ratings when you buy a pair, although any sold in Australia have to conform to an appropriate standard.

The sun can also cause heat exhaustion and sunstroke, so as well as keeping well covered up, stay in the shade if you can. Drink plenty of liquids: on hot days when walking, experts advise drinking a litre of water an hour – which is a lot to carry. Alcohol and sun don't mix well; when you're feeling particularly hot and thirsty, remember that a cold beer will actually dehydrate you.

WILDLIFE DANGERS

Although mosquitoes are found across the whole of the country, malaria is not endemic; however, in the tropical north there are rare outbreaks of similarly transmitted Ross River Fever and Dengue Fever, both of which can be debilitating and recur for life. Medical researchers believe that mosquitoes as far south as Sydney may be carrying Ross River and Barmah Forest virus for the first time – which is reason enough not to be too blasé about mozzie bites. Aeroguard and Rid are the popular brands of insect repellent.

The danger from other **wildlife** is much over-rated: snake and spider bites, and crocodile and shark attacks are widely publicized and an essential part of the perilous Outback myth – nonetheless, all are extremely rare. There are always scares: there was mild hysteria in Queensland in 1996 after a couple of people died from being bitten by **flying foxes** infected with the lyssa virus, so keep away from bats until the virus has been eliminated. Rabies is unknown in Australia.

Apart from never smiling at them, the way to minimize danger from **saltwater crocodiles** (which actually range far inland) is to keep your distance. If you're camping in the bush within 100km of the northern coast between Broome (WA) and Rockhampton (QLD), make sure your tent is at least 50m from waterholes or creeks, don't collect water at the same spot every day or leave any rubbish around, and always seek local advice. Four-wheel drivers should take extra care when walking creeks prior to driving across.

Snakes almost always do their best to avoid people and you'll probably never see one. They're more likely to be out and about in hot weather, when you should be more careful. If you treat them with respect, it's very unlikely you'll be bitten: most bites occur when people try to catch or kill snakes. Don't creep about, do wear boots and long trousers when hiking through undergrowth, collect firewood carefully, and, in the event of a confrontation, back off. **Sea snakes** sometimes find divers intriguing, wrapping themselves around limbs or staring into masks, but they're seldom aggressive. If **bitten** by a snake, use a crepe bandage to bind the limb firmly, then a splint to immobilize it (this slows the distribution of venom into the lymphatic system) and get to a hospital for treatment. Don't clean the bite area (venom around the bite can identify the species, making treatment easier), and don't slash the bite or apply a tourniquet. Despite what you might hear, death from snakebite is extremely rare.

Two **spiders** whose bites can be fatal are the **Sydney funnel-web**, a black, stocky creature found in the Sydney area, and the tiny **redback**, a relative of the notorious black widow of the Americas, usually found in dark, dry locations. January and February are the months in which there is the greatest danger of bites by both. Treat funnel-web bites as for snakebite, and apply ice to redback wounds to relieve pain; if bitten by either, get to a hospital as soon as you can – antivenins are available. **Other spiders** and **scorpions** can deliver painful wounds but are only a problem if you have allergies.

Ticks and **leeches** are the bane of bushwalkers. Some ticks are poisonous and you may want to check yourself over after a hike, but you'll probably feel them – look for local irritation and swelling (usually just inside hairlines) and you'll find a tiny black dot. Kill the tick with kerosene and then, using tweezers, twist and pull it off. Pulling alone will leave the head behind, which might fester. Leeches are gruesome but harmless; insect repellent, fire or salt gets them off the skin. Spraying repellent over shoes and leggings might keep both pests away in the first instance.

The menace from **box jellyfish** (also known as stingers or sea wasps) in summertime tropical sea waters is more realistic – especially as it occurs at a place and time of year when a cooling dip in the sea is just about all you can think of. Their stings leave permanent red weals, and if the weals cover more than half a limb, serious damage could result – possibly even death. Treat victims by dousing the sting area (front and back) with liberal amounts of **vinegar** (*never* rub with sand or towels, or attempt to remove tentacles from the skin – both could trigger the release of more venom); apply mouth-to-mouth resuscitation if needed, and get the victim to hospital for treatment. Don't risk swimming on tropical beaches during the **stinger season** (roughly October to May). Specific **reef hazards** are covered at the start of the chapter on Queensland's tropical coast (p.404).

For more background on Australian fauna, see "Wildlife" on p.1005.

OTHER HEALTH HAZARDS

Australia has one of the lowest rates of **AIDS** infection in the world, largely because the population caught on very early to the need for safe sex, which has been promoted heavily. Infected needles are also a danger, not only among intravenous drug users but also from ear-piercing and tattooing. The Australian National Council on AIDS (ANCA) has centres all over the country, and you'll find AIDS helplines listed in the major cities in this guide.

Other health hazards are far less pressing. **Tap water** is safe to drink everywhere. It doesn't always taste good, but bottled water is commonly available. Although you're unlikely to find yourself in the path of a raging **bushfire**, it helps to know how to survive one. If you're in a car, don't attempt to drive through smoke but park at the side of the road in the clearest spot, put on your headlights, wind up the windows and close the air vents. Although it seems to go against common sense – and your natural instincts – it's safer to **stay inside the car**. Lie on the floor and cover all exposed skin with a blanket or any covering at hand. The car won't explode or catch on fire, and a fast-moving wildfire will pass quickly overhead. If you smell or see smoke and fire while **walking**, find a cleared rocky outcrop or an open space: if the terrain and time permits, dig a shallow trench – but in any event, lie face down and cover all exposed skin.

INFORMATION AND MAPS

Australian tourism abroad is represented by the Australian Tourist Commission, who pro-duce an annual, glossy *Australia, A Traveller's Guide* which gives an excellent introduction to Australia. It details the country region by region, offers travel tips and ways of getting around, and has a useful directory of addresses. You can also get information on the Internet at Gateway to Australia – *www.aussie.net.au.*

More detailed information is available by the sackful once you're in the country. Each state or territory has its own **tourist authority**, which operates information offices throughout its own area and in major cities in other parts of Australia – some are even represented abroad (almost all have London offices, detailed in the box below). A level below this are a host of regional and community-run **visitors centres** and **information kiosks**. Even the smallest Outback town seems to have one – or at the very least a pamphlet rack

AUSTRALIAN TOURIST COMMISSION OFFICES

New Zealand Level 13, 44–48 Emily Place, Auckland 1 (☎09/379 9594).

United Kingdom Gemini House, 10–18 Putney Hill, Putney, London SW15 6AA ("Aussie Helpline" charged at 50p a minute: ☎0990/022000; *www.tourism.gov.au*).

US Visitors should contact the "Aussie Helpline" for tour information (☎847/296-4900).

STATE TOURIST OFFICES IN LONDON

Northern Territory Tourist Commission, 1st floor, Beaumont House, Lambton Rd, London SW20 0LW (☎0181/944 2992; *www.outbackaustralia.demon.co.uk*).

Queensland Tourist & Travel Corporation, 392 Strand, London WC2R 0LZ (☎0171/836 7142; *www.qttc.com.au*).

South Australian Tourist Commission, 1st floor, Beaumont House, Lambton Rd, London SW20 0LW (☎0181/944 5375).

Tourism New South Wales, 2nd floor, Australia Centre, Strand, London WC2B 4LC (☎0990/022000).

Tourism Victoria, 4th floor, Victoria House, Melbourne Place, Strand, London. WC2B 4LG (☎0171/240 7176).

Western Australian Tourist Commission, 4th floor, Australia Centre, Strand, London. WC2B 4LC (☎0171/240 2881).

at the local service station – while larger places will often have two or more rival offices. Remember though, most of these associations only promote subscribing or advertising members – the information they supply is not comprehensive or impartial, although anyone in the tourist business is likely to be involved with a tourism association.

It's also worthwhile asking **fellow travellers** about places they've been to, to give you an idea whether or not you wish to go there. One of the best things about **hostels**, apart from the inexpensive accommodation they offer, is that they act as information points. Almost all of them have **noticeboards** where you'll find local bus sched-

ules, offers of cheap excursions or ride shares, and comments and advice from people who've already passed this way.

MAPS

If you want to obtain maps before you go, the GeoCenter (including NZ) and Nelles **maps of Australia**, both 1:4,000,000, are finely produced, with good topographical detail: the Nelles (printed in northern and southern halves on both sides of the sheet) includes additional detail of major city environs. The Bartholomew and the new Globetrotter (both 1:5,000,000) are the best of the

SPECIALIST BOOK AND MAP SUPPLIERS

UK

London

National Map Centre, 22–24 Caxton St, SW1H 0QU (☎0171/222 4945).

Stanfords, 12–14 Long Acre, WC2E 9LP (☎0171/836 1321); 52 Grosvenor Gardens, SW1W 0AG (☎0171/730 1314); 156 Regent St, W1R 5TA (☎0171/434 4744).

The Travel Bookshop, 13–15 Blenheim Crescent, W11 2EE (☎0171/229 5260).

Edinburgh

Thomas Nelson and Sons Ltd, 51 York Place, EH1 3JD (☎0131/557 3011).

Glasgow

John Smith and Sons, 57–61 St Vincent St, G2 5TB (☎0141/221 7472).

Maps by **mail or phone order** are available from Stanfords (☎0171/836 1321).

NEW ZEALAND

Specialty Maps, 58 Albert St, Auckland (☎09/307 2217).

US

ADC Map and Travel Centre, 1636 first st NW, Washington, DC 20006 (☎1-800/544-2659 or 202/628-2608).

Book Passage, 51 Tamal Vista Blvd, Corte Madera, CA 94925 (☎1-800/999-7909 or 415/927 -0960).

The Complete Traveler Bookstore, 3207 Fillmore St, San Francisco, CA 94123 (☎415/923-1511) and at 199 Madison Ave, New York, NY 10016 (☎212/685-9007). *www.completetraveler.com*

Elliot Bay Book Company, 101 S Main St, Seattle, WA 98104 (☎1-800/962-5311 or 206/624 -6600; *www.elliotbaybook.com\ebbco\).*

Forsyth Travel Library, 226 Westchester Ave, White Plains, NY 10604 (☎1-800/367-7984; *www.forsyth.com).*

Map Link Inc, 30 S La Patera Lane, Unit 5, Santa Barbara, CA 93117 (☎805/692-6777; *www.maplink.com).*

Phileas Fogg's Books & Maps, #87 Stanford Shopping Center, Palo Alto, CA 94304 (☎1-800/533-FOGG; *www.foggs.com).*

Rand McNally, 444 N Michigan Ave, Chicago, IL 60611 (☎312/321-1751); 150 E 52nd St, New York, NY 10022 (☎212/758-7488); 595 Market St, San Francisco, CA 94105 (☎415/777-3131). Note: Rand McNally now has more than 20 stores across the US; call (☎1-800/234-0679) for the address of your nearest store, or for direct mail maps. *www.randmcnallystore.com*

Sierra Club Bookstore, 6014 College Ave, Oakland, CA 94618 (☎510/658-7470; *www.sierraclubbookstore.com).*

Travel Books & Language Center, 4437 Wisconsin Ave, Washington, DC 20016 (☎1-800/220-2665).

CANADA

International Travel Maps & Books, 552 Seymour St, Vancouver BC, V6B 3J6 (☎604/687-3320; *www.itmb.com).*

Open Air Books and Maps, 25 Toronto St, Toronto, ON M5C 2R1 (☎416/363-0719). **Ulysses Travel Bookshop**, 4176 St Denis, Montréal PQ H2W 2M5 (☎514/843-9447; *www.ulysses.ca).*

rest. Any of the specialist map shops listed in the box above should have all of these, together with a reasonable selection of more detailed local maps.

In Australia UBD, Gregory's and AusMap produce national, state, regional and city maps of varying sizes and quality: the first two are the most widely available. BP and the state motoring organizations have regularly updated **touring guides** to Australia, with regional maps, listings, and details of things to see and do – something for the back shelf of the car rather than a backpack.

If you're a member of a **motoring organization** or automobile association, there's a good chance you'll have reciprocal rights with the Australian

equivalent and be entitled to **free maps** and other discounted services. Each state has its own organization (they're listed in the Australian Tourist Commission's guide) and most are excellent – you'll need to bring proof of membership along to take advantage.

The whole country is now covered by 1:50,000 topographical sheets, suitable for hiking or travel in remote areas. You can get them at government mapping agency offices or official government bookshops (in major cities) or take a look at them at a library in the nearest major town; they're also available by mail from the **National Mapping Agency**, PO Box 31, Belconnen, ACT 2616.

GETTING AROUND

Australia's huge scale makes the distances, and how you conquer them, a major feature of any stay in the country. In general, public transport will take you only along the major highways to capital cities, the bigger towns between them, and popular tourist destinations; to get off the beaten track you'll have to consider driving or hitching. Regular long-distance bus, train and plane services can be found under "Travel details" at the end of each chapter, with local buses and trains covered in the main text.

PLANES

Flying isn't particularly cheap, but it can begin to seem a bargain when you take into account the time saved, and the money you'll spend on incidentals during a long bus or train journey. The **best-value** flights are, not surprisingly, the most popular – between state capitals and major towns in the southeast; flying to remote Outback locations on private local services such as **mail runs** can be an expensive business. The two main domestic airlines are Qantas and Ansett flying major routes, with the moderate-sized Kendell, using smaller craft, covering more regional areas of NSW, Victoria and South Australia and having recently taken over Ansett's routes to Tasmania. Then there are smaller, regional airlines in each state such as Airlines of South Australia, or Hazelton in NSW.

If you do expect to fly a fair amount, there are a number of **passes** that can save money, such as

the Qantas Boomerang Pass or Ansett G'Day Pass. The **Ansett G'Day Pass** entitles you to discounted internal flights, with further discounts if your international flight is with Air New Zealand or Singapore Airlines: the pass must be purchased outside Australia, and you need to book a minimum of two flights (up to a maximum of ten). Tickets cost £103 (£88 discounted; US$175) for destinations within the same zone: for example, Sydney–Hobart, and £127 (£110 discounted; US$220) for longer flights such as Sydney–Perth. The **Qantas Boomerang Pass** is discounted with a Qantas or British Airways international ticket but otherwise has the same conditions and fares. You can also make substantial **savings** by booking internal flights with Ansett and Qantas before you leave as add-ons to an international ticket, though if you want more than two longer distance flights, an airpass is better value. A one-way ticket bought in this way with Ansett or Qantas from Sydney to Melbourne costs about £75 ($115), from Sydney to Perth £190 ($285). British Airways and Qantas often have special deals with their tickets allowing you to take two extra stops for around £50 each. Once in Australia, Qantas also offers the Discover Australia fare which gives you around a thirty percent discount on the full fare on all domestic Qantas routes on production of your international air ticket (which need not be a Qantas ticket). However, buying a discounted full fare ticket, is not the cheapest option: this is a 21-day advance purchase return. For example, Sydney to Melbourne return with a Discover Australia fare would cost $404 ($576 full fare) but with an APEX 21-day advance purchase it would cost around $239. One-way tickets can be bought as 5-day advance purchases – from $259 for Sydney to Melbourne, while a Discover Australia fare on this route one-way would be $202.

Travellers from New Zealand can take advantage of the Qantas/Air New Zealand See Australia pass, which gives substantial discounts on flights within the eastern states of Australia, such as Sydney–Cairns for A$200 instead of

---

DOMESTIC AIRLINES
Ansett ☎13 1300
Qantas ☎13 1313

A\$570. For longer flights, or simply more flexibility, Airpass coupons (minimum purchase two) allow single, direct flights, with each coupon costing A\$200 (excluding Western Australia, Alice Springs and Ayers Rock) or A\$250 (with no restrictions).

Once you're in Australia, there's the usual range of APEX and other restricted **fares** (mentioned above), including student and pensioner reductions. Qantas and Ansett's **backpacker fares** are available to anyone with a YHA or VIP card (see p.42) if you buy a minimum of three flights and represent a substantial discount – a useful adjunct to an open-jaw ticket.

Another type of flight offered all over Australia is brief **sightseeing** or joyrides. Everything is covered, from biplane spins above cities (cricket-lovers may wish to re-create David Gower's infamous escapade) to excursions to the Great Barrier Reef and flights over well-known landscapes. The last, especially, can be worthwhile, enabling you to see things that are inaccessible or impractical to reach overland. **Aircruising Australia** (☎02/9693 2233) offers a 12-day tour by air which takes in the main sights; the price of around £3000 per person (US\$4799) includes accommodation, meals and guides. **Oz Experience** (Sydney ☎02/9221 4711, rest of Australia ☎1300/301 359) offer an Air-Bus Pass where you fly one-way around Australia with Qantas and bus the other in off the beaten track routes with driver-guides; for example, the cheapest \$545 "Cobber Rama" allows you to fly from Sydney to Cairns and then bus down the coast from Cairns to Sydney with unlimited stops (min 9 days, max six months), while the priciest lets you fly Sydney to Darwin, bus Darwin to Alice, fly Alice to Cairns and then bus Cairns to Sydney (minimum 13 days, maximum one year).

TRAINS

Trains are not the most obvious way to get around Australia, which has a limited network, but there are a couple of wonderful, epic journeys to be made. The populous southeast, at least, does have a reasonably comprehensive service: **interstate railways** link the entire east coast from Cairns to Sydney, and on to Melbourne and Adelaide. The two great journeys, though, are the coast-to-coast **Indian Pacific** (Sydney–Perth; 65hr; seat only \$400, sleeper \$823, first class with meals \$1262) and the **Ghan** (Adelaide–Alice Springs; 20hr; seat \$170, sleeper \$351, first class with meals \$539). Like much of the national net-

work, both these routes have been losing money for years, and the plan now is to make these journeys unapologetically upmarket (and therefore expensive) – a down-under answer to the Orient Express. A real partnership between the Venice-Simplon-Orient-Express has created the **Great South Pacific Express** (in Australia free call ☎1800/677 777), which commenced in December 1998; the luxury tourist train runs year-round from Sydney up the east coast to Cairns. The entire journey takes four nights or can be done in components (the 3-day Brisbane to Cairns component, with all meals and sightseeing, costs \$2430, while the entire trip will set you back \$3720). Other than these, there are a couple of inland tracks in Queensland – to Mount Isa and Longreach – and suburban networks around some of the major cities. Only around Sydney does this amount to much, with decent services to much of New South Wales. There are no passenger trains in Tasmania.

The advantages of travelling by train rather than bus are comfort, conversation and leisure; disadvantages are the slower pace, higher price and potential booking problems – Queensland trains, for instance, travel at about 60kph and require at least a month's advance booking during the holiday season. The famous long-distance journeys can also be booked solid, so you'd be wise to reserve a place before you leave home if this is a major part of your plans (Rail Australia agents are listed overleaf). Sample one-way fares from Sydney are Melbourne \$96 (sleeper \$229), Adelaide \$152 (sleeper \$303), Perth \$400 (sleeper \$823), Alice Springs \$322 (sleeper \$654), Brisbane \$96 (sleeper \$229) and Cairns \$135 (sleeper \$165).

Rail passes include the Austrailpass, which must be bought outside Australia and gives unlimited travel for fourteen, twenty-one or thirty consecutive days on all state-owned railways, including suburban links around state capitals; prices cost £237 (US\$408) for fourteen days, £307 (US\$528) for twenty-one days and £370 (US\$638) for thirty days. The Austrail Flexipass lets you linger without wasting your ticket: eight days of travel within a six-month period, for example, costs around £196 (US\$338) you can also choose 15, 22 or 29 days). These passes are for international travellers only and must be bought before you arrive in Australia. To be sure that you can make full use of your pass, it's advisable to book your route when you buy it. Western Australia, Victoria, New South

Wales and Queensland also have their own passes available through main stations, but check any travel restrictions before buying – interstate routes do not overlap as far as passes are concerned.

BUSES

Travelling by **bus** is almost certainly the cheapest way to get around, although it's rarely a very satisfactory one. There's a lot to be said against spending much of your trip staring at the passing landscape from a cramped seat with a Nintendo device jabbering in your ear. And even though the bus network is a great deal more comprehensive than the train network, it will still let you down if you hope to escape the tourist trail. Relying on the major operators (as you may have to do if you have a bus pass) will restrict you to the main highways between cities, and may mean arriving at smaller places in the middle of the night. On the other hand bus services are regular and good value, and vehicles are about as comfortable as they could be, with reclining seats, air-conditioning, toilets and videos: the real problem is having all these things work for the entire duration of your trip. If possible, try and plan for a stopover after every twenty hours on a bus – if you try stoically to sit out a two-day trip, you'll be in a foul mood when you reach your destination.

The main **interstate bus company** on the mainland is **Greyhound Pioneer Australia** (Australia-wide ☎13 2030; *www.greyhound.com.au*); its main competitor, **McCafferty's** (Australia-wide ☎13 1499; *www.mccaffertys.com.au*), is limited to the eastern states. **Tasmania** is thoroughly covered by Redline and Wilderness Transport, and a full breakdown of fares and passes can be found on pp.000–000. **Fares** vary according to the popularity of the route and quality and speed of the road, and there are often special offers – it's always worth shopping around; sample one-way fares from Sydney with Greyhound are: Melbourne $60, Adelaide $96, Perth $295, Alice Springs $230, Darwin $376, Brisbane $70 and Cairns $222. Return fares are, at best, only marginally cheaper than two singles.

By far the most popular option is to buy a **bus pass**. The Aussie Kilometre Pass is the most flexible as it allows you unlimited travel in any direction up to the number of kilometres purchased over a twelve-month period; the kilometres can also be used on Greyhound Pioneer tours. The passes range from 2000km ($185; which would get you from Brisbane to Cairns, for example) to 20,000km ($1400). The Aussie Day Pass allows unlimited travel for between 7 to 21 non-consecutive days (24-hr periods) within a specified period: 7-, 10- and 15-day are valid for 30 days, while 21-day passes are valid for 60 days; prices range from $499 for 7 days to $982 for 21 days. There are also Aussie Explorer pass options that allow either six or twelve months (depending on distance) to cover a specified route (Melbourne–Cairns for $300, for example, or even a circuit right round Australia, with limitless stopovers, for $1555), and they incorporate regional tours. McCafferty's has a range of eight Travel Australia passes: the "Best of the East and Centre" pass includes their entire network on the mainland, is valid for twelve months and costs $820; there are also a number of point-to-point passes, such as Melbourne–Cairns "Follow the Sun" lasting for six months and costing $295. Tasmania has its own passes offered by Tasmanian Wilderness Transport (*www.tassie.net.au/wildtour*), whose coverage, however, is not comprehensive though the passes include an entitlement to a third off Redline Coaches services; passes cost from $99 for 5 days travel in 7 days to $220 for 30 days travel in 40 days.

Substantial **discounts** (ten percent, or fifteen percent if you buy your ticket before entering Australia) are available on many fares if you have a YHA, ISIC or recognized backpacker card such as VIP or Nomad's (see p.42) or if you are a pensioner.

Oz Experience (see above and below) offers combined Air-Bus passes which can speed up the process but also offer plenty of time down on the ground. They also offer bus-only passes (see box p.34). In a similar vein, **Wayward Bus'** excellent tours can also be used as hop - on hop-off transport within a six-month period (see box p.34). Other more localized bus services have also started to offer passes. **Premier Motor Service/Pioneer Motor Service** (☎1300/368 100) have their own bus passes on their more limited range of two routes going along the north and the south coast from Sydney. On their Sydney to Brisbane route (3 services daily), an Ocean Pass gives you one stop en route for $69 (students, YHA/VIP $55), while the Premier Pass offers unlimited stops in one direction for $88/$79. On their Sydney to Eden route (2–3 services daily)

they have a South Coast Pass (one stop; $50/$44) and a Getaway Pass (unlimited stops in one direction; $75/$60). Passes last for three months.

ONE-WAY TOURS

The big bus companies exist to transport as many passengers as quickly as possible from A to B. If you want more than a fleeting look at what you're passing, a **one-way tour** may be a lot more fun. These tours, usually in minibuses, tend to be more leisurely and detour to attractions along the way; groups are usually quite small (ten to eighteen people) and the driver/guides are mostly knowledgeable locals – see the box on p.34 for a selection of operators plus boxes on pp.172-173 ("Tours from Sydney"), p.810 ("Tours from Melbourne") and p.701 ("Tours" under Adelaide "Listings"). More conventional tours, starting from and returning to the same place, are mentioned in the "Listings" sections of the relevant accounts and in other interest boxes throughout the guide.

DRIVING

Having **your own vehicle** really allows you to explore Australia, filling the public transport void away from the cities and allowing you to get to the national parks, the isolated beaches and the ghost towns that make the country such a special place. If your trip is a long one – three months or more – then **buying a vehicle** may well be the cheapest way of seeing Australia. On shorter trips you should consider **renting** – if not for the whole time, then at least for short periods between bus rides, thereby allowing you to explore an area in depth.

Most foreign **licences** are valid for a year in Australia. An International Driving Permit (available from national motoring organizations) may be useful if you come from a non-English-speaking country. **Fuel** prices start at around 66¢ per litre for "super" (standard) or unleaded, with diesel slightly cheaper: prices can double at remote roadhouses, and you can expect a ten to fifteen percent increase in Outback areas. The **rules of the road** are similar to those in the US and UK. Most importantly, **drive on the left** (as in Britain), remember that seatbelts are compulsory for all, and maximum **speed limits** outside built-up areas are around 100kph, except in the Northern Territory where common sense and horsepower are your only limits between towns; in all built-up areas, the speed limit is 60kph. Whatever else you do in a vehicle, avoid **drinking and driving**. In what has been a relatively successful campaign to lower Australia's frighteningly high road death toll, random breath tests are common, especially during the Christmas season and on Friday and Saturday nights. The Australian media are lovingly obsessed with comparing annual figures from road deaths.

Main **hazards** are fatigue, losing control on dirt roads, and the presence of animals on the road – a serious problem everywhere (not just in the Outback) at dawn, dusk and night-time. Beware of fifty-metre-long **road trains**: these colossal trucks can't stop quickly or pull off the road safely, so if there's the slightest doubt, get out of the way; only overtake a road train if you can see well ahead and are certain that your vehicle can manage it. On dirt roads be doubly cautious, or just pull over and let the road train overtake you.

ROADS, OUTBACK DRIVING AND BREAKDOWNS

Around the cities the only problem you'll face is inept signposting, but interstate main roads – even Highway 1, which circles the country – aren't always great, and some of the minor routes are awful. **Conditions**, especially on unsealed roads, are unpredictable and some roads can be impassable after a storm, so always seek reliable advice (from the local police or a roadhouse) before starting out. Make it clear what sort of vehicle you're driving and remember that their idea of a "good" or "bad" road may be radically different from yours. Some "4WD only" tracks *might* be navigable in lesser transport with a skilled driver – high ground clearance, rather than four driven wheels, is often the crucial factor.

Rain and floods – particularly in the tropics and central Australia – can close roads to all vehicles within minutes, so driving through remote

---

SOME SAFARIS AND ONE-WAY TOURS

Heading Bush (Free call ☎1800/639 933, fax 08/8648 6655; *www.headbush.mtx.net*). Adelaide–Alice Springs in ten days, via Flinders Ranges, Oodnadatta Track, the Simpson Desert, Ayers Rock, the Olgas, Kings Canyon and Alice. Tour operated by Andu Lodge in Quorn (see p.753) and emphasizes Aboriginal heritage. All buses are 4WD, with seating for a maximum of ten people. All meals vegetarian. Departures every Monday; $750. They also offer a 2-day express return to Adelaide for $79, including overnight accommodation in Coober Pedy.

Oz Experience (Sydney ☎02/9368 1766, Australia-wide ☎1300/300 028 *www.ozex.com.au*). Eleven unlimited stop routes which you can follow over six months, including Sydney–Cairns ($295), Cairns–Adelaide ($460), Sydney–Melbourne ($165), Melbourne–Adelaide ($165) and Adelaide–Alice ($215), with plenty of stops at wineries, beaches, national parks and cattle stations. There are four twelve-month passes – $795 for Sydney up the north coast to Cairns then inland to Alice and up to Darwin to $1275 for a complete circuit from Melbourne to Darwin. All routes are indirect and take you to out-of-the-way places. Five percent discount for YHA/VIP cardholders on some services.

Wallaby Tracks Adventure Tours (Free call ☎1800/639 933, fax 08/8648 6655). Pick-up in Adelaide for a three-day Flinders Ranges tour, investigating Aboriginal sites, camping out, and bushwalking around Quorn and Wilpena. Leaves Tuesday; $250. Tour operated by Andu Lodge in Quorn (see p.753).

Wayward Bus (Free call ☎1800/882 823; *www.waywardbus.com.au*). The excellent long established Wayward Bus, based in Adelaide, does a series of one-way and circuit trips in eastern, central Australia and Western Australia. The bus seats twenty people, with the driver acting as your guide, and the price includes transport only – you can choose to stay at hostels, campgrounds or motels en route, depending on your budget. You can hop on and off where you like over a six-month period. Routes include Melbourne–Adelaide via the Great Ocean Road and the Coorong (three days for $150, four days for $200), Adelaide–Perth Outback and coastal camping adventure (twelve days for $840), Sydney and Melbourne via the Blue Mountains, Canberra and the Australian Alps (five days for $190), and Adelaide to Sydney on a "Fruit Bowl" trip aimed at working backpackers, taking in four fruit-growing areas in NSW, Victoria and SA ($190; 4 days). A circuit trip from Sydney to Canberra takes in the Blue Mountains in one direction and the Southern Highlands in the other ($110; 2 days).

regions in the wet season will be prone to delays. Several remote and unsealed roads through central Australia (the Sandover and Plenty highways, the Oodnadatta, Birdsville and Tanami tracks, and others) are theoretically open to all vehicles, but unless you're well equipped with a tough car, don't attempt a crossing during the summer, when extreme temperatures place extra strain on both driver and vehicle.

On **poor roads and dirt tracks**, the rules are to keep your speed down to a maximum of 80kph, stick to the best section and never assume that the road is free from potholes, eroded cattle grids, sand, rocks or oncoming traffic. Long corrugated stretches are a major bugbear and can literally shake the vehicle apart – check radiators and fuel tanks for cracks afterwards; reducing tyre pressures slightly softens the ride but can cause the tyres to overheat at high speeds, making them more prone to punctures. Windscreens are often shattered by flying stones from passing traffic, so slow down and pull over to the left. Fine "bulldust" fills potholes, obscures hazards and invades the car. Dirt tracks are often deeply rutted, and exposed tree roots can burst tyres if you drive over them too fast.

At all times carry plenty of **drinking water, fuel** and food, and tell someone reliable your timetable, route and destination, so that a rescue can be organized if you don't report in. Carry a detailed, recent **map** and don't count on finding regular signposts. In the event of a **breakdown** in the Outback, always stay with your vehicle: it's visible to potential rescuers and you can use it for shade; in any case, you risk finding it stripped when you return with a tow truck if you're stranded on an isolated road. As a last resort, burn a tyre – the black smoke will be distinctive from the average bushfire.

CAR RENTAL

To **rent** a car you need a full, clean driver's licence; usually, a minimum age of 21 is stipulated by the major car-rental companies, rising to 25 for 4WDs. Check on any mileage limits or other restrictions, extras, and what you're covered for in an accident, before signing. The multinational operators Hertz, Budget, Avis and Thrifty have offices in the major cities, but outside the big cities lack of competition makes their **standard rates** expensive at $70–90 a day for a sedan; long-term rental, specials and even plain bargaining can bring this down to a more affordable level. National has offices in Melbourne, Brisbane, Cairns, the Gold Coast and Surfers Paradise, and Holiday has several branches throughout the country. **Local firms** – of which there are many in the cities – are almost always better value, and the bottom-line "rent-a-bomb" agencies go as low as $12 a day; however, these places often have restrictions on how far away from base you're allowed to go. **One-way rental** might appear handy, but is usually very expensive: at least $200 extra for the drop-off fee. If you're simply trying to get from one place to another, you could try offering to **relocate** any vehicles they may have from other cities (ie returning someone else's one-way). They'll have regular drivers to do this, but being politely persuasive and claiming previous experience might get you massive reductions. As a rule, cars are needed in the southern cities as the Wet hits the tropics towards the end of the year. For more advice, see the box on p.37. From New Zealand, pre-booking a rental car will cost you at least NZ$280 per week, including insurance and tax – though rates will be considerably higher than this away from the main cities. However, you may get a cheaper deal during slack periods or as part of a fly-drive package (see p.8). To reserve a rental car from the UK, USA or Canada, contact the companies listed in the box on p.37.

Four-wheel drives are best used for specific areas rather than long term, as rental costs are steep, starting at around $100 a day. Some 4WD agents actually don't allow their vehicles to be driven off sealed roads, so check the fine print first. An increasing number of places offer **campervans** and **motor homes** to rent, and with fierce competition prices start at around $80 a day with unlimited kilometres – amazing value when you consider the independence, comfort and the saving on accommodation charges. Although, like cars, they are limited to sealed roads, campervans give you the chance to create your own tour of a lifetime across Australia. Their only drawback is that you can get pretty cranky spending all day *and* all night in the same compact vehicle; raised-roof or poptop models are more tolerable (as is the occasional night in a motel). Remember, too, that the sleeping capacity stated in the adverts (especially on the larger vehicles) is an absolute maximum, which you wouldn't want to endure for too long.

FOUR-WHEEL DRIVING SOME HINTS

The Outback is not the place to learn how to handle a 4WD, and you should know what you're doing before disappearing off the map. Many novice four-wheel drivers assume that their vehicles are unstoppable, all-terrain machines and soon get stuck through lack of technique and experience. In addition to the **spares** listed on p.00, you'll want a shovel, hi-lift jack and gloves. In addition to the many "how to" manuals easily found in bookshops, try and get a copy of *Off Road Sense* produced by Dunlop (Dunlop Tyres, PO Box 100, Port Melbourne, VIC 3207). This illustrated booklet clearly spells out the practicalities of off-road driving without confusing the beginner with technical jargon. If you're planning a long off-road tour, *Explore Australia by Four-Wheel Drive* (Viking) will suit recreational drivers. In remote areas you may want to rent a **two-way HF radio** tuned to the Royal Flying Doctor Service – contact the state motoring association or National Parks and Wildlife Service for details. The following basic hints should help; see also the advice on creek crossings on p.469.

• Be aware of your limitations, and those of your vehicle.
• Know how to operate everything – including how to change a tyre – *before* you need it.
• Always cross rivers and very sandy or muddy sections on foot first.
• Don't persevere if you're stuck – avoid wheel spin and reverse out.
• Reducing tyre pressure by up to seventy per cent dramatically increases traction in mud or sand, but risks punctures and causes over heating at higher road speeds.

• If stuck, clear all the wheels with a shovel, create a shallow ramp (again, for *all* wheels), engage four-wheel-drive and lower tyre pressures if necessary, and drive out in low-range second or third gear.
• Keep to tracks – avoid unnecessary damage to the environment.
• Driving on beaches can be great fun, but treacherous – observe other vehicles' tracks and be aware of tidal patterns.

BUYING A CAR

Buying a used vehicle needn't be an expensive business and a well-kept car should resell at about two-thirds of the purchase price at the end of your trip – if you're lucky, or a skilful negotiator, you might even make a profit.

If you don't know your axle from your big end, **car yards** can save you a lot of hassle and provide welcome advice: in Sydney, they're the most common place to buy a used vehicle, and some even cater specifically to travellers (see p.164). Assuming you have a little time and some mechanical knowledge, however, you'll save money by buying **privately**; unless you're returning to your starting point, a **buy-back guarantee** (offered by some car yards and dealers) is usually a guarantee to pay you a fraction of the car's potential value. Adverts in the local newspapers and hostel notice boards in main exit points from Australia are the best places to start. One of the great advantages of buying from a **fellow traveller** is that you might get all sorts of gear thrown in – jerrycans, camping gear and many of the spares listed on pp.37–38. The disadvantage is that the car may have had a hard life circumnavi-

gating the country while being maintained on a backpacker's budget.

A thorough **inspection** is worthwhile. **Rust** is one thing to watch for, especially in the tropics where humidity and salt air will turn scratches to holes within weeks – look out for poorly patched bodywork. Take cars for a spin and check the engine, gearbox, clutch and brakes for operation, unusual noises, vibration and leaks; repairs on some of these parts can be costly. Don't expect perfection, though: worn brakes and tyres, grating wheel bearings and defective batteries can be fixed inexpensively. If repairs are needed, it gives you a good excuse to haggle over the price. All **tyres** should be the same type and size, especially on 4WDs. If you lack faith in your own abilities, the various state automobile associations offer rigorous **pre-purchase inspections** for about $90 – not too much to pay if it saves you from buying a wreck.

If you're buying privately (or from an unscrupulous dealer) you should also check the requirements of the state transport department: in most states you'll need a **roadworthiness certificate** to have the vehicle transferred from its previous owner's name to yours. This means having a garage check it over; legally, the previous owner should do this, and theoretically it guarantees that the car is mechanically sound – but don't rely on it. You then proceed to the local Department of Transport with the certificate, a receipt, your driver's licence and passport; they charge a percentage of the price as stated on the receipt to register the vehicle in your name.

If the annual **vehicle registration** is due, or you bought an interstate or deregistered vehicle ("as is", without number plates), you'll have to pay extra for registration, which is dependent on the engine size and runs into hundreds of dollars. Note that cars with interstate registration can be difficult to sell: if possible, go for a car with the registration of the state where you anticipate selling. Registration includes the legal minimum third-party personal **insurance**, but you might want to increase this cover to protect you against theft of the vehicle (for around $70), or if you've bought something more flash go the whole way with comprehensive motor insurance. Joining one

of the **automobile clubs** for another $50 or so is well worth considering for peace of mind. Each state has their own, but membership is reciprocal with overseas equivalents: you also get benefits such as free or discounted maps.

EQUIPPING YOUR CAR

Even if you expect to stick mostly to the main highways, you'll need to carry a fair number of **spares**: there are plenty of very isolated spots, even between Sydney and Melbourne. A proper tow rope is vital; passing motorists are far cheaper than tow trucks. In addition – and especially if your vehicle is past its prime – you should have a set of spark plugs, points, fuses, fuel filters (for diesels), fuel lines, fan belt and radiator hoses – you need to check all these anyway and might want to replace them as a matter of course and keep the originals as backups. A selection of hose clamps, radiator sealant, putty for leaking tanks, water-dispersing spray, jump leads and a board to support the jack on soft ground may also come in handy. Again, if the car is old, establish its engine

---

RENTAL RESERVATIONS

CARS

UK

Avis ☎0990/900500
fax 0134/4485616

Budget ☎0800/181181
fax 01442/276044

Hertz ☎0990/996699
fax 0161/4989325

Holiday Autos ☎0990/300405
fax 300445

USA AND CANADA

Avis ☎1-800/331-1084
Budget ☎1-800/527-0700
Hertz ☎1-800/654-3001;
Kemwel Holiday Autos ☎1-800/422-7737
National ☎1-800/CAR-RENT

NEW ZEALAND

Avis ☎09/526 2847
Budget ☎09/375 2222

CAMPERVANS AND MOTOR HOMES

Britz Australia (in the UK ☎0990/143609, fax 0990168309, *info@britz.com.au*; in Australia ☎03/9483 1888; fax 9416 2933; *www.britz.com*). Long-established, German-owned company whose high-roofed Land Cruisers are a common sight all around the country. These 4WD models are well equipped, with long-range tanks and even a kitchen sink, but leaf-sprung suspension can be tiring. Also rents out Koala campervans and motor homes holding from two to six people.

Budget Campervan Rentals (in Australia ☎03/9483 1849, fax 9416 2933). Chasing Britz

Australia's lead with a similar range of well-equipped vehicles.

NQ Rentals (in the UK ☎0181/715 1590, fax 715 1591; in Australia ☎07/7053 1875, fax 7032 2068, free call ☎1800/899 558; *www.campervansaust.com.au*). A Cairns-based campervan company with agents in all major mainland cities. Vans from $80 a day, motor homes $150 a day.

Branches of the big chains and local firms are detailed in "Listings" sections throughout the guide.

oil consumption early on; a car can carry on for thousands of kilometres guzzling oil at an alarming rate, and if the level drops too much the engine is ruined. If you're confident, get a *Gregory's* workshop manual for your vehicle; even if you're not, carry these spares anyway – someone who knows how to use them might stop. Whatever else, always carry **jerrycans** with enough water and fuel to get you to the next garage after a mishap. For ordinary cars, the cheapest place to **buy spares** is at a supermarket – head for the racks of any branch of K-Mart or Coles.

Before you set off, check battery terminals for corrosion, and the battery for charge – buy a new one if necessary; don't risk money on a secondhand item. Carry *two* spare tyres; **off-road drivers** in remote regions should add to the list a puncture repair kit, bead breaker and tubes – and know how to use them. Keeping tyres at the correct pressure and having a wheel balance/alignment will cut down wear. Change the oil and filter, clean or replace the air filter and check the radiator for coolant/antifreeze.

MOTORBIKING

Motorbikes, especially large-capacity trail bikes, are perfect for the Australian climate and an inexpensive compromise between conventional vehicles and 4WDs, although long distances place a premium on their comfort and fuel range. Mid-1980s 600cc Japanese trail bikes, such as **Yamaha**'s trendsetting XT600 Ténéré, sell for around $3000 and allow 100kph on-road cruising with adequate off-road agility and readily available spares. A **Honda** XL600V Transalp is much more comfortable on the road and OK on gravel. The choice of tyres is crucial to off-road performance. Pirelli MT21 tyres are widely regarded as the best-compromise tyre for road and track, but always carry a complete puncture repair kit and a spare tube – and know how to use them. The *Adventure Motorbiking Handbook* (Compass Star) is a definitive manual to motorbiking off the beaten track and includes a regional rundown of Australia's Outback biking highlights.

If it's likely that you'll return to your starting point, look out for dealers offering **buy-back** options, which guarantee a resale at the end of your trip; bikes can be more difficult to sell than cars. You're going to need a helmet and, especially if you're heading **off-road**, plenty of water-carrying capacity. It's also essential that you know what you're doing: the Outback is not somewhere you can afford to have things go wrong. Travelling alone can be risky, and **night-riding** is plain dangerous, with poor surfaces hard to judge and kangaroos liable to bounce out of nowhere.

Motorbike **rental** – usually available only in the cities – is expensive: at least the same price

---

BEST SECONDHAND BUYS

Big-engined, mid-1970s or later, Holden Kingswood or Ford Falcon station wagons are the **ideal travellers' cars**: roomy, reliable, mechanically simple and durable, with spares available in just about any city supermarket, roadhouse or wrecker's yard. At the bottom end, **$1000** plus some luck should find you some kind of old car that runs reliably. Chances are, if a vehicle has survived this long, there's nothing seriously wrong with it and you should be able to nurse it through a bit further. Also, real bargains can be secured from travellers desperate to get rid of their vehicle before flying out. Ideally, though, you should plan to pay at least **$4000** in total for a sound, fully prepared and equipped vehicle. Manual transmission models are more economical than automatic, with the four-speed versions superior to the awkward, three-speed, steering-column-mounted models. Smaller and less robust, but much more economical to run, are old Toyota Corollas or other Japanese station wagons, suitable for one or two people travelling light.

Four-wheel drives are expensive, and, with poor fuel economy and higher running costs, worth it only if you have some serious off-roading planned. Toyota FJ or HJ Land Cruisers are Outback legends, especially the long-wheelbase (LWB) models: tough, reliable and with plenty of new and used spares all over the country. If nothing goes wrong, a **diesel** (HJ) is preferable to a **petrol** (FJ) engine, being sturdier and more economical – although all Toyota engines, particularly the six-cylinder FJs, seem to keep on running, even if totally clapped-out. The trouble with diesels is that problems, when they occur, tend to be serious and repairs expensive; also, lower revs mean slower acceleration which can cause a problem in mud or going up hills. Generally, you're looking at **$6000–12,000** for a reliable twelve-year-old model.

MOTORCYCLING IN AUSTRALIA: USEFUL WEB SITES

Honda V-twins Adventure Club
www.geocities.com/MotorCity/Track/4459/
Australian-based club dealing with Africa Twins, Transalps and the little known 750 XLVs. If you own or are interested in these Hondas – a good choice for smooth adventuring, the way singles never are – pay them a visit. Plenty of links to other Australian sites too.

Adventure Motorbiking web site
www.compass-star.co.uk/AMW.htm

Complements the *Adventure Motorbiking Handbook* with regular updates and many links, but not Australia specific.

Australian Rides
www.smople.thehub.com.au/~adm/aml/html/rides.html
Homepage with state by state rundown of roads and highlights. Good overview for those thinking of riding down under.

as a car. A better alternative is a **motorbike tour**: these take various forms, from ones where you provide the bike and the tour consists of an itinerary, company on the road and a support vehicle (check out the bimonthly *Side Track* magazine once in Australia), to a quick blast on the back of a Harley Davidson (see "Listings" section throughout the guide for details of operators).

CYCLING

Cycling, and especially cycle-racing, is popular in Australia, and even if you're not a triathlete bent on pedalling between Sydney and Perth, bicycles are easily ferried between the places where you'd want to use them. Mountain bikes are ideal for rougher country, but lighter and more efficient tourers are better if you're attempting any long-distance travel on main roads. Most cities have well-defined cycle routes and bike lanes; helmets are compulsory, though the law is not always enforced in rural areas. **Renting** and finding **spares** is no trouble in capital cities and larger country towns.

If you're **bringing your own** bike, international airlines usually overlook the odd extra kilo if the bike is properly packaged; ask first – though it's often the airport check-in counter which has the last word. On **internal flights** you'll need to have the handlebars and pedals turned in, the front wheel removed and strapped to the back, and the tyres deflated; some airlines consider bikes as two pieces of excess baggage and charge accordingly (excess baggage is usually insured against damage up to a maximum of $1600 damages, so you might want to extend this). **Trains** have fixed rates for carrying bikes (depending on the route) and you'll save on **bus** charges by disassembling and packing your bike

flat. See "Books" (p.1020) for specialist guides to cycling in Australia.

HITCHING

Recent events – primarily the 1992 "backpacker murders" – have drastically changed Australian attitudes to hitching. The gruesome murders attracted worldwide publicity, both for their shock value and for the seemingly indiscriminate choice of victims: men and couples seemed as likely a target as lone women, allaying several hitchhiking myths. The official advice is **don't**: with so many affordable forms of transport available, there's no real need to take the risk.

If you must do it, never hitch **alone**, and always avoid being dropped in the middle of nowhere between settlements. In rural areas people seem more willing to stop, but long, isolated stretches of road don't make this the safest country to hitch in; as usual, **women** are at greatest risk. Remember that you don't have to get into a vehicle just because it stops: choose who to get in with and don't be afraid to ask questions before you do get in, making the arrangement clear from the start. Ask the driver where he or she is going rather than saying where you want to go. Try to keep your pack with you; having it locked in the boot makes a quick escape more difficult.

A much better method is lining up lifts through **hostel notice boards** (though this means sharing fuel costs). This option gives you the chance to meet the driver in advance, and – as a fellow traveller – he or she will most likely be stopping to see many of the same sights along the way. In out-of-the-way locations, roadhouses are a good place to head, as the owners often know of people who'll be heading your way.

The best way to ensure your **safety**, apart from exercising your judgement and common sense, is to make concrete arrangements before your departure and stick to them. Hostel managers are well aware of the possible danger to young women departing across the Outback with new acquaintances or undertaking work on remote stations, and will gladly receive – or better still – make calls to ensure your safe arrival.

ACCOMMODATION

Australians love to move around, and finding somewhere to bed down is rarely a problem, even in the smallest of places. However, on the east coast it's a good idea to book ahead for Christmas and Easter holidays, and in some places (the Gold Coast for instance) there are price rises and room shortages even at weekends.

Watch out for the term "**hotel**", which does not necessarily mean the same in Australia as it does everywhere else in the world. Traditionally, an Australian hotel was a place to drink – a pub – and although they were legally required to provide somewhere for customers to sleep off a skinful, the accommodation was not necessarily salubrious. Today, plenty of hotels have cleaned up their act and do offer pleasant rooms; these are the ones highlighted in this guide. However, the majority of them are still primarily places to drink, can be loud and drunken, and are not necessarily enticing places to stay.

The other side of this coin is that many places that would call themselves hotels anywhere else prefer to use another name – hence the reason for so many **motels** and **resorts**, and in the cities "**private hotels**" or (especially in Sydney) "**bou-**

tique hotels" that tend to be smaller and more characterful places to stay – more like guest-houses than hotels. There are also a growing number of **bed and breakfast** places (B&Bs) and **farmstays** where you can join in with farm life.

Other categories of accommodation worth looking into are the huge array of excellent **hostels** and "**backpackers**", **caravan parks** that offer accommodation in the form of permanent on-site vans and cabins or chalets as well as campervan facilities and tent spaces, and **self-catering apartments** or, in country areas, cabins and cottages.

HOTELS AND MOTELS

Cheaper Australian **hotels** are generally pubs offering only rudimentary lodgings. On the downside, rooms tend to be basic – no TV, and shared bathrooms and plain furnishings – and aren't always the best choice for peace and quiet. In country areas hotels are often the social centre of town, especially on Friday and Saturday nights. But with double rooms at around $30–50 and singles at $20–35 (often with breakfast included), for two or more people sharing they can be better value – and more private – than hostel accommodation; many now also offer special **backpacker deals** in newly kitted-out dorms. **Motels** are typically a comfortable, bland choice, often found on the edge of town to catch weary drivers, and priced on average at $50–70 for a double room with TV and bath, not including breakfast. They rarely have single rooms, but they may have larger units for families, often with basic cooking facilities.

In cities, you're far more likely to come across a hotel in the conventional sense. The cheaper of these may well describe themselves as "**private hotels**" to distinguish themselves from pubs, the decisive factor being the absence of a public bar. Some of these, especially in inner cities, can be rather sleazy, but others are very pleasant, family-run guesthouses. Double rooms might cost anything from $35 to $70, and there are often singles available at about two-thirds of this price. More expensive hotels are much as you'd expect: in the cities most of them are standard places with all the usual facilities, aimed at the business community; in resorts and tourist areas they're more like upmarket motels. Prices might be anything from $70 to $300 or more in five-star establishments: a typical city three-star will probably cost you $100–150. Similar places in a resort or country area charge $80–120.

There are numerous nationwide hotel and motel chains that give certain guarantees of standards, among them familiar names such as Best Western and Travelodge, as well as Australian ones such as Budget, Golden Chain and Flag. All have directories of their members, which you can use to plan ahead. Flag goes one further, with a discounted **hotel pass** (sold outside Australia only) – actually pre-paid vouchers in one of six categories for Flag's four hundred or so properties across the country. While you might find it rather restrictive to use them for your whole stay, they offer good value and can be used to ensure that you have a reservation on arrival, or at anywhere else you know you'll be spending some time.

RESORTS AND SELF-CATERING UNITS

You'll find establishments calling themselves **resorts** all over Australia, but the term is not a very clearly defined one. At the bottom end, price, appearance and facilities may be little different to those of a motel, while top-flight places can be exclusive hideaways costing hundreds of dollars a night. Originally the name implied that the price

was all-inclusive of accommodation, drinks, meals, sports and anything else on offer, but this isn't always the case. These places tend to be set in picturesque locations – the Barrier Reef islands swarm with them – and are often brilliant value if you can wangle a stand-by or off-season price.

Self-catering or self-contained **units**, **apartments** or **country cabins** can be a very good deal for families and larger groups. The places themselves range from larger units at a motel to purpose-built apartment hotels, but are usually excellent value. Cooking facilities are variable, but there'll always be a TV and fridge; linen (generally not included) can sometimes be rented for a small extra charge.

FARMSTAYS AND BED & BREAKFAST

Another option in rural areas are **farmstays** on working farms and **B&Bs** or **guesthouses**, the last two predominantly in the south and east. Both offer a more homely atmosphere, though B&Bs especially can be anything from someone's large home to your own colonial cottage – ask what the "breakfast" actually includes. Farmstays are even more variable, with some offering very upmarket comforts while at others you make do with the basic facilities in vacant shearers' quarters; their attraction is that they are always in out-of-the-way locations, and you'll often get a chance to participate in the working of the farm, or take advantage of guided tours around the property on horseback or 4WD.

HOSTELS

There's a huge amount of **budget accommodation** in Australia, and though the more shambolic

---

ACCOMMODATION PRICES

All the accommodation listed in this book has been categorized into one of eight price bands, as set out below. Apart from band ①, these represent the cost of the cheapest available double or twin room in **high season**; single rooms are generally about two-thirds the price of doubles. However, there's a variety of different types of accommodation on offer – sometimes under the same roof: band ① is used only for hostels and backpackers' accommodation, where it refers to a bed in a dorm; for units, cabins and vans the code covers the cost of the entire unit, which may sleep as many as six people.

In the lower categories, most rooms will be without private bath, though there's usually a washbasin in the room. From band ⑤ upwards you'll probably have private facilities. Remember that many of the cheaper places may also have more expensive rooms with en-suite facilities.

① Under $18	⑤ $61–74
② $19–30	⑥ $75–94
③ $31–45	⑦ $95–124
④ $46–60	⑧ $125 upwards

YHA, VIP AND NOMAD PASSES

If you're travelling on a budget, it's well worth laying your hands on an **International YHA card** (purchased from your national youth hostel association before you leave home, or available in Australia from $44). The other option is a **VIP card** (the Backpacker Resorts equivalent) or a Nomads **Dreamtime card**, either of which costs $25 from member hostels. Both of these give you members' rates on accommodation at participating hostels – usually ten percent off – and also entitle you to a wide range of other **discounts**, on everything from bus tickets and tours to phone calls, museum entry fees and meals. After joining, all three organizations will provide directories of participating accommodation and services. You can get the latest information on VIP via their Web site: *www.backpackers.com.au*.

operations don't survive for long, standards are still variable. Official YHA **youth hostels** are pretty dependable, and many of their depressingly regimented rules and regulations have been dropped in the face of competition, especially from the firmly established **Backpacker Resorts/VIP** network and **Nomads**, whose **membership cards** are as useful and widely known as the YHA equivalent.

At their best, **hostels and backpackers' accommodation** – both names are widely used, and don't necessarily imply membership of any organization – are excellent value and are good places to meet other travellers and plug into the grapevine. There's often a choice of dormitories, double or family rooms, plus bike rental, kitchen,

games room, TV, a pool, and help with finding work or organizing trips. Many have useful noticeboards, organized activities and tours. At their worst, their double rooms might be poorer value than local hotel accommodation, and some are simply grubby, rapid-turnover dives – affiliation to an organization does not ensure quality.

Most hostels provide blankets, but they don't always include **sheets**; you usually pay extra to rent them, so it's a wise precaution to carry a sheet sleeping bag. Expect to pay between $15 and $20 a night for a bed in a dorm, or $30 to $40 for a double room.

CAMPING, CARAVAN PARKS AND ROADHOUSES

Perhaps because Australian hostels are so widespread and inexpensive, simple tent **camping** is an option little-used by foreign travellers. Australia has some remarkably hard ground, so vital **equipment** includes ground mats and a range of pegs – some wide for sand, others narrow for soil. A hatchet for splitting firewood is light to carry and doubles as a hammer. Fuel stoves are recommended, but if you do build a fire, make sure it doesn't get out of control – and always observe any fire bans. In national parks, **bushcamping** is often the only option for staying overnight: some park sites have hot showers, drinking water and toilets; others provide absolutely nothing. Prices depend on state policy and site facilities, and you'll usually need a permit from the local NPWS (National Parks and Wildlife Service) office, details of which are given throughout the guide.

Camping rough by the road is not a good idea, even if you take the usual precautions of

YOUTH HOSTELS ASSOCIATIONS

England and Wales Youth Hostels Association (YHA), Trevelyan House, 8 St Stephen's Hill, St Albans, Herts AL1 2DY (☎01727/845047). London shop and information office: 14 Southampton St, London WC2E 7HY (☎0171/379 0597).

Northern Ireland Belfast International Youth Hostel, 22–33 Donegall Rd, Belfast BT12 5JN (☎01232/324733).

Scotland Scottish Youth Hostels Association, 7 Glebe Crescent, Stirling FK8 2JA (☎01786/891 400).

Ireland An Óige, 61 Mountjoy Square, Dublin 1 (☎01/830 4555).

US Hostelling International-American Youth Hostels (HI-AYH), 733 15th St NW, Suite 840, PO Box 37613, Washington, DC 20005 (☎202/783 6161; *www.hiayh.org*).

Canada Hostelling International/Canadian Hostelling Association, Room 400, 205 Catherine St, Ottawa, ON K2P 1C3 (☎613/237-7884 or 1-800/663-5777).

Australia Australian Youth Hostels Association, Level 3, 10 Mallet St, Camperdown, NSW 2050 (☎02/9565 1325).

New Zealand Youth Hostels Association of New Zealand, PO Box 436, Christchurch 1 (☎03/379 9970).

setting up away from the roadside and avoiding dry riverbeds. If you have to do it, try and ensure you're not too visible: having a group of drunks pitch into your camp at midnight is not an enjoyable experience. Animals are unlikely to pose a threat, except to your food – keep it in your tent or a secure container, or be prepared to be woken by their nocturnal shenanigans.

In towns, there's often a choice between basic **council campsites** and better **caravan parks**, which will not only have space to pitch a tent but will also have hook-up facilities for campervans and probably a store; some even offer pools and all the facilities of a mini-resort. Many have **on-site vans** (caravans with cooking facilities but no toilet) or **cabins** (with bath or shower and often a TV): these can be very good value and are often available even when all the hotel and motel rooms have been filled up. The main problem is that linen – sheets, towels, etc – is usually not included, though you may be able to rent it. Expect to pay between $3–10 for an unpowered site, or upwards of $15 per person for a van or cabin. Highway **roadhouses** are similar, combining a range of accommodation with fuel and restaurants for long-distance travellers.

FOOD AND DRINK

Australia is almost two separate nations when it comes to food. In the cities of the southeast – especially Melbourne – there's a range of fantastic, cosmopolitan and inexpensive restaurants and cafés featuring almost every imaginable cuisine. Here there's an exceptionally high ratio of eating places to people, and they survive because people eat out so much – three times a week is not unusual. Remote country areas are the complete antithesis of this, where the only thing better than meat pies and microwaveable fast food are the plain, unexciting counter meals served at the local hotel or – if you're lucky – a slightly more upmarket bistro or basic Chinese restaurant.

Traditionally, Australian food found its roots in the English overcooked-meat-and-three-veg "common-sense cookery" mould. Two things have rescued the country from its culinary destitution: immigration and an extraordinary range of superb, locally produced fresh ingredients that not even the most ham-fisted chef could ruin. Various ethnic cuisines are briefly discussed below, but in addition to introducing their own cuisine, immigrants have had at least as profound an effect on mainstream Australian food. "Contemporary Australian" cuisine is an exciting blend of tastes and influences from around the world – particularly Asia and the Mediterranean – and many not specifically "ethnic" restaurants will have a menu that includes properly prepared curry, dolmades and fettuccini alongside steak and prawns. This healthy, eclectic – and above all, fresh – modern Australian cuisine has a lot in common with Californian cooking styles, and both go under the latest trendy banner of "Pacific Rim cuisine".

AUSTRALIAN FOOD

Meat is plentiful, cheap and excellent: steak forms the mainstay of the pub counter meal and of the ubiquitous **"barbie"**, or barbecue – as Australian an institution as you could hope to find. Even if no one invites you along to one, you can still enjoy a barbie: free or coin-operated electric barbecues can be found in car parks,

INFAMOUS AUSTRALIAN FOODS AND "ESKY"

Damper Sounding positively wholesome in this company, "damper" is the swagman's staple – soda bread baked in a pot buried in the ashes of a fire. It's not hard to make after a few attempts – the secret is in the heat of the coals and a splash of beer.

Lamington A chocolate-coated sponge cake rolled in shredded coconut.

Pavlova (pav) A dessert concoction of meringue with layers of cream and fruit; named after the eminent Russian ballerina.

Pie floater The apotheosis of the meat pie; a "pie floater" is an inverted meat pie swamped in mashed green peas and tomato sauce; found especially in Queensland and South Australia.

Vegemite Regarded by the English as an inferior form of Marmite and by almost every other

nationality with total bemusement, Vegemite is an Australian institution – a strong, dark, yeast spread for bread and toast.

Witchetty (witjuti) grubs About the size of your little finger, witchetty grubs are dug from the roots of mulga trees and are a well-known Australian bush delicacy. Eating the plump, fawn-coloured caterpillars live (as is traditional) takes some nerve, so try giving them a brief roasting in embers. They're very tasty either way – reminiscent of peanut butter.

Esky Eskies are insulated food containers varying from handy "six-pack" sizes to cavernous sixty-litre trunks capable of refrigerating a weekend's worth of food or beer. No barbie or camping trip is complete without a couple of eskies. The brand name "Esky" has been adopted to describe all similar products.

campsites and beauty spots all over the country. As well as beef and lamb, you may also find **exotic meats**, especially in the more upmarket restaurants. Emu, buffalo, camel and witchetty grubs are all served, but the two most common are **kangaroo**, a delicious, tender and virtually fat-free meat, and **crocodile**, which tastes like a mix of chicken and pork and is at its best when simply grilled. At the coast, and elsewhere in specialist restaurants, there's tremendous **seafood** too: prawns and oysters, mud crabs, Moreton Bay bugs and yabbies (sea- and freshwater crayfish), lobsters, and a wide variety of fresh- and seawater fish – barramundi has a reputation as one of the finest.

Fruit is good, too, from Tasmanian apples and pears to tropical bananas, pawpaw (papaya), mangoes, avocados, citrus fruits, custard apples, lychees, pineapples, passion fruit, star fruit and coconuts – few of them native, but delicious nonetheless. **Vegetables** are also fresh, cheap and good; note that aubergine is known as eggplant, courgettes as zucchini and red or green peppers as capsicums.

Vegetarians might assume that they'll face a narrow choice of food in "meatocentric" Australia, and in the country areas that's probably true. But elsewhere most restaurants will have one vegetarian option at least, and in the cities veggie cafés have cultivated a wholesome, trendy image that suits Australians' active, health-conscious nature.

ETHNIC FOOD

Since World War II wave after wave of immigrants have brought a huge variety of **ethnic cuisines** to Australia: first North European, then Mediterranean and most recently Asian.

CHINESE

Chinese restaurants were on the scene early in Australia – a result of post-goldrush Chinese enterprise – and Sydney, Melbourne and Darwin have Chinese connections dating back to the 1850s. The Chinese restaurants you'll find in most of the country tend to be rather old-fashioned and heavily reliant on MSG, but they're often the only alternative to Australian food. In contrast, the Chinatown area of big cities will provide a chance to sample some regional Chinese dishes as well as the usual Cantonese fare.

Two specialities served in Chinese restaurants are **yum cha** (or dim sum), lots of little titbits such as steamed buns and dumplings served from trolleys; and **steamboat**, an Asian version of fondue. Both are tasty and extremely good value for money – especially for a group.

OTHER ASIAN CUISINES

Since the 1970s a new wave of immigrants from Southeast Asia has further energized Australian cuisine. **Vietnamese** restaurants not only offer some of the cheapest meals anywhere but also combine fresh ingredients with sophisticated French influences from colonial days; with your meal comes a plate of red chillies, lemon wedges and crunchy beansprouts.

There are numerous **Malaysian** and **Indonesian** restaurants and market stalls, where hearty noodle soups and satays with hot peanut sauce are served up. Hawker-style stalls in city food courts often serve laksa, a huge bowl of hot and spicy coconut-milk-based soup full of noodles, tofu and chicken or prawns.

The biggest success of them all, however, are the **Thai** restaurants, and it's hard to believe that they've been around for less than fifteen years. Dishes can be fiery, yet subtly flavoured, with ingredients such as basil, lemongrass, garlic, chilli and coriander.

Because so much fresh seafood is available in Australia, **Japanese** food is more accessible – and less expensive – that it is in many other countries. There may not be a large Japanese population, but there are a huge number of Japanese visitors – and plenty of places catering for them (you'll find lots on the Gold Coast, for example).

Mongolian barbecues sound like a short-lived novelty but in fact are quite good: an unusual, fast and inexpensive complement to the already diverse Asian food culture. Thinly sliced meat or seafood is added to a selection of sliced vegetables and stir-fried in a soy-type sauce before your eyes on a giant wok – a Mongol warrior's shield is said to have been the original cooking utensil.

ITALIAN – AND COFFEE

The **Italian** influence on Australian cooking has been enormous. Second in number only to the English as an ethnic group, the Italians brought with them their love of food, which was a perfect complement to the Australian climate and way of life, and from the 1950s pizzerias, espresso and *gelati* bars, and the then-exotic taste of garlic,

BUSH TUCKER

The first European colonists decided that the country was not "owned" by the Aborigines because they didn't systematically farm the land. As many frustrated pastoralists later came to realize, the Aboriginal way of life was the best suited to Australia's erratic seasons, which don't lend themselves to European farming methods with any degree of long-term security. Instead, Aborigines followed a nomadic lifestyle within extensive tribal boundaries, following seasonal game and plants and promoting both by annually burning off grassland.

Along the coast people speared turtles and dugong from outrigger canoes, caught fish in stone traps, piled oyster shells into giant middens, and even co-operated with dolphins to herd fish into shallows. Other **animals** caught all over the country were possums, snakes (highly prized), goannas, emus and kangaroos. These animals were thrown straight onto a fire and cooked in their own juices, and their skins, bones and fat were sometimes used as clothing, tools and ointment respectively. More meagre pickings were provided by honey and green ants, water-holding frogs, moths and various grubs – the witchetty (or *witjuti*) being the best known. Foot-long ooli worms were drawn out of rotten mangrove trunks and tiny native bees were tagged with strands of spider web and then followed to their hives for honey; another sweet treat was mulga resin, picked off the tree trunk.

Plants, usually gathered by women, were used extensively and formed the bulk of the diet. The cabbage palm, sea almond, mangrove seeds, pandanus and dozens of fruits, including tropical coconuts, plums and figs, all grew along the coast. Inland were samphire bush, wild tomatoes and "citrus", grasstree hearts, cycad nuts (very toxic until washed, but high in starch), native millet, wattle seeds, waterlily tubers, *nardoo* seeds (a water fern), fungi, macadamia nuts, quandongs, and bunya pine nuts – the last had great social importance in southern Queensland, where they were eaten at huge feasts. In Queensland's far north you'll find one of the few surviving traditional styles of cooking, the Torres Strait Islander *kup maori* – meat and vegetables wrapped in banana leaves and roasted in an underground oven.

It's tempting to **taste** some bush foods, and a few outlets (see *Koori Gugidjela Restaurant* in the Grampians, p.864) are now experimenting with them as ingredients; otherwise you'll need expert guidance, as many plants are poisonous. A few tours and safaris (particularly in the Northern Territory) give an introduction to living off the land; for further reading, try *Bush Tucker: Australia's Wild Food Harvest* by Tim Low (Angus & Robertson Aus).

were conquering palates countrywide. One particularly Australian metamorphosis is **focaccia**, now a staple of every city café and even beginning to make an appearance in country towns. A flat bread with a nubbly golden top, it's cut horizontally, filled and then toasted to make a delicious sandwich.

Australia can also thank the Italians for elevating **coffee** to a pastime rather than just a hot drink. Nowadays every suburban café has an espresso machine, and it's not just used to make cappuccino. Other **styles of coffee** have adopted uniquely Australian names: a "flat white" is a plain white coffee, a "cafe latte" is a milkier version usually served in a glass (like cappuccino without the froth), a "long black" is a regular cup of black coffee, and a "short black" is an espresso – transformed by a splash of milk into a *macchiato*. A cappuccino costs around $2 to $2.50.

OTHER EUROPEAN AND MIDDLE EASTERN

Melbourne is Australia's food capital, with its legendary **Greek** population among the many European influences in the city. As well as taverna-style Greek restaurants, souvlaki/bars, with spiced lamb rotating on a spit, abound. **Turkish** and **Lebanese** takeaways use a similar ingredient for their spicy filled rolls, while some Turkish places also offer *pides*, small, simple but spicy variants on a pizza. Lebanese restaurants are especially good for **vegetarians**, with falafel rolls (pitta bread stuffed with chickpea patties, hoummous and tabbouleh) making an inexpensive, filling meal.

Central European influences are most obvious in baking, particularly in Melbourne, where there is a large **Jewish** community made up of immigrants from prewar Poland, and there are also a few **Polish** restaurants serving solid, peasant-style dishes. **German** influences are most prominent around Adelaide – as well as at deli counters throughout the country, where you'll find an abundance of Australian-made salamis and sausages.

PLACES TO EAT

Restaurants are astonishingly good value compared with Britain and North America, particularly as many restaurants are **BYO** (bring your own): you buy your own wine or beer and bring it with you – you're rarely far from a bottle shop (the Australian term for an off-licence or liquor store). There may be a small corkage fee, but it's still better than paying inflated restaurant prices for your

drink: even many licensed restaurants also allow you to BYO. You should have no problem finding an excellent two- or three-course meal in a BYO restaurant for $20 or less, though a main course at a moderate restaurant is around $14–18. There are also lots of excellent **cafés and coffee shops** – Italian ones (see above), continental patisseries/bakeries, and places that serve English-style Devonshire (cream) teas and cakes. In the cities and resorts, cafés will be open from early in the morning until late at night, serving food all day; in the country, they may stick more or less to shop hours.

The hotel **counter meal** is another mainstay, and at times may be all that's available: if it is, make sure you get there in time – meals in pubs are generally served only from noon to 2pm and again from 6 to 8pm, and rarely at all on Sunday evening. The food – served at the bar – will be simple but substantial and inexpensive (usually around $10 or less): steak, salad and chips, and variations on this theme. Slightly upmarket from this is the hotel **bistro** or restaurant in a motel, where you sit down to be served much the same food, those places often have a help yourself salad bar, too, which is always a good alternative for vegetarians. Usually the most expensive thing on the menu is a huge steak for $12–15.

Fast food is widely available, with all the usual burger, pizza and chicken places offering a quick bite for as little as $5. Fish (usually shark or snapper) and chips can be excellent in coastal regions. In cities and bigger resorts you'll find fantastic fast food in **food courts**, often in the basements of office buildings or in shopping malls, where dozens of small stalls compete to offer Thai, Chinese, Japanese or Italian food as well as burgers, steaks and sandwiches. On the road, you may be reduced to what's available at the **roadhouse**, usually the lowest common denominator of reheated meat pies and microwaved ready meals.

DRINKING

Australians have a reputation for enjoying a drink, and **hotels** (also sometimes called taverns, inns, pubs and bars) are where it mostly takes place. Traditionally, public bars are male enclaves, the place where mates meet after work on their way home, with the emphasis more on the beer and banter than the surroundings (see also "Women and Sexual Harassment", p.58). While changing attitudes have converted many city hotels into comfortable, relaxed bars, many Outback pubs are still pretty spartan and daunting for strangers of either sex, but you'll find barriers will come down if you're prepared to join in the conversation.

Friday and Saturday are the serious **party nights**, when there's likely to be a band and – in the case of some Outback establishments – literally everybody for a hundred kilometres around jammed into the building. **Opening hours** vary from state to state; they're usually 11am to 11pm, but are often much later, with early closing on Sunday. Some places are also "early openers", with hours ranging from 6am to 6pm.

For take-out sales, liquor stores or off-licenses are known as **bottle shops**. These are usually in a separate section attached to a pub or supermarket – you cannot normally buy alcohol from within supermarkets or grocery stores. There are also **drive-in bottle shops** attached to pubs where locals can load "slabs" of beer directly into the boot of their car; these solve the question of parking, though aren't totally the lazy option as you normally have to get out of the car to make your selection.

BEER

As anyone you ask will tell you, the proper way to drink **beer** in a hot country such as Australia is ice cold (the English can expect to be constantly berated for their supposed preference for warm beer) and fast, from a small container so it doesn't heat up before you can down the contents. Tubular foam or polystyrene **coolers** are often supplied for **tinnies** (cans) or **stubbies** (short-necked bottles) to make sure they stay icy. Glasses are always on the small side, and are given confusingly different names state by state. The standard ten-ounce (half-pint) serving is known as a **pot** in Victoria and Queensland, and a **middie** in NSW and WA, where the situation is further complicated by the presence of fifteen-ounce **schooners**. A **carton** or slab is a box of 24 tinnies or stubbies, bought in bulk from a bottle shop and always cheaper when not chilled (a "Darwin stubby", with typically Territorian eccentricity, is two litres of beer in an oversized bottle).

Australian beers are lager- or pilsner-style, and even the big mass-produced ones are pretty good – at least once you've worked up a thirst. They're considerably stronger than their US equivalents, and marginally stronger than the average British lager at just under five percent alcohol. Fosters is

everywhere, of course, but each state has its own label and there are fierce local loyalties, even though most are sold nationwide: Fourex (XXXX) (see p.349) and Powers in Queensland; Swan in Western Australia; Coopers in South Australia; VB in Victoria; Tooheys in New South Wales; Bogues in Tasmania. Almost all of these companies produce more than one beer – usually a light low-alcohol version and a premium "gold" or bitter brew. There are also a number of smaller "boutique" breweries and specialist beermakers: Tasmania's Cascade, WA's Redback or Matilda Bay, Cairns's Draught and Eumundi from Queensland are more distinctive but harder to find. Larger bottle shops might have **imported beers**, but outside the southern capitals (where Irish pubs serve Guinness) it's rare that you'll find anything foreign on tap.

WINES AND SPiRITS

Australian **wines** have long been appreciated at home, and it's not hard to see why; even an inexpensive bottle (around $10) will be better than just drinkable, while pricier varieties compare favourably with fine French wines. A mid-range bottle of wine will set you back about $14. The secret is to be a bit adventurous: you're extremely unlikely to be disappointed. Even the "chateau cardboard" four-litre bladders or wine casks that prevail at parties and barbecues are perfectly palatable.

The biggest wine-producing regions are the Hunter Valley in New South Wales (see p.185) and the Barossa Valley in South Australia (see pp.704–711), but you'll find smaller commercial vineyards as far north as Stanthorpe in Queensland and in southwest Western Australia; all are detailed in the text of the guide. If you **buy** at these places you'll be able to sample in advance, though there's occasionally a charge for tasting to discourage overly enthusiastic visitors from just trying everything and then moving on elsewhere (see the box "Wine tasting tips" on p.705). Most bottle shops will in any case have a good range of very reasonably priced options.

The Australian wine industry also makes **port** and **brandy** as a sideline, though generally these are not up to international standards. Two excellent dark **rums** from Queensland's sugar belt are well worth tasting, however: the sweet, deliciously smoky Bundaberg (see p.400) and the more conventionally flavoured Beenleigh. They're of average strength, normally 33 percent alcohol, but beware of "overproof" variations, which will have you flat on your back if you try to drink them like ordinary spirits.

SOFT DRINKS

Various colas, Sprite, 7-Up, Fanta and a couple of home-produced brands — Bundaberg ginger beer and Cascade's Tasmanian apple juice — are the soft alternatives to alcohol. Bottled **fruit juices** come in every style, and in the tropics (and trendy city cafés) you can often get freshly squeezed juices made from familiar and not-so-familiar fruits. There's also a range of **spring waters** from several sources along the Great Dividing Range — a relief at times from the heavily chlorinated tap water. Sickly **flavoured milk** is another national institution: every store's fridge will be packed with different flavoured cartons.

MAIL AND PHONES

Australia may be far away to some but efficient international communication has enabled the visitor from abroad to be in contact wherever they are. To ensure you're not waking somebody up when phoning, see p.67 for the relevant time zone.

MAIL

Every town of any size will have a **post office**, and where there isn't one there'll be an **Australia Post agency**, usually at the general store. Post offices and agencies are officially open Monday to Friday 9am to 5pm. Agencies might have an hour off during the day for lunch or close early, and big city GPOs sometimes open late or on Saturday morning. Out in the country it's rare to see postboxes, so you'll usually have to take your mail to the nearest post office or agency.

Domestically, the mail service has a poor reputation, at least for long distances: it can take a week for a letter to get from Wittenoom (WA) to Wagga Wagga (NSW), though major cities have a guaranteed express delivery service to other major cities — worth the expense for important packages. On the other hand **international mail** is extremely efficient, taking five to ten days to reach Europe, Asia and the US, depending on where it's posted. **Stamps** are sold at some newsagents and general stores, as well as post offices and agencies. A standard letter or postcard within Australia costs 45¢; printed aerogrammes for international letters anywhere in the world cost 70¢; postcards cost 95¢ to the US and Canada, $1 to Europe; regular letters start at $1.05 to the US and Canada, $1.20 to Europe. If you're sending anything bigger in or outside Australia, there are many different ways to do it — all at different prices; get some advice from the post office. Large **parcels** are reasonably cheap to send home by surface mail, but it will take up to three months for them to get there.

You can receive mail at any post office or agency: address the letter to **Poste Restante** (add "GPO" or "Central Post Office" for cities, unless you have the address of a particular branch), followed by the town, state and post code. You need a passport or other ID to collect mail, which is kept for a month and then returned; it's possible to get mail redirected if you change your plans — ask for a form at any post office. Some smaller post offices will allow you to phone and check if you have any mail waiting.

Most **hostels and hotels** will also hold mail for you if it's clearly marked, preferably with a date of arrival, or holders of **Amex** cards or travellers' cheques can have it sent to American Express offices. Another option is **Travellers' Contact Point**, 428 George St, Sydney (☎02/9221 8744; *www.travellers.com.au*), which operates a mail and message service with far more flexibility than poste restante: for a $40 fee, they'll hold and forward your mail as directed by you while travelling around Australia, up to a maximum of twelve months, and also offer free extras such as a voicemail phonecard. For an additional $5 they'll even give you an email account with fifteen minutes' access a day.

PHONES

Post offices (but not agencies) always have a bank of **telephones** outside; otherwise head for the nearest bar or service station – you'll even find solar-powered, satellite-connected booths in the Outback. Most public telephones now take **phone cards**, which are sold through newsagents and other stores for $5, $10, $20 or $50. There are also some older coin-operated boxes, and newer call boxes which take credit cards (though many do not take Mastercard) and bank cards. You can make **international calls** from virtually any of them, though it's a great deal easier with a card; instructions are provided. Many bars, shops and restaurants also have **payphones**, although they may cost more than a regular call box. In cities there are **telecom offices** with calling rooms, where you can talk privately in quiet surroundings, and also check phone directories and time differences; elsewhere post offices may be able to help. Following deregulation, Telstra has been joined by Optus, and competition has seen some good-value off-peak and holiday rates appear from time to time, especially for overseas rates – you'll see prominent adverts for these in the papers or on TV when they're available.

OPERATORS AND INTERNATIONAL CODES

OPERATOR SERVICES

Local Directory Assistance	☎013		☎011 from private phone
National Directory Assistance	☎0175		
International Directory Assistance	☎0103	International Operator	☎0107 from payphone
Operator	☎0176 from payphone		☎0101 from private phone

INTERNATIONAL CALLS

To call Australia from overseas dial the international access code (☎00 from the UK, ☎011 from the USA and Canada), followed by ☎61, the area code minus its initial zero, and the number. To dial out of Australia it's ☎0011, followed by the country code, then the area code (without the zero, if there is one), followed by the number:

UK ☎0011 44	Ireland ☎0011 353
USA and Canada ☎0011 1	New Zealand ☎0011 64

COUNTRY DIRECT

UK		**CANADA**	
British Telecom operator	Freecall☎1800/881 440	Teleglobe	Freecall☎1800/881 490
automatic	Freecall☎1800/881 441	**IRELAND**	
Mercury	Freecall☎1800/881 417	Telecom	Freecall☎1800/881 353
US		**NEW ZEALAND**	
AT&T	Freecall☎1800/881 011	Clear	Freecall☎1800/124 333
LDDS Worldcom	Freecall☎1800/881 212	Telecom	Freecall☎1800/881 640
MCI	Freecall☎1800/881 100		
Sprint	Freecall☎1800/881 877		

Crediphones accept most major credit cards such as Amex, Visa and Diners International, and can be found at international and domestic airports, central locations in major cities, and many hotels. Call boxes do not accept incoming calls. You can make **reverse charge** calls through the operator (☎0176 from public phones, ☎011 from private ones), but it's easier with **Country Direct** which, for the price of a local call, will connect you directly to an operator in the country you're calling (numbers are listed in the box on p.49). **Country Direct** allows you to speak directly with an operator in your home country. Cash is not needed, as the call is charged to the receiving number or to your own phone credit card. Country Direct calling cards are available through hotels, travel agents and tour operators.

Rates for calls within Australia are cheapest in the evenings from Monday to Saturday, and all day Sunday; local payphone calls cost only 40¢, allowing you to talk for as long as you like. Many businesses and services operate **free call** numbers, prefixed ☎1800, while others have six-digit numbers beginning ☎13 that are charged at the local-call rate. Numbers starting ☎0055 are private information services (often recorded), costing between 35¢ and 70¢ a minute, but with a minimum charge of 40¢ from public phones. **International calls** have different hours for cheap rates, depending on the destination, but weekends will almost always be cheaper. Prices are reasonable – a call to Britain or North America costs between $1.03 and $1.35 a minute.

THE MEDIA

The Murdoch-owned *Australian* is Australia's only national daily newspaper; aimed mainly at the business community, it has good overseas coverage but local news is often built around statistics. Each state (or more properly, each state capital) has its own daily paper – sometimes more than one – ranging from Queensland's vapid, reactionary *Courier Mail* to the more thoughtful *Sydney Morning Herald* and Melbourne's venerable *The Age*. The last two, both Fairfax-owned are probably the most objective of Australia's papers and are also widely available across much of the country.

Local papers are always a good source of listings, if not news. You should be able to track down some **international papers**, or their overseas editions – British, American, Asian and European – in the state capitals. The weekly *Time Australia* and *Newsweek/Bulletin* are the current affairs **magazines**. The monthly *HQ* focuses on literature, the arts and current affairs from a younger but sophisticated international and Australian perspective, while *Juice* is an intelligent and amusing music/popular culture mag. If you're interested in wildlife, pick up a copy of *Geo* or the bimonthly *Australian Geographic* (related only in name to the US magazine) for some excellent photography and in-depth coverage of Australia's remoter corners.

There are some excellent glossy Australian-focused adventure travel magazines, too, like the Victorian based monthly *Expanse* and the quarterly *Wild*. You'll find Australian versions of all the fashion mags, from *Vogue* to *Elle*, plus enduring and endearing publications like the *Australian Women's Weekly* (now monthly) which is well-known for its excellent recipes, and gossipy magazines like *Who Weekly* featuring the lowdown on the antics of international and Australian celebs. On a different note, the Australian version of *The Big Issue*, produced out of Melbourne, is called *The Big Issue Australia* and has been operating since 1996. Vendors are homeless, ex-homeless or long term unemployed and make half of the $2 cover price.

Australia's first television station opened in 1956 and the country didn't get colour television until 1974 – both much later than other Westernized countries. Australian **television** isn't particularly exciting unless you're into sport, of which there's plenty, and commercial stations put on frequent commercial breaks – with often annoyingly unsophisticated advertisements – throughout films. There are Australian content rulings which mean that there are a good amount of Australian dramas, series and soap operas, many of which go on to make it big overseas, from *Neighbours* and *Home and Away* to *Blue*

Heelers. However, there's a predominance of American programmes and lots of repeats. Australian TV is also fairly permissive in terms of sexual content compared to the programming of Britain or North America. There are three predictable commercial stations (in the cities these are Channel Ten, Channel Nine and Channel Seven but they have different numbers in the countryside). Channel Nine aims for an older market with more conservative programming, while Channel Ten tries to grab the younger market with some good comedy programmes including *Good News Week* and the irreverent talk show *The Panel*. In addition, there is also the more serious **ABC** (or Channel Two) – a national, advertisment-free station still with quite a British bias, showing all the best British sitcoms and mini-series – and the livelier **SBS**, a government-sponsored, multi-cultural station, which has the best coverage of

world news, as well as interesting current affairs programmes and plenty of foreign-language films (and now carefully timed advertisements which fit into the upmarket end of the scale). In more remote areas you will not be able to access all five channels and often only ABC and SBS are receivable. There are two pay TV stations, Optus and the Murdoch-owned Foxtel, though the pay - TV culture is not firmly established yet as in other countries, and even expensive hotels often still only have terrestial TV.

The best **radio** is on the various ABC stations, both local and national. **ABC Radio National** – broadcast all over Australia – offers a popular mix of arty intellectual topics, and another ABC station, **2JJJ** ("Triple J"), a former Sydney-based alternative rock station, is aimed at the nation's youth and is available across the country in only slightly watered-down form.

OPENING HOURS, HOLIDAYS AND FESTIVALS

open every day or at least through the week plus weekend mornings; urban information centres are more likely to conform to normal shopping hours.

Tourist attractions – museums, galleries and attended historic monuments – are often open daily, although rural communities may often have erratic opening hours – particularly in the north during the tropical Wet; specific opening hours are given throughout the guide.

NATIONAL HOLIDAYS

In addition to the holidays listed below, every state has its own bank holidays – generally two or three a year, or more. When the official holidays fall at the weekend, there may be an extra day off immediately before or after, and these can again vary from state to state.

New Year's Day

Australia Day
    (January 26 or Monday following)

Good Friday

Easter Monday

Anzac Day (April 25)

Christmas Day

Boxing Day

Shops and services are generally open Monday to Friday 9am to 5pm and until lunchtime on Saturday. In cities and larger towns, many shops stay open late on Thursday or Friday evening – usually until 9pm – and all day Saturday.

In remote country areas **roadhouses** provide all the essential services for a traveller and, on the major highways, are open 18 or even 24 hours a day. In tourist areas – even ones well off the beaten track – **tourist offices** are often

FESTIVALS

Besides the major events listed below, there's a host of smaller, local events many of which are detailed throughout the guide. The Christmas and Easter holiday periods, especially, are marked by celebrations at every turn, all over the country.

JANUARY

Festival of Sydney, NSW. A month of festivities, with something for absolutely everyone.

Montsalvat Jazz Festival, Eltham, VIC. Australia's premier jazz festival, which takes place on the Montsalvat Estate over Australia Day weekend; book well ahead.

Tamworth Country Music Festival, Tamworth, NSW. A week of Slim Dusty and his ilk, culminating in the Australian Country Music Awards.

FEBRUARY

Sydney Gay and Lesbian Mardi Gras, NSW. Sydney's proud gay community's festival begins at the end of February and lasts three weeks, ending with an extravagant parade and an all-night dance party.

Festival of Perth, WA. A month of "low-brow arts" at venues all over the city.

Bindoon Rock Festival, Bindoon, WA. WA's answer to Woodstock or Reading, with some visiting overseas bands.

MARCH

Adelaide Arts Festival, SA. The country's best-known and most innovative arts festival (biennial, in even years); not to be missed.

Melbourne Moomba Festival, VIC. Eleven days of partying, beginning and ending with fireworks and lots of fun in between.

APRIL

Barossa Valley Vintage Festival, SA. Biennial (odd years) Germanic festival set in the country's viticultural heart.

Melbourne International Comedy Festival, VIC. Opening on April Fools' Day, comics from around the world gather for three weeks.

MAY

Bangtail Muster, Alice Springs, NT. Nutty parades and Outback silliness.

JUNE

Melbourne International Film Festival, VIC. The country's largest and most prestigious film festival, lasting two weeks.

Sydney International Film Festival, NSW. Also an important film festival, running for over two weeks in June and based at the glorious *State Theatre*.

Barunga Sports Festival, Beswick Aboriginal Land, NT. A rare and enjoyable chance to encounter Aboriginal culture in the NT. No alcohol.

HOLIDAYS

Contrary to popular opinion and Australia's commendably relaxed interpretation of the work ethic, there are surprisingly few nationwide **public holidays** – and even when you add in the state ones (two or three per state, about eight in the Northern Territory), Australia lags behind most European countries in having official days off.

Watch out for **school holidays**, when seaside resorts can be transformed into bucket-and-spade war zones and the roads are jammed with station wagons full of holidaying families. Dates vary from year to year and state to state, but generally people are on the move for six weeks from mid-December (January is worst, as many people stay home until after Christmas), two weeks around Easter, and another couple of weeks in June or July.

Cape York Aboriginal Dance Festival, QLD. Three-day, alcohol-free celebration of authentic Aboriginal culture. Biennial in odd-numbered years.

JULY

Camel Cup, Alice Springs, NT. Camel-racing down the dry Todd River.

Darwin Beer Can Regatta, NT. Mindil Beach is the venue for the recycling of copious empties into a variety of nutty seacraft. Also a thong-throwing contest; Territorian eccentricity personified.

AUGUST

Shinju Matsuri Festival, Broome, WA. Probably the most remote big festival, which doesn't stop the town being packed for this Oriental-themed pearl festival.

Mount Isa Rodeo, Mount Isa, QLD. Australia's largest rodeo – a gritty, down-to-earth encounter with bulls, horses and their riders.

SEPTEMBER

Bathurst 1000 Road Races, Bathurst, NSW. Australia's premier weekend of car and bike street racing.

Birdsville Races, QLD. Once a year the remote Outback town of Birdsville (population 120) comes alive for a weekend of drinking and horse-racing – a well-known and definitive Australian oddity.

Warana, Brisbane, QLD. Huge, two-week arts festival centred in the city's Botanic Gardens with food, wine, beer, music, writing and children's events topped off with fireworks and a wacky *Concours de Decadence*.

Melbourne International Festival of the Arts, VIC. Two-week celebration of visual, performing and written arts in venues all over the city.

OCTOBER

Henley-on-Todd Regatta, Alice Springs, NT. Wacky races in bottomless boats running down the dry Todd riverbed; the event is heavily insured against the river actually flowing.

Manly Jazz Festival, Sydney, NSW. Three-day jazz festival with artists from all over the world.

NOVEMBER

Australian Grand Prix, Melbourne, VIC. Formula One street-racing which follows a week of partying; formerly held in Adelaide, now relocated to Albert Park in Melbourne.

Melbourne Cup, Flemington Racecourse, VIC. 130-year-old horse race which brings the entire country to a standstill around the radio or TV.

DECEMBER

Sydney to Hobart Yacht Race, Sydney, NSW. Crowds flock to the harbour to witness the start of this classic regatta which departs Sydney on Boxing Day and arrives in Hobart three days later.

The **Christmas holidays** and **New Year's Eve** are celebrated with gusto everywhere.

FESTIVALS

The nationwide selection of festivals listed in the box above all include, necessitate, and are in some cases the imaginative product of, prolonged beer-swilling. Why else would you drive to the edge of the Simpson Desert to watch a horse race? (See "Birdsville".) Also, all cities and towns have their own agricultural festivals ("shows") which are high points of the local calendar.

More seriously, each mainland capital tries to elevate its sophistication quotient with a regular celebration and showcase of art and culture, of which the biennial Adelaide Arts Festival is the best known.

OUTDOOR ACTIVITIES

Though the cities are fun, what really makes Australia special is the great outdoors: the vast and remote wilderness of the bush, the legendary Outback, and the thousands of kilometres of unspoilt coastline. There's tremendous potential here to indulge in a huge range of outdoor pursuits – hiking, fishing, surfing, diving, even skiing – especially in the multitude of national parks that cover the country. Further information on all of these is available from local tourist offices, which publicize what's available in their area; from the National Parks and Wildlife Service (NPWS), who have detailed maps of parks with walking trails, climbs, swimming holes and other activities; and from specialist books (see p.1032 for a selection). In addition, virtually any activity can be done as part of an organized excursion, often with all the gear supplied. If you want to go it alone you'll find plenty of places ready to rent or sell you the necessary equipment, along with some friendly advice. Before indulging in adventure activities, check your insurance cover (see pp.18–19).

As with any wilderness area, the Australian interior does not suffer fools, and the coast conceals dangers too: sunstroke and dehydration are risks everywhere, with riptides, currents and unexpected king waves to be wary of on exposed coasts. In the more remote regions isolation and lack of surface water compromise energetic outdoor activities such as bushwalking or mountain biking, which are probably better indulged in the cooler climes and more populated locations of the south.

BUSHWALKING

Bushwalking in Australia doesn't mean just a stroll in the bush, but refers to self-sufficient hikes, from a day to a week or longer. It's an extremely popular activity nationwide, and you'll find trails marked in almost every national park, as well as local bushwalking clubs whose trips you may be able to join. In any tourist area you'll also find experienced guides.

It's essential to be properly equipped for the conditions you'll encounter – and to know what those conditions are likely to be. Carry a map (often on hand at the ranger station in popular national parks), know how the trail is marked, and stay on the route. If your trip is a long one, let someone know where you're going, and confirm to them that you've arrived back safely – park rangers are useful contacts for this, and some will insist on it anyway. The essentials, even for a short walk, are adequate clothing including a wide-brimmed hat, enough food, and, above all, water. Other things you really shouldn't be without are a torch, matches or lighter, penknife, sunblock, insect repellent, toilet paper, first-aid kit, and a whistle or mirror to attract attention if you get lost. A lot of this gear can be rented, or bought cheaply at disposal stores, which can often also put you in touch with local clubs or specialists.

Long-distance tracks exist mostly in the south of the country, with Tasmania's wilderness areas being perhaps the most rewarding for bushwalking location; the eighty-kilometre Overland Track from Cradle Mountain to Lake St Clair is the island's best-known trail. On the mainland, the Blue Mountains, a two-hour train ride from Sydney, the Snowy Mountains further south, and Victoria's spectacular Grampians are all popular regions for longer, marked walks.

South Australia's Flinders Ranges, 300km north of Adelaide, are accessible along the Heysen Trail from the Fleurieu Peninsula, the walk into the thousand-metre-high natural basin of Wilpena Pound being the highlight. In vast Western Australia, only the southwestern corner can offer extended walks: the 640-kilometre Bibulman Track, an old Aboriginal trail passing through the region's giant eucalypt forests, is signed all the way from Walpole to Perth. An hour's drive north of Albany, the peaks of the Stirling Ranges, almost a thousand metres high, also offer some spectacular trails. In the Northern Territory, Litchfield Park, two hours south of Darwin in a croc-free tableland fringed with perennial springs, has some satisfying bushwalks in the dry season; while the Larapinta Trail, along the MacDonnell Ranges west of Alice Springs, is being extended each year. Queensland's rainforested coastal strip offers plenty more opportunities for walks, including the Mount Tamborine-Lamington

BUSH ESSENTIALS

Three things above all:

Fire: the driest continent on earth is covered by vegetation specifically evolved to make use of regular conflagrations, and is always at risk from **bushfires**. Sydney's **Black Friday** fires of 1994 saw the city ringed with burning bushland and, even in wet years, there's a constant red alert during summer months. Always use an established fireplace where available, or ideally dig a shallow pit and ring it with stones. Keep fires as small as practicable, and make absolutely sure that even embers are smothered before going to sleep or moving on. Never discard burning cigarette butts from cars. Periodic **total fire bans** – announced in the local media when in effect – prohibit any fire in the open, including wood, gas or electric barbecues, with heavy fines for offenders. Check on the local fire danger before you go bushwalking – some walking trails are closed in the riskiest periods (summer in the south; the end of the dry season

– Sept/Oct – in the north). If driving, carry blankets and a filled water container, listen to your car radio and watch out for roadside fire danger indicators. If the worst happens, there are practical ways of surviving a bushfire.*

Water: carry plenty with you and do not contaminate local water resources. In particular, soaps and detergents can render water undrinkable and kill livestock and wild animals. Avoid washing in standing water, especially tanks and small lakes or reservoirs.

Waste: take only photographs, leave only footprints. That means carrying all your rubbish out with you – never burn or bury it – and making sure you urinate (and bury your excrement) at least 50m from a campsite or water source.

*See "Health", pp.25-27, for potential bushwalking hazards and advice on how to deal with them – including ways to survive if caught in a bushfire.

area in the south, and around northern **Atherton Tablelands** and **Hinchinbrook Island**.

WATER SPORTS

The oceans and seas around Australia are a national playground and are not just for tanning or playing volleyball on the beach. Always take local advice on the waves, which must be treated with respect. If possible, **swim** from a patrolled beach, between the flags: raise one hand if you get into difficulty, and clear the water if a siren sounds – it could signal dangerous waves, a shark sighting or a swarm of bluebottles (stinging jellyfish). Enjoying the water doesn't necessarily involve any special effort or equipment, but if you want it, there are plenty of activities on offer. Probably the easiest to get into is **surfing**, starting with bodysurfing and progressing to boogie-boards (small boards that you lie on) and then on to full-scale surfboards. Surfing is popular everywhere, but don't expect the local surfie community to be too friendly at first – they're often very cliquey. Seaside hostels often have boards which they loan out free. **Windsurfing** and **sailing** are also extremely popular, and you'll be able to rent equipment and get instruction in almost any resort. Other water sports include **white-water rafting**, **sea-kayaking** and **canoeing**.

The Great Barrier Reef is one of the world's great **scuba-diving** meccas, with some other lesser-known but excellent sites around the country – such as West Australia's Ningaloo Reef – beginning to attract attention. Dive facilities in Australia are of a high standard, and scuba courses are not that expensive, though if you simply want to try it once there are plenty of people offering closely supervised "resort dives". Good **rental gear** is widely available, but if you're bringing your own, check for compatibility problems; yokes are the Australian norm, so if your first-stage fitting is DIN (likely in Europe and the UK), you'll need an adaptor. **Snorkelling** is the low-tech alternative, and still allows you to get dramatically close to the aquatic life around the Reef.

Fishing is an Australian obsession – on rivers and lakes, off piers or small boats ("tinnies"), or out at sea where marlin and other game fish are caught. Again, all the equipment – even boats – can be rented in most good fishing areas. Barramundi, renowned for its fighting qualities, is the thing to go for up north.

OTHER PURSUITS

The craze for **bungee jumping** has, not surprisingly, caught on with Australia's hard-core thrillseekers: Cairns in northern Queensland is a good place to try it in a spectacular setting, or there are cranes to jump from in plenty of other places. **Rap jumping** is a newer version that essentially involves abseiling headfirst at very high speed down sheer cliff faces. Alice Springs' wide-open spaces make it the country's **hot-air-ballooning** centre and also a base for **camel treks** through the surrounding desert.

More regular **riding**, on horseback, is offered all over the country – anything from a gentle hour at walking pace to a serious cattle roundup. **Cycling** and **mountain biking** are tremendously popular too, as well as being a good way of getting around resorts; many hostels rent out bikes, and we've listed other outlets throughout the text.

Australia's wilderness is an ideal venue for extended **off-road driving** or **dirt-bike riding**, although permission may be needed to cross station- and Aboriginal-owned lands, and the fragile desert ecology should be respected at all times. Northern Queensland's Cape York and WA's Kimberley are the most adventurous destinations, 4WD-accessible in the dry season only. The **great Outback tracks** pushed out by explorers or drovers, such as the Gunbarrel and Sandover highways and the Tanami, Birdsville and Oodnadatta tracks, are technically mostly two-wheel driveable in dry conditions, but can be hard on poorly prepared vehicles; only WA's two-thousand-kilometre Canning Stock Route demands a 4WD and an enormous fuel range, effectively ruling out motorbikes.

Finally, you may not associate Australia with **skiing**, but there's plenty of it in the 1500-metre-high Australian Alps on the border of Victoria and New South Wales, based around the winter resorts of Thredbo, Mount Hotham and Perisher.

Europeans tend to be sniffy about Australian skiing, and certainly it's limited, with a season that lasts barely two months – July and August – and very few challenging runs. The one area where it does match up to Europe is in the prices. On the other hand it's fun if you're here, and the relatively gentle slopes of the mountains are ideal for **cross-country skiing**, which is increasingly being developed alongside downhill.

NATIONAL PARKS

The Australian **National Parks and Wildlife Service** is split into federal and state bodies, the federal organization dealing with international problems such as whaling and how to make use of Antarctica, and occasionally arbitrating between the otherwise independent state departments. The state bodies actually run the parks day-to-day – and each tends to be called something slightly different, though throughout the guide we've usually referred to them as NPWS. The seven-hundred-odd national parks range from suburban commons to the Great Barrier Reef and from popular hiking areas within striking distance of the big cities to wilderness regions which require days in a 4WD simply to reach. They protect everything within their boundaries: flora, fauna and landforms as well as Aboriginal art and sacred sites.

Fees are variable. Some parks or states have no fees at all, some charge for use of camping facilities, while others require permits bought in advance. If you're **camping** you can usually pay on site, but booking ahead might be a good idea during the Christmas and Easter holidays. Nearby resorts or alternative accommodation are always independently run, rather than by the NPWS.

SPORT

Australians are sports mad, especially for the ostensibly passive spectator sports of cricket, Aussie Rules football, rugby (league or union), tennis or any type of racing, from cockroach to camel. No matter what it is, it'll draw a crowd – with thousands more watching on TV – and a crowd means a party. Even unpromising-sounding activities such as surf lifesaving and yacht racing (the start of the Sydney to Hobart race just after Christmas is a massive social event) are tremendously popular. And of course, the Olympics will be held in Sydney in 2000 – for details, see the Sydney account on p.74-76.

It's hard to escape sport in Australia: people talk about it all the time; sporting news fills up the newspapers; events and commentary are constantly broadcast on TV and radio; and it's a huge source of national pride. The wintertime **football** (footy) season in Australia lasts from March to September; in summer **cricket** is played from October to March.

Footy comes in several varieties. Before World War II, **soccer** was played by British immigrants but with postwar immigration it was branded as "ethnic", as new clubs became based on the country of origin of the players: Australian Rules (see below) was considered the game "real Australians" played. More than fifty percent of Australia's twelve league soccer clubs evolved from communities of postwar immigrants – mainly Italians, Greeks and Yugoslavs – and David Hill, the former chairman of Soccer Australia, believed that their fervent nationalism has marginalized the game; his mid-1990s ban on clubs that included national flags in their logos won support as well as accusations of the pursuance of a policy of "ethnic cleansing". Getting the national team, the Socceroos, to play for the World Cup is seen as the best way to create interest in the sport on a national level. To this end, the once-famous English footballer Terry Venables was appointed coach in the wake of his success in managing England to the semi-finals of the European Championships (Euro '96), training the Socceroos for their qualifying rounds to enter the 1998 World Cup in France. However, they drew to Iran and went out on away goals and didn't make it to France. The first big event

at the new Olympic Stadium in Sydney in June 1999 will be the match between the Socceroos and a world-star cast Fifa 11 team coached by Aimé Jacquet, who led the French team to victory in the 1998 World Cup. **Rugby union**, despite the huge success of the Wallabies national team, is also very much a minority interest domestically. The introduction of a Super 12 competition, involving teams from Australia, New Zealand and South Africa, has generated a much greater interest in what was formerly an elitist sport.

Australian Rules ("Aussie Rules") football dominates Victoria, South Australia and Western Australia. It's an extraordinary, anarchic, no-holds-barred, eighteen-a-side brawl, most closely related to Gaelic football and known dismissively north of the Victorian border as "aerial ping pong". The ball can be propelled by any means necessary, and the fact that players aren't sent off for misconduct ensures a lively, skilful and, above all, gladiatorial confrontation. Aussie Rules stars have delightful sobriquets such as "Tugger" and "Crackers", and their macho garb consists of tiny butt-hugging shorts and a biceps-revealing tank top. The game is mostly played on cricket grounds, with a ball similar to that used in rugby or American football. The aim is to get the ball through the uprights for a goal (six points). There are four 25-minute quarters, plus lots of time added on for injury. Despite the violence on the pitch (or perhaps because of it), Aussie Rules fans tend to be loyal and well behaved. Victoria has traditionally been the home of the game, and Victorian sides are expected to win the AFL Flag, decided at the Grand Final in September, as a matter of course.

In New South Wales and Queensland **Rugby League** attracts the fanatics, especially for the hard-fought **State of Origin** matches. The thirteen-a-side game is one of which the Australians seem permanent world champions, despite having a relatively small professional league. Recently, the game has been split down the middle – there are now two rival competitions – the traditional Australian Rugby League (ARL) and the Murdoch-owned Super League. One of the sadder consequences of this media-inspired revolution has been the loss of some of the traditional inner-city clubs through mergers. The common view is that the game cannot support the number of teams required for two competitions. Many people also resent the way in which this one-time bastion of working-class culture has been co-opted by pay TV.

Summertime **cricket** is a great spectator sport – for the crowd, the sunshine and the beer as much as the play. Every state is involved, and the three- or four-day Sheffield Shield matches of the interstate series are interspersed with one-day games and internationals, as well as full five-day international test matches. Interest in the five-day matches has been revitalized by Australia's recent victories against all-comers: the 1996–97 cricket season saw the home side convincingly defeat the West Indies, who had reigned supreme in world cricket for the best part of twenty years. In 1998 they beat South Africa and England, but really consolidated their position of World Champion when they beat Pakistan in Pakistan itself.

The international competition that still arouses greatest interest is that between Australia and England – **The Ashes**. Having been around for 120 years, this is perhaps the oldest rivalry between nations in international sport. The "trophy" competed for has an interesting provenance. In 1077 an English touring side was soundly beaten by the locals in Melbourne. As a consequence, the London *Times* was moved to report, in a mock obituary, on the "death of English cricket". The funeral ceremony involved the cremation of a set of bails, which were then preserved in a funerary urn. Each time the two countries compete, this is the trophy that is up for grabs (though the urn itself never actually leaves Lord's cricket ground in London) and a new crystal trophy actually goes to the winners.

Minor sports are followed with no less avid attention, and there are plenty of them, including horse-racing and trotting, motor-racing, swimming, athletics, tennis – you name it. One peculiarly Australian institution is the **surf carnival**, when teams of volunteer lifesavers demonstrate their skills – this makes for a great day out on the beach. **Surfing** itself can also be a competitive sport, with the Eastertime World Championships held at Bell's Beach, southwest of Melbourne, and November's Margaret River Classic, south of Perth, both good opportunities to catch some hot wave-riding action. Inland, many rural towns have a **speedway track** occupying a tract of wasteland, where at weekends motor-headed hoons demonstrate their dirt-tracking skills in souped-up utes or motorbikes; a dusty, noisy and merry focus for the entire community and passers-by.

WOMEN AND SEXUAL HARASSMENT

The stereotyped image of the Aussie male is of a boozy bloke interested in sport, his car and his mates, with his girlfriend a poor

fourth. And it's not far wrong: the Australian ethos of mateship has traditionally excluded women – the hard, tough life of the early days of white settlement, when women were scarce, fostered a male culture that's to some extent still current. Another legacy of pioneering times is the reputation of Australian women for being robust and practical.

In the main **cities**, attitudes are generally enlightened and "new men" are gaining ground, but in the more remote country and **Outback areas**, the older attitudes are more tenacious and sexual harassment can be commonplace – if rarely threatening. Men driving by in cars, in particular, are notorious for shouting out crude comments and sexual remarks as a woman walks by, and catcalling from groups of men in the street can be intimidating.

Meeting Australian men **socially**, as individuals, you'll often find that their brusque, offhand exterior conceals a surprisingly helpful and kind nature; they're also, on the whole, honest and upfront.

SEXUAL EQUALITY AND ATTITUDES

In public life, Australia has one of the best records for **sexual equality** in the world. It was the second country to give women the vote (after New Zealand in 1893), and the fact that this happened a year after federation in 1901 shows that the intention was for women to take a full role in the new nation. In the 1970s and 1980s Australia kept pace with the worldwide **feminist movement** (indeed, with Germaine Greer, it helped lead it): the first big milestone – equal pay for equal work – was finally achieved in 1974. Equal opportunities legislation and affirmative action schemes for employment have been widely adopted: today, nonsexist language is the norm for newspapers and officialdom.

However, corresponding changes in attitudes have not always kept pace with all of this. At about the same time that women achieved equal pay, the **public bars** of hotels, which had traditionally refused to serve women, were being stormed by women's groups. Today, a woman can be served a drink anywhere in the country, but the way that Australian pubs are set up – with two separate bars – continues to reflect the old bias; you'll still see signs saying "Ladies' Lounge", and if you want to go to the women's toilets you'll have to walk a long way from the public bar. **Outback and country pubs** are still very much male bastions, and any woman travelling on her own would do well to avoid them, thus escaping the full blast of misogyny.

WOMEN ALONE

Avoiding pubs is all very well, but **hotels** are often the cheapest and sometimes the only places to stay in **small towns**. The major drawback is that pub accommodation is often full of single male workers from other towns, or old men who are permanent boarders, so roaming corridors late at night in search of the toilet can be an unpleasant experience. That said, the management is usually friendly, and most country pubs are family-run. **Bed and breakfast** establishments and **guesthouses** provide a more homelike, friendly environment, unlike the inevitably impersonal **motels** where a stay can be a potentially lonely experience. **Caravan parks** and **campsites** tend to be safe, family-dominated environments and are a

good bet if you have your own transport – and sleeping bag. In larger towns and cities, **hostels** are where you're most likely to meet like-minded women travelling alone. Easy-going Australian attitudes mean that dorms in backpackers' hostels (never YHA hostels) are often mixed sex. There's usually at least one female-only dorm and if this is really important to you, you should ask about it in advance or when you check in.

Best of all for making contact with locals and generally getting involved are **farmstays** (which needn't be expensive if you stay in shearers' quarters and the like) or the experience of being a WWOOF (Willing Workers on Organic Farms; see p.65). Before going to work or to stay on remote **Outback stations**, try to find out as much about the setup as possible, for you could end up being the only woman among a group of men – which could create potentially uncomfortable situations.

RAPE AND SERIOUS TROUBLE

If the worst happens, it's best to contact a **Rape Crisis Line** before going straight to the police; all major cities (see the "Listings" sections of city accounts in this guide) have them and there's always a free-call line if you're in the country. Women police officers form a large part of the force, and in general the police deal sensitively with sexual assault cases.

To **avoid** physical attack, don't get too relaxed about Australia's friendly, easy-going attitude. The usual defensive tactics apply. In the cities at night, buses or trams are generally safer than trains – on the train, always sit next to the guard in the carriage. Pick somewhere to stay that's close to public transport so you don't have to walk far at night – an area with busy nightlife may well be safer than a dead suburban backstreet. If you're going to have to walk for long stretches at night, take a cab unless the streets are busy with traffic, restaurants and people.

The 1992 "backpacker murders" of hitching travellers just outside Sydney prove that it's not only in remote areas or when travelling alone that **hitchhiking** is dangerous – and that even male company is no safeguard. Hitching is doubly inadvisable for women and, with the wide variety of inexpensive transport options available, is hard to justify. If you must do it, never do it alone – and heed the general advice and warnings given on pp.39-40.

WOMEN'S CONTACTS

All the major cities have good **women's con-tacts**, from resource centres and information lines to health centres where you can often get free pregnancy testing and other help. There's also a lively culture of women's galleries and bookshops; as well as stocking the works of the hundreds of great Australian women writers (see "Books" in Contexts for suggested reading), they'll have copies of feminist journals and good notice boards which often have information about

women-only accommodation. Lesbian maga-zines also carry ads for women's bed and break-fasts and the like – you don't have to be gay to stay. In March, **International Women's Day** provides an excuse for a month-long series of women's events in the cities, culminating in enthusiastically attended street marches.

Specific women's contacts are listed in the city accounts of this guide. For more, check out the White Pages under "Women"; alternatively, the Citizen's Advice Bureau in each city should be able to refer you to relevant organizations.

GAY AND LESBIAN AUSTRALIA

Year by year Australia grows in popularity as a Queer destination. Even as far back as 1832 a Select Committee of the British Parliament noted the popularity of "alternative lifestyles" among the colonists. Today, the beautiful people flock down under, lured by the conducive climate and laidback lifestyle and eager to hang out with the homeboys on balmy beaches and sun-kissed city streets.

Despite its reputation as a macho culture, Australia revels in a large and active **scene**: you'll find an air of confidence and a sense of community that is often missing in other countries – and, what's more, it's friendly and accessible.

The colonists transported English **law** to Australia, but in 1972 South Australia was the first state to enact decriminalization, followed the next year by the ACT and Northern Territory. Surprisingly, Victoria and New South Wales (gen-erally thought of as liberal states) delayed similar legislation until the 1980s. Less surprisingly, Queensland took the plunge only in 1991 while it took a decade of constant petitioning from the Tasmanian Gay and Lesbian Rights Group, and pressure from the Federal Government and the UN Human Rights Committee for the law to change in Tasmania in 1997. In Western Australia there's still an age of consent of 21, whereas the ages of consent in ACT and Victoria (both 16), SA and Tasmania (both 17), are the same as the hetero-sexual age. In the Northern Territory and NSW, the homosexual age of consent is 18. In Queensland, the age of consent for homosexuals depends on the sexual act practised, with anal sex outlawed

until 18 but otherwise 16. Sex between women is either not mentioned in state laws or is covered by the heterosexual age. The foreign partner in a de facto gay relationship can apply to immigrate to or permanently reside in Australia, a much better sit-uation than in many countries, but the current bat-tle Australian gay and lesbian lobby groups are waging is to make same sex relationships com-pletely equal in the eyes of the law as heterosex-ual ones, in terms of marriage, next of kin rights, superannuation and age of consent.

Today, Australia is testimony to the power of the pink dollar, and there's an abundance of gay venues, services, businesses, travel clubs, country retreats and the like.

Australia is definitely the place to watch Men At Work – and at play. **Aussie boys** get a lot of sun and sport – although the scene is a lot more diverse than simply tan and toned muscle, and the community is so large that there's bound to be something for everyone. One thing's for certain: you won't be bored. Just remember to pack your trunks, snorkel and fins, your clubbing gear and some barbecue tongs.

Australian **dykes** are refreshingly open and self-possessed – a relief after the more closed and cliquey scene in Europe. The flip side of their fearlessness is the predominance of S&M on the scene. Maybe the climate has something to do with it, but you'll see a good deal of tattoos and pierced flesh around.

Dyke **scenes** are nothing if not mercurial, and Australia is no exception. We've done our best to list bars, clubs and meeting places, but be

GAY AND LESBIAN CONTACTS

AIDS organizations ACON (AIDS Council of NSW), PO Box 350, Darlinghurst, NSW 2010 (☎02/9206 2000 or free call ☎1800/063 060; *www.acon.org.au*); AIDS Trust of Australia, PO Box 1030, Darlinghurst, NSW 2010 (☎02/9281 0600); Australian National Council on AIDS and Related Diseases (ANCARD), PO Box 9848, Canberra, ACT 2601 (☎02/6289 4381); National Association of People Living with HIV/AIDS (NAPWA), PO Box 876, Darlinghurst, NSW 2010 (☎02/9281 1999, fax 9281 1044).

Personal contacts Country Network, PO Box 192, Subiaco, WA 6904 (☎08/9385 1366; *CountryOz@queer.org.au; www.pinkboard.com.au~countrynetwork*), is a mainly urban gay and lesbian friendship network. Country Oz is an email network linking gay guys in rural Australia.

Press and multimedia Two monthly national gay and lesbian glossy magazines are widely available at newsagents: *Campaign*, 1st floor, 36 Fitzroy St, Marrickville, NSW 2204 (☎02/9550 1546, fax 9516 5625; $6.50); and *Outrage*, 85 King William St, Fitzroy, VIC 3065 (☎03/9926 1122; $5.95). *LOTL (Lesbians on the Loose)*, PO Box 1099, Darlinghurst, 2010 (☎02/9380 6528, fax 9380 6529), is a monthly publication available at lesbian and gay venues. Each major capital has excellent free gay newspapers, like the *Sydney Star Observer* or Melbourne's *Brother Sister* that give the local lowdown. There are also some very useful Web sites, the best of which is *www.outbiz.com.au* for online gay and lesbian

business and community information and links to other sites, including that of the Gay and Lesbian Mardi Gras (see pp.156-157). The ALSO Foundation, based in Victoria (see p.802), also have a good Web site containing their directory: *www. also.org.au*

Tour operator Destination Downunder, Level 10, 130 Elizabeth St, Sydney, NSW 2000 (☎02/9268 2188); Beyond the Blue, Level 6, 300 George St, Sydney 2000 (02/9221 6377, fax 9221 6722; *sales@beyondblue.com.au; www.beyondblue.com.au*). Gay tour operator can arrange packages for the Gay and Lesbian Mardi Gras.

Tourist services AGLTA (Australian Gay and Lesbian Tourism Association), PO Box 208, Darlinghurst, NSW 2010 (☎08/8379 7498, fax 8379 2483) produces the *Gay and Lesbian Tourism Services Directory*. It's free, but there's a small charge for overseas postage.

Travel agents Friends of Dorothy Travel, 2nd floor, 77 Oxford St, Darlinghurst, NSW (☎02/9360 3616; *fod@dot.net.au*); Parkside Travel, 70 Glen Osmond Rd, Parkside, SA 5063 (☎08/8274 1222 or free call ☎1800/888 501); Pride Travel and Tours, 254 Bay St, Brighton, VIC 3186 (☎03/9596 3566, fax 9596 7761); Silke's Travel, 263 Oxford St, Darlinghurst, NSW 2010 (☎02/9380 6244, fax 9361 3729, free call ☎1800/807 860; *silba@magna.com.au*); Tearaway Travel, 52 Porter St, Prahan, VIC 3181 (☎03/9510 6644; *tearaway@bigpond.com*).

---

warned that venues open, change their names, change hands, shut for refurbishment, get relaunched at a new address and finally go out of business with frightening rapidity.

WHERE AND HOW TO GO

Sydney is the jewel in Australia's luscious navel. Firmly established as one of the world's great gay cities – only San Francisco can really rival it – it attracts lesbian and gay visitors from around the world. And if this can be overwhelming at times (the gossip alone has been known to drive people to the other side of the continent), Australia has plenty more to offer. Melbourne closely follows the scene in Sydney, but for a change of pace, take a trip to Brisbane and the Gold Coast. Perth, Adelaide and Darwin all have smaller, quieter scenes.

Away from the cities, things get more discreet, but a lot of **country areas** do have very friendly local scenes – impossible to pinpoint, but easy to stumble across. Australians on the city scene are a friendly bunch, but in a small country town they get *really* friendly, so if there's anything going on you'll probably get invited along.

The **Outback** covers the vast majority of the Australian continent and is, in European terms, sparsely populated. Mining and cattle ranching are the primary employers and they help to create a culture not famed for its tolerance of homosexuality. Tread carefully: bear in mind that Ayers Rock may be 2000km from Sydney as the crow flies, but in many ways it's a million miles away in terms of attitudes.

The **Australian Gay and Lesbian Tourism Association** (AGLTA, see box above for details) is a dynamic organization dedicated to turning Australia into *the* premier destination for gay and lesbian tourists from all over the world. They give their seal of approval to accommodation, resorts, travel agents and promoters that provide the attitude or atmosphere that today's gay globetrotter demands – and their *Gay and Lesbian Tourism Services Directory* covers retreats, guesthouses and country lodges across Australia, not just in the cities.

Each chapter of this guide has specific gay and lesbian listings, with a wealth of information – check out the box on p.156 of Sydney and Around in particular, which has all you need to know to join in the Mardi Gras celebrations.

check out the box on p.156 of Sydney and Around

AIDS

Australia is, by and large, very **AIDS** aware. Safe sex has a prominent place on the scene and you'll probably find that you have an amazing variety and quantity of safe-sex gear thrust upon you as you travel around. Australia responded early to the AIDS threat and the federal government and most state governments have been relatively progressive, funding a range of AIDS organizations.

As you might expect, Sydney has the majority of Australia's AIDS cases, and the support networks are well established here and in the other major cities; again, you'll find local listings in the major city accounts as well as those included in the box overleaf.

POLICE, PREJUDICE AND TROUBLE

"Transportation across the seas", to which judges condemned the petty criminals of two centuries ago, seems to have been a successful policy; Australia today can pride itself on being a relatively crime-free country, although increasingly it is following the American trend in gun-related incidents.

This is not to say there's no petty crime, or that you can leave normal caution behind, but there is less violent crime and theft in Australia, even in the big cities, than in most of Europe or North America, and even so-called "heavy" downtown areas can appear pretty tame. One place where **violence** is commonplace is at the ritual pub "blue" (fight) among known protagonists on a

Friday or Saturday night, but strangers are seldom involved without at least some apparent provocation.

You're perhaps more likely to fall victim to a fellow traveller or an opportunist: **theft** is fairly common in some hostels, while if you leave valuables lying around, or on view in cars, you can expect them to be stolen. Exercise caution, don't forgot your normal streetwise precautions, and you should be fine; in cities at night stay in areas that are well-lit and full of people, look like you know where you are going and don't carry excess cash or anything else you can't afford to lose.

POLICE AND THE LAW

Australia's **police** – all armed – have a thoroughly poor public image and perhaps as a result tend to keep a low profile; you should have no trouble in your dealings with them. Indeed you'll hardly see them, unless you're out on a Friday or Saturday night when they cruise in search of drink-related brawls.

Things to watch out for, most of all, are **drugs**. A lot of marijuana is grown and its use is widespread, but you'd be foolish to carry it when you travel, and crazy to carry any other illicit narcotic. Each state has its own penalties, and though a small amount of grass may mean no more than confiscation or an on-the-spot fine, they're generally pretty tough – especially in Queensland.

When you cross **state borders** you may find that your vehicle will be searched – not just for "firearms, pornography or drugs" but also for fruit and fresh produce, which often cannot be carried from one state to the next (you'll see large signs warning you, and places to dispose of your life-threatening bananas). Driving in general makes you more likely to have a confrontation of some kind, if only for a minor traffic infringement: **drunk driving** is regarded extremely seriously, so don't risk it.

Lesser potential problems are **alcohol** – there are all sorts of controls on where and when you can drink, and taking alcohol onto Aboriginal lands can be a serious offence – **smoking**, which is increasingly being banned in public places; and nude or **topless** sunbathing, which is quite acceptable in many places, but absolutely not in others – follow the locals' lead.

If for any reason you are **arrested** or need help (and you can be arrested merely on suspicion of committing an offence), you are entitled to contact a friend or lawyer before answering any questions. You could call your consulate, but don't expect much sympathy. If necessary, the police will provide a lawyer, and you can usually get legal aid to settle the bill.

PREJUDICE, POLICE AND THE TRAVELLER

Given Australia's record on its treatment of the Aboriginal population, the history of the White Australia policy, and the recent rise of Pauline Hanson's One Nation party on a racist agenda, it comes as little surprise to find that this is a nation where **racial prejudice** is ingrained. As a **black traveller** you're likely to attract attention when you don't particularly want it, and be unable to get it when you do – even to the extent of being refused service in an Outback bar or being unable

---

EMERGENCIES

☎000 is the free emergency telephone number which summons the police, ambulance or fire service.

---

to flag down a cab in a city. Certainly in remote areas, where Aboriginal people are still often treated as second-class citizens at best, black travellers may have an uncomfortable time.

Asians are generally more accepted (in Australia, "Asian" usually means Southeast Asian – the Indian and Pakistani populations are negligible). However, a strong undercurrent of anti-Asian feeling – never too far below the surface in Australia's European history – has recently come out into the open, encouraged by Pauline Hanson's many infamous remarks since her maiden speech in parliament in September 1996. Cliché-ridden, uninformed and simplistic as they are, her statements have struck a chord with some Australians, who feel bewildered and marginalized by the massive socioeconomic changes their country has gone through in the last 25 years. In hard times it's handy to have a scapegoat, and Asians have always been a target for criticism in Australia.

Nevertheless, Australia does have powerful anti-discrimination laws. Any racial discrimination can be reported to the **Human Rights and Equal Opportunities Commission**, who have offices in each state capital (listed in the "Government" section at the front of the White Pages phone book). Although you might not have time (or the desire) to go through the lengthy complaints process, the threat is a useful one, as their powers are considerable. Just don't expect a country policeman to help you – many are part of the problem rather than its solution.

WORK

Most visitors' visas clearly state that no employment of any kind is to be undertaken during a visit to Australia. However, if you've succeeded in getting a Working Holiday Visa (see "Visas and red tape", pp.16-17) and are prepared to try anything – officially for no more than three months at a time – there are plenty of possibilities for finding work. There are also organized work programmes – both paid and voluntary.

In practice this means that the only jobs officially open to you are unskilled, temporary ones. The former Commonwealth Employment Service (CES) has been broken up into competing, semi-privatized employment agencies. One of the largest ones is **Employment National** (Mon–Fri 9am–5pm; ☎13 3444). When you dial this number you will be put through to their nearest local branch. They will usually ask you to come in and register, or send a fax with all your details and a resumé. There are 209 branches all over Australia, including rural areas where there's a lot of seasonal work. What they offer will usually be either **harvesting or farm-labouring jobs** (see box opposite), or in the cities **clerical**, **bar** or **restaurant** jobs, or occasional **factory** work. Look up their database on the Internet: *www.employmentnational.com.au* which lists current availabe jobs.

Another Web site worthwhile perusing is *www.jobsearch.deetya.gov.au*. This database can be accessed from touchscreen computers at Centrelink offices (an agency handling the pay-ment of unemployment benefits with branches all over Australia). Internet cafés and some hostels also provide access to Internet databases – for a fee, of course. **Travellers Contact Point** in Sydney and Melbourne provide many services for travellers, including assistance with finding a job through a **jobsearch centre** (see "Listings", for details). Their Web site address is: *www.travellers.com.au*.

In addition to that, more specialized **employment agencies** are well worth a try in the cities, especially if you have a marketable skill (computer training, accountancy, nursing, cooking and the like). They might have better, higher-paid jobs on their books, though they may be looking for full-time or at least longer-term commitment. Newspaper **job ads** are also worth checking out, especially in smaller local papers. And finally, fellow travellers, **hostel** staff in smaller hostels, and notice boards may be the best source of all, especially in remote areas, some even run their own employment agency or have a permanently staffed employment desk. This is where you'll find out about local opportunities, and the hostels themselves may occasionally offer free nights in lieu of cleaning work – or even pay you for jobs that involve a bit more skill. Some of the hostels in the big cities or in country towns where there is a lot of harvesting work also arrange employment.

Significant long-term **unemployment** is prevalent in Australia, and the days of legendary wages for relentless hard work in mines, on the roads or on prawn trawlers are long gone. Nonetheless, plenty of people still manage to work **illegally**, though visa checks in the major harvest areas (they really do happen!) and tax reforms have made this much harder than it used to be.

ORGANIZED WORK PROGRAMMES

To streamline the process of procuring a working visa, getting to Australia and orienting yourself on arrival, there are several packages aimed at working travellers. BUNAC organizes a **Work Australia** programme that can be combined with their North American programmes, with departures from London between August and December and from Los Angeles in September and October. See opposite for contact details of this and other organizations.

SEASONAL PICKING AND HARVESTING WORK

Listed below are the major **harvest seasons** around the country. Once you're into the harvest season it's possible to move with it around the country, from one product to another, as many people do. There may be lesser harvests and other work in all of these places at any time.

NEW SOUTH WALES

Summer November–April, peaking in February, in the central eastern district around Bathurst, Dubbo and Orange; orchard and other fruits, cotton, onions and asparagus.

Year-round The north coast around Coffs Harbour; bananas.

VICTORIA

Summer November–April, peaking in February, in central northern areas around Shepparton, and also along the Murray River (Mildura, Swan Hill and, to a lesser extent, Echuca); orchard fruits, tomatoes, tobacco, grapes and soft fruits.

QUEENSLAND

Summer December–March, around Warwick, inland on the NSW border; stone and orchard fruits, grapes.

Year-round The southern central coast around Bundaberg and Childers; all kinds of fruit and vegetables.

May–December the central coast around Bowen; fruit and vegetables, especially mangoes at the end of the year.

May–November The northern coast around Ayr and Ingham; sugar cane, bananas and tobacco.

TASMANIA

Summer December–March; orchard and soft fruits, grapes.

SOUTH AUSTRALIA

February–April The Barossa Valley; grapes.

Year-round The Riverland; picking, pruning and packaging citrus and soft fruits.

WESTERN AUSTRALIA

October–June The southwest; grapes and orchard fruits (February–April), plus tractor-driven grain harvesting.

March–November The west coast from Fremantle to Carnarvon; crayfish, prawn and scallop fishing and processing.

May–October The northeast around Kununurra; fruit and vegetable picking and packing.

WORK PROGRAMME CONTACTS

ATCV (Australian Trust for Conservation Volunteers), PO Box 423, Ballarat, VIC 3353 (☎03/3/5333 1483, fax 5333 2166, free call ☎1800/032 501; *info@.atcv.com.au*, *www.atcv.com.au*).

BUNAC (British Universities North America Club), 16 Bowling Green Lane, London EC1R 0BD (☎0171/251 3472, fax 251 0215; *chris.dutton@unac.org.uk*).

Student Uni Travel, Level 8, 92 Pitt St, Sydney, NSW 2000 (☎02/9232 8444, fax 9232 7331). They handle, in Australia, all participants in the BUNAC and USIT programme from the UK, Kilroy from Scandinavia, SWAP groups from Canada and Travel Active from the Netherlands. Services provided include arrival, greeting and orientation, preopened bank accounts and tax file assistance, employment advice and assistance, job placement, travel discounts, free email, free access to word processing computers, and emergency assistance.

Travel Active Programmes, Postbus 107, 5800 AC Venray, The Netherlands (☎031/478 551 900, fax 478 551 911; *info@travelactive.nl*).

WWOOF (Willing Workers on Organic Farms), Mount Murrindal Reserve, Buchan, VIC 3885 (☎ & fax 03 5155 0218; *woof@ozemail.com.au*).Their listings book *The Australian Farm and Cultural Experience* is available direct or from agents (eg Backpackers' Travel Centres; branches of Student Uni Travel) in the capital cities of the Australian states and some other cities in the eastern states (eg Byron Bay, Surfers Paradise, Cairns). The price ($35 single, $40 for a couple) includes work insurance.

TAX

In recent years employers have been threatened with huge fines for offering cash-in-hand labour and, as a result, it's difficult to avoid paying **income tax**, which is levied at 29 percent for earnings under about $26,000 per annum and deducted at source. To become part of the system you'll need a **tax file number** (form available at post offices or taxation offices), which is pretty easy to obtain on presentation of a passport with relevant visa. Your employer will give you a couple of weeks' grace, but not much more – if you don't have a number, after that you'll be taxed at

49 percent. Nowadays it's hard to claim a tax **rebate**, no matter how little you earn; however, it's worth a try, and possibly a visit to a tax adviser. One tip is to tick the "resident" box on the rebate form: you're resident if you're planning to stay a day over six months.

DIRECTORY

BIG THINGS Don't be surprised if, on a long, hot stretch of Queensland highway, you find yourself hitchhiking next to Captain Cook. . . and no, that enormous pineapple on the horizon isn't an alien spacecraft – it's real. Real fibreglass, that is. Big Things are an Australian obsession, and a way for a small town to make a mark on the tourist map. As you travel around the country you'll find giant fruit – the Big Apple, the Big Banana, the Big Strawberry; animals and fish – the Big Lobster, the Big Penguin, the Big Cow; and tourist attractions – the Big Gold Panner and even Big Ayers Rock (far smaller than the real thing, of course). They're places to stop and get a drink or a bite, buy joyously tacky souvenirs and look at an exhibition – but above all they're places to take a photo. No Australian holiday is complete without at least one Big Thing in your album.

CHILDREN Children are well catered for in Australia, and are welcome in the bistros of hotels, with kids' menus and often a children's playroom. Nearly every park has a playground. Many attractions have reduced rates for children or families, and most motels and self-catering accommodation can provide family rooms and special rates.

ELECTRICITY Australia's electrical current is 240/250v, 50Hz AC. British appliances will work with an adaptor for the Australian three-pin plug. American and Canadian 110v appliances will also need a transformer.

EMERGENCIES Dial ☎000.

GAMBLING Australians are obsessive about gambling, though legalities vary from state to state. Even small towns have their own racetracks and there are government TAB betting agencies everywhere; you can often bet in pubs too. Many states have huge "casinos" and clubs open to anyone, with wall-to-wall one-armed bandits (poker machines or "pokies"); there are also big state lotteries.

LAUNDRIES Known as Laundromats, these are rare outside urban centres. Hostels, motels and caravan parks will often have a laundry area with a washing machine (coin-op). Fancy hotels, of course, will do it for you.

PUBLIC TOILETS Towns and cities are very well supplied with public facilities in civic-minded Australia. They're found in parks and at council and tourist offices in country areas, and in shopping arcades, train stations and department stores in the cities. Most roadhouses offer showers as well as toilets, usually for a small payment.

SEASONS Don't forget that in the southern hemisphere the seasons are reversed. Summer lasts from November to February, winter from June to September. But of course it's not that simple: in the tropical north the important seasonal distinction is between the Wet (effectively summer) and the Dry (winter) – for more on their significance to travellers, (see p.xv)

STUDENT CARDS These are well worth having (if you're eligible) for discounts on travel, tours, museum entry, etc. Backpackers of any age or status who can produce a YHA or VIP membership

METRIC CONVERSION TABLE

1 metre (m) = 100cm 1 kilometre (km) = 1000m	1 centimetre (cm) = 0.394in 1 metre = 39.37in 1 kilometre = 0.621 miles	1 inch (in) = 2.54cm 1 foot (ft) = 30.48cm 1 yard (yd) = 0.91m 1 mile = 1.610km
1 hectare = 10,000 square metres	1 hectare = 2.471 acres	1 acre = 0.4 hectares
	1 litre = 0.22 UK gal 1 litre = 0.26 US gal	1 UK gallon (gal) = 4.55 litres 1 US gallon (gal) = 5.46 litres
1 kilometre (km) = 1000m	1 gram (g) = 0.035oz 1 kilogram = 2.2lb	1 ounce (oz) = 28.57g 1 pound (lb) = 454g

card (see p.42) are entitled to many of these discounts.

TAX At the moment there is no direct sales tax or VAT in Australia. However, the present coalition government (Liberal/National) is proposing the introduction of a Goods and Services Tax (GST). This tax is a contentious issue. At the time of writing the legislation has yet to be put before the parliament and the outcome is uncertain.

TIME ZONES Australia has three time zones: Eastern Standard Time (TAS, VIC, NSW, QLD), Central Standard Time (SA, NT) and Western Standard Time (WA). Eastern Standard Time is ten hours ahead of GMT (Greenwich Mean Time) and fifteen hours ahead of US Eastern Time. (When it's 10pm in Sydney, it's noon in London, 7am in New York and 4am in Los Angeles – but don't forget daylight saving, which can affect this by two hours either way.)

Central Standard Time is thirty minutes behind Eastern Standard, and Western Standard two hours behind Eastern. Daylight saving (October–March) is adopted everywhere except QLD, NT and WA; clocks are put forward one hour.

TIPS Tipping is not customary in Australia, and cab drivers and bar staff don't expect anything. In fact, cab drivers often round the fare down rather than bother with change. In cafés and restaurants you might leave the change – only very fancy establishments expect ten percent.

WEIGHTS AND MEASURES Australia has been fully metric since the early 1970s and is thoroughly adapted to kilometres, kilograms, litres and degrees Celsius. Shoe sizes are unique to Australia, while dress sizes are the same as in the UK (US 8 is equivalent to Australian 10). See the conversion table above.

PART TWO

THE

GUIDE

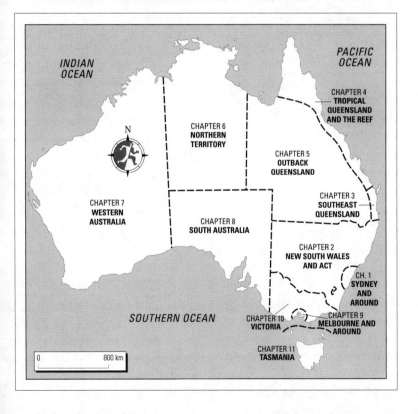

CHAPTER ONE

SYDNEY AND AROUND

Flying into Sydney provides the first close-up snapshot of Australia for most overseas visitors: toy-sized images of the Harbour Bridge and the Opera House, tilting in a glittering expanse of blue water. The Aussie city par excellence, Sydney stands head and shoulders above any other in Australia. Taken together with its surrounds, it's in many ways a microcosm of Australia as a whole – if only in its ability to defy your expectations and prejudices as often as it confirms them. A thrusting, high-rise business centre, a high-profile gay community and inner-city deprivation of

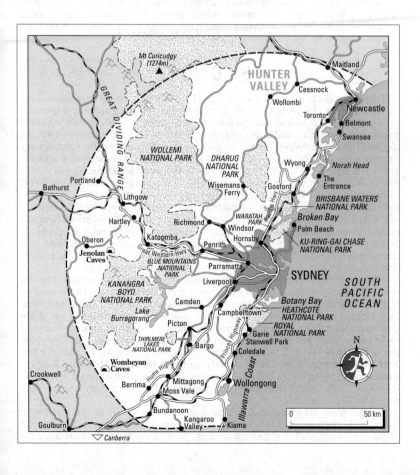

unexpected harshness are as much part of the scene as the beaches, the bodies and the sparkling harbour. The sophistication, cosmopolitan population and exuberant nightlife of Sydney are a long way from the Outback, and yet Sydney has the highest Aboriginal population of any Australian city.

The area around – everything in this chapter is within day-trip distance – offers a taste of virtually everything you'll find in the rest of the country, with the possible exception of desert. There are magnificent **national parks** and native wildlife – Ku-Ring-Gai Chase and Royal being the best known of the parks, each a mere hour's drive from the centre of town – and beyond them stretch endless ocean **beaches**, great for surfers, and more enclosed waters for safer swimming and sailing. Inland the **Blue Mountains**, with three more national parks, offer isolated bushwalking and scenic viewpoints. On the way are historic colonial towns that were among the earliest foundations in the country – Sydney itself, of course, having been the very first.

The commercial and industrial heart of the state of New South Wales, especially the central coastal region, is bordered by **Wollongong** in the south and **Newcastle** in the north. Both are synonymous with coal and steel, but the smokestack industries that supported them for decades are now in severe decline. This is far from an industrial wasteland, though: the heart of the coal-mining country is the **Hunter Valley**, north-west of Newcastle, but to visit it you'd never guess, because this is also Australia's oldest and arguably its best-known wine-growing region.

SYDNEY

SYDNEY has all the vigour of a world class city – with the year 2000 Olympics being its coming-of-age ceremony. Certainly development is continuing apace in preparation for the three weeks of international scrutiny in September, with a greatly improved transport infrastructure and a furious rash of luxury hotels adding themselves to the skyline. The City of Sydney Council is spending $200 million to improve and beautify the city streets, public squares and parks with everything from sculpture walks to smartly designed new street furniture. The feeling back home and abroad is that Sydney is evolving from a regional centre to an international city, with the reputation of its restaurants in particular turning the lingering cultural sneers to swoons. It seems to have the best of both worlds – twenty minutes from Circular Quay by bus, the high-rise office buildings and skyscrapers give way to colourful inner-city suburbs where you can get an eyeful of sky and watch the lemons ripening above the sidewalk and to the centre's north and south are corridors of largely intact bushland where many have built their dream homes. In the summer the city's hot offices are abandoned for the remarkably unspoilt beaches strung around the eastern and northern suburbs.

It's also as beautiful a city as any in the world, with a **setting** that perhaps only Rio de Janeiro can rival: the water is what makes it so special, and no introduction to Sydney would be complete without paying tribute to one of the world's great **harbours**. Port Jackson is a sunken valley which twists inland to meet the fresh water of the Parramatta River; in the process it washes into a hundred coves and bays, winds around rocky points, flows past the small harbour islands, slips under bridges and laps at the foot of the Opera House. If Sydney is seen at its gleaming best from the deck of a harbour ferry, especially at weekends when the harbour's jagged jaws fill with a flotilla of small vessels, racing yachts and cabin cruisers, it's seen at its most varied in its lively neighbourhoods. Getting away from the city centre and exploring them is an essential part of Sydney's pleasures.

It might seem surprising that Sydney is not Australia's capital: the creation of Canberra in 1927 – intended to stem the intense rivalry between Sydney and Melbourne – has not affected the view of many Sydneysiders that their city remains the

ACCOMMODATION PRICES

All the accommodation listed in this book has been categorized into one of eight price bands, as set out below. The rates quoted represent the cheapest available double or twin room in high season – except for category ③, which indicates per-person rates for a dorm bed, and the categories given for units, cabins and vans, which represent the daily charge for the whole unit.

① Under $18	② $19–30	⑤ $61–74	⑥ $75–94
③ $31–45	④ $46–60	⑦ $95–124	⑧ $125 upwards

for more accommodation details, see pp.40–43.

true capital of Australia, and certainly in many ways it feels like it. The city has a tangible sense of history: the old stone walls and well-worn steps in the backstreets around The Rocks are an evocative reminder that Sydney has more than two hundred years of white history behind it.

Some history

The early history of Sydney is very much the history of white Australia, right from its founding as a penal colony, amid brutality, deprivation and despair. In January 1788 the **First Fleet**, carrying over a thousand people, 736 of them convicts, arrived at **Botany Bay** expecting the "fine meadows" that Captain James Cook had described eight years earlier. In fact what greeted them was mostly swamp, scrub and sand dunes: a desolate sight even for sea-weary eyes. An unsuccessful scouting expedition prompted Commander Arthur Phillip to move the fleet a few kilometres north, to the well-wooded Port Jackson, where a stream of fresh water was found. Based around the less than satisfactory Tank Stream, the settlement was named **Sydney Cove** after Viscount Sydney, then Secretary of State in Great Britain. In the first three years of settlement, the new colony nearly starved to death several times; the land around Sydney Cove proved to be barren. When supply ships did arrive, they inevitably came with hundreds more convicts to further burden the colony. It was not until 1790, when land was successfully farmed further west at **Parramatta**, that the hunger began to abate. Measure this suffering with that of the **Eora Aborigines**: their land had been invaded, their people virtually wiped out by smallpox, and now they were stricken by hunger as the settlers shot at their game – and aimed their guns at the Eora themselves as the colonists moved further inland.

By the early 1800s Sydney had become a stable colony and busy trading post. Army officers in charge of the colony, exploiting their access to free land and cheap labour, became rich farm-owners and virtually established a currency based on rum. The **military**, known as the New South Wales Corps (or more familiarly as "the rum corps"), soon became the supreme political force in the colony in 1809, even overthrowing the governor (mutiny-plagued Captain Bligh himself). This was the last straw for the government back home, and the rebellious officers were finally brought to heel when the reformist Governor **Lachlan Macquarie** arrived from England with forces of his own. He liberalized conditions, supported the prisoners' right to become citizens after they had served their time, and appointed several to public offices.

By the 1840s the transportation of convicts to New South Wales had ended, the explorers Lawson and Blaxland had found a way through the Blue Mountains to the Western Plains and gold had been struck in Bathurst. The population soared as free settlers arrived in ever-increasing numbers. In the Victorian era Sydney's population became even more starkly divided into the **haves** and the **have-nots**: self-consciously replicating life in the mother country, the genteel classes took tea on their verandahs and erected grandiloquent monuments such as the Town Hall, the Strand Arcade and

OLYMPIC CITY 2000

Sydney proudly beat Beijing and Manchester in the chase for the **Olympics** in the year 2000 – and don't think you will be allowed to forget the fact while you're here, or indeed anywhere in Australia. The Sydney 2000 theme is hard to escape, seen in various forms of advertising throughout the country. The impact on Sydney is equally all-embracing, with roughly fifty years' worth of development compressed into four years. All of this is for just sixteen days of pure sporting achievement held between September 15 and October 1 2000.

Facts and figures

The City of Sydney Council have been spending $200 million on improving and pret-tifying the city's streets, squares and parks while a further $2.5 billion of public money is funding major road and rail projects to prepare Sydney for the Olympics, spear-headed by ORTA (Olympic Roads and Transport Authority). There is a $365 million project to improve Sydney Airport (airport traffic is expected to double during the Olympics). This does not include the $650 million being spent on the long overdue 10km underground rail link from the airport to the city, allowing Sydney to have the same airport transport infrastructures as other major cities. Other **public transport** includes the $93 million rail link to the **Olympic Park Station** gateway to the venues at Homebush Bay. No private vehicles will be allowed on the site during the Olympics, and even taxis will be banned from within a certain radius, leaving public transport as the only alternative. Around 15,000 athletes and team officials will pour into the coun-try, as well as something like 9000 staff of 175 foreign broadcasters, and then there are the expected quarter of a million spectators, with ticket sales (from mid-1999) hop-ing to generate around half a billion Australian dollars. Ticket prices will range from A$10 for football and baseball preliminaries to A$1000 for category "A" tickets to the opening and closing ceremonies. The majority of tickets will be less than $100; ath-letics and swimming tickets, for example, will start from $35. Hopefully there will be room to fit in all the extra visitors during the Olympic frenzy, but there are contin-gency plans to anchor cruise ships to increase capacity while a residential accommo-dation programme will find apartments to rent and rooms for visitors in private homes.

Background

Sydney's **Olympic logo**, with the inevitable boomerang replacing the Olympic rings, was launched in September 1996 at Darling Harbour amid fireworks. Though the logo may be inspired by indigenous culture, Aboriginal spokespeople have suggest-ed that Aboriginal groups might resort to political tactics, such as asking black nations to boycott the Games, if their issues are not taken more seriously. The tradi-tional owners of Uluru stirred things up further when they requested $60,000 to host the start of the 100-day Olympic torch relay, which will involve 2,500 escort runners and cover every state and territory. The failure of the **Sydney Organising Committee for the Olympic Games (SOCOG)** to select an Aboriginal committee member to replace an exiting member in highlighted the embarrassing political infighting typical of SOCOG which has also been the critical media spotlight over budget overruns and inflated salaries for bureaucrats. Olympic controversy deep-ened in January 1999 when the scandal of the evidence of bribery surrounding Salt Lake City's winning bid for the 2002 Winter Games focused scrutiny on Sydney's dealings.

What to see and where

While the world might imagine a backdrop of Opera House and Harbour Bridge, the main focus of events will be far removed from the glamour of Sydney's harbour, at Homebush Bay, a fairly down-at-heel working-class area in the city's west. There's a cer-tain logic to the choice, as Homebush Bay is virtually the geographical heart of a city that spreads ever westward, with the extensive riverfront Bicentennial Park nearby and some heavy-duty sporting facilities already in place just across on Australia Avenue.

The $470 million Olympic project at **Homebush Bay** is centred around the 110,000-seat **Olympic Stadium**, the largest ever outdoor Olympic venue, which will witness the opening and closing ceremonies, track and field events, and marathon and soccer finals. Other projects on site are a 16-court Tennis Centre, an Archery Centre, and an indoor Multi-Use Arena. The Sydney Showground at the site will host the softball, the existing State Hockey Centre has been upgraded, and the Sydney International Athletic Centre and the Sydney International Aquatic Centre (see below) will host their respective sports. The pentathlon is set to be contested across the road from the Olympic site at Bicentennial Park.

Other Olympic events around town will take place at more picturesque locations, like the beach volleyball at Bondi Beach and sailing at the revamped Rushcutters Bay Marina. The marathon will commence at North Sydney, heading across the Harbour Bridge through the city to Centennial Park and Anzac Parade, thence back to the city then across Glebe Island Bridge, finishing at the Olympic Stadium, while the road cycling races will terminate at Bronte Beach. Darling Harbour will be quite a focus, with basketball at the Entertainment Centre, boxing, judo, table tennis and tae kwon do at the Exhibition Centre, and weightlifting at the Convention Centre. Moore Park will see football events in the Sydney Football Stadium and fencing in the former Showground pavilions. Further afield, water polo will be held at the revamped Ryde Pool complex, mountain-biking at Fairfield City Farm while rowing events will take place at Penrith Lakes. Several newly built sporting venues will host sports on Sydney's western outskirts: a cycling velodrome at Bankstown, a Shooting Centre in Liverpool, a softball centre in Blacktown, and an Equestrian Centre at Horsley Park.

A green-friendly **Athlete's Village** will house athletes and officials; more than half of the modular dwellings, will be moved and reused elsewhere afterwards. Alongside the village is a new solar powered suburb, **Newington**. Private tenants will already be in occupation during the Olympics, while the remaining Olympic dwellings will be incorporated into the suburb later. Besides building work there is the landscaping of the grounds – many trees taken off site during building will be put back on, and ninety-five percent of plants will be native. A large percentage of the site is being created as the 440-hectare **Millennium Parklands** with the old brickpit, home of the endangered green and gold frog, at its centre.

If you want to check out where the main Homebush action will be, you can visit the **Homebush Bay Information Centre** (daily 9am–5pm; free; ☎02/9735 4800), giving up-to-the-minute information about the development of the site and its facilities. There's a separate souvenir shop (daily 10am–4pm) selling Olympic paraphernalia. Head for Australia Avenue to the **State Sports Centre** (daily 8.30am–10pm; ☎02/9763 0111; 24hr information line ☎1902/260 690, 50¢ per minute), where you can visit the **NSW Hall of Champions** (same hours as centre; free; the Hall of Champions is closed when events are being held at the the the State Sports Centre, so call the latter before setting out) devoted to the state's sporting heroes. Australia Avenue is home to the **Sydney International Aquatic Centre** (Mon–Fri 5am–10pm, Sat & Sun 6am–7pm; $4.50; ☎02/9752 3666) where the swimming events will be based; you can hop in the water and try out the facilities from the competition pools to the landscaped leisure pools with their fountains and slides.

How to get there

To get out to the Olympic site, from Strathfield station you can take bus #401–404 to the Homebush Bay Olympic Centre, the State Sports Centre and the Athletic Centre (every 15–30min from 6am to 10pm; 10min); on weekends the #401 service is only offered in the evenings (every 30min 6.35–10.05pm) and you should take the train to Olympic Park Station. Bus-only tours of the Olympic site, providing information about current facilities and those planned, leave the Homebush Bay information centre every half hour from 10am to 1pm ($5; 45min; entry to sites and venues isn't included;

box continued overleaf . . .

☎02/9735 4800 for more information). You can take a combined RiverCat Cruise from Circular Quay to Homebush Bay and a bus tour at the Olympic Park site including a visit to the information centre (Mon–Fri 10am, 11am, noon, 1pm, 1.30pm; tour 1hr; $15; tickets from Wharf 5; ☎02/9207 3170); an extended weekend tour also includes the Aquatic Centre (Sat & Sun 10.35am & 12.25pm; $22).

Information

If you feel that Homebush is too far to travel, you can find out more about the Olympic plans by checking out various IBM-sponsored Olympic Information Kiosks in prominent places around town For more serious information, contact the Sydney Organising Committee for the Olympic Games (SOCOG), GPO Box 200, Sydney, NSW 2001 (☎02/9297 2000, fax 9297 2817) or the Olympic Co-ordination Authority, GPO Box 5341, Sydney, NSW 2001 (☎02/9228 3333, fax 9228 5551), or check the useful Olympic Web site (*www.sydney.olympic.org*).

the Queen Victoria Building in homage to English architecture of the time. Meanwhile, the poor lived in slums where disease, crime, prostitution and alcoholism were rife. An outbreak of the plague in The Rocks at the turn of the century made wholesale slum clearances unavoidable, and with the demolitions came a change in attitudes. Strict new vice laws meant the end of the bad old days of backstreet knifings, drunken taverns and makeshift brothels.

Over the next few decades, Sydney settled into comfortable suburban living. The metropolis sprawled westwards, creating a flat, unremarkable city with no real centre, an appropriate symbol for the era of shorts and knee socks and the stereotypical, barbecue-loving Bruce and Sheila – an international image which still plagues Australians. Sydney has come a long way since the parochialism of the 1950s, however: the cultural clichés of cold tinnies of beer and meat pies with sauce have at last been tossed out, giving way to a city confident in itself and its culinary attractions too. Skyscrapers at the city's centre have rocketed heavenward and constructions such as the Centrepoint Tower and the Opera House reflect the new dynamism. Today, Sydney's citizens don't look inward – or even to England. Thousands of immigrants from around the globe have given Sydney a truly international air and it's a city as thrilling and alive as any.

Arrival and information

The classic way to **arrive** in Sydney is, of course, by ship, cruising in under the great coathanger of the Harbour Bridge to tie up at the docks alongside Circular Quay. Unfortunately you're not likely to be doing that, and the reality of the functional airport, bus and train stations is a good deal less romantic.

By air

Sydney's **Kingsford Smith Airport**, commonly referred to as "Mascot" after the suburb where it's located, near Botany Bay, is barely 8km south of the city (international flight arrivals and departures ☎1900/951 850, 75¢ per min; Airport Travellers Information ☎02/9669 5111). Domestic and international terminals are on opposite sides of the airport, linked by the free Long-Term Car Park Shuttle Bus (every 30min) or you can take the Airport Express bus (see box opposite) for $2.50; see box on p.77 (opposite) for details of **bus services** into the city, inner-city and to the northern and eastern beaches. There are also a few services that can get you straight out of Sydney and to the Central Coast, the South Coast or the Southern Highlands. If you arrive before around May 2000, expect some disruption/confusion with the upgrading of the

AIRPORT BUSES

STATE TRANSIT
Airport Express (☎13 1500) buses (green-and-yellow) link the domestic and international terminals ($2.50), and shuttle to and from the city centre, and Kings Cross, Glebe and Bondi on four different routes, picking up and setting down at various stops. Fares on all routes are $6 one-way and $10 return (return valid for two months). Operating daily between about 5am and 11pm: the #300 runs to Circular Quay via Central Station and George Street and back every ten minutes; the #350 runs to Central Station and Kings Cross every twenty minutes. Operating every 30min between about 7am and 9pm, the #351 to Bondi goes via the University of NSW, Randwick, Coogee and Bronte while the #352 runs to Glebe. Tickets can be bought on board and at the **New South Wales Travel Centre** in the international terminal (see p.76), where you can also buy tourist bus passes – the Sydney Pass (see p.75) includes return airport–city transfer.
State Transit also has some ordinary commuter routes serving the airport that may be useful: the only daily service is the Metroline #400 which goes frequently to Bondi Junction via Maroubra and Randwick in one direction, and to Burwood in the other; the #100 route runs Monday to Friday only going to the northern beach suburb of Dee Why via the city, North Sydney, Neutral Bay and Cremorne Junction between 6.25am and 6.30pm. Tickets on these routes cost a maximum of $4.60; regular weekly travel passes can be used but these cannot be purchased at the airport (see p.76-77).

SHUTTLE SERVICES – SYDNEY AREA
Jetbus (☎0500/886008 to book a pick-up from your accommodation). Mini-bus service operating continuously from the airport to and from the eastern beaches: Bondi, Coogee, Randwick, Clovelly and Bronte; dropping off at all hostels, motels and hotels; $8. Service leaves when the bus is full.
Kingsford Smith Transport/Sydney Airporter (☎02/9667 3221 or 9667 0663 to book a pick-up from your accommodation). A private bus service, will drop you right at the door of your hotel or hostel in the area bounded by Kings Cross, Darling Harbour, Glebe and Double Bay. Service leaves when the bus is full; $6 one-way, $11 return.
Northern Beaches Airport Shuttle (☎02/9913 9912, fax 9970 5248). Mini-bus service from the international and domestic terminals to northern beaches destinations, including Manly, Whale Beach and Palm Beach, dropping off at your chosen accommodation. You must book in advance giving the day, time and flight and they will designate a waiting point. Manly $20 per person, Palm Beach $30 (cheaper rates for couples and groups).

COACH SERVICES – CENTRAL COAST, SOUTH COAST AND SOUTHERN HIGHLANDS
Central Coast Airbus (☎02/4332 8655) has a scheduled #747 service that runs to the Central Coast (Terrigal and Bateau Bay; 2hr15min–2hr 30min; $18) via the northern suburbs, taking in Pymble, Turramurra, Hornsby, Asquith, Mount Colah, Mount Ku-Ring-Gai and Berowa (Mon–Fri 8am, 9.30am, 11.30am, 2.30pm, 3pm, 3.30pm, 4pm, 4.45pm & 5.45pm, Sat & Sun 9.30am & 4pm).
Premier Motor Service (☎1300/368 1000, Eden ☎02/4423 5233, fax 4421 0068). Daily at 9.45am & 4.30pm, and Mon–Fri at 7.45am from the domestic terminal, 15 minutes later from the international terminal to south coast towns as far as Bega ($44), the 9.45am and 4.30pm service continuing on to Eden ($49).
Prior's Scenic Express (☎02/4472 4040 or free call ☎1800/816 234). Mon, Tues, Thurs, Fri & Sat from the airport (international 7.30am; domestic 7.40am) if booked in advance to the Southern Highlands thence to Moruya or Narooma (not Sat) via the south coast; $26 one-way.

airport in time for the Olympics. $365 million is being spent on the project, including a new rail link. The **Airport Link Underground Railway** is due to open in May 2000; it will connect Sydney Airport to the city circle train line. The journey to the city will take just over ten minutes, with an optimistic frequency of every seven minutes at peak times. A **taxi** ride from the airport to the city centre or Kings Cross costs $20–25, depending on traffic; between the domestic and international terminals it's around $8.

Bureau de change offices at both terminals are open daily from 5am until last arrival (and also sell phonecards) with rates comparable to major banks. On the ground floor (arrivals) of the international terminal, the **New South Wales Travel Centre** (☎02/9667 6050; daily 5am until last arrival) can arrange car rental and onward travel – it's licensed to sell train and bus tickets – and book hotels (but not hostels) anywhere in Sydney and NSW free of charge. The **accommodation bookings** here are at stand-by rates, faxed to them everyday, so it's possible to get a good deal – but only face to face (no telephone bookings). Most hostels do, however, advertise on an adjacent notice board, the "Backpacker Accommodation Directory"; there's a freephone line for reservations, and many of them will refund your bus fare.

By train and bus

All local and interstate **trains** arrive at **Central Station** on Eddy Avenue, south of the city centre. From here, and neighbouring **Railway Square** you can hop onto nearly every major bus route, and from within Central Station you can take a CityRail train to any city or suburban station. See "City transport" on p.79 for more details.

All **buses** to Sydney now arrive and depart from Eddy Avenue and Pitt Street bordering Central Station. The area is well set up with decent cafés, a 24-hour police station and a huge new YHA hostel (see p.87), as well as the **Sydney Coach Terminal**, on the corner of the two streets (daily 6am–10pm; ☎02/9281 9366). The terminal also has telephones, luggage lockers ($4, $6 or $8 per 24hr, depending on size), toilets, and a waiting room. The 'Traveller's Information Service (☎02/0000 0111) in the coach terminal can make hotel **accommodation bookings** at stand-by rates while a range of hostels advertise on an adjacent notice board with free phones for direct reservations; many of them will also provide free pick-ups (usually from Bay 14). You can purchase coach tickets and passes from the Information Service as well as Sydney Passes, and arrange harbour cruises and other tours. Greyhound Pioneer and McCafferty's also have separate ticket offices/departure lounges on Eddy Avenue.

Information

There's no shortage of places offering **information** about Sydney. The New South Wales Travel Centre at the international airport terminal offers the most comprehensive service (above), with maps and brochures, accommodation reservations (face to face only, at stand-by rates) and transport bookings for Sydney and the rest of New South Wales. Ask for *Sydney: The Official Book of Maps*, a free booklet with seventeen excellent maps of Sydney's various areas and its surroundings plus a CityRail and ferry plan, and the useful *Sydney Airport Arrivals Guide*. The main central tourist office is the **Sydney Visitor Centre** in The Rocks at 106 George St near Circular Quay (daily 9am–6pm; ☎02/9255 1788; also see p.102), offering a similar range of literature; they also have a self-service budget accommodation booking board with free phones directly linked to the listed hotels. Otherwise, tourist information is supplied by the **Darling Harbour Visitor Information Centre** (see p.114), or **Sydney Visitors Information** (Mon–Fri 9am–5pm; ☎02/9235 2424), a small information kiosk at Martin Place, or the tourist office at Manly (see p.135). The City of Sydney Council has introduced the **City Host Programme** with three information kiosks open daily at Circular Quay, Martin Place and Town Hall, with staff providing brochures, maps and information. Several free monthly **listings magazines** are worth picking up at tourist offices: *This Week in Sydney* is probably the best for general information, while *Index* is good for details of cultural activities. *TNT Magazine* is the best of an array of publications aimed at **back-**

packers, giving the lowdown on Sydney on the cheap, while **hostel notice boards** themselves act as an informal network, advertising everything from cars and international plane tickets to backpacks, camping gear and rides to other cities.

City transport

Sydney's public transport network is reasonably good, though the system relies heavily on buses and traffic jams can be a problem. There are buses, trains, ferries, a light rail system and the city monorail to choose from, plus plenty of licensed **taxis** (flag them down – they're vacant if the rooftop light is on; see "Listings", p.167, for cab rank locations and phone numbers). Trains finish around midnight, as do most regular buses, though several services running towards the eastern and northern beaches, such as the #380 to Bondi Beach, the #372 and #373 to Coogee and the #151 to Manly, run through the night. Otherwise a pretty good network of **Nightride buses** follow the train routes to the suburbs, departing from Town Hall Station (outside the Sydney Electricity Building on George Street) and stopping at train stations (where taxi ranks fine-tune the getting home process). You can use return train tickets, Railpasses and Travelpasses on board the nightbuses or else buy a ticket from the driver. If you're staying for more than a few days, a weekly **Travelpass** is a worthwhile investment (see box on p.83). For public transport information, routes and timetables call ☎13 1500 (daily 6am–10pm; *www.sydneytransport.net.au*).

Buses

Within the central area, **buses,** hailed from yellow-signed bus stops, are much the most convenient and widespread mode of transport, and in general they cover more of the city than the trains. With few exceptions buses radiate from the centre: major interchanges are located at Railway Square near Central Station, especially for the southwest routes; at Circular Quay for a range of routes; from York and Carrington streets outside Wynyard Station for the North Shore; and Bondi Junction Station for the eastern suburbs and beaches. The only west–east bus route is the Metroline #400, which goes from Burwood through to Bondi Junction via the airport (see box on p.77). **Tickets**, costing from $1.20 for up to two sections, $2.50 (the most typical fare) for up to nine sections and rising to $4.60 according to the distance travelled, can be bought on board from the driver. If you're going to use the bus network more than occasionally, substantial discounts are available with TravelTen tickets and other travel passes (see box on p.83). These must be validated in the green ticket reader by the front door. You can get bus **information**, **timetables** and **passes** from a few handy booths: at Carrington Street, Wynyard (Mon–Fri 8am–6pm, Sat 9am–2pm), at Circular Quay on the corner of Loftus and Alfred streets (Mon–Fri 8am–8pm, Sat & Sun 9am–6pm), at the Queen Victoria Building on York Street (Mon–Fri 8am–6pm, Sat 9am–2pm), at Bondi Junction bus interchange (Mon–Fri 7.15am–5pm, Sat 7.30am–2.30pm) and at Manly Wharf (Mon–Fri 7am–6pm, Sat & Sun 8am–4pm). Sydney buses have their own Web site: *www.sydneybuses.nsw.gov.au*.

Trains

Trains, operated by **CityRail** (see map on p.81), will get you where you're going faster than buses, especially at rush hour and when heading out to the suburbs, but you need to transfer to a bus or ferry to get to most harbourside or beach destinations. There are five train lines, each of which stops at Central and Town Hall stations. The underground City Loop is very useful, linking Central Station, Town Hall, Wynyard, Circular Quay, St James and Museum, and allowing you to connect with the rail system from almost anywhere in the centre. The only other underground route, running from Bondi

Junction, through Edgecliff, Kings Cross, Martin Place, Town Hall, Central and Redfern, then overland to the beach at Cronulla, is handy for tourists. In addition there are two new train links, one to the Olympic site at Homebush Bay, and the **new Southern Railway**, a 10km underground rail link from the airport to Central Station and the city circle, due for completion by May 2000 (for more information contact Airport Link on ☎02/9384 1000). Trains run from around 5am to midnight, with **tickets** starting at around $1.60 on the City Loop and for short hops; you can save money by buying off-peak returns after 9am and all weekend.

Automatic ticket machines (which give change) and barriers (if you have a magnetic ticket insert it, otherwise show your ticket at the gate) have been introduced just about everywhere. No excuses will be accepted if you don't have a ticket or have overridden your fare, with fines at $150. Following incidents on late evening trains, all platforms have been painted with designated "nightsafe" waiting areas and all but two or three train carriages are closed after about 8pm, enforcing a cattle-like safety in numbers. At other times, if the train is deserted, sit in the carriage nearest the guard, marked by a blue light. **CityRail** has its own Web site: *www.cityrail.nsw.gov.au*.

Ferries

Sydney's distinctive green-and-yellow **ferries** are the fastest means of transport from Circular Quay to the North Shore, and indeed to most places around the harbour. Even if you don't want to go anywhere, a ferry ride is a must, for it gives you a chance to get out on the water and see the city from the harbour. There's also a **hydrofoil** which goes to Manly, the JetCat, a speedy catamaran that gets you there in half the time, but with less charm.

There are ferries going off in various directions from the wharves at Circular Quay (see map on p.82); cruises depart from Wharf 6. The last ferry service from Circular Quay to Manly is at 7pm after which time the faster JetCats operate until midnight, 11pm on Saturdays. Other ferry routes, such as those to Parramatta and Pyrmont Bay, also operate only until early evening, while ferries to locations including Neutral Bay and Balmain continue to around 11.30pm. Except for the Manly ferry, services on Sunday are greatly reduced and often finish earlier. Timetables for each route are available at Circular Quay.

One-way fares are $3.20 ($4 for the Manly Ferry); return fares are doubled. The pricier JetCat to Manly is $5.20, while the RiverCat to Parramatta is $5. Once again, the various Travelpasses and FerryTen tickets can be a good deal – see box on p.83 for complete details. Sydney Ferries have their own Web site: *www.sydneyferries.nsw.gov.au*.

A private company, Hegarty's Ferries (☎02/9206 1167), also operate their own blue-and-white boats to Milsons Point, Lavender Bay and McMahons Point from Wharf 6 ($2.40; ten trips $17).

Monorail

The **Monorail** (☎02/9552 2288) is essentially a tourist shuttle designed to loop around Darling Harbour every 3–5 minutes, connecting it with the city centre. Thundering along tracks set above the older city streets, the monster rail – as many locals know it – doesn't exactly blend in with its surroundings. Still, the elevated view of the city, particularly from Pyrmont Bridge, makes it worth investing $2.50 (day-pass $7) and ten minutes to do the whole circuit with its seven stops (see "Central Sydney" map on pp.96–97; Mon–Wed 7am–10pm, Thurs–Sat 7am–midnight, Sun 8am–10pm, May–October Thurs until 10pm).

Light Rail

Sydney Light Rail (SLR) – a **light rail system** funded jointly by the state government and by private backers – has been operating since mid-1997 on a route which runs from

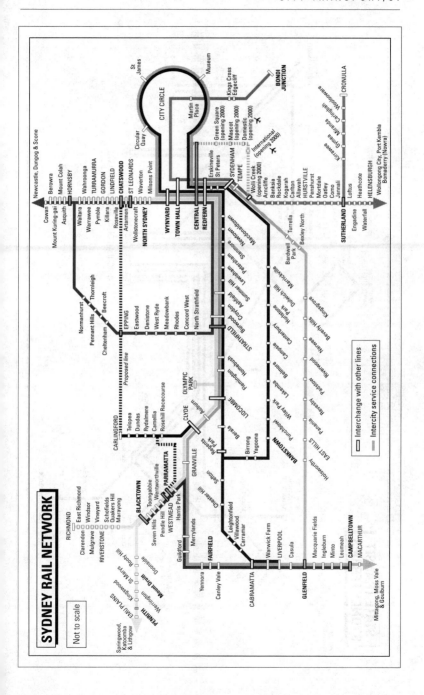

SYDNEY RAIL NETWORK

Not to scale

Interchange with other lines
Intercity service connections

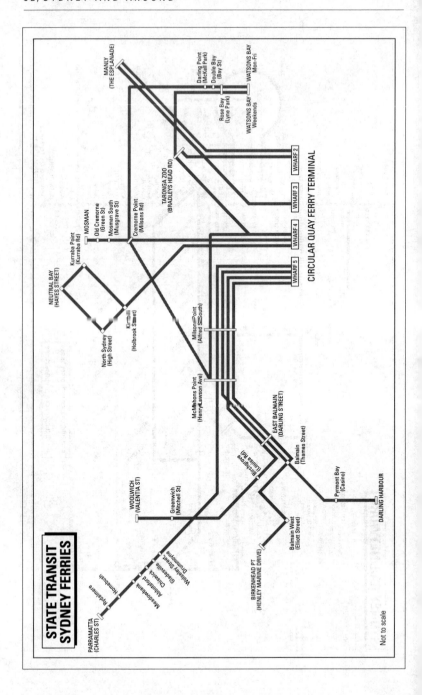

STATE TRANSIT
SYDNEY FERRIES

CIRCULAR QUAY FERRY TERMINAL

WHARF 2
WHARF 3
WHARF 4
WHARF 5

MANLY (THE ESPLANADE)

Darling Point (McKell Park)
Double Bay (Bay St)
Rose Bay (Lyne Park)
WATSONS BAY Mon-Fri
WATSONS BAY Weekends

TARONGA ZOO (BRADLEYS HEAD RD)

MOSMAN
Old Cremorne (Green St)
Mosman South (Musgrave St)
Cremorne Point (Milsons Rd)

Kurraba Point (Kurraba Rd)

NEUTRAL BAY (HAYES STREET)

North Sydney (High Street)

Kirribilli (Holbrook Street)

Milsons Point (Alfred St South)

McMahons Point (Henry Lawson Ave)

EAST BALMAIN (DARLING STREET)

Balmain (Thames Street)

Birchgrove (Louisa Rd)

Balmain West (Elliott Street)

BIRKENHEAD PT (HENLEY MARINE DRIVE)

Greenwich (Mitchell St)

WOOLWICH (VALENTIA ST)

Pyrmont Bay (Casino)

DARLING HARBOUR

PARRAMATTA (CHARLES ST)

Rydalmere

Homebush

Meadowbank
Abbotsford
Chiswick
Gladesville
Wolseley Street
Drummoyne

Not to scale

TRAVEL PASSES

In addition to single-journey tickets, there's a vast array of **travel passes** available. The most useful for visitors are outlined below; for more **information** on the full range of tickets and timetables, phone the Bus, Train, Ferry InfoLine (☎13 1500; daily 6am–10pm; *www.sta.nsw.gov.au*).

Passes are sold at most **newsagents** and at **train stations**; the more tourist-oriented Sydney Passes and Sydney Explorer Passes can be bought on-board the Explorer buses, at the **airport** (from the NSW Travel Centre and the STA booth in the international terminal and from State Transit ground staff in the domestic), at State Transit Info booths from the Sydney Visitor Centre in The Rocks (see p.102), and at some Countrylink offices as well as at railway stations.

TOURIST PASSES

Sydney Explorer Pass (one-day $25, child $18, family pass $68) comes with a map and description of the sights, and includes free travel on any State Transit bus within the same zones as the Explorer routes. The red **Sydney Explorer** (daily 8.15am–5.25pm; every 15min) takes in all the important sights in the city and inner suburbs, and you can hop on and off at any of the 24 stops. The blue **Bondi & Bay Explorer** (daily 9.15am–4.20pm; every 25min) covers the waterside eastern suburbs; nineteen stops en route include Kings Cross, Paddington, Double Bay, Vaucluse and the beaches of Bondi, Bronte, Clovelly and Coogee. A two-day Twin Ticket ($45, child $35, family $120) allows you to use both bus services over two days in a seven-day period.

Sydney Pass (three, five or seven days' travel within a seven-day period for $70, $95 and $110 respectively; children $60/$80/$95, family rates $200/$270/$315) is valid for all buses and ferries including the above Explorer services, the ferry and JetCat to Manly, the RiverCat to Parramatta and a return trip to the airport valid for two months with the Airport Express bus (make sure you buy it at the airport). It also includes four narrated harbour cruises, one of them in the evening, and travel on trains within a central area.

BUSES, TRAINS AND FERRIES

Travelpasses buy unlimited use of buses, trains and ferries and can begin on any day of the week. Most useful are the **Red Travelpass** ($23 a week), valid for the city and inner suburbs, and inner harbour ferries (not the Manly Ferry or the RiverCat beyond Meadowbank); and the **Green Travelpass** ($29), which allows use of all ferries – except JetCats before 7pm. Passes covering a wider area cost between $32 and $47 a week, and monthly passes are also available.

DayRover tickets ($16 off-peak to $20 peak) are also available for unlimited travel on all services offered by CityRail and State Transit.

BUSES AND TRAINS

Cityhopper tickets give one day's unlimited train and bus travel in the area between Central Station, Darling Harbour, Redfern, Moore Park, Kings Cross and North Sydney for $6.60; the off-peak fare is $5.40 (Mon–Fri after 9am and any time at weekends and public holidays).

BUSES AND FERRIES

DayPass provides all-day bus and ferry transport as far afield as you like for $12. Travelpasses for buses and ferries consist of the **Blue Travelpass** ($20 a week), which gives you unlimited travel on buses in the inner-city area and on inner harbour ferries but cannot be used for Manly or beyond Meadowbank; the **Orange Travelpass** ($26), which gets you further on the buses and is valid on all ferries; and the **Pittwater Travelpass** ($37 a week) which gives unlimited travel on all buses and ferries. These travelpasses start with first use rather than on the day of purchase.

BUSES

TravelTen tickets represent a 45 percent saving over single fares by buying ten trips at once; they can be used over a space of time and for more than one person. The blue ver-

box continues overleaf . . .

sion ($8.80) lets you ride up to two sections per validation (it's one section from Central Station to Circular Quay, for example, and two sections from Queen Street Woollahra to Bondi Junction), while a Red TravelTen ($17.60) allows you to travel up to nine sections per ride (Leichhardt to Town Hall is five sections), and there are three other colour-coded TravelTens for greater distances.

Two Zone Travelpass comes in a bus-only variant for $20 a week for adjacent bus zones.

BusTripper offers a day's unlimited bus travel for $7.80.

FERRIES

FerryTen tickets, valid for ten single trips, start at $19 for Inner Harbour Services, go up to $30 for the Manly Ferry, and peak at $44 for the JetCat services.

TRAINS

Rail Weekly tickets allow unlimited travel between any two nominated stations and those in between, with savings of about twenty percent on the price of five return trips.

Central Station to the Pyrmont peninsula (see "Central Sydney" map on pp.96–97); there are plans to extend it to Circular Quay in one direction and Leichhardt in the other. There are ten stops on the route, which links Central Station with Chinatown, Darling Harbour, Star City Casino, the fish markets at Pyrmont and Wentworth Park. The air-conditioned light rail vehicles can carry two hundred passengers, and are fully accessible to disabled commuters and people with prams with their wide doors, roomy aisles and low steps. The service operates 24-hour (as it takes in the casino), at five- to seven-minute intervals during peak periods on weekdays and weekends and every ten to twelve minutes at other times. For more information, contact SLR on (☎02/9660 5288). Tickets can be purchased at vending machines by the stops. The route is divided into two zones, with Central Station to Convention as Zone One and Pyrmont Bay to Wentworth Park as Zone Two. Fares are pricey (single Zone 1 ticket $2, return $3; single Zone 2 ticket $3, return $4; day-pass $6; weekly ticket $16). You can buy a TramLink ticket from any CityRail station and this combines a rail ticket to Central Station with an SLR ticket; price depends on which train station you buy your ticket from.

Accommodation

There are a tremendous number of places to stay in Sydney, and fierce competition helps keep prices down. Finding somewhere to stay is usually only a problem just before Christmas and throughout January, and in late February/early March during the Gay Mardi Gras: at these times you'll definitely need to **book ahead**. There'll be problems finding accommodation during the Olympics in September 2000, when prices will go up. All types of accommodation offer a (sometimes substantial) discount for **weekly bookings**, and may also cut prices considerably during the **low season** (from autumn to spring, school holidays excepted); it's always worth asking. A ten percent **bed tax** has been introduced for city centre (including Kings Cross) and North Sydney municipality hotels (not hostels) by the NSW government.

The larger **international hotels** in The Rocks and the CBD charge around $150–220 for a double room but if you head downtown to the area around Central Station you can find a four-star for $140; if you have a car even the five-star hotels seem to charge around $15 a day for parking. Even the least expensive hotels in the city, often above **pubs** and sharing bathrooms, start from $80. Rates in Kings Cross are much cheaper than in the city centre, with rooms in **private hotels** available for $50–60 and in three- or four-star hotels at around $130. **Motels**, such as ones we've listed in Glebe, Surry Hills and Bondi, charge $80–95. There is now an increasing number of mid-range "boutique" hotels and **guesthouses**, mostly away from the centre, which tend to be smaller, more characterful places to stay, charging around $95–140. **Serviced holiday apartments** can be very good value for a group, but are generally heavily booked.

Despite the number of **hostels** all over Sydney and the rivalry between them, standards are very variable and, in Kings Cross especially, can unfortunately be very low. As the scene changes rapidly, it's worth getting the latest news from other travellers. Rates are pretty standard – in summer about $18–20 for a dorm bed ($18–23 all year at YHAs) and $40–48 for a double (around $65 for an en suite), with rates dropping as low as $13 for a dorm bed in winter; plus $10–20 key deposit which will be refunded upon departure. If you're staying longer, weekly rates can often save you the cost of a night's stay, about $100–120 weekly for a dorm room. All hostels have a laundry, kitchen, and common room with TV unless stated otherwise. Office hours are generally restricted, typically 8am–noon and 4.30–6pm so it's best to call first and arrange an arrival time; we have indicated where places have longer reception hours.

If you're staying for any length of time, you might want to consider a **rental** or **flat-share** as an alternative to hotels or hostels. The best place to look is in Saturday's real-estate section of the *Sydney Morning Herald* or on café notice boards, especially in Newtown, Glebe and Bondi. Most rooms go from about $110 per week (rent is usually two weeks in advance, plus a deposit of four weeks' rent). The best areas for good, cheap apartments are Bondi and around the universities in Glebe, Newtown and Randwick: check on the notice boards at Sydney University and the University of NSW. **Homeshare Flatmates**, 127 York St, Darlinghurst (☎02/9261 3146), is a reliable agency that can help you find a flatshare for a $65 fee.

There are no **campsites** or caravan parks close to the centre; the nearest are at the suburbs of Rockdale, 13km south of the city, and North Ryde, 14km northwest (see box below).

Where to stay

The listings below are arranged by area. For short visits, you'll want to stay in the **city centre** or the immediate vicinity: The Rocks, the Central Business District (CBD) and Darling Harbour have the greatest concentration of expensive hotels while the area around Central Station and Chinatown known as Haymarket, has a glut of cheaper

---

CAMPSITES AROUND SYDNEY

It's possible to camp in the area around Sydney, or stay in one of several well-equipped caravan parks. The ones listed below are some of the best. Camping will cost $15–20 for two people in an unpowered site.

Lane Cove River Caravan Park, Plassey Rd, North Ryde, 14km northwest of the city (☎02/9888 9133, fax 9888 9322). Wonderful bush location beside Lane Cove National Park, right on the river, in Sydney's northern suburbs. Facilities include a bush kitchen with fridge and swimming pool. Train to Chatswood then bus #550 or #551. En-suite cabins ⑤.

Lakeside Caravan Park, Lake Park Rd, Narrabeen, 26km north of the city

(☎02/9913 7845, fax 9970 6385). Bus #190 or #L90 from Wynyard and then a 10min walk. Great spot by Narrabeen Lakes on Sydney's northern beaches. Free gas barbecues, camp kitchen and a nearby shop. Cabins ⑤–⑦.

Sheralee Tourist Caravan Park, 88 Bryant St, Rockdale, 13km south of the city (☎02/9567 7161). Train to Rockdale station, then a 10min walk. Small park with camp kitchen; on-site vans ③.

more downmarket places. **Kings Cross** is still very much the travellers' centre, with more backpackers' accommodation and cheaper hotels than elsewhere – it's a ten-minute walk from the city, has its own train station, and makes a convenient base if you don't mind the sleaze and the all-night partying. The adjacent suburbs of **Woolloomooloo**, **Potts Point** and **Elizabeth Bay** move gradually upmarket, and what little you lose in terms of accessibility, you gain in peace and quiet. To the west, **Glebe** is another slice of prime backpackers' territory, featuring a large YHA hostel, as well as several other backpackers' places and a number of small guesthouses.

If you're staying longer, consider somewhere further out, on the **North Shore**, where you'll get more for your money and more of a feel for Sydney as a city. **Kirribilli**, **Neutral Bay** or **Cremorne Point** offer some serenity and maybe an affordable water view as well: they're only a short ferry ride from Circular Quay. Large old private hotels out this way are increasingly being converted into hostels, particularly on Carabella Street in Kirribilli. **Manly**, tucked away in the northeast corner of the harbour, is a sea-side suburb with ocean and harbour beaches, just thirty minutes from Circular Quay by ferry.

Nowhere but in Sydney could you stay at such great beachside locations so close to the city as **Bondi** and **Coogee Beach**, both with concentrations of hostels and budget accommodation.

The CBD and The Rocks

Grand Hotel, 30 Hunter St, City (☎02/9232 3755, fax 9232 1073). Close to Wynyard Station, with several floors of accommodation above one of Sydney's oldest, but not necessarily nicest, pubs (open until 3am Thurs–Sat). Rooms themselves, sharing bathrooms, are fine - all brightly painted, with colourful bed covers, lamps, fridge, TV, fan, heating and ceiling fans. ⑥.

Lord Nelson Brewery Hotel, corner of Argyle and Kent streets, The Rocks (☎02/9251 4044, fax 9251 1532). B&B in a historic pub. The ten very smart Colonial-style rooms, recently renovated, and with all mod-cons, are mostly en suite. Price varies according to size and position ($150–180): best is the corner room with views of Argyle Street. Meals served in the upmarket brasserie. ⑦.

Old Sydney Park Royal, 55 George St, The Rocks (☎02/9252 0524, fax 9251 0393). Four-star in a great location right in the heart of The Rocks, with impressive architecture; eight levels of rooms ($195–225) around a central atrium creates a remarkable feeling of space. The best rooms have harbour views but the rooftop swimming pool (plus spa and sauna) also gives fantastic vistas. Not a tour group hotel so it manages to keep its personal touch; 24hr room service. ⑧.

Palisade Hotel, 35 Bettington St, Millers Point (☎02/9247 2272). Magnificent tiled pub standing like an observatory over the old and new of Millers Point. Similarly, the hotel manages to keep old style charm and simplicity – the bar downstairs is very down to earth – but there's a stylish contemporary restaurant upstairs. Clean, cute rooms – share bathroom – have a bright old-fashioned feel. Some have fantastic views over the inner harbour and Harbour Bridge. ⑥.

The Regent, 199 George St, City (☎02/9238 0000, fax 9251 2851). One of Australia's best hotels, this classy, modern five-star, is superbly located by The Rocks with views of the Harbour Bridge and the Opera House. While there are certainly other more luxurious hotels in Sydney, the *Regent* has the best reputation for personal service. All this comes at a price – $220 minimum, $310 more likely. ⑨.

The Russell, 143a George St, The Rocks (☎02/9241 3543, fax 9252 1652). Charming, small National Trust-listed hotel. Rooms have Colonial-style decor; some are en suite but the small shared bathroom options are very popular – and at $110 are a great price for the area. Other rooms range from $150–220, the best with views of the Quay. Sunny central courtyard and a rooftop garden, sitting room and bar, and downstairs restaurant for the continental breakfast. B&B. ⑦–⑧.

Sydney City Centre Serviced Apartments, 7 Elizabeth St, Martin Place (☎02/9223 6677, fax 9235 3432). Fully equipped apartments with kitchenette, TV, video, fans; basic, but in an excellent location. No weekly rate. ⑥.

Wynyard Vista Hotel, 7–9 York St, City (☎02/9274 1222, fax 9274 1274). Central position for both the CBD and The Rocks. Recently refurbished 22-storey high-rise hotel has the usual motel-style rooms but it excels with its spacious studios. These come with kitchen area, CD player, voicemail, and a safe. Small gym; 24hr room service; pleasant café-brasserie. Cheaper weekend packages available though normal rates start from $175. ⑨.

Darling Harbour, Haymarket and Ultimo

Aarons Hotel, 37 Ultimo Rd, Haymarket (☎02/9281 5555, fax 9281 2666). Large, recently renovated hotel in a lively position, with its own modern café downstairs where a light breakfast is served. Though the rooms are charmless and cheaply furnished, they're comfortable en suites, all with TV, ceiling fan or air-con. The least expensive are internal, small and box-like, with skylight only, while the pricier courtyard rooms have air-con. Room service, 24hr reception. B&B. ⑤–⑧.

Carlton Crest, 169–179 Thomas St, Haymarket (☎02/9281 6888, fax 9281 6688). Architecturally interesting, this modern 18-storey tower is fronted by the old-fashioned facade of the site's former hospital. In a quiet street but right near Chinatown and Central Station, the hotel also has a relaxed atmosphere. The modern decor is plain enough to suit all tastes. Small heated outdoor swimming pool with views to Darling Harbour, plus a spa, and terrace garden with BBQ area. 24hr room service. Rates from $179. ⑨.

The George, 700A George St, Haymarket (☎ & fax 02/9211 1800). Budget private hotel on three floors opposite Chinatown. Though the key deposit and payment-in-advance are off-putting, the bargain-priced rooms – all but two sharing bathrooms – are clean and acceptable. Facilities include a small combined kitchen and TV room and a laundry. ④.

Glasgow Arms Hotel, 527 Harris St, Ultimo, opposite the Powerhouse Museum (☎02/9211 2354, fax 9281 9439). Handily positioned for Darling Harbour, with rooms – nicely decorated, all air-con and en-suite plus TV and radio – situated above a very pleasant pub with courtyard dining. The bar usually shuts around 10pm so noise levels aren't a worry. Light breakfast included. ⑦.

Goldspear Hotel, Capitol Square, Campbell and George streets, Haymarket (☎02/9211 8633, fax 9211 8733). One of the centre's most affordable four-stars (rooms from $140), doesn't cater to tour groups, and is small enough not to feel impersonal. Decor in the rooms is modern if a little chintzy. In an excellent location right next to the Capitol Theatre and cafés; it also has its own restaurant serving Asian and European food. Price includes buffet breakfast and free access to a gym. ⑧.

Sydney Central YHA, corner of Pitt and Rawson streets, opposite Central Station (☎02/9281 9111, fax 9281 9199; *sydcentral@yhansw.org.au*). Centrally located and completely refurbished listed building, transformed into a snazzy hostel; over 500 beds – spacious four-share dorms and share bathroom or en-suite twins and doubles. Wide range of amenities, including employment desk, travel agency, rooftop swimming pool, sauna, barbecue area, video and TV lounges, kitchens, and dining and lounge areas. 24hr reception. Licensed bistro plus a cute bar, *Scubar*. Some parking available. Maximum stay fourteen days. Rooms ④–⑤, dorms $20–23 ②.

Westend Hotel, 412 Pitt St, City (☎02/9211 4822, fax 9281 9570). Old-style hotel with tastefully decorated en-suite rooms, all with TV and air-con. No double-glazing though – traffic can be a bit noisy. Very helpful management; 24hr reception. Bar and bottle shop attached. Airport bus stops outside. ⑦.

Kings Cross and around

The Kings Cross area – neighbouring Potts Point, Woolloomooloo and Elizabeth Bay – has a concentration of hostels, which are listed separately, as well as cheaper hotels, though there are some upmarket choices too. Some hotels also offer a few dorm beds, so check the hotel listings too. It's best avoiding any hostels or cheap hotels that spring up on Darlinghurst Road, the hardcore strip; the parallel, leafy Victoria street and the backstreets have a contrastingly pleasant atmosphere. See p.124-125 for an account of the area.

Hotels

Bernly Private Hotel, 15 Springfield Ave, Kings Cross (☎02/9358 3122, fax 9356 4405). All rooms recently refurbished with TV, sink, and fridge, and are available en-suite and with air-con or share bathroom; also a few dorms. Facilities include a tidy kitchen and TV lounge and a big sunroof with deck chairs and a view of the Harbour Bridge. 24hr reception, good security and courteous service. Good single rates. Rooms ④, en-suite ⑤, dorms ①.

Challis Lodge, 21–23 Challis Ave, Potts Point (☎02/9358 5422, fax 9357 4742). Nice old mansion, friendly and in a quiet location. All rooms have TV, fridge and sink; some en-suite; laundry available. Good single and family rooms, as well as the usual twins/doubles. ④.

Cross Court, 201–203 Brougham St, Kings Cross (☎02/9368 1822, fax 9358 2595). In a terrace house in a leafy side street. New, spacious doubles, plus good value small singles, all with fridge, TV, ceiling fans, lamps. Rooms at the rear have fantastic views over the city, and an apartment has its own balcony. There's also six-bed dorms but no common room or kitchen. The drawback is it's near a noisy, late-closing pub. Rooms ④, apartment ⑦, dorms ②.

Gazebo Hotel Tower, 2 Elizabeth Bay Rd, Elizabeth Bay (☎02/9358 1999, fax 9356 2951, free call ☎1800/221 495). Once one of the city's finest, this circular high-rise has come down in the world a bit but it's still pretty swish (rooms from $130). Worth it if you get one of the rooms with a harbour view. Swimming pool. Free parking is usually available. ⑧.

Highfield Private Hotel, 166 Victoria St, Kings Cross (☎02/9326 9539, fax 9358 1552). Run by Scandinavians, this is a very clean, modern, safe though slightly impersonal place. Rooms are well-equipped with fans, heating and sinks. Also three-bed dorms. Tiny kitchen/common room with TV. Rooms ③–④, dorms ①–②.

Kirketon Hotel, 229–231 Darlinghurst Rd, Kings Cross (☎02/9332 2011, fax 9332 2499). Totally renovated hotel is now top in the fashion stakes helped by big name Australian designers creating the interiors. On the ground level, stylish restaurants and bars beckon, while the forty rooms boast every luxury, from toiletries by Aveda to mohair throw rugs, and CD players. You may not be as beautiful as the staff, but service is slick and 24hr. The price is a cool $170–250. ⑧.

Madison's Ward Avenue, 6–8 Ward Ave, Elizabeth Bay (☎02/9357 1155, fax 9357 1193). Slickly modern three star hotel with correspondingly contemporary rooms, all en-suite. Undercover parking included in the rates. ⑦.

Montpelier Private Hotel, 39a Elizabeth Bay Rd, Elizabeth Bay (☎ & fax 02/9358 6960). Long-established private hotel, moderately priced, simple and clean. Singles and doubles both come with TV, fridge and coffee-making facilities; shower and toilets are down the hall. Great value and central location. ③.

Sydney Star Accommodation, 275 Darlinghurst Rd, Darlinghurst (☎02/9331 8501, fax 9380 6901). Individually styled, clean and nicely painted self-catering rooms in two adjoining terraces with a lovely courtyard. Rooms in the first terrace share bathrooms, while in the second they're en-suite, all have air-con. Each room has a microwave, sink, kettle, fridge and TV. If you stay a month or more rates are reduced by more than half. ⑥.

Victoria Court Sydney, 122 Victoria St, Kings Cross (☎02/9357 3200, fax 9357 7606). Boutique hotel in two interlinked Victorian terraced houses; very tasteful and quiet. En-suite rooms with all mod cons, some with balconies; buffet breakfast included and served in the conservatory. Security parking a bonus. ⑦.

Woolloomooloo Waters, 88 Dowling St, Woolloomooloo (☎02/9358 3100, fax 9356 4839). Studio apartments with balcony views over Woolloomooloo Bay or the city; light breakfast included. Has a pool, spa and restaurant – all this means it's $155 plus. ⑧.

Hostels

Backpackers Headquarters, 79 Bayswater Rd, Kings Cross (☎ & fax 02/9331 6180). Modern, light and clean hostel well-run by very courteous management. Large, partitioned dorms with firm mattresses, fans, heaters and mirrors; only two doubles. Usual amenities plus sundeck and barbecue area on the rooftop. Excellent security. Rooms ③–④, dorms ①–②.

Eva's Backpackers, 6–8 Orwell St, Potts Point (☎02/9358 2185, fax 9358 3259). Recommended family-run hostel with colourfully painted, clean rooms, some of them en-suite. 24hr reception and rooftop garden with barbecue area – and fantastic views over the city. Rooms ③–④, dorms ①–②.

Forbes Terrace, 153 Forbes St, Woolloomooloo (☎02/9358 4327, fax 9357 3652). Top-class upmarket hostel, well-run and clean; very friendly, with good weekly terms. Rooms ③–④, dorms ①–②.

Funk House, 23 Darlinghurst Rd, Kings Cross (☎02/9358 6455, fax 9358 3506; *funkhouse@bigpond .com*). With different murals on every door – Acid art, Aboriginal and cartoons – and upbeat music playing in the corridors and showers, this very colourful place has a relaxed vibe. Not too squeezy either, with three- and four-bed dorms. Doubles and twins come with fridge and TV. Free lifts to Bondi in the summer. Also licensed travel agents. Rooms ③–④, dorms ①–②.

Jolly Swagman, headquarters at 27 Orwell St (☎02/9358 6400, fax 9331 0125, free call ☎1800/805 870; *www.jollyswagman.com.au*); 144 Victoria St, Kings Cross (☎02/9357 4733); and 16 Orwell St (☎02/9358 6600). Three hostels run by the same team. Colourful, clean and lively, with good notice boards and work connections. They run their own events from sporting teams to pub crawls plus tours. Along with the usual communal facilities, every room has its own fridge and lockers; four- to six-bed dorms. At the 27 Orwell St headquarters there's a 24hr reception, Internet access and a cheap café. Rooms ③–④, dorms ①.

Original Backpackers, 160–162 Victoria St, Kings Cross (☎02/9356 3232, fax 9368 1435; *oakey@giga.net.au*). The first backpackers' hostel in the Cross, in an 1887 mansion. There's a choice of simple, well-maintained rooms and three- to ten-bed dorms – the best one leading off the huge balcony. Ask about rooms in the two smaller terraced houses nearby. Pleasant outdoor courtyard, cable TV and lots of job contacts. Happy to cater for families. Rooms ③, dorms ①–②.

The Pink House, 6–8 Barncleuth Square, Kings Cross (☎ & fax 02/9358 1689, free call ☎1800/806 384; *theglobe@qd.com.au*). Attractive Art Deco mansion with big dorms and a few doubles, and all the expected amenities plus cable TV in the common room and a café. Friendly, very peaceful place but close to the action. YHA-associated. Rooms ③, dorms ①–②.

Rucksack Rest, 9 McDonald St, Potts Point (☎ & fax 02/9358 2348). Small, well-run private hostel which benefits from a friendly atmosphere and quiet location. Facilities include a barbecue area. Rooms ③, dorms ①–②.

Traveller's Rest, 156 Victoria St, Kings Cross (☎02/9358 4606, fax 9358 4531). Efficiently run by the helpful owner, this place is very popular with long-stayers who are well provided for and given good-value weekly rates. Decent twins and doubles; triple rooms available on a share basis as dorms – all with TV, fan, phone with a voicemail, fridge, kettle, sink and table and chairs. Usual shared facilities plus a yard for smokers. Rooms ③, dorms ①.

Surry Hills, Darlinghurst, Paddington and Woollahra

Alfred Park Private Hotel, 207 Cleveland St, Surry Hills (☎02/9319 4031). Small, private hotel close to Central Station with some dorm accommodation, the rooms share bathroom or are en-suite. There's a courtyard to sun in, and facilities include a communal kitchen, laundry, and car park. Rooms ④, dorms ①.

Camelot Inn, 358a Victoria St, Darlinghurst (☎02/9331 7555, fax 9331 2519). Studio apartments for up to five people located on a lively, restaurant-filled street. Parking available. ⑥.

City Crown Lodge, 289 Crown St, corner of Reservoir St, Surry Hills (☎02/9331 2433, fax 9360 7760). A fairly typical motel but well-located offering en-suite units with heating, fan and small kitchenette. Free in-house movies. Some parking space: enter on Reservoir St. ⑥.

Hughendon Hotel, 14 Queen St, Woollahra (☎02/9363 4863, fax 9362 0398). Old-fashioned guesthouse, built in 1876, situated opposite Centennial Park. Expensive en-suite singles and doubles with rates ranging from $140 to $175, depending on size of room. There are also suites for $250; breakfast included. ⑧.

Kangaroo Bakpak, 665 S Dowling St, Surry Hills (☎02/9319 5915). Small, clean and very friendly backpackers' hostel. Enormous dorms and generally untidy, but the atmosphere compensates. ①.

L'Otel, 114 Darlinghurst Rd, Darlinghurst (☎02/9360 6868, fax 9331 4536). Stylish, small hotel with sixteen rooms, all en-suite with TV, video, mini-bar and ceiling fans with rates from $140 to $160. Trendy bar and brasserie downstairs befitting its position on a prime café strip. ⑧.

Medina on Crown, 359 Crown St, Surry Hills (☎02/9360 6666, fax 9361 5965). Stylishly decorated one- or two-bedroom serviced apartment, with air-con, lounge suite, dining area, TV, video and telephone. Well-equipped kitchen, laundry and balcony, and a café, gym, sauna and swimming pool downstairs. 24hr reception and free undercover parking. ⑧

Oxford Koala Hotel, corner of Oxford and Pelican streets, Darlinghurst (☎02/9269 0645, fax 9283 2741). Multistoreyed motel overlooking Hyde Park. The fully equipped apartments are good for families, and the complex has a swimming pool. Room service. ⑦–⑧.

Sullivans Hotel, 21 Oxford St, Paddington (☎02/9361 0211, fax 9360 3735). Large, private hotel in a trendy location, run by staff tuned into the local scene. Comfortable, modern en-suite rooms with TV and telephones. Free (but limited) parking, swimming pool, in-house movies, 24hr reception and a café open for breakfast. ⑦.

YWCA, 5–11 Wentworth Ave, Darlinghurst (☎02/9264 2451, fax 9283 2485). Great location just off Oxford Street. Double or twin rooms with en-suite or shared bathrooms, plus singles sharing bathrooms ($60) and four-bed dorms. En-suite rooms come with a TV, or there are TV lounges. There's no kitchen, but facilities include a café (open 7am–8pm), and a laundry. Rooms ⑥–⑦, dorms ②.

Glebe and Newtown

Alishan International Guesthouse, 100 Glebe Point Rd, Glebe (☎02/9566 4048, fax 9525 4686). Japanese-owned, beautifully restored old villa offering chintzy double en-suite rooms with a couple having a Japanese aesthetic, as well as spotless four-bed dorms. Facilities include a kitchen, spa, and an airy common room with its own barbecue area. Rooms ⑥, dorms ②.

Australian Sunrise Lodge, 485 King St, Newtown (☎02/9550 4999, fax 9550 4457). Inexpensive, tastefully furnished and well-managed small, private hotel with kitchen. Sunny single and double rooms, all with TV, fridge and toaster, most with bath and balcony. Family rooms available. Rooms ④, en-suites ⑤.

Billabong Gardens, 5–11 Egan St, off King St, Newtown (☎02/9550 3236, fax 9550 4352). In a quiet street but close to the action, and run by a friendly team, this purpose-built hostel is arranged around a peaceful inner courtyard with swimming pool. It offers clean dorms (up to 6-bed), rooms and motel-style en-suites. Communal facilities include a gym, pool table and Net access. Undercover car park (but $5 night). Rooms ④, en-suite ⑤, dorms ①.

Glebe Point YHA, 262 Glebe Point Rd, Glebe (☎02/9692 8418, fax 9660 0431, *glebe@yhansw.org.au*). Reliable YHA standard with impeccably helpful, patient staff. Private rooms as well as four-bed dorms. Facilities include a sunroof, pool table, TV and video lounge, and luggage storage. Lots of activities organized. Reception 7am–11pm. Rooms ④, dorms ②.

Glebe Village Backpackers, 256 Glebe Point Rd, Glebe (☎02/9660 8133, fax 9552 3707, free call ☎1800/801 983). Three large old houses with a mellow atmosphere, feeling more like a guesthouse than a hostel, and staffed by young locals who know what's going on around town. Double and twin rooms as well as dorms. Relaxing alfresco café overlooking the street, shady courtyard and a travel agency. Rooms ④, dorms ①–②.

Nomads Forest Lodge Hotel, 117 Arundel St, Forest Lodge, near Glebe (☎02/9660 1872, fax 9552 1053; bus #470 from Central). Hostels above pubs can be dodgy but this one is clean and well-run. Mostly two- or four-bunk dorms, plus two doubles, all with lockers and linen; small all-in-one kitchen/TV/common room. No laundry. The pleasant pub, with a laid-back café attached, is in a quiet street, and closes at 11pm. Dorms ①.

Rooftop Motel, 146 Glebe Point Rd, Glebe (☎02/9660 7777, fax 9660 7155). Reasonably priced motel with 24hr reception, right in the thick of things; barbecue, swimming pool and babysitting services available. Parking included. ⑥–⑦.

Tricketts Bed and Breakfast, 270 Glebe Point Rd, Glebe (☎02/9552 1141, fax 9692 9462). Luxury B&B accommodation in an 1880 mansion; en-suite rooms furnished with antiques and Persian rugs. The lounge, complete with a billiard table and leather armchairs, was originally a small ballroom. The price for all this ($140) is excellent, especially as it includes a generous breakfast. ⑧.

Hotel Unilodge, corner of Broadway and Bay streets, near Glebe (☎02/9338 5000, fax 9338 5111, free call ☎1800/500 658). Converted from a former department store, with some striking original fixtures, this hotel has a luxury feel but rates can be reasonable (from $145). Self-catering rooms, some sleeping up to five, are comfortably furnished, with kitchenettes and voicemail phones. There's a small gym, lap-pool, spa and sauna, rooftop running track and BBQ. 24hr reception, and 24hr convenience store and food court in the foyer. Children under 12 free. Parking $5 day. ⑧.

Wattle House Hostel, 44 Hereford St, Glebe (☎02/9692 0879, fax 9660 2528). Small, cosy and clean privately owned hostel in a restored terrace house on a quiet street. Four-bed dorms and well-furnished doubles. Rates include linen and towels. Rooms ④, dorms ②.

Bondi Beach

Bondi Beach Guesthouse, 11 Consett Ave, off Lamrock Ave (☎02/9389 8309). Central but surprisingly quiet location. Definitely a budget option but clean and simple rooms with TV, and fridge; communal bathrooms, kitchen and laundry, and a very pleasant shady courtyard. Sharing available for backpackers, maximum three-share. Rooms ③, dorms ①.

Bondi Beachside Inn, 152 Campbell Parade (☎02/9130 5311, fax 9365 2646). Multistoreyed motel positioned right on the beach: all the rooms – clean, modern and air-con – have balconies, and half have ocean views. Motel units with kitchenettes available and a two-bedroom apartment. Free security parking and 24hr reception. ⑤–⑧.

Indy's at Bondi, 35a Hall St (☎02/9365 4900, 24hr mobile 0413/836681, fax 9365 4994). Justifiably popular, this spacious hostel feels like a friendly student share-house – except it's well-organized and there's every amenity: including a pool table, phone with voicemail, outdoor area with seating, excellent security and free use of surfboards and bike. Social events and trips organized; also travel bookings. Dorms only here (four- to eight-bed) – couples and families can stay at their annexe, *Couples on the Beach*, opposite the beach at North Bondi, where all rooms have TV, and there's a small kitchen but no common room – you can sit out on the roof. Rooms ③, dorms ①.

Plage Bondi, 212 Bondi Rd (☎02/9387 1122, fax 9389 1266). Excellent-value serviced motel studio apartments. Air-conditioned units all have clean modern furniture, TV, telephone, kitchen and a balcony with sea view. Best of all is the rooftop pool. Laundry on each floor. Cheaper rates if you stay a week or more. Parking included. ⑦.

Ravesi's, corner of Campbell Parade and Hall St (☎02/9365 4422, fax 9365 1481). Swanky boutique hotel: most rooms (all en-suite) have sea views and small balconies. Rooms range in price from $99 to $275 for the top-floor penthouse; best are split-level suites with their own private terrace ($170–195). It's a well-regarded restaurant, making a great place for breakfast with glorious sea views. Room service. ⑥–⑧.

GAY AND LESBIAN ACCOMMODATION

You won't encounter any problems booking into a regular hotel as gay men or lesbians, but here are several places that are particularly gay friendly or close to Oxford Street. For **flat shares** check the community press and café notice boards or try an agency: Sharespace, 263 Oxford St, Darlinghurst (☎02/9360 7744), deals with gay and lesbian shares for a $75 fee, as does the slightly cheaper Share-A-Home, 127 York St, City (☎02/9267 9824; $65 fee).

Dorchester Inn, 38 Macleay St, Potts Point (☎02/9358 2400, fax 9357 7579; *dorchester@one.net.au*). Apartments, with full kitchen facilities including microwave. ⑦.

Helen's Hideaway, Address and rates provided on inquiry (☎02/ 9360 1678, fax 9360 4865). Lesbian-owned bed and breakfast catering only for women, featuring well-designed rooms, elegant dining room and roof balcony. Only minutes from Oxford Street.

Pelican Private Hotel & 415 on Bourke Street, 411 Bourke St, Darlinghurst (☎ & fax 9331 5344; *www.rainbow.net.au/-pelican*). Comfortable budget accommodation in one of Sydney's oldest gay guesthouses. Appealing rooms with TV and fridge, but you have to share facilities. Rate includes continental breakfast. ④.

Sydney Manor House Boutique Hotel, 86 Flinders St, Darlinghurst (☎02/9380 6633, fax 9380 5016; *manor@rainbow .net.au*). This wonderfully restored building, the residence of Sydney's first Lord Mayor, is gay-owned and run for mostly men. The marvellous rooms have wooden decks overlooking the courtyard, where there's a heated pool and spa. Licensed restaurant and bar. Continental breakfast included. ⑦.

Wattle Private Hotel, 108 Oxford St, corner Palmer St, Darlinghurst (☎02/9332 4118, fax 9331 2074). You can't get any closer to the action, and although the rooms aren't flash, they're clean. Ask for the room on the roof, which opens out to the garden with spectacular city and harbour views. Continental breakfast included. ⑥–⑦.

Thelellen Lodge, 11a Consett Ave (☎02/9130 1521 or 9130 1521, fax 9365 6427). Budget accommodation in a big two-storey house in a quiet tree-filled street but close to the action. Fifteen rooms, all sharing bathrooms, come with TV, air-con, fridge, toaster, plus there's a kitchen and laundry. Small sunny courtyard outside with trees and a big sundeck upstairs. Cheaper single room rates available. ③.

Coogee and Randwick

Coogee Bay Boutique Hotel, 9 Vicar St, Coogee (☎02/9665 0000, fax 9664 2103). New hotel attached to the rear of a pub, the older, sprawling *Coogee Bay Hotel*. Rooms – all with balconies, half with ocean views – look like something from *Vogue Interior*; luxurious touches include marble floors in the bathrooms. Mini-bars and in-room safes, data ports, fax, voicemail and continental breakfast are also part of the deal ($135 to $175). Cheaper rooms ($99–109) in the old hotel are noisy on weekends but are just as stylish; several offer splendid water views. Parking included. 24hr reception. The pub has an excellent brasserie, several bars and a nightclub. ⑦–⑧.

Coogee Beach Backpackers, 94 Beach St, Coogee (☎02/9315 8000, fax 9664 1258). Clean, attractive rooms and dorms in four characterful neighbouring houses, with balconies overlooking the ocean. Each house has a well-equipped kitchen, and common room, and there are several gardens. Congenial and well managed, it's the best of the bunch. Rooms ③–④, dorms ①–②.

Coogee Beach Wizard of Oz, 172 Coogee Bay Rd (☎02/9315 7876, fax 9315 8974). Hostel in a big old Californian-style house with a huge verandah and wooden floors. Run by a friendly local couple, this is a quieter option. Spacious dorms with ceiling fans. Couples should head for their sister establishment, *Sydney Beachside*, which has doubles. TV/video room, dining area, modern kitchen and an outdoor courtyard. Dorms ①.

Coogee Bunkhouse, 15 Waltham St, Coogee (☎02/9665 9254, fax 9665 9254, free call ☎1800/657 122). Spacious Victorian terrace house, bright and well-run, offering six-bed dorms. Common room downstairs with TV and a quiet room for reading and writing. BBQ and laundry out back. Free pick-up if you stay a minimum of two nights. ①–②.

Indy's Beachside Backpackers, 302 Arden St, Coogee (☎02/9315 7644, fax 9365 4994). Small hostel with a laid-back atmosphere that feels more like a share house. Mostly four-bed dorms; no doubles. Rates include a light breakfast. Cheap day-trips to the countryside arranged. ②.

The Royal, corner of Perouse Rd and Cuthill St, Randwick (☎02/9399 3000 or 9399 3039, fax 9399 8181). Big, historic pub (listed by the National Trust), with fairly upmarket rooms, all sharing bathrooms except for one en-suite. Good transport to the city and beaches. ⑤.

Surfside Backpackers Coogee, 186 Arden St, Coogee (☎02/9315 7888, fax 9315 7892). On Coogee's main drag, above *McDonald's*, and opposite the beach, with great views from its high balconies. Well-rated, clean, modern facilities but a tower-block feel. Double rooms available in winter only. Dorms ②.

Sydney Beachside, 178 Coogee Bay Rd, Coogee (☎02/9315 8511, fax 9315 8974). Same management as *Wizard of Oz* (above), but more budget accommodation than backpackers. The airy, old two-storey house is pleasantly renovated, with wooden floors. All rooms and dorms (four-bed) come with TV but share bathrooms. Doubles and family rooms get linen, duvets and a fridge. Small kitchen but no common room. Up the hill from the beach but handy for shops and the supermarket; Rooms ③–④, dorms ①.

North Shore

Cremorne Point Manor, 6 Cremorne Rd, Cremorne Point (☎02/9953 7899, fax 9904 1265). Huge restored Federation-style villa with very cheap singles and good-value doubles run by a friendly couple. Most rooms are en-suite with TV, fridge and some have harbour views. There's a communal kitchen and a laundry. Rate includes continental breakfast. ⑦.

Elite Private Hotel, 133 Carabella St, Kirribilli (☎02/9929 6365, fax 9925 0999). Bright place surrounded by plants offering good, standard rooms with TV and fridge; some have a harbour view and all share bathrooms. Small communal cooking facility but no laundry. Only minutes by ferry from the city (to Kirribilli wharf) and near Milsons Point train station. ④.

Glenferrie Boutique Hotel, 12a Carabella St, Kirribilli (☎02/9955 1685, fax 9929 9439). Another made-over Kirribilli mansion, clean, light and secure with 24hr reception. Rates include a buffet breakfast and three-course dinner, whether you're in a four-share dorm, single, double or family room (all share bathroom). Facilities include a TV lounge and laundry. Ferry to Kirribilli wharf or train to Milsons Point. Rooms ⑦, dorms ③.

Kirribilli Court Private Hotel, 45 Carabella St, Kirribilli (☎02/9955 4344, fax 9929 4774). Inexpensive dorms and private rooms (all shared bathroom) in an old mansion with harbour views; communal kitchen, dining room and TV lounge with cable. Weekly rates available. Rooms ③, dorms ①.

North Sydney Lodge, 310 Miller St, North Sydney (☎02/9955 1012, fax 9955 4212). Two-storey mansion with balconies in a quiet location opposite a park. En-suite rooms or family studios sleeping four, all with air-con, TV, hot drinks and telephone. Shared kitchen and laundry facilities; breakfast available. ⑥–⑦.

Manly and the northern beaches

Avalon Beach Hostel, 59 Avalon Parade, Avalon (☎02/9918 9709). Located at one of Sydney's best – and most beautiful – surf beaches, the plan of this specially built hostel is certainly conducive to year-round relaxation with warming fireplaces, balconies to take the breeze and plenty of greenery to gaze at. Surfboard and bike rental available. ①.

HOLIDAY APARTMENTS

The following places rent out apartments, generally for a minimum of a week. Expect to pay between $350 and $600 per week, depending on the size and the season; all are completely furnished and equipped – though occasionally you're expected to provide linen and towels: check first. Many hotels (some called apartment hotels) and all hostels also have self-catering facilities – see main listings for details.

Enochs Holiday Flats (☎02/9388 1477, fax 9388 1353). All close to Bondi Beach; one- or two-bedroom apartments sleeping four to six people. $400–820 weekly, depending on the size and season.

Kings Cross Holiday Apartments, 169 William St, Kings Cross, Sydney, NSW 2011 (☎02/9361 0637, fax 9331 1366). One-bedroom apartments in this very central location, with accommodation for up to five. Linen and towels included, and though the apartments aren't serviced, a washing-machine and dryer are provided in the kitchen. $520 weekly (for two adults and two children; extra guests $10 each per day), cheaper in winter and longer-term rates are negotiable.

Kirribilli Lodge, 33 Fitzroy St, Kirribilli, NSW 2061 (☎02/9955 0821, fax 9929 6986). Well set-up apartments for two people in a pleasant harbourside suburb. $350 weekly, but with an extra one-off cleaning fee of $45. Linen included.

Manly National, 22 Central Ave, Manly, NSW 2095 (☎02/9977 6469, fax 9977 3760). One- and two-bedroom apartments accommodate up to four people;

swimming pool; linen not supplied. One-bedroom $450–585 weekly, two-bedroom $550–695.

Medina Executive Apartments, Head office, Level 1, 355 Crown St, Surry Hills, Sydney, NSW 2010 (☎02/9360 1699, fax 9360 7769). Upmarket studio or one-, two- and three-bedroom serviced apartments with resident managers and reception in salubrious places. Various locations in the eastern suburbs include Elizabeth Bay, Double Bay, Paddington and Randwick, on the lower North Shore at Crows Nest, and at North Ryde handy for Macquarie University. All include undercover parking. From $850 weekly upwards. See also *Medina on Crown*, p.89.

The Park Agency, 190 Arden St, Coogee (☎02/9315 7777, fax 9665 7777; *www.parkpm.com.au*). Very friendly staff who offer several spacious well set-up studio apartments right opposite the beach for $400 per week, and further away from the surf from $250 per week. All fully furnished including linen, blankets and washing-machine.

Jonah's, 69 Byna Rd, Palm Beach (☎02/9974 5599, fax 9974 1212). Indulge yourself by staying at this small 1920s resort with period decor and surrounding tropical-feel gardens (rates from $240). Wonderful ocean views to enjoy while eating the scrumptious breakfast on the terrace. Its restaurant has a reputation as one of Sydney's best. Dinner and B&B packages available. ⑧.

Manly Backpackers Beachside, 28 Raglan St, Manly (☎02/9977 3411, fax 9977 4079). Modern purpose-built two-storey hostel one block from the surf; well run, though the management can be a little brisk, as the very early 9.30am check-out with a $5 penalty indicates. Clean twin and double rooms – some en-suite – plus small three-bed dorms (six-bed is largest). Best dorm is the one at the front with a balcony. Outside terrace with BBQ; free boogie-boards. Rooms ④, dorms ①.

Manly Beach Resort Backpackers, 6 Carlton St, Manly (☎02/9977 4188, fax 9977 0524). Located one block from the beach. Clean, non-smoking four- to six-bed en-suite dorms and a few very reasonable doubles. There is also a more upmarket motel section. The attached café is good for breakfast. 24hr reception. Rooms ③, motel ⑦, dorms ①.

Manly Pacific Park Royal, 55 North Steyne, Manly (☎02/9977 7666, fax 9977 7822). Beachfront multistoreyed four-star hotel with 24hr reception, room service, spa, sauna, gym and heated rooftop pool – all at a price: over $190, and more for an ocean view ($220). ⑧.

Periwinkle Guesthouse, 18–19 East Esplanade, corner of Ashburner St, Manly (☎02/9977 4668, fax 9977 6308). Pleasant B&B near Manly Cove, close to the ferry terminal and shops. Rooms have fridge and fans. Facilities include a communal kitchen and car park. Several en-suites available, with larger rooms suitable for families or groups. ⑦.

Sydney Beachhouse YHA, 4 Collaroy St, Collaroy Beach (☎02/9981 1177, fax 9981 1114; *sydneybeachouse.com.au*). At last Sydney has a beachside YHA hostel. Purpose built, it's suitable for year-round enjoyment with a heated swimming pool plus open fireplaces, video lounge and games and pool rooms. Four- to six-bed dorms plus several doubles (some en-suite) and family rooms. Free use of surfboards, boogie-boards and bikes, and surfing lessons for weekly guests. Trips organized in clude the popular jaunt to the Home and Away filming location. Shuttle bus from Sydney Central YHA. Rooms ④, dorms ②.

Wharf Backpackers, 48 East Esplanade, Manly (☎ 02/9977 2800, fax 9977 2820). Wonderfully quirky but well-run hostel, directly opposite the ferry terminal, really gets into the concept of outdoor living. The big back garden becomes another living area, with a kitchen and TV, tables and oversized chess set, and pet rabbits roaming freely. Though room for 100 guests, there are several kitchens and TV rooms so it never feels too crowded – and it is popular. Colourfully painted dorms – four-, six- and eight-bed – have ceiling fans and heaters. Doubles and twins come with TV. Free bikes, body-boards and wetsuits; surfboards for rent. Good local work contacts. Rooms ③, dorms ①.

The City

Port Jackson carves Sydney in two halves, linked by the Harbour Bridge and Harbour Tunnel. The **South Shore** is the hub of activity, and it's here that you'll find the **city centre** and most of the things to see and do. Many of the classic images of Sydney are within sight of **Circular Quay**, making this busy waterfront area on Sydney Cove a logical – and pleasurable – point to start discovering the city, with the **Opera House** and the expanse of the Royal Botanic Gardens to the east of Sydney Cove and the historic area of **The Rocks** to the west. By contrast, **Darling Harbour**, at the centre's western edge, was redeveloped in the late 1980s as a tourist and entertainment area and is a gleaming, if slightly tawdry, showcase for the new Sydney.

Circular Quay

At the southern end of Sydney Cove, **Circular Quay** is the launching pad for harbour and river ferries and sightseeing boats, the terminal for buses from the eastern and southern suburbs, and a major suburban train station to boot. Circular Quay itself is always bustling with commuters during the week, and with people simply out to enjoy

HARBOUR CRUISES

There's a wide choice of **harbour cruises**, almost all of them leaving from Jetty 6, Circular Quay and some from Darling Harbour. Before you part with your cash, however, consider if this is what you really want: apart from the running commentary (which can be rather annoying), most offer nothing that you won't get on a regular harbour **ferry** for a lot less. The best of the ordinary trips is the thirty-minute ride to **Manly**, but there's a ferry going somewhere at almost any time throughout the day. If you really want to splash out, you could take a **water taxi** ride – Circular Quay to Watsons Bay, for example, costs $35–45 for the first passenger and then an additional $5 for each extra person; a water taxi pick-up point is located on the pier at Campbells Cove but pick-ups are available from any wharf if booked in advance. Try Taxis Afloat on ☎02/9955 3222.

The **Australian Travel Specialists** at Jetty 2 and 6, Circular Quay, the Harbourside Shopping Centre at Darling Harbour and Manly Wharf (☎02/9247 5151 or 9555 2700) book all cruises. Those offered by State Transit – **Sydney Harbour Ferry Cruises** – seem to offer the best value: choose between the Morning River Cruise (daily 10am & 11.15am; 1hr; $12), the recommended Afternoon Harbour Cruise to Middle Harbour and back (Mon–Fri 1pm, Sat & Sun 1.30pm; 2hr 30min; $17.50), or the Harbour Lights Cruise in the evening (Mon–Sat 8pm; 1hr 30min; $15).

Captain Cook Cruises at Jetty 6 (☎02/9206 1111) offers a vast range of cruises including morning and afternoon "Coffee" Cruises into Middle Harbour (daily; 2hr 20min; $32), a lunch cruise ($44), a daily range of rather expensive Dinner Cruises (all-inclusive of three-course meal with drinks from $58; Opera Afloat with opera singers accompanying a four-course dinner for $89), and a Harbour Highlights Cruise (daily 9.30am, 11am, 2.30pm, 4pm; 1hr 15min; $18; option of getting off at Darling Harbour on the 11am, 2.30pm and 4pm trips). They also have a hop-on, hop-off Sydney Harbour Explorer (9.30am–3.30pm; $20; combined ticket with the zoo or the aquarium is $32) circuiting between Circular Quay, the Man O' War jetty at the Opera House, Watsons Bay, Taronga Zoo and Darling Harbour (with two stops – the Harbourside Shopping Centre and the Aquarium).

Matilda Cruises, based in Darling Harbour (Aquarium Wharf, Pier 26; ☎02/9264 7377), offer various cruises; all depart from Darling Harbour (times given) but pick up from Circular Quay later. Its **Sail Venture** trips are on sailing catamarans and all feature a meal or refreshment of some sort: Coffee Cruises gets you a cappuccino and biscuits (9.30am & 3.05pm; 2hr; $24); there's a buffet on the Luncheon Cruise (12.15pm; 2hr; $48), while the pricey Dinner Cruise allows you to chow down on four courses (7pm; 3hr 30min; $90). They also offer the **Rocket Harbour Express Cruise**, a one-hour trip stopping at the Aquarium wharf at Darling Harbour, Man O' War jetty at the Opera House, Commissioners Steps at Circular Quay West, and Taronga Zoo, whizzing past Watsons Bay for a look; you can get off at the stops and rejoin later cruises (commencing from Darling Harbour, every 30min 9.30am–4.30pm; $16). There is also a straight Matilda Ferry service shuttling between Darling Harbour, the casino and Circular Quay ($3.25 one-way).

If you're feeling romantically inclined, or mutinous, you might fancy sailing with the **Bounty** (office at 29 George St, The Rocks; ☎02/9247 1789), a replica of Captain Bligh's ship made for the film starring Mel Gibson. It embarks at Campbells Cove, The Rocks, for various cruises daily, most involving food and entertainment; cheapest is the Sunday brunch (10–11.30am; $45) while the splurge is the nightly dinner cruise (7–9.30pm; three-course buffet and entertainment, drinks extra; $80).

With **Sydney by Sail** (bookings ☎02/9552 7561; *www.sydneysail.com*), you can enjoy the harbour like many lucky locals do – from on board a yacht. Groups are small (up to 12) and if you're interested the skipper will even show you some sailing techniques. There are shorter sails to Port Jackson ($49; 1hr 30min) and longer ones going further into surrounding inlets ($89; 3hr); call for times. Departures are from the National Maritime Museum at Darling Harbour, with free entry to the museum thrown in with the sail (normally $9). Experienced sailors can charter the yachts (from $300 half-day to $1200 for a weekend). Another sailing experience is offered by **Sail Svanen** (☎02/9698 4456), moored at Campbells Cove next to the Bounty: this sailing ship offers day sails on the harbour for $79, including morning tea and lunch, or longer overnight sails to Broken Bay ($240).

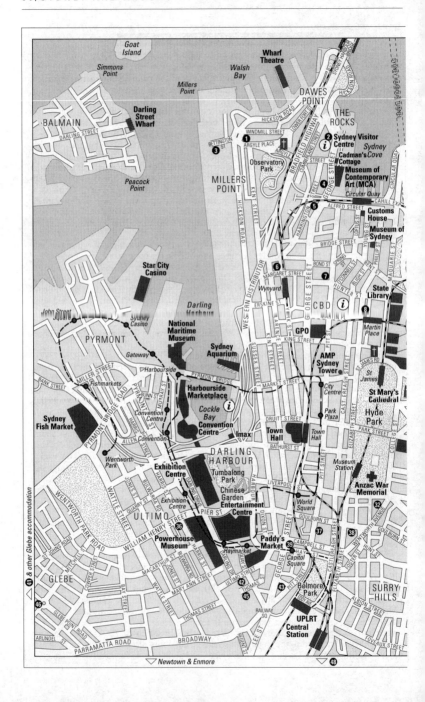

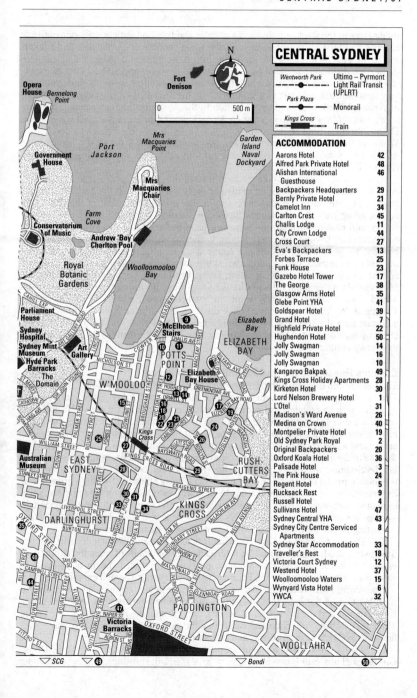

CENTRAL SYDNEY

Wentworth Park - - ● - - ● - -	Ultimo – Pyrmont Light Rail Transit (UPLRT)
Park Plaza ─────●─────	Monorail
Kings Cross ────────	Train

ACCOMMODATION

Aarons Hotel	42
Alfred Park Private Hotel	48
Alishan International Guesthouse	46
Backpackers Headquarters	29
Bernly Private Hotel	21
Camelot Inn	34
Carlton Crest	45
Challis Lodge	11
City Crown Lodge	44
Cross Court	27
Eva's Backpackers	13
Forbes Terrace	25
Funk House	23
Gazebo Hotel Tower	17
The George	38
Glasgow Arms Hotel	35
Glebe Point YHA	41
Goldspear Hotel	39
Grand Hotel	7
Highfield Private Hotel	22
Hughendon Hotel	50
Jolly Swagman	14
Jolly Swagman	16
Jolly Swagman	10
Kangaroo Bakpak	49
Kings Cross Holiday Apartments	28
Kirketon Hotel	30
Lord Nelson Brewery Hotel	1
L'Otel	31
Madison's Ward Avenue	26
Medina on Crown	19
Montpelier Private Hotel	40
Old Sydney Park Royal	2
Original Backpackers	20
Oxford Koala Hotel	36
Palisade Hotel	3
The Pink House	24
Regent Hotel	5
Rucksack Rest	9
Russell Hotel	4
Sullivans Hotel	47
Sydney Central YHA	43
Sydney City Centre Serviced Apartments	8
Sydney Star Accommodation	33
Traveller's Rest	18
Victoria Court Sydney	12
Westend Hotel	37
Woolloomooloo Waters	15
Wynyard Vista Hotel	6
YWCA	32

themselves at the weekend. Restaurants, cafés and fast-food outlets stay open until late at night and buskers entertain the crowds, while vendors of newspapers and trinkets add to the general hubbub. The sun reflecting on the water and its heave and splash as the ferries come and go make for a dreamy setting – best appreciated over an expensive beer and some oysters at a waterfront bar. For intellectual stimulation, you need only look beneath your feet as you stroll along: the inscribed bronze pavement plaques of **Writers' Walk** provide an introduction to the Australian literary canon. There are short biographies of writers ranging from Miles Franklin, author of *My Brilliant Career*, through Booker Prize winner Peter Carey and Noble Prize awardee Patrick White, to the feminist Germaine Greer, and quotable quotes on what it means to be Australian. Notable literati who've visited Australia also feature: Joseph Conrad, Charles Darwin and Mark Twain.

Having dallied, read, and taken in the view and the crush of people, the next thing to do is to embark on a sightseeing **cruise** or enjoy a ferry ride on the harbour (see box below). Staying on dry land, you're only a short walk from most of the city-centre sights, along part of a continuous foreshore walkway beginning under the Harbour Bridge and passing through the historic area of Sydney's first settlement The Rocks, and extending beyond the Opera House to the Royal Botanic Gardens. The Gardens boast some wonderfully picturesque picnic spots – all the necessaries, including bubbly and fresh prawns, can be purchased at the quay. Besides ferries, Circular Quay still acts as a passenger terminal for ocean liners; head in the opposite direction past the Museum of Contemporary Art to Circular Quay West. It's a long time since the crowds waved their hankies regularly from the rust-coloured **Sydney Cove Passenger Terminal**, looking for all the world like the deck of a ship itself, but you may still see an ocean liner docked here; even if there's no ship, take the escalator and the flight of stairs up for excellent views of the harbour. The rest of the terminal is now given over to swanky restaurants.

Customs House and the Justice and Police Museum

The railway and the ugly Cahill Expressway block views to the city from Circular Quay. They also impede a cohesiveness between the quay and Alfred Street, immediately opposite, with its architectural gem, the sandstone and granite **Customs House**. First constructed in 1845 and redesigned in 1885 by the colonial architect James Barnet, to give its current Classical Revival-style facade. It houses a wonderfully varied cultural centre and a collection of indigenous art from the Australian Museum (see p.110). On the fourth floor, the **City Exhibition Space** keeps pace with the sometimes bewildering development of Sydney in time for the Olympics and beyond with a full scale up-to-the-minute model of the city and a multimedia display following Sydney's growth from its inception to the 1930s. The space is blessed with eateries too: on the fifth floor, a contemporary brasserie *Section 51*, comes with wonderful views, on the ground floor, take a coffee at *Caffe Bianchi*, or eat oysters and have a beer at *Quay Bar*, which has alfresco seating on the newly landscaped Customs House Square out front.

The **Djamu Gallery** on Level Two (daily 9.30am–5.30pm; $8 includes admission to the Australian Museum – see p.110; ☎02/9320 6429 for details of changing exhibitions) is an extension of the Australian Museum, providing the space to finally do justice to its vast collection of indigenous art. Four rooms show separate themed exhibitions, which – maximizing an inventive approach – last for three to four months, stressing the cultural heritage of the indigenous people of Australia and surrounding regions such as New Zealand and the Torres Strait Islands, and introducing new artists to the public. The level is shared with **Balarinji Australia**, the indigenous design studio whose work famously enlivens several Qantas and British Airways 747s.

On Level 3 the **Centre for Contemporary Craft** has its exhibition space, **Object Galleries** (Tues–Sun 10am–5pm; free; ☎02/9247 9126), showing changing exhibitions of Australia's best artisans. On the ground floor, Object Stores is the retail outlet (Mon–Fri 10am–5.30pm, Sat & Sun noon–5pm), selling beautifully designed glass, ceramics, woodwork and jewellery, all labelled with the artisan and the state of origin.

A block east of Customs House, on the corner of Phillip Street, the **Justice and Police Museum** is housed in the former Water Police station (Sat & Sun 10am–5pm except Jan Sat–Thurs 10am–5pm; $6); an 1858 sandstone building, its verandah decorated with some particularly fine ironwork. The crime displays, including some truly macabre death masks, are shown within the context of a late nineteenth-century police station and court mock-up.

Museum of Contemporary Art

The **Museum of Contemporary Art** (daily 10am–6pm; $9 all-day ticket; free tours daily 11am & 2pm; for details of special exhibitions and events call ☎02/9252 4033; *www.mca.com.au*), on the western side of Circular Quay with another entrance on George Street (no. 140), is one of the city's most exciting museums. Developing out of a bequest to Sydney University by the art collector John Power in the 1940s, the growing collection finally found a permanent home in 1991 in the former Maritime Services Building. The striking Deco-style 1950s building is now a temple to international twentieth-century art, with an eclectic approach encompassing lithographs, sculpture, film, video, drawings and paintings ranging from Andy Warhol to Aboriginal art. The MCA also has an inventive line in themed exhibitions, on topics such as contemporary Japanese art, popular culture in the Fifties, or simply Television. The museum's superbly sited, if expensive, café (Mon–Fri 11am–5pm, Sat & Sun 9am–5pm) has outdoor tables overlooking the waterfront, and the well-stocked bookshop is worth a browse.

The Opera House

The **Sydney Opera House**, such an icon of Australiana that it almost seems kitsch, is just a short stroll from Circular Quay, by the water's edge on Bennelong Point. It's best seen in profile, when its high white roofs, at the same time evocative of full sails and white shells, give the building an almost ethereal quality. Despite its familiarity, or perhaps precisely because you already feel you know it so well, it's quite breathtaking at first sight. Close-up, you can see that the shimmering effect is created by thousands of white tiles carefully fitted together to cover the sails: much like bathroom tiles, they need frequent regrouting to keep the Opera House waterproof. Inside the shell is a large Concert Hall, used for symphony concerts, chamber music, opera, dance and pop concerts, a smaller Opera Theatre for opera, ballet and dance, and two theatres, the Drama Theatre and the Playhouse, plus restaurants, bars, a cinema, an Aboriginal artists' gallery and a library. Locals have discovered other uses for it besides all this culture: its sloping sides, easy to crawl up before they slant off precariously, make a fine slippery dip after a beery picnic and cricket match in the Royal Botanic Gardens opposite; more determined outdoor types have attempted to abseil it.

Now almost universally loved and admired, it's hard to believe quite how controversial a project this was during its long haul from plan, as a result of an international competition in the late 1950s, to completion in 1973. The building's twenty-fifth birthday was celebrated with free concerts and much hoo-ha in October 1998 and the announcement of a $66 million ten-year plan to renew and modify the interior, re-focusing media attention on past mistakes. For sixteen years, construction was plagued by quarrels and scandal, so much so that the Danish architect, **Jørn Utzon**, who won the competition aged 38, was forced to resign in 1966 after nine years working on the project. Some put it less kindly and say he was hounded out of the country by politicians – the newly elected Askin government disagreeing over his plans for the completion of

THE TOASTER

The latest controversy to surround the Opera House has been the ugly building going up alongside it, the **East Circular Quay apartments**, dubbed "the toaster" by locals, and described by Robert Hughes, the famous expat Australian art critic and historian, author of *The Fatal Shore*, as "that dull brash, intrusive apartment block which now obscures the Opera House from three directions". This hideous high-rise luxury apartment block was somehow approved by Sydney Council but no one can understand why as it is universally considered an eyesore, indeed obscuring one of the world's great buildings, spoiling a wonderful view, and depriving some very majestic Moreton Bay figs their sunlight in the adjoining Botanical Gardens.

There were huge public protests before and during construction but work went ahead. The public temper towards the project is seen clearly in the continuous letters to the *Sydney Morning Herald*. So hated are the apartments that there have been calls for the Prime Minister to dip into the Federation Fund, amassed for the country's 2001 celebrations of a century of Federation, to buy and demolish the building. The price of destruction would be high: the Sydney Lord Mayor, Frank Sartor, estimates it would cost $400 million to purchase and pull down the building. It has cost developers $200 million to build the 237-unit complex and by January 1999, twenty-five units had been sold, with prices ranging from $2.2 to $5.55 million. For the moment, the eyesore will have to stay put.

the interior – and xenophobic architects. Seven years and three Australian architects later the interior was finished, but it has always been felt to be acoustically – and aesthetically – not up to scratch even though the final price tag was $102 million – well over ten times the original estimate. The elderly Utzon, now living in Majorca, was invited by the NSW premier to be the principal consultant on the interior modification, which would have given him the final authority for all design decisions. It's hard to tell whether this was just a gesture of goodwill to make up for past slights to the architect, or a real attempt to finally realize his full design, but Utzon, now in his eighties, has agreed

If you're not content with gazing at the outside – much the building's best feature – and can't attend a performance, there are **guided tours** available (daily 9am–4pm, every 30–40min; 1hr; $9; tickets from the Lower Concourse; ☎02/9250 7111). On Sunday afternoons there are always free outdoor concerts on one of the forecourts, ranging from jazz, classical, folk to rock (☎02/9250 7111 for details, or pick up the *Sydney Opera House Diary*); Sundays are further enlivened by the **Tarpeian Markets** in the forecourt (10am–4pm), with an emphasis on crafts. Best of all, attend an evening performance: the building is particularly stunning when floodlit and, once you're inside, the huge windows come into their own as the dark harbour waters reflect a shimmering image of the night-time city – interval drinks certainly aren't like this anywhere else. You could also choose to eat inside at what is considered to be one of Sydney's best restaurants, *Bennelong* (☎02/9250 7548), overlooking the city skyline, take a drink at its stylish cocktail bar or order a few pricey oysters from the adjoining *Crustacea Bar*.

The Harbour Bridge

The charismatic **Harbour Bridge**, in the opposite direction from Circular Quay, has straddled the channel dividing North and South Sydney since 1932; today it makes the view from Circular Quay complete. The largest arch bridge in the world when it was built, its construction costs weren't paid off until 1988. There's still a $2 toll to drive across, though, payable only when heading south; you can walk or cycle it for free. Pedestrians should head up the steps to the bridge from Cumberland Street, reached from The Rocks via the Argyle Steps off Argyle Street (see p.103), and walk on the eastern side (the western side is the preserve of cyclists). The ever-increasing volume of traffic in recent years proved too much for the bridge to bear, and a harbour **tunnel** (also $2 heading south) has been built, starting south of the Opera House.

The bridge demands full-time maintenance, protected from rust by continuous painting in trademark steel-grey. One of Australia's best-known comedians, Paul Hogan of *Crocodile Dundee* fame, worked as a rigger on "the coathanger" before being rescued by a New Faces talent quest in the 1970s. To check out Hoge's vista, you can now follow a rigger's route and climb the bridge without getting arrested – once the favoured illegal occupation of drunken uni students. In November 1998 **Bridge Climb** began their well-publicized plan of taking small, specially equipped groups (maximum ten) to climb to the top of the bridge (☎02/9240 1111 or bookings through the Australian Travel Specialists; tours every 10–20min, 7.45am–3.05pm extended to 4.25pm during Daylight Saving; must be over 12; $98; you can just turn up but it's safer to book, particularly on weekends). Though the experience takes three hours, only two hours is spent on the bridge, gradually ascending and pausing while the guide points out landmarks and offers interesting background snippets. The hour spent checking in and getting kitted up at the "Base" at 5 Cumberland St, The Rocks, makes you feel as if you are preparing to go into outer space, as do the grey Star Trek-style suits specially designed so that you blend in with the bridge – no colourful crawling ants to spoil people's view at ground-level. It's really not as scary as it looks – there's no way you can fall off, harnessed as you are into a cable system, and this can calm a normal fear of heights, though phobics beware. The only thing of your own you can take up are your glasses, attached to your suit by special cords – everything from handkerchiefs to caps are provided and similarly attached. This precaution that nothing be dropped onto cars or people below means you can't take your camera with you. Since this has to be one of the world's greatest **photo opportunities**, this is annoying, and although you get one group photo on top of the bridge free with the price of the climb, the group – of jolly strangers, arms akimbo – crowds out the background. To get a good shot showing yourself with the splendours of the harbour behind, you'll need to fork out $12.95 for one large photo or $24.95 for four different small ones, taken by the guide.

If you can't stomach (or afford) the climb, there's a **lookout point** (daily 10am–5pm; $2; 5min walk from Cumberland Street then 200 steps) actually inside the bridge's southern pylon where, as well as gazing out across the harbour, you can study a photo exhibition on the bridge's history.

The Rocks

The Rocks, immediately beneath the bridge, is the heart of historic Sydney. On this rocky outcrop between Sydney Cove and Walsh Bay, Captain Arthur Phillip pro-

LUNA PARK

Looking across from the Harbour Bridge to the north side of the harbour, you can't miss the huge laughing clown's face that belongs to **Luna Park** on Lavender Bay at **Milsons Point**. Built at the height of the amusement park era, it's been a feature of Sydney since the 1930s; it was closed down for several years until its grand reopening in 1995 with a new clown's face – the eighth since Luna Park began – closely resembling the 1950s model. Unfortunately, the noise from the state-of-the-art rollercoaster upset nearby residents who'd grown used to peace and quiet, and the park promptly closed again, losing developers millions of dollars. If it does reopen, it's well worth checking out the murals in Coney Island, a sort of indoor funfair within a funfair, which were restored by local artists to their 1930s glory.

claimed the establishment of Sydney Town in 1788, the first permanent European settlement in Australia. Within decades, the area had become little more than a slum of dingy dwellings, narrow alleys and dubious taverns and brothels. In the 1830s and 1840s, merchants began building fine stone warehouses here, but as the focus for Sydney's shipping industry moved from Circular Quay, the area fell into decline. By the 1870s and 1880s, the notorious Rocks "pushes", gangs of "larrikins" (louts), mugged passers-by and beat each other up: the narrow street named **Suez Canal** was a favourite place to hide in wait. Some say the name is a shortening of Sewers' Canal, and indeed the area was so filthy that whole streetfronts had to be torn down in 1900 to contain an outbreak of the bubonic plague. It remained a run-down, depressed and depressing quarter until the 1970s, when there were plans to raze the historic cottages, terraces and warehouses to make way for office towers. However, due to the foresight of a radical building workers' union which opposed the demolition, the restored and renovated **historic quarter** is now one of Sydney's major tourist attractions and, despite a passing resemblance to a historic theme park, it's worth exploring.

There are times, though, when the old atmosphere still seems to prevail: Friday and Saturday nights in The Rocks can be thoroughly drunken, and there's frequently **trouble** – so much so that there's a prominent police station, police often patrol on horseback and the installation of CCTV is planned for The Rocks and neighbouring Circular Quay. New Year's Eve is also riotously celebrated here, to the backdrop of fireworks over the harbour.

Information, tours and transport

The best place to start your **tour** of The Rocks is the **Sailors' Home**, at 106 George St, built in 1864 to provide decent lodgings for visiting sailors as an alternative to the brothels and inns in the area. The building housed sailors until the early 1980s but is now the **Sydney Visitor Centre** (daily 9am–6pm; ☎02/9255 1788), which at street level supplies tourist information (including a guided tour leaflet selling for $1). There is also a budget accommodation booking board with direct freephone access to the various establishments detailed. On the two galleried levels information is provided about the history and sights of The Rocks along with a re-creation of the original sailors' sleeping quarters. The centre is also the starting point for guided **walking tours** (Mon–Fri 10.30am, 12.30pm & 2.30pm, Sat & Sun 11.30am & 2pm; 1hr 15min; $12; ☎02/9247 6678 for more information). You can take the walking tour as part of the Rocks Ticket ($46), sold here, which also entitles you to a meal (at *Pancakes on the Rocks*), entry to the Museum of Contemporary Art (see p.99), and a harbour cruise with Captain Cook Cruises. A separate night-time **Ghost tour** offered by Unseen Sydney Walking Tours (Tues & Thur–Sun at 6.30pm at an appointed place in Circular Quay; 1hr 30min; $15 or $10 YHA members; ☎02/9555 2700; *www.unseensydney.com.au*) is well worth the money, a history tour with a chilling angle, led by an entertaining, theatrical storyteller. The small sandstone house next to the information centre, at 110 George St, is **Cadman's Cottage**, the oldest private house still standing in Sydney, built in 1816 for John Cadman, ex-convict and Government coxswain. It's now the **National Parks and Wildlife Service** bookshop and information centre (daily 9am–5pm; ☎9247 5033), primarily providing information about Sydney's national parks and taking bookings for trips to Fort Denison and other harbour islands.

The corner of Argyle and Kent streets, Millers Point is a terminus for several useful **bus routes** so you can aim to walk here and then catch a bus back: routes #431–434 go along George Street to Railway Square thence to varying locations including Glebe and Balmain while #339 goes to the eastern beaches suburb of Clovelly via George Street in the City and Elizabeth and Albion streets in Surry Hills.

Exploring The Rocks: from Campbells Cove to the Argyle Cut

Just exploring the narrow alleys and streets hewn out of the original rocky spur is the chief delight of The Rocks, a voyage of discovery that involves climbing and descending several stairs and cuts to different levels. A set of steps alongside The Sydney Visitor Centre leads down to the waterfront and the Overseas Passenger Terminal (see p.102). Head north from here along the waterfront walkway to **Campbells Cove**, where **Campbell's Storehouses** is fairly representative of The Rocks' focus on eating and shopping for souvenirs, clothing and arts and crafts in beautifully restored 1830s stone warehouses, once part of the private wharf of the merchant Robert Campbell (for details of restaurants see "Eating and Drinking", beginning on p.139). A replica of Captain Bligh's ship, the *Bounty*, is moored here between cruises (see p.95), adding a Disney-ish atmosphere, while a luxury hotel, the *Park Hyatt*, overlooks the whole area. Climb the **Customs Officer's Stairs** from Campbells Cove to Hickson Road, from where it's a short walk to Dawes Point (see below) beneath the Harbour Bridge, or browse in the road's **Metcalfe Stores**, another storehouses-turned-shopping complex, this time dating from around 1912. Exit from the old bond stores onto George Street, where at weekends you can further satisfy your shopping urge at **The Rocks Market** (Sat & Sun 10am–5pm), which takes over the entire Harbour Bridge end of the street with more than a hundred stalls selling bric-a-brac, jewellery, antiques and arts and crafts mostly with an Australiana/souvenir slant; the market is sheltered from the sun and rain by huge sails, and there's usually some live entertainment.

There's more shopping at the **Argyle Stores**, on the corner of Argyle and Playfair streets, a complex of decidedly more tasteful and upmarket boutiques (including an outlet of the fashionable Australian jewellery-makers Dinosaur Designs) in a beautifully restored set of former bond stores arranged around an inner courtyard; on the top floor you can take in great views from the bar of *Bel Mondo* (see p.140), a pricey Italian restaurant (also accesses from Gloucester Walk, see below). The Argyle Stores is just near the impressive **Argyle Cut**, which slices through solid stone to The Rocks' other half, Millers Point (see p.104). The cut took eighteen years to complete, carved first with chisel and hammer by convict chain gangs who began the work in 1843; when transportation ended ten years later the tunnel was still unfinished, and it took hired hands to complete it in 1859. Walk up the **Argyle Steps** and along the narrow brick pedestrian walkway of peaceful **Gloucester Walk**, where you'll find a strange mixture of bureaucracy, trendiness and alternative culture. There's also a tiny new sculpture park, **Foundation Park**, which is a delight to stumble across: remains of cottage foundations were recently discovered here and they have been used as the basis for installations of sculptures of Victorian furniture. En route back to the northern end of George Street have a drink at *The Mercantile*, one of Sydney's most well-known Irish hotels (see p.151). Gloucester Walk also leads to the pedestrian entrance of the Harbour Bridge on **Cumberland Street**, the location of a couple of fine old boozers, the *Glenmore* and the *Australian* (see pp.150–151). From the latter, head down **Gloucester Street**; at nos. 58–64 is the **Susannah Place Museum** (Sat & Sun only 10am–5pm; $6; ☎02/9241 1893), a row of four brick terraces built in 1844 and continuously occupied by householders until 1990; it's now a "house museum" (including a re-created corner store) which traces the domestic history of Sydney's working class.

The old wharves and Fort Denison

At the end of George Street, under the Harbour Bridge, **Dawes Point** separates Sydney Cove, on the Circular Quay side, from **Walsh Bay** and the old piers; the park here is a favourite spot for photographers. Looking out past the Opera House, you can see **Fort Denison** on a small island in the harbour: "Pinchgut", as the island is still known, was originally used as a special prison for the tough nuts the penal colony could-n't crack. During the Crimean Wars in the mid-nineteenth century, however, old fears of a Russian invasion were rekindled and the fort was built as part of a defence ring around the harbour. For those interested in Australian history, there are tours organized by the NPWS from Circular Quay. Tours are booked through and meet up at Cadman's Cottage (see p.102; ☎02/9247 8861). There are day-time tours (Wed 11.30am & 1.30pm, Sat 11.45am & 1.45pm, Sun 11.45am & 1.45pm; $12; 2hr 30min) and longer sunset tours (Thurs & Fri 5.30pm, Sat 6pm; $14; 3hr), where you get some extra time to relax and enjoy the view – you're encouraged to bring some nibbles and a bottle of wine.

If you want to rest your legs in more genteel surroundings, go a bit further along Hickson Road to the **Wharf Theatre** (Pier 4/5), home to the Sydney Theatre Company and the Sydney Dance Company as well as about twenty other smaller arts organizations. From the restaurant and its bar you can revel in the sublime view across Walsh Bay to Balmain, Goat Island and the North Shore, or get closer to the water (and the arts work-ers) at the cute little *Dance Café* on the ground floor. The exhibition of posters of past pro-ductions in the hallway leading to the theatre restaurant might even tempt you to come back for a Sydney Theatre Company performance (see p.159). Guided tours of the the-atre, including the costume department and a peek at set construction, are also available (Thurs 10am or by arrangement; 1hr; $5; ☎02/9250 1777).

Millers Point and Observatory Park

Beyond the wharves, looking towards Darling Harbour, **Millers Point** is a reminder of how The Rocks used to be – with a surprisingly real community feel so close to the tourist hype of the Rocks, as much of the housing is government or housing association-owned. Of course, the area has its upmarket pockets, like the very swish *Observatory Hotel* on Kent Street, but for the moment, however, the traditional street-corner pubs and shabby terraced houses on the hill are reminiscent of the raffish atmosphere once typical of the whole area, and the mostly peaceful residential streets are a delight to wander in.

Reach the area through the Argyle Cut (see p.103) or from the end of George Street, heading onto **Lower Fort Street**. The **Colonial House Museum**, 53 Lower Fort St (daily 10am–5pm; $1), takes up the bottom two floors of a residential terrace house (1883) where local character Shirley Ball has lived for over 50 years; her collection – a labour of love rather than a commercial enterprise – is crammed into six rooms, and includes period furnishings, hundreds of photographs of the area, etchings, artefacts and models. Continue to wander up Lower Fort Street and stop for a drink at the **Hero of Waterloo** at no. 81 (see p.151), built from sandstone excavated from the Argyle Cut in 1844, then peek in at the place of worship for the military stationed at Dawes Point fort from the 1840s, the **Garrison Church** (officially Holy Trinity Church; daily 9am–5pm) on the corner of Argyle Street (daily 8am–6pm). Next to the church, the volunteer-run **Garrison Gallery Museum** (Tues & Wed, Fri & Sat 11am–3pm, Sun noon–4pm; free) is housed in what was once the parish schoolhouse – Australia's first Prime Minister, Edmund Barton, was educated here and the collection of turn-of-the-century pho-tographs, complete with images of ragged barefoot children and muddy dirt roads gives a good indication of the conditions of his tutelage. Beside the church, Argyle Place has some of the area's prettiest old terrace houses.

From here, walk up the steps on Argyle Street opposite the church to **Observatory Park** with its shady Moreton Bay figs, park benches and lawns, for a marvellous hilltop view over the architecture below and the whole harbour in all its different aspects – glitzy Darling Harbour, the new Glebe Island Bridge in one direction and the old Harbour Bridge in the other, gritty container terminals, ferries gliding by – and on a rainy day enjoy it from the bandstand which dominates the park. It's also easy to reach the park from the **Bridge Stairs** off Cumberland Street by the Argyle Cut.

The Italianate-style **Observatory** from which the park takes its name marked the beginning of an accurate time standard for the city when it opened in 1858, calculating the correct time from the stars and signalling it to ships in the harbour and Martin Places's GPO by the dropping of a time ball in its tower at 1pm every day – a custom which still continues. Set amongst some very pretty gardens, the Observatory has been a **museum of astronomy** (daily 10am–5pm; $5) since 1982 and the excellent, modern museum is well worth a visit. A large section is devoted to the Transit of Venus, the rare astronomical event (about twice every century), the observation of which prompted Captain Cook's 1769 voyage of exploration, which led to the charting of Australia's east coast. The extensive exhibition of astronomical equipment, both obsolete and high-tech, includes the telescope installed under the copper dome to observe the 1874 Transit of Venus and still working. Another highlight, in the "Stars of the Southern Sky" section are three animated videos of Aboriginal creation stories, retellings of how the stars came to be, from the Milky Way to Orion. Every evening you can view the southern sky through telescopes and learn about the Southern Cross and other southern constellations (times vary with season; 2hr tours include a lecture, film, exhibition, guided view of the telescopes and a look at the sky, weather permitting; booking essential on ☎02/9217 0485, usually up to a week in advance; $8); there's also a small planetarium which is only used during night visits when the sky is not clear enough for observation.

Also in the park is the **National Trust Centre**, located in the former military hospital (1815) south of the Observatory. The rear of the building, purpose built as a school in 1850 in neo-Regency style, houses the **S. H. Ervin Gallery** (Tues–Fri 11am–5pm, Sat & Sun noon–5pm; free; ☎02/9258 0123 for details of special exhibitions), the result of a 1978 bequest by Ervin of a million dollars to devote to Australian art; the changing thematic exhibitions, around eight per year, are of scholarly non-mainstream Australian art, focusing on subjects such as Aboriginal or women artists. There's also a café (Tues–Fri 11am–3pm, Sat & Sun 1–5pm), and a specialist bookshop (Tues–Fri 9am–5pm, Sat & Sun noon–5pm) where you can pick up leaflets about other historic buildings and settlements in New South Wales.

City Centre

From Circular Quay south as far as King Street is Sydney's **Central Business District**, often referred to as the **CBD** with **Martin Place** as its commercial nerve centre. A pedestrian mall lined with imposing banks and investment companies (check out the splendid marbled interior of the National Australia Bank), Martin Place has its less serious moments at summer lunchtimes, when street performances are held at the little amphitheatre, and all year round stalls of flower and fruitsellers add some colour. The vast **General Post Office** broods over the George Street end of the place in all its Victorian-era pomp; the upper floors are being developed into yet another luxury hotel. The other end of Martin Place emerges opposite the old civic buildings on lower Macquarie Street (see p.111). The cramped streets of the CBD itself, overshadowed by office buildings, have little to offer as you stroll through. For some impression of the commerce going on here a crowd gathers outside the **Australian Stock Exchange** opposite Australia Square at 20 Bond St to gaze at the computerized display of stocks and shares through the glass of the ground floor. For a glimpse at how all this wealth might be spent, stroll over to Sydney's most upmarket shopping centre, **Chifley Plaza**, on the corner of Hunter and Phillip streets, where you'll find Kenzo, Max Mara and other exclusive labels; a huge stencil-like sculpture of former Australian Prime Minister Ben Chifley, by artist Simeon Nelson, was recently installed in the pleasant palm-filled square outside.

Museum of Sydney

North of Martin Place, on the corner of Bridge and Phillip streets, the **Museum of Sydney** (daily 9.30am–5pm; ☎02/9251 5988 for exhibition details; $6), is a museum devoted to the city. The site itself is the reason for the museum's existence, for here from 1983 a ten-year archeological dig unearthed the foundations of the first Government House built by Governor Phillip in 1788 and home to eight subsequent governors of NSW before it was demolished in 1846. The museum is totally original in its approach, presenting history in an interactive manner, through exhibitions, film, photography and multimedia. It's all very evocative and thought-provoking but you may come away feeling less well informed than you expected. A key feature of the museum are the special exhibitions – about four each year – so it's worth finding out what's on before you go.

First Government Place, a public square in front of the museum, preserves the site of the original Government House: its foundations are marked out in different coloured sandstone on the pavement. The museum itself is built of honey-coloured sandstone blocks, using the different types of tooling available from the earliest days of the colony right up to modern times: you can trace this development from the bottom to the top of the facade. Near the entrance, **Edge of the Trees**, an emotive sculptural installation which was a collaboration between a European and an Aboriginal artist, conveys the complexity of a shared history that began in 1788. You walk among massive pillars – some inscribed with the names of First Fleeters or Eora tribespeople or their words, while others have glass panels through which you can see human hair or other organic matter – while listening to the haunting, evocative sounds of Eora words. Entering the museum, you hear a dramatized dialogue between the Eora woman Patyegarang and the First Fleeter Lieutenant Dawes, which gives a strong impression of two cultures meeting yet not understanding each other. Beneath your feet you can see, through perspex, the excavated foundations of Government House.

If you decide to pay to get into the rest of the museum, it's best first to go upstairs to the **auditorium** on level 2 and watch the fifteen-minute video explaining the background and aims of the museum. Back on level 1 a video screen, extending up through all three levels, shows images of the bush, sea and sandstone Sydney as it was before the arrival of Europeans, and elsewhere in the museum other exhibits, such as benches with inlays of spotted gum, are evocative of the bush. On level 2, recordings of Sydney Kooris (Aboriginal people) are combined with video images and sound to help the viewer reflect on contemporary experience. The **Collectors Chests** allow you to really familiarize yourself with history, as you can slide open the glass and steel drawers to examine various found fragments. The dark and creepy **Bond Store** on level 3 is the storytelling part of the museum, where holographic "ghosts" relate tales of old Sydney as an ocean port. On the same level, a whole area is devoted to some rather wonderful **panoramas** of Sydney Harbour with views of the harbour itself from the windows.

There is also an excellent **gift shop** with a wide range of photos, artworks and books on Sydney. Quite separate from the museum is the expensive, licensed *MOS café*, on First Government Place; usually filled with lawyers at lunch time, it's agreeably peaceful for a (reasonably priced) coffee at other times.

King Street to Liverpool Street

Further south from Martin Place, the streets get a little more interesting. The rectangle between Elizabeth, King, George and Park streets is Sydney's prime shopping area, with a number of beautifully restored **Victorian arcades** (the Imperial Arcade, Strand Arcade and Queen Victoria Building are all worth a look) and Sydney's two **department stores**, the very upmarket David Jones on the corner of

Market and Elizabeth streets, established over 160 years ago, and the more populist but still quality-focused Grace Bros on Pitt Street Mall.

The landmark **AMP Centrepoint Tower** (daily 9am–10.30pm, Sat until 11.30pm; viewing gallery $10), on the corner of Market and Pitt streets, a giant golden gearstick thrusting up 305m, is the tallest poppy in the Sydney skyline – and its observation level is the highest in the entire southern hemisphere, though management must ruefully admit the tower's height is just beaten by the spire of the Sky Tower in Auckland, New Zealand, which is 23m taller. The 12- to 16-metre-high steel Olympic **sculptures** on top of the tower, colourfully lit up at night, were dramatically put in place by helicopter in July 1998 and will remain there until the end of November 2000. Meanwhile, if you're around before September 2000, a giant clock counts down the days until the big event, while an electronic message panel, facing west in the direction of Homebush Bay, blats out Olympic info and details of city events. The 360° view from the observation level is especially fine at sunset, and on clear days you can even see the Blue Mountains, 100km away. Another way to enjoy the all-round view – without moving – is from the inevitable **revolving restaurants** on the two floors below: level 2 features an all-you-can-eat buffet from $34–40, while the more upmarket à la carte venue on level 1 will cost $50 plus (bookings on ☎02/8223 3800).

Nearby, at the corner of Market and George streets, a couple of fine old buildings provide a pointed contrast. If heaven has a hallway, it surely must resemble that of the restored **State Theatre** on Market Street, host to the Sydney Film Festival (see p.108). Step inside and take a look at the ornate and glorious interior of this picture palace opened in 1929 – a lavishly painted, gilded and sculpted corridor leads to the lush, red and wood-panelled foyer. To see more of the lavish interior (decorations include crystal chandeliers in the dress circle), you'll need to attend the film festival or other events held here, such as concerts and drama, or if you're really keen you can go on a self-guided tour (details on ☎02/9373 6655). The stately **Queen Victoria Building** nearby, in the block between George and York streets, is another of Sydney's finest – but this hasn't stopped Sydneysiders, with characteristic disrespect, from abbreviating it to the QVB. Originally built as a market hall in 1898, the restored QVB was reopened as an upmarket shopping arcade in 1986 (shopping hours Mon–Sat 9am–6pm, Thurs until 9pm, Sun 11am–5pm but you can walk through the building 24hr). The interior is magnificent, with its beautiful woodwork, elevated walkways and antique lifts; Charles I is beheaded on the hour, every hour, by figurines on the ground-floor mechanical clock. From Town Hall Station you can walk right through the basement level (mainly bustling food stalls) and continue via the Sydney Central Plaza to Grace Bros Department Store, emerging on Pitt Street without having to go outside – very cooling on a hot day. Another underground tunnel will link the QVB with Gowings. From the basement up, the four levels of the QVB become progressively upmarket; the third level is worth visiting for its boutiques featuring the work of new young Australian designers. There's also a guided **tour** of the building from the tour desk on the ground floor (Mon–Sat 11.30am & 2.30pm, Sun noon; $5; 1hr; bookings on ☎02/9264 9209) which delves into its architecture and history.

In the realm of architectural excess, however, the **Town Hall** is king – you'll find it a block further up George Street, at the corner of Druitt Street. It was built during the boom years of the 1870s and 1880s as a homage to Victorian England, and has a huge organ inside its Centennial Hall, giving it the air of a secular cathedral. Throughout the interior different styles of ornamentation compete for attention in a riot of colour and detail; the splendidly dignified toilets are a must-see (for tours ring Centrepoint Tours ☎02/9231 4629). Concerts and theatre performances (details on the City Infoline Mon–Fri 9am–6pm; ☎02/9265 9007) set off the splendiferous interior perfectly. Next door, on the corner of Bathurst Street, the Gothic Revival Anglican **St Andrews Cathedral**, is undergoing an expensive interior restoration.

FILM FESTIVALS

The **Sydney Film Festival**, held annually for two weeks in **early June**, is an exciting programme of features, shorts, documentaries and retrospective screenings from Australia and around the world: there are some seventy features and over a hundred shorts and documentaries in all. Founded in 1954 by a group of film enthusiasts at Sydney University, the festival struggled with prudish censors and parochial attitudes until freedom from censorship for festival films was introduced in 1971. From the early, relaxed atmosphere of picnics on the lawns between screenings and hardy film-lovers crouching under blankets in freezing prefabricated sheds, it has gradually moved off-campus, to find a home from 1974 in the magnificent State Theatre (see overleaf). Films are also shown at the Pitt Centre and some other cinemas around town.

The festival is mainly sold on a subscription basis – the only single **tickets** are for special events and cost around $16 while the next cheapest option is the Flexipass, getting you three films for around $21. Otherwise, a Red Pass covers the first week, a Blue Pass the second (both $110 dress circle; $180 stalls). Gold subscriptions for a whole fortnight cost $180–245. For more information, call or drop into the Festival office at 405 Glebe Point Rd, Glebe (Mon–Fri 9am–5pm; ☎02/9660 3844 or 9660 0252, fax 9692 8793; *www.sydfilm-fest.com.au*), or write to PO Box 950, Glebe, NSW 2037.

There are also two short film festivals in the summer with a young feel and the sort of irreverent approach which once fuelled the Sydney Film Festival. Stars above and the sound of waves accompany the week-long **Flickerfest International Short Film Festival** (☎02/9211 7133; *flickerfest@bigpond.com*), held in early January, in the amphitheatre of the Bondi Pavilion and showing foreign and Australian productions, including documentaries. The **Tropfest** is a competition festival for short films held annually around the end of February; its name comes from the *Tropicana Café* (see p.145) on Victoria Street, Darlinghurst, where the festival began almost by chance in 1993 when young actor, John Polsen, forced his local coffee spot to show the short film he had made. He pushed other filmmakers to follow suit, and the following year a huge crowd of punters packed themselves into the café to watch around twenty films. These days the entire street is closed to traffic to enable an outdoor screening, while cafés along the strip also screen films on TVs inside and notables such as Nicole Kidman have turned up to watch the proceedings. The festival has grown enormously over the years, and screenings have subsequently been removed to The Domain. Films must be specifically made for the festival and be up-to-the-minute. To this end, an item is mentioned a few months in advance of the entry date which must feature in the shorts; in 1997 it was pickles, in 1998 a kiss, and in 1999 chopsticks. For more details, contact Tropfest, Suite 24, 2A Bayswater Rd, Kings Cross, NSW 2011 (☎02/9368 0434, fax 9356 4531; *www.tropfest.com.au*).

Other less high-profile film fests include the **Women on Women Film Festival** (WOW; Women in Film and Television, Sydney Film Centre, corner Oatley Road and Oxford Street, Paddington, NSW 2021; ☎02/9332 2408, fax 9380 4311; single $11.50, day $29, weekend pass $49), held over three days in late September at the Chauvel Cinema, Paddington (see p.160). There is also a gay and lesbian film festival in late February (see p.157).

Down to Chinatown

Between Town Hall and Central Station, **George Street** becomes increasingly down-market but along the way you'll pass Chinatown and Paddy's Market both in the area known as **Haymarket**, and just beyond is Darling Harbour (see p.113). The short stretch between the Town Hall and Liverpool Street is for the most part teenage territory, a frenetic zone of **multiscreen cinemas**, pinball halls and fast-food joints; *Planet Hollywood* also attracts a keen stream of youngsters. The stretch is trouble-prone on Friday and Saturday nights when there are pleasanter places to choose to catch a film (see cinema listings p.159). Things change pace at Liverpool Street, where Sydney's

Spanish corner consists basically of a clutch of Spanish restaurants (see pp.140-141 for recommendations) and the *Spanish Club*.

Sydney's **Chinatown**, is a more full-blooded affair than Spanish corner – through the Chinese gates, **Dixon Street Mall** is the main drag, buzzing day and night as people crowd into numerous restaurants, pubs, cafés, cinemas, food stalls and Asian grocery stores. Towards the end of January or in the first weeks of February, Chinese New Year is celebrated here with gusto: dragon and lion dances, food festivals and musical entertainment compete with the noise and smoke from strings of Chinese crackers. The return of Hong Kong to China in 1997 has resulted in massive investments of Hong Kong money in Australian enterprises, including Australia's biggest restaurant, the *Kam Fook* in Chinatown (see p.141). The **Chinese Garden** (Mon–Fri 9.30am–5.30pm, Sat & Sun 9.30am–6pm; closes 1hr earlier in winter; $4), just on the edge of Chinatown at the southern fringes of Darling Harbour, was completed for the Bicentenary Festival in 1988 as a gift from Sydney's sister city Guangdong; the "Garden of Friendship" is designed in the traditional southern Chinese style. As you wander the miniature landscape, plaques in delightfully formal language tell you how best to experience and understand the various viewpoints. Although not large, it feels remarkably calm and spacious – a great place to retreat from the commercial hubbub to read a book, smell the fragrant flowers that attract birds and listen to the lilting Chinese music that fills the air. The balcony of the traditional tearoom offers a bird's-eye view of the dragon wall, waterfalls, a pagoda on a hill and carp swimming in winding lakes.

The area immediately south of Chinatown is enlivened every Saturday and Sunday by Sydney's oldest market, frenetic **Paddy's Market** (Fri, Sat & Sun 9am–4.30pm), in its undercover home at the corner of Thomas and Quay streets, next door to the Entertainment Centre. It's a good place to buy cheap vegetables, seafood, plants, clothes and bric-a-brac. Above the old market, a new multilevel shopping mall has been built, the **Market City Shopping Centre** with a very Asian feel – you could easily imagine yourself in one of the air-conditioned centres of Bangkok or Kuala Lumpur; there's an excellent Asian food court (see p.141) on the top floor next to the Reading multiscreen cinema.

The historic precinct: Hyde Park, College Street and Macquarie Street

Lachlan Macquarie, reformist governor of New South Wales between 1809 and 1821, gave the early settlement its first imposing public buildings, clustered on the southern half of his namesake Macquarie Street. He had a vision of an elegant, prosperous city – although the Imperial Office in London didn't share his enthusiasm for expensive civic projects. Refused both money and expertise, Macquarie was forced to be resourceful: many of the the city's finest buildings were designed by the ex-convict architect Francis Greenway and paid for with rum-money, the proceeds of a monopoly on liquor sales. Hyde Park was fenced off by Governor Macquarie in 1810 to mark the outskirts of his township, and with its war memorials and church, and peripheral museum and Catholic cathedral, is still very much a formal city park.

Hyde Park

From the Town Hall, it's a short walk east to **Hyde Park** along Park Street, which divides the park into two sections, with the Anzac Memorial in the southern half, and the Sandringham Memorial Gardens and Archibald Fountain in the north, overlooked by St James's Church across the northern boundary. From Queens Square, **St James's Church** (daily 9am–5pm) marks the entry to the park – the Anglican church, completed in 1824, is Sydney's oldest place of worship. It was one of Macquarie's schemes built to ex-convict Greenway's design, and the architect originally planned it as a courthouse – you can see how the simple design has been converted into a graceful church. It's worth popping into the crypt to see the richly coloured Children's Chapel mural painted in the 1930s. Behind St James train station, the **Archibald Fountain** commemorates the association of Australia and France during World War I and near here is a **giant chess set** where you can challenge the locals to a match. Further south near Park Street, the Sandringham Memorial Gardens also commemorate Australia's war dead, but the most potent of these monuments is the famous **Anzac Memorial** at the southern end of the park. Fronted by the tree-lined Pool of Remembrance, the thirty-metre-high cenotaph, unveiled in 1934, is classic Art Deco right down to the detail of Raynor Hoff's stylized soldier figures solemnly decorating the exterior.

College Street: the Australian Museum and St Mary's Cathedral

Facing Hyde Park across College Street, at the junction of William Street as it heads up to Kings Cross, the **Australian Museum** (daily 9.30am–5pm; $5, students & YHA $3, ages 5–15 $2, families $12; the $8 combined ticket with the Djamu Gallery is only available from the Djamu itself – see p.98; 30min tours 10am–3pm on the hour) is primarily a museum of natural history, with an interest in human evolution and Aboriginal culture and history. The collection was founded in 1827, but the actual building, a grand sandstone affair with a facade of Corinthian pillars, wasn't fully finished until the 1860s and was extended in the 1980s. The core of the old museum are the three levels of the **Long Gallery**, Australia's first exhibition gallery, opened in 1855 to a public keen to gawk at the colony's curiosities. Many of the classic displays of the following hundred years remain here, Heritage-listed, contrasting with a very modern approach in the rest of the museum.

On the **ground floor**, the impressive **Indigenous Australian** exhibition looks at the history of Australia's Aboriginal people from the dreaming to more contemporary issues of the "stolen generation" and the freedom rides, through a diverse range of approaches, from audiovisual personal views to displays of cultural artefacts. The ground-floor level of the Long Gallery houses the **Skeletons** exhibit, where you can see a skeletal human going through the motions of riding a bicycle, for example. **Level 1** is devoted to minerals, but far more exciting are the disparate collections on **level 2** – especially the Long Gallery's **Birds and Insects** exhibit. There are chilling contextual displays of dangerous spiders such as redbacks and funnelwebs, and you can press buttons to illuminate certain specimens of birds and hear the corresponding bird cry. Pass through this section to the new **Biodiversity: life supporting life** exhibition. It looks at the impact of environmental change on the ecosystems of Australian animals, plants, and micro-organisms, around eighty percent of which do not naturally occur elsewhere, giving the country one of the highest levels of so called biodiversity. In the newer section, the **Discovery Centre** is a hands-on hive of activity for children, while **Search and Discover** is aimed at adults, an identification centre for any creepie crawlies you might come across, with Internet access and books to consult. The **Human Evolution** gallery, also in the new section, traces the development of fossil evidence worldwide and ends with an exploration of archeological evidence of Aboriginal occupation of Australia. A separate section deals with fossil skeletons of dinosaurs and giant marsupials: best of all is the model of the largest of Australia's megafauna, the wombat-like Diprotodon, which may have roamed the mainland as recently as ten thousand years ago.

Stanley Street, off College Street just south of the museum, has a cluster of cheap Italian cafés and restaurants (see p.144-145), and nearby Crown Street features Sydney's version of the *Hard Rock Café*. North up College Street is Catholic **St Mary's Cathedral**, overlooking the northeast corner of Hyde Park. The huge Gothic-style church opened in 1882, though the foundation stone was laid in 1821. The cathedral will at last gain the twin stone spires originally planned by architect William Wardell in 1865 for the two southern towers, with $8 million of the project funded by State and Federal Governments. The cathedral will, also gain an impressive new forecourt – a pedestrianized terrace with fountains and pools with the consolidation of two traffic-isolated parks into the large **Cook and Phillip Park** (see overleaf) which will include a recreation centre with a 50m swimming pool and a gym. The remodelling will also create a green link to The Domain.

Macquarie Street

The southern end of Governor Macquarie's namesake street is lined with the grand edifices that were the result of his dreams for a stately city: Hyde Park Barracks, Parliament House, the State Library and the hospital he and his wife designed. Macquarie Street neatly divides business from pleasure, separating the office towers and cramped streets of the CBD from the open spaces of The Domain and the Royal Botanic Gardens (see p.113).

Sandstone **Sydney Hospital**, the so-called "Rum Hospital", funded by liquor-trade profits, was Macquarie's first enterprise, commissioned in 1814 and therefore one of the oldest buildings in Australia – apart from the central section, which collapsed and was rebuilt at the end of the century. You can take a short cut through the grounds to The Domain (see p.112) and across to the Art Gallery of NSW (see p.112). One of the original wings of the hospital is now **NSW Parliament House** (Mon–Fri 9.30am–4pm; free guided tours Mon & Fri, at 10am, 11am & 2pm; Tues–Thurs, question time at 2.15pm; call ☎02/9230 2111 to check), where as early as 1829 local councils called by the governor started to meet, making it by some way the oldest parliament building in Australia. Varied exhibitions in the foyer change about every fortnight – all represent community or public sector interests and range from painting, art and craft, and sculpture to excellent photographic displays. You can listen in on question time when the Parliament is sitting. The other wing was converted into a branch of the **Royal Mint** in response to the first Australian goldrush and for some time served appropriately as a museum focusing on gold mining and heritage; the museum closed in 1997 and there are plans to reopen the wing as a community space.

Next door, the **Hyde Park Barracks** (daily 9.30am–5pm; $6), designed by convict-architect Francis Greenway, was built in 1819, again without permission from London; the building is now a museum of the social and architectural history of Sydney, giving an insight into convict life during the early years of the colony and the lives of nineteenth-century immigrant women, plus excellent temporary historical exhibitions (☎02/9223 8922 for details).

The **State Library of New South Wales** (Mon–Fri 9am–9pm, Sat & Sun 11am–5pm; Mitchell Library closed Sun) completes the row of public buildings on the eastern side of Macquarie Street. This complex of old and new buildings includes the 1906 sandstone **Mitchell Library**, with an imposing Neoclassical facade gazing across to the greenness of the Botanic Gardens. Its archive of old maps, illustrations and records relating to the early days of white settlement and exploration in Australia includes the **Tasman Map**, drawn by the Dutch explorer Abel Tasman in the 1640s. Pop into the foyer and look at the floor-mosaic which replicates his curious map of the continent, still without an east coast, and its northern extremity joined to Papua New Guinea. A glass walkway links the library with the modern building housing the General Reference Library. Free exhibitions relating to Australian history and literature are a regular feature of its vestibules while lectures, films and video shows take place regularly in the **Metcalfe Auditorium** (call ☎02/9273 1414 for details). You can refresh yourself at the recommended café or browse in the library's bookshop, which has the best collection of Australia-related books in Sydney.

The Domain and the Royal Botanic Gardens

The new Cook and Phillip Park fills in the gap between Hyde Park and **The Domain**, a much larger, plainer open space that stretches from behind the historic precinct on Macquarie Street to the waterfront, divided from the Botanic Gardens by the ugly Cahill Expressway and Mrs Macquaries Road. In the early days of the settlement, The Domain was the governor's private park; now it's a popular place for a stroll or a picnic, with the Art Gallery of New South Wales, an outdoor swimming pool and Mrs Macquaries Chair to provide distraction. The park has lots of shady trees and during the week it's very animated, with city workers sprawling on the grass eating their sandwiches while more energetic types jog, kick around a football or play lunch-time volleyball. On Sundays, assorted cranks and revolutionaries assemble here for **Speakers' Corner**, and every January thousands of people gather on the lawns to enjoy the free open-air opera and concerts of the Sydney Festival (see p.52).

Art Gallery of New South Wales

Beyond St Mary's Cathedral, Art Gallery Road runs through The Domain to the **Art Gallery of New South Wales** (daily 10am–5pm; free except for special exhibitions; ☎02/9225 1744 for times of free tours), whose collection was established in 1874. The original part of the building (1897) is an imposing Neoclassical structure with a facade inscribed with the names of important Renaissance artists, and principally contains the large collection of European art dating from the eleventh century to the twentieth; extensions were added in 1988 which doubled the gallery space and provided a home for mainly Australian art. On level 1, the **Yiribana Gallery** was opened in 1994, devoted to the art and cultural artefacts of Aboriginal and Torres Strait Islanders; one of the most striking exhibits is the **Pukumani Grave Posts**, carved by the Tiwi people of Melville Island. There is a highly recommended half-hour performance in this gallery (Tues–Sat noon) of dance and didgeridoo by an indigenous Australian who also gives a talk about his people. Combine this with the free one-hour tour of the indigenous collection (Tues–Fri 11am, Sat & Sun 1pm) for maximum enlightenment. Other highlights include some classic **Australian paintings** on level 4: Tom Roberts' romanticized shearing-shed scene *The Golden Fleece* (1894) and an altogether less idyllic look at rural Australia in Russell Drysdale's *Sofala* (1947), a depressing vision of a drought-stricken town. On level 5, the **photographic collection** includes Max Dupain's iconic *Sunbaker*, an early study of Australian hedonism. Although dating from 1937, the boldly abstracted image of a sun-worshipper lying on the beach looks as if it could have been taken in the 1990s.

In addition to the galleries, there is also an auditorium (used for art lectures), an excellent bookshop, a coffee shop on level 2, and a well-regarded restaurant on level 5 that attracts Sydneysiders for its food and atmosphere.

Mrs Macquaries Chair and the "Boy"

Beyond the Art Gallery, an overpass used to give a good view of the speeding traffic of the ugly 1960s Cahill Expressway but largely as the result of lobbying by the Art Gallery itself, a large section of the expressway has been covered over and grassed. The landscaping greatly reduces the problem of noise and fumes, and no longer disgraces the beginning of one of Sydney's most scenic routes – Mrs Macquaries Road, built in 1816 at the urging of the governor's wife, Elizabeth. The road curves down from Art Gallery Road to Mrs Macquaries Point, which separates idyllic Farm Cove from the grittier Woolloomooloo Bay. At the end is the celebrated lookout point known as **Mrs Macquaries Chair**, a seat fashioned out of the rock, from which Elizabeth could admire her favourite view of the harbour on her daily walk in what was then the governor's private park. (The point is now enlivened during January's Sydney Festival by an outdoor cinema.) On the route down to the point, the **Andrew "Boy" Charlton Pool** is an open-air, saltwater swimming pool safely isolated from the harbour waters (☎02/9358 6686; daily Sept–April 6.30am–8pm; $2.50) on the Woolloomooloo side of the promontory, with excellent views across to the engrossingly functional Garden Island Naval Depot; "the Boy", as the locals fondly call it, is a popular hangout for groovy Darlinghurst types and sun-worshipping gays, who descend the McElhone Stairs from Victoria Street in Kings Cross to get here (via Woolloomooloo).

The Royal Botanic Gardens

The **Royal Botanic Gardens** (daily 7am–sunset; free), established in 1816, occupy the area between this strip of The Domain and the Opera House, around the headland on Farm Cove where the first white settlers struggled to grow vegetables for the hungry colony. Today's gardeners are much more successful, judging by the well-tended flower beds, lawns and ponds. There are examples of trees and plants from all over the world, although it's the huge, gnarled native Moreton Bay Figs that stand out. The gardens provide some of the most stunning **views** of Sydney Harbour and are always crowded with workers at lunch time, picnickers on fine weekends, and lovers entwined beneath the trees or in the popular café/restaurant. At dusk fruit bats fly overhead in noisy groups and possums begin to riot.

Many **paths** run through the gardens. A popular and speedy route is to start at the northern gates near the Opera House and stroll along the waterfront path to the gates which separate it from The Domain, through here and up the **Fleet Steps** to Mrs Macquaries Chair (see opposite). Within the northern boundaries of the park, the sandstone mansion glimpsed through a garden and enclosure is the Gothic Revival **Government House** (built 1837–45), seat of the governor of New South Wales, and still used for official engagements by the Governor who now lives in a private residence. The stately interior has limited opening hours (Fri–Sun 10am–3pm; free guided tour 45min; ☎02/9931 5222 for more details) but you are free to roam the grounds (daily 10am–4pm). Further south, just inside the gardens at the end of Bridge Street, the **Conservatorium of Music** is housed in what was intended to be the servants' quarters and stables of Government House. Public opinion in 1821, however, said the imposing castellated building was far too grand for such a purpose and a complete conversion, including the addition of a concert hall, gave it a loftier aim of training the colony's future musicians. Conservatorium students have traditionally given free lunchtime recitals every Tuesday and Friday at 1.10pm during term time. While renovations take place at the Conservatorium (with a planned reopening in January 2000), recitals are given elsewhere; see p.158 for details.

Below the Conservatorium, the remaining southern area of the gardens has a Herb Garden, a cooling Palm Grove established in the 1860s, a popular café by the duckponds, and the **Sydney Tropical Centre** (daily 10am–4pm; $2) where a striking glass pyramid and adjacent glass arc respectively house native tropical plants and exotics. Unfortunately, the pyramid has mysteriously begun to shatter and at the time of writing it was closed for an indeterminate period; in the meantime the admission price has been reduced by $3 for the arc only (call ☎02/9231 8125 for the latest information). At an entrance to the park in the southeast corner you'll find the **visitors centre** (daily 9.30am–4.30pm), where free **guided tours** of the gardens commence (daily 10.30am; 1hr–1hr 30min; no bookings required).

Darling Harbour and around

Darling Harbour is, in some ways, a thoroughly stylish redevelopment of the old wharves around Cockle Bay – the glistening water channels that run along Palm Avenue are a great piece of modern design – but many Sydneysiders sneer at it as a soulless, tacky and touristy kind of place, contrasting with the engrossing reality of adjacent Chinatown (see pp.108-109). Certainly, the 1980s development still puts commercial values foremost and the **Harbourside Shopping Centre**, with its souvenir shops and burger bars, is perhaps the biggest attraction and the worst offender. Facing the shopping centre across the water, the **Cockle Bay wharf** development is a contrastingly upmarket restaurant precinct opened in an attempt to revitalize the area and lure in the locals, with a huge 2000-capacity nightclub (*Home*, see p.154), and eight restaurants and cafés. The whole idea behind the development is to drag the CBD screaming and kicking down to the much-maligned Darling Harbour. Behind the development, and accessible from it, is the new **Darling Park**, with paths laid out in the shape of a waratah flower. Meanwhile though the Harbourside Shopping Centre has been given a $60 million refurbishment, its ground floor is still dominated by a noisy video game parlour, most shops still sell tacky souvenir stuff and its touristy *Ettamogah* pub serves up Aussie tucker, a thousand miles from the attempts at sophistication across the water. Persist in trudging through to find its one gem, **Gavala Art** (daily 10am–7pm), a one hundred percent Aboriginal-owned and operated store selling Aboriginal-designed art, clothing and accessories plus music; ask about the free talks on Aboriginal art and the dance performances ($15) held here. Behind the shopping centre, the western side of Darling Harbour is dominated by rather ugly modern chain hotels – the *Novotel*, *Hotel Ibis* and *Grand Mercure* – providing the view for the stylish Cockle Bay wharf diners.

Still, Darling Harbour and the surrounding areas of Haymarket, Ultimo and Pyrmont have plenty else to offer: museums, an Aboriginal cultural centre, an aquarium, entertainment areas, an IMAX cinema, a children's playground, a high-tech amusement park, gardens, and a convention and exhibition centre.

To **get to Darling Harbour** you could walk – it's only ten minutes on foot from the Town Hall; from the Queen Victoria Building walk down Market Street, along the overhead walkway and across Pyrmont Bridge. Further south there's a pedestrian bridge from Bathurst Street or you can cut through on Liverpool Street to Tumbalong Park both bringing you out near the Chinese Garden. Alternatively, the **monorail** (see p.80) runs from the city centre to one of three stops around Darling Harbour, and has the views to recommend it. Getting there by **ferry** from Circular Quay gives you a chance to see a bit of the harbour, and to stop over at Balmain en route: State Transit ferries leave from Wharf 5, Circular Quay (about every 45min Mon–Fri 8am–7.30pm, less often Sat & Sun; $3.20), calling at McMahons Point, Darling Street Wharf in Balmain and Sydney Aquarium in Darling Harbour. Alternatively you could take the Matilda Ferry which runs from the Commissioners Steps, Circular Quay West, outside the Museum of Contemporary Art via the Star City casino at Pyrmont to the Aquarium Wharf (roughly every 25min, 9am–6.30pm, later Fri–Sun; $3.25 one-way). By ordinary bus, from Circular the #456 goes to Darling Harbour, the casino and the Powerhouse Museum. There's actually quite a bit of walking involved getting around the large site and if you're exhausted, or just for fun with kids, you might consider hopping on board the dinky Darling Harbour People Mover Train (adult $2.50; daily: summer 10am–6pm, winter 10am–5pm; full circuit 20min) leaving every fifteen minutes from various points around Darling Harbour. The **Darling Harbour Super Ticket** ($29.90; ☎02/9262 2300) includes rides on the monorail, a two-hour cruise with Matilda Cruises, entry to the Aquarium and the Chinese Garden, a meal at the Aquarium's café and discounts at the IMAX Cinema, the Powerhouse Museum and on the People Mover train.

To find out what's on, visit the **Darling Harbour Visitor Information Centre** (daily 9.30am–5.30pm; ☎02/9286 0111), next door to the IMAX cinema. There are always festivals and events, particularly during school holidays.

Around the water

The Southern Promenade of Darling Harbour is dominated by the **Panasonic IMAX Theatre** (☎02/9281 3300; $14). Its giant cinema screen has a constantly changing programme from their 100-film library; the emphasis is on scenic wonders such as Mount Everest, shown in stunning clarity with wraparound sound. Other Darling Harbour visual onslaughts include **Aquamagic**, a free night-time laser show projected onto a semicircular water screen on Cockle Bay (Wed–Sun: summer 8.10pm & 9.10pm, winter 7.10pm & 8.10pm; 25min).

The Cockle Bay wharf development extends along the eastern promenade of Darling Harbour from the IMAX cinema to **Pyrmont Bridge**, which was "the world's first electrically operated swing span bridge", and is now a pedestrian walkway across Cockle Bay, linking the two sides of the harbour. Beside the bridge is the **Sydney Aquarium** (daily 9.30am–10pm; $15.90; also an Aquarium Pass including STA ferry from Circular Quay $19.20; also see Darling Harbour Super Ticket, opposite). You can also visit the aquarium with Captain Cook Cruises from Wharf 6 at Circular Quay (for details see box on p.95). If you're not going to get the chance to explore the Barrier Reef, the aquarium makes a surprisingly passable substitute. Head straight for the underwater walkway where you can wander in complete safety among sharks, wobbegongs, stingrays and eely things. Upstairs are freshwater fish from the Murray–Darling basin, Australia's biggest river system, while another area features exotic species from the warmer waters further north, and the colourful and bizarre world of the Great Barrier Reef. Sadly though, some of the aquarium's tanks are rather small and you can't blame the seals for looking bored with their unstimulating pool.

On the western side of Pyrmont Bridge the **National Maritime Museum** (daily 9.30am–5pm; $9; guided tour of *HMAS Vampire* $6), with its distinctive modern architecture topped by a wave-shaped roof, highlights the history of Australia as a seafaring nation. However, it goes beyond maritime interests to look at how the sea has shaped Australian life, covering everything from immigration to beach culture and Aboriginal fishing methods. Highlights include the "Merana Eora Nora – First People" exhibition which delves into indigenous culture and "Navigators – Defining Australia" which focuses on the seventeenth-century Dutch explorers. The museum also hosts excellent temporary exhibitions – past ones have looked at immigration to Australia (for latest details call ☎02/9552 7777). There's also a library, auditorium and shop. Outside are its own wharfs, with twelve vessels moored – from an old navy destroyer, the *Vampire*, to a Vietnamese refugee boat. There is a pleasant alfresco café here, which you don't have to enter the museum to use, with views of the boats.

Tumbalong Park and around

Tumbalong Park, inland between the Exhibition Centre and the Chinese Garden, and reached from the city via Liverpool Street, is the "village green" of Darling Harbour and serves as a venue for open-air concerts and free public entertainment. The area surrounding it is perhaps Darling Harbour's most frenetic – at least on weekends during school holidays – as most of the attractions are aimed at children. The tasteful and calm aesthetic of the Chinese Garden (see p.109), on the east side of the park, contrasts quite violently with the **Darling Walk** retail and entertainment centre on the park's north side. Dominating the centre is an indoor theme park, **Sega World** (Mon–Fri 11am–10pm, Sat & Sun 10am–10pm; unlimited rides $25, child $20; ☎02/9273 9273; *www.segaworld.com.au*), a colourful structure which looks like a cross between a giant Lego building and a circus tent. Time-zones are the theme, with the rides (nine of them, including a rollercoaster and a virtual reality experience), entertainment (a 360° theatre), and video games (over 200 of them).

Also in the Darling Walk complex is the new **National Aboriginal Cultural Centre** (daily 9.30am–8pm; free; admission to 45min dance performances at 11am, 1pm, 4pm & 6pm; $14.50). Firmly aimed at tourists, the centre's overt commercialism is a shock if you've visited other excellent Aboriginal cultural centres. Its title is perhaps too grand a claim – the centre is really a commercial art gallery and shop with a performance place attached. There is no interpretive material displayed and the overpriced 45-minute dance performance, amongst shaky sets, is amateurish. The art exhibitions, mostly paintings, change monthly and a whole range of Aboriginal-made products, including didgeridoos, are on sale.

Ultimo: the Powerhouse Museum and around

From Tumbalong Park, a signposted walkway leads to **Ultimo** and its **Powerhouse Museum** on Harris Street (daily 9.30am–5pm; $8, children $2, free first Sat in month; free tours daily, call ☎02/9217 0100 for details; monorail to Haymarket). Located, as the name suggests, in a former power station, this is arguably the best museum in Sydney, a young and exciting place with fresh ideas. The museum was opened here in 1988 but was originally founded in 1880: its main function has always been to collect, care for and interpret "material culture". This notion is open to a wide interpretation and, unusually, the museum combines arts and sciences, design, sociology and technology under the same roof – and even fashion, with the much-anticipated "Fashion of the Year" display every November. The displays are varied, and there's something for everyone here, presented with an interactive approach that means you'll need hours, or several trips, to investigate the 5-level museum properly. There's always one or two special exhibitions too, which might range from showcasing a new young Australian designer to fabulous Korean costumes. The entrance level is dominated by the huge **Boulton and Watt Steam Engine**, first put to use in 1875 in a British brewery; still operational, the engine is often loudly demonstrated. The **Kings Cinema** on level 3, with its original Art Deco fittings, suitably shows the sorts of newsreels and films a Sydneysider would have watched in the 1930s. Judging by the tears at closing time, the special childrens' circus have proved a great success. On level 5, there's a licensed restaurant, colourfully painted with bright Ken Done flower shapes, with a more inexpensive courtyard cafeteria downstairs. The souvenir shop is also worth a browse for some unusual gifts.

Three blocks north, at 320 Harris St, the **Motor Museum** (public holidays, Wed–Sun & daily during school holidays 10am–5pm; $10; monorail to Convention) houses around 160 vehicles on three levels. The usual mix of vintage cars and 1950s American-style cruisers, it also has a comprehensive collection of Australian automobilia.

Pyrmont: Star City and the Sydney Fish Market

Frantic redevelopment is taking place at **Pyrmont**, the once dilapidated suburb jutting out into the water between Darling Harbour and Blackwattle Bay, Sydney's answer to Ellis Island in the 1950s when thousands of immigrants disembarked at Pier 13 – then the city's main overseas passenger terminal. With the NSW government selling $97 million worth of property, this is one of the biggest concentrated sell-offs of land in Australia. The former industrial suburb, which had a population of only nine hundred in 1988, is in the process of being transformed into a residential suburb of twenty thousand over the coming decade with $2 billion worth of investment. The approach to the spectacularly cabled **Glebe Island Bridge** – Sydney's newest – cuts through Pyrmont and saves between fifteen and twenty minutes' travelling time to Sydney's inner west. The area has certainly become glitzier, with Sydney's new casino, Star City, and two TV companies – Channel Ten and Foxtel – now based here.

Beyond the Maritime Museum, on Pyrmont Bay is **Star City**, the spectacularly tasteless new Sydney casino (☎1300/300 711 for more information), open 24-hours a day. As well as the casino, the building houses two theatres, fourteen restaurants, cafés and theme bars, and a nightclub. A free 24-hour shuttle bus (see opposite) attempts to lure punters here from Kings Cross. It's certainly a place to come for late night eats, with some quite good value places like the *City Noodle Café*, which stays open until 2am. Add to this ATMs, ice-cream outlets, souvenir shops and small supermarkets and a mini universe is created. The casino interior itself is a riot of giant palm sculptures, a big silver tree, prize cars spinning on rotating bases, ochre columns, Aboriginal painting motifs on the ceiling, a carpet of Australian critters scurrying across a red desert-coloured carpet, and an endless array of poker machines flashing beneath what look like Christmas lights. To **get to the casino** by bus, you can take the #888 from Circular Quay via George Street and Town Hall, #443 from Circular Quay via Phillip and Market streets and the QVB on York street, or the free blue-and-white Star City shuttle bus, Casino Shuttlebus (free call ☎1800/681 500; every 30min through 24hr from various locations in Kings Cross; every 30min after 4.15pm from Circular Quay). The light rail (see p.80-84) pulls in underneath the building.

The main reason to visit this area, though, is the **Sydney Fish Market**, on the corner of Pyrmont Bridge Road and Bank Street (daily 7am–4pm; ☎02/9660 1611), only a ten-minute walk via Pyrmont Bridge Road from Darling Harbour. Now a popular tourist attraction, it's a frenetic, early-morning spectacular – a gathering of boats from the Sydney fishing fleet, cargo boats, fishermen and buyers. The market is the second-largest seafood market in the world for variety of fish, after the massive Tsukiji market in Tokyo. You need to visit early to see the **auctions** (Mon–Fri only, with the biggest auction floor on Friday; the buyers begin viewing the fish at 4.30am and auctions begin 5.30am but public viewing platform opens 7am), buyers log into computer terminals to register their bids. A two-hour early morning tour of the selling floor and a hands-on cookery class – making yourself a fishy breakfast – is a good way to get amongst it (held about once a month; $38 per person includes the tour, ingredients, tuition and the meal).

You can take away oysters, prawns and cooked seafood and eat picnic-style on waterfront tables. Everything is set up for throwing together an impromptu meal – there's a nearby bakery, a deli, a bottle shop and a grocer. Alternatively, you can eat in at the fish restaurant, *Doyles* (see also p.140), an excellent sushi bar, or have dirt-cheap fish and chips at the *Italian Fish Market Café*, where you can also come for an excellent very early morning coffee (Mon–Fri 4am–4pm, Sat & Sun 5am–5pm); retail shops open at 7am. Apart from the morning tour, above, you can learn to cook seafood here, from Thai-style to French provincial, under the expert tuition of well-known local chefs at the **Sydney Seafood School** (same phone number as market above).

To **get to** the fish market by public transport, take the Light Rail service from Central to Fish Market station on Miller Street, near the entrance to the market. By bus, take #501 from outside the Sydney Electricity Building, on the corner of George and Bathurst streets opposite the Town Hall, which stops right outside on Bank Street; otherwise take bus #443 from the Queen Victoria Building, and it's a five-minute walk from the corner of Harris Street and Pyrmont Bridge Road. Otherwise it's a five-minute walk from Darling Harbour; from the Maritime Museum take Pyrmont Bridge Road straight there.

Inner western suburbs

West of the centre, immediately beyond Darling Harbour, the inner-city areas of **Glebe** and **Newtown** surround Sydney University, their vibrant cultural mix enlivened by large student populations. On a peninsula north of Glebe and west of The Rocks, **Balmain** is a gentrified working-class dock area popular for its village atmosphere, while en route **Leichhardt** is the focus of Sydney's Italian community.

Glebe

Glebe, right by Australia's oldest university, has gradually been evolving from a café-oriented student quarter to more upmarket thirtysomething territory with a New Age slant. Indeed, it's very much the centre of alternative culture in Sydney, with its yoga schools, healing centres to places selling organic vegetables. **Glebe Point Road**, the focal point of the area, is filled with an eclectic mix of cafés with trademark leafy court-

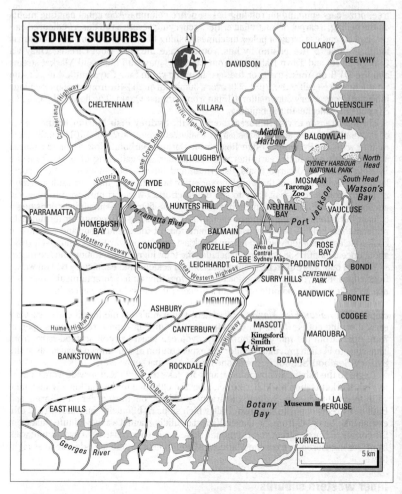

yards, restaurants, bookshops and secondhand and speciality shops as it runs uphill from **Broadway**, becoming quietly residential as it slopes down towards the water of Rozelle Bay. The side streets are fringed with renovated two-storey terraced houses with white iron lacework verandahs. Not surprisingly, Glebe is popular with backpackers: there is a good YHA hostel among others (see "Accommodation", p.90), an Internet café and even a backpackers' travel centre; for **longer stays**, check the many café notice boards for flat shares. However, a new element is altering Glebe's laid-back, almost villagey feel, the brand-new **Broadway Shopping Centre** on nearby Broadway, though it certainly is handy if you're staying in the area, with its supermarkets, speciality food shops, huge food court, record and bookshops, and stores selling everything from clothes and shoes to luggage and with a 12-screen cinema. It's linked to Glebe by an overhead walkway from Glebe Point Road opposite one of the street's favourite cafés, *Badde Mannors*.

Just before the beginning of Glebe Point Road, on Broadway, the recently reland-scaped **Victoria Park** has a very pleasant, heated, outdoor swimming pool (Mon–Fri 6am–7.15pm, Sat & Sun 7am–5.45pm; $2.50), with a sophisticated café. Next door to the park, as Broadway turns into **Parramatta Road**, is one of the main gates to **Sydney University**, Australia's oldest tertiary educational institution, inaugurated in 1850. You can freely walk through the gates and wander through the pleasant grounds which take up a suburb-sized area between Parramatta Road, and City Road running up to King Street, Newtown (see below).

Glebe itself is at its best on Saturday, when **Glebe Market** (which takes place on the shady primary school playground a couple of blocks up from Broadway) is in full swing. The market is shady, relaxed and quietly sociable, like Glebe itself. On sale are mainly clothes and accessories – funky new and secondhand stuff, beach dresses, cute hand-bags, jewellery – plus plants, records and CDs, mobiles, the inevitable crystals, and a bit of bric-a-brac, but the food stalls are disappointing.

At no. 49 Glebe Point Rd, you'll find the excellent **Gleebooks** – one of Sydney's best-loved bookshops and the focus of Glebe's literary and academic aspirations, with regular readings and talks upstairs (call ☎02/9660 2333 for details or pick up a pro-gramme inside). The original Gleebooks, now selling secondhand and children's books only, is worth the trek farther up at 191 Glebe Point Rd, past St Johns Road and Glebe's pretty park. A few blocks on from here, the action stops and Glebe Point Road trails off into a more residential area, petering out at **Jubilee Park** with characterful views across the water to boats and Rozelle Bay's container terminal. The pleasantly landscaped waterfront park, complete with huge shady Moreton Bay fig trees and a children's playground, offers an unusual view of far-off Sydney Harbour Bridge framed within Sydney's newest, the fanciful Glebe Island Bridge. Drop in to **Blackwattle Studios**, across from the park at 465 Glebe Point Rd where artists, designers and craftspeople, and even architects and a film production studio, operate from this old industrial waterside building. This corral of creative types hog the big table at the studio's insouciant café, the *Blackwattle Canteen* (see p.142), but the pub-lic can also enjoy the food and the water views. You're also welcome to wander around the rest of the building; some studios have windows displaying work, while others splurge on a showroom.

Buses #431, #433 and #434 run to Glebe from Millers Point, George Street and Central Station; #431 and #434 run right down the length of Glebe Point Road to Jubilee Park, with the #434 continuing on to Balmain, while the #433 runs half-way turning at Wigram Road and heads on to Balmain. Otherwise it's a fifteen-minute **walk** from Central up Broadway to the beginning of Glebe Point Road.

Newtown and around

Newtown, quite a bit further to the southwest, is another up-and-coming inner-city sub-urb. What was once a working-class district – a hotchpotch of derelict factories, junk-yards and cheap accommodation – has been transformed into a trendy but still offbeat and alternative area. Newtown is characterized by its large gay and lesbian population, its rich cultural mix and a healthy dose of students and lecturers from nearby Sydney University amongst the young homebuyers. It has an enviable number of great cafés and diverse restaurants, especially Thai and Vietnamese. A big part of the changing face is no doubt due to the Dendy Cinema complex, more like a cultural centre than just a film theatre, with its attached bookshop, excellent record store, and streetfront café, all open daily and into the night.

The main drag, **King Street**, is filled with unusual secondhand, funky fashion and spe-ciality shops; during the **Newtown Festival** (early Oct to early Nov; *www.newtownfestival .org.au*) various shop windows let themselves be taken over by young, irreverent and in-your-face art. On the book front, check out Gould's Book Arcade at no. 32, the vast and chaotic secondhand book warehouse that is a Sydney institution, browsable until midnight. Head towards Faster Pussy Cat, at no. 433, for wild retro accessories including lurid B-grade books and cat's-eye sunnies, while C's Flashback at no. 180 has a fab range of loud Hawaiian shirts amongst its racks. Veer off King Street for Pretty Dog, at 1 Brown St, which is open daily for a good range of retro secondhand gear out back, while up front you'll find over-the-top club and streetwear.

King Street becomes more quiet on the **St Peters** side of the train station, but it's well worth strolling down to look at the more unusual speciality shops (buttons, ribbons, train memorabilia, cowboy high-style).

So far **Enmore**, which begins along Enmore Road, stretching west from King Street, opposite Newtown station, has escaped gentrification, with the result that the migrant population hasn't been squeezed out by higher rents and more expensive leases. The Thai grocery stores share the road with a Turkish belly-dancing school, Chinese laundry, Fijian grocer and Italian deli, while the Greek community is represented by a barber, a bakery and a darkly lit men's club whence drifts the sound of clicking dominoes. It's generally much quieter than Newtown, except when Massive Attack or another big band is playing at the **Enmore Theatre**.

Erskinville Road, stretching from the eastern side of King Street marks the beginning of the adjoining suburb of, **Erskineville** is a popular gay locale; the *Imperial Hotel* here at 35 Erskineville Rd (see also p.155), which has long hosted popular drag shows, now trades on its fame as the starting point of the gang in the hit film *Priscilla Queen of the Desert* with Friday and Saturday night Priscilla tributes (10.30–11.30pm).

Buses #422, #423, #426 and #428 run to Newtown from Circular Quay via Castlereagh Street, Railway Square and City Road. They all go down King Street as far as the station, where the #400 continues to St Peters and the others turn off to Enmore and Marrickville. You can also get here by **train** from Central Station and the city circle.

Balmain, Leichhardt and Rozelle

Balmain, directly north of Glebe, is less than 2km from the Opera House, by ferry from Circular Quay to Darling Street wharf. But, stuck out on a spur in the harbour and kept apart from the centre by Darling Harbour and Johnston's Bay, it has a degree of separation that has helped it retain its slow, villagey atmosphere and made it the favoured abode of many writers and filmmakers. Like better-known Paddington, Balmain was once a working-class quarter of terraced houses that has gradually been gentrified. The docks at White Bay are still important, though, and Balmain hasn't completely forsaken its roots, and the area has a good mix of people. Darling Street rewards a leisurely stroll, with a bit of browsing in its speciality shops (focused on clothes and gifts), and grazing in its restaurants and cafés. It, and the surrounding backstreets, are also blessed with enough watering holes to warrant a pub crawl – two classics are the *London Hotel* on Darling Street (see p.151) and the *Exchange Hotel* on Beattie Street (see p.151). The best time to come is on Saturday, when a lively **market**, together with some exotic food stalls, occupies the grounds of St Andrews Church (7.30am–4pm), on the corner opposite the *London Hotel*. For long light, stunning sunsets and wow-worthy real estate, meander down the backstreets towards water-surrounded **Birchgrove** on its finger of land, where Louisa Road leads to Birchgrove wharf; from here you can catch a ferry back to Circular Quay, or stay and relax in the small park on Yurulbin Point.

It's almost an hour from The Rocks to Balmain by the #440 bus, via **Leichhardt**, Sydney's "Little Italy", where the famous **Norton Street** strip of cafés and restaurants runs off ugly **Parramatta Road**. Leichhardt is very much up and coming – shiny, trendy, Italian cafés keep popping up all along the strip, in the wake of the new upmarket cinema complex, The Palace, with its attached record store, bookshop and Internet

GOAT ISLAND

Just across the water from Balmain East, **Goat Island** is the site of a well-preserved gunpowder magazine complex. The sandstone buildings, including a barracks, were built by two hundred convicts between 1833 and 1839. Treatment of the convicts was harsh: eighteen-year-old Charles Anderson, a mentally impaired convict with a wild, seemingly untameable temper who made several attempts to escape, received over twelve hundred lashes in 1835 – and if that wasn't enough, he was sentenced to be chained to a rock for two years in an attempt to control him, a cruel punishment even by the standards of the day. Tethered to the rock, which you can still see, his unhealed back crawling with maggots, he slept in a cavity hewn into the sandstone "couch". Sydneysiders would row up and tease him for entertainment. Eventually Anderson ended up on Norfolk Island (see p.292), where under the humane prisoner reform experiments of Alexander Maconochie, the feral, abused 24-year-old made a startling transformation. The island is looked after by the NPWS, who run various **tours** with Sydney Ferries (bookings essential, call ☎02/9247 5033), making the most of the island's gruesome history and its present use as the shooting location for the popular TV series *Water Rats* about the water police. Tours range from a Heritage Tour (Mon, Fri & Sat 1pm; $11), a picnic tour (Sun 11.30am; BYO picnic), and a *Water Rats* tour checking out film sets (Wed noon; $13). There are also night time **ghost tours** for over-12s only (Sat 6pm; $16) and less frequent ones for children (last Fri month 6pm; $16).

café, and another bookshop complex plus a shopping centre are under construction. However, the two most authentic Italian cafés, the low-key *Caffe Sport* (see p.143) at the Parramatta Road end, and the lively and much-loved *Bar Italia* (see p.143), a fifteen-minute walk further down Norton at the extent of the tempting array of eateries, are still the best. From Leichhardt, the #440 bus continues to Darling Street, which runs from **Rozelle** right down to Balmain's waterfront. Rozelle, once very much the down-at-heel, poorer sister to Balmain, is now emergently trendy with the Sydney College of the Arts and the Sydney Writers' Centre based here as well as lots of cafés, bookshops, speciality shops, gourmet grocers, restaurants and designer home-goods stores. Its pubs have also emerged from their stuporific gloom with glass fronts and breezy decor, like the once seedy *Sackville Hotel* at no. 599 with its *Bistro Deux* and its *Lime Bar*. Further on towards Balmain, Elkington Park has the quaint **Dawn Fraser Swimming Pool** (Oct–April 7.15am–5.30pm; $2), an old-fashioned harbour pool named after the famous Australian Olympic swimmer.

To **get to** Balmain, you can catch a ferry from Circular Quay to Darling Street wharf, in Balmain East where buses wait to take you up Darling Street to Balmain proper. Buses #433 and #434 run out to Balmain via George Street, Railway Square and Glebe Point Road and down Darling Street, or a faster bus is the #442 from the QVB, which crosses the new Glebe Island Bridge and heads to Balmain wharf. Birchgrove can be reached via ferry from Circular Quay or on the #441 from the QVB. To get to Leichhardt you can take bus #436, #437, #438 or #440 from George Street in the city via Rozelle.

Inner eastern suburbs

To the east, **Surry Hills**, **Darlinghurst** and **Paddington** were once rather scruffy working-class suburbs, but they have been taken over and revamped by the young, arty and upwardly mobile. **Kings Cross** is home to Sydney's red-light district as well as many of its tourists, while in adjacent **Woolloomooloo** container ships tie up at the docks. Further east, the "Cross" fades into the more elegant suburbs of **Potts Point** and **Elizabeth Bay**, which trade on their harbour views.

Surry Hills and Redfern

Surry Hills, directly east of Central Station from Elizabeth Street, was traditionally the centre of the rag trade, which still finds its focus on Devonshire Street. Rows of tiny terraces once housed its original poor, working-class population, many of them of Irish origin. Considered a slum by the rest of Sydney, the dire and overcrowded conditions were given fictional life in Ruth Park's *The Harp in the South* trilogy (see "Books", p.1029), set in the Surry Hills of the 1940s. The area became something of a cultural melting pot with European postwar immigration, and doubled as a grungy, studenty, muso heartland in the 1980s. By the mid-1990s, however, the slickly fashionable scene of neighbouring Darlinghurst and Paddington had finally taken over Surry Hills' twin focal points of parallel **Crown Street**, filled with cafés, swanky restaurants – like *MG Garage* (see p.144), where you eat parked among posh cars – funky clothes shops, and designer galleries, and leafy **Bourke Street**, where a couple of Sydney's best cafés lurk among the trees. As rents have gone up, only **Cleveland Street**, running west to Redfern and east towards Moore Park and the Sydney Cricket Ground (see box on p.124), traffic-snarled and lined with cheap Lebanese and Turkish restaurants, retains its ethnically varied population.

A good time to visit Surry Hills is the first Saturday of the month when a lively **flea market**, complete with tempting food stalls, takes over the small Shannon Reserve, on the corner of Crown and Fouveaux streets, overlooked by the **Clock Hotel**. The hotel, which has expanded out of all recognition from its 1840s roots, is emblematic of the new Surry Hills. The landmark clock tower was added in the 1960s, and the hotel has been made over with a swish pool restaurant and cocktail bar to attract a far different crowd from the rough and ready pool-playing crew of recent years, though the pool room is still popular. The artistic side of Surry Hills can be experienced nearby at the **Brett Whitely Studio** at 2 Raper St (Sat & Sun 10am–4pm; $6); walk about three blocks further south down Crown Street, and it's off Davies Street. Whitely was one of Australia's best-known contemporary painters who had gained international recognition by the time he died of a heroin overdose at the age of 53; his work expresses his wild visions of himself and of Sydney. In the mid-1980s Whitely converted this one-time factory into a studio and living space. Since his death it's become a public gallery administered by the Art Gallery of New South Wales, showing his paintings and the work of other artists, plus Whitely memorabilia.

Surry Hills is a short **walk** uphill from Central (Devonshire Street or Elizabeth Street exit); take Fouveax or Devonshire Street and you'll soon hit Crown, or it's an even quicker stroll for Oxford Street, Darlinghurst, heading south along Crown or Bourke streets.

Just beyond Surry Hills, and only 2km from the glitter and sparkle of Darling Harbour, **Redfern** is Sydney's underbelly. Around the **Everleigh Street** area, Australia's biggest urban Aboriginal community lives in "**the Block**", a squalid streetscape of derelict terraced houses and rubbish-strewn streets not far from Redfern train station – the closest Sydney has to a no-go zone. The Aboriginal Housing Company, set up as a co-operative in 1973, has been unable to pay for repairs and renovation work, in shocking contrast to Paddington's cutesy restored terraces and the harbourview mansions of Sydney's rich and beautiful. Recently the Company began knocking down derelict houses and relocating people which has upset many residents who want to keep the community together.

Darlinghurst, Paddington and Woollahra

Oxford Street, from Hyde Park to Paddington and beyond, is a major amusement strip. Waiting to be discovered, here and in the side streets, is an array of nightclubs, restaurants, cafés and pubs. Around **Darlinghurst**, Oxford Street is the focus of Sydney's very active gay and lesbian movement. Hip and bohemian, Darlinghurst mingles seediness with a certain hedonistic style: some art students and pale and wasted clubbers never leave the district – save for a coffee at the Cross or a swim (in black cozzies and cat's-eye sunglasses, of course) at "the Boy" in The Domain (see p.112). There's another concentration of cafés, restaurants and fashion on Liverpool Street, while Victoria Street is a classic pose strip with the legendary, street-smart *Coluzzi Bar* (see p.144). At 148 Darlinghurst Rd, the **Sydney Jewish Museum** (Mon–Thurs 10am–4pm, Fri 10am–2pm, Sun 11am–5pm; $6) is housed in the old Maccabean Hall, which has been a Jewish meeting point for over seventy years. Sixteen Jews were among the convicts who arrived with the First Fleet, and the high-tech, interactive museum explores over two hundred years of Australian Jewish experience; one of its permanent exhibitions covers the Holocaust. There's also a café dishing up kosher cuisine.

Paddington, a slum at the turn of the century, became a popular hangout for hipsters during the late 1960s and 1970s. Since then, yuppies took over and turned Paddington into the smart and fashionable suburb it is today: the Victorian-era terraced houses, with their iron-lace verandahs reminiscent of New Orleans, have been beautifully restored. Many of the terraces were originally built in the 1840s to house the artisans who worked on the graceful sandstone **Victoria Barracks** on the southern side of Oxford Street, its walls stretching seven blocks, from Greens Road to just before the Paddington Town Hall on Oatley Road. **Shadforth Street**, opposite the entrance gates, has many examples of the original artisans' homes. Though the barracks are still used by the army, there are free guided tours (Thurs 10am) – complete with army band – while a small **museum** is open to visitors (Sun 10am–3pm). On the other side of Oxford Street the small, winding, tree-lined streets are a pleasant place for a stroll and offer tantalizing glimpses of the sparkling waters of the harbour – and a chance to wander into the many small art galleries or to take some liquid refreshment. Head via Underwood and Heeley streets to **Five Ways**, where you'll find cafés, speciality shops and a typically gracious old boozer, the *Royal Hotel* (see p.152), or more shops on Elizabeth Street running off Oxford Street. But the main action is, of course, on Oxford Street, most lively on Saturday from 10am to around 4pm, when the crowds descend on **Paddington Market** in the church grounds at 395 Oxford St. As well as being a prime spot to show off and hang out, it's a sure-fire source of great presents, with leather goods, jewellery and clothes – old and new – at the top of the list. Even if you're hard up, it's worth a visit just to browse – the atmosphere, music and buskers come free, and the food is cheap and tasty.

Woollahra, along Oxford Street from Paddington, is even more moneyed but contrastingly staid, with severely expensive **antique shops** along Queen Street replacing the wackier style of Paddington. South of Paddington and Woollahra lies the green expanse of **Centennial Park**, opened to the citizens of Sydney at the Centennial Festival in 1888 (the bicentennial version was opened at Homebush in 1988). With its vast lawns, rose gardens and extensive network of ponds it resembles an English country park, but is reclaimed at dawn and dusk by distinctly Antipodean residents, including possums and flying foxes. The park is crisscrossed by walking paths and tracks for cycling, roller-blading, jogging and horse-riding: you can rent a bike or rollerblades or hire a horse (see "Listings", p.162, for details) and then recover from your exertions in the café or in the finer months stay on until dark and catch an outdoor film with the Moonlight Cinema (see p.159). Adjoining **Moore Park** has facilities for tennis, golf, grass-skiing, bowling, cricket and hockey; it is also home to the **Sydney Cricket Ground**, the Sydney Football Stadium and the new **Fox Studios** site, built in the old Showgrounds (see overleaf).

Transport heading in this direction includes **buses** #380 and #382 from Circular Quay which both run up Elizabeth Street and along Oxford Street. The #378, from Central Station, also heads along Oxford Street. Bus #389 from Circular Quay runs via Elizabeth and William streets in the city and along Glenmore Road and Hargrave streets, Paddington, to emerge on Oxford Street.

MOORE PARK: THE SYDNEY CRICKET GROUND AND FOX STUDIOS

The venerated institution of the **Sydney Cricket Ground (SCG)** in **Moore Park**, south of Oxford Street, Paddington, has earned its place in cricketing history for Don Bradman's score of 452 not out in 1929, and for the controversy over England's bodyline bowling techniques in 1932. Ideally, proceedings are observed from the lovely 1886 Members Stand, while sipping an icy gin and tonic – but unless you're invited by a member, you'll end up elsewhere, probably drinking beer from a plastic cup. Cricket spectators aren't a sedate lot in Sydney, and the noisiest barrackers will probably come from "the Hill" – or the Doug Walters stand, as it's officially known. Still the cheapest spot to sit, the concreted area was once a grassy hill where rowdy supporters threw empty beer cans at players and each other, but beer is now strictly rationed. The Bill O'Reilly Stand gives comfortable viewing until the afternoon, when you'll be blinded by the sun, whereas the Brewongle Stand provides consistently good viewing. Best of all is the Bradman Stand, with a view directly behind the bowler's arm, and adjacent to the exclusive stand occupied by members, commentators and ex-players. The Test to see here is, of course, **The Ashes** (see p.58); the Sydney leg of the five tests, each for five days, begins on New Year's Day. For information, scores, prices and times, call Match Information on ☎0055/63132. You can buy tickets at the gates on the day subject to availability, or purchase them in advance from Ticketek (☎02/9266 4800).

Die-hard cricket fans can actually go on a **tour** of the SCG on non-match days (Mon–Sat 10am, 1pm & 3pm; 1hr 30min; $18; ☎02/9380 0383). The tour also covers the **Sydney Football Stadium** next door, where **State of Origin** Rugby League is played, coverage of which consistently produces the highest ratings on Australian television.

Also within Moore Park, immediately southeast of the SCG, the new **Fox Studios** have been constructed within the old Showgrounds site, where the Royal Agricultural Society held its annual **Royal Easter Show** for over a century. In 1998 the huge show took place for the first time at the new $380 million Sydney Showground at the Olympic site at Homebush Bay. In order to use the Showgrounds as a film studio, the significant heritage features of the site had to be preserved. This was not difficult: the 60-acre site was already a world unto itself, complete with road systems, gardens, pavilions – many of them quite grand – and a huge show ring, all of which the film studios will make use of. The **Professional Studio**, opened in May 1998, takes up over half the site and has facilities for both film and television production, with six high-tech stages and industry tenants on-site providing everything from casting services to stunt professionals. *Babe: Pig in the City* was made here for Universal Pictures and yet more of the *Star Wars* saga will be filmed on-site. The rest of the site is planned to open in late 1999. The public will be able to take a peek at film or television sets in action from an elevated walkway running from the **Fox Studios Backlot**. The tours from here will mainly show behind the scenes film techniques married with an interactive approach that allows visitors to become part of the cinematic action. For times and prices call Fox Studios on (☎02/9383 4000). A separate area will be freely open to the public – the **Entertainment and Retail Precinct**. A mega state-of-the-art sixteen-screen **cinema complex** will be the focus, with twelve screens in an Art Deco-style building paying homage to the picture palaces of the 1930s, and four screens showing less mainstream films in another building. The old **Show Ring**, once the preserve of wood-chopping competitions and rodeo events, will be used for a range of entertainment, from open-air cinema to circuses, and will be surrounded by shops, cafés and restaurants.

To **get to** the SCG or the Studios you can take a bus from Central Station (#372, #393 or 395) or from Elizabeth Street in City, before Museum Station (#390, # 391, #394, #396 or #398). Alternatively you could take a bus to Oxford Street, Paddington (see above) and then walk.

Kings Cross, Woolloomooloo and Potts Point

The preserve of Sydney's bohemians in the 1950s, **Kings Cross** became an R&R spot for American soldiers during the Vietnam war, and is now Sydney's red-light district, its streets prowled by prostitutes, junkies, drunks, strippers and homeless teenagers. It is also a bustling centre for backpackers and other travellers, especially around leafy and quieter Victoria Street; the two sides of "the Cross" (as locals call it) coexist with little trouble, though some of the tourists seem a little surprised at where they've ended up, and it can be rather intimidating for lone women.

The Cross can *seem* heavy but the constant flow of people makes it relatively safe, and it's always lively, with places to eat and drink that stay open all hours. Climbing up William Street from Hyde Park, **Darlinghurst Road** beckons with its giant neon Coca-Cola sign. At weekends, an endless stream of ice-cream-licking suburban voyeurs trawl along the Darlinghurst Road strip past the El Alamein fountain in Fitzroy Gardens to **Macleay Street**, as touts try their best to haul them into tacky strip-joints and sleazy nightclubs. Kings Cross is much more subdued during the day, with a slightly hung-over feel to it: local residents emerge and it's a good time to hang out in the cafés. Every Sunday there's a small art and crafts market in the Fitzroy Gardens by the fountain. South Sydney Council has produced a free **Kings Cross Walking Tour** map available from the library off Fitzroy Gardens (or downloaded from *www.kingscross.nsw.gov.au*), which points out some of the Art Deco architecture the area is known for and provides some background history.

All around the Cross, and indeed very close by, are quiet, upmarket pockets. Towards the harbour, **Potts Point** becomes more peaceful and more expensive the closer you get to exclusive Elizabeth Bay (see p.126). **Woolloomooloo** occupies the old harbourside quarter back towards the city, between the docks and William Street. Once a narrow-streeted slum, it's slowly being spruced up; reach it by foot from Kings Cross by taking the **McElhone Stairs** or the **Butlers Stairs** from Victoria Street. There are some rowdy pubs here, as well as the legendary *Harry's Café de Wheels* on Cowper Wharf Road, a 24-hour pie-cart operating since 1945. Famous for Pea and Pie floaters, *Harry's* has become a gathering place for Sydney cabbies and hungry clubbers in the early hours of the morning.

You can get to Kings Cross by **train** (Eastern Suburbs line) or **bus** (#311, #324, #325 or #327 from Circular Quay; many others from the city to Darlinghurst Road), or it's not too far to walk: an uphill walk straight up William Street from Hyde Park. For a quieter route, you could head up from The Domain via Cowper Wharf Road in Woolloomooloo, and then up the McElhone Stairs to Victoria Street.

The Harbour

Loftily flanking the mouth of Sydney Harbour are the rugged sandstone cliffs of North Head and South Head, providing spectacular viewing points across the calm water to the city 11km away, where the Harbour Bridge spans the sunken valley at its deepest point. The many coves, bays, points and headlands of Sydney Harbour, and their parks, bush-land and swimmable beaches are rewarding to explore. However, harbour beaches are not as clean as ocean ones, and after storms are often closed to swimmers (see pp.129-130). Finding your way by ferry is the most pleasurable method: services run to much of the **North Shore** and to harbourfront areas of the **eastern suburbs**. The eastern shores are characterized by a certain glitziness and are the haunt of the nouveaux rich-es, while the leafy North Shore is very much old money. Both sides of the harbour – the North Shore in particular – have pockets of bushland (and five islands, two of which – Goat Island and Fort Denison – can be visited on tours; the other three, Shark Island, Clark Island and Rodd Island, are bookable for picnics but you must provide your own transport) which have been incorporated into **Sydney Harbour National Park**; the NPWS publish an excellent free map detailing the areas of the national park and its many walking tracks (☎02/9337 5511 for general information or visit Cadman's Cottage in The Rocks or NPWS office in Neilson Park – see p.102 and p.126 respectively).

Elizabeth Bay to South Head

The suburbs on the hilly southeast shores of the harbour are rich and exclusive. A couple of early nineteenth-century mansions, Elizabeth Bay House and Vaucluse House, are open to visitors, giving an insight into the lifestyle of the pioneering upper crust. **Buses** #324 and #325 from Circular Quay via Pitt Street, Kings Cross and Edgecliff cover the places listed below, heading to Watsons Bay via New South Head Road; #325 detours at Vaucluse for Nielson Park.

Elizabeth Bay and Rushcutters Bay

Barely five minutes' walk northwest of Kings Cross, **Elizabeth Bay** is nevertheless a well-heeled residential area, centred around **Elizabeth Bay House**, at 7 Onslow Ave (Tues–Sun 10am–4.30pm; $6; bus #311 from either Railway Square or Circular Quay, or walk from Kings Cross station), a grand Regency residence with fine harbour views, built in 1832. Heading southeast, you're only a few minutes' walk from **Rushcutters Bay Park**, wonderfully set against a backdrop of the yacht- and cruiser-packed marina in the bay. Gangs of picnickers book out the **tennis** courts at Rushcutters Bay Tennis Centre (☎02/9357 1675 for bookings; daily 8am–9 or 10pm; courts $14 per hour, $16 after 4pm and on Sat & Sun; racket rental $3), feasting in between sets. If you don't have anyone to play, the friendly managers promise a hitting partner thrown in with the court; there's a nice little coffee bar too (open Mon–Fri 9am–6pm, Sat & Sun 8am–6pm).

Double Bay and Rose Bay

Continuing northeast to **Darling Point**, McKell Park provides a wonderful view across to **Clarke Island** and **Bradleys Head**, both part of Sydney Harbour National Park; follow Darling Point Road (or take bus #327 from Edgecliff Station). The next port of call is **Double Bay**, dubbed "Double Pay" for obvious reasons. The noise and traffic of New South Head Road are redeemed by several excellent antiquarian and secondhand bookshops (see p.148), while in the quieter "village" are some of the most exclusive shops in Sydney, full of imported designer labels and expensive jewellery. The eastern suburbs socialites meet on Cross Street, where the swanky pavement cafés are filled with well-groomed women in Armani outfits sipping coffee, their Mercedes and Rolls-Royces illegally parked outside. If all this sounds like a turn-off, Double Bay's real delight is **Redleaf Pool** (daily Sept–May dawn–dusk; free), a peaceful, shady harbour beach – one of the cleanest – enclosed by a wooden pier you can wander around, dive off or just laze on; there's also an excellent café famed for its fruit salad and cappuccino. A ferry from Circular Quay (Wharf 2) stops at both Darling Point and Double Bay; otherwise catch bus #324 or #325, also from Circular Quay.

The ferry to **Rose Bay** (Circular Quay, Wharf 2) gives you a chance to check out the waterfront mansions of **Point Piper** as you skim past. Rose Bay itself is quite a haven of exclusivity, with the verdant expanse of the members-only Royal Sydney Golf Course. Directly across New South Head Road from the course, waterfront **Lyne Park** provides welcome distraction in the form of a **seaplane** service: based here since the 1930s, the planes are quite a sight as they take off and land on the water (see "Listings", p.162). Rose bay is also a popular **windsurfing** spot, and you can rent equipment to join in from Rose Bay Aquatic Hire (see p.167).

Nielson Park and Vaucluse

Sydney Harbour National Park emerges onto the waterfront at Bay View Hill, where the 1.5km **Hermitage walking track** to Nielson Park begins; the starting point, Bay View Hill Road, is off South Head Road between the Kambala School and the Rose Bay Convent (on bus routes #324 and #325). The walk takes about an hour, with great views of the Opera House and Harbour Bridge, some lovely little coves to swim in and a pic-nic ground and sandy beach at yacht-filled **Hermit Point**. Extensive, tree-filled **Nielson Park**, on Shark Bay, is one of Sydney's delights (don't worry about Shark Bay's ominous name – it's netted), a great place for a day-time swim, a night-time skin-ny-dip, a picnic, or refreshment at the popular café. Within the park, the decorative Victorian-era mansion, **Greycliffe House**, built for William Wentworth's daughter in 1852 (see below), is now the headquarters of Sydney Harbour National Park; pop in for information on other waterfront walks.

Beyond Shark Bay, Vaucluse Bay shelters the magnificent **Vaucluse House** and its large estate on Wentworth Road (Tues–Sun 10am–4.30pm and public holiday Mondays; $6), with tearooms in the grounds for refreshment. The house's original owner was the explorer and reformer William Wentworth, who was a member of the first party to cross the Blue Mountains. In 1831 he invited four thousand guests to Vaucluse House to celebrate the departure of the hated Governor Darling – the climax of the evening was a fireworks display which burned "Down with the Tyrant" into the night sky. To get there, walk from Nielson Park along Coolong Road, or take bus #325 right to the door.

Watsons Bay to South Head

Narrow **Parsley Bay**, crossed by a pedestrian suspension bridge, follows Vaucluse Bay to **Watsons Bay** (accessible by ferry from Wharf 4 at Circular Quay), on the now nar-row finger of land culminating in South Head. Once a fishing village, the suburb has retained a villagey feel with old fishermen's cottages still found on the narrow streets. These associations make an appropriate location for one of Sydney's most popular fish restaurants, *Doyles*, right out on the bay by the old Fishermans Wharf, with superb views and food (see p.140). For less expensive views, settle in at the bayfront beer gar-den of the adjacent *Watsons Bay Hotel*. More spectacular views from the ocean cliffs are just a two-minute walk away through grassy Robertson Park, across Gap Road to **The Gap**, whose high cliffs are a well-known place to commit suicide. This is where bus #325 terminates, but a **walking track** leads from here to South Head through another chunk of **Sydney Harbour National Park**. From The Gap the track heads back to the bay side, past **Camp Cove**, a tiny palm-fronted beach popular with families. If you'd pre-fer to swim *au naturel*, continue on the track to the next bay just on the harbour side of South Head, to reach Sydney's best-known **nude beach**, Lady Jane (officially "Lady Bay" on maps). Unfortunately tour boats cruise past all weekend – Cobblers Beach in Middle Harbour (see p.128-129) is a better bet for privacy. From Lady Bay, it's about a fifteen-minute walk along the track to **South Head**, the lower jaw of the harbour mouth affording fantastic views of Port Jackson and the city.

The North Shore

The **North Shore** is generally more affluent than the South. **Mosman** and **Neutral Bay** in particular have some stunning waterfront real estate, priced to match. It's sur-prising just how much harbourside bushland remains intact here: "leafy" just doesn't do it justice. A ride on any ferry lets you gaze at beaches, bush, yachts and swish har-bourfront houses and is one of the chief joys of this area – even if the lucky people who live "on the other side of the bridge" and use the ferry to commute keep their eyes firmly glued to their newspapers. Many North Shore office staff don't even need to get to the other side to go to work: **North Sydney** itself, just across the bridge, is quite a corporate high-rise centre in its own right.

Just east of the Harbour Bridge and immediately opposite the Opera House, **Kirribilli** and adjacent **Neutral Bay** are mainly residential areas, although Kirribilli hosts a great **market** on the last Saturday of the month in Bradfield Park. On Kirribilli Point, the current Prime Minister, John Howard, lives in an official residence,

Kirribilli House rather than in Canberra. Admiralty House, next door, is the Sydney home of the Governor General. The highlight of North Shore drinking is the shady **beer garden** at Neutral Bay's *Oaks Hotel* on Military Road. Bush-covered **Cremorne Point**, which juts into the harbour here, is also worth a jaunt. Catch the ferry from Circular Quay and you'll find a quaint open access sea pool to swim in by the wharf; from here, you can walk right around the point to Mosman Bay (just under 2km; see below), or in the other direction, past the pool, there's a very pretty walk along **Shell Cove** (1km).

Mosman: Taronga Zoo and Bradleys Head

Mosman Bay's seclusion was first recognized as a virtue during its early days as a whaling station, since it kept the stench of rotting whale flesh from the Sydney Cove settlement. Now the seclusion is a corollary of wealth. The ferry ride into the narrow, yacht-filled bay is a choice one – get off at Mosman Wharf, not South Mosman (Musgrave Street) – and fittingly finished off with a beer at the unpretentious *Mosman Rowers' Club* (visitors welcome).

What Mosman is most famous for, though, is **Taronga Zoological Park** on Bradleys Head Road, with its superb hilltop position overlooking the city (daily 9am–5pm; $16, child $8.50, family $41, $21 Zoo Pass from Circular Quay including return ferry, bus and entry, child pass $10.50; Australian wildlife tours 10.10am, 11.10am & 1.10pm, no booking needed). The zoo houses bounding Australian marsupials, native birds (including kookaburras, galahs and cockatoos), and sea lions and seals from the sub-Antarctic region. You'll also find all the usual exotic beasts from around the world, including two rare snow leopards. The zoo is best reached by taking the ferry from Wharf 2 at Circular Quay to the Taronga Zoo wharf. Though there's a lower entrance near the wharf on Athol Road, it's best to start your zoo visit from the upper entrance so you can wind your way downhill and exit for the ferry: State Transit buses meet the ferries for the trip uphill. You can also get to the zoo on bus #247 from Wynyard.

Beyond the zoo, at the termination of Bradleys Head Road, **Bradleys Head**, at the point of a finger extending into the harbour, is marked by an enormous mast that towers over the rocky point. The mast once belonged to *HMS Sydney*, a victorious World War II battleship, long since gone to the wrecker's yard. It's a peaceful spot with a dinky lighthouse and, of course, a fabulous view back over the south shore. A colony of ring-tailed possums nests here, and boisterous flocks of rainbow lorikeets visit. The headland comprises another large chunk of **Sydney Harbour National Park** and you can walk to Bradleys Head via the six-kilometre Ashton Park **walking track** which starts near the ferry wharf, opposite the zoo entrance, and continues beyond the headland to Taylors Bay and Chowder Head, finishing at **Clifton Gardens**, where there's a jetty and sea baths on Chowder Bay. A now defunct military reserve separates Chowder Bay from another chunk of Sydney Harbour National Park on Middle Head (see opposite).

Middle Harbour

Middle Harbour is the largest inlet of Port Jackson, its two sides joined across the narrowest point at **The Spit**. The Spit Bridge opens regularly to let tall-masted yachts through – much the best way to explore its pretty, quiet coves and bays; several cruises pass by (see box on p.95). The area also hides some architectural gems: the 1889 bridge leading to **Northbridge**, which Jan Morris in *Sydney* (see Contexts, p.1021) describes rather fancifully as "an enormously castellated mock-Gothic bridge, with hefty towers, arches, crests and arrow-slits, such as might have been thrown across a river in Saxe-Coburg by some quixotic nineteenth-century princeling"; and the idyllic enclave of **Castlecrag**. The latter was designed in 1924 by **Walter Burley Griffin**, fresh from planning Canberra and intent on building an environmentally friendly suburb – free of the fences and the red-tiled roofs he hated – that would be "for ever part of the bush".

Between Clifton Gardens and Balmoral Beach, a military reserve and a naval depot block coastal access to both **Georges Head** and the more spectacular **Middle Head**, although they can be reached by road. However, the military have mostly withdrawn from the site, and plans to build new housing there have met with fierce protests. On the Hunters Bay side of Middle Head, tiny **Cobblers Beach** (ferry to Cremorne, then bus #204, or bus #206 direct from outside the Queen Victoria Building) is officially nude, and is a much more peaceful, secluded option than the more famous Lady Jane at South Head (see p.127).

The bush setting provided by Middle Head helps lend **Balmoral**, on Hunters Bay, the peaceful secluded air that makes it so popular with families (it's netted, too, which helps). There's something very Edwardian and genteel about palm-filled, grassy Hunters Park and its bandstand, which is still used for Sunday jazz concerts or even Shakespeare recitals in summer. The antediluvian air is added to by the pretty white-painted **Bathers Pavilion** at the northern end, now converted into a restaurant and café (see p.148). There are really two beaches at Balmoral, separated by **Rocky Point**, a noted picnicking spot reached by a decorative footbridge. The low-key esplanade has some takeaway shops, a quiet café, an excellent fish-and-chip shop, and a fine bottle shop. South of Rocky Point, the "baths" – actually a netted bit of beach with a board-walk and lanes for swimming laps – have been here in one form or another since 1899; you can rent sailboards, catamarans and take lessons from the neighbouring boat shed (see p.167). To get to Balmoral, catch a ferry from Circular Quay to Athol Wharf and then bus #238 via Bradleys Head Road, or the ferry to Musgrave Street wharf, Mosman, then bus #233 or #257 via Military Road.

The hillside houses overlooking Balmoral have some of the highest price tags in Sydney: for a stroll through some prime real estate, head for **Chinamans Beach**, via Hopetoun Avenue and Rosherville Road. Famous residents include Ken Done, the artist who found fame with colourful impressionistic harbour scenes that now adorn duvet covers and wine bottles – and every souvenir shop in town.

Crossing the Spit Bridge, you can walk all the way to Manly Beach along the ten-kilometre Manly Scenic Walkway (see p.135), while bus #144 runs from Spit Road to Manly Wharf, taking in a scenic route uphill overlooking the Spit marina.

Ocean beaches

Sydney's **beaches** are among its great natural joys, key elements in the equation that makes the city special. The water and sand seem remarkably clean – people actually fish in the harbour, and don't just catch old condoms and plimsolls – and at Long Reef, just north of Manly, you can find rock pools teeming with starfish, anemones, sea-snails and crabs, and even a few shy moray eels.

Don't be lulled into a false sense of security, however: the beaches do have **perils** as well as pleasures. Some beaches are protected by special shark nets, but they don't keep out stingers such as bluebottles, which can suddenly swamp an entire beach; listen for loudspeaker announcements that will summon you from the water in the event of shark sightings or other dangers. Pacific **currents** can be very strong indeed – inexperienced swimmers and those with small children would do better sticking to the sheltered **harbour beaches** or **sea pools** at the ocean beaches. Ocean beaches are generally patrolled by **surf lifesavers** during the day between October and April (all year at Bondi): red and yellow flags (generally up from 6am until 6 or 7pm) indicate the safe areas to swim, avoiding dangerous rips and undertows. It can't be stressed strongly enough that you must try to swim between the flags – the summer of 1998–99 witnessed several drownings in strong surf. If you do get into difficulty, stay calm and raise one arm above your head as a signal to be rescued. It's hard not to be impressed as **surfers** paddle out on a seething ocean that you wouldn't dip your big toe in, but don't follow them unless you're confident you know what you're doing. Surf schools can teach you the basic skills and enlighten you on surfing etiquette and lingo; Let's Go Surfing (☎02/9665 4473) is based around Bondi, while Manly Surf School (☎02/9977 3777) covers the northern beaches. Listen to radio station 2MMM (FM 104.9 MHz) for the **surf report** at 7am, 9am and 3.40pm on weekdays and 7am, 9am and noon on weekends.

It's easy to underestimate the strength of the southern **sun**: follow the local slogan and Slip (on a shirt), Slop (on the sunblock), Slap (on a hat). The final hazard, despite the apparent cleanliness, is **pollution**. After storms, currents and onshore breezes wash up sewage and other rubbish onto certain beaches making them (as signs will indicate) unsuitable for swimming and surfing. Harbour swimming spots in Port Jackson, Botany Bay and Pittwater and southern ocean beaches are the worst performers. South Sydney beaches suffer from the cliff-face sewage outfall on the Kurnell Peninsula with deceptively pretty Boat Harbour Beach consistently the most polluted. A recent pollution survey rated Sydney's cleanest beaches with Bondi coming out on top, but all the others were northern beaches including Palm, Whale, Bilgola, Newport, Bungan, Mona Vale, North Narabeen, Long Reef, North and South Curl Curl, Freshwater and North Steyne. To check pollution levels, call the Beachwatch Information Line on ☎02/9901 7996.

A final note: topless bathing is allowed on many beaches but frowned on in others, so if in doubt, do as the locals do. There are two official nude beaches around the harbour (see pp.127 and 129).

Bondi and the eastern beaches

With brash **Bondi Beach** as their epicentre, Sydney's Eastern beaches stretch from South Head down to Maroubra. North of Bondi, **Watsons Bay** (see p.146), once a fishing village, harbours Sydney's most famous seafood restaurant and there are spectacular views from **The Gap** in another chunk of Sydney Harbour National Park. Heading south from Bondi, you can walk right along the coast to its smaller, less brazen but very lively cousin **Coogee**, passing through gay favourite **Tamarama**,

---

CHRISTMAS DAY ON BONDI BEACH

For years backpackers and Bondi Beach on **Christmas Day** were synonymous. The beach was transformed into a drunken party scene, as those from colder climates lived out their fantasy of spending Christmas on the beach under a scorching sun. The behaviour and litter had been getting out of control over several years, and after riots in 1995, and a rubbish-strewn beach to clean up, the local council is now strictly controlling the whole performance – but with the idea of trying to keep a spirit of goodwill towards the travellers while also tempting local families back to the beach on what is regarded as a family day. In 1996 alcohol was banned from the beach for the first time, with a strong police presence and on-the-spot confiscations, so even locals couldn't enjoy a bottle of beachfront bubbly. However, a big beach party was organized for the backpackers: a large area of sand was fenced off, with a bar, bands, food and entertainment. There was a $10 entry fee to get into "the cage", which included sophisticated accessories such as a plastic middy glass on a string to hang around people's necks. By 1998 the fee had hiked up to $15 and the cage was a great deal less popular, with only 3000 crammed into it at the height of the festivities, with another 30,000 abstainers, including a greater proportion of the desired family groups, remaining outside. The great drunken backpacker clan had dispersed to other beaches, notably Coogee further east. Waverly Council (☎02/9369 8000) is not sure whether to dispense with organized proceedings in future, though the alcohol ban will certainly remain in place. It looks to be the end of an era.

family-focused, café cultured **Bronte**, narrow **Clovelly** and **Gordons Bay,** the latter with an underwater nature trail. Randwick Council have designed the "Eastern Beaches Coast Walk" from Clovelly to Coogee and beyond to more downmarket **Maroubra**; with stretches of boardwalk and interpretive boards detailing environmental features. Randwick Council provide a free guide-map detailing the Coogee to Maroubra walk, which can be picked up from the council's Customer Service Office, 30 Francis St, Randwick (☎02/9399 0999), or from Coogee at the beachfront Coogee Kiosk, Goldstein Reserve, Arden Street opposite *McDonalds.*

Bondi Beach

Bondi Beach is synonymous with Australian beach culture, and indeed the mile-long curve of golden sand must be one of the best known beaches in the world. It's the closest ocean beach to the city centre; you can take a train to Bondi Junction and then a ten-minute bus ride, or drive there in twenty minutes (parking is another story). Big, brash and action-packed, it's probably not the best place for a quiet sunbathe and swim, but the sprawling sandy crescent really is spectacular. Red-tiled houses and apartment buildings crowd in to catch the view, many of them erected in the 1920s when Bondi was a working-class suburb. Although still residential, it has long since become a popular gathering place for backpackers from around the world (see box opposite), though the charm has begun to wear off and many have headed south to Coogee or north to Manly, especially as it is now an alternative to the city centre for suburban teenagers to make weekend whoopee, sometimes a little too aggressively.

The beachfront **Campbell Parade** is both cosmopolitan and highly commercialized, lined with cafés and shops. A lot of money has recently been spent improving the congested Parade, widening the footpaths and landscaping, so that sidewalk dining is now the norm and a pedestrian's experience is a whole lot pleasanter. Further developments may include an underground train line extending from Bondi Junction.

For a gentler experience, explore some of the side streets, such as **Hall Street**, where you'll find an assortment of kosher bakeries and delis that serve the area's Jewish community, as well as some of Bondi's best cafés.

Surfing is part of the Bondi legend, the big waves ensuring that there's always a pack of damp young things hanging around, bristling with surfboards. However, the beach is carefully delineated, with surfers using the southern end of the beach – so you shouldn't have to fear catapulting surfboards. There are two sets of flags for swimmers and boogie-boarders, with families congregating at the northern end near the sheltered saltwater pool (free), and everybody else using the middle flags. The beach is netted and there hasn't been a shark attack for over forty years. If the sea is too rough, or if you want to swim laps, there is a seawater swimming pool at the southern end of the beach under the Bondi Icebergs Club building entrance on Notts Avenue ($1 entry). **Topless bathing** is allowed at Bondi – a long way from conditions right up to the late 1960s when stern beach inspectors were constantly on the lookout for indecent exposure. In fact, so blasé are the attitudes here that every January, as part of the Sydney Fringe Festival, a sunset **nude surfing competition** is held: crowds turn out to watch, everybody has a great laugh and TV cameras film the whole thing and show it on the nightly news. If you want to join in the sun and splash but don't have the gear, Beached at Bondi, below the lifeguard lookout tower, rents out everything from umbrellas, wetsuits, cozzies and towels to surfboards and body-boards. They also sell hats and sunblock – or a spray of sunscreen for a couple of dollars – and have lockers for valuables.

Between Campbell Parade and the beach, Bondi Park slopes down to the promenade, and is always full of sprawling bodies. Along the promenade there are two board ramps for **rollerblading** and **skateboarding**. The focus of the promenade is the arcaded, Spanish-style **Bondi Pavilion**, built in 1928 as a de luxe changing-room complex and now converted to a **community centre** hosting an array of workshops, classes and events, from drama and comedy in the theatre and the Seagull Room (the former ball-room) to day-time dance parties and outdoor film festivals in the courtyard (programme details on ☎02/9130 3325 Mon–Fri, ☎02/9368 1253 Sat & Sun). The pavilion is now also the base for the Sydney Fringe Festival in January. Downstairs in the foyer, photos of Bondi's past are worth checking out, with some classic beach images of men in 1930s bathing suits, and there's an excellent **souvenir shop** (daily 9.30am–5.30pm) which uti-lizes lots of old-fashioned Bondi imagery. There's even a community access **art gallery** (daily 10am–5pm) featuring changing exhibitions by local artists.

Another Bondi institution is the blue-painted building of the **Bondi Icebergs Club** (see also p.153), above the southern end of the beach on Notts Avenue, which has been part of the Bondi legend since 1929. Members swim throughout the winter, and media coverage of their plunge, made truly wintry with the addition of chunks of ice, heralds the first day of winter.

In September, the Festival of the Winds, Australia's largest **kite festival**, takes over the beach. On Sunday the **Bondi Beach markets** (10am–5pm), in the grounds of the primary school on the corner of Campbell Parade and Warners Avenue facing the northern end of the beach, place great emphasis on groovy fashion and jewellery.

You can reach Bondi on **bus** #380, #382 and #389 from Circular Quay via Oxford Street and Bondi Junction, or take the train directly to Bondi Junction, then transfer to these buses or to the #361 or the #365.

Tamarama to Gordons Bay

Many people find the smaller, quieter beaches to the south of Bondi more enticing, and it's a popular walk or jog right around the oceanfront and clifftop **walking track** to Clovelly (about 2hr) which also includes a fitness circuit, so you'll see plenty of joggers en route. Walk past the Bondi Icebergs Club on Notts Avenue (see above) round Mackenzies Point, through Marks Park, until you reach the modest and secluded **Mackenzies Bay**, with con-venient large slabs of rock on which to leave your towel. Next is **Tamarama Bay**, a deep, narrow beach favoured by the smart set and a hedonistic gay crowd ("Glamarama" to the locals), as well as surfers (who stay further out in the water) with its own small Surf Life Saving Club (SLSC). Topless bathing is the norm for women here.

Apart from the SLSC, where you can even take in a drop-in yoga class, the intimate beach has a popular beachside café. However, if you don't feel like stretching yourself on the sand, or in fact you can't bear to come in contact with the gritty stuff, a new

---

BONDI'S SURF LIFESAVERS

Surf lifesavers are what made Bondi famous; there's a bronze sculpture of one outside the Bondi Pavilion. The surf lifesaving movement began in 1906 with the founding of the Bondi Surf Life Bathers' Lifesaving Club in response to the drownings that accompanied the increasing popularity of swimming. From the beginning of the colony, swimming was harshly discouraged as an unsuitable bare-fleshed activity. However, by the 1890s swim-ming in the ocean had become the latest fad, and a Pacific Islander introduced the con-cept of catching waves or **bodysurfing** that was to become an enduring national craze. Although "wowsers" (teetotal puritanical types) attempted to put a stop to it, by 1903 all-day swimming was every Sydneysider's right.

The bronzed and muscled surf lifesavers in their distinctive red and yellow caps are a highly photographed, world-famous Australian image. Surf lifesavers (members of what are now called Surf Life Saving Clubs, abbreviated to SLSC) are volunteers working the beach at weekends, so come then to watch their exploits – or look out for a surf carnival; lifeguards, on the other hand, are employed by the council and work all week during swimming season (year-round at Bondi).

Riviera-style service (bookings on free call ☎1800/232 242) offers chaise lounges, umbrellas, fluffy white towels, and attendants bringing cold towels, spring water and snacks from the café, all for $10 an hour. Nothing like this service has ever been seen in egalitarian Sydney, and it's causing something of a stir. The beach is a 15-minute walk from Bondi, or if you want to come here directly, it's a 300m-walk from the #380 bus (from Circular Quay or Oxford Street) alighting at Fletcher Street, or hop on bus #360 or #361 from Bondi Junction.

Walk through Tamarama's small park and follow the oceanfront road for five minutes to the next beach around, **Bronte Beach** on Nelson Bay. More of a family affair with a large green park, a popular café strip and sea baths, it's also easily reached on bus #378 from Central Station via Oxford Street and Bondi Junction. The **northern end** as you arrive from Tamarama has inviting flat rock platforms, popular as fishing and relaxation spots, and the beach here is cliff-backed, providing some shade. The valley-like **park** beyond is extensive and shady; in foreground a **mini-train ride** for small children ($1.50) has been operating here since 1947 while further back there's an imaginative children's playground. At the **southern end** of the beach, palm trees give a suitably holiday feel against blue water views as you relax at one of the outside tables of Bronte Road's wonderful café strip, with a clutch of eight – and a fish and chip shop – to wander past and choose from. Back on the water at this end, a natural rock enclosure makes a calm area for kids to swim in, and there are rock ledges to lie on around the enclosed sea swimming pool known as **Bronte Baths** (open access; free).

From Bronte, it's a pleasant five-minute walk past the baths to **Waverly Cemetery**, a fantastic spot to spend eternity. Established in 1877, it contains the graves of many famous Australians, with the bush poet contingent well represented. **Henry Lawson**, described on his headstone as poet, journalist and patriot, languishes in section 3G 516, while **Dorothea Mackeller**, who penned the famous poem "I love a sunburnt country", is in section 6 832–833. Beyond here – another five-minute walk – on the other side of the ominously named Shark Point, is the channel-like **Clovelly Bay**, with concrete platforms on either side and several sets of steps leading into the very deep water. Rocks at the far end keep out the waves and the sheltered bay is popular with lap-swimmers. On Sunday afternoons and evenings, the nearby *Clovelly Hotel* is a popular hangout for locals and travellers, with free live music. To get to Clovelly directly, take bus #339 from Millers Point via Central Station and Albion Street, Surry Hills, #340 from Millers Point via Taylor Square in Darlinghurst, #329 from Bondi Junction or the weekday peak hour X39 from Wynyard.

From Clovelly you can rock-hop around to equally narrow **Gordon's Bay**, though this can be a little tricky – backed by high sandstone cliffs with some rocky tunnels to pass through – and without local knowledge you might be better off sticking to the road route along Cliffbrook Parade. The rocks are a peaceful fishing spot, or locals choose secluded rocks to sunbathe on, and rescuing stranded tourists tends to shatter the equilibrium. Unsupervised, undeveloped Gordons Bay itself is not a pretty beach; however, there are plenty of agreeable rocks to sit on, and another world exists beneath the sheltered water: the protected **underwater nature trail** makes it diving/snorkelling heaven (see "Listings", p.167 for diving operators). From here, a walkway leads around the waterfront to Major Street and then onto **Dunningham Reserve** overlooking the northern end of Coogee Beach; the walk to Coogee proper takes about fifteen minutes in all.

Coogee

You could say that the battle for Bondi to keep its local feel has already been lost when you compare it to **Coogee**, another popular seaside resort. The hustle, bustle and agro of the city has already truly arrived at Bondi, and while Coogee has a lively bar, café, restaurant and backpacker scene, and some big hotels, there's just something more laid-back, community-oriented and friendly about it – and it's not teeming with pseudo-trendy people. With its hilly streets of Californian-style apartment blocks looking onto a compact pretty beach enclosed by two cliffy green-covered headlands, Coogee has a snugness that Bondi just can't match. Everything is close to hand: beachfront Arden Street has a down-to-earth strip of cafés that compete with each other to sell the cheapest cooked breakfast (about $5), while the main shopping street, Coogee Bay Road, running uphill from the beach, has a choice selection of coffee spots and eateries, plus a big supermarket.

The ugly high-rise *Holiday Inn* spoils the southern end of the beach but the hotel's *Pier Bar* has fabulous views over the water. Other Nineties developments were more aesthetically successful: the imaginatively modernized promenade is a great place to stroll and hang out. Between it and the medium-sized beach is a grassy park with free electric barbecues, picnic tables and shelters. The beach is popular with families (there's an excellent children's playground at the southern end) and young travellers, as there's a stack of backpackers' hostels here (see "Accommodation", p.91-92). However, one of Coogee's chief pleasures are its baths, beyond the southern end of the beach. The first, McIvers Baths, for women and children only, is known by locals as **Coogee Women's Pool** (noon–5pm; 20¢); it's suitably secluded, with plenty of hidden rocks for nude sunbathing if you prefer. Opposite the entrance to the women's pool Grant Reserve has a full-on adventure playground. Just south of the women's pool, **Wylie's Baths**, a saltwater pool on the edge of the sea, is at the end of Neptune Street (7am–7pm; $2) with big decks to lie on, and solar heated showers.

You can reach Coogee on **bus** #373 from Circular Quay via Randwick, or #372 from Eddy Avenue, outside Central Station; journey time from Central is about 25min. There are also buses from Bondi Junction via Randwick: #314 and #315.

Immediately south of Wylie's, **Trenerry Reserve** is a huge green park jutting out into the ocean; its spread of big flat rocks offer tremendous views and make a great place to chill out. Probably the most impressive section of Randwick Council's **Eastern Beaches Coast Walk** commences here. The council are attempting to regenerate the native flora, and the walk, sometimes on boards, is accompanied by interpretive panels detailing the surrounding plant- and birdlife. Steps lead down to a rock platform full of small pools – you can wander down and look at the life within, and there is a large tear-shaped pool you can swim in. It's quite thrilling with the waves crashing over but be careful of both the waves and the blue-ringed octopus found here. At low tide you can continue walking along the rocks around Lurline Bay – otherwise you must follow the streets inland for a bit, rejoining the waterfront from Mermaid Avenue. Jack Vanny Memorial Park is fronted by the great cliffy rocks of Mistral Point, a great spot to sit and look at the water, and down by the water the **Mahon Pool**, a small, pleasant sea pool (free; open access), with waves crashing at the edge and surrounded by great boulders, has an unspoilt secluded feel. The the isolated *Pool Caffe* across the road makes a wonderful lunch or coffee spot.

Manly and the northern beaches

Manly, just above North Head at the northern mouth of the harbour, is doubly blessed with both ocean and harbour beaches. When Captain Arthur Phillip, the commander of the First Fleet, was exploring Sydney Harbour in 1788, he saw a group of well-built Aboriginal men onshore, proclaimed them to be "manly" and named the cove in the process. During the Edwardian era it became fashionable as a recreational retreat from the city, and the promotional slogan of the time "Manly – seven miles from Sydney, but a thousand miles from care" still holds true today. The area has become quite a travellers' centre in recent years with a whole host of some of Sydney's best backpackers' hostels. An excellent time to visit is over the Labour Day long weekend in early October, when there is a **Jazz Festival** with free outdoor concerts featuring musicians from around the world. Beyond Manly, the **northern beaches** continue for 30km up to Barrenjoey Heads and **Palm Beach**.

Manly

A day-trip to Manly, rounded off with a dinner of fish and chips, offers a classic taste of Sydney life. The ferry trip out here has always been half the fun: the legendary Manly Ferry service has been running from Circular Quay since 1854, and the huge old boats come complete with snack bars selling the ubiquitous meat pie. Ferries terminate at Manly Wharf in Manly Cove, near a small section of harbour beach with a netted-off swimming area popular with families. Like a typical English seaside resort, Manly Wharf has always had a **funfair**: although it's been modernized into a sort of two-storey shopping mall, a colourful ferris-wheel and merry-go-round still light up the waterfront. From the wharf, walk west, either along the beach with the pool or along West Esplanade to **Oceanworld** (daily 10am–5.30pm; $14.50, family ticket $34; Ocean Pass including return ferry to Manly, adult $20.50, family $54; ☎02/9949 2644), where clear acrylic walls hold back the water so you can saunter along the harbour floor, gazing at sharks and stingrays. Enquire about the possibility of diving amongst the sharks – such foolhardiness is organized for brave folk. The original vividly painted aquarium now houses an art gallery.

Many visitors mistake Manly Cove for the ocean beach, which in fact lies on the other side of the isthmus, 500m down The Corso, Manly's busy pedestrianized main drag. The ocean beach, **South Steyne**, is characterized by the stands of Norfolk pine which line the shore. Here you'll find the **Manly Visitor Information Centre** (daily 10am–4pm; ☎02/9977 1088). A six-kilometre-long cycle path (shared with pedestrians) begins at the visitor centre and runs north to Seaforth, past North Steyne Beach and Queenscliff. You can rent bikes from the Australian Travel Specialists at Manly Wharf (half-day $15, full-day $25). For a more idyllic beach than the long stretch of South Steyne, follow the footpath from the southern end of the beach around the headland to Cabbage Tree Bay, with two very pretty, green-backed beaches at either end – **Fairy Bower** to the west and **Shelley Beach** to the east.

Belgrave Street, running north from Manly Wharf, is Manly's alternative strip, where you'll find some good cafés tucked away, interesting shops to browse, yoga schools, and the Manly Environment Centre.

A wonderful long-distance seaside walk starts at Manly Cove. The **Manly Scenic Walkway** follows the harbour shore inland from Manly Cove all the way back to Spit Bridge on Middle Harbour, where you can catch bus #180 back to Wynyard Station in the city centre (20min). The eight-kilometre walk takes you through a section of **Sydney Harbour National Park**, past a number of small beaches and swimmable coves, Aboriginal middens and some subtropical rainforest. The entire walk takes three to four hours but is broken up into six sections with obvious exit/entry points if you're not up to doing the whole thing; pick up a map from the Manly Visitor Information Centre (above) or NPWS offices (p.166 "Parks and wildlife").

Ferries leave wharves 2 and 3 at Circular Quay for Manly approximately twice an hour ($4) and take half an hour. The last ferry service from Circular Quay is at 7pm after which time the faster JetCats operate until midnight, 11pm on Saturdays. The JetCat ($5.20) goes twice as fast as the regular ferries but is about half as much fun. After it finishes, night bus #150 runs from Wynyard Terminal. Day-trippers can buy an OceanPass (see above), which includes return ferry rides.

North Head

You can take in more of the Sydney Harbour National Park in the other direction, too: grab the #135 **bus** from Manly Wharf (10–14 daily; last bus returns 3.56pm Mon–Fri, Sat & Sun 4.26pm) to **North Head**, the harbour mouth's upper jaw, and follow the short circuitous Fairfax Walking Track to three lookout points including the **Fairfax Lookout** for splendid views. If you have your own car, there's also parking ($3 hour, $5 day), and you can drop in en route to the NPWS office (daily 9am–4.30pm), a kilometre of so before the lookouts, to pick up free information leaflets.

Smack bang in the middle of all this national park is a military reserve with its own National Artillery Museum (Wed, Sat & Sun noon–4pm; $4) sited in the historic **North Fort**, which consists of a curious system of tunnels built into the headland.

There's more history at the old **Quarantine Station**, on the harbour side of North Head, used from 1828 until 1984: arriving passengers or crew who had a contagious disease were set down at Spring Cove to serve a spell of isolation at the station, all at the shipping companies' expense. Accordingly, First Class passengers received first class accommodation and treatment while those in steerage had to cook their own dinner. Sydney residents, too, were forced here, most memorably during the plague which broke out in The Rocks in 1900, when 1832 people were quarantined (104 plague victims are buried in the grounds). The site, its buildings still intact, is now looked after by the NPWS who offer **guided history tours** (daily 10.40am; 1hr 30min; $10; booking essential ☎02/9977 6522), giving an insight not only into Sydney's immigration history but the evolution of medical science in the past century and a half, often in gory detail. The tours, which co-ordinate with the #135 bus from Manly Wharf (return bus trip included in the price), provide the only opportunity to get out to this beautiful isolated harbour spot with its views across to Balmoral Beach. The night-time **ghost tours** (Wed & Fri–Sun; 3hr; $20, including tea and damper) are very popular; children under twelve have a less frequent – and not so hair-raising – Kids Ghost Tour ($10 child or adult; 2hr; no supper). Unfortunately, no public transport is available for the night-time visits: without your own vehicle you'll have to catch a taxi.

The northern beaches

Freshwater, just further than Manly, sits snugly between two rocky headlands on Queenscliff Bay, and is one of the most picturesque of the northern beaches. There's plenty of surf culture around the headland at Curl Curl and a walking track at its northern end, commencing from Huston Parade, which will take you above the rocky coastline to the curve of **Dee Why Beach**. Dee Why provides consistently good surf, while its sheltered lagoon makes it popular with families. Beyond the lagoon, windsurfers gather around **Long Reef**, where the point is surrounded by a wide rock shelf creviced with rock pools and protected as an aquatic reserve – well worth a wander to peek at the creatures within. The long, beautiful sweep of **Collaroy Beach** now with a popular new YHA (see p.93-94), shades into **Narrabeen Beach**. Narrabeen is an idyllic spot backed by the extensive, swimmable and fishable **Narrabeen Lakes** popular with anglers and families and it offers a good campsite by the lakes (see box on p.85). Beyond Narrabeen, **Mona Vale** is a long, straight stretch of beach with a large park behind and a sea pool dividing it from sheltered **Bongin Bongin Bay** whose headland reserve, and rocks to clamber on, make it ideal for children.

After Bongin Bongin Bay the Barrenjoey Peninsula commences, with calm Pittwater (see p.169-170), on its western side and ocean beaches running up its eastern side until it spears into Broken Bay. Bus #190 and #L90 run up the peninsula from Wynyard to Avalon, continuing to Palm Beach via the Pittwater side. **Newport**, boasts a fine stretch of ocean beach between two rocky headlands; on Sunday crowds gather to listen to live jazz in the beer garden of the *Newport Arms* on Kalinya Street, overlooking Heron Cove on Pittwater. Unassuming **Bilgola Beach**, next door to Newport, is one of the prettiest of the northern beaches. From here, a trio of Sydney's best beaches, for both surf and scenery, run up the eastern fringe of the mushroom-shaped peninsula: **Avalon** and **Whale Beach** are less fashionable than Palm Beach, but rather cleaner – popular surfie

territory. The people pf Avalon memorably rejected the proposed filming of a series of
Baywatch in early 1999, though the beach did feature in a tacky *Baywatch* special. **Palm
Beach**, living up to its name, is a hangout for the rich and famous: you can even get
here by Hollywood-style seaplane from Rose Bay (see p.126). Palm Beach residents
aren't as concerned about the film cameras: the beach also leads a double life as
"Summer Bay" in the famous Aussie soap *Home and Away*, with the Barrenjoey
Lighthouse and headland regularly in shot; you can also go on the phenomenally popular "Summer Bay" location tour with Collaroy YHA. The bush-covered headland is
actually an outpost of Ku-Ring-Gai Chase National Park (see p169), the bulk of which is
across Pittwater, and can be visited courtesy of Palm Beach Ferries (☎02/9918 2747;
cruise $25, leaving Palm Beach at 11am, back at 3.30pm; general transport to Pittwater
and to Patonga; hourly 9am–5pm, Sun 9am–6pm; $7 one-way).

The northern beaches can be reached by regular **bus** from Wynyard in the city or
from Manly.

Botany Bay

The southern suburbs of Sydney, arranged around huge **Botany Bay**, are seen as the
heartland of red-tiled-roof suburbia, a terracotta sea spied from above as the planes
land at **Mascot**. Clive James, the area's most famous son, hails from Kogarah –
described as a 1950s suburban wasteland in his tongue-in-cheek *Unreliable Memoirs*
(see p.1021). The popular perception of Botany Bay is coloured by its proximity to an
airport, a high-security prison (Long Bay), an oil refinery, a container terminal and a
sewerage outlet. Yet the surprisingly clean-looking water (pollution levels are high,
however) is fringed by quiet, sandy beaches and the marshlands shelter a profusion of
birdlife. Whole areas of the waterfront, at **La Perouse**, with its associations with eighteenth-century French exploration, and on the **Kurnell Peninsula** where Captain
Cook first put anchor, are designated as part of **Botany Bay National Park**, and large
stretches on either side of the Georges River form a State Recreation Area.

La Perouse

La Perouse, tucked into the northern shore of Botany Bay where it meets the Pacific
Ocean, contains Sydney's oldest Aboriginal settlement, the legacy of a mission. The
suburb took its name from **Laperouse**, the eighteenth-century French explorer, who
set up camp here for six weeks, briefly and cordially meeting Captain Arthur Phillip,
who was making his historic decision to forgo swampy Botany Bay and move on to Port
Jackson; after leaving Botany Bay, the Laperouse expedition was never seen again. A
monument erected in 1825 and an excellent museum (see overleaf) between them tell
the whole fascinating story.

The surrounding headlands and foreshore have been incorporated into the northern
half of **Botany Bay National Park** (no entry fee; the other half is across Botany Bay
on the Kurnell Peninsula, see p.138), with a **visitor centre** (☎02/9311 3379) in the
same building as the Laperouse Museum (below) where details of potential walks are
available including a fine one past Congwong Bay Beach to Henry Head and its lighthouse (5km return). The verandah of the *Boatshed Café*, on the small headland between
Congwong and Frenchmans bays, sits right over the water with pelicans floating about
below; it's an idyllic spot for a cappuccino. La Perouse is at its most lively on **Sunday**
(and public holidays) when, following a tradition established at the turn of the century,
Aboriginal people come down to sell boomerangs and other crafts, and demonstrate
boomerang throwing, and snake-handling skills are on display from 1.30pm. There are
also tours of the nineteenth-century fortifications on **Bare Island** (Sat, Sun & public

holidays 12.30pm, 1.30pm, 2.30pm & 3.30pm; $7; no booking required, wait at the gate to the island), joined to La Perouse by a walkway.

To **get to** La Perouse, catch bus #394 from Circular Quay or #393 from Railway Square (Sun only), or take the #L94 express from Circular Quay.

The Laperouse Museum

"At least, is there any news of Monsieur de Laperouse?"

Louis XVI, about to be guillotined, 1793

The **Laperouse Museum** (Tues–Sun 10am–4pm; $5), run by the NPWS, sits on a grassy headland between the pretty beaches of Congwong Bay and Frenchmans Bay. The large burgundy-coloured building was converted into a museum in 1988 as a bicentennial project. Tracing Laperouse's voyage in great detail, the displays are enlivened by relics from the wrecks, exhibits of antique French maps and copies of etchings by the naturalists on board. The voyage was commissioned by the French king Louis XVI in 1785 as a purely scientific exploration of the Pacific to rival Cook's voyages, and strict instructions were given for Laperouse to "act with great gentleness and humanity towards the different people whom he will visit".

After an astonishing three-and-a-half-year journey through South America, the Easter Islands, Hawaii, the northwest coast of America, and past China and Japan to Russia, the *Astrolabe* and the *Boussole* struck disaster – first encountering hostility in the Solomon Islands and then in their doomed sailing from Botany Bay, on March 10, 1788. Their disappearance remained a mystery until 1828, when relics were discovered on Vanikoro in the Solomon Islands, the wrecks themselves were found only in 1958 and 1964.

A recent addition to the museum is a new exhibition which looks at the Aboriginal history and culture of the area.

The Kurnell Peninsula and Cronulla

From La Perouse, you can see across Botany Bay to Kurnell and the red buoy marking the spot where Captain James Cook and the crew of the *Endeavour* anchored on April 29, 1770 for an eight-day exploration. Back in England, many refused to believe that the uniquely Australian plants and animals they had recorded actually existed – the kangaroo in particular was thought to be a hoax. **Captain Cook's Landing Place** is now the south head of **Botany Bay National Park**, where the informative **Discovery Centre** (Mon–Fri 10am–4pm, Sat & Sun 9.30am–4.30pm; $7.50 fee per car; ☎02/9668 9111) looks at the wetlands ecology of the park and tells the story of Cook's visit and its implications for Aboriginal people. Indeed the political sensitivity of the spot which effectively marks the beginning of the decline of an ancient culture has led for a search for an Aboriginal name for the park. One suggestion has been "Gillingarie" from the language of the original Dharawal people of the area, which means "land that belongs to us all". Set aside as a public recreation area in 1899, the heath and woodland is unspoilt and there are some secluded beaches for swimming; you may even spot parrots and honeyeaters if you keep your eyes peeled. To get here by **public transport**, take the train to Cronulla and then route #987 of Kurnell Bus Services (☎02/9524 8977).

On the ocean side of the **Kurnell Peninsula** is Sydney's longest beach: the ten-kilometre stretch begins at **Cronulla** and continues as deserted, dune-backed **Wanda Beach**. This is prime surfing territory – and the only Sydney beach accessible by train (Sutherland line from Bondi Junction; surfboards carried free). From Cronulla, you can catch a ferry to Bundeena in the Royal National Park (see pp.198-199).

Eating and drinking

Sydney boasts an extraordinary number of food stalls, cafés, takeaways, restaurants and pubs serving food as well as drink, only a fraction of which are listed here. Check out the "Pubs and bars" listings on p.150 for more casual eats. Be adventurous, as quality is uniformly high, with fresh ingredients and imaginative cuisine on offer. The restaurant scene is highly fashionable, and businesses rise in favour, fall in popularity and close down or change names and style at an astonishing rate.

Most of the inner suburbs are just a few minutes away by bus, train, ferry or taxi, and there you'll generally find better, less expensive and more enjoyable places to eat and drink. Sydney has a fully fledged café culture, most notably in Darlinghurst, Glebe, Newtown and the eastern beaches of Bondi, Bronte and Coogee. There are also fantastic places to eat further out in the suburbs: one of the best is **Cabramatta**, where Sydney's Vietnamese community makes its home. To get there, take the train from Central Station (fourteen stops) and you'll find a glut of excellent restaurants on Park Road and John Street, just west of Cabramatta Station.

All restaurants in the following listings are open daily for lunch and dinner, unless otherwise stated, and the more specific café times are given (most are open for breakfast, which is one of Sydney's most popular meals).

The city centre and The Rocks

The cafés and food stalls in the business and shopping districts of the city centre cater mainly for lunchtime crowds, and there are lots of **food courts** and stalls serving fast food and snacks. Check out the selection in the basement of the **Queen Victoria Building** (see p.107) and the **MLC Centre** near Martin Place, in the first floor of the **Hunter Connection** shopping arcade, 310 George St, opposite Wynyard Station, and the ground floor of the **Quayside Shopping Centre** at Circular Quay, off Alfred Sreet. The classiest of them is probably the foodie's paradise in the basement of the **David Jones** department store on Market Street, where a number of counters serve rather pricey snacks and titbits; Many museums and tourist attractions also have surprisingly good **cafés** – notably the Museum of Contemporary Art, the Australian Museum, the Hyde Park Barracks and the Art Gallery of New South Wales.

There are several good **pubs** in The Rocks (see p.150-151), many of which serve some kind of food, but for the most part the area around the harbour has a choice of expensive restaurants or average fast food.

Cafés and brasseries

City Extra, Circular Quay. Licensed 24hr coffee shop with a stop-the-press theme – and of course, newspapers for customers to read. Breakfast is served round the clock plus burgers, pasta, steaks and desserts. Quay-side seating too.

Corto, 10 Barrack St. Stylish little espresso bar in a real hideaway spot from city havoc. Excellent big coffees and friendly young staff. You can munch on Turkish bread (or ordinary), sandwiches or mini pizzas. Mon–Fri 7am–4.30pm.

Glass House Café, Level 7, State Library, Macquarie St. Airy and with masses of plants, this glass-roofed space is a relaxing spot for lunch or just coffee and cake. The inexpensive menu changes often. Mon–Fri 10am–4.30pm, Sat & Sun 11am–3.30pm.

Paradiso, Shop 1, 7 Macquarie Place. Stylish outdoor café close to Circular Quay. Fab spot on an historic square with big shady trees, or sit inside on stools and listen to jazzy music on a wet day. Attracts a working crowd who plunge in for great coffee, *pizzetta* and focaccia. Mon–Fri 7am–4.30pm. Other *Paradiso*'s around town have varying hours, some have a licence.

Pavilion on the Park, 1 Art Gallery Rd (☎02/9232 1322). On the edge of The Domain, this total-ly round building, circa 1960s, has had its interior recently redesigned to stunning effect. With a kiosk, a café section and an upmarket restaurant, this well-reviewed place has something for every-one. Café daily 9am–5pm; restaurant closed Sat lunch and Sun–Wed dinner. Licensed.

Rossini, between wharves 5 & 6, Circular Quay. Quality Italian fast food alfresco while you're wait-ing for a ferry or just watching the Quay. *Panzerotto* – big, cinnamon-flavoured and ricotta-filled doughnuts – are a speciality. Pricey but excellent coffee. Daily 7am–11pm. Licensed.

Sailors Thai Canteen, 106 George St, The Rocks. The cheaper version of the much-praised, pricey downstairs restaurant (☎02/9251 2466 for bookings), housed in the restored Sailors' Home. Its ground-level canteen with a long stainless steel communal table looks onto an open kitchen, where the chefs chop away to produce simple one-bowl meals. Licensed.

Sydney Cove Oyster Bar, Circular Quay East. It's hard not to be lured into this place on a stroll to the Opera House. The waterfront tables provide a magical location to sample Sydney Rock Pacific oysters (around $17.50 a dozen). There's other seafood as well, or just come for coffee, cake and the view. Mon–Wed 11am–10.30pm, Thurs–Sat 11am–midnight, Sun 11am–8pm.

Restaurants

bel mondo, Level 3, the Argyle Department Store (☎02/9241 3700). With fabulous views over The Rocks and the harbour, the North Italian food served here is probably the best of its kind in Sydney. A sophisticated crowd eats here, but for less cash you can get views and similar food at the fash-ionable *Anti-Bar* at the front. Very expensive; licensed. Restaurant closed Sat & Sun lunch, bar closed Sat lunch.

Doyles on the Quay, Overseas Passenger Terminal, Circular Quay West (☎02/9252 3400). Downtown branch of a Sydney seafood institution; pricey but excellent, with great harbour views from the outdoor waterfront tables. You'll probably need to book. Licensed.

Kables, *The Regent Hotel*, 155 George St (☎02/9255 0266), World-class hotel restaurant with won-derful service and elegant surroundings, placing an emphasis on fresh Australian produce. Expensive, but the $42.50 two-course set lunch, including coffee and parking, is a good deal. Licensed. Lunch Tues–Fri, dinner Tues–Sat.

Quay, Sydney Cove Passenger Terminal, Circular Quay West (☎02/9251 5600). Fabulous views, and a French chef means it's posh and very pricey. Bookings essential; licensed. Closed Sat & Sun lunch.

Rockpool, 109 George St, The Rocks (☎02/9252 1888). Rated as one of Sydney's most glamorous dining spots, with celebrities filing in to eat the raved-about seafood and contemporary creations. Set menu lunches are between $55 and $65, but dinner mains are around $38, this is definitely splurge material. Closed Sun & lunch Sat.

Wharf Restaurant, Pier 4, Hickson Rd, The Rocks (☎02/9250 1761), next to the Wharf Theatre. Enterprising modern food, including at least one vegetarian dish, served up in an old dock building with heaps of raw charm and a harbour vista; bag the outside tables for the best views. Cocktail bar open from noon until end of evening performance. Expensive. Closed Sun.

Haymarket, Chinatown, Darling Harbour and around

The southern end of George Street has plenty of very cheap restaurants, of variable quality. Chinatown around the corner is a better bet: many places here specialize in *yum cha* (or dim sum as it's also known). There are inexpensive licensed Asian food courts, serving everything from Japanese to Vietnamese, and of course Chinese food, in the Sussex Centre (1st floor, 401 Sussex St, daily 10am–9pm); Dixon House (basement level, corner Little Hay and Dixon streets; daily 10.30am–8.30pm); the Harbour Plaza (basement level, corner Factory and Dixon streets; daily 10am–10pm); but the best is on the top floor of the Market City Shopping Centre, above Paddy's Market at the cor-ner of Quay and Thomas streets (daily 8am–10pm). There are several late-night and all-night eating options in Chinatown. A few blocks back toward the city centre, there's a good array of Spanish eateries on Liverpool Street. At Darling Harbour, the Harbourside Shopping Centre has an indifferent food court, best avoided, but there are some excellent takeaway food outlets near Sega World including a kebab place, a Mexican and an excellent Japanese sushi bar. Beyond here, you can eat fantastically well at the Sydney Fish Market (see p.116-117).

Cafés, pubs and cheap eats

Bella Ciao, Shop 5, 187 Thomas St, corner Quay St. Hard to find – look for a sign – but worth the hunt, as a real café culture spot in this part of town is unusual. Breakfast, served until 2pm, includes such yummies as blueberry bagels with fresh ricotta and the legendary Hank's jam as well as the excellent Italian coffee. Mon–Fri 7am–6pm, Sat 8.30am–2pm.

Glasgow Arms Hotel, 527 Harris St, Ultimo, opposite the Powerhouse Museum. Very pleasant pub with leafy courtyard dining. Sat dinner only and Sun restaurant is closed.

Grand Taverna, *Sir John Young Hotel*, corner of Liverpool and George streets, Haymarket. Spanish food, including tapas, at the heart of the Spanish quarter. Authentically lively atmosphere and no-frills setting for some of the best paella and sangria in town. Closed Sun.

Ippon Sushi, 404 Sussex St, Haymarket. Fun, inexpensive Japanese sushi train downstairs, with a revolving choice of delectables from $1 to $4. Licensed and BYO. Daily 11am–10.30pm.

McLuksa, Level 3, Market City Shopping Centre. This food court café serves genuine Singaporean, Malaysian and Indonesian food. The spicy coconut noodle soups ($5–7.50) which give it its name are delicious. Very helpful patient staff will talk you through the food on offer. Daily 10am–8pm.

Pho Pasteur, 709 George St. Very popular casual Vietnamese eatery: quick, fresh and authentic. Great noodles soups for $5. Daily 10am–9pm.

Roma Caffe, 191 Hay St, Haymarket. The *Roma* has been in the area for over 35 years offering fabulous coffee, great breakfasts and a huge gleaming display of wicked Italian desserts, plus delicious focaccia and fresh pasta – try the home-made pumpkin tortellini. Mon–Sat 8am–6pm.

Tai Pei, Shop 2, Prince Centre, 8 Quay St, Haymarket. Tiny, congenial and cheap Taiwanese eatery offering generous servings; great dumplings from $4–6, and tofu (with pork – like most things on the menu) is very tasty. Daily 11am–9pm.

Restaurants

Ampersand, Cockle Bay development, Darling Harbour (☎02/9264 6666). On the roof terrace of the new Cockle Bay restaurant precinct, *Ampersand* offers wonderful views and French-style dining with an emphasis on local produce. Very expensive; licensed. Closed Sat lunch & Sun dinner.

BBQ King, 18–20 Goulburn St, Haymarket (☎02/9267 2433). Unprepossessing but perpetually crowded Chinese restaurant specializing in barbecued meat but there is also, surprisingly, a big vegetarian list on the menu. Inexpensive to moderate; licensed. Daily 11.30am–2am.

Bodhidharma, Capitol Square, 730–742 George St, Haymarket (☎02/9211 8966). In a smart modern "Eat Street" arcade attached to the Capitol Theatre, *Bodhidharma* is the vegetarian/vegan option. Organic and biodynamic produce is used, with not a hint of quiche on the menu which embraces Mediterranean, Asian and even bush tucker. Cheap to moderate; licensed.

Capitan Torres, 73 Liverpool St (☎02/9264 5574). An atmospheric Spanish place, specializing in seafood – a fresh display helps you choose – and paella; licensed. Sit downstairs at the bar or upstairs in the restaurant.

Kam Fook Sharks Fin Seafood Restaurant, Level 3, Market City complex, corner of Quay and Haymarket streets, Haymarket (☎02/9211 8988). The long name matches the size of this Cantonese establishment, officially Australia's largest restaurant, seating over eight hundred people. You can eat some of the best *yum cha* in Sydney here, and you'll have to queue for it if you haven't booked. Moderate to expensive; licensed. *Yum Cha* Mon–Fri 10am–5.30pm, Sat & Sun 9am–5.30pm, dinner nightly.

Lam's Seafood Restaurant, 3rd Floor, 35 Goulburn St, Haymarket (☎02/9281 2881). A Chinatown institution that's a great place for seafood steamboats as dawn approaches. Moderate. Licensed and BYO. Daily noon–4am.

The Malaya, 761 George St, Haymarket, near Railway Square (☎02/9211 0946). Popular, veteran Chinese–Malaysian place, serving some of the best, most authentic and spicy *laksa* in town. Moderately priced; licensed. Closed Sun.

Wokpool, Darling Harbour, next door to the IMAX Theatre (☎02/9211 9888). Stylish combination of upmarket but affordable noodle bar at the front and swish modern Asian seafood-focused restaurant beyond. The four-level branch at 155 Victoria St, Potts Point (no bookings; dinner only, closed Sun) is terribly fashionable.

Glebe

In Glebe you'll find both cheap and upmarket restaurants, ethnic takeaways, delis and a string of good cafés. **Glebe Point Road** is dominated by bookshops and cafés – with a cluster of particularly good cafés at the Broadway end. No one cuisine dominates: café fare is eclectic with plenty of choice for vegetarians, and Indian, Lebanese and Thai eateries rub shoulders. A delightful feature of Glebe cafés are their leafy courtyards and gardens.

Badde Manors, 37 Glebe Point Rd. Vegetarian corner café with a wonderful light-and-airy ambience and laid-back staff; always packed, especially for weekend brunch. One of the best cafés on this strip. Inexpensive. Mon–Fri 8am until midnight, Sat & Sun 9am–1am.

Blackwattle Canteen, Blackwattle Studios, 465 Glebe Point Rd. Stunning views from this unpretentious artists' cafe right at Glebe Point; big windows look out to the Glebe Island Bridge. Expect great coffee, home-made cakes and generous servings from the simple menu and lots of breakfasty stuff. Mon–Fri 8am–4pm, Sat & Sun 9am–4pm.

Borobudur, 123–125 Glebe Point Rd (☎02/9660 5611). Value-for-money Indonesian with an outdoor courtyard and courteous service. Dinner only Mon–Sat. Licensed and BYO.

Dakhni, 65 Glebe Point Rd (☎02/9660 4887). A range of Indian dishes from tandoori through to delicious south Indian vegetarian *masala dosai* (filled pancakes). Tasteful blue and coral decor but not as expensive as it looks, with a meat or vegetarian *thali* around $12, plus it's BYO. A popular spot, so book. Closed Mon–Wed lunch.

Darling Mills, 134 Glebe Point Rd (☎02/9660 0600). Innovative modern Australian cuisine with fresh herbs and floral ingredients grown on the premises, served in an old sandstone building in a leafy garden; licensed. Very posh – an expensive treat.

Iku, 25a Glebe Point Rd (also at 168 Military Rd, Neutral Bay and 279 Bronte Rd, Waverly). Healthy – but delicious – macrobiotic meals and snacks, all vegetarian or vegan. Meditative interior and outdoor dining area – both non-smoking. Daily 11am–9pm, Sun to 8pm.

Lolita's, 29 Glebe Point Rd. The place for a big weekend breakfast (Sat & Sun 9am–1pm), with a great deck to soak up the sun and an upstairs balcony to hang out on. Mon–Fri 10am–10pm, Sat & Sun 9am–10pm.

No Names, *Friend in Hand Hotel*, 58 Cowper St. Excellent, inexpensive Italian restaurant hidden at the back of the pub, with generous pasta meals from $7.50 and meaty main courses like schnitzels from $9. Restaurant closed Sun lunch. The pub is a popular haunt for backpackers, and sometimes lays on entertainment, from poetry nights to Irish folk music.

Well Connected Café, 35 Glebe Point Rd. Glebe's Internet café ($12 per hour, or 5min blocks); the best place to eat and work is upstairs on the huge front verandah. The menu features tasty sandwiches made with Turkish bread. Mon–Fri 8am–11pm, Sat & Sun 10am–11pm.

Newtown

On the other side of Sydney University from Glebe, **King Street** in Newtown is lined with cafés, takeaways and restaurants of every ethnic persuasion; there are some particularly good Thai and Vietnamese places here.

El Bahsa Sweets, 233 King St. Lebanese coffee lounge with some of the best coffee on King Street: try it with some Lebanese sweets, all home-made. Daily until 11pm, later at weekends.

Feel Cafe, 165 King St. Popular, bright and bubbly café with multicoloured walls covered with art for sale, all of which makes this small place feel more like a busy bar. As well as coffee and cake, you can eat tasty meals here from scallop rissotto through to sirloin steak. Garden courtyard outside. BYO. Daily 8am–midnight.

George's Cafe, 222 King St. *George's* is late night – or all night – cake heaven with such delights as mango and passionfruit coconut cake to choose from ($6 for a healthy slice). Lots of cheesecakes and pancakes also feature. Enjoy from comfy booth-style seating. Sun–Thurs 10am–midnight, Fri & Sat 24hr.

Le Kilimanjaro Fast Food Eatery, 280 King St. Senegalese-run place but the authentic and simple dishes span Africa – from West African marinated chicken to North African couscous. Casual and friendly atmosphere. BYO.

Old Saigon, 107 King St (☎02/9519 5931). Vietnamese food with French, Thai and Japanese influences. Saigon memorabilia cover the walls of this cosy restaurant run by a former war correspondent and his Vietnamese wife. Reasonably priced. Licensed and BYO. Lunch Wed–Fri, dinner Tues–Sun; closed Mon.

Steki Taverna, 2 O'Connell St, off King St (☎02/9516 2191). Atmospheric and moderately priced Greek taverna, with live music and dancing at weekends – when you'll need to book. Dinner Wed–Sun.

Sumalee, courtyard of the *Bank Hotel*, 324 King St, next to Newtown Station (☎02/9565 1730). Great Thai restaurant in a pub. Eat in the leafy beer garden. Closed Mon.

Tamana's North Indian Diner, 196 & 236 King St. Very cheap, absolutely delicious fast meals to eat in or take away.

Thai Potong, 294 King St (☎02/9550 6277). King Street's best Thai; excellent service and moderate prices. Essential to book on the weekend. Closed Mon lunch.

Thanh Binh, 111 King St (☎02/9557 1175). With a celebrated original in Cabramatta (see p.139), the food at this Newtown offspring is just as fresh, delicious and inexpensive. There are a huge range of noodles to choose from. Licensed and BYO. Closed lunch Mon–Wed.

Balmain, Rozelle and Leichhardt

Further west is **Leichhardt**, Sydney's "Little Italy", which has a concentration of cafés and restaurants on **Norton Street**, while the **Darling Street** strip of restaurants runs from up-and-coming **Rozelle** to already upmarket **Balmain**.

Bar Italia, 169 Norton St, Leichhardt. Like a community centre with the day-long comings and goings of Leichhardt locals, positively packed at night. The focaccia, served during the day, comes big and tasty, and coffee is spot-on. Best gelato in Sydney; pasta from $6.50, and the extra night-time menu includes more substantial meat dishes (nothing over $12). BYO. Sun & Mon 10am–midnight, Tues–Thurs 9am–midnight, Fri 9am–1am, Sat 10am–1am.

Caffe Sport, 2a Norton St, Leichhardt. One of the original Norton Street cafés decorated with Italian sporting paraphernalia. Very casual, very Italian and very friendly. Extremely good prices and generous helpings of focaccia. Daily from 7am (Sun 8am) to early evening.

Canteen, 332 Darling St, Balmain. Airy, simply styled café with whitewashed walls inside the old Working Men's Institute; eggy breakfasts are popular here, particularly on weekends when customers spill onto the street. Mon–Sat 7am–5pm, Sun 8am–5pm.

Frattini, 122 Marion St, Leichhardt (☎02/9569 2997). One of the best Italian restaurants in Little Italy run by a genial family. Modern airy space, but white tablecloths and old-fashioned service. The fish, with daily specials, is recommended here, especially the whitebait fritters. BYO. Moderate. Closed Sat lunch.

Harvest, 71 Evans St, Rozelle (☎02/9818 4201), also a branch at 152 Jersey Rd, Woollahra (☎02/9328 1939; Sunday lunch, dinner Wed–Sat). Vegan and vegetarian restaurant dipping into Vietnamese, Japanese, Italian and a whole range of cuisine at a moderate price. Food is delicious, desserts decadent and the coffee gets the thumbs up. Non-smoking. BYO. Dinner only; closed Sun.

Tetsuya's, 729 Darling St, corner of Cambridge St, Rozelle (☎02/9555 1017). Tetsuya Wakuda is one of Sydney's star chefs, creatively presenting Japanese/French-style fare. There's a six-course *dégustation* dinner menu at $100, or a five-course lunch for $70. Licensed and BYO; book in advance. Closed Sat dinner, Sun & Mon.

Surry Hills and Redfern

Just east of Central Station, **Elizabeth and Cleveland streets** in Surry Hills, running down to Redfern, are traditionally the domain of Turkish and Lebanese restaurants, which are among the cheapest in Sydney, and almost all BYO. Several Indian restaurants have recently made an appearance too. **Crown Street** in Surry Hills harbours several interesting cafés and some upmarket restaurants.

Abdul's, corner of Cleveland and Elizabeth streets, Surry Hills. Good-value, somewhat grungy Lebanese place. A late-night after-pub institution; eat in or takeaway.

Café Niki, corner of Bourke and Nobbs streets, Surry Hills. Corner café with a relaxed ambience, which manages to feel groovy but not pretentious. The place buzzes with young staff. Cheap and delicious food: best are their soups and focaccia plus excellent coffee. Mon–Fri 7am–10pm, Sat 8am–10pm, Sun 8am–6pm.

Dhaba House, 466 Cleveland St, Surry Hills (☎02/9319 6260). Downmarket decor matches the cheap prices at this invariably crowded Indian restaurant, but the dishes are above average in quality. BYO. Lunch Wed–Sun, dinner nightly.

Erciyes, 409 Cleveland St, Redfern (☎02/9319 1309). Among the offerings of this busy Turkish restaurant is delicious *pide* – a bit like pizza – available with a range of toppings, many vegetarian. Belly dancing Fri & Sat nights. BYO. 11am–midnight; closed Mon.

La Passion du Fruit, 633 Bourke St, corner of Devonshire St, Surry Hills. The best brunch in town is served at this bright and friendly place with interesting salads, sandwiches and light meals. Mon–Sat 8am–5pm.

Maltese Cafe, 310 Crown St, Surry Hills. Café serving reasonably priced food, especially delicious *pastizzi* – flaky pastry pockets of ricotta cheese, plain or with meat, spinach or peas.

MG Garage, 490 Crown St, Surry Hills (☎02/9383 9383). Flash restaurant which doubles as a car showroom with MG cars sharing the dining room. The modern Australian fare on offer is superb, and if you can afford it, this makes a fun night out; licensed. Next door neighbour *Fuel* is the cheaper café/bistro version. *MG Garage* closed Sun & lunch Sat; *Fuel* open Mon–Fri 10am–10.30pm, Sat 8am–10.30pm, Sun 8am–8.30pm.

Mohr Fish, 202 Devonshire St, Surry Hills. Tiny but stylish fish-and-chip bar with stools and tiled walls. BYO. Mon–Sat 10am–10pm, Sun 10am–9pm.

Nepalese Kitchen, 481 Crown St, Surry Hills (☎02/9319 4264). The speciality here is goat curry, served with some *achars*, freshly cooked relishes which traditionally accompany the mild Nepalese dishes, highlighting flavours. There's also a whole range of vegetarian options. Cosy, calming atmosphere, with traditional music playing. Dinner nightly. BYO.

Prasit's Northside Take-away, 395 Crown St, & **Prasit's Northside on Crown**, 413 Crown St, Surry Hills (☎02/9319 0748). The two *Prasit's* outlets on Crown are a storming success: be prepared for some great Thai taste sensations amongst the bold purple colour scheme. Since entrees are available cheaply by the piece, you can attempt to work your way through their delicious repertoire; plenty of vegetarian options too. Takeaway can squeeze diners out front on stools, with a few more places upstairs. Both BYO. Takeaway closed Mon; restaurant open lunch Thurs & Fri, dinner Mon–Sat.

Sushi-Suma, 419 Cleveland St, Surry Hills (☎02/9698 8873). That this small, noisy Japanese restaurant is extremely popular with Japanese locals and visitors says it all. You'll need to book a table to avoid disappointment. Moderate. Closed Mon & lunch Sat & Sun.

Darlinghurst and East Sydney

Oxford Street is lined with restaurants and cafés from one end to the other. **Taylor Square** and its surround is a particularly busy area, with lots of ethnic restaurants and several pubs. **Victoria Street** in Darlinghurst has a thriving café scene. East Sydney, where Crown Street heads downhill from Oxford Street towards William Street, has some excellent Italian restaurants and coffee bars – particularly on **Stanley Street**.

Balkan Seafood Restaurant, 215 Oxford St, Darlinghurst (☎02/9331 7670). Croatian/Italian cuisine. A Darlinghurst institution: fish and seafood is the best choice, but you can also get huge schnitzels and other continental meat dishes. Bustling atmosphere, moderate prices. BYO. Tues–Sun dinner.

Bar Coluzzi, 322 Victoria St, Darlinghurst. Famous Italian café run by a genial former boxer. Tiny and always packed, with impromptu opera-singing from the patron, and the characterful crew of regular customers spilling out onto stools on the pavement. You can watch the carryings-on from a safe distance at the trendier, though equally tiny and very popular *Parmalat* next door. Daily 5am–7.30pm.

Betty's Soup Kitchen, 269 Crown St, Darlinghurst. Soup is the speciality ($5.50), and makes for a cheap meal, served with damper. Salads, pies, nachos and desserts too. Nothing over $9. BYO.

Bill and Toni, 72–74 Stanley St, East Sydney. Atmospheric, cheap Italian restaurant upstairs with balcony tables. Queue to get in. The café downstairs is a popular Stanley St local (daily 7am–midnight) and serves tasty Italian sandwiches. BYO.

Fez Cafe, 247 Victoria St, corner of Liverpool St, Darlinghurst. With its corner position and cushioned window seats, this Middle Eastern and North African café is a favoured Darlinghurst hangout. You can start the day with a breakfast of sweet couscous here and end it with a spicy lamb *tagine*. Licensed and BYO. Mon–Fri 7am–10.30pm, Sat & Sun 8am–10.30pm.

Fishface, 132 Darlinghurst Rd, Darlinghurst. Best market buys of fish, and a chance to taste some unusual varieties (imaginatively cooked), served at fish-shop-style, stool-height tables and benches. BYO. Dinner nightly, lunch Sun only.

Forbes Ristorante, 155 Forbes St, near William St, East Sydney (☎02/9357 3652). Extremely good value – pleasant atmosphere, courtyard tables, good Italian food, coffee and cakes.

fu-manchu, 249 Victoria St, Darlinghurst. Perch yourself on red stools at stainless-steel counters and enjoy stylish but inexpensive Chinese and Malaysian noodles. Non-smoking and BYO.

Govinda's, 112 Darlinghurst Rd, Darlinghurst. Excellent, cheap Indian vegetarian restaurant, in the Hare Krishna centre. All-you-can-eat $13.90 specials with a film thrown in – they have their own cinema (see p.160). Dinner nightly.

Le Petit Crème, 118 Darlinghurst Rd, Darlinghurst. Popular French café serving huge filled baguettes, steak and *frites*, omelettes, *pain au chocolat* and big bowls of *café au lait*; bread and pastries are baked on the premises. Mon–Sat 7am–3pm, Sun 8am–3pm.

Tropicana Café, 227b Victoria St, Darlinghurst. The birthplace of the Tropfest film festival (see p.108). Still a good place to hangout and pose on the weekend. For $6 the huge Trop salad could fuel you all day.

Una's Coffee Lounge, 340 Victoria St, Darlinghurst. Cosy café that's been here for years dishing up schnitzel and other German dishes that are cheap, plentiful and tasty. The big breakfasts, complete with potato, are very popular. BYO. Mon–Sat 6.30am–11pm, Sun 8am–11pm.

Kings Cross, Potts Point and Woolloomooloo

Many of the coffee shops and eateries in the Cross cater for the tastes (and wallets) of the area's backpackers, though there are also several stylish restaurants particularly in Potts Point. Most are also open late.

Bayswater Brasserie, 32 Bayswater Rd, Kings Cross (☎02/9357 2177). Busy, lively, upmarket brasserie consistently rated for its interesting modern food. Expensive; licensed. Closed Sun.

Cafe Hernandez, 60 Kings Cross Rd, Potts Point. Argentinian-run 24hr coffee shop, open daily, is relaxed and friendly. You can dawdle here for ages and no one will make you feel unwelcome. Popular with taxi drivers and a mixed clientele of locals. Spanish food is served: *churros*, tortilla, *empanadas* and good pastries but the coffee is really the focus.

Cicada, 29 Challis Ave, Potts Point (☎02/9358 1255). One of Sydney's star chefs, Peter Doyle, dishes up French-style food – with the odd cross-cultural reference creeping in – in very civilized surrounds. You can eat on the balcony of the pretty Victorian building. Expensive; licensed. Lunch Wed–Fri, dinner Mon–Sat.

Darley Street Thai, 28–30 Bayswater Rd, Kings Cross (☎02/9358 6530). The most highly esteemed Thai restaurant in Sydney. If you really want to see what the chefs can do with flavours and textures, try the set menu at $70 each. Very expensive but worth a blowout; licensed. Dinner nightly.

Roy's Famous, 176 Victoria St, Kings Cross. A congenial open-front café and favourite hangout, looking onto the leafy, action-packed travellers' street. Daily 9am until late. Licensed and BYO.

Tilbury Hotel, corner of Forbes and Nicholson streets, Woolloomooloo (☎02/9368 1955). Great pub with traditional pub grub – lots of steaks – plus more exotic dishes, accompanied by cabaret-style entertainment.

A Touch of Thai, 230 William St, Kings Cross. Tiny frenetic Thai café with friendly young staff cooking in the open kitchen to the sugary strains of Thai pop music. Food is inexpensive and delicious with an inventive line in daily specials.

Venice Beach Restaurant, 2 Kellet St, Kings Cross (☎02/9326 9928). In a big Victorian terrace house with a courtyard and a cushion room, this is a seriously stylish cheap eat. All entrees are $4.90 including half-dozen oysters, and mains range from pasta ($6.90) to steak ($9.90). A giant char-grilled seafood platter feeding two costs $30. Daily 5pm until late.

The Woolloomooloo Woodshed, 132 Forbes St, Woolloomooloo (☎02/9357 1978). All-Australian restaurant – grilled lamb chops or juicy steaks with chips and salad served amongst woolshed memorabilia. Closed lunch Sat & Sun.

Paddington

As **Oxford Street** continues through Paddington, it becomes gradually more upmarket; the majority of restaurants here are attached to gracious old pubs.

Grand National Hotel, 161 Underwood St, corner of Elizabeth St (☎02/9963 4557). One of the best pub-restaurants in Sydney dishing up imaginative fare, but with old-fashioned attentive service. Booking essential at weekends. Expensive. Lunch Wed–Sun, dinner nightly.

Paddington Inn Bistro, 388 Oxford St (☎02/9361 4402). Busy upmarket pub-bistro with an extensive and eclectic menu.

Royal Bar & Grill, *Royal Hotel*, 237 Glenmore Rd, off Five Ways. Pub-restaurant serving generous portions of meaty modern Australian fare. Smart interior and staff. Eating on the verandah is a real treat, but places fill fast – and they don't take bookings.

Sloane Rangers, 312 Oxford St (☎02/9331 6717). The emphasis is on good, unusual vegetarian food, moderately priced but some meatier dishes have slipped onto the menu. Recently renovated with stone floors and a gleaming espresso bar, and now open on to the street to check out all the Saturday market action or for more peace try the courtyard. Nothing over $11. BYO. Daily 7am–6pm.

Bondi and Watsons Bay

Bondi is a cosmopolitan centre with the many Eastern European and Jewish people giving its cafés a continental flair; there are also some fantastic kosher restaurants, delis and cake shops. The Bondi Beach area is full of cheap takeaways, fish and-chip shops and beer gardens, as well as some seriously trendy cafés and restaurants, several of them at the quieter northern end of Campbell Parade. To the north, **Watsons Bay** is known for its famous seafood restaurant.

Bondi Tratt, 34b Campbell Parade, Bondi Beach (☎02/9365 4303). Considering the setting overlooking the beach, not at all expensive. Serves Italian food and is invariably buzzing. Daily from 7am–11pm. Licensed and BYO.

Burgerman, 249 Bondi Rd, Bondi. Gourmet burgers to slaver over. Busy takeaway service and small eat-in area. Daily noon–10pm.

Doyles on the Beach, 11 Marine Parade, Watsons Bay (☎02/9337 1350); also **Doyles Wharf Restaurant** (☎02/9337 1572). The original of the great Sydney institution is the first of these, but both serve great seafood and have views of the city across the water. A water taxi can transport you from Circular Quay to Watsons Bay. Expensive. Daily lunch and dinner.

Gelato Bar, 140 Campbell Parade, Bondi Beach. This is actually a Hungarian-run place that's been serving up Eastern European dishes and cakes for over thirty years to satisfied customers; and gelato too, of course. Gleaming coffee-lounge decor. Daily 8am–midnight.

Lamrock Cafe, 72 Campbell Parade, corner Lamrock Ave. Stalwart Bondi café, invariably buzzy. The unpretentious local crowd come for the magnificent ocean views, the uncomplicated food – *panini* sandwiches, salads, pasta, burgers and fish and chips – and the breakfasts. You can even have a cocktail with your brunch – try the scarily named "Shark Attack", their version of a Bloody Mary.

Le Paris Go Café, corner Hall St and Consett Ave, Bondi Beach. French-run café in a sunny spot with cushioned benches on the street. Inside, jazzy music plays and customers soak up the congenial ambience – and play chess. Excellent croissants which can be teamed with bowls of coffee, and other French snacks from *croque monsieur* to salad *niçoise*. Mon–Sat 7am–5pm, Sun 8am–5pm.

Noodle King, corner of Campbell Parade and Hall St, Bondi Beach. Delicious fresh-cooked Thai, Chinese and Malaysian noodles; generous portions for around $8. There's a small eat-in area but the emphasis is on takeaways.

The One That Got Away, 163 Bondi Rd, Bondi. Award-winning fish shop which even sells kosher fish, also cooks up fish and chips and has a small eat-in section. Their unusual yam chips are recommended. Daily 10am–9pm.

The Red Kite, 95 Roscoe St, Bondi Beach. Funky vegetarian café just back from Campbell Parade attracting a young crowd. Fresh, imaginative food and freshly squeezed juices. Daily 8am–6pm.

Sean's Panorama, 270 Campbell Parade, Bondi Beach (☎02/9365 4924). Inventive food from one of Sydney's best chefs, Sean Moran. A funky café on the weekend, at night (except Sun) it's a restaurant, with two- or three-course set menus (around $35–40). The weekend breakfasts run from 7am to 3pm and shade into the Mediterranean-inspired lunches. BYO. Bookings for dinner only.

The Sports Bard, 32 Campbell Parade, Bondi Beach. Fun young brasserie decorated with sporting memorabilia and pool table out back. Refreshingly simple food – fish, meat, roast chicken at moderate prices. Licensed and BYO. Mon–Fri 5pm–midnight, Sat & Sun 10am–midnight.

Coogee and Bronte

South of Bondi, **Bronte's** beachfront café strip is wonderfully laid-back, and **Coogee** has a thriving café scene which is friendlier and more easy-going than Bondi's.

Barzura Cafe Ristorante, 62 Carr St, Coogee (☎02/9665 5546). Fantastic spot providing up-close ocean views. Both a café and a fully fledged restaurant, with wholesome breakfast until 1pm, snacks until 7pm, and restaurant meals – like seafood spaghetti or kangaroo fillets – served at lunch and dinner. Unpretentious though stylish service encourages a local crowd. Moderate; licensed and BYO. Daily 7am–11pm.

The Beach Pit, 211 Coogee Bay Rd, Coogee (☎02/9665 0068). Really enjoyable café restaurant with Coogee's trademark informality and friendliness. Small but succulent menu has European and Asian influences and plenty of fish and seafood on offer; dishes are generous, well-priced and presented. Book on weekends. Noon–10pm, Sun 10am–9pm. Closed Tues & Wed. BYO.

Bronte Café, 467 Bronte Rd, Bronte. One of the original cafés on this bustling strip is still among the best. Enjoy the view across Bronte Beach and kick back. Good café food, particularly the homemade cakes. Busy at weekends. BYO. 10am–6pm; closed Mon–Wed.

Coogee Bay Hotel Beach Brasserie, 212 Arden St, Coogee. Very reasonably priced pub food, with an interesting menu featuring dishes like roasted Moroccan chicken breast. Traditionalists can cook their own steaks on the barbie. Daily 7am–10pm.

Globe, 203 Coogee Bay Rd. Really relaxed local; fold-back windows let in the light and the street, and vividly coloured paintings on walls add atmosphere. Newspapers to read and good coffee. Food is interesting and healthy, from gourmet sandwiches to main meals with a Mediterranean feel. Mon–Sat 8am–6pm, Sun 9am–6pm.

Regal Pearl Seafood Restaurant, Level 3, Coogee Palace, 169 Dolphin St, Coogee (☎02/9665 3308). Eat under the renovated dome of the original Coogee Palace. Better and cheaper seafood than in Chinatown – plus ocean views. Licensed. A great spot for *yum cha*, available daily 11am–3pm; dinner from 6pm.

Sari Rasa, 186 Arden St, above *McDonald's*, Coogee Beach (☎02/9665 5649). A mostly Indonesian menu, plus delicious Malaysian and Indian specialities, accompanied by ocean views – some tables outside on the balcony. Generous servings and low prices; BYO. Daily noon–3pm & 6pm–late.

North Shore and Manly

Military Road, running from Neutral Bay to Mosman, rivals and perhaps outdoes all the gourmet streets south of the harbour. The string of excellent restaurants tends to

SHOPPING

Most stores are **open** Monday to Saturday 8.30am–5.30pm, with Thursday and Friday late-night shopping until 9pm. Many of the larger shops and department stores in the city are open on Sunday 10am–5pm, as are shopping centres at tourist centres such as Darling Harbour. Apart from its old arcades and two department stores, David Jones and Grace Bros (see pp.106-107), the city centre also has six sparkling modern multilevel shopping complexes where you can hunt down women's clothes and accessories without raising a sweat, among them Skygarden (between Pitt and Castlereagh streets) and Centrepoint on Pitt Street Mall, on the corner of Market Street. For more interesting **fashion**, Oxford Street in Paddington (see pp.122-123) is the place, along with the **Strand Arcade** (see p.106) in the city, and some one-off finds on Crown Street in Surry Hills such as Wheels & Doll Baby at no. 259 and Dangerfield at no. 330; for cheaper styles and interesting junk, try King Street in Newtown (see p.119). If you want to peek at expensive Australian designer fashion, head for the two upper levels of the Queen Victoria Building (see p.107). There are several outlets for samples and seconds of Australian-made fashions on Regent Street in Redfern. To go with the outfits, funky Australian **jewellery** can be found in the Strand Arcade at Dinosaur Designs (also at Argyle Stores, The Rocks, see p.103), and at Love and Hatred. For **beauty** products, Jurlique in the Strand Arcade sells its own pure, hypoallergenic Australian-made skin and hair products; check the department stores for homegrown Poppy Lipsticks. The city centre's most glamorous shopping centre is Chifley Plaza on the corner of Hunter and Phillip streets in the Chifley Tower with the most exclusive labels from around the world such as Kenzo and Max Mara. Otherwise head for the exclusive boutiques of Double Bay (see p.126).

For Australian workwear the place to head for is **Gowings**, on the corner of Market and George streets a beloved Sydney institution for 125 years and a delightfully old-fashioned **menswear** department store. It has everything a bloke (and even a sheila) could want, from Bonds T-shirts to Speedo swimwear, Blundestone boots and a range of felt hats at the best prices in town – plus cheap haircuts. Two other branches are at 319 George St, Wynyard (with a rooftop café) and 82 Oxford St, Darlinghurst. There's also a newer branch on Oxford St, Darlinghurst. The quality **bush outfitters** R. M. Williams, 389 George St (and also at the airport, with similar prices), are great for moleskins and Drizabones and superb leather riding boots. For the widest range of Akubra hats, check out Strand Hatters in the Strand Arcade. If it's **surfwear** you're after, head for Mambo, 17 Oxford St, Paddington, or Hot Tuna at no. 180.

The Rocks is heaving with **Australiana** and **arts and crafts** souvenirs. Tourists flock to Ken Done's emporium here at 123 George St and 1–5 Hickson Rd (in the restored Australian Steam and Navigation Building) to buy his colourful designs, which feature Sydney's har-

be expensive, but there are a number of bakeries, tempting pastry shops and well-stocked delis. On Sunday afternoon the **North Sydney Noodle Market** takes place at 234 Miller St. **Manly** offers something for every taste and budget, though cheap and cheerful is its forte; there are some good cafés tucked away on **Belgrave Street**.

Bathers Pavilion, The Esplanade, Balmoral Beach (☎02/9968 1133). It's worth indulging in some beach-house-style dining (delicious seafood) in this one-time changing shed. Weekend breakfast (with champagne) is a chic/casual North Shore ritual. Licensed. Less expensive is the tiny cranny of a café which provides peace, light, views and excellent coffee.

Brazil Café, 29 Belgrave St, corner of West Esplanade, Manly (☎02/9977 3825). A classy surf-front café that's more Italian/eclectic than Brazilian, and transforms into a pricey restaurant in the evenings. A popular local hangout, particularly for the breakfasts (and famed Sunday brunch). Daily 8am–midnight.

Café Tunis, 30 South Steyne, Manly (☎02/9976 2805). Beachfront restaurant, inside it's airy and cool, with tiled floors. The Cous Cous Royale is the main dish here, or you could opt for the tasty toasted *pide* sandwiches; servings are severely filling. Delicious drinks like Lime and Rosewater go well, or there's wine by the glass. Moderate. Daily 7am–9pm. Licensed and BYO.

bour, boats and flowers on such items as duvet covers. The Rocks is also a focus for **Aboriginal art** (see "Galleries and exhibitions", p.160) and is the location of Balarinji (1st floor, Argyle Stores, Argyle Street), an Aboriginal-owned clothing and accessory company that is the sponsor of the Aboriginal athlete Cathy Freeman. A great place to buy **boomerangs** is from Duncan MacLennon's Boomerang School, 200 William St (Mon–Sat 9am–6.30pm, Sun 2–6pm). The boomerangs sold here are mostly authentic, made by Aboriginal artisans from around Australia. Duncan has been giving free boomerang-throwing lessons every Sun (10am–noon), in Yarranabbe Park near Rushcutters Bay, since 1958.

The best place to head for a take-home sample of the **Australian music** scene in all its variety, from Aboriginal through to indie and jazz, is Sounds Australian, Shop 33, The Rocks Centre, 16–23 Playfair St, The Rocks; the retail arm of the Australian Music Centre with very knowledgeable staff – you can listen before you buy. They have their own Web site; *www.amcoz.com.au/amc*.

Two of the biggest **bookshops** in the city are Abbey's, 131 York St, and Dymocks, 428 George St, both open daily. The more frenetic Dymocks is on several floors with an impressive Australian selection, and even has a café; Abbey's is better for relaxed browsing, with more of a literary feel. Gleebooks, 49 Glebe Point Rd, Glebe, is one of Australia's best bookshops, specializing in academic and alternative books, contemporary Australian and international literature, and is open daily until 9pm; book launches and other literary events are regularly held upstairs and the Web site has excellent reviews (for details of events call ☎02/9660 2333; *www.gleebooks.com.au*). Ariel has two large, lively and hip branches, one at 103 George Street, The Rocks and 42 Oxford St, Paddington; both branches are open daily until midnight. The Travel Bookshop at 175 Liverpool St (closed Sun) is the place to head for maps, guides and travel journals plus a good selection of Australiana. Secondhand books can be found at Glebe and Paddington markets, at Gleebooks Second Hand Books, 191 Glebe Point Rd (daily until 9pm); Lesley McKays Bookshop, 346 New South Head Rd, Double Bay (until midnight); and in the secondhand bookshops on King Street, Newtown, in particular check out the amazingly chaotic piles of books at Gould's Book Arcade, 32–38 King St, Newtown (daily 7am–midnight).

On a more mundane level, there are two handy **supermarkets** in the city centre: with extended opening hours, one is in the basement of Woolworths Metro on the corner of Park and George streets, above Town Hall Station (Mon–Wed 7am–8pm, Thurs & Fri 7am–9pm, Sat 9am–6.30pm, Sun 10am–5.30pm) and Coles Express, Level 2, Wynyard Station (daily 6am–midnight). In the suburbs, large supermarkets such as Coles stay open daily until about 10pm, and there are plenty of 24-hour 7-Eleven convenience stores in the inner city and suburbs. For delicatessen items, look no further than the splendid food hall at David Jones (see pp.106-107).

Gourmet Pizza Kitchen, 199–207 Military Rd, Neutral Bay (☎02/9953 9000). Spacious, popular place. The name says it all.

Indian Empire, 5 Walker St, North Sydney (☎02/9923 2909). Spectacular view of the city across Lavender Bay, plus everything you'd expect from a good Indian restaurant. BYO. Closed Sat & Sun lunch. Mains $9.90–13.90.

Jipang, 37 The Corso, Manly (☎02/9977 4436). Excellent Japanese noodle house; very inexpensive. BYO. Closed Mon.

Just Hooked, 236 Military Rd, Neutral Bay. A small range of delicious fresh fish (five starters, five main courses) in a classy version of a classic fish shop, with white-tiled walls and high stools. BYO. Dinner nightly, lunch Fri only.

Maisys Cafe, 164 Military Rd, Neutral Bay. Cool hangout on a hot day (or all night: open 24hr), with funky interior and music, smiling staff – and smoking is allowed! Good for breakfast – from croissants to bacon and eggs – or delicious Maltese *pastizzi* plus soups, burgers, pasta and cakes. Not cheap but servings are generous. BYO.

Somi's, 48 Victoria Parade, corner South Steyne, Manly (☎02/9977 7511). Inexpensive Thai restaurant across from the beach with an appropriately fresh and delicious range of spicy seafood dishes on the menu. Licensed and BYO.

Twocan, 27 Belgrave St, Manly (☎02/9977 1558). Colourful Latin American decor on the walls and yummy modern Australian Mediterranean-slanted, on the menu. The desserts here are divine. BYO. Closed Sun, Mon & lunch Sat.

Watermark, 2a The Esplanade, Balmoral Beach (☎02/9968 3433). For a memorable Sydney meal, both for location and food, you can't go wrong here. Chef Kenneth Leung is well-known for his fusion of Eastern and Western cooking styles and ingredients, there's views right across the water, a terrace to dine under the sun or stars, a stylish interior and fabulous service. Very expensive; licensed.

Entertainment, nightlife and culture

There's an awful lot going on in Sydney, especially at the level of bands in sweaty pubs and club nights in upstairs rooms, and a diverse arts scene. It's easy enough to find out exactly **what's on**: in addition to the rather bland monthly programmes distributed by various tourist organizations, you'll find comprehensive listings of film, theatre and music events in "Metro", a supplement in Friday's *Sydney Morning Herald*, "Time Out", a weekly entertainment lift-out in Sunday's *Sun-Herald* or "Seven Days", a *Daily Telegraph* pull-out every Thursday. For more alternative goings-on – clubbing, bands, fashion, music and the like – there is a plethora of **free listings magazines** which can be found lying around in the cafés, record shops and boutiques of Paddington, Glebe and Kings Cross, such as *On the Street*, *Revolver* and *Drum Media* with their weekly band listings and reviews, and *3D World* and *Beat* covering the dance scene. Also check the useful Internet site *www.sydney.citysearch.com.au*.

Ticketek is the main **booking agency**, with branches located at 195 Elizabeth St, inside Grace Bros department store at the corner of George and Market streets, and within the Entertainment Centre; bookings on ☎02/9266 4800. There's also Ticketmaster, 1st floor, 66 Hunter St (☎02/9320 9000). For theatre, concerts, opera and ballet you can always try for cheap, same-day tickets at the **Halftix** kiosk in Martin Place (Mon–Sat noon–6pm; personal callers only and payments in cash); they also sell regular tickets.

Pubs and bars

The differences between a restaurant, bar, pub and nightclub are often blurred in Sydney, and one establishment may be a combination of all these under one roof. The list below consists mainly of traditional old **hotels**, though even at most of these there'll be some kind of food available, and they may even occasionally lay on entertainment. For a guaranteed drink any time, head for Kings Cross. A recent relaxing of licensing laws also means restaurants will be able to serve drinks to non-diners.

City centre and The Rocks

Australian Hotel, 100 Cumberland St, The Rocks. Convivial corner hotel with crowded outside tables. Inside, original fittings give a lovely old-pub feel. Known for its Bavarian-style draught beer brewed in Picton (see p.202), plus gourmet pizzas.

Bar Luca, 52 Phillip St, Circular Quay. Trendy city bar – all natural woods, mellow-coloured walls, and fresh flowers. It also doubles as an Italian café, with breakfast from 7am and main meals through the day; you can also just come in for a drink or coffee and cake. Closed Sat & Sun.

Craig Brewery, Harbourside Shopping Centre, Darling Harbour. Popular place with three bars and an open-air restaurant. After-work happy hour with cheap beer on weeknights.

Customs House Bar, Macquarie Place, off Bridge St, City. A nice spot on a square with palm trees and statues. Customers have been enjoying a drink here since 1826. Very popular with city workers, with tables outside on the square. Cheap lunches $3.50–9.50. Closed Sat & Sun.

Forbes Hotel, corner of King and York streets, City. Atmospheric, turn-of-the-century corner hotel with a lively downstairs bar. Upstairs is more sedate, with a pool table and plenty of window seating

– the best spot is the tiny cast-iron balcony, with just enough room for two. Very popular Thurs & Fri nights. Fri & Sat to 3am.

Glenmore Hotel, 96 Cumberland St, The Rocks, opposite the entrance to the Harbour Bridge pedestrian walkway (☎02/9247 4794). Unpretentious, breezy pub perched over The Rocks, with great views from large windows in the public bar and spectacular ones from the rooftop beer garden. A good refresher before or after the bridge walk, and serving up reasonably priced pub grub. Reached from the Argyle Steps.

Hero of Waterloo, 81 Lower Fort St, Millers Point, The Rocks. One of Sydney's oldest pubs, built in 1843 from sandstone dug out from the Argyle Cut (see p.103), this place has plenty of atmosphere. Open fireplaces make it a good choice for a winter drink, and it serves simple meals.

Lord Nelson Brewery Hotel, corner of Argyle and Kent streets, Millers Point, The Rocks (☎02/9251 4044). Licensed in 1841, this very old pub serves beer brewed on the premises, plus bar food daily and upmarket meals from its first floor brasserie (lunch Mon–Fri, dinner Mon–Sat). Ask for a tour of the brewery.

The Marble Bar, *Hilton Hotel*, 259 Pitt St, City. A sightseeing stop-off as much as a good spot for a drink amongst high Victorian decor featuring Italian marble. This was the original 1893 basement bar of the *Tattersalls Hotel*, which was replaced by the *Hilton* in 1973. Pricey drinks but happy hour 5–7pm. Free jazz or blues Tues–Sun.

Mercantile Hotel, 25 George St, The Rocks. High-spirited Irish pub where you can get Sydney's best-poured Guinness; bistro meals and weekend outdoor café.

Orient Hotel, corner of George and Argyle streets, The Rocks. Perennially popular, and one of The Rocks' liveliest boozers, with several bars to choose from. Heaving on weekends, when the more upmarket first floor cocktail bar is bound to be the most sedate option. Open until 2am, until 4am Fri and Sat night.

Pumphouse Tavern, 17 Little Pier St, Darling Harbour. Pleasant, restored pub with a beer garden at the edge of Darling Harbour – counter meals available; pool tables.

Slip Inn, 111 Sussex St. On three levels overlooking Darling Harbour, this huge place has several bars, a bistro and a nightclub. It attracts a young, more style-conscious afterwork crowd but is popular on weekends too. The front bars have a pool room, while downstairs a boisterous beer garden fills up on sultry nights, with a quieter, more sophisticated bar beside it. Excellent wine list, with lots available by the glass. Expensive pub food and gourmet pizzas by day, tasty contemporary fare in the bistro by night. Live jazz Thurs night, DJs Fri night.

Inner west

Bank Hotel, 324 King St, next to Newtown Station. Stylish pub – always packed and open late. Pool table out front, cocktail bar out back and a big beer garden downstairs (with Thai restaurant).

Exchange Hotel, corner of Beattie and Mullens streets, Balmain. Classic Balmain boozer, a backstreet corner pub with the largest balcony ever, perfect for sitting out at and drinking the weekend early morning Bloody Mary specials.

London Hotel, 234 Darling St, Balmain. Convivial British-style pub, with stools to perch on on the high verandah, overlooking the Saturday market. Attracts a typically mixed Balmain crowd.

Marlborough Hotel, 145 King St, Newtown. A spacious pub popular with students from nearby Sydney University. Often has bands on Fri and Sat nights, but the comfy lounge is a quiet place to talk. There's also a great beer garden and a good Italian restaurant.

Monkey Bar, 255 Darling St, Balmain. Stylish bar with an atrium covered restaurant area overlooked by the bar. Twenty- and thirtysomething professionals come for a drink here, amongst loud music in a crowded space. There's a small stage for the free live music – blues, soul, jazz or acoustic rock – Wed, Fri, Sat nights and early Sunday evening. Bar menu $10–12.

Nag's Head Hotel, corner of Lodge St and St Johns Rd, off Glebe Point Rd. A good place for a quiet drink – no pool tables, no pokies – with British beers (pints available) and atmosphere; calls itself a "posh pub". Its bistro also dishes up excellent steaks and other grills.

Kings Cross, Darlinghurst and Potts Point

Bourbon and Beefsteak Bar, 24 Darlinghurst Rd, Kings Cross. Legendary 24hr Kings Cross drinking hole. Come here for a steak breakfast and a Bloody Mary after a night out.

Darlo Bar, corner of Darlinghurst Rd and Liverpool St, Darlinghurst. Traditional Cross meeting place with a lounge room atmosphere – comfy colourful chairs and sofas. Drinks aren't expensive, with a range of reasonable house wines also on offer. You can order here from the menu of near-by *Fish face* (see p.145), and they'll fetch the food for you. The sole pool table is always in action.

Green Park Hotel, 360 Victoria St, Darlinghurst. Always lively, packed and cruisy at night with a regular crowd. Getting ever younger: past crews tend to move onto the *Darlo Bar* around the corner which may be more your taste. The stash of pool tables are a big part of the attraction.

International Bar, 14th floor, *Top of the Town Hotel*, 227 Victoria St, Darlinghurst. Try to come here for just one drink to admire the fantastic view of the Sydney skyline. Get dressed up in your most stylish gear, but don't be disappointed if you're turned away from this beautiful people's bar, which opened in the 1960s and is now trendy again after several cheesy years. The price of beer here is steep ($7) and the bar snacks include Russian caviar.

Judgement Bar, *Courthouse Hotel*, 189 Oxford St, Darlinghurst. Overlooking Taylor Square, the upstairs bar of this pub can, and often does, open 24hr; your punishment may be ending up here with a very assorted selection of nightbirds, from young clubbers to old drunks.

Soho Bar, 171 Victoria St, Potts Point. This trendy pub is a good place for a chat. Most locals head for the upstairs bar (Tues–Sun nights only) to hang out on the back balcony and play pool.

Paddington and Surry Hills

Bar Cleveland, corner of Cleveland and Bourke streets, Surry Hills. Huge plate glass windows have opened this pub onto the busy, gritty street of traffic, Turkish takeaways and secondhand clothes shops – and punters have packed it ever since for an authentic urban brew.

Bentley Bar, 320 Crown St, Surry Hills. Perennially popular pre- and post-clubbing venue. Dark, noisy and packed. DJs Mon, Wed, Thurs & Sun nights.

Cricketers Arms, 106 Fitzroy St, Surry Hills. A good cross-section of people frequent this pub: old fellas watching sport on TV and young folk playing pool, plus a snazzy selection of CDs blaring out from behind the bar.

Dolphin Hotel, 412 Crown St, Surry Hills. Fashionably renovated pub; the lounge bar doubles as a café, while the public bar is as down-to-earth as ever. Upstairs, the tiny bar, overlooking the stunning architecture of the *Dolphin*'s restaurant, is a good spot for a chat and a glass of wine.

O'Bar, *Clarendon Hotel*, 156 Devonshire St, corner of Waterloo St, Surry Hills (☎02/9319 6881). The name comes from the perfectly round bar of this upmarket pub. This is a good place for a chat, especially over a bottle of wine from its varied list or over their excellent food. Alternatively it's the perfect early evening watering hole before eating on nearby Crown St.

Paddington Inn Hotel, 338 Oxford St, Paddington. Slick, crowded and expensive; packed out on Saturdays as it's opposite the market. The bistro is also recommended (see p.146).

Palace, corner of Flinders and South Dowling streets, Surry Hills. Tastefully distressed decor in the noisy smart-set hangout downstairs, with a tiny eating area for the well-recommended kitchen. Several rooms of pool tables upstairs are the star attraction.

Royal Hotel, 237 Glenmore Rd, Paddington. The original renovated Paddington pub.

Bondi

B.B's, 157 Curlewis St, Bondi Beach. A feral wine bar, *B.Bs* looks and feels as if squatters have taken over the Duke's private den. Welcoming and with free live music every night. The bands are of varied quality but unvarying enthusiasm. Good-value meals. Mon–Fri from 5pm, Sat & Sun from 4pm.

Beach Road Hotel, 71 Beach Rd, Bondi Beach. Huge, stylish decorated pub with a bewildering range of bars and a beer garden. Popular with travellers, but with its good vibe, even the goatee and black frame glasses brigade are starting to give it a sniff. Entertainment, mostly free, comes from DJs playing mellow grooves, rock bands and a jazz supper club. The hotel also has a cheap Italian bistro, *No Names*, and an upmarket contemporary Australian restaurant.

Bondi Hotel, 178 Campbell Parade, Bondi Beach. Huge pub dating from the 1920s, with many of its original features intact. Sedate during the day but at night an over-the-top, late-night backpackers' hangout. Mon–Sat until 4am.

Bondi Icebergs Club, 1 Notts Ave, Bondi Beach. Totally unpretentious place for a cheap beer – but with the most stunning views in Bondi, right over the southern end of the beach where you can watch surfers catch their waves. To guarantee entry as a non-member of the club, bring a passport or other ID to prove you're an out-of-towner. A good time to drop in is Sunday afternoon, with live music 4–8pm.

Live music: jazz, blues and rock

Though the live music scene in Sydney has passed its boom time, it's still vibrant, regularly churning out world class talent as well as nourishing a steady stream of local, interstate and overseas acts passing through every month, peaking in summer with a well-established open-air festival circuit. Pub bands and clubs are often free, especially if you arrive early; if there is a charge, it's usually between $5–10, with $12–15 the uppermost price for smaller international acts, or the latest interstate sensation. Early Sunday evenings are laid-back, from about 6–10pm is a mellow time to catch some music, particularly jazz, around town.

The **venues for major events**, with bookings direct or through Ticketek or Ticketmasters (see p.150) are the Entertainment Centre at Haymarket near Darling Harbour (enquiries and credit-card sales ☎02/9266 4800); the Capitol Theatre, 13 Campbell St, Haymarket (☎02/9266 4800); the Enmore Theatre, 130 Enmore Rd, just up from Newtown (☎02/9550 3666); and the centrally located Metro Theatre, 624 George St (☎02/9264 2666).

There are several big outdoor rock concerts through the year. **Homebake** (around $40; *www.homebake.com*) a huge annual open-air festival in The Domain in early December with an all-Australian cast; includes food and market stalls, rides and a line-up of thirty underground Australian bands. The **Big Day Out** on Australia Day (Jan 26; around $65), at the showground at Homebush Bay, features big international names like the Manic Street Preachers and Marilyn Manson as well as local talent with several stages and dance floors.

The Basement, 29 Reiby Place, Circular Quay (☎02/9251 2797; *www.basement.com.au*). A great place to see jazz, acoustic and world music as well as a roster of the world's most renowned blues performers. The best way to take in a performance is to book a table and dine in front of the low stage.

Bridge Hotel, 135 Victoria Rd, Rozelle (☎02/9810 1260). A legendary inner west venue specializing in blues and pub rock, with international but mostly local acts. Also has a good pub theatre and comedy nights.

Cat and Fiddle Hotel, 456 Darling St, Balmain (☎02/9810 7931). Smallish venue with high standards attracting informed indie rock audiences who savour the best of interstate music along with local gonnabe's. Music every night of the week.

Excelsior Hotel, Pyrmont Bridge Rd, Glebe (☎02/9660 7479). A modest pub, it truly has one of the best atmospheres for experiencing Sunday afternoon rock in Sydney. The upstairs pool room with interior balcony is a great feature and it offers good food. Usually free.

Excelsior Hotel, 64 Foveaux St, Surry Hills (☎02/9211 4945). Musos pub – songwriters and jamming nights are part of the nightly live music line-up, mostly free. Bistro, and bar until 3am Fri and Sat.

The Globe, 379 King St, Newtown (☎02/9519 0220). The epicentre of Newtown's – and perhaps Sydney's – musical subculture. Top bands rub shoulders with DJs and the venue isn't above putting on the occasional theme/retro night. The venue often has free entry but otherwise be prepared to pay $6–10. Big line-ups Thurs–Sun and more intimate gigs Mon–Wed.

Harbourside Brasserie, Pier One, Hickson Rd, Millers Point (☎02/9252 3000; *www.ozemail.com.au/~harbrass*). Great location on the harbour near The Rocks; jazz, blues, soul, fusion, world music or cabaret from 10pm Mon–Sat, Sun music from 4pm, and Latin Dance club from 8pm. Discriminating crowd, mellow atmosphere.

Hopetoun Hotel, 416 Bourke St, corner of Fitzroy St, Surry Hills (☎02/9361 5257). "The Hoey" is one of Sydney's best venues for the indie band scene, with music Wednesday to Sunday in the small and inevitably packed front bar. There's also a packed pool room, a drinking pit in the basement, and an ambitious little restaurant. Free Mon–Wed; no music Sun. Closes midnight.

Iron Duke Hotel, 220 Botany Rd, Alexandria (☎02/9990 9988). Hard rock venue with big line-ups of amp-crashing local, interstate and international bands Tues–Sun. A crowd of the inner city music cognoscenti make it a genuine Sydney rock experience.

Round Midnight, 2 Roslyn St, Kings Cross (☎02/9356 4045). Cooking late-night jazz and blues venue; Tues–Sun from 9pm.

Selina's, *Coogee Bay Hotel*, 212 Arden St, Coogee Bay (☎02/9665 0000). Woeful acoustics and restricted views, but a dearth of competition has seen *Selina's* survive as one of the larger venues.

Clubs

Many of Sydney's best clubs are at **gay** or **lesbian** venues: although these are listed separately, the divisions are not always that clear – many are **theme places**, and may have a gay night one day, lesbian the next and straight the following night. *DCM* (see opposite) in particular is a good one. A long strip of thriving clubs stretches from Kings Cross to Oxford Street and down towards Hyde Park. As anywhere, the scene can be pretty snobby, with door people at some places vetting your style. Admission ranges from $10 to $20.

Cauldron, 207 Darlinghurst Rd, Darlinghurst (☎02/9331 1523). Stalwart club that's as popular as ever with a new generation of well-heeled Eastern Suburbs types. High energy dance Wed, Fri & Sat, retro Thurs.

Club 77, 277 William St, East Sydney (☎02/9361 4981). Retro nights, techno beats and house sounds provide a hands-in-the-air rave atmosphere. The club stops just short of allowing entry to any old goose who wanders up with a bottle of lucozade and a foldable anorak, so you may have to queue, but without too much anxiety. Mood is largely all-night party and the drinks are only a little above pub prices.

Home, Cockle Bay Wharf, Darling Harbour (☎02/9266 0600). The latest and first really BIG club venture in Sydney. Its cool, cavernous interior, with a 2000-capacity and acre or two of floor space thunder to the feet of several suburbs' youth. The decks are often manned by name DJs but you get the feeling the crowd don't know or don't care too much. There's a mezzanine to witness rather than participate, and a chill-out room. Drinks are expensive, staff beautiful.

Palladium, corner of Darlinghurst Rd and Roslyn St, Kings Cross (☎02/9331 0127). The *Palladium* radiates a great vibe and offers a succession of cool nights for a variety of different crowds, from lounge cruisers to suburban breakdancers. Sunday Night's Tender Trap is a lounge favourite where non-clubbers rub nylon shirts with the more hard core polyester smoothies and produce just the right amount of static.

Powercuts Reggae Club, 150 Elizabeth St, City (☎02/9264 5380). Sydney's only reggae club; Fri & Sat only 10pm–4.30am.

Q Bar Pool Club, 44 Oxford St, Darlinghurst (☎02/9360 1375). Pool tables en masse and video games plus a dance floor, make a popular combination.

Rhino Bar, 24 Bayswater Rd, Kings Cross. Cheap drinks and a relatively relaxed door policy mean that the *Rhino Bar* is popular with a crowd that likes to have fun and party. Good dancers and joggers mix on a smallish floor, jiving to a pleasing mix of dub and house grooves. The atmosphere throughout is lively, if a little beery in the front bar.

Sublime, 244 Pitt St, City (☎02/9264 8428). Purpose-designed basement club very popular with just about everyone as it caters for all with a successful selection of different theme nights. A hard house feel is the bedrock for a serious club experience and the vast dance area is crammed with hard core clubbers.

Sugareef, 20 Bayswater Rd, Kings Cross (☎02/9357 7250). After the sweaty writhing of *Rhino*, *Sugareef* presents a more distilled atmosphere. With plenty of space to recline and think about your hairstyle and shoes, conversation is possible because the acid jazz house sounds just about manage to maintain the pulse. Popular pool table too.

Underground Café, 22 Bayswater Rd, Kings Cross (☎02/9368 1067). An increasingly popular venue in the middle of Bayswater Rd's club strip. This subterranean enclave contains a mix of fashion-conscious travellers and a sprinkling of youthful locals listening to progressive house, big beats and a little garage. Often guest national and international DJs. Thursday has a special $2 entry and cheap drinks.

Gay bars and clubs

One of the best things about Sydney's scene is that, apart from a few pubs in the inner west, it's all concentrated in one area. So you can do what's known as bar-hopping – start at the *Albury* and keep on going, for days if you like! Sydney never closes – there's always somewhere else to go.

Albury Hotel, 6 Oxford St, Paddington. If you like drag shows, and even if you don't, you should visit the *Albury* to see an energetic, well-choreographed, free performance. Gay boys, (some) lesbians, straight girls with their boyfriends and drag queens. Mon–Fri 2pm–2am, Sun 2pm–midnight.

The Barracks, corner of Bourke and Flinders streets (enter from rear door in Patterson Lane), Surry Hills. Strictly for men, this venue started off being a haunt for leather men and "bears", but it's appeal is broadening. No point getting here until after 11pm. The focus is the pool tables at the back. Bring a torch. Daily 5pm–3am.

Beaucamp Hotel, 267 Oxford St, Darlinghurst. Traditional Aussie pub decor with a mainly male, rough trade crowd. Especially worth visiting on Sunday afternoons. Daily noon till midnight.

DCM (Don't Cry Mama), 33 Oxford St, Darlinghurst. Young, fast and mainly gay. Like most Sydney clubs, this doesn't really liven up till after midnight when you can be assured of a wild night of dancing. $10 cover charge.

Gilligans, First floor, 134 Oxford St, Darlinghurst. Upstairs above the *Oxford*, but a different scene from below. It's a cocktail bar which attracts a mixed crowd of gay boys, lesbians and the straight party set. 5pm till late.

Imperial Hotel, 35 Erskineville Rd, Erskineville. This is the pub out of the movie *Priscilla Queen of the Desert*, and it's notorious as a late-night venue where anything can happen. Here you'll find lesbians, gay men, drag queens and straights. There are shows on weekends and a cellar dance bar. Noon till late, until 8am on weekends.

Midnight Shift, 85 Oxford St, Darlinghurst. A large drinking and cruising space for (mainly) gay men, and a "locker room" out the back. Commonly known as "The Shift", this is the mainstream club for gay men. In the early hours of Sunday morning you can hardly move on a dance floor full of gym-pumped men, sweating it out with their shirts off. There's a $15 cover charge on Saturday nights. Mon–Fri noon–6am, Sat noon–2am, Sun 2pm–10am; club nights Thurs–Sun from 11pm.

Newtown Hotel, 174 King St, Newtown. It's a 20-minute taxi ride, but a thousand miles from Oxford Street. A mix of Newtown lesbians and gays, with drag shows from Tuesday to Sunday, and pool tables. Mon–Sat 11am–midnight, Sun 11am–10pm.

Oxford Hotel, 134 Oxford St, Darlinghurst. Macho pillar of the Sydney gay community. Come here after the *Albury*, for a change of pace. You'll notice the lights are a bit dimmer, and it's mainly for gay men, but this pub is particularly busy on Friday and Saturday nights. Livens up after 11pm.

Phoenix, *Exchange Hotel*, 34 Oxford St, Darlinghurst. This underground "alternative" dance club is a happy mix of gay men and dykes, who go wild to some groovy music (Tues, Thurs & Sun from 11pm).

Stonewall Hotel, 175 Oxford St, Darlinghurst. The newest pub on the strip, which is a big hit with young gay men and their female friends. You can expect theme nights like gay bingo, Mr Gay Sydney heats or go-go dancing championships. There's a cocktail bar and a nightclub (Fri & Sat 11pm–5am). "Riot Girls" is the theme for lesbians on Thursday nights. Daily noon–5am.

Taxi Club, 40 Flinders St, Surry Hills. Last stop. If you've made it here, congratulations, you're a true bar hopper. It's a Sydney legend, but don't bother before 2 or 3am, and you will need to be suitably intoxicated to appreciate it fully. There's a strange blend of drag queens, taxi drivers, lesbians, boys (straight and gay) to observe, and the cheapest drinks in gay Sydney. You have to be a member, but simply ask to join at the door.

GAY AND LESBIAN SYDNEY

Sydney is undisputably one of the world's great gay cities – indeed, many people think it capable of snatching San Francisco's crown as the Queen of them all. There's something for everyone – whether you want to lie on a beach during the warmer months (April–Oct) or party hard all year round. Gays and lesbians are pretty much accepted – particularly in the inner-city and eastern areas. They have to be – there's too many of them for anyone to argue. A big drawcard is the month-long Sydney Gay and Lesbian Mardi Gras festival in February. After the hundreds of arts and community events, there's the famous party, held the last weekend in February or the first in March.

But don't despair if you can't be here for Mardi Gras. The city has many more parties, and much more to offer. The main gay area is **Oxford Street**, Darlinghurst, where you will find a strip of gay restaurants, coffee shops, bookshops and bars. But there are a few pubs in the inner-west suburbs of Newtown, Erskineville and Leichhardt (Dykeheart), areas also worth visiting for their gay/lesbian/groovy café and street scenes. Although the bar and club listings below have been split into separate gay and lesbian listings, the scene thankfully doesn't split so neatly into "them and us".

If you've come for the sun, popular gay beaches are Tamarama (see p.133), Bondi (pp.130-132), and "clothing optional" Lady Jane, at Watsons Bay (p.127), while pools of choice are Red Leaf harbour pool at Double Bay (p.126) and the appropriately named Andrew "Boy" Charlton pool in The Domain (pp.112-113). The Coogee Women's Baths, at the southern end of Coogee Beach (pp.113-114) is popular with lesbians.

MARDI GRAS AND SLEAZE

From a Queer perspective the best time of year to visit Sydney is February, when the Sydney Gay and Lesbian Mardi Gras takes over the city and the already huge gay population is flooded by pilgrims from within and without Australia. Four weeks of exhibitions, performances and other events represent the largest lesbian and gay arts festival in the world, paving the way for the main event, an exuberant night-time **parade** down Oxford Street, when up to 500,000 gays and straights jostle for the best viewing positions. Participants devote months to the preparation of outlandish floats and outrageous costumes at Mardi Gras workshops. Even longer is devoted to the preparation of beautiful bodies in Sydney's packed gyms. Vanity apart, fitness is a necessity for the all-night dance party which follows the parade (about $75 per ticket, plus membership cost). The party is held in five differently themed dance spaces at the old Showgrounds site and there are usually several international acts.

The **Mardi Gras Guide**, available from mid-December, can be picked up from bookshops, cafés and restaurants around Oxford Street or at the Mardi Gras office (see opposite). Also, look out for the *Sydney Morning Herald*'s "Gay and Lesbian Mardi Gras Guide" in the first week of February.

You have to plan ahead if you want to get a ticket to the world's best party. The purchase of **party** tickets is restricted to "Mardi Gras members" in order to keep out troublemakers and "to guard the gay and lesbian nature of the parties". There is an annual membership fee (around $35) or a cheaper associate/international membership for those who live outside Sydney (around $10). Tickets often sell out by the end of January. There are special provisions for overseas visitors: to be sure of a **ticket** (restricted to one only for associate/international members), it's best to telephone, fax or email Sydney Gay and Lesbian Mardi Gras Ltd (see opposite for details), and ask for the current procedure. Once you've

LESBIAN NIGHTSPOTS

Also see the gay bars and clubs overleaf, particularly the *Stonewall Hotel* which has a specific "Riot Girls" night on Thursday, the *Albury Hotel*, *Newtown Hotel*, *Imperial Hotel*, *Gilligans* and the *Taxi Club*.

Bank Hotel, 324 King St, next to Newtown Station. This stylish bar has become a dyke favourite. The Wednesday night women's pool competition draws large crowds.

given credit card details, they'll post it to you, or hold it for collection. Full members can buy several tickets so, if all else fails, once you're on the ground ask around and you may find someone with a spare ticket.

For more information, ask at the **Mardi Gras office**, 21 Erskineville Rd, Erskineville, NSW 2043 (Mon–Fri 10am–6pm; ☎02/9557 4332, or fax 9516 4446; *www.mardigras .com.au*). For credit card bookings for festival events visit *www.ticketek.com.au*.

Sydney just can't wait all year for Mardi Gras, so the **Sleaze Ball** is a very welcome stopgap in September/October. Similar to the Mardi Gras party, it's held at the former Showground site, and goes on through the night. Tickets are organized by Mardi Gras Ltd and are likewise restricted to members.

Finally, a **Gay and Lesbian Film Festival** forms part of the Mardi Gras programme; it runs for two weeks from mid-February at various venues around town.

GROUPS AND INFORMATION

Press The Bookshop, 207 Oxford St, Darlinghurst (☎02/9331 1103). A good starting point to getting to know gay Sydney is The Bookshop, which has a complete stock of gay and lesbian-related books, cards and magazines. The staff are friendly and ready to help in any way they can. You can pick up the two free gay and lesbian weeklys, *Sydney Star Observer* (2nd floor, 94 Oxford St, Darlinghurst; ☎02/9380 5577) and *Capital Q* (Suite 5, Level 5, 15–19 Boundary St, Rushcutters Bay; ☎02/9332 4988), also available from venues and gay-friendly businesses in the eastern suburbs and inner west. These newspapers will tell you where and when the weekly dance parties are being held, and where you can buy tickets. *LOTL* (*Lesbians on the Loose*, PO Box 798, Newtown, NSW 2042; ☎02/9380 6529), is a free, non-glossy monthly magazine also available in The Bookshop and cafés of Newtown and Glebe.

Support networks Gay & Lesbian Counselling Service of New South Wales, GLCS Centre, 197 Albion St, Surry Hills (PO Box 334, Darlinghurst, NSW 2010); counselling line ☎02/9360 2211 (daily 4pm–midnight); What's On (☎02/9361 3655; 24hr recorded message). Lesbian Line (☎02/9550 0910 Fri 6–10pm, or recorded 24hr information). AIDS Council of NSW (ACON), 9 Commonwealth St, Surry Hills (☎02/9206 2000). Bobby Goldsmith Foundation for AIDS and AIDS Related Diseases, Level 4, 16 Victoria St, Darlinghurst (☎02/9860 9755). Sydney AIDS Hotline/NSW AIDS line (☎02/9332 4000 or free call ☎1800/451 600). Albion Street Centre, 150–154 Albion St, Surry Hills (☎02/9332 1090); counselling, testing clinic, information and library.

TRAVEL AGENTS

FOD Travel, Level 2, 77 Oxford St, Darlinghurst (☎02/9360 3616, fax 9332 3326). Offers special tours designed for gays and lesbians, and can advise about travel during Mardi Gras.

Jornada, Level 1, 263 Liverpool St, Darlinghurst (☎02/9360 9611, fax 9326 0199; *www.jornada.com.au*). The largest tour operator for the Mardi Gras. Can organize trips up north for gay travellers.

Silke's Travel, 263 Oxford St, Darlinghurst (☎02/9380 6244, fax 9361 3729, free call ☎1800/807 860; *silba@magna.com.au*). Offers advice and bookings for domestic and international travel, and accommodation from a gay perspective.

See also p.91 for gay- and lesbian-friendly places to stay, and pp.154 and 157 for a low-down on the club scene and listings of specifically gay and lesbian venues.

Leichhardt Hotel, corner of Short and Balmain roads, Leichhardt. Popular lesbian watering hole. Sun–Tues noon–10pm, Wed–Sat 10pm–midnight.

On the Other Side, *NV Nightclub*, 163 Oxford St, Darlinghurst. Mainly lesbian party night. Happy hour 9–10pm. $5 entry.

Spicy Friday, *Lansdowne Hotel*, 2–6 City Rd, Broadway (☎02/9211 2325). The crowd is about 80 percent lesbian at this funky soul and cabaret theme night. Pool tables and upstairs chill-out lounge. $5 cover charge.

Classical music, theatre and dance

Sydney's **arts scene** is vibrant and extensive. **Prices** for mainstream theatre and music performances are fairly high, upwards of $25, with a classical concert at the Opera House costing around $50 – and you don't get cheap seats for restricted views. Tickets in smaller, fringe venues cost around $18. Half-price same day tickets are available from Halftix (see p.150). The Sydney Symphony Orchestra plays at the Town Hall, St Jame's Church or the Opera House while the Australian Ballet (prices $45–75) performs at the Opera House and the Capitol Theatre. The Australian Music Centre in The Rocks publishes a handy free bimonthly fold-out programme of classical and experimental music performances Australia-wide. Also useful is the free booklet *Sydney Arts and Cultural Guide*, published every six months with details of current and forthcoming theatrical productions and classical concerts, available from tourist offices.

The free outdoor performances in The Domain, under the auspices of the Sydney Festival, are a highlight of the year, as crowds gather to enjoy the music with a picnic. Check the *Sydney Morning Herald*'s "Metro" to find out what's on at the venues below.

Concert halls

Conservatorium of Music, off Macquarie St (concert department ☎02/9351 1263), set back in the Royal Botanic Gardens; its temporary home, until January 2000, is at Bay 4, Australian Technology Park, Garden Street, Eveleigh, a 2-minute walk from Redfern Station. Conservatorium students have traditionally given free lunch-time recitals every Wednesday and Friday at 1.10pm during term time. While renovations continue at Macquarie St, the Tuesday recital takes place at St Andrews Cathedral next to the Town Hall, and Friday's is at the Australian Technology Park. Staff and students also give other concerts, both free and ticketed (up to $25) at various venues around town; a programme is available from the music school. See p.113 for more details.

Eugene Goosens Hall, ABC Centre, Harris St, Ultimo (☎02/9333 1500). 320-seat auditorium with state of the art acoustics within the radio headquarters of the ABC; mainly new music. The Sydney Spring International Festival of New Music is held here for four weeks from the end of August.

Sydney Opera House, Bennelong Point (☎02/9250 7777; box office Mon–Sat 9am–8.30pm, Sun 9am–4pm). The Opera House is, of course, *the* place for the most prestigious performances in Sydney, hosting not just opera and classical music but also theatre and ballet in its many auditoriums. Forget quibbles about acoustics or ticket prices (classical concerts from $52) – it's worth going just to say you've been. See p.99 for more details.

Town Hall, corner of Druitt and George streets (☎02/9265 9230). Centrally located concert hall. See p.107 for more details.

Theatre and dance

Aboriginal and Islander Dance Theatre (☎02/9252 0199). Established in 1976, the famous training company for young Aboriginal and Islander dancers, based in The Rocks, puts on about three productions per year at various venues; call for times and locations.

Bangarra Dance Theatre, Pier 4, Hickson Rd, Millers Point, The Rocks (☎02/9251 5333). Formed in 1989, Bangarra's innovative style fuses contemporary movement with the traditional dances and culture of the Yirrkala Community in Arnhemland. Based at the same pier as the Wharf Theatre but performing at other venues in Sydney and touring nationally and internationally.

Belvoir St Theatre, 25 Belvoir St, Surry Hills (☎02/9699 3444). Highly regarded two-stage venue for a wide range of contemporary Australian and international theatre.

Capitol Theatre, 13 Campbell St, Haymarket (☎02/9266 4800). Built as a de luxe picture theatre in the 1920s, the theatre was saved from demolition and beautifully restored in the mid-1990s. The 2000-seater now hosts big-budget musicals and ballet, watched from beneath its best feature, the deep blue ceiling spangled with the stars of the southern skies.

Ensemble Theatre, 78 McDougall St, Milsons Point (☎02/9929 0644). Australian contemporary and classic plays.

The Footbridge Theatre, Parramatta Rd, University of Sydney, Glebe (☎02/9692 9955). Rich and varied repertoire: from *Cabaret* to Shakespeare.

Her Majesty's Theatre, 107 Quay St, Haymarket, near Central Station (☎02/9266 4820). The place to see those big musical extravaganzas imported from the West End and Broadway.

Marion Street Theatre, 2 Marian St, Killara (☎02/9498 3166). Broadway, West End and Australian comedies and popular drama. Bookings are essential for the popular 1pm Saturday matinee for kids (3–10 year olds; also school holidays Mon–Fri 10.30am & 1pm).

The Playhouse and **Drama Theatre**, both at the Sydney Opera House, Bennelong Point (☎02/9250 7777; box office Mon–Sat 9am–8.30pm, Sun 9am–4pm). Modern and traditional plays, and dance.

Theatre Royal, MLC Centre, King St, City (☎02/9320 9191). Imported musicals and blockbuster plays.

Wharf Theatre, Pier 4, Hickson Rd, Millers Point, The Rocks (☎02/9250 1777). Home to the highly regarded Sydney Theatre Company, producing Shakespeare and modern pieces, and also to the Sydney Dance Company. Atmospheric waterfront location, with a well-regarded restaurant, bar and café, from which to check out the views.

Fringe theatre, comedy and cabaret

Sydney's first **Sydney Comedy Festival** (*www.comedy.com.au*) was held in October 1998 as a rival to Melbourne's (see p.804) and should become an annual event at various venues around town (but based primarily at the Comedy Cellar – see below). Also see the *Bridge Hotel* (p.153) which has irregular comedy nights.

Comedy Cellar, Off *Broadway Hotel*, corner of Bay St and Broadway (☎02/9552 2999). Comedy seven nights a week from 8.30pm in this cavernous modern venue. Try-out nights are on Mondays plus a varied programme of international, interstate and local comedians. An all-in-one venue with a restaurant upstairs and DJs Mon–Sat after the shows. Tickets $15–20.

Comedy Store, 450 Parramatta Rd, corner Crystal St, Petersham (☎02/9564 3900; bookings recommended). International (often American) and Australian stand-up comics and meals Tues–Sun. Pub open 5pm–midnight.

New Theatre, 542 King St, Newtown (☎02/9873 3575). Professional and amateur actors (all working without pay) perform contemporary pieces with socially relevant themes. Tickets average $22.

NIDA Theatre, 215 Anzac Parade, Kensington (☎02/9697 7613). Australia's premier dramatic training ground – the National Institute of Dramatic Art – where the likes of Mel Gibson, Judy Davis and Colin Friels started out also offers student productions for talent-spotting. Tickets $18.

The Performance Space, 199 Cleveland St, Redfern, opposite Prince Alfred Park (☎02/9319 5091). Stages experimental performances.

Stables Theatre, 10 Nimrod St, Darlinghurst (☎02/9361 3817). Has a mission to develop and foster new Australian playwrights. Around $18.

Theatresports (☎02/9281 7666; bookings ☎02/9699 3444). Improvised genius with teams competing against each other. The theatrical games are at Belvoir St Theatre most Sunday evenings (see opposite), or occasionally at other venues around town. Tickets cost about $16.

Cinemas

The commercial movie centre of Sydney is on George Street, south of the Town Hall, where you'll find Hoyt's (☎02/9267 9877), Village (☎02/9264 6701), and Greater Union (☎02/9267 8666); the last has another complex, the Pitt Centre, nearby at 232 Pitt St. There is also a brand-new Hoyt's multiplex at the Broadway Shopping Centre, on Broadway near Glebe (☎02/9211 1911), and another new mainstream multiplex, Reading Cinemas, at Level 3, Market City Shopping Centre, Haymarket (☎02/9280 1202). Tuesdays are reduced-price (around $7) here and at all three chains, including their suburban outlets. In the summer, an open-air cinema glows in the hot dark: the Moonlight Cinema, in the Centennial Park Amphitheatre (Oxford St, Woollahra entrance; Tues–Sun, films start 8.45pm, tickets from 7.30pm or via Ticketmaster on

☎13 6100), showing classic, arthouse and cult films. See p.108 and p.162 for details of Sydney's annual film festivals.

Chauvel Twin Cinema, Paddington Town Hall, corner of Oatley Rd and Oxford St, Paddington (☎02/9361 5398). Varied programme of Australian and foreign films plus classics. Discounts on Monday and Tuesday.

The Dendy, MLC Centre, Martin Place (☎02/9233 8166). Dendy rhymes with trendy: cinema, café, bar and pool room complex; daily noon–midnight. Plus a wildly decorated branch within the music venue *Metro* at 624 George St (☎02/9264 1577), complete with trompe l'oeil, and the newest addition, Dendy Newtown, 261 King St (☎02/9550 5699), with attached café, bar and bookshop. Prestige new-release films. $7.50 on Mon.

Encore Cinema, 64 Devonshire St, near Central Station, Surry Hills (☎02/9281 6493). Programme of retro, cult, camp and trash films; also late-night films Fri and Sat night. The foyer café is open late. Occasional Hip Hop Culture nights combining films and live DJs.

Globe Cinema, 200 Parramatta Rd, Stanmore (☎02/9569 0488). Good mix of mainstream, cult and independent films, often screening with shorts; look out for the odd event such as director talks. Cheap prices plus $7.50 Sunday double bills and $6 bargain days. Licensed bar.

Govinda's Movie Room, 112 Darlinghurst Rd, Darlinghurst (bookings ☎02/9380 5162 or 9360 7853 for recorded programme information). Run by the Hare Krishnas, (but definitely no indoctrination) it shows two films every night from a range of classics and recent releases. The $14 movie and dinner deal (vegetarian buffet) is popular and you may need to book (see p.145).

Hayden Orpheum Picture Palace, 380 Military Rd, Cremorne (☎02/9908 4344). Charming heritage-listed four-screen cinema built in 1935 with the splendid Art Deco interior intact as is the old-fashioned friendly service. The main cinema has never dispensed with its Wurlitzer organ recitals preceding the Saturday and Sunday night films. Mainstream and new releases. $7 on Tuesday

Palace Cinemas is a chain of four inner-city cinemas showing foreign language arthouse and new releases; $7.50 on Monday. The cinemas are: Academy, 3a Oxford St, corner of South Dowling St, Paddington (☎02/9361 4453); Verona, 17 Oxford St, corner of Verona St, Paddington (☎02/9360 6099), with a groovy bar/café; Norton, 99 Norton St, Leichhardt (☎02/9550 0122), the newest with bookshop and cybercafé; and Walker, 121 Walker St, North Sydney (☎02/9959 4222).

Panasonic Imax Theatre, Southern Promenade, Darling Harbour (☎9281 3300). State-of-the-art giant cinema screen showing four films designed to thrill your senses, at $13.95 a go.

Art galleries and exhibitions

"Metro" (see p.150) has comprehensive listings of all the art galleries and current exhibitions – which tend to be concentrated in Paddington, and there are at least four small galleries on King Street, Newtown.

Aboriginal and Tribal Art Centre, 1st floor, 117 George St (☎02/9247 9625). Huge collection of traditional Aboriginal art from around Australia. Daily 10am–5pm.

Artspace, The Gunnery Arts Centre, 43–51 Cowper Wharf Rd, Woolloomooloo (☎02/9368 1899). In a wonderful location, showing provocative young artists. Tues–Sat 11am–6pm.

Australian Centre for Photography, 257 Oxford St, Paddington (☎02/9332 1455). Photographic exhibitions. Tues–Sat 11am–6pm.

Dreamtime Gallery, Shop 35, The Rocks Centre, 12–26 Playfair St, The Rocks (☎02/9247 1380). Traditional Aboriginal art including didgeridoos (live didj played weekends). Also a branch at the Opera House. Daily 9.30am–5.30pm.

Hogarth Aboriginal Art Gallery, 7 Walker Lane, Paddington (☎02/9360 6839). Extensive collection of work by contemporary Aboriginal artists, both tribal and urban and special exhibitions. Tues–Sat 11am–5pm.

Ivan Dougherty Gallery, corner of Albion Ave and Selwyn St, Paddington (☎02/9385 0726). National and international contemporary art; forums and performances sponsored by the College of Fine Arts, University of NSW. Mon–Fri 10am–5pm, Sat 1–5pm.

Josef Lebovic, 34 Paddington St, Paddington (☎02/9332 1840). Renowned print and graphic gallery specializing in Australian and international prints from the nineteenth and twentieth centuries, as well as vintage photography. Tues–Fri 1–6pm, Sat 11am–5pm.

Lewis Morley Photographers Showcase Gallery, 76 Parramatta Rd, Stanmore (☎02/9516 5191). Lewis Morley is the British photographer who took the famous photo of Christine Keeler in the 1960s; he decamped to Australia in the early 1970s. Changing exhibitions of international and Australian photographers. Thurs & Fri 11am–4pm, Sat & Sun 11am–5pm.

The Performance Space, 199 Cleveland St, Redfern, opposite Prince Alfred Park (☎02/9698 7235). Experimental multimedia and plastic arts: installations, sculpture, photography and painting. Wed–Fri noon–6pm, Sat noon–5pm.

Ray Hughes Gallery, 270 Devonshire St, Surry Hills (☎02/9698 3200). Has a stable of high-profile contemporary Australian and New Zealand artists. Openings monthly, with two artists per show. Tues–Sat 10am–6pm.

Roslyn Oxley, 8 Soudan Lane, Paddington (☎02/9331 1919). Avant-garde videos and installations among the Australian and international offerings. Tues–Fri 10am–6pm, Sat 11am–6pm.

Festivals and events

The Sydney year is interspersed with festivals and events of various sorts that reach their peak in the summer. The City of Sydney Council has a City Infoline (☎02/9265 9007) for details of events year round or you can consult their Web site (*www.sydneycity.nsw.gov.au*). The **New Year** begins with a spectacular **fireworks** display from Harbour Bridge, filling the sky above the city centre and Darling Harbour. There's a brief hiatus of a week or so until the annual **Festival of Sydney**, an exhaustive and exhausting arts event that lasts for the rest of **January** and ranges from opera-in-the-park, concerts, plays, and outdoor art installations to circus performances. About fifty percent of the events are free and are based around urban public spaces, focusing on Circular Quay, The Domain and Darling Harbour; the remainder – mostly international performances – can cost a packet. The general programme is usually printed in the *Sydney Morning Herald* in October while a full 80-plus-page programme is available nearer the time. There's also a **fringe festival** based at the Bondi Pavilion. From Boxing Day to the end of January, Darling Harbour hosts its own festival, linked with the Festival of Sydney. Most of the attractions are aimed at children, but there's also a free promenade jazz festival.

Australia Day on January 26 is a huge celebration in Sydney, with activities focused on the water. There's the Coca-Cola Amatil Marathon, where Sydney's passenger ferries race from Fort Denison to the Harbour Bridge, the Tall Ships Race, from Bradley's Head to the Harbour Bridge, a 21-gun salute fired from the Man O'War steps at the Opera House, and an aerial display of military planes. The **Australia Day Regatta** takes place in the afternoon, with hundreds of yachts racing all over the water, from Botany Bay to the Parramatta River. There are also events at The Rocks and Hyde Park, and at Darling Harbour, where the day culminates at around 9pm with a fireworks display. In addition, many museums let visitors in for free. Besides all this, there are at least two outdoor music events to choose from. An all-day outdoor rock concert, **Survival** (☎02/9331 3777), which celebrates Aboriginal culture and acts as an antidote to the mainstream white Australia Day festivities is held at Waverly Oval near Bondi. On the same day the **Big Day Out** is a huge outdoor rock concert, held at the Showground at Homebush Bay, featuring around 50 of the best local and international acts (tickets around $65).

An entirely different side of Sydney life is on view at the impressive summer **Surf Carnivals**, staged regularly by local surf lifesaving clubs; check the newspapers for details.

At the end of **February** the city is engulfed by the **Sydney Gay and Lesbian Mardi Gras** (see pp.156-157). Another big event is the **Royal Easter Show**, an agricultural and garden show in late **March/early April**, based at the Sydney Showground at Homebush Bay. For twelve consecutive days (with the second weekend always the Easter weekend) there is a frantic array of amusement-park rides, fireworks, parades of prize animals, a rodeo and wood-chopping displays – it's when the country comes to the city.

The **International Film Festival** takes over many of the city's screens in **June** (see box on p.108); and the **City to Surf Race**, an eight-kilometre fun run from the city to Bondi, happens every **August**. In spring, from September to early October, **Carnivale** (free call ☎1800/064 534) celebrates "vibrant collaborations in the fields of theatre, music and dance". The Labour Day weekend in early **October** is marked by the **Manly International Jazz Festival** (☎02/9977 1088), with several free outdoor, waterfront events and a few indoor concerts charging entry. This is followed by the very Italian **Blessing of the Fleet** at Darling Harbour (☎02/9286 0100). Every alternate (even-numbered) year, the **Biennale of Sydney**, takes place over six weeks from mid-September until early November, with provocative contemporary art exhibitions at various venues and public spaces around town.

The year is brought to a close by the **Sydney to Hobart Yacht Race**, when it seems that half of Sydney turns up at or on the harbour on December 26 to cheer the start of this classic regatta and watch the colourful spectacle of two hundred or so yachts setting sail for a 630-nautical-mile slog.

Listings

Airlines (domestic) Aeropelican (☎13 1300), to Newcastle; Ansett Australia (2nd floor, 55 Oxford St, 19 Pitt St and 32 Martin Place; ☎13 1300), Australia-wide; Eastern Australia Airlines (☎02/9693 1000), to Armidale, Canberra, Coffs Harbour, Dubbo, Grafton, Lord Howe Island, Moree, Narrabri, Newcastle, Port Macquarie, Tamworth and Taree; Hazelton Airlines (☎13 1713), to Albury, Armidale, Bathurst, Broken Hill, Casino, Cobar, Cudal, Dubbo, Griffith, Lismore, Merimbula, Moruya, Mudgee, Narrandera, Orange, Parkes and Wagga Wagga; Impulse Airlines (☎13 1381), to Glen Innes, Inverell, Kempsey, Newcastle and Port Macquarie on the north coast; International Aviation (free call ☎1800/810 008), to Broken Hill and Mildura; Kendell Airlines (☎13 1300), daily services to Albury, Ballina, Coffs Harbour and Wagga Wagga; Qantas (70 Hunter St, corner of Phillip St; ☎13 1313), Australia-wide; Sydney Harbour Seaplanes (Lyne Park, Rose Bay; free call ☎1800/803 558), to Newcastle and Port Stephens; Tamair (free call ☎1800/647 878), to Tamworth.

Airlines (international) Aeroflot, 44 Market St (☎02/9262 2233); Aerolineas Argentinas, Level 2, 580 George St (☎02/9283 3660); Air Canada, Level 12, 92 Pitt St (☎02/9232 5222); Air Lanka, 64 York St (☎02/9321 9234); Air New Zealand, 5 Elizabeth St (☎13 2476); Air Niugini, Level 3, 100 Clarence St (☎1300/361 380); Alitalia, 118 Alfred St, Milsons Point (☎02/9922 1555); All Nippon (ANA), Level 32, Chifley Tower, 2 Chifley Square (☎02/9367 6700); British Airways, 201 Kent St (☎02/9258 3200); Canadian Airlines, Level 8, 80 Clarence St (☎1300/655 757); Cathay Pacific, 8 Spring St (☎13 1747); Continental, 64 York St (☎02/9244 2242); Delta, Level 9, 189 Kent St (☎02/9251 3211); Finnair, 64 York St (☎02/9244 2299); Garuda, 55 Hunter St (☎1300/365 330); Japan Airlines, Level 14, 201 Sussex St (☎02/9272 1111); KLM, 5 Elizabeth St (☎02/9231 6333); Lauda Air, Level 11, 143 Macquarie St (☎02/9251 6155); MAS-Malaysian Airlines, 16 Spring St (☎13 2627); Olympic, 3rd floor, 37–49 Pitt St (☎02/9251 1048); Qantas, 70 Hunter St, corner of Phillip St, and 468 Oxford St, Bondi Junction (☎13 1211); Royal Brunei, Suite 5208, MLC Centre, 19 Martin Place (☎02/9223 1566); Sabena, 64 York St (☎02/9344 2135); Scandinavian Airlines, 350 Kent St (☎02/9299 9800); Singapore Airlines, 17 Bridge St (☎13 1011); Swissair, 33 Pitt St (☎02/9232 1744); Thai International, 75 Pitt St (☎02/9251 1922); United, Level 5, 10 Barrack St (☎13 1777).

American Express, 92 Pitt St (Mon–Fri 8.30am–5.30pm, Sat 9am–noon; ☎02/9239 0666). Lost or stolen travellers' cheques ☎02/9271 1111.

Banks and foreign exchange Main branches of banks are mostly in the CBD, around Martin Place; hours are Mon–Thurs 9am–4pm, Fri 9am–5pm, with some suburban branches open later and on Saturday. ANZ, 20 Martin Place (☎02/9227 1911); Commonwealth Bank, 48 Martin Place (☎02/9378 2000); National Australia Bank, 300 Elizabeth St (☎02/9215 6789); Westpac, AMP Centre, 50 Bridge St (☎13 2032). Money can also be exchanged at American Express (see above); Thomas Cook, 175 Pitt St (☎02/9231 2523); Singapore Money Exchange, Eddy Ave (Mon–Sat 9am–7pm, Sun 9am–6pm); Travelex Australia, 37–49 Pitt St (daily 8am–6.45pm; ☎02/9241 5722); Western Union, 182 George St (daily 8.30am–5pm; ☎02/9241 2372).

Bus companies Central Coast Airbus (☎1300/367 470); Firefly Express (☎02/9211 1644), to Melbourne and Adelaide; Great Lakes Coaches (☎02/4983 1560), daily to Forster via Newcastle; Greyhound Pioneer, ticket offices at Eddy Ave, Central Station (☎02/9212 1500, nationwide reservations ☎13 2030); Keans Travel Express (Sydney ☎02/9281 9366, Muswellbrook ☎02/6543 1322), daily Sydney to Hunter Valley including Cessnock and Muswellbrook; McCafferty's (ticket office at Eddy Ave, Central Station; ☎02/9212 3433; nationwide reservations ☎13 1499), to Melbourne and Adelaide, Brisbane and Queensland; Murray's (Overseas Passenger Terminal, Circular Quay; ☎13 2251), to Canberra three times daily from Circular Quay, Central or Strathfield; Pioneer Motor Service (Shop 1, Sydney Coach Terminal, Eddy Ave; ☎1300/368 100), Sydney to Brisbane via the north coast with stops including Byron Bay (a pass is available – see "Basics" p.32); Port Stephens Coaches (☎02/9281 9366 or free call ☎1800/045 949), daily to Port Stephens at 2pm from Bay 14 Eddy Ave via the outskirts of Newcastle; Premier Motor Service (☎1300/368 100), daily to Bega via the south coast, with one service daily continuing on to Eden (a pass is available – see "Basics" p.33); the service is also available from the airport, both domestic and international terminals. Prior's Scenic Express (☎02/4472 4040 or free call ☎1800/816 234), five times weekly from the airport (bookings only) and Central Station to the Southern Highlands including Kangaroo Valley, thence to Moruya or Narooma via the south coast.

Bus terminal Sydney Coach Terminal, corner of Eddy Ave and Pitt St, next to Central Station (daily 6am–10.30pm; ☎02/9281 9366).

Bus tickets Make bookings at the Traveller's Information Service at the bus terminal (☎02/9281 9366), at one of the Bus Booking Centres with locations at the corner of Springfield and Orwell streets, Potts Point (☎02/9368 0299), and Shop 526, Royal Arcade, below the *Hilton Hotel*, 255 Pitt St (☎02/9264 3691); at Backpackers Travel Centre, Bronka Arcade, 157 Oxford St, Bondi Junction (☎02/9369 1331) and the Imperial Arcade, Pitt St near Centrepoint (☎02/9231 3699); or direct with the bus companies listed above.

Campervans and 4WD rental Australian Outback 4 Wheel Drive Hire Co., 184 Elizabeth St, City (☎02/9281 9676); Brits Australia (182 O'Riordan St, Mascot; ☎02/9667 0402 or free call ☎1800/331 454), campervans, 4WDs and camping gear, one-way to Adelaide, Alice Springs, Brisbane, Cairns, Darwin, Melbourne and Perth; Campervan Rentals (31/9 Ward Ave, Kings Cross; ☎02/9326 9865), fully equipped vehicles; Daytona Rentals (164 Parramatta Rd, Ashfield; ☎02/9797 0166), affordable 4WD rates; Jay & Jay Campervan Rentals (94 Bryant St, Padstow; ☎02/9773 4349), campervans and motor homes; Koala Camper Rentals (182 O'Riordan St, Mascot; ☎02/9599 3533 or free call ☎1800/998 029), campervans and 4WDs, one-way deals to Adelaide, Alice Springs, Brisbane, Broome, Cairns, Darwin, Melbourne and Perth; Maui (9 Wollongong Rd, Arncliffe; ☎02/9597 6155 or free call ☎1800/227 279), two-, four- and six-berth campervans and converted 4WDs with one-way rentals available between Sydney and other depots: Adelaide, Alice Springs, Brisbane, Cairns, Darwin, Melbourne and Perth; Sunseeker Campervans (9 Wollongong Rd, Arncliffe; ☎02/9597 6445), one-way rental available to Adelaide, Alice Springs, Brisbane, Cairns, Darwin, Melbourne and Perth. Travellers Auto Barn (see "Cars – buying and selling" overleaf) also offer budget campervan rental from $65 per day.

Camping equipment and rental Kent St in the city behind the Town Hall is nicknamed "adventure alley" for its preponderance of outdoor equipment stores; the best-known is Paddy Pallin at no. 507. Cheaper options include disposal shops such as Boss Disposals, 708 George St, and Mitchell King Disposals, 323 and 327 Pitt St, and suburban K-Mart stores and hostel notice boards. Only a few places rent gear, mostly based in the suburbs, with weekend rent of a backpack or sleeping bag from $15 each, and a tent from $20: try Alpsport, 1045 Victoria Rd, West Ryde (☎02/9858 5844) or Tramping 'n' Camping, 30 Bronte Rd, Bondi Junction (☎02/9387 4095).

Car rental There are scores of car-rental firms in Sydney, and most of them seem to have a branch in William St, Kings Cross. The big four, with expensive new model cars, are also at the airport, charging from around $55–70 for a small manual: Avis, airport (☎02/9353 9000) and 214 William St, Kings Cross (☎02/9357 2000); Budget (☎13 2727), 93 William St, Kings Cross (☎02/9339 8888); Hertz (☎13 3039), airport and elsewhere including corner of William and Riley streets, Kings Cross; Thrifty, airport (☎02/9669 6677) and elsewhere, including 75 William St, Kings Cross (☎02/9331 1385). There are cheaper deals with Airport Rent a Car/Advantage, 12 Princes Highway, Arncliffe (☎02/9599 3000; *www.car-rentals.net.au*); Bayswater, 120 Darlinghurst Rd, Kings Cross (☎02/9360 3622), which has low rates including insurance, but limited km; Kings Cross Rent-a-Car, 169 William St, Kings Cross (☎02/9331 1366), which is open daily and has low rates, but insurance is extra; and Network, which has several branches, including 51 William St, Kings Cross (☎02/9361 0022), offering good-value one-way rentals. The Jalopy Shoppe, 690 Parramatta Rd, Croydon (☎02/9798 8666), rents and sells cars; and Rent-a-Ruffy, 33 Pittwater Rd, Manly (☎02/9977 5777), has cheap, older-model cars.

CARS – BUYING AND SELLING

Sydney is the most popular place to buy a car or campervan in which to travel around Australia; the information below is specific to buying a car in NSW – for general background on buying and selling a car, see Basics p.36.

Before you start looking for wheels, pick up the NRMA's complimentary *Worry Free Guide to Buying a Car* from the NRMA offices at 388 George St, City or 17 Newland St, Bondi Junction (☎13 2132). If you're a member of a motoring association overseas, you'll have reciprocal membership of the NRMA (otherwise there's a $40 initial joining fee then the annual charge is $46), which entitles you to roadside assistance and a $125 inspection and appraisal of a potential purchase (call ☎02/9892 0355 to book a vehicle inspection). The *Weekly Trading Post,* out every Thursday, has a big secondhand car section and it's worth checking through this to get a general idea of prices of cars bought direct from sellers; it's good also if you know a fair bit about cars and want to go it alone (see "Getting Around" in Basics for general advice), though you would probably need to rent a car to get to most of the far-flung suburban locations. The *Sydney Morning Herald's* Friday edition has a "Drive" supplement which has full-page ads for secondhand dealers and private used cars for sale at the pricier end of the secondhand market. Demand to see the pink slip (certificate of roadworthiness), as it proves the car is safe. If you're seriously thinking about buying, call ☎02/9600 0022 to check the validity of NSW-registered cars; quote registration, engine and chassis numbers and they will inform you of any payments owing or unpaid parking fines. Call the Roads and Traffic Authority (RTA; ☎13 2213) to double-check that the registration has not been cancelled.

As Sydney is the first place where most tourists arrive, the city is well-equipped with dealerships who will arrange to **buy back** your vehicle at the end of your trip for a 30–50 percent buy-back (see "Getting Around" in Basics for general advice). These include Auto **Becker**, 752 Parramatta Rd, Lewisham 2049, near Lewisham Station (☎02/9568 4455, fax 9337 4202); **Jalopy Shoppe**, 690 Parramatta Rd, Croydon 2132 (☎02/9798 8666, fax 9797 9604); **Travellers Auto Barn**, 177 William St, Kings Cross (☎02/9360 1500; *www.travellers-autobarn.com.au*); and **Travel Car Centre** (54 Orchard Rd, Brookvale 2100; ☎02/9905 6928; *www.travelcar.com.au*), which has higher-range cars starting around the $5000 mark, all eight years or younger – campervans and 4WDs are a speciality.

The Backpackers Car Market, Kings Cross Car Park, Level 2, Ward Ave (daily 9am–6pm; ☎02/9358 5000, fax 9358 5102 or free call ☎1800/808 188; *www.carmarket.com.au*) is the only place where it's legal for travellers to resell their cars at the Cross – selling on the street is not allowed. Dealers are barred, fees for sellers, if you have a pink slip, are set at $15 per day or $35 per week; inspection reports for the seller cost around $23 – call the car market for recommended mechanics. One of the advantages of the **car market** for sellers is that it's one of the few places where you will be able to sell a car registered in another state. Many of the vehicles come ready equipped with camping gear and other extras at good prices: get here early for the best choice. But think carefully about whether you really want to buy a car that's already done the rounds of Australia. The guys will advise you and help with the paperwork, and they'll even oversee the exchanging of the contract to make sure everything's done properly, and arrange third-party property **insurance** ($190 for 3 months, $340 for 12 months) – the NRMA refuses to provide cover for overseas travellers. Another car market is held on Sunday at Flemington Market opposite Flemington Station, Austen Ave entrance (8am–4pm; ☎02/9818 3085), but is better for buying than selling: if you're trying to sell a vehicle that's travelled around Australia, particularly if the clock is past 200,000km, local buyers won't be interested; besides, fees for sellers are steep at around $60 per day (no bookings required).

Consulates Embassies are all in Canberra (see p.223), and it's usually easier to call them than to go to the consulates in Sydney. British Consulate General, Level 16, Gateway Building, 1 Macquarie Place (☎02/9247 7521); Canadian Consulate General, Level 5, 111 Harrington St (☎02/9364 3000); US Consulate General, Level 59, MLC Centre, 19–29 Martin Place (☎02/9373 9200).

Cycling The narrow maze of streets in Sydney's CBD and its traffic congestion, plus the fair number of hills in town, mean that cycling has never been as popular here as in Melbourne or Adelaide with their flat, wide streets, although more cycle lanes are beginning to appear. Bicycles are carried free on trains outside of peak hours (Mon–Fri 6–9am & 3.30–7.30pm) and on ferries at all times if there is room in the bicycle racks. The Roads and Traffic Authority (RTA; ☎13 2213) has some brochures listing bicycle routes which they will post out, but the best source of information is Bicycle NSW, with an office and attached bookshop at Level 2, 209 Castlereagh St, corner of Bathurst St (Mon–Fri 9am–5.30pm; ☎02/9283 5200). Two of their useful publications you can buy here are *Cycling Around Sydney* ($10) and *Discovering NSW and Canberra Bike and Walking Paths* ($18). Some recommended central bicycle shops for repairs and equipment include Clarence Street Cyclery, 104 Clarence St (☎02/9299 4962; mountain bikes); Wooleys Wheels, 82 Oxford St, Paddington (☎02/9331 2671); and Inner City Cycles, 31 Glebe Point Rd, Glebe (☎02/9660 6605). The cheapest **bike rental** is at Centennial Park Cycles, 50 Clovelly Rd, Randwick (☎02/9398 5027; open daily) with mountain bikes for $8 an hour, standard bikes and bikes for kids $6; Clarence Street Cyclery hire mountain bikes ($65 day, $110 weekend), as do Inner City Cycles ($30 per 24hr, $50 weekend; open daily).

Cycle Tours Australia offer a guided bike tour of Sydney (free call ☎1800/353 004 or book through YHA Travel; $45; 5hr; tours meet Sat & Sun outside Sydney Central YHA at 9am and head for the Sydney Cricket Ground, Centennial Park, Bronte Beach, Bondi and Watsons Bay concluding with a ferry trip to Circular Quay.

Didgeridoos You can make your own didgeridoo, and learn to play it, with Dreamtime Experience (☎02/9130 7650; Sundays only at Bondi Pavilion) and at $150 (including lunch) it's cheaper than buying a didgeridoo from a souvenir shop (from around $180). Matthew Lee, who takes the all-day workshop, learnt the craft from two years in Arnhemland.

Disabled travellers ACROD NSW, 24 Cabarita Rd, Cabarita, NSW 2137 (☎02/9743 2699, fax 9743 2899); People with Disabilities NSW (☎02/9319 6622). Barrier Free Travel, 36 Wheatley St, North Bellingen, NSW 2452 (☎ & fax 02/6655 1733), is a travel consultant service that can plan trips and give advice for a fee; they also publish a useful guide to Sydney, available direct or from the NSW Tourism Commission. Randwick Council (Customer Services, 30 Francis St, Randwick, NSW 2031; ☎02/9399 0999) make a real effort to get wheelchair people into the water, with wheelchair accessible ramps at Clovelly and Malabar beaches; they also publish a series of mobility maps which they will post out. For taxis, try Wheelchair Accessible Taxis (☎02/9332 0200) or ABC (☎13 2522). For more detailed information see p.21.

Emergency ☎000 for fire, police or ambulance.

Hospitals Sydney Hospital, Macquarie St (☎02/9382 7111); St Vincents Hospital, corner of Victoria and Burton streets, Darlinghurst (☎02/9339 1111).

Immigration Department of Immigration and Multicultural Affairs, 88 Cumberland St, The Rocks (☎02/9258 4555).

Internet access You can access the Internet for free at the State Library, Macquarie St (see p.111); two terminals are reserved for 15-minute usage bookable in person on the day, while two others are kept for 1-hour usage and are bookable over the phone with a waiting list of about a week in advance. Many local libraries also offer free or discounted Internet access but only to members. The City of Sydney Public Library (see "Libraries" overleaf) offers Internet access to non-members for $8 per hour (1hr booking only available) but it needs to be booked in advance in person. Many backpackers hostels have Internet terminals, and dedicated Internet places have sprung up all over Sydney, with a glut of places around Kings Cross. Global Gossip, open daily 8am–midnight, has two offices: 770 George St and 111 Darlinghurst Rd, Kings Cross; rates range from $2 per 10min to $10 per hour. *Internet Café* at Level 1, *Top of the Town Hotel*, 227 Victoria St, Darlinghurst (Mon–Fri 10am–8pm, Sat 11am–6pm), charges only $6 per hour. Kinko's, 175 Liverpool St, opposite Hyde Park, is open 24hr but charges $15 per hour. *Surfnet Café Manly*, 5a Market Lane, off The Corso, Manly (daily 10am–10pm; from $2 per 10 min to $8 per hr), is one of the cheapest as is the cybercafé at Shearer's Bookshop, 99 Norton St, Leichhardt (Mon–Fri 10am–10pm, Sat 10am–11pm, Sun 10am–7pm from $2 per 15min to $8 per hour). *Phone.Net.Café*, 73–75 Hall St, Bondi (daily 9am–9pm; from $1 per 5min to $10 per hr) is a lively café haunt in its own right, as is the *Well Connected Café* in Glebe (see p.142).

Left luggage Cloakrooms at Town Hall Station and Central Station (country trains) are both open Mon–Sat 9am–4.40pm ($1.50 per 24hr); also lockers at the airport and the Sydney Coach Terminal (both $4 per 24hr).

Libraries City of Sydney Public Library, just behind the Town Hall on Sydney Square (Mon–Thurs 9am–7pm, Fri 9am–6pm, Sat 9am–noon; ☎02/9265 9470). Also see the State Library, p.111.

Maps The Map Shop, Land Information Centre, 23 Bridge St (☎02/9228 6111), a wide range of maps including touring, National Park and bushwalking maps.

Markets The two best markets are the Paddington Market on Saturday and the more downbeat weekend market on Glebe Point Rd (see p.123 and p.119, respectively). The Balmain Market (Sat 7.30am–4pm; see p.120) at St Andrews Church, Darling St, Balmain, is similar to Glebe in atmosphere. The Rocks Market (Sat & Sun 10am–5pm; see p.103), on George St (Harbour Bridge end), is more touristy but worth a look, while Paddy's Market (Fri, Sat & Sun 9am–4.30pm; see p.109), in Haymarket near the Entertainment Centre and Chinatown, is Sydney's oldest, selling fruit and veg, deli products, meat and fish, plus large quantities of bargain-basement clothes and toys.

Medical centres Broadway Medical Centre (185–211 Broadway near Glebe; ☎02/9212 2733), general practitioners open Mon–Sat, no appointment necessary; Skin Cancer Centre, Ground floor, 403 George St (☎02/9262 4877); Sydney Sexual Health Centre, Nightingale Wing, Sydney Hospital, Macquarie St (☎02/9382 7440), free tests, counselling and condoms; Travellers Medical and Vaccination Centre, 7th floor, 428 George St (☎02/9221 7133).

Motorbikes Wentworth St in the city has a concentration of motorbike salesrooms for new models. For secondhand motorbikes there's Sydney Motorcycle Hire, at 23 Euston Rd, Alexandria, NSW 2015 (☎02/9565 5788; *www.dropbears.com.au*), where you can also rent bikes – from $38 per day, helmet $4 extra. Maverick Motorcycles, 133 Parramatta Rd, Homebush, NSW 2140 (☎02/9746 2005, fax 9746 2006), specializes in selling and exchanging travellers' motorbikes – a free helmet with every one; also swaps for cars.

NRMA Head office, 388 George St (☎13 2132). Road maps of NSW and other states, a useful map of Sydney and other cities, comprehensive accommodation directories and lots more information, much of it free to members of associated organizations. There's also a handy free Australia-wide accommodation booking service (Mon–Fri 8am–7pm, Sat 8.00am–1.00pm; ☎13 1122)

Parks and wildlife information The NPWS (Cadman's Cottage, 110 George St, The Rocks; ☎02/9247 8861) has details on Sydney Harbour National Park and books tours to its islands; they do not arrange camping permits. There are also NPWS offices at Nielson Park (see p.126), North Head (see p.135), La Perouse (see p.137) and Botany Bay National Park (see p.137). The Sydney Map Shop, part of the Surveyor-General's Department (23–33 Bridge St; ☎02/9228 6111) sells detailed bushwalking maps of NSW.

Pharmacy Blake's Pharmacy, 28 Darlinghurst Rd, Kings Cross (daily 8am–midnight; ☎02/9358 6712). Late-night pharmacy information ☎02/9235 0333.

Police Headquarters at 14 College St (☎02/9339 0277); emergency ☎000.

Post office The GPO building on Martin Place will be reopening sometime in early 2000. In the meantime, the General Post Office is located across the road, at 130 Pitt St (Mon–Fri 8.15am–5.30pm, Sat 9am–1pm). Poste restante will remain permanently at the post office in the Hunter Connection shopping mall at 310 George St (Mon–Fri 8.15am–6pm), opposite Wynyard Station. Log your name in the computer to see if there is any post for you before queueing. The address to receive mail is still: Poste Restante, Sydney GPO, Sydney NSW, 2000.

Public holidays Sydneysiders like days off, and in addition to the Australia-wide public holidays (see Basics, p.51), the following are celebrated only in NSW: Bank Holiday – first Monday in August; Labour Day – first Monday in October; Queen's Birthday – first Monday in June.

Swimming pools Most pools are outdoors and unheated, and open from the long weekend in October until Easter; entry fees are between $2 and $3. The best pool, and open all year, is the heated North Sydney Olympic Pool, Alfred South St, Milsons Pl. (Mon–Fri 5.30am–9pm, Sat & Sun 7am–7pm), an outdoor pool (covered in winter), near the water's edge – an easy walk from Milsons Point train station. Another heated outdoor pool is at Victoria Park, City Rd next to Sydney University (Mon–Fri 6am–7.15pm, Sat & Sun 7am–5.45pm). Inner-city outdoor pools are at Prince Alfred Park, Chalmers St, Surry Hills (daily 6.30am–8pm) and the Andrew "Boy" Charlton in The Domain (see p.112). The brand new 50m swimming pool at Cook and Phillip Park, cnr of William and College streets, was not yet open at the time of writing; for details call ☎02/9265 9560. For the ultimate swimming experience, head out west to the Olympic site for the Sydney International Aquatic Centre (Mon–Fri 5am–10pm, Sat & Sun 6am–7pm; $4.50); it's very popular with kids with an area with waves and slides.

Taxis ABC (☎13 2522); De-Luxe Cab Company (☎02/9361 8222); Legion (☎13 1451); Premier (☎13 1017); RSL (☎13 1581); Taxis Afloat (harbour water taxis ☎02/9955 3222); Taxis Combined Services (☎02/9332 8888). The three major cab ranks are outside the *Regent Hotel*, George St, The Rocks; on Park St outside Woolworths, opposite the Town Hall; and at the Pitt St entrance to Central Station.

Telephones For peace and quiet, the Telstra Pay Phone Centre, 231 Elizabeth St, City (Mon–Fri 7am–11pm, Sat & Sun 7am–5pm) has private booths but is unattended so buy a phonecard or get change first. Global Gossip, 770 George St, Haymarket and 111 Darlinghurst Rd, Kings Cross, offer discount-rate international calls; both branches are open daily 8am–midnight.

Trains All out-of-town trains depart from the country trains terminal of Central Station. Information and booking 6.30am–10pm (☎13 2232). There are Countrylink Travel Centres at Central Station (☎02/9379 5036); Transport House, 11–31 York St (☎02/9224 4744); in the Queen Victoria Building Arcade at Town Hall Station (☎02/9379 3600); and at Circular Quay (☎02/9224 3400) and Bondi Junction Station (☎02/9379 4792). Interstate trains should be booked as early as possible, especially the *Indian Pacific* and Brisbane–Cairns trains.

Travel agents All Planet Travel, 11 Glebe Point Rd, Glebe, near Broadway (☎02/9556 1499; *www.allplanet.com.au*); do everything from international flights to bus passes. Backpackers Travel Centre, Shop 33, Imperial Arcade, near Centrepoint, Pitt St (☎02/9231 3699); Flight Centre, 52 Martin Place (☎02/9235 0166), also at several other locations, offer cheap domestic and international air tickets. STA Travel has many branches, including Shop 205, Broadway Shopping Centre, Bay St, Broadway (☎02/9211 2563) which is open daily. YHA Travel, 422 Kent St, behind the Town Hall (☎02/9261 1111) also has a branch at Sydney Central YHA, 11 Rawson Place off Eddy Ave (☎02/9281 9444) with excellent Sydney tours. For details of tours from Sydney.

Water sports Rose Bay Aquatic Hire, 1 Vickery Ave, Rose Bay (☎02/9371 7036) rents out catamarans ($25 first hour, $15 thereafter), windsurfers ($15 per hour), and motorboats (weekends $40 for the first two hours, $10 for each subsequent hour, plus charge for petrol; midweek $40 half-day, $60 full-day). Balmoral Windsurf, Sail and Kayak School is open all year at the Balmoral boatshed, southern end of the Esplanade, Balmoral (☎02/9960 5344), and rents out sailboards (from $20 per hour), kayaks ($10 hour) and catamarans ($30 hour) as well as giving sailboarding lessons (6hr sailboarding course over two mornings $150). Northside Sailing School, Spit Bridge, Mosman (☎02/9969 3972; *www.northsidesailing.com.au*) specializes in weekend dinghy sailing courses on Middle Harbour during the sailing season (Sept–April); tuition is in groups of up to four and the two-day course costs $280. They offer boats for rent (daily during the season) for $25 for the first hour and $15 for subsequent hours. Scotland Island Sailing School (☎02/9999 2285) gives two-day sailing courses on Pittwater from $200, year round, training on a 20ft small sloop with a chance to try out some old-fashioned sailing on a schooner. Experienced sailors can charter yachts from Sydney by Sail (☎02/9552 7561; *www.sydneysail.com*). Natural Wanders Sea Kayak Adventures (☎02/9555 9788) arranges sea-kayaking in the harbour and lessons for beginners.

One of the best places to dive is at Gordon's Bay in Clovelly, a declared inter-tidal protected area, and off the North and South Heads. Prodive Coogee, 27 Alfreda St, Coogee (☎02/9665 6333), offer boat and shore dives anywhere between Camp Cove and La Perouse (double boat dive with gear $135, double shore dive $105). Cronulla Dive Centre, 40 Kingsway, Cronulla (☎02/9523 7222) do local shore dives including Shiprock and the Botany Bay National Park on the Kurnell Peninsula on weekends; dives are free but gear rental costs $45 per day. They also organize dives and weekends away up and down the NSW coast. Dive Centre, 10 Belgrave St, Manly (☎02/9977 4355), offer shore dives to Shelley Beach, Fairlight, Little Manly and Harboard plus boat dives off North and South Head (boat dive with full gear $70, shore dive with gear $50).

Wine The Australian Wine Centre, at George and Alfred streets, Circular Quay, sells more than a thousand wines from around Australia. Mon–Sat 9.30am–6pm, Sun 10am–4pm.

Women The big events are the Reclaim the Night march in late November and events around International Women's Day in March. Contact the Women's Information and Referral Service (free call ☎1800/817 227 Mon–Fri 9am–5pm) for information on this and women's organizations, services and referrals, or try The Women's Library, 8–10 Brown St, Newtown (☎02/9557 7060; Tues–Fri 11am–8pm, Sat & Sun 11am–5pm), which collects and lends feminist and lesbian literature. The more academic Jesse Street National Women's Library (☎02/9896 3927; Mon–Fri 10am–2pm) is in the Town Hall; it is an archive collecting literature and material detailing Australian women's history and writing. The Feminist Bookshop is tucked away in Orange Grove Plaza on Balmain Rd, Lilyfield (☎02/9810 2666). For medical advice, contact the Women's Health Clinic, 139 Macquarie St, City (☎02/9247 1555).

Work If you have a working holiday visa, you shouldn't have too much trouble finding some sort of work in Sydney. Offices of the government-run Centrelink (☎13 2850), have a database of jobs; the most central offices are at George and Redfern streets, Redfern; 137 Crown St, Darlinghurst; and Level 6, Carousel Centre, Bondi Junction. The private agency Troy's (Level 1, 89 York St; ☎02/9290 2955), specializes in the hospitality industry. If you have some office or professional skills, there are plenty of temp agencies that are more than keen to take on travellers: flick through "Employment agencies" in the Yellow Pages. For a whole range of work, from unskilled to professional, the multi-national Manpower is a good bet (☎13 2502). Otherwise, scour hostel notice boards and the *Sydney Morning Herald* – Saturday's edition is best.

AROUND SYDNEY

If life in the fast lane is taking its toll, Sydney's residents can easily get away from it all. Right on their doorstep, golden beaches and magnificent national parks beckon, inter-woven with intricate waterways. Everything in this part of the chapter can be done as a day-trip from the city, although some require an overnight stay to explore more fully. See the box on pp.172–73 for some of the huge variety of tours on offer.

North of Sydney the Hawkesbury River flows into the jagged jaws of the aptly named **Broken Bay**, which streaks across the map like a bolt of lightning. The entire area is surrounded by bush, with the huge spaces of the **Ku-Ring-Gai Chase National Park** in the south and the **Brisbane Waters National Park** in the north. Beyond Broken Bay, the **Central Coast** between Gosford and Newcastle is an ideal spot for a bit of fishing, sailing and lazing around. **Newcastle** is more attractive than its reputa-tion as a coal and steel city might suggest. Immediately beyond, however, are the beau-tiful vineyards of the **Hunter Valley**, which make a great day out, with visits to winer-ies interspersed with some gentle driving on country roads.

To the **west**, you escape suburbia to emerge at the foot of the beautiful **Blue Mountains**, where the scenic Hawkesbury-Nepean river valley is home to historic rural towns such as **Richmond** and **Windsor**.

Heading **south**, the **Royal National Park** is an hour's drive away, while on the coast beyond are a string of small, laid-back towns – Waterfall, Stanwell Park, Wombarra – with beautiful, unspoilt **beaches**. The industrial city of **Wollongong** and neighbouring **Port Kembla** are impressively located between the Illawarra Escarpment and the sea, but of paltry interest to visitors, although more interesting spots cluster around. Inland, the **Southern Highlands** are covered with yet more national parks, punctuated by pleasing little towns such as **Bundanoon** and **Berrima**.

North

The **Hawkesbury River** widens and slows as it approaches the South Pacific, joining Berowra Creek, Cowan Creek, Pittwater and Brisbane Water in the system of flooded valleys that form **Broken Bay**. The bay and its surrounding inlets are a haven for anglers, sailors and windsurfers, while the surrounding bushland is virtually untouched. Three major national parks surround the Hawkesbury River: **Ku-Ring-Gai Chase** in the south, **Brisbane Waters** facing it across the bay, and **Dharug**, inland to the west.

The **Pacific Highway** up here, partly supplanted by the Sydney–Newcastle Freeway, is fast and efficient, though not particularly attractive until you're approaching Ku-Ring-Gai Chase; if you want to detour into the park or towards Brooklyn, don't take the free-way. The **rail** lines follow the road almost as far as Broken Bay, before they take a scenic diversion through Brooklyn and Brisbane Waters to Woy Woy and Gosford.

Ku-Ring-Gai Chase National Park

Ku-Ring-Gai Chase is much the best known of New South Wales's national parks and, with the Pacific Highway running all the way up one side, is also the easiest to get to. The bushland scenery is crisscrossed by walking tracks, which you can explore to seek out Aboriginal rock paintings, or just to get away from it all and see the forest and its wildlife. Only 24km from the city centre, the huge park's unspoilt beauty is enhanced by the presence of water on three sides: the Hawkesbury, its inlet Cowan Creek, and the expanse of **Pittwater**, an inlet of Broken Bay. From Palm Beach you can take a boat cruise (see p.171) through all these waters to the park's most popular picnic spot at **Bobbin Head**, with a colourful boat marina. At the **Kalkari Visitor Centre** (daily 9am–5pm), on the Ku-Ring-Gai Chase Road, you can watch videos about the area's Aboriginal heritage and the wildlife you might encounter, pick up information about walks in the park or take a guided walk led by volunteers. The Birrawanna Walking Track leads from here to the park headquarters, which can also be approached by car further along Ku-Ring-Gai Chase Road. The NPWS **Bobbin Head Information Centre** (daily 9am–4pm; ☎02/9457 1049) is located inside the Art Deco *Bobbin Inn* which also has a very pleasant restaurant, popular for weekend breakfasts and Sunday afternoon jazz. There are four road entrances to the park and $7.50 entrance fee for cars. Without your own transport, the best way to get here are the ferries to the Pittwater side, or by train to Turramurra Station and then a private Hornsby Bus #577 (☎02/9457 8888) to the Bobbin Head Road entrance; some buses continue down to Bobbin Head itself.

Waratah Park and Pittwater

One of Sydney's oldest wildlife reserves, **Waratah Park** (daily 10am–5pm; $12.90, family $34; koala cuddling hourly 11am–4pm & 4.30pm; ☎02/9968 1111) sits in the middle of this stunning scenery on Namba Road, off Mona Vale Road. Waratah is most famous as the home of **Skippy**, the bush kangaroo, television's first marsupial star: you can still see Skippy (or at least her fifth- or sixth-generation descendant) amongst the free-ranging kangaroos, and visit the Ranger Station where most of the filming was done. To get here, take the train to Chatswood (North Shore line) and then bus #284 from stand "S" of the interchange (☎02/9450 1236 for times).

From West Head at the northeastern corner of Ku-Ring-Gai Chase, there are superb views across Pittwater to the Barrenjoey Lighthouse at Palm Beach (see p.137). The **Garigal Aboriginal Heritage Walk** (3.5km circuit) heads from West Head Road to the Aboriginal rock engravings and hand art, the most accessible Aboriginal art site in the park. The only place to **camp** is *The Basin* (☎02/9451 8124 for bookings) on Pittwater, reached via the Palm Beach Ferry Service from Barrenjoey Road, Palm Beach wharf (departing hourly 9–11am & 1–5pm, Sat & Sun until 6pm; $7 return; ☎02/9918 2747 to check times; see p.137 for Palm Beach account). Facilities at the site are minimal so bring everything with you.

If you want to stay here in rather more comfort, there's a very popular **YHA hostel** (☎02/9999 2196, fax 9997 4296; rooms ③–④, dorms ①–②; phone bookings essential and well in advance for weekends) at Halls Wharf. It's one of New South Wales' most scenically sited – a rambling old house surrounded by bush and with a verandah where you can feed rainbow lorikeets and look down onto the water; sailing lessons can also be arranged. You must bring everything with you – the last food (and bottle) shop is at Church Point where the ferry departs to Halls Wharf (last departure Mon–Fri 7.15pm, Sat & Sun 6.30pm; call ☎02/9999 3492 for times; $6 return) or there's a 24-hour service with Pink Water Taxi (☎018/238 190). The same friendly ferry service can also get you to and from **Scotland Island** at the southern end of Pittwater, which it stops at on the 40-minute round trip from Church Point. The bush-clad island is residential only with no sealed roads or shops, just a school, a kindergarten and a bush fire brigade. There are two **direct buses** to Church Point: #E86 from Central Station or #156 from Manly Wharf. It's then a ten-

MORE CUDDLY KOALAS

If meeting Skippy and cuddling the koalas at Waratah is your kind of thing – and who could resist – there are several other hands-on wildlife experiences around Sydney you might like to try.

The **Koala Park Sanctuary** (daily 9am–5pm; adults $10, children 4–14 $5, under 4s free) was established as a safe haven for koalas in 1935 and has since opened its gates to many other Australian natives – wombats, possums, kangaroos and birds of all kinds. Koala patting sessions are held daily at 10.20am, 11.45am, 2pm and 3pm. It's around 25km north of Sydney, not far from the Pacific Highway on Castle Hill Road, West Pennant Hills. To get here on public transport take the train from Central Station to Pennant Hills and then bus #651 or #655 towards Glenorie (Mon–Sat).

At **Featherdale Wildlife Park** (daily 9am–5pm; $12, children 4–14 $6, under 4s free, family $30), cuddly koalas are the special attraction. Although they're generally placid, koalas have claws like Edward Scissorhands, so don't forget that wild koalas can turn nasty. Featherdale is at 217 Kildare Rd, Doonside, 30km west of Sydney off the Western Highway between Parramatta and Penrith; take the train to Blacktown Station (Emu Plains line) and then bus #725.

Australia's Wonderland (☎02/9830 9167) is not far away, a huge family entertainment complex encompassing shows, giant waterslides, roller-coasters and the **Australian Wildlife Park** (☎02/9830 9167), where the "meet the animals" experience includes koalas, kangaroos, echidnas, wombats, emus, goannas, saltwater crocodiles (from a discreet distance) and forest birds in simulated natural habitats – it's wildly popular with children. The complex is open daily from 10am to 5pm. Entry to the wildlife park costs $13 ($9 for children 4–12), or $37 ($26 for children) for the whole complex, including all rides and events. Australia's Wonderland is on Wallgrove Road, Rooty Hill again not far off the M4 approaching Penrith. To get there by public transport, take a train to Rooty Hill Station (on the Emu Plains line) and get a special Busways service (☎02/9625 8900 for times) from outside the Commonwealth Bank. Alternatively, AAT Kings (☎02/9252 2788) offers a bus transfer and admission package.

minute uphill walk. Alternatively, bus #190 from Wynyard runs up the coast to Newport, where you can have a drink at the *Newport Hotel* and then catch a water taxi.

The Hawkesbury River

One of New South Wales' prettiest rivers, with bush covering its banks for much of its course and some interesting old settlements alongside, the **Hawkesbury River** has its source in the Great Dividing Range and flows out to sea at Broken Bay. For information about the many national parks along the river, contact the NPWS in Sydney (☎02/9247 8861) or at 370 Windsor Rd in Richmond (☎02/4588 5247). Short of chartering your own boat, the best way to explore the river system is to take a cruise (see box opposite).

Upstream: Wisemans Ferry

The first ferry across the Hawkesbury River was opened by Solomon Wiseman in 1827, some way inland at the spot now known as **WISEMANS FERRY**. The crossing forged an inland connection between Sydney and the Hunter Valley via the convict-built Great North Road. Unfortunately, travellers on this isolated route were easy prey for marauding bushrangers and it was largely abandoned for the longer but safer coastal route. Today it's a popular recreational spot for day-trippers – just a little over an hour from Sydney by car, and with access to the **Dharug National Park** over the river by a free 24-hour car ferry. Dharug's rugged sandstone cliffs and gullies shelter Aboriginal rock engravings which can be visited only on ranger-led trips during school holidays; there's a **camping** area at Mill Creek (call Gosford NPWS on ☎02/4324 4911 for details of both walks and camp-

EXPLORING THE HAWKESBURY RIVER SYSTEM

Brooklyn, just above the western mass of Ku-Ring-Gai Chase National Park, and easily reached by train from Central, is the base for Hawkesbury River Ferries (☎02/9985 7566) whose River Boat Mail Run still takes letters, as well as tourists, up and down the river. Departures are from Brooklyn Wharf on Dangan Road (Mon–Fri 9.30am, connecting with the 8.16am train from Central Station in Sydney and 8.17am from Gosford; Wed & Fri 1.30–4pm; $25 including morning tea, or good-value combined train-boat ticket; booking essential). Hawkesbury River Ferries also offers two-hour coffee cruises towards the mouth of the river (Mon, Tues & Thurs 1.30pm, Sat 11am & 1.30pm, Sun 11am; $12), as well as a standard ferry service to Patonga at the edge of Brisbane Waters National Park (Mon–Thurs departs Brooklyn 1.30pm, departs Patonga 2.15pm; Sat Brooklyn 11am & 1.30pm, Patonga 11.45am & 2.15pm; Sun Brooklyn 11am & Patonga 11.45am; $5 one-way, $10 return; bikes $2).

Gosford's Public Wharf is the starting point for the *MV Lady Kendall* (☎02/4323 1655 for details; bookings essential), which cruises both Brisbane Water and Broken Bay (Mon–Wed, Sat & Sun, daily during school & public holidays, 10.15am & 1pm; 2hr 30min).

Windsor is the base for Windsor River Cruises (☎02/9831 6630), with cruises Sun & Wed only: the coffee cruise (2hr 15min; $15), the Bridge to Bridge cruise from Windsor to Kangaroo Point in Brooklyn ($55 includes lunch at Wisemans Ferry; 8.30am–5.30pm), and the Tizzana Winery cruise including wine tasting and a smorgasboard lunch ($50; 6hr).

Woy Woy is also a port of call for the *MV Lady Kendall* (see above) at 10.35am and 12.10pm.

KAYAKING

Hawkesbury Kayak Tours (☎02/9875 2287). Day-trips from various Hawkesbury locations; no experience necessary.

BOAT AND HOUSEBOAT RENTALS

The **Hawkesbury Boating Centre**, on Dangar Road, opposite the railway station in Brooklyn (☎02/9985 7252) hires out small boats which seat up to eight people. For houseboats, the **New South Wales Travel Centre** in Sydney (☎02/9667 6050) has details of operators such as Ripples Houseboats, 87 Brooklyn Rd, Brooklyn (☎02/9985 7788), which sleep up to six people from around $600–850 for a weekend or $650–1100 for five days, depending on the season; and Able Hawkesbury River Houseboats, on River Road in Wisemans Ferry (free call ☎1800/024 979), with prices starting from just under $1000 per week for six people (BYO linen).

ing bookings, which are essential for weekends and holiday periods). Open to walkers, cyclists and horse-riders but not fume-belching vehicles, the **Old Great North Road** was literally carved out of the rock by hundreds of convicts from 1829; you can camp en route at the Ten Mile Hollow camping area. Driving north of Wisemans Ferry by car along **Settlers Road**, another convict-built route, you'll come to **St Albans**, where you can partake of a cooling brew (or stay a while) at a pub built in 1836, the hewn sandstone *Settlers Arms Inn* (☎02/4568 2111; all rooms en-suite; ⑦). The pub is set on two-and-a-half acres and much of the fruit and vegetables for the delicious home-cooked food is organically grown on site.

Other **accommodation** for a river retreat includes the blue-painted *Wisemans Ferry Inn* on the Old Great North Road (☎02/4566 4301; ④–⑤), an old inn dating partly from 1817, with characterful rooms upstairs sharing bathrooms and en-suite motel-style rooms outside at the back. Bistro meals are served daily and there's entertainment on Sunday afternoons. *Del Rio Riverside Resort* (☎02/4566 4330, fax 4566 4358; all en-suite cabins ⑤–⑥), in Webbs Creek across the Webbs Creek ferry, 3km south of Wisemans Ferry, which is a campsite with a Chinese restaurant, swimming pool, tennis court and

TOURS FROM SYDNEY

Tours from Sydney span the range from a day spent staring out the window of a bus to two days canyoning in the Blue Mountains. Listed below are a couple of regular bus-tour operators, but you'll almost certainly have a better time with one of the outfits who specialize in small-group tours, quite often with an emphasis on physical activities such as bushwalking, horse-riding, white-water rafting or abseiling. Many hostels organize their own trips – most often to the beach – which are usually fun and tremendously good value. YHA and VIP card holders are offered substantial discounts on many tours – we have quoted full prices only.

One-way tours can be the next best thing to going by car: small groups in minibuses travel from Sydney to Melbourne (for example), taking detours to attractions along the way that you'd never be able to reach on public transport.

RETURN TOURS

AAT Kings (☎02/9252 2788). One of the largest operators, its big-group bus tours cover city sights, wildlife parks, the Blue Mountains, Jenolan Caves, the Hawkesbury River and the Hunter Valley. Admissions and hotel pick-ups and drop offs included in price.

Aussie Bush Discoveries (☎02/9622 1557, bookings on ☎0418/962 215; *ausbush@mpx.com.au*). Guided by a qualified biologist, these minibus tours to the Blue Mountains include a wildlife park, a gentle bushwalk and a boomerang-throwing lesson. Pick-ups from Circular Quay at 7.30am; return from Parramatta by RiverCat ferry. Maximum ten people per group; $125 per person.

Blue Mountains Canyon Tours (☎ & fax 02/9371 5859; *www.chilli.net/~canyon*). Exploring the Blue Mountains' deep canyons requires a thrilling mixture of abseiling down waterfalls, swimming through cave slots, bushwalking and rock climbing. Wet canyoning is offered Oct–April, dry canyoning is available all year. Depending on the area or the number of abseils, trips range from $79–219.

CityRail (☎02/9217 8812). Day-trips by rail can be very good value, generally covering all transport and entry fees – trips include the Blue Mountains, and the Hawkesbury River (which includes a cruise). Details and tickets from CityRail at Circular Quay or Central Station.

Kangaroo Valley Expeditions (☎ & fax 02/4465 1438, free call ☎1800/651 438 or book through YHA Travel). Small group minibus weekend camping trips (Fri 7pm–Sun 7pm; $195 all inclusive). Base camp overlooks Kangaroo Valley River, and there's a swimming pool. Activities include an exploration of Kangaroo Valley Village, Morton National Park, and canoeing on the river.

Motorcycle Tours (☎02/9545 4321). Trips to anywhere you fancy around Sydney on Harley-Davidsons; 2hr $140, full day $395.

White Thunder Adventures (☎02/9905 9314 or 9989 8400). Day-trips include white-water rafting on the Shoalhaven River, abseiling at Diamond Bay in Vaucluse, or canyoning in the Blue Mountains; all around $120.

Wildframe (☎02/9314 0658; *wildframe@S054.aone.net.au*). Two tours to the Blue Mountains, the first for fit walkers, the second for lazier types. The Grand Canyon Eco-tour is a small group bushwalk (max 16) through the Grand Canyon. You'll see kangaroos

golf course. Better still is *Rosevale Farm Resort*, 3km along Wisemans Ferry Road en route to Gosford (☎02/4566 4207; on-site vans ③–④), with inexpensive camping in extensive bushland close to Dharug National Park. For considerably more luxury, check out houseboat rentals (see box overleaf).

The Upper Hawkesbury: Windsor and Richmond

About 50km inland from Sydney and just a few kilometres apart, Windsor and Richmond are two of five towns founded by Governor Macquarie in the early nineteenth century to capitalize on the fertile, well-watered soil of the Upper Hawkesbury River area. You can in the national park and learn how to throw a boomerang; full-day tour (8am–6pm; $55) with pick-ups from Kings Cross and city accommodation. The Blue Mountains Bush Tour ($76) is a more relaxed day with short bushwalks and lunch at Jemby-Rinjah eco-lodge (see p.193), plus the kangaroos and boomerang throwing.

Wonderbus (☎02/9555 9800, or bookings at the YHA office ☎02/9261 1111 or through YHA hostels; *www.wonderbus.com.au*). Good-value day tours to the Blue Mountains, including wildlife-watching at morning or dusk and a satisfying bushwalk ($60). The day-trip can be extended into an overnight package including abseiling ($180), a trip to the Jenolan Caves ($170) or horse-riding ($230). Another day-tour goes to the Hunter Valley and Port Stephens – wine tasting followed by a dolphin cruise ($99).

ONE-WAY TOURS

Ando's Outback Tours (☎02/9559 2901 or free call ☎1800/228 828; *www.outback-tours.com.au*). Popular five-day tour from Sydney to Byron Bay but taking an inland route, getting well off the beaten track and out bush; $369, everything included; a $40 return to Sydney or a $30 transfer to Brisbane are available if you want; tours leave every Sun; book well in advance.

Oz Experience (Australia-wide ☎1300/300 028; Sydney ☎02/9368 1766; *www.ozex.com.au*). A cross between transport and tours that go a little off the beaten track, with a hop-on, hop-off component lasting six months aimed at young independent travellers. Their scheduled routes include Sydney to Cairns in six days ($245) and Sydney to Melbourne in four days via the south coast, Canberra, the Snowy Mountains and Phillip Island ($165).

Pioneering Spirit (free call ☎1800/672 422). Another tour that heads to beach-heaven Byron, this three-day excursion goes via the Hunter Valley for a spot of wine-tasting; $175 including meals, accommodation and entry fees (or $220 if you want to return to Sydney). Departs Sydney every Friday.

Surfaris (free call ☎1800/634 951; *www.bay.web.com.au/surfaris*). Excellent six-day surfing trip, Sydney to Byron Bay; you're taught how to surf and judge the waves and more experienced folk often come along for the ride. Price ($385) includes gear, lessons, secluded camping by the beach with a chance to spot wildlife.

Wayward Bus (free call ☎1800/882 823; *www.waywardbus.com.au*). The excellent long-established Wayward Bus, based in Adelaide, offers three off-the-beaten tracks trips from Sydney with the option of hopping on and off over a six-month period. The bus seats twenty people, with the driver acting as your guide; price includes transport only – you can choose to stay at hostels, campsites or motels en route, depending on your budget. The five-day Over the Top Tour runs between Sydney and Melbourne via the Blue Mountains, Jenolan Caves, Bathurst, Cowra, Canberra, Victoria's Alpine Way and through Beechworth and Bright to Melbourne ($190). You can take a shortened three-day version to Canberra ($140). The Fruit Bowl trip from Sydney to Adelaide is aimed at getting working backpackers fruitpicking jobs; as well as dropping in on Katoomba and the Jenolan Caves, it takes in four fruit-growing areas in NSW, Victoria and SA ($190; 4 days). The Circuit trip follows the same route as the Over the Top Tour to Canberra, then heads through the Southern Highlands back to Sydney ($110; 2 days). For other Wayward Bus tours from Melbourne and Adelaide, see p.810 and p.701.

take a **train to** Windsor and Richmond from Central Station in Sydney via Blacktown. **WINDSOR** is probably the best preserved of all the historic towns in the riverlands, witj a lively centre of narrow streets, spacious old pubs and numerous historic colonial buildings. **The Hawkesbury River Museum and Tourist Information Centre on** Thompson Square (daily 10am–4pm; 02/4577 2310; museum $2.50) is a good place to start exploring, and the *Macquarie Arms Hotel,* claimed to be the oldest in Australia, is the best place to end up for a cool beer. From Windsor, Putty Road (route 69) heads north through beautiful forest country, along the eastern edge of the Wollemi National Park (see p.191), to Singleton in the Hunter Valley (see p.181)

RICHMOND's attractions include an old graveyard and settlers' dwellings, plus its unspoilt riverside setting. Cinema buffs could take in a bargain-priced film at the Regent Twin Cinema (☎02/4578 1800; Mon–Sat $7, Sun $5), a classic, beautifully decorated old theatre. **Moving on**, the Bells Line of Road (Route 40), from Richmond to Lithgow via Kurrajong, is a great scenic drive; all along the way are fruit stalls stacked with produce from the valley. There's a wonderful view of the Upper Hawkesbury Valley from the lookout point at Kurrajong Heights, on the edge of the Blue Mountains, and you can take it all in from the *Balcony View Café* (☎02/4567 7498). Another scenic drive from Richmond to the Blue Mountains, emerging near Springwood (see p.189), is south along the Hawkesbury Road, with the Hawkesbury Heights Lookout halfway along providing panoramic views. Not far from the lookout is the brand-new solar-powered *Hawkesbury Heights YHA Hostel* (☎02/9261 1111; ③), with more views from its secluded bush setting, and no chance of overcrowding with only two beds in each of the six rooms.

The Central Coast

The shoreline between Broken Bay and Newcastle, known as the **Central Coast**, is characterized by large **coastal lakes** – saltwater lagoons almost entirely enclosed, but connected to the ocean by small waterways. The northernmost, **Lake Macquarie**, is the biggest saltwater lake in New South Wales. People in a hurry can bypass the Central Coast altogether on the Sydney–Newcastle Freeway, which runs some way inland, but to see a bit more of the coastal scenery and the lakes, stay on the old Pacific Highway. A further detour would take you from Gosford to **Terrigal** and then right along the narrow coastal strip via **The Entrance** and **Budgewoi** to rejoin the Pacific Highway at **Elizabeth Bay**. The fit and intrepid can get here by bike: from Manly, head up the northern beaches, hop on the Palm Beach Ferry Service from Barrenjoey Road, Palm Beach wharf (☎02/9918 2747; see p.137 for Palm Beach account), to Patonga, then continue up through Woy Woy and Gosford to the coast. Otherwise you can take the **train** to Gosford or Woy Woy, following a very scenic route. You can get to the area direct from Sydney airport: the Central Coast Airbus (☎02/4332 8655) provides several services daily (also picking up in the city centre): stops include Gosford, Erina, Terrigal and The Entrance. For **tourist information** on the whole region, and accommodation bookings, call Central Coast Tourism (free call ☎1800/806 258). Within the Central Coast area there is a well-developed **bus service**, run by a collection of operators: Busways Peninsula (☎02/4362 1030), Busways Central Coast (☎02/4392 6666), Gosford Bus Service (☎02/4325 1781), Peninsula Bus Lines (☎02/4324 1255 or 4362 1188) and The Entrance Red Bus Services (☎02/4332 8655). You can also take a **ferry** from Palm Beach to Patonga and walk from there to Pearl Beach. For **taxis**, call Central Coast Taxis (☎13 1008).

Gosford and around

To get anywhere on the Central Coast, you need to go through **GOSFORD**, perched on the north shore of Brisbane Water and just about within commuting distance of Sydney. Its proximity to the city has resulted in uncontrolled residential sprawl along much of the Central Coast, which has put a great strain on the once-unspoilt lakes. Although there's plenty of accommodation in and around Gosford – details from **Central Coast Tourism**, near the train station at 200 Mann St (Mon–Fri 9am–5pm, Sat 9.30am–3pm, Sun 10am–2pm; ☎02/4385 4074) – there's not much incentive to stay. The main reason to come is that it's the gateway to two excellent national parks, and it offers an insight into Sydney's past in the form of Old Sydney Town. Beyond the national parks, Pearl Beach and nearby Patonga are idyllic beach retreats.

Old Sydney Town (Wed–Sun, daily during school & public holidays, 10am–4pm; $17), southwest of Gosford just off the Pacific Highway, is a reconstruction of Sydney as it looked in the early years of the penal settlement. "Everyday" scenes, such as a convict's escape or a flogging, are acted out, and a token gesture towards Aboriginal culture has been made in the form of a Koorie Trading Post, which sells souvenirs. Most tour buses include Old Sydney Town in their itineraries. Take Peninsula Bus Lines #38 to Old Sydney Town from Gosford.

Brisbane Waters National Park, immediately south of Gosford, is the site of the **Bulgandry Aboriginal engravings**, which are of a style unique to the Sydney region, with figurative outlines scratched boldly into sandstone. The site, no longer frequented by the Guringgai people – whose territory ranged south as far as Sydney Harbour and north to Lake Macquarie – is 7km southwest of Gosford off the Woy Woy Road. Tiny **Bouddi National Park** is 20km southeast along the coast, at the northern mouth of Broken Bay, and is a great spot for bushwalking with camping facilities at Putty Beach, Little Beach and Tallow Beach: book through the NPWS office at 207 Albury St, Gosford (☎02/4324 4911), which also has information on both parks.

Surrounded by Brisbane Waters National Park, undeveloped **PEARL BEACH** is a small community which expands on weekends. There are holiday houses to rent, but no other accommodation. The settlement doesn't even have a bottle shop. Besides a popular café and a beachfront licensed restaurant (*Pearls on the Beach*; ☎02/4342 4400; licensed & BYO, bookings advised, closed Mon–Wed, no dinner Sun), there's a general store (daily 8am–6pm) also selling petrol, a real estate agent who can arrange holiday lets (☎02/4341 7555, fax 4341 9665; around $400–700 per week), and some tennis courts. The community is classified and zoned residential so there can be no commercial development – and that's the way people here like it, peaceful, and decidedly friendly. The very pretty, sheltered beach, popular with families, has a relaxing open access saltwater pool at one end (perfect for a discreet night-time skinny-dip). You can walk from the end of Crystal Avenue to the neighbouring beach settlement of **PATONGA** visiting a lookout and the **Crommelin Native Arboretum** en route. The walk takes about 45min and the best day to undertake it is the last Sunday of the month when the **Patonga Beach market** is held (8am–4pm) with arts and crafts, food stalls and buskers. You can also get to Patonga by taking a ferry from Palm Beach (see p.137).

To get to Pearl Beach or Patonga, you can take the Busways Peninsula **bus** (☎02/4362 1030) from Woy Woy train station.

Terrigal, Avoca Beach and The Entrance

Twelve kilometres southeast of Gosford, **TERRIGAL** is one of the most enjoyable spots on the Central Coast, a family-oriented beach resort with foodie and New Age inclinations. **Central Coast Tourism** at Rotary Park, Terrigal Drive (summer daily 9am–5pm, winter closed Sun; ☎02/4385 4074), is a good source of information on the whole region, and does free **accommodation** bookings. If you're after a holiday unit (around $350–950 weekly, depending on season and number of rooms) contact Hunters Real Estate, 104 Terrigal Esplanade (☎02/4384 1444). The de luxe YHA-affiliated *Terrigal Beach Backpackers Lodge*, at 12 Campbell Crescent (☎ & fax 02/4385 3330; *rockwell@enterprise.net.au*; rooms ③, dorms ①), is only one minute's walk from the beach, and is run by a friendly, well-travelled Canadian. Bikes and boogie-boards are provided free. Terrigal is a popular spot for sailboarding: contact Terrigal Sailboard Hire (☎02/4365 2355) if you want to join in.

Terrigal does well on the **eating** front, with plenty of adventurous cafés along the Esplanade such as *The Boatshed* at no. 84 specializing in good value all-day breakfasts and gourmet sandwiches and burgers. The best café, however, is tucked away in Church Street near the hostel: *Patcino's*, a small corner place offering good cakes and excellent coffee, with an Indonesian chef taking over at the weekend (Fri and Sat 6–9pm; bookings ☎02/4385 1960). The best **restaurant** meal, with fabulous views, is at the eastern end of the beach at *The Gallery*. The really delicious contemporary food has a

Mediterranean/Middle Eastern twist, and desserts are delicious. If it's beyond your budget, then *Haven Seafood* is just nearby for fish and chips. To **get** to Terrigal, take Peninsula Bus Lines #80, #81 or #82 from Gosford; #81 also links Terrigal and Avoca Beach.

Six kilometres to the south, and altogether quieter, **AVOCA BEACH** is especially popular with surfers. A large, crescent-shaped and sandy beach between two headlands, it has its own surf lifesaving club – and a safe children's rock pool. Its pleasant small-town atmosphere is enhanced by the cute Avoca Beach Theatre on Avoca Drive (☎02/4382 2156), a surviving early-1950s cinema that has changed little. **Accommodation** is limited to a couple of motels and one caravan park, *The Palms*, at 160 The Round Drive (☎02/4382 1227; cabins ⑤). The best bet is to rent holiday units – call George Brand Real Estate (☎02/4382 1311) for stacks of listings; weekly rental rates start at $350. A good place to hang out on the beachfront is the *Beachfront Café and Restaurant* (☎02/4382 1622; daily 9am–late), with suitably fishy dishes. The café also lays on weekend entertainment, ranging from bands to poetry readings.

Avoca Beach offers endless opportunities for **outdoor activities**. Central Coast Adventures (☎02/4381 0326) organizes abseiling and canyoning; Central Coast Kayak Tours (☎02/4381 0342) does kayaking trips from $75; and Central Coast Surf School (☎02/4382 1541) gives lessons (1hr 30min; $15, including gear) on weekends at local beaches. Peninsula Bus Lines serves Avoca Beach: take **bus** #79 from Gosford.

Further north, Tuggerah and Munmorah lakes meet the sea at **THE ENTRANCE**, a beautiful spot with water extending as far as the eye can see. Naturally it's a favourite fishing spot – and with swarms of **pelicans**, which turn up for the afternoon fish-feeds daily at 3.30pm (free) at Memorial Park, near the visitor centre (see below). The beaches and lakes along the coast from here to Newcastle are crowded with caravan parks and motels, and with places offering the opportunity to fish, windsurf, sail or waterski, although less attractive than places further north, they make a great day-trip or weekend escape from Sydney. Pro Dive Central Coast, 96 The Entrance Rd (☎02/4334 1559), arranges **scuba-diving** lessons, daily boat dives and rents out snorkelling and dive gear. The **Entrance Visitors Centre**, Marine Parade (daily 9am–5pm; ☎02/4385 4074), can help with **accommodation**.

Newcastle

NEWCASTLE is a blue-collar town enlivened by its waterside location, and with an alternative feel provided by a big dose of surf culture and a large student community. New South Wales' second city, with a population of around a quarter of a million, it suffers from comparison with nearby Sydney and from denigration by Sydneysiders who may never have set foot here. In fact, it has plenty going for it, especially as it's recently had a much-needed facelift: years of accumulated soot has been scraped off its stately buildings, riverside gardens have been created in front of the city centre, and an old wharf has been converted into a waterside entertainment venue. The BHP steelworks, the docks and the slag heaps still loom in the background but, for a major industrial and port city, Newcastle is surprisingly attractive. You might not choose to spend your entire holiday here, but it can be a good base for excursions, particularly to the nearby Hunter Valley (see p.181). The surf beaches are wonderful, and there are some more sheltered sandy beaches around the rocky promontory at the mouth of the Hunter.

Newcastle was founded in 1804 for convicts too hard even for Sydney to cope with, but the river is the real reason for the city's existence. Coal was brought down it from the fields of the Hunter Valley, to be exported around the country and indeed around the world; coal exports are still an important source of income, and the proximity of the mines encouraged the establishment of other heavy industries. In recent years Newcastle made world headlines, when Australia's worst earthquake struck the area two days after Christmas in 1989, killing twelve people and destroying several buildings.

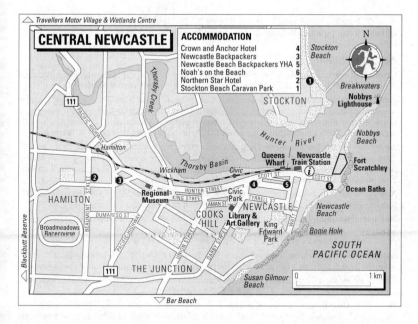

Rebuilding has been imaginative – for example, the use of colourful mosaics in the pavement of Beaumont Street in Hamilton, one of the hardest-hit areas.

Arrival, public transport and information

If you're not driving, you'll arrive by train at Newcastle **train station**, right in the heart of the city on Scott Street, or by bus at nearby Watt Street. A novel way to arrive (or depart) right on Newcastle Harbour is by **seaplane** (see p.162).

Heading west from Newcastle train station, Scott Street eventually becomes Hunter Street, the city's main street. Newcastle's hub is the pedestrianized Hunter Street Mall, with its large department stores and shops. Continuing west along Hunter Street, the Civic train station marks the city's cultural and administrative district focused around City Hall and Civic Park. A short walk south of here is an area called Cooks Hill, focused on café- and restaurant-lined Darby Street; the other eat street is Beaumont Street in Italian-dominated Hamilton, 3km west of the city.

It's easy to get around using Newcastle's **public transport** system. Newcastle Bus and Ferry Services (☎02/4961 8933) has an information booth at the west end of Hunter Street Mall on the corner of Perkins Street; bus fares are time-based with a one-hour ticket, allowing transfers, costing $2, an all day bus and ferry ticket costs $6; all can be bought on board. The one ferry operating goes to Stockton, departing from Queens Wharf (Mon–Sat 5.15am–11pm or midnight, Sun 8.30am–8.30pm; $1.40 one-way, $2.80 return). Two passenger train lines have several suburban stops, the most useful heading southwest from Newcastle Station (towards Sydney), with handy stops at Civic (for Darby Street) and Hamilton (for Beaumont Street), the other line runs northeast (towards Maitland). Weekly passes, combining bus and ferry ($26) or bus, ferry and train ($35) are also available from selected newsagencies.

The extremely helpful **Newcastle Tourist Information** (Mon–Fri 9am–5pm, Sat & Sun 10am–3.30pm; ☎02/4929 9299 or free call ☎1800/654 558; *www*

.hunter_region.org.au) is at 92 Scott St, east of the station towards the beach. Disabled travellers can pick up the useful *Newcastle Mobility Map* from here.

Accommodation

Crown and Anchor Hotel, corner of Hunter and Perkins streets, next to David Jones department store (☎02/4929 1027, fax 4927 0161). Inexpensive rooms in a pub; central location. ③.

Newcastle Backpackers, 42 and 44 Denison St, Hamilton (☎02/4969 3436). A home-style hostel in two houses run by a friendly young family. Although it's some distance from the beach, the owner runs people down most days for free surfing lessons, boards included. Located 3km from the city centre (in possibly Newcastle's trendiest area), but take bus #260 or call for a pick-up. Rooms ③, dorms ①.

Newcastle Beach Backpackers YHA, 20 Pacific St, corner of King St (☎02/4925 3544, fax 4295 3944; *yhanewcastle@hunterlink.net.au*). New YHA in an impressively restored, spacious Queen Anne-style building just 250m from the surf and right in the centre of town. There are four-bed, doubles, twins and family rooms. Internet access. Rooms ③, dorms ①.

Noah's on the Beach, corner of Shortland Esplanade and Zara St (☎02/4929 5181, fax 049/265 208). Most rooms in this upmarket, modern motel have ocean views, and there's room service. ⑦–⑧.

Northern Star Hotel, 112 Beaumont St, Hamilton (☎02/4961 1087, fax 4961 2944). Has a great location on a restaurant- and café-lined street northwest of the centre. All rooms are en-suite, spacious, clean and have fridges, TV, tea and coffee facilities and ceiling fans. ⑤.

Stockton Beach Caravan Park, Stockton Beach (☎02/4928 1393). Picturesquely sited on an extensive beach, and only a ferry ride from the centre (but a much longer car ride). On-site vans ④.

Travellers Motor Village, 295 Maitland Rd, Mayfield West (☎02/4968 1394). Campsite with units for rent, about 7km northwest of the centre. Cabins ⑤, villa ⑥.

West End Guesthouse, corner of Hunter and Stewart streets (☎02/4961 4446). A well-priced imaginatively decored guesthouse. Small enough (seven rooms, all en-suite) to have a personal touch and lots of advice provided. TV lounge, kitchen, rooftop terrace and BBQ. ③.

The City

Newcastle has whole streetscapes of beautiful **Victorian terraces** that would put Sydney's to shame – pick up a *Newcastle City of Heritage and Enterprise* map for $1.95 from the tourist office, or the briefer (and free) *Newcastle Town Walk*, to guide you around some of the old buildings. A couple of buildings in **Newcastle Harbour Foreshore Park** show the trend for the city's wealth of disused public architecture: on one corner of the park stands the beautiful Italianate brick **Customs House**, now a well-regarded café, bar and restaurant, with a tall watchtower. Nearby is the wooden two-storey **Paymasters House**, where you can sit with a coffee in its fine verandah café and contemplate the water.

The restored **Queens Wharf**, a landmark with its distinctive observation tower, is located on the south bank of the Hunter River. It's linked to the city centre by an elevated walkway from Hunter Street Mall and boasts *The Brewery*, a popular, stylish waterfront drinking spot. A **ferry** goes from here to Stockton which has a caravan park and beach. From the nearby Merewether St Wharf you can take a cruise on **William the Fourth** (third Sunday of the month; 11am & 2pm; 1hr 30min; $20; ☎02/4926 1200), a reproduction of the first Australian-built coastal paddlewheel steamship. It's also quite a sight to watch the **seaplanes** from Sydney land nearby the two wharfs.

Besides Newcastle's waterside attractions, there are a few other places that might be of interest. The **Newcastle Regional Museum**, 787 Hunter St (Tues–Sun 10am–5pm, daily during school holidays; free), housed in what began as a brewery in the 1870s, focuses on the history of the mining and steel industries of the area; the Supernova hands-on science centre is attached, much the best thing about the museum. If you're at a loose end, the **Newcastle Regional Art Gallery**, on Laman Street near Civic Park (Tues–Sun 10am–5pm; free), usually has an interesting temporary exhibition in addition to its permanent display.

Beaches and wildlife reserves

The city centre, positioned on a narrow length of land between the Hunter River to the west and the Pacific Ocean to the east, has several popular and pleasantly low-key beaches close by. **Newcastle Beach**, only a few hundred metres from the city on Shortland Esplanade, has patrolled swimming between flags, a sandy saltwater pool perfect for children, shaded picnic tables and good surfing at its southern end. It is a working harbour and the container ships and tugs on the horizon manage to look interesting rather than unlovely. At the northern end, the beautifully painted Art Deco-style **Ocean Baths** (daily 6am–2pm, until 6pm in spring and 10pm in summer; closed in winter; supervised; free) houses the changing pavilions for the huge saltwater pool, which has its own diving board.

Overlooking the water north of Newcastle Beach, **Fort Scratchley**, built in the 1880s, houses a maritime and military museum (Tues–Sun noon–4pm but check on ☎02/4929 2588 as it's volunteer-run; free). Beyond the fort is the long, uncrowded stretch of **Nobbys Beach**, with a lovely old beach pavilion. A walkway leads to Nobbys Head, where there is a nineteenth-century lighthouse and where you have views over the river to the port and the city.

If you follow Shortland Esplanade south from Newcastle Beach, you'll come to the huge expanse of King Edward Park, with good walking paths and cliff views over this rocky stretch of waterfront. One section of the rock ledge holds Australia's first manmade ocean pool, the **Bogie Hole**. Chiselled out of the rock by convicts in the early nineteenth century for the Military Commandant's personal bathing pleasure, it's still a fine spot for a swim. The cliffs are momentarily intercepted by **Susan Gilmore Beach** – secluded enough to indulge in some nude bathing. **Bar Beach** follows around the rocks, and it's a popular surfing spot, floodlit at night. More rocks separate it from the longer **Merewether Beach** next door, the southern end of which has a fabulous ocean baths, great for salty laps, and a separate children's pool. The *Merewether Hotel*, overlooking the beach, is a fine place to pause and have a drink.

Blackbutt Reserve is a large slab of bushland in the middle of Newcastle suburbia in New Lambton Heights about 10km southwest of the city (daily 9am–5pm; free), consisting of four valleys, including a remnant of rainforest, creeks, lakes and ponds and 20km of walking tracks to explore them. En route you'll see kangaroos, koalas, wombats, emus and other native animals in the reserve's wildlife enclosures. To get there, take the **train** to Kotara and walk to the Carnley Avenue entrance or take **bus** #216 or #217 via Kotara; for the entrances on Lookout Road you can take bus #363. As it's a little hard to find the tourist office produces a helpful free map which you might like to get first. Northwest of the city, the **Wetlands Centre**, Sandgate Road, Shortland (daily 9am–5pm; $2 donation), is situated on the wetlands of Hexham Swamp by Ironbark Creek and is home to a mass of birdlife. There are walking and cycling trails here, and the more intrepid can rent canoes from tourist information. You can reach the *Wetlands Centre* by train from Newcastle to Sandgate, from where it's a ten-minute walk.

Cafés and restaurants

The two streets to head for are **Darby Street**, close to the city centre, which has a multicultural mix of restaurants and some fairly hip cafés as well as some secondhand bookshops and retro clothes stores to browse in between coffees; and **Beaumont Street** in Hamilton, northeast of the city centre (take the train to Hamilton Station or bus #260), where there is a concentration of Italian places, as well as Turkish, Lebanese, Dutch and Indian.

Al-Oi-Thai, Shop 2, 50 Beaumont St (☎02/4969 1434). Delicious traditional Thai food served in stylish surrounds is justifiably popular. Lunch Wed–Sat, dinner Tues–Sun; BYO. Fronted by a cheaper express noodle bar serving superb noodle soups and fried noodles. There is another *Al-Oi-Thai* at 133 Darby St.

Dolomiti Gelato, 79 Beaumont St, Hamilton. Great home-made *gelati*, plus pasta and focaccia in a typically casual Italian café. Closed Sun.

Goldbergs' Coffee House, 139 Darby St. Popular, buzzy café is big and airy with modish green walls and polished wooden floors. The emphasis is on the excellent coffee, plus very reasonably priced eclectically modern meals. 8am–midnight. Licensed.

Italian Centre Restaurant, 44 Beaumont St, Hamilton (☎02/4961 4656). Good, authentic food in a homely restaurant above the Italian community centre. Upstairs balcony to sit out on. Closed Mon. Licensed.

Little Swallows Café, 54 Beaumont St, Hamilton (☎02/4969 2135). Simple place, a favourite daytime coffee hangout for Italian locals presided over by the friendly owner Paolo. Captures the earthy feel of a traditional Italian trattoria, with suitably generous portions. Daily 9am–10pm. BYO.

Market Square Foodcourt, upstairs in the Hunter Street Mall. Best place in the city centre, with a good range of food bars – Italian, Chinese, kebabs, roasts – and mightily generous salad sandwiches and fresh juices at the *Oak Dairy Bar*. Mon–Sat 8am–5pm, Thurs until 9pm.

Scott Street Café Restaurant, 19 Scott St (☎02/4927 0107). Smart, minimalist restaurant close to Newcastle Beach. The small seasonal dinner changes every six weeks, with contemporary-style dishes like King Prawn risotto with coriander and chilli to slaver over. BYO. Brunch Sat & Sun 10am–3pm, dinner Mon–Sat from 6pm.

Splash, 126 Darby St. Freshly cooked budget takeaway seafood; tempura prawns and crumbed calamari are among the offerings. Mon–Thurs 4.30–8.30pm, Fri–Sun 11am–9pm.

Taj Takeaway, 120 Darby St. Quick and tasty Indian takeaway – and also a grocery. Daily 7am–11pm.

Taters, 78 Darby St. Stuffed baked potatoes, with a variety of fillings from seafood to chilli con carne with nachos. Great salads too. Daily till 8pm.

Vega Café, 131 Darby St. Ventures beyond the usual clichéd veggie burgers to produce meat-free dishes inspired by Indian, Lebanese, Moroccan, Italian, Thai and Indonesian cuisines. Cute little space with colourful walls and ceiling fans.

View Factory, corner of Scott and Telford streets (☎02/4929 4580). This brasserie/café/gallery near the waterfront is arty, airy and slick. All the café favourites from big breakfasts to focaccia and nachos plus a pricier restaurant menu (nightly from 6pm) making creative use of seafood and fine ingredients. There's even a pool table. Licensed.

Drinking and nightlife

For listings, check out the "That's Entertainment" in Wednesday's *Post*. During term time, the students of Newcastle University add a lot of life to the city, but there is always a thriving **live music** scene. On Friday and Saturday nights the city pubs on Hunter Street, parallel King Street and perpendicular Watt Street all have bands, many of them free.

The Bar on the Hill, Newcastle University campus at Callaghan (☎02/4921 5000). Hosts live bands; all welcome. Take bus #260.

Beaches Hotel, opposite Merewether Beach (☎02/4963 1574). The only place to go on a Sunday night; live bands.

The Brewery, 150 Wharf Rd. Popular waterfront drinking hole which has a crowded bistro.

Hotel Delany, 134 Darby St. Stylish renovated pub popular with the business crowd with several bars and a bistro; free rock bands out back Wed–Sat, and a more genteel keyboard player in the front bar Thurs from 6pm.

The Kent, corner of Cleary and Beaumont streets, Hamilton. Beautifully renovated old pub and jazz venue (Wed, Sat & Sun) with leadlighting. Busy every night, but with several refuges, including a wonderful plant-filled beer garden and a great bistro. Pool comp Mon nights, Trivia Tues.

Newcastle Workers Club, corner of King and Union streets (☎02/4926 2700). Big gigs by touring bands.

Entertainment and culture

The area known as "the cultural precinct", near Civic Park on King, Hunter and Auckland streets, is the location for three refurbished Art Deco venues; pick up a monthly calendar from the tourist office for details of what's on. The **Civic Theatre** (☎02/4929 1977) hosts mainly big-budget musicals and theatre. At the **University Conservatorium of Music**, on

Auckland Street (☎02/4929 4133), there are often free lunchtime concerts as well as evening performances, while the grand **City Hall** (☎02/4929 9370) has occasional classical music events. **Film** buffs should head for the small, single screen Kensington Cinema, 299 Hunter St, opposite Civic Station or the three-screen Showcase City Cinemas, 31–33 Wolfe St, off Hunter Street Mall (☎02/4929 5019), both show arthouse and mainstream releases.

Listings

Banks and exchange Commonwealth Bank, Hunter Street Mall, has foreign exchange.

Car rental Ara (☎02/4962 2488), from $49 including standard insurance, with 100km mileage; Thrifty (☎02/4942 2266).

Environment The Wilderness Society, 59 Hunter St, opposite the post office (☎02/4929 4395).

Left luggage The train station has a luggage room (daily 8am–5pm; $1.50 per article).

Post office Newcastle GPO, Hunter St, NSW 2300 (Mon–Fri 8am–5pm; ☎02/4926 1922).

Taxi Taxi Services (☎02/4962 2622).

Tours Hunter Vineyard Tours (☎02/4991 1659) are excellent and good value; they do pick-ups from Newcastle for an extra charge; see p.182 for details. For Hunter Valley Day Tours (☎02/4938 5031) see p.182.

Trains Newcastle Station enquiries ☎02/4962 9119.

Travel Agent Newcastle Travel, 68 Hunter St, corner Watt St (☎02/4926 1855). Sells bus tickets for coaches going up the North Coast.

The Lower Hunter Valley

In Australia (and, increasingly, worldwide) the **Hunter Valley** is synonymous with fine **wine**. The first vines were planted 150 years ago and are mainly the two classic white-wine varieties of Semillon and Chardonnay, with Pinot Noir and Shiraz dominating the reds. In what seems a bizarre juxtaposition, this is also a very important **coal-mining region**: in the upper part of the valley especially (see p.168), the two often go hand-in-hand. By far the best-known area, however, is in the Lower Hunter Valley around the old country town of Cessnock. Even the town's jail has its own vineyard, and the prisoners have produced some prize-winning wines. One of the appeals of the Hunter Valley wine country is the bush and farming feel of the place with the vast plantings of vineyards seemingly lost among bushland, forested ridges, red-soiled dirt tracks, and paddocks with grazing cattle.

CESSNOCK itself is much the best place to base yourself if you plan to stay overnight, while most of the vineyards are clustered around nearby **Pokolbin**. Pick up the excellent free fold-up maps and brochures on the Hunter Valley from the NSW Travel Centre in Sydney or the **Cessnock Visitors Centre**, at Turner Park, Abedare Road (Mon–Fri 9am–5pm, Sat 9.30am–5pm, Sun 9.30am–3.30pm; ☎02/4990 4477; *www.winecountry.com.au*); the latter can also book accommodation. If you're going to tour the wineries, try and do so during the week; at weekends both the number of visitors and the prices go up. In February, when the place is flooded with wine-lovers enjoying the Dionysian delights of the **Hunter Valley Vintage Festival**, accommodation is impossible to find. Another lively time is October, when Wyndham Estate hosts **Opera in the Vineyards** (free call ☎1800/675 875), followed by the **Jazz in the Vines** Festival (☎02/4938 1345) based at Tyrell's.

Getting there and around

To get to Cessnock, catch a train from Central to Maitland or Newcastle and then a bus to Cessnock with Rover Motors (☎02/4990 1699). Alternatively, Keans Travel Express (Sydney ☎02/9281 9366; Muswellbrook ☎02/6543 1322) goes direct from Sydney to the Hunter Valley once daily (terminating at Scone), taking just over two hours with stops including Kurri Kurri, Neath, Cessnock, Pokolbin and Muswellbrook.

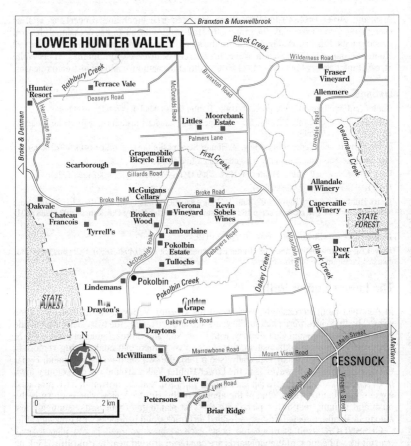

LOWER HUNTER VALLEY

If you're without transport (there's no public transport to the wineries) – or don't want to meander unintentionally off-road after excessive wine-tasting – **vineyard tours** are a good option. Most are exhausting return trips from Sydney (see box p.172) but a local operator, Hunter Vineyard Tours (☎02/4991 1659) runs bus tours (small groups only) visiting five well-chosen wineries over six hours, all offering tastings ($29, including pick-up from Cessnock; with Newcastle or Maitland pick-ups $34; $16 extra with lunch). The more expensive Hunter Valley Day Tours (☎02/4938 5031) will tailor-make tours to also include surrounding scenic areas such as Barrington Tops. Pedal power is also popular: either **rent bikes** from Grapemobile, on the corner of McDonalds and Gilliards roads, Pokolbin (☎ & fax 02/4991 2339; $25 per day, $15 half-day), or go on their **bicycle tour**, also taking in six wineries ($89).

Around Cessnock

Cessnock lies more or less due west of Newcastle, in an area of small creeks and tributaries of the Hunter River. But even in the main valley of the Hunter, followed by the New England Highway as it heads up towards the mountains of the Great Dividing Range and the New England Plateau, the impression is overwhelmingly rural, with green meadows and pastures interspersed with cornfields, vegetable patches and, of course, vineyards. Old mansions and sleepy hamlets, dating back to colonial times, complete the seemingly idyllic pastoral scene. Yet nearby coal is extracted from several enormous open-cast mines to feed Newcastle's power stations.

The area is dotted with interesting old country towns: even **MAITLAND** and **SINGLETON**, two of the main centres of the coal industry, boast historic buildings that help retain a beguilingly colonial flavour. Maitland, 25km northwest of Cessnock, is in fact a throughly historic place – an early convict foundation that in the nineteenth century became one of the most important towns in early Australia. There's an excellent state-of-the-art **tourist information centre** in Ministers Park on the corner of the New England Highway and High Street (☎02/4933 2611), and in both towns the old jails have been converted into local history museums. Only 6km from Maitland, **MORPETH** is a picturesque river town that was an important Hunter Valley river port 150 years ago; today the old buildings house art galleries and craft shops.

WOLLOMBI, a historic homesteading settlement some 30km south of Cessnock, is the gateway to the Hunter Valley on the scenic inland route from Sydney, which involves leaving the freeway at Calga and heading north via Mangrove and Bucketty. The *Wollombi Tavern*, home of Dr Jurd's Jungle Juice (have a free taste and find out), makes a fine refreshment stop – sitting out on the wooden verandah looking over the creek to trees, fields and hills beyond is a real pleasure. Wollombi was once a ceremonial meeting place, and there are **Aboriginal rock carvings** and cave paintings throughout the area, some of which can be visited on horseback through the Wollombi Horse Riding Centre (☎02/4998 3221; 1hr 30min–2hr; $30), 4km past the *Wollombi Tavern* on the Singleton Road. The **New Gokula Farm**, halfway between Cessnock and Wollombi on the Wollombi Road (☎02/4998 1800), is a Hare Krishna farming community that puts on a free vegetarian feast at noon on Sunday; ask about staying in their guesthouse – a very peaceful spot flanked by bush-covered hills.

Moving on from the valley, it's an easy detour to **Barrington Tops National Park** (see p.246), north from Singleton and Maitland, or the **Chichester Dam**, slightly closer at hand in the same direction, surrounded by beautiful mountain and forest scenery, and inhabited by melodic bellbirds.

Accommodation

Since the Hunter Valley is a popular weekend trip for Sydneysiders, accommodation **prices** invariably rise on Friday and Saturday nights when many places only offer two-night deals. If you're going to be here at a weekend, or during the February vintage festival, advance **booking** is essential. Most of the accommodation is around Pokolbin, at the centre of the vineyards, 12–15km northwest of Cessnock.

Belford Country Cabins, 659 Hermitage Rd, Pokolbin (☎02/6574 7100). Family-run, fully equipped wooden bungalows for up to eight people. Great bushland location, small pool and playground. ⑤–⑥.

Bellbird Hotel, 388 Wollombi Rd, 5km southwest from the centre of Cessnock (☎02/4990 1094). Great classic country pub, circa 1908, with wide iron-lace. Bistro, pretty beer garden and children's playground. Rates include a generous cooked breakfast. ④, Sat ⑥.

Black Opal Hotel, 216 Vincent St, Cessnock (☎02/4990 1070). Pub accommodation that feels upmarket but is actually inexpensive. ③, Fri & Sat ④–⑤.

Cessnock Valley View Caravan Park, Mount View Rd, 2km northwest of Cessnock (☎02/4990 2573). Site with barbecues and pool. Cabins ④, on-site vans ②.

The Convent, Halls Rd, Pokolbin (☎02/4998 7764, fax 4998 7323). The swankiest place to stay in the Hunter Valley, but at a price (from $260 per night). The guesthouse has heaps of cosy cachet, fireplaces and low beams, and was converted from an old convent, and is part of the Peppertree winery. Attached is the fine-dining restaurant, *Roberts at Peppertree*. ⑧.

Elfin Hill Motel, Marrowbone Rd, Pokolbin (☎02/4998 7543, fax 4998 7817). Friendly, family-run hilltop motel with extensive views. Comfortable units in timber cabins, all air-con and recently renovated. Facilities include a saltwater pool and barbecue area. Breakfast available. ⑤, Fri & Sat ⑦.

Neath Hotel, Cessnock Rd, Neath, 6km east of Cessnock (☎02/4930 4270). B&B in a nicely furnished historic pub, listed by the National Trust. ④, Fri & Sat ⑤.

Pokolbin Cabins, Palmers Lane, Pokolbin (☎02/4998 7611). In the midst of the wineries, this extensive complex has two- and three-bedroom log cabins and five-bedroom homesteads, fully equipped with everything from linen to firewood. Swimming pool and tennis court in the shady grounds. ⑥.

Sussex Ridge, off Deaseys Rd, Pokolbin (☎02/4998 7753, fax 4998 7359). Guesthouse in a classic two-storey, tin-roofed homestead among extensive bushland, with great views from the balcony. All rooms are en-suite and facilities include two communal lounge areas with open fires, an outdoor barbecue area and a swimming pool. B&B ⑥, Fri & Sat ⑦.

Tallawanta Resort, Broke Rd, Pokolbin (☎02/4998 7854, fax 4998 7845). Modern combined motel and hotel complex overlooking vineyards with a bar, bistro, bottle shop, pool, spa and tennis courts. One room is accessible to disabled guests. B&B ⑤, Fri & Sat ⑧.

Wentworth Hotel, 36 Vincent St, Cessnock (☎02/4990 1364). Large old country pub with original wooden fixtures circa 1914. Rooms are clean and spacious with washbasin, fan and heating, and rates include a continental breakfast. B&B ④.

Wollombi Horse Riding Centre, Singleton Rd, 4km past the *Wollombi Tavern* (☎ & fax 02/4998 3221). Barnstay accommodation in bunks, with kitchen, lounge area, fuel stove, verandah and barbecue. Rates include linen, semi-stocked kitchen and sole run of the facilities. Also riverside camping. ④.

Eating and drinking

Most of the many excellent (and pricey) Hunter Valley restaurants are attached to the various wineries or are among the vineyards, rather than in the towns, while the Hunter's large old pubs dish out less fancy but more affordable grub. Every year over a mid-May weekend several wineries along and around Lovedale Road team up with local restaurants to host the **Lovedale Long Lunch** (☎02/4930 7611), with wine and gourmet food served amongst the vines. You can taste free samples of The Hunter Valley Cheese Company's handmade wares, or buy some to accompany a picnic, at the McGuigan Bros Winery, Broke Road, Pokolbin.

Amicos, 138 Wollombi Rd, Cessnock (☎02/4991 1995). A popular cheap eat, this BYO restaurant serves Italian and Mexican food in a casual atmosphere, $5 pasta night Mon. Daily from 6pm.

Baron's Restaurant, at the *Neath Hotel* (☎02/4930 4270). Antique-filled restaurant in a historic pub. Fri & Sat nights only.

Bellbird Hotel, 388 Wollombi Rd, 5km from the centre of Cessnock. Vast old-fashioned pub full of country characters. Eat inexpensive no-frills bistro food in the very pleasant vine-covered and flower-filled beer garden with adjacent children's playground.

Blaxlands Restaurant, Broke Rd, Pokolbin (☎02/4998 7550). More than a hundred wines from the Hunter Valley are available at this well-regarded restaurant in an 1829 sandstone cottage. You can eat outside on the verandah. Expensive. Booking advised.

Café Enzo, Peppers Creek Antiques, Broke Rd, Pokolbin (☎02/4998 7233). Courtyard café with a light Mediterranean menu and excellent Italian-style coffee. Wed–Sun 10am–5pm.

Café Max, McDonalds Rd, Pokolbin (☎02/4998 7899). Above The Small Winemakers Centre (see box opposite), with balcony views of vineyards and far-off hills. An eclectic lunch menu. BYO. Daily 10am–5pm.

Chez Pok, *Pepper's Guesthouse*, Ekerts Rd, Pokolbin (☎02/4998 7596). Highly regarded restaurant stylishly using local produce. The views overlooking vineyards are very pretty as is the antique-filled cottage interior. Daily breakfast to dinner. Expensive.

Hermitage Restaurant, Hunter Estate, Hermitage Rd, Pokolbin (☎02/4998 7777). Pleasant, rustic-style dining room; menu focusing on produce from New South Wales, imaginatively cooked; Expensive. BYO and licensed. Dinner nightly.

The Hoot Café, 115 Vincent St, Cessnock (☎02/4991 2856). Sydney style and prices in this bright and airy café with ceiling fans whirring and soul music playing. Gourmet sandwiches, croissants, tasty cakes, good coffee and delicious stuffed potatoes. Mon–Fri 8am–4pm, Sat 8am–1pm.

HUNTER VALLEY WINERIES

More than sixty wineries cluster around the Hunter Valley, and almost all of them offer tastings and are interesting to visit. The most-visited are in the lower part of the valley, near Pokolbin, but there are also a few gems in the upper valley, around Wybong and Denman, west of Muswellbrook. See the box on p.705 for some wine-tasting tips. Below are a few of our favourites or ones that offer tours.

Allandale Winery, Lovedale Rd, Pokolbin (☎02/4990 4526). A very picturesque small winery established in 1978; it's set on a hill, with great views overlooking the vineyard, the Lower Hunter and the Brokenback Range. They're happy for you to visit during vintage time, when you can see the small operation in action; try their prize-winning Chardonnay. One of the best. Mon–Sat 9am–5pm, Sun 10am–5pm.

Cruikshank Callatoota Estate, Wybong Rd, Wybong, Upper Hunter Valley, 18km north of Denman (☎02/6547 8149). Winemaker John Cruikshank is a real character who unapologetically makes only red wine, which he loves. Barbecue facilities and winery tours. Daily 9am–5pm.

Drayton's Family Wines, Oakey Creek Rd, Pokolbin (☎02/4998 7513). A very friendly, down-to-earth family winery, established for over 140 years. In that time they've become well known for their ports; you might be lucky and get a taste of Old Decanter Port, aged 21 years. Barbecue facilities and a children's play area too. Mon–Fri 8am–5pm, Sat & Sun 10am–5pm.

Hermitage Road Cellars and Winery, Hunter Resort, Hermitage Rd, Pokolbin (☎02/4998 7777). The largest commercial winery, lacking in atmosphere but offering informative wine tours: booking essential. Daily 10am–5pm; tour 11am & 2pm.

Kevin Sobels Wines, corner of Broke and Halls roads, Pokolbin (☎02/4998 7766). Set up in 1992, the welcome at this small, simple winery is wonderfully down-to-earth, and includes a greeting by Bacchas, the resident St Bernard. The building itself is a real treat, all timber and glass but with a very home-made, slightly wonky feel. Outside there are picnic tables. Daily 9am–5pm.

Lindemans Wines, McDonalds Rd, Pokolbin (☎02/4998 7684). One of the best-known names in the valley; Dr Lindeman first planted vines in the valley in 1842. Its museum has a collection of winemaking paraphernalia. Mon–Fri 9am–4.30pm, Sat & Sun 10am–4.30pm.

Reynolds Yarraman, Yarraman Road, Wybong, Upper Hunter (☎02/6547 8127). Tucked away in the upper valley, but worth seeking out for the best location of all the wineries. Convict-constructed sandstone buildings, circa 1837, and excellent, prize-winning wines. There's also a café open weekends. Mon–Sat 10am–4pm, Sun 11am–4pm.

Rosemount Estate, Rosemount Rd, Denman, Upper Hunter (☎02/6547 2467). Producer of some of Australia's best-known, award-winning wines, and with an excellent vineyard brasserie (closed Mon). Mon–Sat 10am–4pm, Sun 10.30am–4pm.

Scarborough Wine Co, Gilliards Rd, Pokolbin (☎02/4998 7563). Small, friendly winery specializing in Chardonnay. Pleasantly relaxed sit-down tastings are held in a small cottage on Hungerford Hill with wonderful valley views. Daily 9am–5pm.

Tamburlaine Wines, McDonalds Rd, Pokolbin (☎02/4998 7570). The jasmine-scented garden outside gives a hint of the flowery elegant wines within. Only a small range of wines – too small even for the domestic market, so you must buy here. Tastings are well orchestrated and delivered with a heap of experience. Daily 9.30am–5pm.

Tyrrell's Family Vineyard, Broke Rd, Pokolbin (☎02/4998 7509). The oldest independent family vineyards, producing consistently good wines. The tiny ironbark slab hut, where Edward Tyrrell lived when he began the winery in 1858, is still in the grounds, and the old winery with its cool earth floor is much as it was. Set against the Brokenback Range, the setting is as spectacular as the wines. Mon–Sat 8am–5pm, with tour Mon–Fri 1.30pm.

Verona Vineyard & The Small Winemakers Centre, McDonalds Rd, Pokolbin (☎02/4998 7668). Sells wines produced by four other small vineyards – Broke Estate, Inglewood, Reynolds Yarraman and Simon Whitlam; the $2 tasting charge levied on some wines is refunded on purchases. Excellent café (see opposite). Daily 10am–5pm.

Il Cacciatore, Hermitage Lodge, corner of McDonalds and Gilliards roads, Pokolbin (☎02/4998 7639). Excellent upmarket Italian restaurant with a wide choice, including fish dishes. Desserts like chocolate pasta ensure that the place is packed. Licensed and BYO.

Roberts at Pepper Tree, Halls Rd, Pokolbin (☎02/4998 7330). Attached to *The Convent* (see "Accommodation", p.183), this is the place to head for a treat in a beautiful old farmhouse filled with flowers. French rustic-style food emerges from wood-fired ovens. Expensive; licensed.

Rothbury Café, Rothbury Estate, Broke Rd, Pokolbin (☎02/4998 7363). A good, unpretentious lunch spot overlooking the vineyards of this winery. Reasonably priced pizza and pasta of the day plus interesting modern Australian dishes; wine at cellar-door prices. Lunch daily.

West

For fifty years, Sydney has been sliding ever westwards in a monotonous sprawl of shopping centres, brick-veneer homes and fast-food chains, in the process swallowing up towns and villages, some of which date back to colonial times. The first settlers to explore inland found well-watered, fertile river flats, and quickly established agricultural outposts to support the fledgling colony. **Parramatta**, **Liverpool**, **Penrith** and **Campbelltown**, once separate communities, have become satellite towns inside Sydney's commuter belt. Yet, despite Sydney's advance, bushwalkers will find there's still plenty of wild west to explore. Three wildlife parks keep suburbia at bay, and the beauty of the **Blue Mountains** are a far cry from the modernity of Sydney.

Parramatta and Penrith

Situated on the Parramatta River, a little over 20km upstream from the harbour mouth, **PARRAMATTA** was the first of Sydney's rural satellites – the first farm settlement in Australia, in fact. The fertile soil of "Rosehill", as it was originally called, saved the fledgling colony from starvation with its first wheat crop of 1789. It's hard to believe today, but dotted here and there among the malls and busy roads are a few remnants from that time – eighteenth-century public buildings and original settlers' dwellings that warrant a visit if you're interested in Australian history.

You can call in to Parramatta on your way out of Sydney – a rather depressing drive along the ugly and congested Parramatta Road – or endure the dreary thirty-minute suburban train ride from Central Station. But much the most enjoyable way to get here is on the sleek RiverCat ferry from Circular Quay up the Parramatta River (1hr; $5 one-way). The wharf at Parramatta is on Phillip Street, a couple of blocks away from the helpful **Parramatta Visitors Centre** on the corner of Church and Market streets (Mon–Fri 10am–4pm, Sat 9am–1pm, Sun 10.30am–3.30pm; ☎02/9630 3703), which hands out free walking route maps.

Parramatta's most important historic feature is the National Trust-owned **Old Government House** Tues–Fri 10am–4pm, Sat & Sun 11am–4pm; last admission 3.30pm; $5) in **Parramatta Park** by the river. Turn left onto Marsden Street from the visitors centre, cross the river, then go right onto George Street. Entered through the 1885 gatehouse on O'Connell Street, the park – filled with native trees – rises up to the gracious old Georgian-style building, the oldest remaining public edifice in Australia. It was built between 1799 and 1816 and used as the Viceregal residence until 1855; one wing has been converted into a pleasant teahouse. The three other main historic attractions are close together: from Parramatta Park, follow Macquarie Street and turn right at its end onto Harris Street. Running off here is Ruse Street, where the aptly named **Experiment Farm Cottage** (Tues–Thurs 10am–4pm, Sun 11am–4pm; $5, free for National Trust members), at no. 9, was built on the site of the first land grant, given in 1790 to reformed convict James Ruse. On parallel Alice Street, at no. 70, **Elizabeth Farm** (daily 10am–5pm; $6) dates from 1793 and claims to be the oldest surviving home in the country. The farm was built and run by the Macarthurs, who bred the first of the merino sheep that made Australian wealth "ride on a sheep's back"; a small café here serves refreshments. Nearby **Hambledon Cottage** on Hassel Street (Wed, Thurs, Sat & Sun 11am–4pm; $3), built in 1824, was part of the Macarthur estate.

Continuing west, the Western Highway and the rail lines head on to **PENRITH**, the most westerly of Sydney's satellite towns, in a curve of the Nepean River at the foot of the Blue Mountains (on the way out here you pass a couple of wildlife parks; see box on p.170). Penrith has an old-fashioned Aussie feel about it – a tight community that is immensely proud of the Panthers, its boisterous rugby league team. From town you can take in the splendour of the spectacular **Nepean Gorge** from the decks of the paddle steamer *Nepean Belle* (bookings ☎02/4733 1274; range of cruises from $12 for 1hr 30min) or head 24km south to the **Warragamba Dam**. The dam has created the huge reservoir of **Lake Burragorang**, a popular picnic spot with barbecues and a kiosk, and some easy walking trails through the bush.

The Blue Mountains region

The section of the Great Dividing Range nearest Sydney gets its name from the blue mist that rises from millions of eucalyptus trees and hangs in the mountain air, tinting the sky and the range alike. In the early days of the colony, the **Blue Mountains** were believed to be an insurmountable barrier to the west. The first expeditions followed the streams in the valleys until they were defeated by cliff faces rising vertically above them. Only in 1813, when the explorers Wentworth, Blaxland and Lawson followed the ridges instead of the valleys, were the mountains finally conquered, allowing the western plains to be opened up for settlement. The range is surmounted by a plateau at an altitude of more than 1000m where, over millions of years, rivers have carved deep valleys into the sandstone, and winds and driving rain have helped to deepen the ravines, creating a spectacular scenery of sheer precipices and walled canyons. Occasional landslides are a reminder that the process of erosion is still underway. Before white settlement, the Daruk Aborigines lived here, dressed in animal-skin cloaks to ward off the cold. An early coal-mining industry, based in Katoomba, was followed by tourism which snowballed after the arrival of the railway in 1868. By 1900, the first three mountain stations of Wentworth Falls, Katoomba and Mount Victoria had been established as fashionable resorts, extolling the health-giving benefits of eucalyptus-tinged mountain air.

All the villages and towns of the romantically dubbed "**City of the Blue Mountains**" – Glenbrook, Springwood, Wentworth Falls, Katoomba and Blackheath – lie on a ridge, connected by the Great Western Highway. Around them is the **Blue Mountains National Park**, the fourth-largest national park in the state and to many minds the best. The region makes a great weekend break from the city, with stunning views and clean air complemented by a wide range of accommodation, cafés and restaurants, a few good shops and even some entertainment. But be warned: at weekends, and during the summer holidays, Katoomba is thronged with escapees from the city, and prices escalate accordingly. Even at their most crowded, though, the Blue Mountains always offer somewhere where you can find peace and quiet, and even solitude – the deep gorges and high rocks make much of the terrain inaccessible except to bushwalkers and mountaineers. Climbing schools offer weekend courses in rock-climbing and abseiling for both beginners and experienced climbers.

Transport and information

Public transport to the mountains is quite good but your own vehicle will give you much greater flexibility once you've arrived, allowing you to take detours to old mansions, cottage gardens and the lookout points scattered along the ridge. **Trains** leave

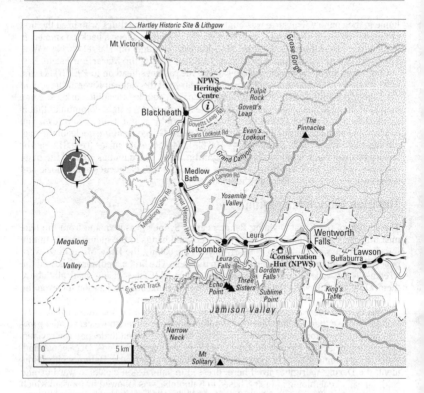

from Central Station to Mount Victoria and follow the highway, stopping at all the major towns en route (frequent departures until about midnight, no booking required; 2hr; $9 one-way to Katoomba). If you're dependent on public transport, Katoomba makes the best base: facilities and services are concentrated here, and there are **local buses** to attractions in the vicinity and to other centres. The Katoomba–Woodford Bus Co (☎02/4782 4213) links Katoomba with Leura, Wentworth Falls, Bullaburra, Lawson, Hazelbrook and Woodford. Mountainlink (☎02/4782 3333) has three routes, one linking Katoomba with Medlow Bath, Blackheath and Mount Victoria, one heading from Katoomba Street to Echo Point, and another going from Katoomba to Leura and Gordon Falls. Buses leave town from Katoomba Street outside the *Carrington Hotel*. Another way to get around is with the hop-on, hop-off Blue Mountains Explorer Bus, which links the main tourist spots around Katoomba and Leura on weekends. The bus is run by Fantastic Aussie Tours, whose office is at 283 Main St, Katoomba (☎02/4782 1866), by the train station; for full details of times and fares, see "Tours" on p.196.

  GLENBROOK, the gateway to the Blue Mountains, has the **Blue Mountains Information Centre**, on the Great Western Highway (daily 9am–5pm; ☎02/4739 6266; *www.bluemts.com.au*), the place to pick up a huge amount of information about the area, including the very useful *Blue Mountains Wonderland Visitors Guide*, which has several detailed colour maps of the area and its towns. Other handy free publications include *This Month in the Blue Mountains*, a what's on guide. The other official tourist information centre is at **Echo Point**, near Katoomba (see p.191); neither office books

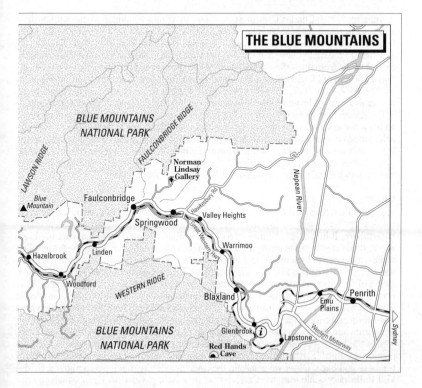

accommodation but they do issue vacancy listings. The **NPWS** has ranger stations at Wentworth Falls (see below) and Blackheath (see p.192) where you can get comprehensive walking information.

Springwood to Wentworth Falls

Eleven kilometres west of Glenbrook, **SPRINGWOOD** is home to many of the artists who have settled in the mountains, and there are numerous shops selling antiques and arts and crafts. Further west is **FAULCONBRIDGE**, where it's well worth visiting the exhibition of paintings and drawings at the **Norman Lindsay Gallery**, 14 Norman Lindsay Crescent (daily during school holidays, otherwise Fri–Sun 11am–5pm; $6). The controversial artist and poet, whose nude studies scandalized Australia in the 1930s and whose story was told in the 1994 film *Sirens* (with Elle McPherson as one of the life models), spent the last part of his life here.

The small village of **WENTWORTH FALLS**, named after the explorer William Wentworth, is home to the restored nineteenth-century **Yester Grange** (Mon–Fri 10am–4pm, Sat & Sun 10am–5pm; $5), filled with Victorian-era antiques and a fine watercolour collection, its neat gardens set off by their rugged bush backdrop (and there's a good tearoom). Nearby, a signposted road leads from the Great Western Highway to the **Wentworth Falls Reserve**, with superb views of the waterfall tumbling down into the Jamison Valley. You can reach this picnic area from Wentworth train station by following **Darwin's Walk** – the route followed by the famous naturalist in 1836. Of the view, which has changed little, Charles Darwin wrote, "If we imagine a winding harbour, with its deep water surrounded by bold cliff-like shores, laid dry, and a forest sprung up on its sandy bottom, we should then have the appearance and structure here exhibited. This kind of view was to me quite novel, and extremely magnificent." Most of the other bushwalks in the area start from the **Valley of the Waters Conservation Hut**, about 3km from the station at the end of Fletcher Street. Bus services are infrequent; a taxi from the station costs $6. The NPWS hut (daily 9am–5pm; ☎02/4757 3827) is in a fantastic location overlooking the Jamison Valley. From its wonderful *Conservation Hut Café* you can take full advantage of the stupendous views through the big windows or from the deck outside, and in winter an open fire crackles in the grate. A wide selection of bushwalks, detailed on boards outside, ranges from the two-hour **Valley of the Waters track**, which descends into the valley, to an extended two-day walk to **Mount Solitary**. One of the most rewarding is the quite strenuous, six-kilometre **National Pass**, a one-way walk which will conveniently get you back to the train station and takes in Wentworth Falls en route.

Leura

Just two kilometres east of Katoomba, the more upmarket **LEURA**, packed with great cafés, art galleries and small boutiques, retains its own distinct identity and a real village atmosphere. It helps that the main street – The Mall – is quite secluded from the highway and its green median strip practically qualifies as a small park. Even the flower-filled station manages to look pretty, and indeed Leura is renowned for its beautiful **gardens**, some of which are open to the public during the **Leura Gardens Festival** (early to mid-Oct; $10 for visits to around eight gardens; details on ☎02/4739 6266). Open all year round, though, is the beautiful **Everglades Gardens** (daily 9am–sunset; $5) situated in the grounds of an elegant mansion at 37 Everglades Ave. There are enjoyable views from its formal terraces, with a colourful display of azaleas and rhododendrons, an aboretum, and peacocks strutting among it all. Not far from the village, the flowers give way to the bush: less tame scenery, such as **Leura Cascades**, can be viewed from the picnic area on Cliff Drive; to see it at closer quarters, take the two- to three-hour walk to the base and back. Other waterfalls in the area include the much-photographed **Bridal Veil Falls**, accessible from the Cascades picnic area, and **Gordon Falls**, which you can walk to from Lone Pine Avenue. To the east of Gordon Falls, Sublime Point Road leads to the aptly named **Sublime Point** lookout, with panoramic views of the Jamison Valley. A popular walking track from Leura Falls is the Federal Pass, which skirts the cliffs between here and **Katoomba Falls** (6km one-way; 2hr 30min).

Katoomba and around

KATOOMBA, the biggest town in the Blue Mountains and the area's commercial heart, is also the best located, though for all its surrounding charms, café culture and vintage clothes shops it can still seem a little raw and characterless. When the town was discovered by fashionable city dwellers in the late nineteenth century, the grandiose *Carrington Hotel*, prominently located in lands near the train station, was the height of elegance, with its leadlighting and wood panelling. After sitting empty and derelict for years, it has finally been renovated and now has accommodation, a restaurant and two cocktail bars. However, the Savoy Theatre opposite is still closed and continues to lend an air of slight neglect.

Katoomba's newest attraction, opened in late 1995, is a huge six-storey cinema screen, the **Edge Maxvision Cinema**, at 225–237 Great Western Highway (☎02/4782 8928). Maxvision is an Australian company, and the cinema was created as a venue to show *The Edge – The Movie*, a stunning and moving introduction to the ecology of the Blue Mountains – and the joys of canyoning (daily 10am, 11.40am, 12.30pm 2.50pm, & 5.15pm; $12.50). The forty-minute-long film took a year to complete and cost $2.25 million to produce for its giant screen format. Its highlight is the segment about the "dinosaur trees", a stand of thirty-metre-high **Wollemi Pine**, previously known only from fossil material over sixty million years old. The trees – miraculously still existing – survive deep within a sheltered rainforest gully in the **Wollemi National Park**, north of Katoomba, and they made headlines when they were first discovered in 1994 by a group of canyoners. To film the pines, whose exact location is kept secret, it was necessary to work closely with the NPWS; there is an informative NPWS display in the cinema lobby.

A 25-minute walk south from the train station (or by the Mountainlink bus departing daily 8am–2pm from outside the Savoy Theatre) will bring you to **Echo Point**, the location of the information centre (daily 9am–5pm; ☎02/4782 0756). From here you have breathtaking vistas that take in the Blue Mountains' most famous landmark, the **Three Sisters** (910m). These three gnarled rocky points take their name from an Aboriginal Dreamtime story which relates how the Katoomba people were losing a battle against the rival Nepean people: the Katoomba leader, fearing that his three beautiful daughters would be carried off by the enemy, turned them to stone, but was tragically killed before he could reverse his spell. They have stood here ever since, subjected to the

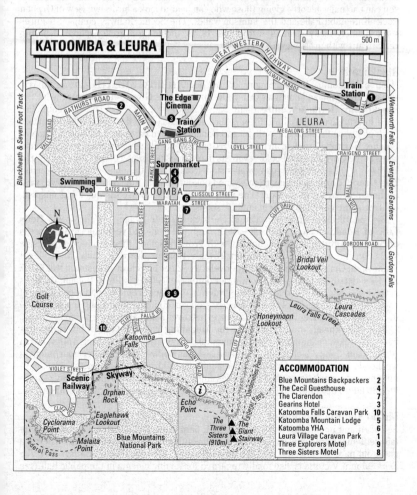

KATOOMBA & LEURA

0   500 m

GREAT WESTERN HIGHWAY
RAILWAY PARADE

Blackheath & Seven Foot Track

BATHURST ROAD
VALLEY ROAD
MAIN ST
PARKES STREET

The Edge Cinema
Train Station

LEURA
MEGALONG STREET
LOVEL STREET
CRAIGEND STREET

GANG GANG STREET
Supermarket
PINE ST
GATES AVE
CLISSOLD STREET
WARATAH STREET

Swimming Pool
KATOOMBA

Train Station

Wentworth Falls
Everglades Gardens
Gordon Falls

THE MALL
CLIFF DRIVE

CASCADE STREET
KATOOMBA STREET
LURLINE STREET

N

CLIFF DRIVE
GORDON ROAD

Bridal Veil Lookout

Golf Course

CLIFF FALLS RD

Katoomba Falls

Honeymoon Lookout

Leura Falls Creek

Leura Cascades

VIOLET STREET
Scenic Railway
Skyway

Orphan Rock

ECHO POINT ROAD

Echo Point

Federal Pass
Dardanelles Pass

CLIFF DRIVE

Cyclorama Point
Eaglehawk Lookout

Malaita Point

Federal Pass

Blue Mountains National Park

The Three Sisters (910m)
The Giant Stairway

ACCOMMODATION

Blue Mountains Backpackers	2
The Cecil Guesthouse	4
The Clarendon	7
Gearins Hotel	3
Katoomba Falls Caravan Park	10
Katoomba Mountain Lodge	5
Katoomba YHA	6
Leura Village Caravan Park	1
Three Explorers Motel	9
Three Sisters Motel	8

indignities of thousands of tourist cameras and persistent abseilers and kept awake at night by spectacular floodlighting. The Three Sisters are at the top of the **Giant Stairway**, the beginning of the very steep stairs into the three-hundred-metre-deep **Jamison Valley** below, where there are several walking tracks to places with such intriguing names as **Orphan Rock** and **Ruined Castle**. There's a popular walking route, taking about two hours and graded medium, down the stairway and part way along the **Federal Pass** to the **Landslide**, and then on to the Scenic Railway (see below) which you can take back up to the ridge.

If you want to spare yourself the trek down into the Jamison Valley – or the walk back up – take the **Scenic Railway** at the end of Violet Street (daily 9am–5pm; last train up leaves at 4.50pm; $3, $4.50 return). Originally built to carry coal, this funicular railway glides down an impossibly steep gorge to the valley floor. Even more vertiginous is the **Skyway** (daily 9am–5pm; $4.50), a rickety-looking cable-car contraption that starts next to the railway and travels 350m across to the other side of the gorge and back again – you can't actually get off – giving those who can bear to look a bird's-eye view of Orphan Rock, Katoomba Falls and the Jamison Valley. The Scenic Railway complex features some divinely tacky structures from the 1970s, including a greasy-spoon **revolving restaurant** with great views.

Blackheath

North of Katoomba, there are more lookout points at **BLACKHEATH** – just as impressive as Echo Point and much less busy. One of the best is **Govetts Leap**, near the NPWS **Blackheath Heritage Centre** (daily 9am–4.30pm; ☎02/4787 8877). The centre has good interpretive material on history, flora and fauna, as well as practical information (with plenty on the adjacent Wollemi and Kanangra Boyd parks too). The two-kilometre **Fairfax Heritage Track** from the NPWS Centre is wheelchair- and pram-accessible and takes in the Govett's Leap Lookout with its marvellous panorama of the Grose Valley and Bridal Veil Falls. Although many walks start from the centre, one of the most popular, **The Grand Canyon**, begins from Evans Lookout Road at the south end of town, west of the Great Western Highway. The village of Blackheath itself is quiet and unspoilt, offering some good browsing in antique shops.

Beyond Blackheath, drivers can circle back towards Sydney via the scenic **Bells Line of Road**, which heads back east through the fruit- and vegetable-growing areas of Bilpin and Kurrajong to Richmond, with growers selling their produce at roadside stalls. On the way you'll pass **Mount Tomah Botanic Garden** (daily: March–Sept 10am–4pm; Oct–Feb 10am–5pm; $5 per vehicle, $2 per bicycle or pedestrian; ☎02/4567 2154 for details of free guided tours), an outpost of Sydney's Royal Botanic Gardens since 1987. There's a rhododendron garden, a display of conifers, and a collection of southern hemisphere cool-climate species. You can continue west along the Bells Line of Road to the Zig Zag Railway at Clarence, just over 35km away (see p.196).

From Blackheath you can also take the **Megalong Valley Road** southwest into this beautiful valley, calling in to visit the marsupials and emus at **Megalong Valley Farm** (daily 10am–5pm; $3, child $2). The farm also has horse-riding ($20 per hour) and, on weekends and holidays, farm activities aimed at children, such as tractor rides, cow-milking and a stock-horse show. Activities run from 10.30am to 3.30pm (full day of activities $9 adult, $6 child, $25 family), and there is a kiosk where you can buy lunch.

Mount Victoria and around

Secluded and homely **MOUNT VICTORIA**, 6km from Blackheath and the last mountain settlement proper, is the only one with an authentic, unspoilt village feel. There's a great old pub, the *Imperial*, and the best scones on the mountain at the *Bay Tree Tea Shop*. Mount Victoria is also fondly regarded for its tiny cinema in the public hall (see p.196), where the patron introduces the varied films and defends his choice. Worth a browse are several antique shops and a cluttered antiquarian and secondhand book-shop. Some short **walks** start from the Fairy Bower Picnic area, a ten-minute walk from the Great Western Highway via Mount Piddington Road: get details from any Blue Mountains tourist office, or ask at the *Victoria and Albert Guesthouse* (see overleaf).

The **Hartley Historic Site** (daily 10am–1pm & 2–4.30pm) lies at the foot of the scenic Victoria Pass in the small valley of the River Lett, 11km from Mount Victoria. It's a well-pre-served nineteenth-century village, which began to develop as settlers headed west and forged roads through the mountains. The need for a police centre led to the building of a courthouse here in 1837, and the village of Hartley developed around it until it was bypassed by the Great Western Highway in 1887. It's free to look at the site, but to enter the buildings – only the courthouse is currently visitable – you have to take a guided tour (cour-thouse tours 10am, 11am, noon, 2pm & 3pm; 20min; $4). There is no transport to the site.

Blue Mountains accommodation

Accommodation rates rise on Friday and Saturday nights, so you should aim to visit on weekdays when it's quieter and cheaper. The tourist office (☎02/4739 6266) doesn't do bookings but they can advise you of vacancies. **Katoomba** is the obvious choice for those arriving by train, particularly for those on a budget since it has four **hostels** to choose from, but if you have your own transport you can indulge in some of the more unusual and characterful guesthouses in **Blackheath** and **Mount Victoria**.

HOTELS, MOTELS AND GUESTHOUSES

The Cecil Guesthouse, 108 Katoomba St, Katoomba (☎02/4782 1411, fax 4728 5364). Very central choice, but back from the main drag, which makes it peaceful. Has an old-fashioned 1940s atmosphere, with log fires, games room and tennis courts, plus modern touches such as a spa. No en-suite rooms. A hearty breakfast is included. Meals served. B&B ⑥, weekends ⑦.

The Clarendon, corner of Lurline and Waratah streets, Katoomba (☎02/4782 1322, fax 4782 2564). Classic 1920s guesthouse with its own bar and restaurant, and cabaret weekends. Nice firm beds and mostly en-suites. The guesthouse rooms are best – avoid the fairly unattractive, Seventies-style motel rooms. Budget rooms without bathroom are available. ④–⑦.

Cleopatra Guesthouse, Cleopatra St, Blackheath (☎02/4787 8456, fax 4787 6092). A highly salu-brious, gay-friendly guesthouse. The price includes luscious meals at breakfast and dinner in the attached restaurant, which is probably the best – and most expensive – in the mountains. ⑧.

Glenella, 56 Govett's Leap Rd, Blackheath (☎02/4787 8352, fax 4787 6114). Guesthouse in a charm-ing 1905 homestead with a well-regarded restaurant. Rooms are furnished with antiques. Breakfast included. ⑦, weekends ⑧.

Hydro-Majestic Hotel, Great Western Highway, opposite Medlow Bath train station, 7km west of Katoomba (☎02/4788 1002, fax 4788 1063). Luxurious, Art Deco hotel restored to its former glory. Breakfast included; bar and restaurant. Magnificent views. All rooms are en-suite with hot drinks and telephone. TV is banished to the guest lounge. ⑧.

Hotel Imperial, Station St, Mount Victoria (☎02/4787 1233, fax 4787 1461). Nicely restored country pub with beautiful leadlighting and good food. B&B, with some en-suite rooms. ⑥–⑦, weekends ⑦–⑧.

Jemby-Rinjah Lodge, 336 Evans Lookout Rd, Blackheath (☎02/4787 7622, fax 4787 6230). Award-winning accommodation, calling itself an "eco-lodge", with good links with National Park rangers and bushwalks organized for guests who stay in distinctive timber cabins, with wood fires, in bushland near the Grose Valley. Cabins sleep up to six people; no linen but duvets sup-plied. ⑤, weekends ⑦.

Kanangra Lodge, 9 Belvedere Ave, Blackheath (☎02/4787 8715, fax 4787 7563). Small, peaceful B&B with four rooms, all en-suite. Full hot breakfast. Open fireplaces in its cosy lounges, and a large garden outside. ⑥.

Three Explorers Motel, 197 Lurline St, Katoomba (☎02/4782 1733, fax 4782 1146). Well-run, three-star place a cut above the usual charmless motel, on two levels with tastefully decorated units. Spa rooms plus large family suites. Great spot near Echo Point. ⑥, weekends ⑧.

Three Sisters Motel, 348 Katoomba St, Katoomba (☎02/4782 2911, fax 4782 6263). Small, old-style red-brick motel units, but clean, well-equipped and run by an amiable couple. Continental breakfast included. Excellent location near Echo Point. ⑤, weekends ⑥–⑦.

Victoria and Albert Guesthouse, Station St, Mount Victoria (☎02/4787 1241, fax 4787 1588). Classy but friendly place with Art Deco features. Rooms are large and there's a bar, café, restaurant, pool, spa and sauna. Breakfast included. ④, weekends ⑤.

HOSTELS AND CAMPING

Blue Mountains Backpackers, 190 and 194 Bathurst Rd, Katoomba (☎02/4782 4226, fax 4782 4236). Two shabby but comfortable bungalows near the station, one with dorms sleeping six to ten. Separate TV/video rooms, a small kitchen, free tea and coffee and lifts to bushwalks. The owners also have an adventure company offering tours and activities. Rooms ③, dorms ①.

Gearins Hotel, 273 Great Western Highway, Katoomba (☎02/4782 4395, fax 4782 4730). A large Victorian-era hotel with a 1930s facade. Plenty of rooms upstairs, many converted into clean, four-bed dorms with lockers. Linen and bedding included, and free tea and coffee in the TV lounge. There's no kitchen, though, and the music from the pub below might bother you. Rooms ②, dorms ①.

Katoomba Falls Caravan Park, Katoomba Falls Rd, Katoomba (☎02/4782 1835). A good location near the falls. Cabins ③–④.

Katoomba Mountain Lodge, Church Lane, off Katoomba St, Katoomba (☎ & fax 02/4782 3933). Central budget accommodation with great views over the town from its verandah, TV room and some bedrooms. Four-bed dorms and attractive doubles (all share bathrooms) with window seats. Small kitchen, and large dining room with free tea and coffee. Breakfast and dinner available. Rooms ④–⑤, dorms ①.

Katoomba YHA Hostel, 66 Waratah St, corner of Lurline St, Katoomba (☎02/4782 1416, fax 4782 6203; *bluemountains@yhansw.org.au*). Large, pleasant hostel in a charming old guesthouse with wood-combustion fires and a games room. Rooms are ensuite and linen is supplied. Convenient for both town centre and Echo Point walks. Mountain-bike rental for guests and abseiling and Jenolan Caves trips arranged. Internet access. Reception open all day. Rooms ③–④, dorms ①–②.

Leura Village Caravan Park, Great Western Highway at The Mall, Leura (☎02/4784 1552). Conveniently located right near the train station and shops, with heated indoor pool and TV lounge. Cabins ④, on-site vans ③.

Blue Mountains food, drink and entertainment

Cuisine in the Blue Mountains has gone way beyond the ubiquitous "Devonshire teas", with some well-regarded restaurants, and a real café culture in Katoomba and Leura; don't forget the NPWS-run *Conservation Hut Café* (see p.190) with tremendous views over the Jamison Valley. The best place for a civilized **drink** is the *Carrington Bar* on Katoomba Street, which features a piano player on Friday nights and jazz on Saturday; or you could try your luck at *The Clarendon*'s salubrious little bar, mostly reserved for guests, where there are also cabaret acts. On the other side of the railway line, the huge *Gearins Hotel* is a hive of activity, with several bars where you can play pool and see bands, and it stays open very late.

Arjuna, 16 Valley Rd, just off the Great Western Highway, Katoomba (☎02/4782 4662). Excellent, authentic Indian restaurant. A bit out of the way, but positioned for spectacular sunset views, so get there early. Good veggie choices too. BYO; non-smoking. Evenings from 6pm; closed Tues & Wed.

Avalon Restaurant, upstairs at 98 Main St, Katoomba, opposite the station (☎02/4782 5532). A stylish restaurant with the ambience of a quirky café, located in a warehouse-style space. There's even a smoking room to retire to. Moderately expensive menu, but generous servings and huge desserts to die for. BYO. Dinner daily, plus lunch Thurs, Fri & Sun.

The Bakery Café, 179 The Mall, Leura. A tiny but thriving place consisting of a counter with a few stools – and heavenly bakery products to consume with excellent coffee. Daily 7.30am–7.30pm.

Bay Tree Tea Shop, Station St, Mount Victoria. A family-run place in a converted Victorian cottage, and the best place in the mountains for scones and pots of real leaf tea. Open 10.30am–5pm; closed Wed–Fri.

The Blues Café, 57 Katoomba St, Katoomba. Bakery and cosy vegetarian café – this place has been going for years and is as popular as ever. Daily 9am–9pm.

Brad's Mountain Deli, 134 The Mall, Leura. A big range of food at reasonable prices makes this a popular one with the locals, and the big window overlooking the street means people watch all day. Good value sandwiches, yummy home-baked cakes, and friendly staff. Mon–Fri & Sun 9am–6pm, Sat 8am–6pm.

Glenella, 56 Govett's Leap Rd, Blackheath (☎02/4787 8352). An award-winning restaurant, good for a splurge – you can eat on the terrace, surrounded by a beautiful garden.

House of Penang, 183 Katoomba St, Katoomba. Chinese and Malaysian fast-food joint with a few eat-in tables. Delicious laksa noodle soups for around $6.50. Daily 10am–10pm.

Hydro-Majestic Hotel, Great Western Highway, opposite Medlow Bath train station, 7km west of Katoomba (☎02/4788 1002). Turn-of-the-century spa atmosphere, with scintillating views of the Megalong Valley, especially from the bar and beer garden balcony. Café open daily 9.30am–7pm, longer hours at the weekend.

Hotel Imperial, Station St, Mount Victoria, opposite the post office. Good-value, filling and tasty bistro meals can be eaten in the foyer, ballroom, verandah or garden of this classic old-fashioned country-style pub. Also serves coffee and cakes. Food served daily 8am–8.30pm.

Landseers, 178 The Mall, Leura. Tiny café with a very striking, cosily dark interior – or you can sit outside in the courtyard. Substantial sandwiches, soups and lasagne, plus delicious home-made cakes and puddings. Daily 7.30am–5pm.

The Paragon Café, 65 Katoomba St, Katoomba. Known for its fabulous handmade chocolates and sweets – check out the window and the counter display – and its wonderful National Trust-listed Art Deco interior complete with cocktail bar. They do meals, but you're better off buying chocolate or having a coffee and a gawk. Licensed. Tues–Sun 10am–4pm.

Parakeet Café, 195b Katoomba St, Katoomba. Eclectic, colourful café, its walls covered with paintings by local artists. There are separate rooms for smokers and non-smokers, so you can happily puff away. Simple, inexpensive food and hearty soups are the favourite here. Daily 7am–9.30pm, later Fri & Sat night when there is live music.

Patisserie Schwarz, Renae Arcade, 30 Station St, Wentworth Falls. German-style pastries to eat in or take away. Ideal to replenish your energies after a bushwalk. Closed Tues.

Siam Cuisine, 172 Katoomba St, Katoomba (☎02/4782 5671). Crowded, inexpensive Thai restaurant with $6 lunchtime specials. BYO. Tues–Sun 11.30am–2.30pm & 5.30–10pm.

Victoria and Albert, Station St, Mount Victoria (☎02/4787 1241). Civilized verandah café (Thurs–Sun 10am–5pm), plus a highly recommended restaurant in a wonderful old dining room, open nightly. Bookings preferred for non-residents.

Woodstack Café, 6 Katoomba St, Katoomba, opposite the station. A colourful, light, gay-friendly café attracting a young local crowd. Healthy breakfasts or fry-ups are available, plus affordable soups, burgers, Italian sandwiches, steaks, chicken and good coffee. Occasional live music. Daily 8 or 9am–10pm, until midnight Fri–Sun.

Zuppa, 36 Katoomba St, Katoomba (☎02/4782 9247). Katoomba's trendiest café – amiable staff, Art Deco interior, generous servings. Nothing over $7 during the day; different menu on Fri and Sat night (bookings advised) but never more than $15. Live music Fri night. Daily 8am–5pm and Fri & Sat night to 11pm.

Listings

Adventure activities Australian School of Mountaineering (at Paddy Pallin, 166b Katoomba St; ☎02/4782 2014), Katoomba's original abseiling outfit, offering courses (daily; $79 including lunch) plus a programme of canyoning, climbing, and bush-survival courses. Canyoning is the big thing with Blue Mountains Adventure Company (84a Main St; ☎02/4782 1271), with beginners'canyoning and abseiling trips for $89–99 (full day, including lunch), rock-climbing, mountain-biking and caving. Great Australian Walks (☎02/9555 7580), offer guided walks in the Jenolan Caves area and along the Six Foot Track. High 'n' Wild Mountain Adventures (3/5 Katoomba St; ☎02/4782 6224 or book through YHA Travel), has a consistently good reputation, for beginners' abseiling courses ($49 including lunch) plus canyoning ($65), rock-climbing ($55) and wilderness walks (from $49).

Bike rental Cycle Tech (Gang Gang St, opposite the station, Katoomba; ☎02/4782 2800), mountain bikes $15 half-day, $25 full-day and de luxe front suspension versions for $25/$45. The YHA rents bikes to guests.

Bookshops There are several interesting secondhand bookshops on Katoomba St, Katoomba, and in the other villages. New books can be bought at the very literary Megalong Books, 183 The Mall, Leura (☎02/4784 1302).

Bus services Katoomba–Leura bus service (☎02/4782 3333); Mountainlink (☎02/4782 4213).

Camping equipment If you haven't got your own gear, you must rent it in Sydney before you come up (see Sydney "Listings", p.163). Paddy Pallin, 166b Katoomba St (☎02/4782 4466), sells all camping gear and a good range of topographic maps and bushwalking guides.

Car rental Cales Rentals, 136 Bathurst Rd, Katoomba (☎02/4782 2917); Cullen, 60 Wilson St, Katoomba (☎02/4782 5535); Thrifty (☎02/4784 2888).

Cinemas The Edge, 225–237 Great Western Highway, Katoomba (☎02/4782 8928), shows new-release feature films on a giant screen (cheap tickets Tues $6; see p.190 for Maxvision details). Mount Vic Flicks, Harley Ave, off Station St, Mount Victoria (☎02/4787 1577), is a quaint local cinema in an old hall showing a fine programme of prestige new releases and independent films (Thurs–Sun, daily during school hols; cheaper tickets Thurs).

Horse-riding The Packsaddlers, Green Gully, Megalong Rd, Megalong Valley (☎02/4787 9150), offers one-hour rides up to the mountains ($20) or one-day or overnight (with camping) excursions down to the Coxs River; accommodation available on-site in well-equipped cabins. Werriberri Trail Rides, Megalong Rd, Megalong Valley (☎02/4787 9171), offers horse-riding for all abilities, pony rides for children and two-day camp-outs.

Hospital Blue Mountains District Anzac Memorial, Katoomba (☎02/4782 2111).

Laundry The Washing Well, K-Mart car park, Katoomba. Daily 7am–7pm.

Pharmacies Smith Hayden, 159 Macquarie Rd, Springwood (☎02/4751 2963; Mon–Fri 8.30am–9pm, Sat & Sun 9am–7pm); Greenwell & Thomas, 145 Katoomba St, Katoomba (☎02/4782 1066; Mon–Fri 8.30am–7pm, Sat & Sun 8.30am–6pm; deliveries available).

Post office Katoomba Post Office, Pioneer Place opposite Coles supermarket, off Katoomba St, Katoomba, NSW 2780.

Supermarket Coles, Pioneer Place off Katoomba St, Katoomba. Daily 6am–midnight.

Swimming pool Katoomba Aquatic Centre, Gates Ave, Katoomba (☎02/4782 2192). Olympic-sized outdoor pool but heated to 26°C, plus a heated children's pool. $2 entry includes free hot showers. Oct–Easter approximately 8am–6pm (extended hours in high summer).

Taxis Taxis wait outside the main Blue Mountains train stations to meet arrivals; otherwise call Katoomba Radio Cabs (☎02/4782 1311) or Blue Mountains Taxis (☎02/4759 3000).

Tours Most tours of the Blue Mountains start from Sydney; see box on pp.172–173. From Katoomba the Blue Mountains Explorer Bus, offered by Fantastic Aussie Tours, 283 Main St, Katoomba (☎02/4782 1866), provides a weekend hop-on, hop-off service linking the Leura, the Three Sisters, the Skyway and other lookouts via 18 stops (departs Katoomba hourly 9.30–11.30am then 12.20pm, 1.40pm, and hourly 2.30–4.30pm; day-ticket $18). They also have a "Blue Mountains Highlights" half-day coach tour ($34) including a short bushwalk. The same company does a day-tour to the Jenolan Caves (daily $64–73) and a combined bushwalk and cave visit ($85), plus adventure caving ($85) and a half-day 4WD tour of the Blue Mountains National Park ($68); they also do a full-day tour which takes in the Mount Tomah Botanic Gardens (see p.192) and the Zig Zag Railway (see below) for $55. Wonderbus (☎02/9555 9800) and Katoomba YHA (☎02/4782 1416) also do less touristy Jenolan Caves tours from Katoomba (both around $50).

Trains Katoomba Station general enquiries ☎02/4782 1902.

Lithgow and the Zig Zag Railway

LITHGOW, on the Great Western Highway 11km northwest of Hartley, is a charming coal-mining town nestled under bush-clad hills, with wide leafy streets and some imposing old buildings. The reason most people come to Lithgow, though, is for the **Zig Zag Railway**, situated about 13km east of the town on the Bells Line of Road, Clarence (from Clarence Mon–Fri 11am, 1pm & 3pm, Sat, Sun & holidays 10.30am, 12.15pm, 2pm & 3.45pm. From the Zig Zag platform add 40min to these times; $12; no bookings required but to check times call ☎02/6353 1795). In the 1860s engineers were faced with the problem of how to get the main western railway line from the top of the Blue Mountains down the steep drop to the Lithgow Valley, so they came up with a series of zigzag ramps. These fell into disuse in the early twentieth century, but tracks were relaid by rail enthusiasts in the 1970s. Served by old steam trains, the picturesque line passes through two tunnels and over three viaducts. You can stop at points along the way and rejoin a later train. Public **transport** runs regular services between Sydney and Lithgow (via Katoomba and Mount Victoria) and will stop at a Zig Zag platform on request – remember to ask the guard to let you off. People with their own transport normally catch the train from Clarence. There are plenty of **motels** in and around Lithgow – and the helpful **tourist visitors centre**, 184 Mort St (daily 9am–5pm; ☎02/6353 1859) can book accommodation for you.

Kanangra Boyd National Park and the Jenolan Caves

Kanangra Boyd National Park shares a boundary with the Blue Mountains National Park. Further south than the latter, much of it is inaccessible and it surrounds Warragamba Dam, a protected water source, but you can explore the rugged beauty of **Kanangra Walls**, where the Boyd Plateau falls away to reveal a wilderness area of creeks, rivers, deep gorges and rivers below. Reached via Jenolan Caves, there are three walks from the car park at Kanangra Walls, a short lookout walk, a waterfall stroll and a longer plateau walk; contact the NPWS in Oberon for details (☎02/6336 1972). You can get to **Oberon**, a timber-milling town and the closest settlement to Kanangra, by Countrylink bus from Mount Victoria (3 weekly).

The **Jenolan Caves** lie 30km southwest across the mountains from Katoomba on the far edge of the Kanangra Boyd National Park – over 80km by road – and contain New South Wales' most spectacular limestone formations. There are nine "show" caves with entry prices ranging from $12 to $20 (daily, guided tours every 30min 9.30am–5pm). If you're coming for just a day, plan to see one or two caves: the best general cave is the Lucas Cave ($12), and a more spectacular one is the Temple of Baal ($14). Visitors are treated to stalactites and stalagmites that have tortured themselves into extraordinary agglomerations and have been given names, such as the "Sword of Michael" and "Gabriel's Wing" (in the Temple of Baal Cave) and the "Minaret" (in the River Cave), which require the usual feat of the imagination. The system of nine limestone caves is surrounded by the **Jenolan Caves Reserve**, a fauna and flora sanctuary with picnic facilities and walking trails to small waterfalls and lookout points. There's no public transport to the caves, but many Blue Mountain tours include them on their itinerary.

You can actually **walk** from Katoomba to the Jenolan Caves; the 42-kilometre-long **Six Foot Track** through the bush begins at the Explorers Tree next to the Great Western Highway about 2.5km west of Katoomba train station; you'll need to allow two to three days for the one-way walk, and you're advised to carry plenty of water. The track, which finishes near *Jenolan Caves House* (see overleaf), was originally cut as a bridle path in 1884 to provide access to the caves from Katoomba, and was described in an 1894 tourist guide as "steep in places, but the romantic beauty of the surroundings amply compensates for the roughness of the ground". There are four basic **campsites** along the way, plus well-equipped cabins at Binda Flats reached by car from Jenolan Caves Road, sleeping six to eight people (min two nights ⑥). Book the cabins through Jenolan Caves Trust (☎02/6359 3311), who will also supply details and **information** on guided walks, while Glenbrook NPWS information centre can provide more information on camping. Fantastic Aussie Tours, 283 Main St, Katoomba (☎02/4782 1866), provides a daily transfer service ($36) for bushwalkers on the Six Foot Track; you can leave your car in their depot. The same service will get you from Katoomba to the Jenolan Caves (2hr; departs Katoomba 10.30am; departs Jenolan Caves 3.45pm), designed as an overnight rather than a day return service; otherwise Fantastic Aussie Tours offers day tours from Katoomba, as do several other operators (see Blue Mountains listings p.195) or there are many tours from Sydney (see pp.172-173).

The focus of the area, apart from the caves themselves, is the rather romantic *Jenolan Caves House*, a beautiful old hotel (☎02/6359 3304, fax 6359 3388; ⑦–⑧) which found fame as a honeymoon destination in the 1920s. If you decide to indulge, make sure you get one of the characterful older rooms rather than one in the new annexe; food in the restaurant is good and plentiful; dinner plus bed and breakfast packages are available. Other **places to stay** in the area include the peaceful and pleasant *Forest Lodge*, 7km southeast of the caves on Caves Road, Oberon Plateau (☎02/6335 6313; ⑦), where all rooms are en-suite; and the modern, prize-winning *Porcupine Hill Jenolan Cabins*, Oberon Road, 5km west of Jenolan Caves (☎ & fax 02/6335 6239; ⑥), whose very reasonably priced well-equipped two-bedroom timber cabins with wood-fires accommodate six (bring your own linen) – all with magnificent views over the Blue Mountains National Park, Kanangra Boyd National Park and the Jenolan Caves Reserve.

South

Once you escape Sydney's uninspiring outer suburbs, the journey south is very enjoyable. Beyond Botany Bay and Port Hacking, the Princes Highway and the Illawarra railway hug the edge of the **Royal National Park** for more than 20km. South of the park, the railway and the scenic Lawrence Hargrave Drive (Route 68) follow the coast to Wollongong. There's impressive cliff scenery as you pass through **Scarborough**, **Wombarra** and **Thirroul**, tiny seaside villages with a station, lovely local beaches and not much else. Just south of **Otford**, hang-gliders swoop down from the top of Lawrence Hargrave Lookout to **Stanwell Park**'s sandy beach. Between **Wollongong** and **Nowra**, the ocean beaches of the Leisure Coast are popular with local holiday-makers, while fishermen, windsurfers and yachtsmen gather at **Lake Illawarra**, a huge coastal lake near **Port Kembla**. A few kilometres further down the coast is the famous, and often lethal, blowhole at **Kiama**.

Inland, west of Wollongong, Sydney's drinking water is stored in the Cataract and Cordeaux **reservoirs**, surrounded by picnic and leisure areas. Further southwest, past **Kangaroo Valley**, the softly rolling hills of the **Southern Highlands** are dotted with old country towns such as **Berrima** and **Bundanoon**, the latter overlooking the wild and windswept crags of **Morton National Park**.

Transport down south is good, with a frequent train service operating between Sydney and Nowra, stopping at most of the coastal locations detailed below. The main bus service is Pioneer Motor Service, which stops at Wollongong and Kiama en route to Bega and Eden (☎02/4423 5233; 3–4 daily Mon–Fri, 1 daily Sat & Sun). Greyhound Pioneer (☎13 2030) has a daily Sydney–Melbourne coastal route (departing 11.30am) which also stops at Wollongong and Kiama. There are also several local bus companies in the region; these are detailed in the accounts below.

The Royal and Heathcote national parks

The **Royal National Park** is a huge nature reserve right on Sydney's doorstep, only 36km south of the city. Established in 1879, it was the second national park in the world (after Yellowstone in the USA). The railway between Sydney and Wollongong marks its western border, and from the train the scenery is fantastic – streams, waterfalls, rock formations and rainforest flora fly past the window. If you want to explore more closely, get off at one of the stations along the way – Loftus, Engadine, Heathcote, Waterfall or Otford – all starting points for walking trails into the park. On the eastern side, from Jibbon Head to Garie Beach, the park falls away abruptly to the ocean, creating a spectacular coastline of steep cliffs broken here and there by creeks cascading into the seas and little coves with fine sandy beaches. **Walking tracks** abound: the popular walk from Otford down to the secluded beachfront **Burning Palms** takes about two hours one-way, though camping is no longer allowed here, but the ultimate trek is the spectacular 26km **Coastal Walk** which takes in the entire coastal length of the park. Give yourself two days to complete the walk, which you can begin at either Otford or Bundeena, camping overnight. A good book to buy is the *Royal National Park on Foot* by Alan Fairley ($8.95; Enviro Books), and try to get a copy of the *Royal National Park* map ($5.50); both are available at the NPWS Visitor Centre (below).

You can also drive in at various points ($7.50 entry; gates open 24-hour except at Garie Beach, where they shut at 8.30pm); coming in at the northern end, reached by turning off the Princes Highway south of Loftus, you can visit the **NPWS Visitor Centre** (daily 8.30am–4.30pm; ☎02/9542 0648), about a two kilometre walk from Loftus train station if you're walking. The easy one-kilometre track from here to the Bungoona Lookout boasts panoramic views and is wheelchair-accessible. Cars are allowed right through the park, exiting at **Waterfall** on the Princes Highway or **Stanwell Park** on Lawrence Hargrave Drive. Not far south of the NPWS centre, **Audley** is a picturesque picnic ground on the Hacking River, where you can rent a boat or canoe for a leisurely paddle. Deeper into the park, on the ocean shore, **Wattamolla** and **Garie beaches** have good surfing waves; the two beaches are connected by a walking track. A stroll along Jibbon Beach will bring you to some rock engravings of the Dharawal people, one of about eighty **Aboriginal art sites** around Port Hacking.

There's a small, very basic but secluded YHA **youth hostel** inside the park 1km from Garie Beach (book in advance at any YHA hostel; key must be collected from Waterfall; ①), with no electricity or showers. There are also a number of **bushcamps** which require a permit (free) from the vistor centre – telephone in advance. The permit is then posted out to you, which can take up to five days and is awkward for travellers. If you decide to camp more spontaneously, still telephone here and they can tell you if there are any spaces and give you a permit number. You can of course just sidestep bureaucracy but you may not be able to find a space at a site.

There are **kiosks** at Audley, Wattamolla and Garie Beach. An interesting alternative way to get here is by **ferry** from the southern beachside suburb of Cronulla (see p.117) at Tonkin Street wharf just below the train station: Cronulla National Park Ferries (☎02/9523 2990; $2.40; hourly: April–Oct Mon–Fri 8.30am–5.30pm Nov–March Mon–Fri 5.30am–6.30pm except 12.30pm, Sat & Sun 8.30am–6.30pm) take half an hour to cross Port Hacking to the small town of **Bundeena** at the park's northeast tip where there's a good **campsite** at the *Bundeena Caravan Park* (☎02/9523 9520; cabins ③–④). The ferry company also offers narrated three-hour cruises of Port Hacking (Mon, Wed, Fri & Sun 10.30am; 3hr; $10).

Heathcote National Park, across the Princes Highway from the Royal National Park, is much smaller and quieter. This is a serious bushwalkers' park with no roads and a ban on trail bikes. The best **train** station for the park is Waterfall, from where you can follow a twelve-kilometre trail through the park, before catching a train back from Heathcote. On the way you pass through quite a variety of vegetation and alongside several swimmable pools, the carved sandstone of the **Kingfisher Pool** making it the most ravishingly picturesque. By **car**, you can reach the picnic area at Woronora Dam on the western edge of the park: turn east off the Princes Highway onto Woronora Road. **Camping** permits are available from the NPWS Visitor Centre (see above).

Wollongong and around

Although it's New South Wales' third-largest city, **WOLLONGONG** has more of a country-town feel, with the students of Wollongong University giving it extra life in term time. Eighty kilometres south of Sydney, it's essentially an industrial centre (Australia's largest steelworks is at nearby Port Kembla) but with a few natural attractions to make it worth visiting – such as the **Illawarra Escarpment**, which rises dramatically beyond and provides a lush backdrop to the city.

The highlight of the city itself is **Wollongong Harbour**, with its maritime feel enhanced by a fishing fleet in Belmore Basin, a fish market, a few seafood restaurants, and a picturesque nineteenth-century lighthouse on the breakwater. On either side are Wollongong's central **surf beaches**: choose North Beach for the best surf, the harbour beaches for more gentle swimming. There's not really much to see in the **city centre**, which has been swallowed up by a giant shopping mall on Crown Street, but if you want to kill a few hours, visit the **City Gallery**, on the corner of Kembla and Burelli streets (Tues–Fri 10am–5pm, Sat & Sun noon–4pm; free), a regional art centre showing changing exhibitions plus a permanent collection with an emphasis on contemporary Aboriginal and colonial Illawarra artists. Wollongong is also home to the vast **Nan Tien Buddhist Temple**, the largest in Australia, on Berkeley Road, Berkeley, south of the centre and reached from Wollongong by train. The temple offers monthly two-day meditation retreats in the temple for $70 (☎02/4272 0600 for details).

If you're **driving from Sydney**, the quickest route to take is the Princes Highway past Heathcote and the Royal National Park, avoiding the coast. However, a more scenic coastal and bush route involves driving through the Royal National Park, emerging above the cliffs at **Otford**. A few kilometres on is the impressive clifftop lookout on **Bald Hill** above Stanwell Park – you'll see not only the vista but also the breathtaking sight of **hang-gliders** taking off and soaring down. You can join in with the Sydney Hang Gliding Centre (☎02/4294 4294; *www.hanggliding.com.au*) and take tandem flights with an instructor for around $150, available daily depending on the weather; the centre also runs courses. At **Coalcliff** the *Imperial Hotel* is a must for an en-route drink, no it sits right on the cliff's edge. By the time you get to **Austinmer** you're at the base of the stunning cliffs and into some heavy surf territory; another drinking hole here is the legendary *Headlands Hotel*, which also offers budget accommodation (see p.201). A few kilometres further on, **Thirroul** is the spot where the English novelist D.H. Lawrence wrote *Kangaroo* during his short Australian interlude. The appropriately named **Sublime Point**, on the Bulli Pass at the Illawarra Escarpment, is a place to stop for fantastic views. If you have your own transport you can explore the escarpment using the **walking tracks** on Mount Kembla and Mount Keira, about 10km from Wollongong.

Practicalities

The best and cheapest way to get to Wollongong from Sydney is by **train** (departs Sydney Central Station or Redfern every 30min most of the day), which hugs the coast and stops at most of the small towns en route; Wollongong Station is right in the centre just off Crown Street. Pioneer Motor Service has three to four services on weekdays and two a day at weekends, while Greyhound Pioneer runs one daily bus service, leaving Sydney at 11.30am and returning from Wollongong at 11.50am. **Tourism Wollongong**, near the mall at 93 Crown St (Mon–Fri 9am–5pm, Sat & Sun 10am–4pm; ☎02/4228 0300), provides information and can advise on **accommodation**. The *Boat Harbour Motel,* on the corner of Campbell and Wilson streets (☎02/4228 9166, fax 4226 4878; with views ⑦, without ⑤), has comfortable and spacious rooms, some with sea views; more upmarket is Wollongong's five-star *Novotel Northbeach*, 2–14 Cliff Rd, North Wollongong (☎02/4226 3555, fax 4229 1705; ⑧), including full breakfast). Dorm rooms as well as singles and twins, some en-suite, are available at *Keiraleagh House*, 60 Kembla St (☎02/4228 6765; room ③, dorm ①, both include a light breakfast), in an old mansion converted to provide accommodation for students and backpackers, a few blocks back from the beach. A garden with a barbecue area makes for happy mingling between students and travellers. There's nowhere central to **camp** in Wollongong, but the two caravan parks to the north are right on the beach: *Corrimal Beach Caravan Park* is on Lake Parade in Corrimal, 6km north at the mouth of Towradgi Lagoon (☎02/4285 5688; cabins

④–⑧)); while *Bulli Beach Caravan Park* is 11km north of town on Farrell Road, Bulli, 11km north (☎02/4285 5677). In Austinmer the *Headlands Hotel*, on Headlands Avenue (☎02/4267 1146; ③), has inexpensive – dilapidated, but clean – rooms but with stunning views overlooking the water. Food is available from the cheap pub bistro at lunchtime.

Wollongong isn't really renowned for its **food**. There is a concentration of cafés on Kembla Street, just down from *Keiraleagh House*: the wildly painted *Stella Lunar Café* here is a popular choice with students, with its vegetarian menu and alternative feel. *Tannous*, on the corner of Crown and Corrimal streets, serves cheap and generous Lebanese food including falafel rolls and plenty of Lebanese sweets (daily 8am–midnight). Wollongong's most well-regarded eatery is *Sweetlips Café*, 50 Crown St (closed Sun & Mon), with a vivid colour scheme, outdoor seating, and a Mediterranean menu; come here for a full meal or just an espresso.

Kiama and around

Of the coastal resorts south of Sydney, **KIAMA** is probably the most attractive – though if you want more than a day- or overnight trip to the beach, you'd be better off continuing down to Nowra and beyond (see p.234). A small resort and fishing town, Kiama is famous for its star attraction, the **Blowhole**, a five-minute walk from the railway station on Blowhole Point. Stemming from a natural fault in the cliffs, the blowhole explodes into a waterspout when a wave hits with sufficient force. It's impressive, but also potentially dangerous: freak waves can be thrown over 60m into the air and have swept several over-curious bystanders into the raging sea – so stand well back. The **Kiama Visitor Information Centre**, nearby on Blowhole Point Road (daily 9am–5pm; ☎02/4232 3322 or free call ☎1800/803 897), supplies details of other local attractions such as **Cathedral Rocks**, a few kilometres to the north, whose rocky outcrops drop abruptly to the ocean.

Between the rocks there are some good sandy beaches, one of the best of which is **Seven Mile Beach**, with its own small oceanfront **national park**, about 15km south of Kiama.

West of Kiama, a steep road leads to **Mount Saddleback Lookout**, from where on a clear day you can get an incredible view of the entire coast – from the Royal National Park in the north to Jervis Bay in the south. Further west, about 14km from Kiama, is the **Jamberoo Recreation Park** (Sat, Sun & school and public holidays only 10am–5pm; $20) – a mixed bag of offerings including chairlifts, bobsleds, giant waterslides and a barbecue area. Beyond Jamberoo you can head north to join the Illawarra Highway, and follow that inland to **Macquarie Pass**, the gateway to the Southern Highlands. The **Macquarie Pass National Park** is one of the southernmost stands of Australia's subtropical rainforest; there's a car park on the road from where the Cascades Walk takes you on a 2km loop through the forest. Alternatively, Jamberoo Mountain Pass Road heads to Robertson on the Illawarra Highway via the **Budderoo National Park** where the **Minnamurra Rainforest Centre** (daily 9am–5pm, boardwalk and track closes 4pm; ☎02/4236 0469), offers an elevated boardwalk and walking track through cabbage tree palms, staghorn ferns and impressive Illawarra fig trees to the upper **Carrington Falls**. The impressive falls are 8km east of Robertson by road, and are worth a detour: a turn-off from the Jamberoo Mountain Pass Road leads to lookout points over the waterfalls.

If you want to **stay** in this area you'll find plenty of motels strung out along the highway. Alternatives in Kiama include *Kiama Backpackers*, 31 Bong Bong St, very close to the train station and right near the beach (☎ & fax 02/4233 1881; rooms ③, dorms ①), a hostel whose owner sometimes offers free trips to the surrounding areas on a quiet day; the *Grand Hotel*, corner of Manning and Bong Bong streets (☎02/4232 3782; weekdays ③, weekends ④), for budget-priced old-fashioned pub accommodation; the pub restaurant serves decent filling meals lunch and dinner daily. The closest campsite to the centre is at *Blowhole Point Caravan Park* right near the Blowhole (☎02/4232 2707; on-site vans ③, cabin ④, extra $5 weekends), while *Easts Van Park*, on Easts Beach a couple of kilometres south of Kiama (☎02/4232 2124, fax 4233 1009; basic cabins ④, en-suite ⑤; two night minimum), is handy for the beach with safe, sheltered swimming. In Gerringong there's *Nestor House*, a YHA hostel on Fern Street (☎ & fax 02/4234 1249; ①) just 250m from Werri Beach (dorms only), and also *Werri Beach Holiday Park*, Werri Beach, Gerringong (☎02/4234 1285; on-site vans ④, cabins ⑤–⑥; two night minimum), which benefits from a great location at the northern end of Seven Mile Beach, between Crooked River and the sand; canoes can be rented.

Inland: the road to Canberra

If you want to take your time getting to Canberra, there are a number of worthwhile diversions off the speedy South Western Freeway (Route 31), the main road inland which eventually joins up with the Hume Highway. Camden Valley Way heads west from the freeway to **CAMDEN** on the Nepean River, where John Macarthur pioneered the breeding of Merino sheep in 1805. The town still has a rural feel and several well-preserved nineteenth-century buildings, the oldest of which dates from 1816. En route, you'll pass **Mount Annan Botanical Garden** (daily: April–Sept 10am–4pm; Oct–March 10am–6pm; $5 per car, $2 per cyclist or pedestrian). Actually the native-plant section of the Royal Botanic Gardens in Sydney, this outstanding collection of flora is the largest of its kind in Australia. The garden is 57km southwest of Sydney and can be reached by a combination of CityRail train to Campbelltown, and then Busways (☎02/4625 8922).

From Camden, Remembrance Drive leads to **PICTON**, a small farming town cradled by hills; you can get here by train from Sydney or with Picton Coaches (☎02/4677 1564) from Campbelltown or Wollongong, via Bargo, Tahmoor and Thirlmere. Picton is a good spot for a drink at the 1839 sandstone *George IV Inn*, which brews its own beer by a traditional German method; you can imbibe in the shady beer garden and indulge in one of their legendary seafood platters. Eleven kilometres south of Picton, the five connected freshwater lakes that make up **Thirlmere Lakes National Park** are named in the language of the Gandangarra Aborigines. Lake Couridjah is best for swimming, surrounded by unspoilt bushland and plenty of birdlife. Continuing along Remembrance Drive, it's 8km to the **Wirrimbirra Sanctuary** at **Bargo** (daily 8am–5pm; free), a peaceful bushland spot run by the National Trust, with a field studies centre, a native nursery, bushwalking trails, and pools to swim in and engage in a bit of platypus-spotting at dawn or dusk. You might also see wallabies, kangaroos, wombats, brush-tailed possums and goannas, along with 150 different species of birds. There are basic **cabins** to stay in (☎02/4684 1112; ②), and outside there's a big open fireplace to sit around, which comes into its own in April when local musicians gather for the annual Brush with the Bush weekend. If you don't have your own **transport**, you can get here by taking the train from Sydney to Bargo and then walking a couple of kilometres.

The Southern Highlands

From Bargo, there are a couple of detours worth taking on the old road south, the Hume Highway, through the picturesque Southern Highlands which have been a favourite weekend retreat for Sydneysiders since the 1920s. Marking the beginning of the Highlands is **MITTAGONG**, a small agricultural and tourist town 110km south of Sydney, mostly visited on the way to the limestone **Wombeyan Caves** (daily 8.30am–4pm; $12 guided tour of one cave, $20 for two caves, cheaper family rates available; 1hr 30min) in the nearby hills. The route to the five caves begins 4km south of the town off the highway and winds upwards for 65km. Fairly special high-country scenery helps to distract you from the bumpiness of the partly unsealed road. There's a **campsite** near the caves (☎02/4853 5976; min two nights for cottages and cabins; cottages $90, cabins $60, ④–⑤, on-site vans $45 ③). For more on accommodation in the area – and a free booking service – contact **Tourism Southern Highlands** (daily 8am–5.30pm; ☎02/4871 2888) in Winifred West Park on the Hume Highway; they also have masses of information on bushwalks of varying lengths. The Southern Highlands is well served by **transport**, with a frequent train service between Sydney and Canberra stopping at Picton, Mittagong, Bowral, Moss Vale, Bundanoon and Goulburn. Priors Scenic Express (☎02/4472 4040 or free call ☎1800/816 234) from Sydney also goes to Mittagong, Bowral and Moss Vale (daily during school holidays, otherwise Mon & Tues, Thurs–Sat) while Berrima Coaches provides a local bus service (☎02/4871 3211).

Mittagong and neighbouring **BOWRAL**, 6km southwest, while less pretty than other Highland bases such as Berrima and Bundanoon, share a stash of impressive **restaurants**. At Mittagong, *Thonburi*, 60 Bowral Rd (lunch Wed–Sun, dinner daily; BYO and licensed; ☎02/4872 1511), serves delicious traditional Thai meals in an elegant setting, while *The Blue Cockerel*, 95 Hume Highway (dinner Tues–Sat; licensed and BYO; ☎02/4872 1677), is a busy bistro serving modern Australian food with a French twist. In Bowral, *The Catch*, 250 Bong Bong St (lunch Wed–Sun, dinner Wed–Mon; licensed and BYO), is a city-style brasserie focusing on fish, plus wood-fired gourmet pizzas; further down the same street, in the Empire Cinema complex, you can have the best coffee in town at *Coffee Culture* (Mon–Thurs 8.30am–5.30pm, Fri & Sat 8.30am–9.30pm). After scoffing in Bowral, cricket fans might like to check out the **Bradman Museum** on Judo Street (daily 10am–4pm; $7), which details the career of the famous Australian cricketer Don Bradman and the history of The Ashes.

The picturesque village of **BERRIMA**, 123km southwest of Sydney, is a bit further on from Mittagong. The *Surveyor General Inn*, one of an excellent complement of well-preserved and restored old buildings, has been serving beer here since 1835 – making it a good enough reason to indulge. Suitably refreshed, you can check out some of the other sights: inside the 1838 sandstone **courthouse**, on the corner of Argyle and Wiltshire streets (daily 10am–4pm; $3), is the **Visitor Centre**, while across the road is the old **Berrima Gaol**, which once held the infamous bushranger Thunderbolt – and also has the dubious distinction of being the first place in Australia where a woman was executed. Continue up Wiltshire Street from the courthouse to get to the **River Walk**, the end of which is marked by a fine reserve with picnic tables – and camping too. Other **accommodation** includes a slather of B&Bs in pretty, old stone cottages such as *Parsley Cottage* (☎ and fax 02/4877 1427; ⑦ midweek, 2-day minimum weekend $250) and *Waldon Wood* (☎02/4877 1164; ⑥). Motels here are also fairly salubrious: the *Berrima Bakehouse Motel* (☎02/4877 1381, fax 4877 1047; ⑤, Sat ⑦), on the highway at the corner of Wingecarribee Street, is a modern brick building but with the bonus of a peaceful, pleasant garden leading down to the river and a saltwater pool; the *White Horse Inn* in Market Place (☎02/4877 1204; ⑤–⑦) is a large old 1832 sandstone hotel with accommodation in modern motel units in the garden. The old building is a **restaurant** with various eating areas, ranging from small fire-placed rooms overlooked by dour portraits to the cool cellar or the green gazebo out back.

Five kilometres from Moss Vale on the Hume Highway is the turn-off south to **BUNDANOON**, famous for its annual April celebration of its Scottish heritage. Exploiting the autumnal atmosphere of mist and turning leaves, Bundanoon becomes Brigadoon for a day, overtaken by Highland Games – Aussie-style. Even if you miss the frivolity, it's an attractive spot set in hilly countryside scarred by deep gullies and with splendid views over the gorges and mountains of the huge **Morton National Park**. The park, and Bundanoon, have traditionally been a mecca for cyclists, with the long-established Ye Olde Bicycle Shop renting out bikes at very reasonable rates (Mon–Wed & Fri 10am–4.30pm, Sat & Sun 9am–5pm; $8 per hour, $15 half-day, $20 full-day; ☎02/4883 6043). It also must be one of the few bike shops in the world with its own espresso machine (lunches and cakes also available). A recommended evening activity is a visit to **Glow Worm Glen**; after dark the small sandstone grotto is transformed by the naturally flickering lights of these creatures. It's a 25-minute walk from town via the end of William Street, or an easy forty-minute signposted trek from Riverview Road in the park. Set off at sunset, armed with a torch.

Bundanoon has a classic, well-preserved **train** station which is a pleasure to arrive at from Sydney or Goulburn. The *Lynbrook YHA* **hostel**, Railway Avenue (☎ & fax 02/4883 6010; rooms ③, dorms ①), is a spacious Edwardian-era guesthouse complete with open fireplaces; the enthusiastic managers dish out loads of information and organize activities such as theme night meals. If you're after a **B&B**, the central *Gasthof Old Heidelberg*, on the corner of Penrose Road and Anzac Parade (☎02/4883 6242; ④), is the best value with a German restaurant if you're after some hearty fare (dinner Wed–Sun; mains around $17). Recommended **places to eat** are the *Post Office Restaurant*, on Railway Parade opposite the station (☎02/4883 6354), dishing up modern Australian cuisine by night (dinner Wed–Sat; mains $18) and doubling as a café during the day (Thurs–Sun 10.30am–3pm). The *Bundanoon Hotel*, on Erith Street near the train station, is a quaint little country pub which serves up plain, affordable food and is a friendly spot for a drink. There's a supermarket on Railway Terrace open daily until 9pm.

Kangaroo Valley

Between Nowra on the coast and Moss Vale on the inland road, **Kangaroo Valley** is a popular spot for weekenders from Sydney – a lovely, hidden valley situated between the lush dairy country of Nowra and the Southern Highlands. Coming from the coastal end, a narrow, winding country road climbs 700m up Cambewarra Mountain, with superb coastal panoramas along the way. **KANGAROO VALLEY** village has tearooms and a **Pioneer Settlement Museum** (daily 9.30am–4.30pm; $3) with an attached bush-walk and a **market** held in the grounds on the last Sunday of the month. From here the drive continues across the old sandstone Hampden Suspension Bridge over the Kangaroo River, to the Barrengarry plateau. Allow yourself to be waylaid at **Fitzroy Falls**, at the northeast edge of **Morton National Park**, where a short walk from the car park takes you to a waterfall plunging 80m into the valley below. The **NPWS Visitor Centre** here (daily 8.30am–5pm; ☎02/4887 7270) has been designed on a sandstone and water theme, with a deck built around existing trees. The complex includes an excellent café, and there's disabled access to the falls. Detailed information about walking tracks in the surrounding area is available, and the office issues **camping** permits for the nearby bushcamp at Yarrunga Creek. If you want to camp in rather more comfort, try the *Kangaroo Valley Tourist Park*, Moss Vale Road (☎02/4465 1310; cabins ③–⑥), on the banks of the Kangaroo River about a kilometre from the village centre, with canoes and kayaks to get you on the water. This is above all **B&B** territory: *Tall Trees Bed and Breakfast*, 8 Nugents Creek Rd, 1km east from the village (☎02/4465 1208; ⑥ midweek, ⑧ weekend, min two nights), boasts a guest lounge with log fires, serves a full country breakfast on a patio with views across the valley, and there's also a self-contained studio with a spa, woodfire and kitchen (breakfast basket supplied; ⑧). Near **BERRY**, the *Tara Country Retreat*, 219 Wattamolla Rd (☎02/4464 1472, fax 4464 2265; ⑤–⑧, cottage ⑦–⑧), is a **gay and lesbian friendly** guesthouse set in farmland and adjoining a nature reserve, and a 20-minute drive to Seven Mile Beach; camping is also available. On site there's a swimming pool, spa, steam room, games room and video library. Room rates include a continental breakfast, and evening meals are available at $20 per head. A separate two-bedroom cottage is also available.

You can get to Kangaroo Valley from Sydney on Priors Scenic Express (☎02/4472 4040 or free call ☎1800/816 234); departing from the airport at 7.30am (if booked), it picks up at Central Station at 8.20am and goes to Kangaroo Valley (daily during school holidays, otherwise Mon & Tues, Thurs–Sat); a half-hour stop is scheduled at Fitzroy Falls.

travel details

Sydney is very much the centre of the Australian transport network, and you can get to virtually anywhere in the country from there on a variety of competing services. The following list represents a **minimum**; as well as the dedicated services listed below, many places will also be served by long-distance services stopping en route.

Trains

Sydney to: Adelaide (*Indian Pacific* 2 weekly, Mon & Thurs 2.40pm; 27hr 30min); Brisbane (1 daily; 16hr); Canberra (3 daily; 5hr); Dubbo (1 daily; 6hr 40min); Goulburn (8–10 daily; 3hr); Katoomba (22–30 daily; 2hr); Maitland (1 daily; 2hr 30min); Melbourne (1 daily; 10hr 20min; plus daily bus/train Speedlink via Albury; 12–13hr); Murwillumbah (1 daily; 13hr 35min); Newcastle (20–25 daily; 2hr 30min); Perth (*90.* 2 weekly, Mon & Thurs 2.40pm; 60hr); Richmond (18–25 daily; 1hr 15min); Windsor (18–25 daily; 1hr 15min); Wollongong (15–25 daily; 1hr 40min).

Buses

Sydney to: Adelaide (2–3 daily; 20hr); Albury (2 daily; 8hr 30min); Armidale (2 daily; 8hr 30min); Batemans Bay (3 daily; 5hr 20min); Bathurst (2–3 daily; 4hr); Bega (2–3 daily; 8hr); Bowral (5 weekly; 2hr 35min); Brisbane (8–12 daily; 15–17hr, with connections to Cairns and Darwin); Broken Hill (2–3 daily; 15hr 30min); Byron Bay (8 daily; 12hr 30min); Canberra (3 daily; 4hr); Cessnock (1 daily; 2hr 20min); Coffs Harbour (8 daily; 8hr 30min); Eden (4 daily; 8hr 30min–9hr 30min); Glen Innes (2 daily; 10hr); Grafton (2 daily; 10hr); Kangaroo Valley (5 weekly; 4hr); Melbourne (5 daily; 12–18hr); Mildura (2–3 daily; 16hr); Mittagong (5 weekly; 2hr 30min); Moss Vale (5 weekly; 2hr 45min); Muswellbrook (1 daily; 3hr 30min); Narooma (4 weekly; 8hr); Newcastle (8 daily; 3hr); Nowra (3 daily; 3hr–4hr 20min); Perth (2–3 daily; 52–56hr); Port Macquarie (8 daily; 7hr); Port Stephens (1 daily; 4hr); Scone (1 daily; 3hr 50min); Tamworth (2 daily; 7hr); Taree Tenterfield (2 daily; 11hr 30min).

Flights

Sydney is the main international point of entry into Australia with flights from all around the world. It is also the centre of the domestic network, and you can fly to virtually anywhere in the country from here. Major services include:

Sydney to: Adelaide (20 daily; 2hr 30min); Alice Springs (4 daily; 2hr 40min); Ayers Rock Resort (2 daily; 3hr); Brisbane (20 daily; 1hr 15min); Cairns (15 daily; 2hr 40min); Darwin (3 daily; 4hr); Dubbo (3–5 daily; 1hr); Hobart (8 daily; 1hr 30min); Lismore (2—3 daily; 1hr 35min); Lord Howe Island (6 weekly; 2hr 20min); Melbourne (20 daily; 1hr 10min); Newcastle (Mon–Fri 4 daily; 40min); Perth (10 daily; 4hr); Port Stephens (Mon–Fri 1 daily; 1hr).

CHAPTER TWO

NEW SOUTH WALES AND ACT

N ew South Wales is Australia's premier state in more ways than one: it's not only the oldest of the five states, but it's the most densely populated too. Including Sydney, New South Wales covers an area about twice the size of Britain, with roughly a tenth of its population; not a very big state by antipodean standards, but its six and a quarter million residents constitute one-third of the country's population. Their distribution is wildly uneven: few live in the Outback or the rural regions, and the vast majority are absorbed by the urban and suburban sprawl on the coast. The state's Aboriginal population is about forty thousand, approximately one-fifth of the total living in Australia. This chapter also covers the Australian Capitol Territory (ACT), which was carved out of NSW at the beginning of this century as an independent base for the new national capital, Canberra.

When Lieutenant James Cook claimed New South Wales for Great Britain in 1770, naming it after a land that he'd apparently never visited – and to which it bears strikingly little resemblance – he could have hardly foreseen what would become of it. And indeed the early years, of penal settlement and timid encroachment into the fringes of the coastal area around Sydney, were hardly a promising start. But with the discovery of a passage through the Blue Mountains in 1813 (see p.187), the rolling plains of the west were opened up. Free (non-convict) settlers – **squatters** – appropriated vast areas of this rich pastureland, making immense fortunes off the backs of sheep. When **gold** was discovered near Bathurst in 1851, and the first goldrush began, New South Wales' fortunes were assured. Although penal transport ceased the following year, the population continued to increase rapidly and the economy boomed as fortune-seekers arrived in droves. At much the same time, Victoria broke off to form a separate colony, followed by Queensland in 1859. The much-reduced borders that New South Wales has today were defined in 1863.

There are over a thousand kilometres of **Pacific coastline** in New South Wales, from subtropical **Tweed Heads** in the north to temperate **Eden** in the south. The year-round mild climate, together with the ocean and the **beaches**, draws visitors pretty much all the time – though it's the summer holiday season that brings thousands of Australians to the coast to enjoy the extensive surf beaches and the numerous more sheltered waters, in bays, river mouths and inlets, and in a series of salt lagoons or "coastal lakes", protected behind a narrow spit from the force of the ocean waves. **South of Sydney** the coast is relatively undeveloped, and there's a string of low-key family resorts and fishing ports, great for water sports and fishing. To the **north** the climate gradually becomes warmer, and the coastline more popular – the series of big resorts up here includes **Port Macquarie** and **Coffs Harbour**, but there are also less-developed places where you can escape it all. One of the most enjoyable beach resorts in Australia is **Byron Bay**, which, despite increasing popularity, has managed to retain its

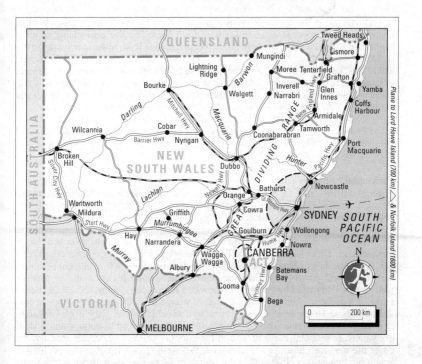

slightly offbeat, alternative appeal, which radiates from the still-thriving hippie communes of the lush, hilly **North Coast Hinterland**. We've also included in this chapter the Pacific islands far off the north coast of New South Wales: subtropical **Lord Howe Island**, 700km northeast of Sydney and roughly parallel to Port Macquarie, and **Norfolk Island**, 900km further northeast and actually closer to New Zealand, inhabited by the descendants of the mutiny on the *Bounty*.

The **Great Dividing Range** runs parallel to the coastline – often very close – splitting the state in two. In the north, the gentle **New England** stretch of the range comprises tablelands ideal for sheep- and cattle-farming; where this plateau falls away steeply towards the coast are some of the few remaining pockets of dense – at times impenetrable – primeval **forest**: the Big Scrub that drove the early settlers to despair. To the south is the Australian Capital Territory where **Canberra**, the nation's capital and a city struggling to shed its dull image, is the gateway to the **Snowy Mountains**. Here the range builds to a crescendo as **Mount Kosciuszko** (Australia's highest at 2228m) marks the peak of the Australian Alps. In winter there's skiing here, but the mountains are perhaps even better in summer, when the national park that covers most of them offers some unbeatable hiking. Unsurprisingly, it's not so warm up in the mountains of the Great Dividing Range: in summer the cooler days and the drop in temperature at night offer a welcome respite from the coastal heat and humidity. In winter, however, it can be genuinely freezing, with snow even falling near the Queensland border in Tenterfield.

West of the range, rich agricultural country gradually fades into desert-like Outback regions where the mercury can climb well above the 40°C mark in summer, while mild winter days are followed by very cold, frosty nights. West of Canberra, between the three rivers of the Murrumbidgee, the Darling and the Murray (the last dividing NSW from Victoria), is the fertile **Riverina**. Beyond New England, the flat, black-soiled plains of the **northwest** head through cotton country to the opal-mining town of **Lightning Ridge**. It's a uniquely Australian experience to leave Sydney, cross the extraordinarily scenic Blue Mountains and be gradually sucked into this vast emptiness, where the "**back o' Bourke**" is synonymous with the Outback. The mining settlement of **Broken Hill**, almost at the South Australian border, is the obvious destination, a gracious city surrounded by the desert landscape of *Mad Max* and home to the classic Outback institutions of the School of the Air and the Flying Doctor Service.

New South Wales still has a fairly extensive **rail** network, although Countrylink, as it's called, has replaced many services with buses. A one-month $249 unlimited Discovery Pass will get you just about anywhere in the state on this system (call ☎13 2232 for reservations).

Parks and wildlife

Throughout the state there are magnificent **national parks** and wilderness areas. Before European settlement, the **northeastern** corner of New South Wales was covered by dense subtropical rainforest. It's this that you can visit along the escarpment of the Great Dividing Range, though often only the very edge of these national parks or forests can be reached by road or track, while the interior is accessible only to hardy bushwalkers. These forests are inhabited by many types of parrots, and occasionally by bell birds and bower birds, brush turkeys, and marsupials such as ringtail possums, bandicoots and padimelons. **Further south**, the slightly higher altitudes and the plateaus are dominated by eucalypt forest with a more open canopy, and by less dense eucalypt woodland – the preferred habitat of wombats, wallabies, other types of possum, koalas and a few small marsupials, as well as echidnas and platypuses, kookaburras, magpies and parrots. The **Snowy Mountains** are covered by snow gums, a slow-growing, cold-resistant eucalypt, and in the summer clusters of delicate wild flowers cover the mountain hillsides and meadows. Where the forest is not protected, lumber is still big business in NSW, and is the source of fierce clashes between environmentalists and the towns that make their living from the timber trade. To the **west**, kangaroos, wallabies and emus roam the wide plains, and with a bit of luck a wedge tailed eagle can be sighted. Parks here tend to encompass vast areas of desert or places marked out by extraordinary geological formations. The far southwest corner is part of the **Mallee** – a sandy, semi-arid area covered by the eucalypt shrubs that lend the area its name. Here the mallee fowl build the incubation mounds for their eggs in the sand.

The **National Parks and Wildlife Service** (NPWS) has **entrance fees** to many of its parks – usually $5–12 per car and $4 for motorcyles (often on an honour system when there is no ranger station). If you intend to go bush often in NSW you can buy an annual pass for $50 ($30 for motorbikes), which includes all parks except Kosciuszko. Because of its popularity as a skiing destination, entrance to Kosciuszko is a steep $12 per car per day, perversely levied in summer too – so if you plan on spending any length of time here, or are going to visit other parks as well, consider the $60 annual pass which covers entry to all parks, including Kosciuszko. Permits can be bought at NPWS offices and some park entry stations, or by mail (include your vehicle type and its registration number), from The Cashier, NSW National Parks and Wildlife Service, PO Box 1967, Hurstville, NSW 2220, or over the phone using a credit card (☎02/9585 6333).

You can **camp** in most national parks. Bush camping is generally free, but where there is a ranger station and a designated campsite with facilities, fees are charged, usually around $5 per site. If the amenities are of a high standard, including hot showers and the like, or if the spot is just plain popular, fees can be as high as $15 per tent. Open fires are banned in most parks and forbidden everywhere on days when there is high danger of fire, and while there are often electric or gas barbecues in picnic areas, you'll need a fuel stove for bush camping.

AUSTRALIAN CAPITAL TERRITORY

In the 1820s the first European squatters settled in the valleys and plains north of the Snowy Mountains and established family dynasties on their prosperous grazing properties. Until the turn of the century, however, this remained a remote rural area. When the Australian colonies united in the **Commonwealth of Australia** in 1901, a capital city had to be chosen, with Melbourne and Sydney the two obvious and eager rivals. After much wrangling, and partly in order to avoid having to decide on one of the two, it was agreed to establish a brand-new capital instead: Melbourne was to be the seat of the provisional government until the new capital was completed and the government departments had moved there. A provision in the Constitution Act decreed that the seat of government was to be in the state of New South Wales and not less than one hundred miles from Sydney. In 1909 Limestone Plains, a plain south of Yass surrounded by mountain ranges, was chosen out of several possible sites as the future seat of the Australian government. An area of 2368 square kilometres was excised from the state of New South Wales and named the **Australian Capital Territory** (ACT). The ACT officially included an adjunct at Jervis Bay (see p.234), on the coast south of Nowra, to give Australia's capital its own access to the sea and a naval base. The name for the future capital was supposedly taken from the language of local Aborigines: **Canberra** – the meeting place.

Canberra is situated on a high plain (600m above sea level) and, unlike the coastal cities, experiences four distinct seasons. In summer, the average temperatures are 27°C maximum during the day and 12°C minimum at night; in winter they drop from an average of 12°C maximum during the day to freezing point (and below) at night. Spring and autumn can be really delightful, though. The mountain ranges to the west and south of the city rise up to 1900m and are snow-covered in winter.

Canberra

In 1912 Walter Burley Griffin, an American landscape architect from Chicago, won the international competition for the design of the future Australian capital: his plan envisaged a garden city for about 25,000 people, which took into account the natural features of the landscape. There were to be five main centres, each with separate city functions, located on three axes: land, water and municipal. Roads were to be in concentric circles, with arcs linking the radiating design. Construction started in 1913, but political squabbling and the effects of World War I prevented any real progress being made. Little building had been done, in fact, by the time Griffin left the site in 1920, and only in 1927 was the provisional parliament building officially opened. By 1930 some one thousand

---

ACCOMMODATION PRICES

All the accommodation listed in this book has been categorized into one of eight price bands, as set out below. The rates quoted represent the cheapest available double or twin room in high season – except for category ①, which indicates per-person rates for a dorm bed, and the categories given for units, cabins and vans, which represent the daily charge for the whole unit.

① Under $18	⑤ $61–74
② $19–30	⑥ $75–94
③ $31–45	⑦ $95–124
④ $46–60	⑧ $125 upwards

For more accommodation details, see pp.41-43.

families had settled in the capital. Then the Depression set in, World War II broke out and development slowed again. After more years of stagnation, the National Capital Development Commission (NCDC) was finally established in 1958, and at last growth began in earnest.

In 1963 the Molonglo River was dammed to form a lake 11km wide, the artificial **Lake Burley Griffin** that is the centrepiece of modern **CANBERRA**. Numerous open spaces and public buildings came into existence, as a real city started to emerge. Slowly, the **Civic Centre** near London Circuit began to live up to its name. The **population** grew rapidly, from fifteen thousand in 1947 to over one hundred thousand in 1967; today, more than three hundred thousand people live in Canberra. This population growth has been accommodated in satellite towns with their own centres: **Woden**, 12km south of the Civic Centre, was built in the mid-1960s; five years later **Belconnen** was added in the northwest; and in the mid-1970s **Tuggeranong** in the south. It was this sprawl that fostered Canberra's image as "a cluster of suburbs in search of a centre".

Inevitably, modern Canberra is mainly a city of civil servants and administrators. There are plenty of service industries – especially ones aimed at feeding and watering all those politicians and visitors – but little real industrial activity. Canberra recently gained self-government, with only the Parliamentary Triangle remaining under federal control; the self-financing responsibilities that this entails have placed a premium on tourism revenues. And indeed, the main reason to come to Canberra is for the **national museums and institutions** you can visit – top of the list is the **National Gallery**, and the stunning **New Parliament House**, opened in 1988 and certainly one of the principal tourist sights, with its original architecture intended to blend into the landscape. Canberra is also trying very hard to present an image to counter its reputation as the domain of dull bureaucrats. It hasn't succeeded yet: most Australians still regard Canberra as "pollie city" – a frosty, boring place where politicians (the lowest form of human life) and public servants (only marginally higher on the evolutionary scale) live it up at the expense of the hard-done-by Australian taxpayer. They also complain about its concentric circular streets, which can make driving here seem like a Kafkaesque nightmare, and about the contrived, neat-as-a-pin nature of the place.

But the image-makers have a point, and Canberra is a far more pleasant place than it's usually given credit for. The city has wide open spaces and many **parks** and gardens, with the impressive architecture housing the national institutions set in astonishingly well-groomed surroundings, so that you can pad barefoot through the grass from the National Gallery to the National Library, peacefully admiring the gum trees. Right on its doorstep are forests and **bushland**, with unspoilt wilderness just a bit further afield in the Brindabella Ranges and the Namagdi National Park; skiing in the Snowy Mountains or surfing on the coast are only a few hours away. To appreciate the city, you really need a vehicle of some kind – things are very spread out, and at the weekend especially (when many residents leave and the city is quite dead) public transport is extremely limited. You'll find that the dispersed nature of the city means that you can easily park your car, often for free, at the main sights. Cycling is very popular and renting a bike – to take advantage of the excellent network of bike paths – is strongly recommended (see "Listings" on p.223).

Canberra's **nightlife** is also a great deal better than you might expect considering its reputation, in term time at least: the two universities here (and the Duntroon Military Academy for officer material) means there's a large and lively **student population** (good news for those who have student cards, as most attractions offer hefty discounts). The city is said to have more restaurants per capita than any other in Australia – which is saying something – and there are plenty of pubs and nightclubs

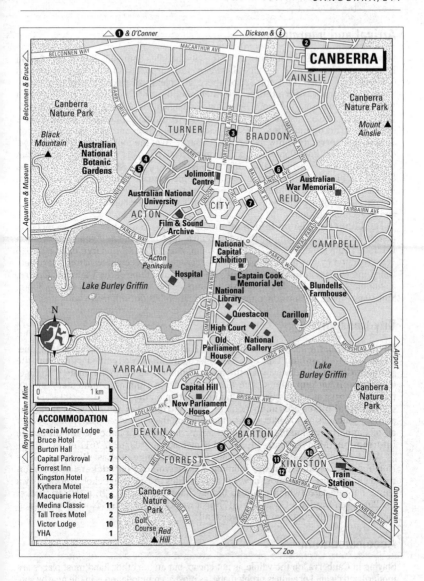

△ ❶ & O'Conner   △ Dickson & ⓘ

❷

CANBERRA

BELCONNEN WAY

MACARTHUR AVE

AINSLIE

Canbera
Nature Park

Canberra
Nature Park

Mount ▲
Ainslie

BARRY DRIVE

TURNER   BRADDON
❸

Black
Mountain
▲

**Australian
National
Botanic
Gardens**

❹
❺

**Jolimont
Centre**

❻

**Australian
War Memorial**

**Australian National
University**

CLUNIES ROSS ST

**Film & Sound
Archive**

CITY

❼

REID

FAIRBAIRN AVE

ACTON

PARKES WAY

**National
Capital
Exhibition**

PARKES WAY

CAMPBELL

Acton
Peninsula

Hospital

**Captain Cook
Memorial Jet**

**Blundells
Farmhouse**

Lake Burley Griffin

**National
Library**

Questacon

Carillon

MORSHEAD DR

High Court

**Old
Parliament
House**

**National
Gallery**

KINGS AVENUE

Lake
Burley
Griffin

N

YARRALUMLA

CAPITAL CIRCLE

Capital Hill

Canberra
Nature
Park

0   1 km

ADELAIDE AVE

BRISBANE AVE

**New Parliament
House**

STATE CIRCLE

DEAKIN

❽

BARTON

❾

FORREST

MELBOURNE AVE

❶❶

❶❷

❶❶

KINGSTON

**Train
Station**

CANBERRA AVE

Canberra
Nature
Park

CANBERRA AVE

Golf
Course Red
▲ Hill

HUGEER WAY

▽ Zoo

ACCOMMODATION	
Acacia Motor Lodge	6
Bruce Hotel	4
Burton Hall	5
Capital Parkroyal	7
Forrest Inn	9
Kingston Hotel	12
Kythera Motel	3
Macquarie Hotel	8
Medina Classic	11
Tall Trees Motel	2
Victor Lodge	10
YHA	1

to choose from, too. Many of them, though, are tucked away in hidden corners of the city or in the satellite towns. Surprisingly perhaps, Canberra also holds the dubious title of Australia's **porn** capital, due to its liberal licensing laws which legalize and regulate the sex industry. There's even an alternative tour available aboard the *Love Bus* which explores Canberra's seedier side (see "Listings" on p.224).

Arrival and information

Canberra's **airport**, about 7km east of the city, handles domestic flights only. Action Buses runs an hourly service between the airport and the city (Mon–Fri 6.55am–10pm; ☎13 1710) for $2, or there are plenty of **taxis**, charging roughly $10–12. The main **train station** is located southeast of the centre, on Wentworth Avenue in Kingston, and from here taxis are again the easiest way to get where you're going; trains also stop at the suburb of Queanbeyan, in NSW, where there's some cheap accommodation. Most interstate **buses** drop and pick up at the handy **Jolimont Centre**, downtown at 67 Northbourne Ave; the modern centre has showers, lockers ($4; until 9pm only), a TV room, snack bar, post office and an excellent travel bookshop, which also offers everything from Australia-wide tours to Canberra city bus tickets, as well as some tourist information and maps. Additionally, the centre has ticket offices for the train, airline and bus companies. There is a free direct telephone line to the tourist office (see below), to taxi companies and to accommodation.

The **Canberra Visitor Information Centre**, the main tourist office, is inconveniently located about 2km north of the centre, on Northbourne Avenue in Dickson (Mon–Fri 9am–5pm, Sat & Sun 8.30am–5pm; ☎02/6205 0044 or free call 1800/026 166), reached by bus #380; it books tours, transport and accommodation. More central is the **tourist information booth** on the ground floor of the Canberra Centre, a shopping mall on Bunda Street (Mon–Thurs & Sat 9am–5.30pm, Fri 9am–7.30pm, Sun 10am–4pm); it provides maps and information but doesn't make bookings.

City transport

The handy Murray's **Canberra Explorer Bus** (☎13 2251; hourly 11am–3pm; one-day ticket $18, four-hour tour $12; YHA discounts) does a circuit, starting from the Jolimont Centre and covering all the major sights – a 25-kilometre route with nineteen drop-off/pick-up points. The driver provides a running commentary on the places you pass as well as background information on the city.

Municipal buses are run by Action. The **day-trip ticket** ($6.70), valid all day for as many journeys as you like, is ideal for using on these services. Other buses cover all of Canberra, including the satellite towns: for details, phone Action **timetable information** (Mon–Sat 6am–11pm, Sun 8am–5.30pm; ☎02/6207 7611 or 13 1710).

Most Action buses start at the City Bus Interchange, at East Row just across Northbourne Avenue from the Jolimont Centre; you can buy **tickets** at the information kiosk here, or at most newsagents. Besides the day-trip ticket, you can pay a single flat-rate fare (which can also be purchased on board; $2), a four-trip ticket ($7.20), a ten-trip Fare Go ticket ($17) or a weekly ticket ($29). Note that bus services are severely curtailed at the weekend.

Accommodation

Staying in Canberra, on the whole, is not cheap, but on the other hand most places are modern and clean. Location is problematic, as most accommodation is in the nearby suburbs rather than the centre. One of the best locations is **Kingston**, a salubrious, café-filled suburb close to the train station, and also within walking distance of the Parliamentary Triangle attractions. **Hotels** and **motels** rarely charge less than $65 for a double, although guesthouses often have more reasonable rates. Canberra has an excellent, modern youth **hostel**, and out-of-term inexpensive B&B is available in several student halls of residence. Accommodation in the neighbouring city of **Queanbeyan**, 14km away, costs on average $10–20 less, so we've listed a couple of suggestions there, too.

Hotels, motels and guesthouses

Acacia Motor Lodge, 65 Ainslie Ave, Braddon (☎02/6249 6955, fax 6247 7058). Very central motel in a leafy street near the war memorial. A light breakfast is included. Bus #33 or #38. ⑤.

Blue & White Lodge, 524 Northbourne Ave, Downer, 5km north of the city (☎02/6248 0498, fax 6248 8277). B&B with well-equipped rooms – TV, fridge, heating, air-con and tea-making facilities; mostly shared bathrooms. Bus #39 or #50. ④–⑤.

Capital Parkroyal, 1 Binara St, Civic (☎02/6247 8999, fax 6257 4903). Central, four-star hotel with all the conveniences you'd expect, including room service, swimming pool, sauna and gym. ⑧.

Forrest Inn, 30 National Circuit, Forrest (☎02/6295 3433, fax 6295 2119). Modern motel in the embassy area next to the pretty Serbian Church offering air-con units. Bus #35 or #36. ⑥.

Kythera Motel, 98 Northbourne Ave, Braddon (☎02/6248 7611, fax 6248 0419). Well-equipped rooms with heating and air-con and a swimming pool to cool off even further. Bus #39 or #50. ⑤.

Macquarie Hotel, 18 National Circuit, Barton, 6km southeast (☎02/6273 2325, fax 6273 4241). Comfortable place with heating; all rooms share bathroom. Includes a cooked breakfast, with dinner available. Weekly rates offered. Bus #310, #311 or #360. ④.

Medina Classic, 11 Giles St, Kingston (☎02/6239 8100, fax 6239 7226). Upmarket one-, two- or three-bedroom self-catering serviced apartments with fully equipped kitchens (except for a couple of smaller apartments), popular with families. Facilities include reception, swimming pool, spa, gym and undercover parking; bike rental available. Bus #38. ⑧.

Parkview Lodge, 526 Northbourne Ave, Downer, 4km north (☎02/6248 0655, fax 6247 6166). A recommended non-smoking B&B near Southall Park; rooms with TV, fridge, heating and tea-making facilities, all en suite and some with whirlpool. Bus #39 or #50. ⑤.

Sunrise Motel, 9 Uriarra Rd, Queanbeyan (☎02/6297 2822, fax 6297 2978). Value-for-money motel with lots of extras: air-con, videos and swimming pool. ④.

Tall Trees Motel, 21 Stephen St, Ainslie (☎02/6247 9200, fax 6257 4479). Pleasant, upmarket motel in quiet shady grounds. Laundry. Bus #38. ⑥.

Hostels and college accommodation

ANU student accommodation: Bruce Hall (☎02/6267 4000), Burton & Garran Hall (☎02/6267 4333), Fenner Hall (☎02/6279 9000), Ursula College (☎02/6279 4300). Located around the Australian National University campus in Acton, just west of the city centre; most rooms are singles, but there are also a few twins. ②–④.

Canberra YHA Hostel, 191 Dryandra St, O'Connor (☎02/6248 9155, fax 6249 1731). A large, modern institutionalized hostel backing onto extensive bushland. Reception open daily 7am–10pm, with a small shop for supplies as well as bike rental. Ten minutes from the centre on bus #35. Due to the distance from the centre, they refund $7 of your taxi fare to get to the hostel (present your receipt on arrival). Rooms ③, dorms ①.

Kingston Hotel, Canberra Ave, corner of Giles St, Kingston, 6km southwest (☎02/6295 0123). A lively pub with shabby backpackers' accommodation; facilities include a kitchen. Cheap pub grub counter meals available. Bus #38 or #84. ①.

Victor Lodge, 29 Dawes St, Kingston, 4km southwest (☎02/6295 7777). A small, friendly, family-run backpackers' hostel/guesthouse. Clean, bright rooms with heating, washbasin, and desks in the singles; rates include linen and duvets. Facilities include baths, showers, fridge, laundry, TV room and barbecue area, but no kitchen. Bicycle and car rental; city pick-ups and drop-offs. Bus #38 or #84. Rooms ③, dorms ①.

Camping and caravan parks

Canberra Carotel, Federal Highway, Watson, 6km north (☎02/6241 1377). Park with a swimming pool and café. Campsites and holiday apartments (for up to six people). Bus #36. Cabins ④, on-site vans ③.

Crestview Tourist Park, 81 Donald Rd, Queanbeyan (☎02/6297 2443). Facilities include a swimming pool and shop. Camping space, plus cabins ③–④.

Federal Highway Tourist Park, Federal Highway, Sutton, NSW, 12km northeast (☎02/6241 6411). Good facilities – swimming pool, tennis courts, licensed bistro and supermarket. Cabins ④.

White Ibis Tourist Village and Caravan Park, Bidges Rd, off the Federal Highway, Sutton, NSW, 12km northeast (☎02/6230 3433). Good site with pool, tennis court and kiosk selling the essentials. Cabins ④.

The City

Strictly planned as it is, Canberra is a straightforward place to find your way around – though distances are such that only in the very centre will you want to do much walking, and even there it can be something of a test of fitness. The eleven-kilometre-wide **Lake Burley Griffin** pretty much marks the heart of the city, with several lakeside places of interest both north and south. North of the lake is the city centre proper, the **Civic Centre**, or "Civic" for short, which houses shops, restaurants, cafés, pubs, cinemas and theatres, as well as the GPO and the tourist information office. The campus of the **Australian National University** (ANU) is just to the west of the centre in the suburb of Acton, and you'll also find the **National Film and Sound Archive** here. Beyond Acton, the **National Botanic Gardens** sit at the flanks of the 806-metre **Black Mountain**, topped by the distinctive Telecom Tower and just one of many scattered sections of the **Canberra Nature Park**. East of the centre is the **Australian War Memorial**, solemnly gazing back along monument-lined **Anzac Parade** to the **Parliamentary Triangle**, south of the lake, with the old Parliament House overlooked by the New Parliament House on Capital Hill. This political quarter, linked to the city centre by the **Commonwealth Avenue Bridge**, is where you'll find the government offices and national cultural institutions, and is the part of Canberra that is of most architectural interest. Fronting the lake, strung along King Edward Terrace, are four impressive modern public buildings: the **National Library**, **Questacon** (the National Science and Technology Centre), the **National Gallery** and the **High Court**. The prime minister himself resides at The Lodge in **Yarralumla**, at the foot of Capital Hill, while most of the foreign embassies – intended to resemble the vernacular architecture of their home countries – cluster around Yarralumla and Forrest.

Questacon and the National Library

Crossing the Commonwealth Avenue Bridge from the city centre, you turn left onto King Edward Terrace. Immediately before you is **Questacon – the National Science and Technology Centre** (daily 10am–5pm; $8, children $4), a "hands-on" museum opened in 1988 as a joint Australian/Japanese bicentennial project. The centre's six galleries are arranged around a 27-metre-high drum at the core of the building, and are linked by a continuous spiral walkway. There are some free interactive exhibits in the foyer if you just want a taste, but it's a good place to keep children occupied.

BLUE POLES

The National Gallery's most valuable foreign work of art is **Blue Poles** by the American painter **Jackson Pollack**. The monumental abstract painting was bought by the Labor government in 1973 for A$1.3 million, which at the time was a world-record price for a contemporary American painting. The Australian press immediately vilified the painting as seeming to be the work of drunks and an emblem of the liberal excesses of the Whitlam era (see "A History" p.997 in Contexts). However, the painting was recently loaned to the Museum of Modern Art in New York to feature in a Pollack retrospective as one of the artist's most significant works; the museum's chief curator, Kirk Varnedoe, expressed that he would love to have this masterpiece as part of the permanent collection. Though not for sale, if it were to be put on the market today bidding would start at at least A$45 million.

Looming behind the science centre is one of the country's most important institutions, the **National Library** (Mon–Thurs 9am–9pm, Fri & Sat 9am–5pm, Sun 1.30–5pm; free guided tours Tues–Thurs 2pm), whose Reading Room has a comprehensive selection of overseas newspapers and magazines. There are also exhibitions of rare books in the foyer, and usually some kind of interesting temporary display, including items from the pictorial collection comprising about forty thousand items; you can view any of those not on display via an interactive touch-screen system in the foyer. The library's *Brindabella Bistro* is a good place to stop for a cappuccino and a snack – it's open until half an hour before the library closes.

The High Court of Australia

From the library, it's a pleasant walk about 500m east along lakefront Parkes Place to the **High Court of Australia** (daily 9.45am–4.30pm), the highest authority in the Australian judicial system, set in an appropriately grandiose, glass-fronted edifice with a stylized waterfall running alongside the walkway up to the entrance. Its functions are to uphold and interpret the constitution and to hear cases referred from the lower courts, which involves delivering about seventy judgements a year. Visitors can watch a short video that explains the court's function and examines two of its landmark cases: its 1983 ruling that saved Tasmania's wild Franklin River from damming as part of a hydroelectric scheme, and its finding on the 1992 land rights case Mabo versus Queensland – a momentous decision that overturned the British legal concept of *terra nullius* whereby Australia was considered uninhabited prior to white settlement in 1788. The Great Hall and three courtrooms are also worth looking at – and there's a licensed café upstairs.

The National Gallery

One of the major attractions in Canberra is the **National Gallery** (daily 10am–5pm; $3; free daily 1hr guided tours of Australian art 11am & 2pm, international art same hours, Aboriginal and Torres Straits Island art Thurs & Sun 11am), situated on Parkes Place immediately east of the High Court, to which it is linked by a footbridge. Occupying twelve galleries spread over three floors, the collection explores the art of Africa and the Americas, Asia and Europe from ancient to modern (with a fairly good collection of modern European and North American art, including works by Monet, de Chirico, Magritte and Tanguy), but the core of the national collection is Australian. There are also regular special exhibitions and international touring shows (admission charge).

For most visitors, the highlight is the **Art of Aboriginal Australia and Torres Strait Islands** gallery on the entrance level; the collection is extensive and every six months a new display is mounted, ranging from traditional bark paintings from the Northern Territory to politically aware contemporary work in different media. On permanent display is the **Aboriginal Memorial 1988**, which pays homage to the Aboriginal people who since 1788 have lost life, land and culture; the memorial comprises two hundred termite-hollowed logs representative of the culture's log coffins, painted with totemic designs by over forty artists from around Ramingining in Central Arnhem Land.

On the upper level, the **Australian Art** gallery explores the country's visual arts, from colonial to contemporary. Most striking are the 25 paintings in Sidney Nolan's celebrated *Ned Kelly* series, painted in the 1940s. Other works on permanent display include Russell Drysdale's *The Drover's Wife* (1945), probably his best-known painting.

Outside is a living fern-tree sculpture by Australian artist Fiona Hall, and a **Sculpture Garden** overlooking Lake Burley Griffin. Also visible and audible from here is the **Carillon** stranded on Aspen Island, whose three bell towers with 53 bronze bells were a gift from the British government to mark Canberra's fiftieth birthday. It's pleasant to sit on the lawns under a shady tree by the lake and listen to the recitals (Wed 12.30–1.30pm & Sun 2.45–3.30pm). On summer evenings, concerts and other events, such as open-air film screenings, sometimes take place here to coincide with special exhibitions.

The Old and New Parliament houses

Away from the lake, on King George Terrace at the foot of Capital Hill, is the **Old Parliament House** (daily 9am–4pm; $2; tours every 30min), whose grounds became the site of a live-in Aboriginal protest for land rights (dubbed the **Tent Embassy**) for over six months in 1972. Twenty years later a second tent embassy was erected, to protest the fact that Aboriginal land rights had still not been achieved, and it remains there still, flying the Aboriginal flag.

The simple white Neoclassical building was the seat of government from 1927 until 1988, but it was only ever meant to be a provisional parliament house for fifty years; a **tour** of the "wedding cake" – either before or after seeing the New Parliament House to allow comparisions – provides a fascinating insight into how crowded and inconvenient the building actually was. Presently, the **National Portrait Gallery** ($2) uses the building for exhibitions, making it something of a treasure trove to visit. Outside, you can wander in the **Senate Rose Garden** or visit the National Archives of Australia, Queen Victoria Terrace which has socio-historical exhibitions (daily 9am–4pm; free).

Merging onto Capital Hill itself is the **New Parliament House**, with its grass-covered contours (daily 9am–5pm, extended hours for Parliamentary evening sessions; free guided tours 9am–4.30pm every 30min; information line ☎02/6277 5399). The stunning angular design of the exterior, topped by a sputnik-like flagpole, is matched by the interior, which represents the best in Australian art and design. You can wander about inside unattended but the excellent guided tour is recommended, helping you to come to grips with the amount of work that went into a building which employs three people just to change the lightbulbs. The first-floor theatre screens hourly films about the construction of the building, including interviews with architects and artisans. There's an excellent café (daily 10am–4.30pm) with an outdoor area with views across to Old Parliament House.

An **international competition** for a new Parliament House was launched in 1980, the brief being to create a building true to Walter Burley Griffin's vision of a city nestling in the natural folds of the land. The resulting building (opened in May 1988) was the startling design of Romaldo Giurgola, an American-based Italian architect. You're free to walk over, loll on, and even roll down the grassy ramps covering the building, while perhaps ironically contemplating the idea that you are dancing on the heads of the politicians below. Outside the ground-floor entrance level is a **mosaic** by the Aboriginal artist Michael Tjakamarra Nelson – a piece that conveys the idea of a sacred meeting place. Inside, the impressive **foyer** is dominated by grand marble staircases and over forty columns speckled grey-green and brown representing both a eucalypt forest and the marble columns used by European settlers when they built. The floors are made of native woods, and the walls feature marquetry panels detailing native plants.

Beyond the foyer, the **Great Hall** is dominated by a vast twenty-metre-high tapestry based on a painting of the same dimensions by **Arthur Boyd**; in a richly symbolic landscape, the opposing forces of life and death meet in blackened trees set against a powerful sky. Other chambers are adorned with paintings by artists such as Albert Tucker, Sidney Nolan and Ian Fairweather, as well as portraits of political figures, photographs, and ceramics. Important documents in the country's political history are also on display, as is an exhibition on Federation and a display outlining the Australian political system.

THE ANZACS

Travelling around Australia you'll notice almost every town – large or small – has a war memorial dedicated to the memory of the Anzacs, the **Australia and New Zealand Army Corps**.

When war erupted in Europe in 1914, Australia was overwhelmed by a wave of pro-British sentiment. On August 5, 1914, one day after Great Britain had declared war against the German empire, the Australian prime minister summed up the feelings of his compatriots: "When the Empire is at war so Australia is at war." On November 1, 1914, a contingent of twenty thousand enthusiastic volunteers – the **Anzacs** – left from the port of Albany in Western Australia to assist the mother country in her struggle.

In Europe, Turkey had entered the war on the German side in October 1914. At the beginning of 1915, military planners in London (Winston Churchill prominent among them) came up with a plan to capture the strategically important Turkish peninsula of the Dardanelles with a surprise attack near **Gallipoli**, thus opening the way to the Black Sea. On April 25, 1915, sixteen thousand Australian soldiers landed at dawn in a small bay flanked by steep cliffs: by nightfall, two thousand men had died in a hail of Turkish bullets from above. The plan, whose one chance of success was surprise, had been signalled by troop and ship movements long in advance; by the time it was carried out, it was already doomed to failure. Nonetheless, Allied soldiers continued to lose their lives for another eight months without ever gaining more than a feeble foothold.

In December, London finally issued the order to withdraw. Eleven thousand Australians and New Zealanders had been killed, along with as many French and three times as many British troops. The Turks lost 86,000 men.

Official Australian historiography continues to mythologize the battle for Gallipoli, elevating it to the level of a national legend on which Australian identity is founded. From this point of view, in the war's baptism of fire, the Anzac soldiers proved themselves heroes who did the new nation proud, their loyalty and bravery evidence of how far Australia had developed. It was "the birth of a nation", and at the same time a loss of innocence, a national rite of passage – never again would Australians so unquestioningly involve themselves in foreign ventures.

Today the legend is as fiercely defended as ever, the focal point of Australian national pride, commemorated each year on April 25, **Anzac Day**. To outsiders, it may seem like a one-battle flag-waving ceremony, and the question of why a futile battle in someone else's interests would occupy such a central place in the country's conscience may occur to the visitor. However, the ceremony is akin to Britain's Remembrance Day and the USA's Veterans' Day, all solemn occasions when one is asked to reflect on the sacrifices made by those who fought in all wars.

When Parliament is in session – usually from seventy to eighty days a year – you can sit in the public gallery and watch the proceedings in the House of Representatives (the lower chamber of Parliament) or the Senate (the upper chamber of the legislature); **Question Time** at the House of Representatives (3pm) makes for good viewing, though it's also the most popular time; to guarantee a seat, book in advance on ☎02/6277 4889. There are always plenty of seats for Question Time at the Senate (2pm).

The diplomatic quarters and the mint

After visiting the New Parliament House, a trip among the upmarket suburban homes in Canberra's diplomatic quarters – **Yarralumla** and **Forrest** – completes the political sightseeing tour. The consuls and high commissions were asked to construct buildings that deployed the typical architecture of the countries they represent. The result is an international compendium of architectural styles. Some of the eye-catching national designs worth looking out for include the American Embassy's plantation-style mansion, and the embassies of Thailand, Indonesia (with a small cultural centre), the People's Republic of China and Papua New Guinea.

At the **Royal Australian Mint**, a few kilometres to the southwest on Denison Street, Deakin (Mon–Fri 9am–4pm, Sat & Sun 10am–3pm; free), you can watch money being "made" on weekdays and acquire a few items for your coin collection at the Collectors' Shop.

Lake Burley Griffin

Back across the Commonwealth Avenue Bridge, the northern shores of Lake Burley Griffin have plenty to offer. At the furthest western end of the lake, by the Scrivener Dam on Lady Denman Drive, is the **National Aquarium**, opened in 1989 (daily 9am–5.30pm; $10). Visitors walk through tunnels of acrylic glass while sharks, stingrays and other creatures glide past, only an arm's-length away. Other tanks and exhibits present the ecosystem of the Great Barrier Reef, and contain freshwater fish, sea snakes, marine turtles and saltwater crocodiles. Yarramundi Reach, a couple of kilometres closer to the city centre on Lady Denman Drive, is the site of the **National Museum of Australia Visitor Centre** (Mon–Fri 10am–4pm, Sat & Sun 1–4pm; free). The museum's permanent home is currently under construction, and a short film screened at the centre outlines the ambitious project to house the two hundred thousand artefacts in the collection. The new $100 million museum will occupy a prime lakefront site on the Acton Peninsula and should be completed by 2001, the centenary of Federation.

Just east of the Commonwealth Avenue Bridge, you'll pass the **National Capital Exhibition** at Regatta Point (daily 9am–5pm; free), comprising a small theatre, displays and models depicting Canberra's development from the cattle and sheep pastures of the nineteenth century to its modern incarnation as capital city. There's a great view from the terrace, though on windy days you have to beware of the spray from the **Captain Cook Memorial Jet** (10am–noon & 2–4pm, also 7–9pm during daylight saving), which spurts a column of water 140m into the air. The jet, built in 1970 to mark the bicentenary of Captain Cook's "discovery" of Australia, costs over $125 an hour to run – hence the limited operating times.

Further east is one of the few historic buildings in the city: **Blundells Cottage**, on Wendouree Drive in Kings Park (daily 10am–4pm; $2), serves as a reminder of the farming industry that flourished here before Canberra became the capital. Built in 1860, this simple farmhouse once housed workers from a sheep station, and has been preserved as a small museum. Almost due south of here is the **Carillon** (see p.215), across the lake from the National Gallery.

The Australian War Memorial and Mount Ainslie

To the east of the city, the massive, domed building perched at the base of Mount Ainslie, at the far end of **Anzac Parade** (its length lined with smaller war memorials), is the **Australian War Memorial** (daily 10am–5pm, school and public holidays from 9am; free guided tours at 10am, 10.30am, 11am, 1.30pm & 2pm). At the same time as commemorating the 102,000 Australian soldiers who lost their lives in seven wars in the last hundred years, most movingly in the Hall of Memory, this is also a military museum, depicting war through miniature battle dioramas and old aircraft. Although it's the most visited museum in Australia, with an average of about a million visitors a year – many of them motivated by patriotism – this mixture makes for slightly uneasy viewing: it's an unquestioningly heroic past that's constructed here, with the Anzac legend as its most illustrious episode. However, the museum does have some intriguing temporary exhibitions – past ones have looked at the Boer War, for example – which do make the point about Australians fighting for interests which were actually remote to them. For something more life-affirming, the picnic grounds in bushland behind the memorial yield the beginning of a walk to the summit of Mount Ainslie – really a large round hill and part of Canberra Nature Park (see p.220) – where a lookout provides a perfect view over the city and the Parliamentary Triangle.

ANU and the National Film and Sound Archive

The green, spacious **Australian National University** campus (ANU), just west of the city centre in **Acton**, is a pleasant place to wander. The two small **anthropological museums** at the Hope Building on Ellery Crescent are open to the public (Mon–Fri 9am–4pm; free), and there are also the usual student activities, concerts and plays: for information about current and forthcoming events phone the recorded weekly diary on ☎02/6249 0742. Within the grounds of the ANU campus, on McCoy Circuit, the **National Film and Sound Archive** is the most comprehensive collection of Australian sound and screen recordings in existence, dating back to the 1890s. One of the highlights of a visit here is an interactive exhibition (daily 9am–5pm; $5.50), where (via infrared lights) special headphones tune in to the frequency of each display as you pass. A highlight of the exhibits is the yellow car that split in two in the 1986 film *Malcolm* (see "Australian Film", p.1011); the scene is replayed on a video screen. Past eras come alive at the touch of a button, providing archival footage of various towns in Australia. A wildcard display of Australian TV ads features some real humdingers from the 1970s, and you can watch fascinating snippets from old newsreels in a small projection room.

Black Mountain and around

The **National Botanic Gardens** (daily 9am–5pm; free guided tours Mon–Fri 11am, Sat & Sun 11am & 2pm), on the flanks of Black Mountain, are well worth a diversion from the city centre – beautiful in themselves and an excellent introduction to Australian flora. About six thousand species of native plants have been planted here in ecological niches, including an example of Sydney Basin flora, some mallee shrubland, and rainforest species growing in a shady, watered gully. There are hundreds of different types of eucalypts, banksias and proteaceas, as well as tree ferns and even an Aboriginal trail. The main entrance is on Clunies Ross Street, beyond the university area, and there's a visitor information centre (daily 9.30am–4.30pm; ☎02/6250 9450) with leaflets for self-guided tours, displays and videos, and a small bookshop; nearby there's a pleasant coffee shop (same hours).

While you're here, you should take the opportunity to drive up to Black Mountain, which rises about 200m above Canberra. On clear days, the panoramic view of Canberra and across the ACT from the 58-metre-high viewing platform at the **Black Mountain Telstra Tower** (daily 9am–10pm; $3) is magnificent. The tower also has a café and a revolving restaurant (advance booking recommended on ☎02/6248 6162) for families, serving smorgasbord. Both gardens and tower are on the route of Action bus #904, which also goes to the aquarium (see p.218).

North of Black Mountain, the **Australian Institute of Sport**, on Leverrier Crescent in Bruce (☎02/6252 1444; tours with an AIS athlete Mon–Fri 11.30am & 2.30pm, Sat & Sun 10am, 11.30am, 1pm & 2.30pm; 1hr 30min; $7; bus #431), is a manifestation of Australia's craze for sport. The ultra-modern, multimillion-dollar complex was established in 1981 with the aim of churning out world-class athletes, and a visit is particularly relevant with the Sydney 2000 Olympics. The Sportex interactive sports exhibition gives you the chance to test your sporting prowess, and there's a café and a shop selling souvenirs and sports clothing – just in case you decide to take advantage of the facilities (at an extra charge): a heated pool, spa and sauna, and indoor and outdoor tennis courts.

Canberra Nature Park

The bush hills and ridges which intersperse Canberra's suburbs make up the **Canberra Nature Park**, which has many walking tracks to explore. You can pick up maps and guides from the ACT Government Information Shop Front, Saraton Building, East Row, Civic, or call the park headquarters for more information on ☎02/6207 2090. The park actually comprises many sites, one of the most accessible being the Bruce/O'Connor Ridge section, across Belconnen Way from the Black Mountain area of the park; from here, several walking tracks head through bushland, including one that runs right behind the well-positioned youth hostel.

Eating and drinking

All cuisines imaginable are represented somewhere in Canberra and the surrounding suburbs, and if you have the time it's well worth getting out of the centre to explore some of them. Woolley Street in **Dickson** is the best suburban street to head for, crammed as it is with a variety of Asian restaurants and supermarkets. The well-off areas of **Manuka** and **Kingston**, near New Parliament House, have gourmet delis and fine restaurants. **Civic** itself is well served with places to eat, especially in the pedestrian mall around Garema Place. In addition to the restaurants listed here, Canberra's many clubs (see "Entertainment and nightlife", p.221) also serve very inexpensive meals in a typical Aussie atmosphere. **Cafés** are plentiful around the centre, with a particular concentration on Bunda Street, near the cinemas. On the ground level of the City Market shopping mall, on the corner of Bunda Street and Ainslie Avenue, there's an excellent food court, as well as a large supermarket, both open daily. Most local buses go from the City Bus Interchange to the suburbs listed below (see "City transport", p.212, for details).

Cafés and food courts

Ali Baba, corner of Petrie Plaza and Bunda St. A simple Lebanese takeaway with outside tables. Daily to 10pm, very late Fri & Sat.

ANU Union, Union Crescent, Acton. The students' union has a restaurant, a café and a super-cheap bistro specializing in Asian food. BYO. Mon–Fri lunch and dinner.

The Café, Barrine Drive, west of the Commonwealth Avenue Bridge, next to Mr Spokes Bike Hire. In a lovely spot by the lake. Open daily from 9am.

Café Essen, Garema Arcade. A groovy, gourmet coffee house with unusual, good value brunches and live music on Sundays. Open daily from 7.30am.

Caffe della Piazza, 19 Garema Place. A lively, people-watching place spilling out into the square, with sidewalk tables. Great Italian coffee, focaccia, pizza and pasta. Licensed.

Glebe Park, 15 Coranderk St, at the southern end of Bunda St. A choice of inexpensive food stalls – Lebanese, Indian and more – a café and a pub under one roof. Daily 10.30am–8.30 or 9pm.

Gus' Café, Bunda St, next to Center Cinema. Canberra's best café serves inexpensive light meals, and fresh soups with lots of choice for vegetarians. Tables outside under vines and a huge tree; magazines and newspapers to read. Popular with students and an arty crowd. Open daily 7.30am–11pm.

Mother's Café, Bunda St. Gourmet burgers and yummy baked goods. Open daily.

Pancake Parlor, corner of East Row and Alinga St. Open 24hr Fri–Sun, which is its main attraction. Mon–Wed 7am–late.

Waffles Patisserie and Bakery, 102 Alinga St, near the Jolimont Centre. Quality cakes and breads and healthy slices make good breakfast fare. Mon–Fri from 7.30am, Sat from 8am. Closed Sun.

Restaurants

Anarkali Pakistani Restaurant, corner of London Circuit and Akuna St (☎02/6247 6135). An excellent, affordable curry house. Licensed. Closed Sat & Sun lunch.

Australian Pizza Kitchen & Brewery, Lower Ground Floor, corner of London Circuit and East Row. Gourmet pizzas plus Canberra's only "boutique brewery", where beer is brewed on the premises. Pleasant courtyard.

The Chairman and Yip, 108 Bunda St (☎02/6248 7109). A stylish, good-humoured Chinese restaurant, its walls adorned with Mao paraphernalia; a "workers lunch" costs $12.50.

Delicateating, O'Connor Shopping Centre, Macpherson St. Trendy, delicatessen-style place tending towards Italian cuisine, and conveniently located near the youth hostel. Mellow yellow walls and tables outside. BYO. Mon–Fri 10am–10pm, Sat & Sun 9am–10pm.

Fringe Benefits Brasserie, 54 Marcus Clarke St (☎02/6247 4042). Stylish restaurant with an extensive wine cellar. Licensed. Closed Sun.

Gundaroo Pub Restaurant, Cork St, Gundaroo. Features "typical Outback Aussie atmosphere" with dishes such as kangaroo-tail soup, roast and three veg, or damper and billy tea.

Karuna House, 32 Archibald St, Lyneham. Oriental-style vegetarian restaurant at the Sakyamuni Buddhist Centre; $10 buffet dinner Tues–Sun, or $7 lunch at weekends.

Little Saigon, corner of Alinga St and Northbourne Ave (☎02/6230 5003). Large, busy, cheap and tasty Vietnamese restaurant. Advisable to book on weekends. Open daily 9am–3pm & 5–10.30pm.

Mama's Café and Bar, 7 Garema Place. Decent, usually crowded, Italian restaurant with outside tables. Daily 10am–late.

Montezuma's Mexican, FAI House, 197 London Circuit. Loud and popular, with live entertainment Fri–Sun. Licensed. Closed Mon.

The Oak Room, *Hyatt Hotel*, 1 Commonwealth Ave, Yarralumla (☎02/6270 1234). Expense-account territory: suitably refined old-school dining. Blokes need a tie at dinner. Licensed. Closed Sun & Mon.

Ottoman Cuisine, First floor, Shop 8, Franklin St, Manuka (☎02/6239 6754). An excellent Turkish restaurant that's a little more expensive than the Sydney equivalent, but worth it. Particularly delicious seafood. Licensed & BYO. Closed Sun.

Red Sea Restaurant, 128 Bunda St (☎02/6257 6633). African restaurant serving Eritrean and Moroccan cuisine – stews, couscous and the like. A club here gets kicking after 9pm, sometimes with live African music. Licensed and BYO. Tues–Fri lunch, Tues–Sun dinner.

Three Mothers Thai, Petrie Plaza off Garema Place (☎02/6249 8900). A modern, trendy brasserie-style Thai, very reasonably priced and with speedy service. BYO. Daily 10.30am–10pm.

Entertainment and nightlife

There's plenty happening in Canberra, and if it all sometimes seems rather "worthy", that's made up for by the liveliness of the student scene and by liberal licensing laws. For current events, the daily *Canberra Times* is your best bet: the most extensive **listings** are published every Thursday in a cultural and entertainment supplement, *Good Times*. For details of bands and clubs, pick up a copy of *BMA*, a free monthly music magazine. The visitor information centre and most hotels also distribute the quarterly booklet *Canberra What's On*, which lists major cultural events.

Nightclubs, pubs and music

There are several **nightclubs** in Canberra, including *Pandora's*, on the corner of Mort and Alinga streets, with two floors of dance music, disco and rock; and *The Private Bin*, on the corner of Northbourne Avenue and East Row, where the city's public servants let their hair down. Also worth checking out is *Club Asmara*, 128 Bunda St, an African-run joint with live African music and Latin nights, popular with the thirty-something set.

In the centre, the best **pub** for a drink is the tiny *Phoenix Pub*, 23 East Row, which attracts a grungey crowd and has feral live bands. Popular with locals and tourists alike is the large Irish theme pub *P. J. O'Reilly's*, at the corner of West Row and Alinga Street, which also has a reasonable restaurant and snack menu (daily 11am–10pm). An equally Irish pub, with Guinness on tap, pork pies and occasional live music is the *Wig & Pen*, in the Canberra Arcade. A good pub away from the centre is *Maddie's Bar*, in the *Kingston Hotel*, 73 Canberra Ave, Kingston; it's popular with travellers because of the nearby hostel, and is open Wed–Sat until 4am. The *ANU Bar*, on Childers Street at the ANU campus in Acton, entertaining six thousand or so students, is invariably the best place for **rock bands** of all sorts, with live performances at least a couple of times a week during term time (☎02/6249 5010 for details), while the *Canberra Workers Club* (☎02/6248 0399) hosts big touring bands, with cheap drinks until midnight. Clustered around Garema Place in the city centre are several bars and dance venues, including the *Red Room* (above *Caffe della Piazza*) with cocktails and one-off poetry nights in a loungey, rougey setting; *Gypsy Bar*, 131 City Walk, with live bands performing ($8 entry fee); *Liquid Lounge* (underneath *Antigo Café*) a commercial top 40 dance club, and *Heaven*, at Petrie Palace, the best dance club, popular with Canberra's gay set ($5–10).

However, the music you're most likely to hear in Canberra is **jazz**. *Déjà Vu*, the upstairs bar at the Canberra Casino, 21 Binara St (☎02/6257 7074), regularly hosts big-name jazz bands. For something more intimate, jazz can be heard on Sunday night from 7pm at *Tilleys*, an ambient café/bar/gallery in Lyneham at 96 Wattle St; more mainstream jazz is played on Thursday at *Olims's Canberra Hotel*, corner of Limestone and Ainslie avenues, Braddon, and at *The Contented Soul*, Woden Town Square, Woden. The *Canberra Yacht Club*, Lotus Bay, Coronation Drive, Yarralumla, has more middle-of-the-road entertainment on Friday night, featuring a singer and guitarist. On Saturday evening the *Pot Belly Bar*, Weedon Close, Belconnen, has **folk** and **blues**, but a younger, hipper crowd hangs out at *Gypsy Bar and Brasserie*, 9 East Row, for the live blues, R&B, folk and acoustic nights. **Classical music** performances are staged sporadically at the Canberra Theatre Centre in Civic Square (☎02/6257 1077), and regularly at the Canberra School of Music, Llewellyn Hall (☎02/6249 5700).

Theatre and cinema

The main **drama** venue in the capital is the impressive Canberra Theatre Centre on Civic Square (☎02/6257 1077). In addition to a broad range of plays, its several theatres also host concerts, dance performances and readings – it's always worth finding out what's going on here. In addition there are a number of active independent theatre groups based at the Gorman House Community Arts Centre on Ainslie Avenue, Braddon (☎02/6249 0448 for information and bookings), performing here in the Currong Contemporary Arts Theatre. The Skylark Puppet & Mask Theatre is based at Strickland Crescent, Deakin (☎02/6285 1121). *Tilleys* in Lyneham (see "Nightclubs, pubs and music", p.221) also hosts cabaret programmes, as does the *School of the Arts Café*, 108 Monaro St, Queanbeyan (☎02/6297 6857), worth checking out for its new plays by fringe theatre groups, as well as its live music and comedy acts – all from Thursday to Saturday.

As for **cinemas**, the Center Cinema on Bunda Street (☎02/6249 7979; cheap day Tues and after 6pm Sun) is probably the best of the regular commercial choices, with Saturday late shows at 11pm, while the Electric Shadows Cinema, Akuna Street (☎02/6247 5060; cheap day Wed $8), shows the best in world cinema, and has a book-shop and café-bar.

Clubs

Numerous **clubs**, most of which admit visitors, are one of the features of Canberra life. They often serve inexpensive meals, and may also organize live music, film evenings, parties or comedy shows – all in the hope of luring visitors to gamble their money away on the one-armed bandits. One of the biggest is the *Canberra Workers Club* on Childers Street (☎02/6248 0399): it boasts a bistro serving meals every day, regular discos, and darts and pool as well as pokies. The *Canberra Tradesmen's Union Club*, 2 Badham St, Dickson (☎02/6248 0999), has a sauna, gym and squash courts, an observatory with an astronomical officer on duty (dusk until about 12.30am), and a Bicycle Museum (daily 9am–midnight); you can even dine in a restored tram, or have your hair cut in a 1920s-style barber shop. The attractions are all free, but children have to leave by 8pm, when the sinful poker machines rev up. The *Canberra Labor Club*, Chandler Street, Belconnen (☎02/6251 5522), serves meals daily and offers bingo as well as occasional disco or rock nights.

Listings

Airlines Ansett, Jolimont Centre, 65 Northbourne Ave (☎02/6245 7715, reservations ☎13 1300); Qantas Travel Centre, Jolimont Centre, 65 Northbourne Ave (☎13 1313).

Airport bus For airport transport call ACT Minibuses (☎02/6250 8211).

American Express 185 City Walk, corner of Petrie Plaza (☎02/6247 2333).

Banks The city branches of the bigger banks are open Mon–Thurs 9.30am–4pm, Fri until 5pm: ANZ, 19 London Circuit; Commonwealth Bank, corner of London Circuit and Ainslie Ave; National Australia Bank, corner of London Circuit and Ainslie Ave; Westpac, corner of Alinga and Mort streets.

Bike rental Canberra Bike Rental (☎02/6241 2216, 24hr phone booking); The Gecko Gang (☎02/6254 8047); Wombat Mountain Bikes (☎02/6285 4058, after hours ☎02/6288 2753; $40 per day). A pleasurable bicycle path goes all the way around Lake Burley Griffin: to enjoy it, contact Mr Spokes Bike Hire (☎02/6257 1188; $8 per hour), right on the water at Barrine Drive, Acton.

Buses For local bus information phone Action timetable information (Mon–Sat 6am–11pm, Sun 8am–5.30pm, ☎02/6207 7611), or call at the kiosk at the City Bus Interchange, 11 East Row. Long-distance services, including state-owned Countrylink and V/Line, use the Jolimont Centre, 65 Northbourne Ave, as their terminal. You can buy tickets direct here from the Countrylink Travel Centre (☎02/6257 1576; Countrylink to Eden and Cootamundra, V/Line to Wodonga and Sale); Greyhound Pioneer (Canberra terminal ☎02/6257 4424; central reservations ☎13 2030) and Murrays Coaches (☎02/6295 3611; to Sydney, Wollongong, Batemans Bay and the Snowy Mountains). Travellers Maps and Guides (closed Sun) at the Jolimont Centre is an authorized travel agent selling bus tickets for the remaining bus companies: McCafferty's (☎13 1499; to Sydney and Melbourne); Capital Coaches (☎02/6292 9412; west and northwest to Orange, Dubbo, Bathurst, Young and Cowra); Cooma Buslines (☎02/6452 1259; to Cooma); Rendell Coaches (☎02/6884 4199; to Dubbo); and Sid Fogg's (☎02/4928 1088 or free call ☎1800/045 952; to Newcastle).

Car rental Inexpensive deals are available from Network Rent-a-Car (☎02/6231 5095); Rent-a-Dent (☎02/6257 5947), which also rents campervans; and Rumbles Rent-a-Car (☎02/6280 7444). Others, mostly clustered on Lonsdale St in Braddon, with additional locations at the airport, are Avis (☎02/6249 6088, airport ☎02/6249 1601); Budget (☎02/6257 2200, airport ☎02/6257 1305 or 13 2848); Hertz (☎02/6257 4877, airport ☎02/6249 6211); and Thrifty (☎02/6247 7422, airport ☎02/6248 9081).

Embassies and high commissions There are 67 in Canberra (all the following are in Yarralumla, unless otherwise stated): Canada, Commonwealth Ave (☎02/6273 3844); Germany, 119 Empire Court (☎02/6270 1911); Indonesia, 8 Darwin Ave (☎02/6273 3222); Ireland, 20 Arkana St (☎02/6273 3022); Malaysia, 7 Perth Ave (☎02/6273 1543); Netherlands, 120 Empire Circuit (☎02/6273 3111); New Zealand, Commonwealth Ave (☎02/6273 3611); Norway, 17 Hunter St (☎02/6273 3444); Papua New Guinea, Forster Crescent (☎02/6273 3322); Singapore, 17 Forster St (☎02/6273 3944); Sweden, 5 Turrana St (☎02/6273 3033); Switzerland, 7 Melbourne Ave, Forrest (☎02/6273 3977); Thailand, 111 Empire Circuit (☎02/6273 1149); UK, Commonwealth Ave (☎02/6270 6666); USA, 21 Moonah Place (☎02/6270 5000).

Emergency ☎000 for fire, police or ambulance.

Environmental contacts The Environment Centre, Kingsley St, Acton (☎02/6247 3064), is a library and archive on environmental topics as well as a book and gift shop (Mon–Fri 9am–5pm). The Wilderness Society Shop, 16 Garema Place (☎02/6249 8011), is a book and gift shop with information about the local environment.

Festivals The big event of the year is the Canberra Festival – the anniversary of the city's foundation – celebrated with concerts, theatre, exhibitions, street parades and fireworks for ten days from the beginning of March. It's followed in late March by Word Fest, a writers' festival held at ANU (programme available from January; details on ☎02/6249 7068). The Royal Canberra Show is an agricultural fair lasting three days over the last weekend in February, while the Floriade is a spring festival marked by floral displays, theatre, music and the like, from mid-September to mid-October.

Galleries Good private galleries include the Chapman Gallery, 31 Captain Cook Crescent, Manuka (Wed–Sun 11am–6pm; ☎02/6295 2550), specializing in Aboriginal art; and the Beaver Galleries, 81 Denison St, Deakin (Wed–Sun 10.30am–5pm; ☎02/6282 5294), for paintings, sculpture, jewellery and furniture.

Gay and lesbian Canberra Gayline ☎02/6247 2726 (nightly 6–10pm); Gay Contact ☎02/6257 2855 (same hours).

Horse riding Brindabella Valley Trails, 19 Sabine Close, Garran (☎02/6281 6682), offers riding in the Brindabella Ranges close to Kosciuszko National Park.

Hospitals Royal Canberra Hospital, Lennox Crossing, Acton (☎02/6243 2111); John James Memorial Hospital, Strickland Crescent, Deakin (☎02/6281 8100).

Markets Gorman House Arts and Crafts Market, Gorman House Arts Centre, Ainslie Ave, Braddon (Sat 10am–4pm; bus #302, #303 or #385), is a community market where items such as pottery, hand-painted T-shirts, bric-a-brac and secondhand clothes are sold; Fyshwick Markets, Dalby St (Thurs–Sun 8am–5.30pm), is a large market for fruit, vegetables, meat, fish, cheeses, deli goods and flowers.

Nature reserves Information on ACT parks and reserves from Canberra Nature Park (☎02/6207 2090) and ACT Parks and Conservation Service (☎02/6237 5120). For Namadgi National Park, which takes up virtually the whole southern half of the ACT, and nearby national parks in NSW, contact the Australian National Parks and Wildlife Service, 153 Emu Bank, Belconnen (☎02/6250 0200).

NRMA (National Roads and Motorists Association), 92 Northbourne Ave, Braddon, or Belconnen Mall, Belconnen (☎13 2132). Publishes a very useful map of Canberra and the ACT, free to members. Touring and accommodation enquiries ☎13 1122.

Police ☎02/256 7777.

Post office Alinga St, Canberra, ACT 2600 (☎02/6209 1370). Mon–Fri 9am–5pm.

Rape Crisis Centre ☎02/6247 2525; 24hr.

Scenic flights Vee H Aviation (☎02/6248 6766) charges from about $40 per person for 35–40min.

Shopping Shopping hours are Mon–Thurs 9am–5.30pm, Fri 9am–9pm, Sat 9am–noon. Shops in the Canberra Centre are open daily. In the city centre the shopping focus is on Bunda St, with department stores such as David Jones and Grace Bros, and a comprehensive Target. The shops and supermarket at City Market, on the corner of Bunda St and Ainslie Ave, are also open daily. There are late-opening supermarkets in the shopping centres of the satellite towns.

Taxis Aerial Taxis (☎02/6285 9222); Queanbeyan Taxi Co-operative, Queanbeyan (☎02/6297 3000). There is a taxi rank on Bunda St outside the Center Cinema.

Tours and cruises Murrays, the Jolimont Centre, 67 Northbourne Ave (☎02/6295 3611), has half- or full-day bus tours around Canberra and to the Snowy Mountains; Bunyip Bush Safaris (☎02/6255 1472), arranges trips for small groups to the Snowy Mountains and further afield to the national parks of southeast Australia from $64 for a full day; Round About Tours (☎02/6249 6006) specialize in bush walks in the Tidbinalla Nature Reserve from $48; Ultimate Tours (☎02/6291 8117), does sightseeing trips in and around Canberra from the back of a Harley Davidson; Wild Things Tours (☎02/6254 6303), has half-day tours into Namadgi National Park for guaranteed Eastern Grey kangaroo-spotting, $19, including billy tea, pick-ups and drop-offs. Australia Capital Tours (☎02/6284 7160) offers 90min cruises twice daily ($15) in the Central Basin of Lake Burley Griffin, with additional evening cruises in summer. *The Love Bus* (☎02/6282 6733) takes you on a "Route 69" nighttime cruise around Canberra's red light district, with an experienced guide. The tour nips around town in party hen-night mode visiting a wide variety of cheeky hotspots.

Trains The Xplorer train links Canberra and Sydney (3 daily; 4hr) via Queanbeyan, Bungendore, Goulburn, Bundanoon, Moss Vale, Bowral and Mittagong. Ticket sales and information at the Countrylink Travel Centre, Jolimont Centre, 67 Northbourne Ave (☎02/6257 1576), and at the train station in Kingston (☎02/6239 0133).

Travel agents Canberra Flight Centre, City Walk Arcade, 2 Mort St, Civic Mon–Sat 9am–5pm (☎02/6247 8199); STA Travel, 13–15 Garema Place, Civic (Mon–Sat 9am–5pm; ☎02/6247 8633).

Women Women's Information and Referral Centre, ground floor, North Building, London Circuit (Mon–Fri 9am–5pm; ☎02/6205 1075).

The Opera House and Circular Quay, Sydney

An archetypal outback pub, Silverton, NSW

River Red Gums on the Murray River, NSW

New Parliament House, Canberra, ACT

Desert sculptures, Broken Hill, NSW

Sub-tropical rainforest,
Nightcap National Park, NSW

Norfolk Island's famous pines

Terrace house, Paddington, Sydney

The Big Merino, Goulburn, NSW

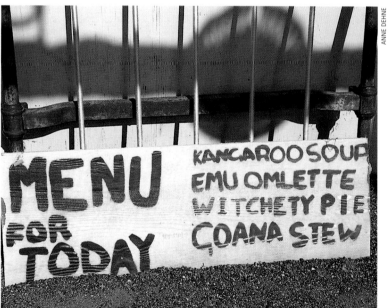

Mungo Woolshed, Mungo National Park, NSW

Plat du jour at a bush pub in Lightning Ridge, NSW

Around Canberra

The residents of Canberra live with nature right on their doorstep: the numerous **picnic grounds** and **bushwalking trails** in the state reserves and national parks are only about half an hour's drive from the city centre. Be warned, though, that at the height of summer, when there is a high risk of bushfires, a total fire ban is declared and all the nature reserves and national parks are closed (call ☎02/6207 8600 to check).

Bushland aside, the environs of the capital can also lay claim to historic **homesteads and villages**, private zoos, a former goldmining town and a few **wineries**, some of them across the border in New South Wales.

South

Just 4km south from Canberra's New Parliament House is the private, open-range **Mugga Lane Zoo** (Mon–Fri 9am–4pm, Sat & Sun 9am–5pm; $7.50), at Mugga Lane, off Hindmarsh Drive, Symonston. Here you can see kangaroos, wallabies and wombats, as well as dingoes and emus. Leaving the city further behind, the Tharwa Road follows the course of the **Murrumbidgee River** as it approaches Tharwa. Thirty-two kilometres from Canberra, at the southern end of the Tuggeranong Valley, the convict-built **Lanyon Homestead** (Tues–Sat 10am–4pm, grounds open to 5pm; admission to grounds free, $3 for house, $5 including gallery) dates back to the earliest European settlement of the region. Thoroughly refurbished by the National Trust, it now houses a small display outlining the history of the area before Canberra existed, but the real reasons to come are the house itself and the **Sidney Nolan Gallery** next door, where works by the famous Australian painter are on permanent display alongside changing exhibitions of contemporary Australian art. There's no public transport out here.

Beyond the Lanyon Homestead and Tharwa, old cottages on the Naas Road, overlooking the river, house the galleries and antique shops of the **Cuppacumbalong Craft Centre** (Wed–Sun & holidays 11am–5pm). Nearby, a small, licensed café serves hearty meals and local cider, and there's also a spot nearby where you can swim in the river.

Namagdi National Park

Namagdi National Park occupies almost half of the ACT, largely made up of wilderness areas in the west and southwest. Its mountain ranges and high plains, rising to 1900m, have a far more severe climate than low-lying Canberra and give rise to the Cotter River and many smaller streams. In the northwest, the Corin Road leads to Corin Dam, while in the south the partly surfaced Bobyan Road cuts right through the national park, emerging beneath the Snowy Mountains in the south (the park abuts the Kosciuszko National Park along the state border). There are picnic grounds and bush campsites by the Orroral River and near Mount Clear in the south.

The **Namagdi Visitors Information Centre**, 3km south of Tharwa on the Naas Road (daily 9am–4pm; ☎02/6237 5222; in emergency call ranger on ☎02/6281 5878), has displays and videos about the park, and also provides detailed information on bushwalking tracks and emergency shelters in the remote areas.

West: Tidbinbilla Nature Reserve and Cotter Reserve

The small **Tidbinbilla Nature Reserve**, to the southwest of the city (daily 9am–6pm, later during daylight saving), is an enjoyable place with relatively easy walks, and some wheelchair-accessible paths. In the area around the park entrance and information centre

(Mon–Fri 11am–3pm, Sat & Sun 9am–6pm; ☎02/6237 5120) kangaroos and wallabies roam in spacious bush enclosures, and you can also see koalas and lots of birds. Picnic grounds are dotted all along the sealed road that leads through the reserve, and on long weekends and during the school holidays it's a busy place, especially popular with families. The **Tidbinbilla Deep Space Tracking Station** (visitors centre open daily 9am–5pm, summer to 8pm; free) sounds like every child's dream, though in fact the displays of spacecraft and highly sensitive communications equipment are not as exciting as you might have hoped. Operated in conjunction with NASA, the purpose of the station is to pick up even the most obscure signals from outer space; there are only two others in the world with the same range as Tidbinbilla – one near Madrid, the other in Goldstone, California.

Southwest of here, Corin Road turns off the Tidbinbilla Road towards the **Corin Forest** (winter daily 8am–10pm; otherwise Wed, Sun & holidays 10am–6pm; ☎02/6247 2250) and reservoir, a popular recreation spot in the hills, with many walking trails, picnic grounds and barbecue facilities. In winter you can ski on artificial snow and during school holidays special activities are organized for children.

Cotter Reserve

The **Cotter Reserve**, near the Cotter Dam, 22km west of the city, is another popular spot for short weekend outings. Here, around an artificial lake that was the original reservoir built to serve the new capital, you'll find picnic grounds, a restaurant and a **campsite** (☎02/6288 4930). The **Murrumbidgee River** nearby is suitable for swimming. On the way to the Cotter Reserve you pass the **Mount Stromlo Observatory** (visitors gallery open daily 9am–4.30pm; free; ☎02/6249 5111), about 16km from Canberra. The giant silver dome houses the telescopes of the ANU's Department of Astronomy; inside the complex, there are photographic displays and textual information on various aspects of astronomy, and you can see some of the viewing equipment. There's no public transport out here. Enquire at the above number for viewing nights.

North

Leaving Canberra by the Barton Highway to the north, the first place of interest is **GINNINDERA**, approximately 9km out. It's a rather consciously touristy village with a few arts and crafts shops and *The Green Herring* restaurant in a log hut. Just before Ginnindera, on Gold Creek Road, the **National Dinosaur Museum** (daily 10am–5pm; $7.50) is not a big, government-run museum as the name might suggest, but rather a private collection of replica skeletons and some bones and fossils. Other local tourist attractions include **Cockington Green** (daily 9.30am–4.30pm; $6), a miniature model English village; and the **Artgems Gallery** (daily 10am–5pm) in the village, with exhibits of paintings, gems (especially opals and crystals), and local arts and crafts. **HALL**, 3km north of Ginnindera, is a similar village with a few shops and a restaurant, and another Artgems Gallery.

More or less opposite the turn-off for Hall, the Wallaroo Road heads west towards the New South Wales border. Not far down the road, at Woodgrove Close, is Brindabella Hill Wines (☎02/6230 2583), where you can sample some of the local "cool climate" vintages. There are more wineries around **MURRUMBATEMAN**, north along the Barton Highway into NSW between Canberra and the large country town of Yass (see p.310); full lists are available from the tourist office.

The Federal Highway

Northeast of Canberra, the Federal Highway crosses into NSW shortly after leaving the city. The first of the sights along this way is the **Bywong Town Mining Village** (daily 10am–4pm; tours 11am, 1pm & 3pm; $7), where a brief goldrush at the end of the nineteenth century has left shafts and some old mine workings. The gold-diggers' camp has been reconstructed with some serious attention to historic detail, and it's well worth stopping in if you're passing by; you can also try your hand at panning, and there are picnic and barbecue areas. The mining village is on Bungendore Road, further down which lies the attractive village of **BUNGENDORE**, with a pottery, woodturner, café and shops arranged around the village green. Heading on, you can circle back round to Canberra via Queanbeyan, or strike east, a scenic drive that takes you through **BRAIDWOOD** – which has more antiques and crafts shops, and a fine old hotel – towards the coast at Batemans Bay (see p.236).

SOUTHERN NSW

There are two quite separate parts to the southern half of New South Wales, just as there are to the state as a whole: the coast, and the mountains and hinterland beyond them. The **south coast**, with its green dairylands, is delightful in a quiet sort of way – an area for fishing or surfing or relaxing on the beaches, with no huge resorts or commercial developments. Inland, the **Snowy Mountains** constitute the Dividing Range's highest peaks; they have Australia's best skiing and, in summer, some fine bushwalking. Beyond the mountains, the southwest is dull farming country – you're better off crossing to the riverlands of Victoria, or driving straight through.

The direct route from Sydney to Melbourne is via the inland **Hume Highway**, from which you can easily detour to Canberra or the Snowy Mountains. There's a four-lane freeway from Sydney to Moss Vale, and the rest of the way it's a normal two-lane road with occasional overtaking lanes, but very winding between Yass and Albury. It is also very busy, with heavy truck traffic, and most of the time quite boring – a potentially lethal combination. It takes roughly twelve hours to drive straight through from Sydney to Melbourne, which is fine if you're sharing the driving, but otherwise allow two days.

The coastal route, the **Princes Highway**, is slightly longer but much more attractive in terms of scenery. Give yourself two or more days if you want to appreciate the surf, the sandy beaches, and the mountains, valleys and forests that back this beautiful stretch of the coast.

Most **buses** run via the Hume Highway, usually with a detour to Canberra; the **train** follows largely the same route.

The Snowy Mountains

The **Snowy Mountains** are just one section of the alpine highlands that spread across the southeast corner of the Australian continent. The Australian Alps sprawl from Mount Buller, Mount Bogong and Mount Beauty in northeast Victoria via the Crackenback Range in New South Wales to the township of Cooma; though it's a continuous massif, only the New South Wales section is strictly known as the Snowy Mountains. **Mount Kosciuszko**, at 2228m the highest mountain in mainland Australia, is located close to the Victorian border in the far southeast. It was named in 1840 by the Polish-born explorer Paul Strzelecki after the Polish freedom fighter General Tadeusz Kosciuszko, and, although Strzelecki stressed he was "in a foreign country and on a foreign ground", he couldn't resist giving it its name "amongst a free people who appreciate freedom". The **Kosciuszko National Park** which surrounds the peak includes most of the Snowy Mountains region, and almost everything of interest. To the north and east of **Cooma** – the main approach to the range – the treeless, brownish-yellow **Monaro High Plain** is sheep country famous for the quality of its Merino wool.

SKIING IN THE SNOWY MOUNTAINS

The easiest option is to arrange a **ski package** departing from Sydney – always check exactly what's included in the price. Recommended operators include Kosciuszko Accommodation Centre (☎02/6456 2022 or free call 1800/026 385), who can put together a low-season basic weekend package including transport by bus, national park entry, ski rental, lift and lessons, and two nights' accommodation, dinner and breakfast for $249; similar deals can be arranged through Alpine World (see below).

A one-day **ski-lift pass** starts from about $32 at Selwyn, $60 at Charlotte Pass and $62 at Thredbo and Perisher Blue, and beginners' one-day group lessons cost around $75. Resorts are generally pretty child-friendly, particularly at Charlotte Pass where the homely and old-fashioned *Kosciuszko Chalet* (free call ☎1800/026 369) offers free childcare throughout the ski season; Paddy Pallin at Jindabyne (☎02/6456 2922 or free call 1800/623 459) has several cross-country skiing sessions, including an easy three-hour introduction aimed at family groups (adults $35, children $25).

Another good source of information on the latest deals is Inski, a popular ski shop with its own attached ski travel agency, Alpine World, at 46 York St, Sydney (☎02/9290 2688).

Compared to the high mountain ranges of other continents, the "roof of Australia" is relatively low and, despite the name, the flattened mountaintops lie below the line of permanent snow. After heavy snowfalls in winter, however (roughly from the end of June to the beginning of October), winter-sports fans from all over southeast Australia congregate at the **ski resorts** in the Mount Kosciuszko area – Perisher Blue Resort, Thredbo, Mount Selwyn and Charlotte Pass. It's not the most exciting skiing in the world – there are few challenging runs – and prices are hiked up to ridiculous levels as the resorts attempt to make their living during a very short season. Selwyn, a family resort, which is generally half the price of other resorts in the region, is one cheap alternative. Only the most fanatical European winter-sports enthusiast would come here especially to ski, but if you're passing it can be an enjoyable diversion. This is also an ideal area for cross-country skiing, an increasingly popular pursuit. In summer it's a different story: price levels return to normal, the towns and resorts are not quite so crowded, even sleepy, and there are fabulous walks and mountain scenery to be enjoyed. Perisher and Selwyn almost completely close down, but Thredbo operates ski-lifts throughout the year, transporting hikers and sightseers to mountaintops from where they can embark on short or extended bushwalks across the wildflower-covered high country. There are plenty of opportunities for horse-riding, too, mountain-biking and trout-fishing or white-water rafting in the crystal-clear mountain streams.

The system of roads which made possible the existence of the townships and ski resorts was established by the **Snowy Mountains Hydroelectric Scheme**. This gigantic engineering project to harness the waters of the Snowy Mountains for hydroelectric power and irrigation was begun in the 1950s. Tunnels were dug under the mountains, rivers redirected and dams built. Many postwar immigrants from middle and southern Europe found their first jobs on the "Snowy"; some lost their lives here. Twenty-five years and about $800 million later, in 1974 the project was completed: seven power stations now utilize the waters of the Upper Murrumbidgee, Tumut and Snowy rivers to generate electricity and provide New South Wales, the ACT and Victoria with power. The scheme's generating capacity is about eighteen percent of the total for southeast Australia, while the water of the redirected rivers is used for irrigation right across New South Wales, Victoria and South Australia.

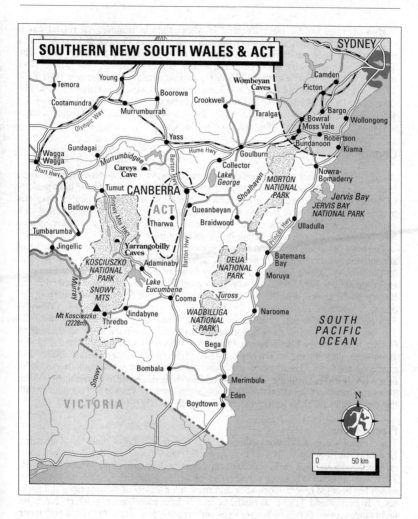

SOUTHERN NEW SOUTH WALES & ACT

Getting around

The most important of the area's roads is the **Snowy Mountains Highway**, which leads straight across the mountain ranges and through the national park from Cooma to Tumut and Gundagai. If you want to see more of the alpine scenery, the **Alpine Way** offers a spectacular circuit, turning off the highway at Kiandra in the heart of the park and heading via Khancoban and Geehi to Thredbo. Nine kilometres of the route – around Geehi – consists of rutted gravel road: you don't need a 4WD, but you will need lots of time. In winter, check road conditions before driving anywhere, even on the Snowy Mountains Highway; on the Alpine Way and on Kosciuszko Road (after Sawpit Creek) **snow chains** must be carried between June and October, and the roads might be closed altogether.

Bus services are far more frequent in winter than in summer – a **rental car** is strongly recommended for summer sojourns. Greyhound Pioneer (☎13 2030) has a daily service between Sydney, Canberra, Cooma, Jindabyne, Perisher Valley and Thredbo, with additional services in the winter. Additional winter-only bus services include Murrays Coaches (☎02/6295 3611) and Adaminaby Bus Service (☎02/6454 2318) between Cooma, Adaminaby and Mount Selwyn ski resort. Perisher Blue Skitube (free call ☎1800/654 681; see p.231 for more details) is a railway specially designed for skiers, but it also operates for bushwalkers in the summer months, linking the ski areas of Bullocks Flat, Perisher Valley and Mount Blue Cow.

Cooma

Because of its location at the intersection of two highways – the Monaro Highway south from Canberra and the Snowy Mountains Highway from the coast to the high peaks – **COOMA** is the obvious base for trips into the Snowy Mountains. Although it functions mainly as a service centre for skiers, it's also an attractive place in its own right, with a number of fine old buildings, notably on Lambie and Vale streets – the visitors centre (see below) has a brochure detailing buildings of interest.

The town has really come into its own since the 1950s, when it took on the mantle of administrative centre for the hydroelectric scheme. Many of the migrants who worked on the "Snowy", as it's known – particularly those who arrived from central Europe – ended up settling here, making it a fairly cosmopolitan town. If you're interested in the history of the project and the technical details, check out the **visitors centre** of the Snowy Mountains Authority, on the Monaro Highway in North Cooma (Mon–Fri 8am–5pm, plus Sat & Sun during school holidays 8am–1pm; free; free call ☎1800/623 776 for details of guided visits to various power stations). That's about all there is to Cooma, except for the **Llama Farm**, 19km out of town on the Adaminaby Road (Fri–Sun 10am–4pm, daily during school holidays; $10, children $5), where llamas, alpacas and guanacos are bred. Llamas aside, the Snowy Mountains are traditionally regarded as prime **horse-riding** country. The long-established Yarramba Trail Riding at Berridale, 34km southwest of Cooma (☎02/6456 3150), offers escorted rides at $20 per hour or full-day picnic rides ($75), as well as extended camping safaris ($165 for two days).

Practicalities

The helpful **Cooma Visitors Centre**, 119 Sharp St (daily: June–Oct 7am–6pm; Nov–May 9am–5pm; ☎02/6450 1742 or free call 1800/636 525), has detailed information on Kosciuszko National Park, plus farmstays, horse-riding and fishing safaris, and offers a free accommodation booking service. Pick up a copy of the free monthly *Snowy Times*, which has detailed resort information and maps, plus listings of skiing prices and packages. Harvey World Travel, 96 Sharp St, is a helpful **travel agency** which can book flights out, provide details of bus services and arrange local tours (☎02/6452 4677); **car rental** is available from Thrifty, 1/30 Baron St (☎02/6452 5300).

Accommodation can be hard to come by in the ski season, when everything, especially the motels, is booked up pretty early, but the rest of the year you shouldn't have too many problems. Good options include the inexpensive and central *Royal Hotel*, on the corner of Lambie and Sharp streets (☎02/6552 2132; ③): built in 1858, it has loads of character – many of the rooms have French windows opening onto the huge balcony. The family-run *Bunkhouse Motel*, 28–30 Soho St (☎02/6452 2983; rooms ③, dorms ①), is a guesthouse-style backpackers' with dorms and lots of en-suite singles. The good-value *Swiss Motel*, 34 Massie St (☎02/6452 1950; ③), also has holiday apartments on offer (⑤) – and there are plenty of other motels nearby. *Snowtels Caravan Park*, Snowy Mountains Highway (☎02/6452 1828; apartments ④–⑦, cabins ③–⑤, on-site vans ②–③), with a tennis court and communal kitchen, is probably the best of the campsites.

Out of town, you can get away from it all with **farmstay** accommodation: *Rose Valley Station*, 8km along the unsealed Rose Valley Road, after heading 14km northeast along the Monaro Highway (☎02/6452 2885; ⑧), has cottages sleeping up to six; *Warreen Farm Holidays*, 37km east (☎02/6453 3272; ③), provides accommodation in a self-catering cabin on a sheep and cattle property; and *Litchfield Holiday Farm*, Carlaminda Road, 21km east (☎02/6453 3231; ⑧), is a riverfront sheep and horse property, whose rates include all meals and horse-riding.

Cooma's not really a foodie sort of town. The best place to **eat** is *Café Upstairs*, 121 Sharp St, next door to the tourist office. A cross between a café and a licensed brasserie, it serves everything from hamburgers to trout and good-value pasta dishes – plus decent espresso – and is open daily from noon to midnight, and on weekends until 2am. Other good cafés include the BYO *Terry's*, 112 Sharp St, the new *Sharp Food*, 122 Sharp St and *Mystic Munchies*, 161 Sharp St. Inexpensive **pub meals** can be had at the bistro of the *Australian Hotel*, 137 Sharp St.

Kosciuszko National Park and around

The largest national park in New South Wales, **Kosciuszko National Park** extends 200km north to south, from Tumut to the Victorian border, encompassing an area of some 6500 square kilometres. The scenery includes almost all of the high country, with ten peaks above 2100m, forested valleys and a treeless plateau with glacial lakes, as well as the headwaters of Australia's biggest river system, the Murray–Murrumbidgee. The main centres are the lakeside resort of Jindabyne, just outside the eastern boundary of the park, and the ski resort of Thredbo, 30km further west along the scenic Alpine Way, actually in the national park. Perisher and Mount Blue Cow can be reached via the Skitube from Bullocks Flat, roughly midway between Jindabyne and Thredbo.

If you're driving through, there's a **fee** of $12 per car per day or $3.50 per motorbike – so if you plan to stay more than a day or two and especially if other national parks are on your itinerary, the annual national park pass ($60) may be a good investment (see p.619 for details). Arriving by bus, you'll still have to fork out a one-off payment of $4. Note that **parking** is heavily restricted throughout the park, and can reach crisis point in Thredbo – if you've come by car it might be worth paying extra for accommodation with space to park.

The **National Parks and Wildlife Service** has its headquarters in Jindabyne (daily 8.30am–4.30pm; ☎02/6456 2444), a $5.4 million complex featuring red-gum interiors and including a tourist information office, theatre, café and bus station. It offers a comprehensive service, with leaflets about walking trails in the national park, activities such as ranger-guided tours, details of campsites, as well as maps for sale and a display on the natural features of the park. There are also NPWS **ranger stations** at Perisher Valley (☎02/6457 5214; winter only), Khancoban (☎02/6076 9373) and Tumut (☎02/6947 4200).

Bushwalking in the park

Some of the country's most interesting and beautiful **bushwalking tracks** pass through the area. One of the most accessible of these is the walking trail around **Mount Kosciuszko**. The **chair-lift** from Thredbo (see overleaf) will take you up to Crackenback station on the edge of the plateau; the actual summit is about 6km from here, though it seems barely higher than the surrounding country, or you can walk 2km to **Mount Kosciuszko Lookout** for panoramic views. Another good way up to the high country is to take the **Skitube** from Bullocks Flat on the Alpine Way (see p.231), a funicular railway that leads uphill and through a tunnel to Perisher Valley and Mount Blue Cow (which has a bistro and art gallery), where more fine trails await. Even if you plan only a brief walk of an hour or so, bear in mind that the weather up here is very fickle, and pack a sweater and some rain protection.

Jindabyne and Thredbo

A resort town at the man-made lake of the same name, **JINDABYNE**, 63km west of Cooma, is the jumping-off point for the ski resorts of Thredbo, a further 30km west, and Guthega, or up the Kosciuszko Road to Smiggin Holes and Perisher Valley (these two are also accessible by the Skitube – ☎02/6456 2010 to check times which vary throughout the year; $13–19 return). Jindabyne itself is entirely new, having been relocated when the Snowy Mountains Scheme dammed the Snowy River and drowned the first settlement, and the lake is now its main attraction: there's good fishing, and in summer you can also swim and sail – most equipment is available to rent in the town. The **Snowy River Information Centre** is within the NPWS headquarters here (daily 9am–5pm; ☎02/6456 2444).

From Jindabyne, the Alpine Way continues into the national park and up to **THREDBO**, a compact and attractive village, squeezed into a narrow valley beside the road and the Crackenback River, with alpine-style houses huddled against the mountainside. In winter it offers the best and most expensive skiing in Australia, but unlike the other resorts, it is also reasonably lively in summer and – with its Crackenback **chair-lift** (daily 8.30am–4pm; $17.00 return) giving easy access to the high country – makes a good base for bushwalking and other explorations. The *Thredbo Resort Centre* (☎02/6459 4198 or free call 1800/020 589) can advise on chair-lift timetables and provide other tourist information. There are several annual events in the Thredbo calendar. The two musical highlights are the three-day Thredbo **Blues Festival** in mid January and, in early May, the four-day **Jazz Festival** with gigs all over the village.

Yarrangobilly Caves and Kiandra

The **Yarrangobilly Caves**, a system of about sixty limestone caves at the edge of a rocky plateau surrounded by unspoiled bushland, are one of the few specific sights in the park, they're 6.5km off the Snowy Mountains Highway near Kiandra, 113km north of Cooma and 70km south of Tumut. There are several guided tours daily to the **North Glory**, **Jersey** and **Jillabenan Caves** (the last is wheelchair-accessible; $10; ☎02/6454 9597 for tour times). A fourth cave, the **Glory Hole Cave** (daily 10am–4pm; $6), can be explored on a self-guided tour. From walking trails along the edge of the rock plateau there are panoramic views of the Yarrangobilly Gorge, and a steep trail leads from the Glory Hole car park to a thermal pool at the bottom of the gorge near the Yarrangobilly River. The spring-fed pool, which you can swim in (for free), has a year-round constant temperature of 27°C.

KIANDRA itself is a ghost town, but the detailed interpretive boards of the Heritage Trail will help you find your way through the remaining ruins on this desolate, windswept spot – the extensive plains in the northern part of the park are too cold for any trees to survive. It's hard to believe that fifteen thousand prospectors camped here during the goldrush of 1860; the short-term rush left behind a town of about three hundred people who eked out a living mining and grazing.

Accommodation

In winter, **rooms** are at a premium – despite the plethora of holiday apartments and motels, accommodation is almost impossible to come by without a reservation. In summer, the situation is less dire, and you should have little difficulty finding somewhere in one of the resorts, or at motels on the fringes of the park – such as at Tumut in the north or even back in Cooma (see p.230). Most accommodation in Thredbo can be **booked** through the *Thredbo Resort Centre* (☎02/6459 4198 or free call 1800/020 589) or Thredbo Accommodation Services (free call ☎1800/801 982); the Snowy River Information Centre in Jindabyne (☎02/6456 2444) also handles accommodation bookings.

Alpine Inn, Alpine Way, Khancoban (☎02/6076 9471). The *Alpine Inn* offers motel-style accommodation attached to a great pub and restaurant. ④–⑥.

Fishermen's Lodge, Alpine Way, Khancoban (☎02/6076 9471). Under the same management as the *Alpine Inn*, this lodge caters to backpackers with inexpensive single rooms, plus activities such as horse-riding and white-water rafting; they also rent out fishing gear, boats and canoes. ①.

Kasees Mountain Lodge and Apartments, Banjo Drive, Thredbo (☎02/6457 6370). One of several lodges and motels along Banjo Drive, this one boasts a pool, sauna, and bargain summer rates. Summer ②–④, winter ③–⑤.

Kosciuszko Mountain Retreat, Sawpit Creek, near the park headquarters (☎02/6456 2224, fax 6456 1415). Tent sites, and cabins and chalets sleeping six, set among a forest of snow gums. Advance booking recommended, especially in winter when prices rise. Chalets ⑥, cabins ④.

Nettin Chalet, 24 Nettin Circuit, Jindabyne (☎02/6456 2692, fax 6456 1115). Motel-style units, all with private balconies boasting lake and mountain views. Facilities include a bistro, bar, spa and sauna. Summer ⑥, winter ⑧.

Riverglade Caravan Park, Snowy Mountains Highway, Tumut (☎02/6947 2528). Camping and cabins by the river, with kiosk and barbecue. Cabins ④.

Snowline Caravan Park, junction of Alpine Way and Kosciuszko Rd, Jindabyne (☎02/6456 2099). Camping or cabins, and good facilities, including spa, sauna, café-restaurant and boat rental. Cabins ③–⑧.

Snowy Valley Motel, Kosciuszko Rd, 9km east of Jindabyne (☎02/6456 7138 or 6456 7180). Motel with indoor swimming pool and sauna, as well as meals for residents and non-residents. Lots of big family rooms sleeping five – ask about backpackers' specials in these. ④–⑤.

Thredbo Alpine Hotel, Friday Drive, (free call ☎1800/026 333, fax 02/6459 4201) Large luxury hotel complex in the centre of the village, close to the chairlift. Wine bars and the resort's only nightclub. ⑧.

Thredbo YHA Lodge, 8 Jack Adams Pass, Thredbo (☎02/6457 6376, fax 6457 6043; *thredbo@yhansw.org.au*). A modern hostel, with reception open 7–10am and 4.30–9pm. Between June and September, bookings must be made in writing through the YHA head office in Sydney (☎02/9261 1111). En-suite rooms ⑥,winter only $38–55 per person. summer dorms ①.

The South Coast

The south coast of New South Wales is relatively quiet and relaxed, its numerous bays, coastal lakes and inlets interspersed with unspoiled, sandy beaches, small fishing villages and seaside resorts. During the summer months, especially from Christmas to the end of January, a lot of holiday-makers escape here from the "big smoke" up north, or come up from Victoria: the towns can get busy then, especially the **Shoalhaven area** around **Nowra** and **Batemans Bay**, and **Merimbula**. But don't expect glamorous resort hotels and entertainment Queensland-style – it's all rather low-key and family-oriented. There are a few wildlife and amusement parks to keep the children happy, and plenty of opportunities for traditional outdoor pursuits. (One of the region's highlights is the awesome **Pebbly Beach**, 20km from **Ulladulla**, where a tame kangaroo colony lives right on the sand dunes.) Exposed parts on this stretch of the coast are battered by powerful waves that are perfect for **surfing**, while the calmer waters of the numerous coastal lakes, bays and inlets are suited for **swimming**, windsurfing, sailing or paddling your own canoe. There's great **fishing** too, in the rivers and lakes, as well as the inevitable deep-sea season, when game-fishers set out to tussle with marlin. Away from the ocean there's some superb, rugged scenery and great bushwalking and horse-riding in the forest-clad, mountainous hinterland. When summer holidays are over, even the bigger towns revert back to an unassuming, laid-back lifestyle, and the weather is mild enough to enjoy them pretty much year round.

Most of the way down the coast, the **Princes Highway** runs a few kilometres inland. Away from the towns, apparently obscure turn-offs from the highway often lead to beautiful and secluded beaches – it's worth taking some time to make your own discoveries. Heading towards **Canberra** there are three main routes from the coast: through Kangaroo Valley (see p.204), continuing via Moss Vale (or Bundanoon) and Goulburn; the Capital Highway from Batemans Bay; or the Snowy Mountains Highway from Bega via Cooma.

Transport links from Sydney, Canberra and Melbourne to the south coast include Greyhound Pioneer's daily Sydney–Canberra route via the coast as well as a daily Canberra–Nowra service; the Sydney–Eden route offered by Pioneer Motor Services (☎02/4421 7722); Countrylink services (☎13 2232) from Canberra to Eden daily; Murray's (☎13 2251) daily route from Canberra to Narooma with several stops including Batemans Bay and Moruya, and from Canberra to Sydney via Batemans Bay, Ulladulla and Nowra; Premier's (☎1300/368 100) daily Sydney to Eden service and Priors (☎ free call 1800/816 234) Southern Highlands–South Coast express, between Sydney and Narooma via Mittagong and Kangaroo Valley. From Melbourne, the *Sapphire Coast Express* (☎02/4473 5517) runs twice weekly to Batemans Bay, stopping at such places as Eden, Merimbula and Bega.

Nowra–Bomaderry

Straddling the wide Shoalhaven River, the twin town of **NOWRA–BOMADERRY** is the centre of the Shoalhaven holiday region: Bomaderry is situated north of the river, Nowra south. The river here is great for sailing, windsurfing and boating in general, while the coast, 13km away, is dotted with popular holiday settlements and numerous beaches. **Shoalhaven Heads** north of the river mouth, **Greenwell Point** in the south, **Huskisson** at Jervis Bay (see p.234) and **Sussex Inlet** are all easily accessible on good roads, although public transport doesn't run this far. Possible inland trips include a one-hour tour to the top of nearby Mount Coolangatta with Australian Bushmobile Tours (☎02/4423 0495; $10).

For further information on the beaches and how to get to them, and on local accommodation, stop first at the **Shoalhaven Tourist Centre**, 245 Princes Highway, in Bomaderry (daily 9am–5pm; ☎02/4421 0778 or free call 1800/024 261). **Accommodation** includes an abundance of motels, and two hostels/guesthouses. Rooms at *Armstrong's Guesthouse*, 30 Junction St (☎02/4421 2084, fax 4423 6876; rooms ④, dorms ①), share bathrooms but they're reasonably priced, plus there's a YHA hostel section in two cabins. *Riverhaven Guesthouse Backpackers* is on a riverfront landscaped property but only one block from the shops, by the bridge at 1 Scenic Drive (☎02/4421 2044, fax 4421 2121; ①–④); facilities include a kitchen and swimming pool. You can camp at the central, riverside *Shoalhaven Caravan Village*, Terrara Road, Nowra (☎02/4423 0770; cabins ③–④), with its own pool and tennis courts and bikes available to rent. There's not much by way of **restaurants** or **nightlife** in Nowra but it does have one alternative hangout, the *Tea Club*, 46 Berry St (☎02/4422 0900; closed Sun & Mon) a veggie café with a bohemian feel, artworks for sale, drumming workshops (Thurs eve) and bellydancing displays (Sat eve).

Jervis Bay

Just southeast of Nowra, the sheltered waters of **Jervis Bay**, (pronounced "Jarvis") by a political quirk, are technically part of the ACT, in order to provide Canberra with access to the sea. The beautiful coast of the **Jervis Bay National Park**, at the southeast arm of the bay, is very popular, with its rugged cliffs facing the pounding ocean and tranquil beaches of dazzling white sand and clear water within the confines of the bay, while inland heaths, wetlands and forests offer strolls and bushwalks; details are available from the **visitor centre** (☎02/4443 0977) as you enter the park. There are a couple of **campsites** (bookings essential in summer ☎02/4443 0977): the more secluded and small *Cave Beach* on Wreck Bay is the most sought-after site, despite its cold showers; the larger, more expensive *Greenpatch*, on a creek by Jervis Bay, has the benefit of hot showers, and cars can be parked at each tent site. Holiday-unit accommodation, sleeping up to six, is available on Ellmoos Road, at *Kullindi* (☎ & fax 02/4441 2897; ⑥), and at *Lumeah* (☎02/4441 2018, fax 4441 0021; ⑥), with weekly-only rates in summer at around $850.

The **Wreck Bay Aboriginal Community**, which has land in the middle section of the park, organizes a summer cultural interpretation programme, Wreck Bay Walkabouts (bookings and information ☎02/4442 1166), which covers diet and medicines, archeology and wildlife; plus there's the recommended Barry's Bushtucker Tours (☎02/4442 1168). **Jervis Bay Botanic Gardens** (Mon–Fri 8am–4pm, Sun 10am–5pm, closed Sat except Dec–April 10am–5pm; free), on Cave Beach Road, is an annexe of Canberra's Australian National Botanic Gardens and has specimens of plants from around Australia, including a pleasantly cool rainforest gully. Heading south from Sydney to Jervis Bay, 10km south of Nowra, down the turn-off for Huskisson takes you to Marayong Park Emu Farm, 132 Jervis Bay Rd, (Wed–Sun 10am–4pm: guided tours and emu feeding sessions 10.30am, 11.30am, 1.30pm & 2.30pm; ☎02/4447 8505).

On the western shores of Jervis Bay, 21km southeast of Nowra, **HUSKISSON** is an old town that's a popular tourist spot, with several beachside campsites: the council-run *Huskisson Beach Tourist Park*, Beach Street (☎02/4441 5142; cabins ④–⑧), has a playground and tennis courts; or try *Huskisson White Sands Tourist Park*, corner of Nowra and Beach streets (☎02/4441 6025; cabins ③–⑦). A friendly B&B is *Clovelly Cottage*, 12 Tomerong St (☎02/4441 7551; ⑥). The focus of the town is the beachfront *Huskisson Hotel*, which has a good bistro and plenty of pool-playing opportunities. **Sea-life** watching tours are available all year, and there's an eighty percent success rate of seeing whales and other marine life with Dolphin Watch Cruises, 50 Owen St (☎ free call 1800/246 010; tours depart Tues & Thurs–Sun at 11am & 1pm; $25). Huskisson is also a good base for **diving** into the pristine waters of Jervis Bay. Contact ProDive (☎02/4441 5255) for details of one-off dives ($70 including gear) and packages including accommodation ($339).

Ulladulla

In the 1930s many Italian fishermen settled in the small fishing village of **ULLADUL-LA**, and they're still a strong influence on the atmosphere of this tranquil outpost: the traditional Blessing of the Fleet continues to be celebrated every Easter at the harbour breakwater. It's a beautiful area, dominated by the sandstone plateau of the **Morton National Park**, rising steeply to the west of town. Mostly this is an inaccessible barri-er, but there's a good bushwalk to the top of the 719-metre **Pigeon House Mountain** in the Budawang Range; the walk there and back takes about four hours and is accessed from the Princes Highway, via a turn-off 8km south of Ulladulla. Along the coast in both directions are attractive river mouths, beaches and lakes: among those worth visiting are pretty **Lake Conjola**, 10km to the north; **Lake Burrill**, 5km to the south; and **Lake Tabourie**, 13km to the south – all are popular with fishermen, canoeists and campers. Around Ulladulla there are also some quaint country towns worth visiting. **Mollymook**, 3km to the north, has some sensational surfing sites and hiking trails and a few kilometres further on there's lots to see and do in the village of **Milton**, home to numerous antique shops, craft shops and cafés. This region provides a relaxing weekend escape from Sydney or a worthwhile stopover en route to or from Melbourne, but you really need your own transport to appreciate the area and to get off the main roads onto some of the scenic drives.

Tourist information is available from the Civic Centre on the highway (Mon–Fri 10am–5pm, Sat & Sun 9am–5pm; ☎02/4455 1269). They can advise you on **accommodation**, and the local Chamber of Commerce also operates a central reservations hotline (☎02/4454 4434). Places to stay include the *Quiet Garden Motel* on a rocky promontory at 2 Burrill St (☎02/4455 1757; ④–⑥); the elegant *Ulladulla Guesthouse*, near the harbour at 39 Burrill St (☎ & fax 02/4455 1796; ④–⑦), which has a spa and sauna; the *South Coast Backpackers*, 63 Princes Highway (☎02/4454 0500; rooms ③, dorms ①), a small, renovated hostel providing lifts to Pigeon House Mountain, Jervis Bay, or Murramarang National Park, or you can rent a bike or canoe from them. The *Beach Haven Tourist Resort*, on Princes Highway in Ulladulla South (☎02/4455 2110 or 4455 1712; holiday apartments ④–⑥, cabins ④, on-site vans ②–③), boasts a beachfront location, complete with swimming pools, spa and tennis courts. There's also a council-run caravan park on South Street, close to the beach, *Holiday Haven* (☎02/4455 2457; on-site vans ②–③).

In terms of **activities**, there's swimming at the free sea-water pool by the wharf, or open-water scuba courses run by Ulladulla Divers Supplies, Watson Street (☎02/4455 5303). The local Aboriginal community has also constructed an interesting cultural trail, the Coomee Nulunga (☎02/4455 5883). Access is via Deering Street, opposite the Lighthouse Oval car park. The track meanders through eucalypts and heath flowers to a viewing platform over the ocean, and then on to a secluded beach. Guided tours ($5) are offered by local Aborigines, and include boomerang throwing, didgeridoo playing and dreaming stories.

There are a couple of good Italian places to **eat** in the town, including *Carmello's* on Green Street (☎02/4455 4099) open daily for lunch and dinner, and *Tory's Seafood*, 30 Watson St (☎02/4454 0000), by the wharf (daily for dinner plus Sun lunch). *Cookaburra's*, 10 Watson St (☎02/4454 1443) is an ambient, BYO restaurant with waterfront views serving innovative Asian and Cajun-inspired seafood and poultry dishes (closed Thurs). The *Harbourside Restaurant*, 84 Princes Highway (☎02/4455 3377) specializes in modern Australian cuisine and fresh seafood open daily and is licensed and BYO. There's also a Thai restaurant, *Supreeya's* upstairs at the Centre Court Complex on the corner of Deering and St Vincent streets.

Batemans Bay and around

BATEMANS BAY, at the mouth of the Clyde River and the end of the highway from Canberra, is a favourite escape for the landlocked residents of the capital, just 152km away. It's not the most exciting place on the coast, but since it's a fair-sized resort, there's plenty to do. Around Batemans Bay itself you can take a **cruise** on the Clyde River with one of several companies, including Clyde River Cruises (☎02/4478 1005; $15 for 3 hours to Nelligen and back), Blue Dolphin Cruises (☎02/4472 4220; $25 for two hours), or Merinda Cruises (☎02/4472 4052), departing daily from the wharf at 11.30am for a three-hour tour ($12) including a stopover up-river in the historic township of **Nelligen** with arts and crafts and a nice café. Alternatively, you can board one of the little trains that run through the woodlands of the **Birdland Sanctuary**, 55 Beach Rd (daily 9am–5pm; $8.50), for a closer look at the birds and native animals.

In the **Murramarang National Park** (ranger ☎02/4478 6006), a small coastal strip just north of town, there are campsites at **Pretty Beach**, **Pebbly Beach** and **Durras Beach** – popular not only with campers but also with kangaroos, which come here at dawn or dusk to frolic on the beach. Rumour has it that they even enjoy body surfing. You can stay at *Murramarang Resort* (☎02/4478 6355; cabins and on-site vans; ④) where there's bike and canoe rental available, plus organized geology walks, lake rides and fishing cruises, or at **Pebbly Beach** where there's a basic campsite (☎02/4478 6006).

BURNUM BURNUM: ABORIGINAL ACTIVIST

Wallaga Lake is the birthplace of one of Australia's most important Aboriginal figure-heads, the elder named **Burnum Burnum**, an ancestral name meaning great warrior. He is best known for his flamboyant political stunts, which included planting the Aboriginal flag at Dover to claim England as Aboriginal territory in Australia's bicentennial year, 1988, highlighting the dispossession of his native country. He was born under a sacred tree by Wallaga Lake in January 1936. His mother died soon afterwards and he was taken by the Aborigines Protection Board and placed in a mission at Bomaderry, constituting one of the "stolen generation" of indigenous children removed from their families in this period. After graduating in law and playing professional rugby union for New South Wales, he became a prominent political activist in the 1970s. He was involved in various environmental and indigenous protests, including erecting the "tent embassy" outside the Federal Parliament in Canberra (see p.216), and standing twice, unsuccessfully, for the senate. Burnum Burnum died in August 1997 and his ashes were scattered near the tree where he was born.

From **MOGO**, 10km to the south, you can visit the open-air **Old Mogo Town** museum (daily 9am–5pm during school holidays, otherwise Fri–Sun 10am–4pm; $6), a reconstruction of a mid-nineteenth-century goldrush town near an old gold mine. The best time to come, however, is Sunday morning when there's a bric-a-brac **market** held here. Twenty-five kilometres south of Batemans Bay, just before **Moruya**, a small, unsealed road turns off the highway to the west, heading through a pretty valley and then up over hills at the edge of the remote **Deua National Park** to the former goldrush town of **Araluen** where, between 1868 and 1872, about fifteen thousand prospectors congegrated in the hope of striking it lucky.

Batemans Bay Tourist Information is on Princes Highway, at the corner of Beach Road (daily 9am–5pm; ☎02/4472 6900 or free call 1800/802 528). As you'd expect of a resort, **accommodation** consists mainly of motels and a wide range of holiday units; most of the latter require a minimum week's booking during peak summer times. Try *Bay Surfside*, 7km out of town at 662 Beach Rd (☎02/4471 1275; ④–⑥), whose units sleep up to six and have all mod cons. There's camping at eight caravan parks including the *Coachhouse Marina Resort*, by the beach on Beach Road 1km south of town (☎02/4472 4392; cabins ④–⑦, on-site vans ③–⑥), with a pool and tennis court; and *Batemans Bay Tourist Park* (☎ & fax 02/4472 4972; cabins ③–⑥, on-site vans ②–④, dorms ①), close to town (but not the beach) and with a YHA hostel section attached. *Mogendoura Farm*, on Hawdons Road, 8km west of Moruya on the Moruya River (☎02/4474 2057; ⑤–⑥), offers cottage farmstays with horse-riding, canoeing and bush-walking opportunities; minimum booking is two nights.

There's a range of **restaurants** in Bateman's Bay, mainly with fish and seafood-based menus. *Rafters*, 28 Beach Rd has a relaxing, intimate atmosphere, with à la carte dining and vegetarian options. On the promenade, *Seagulls* serves rather overpriced seafood and steaks, but the sweeping waterfront views may make it worth the extra expense (closed Tues; ☎02/4472 0253) while the *Starfish Deli* also has a marine panorama with a modern menu, including a variety of wood-fired pizzas and many veggie dishes. *Jameson's on the Pier* offers fine dining on fresh fish and is set on its own jetty opposite the promenade, jutting out over the river.

Narooma and around

A small fishing village surrounded by beautiful beaches, bays and coastal lakes, **NAROOMA** lies at the heart of an area famous for its succulent **mud oysters**. You can canoe and windsurf on the **Wagonga Inlet** or sail to **Montague Island** – an offshore sanctuary for sea birds, seals and penguins. If you actually want to disembark at the island, you'll have to join a tour organized by the NPWS in Narooma (π02/4476 2888; tours daily winter 3.30pm, summer 6.30pm though morning tours are sometimes available; 3hr; $60), since it's a protected wildlife reserve. Southern right and humpback **whales** have begun to reappear in the bay between September and November, and tour operators also organize whale-watching tours in the event of any sightings; you can book at the **visitors centre** on the highway (daily 9am–5pm; π02/4476 2881). **Cruises** cost $30–40 for a 2–3 hour trip, including a visit to Montague Island to see the seal colonies. The visitors centre can also book you on a scenic cruise aboard the *Wagonga Princess* (π02/4476 2665) a century-old pine ferry which winds its way in and out of secluded bays on the river, stopping off for a guided rainforest walk and oyster tasting session ($18 for a 3hr tour). **Diving** can be found off Montague Island all year, organized by Ocean Hut, 123 Princes Highway (π02/4476 2278) costing $45 for one dive and $60 for two (Jan–Apr grey nurse sharks and tropical fish; Aug–Dec mainly seal-spotting).

In Narooma there's a popular, cosy YHA **hostel**, *Bluewater Lodge*, 11–13 Riverside Drive (π02/4476 4440, fax 4476 3492; *naryha@sei.net.au*; rooms ③–④, dorms ①), a renovated period building, complete with polished wood floors, and an open verandah facing the waterfront; cheap bike and canoe rental and free fishing gear can be used. Good **motels** and resorts include *Forsters Bay Lodge Motel*, Forsters Bay Road (π & fax 02/4476 2319; ④); *Tree Motel*, 213 Princes Highway (π02/4476 4233; ④–⑤), which has a pool and barbecue; and the beachside *Island View Beach Resort*, on the highway 3km south of town (π02/4476 4600; cabins ③–⑧). *Pub Hill Farm*, Scenic Drive, 8klll ʍuɪt of Narooma (π02/4476 3177, fax 4476 3153; ⑤), is a farm-style B&B which has a couple of en-sulic ʍonms and offers a baby-sitting service. *Clark Bay Farm* (π02/4476 1640; ⑤–⑦) offers disabled-access accommodation, with electronically activated doors and beds. *Lynch's Hotel*, on the Princes Hlghway (π02/4476 3022; ③), serves contemporary Australian **meals** daily, including the local oysters in its recommended restaurant.

There are several **bistros** at the Marina on Riverside Drive at Forsters Bay, including the sumptuous *Simply Seafood* (lunch Tues–Sun, dinner Tues–Sat; π02/4476 2403), and the less pricey *Quarterdeck* next door. *Rockwalls* on Campbell Street has à la carte seafood specials, costing around $15 for main courses (closed Sun & Mon; π02/4476 2040). *Casey's Café* at the top of the town's hill, on the corner of Canty and Wagonga streets (π02/4476 1241) is the best place for a coffee, also serving healthy, hearty food. Narooma's **nightlife** doesn't extend much beyond the vast *Golf Club* on Balinga Street (daily 10am–10pm; π02/4476 2522), with pool tables and poker machines, serving the latest drink in town. If you're in need of a film fix, there is a delightfully preserved Kinema picture theatre worth visiting – an original cinema from 1926 screening modern movies on Friday and Saturday evenings and Sunday matinees (daily showings, except Mondays, during school holidays and the Dec/Jan holiday season).

A thriving local **Koorie** community, run their own Umbarra Aboriginal Cultural Centre (π02/4473 7232, fax 4473 7169) at **Wallaga Lake**, 25km south of Narooma. They operate tours to local sacred sites, including Gulaga (Mt Dromedary), with hands-on activities such as painting with ochres, building bark huts and sampling bush tucker and traditional medicine. (As some of their tours traverse aboriginal lands, special permits are required for external visitors planning on visiting these areas independently.) They also have a cruise with commentary on Wallaga Lake, one of the largest saltwater lakes on the Australian coast. The lake's black duck is the sacred totem for the local aboriginal community. Entry to the centre is free; activities and tours range from $6 to $45.

Tilba Tilba

Continuing south, take a break in the picturesque mountain villages of **TILBA TILBA** and **CENTRAL TILBA**, 17km south of Narooma, where time seems to have stood still – and various craft shops and workshops are ready and willing to exploit the olde worlde ambience. It's an area famous for its cheeses, and is also a little-known wine-growing region: Central Tilba's hundred-year-old **ABC Cheese Factory** is open for visits – and free tastings (daily 9am–5pm), and you can follow this up with some wine tasting at Tilba Valley Winery, signposted off the Princes Highway, 5km north of town (Mon–Sat 10am–5pm, Sun 11am–5pm; ☎02/4473 7308). Situated on Corunna Lake, the working family vineyard and winery is an idyllic spot for a ploughman's lunch on the terrace or a picnic on the grounds, overlooking a lake. Try the unusual local mead made at the winery.

The *Dromedary Hotel*, on Bates Street in Central Tilba (☎ & fax 02/4473 7223; ④), is a quaint, historic pub with open fires; counter **meals** are served and there's **B&B** accommodation. The nearby *Rose & Sparrow Café* offers cream teas and light meals but is self-consciously twee. If you're feeling energetic you can follow the walking trail which starts from Pam's Store in Tilba Tilba and leads through a forest to the summit of **Mount Dromedary**, at almost 800m. The hike there and back is about 11km, and you should allow five to six hours – or go for the lazy option, with a horse from Mount Dromedary Trail Rides (☎02/4476 3376; 3hr; $45).

Bermagui

There's a delightful scenic detour along the coast: turn off the highway just after Tilba Tilba and after 8km you reach **BERMAGUI**, on both the Bermagui River and sheltered Horseshoe Bay. Bermagui attracts quite a few game-fishing fanatics, thanks to its associations with Zane Grey, the American writer of Westerns and a legendary marlin fisherman. There are several big-game fishing tournaments annually, and charter boats offer trips to catch black marlin, yellow fin tuna and other big fish. In addition to several **motels**, there's the friendly, family-run *Blue Pacific Hostel* at 73 Murrah St (☎02/6493 4921; rooms ②, dorms ①), which can arrange fishing charters. Other alternatives are the pleasant old *Bermagui Hotel*, Lamont Street (☎02/6493 4206; ③), serving decent meals; *Elite Holiday Flats*, 84 Murrah St (☎02/6493 4274; ④); or the central *Zane Grey Caravan Park* on Lamont Street (☎02/6493 4382; cabins ③–⑤). The **Bermagui Information Centre** is part of the BP Service Station at 8 Coluga St (daily 7am–7pm; ☎02/6493 4174). There's no **bank** in town but you can get money from EFTPOS at the supermarket and an ATM machine in the *Country Club*, which also serves **meals**. Besides the club and pub, eating choices include a Thai restaurant and a pizzeria, but *Roly's Wharf Restaurant* is the best place to try Bermagui's legendary fish catches.

Further south, unsealed tracks branch off the coast road to **Mimosa Rocks National Park**, where there are opportunities for bushwalking and swimming. There are NPWS **campsites** at Middle Beach, Picnic Point and Argannu Beach (☎02/6476 2888 for details and bookings).

Bega and around

Lush green meadows, munching cows, wide valleys and mountains in the background – you could almost mistake this pastoral scenery for somewhere in the foothills of the Swiss Alps. Certainly the area around **BEGA** is prime dairy country: at the **Bega Cheese Factory & Heritage Centre**, Lagoon Street, North Bega (daily 9am–5pm; ☎02/6492 1444), you can watch the famous local cheese being made, and try a few samples. Scenery and cheese apart, there's no great reason to come here, but it's a convenient stopover, handy for the junction of the Princes Highway with the Snowy Mountains Highway. In town, the **Historical Museum**, on the corner of Bega and Auckland streets (Mon–Fri 10.30am–4pm, holidays also Sat 10am–noon), has regional memorabilia and photos. For more on local attractions, including the Grevillea Winery, check out the **Bega Tourist Information Centre**, 91 Gipps St (Mon–Fri 9am–5pm, Sat & Sun 10am–2pm; ☎02/6492 2045).

The small, pleasant *Bega YHA* on Kirkland Crescent (☎02/6492 3103; reception hours 4–8pm; rooms ③, dorms ①) is built from mud bricks. Less earthy accommodation can be found at the *Grand Hotel*, 236 Carp St (☎02/6492 1122; ④), which has motel-style pub accommodation, as well as counter **meals** during the week. Campers can head for *Bega Caravan Park* on the Princes Highway (☎02/6492 2303; cabins and units ③–④, on-site vans ②–③).

Candelo and Tathra

CANDELO, reached by a country road off the highway 11km south of Bega, is a pretty village where you can browse in the galleries and craft shops, have a cream tea at one of the tearooms, or a drink in the preserved *Candelo Hotel* on Sharp Street (☎02/6493 2214; ③), which also has **rooms** and good counter meals. Other accommodation options include the self-contained units at *Bumblebrook Farm*, Kemps Lane, 4km northwest of Candelo (☎02/6493 2238, fax 6493 2299; ⑤), although you can also take advantage of room service or dine in the homestead.

Heading on from Bega, an alternative route to Merimbula takes you along the coast road via the small holiday and fishing village of **TATHRA**. Accommodation ranges from the motel-style units at the *Tathra Hotel Motel* on Bega Street (☎02/6494 1101; ④–⑥), to the *Tathra Beach Tourist Park*, right by the beach on Andy Poole Drive, 2km from the centre (☎02/6494 1302; cabins ③–⑤, on-site vans ③) – or a the timber cottages at *Kianinny Park Cabins* on the Snowy Mountains Highway, 2km west of town (☎02/6494 1990 or free call 1800/064 225; ⑤–⑧), a family place with a saltwater pool. **Tourist information** is dispensed at the helpful Tathra Wharf Trading Post right on the wharf (☎02/6494 4062; usually 7.30am–8pm), an all-purpose place which also rents out fishing, diving and surfing gear, and has a decent café; there's a **maritime museum** upstairs (daily 8am–5pm; $1.50).

Just to the south, coastal **Bournda National Park** features stunning beaches, brackish lagoons and freshwater lakes: there are NPWS **campsites** at Hobart Beach on the southern end of Wallagoot Lake (book well ahead from December to Easter; ☎02/6494 1209 or 6496 1434).

Merimbula

The pretty township of **MERIMBULA** attracts a lot of holiday-makers from Victoria because of its accessibility, year-round temperate climate and good beaches. Between tanning sessions, you can cruise Merimbula Lake (actually the wide mouth of the Merimbula River) and Pambula Lake with several different companies for around $20 for two hours: Sinbad Cruises (book at the tourist centre) are recommended for their interesting commentary on Aboriginal history and oyster cultivation, while Merimbula Marina (☎02/6495 1686) offers $20 dolphin cruises. There are also whale-watching tours (Sept–early Dec) costing $40 for 4 hours. Cruises and boat rental can both be arranged at the **Merimbula Tourist Information Booking Service**, Beach Street (daily 9am–4pm, school holidays until 5pm; ☎02/6495 1129); they also have info on lots of other activities in the area, including 4WD forest tours and horse-riding. If the Sinbad cruise kindles an interest in the Aboriginal culture of the area, look up Umburra Cultural Tours (☎02/4473 7232), run by the local land council based at Wallaga Lake and led by Koorie guides (for more details, see the Narooma section).

By **bus**, you can get to Merimbula from Canberra, Cooma or Eden with Countrylink, from Sydney or Melbourne with Greyhound Pioneer, and from Sydney or Eden with Pioneer Motor Service. Hazelton (☎13 1713) **flies** to Merimbula from Sydney at least twice daily and Kendell Airlines (☎13 1300) flies twice daily from Melbourne.

There are several places to **eat** out, including the *Waterfront Café*, on the promenade by the tourist office, which has a seafood and snack menu (daily: March–Dec 8am–5pm; Jan–Feb 8am–midnight). Also on the promenade, the *Lakeside Café* is open for lunch and dinner serving assorted fish dishes and some veggie options, and the *Lakeview Hotel* on Market Street has a bistro open for lunch and dinner. Merimbula has several good Asian restaurants, particularly the cheap *Thai Noodle House* at 15 Market St (daily 11am–8.30pm) and *Bahn Thai* at 17 Merimbula Drive (☎02/6495 4555) open daily for dinner. Opposite each other in the shopping centre on Princes Highway, try *Saigon Palace* (☎02/6495 3255) for Vietnamese cuisine, or *Pedro's* for Mexican meals.

Accommodation

Though there are dozens of **motels** (④–⑤, depending on the season) and **holiday apartments**, all of them can be heavily booked during the summer holidays, when many holiday apartments accept only weekly bookings with rates starting at around $220. There's a freephone booking service run by the local Chamber of Commerce (free call ☎1800/150 457) covering all grades of accommodation. The places listed below may have space at short notice.

Kalorama Caravan Park, Millingandi Rd, Pambula (☎02/6495 6366). Swimming pool, toddlers' pool and tennis court. Cabins ③, on-site vans ②.

Mandeni Resort, Sapphire Coast Drive, 7km north (☎02/6495 9644, fax 6495 9668). Fully equipped timber cottages in a bushland setting, sleeping a maximum of six. Facilities include tennis courts, two swimming pools, a golf course and many walking trails. Weekly bookings only, $340–1070 per cottage.

South Haven Caravan Park, Elizabeth St, between Merimbula Lake and the beach (☎02/6495 1304). Sauna, heated pool, tennis and squash courts. Cabins from ③; units from $280 weekly.

Wandarrah YHA Lodge, 8 Marine Parade (☎02/6495 3503, fax 6495 3163). A modern, purpose-built youth hostel close to both the beach and lake. Lots of organized activities and outings, friendly, knowledgeable staff and free pick-up from bus or plane. Rooms ③, dorms ①.

Woodbine Park Cabins, Sapphire Coast Drive, 7km north (☎ & fax 02/6495 9333). Wooden cabins in a bushland setting, sleeping a maximum of six. Swimming pool, tennis court and golf course. $220–860 per week per cabin.

Eden – and heading inland

EDEN, on Twofold Bay, is pretty much the last seaside stop before the Princes Highway heads inland towards Victoria. As well as the bus services mentioned on p.234, Eden can be reached from Bega and Merimbula on Edwards Bus Services (☎02/6496 1422) from Sunday to Friday, and from Canberra daily. In 1818 the first whaling station on the Australian mainland was established at Eden, and **whaling** remained a major industry until the 1920s. For information on the local area, call in at the **Eden Visitors Centre** on the highway (Jan & Feb daily 9am–5pm; March–Dec Mon–Fri 9am–4pm, Sat & Sun 9am–noon; ☎ & fax 02/6496 1953).

Today Eden is touristy in a quiet sort of way, with good fishing, and there are plenty of reminders of the old days, the best of which is the **Killer Whale Museum** on Imlay Street (Mon–Sat 9.15am–3.45pm, Sun 11.15am–3.45pm; $4); as well as whaling, it looks at the fishing and timber industries which still contribute to Eden's livelihood. At the information centre you can also book **cruises** on Twofold Bay and further out to sea – with luck, penguins, dolphins and, in winter, even whales might be sighted. There's more on the important and controversial timber industry at the **Harris Daishowa**

Chipmill, which gobbles up thousands of eucalypts from the surrounding forests and transforms them into wood chips for export to Japan. The **visitors centre** at Edrom Road (daily 8am–5pm; free guided mill tour Thurs 10.30am, book in advance on ☎02/6496 1303) presents an exhibition and slide show about the local timber industry, past and present – no prizes for guessing whose side they're on in the forestry debate.

The forests themselves may seem a more attractive option, and as you head south you become increasingly surrounded by the vast temperate rainforests that characterize southeastern Australia. Roads lead off the highway in both directions into the magnificent **Ben Boyd National Park** (NPWS Eden office ☎02/6495 4130), which hugs the coast to the north and south of Eden, offering good camping, walking and beaches. Inland, the summit of **Mount Imlay** can be reached by a three-kilometre walking track which starts at the picnic grounds at Burrawang Forest Road, 14km south of Eden. The steep, strenuous ascent is rewarded by a panoramic view over the coast and across the dense forests of the hinterland onto the Monaro plain. An excellent way to explore the mountain and forest is on horseback with Leo's Eagle Rest Rides (☎02/6495 7124; 2hr; $25). At **BOYDTOWN**, 9km south of Eden, take a look at the mock-Tudor **Seahorse Inn**, which nowadays houses a small museum of local history as well as tearooms, a restaurant and a hotel (see below).

Accommodation

Hotel Australasia, Imlay St (☎02/6496 1600). Budget accommodation in an old pub, catering mostly to backpackers; counter meals available. Rooms ②–③, dorms ①.

Bayview Motor Inn, Princes Highway (☎02/6496 1242, fax 6496 1273). Deluxe motel with room service, swimming pool and spa. ⑥.

Fountain Caravan Park, Princes Highway (☎02/6496 1798). Decent site with swimming pool and camp kitchen. Cabins ⑤, on site vans ⑦

Seahorse Inn, just off the Princes Highway in Boydtown (☎02/6496 1361). A mock-Tudor inn offering B&B, with a tennis court, tearooms and restaurant. ⑥–⑧.

Shadrack Resort, Princes Highway, Legges Beach, 4km south of Eden (☎02/6496 1651, fax 6496 1671). An attractive complex in a bushland setting on the beach. Cabins ③–⑤.

Twofold Beach Caravan Park, Princes Highway, 7km south of Eden (☎02/6496 1572). Beachside location with pool. Cabins ⑤–⑥, on-site vans ②–③.

Wonboyn Lake Resort, 40km south of Eden (☎02/6496 9162, fax 6496 9100). A scenic location off the beaten track at Lake Wonboyn. Swimming pool, spa, shop, boat-ramp, canoe and boat rental; beach nearby. Cottages ④–⑧.

NORTHERN NSW

Northern New South Wales may have nothing to match the majesty of the Snowy Mountains, as the Dividing Range falls away to the lower slopes that protect the **New England Plateau**, but the World Heritage-listed temperate and subtropical areas of the range's northeast end harbour sixteen pockets of rainforest which more than compete in terms of natural beauty. In many ways the north is more varied than the south, offering a taste of everything: big resorts and empty beaches on the coast, with alternative-lifestyle villages and communes in the hinterland beyond; lovely parks and forests on the steep slopes behind the coast; and further inland quietly attractive agricultural country, dotted with interesting old towns.

The roads are generally in fairly good condition, but the busy **Pacific Highway** is not the best of them. Though it's gradually being upgraded and widened, with the addition of much-needed overtaking lanes, sections of this winding coastal road are still alarmingly narrow considering the weight of traffic and the big trucks that use it; bus services on the highway almost invariably run late. The inland route on the **New England Highway** via Muswellbrook, Tamworth and Armidale is a faster alternative if you're heading straight for Brisbane – plenty of buses go this way too.

The North Coast

The coast from Sydney north to the Queensland border is more densely populated and much more touristy than the southern coast. Popular holiday destinations are strung up the coast north from Newcastle (see p.176). **Port Stephens**, **Port Macquarie**, **Coffs Harbour** and the twin city of **Tweed Heads**–Coolangatta, straddling the state line, attract local tourists as well as overseas visitors. The subtropical part of the coast, from Coffs Harbour north, is much the most attractive: since the 1970s the area around **Lismore**, **Byron Bay** and **Murwillumbah** has been a favoured destination for people from the southern cities seeking an "alternative" lifestyle. This movement has left in its wake not only disillusioned hippie farmers (as well as a few who've survived with their illusions intact) but also a firmly established artistic and alternative scene.

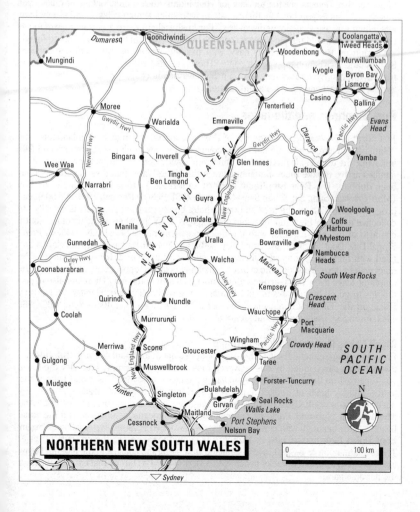

NORTHERN NEW SOUTH WALES

0   100 km

▽ *Sydney*

As in the south, the **coastline** consists of myriad inlets, bays and coastal lakes, interspersed by white, sandy beaches and rocky promontories. Parallel to the coast, the rocky plateaus of the **Great Dividing Range** rise steeply from the plain; so steep is the eastern edge of this range, indeed, that it defied even the efforts of the early foresters, so that to this day the hills remain densely wooded. A handful of townships still depend on the timber industry, but most **forest** areas are now protected as either national parks or state forests. From the highlands, numerous streams tumble down from the escarpment in mighty waterfalls, and once on the coastal plain they flow together to form short, very wide and fast-flowing rivers. In the fertile river valleys the predominant agricultural activity is cattle breeding, while in the north subtropical and tropical agriculture takes over, especially the cultivation of bananas.

In essence, the further you go, the better this coast gets – the northeast corner is one of the most scenic areas in the state, its remote country roads well worth exploring. If the bigger coastal resorts are too touristy for your liking, there's no shortage of quiet, even lonely, beaches as you head further up, along with small fishing villages and sleepy hamlets inland that are virtually undiscovered. For bushwalkers there are vast areas of totally remote, rugged, wild terrain to explore in the national parks of the Great Dividing Range.

Getting up the north coast is easy, with frequent **train** and **bus** services between Sydney and Brisbane stopping en route. There are also some excellent one-way tours from Sydney to Byron Bay (see box on p.266). Kirklands (☎02/9281 2233) runs between Sydney and Brisbane via Ballina and Lismore.

Port Stephens and the lakes

Just north of Newcastle, the wide bay of **Port Stephens**, which extends inland for some 25km, offers calm waters and numerous coves ideal for swimming, water sports and fishing, while the ocean side has good surf and wide, sandy beaches. In January thousands of families arrive to take their annual holiday in the "Blue Water Paradise", as the area has been dubbed. The **Port Stephens Visitors Centre**, at Victoria Parade in Nelson Bay (Mon–Fri 9am–5pm, Sat & Sun 9am–4pm; ☎02/4981 1579 or free call 1800/808 900), can provide information on the area and make hotel bookings. Port Stephens is actually the collective name for the main township of **NELSON BAY**, perched at the tip of the southern arm of the bay, together with the quieter settlements of Shoal Bay, Soldiers Point, Fingal Bay, Boat Harbour and Anna Bay. Although Nelson Bay is highly developed and filled with high-rises, you can still enjoy the simple pleasure of **dolphin-watching** in the quiet waters here. Most dolphin cruises, which give you the opportunity to swim with the dolphins, leave from **Tea Gardens** on the northern arm of the bay. There are also opportunities to go on bush walks to spot **koalas** in the wild at Tilligery Habitat, 14 Tilligery Plaza, on the Tilligery Peninsula (Mon–Sat 9.30am–4.30pm, Sun 10am–2pm; ☎02/4982 4441; tours $8). Daily guided tours leave at 10.30am and 2pm.

Myall Lakes National Park and around

From Port Stephens the Pacific Highway continues north for about 40km to **Bulahdelah**, a small town surrounded by bush-covered hills and rocky outcrops. Just after the town, you turn east on the Lakes Highway towards the coast, past Myall Lake and Lake Wallis to the holiday town of Forster–Tuncurry. At Bungwahl a turn-off leads down mostly unsealed roads to **SEAL ROCKS**, a remote fishing village and the only settlement in the **Myall Lakes National Park**. Its national park status means it's unspoilt, and the small beach is truly beautiful with crystal-clear waters marooned between two headlands. **Sugar Loaf Point Lighthouse**, built in 1875, is a ten-minute stroll away; the grounds (Tues & Thurs 10am–noon & 1–3pm) offer a fantastic view along the coast, and the lookout below leads down to a deserted, rocky beach with a view of the 4WD track that extends through the national park.

From Bulahdelah itself, Myall Way heads via a toll ferry (daily 8am–6pm) to more deserted spots along the lakeshore, the most popular being **Mungo Brush**, where an easy walking track (30min return) heads through the littoral rainforest – a variant adapted to salty and harsh seafront conditions, with a low canopy. A more challenging 21-kilometre walking track leads from here to **Hawks Nest**, on Port Stephens Bay and the Myall River, linked by a bridge across the river to Tea Gardens.

North of Seal Rocks, the tiny **Booti Booti National Park** is located between Cape Hawke and Charlotte Head. Ten kilometres further north, a bridge connects the twin cities **FORSTER–TUNCURRY** on the spit of land that separates **Lake Wallis** from the ocean. The lake is very pretty, surrounded by trees and with bush-covered **Corrie Island** at its centre. Forster is famous for its **oysters**, and for its playful resident **dolphins**. The lake itself is superb for fishing and swimming – you can rent houseboats as well as dinghies, canoes and windsurfers. The abundant seafood made the spot attractive to the local Aboriginal people, the Wallamba, and their descendants can take you on a tour of significant sites (see "Listings", p.246).

Practicalities

Port Stephens, Forster–Tuncurry and Myall Lakes National Park are not the easiest places to reach on public **transport**. Long-distance Sydney–Brisbane buses, such as Greyhound Pioneer, tend to stop only at Raymond Terrace or Karuah on the Pacific Highway (a few stop at Bulahdelah). But there are reasonably good connections to Newcastle and Sydney with Port Stephens Buses (☎02/4981 1207), which stop daily at Nelson Bay, Shoal Bay and Fingal Bay, from where local buses run to Boat Harbour, Anna Bay and Soldiers Point. Also, Great Lakes Coaches (☎02/4983 1560), runs weekdays only to Tea Gardens, Hawks Nest, Bulahdelah, Forster and on to Taree. Both the **Port Stephens Visitors Centre** (see p.244) in Nelson Bay and the well-organized **Great Lakes Visitors Centre** at Little Street in Forster (daily 9am–5pm; ☎02/6554 8799) can provide you with stacks of information and can book accommodation and tours. A good place to **eat** in Forster–Tuncurry is the *Lakeside Tavern*, near the K-Mart shopping village, which serves fresh, good-value seafood. As for **accommodation**, there are scores of motels and even more holiday apartments to choose from in the area, though they may insist on weekly bookings during the holiday season. If you want to stay within the national park itself, **camping** is the way to go. **Houseboats** are also an option (see "Listings" below).

Forster Dolphin Lodge (YHA), 43 Head St, Forster (☎ & fax 02/6555 8155). Just 2min from the beach and the ocean baths, this lodge/hostel has plenty of doubles, as well as dorms. Facilities include communal kitchens, a barbecue area and laundry. Free use of bikes, fishing gear and surf- and boogie-boards. Rooms ③, dorms ①.

Halifax Holiday Park, Beach Rd, Little Beach, 2km east of central Nelson Bay (☎02/4981 1522). A well-outfitted beachside campsite with camp kitchen, barbecues and kiosk. Cabins ③–⑥.

Karen Court Holiday Flats, 27 Townsend St, Forster (☎02/6554 6856). Self-contained apartments for up to five people, sharing a swimming pool and garden. Minimum stay of two nights. ③–⑤.

Myall Shores, Bombah Point, 16km east of Bulahdelah in the Myall Lakes National Park (☎02/4997 4495). Campsite with restaurant, shop and boat-ramp, plus bushwalks, 4WD tours and cruises on offer. Cabins ④–⑤, bungalows ③–④.

Samurai Beach Bungalows, Frost Rd, corner of Robert Connell Close, Anna Bay (☎02/4982 1921). A backpackers' hostel in an idyllic and quiet bushland setting; cabins are arranged around an undercover "bush" kitchen. Free use of boards and bikes and surfing excursions to nearby beaches. Port Stephens Buses from Sydney or Newcastle stops outside. Rooms ②, dorms ①.

Seal Rocks Camping Reserve, Seal Rocks (☎02/4997 6164). Small site just across from the beach; all sites unpowered. Bookings essential during school holidays. On-site vans ③.

Smuggler's Cove Holiday Village, 45 The Lakes Way, 2km south of Forster (☎02/6554 6666). Lakeside campsite with camp kitchen, pool and children's playground. Cabins ②–⑥.

Thurlow Lodge, Thurlow Ave, Nelson Bay (☎02/4981 1577). Central self-catering units sleeping up to six, with a communal swimming pool. From $200–600 per week.

YHA Shoal Bay/Shoal Bay Motel, 61 Shoal Bay Rd, Shoal Bay (☎02/4981 1744). Beachfront motel that also runs a small YHA section – non-members welcome. Sauna and spa; advance booking recommended. Motel rooms ⑤, YHA rooms ④, dorms ①–②.

Listings

Cruises Dolphin-watching jaunts are organized by Dawson's Scenic Cruises (☎02/4982 0444; 2hr; $16) at Nelson Bay; Dolphin Watch Cruises (☎02/6554 7478; 2hr 30min; $30) at Forster; and Myall River Charter Cruises (☎02/4997 1084) at Tea Gardens (daily 10am; 3hr; $18) and Nelson Bay (Wed & Sun 11am; 2hr; $14). General two-hour cruises on Wallis Lake, Forster, with Amaroo Scenic Lake Cruises (mobile phone ☎0419/333 445; office opposite post office).

Gallery Towabba Art, 10 Breckinridge St, Forster. An Aboriginal art collective where you can see and buy local work. Also see "Tours" below.

Houseboats Several operators, including Myall Lakes Houseboats, 90 Crawford St, Bulahdelah (☎02/4997 4221); and Tea Gardens Houseboats, Marine Drive, Tea Gardens (☎02/4997 0555). Weekly rates from $530 to more than $2000, weekends $350 to $470.

NPWS Lot 5, Bourke St, Raymond Terrace (☎02/4987 3108).

Taxis Forster–Tuncurry Radio Taxis (☎13 1008); Nelson Bay Taxi Services (☎02/4981 1210); Raymond Terrace Taxis (mobile phone ☎018/686 541).

Tours Towabba Tours (bookings ☎02/6555 5411) offers an Aboriginal-led walking tour to significant Wallamba sites around Forster, including a bush-tucker lunch and a visit to Towabba Art (see above), departing from the Great Lakes Visitors Centre (Mon 10am; 3hr; $30).

A detour inland: Barrington Tops

There's equally attractive scenery inland, and the drive from Forster via Nabiac, Krambach and Gloucester to the **Barrington Tops National Park** ($7.50 entry per car), for example, makes an enjoyable day-trip. On the way up to the country town of Gloucester it's gently hilly farming country; from here, unsealed roads lead to various scenic spots in the national park – the Barrington Road towards Scone (see p.278), or the Gloucester Tops road to the park's southwestern section. You can also approach it via the Hunter Valley from Maitland via Dungog. The closest you'll get to the park via public transport is on the train from Sydney or Newcastle to Dungog or Gloucester; the *Barrington Guest House* (see below) does free pick-ups from Dungog.

The Barrington Tops themselves are two high, cliff-ringed plateaus, Barrington and Gloucester, that rise steeply from the surrounding valleys. The World Heritage-listed national park was declared in 1969 and protects the catchment areas of six streams that feed the Manning and the Hunter rivers. The changes in altitude are so great – the highest points are Mount Barrington (1555m) and Polblue Mountain (1577m) – that within a few minutes you can pass from areas of subtropical rainforest to warm and cool temperate rainforest, and then to high, windswept plateaus covered with snow gums, meadows and subalpine bog. Up on the plateau, snow is common from the end of April to early October, while heavy fogs and rains are possible at virtually any time.

The **Great Lakes Visitors Centre** in Forster (see p.245) can help with specific routes or organized 4WD tours into the national park; one company running such tours is Manning Valley 4WD Tours (☎02/6553 5977; $75 including morning and afternoon tea and barbecue lunch; pick-ups from Forster, Taree or Sydney). There are plenty of picnic grounds and scenic **lookouts** in the park, plus several **campsites**, some of which are accessible only by 4WD. The main camping area, reached by car, is in the Gloucester River area, with barbecues, toilet and water (no showers; $5 per site). You don't need to book, but for more information contact the NPWS in Raymond Terrace (☎02/4987 3108). A good camping alternative, with hot showers, is *Riverwood Downs*, just outside the park in the Monkerai Valley, 30km south of Gloucester (☎02/4994 7112; ②). The closest **accommodation** to the park is the expensive *Barrington Guest House* in Salisbury, about 40km from Dungog (☎02/4995 3212; ⑧), which charges between $80 and $90 per person (shared bathroom or en suite), including meals and activities from bushwalking to horse-riding. A cheaper alternative is *Barringtons Country Retreat* on Chichester Road, 23km north of Dungog (☎02/4995 9269, fax 4995 9279; ⑦), which has a pool, spa and horse-riding on offer (meals or self-catering available).

The Manning Valley: Taree and around

TAREE, on the Pacific Highway north of Forster–Tuncurry, is a quiet riverside town and the main centre of the fertile, scenic Manning Valley. Served by trains and buses from Sydney and Brisbane, it's a pleasant alternative to the touristy hustle and bustle of Port Macquarie, the next stop north (see below), and especially good as a base for some gentle exploration of the hills, forests and deserted beaches.

The very helpful **tourist office**, on the old Pacific Highway in Taree North (daily 9am–5pm; ☎02/6552 1900), has detailed leaflets describing forest drives, most of which lead to the high plateau where waterfalls abound. **River cruises**, Taree's main attraction, are organized by Manning River Marina and Boat Hire (☎02/6553 2683; 3hr; $15). There's the usual abundance of **motels** along the highway, such as the *Pacific Motel*, 500m north of town (☎02/6552 1977; ④), with air-conditioned rooms and a swimming pool. Cheaper options include the *Royal Bar* (☎02/6550 0255; ①) with counter food and music on weekends, and the *Exchange Hotel* on Victoria St (①) is close to the river for boating. *Fotheringham's Hotel* at 236 Victoria St (☎02/6552 1153; ②) is a pleasant old pub and restaurant, with all rooms newly decorated but no en suites; and the *Twilight Caravan Park*, Pacific Highway, 3km north of town (☎02/6552 2857; cabins ③, on-site vans ②) has a saltwater pool, barbecues and kiosk. If you want to stay aboard a houseboat contact Manning River Holidays Afloat (☎02/6552 6271) who have moored and moving boats available for rent.

Along the route from Taree to Port Macquarie, there are a number of worthwhile detours. One of the most impressive waterfalls on the whole coast is the 160-metre-high **Ellenborough Falls**, about an hour's drive northwest of Taree beyond Wingham on the Bulga Forest Drive – unsealed much of the way. From the main Pacific Highway at Moorland, a road turns off to the small **Crowdy Bay National Park**, situated between Crowdy Head and the lofty Diamond Head, whose landscape includes heathlands, swamp, lagoons, woodlands, forests and sand dunes, all enlivened by prolific birdlife. Back on the Pacific Highway, there is a convenient gateway tourist office fuelling drivers with free tea and coffee at **Kew**, between Taree and Port Macquarie; turn right at the *Kew Hotel* for the more interesting route that hugs the coast.

Port Macquarie

PORT MACQUARIE, at the mouth of the Hastings River, was established in 1821 as a place of secondary punishment for convicts who had committed offences after arrival in New South Wales, as well as for hardened criminals from Britain. By the late 1820s, however, the spread of population meant that this was no longer an isolated outpost, so the penal settlement was closed and the area was opened up to free settlers. The convicts who were still considered incorrigible were sent off to either Moreton Bay in the Brisbane area, or to remote Norfolk Island (see p.292).

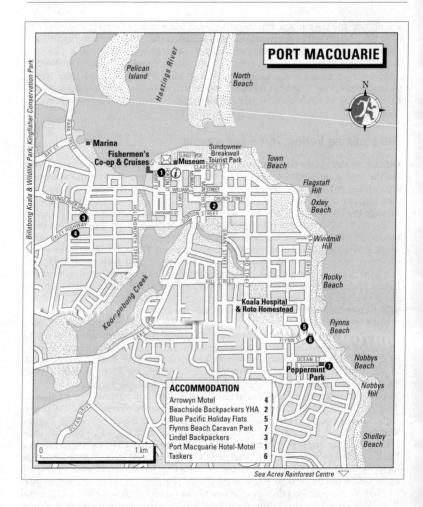

PORT MACQUARIE

ACCOMMODATION

Arrowyn Motel	4
Beachside Backpackers YHA	2
Blue Pacific Holiday Flats	5
Flynns Beach Caravan Park	7
Lindel Backpackers	3
Port Macquarie Hotel-Motel	1
Taskers	6

As with many other northern coastal ports, the **harbour** was unreliable and its approaches difficult, so for more than a century the town failed to live up to its early promise of commercial success. Prosperity and expansion finally came only with the tourism boom, which started in the early 1970s and shows no signs of abating; with a population of about thirty thousand, Port Macquarie is now one of the fastest-growing towns on the north coast of New South Wales, particularly popular with older people from the southern cities who want to spend their retirement years in a sunny place with a moderate climate. The result is that much of "The Port" has the featureless look of just another Australian suburb; more accurately, you might say it's a series of **suburbs** sprawling along the beaches, forever encroaching further on the bush.

For visitors, in addition to the obvious scenic attractions – long, sandy beaches that start right in town and extend far along the coast, and forests and mountains in the hinterland – there's also plenty laid on in and around the town itself: amusement parks, mini-zoos, nature parks, cruises on the Hastings River and connecting waterways, horse-riding, and, above all, water sports and fishing.

Arrival and information

As a popular resort, Port Macquarie is well served by transport from Sydney, Tamworth (see p.279) and Brisbane, although not all **buses** make the detour from the Pacific Highway, so check carefully. Buses drop you off outside the tourist information office. **Trains** stop in Wauchope, 22km west, from where there's a Countrylink bus connection with Port Macquarie Bus (☎02/6583 3079). You can also **fly** into Port Macquarie from Sydney with Eastern Australian (☎13 1313). Horton Street is the main downtown street, running north to the Hastings River. The helpful and friendly **tourist information office** (Mon–Fri 8.30am–5pm, Sat & Sun 9am–4pm; ☎02/6583 1293, accommodation and tour bookings free call ☎1800/025 935), on Clarence Street paralleling the river, will also mind your bags free of charge if you've time to kill. The town's attractions and beaches are far flung, and transport isn't the best. You can get around town on Port Macquarie Bus Service (☎02/6583 2161), which has eleven different routes running mainly in the daytime Monday to Friday, with some services on Saturday. Only bus #334 to Wauchope runs daily. Waits are long between buses (often an hour or more), so a timetable – available from the tourist information office – is vital. Otherwise the best option is **cycling** (see "Listings", p.251).

Accommodation

With sixty motels and holiday apartments in town, you're not going to be hard-pressed to find somewhere to stay; the cheaper, older motels are mostly found on Gordon Street, with the average double going for $50.

Arrowyn Motel, 170 Gordon St (☎02/6583 1633, fax 6583 3040). Simple, inexpensive motel with a communal kitchen/dining area and outside barbecue. Within walking distance of the river and Main Beach. ④.

Beachside Backpackers, 40 Church St (☎ & fax 02/6583 5512). Central, family-run, friendly YHA hostel, recently renovated with kitchen/TV/video room and BBQ on the patio. Free pick-up from the bus terminal. Small gym area; free bikes, boogie- and surfboards, with free surf lessons every morning. Dorms ①.

Blue Pacific Holiday Flats, 37 Pacific Drive, Flynns Beach (☎02/6583 1686). Apartments near the beach, sleeping up to six. Small kitchen, and TV. ③–⑤.

Flynns Beach Caravan Park, 22 Ocean St, 2.5km from the centre (☎02/6583 5754). A good camping option for people with no transport, as they will pick up travellers from the bus terminal. On-site vans ②–③.

Lindel Backpackers, Hastings River Drive, corner of Gordon St (☎ & fax 02/6583 1791). Top-class hostel in one of the oldest houses in town, an 1888 Victorian Gothic building. Clean, friendly and family-run, with a barbecue area and swimming pool, plus free use of bikes, surfboards and fishing gear. Book in advance for free pick-up service from the bus terminal; free trips by shuttle-bus to the koala hospital and beaches. Rooms ②, dorms ①.

Ocean Beach Flats, 2 Bundella Ave, Lake Cathie, about 15km south (☎02/6585 5292). Apartments for a maximum of five people, close to the lake and beach with shops nearby; BYO linen. ④.

Port Macquarie Hotel-Motel, Clarence St, opposite the post office (☎02/6583 1011, fax 6583 5822). Clean, good-value hotel rooms with or without bath, in a pub overlooking the river. Also some motel rooms. Good beer garden and bistro. Motel ④, hotel ②–③.

Rainbow Beach Holiday Village, Beach St, Bonny Hills, about 23km south (☎02/6585 5655). Spacious, beachside camping complex in a bushland setting, with solar-heated pool, playground, barbecue and shop. On-site vans ③, cabins ④, cottages ⑤.

Sundowner Breakwall Tourist Park, right on the riverfront (☎02/6583 2755). Park offering shops, amenities and a palm-fringed pool; on-site caravans ③, cabins ⑤.

Taskers, 14 Flynn St, opposite Flynns Beach (☎02/6583 1520). Nice, shady complex with pool, children's playground and barbecue. Cabins ③–⑦.

The Town and around

Port Macquarie has a history of destroying reminders of its past. The only surviving remnants are **St Thomas' Church** (1824–28) on Hay Street; the **courthouse** on Clarence Street (Mon–Fri 10am–3pm; free), built in 1869 and refurbished accordingly; the **Historical Museum** opposite (Mon–Sat 9.30am–4.30pm, Sun 1.30–4.30pm; $4), which has an extensive and well-presented collection of documents and memorabilia dealing with the history of the Hastings River area; and there's also a **Maritime Museum** at 6 William St (Mon–Sat 11am–3pm $2) with model ships, nautical paintings and artefacts. The 1890s **Pilots Boatshed Museum** at Town Wharf (Tues–Sat 10am–2pm; $1) also has a small collection covering the history of maritime and river wrecks. Several **river cruises** leave from the **Fishermen's Co-op** at the beach end of Clarence Street (see "Listings", p.251). The river foreshore provides a pleasant place for a peaceful sunset stroll and you can watch the pelican colony begging for tiddlers from the local anglers.

Perhaps the best of the attractions is the **Kooloonbung Creek Nature Park**, a large bushland reserve remarkably close to the town centre. From the entrance at the corner of Horton and Gordon streets, you step onto trails among casuarinas, mangroves and eucalypts, or sweat through a small patch of rainforest, and it's amazingly easy to believe that you're lost in the wilderness of the Australian bush, rather than minutes from the main road. The eastern part of the nature reserve is accessible to wheelchairs, and at the **old cemetery** near the main entrance a few graves of pioneer settlers have been preserved.

On the ocean-facing side of town, Port Macquarie's three flagged, patrolled **beaches** are Town Beach, Flynn's and Lighthouse. The **Sea Acres Rainforest Centre** (daily 9am–4.30pm; $8.50, $22 family; free guided walks every 45min), south of the town on Pacific Drive, is impressive, conveying an urgent environmental message about the fast-disappearing coastal rainforest of New South Wales which you can learn about in the ecology display room and enviro-theatre. The centre comprises three different types of rainforest, which can be inspected at close quarters from a boardwalk (again wheelchair-accessible).

Back towards the town centre, on Lord Street, **Roto** is a fine nineteenth-century homestead, with Australia's only **koala hospital** in its grounds (both open daily 9am–5pm; free, donations welcome; check feeding times on ☎02/6584 1522). Run and financed by volunteers, the hospital takes in disease-stricken koalas, as well as road casualties – a sad consequence of Port Macquarie's suburban sprawl.

If you've not had your fill of cuddly animals, the **Billabong Koala & Wildlife Park**, 233 Oxley Highway (daily 9.30am–4.30pm; $7.50), advertises cute kangaroos that can be hand-fed and koalas that can be patted and embraced. There's also the **Kingfisher Conservation Park**, on Kingfisher Road (daily 9am–5pm; $7), home to over four hundred animals, some of which are threatened by extinction. **Peppermint Park**, corner of Pacific Drive and Ocean Street (Tues–Sun 10am–5pm, daily during school holidays; $11.90 adult or child, $39.80 family), is a typical amusement park, with giant waterslides, a mini-golf course and a roller-skating rink; the admission fee is high, but includes all attractions.

Eating, drinking and nightlife

As you'd expect in a resort of this size, there are plenty of places to **eat**, and particularly fast-food outlets: not surprisingly, seafood and fish predominate and the local oysters really must be tried. *Macquarie Seafoods*, centrally located on the corner of Clarence and Short streets, is the best place for takeaway fish and chips. You can also buy fresh fish and seafood from the **Fishermen's Co-op** at the end of Clarence Street in the town wharf area and cook it yourself. *Scampi's*, at the Marina on Park Street, just west of the town centre (BYO; nightly dinner plus lunch in summer), is one of the most enjoyable of several seafood restaurants. *Sassies*, in the Shores City Mall on nearby Bay Street (BYO; closed Mon lunch & Sun), is a café-restaurant specializing in innovatively prepared local produce. *Toro's Mexican Cantina* at 22 Murray St (☎02/6583 4340) has build-your-own burritos and tacos in the evenings only, while *Spicy Kruthai* on the corner of Clarence and Hay streets (☎02/6583 9043) has reasonably priced Thai seafood and stir-fries. One above the other at 74 Clarence St on the waterfront, is *Crays Seafood Restaurant*, a pricey establishment although it does have decent lunchtime deals, and *Al Dente Italian* (☎02/6584 1422) open for lunch and dinner offering risottos and seafood chowders. The Port Central Shopping Centre, behind the tourist information office on Clarence Street, has an excellent food court on the second floor; choices include fresh, healthy fare from the *Pure and Natural Food Co*, and excellent coffee and cakes at *The Coffee Club* – both open daily. The new *Cosmopolitan Caffe*, on the corner of Clarence and Short streets is a sidewalk café with an extensive list of flavoured coffees plus lunchtime nachos and sandwiches, while nearby *Café 66* at 66 Clarence St (☎02/6583 7885) has pasta and focaccia at lunchtime and a patio popular with evening diners. For a taste of the tacky, *Carz* is a car-theme restaurant serving American-inspired food, from burgers to bugtails (free call ☎1800/022 088).

The *Macquarie Hotel*, opposite the tourist information office, on the corner of Clarence and Horton streets, is a good **drinking** spot with a riverfront location and lots of different bars; bands play here Wednesday and Saturday. The attached nightclub, *Lachlan's*, has a pool competition on Wednesday, dance parties on Thursday and Friday, and live bands on Saturday. Other nightclubs are *TC's*, on William Street, popular with the 18–25 set; and *Down Under*, on Short Street next to Coles supermarket, a tiny underground place for the over-thirties.

There are now a few **wineries** in the area: Cassegrain Winery, on the Hastings River on Fernbank Creek Road off the Pacific Highway south of town (daily 9am–5pm), has a particularly pleasant restaurant on a verandah overlooking the vineyards.

Listings

Bike rental Graham Seers Cyclery, Port Marina, Park St (☎02/6583 2333).

Buses Long-distance buses on the Sydney–Brisbane route stop outside the tourist information office. Kings Bus Service (☎02/6562 4724) runs between Port Macquarie and Tamworth via Kempsey, Macksville, Nambucca Heads, Urunga, Coffs Harbour, Bellingen, Dorrigo, Armidale, Uralla and Walcha three times a week. As well as running around town, Port Macquarie Bus Service (☎02/6583 2161) also serves Wauchope and Kempsey.

Camels Rides on Lighthouse Beach (bookings through the tourist information office on ☎02/6583 1293 or call ☎02/6583 7650; $12 for 20min, $22 per hour).

Car rental Budget, William St (☎02/6583 5144); Economical Rent-a-Car, 190 Oxley St (☎02/6581 1020); Hertz, 73 Hastings River Drive (☎02/6583 6599); or Thrifty at the airport (☎02/6584 2122).

Cruises Cruises depart from the Clarence Street Wharf: *MV Port Venture* cruises up the Hastings River (1–2 daily; 2hr; $15); Pelican River Cruises departs from the Fishermen's Co-op Wharf to the everglades in Limeburners Creek National Park and an oyster farm for tastings (Mon–Fri 10am, Sat & Sun 2pm; 2hr 30min–5hr; $30); *Fanta Sea II* explores the Hastings River, often encountering dolphins (☎015/256 742; daily 10am & 2pm; $15); the *Wentworth*, a 50-year-old wooden boat offers a cruise ($10; 2hr); and the Waterbus Everglade Tours offer an Explorer Cruise (daily 2pm; 2hr 30min; $20) among others.

Hospital Port Macquarie Hospital, Wright's Rd (☎02/6581 2000).

Internet Café *Felglow Internet Coffee Lounge* at 4–16 Clarence St has cheap cakes and coffee and charges $4.75 per half hour for Internet use: *admin@felglow.com.au*. Mon–Fri 9am–6pm, Sat 9am–5pm.

Police ☎02/6583 0199.

Post office Port Macquarie Post Office, Clarence St, NSW 2444.

Surfing The Paradise Surf Centre at 49 Horton St (☎02/6583 6062) sells surfboards and gear as well as organizing lessons and day-trips on request.

Taxis Port Macquarie Taxicabs (☎02/6581 0081); Wauchope Radio Taxicabs (☎02/6585 2100). There is a taxi rank on Horton St.

Tours There are several day-tour operators to the hinterland, but the least touristy is East Coast Mountain Safaris (☎02/6584 2366), a 4WD tour where you learn about local flora and fauna and visit Ellenborough Falls and Wilson River Reserve (full-day $73, including barbecue lunch and morning tea; a half-day tour for $43 – not including lunch – takes in coastal mountain lookouts). You can get to South West Rocks with Southern Cross Tours (☎02/6581 2181; Wed & Fri 9am–4.30pm; $38 including barbecue lunch and entry fees).

Trains The XPT links Wauchope and Sydney (3 daily; 6hr).

Water sports Several companies operate parasailing, fishing charters and jet-ski tours on the river and ocean, including Watersports World (☎02/6583 9777) and Port Water Sports (☎0412 234509).

Heading inland: Wauchope

Surrounded by forest, the pretty little village of **WAUCHOPE** (pronounced War-hope), 22km west of Port Macquarie, makes an enjoyable contrast to the coast. Through working exhibits, the open-air museum of **Timbertown**, 3km from the village (daily 9.30am–3.30pm; $16), depicts life as it must have been in the isolated timber settlements 150 years ago. Timber logs are pulled over muddy roads to saw-pits, where they are cut and shaped, the bakery bakes and sells bread fresh from the oven, and many other aspects of Victorian life are re-enacted. North of Wauchope, the **Wilson River Rainforest R**_____'s picnic grounds are a popular destination for day-trips from Port Macquarie. Another feature of Wauchope is the large separatist lesbian community that lives in the vicinity – something strangely absent from the tourist literature.

Basic pub **accommodation** and counter meals can be had at the *Hastings Hotel*, on the corner of High and Cameron streets (☎02/6585 2003; ②). The delightful *Mount Seaview Resort*, on the Oxley Highway towards Tamworth (☎02/6587 7155, fax 6587 7195, free call ☎1800/818 804; resort ⑤, lodge ④), a cattle station on the Hastings River, offers farmstays and campsites as well as rooms; there's a bar, restaurant and tennis court, and the resort organizes very popular cross-country horse-riding (available also for non-guests; 9am daily; $15 per hour) and 4WD tours. You can also swim in the river here. They will pick up guests from Wauchope train station or Port Macquarie airport.

You can get to Wauchope daily on Steinhardt's Port Macquarie Bus Service (☎02/6583 2161); on weekdays the 9.20am service goes directly to Timbertown, returning at 2.30pm (around $5).

The coast north to Nambucca Heads

The coastline between Port Macquarie and Nambucca Heads, 115km north, has some magic spots. **KEMPSEY**, a large service town on the Macleay River, 49km from Port Macquarie, is home to a prominent Aboriginal population: **the Dunghutti** people. The first white settlers moved into the area five years after the explorer John Oxley entered the Macleay River area in 1818. Between 1830 and 1850 the Dunghutti put up resistance to the settlers, and several Aboriginal massacres resulted. By the 1850s resistance was so widespread that native police were called in to stop the fighting. In the following decade Aboriginal reserves were established, and a degree of self-determination existed from the 1890s when several Aboriginal farms were set up, but the people were pushed off the farms after World War I. The Dunghutti were still holding traditional ceremonies as late as the 1940s. Their ability to demonstrate continuous links with their land led in 1996 to a successful claim for Native Title for a portion of land at **CRESCENT HEAD**, 21km northeast from Kempsey along a good sealed road, although they will hold title only temporarily. There are some wonderful waterfront **campsites** here: Crescent Head Tourist Park (☎02/6566 0261), which also has some very pleasant verandah-fronted wooden chalets (③–⑥); and *Delicate Nobby Camping Ground* (☎02/6566 0144), which is in extensive but secluded bushland, ten minutes' drive from the township. Meandering back and then away from the Pacific Highway, you come to the coastal **Hat Head National Park** and the small town of **SOUTH WEST ROCKS**, perched on a picturesque headland. Three kilometres east on **Trial Bay**, the **Arakoon State Recreation Area** has as its centrepiece **Trial Bay Gaol** (daily 9am–5pm; $3). Classified as a public works prison in which prisoners could learn a trade, the jail was considered progressive when it was established in 1886. Built from local granite, it's certainly an impressive construction – the massive outer walls surround an extensive complex of buildings and are supported by high buttresses with four watchtowers. The prison was closed in 1903, but reopened during World War I when it was used as an internment camp for over five hundred internees – including some Buddhist monks from Ceylon, though most of those held here were German.

Nambucca Heads

About 100km away, via the Pacific Highway, the casual resort town of **NAMBUCCA HEADS** makes a good base for trips to the rivers, mountains and forests of the hinterland; it's also a great place to break the long haul from Sydney to Brisbane – whether you're travelling by car, bus or train (the train station is on Bowra Street, about 3km from the centre). From the headlands near the town centre there are fantastic views of the mouth of Nambucca River, and of the seemingly endless sweep of sandy beaches that stretch both north and south from here. There's fishing, windsurfing and canoeing available to take advantage of the gentler waters at the river mouth, and some excellent surf on the ocean beaches. From vantage points at **Scotts Head**, a popular surfing spot, whales can sometimes be sighted during their southern migration (Aug–Oct).

For information on these and other activities around town (including white-water rafting and horse-riding), call in at the **visitor information centre** on the Pacific Highway at the southern entrance to town (daily 9am–5pm; ☎02/6568 6954). Here you can book **accommodation**; motels and apartments are generally better value here than in Port Macquarie or Coffs Harbour. Try the *Nirvana Village Motel*, Riverside Drive (☎02/6568 6700); ③–④), with a pool and barbecue; the renovated family-run *Scotts Guesthouse*, 4 Wellington Drive (☎02/6568 6386, fax 6569 4169; en-suite B&B ④); or the *White Albatross Holiday Centre*, Wellington Drive (☎02/6568 6468; cabins ③, on-site vans ②), in an attractive location and with facilities including a tennis court, tavern, café and children's playground. The best of the budget options is *Nambucca Backpackers*, 3 Newman St (☎ & fax 02/6568 6360; rooms ③, dorms ①), a small, cosy, family-run hostel with free use of boogie-boards, snorkelling and fishing gear and pick-up from the bus terminal or train station. A good place to **eat** is *Johnny's Pizza*, in the town centre on Kent Street, serving delicious gourmet hot dogs, salad sandwiches and pizzas, while *Nirvana Sawasdee*, next door to the tourist office, is a traditional Thai restaurant that makes good use of fresh local seafood. Singapore-Malay and Chinese dishes are on offer at *Ken Leong's* at the *Nambucca League's Club* by Coronation Park (☎02/6568 7415).

Nambucca Heads is on the main Sydney–Brisbane bus and train routes; Kings Bus Service (☎02/6562 4724) runs to Port Macquarie or Tamworth and back three times a week. **Local buses** leave from Bowra Street outside the police station: Newman's Coaches (☎02/6568 1296) operates Monday to Friday only between Nambucca Heads and Coffs Harbour via Bowraville; Jessups Bus Service (☎02/6653 4552) goes on schooldays only to Coffs Harbour via Urunga and Bellingen; and Joyce's (☎02/6655 6330) goes to Urunga, again on schooldays only.

Heading inland from Nambucca, it's about half an hour's drive to the picturesque former timber town of **BOWRAVILLE**, where you can rest up in the old pub, now renovated to its former glory, and browse in a few arts-and-crafts shops and the jumble of Gleeson's Second Hand Store. *The Phoenix Gallery & Tea Rooms* is a pleasant refreshment stop. From here, you can travel on unsealed forest roads to the small, alternative town of Bellingen (see below), although it's more easily reached on the sealed road which turns off the Pacific Highway after Urunga.

The Bellinger River and around

URUNGA, 20km north from Nambucca Heads, is a pleasant beachside spot where the Bellinger and Kalang rivers meet the sea. Seven kilometres further along the Pacific Highway is the turn-off to **MYLESTOM**, which occupies a stunningly beautiful spot on the wide Bellinger River. You can take advantage of its riverside setting at the Alma Doepel Reserve's sheltered, sandy river beach, which has changing rooms and showers. Two minutes' walk to the east is a gorgeous sweep of surf beach – often gloriously deserted – which is patrolled on summer weekends and school holidays. You can walk along the beach to **Bundagen**, an alternative, environmentally friendly community that welcomes visitors.

A great **place to stay** in Mylestom is the *Riverside Lodge*, on River Street facing Tuckers Island (☎02/6655 4245; rooms ②, dorms ①). Although there's no transport here, Bill, the friendly owner, will pick guests up from Urunga or Coffs Harbour. The lodge has the comfortable, relaxed feel of an Indonesian guesthouse; all the rooms are well furnished with desks, lamps and armchairs. You can use the lodge's bicycles, boat and kayaks. Other **facilities** in Mylestom are limited: a post office with supplies and EFTPOS, a decent Chinese **restaurant**, and a swanky riverfront brasserie called *Beaches* (with a handy bottle shop).

Bellingen

Just after Urunga, the turn-off west heads through the verdant Bellinger River valley for 12km to **BELLINGEN**, a relaxed little town with a strong alternative bent, full of arts-and-crafts outlets and workshops, cafés and thriving small businesses. Just before town, the **Old Butter Factory**, a renovated dairy, holds a complex of several craft shops where you can check out the work of local artisans, plus a chilled-out café and a massage and float tank centre ($45 for a 2hr combo pamper). In town there's a **Historical Museum** at Hyde Street (Tues–Sun 10am–4pm; $1) containing local memorabilia which charts the development of the district from 1860. Also on Hyde Street, The Yellow Shed is a crafts outlet worth a peek. Bellingen also has an interesting monthly **market**, held on the third Saturday of the month (7am–2pm) in Bellingen Park, with buskers, crafts and organic food stalls. There's more shopping at the **Hammond and Wheatley Emporium** on Hyde Street, a glorious old restored department store with an Aladdin's cave of locally-produced jewellery, artefacts and artworks. Each year Bellingen hosts a lively **jazz festival** (☎02/6655 9345, fax 6655 1053; *belljazz@midcoast.com.au*) over the third weekend in August, followed by the newly launched three-day Global Festival of world music over the October long weekend. For a cooling break from crafts and culture, you can swim in the waterholes of the Bellinger and Never Never rivers.

More **information** on the town and surrounding area is available at Bellingen Travel, Shop 1, 42 Hyde St (☎02/6655 2055), which has details of rafting, bushwalking and other tours and acts as an agent for Countrylink. The creekfront *Bellingen YHA Backpackers*, 2 Short St (☎02/6655 1116, fax 6655 1358; *belloyha@midcoast.com.au*; rooms ③, dorms ①), is one of the best **hostels** around, a beautiful two-storey building with a huge bal-

cony facing a rainforest island full of jacaranda trees that come alive at dusk with the stir-
rings of fruit bats; you can even camp out the back if you prefer. There's a free pick-up
from Urunga railway station and you can get lifts to Dorrigo for $10. They also offer
canoes and bikes for rent, plus a BBQ. Otherwise, there's the *Rivendell Bed and
Breakfast*, centrally located at 10 Hyde St (☎ & fax 02/6655 0060; ⑤); or the more
secluded and luxurious *Fernridge Cottage*, just over 4km out of Bellingen on the
Dorrigo Road (☎ & fax 02/6655 2142; ⑥), which you have all to yourself for a minimum booking of two nights. The *Bellingen Valley Motor Inn* (☎02/6655 1599, fax
6655 1824; ⑤–⑦) is also in a green expanse on the way to Dorrigo, but only 1km out
of town, with room service, a swimming pool, spa, playground and barbecue. You
can **camp** at the *Bellingen Caravan Park* on Dowle Street, North Bellingen
(☎02/6655 1338).

The town is full of great **cafés**. *Lodge 241*, an art gallery-cum-café on Short Street
serves some of the best coffee in town and interesting, wholesome lunches. The light
and airy *Carriageway Café*, 75 Hyde St, serves simple and affordable city fare – melts,
burgers, gourmet sandwiches, bagels and croissants; at the back, a polished wooden
staircase heads upstairs to an art gallery. On Church Street, the spacious *Cool Creek
Café* has a folksy ambience and an extensive veggie menu, as well as lasagne, and
bacon and eggs for breakfast. Next door, *The Good Food Shop* is a real find for wholefood supplies; it also serves good lunches. *McNally House* on Hyde Street (☎02/6655
6344; Tues–Sat eve only) is a BYO restaurant in a cute cottage, with a mixed menu
run by Swiss chefs. The town has only one **pub**: the animated *Federal Hotel*, on Hyde
Street, with live music (usually free) from Thursday to Sunday.

Interstate buses do not detour into Bellingen; the nearest drop-off point is Urunga
or Coffs Harbour, from where Jessups Bus Service (☎02/6653 4552) runs here on
schooldays. You can also reach Bellingen on Kings Bus Service (☎02/6562 4724),
which operates three times a week between Port Macquarie and Tamworth.

Inland to Dorrigo

The Dorrigo Road from Bellingen follows the beautiful Bellinger River, with bewitch-
ing green hills in the distance and fat cows grazing in lush riverside fields, passing
through **THORA**, and its roadhouse with the pleasant *River Bend Café* attached.
Beyond Thora, the scenic road winds ever more steeply through the **Dorrigo
National Park**, a startlingly beautiful rainforest remnant of an area that was once similarly heavily forested; however, the lure of the valuable Australian cedar – "red gold"
– left most of the plateau cleared by the 1920s. The ultramodern **National Park
Visitor Centre** (daily 9am–5pm; ☎02/6657 2309) has a detailed interpretive display
that goes through this sorry saga, with some insights into the life of the north coast
Aboriginal people, and some examples of red cedar furniture. The *Canopy Café* here,
with wonderful views, serves light lunches and afternoon teas until 4pm. Starting at
the visitor centre, the **Skywalk** is easily the most spectacular of the walks and the least
strenuous, a wooden walkway stretching out high over the rainforest canopy, enabling
you to look down on the forest and out over the surrounding landscape and distant
hills. The walkway is open 24 hours, to allow observance of the forest's nocturnal creatures. Other trails will take you to some of the park's best features, including a number of beautiful waterfalls – there are comprehensive information boards at the centre,
or pick up some leaflets for details.

DORRIGO itself is an old settlement on the eastern edge of the New England
Plateau, a classic small country town typified by the old-fashioned air and 1950s
Formica fittings of *Nick's Café* on Hickory Street, which serves scones and pots of
tea. There's plenty of **accommodation** here: the wide-verandahed *Hotel Dorrigo*
(☎02/6657 2016, fax 6557 2059; ①–③) has basic hotel and fancier motel-style rooms,

as well as dorm accommodation, while *Dorrigo Mountain Resort*, 1 Bellingen Rd (☎02/6657 2564), close to the national park, has camping and a range of cabins (②–④). There are also plenty of farmstays in the area; get full details from the **tourist information** service at 36 Hickory St (daily 10am–4pm; ☎02/6657 2486).

The only way to get to Dorrigo on public transport is with Kings Bus Service (☎02/6562 4724), which runs three times a week between Port Macquarie and Tamworth; you can catch it from Bellingen. The bus follows the road west from Dorrigo cutting cross-country, past several more national parks, towards Armidale (see p.281).

Coffs Harbour

Back on the main coastal highway, **COFFS HARBOUR** – or "Coffs" – divides neatly into two separate parts. One half is a modern town snuggled close to the hills near the Pacific Highway – this is the centre of town, with the shopping mall, post office and all other facilities. The other part is the jetty area around the train station and the man-made harbour. Although Coffs Harbour depends almost as much on tourism as Port Macquarie, the suburban sprawl of retirement homes and holiday apartments, hotels and motels is somehow not as noticeable here; instead the dramatic coastal landscape manages to hold sway. At this point the mountains and hills of the Great Dividing Range fall almost directly into the South Pacific Ocean, and glorious white, sandy beaches stretch endlessly along the coast, from the town **beaches** of Boambee Beach and Jetty Beach through Park Beach and Diggers Beach, up to northern strands such as Emerald (see p.259). There are several small islands offshore with fringing coral reefs designated as marine reserves; the plethora of fish around these makes diving a popular activity. In summer, the cool, rainforest-clad mountains with crystal-clear creeks and tumbling torrents offer a welcome respite from the heat and humidity of the coast.

Arrival and information

All long-distance **buses** stop on Moonee Street, on the corner of Grafton Street; the **train station** (☎02/6651 2757) is by the harbour. You can also fly into Coffs with Eastern Australian, Ansett and Impulse; the airport is about 5km south and you can rent a car at one of the airport desks, or take a **taxi** into town (about $5). However, if you've booked accommodation you can probably arrange to be picked up. Given the split of Coffs into two halves, the distances you have to cover are considerable, and the **local bus service**, which runs between the town centre, Coffs Jetty and Park Beach (Coffs Harbour Bus Lines, ☎02/6652 2686; timetables from the visitor information centre), is barely adequate, so you may find yourself having to take taxis. Alternatively, you could rent a bike or car – see "Listings" on p.260 for details. To get to the beaches north of Coffs, take Ryan's Bus Service, which goes to Woolgoolga via Sapphire, Moonee Beach and Emerald Beach (☎02/6652 3201; Mon–Fri 5 daily, Sat 2 daily).

The City Centre Mall, right in the centre off Grafton Street (as the Pacific Highway is called in town), is very much the heart of Coffs, and most facilities and much of the accommodation are nearby. Unfortunately, the **visitor information centre** (daily 9am–5pm; ☎02/6652 1522) is not exactly centrally situated, positioned as it is for drivers' convenience on the corner of Marcia Street and Woolgoolga Road (the Pacific Highway) on the north side of town. The National Parks and Wildlife Service (☎02/6651 9522) has an office in the GIO building at 24 Moonee St, and a branch at the jetty on Orlando Street, providing information on the marine reserve and rangers tours of Muttonbird Island. State Forests also has an information centre and shop at 130 W High St (☎02/6652 0111) with camping maps available covering the mid-north coast region.

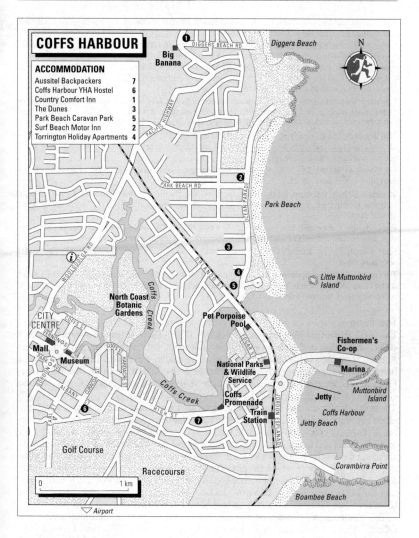

COFFS HARBOUR

ACCOMMODATION

Aussitel Backpackers	7
Coffs Harbour YHA Hostel	6
Country Comfort Inn	1
The Dunes	3
Park Beach Caravan Park	5
Surf Beach Motor Inn	2
Torrington Holiday Apartments	4

Accommodation

Coffs has everything from international resort hotels down to caravan parks. During the summer and Easter holidays the place is packed, and weekly **bookings** are preferred or even compulsory. As trains and buses from Sydney arrive in the late evening, it's wise to book in advance in any case, especially as the **hostels** will pick you up if notified. The cheapest **motels** are on the south side of town; **resorts** sometimes have bargain off-season rates, too. The visitor information centre has a free-call **reservations** line ☎1800/025 650.

Aussitel Backpackers, 312 High St (☎02/6651 1871, fax 6651 5335). Large, well-equipped hostel with a clean communal kitchen and heated pool; free use of bikes, surf- and boogie-boards and canoes, and lots of activities including an inexpensive dive course. Free pick-up from the bus terminal and train station. Rooms ③, dorms ①.

Coffs Harbour YHA Hostel, 110 Albany St (☎ & fax 02/6652 6462). Friendly, active hostel, handy for the town centre with lifts every morning to the beach and other attractions. Kiosk with basic foodstuffs, garden with a pool, barbecue, plus bike rental, free surf- and boogie-boards and fishing gear. Surf lessons and special rate dive courses arranged ($150). Free pick-up from bus terminal, train station and airport. Rooms ③, dorms ①.

Country Comfort Inn, Pacific Highway, 4km north (☎02/6652 8222, fax 6652 3832). One of Coffs' most popular resorts, right next to the Big Banana. It's not exactly cheap, but is good value for money, with tennis courts, pool, sauna, restaurant and bar. All rooms are air-con. ⑥–⑦.

The Dunes, 28 Fitzgerald St, off Ocean Parade (☎02/6652 4522, fax 6652 3308). A fancy complex of one-, two- and three-bedroom serviced apartments near Park Beach, with a heated pool, tennis courts, spa and sauna. ⑥.

Go Bananas Motel, 53 Pacific Highway, Woolgoolga, 10km north (☎02/6654 1424). The cheapest motel in the area. ②–④.

Moonee Beach Caravan Park, 12km north off the Pacific Highway (☎02/6653 6552). Magic camping spot in bush surroundings, with beach, estuary and headlands to explore. Cabins ③–④, on-site vans ②–③.

Park Beach Caravan Park, Ocean Parade (☎02/6652 3204). Huge, well-run beachfront campsite, with barbecue facilities and children's playground. Cabins ③, on-site vans ②.

Surf Beach Motor Inn, 25 Ocean Parade (☎02/6652 1872, fax 6652 1498). Good-value motel with pool. ④–⑥.

Torrington Holiday Apartments, 27 Boultwood St (☎02/6652 7546, fax 6652 8505). On a quiet street close to Park Beach. Fully self-contained apartments ideal for families, with a playground, swimming pool, spa and sauna. ④–⑥.

The Town

The small **Historical Museum**, at 191 High St (Tues–Thurs & Sun 1.30–4pm; $2), has a collection of relics and tools owned by early pioneers and cedar-getters, as well as local Aboriginal artefacts of the **Gumbaingirr**, whose boundaries extended from the Nambucca River north to the Clarence River, and inland to the foothills of the Great Dividing Range. From the museum, it's only a short distance to the magnificent **North Coast Botanic Gardens**, with an entrance on Hardacre Street, just off High Street (daily 9am–5pm). These delightfully tranquil subtropical gardens are located on a triangle of land surrounded on two sides by **Coffs Creek** and feature a mangrove boardwalk and a slice of rainforest. A charming **creek walk** and **cycle trail** begin just near the town centre at Rotary Park on Coffs Street and head 5.4km to Muttonbird Island (see below); the final thirty minutes are along the northern breakwater – detailed maps are available from the visitor information centre. The new development of **Coffs Promenade**, along the creek towards Coffs Jetty, contains crafts and speciality shops as well as an ice-cream parlour, a café and restaurant, the last two with outdoor tables overlooking the tranquil, tree-lined creek. You can rent bikes here (see "Listings" on p.260), as well as canoes ($20 half-day, $35 full-day).

The **Fishermen's Co-op**, on the northern breakwater of the harbour, sells fresh fish; the wharf here is also the departure point for most of Coffs' cruises (see p.229). Beyond the boat-filled marina is **Muttonbird Island Nature Reserve**, high enough to offer fantastic views of Coffs Harbour and the southern and northern beaches. There's plenty of birdlife too, with an interpretive walk describing the lifestyle of the oily, migratory birds who come here to nest in summer. The best time to come is at sunset, when you can watch the muttonbirds return to their nests. You can sometimes see dolphins frolicking close to the island. If you want to see domesticated dolphins (and seals) being put through their paces, visit the misleadingly named **Pet Porpoise Pool**, between Coffs Jetty and Park Beach ($9.80, children $4.70, family ticket $30; performances 10.30am & 2.15pm; 1hr 30min), which seems stuck in a 1970s time warp; there's also a small aquarium with sharks, other marine animals and a reef tank.

Banana plantations indicate that at Coffs you're entering a subtropical climatic zone. The cultural influence of nearby Queensland becomes apparent, too, in tourist attractions such as the **Big Banana** (daily 9am–5pm), a huge, bright-yellow concrete banana, 3km north of Coffs on the Pacific Highway, advertising a "horticultural theme park". It's free to walk through the banana and look at displays dealing with early pioneer life in the district and Coffs Harbour's $70-million-a-year banana industry. There are several tours of the plantation (by bus 30min–1hr, $3.50–5.50; by monorail 1hr 30min, $6.50–9.50), which show you packing sheds and hydroponics glasshouses, as well as a space station and an Aboriginal Dreamtime Cave. A new attraction is a toboggan ride ($4), which whizzes 720m down through the steep hillside plantations. For the complete banana experience, stop in at the milk bar, which serves bananas in every conceivable way. The souvenir shop next door is crammed with lurid yellow objects such as banana pencil sharpeners and "Bananas in Pyjamas".

Around Coffs Harbour

An hour's drive inland from Coffs, on Bushmans Range Road at Lowanna, 42km northwest, is **George's Gold Mine** (Wed–Sun 10.30am–3pm, daily during school holidays; $8.50), where you can take a tour of a gold mine and look at the old stamper battery that was used to crush the ore. There are also picnic grounds, barbecues and walking trails through the rainforest.

To the north of Coffs is a string of fantastic sandy beaches. **Sapphire Beach**, 9km north, has an **environment centre** (daily 10am–5pm) with a relaxing café. **Moonee Beach Reserve**, 3km further, is in beautiful bush surroundings with a winding creek that has safe swimming – but beware of strong currents at its mouth. The reserve has plenty of shade, picnic tables and barbecues, making it a great spot for picnics. There's a caravan park here (see "Accommodation", p.265), and little else except for a small shop which sells supplies, good fish and chips and hamburgers. About 8km further on, the relatively unspoilt **Emerald Beach** is popular with surfers; it's very picturesque, with a small island offshore.

At **WOOLGOOLGA**, another 10km or so north on the Pacific Highway, a gleaming white **temple** is evidence of the large Sikh population which settled here in the early 1970s. There's also the **Raj Mahal**, an emporium selling crafts, clothes and jewellery, plus a pricey Indian **restaurant** – the *Temple View*, opposite the temple, is better value. Woolgoolga is also a popular seaside holiday resort, with excellent surfing on the ocean beach, while the calmer waters of **Woolgoolga Lake** to the north offer swimming and boating opportunities. Eight kilometres north of Woolgoolga, **Corindi Beach** is the site of the **Yarrawarra Aboriginal Cultural Centre** (Mon–Fri 7.30am–3.30pm, Sat & Sun 10am–2pm; bookings required for guided walks ☎02/6649 2515), which provides a focus and employment for the **Gumbaingirr** people in the area. There's an arts and crafts shop, bush-tucker café, and a native bush-tucker medicine nursery with plants for sale. Guides can take you on a Bush-tucker Walk or a tour through local sites (both 2hr; $6) or you can opt for a full day including a bush-tucker lunch ($28). After Corindi Beach, the road turns inland towards Grafton (see p.261); for more beaches, take the first turn off the Pacific Highway and follow a short road northeast for 6km to reach the coast again at **Red Rock** and the beginning of the **Yuraygir National Park** (detailed on p.262).

Eating, drinking and nightlife

For **coffee** and gourmet **snacks** and cakes, head to the creek for the *Up the Creek Café*, on the Promenade, or in town at the Mall end, to *Icehouse Café & Ice-creamery* at 181 High St (closed Sun). Coffs Harbour also has its own Internet café, *Happy Planet* (closed Sun), above the unfortunately named Athletes Foot shoe store in the City Centre Mall.

For more extensive **eating** try High Street, particularly at either end – around the City Centre Mall and nearby Grafton Street, and down in the block or so before Coffs Jetty. At the ocean end of High Street, on the corner of Camperdown Street, the *Pier Hotel* has a bistro with good, inexpensive counter meals (daily 7–9am, noon–2pm & 6–9pm); *Fisherman's Katch*, at no. 386, serves excellent seafood. Also in the harbour area of town, *Tahruah Thai Kitchen*, 360 High St (☎02/6651 5992), is recommended for its spicy stir-fries. On this stretch of High Street you'll find a plethora of good restaurants, including *Tandoori Oven*, no. 384, (☎02/6652 2279) with tasteful, marine-inspired decor and a menu to match, along with good value vegetarian thalis. *Tequila* at 24 High St (☎02/6652 1279) serves Mexican food and margaritas while *Maria's*, no. 368, is an Italian BYO with pasta, pizza and seafood chowders. For French-style cuisine, try *Peter's Peppermill* at 372 High St ☎02/6652 5855), with specialities such as barramundi in chardonnay sauce (closed Sun & Mon). Chinese food is available at the *Golden Crown* (☎02/6651 6787) serving a large selection of seafood stir-fries (Tues–Sat eve only). Innovative, international food with a hefty price-tag can be found at *Passionfish Brasserie*, 384 High St (☎02/6652 1423; closed Sun & Mon). Down at the Marina, the *Tide & Pilot Brasserie* (☎02/6651 6888) has expensive seafood specials with waterfront views while the *Iguana Beach Café* at the Yacht Club, at the Marina (☎02/6652 5725) serves up a "taste of the tropics".

Nightlife in Coffs is lively in summer, but very mainstream. There are generally live bands playing cover versions at some venue around town from Wednesday to Sunday, usually with free entry. On Friday and Saturday nights the *RSL Club*, on the corner of Vernon Street and the Pacific Highway, has two bands and a disco, free entry and very cheap drinks until 2am. The *Plantation Hotel*, 88 Grafton St, puts on live bands three nights a week. For a more sedate drink, the *Greenhouse Tavern*, on the corner of Bray Street and the Pacific Highway, lets you sip in a reasonable approximation of tropical rainforest surroundings in its gazebo. There is one dressy nightclub, the lively *Saloon Bar*, on The Mall at no. 76.

Listings

Bike rental Promenade Leisure Hire, Coffs Promenade, Coffs Creek, 321 High St (☎02/6651 1032), charges $8 per hour, $20 half-day, $35 full-day; also canoe rental.

Buses Besides the interstate services, there's Jessups Bus Service (☎02/6653 4551) to Bellingen, Urunga and Nambucca Heads; Watsons City Link (☎02/6654 1063) to Grafton via Red Rock and Woolgoolga (5–8 services Mon–Fri); and Sawtell Coaches (☎02/6653 3344) to Sawtell, 6km south. Coffs Harbour Coaches (☎02/6652 2877) offer air-con tours to Bellingen, Dorrigo and Nambucca Heads.

Canoeing Wild Water Adventures (☎02/6653 4469) organizes full-day canoeing trips on the Bellinger River for $85 including gourmet lunch.

Car rental All-Ways (☎02/6652 1811); Coffs Harbour Rent-a-Car (☎02/6652 5022); Hertz (☎02/6651 1899); Thrifty (☎02/6652 8622); Coffs Harbour Rent-a-Wreck (☎02/6651 7933).

Cinemas Coffs Cinema, Bray St (☎02/6651 6444); Coffs Harbour Cinema Centre, Vernon St (☎02/6652 2233), the latter half-price Monday to Friday before 6pm and all day Tuesday.

Cruises Pacific Explorer (mobile phone ☎018/663 815) runs whale-watching cruises on a sailing vessel June–Nov; regular cruises during summer. *Spirit of Coffs Harbour*, a large catamaran, offers a 3.5hr whale-watching tour for $35.

Diving The Solitary Islands Marine Reserve, five islands and several islets north of Coffs, is the largest marine reserve in NSW; the mingling of tropical and temperate waters means that there's a huge variety of sealife, described in a range of excellent leaflets, available from the visitor information centre or the Fisheries office (☎02/6652 3977). Jetty Dive Centre, 398 High St, at the harbour (☎02/6651 1611), offers dives for beginners and advanced divers at the coral reefs around South Solitary Island, costing from $65 for two dives, as does Divers Depot (☎02/6652 2033) at the Marina and Pacific Blue Dive Centre (☎02/6652 2759) at the Promenade. Both hostels arrange inexpensive snorkelling expeditions and scuba courses.

Horse-riding Valery Trails, 20km southwest of Coffs (☎02/6653 4301): turn off the Pacific Highway at Bonville. Closer to Coffs, Wyndyarra Estate (☎02/6653 8488) offer horse rides for $30 (plus pick-up $5).

Hospital High St, near *Aussitel Backpackers* (☎02/6652 2866).

Laundry Marina Laundrette at the jetty has the best views whilst you wait for your whites. Open daily 8am–8pm.

Markets Sunday-morning markets are held at the Jetty Village Shopping Centre, on Coffs Jetty (8am–2pm), and in the Big W car park, on the corner of Castle and Vernon streets (same hours).

Police ☎02/6652 0299.

Post office In the arcade off the Grafton Street Mall, NSW 2450.

Scenic flights Pacific Eagle Airlines (☎02/6651 2523) charges from $59 per person for a one-hour flight.

Surfing East Coast Surf School, based at Diggers Beach (☎02/6651 5515), is an excellent place to learn to surf in small groups. Introductory 2hr lesson ($22) or three classes ($45); includes surfboard and wetsuit. Write for details of their excellent-value three-day surf camps: PO Box 6336, Coffs Harbour, NSW 2450.

Taxi ☎13 1008.

Tours 4WD Adventure Safaris (☎02/6653 6686) does half- and full-day tours including George's Gold Mine, plus canoeing and horse-riding; Mountain Trails 4WD Tours (☎02/6655 7117) operates recommended half- and full-day 4WD adventures along remote tracks to banana plantations, waterfalls and the rainforest, weekend trips to Dorrigo and mountain country, and wildlife tours at night; Gambaarri Tours (☎02/6655 4195) runs Aboriginal cultural tours with a local guide to Red Rock and the Yarrawarra Cultural Centre, plus other tours from Nambucca Heads and Bellingen (all $45, including bush tucker).

Travel agent Kelly Travel, at the corner of High and Moonee streets (☎02/6651 2747; *kellytravel@key.net.au*) is a discount flight agent for Qantas and STA Travel.

White-water rafting Coffs Harbour is one of the few places on the east coast where you can go rafting, though after a dry winter the rivers can be low. The best outfit is White Water Rafting Professionals (☎02/6651 4066; around $125 per day).

Grafton and around

Between Woolgoolga and Ballina the Pacific Highway runs inland, and the unspoilt coast between the two towns consists of a series of national parks to which access is gained by a few intermittent side roads. **GRAFTON**, an 83-kilometre drive along the Pacific Highway from Coffs Harbour, is a peaceful district capital on a bend of the wide **Clarence River**, which almost encircles the city and occasionally floods it. The "Big River" is the largest river system on the north coast and, with its tributaries, drains a vast area of northern New South Wales. An afternoon sitting on the balcony of the *Crown Hotel*, sipping a beer and watching the majestic river roll by, is truly well spent. Northeast of Grafton, the river widens as it approaches the ocean and branches out into a network of waterways and channels. There are more than a hundred river islands, on many of which sugar cane is grown.

Grafton is proud of its wide, tree-lined streets and has the air of a genteel, old-fashioned town. In spring, when the jacaranda and flame trees are ablaze with purple, mauve and red blossoms, they even have a **Jacaranda Festival** to celebrate them (last week of Oct and first week of Nov). Out of festival time this is a quiet place, where the main attraction is cruising on the river or visiting some of the historic buildings preserved by the National Trust. **Schaeffer House**, 190 Fitzroy St (Tues–Thurs, Sun 1–4pm; $2), has a collection of beautiful china, glassware and period furniture donated to the Trust over the years, while **Grafton Regional Gallery**, 158 Fitzroy St, houses the Regional Art Gallery (Tues–Sun 10am–4pm; donation), and has a pretty garden café.

Practicalities

Call in at the **Clarence River Tourist Association**, on the Pacific Highway at the corner of Spring Street, South Grafton (daily 9am–5pm; ☎02/6642 4677), which can give you information on scenic drives, river cruises, and the national parks that surround Grafton; there's also a centrally located NPWS office at 49 Victoria St (☎02/6642 0613), in the State Office Block. **Long-distance buses** stop near the tourist association, and Harvey World Travel, 54 Prince St (☎02/6640 3910), can provide timetables and make reservations. Watsons City Link (☎02/6654 1063), a **local bus** service, leaves from the city centre in the direction of Coffs Harbour via Red Rock and Woolgoolga (Mon–Fri), and the Grafton–Yamba Bus Service (☎02/6646 2019) runs north to Yamba. There's plenty of **accommodation**: try the *Grafton Hotel*, 97 Fitzroy St (☎02/6642 2000; ③), a good pub offering beds and counter meals; or the *Crown Hotel-Motel*, 1 Prince St (☎02/6642 4000), for hotel rooms with a river view or ground-level motel units (②–④). If you want a swimming pool, spa and all the mod-cons, check out the more expensive *Fitzroy Motel*, 27 Fitzroy St (☎02/6642 4477; ⑤), 500m east of the centre. For **camping**, head for South Grafton to the well-equipped *Glenwood Tourist Park* on Heber Street (☎02/6642 3466; cabins ③–④). A good place to **eat** is *Crabba Jack's Takeaway*, 79 Fitzroy St, for fresh fish and chips and seafood. Across the street at no. 100, *Big River Pizza* (☎02/6643 1555 for deliveries) is also recommended, and it's usually open when most places have closed.

Around Grafton

From Grafton it's 47km **northeast** on the Pacific Highway, paralleling the Clarence River, to **MACLEAN** a small delta town which proclaims its Scottish heritage with street signs in Gaelic. From the Maclean lookout on Wharf Street, 2km from the centre, panoramic views of the coast, bushland, canefields, river islands and the town itself can be enjoyed. A few kilometres further north, you can turn east off the highway in the direction of the twin towns of **YAMBA** and **ILUKA** – increasingly popular holiday spots facing each other across the mouth of the river. Clarence River Ferries shuttles between the two communities (4–5 daily; $3; also cruises to river islands; ☎018/664 555). In Yamba, *Backpackers at the Pacific Hotel*, 1 Pilot St (☎02/6646 2466; ②), is in a great old pub right on the beach, and offers very cheap singles and twins; ask about lifts to Byron Bay. You can get to Yamba on public transport with the Grafton–Yamba Bus Service (at least 3 daily; ☎02/6646 2019).

A few kilometres south of Yamba is **Yuraygir National Park**, with several basic but attractive NPWS campsites ($5 per site, details from Grafton NPWS – see above) surrounded by isolated beaches and placid lake systems. North of Iluka, between the town and Bundjalung National Park, the **Iluka Nature Reserve** contains within it a World Heritage-listed **rainforest remnant**, one of sixteen such areas in northern New South Wales. **Bundjalung National Park** itself has a long coastline on the Coral Sea, as well as the sheltered inland waterways of the Esk River; **camping** is available at Woody Head, a site very popular with anglers (bookings advised; ☎02/6646 6134). Just north of Bundjalung, the town of **EVANS HEAD** has a range of accommodation and shops, plus boat rental outlets. The tropical climate begins to make its presence felt here, with sugar cane growing by the roadside.

West from Grafton, the **Gwydir Highway** takes you to Glen Innes, 160km away on the New England Plateau. En route it passes the rugged and densely forested adjoining **national parks** of Gibraltar Range and Walshpool. **Gibraltar Range** is an elevated plateau 1200m above sea level, scattered with huge granite outcrops and intersected by deep gorges, and is famous for its wild flower displays of Christmas bells and waratahs in late summer. There's a **visitors centre** on the highway at Dandahra Picnic Area and a gravel road leads from here into the park, where you'll find walking tracks, lookout points and waterfalls. **Walshpool National Park** is very remote, a wilderness park on the eastern escarpment of the New England Tableland. Its **rainforest** is worth visiting, and there are picnic facilities, walks and camping at Coombadjha Creek – reached via the Coombadjha Road off the Gwydir Highway, 88km from Grafton.

Ballina

The old port of **BALLINA**, at the mouth of the Richmond River, experienced a short-lived goldrush in the 1880s, but it has few reminders of this era and is now mostly a holiday town, with some pleasant beaches and the opportunity to take river trips to Lismore (see p.273) and other destinations. Neither has it escaped the clutches of the "big things", with the **giant prawn** marking the entrance to town, just off the highway from Grafton. It's a fairly conservative cousin to nearby Byron Bay, although the fact that you're entering New Age territory is obvious by the outskirts of Ballina, where the **Thursday Plantation** (daily 9am–5pm; free; patio café & gift shop), 4km north on Gallans Road, east of the Pacific Highway, was the first commercial **tea tree** plantation, producing the all-healing tea tree oil and its products. One of the highlights of the town is a lively **market,** held on the third Sunday of the month at the town's Fawcett Park.

There's a cycling and walking track (20min walk) from the centre of town along the sea wall to the beach. In Las Balsas Plaza, on River Street, is a small **maritime museum** (daily 9am–4pm; free), whose exhibits include the *Atzlan*, a balsa raft that made it across the Pacific from Ecuador in 1973 as part of the Thor Heyerdahl-inspired Las Balsas expedition. The **tourist information centre** (daily 9am–5pm; ☎02/6686 3484, fax 6686 0136; *balinfo@om.com.au*) is in the same plaza. **Accommodation** includes the *Ballina Travellers Lodge Motel*, 36–38 Tamar St (☎02/6686 6737, fax 6686 6342; rooms ④, dorms ①), with a YHA hostel section; it's modern and family-run, with a swimming pool and free use of bicycles, fishing rods, surf- and boogie-boards. *Ballina Gardens Caravan Park*, 3km north on the Pacific Highway (☎02/6686 2475; cabins ②–③), also has a pool and is one of the better places to **camp**. If you have a car, though, the prime spot to pitch a tent is at *Flat Rock Camping Ground* (☎02/6686 4848), on the Coast Road 5km east of Ballina; right on the beach, this unspoilt site is for tents only and there's no electricity, so it's very peaceful – hot showers supply a touch of comfort.

Ballina has quite a lively summer **nightlife**: the *Henry Rous Tavern*, on River Street, has a popular café and hosts occasional bands, while the *Australian Hotel*, on the corner of Cherry and River streets, is more sedate, with jazz, piano music and a pleasant beer garden. Both pubs have recommended **bistros**, while *Ripples* at the *El Rancho Motor Inn*, on the corner of Fox and Cherry streets (☎02/6686 3333; licensed; closed Sun), serves up seafood, crocodile and other native critters. There's also *Mexican del Rio* at 196 River St (☎02/6686 2775; licensed), and the adjacent *Ping Sun Chinese Restaurant* (☎02/6686 3292). The best place for brunch is *Shellys on the Beach* at Shellys Beach, for great ocean views and healthy, creative cooking; follow the bridge and sea wall 2km out of town.

Ballina is connected by the long-distance Kirklands **bus** (☎02/6622 1499) to Brisbane via Lismore, Lennox Head and Evans Head. **Local** services include Blanch's (☎02/6686 2144) to and from the airport east of town, and to Lennox Head, Byron Bay and Mullumbimby. To get around, you can rent a **bike** from Jack Ransom Cycles, 16 Cherry St (☎02/6686 2180); rental **cars** are available from North Coast Rent-a-Car (☎02/6686 9966).

Lennox Head

The best of the **surf beaches** are those around the small town of **LENNOX HEAD**, 11km north of Ballina, a relaxed resort with a small shopping centre, some good cafés and restaurants and a lively pub. Lennox rates among the top ten surfing spots in the world and professionals congregate here for the big waves in May, June and July. Adding to Lennox Head's appeal is the calm, fresh water of **Lake Ainsworth** close to the beach: stained dark by the tea trees around its banks, it's a popular swimming spot for families seeking refuge from the crashing surf; and the soft, practically medicinal water is wonderful for your skin. Lennox Head Sailing (☎02/6687 6010), on the lake, rents out sailboards and can arrange lessons.

Ideally situated between the lake and the beach, *Lennox Head Backpackers*, 2–3 Ross St (☎02/6687 7636; rooms ③, dorms ①), is a relaxed place where massage and aromatherapy are available in-house; there's free use of boards and fishing gear, as well as bargain rental of windsurfers and catamarans. Also in a prime position is the *Lake Ainsworth Caravan Park* on Pacific Parade (☎02/6687 7249; cabins ③–④). The Mexican **food** at *Pancho Villa*, Ballina Street (☎02/6687 6171; BYO; Mon–Thurs & Sun dinner), is popular with surfies; *Lennox Head Chinese*, 63 Ballina St (BYO; daily from 5pm), is also recommended. The *Lennox Point Hotel* serves great pub food with a Mediterranean slant, and hosts bands on Thursday, Friday and Saturday nights.

Since Lennox Head is off the Pacific Highway, only one Greyhound **bus** a day makes it out here; Kirklands also stops in town daily, and there are local services to and from Byron Bay (see below).

Byron Bay and around

Situated at the end of a long sweeping bay, the township of **BYRON BAY** boasts 30km of almost unbroken sandy beaches. Formerly a working-class coastal town of dilapidated weatherboard cottages, best known for its abattoir, it's now a thriving resort, first discovered by the surfies, then the hippies and more recently by better-heeled travellers. The New Age legacy lives on, and Byron Bay's charms have not gone unnoticed in backpackers' circles either, while in summer it can seem like Sydney-by-the-sea, as half of Paddington and Darlinghurst arrive en masse to escape the city. For the moment, however, it remains a special and enjoyable place – small, picturesque, with an oddball but equable local community and a splendidly scenic setting. The locals, despite being permanently outnumbered, seem far from overwhelmed. One of Byron's charms is its lack of retail chain outlets; instead, small, often alternative, local businesses are the norm.

Arrival and information

If you come by **train**, you'll arrive right in the heart of town on **Jonson Street**, the main thoroughfare. Not all north coast **buses** stop at Byron Bay; however, those that do will also drop you here, or else a little way north near the junction of Jonson and Lawson streets (see "Listings" for details of bus companies and booking agents, on p.271). The closest **airports** are at Ballina, 39km south (from where you can get a bus connection with Kirklands, see p.262), or Coolangatta, 109km north in Queensland; Byron Bay Connection buses link up with both airports (☎02/6685 5980; Ballina from $20, Coolangatta from $50).

Check out the helpful **Byron Bay Tourist Information Centre**, staffed by volunteers at 80 Jonson St, next to the train station (daily 9am–5pm; ☎02/6685 8050). You'll be able to pick up an excellent range of printed information here about accommodation (free booking service), eating, national parks, scenic drives, sights, activities and tours. A *Disabled Access Guide* is also available. An alternative for information is the recently renovated Byron Bus & Backpacker Centre, next to the information centre (daily 7am–midnight; ☎02/6685 5517), which books tours, activities, accommodation, bus tickets, car rental and arranges freight.

Accommodation

There are plenty of places to stay in Byron Bay, but that doesn't mean it's easy to find a bed. During December and January especially, demand for accommodation in all categories far exceeds supply, and it's essential to book well in advance. A1 Accommodation, 69 Jonson St (☎02/6685 7523), will make bookings for all accommodation free of charge. The **hostels** in Byron Bay are among the best in Australia, but prices rise dramatically in summer; if you're part of a group, **holiday apartments** (booked through A1 Accommodation and real estate agents in town) might be a more practical option. If all places in town are full, you may strike it lucky in the surrounding area – either towards **Brunswick Heads**, about 18km further up the coast (see p.268), or in the quiet town of **Mullumbimby**, just inland at the foot of Mount Chincogan on the Brunswick River.

MOTELS, HOTELS, GUESTHOUSES AND APARTMENTS

Beach Hotel, corner of Jonson and Bay streets (☎02/6685 6402, fax 6685 8758). Brand-new luxury waterfront hotel. Spacious, tasteful units with patios or balconies. Outdoor heated pool and spa set among greenery. ⑧.

Brunswick Hotel, Mullumbimby St, Brunswick Heads (☎02/6685 1236). Bargain accommodation in a restored riverfront pub; counter meals and live music. ③.

Byron Bay Beach Club, Bayshore Drive, 3km north (☎02/6685 8000, fax 6685 6916). Lovely complex of serviced wooden chalets with self-contained cooking facilities and TV. The resort-style extras include a pool, bar, restaurant, tennis courts and golf course. ⑥–⑧.

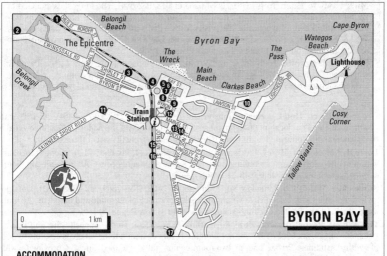

ACCOMMODATION

Aquarius Backpackers Resort	9	Blue Iguana Beachouse	6	First Sun Caravan Park	4
Arts Factory Lodge	11	Byron Bay Bunkhouse	13	Great Northern Hotel	8
Backpackers Holiday Village	15	Cape Byron Lodge	17	J's Bay YHA	14
Backpackers Inn	3	Cape Byron Van Village	2	Lord Byron Resort Motel	16
Beach Hotel	5	Cape Byron YHA	12	Main Beach Backpackers	7
Belongil Beach House	1	Clarkes Beach Caravan Park	10		

TOURS FROM BYRON BAY

There are many tours to the rainforest, waterfalls and national parks in the hinterland around Byron Bay (see "Far North Coast Hinterland", for details of destinations mentioned). All tours and activities can be booked at Byron Bus & Backpacker Centre, next to the tourist office (daily 7am–midnight; ☎02/6685 5517). Below are listed some of the more specialist and unusual tour operators.

Byron Bay Dreamtime Journey (☎02/6680 8505). Aboriginal cultural experience run by local indigenous people. Cave and waterfall tours with bush tucker tastings, $49; didjeridoo-making workshops and lessons from $100.

Byron Bay Motorcycle Tours (☎02/6685 6304). Whizz around the beaches and hinterland on the back of a Harley Davidson (30min for $35, half-day for $155; summer only).

Byron Bay Sea Kayaks (☎02/6685 5830). Dolphin-watching from sea level in 2-person boats ($30 including breakfast or afternoon tea).

Byron Beach Rider (☎02/6684 7499). Horseback jaunts on isolated beaches in the Byron area (daily; 2hr tours from $40).

Excellent Adventures (☎02/6687 1092). One-day canoe safaris on the Brunswick River, from Mullumbimby to Brunswick Heads, with opportunities to see plenty of birdlife ($50, including picnic lunch).

Jim's Alternative Tours (☎02/6685 7720). Tours aimed at presenting a positive, accurate portrayal of the hinterland "back to the land" movement. The "Big Wet" tour visits Nimbin, and Holy Goat Ranch, one of Australia's best examples of permaculture, then takes in Protestors Falls and Minyon Falls, with opportunities for swimming ($30). It can also help transport you to the Sunday markets at The Channon ($10) and Bangalow ($5), with more flexible times than other operators.

Mick's Bay to Bush Tours (☎02/6684 0253 or 018/662 684). The longest-established of Byron Bay's alternative tours, with a bit of a personal touch: the popular Rainbow Trip, taking in Nimbin and Minyon Falls, also visits Mick's dad's house for tea and muffins (Mon, Wed & Fri 9am–6pm; $30). Plus a Nimbin & Bush Day Out (Tues, Thurs & Sat 9am–6pm; $30), commune tour and transport to north coast markets.

Rapid Rafting (☎02/6685 8687) and **Whitewater Rafting** (☎02/6685 4469). Two-day white-water rafting on the Gwydir River (grade 4 & 5) with overnight camping in the hinterland. Departs daily, depending on the weather at 10am, returns 8pm following day ($109).

Great Northern Hotel, corner of Jonson and Byron streets (☎02/6685 6454). No-frills pub rooms in an excellent location on the main street. The noise from the bands playing below make this place one for confirmed night owls. Cheap single rates, particularly off-season. ③.

Lord Byron Resort Motel, 120 Jonson St (☎02/6685 7444, fax 6685 7120). Central location, with amenities including a swimming pool, spa, sauna and tennis court. All units air-con. Some serviced apartments available (with fans only). ⑥–⑧.

Sunseeker Motel, 100 Bangalow Rd, 1.5km south (☎02/6685 7369, fax 6685 5181). Cottage-style motel units with balconies or verandahs. Saltwater pool, playground and barbecue. All units sleep six and have limited cooking facilities. Close to Tallow Beach. ⑥.

The Wheel Resort, Broken Head Rd, Suffolk Park, 3.5km south, opposite the golf course (☎02/6685 6139, fax 6685 8757). A prize-winning resort designed to be totally accessible to people with disabilities. Private one- or two-room cabins, fully equipped (linen is provided), with verandah and TV. There's a swimming pool with ramp. Set in a rainforest with easy access to the beach. Cabins from ⑦, cheaper weekly rates.

HOSTELS

Aquarius Backpackers Resort, 161 Lawson St (☎02/6685 7663, fax 6685 7439; *aquarius@om.com.au*). Newly renovated motel with self-contained units with kitchenettes. Pool,

BBQ area, café, bar, free use of bikes and boogie-boards. Email, Internet and currency exchange facilities are also available. Rooms ③, dorms ①.

Arts Factory Lodge, Skinners Shoot Rd (☎02/6685 7709, fax 6685 8534; *artsfact@om.com.au*). A two-storey, balconied wooden building in a bushland creek setting. Pleasant dorms sleep four or six, and alternative accommodation is in tepees and canvas huts by the creek; there's also a camping area. Pool and free bikes; no children. Lots of New Age music events, plus yoga classes. Advance booking required for pick-ups from train or bus. Huts ③, dorms ①.

Backpackers Holiday Village, 116 Jonson St (☎02/6685 8888, fax 6685 8777). One of the most central and long-established hostels, this place is clean, friendly and well equipped, with a solar-heated swimming pool, spa and barbecues. Free bikes, boards and luggage storage. Rooms ③, dorms ①.

Backpackers Inn, 29 Shirley St (☎02/6685 8231, fax 6685 5708). Arranged around a central courtyard. Facilities include a communal kitchen, swimming pool, barbecue and volleyball court. Free bikes and boards. Rooms ③, dorms ①.

Belongil Beach House, Childe St (☎02/6685 7868, fax 6685 7445). Beautiful complex in the style of a Balinese resort, with spacious, cool, high-ceilinged timber cottages around a land-scaped garden. Out of town, but with a prime beachside location. Parking and free bikes and boards available. Apartments ⑤, rooms ③, dorms ①.

Blue Iguana Beachhouse, 14 Bay St (☎02/6685 5298). In a lovely old bungalow with a veran-dah. It's small enough to feel personal – a place to relax, listen to music and barbecue on the deck among the hibiscus. Double, twin and four-share rooms, all en suite. Rooms ③–④, dorms ①–②.

Byron Bay Bunkhouse, Carlyle St (☎ 02/6685 8311). Large, laid-back hostel with dorms only. There are two storeys with the one below containing the *Spice Café* serving up regular caff food. Dorms ①.

Cape Byron Lodge, 78 Old Bangalow Rd (☎ & fax 02/6685 6445). Has a swimming pool and attractive garden. A 15min walk from town or take the shuttle bus; a 10min walk to Tallow Beach. Rooms ③, dorms ①.

Cape Byron YHA Hostel, corner of Middleton and Byron streets (☎02/6685 8788, fax 6685 8814). Large, central hostel which feels more like a resort hotel. Facilities include a pool; also free bikes and boogie-boards. Rooms ③, en-suite ④, dorms ①.

J's Bay YHA Hostel, 7 Carlyle St (☎02/6685 8853, fax 6685 6766, free call ☎1800/678 195; *jbay@nor.com.au*). Brand-new, airy, resort-style hostel with two central courtyards, one with barbe-cue and outdoor eating area, the other with heated saltwater pool. Extras include free boards and bikes and a TV room with videos. Many rooms are en-suite. Rooms ③, dorms ①.

Main Beach Backpackers, corner of Lawson and Fletcher streets (☎ 02/6685 8695). Old Council chambers converted to a hostel, complete with pool, car-parking, Internet access and secure lockers in every room. In-house psychic does readings on Monday nights. Rooms ③, dorms ①.

CAMPSITES

Cape Byron Van Village, Ewingsdale Rd, 2km northwest (☎02/6685 7378). Pool and tennis court; 10min walk to Belongil Beach. Cabins ④–⑤.

Clarkes Beach Caravan Park, off Lighthouse Rd (☎02/6685 6496). Only 1km west of town, and right on the beach. Cabins ④–⑤.

Ferry Reserve Caravan Park, Pacific Highway, Brunswick Heads (☎02/6685 1872). Pleasant campsite near the river, with a kiosk and barbecue. Cabins ③.

First Sun Caravan Park, Lawson St (☎02/6685 6544). Very central, overlooking Main Beach. Cabins ③–⑤.

Maca's Camping Ground, Main Arm Rd, near Mullumbimby (☎02/6684 5211). Campsite in the bush. Communal kitchen and dining room, plus laundry; tents for rent.

Suffolk Park Caravan Park, Alcorn St, Suffolk Park, 5km south (☎02/6685 3353). Good location in a shady setting on Tallow Beach. Cabins ②–④.

Terrace Caravan Park, The Terrace, Brunswick Heads (☎02/6685 1233). Shady spot by the river, near the beach. Cabins ③–⑤.

The Town and around

There's plenty of opportunity to soak up local atmosphere – and the often bizarre mix of countercultures as surfie meets soap starlet meets hippie – simply by wandering the streets. Probably the best place to take it all in is on the first Sunday of each month at the **market**, on Butler Street behind the train station, a huge affair containing everything from leather handbags to organic veggies. If you want to explore, one of the first places to visit is the **lighthouse** on the rocky promontory of **Cape Byron**, where there's a small nature reserve (8am–5.30pm). The cape includes the easternmost point of the Australian mainland and is a popular spot to greet the dawn, but don't worry if you're not an early riser – the views from the cape and the lighthouse reserve are fabulous anytime, and there's an excellent circular **walking track** from the lighthouse. With a bit of luck you'll see **dolphins**, who like to sport in the surf off the headland, **humpback whales**, which pass this way heading north to warmer waters in June or July and again on their return south in September or October, and maybe some **sharks**.

Main Beach in town is as good as any to swim from, and usually has relatively gentle surf. One reason why Byron Bay is so popular with surf freaks is because its beaches face in all directions, so there's almost always one with a good swell; however, you can usually find somewhere for a calmer swim.

East of Main Beach, you can always find a spot to yourself on the less sheltered stretch of **Belongil Beach**, from where there's sand virtually all the way to **BRUNSWICK HEADS**, a quieter, more family-oriented resort located between the mouth of the Brunswick River and Simpson's Creek, with a long crescent of beach on the ocean side. The grassy riverfront area is a good spot for children, with several playgrounds and picnic areas. The attractive 1930s-style *Brunswick Hotel* has a popular beer garden facing the river, packed on Sunday afternoon when there's free live music outdoors.

Back in the other direction, Main Beach curves round towards Cape Byron to become **Clarkes Beach**. This and neighbouring **Wategos Beach** – beautifully framed between two rocky spurs – face north, and they usually have the best surfing. On the far side of the cape, **Tallow Beach** extends towards the **Broken Head Nature Reserve**, 6km south of the town centre at Suffolk Park; there's good surf at Tallow just around the cape at Cosy Corner, and also at Broken Head. From the car park here, a short stroll through rainforest leads to the secluded, nudist **Kings Beach**, one of several isolated stretches of sand out this way.

When you tire of lazing on the beach and admiring the sea from above, you can take your explorations one step further and head underwater. The diversity of marine life in the waters of Byron Bay make it second only to the Great Barrier Reef as a place to **dive** on the east coast. Tropical marine life and creatures from warm temperate seas mingle at the granite outcrop of **Julian Rocks Aquatic Reserve**, 3km offshore; by far the most popular spot here is the **Cod Hole**, an extensive underwater cave inhabited by large moray eels and other fish. Between April and June is the best time to dive, before the plankton bloom (see "Listings" on p.271 for information on dive schools).

Eating

There's a multitude of places selling food in Byron Bay, and the standard is generally pretty high. A café society exists, although cafés don't usually stay open late – even in summer. Lots of alternative cafés offer delicious health foods and vegetarian dishes, and there are plenty of takeaways and fish-and-chip shops, as well as restaurants that serve everything from Japanese to Indian. All have extended opening hours in the peak summer period.

Athena Taverna, Lawson St (☎02/6685 6810). A very popular Greek restaurant, with casual atmosphere and tables outside. Moderate prices. BYO. Tues–Sat 6.30–10pm.

Bay Kebabs, corner of Jonson and Lawson streets. Generous falafel rolls and gourmet kebabs are the thing to have here. Eat sitting on the stools inside, or take away. Daily 10am until late.

ALTERNATIVE AND ARTISTIC BYRON BAY

Byron Bay offers a truly wide variety of alternative therapies, extensive browsing in New Age bookshops, a wealth of crystals, and a future foretold through palmistry and tarot readings – all underlaid with a good dose of capitalism as prices for massages and tarot readings are hiked up during the lucrative summer months. The alternative culture attracts artists and artisans in droves, and galleries and artists' studios abound.

The **Community Centre**, at 69 Jonson St (☎02/6685 6807; *bbcc@mullum.com.au*), opposite the train station, is hard to miss with its bright figurative mural, and has great notice boards packed with information on everything from Celtic Shamanism to Tibetan healing workshops. One of the best New Age emporiums is the **Crystal Temple** at 87 Jonson St, flogging crystals, books, tapes and jewellery. They also have a wide range of alternative therapies on offer. At the rear of the *Belongil Beach House* on Childe Street, the Relax Haven (☎02/6685 8304) has a float tank (1hr float, $25) and massage available ($40 per hour); or the more central Samadhi Flotation Centre, 107 Jonson St (☎02/6685 6905), offers the same, plus classes, workshops and a resident naturopath and homeopath. Quintessence, Shop 8, 11 Fletcher St (☎02/6685 5533), offers aromatherapy massage and reflexology.

The **Byron Bay market**, held on the first Sunday of each month on Butler Street, behind the train station, is the best way to become acquainted with the arts and crafts of the area (if you miss it, there's others at The Channon on the second Sunday, Mullumbimby on the third Saturday, Uki on the third Sunday and one at the showground at Bangalow, 13km southwest, on the fourth Sunday of each month). The **Arts Factory**, on Skinners Shoot Road, has several artists' workshops which you can visit (Tues–Sun 10am–3pm), and the **Byron Craft Market** is held here every Saturday (8.30am–3pm) with a courtesy bus (9.30am–3.30pm) from the community centre on Jonson Street. **The Epicentre**, on Border Street, near Belongil Beach, has several outlets and resident artists and craftspeople, plus a large art gallery showing the work of local artists ($1 donation). Beyond here, northwest of town along Ewingsdale Road, **Byron Bay Industrial Estate**, between Banksia Drive and Acacia Street, has a host of artisans producing everything from leathergoods to hats; the most highly regarded creative talents here are the glassblowers at **Colin Heaney's Hot Glass Studio** (gallery daily 10am–4pm, demonstrations Mon–Fri 9am–3pm). Back in town, one of the best alternative shops is Cat's Recycled Emporium, Shop 1/3, Lawson St, which sells a mixture of clothes and art, most made locally – everything from groovy beach dresses to mobiles made of cutlery. Also check out Love Hemp, Shop 2, Byron Street, devoted entirely to hemp clothing.

Byron Bay is host to an Australian **Writers' Festival** featuring established and budding writers, readings and signings during the last week of July; contact the Northern Rivers Writers' Centre, PO Box II41, Lismore, NSW 2480 (☎02/6622 3599, fax 6622 7035).

The Beach Café, Clarkes Beach (dinner reservations ☎02/6685 7598). The best place for breakfast, from 7.30am. Serves dinner in the summer.

Belongil Beach Café, Childe St, next to *Belongil Beach House*. Another great oceanfront place for breakfast, lunch and dinner, though the sea view is behind beachfront bush. There are outside tables, where customers are sometimes serenaded by free music. BYO. Daily 8am–9pm.

Byron Thai, 32 Lawson St (☎02/6685 8453). Excellent Thai restaurant with a palm-garden dining area. Loads of choice for vegetarians. Moderate prices. Licensed. Dinner daily from 5.30pm.

The Byronian, 58 Jonson St. This café, frequented by locals, has a lively atmosphere with lots of chat over good coffee. An attractive front courtyard next to a green park. Early, good-value breakfasts. BYO. Daily 7.30am–5.30pm.

Cocomangas, 32 Jonson St (☎02/6685 8493). Philippines-inspired restaurant which turns into a dance spot with theme nights after dark (Mon is 70s night). Mon–Sat 6pm–3am.

Earth 'n' Sea Pizzas, corner of Lawson and Jonson streets. A favourite place to eat in Byron. Toppings are unusual and imaginative: try "Mullumbimby Madness", with mushrooms, of course. Generous and affordable pasta. BYO and licensed. Daily from 5.30pm; $10 all-you-can-eat special on Wednesday nights.

Ginelli Ristorante Italiano, 36 Jonson St (☎02/6684 7179). Pricey pasta and à la carte; good for a splurge. Thurs–Sun 6–10pm.

Koo Café, Marvell St (☎02/6685 5711; *koocafé@om.com.au*). This relaxed little place is one of the best cafés in the centre, and probably the cheapest, with a terminal to surf the Internet and outside tables where you can enjoy your food. The menu includes Italian sandwiches and lasagne, and the coffee is good. Mon–Fri 8am–5pm, Sat 8am–3pm.

Lightwork Café, 50 Jonson St. Café catering for locals with hearty breakfasts as well as snacks and cakes at outdoor courtyard tables. Licensed. Mon–Sat 8.30am–5pm, Sun (market day) 9am–5pm.

Misaki Byron, 11 Fletcher St (☎02/6685 7966). An excellent Japanese restaurant, in a pleasant brick courtyard, serving everything from sushi to noodles. Expensive, but BYO; bookings required. Tues–Sat 6–10pm, daily during school holidays.

Oh! Delhi, Bay Centre Arcade, upstairs, 6 Lawson St (☎02/6685 6251). Byron's best curry house and takeaway. BYO and licensed. Nightly dinner, with live Indian music and belly-dancing Thurs, Fri & Sat.

The Piggery Supernatural Food, Arts Factory, Skinners Shoot Rd. Don't be fooled by the name – this is a popular vegetarian place in a spacious setting, retaining the open rafters of the building's early days as – ironically – a meatworks. BYO. Nightly dinner.

Ringo's, 29 Jonson St. One of Byron's most popular cafés, with probably the cheapest food in town. Serves everything from simple salad sandwiches to lasagne or curry, with lots of vegetarian options. There's a notice board advertising events around town, and a secondhand bookshop out back. BYO. Daily 8.30am–9pm.

Strictly Vego, The Plaza, Jonson St. Attached to *The Car Park* nightclub, but with its own separate identity. Has a delectable smorgasbord of fresh, meatless cuisine – fill your own plate for around $7, or fill your face for a tenner. Leafy courtyard too. Daily noon–9pm.

Thai Noodle Bar, 24 Jonson St. Moderately-priced fresh noodles wok-fried; you select the fresh ingredients. Also Malaysian-style laksa (noodle soup). Good selection of vegetarian dishes. Small bar-style eating area, but primarily a takeaway place. Mon–Sat 10am–6pm.

Toscani's Ristorante, corner of Jonson and Marvell streets (☎02/6685 7320). A sophisticated Italian restaurant in an architecturally innovative building. Doubles as a café, with every imaginable kind of Italian coffee. Expensive, though there are coffee and cake specials. Licensed; noon–midnight. Live music on Wed; closed Sun.

Entertainment and nightlife

The weekly free community newspaper, *The Byron Shire Echo*, has a comprehensive gig guide. There's plenty of activity in summer: **New Year's Eve** is such a big event that the council has taken to closing the town off – so come early. The huge outdoor **Annual Byron Bay Arts and Music Festival** is normally held for three days in early January but may be moving to February; it takes over Belongil Fields with several stages, a rave field, an all-night cinema, a food fair, market stalls and workshops; to find out exact dates, call the tourist information centre (☎02/6685 5980). Tickets can be bought in advance from independent record outlets around Australia.

Beach Hotel, corner of Jonson and Bay streets (☎02/6685 6402). Owned by John Cornell, who played Paul Hogan's sidekick in a 1970s Australian comedy series, this big and smart pub is superbly sited right opposite Main Beach with a huge terrace beer garden, bistro and restaurant, and attracts a cross-section of locals. Live music (often free), including jazz sessions on Sunday afternoon.

The Car Park, The Plaza, Jonson St (☎02/6685 6170). Late-night techno dance club – Byron's best.

Chincogan Tavern, Burringbar St, Mullumbimby (☎02/6684 1550). Bands on Friday night.

The Epicentre, Border St, Belongil Beach (☎02/6685 6789). A multipurpose performance space hosting everything from dance parties, comedy festivals and Aboriginal dance troupes to international and Australian musicians and singers, plus visiting gurus. This is a non-smoking venue and many, though not all, of the gigs are alcohol-free.

Great Northern Hotel, Jonson St (☎02/6685 6454). Something for everyone: a front room with pool tables, a typically blokish public bar and *The Backroom*, a large stylish space that doubles as an Italian restaurant and a music venue with big-name Australian bands playing three or four times a week. Open till 1am nightly.

Pighouse Flicks, Old Piggery, Skinners Shoot Rd (☎02/6685 5828). "The Byron Cinema Experience" shows a hand-picked bill of latest-release films with the emphasis on the quirky and the first-rate, with two to three films nightly and deck chairs or sofas for seating. The price is $7.50 per film with a discount if you eat first at their great vegetarian restaurant.

Railway Friendly Bar, next to the train station, Jonson St (☎02/6685 7662). A small pub that's a popular and noisy haunt of locals and travellers alike. It has quaint train-carriage decor, great counter meals, a beer garden, and free live music nightly 6.30–9.30pm.

Listings

Bike rental Many hostels have either free or rentable bikes for guests; otherwise try Byron Bay Bicycles, Shop 5, The Plaza, Jonson St (☎02/6685 6315), or Let's Go Bikes, 93 Jonson St, opposite Woolworths (☎02/6685 6067; also rollerblades) – both charge around $12 per day for a basic bike and up to $18 for a mountain bike. A cycling track runs from Byron to Suffolk Park via Broken Head nature reserve (8km one-way). Hinterland tours with Backcountry Cycling (see box on p.266).

Buses Booking for McCafferty's, Greyhound Pioneer and Premier, through Byron Bus & Backpacker Centre, 52 Jonson St (☎02/6685 5517). Kirklands goes daily to Brisbane, and to Ballina (with stops at Murwillumbah and Tweed Heads), also daily to Lismore and Casino; bookings through Cape Byron Travel, 6 Lawson St (☎02/6685 6262). Blanch's Coaches (☎02/6686 2144) runs south to Ballina via Suffolk Park, Bangalow and Lennox Head, and north to Mullimbimby. Brunswick Valley Coaches (☎02/6685 1385) goes north to Brunswick Heads and Mullimbimby.

Car rental Hertz (☎02/6685 6522); Byron Car Rentals (☎02/6685 6345) Earth Car Rental (☎02/6685 7472) charges from $35 per day.

Diving Most dive schools offer complete scuba-diving courses, together with more affordable one-day courses and daily snorkelling trips (around $30). Byron Bay Dive Centre & Bayside Scuba, corner of Lawson and Fletcher streets (☎02/6685 7149 or free call 1800/243 483), also does a good-value, one-day course for $95 including all equipment; Sundive, Middleton St (☎02/6685 7755), is a small, friendly outfit. If you're already trained, one dive at Julian Rocks, with gear, costs from $65, two dives $105, night dives $45.

Environment Byron Bay Environment Centre, Shop 10, The Plaza (☎02/6685 7066).

Gay and lesbian information Tropical Fruits is a social group for gays and lesbians, holding dance parties every few weeks in halls around the area; the Fruitline (☎02/6622 4353) gives recorded information on upcoming events.

Hang-gliding Tandem take-offs from Byron's lighthouse point. Call Skylimit Sports Aviation (☎02/6684 3711) for aeronautical info.

Horse-riding Barongarook, Upper Wilsons Creek (☎02/6684 0237), has rides through rainforest, suitable for beginners and experienced riders ($45 half day, $85 full day, pick-up from Byron $5); Seahorses Riding Centre, 9 Boarder St (☎02/6680 8155), offers lessons ($60 per half day). Rides include beach, rainforest, sunrise and sunset tours ($45); Tiny's Tours (☎014/814 464) organizes rides along 9km of Tallow Beach ($30 half day).

Hospital ☎02/6685 6878.

Laundries You can use the laundry at most accommodation; otherwise try Byron Dry Cleaners and Laundrette, 42 Jonson St (daily 7am–7pm) with service washes available, or the unattended self-service laundry on Marvell St (Mon–Fri 6am–7pm, Sat & Sun 6am–6pm).

Left luggage Byron Bus & Backpacker Centre, next to the tourist information centre, will mind bags for 24 hours for $3 (daily 7am–6.30pm).

Post office Next door to the Community Centre on Jonson St (postcode NSW 2481).

Surfing Many hostels provide free boards. For surf lessons the best outfits are the highly profes-sional East Coast Surf School (☎02/6685 5989, ☎015/257 243; $20 for 2hr, pick-up from accom-modation; $68 for a three-day course; $110 for a weekend surf camp), with safety-conscious sports science graduates teaching not just technique but how to read the surf; Byron Surf School, corner of Lawson and Fletcher streets (☎02/6685 7536 or free call ☎1800/707 274), rents out surf gear and also offers 3hr lessons from $25 with free pick-ups daily for classes at 9am, 11am and 2pm.

Taxi Byron Taxi (☎02/6685 5008). There's a taxi rank on Jonson St, opposite the *Great Northern Hotel*.

Travel agent Byron Bay Travel Centre, Shop 4, 52 Jonson St (☎02/6685 6733), is a general travel agent and STA agent which deals with bus bookings and passes; also sells YHA and VIP membership. Jetset, corner of Jonson and Marvell streets (☎02/6685 6554) can revalidate tickets and book international and domestic flights.

Tweed Heads

From Brunswick Heads, the Pacific Highway heads around 30km inland to Murwillumbah (see p.276) and then a further 30km to the coast at **TWEED HEADS**. Although officially still part of New South Wales, Tweed Heads – the twin city of Coolangatta in Queensland (see p.373) – is for all practical purposes part of the **Gold Coast**. It certainly looks the part: high-rise buildings, concrete apartment blocks and shopping centres vie for space with grandiose club buildings and a roadscape of advertising billboards in gaudy colours. From the shore the jagged skyline of Surfers Paradise can be seen in the distance.

In its favour, it does have lots of places to stay (motels are cheaper here than further north), and even more opportunities to eat and drink – not to mention the opportunity to **gamble**, an activity that was once banned in Queensland. **Clubs** and casinos opened up just across the border to cash in: one of the biggest, brightest and longest-established of these is the *Twin Towns RSL Club* (☎07/5536 2277) on Wharf Street, whose special offers on cheap food and drink can be a good deal, so long as you don't lose too much in the machines along the way.

One of the few other attractions is the **Minjungbal Aboriginal Cultural Museum**, on Kirkwood Road in South Tweed Heads (daily 10am–4pm; $6), where detailed exhibits and videos illustrate how Aboriginal people lived on this stretch of the coast; near the museum, a signposted boardwalk leads past an old bora ring – a sacred site used in initiation ceremonies. Ironically, the **Captain Cook Memorial Lighthouse** on **Point Danger** celebrates the very event that signalled the demise of Aboriginal culture in these parts: right at the state border, it was erected for the Cook bicentenary celebrations in 1970. Cook gave Point Danger its name after nearly running aground on it, and **Mount Warning** (see p.273) got its name at the same time – as a landmark to help sailors navigate around the point.

Practicalities

The **Tweed Tourist Information Centre** is at 4 Wharf St (Mon–Fri 9am–5pm, Sat 9am–3.30pm; ☎07/5536 4244); they also have information on the rest of the Gold Coast. The **transport** situation merely serves to emphasize Tweed Heads' functional integration into the Gold Coast: arriving at Coolangatta airport, buses generally make a beeline for the resort strip in Queensland; Kirklands stops at Coolangatta Transit Centre en route between Lismore and Brisbane; Surfside Buslines (☎07/5536 7666) runs local services up and down the Gold Coast, and to Murwillumbah. Should you want to **stay**, there are dozens of motels, caravan parks and holiday apartments strung out along the highway, though there's even more choice over the border and you're probably better off continuing on to Surfers Paradise (see p.366) for the full Gold Coast experience – if that's what you're after. For something less crass, head 20km south down the Coast Road to **Cabarita Beach** near Bogangar where you'll find *Emu Park Backpackers Resort* (☎02/6676 1190; rooms ③–④, dorms ①), a good **hostel** which has free use of bikes and boards, surfing lessons and trips to Mount Warning; the village has a pub and several eating places. Back in Tweed Heads itself, it's not hard to find something to **eat**: if the clubs don't appeal, head for oceanfront Marine Parade, where there's everything from takeaway pizza to *Reggae's* (☎07/5599 0000) in the new *Calypso Plaza Resort*.

Far North Coast Hinterland

The beautiful area inland from the far north coast, between artist-filled **Lismore** in the fertile Richmond River valley to the south, and staid **Murwillumbah** in the even lusher valley of the Tweed River near the Queensland border, is known as the **Far North Coast Hinterland**. But pioneers dubbed this region – once covered in **rainforest** that included species of flora extant from the era of the ancient supercontinent of **Gondwanaland** – the Big Scrub. The hinterland's three national parks, plus several reserves, are **World Heritage-listed**, protecting pockets of rainforest which the settlers never managed to log, and which protesters helped to save in the first successful anti-logging demonstration in Australia, in 1979.

Mount Warning – Wollumbin or "cloud catcher" to the Bandjalung Aborigines – is what remains of the central magma chamber of a four-thousand-square-kilometre, shield-shaped volcano; from this 1157-metre peak, where the sun's rays first strike Australia, dazzling views reveal the area's geographic features. **Mount Warning National Park** rises in the middle of a massive **caldera** eroded on the eastern side into a huge bowl, where the Tweed River flows to the sea through the mostly agricultural patchwork of the valley floor. The northwest rim section consists of the McPherson and Tweed ranges, in the **Border Ranges National Park**; the southern section is within the **Nightcap National Park**, near countercultural **Nimbin**, and **The Channon** – one of many villages in "the hills" and famous for hosting the largest, most colourful **market** in the area.

Justice Bus Service (☎02/6621 2307) runs daily between Lismore and Murwillumbah via Nimbin. From Byron Bay, there are several tours of the hinterland, and those that stop at Nimbin can be a convenient way to get there (see p.275).

Lismore and around

On the Bruxner Highway 65km inland from Ballina, **LISMORE** is the principal town of northeast New South Wales and the commercial focus of the fertile Richmond River valley, surrounded by prosperous dairy and farming country. This is one of the most densely populated rural areas in Australia, and has been since the early days of the colony. In the nineteenth century Lismore was an important river port for the **timber** trade, as lumberjacks cut their way through the dense forest of the valley – the so-called Big Scrub – before moving up to the steep slopes of the McPherson Ranges near the Queensland border. Local red cedar, especially, was much sought after. There's still a fair amount of forestry in the region, but these days the economic mainstay is dairy farming and cattle breeding, along with a rapidly growing tropical agriculture sector: bananas, sugar cane, avocados, tropical fruit and macadamia nuts.

For all the intense agriculture, however, this is not your typical Ocker backwater; the city of 46,000 even has its own **Southern Cross University**, which includes a Koala Hospital on its grounds. Since the alternative-lifestyle seekers discovered the northeast in the 1970s, **cultural life** has flourished and jewellers, potters, painters, graphic artists, sculptors and other arts-and-crafts people who have settled here have established a whole network of shops and galleries where they can sell their work. Every weekend they all come together for Lismore's **Art and Craft Expo**; at other times the **Regional Art Gallery**, 131 Molesworth St (Tues–Sat 10am–5pm; free), is the best place to get an overview, displaying a mixture of travelling exhibitions on the downstairs level with a selection of local works of art for sale upstairs. Though recent works are normally on show, from time to time the gallery displays its permanent collection of Australian art from the 1950s and 1960s. The **Historical Museum**, on the same street (Mon–Fri 10am–4pm), houses an interesting, if somewhat motley, collection of pioneer relics and photographic records of the region's history. An annual **Folk**

Festival with the best of the local and national bands takes place over the October long weekend.

Practicalities

Lismore is the home base of Kirklands **buses**, whose service is the only one to stop here on the Sydney–Brisbane route; their terminal is on Molesworth Street (☎02/6621 9299). Lismore is also on a branch line of the Sydney–Murwillumbah **train** route; trains from Brisbane call in at Casino, 31km southwest (see p.275), from where there's a connecting bus. You can **fly** from Sydney with Hazelton (☎02/6622 3113); if you've booked accommodation, you'll normally be picked up from the airport; there are **car rental** desks here, as well as several agencies on Dawson Street, including Lismore Rent-a-Car at no. 100 (☎02/6621 4118). For details of what's going on locally, head for the Lismore **Visitor and Heritage Centre**, at the corner of Molesworth and Ballina streets (daily 9am–4.30pm; ☎02/6622 0122), where there's also an indoor rainforest display, a cultural gallery with the works of 100 artists and craftspersons and a history exhibit; ask here about **river cruises** to Ballina (or see p.263).

There's a wide range of **accommodation** choices in the Lismore region, including hostels, hotels, motels, B&Bs and caravan parks most of which can be booked through the Visitor and Heritage Centre. The friendliest place to stay is the *Currendina Travellers Lodge*, 14 Ewing St (☎02/6621 6118, fax 6622 8090; rooms ③, dorms ①), a pleasant **hostel** which will pick you up from the bus, train station or airport, or from Byron Bay by arrangement – they also organize tours to the surrounding national parks. The *Metropole Hotel*, 98 Keen St (☎02/6621 4910; ②), has simple pub accommodation and serves bistro and counter meals. A couple of kilometres south of town, the *Lismore Lake Caravan Park*, Bruxner Highway (☎02/6621 2585; cabins ③), has inexpensive campsites, a pool, barbecue, children's playground and small shop.

Lismore isn't a bad place to **eat**, and has a couple of excellent cafés and cosmopolitan restaurants. The favoured haunt of artists is *Caddies Coffee Company*, at 20–24 Carrington St, which has excellent bagels, *panini*, salads and coffee. The *Fundamental Food Bar* nearby focuses on healthy organic fodder. If pasta's more tempting, there are a number of fine Italian establishments, including *Pauplettes* on Ballina Street (☎02/6621 6135) for à la carte dining, *Café Giardino* on Keen St (☎02/6622 4664) or *Giovanni's* on Molesworth Street (☎02/6621 6566) overlooking the Wilson's River.

The presence of students means there's some **nightlife** in Lismore. *Maggie Moore's*, 29 Molesworth St, is a pub that hosts bands Thursday, Friday and Saturday. Most of the pubs feature live bands throughout the week, and the area is developing a bit of a reputation for its local musical talent. There are also a couple of nightclubs: the best music is played at the *Powerhouse* on Molesworth Street, and there's the more mainstream but very popular *Legends* at the *Oakes Hotel*, 55 Keen St. For other diversions, there's a four-screen **cinema** in town, on the corner of Keen and Zadoc streets (☎02/6622 4350).

Around Lismore

To explore the country **around Lismore** you really need your own vehicle, though tours do depart from Byron Bay (see p.266). Most Sundays there's a **market** in at least one of the villages, providing a taste of the area's colourful alternative lifestyle – the big ones are in the hilltop village of The Channon on the second Sunday of the month, and in Nimbin on the last (see below). The halls in the various towns have dances and live music, and you may be lucky enough to be invited to a legendary hill party involving live bands, fire-eaters and drumming and dancing till dawn – there's usually one happening somewhere every weekend.

CASINO, around 30km southwest of Lismore, is a small country town on the Richmond River from where route 91 follows the rail lines south towards Grafton, or north through **KYOGLE**, with its Buddhist temple and retreat, into Queensland. One of the most scenic drives in New South Wales is the short round-trip over the mountainous, winding country roads north and northeast of Lismore to Nimbin (see below), The Channon (see below), and Clunes, and then via Eltham and Bexhill, with superb views from the ridges and hilltops. Accessible via Nimbin, with the peak of Mount Nardi (800m) visible 12km beyond the town, is **Nightcap Range National Park**, a World Heritage-listed park with several walking trails from the summit.

Nimbin and around

NIMBIN, site of the famed Aquarius Festival which launched Australian hippie culture in 1973, is understandably more reluctant than most towns to move out of its 1970s time warp; its house facades and shopfronts are painted in lurid, psychedelic designs, its small stores sell health food, incense sticks and patchouli oil, and many of the locals have stuck to their 1970s dress code too. Yet the range of Nimbin's cafés and restaurants certainly marks it as a place of the 1990s. Most visitors may want to get out of town as quickly as possible, for you'll invariably be hit up for a dope deal or something stronger once you set foot on the street; some find this threatening (although a simple "no thanks" is enough to deter them), while for others it's the ulterior motive for coming here.

Something akin to a "hippie hall of fame", the **Nimbin Museum** at 62 Cullen St (hours as they please but usually daily; ☎02/6689 1123; $2 donation) is certainly worth a visit. It's a weird and wonderful living museum run by hippies, with plenty of local history relating to the Aquarius Festival, Bundjalung Aboriginal culture, and a huge stone phallus in the centre of one room. Ask here about the **Annual Hemp Mardi Gras and Drug Law Reform Festival**, held around May 1; the place is booked up well in advance so be prepared to camp. If you have affinities with the Green movement, the **Nimbin Environmental Centre**, also on Cullen Street, might interest you: they publicize and campaign on environmental issues, and can also arrange visits to the **Permaculture Centre**, a showcase for a system of sustainable agriculture that is gaining ground worldwide but especially in developing countries. The **Hemp Embassy** down the lane next to the pub is worth a visit too for it's display on the uses of hemp.

THE CHANNON, a 26-kilometre drive southwest of Nimbin, is a pretty village on the banks of **Terania Creek** with a well-known monthly market, and a tavern, teahouse, craft shop and art gallery in an old butter factory. A fourteen-kilometre drive along the unsealed Terania Creek Road brings you to **Protestors Falls**, perhaps the Nimbin area's most famous environmental attraction, saved by a 1979 protest that was dubbed a "hippie guerrilla struggle" by a *Rolling Stone* article of the period. The first successful anti-logging campaign in Australia saved this rainforest valley filled with ancient brush box trees. The falls, named after the dispute, are a seven-hundred-metre walk from the picnic area, and the waterhole underneath is perfect for swimming. You are permitted to **camp** for one night only at Terania Creek – but no open fires are allowed; otherwise you can head back to The Channon, where you can stay at the village campsite on the banks of the creek (☎02/6689 6321) or at *Terania Park* (☎02/6688 6121), a scenic caravan park with cabins and campsites. Terania Creek is near the western edge of **Whian Whian State Forest**; on the forest's southeastern edge (reached via Mullumbimby or Dunoon), further watery delights are provided by the one-hundred-metre cascade of **Minyon Falls**.

Practicalities

There are a number of **places to stay** in and near Nimbin. *Nimbin Backpackers Granny's Farm* YHA hostel (☎02/6689 1333; rooms ②, dorms ①), very close to town but in a peaceful farm setting, is an easy-going place with log fires in winter and a swimming pool in summer; you can choose to camp or stay in the farm's own tepee. The other hostel option is the equally good *Rainbow Retreat* (☎02/6689 1262; ①), in a bush setting by Goolmanger Creek with a swimming hole nearby; it's more intimate and you end up feeling like a personal guest of the friendly owner. The very comfortable, nicely decorated *Grey Gum Lodge*, 2 High St (☎ & fax 02/6689 1713; ④), is a guesthouse right in town, with its own excellent restaurant and a saltwater swimming pool. The *Nimbin Motel*, 413 Croften Rd (☎02/6689 1420; ③), 4km north of town near Nightcap National Park, has a small pool. At *Haven Earth* (☎02/6689 7297), 12km north of town on Lillian Rock Road in Lillian Rock, you can stay in wooden chalets (④), and watch the wild lorikeets that come to feed here.

Nimbin's main strip, Cullen Street, is full of good **places to eat**. The once-legendary *Rainbow Café* began operating in 1973 but closed down for a while in the mid-1990s; it's now reopened, but locals prefer to hang out at *Ricks Café*. *Nimbin Pizza and Trattoria* serves up generous servings of pizza, pasta and salad nightly from 5pm.

In terms of **nightlife and entertainment**, Nimbin's only drinking hole is the *Freemason's Hotel* on Cullen Street, which sees plenty of action (the bistro also serves good counter meals). The cultural heart of town is the small Bush Theatre (☎02/6689 1111), over the bridge opposite *Granny's Farm* hostel. Movies are shown here at weekends: call or check town notice boards for details. During intermission everyone heads next door to the *Mulgum Café* to sit on the grass and eat fruit salad and ice cream from china bowls.

Murwillumbah and around

The next major stop on the Pacific Highway is **MURWILLUMBAH**, a quiet, inland town on a bend of the Tweed River, a little over 30km north of Byron Bay, which makes a good base for exploring some of the beautiful Tweed Valley and the mountains that extend to the Queensland border.

Murwillumbah is the terminus of the coastal branch **rail** line from Sydney (one train daily in each direction), and almost all buses on the north coast route stop here. The **tourist information** office on Alma Street (Mon–Fri 9am–5pm, Sat 9am–4pm, Sun 10am–3.30pm; ☎02/6672 1340) has information about the immediate area, and about several other magnificent national parks and state forests in the vicinity. It's worth dropping by the **Tweed River Regional Art Gallery** on Tumbulgum Road, by Nicholls Park on the river (Wed–Sun 10am–5pm; free). It displays the winners of the Doug Moran National Portrait Prize, which originated here, as well as the work of local artists and travelling exhibitions.

The Tweed Valley and the surrounding area close to the Queensland border are among the most beautiful in New South Wales, ringed by mountain ranges that are actually the remains of an extinct volcano. Some twenty million years ago a huge shield **volcano** (a flat, shield-shaped landform rather than a cone-shaped peak) spewed lava through a central vent onto the surrounding plain. Erosion carved out an enormous bowl around the centre of the resultant mass of lava, while the more resistant rocks around the edges stood firm – these are now the **Nightcap**, **Border** and **McPherson ranges**, the outer rim of a vast bowl. Right at its heart is **Mount Warning** (1150m), the original vent of the volcano, whose unmistakeable, twisted profile rises like a sentinel from the Tweed Valley. A well-marked **bushwalking track** leads to the top from a car park just off the national park access road, itself a turn-off from the road to Uki, southwest of town. The path is extremely steep in its final stages (allow at least 4hr there and back) but you're rewarded by a sweeping view over the ranges of the volcanic rim and across the Tweed Valley to the Pacific.

There's a less strenuous, signposted 64-kilometre scenic drive through the **Tweed Valley**, which takes in some of its best features. A patchwork of sugar-cane fields and tropical fruit plantations is testimony to the fertility of the volcanic soil; there's even a tea plantation. Between the villages of Tumbulgum and Duranbah, the **Big Avocado** lures the wild-at-heart towards Avocado Adventureland on Duranbah Road (daily 10am–5pm; free admission, train and bus rides extra), a plantation that grows avocados, macadamia nuts and many kinds of tropical fruit, and has been turned into a miniature theme park where you can ride through the plantation in open-air buses and miniature trains, or cruise around on man-made "tropical canals". There are canoes and aqua-bikes for rent, an animal park and playground, a restaurant and café, as well as a fruit market selling plantation produce. Slightly less commercial are the tours given during the cane-harvesting season at **Condong Sugar Mill**, on the Tweed River about 5km north of Murwillumbah (guided tours July–Nov Mon–Fri 9am–3pm; $4). The turn-off for the **Tree Tops Environment Centre** (daily 10am–5pm; free) is opposite the sugar mill; the centre is the home of Griffith Furniture, which creates beautiful designs from salvaged native timber such as red cedar, using traditional timber-working techniques that you can observe in the workshop. Halfway between Nimbin and Murwillumbah, **UKI** is a pretty little village with views of Mount Warning; there's a small relaxed **market** on the third Sunday of each month in the grounds of the Community Centre. A stall sells locally grown organic coffee, or you can sample some at the Uki Trading Post (daily 9am–5pm).

Practicalities

Places to stay in Murwillumbah include the *Tweed River Motel* (☎02/6672 3933; ⑤), on the Pacific Highway not far from the train station, but in a good riverfront location and with a swimming pool, barbecue and playground; you can also rent surf-skis or paddles. *Mount Warning Murwillumbah Backpackers*, 1 Tumbulgum Rd (☎02/6672 3763; rooms ③, dorms ①), is a small YHA hostel in an old house on the river with access for swimming; you can rent their bikes or use their canoes for free. You can make the most of the countryside by staying in rural or farmstay accommodation. *Midginbil Hill Holiday Farm* (☎02/6679 7158, fax 6679 7120; lodges ⑧, bunkhouses ①, plus camping), is a cattle station 30km west near Mount Warning, offering activities such as horse-riding, canoeing and archery. *Forest Hideaway Units* on Byrill Creek Road, near Uki (☎02/6679 7139; ④), are small, motel-style units each with a double bed and bunks, fridge and cooking facilities, and there's a swimming pool, while the *Bushwalker Cabins* near Doon Doon, Nightcap Pass, 30km from Uki (☎02/6679 9133; ③), are simpler cabins with bunks and cooking facilities.

Places to eat include the old-fashioned *Austral Café*, an eat-in bakery on Main Street. *Govinda's Natural Foods*, at no. 91, is run by Hare Krishna devotees and serves exclusively vegetarian food but with Italian, Chinese and other influences besides the predominantly Indian flavour. The *Riverview Hotel*, 267 Pacific Highway, has a passable, inexpensive bistro serving hamburgers, steaks and pasta, with a verandah overlooking the Tweed.

The New England Plateau

The **New England Plateau** rises parallel to the coast in the northeast of New South Wales, extending from the northern end of the Hunter Valley to the Queensland border. At the top it's between 1000m and 1400m above sea level, and on the eastern edge an escarpment falls away steeply towards the coast. This eastern rim consists of steep slopes and precipitous cliff faces, deep gorges and thickly forested valleys, and because of its inaccessibility has remained a largely undisturbed wilderness. Streams and rivers from the highland tumble over the rocks, and in numerous mighty waterfalls pour into narrow gorges. On the plateau itself the scene is far more peaceful, as sheep and cattle graze on the undulating highland. Because of the altitude, the **climate** up here is fundamentally different from the subtropical coast, a mere 150km or so away: winters are cold and frosty, with occasional snowfalls, while in summer the fresh, dry air can offer welcome relief after the heat and humidity of the coast. Even during a summer heatwave, when the daytime temperature might reach 30°C, the nights will be pleasantly cool. Perhaps it was this that attracted the mainly Scottish immigrants who – despite the name – transformed the New England highland into pastures in the last century.

The **New England Highway**, one of the main links between Brisbane and Sydney, runs north through New England, passing all the major towns – Tamworth, Armidale, Glen Innes and Tenterfield. From any of these, good, sealed roads branch off towards the coast, and it's these minor roads that are especially worth exploring, with turn-offs leading to gorges, waterfalls and scenic lookouts. The area around Glen Innes and Inverell is rich in gemstones, yielding industrial diamonds, zircons and, above all, sapphires. Farms and stations all over the highlands provide farmstay accommodation, offering horse-riding and other activities.

The area is well serviced by **bus**: Greyhound Pioneer and McCafferty's have daily services between Sydney or Canberra and Brisbane and between Brisbane and Melbourne, both via New England; Keans Travel (☎02/9281 9366) operates daily between Sydney and Tenterfield via the Upper Hunter Valley; and Kings Bus Service (☎02/6562 4724) runs three times a week between Port Macquarie and Tamworth via Nambucca Heads, Coffs Harbour, Bellingen, Dorrigo, Armidale, Uralla and Walcha. There is also a daily **train** service between Sydney and Armidale via Tamworth.

The Upper Hunter Valley

The upper end of Hunter Valley is Australia's main horse-breeding and thoroughbred area – indeed it claims to deal in as much horseflesh as anywhere in the world, with at least thirty stud farms. There are cattle- and sheep-breeding stations up here, too, while the fertile soils of the Upper Hunter also yield a harvest of cereals and fruits including, of course, grapes – see the box on p.185 for a sampling of Hunter Valley wineries.

The pretty township of **SCONE** is at the centre of the Hunter Valley horse trade, and you can get further details of the business from the **tourist information centre** on the corner of Susan and Kelly streets (Mon–Fri 9am–5pm, Sat & Sun 10am–3.30pm; ☎02/6545 2907). The best time to visit, when everything's open, is during **Scone Horse Week** – ten days in the middle of May – which features local prize specimens in horse shows, rodeos and races, along with more general cultural and artistic events.

Glenbawn Dam, 15km east of Scone, makes a pleasant excursion. The dam holds back the waters of the Upper Hunter, storing up to 750,000 million litres for irrigation purposes. **Recreation facilities** at the reserve here include accommodation and boat rental: the lake is great for water-skiing, canoeing, sailing and fishing. Despite all the emphasis on horses, this is one of the few places where horse-riding is actually offered, departing on Sunday only from *Lake Glenbawn Resort Village* (☎02/6543 7752). Next to the kiosk, a small **museum** (Sun and holidays only) exhibits relics from early pioneering days in the Hunter Valley. For a fine day-trip you can continue past the dam and climb to the plateau of the Barrington Tops (see p.246) to the national park of the same name, or you can go on towards the coast via Gloucester (about 150km from Scone).

Northeast of Scone is polo country, the haunt of mega-rich Australians such as the media mogul Kerry Packer. If you fancy watching the elitist sport in action, there are polo grounds at **GUNDY** and at **ELLERSTON**. At Gundy, you can have a drink at the classic green-tin-roofed *Linga Longa Hotel*. In between Gundy and Ellerston, **Belltrees** is the family estate of the White family, who gave the world the Nobel prize-winning novelist **Patrick White**. Belltrees Station is a collection of buildings, including the 1832 Semphill Cottage, set among pepper trees; there's even a small school established in

1879. Further along is the White mansion where the family still live, and if you can afford it you can stay at the country house next door, or in the mountain retreat where in later life Patrick White used to escape when he returned home to visit (country house $165 per person per night, including breakfast, dinner and tour of the property; mountain retreat $195 per person per night, including all meals and 4WD transfers; ☎02/6545 1688 or fax 6546 1122 for bookings); polo tuition can be arranged as part of your stay.

Heading on towards the heart of the New England Plateau, you pass **Burning Mountain** about 20km north of Scone, near the village of Wingen. The smoking vents do not indicate volcanic activity but rather a seam of coal burning 30m under the surface: the fire was ignited naturally, perhaps by a lightning strike or spontaneous combustion, over a thousand years ago. The area, protected as a nature reserve, can be reached via a signposted **walking trail** that starts at the picnic grounds at the foot of the hill, just off the New England Highway; pick up the informative NPWS guide to the area's walking tracks from any NPWS office. Fourteen kilometres north of Wingen, **MURRURUNDI** marks the end of the Upper Hunter Valley. It's a pretty spot, enclosed by the Liverpool Ranges, and the *Café Telegraph* here makes a good refreshment stop, with seats outside in the garden with the creek flowing past.

Practicalities

Trains from Sydney (four daily) and Newcastle (one daily) stop at Scone. Greyhound Pioneer and McCafferty's **buses** pass through Scone, while a Countrylink bus runs daily to Moree.

Places to stay in this area are widely scattered. Right in Scone the *Royal Hotel-Motel*, 119 Kelly St (☎02/6545 1722, fax 6545 3245; ②–④), offers simple pub accommodation or fancier motel units – it also serves good counter meals. About halfway to Glenbawn Dam, on Segenhoe Road, is a delightful YHA **hostel** (☎02/6545 2072; rooms ③, dorms ①) in a former school; you can rent bikes here to explore the countryside. Right at the lake, the *Lake Glenbawn Resort Village* (☎02/6543 7752; ④–⑤) has camping and three-bedroom cottages. Heading north, *Ethel Cottage* in Wingen offers farmstay-style B&B lodgings in a self-contained heritage cottage (☎ & fax 02/6545 0300; ⑤). In Murrurundi, *Creative Escapes*, an artist-run B&B guesthouse in a former bank on the New England Highway (☎ & fax 02/6546 6541; ⑤), offers the chance to make pottery or paint in studios set in a large garden with views of the Liverpool Ranges; the rooms are all painted in beautiful colours and furnished with works of art, and an excellent dinner ($25) is available. There's also the basic *Murrurundi Motel* (☎02/6546 6082; ④), right on the highway in Murrurundi. For something to **eat** in Scone, head for *The Station Gallery and Café* in the old station waiting room, where Italian-style food is served; best of all are the chunky cakes with lashings of cream, and naturally enough scones. For entertainment, Scone's **Civic Theatre** (☎02/6541 1569) is an Art Deco movie palace with displays of memorabilia in the foyer.

Tamworth and around

TAMWORTH is the first city on the New England Plateau proper, a fair-sized place that's proud of its public buildings, parks and gardens. It also likes to refer to itself as the "City of Lights", having been the first in Australia to be fitted with electric street lighting, in 1888. To most Australians, however, Tamworth means **country music** – it's a sort of antipodean Nashville. The twelve-metre-high golden guitar in front of the **Tamworth Country Centre** (daily 9am–5pm; $4), on the southern edge of town, sums up the town's role as the C&W capital of Australasia. Inside the centre, you'll find waxwork figures of the great Australian country stars such as Chad Morgan, Buddy Williams, Smoky Dawson and his horse Flash, Slim Dusty, Reg Lindsay and Tex Morton. The ladies aren't forgotten, and their "country meets disco" outfits are even more over the top than the men's – check out Jean Stafford, "the glamorous Tasmanian", and the McKeen sisters in red corduroy A-line skirts with matching waistcoats. Take your camera in and snap some hilarious pictures with the stars. There's also a slightly incongruous collection of gems and minerals from the region – no rhinestones though. Afterwards, the *Longyard Hotel* next door is a handy place to weep in your beer for a while and, once a year, for a week at the end of January, it becomes the focus of the **Tamworth Country Music Festival** when fans from all over the country descend, packing out camping spots. The town is given over to starry-eyed buskers, Akubra hats and cowboy boots, and every pub, club and hall in town hosts music gigs, record launches and bush poetry, culminating in the presentation of the Australian country music awards. Further information and bookings from BAL Marketing (☎02/6762 2399) or the visitors centre (see below). The final piece of the country puzzle is found at the corner of Brisbane Street and Kable Avenue, where the **Hands of Fame** cornerstone bears the palm-prints of more country greats. A glorious spoof, the Noses of Fame memorial, can be savoured over a beer at the *Tattersalls Hotel* on Peel Street.

Don't give up on Tamworth entirely if country music isn't your thing. The new **Powerstation Museum** at 216 Peel St (Tues–Fri 9am–1pm, Sat & Sun by arrangement; free), celebrates those pioneering street lights, and there are numerous art galleries and crafts studios around town: the **Tamworth City Gallery**, housed in the Guy Kable Building on Marius Street (Mon–Fri 10am–5pm, Sat 9–11.30am, Sun 1–4pm; free) has a surprisingly good permanent exhibition. Natural attractions include the **Oxley Lookout and Nature Reserve** at the end of White Street, with panoramic views of the city and the Peel River Valley, and **Lake Keepit**, 56km northwest of the city, where you can rent boats and mess about on the water.

The former goldmining township of **NUNDLE** lies some 60km southeast of town in the "hills of gold" – people still visit with picks, shovels and sieves in the hope of striking it lucky, and you can join them for a day. You no longer need to buy a fossicking licence but it's still worth dropping by the General Store on Jenkins Street; they'll point you in the right direction to start digging.

Practicalities

The big **Tamworth Visitors Centre** (Mon–Fri 8.30am–4.30pm, Sat & Sun 9am–3pm; ☎02/6768 4461) is on the corner of Peel Street and Scots Road. Tamworth is well serviced by **bus**: Greyhound and McCafferty's run daily between Sydney or Canberra and Brisbane and between Brisbane and Melbourne. Kings Bus Service (☎02/6562 4724) runs three times a week between Port Macquarie and Tamworth via Nambucca Heads, Coffs Harbour, Bellingen, Dorrigo, Armidale, Uralla and Walcha. **Local buses** can get you to Nundle (Peel Valley Coaches ☎02/6766 4418) and Gunnedah (McPhersons Coaches ☎02/6767 7190), while Countrylink buses serve Narrabri, Moree, Armidale, Walcha, Inverell and Dubbo. A **train** arrives from Sydney daily en route to Armidale.

ACCOMMODATION

As you drive into Tamworth you'll pass a string of **motels** on the New England Highway – the only time you might have trouble finding a room is during the festival, when everything's booked out. There's a friendly, new *Country Backpackers* at 169 Marius St, opposite the railway station (☎02/6761 2600; rooms ③, dorms ①) or the *Tamworth Hotel* on Marius Street, in the centre of town, offers simple pub accommodation and good counter meals (☎02/6766 2923; ③). If, however, you feel like staying somewhere a little more luxurious, the *Powerhouse Boutique Hotel*, on the New England Highway 1.5km northeast of the centre (☎02/6766 7000, fax 6766 7748; ⑦), has four-star facilities – room service, gym, swimming pool and sauna – but plenty of old-fashioned charm. The closest place for **campers** and caravanners is the *Paradise*

Caravan Park, Peel St (☎02/6766 3120; cabins ④, on-site vans ②–③), on the river about five minutes' walk from the main part of town. Further out, you could try the *Thunderbird Caravan Park*, 6km north (☎02/6760 9356; cabins ③, on-site vans ②), or the bigger *City Lights Caravan Park*, 6km south (☎02/6765 7664; cabins ④, on-site vans ②–③), which has a swimming pool; both are on the New England Highway. In **Nundle** there are rooms and meals at the historic *Peel Inn* on Jenkins Street (☎02/6769 3377, fax 6769 3307; ③), where they also organize gold-panning. If you want a taste of life on a sheep and cattle station, there's *Echo Hills Station*, 45km east of Tamworth at Mulla Creek (☎02/6769 4214, fax 6769 4242, free call ☎1800/810 243; dorms ①); they pick you up for stays of over two days, if arranged in advance. Meals are available ($15 per day) or you can use their kitchen. There's horse-riding and 4WD tours, as well as mustering cattle and sheep (all activities $25 per day). The station also offers popular **Jackeroo and Jilleroo courses** to enable you to get work as a rouse-about (or just for the unique experience); on the week-long residential course ($374) you learn to ride and groom horses, shear and throw fleeces, and go out mustering.

ENTERTAINMENT
There are a couple of recommended **cafés** in Tamworth: the *Old Vic Café*, 261 Peel St (Mon–Sat 9am–5pm, Sun 9am–2.30pm), and the *Weswal Gallery*, 192 Brisbane St (daily 10am–4.30pm). Outside festival time, you'll be disappointed if you think the town's **clubs and pubs** constantly resound to C&W twangings, but you can catch some acts on Thursday evening at the *Tamworth RSL Club* on Kable Avenue, and on Sunday evening at the *West Tamworth Leagues Club* on Phillip Street; on Sunday after-noon the *Longyard Hotel*, behind the *Golden Guitar* in South Tamworth, puts on country music for free.

Armidale

The university city of **ARMIDALE**, halfway between Sydney and Brisbane, is some-thing of a rarity in Australia, where most universities are based in the state capitals. About four thousand students are enrolled at the **University of New England**, which, together with a couple of famous boarding schools, provides an unexpected academic aspect in a place so far "up country". Armidale is a city of some natural beauty, espe-cially in autumn when, with its church spires and many parks, it is embedded in a sea of red and golden leaves. At around 1000m, the climate is unpredictable and can be decidedly brisk in winter.

Beardy Street, the town centre's pedestrian mall, is flanked by quaint Australian coun-try pubs with wide, iron-lace verandahs, and is an excellent place to start exploring. On the last Sunday of the month the mall comes alive with a 150-stall market complete with buskers, and the mall's cafés open their doors. One of the best ways to get around town is by **bike**: there's a signposted city tour, as well as a bike path to the **university cam-pus**, 5km northwest of the city, where there are two small specialized museums (both free), a kangaroo and deer park, and the historic Booloominbah homestead, built in the 1880s as a fashionable gentlemen's residence and now housing the principal adminis-tration office. Back in the city centre, the **New England Regional Art Museum** on Kentucky Street (daily 10.30am–5pm; free) is worth a visit for its two collections of Australian art. Foremost is the Hinton Collection, a group of paintings from the 1880s to the 1940s that includes works by Arthur Streeton and Tom Roberts. The Coventry Collection, focusing on the second half of the twentieth century, also has some impor-tant works, among them a wild self-portrait by Brett Whitely. Next door, the arresting modern building with the distinctive ochre-coloured tin roof is the Aboriginal-run **Aboriginal Centre and Keeping Place** (Mon–Fri 9am–5pm, Sat & Sun 2–5pm; $3), an educational, visual and performing arts centre that aims to foster the renewal and continuity of Aboriginal culture. Artefacts and interpretive material are on permanent display, and special exhibitions are shown; crafts, Aboriginal-designed clothes and other items are for sale in the gift shop. You might also want to visit the Armidale **Folk Museum**, at the corner of Rusden and Faulkner streets (daily 1–4pm; free), which has a collection of artefacts from the New England region and displays on local history.

Practicalities

Armidale has a helpful **Visitors Information Centre** at 82 Marsh St (Mon–Fri 9am–5pm, Sat 9am–4pm, Sun 10am–4pm; ☎02/6772 4655). For details of the area's national parks (see below), head for the NPWS in the McCarthy Building, 87 Faulkner St (☎02/6773 7211). The **bus** terminal is just by the information centre. Plenty of places offer **car rental** if you plan to explore the surrounding countryside, among them Budget (☎02/6771 1535) and Realistic Car Rentals (☎02/6772 3004). **Bikes** can be rented from Armidale Bicycle Centre, 248 Beardy St (☎02/6772 3718). For **taxis**, call Armidale Radio Taxis (☎13 1008).

The *Wicklow Hotel*, or "Pink Pub" as it's more familiarly known (☎02/6772 2421), on the corner of Marsh and Dumaresq streets opposite the bus terminal, caters for weary travellers with **accommodation** (rooms ②, dorms ①). Other pubs include *Tattersalls Hotel*, 174 Beardy St (☎02/6772 2247; ③), and the *Royal Hotel* on the corner of Marsh Street (☎02/6772 2259; ③). There are over twenty motels in Armidale: the information centre has the full list with prices. The most central upmarket choice is the *Cattlemans Motor Inn*, 31 Marsh St (☎02/6772 7788, fax 6771 1447; ⑦). For a taste of tranquillity, *Glenhope* on Red Gum Lane is an elegant B&B homestead set in a valley 11km northwest from the city (☎02/6772 1940; ④). The cheapest motels are on the edge of the city: try the *Armidale Rosevilla*, off the New England Highway 3km north of the centre (☎ & fax 02/6772 3872; ③). Further out, try *Pembroke Caravan and Leisure Park*, Grafton Street, on the corner of Cooks Road, 2km east of town (☎02/6772 6470, fax 6772 9804; cabins ③–⑥, on-site vans ②–③, YHA dorms ①), which has a swimming pool and tennis court; or *Highlander Van Village*, 76 Glen Innes Rd, 2km north of town (☎ 02/6772 4768; cabins and units ③–④, on-site vans ②–③), which has similar facilities.

Good, inexpensive **counter meals** are served at many of the grand old pubs on Beardy Street, including the *New England Hotel* and the *Imperial*. There are several Chinese **restaurants** in town, including *Mekong* in the Beardy Street Mall. *Jean Pierre's*, also in the mall (BYO), has a French chef and is one of Armidale's more exotic restaurants. *Eagle Boys Pizza* on Rusden Street (☎02/6772 2577 for deliveries) is open until late. The student population contributes to a café society of sorts: the light and airy *Café Midalé*, 173 Beardy Street Mall, serves up Italian-style food – focaccia, *panini* and pasta of the day, while *Rumours*, further down the mall, offers good, inexpensive meals and sandwiches, plus a decent breakfast served until noon (both places Mon–Fri 8.30am–5.30pm, Sat until 2pm).

For an evening's **entertainment** visit the Belgrave Twin Cinema (☎02/6772 2856), which screens mainstream and alternative films, and has a café open until late.

Around Armidale

Surrounded by national parks and wild mountain scenery, Armidale makes a good base to stop over for a few days and explore, or perhaps try your hand at a spot of fossicking. The **New England National Park**, 85km east on the Waterfall Way, and the several patchwork sections of the **Oxley Wild Rivers National Park**, exploit the beauty of the eastern edge of the plateau; gorges and spectacular waterfalls abound, although the falls may diminish to a trickle during prolonged dry spells. The most impressive of them are the **Wollomombi Falls**, just over 40km east of Armidale, off the road to

THE MYALL CREEK MASSACRE

In the first decades of the nineteenth century, when European settlers started to move up to the highlands and to use Aboriginal-occupied land on the plateau as sheep and cattle pasture, many of the local Aborigines fought back. Time and again bloody skirmishes flared up. The **Myall Creek massacre** is one of the few that has found a place in the history of white Australia, while innumerable others were never mentioned in genteel pioneer circles and have subsequently been erased from public memory.

For Aboriginal people, expulsion from the lands of their ancestors amounted to spiritual as well as physical dispossession, and they resisted as best they could: white stockmen staying in huts far away from pioneer townships or homesteads feared for their lives. In 1837 and 1838, Aborigines repeatedly ambushed and killed stockmen near the Gwydir and Namoi rivers. Then, during the absence of the overseer at Myall Creek Station, near present-day Inverell, twelve farm hands organized a raid in retribution, killing 28 Aborigines. In court, the farm hands were acquitted – public opinion saw nothing wrong with their deed, and neither did the jury. The case was later taken up again, however, and seven of the participants in the massacre were sentenced to death on the gallows.

Dorrigo; among the highest in Australia, they plunge 225m into a gorge. Nearby are the Chandler Falls, while **Ebor Falls**, a stunning double drop of the Guy Fawkes River in the national park of the same name, can be viewed from platforms just off Waterfall Way, another 40km beyond Wollomombi. Between Wollomombi and Ebor, **Point Lookout** in the New England National Park offers a truly wonderful panoramic view across the forested ranges. The road to the lookout is unsealed gravel, but is usually in reasonable condition, and there are simple **cabins** and bush **campsites** where you can stay overnight: phone the NPWS in Dorrigo for bookings (☎02/6657 2309). The rest of the park is virtually inaccessible wilderness.

On the way back to Armidale, you could detour through the goldrush ghost town of **HILLGROVE**, where the old school has been converted into a **museum** (daily 10am–5pm; free) displaying old mining equipment and trying to re-create the lifestyle of the once-prosperous settlement. **URALLA**, 22km south of Armidale, is another old gold town, though in this case it has managed to hang on, with a population of a couple of thousand. The Historic Building Walk will take you past the town's highlights, including **McCrossin's Mill Museum** (daily noon–5pm; $3.50), an old three-storey flour mill on Salisbury Street. Fossicking is still possible at the old Rocky River diggings: enquire at the **Tourist Information Centre**, New England Highway (daily 10.30am–4.30pm; ☎02/6778 4496); or you can go on tour with **Uralla Goldfield Tours** (☎02/6772 6828). Gold apart, Uralla's other claim to fame is that **Captain Thunderbolt**, the bushranger who terrorized the New England region in the nineteenth century, was shot dead here in 1870, after a furious battle in the swampy country southeast of Uralla – an event commemorated by the bronze statue of Thunderbolt and his horse on the corner of Bridge and Salisbury streets.

Southeast of Armidale, towards Walcha, **Dangars Lagoon** is a wetland region visited by more than a hundred different kinds of bird; a hide is provided for spotters. **Dangars Falls** and a network of twenty walking tracks and lookouts around **Dangars Gorge** are only 22km from Armidale on a minor road. Beyond these, about 20km east of Walcha, a turn-off from the Oxley Highway leads to **Apsley Gorge** and two more waterfalls in another section of the Oxley Rivers park. In **WALCHA** itself, 65km southwest of Armidale, there are the usual pioneer museums, but more interesting is the **Amaroo Museum and Cultural Centre** on Derby Street (Mon–Fri 9am–5pm), which displays arts and crafts made by local Aboriginal people.

West of Armidale, 27km along the Bundarra Road, is the Mount Yarrowyck Nature Reserve where an **Aboriginal rock-art site** can be accessed via a 3km circuit walk.

Glen Innes and around

GLEN INNES, the next major stop north on the New England Highway, about 100km from Armidale, is another pleasant town in a beautiful setting. Although agriculture is still important up here, you begin to see more and more evidence of the gemfields – sapphires are big business, as, to a lesser extent, is tin mining. In the centre, on Grey Street especially, numerous century-old public buildings and parks have been renovated and spruced up. There's some fine country architecture including a couple of large corner pubs, their verandahs decorated with iron lace. The **Land of the Beardies Museum** (Mon–Fri 10am–noon & 2–5pm, Sat & Sun 2–5pm; $4), in the town's first hospital on Ferguson Street, takes this feeling for the past further, displaying pioneer relics, period room settings and a reconstructed slab hut. The name alludes to the two hairy men who settled the area in the last century, and it's a title the town's proud of, along with the Scottish connections reflected in the name of the town itself and in many of its streets, which are rendered in both English and Gaelic. The local granite **Australian Standing Stones** at Martins Lookout, Watsons Drive, are based on the Ring of Brodgar in Scotland, and are intended to honour the "contribution of the Celtic races to Australia's development"; there's a great picnic and barbecue area with granite seats and tables, echoing the stones themselves. The strongly Celtic nature of Glen Innes is counterbalanced by the town's department store, Kwong Sing & Co, which has been run by the same family of Chinese origin since 1886.

In early November, Glen Innes celebrates the **Land of the Beardies Bushfestival**, with everything from a beard-growing contest and shopping-trolley derby to dances, street parades and arts-and-crafts exhibits. More details, including help with rooms, are available from the **Glen Innes & District Visitors Centre,** 52 Church St, as the New England Highway is called when it passes through town (daily 9am–5pm; ☎02/6732 2397); there's a café, *The Celtic Kitchen* in the centre serving soda bread and smacks, and the 24-hour **bus terminal** is also attached. Good **accommodation** options include the air-conditioned *Central Motel*, Meade Street, opposite the post office (☎02/6732 2826, fax 6732 1624; ④); the fancier (though not air-con) *Rest Point Motel* on Church Street, 1km south of the centre (☎02/6713 2255, fax 6732 1515; ⑤), with a swimming pool and extensive landscaped grounds; the well-equipped *Poplar Caravan Park*, 15 Church St (☎02/6732 1514; cabins ③, on-site vans ②); and *Blue Sapphire Caravan Park*, corner of Church and Grafton streets (☎02/6732 1590; cabins ③, on-site vans ②). For sustenance, try the unimaginatively named *Tea and Coffee Shop* on Grey Street, a cosy **tearoom** with loads of choice including Dutch pancakes, an array of interesting sandwiches, savoury croissants and hot breakfasts. The *One Eighty Nine Coffee Lounge*, at 189 Grey St, has a more down-to-earth menu, including hamburgers. The best Chinese **restaurant** is *Dragon Court*, at no. 173 (licensed; lunch and dinner daily).

Inverell

The area between Glen Innes and **INVERELL**, 67km to the west, is one huge gemfield. Industrial diamonds, garnets, topaz, zircons and three-quarters of the world's sapphires are mined in the area. Inverell is also known as "Sapphire City", and at the **Dejon Sapphire Centre**, on the Gwydir Highway, 18km east of town, you can watch the gems being mined, washed, sorted and cut (daily 9am–5pm; mine tours 10.30am & 3pm). The showroom has a display of sapphires in 155 colours, from pale blue and green, to gold, lemon and pink. If you want to try your luck, you'll need to contact the **tourist office** on Campbell Street (Mon–Fri 9am–4pm, Sat 9am–noon; ☎02/6722 1693), which can direct you to the designated areas. If you want to **stay** over and wait for that big strike, try the *Royal Motel-Hotel*, 260 Byron St (☎02/6722 2811; ④), which has air-conditioned en-suite rooms and serves counter meals, or *Sapphire City Caravan Park* on Moore Street (☎02/6722 1830; cabins ③, on-site vans ②).

Tenterfield and around

Less than 20km from the Queensland border, **TENTERFIELD** marks the northern end of the New England Plateau. Although only a small town, it has a confirmed place in Australian history, being the birthplace of the Australian Federation. This title was earned when, in 1889, the Prime Minister of New South Wales, Sir Henry Parkes, made his famous Federation speech here, advocating the union of the Australian colonies; twelve years later the Commonwealth of Australia was inaugurated. A small **museum** (Sat & Sun 2–4pm; $2) in Centenary Cottage recalls the occasion and displays other items of local interest.

As throughout the region, however, the real attractions of Tenterfield lie outside town – undulating pastures and orchards, remnants of stands of eucalypt and rainforests, and rugged granite hills. **Bald Rock**, in a national park of the same name near the Queensland border, about 30km northeast of Tenterfield, is Australia's second-largest monolith, after Uluru (see p.587), but a grey granite version, 213m high. It can be climbed from its northeast side, and from the summit there are all-round views taking in both states. The excursion to Bald Rock fits in nicely with a visit to 210-metre-high **Boonoo Boonoo Falls**, set in another national park 32km north of Tenterfield. Access is via a gravel road which can be a bit rough, but it's worth it, and there's a beautiful picnic area. The NPWS occasionally offers tours to both national parks: details are available from the **Tenterfield Visitors Centre**, New England Highway (Mon–Fri 9.30am–5pm, Sat 9.30am–5.30pm, Sun 9.30am–4pm; ☎02/6736 1082). Woollool Woollool Aboriginal Cultural Tours (☎018/669 048 for prices and times) also operates tours to the parks, conducted by trained Aboriginal guides, which look at the relics and visit the ghost town of Boonoo Boonoo; they also visit Bald Rock – tours go Wednesday to Monday and pick up and drop off at the Tenterfield YHA hostel.

Accommodation in Tenterfield includes the central *Commercial Hotel*, 288 Rouse St (☎02/6736 1027; ②), where you can also get counter meals. *Tenterfield YHA Lodge*, 2 Manners St (☎02/6736 1477; rooms ③, dorms ①, cabins ③, on-site vans ②), is an old country hotel surrounded by parklands, incorporating a caravan park and a small hostel.

PACIFIC ISLANDS: LORD HOWE AND NORFOLK

Lord Howe Island, 700km northeast of Sydney, and roughly in line with Port Macquarie, is actually a far-flung part of New South Wales, on the world's southern-most coral reef. Its nearest neighbour is **Norfolk Island**, 900km further northeast – an external independent territory of Australia, though geographically closer to New Zealand. The approach to tourism of the two subtropical islands couldn't be more different: Lord Howe is the perfect ecodestination, attracting outdoor types, and is very sophisticated in terms of food and accommodation, while Norfolk Island mostly disregards its natural beauty to concentrate first on its status as a tax haven and a magnet for Australian pensioners who come for its duty-free shopping, and second on its fascinating history as a tough convict settlement and then as the home for many of the descendants of the *Bounty* mutineers after they had left Pitcairn Island.

Getting there

It's not cheap to get to **Lord Howe Island**: you can **fly** with Eastern Australian Airlines from Sydney at least six times weekly, or with Sunstate from Brisbane twice weekly (book both through Qantas on ☎13 1313) for about $860 return; note that the Lord Howe Island Board (for information call ☎02/6563 2066, fax 6563 2127) charges a $20 service levy which is included in your airline ticket. It's much easier to go on a **package tour** with Pacific Unlimited Holidays in Sydney (☎02/9290 2266, fax 9232 8150), or Pinetrees Travel (free call ☎1800/226 142) but the lowest you can expect to pay for a week is about $1279. Overseas visitors can also fly to Lord Howe as an add-on sector fare on an airpass. The Qantas-linked Norfolk Jet Express (☎13 1313) flies to **Norfolk Island** from Sydney and Brisbane three to five times a week, while the Ansett-partner Flight West (☎13 1314) operates three flights a week from Brisbane. Packages, available through Fastbook Pacific Holidays (☎1300/361153), offer the best value – from $890 for five days; note there's a $25 departure tax from Norfolk. Fastbook can also arrange flights between the two islands with Tasman Australian Airlines. Air New Zealand flies twice weekly **from Auckland** to Norfolk Island, which may soon become an optional stopover on the route between Australia and New Zealand.

Lord Howe Island

I would strongly urge preserving this beautiful island from further intrusions of any kind...
Government Expedition, 1882

On the UNESCO World Heritage list since 1982 because of its rare birds and plant life, and its coral reef in unpolluted and virtually untouched waters, **LORD HOWE ISLAND** is the ultimate destination for ecotourists. The island's preservation was assured by Victorian-era descriptions of "this gem of the sea" when reports were brought back to the Australian mainland regarding the progress of the multiracial settlers who had arrived in the 1830s. Even today only a tenth of the land has been cleared for cultivation or grazing, and two-thirds of the island is designated as **Permanent Park Reserve**. Only 11km long and just under 3km across at its widest point, the crescent-shaped subtropical island is covered with **kentia palm plantations**, which represent the island's only industry other than tourism. With a population of just 280, only 400 visitors are allowed on the island at any one time; to enforce this limit, accommodation has to be booked in advance. There is only one short road and, although some locals have vehicles, people get around mainly by bicycle, boat or on foot.

As you fly in, you have a stunning view of the whole of the volcanic island: the towering summits of rainforest-clad **Mount Gower** and **Mount Lidgbird** at the southern end, the narrow centre with its idyllic lagoon and a **coral reef** extending about six kilometres along the island's west coast, and a group of tiny islets off the coast at the lower northern end of the island providing sanctuary for the prolific **birdlife** – the island's 32 species make this a heaven for ornithologists.

One of the first things you notice about the island is how easy-going and laid-back the local people are: many prefer to go barefoot. The emphasis is on tranquillity and visitors are mostly couples and families – there are no rowdy nightclubs here. Though it's expensive to get to the island, once here you'll find that cruises, bike rental and eating out are all relatively affordable. The island's **climate** is subtropical, with temperatures rising from an average low of 16°C to 19°C in winter, 26°C in the summer, and an annual rainfall of 1650mm. It's cheaper to visit in the winter, though many places are closed and there's usually a lot more rain and wind.

Some history
Although the ship *Supply* discovered Lord Howe Island in 1778 on a journey from Sydney to found a colony on Norfolk Island, the island was not actually settled for another 55 years. These first **settlers**, who arrived in 1833, were three white men,

with Maori women and boys, and the group earned their livelihood by providing whaling vessels with provisions. Other settlers arrived in the 1840s, but in 1853 two white men came with three women from the Gilbert Islands, and it is from this small group that many of Lord Howe's present population is descended. In the 1840s and 1850s the island continued to serve as a stopover for **whaling ships** from the USA and Britain, with as many as fifty ships a year passing through. In 1882 a government expedition from the mainland recommended that, in order to preserve the island, no one other than the present "happy, industrious" leaseholders and their families be allowed to make permanent settlement.

With the decline of whaling, economic salvation came in the form of the "thatch" palm, one of the four endemic species of the **kentia palm**. Up to this time used as roofing for the islanders' homes, it now began to be exported to Europe and the USA as a decorative interior plant, which helped to boost the island's economy. Then, in 1918 the kentia industry was devastated by the introduction of **rats**, which escaped onto the island from a ship. **Tourism**, though, was eventually to become the mainstay of the island. Lord Howe had been a popular stopover on the cruise-ship circuit before World War II, and after the war it began to be visited by holiday-makers from Sydney, who came by seaplane.

Today, rats still pose a hazard to the palms, but the **kentia industry** is nonetheless in resurgence, run by the Lord Howe Island Board under the auspices of the government of New South Wales, with profits going towards the preservation of the island's unique ecosystem. Seeds are no longer exported but instead cultivated in the Lord Howe Island Board's own **nursery**, which sells two-and-a-half million plants annually, mainly to Europe and North America. You can visit the nursery on guided walks with Ron's Rambles or Jim's Tours (book at Thompson's General Store, see below); they also grow seedlings here for regeneration around the island.

Practicalities

There's no official transport from the **airport**, located in the narrow central part of the island, but wherever you're staying, you'll be met on arrival by the lodge-owner. Crossing the centre of the island, **Ned's Beach Road** has a cluster of shops and services. The **visitors centre** here (Mon–Fri 9am–12.30pm; ☎02/6563 2114, fax 6563 2127) has information on the natural history of the island, with plenty of free brochures about wildlife and plants, plus an excellent twenty-minute audiovisual presentation; outside there's an information hut with details of tours and activities and an excellent map of the island showing coral reefs and diving holes; a weather report is also posted daily. Most activities can be booked next door at Thompson's **General Store** (☎02/6563 2010) – it's advisable to sign up in advance for cruises.

Another worthwhile stop is the **Lord Howe Historical Museum**, opposite Lagoon Beach on the corner of Middle Beach Road and Lagoon Road (daily 2–4pm; $4). As well as detailing the history of Lord Howe Island from its discovery to the present day, the museum also sells the useful World Heritage Map ($8), which has a guide, **maps**, details of **walks** and bird-watching information. Another good buy is the useful *Ramblers Guide to Lord Howe Island* ($6), which covers all the walks on the island in much greater detail. You'll also find a **post office** (Mon–Fri 9am–5pm, closed lunch 1–2pm), which acts as a Commonwealth Bank agent ($3 processing fee), a Westpac **bank** (Mon–Fri 10am–noon & 2–4pm) and a community hall-cum-summer cinema here. There's another store, Joy's Shop (daily 9am–6.30pm), on Middle Beach Road opposite *Leanda Lei Apartments*, which sells liquor and cigarettes, though the cheapest place to get alcohol is the Liquor Store, off Lagoon Road further east. The State Bank (Mon–Fri 10am–12.30pm & 2–4.30pm) is also located off

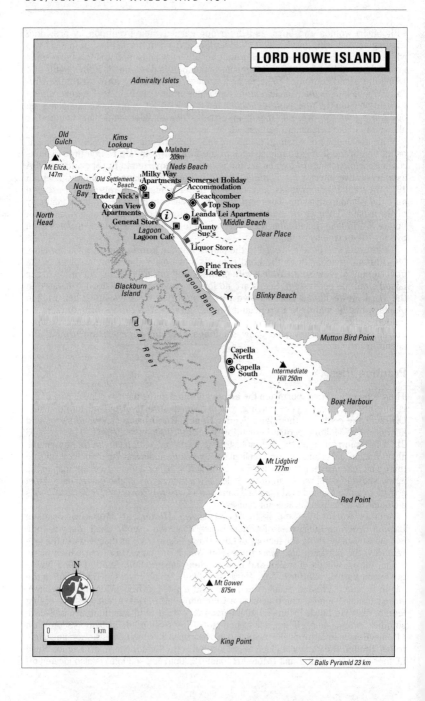

LORD HOWE ISLAND

Admiralty Islets

Old Gulch

Kims Lookout

Malabar 209m

Neds Beach

Mt Eliza 147m

Old Settlement Beach

Milky Way Apartments

Somerset Holiday Accommodation

North Bay

Trader Nick's

Beachcomber

Top Shop

Ocean View Apartments

Leanda Lei Apartments

North Head

General Store

Middle Beach

Aunty Sue's

Clear Place

Lagoon

Lagoon Café

Liquor Store

Blackburn Island

Pine Trees Lodge

Lagoon Beach

Blinky Beach

Coral Reef

Mutton Bird Point

Capella North

Capella South

Intermediate Hill 250m

Boat Harbour

Mt Lidgbird 777m

Red Point

Mt Gower 875m

N

0   1 km

King Point

▽ Balls Pyramid 23 km

LORD HOWE ECOLOGY

Seven million years ago a volcanic eruption on the sea floor created Lord Howe Island and its 27 surrounding islets and outcrops – the island's boomerang shape is a mere remnant of the massive shield volcano, mostly eroded away by the sea. While much of the **flora** on the island is similar to that of Australia, New Zealand, New Caledonia and Norfolk Island, the island's relative isolation has led to the evolution of **new species** – of the 241 native plants found here, 105 are endemic, including the important indigenous **kentia palm** (see p.287).

Similarly, until the arrival of settlers, fifteen species of **land birds** (nine of which are now extinct) lived on the island, undisturbed by predators and coexisting with migrating seabirds, skinks, geckos, spiders, snails and the now-extinct giant horned turtle. However, in the eighteenth century Lord Howe became a port of call for ships en route to Norfolk Island, whose hungry crews eradicated the island's stocks of **white gallinule** and **white-throated pigeon**. The small, plump and flightless **woodhen** managed to survive, protected on Mount Gower, and an intensive captive breeding programme in the early 1980s has more than doubled numbers of the species to 66. About one million **seabirds** – fourteen species – nest here annually: as well as being one of the few known breeding grounds of the **providence petrel**, the island also has the world's largest colony of **red-tailed tropic birds** and is the most southerly breeding location of the **sooty tern**, the noddy tern and the masked booby.

The cold waters of the **Tasman Sea**, which surround Lord Howe, host the world's southernmost **coral reef**, a tropical oddity which is sustained by the warm summer currents that sweep in from the Great Barrier Reef. There are about sixty varieties of brilliantly coloured and fantastically shaped coral, and the meeting of warm and cold currents means that a huge variety of both tropical and temperate fish can be spotted by snorkellers in the crystal-clear waters. Some of the most colourful species include the yellow **moon wrasse** and the yellow-and-black **banner fish**. Unique to Lord Howe is the **doubleheader**, with its bizarre, bulbous forehead and fat lips. Beyond the lagoon, the water becomes very deep, with particularly good **diving** in the seas around the **Admiralty Islets**, which have sheer underwater precipices and chasms. The diving season lasts from May to September (for information on dive companies, see p.292).

Lagoon Road. The place where the locals **shop** is the Top Shop, tucked away on Skyline Street, off Mutton Bird Drive; here you can get fresh meat and vegetables, which are flown in daily from Port Macquarie. There are no ATMs on the island, so bring cash with you, although in emergencies some establishments, including Larrups clothes and beachwear shop and the *Lagoon Café* can give cash out on EFT-POS or credit cards to customers.

Transport

The island has only one **road** and relatively few cars. There are no streetlights so you'll need to bring a torch with you, or buy one from Joy's Shop, if you want to venture out at night. There's no regular bus service, but lodge hosts and restaurants will often pick up and drop off customers. Otherwise, Wilson's (see below) can do pick-ups and drop-offs. The most common ways to get around are by **bicycle**, boat or just plain walking. There are plenty of places to **rent bikes** but again the drawback is that they don't have lights, so if you want to ride at night attach a torch. *Leanda Lei Apartments* (☎02/6563 2195) rents out mountain bikes for $7.50 per day, $50 per week, but note that guests have preference. Otherwise, the main outlet is Wilson's Bike Hire, opposite Lagoon Beach (☎02/6563 2045; $3 per day plus $1 for helmets, minimum charge of $5 per day), but be warned that their bikes are basic, with no gears – and there are some steep hills on the island. Both Wilson's and *Leanda Lei* also rent **cars** ($40–50 per day plus 20¢ per km).

Accommodation

Since you need to have an accommodation booking before you can buy a flight, package tours are the most convenient option. Most of the accommodation on Lord Howe Island is **self-catering** (otherwise full board is available) and of a good standard, including TV and usually a laundry.

Beachcomber (☎02/6563 2032, fax 6563 2132). Studio apartments including breakfast (some larger suites available with self-catering facilities) in a central location amongst palm-trees. Owned by long-established island family; suitable for couples with kids. ⑦.

Capella South (☎02/6563 2008, fax 6563 2158). Towards the southern end of the island, above Salmon Beach and overlooked by Mount Gower and Mount Lidgbird. Nine stylish, breezy rooms with fantastic views, hip *Mambo* furnishings and interior design and large bathrooms. TVs, torches and mountain bikes also provided. Restaurant and bar on site. ⑧.

Capella North (☎02/6563 2113, fax 6563 2158). This is run by the same people as *Capella South*. It's a simpler version than the above and is opposite the lagoon, offering self-contained units. ⑦.

Leanda Lei Apartments (☎02/6563 2195, fax 6563 2095). Studio or one- or two-bedroom self-catering apartments. The friendly owners can rent you a bike or a car, and will drop off at restaurants in the evening. In the middle of the island, set in nicely manicured grounds with barbecues; close to shops, restaurants and Lagoon Beach. ⑧.

Milky Way Apartments (book through Fast Bookings in Sydney: ☎02/9958 2799, fax 9958 2079). Set amid native forests by Old Settlement Beach at the northern end of the island. One of the best spots, surrounded by bird-filled green forests. All units have balconies. ⑧.

Ocean View Apartments (☎02/6563 20458, fax 6563 21251). Very pleasant, old-fashioned place, with a sunny garden, tennis court and a common room with pool tables. There *is* a view of the sea at the end of the driveway, but not from the rooms. ⑧.

Pine Trees Lodge (☎02/6563 2177, fax 6563 2156). The island's original resort, set in extensive grounds filled with native palms and hundred-year-old Norfolk Island pines. A pleasant, old-fashioned homestead with a guest lounge, verandah, courtyard and tennis court. Palm units are motel-style, each with a small verandah. The newer garden cottages are better, with courtyards, separate bedrooms and living rooms. The lodge has its own boatshed and deck on Lagoon Beach. Bikes rented for $4 per day. Package tours only ($1595 per person per week, including flight, accommodation and all meals).

Somerset Holiday Accommodation (☎02/6563 2061, fax 6563 2110; *somerset.lhi@bigpond.com*). The largest self-contained apartments complex on the island, conveniently located with BBQs for self-catering, which also have kitchenettes. ⑧.

Trader Nick's (☎02/6563 2022, fax 6563 2002; *traders@nor.com.au*; ⑧). Seven suites with separate living and private decks nestling in among the kentia forest.

Eating and drinking

Bookings are essential at all **eating** places for evening meals. An essential **lunch** or snack stop is the centrally-situated *Lagoon Café* (daily 11.30am–6pm) on Lagoon Road, offering affordable salads, speciality burgers, focaccia and daily fish specials. They also have an alfresco tapas and cocktails evening event at the once-weekly *Zoo Bar* (theme night varies each season). Thompson's General Store also does takeaway fish and beef burgers at lunchtime (closed Wed & Thurs in winter). The best **restaurants** on the island are *Aunty Sue's* (☎02/6563 2177; closed Mon), a relaxed place with tables outside on the deck and a lively atmosphere, where the menu features generous portions of traditional dishes such as quail and kingfish, and *Williams at Trader Nick's* (☎02/6563 2022) a casual fine dining venue with innovative local speciality dishes such as fruit and nut stuffed chicken breast. *Shores Restaurant* at the *Blue Lagoon Lodge* on Neds Beach Road (☎02/6563 2043 or 6563 2020; closed Wed & Thurs) also has great contemporary Australian cuisine in an artistic setting. For a typical island fish fry, *Beachcomber* (☎02/6563 2032), is the place to come at 7pm on Wednesday or Sunday night; a buffet-style meal including a rather unusual marshmallow, coconut and mandarin salad costs $25. There's no pub on the island, but the closest thing to a **bar** is the *Bowling Club* where the locals hang out daily between 5pm and 8pm; for local swingers there's a disco held here every Friday night (8.30pm–midnight).

The island

At the island's **northern end**, you can walk, stopping at various lookout points, all the way from Old Settlement Beach on the western side to Ned's Beach on the east. From the streamside picnic area at **Old Settlement Beach**, it's just over 2km to the summit of **Mount Eliza** (147m). If you want to save time, you can take a boat to **North Bay** with Islander Cruises (see below) and begin the walk from there – the return walk will then take only an hour. The summit is the most accessible place to see **sooty terns** in their southernmost breeding grounds. When the colony visits the island between August and March each female lays a single speckled egg on the bare ground, which means that the actual summit has to be closed for the birds' protection. Back at the base, a short five- or ten-minute walk through forest from **North Beach** (good for swimming and snorkelling on North Reef) leads to **Old Gulch**, a beach of boulders, where at low tide you can rock-hop to the **Herring Pools** at the base of the cliff front and examine the colourful marine life. From **Ned's Beach** (see below) the walk to **Malabar Hill** (209m) gives access to one of the world's largest nesting concentrations of **red-tailed tropic birds**, who between September and May make their homes in the crannies of the cliff face below, laying only one egg and looking after the chick for twelve weeks until it can fly. It's fascinating to watch the white-and-red birds' unusual and rather balletic backwards-dancing through the air. From here, you can head along the cliff edge to **Kim's Lookout** (182m), which provides a good view of the settlement and the lagoon beaches and islets at this end of the island, and from where it's just over a kilometre back to Old Settlement Beach (or you can continue on to North Beach and Mount Eliza). In the **centre of the island** there are other walks to take: from Middle Beach to the Clear Place; from Blinky Beach, the island's main surfing spot, to **Transit Hill** (121m); and from near the airstrip to the summit of **Intermediate Hill** (250m); and two longer walks from the base of Intermediate Hill to **Boat Harbour** or to the base of **Mount Lidgbird** (777m).

The ultimate view, however, is at the **southern end** of the island, where the lofty summit of **Mount Gower** (875m) gives vistas over the whole island and out to sea towards **Balls Pyramid** (548m), a rocky outcrop 23km from Lord Howe. The mountain is high enough to have a true **mist forest** on its summit, with a profusion of ferns, and tree trunks and rocks covered in mosses. This very strenuous walk can be undertaken only with a licensed **guide** (Jack Shick ☎02/6563 2218; $25; bring your own lunch). The track to the top was blazed by botanists in 1869, who took two days to get there, but they were rewarded with the discovery of a plant seen nowhere else on earth – the **pumpkin tree**, bearing fleshy orange flowers. You can see other rare endemic plants here, such as the island apple and the blue plum, as well as birds such as the providence petrel and the woodhen. On average, the return walk takes eight hours; it's graded medium to hard and you'll need to be fit and have a good pair of walking boots. It's not for the faint-hearted: one section of the walk runs precariously along a narrow cliff face above the sea, and in parts the track is so steep that you must haul yourself up by ropes. To join the walk, you have to be at the Little Island gate on the south of the island by 7.30am. Transport is not provided; it takes about 25 minutes to cycle from the north end or you could call Wilson's (☎02/6563 2045) who might be able to provide a lift.

Water-based activities

Besides bushwalks, the island has some sensational swimming, snorkelling and diving sites. The water's combined temperate and tropical sealife make local double-headed wrasse, lobsters and angel-fish a common sight. Among the cruises on offer, the **glass-bottom boat cruises** from Lagoon Beach, which take about twenty passengers, are good value at $15 for two hours (book at Thompson's General Store); included are opportunities to snorkel at **Erscotts Hole**, with gear and wetsuits provided, and hand-feeding of fish, including a friendly old double-headed wrasse.

Islander Cruises can take you to North Bay, combining a **snorkelling** excursion around the 1965 wreck of the *Favourite* (where three-stripe butterfly fish have made their home) with bushwalks up to Old Gulch or up to the summit of Mount Eliza (☎02/6563 2021; 10am–4pm; $25 including morning and afternoon tea, BYO lunch; no tour July & Aug).

There's more stunning snorkelling at Sylphs Hole, off Old Settlement Beach, and on the east side of the island at Ned's Beach, where snorkelling sets can be rented on an honesty-box system ($2 per hr, $4 half day, $6 full day, $30 per week; wetsuit $3 for 30min, $6 for 1hr). At 5pm every day Ned's Beach is the site of a **fish-feeding** frenzy, when a local man throws fish scraps into the water, attracting a throng of big trevally and reef sharks. Stay here until dusk and you can observe **muttonbirds** en masse darkening the sky as they come home to roost. This experience can be a bit frightening, as they fly low through a forest of enormous **banyan trees** whose tangle of aerial roots descends to the ground.

Fishing trips can be arranged with Lulawai (☎02/6563 2195; $50 half day), who guarantee you some fish, which the crew will prepare for you to barbecue later. If you're interested in **diving** in the waters around Lord Howe, contact Howea Divers (☎ & fax 02/6563 2290), a recommended outfit run by a local. As well as advanced dives and tuition, they offer novices the chance to dive either off boats or from the shore for $90. Pro-Dive also has an outlet on the island, with packages bookable through their Sydney central reservations (☎02/9232 5733, fax 9232 5788).

Norfolk Island

Just 8km long and 5km wide, tiny isolated **NORFOLK ISLAND**, an External Territory of Australia located 1500km due east of Brisbane, nevertheless has had an eventful history, linked with early convict settlements and later with the descendants of Fletcher Christian and other "mutiny-on-the-*Bounty*" rebels and their Tahitian wives who had outgrown Pitcairn Island. It's a beautiful, unique island, forested with grand indigenous pine trees, and with a mild subtropical climate ranging between 11°C and 18°C in the winter and from 19°C to 20°C (with high humidity) in the summer. Nowadays the island's **tax-haven** status makes it a refuge for millionaires, with thirteen of them living on the island including the Australian novelist Colleen McCullough. The island's history is exploited to the full for Norfolk's tourists, who spend a fortune in the numerous duty-free stores; there's a big philatelic industry too.

The island mainly attracts honeymooners or retired Australians and New Zealanders lured by the quiet life and the inexpensive shopping (known collectively as the "newly weds and nearly deads"). Even the most frequent visitors require a passport to visit the island, which has its own government, a nine-member Legislative Assembly, and an administrator appointed by the Australian Governor General. A thirty-day **visitor permit**, extendable to 120 days, is granted automatically on arrival. The island has no income tax, finances being raised from sources such as departure tax ($25) and a road levy included in the price of petrol. There's a $500 fine for working illegally, but finding **work** here through the right channels is not impossible: many of the 1800 residents (who are not entitled to the dole) hold down two or three jobs, and employment for school-leavers is guaranteed, often in the two tacky sound-and-light shows that tell the story of the mutiny on the *Bounty* and the convict era. Most of the local people remain unaffected by tourism, maintaining their friendly, good-humoured attitude, their ridiculous nicknames and the remnants of their dialect, **Pitcairn**, a mixture of old West Country English and Tahitian (see p.293).

Much of the land is cleared for cultivation, as islanders have to grow all their own fresh food to keep the island disease-free; cattle roam freely on the green island and are given right of way, creating a positively bucolic atmosphere. Scenic winding roads provide access to the **national park** and the **Botanic Garden** in the northern half of the island, which together cover twenty percent of Norfolk's area. It's here that you get an idea of how the entire island originally looked, as you roam through the best of the remaining subtropical rainforest. Norfolk Island is also an ornithologist's paradise, with nine endemic **landbird** species, including the endangered **Norfolk Island green parrot** with its distinctive chuckling sound. The two small islands immediately south of Norfolk, Nepean and Phillip islands, are important **seabird** nesting sites.

Some history

A violent volcanic eruption three million years ago produced the Norfolk Ridge, extending from New Zealand to New Caledonia (Norfolk Island's closest neighbour, 700km north), with only Norfolk Island and the smaller adjacent and uninhabited **Phillip** and **Nepean islands** remaining above sea level. **Captain Cook** "discovered" the island in 1774, but it's now believed that migrating Polynesian people had lived here for hundreds of years prior to his visit. Cook recommended that the island be secured for the British Crown, seeing value in its vegetation: the tall **Norfolk pines** he thought would make fine ships' masts, with accompanying sails woven from the native **flax**. Norfolk Island was settled in 1788, only six weeks after Sydney, with the idea of establishing a free settlement - of the 23 original settlers, 15 were convicts. However, plans to use the fertile island as a base to grow food for the starving young colony of Australia foundered when, in 1790, a First Fleet ship, the *Sirius*, was wrecked on a reef off the island, highlighting the problem, which still exists today, of its lack of a navigable harbour. This **first settlement** was judged a failure when its wood proved not to be strong enough for masts and it was finally abandoned in 1814. Most of the buildings were destroyed to discourage settlement by other powers, and many free settlers were granted land in New Norfolk in Tasmania (see p.927).

Norfolk's isolation was one of the major reasons for its **second settlement** (1825–55) – as a **prison** rather than a productive island, described officially as "a place of the extremest punishment short of death". Some of the imposing stone buildings designed by Royal Engineers still stand in **Kingston**, on the southern coast of the island. There were up to two thousand convicts on the island, overseen by sadistic commandants who had virtually unlimited power to run the settlement and inflict punishments as they saw fit. Only under the command of the enlightened reformer Captain Maconochie (1840–44) was there some improvement in prisoners' conditions.

Norfolk Island was again abandoned in 1855, but this time the buildings remained and were used a year later during the **third settlement**, which consisted of 194 Pitcairn Islanders (the entire population of the island), who left behind their overcrowded conditions to establish a new life elsewhere. The new settlers had only eight family surnames among them – five of which (Christian, Quintal, Adams, McKoy and Young) were the names of the original mutineers of the *Bounty*. These names – especially Christian – are still common on the island, and today about one in three islanders can claim descent from the mutineers. The building of an airport during World War II, and the arrival of television have helped greatly to reduce Norfolk's linguistic isolation, though these descendants still speak some Pitcairn to each other. Listen for expressions such as "Whataway?" ("How are you?") and "Webout you gwen?" ("Where are you going?"). **Bounty Day**, the day the Pitcairners arrived, is celebrated in Kingston on June 8.

Practicalities

For information and **bookings** in advance, contact the Norfolk Island Government Tourist Bureau, Australian office, PO Box 523, Turramurra, NSW 2074 (☎02/9983 0939, fax 9983 0949). Ansett (see p.286) offer package deals which include flights, accommodation and car rental, operating four weekly services from Brisbane. Norfolk Jet Express, affiliated with Qantas (☎13 1313), flies from Brisbane five days a week, and from Sydney six days a week.

All tourist facilities are based in the main town of **Burnt Pine**. Here, in the Bicentennial Complex on Taylors Road, you'll find the **Norfolk Island Visitor Information Centre** (☎6723/22147, fax 23109), which can book tours and activities, plus the liquor bond store (which sells discounted alcohol on production of your airline ticket), the **post office** and the Communications Centre, where you need to go to make international **phone calls**. There are two **banks** on the main street, Westpac and Commonwealth, the Commonwealth has an ATM.

Accommodation and transport

A lot of **accommodation** is in 1970s-style motels, but the island is gradually upgrading its image and now boasts some quaint, faithfully restored five-star cottages. The two most stunning places to stay are *Christians of Buck Point* (☎6723/22282, fax 23582; *christians@ni.net.nf*; ⑧), a well-renovated historic property sleeping up to six, with floorboards and wooden doors from the original convict quarters in Kingston, and *Tintoela* (☎6723/22946, fax 23376; ⑧), a large, luxury wooden house, and adjacent cottage sleeping up to ten, with panoramic views of Cockpit Valley and the ocean. Some of the more attractive motels include *Whispering Pines Luxury Cottages* on Grassy Road (☎6723/22114, fax 23014; ⑧), which offers two-bedroom units with garden views over the sea, *Shearwater Millionaire's Hideaway* (☎6723/22539, fax 23359; ⑧), offering upmarket self-contained accommodation on extensive grounds overlooking the water near Bumbora Reserve; the well-appointed *Crest Apartments*, near Kingston (☎6723/22280, fax 22977; ⑥), which have fully equipped kitchens and excellent views over to Phillip Island; and *Knobbs Apartments* (☎6723/22204, fax 23204, ⑦), in semi-bushland at the base of Mount Pitt. The *South Pacific Resort* (☎6723/23507, fax 23508; ⑦) is a recommended hotel close to Burnt Pine, with a bar, restaurant, swimming pool and pleasant green grounds.

There's no public transport on Norfolk Island, so getting around by **car** is much the best option. Many accommodation places offer a car as part of the package or give you a big discount on **car rental**. It's very cheap anyway, from just $20 per day with Norfolk Island Rent-a-Car (☎6723/22656) or Martin's (☎6723/22021). No one's bothered about seat belts or even driving mirrors, and the maximum speed limit is only 50kph (40kph in town). There are also a limited number of **bikes** for rent, which can be arranged through the tourist office, or by calling Bill's Push Bike Hire (☎6723/22551) or Wilson's Hire Service (☎02/6563 2045; $3 per day).

Tours

For **tours**, Jimbo's 4WD Tours (☎ & fax 6723/22693) are a good introduction to the island's ecology ($22), and they also offer cruises around the island; Pinetree Tours (☎6723/22422), with an office on the main street next to the Commonwealth bank, offers a slew of pricey tours including an extensive introductory half-day bus tour of the island ($20). Bounty Excursions (☎6723/23693) cover a range of cultural and historic sites, including a convict ruins tour (Mon & Thurs afternoons; $16) and a panoramic Norfolk Discovery outing (daily; 3.5hr; $18). The island is surrounded by a coral reef and pristine waters, making at least one waterborne tour a must. There are several glass-bottomed **boat cruises** on Emily Bay, including one on the *Emily Queen* (☎6723/22225; 1hr; $12) which operates at 9 and 10am. **Snorkelling** and **diving** gear – and fishing rods – are available for rent. Ask at the tourist office, or call Norfolk Land and Sea (☎6723/23418) for fishing trips, or Bounty Divers (☎6723/22751) at the Village Centre who run PADI courses and have dive charters ($65 per dive, including gear).

A pleasant way to get around is on **horseback**; try Silky Oaks (☎6723/22291; from $15 for a sunset ride), just down from the Botanic Gardens, which has its own tearoom in a shady, flower-filled garden.

Eating, drinking and entertainment

Norfolk Island **food** is plain and fresh, with an emphasis on locally caught fish and home-grown seasonal produce. Tahitian influence remains in the tradition of the big fish frys, and in some novel ways of preparing bananas. As most accommodation is self-catering, you'll want to head to the Foodland Supermarket in Burnt Pine (daily to 6pm); most of the products on the shelves are from New Zealand, and the small range of fruit and veg available reflects what is grown on the island – you won't find the variety you would else-where. On Sunday afternoon fresh fish is sold at the Kingston pier.

The **clubs** on the island provide good places to eat, drink and mingle with the locals. Facing each other across Burnt Pine's main street are the *Sports and Workers Club* (daily lunch, Mon & Sat 5.30–7pm dinner) and the *Norfolk Island Bowling Club* with a daily bar and food (lunch Sun–Fri, dinner Tues & Thurs, fish frys Wed & Sun, $10). The *Golf Club* in Kingston has a popular bar which also serves meals, while the nearby Royal Engineers Office has a café serving tea and cakes. The only **pub** is the *Brewery*, oppo-site the airport, with local ales such as "Bee Sting" and "Bligh's Revenge", pool tables and a rough, late night crowd which can be a bit intimidating for single women.

The *South Pacific Island Resort* has a big fish fry on Sunday from 6pm ($15), while on other nights an ordinary brasserie menu is available from 5.30pm. The best **restaurants** are *Branka House*, in a restored nineteenth-century homestead on Rocky Point Road near the airport (☎6723/22346; closed Sun & Mon) and *Mariah's* at Hillcrest Gardens Hotel, Taylors Road (☎6723/22255; closed Mon & Tues) for à la carte dining and a special Sunday carvery, with spectacular views of Phillip Island. *James' Place* at New Cascade Road in Burnt Pine (☎6723/23039; closed Wed) has innovative, Asian-influenced and veg-etarian dishes. A superb spot for lunch is *Café Pacifica* (☎6723/23210) on Cutters Corn Road, set in a leafy nursery and serving exquisite brunches and afternoon teas.

The island

At the centre of the island is its only significant settlement, **BURNT PINE**, a fairly mod-ern affair crammed with shops selling everything from Lancôme cosmetics through to Sanyo stereos, all at duty-free prices; most shops are closed on Wednesday and Saturday afternoons and all day Sunday. The island's information centre, banks and post office are all here – see "Practicalities", p.298.

On the south coast, contrastingly picturesque **KINGSTON** is the sightseeing focus of the island; it's also Norfolk's administrative centre, with the Legislative Assembly meeting in the military barracks, and the old colonial Government House now home to the island's Administrator. There is an excellent view from the **Queen Elizabeth Lookout** (opened by the Queen in 1974, the bicentenary year of the discovery of the island) over the **Kingston and Arthur's Vale Historic Area** and the poignant seafront **cemetery**, con-taining a number of graves from the brutal second settlement. You can wander freely around the cemetery and the grounds, which have detailed interpretive boards, but it's very expensive to visit the remaining buildings and their museums: you can tour the build-ings separately (prices given below) or with a combined ticket ($16) which allows multi-ple access to all sites spread over several days.

Quality Row bears some of the world's most impressive examples of Georgian **mili-tary architecture**, and looking at the buildings now it's difficult to imagine the suffering that took place behind their walls. Here the **Archeological Museum** (daily 1–4pm; $5), where ongoing research is carried out, is located in the basement of the former

Commissariat (1835), the upstairs of which was converted by the Pitcairners to All Saints Church. Close by, in the **House Museum** (daily 1–4pm; $5), there are examples of Norfolk pine furniture made by convicts. The worthwhile **Social History Museum** (daily 9.30am–4.30pm; $5), located in the pier store, outlines the story of the island through its three settlements. Perhaps most interesting, though, is the **Maritime Museum** (daily 9.30am–1pm; $5) in what was once the Protestant chapel; various artefacts recovered from the 1790 wreck of the *Sirius* are on display, including its huge anchor, but more compelling is the *Bounty*-related paraphernalia brought here by Pitcairners, including the ship's cannon and even the kettle that was used on Pitcairn Island for everything from fermenting liquor to boiling sea water for salt. Near the museum you can watch cargo being towed ashore to the small jetty – even cars have to come this way, as there are no wharves. The Kingston area is also the site of the sports oval, the golf course and the island's main swimming **beaches**, protected by a small reef: immediately in front of the walls of the ruined barracks, which local people use for shade and wind shelter while picnicking, is **Slaughter Bay**, which has a sandy beach dotted with interestingly gnarled and eroded basalt rock formations; the small bit of coral reef is excellent for **snorkelling**, and at low tide you can take a cruise in a glass-bottomed boat (see "Practicalities"). Nearby, the more sheltered Emily Bay is a safe swimming area, backed by a large pine forest.

In **Bumbora Reserve**, just west of Kingston, reached by car via Bumbora Road, you can see the natural regrowth of Norfolk pines; from the reserve you can walk down to Bumbora Beach, a shady little beach where you'll find some safe pools for children to swim in at low tide. There's another track down to **Crystal Pool**, which has more swimming and snorkelling.

West of Burnt Pine, along Douglas Drive, you'll find the exquisite **St Barnabas Chapel**, once the property of the Melanesian Mission (Anglican), which relocated gradually here from New Zealand between 1866 and 1921 with the aim of educating Western Pacific people in trades and education. The chapel's rose window was designed by William Morris and some other windows are by Sir Edward Burne-Jones, with the altar carved by Solomon Islanders.

On the **west coast** there's a scenic picnic area with tables and barbecues high over **Anson Bay**, from where it's a satisfying walk down to the beach. Immediately north of here, the **national park** has 8km of walking trails, many of them old logging tracks. Many walks start from **Mount Pitt** (320m), a pleasing drive up a fairly narrow and winding sealed road surrounded by palms and trees – worth it for the panoramic views. The most enjoyable walk from here is the three-kilometre route to the **Captain Cook Memorial** (1hr 45min), which starts as a beautiful grassy path but soon becomes a downward-sloping dirt track with some steps. Just south of the national park, on Pitt Road, the rainforest of the **Botanic Gardens** is worth a tranquil stroll. Here you can observe the forty endemic plant species including the pretty native hibiscus, the native palm, and the island's best-known symbol, the **Norfolk pine**, which can grow as high as 57m with a circumference of up to 11m. Both parks are permanently open, but camping is not allowed in either. The island also has an eco-tourism attraction, A Walk in the Wild, at Grassy Road (daily 2–5pm; free), educating visitors about the fragile, disappearing rainforest and its birdlife.

WEST OF THE GREAT DIVIDING RANGE

Western New South Wales is a very different proposition from the other parts of the state. For a start, there's hardly anyone living here. Beyond the Great Dividing Range are a few towns with a pioneer heritage, such as **Bathurst** and **Dubbo**, where there are still small agricultural communities and green fields; beyond them it begins to get increasingly desolate and arid, and even apparently large towns turn out to be tiny communities.

Out beyond the Blue Mountains, the **Great Western Highway** takes you as far as Bathurst; from there the **Mid-Western Highway** goes on to join the **Sturt Highway**, which heads, via Mildura on the Victorian border, to Adelaide. Any route west is eventually obliged to cross the **Newell Highway**, the direct route between Melbourne and Brisbane that cuts straight across the heart of central New South Wales. The most exciting Outback routes head north and west, though, passing through Dubbo, at the junction of the Newell and **Mitchell** highways, and then plunging into real isolation: north to **Lightning Ridge** or **Bourke** and western Queensland, or west on the **Barrier Highway**, right across the state to **Broken Hill**, almost at the South Australian border.

Bathurst, Dubbo and the central west

The gracious city of **BATHURST**, elegantly situated on the western slopes of the Great Dividing Range 209km west of Sydney, is Australia's oldest inland settlement. Its beautifully preserved nineteenth-century architecture makes it worth a weekend visit from Sydney, to browse the antique shops and mellow out in one of the city's many cafés. The settlement was first founded by Governor Macquarie in 1815, but Bathurst remained nothing more than a small convict and military settlement for years, only slowly developing into the main supply centre for the surrounding rich pastoral area. It was the discovery of **gold** nearby at the Lewis Ponds Creek at Ophir in 1851 (see p.301), and more later the same year on the Turon River, that resulted in a goldrush which changed the life of the town and the colony for ever. Soon rich fields of alluvial gold were discovered in every direction and, being the first town over the mountains for those on the way to the goldfields, Bathurst prospered and grew. The population increased dramatically: in 1885 Bathurst was proclaimed a city, and in the late 1890s it was even proposing itself (unsuccessfully) as the site for the capital of the new Commonwealth of Australia.

Although there's still the odd speck of gold and a few gemstones (especially sapphires) in the surrounding area, modern Bathurst has reverted to its role as a community in the centre of some of the richest agricultural land in New South Wales, a pastoral and fruit- and grain-growing district. It's also a tertiary education centre, with many students attending the Mitchell campus of Charles Sturt University. For anyone heading west, it's still the first stop beyond the mountains, and the gateway to the Outback. In October, visitors are also drawn to the big annual motor-racing meeting – centred around the famous **Bathurst 1000** endurance race – at the Mount Panorama Racing Circuit.

The City

Because of its cool climate – proximity to the mountains means it can be cold at night and sometimes snowy in winter – and a scattering of grand nineteenth-century buildings, the town has a very different feel to anywhere on the coast or on the baking plains further west.

Pick up a map from the modern **visitors centre** at 28 William St (daily 9am–5pm; ☎02/6332 1444) to help you find some of the stately mansions scattered around that bear testimony to Bathurst's former wealth; one of their pamphlets outlines an entertaining self-guided walk through the historic city centre. The old **courthouse** on Russell Street, built in 1880, makes a good place to start exploring, and there's also an interesting little **museum** tucked away in the east wing (Tues, Wed & Sun 10am–4pm, Sat 9.30am–4.30pm, or by appointment ☎02/6332 4755; $1), which displays relics and archives of regional pioneer history along with some interesting Aboriginal artefacts.

The **Regional Gallery**, 70 Keppel St (Mon–Fri 10am–5pm, Sat 10am–1pm & 2–5pm, Sun 2–5pm; free), is a fine provincial art gallery which has a very good ceramic collection and paintings by Lloyd Rees, as well as regular special and travelling exhibitions. **Machattie Park**, further north up Keppel Street, on the corner of William Street, offers a chance to relax amid landscaped Victorian-era gardens with duck ponds and spreading shady trees; there's also a Fern House, and a Begonia House which has an impressive display from mid-February to Easter. Look out, too, for **Ben Chifley's Cottage** at 10 Busby St (Mon–Sat 2–4pm, Sun 10am–noon; $2.50), once the residence of Bathurst's most famous son, who was born to a blacksmith and his wife in south Bathurst in 1885, and was Prime Minister of Australia between 1945 and 1949.

Further afield, a drive up to **Mount Panorama** and its famous racing circuit provides, as you might expect, panoramic views of the city: there's the **National Motor-Racing Museum** on Pit Straight (daily 9am–4.30pm; $5), at the beginning of the racing circuit, featuring famous racing cars and bikes, along with photographs and memorabilia from the races. **Sir Joseph Banks's Nature Park** (daily 9am–3.30pm; $3) occupies the summit of the hill, enabling native birds and animals, including wallabies, kangaroos and koalas, to enjoy the vistas from a large area of bushland; the visitors centre houses an aquarium and a reptile collection. Not far away, the **Bathurst Gold Fields** on Conrod Straight (Mon–Fri 10am–4pm; guided tours $8 ☎02/6332 2022), a reconstruction of a former gold-mining area, are worth a visit if you're not going to make it to one of the actual gold towns further out. Goldrush mining methods are demonstrated and explained, and you can even take individual lessons in gold-panning. A bit further out, the **Bathurst Sheep and Cattle Drome** on Limekilns Road, 8km northeast of the city, has an educational and entertaining show (daily at 11.30am, extra shows during school holidays; $10, children $6; ☎02/6337 3634 for details) covering everything you always wanted to know about sheepshearing and milking cows.

Practicalities

Accommodation is relatively expensive here, but try the *Park Hotel* at the corner of George and Keppel streets (☎02/6331 3399; ④) for comfortable B&B and motel-style units. There are a dozen or more motels along the highway, as well as holiday units at *Rossmore Park Farm Holidays*, at the Bathurst Sheep and Cattle Drome (see above; ☎02/6337 3634, fax 6337 3441; ⑥), and **camping** at *East Bathurst Holiday Park*, on the highway in Kelso, 5km east (☎02/6331 8286; on-site vans and cabins ③). One budget option is the *Family Hotel* on the corner of Bentick and Russell streets (☎02/6334 2414; ①), which is clean and cheap, but the pub below features topless girls on Thursday and Friday nights. Otherwise the *Edinboro Castle* at 134 William St (☎02/6331 5020; ③) has reasonably-priced singles and doubles as does the nearby *Knickerbox Hotel* at 110 William St (☎02/6332 4500; ③–④) which also includes breakfast. For a splurge, the best suites are at the lavish *Royal Hotel* at 108 William St (☎02/6332 4920, fax 6332 3132; ⑦), the town's jewel-in-the-crown heritage building. The owners also rent other properties in Bathurst, including the cute *David Jones Cottage* which sleeps up to eight people (④–⑦).

There's a variety of **restaurants** in the city centre, including Thai, Indian and modern Australian cuisine. Most of the town's pubs also serve counter meals or have bistros at the back. The *Yoga Tandoori House* at 94 Bentick St (☎02/6332 3320; lunch Mon & Wed–Sat, dinner daily) has an extensive selection of curries including many veggie ones. For à la carte dining, try *Lamplighters* at 126 William St (☎02/6331 1448; closed Sun) with blackboard specials and old world charm. In a similar vein, *Vines Cottage* at 142 William St (☎02/6331 6470; closed Sun) has some more unusual fare, including dishes like kangaroo in port and blackberry sauce. In the *Royal Hotel* building, the *Heritage Royal Coffee House* has superb coffee and cakes, while *Crêpes Royale* serves French-inspired dishes from morning tea, to dinner (closed Mon). *Zegelers*

Café at 52 Keppel St (☎02/6332 1565), close to the train station, has good lunches in a leafy courtyard and cosy, candlelight dinners in the evening.

Due to the presence of so many students, Bathurst has a reasonable **nightlife**, centering mainly on the pubs close to the univeristy. Particularly popular is the *Oxford Tavern* on the corner of William and Piper streets, opposite the enormous *Leagues Club*. Friday is club night, featuring guest DJs at the *Site* on George Street ($6 entry).

Around Bathurst

The area **around Bathurst**, heading towards the Mudgee wine country, is dotted with semi-derelict villages and ghost towns dating back to the goldrushes of the nineteenth century. A scenic drive to the north via Peel and Wattle Flat leads to the tiny, picturesque village of **SOFALA**, 35km north of Bathurst on the Turon River, en route to Mudgee. Gold was found in the river here in 1851, just three weeks after the very first gold strikes in Australia, and today the narrow, winding main street still follows the course of the river. A good spot for a drink is the *Sofala Royal Hotel*, a classic wooden pub with a big balcony; they also offer meals, and **rooms** (☎02/6337 7008; ④) with a period flavour. There's basic **tent** space at the *Village Camping Area* on Clarke Street (☎02/6337 8206).

From Sofala, a very narrow, bone-rattling unsealed road follows the Turon River towards **HILL END**, an even more important goldrush site located on a plateau above the Turon Valley, 86km from Bathurst. In 1870, Hill End was the largest inland centre in New South Wales, a booming gold-mining town with a population of about twenty thousand, with 53 hotels, plus all the accoutrements of a wealthy settlement. Within ten years, however, gold production had faltered and Hill End had already become a virtual ghost town. It stayed that way until 1967, when the area was proclaimed a historic site and huge efforts were made to restore and preserve the town. You can pick up a leaflet at the NPWS **visitors centre** in the old hospital (daily 9.30am–12.30pm & 1.30–4.30pm; ☎02/6337 8206), where there is also a small museum ($2), and take a self-guided walk around the village, or rent some equipment and try your hand at panning or fossicking. There's an underground **mine tour** daily at 1pm ($4.50) and a gold-panning tour at 11am ($3). You can **stay** in the *Royal Motel* here (☎02/6337 8261, fax 6337 8393; ③) and **eat** in the restaurant. There is also a B&B, as well as **camping** areas run by the NPWS.

Another enjoyable excursion, this time to the south, takes in the former gold-mining towns of Rockley, 35km south of Bathurst, and Trunkey Creek, and then continues to the spectacular **Abercrombie Caves**, 72km south of Bathurst in the middle of a large nature reserve. The principal and most impressive cavern, the **Grand Arch** (self-guided tours daily 9am–4pm, $10), is 221m long, about 39m wide at the north and south entrances, and in some places over 30m high – it's said to be the largest natural limestone arch in the southern hemisphere. More than eighty other caves are dotted around the reserve. In one of them, miners constructed a dance floor more than a century ago, and concerts or church services are still held here occasionally. Also within the reserve are old gold mines, and swimming holes in **Grove Creek**, which runs right through the reserve, plunging more than 70m over the Grove Creek Falls at the southern edge. There's a **camping area** on the shore (☎02/6368 8603; cabins ③; blankets and pillows included), complete with a public fossicking ground.

Mudgee and the wine country

The large old country town of **MUDGEE**, in the Kamilaroi language meaning "the nest in the hills", is the centre for an often-overlooked wine region about 120km north of Bathurst. The town is set along the lush banks of the Cugewong River, and the countryside appears to have more grazing cows and sheep than vineyards. The wines, once referred to as "Mudgee mud", have improved in the past few years: the Cabernet

MUDGEE WINERIES SIX OF THE BEST

Botolabar, Botolabar Lane (Mon–Sat 10am–5pm, Sun 10am–3pm; ☎02/6373 3840). An organic winery with self-guided tours (40min). Tastings on a shady terrace; picnic area and barbecues.

Craigmoor Winery, Craigmoor Road (Mon–Sat 10am–4.30pm, Sun 10am–4pm; ☎02/6372 2208). The original 1859 cellar, a vast space with a huge open fireplace, has a tin roof held up by tree-trunk beams. Upstairs is an equally characterful, expensive restaurant (daily lunch, Fri & Sat dinner), while outside, views of hills and vineyards are fronted by peaceful lawns fragrant with flowers and a perfect cricket pitch.

Lawson Hill Estate, Lawson Hill Drive (daily 9.30am–5pm; ☎02/6373 3953). A small, family-owned winery above the Henry Lawson memorial, on the site of the Australian poet's boyhood home. Friendly, low-key tasting is in the hilltop tin shed where the wine is made.

Miramar Wines, Henry Lawson Drive (daily 9am–5pm; ☎02/6373 3874). Atmospheric tastings among old cobwebbed casks. The well-respected wine maker, Ian MacRae, established the winery in 1977; he's serious about his wines, and specializes in delicious whites.

Montrose Winery, Henry Lawson Drive (daily 10am–4.30pm; ☎02/6373 3883). The largest and best known of Mudgee's wineries: particularly for its Poets Corner, a good table red, and its prize-winning Chardonnays, Cabernets and Shiraz. The modern white, brick building covered in ivy has picnic tables outside and beautiful views.

Pieter Van Gent, Black Springs Road (Mon–Sat 9am–5pm, Sun 11am–4pm; ☎02/6373 3807). Tastings in a delightful setting: beautiful nineteenth-century choir stalls on cool earth floors, overshadowed by huge old barrels salvaged from Penfolds. Try their Pipeclay Port, a tawny port aged in wood, a blend of various vintages. The winemaker is Dutch, and the herbs he uses in his traditional vermouth are specially imported from Holland.

Sauvignon and Shiraz wines are the tastiest, although the area's Chardonnays are gaining a good reputation. You can reach Mudgee via Hill End, but it's a bumpy unsealed route, and you're better off approaching via Sofala on an 88-kilometre sealed road (except for a small section) – watch out for sheep.

When you arrive, head for the **tourist information centre** at 84 Market St (Mon–Fri 9am–5pm, Sat 9am–3.30pm, Sun 9.30am–2pm; ☎02/6372 5875) to pick up a copy of the *Mudgee Region Visitors' Guide*, which has detailed winery information and maps. Mudgee's proximity to Sydney means that **accommodation** is booked out at weekends, when it's best to call in advance. Some suggestions are the central *Woolpack Hotel* at 67 Market St (☎02/6372 1908, fax 6372 6782; ②), with mediocre shared-bathroom pub rooms; the more upmarket but equally central *Wanderlight Motor Inn*, 107 Market St (☎02/6372 1088, fax 6372 2859; ⑤), which has a pool and spa and some units adapted for disabled travellers; and the *Parkview Guest House*, 99 Market St (☎02/6372 4477; ⑦), a quiet, centrally located B&B built in 1859. Other heritage houses worth staying at for the charm factor include *Bleak House*, 7 Lawson St (☎02/6372 3030; ⑦) with private verandahs overlooking the Cugewong River, and the *Lauralla Historic Guesthouse*, Lewis and Mortimer streets (☎02/6372 4480, fax 6372 3320; ⑦) a classic Victorian-style home offering "murder mystery" and wine weekends. **Campers** should go to the *Cooinda Caravan Village*, corner of Bell Street and Gulgong Road, 1.5km west of the centre (☎02/6372 1236), which has a pool, kiosk and barbecues. Mudgee isn't really a town in which to eat out, so your best bet for a meal is the **pub food** at places such as the *Lawson Park Hotel*, a great old country pub on Church Street, which does roasts on Monday and Tuesday and pasta specials on Wednesday night for $6–7. You could also lunch at one of the wineries such as Craigmoor (see box above); or try *Renditions* (Wed–Sun only), the new tearooms attached to the *Parkview Guest House*, for refreshments on the verandah or in the courtyard.

Orange, Forbes and Parkes

ORANGE, on the Mitchell Highway en route from Bathurst to Dubbo, is a small city on the eastern slopes of Mount Canabolas; coming from Bathurst, the drive is a pleasant one through undulating countryside, with the valley opening up before you. Orange is a pretty place full of trees, including many European varieties; it claims to have four distinct seasons, and the chilly winter always sees one or two snowfalls. Its major industry is **apple growing**, based in the apple orchards southwest of the town. You can find apple-picking **work** here from late February or early March for a period of about six weeks, while cherry picking takes place from late November to early January; contact the Employment National (☎13 3444). Many growers have rough accommodation on their properties but demand often outstrips supply, so bring a tent. The **Orange Visitors Centre** on Byng Street (Mon–Fri 9am–5pm, Sat & Sun 9am–4pm; ☎02/6361 5226) has information on local attractions, which include the **Ophir diggings**. The first gold field in Australia, established in 1851 and only 30km north of Orange, the site is still much as the diggers left it – beware of open shafts.

Orange prides itself on being rather cosmopolitan, and it has quite a **café** society and some well-regarded **restaurants**. Try *Scottys* at 202a Summer St, which prepares gourmet sandwiches; *Union Bank Café* at 84 Byng St, which has a good range of vegetarian dishes; *Beau's on Byng*, further up the street at no. 123 (three courses for $25; BYO; closed Sun & Mon), a restaurant featuring local produce; or *Café 48*, 48 Sale St (BYO), for its praiseworthy Southeast Asian curries. A recommended place both to **stay** and eat is the *Metropolitan Hotel* at 107 Byng St (☎02/6362 1353, fax 6361 3806; ④), just up from the tourist office. It's a huge old-fashioned country pub built in 1872, with a wooden verandah where you can sit and eat barbecued dishes, hot potatoes, damper and salad. Rooms are clean and nicely decorated, and all have TV but no ensuite facilities. Pickers could consider the two **caravan parks**, both a few kilometres from the centre; to the north, the *Colour City Caravan Park* on Margaret Street (☎02/6362 7254; cabins ③); and to the east, the *Canabolas Caravan Park*, 166 Bathurst Rd (☎02/6362 7279; cabins ③).

Forming a triangle, with Orange at the apex, Forbes and Parkes to the west are also important regional towns. **FORBES**, on the Lachlan River, is a graceful old town famous as the stomping ground of the nineteenth-century bushranger **Ben Hall**, who is buried in the Forbes Cemetery. **PARKES**, 33km to the northwest along the Newell Highway, is well known for its **Observatory** which has a 64-metre radio telescope. The observatory's **visitors centre** (daily 8.30am–4.15pm; free) has a half-hour audiovisual presentation, The Invisible Universe (daily 8.30am–3.30pm; every 30min; $3).

Cowra

COWRA, on the banks of the Lachlan River, 107km southwest of Bathurst along the Mid-Western Highway, is famous as the location of the **Cowra Breakout** during World War II. The breakout of August 5, 1944 saw the escape of 378 Japanese prisoners of war armed with baseball bats, staves, homemade clubs and sharpened kitchen knives – those who were sick and remained behind hanged or disembowelled themselves, unable to endure the disgrace of capture. It took nine days to recapture all the prisoners, during which four Australian soldiers and 231 Japanese died. The breakout was little known until the publication of Harry Gordon's excellent 1970s account *Die Like the Carp* (recently republished as *Voyage of Shame*; see "Books", p.1024).

You can see the site of the prisoner-of-war camp, now just ruins and fields, on Sakura Avenue on the northeast edge of town. The graves of the Japanese, who were buried in Cowra, were well cared for by members of the local Returned Servicemen's League, a humanitarian gesture which touched Japanese embassy officials who then broached the idea of an official **Japanese War Cemetery**. Designed by Shigeru Yura, the tranquil burial ground is further north, on Doncaster Drive. The theme of Japanese–Australian friendship and reconciliation continued in Cowra with the establishment of the **Japanese Garden** (daily 8.30am–5pm; $6) in 1979 with funding from Japanese and Australian governments and companies. The large garden, designed by the internationally known Ken Nakajima to represent the landscape of Japan, is set on a hill overlooking the town, on a scenic drive running north off Kendal Street, the main thoroughfare. Cherry and other flowering trees blossom and their leaves change colour with the autumn, mirroring the northern hemisphere's change of seasons. It's very peaceful and idyllic here: cooling on a hot day, with the shade and the sound of the stream burbling through the garden. A further anti-war symbol in Cowra is the **World Peace Bell** in Civic Square; and the planting of an avenue of cherry trees connecting the war cemeteries, the POW campsite and the Japanese Garden. The introduction of the **POW Theatre**, at the Cowra Vistors Centre, is another attraction explaining the war years, the breakout and the reconciliation process since then.

For more information on the town, and **accommodation** options if you want to stay, head for the very helpful **Cowra Visitors Centre**, at the corner of Grenfell and Borowa roads on the Mid-Western Highway (daily 9am–5pm; ☎02/6342 4333), near the large riverside park. There are lots of **vineyards** in the Cowra area – actually more than in Mudgee – but no wineries; instead, grapes are sent off to large wineries elsewhere to be made into wine. Their origin is often revealed by their names, such as Richmond Grove Cowra Wine. The region is best known for Chardonnay: to taste the product of the local grapes, head for the Quarry Cellar, 5km from Cowra on the Boorowa Road (☎02/6342 3650; closed Mon); the attached restaurant (Thurs–Sat dinner) also does Devonshire teas and inexpensive light lunches of pasta and salads. If you're interested in the possibility of some **grape-picking** work, contact the Employment National (☎13 3444).

Young

Seventy kilometres southwest of Cowra along the Olympic Way, the hilly town of YOUNG is a good spot to pick up some **cherry-picking** work during the season (approximately six weeks from the first week of November). Being monotonous rather than strenuous, the work attracts a genteel crowd and is popular with retired Queenslanders. If you just want to pick your own and have a look at some orchards and packing sheds, there are a number of them on the way into town from Cowra; you could also contact the Employment National on Boorowa Street (☎02/6382 3366). The long weekend in October generally coincides with the time when the **cherry blossoms** are in full bloom – a glorious sight. There's even a Cherry Festival each year, in late November/early December. There are also several vineyards on the slopes of the undulating area, which is becoming known as the Hilltops wine region; one worth visiting is the small, family-run **Woodonga Hill Winery**, 10km north of Young on the Olympic Way (daily 9am–5pm; ☎02/6382 2972).

Young also has some significance as the site of the notorious **Lambing Flat Riots**, described in every Australian history book. A former gold-mining centre known then as Lambing Flats, the town was the site of racist riots against Chinese miners in June 1861. As the gold ran out, European miners resented what they saw as the greater success of the more industrious Chinese. Troops had to be called in when the Chinese were chased violently from the diggings, beaten, their pigtails cut off, and their property destroyed. Carried at the head of the mob was a flag, painted on a tent flysheet, with the Southern Cross in the centre, and "Roll Up, Roll Up, No Chinese" lettered in the manner of a circus flyer. You can see the original flag, and other exhibits relating to the riots, in the **Lambing Flat Folk Museum** (daily 10am–4pm; $2), located on the Olympic Way, just south of Boorowa Street. For more information, including lists of accommodation and where to eat, contact the **Young Visitors Centre**, 2 Short St (Mon–Fri 9am–5pm, Sat & Sun 10am–4pm; ☎02/6382 3394). A recommended **farmstay** outside town is *Old Nubba School House* (☎02/6943 2513; ⑤–⑥), halfway between Young and Cootamundra on the Olympic Highway; the peaceful self-contained accommodation, a former schoolhouse in the grounds of the friendly family farm, sleeps up to six and breakfast provisions are included.

Dubbo

DUBBO, an Aboriginal word meaning "red earth", is a self-styled "Wild West" country city on the banks of the Macquarie River, 420km northwest of Sydney and about 200km from Bathurst. The regional capital for the west of the state, it supports many agricultural industries and is located at a vital crossroads where the Melbourne–Brisbane **Newell Highway** meets the **Mitchell Highway** and routes west to Bourke or Broken Hill.

As such, it's well used to people passing through, but not staying long. If you do stop, drop by the **Western Plains Zoo** on Obley Road, 5km south of town off the Newell Highway (daily 9am–5pm $16; keeper talks Sat, Sun & school holidays at 10.30am, 11.30am, 1.30pm, 2pm & 3pm; 2hr zoo walks Sun at 6.45am, $2.50 plus zoo admission). If you're planning on visiting more than one attraction in Dubbo, then a "ZooPlusII" pass ($22) available from the Visitors Centre is a worthwhile investment, allowing you entry to three sites. The vast, open-range zoo features expansive landscaped habitats, through which many Australian animals are free to roam; other animals from five continents are kept in natural surroundings, separated from the public by moats or creeks rather than fences wherever possible. The zoo is crisscrossed by walking and cycling paths: especially during the hot months, the best idea is to get up early in the morning and set off early – by noon, the temperatures can become unbearable and the animals sometimes slink off out of sight into the shade. There is no public transport to the zoo, so cycling there, and around the zoo itself, is a good option: Wheeler Cycles, 193 Brisbane St (☎02/6882 9899), rents out bikes; electronic carts and bikes can also be rented at the zoo itself ($8 for 4-hour bike hire). If you prefer to walk, there's a pleasant cycle track following the river which takes around an hour on foot from the city centre. Otherwise, Langley's Dubbo Day Tours (☎02/6884 5333) do pricey escorted bus tours (Wed & Sun 9.30am–1.30pm; $40 including pick-up from accommodation), or you can take a taxi (Radio Cabs ☎13 1008).

The state's largest **Livestock Market**, 3km north out of town on the Newell Highway, auctions sheep and cattle every Monday, Thursday and Friday (unloading from 8.30am). It's worth a visit just to see the local farmers decked out authentically in their Akubra hats and Drizabone coats, and to get the authentic smell of country life. The YHA gives lifts to the market to its guests on request.

If you have another hour to spare, head for the **Old Dubbo Gaol** on Macquarie Street in the centre of town (daily 9am–4.30pm; $5). A hundred years ago, this fortress-style building housed some of the most notorious criminals of the west, and today it glories in the details of nineteenth-century prison life, with loving attention to the macabre: the gallows, the hangman's kit and the careers of some of those who were executed here. In the cells, life-size (and convincingly lifelike) animatronic models of convicted criminals tell the stories of their lives and condemned futures.

The **Dubbo Museum** at 234 Macquarie St (daily 10am–4.30pm; $5) has an extensive and somewhat chequered collection of items of regional history. There are agricultural and transport exhibits, a colonial kitchen, musical instruments, a dentist's surgery and the re-creation of a village square complete with drapery store, bootmaker, barber and blacksmith. Also worth a look-in is the National Trust property **Dundullimal Homestead** (daily 9am–5pm), 2km past the zoo on Obley Road. An 1840s slab house with stone stables, it now houses a craft shop and mini farm, and you can sometimes see the odd cowboy riding oxen rodeo-style. A visit here is best combined with a "hayride" on a truck and cruise on the Macquarie River, stopping in at the property for afternoon teas. Tours cost $15, bookable through the visitors centre.

The Dubbo **Regional Gallery** at 165 Darling St (Tues–Sun 11am–4.30pm) has a kitsch collection of animals represented in art, including, suprisingly, an exceptional painting of a fox by the noted Australian artist Arthur Boyd. They also have a rotating cultural programme, including indigenous works at times.

Practicalities

As it's a crossroads, Dubbo's 24-hour **bus** terminal, on the corner of Erskine and Darling streets, is busy with daily connections to Brisbane, Sydney, Melbourne and Adelaide, and buses three times a week to Canberra and Newcastle. Just across the railway line is the **train station**, terminal for the XPT to and from Sydney. Countrylink buses leave here for Bourke and Lightning Ridge. You can also **fly** to Dubbo with Hazelton (☎13 1713) and Eastern Australia (☎13 1313) from Sydney; Hazelton also flies to Broken Hill from here, and Air Link (☎02/6884 2435) has other Outback/northwest connections: to Bourke, Brewarrina, Cobar, Coonamble, Lightning Ridge, Nyngan and Walgett. Dubbo Rent-a-Car (☎02/6884 2800) rents vehicles from $30 a day. The helpful **Dubbo Visitors Centre** (daily 9am–5pm; ☎02/6884 1422) is set in a riverside park at the corner of Erskine and Macquarie streets, just off the Newell Highway. As well as giving out good free maps and information, the centre sells discounted "ZooPlusII" tickets.

As you'd expect there are plenty of **motels**, with the majority on the Mitchell Highway (called Cobra Street as it passes through town). A couple of the better-value ones are the *Merino Motel*, 65 Church St, 200m south of the city centre (☎02/6882 4133; ④), and the *Across Country Motel*, on the corner of the Newell Highway and Baird Street (☎02/6882 0877, fax 6882 0480; ⑤). Two old **hotels** downtown offer a bit more character: the rowdy *Civic Hotel*, on the corner of Tabralgar and Darling streets (☎02/6882 3688; ③), has the cheapest rooms in town, or there's the more civilized *Castlereagh Hotel*, on the corner of Brisbane and Tabralgar streets (☎02/6882 4877; ③). The most salubrious pub-hotel in town is the *Amaroo Hotel*, 83 Macquarie St (☎02/6882 3533, fax 6884 2601; ⑤), which has renovated rooms and includes a cooked breakfast. *Mayfair Cottage*, 10 Baird St (☎02/6882 5226; ⑥), is a good choice, and has a separate guest wing and a pool. The *Dubbo YHA Hostel*, at 87 Brisbane St (☎02/6882 0922; rooms ②, dorms ①), is a cosy and welcoming family-run hostel within walking distance of the train station and the city centre; they also rent bikes ($6) and sell discounted zoo tickets. **Campsites** include *Dubbo City Caravan Park* on Whylandra Street, 2km west (☎02/6882 4820; cabins ③–④, on-site vans ②), and *Poplars Caravan Park*, overlooking the river near the city centre on Lower Bultje Street (☎02/6882 4067; cabins ③, on-site vans ②).

Dubbo has developed a bit of a **café society**. The self-consciously trendy *Echidna Café*, 177 Macquarie St, serves expensive contemporary Australian cuisine, but you can just drop in for an excellent coffee. The *Grapevine Café*, 144 Brisbane St, is more low-key – a relaxing place with generous portions and breakfast served until noon at the weekend. For fresh bread and cakes, try the *Village Hot Bake* on Darling Street, by the railway station, a bustling bakery on two levels, also serving pies, fries and pizzas. If you crave the usual country-town fare, the *Amaroo Hotel* has the best **bistro** in Dubbo. There are also several **restaurants** at the bottom end of the main shopping area, including the recommended *Darbar* at 215 Macquarie St (☎02/6884 4338), a tandoori house located in an old sandstone basement.

The Northwest

From Dubbo the **Newell Highway**, the main route from Melbourne to Brisbane, continues through the wheat plains of the northwest, their relentless flatness relieved by the ancient eroded mountain ranges of the **Warrumbungles**, near Coonabarabran, and **Mount Kaputar**, near Narrabri, with the **Pillaga Scrub** between the two towns. Clear skies and the lack of large towns with their attendant lights make the area ideal for the **telescopes** that stare into space at both Coonabarabran and Narrabri. The thinly populated northwest has a relatively large percentage of Aborigines, peaking in the largest town of **Moree**. In 1971 Charles Perkins, an Aboriginal activist, led the **Freedom Ride**, a group of thirty people – mostly university students – who bussed through New South Wales on a mission to root out racism in the state. The biggest victory was in Moree itself when the riders, facing hostile townsfolk, broke the race bar by escorting Aboriginal children into the public swimming pool.

The **Namoi Valley** – extending from Gunnedah, just west of Tamworth, to Walgett – with its rich black soil, is **cotton country**. Beyond Walgett, just off the sealed Castlereagh Highway that runs from Dubbo, is **Lightning Ridge**, a scorching-hot opal-mining town relieved by the hot **artesian bore baths** which are a feature of the northwest.

Coonabarabran and the Warrumbungles

COONABARABRAN is a touristy little town on the Castlereagh River, 160km north of Dubbo via the Newell Highway, and 465km northwest of Sydney. People come here for bushwalking and climbing in the spectacular Warrumbungles, an ancient mountain range 35km to the west, to gaze at stars in the clear skies, and to bring their dinosaur-fixated children to look at giant tacky models of the prehistoric beasts.

By virtue of its proximity to the **Siding Spring Observatory Complex** (daily 9am–4pm; $5), perched high above the township on the edge of the Warrumbungle National Park, Coonabarabran considers itself the astronomy capital of Australia. The skies are exceptionally clear out here, due to the dry climate and a lack of pollution and population. The giant 3.9-metre optical telescope (one of the largest in the world) can be viewed close up from an observation gallery, and there's an astronomy exhibition, complemented by hands-on exhibits and a video show. There's no public transport here, but the school bus passes by – ask at the visitors centre (see below). You can't actually view the stars at Siding Spring, but the **Skywatch Observatory** (daily 2–10pm; book before dusk on ☎02/6842 2506) on Timor Road, 2km from town on the way to the Warrumbungles, has night viewing through its modern telescope, plus a planetarium and computer space-simulation programs.

More down-to-earth attractions are on offer at **Crystal Kingdom** on the Newell Highway just north of the town centre (daily 8am–5pm; $2), where there's a display of Warrumbungle minerals including a sparkling crystal cave, and at **Miniland** theme park (daily 9am–5.30pm; $10), on the way to the Warrumbungles. The main attractions at the latter are the life-size animated **dinosaurs**, but there are also birds and animals, a playground with paddle boats and bumper cars, a mural of the Warrumbungles, and a fantasy Stone-Age trail through the complex.

Warrumbungle National Park

The rugged **Warrumbungles** are ancient mountains of volcanic origin with jagged cliffs, rocky pinnacles and crags jutting from the western horizon. The dry western plains and the more moist environment of the east coast meet at these ranges, with plant and animal species from both habitats coexisting in the park. Warrumbungle means "crooked mountains" in an Aboriginal language, and the park was in fact bordered by three different language groups – the Kamilaroi, the Weilwan and Kawambarai. Evidence of Aborigines' past visits is common, with stone flakes used to make tools indicating old campsites. The **Warrumbungle National Park** is spectacular, especially in spring when the wild flowers in the sandstone areas are in bloom. The most popular months with visitors are April, September and October: it's really just too hot for walking here in summer, and the cold winters sometimes bring snow. If you do come in the hot months, remember to take plenty of water when you go walking, and something warm for the nights, which get quite cool.

The **visitors centre**, at John Street, (daily 8.30am–4pm; ☎02/6842 1441) has hands-on displays and detailed maps of walking tracks. The wheelchair-accessible bitumen **Gurianawa Track** makes a short circuit around the centre and overlooks the flats where Eastern Grey Kangaroos gather at dusk. Another good introduction to the park is the short **White Gum Lookout Walk** (1km), with panoramic views over the ranges that are particularly dramatic at sunset. However, the ultimate – for the reasonably fit only – is the 14.5-kilometre **Grand High Tops Trail** along the main ridge and back. The walk begins at the kangaroo-filled Camp Pincham and follows the flat floor of Spirey Creek through open forests full of colourful rosellas and lorikeets, and lizards basking on rocks. As the trail climbs, there are views of the three-hundred-metre-high Belougery Spire, and more scrambling gets you to the foot of the **Breadknife**, the park's most famous feature, thrusting 90m up into the sky. From here the main track heads on to the rocky slabs of the Grand High Tops, with tremendous views of most of the surrounding peaks and with the possibility of spotting a wedge-tailed eagle soaring above. Experienced walkers could carry on to climb Bluff Mountain and then head west for Mount Exmouth (1205m), the park's highest peak; both are great spots from which to watch the sunrise. The Warrumbungles are very popular with **rock climbers**, who are allowed to climb anywhere except the Breadknife; permits are required. There isn't any public transport to the Warrumbungles.

Practicalities

Coonabarabran's **visitors centre** on John Street (daily 9am–5pm; ☎02/6842 1441) has tourist information and can book accommodation and tours such as **scenic flights** over the Warrumbungles ($55 for 30min, minimum of two) and special visits to out-of-the-way places, including Aboriginal sites, with Coona Country Tours (from $80 per person).

Accommodation in the national park itself is limited to **campsites**, some of which have hot showers, electric barbecues and fireplaces (note that wood is not supplied, and there's a fine for collecting it in the park), while others are more basic. Bookings aren't necessary for any of the sites, but you will need to bring provisions. Between the park and Coonabarabran, the *Warrumbungles Mountain Motel* on Timor Road, 19km from town (☎02/6842 1832, fax 6842 2944; ④), is set in bushland on the Castlereagh River. Rooms have extra bunks and kitchens, so are good for families or small groups; there's also a small saltwater pool and a playing field. Also along Timor Road (16km from town), nestled under Bulleamble Mountain, is the *Tibuc* farm (☎02/6842 1740; ②–⑤), where self-contained cabins here vary from quite to extremely basic; there are reductions for longer stays. There are plenty of alternatives in town: the *All Travellers Motor Inn* on John Street (☎02/6842 1133, fax 6842 2505; ④–⑥), with air-conditioning and disabled-accessible rooms, or the *Imperial Hotel* (☎02/6842 1023; ③) and the *Royal Hotel* (☎02/6842 1816; ③) on the same street. Along the Oxley Highway you'll find the *Wayfarer Caravan Park* (☎02/6842 1773; cabins ③, on-site vans ②) and the shady *John Oxley Caravan Park* (☎02/6842 1635; cabins ③, on-site vans ②).

Good **places to eat** in town are all on John Street. The bright and airy *Jolly Cauli*, at no. 30, has a wide choice of dishes, delicious coffee and homemade cakes. *The Lunch Box* does inexpensive midday meals, the *Imperial Hotel* has the best counter meals, and the *Golden Sea Dragon* serves up reliable Chinese food.

The Namoi Valley: cotton country

On the Oxley Highway, 76km west of the New England city of Tamworth, **GUNNEDAH**, with a population of over eight thousand, is one of the largest towns in the northwest. The town's claim to fame is as the inspiration for the Australian poet Dorothea MacKellar (1885–1968) and her patriotic verse *My Country*, in which she pledged her undying love for what was then – and still is now – a drought-stricken land. The opening stanza is familiar to most Australians, who learnt it by rote at school:

> *I love a sunburnt country*
> *A land of sweeping plains*
> *Of ragged mountain ranges*
> *Of drought and flooding rains...*

Gunnedah has one of the healthiest **koala populations** in the state: your best chance of spotting one, wedged high in the trees, is from the Bindea Walking Track that starts at the **information centre** in Anzac Park (Mon–Fri 9am–5pm; ☎02/6742 4300). Should you want to stay, try the *Billabong* **motel** on Conadilly Street (☎02/6742 2033; ④), by the main shopping centre – it's handy and economical, with well-equipped, air-conditioned rooms and a swimming pool. The nearest **caravan park** is 1km east of town on Henry Street (☎02/6742 1372; cabins and on-site vans ②). Besides the usual pub bistros you can **eat** in more style at *Sabatinas Italian Restaurant* at the *Regal Hotel* or at *Mackellar Restaurant* at the *Overlander Motel* which offers basic, good value meals.

While Gunnedah does have some cotton crops, **NARRABRI**, 97km northwest via the oddly named communities of Boggabri and Baan Baa, is recognized as the commercial centre of cotton growing. A little smaller than Gunnedah, the town has a prosperous feel. The **tourist information centre**, on Tibbereena Street (Mon–Fri 9am–1pm & 2–5pm, Sat & Sun 9am–noon; ☎02/6792 3583), can give you the times to go and see the five linked dishes of the **Australia Telescope** complex, 24km west on the Yarrie Lake Road. Opening times depend on what they're tracking, but the centre is staffed Monday to Friday from 8am to 4pm, entry is free and there are lots of computer models to play with. The other main attraction around Narrabri is **Mount Kaputar National Park**. The drive into the park to the 1524-metre **lookout** – with its panoramic views encompassing the vast Pillaga Scrub, the Warrumbungles and the New England Tablelands – is steep, narrow and unsealed (call ☎02/6792 1147 for road conditions). There are eleven marked bushwalking trails in the park, with brochures available from the **NPWS office** in Narrabri at 165 Maitland St (☎02/6792 4724), or the **visitors centre** at **Dawsons Spring** campsite and picnic area, although the latter is not permanently staffed. The **camping** facilities at *Dawsons Spring* include hot showers, and there are a couple of cabins with bathroom, kitchen and wood stove (reservations via NPWS on ☎02/6792 4724; ③). The most striking geological feature of the park is **Sawn Rocks**, a basalt formation which looks like a series of organ pipes; it's reached via the northern end of the park on the unsealed road heading to Bingara.

If you want to **stay** in Narrabri itself, or **eat** something, the *Club House Hotel*, 87 Maitland St (☎02/6792 2027; ③), fits the bill on both counts, with a decent Italian restaurant (Tues–Sat dinner only) upstairs, and plainer pub meals downstairs. For a snack, Watson's Bakery on Maitland Street serves good-quality pies and sandwiches to take away.

The drive from Narrabri to **WEE WAA**, roughly 40km west, warns of your entry into redneck territory – the roadside glitters with shattered bottles thrown from speeding cars. Wee Waa was where the Namoi cotton industry began in the 1960s, and the large cotton "gins" or processing plants are located here. During the picking and growing season (April–July) free guided tours leave Namoi Co-op (daily 10.30am & 2.30pm; 1hr 30min–3hr 30min), but you'll need your car to get around the various areas. If you can stand the rather raw, dispirited town and the blazing summer heat, there's **cotton-chipping** work here in abundance in December and January; ask at one of the two pubs on Rose Street, the main drag, and someone will send you in the right direction. From Wee Waa you can head west to Walgett and on to Lightning Ridge.

Lightning Ridge

The population of **LIGHTNING RIDGE**, 74km north of **Walgett** on the Castlereagh Highway (the road is fully sealed, but note that there's no place to stop for fuel between the two), is officially 2500 but unofficially it's reckoned to be about 7000. The reason for its existence – and the reason why people come here in numbers – is the opal. Amid this harsh landscape scarred by holes and slag heaps, Lightning Ridge's opal fields are the only place in the world where the extremely valuable **black opal** can consistently be found. This one attraction is heavily exploited by opal galleries and **mines** you can visit, among them the Big Opal, 3 Mile Rd (daily 9am–5pm; free; tour 10am, $8), which has demonstrations of opal-cutting and guided tours of an underground mine; Spectrum Opal Mines, Bald Hill Road (daily 9am–5pm; free), a centre displaying solid opals in an underground showroom with a film about opal-mining shown on the hour; and the Walk-in Mine, 1 Bald Hill Rd (daily 9am–5pm; tour 9am, $5), which has a mining display and tours to an underground mine. There are also clearly demarcated fossicking areas where you can try your luck at finding opals – but don't do it anywhere else, or you may stray onto others' claims. Recover afterwards in the 52°C water of the **Hot Artesian Bore Baths** on Pandora Street (open 24hr; free). More cooling is the Olympic Pool on Gem Street (end Sept to Easter daily 10am–8pm), particularly appealing in the scorching heat since parts of the pool are shaded from the sun. The **Goondee Aboriginal Keeping Place** on Pandora Street (☎02/6829 2001 for opening times which vary) has Aboriginal artefacts and information on bush tucker.

Practicalities

The **tourist information centre** in Lightning Ridge is in the new Miners Associated building on Morilla Street (☎02/6829 1466, fax 6829 0565, free call ☎1800/639 545) and has opal-buying rooms attached – ask for the useful booklet *Walgett Shire and the Lightning Ridge Opal Fields*, which contains a handy guide to buying opals. The centre can also fill you in on **accommodation** possibilities (all have air-con rooms), which include the *Black Opal Motel* on Opal Street (☎02/6829 0518, fax 6829 0884; ⑤), the *Wallangulla Motel*, on the corner of Morella and Agate streets (☎02/6829 0542; ④–⑤), and *Lightning Ridge Motor Village* on Onyx Street (☎02/6829 0304, fax 6829 0306; ⑤), which also has tent sites. The best place to **camp**, though, is *Crocodile Caravan and Camping Park*, Morilla Street (☎02/6829 0437; ③), which has a pool and spa and air-con cabins. Full **banking** facilities are available at Westpac on Morella Street.

The Hume Highway and the Riverina

The rolling plains of southwestern New South Wales, spreading west from the Great Dividing Range, are bounded by two great rivers: the Murrumbidgee to the north and the Murray to the south, the latter forming the border with the state of Victoria. This area is known as the **Riverina**, a name that conjures up a certain rural romance, suggesting a country Australia little visited by tourists – except those en route to Melbourne along the **Hume Highway**, which cuts a fume-filled swath through the southwest. If you're looking for work on the land, you've a reasonable chance of finding it here. The land the explorer John Oxley described as "uninhabitable and useless to civilized man" began its transformation to fertile fruit bowl when the ambitious **Murrumbidgee Irrigation Scheme** was launched in 1907, and the area around **Griffith** and **Leeton** now produces ninety percent of Australia's rice, most of its citrus fruits and twenty percent of its wine grapes. The capital of the central Riverina is **Wagga Wagga**, Australia's largest inland city. Along the Upper Murray, the main towns are on the Victorian side of the river (and are covered in the Victoria chapter), but you may drop into **Albury** en route to Melbourne on the Hume, or into **Wentworth** as a day-trip from Mildura or on the way to or from Broken Hill on the Silver City Highway.

The Hume Highway: Goulburn to Albury

If you want a quick route to Melbourne from Sydney, or vice versa, you'll inevitably end up on the rather tedious **Hume Highway**, which passes through the Southern Highlands, the Riverina and across the Murray River. Over the years the highway has been improved, but though this is one of Australia's main arteries between its two largest cities, it still narrows to one lane either way in parts. Choked with trucks, particularly at night, accidents are not infrequent, so keep your wits about you. Following are the main stopping points along the way in New South Wales (for Sydney to Goulburn, see p.204) and some suggestions for food, accommodation and breaks.

Goulburn and around

Now bypassed by the Hume Highway, **GOULBURN** is still the traditional stop-off point en route to Canberra. It's a large regional centre for the surrounding area, and for a quality **wool industry** which was established in the 1820s. The town, with its wide streets, has a conservative country feel, but boasts city facilities and some large and impressive public buildings. Goulburn's connection to sheep, and one kind in particular, is made obvious to the public with the **Big Merino** (daily 8am–8pm). Another of Australia's unashamedly tacky "big things", the fifteen-metre-high sheep proudly stands next to the Ampol service station on the Old Hume Highway; the first floor has a wool industry display, and on the third level you can look out over the town through the sheep's eyes. To get closer to the real thing, head for the long-established **Pelican**

THE HUME AND HOVELL WALKING TRACK

This long-distance walk starts at **Gunning**, on the Hume Highway 50km east of Goulburn, and runs over 400km southwest **to Albury**, retracing as closely as possible the route taken on foot by the two eponymous explorers in the spring and summer of 1824 on their expedition from Sydney to Port Phillip, the site of what was to become Melbourne. The walk takes about fifteen to twenty days but the layout – a Bicentenary project – allows for half-day, full-day and weekend walks. There are several free leaflets detailing different chunks, available from the Department of Conservation and Land Management in Sydney (☎02/9228 6111), Goulburn (☎02/4823 0665) and Wagga Wagga (☎02/6921 2503); the *Hume and Hovell Walking Track Guidebook* by Harry Hill (Crawford House Press, Bathurst, $19.95) is also useful.

Sheep Station on Braidwood Road, 10km south of town (☎02/4821 4668, fax 4822 1179; booking essential for tours, price dependent on number of people; accommodation in bunkhouses ③, plus camping), which has been in the same family since 1827. Tours include a shearing demonstration and the chance to see some sheepdogs being put through their paces.

There are several historic places to visit in Goulburn, including the National Trust property **Riversdale**, an 1840 coaching inn on Maud Street (Fri, Sun and holidays 10am–4pm, at other times by appointment ☎02/4821 4741), but the most interesting is the **Old Goulburn Brewery** on Bungonia Road (daily tastings from 11am), which has been brewing traditional ales and stouts since 1836. Details of other old properties can be obtained from the **Goulburn Visitors Centre**, next to the very impressive 1887 courthouse and opposite the shady, flower-filled Belmore Park, on Montague Street (daily 9am–5pm; ☎02/4823 0492); they also have a list of accommodation.

The classic place to **eat** in Goulburn, obligatory when passing through on the way to Canberra, is the *Paragon Café*, at 174 Auburn St, open daily for lunch and dinner. A bastion of good, filling food – inexpensive breakfasts, great hamburgers, steaks, fish, veal, pasta and pizza – it's been here for around fifty years and retains its 1940s-era fittings – it's also licensed.

The most intriguing place to **stay** in the area is at the **Yurt Farm**, 20km out of town on Grabben Gullen Road (☎02/4829 2114; $15 as a helper with four hours' work per day required, but all meals included; $11 in a yurt overnight, plus $6 for a meal; or as part of a WWOOF placement, see p.65). A yurt, in its original form, is a Mongolian round leather tent, and the concept was enthusiastically adopted and adapted by Californian New Agers. The ones here are mostly of wood and are portable prefab buildings in the Californian mould – solar-powered, naturally lit and wood-heated. Essentially a sheep property, the yurt village has several yurts each with a different function, providing an educational centre for groups of children to help them become more self-sufficient and environmentally aware. If you want to stay, you must call in advance; if you don't have your own transport, someone can pick you up.

The **Bungonia State Recreation Area**, 25km east of Goulburn, covers a rugged strip of the Southern Tablelands containing some of the deepest **caves** in Australia. The spectacular limestone Bungonia Gorge and the Shoalhaven River are two of its physical attractions.

Yass and the Burrinjuck State Recreation Area

YASS dates back to 1821 when Europeans first entered the area. Prior to this, the area had a high Aboriginal population, who gave the town its name, "yharr", meaning running water. On the outskirts of Yass as you exit the Hume Highway onto the Yass Valley Way from Goulburn (87km away) is the National Trust-owned **Cooma Cottage** (Wed–Mon 10am–4pm; $4), the former home of the famous explorer **Hamilton Hume**, set in rolling countryside stocked with sheep. The well-preserved nineteenth-century homestead's architectural interest is outweighed by the excellent interpretive material on Hume and his expeditions. Hume was different from many of his contemporaries in that he was born in Australia – in Parramatta, to free settlers in 1797. His explorations relied on his knowledge of the bush: he befriended Aborigines who taught him their skills and language, which made him infinitely better prepared than those equipped only with romantic notions. His first expedition was at the age of 17, accompanied by his brother and his Aboriginal friend Doual, and the trio discovered prime grazing lands in the Southern Highlands. Three years later he led the Goulburn Plains expedition, and pushing further afield in 1821 he discovered the rich and productive Yass Plains, where he settled in later life. Hume's best-known exploration was when he paired with Hovell, an English sea captain, to head for Port Phillip Bay; you can follow in their footsteps on the Hume and Hovell

Walking Track (see box on p.309). He also assisted Sturt in tracing the Murray and Darling rivers. The Tourist Information Centre (daily 9am–5pm; ☎02/6226 2557, fax 6226 1509, *yasstourism@interact.net.au*) has maps outlining a 2km informative walk, and the **Hamilton Hume Museum** (Sat & Sun and school holidays; $2) contains displays on what the town looked like back in the 1890s. The old **Tramway** in the centre of town features the smallest platform in Australia (open Sunday afternoons only; $3).

Continuing along the Hume Highway, 27km south of Yass is a turn-off to the **Burrinjuck Waters State Park**, and from here it's a 25km drive on a sealed road to the bushland park set around Burrinjuck Dam, with camping and picnic areas filled with kangaroos and chirping rosellas (☎02/6227 8114; cottages ⑤, on-site vans, units and tent sites ③). There is a **riverboat cruise** most weekends in summer on the *Lady BJ* (☎02/6227 7270; 2hr; $14) up to the dam and across the main basin. **Wee Jasper** is a picturesque village located on the backwaters of Burrinjuck Dam, with a basic **campsite** (☎02/6227 9626). From here you can visit **Carey's Caves** and see some of Australia's most spectacular limestone rock formations (Fri–Mon 9am–5pm; other times by appointment ☎02/6227 9622; $8).

Turning off the Hume Highway at **Bowning** brings you to the peaceful village of **Binalong**. Australia's best known poet, Banjo Patterson, spent much of his childhood here, attending the local school. Binalong railway station was used to transport gold from nearby Lambing Flats (Young), which made it a lucrative area for bushrangers. The grave of the daring bushranger "Flash" Johnny Gilbert, a member of a local outlaw gang is along the side of the road to Harden.

Gundagai and Holbrook

One hundred and four kilometres from Yass, **GUNDAGAI** sits on the southern banks of the Murrumbidgee, at the foot of the rounded bump of Mount Parnassus. The town was once situated on the alluvial flats north of the river, despite warnings from local Aborigines that the area was prone to major flooding, and old Gundagai was the scene of Australia's worst flood disaster in 1852 when 89 people drowned. The relocated Gundagai, on the main route between Sydney and Melbourne (until bypassed by the Hume Highway), became a favoured overnight stopping point, with the bullock wagons which took the pioneers into the interior favouring a camping spot out of town at Five Mile Creek. A large punt was the only means of crossing the Murrumbidgee from 1849 until the Prince Alfred Bridge was erected in 1867; although now closed to traffic, the pretty wooden bridge can still be crossed by pedestrians. Gold was eventually discovered here, and by 1864 Gundagai had become a boom town, preyed upon by the romantically dubbed bushranger **Captain Moonlight** who was eventually captured and tried at the Gundagai courthouse in 1879.

Perhaps this colourful history and the road-much-travelled appeal of Gundagai explains why the town features so often in Australian verse and folk song, finding immortality through a Jack Moses poem, in which "the dog sat on the tuckerbox, nine miles from Gundagai" – and stubbornly refused to help its master pull the bogged bullock team from the creek. Somehow the whole image became elevated from that of a disobedient hound and a fed-up, cursing teamster to a symbol of the pioneer with a faithful hound at his side. As a consequence, a **statue** of the dog was erected at the original five-mile point: it's actually a very pleasant place to take a break from the rigours of the road, with a shady picnic area and undulating fields and hills beyond. Inside the **tourist centre** here, there's a range of cheerfully tacky souvenirs plus the rare opportunity to send a postcard with a special "dog on the tuckerbox" postmark.

In the town itself, the **Gundagai Tourist Information Centre** (Mon–Fri 8am–5pm, Sat & Sun 9am–noon & 1–5pm; ☎02/6944 1341) can help you find somewhere to stay if need be – and also sells a tape of several folk songs featuring Gundagai, including *Along the Road to Gundagai*, from which every Australian remembers only the tuneful snatch "There's a track winding back, to an old-fashioned shack, along the road to Gundagai". Also at the information centre, you can see (for $1) the **miniature Baroque cathedral** by Frank Rusconi, the sculptor who created the statue of the noble dog. The cathedral, a project that required complete patience and precision, took 28 years to build; constructed with absolutely no plans of any sort, it is made from thousands of pieces of twenty different kinds of New South Wales marble. Satisfying more mundane appetites, *Bidgee Cakes*, at 198 Sheridan St, bakes traditional tarts using free-range eggs, and sells lamb sausage rolls plus honey rolls made from local honey.

Sixty-eight kilometres north of Gundagai, **HOLBROOK** is a recommended food break on the drive to Melbourne (or Sydney), being roughly halfway. It's twinned with Wodonga that heads through town. The *Holbrook Bakery* dishes out delicious beef and curry pies, and the *Scrummy Buns Bakery* across the road sells more unorthodox pies filled with crocodile, emu, kangaroo and rabbit – plus cappuccino and continental cakes. Perhaps these great bakeries are a legacy of a German past: settled by Germans in the 1860s, Holbrook was called Germantown right up until World War I, when anti-German feeling warranted a name change.

Albury and around

The small city of **ALBURY** on the Murray River is a major stopover point on the route between Sydney and Melbourne, being roughly halfway. It's twinned with Wodonga across the river in Victoria, and although Albury is the major centre, the principal information centre is on the Wodonga side – **Gateway Tourist Information Centre** on the Hume Highway (daily 9am–5pm; ☎02/6041 3875). You can also pick up tourist information from the **Albury Regional Museum** (daily 10.30am–4.30pm; free; ☎02/6021 4550) on the Hume Highway in what was once the *Turks' Head Hotel* – opportunistically sited here when the river was crossed by punt; changing exhibitions now focus on the social history of the region. The museum is set in **Noreuil Park**, a peaceful spot looking across to a bush-covered riverbank in Victoria. People lie about under the large gum trees – one of which was marked by the explorer Hovell at the point where he and Hume crossed the Murray – and swim in the river. You can also take to the water with a **cruise** on a replica paddle steamer (mid-Sept to mid-April Wed–Sat, daily during school holidays, 10am, noon & 2pm; $8–9.50; ☎02/6021 1113). Another pleasant place to stretch your legs is in the **Albury Botanical Gardens** at the Dean Street end of Wodonga Place. Established in 1877, the gardens hold some impressive old trees, including a huge 41-metre Queensland kauri pine; palm trees and flowerbeds fill a small grassy park, and the short fern walk is pleasantly cooling.

The **Albury Regional Art Centre** is at 546 Dean St (daily 10.30am–5pm; free), in the decorative old town hall. The gallery's speciality is photography, but it also has a sizeable collection of Russell Drysdale's sketches and studies for paintings; the Australian artist (1912–1981) lived in the area in the 1920s and married into an Albury family. The town has its own extraordinary troupe of performers: **The Flying Fruit Circus** (☎02/6021 7044 to find out when they're performing locally), which began in 1979 as a local circus project to teach acrobatics to schoolchildren and went on to become a national success.

Albury has a good range of places to **stay** for the night, which the tourist office can book for you. There's even a **hostel**, the comfortable, activity-focused *Albury Backpackers*, on the corner of David and Smollett streets, one block from the main street (☎02/6041 1822, fax 6021 6335; rooms ②, dorms ①). They offer free use of bikes, rent canoes and can arrange canoe trips, and can also help line up **fruit-picking work**; if you call, they'll also pick you up from your train or bus. *The Globe Hotel* at 586 Dean St also has backpacker-style accommodation, some of which are en suite (①–②). There's also a YHA at *Albury Motor Village,* 372 Wagga Rd (Hume Highway), Lowington (☎02/6040 2999), situated at a caravan park with a pool, 5km out of town.

The most upmarket place to stay is the *Carlton Country Comfort*, on the corner of Dean and Elizabeth streets (☎02/6021 5366, fax 6041 2848; ⑦), with a swimming pool, sauna, gym, spa and room service. One of the best-value motels is the *Albury Viscount Motor Inn*, on the Hume Highway 1km south of the centre (☎02/6021 2444; ④), which has air-conditioned units and a swimming pool. **Campers** are catered for at *Trek-31 Tourist Park*, 8km north on the highway (☎02/6025 4355; cabins ④, on-site vans ③).

Dean Street is the main street for **food**: *Café Victor* serves up wood-fired pizzas, while the *Pancake Parlour*, with its outdoor tables, is a satisfying and inexpensive place offering focaccia and pancakes. *Rama's Curry Kitchen* in the *Globe Hotel*, at no. 586, is an authentic, affordable Indian place with a good range of spicy vegetarian dishes. The *Electra Café* on the corner of Dean and Macaley streets has a funky retro vibe, and serves a variety of internationally-influenced meals on kitsch crockery (Mon–Sat 10am–10pm, Sun 10am–3pm; live music on Tues). An alternative way of getting a feed is to visit the **Hume Weir Trout Farm**, a pleasant spot with landscaped gardens and waterfalls off the Riverina Highway (daily 9am–dusk; $5), where the entry fee includes rods so that you can catch your own freshwater trout; there are barbecues here to cook the fish, although you must pay for the catch by the kilo. Albury is positioned in prime dairy country and you can try some of its produce at the **Haberfield Dairy**, 470–482 Hovell St (Mon–Fri 10am–5pm, Sat 9am–1pm), renowned for its Swiss-style cheeses.

About 10km north of Albury on the Hume Highway, the larger-than-life *Ettamogah Pub* is a parody of an Outback pub, straight out of a sketch by the Aussie cartoonist Maynard, although the precariously askew hotel really does serve drinks. Walk up the slanting staircase to the veering verandah where there are great views of the surrounding countryside. A touristy tin shack in the back flogs souvenirs.

The Murrumbidgee Irrigation Area

Irrigation has transformed the area northwest of Albury, between the Lachlan and the Murrumbidgee rivers, into a fertile valley full of orchards, vineyards and rice paddies, cut through with irrigation canals. The **Murrumbidgee Irrigation Area** (or **MIA**) extends over two thousand square kilometres, a mostly flat and – from ground level at least – featureless landscape that nonetheless is responsible for producing most of Australia's rice, approximately eighty percent of New South Wales's wine grapes, and sixty percent of its citrus fruits. The water for the irrigation area is stored in Burrinjuck and Blowering dams and flows over 400km down the Murrumbidgee River to Berembed Weir, before being diverted into the main canal, which is 155km long and feeds a network of 1450km of supply canals.

Probably the main reason you'll visit this off-the-beaten-track area is to find **work**, which there is in abundance for the intensive fruit-picking season from December to April – plus a considerable picking of Valencia oranges throughout the year as the largest citrus-growing area in Australia. At the peak season there are up to three thousand jobs going begging. The season starts in August with oranges, which are picked right through to March, then onions in November, and stonefruit, prunes and melons from December to March, overlapping with the grape harvest in February and March. Pay is calculated according to the amount picked and, basing yourself in Griffith or Leeton, you'll need your own transport – if only a bicycle – since the orchards are up to 10km outside town. To avoid the possibility of a wasted trip, due to a late season or a poor crop, it's essential to check with Employment National (☎13 3444) before turning up.

Griffith

Citrus orchards line the way into **GRIFFITH**, with a range of low hills in the background. The major centre of the MIA, it's known for its large **Italian population** and their enduring cultural life, despite the fact that some of the families arrived here around the time of World War I. More came in the 1920s, having already tried mining in Broken Hill, and the area attracted post-World War II Italian immigrants as well. Needless to say, a string of excellent Italian cafés and restaurants line the tree-filled main street of Banna Avenue, and the majority of **wineries** are run by Italian families. Designed by Walter Burley Griffin, the landscape architect from Chicago who was responsible for Canberra (see p.209), the city has since grown beyond his plan.

For free maps and information, head for the **Griffith Visitors Centre**, on the corner of Jondaryan and Banna avenues (Mon–Fri 9am–5pm, Sat 9am–3pm, Sun 10am–2pm; ☎02/6962 4145). During the week, they can arrange for you to hop on a school bus-run (7–9am & 3.30–5pm) to see the surrounding district, its rice paddies, citrus and stonefruit orchards and vineyards, for around a dollar. An even better way to get an overview of the area is to head for **Scenic Hill**, the escarpment that forms the northern boundary of the city. The **Sir Dudley de Chair's Lookout** gives a panoramic view of the horticultural enterprises below. Immediately beneath this rocky outcrop, is the **Hermit's Cave** where Valerio Recetti, an Italian immigrant, lived alone and quite undetected for ten years until an accident in 1935. Working only at night and early in the morning, he made a home in the caves he found in the cliff, and created cliffside gardens. One cave contained a small shrine where you can still see a painted cross. During World War II he was interned in Hay (around 150km to the west of Griffith) – as were most of the local Italians – and in 1952 he returned to Italy, where he died.

Pioneer Park, in an extensive bushland setting 1.5km west of the lookout and 2km from the city centre (daily 8.30am–5pm; $5), has 36 buildings re-creating the era of the early MIA. The most interesting part is "Bagtown", a reconstruction of an early makeshift town built in 1919 to meet the needs of the Murrumbidgee Irrigation Area canal workers and pioneer farmers, and so-called because the homes were made of hessian cement bags with corrugated iron roofs.

There are sixteen **wineries**, many Italian-run, in the area surrounding Griffith. Nine are open to the public, and detailed in the *Griffith Visitors' Guide* booklet available from the visitors centre. The very first winery, McWilliam's, was established in 1913 and holds tastings in a building resembling a wine barrel (Mon–Sat 9am–5pm); there are barbecues in the grounds. Several other wineries have been around for more than fifty years, dating from the post-World War I influx of Italian immigrants. One of these is Rossetto Wines on Rossetto Road, off Leeton Road (Mon–Sat 8.30am–5.30pm). Still run by the same family, it's a down-to-earth, friendly concern known for its muscats and ports.

The *Pioneer Park* has bunkhouse **accommodation** for backpackers and fruit-pickers (☎02/6962 4196; ①, cheap weekly rates), but it's a long uphill walk out of town, with no public transport. Most pickers camp or stay in caravans at the *Griffith Tourist Caravan Village*, 919 Willandra Ave, 2km south of the centre (☎02/6964 2144, fax 6964 1126; on-site vans ②–③); the *Griffith Caravan Park*, on the Leeton Road, 3km east (☎02/6962 3785); or the cheap and basic campsite at the showground on the edge of town. For a bit more comfort, the popular *Victoria Hotel*, 384 Banna St (☎02/6962 1299, fax 6962 1081; ②, with bargain weekly rates), has basic rooms, but there's a TV lounge with tea and coffee provided, a cool covered courtyard, counter lunches downstairs, and a bistro Thursday and Friday nights. You could also try the central *Crown Hotel* on Kooyoo Street (☎02/6962 1011; ④), which has air-conditioned rooms.

There's no shortage of good Italian places to **eat and drink** on Banna Avenue, with the pavement tables of the *Bassano Café* (Mon–Thurs 8am–6pm, Fri–Sun 8am–10pm) a good place to sample excellent coffee and delicious focaccia; you can also get pasta, homemade *gelati*, pastries and biscuits. The much cheaper cafeteria-style *Bertoldo's Pasticerria* has budget-priced and filling pasta dishes. Casual meals are served at the *Belvedere Restaurant and Pizza*, 494 Banna Ave, while *La Scala*, at no. 455 (Tues–Sun

6pm–midnight), is a more upmarket (licensed) and expensive choice. *Romeo & Giulietta*, 40 Mackay Ave, uses a wood-fired oven for its delicious pizzas.

Around Griffith

Fifty-nine kilometres southeast of Griffith, **LEETON** is the third-largest town in the MIA, with a quarter of its population of Italian extraction; like Griffith, it was designed by Walter Burley Griffin. For information on the area and details of visiting its **rice mill**, head for the **Leeton Visitor Information Centre** on Chelmsford Place (Mon–Fri 9am–5pm, Sat & Sun 9.30am–12.30pm; ☎02/6953 2832). There are two **caravan parks**, both 2km southeast: the *Leeton Caravan Park*, on Yanco Avenue (☎ & fax 02/6953 3323), caters best for fruit-pickers with basic vans at $90 per week, but also has on-site vans (②) and en-suite cabins with TV (③); while the *Gilgal Family Holiday Centre*, on Corbie Hill Road (☎ & fax 02/6953 3882; cabins ③, spacious cottage ③, vans ②), caters more for tourists with a better range of facilities. The large, tree-filled property at *Gilgal* is also a great spot to pitch a tent, with cheap rates for pickers. Despite the Italian population, Leeton feels less cosmopolitan than Griffith, but you can nevertheless enjoy an Italian **meal** at the *MIA Social Club* on Racecourse Road (daily from 3pm; ☎02/6953 4357).

Twenty-five kilometres northeast of Griffith is the **Cocoparra National Park** in the woodland-covered Cocoparra Range. Enquire about camping and bushwalking at the NPWS office, 105 Banna Ave, Griffith (☎02/6967 8159). Much further away, on the flat plains 185km northwest of Griffith, is **Willandra National Park**, reached via **Hillston** (64km from Griffith) on the unsealed Hillston–Mossgiel Road. The park was created in 1971 from a section of the vast Big Willandra pastoral station, a famous stud Merino property which had operated since the 1860s, and now has several temporary wetland areas. As well as enabling you to experience the semi-arid riverine plains country at close quarters, a visit to the 1918 **homestead** gives an insight into station life and the wool industry. Wet weather makes all the roads to Willandra impassable, so check first with the **park office** in Hillston (☎02/6967 9159; this is also the number for **accommodation bookings**, with shared rooms available in shearers' quarters ①) – and take extra supplies in case you get rained in.

Narrandera

Thirty kilometres southeast of Leeton, at the junction of the Sturt and Newell highways, **NARRANDERA** is a popular overnight stop en route from Adelaide to Sydney, or Melbourne to Brisbane. It's actually a very pleasant place to take a break, set on the Murrumbidgee River with streets lined with tall native and deciduous trees owing to the foresight of the pioneer settlers; its white cedars, which blossom in November, are particularly beautiful.

A good place to cool down is **Lake Talbot**, a willow-surrounded expanse of water flowing from the Murrumbidgee River. Right next to the lake, with just a grassy bank between them, is the splendidly sited *Lake Talbot Holiday Complex* (third weekend in Oct to third weekend in April, Mon–Fri 5.30–8am & 10am–9pm, Sat & Sun 10am–9pm; adults $2, children $1). The complex is very family-friendly, with picnic areas and barbecues, various watery slides at 20–80¢ a go, children's pools and an Olympic-sized **swimming** pool. Nearby, a reserve along the river has been declared a **koala regeneration area** for a disease-free colony of koalas; to get there, follow the **Bundidgerry Walking Track** around Lake Talbot and the Murrumbidgee River. Free maps of the track are available at the **Narrandera Tourist Information Centre**, in Narrandera Park on the Newell Highway (Mon–Fri 9am–5pm, Sat & Sun 10am–4pm; ☎02/6959 1766). Fishing fanatics could try out the lake or river for some Murray cod, yellowbelly or silverbeam; fish abound in the river, and 5km east of Narrandera, off the Sturt Highway, the **John Lake Centre** at the Inland Fisheries Research Station (Mon–Fri 9am–4pm; guided tours

10.30am; $5), carries out research into the species of the Murray, Murrumbidgee and Darling rivers.

The best place to **stay** in Narrandera is the *Star Lodge*, on the corner of Whitton and Arthur streets (☎02/6959 1768, fax 6959 4164; rooms ③, dorms ①). Classified by the National Trust, the building retains many of its original 1916 features and is now a fine B&B and hostel run by a friendly couple. East Street is the main street for hotels and motels, with several classic iron-lace-verandahed country hotels, all offering accommodation. The real bargain is the *Royal Mail Hotel* on East Street (☎02/6959 2007; ②), or try the *Mid Town Motor Inn* on the corner of East and Larmer streets (☎02/6959 2122, fax 6959 3271; ④), which has a swimming pool. Another good spot is the shady *Lake Talbot Caravan Park*, well positioned above the lake and pool (☎02/6959 1302; cabins ③, on-site vans ②). The best place for a **meal** is the large old *Narrandera Hotel*, the last pub on East Street near the Murrumbidgee canal.

Wagga Wagga

WAGGA WAGGA, known simply as "Wagga" to the locals, is the most populous inland city in Australia with around 55,000 inhabitants, but it still has the appearance of a slow and solid country town. Its curious name comes from the Widadjuri, the largest of the New South Wales Aboriginal peoples: Wagga means crow and its repetition signifies the plural. Set on the Murrumbidgee River just under 100km east of Narrandera, with a beautiful sandy river beach to swim in close to the main street, it is the capital of the Riverina region, with its own **university**, Charles Sturt, boasting a well-regarded wine course and its own on-campus **winery** which is open for tastings and cellar door sales (Mon–Fri 10am–4pm, Sat & Sun 11am–4pm; ☎02/6933 2435), an ABC radio station, and a regional theatre.

Wagga's main attractions, though, are on the edge of the city. To the south, about a half-hour hike by foot, are the impressive **Botanic Gardens** at the base of Willans Hill, a huge place with such attractions as a walk-through bird aviary where over three hundred species flit about, a children's petting zoo (aviary and zoo daily 9am–4pm; free), bush trails and picnic areas, specialist gardens of cacti and succulents, and a Chinese-style garden, plus a kiosk café. On the first and third Sunday of each month, a model train takes children around about for 80¢ a ride. There's a **Historical Museum** on Lord Baden Powell Drive, by the Botanic Gardens (Tues & Wed, Sat & Sun 2–5pm) with a hotchpotch collection of old farm machinery, printing presses and a display of over 200 door knockers. Further to the south, the artificial **Lake Albert** is a popular spot for water-skiing. Canoe cruises are also available down by the Murrumbidgee River (☎02/6925 5807).

Back in the centre, the **City Art Gallery**, 40 Gurwood St (Tues–Fri 11am–5pm, Sat 10am–5pm, Sun 2–5pm; free), is home to the National Art Glass collection, a stunning array of contemporary glass pieces, and the Carnegie Print Collection, with over five hundred originals from innovative Australian printmakers from 1940 on; if you're lucky, Sally Robinson's vivid *Kakadu* series might be on display.

On Sunday mornings a bit of life is sparked by the **markets** (7.30am–noon), at the Grace Bros car park on O'Reilly Street, which have secondhand clothes and books, crafts, local produce and cakes on sale. The **Ngungilanna Culture Centre**, 11 Gurwood St (Mon–Sat 9am–5.30pm; ☎02/6921 8982), is also worth checking out: run by the Wagga Advancement Aboriginal Corporation, it sells locally made crafts and clothes, as well as books, cards and paintings from around Australia.

Practicalities

Roughly halfway between Sydney (470km) and Melbourne (435km), Wagga is just off the Sturt Highway, the main route between Adelaide and Sydney. Interstate **buses** heading to and from Brisbane, Sydney, Adelaide, Melbourne and Canberra all pass through, stopping at the Greyhound Pioneer Interstate Terminal, on the corner of Gurwood and Trail streets (☎02/6921 1977). To **get around**, you can rent bikes from Kidson's Cycles at 107 Fitzmaurice St (☎02/6921 4474), or a car from Avis, on the corner of Edwards and Fitzharding streets (☎02/6921 9977). Baylis Street, the main strip (and Fitzmaurice Street, its continuation), extends from the train station to the bridge spanning the Murrumbidgee River.

The **Wagga Wagga Visitors Centre**, on Tarcutta Street, close to the river (daily 9am–5pm; ☎02/6923 5402), dispenses free handy driving maps. It doesn't book **accommodation**, but does have information about **farmstays** in the surrounding countryside. In town, the old *Romano's Hotel*, on the corner of Sturt and Fitzmaurice streets (☎02/6921 2013; ③), has been beautifully renovated; rooms are decorated in turn-of-the-century style, and some have showers. *The Tourist Hotel*, 97 Fitzmaurice St (☎02/6921 2264; ③), has no-frills pub doubles, while *The Manor Guesthouse*, 38 Morrow St (☎02/6921 5962; ⑤), is a good B&B next to the beautiful riverfront park. The best-situated **caravan park** is the shady and peaceful *Wagga Wagga Tourist Park*, Johnston Street (☎02/6921 2540; on-site vans and cabins ③), right on the town beach and five minutes' walk from the main shops.

The Baylis/Fitzmaurice strip and its side streets provide fertile **eating** ground. Wagga Marketplace, a new mall on Baylis Street near the station, has a gleaming food court. For a snack, *Café Delish* at 14 Baylis St (Mon–Fri 8.30am–5pm, Sat & Sun 8.30am–3pm) has sandwiches, fresh juices and snacks. Other places to eat include the *Bahn Thai* **restaurant** at the *Club Motel*, 73 Morgan St, for authentic Thai cuisine, including a good selection for vegetarians (BYO), and the *Kebab Place Restaurant*, 152 Fitzmaurice St (BYO; Tues–Sat 11am–midnight), for really tasty Lebanese food. *Romano's Hotel* (see above) has a modern and very stylish café/bar that makes a decent espresso and serves breakfast all day, and the slick *Victoria Hotel* at 55 Baylis St has an extensive bistro menu and upstairs balcony open Friday and Saturday nights. Head for the popular *Café Europa* (closed Sun), 44 Johnston St, for affordable pasta and pizza, or *Il Corso* at 16 Baylis St (closed Mon) for more upmarket Italian dinners made to order in an open marble kitchen. For Mexican, try *Montezuma's* cosy wooden cantina at 85 Baylis St (lunch Wed–Fri, dinner Tues–Sun). The town's trendiest watering hole – frequented by ABC radio staff – is *No 96*, at 96 Fitzmaurice St, a wine bar that serves brasserie-style meals. On the other side of the street, at no. 97, *The Tourist Hotel* has a great place to eat out back; *Bernie's Veggie Restaurant* (lunch Wed–Fri, dinner Wed–Sat), serving an array of sumptuous, cheap meals, in an open-fire room with retro decor.

Wagga also has several huge **clubs** which provide free courtesy buses. *Wagga RSL*, on the corner of Dobbs and Kincaid streets, also has a Chinese restaurant and Friday-night piano bar, while the *Wagga Leagues Club*, Gurwood Street, has a good brasserie and live entertainment every Saturday. *Maddison's* nightclub at 146 Fitzmaurice St (Wed–Sat) is Wagga's in-vogue venue for bands and student shenanigans, whilst the *Black Swan Hotel* (alias "The Muddy Duck") in North Wagga, close to the university, is also popular with the student population.

The lower Murray: Albury to Wentworth

Following the **lower Murray River** between Albury (see p.312) and the South Australian border, there's little of interest on the New South Wales side until the old port town of **Wentworth** and its surrounding storehouse of ancient Aboriginal history around **Lake Victoria** and in the remote **Mungo National Park**. The main centres are on the Victorian side of the river, Mildura (see p.869) and Echuca (see p.874) chief among them, although the NSW riverside towns of **Tocumwal** and **Corowa**, not far from Albury, are pleasant enough.

Corowa and Tocumwal

Following the river, it's 56km from Albury northwest to **COROWA**, across the Murray from Victoria's **Rutherglen wine region** (see p.891). Blue flags flying all over town proclaim it to be the birthplace of Federation, since the Federation Conference of 1893 was held at Corowa's courthouse. The **Corowa Tourist Information Centre** is in the cream-coloured former train station on John Street (Mon–Sat 9.45am–4.30pm; ☎02/6033 3221) and can give you information about river cruises on the *MV Lynne Maree* (Sat, Sun & holidays 10am–2pm; 1hr; $10; ☎02/6033 2846). There are stacks of **motels** in town offering very reasonable accommodation, such as the *Corowa Murray View* at 193 River St (☎02/6033 2144, fax 6033 1625; ④), with a swimming pool, spa and barbecues (some rooms have a private garden courtyard). **Campers** could try the *Ball Park Caravan Park*, by the Murray on Bridge Road (☎02/6033 1426; cabins and vans ③), or the *Lake Talbot Caravan Park* (☎02/6959 1302; tent pitches and vans ③). There are several places on the main street where you can get a **meal**, including the *Star Hotel*, which does a good-value roast of the day; the *Royal Hotel*, which serves up decent counter food; and the *Old Corowa Bakehouse*, a popular café/bakery that opens early.

On the way to Tocumwal, which is just under 80km from Corowa, there's a **boomerang factory** at **BAROOGA** called the Binghi Boomerang, where you can watch boomerangs being made and try them out yourself (call ☎03/5873 4463 for times). **TOCUMWAL** itself ("Toc" to locals) is a small, pleasant river town: its **Foreshore Park**, just behind the main street, is peaceful and shaded by large gum trees, and there's a sandy river beach only ten minutes' walk away. In front of the park, there's a rather tacky fibreglass model of a huge Murray cod, and alongside is the **Tocumwal Tourist Centre** (daily 9am–5pm; ☎03/5874 2131), which provides information about the area and can book rides in a glider that flies over the Murray.

Tocumwal has some classic old **country hotels**, most notably the *Tocumwal Hotel* on Deniliquin Street (☎03/5874 2025; ③), a single-storey hotel built in 1861, fronted by palms and an iron-lace verandah. Next door is Central Store Antiques, with good tearooms at the back serving scones, jam and cream or reasonably priced sandwiches and light meals. The best place to **camp** is the riverfront *Bushlands on the Murray* (☎03/5874 2752; cabins ④), right on the swimming beach

Wentworth and Lake Victoria

Once a thriving river port, **WENTWORTH** is now a sleepy old town overshadowed by nearby Mildura, 31km back along the Sturt Highway and across the Murray River in Victoria. Located at the junction of the Murray and the Darling, the "two rivers" town was for seventy years the centre of river trade between New South Wales, Victoria and South Australia. The extension of the railway at the turn of the century bypassed Wentworth, however, and at the same time killed off much of the river trade. Nowadays the town makes a pleasant stopover en route to or from Broken Hill, 261km north on the sealed **Silver City Highway**, or a brief excursion from Mildura (in Victoria). Enquire at the **tourist information centre**, Shop 4, Wentworth Place, Adams Street (daily 9am–5pm; ☎03/5027 3624), about river cruises on the *MV Loyalty*, built about 1914 (or direct on ☎03/5027 3330). You could visit the **Wentworth Gaol** on Beverly Street (daily 10am–5pm; $5), built of handmade bricks in 1879, but the interpretive displays consist of bits of curling cardboard and dejected dummies, making it hardly worth the entrance fee. Opposite, **Pioneer World** (daily 10am–5pm; $4) is a folk museum exhibiting items related to Aboriginal and European history of the area, and very tacky models of large animals. You can also take a tour through citrus groves at **Orange World** in Mourquong, back towards Mildura (9am–4pm; closed Sat; guided tractor tours 10.30am & 2.30pm; 1hr; $6).

The Aboriginal land council in Wentworth organizes visits to significant **Aboriginal sites** around Lake Victoria to the west, and Mungo National Park (see below) among the dry salt lakes to the northeast. The tours are run by Harry Nanya Tours at Shop 10, Wentworth Place, Sandych Street (☎03/5027 2076), and are accompanied by accredited Barkindji guides. Ancient Aboriginal graves were recently discovered at **Lake Victoria** – the Barkindji had always spoken of their existence. In April 1994, the partial draining of the eleven-square-kilometre lake revealed skeletons buried side by side and in deep layers; some of the estimated ten thousand graves date back six thousand years, in what is believed to be Australia's largest pre-industrial burial site – surpassing any such finds in Europe, Asia or North and South America. The site also challenges the premise that Aboriginal lifestyles were solely nomadic, suggesting that here at least they lived in semi-permanent dwellings around the lake.

Among the places to **stay** in Wentworth, the luxury apartments at the *Red Gum Lagoon*, 210 Adams St (☎03/5027 2063; ⑥), are wonderful, offering free use of canoes and rowboats on the lagoon itself. Another good waterfront choice is the *Willow Bend Caravan Park* on Darling Street (☎03/5027 3213; cabins ③, on-site vans ②), right near the shops but also at the confluence of the Darling and Murray rivers, where there are plenty of trees – watch out for ferocious possums, though. You can get out on the water by renting a **houseboat** from *Twin Rivers Houseboats* at 1 William St (☎03/5027 3026; sleeps up to six; $620–1200 per week).

Mungo National Park
Mungo National Park, in the far southwest of New South Wales, is most easily reached from the river townships of Wentworth (see above) or Mildura (over the Victorian border, about 110km away – see p.869); organized tours run from both towns. If you want to tackle it on your own, you'll need a 4WD. The park is part of the dried-up **Willandra Lakes System**, a UNESCO World Heritage area in recognition of its Aboriginal legacy and record of past climates preserved in the landscape. The Willandra Lakes contain the longest continuous record of Aboriginal life in Australia, dating back more than forty thousand years. During the Ice Ages, between forty thousand and fifteen thousand years ago, the system formed a vast chain of freshwater lakes strung along Willandra Creek, then the main channel of the Lachlan River, flowing into the Murrumbidgee. The waters teemed with fish, attracting waterbirds and mammals, while Aborigines camped at the shores of the lake to fish and hunt, and buried their dead in the sand dunes. When the lakes started drying out fifteen thousand years ago, Aborigines continued to live near soaks along the old river channel. The park covers most of one of these dry lake beds, and its dominant feature is a great, crescent-shaped dune (a lunette), at the eastern edge of the lake, commonly referred to as the **Walls of China**. Elsewhere, the vegetation consists of saltbush on the lake floors and mallee (a low-growing, scrubby type of eucalypt) on the dune fields. Casuarinas grow on the sand plains, and western grey and red kangaroos can sometimes be seen.

The **visitors centre** (☎03/5023 1278), by the southwest entrance to the park, has a very informative display about the geological and Aboriginal history of the national park, and nearby the impressive old **Mungo Woolshed** is open for inspection. From there it's a short drive to the lookout point on the rim of the lake, the former shore, from where you can look across the dry lakebed to the Walls of China. A signposted track takes you on a return trip across the lake floor to the Walls of China, then over the dune and to the northwest part of the park. At sunset, or on nights with a full moon, the scenery takes on an eerie, otherworldly quality.

If you want to **stay** nearby, beds in the former shearers' quarters, or at NPWS campsites in the park, can be booked in advance through the visitors centre. Otherwise, try *Mungo Lodge* on Arumpo Road (☎03/5029 7297; ⑤), which has motel units and self-contained cottages as well as a licensed restaurant.

Back o' Bourke: the Outback

Once you're past Dubbo, you're really getting away from the populated coast and moving towards the red plains that make western New South Wales the quintessential Australian Outback. The searing summer heat makes touring uncomfortable from December to February, and you'd be well advised to visit at a cooler time of year. **Bourke**, about 370km along the sealed **Mitchell Highway**, is generally considered the turning point; venture further and you're into the land known as "Back o' Bourke" – the back of beyond. The Mitchell passes through **NYNGAN**, at the geographical centre of New South Wales and 133km from Dubbo, where the sealed **Barrier Highway** heads west for 584 sweltering kilometres, through Cobar and Wilcannia, to Broken Hill. Flood-prone Nyngan, on the eastern bank of the Bogan River, is a sizeable (compared to what you'll find beyond), old-fashioned country town where you can refuel and freshen up. There's a small, shady park on Main Street where you can slump at picnic tables, or you can visit *Arnold's Take Away* at 133 Main St – a spacious café where generous pots of tea help to quench thirst and a ceiling fan manages to circulate a bit of air.

Bourke and around

BOURKE is mainly known for its very remoteness, and this alone is enough to attract tourists; once you've crossed the North Bourke Bridge that spans the **Darling River**, you're officially "out back". If you want to have a drink in the "Back O' Bourke" without pressing too far into the endless, scarcely populated plains all around, try the *North Bourke Hotel*, a shabby, wooden, green-tin-roofed Outback pub where bush poets congregate once a year during the annual **Mateship Festival** weekend normally held in late September (details from the information centre). The lively festival began in 1993 to mark the centenary of the poet **Henry Lawson**'s stay in Bourke during a particularly harsh drought. Discovering mateship in hardship was but a microcosm for the fierce nationalism that arose in 1890s depression and drought-struck Australia. Work was scarce and Lawson often slept out in the town's Central Park, where a plaque is dedicated to him and to two other bush poets who lived in the area at around the same time – Will Ogilvie and **Breaker Morant**, the latter executed during the Boer War. Another famous resident was the well-known ophthalmologist **Fred Hollows**, who began working here in the 1970s with local Aborigines suffering from cataract blindness. As a result of his work the number of cases of incurable blindness among Aboriginal peoples throughout Australia has been halved. Hollows was buried in the town in 1993.

Bourke was a bustling river port from the 1860s to the 1930s, and there are some fine examples of riverboat-era architecture, including the huge reconstructed **wharf** which can be explored – from here a track winds along the magnificent, tree-lined river. A new port with paddle steamer cruises is under development. Thanks to irrigation with Darling River water, crops as diverse as cotton, lucerne, citrus, grapes and sorghum are successfully grown here despite the 35°C summer heat, while Bourke is also the commercial centre for a vast sheep- and cattle-breeding area: to the north there are rich grazing lands across the Queensland border around Cunnamulla and Charleville.

With a population of three thousand (approximately twenty-five percent Aboriginal), Bourke acts as a base for regional services and welfare. Unfortunately, there is sporadic trouble involving alcoholism and aimless youngsters, and after dark the atmosphere can be a bit disturbing. Visitors are best off drinking in the *Port o' Bourke Hotel* (see below), the *Oxley Club* or *Bowling Club,* and avoiding the *Post Office Hotel.*

Practicalities

The **information centre** is inside the former train station on Anson Street (☎02/6872 2280). It can provide "**Mud Maps**", roughly drawn maps marking places of interest off the beaten track in the surrounding area: but bear in mind that these destinations could be as far as 200km away. It can also arrange Back o' Bourke tours (Mon–Sat 2–5pm; 3hr tour covering vineyards and Aboriginal sites; $15). Except for the Mitchell Highway, all roads mentioned below are unsealed; ask about conditions at the information centre.

Countrylink buses arrive here from Dubbo four times weekly, and you can also fly here with Hazelton, four times weekly, from Sydney via Dubbo. **Accommodation** in town includes the pleasant, renovated *Port o' Bourke Hotel* on Mitchell Street (☎02/6872 2544; ③), which has air-conditioned rooms, some sharing a bath, some en suite, and the *Bourke Riverside Motel*, 3 Mitchell St (☎02/6872 2539; ④), with a swimming pool. The *Back o' Bourke Backpackers*, on the corner of Oxley and Sturt streets (☎02/6872 3009; ①), is essentially a boarding house for local workers. However, the non-resident manager is very obliging and can help you find work harvesting tomatoes, onions and grapes between November and February and cotton-chipping between December and February. For **camping**, try *Kidman's Camp* (☎02/6872 1612). A better way to see how life is lived out here is to stay on an **Outback station**; the information centre has details of stations that take visitors, among them Comeroo Camel Farm (☎02/6874 7735), a unique experience with artesian hot bores, river waterholes with yabbying and fishing opportunities, and resident buffalo and ostriches.

For **food** and **drink**, the *Port o' Bourke Hotel* (see above) is the best place in town. Its fine dining room (Tues–Sat nights) is reminiscent of grander days, while you can eat counter meals (Mon–Sat) out in the shady beer garden.

West and north of Bourke

West of Bourke, it's 193km to the small settlement of **WANAARING**, past a reconstruction of **Fort Bourke**, built by Major Mitchell in 1835 as a secure depot to protect his stocks from Aboriginal people, while he explored the Darling River. Near Fort Bourke is the kibbutz-like **Cornerstone Community**, a cotton-farming operation and teaching centre run by Christians; they put a lot of effort into the local community, including running the tourist office, and visitors are welcome.

Northwest, the road runs 215km to **HUNGERFORD**, on the Queensland border, and the **Dingo Fence** (see p.335). En route, there's fuel, **food** and **accommodation** at the *Warrego Hotel* (☎02/6874 7540; ③) in **Ford's Bridge** on the Warrego River. The state border bisects Hungerford, which consists of little more than a couple of houses, a post office and a pub. Make sure you shut the steel dingo-proof fence behind you when you drive through: there's a $1000 fine if you don't. The heart of the town is the corrugated-iron *Royal Mail Hotel* (☎02/6755 4093; ③), just near the fence in Queensland: you can buy fuel, bread, milk and meat here, excellent **meals** are served until 9pm, and the friendly owners are happy to give advice. You can also **stay** in the bedrooms running along the front verandah, the caravan or bunkroom in the back, or camp. Fun is provided by **dingo-tossing competitions** on the highway at the front of the pub: since traffic is sparse and has to pause at the gate, it's an ideal spot to hurl a stuffed effigy of a dingo as far as you can.

Heading directly **north** from Bourke, the sealed Mitchell Highway goes right up to just past Charleville in Queensland (see p.484). **BARRINGUN**, on the border 135km from Bourke, is worth a visit just to have a drink at the remarkably genteel *Tattersalls Hotel*, set amid a flower-scented garden, once frequented by Breaker Morant. The hotel serves only snacks and doesn't have any accommodation. Across the road and closer to the border is the painted tin shed that comprises the *Bush Tucker Inn* (☎02/6874 7584; ③), which has **meals**, rooms, fuel and camping space.

South and east of Bourke

Because the empty, featureless plains seem to extend in all directions, the elongated rise of **Mount Gunderbooka** (498m), about 70km **southwest** of Bourke en route to Cobar, likened to a mini-Ayers Rock, is striking. It was also of great cultural significance to the Aboriginal people of the area, with semi-permanent waterholes and caves; several **cave paintings** can be seen; contact the National Parks and Wildlife Services for details (☎02/6872 2744).

Twenty-eight kilometres **east** of Bourke, en route to Brewarrina, is a turn-off south to **Mount Oxley**, climbed by the explorers Sturt and Hume in 1829 to herald the white settlement in the area. It's on private property, so you must first pick up a key from the information centre in Bourke. The town of **BREWARRINA** (locals call it "Bree"), 100km east of Bourke on the Barwon River, has a large Aboriginal population. The abundant fish stocks in the river made the area a natural fishery for the original population and the **fish traps** – of large, partly submerged boulders – can still be seen in the river. The excellent **Aboriginal Cultural Museum** (call ☎02/6839 2421 for opening hours), located near the ancient fisheries in an earth-covered building similar to an Aboriginal shelter, explains the history of the area's Ngemba people and offers walkabout **tours**.

Cobar

Since copper was discovered here in 1869, **COBAR**, just under 160km south of Bourke and the first real stop on the Barrier Highway between Nyngan and Broken Hill, has experienced three mining booms. Today, it's home to the vast **CSA Mine**, said to be the most highly mechanized in Australia, extracting about 850,000 tonnes of copper every year. Earlier booms resulted in a number of impressive public buildings among them the 1882 **courthouse** and the police station, as well as the *Great Western Hotel* on Marshall Street, whose iron-lace verandahs are said to be the longest in the state. Cobar's most recent industry is **emu farming**: as more and more restaurants serve up bush tucker, the big birds are in demand. None of these things add up to a very compelling reason to visit; you stop here – if at all – to refuel before driving the long stretch to Wilcannia.

For more about the town, head for the **Cobar Regional Museum** (Mon–Fri 8am–5pm, Sat & Sun 10am–5pm; $3) on Marshall Street, which is also the local **tourist office** (☎02/6836 2448). They can tell you about above-ground tours of the CSA mine (by arrangement on ☎02/6836 2001; free) and provide "Mud Maps", roughly drawn maps showing places of interest around Cobar that are difficult to reach. Chief of these, and arguably one of the most significant **Aboriginal rock art** locations in New South Wales, is the **Mount Grenfell Historic Site**, a 72-kilometre drive northwest of town. The rocky ridge contains three art sites with over a thousand motifs – human and animal figures, including the emus which you're still likely to see around the site, plus abstract designs and hand stencils. Older layers are visible beneath the more recent pigments, but there's no way to tell exactly how old the art is. The adjacent semi-permanent waterhole explains the significance of the site for the **Wongaibon people**. The NPWS in Cobar, at 19 Barton St (☎02/6836 2692), hands out a leaflet detailing the site, with its picnic and barbecue areas, toilets and limited water, plus a five-kilometre signposted return **walk** to the top of the ridge. To reach the site, head west along the Barrier Highway for 40km, then 32km north along a gravel road past Mount Grenfell Homestead to the picnic site.

There are a number of **motels** along the highway in Cobar; two to try – both with air-conditioning and pools – are the *Hi-way Motel* (☎02/6836 2000, fax 6836 1409; ⑤) and the *Cross Roads Motel*, at the corner of Bourke and Louth roads (☎02/6836 2711; ④); alternatively, there's the *Cobar Caravan Park* (☎02/6836 2425; cabins ③, on-site vans ②).

Wilcannia and around

The next major town on the Barrier Highway is **WILCANNIA**, 260km west of Cobar. The former "Queen City of the West" was founded in 1864 and towards the nineteenth century was a major port on the Darling River, from where produce was transported by paddle steamers and barges down the Darling–Murray river system to Adelaide. Droughts, the advent of the railways and the motor car put an end to the river trade, and today the ruins of the docks and the old lift-up bridge, along with a few impressive public buildings – the post office, police station, courthouse, Catholic convent and Athenaeum Museum (daily 9am–5pm) which houses the **tourist centre** (☎08/8091 5909) – are reminders of the once-prosperous era. Nowadays Wilcannia survives as a service centre for a far-flung Outback population, with its banks, shops, motels and service stations. You are welcomed into town by the black, red and yellow Aboriginal flag attesting to the fact that around eighty percent of the population are indigenous. There's an Aboriginal arts-and-crafts shop (irregular hours) on the same street as the town's imposing sandstone buildings. Sadly, alcoholism is a big problem in Wilcannia, and is the cause of sporadic violence (although not generally directed towards visitors).

Most visitors don't stop in Wilcannia for long, but if you need somewhere **to stay**, try the *Wilcannia Motel* (☎08/8091 5802; ⑤) or *Grahams Motel* (☎08/8091 5040; ④), both situated on the Barrier Highway. If you want to experience Outback life, head 85km southeast of Wilcannia along the unsealed Cobb Highway to **Yelta Station** (☎08/8091 9467, fax 8091 9444; ⑧), a sheep and cattle property run by Bill and Chris Elliot. The family take only one set of guests at a time, camping or staying in fully equipped shearers' quarters (③). You can reach the station by two-wheel drive, unless it's been raining – in which case the road is generally closed.

Heading north or south of Wilcannia you can follow the river along one of Australia's last great 4WD adventures – The Darling River Run – 829kms of Outback history, heritage and landscape running between Brewarrina and Wentworth. Further information on the Run is available from Bourke Information Centre (☎02/6872 2280).

You can travel the Darling River upstream **northwest** of Wilcannia all the way to Bourke (see p.320), just under 300km, on unsealed roads that closely follow the east and west banks with crossings at the settlements of Tilpa and Louth. Station properties dot the riverfront, including Mount Murchinson Station, on the west side of the river 30km north of Wilcannia, said to have once been managed by the son of Charles Dickens. At **TILPA**, 130km north of Wilcannia, there's a classic Outback pub, the 1890s *Tilpa Hotel* (☎02/6837 3928; ③), where you can find **meals, accommodation** and **fuel**, and for a $2 donation towards the Royal Flying Doctor Service, you can immortalize your name on the pub's tin wall. Ninety-three kilometres further on, at **LOUTH**, *Shindy's Inn* sells diesel and petrol and has basic accommodation in cabins (☎02/6874 7416; ③).

White Cliffs

From Wilcannia, you can branch off the Barrier Highway, heading north along a road partly sealed for 30km, and then graded gravel for the final 67km to the **opal fields** at **WHITE CLIFFS**, 97km away. Besides opals, White Cliffs is famous for the extraordinary summer heat, and for the way in which the miners have avoided it since the 1890s (when about four thousand lived here) – many of the approximately two hundred residents live underground in so-called "dug-outs", where it's cool in summer and warm in winter. There are all sorts of underground attractions, as well as a high-tech attempt to exploit the climate in the form of an experimental solar power station. For the authentic underground experience, there are two places to stay: the original *White Cliffs Dug-Out Motel* (☎08/8091 6647, fax 8091 6654, free call ☎1800/021 154; ⑤), which comes complete with licensed restaurant and outdoor swimming pool; all bathroom facilities are shared, as is also the case at the only subterranean B&B, *PJs* (☎08/8091 6626; ⑤). Cheaper, above-ground options are the *White Cliffs Hotel* (☎08/8091 6606, fax 8091 6782; ③) and the *Family Inn* at the Post Office (☎ & fax 08/8091 6645). If you can bear the heat, there's also **camping** (with hot showers) at Opal Pioneer Reserve, close to town. **Tourist information** is available at the White Cliffs General Store (☎ & fax 08/8091 6611).

There are several **tours** to White Cliffs from Broken Hill (see p.332); otherwise you'll need your own transport to get here. The only fuel stop between Wilcannia and Broken Hill is at the *Little Topar Hotel*, roughly halfway along the 195-kilometre stretch of the Barrier Highway.

Broken Hill

The ghosts of mining towns that died when the precious minerals ran out are scattered all over Australia. **BROKEN HILL**, on the other hand, celebrated its centenary in 1988, and its famous "**Line of Lode**", one of the world's major lead-silver-zinc ore bodies and the city's *raison d'être*, still has a little life left in it after being mined continuously for over 110 years. Inevitably, Broken Hill revolves around the mines, but in the last decade it has also evolved into a thriving arts centre, thanks to the initiative of the **Brushmen of the Bush**, a painting school founded by local artists Pro Hart, Hugh Schulz, Jack Absalom, John Pickup and the late Eric Minchin. Diverse talents have been attracted to Broken Hill, and their works are displayed in galleries scattered all over town. Some may be a bit on the tacky side, but others are interesting, unique, even excellent, and it's well worth devoting some time to gallery-browsing. The city was also the memorable location for several scenes of the drag-queens-run-riot-in-the-Outback film *Priscilla Queen of the Desert* which was shot here in 1993.

Almost 1200km west of Sydney and about 500km east of Adelaide, this surprisingly gracious Outback mining town, with a feel and architecture reminiscent of the South Australian capital, and with a population of around 21,000, manages to create a welcome splash of **green** in the harsh desert landscape that surrounds it. Extensive revegetation schemes around Broken Hill have created grasslands that, apart from being visually pleasing, help contain the dust that used to make the residents' lives miserable. It's aided by a reliable water supply – secured for the first time only in 1953 – via a one-hundred-kilometre-long pipeline from the Darling River at Menindee. The city is also a convenient base for touring far northwest New South Wales and nearby areas in South Australia.

Remember to adjust your watch: Broken Hill operates on South Australian **Central Standard Time**, half an hour behind the rest of NSW. All local transport schedules are in CST, but you should always check.

Arrival, information and accommodation

Arriving in Broken Hill by bus or train, you'll be pretty centrally placed. The **bus terminal** (☎08/8088 4040, or for 24hr reservations ☎13 2030) is behind the useful **tourist information centre**, at the corner of Bromide and Blende streets (daily 8.30am–5pm; ☎08/8087 6077; *www.murrayoutback.org.au*), where you can pick up a map ($2) for a self-guided Heritage Walk along Argent and Blende streets, or get information on the guided walking tour which delves into the city's history (Mon, Wed, Fri & Sat 10am; no tour late Dec to early Feb; 1hr 30min–2hr; donation). The **train station** is on Crystal Street, just a block below Argent Street – though unless you're travelling in style on the Sydney–Perth *Indian Pacific*, you'll actually come into the city on a Countrylink bus. The **airport** is about 5km south of town; there is no shuttle bus – a taxi costs just under $10 and there are usually a few waiting; alternatively you can arrange to have a hire car waiting (see p.331). In addition to what's on offer at the tourist information centre, you can pick up advice on nearby attractions from the district **NPWS** office at 183 Argent St (Mon–Fri 8am–4.30pm; ☎08/8088 5933).

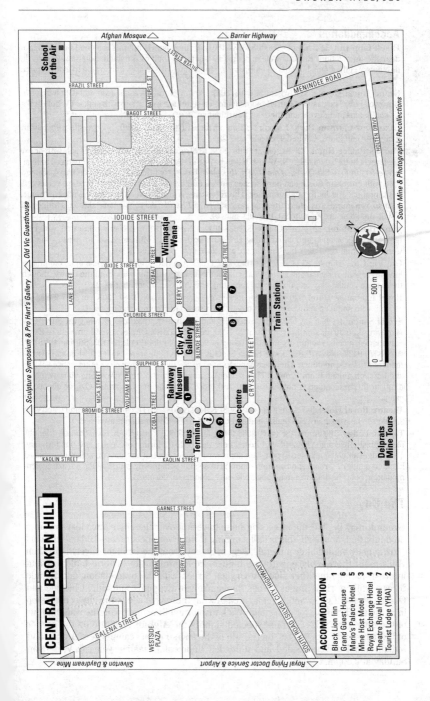

CENTRAL BROKEN HILL

ACCOMMODATION
Black Lion Inn   1
Grand Guest House   6
Mario's Palace Hotel   5
Mine Host Motel   3
Royal Exchange Hotel   4
Theatre Royal Hotel   7
Tourist Lodge (YHA)   2

Accommodation

Black Lion Inn, 34 Bromide St (☎08/8087 4801). If the hostel is full this is a good budget option near the bus station. Basic but clean rooms in a separate half of the lively hotel away from the pub noise; ceiling fans but shared bathrooms. Single rates of $18 are comparable to a dorm price. ②.

Grand Guest House, 317 Argent St (☎08/8087 5305). Central, pleasant accommodation in a two-storey ex-pub. The pastel-coloured rooms (some en-suite) are well set-up with sinks, TV, hot drinks, air-con, lamps and duvets and there's a guest lounge. ④–⑤.

Lake View Caravan Park, 1 Mann St, 3km northeast (☎08/8088 2250). A large site with a swimming pool and kiosk. Cabins ③, on-site vans ②.

Mario's Palace Hotel, 227 Argent St (☎08/8088 1699, fax 8087 6240). Vast corner pub with one of the largest hotel balconies in NSW, also has to be one of the state's most eccentric. Featured to hilarious effect in *Priscilla Queen of the Desert*, this place has every available wall and ceiling space covered with murals of Australian bush scenes plus an outburst of a Botticelli-style Birth of Venus ceiling mural painted by the Italian owner. The rooms are a kitsch lover's dream; the most extreme, with its own mural, was where the drag gang stayed in *Priscilla*. All rooms have air-con, a fridge and a sink and some are en suite. ④, Priscilla suite ⑤.

Mine Host Motel, 120 Argent St (☎08/8088 4044, fax 8088 1313). Recently renovated, with contemporary decor and comfort including air-con; there's also a swimming pool to splash about in. Central location right near the bus station, and close to clubs and pubs. ⑥.

Old Vic Guesthouse, 230 Oxide St (☎08/8087 1169). A comfortable guesthouse in an old bungalow with a wide verandah; all rooms share the bathroom. It's a 15min walk from the centre, though there are a couple of good pubs nearby for eating and drinking opportunities. ④.

Royal Exchange Hotel, 320 Argent St, corner of Chloride St (☎08/8087 2308, fax 8087 2191). An old pub with some en-suite rooms, but mostly the usual pub accommodation. ③–④.

Scotia Sanctuary, halfway between Broken Hill and Wentworth, 163km south along the Silver City Highway, then 30km southwest (☎02/5027 1200, fax 5027 1294). One of several projects of Earth Sanctuaries, a conservation organization based in South Australia (PO Box 1135, Stirling, SA 5152; ☎08/8370 9422, fax 8370 8332), the Scotia Sanctuary protects the rare Mallee fowl in an environment of Mallee sand dunes. There are opportunities to see the birds, as well as other native wildlife and flora, on guided tours (from $10 per person), and you can stay here (providing your own bedding) in the well-equipped homestead (④) and more basic shearers' quarters (①), or choose to camp.

Theatre Royal Hotel, 347 Argent St (☎08/8087 3318, fax 8087 3511). Nineteenth-century pub with simple rooms, which are air-conditioned and come with TV. Cheap singles available. ③.

Tourist Lodge, 100 Argent St (☎08/8088 2086, fax 8087 0511; *mcrae@pcpro.net.au*). A friendly, clean guesthouse and YHA-affiliated hostel near the tourist information centre and bus terminal. The budget air-con guesthouse rooms are popular with older Australians and young families; shared kitchen/dining/TV room and common room. YHA section with mostly twin, double or triple accommodation. Solar-heated swimming pool; bike hire. Rooms ③, dorms ①.

The City

Green it may be, but the huge slag heap towering over the city centre leaves you in no doubt that, above all, this is still a mining town. Even the streets – laid out in a grid – are mostly named after minerals: Argent Street (from the Latin for silver) is Broken Hill's main thoroughfare, with the highest concentration of historic buildings and interest; parallel to either side are Crystal Street, with the train station, and Blende Street, while at right angles across the centre run Bromide, Sulphide, Chloride and Oxide streets. If you want to get an idea of what there is to see in the city centre, stop in at the tourist office for a Heritage Walk map or get information on the walking tour of the town (see p.324). An unexpected sight is the **Afghan Mosque** on the corner of Williams and Buck streets, on the site of the former camel camp where Afghan and Indian camel drivers loaded and unloaded their camel teams; you can visit it on Sunday at 2.30pm.

Public transport in Broken Hill is poor – the tourist office can provide a combined timetable and route map of the Broken Hill Town Bus Service (☎08/8087 3311) with four routes operating infrequently within the city only (Mon–Fri 8am–5.15pm; fares start from $1).

Mines and minerals

One thing you shouldn't miss in Broken Hill is an underground mine tour. You can do it right in town at the disused Delprats mine, or further out at the Daydream Mine. At **Delprats** (tours Mon–Fri 10.30am, Sat 2pm, more during school holidays, arrive 15min before start; 2hr; $23) you don a miner's hat, boots and a heavy belt with batteries for your helmet light, before descending in the miners' cage – jammed with thirty or more people – 130m below the surface. Here, former miners working as guides will take you on a tour through the system of tunnels (stopes), describing and demonstrating how miners used to work in the bad old days, and how the work is done now. The **Daydream Mine** (daily 10am–3.30pm; tours on demand; 1hr; $10), which operated between 1882 and 1889, is 20km out of Broken Hill on the Silverton Road – turn right at the sign and follow the thirteen-kilometre dirt road; tours here are similar, but half as long and a little tamer. Both tours can be booked through the tourist information centre, but without your own transport, you'll need to go on a bus tour for the Daydream Mine (see box on p.332).

MINING AND UNIONISM IN BROKEN HILL

The story of Broken Hill began in 1883 when a German-born boundary rider from Mount Gipps station, Charles Rasp, pegged out a forty-acre lease of a "broken hill" that he believed was tin. A syndicate of seven was formed, founding the **Broken Hill Proprietary** (BHP) to work what turned out to be rich silver, lead and zinc deposits. Broken Hill's mines, dominated by BHP until they withdrew operations in 1939, have contributed greatly to the wealth of Australia: the deposit, more than 7km long and up to 250m wide, is thought originally to have contained more than three hundred million tonnes of sulphide-rich ore. Even now there's said to be ten years left in the "Line of Lode", though only one mining company, **Pasminco**, is currently working it.

In the early years, living and working **conditions** for the miners were atrocious. The climate was harsh, housing was poor and diseases such as typhoid, scarlet fever and dysentery – to say nothing of work-related illnesses such as lead poisoning, and mine accidents – contributed to a death rate almost twice as high as the average in New South Wales. The mine and the growing town rapidly stripped the landscape of timber, leaving the settlement surrounded by a vast, bleak plain. Dust storms were common. Not surprisingly, perhaps, Broken Hill was at the forefront of **trade union** development in Australia, as the miners, many of them recent immigrants, fought to improve their living and working conditions. It was their ability to unite that ultimately won them their battles, above all in the Big Strike of 1919–20, when, after eighteen months of holding out against the police and strikebreakers, major concessions were won from BHP. Not that the trade union movement at Broken Hill should be viewed through too-rosy glasses. The union, which effectively ran the town in conjunction with the mine companies, was also a bastion of racism and male supremacy, though the interpretive boards at the tourist information centre glorify this as "mateship". Non-white persons were not tolerated in town, nor were working women who happened to be married. Even now, these attitudes have not altogether disappeared.

Despite the life left in Broken Hill's mineral deposits, the future is none too certain. With modern mining technology the ore is removed faster, and the numbers employed are lower. Between 1970 and 1975, about 4000 people were employed in the mines. By the early 1980s this number had been reduced to 2500, and less than 700 work there now. The population continues to gradually decrease and every few years another of the city's many pubs closes down.

If you can't face going underground, it's now possible to take an overground tour of the old **South Mine** which commenced operations in 1888 and closed in 1972. Accessed via Eyre Street in Broken Hill South, the site is being developed for visitors with a $4.6 million Federal Government grant. Ambitious plans include a miners' memorial site and cable car to go right across the old open cut workings, with the majority of the work to be finished by 2001. For the moment, however, the tours offered – which concentrate on the old ambulance room and BHP's rather horrific safety record – are rather haphazard and not particularly value-for-money (☎08/8088 6000 or the tourist office for details). If you've proven your interest in mining history by making it out to South Mine, you might like to combine it with a visit to the nearby **Photographic Recollections**, also on Eyre Street (Mon–Fri 10am–4.30pm, Sat & Sun 1–4.30pm; $4). This privately-run but not in the least amateurish exhibition provides a pictorial history of Broken Hill, with over 600 photographs accompanied by well-researched and -written text which delves into mining, union and social history. The location itself, in the former Central Power Station, tells a story of the city's very Outback past; from the 1930s Broken Hill produced all its power here until as late as 1986 when it finally went on the national grid.

There are three other mining related attractions in the city. A visit to the bizarre but wonderful **White's Mineral Art Gallery and Mining Museum**, 1 Allendale St (off Silverton Road; daily 9am–6pm; $4), might well be the next best thing to going underground. The art section is pretty extraordinary, consisting mainly of collages of crushed minerals depicting Broken Hill scenes – mining, historic buildings and the Outback. And at the back there's a walk-in underground mine, re-created so convincingly that it genuinely looks and feels like the real thing: inside, you're given an entertaining lecture, with videos and models, on the history of Broken Hill and its mines. A shop at the front of the museum sells minerals, opals, jewellery and pottery. The **Railway, Mineral and Train Museum** (daily 10am–3pm, $3), opposite the tourist information centre, which features an extensive mineral collection as well as old railway machinery and memorabilia including the fittings from the bedroom of the *Maidens Hotel* in Menindee where the explorers Burke and Wills stayed on their ill-fated expedition (see p.486 and p.758). Finally, the **Geocentre**, in a nineteenth-century bond store on the corner of Bromide and Crystal streets (Mon–Fri 10am–5pm, Sat & Sun 1–5pm; $3), looks at Broken Hill's geology, mineralogy and metallurgy. At the back is an example of a tin miner's shed – you can imagine what the heat must have been like in summer, or experience it yourself if you're foolhardy enough to come out here at that time of year.

Art and the Outback

There's not only indoor art in galleries in Broken Hill; the city is full of public murals and outdoor sculpture. Pick up the Broken Hill Art Trail fold-out poster ($2), which has colour photographs and maps, from the Broken Hill City Art Gallery (below).

Broken Hill's artistic side is perhaps best expressed at the **Broken Hill City Art Gallery** (Mon–Fri 10am–5pm, Sat & Sun 1–5pm; $3), in the Entertainment Centre on Chloride Street, where there's an excellent representative collection of artists from Broken Hill. Established in 1904, it's the second-oldest gallery in the state – after the Art Gallery of New South Wales in Sydney – with a small collection of nineteenth- and early twentieth-century paintings. It's the recent work that's interesting, though, including a Sidney Nolan and a John Olsen, as well as the works of the "Brushmen of the Bush" (though sometimes these might be moved to make way for special exhibitions). One of the highlights of the gallery is the spectacular **Silver Tree**, a 68-centimetre-high figurine, wrought of pure silver from the Broken Hill Mines, depicting five Aborigines, a drover on horseback, kangaroos, emus and sheep gathered under a tree. Also on display are sculptures created by artists who participated in the 1993 Sculpture Symposium at The Living Desert (see below).

Pro Hart's Gallery, at 108 Wyman St (Mon–Sat 9am–12.30pm & 1.30–5pm, Sun 1.30–5pm; $4), should also be visited. Pro Hart is a former Broken Hill miner turned artist and national celebrity who claims that his only artistic influences were the colours and subjects he saw on his family's sheep station where he grew up, which he then turned into illustrations that decorated his correspondence lessons. His trademark humorous Outback scenes depict events such as race meetings or backyard barbecues, all featuring lively figures in a caricature style. The gallery's three cramped levels are said to hold the largest private art collection in Australia, with a truly astounding collection of the artist's own work as well as works by other Australian painters – Tom Roberts, Sidney Nolan and Albert Namatjira among them – although not necessarily their best. A collection of sculptures done by Hart are in a lot across the road – you can check them out for free. Also in the city centre are the **Ant Hill Gallery**, at 24 Bromide St (Mon–Sat 9am–5pm, Sun 1.30–5pm), just opposite the tourist centre, and the **Art of Broken Hill Gallery**, at 219 Argent St (Mon–Fri 10am–6pm, Sat 10am–1pm, Sun 1–5pm); both display a variety of local artists' works, while the Ant Hill Gallery is the only place in Broken Hill where you can buy Pro Hart's paintings.

Community-based **Wiimpatja Wana Aboriginal Crafts**, 84 Oxide St (Mon–Fri 9am–5pm), is the most interesting of the crafts outlets, with a workshop out back where you can watch the artists at work between 9am and 3.30pm making traditional wooden tools, weapons and musical instruments. Wood is gathered (not felled) from as far afield as Wilcannia, and each type has a specific purpose: didgeridoos are made from sections of mallee gums eaten hollow by termites, clapping sticks and nulla nullas are made from mulga, bowls from burls of river red gums, carved snakes from small mulga roots gathered from riverbanks, and brooches from prickly wattle or "purple wood".

Six kilometres out of town, the **Sculpture Symposium** in **The Living Desert Reserve** is the most stunning of Broken Hill's art exhibits, a reserve in the eroded Barrier Ranges desert region that is the location of a group of sculptures carved from Wilcannia sandstone boulders. The twelve artists involved in their creation were part of a sculpture symposium in 1993 and were drawn from diverse cultures – two from Mexico (including an Aztec Indian), two from Syria, three from Georgia (in the Caucasus), and five Australians, including two Bathurst Islanders – and this is reflected in the variety of their works. The pieces from the Georgian artists are particularly fine: Badri Sulushia's Outback Madonna and Child; Valerian Jiiya's Cubist interpretation; and Jumber Jikiya's horse's head, a tribute to the rare breed of Georgian horses slaughtered under Stalin's orders. Nastra Luna of Mexico badly injured his hands and his piece became a collective effort, depicting a soaring eagle, with the hands of the other sculptors who helped him imprinted in the rock. The Aboriginal artist Badger Bates, from Broken Hill, was inspired by the stone carvings of his ancestors, and his piece shows two rainbow serpents travelling north. The best time to visit the sculptures is at sunset when the light is magical and you can really soak up the atmosphere. It's a pleasant fifteen-minute walk up the hill from the car park to the sculptures; you can also drive right up, but because of unfortunate bouts of vandalism in the past you must first go to the tourist information centre in town, get a key to the gate ($10 deposit) and pay $5 per car. A $1 information brochure about the sculptures is available from the tourist office.

The Royal Flying Doctor service and the School of the Air

Broken Hill offers an excellent opportunity to visit two Australian Outback institutions, the **Royal Flying Doctor Service** (RFDS) and the School of the Air. The RFDS, at Broken Hill Airport, offers guided tours (Mon–Fri 9am–noon & 1–5pm, Sat & Sun 10am–noon & 1–4pm; ☎08/8088 0777; it's best to buy your ticket in advance from the tourist office as places are limited; $3), with an accompanying video and talk. In the headquarters you'll see the radio room where calls from remote places in New South Wales, South Australia and Queensland are handled before going out to the hangar to see the aircraft. The increasing popularity of the tours is due to the Australian television series *The Flying Doctors*, which is shown worldwide, and since a third of the annual budget of $30 million has to come through fund-raising – the rest of the money is from the State and Federal governments – whatever you spend on the tour and at the souvenir shop here is going to a good cause.

In many ways the **School of the Air** is also indebted to the RFDS: lessons for children in the Outback, in a transmission area of 1.8 million square kilometres, are conducted via RFDS two-way radio. The service was established in 1956 to improve education for children in the isolated Outback, and today visitors listen to the first hour's transmission in a schoolroom surrounded by childrens' artwork (Mon–Fri, term time only 8.30am; book in advance at the tourist centre; $2). It's frighteningly like being back at school yourself, with jolly primary-school teachers hosting singalongs; what comes out of the radio is a static squawk, but the children in the far-flung areas seem to enjoy it.

Eating, drinking and nightlife

Broken Hill still has the proverbial **pub** on every corner – most of them serve inexpensive counter meals as well as ice-cold beer on tap. Broken Hill has always been a legendary drinking hole, once having over seventy hotels. Many have been converted to other uses, but at the time of writing there were still twenty-three hotels licensed to operate and a pub crawl is highly recommended. Some places to include for an early drink, are the kitsch-crammed *Mario's Palace*, 227 Argent St, which memorably featured in *Priscilla Queen of the Desert*, the *West Darling Historic Hotel*, 400 Argent St, popular on Friday nights (until midnight); the *Black Lion Inn*, 34 Bromide St, good any time (after midnight Tues–Sat but Fri & Sat till 4am) but especially during happy hour at the cocktail bar done out like an underground mine, and the *Theatre Royal Hotel*, 347 Argent St (after midnight Mon–Sat, Sun to 8pm), which hosts occasional bands.

Another option is to sample the local culture at one of the numerous **clubs**. These make most of their money out of gambling – with snooker tables, darts and endless parades of one-armed bandits – and they're happy to draw their customers in and keep them playing by tempting them with cheap food, and quite often live entertainment. Best known is the *Barrier Social Democratic Club* (*Demo Club* to the locals) at 214 Argent St (☎08/8088 4477) with $5 daily meal specials including a well-assorted salad bar plus great, inexpensive breakfasts (7–9am). You could also try the *Broken Hill Legion Club*, 166–170 Crystal St (☎08/8087 4064); or the *Broken Hill Musicians Club*, 276 Crystal St (☎08/8088 1777), which has inherited Broken Hill's famous **Two Up School**, once an illegal back-lane gambling operation.

Apart from the pubs and clubs, there are several good **cafés and bakeries** on Argent Street where you can get something to eat and drink – restaurants aren't really Broken Hill's style. *Ruby's Coffee Lounge*, at no. 373, near the corner of Oxide Street (closed Sun), places the emphasis on healthy food, with a few vegetarian dishes always on offer and lots of baked goodies. Cosy *Charlotte's* at no. 317, opposite the post office, is reckoned to serve the town's best cappuccino and there's a well-assorted range of cakes, muffins and slices to go with your foamy brew. *Stope Café* at no. 343 (Mon–Sat 9am–10pm; ☎08/8087 2637) is a city-style café with a decor of burnt orange walls, blue ceiling, big open doors and wooden floors, but unfortunately the standard of its coffee doesn't match the interior. Their open toasted sandwiches, however, are huge, tasty and cheap; a separate, pricier night-time restaurant menu features grills, pasta and salads. For **grocery** supplies, visit the International Store, 71 Oxide St (daily 7am–midnight), or the Big W supermarket, Westside Plaza, Galena Street (open daily).

Listings

Airlines Hazelton (flying to Sydney and Dubbo Sun–Fri), Kendell (flying to Adelaide daily) and International Aviation (flying to Sydney and Mildura daily); all can be booked through Traveland at 350 Argent St (☎08/8087 1969).

Bike rental Johnny Windham, 135 Argent St (☎08/8087 3707), rents mainly mountain bikes; $5 per day, $25 per week, plus obligatory helmet $2; closed Sat & Sun. The Tourist Lodge hires bikes to guests at similar rates.

Bookshops ABC Centre, 309 Argent St, specializes in local history and the Outback (☎08/8088 1177). For secondhand books, try W Book Exchange, 320 Chloride St, corner of Thomas St (☎08/8087 3383).

Car rental Avis, 121 Rakow St (☎08/8087 7532); Budget, 338 Crystal St (☎13 2727); Hertz, at the tourist information centre (☎08/8087 2719); and Thrifty, 190 Argent St (☎08/8088 1928); all have desks at the airport too. Cheaper deals are available at Holmes' Hire, 475 Argent St (☎08/8087 2210), with older cars from $50 per day and 4WDs from $100.

Cinema Village Silver City Cinema, 41 Oxide St (☎08/8087 4569).

Hospital Broken Hill Base Hospital and Health Services, 176 Thomas St (☎08/8088 0333).

Laundry Oxide Street Laundrette, 241 Oxide St. Service washes available, with free pick-up and delivery (☎08/8088 2022).

Pharmacy Amcal Chemist, Westside Plaza, Galena St (☎08/8088 4800), has an after-hours emergency number (☎08/8088 5639) but the most central pharmacy is Peoples CP Chemist, 323 Argent St (☎08/8087 3326).

Post office Corner of Argent and Chloride streets, NSW 2880.

Swimming pool There are two municipal outdoor pools: Alma Pool, Voughtman St, South Broken Hill (☎08/8091 5059; $2), which is open mid-Nov to late March only, daily 9am–6pm; and North Pool, north of the centre on McCulloch St (☎08/8787 6690), which is heated in winter (daily: April–Oct 6–8.30am & 10.30am–6pm; Nov–March 6–8am & 9am–10pm; $2).

Taxis Yellow Radio Cabs (☎08/8088 1144). Taxis work out to be very expensive; eg $8 just to get from the centre to the South Mine.

Tours See box p.332.

Excursions from Broken Hill: Silverton

The ghost town of **SILVERTON**, just 25km northwest of Broken Hill on a good road, makes a great day out. Take note that there is no fuel available at Silverton. If the scene looks vaguely familiar, you probably have seen it before: parts of *Mad Max II* were shot around here, and the **Silverton Hotel** (daily 8.30am–9.30pm, though they often close earlier) has appeared as the "Gamulla Hotel" in *Razorback*, the "Hotel Australia" in *A Town Like Alice*, and "Juanita's Diner" in *Fiddlers Green* with Don Johnson. It also seems to star in just about every commercial – usually beer-related – that features an Outback scene. The stark impact of the pub, with barren, red earth stretching endlessly to the horizon, has been somewhat diminished by the greening of the desert, but it's still the ultimate Outback image and a must for every photo collection. The pub has its own collection, the lower walls covered with snapshots from the various film shoots, the upper walls piled high with an assortment of beer cans and old bottles. In some ways it feels like a milk bar, with a fridge full of cold soft drinks, a tea urn, and the only available food some limp sandwiches, pies and pasties, rather than the usual counter meals. But in the tradition of all Outback pubs, it has its own in-jokes; you'll find out what all the laughter is about if you ask to "take the test".

Taking the **Silverton Heritage Trail**, a two-hour stroll around town marked by white arrows, is a good way to work up a thirst. But it's far too hot to attempt in the summer, and is best undertaken during the cooler months. Along the way it'll take you past the old **Silverton School Craft Centre**, and the 1889 vintage **Silverton Gaol Museum** (daily 9.30am–4.30pm; $2), with the usual collection of relics from pioneer days and

TOURS FROM BROKEN HILL

There are a big range of tours on offer, from scenic flights to 4WD tours, all of which can be booked from the tourist information office (see p.324). Most include a pick-up and return service to and from your accommodation.

AIR CHARTERS AND SCENIC FLIGHTS

If you have a bit of cash to spare, small aircraft are an excellent way of getting around, covering the enormous distances quickly and in relative comfort.
Crittenden Air, Airport Terminal (☎08/8088 5702). Tour flights to Tibooburra ($285), White Cliffs ($210), as well as several more local scenic tours. Bush mail-run with the Flying Postman, including lunch and tour of White Cliffs, leaves Sat 6.30am ($230).

BUS TOURS

These tend to be overpriced, given that many tours merely provide transport to places that could be more enjoyably visited with a rental car or bike, or even by taxi. Tours are more frequent between early April and the end of November, and have reduced schedules during the hot summer months.
Broken Hill Cockatoo Tours (☎08/8087 7701). Half-day tours ($35) to Silverton, the Daydream Mine, Delprats Mine, or city art galleries plus the Sculpture Symposium; a day-tour is also offered to Menindee Lakes and Kinchega National Park ($80).
Silver City Tours (☎08/8087 3310). Excursions to Royal Flying Doctor Service ($15), School of the Air ($15), White's Mineral Art Gallery and Mining Museum ($15); half-day tours of city sights and Pasminco mining lease ($26), art galleries and the Sculpture Symposium ($29), Silverton ($29); day-tours, including lunch, to White Cliffs ($99), Menindee Lakes, Kinchega National Park and Tandou Irrigation Farm ($79), and Mutawintji National Park ($79).

FOUR-WHEEL-DRIVE TOURS

Alf's 4WD Safaris (☎08/8087 8108). Overnight two-day camping tours to Kinchega and Menindee national parks, and to Mutawintji National Park; three-day trips to Tibooburra and around, or extended to six days following the footsteps of Burke and Wills – Coopers Creek, Dig Tree, Burke's grave and Innamincka. Two-day trips from $280, extra days $140.
Corner Country Adventure Tours (☎08/8087 75142 or outside Broken Hill free call ☎1800/763 440). Longer 4WD trips, including a four-day/three-night trip to all four national parks detailed in the following pages ($710), or tailor-made excursions as far afield as the Birdsville Track.
Goanna Safari (☎08/8087 6057; *www.goanna-safari.com.au*). Recommended tours with a well-informed guide who is not in a rush; maximum four people in the group. One-day tours ($95); to Poolamacca Station, a sheep station 60km north of Broken Hill; Menindee lakes and Kinchega National Park; Mutawintji National Park including the Aboriginal art sites; the Dog Fence; or closer to home a round-up of the Royal Flying Doctor Service, Silverton, and the Sculpture Symposium. Two-day safari to White Cliffs, staying in a dug-out motel ($340), or extending to three days and including Mutawintji ($510). Tibooburra and Camerons Corner are taken in on another two-day trip (also $340). Short trips out to The Living Desert sculpture site (minimum $10, cheaper depending on numbers) are also available.

Outback stations, plus mining equipment. There's a burgeoning art scene here, too, with four galleries to browse through. **Peter Browne's Gallery** (daily 9am–5pm), in an 1884 house on a hill, is worth a look for its uniquely original decoration and the humorous paintings of bush scenes, koala-shearing, kookaburras boiling the billy, and Browne's trademark emus with huge, saucer-shaped eyes. Also interesting is Albert Woodcroffe's and Bronwen Standley's **Horizon Gallery** (daily 9am–6pm), opposite the pub. The husband and wife team paint in a similar style, creating their trademark horizon paintings, mainly in acrylics – finely detailed works that really capture the sense of space and the seemingly endless skyline.

One of the most enjoyable things to do while in Silverton is to go on a camel tour. The Cannard family who run the **Silverton Camel Farm** (☎08/8088 5316), come from a long line of camel trainers and have forty working camels on their farm. They attend to the camels in every way, including making their leather saddles, breaking them in and pegging their noses. You can't miss the camel farm on the way into Silverton, with the shapes of camels looming like desert mirages. You can exercise a whim and hop on for fifteen minutes ($5), or trot for an hour along the nearby creek ($20), but the best experience is the sunset trek (2hr; $40), a ride to the Mundi Mundi Plain to look at the setting sun and a return trip under the night stars accompanied by a pack of lively dogs. Longer safaris into the desert are also on offer, from one to three days ($80–270).

Beyond Silverton, the road continues a further 14km to the **Umberumberka reservoir**, Broken Hill's only source of water until the Menindee Lakes Scheme was set up. There's a signposted lookout area which makes a nice picnic spot. A few kilometres further on you reach the **Mundi Mundi Plains Lookout**. Here, the undulating plateau you have been driving across descends gradually to a vast plain, and on clear days you can see in the distance the blurred outline of the northern Flinders Ranges in South Australia. This spot is where, at the end of *Mad Max II*, Mel Gibson tipped the semitrailer.

If you want to stay in Silverton, your only choice is to **camp** at Penrose Park, where there's a shower, toilets and barbecue; rates are nominal – ask at the house there or call ☎08/8088 5307.

Kinchega National Park and the Menindee lakes

Flat **Kinchega National Park** is situated among the **Menindee lakes**, near the township of **MENINDEE**, southeast of Broken Hill. There's a sealed road for the 110km to Menindee and the park entrance, and gravel roads thereafter; before you go, visit the Broken Hill NPWS to get information about road conditions (see p.324), or ask at the **Menindee Tourist Information Centre** (Mon–Fri 9am–5pm, Sat & Sun 10am–1pm; ☎08/8091 4274), where a detailed, hand-drawn "Mud Map" of the lakes area, showing areas of interest, is available free of charge. The Menindee lakes are an extensive, natural oasis, feeding the Darling and Murray rivers and, most importantly, supplying water to Broken Hill; they're also a big recreation area, with facilities for camping, powerboating, water-skiing, sailing, swimming and fishing. The waters protected by the Kinchega National Park, **Menindee Lake** and **Cawndilla Lake**, are a haven for **waterbirds**; a common sight are little black cormorants (commonly known as shags), floating in feeding flocks alongside pelicans, with whom they hunt co-operatively. There's an **information** shelter 5km into the park and a normally unmanned visitor information centre about 10km further on near the **Kinchega Woolshed**. Kinchega Station was one of the first pastoral settlements in the area in 1850 and was worked until 1967; you can explore it by following the signposted woolshed **walk**. Accommodation is available in the shearers' sheds here (①; book at Broken Hill NPWS), or at the thirty river campsites ($5 payable on site) scattered through the river-red-gum woodland along the river – including the site of Burke and Wills's base camp from late October 1860 until late January 1861 (a tree marks the spot). The main camping area, with toilets, is on the shores of Cawndilla Lake, with its sandy beaches and good swimming.

Burke and Wills stayed in Menindee at the *Maidens Hotel*, Yartla Street (☎08/8091 4208, fax 8091 4300; ②), on their ill-fated trip north in 1860 (see box on p.486). Unfortunately the room in which they stayed is now full of poker machines, but there is some interpretive material in the hotel (the room's fittings are now in the

Railway Museum in Broken Hill; see p.327), and the green courtyard's a good place for a drink or a counter meal. Otherwise, you can stay at the *Burke & Wills Motel* opposite (☎08/8091 4313, fax 8091 4406; ④), or camp in relative comfort at the *Menindee Lakes Caravan Park* on Lakes Shore Road, 5km northwest of town (☎08/8091 4315; on-site vans ②), which has a kiosk and grocery store. If you don't have transport, you can take a **day-tour** out here from Broken Hill; the best is with Goanna Safari (see box on p.332).

Mutawintji National Park

Mutawintji National Park (formerly Mootwingee National Park), 130km northeast of Broken Hill in the Bynguano Ranges, has totally different and perhaps even more fascinating scenery to offer: secluded gorges and quiet waterholes that attract a profusion of wildlife. The main attractions of the park are the ancient galleries of **Aboriginal rock art** in the caves and overhangs; you can only visit these accompanied by an Aboriginal tour guide (Wed & Sat 11am Eastern Standard Time; no bookings required; $15; 2hr; special tours by arrangement ☎08/8088 7000) – there are no tours in the hot summer months. While on the tour you get to visit the **Mutawintji Cultural Resource Centre**, with brightly painted murals depicting Aboriginal myths. There's a **camping** area at Homestead Creek, among river red gums at the entrance to Homestead Gorge (camping is payable on site; $5) and a number of **walking trails** (including the short wheelchair-accessible Thakaaltjika Mingkana Walk). Access to and within the park is via unsealed gravel roads, and you'll need to bring extra fuel as none is available here. It's normally fine for 2WD vehicles, but check locally, as the roads can quickly become impassable after even a light rain; bring extra food just in case. The NPWS office in Broken Hill (see p.324) can provide other information. You can also get here from Broken Hill with Goanna Safari; a bushwalk (2hr 30min) is part of their excellent tour (see p.332).

Corner Country: Tibooburra and the Sturt National Park

A remote Outback settlement in the far northwest corner of New South Wales, 337km from Broken Hill, **TIBOOBURRA** can be reached by normal vehicle on a well-maintained dirt road from Broken Hill – the Silver City Highway. You can also reach it from Bourke (see p.320), 454km southwest along various unsealed and mostly deserted roads. After rain, roads may become impassable, and it's important to find out about road and weather conditions before you set out; it's also crucial to carry extra food, water, fuel and spare vehicle parts in case you get stranded later on. (Refer to the tourist information office in Broken Hill or Bourke for advice before leaving.) Tibooburra has been settled for over a hundred and ten years: several stone buildings from the 1880s still remain, the result of a flurried goldrush, which add a bit of architectural charm to the tiny township. The nearby granite outcrops – worthy of a sunset stroll – from which the stone was quarried, gave the town its former name of Granites. Outback institutions are well-represented here: there are some classic pubs (the *Family Hotel* and *Tibooburra Hotel* are detailed below), a hospital serviced by the Royal Flying Doctor Service, and a **School of the Air** similar to the one in Broken Hill; visitors can witness the on-air education service on schoolday mornings from 9am ($2). The **NPWS office** in the town (☎08/8091 3308), attached to the old courthouse (with a display about the town's history) provides visitor information, including the latest on the roads and weather, and camping permits for the national park.

In nearby **Sturt National Park**, a network of roads and tracks is maintained by the NPWS to 2WD standard, but check with the rangers at Tibooburra before setting out. The park's 3500 square kilometres are cut in two by the Grey Range: to the west are the rolling red sand dunes of the Strzelecki Desert, and to the east are the stone-covered, so-called gibber plains extending for hundreds of kilometres. The area supports a number of red and grey kangaroos, emus and lizards.

At the edge of the park, the border between Queensland, New South Wales and South Australia is delineated by the 1.8-metre-high **Dingo Fence**. This, the world's longest fence (4850km), was originally constructed by the Queensland government to stop the invasion of rabbits from the south; it's now maintained to keep dingoes out of sheep-grazing land. The point where the three states meet is known as **Cameron's Corner** and is marked by a post: it's a popular target for travellers, so much so that there's even a shop here, the wittily named *Corner Store* (☎08/8091 3872). As well as dishing up the ubiquitous meat pies and other typical Aussie fillers, they have fuel and can give you useful road advice.

There are a couple of pleasant **hotels**, with welcome air-conditioning, on Briscoe Street in Tibooburra: the *Family Hotel* (☎08/8091 3314, fax 8091 3430; ③) is marginally the fancier with a wall mural by the Australian artist Clifton Pugh, while the *Tibooburra Hotel* (☎08/8091 3310, fax 8091 3406; ④) vies for attention with its wall full of old hats. Both also serve decent counter meals. *The Granites Caravan Park*, at the corner of Brown and King streets (☎08/8091 3305; cabins ③, on-site vans ②), has a refreshing pool.

travel details

Most public transport in NSW originates in Sydney, and the main services are outlined in the "Travel Details" at the end of Chapter 1.

Trains

There are nine main train routes departing from Sydney that pass through the region covered in this chapter; all trains connect with Countrylink buses run by the state rail system to fill in the gaps. Destinations within the area of this chapter are printed in bold type below.

• Sydney–**Albury** (1 daily; 7hr 20min), via **Cootamundra** (5hr) and **Wagga Wagga** (6hr).

• Sydney–**Armidale** (1 daily; 7hr 45min), via **Tamworth** (5hr 40min).

• Sydney–Brisbane (1 daily; 13hr 30min), with stops including **Taree**, **Coffs Harbour** and **Grafton**.

• Sydney–**Canberra** (1 daily; 4hr), via **Goulburn** (2hr 30min).

• Sydney–**Dubbo** (1 daily; 6hr 30min), via **Bathurst** (3hr 30min).

• Sydney–Melbourne (1 daily; 12hr), with stops at **Cootamundra** and **Wagga Wagga**.

• Sydney–**Moree** (1 daily; 8hr 40min), via **Scone** (2hr 55min), **Gunnedah** (6hr 5min) and **Narrabri** (7hr 15min).

• Sydney–**Murwillumbah** (1 daily; 13hr 30min), via **Taree** (5hr), **Wauchope** (6hr), **Coffs Harbour** (8hr 30min), **Grafton** (9hr 30min), **Lismore** (11hr 30min) and **Byron Bay** (12hr).

• The NSW leg of the Indian Pacific linking Sydney and Perth takes in **Condoblin** (10hr 35min from Sydney), **Ivanhoe** (13hr 50min), **Menindee** (16hr 10min) and **Broken Hill** (18hr 20min).

Buses

Albury to: Corowa (3 weekly; 1hr); Cowra (1 daily; 4hr); Echuca (3 weekly; 4hr 15min).

Armidale to: Brisbane (6 daily; 7hr 45min); Port Macquarie (3 weekly; 6hr 15min); Melbourne (2 daily; 18hr 45min); Sydney (4 daily; 8hr); Tamworth (3 daily; 1hr 45min); Tenterfield (2 daily; 2hr 20min).

Bourke to: Dubbo (3 weekly; 4hr 45min).

Broken Hill to: Adelaide (2 daily; 7hr); Cobar (3 daily; 5hr 30min); Dubbo (5 daily; 8hr 30min); Mildura (3 weekly; 4hr); Sydney (2 daily; 16hr).

Byron Bay to: Ballina (3–8 daily; 25min); Brisbane (10–11 daily; 2hr 20min); Coffs Harbour (6 daily; 5hr); Surfers Paradise (6–7 daily; 1hr 5min); Sydney (6 daily; 12hr 15min).

Canberra to: Bairnsdale (3 weekly; 7hr); Batemans Bay (1–2 daily; 2hr 30min); Bega (1 daily; 3hr 30min); Bombala (3 weekly; 3hr 30min); Cooma (1–2 daily; 1hr 50min); Eden (1 daily; 4hr 20min); Melbourne (6 daily; 8hr 30min); Moruya (1–2 daily; 3hr 25min); Narooma (1–2 daily; 4hr 30min); Nowra (1 daily; 4hr 45min); Wagga Wagga (1 daily; 4hr); Wollongong (1 daily; 3hr 25min).

Coffs Harbour to: Byron Bay (6 daily; 3hr 40min); Grafton (5 daily; 1hr 10min); Nambucca Heads (6 daily; 50min); Tweed Heads (1 daily; 6hr 10min).

Coonabarabran to: Adelaide (3 daily; 12hr); Brisbane (4 daily; 19hr); Canberra (3 daily; 5hr 40min); Melbourne (5 daily; 7hr 30min); Sydney (5–6 daily; 8hr 30min–10hr).

Cootamundra to: Dubbo (3 weekly; 4hr 15min); Gundagai (6 weekly; 45min); Tumbarumba (6 weekly; 2hr 45min).

Dubbo to: Bathurst (2 daily; 2hr 45min); Bourke (3 weekly; 4hr 45min); Brewarrina (3 weekly; 5hr 45min); Broken Hill (5 daily; 8hr 30min); Canberra (4 weekly; 6hr 10min); Cobar (3 daily; 3hr 30min); Coonabarabran (3–5 daily; 1hr 50min); Cootamundra (3 weekly; 4hr 15min); Cowra (1–2 daily; 3hr 20min); Griffith (2 daily; 4hr 45min); Lightning Ridge (1 daily; 4hr 50min); Moree (3 daily; 4hr 20min); Orange (2 daily; 2hr 40min); Tamworth (3–5 daily; 4hr); Wagga Wagga (2 daily; 6hr).

Griffith to: Canberra (1 daily; 6hr 15min); Cootamundra (1 daily; 2hr 35min); Hay (1 daily; 3hr 50min); Leeton (1–2 daily; 50min); Narrandera (1–2 daily; 1hr 15min); Wagga Wagga (1–2 daily; 2hr 40min).

Lismore to: Ballina (1–3 daily; 45min); Brisbane (3–5 daily; 3hr); Byron Bay (4–6 daily; 1hr 15min); Casino (2 daily; 25min); Murwillumbah (3–5 daily; 2hr); Nimbin (2–3 daily; 25min); Tweed Heads (3–5 daily; 2hr 45min).

Lithgow to: Bathurst (3–6 daily; 1hr); Coonabarabran (6 weekly; 5hr 30min); Cowra (6 weekly; 2hr 40min); Dubbo (6 weekly; 4hr 30min); Mudgee (1 daily; 2hr 30min); Orange (2–5 daily; 1hr 45min–2hr).

Murwillumbah to: Tweed Heads (4–11 daily; 30min).

Port Macquarie to: Armidale (3 weekly; 6hr 15min); Ballina (5 daily; 6hr); Bellingen (3 weekly; 3hr 15min); Brisbane (5 daily; 10hr 30min); Coffs Harbour (5–6 daily; 2hr 40min); Dorrigo (3 weekly; 3hr 50min); Grafton (5 daily; 4hr 10min); Scone (3 weekly; 10hr 20min); Surfers Paradise (5 daily; 9hr); Tamworth (3 weekly; 8hr 30min).

Tamworth to: Cessnock (1 daily; 4hr); Dorrigo (3 weekly; 4hr 10min); Gunnedah (2 daily; 1hr); Inverell (1 daily; 3hr 40min); Port Macquarie (3 weekly; 8hr 30min); Scone (2 daily; 2hr 15min); Tenterfield (2 daily; 4hr 30min).

Flights

Armidale to: Brisbane (1–2 daily; 1hr 10min); Coolangatta (3 weekly; 50min); Sydney (1–3 daily; 1hr 10min).

Ballina to: Brisbane (1–3 daily; 45min); Sydney (3 daily; 1hr 10min).

Bourke to: Sydney (5 weekly; 3hr).

Broken Hill to: Adelaide (1–4 daily; 1hr 40min); Dubbo (6 weekly; 2hr); Mildura (6 weekly; 1hr 30min); Sydney (2–4 daily; 3hr 45min).

Canberra to: Ballina (2–3 daily; 4hr 40min); Coffs Harbour (4–6 daily; 3hr 20min); Dubbo (1–2 daily; 2hr 15min); Grafton (1–2 daily; 2hr 30min); Lismore (1–4 daily; 4hr 10min); Moree (1–2 daily; 3hr 55min); Narrabri (1–2 daily; 3hr 15min); Newcastle (3–4 daily; 2hr 10min); Port Macquarie (3–9 daily; 2hr 25min); Sydney (6–25 daily; 35min); Tamworth (4–8 daily; 2hr 25min).

Coffs Harbour to: Brisbane (2 daily; 45min); Sydney (3–5 daily; 55min).

Dubbo to: Bourke (5 weekly; 1hr 40min); Brewarrina (3 weekly; 1hr); Broken Hill (6 weekly; 2hr); Cobar (1–3 a day, Sun–Fri; 1hr); Lightning Ridge (1–2 a day, Mon–Fri; 1hr 40min); Nyngan (4 weekly; 30min); Sydney (3–7 daily; 1hr); Walgett (5 weekly; 1hr 10min).

Lismore to: Brisbane (2–3 daily; 25min); Sydney (5–8 daily; 1hr 50min).

Lord Howe Island to: Brisbane (6 weekly; 2hr); Sydney (6 weekly; 2hr).

Norfolk Island to: Brisbane (6 weekly; 2hr 10min); Sydney (5 weekly; 2hr 30min).

Port Macquarie to: Brisbane (3–6 daily; 1hr); Coffs Harbour (2–3 daily; 25min); Sydney (6 daily; 55min).

Tamworth to: Brisbane (4–12 daily; 2hr 20min); Cobar (8 weekly; 1hr); Melbourne (2–3 daily; 3hr 20min); Mildura (6 weekly; 1hr 30min); Sydney (3–8 daily; 1hr).

Taree to: Port Macquarie (1–2 a day, Mon–Sat; 20min); Sydney (3 daily; 55min).

CHAPTER THREE

SOUTHEAST QUEENSLAND

The coast of southeast Queensland consists of an eight-hundred-kilometre stretch between the New South Wales border and Fraser Island containing many of the classic features that lure visitors to Australia's second-largest state. Surf rolls in to long, sandy beaches, backed by vibrant towns in exotic settings; behind them, the land rises a thousand metres or more to lush, rainforest-clad plateaus. It's one of Australia's busiest tourist venues, a factor which will be central to your impressions of the region: some love the hype and pace; others loathe it for the same reasons and despair of ever finding an untramped corner.

However, although the **Gold Coast** undoubtedly lives up to its glitzy image, it occupies a mere fraction of the region. If its thoroughly trampled and predictable "drunken backpackers" trail isn't your scene, you can wrench yourself free, and, with a little imagination and planning, get off the beaten track into some more diverse and surprising parts of the area – there are plenty of serene refuges from the bustle and hype. An hour away, the **Scenic Rim**'s green heights may be crowded at times but provide the perfect antidote to the concrete coast; remoter sections of this chain of **national parks** offer a challenge for even experienced bushwalkers. Heading north, fruit and vegetable plantations behind the gentle **Sunshine Coast** benefit from rich volcanic soils and a subtropical climate; while offshore looms **Fraser Island** where huge forested dunes, freshwater lakes and sculpted coloured sands form the backdrop for exciting safaris in a 4WD.

Brisbane, Queensland's capital, is in the state's southeastern extremity, between the Gold and Sunshine coasts, but seems curiously unaffected by either. Though it was by far the largest settlement in Queensland at the time of the state separating from New South Wales in 1859, the choice of Brisbane as capital proved unpopular with the northern pioneers, who felt that the government was too far away to understand, or even care about, their needs. These needs centred around the north's sugar plantations and the use of Solomon Islanders for labour, a practice the south equated with **slavery** and finally banned. This resulted in demands for further separation, this time between tropical Queensland and the southern part, and although this never happened, there's a definite division between the two which is felt in more than just the climate: the remoteness of northern settlements from the capital has led to local self-sufficiency and made Queensland far less centralized than other states.

After World War II, when General Douglas MacArthur used Brisbane as his headquarters to co-ordinate attacks on Japanese forces based throughout the Pacific, Brisbane stagnated, earning – along with the rest of Queensland – a reputation as a dull, underdeveloped backwater. During the 1970s and early 1980s, the stranglehold of a strongly conservative National Party government, led by the charismatic **Johannes Bjelke-Petersen** (always known simply as "Joh"), did nothing to enhance the city's

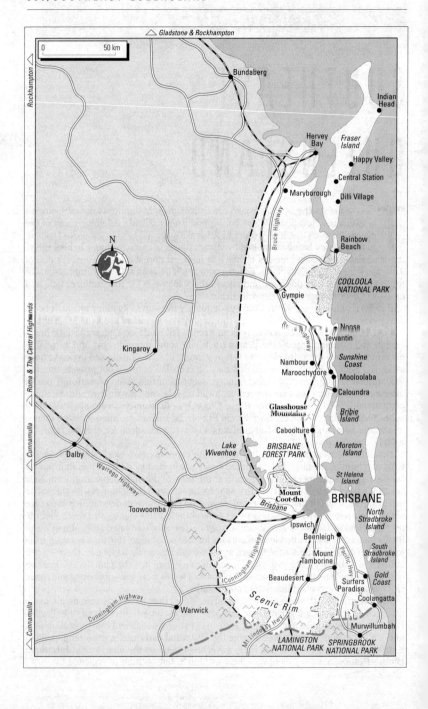

△ Gladstone & Rockhampton

0   50 km

Rockhampton

Bundaberg

Indian
Head

Hervey
Bay

Fraser
Island

Happy Valley

Central Station

Maryborough

Dilli Village

Bruce Highway

Rainbow
Beach

COOLOOLA
NATIONAL PARK

Gympie

Noosa
Tewantin

Bruce Highway

Roma & The Central Highlands

Kingaroy

Sunshine
Coast

Nambour
Maroochydore

Mooloolaba

Caloundra

Cunnamulla

Glasshouse
Mountains

Bribie
Island

Caboolture

Lake
Wivenhoe

BRISBANE
FOREST PARK

Moreton
Island

Dalby

Warrego Highway

St Helena
Island

Mount
Coot-tha

BRISBANE

Toowoomba

Brisbane

North
Stradbroke
Island

Ipswich

Beenleigh

Cunningham Highway

Mount
Tamborine

Pacific Hwy

South
Stradbroke
Island

Beaudesert

Surfers
Paradise

Gold
Coast

Cunnamulla

Cunningham Highway

Warwick

Scenic Rim

Coolangatta

Murwillumbah

Mt Lindesay Hwy

LAMINGTON
NATIONAL PARK

SPRINGBROOK
NATIONAL PARK

ACCOMMODATION PRICES

All the accommodation listed in this book has been categorized into one of eight price bands, as set out below. The rates quoted represent the cheapest available double or twin room in high season – except for category ①, which indicates per-person rates for a dorm bed, and the categories given for units, cabins and vans, which represent the daily charge for the whole unit.

① Under $18	⑤ $61–74
② $19–30	⑥ $75–94
③ $31–45	⑦ $95–124
④ $46–60	⑧ $125 upwards

For more accommodation details, see p.40-43.

image. Citing issues of law and order to justify granting the police sweeping powers, he created a repressive and domineering government, characterized by his own peculiar, slippery oratory. He finally became the victim of his own devices after initiating the Fitzgerald Inquiry – an investigation into government corruption – which implicated his cabinet in a variety of offences and forced him from office. As if to remove all trace of his rule, Brisbane underwent a thorough facelift before hosting the 1988 **World Expo**, when eighteen million visitors came to experience "Leisure in the Age of Technology". Not least for locals, who treated it as something of a coming-out party, the Expo provided a real boost after years of tedium and today, under the public-spirited mayor **Jim Soorely**, the city has become an increasingly busy and pleasant place to spend some time.

As a major tourist destination, Queensland's south coast seldom presents travel or accommodation problems, and in many places the only trouble is making some sort of choice between the vast array of options. However, during **busy periods** – the Easter and Christmas holidays, and weekends – there are room shortages and price hikes in all accommodation except hostels. This is most pronounced on the Gold Coast, though you'll find a degree of seasonal inflation as far north as Hervey Bay. Book in advance whenever possible, and don't be afraid to bargain outside the peak times.

BRISBANE AND AROUND

By far the largest city in Queensland, **BRISBANE** is not quite what you'd expect from a state capital with almost one-and-a-half million residents. Although there is urban sprawl, and high-rise buildings, slow-moving traffic, crowded streets and the other trappings of a business and trade centre, there's little of the pushiness that usually accompanies them. To urbanites used to a more aggressive approach, the atmosphere is slow, even backward (a reputation the city would be pleased to lose), but to others the languid pace is a welcome change and reflects relaxed rather than regressive attitudes.

The origins of most cities in Queensland are a blend of chance and design; Brisbane is no exception. In 1823, responding to political pressure to shift the "worst type of felons" away from Sydney and the southeast – the further the better – the government sent the Surveyor General **John Oxley** north to find a suitable site for a new prison colony. Sailing into Moreton Bay, he encountered three shipwrecked convicts who had been living with Aborigines for several months; they introduced Oxley to a previously unknown river. He explored it briefly, named it "Brisbane" after the governor of New South Wales, and the next year established a convict settlement at Redcliffe on the coast. This was immediately abandoned in favour of better anchorage further upstream, and by the end of 1824 today's city centre had become the site of Brisbane Town.

Twenty years on, events came full circle. With land scarce in the south, the government was persuaded to move out the convicts and free up the Moreton Bay area to settlers. Immigrants on government-assisted passages poured in and Brisbane began to shape up as a busy **port** – an unattractive, awkward settlement of rutted streets and wooden shacks. The first substantial buildings were constructed only after fire destroyed the centre in 1864. Development was slow and uneven: new townships were founded around the centre at Fortitude Valley, Kangaroo Point and Breakfast Creek, gradually merging into a city.

Brisbane's character arises largely from this lack of formal planning: the city has made the best of circumstances rather than anticipating them. Seen from the river or the top of Mount Coot-tha, Brisbane is attractive enough, with the typical features of any Australian city of a comparable age and size: a historic precinct, museums and botanic gardens. There's a confused blur of old and new, crammed in side by side rather than split into distinct districts, while new suburbs are blithely added to the shapeless edges as the need arises. The residents, too, have a spontaneous manner, partly because many are new to the area. In the early 1990s, economic malaise in Australia's southern states resulted in a steady northward migration of people seeking **work** – or at least finding Queensland a better place to be unemployed – and Brisbane was the obvious first stop. It's still a fairly easy place to find casual, short-term employment, and there's a healthy, unpredictable **social scene**, tempting many travellers to spend longer here than they had planned. Meeting people is easy, too, and whether you enjoy yarning over a beer in a downtown hotel or tracking down an ever-changing nightlife, you've missed out if you don't make a few local contacts. As for exploring further afield, you'll find empty beaches and surf on **North Stradbroke Island** and **Moreton Island** – both easy to reach from the city – as well as subtropical woods in **Brisbane Forest Park**, a twenty-minute drive from the centre.

Arrival and information

Brisbane Airport is located 9km northwest of the centre, at the end of Kingsford Smith Drive. You'll find banks (including ATMs) and luggage lockers at both the domestic and the new international terminals. A **taxi** into the city will cost around $24 for the thirty-minute trip; the SkyTrans bus ($6.50) to the Transit Centre (see below) runs every thirty minutes and connects with all domestic and international flights. The Airporter bus ($28) also meets all flights and delivers you direct to your accommodation on the Gold Coast, avoiding Brisbane altogether.

Buses and **trains** connect with Brisbane's functional **Transit Centre**, located in the heart of the city on Roma Street. On the highest of the three levels are the bus offices, luggage lockers and a **hostel information** desk (Mon–Fri 7am–6pm, Sat & Sun 8am–5pm). The middle floor has an information booth, fast-food joints, a bar, **medical centre** and ATMs, while on the ground floor is the arrival and departure point for **local** and **interstate trains**.

During the day, reaching your accommodation seldom poses any problems as local buses and taxis leave from just outside the Transit Centre, and most hosteliers either meet buses or will pick you up if you call them. You can't always rely on a pick-up **late at night**, however, when it's best to take a taxi. While Brisbane is not as dangerous as most European or American cities of its size, it's still not a good idea to wander around after midnight with your luggage in tow; some areas – particularly Fortitude Valley, and even Queen Street Mall – are best avoided altogether. If you simply must get somewhere and don't have the cab fare, it's worth considering leaving your luggage in the lockers.

ABORIGINAL BRISBANE

John Oxley recorded that the Brisbane Aborigines were friendly; they had looked after the shipwrecked convicts and, in the early days, even rounded up and returned runaways from the settlement. In his orders to Oxley on how to deal with the indigenous peoples, Governor Brisbane admitted, though in a roundabout way, that the land belonged to them: "All uncivilized people have wants . . . when treated justly they acquire many comforts by their union with the more civilized. This justifies our occupation of their lands." But future governors were not so liberal in their views, and things had soured long before the first squatters moved into the Brisbane area and began leaving out "gifts" of poisoned flour and calling in the Native Mounted Police to **disperse** local Aborigines – a euphemism for exterminating them. Bill Rosser's grim account in *Up Rode the Troopers – The Black Police in Queensland* tells the story through dialogues with the grandson of one of the last tribal members in the Brisbane area, and gives a good idea of how communities were split up and scattered by Queensland's Protection Act, which remained in force until the 1970s.

A trace of Brisbane's Aboriginal past is found at the **Nudgee Bora Ring** about 12km north of the centre at Nudgee Waterhole Reserve, at the junction of Nudgee and Childs roads. Last used in 1860, two low mounds where boys were initiated form little more than an icon today, and you'll probably feel that it's not worth the trip. More rewarding are the several **Aboriginal walking trails** at Mount Coot-tha; the City Hall information desk has leaflets on these which explain traditional uses of the area (see "Mount Coot-tha", p.360).

Tourist information

Booths providing city information are located at the airport (Mon–Fri 8.30am–4.30pm, Sat 10am–1pm), on the middle floor of the Transit Centre (Mon–Fri 8am–6pm, Sat–Sun 9am–5pm), halfway down Queen Street Mall (Mon–Thurs 9am–5pm, Fri 9am–7pm, Sat 9am–4pm, Sun 10am–4pm), and in the City Hall foyer (Mon–Fri 8.30am–4.30pm, Sat 10am–1pm). For the rest of Queensland, the **Government Travel Centre**, at 243 Edward St (Mon–Fri 8.30am–5pm, Sat 9.30am–12.30pm; ☎07/3874 2800, fax 3221 5320), has a stock of brochures covering a selection of popular trails and tours, and is also helpful in providing information about out-of-the-way places.

City transport

Brisbane's centre is small and possible to cover on foot, but as the only Queensland city with anything that approaches a decent **transit system**, it offers a level of luxury that's worth taking advantage of. Anywhere further afield is relatively easy to reach with private or public transport.

Buses, trains and ferries

All fares are calculated by zone – the more zones you cross, the more you pay. For example, a single fare in the central zone is $1.40, while a train ticket out to the suburbs costs around $3. One-way tickets can be bought on your journey (bus drivers give change); for several journeys and longer stays it's cheaper to buy a book of tickets or a **pass** from agencies around the city – look for the yellow and white flags outside participating shops. Some passes give discounts for day or off-peak travel (for example, the Day Rover offers unlimited bus travel for a day, ending at midnight, for $7). Others give weekly or monthly discounts, or are valid on all buses, trains and ferries. Southeast Explorer, for example, has several different $8 tickets, each for a day's unlimited travel within a particular area (the city is Area #1). For bus, train or ferry **information** call ☎13 1230.

There are several types of **buses**: you'll make suburban trips on Cityxpress, while the Citybus serves central destinations. Services operate daily roughly between 7am and midnight, with most buses travelling via **Queen Street Bus Station** (below the Myer Centre), where platforms are named after native animals (platypus, koala, etc) and where there's an **information office** open Monday to Friday from 8.30am to 5pm; there are no regular night-time bus services. You can tour central Brisbane's historic attractions on a Citysights open-top **tram** (daily 9am–4pm; $15), which you hail from special stops that are clearly signposted. When you've finished your tour, the ticket is valid on all ferries and buses for the rest of the day.

The electric **Citytrain** network provides a faster service than the buses, but it's not as frequent or comprehensive, and has at times come under heavy criticism from residents for unreliable service. Lines from as far afield as Caboolture and Beenleigh converge on downtown Brisbane, with trains every few minutes, but individual routes to the suburbs may operate only once an hour. The last trains leave **Central Station** on Ann Street at about 11.45pm – timetables are available from ticket offices. Buy **tickets and passes** at most stations.

Revamped in 1996, Brisbane's **ferries** are becoming ever more useful as a way of getting across the city. There are a couple of easy cross-river connections, but the Inner City and City Cat services are the most useful, the latter running at a bracing 27 knots between the University of Queensland campus in the southwest to Bretts Wharf, up towards the airport on Kingsford Smith Drive. **Fares** start at around $1.50 for a single crossing, and most bus passes are also valid. The central departure points for Inner City and City Cat are from South Bank Parklands, Eagle Street Pier and North Quay, next to Victoria Bridge.

Taxis, cars and bikes

During the week, Brisbane's public transport is closed down by midnight, so you may well need a **taxi** if you're out on the town. After dark they tend to cruise round the clubs and hotels; during the day Roma Street is a good place to find one. To call a taxi, try B&W Cabs (☎13 1008), Yellow Cabs (☎13 1924) or Brisbane Cabs (☎13 2211).

Driving is not much fun until you get your bearings. Unfortunately, signs just *at* junctions, rather than well before them, are typical not only of Brisbane but of all of Queensland, and you'd be well advised to get some sort of street directory as soon as possible. Once familiar with the city, there are no great problems, although **parking** is expensive and in short supply in the centre. For details of car rental agencies, see "Listings", p.358.

Cyclists have a good number of bike routes from which to choose. Maps are available from libraries and city council offices. Some hostels loan bikes, but they can be easily rented elsewhere – again, see "Listings".

Accommodation

Usually beds are scarce only during major Rugby League events and the Brisbane Show (the "Ekka") in August. The most expensive places are in the city centre, with hostels spread around Petrie Terrace, Fortitude Valley and over the river in South Brisbane. If you're staying for a while, ask about **weekly rates**, which might amount to one free night in seven; prices at more upmarket places may also drop at weekends and outside peak season, due to the scarcity of business customers and competition from the Gold Coast.

Brisbane's **backpackers' hostels** are pretty dependable, with most offering doubles as well as the usual dormitory beds. Many have entertainment, bikes for rent or loan, pools and courtesy buses on arrival (and sometimes departure), and can arrange work connections.

City centre and Petrie Terrace

Considering their convenient locations, the following all offer very decent value for money. Petrie Terrace is a ten-minute walk from the Transit Centre – or take bus #144 from opposite the Transit Centre to stop no. 5.

Annie's Shandon Inn, 405 Upper Edward St (☎07/3831 8684, fax 3831 3073). A rather nice, family-run B&B. ④.

Aussie Way Hostel, 34 Cricket St (☎07/3369 0711). Renovated nineteenth-century town house with quiet ambience, large pool, verandahs, balcony and period decor. ①.

Banana Bender, 118 Petrie Terrace (☎07/3367 1157). A small and friendly hostel, with a distinctly "homely" feel. There's a very small kitchen, casual TV lounge and deck-space for dining, but no pool. ①.

Carlton Crest, corner of Roma and Ann streets (☎07/3229 9111, reservations only free call ☎1800/777 123). Standard business hotel with all the usual facilities. ⑦.

City Backpackers, 380 Upper Roma St (☎07/3211 3221, bookings only free call ☎1800/062 572). A small, busy place, with new carpets and new beds in all rooms. Renovations and expansion continue, and with the planned incorporation of a building and car park next door, this is set to become one of Brisbane's largest hostels. ①–③.

Dorchester Inn, 484 Upper Edward St (☎07/3831 2967, fax 3832 2932). Comfortable, self-contained one- to four-bed motel-style apartments. ⑤–⑥.

Heritage Hotel, Edward St (☎07/3221 1999, fax 3221 6895, free call ☎1800/773 700). Topnotch hotel with a grand mix of colonial and modern buildings overlooking the river and Botanic Gardens. ⑧.

Palace, corner of Ann and Edward streets (☎07/3211 2433, fax 3211 2466, free call ☎1800/676 340). Huge hostel, purpose-built in 1911 but completely revamped (except for the ancient lift). Bang in the centre of town – which means that there's no parking space – with a restaurant and rowdy *Down Under Bar* whose noise prompts some travellers to move elsewhere for some sleep. Poky singles, high-ceilinged and spacious doubles, and four- to nine-bed dorms. Rooms ②–③, dorms ①.

Sportsmans Hotel, 130 Leichhardt St, Spring Hill (☎07/3831 2892). Gay-friendly pub with rooms; predominantly male clientele but both sexes welcome. ③.

Yale Inner City Inn, 413 Upper Edward St (☎07/3832 1663, fax 3832 2591). Pleasant and central no-frills B&B. ④.

Yellow Submarine, 66 Quay St (☎07/3211 3424). Small, comfortable hostel in a refurbished 1860s building, which unfortunately backs right onto the train-line. Full kitchen facilities, laundry, barbecue and pool. Friendly owners put on trips and free barbecues, ensuring a sociable atmosphere, and the staff have good work connections. ①–③.

YHA Brisbane City, 392 Upper Roma St (☎07/3236 1004, fax 3236 1947). Sterile but with excellent facilities, including a first-rate budget canteen (open to non-guests). There's a $3-per-night surcharge for non-members. Doubles & twins ③, dorms ①.

Fortitude Valley and New Farm

The Valley's streets are well placed for clubs but can be seedy late at night, although New Farm is quiet enough. Most buses travelling up Adelaide Street pass through the Valley, or you can take the train to Brunswick Street Station. For New Farm, take a bus (#177, #178, #167 or #168) from Adelaide Street.

Atoa House, 95–101 Annie St, New Farm (☎07/3358 4507, bookings only free call ☎1800/062 693). Well-run hostel oriented towards couples, families and students. Good facilities, free laundry and long-stay discounts. Dorms, doubles, triples and self-contained units. Rooms ②–④, dorms ①.

Balmoral House, 33 Amelia St, Fortitude Valley (☎07/3252 1397, fax 3253 5892). A very quiet, secure and clean hostel, handy for Chinatown and Brunswick St; not for partying. ①–③.

Central Brunswick Apartment Hotel, 455 Brunswick St, Fortitude Valley (☎07/3254 1078 or free call ☎1800/622 686). Gay-friendly accommodation in a sparkling new building. Rooms are very comfortable, all with own bath, TV etc, and some apartment-style with kitchen facilities. Shared amenities include spa and gym. ⑥–⑦.

Globetrekkers, 35 Balfour St, New Farm (☎07/3358 1251). A 100-year-old house in a very quiet street. Rooms are nothing flash and facilities are basic, but it's a casual and relaxing place to stay, and the owners are friendly. Dorms ①, doubles ②.

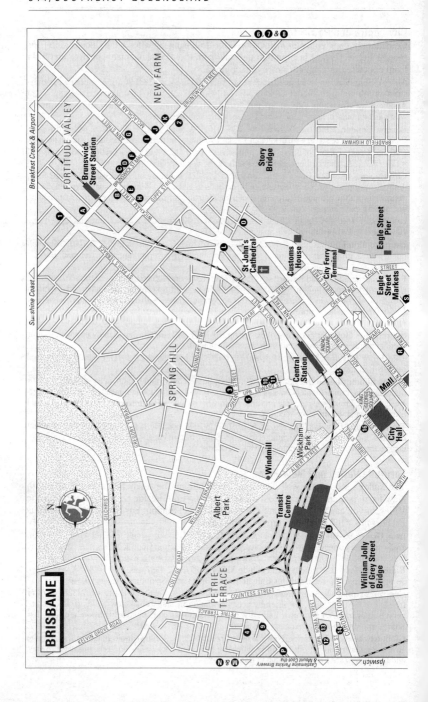

BRISBANE

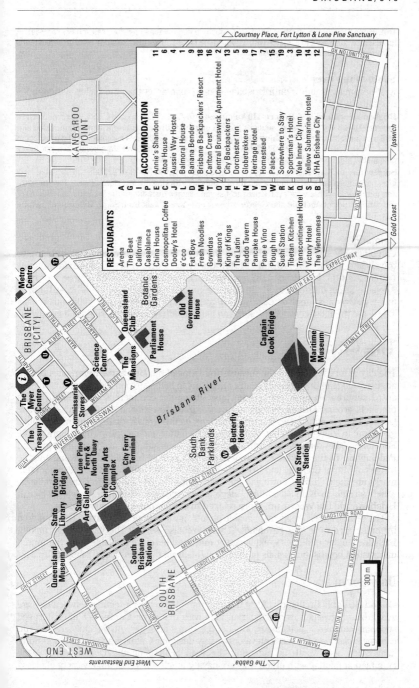

Homestead, 57 Annie St, New Farm (☎07/3358 3538, bookings only free call ☎1800/658 344). A large house converted to a hostel, with a pool shaped like a shamrock. Recently refurbished, it tends towards a party atmosphere. ①–③.

South of the river

Fast becoming trendy, South Brisbane is more upmarket than the Valley, although it's not quite as hip.

Brisbane Backpackers' Resort, 110 Vulture St (☎07/3844 9956, fax 3844 9295, reservations free call ☎1800/626 452). Massive, soulless hostel complex with round-the-clock reception, video surveillance and all facilities, including a licensed travel agent. Booking is essential, but be clear about what you're getting: some travellers have been quoted a low rate over the phone, then put into a dilapidated old house across the road. Rooms ②–③, dorms ①.

Somewhere to Stay, 45 Brighton Rd (☎07/3846 2858 or free call ☎1800/812 398). Reasonable facilities, but nonchalant staff; building and furnishings are showing distinct signs of wear. Pay the extra and get a room with a view over Brisbane's skyline rather than one of the basic dorms. Bus #177 from the corner of Adelaide and George streets, or a 15min walk from South Brisbane or Vulture Street stations. ①–③.

Camping

Camping only saves a dollar or two on the price of a hostel bed, and you still have to travel into town. The **Alpha Motel/Caravan Park**, 1434 Gympie Rd, Aspley (☎07/3263 4011; bus #55 or #182 from the corner of Queen and Creek streets, or from Adelaide Street outside City Hall), is about 10km north on the main highway. If this is full, try *Acres* next door or *Caravan Village*, 763 Zillmere Rd, about 500m further on. These are the most centrally located van parks and have at least a regular bus service.

The City

The city is focused around the meandering loops of the **Brisbane River**, with the triangular wedge of the business centre on the north bank surrounded by community-oriented suburbs. At its heart are the busy, upmarket commercial and administrative precincts around **Queen Street**, an area of glass towers and century-old sandstone facades that extends to the **Botanic Gardens** on the river. Radiating **north**, the polish gives way to less conservative shops, accommodation and eateries around Spring Hill, Fortitude Valley and New Farm, and the aspiring suburbs of Petrie Terrace and Paddington. To the **west** is a blaze of riverside homes at Milton and Toowong and the fringes of Mount Coot-tha and Brisbane Forest Park. **Across the river**, the major landmarks are the Cultural Centre and the Convention Centre, and South Bank Parklands, which stretch to Kangaroo Point. Beyond are the open, bustling streets of **South Brisbane** and the **West End**, more relaxed than their northern counterparts.

The central area is easily manageable on foot: try following the **Tourist Trail**, marked by brass arrows in the pavement. There are also several "heritage" trails linking Brisbane's older buildings – explanatory **maps** of these are available from the tourist information booths. For details of the Citysights tram tour, see "City Transport", p.342.

Downtown

Queen Street is Brisbane's oldest thoroughfare, its southern section between George and Edward streets now a pedestrian mall with the **Myer Centre** – a multistoreyed shopping complex – as its focus. Most of the stores inside are on the chic side but you can, for kicks, ride the glass elevators or buy designer Outback accessories and fluffy koalas. It's also worth investigating the food centres on the Queen Street level, crammed at midday with office workers having lunch. There's a huge variety of classy fast-food outlets, from Asian takeaways to Greek kebab shops, at slightly higher prices than the local hotel food. Outside, the **mall** is always busy with people running errands, window shopping or just socializing. There's usually some kind of entertainment, too: either informal efforts – acrobats, buskers and the occasional soap-box orator – or more organized events such as Aboriginal and Torres Strait Islander dancing or jazz sessions on the small stage about halfway down the street.

City Hall, the Observatory and the business district

North from the mall along Albert Street, you arrive at **City Hall**, facing King George Square: in front of the fountains are bronze sculptures looking like large pieces of futuristic circuitry. A stately building ruined by an ugly clock tower, there's sad irony – and a reflection of former policies – in the triangular sculpture over the portico. A central figure representing the state faces out, arms spread to protect all citizens, while on the left the Aboriginal way of life is depicted "dying out before the approach of the white man". The **City Art Gallery** (daily 10am–5pm; free) inside has a smattering of paintings, pottery and glassware, though it's worth checking to see if there are any temporary exhibitions of work by Australian artists, or if there are any screenings at the tiny cinema. The clock tower is open, too, if you want a view of the city centre (Mon–Fri 8am–5pm; free); access is through the City Hall foyer.

Further up Albert Street is Wickham Park and the grey cone of Brisbane's oldest building, a **windmill** known locally as the **Observatory**, built by convicts in 1829 to grind corn for the early settlement. The original wooden sails were too heavy to turn and for years grinding was done by a treadmill – severe punishment for the convicts who had to work it. Describing the scene in 1836, the Quaker missionary George Walker was quietly appalled: "They work from sunrise to sunset, with a rest of three hours in the middle of the day ... the exertion requisite to keep this up is excessive. I am told the steps of the wheel are sometimes literally wet with the perspiration." The sails, useless for catching the wind, were put to work as gallows before being pulled off in 1850 and, with the convicts gone, the building subsequently became a signal station. It now stands empty, held together with a cement glaze and firmly locked.

East of here lies Brisbane's **business district**, which was heavily developed in the 1980s and left with a legacy of glassy high-rises; the few surviving old buildings are hidden among the modern ones. The copper-domed **Customs House** at the north end of Queen Street harbours the University of Queensland Press, publisher of Peter Carey's surrealistic novels, while rustic **All Saints' Church** on the corner of Wickham Terrace, and Neo-Gothic **St John's Cathedral** on Ann Street, have some elegant stained-glass windows. Sunday morning is made lively by the **Eagle Street Markets** between the river and the road – too trendy for bargains, but not bad for jewellery and leatherwork, clothing and $15 massages.

The historic precinct

The area between Queen Street and the Botanic Gardens contains some of Brisbane's finest architecture, dating from the earliest days of settlement until the late nineteenth century. Between Elizabeth and Queen streets, occupying an entire block, is the former **Treasury** with its classical facade. Built in the 1890s, its grandeur reflects the wealth of Queensland's gold mines (though by this point most were on the decline) and was a slap in the face to New South Wales, which had spitefully withdrawn all financial support from the fledgling state on separation some eighty years previously, leaving it bankrupt. With a twist typical of a state torn between conservatism and tourism, the building is now – appropriately enough – Brisbane's **casino**.

South along William Street, the **Commissariat Stores** is contemporary with the windmill, though in considerably better shape. Originally a granary, it is now a museum

(Tues–Fri 11am–2pm; $2) and headquarters of the Royal Historical Society of Queensland; the knowledgeable staff pep up an otherwise dusty collection of relics dating back to convict times. Brisbane's **Science Centre** (daily 10am–5pm; $7), whose entrance is one block over on George Street, is more interesting to visit. A hands-on approach makes it great fun, especially for children, and very therapeutic if you like to prod and dismantle exhibits instead of merely peering at them through a protective glass case. Favourites include the various optical illusions – try the "swinging bridge", guaranteed to induce nausea though it remains stock-still – and the "Thongophone", a set of giant pan pipes played by whacking the top with a flip-flop. It's all good rainy-day material.

Further south along George Street you pass **Harris Terrace** and **The Mansions**, two of the city centre's last surviving rows of Victorian-era terraced houses, the latter guarded by stone cats on the parapet corners. Nearby, on the corner of George and Alice streets, the **Queensland Club** was founded in 1859, just four days before the separation of Queensland from New South Wales. Heavy walls, columns and spacious balconies evoke a tropical version of a traditional London club; entrance and membership – still barred to women – are by invitation only. Diagonally opposite, **Parliament House** was built to a design by Charles Tiffin in 1864 and presents an appealingly compromised French Renaissance style which incorporates shuttered north windows, shaded colonnades and a high, arched roof to allow for the tropical climate. You can see the grand interior on an hour-long **guided tour** (Mon–Fri 10.30am & 2.30pm; free) and there's access to the chambers when there's no debate in progress.

South of Parliament House, George Street becomes a lane along the western side of the Botanic Gardens. Here you'll find **Old Government House** (variable hours; donation), the official residence of Queensland's governors and premiers between 1862 and 1910. Another of Tiffin's designs, the building is being comprehensively restored to its stately turn-of-the-century condition, beginning with the ground floor; work has started on the main dining room, drawing room and entrance hall. The National Trust offices are in the upper storey.

The Botanic Gardens

Bordered by Alice Street, George Street and the river, Brisbane's **Botanic Gardens** overlook the cliffs of Kangaroo Point and, while more of a park than a botanic garden, provide a generous arrangement of flowers, shrubs, bamboo thickets and greenery that offers an escape from the claustrophobia of the city. Legend has it that the area was once a vegetable patch cultivated by convicts. Formal gardens were laid out in 1855 by Walter Hill, who experimented with local and imported plants to see which would grow well in Queensland's then untried environment. Some of his more successful efforts are the oversized **bunya pines** around the Edward Street entrance at the east end of Alice Street, planted in 1860, and a residual patch of the **rainforest** that once blanketed the area, at the southern end of the park. Mangroves along the river, accessible by a boardwalk, are another native species more recently protected. You can spend summer evenings here at the open-air **stage** listening to classical music recitals. During the day, cyclists flock to the park, as it's at one end of a popular cycling and jogging track that follows the north bank of the river south to St Lucia and the University of Queensland. Free **guided tours** (11am & 1pm Tues–Sun) leave from the rotunda 100m inside the gardens' main entrance, halfway along Alice Street.

The northern suburbs

North of the river, just beyond Brisbane's business district, are several former suburbs which have been absorbed by the city sprawl: Paddington and Petrie Terrace to the west, Spring Hill and Fortitude Valley to the north, and New Farm to the east.

Houses in these areas are popular with Brisbane's aspiring professional class, and while office buildings and one-way streets are beginning to encroach, there's also an older character reflected in the **Queenslander**-style houses (see box overleaf) still standing around Spring Hill and Petrie Terrace.

XXXX – the local brew

Just down the hill from Petrie Terrace, the **Castlemaine Perkins Brewery**, Milton Road, Milton (☎07/3361 7597), has been making Queensland's own beer since 1878, and had no real competition until Powers came on the scene in the 1980s. Their famous yellow-and-red XXXX emblem is almost part of the Queensland landscape: splashed across T-shirts and the roofs of Outback hotels, or on labels on countless discarded bottles and cans that litter everywhere from roadsides to the depths of the Barrier Reef. For enthusiasts, the brewery opens its gates for **tours** (Mon–Wed 11am, 1.30pm, 4.30pm & 7pm; $5), which incorporate a brief rundown on the brewing process and then about thirty minutes during which you watch filmed eulogies and swill beer. Booking ahead by phone between 9 and 11am is essential, because you won't get past the security guards unless your name is on the list.

Fortitude Valley

While the other areas are mainly residential, **Fortitude Valley**'s tangled mix of shops, restaurants, bars and clubs is blossoming into Brisbane's unofficial centre of artistic, gastronomic and alcoholic pursuits. An eclectic mix of the gay, the groovy and the grubby, the Valley is now in stage two of inner-city gentrification, which sees the urban-poor make way for hipsters, artists and students. Stage three – the arrival of yuppies and inflated real estate prices – is probably a few years away, so in the meantime you can enjoy an evening out among Brisbane's young, fun and adventurous. In less than a kilometre, the main thoroughfare of **Brunswick Street** has a dozen nightclubs, an Irish pub, a compact **Chinatown** complete with the usual busy restaurants, stores and martial arts centres, and a burgeoning European **street-café scene**. It's best at weekends; on Saturday there's a secondhand **market** in the mall and the cafés are buzzing. After dark the Valley's streets can still be somewhat menacing, with an element of drug-related petty crime. Although there are usually crowds around until very late, if you've any distance to go on your own after the pubs close, take a taxi.

Breakfast Creek

Named by John Oxley, who tucked into a morning meal here in 1823 on his voyage of exploration upstream, **Breakfast Creek** has shops and a hotel marking an acute traffic bottleneck where the road bridges the creek between the upper reaches of Fortitude Valley and the route to the airport. A pretty, if noisy, spot, looking out over usually placid water to inactive wharves, the real estate in nearby Hamilton and Ascot is becoming quite exclusive. If you're out this way – perhaps going to the airport or heading north – consider looking around **Newstead House**, Brisbane's oldest residence. A low, solid brick and stone building with a slate roof, it was constructed as a private home in 1845 by convict labour, and became the Government House twelve years later. Enlarged by the governor, the house was the focus of social gatherings, and on the nights that balls were held armed police protected the house from attacks by Aborigines. Restored and now open as a **museum** (Mon–Fri 10am–4pm, Sun 2–5pm; $4), the house and grounds are remarkably quiet. As you stand surrounded by century-old furniture, taking in the views across the creek from one of the elegant windows, it's easy to forget how close you are to the city. The house is off Breakfast Creek Road just south of the bridge; to get there by public transport, take bus #117, #190 or #160 to stop 12.

QUEENSLAND HOUSES

There can hardly be a more typical image of rural Queensland than a high-set "Queenslander" surrounded by green fields of sugar cane. A response to the northern climate, these houses come in all shapes and styles but the basic design is a wooden box on piles with a verandah or balcony – the idea being to have a cool flow of air underneath the house to reduce the humidity inside. Traditional colours, now more commonly seen in cities where it's becoming popular to renovate them, are cream, red or green, while older buildings may have corrugated iron awnings, red "bull-nosed" roofs and wooden latticework on porches and eaves. In Brisbane they're generally low-set, but tend to be raised further off the ground as you move up into the tropics – the exception to the rule is at Redcliffe, 12km north of Brisbane, where the pole houses have supports 10m high to compensate for a steep hill.

South Brisbane

Across the river from the city centre, the **Cultural Centre** and its environs – comprising state museum, library, gallery, performing arts complex, convention centre and South Bank Parklands – is Brisbane's most obvious tourist attraction. Immediately south of Victoria Bridge (itself a continuation of Queen Street), it's easily reached by train to South Brisbane Station, while plenty of buses from all parts of the city stop outside the station on Melbourne Street.

Beyond here, the **West End** is South Brisbane's answer to Fortitude Valley, with a similar ethnic mix – Asian, Greek and Italian – but a more genteel atmosphere. There are no sights here as such, but it's worth a visit for the cluster of Asian stores and continental delicatessens, and for an escalating number of inexpensive restaurants and cafés around the hub at Boundary Road and Vulture Street, popular with students from the University of Queensland across the river at St Lucia; see p.354 for details.

Queensland Museum
The Queensland Museum (daily 9.30am–5pm; free, except for special exhibitions) is essentially a natural history museum, but it benefits from a bias towards unorthodox methods of presentation. Wedge-tailed eagles hover overhead, koalas climb the walls and, in the foyer, there's the unsettling experience of walking underneath full-scale models of a family of humpbacked whales suspended from the ceiling. There's an overview of the state's marine environment and western Queensland's fossil beds, including a reconstruction of Queensland's own Muttaburrasaurus and a section of the Lark Quarry **dinosaur trackways**. Above swings a furry pterodactyl, reflecting recent theories that Australia was subject to a cold climate during the era of the dinosaurs. Upstairs, the more recently extinct **megafauna** from the Darling Downs, just west of Brisbane, unexpectedly come to life – a breathing, twitching model of a marsupial lion lounging on a rock at the top of the escalators catches everyone by surprise. Rock hounds and prospective gem hunters will also be interested in the museum's **mineral collection** – dozens of multicoloured rocks from around the state together with information on identifying them in the field.

Ethnographic displays mostly relate to traditional life in New Guinea and Melanesia, with the glaring omission – apart from a handful of tools and a small section on the rainforest tribes from the north – of anything on Queensland's Aboriginal and Torres Strait Islander history. The displays are rounded off by miscellaneous items, including bits and pieces from aviation history and an eclectic collection of period furniture.

State Art Gallery and Library

Queensland's **State Art Gallery** (daily 10am–5pm; free, except for special exhibitions) provides a large, airy space for its wide-ranging collection, which includes a sizeable exhibition of twentieth-century painters. As well as works by visionaries such as Brett Whitely, Arthur Boyd and Sidney Nolan, there are some unusual (and very European) watercolour landscapes by **Aboriginal artists** Walter Ebataringa and Albert Namatjira (for more on the latter, see p.579) alongside a few functional tribal items – dilly bags, headwear and shields – labelled as "art" but somehow out of place here. One of the most interesting pieces in the gallery is a nineteenth-century stained-glass window depicting a kangaroo hunt – a quintessentially Australian theme executed in a very European medium. Other Australian works include the romantic paintings of Tom Roberts and the impressionistic canvases of Frederick McGubbin. Sculpture is scattered throughout the gallery in a somewhat offhand manner, and there's a small collection of high-quality **glass** hidden away in the back.

Equally rewarding is a visit to the **State Library** (Mon–Thurs 10am–8pm, Fri–Sun 10am–5pm), best known for its **John Oxley Library** (closed Sat) on level four which records every aspect of Queensland's past in endless books, journals and photographs. Level three is devoted to music and art; they lend scores and there's even a piano room available for practice. Film buffs should head to level two to sample the video collection and check out the cinema's programme, while there's **free Internet access** via terminals on levels two, three and four – limited, not surprisingly, to one hour a day and booked up several days in advance (for bookings call ☎07/3840 7785).

The South Bank Parklands

The **South Bank Parklands** are a resoundingly successful contrivance, conceived with little rhyme or reason other than that *something* had to be done with the 1988 Expo site. Weekend crowds come to stroll along the river under the trees or to sit on the lawns, watch street performers and stuff their faces full of candy floss and hot dogs – blissfully unconcerned that everything, including the sand around the pool, is imported. Bands play most Saturday nights on the outdoor stage, or at the *Plough Inn*, a restored, century-old pub in the reconstructed cobbled high street; other attractions range from guided tours through the **Butterfly House** (daily 9am–5pm; $8), to exhibits at the **Maritime Museum** (daily 9.30am–5pm; $5), including a ninety-year-old Torres Strait pearling lugger and the World War II frigate *Diamantina*, on show in the dry dock.

Along the river

The sluggish, meandering **Brisbane River** is four hundred million years old, one of the world's most ancient waterways. It flows from above Lake Wivenhoe – 55km inland – past farmland, into quiet suburbs and through the city before emptying 150km downstream into Moreton Bay, behind Fisherman Island. Once an essential trade and transport link with the rest of Australia and the world, it now seems to do little but separate the main part of the city from South Brisbane; though it's superficially active around the city centre, with ferries and dredgers keeping it navigable, most of the old wharves and shipyards now lie derelict or buried under parkland.

If the locals seem to have forgotten the river, it has a habit of reasserting its presence through **flooding**. In February 1893 cyclonic rains swelled the flow through downtown Brisbane, carrying off Victoria Bridge and scores of buildings: eyewitness accounts stated that "Debris of all descriptions – whole houses, trees, cattle and homes – went floating past". This has since been repeated many times, notably in January 1974 when rains from **Cyclone Wanda** completely swamped the centre, swelling the river to a width of 3km at one stage. Despite the grim reminder of the brass plaques marking the depths of the worst floods at Naldham House Polo Club (1 Eagle St, near the markets), some of Brisbane's poshest real estate flanks the river, with waterfront mansions at Yeerongpilly, Graceville and Chelmer. They're all banking on protection from artificial Lake Wivenhoe, completed in 1984, which should act as a buffer against future floods.

Of the various ways to explore the river, the easiest is simply to take a return ride on the City Cat – such a popular, if unofficial, sightseeing trip that the service can be severely overcrowded during holidays. More stylish are the oddly-named *Club Crocodile River Queens*, three-tiered Mississippi-style **paddleboats** decked out in timber and brass, which leave daily from Eagle Street pier; it's a favourite Sunday excursion (daily 10am & 12.45pm, additional Sunday departure 3.30pm; $20–45, depending on level of refreshments), and there are additional evening cruises with full meals (Mon–Sat 7.30pm, Sun 6.30pm; $45 buffet or $55 for seafood); for bookings call ☎07/3221 1300. You can also paddle around the river's upper reaches by **kayak** on one- or two-day expeditions with Wild Escapes (☎07/3357 7222) or Rainbow Safaris (☎07/3396 3141).

Fort Lytton

Surrounded by the pipes and chimneys of the Ampol oil refinery at Wynnum, **Fort Lytton** (Mon–Fri & Sun 10am–4pm, museum open Sun only; $4 entry to fort and museum) is a product of the colonial struggles around the Pacific Rim at the end of the nineteenth century. Only a few days away from French forces on Nouméa (New Caledonia), Queensland felt threatened by competing European empires and developed a string of coastal defences during the 1880s. Brisbane received the best of these: by the turn of the century, the river mouth at Fort Lytton bristled with artillery and a barrage of floating mines. However, the defences were never put to the test and modern warfare made them obsolete. The fort was downgraded to a secondary line of defence after World War I and abandoned altogether in 1945.

As a piece of military history, the buildings look the part: austere concrete bunkers dug into slopes and capped in grass, gun ports trained on the river and an underground tunnel for checking the mines running down to the water. The best time to visit is the first Sunday of each month when the historical museum is open. The **Brisbane Garrison Battery** dresses up in period costume and fires the massive gun at Easter, and again on the Queen's birthday. The fort is at the end of Lytton Road, west of Wynnum at the mouth of Brisbane River; there's no public transport.

Lone Pine Sanctuary

Lone Pine Sanctuary at Jesmond Road, Fig Tree Pocket (daily 8am–5pm; $12), has been a popular day-trip upstream since first opening its gates in 1927. Here you can see a large number of native fauna in their natural state which, in the case of the sanctuary's hundred-odd **koalas**, means being asleep for eighteen hours a day. At close quarters they're revealed as grey cushions wedged into convenient forks in the trees, occasionally waking up for long enough to chew eucalyptus leaves and blink myopically at the crowds. In nearby cages you'll find other slumbering animals: Tasmanian devils, fruit bats, blue-tongued lizards and dingoes. Indeed, about the only active creatures you'll see are birds: as well as the bird cages there's a colony of hyperactive sugar gliders in the nocturnal house. Alternatively, head for the outdoor paddock where tolerant wallabies and kangaroos allow themselves to be petted, fed and occasionally roughed up by visitors.

The best way to reach Lone Pine is to take a ninety-minute **river cruise** past Brisbane's waterfront suburbs with Mirimar Cruises (daily departures 10am from Queens Wharf Road beside Victoria Bridge; return 3.30pm; $15, not including entry to Lone Pine). Free pick-up from your central accommodation is usually possible (for bookings call ☎07/3221 0300). Otherwise, take bus #445 from Adelaide Street all the way to Lone Pine.

Eating

Brisbane has no gastronomic tradition to exploit, but there's a good variety of bars and restaurants all over the city, with a trend towards "Modern Australian" (creative use of local produce, influenced by Asia and the Mediterranean), and a fashionable café society in Fortitude Valley and the West End.

Counter meals and unlimited buffets at hotels are the cheapest route to a full stomach – aim for lunch at around noon and dinner between 5pm and 6pm – or try one of the scores of **cafés** in the centre catering to office workers. The city's **restaurants** open from around 11am to 2pm for lunch, and from 6 to 10pm or later for evening meals; many are closed for one day a week (often Monday).

City centre

Café the Hague, Myer Centre, Level A (next to cinema complex). Dutch-style coffee house, way above the fast-food joints opposite. Try the *poffertjes* – sweet pancakes – and a gourmet coffee for breakfast.

e'cco, 100 Boundary St (☎07/3831 8344). Boasts an impressive awards list that includes Australia's "Restaurant of the Year" for '97 – so you'll have to book, sometimes days ahead. Surprisingly good value, with local favourite "steamed mussels" $12, and most mains around $19. Open for lunch Tues–Fri, dinner Tues–Sat.

Govindas, Elizabeth St. are Krishna-run vegetarian food bar, with a $6 all-you-can-eat menu. Open for lunch Mon–Sat 11.30am–2.30pm, dinner Fri 5.30–7.30pm; there's a $3 banquet every Sunday (5–7pm), but you'll have to sit through a lot of chanting before you actually get to eat.

Jameson's, 475 Adelaide St (☎07/3831 7633). Ostensibly a wine bar, Jameson's reputation now rivals that of *e'cco*. Billed as "Modern Australian", the menu features dishes such as woodside goat's cheese, snail and parsley soufflé, and breast of wood pigeon, all complemented by wine from what is reputed to be Brisbane's most satisfying and extensive cellar. It's one of the only places open late in the city (till 3am) on the weekend and has nightly entertainment (from jazz to hip-hop). Restaurant bookings essential; lunch Mon–Fri, dinner Mon–Sat.

Myer Centre, Queen Street Mall. Heaps of fast food from kebabs to Chinese, all reasonably priced and freshly prepared, but it can be tough finding somewhere to sit at lunch time.

Pancake House, 18 Charlotte St. Open 24hr, this restored church with high-beamed roof and stone floor is an unlikely setting for the consumption of fast food. Portions are on the small side for the $8–10 tag, though the food's not bad and there are vegetarian options.

Pane e Vino, corner of Charlotte and Albert streets. Smart Italian café-restaurant with pavement tables, catering mainly to nearby office executives. Pastas from $12, main courses (lots of fish, chicken and lamb) around $19.

Sushi Station, 142 Elizabeth St, next to *McDonald's*. Good and very authentic Japanese sushi bar and takeaway, featuring low-priced soups, rice, fish, seaweed and green-tea ice cream.

Transcontinental Hotel, Roma St, opposite the Transit Centre. Recommended for its good-value lunchtime smorgasbord during the week, "free beer" happy hour on Monday night, and live music Thurs–Sat.

Victory Hotel, 127 Edward St. Nice beer garden with braziers taking the chill off in winter. The bistro meals are popular with the local business folk.

Petrie Terrace

Casablanca, 52 Petrie Terrace. Inexpensive brasserie and café serving the young and pretentious. Tapas is served at the bar for around $10, and the food is excellent and mouthwateringly spicy, with genuine leanings towards North African cuisine. Taped Brazilian music or live bands provide atmosphere and there's an "open" jam (mostly jazz/funk) on Monday nights.

Fresh Noodles, 49 Caxton St. The name says it all; lots of noodle combinations, soups as well – and there's nothing over $8.

Paddo Tavern, 186 Given Terrace. Respectable pub lunches served every day for only $1.95, leaving you with enough money for a beer or two.

Fortitude Valley

California, 376 Brunswick St. Perfectly preserved 1950s diner, with original coffee cups, Formica-covered tables and hulking jukebox. Only two (men) have managed the "truckie's breakfast" of five eggs, steak, liver, bacon, sausage and tomato: otherwise, a regular cooked breakfast is $7. Open Sun–Wed 6.30am–2.30pm, Thurs–Sat 6.30am till late.

China House, 173 Wickham St. Billed as a seafood restaurant, but the thing to do is join the crowds of Chinese who come for dim sum between 11am and 3pm.

Cosmopolitan Coffee, 322 Brunswick Street Mall. A few doors down from *The Latin* but noticeably more relaxed and downmarket. Something of an institution with Brisbane's café society, and better than the surrounding competition.

Fat Boys, 321 Brunswick Street Mall. The place for an early-morning "heart-starter" after a night out in the Valley, with very good, cheap coffee. Most people opt for the $4 cooked breakfast while reading a newspaper, or just rest their hangover on a street-front table. At other times, try a gourmet pizza, or the soup-with-sourdough will warm you up for only $5. Mon–Wed 6am–midnight; Thurs–Sun 24hr.

King of Kings, 169 Wickham St. Next to *China House*, with a loyal crowd of Sunday *yum cha* patrons. A busy place, popular with the local Chinese community and fast becoming a Valley institution. Open every day.

The Latin, corner of Brunswick and Ann streets. Established upmarket café with street tables outside; marble, tubular aluminium furniture and plenty of space inside.

Tibetan Kitchen, 454 Brunswick St. It's hard to resist any place that advertises "traditional Tibetan, Sherpa, Nepalese foods", but the food here, including the Valley's best *somosas* ($4.90 for four), is tasty and cheap, and served in a very attractive setting. Mains $9–12. Open daily for lunch and dinner.

The Vietnamese Restaurant, 194 Wickham St. With an interior every bit as plain and unassuming as the name over the door, this is an utterly genuine Vietnamese cuisine. Mains around $9; open daily for lunch & dinner.

West End

Bagelo's, corner of Boundary and Vulture streets. Basically a fast-food joint, which does interesting things with every type of bagel from spinach-feta to cinnamon-raisin (all baked on-site and very fresh), plus sandwich combo's. Open daily.

Boundary Street Brasserie, 145b Boundary St. Eclectic menu of grills, noodles and pasta, with the odd "Asian" dish thrown in; nothing over $14. Open 8am for cakes and coffee, live music Fri & Sat nights.

Café Nouveau, 185 Boundary St. Friendly, with Mediterranean-style salads, pasta and seafood for $12–15, and a pleasant courtyard in the back; excellent cakes, too. Open daily 7.30am–late.

Caffé Tempo, 181 Boundary St (☎07/3846 3161). Not sophisticated cuisine, but great Italian-style home cooking, with fresh salads and fine seafood pasta. Most expensive dish is $12.50, and they stay open until the last customer leaves.

Espressohead, 169 Boundary St. Rock posters and weird, nude art adorn the walls of this very casual, sociable café, peopled mostly by students and inner-city hipsters. The coffee is excellent, and the pastas and salads are all in the $6–10 range. Open daily 7.30am–6pm.

King Ahiram, 88 Vulture St. A decent Lebanese takeaway and restaurant; not worth crossing town for, but good for kebabs and sticky Mediterranean desserts if you're in the area.

New Asian, 153 Boundary St (☎07/3846 3569). Forget flashier Vietnamese restaurants in the neighbourhood: this is the best – prawns grilled on sugar cane, deep-fried quail, rice-noodle dishes – all for less than $6 a dish.

Three Monkeys Coffee Shop, 58 Mollison St. Decorated with a funky assortment of African oddments; serves average coffee, awesome cakes, and effortlessly achieves the sort of bohemian atmosphere most coffee shops merely aspire to. Greek-influenced menu with plenty of vegetarian/lentil options, and nothing over $8. Open daily 9.30am–midnight.

Wok On Inn, 94 Boundary St. All kinds of fresh, tasty soups, and noodles in combination with vegies, chicken, beef or prawns; $7–10 for anything on the menu. Open 7 days.

Nightlife, entertainment and culture

The city's entertainment horizons consist of an ever-fluctuating range of clubs, and a sound, if unadventurous, arts scene. The best cross-section of attractions are north of the river in Petrie Terrace – upmarket yet subdued – and in Fortitude Valley, which throbs with the nightclub crowd. South Brisbane and the West End are more down-to-earth.

Pubs, clubs and live music

Brisbane nights were once a byword for boredom. The few places that offered after-dark entertainment were either illegal or lifeless and closed early; locals tended to head to the coast for their weekends. Things have changed, however, and Brisbane has seen a recent explosion of home-grown musical talent, with bands such as Savage Garden, Regurgitator, Custard and Powderfinger putting the city firmly on the Australian pop-culture map. On Friday and Saturday evening the centre is crowded, but the big push is out to the clubs, bars, live venues and restaurants (many with quality entertainment) of a reinvented and revamped Fortitude Valley. The places listed below might be here to stay, but check with music stores, or weekly **free magazines** for up-to-the-minute reviews and listings: *Rave* and *Time Off* for rock and live bands, and *The Scene* for dance venues. There's no standard charge for club entry, and many places offer free nights and special deals. Although some international bands make it as far as Brisbane, most acts you'll see are Australian – for information and tickets, try Rocking Horse, 101 Adelaide St. The **Brisbane Biennial**, held mid-September in alternate (odd-numbered) years, is a showcase of jazz and other music – check with the tourist offices for details.

City centre

Arizona's, *Wintergarden Tavern*, Queen Street Mall. Pretty trendy at present, with cheap drinks on selected nights; open late on Sun.

City Rowers, Waterfront Place, 1 Eagle St. Very much a yuppie hangout. You'll need to be smartly dressed to gain entry and enjoy the evening views over the river.

Crash & Burn, corner of Edward and Mary streets. Independent, very live bands every weekend.

Down Under Bar, at *Palace* backpackers, corner of Ann and Edward streets. Hugely popular and often overtly sexist get-drunk-throw-up-and-fall-down venue for travellers.

Jameson's Restaurant with nightly entertainment in the bar varying from live jazz and Wednesday's "songwriters night" to DJ's playing hip-hop and acid jazz on Friday and Saturday.

Orient Hotel, corner of Queen and Ann streets. Just a regular pub, but a good bet for some local music talent, as it's a place that supports young Brisbane bands.

DRINKS FOR WOMEN: THE REGATTA HOTEL

Though Australian pubs tend towards being all-male enclaves, women were once legally barred to "protect" them from the corrupting influence of foul language. On April 1, 1965, Merle Thornton (mother of the actress Sigrid Thornton) and her friend Rosalie Bogner chained themselves to the footrail of the **Regatta Hotel** bar at Toowong in protest; the movement they inspired led to the granting of "the right to drink alongside men" in the mid-1970s. The pink-and-white colonial hotel is now a trendy place for a drink after work on Friday. It's on the west bank of the river along Coronation Drive, about 2km from the city centre towards St Lucia.

Story Bridge Hotel, 200 Main St, Kangaroo Point. Live bands most nights downstairs at the *Bomb Shelter*, plus cheap drinks and mayhem during weekly "Monday Night Madness". Also hosts the five-day National Beer Festival in July, when around sixty of Australia's finest ales are on offer.

Treasury Tavern, corner of George and Elizabeth streets. Cheap beer and loud music Wednesday, Friday and Saturday; alternative live bands at weekends. Organizes riotous boat cruises from time to time.

Petrie Terrace

Crazies, corner of Caxton and Judge streets (☎07/3369 0555). Cabaret restaurant employing professional actors, where the tone is set by the dress regulations – "Wear what you bloody like; it doesn't worry me" – and the floor show can only be described as original. Go in a group and book well in advance. Prices vary with the season; basic charge is $45 per person.

The Metro, 61 Petrie Terrace. Predictable nightclub and disco – loud, coloured lights, expensive drinks, the works; also occasionally hosts big Australian touring acts.

Paddo Tavern, 186 Given Terrace. Band and disco on Friday night with a crowded beer garden early on in the evening.

Viva, 183 Given Terrace. A gathering of beautiful people and pricey drinks; closed Mon.

Spring Hill

Alliance Hotel, 320 Boundary St. Friday-night DJ sessions with a heavy dose of punk, Gothic, industrial and metal. Open 9pm–3am.

GAY AND LESBIAN BRISBANE

Despite its name, Queensland has long had a reputation for repressive attitudes towards gays and lesbians. However, whereas in 1906 you would virtually be arrested on suspicion of being gay, public attitudes have relaxed considerably in the last few years: homosexuality has been **decriminalized** and anti-discrimination legislation is in force. Today, Brisbane's gays and lesbians are revelling in a loud and energetic scene which gets better every year. In June the Pride Collective hosts the annual **Pride Festival**, a diverse event, with a street march, fair, art exhibitions, a film festival, sports events, general exhibitionism and a dance party – the **Queen's Birthday Ball**. At the **Sleaze Ball** in November there's another opportunity to indulge.

The gay scene is largely clustered around the suburbs of Spring Hill, Fortitude Valley, New Valley, New Farm and Paddington. For up-to-the-moment **information**, listen to Queer Radio, station ZZZ 102.1FM (Wed 6–9pm) or pick up a copy of *BrotherSister* or *Queensland Pride* from gay nightclubs, street distributors and some coffee shops.

Support groups and information
AIDS Gladstone Road Medical Centre, 38 Gladstone Rd, Highgate Hill (☎07/3844 6806), medical services and counselling; Queensland AIDS Council, 32 Peel St, South Brisbane (☎07/3844 1990); QUIV-AA, 191 Brunswick St, Fortitude Valley (☎07/3252 5390), needle exchange and safe-sex gear.
Books Women's Bookshop, 15 Gladstone Rd, Highgate Hill (☎07/3844 6650), stocks the latest lesbian titles.
Counselling and information Gay (☎07/3891 7377), lesbian (☎07/3891 7388); daily 7am–10pm; free call for both ☎1800/249 377.
The Pride Collective PO Box 5159, Woolloongabba, QLD 4102. Organizers of the Pride Festival – write for details.
Queensland Pride PO Box 8151, Woolloongabba, QLD 4102 (☎07/3392 2922). Free monthly publication covering Brisbane and the rest of the state.
Travel Pride Travel (free call ☎1800/808 696). Specialists in gay and lesbian accommodation, bookings and travel.

Note: For gay-friendly accommodation, try *Central Brunswick Apartment Hotel* or the *Sportsmans Hotel* (see Accommodation listings, p.343), while nightlife focuses on *The Beat, Options, The Wickham Hotel, Sportsmans Hotel* and the *Cockatoo Club*) – all listed under "Pubs, Clubs and Live Music".

Options, at the *Spring Hill Hotel*, corner of Leichhardt and Little Edward streets. Two-level gay and lesbian nightclub with bar, dance floor, coffee shop and cabaret stage. Events include drag shows, karaoke, strip nights and sausage sizzles. Young crowd, with women's nights on the second and last Friday of each month – *Options* hosts the "Ms Wicked Queensland" competition. Closed Mon & Tues.

Sportsmans Hotel, 130 Leichhardt St. Gay, lesbian and straight crowds fill the two floors; pool tables, pinball, bottle shop and bistro.

Fortitude Valley

Arena, 201 Brunswick St. Long-established venue hosting popular DJ's and dance parties as well as local and international touring bands.

The Beat, 677 Ann St. Gay and lesbian club, but the clientele is pretty mixed; small, crowded and sweaty inside, with a beer garden outside where you can recharge your batteries on bar food.

The Chelsea, 25 Warner St. Right next to *The Healer*, and yet another converted church; musicians swear by it as a quality "live" venue that supports Brisbane bands.

Cockatoo Club, upstairs at 677 Ann St. Stridently gay venue featuring both indoor and outdoor bars. Open Wed–Sun.

Dooley's, corner of Brunswick and McLachlan streets. Rowdy, popular Irish pub hosting bands of variable quality; territorial male behaviour is the norm in the big pool-hall upstairs

The Healer, 27 Warner St. A renovated ninety-year-old church, which has remained true to its origins by putting the stage at one end and the bar at the other, with rows of seats in between; feels just right for its menu of quality live blues, soul, and R&B.

La Discotheque, 228 Wickham St. Twinned with *The Tube* as the Valley's core dance music venues, and linked to it by a string of people to-ing and fro-ing between the two.

The Press Club, in the *Empire Hotel*, corner of Brunswick and Ann streets. "Members only" club (whatever that means); if you make it past the door gorillas, you'll find leather lounges, big "pouf" cushions to rest your feet on and a huge glam/industrial fan as the centrepiece, all of it enveloped in a relaxed and funky dance beat. Rather a "fabulous" crowd, seeing and being seen, with drinks prices to match. Closed Mon.

Super Deluxe, upstairs from *The Press Club*, in the *Empire Hotel*. Pretentious name for what's actually an attractive room with two bars, and a dance floor populated by a young student crowd. Indie-rock dance tunes (Stone Roses, The Cure, Blur, etc), and no techno. Open Fri & Sat nights only.

The Tube, Wickham St, three doors along from *La Discotheque*. DJ's play a variety of the latest dance tracks.

The Wickham Hotel, corner of Wickham and Alden streets. Reputedly Queensland's most popular gay pub although all are welcome, whether gay or straight. DJ's every night, with cabaret and drag shows as a regular feature.

Zoo, 711 Ann St. A hard-core night out with jazz, local bands and reggae; Wed–Sun 5pm–late.

Film and theatre

Compared with the rest of the state, which tends to get only mainstream commercial successes, Brisbane has some very good cinemas and a varied programme of films. The Classic (963 Stanley St, East Brisbane; ☎07/3393 1066), Dendy (346 George St; ☎07/3211 3244), Schonell (University of Queensland, St Lucia; ☎07/3371 1879) and Village Twin (corner of Brunswick and Annie streets; ☎07/3358 2021) all show contemporary and vintage foreign-language and "offbeat" films. Even the multiscreen Hoyts cinema (☎07/3229 2133), in the Myer Centre, and the luxurious, grand Regent (☎07/3229 5544) further down the mall, are worth checking for unexpected offerings, as is the State Library (☎07/3840 7811). In August the **Brisbane International Film Festival** is in town with a bundle of goodies from around the world shown over a week – contact one of the cinemas for details. Big **theatrical productions** are staged at the Suncorp Theatre (179 Turbot St; ☎07/3221 5177) and the **Performing Arts Complex** (☎07/3846 4646) on the South Bank in the Concert Hall, Optus Playhouse (home of the

Queensland Theatre Company), Cremorne, or Lyric theatres; look out for lower-key lunchtime performances, workshops and foyer exhibitions. The University of Queensland's Cement Box Theatre, over the river at their St Lucia campus (☎07/3377 2240), offers more down-to-earth repertory fare, and there's theatre-in-the-round at La Boite (57 Hale St; ☎07/3369 1622).

Art galleries

Besides the State Art Gallery (see p.351), the most accessible of Brisbane's art show-rooms is the Queensland Aboriginal Creations Gallery at 199 Elizabeth St, whose collectable artefacts – made for the tourist trade but as good as you'll find anywhere – include crafts from the Torres Straits, prints, paintings and books. The gallery contains sculpture, watercolours and batiks – some "conventional", others personal and stylized.

Brisbane's other galleries tend to be somewhat serious. The Institute of Modern Art (608 Ann St, Fortitude Valley; Tues–Fri 11am–5pm, Sat 11am–4pm; free) is typical, with a severe decor enlivened only by various local artists' experiments and travelling exhibitions, while Fire-Works Gallery further along at 678 Ann St, features heavy-handed displays of "Aboriginal Art & Other Burning Issues".

Listings

Airlines Air New Zealand, 133 Mary St (☎07/3853 8340; reservations ☎13 2467); Air Niugini, 99 Creek St (☎1300/361 380); Air Vanuatu, Floor 5, 293 Queen St (☎07/3221 2566); Ansett, 743 Ann St, Fortitude Valley (☎07/3061 0808; 24hr reservations ☎13 1300); British Airways, Level 17, 241 Adelaide St (☎07/3232 3000); Cathay Pacific, 400 Queen St (☎07/3221 6747; reservations ☎13 1747); Flight West, Pandanus Ave, Eagle Farm (☎13 2392); Garuda, 288 Edward St (☎07/3210 0688); Gulf Air, 217 George St (☎07/3867 7188); Japan Airlines, Level 14, 1 Waterfront Place, Eagle St (☎07/3229 9916); KLM, 141 Queen St (free call ☎1800/505 747); Korean Air, 400 Queen St (☎07/3226 6000); Malaysia Airlines, 17th Floor, 80 Albert St (☎13 2627); Qantas, 241 Adelaide St (international ☎13 1211; domestic ☎13 1313); Royal Brunei, 9/25 Mary St (☎07/3221 7757); Singapore, 344 Queen St (☎07/3259 0700); Thai International, 145 Eagle St (☎07/3215 4700); United, 400 Queen St (☎13 1777).

Banks Queensland banking hours are Mon–Fri 9.30am–4pm; major branches in the centre are around Queen and Edward streets.

Bikes Rental and repairs: Brisbane Bike Sales, 87 Albert St (☎07/3229 2433); open daily and late Fri night; rents rollerblades too.

Bookshops American Book Store, 173 Elizabeth St (☎07/3229 4677), has a broad selection; Mary Ryan, Queen Street Mall (☎07/3221 9922), is a good standard bookshop with a coffee shop downstairs; Travel Books, 66 Boundary St, West End (☎07/3846 5432), has a small but comprehensive range of guides and travel literature; Women's Bookshop, 15 Gladstone Rd, Highgate Hill (☎07/3844 6650), stocks the latest lesbian titles.

Buses All ticket desks are on the third floor of the Transit Centre, Roma St. For Queensland and interstate: Brisbane Bus Lines (☎07/3354 3633); Crisp's (☎07/3236 5266); Greyhound Pioneer (☎07/3258 1670); Kirkland's (☎07/3236 5222); McCafferty's (☎07/3236 3035). For Gold Coast and the southeast: Coachtrans (☎07/3236 1000); Suncoast (☎07/3236 1901).

Bushwalking Brisbane Bushwalkers Club, 2 Alderley Ave, Alderley (☎07/3856 4050), 8km west of the centre by train.

Camping supplies K2, 140 Wickham St, Fortitude Valley (☎07/3854 1340); Kathmandu, 144 Wickham St (☎07/3252 8054); and Mountain Designs, 146 Wickham St (☎07/3216 1866), for top-quality camping gear and information; Wilderness Shop, 97 Albert St (☎07/3229 4178), for more general needs.

Canoes There's a good Canoe Trail on Bulimba Creek, east of the city at Wynnum, which includes riverine forest and mangrove habitats. The City Hall information desk has details on the trail and canoe rental.

Car rental You'll pay at least $40 for a single day's rental; longer terms work out from $30 a day. Shop around and read rental conditions before signing. Most places will deliver; minimum age is 21.

Abel, Roma St Transit Centre (☎13 1429); Compass, 728 Main St, Kangaroo Point (☎07/3891 2614); Network Rent A Car, 398 St Pauls Terrace, Fortitude Valley (☎07/3252 1599 or free call ☎1800/077 977); NQ Australia, 24 Violet St, Eagle Farm (☎07/3268 5800), for campervans; Shoe Strings, 360 Nudgee Rd, Hendra (☎07/3268 3334); Thrifty, 325 Wickham St, Fortitude Valley (☎07/3252 5994).

Consulates Austria, 30 Argyle St, Breakfast Creek (☎07/3262 8955); Belgium, Level 5, 160 Edward St (☎07/3229 0244); Bolivia, 210 Queen St (☎07/3221 1606); Britain, 1 Eagle St (☎07/3236 2575); Chile, 204 Baroona Rd, Rosalie (☎07/3368 4073); Denmark, 180 Queen St (☎07/3221 8641); France, 10 Market St (☎07/3229 8201); Germany, 10 Eagle St (☎07/3221 7819); Greece, 215 Adelaide St (☎07/3228 3292); Italy, 10 Eagle St (☎07/3229 8944); Japan, 12 Creek St (☎07/3221 5188); Netherlands, 101 Wickham Terrace (☎07/3839 9644); New Zealand, 288 Edward St (☎07/3221 9933); Norway, 301 Wickham St, Fortitude Valley (☎07/3854 1855); Papua New Guinea, Level 1, 99 Creek St (☎07/3221 7915); Philippines, 126 Wickham Terrace, Fortitude Valley (☎07/3252 8215); Solomon Islands, 97 Creek St (☎07/3221 7899); Spain, 25 Mary St (☎07/3221 8571); Sri Lanka, 70 Roscommon Rd (☎07/3865 1090); Sweden, 1 Eagle St (☎07/3221 9797); Switzerland, 11 Ross St, Newstead (☎07/3257 1666); Thailand, 101 Wickham Terrace (☎07/3832 1999).

Disabled travellers The Disability Information and Awareness Line (DIAL) maintains a database of accessible accommodation and other facilities throughout Queensland (☎07/3224 8444, or outside Brisbane free call ☎1800/177 120; *dial@fsaia.qld.gov.au*).

Diving Nearest dive sites to Brisbane are off North Stradbroke and Moreton islands; details on pp.363-364. South Bank Dive & Hire, Stanley St (☎07/3844 7160, fax 3844 1351), and Nautilus Scuba, 504 Lutwyche Rd (☎07/3857 1440), can cater to all your needs.

Emergencies Dial ☎000 and ask for Fire, Ambulance or Police.

Gay and lesbian Brisbane See box on p.356.

Hospitals/medical centres Roma Street Medical Centre, Level 2, Transit Centre (☎07/3236 2988); Royal Brisbane, Herston Rd, Herston (☎07/3253 8111; buses #126, #144 or #172 from outside City Hall); Travellers' Medical Service, Level 1, 245 Albert St (☎07/3211 3611, fax 3211 3771); Mon–Fri 7.30am–7pm, Sat 9am–5pm, Sun 10am–4pm, for general services, vaccinations and women's health.

Left luggage At the airport, Transit Centre and in the basement of the Myer Centre.

Maps Royal Automobile Club of Queensland's series (free to members from all RACQ centres) covers 4WD-only tracks; Sunmap (Floor 2, State Government Building, corner of Adelaide and Edward streets), the state mapping department, sells general-purpose and detailed survey maps; World Wide, 187 George St, stocks a comprehensive range of maps, atlases and travel guides for Queensland and beyond.

Markets Eagle St (Sun until 3pm) and Brunswick Street Mall (Sat until 4pm) for bits and pieces; South Bank Parklands (Fri night, Sat & Sun until around 4pm) for clothing, arts & crafts and a family atmosphere; Riverside Centre (Sundays only) is more "arty" than the rest.

National Parks and Wildlife Service (NPWS) 160 Ann St (☎07/3227 8185). Officially the Department of Environment in Queensland; plenty of fluffy toys and general information about the state's national parks.

Pharmacies Transit Centre Pharmacy (☎07/3236 3055; open from 7am); Day & Night Pharmacy, Queen Street Mall (Mon–Sat 8am–9pm, Sun 10am–5pm).

Police Queensland Police Headquarters is opposite the Transit Centre on Roma St (☎07/3364 6464).

Post office GPO, 261 Queen St (☎07/3405 1202 or 3405 1448); bring photo ID to collect poste restante. Mon–Fri 7am–6pm; (Myer Centre PO open Sat 9am–4pm, Sun 10.30am–4pm, and until 9pm on Fridays).

RACQ 300 St Pauls Terrace, Fortitude Valley (☎07/3361 2556, breakdown service ☎13 1111).

Sailing A B Sea Sailing School, Manly (☎07/3396 3994), runs one- to eight-day certified training courses aboard their cruise/racer *Red Rizla*; Bay Dolphin (☎07/3821 4470) offers a full-day sailing between the mainland and North Stradbroke Island for $64.

Sheepshearing The Australian Woolshed's highly polished performance includes a parade of trained sheep (a rarity in itself), a shearing demonstration, morning tea and sheepdogs putting startled flocks through their paces. They're west of town at 148 Samford Rd, Ferny Hills (☎07/3351 5366); shows start at 8am, 9.30am, 11am, 1pm & 2.30pm; $12 per person. Take the train to Ferny Grove, turn right out of the station past *Ferny Grove Tavern* and it's about an 800m walk.

Skydiving Ripcord Skydivers (☎07/3399 3552) offer tandem and solo training.

Sport Queensland's sport is Rugby League, and ANZ Stadium is the new home of the Brisbane Broncos, though their traditional stomping ground is Suncorp Stadium (Lang Park), near the XXXX brewery in Milton. The event of the year is the State of Origin series in May or June. Cricket matches are played at "The Gabba", Vulture St, and the Queensland Reds rugby union team play at Ballymore oval. Tickets are usually easy to get at the games.

Telephones International payphones are located in the arcade beside the GPO at 261 Queen St.

Tours Allstate Scenic Tours (☎07/3285 1777), day-trips to Green Mountain at Lamington National Park; Australian Day Tours (☎1300/363 436), day-tours to Sunshine Coast, Stradbroke Island and around Brisbane City; Backtracks (☎07/5573 5693), to Lamington and Springbrook national parks; Downunder Tours (PO Box 149, Maryborough, QLD 4650; free call ☎1800/072 535) has several all-inclusive, luxury bus packages from Brisbane – from a four-day excursion to Carnarvon Gorge to a 22-day Gulf Savannah, Reef and Outback tour; Far Horizons (☎07/3284 5475), day-trips to Lamington and Springbrook national parks; Sunrover (☎07/3203 4241), three- to six-day 4WD safaris to Moreton Island, Carnarvon Gorge and Fraser Island; Wonderful Drive (☎07/3300 6933), full- and half-day tours to the Australian Woolshed, Brisbane Forest Park and elsewhere.

Trains Queensland and interstate trains leave from the Transit Centre's ground floor; for rail information call ☎13 2232.

Travel agents Discounted air fares and other travel arrangements from: Flight Centre, 181 George St (☎07/3229 0150); Jetset Travel, 189 Adelaide St (☎07/3227 1777); STA, 111 Adelaide St (☎13 1776); Trailfinders, 91 Elizabeth St (☎07/3229 0887). There's also the Backpackers Travel Centre at 138 Albert St (☎07/3221 2225), and a YHA office at 154 Roma St (☎07/3236 1680).

Women's Brisbane Contact Women's Infolink, 56 Mary St (free call ☎1800/177 577).

Working Popular with job-hunters, Brisbane offers fairly good employment prospects, if you're not too choosy. Regular employment agencies may actively discourage travellers, however several hostels now run very effective ad hoc agencies themselves, matching up people with a variety of casual jobs. There is always a full amount of casual labour needed to prepare the Exhibition Grounds about eight weeks before the "Ekka" in August.

Outer Brisbane and Moreton Bay

With the grossly hyped Gold Coast and Hinterland for competition, it's not surprising that few people bother with the country immediately surrounding Brisbane. Only 5km to the west, the city is hemmed in by **Mount Coot-tha's** botanic gardens and the foothills of **Brisbane Forest Park**, which covers the green, wet heights of the D'Aguilar Range and stretches to the edge of **Lake Wivenhoe**.

In the opposite direction, coastal suburbs provide access to the shallow waters of **Moreton Bay**, famous throughout Australia as the home of the unfortunately named Moreton Bay Bug, which is actually a small, delicious lobster-like crustacean. While Brisbane is hardly noted for its beach life, with muddy shorelines attracting mangroves rather than sun worshippers, the largest of the bay's islands, **Moreton** and **North Stradbroke**, are generously endowed with sand, and are just the right distance from the city to make their beaches accessible but seldom crowded. The island of **St Helena** is not somewhere you'd visit for sun and surf, but its prison ruins recall the convict era and can be an interesting day-trip. In the bay itself, look for dolphins, **dugong** (sea cows) and humpbacked **whales**, which pass by in winter en route to their calving grounds up north.

For organized **transport and tours** into the area, check the following individual accounts, as well as under "Tours" in the Brisbane "Listings" above.

Mount Coot-tha

The lower slopes of **Mount Coot-tha** are the setting for Brisbane's second **Botanic Gardens**, a popular place for a Sunday picnic located on Sir Samuel Griffith Drive

(Mon–Sat 8am–5pm; free; bus #471 from Adelaide Street runs hourly from 9.15am–3.15pm). Careful landscaping and the use of enclosures create varying climates – dry pine and eucalypt groves, a cool subtropical rainforest complete with waterfalls and streams, and the elegant **Japanese Gardens**. In summer, the **tropical plant dome** seems an unnecessary feature in an already sweltering climate; inside, the floor is almost completely occupied by a pond – stocked with fish – and is overshadowed by towering tropical greenery dripping with moisture. Worth hunting out are the jade vine's extraordinary flowers and the lotus lily's flat pads, usually found much further north.

The other dome in the gardens does duty as a **planetarium** (call ☎07/3403 2578 for current entry fee and timetable of events). While the foyer display is dry and dated, the show itself, which you view lying back under the dome's ceiling, is an interesting observation of the key features of Brisbane's night sky.

After visiting the Botanic Gardens most people head up the road to the **summit** for panoramas of the city and, on a good day, the Moreton Bay islands. **Walking tracks** from here make for moderate hikes of an hour or two through dry gum woodland, and include several **Aboriginal trails** – the best of which branches off the Slaughter Falls track and points out plants and their uses as food, artefacts and hunting poisons. Pamphlets on the tracks are available from the Botanic Gardens library (Tues–Fri 9.30am–4.30pm, Sat 10am–noon) and the information desk in the foyer of Brisbane's City Hall.

Brisbane Forest Park

If your plans don't include seeing any other forests in the southeast, take advantage of **Brisbane Forest Park**'s proximity to the city. While lacking the sustained beauty of Lamington and the Scenic Rim, it contains substantial tracts of virgin forest, and is well stocked with wildlife, pretty lookouts and easy walking tracks. A day is ample time to look around, or you could make the park the first stage of a scenic circuit from Brisbane via Lake Wivenhoe and Toowoomba.

There are a dozen or more places to head for within the park's approximately 280-square-kilometre boundaries. The pick of these include **Bellbird Grove** (4km from Park Headquarters), containing another of the city's Aboriginal trails with an outdoor museum of bark huts housing more information on traditional plant uses; **Boombana**'s one-kilometre rainforest circuit, complete with moss-covered logs, towering buttressed trees, and optimistic signs identifying birds you should encounter; and **Maiala National Park** (30km into the park), a fascinating tract of subtropical forest similar to Lamington's, where palms, figs and other giant trees compete for light, vines tangle up the forest floor and gullies guide fast-flowing creeks. Between these enclaves are the townships of Mount Nebo and Mount Glorious, as well as **Manorina Bush Camp**, the park's sole campsite (see "Practicalities" overleaf).

There's plenty of **wildlife** to be encountered along the park's many kilometres of **walking tracks**. Catbirds snarl at each other in the rainforest, while male satin bowerbirds woo females with an elaborate tunnel made from grass and decorated with blue objects (Queensland dairies changed the colour of their plastic bottle lids when it was suggested that bowerbirds might throttle themselves on them). At night, you'll see wallabies on verges, glider possums around flowering trees in open woodland, echidnas scraping through leaf litter for ants, and possibly the bandy-bandy, a timid snake boldly striped in black and white, which forms vertical hoops with its body when frightened.

Lake Wivenhoe was created in the late 1970s to stop the Brisbane River flooding the city – the last of a series of floods struck in 1974. Its southern end is just visible from an outlook on the western edge of the **D'Aguilar Range**, about 10km west of Maiala, that gives a sweeping view down wooded hills to the drier country of the southwest. A road links the park with the Brisbane Valley Highway and if you're heading west, you can get to Toowoomba (see p.476) via the Wivenhoe Dam (140km) – a slower-paced, far more scenic route than the alternative Warrego Highway.

Practicalities

While by **bus** (Cityxpress #506 from Albert Street) you can come within 500m of the park gates via **The Gap**, 5km west of the city, you really need your own **car** to get around – or you could take a **guided tour**. The **Park Headquarters** at Walkabout Creek (Mon–Fri 8.30am–4.30pm, Sat & Sun 9am–5pm; ☎07/3300 4855) makes a good first stop for maps, information, details of tours and, if you want to **camp out**, a permit. The only **accommodation** in the park is the rather rudimentary *Manorina Bush Camp*, whose facilities comprise barbecues, pit toilets and water; note that the nearest source of supplies is 3km away, at Mount Nebo. In general, spring is the best time to visit; animals are active, many plants are in flower and rain is infrequent. It can be cold at night in winter, with low cloud.

Below the headquarters is the **Walkabout Creek Wildlife Centre** (daily 9am–4.30pm; $3.50), an idealized creek system where lungfish, turtles, snakes and frogs coexist with few of the stresses they'd encounter living this close together in the wild. Everything is well labelled and it's unlikely you'll ever get better views of crayfish mincing over the gravel at the bottom of the stream or water dragons sunning themselves on rocks. The centre also has a noisy walk-through aviary, as well as a collection of platypuses and a nocturnal house.

St Helena Island

Small, low and triangular, **St Helena Island** sits 8km from the mouth of the Brisbane River. Once the hunting ground of local tribes, the island took its name from a parallel drawn with the exile of Napoleon Bonaparte to St Helena in the South Atlantic – in 1828 an Aborigine known as Napoleon was dumped here after he became too troublesome for the jail at Dunwich on North Stradbroke Island. Forty years later, the spectre of overcrowding in mainland prisons prompted the government to turn St Helena Island into a penal settlement, and after clearing rainforest for timber and to prevent escapes, gardens were planted and houses built from coral blocks and clay. In some respects it was a model system: prisoners were taught a trade and were even paid for their labour, and there were only three escapes in 65 years. The government found it particularly useful for political troublemakers, such as the leaders of the 1891 shearers' strike and, with more justice, a couple of slave-trading "Blackbirder" captains.

A **tour** of the prison island, endearingly tagged the "Hell Hole of the South Pacific" during its working life, leaves you thankful you missed out on the "good old days". A clue to why there were so few escapes is provided by the rusty swimming enclosure at the jetty, which was constructed to protect warders from the sharks whose presence was actively encouraged around the island. Evidence of the prisoners' industry and self-sufficiency is still to be seen in the stone houses, as well as in the remains of a sugar mill, paddocks, wells and an ingenious lime kiln built into the shoreline. The Deputy Superintendent's house has been turned into a bare **museum**, displaying a ball and chain lying in a corner, and photographs from the prison era. Outside, the gardens that once produced prize-winning olive oil are now sparse, and the two cemeteries have been desecrated: many headstones were carried off as souvenir coffee tables, the corpses dug up and sold as medical specimens. The remaining stones comprise simple concrete crosses stamped with a number for the prisoners, or inscribed marble tablets for the warders and their children. The last inmate left in 1933.

Cat-o'-Nine-Tails (☎07/3393 3726) offers **day-trips** ($38 including lunch; departing 11am and returning 4pm) and **night-tours** ($79) to the island several times a week, the latter including a three-course meal and a theatrical sound-and-light show on the island. Boats leave from the public jetty in the suburb of **Manly**, a ten-minute walk from Manly train station. Call in advance to find out exact days and make bookings.

Moreton Island

A narrow band of stabilized sand dunes 38km long, **Moreton Island**'s faultless beaches are distinctly underpopulated for much of the year – making it perfect for a day or two of surfing, fishing or camping. The easiest way for pedestrians to reach the island is on the *Tangalooma Resort* **ferry** (daily 10am; ☎07/3268 6333; $30 return), which leaves from the terminal at the end of Holt Street, off Kingsford Smith Drive at Pinkenba. A **courtesy bus** (daily 9.15am) leaves from the McCafferty's bay on the third floor of the Roma Street Transit Centre. The alternatives are to take the similarly priced *Moreton Venture* (☎07/3895 1000), also to Tangalooma, or the Combie Trader **barge** and vehicle transport to Bulwer (☎07/3203 6399) – call for timetables and departure points.

Four-wheel-drive tours organized by Combie Trader and Sunrover Expeditions (☎07/3203 4241) last from one to three days. Taking your own **vehicle** to the island, whose sand tracks are 4WD-only, will cost at least $150 return. The rules of the road are the same as on the mainland; check tide times before driving on the beach, and be aware that pedestrians may not hear you above the sound of the surf. **Supplies** on the island are expensive and limited to Bulwer and Kooringal, so you need to be self-sufficient and have enough water if you are camping. There are no banks. And before you go in the water, remember that the beaches aren't patrolled and there are no shark nets. The worst times to visit are at Christmas and Easter, when up to a thousand vehicles crowd onto the island all at once.

The island has designated campsites at Tangalooma and Ben-Ewa (3km towards Bulwer) on the west coast and Blue Lagoon and Eagers Creek on the east side, you can **camp** anywhere along beaches except where there are signs asking you not to. Permits are available from barge operators or on site for $3.50 per person per night.

Around the island

Most people arrive at **TANGALOOMA**, midway along the island's west coast, where a set of wrecks, deliberately sunk to create an artificial harbour but now swamped in sand, become a fine **snorkelling** site at high tide. Nearby is *Tangalooma Resort* (PO Box 4009, Eagle Farm; bookings ☎07/3268 6333, resort 3408 2666; ⑥), which has parts of a former whaling station incorporated into its buildings. Pleasantly shaded and busy at weekends and holidays, it's the only place on the island that has a restaurant and serves cold drinks – respectable dress required. There's also a national parks **campsite** here (with water, showers and toilets), which gets as crowded as anywhere on the island. A three-kilometre track heads south from Tangalooma to the **Desert**, where the dunes are a great place to try sand-tobogganing.

With your own vehicle, or if you don't mind hiking, take the ten-kilometre track from Tangalooma across to Moreton's more attractive **eastern side**; generally less crowded, the beach also has good surf. You end up at Eagers Creek, where there's another campsite and a five-kilometre return trip up **Mount Tempest**'s 280-metre peak – an exhausting climb. Head 10km north up the beach, and you'll find **Blue Lagoon**, the largest of the island's freshwater lakes, only 500m from the beach and adjacent to the smaller, picturesque **Honeyeater Lake**. Blessed with shady trees, the dunes behind the beach make an ideal place to camp, and the site is supplied with water, showers and toilets. **Dolphins** come in close to shore – a practice that Moreton's Aborigines turned to their advantage by using them to chase fish into the shallows. Writing in the 1870s about his life in Brisbane, Tom Petrie reported that the Ngugi men would beat the surf with their spears, and:

By and by, as in response, porpoises would be seen as they rose to the surface making for the shore and in front of them schools of tailor fish. It may seem wonderful, but they were apparently driving the fish towards the land. When they came near, [they] would run out into the surf, and with their spears would jab down here and there at the fish, at times even getting two on one spear, so plentiful were they.

Moreton's **northern end** is about 9km wide, covered in ferns, grasstrees, paperbark and banksias around the shore, and dense scrub inland. The landing point here is **BULWER**, a cluster of weatherboard "weekenders" and a **store** stocking fuel and beer and providing basic **accommodation** in six-person units (☎07/3203 6399; ⑤). The beach is the only "road" south to Tangalooma, while vehicle tracks cut across to Honeyeater Lake and to the island's northeastern corner, **North Point**, where adjacent dunes form near-vertical cliffs, and fresh water, brown with tannin, seeps out into lagoons. Around from North Point, rocky **Cape Moreton** is capped by a red-and-white lighthouse, built between 1857 and 1928 and still operating. There's a museum in the house below and fine views down the east coast from adjacent cliffs.

The **south end** of the island mostly consists of exposed dunes, some covered in scrub and others forming white "blows", which are destabilized, shifting hills that slowly roll over forests. Right at Moreton's southern tip, **KOORINGAL** is a sleepy version of Bulwer and has a store offering fuel, supplies and drinks from their bar (☎07/3409 0170; open daily 8am–midnight), as well as holiday units that sleep up to six (☎07/3409 0298 or ☎3409 0105; ⑥–⑧). From Kooringal, diversions include the twelve-kilometre return trip to **Big and Little Sandhills** via Toompani beach and eerie, long-dead stands of trees in the wake of the dunes. Take plenty of water.

There's decent **diving** around the deepest points of Tangalooma's wrecks but **Curtain Reef** is superior: an artificial conglomeration of barges, tugs, cars and tyres encrusted with shells, it attracts all types of marine life including sharks, dolphins, groupers and huge rays. Contact *Tangalooma Resort* for seasonal details, transport and rental gear, or see "Diving" in the Brisbane "Listings", p.359.

North Stradbroke Island

North Stradbroke Island is, at 40km long, the largest and most established of the bay's islands, with sealed roads and the fully serviced townships of Dunwich, Amity and Point Lookout. Ninety percent of "Straddie" is given over to mining **rutile** (titanium oxide), and the majority of the 3200 residents are employees of Consolidated Rutile Ltd. The mine sites south of Amity, and in the central west and south, are far from exhausted but their future is precarious, thanks to an oversupply on the world market. Other industries focus on timber, a by-product of preparing land for mining, and, increasingly, tourism.

Transport to the island leaves from Toondah Harbour at Cleveland, with Stradbroke Ferries (☎07/3286 2666) crossing to Dunwich eleven ten times daily (return fares $10 per person by water-taxi; $69 per car by barge); bus connection from Brisbane's Transit Centre to the ferry costs $8 return. Also, watch out for good-value package deals from various sources, such as the free **courtesy bus** (not including ferry fare) from Brisbane run on Monday, Wednesday and Friday by *Stradbroke Island Guesthouse* – call them first to book.

Some roads on Stradbroke are open to mining vehicles only, so drivers should look out for the signs. Off-roading through the centre is ill-advised: quite apart from the damage caused to the dune systems, the sand is very soft and having your vehicle pulled out can be very expensive.

Dunwich to Main Beach

Unless you need to fuel up or visit the bank, there's little to keep you at **DUNWICH**, Straddie's ferry port. Two sealed roads head out of town, east through the island's centre towards **Main Beach**, or north to Amity and Point Lookout. The road through the centre passes two **lakes**, the second and smaller of which, Blue Lake, is a national park and source of fresh water for the island's wildlife, which is most plentiful early in the morning. Beyond Blue Lake you have to cross the **Eighteen Mile Swamp** to reach Main Beach and, though there's a causeway, the rest of the route is for 4WDs only. You can **camp** behind the beach anywhere south of the causeway (north of it is mining company land), but be prepared for the mosquitoes that swarm around the mangroves; the southernmost point, looking over to South Stradbroke Island (see p.372), is an angling and wildlife mecca, with birdlife and kangaroos lounging around on the beaches.

The Top End

Heading north from Dunwich, it's 10km to where the road forks left to Amity and right to Point Lookout: **AMITY** is a sleepy place built around a jetty, while **POINT LOOKOUT** is where most visitors end up if they don't want to camp. Nineteen kilometres from Dunwich, Point Lookout spreads out around Stradbroke's single rock headland, overlooking a string of beaches. Stretched out along the road are a pub, takeaway pizza place, a store, some cafés and various types of **accommodation**. Top of the range are *Anchorage Village Resort* (☎07/3409 8266; ⑧), a comfortable, motel-like option, and *The Islander* (☎07/3409 8388; ⑤–⑦), with motel rooms and two-bedroom units. At the other end of the scale, *Stradbroke Island Guesthouse* (☎07/3409 8888, fax 3409 8715; ①) and the smaller *Straddie Hostel* (☎07/3409 8679; ①) both have dorm beds, plus free loans of surfboards, bikes and fishing gear; they also organize 4WD- , walking- and trail-riding trips. *Stradbroke Tourist Park* (☎07/3409 8127; four- to six-person cabins ④) is the best of the local **caravan parks**, or you can camp on the foreshore west of Rocky Point's beach access road.

The **beaches** here are good. **Flinders** runs west of Amity; **Home** and **Cylinder** between here and Cylinder Headland are both patrolled and, therefore, crowded during holiday weekends. If you don't mind swimming in unwatched waters, head for **Deadman's Beach** or **Frenchman's Bay**. On the headland above, there are fine views and the chance to see loggerhead turtles and dolphins; from the walking track around North Gorge down to Main Beach you might see whales – if you have binoculars. Offshore, Stradbroke's **dive sites** around Flat and Shag rocks are renowned for groups of grey nurse sharks, moray eels and butterfly cod. Stradbroke Island Scuba Centre (☎07/3409 8715, fax 3409 8588) discount their five-day dive course through the hostels.

THE GOLD COAST

Beneath a jagged skyline shaped by countless high-rise beachfront apartments, the **Gold Coast** is Australia's Miami Beach or Costa del Sol, a striking contrast to Brisbane, only an hour away. As a point of entry into Queensland it could hardly provide a less typical picture of the rest of the state. Aggressively superficial, it's not the place to go if you're seeking peace and quiet: the endless succession of nightclubs, bars and theme parks provide raucous, relentless entertainment. It can be enjoyable for a couple of days – perhaps as a weekend break from Brisbane – but there's little variation on the beach and nightclub scene and if you're concerned that this will leave you jaded, bored or broke you might well be better off avoiding this corner of the state altogether.

The coast forms a virtually unbroken beach 40km long, from **South Stradbroke Island** past **Surfers Paradise** and **Burleigh Heads** to the New South Wales border at

Coolangatta. Surfers Paradise has the highest concentration of people and skyscrapers; as you head south through the strip of motels and shops the pace slows (relatively) and it's easier to find some unoccupied sand. The beaches are still touted as the main attraction, though they've become a backdrop to more commercial interests, and they swarm with bathers and board-riders all year round. **Surfing** blossomed along the coast in the 1930s and still pulls in veterans and novices; learning is as easy as renting a board and trying it out. Coolangatta, Burleigh Heads and South Stradbroke have the best waves and definitely the more serious surfies, but you'll find rideable swell all the way along the coast.

With around three hundred days of sunshine each year there's little "off-season" as such. **Rain** can, however, fall at any time during the year, including midwinter – when it's usually dry in the rest of the state – but even if the crowds do thin out a little, they reappear in time for the Gold Coast **Indy car race** in October, and then continue to swell, peaking over Christmas and New Year.

Getting there and around

From Brisbane, Coachtrans runs at least forty services daily from the Transit Centre ($12), taking about ninety minutes to get to Surfers Paradise, and slightly over two hours to Coolangatta. Their Airporter service ($28) meets all flights arriving at Brisbane's domestic and international terminals, and delivers direct to Gold Coast accommodation. If you're **driving**, head down Vulture Street onto the **Gold Coast Highway**, where there's a detour at Beenleigh to Queensland's oldest rum distillery at the *Beenleigh Tavern* (tours at 11am, noon, 1pm & 2pm; ☎07/3287 2488); it started in 1860 as a pirate business on the Albert River.

Coming up **from New South Wales**, the coastal highway enters Queensland at Coolangatta, where you'll also find the Gold Coast Airport. Airport Transit **shuttle buses** run to all points between the airport and Surfers Paradise for $9 one-way, $14 return (call ☎07/5588 8747 for information).

The Gold Coast Highway is covered by a 24-hour **local bus** service (Surfside Buses) running between Coolangatta and Southport, north of Surfers Paradise. The whole journey costs around $5; you'll save money with a **day rover** pass for multiple trips. Otherwise you'll need to take a **taxi** or **rent** a vehicle; there are more details in accounts of the individual resorts.

Surfers Paradise

Spiritually, if not geographically, **SURFERS PARADISE** is at the heart of the Gold Coast, the place where its aims and aspirations are most evident. For the residents, this involves making money by providing services and entertainment for tourists; visitors reciprocate by parting with their cash. All around and irrespective of what you're doing – shopping for clothes, sitting on the beach, partying in one of the frenetic nightclubs or even finding a bed – the pace is brash and glib. Don't come here expecting to be allowed to relax; subtlety is non-existent and you'll find that enjoying Surfers depends largely on how much it bothers you having the party mood rammed down your throat.

Beaches here have been attracting tourists since late in the nineteenth century, though the town only started developing along commercial lines during the 1950s when the first multistoreyed **beachfront apartments** were built. The demand for views over the ocean led to ever-higher towers which began to encroach on the dunes; together with the sheer volume of people attracted here, this soon caused serious **erosion** problems along the entire coast. Attempts to stabilize the foreshore with retaining walls, groynes and sand pumping from offshore have had little long-term success. But this hardly seems to matter. Although Surfers Paradise is a firm tribute to the successful marketing of the ideal Aussie lifestyle as an eternal beach party, most people would probably say that they come here not for the beaches but simply because everyone else does.

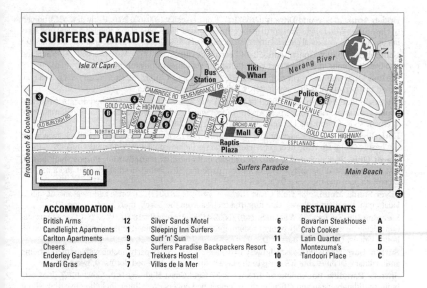

ACCOMMODATION				RESTAURANTS	
British Arms	12	Silver Sands Motel	6	Bavarian Steakhouse	A
Candlelight Apartments	1	Sleeping Inn Surfers	2	Crab Cooker	B
Carlton Apartments	9	Surf 'n' Sun	11	Latin Quarter	E
Cheers	5	Surfers Paradise Backpackers Resort	3	Montezuma's	D
Enderley Gardens	4	Trekkers Hostel	10	Tandoori Place	C
Mardi Gras	7	Villas de la Mer	8		

Arrival, information and security

Surfers' **bus station** (☎07/5531 6400) is on Beach Road on the corner of the highway, one street down from Cavill Avenue. Here you'll find **luggage lockers**, **bus company desks** and an **accommodation information** counter. If the hostel you want isn't listed, call them for a **free pick-up**, and don't be surprised if, while walking around with your luggage, hostel minibuses stop for you as they pass. The **tourist information office** is on Cavill Avenue (Mon–Fri 8am–5pm, Sat 9am–5pm, Sun 9am–3.30pm).

Security is worth bearing in mind. Many people migrate to Surfers in search of an easier life, only to find themselves homeless and hard up. Don't leave vehicles unlocked at any time, don't take valuables onto the beach, and don't wander alone at night; muggings are common, especially around nightclubs – so take advantage of the courtesy buses run by hostels. The situation definitely gets worse around the peak times of Christmas and Easter.

Accommodation

You need to **book** all **accommodation** in advance. Typically quiet early on, the **hostels** come to life late in the day and you won't be left in peace until you've signed up for trips to nightclubs, parties and beach events. They've all struck deals with various clubs for cheap entry and drinks, and all have much the same facilities – pool, dormitories, kitchen, TV and loans of surfboards. Many places don't encourage long stays, but it may be worth asking about weekly rates. **Motels**, on the other hand, sometimes insist on a minimum three-day stay – during quieter times bargaining may get you a reduced rate. Peak-season motel rates range from $55 to a few hundred dollars a night; during off-season and midweek, rooms are considerably cheaper. Expect to pay more for ocean views. There are simply too many possibilities to give a comprehensive list; those below are central and good value. If you want to **camp**, you'll have to head south to the quieter sections of the Gold Coast.

Aquarius, 44 Queen St, Southport (☎07/5527 1300 or free call ☎1800/229 955). A brand new, purpose-built hostel ready to open as this book went to press. Facilities include TV on each floor (in a tiny sitting area), pool and communal kitchen; small four- and six-bed dorms. ①.

British Arms, 70 Seaworld Drive (☎07/5571 1776 or free call ☎1800/680 269). Fairly new YHA property, close to Sea World about 5km north of the centre. Good facilities, plus a lively English bar and grill serving up pub fare, occasional entertainment, and a range of beers till late; dorms ①, doubles and twins ③.

Candlelight Holiday Apartments, 22–24 Leonard St (☎07/5538 1277). Very pleasant, self-contained one-bedroom units in a quiet street close to the bus station; very helpful and friendly owners. ⑤.

Carlton Apartments, corner of Northcliffe Terrace and Clifford St (☎07/5538 5877). Self-contained two-person units in a seven-storey building on the beach. ⑥.

Cheers, 8 Pine Ave (☎07/5531 6539 or free call ☎1800/636 539). Basic four-bed dorms, twins and doubles, all at the same price per person – a fact which reflects the laid-back and egalitarian management style. Communal kitchen and bathrooms, pool and a casual bar. ①.

Enderley Gardens, 38 Enderley Ave (☎07/5570 1511). Self-contained units, one block away from the beach, 10min from the heart of Surfers; facilities include pool, spa and tennis court. ⑤.

Mardi Gras, 28 Hamilton Ave (☎07/5592 5888 or free call ☎1800/801 230). Purpose-built hostel, just over a year old. Security building and car park; facilities include a small kitchen and a bar, but there's no pool and the place feels a bit sterile. Tiny twins ③, four-bed dorms ①.

Silver Sands Motel, 2985 Gold Coast Highway (☎07/5538 6041). Low-rise and pleasant, despite a location on the main highway. One hundred metres from the beach; there's a pool, too. ⑥.

Sleeping Inn Surfers, 26 Whelan St (☎07/5592 4455 or free call ☎1800/817 832). Close to bus station; nicely furnished, quality budget accommodation in self-contained units, all with TV and free in-house videos. Doubles ④, dorms ①.

Surf 'n' Sun, 3323 Gold Coast Highway (☎07/5592 2363). Noisy party hostel, with cramped rooms and ordinary facilities, but it's close to the beach and centre. Five-bed dorms ①, twins ③.

Surfers Paradise Backpackers' Resort, 2837 Gold Coast Highway (☎07/5592 4677). Purpose-built, sparklingly clean and efficient; the price per bed covers everything, including use of washing machines. It's a large place and rooms are spacious. ①.

Trekkers Hostel, 22 White St, Southport (☎07/5591 5616). Beautifully restored old house 3km from the centre; comfortable, and with heaps of deals and trips. Staff are particularly friendly and welcoming, and their weekly barbecue is cheap and good fun. Price includes a basic breakfast. ①.

Villas de la Mer, corner of Markwell Ave and Northcliffe Terrace (☎07/5592 6644, fax 5592 6324). Attractive apartments in a three-storey security complex, with ocean views from upper levels. Rooms are simple but modern and well furnished. Two- and three-bedroom apartments. ⑦–⑧.

The City – and theme parks

Downtown Surfers Paradise is a thin ribbon of partially reclaimed land between the ocean and the **Nerang River** which – as the Broadwater – flows north, parallel with the beach, past **the Spit** and South Stradbroke Island into the choked channels at the bottom end of Moreton Bay. Reclaimed land in the river forms islands whose names reflect the fantasies of their founders – Isle of Capri, Sorrento, Miami Keys – and which have become much-sought-after real estate.

From its dingiest club to its best restaurant, Surfers exudes entertainment, and at times – most notoriously at New Year and Christmas – you can spend 24 hours a day out on the town. Another thing you'll spend is money; the only free venue is the beach and with such a variety of distractions it can be financial suicide venturing out too early in the day. The city is full of tourists staggering around at noon, with terrible hangovers and empty wallets, complaining how expensive their holiday has become. The area around **Cavill Avenue** is a bustle of activity from early morning – when the first surfers head down to the beach and the shops open – to after midnight, when there's a constant exchange of bodies between **Orchid Avenue**'s bars and nightclubs. If you spend any length of time in town, you'll get to know the district intimately. The block between the sea and Orchid Avenue is a **mall**, given over to snack bars, coffee houses and shopping arcades; you can pick up a cheap T-shirt or play a game of chess at one of the outdoor tables. **Raptis Plaza** here is a collection of exotic eateries overlooked by a replica of Michelangelo's *David*.

Across the Esplanade, the **beach** is all you could want as a place to recover from your night out. In early afternoon, the sun moves behind the apartment buildings, but you

---

SURFING THE GOLD COAST

As locals will tell you, the Gold Coast has some of the best surfing beaches in the world. And in terms of consistency this might be true – on any given day there will be rideable surf somewhere along the coast – with 200-metre-long sand bottom point breaks and rideable waves peaking at about four metres in prime conditions. The area is known for its **barrels**, particularly during the summer cyclone season when the winds shift around to the north; in winter the swell is smaller but more reliable, making it easier to learn to surf. A rule of thumb for finding the best surf is to follow the wind: north when the wind blows from the north, south when it comes from the south. Generally, you'll find the best swell along the southern beaches, and on South Stradbroke Island. While sharks might worry you, more commonplace hostility is likely to come from the local surfies who form tight-knit cliques with very protective attitudes towards their patches.

On the subject of **sharks** and **general safety**, all beaches as far north as Surfers are patrolled; look for the signs. Sea temperatures range between 26°C in summer and 17°C in winter, so a 2–3mm wetsuit is adequate. Hard-core surfies come for Christmas and the cyclone season, though spring is really the busiest time. You'll find competitions or events on most weekends, advertised through local surf shops.

---

can escape the shadows by moving up to Main Beach. If you're feeling energetic, seek out a game of volleyball or head for the surf: the swell here is good in a northerly wind, but most of the time it's better for boogie-boards. North of Main Beach, **the Spit**'s attractions include the world's first "Versace hotel" – a six-star edifice currently under construction, to be fitted out with all things Versace – and **Sea World** (daily 10am–5pm; ☎07/5588 2222; $41, family rates; access on the Surfside Bus from the highway), the longest running of the Gold Coast's theme parks. Besides various stomach-churning rides, the park features immaculately trained dolphins and killer whales, and helps rehabilitate stranded wild dolphins for later release. Your stomach can be churned some more at the **bungee jump**, next to Sea World on the west bank of the Spit (for bookings call ☎07/5531 1103; $49), though this is a dismal way to do it – from a wire cage hauled to the required height by a crane. As an alternative, you might try "Rocket Bungee", which sling-shots you into the air from the corner of Palm Ave and Gold Coast Highway (☎07/5570 2700; $25).

The other theme parks are out of town. **Dreamworld** (daily 10am–5pm; info ☎07/5588 1111; $41, family rates), on the Pacific Highway at Coomera, 17km north of Surfers Paradise, has a violent double-loop roller coaster and a fairground atmosphere, as well as a collection of tigers that includes the world's first white tiger born in captivity. Baby tigers are reared by humans before being released into a large enclosure; this may be as close as they'll get to the wild, but at least here they're protected from poachers. **Movie World** (daily 10am–5pm; info ☎07/5573 3999; $41, family rates), also on the Pacific Highway, 14km north of Surfers, is a slice of Hollywood featuring studio tours, and western and stunt shows. Near Movie World, **Wet 'n' Wild** (daily 10am–4.30pm or later; ☎07/5573 2277; $21) has a series of pools linked by vicious water slides – the back-breaking "twister" and the 25-metre-tall, high-speed slide alone are worth the entrance fee.

Eating

Some of the beachfront resorts offer bargain all-you-can-eat **breakfasts**, while during the rest of the day there's always something to eat at the **cafés** and **snack bars** along Cavill Avenue and the Esplanade. **Restaurants** are geared towards the exotic, although some offer early-bird specials in the evening before a certain hour. More and more people are heading to convenient takeaway and burger joints out of Surfers to eat – south to the area around Broadbeach Mall, or north to Tedder Avenue, in Southport, where there's usually a Porsche or two parked along the trendy café strip. For supplies, there's a **supermarket** downstairs in the Paradise Centre (on Cavill Avenue mall) and a 24hr Night Owl store on the highway near Trickett Street.

Bavarian Steakhouse, corner of Gold Coast Highway and Cavill Ave (☎07/5531 7150). Theme restaurant on several floors with counter-meal prices; about $17 for steak, salad and fries.

Crab Cooker, corner of Gold Coast Highway and Thornton St (☎07/5538 6884). Good, Australian-style fresh seafood restaurant where a plate of prawns, bugs and fish costs around $23, and their famous mud crabs start at $40. Lunch from noon, dinner from 5.30pm.

Dracula's, 1 Hooker Blvd, Broadbeach (☎07/5575 1000). Gothic cabaret restaurant open Tues–Sat from 6pm; $45 per head ($52 on Saturday); advance booking and payment essential.

Latin Quarter, Elkhorn Ave (☎07/5592 3162). Serious "Mediterranean" restaurant, with a mouth-watering chicken *boscaiola*. Open for lunch Tues–Sun, daily for dinner from 5.30pm.

Montezuma's, 8 Trickett St, under the Aloha Tower (☎07/5538 4748). A cramped Mexican restaurant, but the food's fresh and spicy. $18 will fill you up; open for lunch and dinner.

Sumo, Raptis Plaza. Japanese takeaway known for its fair prices and large portions, from seafood tempura ($9.50) down to humble buckwheat noodle soup ($5).

Tandoori Place, 7–9 Trickett St (☎07/5592 1004). Fast-food ambience, but actually better than first impressions would suggest; their sweet curries are engagingly different. Nothing over $15, and most main dishes around $12.

Entertainment

Find out **what's on** through the hostels or by word of mouth; the free weekly magazines *Point Out*, *Look* and *Wot's On* are simply business directories. If you are desperate for an injection of culture amid all the brash goings-on, check out the programme at the Arts Centre, 135 Bundall Rd (☎07/5581 6900) where there's a theatre, gallery, restaurant and bar. You'll find **cinema** complexes on the corner of Clifford Street and Gold Coast Highway (☎07/5575 3355), as well as inside Pacific Fair Shopping Centre, Mermaid Beach (☎07/5575 3355) and Australia Fair shopping centre, Southport (☎07/5531 2200).

Realistically, though, it's Surfers' **clubs** that provide most of the nightlife. Initially, particularly if you're staying at a hostel or have picked up a **free pass** somewhere, your choice will most likely be influenced by the various deals on entry and drinks. The places listed below have been around for a while and have a dependable reputation; none is especially chauvinistic, though places do change. Opening times are from around 6pm until 3am or later.

Benson's, 22 Orchid Ave (☎07/5538 7600). Boasts one of the few surviving dance floors that lights up, *Saturday Night Fever*-style. Mostly "alternative" music, very little dance/techno. Closed Mon & Tues.

Berlin Bar, on a lane off Orchid Ave. A bit discreet and stylish for Surfers, with a more civilized scene than you find elsewhere; well-heeled 20–35 crowd being slinky and sexy to Seventies disco and funk tunes. Pricey drinks, no cover charge.

Cocktails and Dreams, Orchid Ave. Seventies nights on Tuesday from 8pm; nightly rhythm and blues at the *Bourbon Bar*; cheap drinks and extended happy hours. Closed Wed.

The Party, at *The Mark*, Orchid Ave. Live rock bands Fri & Sun (often with a $5 cover charge); DJs for the rest of the week.

Penthouse, Orchid Ave. Four floors comprise main dance floor, "R&B room", pool tables and a piano bar. $5 cover charge, generally waived for "backpackers".

Rose and Crown, Raptis Plaza, Cavill Ave (☎07/5531 5425). Surfers' "local" pub; entertainment varies from decent local bands to DJs and strip shows (male & female).

Shooters, right beside *Cocktails and Dreams*. Crowds heading for more serious dance spots start out here for a game of pool and a few drinks.

Surfers Beergarden, Cavill Ave, opposite Orchid Ave. Live music with local and interstate band talent on Thursday and Saturday nights.

THE GOLD COAST INDY

Despite financial and sponsorship problems, the **Gold Coast Indy** car race every October is Surfers' premier "event" of the year. The biggest fans of the race – first held in 1990 and boosted by Nigel Mansell's 1993 Indy debut – are the businesses that benefit from the longer tourist season it creates; other locals are somewhat ambivalent about the disturbance it causes to everyday life. The track takes in a section of the Pacific Highway between Breakers Street and View Avenue and completes the circuit along the Esplanade. Trackside passes range from $20 for general entry to $450 for reserved seating while watching the race on closed-circuit TV; one way around this is to find a room overlooking the race circuit. While you pay top prices for booking in advance, if you start looking about a week before the race, prices are far lower; with only days to go, it's not unknown for motels on the track to charge as little as $55, but you run the risk of ending up without accommodation. The only way you'll get this kind of deal (they won't be advertised) is by walking around to motels along the circuit and bargaining hard.

Listings

Airlines Offices are near Cavill Ave: Ansett, 13–19 Beach Rd (☎13 1300); Qantas, 3047 Gold Coast Highway (☎13 1312).

Banks and exchange American Express, 16 Orchid Ave (☎07/5526 9152); ANZ, 3232 Gold Coast Highway (☎07/5531 6444); Commonwealth, 3206 Gold Coast Highway (☎13 2221); Thomas Cook, Paradise Centre, Cavill Ave (☎07/5531 7770).

Boat and jet-ski rental Tiki Village Boat Hire at the river end of Cavill Ave (☎07/5538 0022), and Captain Barb-E, Ferny Ave (☎07/5531 6176) – the latter has self-drive launches from $10 per hour (based on daily rental).

Bookshops Hooked on Books, Paradise Centre, Cavill Ave.

Buses Coachtrans (☎07/5588 8777); Greyhound Pioneer (☎07/5531 6677); McCafferty's (☎07/5538 2700).

Car rental Competition keeps prices low, but advertised prices are often for long rentals, and exclude insurance and mileage charges: Betta Rent-a-Car, 108 Ferny Ave (☎07/5538 5559), from $35 a day; Red Back Rentals, inside the bus station, Beach Rd (☎07/5592 1655), from $30 a day; Thrifty (☎07/5538 6511) from $29 a day.

Cruises The following explore the Nerang River and seafront on 1hr–half-day cruises. *Aquabus* (☎07/5539 0222), a unique amphibious bus, departs several times daily from Orchid Ave for a 75min trip ($30); *Island Queen* (☎07/5592 2332) has free accommodation pick-up and return, meals available, and evening cruises; *Jungle Queen* (☎07/5594 5467) offers 2hr and evening dinner cruises in a forty-year-old ex-Daintree River ferry; Wobbegong (☎07/5527 7706) runs 3hr guided canoe trips in the calm upper reaches of the Nerang. See overleaf for trips to South Stradbroke Island.

Flights Airwaves (☎07/5564 0444) has 15min to full-day sightseeing excursions from $35 per person; Vintage Flights (☎07/5538 9083) offers authentic Tiger Moth capers along the coast.

Hospitals Gold Coast Hospital, Nerang St, Southport (☎07/5571 8211).

Pharmacy Galleria Shopping Plaza, corner of Elkhorn Ave and Gold Coast Highway (☎07/5592 1321); open 7am–midnight.

Post office Main post office is in the Paradise Centre, Cavill Ave (☎07/5539 9407).

Surf rental Surfworld, Paradise Centre, off Cavill Ave (☎07/5538 4825). Typical prices are $20 a day for board rental, plus credit card deposit.

Taxis ☎13 1008.

Tours Some hostels organize tours of the Scenic Rim, or try the following for day-trips to the Hinterland (Lamington, Natural Bridge, Mount Tamborine and Binna Burra), Sunshine Coast (Noosa, The Big Pineapple or Mooloolaba) and Brisbane (most offer free pick-ups): Aires (☎07/5594 9933); Backtracks (☎07/5573 5693), to Lamington and Springbrook national parks; Coachliner (☎07/5534 9977); Coachtrans (☎1300/361 788); Mountain Coach Company (☎07/5524

4249); Pacific Tours (☎07/5596 0350); Rob's Rainforest Explorer (☎07/3357 7061 or mobile ☎019/496 607); Scenic Hinterland Tours (☎07/5545 2030, fax 5545 2503). Mountain Trek Adventures (☎07/5536 1700) run 4WD day-tours around the Hinterland.

South Stradbroke Island

South Stradbroke Island is a twenty-kilometre-long, narrow strip of sand, separated from North Stradbroke Island by the 1896 cyclone and, as apartment buildings edge closer, doomed to become an extension of the Gold Coast. For now, though, Stradbroke's relatively isolated and quiet beaches offer something of an escape from the mainland, though most day-trippers come over simply to get plastered in the bar at **South Stradbroke Island Resort** (☎07/5577 3311; cabins ⑥). Alternatively, you can enjoy the fine **surf** along the southeast shore (though local surfies are notoriously protective) or **fish** in the Jumpinpin Channel between here and North Stradbroke.

Day cruises to the resort cost around $60 including lunch, with evening booze cruises about $50; operators include *Island Queen* (see "Cruises" under Gold Coast "Listings" overleaf) and Jetaway (tickets and departure details from "The Hut" information booth, corner of Ferny and Cavill avenues; ☎07/5538 3400). A cheaper alternative ($25 or less) is the **resort ferry** (10.30am–4.30pm; Runaway Bay Marina, 5km north of Surfers on Bayview Street, but no public transport).

Surfers Paradise to Currumbin

The central section of the Gold Coast lacks any real focus. Haphazardly developed and visually unattractive, it exists very much in the shadow of Surfers Paradise, and can't match its intensity. The highway is just a continuous maze of crowded, multi-lane traffic systems and drab buildings which lose momentum the further south you drive, but once you leave the road there are beaches, two **wildlife sanctuaries** and – unbelievable amid all the commotion and noise – Burleigh Heads' tiny **national park** which preserves the coast's original environment.

Burleigh Heads: the last rainforest
The Gold Coast's bitumen and paving was, fifty years ago, dense eucalypt and vine forest. The last bit of forest is preserved in a tiny, fragile **national park** about 10km south of Surfers Paradise at **BURLEIGH HEADS**. Entrance is on foot from the car park on the Esplanade, or turn sharply at the lights below the hill just south of the headland for the **visitors information centre** (daily 9am–4pm; ☎07/5535 3032).

Geologically, Burleigh's headland stems from the prehistoric eruptions of the Mount Warning volcano, 30km to the southwest. Lava surfaced through vents, cooling to hard basalt which was extruded into tall hexagonal columns, now mostly tumbled and covered in vines. Rainforest colonizes the richer volcanic soils, while stands of red gum grow in weaker sandy loam; along the eastern seafront there's a patch of exposed heathland bordered by groups of pandanus, and a beach along the mouth of Tallebudgera Creek. This diversity is amazing considering the minimal space, but urban encroachment has seriously affected the wildlife. Butterflies and **birds** are the most obvious inhabitants – on the heathland look out for the fairy wren's telltale black and red pattern – but the gums also support a small koala population (though, notoriously sensitive to disturbance, they often make themselves scarce). The area's natural resources once attracted Yugumbir **Aborigines**, indicated by a few mounds of half-buried shells up on the headland, whose history is brought to life on a "Kaila" tour – book through the park visitors centre.

More of the same awaits you 2km inland at **David Fleay Wildlife Park**, West Burleigh Rd (daily 9am–5pm; $9.50; take the Surfside Bus). The late David Fleay was the first person to persuade platypus to breed in captivity and the park has a special section devoted to this curious animal. The **free guided tours** are worthwhile; take advantage of their night **spotlight** and daily **Aboriginal** talk. Outside the parks, Burleigh's main attraction is **surf** around the headland, but the rocks make it rough for novices. For **accommodation**, *Burleigh Beach Tourist Park* is nicely sited next to the national park, while the *Burleigh Hotel* (☎07/5535 1000; ③), on the Esplanade, offers standard motel units and $10 meals.

Currumbin Beach and Sanctuary

A further 6km past Burleigh Heads, **CURRUMBIN BEACH** is a nice, relatively undeveloped stretch of coast between Elephant Rock and Currumbin Point, and with a breeze there are usually some decent rollers to ride. Just to the north, **PALM BEACH** is more sheltered. *Vikings*, in the surf club building below Elephant Rock, serves Chinese food, or you can fill up on regular pub fare at the *Palm Beach Surf Club*.

Currumbin Sanctuary, on Tomewin Street (daily 8am–5pm; $16), was started in 1946 by Alex Griffiths, who foresaw the decline of the coastal environment and developed the seventy-acre park as a wildlife refuge. Forest, lake and grassland fairly bustle with native fauna. There are the usual feeding times and tame kangaroos but the park's strongest point is the beautiful natural surroundings, best experienced from the **elevated walkways** through the forest, where you'll see koalas, tree kangaroos and birds at eye-level.

Coolangatta

On the Queensland border 10km south of Currumbin, **COOLANGATTA** merges seamlessly with Tweed Heads (in New South Wales; see p.272) along Boundary Road. With little to tell them apart – other than the sudden proliferation of "Adult Shops" over the border in New South Wales – you'll probably make the crossing between states without realizing it. Unless it's New Year, when everyone takes advantage of the one-hour time difference between the states to celebrate twice, most travellers bypass Coolangatta completely; in doing so, they miss some of the best surf, least crowded beaches and the only place along the Gold Coast which can boast a real "local" community.

Coolangatta is set out one block back from the beach along **Griffith Street**, where you'll find banks, shops and very little in the way of high-density development. Even the motel towers on Point Danger are well spaced, and the general ambience harks back pleasingly to small-town seaside life in the early 1960s. **Marine Parade** fronts the shore, the view north over sand and sea ending with the jagged teeth of the skyscrapers on the horizon at Surfers Paradise.

Straddling the border at Point Danger, the **Captain Cook Memorial Lighthouse** forms a shrine where pillars enclose a large bronze globe detailing Cook's peregrinations around the southern hemisphere (see also p.992). Twenty-five metres below, surfers in their colourful wetsuits make the most of Flagstaff Beach's swell – at weekends this area is very crowded.

Coolangatta's daytime action is in the **surf**, the best being between Point Danger and Kirra Point (the latter nominated by world surfing champion Kelly Slater as his favourite break), or at Flagstaff, across the state border in Tweed Heads – exactly where depends on the wind. Greenmount, effectively Coolangatta's town beach, is fairly reliable and is a good beach for beginners; Snapper Rocks and Point Danger further down the peninsula are for the more dedicated. For sun worshippers, Coolangatta beach, just north of Greenmount, is fine if you're staying nearby, but the six-kilometre stretch of sand further up, beyond Kirra Point, is wider and less crowded. **Surfing supplies and rentals** are available from Pipedream, Griffith St (☎07/5599 1164), the best place for gear and information about local conditions and competitions, and from Coolangatta Surf, Griffith

St (☎07/5361 1239) and Mount Woodgee, 122 Griffith St (☎07/5536 5937). Surfboard and ski rental is around $20 a day plus credit card deposit. All shops have decent secondhand boards for sale, though local boards tend to be too thin and lightweight to use elsewhere. You might find a bargain in one of the pawnbroker's shops on Griffith Street.

Cook Island and Nine Mile Reef are the main **diving sites**, with two shipwrecks nearby. Of interest are nurse sharks, turtles, canyons and scattered groups of reef fish. Kirra Dive Centre, on the corner of Creek and South streets, Kirra (☎07/5536 6622), and Blue Juice Dive, 127 Griffith St (☎07/5536 6277) charge around $55 plus equipment for two local dives.

Practicalities

The **bus station** (Mon–Fri 7am–5.30pm, Sat 7am–3pm; ☎07/5536 6600) is in downtown Coolangatta, on the corner of Warner and Griffith streets, the latter an extension of the Gold Coast Highway which ends at the border, 1km south at Point Danger. In the other direction, the road jinks sharply around Kirra Point before joining the highway 3km north, outside the Gold Coast Airport, from where Airport Transit (☎07/5588 8747) shuttle buses serve Coolangatta. There's information available at the bus station, or at the helpful **information centre** (Mon–Fri 8am–4pm, Sat 8am–3pm; ☎07/5536 7765) 100m up the road at Beach House, Marine Parade.

If you want to **camp**, Sherry's Disposals, 27–31 Wharf St, Tweed Heads (☎07/5536 3700), has a good range of supplies. For **car rental**, Thrifty, at Coolangatta Airport (☎07/5536 6954), offers prices starting at $35. Tandem Skydive (☎07/5599 1920), offers a thirty-minute course in **skydiving**, after which you're ready for a free-fall parachute jump with an instructor from 2800m. Considering the length of time in the air (approximately 7min) it's far better value ($200) than a bungee jump and for pure terror the experience can't be beaten. For **flight information** call Ansett (☎13 1300). **Taxis** can be booked on ☎13 1008.

ACCOMMODATION

Accommodation is strung out along the highway at Bilinga and Kirra, while the more expensive places are in the apartment buildings overlooking the sea on Marine Parade and Point Danger. For **camping**, try *Kirra Tourist Park*, Charlotte St, Kirra (☎07/5581 7744).

Calypso Plaza, 87–105 Griffith St (☎07/5599 0000 or free call ☎1800/062 189). Sparkling new and expensive resort hotel, with suites and two-bedroom penthouse apartments, right across from Greenmount Beach. ⑨.

Kirra Beach Hotel, across from the beach at Kirra Point (☎07/5536 3311). Ideal location for boardriders. Some rooms are quite spacious, and all have bath, TV & fridge; cheap meals available in the pub bistro. Singles ②, doubles ③.

On the Beach, 118 Marine Parade, Greenmount Beach (☎07/5536 3624). Single or double rooms in self-contained apartments. Tidy and well placed for the town and the beach. ④–⑥.

Sunset Strip Budget Resort, 199 Boundary St (☎07/5599 5517). Superb facilities, including family rooms, huge kitchen and living areas (with three TV's), 20m pool and sundeck; singles ②, doubles ③, triples ④, but no dorms.

YHA, 3km up the coast at 230 Coolangatta Rd/Gold Coast Highway, Bilinga, near the airport (☎07/5536 7644). Helpful management and nicely located for the quieter beaches, though a bit far from Coolangatta itself. ①.

EATING, DRINKING AND NIGHTLIFE

If you're doing your own cooking, there's a 24-hour convenience store inside the Beach House complex beside the *Coolangatta Hotel*, and bigger supermakets across the border at the main shopping centre on Wharf Street, in Tweed Heads (for further information on Tweed Heads, see p.272). There are plenty of **snack bars** along Griffith Street, or check out *Orbansen's Milk Bar* (23 Griffith St) for its less than convincing

1950s decor, which includes a jukebox selector at each table. *Thai Star* or *Sushi Train*, also on Griffith Street, are the best of the Asian restaurants, while a couple of recently-opened noodle bars provide tasty, inexpensive options.

Coolangatta's **nightlife** centres around the pubs – you'll have to rely on posters to find out what's on. Best are sessions at the *Coolangatta Sands Hotel*'s fairly relaxed bar (corner of Griffith and McLean streets) and the *Coolangatta Hotel*'s nightclub (corner of Griffith and Warner streets), which has live music and pool competitions.

THE HINTERLAND AND SCENIC RIM

One hundred and twenty kilometres inland from the coast's jangling excesses, the **Scenic Rim** forms a barrier between the coastal flatlands and the pastoral Darling Downs, encompassing a series of mountainous **national parks**. Here you'll find Queensland's largest expanse of subtropical rainforest and – the main attraction – the **Lamington Plateau**, packed with powerfully beautiful scenery, animals and birds. Whether you're a day-tripper, veteran hiker or just fancy camping in the same spot for a few days, it's not to be missed. Closest to the coast, **Springbrook**'s waterfalls and undeveloped pockets at **Mount Tamborine** make easy day-trips and are thus the most-visited destinations, while tough tracks at the region's extremes in the **Main Range** remain the prerogative of experienced bushwalkers.

The Eastern and Central Rim

The **Mount Tamborine–Lamington** area is covered with a network of graded, well-trodden paths, so you don't have to be particularly skilled at **bushwalking** to enjoy the experience. Come prepared, though – tackling the longer or steeper routes requires some degree of **fitness**; test your endurance on shorter walks first. **Paths** are often well marked but sometimes narrow and slippery with little fencing along cliffs and waterfalls, so **footwear** should have a good grip and, ideally, be waterproof. Rain is a year-round possibility; the most comfortable weather conditions occur between June and November, though everything looks its best in the middle of the wet season with waterfalls in full flood and the greenery shockingly intense. If you do visit during the Wet (Jan–March), you'll have to endure rain, deep and fast-flowing rivers, occasionally closed paths and an unwelcome abundance of insects.

Accommodation is limited to resorts and campsites, so if you're on a tight budget you'll need a tent. Nights in winter (July–Sept) are always cool enough to warrant a sleeping bag and pullover, though after-dark temperatures can drop even in midsummer. Campsites have water and **stores** nearby, but you'll save money by bringing your own supplies. A **fuel stove** is a good idea – collecting firewood in national parks is forbidden, although there are often barbecues with wood supplied. **Access** to the area is easy enough in itself but because of local geography there are few interconnecting roads, making backtracking unavoidable if you want to visit more than one place. If you can, get hold of a vehicle – only Lamington and Mount Tamborine have a regular bus service – and make sure you take a good **road atlas** along, as signposts to the parks are few and far between. **Tours** visit most locations – see "Listings" for Brisbane (p.360) and Surfers Paradise (p.371).

Mount Tamborine

Mount Tamborine's nine fragmentary national parks offer a pleasant introduction to many of the key features of the Hinterland. If you're **driving**, consult a map and aim for

North Tamborine township: from Brisbane (75km), leave the Pacific Highway at Beenleigh; from the coast (45km) turn inland at Nerang or Oxenford. There's a daily Coachliner **bus** service from Surfers Paradise (☎07/5534 9977; $25), but nothing from Brisbane.

The mountain top is moderately cleared and settled, with remaining patches of forest concentrated around the adjoining compact settlements of **NORTH TAMBORINE** and **EAGLE HEIGHTS** – quiet, upmarket escapes from lowland suburbia. North Tamborine's services include a general store, garage and information centre (more reliable than the frequently unattended National Parks office on the Knoll road); Eagle Heights has a post office, but no banks. From North Tamborine it's between four and six kilometres to the most distant **parks**: Cedar Creek in the north and Macrozamia Grove south.

Once the haunt of the Wangeriburra Aborigines, Mount Tamborine's forests were targeted by the timber industry late last century until locals succeeded in getting the area declared as Queensland's first national park in 1908. This event is commemorated by a roadside monument 1km south of North Tamborine, where a three-kilometre track slaloms down to **Witches Falls** through open scrub and rainforest. It's an easy walk, but is more rewarding for the views from the mountain than for the falls themselves, which are only a trickle that disappears over a narrow ledge below the lookout.

The most significant feature of Mount Tamborine's parks is their diversity of native forest types. There's a stand of primitive, slow-growing cycads (see box on p.482) at **Macrozamia Grove**, and a piccabean palm forest at **Palm Grove**, near Eagle Heights, which creates a limpid, eerie gloom. Hidden 20m up in the canopy are elusive **wompoo pigeons**, often heard but seldom seen – despite their vivid purple and green plumage and onomatopoeic call. Closer to North Tamborine, about 1km north, walking tracks at **Joalah** follow Cedar Creek downstream through woodland to a rock pool; look out for giant epiphytic ferns in the canopy and the **Albert lyrebird**, with its fantastically shaped tail and liquid song. For a break from the heat, the refreshingly cold water of **Cedar Creek Falls**, to the north, tumbles into a wide pool – take your swimming gear. Of the other parks, **MacDonald** at Eagle Heights has a very short walk through typical subtropical rainforest; North Tamborine's environmental park has a stand of **flooded gums**; and there are views to the northwest from **the Knoll**'s picnic tables.

Thunder Eggs

Four kilometres from North Tamborine on the Brisbane road, the privately owned **Thunderbird Park** (☎07/5545 1468; camping $6 per person, motel units ⑤, luxury four- and six-person cabins ⑨) exploits the area's volcanic origin. **Thunder eggs** – or geodes – are to be found here in quantity, and an hour or more digging for them in the sun is sufficient to satisfy the average curiosity. Formed when volcanic liquids were drawn into nodules, they appear to be rather unprepossessing lumpy white spheres, but when cut in half and polished the centres are revealed as banded **agates**. Stones from different sites vary in colour and it usually takes a bucketful to find a couple of good examples. As they're not valuable, the real satisfaction comes from digging them out yourself and the thrill of being the first person to open them up. Mining permits cost $5 per session (from *Thunderbird Park*) and you can rent a pick and bucket; they'll also cut and polish your finds for you. Other activities on offer include horseriding, and walks through a small wildlife park populated by kangaroos and other native animals.

Springbrook National Parks

Close to the coast along the New South Wales border, **Springbrook**'s three parks feature abundant waterfalls and swimming holes; though grouped together, access to each section is by a different road. **Mount Cougal** is at the end of a road 21km west of

Currumbin. Rainforest flanks the upper reaches of Currumbin Creek, and a path follows the stream to an abandoned sawmill, past pools and pretty cascades. For higher drama and a short, moderately demanding walk, head for **Purling Brook Falls**, a 30km drive from Burleigh Heads via Mudgeeraba. There's a campsite outside the forest, near the top of the falls, with a store about 4km back along the main road. The 109m falls are very impressive after rain has swollen the flow; a four-kilometre track zigzags down the escarpment and into the rainforest at the base of the falls before curving underneath the waterfall (expect a soaking from the spray) and going back up the other side. In the plunge pool at the foot of the falls, the force of the water is enough to push you under; **swimming** is more relaxed in a couple of pools downstream, picturesquely encircled by lianas and red cedar. A ten-kilometre drive beyond the falls brings you to **Best of All Lookout** and a broad vista south to Mount Warning from the very edge of the Rim.

At **Natural Bridge** a collapsed cave ceiling beneath the riverbed has created a subterranean waterfall. An exciting but very dangerous leap down the falls will take you into the cave: several people have been killed trying it, and the recommended method is simply to walk in through the mouth, 50m downstream. From the back of the cave the forest outside frames the waterfall and blue plunge pool, surreally lit from above; **glow worms** illuminate the ceiling at night. The park is 49km from Burleigh Heads or Southport via Nerang and about 27km from Purling Brook. For a different tour of the area, Numinbah Valley Adventure Trails is highly recommended for half-day **horseback** rides from the base near Nerang to otherwise inaccessible volcanic caves (pickup from Surfers accommodation extra; book on ☎07/5533 4137; $40).

Lamington National Park

The McPherson Range and Lamington Plateau occupy the northwestern rim of a vast caldera centred on Mount Warning, 15km away in New South Wales. This is **Lamington National Park**, an enthralling world of rainforest-flanked rivers, open heathland and ancient eucalypt woods, and its position on a **crossover zone** between subtropical and temperate climes has made it home to a staggering variety of plants, animals and birds, some forming isolated populations of species found nowhere else.

There are two possible **bases**: **Binna Burra** on the drier northern edge, and *O'Reilly's Guesthouse* at **Green Mountain**, in the thick of the forest. Routes come in from Canungra to Green Mountain (37km) and from Beechmont to Binna Burra (10km) – these are narrow, twisting roads cutting through patches of forest and cleared grazing land. From the Gold Coast, turn off at Nerang – roads to both Binna Burra and Green Mountain diverge from here; from Brisbane, leave the highway at Beenleigh – you pass through Canungra to reach Beechmont this way.

Buses from the Gold Coast or Brisbane to either base cost $35 for a day return, or $18 each way if you stay overnight – good value for long stays, but as the journey takes between ninety minutes and three hours (depending on where you start) it's best to rent a car for day-trips. When you buy your ticket, make it clear whether you want to return the same day or another day; it's also possible to walk between Binna Burra and Green Mountain (see overleaf for details), so you might want to arrange to be dropped at one end and collected at the other. Green Mountain can be reached daily from Surfers Paradise with Mountain Coach Company (call first to arrange pick-up; ☎07/5524 4249) and from Brisbane's Transit Centre with Allstate Scenic Tours (☎07/3285 1777; no Saturday service). Binna Burra's only bus is the *Mountain Lodge*'s Gold Coast service (free call ☎1800/074 260 for details).

Lamington has to be explored **on foot**: most of the tracks described below are clearly signposted and **free maps** are available from local NPWS ranger stations. If you're experienced and want to head off along less-defined paths, contact the rangers first for advice.

Binna Burra

It's some time since guests had to walk the last few kilometres through the steep forest to **BINNA BURRA** with their luggage on a horse. Today, upmarket *Mountain Lodge* (lodge ☎07/5533 3622; bookings ☎1800/074 260; ⑦) has cosy wooden cabins and log fires. The only alternative is the **campsite** (☎07/5533 3758) up the road, where you use your own gear or rent one of their on-site tents. Facilities include hot showers and a tearoom aimed at day-trippers, but bread and some basic provisions are also sold. Don't leave food unattended at the campsite – it's infested with brazen scrub turkeys. Hikers can bush camp between February and November; for details contact the **park ranger** (8am–4pm; ☎07/5533 3584) at the station, 1.5km before the lodge.

Both lodge and campsite overlook the Numinbah Valley from woodland on the crown of Mount Roberts, and **walking** anywhere always leaves you with an uphill return journey. The lethargic can simply wander 500m between the campsite and the lodge at **night** with a torch to be rewarded by the sight of groups of wallabies grazing on the verges; commotion in the trees betrays the presence of brushtail possums foraging for flowers and leaves. Try the lodge's unique **senses trail**: blindfolded and following a rope you become aware that there's more to the forest than just a blaze of green – you sense a drop in temperature under the canopy, feel the textures of bark and leaves, and receive wafts of scent from the forest floor.

Of the longer walks, try the easy five-kilometre **Caves Circuit**, which follows the edge of the Coomera Valley past the white, wind-sculpted **Talangai Caves** to remains of Aboriginal camps, strands of *psilotum nudum*, a rootless precursor of the ferns, and a hillside of strangler figs and red cedar. Plunging into another forest below the campsite, the harder **Ballunji Falls** track is a typical compromise between access and terrain, with occasional vertical drops to test sure-footedness. Features on the way include views of **Egg Rock** from Bellbird Lookout, at its most mysterious when shrouded in dawn mists, and a stand of majestic forty-metre-tall box brush trees. Dedicated walkers can extend the track out to **Ships Stern**, an arduous and very dry 21-kilometre return (allow a minimum of 8hr) with some wonderful views off the escarpment. **Dave's Creek Circuit** is similar but about half as long, crossing bands of rainforest and sclerophyll before emerging onto heathland. Look for tiny clumps of red sundew plants along the track, which supplement their nitrogen intake by trapping insects in sticky globules of nectar.

Other longer tracks can be joined together, allowing you to spend days hiking without ever returning to base. Most popular of these is the **Border Track**; a relatively easy 21-kilometre/nine-hour (one-way) path linking Binna Burra with Green Mountain. If you need road transport between the two, the lodge usually runs a free weekly service to *O'Reilly's* for its guests, and will often take others for a fee if there's room – departures depend on demand, so all arrangements have to be made on site.

Green Mountain

Green Mountain's forests are emphatically the best of the entire Scenic Rim. With so much to dazzle the senses here the initial experience is confused, but gradually the various types of plants and trees become familiar, as do the distinct layers between the rainforest floor and canopy. Random rustles and trills resolve into wallabies thumping around tree roots, scrub turkeys scratching up leaf litter and a whipbird's cracking call; it's easy to become lost in the environment's complex structure.

The road from Canungra to **Green Mountain** ends at *O'Reilly's Guesthouse* (☎07/5544 0644, fax 5544 0638, free call ☎1800/688 722; ⑧), a splendid and comfortable place opened in 1926 – bookings are advised at weekends and during holiday periods. The guesthouse has a limited store (with EFTPOS facilities) and a moderately priced restaurant for meals and snacks throughout the day. There's also an exposed NPWS **campsite** with showers; call the **ranger's office** (Mon, Wed & Fri 1–3.30pm, staffed part-time by volunteers on weekends; ☎07/5544 0634) for essential advance booking. If you can't get in here, about 7km down the road the rustic *Mt Cainbable Cabins* (⑦) offers bed and breakfast in four-person cabins, or try the *Canungra Motel* (☎07/5543 5155; ④) at the bottom of the range.

The **birdlife** near the guesthouse is prolific and distracting: you can't miss the chattering swarms of crimson rosellas mingling with visitors on the lawn, and determined twitchers can clock up over fifty species without even reaching the forest – most spectacular is the black-and-gold **regent bowerbird**. But it's worth pushing on to the **treetop walk** just beyond the clearing, where a suspended walkway swings 15m above ground level. At the halfway anchor point you scale a narrow ladder to vertigo-inducing mesh platforms 30m up the trunk of a strangler fig to see the canopy at eye level. Soaking up the increased sunlight at this height above the forest floor, tree branches become miniature gardens of mosses, ferns and orchids. By night the walkway is the preserve of possums and weird stalking insects.

If you manage only one day-walk at Lamington, make it the exceptional five-hour **Blue Pool/Canungra Creek track** (15km), which features all the jungle trimmings: fantastic trees, river crossings, and countless opportunities to fall off slippery rocks and get soaked. The first hour is dry enough as you tramp downhill past some huge red cedars to Blue Pool, a deep, placid waterhole where **platypuses** are sometimes seen on winter mornings; this makes a good walk in itself. After a dip, head upstream along Canungra Creek; the path traverses the river a few times (there are no bridges, but occasionally a fallen tree conveniently spans the water) – look for yellow or red **arrows** painted on rocks that indicate where to cross. Seasonally, the creek can be almost dried up; if the water is more than knee-deep, you shouldn't attempt a crossing and will need to retrace your steps. Follow the creek as far as Elabana Falls and another swimming hole, or bypass the falls; either way, the path climbs back to the guesthouse.

Another excellent trail (17.5km) takes six hours via **Box Creek Falls** to the eastern escarpment at **Toolona Lookout**, on the Border Track to Binna Burra; rewards are a half-dozen waterfalls, dramatic views into New South Wales, and encounters with clumps of moss-covered **Antarctic beech** trees, a strange Gondwanan relict also found in South America. For seasoned, well-equipped walkers, there's a chance to delve into local history by way of an overnight hike to the **Stinson Wreck**. In February 1937 a plane bound for Sydney crashed into dense forest and the survivors were only located due to the incredible efforts of Bernard O'Reilly who, on his own, hiked to the plane from Green Mountain and returned with a rescue party. Nearby is **Westray's grave**, the burial place of one of the passengers who died looking for help, but it is very difficult to reach from Green Mountain. Today most of the wreck has been carted off by souvenir hunters or covered by jungle, but the guesthouse and park rangers can give you advice on the walk and may be able to put you in touch with bushwalkers who've been there.

The Western Rim

In contrast to the obvious charms of the Eastern Rim, the drier **Western Rim** is mainly given over to open eucalypt woods, with the steep peaks covered in heath. With few facilities, it's a place for serious bushwalkers; on weekends you're likely to meet other hikers at the campsites, but the best way to explore is with a **bushwalking club** (see Brisbane "Listings", p.358). Even "easy" routes are fairly demanding, with few neat paths or signposts – so come equipped, don't walk alone, and carry plenty of water. Access is along the Cunningham and Mount Lindesay highways from Boonah or Beaudesert in the east and **Warwick** from the west; there's no public transport.

Mount Barney, Main Range and Mount Mistake

Mount Barney's multiple peaks form an extremely rough region along the New South Wales border, 45km southwest of Beaudesert. From wherever you're approaching, aim for Rathdowney and then take Barney View Road past Bigriggen to **Yellowpinch** campsite. Nearest supplies and alternative camping are at Rathdowney and Bigriggen.

From the car park some 5km from Yellowpinch there's a distinct, hour-long track to the **Lower Portals**, a pool on Barney Creek flanked by vertical cliffs. The only other marked hike (though even for this you might need a topographic map) is the misleadingly named "tourist trail" along the south ridge to the saddle between **Mount Barney**'s peaks: be prepared for an exhausting seven-hour return trip from Yellowpinch. Experienced walkers, with permits and advice from the NPWS about current conditions (PO Box 121, Boonah; ☎07/5463 5041), could camp in the saddle at **Rum Jungle** and climb the peaks in the morning; the eastern peak is the easier of the two and has the better views across to Mount Lindesay's tor, poking above wooded slopes.

Main Range's precipitous terrain and sharp, progressively higher peaks are most directly accessible along the Cunningham Highway at **Cunningham's Gap**, between Brisbane and Warwick, about 90km from Boonah. Here you'll find some of the easier trails: tracks through rainforest along West Gap Creek and ascents of Bare Rock and Mount Mitchell, which you could complete in a couple of hours or a day, depending on your inclination. There's an NPWS **campsite** at the Gap (☎07/4666 1133); call in advance to check on conditions. **Mount Mistake** is an undeveloped park on the junction of three mountain ranges which form the northernmost extent of the Scenic Rim. Walking is said to be tricky but well worth the effort; if you're tempted, contact the NPWS on ☎07/4666 1133.

THE SUNSHINE COAST

The **Sunshine Coast**, stretching north of Brisbane to **Noosa**, is a more pedestrian version of the Gold Coast, where largely domestic tourist development is tempered by, and sometimes combined with, agriculture. Much local character is due to the lack of death taxes in Queensland – something which, together with the pleasant climate, attracts retirees from all over Australia. The towns tend to be bland places, lively enough at Christmas, but out of season you may be hard pushed to find much to do after dark. Even so, the beaches and surf are good, improving in character as you go further north and providing an excuse to linger for a few days. And though you'll find the Hinterland far tamer than it is down south, it still has some arresting landscapes and scattered hamlets rife with Devonshire cream teas and weekend markets.

Without your own **transport**, the easiest way through the area is by **bus** – Sunshine Coast Coaches (☎07/5491 2555) is the local alternative to the national operators – or on a **tour** from Brisbane or the Gold Coast; Brisbane's Citytrain network can take you as far as Caboolture. For the intrepid, Adventures Sunshine Coast (☎07/5444 8824) organizes day-trips **climbing** in the Glasshouse Mountains, **bushwalking** the Obi Obi gorge in the Blackall Range, or **canoeing** the Mooloolah River south of Maroochydore ($75 per person, including lunch and pick-up from lodgings along the coast).

Caboolture to Mooloolaba

Caboolture marks the start of the **SUNSHINE COAST**, 40km north of Brisbane. There's no reason to stop here, but to the north are the **Glasshouse Mountains**: nine dramatic, isolated pinnacles, visible from as far away as Brisbane. Catching sight of them from the sea, Captain Cook named them after their shape and "elevation", a resemblance that's obscure today. You can reach them along the old highway 16km north from Caboolture or off the new one 10km north of Beerburrum; Sunshine Coast Coaches stops at the Glasshouse Mountains turn-off. **Accommodation** and camping in the area is at *Log Cabin Caravan Park* (☎07/5496 9338; cabins ③), south of Glass House Mountains township.

To the Kabi Aborigines, the mountains are the petrified forms of a family fleeing the incoming tide; their names for the peaks are more evocative than Cook's – three are called Tibrogargan, Tibberoowuccum and Beerwah. The peaks themselves vary enormously: some are rounded and fairly easy to scale, while a couple have vertical faces and sharp spires requiring competent climbing skills. It's worth conquering at least one of the easier peaks; the views are superb and the mountains are one of the few really special places on the Sunshine Coast. **Beerburrum**, overlooking the township of the same name, and **Ngungun**, near Glass House Mountains township, are two of the easiest to climb, with well-used tracks; the latter's views and scenery outclass some of the tougher peaks and it will take you only two hours there and back, though the lower parts of the track are steep and slippery. **Tibberoowuccum** must be climbed from the northwest, and the only special equipment you'll need is a map; ask at the *Log Cabin Caravan Park* for directions. The taller mountains – Tibrogargan, Coonowrin and Beerwah (the highest at 556m) – are at best tricky, and Coonowrin should be attempted only by experienced climbers. Contact the NPWS, 61 Bunya Rd, Maleny (☎07/5494 3983), for more information.

Caloundra

CALOUNDRA, opposite **Bribie Island**, has little to offer except **beaches**. Bulcock Beach is central, and tends to collect the crowds; if you don't mind walking, Golden Beach, overlooking Bribie's narrow tip, or Shelly Beach, on the other side of Caloundra Headland, are just as good, and less crowded. The closest **campsite** to the town centre is at the tiny council-run caravan park, five minutes' walk along Burgess Street, a continuation of Bulcock Street where Sunshine Coast Coaches stop; there's another at Shelly Beach if this is full. For **rooms**, try *City & Surf Motel*, across from the bus stop at 6 Cooma Terrace (☎07/5491 2511; ⑤).

Mooloolaba and around

Twenty kilometres north, Maroochydore, Alexandra Headland and Mooloolaba are gradually filling the foreshore between the Mooloolah and Maroochy rivers with an amoeba-like blob of high-rise units. But for once there are things to do to fill in time between sunbathing sessions.

Southernmost is **MOOLOOLABA**, where **Mooloolaba Wharf**, a kitsch tourist attraction with trendy shops and restaurants, is the central focus. Nearby, on Parkyn Parade, **Underwater World** (daily 9am–6pm; $17.90) has superb saltwater and freshwater tanks where barramundi – fish revered by Queensland anglers for their taste and legendary fighting spirit – and inoffensive freshwater crocodiles stare blankly at you through huge windows. For the real thing, Scuba World, on Parkyn Parade, can train you or take you **diving** to local sandstone terrain, where you'll find nudibranch, soft corals and bottom-dwelling sharks, or up to Wolf Rocks for bigger game. Numerous places nearby rent out **surfboards** at around $20 a day. Sixty-minute **canal cruises** ($10), taking in some rather opulent waterfront real estate, operate from the wharf three times a day.

Most of the local **accommodation** is 3km north of Mooloolaba, past **Alexandra Headland**, at **MAROOCHYDORE**. At the bottom end of the market, try *Cotton Tree Caravan Park* on Cotton Tree Parade, Maroochydore (①–③) or *Suncoast Backpackers Lodge* at 50 Parker St, Maroochydore (☎07/5443 7544; ①), a well-organized **hostel**. Another option is the YHA close to the Maroochy River on Schirrmann Drive

(☎07/5443 3151; ③), which is out of the way but offers a free pick-up from Maroochydore, free loans of surfboards, bikes and fishing gear, and free trips to hinterland towns and the Sunshine Coast Brewery for tours and tasting. **Motels** include *Sunshine Motor Inn*, 122 Alexandra Parade, Alexandra Headland (☎07/5443 6899; ④), and *Blue Waters Motel*, 64 Sixth Ave, Maroochydore (☎07/5443 6700; ⑤), both with spacious rooms, sea views and easy access to the beach. **Eating** options huddled along the Esplanade include *Mooloolaba Surf Club*'s smart restaurant (daily noon–2pm & 6–8.30pm, breakfast Sun from 8am) near the wharf, and *Karakas* at no. 59, for fiery Mexican cooking and **live music** through the week. *Mooloolaba Hotel*, also on the Esplanade, hosts rock bands every Friday and Saturday, and opens its doors as a nightclub on Sundays; the *Alexandra Hotel*, on the highway at Alexandra Headland, is another venue for big-name bands.

Nambour to Noosa

Bisected by tramways from surrounding sugar plantations, **NAMBOUR** sits inland from Maroochydore in the centre of the Sunshine Coast's farming community. Five kilometres south between the highway and **Woombye** lurks the Sunshine Plantation (daily 9am–5pm; free except rides; ☎07/5442 1333) overshadowed by its renowned, ridiculous **Big Pineapple**; activities include trips around the plantation on a cane train and, of course, climbing the fibreglass fruit. Sunshine Coast Coaches can bring you here from Nambour.

A two-hour circuit drive from Nambour into the **Hinterland** along the Blackall Range takes you into a rural English-like idyll quite unexpected in subtropical Queensland. Fields are dotted with herds of pied dairy cattle, and "villages" such as **WOODFORD** – with its annual **folk festival** over Christmas and New Year, **MONTVILLE** and **MAPLETON** are thick with potteries and tearooms and occasional long views over rolling green hills to the coast. After rain it's worth stretching your legs to reach a couple of respectably sized **waterfalls** up here: **Kondalilla**, 3km from Montville, with swimming holes along **Obi Obi Creek**; and **Mapleton Falls**, just west of Mapleton, where the river plunges over basalt cliffs.

Approaching from Nambour along the highway, you can reach Noosa by turning coastwards at **EUMUNDI**, a tiny town best known for its **Saturday market**, reputed to be the biggest and best in Australia. An appealing place to overnight here is *Taylor's Damn Fine B & B* (☎07/5442 8685; ⑧), an old Queenslander home filled with an extraordinary array of European "kitsch" and collectables – one separate guestroom is a beautifully renovated railway caboose. Otherwise, the turn-off for Cooroy sees you entering Noosa along the river via Tewantin. Approaching from Maroochydore up the coastal road, the journey is half as long, passing unevenly spaced townships; coming this way, *Coolum Beach Budget Accommodation* at 1862 David Low Way, Coolum (☎07/5471 6666; ①), is a very clean and well laid out place to pull up for a couple of days of beach life.

Noosa

The exclusive end of the Sunshine Coast, **NOOSA** is dominated by an enviably beautiful headland, defined by the mouth of the placid Noosa River and a strip of beach to the south. Popular since surfers first came in the 1960s to ride fierce waves around the headland, the setting compensates for any neon and concrete in town. It's also a starting point for trips to Cooloola National Park and Fraser Island in the Great Sandy Region directly north (see p.392). These tend to overshadow Noosa's own national park on the headland (see p.384) and unless you're a beach addict or board rider you'll probably find that you stay around only long enough to plan your next move.

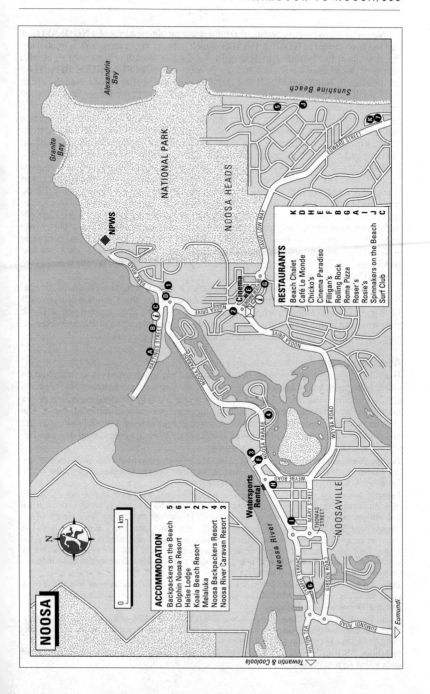

NOOSA

N
0   1 km

ACCOMMODATION

Backpackers on the Beach	5
Dolphin Noosa Resort	6
Halse Lodge	1
Koala Beach Resort	2
Melaluka	7
Noosa Backpackers Resort	4
Noosa River Caravan Resort	3

Watersports Rental

RESTAURANTS

Beach Chalet	K
Café Le Monde	D
Chicko's	H
Cinema Paradiso	E
Filligan's	F
Rolling Rock	B
Roma Pizza	G
Roser's	A
Rosie's	I
Spinnakers on the Beach	J
Surf Club	C

Alexandria Bay

Granite Bay

NATIONAL PARK

NOOSA HEADS

Sunshine Beach

NPWS

Noosa River

NOOSAVILLE

Tewantin & Cooloola

Eumundi

"Noosa" is a loose term covering three merging satellite settlements: **NOOSAVILLE** and the town centre at **NOOSA HEADS**, which between them stretch 7km west along the river from the headland to **Tewantin** – a distinct township in its own right with access to the wilds of Cooloola – and the discreet suburb of **SUNSHINE BEACH** on the headland's south side. You'll find the best sand and surf at **Noosa Beach**, which runs parallel to chic Hastings Street at Noosa Heads, and at the longer, less crowded **Sunshine Beach**; both are patrolled. All three suburbs are connected by a bus service (Sunbus), which goes by every twenty minutes or so between 5am–9pm, with service extended to midnight at weekends. Sunshine Beach Road at Noosa Heads is the main street, with banks, restaurants, shops and a supermarket; Noosaville has stores along the river and a sizeable shopping centre, and there are more shops at Sunshine Beach.

More natural attractions can be found around the Noosa River and in a modest national park. The **Noosa River** deposits low, muddy islands as it passes Tewantin and Noosaville, emptying into the sea at Laguna Bay. In the late afternoon, half of Noosa promenades along Gympie Terrace as the sinking sun colours a gentle tableau: mangroves on the opposite shore, pelicans eyeing anglers for scraps and landing clumsily midstream, and everything from cruise boats to windsurfers and kayaks out on the water. With a spare day you can **cruise** or **canoe** (if you're energetic and start early enough) upstream to shallow lakes **Cooroibah** and **Cootharaba** (see p.388), or just paddle around, fish at the river mouth or rent a **jet ski** and have fun getting soaked (see "Listings" on p.386 for rental outlets).

Noosa's small **national park** is worth a look for its mix of mature rainforest, coastal heath and fine beaches – **Granite Bay** and **Alexandria Bay** ("swimwear optional") have good sand pounded by unpatrolled surf – all reached along graded paths. These start from the picnic area at the end of Park Road (a continuation of Hastings Street), where you'll probably see **koalas** in gum trees above the car park.

Accommodation

Hostels have courtesy buses for beach, town and nightclubs, and all accommodation will help organize tours. **Motels** are concentrated along the river between Noosa Heads and Noosaville; some offer weekly rates which might add up to a free night, but prices double during school holidays. Monolithic upmarket accommodation is as close to the river as possible along Hastings Street. A group of four staying a week or two may get better value – and a slice of luxury – by checking with rental agents about deals on furnished apartments outside holiday periods.

Backpackers on the Beach, 26 Stevens St, Sunshine Beach (☎07/5447 4739, bookings only free call ☎1800/240 344). Quiet, in need of better maintenance, but just two minutes from the beach. Usual facilities, and a large pool (without lounging space). ①.

Dolphin Noosaresort, 137 Gympie Terrace, Noosaville (☎07/5449 7318 or free call ☎1800/072 065). An uninspiring old motel-turned-backpackers' hostel with a pool and TV lounge; dorms in 6–8 bed units (some rooms ludicrously small), each with TV and kitchen; doubles ③–④, dorms ①.

Gagaju (☎07/5474 3522). This is an authentic bush camp near Noosa, with a dozen bunk-beds and space for campers. Created as an eco-friendly "bush experience", everything is built from recycled timber. Canoes and camping equipment, advice on hikes and canoe trips, and fireside bush-poetry readings are among the attractions. Their 3-day canoe trip is highly recommended as an independent adventure experience. Call ahead for directions or pick-up. ①.

Halse Lodge (YHA), 17 Noosa Drive, Noosa Heads (☎07/5447 3377 or free call ☎1800/242 567). Giant, sprawling, immaculate 1888 Queenslander building close to Noosa Beach; definitely not for partying. Doubles ③ and dorms ①.

Koala Beach Resort, 44 Noosa Drive, Noosa Heads (☎07/5447 3355 or free call ☎1800/357 457). Central budget accommodation in dorms and motel units. Nowhere near the beach, and not especially clean, but a party atmosphere and pool, restaurant and bar might compensate. ①.

Melaluka, 7 Selene St, Sunshine Beach (☎07/5447 3663). Somewhat small, brick, self-contained units within sight of the sea. ①.

Noosa Backpackers Resort, William St, Noosaville (☎07/5449 8151 or free call ☎1800/626 673). A small, well-appointed hostel with tours, pool, canoe-, bike- and board-rental. A decent breakfast included, and budget meals on offer from 6pm every night. ①.

Noosa River Caravan Park, Russell St, Noosaville (☎07/5449 7050). Basic campsite and van park (no cabins or on-site vans); tent sites ①.

Eating, drinking and nightlife

Noosa's three communities – surfers, retirees and tourists – seldom share the same enthusiasms; evenings tend to be spent with your own crowd. This doesn't seem to affect the nightlife, though, and eating out in particular is pursued as a serious pastime. Hastings Street has long been the place to dine and be seen in Noosa, but soaring rents have seen some excellent eateries relocate to Noosaville, where you'll now find lots of casual diners checking out the places clustered along Gympie Terrace and Thomas Street.

Beach Chalet, Tingira Crescent, Sunshine Beach (☎07/5447 3944). Trendy spot, where you need to be "intending to dine" to watch the bands.

Café le Monde, Hastings St, Noosa Heads (☎07/5449 2366). Slightly snobbish street atmosphere and a mainly international menu – try the le Monde salad at $13.50. Open 7am for cappuccino; happy hour Mon–Fri 4–6pm; live music evenings except Mon & Wed.

Chicko's, 281 Gympie Terrace, Noosaville. Unquestionably *the* place for fish and chips; open daily 9am–8pm.

Cinema Paradiso, Sunshine Beach Rd, next to the cinema, Noosa Heads. Outdoor eating and good-sized portions of sirloin, rack of lamb and salads from around $13; check out the $18 meal-and-film deal.

Filligan's, 9 Russell St, Noosaville (☎07/5449 8811). Fish and a variety of other tasty dishes with a slight Asian influence (most main courses around $15–17). With an appealingly casual, holiday ambience it's extremely popular, so book ahead. Open for lunch and dinner every day.

Noosa Heads Surf Club, on the beach, Hastings St, Noosa Heads. Evening bistros for under $10 and great views over the beach and bay.

Rolling Rock, Hastings St, Noosa Heads. A busy, sweaty club featuring discos and bands every night.

Roma Pizza, 36 David Low Way, Noosa Heads. Good-value takeaway pizzeria, plus a trattoria-style restaurant featuring used chianti-bottle decorations and inexpensive pizza and pasta meals.

Roser's, 1 Hastings St, Noosa Heads (☎07/5447 3880). One of the better local upmarket seafood restaurants, with barramundi or Moreton Bay Bugs for $19.

Rosie's, Gympie Terrace, near the corner of Albert St, Noosaville (☎07/5449 7888). Tiny and intimate BYO place, with a new menu every week. Popular with locals; mains around $17.

Royal Mail Hotel, Tewantin. Live rock 'n' roll at weekends, late happy hours and dress regulations.

Spinnakers on the Beach, *Sunshine Beach Surf Club* (☎07/5474 5177). Recently refurbished surf club, with a bar, restaurant and unbeatable views. Seafood, steaks, pasta and salad – big servings, all in the $10–15 range.

Listings

Banks Located along Sunshine Beach Rd, Noosa Heads.

Bike rental Koala Bike Hire (☎07/5474 2733) rents mountain bikes for $15 a day, including delivery to your accommodation.

Buses There's no actual bus station for long-distance buses. Drop-off and pick-up points are at the junction of Noosa Parade and Noosa Drive.

Camping supplies and rental Outdoor Store, 28 Sunshine Beach Rd, Noosa Heads (☎07/5447 2688), has all you'll need for Fraser Island and Cooloola.

Car rental Allterrain, Action St, Noosaville (☎07/5449 0877), and Sunshine 4WD (☎07/5447 3702), next to the Noosa post office, have five-seater 4WDs from $150 per day plus deposit. For a conventional runaround vehicle, try Virgin (☎07/5474 5777) or Henry's (☎07/5447 3777).

Cinema Sunshine Beach Rd, Noosa Heads (☎07/5447 5300).

Cruises Cruises: Blue Laguna (☎07/5449 0799), offers lunch while cruising the Noosa River; Everglades Express (☎07/5449 9422) makes half-day excursions up to Lake Cootharaba;

Everglades Waterbus, Harbour Town Complex, Tewantin (☎07/5447 1838), has half-day cruises upriver for $43 – full-day tours for $80 add a 4WD run along Rainbow Beach. Noosa River Cruises, Gympie Terrace, Noosaville (☎07/5449 7362), have day-tours on the river for $50. Tours: Camel Company (☎07/5442 4402) has 1hr to half-day safaris on humpback camel; Seawind Charters (☎07/5447 3042) heads up to prime dolphin co-nurturing spots at Tin Can Bay; Trailblazer (at *Noosa Backpackers Resort;* free call ☎1800/626 673) runs canoe trips to *Gagaju* bush camp, with overnight stay, and 4WD camping trips on Fraser Island.

NPWS Park Rd, at Noosa National Park's picnic area (☎07/5447 3243).

Pharmacy Noosa Heads Day and Night Pharmacy, Hastings St. Daily until 9pm.

Police 48 Hastings St (☎07/5474 5255 or 5447 5888).

Post office Noosa Drive, Sunshine Beach Rd end (Mon–Fri 9am–5pm, Sat 9am–12.30pm).

Surfing equipment and tuition Surf World, Sunshine Beach Rd, Noosa Heads (☎07/5447 3538) for gear; Wavesense (☎07/5474 9076) for training – they can be hard to get hold of, but worth the effort.

Taxi ☎13 1008.

Watersports Pelican Boat Hire, on the river bank at Gympie Terrace (☎07/5449 7239), has canoes and surf skis at $8 for the first hour ($4 per hour after that); Pro Ski (☎07/5449 7740), in the same place, has waterskiing at $65 for 30min, $100 for 1hr, including instruction for novices, and jet skis at $50 for 30min. Kingfisher Boat Hire (☎07/5449 9353), at the Harbour Town Complex in Tewantin, rents out fishing boats with fuel, rods, bait pumps, crab pots, ice boxes and the rest, for around $15 an hour.

THE GREAT SANDY REGION

Halfway between Brisbane and the tropics, the **Great Sandy Region** – the **Cooloola Coast** and **Fraser Island** – consists of giant dunes, forests, coloured sands and fresh water lakes where fishing and four-wheel driving take precedence over the more usual beach activities. But it doesn't have to be a macho tangle with the elements: for once it's relatively easy and inexpensive to hire tents and a 4WD and set off to explore in some comfort. You can venture in for a day, or make a circuit of the region in a week, driving through Cooloola and Fraser, and then back along the highway to return your vehicle.

Europeans were initially unimpressed with this part of the coast, but abundant fresh water, seafood and plants must have supported a very healthy **Aboriginal population**; campfires along the beach allowed Matthew Flinders to navigate Fraser Island at night in 1802. Flinders also coined the region's name by labelling Fraser Island and the Cooloola coast as "the Great Sandy Peninsula" on his maps, though he suspected that Fraser Island was in fact separated from the mainland. The Queensland government declared the area an Aboriginal reserve in the early 1860s but, with the discovery of **gold** at Gympie in 1867, Europeans flocked into the region in their thousands. This influx, and the economic boom that went with it, saved the fledgling Queensland from bankruptcy, but brought the usual conflicts, and the reserve gradually became little more than a holding pen for tribal survivors from all over the state. They were devastated by disease, and the last few were relocated to other reserves around Queensland at the turn of the century so the area could be opened up for recreation.

Sand mining and **logging** are other incendiary topics here and there's a predictable split between conservationists and those people who count on local industries for their livelihood. **Forestry** is a particularly bitter issue; the inland town of Maryborough was built on timber felling, and logging bans have aroused fury at what is seen as a sell-out to the Green movement. Locals, too, once drawn to the area for its natural appeal, now feel crowded out by regulations made to protect the coast from overuse by 4WDs and by drunken campers leaving piles of garbage behind them. While it's unlikely that any of this will have a negative impact on a brief visit, a balance between protection and "development" – a word with almost religious connotations in Queensland – is far from being established.

Getting there

Starting immediately across the Noosa River from Tewantin, the **Cooloola Coast** comprises the beaches and associated inland dunes and woodland stretching 40km north up to Rainbow Beach township. **From Tewantin**, surfaced roads run as far as lakes Cooroibah and Cootharaba, with direct beach access via Tewantin's river ferry at the end of Moorindil Street (daily 6am–9pm or later; cars $4 one-way; pedestrians free). **Rainbow Beach** can be reached on sealed roads from Gympie on the highway. The only direct roads between Tewantin and Rainbow Beach are 4WD-only routes along the beach and interior woodland tracks; without a 4WD you'll have to use the highway. **Access to Fraser Island** is by ferry from Rainbow Beach (Inskip Point) in the south, or Hervey Bay in the north.

   Tours into the area run from Noosa and Hervey Bay, though given the grand scale of the Great Sandy region – 190km from Tewantin to the northern tip of Fraser Island – they're inevitably rushed. The wildlife and overall serenity of the area are elusive, to say the least, unless you get away from the more popular places, camp for the night and explore early on in the day. Assembling a group and hiring a 4WD is one way to do this. Another is simply **walking**, an alternative ignored by almost all visitors, but one which allows unequalled access and intimacy with the region.

   Unless you're on a tour, you'll definitely need **maps**, with many available from local garages and newsagents. Relevant sheets on national parks, available from the NPWS, supplement these. **Drivers** need **tide timetables**, as most beaches are only reliably negotiable at low tide. Rain won't ruin your stay – in fact it makes driving on sand far easier and enhances the colours – though in rough conditions services to Fraser might be cancelled, leaving you stranded.

The Cooloola Coast

Often overlooked in the stampede to reach Hervey Bay and Fraser Island, the **Cooloola Coast** has in fact plenty to see if you take the time. The south is dominated by features of the Noosa River which pools into lakes **Cootharaba** and **Cooroibah** as it nears Tewantin, while stands of commercial timber and dry sclerophyll woodland cover the interior, rising to dunes along the beach stabilized by scrubby heath. The beach runs straight north from Tewantin to **Double Island Point** and then curves west to Rainbow Beach township, where it's backed by vertical, coloured-sand cliffs whose weathered contours and tones constantly change with the shifting sun. Below, the windswept strip of sand separating land from sea becomes a 4WD highway at low tide. Here you'll see brightly coloured flashes of canvas hidden in places where the cliffs are low enough to form a protective foreshore suitable for camping. Most of the beach and interior north of Cootharaba is **national park**, as is the lake's shoreline.

Practicalities

Cooloola's 27km of river can be explored by tour or **canoe** from Noosaville (see Noosa "Listings", p.385) or, for less money, from Boreen Point and Elanda Point townships on Lake Cootharaba. **Four-wheel drive** is essential for the beach, access roads leading to it, and inland tracks after rain – again, see Noosa "Listings" for operators. Conventional vehicles can reach Boreen and Elanda points from Tewantin in the south, and Rainbow Beach from Gympie in the north – both of which are good places to use as bases for day-walks if you don't have the right vehicle.

Hiking, you'll find the easiest path along the beach, but it makes things more interesting if you head inland at some stage. For those well equipped, walking tracks head upstream from Elanda Point, past the top of Lake Cootharaba and along the **Cooloola Wilderness Trail**, or towards the coast – contact the NPWS first.

Accommodation on the southern lake is at *Lake Cooroibah Holiday Park*, PO Box 220, Tewantin (☎07/5447 1225/1706), 2km after the Tewantin ferry, on a good gravel road. Family-oriented, and with every activity from horse-riding to canoeing and tennis, they offer camping ($5 per person) and caravans (④), as well as suites and cottages for up to eight people (⑥–⑧), plus all the associated facilities. At **Lake Cootharaba** there are campsites at Boreen Point and Elanda Point; both rent canoes and boats. **Rainbow Beach** has *Rainbow Beach Holiday Village* (☎07/5486 3222; ①–④), with tents, on-site vans, one-bedroom villas and two-bedroom chalets; *Rainbow Beach Hotel* (☎07/5486 3125; ④) has motel rooms; and *Rainbow Beach Backpackers* (☎07/5486 3288; ①), at *Rainbows Restaurant*, offers budget beds. You can **bush camp** throughout the park. Sites are located along the upper reaches of the Noosa River and wilderness trail, while on the beach you can pitch a tent anywhere south of Little Freshwater Creek and at Freshwater and Double Island Point campsites, run by the NPWS. Details on conditions in the park can be obtained from the Rainbow Beach information centre (daily 7am–6pm; ☎07/5486 3227) or from the national park offices at Rainbow Beach (☎07/5486 3160) or Noosa (see p.386); both offices issue camping permits.

Provisions are available at Boreen Point (fuel, general store, hotel, telephones), Elanda Point (small general store) and Rainbow Beach (post office, fuel, hotel, shops). The hotel just down the road from *Lake Cooroibah Holiday Park* serves good counter meals.

The lakes, river and inland

Cooroibah and its larger and more northerly neighbour **Cootharaba** are joined by a winding six-kilometre stretch of the Noosa River. Placid, and fringed with paperbarks and reedbeds, the lakes look their best at dawn before there's any traffic; they're saltwater and average just 1m in depth, subject to tides. At Cootharaba's top end, Kin Kin Creek and the Noosa River spill lazily into the lake through thickets of mangroves, hibiscus and ti-trees – the so-called **Everglades**. A boardwalk from Kinaba's **information centre** leads to a hide where you can spy on birdlife, and there's more on nearby **Fig Tree Lake**. The picnic area here is a former corroboree ground.

As you head upstream, the river freshens as it winds through the **Narrows** to **Harry Springs Hut** – an easy enough paddle in a canoe, though submerged obstacles require care with an outboard. A campsite on the edge of the rainforest at Harry Springs Hut is a convenient gateway to the park's interior; from here another 8km of river is navigable by canoe, and walking tracks lead off into the bush. The longest of these tracks is the **Cooloola Wilderness Trail**, a three-day, 46-kilometre hike out to the Rainbow Beach Road; clearly marked and not too strenuous, it can become swampy after rain. Best conditions are in September, when it's relatively cool with heathland scattered with wild flowers. Highlights are the first day's trekking through rainforest and mangroves, and the chance of spotting birdlife around waterholes. A good **day-walk** (20km return) follows the river upstream from Harry Springs Hut and then climbs across dunes to Cooloola Sandpatch – a "blow" caused by winds stripping vegetation off a sandhill and destabilizing it. The track starts on the opposite bank from Harry Springs Hut – but come prepared, for you'll have to swim 50m with your clothes in a plastic bag.

The coast

With over 40km of uninterrupted beach at Cooloola you'd think that crowds would hardly be a problem, but there are times when you seem to be constantly dodging oncoming traffic. Having crossed the Noosa River **from Tewantin**, the ferry drops you five minutes' drive from the sea. The powdery foredunes at the end of the road look too small to worry about, but you wouldn't be the first to get stuck driving through them; a **campsite** here has fine views of Noosa, but this close to town things can get busy. From Rainbow Beach township in the north, you can drive (or walk) directly onto the beach or take the vehicle track to **Freshwater Creek** campsite which starts 4km south along Rainbow Beach Road – a rough ride through rainforest along a road scarred and rutted from vehicles that have spun their wheels in the soft sand. Just keep going. There's a similar track to **King's Bore** (about halfway along the coast) off the Lock's Pinch road, with a memorable descent down the side of a blow onto the beach. Drivers should take care to avoid a patch of **quicksand** about 1km south of Freshwater Creek – and remember that there are no exits off the beach between the Tewantin access and Freshwater Creek (30km), so make sure that you have enough time before the tide comes in – the King's Bore track is too steep to use.

Coloured sands are a feature of the region, best seen up along the northern fore-shore near the unremarkable township of Rainbow Beach. Caused by minerals leaching down the cliffs from above leaving broad bands of orange, red and white, the effect is most impressive at a distance; the colours seem less vivid close up but you'll find some curious rounded sculptures formed by the weather. There's also the **shipwreck** of the *Cherry Venture*, grounded up towards Rainbow Beach between Double Island Point and Freshwater Creek in 1973. Sand is piling up on its leeward side and slowly engulfing its rusting frame and funnel.

Heading on, the **Fraser Island ferry** leaves Inskip Point, 10km north of Rainbow Beach, for Hook Point on the island's south coast (daily 7am–4.30pm; $55 return per vehicle, $5 for foot passengers; ☎07/5486 3227); you'll need a **permit** from the NPWS on the Rainbow Beach road (daily 7am–4pm; ☎07/5486 3160), and your own transport to Inskip Point.

Hervey Bay

Back on the highway and heading north from Tewantin, it's a couple of hours to Hervey Bay past **GYMPIE** and **MARYBOROUGH**, historic gold and timber communities and now healthy market towns with handsome stone and wooden period buildings in their centres testifying to their wealthy past. **HERVEY BAY**, a rapidly expanding sprawl of coastal suburbs, has no such pretentions, and the only reason to visit is to join the throng crossing to Fraser Island – or to venture into the bay to spot **whales** in the spring. **PIALBA** is the centre, with shops strung along the Esplanade as it runs 7km from here west through **Scarness** and **Torquay** to **Urangan** harbour; barges to Fraser Island leave from here and from River Heads, 17km south. **Approaching** Hervey Bay from the south, turn off at Maryborough; from the north, leave the highway at Howard. The **bus station** is on the main road into town about 1km from Pialba. Almost every place to stay provides information and makes bookings, but you'll get more reliable, pressure-free help from the **tourist information** office right inside the bus station (☎07/4124 8244; Mon–Fri 6am–5.30pm, Sat–Sun 6.30am–1pm).

Water sports enthusiasts with time to kill might want to take advantage of Torquay Beach Hire, on the Esplanade at Torquay, which has it all – from surf skis to windsurfers and outboard-driven tinnies for a day's **fishing**. More sedentary folk could indulge in a beach bonfire, while nature lovers can search out **echidna** in the vegetation strip between the Esplanade and beach, or visit Natureworld ($10), about 2km back from Pialba on the way to the highway, whose stars include freshwater crocs, snakes, wombats and koalas.

Whale-watching
Humpbacked whales are among the most exciting of marine creatures to encounter: growing to 16m long and 36 tonnes, they make their presence known from a distance by their habit of "breaching" – making spectacular, crashing leaps out of the water – and expelling jets of spray as they exhale. Prior to 1952 an estimated ten thousand whales made the annual journey between the Antarctic and tropics to breed and give birth in shallow coastal waters; a decade later whaling had reduced the population to just two hundred animals.

Now protected, their numbers are increasing and you're fairly likely to see one if you put out to sea between Brisbane and the Whitsundays during the whale-watching season of May to October. The whales' migration brings them close to Hervey Bay between July and September, and the town is particularly well prepared for it: there's an August **Whale Festival**, and operators are always searching for new gimmicks to promote **day cruises** and **flights**. In perfect conditions you'll see whales breach, swim directly under the boat and raise their heads out of the water, close enough to touch. You might also, of course, see nothing at all. Whether all this voyeurism disturbs the animals is unclear, but they seem at least tolerant of the attention paid to them.

For **flights**, try Air Fraser Island (☎07/4125 3600); the cost is from $35 per person (depending on the number of passengers) for a thirty-minute buzz. **Cruises** last for a morning or a full day, cost around $65, and are booked through an agent; some get very crowded – check the boat size and how many will be going. *Princess II* (the smallest vessel), *Islander* (a bit slow and solid), *Tasman II, Hombre* and *Volante III* all come recommended, while *Spirit of Hervey Bay* has the bonus of being a **glass-bottomed** vessel. For the added pleasure of **sailing** out to the whales, make arrangements with the yacht *Stefanie* through your accommodation or other booking services.

Accommodation
Accommodation is packed during the whale-watching season (July–Sept) and at Christmas and Easter (when motel prices double). Most accommodation will pick you up from the bus station. If you're camping, try Urangan's *Harbour Views Caravan Park* at the end of Miller Street (☎07/4128 9374), right next to the harbour, or *Pialba Caravan Park* on the corner of Main Street and the Esplanade on the foreshore in Pialba (☎07/4128 1399; tent sites only).

Bay Bed & Breakfast, 180 Cypress St, Urangan (☎07/4125 6919). Good, home-style accommodation with discounted weekly rates. Double rooms and four-bed "cottage". ③–⑤.

Bayview Motel, 399 Esplanade, Torquay (☎07/4128 1134). Not much to look at from outside, but the rooms are spotless and the friendly owners can't do enough for you; doubles and twins ③.

Beaches, 195 Torquay Rd, Torquay (☎07/4124 1322). Busy party hostel with lively bar/bistro and cheerful staff, one street back from the Esplanade. ①.

Beachside Motor Inn, 298 Esplanade, Scarness (☎07/4124 1999). Comfortable motel units with beach views. ⑤.

Boomerang Beach House, 335 Esplanade, Scarness (☎07/4124 3970). Quiet, tidy rooms. Nothing fancy but good value. Four-person rooms ④.

Colonial Backpackers Resort, corner of Pulgul St and Boat Harbour Drive, Urangan (☎07/4125 1844). Tidy and well-furnished wooden cabins set in bushland near Urangan Harbour, with a bar and restaurant, plus tame wildlife. Campsites also available. ①–③.

Fraser Magic, 369 Esplanade, Torquay (☎07/4124 3488). Friendly, small and well-managed hostel, though a bit run-down these days. ①.

Friendly Hostel, 182 Torquay Rd, Scarness (☎07/4124 4107). Welcoming and secure guesthouse, with small dorms and nice, family atmosphere. ①.

Koala Backpackers, 408 Esplanade, Torquay (☎07/4125 3601). Tatty rooms and large grounds; close to the shops. ①.

Olympus, 184 Torquay Rd, Scarness (☎07/4124 5331). Excellent, purpose-built hostel, with its own whale-watch boat (*Volante III*) and fleet of 4WDs; all units complete with kitchen and TV, and there's a pool. ①.

Playa Concha, 475 Esplanade, Torquay (☎07/4125 1544). Comfortable, beachfront motel surrounded by palms and ferns. ⑤.

Eating

Apart from snack bars and fast-food joints in Pialba, most of the places to eat and spend the evening are along the Esplanade at Torquay.

Curried Away, 174 Boat Harbour Drive, Pialba. Long-established Indian fast-food joint. Dine in, take away or have delivered for free (☎07/4124 0577).

Dolly's, 410 Esplanade, Torquay (☎07/4125 5633). Adorned with 1950s iconography, there's a DJ or live music every night and a range of smorgasbord and all-you-can-eat deals.

Gringo's, 449 Esplanade, Torquay. Good Mexican menu of enchiladas, chilli con carne and nachos, spiced to individual tolerances and with bean fillings as an alternative to meat. Main courses $12–17; open daily from 5.30pm.

Ivey's, 355 Esplanade, Scarness. Burgers, barbecued chicken and chips. Open late.

O'Reileys, 446 Esplanade, Torquay. Savoury pizza, pasta and crepes, but best for fruit pancakes and cream. From $8.

Toucan's, 417 Esplanade, Torquay (☎07/4125 5011). Best-value place in Hervey Bay to treat yourself; menu includes steak, pasta, lamb with pesto sauce, baby octopus and other seafood, with main courses from $14. Open for lunch and on evenings Wed–Sun.

Listings

Banks Most banks are in Pialba, with a few scattered along the Esplanade at Torquay.

Camping and fishing equipment Camping and Leisure, 68 Boat Harbour Drive, Pialba (☎07/4124 2511). Some 4WD operators also rent camping equipment.

Car and scooter rental Hervey Bay Car Rentals (☎07/4125 5534), has non-4WD vehicles from $25 a day plus extras; Bayside, 4 Fraser St, Torquay (☎07/4125 3733), rents scooters at $15 an hour. See "Four-wheel-drive rental" below for 4WDs.

Diving Diver's Mecca, 403 Esplanade, Torquay (☎07/4125 1626 or free call ☎1800/351 626), for shallow-wreck diving and grouper, sea snakes and other marine life.

Flights Air Fraser Island (☎07/4125 3600), $35 per person (group of 6) for day flights to Fraser.

Four-wheel-drive rental Aussie Trax, 56 Boat Harbour Drive, Pialba (☎07/4124 4433 or free call ☎1800/062 275), eight-seaters from $135 a day, including insurance; Bay 4WD Centre, 54 Boat Harbour Drive, Pialba (☎07/4128 2981), two-seaters $85 a day, five- to eight-seaters $140 a day; Rover Rentals, 79 Islander Rd (☎07/4124 3655). See box on p.393 for more on Fraser Island trips.

Laundry Corner of Esplanade and Frank St, Scarness (behind *Dot's Food Bar*); open 7am–7pm.

Pharmacy Day and Night Pharmacy, 418 Esplanade, Torquay (☎07/4125 2733); daily 8.30am–8pm.

Police 146 Torquay Rd, Scarness (☎07/4128 5333).

Post office On the Esplanade, Torquay.

Taxi ☎13 1008.

Tours Full-day tours to Fraser Island start around $65, overnight camping trips about $150. Top Tours (☎07/4125 3933) concentrates on Fraser's north end on their one-day trips, or give a pretty comprehensive coverage to the entire island on a two-day safari; Fraser Venture Tours (☎07/4125 4444) spends a day heading through Central Station to Lake Birrabeen and along the beach as far as the Cathedrals.

Fraser Island

With a length of 123km, **Fraser Island** is the world's largest sand island, but the dry facts do little to prepare you for the experience. Accumulated from sediments swept north from New South Wales over the last two million years, the scenery ranges from silent forests and beaches sculpted by wind and surf, to crystal-clear streams and dark, tannin-stained lakes. The east coast forms a ninety-kilometre razor-edge from which Fraser's tremendous scale can be absorbed as you travel its length; with the sea as a constant, the dunes along the edge seem to evolve before your eyes – in places low and soft, elsewhere hard and worn into intriguing canyons. By contrast, slow progress through the forests of the island's interior creates more subtle impressions of age and permanence – a primal world predating European settlement – brought into question only when the view opens suddenly onto a lake or a bald blow.

The idyllic mood, however, is sobered by a number of factors, most alarming of which is the volume of traffic tearing along the beach and main tracks. The foredunes are trampled and littered with camping detritus, too, and the island has become the epitome of Queensland's environmental conflicts, with conservationists, tour operators, foresters and Aboriginal groups vying for control of resources – at present, Fraser's north end is a national park, with the rest in private hands.

To the Kabi Aborigines, Fraser Island is **Gurri** (or K'gari), a beautiful woman so taken with the earth that she stayed behind after creation, her eyes becoming lakes that mirrored the sky and teemed with wildlife so that she wouldn't be lonely. The story behind the European name is far less enchanting. In 1836, survivors of the wreck of the *Stirling Castle*, including Captain Fraser and his wife Eliza, landed at Waddy Point. Though runaway convicts had already been welcomed into Kabi life, the castaways suffered "dreadful slavery, cruel toil and excruciating tortures", and after the captain's death Eliza was presented as a prize during a corroboree at Lake Cootharaba two months later. She was rescued at this dramatic point by former convict John Graham, who had lived with the Kabi and was part of a search party alerted by three other survivors from the *Stirling Castle*. The exact details of Eliza's captivity remain obscure as she produced several conflicting accounts, but her role as an "anti-Crusoe" inspired the work of novelist Patrick White and artist Sidney Nolan.

Practicalities

It's best to sort out your **crossing to Fraser Island** in advance. Unless on an organized tour, you need a **barge ticket**, **vehicle permit** for the island if driving ($30), plus **camping fees** for national park sites ($3.50 per person a night). All these can be obtained where you rent your vehicle – and are usually covered in package deals – or from barge offices at Urangan and River Heads. You can pre-book for all three ferry services by calling ☎07/4125 4444. Note that you can use return tickets only on the same barge; if you're planning a different exit from the island, you'll have to buy two one-way tickets. Pack insect repellent.

The **Urangan Harbour to Moon Point** (central west coast) barge leaves at 8.30am and 3.30pm, returning at 9.30am and 4.30pm. Returns are $65 for vehicle and driver, plus $5 for passengers; pedestrians pay $15 each way. The Moon Point landing is very difficult, however – unless you have sound 4WD experience, leave from River Heads. The **River Heads to Wanggoolba Creek** barge (access to **Central Station**) departs daily at 9am, 10.15am and 3.30pm, returning at 9.30am, 2.30pm and 4pm. The **Kingfisher Bay** barge leaves River Heads at 7.15am, 9.30am and 2pm, returning at 8am, 12.30pm and 3.30pm; fares are the same as Urangan's. **Pedestrians** are also served by a **high-speed catamaran** from Urangan to *Kingfisher Bay Resort* (5–6 times daily; $30), which includes day use of resort facilities and a free guided walk.

RENTING A 4WD FOR FRASER ISLAND

Fraser Island is simply too large and varied to appreciate fully on a day-trip, and with competition in Hervey Bay keeping prices to a minimum it's a great opportunity to learn to handle a 4WD. See the Hervey Bay "Listings" on p.391 for some recommended out-fits, but from whomever you rent your vehicle, the company should take the time to pro-tect both it and you with a full briefing on the island and driving practicalities.

Conditions include a minimum driver age of 21 and a $500 bond, payable in plastic or cash – note that advertised prices are normally for renting the vehicle only, so tents, food, fuel, and **ferry** and **vehicle permit** for the island are extra, available separately or as part of a **package**. To help cut costs, you'll want to form a **group** of between five and eight, and the easiest way to arrange this is by staying at one of the hostels; they'll organize numbers and provide everything except food and fuel – a three-day, two-night trip works out to about $110 a person.

Getting around

Driving requires a **four-wheel-drive vehicle**; the east beach serves as the main high-way, with roads running inland to popular spots. Other tracks, always slower than the beach, crisscross the interior; main tracks are often rough from heavy use, and minor roads tend to be in better shape. Rain and high tides harden sand surfaces, making dri-ving easier. Most **accidents** involve collisions on blind corners, rolling in soft sand, and trying to cross apparently insignificant creeks on the beach at 60kph – 4WDs are not invincible. Pedestrians can't hear vehicles on the beach and won't be aware of your presence until you barrel through from behind, so give them a wide berth. Road rules are the same as those on the mainland.

Walking is the best way to see the island. There's only one **established circuit**, and even that is very underused, running from Central Station south past lakes Birrabeen and Boomanjin, then up the coast and back to Central Station via lakes Wabby and McKenzie; highlights are circumnavigating the lakes, chance encounters with goannas and dingoes, and the energetic burst up **Wongi Blow** for sweeping views out to sea. A good three-day hike that by each sundown renders you all but unconscious after all that walking across sand, it requires no special skills beyond endurance and the ability to set up camp before you fall asleep.

Essentials and accommodation

Beds need to be booked in advance. Top of the range is the plush *Kingfisher Bay Resort* (free call ☎1800/072 555; ⑧) on the west coast; the more down-to-earth *Fraser Island Retreat* at Happy Valley on the east coast (☎07/4127 9144; doubles, triples and quads ⑧) provides comfortable cabins and good food; *Yidney Rocks Cabins* (☎07/4127 9167; ⑥), just to the south, has basic self-contained, three-bedroom units aimed at fishing groups renting on a weekly basis. Further south, *Eurong Beach Resort* (☎07/4127 9122; ④) has average motel-style rooms, while *Dilli Village* (☎07/4127 9130; ③) has self-contained, four-bed bunkhouses.

With a permit, you can camp anywhere along the eastern foreshore, or if you need facilities, use the national park **campsites** at **Wathumba** on the west coast, or at **Lake Allom**, **Dundubara** and **Waddy Point** (the last two can be booked through most NPWS offices in the region) on the east. Elsewhere there are sites at **Central Station**, **Lake Boomanjin** and **Lake McKenzie** (which is often full by noon). There are pri-vately run campsites at the unfriendly *Cathedral Beach Resort* (☎07/4127 9177) and the nicer *Dilli Village* (see above).

For **supplies**, **HAPPY VALLEY** and **EURONG** have stores, telephones, bars and fuel; there's another store at *Cathedral Beach Resort* but no shops or restaurant at Dilli. You'll save money by bringing whatever you need with you – take the empties home.

Around Central Station

Most people get their bearings by making their first stop at **Central Station**, an old logging depot with campsite, telephone and information hut under some monstrous bunya pines in the middle of the island, directly east of River Heads on the mainland. You'll certainly see **dingoes** here; *don't* feed them, as the expectation of hand-outs makes them aggressive. As there are no domestic dogs on the island, Fraser's dingoes are considered to be Australia's purest strain.

From the station, take a stroll along **Wanggoolba Creek**, a magical stream so clear that it's hard at first to see the water as it runs across the forest floor. Apart from encounters with swimming dingoes or slender pythons drowsing on a branch, it's a botanic walk past some prehistoric *angiopteris* ferns to **Pile Valley** where **satinay trees** humble you to insignificance as they reach 60m to the sky. They produce a very dense timber, durable enough to be used as sidings on the Suez Canal – and are consequently in such demand that the trees on Fraser have almost been logged out.

There are several **lakes** around Central Station, all close enough to walk to and all along main roads. Nine kilometres north (track distance), **McKenzie** is the most popular on the island, and often very crowded: ringed by white sand with clear, tea-coloured water reflecting a blue sky, it's a wonderful place to spend the day. To the south, **Birrabeen** (8km) is mostly hemmed in by trees, while **Boomanjin** (16km) is open and geologically "perched" in a basin above the island's water table. There's a fine campsite and communal fireplace here, attended by tame goannas.

East Beach

Seventy-Five Mile Beach on the east coast is one of the busiest strips of sand you'll ever encounter. Vehicles hurtle along, pedestrians and anglers hug the surf, and tents dot the foredunes; this is what beckons the crowds over from the mainland. Sights along the way include **sand** in all its different forms: **Hammerstone Blow**, 6km north of Eurong, is slowly engulfing **Lake Wabby**, a small but deep patch of blue below the dunes – another century and it will be gone. At **Rainbow Gorge**, about 5km south of Happy Valley, a short trail runs between two blows, through a hot, silent desert landscape where sandblasted trees emerge denuded by their ordeal. Incredibly, a dismal spring seeps water into the valley where the sand swallows it up; "upstream" are the gorge's stubby, eroded red fingers. A path leads in, but if you went you'd only be contributing to the vandalization of the brittle structure.

Six kilometres north of Happy Valley you cross picturesque **Eli Creek**, where water splashes briskly between briefly verdant banks before spilling into the sea. Sand-filtered, it's the nicest swimming spot on the island, though icy-cold. Back on the beach, another 4km brings you to the *Maheno*, wrecked in 1935 and now a skeleton almost consumed by the elements. More striking are the coloured cliffs known as the **Cathedrals**, which run from the wreck north to Indian Head.

The interior, west coast and far north

Fraser's **wooded centre**, a real contrast to the busy coast and popular southern lakes, gets relatively few visitors. It encloses **Yidney Scrub**, the only major stand of **rainforest** left on the island, and although the name doesn't conjure up a very appealing image, the trees are majestic and include towering **Kauri pines**. There's a circuit through Yidney from Happy Valley, taking in **Boomerang** and **Allom** lakes on the long way back to the beach near the *Maheno*. You can camp at Allom, a small lake surrounded by pines and cycads, and completely different in character from its flashy southern cousins. Further north, another road heads in from Dundabara township to **Bowarrady**, a not particularly exciting body of water famed for turtles who pester you for bread – if you can't imagine being pestered by a turtle, try refusing to hand it over.

The island's **west coast** is a mix of mangrove swamp and treacherously soft beaches, both largely inaccessible to vehicles. Rough tracks cross the island via Lake Bowarraddy and Happy Valley to where the Urangan barge lands at **Moon Point**, though there's a better road to *Kingfisher Bay Resort* from the Central Station area. Similarly, most of Fraser's **far north** is inaccessible, with the east coast around **Indian Head** as far north as you can reliably get. The bubbling saltwater pools just north of Indian Head at the **Aquarium** are great fun, and there are some good views from the head itself.

travel details

Trains

Brisbane to: Beenleigh (every 20min; 55min); Bowen (6 weekly; 21hr); Bundaberg (13 weekly; 6hr); Caboolture (every 20min; 1hr); Cairns (4 weekly; 31hr); Charleville (2 weekly; 16hr 25min); Cleveland, for Stradbroke Island (8 daily; 50min); Emerald (2 weekly; 15hr 15min); Gladstone (every 20min; 8hr); Ingham (4 weekly; 26hr 30min); Longreach (2 weekly; 24hr); Mackay (6 weekly; 16hr 30min); Maryborough (13 weekly; 3hr 45min–5hr); Proserpine (6 weekly; 19hr); Rockhampton (13 weekly; 11hr); Roma (2 weekly; 3hr 30min); Sydney (1 daily; 14hr); Toowoomba (2 weekly; 3hr 30min); Townsville (6 weekly; 23hr); Tully (4 weekly; 27hr 30min).

Buses

Brisbane to: Airlie Beach (9 daily; 18hr); Beenleigh (8 daily; 40min); Bundaberg (9 daily; 6hr); Burleigh Heads (8 daily; 1hr 50min); Caboolture (2 daily; 45min); Cairns (9 daily; 27hr); Caloundra (9 daily; 1hr 10min); Charleville (2 daily; 10hr 35min); Coolangatta (8 daily; 2hr 10min); Hervey Bay/Pialba (8 daily; 4hr 40min); Lamington National Park (1 daily; 3hr); Longreach (2 daily; 16hr); Mackay (9 daily; 15hr 30min); Maroochydore (5 daily; 2hr 5min); Maryborough (11 daily; 4hr); Mount Isa (2 daily; 25hr); Nambour (9 daily; 1hr 30min); Noosa (4 daily; 2hr 50min); Roma (3 daily; 7hr 20min); Surfers Paradise (every 30min; 1hr 30min); Sydney (10 daily; 16hr); Toowoomba (8 daily; 2hr 15min); Townsville (9 daily; 21hr 30min); Tully (8 daily; 25hr 30min); Winton (2 daily; 18hr).

Hervey Bay to: Brisbane (8 daily; 4hr 40min); Caboolture (3 daily; 4hr 10min); Caloundra (8 daily; 3hr 20min); Maroochydore (2 daily; 4hr);

Maryborough (8 daily; 30min); Nambour (8 daily; 3hr); Noosa (3 daily; 3hr 15min).

Noosa to: Brisbane (5 daily; 2hr 50min); Caloundra (5 daily; 1 hr); Hervey Bay (6 daily; 3hr 10min); Maroochydore (3 daily; 35min); Maryborough (6 daily; 2hr 35min).

Surfers Paradise to: Brisbane (60 daily; 1hr 30min); Burleigh Heads (every 10min; 30min); Coolangatta (every 10min; 1hr) Lamington National Park (2 daily; 1hr 30min); Sydney (8 daily; 15hr 30min); Tamborine Mountain (1 daily; 1hr); Toowoomba (2 daily; 3hr 30min).

Ferries

Brisbane to: Moreton Island (1 daily; 2hr); North Stradbroke Island (11 daily; 30min); St Helena (3 or more weekly; 2hr).

Hervey Bay to: Fraser Island (8 daily; 30min–1hr).

Rainbow Beach/Inskip Point to: Fraser Island (daily, on demand; 45min).

Surfers Paradise to: South Stradbroke Island (3 or more daily; 30min).

Flights

Brisbane to: Adelaide (15 daily; 3hr 30min); Alice Springs (6 daily; 4hr 30min); Cairns (14 daily; 2hr 10min); Canberra (at least 7 daily; 2hr); Darwin (at least 6 daily; 3hr 40min); Gold Coast/Coolangatta (at least 4 daily; 25min); Hervey Bay (5 daily; 1hr 15min); Hobart (at least 9 daily; 3hr 50min); Melbourne (16 daily; 2hr 25min); Perth (12 daily; 5hr); Sydney (29 daily; 1hr 35min); Townsville (6 daily, 1hr 50min).

Gold Coast/Coolangatta to: Adelaide (12 daily; 3hr 35min); Brisbane (at least 5 daily; 25min); Cairns (at least 5 daily; 3hr 40min); Canberra (12 daily; 2hr 40min); Darwin (3 daily; 7hr 25min); Hobart (9 daily; 6hr 10min); Melbourne (17 daily; 3hr 35min); Perth (11 daily; 6hr); Sydney (18 daily; 1hr 15min); Townsville (at least 2 daily; 3hr 10min).

Hervey Bay to: Brisbane (5 daily; 1hr 15min); Cairns (at least 2 daily; 4hr); Townsville (at least 1 daily; 4hr).

CHAPTER FOUR

TROPICAL QUEENSLAND AND THE REEF

The move towards, and into, Queensland's **tropical coast** is far more obvious than simply passing the Tropic of Capricorn marker at **Rockhampton**. North of Hervey Bay the landscape begins to get brown as the temperature rises, and though there's still an ever-narrowing farming strip hugging the coast, the Great Dividing Range edges coastwards as it progresses north, dry at first but gradually acquiring a green sward which culminates in the steamy, rainforest-draped scenery around **Cairns**. Along the way are scores of beaches, vivid archipelagos of **islands**, and regularly spaced cities, including **Townsville**, north Queensland's largest. There is also a wealth of **national parks**, some – such as **Hinchinbrook Island** – with superb walking trails, and others where you might encounter rare or unusual wildlife. Moving north of Cairns, rainforested ranges ultimately cede to the savannah of the huge, triangular **Cape York Peninsula**, a sparsely populated setting for what is widely regarded as the most rugged 4WD adventure in the country.

The transition between Queensland's southeast (see Chapter 3) and the tropics is also reflected offshore, with the appearance of the **Great Barrier Reef**, among the most beautiful and extensive coral complexes in the world. The reef, which begins to make its presence felt round the level of Bundaberg, drastically changes the nature of the coastline by blocking incoming surf and producing currents that deflect ocean-borne sand far out to sea. As a result, most **islands** north of Fraser are **continental**, formed when the peaks of ranges were drowned by rising waters at the end of the last Ice Age, creating abrupt coastlines and coral rubble beaches entirely different in character from the southeast's sandy formations. On the reef's outer edge, however, small isolated sand islands (**cays**) form, which tend to become encircled by fringing coral reef – these are particularly a feature of the southern reef. Further north, the cays thin out, while the main body of the reef thickens into thousands of individual shoals as it ventures nearer the coast. Whether cay or continental, many of these islands are close enough to ports for a day-trip, but for a real change of pace, try camping on one for a week or splashing out on a comfortable resort. **Divers** are well catered for, but novices needn't miss out on the best of the coral, which is within snorkelling range of the surface.

Access is along the **Bruce Highway** to Cairns, which is then briefly replaced by the **Cook Highway**, until notions of "main roads" begin to fall apart north of Mossman. Beyond here lie the jungles of the **Daintree**, the outpost of **Cooktown** and the beginnings of seasonal roads, humble tracks and the savannah wilderness of the Cape York Peninsula. Frequent **bus** and **train** services stop at all centres between Bundaberg and Cairns, but ideally you'll either be **driving** or willing to hitch to those places that the travel brochures have overlooked. Among the region's peculiar hazards are the slow, endless **sugar cane trains** that cross roads during the crushing

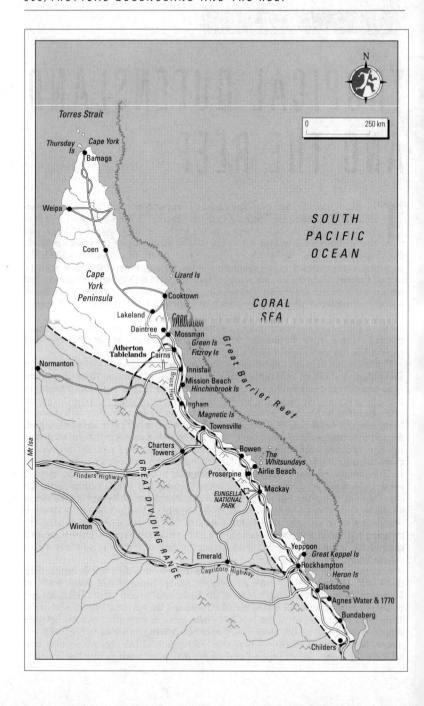

N

0   250 km

Torres Strait

Thursday Is Cape York
Bamaga

Weipa

Coen

Cape York Peninsula

Lizard Is

Cooktown

Lakeland

Daintree Mossman
Green Is
Fitzroy Is

Atherton Tablelands Cairns

Normanton

Innisfail

Mission Beach
Hinchinbrook Is

Ingham

Magnetic Is
Townsville

Charters Towers

Bowen
The Whitsundays

Proserpine Airlie Beach

EUNGELLA NATIONAL PARK Mackay

Flinders Highway

△ *Mt Isa*

GREAT DIVIDING RANGE

Winton

Emerald

Capricorn Highway

Yeppoon
Great Keppel Is
Rockhampton
Heron Is

Gladstone
Agnes Water & 1770

Bundaberg

Childers

SOUTH PACIFIC OCEAN

CORAL SEA

Great Barrier Reef

Bruce Hwy

ACCOMMODATION PRICES

All the accommodation listed in this book has been categorized into one of eight price bands, as set out below. The rates quoted represent the cheapest available double or twin room in high season – except for category ①, which indicates per-person rates for a dorm bed, and the categories given for units, cabins and vans, which represent the daily charge for the whole unit.

① Under $18	⑤ $61–74
② $19–30	⑥ $75–94
③ $31–45	⑦ $95–124
④ $46–60	⑧ $125 upwards

For more accommodation details, see p.40-43.

---

season (roughly June–Dec); crossings are often (but not always) marked by flashing red lights.

Winters are dry and pleasant, but the summer climate (Dec–April) can be oppressively humid, with unpredictable **cyclones** bringing torrential rain and devastating storms making roads on Cape York impassable and sometimes even severing the coastal highway. To avoid the worst of the **crowds** at key places such as the Cairns region or the Whitsunday Islands, come as soon as the wet season is over (late April).

THE SOUTHERN REEF

Outside the tropics, the Barrier Reef is represented by the **Capricorn** and **Bunker** groups, a string of cays about 80km offshore from the ports of **Bundaberg** and **Gladstone**. Fundamentally different in character from towns further south in Queensland, these places are primarily farming and residential centres; you'll notice a change in the climate, which gets increasingly dry as you near the tropics. Bundaberg lies 50km off the Bruce Highway from Childers (south) or Gin Gin (north); Gladstone is 20km off the highway about 170km north of Gin Gin. Both are on the train line.

You enter the region through the pretty, one-horse town of **CHILDERS**, where the down-to-earth *Palace Hostel* (☎07/4126 2244; ①), 72 Churchill St, is becoming a popular alternative to Bundaberg for finding **farm work**. The place is managed by locals, who have good employment connections and will do their best to find you a job.

Bundaberg and offshore

Despite being surrounded by canefields and tomato farms, **BUNDABERG** has the atmosphere of a town in Outback Queensland rather than on the coast; even the **Burnett River** doesn't really manage to add much colour or relieve the heat. Famous throughout Australia for its **rum**, the town is otherwise a busy, humdrum sort of place, and its value as a jumping-off point for trips to Lady Elliot and Lady Musgrave **islands** is scarcely advertised. Apart from the reef, its most likely attraction is the chance of finding seasonal **work** (year-round, except Dec–Jan) picking mandarins, tomatoes, snow peas and zucchini. During the summer, biologists come to watch **marine turtles** lay their eggs on the beaches.

The town and around

"Bundie" is synonymous with dark rum throughout Australia and if you believe their advertising pitch, Bundaberg's **rum distillery** on Whittered Street, about 2km east of the town centre along Bourbong Street (tours Mon–Fri 10am, 11am, noon, 1pm, 2pm & 3pm; Sat & Sun 10am, 11am, noon, 1pm & 2pm; $5), accounts for half the rum consumed in Australia each year. Fans relish the opportunity to wallow in the overpowering pungency of raw molasses on a tour of the distilling process. Molasses – cane syrup after the sugar is removed – is diluted and heated in huge settling tanks to kill any rogue microbes and to separate out any impurities; yeast is then added to metabolize alcohol. After being distilled twice, raw rum with a spirit content of 78 percent is left to mature to full flavour for two years in white-oak vats before being coloured, diluted and bottled. The tour ends, of course, with a **free sample** but you probably won't need to drink much after inhaling the fumes in the vat sheds, where cameras are prohibited in case a flash ignites the vapour. This isn't groundless paranoia: the distillery was gutted by fire in 1936.

Flying 1270km from Sydney to Bundaberg in 1921, **Bert Hinkler** set a world record for continuous flight in a light aircraft, demonstrating its potential as transport for remote areas and leading to the formation of Qantas the following year. It was quite an achievement in his *Baby Arvo* – all flimsy wires and canvas; there's a replica inside the tourist office on Bourbong Street. In 1983, the house where Hinkler lived at the time of his death in Southampton, England, was rescued from demolition and transported to Bundaberg as a shrine to his feat. Today **Hinkler House** (daily 10am–4pm; $2) sits in the **Botanic Gardens** 4km from the centre over the Burnett Bridge towards Gin Gin, sharing its desirable surroundings with a Sugar Museum, Historical Museum and a steam train (all $2). Outside the house, landscaped gardens flank ponds where Hinkler was supposedly inspired to design aircraft by watching ibises in flight.

The **Mystery Craters** on the Gin Gin road, 27km from Bundaberg (daily 8am–5pm; $3.50) are 35 pits ("craters" is more evocative than accurate) that have

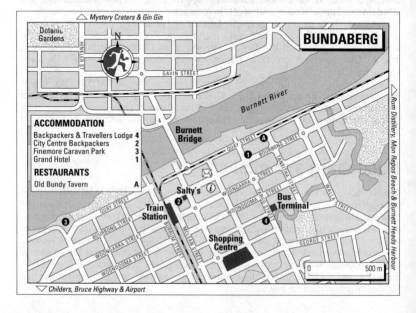

baffled geologists since their discovery on a pineapple plantation in 1971. Between two and three metres wide and excavated to a depth of only about one metre they are, essentially, holes in someone's back yard; you may think the reward doesn't merit the journey.

Mon Repos Beach and Turtle Rookery

Mon Repos Beach is 15km east of Bundaberg, near the suburb of Bargara. Once the site of a French telegraph link to New Caledonia, today its reputation rests on being Australia's most accessible **loggerhead turtle rookery**. From October to March, females clamber laboriously up the beaches after dark, excavate a pit with their hind flippers in the sand above the high-tide mark, and lay about a hundred parchment-shelled eggs. During the eight-week incubation period, the ambient temperature will determine the sex of the entire clutch. The endearing, rubbery-brown youngsters hatch at night and head for the sea. Normally they'd run a gauntlet of predators, but at Mon Repos human intervention raises their chances. Even so, only a handful reach maturity at fifty years old, and they return to lay their eggs on the beach where they themselves originally hatched. Since 1980 the rookery population has been halved – most likely due to net-trawling offshore. The NPWS run nightly **guided tours** ($4) from November to March. In season, about a dozen turtles lay each night, and watching the young leave the nest and race towards the water is both comical and touching – your chances of seeing both in one evening are best during January. Most accommodation places can book you on a tour and arrange transport, or you can enquire about local buses at the tourist information office (see below).

Practicalities

Bundaberg lies south of the Burnett River, with the port at **Burnett Heads** and satellite suburbs – Bargara, Innes Park, Elliot Heads – spreading along the coast about 15km to the east. Bourbong Street, the main thoroughfare, parallels the river. The **bus terminal** is on Targo Street, and the **train station** is half a kilometre west on McLean Street; both streets cross Bourbong. The **tourist information office** (Mon–Fri 8.30am–4.45pm, Sat–Sun 10am–1pm; ☎07/4153 9289) is at 186 Bourbong St.

Central **accommodation** options include the *Grand Hotel* on 89 Bourbong St (☎07/4151 2441; ③), which has basic beds and inexpensive meals; the *Backpackers & Travellers Lodge*, opposite the bus terminal on Targo Street (☎07/4152 2080; ①), a clean but usually full hostel; and the rough-and-ready *City Centre Backpackers,* 216 Bourbong St (☎07/4151 3501; ①) near the train station, that's efficiently-run but afflicted by traffic noise. Both hostels specialize in finding seasonal farm work for travellers and most residents are there to work. The closest **campsite** is *Finemore Caravan Park* (☎07/4151 3663; ③), on Quay Street. At Mon Repos Beach, near Bargara, try the first-rate beachfront *Turtle Sands Caravan Park* (☎07/4159 2340), right next to the turtle rookery and complete with an aspiring **restaurant**, cabins (③) and tent sites. In Bargara, at 6 Trevors Rd, is *Kelly's Beach Resort* (☎07/4154 7200 or free call ☎1800/246 141; cabins ⑦), whose self-contained units are a good deal for groups. Everywhere will be full over the Christmas holidays, and the hostels are reluctant to take advance bookings except in the quieter months from January to March.

The cafés and hotels along Bourbong Street are about the only places in town that provide good **food** and after-dark entertainment; try the *Grand Hotel*'s spread, which is geared towards grills, or the good-value counter meals at the *Old Bundy Tavern*, at the junction of Quay and Tantitha streets.

Listings

Airlines Ansett (☎13 1300); Sunstate (☎13 1313).

Airport On the Bundaberg–Childers road, about 4km from the city centre.

Banks At various locations along Bourbong St.

Buses Greyhound Pioneer (☎13 2030); McCafferty's (☎07/4152 9700).

Camping equipment Bundaberg Camping World, 15 Takalvan St (☎07/4151 5436).

Diving Sites include Nudibranch Park, the encrusted wreck of a Beaufort bomber, and Evan's Patch, where you can see groupers, pelagics and sea snakes. Decent shore diving in the area makes Bundaberg a very cheap place to learn (four-day open-water courses start at just $149): best is Salty's, 208 Bourbong St (☎07/4151 6422, fax 4152 6707), near the *City Centre Backpackers*, who have their own boat; Aqua Scuba, next to the bus terminal on Targo St (☎07/4153 5761), is a good alternative.

NPWS Government Office Building, 46 Quay St, near the Burnett Bridge (☎07/4153 8620). All camping on southern reef islands must be arranged through the Gladstone office – see opposite.

Post office 157b Bourbong St (☎07/4153 2700).

Shopping centre Maryborough St.

Taxi ☎07/4151 2345.

Train station McLean St (☎07/4153 9724; bookings ☎13 2232).

Lady Elliot Island

The southern outpost of the Great Barrier Reef, **Lady Elliot Island** has suffered over the years from phosphate mining and the effects of feral goats. In their wake, vegetation is returning, with soft leaved pisonia trees asserting themselves over a bed of pulverized coral rubble, sand, and – in common with all the southern cays – a thick layer of **guano**, courtesy of the generations of birds which have roosted here. The elegant **lighthouse** was built in 1866 after an extraordinary number of wrecks on the reef; on average, one vessel a year still manages to come to grief here. Wailing shearwaters (muttonbirds) and the occasional suicide of lighthouse staff didn't endear the island to early visitors, but it has since become a popular escape with those who value the very remoteness that once haunted those stationed here.

One of the main reasons to come to Lady Elliot is to go **diving and snorkelling**, and the area certainly has its moments: visibility is always above 20m, and all year round you've a good chance of encountering **loggerhead turtles** and graceful, gigantic **manta rays**. Shore dives cost $25 for the first two, then $10 for each dive on the same day; boat dives cost $35, a night dive $45.

The island can only be reached **by air** on daily flights from Bundaberg with Sunstate (day return $185, including use of resort facilities, snorkelling gear and glass-bottom boat; 2-night packages from $360; ☎13 1313). Accommodation at **Lady Elliot Island Resort** (reservations free call ☎1800/072 200, information ☎07/4125 5344; ⑤–⑧) is comfortable, if not opulent, with meals (but not flights) included in the rates; better value are packages that include airfare and stand-by bookings.

Lady Musgrave Island

Lady Musgrave Island is a pretty place where encircling coral forms a large turquoise lagoon scattered with trawlers, its trees home to nesting colonies of **black noddies** between November and February. **Diving** the shallow coral outcrops is pretty tame, but it is worthwhile **snorkelling**, and seasoned divers may be able to visit the more exciting outer lagoon walls. Lady Musgrave is the best of the southern cays on which to **camp**, although light sleepers will want to avoid a stay during the tern nesting season.

Day **cruises** on *MV Lady Musgrave* depart from Bundaberg Port Marina (Mon–Thurs & Sat 8.30am; $108 day return, $216 if you stay over), about thirty minutes' drive from Bundaberg. The booking office is at the marina (☎07/4159 4519) and the staff can organize a **bus pick-up** from your accommodation ($7). **Private tours** also run from the settlement of 1770 – see below for details. The island has no facilities, although you can arrange with *MV Lady Musgrave* to bring fresh provisions if you're staying for a while – for practical details see the "Island camping" box on p.406.

Agnes Water and 1770

On the coast 100km north of Bundaberg, but most easily reached along the bumpy 65-kilometre road which leaves the highway at **Miriam Vale**, the tiny settlements of **AGNES WATER** and nearby **1770** mark where Captain Cook first set foot ashore in Queensland on May 24, 1770. It's a pretty area, and one of the few undeveloped places along the Queensland coast that can be reached without a 4WD. If you don't have your own transport, you can take a **bus from Bundaberg** leaving on Tuesday at 1.30pm from outside Sugarland Shoppingtown ($20 return). Nearby attractions include the mangrove, fan palm and paperbark wetlands at **Eurimbula National Park**, whose dirt tracks are usually negotiable to vehicles other than 4WDs in dry conditions, and the coast at Agnes Water, which has Queensland's northernmost official **surfing beaches** – though with the reef's lower reaches offshore, don't expect too much from the waves. 1770 is also the closest point on the mainland to the southern cays, from where there is regular transport to two Barrier Reef islands.

Agnes Water itself consists of a service station, a few stores and a smattering of houses set a few hundred metres back from the sea, while 1770 is even smaller, occupying the foreshore of a narrow promontory some 6km north. In 1770, the *Captain Cook Holiday Village* (☎07/4974 9219) has **rooms** and dorms (①–③), a store, bar and bistro, but the nearby beach is not a good place to go paddling – heed the signs warning you about stonefish. For Eurimbula, head 10.5km back towards Miriam Vale from Agnes Water, where you'll see the track and national park sign to the north of the road. Bring all supplies with you, so you can **bushcamp** about 15km inside the park in the dunes behind **Bustard Beach** – ask at the Agnes Water service station for directions.

Apart from a quiet natural beauty, what makes the whole area so appealing is the number of local **tour operators**, all ready to take you around the wilds. *The Larc* (☎07/4974 9422) is an **amphibious bus** that explores the coastline. With advance notice and camping permits from the Gladstone NPWS, you can even take a **water taxi** (☎07/4974 9077) to Lady Musgrave Island at around $200 return, which includes snorkelling gear and water containers (for island details see p.402-407).

Gladstone and nearby islands

GLADSTONE is a busy port, and also the site of the Boyne Island processing plant which refines aluminium from ore mined at Weipa on the Cape York Peninsula. Glaringly hot, it's not an unfriendly place, and there's no reason to stop here unless you're trying to reach the reef. In fact, if you're planning to camp on any of the southern cays, it's here that you need to make arrangements – through the **NPWS office** (136 Goondoon St; ☎07/4972 6055; Mon–Fri 8.30am–5pm).

The main strip is Goondoon Street, where there's a "mall" – just the usual high-street shops, post office and banks – and a couple of hotels and motels. You'll find a helpful

THE GREAT BARRIER REEF

The **Great Barrier Reef** is to Australia what rolling savannahs and game parks are to Africa, and is equally subject to the corniest of representations. "Another world" is the commonest cliché, which, while being completely true, doesn't begin to describe the feeling of donning mask and fins and coming face to face with extraordinary animals, shapes and colours. There's so little relationship to life above the surface that distinctions normally taken for granted – such as that between animal, plant and plain rock – seem blurred, while the respective roles of observer and observed are constantly challenged by shoals of curious fish following you about.

Beginning with Lady Elliot Island, off the coast from Bundaberg, and extending 2300km north to New Guinea, the Barrier Reef follows the outer edge of Australia's continental plate, running closer to land as it moves north: while it's 300km to the main body from Gladstone, Cairns is barely 50km distant from the reef. Far from being a continuous, unified structure, the nature of the reef also changes along its length, forming long **ribbons** north of Cairns, concentrated groups of low sand **cays** further south, and **fringing reef** around islands. All of it, however, was built by one animal: the tiny **coral polyp**. Simple organisms, related to sea anemones, polyps huddle together like building blocks into modular colonies – corals – which form the framework of the reef's ecology by providing food, shelter and hunting grounds for larger, more mobile species. Around their walls and canyons flow a bewildering assortment of creatures: large rays and turtles "fly" effortlessly by, fish dodge between caves and coral branches, snails sift the sand for edibles, and brightly coloured nudibranchs dance above rocks.

The reef is administered by the **Marine Parks Authority**, which gamely tries to battle against – or at least gauge – the effects of overfishing, industrial and agricultural pollution, and tourism. Under funding, and the lengthy study time required to find practical long-term solutions for the reef's protection, mean that little has been achieved to date. The most obvious signs of damage – broken and dead coral – are probably due to the sheer volume of visitors, with divers bumping against outcrops and boats dropping anchors. A popular villain, the **crown of thorns starfish**, undoubtedly causes severe destruction during cyclic plagues, but not enough to account for the level of damage you'll see. Don't let this put you off going – damage is restricted to only a handful of sites, and overall the reef is still healthy. But it's clear that the reef needs to be treated with respect if it is to retain its natural wonder. In order to minimize damage, visitors should take care not to stand on shallow reefs when snorkelling, and always avoid touching coral; even if you don't break off branches, you'll certainly crush the delicate polyps.

DIVING AND OTHER WAYS OF SEEING THE REEF

If you have the money, **scuba diving** is the best way to come to grips with the reef, and **dive courses** are on offer right along the coast. **Five days** is the minimum needed to safely cover the course work – three days' pool and theory, two days at sea – and secure you the all-important C-card. The quality of training and the price you pay vary enormously. Cheaper courses tend to have a higher student-to-instructor ratio, which means that problems can go unnoticed for longer; less importantly, island reefs are used rather than the main reef. The best deals are to be had where the tourists go – Airlie Beach or Cairns – but you'll also find a higher proportion of more dubious courses in these places. With adequate funds and time, you're better off learning away from these centres and then diving them once you're qualified. Another consideration is whether you ever plan to go diving again: if this seems unlikely, **resort dives** (a single dive with an instructor) will set you back only $50 or so, and they're usually available on day-trips to the reef and island resorts.

information centre (Mon–Fri 8.30am–5pm, Sat–Sun 9am–5pm) inside the ferry terminal, at the marina. A casual, basic **hostel** is hidden away at 12 Rollo St (☎07/4972 5744; ①); to get there, go to the marina end of Goondoon Street, turn left and it's three

While the extra weight will be a drag between dives, **qualified divers** can save on rental costs by bringing some gear along; tanks and weightbelts are normally covered in dive packages but anything else is extra. You need an alternative air source, timer, C-card and log book to dive in Queensland (the last is often ignored but some places insist, especially for deep or night-time dives).

Snorkelling is a good alternative to diving: you can pick up the basics in about five minutes and with a little practice the only thing you sacrifice is the extended dive time that a tank allows. If you think you'll do a fair amount, buy your own mask and snorkel – they're not dramatically expensive – as rental gear nearly always leaks. Look for a silicone rubber and toughened glass mask and ask the shop staff to show you how to find a good fit. If getting wet just isn't for you, try glass-bottomed boats or "subs", which can still turn up everything from sharks to oysters.

REEF HAZARDS

Stories of shark attacks, savage octopuses and giant clams all make good press, but are mostly the stuff of fiction and lurid exaggeration. However, there are a few things at the reef capable of putting a dampener on your holiday, and it makes sense to be careful. **Coral and shell cuts** are the commonest of mishaps, and become infected if not treated immediately by removing any fragments and dousing with antiseptic. **Tropical ear** is a fungal infection of the ear canal and can be very painful in its advanced stage. Treatment is with ear drops and if you think you might be susceptible, use them anyway after getting wet. **Animals** to avoid tend to be small (3–15cm). Shore divers might encounter the dangerous **box jellyfish** (see warning on p.26). Jellyfish found at the reef can cause nausea and raise a painful weal, but they're not life-threatening – wearing a Lycra "stinger suit" or full wetsuit with hood ensures protection. Some **corals** can also give you a nasty sting, but this is more a warning to keep away in future than something to worry about seriously.

In fact, the best protection at the reef is simply to look and not touch, as nothing is actively out to harm you. Brightly patterned, conical **cone shells** are home to a fish-eating snail armed with a poisonous barb which has caused fatalities in people who've picked them up. Don't: there is no "safe" end to hold them. Similarly, the shy, small, **blue-ringed octopus** has a fatal bite and should never be handled. **Stonefish** are nightmarish creatures, so well camouflaged that they're almost impossible to distinguish from a rock or lump of coral. They spend their days immobile, sucking in anything small and edible that floats past, and protected from reprisals by a series of poisonous spines along their back. If you tread on one, you'll end up in hospital – an excellent argument against reef-walking. Of the larger animals, **rays** are timid, flattened fish with a sharp spine capable of causing deep wounds – don't swim close over sandy floors where they hide. The most commonly encountered **sharks** are the black-tip and white-tip varieties, and the bottom-dwelling, aptly named carpet shark, or wobbegong – all of these are small and inoffensive unless hassled.

REEF TAX

The Marine Parks Authority introduced a reef tax (currently $4 per person per day) in April 1998 to help fund monitoring and management of human impact on the reef. On most tours and boat trips, you will be required to pay reef-tax in addition to the cost of the tour (unless it has been included in the price). A three-day dive trip, for example, will incur tax of $12. You may feel a little annoyed at having to fork out the extra money, especially if you've already paid quite a lot for your trip but; this is simply a "user-pays" system to help ensure that the reef is maintained for everyone to experience and enjoy.

streets down past a small real estate agent, or give them a call and they'll pick you up when you arrive. *Gladstone Reef Hotel*, 38 Goondoon St (☎07/4972 1000; ⑥), has ordinary **motel** rooms and good views from a rooftop pool. **Cafés** in the mall range from

---

ISLAND CAMPING

Campers intending to stay over on undeveloped southern reef cays need to organize permits and transport well in advance, particularly for the Christmas and Easter periods, and to contact the boat operator a few days before departure to check on weather conditions – rough seas can suspend services to the islands. **Camping permits** are only issued by the Gladstone NPWS (see p.403), and you need to be entirely self-sufficient: take food, at least five litres of water per person per day, a fuel stove (wood fires are prohibited), waterproof tents and sand pegs, shovels, first-aid kit, a radio (for weather forecasts), spare batteries, garbage bags and emergency rations for at least two extra days.

Munchies at 46 Goondoon St, a cheap and cheerful Mexican place with budget lunches during the week, to *Swaggy's*, 52 Goondoon St, where you can spoil yourself with native cuisine – emu, crocodile, kangaroo – at gourmet prices. Hotel **entertainment** is patchy: mud wrestling and live bands seem to be standard fare.

Diving can be arranged through Gladstone Diving at Last Wave Watersports, 16 Goondoon St (☎07/4972 9185). They take qualified divers out for the weekend (Fri–Sun; $320), and offer a seven-day dive course for $395 all-inclusive. It's good value given that, on a budget, this is the only way you'll get to see Heron reef.

Tryon and Masthead islands

Remote both in feel and location, **Tryon** and **Masthead** islands remain virtually undisturbed, with limited numbers of campers permitted at any one time. Masthead takes about an hour to walk around, and Tryon is even smaller. Both are valuable **nesting sites** for turtles, burrowing brown shearwaters (muttonbirds), tree-roosting black noddies and mixed colonies of black-naped, roseate and crested terns nesting in the open. The ruckus generated can be quite disturbing, but in the right frame of mind this all becomes part of the experience. Don't overlook the reef's **snorkelling** or **fishing** if you have the gear, though bear in mind that certain sections of reef are protected zones where fishing is prohibited – check first with the NPWS in Gladstone.

The only way to reach Tryon and Masthead from Gladstone is by **charter boat**, and at $3000 minimum, you'll need to get a group together for it to be financially viable: call Gladstone Marina Bait & Tackle Shop (☎07/4972 7283) for leads on available boats. Check the "Island camping" box above for practical details.

Heron Island

Famous for its diving, **Heron Island** escaped the depredations of goats and guano hunters earlier this century and, though a turtle-canning factory operated on the island for several years, it has survived more or less intact. Small enough to walk around in a relaxed thirty minutes, about half the cay is occupied by a comfortable **resort** and **research station**, the rest covered in groves of pandanus, coconuts, and shady pisonias, whose sticky seeds are unwittingly spread between islands on the backs of birds. Patches of long grass hide ground-dwelling **rails** (moorhen-like birds) which rocket from underfoot. And **herons** *do* stalk around the coral tops at low tide, fishing the pools – they're typically white, but a black form also frequents the area. Where the trees thin out, sand takes over, ringing the island.

As you move deeper into the water, you see coral starting to grow immediately below the tide line, and you can literally walk off the beach and into the reef's maze of coral, or swim along the shallow walls looking for action. The eastern edges of the lagoon are good for snorkelling at any time, but **diving** must be arranged through the resort (see

"Practicalities" below), which charges $44 for a standard dive, and $65 to venture out at night; equipment is extra. Dive **packages** save a few dollars if you're staying long enough to take advantage of them, and you can make two dives daily for free during June. Serious dive-fiends should listen out for news on the **dive festival** which was once a biannual event. It might not be held until 2001, but when it does take place there will be a chance to rub shoulders with visiting veterans and pick up workshop hints on equipment use and photography (check with Gladstone's travel agents, listed under "Practicalities", below).

A drift along the wall facing Wistari reef to Heron Bommie covers about everything you're likely to encounter. The coral itself took a pounding in 1992 when a cyclone hit at low tide with the reef exposed, yet the amount of life is astonishing: tiny boxfish hide under ledges; turtles, cowries, wobbegong, reef sharks, moray eels, butterfly cod and octopuses secrete themselves among the coral; manta rays soar majestically, and larger reef fish gape vacantly as you drift past. The Bommie itself makes first-rate **snorkelling**, with an interesting swim-through if your lungs are up to it, while the Tenements along the reef's northern edge are good for bigger game – including sharks.

Practicalities

There is a price to pay for all this natural wonder, namely no day-trips and no camping. The P&O-owned resort (reservations ☎13 2469; island reception ☎07/4972 9055; ⑧) is excellent but its rates, coupled with the ferry charge ($150) place it well outside the budget bracket. **Stand-by fares** (booked no more than 48 hours in advance; $110) offered by travel agents in Gladstone are worth looking into – try Traveland, 124 Goondoon St (☎07/4972 2288). **Ferries** leave from Gladstone Marina daily at 11am, except at Christmas; there's a **car lockup** here ($8 a day) operated by the tackle shop (8am–5pm).

THE TROPICS: ROCKHAMPTON TO CAPE YORK

Rockhampton marks the start of the tropics, but with the exception of the Mackay region, it's not until you're well past the line and north of **Townsville** that the tropical greenery associated with north Queensland finally appears. Then it comes in a rush, and by the time you've reached **Cairns** there's no doubt that the area deserves its reputation: coastal ranges covered in rainforest and cloud descend right to the sea. **Islands** along the way lure you with good beaches, hiking tracks and opportunities for snorkelling and diving: the **Keppels** near Rockhampton, the **Whitsundays** off Airlie Beach, **Magnetic Island** opposite Townsville, **Hinchinbrook** and **Dunk** further north. Cairns itself serves as a base for exploring highland rainforest on the **Atherton Tablelands** and coastal jungles in the **Daintree**, and for trips onto the **Cape York Peninsula** and, of course, out to the most accessible sections of the **Great Barrier Reef**.

Rockhampton and around

ROCKHAMPTON straddles the Tropic of Capricorn, an hour north of Gladstone, and was founded by accident. A false goldrush in 1858 left hundreds of miners stranded at a depot 40km inland, on the banks of the sluggish **Fitzroy River**; their rough camp below **Mount Archer** was soon put to use by local stockmen as a convenient port. The iron trelliswork and sandstone buildings fronting the river stand as a testament to the balmy 1890s, when money was pouring into the city from central Queensland's pros-

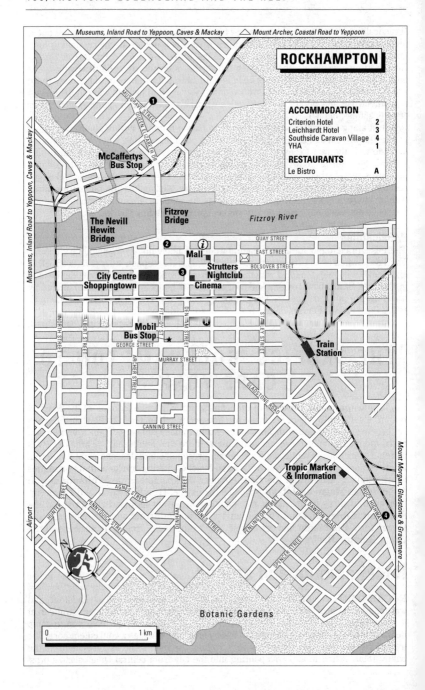

△ *Museums, Inland Road to Yeppoon, Caves & Mackay*   △ *Mount Archer, Coastal Road to Yeppoon*

ROCKHAMPTON

ACCOMMODATION

Criterion Hotel	2
Leichhardt Hotel	3
Southside Caravan Village	4
YHA	1

RESTAURANTS

Le Bistro	A

McCaffertys Bus Stop

The Nevill Hewitt Bridge

Fitzroy Bridge

Fitzroy River

QUAY STREET

EAST STREET

BOLSOVER STREET

Mall

City Centre Shoppingtown

Strutters Nightclub

Cinema

Mobil Bus Stop

GEORGE STREET

MURRAY STREET

Train Station

CANNING STREET

GLADSTONE ROAD

Tropic Marker & Information

AGNES STREET

AGNES STREET

SPENCER STREET

Botanic Gardens

0   1 km

perous cattle industry and the gold and copper mines at nearby **Mount Morgan**. Appallingly humid summers convince most visitors to use the city simply as a springboard for the adjacent Capricorn Coast (see p.412), but there are a few unusual diversions: an Aboriginal version of history at the **Dreamtime Centre**; a group of **limestone caves** which you can explore with or without a guide; and the mining town of Mount Morgan itself.

The City and surroundings

It doesn't take long to look around the city. The **Tropic Marker** at its southern entrance is just a spire informing you of your position at 23° 26' 30" S. And, apart from a riverside stroll to take in the architecture or the brown-stained boulders in midstream that gave the city its name, that's about it – though there are turn-of-the-century buildings around, as well as the very pleasant **Botanic Gardens**, whose main entrance is on Spencer Street.

About 5km north on the Bruce Highway, the **Dreamtime Cultural Centre** (daily 10am–3.30pm; tours with an Aboriginal guide from 10.30am; $11) was built in 1988 both to educate visitors and as a cultural focus for Torres Strait Islanders and central Queensland Aborigines. Inside, chronological and Dreamtime histories are intermingled, with a broad dissection of the archeology and mythology of Carnarvon Gorge (see p.481). Outside, surrounded by woodland, modern gunyahs (shelters of bark and branches) and stencil art, you'll find an unlikely walk-through dugong, and the original stone rings of a **bora ground** which marked the main camp of the Darumbal, whose territory reached from the Keppel Bay coastline inland to Mount Morgan. The tour also introduces plant usage, plus boomerang, dance, and didgeridoo skills – audience participation is definitely encouraged.

Rockhampton also has a couple of staid settlers' museums. **Glenmore Homestead** (Sun only 11am–3pm, unless by group booking; $6, including guided tour) is about 5km north – look for the turning left. The homestead was founded in the 1850s and the buildings remain rare period pieces, from the original beam hut, with gun ports to fend off Aboriginal attacks, to the more substantial homestead. Roughly 4km outside town, the **Heritage Village** (daily 10am–4pm; $9.50) is an eccentric, eclectic collection of such things as vintage cars, whaling cannons and a New Guinea outrigger canoe.

The Caves

The limestone hills 25km north of Rockhampton are riddled with an interesting **cave** system discovered in the 1880s. The caves have few classic stalagmites and stalactites, which need continuous dripping water to form; instead, there are tree roots encased in stone after forcing their way down through rocks, "cave corals" and "frozen waterfalls" – minerals deposited by evaporation after annual floods. The **ghost bat** (Australia's only carnivorous bat) and the **little bent-winged bat** – both now endangered – seasonally use the caves for roosts, and you might catch the odd group huddled together on the ceilings, eyes peering down at you over leaf-shaped noses.

There are three sets of caverns open to the public, all reached by turning off the Bruce Highway at The Caves township. Cross the rail line and bear left, and **Etna Caves National Park** is straight on past a council depot and around to the right. For **Cammoo** (daily 8.30am–5.30pm; self-guided, $7) and **Olsen's** (daily 9am–4pm; guided, $11), turn right after the hotel and follow the billboards. Etna caves are undeveloped but none too extensive; between February and June you can explore on your own (6am to 8pm; take a torch and durable shoes), or between November and February you can go on a **bat tour** (four evenings a week; $6.40) with the NPWS – contact them for details. Cammoo and Olsen's are both quite impressive, with plenty of spotlights and coloured gel illuminating their interiors. Olsen's is generally the more interesting, with some monster caverns and various "adventure" tours. **Bus tours** to Olsen's leave at 9.30am on Monday, Wednesday and Friday from the Arcade Carpark, near the *Leichhardt Hotel* on Bolsover Street (book first on ☎07/4934 2883; $25).

Mount Morgan and Gracemere

Gold was found at **MOUNT MORGAN** in 1880 and the area became one of the richest prospects in Queensland; from the lookout hill across the Dee River, you can still see the 342-metre-deep mine terraces. While gold petered out in the first years of the twentieth century, enough **copper** was found to keep the mine active until 1981. Apart from its deposits, Mount Morgan is famous for its instrumental role in the formation of the BP company, which was founded by William Knox D'Arcy after he had made his money through shares in the mine. The township is 40km south of Rockhampton along Highway 17, and Young's **buses** make the trip four times daily Monday to Friday and twice on Saturday; the last bus back to Rockhampton is at 5.15pm on weekdays and at 1pm on Saturday (call ☎07/4922 3813 for departure points and times).

Although rumours abound that recent exploration and reprocessing could lead to the mines reopening, the town itself seems to have scarcely changed; among the dated pubs and houses it's easy to feel as if you've stepped back fifty years. The only recent intrusion is the crumbling tarmac on the road. A functioning **steam train** and shiny silver fettlers' trolley provide more period ambience (book rides in advance on ☎07/4938 2312), while the **museum** (Mon–Sat 10am–1pm, Sun 10am–4pm), on the corner of Morgan and East streets, has a geology display which includes some plesiosaur fossils, minerals and local history exhibits. Mt. Morgan Goldmine & Dinosaur Cave Tours (☎07/4938 1661) visit the mine and a nearby cave with more bats, and **dinosaur footprints** on the ceiling.

Finally, if you really want to see what makes Rockhampton tick, catch the action at **Australia's largest cattle yards** at **GRACEMERE**, a small town about 9km west of the city towards Emerald along the Capricorn Highway. The weekly Monday sale, starting at 7.30am, can be interesting, but watch out for bigger monthly events and irregular special sales, which pull in some unlikely characters – and whopping brahmin cattle – from out in the boondocks.

Practicalities

Rockhampton is divided by the Fitzroy River, with all services clustered directly south of the **Fitzroy Bridge** along Quay Street and East Street Mall. McCafferty's **buses** stop just north of the bridge, and also across the river at the George Street Mobil service station, 500m south of the centre, where Greyhound Pioneer also pull up. The **train** station is east of the centre on Murray Street. Driving in, the Bruce Highway runs right through town past two pairs of fibreglass bulls (repeatedly "de-balled" by pranksters). **Tourist information** is available from the booth on the highway at the Tropic Marker, or at the more comprehensive and central **Riverside information centre** on Quay Street (Mon–Fri 8.30am–4.30pm, Sat–Sun 9am–4pm; ☎07/4922 5339). Recent reports of nasty incidents involving gangs of Aboriginal teenagers are unfortunately too numerous to ignore; there's no need for paranoia, but do follow local advice and don't walk alone at night.

The pick of the **accommodation** choices are the good-value suites overlooking the river at the historic *Criterion Hotel* on Quay Street (☎07/4922 1225, fax 4922 1226; ③), which occupies the site of Rockhampton's first pub, the *Bush Inn*, built in 1857. Tatty motel-style units are available at the *Leichhardt Hotel* in the centre on Bolsover Street (☎07/4927 6733, fax 4927 8075; ③), where renovations are set to improve standards and boost prices. Budget options include the YHA's well-appointed but dreary and isolated compound north of the river at 60 MacFarlane St (☎07/4927 5288; ①); or the *Southside Caravan Village* on the highway 2km south (☎07/4927 3013; ①–③), with **tent sites**, cramped on-site vans, shop, pool and pick-ups from town. If your only reason for being in Rockhampton is to get to Great Keppel, there's little reason to stay over with Yeppoon and the ferry terminals so close by.

A **steak** of some kind is the obvious choice in Australia's "Beef Capital", and any of the hotels can oblige. There's a smattering of cafés around the mall, while at *Le Bistro* on William Street (Mon–Sat 6.30pm–late), upmarket steak and fish dishes are served along with a couple of vegetarian options, and main courses are about $20. A perch at the *Criterion*'s bar is recommended for steak and beer, and elbow-to-elbow closeness with a few locals. For **nightlife**, there's the cinema on Denham Street, and a nightclub at *Strutters* on the Mall (Wed–Sun 8pm until late) for disco and frequent **live bands**.

Moving on, the Capricorn Highway heads towards Emerald and points west (see *Outback Queensland* beginning on p.474), while the Bruce Highway continues north. The Capricorn Coast is serviced by local **buses**: Young's (☎07/4922 3813) run at least five times daily from Denham Street, near the corner with Bolsover Street, to **Yeppoon** ($13; free for Greyhound pass holders) and all points along the Capricorn Coast; while Rothery's Coaches (☎07/4922 4320) make three daily departures from outside the *Leichhardt Hotel* to **Rosslyn Bay ferry terminal** ($14 return, or $41 including ferry fare to Great Keppel Island).

Listings

Airlines Ansett, 137 East St (☎07/4922 2750 or ☎13 1300); Qantas, 107 East St (☎13 1313). The airport is located at the end of Hunter St.

Banks Branches are located in or around the Queen Street Mall.

Buses Greyhound Pioneer, 91 George St (☎07/4921 1890); McCafferty's, corner of Brown and Linnett streets (☎07/4927 2844); Rothery's, 13 Power St, North Rockhampton (☎07/4922 4320); Young's, 274 George St (☎07/4922 3813).

Camping equipment Campco's, corner of William and Kent streets (☎07/4922 2366).

Car rental Network, corner of George and Archer streets (☎07/4922 2990); Rockhampton Car Rentals, south on the Bruce Highway (☎07/4922 7802); Thrifty, 47 Fitzroy St (☎07/4927 8755).

Diving Capricorn Reef Diving, 189 Musgrave St, North Rockhampton (☎07/4922 7720), gives certification courses from around $380 and offers dive courses around the Keppels. Qualified divers can organize trips to the Bunker and Capricorn groups.

Farm stays *Myella Farm*, The Eather Family, Myella, Barabala, Qld 4702 (☎07/4998 1290, fax 4998 1104), and *Cooper Downs Station*, Dennis Stevenson, Banana, Qld 4702 (☎07/4996 5276), are a couple of hours out of town and offer accommodation, meals and participation in farm life from ⑦ upwards.

Hospital Base Hospital, Canning St, South Rockhampton (☎07/4920 6211).

NPWS A helpful office situated 5km out of town on the Yeppoon–Rockhampton Road (☎07/4936 0511).

Pharmacy CQ Pharmacy, 150 Alma St, next to the cinema (☎07/4922 1621); daily 8am–10pm.

Police Denham St, near the East Street Mall (☎07/4932 1500).

Post office Mall80150 East St Mall (☎07/4927 6566).

RACQ 134 William St (☎07/4927 2255).

Shopping City Centre Plaza on Bolsover St.

State Forestry Department 109 Bolsover St (☎07/4927 6877); permits for access to Byfield National Park (see p.414)

Taxi ☎07/4922 7111.

Trail rides Pony Boys (☎07/4938 1855).

Trains Murray St (☎07/4932 0453).

The Capricorn Coast

Views from volcanic outcrops overlooking the **Capricorn Coast**, east of Rockhampton, stretch across graziers' estates and pineapple plantations to exposed headlands, estuarine mudflats and the **Keppel Islands** 20km offshore. The coastal townships of **Yeppoon** and **Emu Park**, settled by cattle barons in the 1860s, were soon adopted by Rockhampton's elite as places to beat the summer heat. Despite some modern development, the coast retains a pleasantly dated holiday atmosphere and is a good place for independent travel. Everyone heads for the fine beaches at **Great Keppel Island**, but other places – for example, the wilds at **Byfield** – are only just being discovered by visitors and remain largely untouched.

Rockhampton to Yeppoon: coast and inland

There are two routes to Yeppoon from Rockhampton: the coastal **Lakes Creek Road** (immediately north of the Fitzroy Bridge) past Emu Park and Rosslyn Bay, and the direct inland **Yeppoon Road**, off the Bruce Highway, 5km from town (opposite the Dreamtime Centre).

First stop on the **coastal road**, about 25km from Rockhampton, is **Koorana Crocodile Farm** (tours daily at 1pm; $12), where estuarine crocs are bred (*koorana* means "giving birth") to supply the leather industry and restaurants. If the reptiles' ultimate fate doesn't bother you, the tours are interesting – despite a certain amount of showmanship involved in the feeding and meeting of Koorana's "stars". Some of the crocs are penned individually, but most are viewed as manage from the safety of protected boardwalks, raised over the mudflats and ponds where the reptiles bask. With luck you might see babies hatching, bleating as they squeeze themselves out of tiny eggs.

The **sea** appears suddenly at **EMU PARK**, a breezy hillside covered by scattered "Queenslander" houses, a store, hotel and van park. From the cliffs at the **Singing Ship** the wind howls mournful tunes through the wires of this peculiar monument to Captain Cook. There's little to do between here and Yeppoon except take in the seascape; the road runs a gauntlet of units, van parks and campsites as it alternates between twisting headlands and flat beachfront. Possible stops might be at **KINKA BEACH**, where stir-crazy hawksbill turtles endlessly circle the motley aquarium, or **Rosslyn Bay**, where the cliffs have been weathered into hexagonal columns behind the **island ferry terminal and marina** (for details of getting to the islands, see p.413). There are good views from the windswept top; take some lunch to make it worthwhile. Further on, **COOEE BAY** is virtually a suburb of Yeppoon, with an annual "Cooee Competition" when competitors give their tonsils a good airing from Wreck Point.

Following the **inland road**, you'll find the plains dotted with **volcanic plugs**, some of which can be climbed. **Mount Jim Crow** is to the left of the highway, about 15km along the Yeppoon Road; look out for the well-hidden sign to the national park. From the car park, a rough track leads to a small quarry on the left side of the mountain, then follows shallow gullies and water run-offs uphill through some fairly dense scrub. What is really time-consuming is ploughing through the huge, tough webs of the **golden orb weaver spider**, whose thread – dozens of times stronger than silk – is now being used in the production of bullet-proof vests; fortunately, the gigantic female spiders are very timid. A good hour should see you safely at the top admiring the scenery; on the way down don't be tempted to take short cuts, as the rocks are unstable.

Yeppoon

Built around the sheltering hills of Spring Head, **YEPPOON** faces the various Keppel Islands over a blustery expanse of sand and sea. Though busy at Easter and Christmas, it generally keeps a low profile, and residents seem to cherish this tranquillity – to the extent that the *Capricorn International Resort* just along the coast was **bombed** when construction plans overruled local wishes.

All services are on James Street, at right angles to **Anzac Parade** with its seafront **accommodation**. *Tropical Nites Motel*, 34 Anzac Parade (☎07/4939 1914; ④), has small, self-contained rooms, but for views, you're better off at *Hacienda Holiday Units*, 18 Anzac Parade (☎07/4939 1370; ④), a tidy and quiet guesthouse. Friendly *Barrier Reef Backpackers*, 30 Queen St (☎07/4939 4702; four-bed dorms only, ①), has an attractive pool area that catches any afternoon breeze and operates a daily courtesy bus to Rockhampton to meet evening arrivals; call ahead to check exact times. The *Strand Hotel* (☎07/4939 1301; ③), on the corner of Anzac Parade and James Street, offers basic, four-bed units, while the *Blue Dolphin Caravan Park* (☎07/4939 3140), at 74 Whitman St, is relatively sheltered.

Kelly's Bar & Grill, next to the *Tropical Nites Motel*, claims to serve the best steaks in town, while a few doors down, *Pass da Pasta*, in a sprucer setting, is popular for its range of pastas, grills and salads. The **Keppel Bay Sailing Club** occupies two separate premises on opposite corners of Anzac Parade: the original building is still a good venue for a beer along with views of the islands, while the ritzy newer section has a poker-machine-filled restaurant that offers all-you-can-eat lunch ($6.50) and dinner ($9). Another budget option is the *Strand Hotel*'s "kiddies" steak / a fair-sized piece of cow with salad and chips for just $5. Otherwise there's a legion of cafés to choose from along James Street, with weekend entertainment at the Strand Hotel or at *Bonkers Nightclub*, one road back from Anzac Parade on Hill Street.

The Keppel Islands

The eighteen **Keppel Islands** boast white sand so fine that it squeaks when you walk through it, and the sea is an invitingly clear blue – just right for a few days of indolence. Most of the islands are national parks and, with the exception of North and Great Keppel, are very small. Easy access, coupled with a resort and associated facilities, has made **Great Keppel** the most popular, but there are also reefs to snorkel and isolated camping spots on the other islands.

All **access** is from **ROSSLYN BAY**, just off the main road about 8km south of Yeppoon on the coastal route to Rockhampton, with departures from both the **ferry terminal** (☎07/4933 6744), and the nearby new **marina** (☎07/4933 6244). For **Great Keppel**, *Reefcat, Spirit of Keppel* and *Keppel Kat* run a total of four daily return services from the ferry terminal (last leaves Great Keppel at 4.30pm), plus a late service on Fridays; all charge $27 return. The marina is also the place to find transport to **other islands**, or **cruises** beyond them; *Reef Chief* and *Euphoria* are among boats running charter trips (around $75 per person return, depending on passenger numbers). The ferry terminal and marina both have exposed **free parking**, though for protection from salt spray, leave your car undercover at Great Keppel Island Security Car Park ($7 a day), opposite the Rosslyn Bay junction on the main road.

Great Keppel

Arriving at **Great Keppel**, the ferry leaves you on a spit directly in front of the budget **accommodation** choices. *Keppel Haven* (☎07/4933 6744) occupies sheltered, sandy woodland behind Putney Beach, with beds in a pre-fab *Tent Village* (①) or self-contained cabins for up to six (⑧). *Keppel Kampout* (☎07/4939 2131; ⑤) has similar tent accommodation with all meals included in the price, and is specifically aimed at the 18–35s market. The brand new YHA facility (☎07/4927 5288; ①) is yet another tent village; facilities are basic, and the place feels a bit stark and military. *Great Keppel Island Holidays for Backpackers* (☎07/4939 8655; ①) has taken over the old YHA site and spruced it up with a first rate kitchen, and ongoing accommodation improvements. The cheerful owner encourages you to have a "soulful, eco-friendly stay" on the island; snorkelling gear is free, and no one has thus far been asked to pay on any of his impromptu sunrise motor-canoe tours of the island.

Along the beach, the modern and comfortable *Great Keppel Island Resort* (☎07/4939 5044; ③), or rather its *Wreck Bar*, is the island's after-dark social focus; by day, the resort cultivates a family atmosphere and there's a pool for day-trippers. Aside from the YHA and *Backpackers*, all of the above offer substantial savings on **packages** or **stand-by rates**, which are well worth checking out in advance. For food, *Keppel Haven* has a **restaurant** and occasional barbecues, and there's a tearoom at the *Shell House* on Fisherman's Beach. There is also a late-opening **pizza shack** – much frequented after the bar closes.

The main **beaches**, Putney and Fisherman's, are remarkably pleasant considering the number of people lounging on them at any one time, but the effort of a half-hour walk will reward you with some more secluded spots. **Leakes Beach** seldom hosts more than a handful of people; the quickest way there is up a steep path over the point at the rocky end of Putney. Reached on a woodland path past the resort, **Long Beach** attracts a few more sun-worshippers, while snorkellers make the short haul over sand dunes at the western end to shallow coral on **Monkey Beach**. Shell mounds on Monkey Beach were left by Woppaburra Aborigines, who were enslaved and forcibly removed to Fraser Island by early settlers.

Inland is dry, and the paths double as 4WD tracks for the island's few vehicles. For views, take the road behind the resort up a short and steep hill to the lookout. The best walk is the hour-long return trip up **Mount Wyndham**, ending on a cliff with the coast below. Longer excursions to Butterfish Bay, Wreck Beach or Bald Rock Point light-house and back will take at least four hours.

Other Keppels

The only way of getting to these islands is to contact the marina and enquire about boat charters (see p.413); once you're there, there are no **provisions**, and there is (unreliable) **drinking water** only on Humpy and North Keppel. NPWS camping **permits** can be picked up at the Rockhampton (see p.411) or Rosslyn Bay offices.

North Keppel is an undeveloped version of Great Keppel. There's an NPWS camp-site on the west side of the island, behind the dunes at Considine Bay, with a sporadic supply of tank water, showers and toilets; take precautions against sandflies, which are abundant in sheltered spots here, and note that wood fires are banned. A walking track from the group of cabins at the southern end of Considine Beach leads to the reef at Maisy Bay. Just to the south, **Pumpkin Island** is a privately owned area of beach, mangroves and coral with four basic but smart cabins (☎07/4939 2431; ②).

Middle Island is lightly wooded, with an NPWS camping area and **underwater observatory** complete with scenic Taiwanese junk. It's only a short hop from Great Keppel, and you might be able to pick up a day-trip from there to the observatory. If you plan to dive at Olive Head Point, watch out for sea snakes. **Humpy Island**, also off Great Keppel, is popular for fishing and has the best snorkelling reef of all the islands. The hump doesn't do much to protect it from the southeasterlies, which are the main problem with camping here; facilities are similar to those on North Keppel.

The Byfield Coast

Cape York aside, the northernmost stretch of the Capricorn Coast is the wildest area in eastern Australia. The biggest attraction is the scenery and wildlife at **Byfield National Park**, a massive system of tropical and subtropical forests, multicoloured parabolic sand dunes, rivers and swamps fed by underground reservoirs–one of the most unusual stretches of coast in the country. Even so, until disputes over **sand mining** erupted in the 1990s, few people had even heard of it. The lack of public transport means you need your own vehicle to explore.

Twenty kilometres from Yeppoon along the Byfield Road you come across a massive forestry plantation: neatly planted rows of Caribbean pines make for monotonous scenery, though there are two riverside **campsites** among the trees, both with self-registration, toilets, barbecues and tables – **Upper Stoney Creek** is the better. Pick up a free **permit** to use the track into the national park at the **Forestry Office** on the main road; shortly afterwards you reach a crossroads on the edge of the forest. **Nob Creek Pottery**, with its Anagama kiln and fruit trees, is to the left, minuscule **Byfield township** and the Shoalwater Bay Military Zone are straight ahead, and the coast road to the national park is to the right. This twenty-kilometre drive to the coast takes about forty minutes and is only accessible with a **4WD**; the road comes out at **Stockyard Point**, opposite Five Rocks Island's fish beds. If you camp here, note that the dunes are sensitive to erosion and clearing new sites doesn't help the problem. Access along the beaches may be restricted by tides, so check current conditions with the NPWS in Rockhampton.

Mackay and around

Some 360km north of Rockhampton along a famously unexciting stretch of the Bruce Highway, the fertile **Pioneer Valley** makes the **MACKAY** area a pleasant break from

---

SUGAR CANE ON THE TROPICAL COAST

Sugar cane, grown in an almost continuous belt between Bundaberg and Mossman, north of Cairns, is the tropical coast's economic pillar of strength. Introduced in the 1860s, the crop subtly undermined the racial ideals of British colonialists when farmers, planning a system along the lines of the southern United States, employed **Solomon Islanders** – Kanakas – to work the plantations. Though only indentured for a few years, and theoretically given wages and passage home when their term expired, Kanakas on plantations suffered greatly from unfamiliar diseases, while the recruiting methods used by "**Blackbirder**" traders were at best dubious and often slipped into wholesale kidnapping. Growing white unemployment and nationalism through the 1880s, rather than any humanitarian considerations, eventually forced the government to ban blackbirding and repatriate the islanders. Those allowed to stay were joined over the next fifty years by immigrants from Italy and Malta, who mostly settled in the far north and today form large communities scattered between Mackay and Cairns.

After cane has been planted in November, the land is quickly covered by a blanket of dusky green. Before cutting, seven months later, the fields are traditionally **fired** to burn off leaves and maximize sugar content – though the practice is dying out. Cane fires often take place at dusk and are as photogenic as they are brief; the best way to be at the right place at the right time is to ask at a mill. Cut cane is then transported to the mills along a rambling rail network.

The **mills** are incredible buildings, abandoned for half the year, with giant pipes and machinery looming out of makeshift walls. Cane is juiced for raw sugar or molasses, as the market dictates; crushed fibre becomes fuel for the boilers that sustain the process; and ash is returned to the fields as fertilizer. During operations the mills belch out steam around the clock and acquire a strange organic quality when they're lit up at night. You can get to grips with Mackay's **sugar industry** at **Polstone Cane Farm** (tours May–Dec Mon, Wed & Fri 1.30pm; ☎07/4959 7298; $12), where you get a rundown from a tractor-towed wagon; contact them for directions or to arrange a pick-up. **Farleigh Mill** (☎07/4957 4727; $12), north of Mackay, is open for tours during the crushing season (June–Nov Mon–Fri 1pm), and lay on a very popular evening tour (Wed 7pm).

the otherwise dry country between Bundaberg and Townsville. Despite encounters with aggressive Juipera Aborigines, John Mackay was impressed enough to settle the valley in 1861, and within four years the city was founded and the first **sugar cane plantations** were established. Today Mackay radiates a confidence built on sugar and **mining** operations centred inland on the **Bowen Basin coalfields** (see p.490); migrant communities common to the north rub shoulders in town and it's not unusual to hear English, Pidgin and Maltese spoken within earshot of each other. Now marketing itself as "The Natural North", Mackay provides some welcome relief from the east coast "backpackers pub crawl", and with its proximity to unspoilt beaches, plus the delights of **Eungella and Cape Hillsborough national parks,** this is not an area you'll want to miss. Cane plantations surrounding the city offer the chance to tour a mill or photograph a cane fire (see box overleaf), while offshore **Brampton Island** and local **reefs** promise similar attractions to the Whitsundays (see p.424)but without the volume of tourists.

Practicalities

Mackay's centre straddles the crossroads of Victoria Street and Sydney Street, with the **bus station** a short walk away on Milton Street. Both **trains** (station on Connors Road, off Milton Street along Boundary Road or Paradise Street) and **planes** arrive south of town; a taxi will set you back around $8 into town and $25 to Bucasia (for some beachfront accommodation). The **tourist information centre** (☎07/4952 2677) is inconveniently located 3km south of town along the **Nebo Road** (Druse Highway), but you can get help with bookings from accommodation or the bus station.

Accommodation
Nebo Road is a virtual landing strip of neon motel signs; rooms range from $35 to $105, with comfort and facilities according to price. For sun and sand, take the highway towards Townsville and then turn off and follow the signs for **Bucasia**.

Bobby Dazzlers, 64 Wood St (☎07/4957 7286). Smack in the centre of town, with pleasant rooms all recently repainted and carpeted. Doubles and twins, with TV and shared bathrooms, and a huge communal balcony right over Mackay's downtown action. Can get noisy on weekends. ③.

Bucasia Caravan Park, Bucasia Esplanade, Bucasia (☎07/4954 6375). Beachfront camping and units with nice island views. Few amenities, although there is a nearby store. ①–③.

Central Caravan Park, 15 Malcomson St (☎07/4957 6141). Closest park (1km) to the centre of town, though not terribly well kept (vans and caravans ③–④).

Crown & Anchor, River St (☎07/4953 1545). Old fishermen's pub right on the river, with added traveller-friendly communal kitchen and laundry facilities; large wraparound balcony adds to the appeal. Small twins, each with TV, shared bathrooms. ②.

Ko Huna Resort, at Bucasia (☎07/4954 8555 or free call ☎1800/075 128). Casual place with self-contained cabins, restaurant, bar, pool and free pick-up. ⑦.

Larrikin Lodge/YHA, 32 Peel St (☎07/4951 3728). Low-set, comfortable Queenslander house with a pleasant kitchen and laid-back atmosphere, two minutes' walk from the bus station. Phone ahead to arrange check-in outside the office opening hours (7–10am & 5–10pm). Dorms ①, doubles ③.

Paradise Lodge Motel, 19 Peel St (☎07/4951 3644). Right behind the bus station. Friendly owners, comfortable rooms with TV, but no pool. ③–④.

Eating
Mackay has plenty of good, cheap **places to eat**. There are snack bars all around the centre, or try one of the places below for a restaurant meal. Downtown pubs all offer lunch specials – around $3 for a full meal as does *Mackay Leagues Club.*

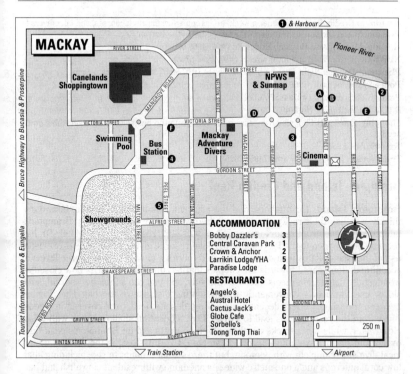

Angelo's, 27 Sydney St. Mediterranean cooking and genuine wood-fired pizzas.

Cactus Jack's, Victoria St (east end). Extraordinarily popular Tex-Mex joint which refuses bookings. Turn up early and prepare to have a few drinks at the bar while waiting for a table.

Coco's Bar & Grill (at the *Austral Hotel*), Victoria St (bus station end). A carnivore's dream, with marinated grilled steaks in 600g, 800g and 1kg servings for $15–20.

Globe Cafe, 36 Sydney St. A good range of coffees and cakes, plus an international menu that includes Belgian beer stew and plenty of salads. Open 10am–11pm; closed Mon evening.

Sorbello's, 168 Victoria St. Good choice for pastas and the typical range of Italian dishes for around $20 per person. Lunch specials Mon–Fri; open for dinner 7 days.

Toong Tong Thai, 10 Sydney St. Long-established Thai restaurant and takeaway with impeccable food, authentically hot and spicy if requested. Around $20 a head for a full meal.

Listings

Airlines Ansett, 113 Victoria St (☎07/4957 4566 or ☎13 1300); Qantas, 105 Victoria St (☎07/4957 4999 or ☎13 1313).

Banks Branches of all major banks are located around the intersection of Sydney and Victoria streets.

Bus terminal Milton St for all buses (☎07/4951 3088).

Camping equipment Great Outdoors Centre, corner of Victoria and Endeavour streets, east end of town (☎07/4957 2000).

Car rental Cut Rate Rentals, 105 Alfred St (☎07/4953 1616), are best, with 200km free for each day of rental – just enough to get you to Eungella National Park and back.

Cinema Multiscreen on Gordon St (☎07/4957 3515).

Diving Mackay Adventure Divers, 153 Victoria St (☎07/4953 1431, fax 4951 1472) make visits to the wreck *Llewellyn*, a seventy-five-year-old steamship submerged in thirty metres of water. They also run trips to Credlin Reef three times a week, offer regular certification courses, and take divers to local islands and the famous Hardline – the very edge of the Barrier Reef.

Hospital Mackay Base Hospital, Bridge Rd (☎07/4968 6000).

NPWS Corner of Wood and River streets (☎07/4951 8788).

Pharmacy Day and Night Pharmacy, 65 Sydney St (☎07/4957 3360); daily 8am–9pm.

Police Sydney St (☎07/4968 3444).

Post office Sydney St (☎07/4957 7333).

RACQ 214 Victoria St (☎07/4957 2918).

Shopping Canelands Shoppingtown, across the road from the bus station, has everything you'll need.

Taxi ☎07/4951 4999.

Train station Boddington St (☎07/4952 7425).

Brampton Island and Credlin Reef

Brampton Island, 1hr offshore, and the adjacent, uninhabited **Carlisle Island** are thickly wooded, their rocky shorelines dotted with pretty coral beaches. Brampton's unobtrusive beachfront **resort** (reservations ☎13 2469; resort ☎07/4951 4499; ⑧), has recently been added to the P&O stable of island resorts, giving resort guests exclusive use of the island. Rates include all meals, and there's a choice between three levels of accommodation geared towards the couples market; the "Kids Club" is now closed. A wonderfully dated train meets guests at the jetty, and you can sunbathe, snorkel, surf-ski or use the pool – conveniently within spitting distance of the bar. The channel between the islands offers decent snorkelling despite dead coral covered in weeds. Away from the resort, paths lead to **Turtle Bay**, a beautiful shallow beach with crisp, clear water, while other tracks cut through pine forests and up Brampton's peak (just over 200m high). Two hours beyond Brampton, **Credlin Reef** is the most touristed local dive site, complete with pontoon, but there's a fair amount to see, including shallow coral outcrops and a one-metre-wide sea anemone with resident clownfish and harlequin tuskfish. More adventurous divers should arrange in advance with Mackay Adventure Divers (see "Listings" on p.417) for access to the nearby **Catacombs**.

Cape Hillsborough and Newry Island

Cape Hillsborough, about an hour's drive north of Mackay, is the site of a pretty beachfront national park with tame wildlife. Offshore from here are the **Newry Islands**, home to the area's last remaining koalas. Reeforest Tours and Jungle Johno offer trips from Mackay to the national park (see below). If you're driving, head towards Townsville and take the signposted Seaforth Road from **The Leap**. This takes its name from events of 1866, when a settler was killed by Aborigines and the police drove an Aboriginal woman over the cliff during reprisals. The woman turned out to be holding a baby in her arms which miraculously survived and was adopted by a local family. *The Leap*, one of Mackay's oldest hotels, is right underneath, and you can contest the details of the story over a cold beer if you're interested. From here the road passes the inevitable canefields on the way to Mount Jukes, before descending to coastal flats. The road to Cape Hillsborough starts a couple of kilometres before **Seaforth** township and branches before the park, the right fork heading to the main area, the left terminating at undeveloped **Smalleys Beach**.

The national park

The main area of the national park is set around a flat, two-kilometre beach bounded by the wooded cliffs of Cape Hillsborough to the north and Andrews Point to the south;

the shallow bay is good for swimming outside the stinger season. Local fauna include bush turkeys and some butch **kangaroos** – they're often on the beach in the early morning, males flexing muscles and chasing does in a parody of the stereotypical Aussie male. Pitch your tent past the **ranger's office** at the sheltered council **campsite** (with water, showers and toilets). Hidden in bushland at the end of the road, *The Cape* (☎07/4959 0152; ④) has cabins, a **store** (which closes at 6pm) and a restaurant.

Trails head out to **Hidden Valley**, a palm forest on a rocky beach where you'll find middens and the outline of an **Aboriginal fish trap**. Dolphins and turtles are often seen from here and from the top of Andrew's Point. Another fine walk is to a **swimming hole** at the foot of the cape, reached either along the beach or by way of a track from the picnic area – see the park ranger for details.

Seaforth and Newry

SEAFORTH is a pleasant township with a store, caravan park and enclosure on the beach to ward off jellyfish. Beyond, the road runs up to **Port Newry** for access to **Newry Island** and uninhabited **Rabbit Island**, both quiet, untouristed locations with few great beaches but dense eucalypt woodland supporting a koala population introduced in the 1920s. Newry Island's **resort** has lately been suffering financial and public relations problems, with tales of female travellers being harassed; check its current status in Mackay before considering a visit. Camping is allowed only on **Outer Newry** and Rabbit islands; you'll first need to arrange a camping permit through the NPWS in Mackay, who'll also give you details on how to get there.

Eungella National Park

At the end of the bitumen, 80km west of Mackay, magical rainforest, mountains and rivers would make **EUNGELLA NATIONAL PARK** (pronounced "young-g'lla") worth the journey even if you weren't almost guaranteed to see **platypuses**. There are two separate sections: lowland swimming holes at **Finch Hatton Gorge** and highland forest at **Broken River**. Finch Hatton's rainforest is authentically tropical, while Broken River's plants are more closely allied with subtropical forests; isolation has produced

---

CANE TOADS

Native to South America, the huge, charismatically ugly **cane toad** was recruited in 1932 to combat a plague of greyback beetles, whose larvae were wreaking havoc with Queensland's sugar cane. The industry was desperate – beetles cut production by ninety percent in plague years – and resorted to seeding tadpoles in waterholes across the north. They thrived, but it soon became clear that toads couldn't reach the adult insects (who never landed on the ground), and they didn't burrow after the grubs. Instead they bred whenever possible, ate anything they could swallow, and killed predators with poisonous secretions from their neck glands. Native wildlife suffered: birds learned to eat non-toxic parts, but snake populations have been seriously affected. Judging from the quantity of flattened carcasses on summer roads (running them over is an unofficial sport), there must be millions lurking in the canefields, and they're gradually spreading into the Northern Territory and New South Wales. Given enough time, they seem certain to infiltrate most of the country.

The toad's outlaw character has generated a cult following, with its warty features and nature the subject of songs, toad races, T-shirt designs, a brand of beer and the award-winning film *Cane Toads: An Unnatural History* – worth seeing if you come across it on video. The record for the largest specimen goes to a 1.8kg monster found in Mackay in 1988.

several unique species, including the Mackay tulip oak, the Eungella honeyeater and the much-discussed but probably extinct **gastric brooding frog**, known for incubating its young in its stomach.

Day-trips to both sections of the park can be arranged from Mackay: Reeforest Tours (☎07/4952 2677; $59), and Jungle Johno (☎07/4959 1822; $55) both run excellent tours, with Johno's personalized, laid-back style and inventive "bush-tucker" yarns appealing particularly to young travellers. Otherwise, rent a car from Mackay (see "Listings" on p.417), head south down the Nebo Road (Bruce Highway) to the city limits and follow the signs.

Finch Hatton Gorge

The Eungella road passes through prime cane country as it runs the length of the **Pioneer Valley**. Some 60km from Mackay, signposts just before Finch Hatton township mark the turn-off to **Finch Hatton Gorge**, 12km from the main road across several fords. Access depends on the season, though generally it's negotiable by all vehicles. Immediately across the first creek, *Platypus Bush Camp* (☎07/4958 3204; bunkbeds ①, or camping at $5 per person), provides the sole **accommodation**: mattress, pillow, amenities and kitchen are supplied, and the rest (including food) is up to you. This is the most authentic rainforest experience you can have anywhere in Queensland: you'll see an astonishing array of bird- and animal-life (including the elusive platypus), sit by a fire under the stars, shower in the rainforest amidst fairy-like fireflies, and be lulled to sleep by a gurgling creek. Both tour operators (see above) can leave you at the bush camp, and collect you when you're ready to leave.

About another kilometre further there is a small tearoom, and then the road ends at a picnic area, with walking tracks leading off into the forest. The gorge winds down the side of Mount Dalrymple as a rocky creek pocked with swimming holes and overshadowed by a hot jungle of palms, vines and creepers – the sort of scenery Hollywood dreams about. **Araluen Falls** (1.5km from the picnic area), a beautiful, if icy, swimming hole and cascade, is the perfect place to spend a summer's day; further up (3km from picnic area) is an even more attractive version at the **Wheel of Fire Falls**.

Eungella township and Broken River

Back on the main road past Finch Hatton township, you climb the range road, once a nightmare track with crumbling edges until cyclone Aivu dropped 120cm of rain in one afternoon in 1989 and the hillside collapsed into the valley. Repair works have widened the road, and though still steep it is now well surfaced. Take an immediate left at the top of the slope and stop for a drink at *Eungella Chalet* (☎07/4958 4509), which has comfortable chalets (twins & doubles with shared bath ②–③), suites ⑤, five-person cabins ⑦) and a swimming pool. It has taken advantage of its 705-metre altitude and installed a hang-glider ramp next to the pool that's used for the sporadically staged **North Queensland Hanggliding Championships** (ask locally for dates). The general store, post office and other buildings, which lie scattered around the top of the road, form the rest of **EUNGELLA** township (the *Hideaway Café*, with its surprisingly international menu and superb apple strudel, is the best place for lunch), while 5km further, through patches of forest and dairy pasture, is **Broken River**. **Accommodation** here is at the *Broken River Mountain Retreat* (☎07/4958 4528; ⑤–⑦) which has four-person cabins with fireplaces. As an alternative, there is an excellent NPWS **campsite** (hot showers and barbecues). Book in advance and pick up **free maps** at the ranger's office (daily 8–9am, 11.30am–12.30pm & 3.30–4.30pm; ☎07/4958 4552). Next door is a **kiosk** open daily for meals and minimal supplies. Be prepared for **rain** – Eungella translates as "Land of Cloud".

Crowded during holidays and weekends, at other times the forest is truly memorable, its quiet, cool interior a naturalist's paradise. The swimming hole downstream from the kiosk is good for a dip during the day and, in winter, becomes a picturesque stage for **platypus watching**; the best vantage points are upstream from the road bridge on the purpose-built platform, or from the bridge itself. Normally fairly timid creatures, here they've become quite tolerant of people, and you're most likely to see them at dawn or dusk. Wander around the picnic area after dark with a torch to see other **wildlife**: feathertail gliders, bettong, possums, grey kangaroos and owlet night-jars. Down by the river you're more likely to come across frogs, cane toads and platy-puses in the evening, while squirrel gliders are sometimes seen in the huge gum trees up along the main road, and pythons use the warm verges to energize before a night's hunting.

The real star of Broken River, though, is the **forest** itself, where ancient trees with but-tressed roots and immensely high canopies conceal a floor of rich rotting timber, ferns, palms and vines. It can be difficult to see animals in the undergrowth but the sun-splashed paths along riverbanks attract reptiles, especially goannas and snakes. Among the best walks is the 8km round trip through the forest to the *Eungella Chalet* (see opposite), and there's a good half-hour circuit from the picnic grounds to **Crystal Cascades**.

On to Whitsunday

PROSERPINE, 123km north of Mackay, is an everyday sugar town on the turn-off from the Bruce Highway to Whitsunday, strangely unaffected by the surge in tourism along the coast. The major transit point for the Whitsunday region, here **trains** are met by Sampson's Buses (☎1300/655 449), which run about seven times a day to Airlie Beach. The main **bus** lines also have services which detour daily to Airlie. The **airport** is 10km south of town; call Sampson's 24 hours in advance to arrange a transfer to or from Proserpine or Whitsunday. Late arrivals can be put up at the *Proserpine Motor Lodge*, 184 Main St (☎07/4945 1788; ④), or the van park on Jupp Street.

Twenty kilometres east off the highway, **WHITSUNDAY** is the cover-all name for **Cannonvale**, **Airlie Beach** and **Shutehaven** (Shute Harbour), thinly sprawling com-munities that twenty years ago were known only to a handful of weekend campers and yachties. Mass tourism discovered the **Whitsunday Islands** (see p.424) in the 1980s and the area enjoyed a boom, but even now nobody comes to Whitsunday to spend time in town; it's just a place to be while deciding which island to visit. Airlie Beach and Cannonvale are the service centres; Shutehaven, from where island ferries generally leave, is 10km on from Airlie, past Cape Conway National Park. Other cruise and dive boats leave from Abel Point Marina in Airlie. Sampson's runs a daily bus from the Wildlife Park (see overleaf) through Cannonvale to Airlie and Shutehaven roughly once an hour from around 6am to 6pm.

Cannonvale, Airlie Beach and Shutehaven

Coming from Proserpine, Whitsunday's first community is **CANNONVALE**, a centre-less scattering of modern buildings fringing the highway for about a kilometre or so, overlooked by luxury homes set higher up on the wooded slopes of the Conway Range. Just around the headland, past **Abel Point Marina**, **AIRLIE BEACH** occupies a beau-tiful position between the sea and pine forests, but despite the name there are only a couple of gritty stretches of sand, which get covered at high tide. Everything is crammed into one short street, **Shute Harbour Road**: the **long-distance bus termi-nal** is at the central car park, in the heart of town, and **local buses** stop halfway down on the bridge.

The main preoccupation in Whitsunday is organizing a **cruise**, but there are a few other distractions. You can rent gear from the **watersports** kiosk on the beach at Airlie, spend the day exploring the coastline in a **kayak** with Salty Dog Sea Kayaking Adventures (☎018/067 913; $65), or hop on the courtesy bus to the **Wildlife Park** (daily 9am–4:30pm; $15), a small zoo 7km towards Proserpine, which has an excellent reptile collection. Next door is Barrier Reef Bungy (☎07/4946 1540; $49), though jumping from a crane is a poor way to do this, even if it is Australia's highest. You can explore the **hills behind Cannonvale** on horseback with Brandy Creek Trail Rides (☎07/4946 6665), 2km past the Wildlife Park, who pick you up from your accommodation and for $41 offer a half-day horseback ride following Brandy Creek through meadow and rainforest. If you don't want to ride, Fawlty Tours runs a similar excursion by bus, including a forest walk and barbecue lunch for $35.

   Conway National Park covers much of the coast facing the islands. Most of it consists of inaccessible mountains and mangroves, but there's a small campsite (NPWS fees apply) on the roadside about 7km from Airlie on Shute Harbour Road. You'll need padding on cold winter nights and you may be pestered by hordes of possums which infest the area. An easy walking track climbs **Mount Rooper** to an observation platform, from where the islands appear as white peaks jutting out of the unbelievably blue sea.

   Ten kilometres past Airlie, **SHUTEHAVEN** (Shute Harbour) is a cluster of houses overlooking the islands – and one of Australia's busiest harbours – from wooded hills above Coral Point; a new yachting complex and booking office hopes to win back business lost to Airlie. There's very limited **parking space** here; undercover facilities are available behind the Shell garage ($9 a day), which also rents tinnies for fishing, and there's an open-air grid at the harbour itself ($7 a day).

The Reef

The Barrier Reef starts about 50km northeast of Airlie; further out than at Cairns but not so heavily touristed, this section has many fair dive locations regularly visited by dive boats (see "Listings" on p.424). Both **Fairey Reefs** and **Black Reef** are good, with a variety of marine life and dive sites, but the best diving is at **Bait Reef**, with patchy coral gardens, shells, maori wrasse and morays. Bommies (massive, isolated coral outcrops) on the outer edge make for good drift diving, and manta rays are often seen at dawn. Other sites include **Hardy**, where there's a pontoon for day-trippers and fringing reefs around the islands themselves – see the island accounts below for details of these.

Practicalities

Unless you arrive during the September **Whitsunday Fun Race** you'll have little trouble finding **accommodation**. All places act as tour agents, some offering reductions or free nights if you book through them, although competition has become so cut-throat that some ruthlessly eject guests found making bookings through other agents. Hostels are usually cramped, but pool, kitchen and room fridges are standard amenities.

   Airlie's **restaurants** are as ubiquitous as its accommodation, with a string of places along the Esplanade or Shute Harbour Road. For self-caterers, there's a **supermarket** near the bridge. **Nightclubs** can legally serve drinks only to those "intending" to eat – but you can intend to eat until you leave.

Accommodation

Motels and resorts often offer **discounted rates** of ten to twenty percent during the low season.

Airlie Cove Van Park, Shute Harbour Rd, 3km towards Shutehaven (☎07/4946 6727). Tidy, green and comfortable van park. ②–③.

Backpackers By The Bay, 12 Hermitage Drive, Airlie (☎07/4946 7267 or free call ☎1800/646 994). Small, comfortably renovated place that's quieter than those in the centre of town and has nice bay views. Dorm beds ①, doubles and twins ③.

Beaches, 362 Shute Harbour Rd, Airlie (☎07/4946 6244 or free call ☎1800/636 630). Brash backpackers' hostel, with plenty of bunks and double rooms available. ①–②.

Bush Village Backpackers Resort, 2 St. Martins Rd, Cannonvale (☎07/4946 6177 or free call ☎1800/809 256). Verging onto bushland at the foot of a hill, this is relatively quiet. The owners rescue injured and orphaned animals, so you'll often find tiny kangaroos and wallabies in their care. Facilities include a kitchen and pool, and prices include breakfast. Dorm beds ①, and attractively renovated doubles ③.

Club Crocodile, Shute Harbour Rd, Cannonvale (☎07/4946 7155). Good-value stand-by resort rooms and pool. Fairly modern place but a little threadbare. ④.

Club Habitat/YHA, 394 Shute Harbour Rd, Airlie (☎07/4946 6312). Tidy dorms and doubles, generally busy and somewhat crowded. ①–③.

Koalas, Shute Harbour Rd, right beside *Wanderers* resort (☎07/4946 6001 or free call ☎1800/800 421). Basic six-bed dorms, each with bathroom and TV. Facilities include a communal kitchen, volleyball court and large pool, in pleasant landscaped grounds. ①.

On the Beach, 269 Shute Harbour Rd, Airlie (☎07/4946 6359, fax 4946 7995). Courtyard motel with some rooms facing out to sea through a palm-and-poinciana-shrouded garden. ⑥.

Reef Oceania Village Resort ("Reef O's"), 3km out of Airlie, 147 Shute Harbour Rd, Cannonvale. (☎07/4946 6137 or free call ☎1800/800 795). Cheapest of the budget options, with 4-, 6- and 8-bed units, some with kitchen and air-con. Price includes an excellent breakfast and a regular shuttle-bus to town (6am–midnight). There's a pool, inexpensive bar/bistro with live music, and a poorly-equipped communal kitchen. ①.

Shute Harbour Motel, Shute Harbour Rd, Shutehaven (☎07/4946 9131). Unpretentious and recently renovated old motel overlooking Shute Harbour. ④.

Whitehaven Holiday Units, 285 Shute Harbour Rd, Airlie (☎07/4946 5710). Extraordinarily quiet, given its central location. Rooms are simply furnished and face out to sea. ⑤.

Whitsunday Backpackers "Club 13", Begley St, on the hill towards Cannonvale (☎07/4946 7376). A slightly dreary warren of time-share apartments converted to a backpackers' hostel. Very small rooms, although some have their own spas, and there are good views of the harbour. ①–②.

Whitsunday Village Resort (*Magnums*), by the bridge on Shute Harbour Rd, Airlie, (☎07/4946 6266 or free call ☎1800/624 634). Tidy self-contained cabins, pleasantly sheltered lawns, comprehensive booking service and a loud bar next door. ①–②.

Whitsunday Wanderers Resort, Shute Harbour Rd, Airlie, Cannonvale end (☎07/4946 6446, reservations only free call ☎1800/075 069). Huge grounds with a generous assortment of leisure facilities – including three pools and two spas – to help while away the day. ⑦.

Eating and entertainment

You'll find a variety of places to **eat** in Cannonvale, Airlie Beach and Shutehaven. However, the best of the lot, as well as the liveliest nightclubs, are in Airlie Beach – especially on Shute Harbour Road.

Airlie Beach Hotel, on the Esplanade. Smartly renovated, incorporating *Mangrove Jack's Cafe* with a tropics-style menu and wood-fired pizzas. Ambience entirely ruined by the poker machines and TAB betting window at rear of pub.

Chatz, Shutehaven end of Shute Harbour Rd, Airlie. Bar and brasserie serving mammoth helpings of grilled and basted meats for around $12. Top-value lunchtime burger for $5.

The Courtyard, 301 Shute Harbour Rd, across from *Chatz*. Award-winning BYO restaurant with seasonal menu. Highly rated by locals. Dinner only (Tues–Sun), around $30 per person.

Hog's Breath Café, Shute Harbour Rd. The original of this chain of Tex-Mex grill restaurants, still serving good grub. Main courses around $18.

KC's, 50 Shute Harbour Rd. Blowout on chargrilled steak and seafood in noisy comfort. Around $20–30 for a full meal.

Magnums, next door to the *Whitsunday Village Resort*, Shute Harbour Rd. Outside bistro open 5–8.30pm for large, inexpensive grills and salads, from a less-than-hygienic kitchen. The seedy bar smells of vomit and has done for years, yet it's still popular.

Morocco's, Shute Harbour Rd, next to *Wanderers Resort*. Cheerful place with a huge video screen, superb view from the terrace and excellent lunch specials. Coral trout recommended for dinner, and the Mediterranean Salad for lunch. Open daily 7am–midnight.

Panache, Shute Harbour Rd, up past the bus terminal. Yet more pasta and fish and beef grills, dressed up in a pricey "European" à la carte-style menu. Main courses around $20.

Tricks Nightclub, Cannonvale end of Shute Harbour Rd. Nightly grind 10pm–late.

Listings

Airlines Ansett, 46 Main St, Proserpine (☎07/4945 1433 or ☎13 1300); Island Air (☎07/4946 9933); Qantas-Sunstate (☎07/4945 1311 or ☎13 1313).

Banks NAB & Commonwealth in Airlie; ANZ & Westpac in Cannonvale.

Boat charters Unless you know exactly what you want, bookings are best made through an agent, such as your accommodation or ABC Travel (see "Information" below). Bareboat charters should be undertaken by experienced sailors only: average wind velocity in the Whitsundays is twenty-five knots, which means serious sailing. Five-person yachts start around $350 a day. Try Australian Bareboat Charters (☎07/4946 9381), Whitsunday Rent-a-Yacht (☎07/4946 9512 or free call ☎1800/075 111) or Queensland Yacht Charters (☎07/4946 7400). Coral Sea Boat Hire (☎07/4946 9843, mobile phone ☎018/182 584) rents six-to-nine metre motor cruisers by the day.

Car and scooter rental Airlie Beach Rentals, Begley St, Airlie (☎07/4946 6110); Tropic Car Hire, 283 Shute Harbour Rd, Airlie (☎07/4946 5216); Thrifty, 406 Shute Harbour Rd, Airlie (☎07/4946 7727).

Dive boats and reef trips All dive shops organize overnight outings for qualified divers; three days and three nights work out to about $400, with ten to twelve dives included. Whitsunday Diver (☎07/4946 5366) zip out to Bait Reef for $120; FantaSea Cruises (☎07/4946 5111) offer a comfortable, high-speed catamaran to the pontoon at Hardy Reef. Island cruises and day-trips can often accommodate divers too – see the box on p.426-427.

Dive schools Beware of bargain dive courses, always ask around, and remember that with diving, there's no substitute for a good training and safety record. Oceania Dive, 257 Shute Harbour Rd (☎07/4946 6032; courses only – no day-trips); Kelly Dive, 1 Esplanade, Airlie (☎07/4946 6122 or free call ☎1800/063 454) have their own, purpose-built dive-boat; and Reef Dive, in the centre of town, across from *McDonald's* (☎07/4946 6508 or free call ☎1800/075 120) all offer certification courses from $320 depending on number of post-qualification dives included.

Doctor Shute Harbour Rd, Airlie, behind Oceania Dive at the Cannonvale end (☎07/4946 6241, after hours ☎018/775 513; Mon–Sat 8am–6pm, Sun 9am–1pm).

Flea market By the creek, for local produce and souvenirs. Sat 8am–noon.

Information Commissioned agents have sprouted everywhere, but for friendly and reliable information and bookings, start with ABC Travel, right next to the bus terminal (☎07/4946 5755). Otherwise try Destination Whitsunday, corner of Shute Harbour Rd and the Esplanade, above an ice-cream shop (free call ☎1800/644 563, fax 07/4946 5008).

NPWS Shute Harbour Rd, 3km out towards Shute on the left of the road (☎07/4946 7022). Island camping permits and a small environmental display.

Pharmacy Airlie Pharmacy, opposite *Magnums* (☎07/4946 6156); daily 8am–6pm.

Police Shute Harbour Rd, Cannonvale (☎07/4946 6445).

Post office In the centre of town, right behind *McDonald's* (☎07/4946 6515).

Taxi Free call ☎1800/811 388.

Work There are three employment agencies in town, none of which is much help to travellers; checking with the hostels may prove more rewarding. The region has a high turnover, but there's also heavy competition, so bring relevant documents. Without Queensland qualifications, you're unlikely to find boat work except as a divemaster, but island jobs can sometimes be found by phoning or walking into a resort and enquiring.

The Whitsundays

The **Whitsunday Islands** look just like the mountain peaks they once were before rising sea levels cut them off from the mainland six thousand years ago. They were sea-

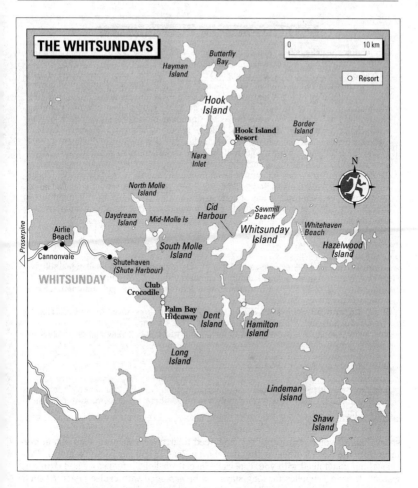

THE WHITSUNDAYS

sonally inhabited by the Ngaro Aborigines when Captain Cook sailed through in 1770; he proceeded to name the area after the day he arrived, and various locations after sponsors of expeditions. Today, dense green pine forests and roughly contoured coastlines give the islands instant appeal, and the surrounding seas bustle with yachts and cruisers. Resorts first opened in the 1930s, but the majority of islands are still undeveloped and controlled by the NPWS, who maintain campsites on thirteen and resorts on four. The few islands left in private hands house another three resorts, while the rest are mainly uninhabited and largely the domain of local yachties. Those covered below all have regular connections to the mainland.

Underlying all the hype, there are two basic ways to explore the Whitsundays – staying on the islands or cruising around them. **Staying** allows you to choose between camping and resort facilities, with snorkelling, bushwalks and beach sports to pass the time. **Cruises** spend one or more days around the islands, perhaps putting ashore at times (check this if it's the islands themselves you want to see) for diving or

CRUISES IN THE WHITSUNDAYS

Day cruises usually take in two or more islands, and offer the chance to experience the thrills of boomnetting* and do some snorkelling; others may concentrate on a single theme, such as whale-watching, fishing or lazing on Whitehaven Beach. **Long cruises** cover much the same territory but at a slower pace, and may give sailing lessons. Experienced groups might consider **chartering a boat** (see "Listings" on p.424 for operators). Some operators will drop and collect **campers** if given advance notice, or you can contact Island Camping Connection (☎07/4946 5255), who charge $35 (minimum of two people) for return runs to beach campsites at North Molle, South Molle, Long Island, Planton and Tancred islands.

The list below is not exhaustive; word of mouth is the best method of finding out about who is still in business, what the current deals are and if operators live up to their advertisements. Things to check for include: how much time is actually spent cruising and at the destination, how many others will be on the cruise, and the size of the vessel. There are scores of beautiful boats, so you'll be swayed by your preference for a performance racing yacht, or a fun trip and lots of deck space on which to lounge. Bear in mind that a cheerful (or jaded) crew can make all the difference, and that weather conditions can affect destinations offered.

DAY-TRIPS: SAILING

Cost $55–65.
Gretel (☎07/4948 0999 or free call ☎1800/675 790). America's Cup challenger, still flying the green and gold "boxing kangaroo" spinnaker; daily to Langford Reef and around.
Illusions (☎07/4946 5255). Catamaran trip includes snorkelling and boomnetting; live music on board every Sunday.
Maxi Ragamuffin (☎07/4946 7777). Twenty-five metre long moor to Blue Pearl Bay (Wed, Fri & Sat) and Whitehaven Beach (Tues, Thurs & Sun).
Nari (☎07/4946 5755). Refurbished 15-metre-long yacht; snorkelling and good deals on scuba diving.

DAY-TRIPS: POWERED VESSELS

Cost $30–70.
Azzurra (☎07/4946 7777). Small, fast powerboat which does the rounds of Whitehaven Beach and Hook Island; ideal if you simply want to get there and do some swimming and snorkelling.

snorkelling. If you're **camping**, you first need to arrange transport, then obtain **permits** from the NPWS office on the Shutehaven Road ($3.50 per person a night). Take everything you'll need with you, especially insect repellent, a fuel stove and **drinking water** – ferrying supplies for long stays can be arranged with cruise boats. **Resorts** sometimes have a higher profile than the islands they're built on; though staying is often beyond budget means, stand-by deals can slash prices and polite bargaining is always worth a try. Most, in any case, allow day-trippers the use of their facilities.

Vessels leave from Shutehaven or Abel Point Marina, and the resort islands all offer relatively expensive return **ferry transfers** to and from the mainland. If you'd like to see more than one island, or plan to camp away from a resort, it's cheaper to choose a **cruise** – for details, see the box above.

Whitsunday Island

The largest island in the group, NPWS-run **Whitsunday Island**, is also one of the most enjoyable, with tropical forests, short walking tracks and the brilliant Whitehaven Beach. On the west side, **Cid Harbour** has three **campsites** above coral and pebble beaches. Dugong Beach is the nicest, sheltered under the protective arms and

Baby J (☎07/4946 6848). Snorkelling at Manta Ray Bay, plus four hours' sunning at Whitehaven.
FantaSea Blue Ferries (☎07/4946 5111 or free call ☎1800/650 851). Range of day trips; also does island transfers.
Ocean Rafting (☎07/4946 1564). Inflatable-hull "raft" which gives you a snorkelling trip, island walk, and sprawl on a beach, all in one day. Highly recommended for a thorough taste of the islands.
Seatrek (☎07/4946 5255). Day transfers to resorts at Hook, South Molle and Daydream islands.
Whitsunday All Over (☎07/4946 6900). A mass of options ranging from simple island transfers to multi-island cruises and coral viewing aboard the *Yellow Sub*.

LONGER TRIPS

Cost $210–300-plus for two-night, three-day outings; departure time is around 9am from Abel Point Marina, returning on day three about 4pm. The basic itinerary is to visit Hook Island via Nara Inlet, then move round to Whitehaven Beach on Whitsunday.
Flying Dutchman (☎07/4946 5299 or free call ☎1800/677 119). Certified divers may want to check out this 18-metre-long "ketch", which offers up to eight dives on its three day trip.
Mollo (☎07/4946 6922 or free call ☎1800/646 146). This sail-catamaran is smaller and less of a party boat than most.
Prosail (☎07/4946 5433). Wide-ranging group of yachts with a variety of safe anchorages for most weather conditions.
Ragamuffin II (☎07/4946 5299). Mono-hull yacht offering sailing lessons and snorkelling.
Southern Cross Sailing Adventures (☎07/4948 0999 or free call ☎1800/675 790). *Siska*: 25-metre-long ocean maxi yacht, winner of races between the UK and Australia; *Southern Cross*: High-speed, 21-metre-long America's Cup challenger; *The Card*: 26-metre-long Whitbread Round-the-World racer.
Tongarra (☎07/4946 6952 or free call ☎1800/639 936). Catamaran with a huge deck for lounging and sleeping; emphasis is on having fun.

*****Boomnetting**: sitting in a large rope hammock stretched above the water at the front of the boat so that you catch the full soaking force of the waves – great fun.

buttressed roots of rainforest trees, and reached by a twenty-minute walk along narrow hill paths from Sawmill Beach, where you'll probably be dropped off if you arrive on a cruise boat; there are no regular ferry services.

On the east side, isolated Whitehaven is easily the finest beach in all the islands. Long, white and still clean despite the numbers of day-trippers and campers, it's a beautiful spot as long as you can handle the lack of distractions. The campsite is above the tide line, with minimal shelter provided by whispering casuarinas. Snorkellers should head down to the far end of the beach facing Hazelwood Island.

Hook Island

Directly north of Whitsunday and pretty similar in appearance, **Hook Island** is the second largest in the group. A daily **ferry** ($25) runs to the low-key backpackers **resort** – really just a set of cabins – and to the **campsite** at the island's southern end; there are also two NPWS sites.

Cruises often pull into **Nara Inlet** for a look at the **Aboriginal paintings** on the roof of a small cave above a tiny shingle beach. Visually unarresting, the art is significant for the net patterns incorporated in its designs, which are otherwise found only at central highland sites. On the rocks below the cave are some more recent graffiti, left by boat crews over the last thirty years.

NPWS runs **campsites** at **Curlew Beach** and **Stonehaven Beach**, both sheltered, pretty and only accessible with your own vessel. The **resort** has no frills but offers doubles and shared-cabin accommodation (☎07/4946 9380; ②–⑤) with fine views over the channel to Whitsunday, a bar, free gas barbecues, a small store and a cafeteria serving meals and snacks. **Campers** utilizing their beachfront sites ($13 per person) can use resort facilities.

Snorkelling on the reef directly in front of the resort is a must; snorkelling gear and surf skis are free (with deposit) to guests. The water is cloudy on large tides, but the coral outcrops are all in fairly good condition and there's plenty of life around, from flatworms to morays and parrotfish. Other opportunities to spy on marine life include the **underwater observatory** (daily 2–4pm; $7) near the resort. Day-cruises run from Airlie to the snorkelling spots and visit the top-rate fringing coral at **Manta Ray Bay**, **Langford Reef** and **Butterfly Bay**.

The Molles, and Planton, Tancred and Denman islands

South Molle Island was a source of **stone** for Ngaro Aborigines, a unique material for tools that have been found on other islands and may help in mapping trade routes. The relaxed **resort** (free call ☎1800/075 080; ⑦) in the north of the island languishes in comfortable surroundings. Rates include guided walks, all sports and facilities, and the ferry from the mainland – but not reef trips. Walking tracks from behind the golf course lead to gum trees and rainforest, encompassing vistas of the islands from the top of Spion Kop and Mount Jeffreys, and some quiet beaches at the south end. There's a daily **ferry** from Shute Harbour ($24 return).

South Molle's resort can sometimes organize a lift to the campsite on uninhabited **North Molle Island**, only 2km away, or contact Island Camping Connection (see box on pp.426-427); the beach here is made up of rough coral fragments, but the snorkelling is fairly good. There are another couple of campsites on **Mid-Molle Island**, joined to South Molle by a low-tide causeway about half a kilometre from the resort.

Tiny **Planton, Tancred** and **Denman islands** are just offshore from South Molle – with no facilities and limited camping at NPWS sites, they're about as isolated as you'll get in the Whitsundays. All three are surrounded by reef, but be careful of strong currents. Again, Island Camping Connection or cruise boats bound for Whitsunday Island may drop you off here.

Long Island

Long Island is exactly that, being not much more than a narrow, ten-kilometre ribbon almost within reach of the mainland forests. There are a few worthwhile hikes through the rainforest to **Sandy Bay** (where there's an NPWS **campsite**) or up **Humpy Point**, and two low-profile **resorts** at the north end of the island. *Club Crocodile Long Island* (free call ☎1800/075 125; packages including meals and transfers ⑦–⑧) at **Happy Bay**, and *Palm Bay Hideaway* (☎07/4946 9233; units or canvas cabins ⑤), half a kilometre south at the island's waist, have similar attractions (a disco, parasailing, water-skiing and a dozen other sports), but the latter's emphasis is more on peace and quiet. Ferries run daily from Shute Harbour to both ($24 return).

Hamilton Island

The apartment buildings dominating the view on **Hamilton Island** are the Gold Coast revisited, and it's interesting to speculate about what will happen to them during the next cyclone. An enormous colony of fruit bats live in the trees behind the waterfront and, apart from the flocks of cockatoos, seem to be the only native wildlife here.

The island is privately owned, and its businesses operate under a lease: development includes a quaint colonial waterfront with hotel, bakery and various other stores, the *Hamilton Island Resort* (free call ☎1800/075 110; ⑧), a small zoo, and so many restaurants, gift shops and sports facilities that the original character of the island has long since vanished. The twin towers of the resort loom over the beach complex, and give the best view of the whole area from one of the external glass lifts taken up to penthouse level. Inside the **beach complex** you'll find one of the pricier places to eat, and lots of signs in Japanese. One of Hamilton's saving graces is the chance of work, in theory advertised through job agencies in Airlie. Phoning the resort and asking if there are any openings may result in an interview (although it's more common to be placed on a "waiting list"), without which there's no point visiting the island.

There's a daily ferry service from Shute Harbour ($38 return).

Hayman, Lindeman and Daydream islands

The extremely high price of accommodation at the **Hayman Island** resort (free call ☎1800/075 175; ⑧), pales into insignificance when compared with the building costs, which topped $300 million. Guests indulge in lush rooms, extravagant Baroque furnishings and underground tunnels so that they don't have to cross paths with the staff, and day-trippers aren't allowed anywhere near the place; although cruises might stop off for snorkelling and diving at **Blue Pearl Bay**, on the island's west coast.

Lindeman Island suffered as a victim of feral goats, though their eradication has seen native plants making a comeback in a small melaleuca swamp and on the wooded northeast side. **Mount Oldfield** offers panoramic views, while other walking tracks lead to swimming beaches on the north shore. The *Club Med* resort (free call ☎1800/801 823; ⑨), Australia's first, has all the services you'd expect.

Daydream Island is little more than a tiny wooded rise between South Molle and the mainland, with a narrow beach running the length of the east side and coral to snorkel over at the north end. The **resort** (☎07/4948 8488; ⑦) offers fine food and hospitality, but its regimental lines dominate views of the island from the sea and detract from an otherwise very pretty scene; day-trippers are tolerated. Ferries run daily from Shute Harbour ($24).

Bowen and the route to Townsville

BOWEN, a quiet settlement an hour north of Proserpine, was once under consideration as the site of the state capital, but it floundered after Townsville's foundation. Today, rather stark first impressions created by the dry terrain and sterile bulk of the saltworks on the highway are offset by a certain small-town charm and some unexpectedly pretty beaches just off to the north. The other attraction is the prospect of seasonal **farm work**: Bowen's mangoes and tomatoes are spoken of in reverential tones, and each April the town's population is swelled by an influx of itinerant pickers. All three backpackers' hostels (see below) can help with finding work, though nothing's guaranteed. There's no public transport in the Bowen area.

The town centre overlooks **Edgecumbe Bay**, at the harbour end of **Herbert Street**, where you'll find the usual range of services and a couple of old colonial exteriors on the **Grand View Hotel** and the Harbour Office; **buses** stop outside Barrier Reef Travel (☎07/4786 2222). Budget **accommodation** consists of *Bowen Backpackers* (☎07/4786 3433; ①) on Herbert Street; *Barnacles* (☎07/4786 1245; ①), around the corner on Gordon Street; and *Trinity's at the Beach* (☎07/4786 4199; pick-up from the centre; ①), located near the beaches (see overleaf) at 93 Horseshoe Bay Rd. There's nothing particularly inspiring about any of these, which act as a base for workers; if you don't plan to work, you're unlikely to stay long. Mid-range options include *Castle Motor Lodge*, 6 Don St (☎07/4786 1322; ④), about the closest to the centre of town. You can **eat** at the *Club Hotel* across from the post office and the late-night **pizza shop** down by the harbour, or stock up at Magees Supermarket on Williams Street and at numerous fruit and vegetable stalls.

Bowen's attractive **beaches** are a couple of kilometres north of the town centre. The best is **Horseshoe Bay**: small, and hemmed in by some sizeable boulders, with good waters for a swim or snorkel. *Horseshoe Bay Resort* (☎07/4786 2564; units ③) makes an excellent base, two minutes' walk from the sea, or you could simply borrow snorkelling gear and a bicycle from one of the hostels and make a day of it.

The Burdekin River and Mount Elliot

Further on up the highway, 115km past Bowen, are the towns of **Home Hill** and **Ayr**, separated by a mill, a few kilometres of canefields and the iron framework of the **Burdekin River Bridge**. The river, one of the north's most famous landmarks, is still liable to flood during severe wet seasons, despite having to fight its way across three weirs and a dam.

North of Ayr, **Mount Elliot** looms on the horizon, the only accessible section of the fragmented **Bowling Green Bay National Park**. The turn-off from the highway is at **ALLIGATOR CREEK** township, about 55km from Ayr. Supplies and fuel are available at the general store here; otherwise press on to the NPWS **ranger station and campsite** (☎07/4778 8203) in a valley at the end of the road (open 6am–6pm only). Huge-eyed geckos in the shower blocks have yet to make an impression on the camp's **cicadas**, whose high-pitched chirp is likely either to drive you mad or lull you to sleep.

Along the valley, the creek widens into a chain of rock pools and deeper channels. The ponds become more private the further you get from camp and though swimmers might attract cruising eels and nibbles from freshwater shrimp, it's pretty idyllic. A couple of **hikes** add variety: you could spend the day rockhopping up **Cockatoo Creek**, or follow **Alligator Creek** to waterfalls that plunge down the mountain. About halfway there, a giant mango tree marks an abandoned farm; after this, the track cuts through and along the creek before ending in forest below the falls. There are a couple of deep pools a short distance up the side, but the rocks above them are too hot to climb during the day.

Townsville

Hot and stuffy **TOWNSVILLE**, sprawling around Castle Hill and Ross Creek, is north Queensland's "capital". The city's detractors unflatteringly describe its two biggest attractions as Magnetic Island and Cairns, but Townsville does have its moments – above all in the muggy, salty evening air and old pile houses on the surrounding hills, which distinguish it as the coast's first really tropical city.

Townsville was founded in 1864 by John Melton Black and **Robert Towns**, entrepreneurs who felt that a settlement was needed for northern stockmen who couldn't reach Bowen when the Burdekin River was in flood. Despite an inferior harbour, the settlement soon outstripped Bowen in terms of both size and prosperity, its development accelerated by **gold** finds inland at Ravenswood and Charters Towers. Today, it's the gateway to the far north, an important military centre and seat of a university, with substantial Torres Strait Islander and Aboriginal communities.

Arrival and information

Townsville's roughly triangular city centre is hemmed in by Cleveland Bay on the north, Ross Creek to the south, and Castle Hill to the west. Oriented northeast and parallel with Ross Creek, **Flinders Street** is the main drag, sectioned into a downtown pedestrian **mall** before running its last five hundred metres as **Flinders Street East**. The **airport** is 5km northwest; a **shuttle bus** ($5) meets most flights, stopping at points around town – phone in advance on ☎07/4775 5544. Long-distance buses stop at the **Transit Centre** on the south side of Ross Creek on Palmer Street, while the **train station** is on the north side of the creek on Flinders Street.

Public **transport** serves the suburbs rather than the sights, though much of what there is to see is central; some hostels have bikes available. An **information** booth and booking agent for all tours (both very helpful) are located in Flinders Street Mall (daily 9am–5pm).

Accommodation

Lodgings are concentrated around the city centre and near the Transit Centre, but hostels and caravan parks will collect you from further afield for the price of a phone call.

Civic House, 262 Walker St (☎07/4771 5381). Clean and helpful, if not wonderfully modern, with a well-equipped kitchen, pool table and table tennis. Ask about deals on dive courses with Mike Ball Dive Expeditions (located next door), and don't miss the free sunset bus-ride up to Castle Hill lookout. ①.

Globetrotters, Palmer St, just down from the bus station (☎07/4771 3242). Small hostel with pool and simple rooms; almost always full. ①.

Great Northern Hotel, corner of Flinders and Blackwood Streets (☎07/4771 6191). Old "Queenslander" pub; downstairs bar has lots of character, and serves huge meals from $7. Rooms have fan or air-con and shared bath. Singles ②, doubles ②–③.

Reef Lodge, 4–6 Wickham St (☎07/4721 1112). The cheapest place in town, with ordinary facilities, but shabby and run-down. ①.

Rowes Bay Caravan Park, Heatleys Parade (☎07/4771 3576). Off The Strand, 3km north of the centre towards Pallarenda, overlooking Magnetic Island across the bay. Very popular, so worth booking in advance. ②–③.

Sheraton Breakwater Casino, Sir Leslie Thiess Drive (☎07/4722 2333). Townsville's top-notch accommodation. This was Queensland's first legal gambling den, famous as an enclave of liberality during conservative years. ⑧.

Sun City Caravan Park, 119 Bowen Rd (☎07/4775 7733, fax 4725 1407). Family-style, self-contained units and holiday cabins with kitchen and TV, located on the Ross River. Also tent sites, each with toilet, shower and laundry. Units and on-site vans ③.

Townsville Centra, Flinders Street Mall (☎07/4772 2477, reservations only free call ☎1800/079 903). Resembles a giant sugar-shaker; comfortable and bland business venue. ⑦.

Transit Centre Hostel, Palmer St, above the bus station (☎07/4721 2322). Minimum space, comfort and security; only worth it if you arrive late at night. ①.

Yongala Motel, 11 Fryer St (☎07/4772 4633). A welcoming place, named after the city's most famous shipwreck, with modern motel rooms joined to a historic old Queenslander with original furnishings. ⑤.

The City and around

Funded by inland gold mines during the late nineteenth century, some of Townsville's architecture is quite imposing. A stroll through the mall and along Flinders Street East, among the unimaginative assortment of pharmacies, newsagents and banks, will reveal a good number of stylishly solid stone facades and iron wraparound balconies on buildings that were formerly shops and warehouses. In

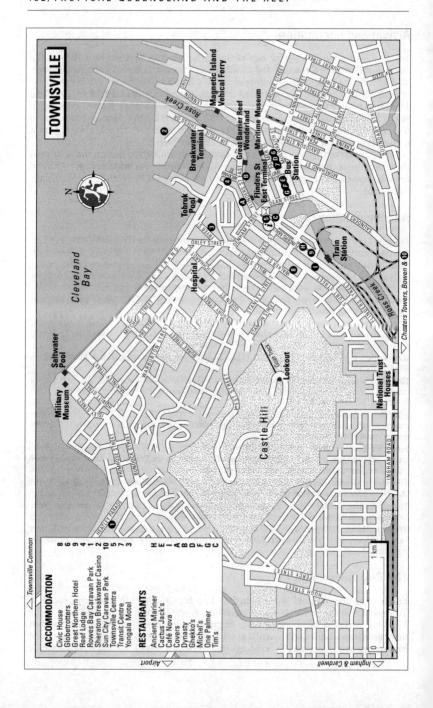

TOWNSVILLE

ACCOMMODATION
Civic House   8
Globetrotters   6
Great Northern Hotel   9
Reef Lodge   4
Rowes Bay Caravan Park   1
Sheraton Breakwater Casino   2
Sun City Caravan Park   10
Townsville Centre   5
Transit Centre   7
Yongala Motel   3

RESTAURANTS
Ancient Mariner   H
Cactus Jack's   E
Café Nova   I
Covers   A
Dynasty   B
Ghekko's   D
Michel's   F
One Palmer   G
Tim's   C

the mall itself, the Perc Tucker Art Gallery (Mon–Thurs, Sat & Sun 10am–5pm, Fri 10am–6pm; free) is one such building, now featuring travelling exhibitions of mainly antique art. More offbeat, modern work by local artists is on view at the Umbrella Gallery, 222 Sturt St (Mon–Fri 10am–4pm). On Sunday the mall hosts **Cotters Market** (8.30am–2pm), which has good local produce.

Castle Hill looms over the city centre. There's a road to the top from Stanley Street; on foot go along Gregory Street to Stanton Terrace and join a walking path of sorts that climbs to the lookout for vistas over the city to the distant Hervey Range and Magnetic Island.

The Strand runs northwest along Cleveland Bay, lined with more old houses and fig trees. About half an hour's walk away, **Kissing Point**, at the far end, is a grassy head-land, with a stretch of sand and accompanying enclosed **saltwater pool** below – very welcome during the scorching stinger season. Above, a **military museum** built into an underground gun emplacement (Mon, Wed & Fri 9am–12.30pm) outlines Townsville's defences during World War II.

More of the city's **tropical architecture** is on show at the National Trust site on Castling Street (Wed 10am–2pm, Sat & Sun 1–4pm; $5), just off Ingham Road, where two 1880s houses have been relocated and fully restored. The wide verandahs and exte-riors are painted in their original greens, reds and browns – not whitewashed, as they're often (erroneously) imagined to have been.

The Great Barrier Reef Wonderland and the Maritime Museum

The **Great Barrier Reef Wonderland**, on Flinders Street East (daily 9.30am–5pm; aquarium $14.80, Omnimax theatre $10), is – without question – Townsville's premier attraction, a blend of illusion and reality that carries you to the outer reef or outer space within moments. The **aquarium** is terrific, with colossal live tanks housing immaculate re-creations of the reef – built out into the harbour and largely self-sustaining. You can watch schools of fish drifting over coral, clown fish hiding inside anemones' tentacles and myopic turtles cruising past. Equally absorbing is a stroll beneath the glass tunnel which houses sharks and other predators, as well as a partial replica of the *Yongala* wreck. Between the main tanks are smaller ones for oddities: sea snakes, deep-sea nau-tiluses, baby turtles and lobster. Upstairs, videos about the reef are shown, and you can handle some inoffensive invertebrates – tiny clams, sea slugs and starfish.

In the **Omnimax theatre** (hourly shows) the film is projected onto a domed ceiling, to create an overwhelming, wraparound image. The construction site next door is in fact the **Museum of Tropical Queensland**, which, when it reopens in 2000, will house the entire marine archeology section of Brisbane's Queensland Museum. A prime fea-ture will be the collection of relics from the wreck of the **Pandora**, a British frigate which hit a remote reef and sank in 1791 while carrying fourteen crew of the *Bounty* from Tahiti to London to stand trial for mutiny.

You'll find more about shipwrecks almost directly across Ross Creek from the Wonderland at the **Maritime Museum** (Mon–Fri 10am–4pm, Sat–Sun 1–4pm; $3) on Palmer Street, near the Transit Centre. It focuses on the story of the **Yongala**, which went down with all hands during a cyclone in 1911, and was finally located intact in shal-low waters in 1958. Other wrecks covered include the Blackbirder vessel *Foam* and the *Gothenburg*, a gold transport which sank near Bowen in 1875; ghoulish salvagers recov-ered the captain's safe and, assuming that corpses loaded with bullion had been eaten by sharks, began to fish for them, spurred on by the prospect of recovering gold from the carcasses.

Townsville Common Environmental Park

The **Townsville Common Environmental Park** (daily 7.30am–7.30pm; free) is 6.5km north of the centre, on the coast at Pallarenda. The **Bohle River** pools into wetlands below the **Many Peaks Range**, a habitat perfect for wildfowl including the brolga, the stately symbol of northern marshes. Less popular – with rice farmers anyway – are huge flocks of magpie geese that visit after rains and are a familiar sight over the city.

You need a vehicle to reach the park, but once there you can get about on foot, although a car or bike makes short work of the less interesting tracks between lagoons. Camouflaged **hides** at Long Swamp and Pink Lily Lagoon let you clock up a few of the hundred or more bird species: egrets stalk frogs around waterlilies, ibises and spoonbills strain the water for edibles and geese honk at each other, undisturbed by the low-flying airport traffic. Bring binoculars.

Cafés and restaurants

Ancient Mariner Seafood Restaurant, 428 Flinders St, near the Stanley St crossroads. All-you-can-eat crumbed squid, bugs, prawns and scallops for $25. Open from 6.30pm.

Cactus Jack's, Palmer St. Tex-Mex burgers, chimichangas and tacos, served amid plenty of noise and neon.

Café Nova, Flinders St, near the station. A student venue, with generous helpings and meals for under $10. Serves huge and tasty salads. Tues–Fri 10.30am–midnight, Sat & Sun 6pm–midnight.

Covers, upstairs at 209 Flinders St East (☎07/4721 4630). A cocktail bar and restaurant that's primarily somewhere to go to be seen. The menu features ordinary grills ($20), and there's a café downstairs. Tues–Sun from 6pm.

Dynasty, 225 Flinders St East. Chinese seafood joint, where you pick your own fish from the tank. $15–20 a head.

Ghekko's, next to the Transit Centre, Palmer St (☎07/4772 5271). Student-training restaurant, with a fine à la carte service and dishes (all under $10) such as chicken and camembert parcels, and mango cheesecake. Wed–Sat noon–3pm & 6–10pm.

Michel's, 7 Palmer St. A mix of Asian and Mediterranean items – pasta, seafood and meats, grills and tandooris, accompanied by a variety of sweet and piquant sauces. Dishes around $20.

One Palmer, 1 Palmer St (☎07/4772 3435). Go "bush" in style at this chic, upmarket bar-and-restaurant, with delicacies such as char-grilled kangaroo flavoured with quandongs. Expensive.

Tim's Surf & Turf, by the bridge, Flinders St. Open-air, riverside restaurant and bar strung along the embankment. Good-value steaks, mango chicken, oysters and seafood (nothing over $15), and the best views in Townsville.

Yongala Restaurant, 11 Fryer St (☎07/4772 4633), next to the motel. Historic, authentically furnished surroundings where you can enjoy live music and good, Greek-influenced food. Appropriately, the building's architect was on the *Yongala* when it sank.

Entertainment

Many of Townsville's hotels have occasional **music**, for which you might have to pay a cover charge. Check *This Month in Townsville*, the local free magazine, for listings. The places listed below are all well established.

Bank, Flinders St East. A sometimes heavy nightclub sporting Corinthian columns, spiked iron railings and bars on the windows.

Bullwinkles, Flinders St East. A venue for hard-core clubbers.

Exchange Hotel, Flinders St East. Run-down pub, but a real locals' watering-hole; occasionally has live bands.

JD's Sports Bar & Grill, Flinders St. Newly decked out in timber, television sets and sports memorabilia; a JD's barstool is the ideal perch for watching big sports events.

Mad Cow, Flinders St East. Pool tables and dancing to "Top 40" – packed on weekends.

Playpen, Flinders St, at the west end of town. Junior relative of the Cairns *Playpen*, with two floors of bars and dance space.

Shamrock Hotel, Palmer St. Very busy hotel opposite the Transit Centre, with cheap meals and a happy hour 6.30–7.30pm; good choice for pool-players.

Listings

Airlines Ansett, 350 Flinders Street Mall (☎07/4727 3666 or ☎13 1300); Qantas, 320 Flinders Mall (☎07/4753 3311 or ☎13 1313).

Banks All located on Flinders Street Mall.

Bookshops Jim's Book Exchange, Shaw's Arcade, The Mall (☎07/4771 6020).

Buses Campbell's Coaches (☎07/4774 5099); Greyhound Pioneer (☎07/4771 2134); McCafferty's (☎07/4772 5100).

Camping supplies Askerns Disposals, opposite the station on Flinders St (☎07/4772 3088).

Car rental Meteor, 333 Ingham Rd (☎07/4779 4422), and Can Do, 194 Flinders St East (☎07/4721 4766), offer deals on one-way rental to Cairns. Rent-a-Rocket, 14 Dean St (☎07/4772 6880), and Thrifty, 635 Sturt St (☎07/4772 4600), charge from around $40 a day.

Diving and reef trips The pontoon at Kelso Reef is the day-trip destination of Pure Pleasure Cruises, whose fast catamaran leaves five times a week from the Great Barrier Reef Wonderland jetty, picking up from Magnetic Island en route ($120); other deals include reef trip plus two nights on Magnetic Island for $125. The region's best dive destination is the coral-encrusted *Yongala*, an early twentieth-century steamer in fifteen to thirty metres of water; this is a fabulous wreck dive, particularly at night. Anchorage is tricky, however, and dives can only be made in good weather. Mike Ball Dive Expeditions, 252–256 Walker St (☎07/4772 3022), and Pro-Dive Townsville (through Great Barrier Reef Wonderland; ☎07/4721 1760, fax 4721 1791) are both well-organized and run qualification courses and three-day trips to the *Yongala* and the outer reef. AIMS – the Australian Institute of Marine Science, 35km south of Townsville (☎07/4753 4211) – sometimes needs volunteers with at least fifteen hours' experience for scientific trips to the reef; you might dive or help with paperwork for the duration.

Hospital Townsville General Hospital, Eyre St (☎07/4781 9211).

Left luggage At the Transit Centre and airport.

NPWS Display and information on regional parks at the Great Barrier Reef Wonderland (☎07/4721 2399). Mon–Fri 9am–5pm, Sat 1–5pm.

Pharmacy Amcal, Flinders Street Mall (☎07/4771 6088).

Police 30 Stanley St (☎07/4760 7777).

RACQ 635 Sturt St (☎07/4721 4888).

Swimming Tobruk Swimming Pool, The Strand, in the parkland on the north side of the road, about 1km west of the junction with Wickham St.

Taxi Stand at Flinders Street Mall (☎07/4772 1555).

Tours Detours (☎07/4721 5977) runs day-trips to Charters Towers, Magnetic Island, Paluma and Ravenswood. Sullivan's, 25 Mandalay Ave, Nelly Bay (☎ & fax 07/4778 5925), arranges two-day 4WD trips to Cairns via the coast and inland.

Travel agents STA Travel, 310 Ross River Rd (☎07/4779 5877).

Magnetic Island

Another island named by Captain Cook in 1770 – this time after his compass played up as he sailed past – **Magnetic Island** is a beautiful triangular granite core about 12km from Townsville. There's a lot to be said for a trip: lounging on a beach, swimming over coral, bouncing around in a moke from one roadside lookout to another, and enjoying the sea breeze and the island's vivid colours. Accommodation and transfer costs are considerably lower than for many of Queensland's other islands, and if you've ever wanted to spot a **koala** in the wild, this could be your chance – they're often seen wedged into gum trees up in the northeast corner of the island.

Seen from the sea, **Mount Cook** hovers above eucalypt woods variegated with patches of darker green vine forest. The north and east coasts are pinched into shallow sandy bays punctuated by eroded headlands and coral reefs, while the western part of the island is flatter and edged with mangroves. A little less than half the island is designated a **national park**, with the settlements of **Picnic Bay**, **Nelly Bay**, **Arcadia** and

Horseshoe Bay – idyllic suburbs of Townsville – dotted here and there along the east coast. Although prices are higher than on the mainland, there's no need to bring any supplies with you.

Arrival and island transport

Ferries leave from the Flinders St East jetty and the Breakwater terminal for Picnic Bay at the island's southernmost point at least ten times daily, with extra departures at weekends (☎07/4771 3855; $13 return); pick up a **timetable** from any information booth. There's no need to book – just buy a ticket at the jetty and hop on board. Some Townsville accommodation sells discounted fares, and island hostels frequently offer deals which include ferry transfers and a few night's accommodation. The *Capricorn Barges* **car ferry** (☎07/4772 5422; $98 for a car and up to six passengers), runs at least three times daily from Ross Street, about a ten-minute walk east along Palmer Street from the Transit Centre.

The island has 35km of road, including a dirt track to West Point and a sealed stretch between Picnic and Horseshoe bays. Magnetic Island Bus Service (☎07/4778 5130) meets all ferries and runs from Picnic Bay to Horseshoe Bay; their **day pass** ($9) allows unlimited travel. The alternatives are to call accommodation in advance for a pick-up, or make use of Moke Magnetic at Picnic Bay mall (☎07/4778 5377), who rent out **bikes**, **scooters** and **mini-mokes**. Mokes are great fun and cost around $35 a day (plus mileage); rental conditions stipulate a minimum driver age of 21 and that you stick to sealed roads. You can, of course, simply **walk** your way around the network of trails, or spend a day **sailing** to hard-to-reach beaches and bays with SunCat Sailing (☎07/4758 1558), who depart Magnetic Island daily for a $49 trip including lunch and afternoon tea.

Accommodation

Magnetic Island's busiest location is **Picnic Bay**, though that's not saying very much. **Nelly Bay** and **Arcadia** are even more relaxed, but the nicest beaches are to be found up around **Horseshoe Bay**. Most lodgings rent out snorkelling gear, bikes, beach gear and water sports equipment, can make tour bookings, and might pick you up if you call in advance.

Picnic Bay and Nelly Bay

Coconuts, Nelly Bay Rd, Nelly Bay (☎07/4778 5777). Shantytown of A-frame cabins and tents right on the beach, with a bistro, poorly-equipped kitchen and a bar. A once-popular party spot that now seems to be in decline, simply for want of better management and maintenance. ①.

Dunoon, The Esplanade, Picnic Bay (☎07/4778 5161). Pleasant, fully-furnished one and two-bedroom apartments with extensive landscaped grounds and pool. ⑥.

Hideaway Budget Resort, 32 Picnic St, Picnic Bay (☎07/4778 5110). Right next to Picnic Bay's hotel, with a small pool and the choice of twin or double rooms only, though you can pay per bed. ③.

Magnetic Island Tropical Resort, Yates St, Nelly Bay (☎07/4778 5955, fax 4778 5601). Exceptionally clean and comfortable chalet-style cabins each with bathroom, in a lovely bush setting. Good-value evening bistro, pool, kitchen, barbecue, plus lots of friendly birdlife. Dorms ①, cabins ③–④.

Palm View Chalets, 114 Sooning St, Nelly Bay (☎07/4778 5596). Totally self-contained and very private A-frame units surrounded by palms and views; advance booking essential. ④.

Travellers No. 1 (*Picnic Bay Hotel*), The Esplanade, Picnic Bay (☎07/4778 5166). Comfortable units and pristine 4–6-bed dorms, each with bathroom. Large pool, beer garden, kitchen and barbecue. New to the backpackers market. Dorms ①, units ④.

Arcadia and Horseshoe Bay

Arcadia Hotel Resort, 7 Marine Parade, Arcadia (☎07/4778 5177). Neat, motel-style units around a pool, plus a bar that aspires to be the island's only nightclub. Organizes dive trips, with equipment. ⑤.

Centaur House, 27 Marine Parade, Arcadia (☎07/4778 5668). This languid, tropical hostel is owner-operated (always a positive) and has recently improved facilities. Quiet, close to shops and with the best snorkelling in the area. ①.

Foresthaven Backpackers, 11 Cook Rd, Arcadia (☎07/4778 5153). Tidy cabins sleeping two to three persons per room, slowly being renovated. In a quiet location just two minutes' walk from the beach. ①.

Geoff's Place, 40 Horseshoe Bay Rd, Horseshoe Bay (☎07/4778 5577). Shaded, busy and frequently chaotic hostel, with a pool, bar and restaurant and reasonable facilities. A party place, currently being improved. ①.

Magnetic North Apartments, 2 Endeavour Rd, Arcadia (☎07/4778 5647). Large apartments sleeping up to six; nothing flash, but good value. ⑤.

Marshall's, 3 Endeavour Rd, Arcadia (☎07/4778 5112). Family atmosphere in this very friendly guesthouse with quiet garden. Breakfast is included and sociable evening barbecues are an optional extra. Three-day discounts are available. ③–④.

The island

After the thirty-minute crossing, the first thing to strike you as you step ashore at **PIC-NIC BAY** is the shade, a welcome contrast to Townsville's parched environment. Picnic Bay is quiet, and an unnecessary pedestrian mall decked out in trendy paving and lighting fortunately fails to dispel the languid atmosphere. Services include an unhelpful **information** booth (Mon–Fri 8am–4.30pm, Sat & Sun 8am–1pm), a **bank**, **post office** and Dee Jay's **store** (with EFTPOS facilities). Places to **eat** include *Andy's Chinese*, which serves huge portions, and *Tropo's Garden Bar* and *Crusoe's Restaurant*, both of which serve grills and salads.

The **beach** has a swimming enclosure and is pretty enough, but it's certainly not the best on the island, so most people head off after sorting out transport. If you want to hang around and fish, you can get tackle from Magnetic Sports on the mall. The island's often-unattended NPWS office (☎07/4778 5378) is at the end of Granite Street, where you'll also find the start of a **walking track** (8km round-trip) out to West Point, a small, assertively private community. The "main" road is closed to rental cars as it ends in a blaze of loose, powdery sand, and the only reason to head out this way is to bird-watch in the mangroves and dry-season lagoons.

Nelly Bay, Arcadia and the Forts

On the east coast, north of Picnic Bay, **NELLY BAY** is simply a sprawl of houses fronted by a fair beach with a little reef some way out. Two streets back is a shopping complex with a supermarket, Mexican restaurant and coffee shop. Bushwalkers can follow the difficult trail up **Mount Cook** from the end of Mandalay Avenue. Forest blocks the view, but take a pen and you can add your name to the list in the metal cylinder left there for the purpose.

A little further along the coast, **ARCADIA** surrounds **Geoffrey Bay** and counts the good-value *Bannister's Seafood Restaurant* among its attractions. **Alma Bay** is a perfect swimming beach hemmed in by cliffs and boulders, and there's good snorkelling over the coral, just offshore. **Diving** here (through the *Arcadia Hotel Resort*) is marred by low visibility, but there are plenty of fish and brain coral, and a disintegrating **ship-wreck**. A walking track from the end of Cook Road leads towards Mount Cook and the track to Nelly Bay, or up to Sphinx Lookout for sea views. At dawn or dusk you might see the diminutive island **rock wallaby** on an outcrop or boulder near Arcadia's jetty.

North of Arcadia the road forks, with the right branch leading to **Radical Bay** and the main road carrying on to Horseshoe. Leave your car at the junction and continue uphill on foot to **the Forts**, built during World War II to protect Townsville from attack by the Japanese. The walking track climbs gently for about 1.5km through gum-tree scenery to **gun emplacements** (now just deserted blockhouses) set one above the other among granite boulders and pine trees. Best views are from the slit windows at the command centre, right at the pinnacle of the hill. Locals rate the woods below the Forts as the best place to see **koalas**, introduced in 1930. They sleep during the day, so tracking them down involves plenty of wandering around – although if you hear ferocious pig-like grunts and squeals, then some lively koalas are not far away.

Horseshoe Bay and Radical Bay

The road ends in the north at **HORSESHOE BAY** on the island's longest beach, with a cluster of shops at its eastern end. Water World here has **jet skis**, **paragliding equipment**, **surf skis** and **boats** for rent. **Koala Park Oasis** (daily 9am–4pm; $8) offers a chance to see and pet this elusive creature and demonstrates why they're so hard to spot in the wild: the comatose grey bundles are perfectly camouflaged against eucalypt bark. Other diversions include wandering around the **Magnetic Mango** fruit plantation, where there's also a café with all kinds of fruit-laden delicacies, or going on a trail ride with **Bluey's Horseshoe Ranch** (☎07/4778 5109; $40 for the popular beach ride, $60 for a half-day ride; advance bookings only).

Walking tracks lead over the headland to Radical Bay by way of tiny **Balding Bay**, arguably the nicest on the island; you can spend a perfect day here snorkelling the coral gardens just offshore and cooking on the hotplate provided. **Radical Bay** itself is small but pretty, half a kilometre of sandy beach sandwiched between two huge, pine-swathed granite fists.

Townsville to Cairns

The character of the coast gradually begins to change beyond Townsville: just an hour to the north the arid landscape that has prevailed since Bundaberg is transformed into dark green plateaus shrouded in cloud. There's superlative scenery at **Wallaman Falls**, inland from Ingham, and also near Cairns as the slopes of the coastal mountains rise up to front the **Bellenden Ker Range**. Forests here once formed a continuous belt almost to Cooktown but logging has thinned them to a disjointed necklace of plantations and national parks. Even so, it seems that almost every side-track off the highway leads to a waterhole or falls surrounded by natural jungle – this is where it really helps to have your own vehicle. There is also a handful of **islands**, including the wilds of **Hinchinbrook**, as well as the **Mission Beach** area between Tully and Innisfail, where you might find regular work on fruit plantations or further opportunities to slump on the sand.

The Paluma Range and Jourama National Park

The change in climate starts some 60km from Townsville, in the **Paluma Range**. The Mount Spec road turns off the highway and climbs a crooked 21km to Paluma township. Halfway there, a solid stone bridge spans **Little Crystal Creek**, which you might want to follow as it burbles over cascades into swimming holes overshadowed by rainforest – look out for large, metallic-blue Ulysses butterflies bobbing around the canopy. **PALUMA** marks the top of the range and the start of trails into the forest. *Ivy Cottage Tearooms* (daily except Mon 10am–4pm) which doubles as the post office, is famous for its lovely garden full of almost-domesticated birds including the normally elusive

Victoria riflebirds, and gorgeous black-and-blue birds of paradise. Paluma's sole **accommodation** is offered by *Misthaven Units* in self-contained cabins (☎07/4721 2060; ④).

Past the turn-off at the dam, the range descends west, leaving the dark, wet coastal forest for open gum woodland. *Hidden Valley Cabins* (☎07/4770 8088; ②–④), 24km past Paluma on a dirt road, provides everything you'll need: spa, pool, beer, meals and packed lunches. Nearby is **the Gorge**, a lively section of river with falls, rapids and pools – drive down in a 4WD or walk the last kilometre.

Back on the coastal highway, you pass *Frosty Mango* roadhouse (daily 8am–6pm), whose exotic fresh cakes and ice creams are made from locally grown fruit, before encountering more aquatic fun at **Jourama Falls**, 20km north of the Crystal Creek junction. After turning west off the highway, the five-kilometre unsurfaced road to Jourama ends at a very pleasant, open NPWS **campsite** (contact Townsville or Ingham NPWS first for booking details), from where an hour-long walking track follows chains across the rocky riverbed to more swimming holes and the falls themselves – which are impressive in full flood but fairly insignificant by the end of the dry season.

Ingham and around

INGHAM, 110km north of Townsville and home to Australia's largest Italian community, is well placed for trips inland to three national parks or for access to the port of Lucinda. The road through the centre is **Lannercost Street**, on which you'll find everything you need; interstate **buses** stop opposite the theatre ten times daily. You can pick up **information** on the area at the Hinchinbrook Visitor Centre (Mon–Fri 8am–5pm, Sat & Sun 9am–2pm), on the corner where the highway from Townsville meets Lannercost Street whilst the NPWS office, which issues **permits** and information about local parks and Hinchinbrook Island, is at 49 Cassady St (PO Box 1293; Mon–Fri 9am–5pm; ☎07/4776 1700). **Accommodation** prospects include the *Palm Tree Caravan Park* (☎07/4776 2403) and *Ingham Motel* (☎07/4776 2355; ④) on the highway at the south entrance to town, or the dubious comforts of a cheap dorm bed at the *Royal Hotel* (①) on Lannercost Street. For the national parks, turn west to **Trebonne** (lucidly marked "This road is not Route 1"); for Lucinda, follow the signs for Forest Beach and Halifax.

Mount Fox, Wallaman Falls and Herbert River

The road divides at Trebonne, the northern branch running 50km to the borders of Lumholtz National Park, the southern route splitting again to Wallaman Falls or Mount Fox. For **Mount Fox National Park**, stay on the sealed road for 55km as it crosses cattle country to the base of this extinct volcano cone. A rocky, loose path climbs to the crater rim through scanty forest; it's hot work, so start early.

The **Wallaman Falls** track initially follows the same road, but soon leaves the bitumen, on a signposted turning to the right, for a dusty forty-kilometre run up the tight and twisting range; heavy rain makes it impassable. Tunnelling through thick rainforest along the ridge, the road emerges at an NPWS **campsite** before reaching the falls lookout. The falls – Australia's highest at 305m – really are spectacular, leaping in a thin ribbon over the sheer cliffs of the plateau opposite and appearing to vaporize by the time they reach the gorge floor. A walk down to the base dispels this impression, as the mist turns out to be from the force of water hitting the plunge pool; platypuses are sometimes seen further downstream on Stony Creek.

Set around the **Herbert River**, the open woodland and pockets of dense rainforest at **Lumholtz National Park** shield rare kangaroos and possums, but the area is of interest mainly for its undeveloped state which makes it the preserve of determined bushwalkers only. A 4WD is needed to reach the **Yamanie Falls** track's trailhead at the end of the road from Trebonne, but contact the NPWS first – you need to know the latest on several **saltwater crocodiles** resident in the river – and come fully equipped for a two-day hike.

Lucinda and the Palm islands

LUCINDA is simply a store and a few homes scattered around a sugar-loading terminal's immense jetty, 25km northeast of Ingham. Most people find themselves here as they return from the hike along Hinchinbrook Island's east coast (see below), but there are a couple of other nearby islands that reward the effort required to get to them. While **Great Palm Island** is an off-limits Aboriginal reserve, both **Orpheus** and **Pelorus** are undeveloped strips of forest and beach surrounded by reef – perfect places for a few days of quiet snorkelling. There are basic NPWS **campsites** on Orpheus and free camping on Pelorus's central beach, but you'll need to take everything with you – especially water. A **boat charter** will cost at least $120, which isn't unrealistic for over several days: contact Jim Judge (PO Box 84, Halifax, Qld 4850; ☎07/4777 8220) or Bill Pearce (48 Patterson Parade, Lucinda; ☎07/4777 8307).

Cardwell

There's very little to **CARDWELL** – just a quiet string of shops on one side of the highway, and the sea on the other – but it's somehow attractive, not least because Hinchinbrook Island hovers just offshore, so close that it almost seems to be part of the mainland; it's also well-placed for waterfall watching and forest walks that could keep you busy for several days. Cardwell has recently been in the news, as property developers and the government have wrangled over the building of a huge resort and marina to the south of town in a "protected" mangrove zone and **dugong** sanctuary. Work proceeds slowly with the aim of doubling tourism in the region, but the resulting increase in marine traffic and the uncontrolled access to Hinchinbrook could be disastrous for this fragile area. The numbers of dugongs (sea cows), once common in the area, and the sea-grass beds on which they feed have declined drastically, though now appear to be stabilizing.

In Cardwell services are spread out for about 2km along the highway, with banks, the post office, supermarket, hotel and the *Seaview Café* (where interstate **buses** stop) near or south of the **jetty**, itself about halfway along. The best of the **accommodation** is north of the jetty at *Kookaburra Caravan Park*, 175 Bruce Highway (☎07/4066 8648; ①–④), which has everything from motel rooms to tent sites and a self-contained hostel block, and free use of bikes, fishing gear and coconuts; and *Cardwell Beachfront Motel*, 1 Scott St (☎07/4066 8776; ④), which nearly faces the sea. Just north of the jetty, the NPWS-run **Rainforest and Reef Centre** (☎07/4066 8601; Mon–Fri 8am–4.30pm, Sat–Sun 8am–noon; free) issues island permits.

Hinchinbrook Island

Across the channel from Cardwell, **Hinchinbrook Island** looms huge and green, with mangroves rising to forest along the mountain range that runs along the island's spine and peaks at **Mount Bowen**. The drier east side, hidden behind the mountains, has long beaches separated by headlands and the occasional sluggish creek. This was Giramay Aboriginal land, and though early Europeans reported the people as friendly, attitudes changed with white settlement and nineteenth-century "dispersals" had the same effect here as elsewhere. The island was never subsequently occupied; apart from an insular resort, Hinchinbrook remains much as it was two hundred years ago.

Bushwalkers explored as best they could until the NPWS were prompted to form the vague paths along the east coast into a thirty-kilometre track. If you are moderately fit and have the slightest interest in hiking, this **East Coast Trail** (or Thorsborne Track) is a must. More adventurous, unmarked routes scale Mount Straloch – site of a USAF B24 **plane wreck** from World War II – and Mount Bowen from the east coast; you'll need permission and advice from the NPWS in Cardwell (see opposite) to tackle these.

The East Coast Trail

The thirty-kilometre **East Coast Trail** is manageable in two days, though at that pace you won't see much. **Trailheads** are at Ramsay Bay in the north and George Point in the south, and the route is marked with orange triangles.

Boats from Cardwell take you through the mangroves of Missionary Bay in the north to a boardwalk that traces the eastern side of the island at the south end of **Ramsay Bay**. The walk from here to **Nina Bay**, which takes a couple of hours, is along a fantastic stretch of coast with rainforest sweeping right down to the sand and Mount Bowen and Nina Peak as a backdrop. If long bushwalks don't appeal, spend a few days here; drinkable water from a creek spills out onto the end of the beach. Otherwise, continue beyond a small cliff at the southern end of Nina, and walk through a pine forest to **Little Ramsay Bay** (drinking water from Warrawilla Creek), which is about as far as you're likely to get on the first day.

Moving on, you rock-hop over boulders at the far end of the beach before crossing another creek (at low tide, as it gets fairly deep) and entering the forest beyond. From here to the next camp at **Zoe Bay** takes about five hours, following creek beds through lowland casuarina woods and rainforest, before exiting onto the beach near Cypress Pine waterhole. A clearing at the southern end of Zoe Bay beside South Zoe Creek marks the campsite, and water bottles can be filled just beyond – but heed the crocodile warnings. This is one of those places where you'll be very glad you brought insect repellent.

Next day, take the path to the base of **Zoe Falls**, then struggle straight up to the cliff top, from where there are great vistas. Across the river, forest and heathland alternate: the hardest part is crossing **Diamantina Creek** – a fast-flowing river with huge, slippery boulders. **Mulligan Falls**, not much further on, is the last source of fresh water, with several rock ledges for sunbathing above a pool full of curious fish. Zoe to Mulligan takes around four hours, and from here to George Point is only a couple more if you push it, but the falls are a better place to camp and give you the chance to backtrack a little to take a look at **Sunken Reef Bay**.

The last leg to **George Point** is the least interesting: rainforest replaces the highland trees around the falls as the path crosses a final creek before arriving at unattractive **Mulligan Bay**. The campsite at George Point has a table and fireplace in the shelter of a coconut grove but there's nothing to see except Lucinda's sugar terminal, and little to do except wait for your ferry.

Practicalities

The usual procedure for the East Coast Trail is to start in the north and walk south to George Point, opposite Lucinda. Hinchinbrook Island Ferries, on the highway opposite the jetty (☎07/4066 8270), can organize transport to and from the island. For $90 return, you land on the north shore of the island, are picked up at George Point and bussed back to Cardwell. Alternatively, a $69 return fare will drop you and pick you up in the north. You'll also need to get NPWS **camping permits** ($3.50 per person a night) in advance. As the number of bushwalkers allowed on the island at any one time is limited to forty-five, the trail is usually booked solid. To be sure of getting a place during Christmas and Easter holidays, aim to book three or four months in advance; otherwise, a month should be enough. **Bookings** can be made through NPWS offices in Cardwell, Ingham and at the Great Barrier Reef Wonderland in Townsville.

Optimum conditions are during winter (June–Oct) but it rains frequently all year. Essentials include water-resistant footgear, pack and tent, a lightweight raincoat and insect repellent; **camping gear** is available from Hinchinbrook Island Ferries and *Kookaburra Van Park*. Although streams with **drinking water** are fairly evenly distributed, they might be dry by the end of winter – take care to collect from flowing sources only. Wood fires are prohibited, so bring a fuel stove. Accommodation and booking agents in Cardwell rent out limited camping gear. Melomys – marsupial mice – sometimes gnaw through tents to reach food; the NPWS have installed metal food stores at campsites, though hanging anything edible from a branch may also foil their attempts. Snakes are also common, if seldom encountered, and you should beware of crocodiles in lowland creek systems.

At the island's northern tip, **Cape Richards** bolds a luxurious **resort** (☎07/4066 8585, reservations and boat connections free call ☎1800/777 021; ⑨), whose charming units are connected by walkways; it's a real treat, if your budget will allow it. An hour's stroll along the track through the forest leads to **Macushla**, a pretty beach with tent sites but no water.

If you'd prefer to spend your time **cruising**, there are a number of options from Cardwell. Hinchinbrook Island Ferries run **day-trips** ($59) to Hinchinbrook or the reef around **Brook** and **Goold islands** – you can camp on the latter. **Bareboats** from Hinchinbrook Rent a Yacht (☎07/4066 8007) work out around $90 per person per day for a group.

Edmund Kennedy National Park and Murray Falls

The **Edmund Kennedy expedition** landed north of Cardwell in May 1848, complete with one hundred sheep and three carts, and set off to walk to Cape York. Slowed by dense vegetation and harassed by local tribes, the party gradually ran out of food and by December Kennedy had left the others while he raced the last 100km with his Aboriginal companion, **Jackey-Jackey Galmarra**. Kennedy was killed by Jadhaigana Aborigines while negotiating a river within sight of the cape; Jackey managed to reach the waiting schooner *Ariel*, which set off down the coast to find only two of the other expedition members still alive. **Edmund Kennedy National Park**, off the highway 22km from Cardwell, marks the spot where the expedition struck inland, and you have to ponder the wisdom of trying to manoeuvre carts through the paperbark and mangrove thickets – romantically described by Kennedy's informant as "wooded hills and green valleys". There are boardwalks and trails here, and views across to Dunk and Hinchinbrook islands from the beach; information can be obtained from the NPWS in the park (☎07/4066 8850).

The road to **Murray Falls**, roughly opposite (with a better-surfaced alternative 10km north), heads 20km past banana plantations to the edge of the Cardwell Range and the falls themselves. There are two **camping areas** here and tracks through the forest to permanent swimming holes and lookouts across the bowl of the valley. The nearest source of supplies is the store on the approach road, some distance from the falls.

Tully, Mission Beach and Dunk Island

Two hundred kilometres north of Townsville, **TULLY** lies to the left of the highway on Mount Tyson's foothills, its 450-centimetre annual rainfall the highest in Australia. Settled by Chinese, who pioneered banana plantations here at the turn of the century, it's nothing special today: cultivated lawns and flowerbeds back onto roaring jungle at the end of Brannigan Street, a constant reminder of the colonists' struggle to keep chaos at bay. *Tully Backpackers* at 19 Richardson St (☎07/4068 2820; ①) and *The Savoy*, 4 Plumb St (☎07/4068 2400; ①), have **work** connections, but most people drive the extra thirty minutes to spend a few days around **Mission Beach**, a peaceful stretch of beach and forest with access to **Dunk Island**.

Mission Beach and around

The Mission Beach area is named after the **Hull River Mission**, destroyed by the savage 1918 cyclone and thence relocated to safer surroundings on Palm Island. After branching east off the highway a couple of kilometres past Tully, a road runs 18km through canefields and patches of rainforest to the seafront, where the area's four disconnected hamlets dot the roadside for 14km. Turning south when you reach the coast takes you 3km to **SOUTH MISSION**, where a monument to the Hull River Mission stands at the original site, signposted off the main road on Mission Drive. Follow the main road to the very end, and you'll find the **Kennedy Walking Track**, which weaves through coastal swamp and forest for a couple of hours to where Edmund Kennedy landed near the Hull River. Heading 8km in the opposite direction past **WONGALING BEACH**'s shopping centre, you reach **MISSION BEACH** itself, a cluster of shops, restaurants and banks, where **buses** set down outside the post office; 6km further north past **Clump Point Jetty** is residential **BINGIL BAY**. Beaches aside, there's an excellent eight-kilometre **walking track** between Mission Beach township and the road back to the highway, where you can tramp through steamy State Forest-maintained **licuala fan palm** and vine greenery; look for **cassowaries**, a blue-headed and bone-crested rainforest version of the emu, whose survival is being threatened as the rainforests are carved up. Many of the forest's larger trees rely on the cassowary as the only beast big enough to eat their fruit and distribute their seeds, meaning that the very makeup of the forest hinges on its presence. Unlike the emu, the cassowary is not at all timid and is quite capable of maiming if provoked: if you are lucky enough to see one in the wild, remain quiet and keep a safe distance.

Mission Beach has a fairly comprehensive set of **shops** and eating places grouped at the south end of Porters Promenade, beginning with the **Post Office** which doubles as a pick-up point for Hostel buses. A **local bus** (☎07/4068 5468) plies between South Mission and Bingil Bay roughly eight times daily between 8.30am and 8.30pm (restricted service Saturday). The tourist **information** office is further along Porters Promenade, close to the **local history centre**. Behind the centre, a cassowary conservation group runs a nursery growing seeds from carefully collected cassowary droppings, with the aim of safeguarding the food supply for future generations of the giant bird.

Accommodation options include the private *Licuala Lodge*, 11 Mission Circle, Mission Beach (☎07/4068 8194; ⑤), a tropical-style guesthouse with airy verandahs; self-contained, modern units around a shady garden and pool at *Mackays*, 7 Porter Promenade, Mission Beach (☎07/4068 7212, fax 4068 7095; ⑥); and beachfront *Castaways Resort*, Pacific Parade, Mission Beach (☎07/4068 7444; ⑥), a comfortable, more upmarket place with large, balconied rooms looking out to sea. The best in the **budget range** is the *YHA/Treehouse Hostel* at Bingil Bay (☎07/4068 7137; ①), a splendid pole-frame house surrounded by forest, though some distance from the beach. Closer to the waterfront are *Scotty's Beachhouse*, 164 Reid Rd, Wongaling (☎07/4068 8676; ①), an excellent, busy place with bunkhouses around a pool and a huge **restaurant**; and *Mission Beach Backpackers*, 28 Wongaling Beach Rd (☎07/4068 8317; ①), whose large dorms are also close to shops and the area's only pub. All the hostels have a pool, kitchen, cheap meals, barbecue nights, guided **rainforest walks** with Giramay Aborigines, **white-water rafting** on the Tully River and bike rental. **Campsites** include *Coconut Caravan Village*, South Mission Beach (☎07/4068 8129), which also has tidy twin-share units (②); and *Hideaway*, Mission Beach (☎07/4068 7104; cabins ③, tent sites ①).

Dunk Island and beyond the Reef

In 1898 Edmund Banfield, a Townsville journalist who had been given only weeks to live, waded ashore on **Dunk Island**. He spent his remaining years – twenty-five of them – as Dunk's first European resident, crediting his unanticipated longevity to the relaxed island life. A tiny version of Hinchinbrook, Dunk attracts far more visitors to its resort and camping grounds. While there is a reasonably satisfying track over and around the island, it's more the kind of place where you make the most of the beach – as Banfield discovered.

Vessels from the Mission Beach area put ashore on or near the jetty, next to a beach rental shop and **canteen** selling sandwiches and hot meals; there's no store on the island. On the far side is the shady NPWS **campsite** (☎07/4068 8199 for permits and details), with toilets, showers and drinking water. Five minutes along the track is the **resort** (☎07/4068 8199; ⑨), a low-key affair well hidden by vegetation. The best places to relax are either on **Brammo Bay**, in front of the resort, or **Pallon Beach**, behind the campsite. Note that the beaches are narrow at high tide and the island is close enough to the coast to attract box jellyfish in season, but you can always retreat to the resort pool.

Before falling victim to incipient lethargy, head into the interior past the resort and Banfield's grave (still carefully tended) for a circuit of the island's west. The full 9km up **Mount Cootaloo**, down to **Palm Valley** and back along the coast is a three-hour rainforest trek, best tackled clockwise from the resort. You'll see green pigeons and yellow-footed scrubfowl foraging in leaf litter, vines, trunkless palms and, from the peak, a vivid blue sea dotted with hunchbacked islands.

Ferries to Dunk cost $22 (see box opposite for details of operators), and you can book directly or through your accommodation. The island is barely fifteen minutes offshore, but even so the tiny water taxis are not really suitable if you have much luggage. **Camping gear** can be rented from the complex next to the post office in Mission Beach; you can also leave surplus equipment with them.

Some distance northeast of Dunk is **Beaver Cay**, the local section of the Barrier Reef, with a sand island and some very pretty coral gardens that make for easy snorkelling or diving. In addition to *Quick Cat* (see box opposite), Friendship Cruises (☎07/4068 7262) at Clump Point Jetty run their old pilot vessel daily to Beaver for a very reasonable $59, which includes free pick-up and lunch (diving by arrangement).

Innisfail and the Bellenden Ker Range

Back on the highway, the next major town is **INNISFAIL**, a busy place on the Johnstone River which has clearly seen better times but is still a good spot to look for **work** picking bananas in season: *Backpackers Innisfail*, 73 Rankin St (☎07/4061 2284; ①), near the bright pink Catholic church, can help if you stay with them. But even if you don't, Innisfail is worth a quick look as a reminder that modern Australia was in no way built by the British alone: there's a huge **Italian community** here, represented by the handful of delicatessens displaying herb sausages and fresh pasta along the central Edith Street. The tiny red **Chinese Confucian temple** (and huge longan tree next to it) was first established in the 1880s by migrant workers from southern China, who cleared scrub and ran market gardens.

Just beyond town, the Palmerston Highway turns off across the bottom end of the Atherton Tablelands, and at about the same point you begin to see the **Bellenden Ker Range**, which dominates the remaining 80km to Cairns. This coastal aspect of the tablelands includes Queensland's highest mountain, **Bartle Frere**. While the two-day return climb through **Wooroonooran National Park** to the 1600-metre summit is within the reach of any fit, well-prepared bushwalker, the path is unformed, which

---

DUNK ISLAND FERRIES

All the ferries detailed below run daily, and all cost $22 return.

Dunk Island Cruises, Clump Point (☎07/4068 7211). Departs 8.45am & 10.30am; can also provide a coach pick-up from Cairns or Innisfail.
Dunk Island Express, Wongaling Beach (☎07/4068 8310). Departs 8am, 9am, 10am, 11am, 12.30pm, 2pm & 4.30pm; last boat leaves Dunk 5pm. Free car lock-up available.
Quick Cat, Clump Point (☎07/4068 7289). Departs 10am; after dropping passengers at Dunk, continues out to Beaver Cay on the Barrier Reef for coral viewing, snorkelling and diving ($125; dives extra).

---

means that you should contact the park ranger (☎07/4067 6304) or the Cairns NPWS in advance (see p.451) for accurate information about the route. To reach the start of the track, leave the highway 19km north of Ingham at one-house Pawngilly and continue for 8km, past Bartle Frere township, to **Josephine Falls**. Even without going any further, the falls – wonderfully enclosed jungle waterslides – are worth the trip. Marked with orange triangles, the climb to the peak passes through rainforest, over large granite boulders and out onto moorland with wind-stunted vegetation. Much of the summit is blinded by scrub and usually cloaked in rain, but there are great views of the tablelands and coast during the ascent.

Further along the highway, there's a detour at **Babinda** to another waterhole at **the Boulders**, where an arm of Babinda Creek forms a wide pool before spilling down a collection of house-sized granite slabs. Cool and relatively shallow, the waterhole is an excellent place to swim and do acrobatics from a rope swing, but belies a more sinister reputation. Several deaths have been caused by subtle undertows dragging people over the falls, so it's advisable to be very careful. Legend has it that an Aboriginal girl was raped here and in reprisal she cursed the pool against men.

Nearing the end of the range at Gordonvale, the tortuous **Gillies Highway** climbs from the coast to lakes Barrine and Eacham on the tableland. Marking the turn-off is **Walsh's Pyramid**, a natural formation which really does look like an overgrown version of its Egyptian counterpart. From here, the last section of the Bruce Highway carries you – in thirty minutes – through the suburbs of Edmonton and White Rock to Cairns.

Cairns

CAIRNS was pegged out over the site of a sea-slug fishing camp when gold was found to the north in 1876, though it was the Atherton Tablelands' tin and timber resources that really established the town and kept it ahead of its nearby rival, Port Douglas (see p.460). The harbour is the focus of the north's fish and prawn concerns, and tourism began modestly when **marlin fishing** became popular after World War II. But with the "discovery" of the **reef** in the 1980s and the appeal of the local climate, tourism snowballed, and Cairns today seems to be little more than a tropical version of the Gold Coast. High-profile development seeks to capitalize on tourism at the expense of what everyone originally came to Cairns to enjoy: a beautiful, unspoiled, lazy **tropical atmosphere**. Wild stories about plans for the city's future abound, and though they may sound far-fetched (such as a tunnel under Trinity Inlet, or reinstating the lost sandy beach), some may be more than rumour. The truth is that nobody can keep up with the pace of change, and based on what *has* happened in the last few years, anything is possible.

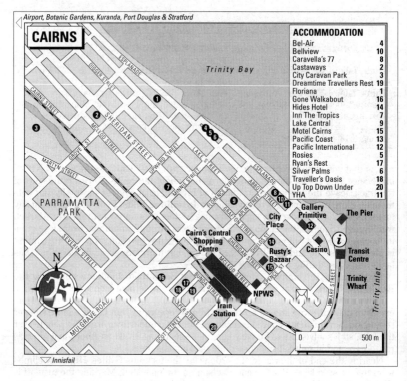

Airport, Botanic Gardens, Kuranda, Port Douglas & Stratford

CAIRNS

Trinity Bay

ACCOMMODATION

Bel-Air	4
Bellview	10
Caravella's 77	8
Castaways	2
City Caravan Park	3
Dreamtime Travellers Rest	19
Floriana	1
Gone Walkabout	16
Hides Hotel	14
Inn The Tropics	7
Lake Central	9
Motel Cairns	15
Pacific Coast	13
Pacific International	12
Rosies	5
Ryan's Rest	17
Silver Palms	6
Traveller's Oasis	18
Up Top Down Under	20
YHA	11

PARRAMATTA PARK

Gallery Primitive   The Pier

City Place

Cairn's Central Shopping Centre

Rusty's Bazaar

Casino

Transit Centre

Trinity Wharf

NPWS

Train Station

0   500 m

Innisfail

For many visitors primed by hype, the city falls far short of expectations. However, if you can accept the tourist industry's shocking glibness and the fact that you're unlikely to escape the crowds, you'll find a great deal on offer and easy access to the surrounding area – the Atherton Tablelands, Cape York and, naturally, the Great Barrier Reef and islands. Used as a base to explore these regions, Cairns can be fun, as long as you accept its limitations.

Arrival and accommodation

Downtown Cairns is the grid of streets behind the Esplanade, overlooking the harbour and Trinity Bay. **Buses** arrive at the end of the Esplanade at **Trinity Wharf Transit Centre**, while the **train station** is 750m away under the new **Cairns Central** development between Bunda Street and McLeod Street (the bus terminal may also move here from Trinity Wharf). If you're staying in a hostel, you'll usually be picked up at the Transit Centre, and possibly from the train and airport if you give advance notice. The **airport** is about 7km north, along the Cook Highway. A **taxi** from the airport into Cairns costs $10; a **shuttle bus** ($4.50) connects with most flights and delivers to all central accommodation. Sunbus, a newly improved **local bus** service, is based at the **Transit Mall** on City Place (Lake Street), and serves several beaches north as far as Ellis Beach; passes are available for a day, week or month. You may also be able to **rent bikes** at your accommodation for getting about, or you could check out the vehicle rental outfits in "Listings" on p.450. If you're after a secondhand car, or want to sell one, head for the Esplanade, scene of an informal trade amongst back-packers.

Unofficial **tourist information centres** abound throughout the centre, each promoting its favourite tours, though all accommodation and many businesses in Cairns can offer much the same. The **Travellers' Contact Point** (daily 9am–6pm) in Shields Street, just north of City Place, gives out basic information for backpackers; it also has a free-for-all notice board and is one of the city's bases for **Internet services** (see "Listings", p.451).

Accommodation

The bulk of lodgings are along the Esplanade, with luxury high-rises overlooking the bay and much of the city's **budget accommodation** between Shields and Aplin streets. If you don't want to party, however, avoid hostels in this area. Expect seasonal **price fluctuations** everywhere, especially at the ruthlessly competitive hostels where there tends to be something of a shortfall despite the quantity of rooms; **book ahead** but beware of committing yourself to a special deal on a longer stay until you've seen the room – you probably won't be able to get a refund. All hostels have kitchens, most have a courtesy bus service, laundry and a pool. There is often scope for haggling over hostel prices, especially when it's quieter (October–April) but bear in mind that competition means slim profits are made on beds: you're only of value while you're still booking tours through the hostel. The nearest **campsite** to the centre is the **City Caravan Park**, at 14 Little St (☎07/4051 1467).

Bel-Air, 157 Esplanade (☎07/4031 4790). Some rooms are stuffy, but it's generally more relaxed than others in the neighbourhood. ①.

Bellview, 85 Esplanade (☎07/4031 4377). Clean and comfortable hostel with good, motel-like facilities; one of the best organized on the Esplanade. ②–③.

Caravella's 77, 77 Esplanade (☎07/4051 2159). A very busy place, with small dorms and a warren of dark corridors and passages. ①.

Castaways, 207 Sheridan St (☎07/4051 1238). Small but sociable hostel, about twenty minutes' walk from the centre, with good facilities including many double and twin rooms and small dorms. ①–③.

Dreamtime Travellers Rest, 4 Terminus St, behind the train station (☎07/4031 6753). A small, clean, friendly hostel about ten minutes' walk from the centre, and the best option after *Gone Walkabout*. Excellent deals on offer to the Atherton Tablelands to stay at their sister hostel at Yungaburra (includes accommodation, transport and activities; see p.458). ①.

Floriana, 183 Esplanade (☎07/4051 7886). Amiable guesthouse overlooking the sea, with Art Deco decor in the reception and small shared units or self-contained rooms and cabins. ⑤.

Gone Walkabout, 274 Draper St (☎07/4051 6160). Cairns' nicest hostel – all the better for being a ten-minute walk from the centre. Small, welcoming and tidy, with a spa pool, air-con dorms or rooms and a very well informed proprietor. ①.

Hides Hotel, corner of Lake and Shields streets (☎07/4051 1266). One of the oldest hotels in town (and formerly the roughest), now totally revamped under the Flag banner. ⑥.

Inn The Tropics, 141 Sheridan St (☎07/4031 1088). Comfortable, upmarket hostel with pool, kitchen, barbecue area and self-contained accommodation. ③.

Lake Central, 137 Lake St (☎07/4051 4933, fax 4051 9716). Modern and smart self-contained units with pool; good central location. ⑧.

Leo's, 100 Sheridan St (☎07/4051 1264). Clean and tidy rooms in an old-style pub converted to a guesthouse; seaside boarding house atmosphere, wooden balcony, small pool and garden. ①–④.

Lillybank, 75 Kamerunga Rd, Stratford (☎07/4055 1123, fax 4058 1990). Very pleasant B&B accommodation off the highway 8km north of the centre. ④–⑤.

Motel Cairns, 48 Spence St (☎07/4051 2271). Certainly nothing elaborate, but close to everything. ③.

Pacific International, corner of Spence St and Esplanade (☎07/4051 7888, fax 4031 1445). Plush high-rise hotel in a prime location close to the casino, restaurants and shops. ⑦.

Rosies, 155 Esplanade (☎07/4051 0235). Secure, informed hostel; rooms are small but otherwise pretty pleasant. ①.

Ryan's Rest, 18 Terminus St (☎07/4051 4734). Another quiet and comfortable budget option west of the train station, in a converted old Queenslander house. ③.

Silver Palms, 153 Esplanade (☎07/4031 6099). Guesthouse with shared facilities and simple rooms. ④.

Traveller's Oasis, 5 Terminus St (☎07/4052 1377). Recently opened hostel in a traditional house in a quiet street. ①.

Up Top Down Under, 164 Spence St (☎07/4051 3636). The best of Cairns' bigger hostels. Cheap meals, helpful staff and enough space to relax. ①.

YHA on the Esplanade, 93 Esplanade (☎07/4031 1919). Crowded, animated hostel, but very pushy with tour bookings. ①–②.

The City

Cairns' strength is in doing, not seeing: there are few monuments, natural or otherwise. This is partly because the Cape York goldfields were too far away and profits were channelled through Cooktown, and partly because Cairns was remote, lacking a rail link with Townsville until 1924; people came here to exploit resources, not to settle. Your best introduction to the region's heritage is at the **Cairns Historical Museum**, Shields and Lake streets (Mon–Sat 10am–3pm; $3), which uses photos and some interesting exhibits to cover maritime history, the Tjapukai and Bama Aborigines from the tablelands, and Chinese involvement in the city and Palmer goldfields.

At **City Place**, the **pedestrian mall** around the museum, you'll find Cairns' souvenir-shopping centre, with limitless quantities of cafés, and shops selling T-shirts, paintings and cuddly koalas. Local orators and performers do their best (or worst) at the small **sound shell** here from time to time, and there are often more professional offerings in the evenings and on holidays. Between Grafton and Sheridan Streets, towards Spence Street, **Rusty's Bazaar markets** (Fri evening, Sat & Sun morning) sell a great range of local produce from crafts to herbs, coffee and fish. Moving from the mall area down towards Trinity Wharf, the shops become more upmarket, though they're still selling essentially the same things; an increasing number of signs target the many Japanese visitors. While you're down this way, drop into Gallery Primitive, 26 Abbott St – though actually a shop, it's virtually a museum of Pacific crafts and well worth a visit. **Trinity Wharf** itself is a lacklustre collection of shops and **cruise terminals**, but you might find solace in the bar above the bus station, which overlooks Trinity Inlet. The *Barrier Reef Hotel*, opposite, is the last of the original rough-and-ready bars; if you're after local colour, this is where you'll find it.

The **casino**, newly opened in 1995 but already debt-ridden – as investors from the Sydney 2000 Olympic Committee discovered too late – faces The Pier, a flashy shopping complex, where many tour and cruise operators have booking offices ready to tempt you with brochures and videos of their activities. An **aquarium** (daily 9am–5pm; $15) here has regular feeding shows and big tanks full of hulking Barrier Reef species such as maori wrasse and potato cod, but the display lacks the punch of those at Townsville (see p.433) and Mooloolaba (see p.381).

In the evenings, the **Esplanade** is packed with people cruising between accommodation and restaurants. Grabbing an early-morning coffee here, you'll witness a quintessentially Australian scene: fig trees framing the waterfront, a couple of trawlers and seaplanes bobbing at anchor in the harbour, and drunks languishing on the benches. Joggers jog, and others promenade along the edge at low tide and watch birds feeding on the mud flats – there's an identification chart in the park. Sand actually covered the seafront until Trinity Inlet was dredged during World War II, and while conservationists are happy with the mangroves, others with plans to restore the beaches are busy pulling them out. The **night market** (daily 5pm–late) on the Esplanade just up from the Aplin Street intersection has a mix of trendy tack and good-quality souvenirs, and a good location near plenty of bars.

Heading out of the centre, the city's natural attractions include the spectacular **Botanic Gardens** (Mon–Fri 8.30am–5.30pm; free) and the adjacent **Mount Whitfield Environmental Park** on Collins Avenue, off the highway near the airport (bus #1B from the transit mall, or a rather dull forty-minute walk). Ringed by suburbia, the rainforest is dense enough for cassowaries and wallabies, and a raised boardwalk track through the wonderfully cool and tranquil atmosphere makes a fine escape from the city. Also worth a look are the **mangrove walks** on the airport road, which, from boardwalks and hides, give you a chance to see the different varieties of mangrove trees, mudskippers and red clawed, asymmetric fiddler crabs. Take some repellent or else give the flies a free lunch.

Eating and nightlife

Cairns has no shortage of places to **eat**. Least expensive are the takeaways between the Esplanade's hostels serving Chinese food, falafel, kebabs and pasta. Some open early while others, such as *La Pizza* on the corner of Aplin Street, never close, switching from fast food during the day and evening to coffee and croissants at dawn. Cairns Central also houses a fast-food plaza upstairs, with a choice ranging from fish and chips to pizza or sushi. If you want to eat in, any of the restaurants listed below offer good value; alternatively, you can stock up at the **supermarkets** on Lake and Sheridan streets, or in Cairns Central.

Openly **drinking** on the streets is now illegal and rigidly enforced in Cairns, but the pub and club culture still thrives. **Clubs** open around 6pm. Most charge $5 entry for bar and disco entertainment, more if there's a band playing; some will collect you from your hostel and throw in a free or discounted meal. Many **pubs** also feature **live music** once a week – reviews and details are in Cairns' free weekly **listings magazine**, *Son of Barfly*. One way to have an unforgettably bad night out is to binge-drink and make yourself an obvious target for **pickpockets** and bag-snatchers who work the nightclubs. More worrying is the increase in reported rapes in recent years – make sure you arrange some form of **safe transport** back to your accommodation.

Cafés and restaurants

Barnacle Bill, 65 Esplanade (☎07/4051 2241). Get in early or book for this popular seafood restaurant, where you choose your lobster and Moreton Bay Bugs from the live tank. Open daily from 5pm; main courses for around $25.

Casa Mia, 82 Sheridan St (☎07/4051 5871). Mediterranean-style garden restaurant with the accent on Spain. From $15 for main courses.

The Chapel, 90 Esplanade. Varied menu and live jazz bands.

Cock & Bull, 6 Grove St, junction with Grafton St. Keg Guinness, good-quality and huge counter meals ($9–12) and a pleasant garden atmosphere.

Gypsy Dees, 41a Shields St (☎07/4051 5530). A mixture of Oriental and European main courses from $16, backed by a bar and live music.

La Fettuccine, 43 Shields St (☎07/4031 5959). Excellent home-made pasta from $13.

Mediterranean Café, 92 Lake St. Best of the mall's snack bars, with good spinach and feta rolls.

Mozart Pastry, 42 Spence St. Top-notch patisserie with crisp strudels, rich cakes and fine coffee.

Red Ochre, 43 Shields St (☎07/4051 0100). Popular upmarket grill restaurant featuring crocodile, emu, kangaroo and other native ingredients – a good place to splash out a little. $18 and up.

Samuel's at the *Playpen*, corner of Lake and Hartley streets. Budget restaurant and salad bar attached to a club.

Taj, 61 Spence St, at the corner of Sheridan St (☎07/4051 2228). Curries ranging from mild to incendiary and including vegetarian options; a $16 thali is served on Wednesday. Open from 6pm.

Woolshed, 22 Shields St. Budget/backpackers' diner. Huge and inexpensive meals, beer by the jug and party fever. Hostels give out vouchers for various meal deals here.

Yama Japanese, corner of Grafton and Spence streets (☎07/4052 1009). Long-running favourite with homesick Japanese visitors; sushi and sashimi $22; teriyaki or tempura $18.

Nightlife

The Beach, corner of Abbott and Aplin streets. Traditional backpackers' haunt, with a huge video screen and a youngish clientele.

Club Trix, 53 Spence St (☎07/4051 8223). Gay bar open Tues–Sun 9pm–late.

Johno's Blues Bar, above *McDonald's* on Esplanade and Shields St (☎07/4031 5008). Cairns' live music mainstay. Even if it's only the house band – and they're not bad – someone plays every night.

Playpen, corner of Lake and Hartley streets. Popular nightclub and disco, with action on most nights.

Listings

Airlines Air New Zealand, airport (☎07/4035 9366); Air Niugini, 4 Shields St (☎13 1380); Ansett, 84 Lake St (☎07/4050 2211); Cape York Air Services, airport (☎07/4035 9399); Flight West, corner of Grafton and Spence streets (☎13 2392); Garuda, *Hilton Hotel*, Wharf St (☎07/4031 2288); JAL, 15 Lake St (☎07/4031 2700); Malaysia, 15 Lake St (☎07/4031 0000); Qantas, corner of Lake and Shields streets (☎07/4050 4000); Singapore, 15 Lake St (☎07/4031 7538).

Banks and exchange Banks are scattered throughout the city centre, mostly around the intersection of Shields and Abbott streets and in Cairns Central. Some hostels on the Esplanade also offer bureau de change facilities, though rates are lower than at the banks.

Bike and motorbike rental and tours Cairns Motorcycle Adventures, 153 Sheridan St (☎07/4051 3522); Cairns Dial a Bike, 147 Sheridan St (☎07/4031 2322) for pedal- and motorbikes delivered to the door; Jolly Frog, 105 Esplanade (☎07/4031 1897).

Books and maps Walkers Bookshop, 96 Lake St (☎07/4051 2410) for general needs. Maps from here, the Department of Lands (Sunmap), 15 Lake St, and Croc Shop, City Place.

Buses Coral Coaches (☎07/4031 7577); Greyhound Pioneer (☎07/4051 3388); McCafferty's (☎07/4051 5899); White Car Coaches/Cape York Coaches (☎07/4051 9533).

Bushwalking Jungle Tours (☎07/4031 1110 or free call ☎1800/817 234), has two- to six-day rainforest and bush trekking adventures in the Daintree and Chillagoe areas; Rare View Tours (contact City Secretarial, Floor 1, Cominos Arcade, 7 Shields St; ☎07/4051 9553) offers Aboriginal-run two-to six-day excursions across the Atherton Tablelands.

Camping equipment Adventure Equipment, 133 Grafton St (☎07/4031 2669); City Place Disposals, corner Shields and Grafton streets; the large outdoor equipment supermarket, Geo Pickers, 108 Mulgrave Rd, corner of Draper St; Wolfies Disposals, 56 McLeod St, for basic equipment and secondhand gear.

Car rental Ausdrive, corner of Aplin and Sheridan streets (☎07/4031 2000); Brits 4WD, 411 Sheridan St (☎07/4032 2611); Delta, 78 Spence St (☎13 1390); Mini Car Rentals, 150 Sheridan St (☎07/4051 6288); NQ Australia, 450 Sheridan St (☎07/4053 1875); Reef Rent-a-Car, 142 Sheridan St (☎07/4031 5500); Rent A Rek, 141 Lake St (☎07/4031 6825); Sugarland, 252 Sheridan St (☎07/4052 1300); Thrifty, 40 Aplin St and at the airport (☎07/4051 8099) .

Cinemas Multi-Screens, 108 Grafton St (☎07/4051 1222), and in Cairns Central; Coral Twin Drive-In, Bruce Highway, about 5km out (all-night sessions $10; ☎07/4054 1005); Palace Independent, 68 Lake St (minimum $30 for four films; ☎07/4031 3607) by subscription only to the End Credits Film Club.

Cruises Kangaroo Explorer, 79 Wattle St, Yorkeys Knob (☎07/4055 8188, fax 4055 7559). Four- to seven-day return cruise/fly packages to Thursday Island via Cooktown and Lizard; economy berths from $1089. (For the lowdown on Reef cruises, see box on p.452.)

Diving See boxes on pp.452–3.

Farmstays *Mount Mulligan Station* (☎07/94 8360). Budget accommodation west of the Tablelands; from $69 for two nights, including courtesy bus from Cairns.

Hospital Base Hospital, northern end of the Esplanade (☎07/4050 6333) or if you have insurance, Calvary Private Hospital, (☎07/4052 5200); 24hr Medical Centre, corner of Grafton and Florence streets (☎07/4052 1119).

Internet cafés are dotted around the centre, and computers are available in several hostels and hotels; around $2 for 10min, $6 an hour.

Left luggage At the airport, train and bus stations; also Tropical Paradise Travel, 29 Spence St ($3 a day).

NPWS in the Government Offices at 10–12 McLeod St (☎07/4052 3096). Open Mon–Fri 8.30am–4.30pm.

Parachuting Paul's (☎07/4035 9666); Jump the Beach (☎07/4050 0671).

Pharmacy Cairns Day and Night Pharmacy, 29b Shields St (☎07/4051 2466). Open daily 8am–9pm.

Police 5 Sheridan St (☎07/4030 7000).

Post office 13 Grafton St (☎07/4051 4200); and upstairs in Orchid Plaza off the Transit Mall, Lake St.

RACQ 112 Sheridan St (☎07/4051 4788).

Shopping Tourist-oriented shops are concentrated close to the Esplanade and around City Place and Lake St, where Aboriginal art galleries and opal shops have lately been springing up, though little is truly local. More authentic are the similarly profuse Digeridoo outlets – the best prices are found in more hidden shops such as The Queensland Aborigine, in the Tropical Arcade off Shields St, opposite the Art Gallery. Moving down Shields St the shops become more general, preparing you for what's on offer at the modern air-conditioned shopping complex in the Cairns Central development. Many shops don't open on Saturdays or Sundays.

Taxis Black and White Cars ☎13 1008. Main cab rank on Lake St, west of City Place.

Tours OZtours (☎07/4055 9535) and Kamp-Out Safaris (☎07/4031 4862) organize trips to Cape York by 4WD, boat and plane, and enjoy reliable reputations. Also getting good reports are Zebra, 89 Esplanade (☎07/4031 7477), to Cape Trib and Bloomfield, and Tropical Horizons (☎07/4058 1244) to Cape Trib, Daintree and the Atherton Tablelands. For some Aboriginal culture try Bama Walkabout Tours, 42 Spence St (☎07/4031 2912), who visit the Boulders at Babinda, Josephine Falls, plus Deeral and Yarrabah communities. Otherwise, for Cape Trib, Daintree and Cooktown, try: Australian Wilderness Safaris (☎07/4098 1766); Northern Exposure (☎07/4051 5111); QLD Adventure Safaris (☎07/4032 0177); Trek North Safaris (☎07/4051 4328); Tropics Explorer (☎07/4055 4555); Wildtrack (☎07/4055 2247). Outfits running trips to the Atherton Tablelands and Chillagoe include Cairns Scenic Tours (☎07/4032 1381) and Wait-a-While Spotlighting Tours (☎07/4033 1153). Kuranda Safaris (☎07/4093 7175) go to Cape York, and you could always join Cape York Air (☎07/4035 9399), for a one-day return run up to Thursday Island with the postman. Check under "Cruises" opposite for other Cape York travel options.

Trail rides Double Horseshoe Ranch (☎015/159 516) offers a full day out and four- to five-hour horseback rides up on the Atherton Tablelands ($118 includes pick-up and barbecue). Mulgrave River Horse Adventures (☎07/4056 3000) has three- to six-hour rides in the bushland and forest around Gordonvale ($69–120; pick-up from Cairns available).

Trains Bunda St, under Cairns Central (☎13 2232).

Travel agents For budget travel and tours try Flight Centre, 24 Spence St (☎07/4052 1077); STA, Central Court, 43 Lake St (☎07/4031 4199); Trailfinders, next to *Hides Hotel*, Shields St (☎07/4041 1199); Tropical Paradise Travel, 51 Spence St (☎07/4051 9533).

Work You may be able to work a passage on barges going to Cape York; check "General Notices" in the *Cairns Post* for openings. For more regular employment try the agencies Latham & Gilbert (☎07/4031 7881) or Black & White (☎07/4031 1128) – turn up looking smart.

Yacht club 4 Esplanade (☎07/4031 2750). Worth contacting for hitching/crewing onwards up to Cape York and to the Torres Strait.

Around Cairns

There's a fair amount to see and do **around Cairns**, most of it reached by turning off the highway north of town. Take one of the various roads west to **Redlynch**, and follow the signs to **Crystal Cascades** (Wongalee Falls), a narrow forest gorge gushing with rapids, small waterfalls and swimming opportunities less than 15km from the city. It's somewhere to picnic rather than explore; you should leave nothing valuable in your car, and heed warnings about the large, pale-green, heart-shaped leaves of "**Dead man's itch**", common on the sides of the paths here; the stories may seem apocryphal but once stung you'll believe them all. Backtracking through Kamerunga, you can drive into the **Barron Gorge** as far as the **power station** (free tours; details ☎07/4051 2213) and then walk through the forests to **Kuranda** (see p.456).

About 10km north of Cairns, the township of **Smithfield** marks the starting point for the Kennedy Highway's ascent to Kuranda. Shortly before, a large complex on the roadside houses both the Kuranda Skyrail **cable-car terminus** (see p.456) and the **Tjapukai Aboriginal Centre** (daily 9am–5pm; $24, $12 child). The centre's hefty admission price isn't bad value, as it includes entry to boomerang and didgeridoo displays, a fine museum, and three separate theatre shows featuring Dreamtime tales and dancing; it's not eye-opening stuff, but is a good introduction to Aboriginal culture.

If you must **bungee jump** in Queensland, then this is the place to do it: from a purpose-built platform surrounded by rainforest in the hills off the coastal highway 5km beyond Smithfield. With airborne time, including rebounds, at only a matter of seconds, it's the climb up to the tower and steeling yourself to take the plunge into what

REEF TRIPS AND DIVE SCHOOLS

The **Reef Cruises** and **Diving** categories below are not mutually exclusive – most outfits offer diving, snorkelling or just plain sailing – but are based on main interests. **Prices** can come down by as much as thirty percent during the low seasons (Feb–April & Nov), depending on how busy operators are, and **stand-bys** can save even more. Get a map and make sure you know where a trip is taking you – parts of the "inner reef", which has suffered most from intensive tourism and can be disappointing, may be described as "outer reef". On trips longer than a day you generally sleep on board.

The Queensland government have been issuing warnings about "expenses only" boat trips offered to backpackers by dubious characters in pubs and clubs followed by sexual harassment once out at sea. If in doubt, find out from any booking office in town if you are dealing with an authorized, registered operator.

REEF CRUISES

YACHTS

Day-trips $49–100; 3 days (2 nights) $350–450

Ocean Free (Silver Sails Cruises Ltd, PO Box 1045; ☎07/4031 6601). Day-trips to the reef around Green Island aboard a nineteen-metre rigged schooner.

Ocean Spirit, 143 Lake St (☎07/4031 2920, fax 4031 4344). Day-trips to Michaelmas and nearby cays on a luxury sail-catamaran.

Santa Maria, PO Box 2483, Cairns 4870 (☎07/4041 1158). Replica nineteenth-century twenty-metre rigged schooner to Thetford and Sudbury reefs.

Vagabond/Investigator (New Image Cruises; ☎07/4033 2664). Seventeen-metre luxury yachts for one to three days' sailing to Moore and Sudbury reefs, Fitzroy and Frankland islands.

POWERBOATS

$90–130 (day-trips only)

Frankland Islands Cruises (☎07/4031 6300, fax 4031 4777). To the Frankland Islands, a group of sand cays, for underwater pursuits; coral here is fair.

Quicksilver, Pier Marketplace (☎07/4031 4299). A lightning-fast service from Port Douglas to Agincourt Reef and the Low Isles, with a connecting shuttle to and from Cairns.

Sunlover Cruises, Trinity Wharf (☎07/4031 1055). High-speed catamaran to Moore and Arlington reefs and Fitzroy Island.

looks like a fishpond that gets the adrenaline going. Contact A.J. Hackett to make book-ings(☎07/4031 1119); the first jump costs $95, but it gets cheaper thereafter, or with various deals such as a half-price nude jump. For more action, there's **white-water raft-ing** in the Barron Gorge – wild fun despite being a conveyor-belt business: as you pick yourself out of the river, the raft is dragged back for the next busload. Agents include Raging Thunder (☎07/4031 1466) and Foaming Fury (☎07/4031 3460) who also cover the less crowded Johnstone and Russel rivers.

Cairns' variously developed **beaches** start 10km north of town (with regular Sunbus connections from the Transit Mall): **Palm Cove** has a full-scale resort, while **Trinity** and **Yorkeys Knob** attract campers and day-tripper crowds with a van park, shops and watersports gear for rent. If you want to escape for a few days, however, get out to **Ellis Beach**, thirty minutes north on the way to Port Douglas, the last stop on Sunbus. You couldn't ask for a finer place to camp, with cabin accommodation at *Ellis Beach Caravan Park* (☎07/4055 3538; units ③) and *Ellis Beach Resort* (☎07/4055 3534; ④).

DIVING

DAY TRIPS

$49–140

Compass, 73 Esplanade (☎07/4051 5777). Good selection of reefs, and a broad, stable budget vessel for windy weather.

Falla (☎07/4031 3488). Old pearling lugger from the Torres Straits; top-value package including snorkelling, diving and storytelling.

Hitch Hiker (☎07/4033 1711). Twenty-metre powerboat to a handful of reef sites; fast trip means more time in the water.

Noah's Ark (☎07/4051 5666). Real budget diving at Michaelmas Cay and Hastings Reef; good value but don't expect any comforts.

Seastar II, 262 Amuller St (☎07/4033 0333). Long-established family-run business with permits for some of the best sections of Hastings and Michaelmas cays. Top value full-day trip allows a good long time in the water.

Tusa Dive (TUSA, corner of the Esplanade and Aplin St; ☎07/4031 1248). A roving permit means each trip could go to any of ten separate reefs.

LONGER TRIPS

Overnight $175–220; 3 days (2 nights) $275–345; longer if desired

Nimrod III, 46 Spence St (☎07/4031 5566). Motorized catamaran with basic or plush cab-ins; four- to seven-day Cod Hole trips where you fly out and cruise back cost $800–1850.

Rum Runner (☎07/4052 1088, fax 4052 1488). Two schooners spending four days at Coral Sea locations or the Cod Hole and Ribbon reefs for around $745; meals are small but otherwise a decent operation.

Taka II (Underwater Camera Centre, 131 Lake St; ☎07/4051 8722, fax 4031 2739). Refurbished trawler with fair facilities, including photographic equipment rental and E-6 processing on board. Four days at the Cod Hole and Ribbon reefs $650–850.

DIVE SCHOOLS

As always, ask around and beware of rock-bottom dealers. Prices vary seasonally but you'll pay around $400 for a five-day Open Water Certification course. The following are long-established and have a sound reputation.

CDC, 121 Abbott St (☎07/4051 0294).

Deep Sea Divers Den, 319 Draper St (☎07/4031 2223).

Down Under Dive, 287 Draper St (☎07/4031 1288).

Pro Dive, Marlin Parade, near Hilton (☎07/4031 5255).

Tusa Dive, corner of the Esplanade and Aplin St (☎07/4031 1248). Also offers Nitrox and rebreather certification courses to divers with Advanced OW/OW2 qualifications.

The Reef and diving

Seeing the **Great Barrier Reef**, either on a cruise or as a diver, is what attracts many visitors to Cairns, and there are so many ways to do this that making a choice can be almost impossible. Broadly speaking, the reef can be classified into three **regions** – inner, outer and island – each somewhat different in character. The **inner reef**, a sheltered section between the outer walls and Cairns, is flat and fairly shallow, a good place for novices. The **outer reef** borders the open sea, so has more dramatic appeal, in the shape of walls, canyons, deeper water and bigger fish. **Island reefs** are generally a blend of inner and outer sites, but have very easy access – again, ideal if you're unsure of your limits.

All regions are visited on **day-cruises**, with vessels ranging from old trawlers to racing yachts and high-speed cruisers. If you want to stay longer, check into an island **resort** or take an extended **dive trip**. One way to choose the right boat is simply to check out the **price**: small, cramped tubs are the cheapest while roomy, faster catamarans are the most expensive. To narrow things down further, find out which serves the best food. Generally, if you've seen the reef or dived before, consider going cheaply; if this is going to be your only visit, pay the extra. Beware of **misleading advertising** when making your choice: despite claims to the contrary, no sailboats can reach the outer reef on a day-trip – it's simply too far away. Before going, or even if you're not, catch the excellent two-hour **Reef Teach** slide show in Cairns at the Bolands Centre, 14 Spence St (Mon–Sat 6.15pm; $12), at which eccentric marine biologist Paddy Colwell gives more essential background than the dive schools and tour operators have time to impart.

You might be a little taken aback by the state of the **coral**: the sheer number of visitors has had a visibly detrimental effect on Cairns' inner reef; further afield, the outer reaches are in better condition, though popular sites are beginning to suffer. From a wider perspective, things are not as bleak as they may first appear: since only a limited number of sites are open to the public, these are inevitably going to be sacrificed in order to minimize the impact on the entire structure. In any case, you'll still see abundant wildlife, ranging from squid to sharks; only seasoned divers are likely to be disappointed.

Dive sites

The dozen or more **inner reef** sites are much of a muchness. Concentrated day-tripping means that you'll probably be sharing the experience with several other boatloads of people, with scores of divers in the water at once. On a good day, snorkelling over shallow outcrops is enjoyable; going deeper, the coral shows more damage but there's plenty of marine life, albeit patchily distributed. **Michaelmas Cay**, a small, vegetated cay, is worth a visit: over thirty thousand sooty, common, and crested terns roost on the island, while giant clams, sweetlips and reef sharks can be found in the surrounding waters. Nearby **Hastings Reef** has better coral, an artificial **wreck** in the making, resident moray eel and maori wrasse, and plenty of starfish and snails in the sand beneath. The two are often included in dive or reef trip packages.

One of the cheaper options for diving the **outer reef** is to take an **overnight trip** (sleep on board) to nearby sections such as **Moore** or **Arlington reefs** – rather generalized terrain, but the advantages over a simple day excursion are that you get longer in the water plus the opportunity for night dives. **Longer trips** venture further from Cairns into two areas: a circuit north to the Cod Hole and Ribbon reefs, or straight out into the Coral Sea. The **Cod Hole**, near Lizard Island (see p.466), has no coral but is justifiably famous for mobs of giant potato cod which rise from the depths to meet you; large sharks, including hammerheads and tigers, have also been encountered. **The Ribbons** are a two-hundred-kilometre string with some relatively pristine locations and good visibility, as are **Coral Sea** sites. Where you'll go on the latter depends on weather, but seasonally you'll find mantas, whales and sharks, along with varied pelagic species.

Green Island and Fitzroy Island

Heart-shaped, tiny and sandy, **Green Island** is the easiest of any of the Barrier Reef's coral cays to reach, making it a near-essential, if expensive, day-trip from Cairns. This, combined with the island's size, means that it can be difficult to escape other visitors, but the forested interior is surprisingly varied and you only need to put on some fins, visit the **underwater observatory** ($5; free admission with some ferry tickets) or go for a cruise in a glass-bottomed boat to see plentiful coral, fish and turtles. Daily **ferries** include *The Big Cat* (☎07/4051 0444; $42) and *Reef Jet* (☎07/4031 5559; $65 including lunch and selected activities), both from the Pier Marketplace; boats run by Great Adventures (☎07/4051 0455; $45–120 depending on vessel) leave from Trinity Wharf. All run **courtesy buses** which will collect you from your accommodation. The recent overhaul of **Green Island Resort** (☎07/4031 3300; ⑧) fuelled much controversy, but in fact the new buildings are carefully hidden and infinitely better than the previous operation, whose leaking sewerage pipes and squalid kitchens were quietly ignored for years. Vegetation removed during construction was restored immediately afterwards and the shifting beaches are typical of all coral cays, not a symptom of disturbance. Five-star rooms now attract long-term guests, and there's a restaurant and pool open to day-trippers, plus plenty of sand to laze on.

    Fitzroy Island is a continental island, not a cay like Green Island, and has a low-key, good-value **resort** (☎07/4051 9588 or free call ☎1800/079 080; bunkhouse ② per person, beach cabins ⑧) set in forest near the shore, from where you can dive on the island's reef. Fitzroy is actually quite large and, away from the resort, there are some good walks through highland greenery where you can escape the sunbathing hordes. Sunlover (☎07/4031 1055) and Great Adventures (see above) operate daily **ferries** to the island from Cairns ($30).

The Atherton Tablelands

The **Atherton Tablelands**, the highlands behind Cairns, are named after **John Atherton**, who made the tin deposits at **Herberton** accessible by opening a route to the coast in 1877. Dense forest covered these highlands before the majority was cleared and given over to dairy cattle, tobacco and grain. The remaining pockets of forest are magnificent, but it's the understated beauty that draws most visitors today, and though **Kuranda** and its markets pull in busloads from the coast, there are several quieter **national parks** brimming with rare species. You could spend days here, driving or hiking through rainforest to crater lakes and endless small waterfalls, or simply camp out for a night and search for wildlife with a torch. For a contrast, consider a side trip west to the mining town of **Chillagoe**, whose dust, limestone caves and Aboriginal art place it firmly in the Outback.

    Drivers can reach the tablelands on the **Palmerston Highway** from Innisfail, the **Gillies Highway** from Gordonvale, or the **Kennedy Highway** from Smithfield to Kuranda. Two stylish and unforgettable ways to ride up to the tablelands are by **train** from Cairns to Kuranda, which twists through gorges and rainforest; and in the green gondolas of the **Kuranda Skyrail cable car**, with a fantastic seven-kilometre/forty-minute aerial view of the canopy between Smithfield and Kuranda – either method costs $25 one-way or $40 return; you could also take advantage of their specially discounted "Skyrail up & train back" package. Numerous **tours** run from Cairns to Kuranda and the tableland highlights. White Car Coaches (from Tropical Paradise

Travel; ☎07/4051 9533) also operates **buses** between Cairns, the tableland towns and Chillagoe, but you really need your own transport to explore at leisure.

Kuranda

A constant stream of visitors arriving from the coast seems to have turned **KURANDA** into a stereotypical resort village – something this once atavistic community was keen to escape. But despite expanding development and heavy market-day tourism, it's hard not to like the place. **Buses**, and the highway, stop at the top of town, **trains** and the Skyrail **cable car** 500m down the hill, with essential services – post office, store (EFT-POS), bank, cafés – laid out between them along Coondoo Street. **Cafés** are legion, but prices are very high – you're better off bringing a packed lunch from the coast.

As it is so accessible from Cairns, Kuranda is not a place where many people stay overnight, and there's little **accommodation**. Just up from the cable-car terminus and **train station** – the latter tastefully decorated with potted orchids and ferns – you'll find the quiet and slowly mouldering *Mrs Miller's Kuranda Hostel*, 6 Arara St (☎07/4093 7355; ①), with a plentiful supply of bunks, large grounds (where you can camp), kitchen and laundry. Around the corner is *The Bottom Pub and Motel* (☎07/4093 7206; ④), also the best place in town for meals and lively Friday nights. Out on the highway, *Kuranda Rainforest Resort* (☎07/4093 7555; ⑤) has a spa and gym (and access by private buses from the coast).

While some stalls operate every day, the **markets** that attract so many tourists open at 9am on Wednesday, Friday and Sunday; the first buses arrive an hour later. Don't ̶e̶x̶p̶e̶c̶t̶ ̶b̶a̶r̶g̶a̶i̶n̶s̶ – the market is a commercial affair hawking crafts, fruit and clothes, set around a fake plane wreck and "rainforest pool". Nearby, forest fauna can be seen close up at the **Butterfly Sanctuary** (daily 10am–3pm; $12), a mix of streams and "feed trees" where giant ulysses and birdwing butterflies are the most obvious of the local species protected by the breeding programme. **Birdworld**, behind the markets (daily 9am–4pm; $9), is a superb aviary with realistically arranged vegetation and nothing between you and a host of rarities such as ecclectus parrots. The **Noctarium**, at the upper end of Coondoo Street (daily 10am–3pm; $9), has a collection of possums, wallabies and bats.

Around Kuranda

Kuranda sits at the top of the **Barron Gorge**, spectacular in the wet season when the river rages down the falls, but otherwise tamed by a hydroelectric dam upstream. Cross the rail bridge next to the station and take a path leading down to the river, where

45-minute **cruises** ($10) depart five times a day; the cruise operators often rent out canoes too. On foot, a dubious **walking track** descends to cold swimming spots along the river from the lookout at the end of Barron Falls Road, 2km from town. Safer trails follow the road beyond the falls to **Wright's Lookout**, then continue to dense forest along **Surprise Creek** and to the **Power Station**. Closer to town, there's another forest walk from the Noctarium to Jumrum Creek (about 1hr) and, opposite the BP garage at the top of Coondoo Street, a huge colony of **flying foxes** to see, hear and smell – but not to touch, since they and other bats have been shown to be carriers of the deadly coleesee virus.

Mareeba

West of Kuranda, rainforest quickly gives way to dry woodland and tobacco plantations, quite a change from the coast's greenery. **Davies Creek** is at the end of a track branching off the road after 25km; paths lead from a campsite to where falls pour over a granite rock face to a pool surrounded by boulders and scrub. The main road continues past a memorial to **James Venture Mulligan**, the veteran prospector who discovered the Palmer River Goldfields (see p.466).

MAREEBA has little going for it, despite being the tablelands' oldest settlement. Byrnes Street has all the shops and banks, while the **motels** and pleasant *Tropical Tablelands Caravan Park* (☎07/4092 1158) are along the highway as you enter town from the south, as is the **information** centre and small museum (daily 8am–4pm; $4). After dark you can tangle with the farming fraternity in one of the hotels, or at **Jimmy D's Night Club** (Thurs–Sat 7pm–3am) on Byrnes Street. **Leaving**, Atherton is 30km south; the **Peninsula Developmental Road** heads north to Mount Molloy; and **Granite Gorge**, another swimming spot, is 12km along Chewko Road (west off Byrnes Street, down Rankin Street, fifth on the left). The AMPOL service station at the north end of town marks the start of the Chillagoe road.

West to Chillagoe

The 150-kilometre road to Chillagoe mysteriously alternates between corrugated gravel and isolated sections of bitumen, but poses no real problem during the dry season. Look for graffiti on boulders (**Top Cat Pass** is a gem) and enticing adverts for the *Almaden Hotel*, whose cool, mirrored, well-supplied bar and beer garden are an incredible oasis in ramshackle, dilapidated **ALMADEN**. From here until Chillagoe's inactive smelter chimney appears from behind an outcrop of rock, the road passes blocks of cut marble awaiting shipment to Italy.

CHILLAGOE dates from 1887, when enough copper ore was found to keep a smelter running until the 1950s; now a gold mine 16km west at **Mungana** seems to keep the place ticking over. Red dust, a service station, oversized motels and general store complete the picture. Arrange **camping** and **cave tours** (daily 9am & 1.30pm) through the post office/NPWS (☎07/4094 7163) down the main street, but check well in advance – the tours may be closed during the wet season and numbers are limited. There are two campsites (tank water and pit toilets), one close to town, the other 7km out near the caves themselves. If you need more luxury, the *Chillagoe Lodge Motel*, 7 King St (☎07/4094 7106; ⑤), has a pool, TV and a sheltered garden, and serves meals.

The caves

Chillagoe's **caves** are ancient coral reefs, hollowed out by rain and broken up into fluted masses half-buried in the scrub. Guides can take you through some, while others are open to solo exploration with instructions from the ranger. The caverns are varied by **limestone sculptures** deposited by evaporation and, unusually for the location, some large **stalagmites**; the best formations are at **Royal Arch, Donna** and **Trezkinn**. Wildlife here includes grey swiftlets and agile pythons, which somehow manage to catch bats on the wing. A **footpath** leads through grassland between the caves, where you'll find echidnas, kangaroos, black cockatoos and frogmouths, the last odd birds whose name fits them perfectly. Given that this is some of the best snake country, solid shoes and trousers ought to be worn. **Balancing Rock** offers panoramic views, with the town hidden by low trees, while obscure **Aboriginal paintings and engravings** have been found near **the Arches**, west at Mungana. Past here, the road continues 500km to Normanton, Karumba and tracks up western Cape York – but it doesn't improve and there's no fuel or help along the way.

Atherton and around

Centrally placed for forays to most of the tablelands' attractions, **ATHERTON** is the only highlands town that has a variety of businesses and accommodation, although it lacks good eating places. Banks, shops and cafés which open very early for breakfast are along Main Street, with a supermarket right at the south end past the post office. **Buses** stop at the junction of Main and Vernon streets. **Accommodation** includes the heavily tiled and hospitable *Atherton Backpackers Hostel*, 37 Alice St, off Vernon Street at the fire station (☎07/4091 3552; ①); green and spacious campsites at the *Woodlands Tourist Park*, just at the edge of town on Herberton Road (☎07/4091 1407); and the *Hinterland Motel*, 44 Cook St (☎07/4091 1885; ⑤). From town, roads head north to Mareeba, south to Ravenshoe and Herberton, and east to lakes and Yungaburra.

Tinaroo, Barrine, Eacham and Yungaburra

Heading east from Atherton towards Yungaburra, turn left to **Lake Tinaroo**, a convoluted reservoir formed by pooling the Barron River's headwaters. An unsurfaced, dry-weather road runs 25km around from the dam to the Gillies Highway, passing **campsites** on the north shore before cutting deep into native forests. It's worth stopping along the way for the short walks to bright green **Mobo Crater** and **Cathedral Fig**, an enormous parasitic strangler fig tree. While common enough in rainforest, one this size – 50m tall and 43m around the base – is extraordinary, with the thick mass of tendrils supporting the crown all fused together like melted wax.

Barrine and Eacham are **maars**, or crater lakes: blue, still circles surrounded by thick rainforest. **Barrine** is the most developed, enough for you to want to escape the crowds around the kiosk and cruise boat (daily at 10.15am, 2pm & 3.15pm; $10) by following a six-kilometre track around the lake past two enormous **kauri pines**, more commonly found in New Zealand and Western Australia. **Eacham**'s circuit is just 4km but otherwise similar, with birds and insects foraging on the forest floor, and frogs, water dragons and inoffensive **amethystine pythons** – Australia's largest snake – often seen sunning themselves around the shores. If this doesn't bother you, both lakes are fine to swim in, though cold.

Heading back towards Atherton, **YUNGABURRA** makes another good base, and consists of an old hotel, a café/store, and pine-and-slate comforts at *On the Wallaby Hostel*, 37 Eacham Rd (☎07/4095 2031; ①–③), run by the *Dreamtime* hostel in Cairns. They organize packages which include canoe and wildlife-spotting trips, and can direct you to local **platypus**-watching sites and **Curtain Fig**, another giant strangler fig tree, on the Atherton road.

The Southern Tablelands: to Ravenshoe and beyond

The Kennedy Highway continues 80km down from Atherton to **Ravenshoe**, the highlands' southernmost town, past **the Crater** at Mount Hypipamee, a 56-metre vertical rift formed by volcanic gases blowing through fractured granite that's now filled with deep, weed-covered water. **Picnic tables** are on the site, as are ridiculously tame Lewins Honeyeaters, and while night brings rare possums and **tree kangaroos** out of the dense forest below, the Crater's soaring popularity with nocturnal tour groups makes it unlikely that you'll see much unless you arrive well after 10pm (camping is prohibited, however). An alternative route from Atherton circles west via **HERBERTON**, a quaint, one-time timber town whose **Historic Village** (daily 10am–4pm; $10) is a meticulous but lifeless collection of about thirty pioneer buildings relocated from elsewhere: a schoolroom, bishop's residence, hotel, Chinese relics, bottle dump – you name it. A sedate way to get there is by the authentically grubby 1920s **steam train** from Atherton's Platypus Park (10.30am Sat, Sun, Wed & holidays; $25 return) which gives you an hour or so before the return trip.

RAVENSHOE, apart from endless explanations for its name, is mainly notable for the *Tully Falls Hotel*, Queensland's highest pub, and **Millstream Falls**, Australia's broadest, 5km away. Southwest, the road drops off the tablelands past steamy upwellings at **Innot Hot Springs** and **Mount Garnet** to the start of the Gulf Developmental Road (see p.509).

Malanda, Millaa Millaa and the Palmerston Highway

About 25km southeast of Atherton, the world's largest **dairy** at **MALANDA** provides milk and cheese for the whole of Queensland's far north, plus most of the Northern Territory and even New Guinea. There's a roadside swimming hole and short rainforest walk starting about 1km back towards Atherton at **Malanda Falls Environmental Park**, and good budget **accommodation** prospects at *Platypus Forest Resort*, 8km east of town at 12 Topaz Rd (☎07/4096 5926; ①), which serves fine food and has outdoor hot tubs.

From Malanda, you can descend to the coastal highway south of Cairns via **Millaa Millaa** and the **Palmerston Highway**. Before you do, there's a **waterfall circuit** starting 2km east of Millaa Millaa, where a fifteen-kilometre road passes three small tumbles and swimming holes; best is **Elinjaa**, with its curtain cave. The highway itself was named after **Christie Palmerston**, a fugitive who hid with Aborigines on the tablelands in the 1870s. Later, appreciation for his trail to Port Douglas bought him a pardon, but he stayed in the bush. The **Palmerston section** of Wooroonooran National Park, which includes the Bellenden Ker Range (see p.444), occupies a huge area north of the highway and is worth a stopover to explore the most extensive, undisturbed spread of Atherton's rainforest – though you'll need some protection from summer flies. A local oddity is the **musky rat kangaroo**, a small, black, uniquely diurnal marsupial common in leaf litter on the forest floor. There's a **campsite** ($3 per person per night) about 27km from Millaa Millaa, from where the best of the walking tracks lead to mossy **Tchupala Falls** and the impressive **Nandroya Falls**, while the highway descends 40km past the park to Innisfail.

Heading north: Cairns to Cape Tribulation

The Daintree and Cape Tribulation, tamed fringes of the Cape York Peninsula, are only a couple of hours' drive north of Cairns on the **Cook Highway**. The highway initially runs in sight of the sea to **Port Douglas** and **Mossman**, a beautiful drive past isolated beaches where hang-gliders patrol the headlands. North of Mossman is the road to **the Daintree**, Australia's largest and the world's oldest surviving stretch of tropical rainforest. World Heritage listing hasn't saved it from development: roads are being surfaced, land has been subdivided, and there's an ever-increasing number of services in place, undermining the wild and remote image depicted in the brochures. While this disappoints some visitors, the majestic forest still descends thick and dark right to the sea, and you can explore paths through the jungle, watch for wildlife, or just rest on the beach. The government has, however, recently allocated funds to buy back and restore the land so there is some hope that developments will stop where they are now.

Day-tours from Cairns will show you the sights, but you really need longer to take in the rich scenery and atmosphere. For once it's not essential to have a vehicle: Coral Coaches (☎07/4031 7577) runs a daily **bus** between Cairns, Cape Tribulation and (weather permitting) Cooktown, which allows multiple stopovers. It's well worth a few extra dollars to go with Tropics Explorer (as far as Cape Trib ☎07/4055 4555) who include several detours for swimming, croc-spotting and sampling the local produce, all with an enthusiastic and informative commentary. If you want to arrive with panache, Quicksilver's (☎07/4031 4299) speedy **catamaran** plies between Cairns and Port Douglas, and also zooms to the outer reef (see pp.452-3).

Port Douglas and Mossman

The turning to **PORT DOUGLAS**, an hour north of Cairns, is signalled by an ostentatious colonnade of West African palm trees. This once pretty fishing village has, with massive investment, been turned into a quaint, upmarket tourist attraction, as is obvious by the huge **Mirage Resort** (☎07/4099 5888; ⑨) off Davidson Street on the way in – host to US President Bill Clinton during his 1996 visit – and a multitude of trendy boutiques. Even so, it's far more relaxed than Cairns and is an alternative base for exploring the area. Less flamboyant lodgings include *4 Mile Beach Caravan Park* on Reef Street (☎07/4099 5001), the pleasant *Port O'Call Lodge/YHA* on Port Street (☎07/4099 5422; ①), with its *Shoestrings Restaurant* and free transfer from either youth hostel in Cairns; the very central *Port Douglas Backpackers* on Macrossan Street (☎07/4099 4883; ①); and *Mango Tree Apartments*, 91 Davidson St (☎07/4099 5677; ⑤), with self-contained units just back from Four Mile Beach.

All services are on the five-hundred-metre-long **Macrossan Street**, which runs between Four Mile Beach and Anzac Park. As in Cairns, a prolific number of businesses offer **tourist information** – the Port Douglas tourist information centre at no. 23 (daily 8.30am–5.30pm; ☎07/4099 5599) can sort out everything from Aboriginal-guided tours of Mossman Gorge to sailing trips and buses to the Daintree. Port Douglas Bike Hire, at no. 40 (☎07/4099 5799), rents **mountain bikes** from $12 a day. **Cafés** and **restaurants** also congregate around Macrossan Street: the *Central Hotel* has **live bands** on Wednesday and at weekends, while the *Court House Hotel* has boozers and dogs sprawled across the verandah, and lunch specials and a barbecue menu in the garden. Between the two, *Iron Bar* has rough-cut timber furniture and a mid-range "surf & turf" menu, while *Mango Jam Café* across the road is open from noon to 2am for wood-fired pizza. At *Catalina*, around the corner on Wharf Street (☎07/4099 5287; Tues–Sun 6.30pm–late), it's worth paying the high prices for delicacies such as coral trout grilled in banana leaves; the restaurant is in a beautiful setting with a verandah shaded by two ancient mango trees.

Anzac Park is the scene of a Sunday-morning **produce market**, good for fruit, vegetables and souvenirs. Near the park's jetty you'll find the whitewashed timber church of **St Mary's by the Sea**, built after the 1911 cyclone carried off the previous structure. Behind, at **Ben Cropp's Shipwreck Museum** (daily 9am–5pm; $5), bronze cannon, teapots and the results of twenty years salvaging are piled around a continuously playing video of Ben's exploits. On the other side of the church, Port Douglas Dive Centre (☎07/4099 5327) visits the **Low Isles**, **Chinaman**, **Tongue** and **Opal reefs**, all decent sites, though in much the same condition as those off Cairns – prices are steeper, too. Quicksilver, based at Marina Mirage attached to the *Mirage Resort* (☎07/4099 5500), also runs a sailing boat to the Low Isles ($95), while its high-speed catamaran will whisk you to the **Agincourt Reef** for the day ($135).

Mossman

MOSSMAN, 14km past Port Douglas, is a quiet town which has hardly changed in the last thirty years; rail lines between the canefields and mill still run along the main street. Ten minutes inland, **Mossman Gorge** looks like all rainforest rivers should; the boulder-strewn flow is good for messing around in on a quiet day but attracts streams of tour buses and car break-ins in peak season. Kuku Yalangi, the local community, put together the Aboriginal **walking trail** here and conduct tours of the gorge explaining history and plant usage.

Continuing north, the road splits left to Daintree township or right for the Daintree Ferry to Cape Tribulation. Backtracking southeast lets you leave the highway and climb to Mount Molloy and the Peninsula Developmental Road – the easier, inland route to Cooktown.

The Daintree

If you detour off the Mossman–Cape Tribulation road to take in the riverside **DAINTREE** township, you'll find that the former timber camp is little more than a place to organize a half-day **crocodile tour** with Daintree Wildlife Safaris (☎07/4098 6125; $30) or a one-hour drift with Daintree River Cruise Centre (☎07/4098 6115; $10), while 4WDs test their mettle on the **CREB Track** to Cooktown (erroneously marked as a proper road on some maps). Most people follow the road to the **Daintree River Ferry** (continuously 6am–midnight; pedestrians $1, vehicles $5) and the start of the mostly sealed 35-kilometre Cape Tribulation road. The river crossing can be very busy, with the cable ferry taking a dozen cars and tour coaches every 30 minutes or so; wait in the café or take a boat trip looking for crocodiles and snakes.

Across the river, you can detour to quiet **lodgings** at **Cape Kimberley** (☎07/4090 7500; ①–⑤), with cabins, campsite and a basic store, or continue 8km through rainforest over the convoluted range to **FLORAVILLE** and **Cow Bay**. Floraville's **café** hands out local advice and doubles as a Commonwealth Bank agent; the **Environmental Centre** in the community explains forest subtleties and local background. **Hostels** don't get any better than the jungle-clad cabins of *Crocodylus Village/YHA* at Cow Bay (☎07/4098 9166; ①–②) where semi-canvas cabins blend into the jungle and bandicoots wander routinely through the bar/dining area built around growing trees; to reach it, turn at the airstrip along Buchannan Creek Road. The hostel can arrange bike rides, sea kayak trips, forest walks, scenic flights and snorkelling/dive trips around Cape Trib and local reefs.

12km further up the main highway, at **Thornton Beach** you'll find sand, a licensed kiosk, rock-bottom prices for camping and a creek said to be "loaded with crocodiles". If this sounds worrying, *Inn the Rainforest* (cabins, camping, supplies; ☎07/4098 9162; ②–⑤), *Lync Haven* (camping, supplies, night walks; ☎07/4098 9155; ②–④) and *Heritage Lodge* (cabins, restaurant, tours; ☎07/4098 9138; ⑤) are all further inland – look for signs along the road.

Plants close in on the **Marrdja Botanical Walk** at **Noah Beach** a few kilometres north, where concrete paths and boardwalks follow the creek through a mixture of forest to mangroves at the river mouth. Look for spiky lawyer cane, lianas twisted into corkscrew shapes where they once surrounded a tree, and the spherical pods of the **cannonball mangrove** – dried and dismembered, they were used as puzzles by Aboriginal peoples, the object being to fit the irregular segments back together. The NPWS has a **campsite** here. Just up the road is *Coconut Beach Resort* (☎07/4098 0033 or free call ☎1800/816 525; ⑦), with an extensive array of facilities including a huge A-frame restaurant requiring "smart tropical dress". Fringing coral comes right up to the shore about 1km to the south.

Cape Tribulation

Cape Tribulation ("Cape Trib") – a forty-minute drive from the ferry crossing – was named when Captain Cook's vessel hit a reef offshore in June 1770. The cleared area below **Mount Sorrow** has a café, store, a boardwalk onto the beach and a **Bat House** (daily approximately 9am–4pm; free), worth a visit to handle tame orphaned flying foxes. **Beds** are available at the often overcrowded *PK's* **hostel** (☎07/4098 0040; ②) which organizes **horse-riding** and **sea-kayaking**, and there are tent sites about 2km along the road at *Pilgrim Sands* **campsite** (☎07/4098 0030) – at least here you'll go to sleep with the sound of surf, not disco music, in your ears.

The area is best explored on foot – for the simple pleasure of walking through the forest with the sea breaking on a beach not five minutes distant. A **path** runs out to the cape, where you may see brilliantly coloured pittas (small, tailless birds with a buff chest, green back and black and rust heads) bouncing around in the leaf litter, or even a crocodile sunning itself on the beach. One way to penetrate the undergrowth away from the paths is to follow small creeks: **Emmagen**, about 6km north, runs halfway up Mount Sorrow and is recommended for its safe swimming holes. Persistence and luck may spot a tree kangaroo, given away during the day by its long tail hanging down like a vine while the animal slouches in the tree tops, asleep.

The Bloomfield Track

The scene of vicious confrontations in 1984 between construction crews and environmentalists who tried unsuccessfully to stop this alternative road to Cooktown being built through virgin forest, the **Bloomfield Track** is completely impassable after rain and other time requires a 4WD. Spanning 80km from Cape Tribulation to where the track joins the Cooktown Road at **Black Mountain**, the exciting section with drastic gradients lies below the halfway mark of the tidal **Bloomfield River**, which has to be crossed at low water. Beyond **Wujal Wujal** community the road flattens out to run past *Home Rule Rainforest Lodge* at **ROSSVILLE** (☎07/4060 3925; ③), which offers inexpensive meals, kitchen facilities and horse-riding, before reaching *The Lions Den* pub at **Helenvale** near Black Mountain (see p.464), about thirty minutes from Cooktown.

THE CAPE YORK PENINSULA AND TORRES STRAIT ISLANDS

The **Cape York Peninsula** points north towards the **Torres Strait** and New Guinea. Tackling the rugged tracks and hectic river crossings on the "Trip To The Tip" is an adventure in itself, as well as a means to reach Australia's northernmost point and the communities at **Bamaga** and **Thursday Island**, so far removed from southern attitudes that they could easily be in another country. But it's not all four-wheel driving across the savannah: during the dry season the historic settlement of **Cooktown**, the wetlands at **Lakefield National Park** and **Laura**'s Aboriginal heritage are only a day's journey from Cairns in any decent vehicle. Given longer you might get as far as **Weipa**, but don't go further than this without off-road transport; while some have managed to reach The Tip in family sedans, most who try fail miserably.

With thousands making the journey between May and October, a **breakdown** won't leave you stranded, but the cost of repairs will make you regret it. **Bikers** should travel in groups and have some off-roading experience. Those without their own vehicle can take **buses** from Cairns to Cape Tribulation or Cooktown and overland **tours** beyond that. There's also a twice-weekly bus to Weipa (when the roads are open), and **flights** or **cruises** up the coast, often calling in at islands on the way. See "Travel details" at the end of this chapter for scheduled services, and "Listings" on p.451 for tour operators.

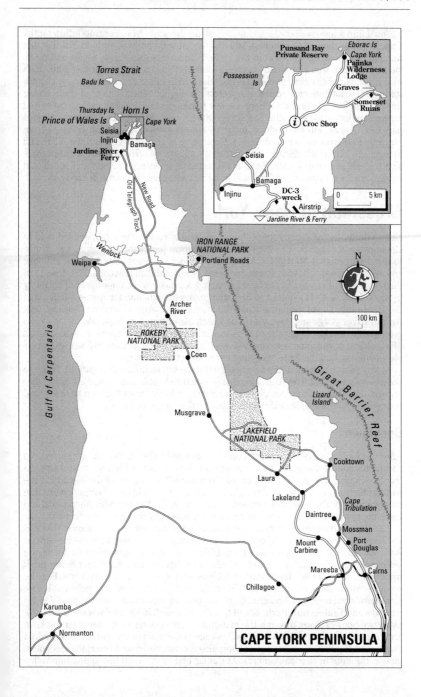

CAPE YORK PENINSULA

You'll find a few roadhouses and motels along the way, but **accommodation** on the Cape is mostly limited to camping, and it's inevitable if you head right to The Tip that one night at least will be spent in the bush. Settlements also supply meals and provisions, but there won't be much on offer so take all you can carry. On this note, don't turn bush campsites into rubbish dumps: take a pack of bin liners and remove all your garbage. **Estuarine crocodiles** are present throughout the Cape: read the warning under "Wildlife" in Contexts. There are few **banks**, so take enough cash to carry you between points – some roadhouses accept plastic. In Cairns, the Department of Lands and RACQ can help with advice on road conditions and **maps**; other maps from Pinevale Publications (try bookshops), Croc Shop at 10 Shields St, and the NPWS fill in local and historical information. Vehicles should carry a **first-aid kit**, a comprehensive tool kit and spares, extra fuel, and a tarpaulin for creek crossings. A winch and equipment for removing, patching and inflating tyres may also come in handy.

Mossman to Cape York

Not as pretty as the coastal tracks but considerably easier, the 260-kilometre road to Cooktown and points north leaves the Cook Highway just before Mossman and climbs to the drier scrub at **MOUNT CARBINE**, a former tungsten mine whose roadhouse and *Wolfram Hotel* (②), with simple but clean rooms, fulfil all functions. The descent of the far side of the range an hour later is rough, a foretaste of the Cape's incredibly dusty byways. **LAKELAND**'s hotel and fuel stop marks the junction for routes north along the **Peninsula Developmental Road** to Laura, but the way to Cooktown lies east, past **Annan River gorge** and the mysterious **Black Mountain**, two huge piles of algae-covered granite boulders near the road. Aborigines reckon the formation to be the result of a building competition between two rivals fighting over a girl, and tell stories of people wandering into the eerie, whistling caverns, never to return.

At this point it's worth a four-kilometre detour south along the **Bloomfield Track** to the *Lions Den* at **HELENVALE**. The *Den* is an old-style pub playing up for tourists during the day but one hundred percent authentic at night, from the iron sheeting and beam decor to those nasty exhibits in glass bottles on the piano.

Cooktown

After the *Endeavour* nearly sank at Cape Tribulation in 1770, Captain Cook landed at a natural harbour to the north, where he spent two months repairing the vessel, observing the "Genius, Temper, Disposition and Number of the Natives" and – legend has it – naming the kangaroo after an Aboriginal word for "I don't know". Tempers wore thin on occasion, as when the crew refused to share a catch of turtles with Aborigines, and Cook commented: "They seem'd to set no value upon any thing we gave them."

The site lay dormant until gold was discovered southwest on the **Palmer River** in 1873, and within months a harbour was being surveyed at the mouth of the Endeavour River for a tented camp known as **COOKTOWN**. A wild success while gold lasted, the settlement once boasted a main street alive with hotels and a busy port doing brisk trade with Asia through thousands of **Chinese** prospectors and merchants. But the reserves were soon exhausted and by 1910 Cooktown was on the decline. Today, Cooktown's main drag, Charlotte Street, is good for random wandering past the old wharves and **Endeavour Park**, site of Cook's landing. A kiosk on the waterfront organizes two-hour **cruises** through the mangroves, and among monuments on the lawn are the remains of defences sent from Brisbane in the nineteenth century to ward off a threatened Russian invasion: one cannon, three cannonballs and two rifles (accompanied at the time by just one officer). At the far end of town, on the Endeavour Valley

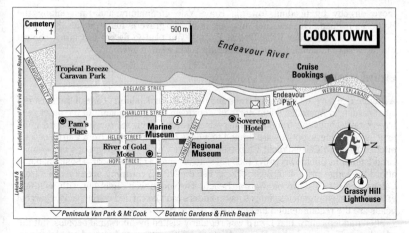

Road, is a Chinese shrine and a **cemetery**, whose most famous resident is Mary Watson of Lizard Island (see overleaf).

The best **views** of the town and river are from the top floor of the old Sisters of Mercy Convent, now a **regional museum** (daily 9.30am–4pm; $5) with a bit of everything: artefacts jettisoned from *Endeavour*, exhaustive local history, a reconstructed joss house, a rundown on pearling around Thursday Island, and the history of the "hopelessly insolvent" Cooktown–Laura railway. Not far away on the corner of Helen and Walker streets, the **Marine Museum** (daily 8.30am–5.30pm; $5) details the 1899 cyclones Mahina and Nachon, which collided north of Cooktown sinking 76 vessels and killing 350 people.

There are more views of the district from the red-and-white corrugated iron cone of **Grassy Hill Lighthouse**, reached on a concrete track from the end of Hope Street. **Mount Cook** is a rather tougher proposition, a two-hour return hike through very thick forest on meagre paths – follow orange triangles from the nondescript starting point that you'll find beyond Ida Street. At the end of Walker Street, the **Botanic Gardens**, founded by Chinese and recently re-established, merge into original paperbark woodland, with a track running to **Finch Beach** on Cherry Tree Bay. Although it is sometimes rated as a safe swimming beach, you should heed the home-made warning signs in pidgin: "Dispela Stap Hia" and a picture of a croc.

Practicalities

The June **Discovery Festival** is a predictably thorough piss-up, but even then **accommodation** shouldn't be too difficult to find. If you're **camping**, the *Tropical Breeze* site near the cemetery is handy for town, but the *Peninsula Van Park* (☎07/4069 5107) has the nicer location, in forest below Mount Cook. *Pam's Place*, Charlotte Street (☎07/4069 5166; ①), is a hostel with inexpensive beds and spacious cooking facilities; while the *Sovereign Hotel* on Charlotte Street (☎07/4069 5400; ⑤), with a pool and beer garden, and the *River of Gold Motel*, corner of Hope and Walker streets (☎07/4069 5222; ⑥), are surprisingly sophisticated alternatives. Numerous cafés and hotels supply **food and drink**; a **supermarket** and grocer are the last source of fresh provisions before Weipa. There's a tourist **information** centre on Charlotte Street (☎07/4069 6100).

Moving on, vehicles other than 4WDs have to head back to Lakeland for Laura and the north. Stronger sets of wheels have the option of reaching Lakefield National Park more directly by heading towards Hope Vale community and then taking the Battlecamp Road. The last fuel this way until Musgrave is found about 33km from Cooktown at Endeavour Falls Tourist Park. If you plan to fly out to Cairns, contact Flight West (☎13 2392); the airstrip is about 10km west of town.

Lizard Island

A granite rise covered in stunted trees and heath, **Lizard Island** is one of the most iso-lated resorts in Australia, 90km north of Cooktown, and within sight of the outer reef. Divers rave about the fringing coral reefs here but, even so, reaching Lizard is an expensive business: options are limited to a daily **flight** on Qantas from Cairns or a lift hitched through Cairns Yacht Club (see "Listings", p.451). Large groups can contact Brad Palmer in Cooktown (☎07/4069 5519) to arrange a charter boat. Those unable to afford the **lodge** (☎07/4060 3999; ⑨) can use the NPWS **camping area** (permits from Cairns; see p.451) down on Watson Beach. The lodge won't help out with anything except in real emergencies, and, as gas cylinders can't be carried on the plane, charcoal beads are the recommended fuel for fires.

Shell middens show that Lizard was regularly visited by Aboriginal peoples, but the island was uninhabited when **Robert Watson** built a cottage and started a sea-slug pro-cessing operation here in the 1870s, accompanied by his wife **Mary** and two Chinese servants. Aborigines attacked the house while Robert was at sea in October 1881, killing one of the Chinese and forcing Mary, her baby and Ah Sam to flee in a water tank; they paddled west for five days before dying of thirst. Her painfully matter-of-fact diary is kept at Brisbane's John Oxley Library, while the tank is on display at the Queensland Museum in Townsville.

Quinkan Country: Laura and the Palmer River

Back on the Peninsula Road, 60km north of Lakeland, **LAURA**'s store-cum-post office, roadhouse and *Quinkan Hotel* (☎07/4060 3255; ⑤) support the two-day **Aboriginal Dance Festival**, an electrifying assertion of Aboriginal identity, held in June of odd-num-bered years. At any time of year you can visit the sandstone caves and ridges at **Split Rock**, 13km south of town, where a steep track leads to a two-hour gallery circuit. Paintings depict animals and startling spirit figures associated with sorcery: spidery, frightening Quinkan with pendulous earlobes, and dumpy Anurra, often with their legs twisted upwards. Other sites show scenes from post-Contact life, depicting horses, rifles and clothed figures; some caves were probably in use until the 1930s. You can find out more through the *Ang-Gnarra Aboriginal Corporation Caravan Park* (☎07/4060 3214) or from Trezise Bush Service/Quinkan Tours (☎07/4060 3236), which has a camp west in the scrub at Jowalbinna (4WD only; ask directions at Laura's *Quinkan Hotel* – see above).

Sites along the **Palmer River**, 80km (8hr) southwest of Laura along a terrible 4WD track, recall the gigantic 1873 goldrush. Mining life was volatile: Aborigines waged guerrilla warfare, and race riots erupted between whites and the Chinese – who at one time outnumbered the entire European population of Queensland and infuriated whites by doggedly extracting gold from "exhausted" claims. The settlements at Maytown and German Bar were abandoned once the gold had gone and today there's virtually noth-ing left except atmosphere; the Cairns NPWS (see p.451) stocks **maps** and permits.

Lakefield National Park

Ideally you'd take at least a week to absorb **Lakefield National Park**'s fifty thousand square kilometres of savannah and riverine flats, drifting between the 21 **campsites**. But even a single night spent here will give you a feel for the Cape's most accessible wilderness area. Apart from the **Old Laura Homestead** – built between 1892 and 1940 and standing abandoned in the scrub on the Laura River – the park's pleasures revolve around outdoor pursuits, fishing and exploring lagoons for wildlife. Lakefield's **crocodile-conservation programme** means you might see both fresh- and saltwater types; birdlife is plentiful and mammals put in an appearance. **Magnetic anthills** are a common landmark: flattened towers aligned north–south to prevent overheating in the noonday sun.

Vehicles other than 4WDs can sometimes manage the rough 170-kilometre track through the park between Laura township and Musgrave Roadhouse. High clearance is needed for other routes, including the Battle Camp road to Cooktown. **Ranger stations** are located along the road at New Laura (southern park, 50km from Laura township), Lakefield (central, 80km) and Bizant (north, 100km). Popular places to camp and watch wildlife are **Horseshoe Lagoon** beyond Old Laura, **12 Mile Hole** near New Laura (4WD only), **Kalpowar Crossing** (near Lakefield, with showers and toilets) and **Hann Crossing**, in the north of the park.

Laura to Iron Range and Weipa

Following the main road, the 300km that stretches between Laura and Archer River passes in a haze of dust, jolts and roadhouses supplying fuel, food, beds and drink. First on the list is **MUSGRAVE** (135km from Laura; ☎07/4060 3229 for road condition check), a converted homestead where the track from Lakefield National Park joins the road, followed by a two-hour roller-coaster ride – look out for "Dip" signs warning of monster gullies – down to **COEN**'s *(S)Exchange Hotel* (107km from Musgrave). Coen's service station handles **camping**, provisions, post office business and banking. The *Homestead Guest House*, on Regent Street, has beds (☎07/4060 1157; ②) and can provide meals, while you can have any car problems fixed at Clark's workshop. The 4WD track continues for another 25km into dry woodland and rainforest and **Mungkan Kaanju National Park**; the ranger station lies 75km west of the main road at Rokeby (☎07/4060 3256), with camping at undeveloped bush sites. Past the park turn-off, **Archer River Roadhouse** (70km from Coen; ☎07/4060 3266) has a camp site and **accommodation** in units (③), as well the last reliable **fuel** on the main road before Bamaga, 400km away. Beyond are routes east to Iron Range (155km) and west to Weipa (190km) – covered below.

Iron Range

You may have seen rainforest before, but you'll have experienced nothing like the magnificent jungle at **Iron Range National Park**, a leftover from the Ice Age link to New Guinea, which hides fauna found nowhere else on the continent – the nocturnal **green python** and brilliant blue-and-red **eclectus parrot** are the best-known species. Four hours' bouncing along a 4WD track from the main road should bring you to a clearing where the army simulated a nuclear strike in the 1960s – fortunately using tons of conventional explosives instead of the real thing. Turning right at the junction here takes you past the **ranger station** (☎07/4060 7170) to **LOCKHART RIVER**, an Aboriginal mission and fishing beach; supplies and fuel are sold here during weekday trading hours. The road left passes two **bush campsites** near the Claudie River and Gordon's Creek crossings before winding up at **PORTLAND ROADS'** few houses and public telephones, overlooking a monument to Edmund Kennedy (see p.442) and the remains of a harbour used by US forces in World War II. There's further camping a few kilometres back towards the junction at **Chilli Beach**, a blustery, tropical setting. There are no stores or any public services at Portland Roads.

Next day, you have the chance to experience something unique on the mainland – **sunrise** and **sunset** over different seas – by taking **Frenchman's Road** to Weipa. This starts 30km back from the Lockhart/Portland junction, crosses the difficult **Pascoe** and **Wenlock** rivers, and emerges on the Peninsula Developmental Road, 2km north of **Batavia Downs**. Head through Batavia and cross more creeks, which look worse than they are, to the main Weipa road; the trip coast to coast might take six to eight hours.

Weipa

Those without a 4WD will have to give Iron Range a miss, but can still reach **WEIPA**, a town of red clay and yellow mining trucks dealing in kaolin and **bauxite**. The area was one of the first in Australia to be described by Europeans: Willem Janz encountered "savage, cruel blacks" here in 1606, a report later reiterated by Jan Carstensz who found nothing of interest and sailed off to chart the Gulf of Carpentaria. Apart from a mission built at **Mappoon** in the nineteenth century, little changed until aluminium ore was first mined in the 1950s and Comalco built the town and began mining.

All the traffic in Weipa gives way to the gargantuan mine vehicles and stays out of the restricted areas. The town comprises mostly company housing, but it does offer long-forgotten luxuries: you can pick up spares for your vehicle at the **auto wreckers** and service station on the way into town; and there's a **supermarket**, a post office and a branch of the Commonwealth Bank just in front of large **campsites** (featuring hot showers and a laundry) where you can unwind and swap tales about the rigours of the trip. The **Albatross Hotel** (☎07/4069 7314; ⑥–⑦) up the road is licensed and looks out over the western sea; fishing trips and **mine tours** can be arranged at the campsite office. Hardened **bikers** should try to catch the August **Croc Run**, Australia's richest and most challenging endurance race which weaves its way through mangroves and creeks.

Around town, the library's **Cape York Collection** contains a unique collection of books and documents relating to the area, while the **Uningan Nature Reserve**, situated on the Mission River, preserves sixteen-metre-high **middens** composed entirely of shells left over from Aboriginal meals – some have been dated to sixteen hundred years ago. Driving is the only way to get here, and guidebooks are available from the campsite. Keep an eye out for crocs while walking around the reserve.

Leaving, there's a barge to Normanton (see p.512) in the Gulf once a week, and there are occasional services to Thursday Island – contact the **travel agent** next to the bank (☎07/4069 7266) or Gulf Freight Services (☎07/4069 8619 or free call ☎1800/640 079). Note that there is **no fuel** between Weipa and Bamaga (340km).

North of the Wenlock

The fast-flowing **Wenlock River**, an hour north of the Weipa junction on the main road, marks the start of the most challenging part of the journey north, with road conditions changing every wet season. The routes divide 42km after the Wenlock: die-hards follow the **Old Telegraph Track**, which has all the interesting scenery and creek crossings; those less certain of their abilities take the longer **New Road** to the east, consisting of 200km of loose gravel and bulldust. The Telegraph Track's lines were dismantled in the wake of satellite communications, and many of the poles have been robbed of their ceramic caps by souvenir hunters. The first travellers of the year build simple rafts and log bridges to cross the creeks; as tracks dry and traffic increases, jarring corrugations and potholes are more likely to pose a problem, constituting a serious test of vehicle strength. There are some fine **creeks** on this route: Bertie's potholes are large enough to submerge an entire vehicle; Gunshot's four-metre vertical clay banks are a real test of skill (use low range first, and keep your foot off the brake); and the north exit at Cockatoo is deceptively sandy. Dozens wipe out on Gunshot every season; for the cautious there's a 24-kilometre detour via open scrub at **Heathlands** to the north side.

CROSSING CREEKS BY 4WD

While Cape York's crocs make the standard 4WD procedure of **walking** creek crossings before driving them potentially dangerous, wherever possible you should make some effort to gauge the waters' depth and find the best route. *Never* blindly follow others across. Make sure all rescue gear – shovel, winch, rope, etc – is easy to reach, outside the vehicle. Electrics on petrol engines need to be waterproofed. On deep crossings, block off air inlets to prevent water entering the engine, slacken off the fan belt and cover the radiator grille with a tarpaulin; this diverts water around the engine as long as the vehicle is moving. Select an appropriate gear (changing it in midstream will let water into the clutch) and drive through at walking speed; clear the opposite embankment before stopping again. If you stall, switch off the ignition *immediately*, exit through windows, disconnect the battery (a short might start the engine) and winch out. Don't restart the vehicle until you've made sure that water hasn't been sucked in through the air filter – which will destroy the engine. If you have severe problems, recovery will be very expensive; see "Basics", p.34.

The two routes rejoin briefly after 75km, then the New Road diverges left 54km to the **Jardine River Ferry** ($80 return includes use of the Injinu campsite at Bamaga), while the Telegraph Track ploughs on past beautiful clear green water and basalt **waterfalls** to Nolans Brook – often necessitating a brief submarine dip – and the hundred-metre-wide **Jardine River**. While this spot was once the only crossing point on the Jardine, the river's width makes the crossing extremely testing, and the likelihood of crocodiles adds to the risks. However, it *is* worth the trip to camp (assuming you have enough fuel) before heading back to the ferry. From there, the last hour to Bamaga passes the remains of a **DC-3** that crashed just short of the airstrip in 1945.

Bamaga

BAMAGA, a community of stilt houses and banana palms founded by Saibai islanders in 1946, owes nothing to suburban values. Around the intersection you'll find a workshop and service station selling **fuel** (Mon–Fri 9am–5pm, Sat 9am–12.30pm, Sun 1.30–3pm), a Commonwealth Bank (Mon–Fri 9.30am–3pm; bank books only), airline offices, a hotel and a **shopping centre** (fresh veggies, National Australia Bank agent, telephones, café and post office). For **accommodation**, turn left at the junction to **Injinu campsite** (Cowall Creek), or right past the shopping centre to the coast at **SEISIA** (Red Island Point). You can stay here at tent sites (①) or in units (④) under palms near the jetty (☎07/4069 3243) and take advantage of showers, laundry facilities, a canteen and fishing safaris. Other services in Seisia include a roadhouse, tackle shop, taxi (☎07/4069 3333) and 4WD rental.

Cape York and Somerset

To make local contacts, stay around Bamaga. To keep with the overland crowd head north to the Croc Shop's information hut, then bear left for the idyllic beach at **Punsand Bay Private Reserve**, a just reward for the trials of the journey, with prefab tents, camping, meals, basic provisions, and a limited repairs service but no fuel (☎07/4069 1722; ②–④). Around here you might spot the rare **palm cockatoo**, a huge, crested black parrot with a curved bill.

You could spend a day recuperating on the beach, or return to the Croc Shop and take the road past the Somerset fork to its end at another **campsite** (shower, water and kiosk) and the exclusive, Aboriginal-owned *Pajinka Lodge* (☎07/4069 2100, bookings free call

☎1800/802 968; ⑦). Follow the footpath through vine forest onto a wild, barren headland and down to a turbulent sea opposite the lighthouse on **Eborac Island**. A sign concreted into an oil drum marks **the tip** of mainland Australia and the end of the journey.

Somerset

Established on government orders in 1864 to balance the French naval station in New Caledonia, **Somerset** was founded by John Jardine, who was succeeded by his son Frank the following year. Frank became a legend on the Cape and tales of his exploits assume larger-than-life proportions (fearless pioneer to some, brutal colonial to others). Though envisaged as a second Singapore, Somerset never amounted to more than a military outpost under constant attack from termites and local tribes. In 1877, after the pearling trade in the Torres Strait erupted into lawlessness, the settlement was abandoned in favour of a seat of government closer to the problem at Thursday Island.

Today, Somerset is a large paddock with only a few cannon, machine parts and mango trees as signs of former habitation; the buildings succumbed to white ants or were moved long ago. Frank and his wife Sana are buried on the beach directly below (standing up, say locals), next to a Chinese cemetery and traces of a jetty into the Adolphus Channel. Exploration of the dense undergrowth above the beach to the left might uncover remains of a **sentry post** and a cave with stick-figure paintings, presumably Aboriginal. Past Somerset, a track continues onto another beach before circling back towards the Croc Shop.

The Torres Strait

Beyond Cape York, barely 200km of sea separates Australia from New Guinea: the **Torres Strait** is an obstacle-strewn stretch named after Luís Vaez de Torres, who navigated the waters in 1606. Prior to European contact, the Strait's islands had developed trade links with Australia and highland New Guinea, which supplied outrigger canoes – no suitable trees grow in the Strait – in exchange for oyster and trochus shell, and heads. Warfare between islands pervaded all aspects of life, and the eastern cult of Malo required human jaws as tribute.

The early nineteenth century saw the first trade with Europeans, who soon discovered the Strait's rich bêche de mer (sea cucumber) and pearl beds and occupied the islands as bases for the industry, decimating the Islanders through violence and disease. Then on July 1, 1871, the **London Missionary Society** landed on Darnley Island. Once Islanders realized that the mission protected them from the more piratical whites, they converted to Christianity at a speed that amazed even the missionaries. The advent of Christianity (known here as the **Coming of the Light**) stabilized communities but also heralded the end of traditional life, as cults were undermined and wages and stores replaced the barter network. Another influential group were **South Sea Island** teachers, who brought their own dance styles and crops, and gradually intermarried with the locals.

The church created **island councils**, but Queensland held the real power with its **segregation laws**, which prevented emigration to the mainland. The only job in the Strait was pearling (for mother-of-pearl), and white boat-owners would have lost their labour pool if Islanders went south. Until World War II the islands made the best of it, but army service overseas gave returning recruits a better understanding of what they deserved from the government, and pressure removed some barriers to migration. The advent of plastics led to the collapse of the mother-of-pearl industry, and the unemployment that followed forced the government to drop all protectionist policies, with the result that by the mid-1970s half the Strait's former population was living on the mainland. The remainder formed a movement to establish an **Islander Nation**, which bore its first fruit on June 3, 1992, when the **Mabo Decision** acknowledged the Merriam as traditional owners of Murray Island, thereby setting a precedent for mainland Aboriginal claims and sending shock waves through the establishment.

Ferries cross regularly between Cape York and Thursday Island, the Strait's administrative centre – which, even on a brief visit, offers a fascinating glimpse into an all-but-forgotten corner of Australia. In theory, travel beyond Thursday (except to neighbouring islands) is forbidden to casual travellers, but the rules are occasionally relaxed.

Thursday Island

A three-square-kilometre speck within sight of the mainland, between Prince of Wales, Hammond and Horn islands, **Thursday Island** wears a few aliases: coined "Sink of the Pacific" for the variety of peoples who passed through in pearling days, the local tag is *Waiben* or (very loosely) "Thirsty Island" – once a reference to the availability of drinking water and now a laconic aside on the quantity of beer consumed. The hotel clock with no hands hints at the pace of life and it's only for events like Christmas, when wall-to-wall aluminium punts from neighbouring islands make the harbour look like a maritime supermarket car park, that things liven up. Other chances to catch Thursday in carnival spirit are during the Coming of the Light festivities on July 1, and for the Island of Origin rugby league matches later in the same month: in one season 25 people were hospitalized, and the spectators often play as big a part in the action as do the teams.

In town there are traces of the old **Chinatown** district around Milman Street, and a reminder of Queensland's worst shipping disaster in the **Quetta Memorial Church**, way down Douglas Street, built after the ship hit an uncharted rock in the Adolphus Channel in 1890 and went down with virtually all the Europeans on board. The Aplin Road **cemetery**, where two of the victims are buried, has tiled Islander tombs and depressing numbers of **Japanese** graves, each marked by a short pillar and kanji inscription. All died diving for pearls. As a by-product of the industry, Japanese crews had accurately mapped the Strait before the last war and it's no coincidence that the airstrip was bombed when hostilities were declared in 1942; fortifications are still in place on Thursday's east coast. Bunkers and naval cannon at the **Old Fort** on the opposite side date from the 1890s.

Practicalities

There are **ferries** to Thursday Island every weekday morning from Cape York (2hr), Punsand Bay (1hr 30min) and Seisia (1hr 15min); prices are around $45 each way. Passing **Possession Island** on the way over, you come within sight of a plaque commemorating James Cook's landing here on August 22, 1770, when he planted the flag for George III and Great Britain. Then it's into the shallow channel between Prince of Wales and Horn islands. Horn has an **airport** (with regular flights to and from Cairns; see p.450) and open-cut gold mine, while **Prince of Wales** is the Strait's largest island, stocked with deer and settled by an overflow population unable to afford Thursday's exorbitant land premiums.

The wharf on Thursday sits below the colonial-style **Customs House**, a minute from the town centre on **Douglas Street**. Here you'll find a **post office** with payphones, the National Australia **bank**, cafés and two of the island's **hotels**: the *Torres* just beats the neighbouring *Royal* as Australia's northernmost bar. Facing the water on **Victoria Parade**, the *Federal* (☎07/4069 1569; ⑤) is fractionally quieter as **lodgings** on a busy night, while on Douglas Street, *Mura Mudh* (☎07/4069 2050; ①) is a good value hostel run by Thursday Islanders. The one-time mainstay, the *Grand* (famous for once briefly accommodating the novelist Somerset Maugham) burned down in 1993. Other facilities include a **travel agent** on the corner of Victoria and Blackall streets (☎07/4069 1264), and a **pharmacy** and **laundry** on Douglas Street. Willie Nelson's T.I. Tours (☎07/4069 1588) meets incoming ferries for a ninety-minute tour of the island ($15).

Travel options

Though you generally need permission from the local council, it's possible that you may be privately invited to other islands in the Strait. While some are within outboard range – "one drum trips" – you're looking at $110 or more each way to fly to anywhere more distant. Far to the east, **Murray Island** (Mer) is enticing for its remoteness and importance in island history. To the north are **Badu**, centre of the Strait's burgeoning crayfish industry, and **Saibai**, a low deltaic island just 16km from the New Guinea mainland. This is the only place in Australia where you can see another country, but regular trading across the Strait has recently included "grass-for-guns" exchanges, and New Guinea is not the place to be caught without a visa.

travel details

Trains

Bundaberg to: Cairns (3–4 weekly; 25hr); Mackay (3–4 weekly; 11hr); Proserpine (3–4 weekly; 13hr 30min); Rockhampton (10 weekly; 4hr 30min); Townsville (3–4 weekly; 17hr).

Cairns to: Bundaberg (6 weekly; 25hr); Kuranda (1–2 daily; 1hr); Mackay (6 weekly; 13hr 20min); Proserpine (5 weekly; 11hr 30min); Rockhampton (10 weekly; 19hr); Townsville (5 weekly; 4hr 40min).

Mackay to: Bundaberg (3–4 weekly; 11hr); Cairns (3–4 weekly; 13hr 20min); Proserpine (3–4 weekly; 2hr 30min); Rockhampton (10 weekly; 5hr 30min); Townsville (3–4 weekly; 7hr).

Rockhampton to: Bundaberg (10 weekly; 4hr 30min); Cairns (3–4 weekly; 19hr); Longreach (2 weekly; 12hr 30min); Mackay (3–4 weekly; 5hr 30min); Proserpine (3–4 weekly; 7hr 40min); Townsville (3–4 weekly; 12hr).

Townsville to: Bundaberg (3–4 weekly; 17hr); Cairns (3–4 weekly; 4hr 40min); Mackay (3–4 weekly; 7hr); Mount Isa (2 weekly; 19hr); Proserpine (3–4 weekly; 4hr 40min); Rockhampton 10 weekly; 12hr).

Buses

For more on services to **Far North Queensland** and **Cape York**, contact Coral Coaches (☎07/4098 2600) or White Car Coaches/Cape York Coaches (☎07/4051 9533).

Airlie Beach to: Bundaberg (6 daily; 11hr 30min); Cairns (6 daily; 9hr 45min); Mission Beach (6 daily; 8hr); Townsville (6 daily; 3hr 30min).

Bundaberg to: Airlie Beach (6 daily; 11hr 30min); Cairns (8 daily; 21hr); Mission Beach (3 daily;

19hr); Townsville (8 daily; 14hr 30min).

Cairns to: Airlie Beach (6 daily; 9hr 45min); Atherton Tablelands (1 daily; 1–3hr); Bundaberg (8 daily; 21hr); Cape Tribulation (daily; 4hr); Cardwell (9 daily; 3hr); Chillagoe (3 weekly; 5hr); Cooktown (5 weekly; 7hr); Laura (2 weekly; 4hr); Mission Beach (3 daily; 2hr); Port Douglas (2 daily; 1hr 30min); Townsville (9 daily; 5hr 20min); Weipa (2 weekly; 14hr).

Mackay to: Airlie Beach (6 daily; 2hr); Cairns (8 daily; 12hr 45min); Dingo (2 daily; 9hr 30min); Emerald (2 daily; 6hr); Mission Beach (4 daily; 23hr); Townsville (8 daily; 5hr 15min).

Rockhampton to: Airlie Beach (6 daily; 6hr 10min); Anakie (3 weekly; 4hr 30min); Cairns (8 daily; 16hr); Longreach (3 weekly; 9hr); Mount Morgan (Mon–Sat 2–3 daily; 2hr); Townsville (9 daily; 9hr 30min); Yeppoon (3–9 daily; 1hr 30min).

Townsville to: Airlie Beach (6 daily; 3hr 30min); Bundaberg (9 daily; 15hr); Cairns (8 daily; 5hr 20min); Cardwell (8 daily; 2hr); Charters Towers (3 daily; 1hr 30min); Mount Isa (3 daily; 11hr 30min); Rockhampton (8 daily; 9hr 30min).

Ferries

Airlie Beach/Shute Harbour to: Daydream Island (1–2 daily; 45min); Hamilton Island (1–3 daily; 1hr); Hook Island (1–2 daily; 1hr 30min); Lindeman Island (2 daily; 1hr 30min); South Molle Island (2 daily; 45min); Whitsunday Island (1 daily; 2hr).

Cairns to: Thursday Island (1 weekly; 36hr)

Cape York to: Thursday Island (Mon–Fri 3 daily; 1hr 15min–2hr).

Cardwell to: Hinchinbrook Island (2 daily; 1–2hr).

Mackay to: Brampton Island (1 daily except Tues & Wed; 1hr).

Mission Beach to: Dunk Island (10 or more daily; 15min).

Rosslyn Bay to: Great Keppel Island (4–5 daily; 45min–1hr).

Townsville to: Magnetic Island (10 or more daily; 45min).

Weipa to: Normanton (1 weekly; 24hr).

Flights

For **Cape York services**, contact: Ansett (☎07/4050 2211) for Cairns-Weipa; Sunstate/Qantas (☎13 1313) for Thursday Island; Flight West (☎13 2392) to Cooktown, Coen, Lockhart River (Iron Range), Weipa and Bamaga; and Aussie Airways (☎07/4035 9309 or free call ☎1800/620 022) for Lizard Island, Cooktown and Cape York. There's also the **Peninsula Mail Run** to these destinations and others; it leaves Cairns

daily before dawn, arriving at Horn Island (Thursday Island) about 11.30am. Contact Cape York Air Services (☎07/4035 9399) to see if there's room for passengers.

Cairns to: Bamaga (1 daily; 2hr 45min); Bundaberg (3–5 daily; 3hr 30min); Lizard Island (1 daily; 1hr); Mackay (1–2 daily; 2hr 45min); Proserpine (6 weekly; 2hr); Rockhampton (1–3 daily; 3hr); Thursday Island (1–2 daily; 2hr); Townsville (2–4 daily; 1hr).

Mackay to: Brampton Island (6 daily; 20min); Cairns (3–4 daily; 2hr 45min); Townsville (4–6 daily; 1hr).

Rockhampton to: Cairns (3–5 daily; 3hr); Great Keppel Island (3–6 daily; 25min); Proserpine (6 weekly; 1hr 40min); Townsville (2–4 daily; 1hr 50min).

Townsville to: Bundaberg (1–5 daily; 3hr 40min); Cairns (4–6 daily; 1hr); Mackay (3–4 daily; 1hr 30min); Proserpine (6 weekly; 50min); Rockhampton (2–4 daily; 1hr 50min).

CHAPTER FIVE

OUTBACK QUEENSLAND

Outback Queensland, the west of the state, is thinly populated by tenacious farming communities swinging precariously between famine and survival, and seems hard to reconcile with the lushness of the wet tropics. The population is concentrated in the relatively fertile highlands along the **Great Dividing Range**, running low behind the coast; on the far side, featureless plains slide over a hot horizon into the fringes of South Australia and the Northern Territory. Almost untouched by overseas visitors, the only places attracting tourists in any numbers are the **Stockman's Hall of Fame** at Longreach, the oases of **Carnarvon Gorge** in the Central Highlands, and the Gulf of Carpentaria's **Lawn Hill Gorge**. But elsewhere the opportunities for exploration are immense, with **precious stones**, **fossils**, **waterholes** and **Aboriginal art** in abundance.

Choosing where to go is often determined by the most convenient starting point. **Main roads** and **trains** head west from the coast at Brisbane, Rockhampton and Townsville; interstate **bus** services from Townsville are good, but otherwise the highways are only partially covered. If you're **driving**, your vehicle must be sound and you should carry essential spares, as even main centres often lack replacements.

Unless you're very experienced and well equipped, you'll find that western **summers** (Dec–April) effectively prohibit travel, with searing temperatures and violent flash floods that can isolate regions (especially in the Channel Country on the far side of the Great Dividing Range) for days or weeks on end. Consequently, many tour companies, information offices and motels simply shut up shop, at least during Jan–Feb. On the other hand, water revives dormant seeds and fast-growing desert flowers, which cover the ground to the horizon in good years. At other times, expect hot days and cool nights, plenty of dust and sparse landscapes.

ACCOMMODATION PRICES

All the accommodation listed in this book has been categorized into one of eight price bands, as set out below. The rates quoted represent the cheapest available double or twin room in high season – except for category ①, which indicates per-person rates for a dorm bed, and the categories given for units, cabins and vans, which represent the daily charge for the whole unit.

① Under $18	⑤ $61–74
② $19–30	⑥ $75–94
③ $31–45	⑦ $95–124
④ $46–60	⑧ $125 upwards

For more accommodation details, see p.40-43.

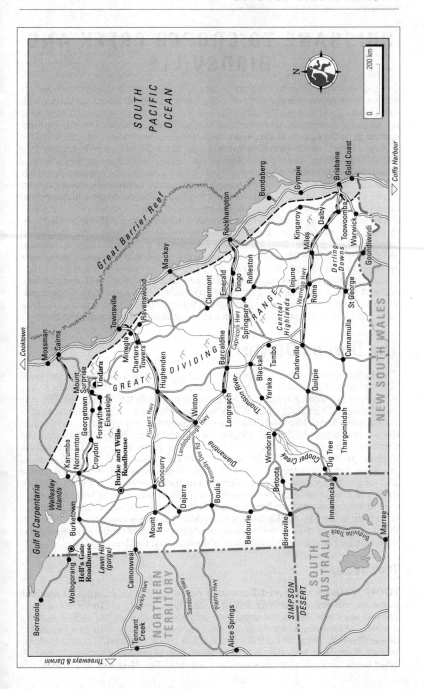

BRISBANE TO COOPER CREEK AND BIRDSVILLE

The thousand-plus-kilometre haul from the coast's comforts to Queensland's remote southwestern corner dumps you tired and dusty on the South Australian border, with some exciting routes down the Birdsville and Strzelecki tracks or through the hostile red barrier of the Simpson Desert yet to come (see *South Australia*). There are two ultimate targets: the outpost of **Birdsville**, with its annual horse races, and the Dig Tree at Nappa Merrie on **Cooper Creek**, monument to the Burke and Wills tragedy (see p.486). The highway scenery is as bleak as you'd expect: after crossing the fertile disc of the **Darling Downs**, the country withers and dries, marooning communities in isolation and hardship. Detour north through Queensland's **Central Highlands**, however, and you'll find a landscape peppered with forested sandstone gorges and **Aboriginal sites** – worth the journey even if you don't go any further.

The most practical route into the area from Brisbane is on the **Warrego Highway**, through Toowoomba, Roma and Charleville towards Quilpie. Roma is the jumping-off point into the highlands; from Quilpie there are largely unsurfaced roads to Birdsville and the Dig Tree. The *Westlander* **train** runs in this direction to Charleville, as do buses en route from Brisbane to Mount Isa.

Running parallel to the south, the **Cunningham Highway** crosses the Downs between Warwick and Goondiwindi (the limit of the **bus** service), then heads out to Cunnamulla. West of Cunnamulla you're heading across oil-, gas- and opal-fields towards the Dig Tree: 4WD is preferable beyond the bitumen and is essential for reaching the Dig Tree.

The Darling Downs

The **Darling Downs** sprawl westwards from the back of the Great Dividing Range behind Brisbane down to the state's southern boundaries. The Warrego Highway climbs a steep escarpment to **Toowoomba** and the Northern Downs, while the Cunningham Highway cuts through Cunningham's Gap to **Warwick** and the south. Highway towns west of Toowoomba – Dalby, Miles and Chinchilla – are unadorned farming centres, and it's more the scenery along the Downs' fringes, particularly at the **Bunya Mountains** and **Girraween**, that warrants a visit. But even as you tear across the Central Downs without stopping, you'll notice that the flat grasslands are clear evidence of Aboriginal custodial practices: created by controlled burning designed to clear woodland and increase grazing land for game, they perfectly suited European pastoral needs. The Downs are relatively fertile and stud farms, dairy, cotton, wool and cereal farming have all been successfully tried at one time or another. Even unwanted plants thrive. During the 1920s millions of acres were infested by **prickly pear**, a South American cactus finally brought to heel by the tiny *cactoblastis* moth in 1930 – a success story of biological control in Queensland to match the later failure of the introduction of the cane toad (see box on p.419).

Toowoomba

TOOWOOMBA is a busy yet dull university city perched on the edge of a six-hundred-metre escarpment, a promising setting it can't quite live up to. To be fair, though, Toowoomba's side streets and numerous gardens *are* pleasant, the stylish houses a reminder of its business wealth in the late nineteenth century. There's a September **flower festival** during which the **tourist office** on James Street/Warrego Highway (daily 8.30am–5pm; ☎07/4639 3797) hands out lists of exhibition gardens to visit. At other times the main attractions are the **Cobb and Co. Museum**, at 27 Lindsay St (daily 9am–4pm; $4), recalling days when intrepid coaches bounced across the Outback delivering mail and passengers; and **Picnic Point** at the top of Tourist Road, offering a café, bar and restaurant as well as picnic space, all with splendid views.

Accommodation prospects include the *Jolly Swagman Caravan Park*, 47 Kitchener Rd (☎07/4632 8735), about 1km east of the centre; *Range Motel*, on Tourist Road (☎07/4632 3133; ③), near the plateau's edge and with fine views; and the more central *Burke and Wills Hotel*, 554 Ruthven St (☎07/4632 2433; ⑤). **Moving on** from Toowoomba, the **New England Highway** runs north to Kingaroy, plied by Polleys Coaches (☎07/5482 2700 for times), and south to Warwick (Crisp's; ☎07/4661 2566). Goondiwindi is three hours southwest with McCafferty's or Greyhound Pioneer, and the Warrego Highway continues west across the Central Downs.

Around Kingaroy: the Northern Downs

KINGAROY is a small town in the heart of peanut country, on the very fringes of the Downs, a couple of hours' drive from Toowoomba and Dalby to the south or Gympie on the coast. A cluster of towering **peanut silos** aptly symbolize the fame Kingaroy owes to **Johannes Bjelke-Petersen**, who farmed nuts here before taking Queensland under his thumb in 1968. His equally charismatic wife Flo made it onto postcards featuring her pumpkin scone recipe – and with a dam, bridge, road and sportsground named after him, not to mention his ominous catch phrase "Don't you worry about that" still echoed in local conversation, Joh is in no danger of obscurity. To get in touch with what Kingaroy is all about, take the fifty-minute **tour** at Kingaroy Toasted Peanuts (☎07/4162 2272; daily at 10am); it's free, but the waft of roasting peanuts is so seductive that you'll probably spend something on fresh nuts. *Kingaroy Caravans* on Walter Road (☎07/4162 1808; cabins ③) is a friendly **place to stay**, while the *Club Hotel* (☎07/4162 2204; ②) offers beds, cheapish meals and occasional live music. Polleys Coaches leaves daily from Kingaroy to Gympie and Toowoomba, while drivers can take the Bunya Highway to Dalby.

The Bunya Mountains

Southwest of Kingaroy, there's a sixty-kilometre section of twisting road along the crumpled **Bunya Mountains** before you reach **Dalby** (see p.479), back on the Warrego Highway. Among general greenery and clusters of unlikely flowers, you'll find enormous **bunya pines**, which once covered large tracts of southern Queensland. Every few years tribal boundaries were overlooked as clans gathered to gorge on the pine seeds. Assisted by loops of vine, the Aborigines scaled the trees and threw down the cones, which gave up their thumb-sized nuts to be eaten raw or roasted. The indefatigable **Ludwig Leichhardt** (see p.994) witnessed such a feast in 1844 and persuaded the government to make the area an Aboriginal reserve, free from logging or settlement. The decree was revoked in 1860 and today the Bunya Mountains contain the last significant stand of pines.

NPWS sites along the road make for good **camping** (ranger's office at Dalby ☎07/4668 3127; advance booking essential during holiday periods), though in winter the mountains are generally several degrees cooler than the plains below. **Walking tracks** lead through the forest to orchid-covered lookouts and waterfalls.

Warwick, Stanthorpe and the Southern Downs

The southern edge of the Darling Downs, also known as Queensland's **Granite Belt**, regularly records the state's coldest temperatures – on a winter's night it drops well below freezing here. Small and relaxed, **WARWICK** makes a fine base for exploring the region. Services are centred around Grafton and Palmerin streets, where sandstone buildings date back to the time when Warwick graziers competed fiercely with Toowoomba's merchants to establish the Downs' premier settlement. The October **rodeo** is about the only time you might experience trouble finding **accommodation**: try *Warwick Tourist Caravan Park*, 18 Palmer Ave, north of town on the highway (☎07/4661 8335; cabins ③), or *Centre Point Motel*, 32 Albion St (☎ & fax 07/4661 3488; ④). Alternatively, you could ask at the **tourist office and art gallery** halfway down Albion Street (Mon–Fri 9am–5.30pm, weekends variable; ☎07/4661 3122).

The **Condamine River**, unimpressive where it flows through town, is part of Australia's longest river system. Originating on the highlands east of Warwick, it joins the Murray/Darling before emptying into the ocean near Adelaide. At **Queen Mary Falls**, 43km from Warwick beyond Killarney, a tributary exits the forest in a plunge off the top of the plateau. A track climbs the cliff from the *Queen Mary Falls* **campsite** (☎07/4664 7151); there's a kiosk, but no shops or transport to the falls.

Moving on, the **New England Highway** runs south to Stanthorpe then over the border to Tenterfield. The Cunningham Highway continues 200km west to **Goondiwindi** and the banks of the Macintyre River, which marks the state border with New South Wales.

Stanthorpe and Girraween

Sixty kilometres south of Warwick, **STANTHORPE** is a quiet town known for the fruit stalls and small-scale **wineries** that throng the highway. Old Caves Winery, just outside Stanthorpe on the New England Highway (☎07/4681 1494), Ballandean Estate by Sundown National Park (☎07/4684 1226) and Bungawarra at Ballandean (☎07/4684 1128) are all making a name for themselves and are open daily – call first to arrange a convenient time.

The surrounding hills are granite, exposed as fantastic monoliths at **Girraween National Park**, 30km south down the New England Highway. There's an NPWS **campsite** here (☎07/4684 5157) with showers and toilets – and the chance of seeing small, shy, active sugar gliders just after dark. Listen for claws clattering over bark and then shine your torch overhead to catch a glowing set of eyes in the spotlight.

With more energy than skill, you can climb several of the giant hills with little risk, as long as rain hasn't made them dangerously slippery. **Castle Rock** (2hr return) is entertaining: initially a gentle incline past lichen-covered boulders in the forest, the track follows a dotted white line into a fissure – look up and you'll see loose rocks balanced above you – before emerging onto a thin ledge above the campsite. Follow this around to the north side and clamber to the very top for superb views of the Pyramids, Sphinx and Mount Norman poking rudely out of the woods. **The Sphinx** and **Turtle Rock** are another thirty minutes from the base of Castle. Sphinx is a broad pillar topped by a boulder, while Turtle's more conventional shape means a scramble, with no handholds on the final stretch. But pat yourself on the back if you make it to the top of the completely bald **South Pyramid** (2hr return) without resorting to hands and knees. Take a well-earned rest at the top and look across to the unscaleable North Pyramid from below **Balancing Rock**, an oval boulder teetering so precariously on its narrow end that you can see underneath to where the support is surely only a few years away from collapse. **Mount Norman**, the park's 1267-metre apex, lies an hour beyond Castle Rock and should only be attempted by experienced climbers; check details with the ranger at Girraween (☎07/4684 5157).

Goondiwindi and St George

Before European settlers put weirs on the Macintyre River in the **GOONDIWINDI** area, it was little more than a string of waterholes and lagoons, attracting a lot of birdlife and inspiring the Aboriginal name Goonawinna – "birds' resting place". The irrigation weirs now supply the huge demands of the local cotton and wheat industries, which proudly boast the largest **silo** in the southern hemisphere, but they haven't discouraged the varied birdlife. The **Old Customs House Museum** at the south end of McLean Street (10am–4pm; closed Tues; $2) has an eclectic gathering of anything old, from preserved snakes to steam engines. It predates the rest of the town and even the wood-paved bridge over the river on the border with New South Wales. Other local attractions include the old water tower on McLean Street. You'll find a **tourist information centre** at the corner of McLean and Bowen streets (daily 9am–5pm; ☎07/4671 2653); Calladoon Street is the place for **shops** and **banks**.

Cheap **camping** and a 24-hour store can be found at *Gundy Star* (☎07/4671 2900) on the Cunningham Highway at the north entrance to town, while there is more central **accommodation** at the *Border Motel*, 126 Marshall St (☎07/4671 1688; ⑤), or *Denn's Caravan Park*, 3 DeLacy St (☎07/4631 1383).

The town's **Bachelors and Spinsters Ball** in October is a night of chaos fuelled by unlimited beer, burgers and bands. You need to sport a tie and look smart; entry is $65.

Two hundred kilometres further west on the Barwon Highway, **ST GEORGE** sits on the banks of the Balonne River and is the administrative centre for the tranquil shire of Balonne. From St George, roads leave in almost every direction, and on your way through the shire every town offers a taste of farming history, wildlife and a relaxed atmosphere. **Information** on the region is available from the Council Offices under the clock tower in the town centre (Mon–Fri 9am–4.45pm; ☎07/4625 3222), and you can **stay** at the *Australian Hotel* (☎07/4625 5000; ①–④) on the river bank. At the back of the Balonne Sports Store, a few doors down from the Council Offices, the proprietor has combined the woodcarving skills of his native Greece with the Aboriginal tradition of emu egg-carving and the wonders of electric lighting to produce a unique display of carved, illuminated **emu eggs** (daily 9am–5pm; ☎07/4625 3490; $2).

The Central Downs and around

To break the unexciting journey west across the Downs from Toowoomba to Dalby, call in at **Jondaryan Woolshed** (daily 9am–4pm; $10), 3km south of the highway from Jondaryan and about 45km from Toowoomba, to look around the collection of old buildings – all relocated from elsewhere, with the exception of the shed itself. Exhibits worth a closer look include a document, dating from 1880, which itemizes some of the schoolmistress's tasks, such as splinting broken legs, wallpapering buildings to keep out snakes and being able to fight off swaggies trying to sleep in the schoolhouse. Make sure you catch one of the **tours** (Mon–Fri 1pm, Sat, Sun & holidays 10.30am & 1.30pm) when the smithy is working, and you can watch sheep shearers at work beneath the vast emptiness of the handcrafted woolshed roof, lit by a bare bulb – a very surreal tableau. There's also **accommodation** in shearers' quarters around the back, with a fire to cook on, hot showers, and the choice of a campsite or bitterly cold tin dorms (①). The next stops over the following 200km are **Dalby**, **Chinchilla** and **Miles**, rural centres devoid of specific attractions but with the usual complement of van park and motel accommodation.

If you have your own transport, two **national parks**, Expedition Range and Isla Gorge, north from Miles off the Leichhardt Highway, are worth investigating: you need to be self-sufficient, competent at orientation and bushwalking – and to contact the ranger first (PO Box 175, Taroom, QLD 4420; ☎07/4627 3358). The massive **Expedition Range** is centred on Robinson Gorge, west of **Taroom** (itself 125km north of Miles) along a ninety-kilometre road that becomes a rough track 20km before the campsite. Rock formations, Aboriginal art and waterfalls lie in tributary canyons, and a couple of the northern gorges are said to have some fine plant fossils, but, even with survey maps, navigation is tricky. Easier to reach, but with the same provisos on getting around, **Isla Gorge** is a small, triangular park right on the highway, 54km north of Taroom. Climb up to the lookout for orientation before descending down the dangerously loose slopes into a maze of offshoot gorges, which you could spend days exploring.

Roma

ROMA, 140km west of Miles, was founded by settlers eager to occupy country made available by the opening up of the Darling Downs in 1862. Once considered for a rail junction to link the east coast with the Gulf of Carpentaria, the town thrives on farming, supplemented by the **oil** and **gas fields** which have been exploited intermittently since the turn of the century.

A typical inland town – tidy, with a slightly dated air lent by the iron decorations and wraparound balconies of its hotels, Roma has a reputation for **cattle markets** – one day-long event saw over $1.6 million change hands; and every Easter there is a **rodeo and carnival**. Romavilla Winery has been producing prize-winning **wine** since 1863 – if you want to buy, it's about a kilometre north of town on the Carnarvon Road, at Quintin Street (Mon–Fri 8am–5pm, Sat 9am–noon & 2–4pm; ☎07/4622 1822).

The Warrego Highway's entry to town from the east is greeted by the **Big Rig**, a drilling rig left as a monument to the oil boom of the 1920s, and beside it the **information centre** (daily 9am–5pm; ☎07/4622 4355). **Accommodation** choices include *Motel Carnarvon*, 18 Northern Rd (☎07/4622 1599 or free call ☎1800/621 155; ④), and the *Starlight Motor Inn* (☎07/4622 2666; ⑤), which both offer standard motel beds; the *Big Rig Caravan Park*, 4 McDowell St (☎07/4622 2538), near the oil bore off the Bowen Road heading east, has welcome hot showers available during sub-zero winter nights. **Restaurants** in Roma are fairly basic, though *Deano's*, at 77 Quintin St, does good steaks. The **train station** is on Station Street at the corner of Charles Street (☎07/4622 9411), and the **bus terminal** is by the BP roadhouse on Bowen Street, as the Warrego Highway is called in town. Tickets can also be obtained from Maranoa Travel, 71 Arthur St (☎07/4622 1409). Heading north, the **Carnarvon Developmental Road** (take Quintin Street from the town centre) gives access to Mount Moffatt and Carnarvon Gorge (see opposite); otherwise the next stops west are Mitchell and Charleville. The **airport** is a small strip a few kilometres outside town.

The Central Highlands

Queensland's **Central Highlands** consist of a broad band of weathered sandstone plateaus along the Great Dividing Range, with spectacularly sculpted sheer cliffs and pinnacles sectioned into a group of **national parks** around **Carnarvon Gorge**, 200km north of Roma. It's an extraordinarily primeval landscape, and one still visibly central to Aboriginal culture; poor pasture left the highlands relatively unscathed by European colonization. Within its boundaries, **Carnarvon National Park** includes the gorge, **Mount Moffatt** and the **Ka Ka Mundi/Salvator Rosa** regions further west. Most people head for Carnarvon Gorge itself, where you'll find the main facilities, the highest concentration of Aboriginal art and arguably the best scenery. For the more adventurous, Mount Moffatt can usually be reached in a non-4WD vehicle; Ka Ka Mundi and Salvator Rosa are well off the beaten track, requiring advance preparation to explore.

Wherever you're going, expect at least 60km of dirt road – which will be closed after heavy rain (most likely Nov–May). Always carry extra rations in case you get stranded for a while and, unless you're desperately short of supplies, stay put in wet weather – you'll only churn the road up and make it harder for others to use. Outside Carnarvon Gorge, remember to allow for enough **fuel** to get you around the park once you're there; it's impossible to drive directly between any of the park's four sections. Summer **temperatures** often reach 40°C, while winter nights will be below freezing. Note that gathering firewood is prohibited inside the park, so stop on the way in or bring a gas stove. The **NPWS district headquarters** are in Emerald (☎07/4982 4555), and regional offices are detailed below.

Carnarvon Gorge

To reach **Carnarvon Gorge** from Roma, head 199km north along the Carnarvon Developmental Road, past Injune to Wyseby Homestead, then 45km west to *Oasis Lodge* (see below) and campsite. The last fuel on the way is at Injune (155km). Guests of the lodge might be able to arrange a ride with the weekly supply truck which leaves at 5am on Friday, returning from Roma at about 2pm; the return trip costs $150 and must be booked on ☎07/4984 4503. Consider detouring 15km east, between Injune and Wyseby, to **Lonesome National Park**, where the ridges above Arcadia Valley provide grand views of both the Carnarvon and Expedition ranges. From **Emerald**, it's 230km south along the Gregory/Dawson highways through Springsure and Rolleston.

As you drive in at dawn, you'll notice the **Consuelo Tableland** standing out magnificently above dark forests as the road crosses the plains below, rising gradually to the foothills on the park's edge before terminating at the mouth of the gorge. Here, **Oasis Lodge** (reservations: via Rolleston, QLD 4702; free call ☎1800/644 150; ⑦) is surrounded by a neat lawn and respectably sized cycad palms; they've comfortable rooms, a bar and a **store** selling basics, fuel and LP gas refills. About 2km further on, in a wilder cycad grove, the NPWS **campsite** is almost always full, despite icy showers; book in advance by calling the **ranger station** (Carnarvon Gorge, Carnarvon National Park via Rolleston, QLD 4702; 8am–5pm; ☎07/4984 4505), which has a payphone, an orientation model of the gorge, **free maps** and a library on the highlands and its wildlife.

Carnarvon Creek's journey between the vertical faces of the gorge has created some magical scenery, where low cloud often blends with the cliffs, making them look infinitely tall. A three-kilometre trail heads downstream between the campsite and

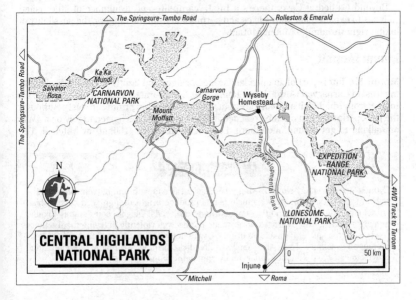

lodge, crossing the creek a few times by means of stepping stones and fallen trees. If you're not prepared to get wet, you can't get past the **swimming hole** here (as cold as the showers, but more fun). **Baloon Cave**, in woodland behind the lodge, shelters some stencil art of hands and boomerangs – easy to reach if unimpressive compared with other sites in the park. Before setting off to find them, climb **Boolimba Bluff** from the campsite for a rare chance to see the gorge system from above; it's a tiring climb but the views from the "Roof of Queensland" make the three-kilometre track worth the effort.

The day-walk (19km return) **into the gorge** takes some beating, with intriguing side gorges: best are the **Moss Garden** (3.5km), a vibrant green carpet of liverworts and ferns lapping up a spring as it seeps through the rockface; the awesomely quiet, claustrophobic **Amphitheatre** (4km), open to the sky and reached by a long ladder from the gorge floor; and **Alijon Falls** (5km), concealing the enchanting **Wards Canyon**, where a remnant group of *angiopteris* ferns hang close to extinction in front of a second waterfall and gorge, complete with bats and blood-red river stones.

Carnarvon's two major **Aboriginal art sites** are the Gallery (5.6km) and Cathedral Cave (at the end of the trail, 9.3km from the campsite), both on the gorge track, though if you keep your eyes open there are plenty more to be found. These are Queensland's most documented Aboriginal art sites, although an understanding of their significance is limited to representational terms. A rockface covered with engravings of vulvas lends a pornographic air to **the Gallery**; other symbols include kangaroo, emu and human tracks. A long, wavy line might represent the rainbow serpent, shaper of many Aboriginal landscapes. Overlaying the engravings are hundreds of coloured stencils made by placing an object against the wall and spraying it with a mixture of ochre and water held in the mouth. Always personal and striking, hands – including children's – form the bulk of the designs, but there are also artefacts, boomerangs and complex crosses formed by four arms. Goannas and mysterious net patterns at the near end of the wall have been painted with a stick. **Cathedral Cave** is larger, with an even greater range of designs, including seashell pendant stencils – proof that trade networks reached from here to the sea – and engravings of animal tracks and nests of emu eggs.

Beyond Cathedral Cave, there's a **bush campsite** and a number of little-visited canyons to explore plus, with advice and permission from the rangers, the possibility of hiking right through to Mount Moffatt.

Mount Moffatt

Mount Moffatt is part of an open landscape of ridges and lightly wooded grassland to the west of Carnarvon Gorge. From Roma, it's a 248-kilometre drive to the campsite via Injune; from Mitchell it's 220km direct (if you're approaching from the west). Although the park perimeter can often be reached in 2WD vehicles, you'll need to rely on a 4WD or walking to get around once there. Last fuel is at Injune (150km) or Mitchell. The

---

CYCADS

Cycads are extremely slow-growing, fire-resistant plants with tough, palm-like fronds – relics of the age of dinosaurs. Female plants produce bright orange seed cones which attract emus to eat them and thereby distribute the seeds. Despite being highly toxic to humans – almost every early explorer made themselves violently ill trying them – these seeds were a staple of highland Aborigines, who detoxified flour made from the nuts by prolonged washing. They also applied "fire-stick farming" techniques, encouraging groves to grow and seed at Carnarvon by annual burning.

access road ends at the **ranger station** (Mount Moffatt, Carnarvon National Park via Mitchell, QLD 4465; ☎07/4626 3581) where you can collect your map of the area, plan any bushwalking and book a site. The campground here has drinking water and toilets.

Mount Moffatt's attractions are spread out, so seeing them involves driving to an area and then walking around. More or less in the vicinity of the ranger station, **the Chimneys** area has some interesting pinnacles. Alcoves in the rockface here once housed bark burial cylinders – look for the stencil of an entire body, arms spread-eagled. **Marlong Arch**, 6km west of the ranger station, is a sandstone arch decorated with handprints and engravings. Five kilometres northeast, a trail leads to **Kookaburra Cave**, named after a weathered, bird-shaped hand stencil.

Further afield, consultation with the ranger might get you access to **Marlong Plain** (10km from the station), a pretty expanse of blue grass surrounded by peaks, and **Kenniffs Cave** (20km), Mount Moffatt's richest site. The Kenniff brothers were cattle rustlers who used the cave as a hideout around 1900, but the cave had been used long before the Kenniffs' time; excavations in 1960 were the first to reveal that Aboriginal occupation of Australia predated the last Ice Age. Art in the cave includes stencils of feet, artefacts and a painted human figure. If you're still in doubt as to the area's significance in Highland Aboriginal culture, visit the **ochre mine** and **bora ring** at **West Branch Camp**. Ochre was used ceremonially in stencilling and body-painting, and mines were a source of trade for tribes who controlled them, while a bora ground was central to male initiation ceremonies. For pure scenery, head east 15km north of the ranger station and follow the track (4WD or on foot) about 7km to the **Mahogany Forest**, a stand of giant stringybark trees. **Mount Moffatt** itself and pink-walled **Devils Canyon**, in the park's southeast, are more difficult to reach – you need to carry reliable maps and have bushwalking skills.

Salvator Rosa and Ka Ka Mundi national parks

Trips to **Salvator Rosa** and **Ka Ka Mundi national parks** demand careful planning, a 4WD and extra supplies, as they are notorious places to get stuck for a week or two after rain. Don't go without first contacting the NPWS at Emerald or PO Box 157, Springsure, QLD 4722 (☎07/4984 1716). Access is from the towns of Springsure (p.490) or Tambo, which are the last places you can get fuel. The parks are bisected by a series of north–south plateaus; east lies Ka Ka Mundi, west is Salvator Rosa. Spring water (don't rely on it) should be boiled and basic maps can be collected when you buy your camping permit from the nearest NPWS.

Ka Ka Mundi National Park is undeveloped and tent sites must be cleared by hand. The access road follows **Jacksons Creek** across brigalow scrub plains ringed by high sandstone escarpments to a campsite at **Bunbuncundoo Springs**, home to a dingo spirit in Aboriginal lore. The presence of ferns suggests that rainforest once covered the area, which now attracts birds and wallabies. The most interesting walking country lies west towards **Cave Hill** and the monolith of **Mount Mooloolong**, dreaded by Aborigines as the home of evil spirits. You'll need a compass and topographic maps to avoid getting lost – and thick clothing to guard against getting spiked on undergrowth.

Salvator Rosa National Park's two tent sites are near the banks of the **Nogoa River** and at **Belinda Springs**, an upwelling into a bed of ferns and reeds. The track ends at **Major Mitchell Springs**, overlooked by **Pyramids** and **Wubin Hill**, both recommended for walks. Wubin is riddled with tunnels, while the open woodland around the Pyramids reminded the explorer Mitchell of canvases by the Italian painter Salvator Rosa – hence the park's name. The best **walking** is along the sandy bed of the Nogoa River, pocked with waterholes and with plenty of birdlife along the banks.

West to Cooper Creek and Birdsville

The last place of any size on the journey west from Roma is **CHARLEVILLE**, terminus for the **train** and a compact, busy town with broad streets, shaded pavements and some solid buildings constructed when the town was a droving centre and staging post for Cobb & Co. It's well known as a victim of contradictory weather – in November 1947 a typical hot summer afternoon was interrupted for twenty minutes as the temperature plummeted and a blast of massive hailstones stripped trees, smashed windows and roofs and killed pets and poultry. In 1990 the town centre was inundated by five-metre-deep floodwaters from the **Warrego River** – a dramatic end to years of drought. At the turn of the century, attempts were made to end another dry spell with **Stiger Vortex Guns**, giant conical contraptions supposed to seed rainclouds. During trials, two of the six guns exploded and the meteorologist who recommended them was run out of town. Only two have survived: one is in the Queensland Museum in Brisbane and the other is outside the Scout Hut on Sturt Street, heading south towards Cunnamulla.

Rooms can be found at the *Charleville Motel* on King Street (☎07/4654 1566; ④–⑤), or head for *Cobb & Co. Caravan Park* off Alfred Street (☎07/4654 1053), a pleasant spot, with hot water, barbecues and a small shop (6am–8pm). All services are clustered around the Wills/Galatea junction on the Quilpie side of town; you can draw **cash** on bank cards at the BP service station opposite the post office. There are the usual coffee shops, and counter **meals** at the *Corones Hotel*, also across from the post office.

Around town, the NPWS complex and **fauna park**, at Park Street on the Roma road (daily 9am–4.30pm; free), is dedicated to studying and preserving local wildlife and features some graceful, yellow-footed rock wallabies; you'll have to head up towards Blackall in a 4WD to see them in the wild. The **Historic House** on Galatea Street, originally a bank, is now a museum with some rooms decorated in period style and showing some elegant architectural touches. **Anglers** can try their luck along the river where the prize catch is large Murray cod, though perch and freshwater catfish are more likely. Get directions to prime fishing spots from the **tourist information centre** (☎07/4654 3057), just south of town on the Cunnamulla Road, who also organize stargazing sessions at the Skywatch Observatory – there are two powerful telescopes and an astronomy chart to guide you. **Bus and train** bookings can be made with

---

BOOMERANGS

Curved **throwing sticks** were once found throughout the world. Several were discovered in Tutankhamen's tomb, Hopi Indians once used them and a 23,000-year-old example made from mammoth ivory was recently found in Poland. Since that time the invention of the bow and arrow superseded what Aborigines call a **boomerang** or *karli*, although they seem to be the only people to have invented returning boomerangs; they were originally used as children's toys but were then modified into decoys for hunting wildfowl. The non-returning types depicted in Carnarvon Gorge show how sophisticated they became as hunting weapons. Usually made from tough acacia wood, some are hooked like a pick, while others are designed to cartwheel along the ground to break the legs of game. Thus immobilized, one animal would be killed while another could be easily tracked to meet the same fate. Besides hunting, the boomerang was also used for digging, levering or cutting, as well as for **musical** or **ceremonial instruments**. At Carnarvon Gorge the long, gently curved boomerangs stencilled on the walls in pairs are not repetitions but portraits of two weapons with identical flight paths; if the first missed, the user could immediately throw the second, knowing how it would move through the air. For the definitive book on the subject, check out Philip Jones's nicely illustrated *Boomerang: Behind an Australian Icon* (Wakefield Press).

Western Travel Service, 37 Wills St (☎07/4654 1260). Charleville lies on the Brisbane–Mount Isa bus route, with at least two services daily in each direction (but no Greyhound service), and also on the Quilpie–Brisbane train line, with two trains a week. **Flights** to Brisbane leave from the tiny strip outside town.

Around Cunnamulla and Quilpie

From Charleville, you can either continue west to Quilpie and the routes to Birdsville or the Dig Tree (see below), or detour south to **CUNNAMULLA,** a nondescript handful of service stations and motels 200km south of Charleville on the Mitchell Highway. There is a helpful **information centre** (☎07/4655 2121) in the old schoolhouse at the end of Jane Street. West towards Thargomindah, 160km from Cunnamulla, are the **Yowah Opal Fields** where shallow deposits yield much-sought-after Yowah Nuts – opalized ironstone nodules. You'll need a Miner's Right ($14.50 from the Mining Office at Cunnamulla's council offices) to start your own diggings. Beware of unfenced vertical shafts, which are practically invisible until you're on your way down: always look where you're going and never step backwards. Yowah has bore water, fuel and a **caravan park** (☎07/4655 4953; cabins ②). Two hundred kilometres southwest of Cunnamulla, on the border with New South Wales, **Currawinya National Park** features lakes, wetlands and associated wildlife in contrast to the semi-arid land more typical of the region. Check on road conditions and camping possibilities with the NPWS ranger (☎07/4655 4001).

QUILPIE is a dusty rail and farming community 200km west of Charleville. Amenities include a baker, butcher, fuel depot, caravan park and the *Imperial Hotel* (☎07/4656 1300; ②–⑤), which can supply basic beds above the bar or quieter units in the back. The hotel serves evening meals between 6 and 7.30pm, and there are a couple of cafés in town which close at about 5.30pm.

Quilpie to the Dig Tree

As there are few signposts, a **map** is essential if you plan to drive from Quilpie to the Dig Tree at Nappa Merrie, 50km from Innamincka in South Australia. Last place to get **fuel** on the 490-kilometre, largely unsealed route lies an hour west of Quilpie at **EROMANGA**. From here you're heading across the stony plains above the huge gas and oil reserves of the Cooper Basin, past the cattle stations of Durham Downs and Karmona, lonely "nodding donkeys" and unaccountably healthy-looking droughtmaster cattle, to the Dig Tree on **Cooper Creek**.

The site of Burke and Wills' stockade (see box overleaf), **Depot Camp 65** is a beautiful shaded river bank alive with pelicans and parrots – it's hard to believe that anyone could have starved to death nearby. **The Dig Tree** is still standing and protected by a walkway, but the three original blaze marks reading "BLXV, DIG 3FT NW, DEC 6 60-APR 21 61" have been cemented over to keep the tree alive. Burke's face was carved into the tree on the right by John Dickins in 1898, and is still clearly visible.

Pressing on, you'll be relieved to know that Innamincka's pub is only 50km away at the top of the **Strzelecki Track** in South Australia (see p.758). If you've made it this far you shouldn't have much trouble with the road.

Quilpie to Birdsville

The long road from Quilpie to Birdsville is a relatively easy journey, manageable in good conditions without a 4WD, though depth markers along the road give an idea of how saturated this **Channel Country** becomes after rain. First stop is **WINDORAH**, a limp settlement of a dozen buildings offering fuel, a post office and an amazingly well-provisioned store. The town last made the news when an errant crocodile was dragged out of the creek and there was talk of having it mounted above the hotel bar. Even without the croc, the *Western Star* **hotel** (☎07/4656 3166; ⑤) is hard to pass by for a cold drink and a look at its collection of old photos; they also might let you **camp** here.

Ruins of the **John Costello hotel** lie 80km further on towards Betoota, opposite a windmill. Tired of riding 30km every morning to round up his stockmen from the bar, the manager of a nearby station had the local liquor licence transferred from the *JC* to his homestead in the 1950s. He pulled the roof off the hotel for good measure, and there's now little left beyond the foundations and some posts.

BETOOTA, 220km from Windorah, is on the verge of crumbling back into the dust, its tiny, century-old adobe hotel opening only once a year for the races and gymkhana. Even then they don't provide beds but there's plenty of room to pitch a tent along the river banks behind. Beyond Betoota the country turns into a rocky, silent plain, with circling crows and wedge-tailed eagles the only signs of life, and it's hard to see what the occasional fence-line or grid is keeping apart. Look for **red sand dunes**, distant outposts of the Simpson Desert. Driving can be hazardous here – you'll pass plenty of wrecks and shredded tyres – but with care (and luck), the Diamantina River and Birdsville are just three hours away.

Birdsville and beyond

Famous for the **horse races** on the first weekend in September, when thousands of beer-swilling spectators pack out the dusty little settlement, at other times

THE BURKE AND WILLS SAGA

In 1860, the government of Victoria, then Australia's richest state, decided to sponsor a lavish expedition to make the first south–north crossing of the continent to the Gulf of Carpentaria. Eighteen men, twenty camels (shipped, along with their handlers, from Asia) and over twenty tons of provisions started out from Melbourne in August, led by **Robert O'Hara Burke** and **William John Wills**. Problems had already begun by the time the party reached Cooper Creek in December. Burke had impatiently left the bulk of the expedition and supplies lagging behind and raced ahead with a handful of men to establish a base camp on Cooper Creek. Having built a stockade, Burke and Wills started north, along with two other members of their team (Gray and King), six camels, a couple of horses and food for three months. Four men remained at camp, led by William Brahe, waiting for the rest of the expedition to catch up. In fact, most of the supplies and camels were dithering halfway between Cooper Creek and Melbourne, unsure of what to do next.

As Burke and Wills failed to keep a regular diary, few details of the "rush to the Gulf" are known. They were seen by Kalkadoon Aborigines following the Corella River into the Gulf, where they found that vast salt marshes lay between them and the sea. Disappointed, they left the banks of the Bynoe (near present-day Normanton) on February 11, 1861, and headed back south. Their progress slowed by the wet season, they killed and ate the pack animals as their food ran out. Gray died after being beaten by Burke for stealing flour; remorse was heightened when they staggered into the Cooper Creek stockade on April 21 to find that, having already waited an extra month for them to return, Brahe had decamped that morning. Too weak to follow him, they found supplies buried under a tree marked "Dig", but failed to change the sign when they moved on, which meant that when the first rescue teams arrived on the scene, they assumed the explorers had never returned from the Gulf. Trying to walk south, the three reached the Innamincka area, where Aborigines fed them fish and nardoo (water fern) seeds, but by the time a rescue party tracked them down in September only King was still alive. The full, sad tale of their trek is expertly told by Alan Moorehead in his classic work *Cooper Creek*, a book well worth tracking down in your library.

BIRDSVILLE promises to be something of an anticlimax, a handful of buildings and ruins where only the hotel and roadhouses seem to be doing business. But unless you've flown in, you'll probably be very glad simply to have arrived intact. The **caravan park** (☎07/4656 3214) comprises a large patch of scrub by the billabong with an amenities block. But if you can live without facilities, camp along the creek or artesian overflow where huge flocks of raucous corellas seem to justify the township's name, although it's more likely a corruption of "Burt's Ville" after the first storekeeper. Given the lack of alternatives, don't be surprised to find the hotel **accommodation** at the *Birdsville Hotel* full (☎07/4656 3244, fax 4656 3262; ⑤); during race weekend, all beds are reserved for the bar staff anyway, so you have to camp. **Provisions** and snacks can be bought from the general store. If you're organizing your own food, prepare the next day's meals after dark when the flies have settled down. You owe yourself at least one drink in the pub; order by 5.30pm if you want a full **evening meal** – the "$15, seven-course takeaway" is a pie and a six-pack.

The **Wirrarrie Information Centre** on Billabong Boulevard (☎07/4656 3300 Mon–Fri 9am–4pm) will give you the lowdown on the state of the various Outback tracks if you're planning to use them, or ask at the pale blue **police station** (☎07/4656 3220) on the other side of the **airstrip** (conveniently laid out next to the hotel). **Monuments** at the airstrip name the various expeditions that have passed through the area, including the Simpson Desert traverse by Ted Coulson and an Aborigine named Peter in 1936. The Information Centre can direct you to another tree blazed by Burke and Wills across the Diamantina, otherwise hard to locate among the scrub, or to attractions in town such as the **old hospital**; originally built as a hotel and now just a stone shell, it operated as the original Australian Inland Mission between 1923 and 1927. The **Birdsville Working Museum**, as its name suggests, is more than just a collection of old stuff; all the exhibits, from petrol pumps and farm machinery to a complete blacksmith's shop are fully restored and regularly operated.

Outside Birdsville there's a stand of slow-growing, old and very rare **Waddi trees**, 14km north on the Bedourie road. They're about 5m tall and resemble sparse conifers wrapped in prickly feather boas with warped, circular seed pods; the wind blowing through the needles makes an eerie noise like the roar of a distant fire. For something more dramatic, head out 33km to **Big Red** at the start of the Simpson Desert crossing. Simpson's largest dune may seem unimpressive from below, but your opinion will change radically if you walk up or try to plant a 4WD on the top. If you're having a hard time getting up the long western face, there is a less steep track immediately on the right, which has a couple of quick turns near the summit. Two-wheel-drive vehicles can often reach the base (check with the police before setting off) and it's worth it to see the dunes, flood plains and stony gibber country on the way.

North of Birdsville, the next substantial settlement, Mount Isa (see p.503), is a lonely 700km further on, with fuel available about every 200km. Those heading west across the Simpson Desert to Dalhousie Springs need a **Desert Parks Pass** ($50) from the Birdsville store; the NPWS office on Graham Street (☎07/4656 3249) provides general information only. Feasible in any vehicle during a dry winter, the 520-kilometre **Birdsville Track** heads from the racecourse down to Marree in South Australia – see pp.759-763 for details of this and the Simpson Desert crossing.

ROCKHAMPTON TO WINTON

Heading west from Rockhampton, the **Capricorn Highway** provides an alternative route to Mount Isa, or simply a break from the trip along the coast. The main attractions in this central section of inland Queensland are the sandstone and forest scenery of the **Blackdown Tablelands**, hunting **sapphires** on the Gemfields, and the

Stockman's Hall of Fame at Longreach – none requiring more than a couple of days' detour from Rockhampton. There's also access from Emerald to Carnarvon Gorge and the Central Highlands. **Historically**, the area is rich: Qantas, the Labor Party and "Waltzing Matilda" originated here, and the district's fossil record includes dramatic dinosaur footprints at **Lark Quarry**. **Buses** connect Rockhampton with Winton, and the **train** travels as far as Longreach.

Into the Northern Highlands

As you move inland the coastal humidity is left behind and the gently undulating landscape becomes baked instead of steamed. Passing the white rubble moonscape atop **Mount Hay**, where you can stay at the van park and fossick for agates, the road loops over low hills before adopting a pattern that becomes ever more familiar: straight for miles and then an unexpected bend. Bottle trees, with their bulbous, thick grey trunks and spindly, thinly leaved branches, herald the drier climate. Gradually, the deep blue platform of the **Blackdown Tablelands** emerges from the horizon, and, by the time you reach **DINGO**, dominates the landscape. Dingo is somewhere to stock up: there's a hotel, van park and a bronze monument to the town's namesake. Heading north towards Mackay, the Dingo–Mount Flora road is direct but uninteresting, skirting the eastern edge of the Bowen Basin's coal mines through fields of sunflowers and corn.

The Blackdown Tablelands

Floating 600m above the heat haze, the **Blackdown Tablelands'** gum forests, waterfalls and escarpments are a delight, a scenic refuge from the dry, flat lands below. A corrugated, unsealed twenty-kilometre **access road** is signposted on the highway 11km from Dingo. National Park campsite bookings can be made through the NPWS in Rockhampton or Emerald, or with the local **ranger** (via Dingo, QLD 4702; ☎07/4986 1964). Outside school holidays you could well have the place to yourself. There's no public transport into the park, but call in advance and catch the McCafferty's bus from Dingo, and **Naomi Hills Cattle Station** (☎07/4935 9121, fax 4935 9239; ①), set at the base of the tablelands, will pick you up at the drop-off point on the highway. They offer accommodation-and-meal packages, run tours round the station and onto the tablelands and regularly cater to the tour-bus crowd – call ahead and check which days are booked if you want peace and quiet.

The track runs flat through open scrub to the base of the range; the climb is steep, twisting and slippery, as "pea gravel" puts in an appearance. Views over a haze of eucalypt woodland are generally blocked by the thicker forest at the top of the plateau, but at **Horseshoe Lookout** there's a fabulous view north and, after rain, **Two Mile Falls** rockets over the edge of the cliffs. From here the road widens and runs past Mimosa Creek, dead-ending at the **Rainbow Falls** car park.

The **Mimosa Creek campground** is excellent, shaded by massive stringybark trees with tank water, tables, toilets, fire pits and a creek to bathe in. At night the air fills with the sharp scent of woodsmoke, and the occasional dingo howls in the distance; with a torch, you might see **greater gliders** or the more active brushtail possum. Watch out for crows that raid unattended tables, tents and cars for anything, edible or not. Temperatures can reach 40°C on summer days, and drop below zero on winter nights.

Walks in the park include the short trip to **Officers Pocket**, a moist amphitheatre of ferns and palms with the facing cliffs picked out yellow and white in the late afternoon; a **circuit track** along Mimosa Creek, past remains of cattle pens and stock huts, to some beautifully clear **ochre stencils** made by Gungaloo Aborigines a century ago; and the park's finest scenery at **Rainbow Falls**, 6km past the campsite. At its glorious best around dawn, this track leads from the car park through an eerie gum forest to the top of the gorge, then follows around to where the creek seeps down steps into the greenery. From the edge you can spy on birds in the rainforest beneath; explosive thumps from below signal rock wallabies tearing across ledges hardly big enough for a mouse. A long staircase descends into a cool world of spring-fed gardens, ending on a large shelf about halfway into the gorge where Rainbow Falls sprays from above into a wide, clear pool. It may be pretty, but the water's paralyzingly cold; for a warmer dip, climb back up the stairs and follow the path to the top of the falls, where the creek runs in full sun and the bed has handy, bath-sized holes to sit in.

Bushwalkers might also head to **Stoney Creek Falls**, although the ten-kilometre round trip off a track between Mimosa Creek and Rainbow Falls, through tinder-dry woodland to magnificent views from the top of the falls, follows a frequently vague path; you'll need directions from the ranger (☎07/4986 1964).

Emerald and around

The road west of Dingo crosses the lower reaches of the **Bowen Basin coalfields** at **Blackwater**, then moves into **cotton country**, signalled by fluffy white tailings along the roadside around **YAMALA**, where there's a **cotton gin** to tour (by appointment ☎07/4982 3888).

EMERALD is a misleadingly named place. This close to the Gemfield towns of Sapphire and Rubyvale, you'd think its origins could be traced to precious stones, but in fact the area was named Emerald Downs by a surveyor who saw its rich green after heavy rains. Ironically, as you'll realize after stopping for a drink every ten minutes, a drier, hotter town would be hard to imagine. Still, as a junction for the mid-west's produce, with roads north to Mackay and south to the Central Highlands, Emerald is a busy place at the heart of a surprisingly productive district: the rich soil supports citrus trees, which attract hundreds of fruit-pickers each season. Despite being around a hundred years old, the town appears quite modern due to rebuilding after a series of disastrous fires in the middle of this century.

Most essential services are on the Capricorn Highway, here called **Clermont Street**, where the main feature is the pristine **station**, built in 1901 and restored in 1986. One road back from this is Egerton Street, where there are **fossil tree trunks** on the lawn outside the town hall; thought to be 250 million years old, they're preserved in great detail, right down to the texture of the bark. The **tourist information** booth at the west end of Clermont Street (Mon–Sat 9am–5pm, Sun 10am–2pm; ☎07/4982 4142) has leaflets on local attractions; at the other end is McCafferty's **bus station** (☎07/4982 2755). **Accommodation** is in the hotels or van parks on Opal Street, although during the April harvest there may be very little room available. Try *Motel 707*, 17 Ruby St (☎07/4982 1707; ④), which has air-conditioned units, a bar in reception and room meals available; the *Meteor Motel*, corner of Opal and Egerton streets (☎07/4982 1166; ④), which has a pool and a good steak restaurant; or the *Explorers Inn Motel* (☎07/4982 2268; ④–⑤), in a quiet spot at the edge of town – it's newer than the rest with comfortable, well-appointed rooms and a salt-water pool.

South to Springsure

Ten kilometres south of Emerald, **Lake Maraboon** has been created by the **Fairburn Dam** as the region's main water supply. Drought conditions over much of the last decade meant water levels dropped, along with the popularity of water sports, but there is still good fishing and bird-watching, and 1998's summer rainfall may mark the start of an encouraging change. All modern amenities and accommodation are provided by the *Sunrover Resort* (☎07/4982 3677, fax 4982 1932; ④), including fuel, a restaurant and a grassed camping area, which is pleasantly situated among trees by the lake.

From Emerald you can reach **Carnarvon Gorge** (see p.481), 200km or so south through the town of **SPRINGSURE**, which is set below the dramatic orange cliffs of **Mount Zamia**, an outcrop of which is called Virgin Rock though weathering since it was named means you can barely see a likeness of the Madonna and Child. From the moment this district was settled, Aborigines put up a strong resistance. At **Rainworth Fort** (9am–5pm; closed Thurs; $3) settlers built a squat stockade of basalt blocks and corrugated iron for protection after "**the Wills Massacre**" when, on October 17, 1861, Aboriginal forces stormed Cullin-la-ringo station and killed nineteen people in apparent retaliation for the slaughter of a dozen Aborigines by a local squatter. White response was savage, spurred on by vigilantes and a contingent of Native Troopers; newspapers reported that "a great massacre has been made among the blacks of the Nogoa". The fort and later structures of **Cairdbeign School and Homestead** are 10km southwest of Springsure and house a few relics of the period.

Springsure and Rolleston (the last stop before Carnarvon Gorge) both have a choice of hotel, motel or caravan park, plus fuel.

The Bowen Basin
North of Emerald, the **Bowen Basin** is largely flat, rough country patterned by acres of giant sunflowers against a horizon of low hills. **Coal-mining** is the mainstay, contributing coal trains and tailing mounds to the scenery. Well-equipped settlements provide shops and housing for miners, but lack character; many residents spend their spare time in Mackay or Rockhampton.

The road through the basin to Mackay (covered by a daily **bus**) runs first to **CLERMONT**, originally a gold-mining town now given over to pastoral pursuits and coal industries. There's a free **mine tour** every Tuesday at 9am (for details call ☎07/4983 1866). After Clermont, the highway passes **Wolf Fang Peak** – famous for its spiders and wallabies, and its fine views – on the way to **MORANBAH**, a confusing system of one-way streets lined with trees and a not-so-obvious town centre, which also acts as a base for weekly tours to local mines; for details call ☎07/4941 7254.

The Gemfields

The country an hour west of Emerald is sparse and always hot, the scrub interrupted only by ugly cleared patches covered in rubble from mining operations. This wasteland masks one of the richest **sapphire fields** in the world and, with hard work, the chances of finding some are good – though you're unlikely to get rich.

The easiest fields to reach are the **Anakie Fields**, with facilities at Anakie, Sapphire and Rubyvale. Anakie township is off the highway about 45km from Emerald; Sapphire is 9km north of Anakie, and Rubyvale a further 8km. Though well worked, the Anakie Fields are the best place for the newcomer to pick up tips; old hands proceed directly to **the Willows**, 27km west of Anakie.

ANAKIE ("permanent water") has no gemfields itself, but gave its name to those at Sapphire and Rubyvale. Unusually pretty, it comprises a van park (☎ & fax 07/4985 4142; ②) with hot showers by the waterhole and a small shop open every day, backing onto a pub, post office and store. The **information centre** near the highway has fuel, licences, rough maps and advice.

In contrast, the country around **SAPPHIRE** looks like a war zone. You'll find a post office-cum-store and houses scattered along the road and an elbow of Retreat Creek, where the first gems were found. *Sunrise Cabins* (☎07/4985 4281; ②–③) are across the road from the medical centre, in sight of the creek. Towards Rubyvale is

Pat's Gem Park with a café, jewellery and craft displays and fossicking lessons for beginners. Down a track opposite the Big Spanner is *Gemini Van Park* (☎07/4985 4280) – a kilometre out from the rest of town, sharing the ramshackle appearance but with a private and better-quality water bore, cold pool, clean shower block and barbecue area which all count for a lot out here. Each evening the owner feeds about fifty rainbow lorikeets, and in the mornings you may find brolgas turning up for breakfast and photo opportunities.

RUBYVALE has several shops, service stations and a few mines to look around: tour groups tend to visit Miner's Heritage (open daily; $5 per person), but cheaper and equally interesting is Bobby Dazzler on the hill as you approach town. The ground beneath each new development here has to be mined first; outdoor tennis courts and the surfaced road were built only after years of wrangling over whether the ground had given up all its treasures. Rubyvale also seems to be the place to pick up on apocryphal stories, such as the one about the largest star sapphire ever found being used as a

GEM MINING

Gems were first discovered in 1870 near **Anakie** but until Thai buyers came onto the scene a century later operations were low-key, and even today there are still solo fossickers making a living from their claims. The most common gems are **zircons, sapphires** and **rubies**. Formed by prehistoric volcanic actions and later dispersed along waterways and covered by sediment, the gems lie in ancient riverbeds and can be identified by a layer of gem-bearing gravel above a clay base. This layer can be up to 15m down, so gullies and dry rivers, where nature has already done some of the excavation for you, are good places to start.

Looking for surface gems, or **specking**, is best after rain, when a trained eye can see the stones sparkle in the mud. It's erratic but certainly easier than the alternative – **fossicking** – which requires a pick, shovel, sieve, washtub full of water and a canvas sack before even starting (this gear can be rented at all the fields). Cut and polished, zircons are pale yellow, sapphires pale green to deep blue, and rubies are of a light pink hue here, but when they're covered in mud it's hard to tell them from gravel, which is where the washing comes in: wet gems glitter like fragments of coloured glass.

You have to be extremely enthusiastic to spend a summer on the fields; the mercury climbs steadily to 42°C, topsoil erodes and everything becomes filmed in dust. The first rains bring floods as the sunbaked ground sheds water, and if you're here then you'll be treated to the sight of locals specking in the rain, dressed in Akubras and Drizabones and shuffling around like mobile mushrooms. Conditions are best as soon after the wet season as possible (around May), when the ground is soft and fresh pickings have been uncovered – not surprisingly, this is also the busiest period.

If this all seems like too much hard work, try a **Gem Park** such as Pat's (see above), where they've done all the digging for you and supply all the necessary gear for about $5. All you have to do is sieve the wash, flip it onto the canvas and check it for stones. There's an art to sieving and flipping, but you're pretty sure to find something, since park owners lace the wash with rejects. Gem parks will also value and cut stones for you. Another break from the business end of a pick is to pay $5, take a **mine tour** and see if the professionals fare any better. In some ways they do – the chilled air 5m down is wonderful – but the main difference is one of scale rather than method or intent.

You need a **fossicker's licence**, available from shops and gem parks, which allows digging in areas set aside for the purpose or on no man's land. The $7.25 licence is valid for two months and gives you no rights at all other than to keep what you find and to camp at fossick grounds. To stake a claim and keep others away you need a **Miner's Right** from the field officer in Emerald (Department of Minerals and Energy, Clerana Centre, Clermont St; ☎07/4982 4011); this also carries obligations to restore the land to its original state and maintain it for two years after quitting the site.

doorstop. You'll also hear plenty more during the annual **August Gemfest** which includes, in odd-numbered years, a **Wheelbarrow Race** when, in imitation of the first pioneering miners, all comers push their one-wheeled transport laden with pick and shovel up the eighteen-kilometre track from Anakie to Rubyvale, pausing only at Sapphire to take on board a bucket of dirt.

The **Willows Gemfield** is still in the making, part mining camp, part township. The immaculate *Willows Caravan Park* (☎ & fax 07/4985 5128; ②) is well shaded, has wangled a liquor licence and acts as a bank agent as well as supplying fuel and digging equipment. The gemfields are just down the track from the park.

The small towns of **Alpha** and **Jericho** are somewhere to freshen up on the journey west along the Capricorn Highway. If you're passing through Jericho on a Saturday night, don't miss the novelty of a **drive-in movie**, with a capacity for thirty-four cars but seating for a further thirty at the back.

Beyond the Range to Winton

Vistas from the rounded sandstone boulders at the top of the Great Dividing Range west of Jericho reveal terrain flat enough to test a spirit level's accuracy. Below, rivers flow to the Gulf of Carpentaria or towards the great dry lakes of South Australia, while unsealed roads run north to Clermont and south to Tambo and Charleville. You'll notice an increase in temperature; flies appear from nowhere, tumbleweeds pile up on fences and trees never seem closer than the horizon. In terms of numbers, sheep are the dominant mammal in these parts, though there are some cattle and even a few people out here.

Barcaldine and Blackall

The only place of any size on the way to Longreach is **BARCALDINE**, 300km from Emerald, an unassuming grid of quiet streets belying an important niche in Australian history. It was near here during the 1885 drought that geologists first tapped Queensland's artesian water, revolutionizing Outback development. The town further secured its place in history during the 1891 **shearing strike** which, though a failure itself, ultimately led to the **formation of the Labor Party**. On the highway, outside the station which became the focus of the dispute, is a granite monument – sculpted to resemble the tips of a pair of shears – to shearers arrested during the strike. Right next to it, the sagging silver trunk of the **Tree of Knowledge** struggles gamely to improve on its 160 years. Sadly, this ghost gum, where shearers rallied a century ago, looks to be on the way out. The **Australian Workers' Heritage Museum** (Mon–Sat 9am–5pm, Sun 10am–5pm; $7) is unmissable underneath a yellow and blue marquee on Ash Street. It has an expanding collection of displays concentrating on the history of the workers' movement after the shearers' strike, as well as videos, artefacts and plenty of sepia-tinted photos covering themes including Outback women and Aboriginal stockmen; the museum rounds out the exhibits at Longreach's Stockman's Hall of Fame (see p.493). Next door to the station, the **information centre** (daily 9am–5pm; ☎07/4651 1724) will direct you to other attractions such as the **Wondae Deer Farm & Wildlife Park**, soon to see the arrival of retired circus lions, tigers and baboons, or the self-styled **Mad Mick's Funny Farm**, which has been restored to its turn-of-the-century condition and is inhabited by friendly, hand-reared animals. The latter is open most mornings from April to September or by arrangement (☎07/4651 1172; adults $7, children $4) and admission includes a ride in a Ford Model-T and tea and damper.

Across the road from the Tree of Knowledge, the shaded verandahs of the *Artesian Hotel* provide a reminder of the value of a reliable watering hole. You can also get a drink and a meal at the *Commercial* and *Union* hotels. **Accommodation** options include the *Ironbark Inn* (☎07/4651 2311; ⑤), *Barcaldine Motel* (☎07/4651 1244; ④) and *Homestead Van Park* (☎07/4651 1308), all on Box Street off the highway on the Longreach side. **Banks** and other services are also on Box Street.

One hour south of Barcaldine on the Landsborough Highway, a sign at **BLACKALL** welcomes you to Merino Country. It was near here in 1892 that Jackie Howe fleeced 321 sheep in under eight hours using hand shears, a still-unbroken record. If you want to visit a **sheep station** to see modern shearers in action, it can be arranged by the **tourist office** just off Shamrock Street on Short Street (Mon–Fri 9am–5pm, Sat–Sun 9am–3pm; ☎07/4657 4637). The town sits on the banks of the usually feeble and often dry (but occasionally five-metre-deep) Barcoo River; an eight-hundred-metre-deep artesian bore provides a more reliable water source. While here, you could visit the steam-driven **woolscour**, built in 1908 and in operation for seventy years; it has been restored recently and is ready to run again as soon as funds are raised (daily: April–Nov 8am–4pm, or check with the tourist office; $5). You could also track down the famous **black stump**, a surveying point used in pinpointing Queensland's borders in the last century and now the butt of many jokes; the original stump has been replaced by a more interesting fossilized one. Near Blackall, **Idalia National Park** preserves Queensland's last population of yellow-footed rock wallabies in the wild. Access details, and long-distance **bus** tickets, are available from Blackall Travel (☎07/4657 4422).

Shamrock Street, shaded by palms and bottle trees (not only bottle-shaped but also full of sugary water for emergency stock-watering), is the main road on which you'll find banks, supplies and a few places to **eat**; if your dress is reasonably smart you can savour good food at the *Blackall Club* (☎07/4657 4711). **Entertainment** is provided by the hotels, such as the *Barcoo*, which has had a recent face-lift. At *Blackall Caravan Park* on Hart Lane you can yarn with other travellers around a huge campfire and be fed pot roasts, billy tea and damper for an extra fee. **Motel** accommodation is available at the brand-new *Acacia Motor Inn* (☎07/4657 6022; ⑤), or the *Blackall Motel* (☎07/4657 4611; ④) at the Barcaldine end of Shamrock Street.

Longreach and the Stockman's Hall of Fame

LONGREACH, 110km west of Barcaldine, is different from other western towns: it's doing more than surviving. This is mainly due to the Stockman's Hall of Fame, an ambitious museum which pulls in busloads of tourists. Yet even before the museum, Longreach was an enterprising settlement with a firm place in history. Ever since the discovery of artesian water it has been a stronghold of cattle- and sheep-farming, but it really took off as the original headquarters of Qantas – their first hangar still stands at the airport.

The Stockman's Hall of Fame (daily 9am–5pm; $15) is a masterpiece, not just in architectural design – a blend of aircraft hangar and cathedral – but in being an encyclopedia of

QANTAS

There's always been contention between Longreach and Winton as to which was the birthplace of **Qantas** – the Queensland and Northern Territories Aerial Service – but the first joy-flights and taxi service flew from Longreach in 1921, pioneered by Hudson Fysh and Paul McGuiness. Their idea – that an airline could play an important role by carrying mail and passengers, dropping supplies to remote districts and providing an emergency link into the Outback – inspired other projects such as the Flying Doctor Service. Qantas stayed at Longreach until 1945, by which time both the company and its planes had outgrown the town.

the Outback right in its heart. Since opening in 1988 its success has silenced critics who underestimated the Outback's widespread appeal. A minor complaint might be that the displays themselves are fairly ordinary, but once you're here the Hall of Fame has achieved its dual aim of bringing people out west and providing background to the development of a vast portion of Australia. Greyhound Pioneer covers the couple of kilometres to the Hall of Fame from Eagle Street; A1 Taxis (free call ☎1800/656 878) and Brooksie's Cabs (free call ☎1800/242 511) can also take you there, or you can walk.

Inside the museum, the Outback is romanticized through videos, slide shows, photographs and exhibits – but this is not just another local museum where anything more than five years old is shown for its own sake. History starts in the Dreamtime and moves on, via a directory of those on the First Fleet, to early explorers and pioneers (including a large section on women in the Outback), ending with personal accounts of life in the bush. Among more day-to-day features are some offbeat selections; if you thought barbed wire was just something to get stuck on, then check out the collection here, with over a hundred types – from the old hook design to modern razor wire. You'd be hard pushed not to find something of interest, be it boxing kangaroos, rodeos, bark huts or tall stories. The library and exhibitions by Outback artists (displayed in the art gallery) are also worth a browse.

Other local activities include **cruises** round waterways and visits to the **Longreach School of Distance Education** (tours at 9am & 10am on school days), out along the highway just past the entrance to the Hall of Fame, where you get a chance to see how three hundred pupils in this remote area are taught via radio. **Tours** of nearby sheep stations offer an insight into Outback life, but the cost can be outrageous in relation to the time spent on the station – check how long is spent in transit. Better value are homestead stays, where you can participate in farm life or simply laze around. Local travel agents or the tourist office can arrange all these.

Practicalities

Longreach is a more active version of Barcaldine, with plenty of spruce old buildings. Eagle Street, where **buses** set down, is the main drag and here you'll find hotels, cafés, **banks**, a cinema and the first well-stocked **supermarket** in a long while. Longreach's **tourist office** (open according to demand; ☎07/4658 3555) is in the replica Qantas office on the corner of Duck Street, opposite the **post office**. Of the half-dozen **hotels**, try the *Lyceum* for counter food, or *Starlight's* for nightlife. The *Longreach RSL Club* also welcomes visitors; you can dine in their inexpensive restaurant, or just settle into a chair in the lounge-bar. There are two **campsites**: *Gunnadoo Van Park* (☎07/4658 1781), on Thrush Road looking across to the Hall of Fame, and *Longreach Caravan Park* (☎07/4658 1770) on Ibis Street. *Hallview Lodge*, 81 Wompoo St (☎07/4658 3777; ③–④), is a friendly **B&B**; or you can indulge in **motel** comforts at either the *Longreach Motel*, 127 Eagle St (☎07/4658 1996, fax 4658 3035; ⑤), or *Longreach Motor Inn* (☎07/4658 2322; ⑥), on Galah Street.

Winton and beyond

Scenery doesn't come blander than on the Longreach–Winton stretch: your only worry as a driver is to keep your foot down and stay awake as the car cruises the empty Mitchell Plains. After 125km there's a turn-off to **Lorraine Station** (☎07/4657 1693; ②–④), a working sheep property open to guests from April to November. Get up before sunrise for an early-morning muster on horseback, or tour the station in a 4WD. Bird-watching, swimming and lounging at the bar are other possibilities.

WINTON is a real frontier town: dust devils blow tumbleweeds down the streets, and the main change over the last fifty years is that 4WDs have superseded the horse as a means of getting around. As an important transport junction and Queensland's largest cattle-trucking depot, Winton has a constant stream of road trains rumbling through it – and conversations overheard in hotels tend to revolve around problems of stock management. Winton has its share of history, too: Qantas held its first meeting here in 1920 and **Waltzing Matilda**, that evergreen ballad, premiered at the *North Gregory Hotel* (see box below). The surrounding countryside is an eerie world of windswept plains and eroded **jump-ups** – flat-topped hills layered in orange, grey and red dust – complete with **opal deposits** at Opalton and a stunning set of **dinosaur footprints** at Lark Quarry.

All **services** (bank, post office and service station with EFTPOS and cash-with-drawal facilities) are around Elderslie Street. If there's a film on, treat yourself to a session in the outdoor **cinema**, at the corner of Cobb Street; the café here stays open until after dark. Or next door, at The Gift and Gem Centre, watch opals being fashioned into jewellery. The best **accommodation** prospects are at the *Matilda Country Caravan Park*, 43 Chirnside St (☎07/4657 1607), or the nearby *Matilda Motel* (☎07/4657 1433; ④).

Further down Elderslie Street, opposite a tepid swimming pool and bronze statue of the jolly swagman, the **Waltzing Matilda Centre** (daily 8.30am–5.30pm; ☎07/4657 1466; $12.50) has some unusual items: a fine display of Aboriginal artefacts, featuring an entire tree with a boomerang half-carved out of its trunk, and an unbelievable bottle collection ranging from poisons to schnapps. The centre also doubles as an **information office** and sorts out **bus** tickets and **tours** to local sights – check with them about road conditions before visiting Opalton or Lark Quarry. For some really ludicrous fun, the **Australian Crayfish Derby**, part of the **Outback Festival** held in September in odd-numbered years, has to be worth a look; the owner of the winning crustacean nets $1500, and the "loser" gets to eat all the competitors. In April the **Waltzing Matilda Festival** involves a rodeo and arts events attracting bush poets to compete with "Banjo" Paterson.

Lark Quarry

It takes about two hours to drive the 120km south from Winton to **Lark Quarry**, dodging kamikaze kangaroos and patches of bulldust, and once you've arrived there's no doubt that this is the rough heart of the Outback. Nor is it surprising to find **dinosaur remains** here: the place looks prehistoric, swarming with flies and surrounded by hills where stunted trees and tufts of grass tussle with rocks for space. A

WALTZING MATILDA

In April 1995, Winton celebrated the centenary of the first public performance of "Banjo" Paterson's ballad **Waltzing Matilda** at the *North Gregory Hotel*, and stirred up a century of gossip and rumour. Legend has it that Christina MacPherson told Paterson the tale of a sheep-rustling swagman while he was staying with her family at nearby Dagwood Station. Christina wrote the music to the ballad, a collaboration which so incensed Paterson's fiancée, Sarah Riley, that she broke off their engagement. While a straightforward "translation" of the poem is easy enough – "Waltzing Matilda" was contemporary slang for tramping (carrying a bedroll or swag from place to place), "jumbuck" for a sheep, and "squatters" refers to landowners – there is some contention as to what the poem actually describes. The most obvious interpretation is of a poor tramp, hounded to death by the law, but first drafts of the poem suggest that Paterson – generally known as a romantic rather than social commentator – originally wrote the piece about the arrest of a union leader during the shearers' strike, and later toned it down. Either version would account for the popularity of the poem, which was once proposed as the national anthem. Australians readily identify with an underdog who dares to confront the system.

hundred million years ago this was a shrinking waterhole across which a carnivorous dinosaur chased a group of various turkey-sized herbivores through the mud to a rockface where it caught and killed one as the others fled back past it. Over three thousand **footprints** have been found recording these few seconds of action, excavated in the 1970s and now protected by an awning and walkway around them. Indentations left by small, amazingly sharp, three-clawed feet – some very light as the prey panicked and ran on tiptoe – stream in all directions, while those left by the larger predator go only one way. Paths lead around to other, buried tracks where the chase ended.

Opalton and Carisbrooke

The Opalton track (110km) from Winton follows the Jundah road for a short way before bearing left. Ten kilometres past Bladensburg Station turn-off is a track on the left to **Skull Waterhole**, named after the "dispersal" of the Goa Aborigines by the Native Mounted Police. Despite this sad history it's an interesting spot, as the water attracts kangaroos, budgerigars and ring-necked parrots, and there are also some **caves** to poke around in.

OPALTON is presently a multicultural area, with Yugoslav and Czech miners, as well as deserters from Coober Pedy in South Australia, reworking century-old diggings with Chinese and Korean finance. You need to be entirely self-sufficient here: the only modern feature is a telephone and there isn't any drinking water. During the summer there won't be any miners either – hotels in Winton are easily preferable to the 40°C-plus temperatures here. Fossicking zones have been established where you can pick over old tailings for scraps. There is a **camping and caravan area**, "washing water", and a small store that's open most days from 10am to 2pm.

If you don't have your own transport, it's worth seeing the area on a **day-tour** from Winton (by arrangement, minimum of four passengers; ☎07/4657 3984; $95) to **Carisbrooke Station,** where you can spend the night in renovated shearer's quarters (②). The trip includes visits to an opal mine and to caves covered in Aboriginal paintings – some abstract, others recognizable outlines of boomerangs and nulla-nullas (clubs).

Onwards

Heading **on from Winton**, the main route follows the **Landsborough Highway** to Cloncurry and Mount Isa (covered by bus) while the **Kennedy Developmental Road** runs west to Boulia. Towards Cloncurry, the **Combo Waterhole** near the low-slung *Blue Heeler Hotel* at Kynuna (165km) provided the inspiration for "Banjo" Paterson's classic poem "Waltzing Matilda" (see box overleaf). It's a fairly typical muddy soak, decorated by trees and beer cans, and with some solid stone weirs built at the turn of the century by Chinese labourers. The other feature on the journey is the *Walkabout Creek Hotel* at **McKINLAY**, used as the rowdy Outback pub in the film *Crocodile Dundee*. The whole building was moved 400m in order to make it more visible to passing tourists lured by the possibility that they might see a new TV series being filmed.

The journey to **Boulia** is a long (335km) continuation of the Winton landscape, with fuel available every 150km and the chance to see the enigmatic **Min Min Light**, an unexplained glowing oval reputedly seen bobbing around the bush at night; in case you miss it, thoughtful townspeople have erected a larger-than-life Min Min model. **BOULIA** consists of a hotel (☎07/4746 3144), van park and roadhouse. From here, Mount Isa is 300km north on bitumen, and Birdsville is 400km south on a mostly reasonable road. If you're really enjoying the ride, Alice Springs is 800km west on the often-used Plenty or less-frequented Donahue "highways". There's fuel every

250km or so, and track conditions improve once you're over the border into the Northern Territory.

THE NORTHWEST

All the major settlements in Queensland's northwest are **mining towns**, spaced so far apart that precise names are redundant: **Mount Isa** becomes "the Isa", **Cloncurry** "the Curry", **Charters Towers** "the Towers", as if nowhere else existed. Scattered across the vast tracts between are geological treasures waiting to be discovered, as well as traces of those who've tried before, and with a 4WD or careful manoeuvring there's plenty to see as you head interstate. Most people never stop to find out, grimly tearing along as fast as possible between Townsville and Three Ways along the **Flinders/Barkly Highway**. It's a shame if time is limited and you're relying on public transport, because Charters Towers' century-old feel and Mount Isa's strange setting are worth a stopover. With the freedom of your own vehicle, there's untramped bush at the **Great Basalt Wall** and **Porcupine Gorge** and the spectacular oasis of **Lawn Hill Gorge**, all a lifetime away from the coast's often banal spirit. With the highway forming the main link between Queensland and the Northern Territory, the major **bus lines** have at least daily services interstate, or there's the twice-weekly *Inlander* **train** between Townsville and Mount Isa.

Gold Country

There's little scenic variation over the two-hour journey from the coast to the heights of the inland range at the community of **Mingela**, but dry scrub at the top once covered seams of ore which had the streets of both Charters Towers and Ravenswood bustling with lucky-strike miners. Those times are long gone – though gold is still extracted from old tailings or sporadically panned from the creek beds – and the towns have survived at opposite extremes: connected by road and rail to Townsville, Charters Towers became a busy rural centre, while Ravenswood, half an hour south of Mingela, was just too far off the track and wasted to a shadow. Detours (☎07/4721 5977) runs day-trips from Townsville to one or the other for about $40.

Ravenswood

As wind blows dust and dried grass around the streets between mine shafts and lonely old buildings, **RAVENSWOOD** fulfils ideas of what a ghost town should look like. Gold was discovered here in 1868 and within two years there were solid brick houses, a frenetic atmosphere and seven hundred miners on Elphinstone Creek working seams of gold, silver and lead ore: "every building in the main street was either a public house and dance house or public house and general store".

The main attraction is to wander between the restored buildings, trying to imagine how the others must have looked; the curator of the **Court House Museum** (10am–3pm; closed Tues) gives entertaining tours of the museum, town and – with sufficient notice – current mining efforts (☎07/4770 2047 to book). Built in 1879, the Post Office today doubles as the town's **store** and fuel supply. Unsurprisingly, the two most complete survivals are **hotels** though how they both keep going with a scattered population of barely a hundred souls is anybody's guess. You'll probably end up in one as the day heats up; the *Imperial* looks the worse for wear but has original wood panelling, mirrors and swing doors on the bar; accommodation is available here (☎07/4770 2131) or at the Top Camp roadhouse (☎07/4770 2188). Across the road attempts are being made to renovate a church and school, still just standing.

Charters Towers and the Great Basalt Wall

Once Queensland's second-largest city, and often referred to in its heyday simply as "the World", **CHARTERS TOWERS** is a showcase of colonial architecture. An Aboriginal boy named **Jupiter Mosman** found gold here in 1871 and within twelve months three thousand prospectors had stripped the landscape of trees and covered it with shafts, chimneys and crushing mills. At first, little money was reinvested – the cemetery is a sad record of cholera and typhoid outbreaks from poor sanitation – but by 1900, despite diminishing returns, Charters Towers had become a prosperous centre. There's been minimal change since then and the population, now mainly sustained by cattle farming, has shrunk to about a third of what it was in its prime. Good times to visit are for the May Day weekend **Country Music Festival**, and the **Rodeo** at Easter.

Just about every building on Gill and Mosman streets catches the eye: a brightly painted police station, the classical elegance of the post office, and the shaded country arcades outside the stores. The courtyard and glass roof at the former Stock Exchange and Assayer's Office now front some quiet shops and a lifeless **mining museum** (daily 9am–4pm). Next door, the solid facade of the **town hall** betrays its original purpose as a bank, which stored gold bars smelted locally; and the next bank along is now a grand facade for The World Theatre and Cinemas. Just down Mosman Street is the **Zara Clark Museum** (daily 10am–3pm; $3), housing an absorbing jumble of everything from old wagons to a set of silver tongs for eating frogs' legs. Further along the road is **Lissner Park**, whose Boer War memorial recalls stories of Breaker Morant, a local executed by the British after shooting a prisoner.

The **Venus Gold Battery**, 5km out of town down Gill Street (tours daily 10am & 2pm; 00), is a fascinating illustration of the monumental efforts needed to separate gold

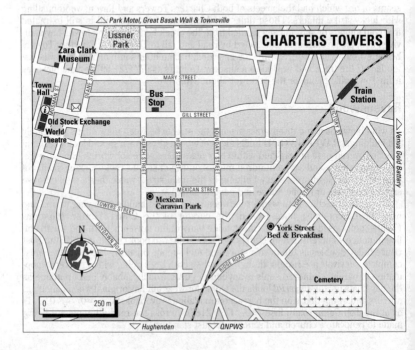

from rock. Abandoned in 1972 after a century of operations, the battery is a huge, gloomy temple to the past, its machinery lying silent and piecemeal around the place. The intention is to restore it to full working order, presumably without re-creating the actual conditions – it was a hideous place, a sweatbox filled with noxious fumes and noise. Ore was ground to a powder in one of the seven massive crushers, mixed with water and passed over a mercury screen. Any gold formed an amalgam and adhered to the mercury, which was then heated in a crucible to leave a pitted nugget and later re-melted with flux to absorb any impurities. Sludge from the mercury screens was soaked in cyanide to leach out more gold, and then the cyanide was neutralized with sulphur and piled up outside. These mounds are now being reprocessed using modern methods to extract the last vestiges of the precious metal.

Practicalities

The main streets are Gill and Mosman, where you'll find everything from supermarkets to banks; **trains** stop at the far end of Gill Street, **buses** halfway along by the Caltex service station. For **accommodation**, the *Mexican Caravan Park*, at the corner of Church and Mexican streets (☎07/4787 1161) on the site of the once-busy Mexican Mine, is shaded and central. In tune with the local atmosphere is *York Street B&B* at 58 York St (☎07/4787 1028; ②–④), a nicely restored old timber building with wide verandahs and a pool. The *Park Motel*, on the corner of Mosman and Deane streets (☎07/4787 1022; ⑤), is also central and comfortable. For **food**, your best bet is to try the hotel dining rooms. There's a Sunday morning **market** in the Stock Exchange building. The **information centre** (daily 9am–5pm), on Mosman, facing down Gill Street, has rough maps and advice on **gold-panning** tours in the area, while Gold Nugget Scenic Tours (Mon, Tues, Thurs & Fri; ☎07/4787 1568; $15) packs the town sights into three hours and may make longer excursions by arrangement.

The Great Basalt Wall

About thirty minutes north of Charters Towers, the Gregory Developmental Road crosses the eastern side of a hundred-kilometre-long **lava flow** known with some justification as the **Great Basalt Wall**. Central sections form an impenetrable band of black boulders, riddled with gullies and caves; aerial surveys show dense vegetation weighed down beneath rubber vines, hiding colonies of fruit bats and hundreds of unconnected saline waterholes. Compasses don't work around basalt and those who've entered the maze are not short on tales about promptly getting lost and wandering around for hours.

You can get an impression of what it's like on the fringes of the wall, at Red Falls and Big Bend. At **Red Falls** (40km along the Developmental Road and then 44km west down a dry-season track) the river runs at right angles to the lava flow; water pours into an Olympic-sized swimming hole and then down a sandy creekbed lined with paperbark trees and overlooked by a bush **campsite**. Walking about 200m further upstream to swim at Silent Hole, you'll see that the riverbed is pocked by the frozen impressions of burst bubbles where gases erupted through the solidifying rock. **Big Bend** (33km north of the Towers and then 2km east) is best reached in a 4WD, though it's not far to walk from the road. This is where the Burdekin River was diverted as lava edged into it, forming a concave cliff and swimming spot at **Echo Hole**. The flows covered an ancient coral reef and you can still pick out some shapes in the limestone rocks where the lava has worn away.

Pentland, Hughenden and around

There's little to see in tiny **PENTLAND**, 105km west of Charters Towers, but the pale sandstone escarpments beyond town, known locally as **White Mountains**, hide some spectacular creek systems and scattered galleries of engraved **Aboriginal art**. Adventure Wildlife & Bush Treks (☎ & fax 07/4788 1126) organizes day-tours round local stations, two- to four-day camping trips ($254–524 per person all-inclusive, or for $10 a day bring your own supplies and 4WD), and three-day hiking excursions around White Mountains ($180 per person).

HUGHENDEN, 140km further along the highway, looks big compared to Pentland. A dozen wide streets, a supermarket, a couple of **hotels** and banks all conspire to make you feel that you've arrived somewhere. The *Grand Hotel* on Gray Street (☎07/4741 1588; ①–③) offers filling meals and budget beds, but the *Rest Easi Motel* (☎07/4741 1633; ①–④) is quieter; you can also **camp** here. *Pete's Country Kitchen*, the **café** before the tracks on the other side of town, has good burgers. Opposite is the service station-cum-bus stop and a newsagent selling yesterday's papers. There are two places to spend time: the **swimming pool** on Resolution Street and a free **museum** and **information** centre (☎07/4741 1021) just past the hotel, dedicated to the Muttaburrasaurus dinosaur, a swamp-dwelling iguanadon. Bones were found at Muttaburra, near Longreach, in 1963 and assembled into a ten-metre-long skeleton after souvenir hunters handed over pieces to the Queensland Museum in Brisbane. It is usually thought to be vegetarian, but its needle-like teeth have prompted a rethink about this type of dinosaur's diet.

More on the regional fossil record is on show 115km west along the highway at **RICHMOND**, whose **Marine Fossil Museum** (daily 8am–5pm; $3) displays the petrified remains of fish, long-necked *elasmosaur*s, and models of a *kronosaur* excavated in the 1920s by a team from Harvard University and now on show in the USA. *Richmonds Caravan Park* has accommodation ranging from tent sites to air-conditioned units (☎07/4741 3772; ①–③).

Porcupine Gorge

Porcupine Gorge is 70km north of Hughenden, along the partially surfaced Kennedy Developmental Road, accessible only if you have your own vehicle (although you can usually scrape by without a 4WD). A deep gash completely invisible among the drab brown scrub until you're virtually in it, it's best seen at the start of the dry season (May–July) before the river stops flowing, when good **swimming holes**, beautifully coloured cliffs and flowering bottlebrush and banksia trees reward the effort of getting there. A **campsite** at the top of the gorge has limited cold water, toilets and nothing else. Look for wallabies on the walk into the gorge, which leads down steps and becomes an increasingly steep, rough path carpeted in loose stones. The white riverbed has been moulded by water into soft, elongated forms, curving into a pool below the orange, yellow and white bands of **Pyramid Rock**. This is the bush at its best: sandstone glowing in the afternoon sun against a deep-blue sky, with animal calls echoing along the gorge as the shadow of the gorge wall creeps over distant woods. Walk along the road at dusk and you'll see groups of kangaroos.

Cloncurry

CLONCURRY, 390km west of Hughenden, is caught between two landscapes, where the flat eastern plains rise to a rough and rocky plateau. Besides being the place where Australia's highest temperature (53.1°C) was recorded, Cloncurry offers glimpses into the mining history that permeates the whole stretch west to the larger and less personal settlement of Mount Isa. Copper was discovered here in 1867 but as the town lacked a rail link to the coast until 1908, profits were eroded by the necessity of transporting the ore by camel to Normanton. This meant that Cloncurry never reflected the quality of its mines: there are no traces of a wealthy past because there never was one.

Buildings at the **Mary Kathleen Memorial Park Museum** (Mon–Fri 7am–4pm, Sat & Sun 9am–3pm; $5) were salvaged from Mary Kathleen, a short-lived uranium mining town between Cloncurry and Mount Isa (see overleaf). The museum is primarily of geological interest, though Aboriginal tools and Burke's water bottle add some historical depth. The mineral collection is a comprehensive catalogue of local ores, fossils and gemstones arranged in long cases. The office gives out information on old mining camps and fossicking details if you feel inspired to try your luck hunting for garnets, copper and maltese crosses (hard, reddish-brown staurolite crystals paired at right angles). Alternatively Wally Robertson (☎07/4742 1606) gives personalized tours of the area including a chance to try fossicking or gold panning. To go on your own you will need a permit from the Department of Mines & Energy in Mount Isa (☎07/4744 6904).

A positive side to Cloncurry's isolation is that it inspired the formation of the Royal Flying Doctor Service. **John Flynn Place**, on the corner of King and Daintree streets (Mon–Fri 7am–4pm, Sat & Sun 9am–3pm; $5), is a monument to the man who pioneered the use of radio and plane to provide a "mantle of safety over the Outback". The exhibition explains how ideas progressed with technology, from pedal-powered radios to assistance from the young Qantas, resulting in the opening in Cloncurry of the first Flying Doctor base in 1928. There is also an art gallery to peruse and gardens to enjoy. A different aspect of Cloncurry's past is evident in the two foreign **cemeteries**. To the left of the highway, before you cross the creek on the way to Mount Isa, a hundred overgrown plots recall a brief goldrush last century when the harsh conditions took a terrible toll on **Chinese prospectors**; equally neglected are the unnamed graves of **Afghans** at the north end of Henry Street, all aligned with Mecca. Afghans were vital to Cloncurry's survival before the coming of the railway, organizing camel trains which carried the ore to Normanton whence it was shipped to Europe – a role now largely forgotten.

Practicalities

At times almost deserted, Cloncurry's **services** are clustered along the highway and a block to the north on Scarr Street. Draw money from the bank or via Lee's Supermarket's EFTPOS facilities. The best of Cloncurry's six **bars** – and serving good meals as well – is the *Wagon Wheel* **motel** (☎07/4742 1866; ⑤), on Ramsay Street; a public house has occupied this same site since 1867. *Oasis Caravan Park* (☎07/4742 1313) has shade, a small store, a saltwater swimming pool and bindi-eye thorns.

From Cloncurry, Mount Isa is just 118km to the west, while the **Burke Developmental Road** heads north to Normanton past several historic roadhouses: **QUAMBY**'s old country hotel with races and an underwear-throwing contest in May; and the **Burke and Wills Roadhouse**, at the junction of the sealed road west towards **Gregory Downs** and Lawn Hill Gorge (see p.508).

Lake Julius is a man-made beauty spot behind the latest of three dams on the Leichhardt River, around 100km northwest of Cloncurry and the same distance from Mount Isa. It's a pleasant spot for fishing or walking in the surrounding hills though the last half of the drive from either direction leaves the highway on a track that's often badly damaged by trucks servicing reopened copper mines near Kajabbi. *Lake Julius Resort* (☎07/4743 2130; ①) has camp sites, dormitories and unadorned cabins sleeping up to eight people (③), which should all be booked in advance.

Cloncurry to Mount Isa

The rough country between Cloncurry and Mount Isa is evidence of ancient upheavals which shattered the landscape and created the region's extensive mineral deposits. While the highway continues safely to Mount Isa past the **Burke and Wills monument** and the **Kalkadoon/Mitakoodi tribal boundary** at Corella Creek, forays into the bush will uncover remains of less fortunate mining settlements. In any vehicle you can manage the brief detour to Mary Kathleen, while with a 4WD you can take the tracks leading through old camps to mineral formations – ask in Cloncurry or Mount Isa about road conditions. Campbell's (see Mount Isa "Listings" on p.506) and Wally Robertson (see overleaf) run safaris from Mount Isa or Cloncurry to parts of the bush drive described below.

Mary Kathleen

About halfway to Mount Isa, the short and steadily crumbling road north to **MARY KATHLEEN** is marked with a small plaque. By all accounts, **uranium** was found here by accident when a car broke down; while waiting for help the driver and his friends tried fossicking and found ore. The two-street town was built in 1956 and completely dismantled in 1982 when export restrictions halted mining. Since then, once-manicured

---

GOING BUSH: CAMPS AND MINES

There are two sections to the bush route between Cloncurry and Mount Isa: first 21.5km from the highway past abandoned camps at Rosebud Dam and Ballara to **Fountain Springs**, then 25km back to the highway past some working copper mines and a maltese cross site. While you might cover the track to Fountain Springs in a normal vehicle, the second section requires a 4WD. It's impossible, however, to predict road conditions and you'll need advice and a **map** from the Cloncurry museum or the RACQ in Mount Isa. If you wish to try your hand at fossicking you will also require a permit from the Department of Mines & Energy in Mount Isa (☎07/4744 6904). Allow an hour to reach Fountain Springs from the highway, and three for the second section.

The **Fountain Springs track** starts south of the highway just over 60km from Cloncurry, opposite a rest area. **Rosebud Dam**, on Corella Creek, is a good place to pick over; there are a couple of waste heaps on the north bank, visible from the creek crossing, and old tins and matchboxes are still to be found around the place. A bottle dump, 50m downstream, might hide an unbroken gem missed by previous collectors. Bear right at the slag heaps 2.5km past Rosebud and continue another 7km to the **Lady J** junction, where you bear left. Two kilometres further on there's an obviously cleared spot; over on a rise in the scrub to the right is a concrete platform and traces of foundations and rail lines. This is **Ballara**, once a depot for ore off to the smelters at Kuridala. Again, long grass hides occasional relics. South from here the long ridge of the **Fountain Range** comes into view on the right. A cleft partway down marks the springs, reached 4km from Ballara. Water oozes into a small waterhole at the foot of perpendicular cliffs, and the mouth of the gorge is marshy and surrounded by trees. You could camp here, or just have a picnic and head back.

Backtracking to Ballara, find the concrete platform and head west (left coming back from the springs) along vague wheel tracks across a fenceline and onto the old railway. From here the track hugs a hill to the right over various gradients, then divides briefly after 2km; the left way passes a tubular cross marking the grave of Thomas Tame, killed while mining in 1912. Another 1.6km past anthills and you're at **Hightville**, surrounded by ridges and mostly lost in the scrub; a few concrete sidings, slag heaps and junk are all that remain. Don't try negotiating the narrow, potholed tunnel; follow the newer track through gullies and rubble to the **Wee McGregor Mine**, which is still worked intermittently for copper – rocks below are stained green with salts from the mine. Four kilometres later the hills recede, and on a small plateau between two ranges you'll find **maltese crosses** carpeting the road. Good specimens are rare and the area is picked over each year; try towards the hillside on the right. After this the track traverses sandy flats between creeks until **Guts Ache Gap**, roughly 10km from the crosses. Onwards, it's 3km to **Mount Frosty** (or **Krusty**), a source of limestone flux for Mount Isa and now a flooded quarry. The highway is two minutes distant, 9km closer to Mount Isa from where you left it.

lawns have run riot, and an occasional bougainvillea and an unkempt row of casuarinas tangling along the access road are the only signs that there were gardens here; in a few years it will all have gone. About a kilometre past the old town the road becomes a dirt track and splits; a kilometre along the right fork a bumpy uphill track leads to the terraces of the open-cast **mine**, now reminiscent of a flooded Greek amphitheatre. On a cloudy day you can be sure that the alarming blue-green colour of the water is not simply a reflection of the sky. Locals maintain it's safe to swim here, and some even claim health benefits.

Mount Isa and around

As the only place of consequence for 700km in any direction, the smokestacks, concrete paving and sterile hills at **MOUNT ISA** assume oasis-like qualities on arrival, despite being undeniably ugly. Though the novelty might have worn off by the time you've had a cold drink, the city has a few points to savour before heading on. There's evidence of the area's **Aboriginal heritage**, a couple of unusual **museums**, tours of the mines themselves, Australia's largest **rodeo** every August and, not least, the fascinating situation and the community it has fostered.

The largest city in the world in terms of surface area – its administrative boundaries stretch as far as Cloncurry – Mount Isa sits astride a wealth of zinc, silver, lead and copper, and owes its existence to these reserves and the need for a staging post for interstate travellers. The city's founding father was **John Miles**, who discovered ore in 1923, established **Mount Isa Mines** (MIM) the next year and began commercial mining in 1925. Originally a settlement of canvas and scrap wood, the city enjoyed a forty-year boom under the benevolent hegemony of MIM until the late 1980s saw a decline in profits. New mining developments such as the new Hilton Mine, north of the city, keep business ticking over, but mines further afield tend to be staffed by workers who live on the east coast and fly in for three-week shifts, staying on site until they take their money home, completely bypassing The Isa.

The City

Having passed so much mining history consigned to the scrub, there's a certain novelty value in exploring Mount Isa's active mines. The **surface tour** ($13) includes a stint looking at videos and pieces of machinery at the **John Middlin Mining Display** on Church Street (daily 9am–4pm; $4) and a bus ride around surface operations. **Underground tours** ($35), from which women were once barred as harbingers of bad luck, descend to see subterranean mining, crushing and the workshops. Book through the tourist office (see p.505) and expect a waiting list of up to a month for the underground tour, or try for a cancellation. This could be your last chance for the real thing – in the next year or so, the tour will be replaced by a replica mine being dug under the **Frank Aston Museum** on Shackleton Street (daily 9am–4pm; $5). At the moment this is partly outdoors and partly underground in a tunnel full of mining memorabilia of a type you'll recognize if you went bush between here and Cloncurry. A staircase rises up through a mineshaft to a walkway above the museum, graced by old cars and mining trucks which look dated in MIM's shadow.

On the Riversleigh Station (see p.508) the lime-saturated waters of the Gregory River have been encapsulating a fossil record since Australia was a teeming tropical forest. Paleontologists have been working at Riversleigh for a decade and have discovered an incredible record of marsupial and mammalian evolution and environmental change between ten thousand and twenty million years ago. The **Riversleigh Fossils Interpretive Centre** on Marian Street (daily 8.30am–5pm; $5) shows how fossils are

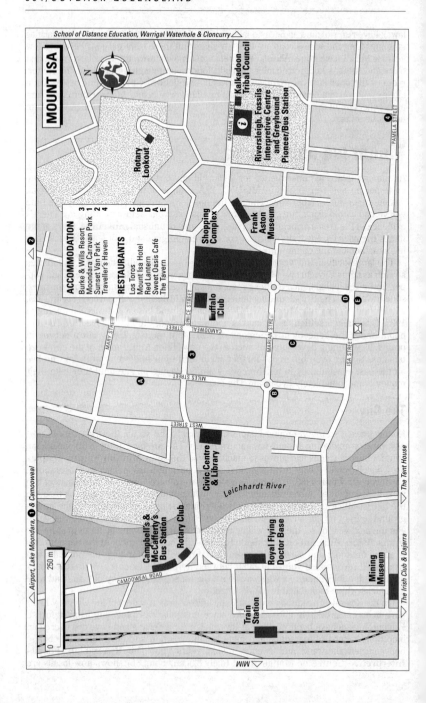

MOUNT ISA

N

School of Distance Education, Warrigal Waterhole & Cloncurry △

Airport, Lake Moondara, ❶ & Camooweal ◁

Rotary Lookout

❷ ◁

ACCOMMODATION
Burke & Wills Resort 3
Moondara Caravan Park 1
Sunset Van Park 2
Traveller's Haven 4

RESTAURANTS
Los Toros C
Mount Isa Hotel B
Red Lantern D
Sweet Oasis Café A
The Tavern E

Kalkadoon Tribal Council

MARIAN STREET

Riversleigh, Fossils Interpretive Centre and Greyhound Pioneer/Bus Station

PAMELA STREET

❹

Shopping Complex

Frank Aston Museum

GRACE STREET

Buffalo Club

CAMOOWEAL STREET

MARIAN STREET

ISA STREET

MARY STREET

MILES STREET

❸

Ⓐ

WEST STREET

Ⓒ

Ⓑ

Ⓓ

Ⓔ

Civic Centre & Library

Leichhardt River

The Tent House ▷

Campbell's & McCafferty's Bus Station

Rotary Club

Royal Flying Doctor Base

CAMOOWEAL ROAD

The Irish Club & Dajarra ▷

Mining Museum

Train Station

MIM ▽

250 m
0

found and reconstructed and explains why this is relevant to modern conservation concerns, which can be more enlightening than a visit to the actual site.

Over the river and left down Camooweal Road is the **Royal Flying Doctor Base** (Mon–Sat 9am–3pm; $2). Ten minutes further south on the corner of Third and Fourth avenues, the National Trust **Tent House** is the last survivor of the city's earliest architecture – a canvas hut with a roof. The **School of Distance Education** (tours at 10am and 11am on school days) is by the Kalkadoon State High School at Abel Smith Parade on the Cloncurry side of town.

Practicalities

Illuminated at night, and with two huge chimneys – the Rotary lookout on Hilary Street gives a good view – **MIM** is the city's major landmark, west of the often dry **Leichhardt River**. The highway runs through town and over the river to the bus station (for McCafferty's and Campbell's services) on Camooweal Road, **trains** stop below MIM, and the **airport** is 7km to the north, where taxis meet arrivals. The city centre is along the highway (Marian and Grace streets) between Simpson and West streets; there's no public transport. The **tourist information office** (daily 8.30am–5pm; ☎07/4743 4066) and the Greyhound Pioneer bus terminal are in the Riversleigh Fossils Interpretive Centre on Marian Street.

Motel accommodation can be found at the *Burke and Wills Resort*, on the corner of Grace and Camooweal (☎07/4743 8000 or free call ☎1800/679 178; ⑥), where somewhat twee rooms decorated in "period" style cluster around a courtyard. Cheaper beds, mostly two to a room, are on offer at *Traveller's Haven*, on the corner of Spence and Pamela streets (☎07/4743 0313; ①), with a free pick-up from bus or train stations. For **camping**, *Sunset Van Park*, 14 Sunset Drive, about 2km north of the centre (☎07/4743 7668), has inexpensive tent sites, while *Moondarra Caravan Park*, 4km from the city off the Camooweal Road (☎07/4743 9780), is plain and tranquil, close to a creek that draws plenty of local birdlife.

Mount Isa's hotels and clubs are the main source of **meals**, though *Red Lantern Chinese*, on the corner of Simpson and Isa streets, is pretty good, if a little expensive. *Los Toros Mexican*, 19 Camooweal Rd, is a friendly family restaurant and serves **real ale** brewed on the premises in Australia's smallest registered brewery. The city boasts members of over fifty nationalities, many of whom have their own clubs with restaurants.

MIM

The **Mount Isa Mines** complex is a land of trundling yellow mine trucks, mountains of slag, intense activity and miles of noisy vibrating pipelines. Above all this the two chimneys trail Mount Isa's signature across the sky, marking the copper mine to the south and separate silver, lead and zinc deposits. Ore is mined almost 2km down by a workforce of twelve hundred; roughly crushed, and hoisted to the surface before undergoing a second crushing, grinding and washing in flotation tanks, to separate ore from waste rock. Zinc is sold as it is, copper is smelted into ingots and transported to Townsville for refining while four-tonne ingots of lead/silver mix are sent to England for the few ounces of silver to be separated. Power for the mines and the entire region comes from MIM's own plant; surplus is sold to the state grid. During nocturnal power failures residents often hike up to the rotary lookout and place bets on which part of town will be reconnected first.

The scale of the process will be brought home to you if you stand under one of the mountains of tailings awaiting future treatment – next to which are humble mounds of green copper ore, bought off a local miner and representing maybe a year's effort – or look down into the depths of the open-cut mine, worked simply for rubble to fill in old shafts. At the edge of the mine the last hole of the original Mount Isa, and site of the first finds seventy years ago, has been left as a memorial.

You'll have to befriend a few locals to find these, but you'll almost definitely end up at the *Irish Club*, on Buckley Avenue 2km south of the centre, where everyone converges for weekend bands and inexpensive food, while the *Rotary Club*, next to Campbell's bus station, hosts an **Oktoberfest**. Closer to the centre the upstairs grill at the bulky *Mount Isa Hotel*, on the corner of Marian and Miles streets, is reliable, and *The Tavern* on Isa Street has excellent-value lunches; look out for other hotels' all-you-can-eat specials or try one of the fast-food outlets on Simpson Street, where you'll also find the flashy new *Buffalo Club* and a shopping complex for **provisions**. For somewhere to unwind, try *Sweet Oasis* café on Miles Street.

Listings

Airlines Air Mount Isa (☎07/4743 2844); Ansett, 8 Miles St (☎07/4749 0240); Flight West, 14 Miles St (☎07/4743 9333); North Western Air (☎07/4743 7720).

Bus station Campbell's (☎07/4743 2006 or free call ☎1800/242 329); Greyhound Pioneer (☎07/4743 6655); McCafferty's (☎07/4743 3685).

Car rental Avis, Marian St (☎07/4743 3733) and at the airport; Four Wheel Drive Hire Service, Simpson St (☎07/4743 6306 or free call ☎1800/077 353); Hertz (☎07/4743 4142) at the airport.

Cinema is on Marian St, corner of West St.

Hospital 30 Camooweal St (☎07/4744 4444).

Internet access from the newsagent at 25 Miles St.

Pharmacy *Corner Pharmacy*, corner of Marian and Miles streets (☎07/4743 3773).

Police 7 Isa St (☎07/4744 1111).

Post office for poste restante, Isa St (☎07/4743 2454); there is another office in Simpson St opposite the shopping complex.

RACQ 13 Simpson St, ☎07/4743 4300.

Taxi ☎07/4743 2333.

Tours Campbell's (☎07/4743 2006 or free call ☎1800/242 329) runs day-tours to local mines and Aboriginal sites, as well as three-day safaris to Lawn Hill Gorge between May and October. Book through the bus station or your accommodation. Bob's Look About Trips (☎07/4743 9523) has a more personalized range of tours of the city and environs for small groups, while Air Mount Isa (☎07/4743 2844) organizes day-trips to Lawn Hill.

Trains ☎07/4744 1202.

Kalkadoon country

The scrub around Mount Isa is thick with abandoned mines, waterholes and Aboriginal sites. Either take a **tour** (see above) or, if you're doing your own driving, check at the tourist office for latest news on road conditions.

The city marks the centre of the territory of the **Kalkadoons**, a tribe often compared with the Zulus for their fierce opposition to white invasion last century. After hounding squatters for ten years with guerrilla tactics, they were all but exterminated in a pitched battle with an army of local settlers and Native Mounted Police near Kajabbi in 1884. Kalkadoon bones littered the region for years, but their stand gained them respect for their organized resistance to Europeans.

Numerous sites around Mount Isa attest to the Kalkadoons' abilities as prolific toolmakers and painters, and it's worth paying the token entry fee to visit their **Tribal Council office** (Mon–Fri 9am–5pm; $1), next to the tourist information office on Marian Street, and talk to the staff. Bear in mind that although it's against the law to alter Aboriginal sites in any way, many local sites have been vandalized and you might find the council evasive.

Warrigal Waterhole, Poison Hole and Lake Moondarra

You need high clearance and care to reach **Warrigal Waterhole**: drive 7km towards Cloncurry from the Tribal Council office on Marian Street, turn right and bear left along a very rough track to reach a parking area 3.4km later, from where you walk past "ripple rocks" to the waterhole. One red figure with strange hair outlined in yellow on the left seems to have escaped damage; not so other figures and symbols, which have melted to ochre smears. The waterhole itself is hemmed in by sheltering rocks, which makes for a cool retreat from the sun.

A flooded open cut mine, **Poison Hole**'s name comes from the surreal appearance of the water, coloured green by copper, but it's actually safe to swim in. Tracks there change each year, but the hole is about ten minutes from the highway, and the turn-off should be roughly 25km back towards Cloncurry; look for signs spray-painted on the road. **Lake Moondarra**, 20km along on a good road (follow the signs from the highway heading towards Camooweal), is less offensively toned, and packed out at weekends with windsurfers and boats. During the week it is nearly deserted and other animals are attracted to the water – goannas, wallabies and flocks of pelicans. By the dam at the north end of the lake, the neat and tidy **Warrina Park** is the unlikely home of peacocks.

Camooweal and Lawn Hill

West of Mount Isa, the **Barkly Highway** continues to Camooweal and the Northern Territory, with an unsealed road, a little over halfway to the state border, heading north off it leading to **Gregory Downs**, **Lawn Hill National Park** and **Burketown**. If you're making for Lawn Hill, ensure you have a **campsite** booked (see p.508 for details) and check the latest **road conditions** – the route via Riversleigh is sometimes 4WD-only or closed, while the Gregory Downs road is fine for most cars if it's dry. Wherever you're driving, fuel up; it's two hundred monotonous kilometres to Camooweal and the fringes of the black-soil **Barkly Tablelands**, and at least twice that to Lawn Hill.

Camooweal and the Caves

There's no way to avoid **CAMOOWEAL** but you might wish there were; the township's atmosphere of lazy aggression is exacerbated by a total lack of charm. The highway from Mount Isa forms the main street, built in 1944 by American servicemen whose names are painted on a rock at the edge of town. You'll find a roadhouse, mechanic, general store (and Westpac agent), post office and hotel – a risky place for a last drink in Queensland. The store's old decor is worth a peek, and murals at the **service station** (with EFTPOS; ☎07/4748 2155) should raise a chuckle; around the back are cabins and a **campsite** with thick grass to raise a tent over. Otherwise, move on.

The best features of the surrounding area are dolomite sinks known as **the Caves**; drive 8km down the Urandangie road south of Camooweal, then turn left and follow the dirt track for about thirty minutes. There's an NPWS **campsite** here with toilets and a fence to keep out marauding cattle. Flocks of gibbering green budgerigars congregate around the creek and, if you can put up with their racket, it's preferable to a night in town. The park's nine **caves** are intriguing terraces, spiralling down 10m before tapering to vertical shafts. The district is riddled with them; one is a roost for **ghost bats**, and another has become famous for its coolabah trees. Caused by tunnels into the water table collapsing at the surface, the shafts continue straight down for anything between 18m and 75m before levelling out into an uncharted system. Instability makes approaching the mouths dangerous, so don't even think about exploring underground.

Heading on from Camooweal there's another track north to Lawn Hill, while 200km south beyond the Caves is **Urandangie** and a 650-kilometre, 4WD "short cut" across to Alice Springs. West, it's a mere ten minutes' drive to the cattle grid separating Queensland from the Northern Territory's time zone and better roads. Next fuel is at the Barkly Homestead, 275km away.

Gregory Downs and Lawn Hill National Park

Hidden from the rest of the world by the Constance Range and a hot ocean of bleached grass, the red sandstone walls and splash of tropical greenery at **Lawn Hill Gorge** seem outrageously extravagant. There's little warning: within moments a land which barely supports scattered herds of cattle is exchanged for palm forests and creeks teeming with wildlife. The **national park** covers two sections: **Riversleigh Fossil Site** and the gorge itself, about 70km from each other, with access either through Riversleigh to the gorge, or direct to the gorge via the **Gregory Downs Roadhouse**. Either way, there's going to be hours of dirt driving, which at its best will be slow going. The Riversleigh route is definitely worth it, but the Gregory Downs track is less remote. This latter track takes you past the **Century Zinc mine**, where work has just restarted; local Aborigines claimed traditional ownership of the region and after several years of negotiations finally accepted a substantial payment for use of the land. While the situation has exacerbated the frustration felt by mining companies and farmers over the legal ambiguities surrounding the 1992 Mabo Decision (see Contexts, p.998), it's evidence that the wishes of Aboriginal communities are now being taken far more seriously.

For either route, leave the Barkly Highway 116km from Mount Isa and head north on the Gregory Downs road. The Riversleigh road diverges left after another 118km; otherwise, stay on track for where routes from Burketown and Cloncurry meet at **GREGORY DOWNS**. At the **pub** here you can have a cold drink, fill up with petrol and have mechanical repairs attended to. On the May Day weekend the pub also organizes a wild **canoe race** down the Gregory River; at other times renting a canoe (☎07/4748 5540) is the best way to seek out local wildlife. For Lawn Hill, head west across the river and follow the 110-kilometre track to the gorge.

Riversleigh Fossil Site

The track from the Barkly Highway/Gregory Downs road to Riversleigh crosses the **Gregory River** three times around Riversleigh Station, which is why you might need a 4WD on this route. The crossings are a foretaste of Lawn Hill – sudden patches of shady green and cool air in an otherwise hostile landscape – and you can **camp** at the third ford, though there are no facilities.

Like Lawn Hill, Riversleigh was once cloaked in rainforest supporting many ancestral forms of Australian fauna. The **fossil finds** here cover a period from twenty million to just ten thousand years ago, a staggering range for a single site and one which details the transitional period from Australia's climatic heyday to its current parched state. Riversleigh may ultimately produce a fossil record of evolutionary change for an entire ecosystem, but don't expect to see much *in situ* as the fossils are trapped in limestone boulders which have to be blasted out and treated with acid to release their contents. A roadside shelter houses a map of the landscape with fossil sites indicated on a rock outcrop nearby where, with some diligence, you can find bones and teeth protruding from the stones.

Lawn Hill Gorge

When **Lawn Hill Creek** started carving its forty-metre-deep gorge, the region was still a tropical wetland but, as the climate began to dry out, vegetation retreated to a handful of moist, isolated pockets. Animals were drawn to creeks and waterholes and people followed the game – middens and art detail an Aboriginal culture at least seventeen thousand years old. The NPWS **campsite** (tank water, showers, toilets) occupies a tamed edge of the creek at the mouth of the gorge and is booked solid between Easter and October (book in advance on ☎07/4748 5572). An alternative campsite is at the pleasant **Adels Grove**, a Savannah Guides post (☎07/4748 5502) 5km from the gorge and run by Barry Kubala, an expert on the gorge's vegetation.

Canoes ($3 per person per hour) let you explore the gorge from the inside. An easy hour's paddle over calm green water takes you from the NPWS campsite between the stark, vertical cliffs of the Middle Gorge to **Indari falls**, an excellent swimming spot with a ramp to carry your gear down. Beyond here the creek relaxes, alternating between calm ponds and slack channels choked with vegetation before slowing to a trickle under the rockfaces of the Upper Gorge. Saltwater crocs are absent from the gorge, but you'll certainly see plenty of **birds** – egrets, bitterns and kites all put in an appearance. Freshwater crocodiles are unlikely to show: since visitor numbers have increased, this timid reptile has retreated to quieter spots, although you might see a "freshie" at dusk in the **Lower Gorge** – a sluggish tract edged in waterlilies and forest where goannas lounge during the day and rare **purple-crowned fairy wrens** forage in pandanus leaves.

In the creek itself are turtles, shockingly large catfish, and sharp-eyed **archer fish** that spit jets of water at insects above the surface. Just how isolated all this is becomes clear from the flat top of the **Island Stack**, a twenty-minute walk from the camp. A predawn hike up the steep sides gives you a commanding view of the sun creeping into the gorge, highlighting orange walls against green palm-tops which hug the river through a flat, undernourished country. The rocks along the banks of the Lower Gorge are daubed with designs relating to the Dingo Dreaming, while fuel drums, tins and middens inside an overhang demonstrate that Lawn Hill has only recently been abandoned by **Aborigines**. This fact was rammed home when a group of fifty people from local communities staged a month-long sit-in at the park in October 1994, demanding joint management – something they'd been promised three years previously. The case is still being milled through the legal system, but it's possible that Aboriginal tour guides may soon be on hand to show you around.

THE GULF OF CARPENTARIA

The great savannahs and intricate river systems of western Cape York and the **Gulf of Carpentaria** were described in 1623 by the Dutch explorer Jan Carstensz as being full of hostile tribes – not surprising, since he'd already kidnapped two men and chased the rest off with musket fire. The Gulf was ignored for centuries thereafter, except by Indonesians gathering sea-slugs to sell to the Chinese, but interest in its potential was stirred in 1841 by **John Lort Stokes**, a lieutenant on the *Beagle* (which had been graced by a young Charles Darwin on an earlier voyage) who absurdly described the coast as "Plains of Promise":

A vast boundless plain lay before us, here and there dotted with woodland isles. . . I could discover the rudiments of future prosperity and ample justification of the name which I had bestowed upon them.

It took Burke and Wills' awful 1861 trek (see box on p.486) to discover that the pastures were deficient in nutrients and that the black soil became a quagmire during the wet season. Too awkward to develop, the Gulf hung in limbo as settlements sprang up, staggered on for a while, then disappeared; even today few places could be described as thriving communities. Not that this should put you off visiting: with few real destinations but plenty to see, the Gulf is a perfect destination for those who just like to travel. On the way, and only half a day's drive from Cairns, the awesome lava tubes at **Undara** shouldn't be missed, while further afield there are **gemstones** to be fossicked, the coast's birdlife and exciting **barramundi** fishing to enjoy, and the Gulf's sheer remoteness to savour.

Two mostly sealed roads head through the region to Normanton and Karumba: the **Gulf Developmental Road**, which starts southwest of Ravenshoe on the Atherton

Tablelands (covered three times weekly from Cairns by Coral Coaches (☎07/4031 7577), which stops at all major settlements and links up with the *Savannahlander* and *Gulflander* trains; ☎07/4041 2295); and the **Burke Developmental Road** from Mount Isa. The Mareeba–Normanton "road", via Chillagoe, is a shattering, unserviced, five-hundred-kilometre track best tackled by well-equipped off-road transport only – as are all the Gulf's remoter stretches. In the **wet season**, flying is the sole option for *any* travel. **Safaris** run from Mount Isa or Cairns (see p.506 and p.451, respectively) if you don't have the right vehicle. There are also two rustic **railways** operating in the Gulf area, from Mount Surprise to Forsayth, and from Croydon to Normanton.

Most visitors to the Gulf need to be reasonably self-sufficient, as there are few banks and accommodation is largely in campsites (no hostels) or pricey hotels. The NPWS are joined by the Savannah Guides, a private organization less altruistic than the government-funded NPWS but no less informed, which runs campsites with rangers to show you around. On a more alarming note, you might also come face to face with the Gulf's two **crocodile** species – take care.

Undara volcano

The **Undara Lava Tubes** are astounding, massive tunnels running in broken chambers for up to 35km from the side of the volcano's low cone. It wasn't until 1989 that the majority of the caves were located and mapped and Undara declared an area of scientific interest, currently run by the Savannah Guides but NPWS-owned. The volcano is on **Yarramulla Station**, ten minutes south of the Gulf Developmental Road, 130km from Ravenshoe. **Accommodation**, bar and restaurant at the Lava Lodge (☎07/4097 1111, cabins ⑥, tent village ②, camping also available) are in eleven restored railway carriages brought over from Mareeba and set up among a thin wattle forest – an eccentric but comfortable idea.

Because the tunnels are hard to enter – and some host a virulent lung fungus – you must take a **tour**. Although not cheap ($26 for a 2-hour introduction, $58 for a half-day, $85 full-day), these are good value considering that, as well as the chance to explore the tubes, you get an intimate rundown on local geology, flora, fauna and history from a member of the Collins family, who've lived on the station for more than a century. There are also some good short **walks** up to lookout points in the low hills above the *Lodge*, and plenty of insect and reptile nightlife if you venture out without a torch – beware of snakes.

Tubes and caves

When Undara erupted 190,000 years ago, lava rivers snaked northwest towards the Gulf. Away from the cone the outside surfaces hardened, forming insulating tubes which kept the lava liquid and allowed it to run until the tubes were drained. These were then covered by later accumulations, and they'd still be unexplored if hot gases hadn't popped holes in the tube ceilings which eventually collapsed, creating a way in.

The edge of the flow is marked by darker soil and healthier vegetation; at cave mouths this becomes rampant, successfully concealing the entrances and making your first view of the tubes something of a shock – what looks like a bush at ground level turns out to be the top of a giant fig tree growing from the cave floor. The caves are decked in rubble and remnant pockets of thick prehistoric vegetation quite out of place among the dry scrub on the surface. **Tool sites** around the cave mouths show that Aborigines knew of their existence, though there's no evidence that they ever ventured in.

Once **inside**, the scale of the 52 tubes is overpowering. Up to 19m high and 900m long, their glazed walls bear evidence of the terrible forces that created them: coil patterns and ledges formed by cooling lava, whirlpools where lava forged its way through rock from other flows, and "stalactites" made when solidifying lava dribbled from the ceiling. Some end in **lakes**, while others are blocked by lava plugs. Animal tracks in the dust indicate the regular passage of kangaroos, snakes and invertebrates, and seasonally you'll encounter twittering colonies of bats clinging to the ceiling, but the overall scale of the tubes tends to deaden any sounds or signs of life.

Mount Surprise and Ambo

MOUNT SURPRISE, 40km from Undara, takes its name from the shock of the local Aborigines when they first saw whites. It's little more than a van park/gem shop/service station (☎07/4062 3153) and **hotel** (☎07/4062 3118; ③); the main point of interest is the anachronistic **Savannahlander train**, which runs in recently renovated splendour from Mount Surprise through Einasleigh and down to Forsayth. You spend the five-hour journey being hauled over rickety bridges in carriages with corrugated-iron ceilings and wooden dunnies – a pastiche of Outback iconography. The train leaves Mount Surprise on Monday and Thursday at around noon, departing Forsayth for the return leg Tuesday and Friday at 7.30am ($35 each way); for an additional $40 you can have dinner and a bed at Forsayth's *Goldfields Hotel* (☎07/4062 5374). The other local attraction lies a bumpy hour's drive north of Mount Surprise at **O'Briens Creek Topaz Field**; you'll need a 4WD. Arthur Griffin lives on the field and, for $10 a head, will organize fossicking trips for anyone turning up by 8.30am at his home, **the Oasis**. You might find a handful of topaz in a couple of hours, and while it's not very valuable, there's pleasure in the hunt.

West of Mount Surprise the road crosses the **Wall**, where expanding gases in a blocked subterranean lava tube forced the ground above it up 20m into a long ridge. The same gaseous expulsion also seems to have cracked open a much deeper seam at **Ambo Springs** on Tallaroo Station. Formed by water 3km down becoming heated and forcing its way to the surface, the clear blue, sulphurous pools gradually accumulate a crusty grey collar around their vent from dissolved lime, which eventually closes the outflow – until the build-up of pressure explodes through to create a new spring. The water emerges at 92°C, but there are some cooler spas that are more comfortable for soaking in. Tallaroo Station itself is open to the public (Easter–Oct daily until 4pm; ☎07/4662 1221; $9).

Einasleigh, Forsayth and around

Much of the dry basalt-and-sandstone country southwest of Mount Surprise can be explored in 2WD vehicles during dry weather – though roads can be very rough – or seen from the *Savannahlander* train (see above). **EINASLEIGH**, 32km west along the highway and then 43km south on a dirt road, consists of an ordinary handful of weatherboard and iron houses, made memorable by the huge, delicious evening meals served at the *Central Hotel* (☎07/4062 5222; ④), and summer dips in **Einasleigh Creek**'s deep basalt gorge. A further 70km of bumpy, unsealed road west (or a slightly more comfortable 40km south off the highway via Georgetown, a tidy settlement 90km from Mount Surprise), **FORSAYTH** is the terminus for the *Savannahlander* and also the last place to stock up before heading bush to a couple of unusual locations. Two hours south in a 4WD through an area of scrub and sandstone, the basic **camp** at **Agate Creek** (☎07/4062 5335; Easter–Oct) caters to agate hunters who scour the creek banks after each wet season and rate this the best site in the world for these semiprecious stones. This may be a matter of opinion but the colours, ranging from honey through to delicate blue, justify the time spent grubbing around with a pick looking for them. **Cobbold Gorge**, at Robinhood Station, 50km south of Forsayth on a passable dirt road, is a recently discovered and starkly attractive oasis inhabited by freshwater crocs and crayfish and surrounded by baking hot sandstone country. **Tours** (☎07/4062 5470; $45–75, advance bookings essential; pick-ups from the region can be arranged) include a 4WD trip around the station and a scout up the kilometre-long gorge in a motorized punt – an excellent way to experience a very remote corner of the Outback.

Croydon

CROYDON, 150km west of Georgetown along the main road, was the site of Queensland's last major **goldrush** after two station hands found nuggets in a fence-post hole in 1885. For a brief period the region received the attention it had always craved. Within five years the railway was built, and lucky miners whooped it up at Croydon's 36 hotels, but by 1900 chaotic management had brought operations to a close. Whether the rush brought any lasting benefits is doubtful: today, mining junk and vacant blocks set the scene and you wonder how close Croydon is to being completely abandoned. All buildings predate 1920; the *Club Hotel* (last of the 36) and general store both have their original fittings and offer directions to other scattered relics. There's plenty of atmosphere, though, and if you're tempted to stay, there's a **van park** on the Georgetown side.

Moving on, you could take the highway to Normanton, 154km west, or – better still – indulge yourself in a nostalgic **train ride** on the *Gulflander* (☎07/4745 1391), which leaves Croydon on Thursday at 8.30am from the station on Helen Street and takes four hours to trundle to Normanton (return departures from Normanton Thurs 8.30am). Fares are $35 one-way, plus an extra $110 to take your car. When the rails and sleepers were unloaded at Normanton's wharves in the nineteenth century they were meant to form the first stage of a line to Cloncurry, but it was redirected to Croydon when gold was found.

Normanton and around

From Cloncurry you can take the Burke Developmental Road 400km north to **NORMANTON**, stopping for a break halfway at the *Burke and Wills Roadhouse* (☎07/4742 5909). Though sealed, the road is really only wide enough for one vehicle, so when you see a road-train coming you'd better be prepared to hit the dirt. **Termite mounds** line the route, changing with the earth from red to grey as you near the coast and becoming more numerous and more like eroded tombstones as you reach Normanton's neatly trimmed cemetery.

Founded on the banks of the Norman River in 1868, Normanton was the Gulf's main port, connected to the Croydon goldfield by rail and Cloncurry's copper mines by camel train, and today the town has an air of faded splendour. The train still runs once a week to Croydon (see above) and also makes daily trips (June–Sept) to local fishing spots. Set in gritty, flat country, Normanton's fortunes declined along with its mineral deposits, and today there's only a collection of stores and service stations, a Westpac **bank** and **post office**, with shop awnings and a handful of trees providing scant shade. **Fishing** for barramundi (check out Norman River Cruises; ☎07/4745 1347) is beginning to brighten the area's prospects, celebrated by the *Gulfland Motel* (☎07/4745 1290; ⑥) under the sign of the "Big Barra" at the south entrance to the town; the motel has a thick lawn and pleasant **rooms**. The *Normanton Van Park* (☎07/4745 1121) provides access to a shower block and the choice of which bit of gravel to camp on. Normanton's **hotels** rate a mention, especially the luridly painted *Purple Pub*, and the *Albion* with its corrugated iron and wooden fittings – both are pretty frenetic watering holes. When you've had enough boozing, Karumba and routes on to western Cape York lie north. To the west is the fuelless, 220-kilometre Burketown road, with features along the way including the site of Burke and Wills' northernmost camp near the Bynoe

River, and the often difficult **Leichhardt River** crossing where the pocket-sized **Leichhardt Falls** contrasts with the aridity of the surrounding sand dunes, deposited each year when the river is in spate.

Reached from Normanton across 70km of cracked, burning saltpan, **KARUMBA**'s tidy gardens are ridiculously suburban and camouflage the remote setting – betrayed the moment you buy a newspaper and realize that it's two days old. Once a candidate for a telegraph connection with Asia, today the single-street township survives, barely, on prawn trawling and fishing. Aborigines shun the area, as many died in a battle nearby – whether in a tribal war or against settlers isn't clear. Luxuries include a **campsite** (*Sunset Park*; ☎07/4745 9277), **store**, Westpac **bank** (Tues & Thurs only), **post office** and the *Karumba Lodge* (☎07/4745 9121; ⑥). Stay out of the infamous *Animal Bar* unless you're extremely serious about drinking and getting into occasional bouts of hand-to-hand combat. For a more relaxing time and the chance of catching something for the pot, contact Graham Sneddon (☎07/4745 9316) to find out about **river cruises** in search of fish, crocs or birds. If you have your own tackle, Karumba Boat Hire (☎07/4745 9205) rents out four-metre-long tinnies from $50 for a half day.

Onwards: the Wellesleys and western Cape York

Gulf Freight Services (☎07/4745 9333 or free call ☎1800/640 079) operates a weekly barge from Karumba to **Weipa** (see p.468 for more on Weipa itself). The journey takes around thirty hours, leaving on Friday and returning Tuesday. A one-way trip costs $210 including meals and cabin; prices for vehicles, which must be containerized, start at $370. Erratic services also go to **Thursday Island** or the Wellesleys, depending on cargo. Domain of the Lardil Aborigines, the **Wellesley Group** comprises two dozen windswept islands north of Burketown with excellent fishing around fragmented coral rubble. Never settled by whites, today they are Aboriginal communities with expensive but basic **resorts** on **Mornington** and **Sweers** islands. Day-flights can be booked through Burketown's post office (see below).

Off-road drivers after wildlife might be tempted by superb **wetlands** on the western edge of the Cape York Peninsula, accessed from the Normanton–Karumba stretch off a 4WD-only, five-hundred-kilometre track which ultimately takes you to Chillagoe (see p.457). Detouring north from it, you'll find the coast thick with creeks, waterholes and animals. **Dorunda Station** (food, drink and limited fuel supplies; ☎07/4745 3477; units ⑤), about 180km up the road, is a working cattle property which arranges **hunting safaris** with cameras or .303s – targets are pigs, fish, birds and crocodiles. There's more of the same even further north at **Mitchell and Alice Rivers National Park**, via the Aboriginal community of Kowanyama. You'll need to take all supplies, an NPWS permit and permission from the community (contact Cairns NPWS on ☎07/4052 3096 for details).

Burketown and beyond

Set on the Albert River, **BURKETOWN** balances on the dusty frontier between grassland and the Gulf's thirty-kilometre-deep, unfriendly coastal flats. Styled Queensland's "Barramundi Capital" after the delicious sports fish, it has a huge road maintenance depot employing most of its 235 inhabitants. Despite lukewarm fame for providing background to Nevil Shute's *A Town Like Alice*, there's little beyond the historic but dodgy *Albert Hotel*, a store, a couple of **fuel pumps** and a post office which also acts as the **tourist information** office and agent for day-flights to the Wellesley Islands (☎07/4745 5111). The store runs a **campsite** but to engage in barra fishing, you'll need your own boat and fishing gear. To rent these, head for **Escott Lodge** (☎07/4748 5577; units ⑤), 16km west, where you can also go riding or mustering, or tour one of the Gulf's cattle stations, which eke out a precarious living. There's a **restaurant** and **bar** at the lodge but no store.

Onwards: The Hells Gate Track

The best road from Burketown heads south for about two hours to **Gregory Downs Hotel** and routes to Lawn Hill and Cloncurry. If you're serious about **fishing** and have a 4WD, however, head west from the Gregory Downs/Burketown road via **Tirranna Roadhouse** (food and fuel facilities) and the Aboriginal community at **Doomadgee**, to the **Hells Gate Roadhouse** (☎07/4745 8258), 50km from the Northern Territory. Fishing information and guided tours can be obtained from the Savannah Guides here, or you could try **Massacre Inlet**, reached from **Wollogorang Station** (☎08/8975 9944) just on the Territory border; they will supply you with a $12 fishing permit as well as camping, motel rooms, meals, beer and the last fuel before Borroloola. Giant anthills, pandanus-frilled waterholes and irregular tides are the rewards – and the area is stacked with wildlife, including **saltwater crocs**.

The road on from Hells Gate improves inside The Territory and once there you shouldn't have any trouble reaching Borroloola (see p.557), 266km down the track.

t r a v e l   d e t a i l s

Trains

Charleville to: Brisbane (2 weekly; 15hr 35min); Quilpie (2 weekly; 4hr 30min); Roma (2 weekly; 5hr); Toowoomba (2 weekly; 12hr).

Charters Towers to: Cloncurry (2 weekly; 11hr 30min); Hughenden (2 weekly; 5hr); Mount Isa (2 weekly; 20hr); Townsville (2 weekly; 2hr 30min).

Croydon to: Normanton (1 weekly; 5hr).

Emerald to: Barcaldine (2 weekly; 6hr); Longreach (2 weekly; 8hr); Rockhampton (2 weekly; 4hr 30min).

Longreach to: Barcaldine (2 weekly; 2hr); Emerald (2 weekly; 8hr); Rockhampton (2 weekly; 12hr 30min).

Mount Isa to: Charters Towers (2 weekly; 15hr 30min); Cloncurry (2 weekly; 4hr 15min); Hughenden (2 weekly; 11hr).

Mount Surprise to: Forsayth (2 weekly; 5hr).

Roma to: Brisbane (2 weekly; 10hr 20min); Charleville (2 weekly; 5hr 10min); Quilpie (2 weekly; 4hr 30min); Toowoomba (2 weekly; 11hr 40min).

Toowoomba to: Brisbane (2 weekly; 3hr 30min); Charleville (2 weekly; 12hr 30min); Quilpie (2 weekly; 18hr 15min); Roma (2 weekly; 6hr 40min).

Buses

Charleville to: Barcaldine (2 daily; 5hr 20min); Blackall (2 daily; 4hr 10min); Brisbane (3 daily; 10hr 40min); Cloncurry (2 daily; 13hr 30min); Longreach (2 daily; 6hr 30min); Mount Isa (2 daily; 15hr); Roma (3 daily; 3hr 40min); Toowoomba (3 daily; 8hr); Winton (2 daily; 9hr).

Charters Towers to: Cloncurry (3 daily; 8hr); Emerald (1 weekly; 6hr 30min); Hughenden (3 daily; 3hr); Mount Isa (3 daily; 10hr); Townsville (4 daily; 1hr 40min).

Emerald to: Anakie (3 weekly; 35min); Barcaldine (3 weekly; 3hr 40min); Charters Towers (1 weekly; 6hr 30min); Clermont (1 daily; 1hr 20min); Dingo (3 weekly; 1hr 35min); Longreach (3 weekly; 5hr 30min); Mackay (1 daily; 4hr 20min); Moranbah (1 daily; 2hr); Rockhampton (3 weekly; 3hr 30min); Springsure (2 weekly; 45min–1hr).

Longreach to: Anakie (3 weekly; 5hr); Barcaldine (2 daily; 1hr); Blackall (2 daily; 3hr 15min); Brisbane (2 daily; 16hr 10min); Charleville (2 daily; 6hr 30min); Cloncurry (2 daily; 6hr 30min); Dingo (3 weekly; 7hr 30min); Emerald (3 weekly; 5hr 30min); Mount Isa (2 daily; 7hr 50min); Rockhampton (3 weekly; 9hr 30min); Roma (2 daily; 10hr 25min); Toowoomba (2 daily; 14hr); Winton (2 daily; 2hr).

Mount Isa to: Barcaldine (2 daily; 9hr); Blackall (2 daily; 11hr 10min); Brisbane (2 daily; 25hr 20min); Camooweal (1 daily; 2hr 10min); Charleville (2 daily; 14hr 40min); Charters Towers (3 daily; 9hr 50min); Cloncurry (3 daily; 2hr 35min); Hughenden (3 daily; 7hr); Karumba (1 weekly; 7hr 10min); Longreach (2 daily; 8hr); Normanton (1 weekly; 6hr 10min); Roma (2 daily; 18hr 20min); Toowoomba (2 daily; 23hr); Townsville (3 daily; 12hr); Winton (2 daily; 6hr).

Roma to: Barcaldine (2 daily; 8hr); Blackall (2 daily; 7hr); Brisbane (2 daily; 7hr); Charleville (2 daily; 3hr 30min); Cloncurry (2 daily; 16hr 20min); Longreach (2 daily; 10hr); Mount Isa (2 daily; 18hr); Toowoomba (3 daily; 4hr 30min); Winton (2 daily; 12hr).

Toowoomba to: Barcaldine (2 daily; 13hr); Blackall (2 daily; 12hr); Brisbane (8 daily; 1hr 50min); Charleville (3 daily; 8hr); Cloncurry (2 daily; 21hr 30min); Coolangatta (2 daily; 3hr 40min); Kingaroy (1 daily except Fri; 3hr); Longreach (2 daily; 14hr 30min); Mount Isa (2 daily; 23hr); Rockhampton (2 daily; 12hr 45min); Roma (4 daily; 5hr); Surfers Paradise (2 daily; 3hr); Warwick (1 daily except Sun; 3hr); Winton (2 daily; 16hr 30min).

Winton to: Barcaldine (2 daily; 3hr); Blackall (2 daily; 5hr 15min); Brisbane (2 daily; 19hr 25min); Charleville (2 daily; 9hr 20min); Cloncurry (2 daily; 4hr 30min); Longreach (2 daily; 2hr); Mount Isa (2 daily; 6hr); Roma (2 daily; 12hr 25min); Toowoomba (2 daily; 17hr).

Flights

Air Mount Isa (☎07/4743 2844) flies Wed morning on a mail run to Lorraine, Gregory Downs, Hells Gate Roadhouse, Lawn Hill and Burketown.

North Western Air (☎07/4743 7720) and Air Mount Isa also have three- and five-seater charter planes.

Charleville to: Brisbane (1 daily; 2hr).

Emerald to: Brisbane (2 daily; 2hr); Cairns (1–2 daily; 6hr 40min); Mackay (5 weekly; 5hr); Maroochydore (1 daily; 4hr 35min); Rockhampton (1–2 daily except Sun; 4hr); Townsville (1 daily except Sat; 4hr).

Longreach to: Brisbane (1 daily; 2hr 25min); Roma (5 weekly; 2hr).

Mount Isa to: Brisbane (1–2 daily; 2hr 15min); Burketown (1 weekly; 1hr 35min); Cairns (1–2 daily; 5hr 20min); Mackay (1 daily except Sun; 8hr); Mornington Island (5 weekly; 1hr 50min); Rockhampton (1–2 daily; 4hr); Townsville (1–3 daily; 2hr).

Roma to: Brisbane (1–2 daily; 1hr 10min); Longreach (4 weekly; 2hr).

Winton to: Townsville (2 weekly; 1hr 25min).`

CHAPTER SIX

NORTHERN TERRITORY

Far in the north of Australia lies a little-known land, a vast half-finished sort of region, wherein Nature has been apparently practising how to make better places. This is the Northern Territory of South Australia . . . The decline and fall of the British Empire will date from the day that Britannia starts to monkey with the Northern Territory.

A.B. ("Banjo") Paterson, 1898

This rather ominous prophecy by the bush balladeer "Banjo" Paterson, author of "Waltzing Matilda", is still the way many Australians view the frontier lands of the **Northern Territory**, usually known as "The Territory", or simply "NT". Even the name conjures up a distant, untamed province and, to an extent, this is so: just over one percent of Australians (170,000) live in an area covering nearly twenty percent of the continent. Until recently this tiny population and lack of economic autonomy explained why The Territory never achieved full statehood, but by the new millennium the NT will have become the **seventh Australian state** (with a few strings still held by the federal government). Not all Australians are sure that the Territory's entrenched "cowboy" government is ready for this responsibility. Incidents like the failed euthanasia bill (quickly quashed by Canberra) and extremes like mandatory sentencing (a fortnight in jail for a first offence, two months for a second, and so on) gives southern liberals the impression that Territorian necks are redder than Ayers Rock at sunset.

Territorians relish this tough, maverick image, as well as the extremes of climate, distance and isolation that mould their temperaments. In this utmost corner of the country, drifters get washed up, fugitives cower and failed entrepreneurs pursue another abortive venture or become politicians. That great Australian institution of the "character" is in his element here, propping up the bars and bolstering the mythology of The Territory's recent lawless frontier history in what Xavier Herbert once described as the "Land of Ratbags". His classic 1938 novel, *Capricornia*, remains a scathing allegorical saga of the early Territorian years, based on Herbert's experience in 1930s Darwin.

Within The Territory's boundaries there's evidence of the most recent colonial presence set among the oldest-occupied Aboriginal sites in Australia. **Darwin**, The Territory's capital, is a prospering tropical town – a year-round temperature in the low thirties compelling a laid-back lifestyle. Travellers the world over flock here to explore the **Top End** (as tropical NT is known), primarily **Kakadu National Park**'s prolific wildlife and the Aboriginal art sites. Adjacent **Arnhemland**, to the east, is Aboriginal Land, too – and out of bounds to casual visitors, although a few tours are now beginning to visit this never-colonized wilderness of scattered communities. Heading south, you arrive at **Katherine**, where nearby gorges within the **Nitmiluk National Park** are the town's principal attraction. At Katherine, the **Victoria Highway** heads west, past the Gregory National Park to Western Australia, while to the south, just beyond the thermal resort of **Mataranka**, a road winds east along the palm-fringed Roper River to the Gulf Country. Here, **Borroloola**, a briefly thriving and lawless outpost, once on the Gulf stock route from northern Queensland, has since been bypassed into oblivion.

By the time you reach **Tennant Creek** you're out of the interminable light woodland and passing pastoral tablelands on the way to the central deserts surrounding **Alice**

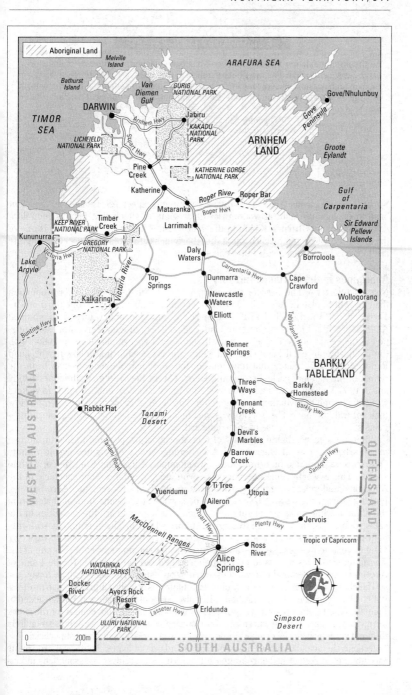

Aboriginal Land

ARAFURA SEA

Melville Island

Bathurst Island

Van Diemen Gulf

GURIG NATIONAL PARK

DARWIN

Gove/Nhulunbuy

Gove Peninsula

TIMOR SEA

Jabiru

Arnhem Hwy

KAKADU NATIONAL PARK

ARNHEM LAND

Groote Eylandt

LICHFIELD NATIONAL PARK

Stuart Hwy

Pine Creek

KATHERINE GORGE NATIONAL PARK

Gulf of Carpentaria

Katherine

Roper River

Roper Bar

Sir Edward Pellew Islands

Mataranka

Roper Hwy

KEEP RIVER NATIONAL PARK

Timber Creek

Larrimah

Kununurra

Victoria Hwy

GREGORY NATIONAL PARK

Daly Waters

Borroloola

Lake Argyle

Victoria River

Dunmarra

Carpentaria Hwy

Cape Crawford

Top Springs

Newcastle Waters

Wollogorang

Kalkaringi

Elliott

Buntine Hwy

Renner Springs

Tablelands Hwy

BARKLY TABLELAND

WESTERN AUSTRALIA

Three Ways

Barkly Homestead

Rabbit Flat

Tanami Desert

Tennant Creek

Barkly Hwy

Devil's Marbles

QUEENSLAND

Barrow Creek

Tanami Road

Sandover Hwy

Yuendumu

Ti Tree

Utopia

Aileron

Plenty Hwy

Jervois

MacDonnell Ranges

Stuart Hwy

Tropic of Capricorn

WATARRKA NATIONAL PARKS

Ross River

Alice Springs

Docker River

Ayers Rock Resort

Lasseter Hwy

Erldunda

Simpson Desert

N

ULURU NATIONAL PARK

0   200m

SOUTH AUSTRALIA

ACCOMMODATION PRICES

All the accommodation listed in this book has been categorized into one of eight price bands, as set out below. The rates quoted represent the cheapest available double or twin room in high season – except for category ①, which indicates per person rates for a dorm bed, and the categories given for units, cabins and vans, which represent the daily charge for the whole unit.

① Under $18	⑤ $61–74
② $19–30	⑥ $75–94
③ $31–45	⑦ $95–124
④ $46–60	⑧ $125 upwards

For more accommodation details, see pp.41-43.

Springs. By no means the dusty Outback town many expect, Alice makes an excellent base to explore the natural wonders of the region, of which that famous monolith, **Ayers Rock** – or **Uluru** – 450km to the southwest, is but one of many. This is one of the finest areas to begin to learn about the Aborigines of the western desert, among the last to come into contact with European settlers.

Aborigines in the Northern Territory

Nearly a quarter of The Territory's inhabitants are Aborigines, a far higher proportion than anywhere else in Australia. Most modern maps show that over one-third of The Territory is "Aboriginal Land", commercially unviable and returned to nominal Aboriginal control following lengthy land claims. This uniquely Territorian demography is the result of the formerly sympathetic federal government's co-operation with the politically powerful Land Councils within the NT, established following the Land Rights Act of 1976. Since that time, one of the most notable victories has been the return of the national park surrounding Uluru (Ayers Rock) to its traditional custodians in 1986. Excepting the national parks, Aboriginal lands are out of bounds to visitors without a permit or invitation, although some roads which cross them are exempt. How their lot will fare once The Territory government – long hostile to Aboriginal rights – gains statehood, is the cause of some concern.

While the overwhelming majority of non-Aboriginal people tend to live in the two major urban centres of Darwin and Alice Springs, most Aborigines live in remote Outback communities, or **outstations**, in self-imposed isolation from modern white society. This is worth remembering before you judge the depressing spectacle of the Aboriginal underclass staggering around Katherine, Tennant Creek and Alice Springs. Estranged from their own "dry" communities, while at the same time alienated from the affluent white society that surrounds them, these people are the casualties of the catastrophic clash of white and Aboriginal culture which, in The Territory, is still within living memory. As Bill Harney, the first ranger at Ayers Rock, observed 35 years ago: "The traveller only sees the ones on the roadway, for should he want to visit one of the Aboriginal Reserves he has to go through a wall of red tape. Thus is the best side of Aboriginal life hidden and the worst exposed to our view." The same is true today.

The chasm between the two vastly different cultures is actually far greater than most visitors realize. The failure of assimilation – the naive policy of the 1950s and 1960s – added to mutual cultural (rather than racial) ignorance makes any meaningful contact for the short-term visitor unlikely. Weary suspicion of patronizing white curiosity, as well as an entirely different strategy in social dealings, render most exchanges awkward and superficial.

Despite the scandal of the "Third World" standards of living, Aboriginal **culture** is thriving. Political clout has encouraged self-determination and a renaissance of cultural pride in the face of overwhelming white control has enabled a self-expression in lifestyle, spirituality and – most obviously to the visitor – arts, crafts and tours. Gradually, progressive outstations are inviting responsible tour operators to visit their settlements, or else are setting up their own operations, so allowing you to experience something of their former way of life – for it must be remembered that even in The Territory no Aborigines live in or off the bush as they once did. Nevertheless, for those interested in getting to the heart of the enigmatic Australian wilderness, the Northern Territory personifies the remote and mythologized Outback, offering enriching and memorable travel: an introduction to a land that has sustained a fascinating and sophisticated culture for at least sixty thousand years.

DARWIN AND THE TOP END

Darwin, The Territory's capital, lies midway along Australia's convoluted northern coast. Most tourists end up spending no more time here than it takes to visit nearby **Kakadu** and **Litchfield national parks**, continue their Australian circuit or fly on to Indonesia. Until recently the city had little appeal to short-term visitors, but things have changed and Darwin is beginning to mature into a worthwhile destination in itself.

Darwin and around

Establishing a European settlement on Australia's remote northern shores was never going to be easy. It took four abortive attempts over a period of 45 years before **DARWIN** (originally called Palmerston) was surveyed in 1869 by the new South Australian state keen to exploit its recently acquired "northern territory". The early colonists' aim was to pre-empt foreign occupation and create a trading post, a "new Singapore", for the British Empire.

Things got off to a good start with the arrival in 1872 of the **Overland Telegraph Line** (OTL), following the route pioneered by explorer **John McDouall Stuart** in 1862, that finally linked Australia with the rest of the world. **Gold** was discovered at Pine Creek while pylons were being erected for the OTL, prompting the inevitable goldrush, and the construction of a southbound railway. After the goldrush subsided, a cyclone flattened the depressed town in 1897, but by 1911, when Darwin adopted its present name, the rough-and-ready frontier outpost had grown into a small government centre, servicing the mines and properties of the Top End. In 1942, just five years after a second cyclone had razed the town, repeated **Japanese air raids** destroyed Darwin yet again – this time at a human cost of hundreds of lives (a fact concealed for years from the jittery nation). The fear of invasion, and an urgent need to get troops to the war zone, led to the swift construction of the Stuart Highway, the first reliable land link between Darwin and the rest of the country.

Three decades of guarded postwar prosperity followed until Christmas Day, 1974, when **Cyclone Tracy** devastated Darwin. For many residents this trauma was the last straw and having been evacuated they never returned. Indeed, the myth of Darwinian resilience is just that: the town has always accommodated a transient, easy-going population, happy to "give it a go" for a couple of years and then move on. The surrounding land is agriculturally unviable and Top End beef (an industry hampered by disease-eradication programmes and foreign competition) is among the poorest in Australia; most beef is exported as live cattle to Asia.

But since the mid-Nineties Darwin has been making a concerted effort to take itself seriously as Australia's commercial "gateway" into Asia. With the help of the tourist boom, kicked off by Kakadu's exposure in the film *Crocodile Dundee*, as well as some

TOP END WEATHER

There is a certain amount of misunderstanding about the tropical climate of the Top End, usually summed up as the hot and humid "Dry" and the hotter and very humid "Wet". Give or take a couple of weeks either way, this is the pattern: the **Dry** begins in April when rains stop and humidity decreases – although this always remains high in the tropics, whatever the season. It may take a couple of months for vehicular access to be restored to all far-flung tracks, but the bush never looks greener, while engorged waterfalls pound the base of the escarpments. From now until October skies are generally cloud-free with daily temperatures reliably peaking in the low thirties, though August nights might cool down to 10°C – sheer agony for seasoned Top Enders but bliss for unacclimatized tourists.

From October until the end of the year temperatures and humidity begin to rise – the dreaded **Build Up**. Clouds accumulate to discharge brief showers, and it's a time of year when the weak-willed or insufficiently drunk can go "troppo" as the unbearable tensions of heat and humidity push them over the edge. Around November promising storms can still be frustratingly dry but often give rise to spectacular lightning shows; Darwin is the world's most lightning-prone city. While rain showers become longer and more frequent towards Christmas – the onset of the **Wet** – access on sealed roads is rarely a problem.

Only when the actual **monsoon** commences at the turn of the year do the daily afternoon storms quickly rejuvenate and then saturate the land. This daily cycle lasts for at least three months and is much more tolerable than you might expect, with a daily thunderous downpour cooling things off from the mid- to the low-thirties. Along with Queensland's Cape York, Darwin's proximity to the equator gives it a true monsoon. Two hundred kilometres south the rains are much less heavy though a Wet is experienced along the coast as far southwest as Derby, WA and Townsville on the north Queensland coast.

Cyclones, sometimes just a week apart, occur most commonly at either end of the Wet and can dump 30cm of rain in as many hours, with winds of 100kph and gusts twice that speed. Frequent updates on the erratic path and intensity of these tropical depressions are given on national and state radio, so that most people are fully prepared if and when the storm actually hits. Some fizzle out or head back out to sea; others can intensify and zigzag across the land, as nearly every community between Exmouth, WA (1996) and Darwin (1974) has found to its cost.

thoughtful refurbishments in Mitchell Street and the Mall, Darwin has shaken off the bland feel of a company town armoured against the climate. A spate of cool new outdoor eateries now allow you to appreciate the tropical ambience so that where once the city centre had all the life of a weekend car park, now it can be as lively as any other Australian capital. There's even talk of the rail line being extended up from Alice and permission has been given to buy up the land to lay the tracks.

Day-trips from Darwin include the popular national parks, Kakadu and Litchfield (see pp.534–546) as well as the Aboriginal-owned Bathurst and Melville islands (see p.533), which are a thirty-minute flight from town. They are Australia's largest islands after Tasmania and are well worth more than just a flying visit, if you can afford it. Also worth a visit are Crocodylus Park (see p.528) and the Territory Wildlife Park (see p.544).

Arrival and information

All flights arrive at **Darwin Airport**, 12km northeast of the city centre. A **shuttle bus** service (☎08/8981 5066 or free call ☎1800/808 507; $6) meets international flights and drops you off at all major hotels or delivers you to the central **Transit Centre** behind

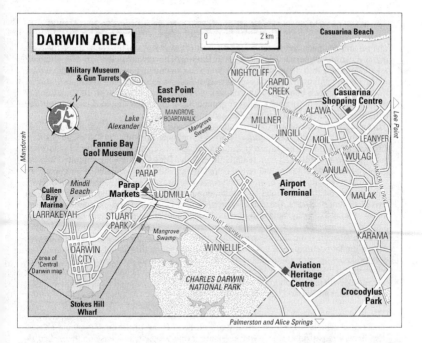

0   2 km

Casuarina Beach

Military Museum
& Gun Turrets

NIGHTCLIFF

East Point
Reserve

RAPID
CREEK

Casuarina
Shopping Centre

MANGROVE
BOARDWALK

TROWER ROAD

ALAWA

Lake
Alexander

Mangrove
Swamp

MILLNER

JINGILI

MOIL

LEANYER

N

Mandorah

Fannie Bay
Gaol Museum

BAGOT ROAD

LEE POINT ROAD

WULAGI

MCMILLANS ROAD

PARAP

ANULA

Mindil
Beach

Parap
Markets

Airport
Terminal

MALAK

Cullen
Bay
Marina

LUDMILLA

LARRAKEYAH

STUART
PARK

STUART HIGHWAY

KARAMA

area of
'Central
Darwin map

DARWIN
CITY

Mangrove
Swamp

WINNELLIE

Stokes Hill
Wharf

CHARLES DARWIN
NATIONAL PARK

Aviation
Heritage
Centre

Crocodylus
Park

Lee Point

VANDERLIN DRIVE

Palmerston and Alice Springs ▽

69 Mitchell St; a **taxi** (☎13 1008) to town from the airport costs about $14. Given the proximity of Indonesia, Darwin is the cheapest place from which to leave Australian soil (see "Listings", p.531, for details).

On the other hand, Darwin is a long way from anywhere in Australia – the bus journey from Cairns takes a gruelling day and a half, including changes, and coming direct from Sydney, Melbourne or Perth, you'd do much better to fly. **Interstate buses** arrive behind the Transit Centre, where you can make reservations for onward journeys.

Five minutes' walk up Mitchell Street, the **Darwin Regional Tourism Association** (daily 9am–5pm; ☎08/8989 4300; *drtainfo@ozemail.com.au*) is the official tourist information outlet and has a **Parks and Wildlife Commission (P&WC)** desk with plenty of material on national parks throughout NT. It's also worth noting that local rental cars booked through the DRTA come with unlimited kilometres (see box overleaf). All around town you'll find several other independent tourist information offices, all competing for their slice of the cake; shop around before you shell out a couple of hundred dollars on a tour. The free booklets *This Week In Darwin* and *Darwin and the Top End Today*, which can be picked up all around town, are mostly rose-tinted advertorials, but are handy for **maps**, including bus routes (see below). A five-hundred-metre radius around Smith Street Mall encompasses Darwin's city centre, catering for most of your needs; there are few attractions in the sea of suburbs spreading towards the north and the east.

City transport

The city's inexpensive **bus service** (maximum fare $2 for all three zones; pay the driver) can deliver you to most corners of Darwin. Services operate daily from around 7am to 8pm, with some routes running until after 11pm on Friday and Saturday.

RENTING AND BUYING A VEHICLE: SOME TIPS

The hit-and-run pace and variable guide quality of many Kakadu tours has made the renting of a car or campervan big business in Darwin. The advantages of **driving yourself** are obvious and with a group of three or four you can end up paying less than with a tour. At the bottom end of the trade, a car can cost as little as $25 a day plus a typical surcharge rate of 25¢ for each kilometre. Alternatively you can pay up to $35 with 100 free kilometres – handy for a day round town – or around $70 a day with unlimited kilometres. The older the cars the company offers, the lower their charges.

Seemingly **special deals** for the standard Kakadu/Litchfield run (eg $200 for three days with 1000km free) are commonly offered, but note that this trip will easily clock up 1200km and clued-in operators price accordingly. As mentioned earlier, it's an open secret in the trade that all cars booked though the DRTA come with unlimited kilometres, no matter what the actual rental company may be charging itself. It's a good offer which most operators stick to and which could work only in a small town such as Darwin.

It's important to understand the limitations of your **insurance** and **where you can drive** conventional cars. Basically, with one or two clearly defined exceptions, you cannot take your $25-a-day sedan on unsealed roads, and any underbody, roof, windscreen and water damage is down to you. Your **insurance obligations** are something that not all companies spell out, but be assured that if you damage their car you end up paying. An additional premium of a few dollars a day can reduce this liability to a few hundred dollars. Local operators know too well that European drivers are unused to the vagaries of driving on cambered dirt roads and that sliding off into the bushes or hitting a tree are common accidents. If you get tempted to take to the dirt, remember that even with the windows shut and air-con on recycle, fine dust will leave a clear message of where you've been.

Bear in mind, though, that whatever you drive and whatever you pay in surcharges, most rental vehicles – even 4WDs – are **uninsured off the bitumen**. If you have an accident here, you pay dearly. It's a way of ensuring that people take it easy on the dirt roads or don't leave the highway at all.

Wherever you go from Darwin **distances** are long. The Territory has Australia's highest death rate on the roads: a combination of drunkenness, fatigue and the dangers of wandering stock and wild animals. New laws and speed traps are desperately trying to reduce this, but avoid trying to pack in a Katherine and Kakadu run in a couple of days, take it easy if driving top-heavy 4WDs on dirt roads and avoid driving at night in rural areas.

Self-contained **campervan** rentals have boomed across Australia over the last few years and in Darwin they are available from $90 a day with unlimited kilometres, although most companies specify a few days minimum rental. The smallest models can get crowded with more than two people, but the savings in accommodation and the independence offered make them a great way to see the parks or even the whole country. Like ordinary cars, campervans must stick to sealed roads unless you opt for the 4WD models.

Many visitors assume a **4WD** will allow them to really see Kakadu but it's not essential. Built to take a beating, a Toyota Land Cruiser will cost around $150 a day and use twice as much fuel as an ordinary car, although the only road in Kakadu where you need a 4WD is the Jim Jim/Twin Falls track (see p.540), which involves crossing Jim Jim Creek. Several vehicles have been lost here over the years and even in a "four-wheeler" some companies may still exclude this track so make sure you ask.

If you're prepared to leave Twin Falls off your itinerary, it's a bit cheaper (if less fun) to rent a so-called **off-road vehicle**, such as the chunky 2WD twin-cab utes supplied by Territory Thrifty Rental Cars. At around $90 per day unlimited you can drive it all around the park without risking the penalty of damaging a flimsy modern town car.

If you're looking to **buy a vehicle**, hostel notice boards are an excellent starting-point, or check out the semi-squatted lot on Mitchell Street behind the Night Markets where many prospective sellers park up.

"Multirider" tickets are also available, giving an extra twenty percent value on buying a $10 or $20 ticket. The **bus terminal** (☎08/8924 7666) is on Harry Chan Avenue, at the bottom of Cavenagh Street, though there's also a major interchange in the shopping centre at Casuarina, in the northern suburbs. Buses leave the city for the suburbs along Cavenagh Street and come back in along Mitchell and Smith streets. They head out as far as Palmerston, Howard Springs and, on weekdays, Humpty Doo, 50km from town on the Kakadu road.

Most hostels and some hotels rent out **bicycles** for $15 a day. Although Darwin is flat, it's also hot and humid, so East Point Reserve, 8km from the centre, is about as far as you'd want to ride for fun. Along Mitchell and Smith streets, a few local **car rental** outfits do battle, with prices starting at around $25 a day, plus a kilometre fee (see box opposite and "Listings", p.531, for more). **Taxis** work out at about a dollar a kilometre and there are plenty cruising around: either hail one on the street or give them a call on ☎13 1008.

Accommodation

Darwin has plenty of **accommodation**, from luxury hotels to hostels galore, and most of it is conveniently central. During the wet season (Jan–March) prices in the upmarket establishments can take a dive, with half-price weekend packages frequently available. In the hostels it seems the price has settled at around $15 a bed, but brief price wars can flare up at any time of the year.

Hotels, motels and apartments

Most **hotels** and **motels** are right in the city centre, with the more prestigious examples found along the Esplanade offering views of the bay. If you're looking for self-catering accommodation, there are several **apartment-hotels** in the centre, but for the most part they're further out.

Asti Motel, 7 Packard Place (☎08/8981 8200, fax 8981 8038). Exemplary large motel with spa, restaurant and pool. ⑥.

Atrium Novotel, 100 Esplanade (☎08/8941 0755, fax 8981 9025). Among the best value of the upmarket hotels along the Esplanade with a foliage-draped atrium and all the comforts and service you'd expect as well as a sea view. ⑧.

Capricornia Motel, 44 East Point Rd (☎08/8981 4055). Small motel out near Fannie Bay, 4km from the centre (bus #4 or #6), with pool and shared cooking facilities. ④.

City Gardens Apartments, 93 Woods St (☎08/8941 2888, fax 8981 2934). Centrally located family units in a tropical setting. Two minutes' walk from Frogshollow Park, five minutes from town. ⑧.

Darwin Central Hotel, Knuckley St (☎08/8944 9000, fax 8944 9100). New All Seasons luxury hotel right by the Mall with spacious rooms and several restaurants and bars. ⑧.

Hotel Darwin, 10 Herbert St (☎08/8981 9211, fax 8981 9575). One of the city's oldest intact buildings, retaining vestiges of colonial charm and an old-fashioned, solid feel. A few good-value rooms, alongside more expensive options. ⑥.

Poinciana Inn, 84 Mitchell St (☎08/8981 8111, fax 8941 2440). Three-star motel right on the grassy Esplanade. ⑤.

Seabreeze Motel, 60 East Point Rd (☎08/8981 8433). Good-value motel in Fannie Bay, 4km from the centre but close to yacht club, museum and beaches. ⑤.

Value Inn, 50 Mitchell St (☎08/8981 4733, fax 8981 4730). Set price, no-frills motel with small ensuite rooms (TV, air-con and fridge) that sleep up to three – a real squeeze but a good deal and there's a pool too. ⑤.

Hostels

The situation for backpackers' **hostels** in Darwin has improved in recent years with the opening of the *YHA* and the *Nomad Backpackers* next door to each other and introducing "East Coast" standards to the Top End. Note that some establishments offer a free pick-up on the airport shuttle if you book with them in advance and also that some places charge a dollar or two extra for beds in air-conditioned rooms or run the air conditioning only at night.

Banyan View Lodge, 119 Mitchell St (☎08/8981 8644, fax 8981 6104). Well-kept twin rooms with fans and fridge and big recreational rooms. Rooms ③, dorms ①.

CWA Hostel, 3 Packard Place (☎08/8941 1536, fax 8941 3305). Not a backpackers' place but a small, shady house in its own grounds for women, couples and families only. Rooms ③, dorms ①.

Darwin City Lodge, 151 Mitchell St (☎ & fax 08/8941 1295). Friendly, family-run, comfortably converted house (with a less attractive annexe) featuring a pool, tour-booking service and lifts uptown. Rooms ③, dorms ①.

Elke's, 112 Mitchell St (☎08/8981 8399, fax 8981 2834). Well-refurbished old house at the quiet end of Mitchell St, with a shady pool and free pick-ups: one of Darwin's better options. Rooms ③, dorms ①.

Fawlty Towers, 88 Mitchell St (☎08/8941 2161, fax 8941 3660). Not the greatest building, but a friendly place with air-con rooms and a pool. Rooms ③, dorms ①.

Frogshollow Backpackers, 27 Lindsay St (☎08/8941 2600, fax 8941 0758). Popular, attractive, tropical building opposite a large park. Still suffers from ill-conceived partitioning making sixteen-bed mixed dorms. Rooms ③, dorms ①.

Gecko Lodge, 146 Mitchell St (☎08/8981 5569, fax 8981 2757). At the far end of Mitchell St, a small, friendly hostel with a small pool, and close to Mindil Beach. Free pick-ups and nightly lifts uptown. Rooms ③, dorms ①.

Globetrotters, 97 Mitchell St (☎08/8981 5385, fax 8981 9096). Ex-motel with four-bed rooms with air-con plus a pool and a bar with live bands. Can't quite shake the daggy feel of a converted motel though. Rooms ③, dorms ①.

Melaleuka Lodge, 52 Mitchell St (☎08/8941 3395, fax 8941 3368). Popular and well-equipped warren of rooms and courtyards right opposite the Transit Centre. Rooms ③, dorms ①.

Nomad Backpackers, 69 Mitchell St (☎08/8949 9772). The old YHA half knocked down and cleverly redesigned with airy decks to eat, chat or sunbake by the pool. Rooms ③, four-share max dorms ①.

YHA, 69a Mitchell St (☎08/8981 3995, fax 8981 6674). Recently refurbished modern, clean and thoughtfully designed hostel resort right by the Transit Centre. Breezy dining area overlooks the pool while rooms are four-share max ①.

Camping and caravan parks

The following **camping** and **caravan parks** are all along the Stuart Highway in Winnellie, between 7km and 14km from the centre. Comments by visitors at the DRTA have not been kind to Darwin's caravan parks and Winnellie itself is a rather godforsaken light-industrial suburb, lying along the southern edge of the airport. Buses #5 and #8 run here from the central bus terminal. From the airport it's only a five-minute taxi ride.

Leprechaun Caravan Park, Airport Gates, Stuart Highway (☎08/8984 3400). Behind a motel of the same name and closest to Darwin, this has a pool and shady tent sites. On-site vans ②.

Overlander Caravan Park, corner of Stuart Highway and McMillans Rd, Berrimah (☎08/8984 3025). Plenty of shade and lawns and close to shops. On-site vans ③.

Shady Glen Caravan Park, corner of Farrell Crescent and Stuart Highway (☎08/8984 3330). Pool and kiosk with tent sites. On-site vans ②.

The City

Present-day Darwin projects north from the end of a stubby peninsula where a settlement was originally established in 1869 on the lands of the Larrakeyah Aborigines. Over the years, the suburbs have spread across the flat, mangrove-fringed headland, but for the visitor most of the points of interest lie between the city and East Point, 8km to the north. Tropical vegetation apart, it's by no means a good-looking city:

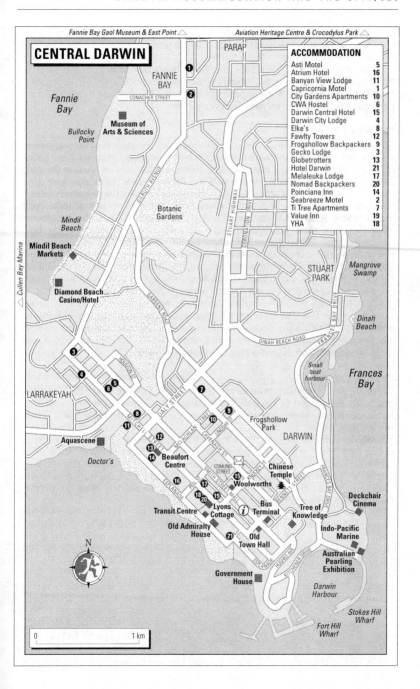

Fannie Bay Gaol Museum & East Point △   Aviation Heritage Centre & Crocodylus Park △

CENTRAL DARWIN

PARAP

FANNIE BAY

CONACHER STREET

Fannie Bay

Museum of Arts & Sciences

Bullocky Point

Botanic Gardens

Mindil Beach

STUART HIGHWAY

CORRIGATION DRIVE

STUART PARK

Mangrove Swamp

Mindil Beach Markets

Cullen Bay Marina △

Diamond Beach Casino/Hotel

GARDEN ROAD

DINAH BEACH ROAD

FRANCES BAY DRIVE

Dinah Beach

Small boat harbour

Frances Bay

LARRAKEYAH

DALY STREET

MITCHELL STREET

Aquascene

Doctor's

MCLACHLAN STREET

CAVENAGH ST

LINDSAY ST

Frogshollow Park

DARWIN

MCMINN ST

Beaufort Centre

THE MALL

SMITH STREET

EDMUND STREET

KNUCKEY ST

BENNETT STREET

FRANCES BAY DRIVE

Woolworths

Chinese Temple

Deckchair Cinema

ESPLANADE

PEEL STREET

Transit Centre

Lyons Cottage

Bus Terminal

Tree of Knowledge

Indo-Pacific Marine

Old Admiralty House

Old Town Hall

HUGHES AVE

KITCHENER DRIVE

Australian Pearling Exhibition

Government House

Darwin Harbour

Stokes Hill Wharf

Fort Hill Wharf

N

0   1 km

ACCOMMODATION	
Asti Motel	5
Atrium Hotel	16
Banyan View Lodge	11
Capricornia Motel	1
City Gardens Apartments	10
CWA Hostel	6
Darwin Central Hotel	15
Darwin City Lodge	4
Elke's	8
Fawlty Towers	12
Frogshollow Backpackers	9
Gecko Lodge	3
Globetrotters	13
Hotel Darwin	21
Melaleuka Lodge	17
Nomad Backpackers	20
Poinciana Inn	14
Seabreeze Motel	2
Ti Tree Apartments	7
Value Inn	19
YHA	18

huge tides create a warm, sludge-filled sea devoid of waves, while repeated destruction from cyclones, air raids and termites has left any surviving colonial architecture discreet and intermittent.

Short of renting a car or a bike, the **Tour Tub** (daily 9am–4pm; day-ticket $18; ☎08/8981 5233) is a fun way to see most of the places detailed below. Departing on the hour from Smith Street Mall, opposite Woolworth's, the minibus trundles along its route allowing you to hop on and off as you please.

The Wharf Precinct

Slow but sure development is refashioning the old wharves and jetty at the southern end of town into a thriving new tourist precinct. *Christo's* seafood restaurant (see "Eating", p.529) set the ball rolling a few years ago by moving into the old shed at the end of **Stokes Hill Wharf** and the eyesore that was the old power station has been demolished. Souvenir shops and alfresco cafés have sprung up along the pier which comes to life on Sunday evenings. Well worth a look is the live coral display at **Indo-Pacific Marine** (daily: April–Oct 10am–5pm; Nov–March 9am–1pm; $12). In the right frame of mind, you could spend hours observing these marine environments, and the regular informative talks will set you straight about corals – the Timor Sea north of Darwin is one of the world's richest and most diverse coral environments, obscured by an over-abundance of tidal silt. In the same building, the **Australian Pearling Exhibition** (Mon–Fri 10am–5pm, Sat & Sun 10am–5.30pm; $7) is a similarly imaginative display, entertainingly describing Darwin's part in northern Australia's pearling exploits.

Round the other side of the harbour, a stairway up the cliff just past the Oil Storage Tunnels (on the Tour Tub itinerary, but about as interesting as they sound) leads up to a viewing point and to **Government House**, built in 1883 after the original residence was devoured by white ants. Rarely open to the public, it's nevertheless a good example of an elegant, though much restored, tropical building.

The City Centre

There are more old buildings on nearby Smith Street. The **Old Town Hall** (1883) was practically demolished by Cyclone Tracy, but its ruins occasionally host outdoor performances by the theatre group based in the stone building, **Brown's Mart**, opposite. In the park behind Brown's Mart is a huge banyan tree known as the **Tree of Knowledge**, while nearby stands the ornate **Chinese Temple** (Mon–Fri 8am–4pm, Sat & Sun 8am–3pm) on Woods Street, near the corner of Bennett Street. Another post-cyclone restoration, using the altar and statues from the 1887 original, this still serves Darwin's Chinese population – considerably diminished since the early days of white settlement, when Chinese labourers were responsible for building virtually everything, including the former railway down to Pine Creek.

From the temple take a walk through the city's commercial heart: the restyled Smith Street Mall or known just as the **Mall** these days. The new look was at the cost of a few trees but there's a **walk-through fountain** which tempts passers-by with a quick plunge and your willpower will be much depleted after a good session at the **Hotel Victoria**. As the erstwhile *Vic*, it was once Darwin's answer to a Wild West saloon and some clients are still having trouble adjusting to the city's pub-gentrification programme. All along and off the Mall several art galleries and gift shops entice you to buy Aboriginal crafts or Australiana. From here, a left turn down Knuckey Street leads to the Esplanade, where two more buildings await inspection. On the left corner is the former **Admiralty House** (Mon–Sat 10am–5pm; free), a tropical-style house elevated on stilts which has survived cyclones and air raids. Opposite, **Lyons Cottage** (daily 10am–5pm; free), a stone bungalow, also dates from the 1920s, with displays of early Territorian history and the Overland Telegraph Line (OTL) in particular. For a diversion step round to the **Mitchell Street Tourist Precinct**. Formerly a backpackers' ghetto it has been redefined with the help of a few outdoor bars and cafés, night markets and occasional entertainment into somewhere to linger rather than loiter.

A pleasant walk along the lawns of the **Esplanade** leads to Daly Street, which marks the very end of the Stuart Highway. From here it's a straight 1500-kilometre run to Alice Springs with only about half a dozen traffic lights on the way. Otherwise, a left turn down Doctor's Gully leads to the ever-popular **Aquascene** (call ☎08/8981 7837 for tide-dependent opening hours; $5), where at high tide scores of catfish, mullet and metre-long milkfish come in to be hand-fed on stale bread (supplied free).

Cullen Bay Marina and the Fannie Bay museums

Walking north down the full length of Smith Street will bring you to a small roundabout and a sign leading down to **Cullen Bay Marina**. Like most marina's around the world there's not much to do here except observe "yachties" fiddling with their boats, envy those who can afford to live here and enjoy a waterside meal or a drink. Apart from taking one of the harbour cruises or the jet shuttle over the harbour to Mandurah's deserted beaches (☎08/8981 7600) that about sums up Cullen Bay, but it's well worth at least one visit just to mingle in the reflected light of the sails and deliberate on your dream vessel.

From the centre it's a two-kilometre walk north to the **Botanic Gardens** (daily 7am–7pm; free), Darwin's main park, housing a large collection of palms as well as a separate Plant Display House (daily 7.30am–4pm). A further kilometre north brings you to the **Museum of Arts and Sciences** (Mon–Fri 9am–5pm, Sat & Sun 10am–5pm; free) on Conacher Street, overlooking Fannie Bay. An excellent museum and art gallery, it's particularly notable for its Southeast Asian perspective, in pleasing contrast to the usual focus on recent white achievements. With an absorbing display of Aboriginal art by the Tiwi people of Bathurst and Melville islands as well as Top End bark paintings and the familiar pointillist style of the Central deserts, there's just enough here to keep your attention without seeing dots yourself. Elsewhere the stuffed remains of "Sweetheart", a five-metre-long rogue crocodile with a taste for outboard engines, are particularly alarming, while the massive boat shed is a mariners' paradise, with boats as diverse as pearling luggers, Indonesian *praus*, Polynesian outriggers and the simplest of bark canoes.

There's also an imaginatively designed exhibition commemorating Darwin's destruction by **Cyclone Tracy**. By 3am on Christmas Day, 1974 – a day that most Darwinians who lived through the cyclone would like to forget – the worst was thought to be over as winds that had raged since midnight began to abate. Instead, the becalmed eye of the storm was passing over the part-ruined city, only to return with even greater fury from the opposite direction. Lampposts were bent flat along the ground, houses were ripped from their piers, and at the Yacht Club mangled remains of boats filled the car park. Mercifully, a low tide meant that only 66 people lost their lives, but Tracy marked the end of old Darwin, psychologically as well as architecturally.

Fannie Bay Gaol Museum (daily 10am–5pm; free; bus #4 or #6), further north along the bay, 5km from the city centre, served as Darwin's prison for nearly a hundred years until 1979. Displayed alongside the grim prisoners' quarters is an old train, a reminder of the thorny issue of Darwin's rail link with the rest of the country. This has been promised by successive campaigning prime ministers and with Darwin's current boom has yet again been resurrected.

On to East Point

Right by the Gaol Museum, the main route (and buses #4 and #6) curves right, while East Point Road continues straight up to the **East Point Reserve**, an area of largely natural bushland that's home to around two thousand wallabies. After a kilometre you pass **Lake Alexander**, a recreational saltwater lake suitable for year-round swimming and, nearby, a **mangrove boardwalk** takes you into the tidal environment.

The road ends 3km from the former prison at the **Military Museum** (daily 9.30am–5pm; $5) and **gun turrets**. Most visitors – and quite a few Australians – are unaware that Darwin was repeatedly bombed by the Japanese in 1942; at the time, news of both the air raids and the thirty thousand enemy troops massed on Timor, awaiting the order to invade, was suppressed. The museum commemorates these events with a short video and some rather staid displays of uniforms, medals and other wartime memorabilia, while in the grounds a collection of neglected World War II guns, aircraft engines and associated hardware quietly rusts away. At the top of East Point, the guns themselves were never actually fired and the huge barrels were eventually sold ten years later as scrap to – ironically – the Japanese. East Point is also an ideal spot to watch the striking hues of Darwin's multichrome sunsets; if driving, watch out for roadside wallabies on the way back.

Aviation Heritage Centre, Crocodylus Park and Charles Darwin National Park

Set in a hangar off the Stuart Highway, on the southeastern edge of the airport, the **Aviation Heritage Centre** (daily 8.30am–5pm; $8; bus #5 or #8) is easily dominated by the huge bulk of a B52 bomber on loan from the US Air Force.

Further down the Stuart Highway, and taking a left at the Berrimah traffic lights, leads you to the crocodile research facility and farm of **Crocodylus Park** (daily 9am–5pm; tours 10nm, m????, 8pm, 015, bus #3) in McMillans Road. No visit to Australia is complete without a close look at these prehistoric-looking beasts and in the croc-filled lagoon you can get within kissing distance of a three-metre man eater should one happen to doze off right by the fence. These usually dormant reptiles are coaxed into action during daily feeding sessions which coincide with the tours and there's an absorbing museum giving you the lowdown on the world of crocs.

Returning along Tiger Brennan Drive you can pay a visit to the new **Charles Darwin National Park**, designated to protect an area of natural bushland against a rash of surrounding development. Along with views onto the city and a few wartime storage hangars, **mangroves** is what it's all about down here. Although not much to look at, mangroves provide a crucial and biodiverse coastal habitat. Nearly eighty percent of the world's many species are found in tropical NT. The trees' salt-tolerant root systems inhibit coastal erosion, filter the water and provide shelter to everything from mud crabs and crocs to pesky sandflies which can waltz through mosquito nets five abreast. Altogether the park's a nice spot for a picnic, a walk or a traffic-free cycle: just don't forget some repellent for the insects.

Darwin's beaches

Several factors exclude Darwin from being the beach resort you might have hoped for. A high tidal range, the fierce tropical sun, sheets of mangroves and the seasonal but deadly menace of stinging box jellyfish (from October to May) – which rules out swimming in the sea at the hottest time of year – mean that, despite its few beaches, you're rarely pushed for a spot to roll out your towel. Traps in the harbour regularly capture *most* of the crocodiles. **Fannie Bay**'s beaches (bus #4 or #6) are closest to the town centre and have a kiosk and water craft rental. However, the **Casuarina Coastal Reserve** (bus #4 or #10; 40min), capping the northern suburbs, has the city's least unattractive sandy stretches, including a "free beach" for nudists. A good place to splash about is **Lee Point**, mainly used by sunset dog walkers and found at the end of Lee Point Road, directly north of the airport.

Eating

There have been big improvements in the ambience of Darwin's restaurants in the last few years. They've finally realized that whatever you're eating, sitting in an open-air tropical environment with a few palms flapping about is far more agreeable than inside an air-con box. Like much of Australia, Asian, Italian, steak and seafood about sums up the options and it's certainly enough to keep your taste buds busy. Adventurous carnivores can tackle exotic meats such as **kangaroo**, buffalo, camel and **crocodile**, though they're often more memorable running about in the bush than on a plate. Ironically, the climate makes it likely that seafood will have been frozen, and so might as well be from Cape Cod as from the Timor Sea. That said, anglers are drawn to the Top End hoping to catch **barramundi** – a bland tasting and overrated "fighting fish"; snapper (aka Red Emperor) is much more flavoursome.

City centre and the wharf area

Café Bella, 9–11 Cavenagh St. Alfresco resto with Italian dishes from early till late.

Capri, 37 Knuckey St. Plush, city-centre coffee bar serving big brekkies and meals with a Mediterranean theme.

Christo's, Stokes Hill Wharf (☎08/8981 8658). Old shed at the end of the pier, offering à la carte Greek and Mediterranean-style seafood and sea breezes.

Coyotes Cantina, Transit Centre, Mitchell St. Mexican dishes on an elevated deck overlooking Mitchell St.

Fish & Chips by Christos, Transit Centre, Mitchell St. Central takeaway outlet of the wharfside resto (see above).

Fisherman's Wharf, Frances Bay Rd. Far away from anything else and for a long time Darwinians' select getaway for cheap seafood and chips.

Galleria Restaurant, Galleria Mall, off The Mall. Superior daytime lunchspot among the many to choose from in the Mall.

Rendezvous, Star Village Arcade, Smith St Mall. Malaysian-flavoured cheap lunch spot.

Roma, Cavenagh St. This classic, Italian-inspired coffee bar serving tasty snacks and breakfasts is an old favourite with Darwinites.

Sizzlers, Cinema Complex, Mitchell St. American-style chain serving steak and seafood with an all-you-can-eat salad bar.

Cullen Bay, Fannie Bay and East Point

Bay Seafood Cafe, Marine Blvd, Cullen Bay. Inexpensive large portions of seafood and chips.

Cornucopia, Museum of Arts and Sciences Complex, Conacher St (☎08/8981 7791). Sunset views from the terrace and a contemporary Australian menu. Moderate prices.

Pee Wees at the Point, East Point Rd. Tucked away in the trees on a grassy terrace overlooking the bay serving up steak and seafood at around $20 plus.

YOTS, Shop 4, 54 Marine Blvd, Cullen Bay. One of a dozen or so restaurants in the marina, this one has a varied and reasonably priced seafood menu and pleasant location. Ideal for a post-cruise evening meal.

Drinking, nightlife and entertainment

Darwin's thirst for alcohol used to be legendary, with statistics for **beer consumption** averaging out at around 230 litres per year for every man, woman and child. Eliminating the largely teetotal children and moderate women drinkers, that meant each grown man knocked back nearly a pair of "slabs" (24-can cartons) each week – fifty percent more than in the rest of Australia, although to be fair, consumption of soft drinks is also well above the national average. In recent years, consumption has eased off considerably, as the NT government, embarrassed by this boozy image, instigated a "Drink Less Live More" campaign, imploring moderation and reducing the price of "lite", low-alcohol beer. They've got their work cut out however as beer-drinking is still considered a prerequisite or indeed the main way of having a good night out in Darwin.

Pubs and bars

Many pubs have responded to changing demands by transforming their functional frontier-town interiors into something more conducive to the new-found clientele of public servants and tourists, and many are no longer no-go areas for unaccompanied women. Nevertheless, the *Hotel Victoria*, ideally positioned in The Mall to attract tourists, can't resist erring towards its tacky roots.

The ageing *Hotel Darwin*, on Herbert Street, milks its neo-colonial image with the *Pickled Parrot* piano bar and airy *Green Room*, and don't turn down an invitation to the "members only" *Yacht Club* in Fannie Bay, a fine spot to watch the sun set over the Timor Sea. Next to the Transit Centre the Guinness-serving *Shenanigan's* brought "Oirishness" to the Territory and has struck the right chord with both locals and visitors. Now there's also *Kitty O'Shea's* at the top of Mitchell Street creating the same sort of hooley but serving food as well. Over the road, *Rourk's Drift* features a bit of wood and brass and calls itself a "British Pub", it's actually something much more continental but not bad for all that. And for a post-tour knees up, the *Kakadu Bar* next to the *Hotel Darwin* on the Esplanade is a popular venue for intoxication.

Clubs and live music

Like Darwin's transient population, things change quickly on the city's **club scene**, with the fortnightly live gig guide *Pulse* keeping abreast of developments and the occasional trend. Along the Esplanade, the *Rattle & Hum* club is desperate to pull in the "backies" with various incentives, while *The Time* nightclub on Edmunds Street has managed to keep the same name for a couple of years which longevity must say something. The **casino** (see below) hosts several diversions, including *Crystals*, a straightforward disco, while karaoke crooning takes off in the early hours at the *Sweethearts Bar*. On Sunday afternoon "Jazz on the Lawn", behind the casino, is strictly middle of the road: there's more spirited jazz on Friday night at the *Hotel Darwin's Green Room*, on Herbert Street.

Theatre, cinemas and the casino

For **theatrical performances**, see what Brown's Mart Community Arts (☎08/8998 5522) is up to, or check out the programme at the Performing Arts Centre (☎08/8198 1222) on Mitchell Street, which hosts top acts and shows from all over the country and even international ones. The five-screen **cinema**, Cinema Darwin, just over the road, has cheap tickets on Tuesday, but take a sweater as the air-con means business; for an alternative to mainstream films, see what's on at the outdoor Deckchair Cinema, on Frances Bay near Stokes Hill Wharf (closed Nov–March).

Down on East Point Road the **casino** (near Mindil Beach; open nightly) is a sawn-off pyramid designed to withstand 350kph winds – and filled with a variety of distractions designed to remove your money just as fast. Don't be put off by the jet-setting image of European casinos; the Australian's love of **gambling** means that anyone can fit in comfortably as long as they're presentable.

Events and festivals

The Dry season sees an upsurge in popular activity as the city shakes off the languor of the Wet. As well as agricultural shows, rodeos and racing, August's **Festival of Darwin** sees bands, plays, parades and all sorts of happenings around the city, and is well worth catching. Late July is the time for the famous **Beer Can Regatta** in Fannie Bay – wacky boat races in sea craft made entirely from beer cans. A genuine manifestation of Territorian eccentricity, this inevitably involves drunken revelries, and there have been attempts by the "Drink Less Live More" brigade to make the event more family-oriented. Also in August, there is more nuttiness during the barefoot **Mud Crab Tying Competition**, a speed event that can cost you your digits.

Markets

Every Thursday night from 5.30pm (May–Oct only) **Mindil Beach Markets** attracts thousands of locals who park, unpack their eskies and garden furniture, and settle in for the sunset. A mouthwatering array of sizzling food stalls from all corners of the earth (but mostly Asia) torments your nostrils, and New Age remedies, handicrafts and teeming humanity round off Darwin's one unmissable event. It's a three-kilometre walk from town through the Botanic Gardens, or a short ride on a #4 or #6 bus from the city centre. Alternatively, call Tour Tub (☎08/8981 5233) or Galaxy Tours (☎08/8932 6222) for a pick-up. **Parap**'s Saturday morning market, on Parap Road (bus #6), or **Rapid Creek market**, off Trower Road on Sunday (bus #6 or #10), are good year-round substitutes, with a smaller food selection, old books and knick-knacks. There is also the recently developed **Night Markets** which have spiced up Mitchell Street.

Listings

Airlines Ansett Airlines, 46 The Mall (☎13 1300), has inexpensive, one-way backpackers' fares to Kununurra and Broome. Garuda (☎08/8981 6422) and Merpati (☎08/8941 1030) have flights to Bali and Kupang, in Timor, both departing four times a week, while Malaysian Airlines (☎08/8941 2323) flies to Singapore twice a week.

Banks All major banks are located in or near Smith St Mall.

Book exchanges Readback Book Exchange in Darwin Plaza off The Mall (Mon–Fri 9am–5pm, Sat 9.30am–1.30pm) offers a good selection of secondhand books including used travel guides. Also try Dusty Covers, Chin Arcade, 29 Cavenagh St (Mon–Fri 10.30am–5pm) for rare Australian first editions.

Buses Greyhound Pioneer, Transit Centre, 69 Mitchell St (☎08/8941 6433) and McCafferty's, corner of Peel and Smith streets (☎08/8941 0911), for journeys within The Territory and out of state. Bus passes can also be purchased at both places, which for longer stays are much better value than ordinary tickets.

Camping equipment The NT General Store, 42 Cavenagh St, has everything you need for going out into the bush, from a new pair of blunnies to mozzie nets, eskies and billies.

Car rental Nifty, 86 Mitchell St (☎08/8981 2112), has mokes for local use from $25 a day; Network, 90 Mitchell St (☎08/8924 0000), also has mokes from $25 a day, plus charge per km. Territory Thrifty Rental Cars, 64 Stuart Highway (☎08/8981 8400), has a huge fleet of vehicles.

Car trouble AANT, 79–81 Smith St (☎08/8981 3837). Vehicle breakdown service, road maps and information. For roadside service call ☎08/8941 0611.

Consulates Indonesia, 18 Harry Chan Ave (Mon–Fri 9am–1pm & 2–5pm; ☎08/8941 0488).

Hospital Royal Darwin Hospital, Rocklands Drive, Casuarina (☎08/8920 7211).

Internet and email The State Library in the Parliament Building gives you half an hour of emailing or an hour of surfing free per day. For surfing only (one hour per day) try the Council Offices library at the end of Cavenagh St by the bus station. Otherwise it's $8 per hour at Oz Books in the Transit Centre or at Multigamer, 20 Knuckley St. All of these are proper computers and not the awkward coin-operated email machines some hostels provide.

Pharmacy 46 Smith St Mall (9am–9pm; ☎08/8981 9202).

Police The main police station is at West Lane, behind Knuckey St (☎08/8981 1866).

Post office 48 Cavenagh St, on the corner of Edmunds St. Open on Saturday morning and with a well-organized poste restante service (☎08/8980 8227).

TOURS FROM DARWIN TO THE TOP END

For the visitor, Darwin itself isn't really a destination of enduring interest, compared to the surrounding countryside. **Kakadu** is the obvious draw, and for many is the primary reason for visiting the Top End, but **Litchfield Park** is nearer, croc-free and a fun day out. While Litchfield remains a popular day-trip, many Kakadu tour operators are now offering two- and three-day tours, providing a less hurried way of enjoying the park. Below are some recommended **tour operators** in the Top End not mentioned elsewhere in the text. Prices fluctuate but generally expect to pay $110 a day. Most of these tours include the $15 Kakadu park entry fee.

Darwin's **harbour** may not be the world's most picturesque inlet but there are a number of ways of making it an enjoyable experience. At Stokes Hill Wharf a **sea plane** and **helicopter** stand by, waiting to fly you over the city while down at the Fishing Boat Harbour off Frances Bay Road a **hovercraft** offers the same thing at a lower altitude. But the best options are either the **yacht**, **catamaran** or **pearl lugger** based at Cullen Bay Marina. A sunset cruise brings you back in time to enjoy an evening meal by the waterfront and in the meantime you'll get an amusing commentary as well as drinks and snacks for your two-hour trip.

Australian Kakadu Tours (AKT; ☎08/8947 3900). Tours for the less active, ranging all over the Top End; up to ten days, costing between $80 and $200 per day.

Blue Banana (☎08/8945 6800). Hop on, hop off, stay as long as you like bus doing a circuit between Darwin, Katherine and Kakadu.

Coo-ee Tours (☎08/8981 6116). Enjoyable twelve-hour waterfall hop through Litchfield and Reynolds River cruise with a dinkum Aussie family.

Darwin Day Tours (☎08/8981 8696). Day- and half-day tours (essentially a bus service plus a cuppa) to the croc farm and Territory Wildife Park.

Foot Print Safaris (☎08/8981 3966). Two- to five-day tours through Kakadu at walking pace. One of the few companies offering this kind of tour at a reasonable price.

Kakadu Adventure Safaris (aka Territory Style Tours; ☎08/8947 2677). Two or three full days in a packed 4WD for the fun-hearted and budget-minded; a longer tour includes Twin Falls.

Kakadu Dreams (☎08/8981 3266). Low-cost, fun, activity tours in another packed 4WD.

Keetleys (☎08/8947 2472). Established tour operator for those who prefer not to rough it too much. One-day Litchfield and Katherine tours or two-day Kakadu tours for $300.

Unchartered Tours (☎08/8976 7160). Mount Bundy Station is near the township of Adelaide River south of Darwin. Riding quads (four-wheeled bikes) all over the station land spotting all sorts of wildlife and raising a fair bit of dust. No experience necessary. Two-hour, four-hour and full-day tours.

Wild Thing (mobile phone ☎015/928 785). All-out one and two-day action and adventure in Litchfield: abseiling, waterfalls, etc.

Wilderness 4WD Adventures (aka Backpackers Australia Tours; free call ☎1800/808 288). Competitively priced two- to five-day tours through Kakadu and Litchfield. Plenty of fun and action with the longer tours always a better deal in the long run.

Willis Walkabouts (☎08/8985 2134). Bushwalking in the Top End, Kimberley and the Centre for committed walkers.

Secondhand stuff City Secondhand and Pawnbrokers, 6 Harriet Place (where Daly crosses Smith St), has some useful used gear such as cameras, bikes, eskies, tools and hats.

Swimming The nearest decent-sized pool is at Ross Smith Ave, Parap (☎08/8981 2662); take bus #6 or #10 from the city centre. Or try Lake Alexander at East Point.

Vaccinations Contact the Travel and Immunization Service, 43 Cavenagh St (☎08/8981 7492), for vaccination service if you're heading for Asia.

The Bathurst and Melville islands

Around six thousand years ago, rising sea levels created the **Bathurst and Melville islands**, 80km north of Darwin. Home of the **Tiwi** Aborigines, the islands are often collectively known as the Tiwi Islands. Differing significantly from mainland Aborigines, with whom they had limited contact until the last century, the Tiwi people's hostility towards all intruders hastened the failure of **Fort Dundas**, Britain's first north Australian outpost (on Melville Island), which lasted just five years until 1829. The Tiwi word for white men, *murantani* or "hot, red face", probably originates from this time.

In just two generations, since a Belgian missionary cautiously established the present-day town of **NGUIU**, on Bathurst, the Tiwi have moved from a hunter-gatherer lifestyle to a commodity-based economy with remarkable ease. Running their own tours and manufacturing their own crafts and garments, they are now seen as an offshore model for successful Aboriginal self-determination.

The **Tiwi Land Council** (☎08/8947 1838) issues permits for visitors to the islands, but doesn't allow individual tourism. Without an invitation, **tours** are the only way to see the islands, and even then you'll see very little. Tiwi Tours (☎08/8981 5115) offers small-group tours of the islands, from $260 for a day-trip, including return flight and permit. It's a bit of a shopping trip, inspecting Tiwi art and craft outlets such as Bima Wear's showroom, but lunch at Taracumbie Waterfall and a visit to an overgrown burial ground, where lopsided crosses mingle with carved *pukamani* burial poles, add some flavour – as does the thirty-minute flight over Van Diemen Gulf. At $460 the **overnight tours** are much more worthwhile. You'll get a chance to go food-gathering with local Tiwi, either offshore or through the bush, making it a refreshingly spontaneous encounter. For more information call in at Aussie Adventure Holidays, on the corner of Smith and Knuckley streets.

The Arnhem Highway to Kakadu

The **Arnhem Highway**, which runs east towards Kakadu, parts company with the main southbound Stuart Highway 10km after Howard Springs. Eleven kilometres from the turning, the small settlement of **HUMPTY DOO** (bus #19 from Palmerston, a suburb of Darwin) has a **pub** renowned for its Sunday sessions; adjacent is the *Hard Croc Café*. Down the road a bit is **Grahame Gow's Reptile World** (daily 8.30am–5.30pm; $5), which displays an array of deadly, and deadly-looking, reptiles. Australia contains over 75 percent of the world's venomous snakes and most of them, as well as pythons and other reptiles, are represented here. Grahame Gow, a world authority on snakes, has been bitten enough times to be thought immune to snake venom.

A few kilometres further on is the turn-off to **Fogg Dam Conservation Reserve**. Originally established in the late 1950s as an experimental rice- and cotton-growing area which was to have transformed The Territory's economy, for various "operational" reasons the whole scheme was a flop. Since then the dam has become successful as a bird sanctuary: early morning or twilight are the best times for spotting jacanas, egrets and geese, as well as pythons who feed on the water rats, goannas and wallabies. There's also a 3.6-kilometre signposted boardwalk through the adjacent woodland and another leading into the lagoon itself. During the Dry, rangers lead night-time walks along the dam.

Back on the highway you'll spot the distinctive observation platform of the **Windows on the Wetlands Visitors Centre** (daily 7.30am–7.30pm), which overlooks the Adelaide River flood plain from the top of Beatrice Hill. On the top floor you can look out onto the flood plain through binoculars, play with interactive displays describing the surrounding ecology and get the full story on the Fogg Dam fiasco.

Adelaide River Crossing: jumping crocodiles

Seeing crocodiles in their natural habitat is one of the Top End's undoubted highlights and at the **Adelaide River crossing**, 64km east of Darwin, you can sign up for the so-called **jumping crocodile cruise**. The familiar appeal "Don't Risk Your Life", posted along northern Australian waterways and shorelines, took on greater significance when in August 1998 part of the Adelaide River Bridge sank into the mud. The temporary closing of the Arnhem Highway soon had a devastating effect on passing trade east of the river, and while divers prepared to inspect the bridge's foundations, the *NT News'* cartoonist Wicking drew a pair of bug-eyed crocs offering "jumping human cruises".

The *Adelaide River Queen* ($30 for a 90min cruise; up to four times daily; check times and availability of seats in advance on ☎08/8988 8144). The cruises involve enticing the river's numerous salties with bits of boney offal, making the business of snapping stunning photographs straightforward and safe. All the crocs have individual personalities, such as the sprightly Mr Reliable or the generally languid nine-hundred-kilogram Hannibal. Sea eagles sometimes swoop in and snatch morsels from the crocs' maw and, whatever your thoughts on the methods or wisdom of encouraging crocodiles to jump 2m out of the water, they are an amazing spectacle.

The Mary River Wetlands

Continuing along the Arnhem Highway, 12km past the *Bark Hut Inn*, the **Old Darwin Road** (also known as the Jim Jim Road) leads southeast into Kakadu. Another 8km further on, the unsealed Point Stuart Road turns north into the **Mary River Wetlands**, ending at the point where Stuart actually reached the sea in 1862. It's an opportunity for those with their own vehicle to explore a wetlands environment no less impressive for not being in Kakadu – indeed as Kakadu's wetlands are largely inaccessible it's your best option. Accommodation is offered at *Wildman River Wilderness Lodge* (☎08/8978 8912, fax 8947 3988; ⑦), a tidy bushcamp around 15km off the Point Stuart Road with large tents or small air-con cabins and a nice bar/restaurant area with a pool. From here you can take a boat tour out to the **Rock Hole**, a lush billabong similar to the better-known Yellow Waters near Cooinda. Another 25km up the road is *Point Stuart Wilderness Lodge* (☎08/8978 8914, fax 8978 8898; four-bed units ⑤–⑥, dorms ①), a less expensive place to spend the night, with a pool, boat tours, gear rental and meals available with advance warning.

Further up the Point Stuart Road is **Shady Camp**. Clouds of mosquitoes make this a miserable place to spend the night but Crocodylus Wildlife Cruises (☎08/8927 0777; $45) can take you to up- or downstream of the barrage which keeps the tide at bay – whichever way you go crocs, and plenty of them, are guaranteed.

Directly south of the *Bark Hut Inn* on the Arnhem Highway, a track leads 2km to the *Annabaroo Billabong* (☎ & fax 08/8978 8971; ①), a rustic collection of airy bush cabins and campsites spread out among the light woodland and including the original, century-old bark hut used by buffalo hunters. It's a lovely, peaceful spot where you can swim and canoe in the billabong, and there's also a small shop and a bar.

Kakadu National Park

A hundred and fifty kilometres east of Darwin you reach the western boundary of **KAKADU NATIONAL PARK**, a unique area of largely unspoilt wilderness and, along with Uluru (Ayers Rock), the most visited natural site in Australia. On UNESCO's World Heritage List, it was brought to worldwide attention when used as a backdrop in the film

CROCODILES

Two distinct types of crocodile inhabit the Top End. Bashful **Johnston** or **freshwater** crocodiles ("freshies") grow up to 3m in length, eat seafood, birds and small mammals, and live exclusively in freshwater rivers and billabongs. Unique to Australia, and distinguishable by their narrow snouts and neat rows of spiky teeth, they look relatively benign and are considered harmless to man. Some swimming areas in Kakadu are known to harbour freshies.

Estuarine, or **saltwater** crocodiles ("salties"), can inhabit both salt and fresh water and are the world's biggest reptiles. Once fully mature (up to 6m long and 1000kg in weight), they have no natural predators other than each other and have been known to "take" (the approved euphemism) buffaloes trapped in the mud – although fishermen and swimmers are a much less strenuously acquired snack. Their broad, powerful snouts and gnarled jawline comprise a fascinating and gruesome sight that has changed little since the time of the dinosaurs 160 million years ago – only then salties were four times bigger than they are now. They are opportunistic hunters, catching their prey in sudden, short bursts of speed and then resuming their customary inactivity for days if not weeks at a time. Apart from the jumping crocs at Adelaide River, most you'll see are inactive, sunning themselves in the mud or cooling off underwater.

Aborigines have lived alongside crocodiles, and eaten them or their eggs, for thousands of years, but earlier this century crocodiles were hunted close to extinction – either for sport, as vermin, or for their skin. Legislation reversed this trend in the mid-1960s though with current conservation, farming and elimination of rogue crocs, it's unlikely the Top End will ever see the really huge five-metre-plus crocs ever again.

The absence of **warning signs** does not guarantee safe swimming (the signs are persistently stolen as souvenirs), nor does the *apparent* absence of salties. Hard enough to spot even when they're above water, crocodiles can lie submerged for hours. In short, unless you're sure it's safe, don't swim. If you're camping, don't prepare fresh meat by the water's edge, and don't collect water from the same place every day. Fatalities are surprisingly rare but all attacks make the front page of the *NT News*. Grisly stories are part of every tour guide's repertoire and are firmly entrenched in Territorian folklore.

Crocodile Dundee. The park derives its name from the Gagudju language group of Aborigines, who number among the area's traditional custodians; the Gagudju Association now manages the park, with the assistance of the Australian National Conservation Agency (ANCA). The association also claims a royalty from the **uranium** mined in Kakadu: along the eastern border with Arnhemland lies fifteen percent of the world's known reserves, and the Ranger Uranium Mine near Jabiru yields around $10 million a year for the association. Indeed, the environmental debate over the proposed mining in the late 1970s was instrumental in the establishment of the park, though controversy erupted again in 1998 over the proposed mining of a new site at **Jabiluka**. Located close to Ubirr, one of the park's most beautiful spots, anti-nuclear graffiti appeared all over Darwin as protesters occupied the site. The situation is still unresolved.

The park's 20,000 square kilometres encompass the entire catchment area of the **South Alligator River**, misnamed by an early British explorer after the river's prolific crocodile population. In its short run to the sea, the river passes through, and creates, a number of varied topographical features. Ravines in the southern sandstone escarpment, itself topped with plateau **heathlands**, shelter scattered pockets of monsoonal **rainforest**, while downstream the more commonly seen **eucalypt woodlands** merge into the paperbark **swamps** and tidal **wetlands** of the coastal fringe.

Within these varied habitats an extraordinary diversity of flora and fauna thrives. Included are 1600 different **plants**, over 10,000 species of **insect**, half The Territory's species of **frog**, a quarter of Australia's **freshwater fish** and over 75 different **reptiles**

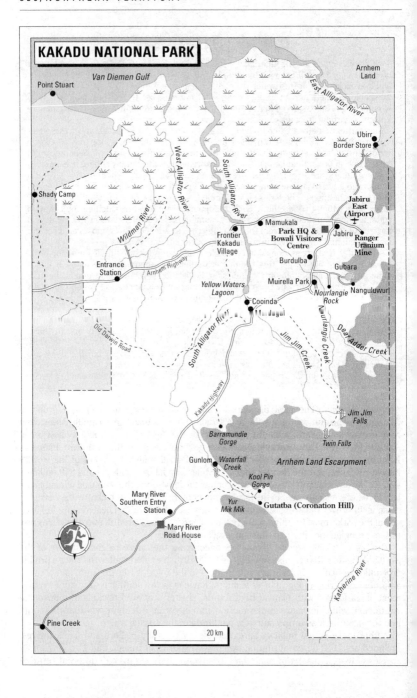

KAKADU NATIONAL PARK

Arnhem Land

Van Diemen Gulf

Point Stuart

East Alligator River

Ubirr
Border Store

West Alligator River

South Alligator River

Shady Camp

Jabiru East (Airport)

Wildman River

Mamukala
Park HQ & Bowali Visitors' Centre
Jabiru
Ranger Uranium Mine

Frontier Kakadu Village

Burdulba

Gubara

Entrance Station

Arnhem Highway

Muirella Park

Yellow Waters Lagoon

Nourlangie Rock

Nanguluwur

Old Darwin Road

Cooinda
Mardugal

South Alligator River

Jim Jim Creek

Nourlangie Creek

Deaf Adder Creek

Jim Jim Falls

Barramundie Gorge

Twin Falls

Kakadu Highway

Gunlom
Waterfall Creek

Arnhem Land Escarpment

Kool Pin Gorge

Mary River Southern Entry Station

Yur Mik Mik

Gutatba (Coronation Hill)

N

Mary River Road House

Katherine River

Pine Creek

0   20 km

– some, such as the freshwater (or Johnston) crocodile, unique to the Top End. A third of Australia's **birds** can also be found in Kakadu, including the elegant Jabiru stork, the similarly large brolga, with its curious courting dance, lily-hopping jacanas, white-breasted sea eagles, which build lifelong nests from heavy sticks, as well as galahs and magpie geese by the thousand. **Mammals** include kangaroos, wallabies, walleroos, 26 bat species, and dingoes – a barkless and incorrigibly wild dog introduced to the continent by Aborigines some five thousand years ago.

With so many interdependent ecosystems, maintaining the park's natural balance has become a full-time job. The **water buffalo**, brought in from Timor early in the last century and one of ten **feral species** found in the park, proliferated so successfully that its wallowing behaviour soon turned the fragile wetlands into saltwater mudbaths. However, concerted bovine eradication in the Top End has left other problems in its wake, not least the aptly named **salvinia molesta weed**. With no buffaloes to eat it, the exotic weed has invaded vast areas of the wetlands, creating a thick, sunlight- and oxygen-depleting mat that chokes all other plant and fish life.

The other ever-present danger is **fire**. Burning off has long been recognized as a technique of land management by Aborigines who lit small, controllable fires as an aid to hunting and to stimulate new plant growth. Today, rangers imitate age-old Aboriginal practice, burning off the drying speargrass during June to preclude bushfires at the end of the Dry, when the desiccated countryside could be devastated by an early electrical storm. Finally, the disastrous effect that Queensland's poison-army of **cane toads** (see p.1013) might have on Kakadu's precious ecology doesn't even bear thinking about.

Ancient rock art

Up to five thousand **Aboriginal art sites** cover the walls of Kakadu's caves and sheltered outcrops, ranging from thirty to over twenty thousand years in age. Most of them are inaccessible to visitors, and many are still of spiritual significance to the three hundred or so Gagudju and other language groups who live in the park. The paintings include a variety of styles, from hand prints to detailed cross-hatched depictions of animals and fish from the rich **Estuarine period** of six thousand years ago. At this time, rising sea levels submerged the land bridge by which Aborigines crossed into Australia. It is not unusual to see paintings from successive eras on one wall: **Contact period** images of seventeenth-century Maccassan fishing *praus* and larger European schooners might be superimposed over depictions of ancient and bizarre spirit-beings. Though partially understood at best, Kakadu's rock art provides a fascinating record of a culture that, as recent excavations at Jinmium on the NT/WA coastal border suggest, might have inhabited the Top End for over 100,000 years.

Visiting the park

It must be stressed that Australia's largest national park is a difficult place to appreciate in one short visit. Access to the park's diverse features is limited, and those expecting to find the air a-flutter with colourful birds and the bush humming with wildlife will be disappointed. Furthermore, at the most popular times of year for visitors, Kakadu is much drier than might be imagined, and most of the wildlife is active only during the early morning, in the evening or at night. The danger from crocodiles and of inadvertent desecration of sacred Aboriginal sites, as well as the harsh terrain, means that the wetlands and especially the escarpment country are best appreciated from a small aircraft, something which can be arranged in Jabiru (see p.539) or through the *Gagudju Lodge* in Cooinda (☎08/8979 2411), with scenic flights for around $100 per hour.

Although Kakadu's Aborigines distinguish six **seasons** throughout the year, to most people it's either the Wet, with up to 1600mm (just over five feet) of torrential rainfall between December and March, or the Dry, an almost complete drought.

The **dry-season months** of June, July and August are the most popular times to visit the park, with acceptable humidity and temperatures and fairly conspicuous wildlife. Towards the end of the Dry, birdlife congregates around the diminishing waterholes, while November's rising temperatures and epic electrical storms – known as the Build Up – herald the onset of the Wet. To see Kakadu during the **Wet** or the early Dry is, some say, to see it at its best: water is everywhere and, while some sights are inaccessible and the wildlife dispersed, the land demonstrates the kind of verdant splendour that people often expect, but fail to find, in the most visited months.

Getting there

The **Arnhem Highway** leaves the Stuart Highway 43km south of Darwin, following which it's a fairly dull 210-kilometre drive to the Park HQ near Jabiru (see below). On the way you'll pass the **park entrance station**, where you pay the $15-per-person entrance fee; tickets are valid for two weeks, and you can leave and re-enter the park as many times as you like during this period. From Jabiru the sealed **Kakadu Highway** heads southwest through to Pine Creek on the Stuart Highway (an alternative entry point into the park if approaching from the south), passing Cooinda, which is pretty much at the heart of the park. Along this road you'll encounter many of Kakadu's best features.

The **Old Darwin Road** (or **Jim Jim Road**), unsealed, but usually passable for robust 2WD-cars in dry conditions, is a good alternative to slogging the full length of the Arnhem Highway. It starts 12km east of the **Bark Hut Inn** on the Arnhem Highway and joins the Kakadu Highway near Cooinda, 100km further on. Entering the park this way you should pay at the Cooinda resort, or at the Park HQ near Jabiru; for both, see below.

Without your own transport you'll have to rely on a **tour** (see box p.532 for some recommended Darwin-based operators). There are **buses** into the park: Greyhound Pioneer operates daily between Darwin, Jabiru, Cooinda and the Kakadu Parklink (free call ☎1800/089 113) runs between the main accommodation centres of the Frontier Kakadu Village, Jabiru and Cooinda. But make no mistake, those trying to see the park using only their bus passes will end up frustrated. You're probably going to be in Kakadu only once, so do it properly. rent a car or join a tour. **Car rental** can be arranged through The Territory Thrifty office at the *Gagudju Crocodile Hotel* in Jabiru (☎08/8979 2552). The **map** you're given when you enter the park is handy, but details only the most popular areas; for the whole picture get yourself a copy of the HEMA 1:400,000 *Kakadu National Park* map ($5.95).

The Park Headquarters and Bowali Visitors Centre

At the eastern edge of the park, 250km from Darwin, near the junction of the Arnhem and Kakadu highways, you arrive at the **Park Headquarters and Bowali Visitors Centre** (daily 8am–5pm; ☎08/8979 2101). The visitors centre is a masterpiece of thoughtful and relevant landscaping and design and should not be missed. Here you can get an official *Visitors' Guide* that suggests how to make the most of your visit, while for further information, *Park Notes*, covering all aspects of the park, are available at the desk. A *What's On* pamphlet has details of the informative ranger-led walks at many of the sites covered below, and the programme of evening slide shows at the caravan parks and resorts.

An innovative walk-through exhibition takes you through a condensed Kakadu habitat, passing across underfloor snakes and under a croc's belly. There's also a range of **videos**, shown near the main desk. A café and gift shop round off the facilities.

Accommodation

Within Kakadu there are resorts near the **South Alligator River** and at **Cooinda**, and a hotel and caravan park at **Jabiru**. There are also seventeen camping areas scattered

all over the park, some accessible only along deliberately unmaintained tracks requiring 4WDs and all ranging from basic sites, which are free, to better-equipped caravan
parks at **Mardugal** near Cooinda, **Muirella Park** near Nourlangie Rock, **Merl** at Ubirr
and at **Gunlom**. In the Dry season, booking ahead at the Park HQ is advisable.

Frontier Kakadu Lodge, Jabiru (☎08/8979 2422, fax 8979 2254). Caravan park (camping available) surrounding a grassed pool and bar area, with plain, four-bed, air-con rooms, shared facilities
and basic kitchen (extra charge for linen). Close to Jabiru and Park HQ. ②.

Frontier Kakadu Village, Arnhem Highway, 2.5km west of South Alligator Bridge (☎08/8979
0166, fax 8979 0147). Attractively landscaped resort/roadhouse (with café and restaurant), but a bit
far from anything except its own Gungarre nature trail. Motel rooms with camping available. ⑧.

Gagudju Crocodile Hotel, Jabiru (☎08/8979 2800, fax 8979 2707). Overpriced crocodile-shaped
hotel popular with coach parties. ⑦.

Gagudju Lodge, Cooinda (☎08/8979 0145, fax 8979 0148). Well-positioned resort near Yellow
Waters and Warradjan Cultural Centre; good campsite, decidedly afterthought air-con cabins and
motel units with a totally inadequate BBQ area, which makes the $15 all-the-veggies-you-can-eat
bistro obligatory unless you have your own cooking gear. Motel units ⑦, cabins ③.

Kakadu Hostel, next to the Border Store near Ubirr (☎08/8979 2232). An old lodge past its prime
but with all facilities; the cheapest bed in Kakadu but popular with mosquitoes too. Open all year
subject to access. ①.

Around the park

If your visit to Kakadu is short, seeing **Ubirr** or **Nourlangie Rock**, taking a **cruise** at
Guluyambi or Yellow Waters and checking out the Bowali Visitors Centre or Warradjan
Cultural Centre will give you a taste of the park, and can just about be fitted into a long
day. However, you can easily spend a week visiting all the spots detailed below, ideally
followed by a return visit six months later to observe the seasonal changes. All the following places are reached off the **Kakadu Highway** which runs southwest from Jabiru
out of the park, joining the Stuart Highway at Pine Creek. Unless indicated, all roads
below are sealed and so accessible to rental cars.

Jabiru and the Ranger Uranium Mine

JABIRU, a couple of kilometres east of the Park HQ, is a company town, originally built
to serve Kakadu's uranium-mining leases before the park was established. There are
four mine leases in the park (and another in Arnhemland) but only one or possibly two
are operating at present. As a result, Jabiru is less than half full of mineworkers and
park employees. There is a **tourist information centre** (☎08/8979 2548), a small
supermarket, a takeaway, bakery, post office and Westpac bank, all found in the **shopping plaza**. You'll also find a **Health and Dental Clinic** (☎08/8979 2018) and a swimming pool (daily 9am–7pm; $2).

Kakadu Air (☎08/8979 2411) operates out of the airport at Jabiru East (as the original town site 6km east of Jabiru is known), offering one-hour **scenic flights** along the
escarpment and wetlands for $100. From Kakadu Air's office you can also take a one-
hour tour of **Ranger Uranium Mine** (daily at 9.15am, 10.15am, 1.15pm & 2.30pm;
$10). However, the mine is nothing more than a pit, pipelines and mysterious-looking
buildings where the ore is processed, while the tour itself is largely a public-relations
litany designed to assuage visitors' misgivings. Australia's only other productive uranium mines are in South Australia and across the park boundary in Arnhemland.

Ubirr and the Guluyambi Cruise

The rock-galleries at **Ubirr**, 43km north of the Park HQ, illustrate the rich food
resources of the wetlands. Fish, lizards, marsupials and the now-extinct Tasmanian
tiger or thylacine are depicted, as well as stick-like Mimi spirits, mischievous beings

said to inhabit cracks in the rock. The **Lookout** offers one of the park's most beautiful views across the East Alligator River to the rocky outcrops of Arnhemland and should not be missed, while the six-kilometre return **Rockholes Walk** along the East Alligator River is one of the few longish walks in the park – a good way to escape the crowds.

Right by the start of the Rockholes Walk you can take a ninety-minute **Guluyambi Cruise** (☎08/8979 2411; $25) along the East Alligator River. A local Aboriginal guide takes you upstream to view the towering escarpment and rock paintings while demonstrating some canny bush trickery and he even gives you a chance to set foot, albeit briefly, on Arnhemland. The dramatic scenery makes it an enjoyable, if not superior, alternative to the better-known Yellow Waters option at Cooinda.

Nourlangie Rock Area

Nourlangie Rock, Kakadu's most accessible and therefore most visited site, is 31km south of the Park HQ. It includes the **Anbangbang Rock Shelter**, where the dry ground preserves evidence of occupation stretching back twenty thousand years; dimples on boulders show where ochre was ground and then mixed with blood for painting. The **Anbangbang Gallery**, nearby, depicts the dramatic figures of Nabulwinjbulwinj, Namarrgon (the Lightning Man) and his wife Barrkinj. Unusually vivid, they were in fact repainted (a traditional and sometimes ritual practice) between 1963 and 1964 over similar but faded designs. The **Lookout** over the Arnhemland escarpment, to the home of Namarrgon, is also the beginning of the twelve-kilometre **Barrk Walk** (see box below). Other places in the Nourlangie Rock area, all signposted, and marked in the *Visitors' Guide*, include **Nanguluwur**, a less popular but fascinating art site 1.5km from the Nourlangie car park, which includes images from the contact period when Aborigines first encountered explorers and settlers. **Nawulandja Lookout** looks onto the imposing hulk of Nourlangie Rock itself, which looms over **Anbangbang Billabong**, one of the locations used in the film *Crocodile Dundee*. During the Dry, a two-and-a-half-kilometre track circumvents the billabong. **Gubara** or Burdulba Springs, an unsealed 13km off the Nourlangie road, is a string of small pools along a palm-shaded creek, itself a hot forty-minute walk from the car park.

Jim Jim Falls and Twin Falls

Although over 100km south of Park HQ, at the end of a tricky 4WD-only track, these two falls are definitely worth visiting; allow two hours for the sixty-kilometre drive from

---

BUSHWALKING IN KAKADU

One of Kakadu's biggest disappointments is the lack of long-distance marked trails. A leaflet at the Park HQ lists twenty marked trails in the park, but most are short **nature trails**, such as the six-kilometre **Rockholes Walk** near Ubirr. Only the twelve-kilometre **Barrk Walk** – a six-hour trek through Nourlangie Rock's backcountry – offers any challenge. Although the trail is marked and gets you into the bush without the need for skilled navigation, it still should not be undertaken lightly.

In the often-overlooked southwest of the park near Gunlom, the **Yurmikmik** area on the edge of the escarpment offers a similar challenge in the unmarked **Motor Car Creek Walk** (11km) and **Motor Car and Kurrundie Creek Circle Walk** (14km; overnight stop recommended). Ask for the *Yurmikmik Park Notes* at the visitors centre. You're more than likely to have the faint track to yourself.

Experienced bushwalkers can apply to Park HQ with proposed itineraries, which need to be approved before a permit is given. Willis Walkabouts (☎08/8985 2134) in Darwin organizes extended bushwalks up in the escarpment country, as does Foot Print Safaris (☎08/8981 3966). For something less strenuous, The Darwin Bushwalking Club (☎08/8985 1484) organizes weekend walks in the Top End and welcomes visitors.

the Kakadu Highway or get an operator like Kakadu Gorge and Waterfall Tours to take you there (☎08/8979 0111; around $200). **Jim Jim Falls** tip 215m straight off the edge of the escarpment and are best caught in the early Dry, as soon as the road reopens – they often stop flowing later and will certainly look less impressive. A rocky, one-kilometre trail leads alongside the large pool to the base of the falls.

Twin Falls is a rough ten-kilometre drive from Jim Jim, including the crossing of Jim Jim Creek, which genuinely does require a 4WD and not just high clearance although they have lately added a firm concrete base under the sands. From the car park it's a short walk and then a swim up the monsoon-forested gorge for another kilometre – an airbed and waterproof containers help here. This little bit of adventure is rewarded by the sight of Twin Falls cascading into a pool edged by an idyllic sandy beach, a beautiful and recently very popular spot to while away the day. The sure-footed can scramble to the top of the falls via the overgrown gully to the right – a difficult climb capped with a view you won't forget in a hurry, but note that fatal accidents have occurred here. Both falls quickly become inaccessible after the first big rains.

Yellow Waters and the Warradjan Aboriginal Cultural Centre

As Jim Jim Creek begins meandering into the flood plains close to the Cooinda resort, 50km southwest of Jabiru, it forms the inland lagoon of **Yellow Waters**. From the car park here, a short walk leads along the edge of the billabong, from where popular **cruises** (five daily; book in advance on ☎08/8979 0145) weave through the lushly vegetated waterways. The early morning cruise (2hr; $28) catches the lagoon and wildlife at their best: heat-of-the-day tours are thirty minutes shorter and a few dollars cheaper.

The turtle-shaped **Warradjan Aboriginal Cultural Centre** (daily 8.30am–5pm), on the Cooinda access road, offers unusually designed interpretive displays on the culture and lore of the local Aborigines, together with an arts and crafts shop. Interesting though it is, it has to be said that the display is not particularly effective at communicating its message and, unless you have some previous understanding of Aboriginal culture, you've forgotten much of what you've seen soon after leaving.

Barramundie Gorge, Gunlom and other beauty spots

Robust cars can manage the twelve-kilometre corrugated track from the Kakadu Highway to **Barramundie Gorge** (also known as Maguk), the best of Kakadu's few swimming holes, 57km southwest of Cooinda. From the car park, a path leads along the creek to the large pool, possibly still the home of a harassed freshie; for its sake rather than yours, keep away from the left bank. The top of the waterfall and more rock pools can be reached by clambering up the tree roots to the right of the falls.

Gunlom (also known as Waterfall Creek) is another *Crocodile Dundee* location, on an unsealed road 36km off the Kakadu Highway, close to the park's southwestern exit. Although the falls don't flow all year, it's a lovely paperbark-shaded swimming spot, and as you can camp here comfortably it's well worth the diversion if entering or leaving via Pine Creek. The steep path at the top of the falls reveals still more pools for an inviting dip.

A right turn at the junction that leads to Gunlom follows on through Koolpin Creek to a locked gate and **Koolpin Gorge**. The key is available from the Southern Entry Station (☎08/8975 4859) on the Pine Creek road where you must leave a $50 deposit. The track to the gorge is definitely for 4WDs, ending just before the actual gorge which begins 1km upstream and continues deep into the escarpment. You can camp here or follow the escarpment on foot to the northwest for 3km to the narrow chasm of **Freezing Gorge** which, you'll be pleased to discover, lives up to its name. Five kilometres past the locked gate is **Gutatba**, a picnic site on the South Alligator River. Also known as Coronation Hill, this is the site of a former uranium mine. To local Jawoyn Aborigines this area is traditionally "Sickness Country", suggesting that even in its natural state uranium proved harmful to human health.

Arnhemland

Individual tourist access into Aboriginal-owned **ARNHEMLAND**, a vast wilderness east of Kakadu, is virtually impossible. By and large, the three thousand Aborigines who live in this remote region, where supplies come in by sea or air, want to be left alone – as they have been for over forty thousand years. In 1963 the Yirrkala of north-western Arnhemland appealed against the proposed mining of bauxite on their land. It was the first such protest of its kind, and included the presentation of sacred artefacts as well as a petition in the form of a bark painting to the government in Canberra. Although unsuccessful on this occasion, their actions brought the issue of Aboriginal land rights to the public eye and paved the way for subsequent successful land claims.

The **Northern Land Council** (Darwin ☎08/8920 5100; Jabiru ☎08/8979 2410) issues expensive permits, allowing a maximum of fifteen tourist vehicles in at any one time. The only major settlement is **Gove/Nhulunbuy**, in the northeast corner, a mining town of no appeal to tourists, and with only basic and overpriced facilities. Nevertheless, Arnhemland is beginning to open up, and not just at exclusive prices. Most visitors are fishermen heading up to **Smith Point**, an approved destination for which permits are booked up months in advance, but Billy Can Tours (☎08/8981 2560) drives you out and flies you back for a three-day tour costing $485 twin share. Davidson's Arnhemland Safaris (☎08/8979 2411) is another established operator offering tours in the Mount Borradaile area for around $300 a day plus flights. Lords of Kakadu (☎08/8979 2567) offers a day-hop into Arnhemland from the Border Store while the best-value tour ($350) seems to be Dreamtime Safaris' four day trip up from Itnhcrline to the Bodeidei camp in southern central Arnhemland (fax 08/8948 0333).

The Cobourg Peninsula

The **Cobourg Peninsula** – encompassing the **Gurig National Park** and **Cobourg Marine Park** – is a largely inaccessible headland clinging to northwestern Arnhemland by a slender isthmus. Although you have to drive through Arnhemland to get there, the peninsula is not part of the Aboriginal-owned reserve. With the failure of Fort Dundas on nearby Melville Island, the British tried again to establish a foothold, first at **Raffles Bay** and later at **Port Essington** (from 1838 to 1849), where the explorer Ludwig Leichhardt arrived in 1844 after his epic overland trek from Moreton Bay in Queensland. Port Essington was abandoned after eleven years due to malarial epidemics, harassment by Aborigines and Indonesian pirates, and – more tellingly – the peninsula's severe climatic extremes, being hotter and wetter than anywhere else in The Territory.

On the peninsula is **Seven Spirit Bay** (☎08/8979 0277), an exclusive low-key "eco-resort" reached by boat or light aircraft offering five-star service and cuisine, with various activities at your disposal. At $200 per person per night for twin-share "habitats" (minimum, and flights are extra), it's the place to politely ignore film stars trying to get away from it all. Alternatively, you can visit this area under your own steam with a 4WD. It's about 260km from the Border Store in Kakadu to **Smith Point** (camping and s/c chalets, ☎08/8979 0263), on the other side of the inlet from *Seven Spirit Bay*. You can get fuel and check in with the ranger at the Gurig Store at **Black Point** (daily 3–5pm; ☎08/8979 0263). For more information ask at the Parks and Wildlife Commission (P&WC) desk in the Darwin Regional Tourist Association office on Mitchell Street (daily 9am–5pm; ☎08/8989 5511).

Along the Stuart Highway

From Darwin the **Stuart Highway** passes early mining and pastoral outposts and is bordered intermittently by overgrown, but still commemorated, airstrips dating from

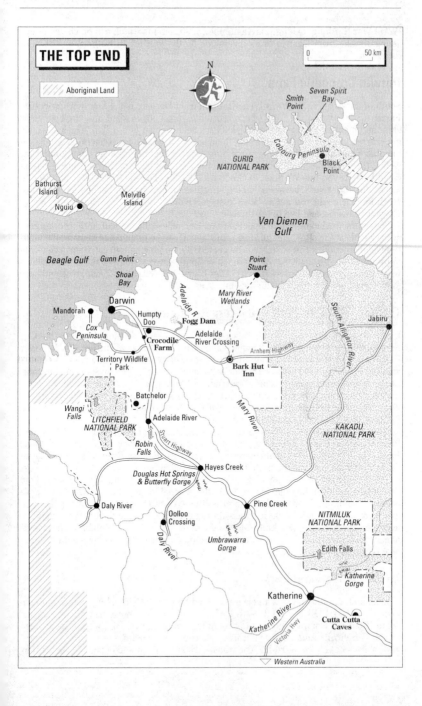

THE TOP END

Aboriginal Land

0   50 km

N

Seven Spirit Bay

Smith Point

GURIG NATIONAL PARK

Cobourg Peninsula

Black Point

Bathurst Island

Nguiu

Melville Island

Van Diemen Gulf

Beagle Gulf

Gunn Point

Point Stuart

Shoal Bay

Adelaide R

Mary River Wetlands

Darwin

Mandorah

Humpty Doo

Fogg Dam

South Alligator River

Jabiru

Cox Peninsula

Crocodile Farm

Adelaide River Crossing

Arnhem Highway

Territory Wildlife Park

Bark Hut Inn

Batchelor

Mary River

Wangi Falls

LITCHFIELD NATIONAL PARK

Adelaide River

KAKADU NATIONAL PARK

Stuart Highway

Robin Falls

Douglas Hot Springs & Butterfly Gorge

Hayes Creek

Daly River

Oolloo Crossing

Pine Creek

NITMILUK NATIONAL PARK

Umbrawarra Gorge

Edith Falls

Daly River

Katherine Gorge

Katherine

Cutta Cutta Caves

Katherine River

Victoria Hwy

Western Australia

World War II. Along its length are a number of attractions which can be visited either as excursions from Darwin or as diversions on the journey to Katherine, 320km to the south.

Darwin Crocodile Farm

South of the Arnhem Highway turn-off, 40km from Darwin, is the **Darwin Crocodile Farm** (daily 10am–4pm; $10) where crocodiles are both studied and bred for their skins and meat as they are at Crocodylus Park near Darwin (see p.528). The lucky ones get scarred at an early age, rendering themselves unsuitable for conversion into $3000 handbags and become breeding stock. Rogue crocs that harass local communities, as well as the sixty odd caught annually in the traps around Darwin Harbour, are also relocated here. If you haven't been to Crocodylus Park in Darwin, this is a good place to learn the difference between salties, freshies and American alligators. Besides, nowhere else could you get as close to such a monster as Burt, the five-metre star of *Crocodile Dundee*, and live to tell the tale.

Souvenirs (including photo opportunities to cradle baby salties) and croc burgers are available at the shop, and **guided tours** set off on the hour, when some of the eight thousand crocodiles and alligators also get fed. It's worth trying to catch the main feeding time (Mon–Fri 2pm, Sat & Sun noon & 2pm), since it's one of the few occasions when the crocs actually move. Darwin Day Tours (☎08/8981 8696) can bring you here four times a week for $25, including entry fee.

Territory Wildlife Park – and termite mounds

Eight kilometres further south down the highway, the turning west to the Cox Peninsula leads to the four-square-kilometre **Territory Wildlife Park** (daily 8.30am–6pm, last admission 4pm; $15), where you can spend a happy couple of hours wandering through a variety of Territorian habitats, which include walk-in aviaries, nocturnal houses and walk-through aquariums. The entry fee – worth every cent – includes free rides on the circulating train, which saves trudging along the four-kilometre roadway. Both Darwin Day Tours (☎08/8981 8696) and Galaxy Tours (☎08/8932 6222) do daily runs out from Darwin.

Twenty kilometres west before the Cox Peninsula road veers north to Mandorah there's a turning onto the corrugated northern approach track to Litchfield National Park (see below). Crossing through the usually dry Finniss River, this track passes fields of **termite mounds**, both fluted "cathedral" mounds, up to 4m high, and so-called "magnetic" or "meridian" mounds. Not often seen in the same vicinity, both designs accomplish their aim of regulating the internal temperature. Magnetic mounds are unusual things: made of digested grass, they're always aligned along a polar axis, and were once thought to be in tune with the earth's magnetic field. In fact, they are arranged so as to present a knife edge to the midday sun, thus maintaining the habitat at a termite-preferred 30°C; you can feel the temperature difference by touching either side of the mound.

Litchfield National Park

"Kaka-don't, Litchfield-do" is an over-simplified quip expressing many people's preference for **LITCHFIELD NATIONAL PARK** over its better-known neighbour. Situated 100km south of Darwin, and roughly 16km west of the Stuart Highway, it encompasses the **Tabletop Range**, a spring-fringed plateau from which issue several permanent and easily accessible **waterfalls**. The whole park is a popular and enjoyable destination,

Uluru (Ayers Rock), NT

Tropical beach, Dunk Island, QLD

Castlemaine Brewery, Brisbane, QLD

A crimson rosella, one of Australia's many colourful parrots, QLD

Agincourt Reef, northern QLD

Tree kangaroo and joey,
Currumbin Sanctuary, QLD

Aboriginal rock painting, Wardaman Country, Victoria River, NT

Sand dunes near Yulara, NT

Yellow Waters, Kakadu National Park, NT

Going hunting, Melville Island, NT

Iron lacework balcony, Brisbane, QLD

Tourist information centre, Port Douglas, QLD

generally free of restrictions, long drives and intangible expectations. It is also croco-dile-free, so you can splash around to your heart's content – a much more attractive prospect than some of the sterile dammed lakes closer to Darwin. **Bushwalking** is encouraged: walkers planning extended hikes should contact the P&WC in Batchelor (see below) for camping permits, as well as information about trails and maps. For details of **organized tours**, which are the only way to see the park without your own transport, see p.532.

Batchelor
BATCHELOR – 8km west of the highway – was originally built to serve the postwar rush to mine uranium at nearby Rum Jungle. In the early 1970s, when large-scale min-ing ceased, the townsfolk managed to resist Rum Jungle's closure. The establishment of the national park in the 1980s gave the town a new lease of life, though don't expect much; just about the only sight of note is a replica of the Gothic **Karlstein Castle**, next to the police station, built by a homesick Czech immigrant. The local **P&WC** (☎08/8976 0282) gives out information on Litchfield National Park. There are a cou-ple of **caravan parks** around Batchelor, but **camping** in the park is generally more appealing (some of the best sites are detailed in the text below). For those who don't want to rough it, the *Rum Jungle Motor Inn* (☎08/8976 0123, fax 8976 0230; ⑥), on Rum Jungle Road, is a comfortable **motel** with a decent restaurant – an alternative to the town's several eateries.

Into the park
There's no admission fee to enter the park, and no visitors centre either, so get all the information you need from the P&WC at the DRTA in Darwin or in Batchelor. Heading into the park from Batchelor you'll pass black soil plains dotted with grey, tombstone-like termite mounds. **Buley Rock Holes**, down a right turn, 38km from Batchelor, are nothing more than a couple of rock pools, but a five-kilometre trail fol-lows the creek from here to **Florence Falls**. A high lookout surveys the twenty-metre falls, which can be reached along a path leading from the car park down to the plunge pool. There's not much room to spread out picnics, but the water is beautifully cool, and a 4WD track leads back to the Batchelor road. **Camping** is permitted at both the rock holes and the falls.

The **Lost City**, off the main road through the park, 6km after the Florence Falls turn-off, is a jumble of unusually weathered sandstone columns. These are interest-ing enough in themselves, but getting to them is the real highlight, as they're at the end of an increasingly difficult, eight-kilometre 4WD track which should not be visit-ed in rented vehicles unless you know how to drive over steep rock steps without damage. The rarely used track, which continues on to Blyth Homestead and Sandy Creek (see below for more on these – and an easier way of getting to them), gets trickier still after the Lost City. Back on the main road through the park, the pool below **Tolmer Falls** is closed to the public, to grant the rare orange horseshoe bat some seclusion. However, the long, slender falls can be appreciated from a fine look-out (signposted off the main road). A two-kilometre path leads from here to an area of pools and minor cascades at the top of the falls, which are swimmable in the Wet, before heading back to the car park.

From the highway a track leads south to **Blyth Homestead** and **Sandy Creek** (or Tjaynera Falls). The abandoned homestead adds some token historic interest to the park, while Sandy Creek (accessible by 4WD only) is a series of falls and a pool surrounded by rainforest, with a **campsite** less than 2km away. From Sandy Creek, the 4WD track con-tinues (with several steep creek crossings) to the Reynolds River – back in crocodile country – and halfway between Daly River (see overleaf) and the Stuart Highway.

Green Ant Creek is a new destination carved out of the bush. From the car park a stiff one hour return walk leads to the top of **Tjederba Falls**, with a pool to cool off in right on the lip of the cascade.

The park's most popular waterfall, with easy access to tree-shaded lawns and a large pool, is **Wangi Falls**, 55km east of Batchelor. There is a sun-warmed natural spa pool near the base of the left-hand cascade, once a sacred site for Aboriginal women and for-bidden to men. Strangely enough, several men, including some trying to save drown-ing women, have perished at Wangi; trilingual signs now warn of the danger, and the pool closes in the Wet when abnormal **undertows** develop. A trail leads through a rain-forest boardwalk (the initial section of which is wheelchair-accessible), up over the falls and down the other side via a **lookout** – a good way to work off lunch. Wangi tends to get overcrowded at weekends and in school holidays, since it has the best-equipped **campsite** in the park.

A corrugated dirt road leads north from Wangi out of the park, past *Penthericks Rain Forest* (waterfalls and quiet **camping**) and across the Finniss River (where "Sweetheart" the crocodile once roamed before falling prey to the taxidermist at the museum in Darwin) and on to the Territory Wildlife Park.

Adelaide River and the Daly River Region

Established during the construction of the Overland Telegraph Line, the town of **ADE-LAIDE RIVER** was the supply head for Darwin's defence during World War II and con-sequently suffered sporadic Japanese bombing after 1942. Today the town, 110km south of Darwin, provides little more than a lunch-stop along the Stuart Highway. You may, however, want to visit the town's **war cemetery** where many of the victims of the air raids are buried. Officially, 243 people died as a result of the eighteen months of Japanese bombing, which began in February 1942, but it is thought that the actual death toll may have been up to four times as high. Enquire at the *Mobil Roadhouse* for **camping** space, or try the *Adelaide River Inn* (✆08/8976 7047; motel rooms ⑤, dorms ①), which also provides counter meals and has a **restaurant**.

Just south of town, the old highway forks west along a rolling 75-kilometre **scenic drive** before rejoining the main road at Hayes Creek roadhouse. After the first 17km you'll come to the turn-off for **Robin Falls**, a pretty little cascade reached after a ten-minute scramble up the creek bed from the car park, while a further 17km marks the turn-off for Daly River.

The Daly River Region

A quiet backwater, 120km southwest of Adelaide River, the **Daly River Region** is best known as an excellent fishing spot. Apart from a twenty-kilometre section, the road is sealed all the way from the highway to the police station at **DALY RIVER** – beyond that it's dirt in all directions. It wasn't always so pleasant: in 1884, four copper miners were killed by local Aborigines. The *Northern Territory News* was apoplectic with indigna-tion, but calmed down enough to reassure its readers that "the right class of men are now on the tracks of the Daly River natives, but we do not expect to hear many partic-ulars of their chase; the less said the better". Two years of punitive "bush riding" fol-lowed until the Wilwonga Aborigines were all but wiped out.

There are no banks or shops here, but you'll find **accommodation** spread out along both sides of the river. The pick of the crop is *Mango Farm* (✆08/8978 2464, fax 8978 2331), signposted a few kilometres over the causeway and offering four-bed cabins (⑤), safari tents and a seven-berth gazebo for backpackers (①), as well as a pool, small bistro, dinghy rental, river cruises and "24-hour power", something to boast about in these parts. Its most outstanding feature, however, is the stand of mature **mango trees** which arch over the whole compound like the vaulting of a Gothic cathedral; in season you'll be woken repeatedly by the thud of mangoes dropping onto the tin roofs. Another good place to stay is the *Woolianna Tourist Park* (☎08/8978 2478; s/c cabins ⑥), on the other side of the river about 30km downstream, with more boats to rent, a pool and **camping**, while the main attraction at the *Daly River Roadside Inn* (☎08/8978 2418; ⑤), in what might be called the "town centre", is a four-metre-long pet saltie called Boris.

Douglas Hot Springs and Butterfly Gorge

Back on the scenic route from Adelaide River, a turn-off leads 35km southwest to **Douglas Hot Springs**, where water bubbles at 40°C out of the sandy creek bed – very agreeable, but often crowded during school holidays. **Camping** costs just $1, but you'll need to collect your firewood on the way in, as the nearby woods have been picked clean. From the springs, a 4WD track leads another 17km to the secluded **Butterfly Gorge**. When you can drive no further, follow the creek upstream on foot, past massive paperbarks and over rocky outcrops to the beautiful, orange-walled gorge and sandy beach. Here you can swim in several rock pools.

Pine Creek and around

Site of The Territory's first goldrush, the small town of **PINE CREEK**, 230km from Darwin, has retained its colonial appearance, making it an unusually appealing stop along the highway. Gold was discovered while digging holes for the Overland Telegraph Line pylons in 1871, and fools rushed in, hoping to pan their way to fortune. Unfortunately the gold was in the rock, not the riverbeds, requiring laborious crushing with heavy stamp batteries – which, for most prospectors, was too much like hard work for unpredictable returns. The subsequent labour shortage was solved by importing cheap Chinese labour, which kept the progressively poorer-quality ore coming for a couple of years until fears of Asian dominance (the Chinese workers outnumbered Europeans eight-to-one by this time) led to their being banned from The Territory in 1888, a shot in the foot for gold production. A modern gold mine now goes at it hammer and tongs, as new technology extracts the remaining deposits. If you're lured by the prospect of easy pickings, Gun Alley Gold Mining Tours (☎08/8976 1221) can give you a chance to try some gold-panning.

Around the town, the various time-worn buildings, such as the 1889 **Old Playford Hotel** and **Old Bakery**, may lead you to contemplate the crucial role of corrugated iron, or "galvo", in the pioneering colonial process. The **Miners Park**, at the northern end of town, displays the crude mining hardware from a hundred years ago and there's a **museum** (Mon–Fri 1–5pm; $2) on Railway Terrace, near the police station, and an old locomotive on the old train station itself. For accommodation there's a **caravan park** with camping, or the *Pine Creek Diggers Rest Motel* (☎08/8976 1442, fax 8976 1458; ⑥) on Main Street. Next to the pub the *Hard Rock Café*, presumably an ore-crushing pun, is the only place to **eat**. Ah Toys general store on Main Terrace is still run by the descendants of its original Chinese owner.

From Pine Creek it's 200km along the sealed **Kakadu Highway** to Jabiru, in the heart of Kakadu National Park, passing the majority of the park's highlights on the way (described in the Kakadu section, pp.534–541). South of town, on the way to Katherine, there are a couple of other diversions within a short drive of the Stuart Highway.

Umbrawarra Gorge and Edith Falls

At **Umbrawarra Gorge**, 22km southwest of Pine Creek along a corrugated track with several dry creek crossings, you can camp for a dollar and walk up the shaded gorge which has pools throughout the year, but **Edith Falls**, halfway to Katherine, 20km east of the highway, is more impressive. The falls, just within Nitmiluk National Park, drop to a large, forest-encircled pool in three stages, around which an adventurous five-kilometre loop **walk** has been completed. There's **camping** at Edith Falls, for a $5 fee. It's also possible to walk to Katherine Gorge from here, along a 66-kilometre trail (see "Nitmiluk National Park", p.551).

KATHERINE TO ALICE

An obligatory stopover (at least for a couple of days) for visitors to the Top End, **Katherine** is a small but rapidly growing regional centre on the southern banks of the Katherine River. It's just 32km from **Katherine Gorge**, the town's primary tourist attraction and itself part of the larger **Nitmiluk National Park**.

West of Katherine, the **Victoria Highway** leads for 500km west to the WA border, passing Timber Creek and the entrance to the 4WD tracks of the **Gregory National Park** on the way. South of town, a dip in **Mataranka**'s thermal pool and a couple of "bush pubs" are the highlights of the 670km to **Tennant Creek**, unless you take the former droving route via **Borroloola** and the Gulf of Carpentaria, to northern Queensland, still a rough track but passable to sturdy cars in the Dry. South of Tennant Creek, only the rotund boulders of the **Devil's Marbles** brighten the string of road-houses along the Stuart Highway, which stretches for just over 500km to Alice Springs.

Katherine

Traditionally home of the Jawoyn Aborigines, the **Katherine River** area must have been a sight for explorer John McDouall Stuart's sore eyes as he struggled north in 1862. Having reached here, he named the river after a benefactor's daughter and within ten years the completion of the Overland Telegraph Line (OTL) encouraged European settlement, as drovers and prospectors converged on the first reliable water north of Alice Springs. In 1926 the railway from Darwin finally spanned the river and "Kath-rhyne", as the die-hard locals still call the town of **KATHERINE**, became established on its present site. It's essentially a "one-street" town, with Tennant Creek the only other place of consequence in the 1500 kilometres between Darwin and Alice.

Arrival, information and getting around

All buses arrive at the **Transit Centre**, at 6 Katherine Terrace (daily 7.30am–6.30pm; ☎08/8972 1044), next to the 24-hour *BP Roadhouse*. Katherine is a busy interchange for buses, with at least one daily arrival or departure for Darwin, Kununurra (WA) and Alice Springs. Just over the road in the middle of a car park you'll find the **tourist information centre** (Mon–Fri 9am–5pm, Sat 8.45am–noon; ☎08/8972 2650; *krta@nt-tech.com.au*), which produces a free guide to the region and can book tickets for the cruise to Katherine Gorge (see p.551). For more detailed information on Nitmiluk, Gregory and Keep River national parks call in at the **Parks and Wildlife Commission** on Giles Street, just over 1km from town, past O'Shea Terrace (☎08/8973 8770). There are **email** facilities at the Katherine Art Gallery at 12 Katherine Terrace. The **airport** is 8km south of town; a **taxi** to Katherine will cost about $15 (☎08/8972 1777 or 8972 1999).

Bikes can be rented at Coopers Cycles on First Street (☎08/8972 1213; $10 per half day, $15 per 24hr); to **rent a car** call Territory Thrifty (☎08/8972 3183).

Accommodation

Thanks to the immense popularity of Katherine Gorge, there's plenty of choice for places to stay in town. The tourist information centre provides a list and current prices of all the town's accommodation; the best options and all the hostels are detailed below.

Motels

Beagle Motor Inn, 2 Fourth St (☎08/8972 3998, fax 8972 3725). The best choice for a cheap motel in town. ⑤.

Paraway Motel, corner of O'Shea and First streets (☎08/8972 2644, fax 8972 2720). The most comfortable motel in the town centre. ⑥.

Hostels

Kookaburra Lodge, corner of Lindsay and Third streets (☎08/8971 0257, fax 8971 1567, free call ☎1800/808 211). Well-converted motel units in spacious grounds with eight-bed air-con dorms and twins, making this currently Katherine's best backpackers' choice by far. Also ping pong, pool and Transit Centre drop-offs. Rooms ③, dorms ①.

Palm Court Backpackers, corner of Giles and Third streets (☎08/8972 2722, fax 8972 1443). Long-neglected old motel with tiny pool and packed eight-bed dorms plus four-bed dorms and twins, all with own bathroom, mini-fridge, TV and lame air-con. Rooms ③, dorms ①.

Victoria Lodge, 21 Victoria Highway (☎08/7892 3464, fax 8971 1738). In between the above two places in standards, with eight- and four-bed dorms, plus twins and cheap moke rental. Rooms ③, four-bed dorms ①.

Caravan parks

Katherine Gorge Caravan Park, Nitmiluk National Park (☎08/8972 1253). Much improved new site right by the gorges but 32km from Katherine. Makes a good base for exploring the park on foot.

Katherine Low Level, Shadforth Rd (☎08/8972 3962). Close to the Low Level Nature Reserve, with free canoes and plenty of shady, grassed sites. On-site vans ③.

Knotts Crossing Resort, 4km down Giles Rd. Well-appointed resort with all sorts of cabins and units, motel rooms and camping. On-site cabins ③.

The Town and around

The Stuart Highway becomes **Katherine Terrace**, the main street, as it passes through town. Along it lie most of the shops and services, including a big Woolworths, giving Katherine a compact – and unexpectedly busy – feel. The **Railway Museum** (Mon–Fri 10am–noon & 1–3pm; donation), housed in the old station on Railway Terrace, isn't really worth the bother. If you want the full story on the town head 3km up Giles Street to the **Katherine Museum** (Mon–Fri 10am–4pm, Sun 2–5pm; $5), just before the old town site at Knotts Crossing, where a few original OTL pylons still remain upright. Inside are displays relating to Katherine's colonial history, including early medical instruments and a biplane from the time when the building did duty as a Flying Doctor base.

Mimi Arts on Lindsay Street is an Aboriginal-owned **gallery** selling carved woodwork, bark paintings and **didgeridoos**, which are indigenous to the Katherine area (before you buy one, check out the box on p.572). Indigenous Creations on Katherine Terrace is another good spot for Aboriginal arts and crafts.

Three kilometres down Victoria Highway are some decidedly **warm springs** first right after the *Red Gum Caravan Park*. From here, it's just a short walk to the **Low Level Nature Park**, a pleasant spot for a stroll, swim or canoe along the pandanus-fringed river, seasonal floods permitting. **Springvale Homestead**, at the end of Shadforth Road, 8km west of the town centre, is a tourist resort based around the oldest homestead in The Territory, built in 1884. The station was at one time run by Ted Ronan, a writer of the wry and romantic school, who helped mythologize the Outback with novels such as *Vision Splendid*. There are free, half-hourly tours of the homestead (May–Oct daily 10am & 2pm) and the local Jawoyn also perform light-hearted **Corroborees** here (May–Sept Mon, Wed & Sat at 8pm; $15); you can eat here, too (see below).

Cutta Cutta Caves, 27km south of town, offer guided tours of two systems, Cutta Cutta and Tindal Cave (hourly 9–11am & 1–3pm; closed at the height of the Wet; $9 for one cave, $15 for both; ☎08/8972 1940). Both display extraordinary subterranean karst features as diverse as they are delicate. Cutta Cutta is the more visually impressive, but Tindal is also the home of the rare orange horseshoe bat and rather alarming stalactite-climbing brown snakes.

Eating, drinking and nightlife

With the gradual improvement in tourist services it is no longer mandatory to go to a hotel to get a good feed, but don't discount this possibility. This is just as well, because the pubs' front **bars** are rough and sometimes rowdy places.

Restaurants and cafés

Buchanan's, *Paraway Motel,* corner of O'Shea and First streets (☎08/8972 2644). Sharing the honours, with *Seasons*, as the best restaurant in town. Around $22 a head.

Café on First, Cinema Complex, First St. A relatively classy new joint open from early till late.

Oroc Room, *Beagle Motor Inn*, 2 Fourth St (☎08/8972 3998). Serves up its namesake, baked, at moderate prices

Jade Café, Katherine Terrace. One of the few lunch spots in town, serving wholesome snacks.

Mekhong Thai, corner of Katherine Terrace and Victoria Highway. Authentic Thai cuisine using home-grown herbs.

Seasons, *All Seasons Frontier Motel*, Stuart Highway, 3km south of town. Eat your heart out from a droolsome à la carte menu of steak and seafood for $20–25 a meal.

Springvale Homestead, Shadforth Rd (☎08/8972 1044). "Bush kitchen" meals coincide with other activities, such as thrice-weekly Aboriginal didgeri-dancing shows and nightly croc-spotting cruises along the Katherine River.

LA NIÑA

As you cross the road bridge into Katherine from the north you'll pass a height scale on the redundant rail bridge alongside. The scale ends at 18 metres above the river but by the evening of January 27, 1998, following an Australia Day few in the town will forget, the engorged Katherine river peaked at a record twenty and a half metres.

This staggering volume of water was the result of two cyclones dumping their load over southern Arnhemland – a Wet season of rain in a few days – and was exacerbated by a king tide from the Timor Sea which backed up the water inland. Just about every business in town was under 2m of water, four lives were lost and a crocodile was spotted cruising lazily past the semi-submerged Woolworths. Within two days the waters dropped away as quickly as they had risen and the evacuated townsfolk returned to their ruined homes and businesses to begin the clean-up. Knee-high silt was shovelled out of shops and motel rooms, while the stench of rotting food and drowned cattle enveloped the town. And yet, with voluntary help from other communities and government aid, the town was on its feet within just a couple of weeks.

The 1990s have seen successive record Wet's in the Top End – partly the consequence of La Niña, El Niño's less well-known and deluge bringing counterpart.

Nitmiluk National Park

The central attraction of the **Nitmiluk National Park** is the magnificent twelve-kilo-metre **Katherine Gorge**, carved by the Katherine River through the Arnhemland plateau. Often described as thirteen gorges, it is in fact one continuous cleft, turning left and right along fault lines and separated during the dry season by rock bars. The spectacle of the river, hemmed in by orange cliffs, makes for a wonderful **cruise** or canoe trip and, unlike Kakadu, Nitmiluk also welcomes bushwalkers along its many marked **trails**.

Travel North (free call ☎1800/089 103) operates **shuttle buses** along the sealed road between Katherine and the gorge for $15 return. The all-new **Park Visitors Centre** (daily 8am–7pm) has interpretive displays on the park's features from the local Jawoyn Aborigines' perspective (they own the park), and provides maps and further information on the trails, including the *Guide to Nitmiluk National Park* ($4.95) with topographical walking maps. It also includes a restaurant, gallery and a model of the gorge system which puts it all in perspective. As you sit on the terrace overlooking the river below, consider that in the catastrophic floods of January 1998 you would have been under a metre of water.

Bushwalks include the 66-kilometre **hike to Edith Falls**, in the park's northwest-ern corner, for which you'll need at least three days, a minimum of two people and a $50 returnable deposit. Away from the gorge itself, the terrain is rough and very dry; be sure to wear sturdy footwear and a hat, and carry plenty of water. As a safety pre-caution, all walkers must **register** ($1; overnight stays $20 refundable deposit) with the rangers at the visitors centre: those on day-hikes must check in again by 6pm.

Exploring Katherine Gorge

Buses from Katherine terminate at the new canoe ramp and jetty designed to save canoeists tangling with the cruise boats heading **up the gorge**. Tickets for cruises are sold at the visitors centre. They've also sorted out safe swimming access, too, and you'll be pleased to know that saltwater crocs are virtually unknown in the gorge. While wait-ing for a cruise, you might want to take the steep, four-hundred-metre walk leading from the jetty to a superb clifftop **lookout** up the river (no need to register for this short walk).

Cruises ply the gorge in a series of boats. Travel North (free call ☎1800/089 103) offers two-hour cruises to the second gorge for $28, a four-hour cruise to the third gorge (the limit during the Wet season when a more powerful jet boat is brought in costing $41) and an eight-hour "safari" (around $71), which includes some rock-hop-ping that demands secure footwear. The relaxed "safari" cruise includes a barbecue lunch, refreshments, plenty of time for swimming and a peep at the sixth gorge; it gets away from the rather busy downstream sections and is highly recommended. There are also exhilarating **helicopter flights** up the gorge (minimum of three people required; $65 per person for 15min, $100 for 25min; ☎08/8971 0700).

Canoeing up the gorge is an option for the more energetic, but don't expect to paddle up to the "thirteenth" in a day; canoeing is hard work for unaccustomed arms and shoulders, especially against the breeze which wafts down the gorge. Nitmiluk Tours (free call ☎1800/089 103) rents solo canoes for $34 a day, $24 per half-day – add about fifty percent for two-person canoes (easier to control and a shared load for beginners). Waterproof containers are provided. The rental period is 8.30am–4.45pm; overnight trips cost a bit less than an extra day's rental. Alternatively, put your own canoe on the river, for a small fee payable at the visitors centre. Expect long sections of canoe-carrying over boulders and successively shorter sections of water as you progress up the gorges. Those determined to reach the thirteenth gorge (which, scenically speaking, is not really worthwhile) will find it easier to leave the canoe at the fifth and swim/walk the last couple of kilometres.

The first permissible overnight **campsite** is Smith's Rock in the fourth gorge (or anywhere upstream from there) – this is regarded as a fair day's paddling and portaging. The best time to canoe the gorge is early in the Dry season, when small waterfalls run off cliff walls and the water level is still high enough to reduce the length of the walking sections.

The Victoria Highway to Western Australia

The **Victoria Highway** stretches for 510km southwest of Katherine to Kununurra in Western Australia. After an initial, dull 125km a narrow sealed road leads south off the highway down to a bleak roadhouse at **TOP SPRINGS** (cabins ⑤), where there's camping and fuel. From here, a dirt road heads west past the legendary **Victoria River Downs** (VRD) station through to Jasper Gorge, rejoining the Victoria Highway east of Timber Creek. Once the country's biggest cattle station, known colloquially as the "Big Run", Victoria River Downs was established in the great droving days of the 1880s, and, like many "unmanageable" properties, is now owned by a business consortium better able to weather the currently depressed market. It still operates over a massive, semi-arid area, with the "homestead" more like a small township, incorporating a post office and shop. The station is also the base of Australia's biggest **heli-mustering** outfit, which pursues the daredevil practice of mustering widely dispersed stock with single-seater helicopters.

From Top Springs, the **Buchanan Highway** (in fact just a dirt road) continues south and west through Wave Hill to **Halls Creek** (WA), a stretch of nearly 700km that should not be undertaken lightly. Wave Hill is notable as the site of the Aboriginal stockmen's strike in 1966, which led to the first successful land claim and the birth of the Aboriginal **Land Rights Movement**.

Back on the Victoria Highway, the road narrows as it enters a picturesque spur of the Gregory National Park (see p.554). The *Victoria River Wayside Inn* (④), at the Victoria River crossing, boasts "the cheapest caravan park in Australia" and twin-share **motel** rooms. It also books **river cruises** (daily April–Oct; $30) on the Victoria River.

Timber Creek

Although little more than a pair of roadhouses/bars with adjacent campsites, **TIMBER CREEK** makes a welcome break on the long run to Kununurra, 300km west of Katherine. Lying on the Victoria River, a century ago it was known as the "Depot",

END OF THE LINE FOR THE BIG RUNS

The iconography of the **Australian cattle industry** is etched deep in the nation's psyche. The romance of the gritty station owner in a crumpled Akubra, his kids educated from the remote homestead by the School of the Air, while triple trailer roadtrains drag tornadoes of dust across the plains, creates a stirring idea of the modern-day pioneer battling against the elemental Outback.

Australia remains the world's largest exporter of beef, but in recent years shrewd business interests from the **USA and Japan** (the latter Australia's biggest overseas market) have bought into the trade – lock, stock and barrel – including everything from stations to abattoirs, packers and shipping companies. This has enabled them to control the price of beef and drive marginal stations over the edge into bankruptcy.

Indeed, it could be said that the days of old-fashioned station dynasties are coming to an end. With cattle fetching only half the prices they did a few years ago, the extravagance of maintaining thousand-kilometre fences and mustering over a vast area with helicopters has been put to the test. Despite the glory associated with the great drovers such as Nat Buchanan and the Duracks, the semi-arid interior and tropical Top End of the Northern Territory produce less beef than New South Wales. Western Australia's Kimberley region similarly glorifies in its great stations, but it's the worst land in the country, cut with seasonal torrents, and with boulder-strewn plains prone to fires and flooding. Many stations haven't mustered for years, leaving their stock to run feral; you'll come across some huge and essentially wild bulls in the Kimberley.

It's far simpler to keep the beasts in enclosed and well-watered paddocks munching decent grass rather than leave them roaming the semi-desert for years. Slow to respond to the dominance of overseas interests in its country's livestock, the **Australian Cattleman's Association** has squandered its members' money on ill-conceived schemes of automated abattoirs rather than attempting to secure the protection of its industry.

Only slowly are consumer's eyes being opened to "non-traditional" meats. **Kangaroos**, now a plague in Australia, have meat leaner than anything a cow can produce, and it tastes virtually the same. Meanwhile, Ian Conway, the half-Aboriginal owner of Kings Creek station near Ayers Rock, raises **camels**, descendants of those introduced as beasts of burden from Afghanistan in the nineteenth century and which were released to roam free with the advent of rail and roads. They are detested by cattle owners, who shoot them on sight; a thirsty mob can drain a tank and run through bovine fences with impunity. Yet one of Conway's disease-free camels can fetch ten times the price of a cow when sold to a private zoo in America or a racing cartel in Oman. When the station gets low on stock they simply drive out into the Gibson Desert for more, capitalizing on a resource which prospers in the Australian desert rather than turning it into a dust bowl.

when the inland port supplied the vast pastoral properties being established throughout the region. But this remote outpost was soon the scene of bitter disputes between the Aborigines and the new landowners. In 1885 a police station was set up at Timber Creek, staffed by two policemen and a black tracker whose task was to patrol an area the size of Tasmania. Diana Bell's harrowing book, *Hidden Histories*, describes the ruthless pastoral occupation of the area from an Aboriginal perspective.

The **museum** (ask around for times and the key; $2) is housed in an early police station, west of the town. It's a familiar display of miscellaneous pioneering relics, retrieved from the surrounding undergrowth and used to illustrate a pithy historical commentary about the region. On a different note, the town has the easternmost examples of the curious, bottle-trunked **boab trees**, similar to Africa's baobabs and according to Aboriginal mythology a once-arrogant tree turned upside down to teach it a lesson in humility. Behind one such tree, a twin-trunked boab on the south side of the highway 4km west of town, lies the miserable **grave** of Tom Lawler (or Lander). He was not the first disillusioned inhabitant of Timber Creek to seek solace in alcohol, and in 1906 got a bullet through his brains, but he is one of the few to get a marked grave. Another boab, **Gregory's Bottle Tree**, on the banks of the Victoria River, was inscribed by the explorer, Gregory, in 1856. A short distance upstream, his ship ran aground and he was forced to make repairs here, giving Timber Creek its name.

Practicalities

Tourist information is dispensed by the ever-spry Max from his office situated between the two pubs (☎08/8975 0850). He will doubtless insist that you undertake his morning boat tour ($35) along the Victoria River, an indefatigable performance of bushcraft, legend and history straight out of vaudeville, which is interrupted at your peril.

Accommodation can be found at the grandly named *Timber Creek Hotel* (☎08/8975 0772; ④), incorporating the *Circle 'F' Caravan Park* and Fogarty's Store, which has camping, cabins and motel rooms. The *Wayside Inn* (☎08/8975 0732; ④) also has camping and cabins, with shared bathrooms. The *Shell Roadhouse* here is open 24 hours.

Eating entails sampling the customary frozen/microwaved roadhouse fare, while the two pubs have all the character of a gym changing-room. During all-nighters at the graffiti-covered *Wayside Inn*, a chummy game of darts gives way to belly-sliding head first off the beer-oiled bar. You might as well enjoy it – it's a sobering 225km to the next pub.

Gregory National Park

GREGORY NATIONAL PARK, The Territory's second-largest park, is entered off the Victoria Highway, 11km east of Timber Creek. Carved out from various pastoral leases, the park exhibits sandstone escarpments and limestone hills covered in light woodland. Because of its remoteness and rough terrain, it's best explored in a suitable **4WD vehicle**, and it's a good idea to call at the **P&WC** office in Timber Creek (turn right just before Watch Creek, west of town; ☎08/8975 0888) to study the large map and get information about conditions. A **permit** is required for the two 4WD tracks (see below), available at the office or from the Park Ranger at **Bullita Outstation** (☎08/8975 0833; see below).

Conventional cars can get as far as **Limestone Gorge**, on a corrugated road 60km south of the entrance. Here you'll find a 25-minute marked walking trail looping up onto the surrounding escarpment, a croc-free billabong and a **campsite**. There's no point in 2WDs going on to the stockyards at Bullita, 6km south of the Limestone Gorge turn-off, unless you want to see the ranger. However, self-sufficient drivers in 4WDs should register here before starting the **Bullita Stockroute**, 90km of scenic limestone outcrops and river crossings, which loops back northwards and involves a full day's driving. **Camping** is permitted at designated spots along the way.

Alternatively, 4WDs can choose to leave the park further south, along the **Humbert River Track** – allow at least six hours for the 112km to the park's eastern boundary, from where you head east along station roads. For another route continue circuitously south to the **Buntine Highway** and Kalkarindji via the **Broadarrow** or **Wickham tracks**. Allow three days from Bullita: the ranger will explain the way (Wickham Ranger Station ☎08/8975 0600). Some sections of this route have some very slow, rocky sections and the tricky Humbert River crossing will challenge the inexperienced even in the Dry. Both the Limestone Gorge and this route are **one-way** only from Bullita, and are closed from December to March.

Keep River National Park and the WA border

West of Timber Creek, the land flattens out into the evocatively named **Whirlwind Plains**, where the East and West Baines rivers frequently cut the Victoria Highway in the Wet. **KEEP RIVER NATIONAL PARK** lies just before the Western Australia border, 185km from Timber Creek. Accessible to all vehicles, it's an easily explored area of dissected sandstone ridges, shallow gorges and Aboriginal art sites, the best of which is **Nganalam**, 24km from the park entrance. Marked trails start from the two **campsites** in the park, and the ranger station (☎08/9167 8827), 3km from the highway, supplies details on longer walks and other attractions.

By now you can hardly have failed to get the message that Western Australia does not want any infested Territorian livestock, produce or honey, or even boxes which have carried those products. The intensively irrigated agricultural area around Kununurra is hoping to remain free from pests found elsewhere in Australia, so eat up your fruit and veg before the border or throw it away. Note, too, that Western Australia is an hour and thirty minutes behind The Territory.

At the **border**, Kununurra (see p.669) is just 40km away.

South to Alice

The 1100km from Katherine, south down the "**Track**" (as the Stuart Highway is known) to Alice Springs, are regarded as something of a no-man's-land for travellers. A flat, arid plain rolls from the Top End's big rivers to the waterholes of the Red Centre. The white population in this region is sparse, and consists largely of individuals who are either unusually tenacious, transient or slowly going "troppo". West of the Track, the vast Aboriginal lands of the Warlpiri and neighbouring groups just about occupy the entire **Tanami Desert**, while to the east are the grasslands of the **Barkly Tableland**, a declining pastoral region extending north to the seldom-visited coast of the **Gulf of Carpentaria**. **Tennant Creek**, just over halfway, can be an expectedly anti-climactic break to a bus journey, and even car drivers tend to press on down the Track before something breaks or wears out. The landscape as seen from the Stuart Highway encourages a kind of agoraphobic urgency (or just plain boredom), while the mind churns repetitively over such imponderables as "just how many anthills *are* there in the Northern Territory?"

Mataranka and the Roper River Region

MATARANKA – just over 100km from Katherine – is a small town, the capital of the tediously hyped "Never Never" country named after Jeanie Gunn's 1908 novel of a pioneering woman's life, *We of the Never Never*, set and later filmed in the region. Site of despised Administrator John Gilruth's planned Northern Territory capital, and of failed experimental stations in the early Federation years, today the town is practically eclipsed by the nearby **Mataranka Homestead** resort, which lures in buses and passing tourists (see overleaf). South of town the **Elsey National Park** leads to the often-overlooked freshwater wetlands of the **Roper River**.

There's not much to the town itself. Outside the *Stockyard Café* you can feed a dollar into the statue of **The Fizzer** to hear the tale of the punctual postman, Henry Peckham of "Never Never" fame, who was tragically drowned in action. Tom Coles' account of his escapades in the Top End between the wars, *Hell West and Crooked*, describes the hair-raising river crossings with pack horses while delivering mail in the Wet season. Invariably the post would be delivered with barely a smudge.

All **accommodation**, along with the supermarket, roadhouses, museum, café and craft shop, is lined up along **Roper Terrace**, the main highway. Both the Shell and Mobil roadhouses have on-site vans and at the town **pub**, the *Old Elsey Hotel* (☎08/8975 4512; ⑤), you'll find motel rooms. The *Territory Manor*, on Martins Road (☎ & fax 08/8975 4516; ⑥), is a plush motel set in its own landscaped grounds, catering for bus tours: it also boasts a caravan park (with camping) as well as the town's only licensed **restaurant**.

Mataranka Homestead

Mataranka Homestead, 6km from town (☎08/8975 4544, fax 8975 4580; cabins ⑥, rooms ④–⑤, dorms ①), was established by Gilruth to raise sheep and horses and is now a popular holiday resort offering an array of recreational activities, including (expensive) bike- and canoe-rental and horse-riding. A replica of the **Elsey Homestead**, used in the 1981 film of *We of the Never Never*, is open for daily tours. The original "Old Elsey Homestead" site and cemetery are south of town, just past the Roper Highway turn-off – of interest only to Jeanie Gunn devotees.

The resort has a bar and bistro, and free nightly entertainment (April–Sept only) as well as a tour-booking service. Accommodation includes self-catering cabins, motel rooms, and three-bed en-suite rooms with air-con. There is also a youth hostel (advance booking recommended) and a campsite. Overland **buses** stop at the homestead, which is signposted to the south of Mataranka.

The **thermal pool**, actually in Elsey National Park (see below), but seemingly part of the resort, is the main attraction – it's free, always open, and the water is a pleasant 34°C. A soak in the palm-shaded, pale blue water is divine, with early mornings or candlelit night-time dips less crowded.

Elsey National Park and the Roper River

A twelve-kilometre road into **ELSEY NATIONAL PARK** (turn off just before the *Homestead*) leads to a more secluded campsite with less of a holiday-camp atmosphere, offering canoe rental and swimming in the (almost croc-free) upper Roper River, as well as a small kiosk.

The **Roper River** itself is difficult to visit independently, since it's barely developed, yet it's as scenic as the wetlands of Kakadu. Brolga Tours in Mataranka (☎08/8975 4538) is your best bet, operating **cruises** along the river from May to October. Their four-hour river tour (around $70) leads you along the river's so-called **Pandanus Avenue** and through some "African Queen"-type channels into the beautiful **Red Lily Lagoon**, the most extensive freshwater wetland in The Territory.

The Roper Highway

A couple of kilometres south of Mataranka, the **Roper Highway** leads east for 185km (the bitumen ends after 140km) to the remote store at **ROPER BAR**. It was here in 1844, during his five-thousand-kilometre trek from Queensland, that naturalist-cum-explorer **Ludwig Leichhardt** dined on fruit bat and built a "bar" (a ford) across the Roper River. You may drive across the slippery bar, but beyond is Aboriginal Land – off-limits without a permit. The store provides the local Aboriginal community and visiting barramundi fishermen with pricey fuel, food and the biggest selection of cheap toys and gobstoppers for 200km. Up behind the store are some self-catering **cabins** (②) or there's a **campsite** 2km back towards the highway. If you go boating or fishing here, take care because you're back in "saltie waters" again.

If you've got this far, you'll have seen the turn-off to Borroloola, 380km away (see opposite). Corrugated enough to test the calmest temperaments, this rarely used route to the Gulf of Carpentaria and Queensland (where the dirt roads deteriorate still further) is passable in the Dry for regular cars in good shape.

Down the Track to Three Ways

LARRIMAH, 72km south of Mataranka, was where the old Darwin railway terminated until 1976 when it closed for good, due to a lack of maintenance following Cyclone

Tracy. Up until then, Larrimah had been a busy road-rail terminus, receiving goods brought up from Alice Springs. Now it's just a fuel stop on the highway.

The *Larrimah Hotel* and *Wayside Inn* comprise a typical **bush pub**, full of eccentricity, old bottles and half-melted Spitfire engines; you can **camp** for free but there's a $2 charge for showers. Over the road, the *Green Park Caravan Site*, part of the *Shell Roadhouse*, has a pool (the five-metre croc gets one to himself) and camping plus a café and shop. At the *Top of The Town*, Angela also offers camping as well as budget **rooms** (①), cabins (③) and "the cheapest slabs in town". You'll need them round here.

Another 89km south brings you to the **Daly Waters Pub**, situated 3km off the highway. Having held a "gallon licence" since 1893, it positively drips with memorabilia including money and women's underwear pinned to the walls: you're welcome to contribute. If you need a break there are cheap and basic **rooms** (③). During the 1930s, when Qantas's Singapore flights refuelled here, world-class aviators used to pop in for a pint, and these days tourists come to marvel at the quaintness of it all and buy the famously offbeat tea towels.

Just beyond here, the **Carpentaria Highway** (technically the circumnational Highway 1) heads off east to Borroloola, 414km away (see below); the turn-off is at the *Highway Inn Roadhouse* (open 24hr). There's a second turn-off, further down the Track, just before *Dunmarra Roadhouse*, where the **Buchanan Highway** heads west to *Top Springs Roadhouse* (185km) and ultimately Halls Creek in Western Australia (see p.667) along almost 800km of unsealed road suitable for sound vehicles only. Dunmarra's drive-through drudgery was livened up a couple of years ago when it received a bizarre shower of fish, although the hoped-for cloud of chips never materialized.

Back on the Track, **Newcastle Waters** can't seem to make up its mind whether it's an historic droving township wanting to encourage tourists or a semi-abandoned ghost town. Right up to the 1950s, when road trains replaced the great cattle drives, it was the junction (hence the *Junction Hotel*) of the Barkly and Murranji stock routes. However, it's of little interest today except to nostalgic drovers.

ELLIOTT is little more than a string of roadhouses with cheap **camping** at the *Mobil Roadhouse* and slightly better facilities at the *Midland Caravan Park* (also the local post office). The *BP Roadhouse* (③) and the *Elliott Hotel* (☎08/8969 2018; ③) both offer simple **rooms**. There are a few shops serving the Jingili Aboriginal communities at either end of town, but apart from filling up with fuel or a counter meal at the pub, there's no earthly reason to stop.

As you leave town to the south, the trees which have blocked the horizon for days recede into shrubs and soon disappear altogether as you approach the deserts of Central Australia. **RENNER SPRINGS** is a roadhouse (rooms ③–④) built after World War II from bits of ex-army junk and recently done up; you can camp here, and eat the same sort of food you were probably offered at the last roadhouse.

On the way to the roadhouse at **THREE WAYS** (open 24hr) watch out for the turn-off to a rocky profile of Churchill's Head and also the **Attack Creek Memorial** – where explorer Stuart was repelled by Aborigines on one of his expeditions. At Three Ways, the **Barkly Highway** heads east to Camooweal, Mount Isa and eventually Townsville, all in Queensland; it's 210km on to the *Barkly Homestead* (6am–1am; ☎08/8964 4549), a roadhouse with all the usual services. From Three Ways, Tennant Creek (see p.559) is just 26km down the road.

Borroloola and the Gulf Country

Situated on the croc-infested **MacArthur River**, which drains the predominantly flat Gulf Savannah lands, **BORROLOOLA** has a colourful history which reads like an exaggerated version of the familiar boom, bust and dribble pattern of so many Outback

THE CLASSICS LIBRARY AND HERMITS OF BORROLOOLA

There are a number of more or less unlikely explanations for Borroloola's improbable **classics library**, including that which starts with a bored policeman's request for reading matter to New York's Carnegie Foundation. In truth, it was a gradual acquisition of nearly two thousand literary classics by the town's MacArthur Institute at the beginning of the century. Termites tucked into the library, a cyclone destroyed the remains and only a handful of books survived, many in "private collections", gathering what must be enormous overdue fees.

In 1963 a boyish David Attenborough made a TV documentary about three **hermits** who had chosen to retreat to the 'Loo. Jack Mulholland came across as a slightly jaded recluse when pressed about "loneliness and . . . women", and the reputedly aristocratic "Mad Fiddler" was too deranged to face the camera, but **Roger Jose** was, and looked like, the real thing. Having devoured the library ahead of the ants, he lived in a water tank with his Aboriginal wife and was a humane if eccentric "bush philosopher" who once observed that "a man's riches are the fewness of his needs". He is buried at the end of the airstrip in Borroloola.

towns. The explorers Leichhardt and Gregory came this way in the mid-nineteenth century, reporting good pasture, and the cattle followed in droves. By the early 1880s, when Tennant Creek and Katherine were still just shacks on the Overland Telegraph Line, the settlement was a wild outpost that even the missionaries avoided. Ships that supplied the OTL in the early 1870s now came upriver with provisions for the hard-living drovers, who were helping stock the pastoral leases right across the north of Australia.

Borroloola was proclaimed, or "gazetted", in 1885 and a new police station was established in an attempt to control the town's lawless urges. Although well watered, the **Great Coast Route** which Borroloola serviced fell victim to the bovine disease of Red Water Fever, after which the southern stock route (today's Barkly Highway) became the favoured droving route. By the turn of the century, just a handful of whites remained in "The 'Loo" and, with their frenzied passing, the four local Aboriginal groups have reclaimed the town and surrounding land, which now serves their communities and outstations.

The only original building to have survived the punch-ups, white ants and cyclones is the **Old Police Station**, now a museum. The key is available from *MacArthur Caravan Park* on Robinson Road – or at least they'll know who has it – and a donation of $2 is welcome. With Borroloola's exceptional white history (see box above), the museum couldn't fail to be fascinating. Read, for example, E. Gaunt's hair-raising account of "The Birth of Borroloola", recalling the sporadic insanity of the early days; it seems the toxic home brew known as "Come Hither", whose label showed a red-eyed Lucifer beckoning malevolently, was to blame. Not surprisingly, the coverage of local Aboriginal history is lightweight.

Practicalities

Although on Aboriginal land, no permit is required to visit the town, which sees a few intrepid tourists and fishermen. Borroloola is mainly on the itinerary of those taking the coast route from Queensland to Darwin or travelling on to Western Australia.

There's plenty of light **air traffic** to and from the town, mostly from Katherine, which otherwise is over 700km away to the northwest by sealed road. Skyport makes mail runs three times a week; the Bulk Discount Store supermarket (☎08/8975 8775) is their agent in Borroloola, and it will cost you about $240 one-way.

By road, Borroloola is easily accessible along the **Carpentaria Highway**, via the *Heartbreak Hotel* at Cape Crawford (see opposite), set at the junction where the single-width **Tablelands Highway** comes up from the main Queensland road. Depending on who you ask, the **dirt road** to **Wollogorang** (a roadhouse with access to coastal inlets) and Hells Gate (Queensland) is either terrible or not bad, but it's bound to be an adventure; the Queensland gulf towns are by no means renowned for their sobriety. The dirt road up to Roper Bar is good until Nathan River, where the corrugations will turn your brain into a froth for about 100km.

Borroloola's isolation makes it an **expensive** place to visit, with little fresh food available and prices (except for fuel) up to thirty percent higher than those you'll find in Katherine. Most facilities are on Robinson Road including a **tourist information centre** at the council offices on the corner of Broad Street (Mon–Fri 8am–4pm; ☎08/8975 8799). As for **accommodation**, the *MacArthur River Caravan Park* charges $10 for a campsite, with cabins from ③ to ⑥ and on-site vans for ①. This is also the home of Croc Spot Tours (☎08/8975 8734), which can run you up and down the river, or out to islands to go fishing, for about $100 a day. The town's **pub**, the *Borroloola Inn* (☎08/8975 8766, fax 8975 8773; ③), has "quiet" and "rowdy" bars and a grassed pool area popular with cane toads on the march for Kakadu. The MacArthur River is renowned for its massive crocodiles, but you can camp for free by the boat ramps along the river, providing you have your own "shower and toilet facilities" and are familiar with croc-etiquette (see box on p.535). There is also a **post office** in town, and a couple of fast-food joints.

The Savannah-Gulf Country

The inviting coast and islands of the **Savannah-Gulf Country** are presently off-limits to independent tourists, hidden away on largely defunct cattle properties or on Aboriginal land. However, because of disastrous over-grazing and a disease-eradication programme which has decimated the herds, station owners right across the north are looking towards tourism to save them, either developing "dude ranches" that take paying guests or exploiting unusual natural features.

The *Heartbreak Hotel* at **Cape Crawford** (☎08/8975 9928, fax 8975 9993) – a bougainvillea-draped roadhouse, 113km southwest of Borroloola – offers helicopter rides to one of the many "**Lost Cities**" (unusual sandstone formations) hereabouts, as well as 4WD tours with Savannah Guides to the waterholes of the Bukalara Ranges. The **Caranbirini Conservation Reserve**, 46km southwest of "the Loo" is one of their destinations: more weird rock formations and a bird-filled lagoon.

Just offshore, northwest of Borroloola, are the **Sir Edward Pellew Islands**, mostly owned by the Mara Aborigines or the subject of land claims in progress. However, the P&WC has acquired **North Island**, creating the **BARRANYI NATIONAL PARK** and turning it into a simple island retreat where you can escape into your own world for a few days – providing you can actually get there. Borroloola's Croc Spot Tours (☎08/8975 8734 or 8975 8721) will give you up-to-date information on how to get there by air or sea.

Tennant Creek

Visitors expect to be disappointed by **TENNANT CREEK**, lying 26km south of Three Ways and the butt of much "nether regions of the Universe" humour. Its appeal to tourists is not immediately apparent, but hang around and you'll discover an unpretentious Outback town, defying stagnation and hoping for prosperity.

John McDouall Stuart came through in the early 1860s, followed by the Overland Telegraph Line ten years later. Pastoralists and prospectors came from the south and east, and in 1933 Tennant Creek was the site of the last major **goldrush** in Australia. This was the time of gritty "gougers", such as Jack Noble and partner Bill Weaber (with one eye *between* them), who defied the Depression by pegging some of the town's most productive claims. Modern methods of gold retrieval have caused a revival in recent years, although tenacity and luck still have much to do with striking it rich. Recently, the near-exhausted Peko mine was assessed one more time and then sold for a song; its new owners drilled a little bit deeper and struck payable gold.

Arrival and information

Tennant Creek is 504km from Alice and 664km from Katherine. The **airport** is about 3km from the centre, at the end of Davidson Street; for a **taxi** into town from the airport, call ☎08/8962 1061 or your chosen accommodation may pick you up. On Paterson Street (the town's main street – essentially the Stuart Highway) you'll find the Transit Centre where interstate **buses** pull in – some buses come through at 3.30am, which doesn't exactly encourage stopovers, although the hostel (see "Accommodation" below) tries to meet all buses; look out for the yellow van.

The visitors centre, **Battery Hill Regional Centre** (Mon–Fri 9am–5pm, Sat 9am–noon; ☎08/8962 3388; *tcrta@topend.com.au*), is at an old mine site 1.5km east along Peko Road. Once here you might as well take the sixty-minute **tour** of the site (at least two daily; $8), which includes an entertaining stroll through a specially built show mine and a chance to appreciate the din of the old stamp battery itself.

Accommodation

Bluestone Motor Inn, Paterson St (☎08/8962 2617, fax 8962 2883). Large, three-star motel at the south end of Paterson St with restaurant and pool. ⑥.

El Dorado, Paterson St North (☎08/8962 2402, fax 8962 3034). One of the town's better motels, with a licensed restaurant and nice pool area. ⑥.

Outback Caravan Park, Peko Rd (☎08/8962 2459). Shady and comfortable caravan park with shop and pool. On-site vans ③, self-contained cabins ④.

Safari Backpackers, Davidson St (☎08/8962 2207, fax 8962 3188). Clean new block with kitchen, TV and functional air-con. Four-bed dorms ①, and other rooms ③–④.

Safari Lodge Motel, Davidson St (☎08/8962 2207). Comfortable motel rooms right in town with the *Dolly Pot Inn* next door. ⑤.

TC Caravan Park, next to the Shell service station, Paterson St (☎08/8962 2325). Recently renovated, the new owners offer good deals. Options include camping, backpackers' cabins ③, on site vans ③ and roomy cabins ④.

Travellers' Rest, Leichhardt St (☎08/8962 2719). The characterful former youth hostel, hopefully still hanging on with an ageing row of two- and three-bed rooms with rattly air-con, a pool and an authentic "Tennant" feel. ①.

The Town and around

With one or two free days on your hands, the limited prospects of Tennant Creek are spread before you. In town, the **museum** (daily 3.30–5.30pm; $2) close to the *Travellers' Rest*, minutely details the history of Tennant Creek, using a chronological time scale starting from the year "0 AS" (After Stuart) and displaying plenty of pioneering relics. On the other side of Anzac Hill, check out the Ngalipanyangu Cultural Centre Aboriginal Arts and Crafts Gallery (Mon–Fri 8.30am–5pm) on Davidson Street, where you'll find a small selection of local dot **paintings and crafts** which are much cheaper than in Alice Springs – this is a place to buy as well as look.

That's about it unless you've got your own vehicle or want to **rent a bike** (see "Listings", opposite), in which case head up Peko Road, past the swimming pool, to the visitors centre and the **tour** mentioned above. Back in town there's also a paved cycle and walking trail out to the **Mary Ann Dam Recreation Area**, 5km north of town, with picnic space, birdlife and swimming in the rather dank reservoir.

Perhaps the best way to spend your time in town is by taking a **tour** of the various abandoned mine sites east of town. Norm's Gold and Scenic Tours (☎08/8962 2719) is highly recommended, giving you the lowdown on gold mining and making the whole business appear more interesting than you might expect. They also do fossicking tours; don't be surprised if you come home with a little nugget. Ten Ant Tours' (☎08/8962 2358) sunset rides to the **Devil's Pebbles** (16km northwest of town) shouldn't be confused with trips to the much more impressive Devil's Marbles (see overleaf) on the road to Alice Springs. On the way to the Pebbles, you pass one of four surviving **telegraph stations**, recently restored as an historic exhibit (☎08/8962 3388 for opening times). If you've come down the Track and not seen an OTL station yet, here's your chance.

Restaurants

With the exception of the *Dolly Pot Inn*, Tennant Creek's eating opportunities mirror the surrounding landscape – an acquired taste. The better places are listed below. Besides these, there are restaurants in the *El Dorado* and *Bluestone* motels.

Dolly Pot Inn, Davidson St (☎08/8962 2824). The Territory's only squash court/restaurant. A bit pricey, but the food is better than average with main courses around $15.

Memorial Club, Schmidt St. At the "Memo" you can sign in and get a decent counter meal to eat in (or take away) for around $10 plus a quiet place for a drink afterwards. Meals noon–2pm and 6pm until late.

Tennant Creek Hotel, Paterson St. Good restaurant attached to one of the town's more tranquil pubs.

Drinking and nightlife

Dedicated drinkers are well looked after, as the town boasts around thirteen licences and two **pubs** where miners and Aborigines come to get smashed as thoroughly as possible. Like a lot of pubs in Outback towns, front bars can become intimidating arenas of flying bottles and vitriol, while the carpeted back bars are for games of pool and benign socializing. Pubs are generally open from 10am to midnight.

The *Goldfields*, on Paterson Street, has a cleared front bar where you can get a good swing at your neighbour without breaking any of the fittings; the back bar is the place to take your mum for a sherry. Over the road, the *Tennant Creek Hotel* has tried to revamp its old mining image with a blues-proof (punch-ups, not John Lee Hooker) front bar and a tamer back bar for a quiet drink, and *Shaft*, the town's only **disco** (Thurs–Sat 11pm–3am), enabling licensed drinking into the night. *Jackson's Bar* is where the legendary beer cart got mired on the way to the original settlement near the telegraph station, sixty years ago. The beer cart wouldn't budge, so the settlement relocated around it, drank it dry and the rest is history.

If you just want a quiet drink don't forget the "Memo" or "Sporties" clubs (the latter on Ambrose Street); at either you can easily sign in as a guest and enjoy the tame if somewhat bland atmosphere.

Listings

Airlines Air North (free call ☎1800/627 474) has daily flights to Darwin and Alice Springs. Tickets can be bought or changed at the newsagent, 54 Paterson St (☎08/8962 2211), just up from the Transit Centre.

Bike rental Bridgestone Tyre Centre, 52 Paterson St (Mon–Sat 8am–5pm; ☎08/8962 2361).

Book exchange Holly's, opposite the swimming pool on Peko Rd.

Bus tickets can be bought or changed at the Paterson St newsagent (see above).

Car rental *Outback Caravan Park*, Peko Rd (☎08/8962 2459), for Hertz; or Ten Ant Tours, Transit Centre, Paterson St (☎08/8962 2358).

Hospital Leichhardt St (☎08/8962 4399).

Pharmacy 50 Paterson St (after hours ☎08/8962 2093).

Police Paterson St, next to the post office (☎08/8962 4444).

Post office Corner of Memorial Drive and Paterson St (☎08/8962 2196).

Supermarket The Food Barn, opposite the post office (daily 8am–6pm).

Swimming pool Peko Rd (Sept & Oct 11am–6pm; Nov–May 6–7.30am & 11am–7.30pm; $1).

Towards Alice and the Centre

The 500km from Tennant Creek to Alice are no more enthralling than the 500km that's gone before, and the places en route, detailed below, are easily visited only by those with their own transport or by especially determined bus travellers.

The **Devil's Marbles**, just over 100km south of Tennant Creek, are a genuine geological oddity, a scattering of huge rounded boulders thought by the local Warumungu Aborigines to be the eggs of the Rainbow Serpent; they're well worth a look, as they're only 2km off the highway. You'll find a spacious camping area and car park with toilets, barbecues and shaded tables, but no water and little firewood. A **helicopter** stands by, offering ten-minute flights for $35 (☎08/8964 1936; minimum of three people required) and Norm's and Ten Ant Tours do day-trips down here from Tennant, if there are enough people. A short drive from the Marbles is the comfortable old roadhouse/pub of **WAUCHOPE** (pronounced "walkup"). **WYCLIFFE WELL**, a little further south, has a good foreign beer selection, a nice park and lake round the back and an alien spaceship in the forecourt. Several UFOs have been seen around here in recent years.

BARROW CREEK, 60km further on, is one of the oldest roadhouses on the Track, originally a telegraph station, and remembered as the site of the **Barrow Creek Massacre** in 1874. It's never quite clear to whom the word "massacre" applied – the two dead and several wounded during an attack on the two-year-old station by the local Kaitej, or those who perished in the two months' "speedy and severe" retribution demanded by the *Northern Territory News*. The pub itself (☎08/8956 9753) has walls daubed in coarse humour, as well as old-fashioned rooms (④) and cheaper cabins (②–③) out back.

At **TI TREE**, an Aboriginal community close to the middle of the continent, the Aaki Colliery sells keenly priced artefacts and paintings produced by local Anmatjera. After another 43km, the **AILERON** roadhouse (②) has the last fuel before Alice and also sells Aboriginal art; in a shrewd marketing ploy, the first beer in the bar is free to backpackers staying overnight.

The Plenty Highway and Tanami Road

Heading towards Alice, the land finally begins to crumple as you near the MacDonnell Ranges. The **Plenty** and **Sandover highways**, which run off the Stuart Highway 66km south of Aileron, head northeast towards Queensland through the scenic Harts and Jervois ranges. Both are passable to sound, well-equipped conventional cars – the Plenty is generally the busier and better maintained. If you're heading down to Birdsville or Winton (Queensland) this way, the Donahue Highway short cut down to Boulia isn't half as bad as maps suggest.

Twenty kilometres north of Alice, the **Tanami Road** leads over 1000km northwest to Halls Creek in Western Australia. Again, the track is easily passable in a 2WD up to the NT/WA border where things can get a little rough and sandy. The longest section without fuel is the 322km from Yuendumu to **Rabbit Flat** roadhouse (closed Tues–Thurs), with the next section to Billiluna station nearly as long at 292km. You can also pop into the art gallery at the desert outstation of **Balgo Hills** (sometimes fuel), 31km south of the Tanami, whose garish and splodgy school of dot paintings is highly distinctive; the turn-off is about 88km on the WA side of the track.

Before embarking on either route, it's worth checking out the condition of the tracks; phone RACQ (for Queensland sections ☎07/3219 0900, Emergency Services in Alice Springs ☎08/8922 3232 or Main Roads Dept WA ☎08/9168 6007); you can also read daily **print-outs** of the track conditions at the tourist information office in Alice Springs (daily 9am–6pm; ☎08/8952 5800). While they shouldn't be considered a time-saving short cut, the Plenty and Tanami tracks are both perfectly feasible in a tough, well-equipped 2WD vehicle, and certainly give a taste of the real Outback you'll never get on the tarmac highway.

ALICE AND THE CENTRE

A land such as this, with its great loneliness, its dearth of life, and its enshrouding atmosphere of awe and mystery, has a voice of its own, distinctly different from that of the ordinary Australian bush.

Ernest Favenc, *Voices in the Desert*, 1905

Set in what is just about the geographical centre of the continent, **Alice Springs** has a population of just 25,000, yet is still the largest settlement of the Australian interior. A clean, modern and compact town in the midst of the MacDonnell Ranges, it makes an excellent base from which to plan trips into the surrounding countryside.

The **Red Centre**, a marketing term coined to describe the area to the south, west and east of Alice Springs, is an historically rich and scenically spectacular region. It includes the lands inhabited by the "Anangu", the more easily pronounceable name for the Aborigines from the Uluru region. The Aborigines around here were fortunate in being among the last to come into contact with white settlers. As a result of this and the necessary strictness of desert nomads' laws, they and their fascinating but arcane culture have survived relatively unscathed. Here, as much as anywhere in Australia, some Aborigines are living the life of their choice on their traditional homelands, and dealing with the neighbouring white culture on their own terms.

Ayers Rock – known to the Anangu as **Uluru** – is Australia's most famous and most visited natural spectacle, and still the primary reason why most people come to the Red Centre. At first sight, even jaded "seen-it-all" cynics will find it hard to take their eyes away from its awesome bulk. But there's much more here than just the Rock, and it's rare in Outback Australia to find such a large region crammed with worthwhile and accessible places of interest. The **West MacDonnells**, a series of rugged ridges cut at intervals by slender chasms or enormous gorges, start right on Alice's doorstep. In the other direction, the **Eastern MacDonnells** are less visited but no less appealing, with the remote tracks of the **Simpson Desert** to the south attracting the intrepid. To the west, **Palm Valley**, now linked to **Kings Canyon** via a good dirt road, can add a few days to a trip which, including the Rock, makes for probably the most memorable tour in the Outback. While most of these places certainly don't need a 4WD vehicle to get to, there are a few enjoyable and easy off-road tracks that can be fun in a rented 4WD; they're detailed in the box on p.580.

When to go

The aridity of the Centre results in extremes of temperature that are best avoided, if at all possible. In the midwinter months of July and August the air is lovely and clear although **freezing nights**, especially around Uluru, are not uncommon. But there's no escaping the **summer heat**: in December and January the temperature may have already reached 40°C by 10am and doesn't drop below 30°C all night. Autumn (April–June) and Spring (Sept & Oct) are ideal times to explore the region in comfort.

Rain is a rare and wonderful thing in the Centre. In Alice, most houses don't have gutters: they would rarely be needed and, in any case, would be unable to cope with the deluge when it comes. Whenever you visit, a sudden storm may temporarily transform the desert into a garden of exquisite flowers as well as cut off access along even the main roads.

Out here a **wide-brimmed hat** is not so much a fashion accessory as a life saver, keeping your head and face in permanent shadow. All but the shortest of walks will also require a **water bottle** and loose, long-sleeved clothing plus lashings of **sun block** on any exposed skin. Australia's many venomous but rarely seen snakes and, more relevantly, rocky tracks and the carpet of prickly spinifex grass that covers one-fifth of the continent, make a pair of **covered shoes or boots** the final elementary precaution to safe and comfortable enjoyment of the Centre.

Alice Springs and around

Most visitors are surprised by the modern appearance of **ALICE SPRINGS**. The bright, clear desert air gives the Outback town a charge you don't find in the languid, tropical north. In Alice, the shopping centre is in the busy town centre and not in some peripheral suburb, and so allusions to Nevil Shute's flyblown *A Town Like Alice*, or even Robyn Davidson's ockersome observations in *Tracks*, have long been obsolete.

The area has been inhabited for at least thirty thousand years by Aranda Aborigines, who moved between the waterhole of Alice Springs (Tjanerilji) and other reliable water sources in the MacDonnell Ranges. But, as elsewhere in The Territory, it was only the Overland Telegraph Line's arrival in the 1870s that led to a permanent settlement here. Following **John McDouall Stuart's** exploratory journeys through the area in the early 1860s, it was the visionary **Charles Todd**, then South Australia's Superintendent of Telegraphs, who saw the need to link Australia with the rest of the empire. The town's river and its tributary carry his name, and the spring that of his wife, Alice.

With repeater stations needed every 250km from Adelaide to Darwin to boost the OTL signal, the site just north of today's town, with its permanent "spring" (actually a billabong on the Todd River), was ideal as a place to erect the necessary buildings. When a spurious ruby rush led to the discovery of gold at Arltunga in the Eastern MacDonnells, **Stuart Town** (the town's seldom-used official name in its early years) became a jumping-off point for the long slog to the riches out east. Arltunga's goldrush fizzled out under desperate conditions, but the township of Stuart remained, a collection of shanty dwellings serving a stream of pastoralists, prospectors and missionaries.

In 1929 the **railway line** from Adelaide finally reached Stuart Town. Journeys that had once taken weeks by camel from Oodnadatta could now be undertaken in just a few days and by 1933, when the town officially took the name Alice Springs, the population had mushroomed to nearly five hundred Europeans. In 1942 the bombing and subsequent evacuation of Darwin saw Alice Springs become The Territory's administrative headquarters and a busy military base, supplying the war zone in the north. After the hostilities ceased, some of the wartime population stayed on and Alice's fortunes continued to grow slowly. In the meantime, wealthy tourists began to visit the mysterious monolith in the desert, southwest of town – for thousands of years a store of sites sacred to the Anangu.

With the reconstruction of the notoriously unreliable rail link from Adelaide and a new, tar-sealed, Stuart Highway completed in the mid-1980s, Alice has only recently attained its present size and unexpected modernity. A **tourist boom** at that time, helped in no small measure by the massive publicity surrounding Azaria Chamberlain's reputed canine abduction at the Rock (as portrayed in the movie *A Cry in the Dark*), has waned a little in recent years, but Alice still remains the undisputed "capital" of the Outback. Even so, the population remains tiny: within a thousand-kilometre radius of "The Alice", as it's affectionately known, there are fewer than forty thousand inhabitants. The town has embraced tourism wholeheartedly and although the continuing improvements of the on-site Ayers Rock Resort has affected trade, Alice still seems set to succeed, primarily because both the town and surrounding area have much to offer, even without the obligatory visit to the Rock.

Arrival, information and transport

The **airport** is 14km south of town. The airport shuttle (☎08/8953 0310) meets incoming flights and costs $9, while a taxi (☎08/8952 1877) will be about twice that amount. Greyhound Pioneer **buses** arrive at the Coles Complex on West Stott Street; McCafferty's buses outside their office on Gregory Terrace, opposite the tourist office. Some of the keener hostels send minibuses to meet incoming buses (as well as some incoming flights). Alice's **train station** – open only when trains are due to arrive – is on George Crescent on the west side of the Stuart Highway, just off Larapinta Drive, about a fifteen-minute walk (or $4 taxi ride) from the town centre.

The **tourist information office** (daily 9am–6pm; ☎08/8952 5800) is in Gregory Terrace at the river end by the library and council offices. Besides all the usual stuff there's also a helpful Parks and Wildlife Commission desk (☎08/8951 5210), providing information on their parks and other services in Central Australia.

Transport

The centre occupies a compact area between the Stuart Highway and Leichhardt Terrace, along the dry Todd River, bordered to the north and south by Wills Terrace and Stott Terrace respectively. Bisecting this rectangle is **Todd Mall**, once the main street, now a relaxing pedestrian thoroughfare lined with alfresco cafés, galleries and souvenir outlets.

The town's sights are scattered, but you can still get around them all in a couple of days on foot. An alternative is to use the green and yellow **Alice Wanderer** (☎08/8952 2111; day-ticket $22), a "hop on, hop off" bus service with commentary, visiting most of the places of interest every seventy minutes. The Yeperenye Shopping Centre, around the corner from the tourist office, on Hartley Street, is the terminus for the **suburban bus** network. This is tailored for shoppers and schoolchildren, which means you'll have to plan your ride around a timetable (available from the tourist office or the Council Offices on Gregory Terrace) rather than just turning up at a bus stop and waiting; of the four main routes, **#1 West** and **#4 South** are the most useful. Otherwise your best bet is to rent a **car** (see "Listings", p.572), or a **bicycle** from any of the hostels, for around $10 a day. There's an enjoyable seventeen-kilometre **paved cycle track** through the bush to Simpson's Gap, starting at Flynn's Grave, 7km along Larapinta Drive, west of the town centre.

Accommodation

There's plenty of choice of accommodation in Alice, most places (except the campsites) are either in the central area or along **Todd Street** and its continuation, **Gap Road** – a fifteen-minute walk from the centre, despite what people may claim. Booking ahead is advisable during the winter school holidays (June & July) or during special events. Note that the price codes given for self-contained apartments are for a unit sleeping between four and six people; they often work out a better deal all round than a motel and are certainly more spacious.

Motels

Diplomat Hotel, 15 Gregory Terrace (☎08/8952 8977, fax 8953 0225, free call ☎008/804 885). Right in town, a large, four-star motel popular with big bus tours. ⑥–⑧.

Frontier Oasis Motel, 10 Gap Rd (☎08/8952 1444, fax 8952 3776, free call ☎008/815 658). Nicely laid-out motel with landscaped pool area, comfortable rooms and a fine restaurant/bar. ⑦.

Territory Inn, Leichhardt Terrace (☎08/8952 2066, fax 8952 7829, free call ☎1800/089 644). Large motel backing onto Todd Mall and about as central as they get. ⑧.

Vista Hotel, Stephens Rd (☎08/8952 6100, fax 8952 1988, free call ☎1800/810 644). Well-equipped, modern four-star hotel tucked under the MacDonnell Ranges with a pool, tennis courts and a good restaurant. ⑧.

Self-contained apartments

Alice Tourist Apartments, corner of Gnoilya St and Gap Rd (☎08/8952 2788, fax 8953 2950, free call ☎1800/806 142). Large, well-equipped apartments at the far end of Gap Rd. ⑤–⑦.

Outback Motor Lodge, South Terrace (☎08/8952 3888, fax 8953 2166, free call ☎1800/896 133). Among the best deals in this category, with more room than many more expensive motels. ⑤.

Swagman's Rest, 67–69 Gap Rd (☎08/8953 1333, fax 8953 0404, free call ☎1800/089 612). Another good-value, self-contained option on Gap Rd. ⑤.

White Gums Holiday Inn, 17 Gap Rd (☎08/8952 5144, fax 8953 2092). Nearest self-contained apartments to town centre. ④.

Hostels

Alice Lodge, 4 Mueller St (☎08/8953 1975). Often-overlooked converted house in a quiet, residential area on the east side of the river, with no parking problems. Long-stay deals, nice garden and pool. Rooms ③, four-bed dorms ①.

Elke's, 39 Gap Rd (☎08/8952 8134, fax 8952 8143, free call ☎1800/633 354). Former s/c apartments with various-sized air-con rooms from twins to eights, each sharing a bathroom and small kitchen with TV. Nice pool area and free breakfasts make up for the lack of a good communal area. Rooms ③, dorms ①.

Melanka Backpackers Resort, 94 Todd St (☎08/8952 4744, fax 8952 4587, free call ☎1800/896 110). Huge complex of central but ageing motel buildings popular with unfussy young backpackers. Has a popular bar, *Skippy's*, and a cafeteria with cheap meals, a pool and even beach volleyball. Avoid the four-bed dorms unless you're a sardine, the eights have more room. Rooms ③, dorms ①.

Ossies Homestead, 18 Warburton St (☎08/8952 2308, fax 8953 2211, free call ☎1800/628 211). Small and friendly hostel in quiet residential street no further than the Gap Rd options, with pet 'roo, pool, bikes and horse rides too. Mixed dorms plus some four- and twin-bed rooms. ①–③.

Pioneer YHA, Todd River end of Parsons St (☎08/8952 8855, fax 8952 4144). The most central location by far, just half a minute from the "Sails" awning (though parking can be a problem). Mostly four-bed air-con dorms, plus a pool and a clean and spacious kitchen. ①.

Toddy's Backpackers, 41 Gap Rd (☎08/8952 1322, fax 8952 1767). Popular large resort next to *Elke's* and with very cheap mixed, eight-bed dorms, smaller dorms and "de luxe" double rooms with bath, fridge and TV. Bargain evening meals with bar, barbecues and occasional entertainment, pool, bikes, tour information and bookings. Rooms ③, air-con dorms ①.

Campsites and caravan parks

Heavitree Gap Outback Resort, Palm Circuit, 2km south of Heavitree Gap (☎08/8952 4866). Smart, newly renovated campsite with powered sites and good facilities and its own pub, *AJ's Tavern*. On-site vans ③.

Stuart Tourist Park, opposite Araluen Centre, Larapinta Drive (☎08/8952 2547). Most central caravan park with regular camping and powered sites. On-site vans ③.

Wintersun Caravan Park, Stuart Highway, 3km north of town. Regular camping and powered sites. On-site vans ③.

The Town

Start your tour of town by nipping up to **Anzac Hill** (off Wills Terrace) for a great view over Alice to the Heavitree Ranges beyond. Next stop is the **Museum of Central Australia** on the first floor of Alice Plaza (Mon–Fri 9am–5pm; $2) right by the **"Sails"** awning where Parsons Street crosses Todd Mall. The museum focuses on regional natural history including displays of gems, fossils and local meteorites, plus a cast of the petroglyphs at Ewaninga (see p.582). Just down Parsons Street is the **Old Courthouse** (daily 10am–2pm; donation), former residence of the governor of southern NT; it now

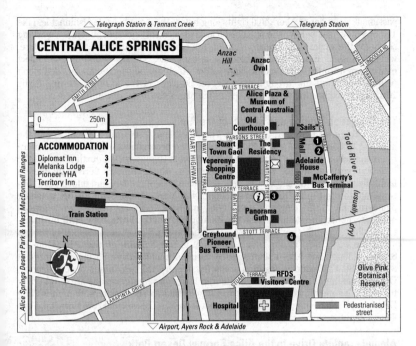

displays the National Pioneer Women's Hall of Fame. Across the street, though barely worth the effort, is the **Residency** and the **Stuart Town Gaol**, the latter Alice's oldest building, dating from 1909.

From the "Sails" awning, a short stroll down the mall will take you past **Adelaide House** (March–Nov Mon–Fri 10am–4pm, Sun 10am–noon; $2), an ingenious convection-cooled building designed by the Reverend John Flynn, founder of the Royal Flying Doctor Service (RFDS). Adelaide House was the first hospital in Central Australia, and also the site of Flynn and Alf Treager's innovative radio experiments using portable, pedal-generated electricity. Inside you'll come across early medical and RFDS memorabilia. If you want to find out more about the RFDS, head down Hartley Street to the **RFDS Visitors Centre** (March–Nov Mon–Sat 9am–4pm, Sun 1–4pm; $3) on Stuart Terrace, which has half-hourly tours including a film describing the work of this unique medical organization, still subsidized by charitable donations.

Next door to Adelaide House is the **John Flynn Memorial Church** and, at 65 Hartley St, you'll find **Panorama Guth** (Mon–Sat 9am–5pm, Sun 2–5pm; $4), a museum and art gallery displaying Henk Guth's eminently forgettable landscapes, as well as original Albert Namatjira watercolours (see p.579 for more on Namatjira's life and the Hermannsburg school of painting he initiated). Much more curious is the collection of rare Aboriginal artefacts found here, including some sacred and totemic objects (*tjuringas*) that you'll rarely see elsewhere. The panorama, from which the gallery takes it name, is a novel if unremarkable painting, 60m in circumference, showing the area around Alice, but the gallery below is a wonderfully comfy and congenial place to snooze through the regional home movies on show.

When you've had enough of artefacts and memorabilia, pack a lunch and cycle out to the **Olive Pink Botanical Reserve** (daily 10am–6pm; donation), just across the causeway on Tuncks Road. Olive Pink, whose life story is about to be made into a film, was a passionate defender of Aboriginal rights long before the issue became fashionable. Like Ted Strehlow (see below) she practised a kind of fanatical "inverted eugenics", working solely for the welfare and preservation of "full blood" tribal Aborigines and their lore, while dismissing those of mixed blood as a lost cause. She also found time to collect native flora from the surrounding lands, all of which can be seen neatly labelled along pathways winding up through the reserve. Displays in the **visitors centre** (daily 10am–4pm) explain the various strategies the plants use to survive in the desert.

The Telegraph Station and School of the Air

The old **Telegraph Station** (daily 8am–7pm, until 9pm Oct–April; $4) is tucked in the hills just to the north of town. Fully restored and accessible along a three-kilometre riverside walk from Wills Terrace (or off the Stuart Highway, 4km north of town), the historic reserve – situated right by the pool from which the town derives its name – faithfully re-creates the settlement's earliest years. There are free and informative thirty-minute **tours** (April–Oct 8.30am–4.30pm; Nov–March 10am–3pm) further detailing pioneering life at the telegraph station – all in all, it's a pleasant place to while away a quiet afternoon. The station is also the starting point of the **Larapinta Trail** bushwalk to Standley Chasm in the Western MacDonnells (see p.575).

On the other side of the Stuart Highway is the **School of the Air** (Mon–Sat 8.30am–4.30pm, Sun 1.30–4.30pm; closed during school holidays; $3, children free), at 80 Head St. Explanatory sessions are offered every thirty minutes on this famous Outback institution, through which children living on remote stations are taught over the radio. It's mostly visited by overseas schoolchildren and teachers, though visiting British royalty have taken a nodding interest at various times, to . From town take bus #3 and alight at stop 5 or 11.

Along Larapinta Drive to the Alice Springs Desert Park

Larapinta Drive heads out through the western suburbs past the Araluen Arts Centre, some 2km from the town, to the new Alice Springs Desert Park, now one of the town's premier attractions. The walk to the Araluen isn't too bad, but check out the new bus service heading this way if you're continuing to the park.

The **Araluen Arts Centre** (daily 10am–5pm; $2), Alice's performing arts and entertainment centre, incorporates a gallery, cinema and theatre. There's usually something interesting on in the gallery or you can look out for the bimonthly What's On sheets available here and around town.

Next to the Arts Centre is the **Ted Strehlow Research Centre** (daily 10am–5pm; $4), which houses an absorbing exhibition dominated by the life and works of Ted Strehlow, son of a Hermannsburg missionary and Aranda initiate, who devoted his life to studying these Aborigines. Betraying their trust in later years, Strehlow disclosed his ceremonial knowledge and sacred objects to his second wife, Kathleen, and a battle now seethes for the return of the material that the late Strehlow collected. Many of the *tjuringas* are locked "for safe keeping" in the centre's vault; some are so sacred that they should only ever be seen by initiated Aranda men.

In response to new cultural centres popping up around the NT, there are plans to reprofile the exhibition's focus away from Strehlow's life and provide more detail on the old ways of the Aranda. For a taste of Strehlow's work, his sixty-page article *Central Australian Religion*, published in 1964, is available at the Arunta Bookshop (see "Listings"); it's a good taster before getting stuck into his weightier *Aranda Traditions* (1947), whose ideas were taken up in the well-known works of Claude Lévi-Strauss.

Around the corner on Memorial Drive, the **Old Connellan Hangar** (daily 9am–5pm; free) houses many of the aircraft that pioneered travel in the Outback. There is a special memorial to the **"Coffee Royale Incident"** of 1929, when the rescuers of missing aviator Charles Kingsford-Smith themselves crashed and perished in the northern Tanami desert. Kingsford-Smith, a national hero, was accused of cynically staging the crash for publicity purposes; the memorial poignantly displays the wreckage of the long-lost *Kookaburra* used in the search. Also on Memorial Drive, the **Alice Springs Memorial Cemetery** includes the graves of pioneer aviator Eddie Connellan, artist Albert Namatjira and the reburied remains of the legendary, luckless prospector Harold Lasseter, after whom the town's casino is rather ironically named.

Alice's latest attraction is the **Alice Springs Desert Park** (daily 7.30am–6pm; $14), phase one of which opened in March 1997. Set right beneath the ranges topped by Mount Gillen, the park is an example of a thoughtful and imaginative design displaying various natural environments of The Territory. Allow yourself at least two hours to fully appreciate the centre's ecology. Shown on the hour, the twenty-minute **film** is actually a little over-portentous, and the real highlight, after you've wandered through various **aviaries** and creek, sand dune and woodland habitats, is the large **nocturnal house** where The Territory's varied, but rarely seen, fauna can be seen scurrying around in moonlit action. The park succeeds in blurring the boundary between the surrounding bush and the fenced interior – there's as much birdlife darting about outside the aviaries as in. Not to be missed.

Eating

For a town with the population of a couple of New York precincts, the **eating opportunities** in Alice aren't at all bad. And some places can turn a meal into an event, such as the dinners served on the old Ghan train once or twice a week (☎08/8955 5047); evenings at *The Winery* (☎08/8955 5133); or a ride out into the bush to crack whips and throw boomerangs, while the damper bakes, with the *Camp Oven Kitchen* (☎08/8953 1411). Alternatively, start the day with a gourmet **champagne breakfast**, having just watched the sunrise from a thousand metres up in a hot-air balloon (see "Tours from Alice" box, overleaf).

Otherwise, Todd Mall is lined with **cafés** providing outdoor seating, and the **pubs** (see "Drinking, nightlife and entertainment" overleaf) supply counter meals for well under $10. Besides the places listed below, some of the **hotels** have good restaurants; a queue of chattering locals is always a good sign.

Cafés and snack bars

Alice Plaza, Todd Mall. Food halls with Asian- and Italian-inspired lunches.

Bar Doppio Mediterranean, Fan Arcade, Todd Mall. Mouthwatering concoctions of trans-Adriatic and Asian dishes with pitta or rice.

Red Rock Bakery, Todd Mall, south end. Good spot for morning croissants and coffee before some serious didge shopping.

Swinger's, Gregory Terrace, opposite the Environment Centre. Snazzy café, with a distinctly "arty/green" feel, serving imaginative snacks and meals.

Restaurants

Al Fresco, Todd Mall, next to the cinema. Delicious pasta and salad dishes with movie-and-meal deals on Monday night.

Dingos, Stott Terrace. Distinctive old building with a "bush meat", seafood and veggie menu.

Lasseters Hotel Casino, Barrett Drive. Lays on a nightly $18 buffet with the best of everything ($21 seafood buffet on Wed) to tempt you onto the pokies. A gourmet bargain for non-gamblers.

Madigans, Alice Springs Desert Park, Larapinta Drive. Top quality bush tucker with a great setting (noon–3pm & 6.30pm–late).

Oscars, Todd Mall Cinema Complex. A classy Italian restaurant offering surprisingly good-value and large portions, mostly under $15.

Overlander Steakhouse, 72 Hartley St (☎08/8952 2159). For the spirit *and* taste of the Outback; the "Drover's Blowout" gives you all your favourite Aussie fauna on a plate.

Scotty's Tavern and **Alice's Restaurant**, Todd Mall. Bar and restaurant serving typical Territorian food (including emu).

Sri Devi, Shop 2, Gregory Terrace. Alice's only Indian restaurant seems to have scared all the competition away with its delicious and varied menu.

Drinking, nightlife and entertainment

Like the surrounding desert, night-time Alice initially appears lifeless. However, something can be found going on somewhere most nights, particularly in the latter half of the week. The fortnightly freebie, *Pulse*, or Alice's daily *Centralian Advocate*, carry details of what's going on.

The *Todd Tavern*, at the top of Todd Mall, is the town's premier **drinking** spot, putting on a jam session until the early hours on Monday night. Thursday night at *Bojangles* on Todd Street is all action and *The Stuart Arms*, right by the "Sails", also

---

TOURS FROM ALICE

A large number of professional **tour operators** offer adventurous, cultural or historic tours throughout the area – some recommended operators are listed below. Just about every hostel and hotel offers a tour-booking service, but if you feel you need more advice, ask at the official tourist information office on Hartley Street on the corner of Gregory Terrace (see "Arrival, information and transport", p.566).

AAT Kings (☎08/8952 1700) and **Holidays NT** (☎08/8953 2897). Day-trips to Uluru for $130 – but you'll regret such a short visit. AAT also offers Eastern MacDonnell tours on demand.

Ballooning Downunder (☎08/8952 8816), **Outback Ballooning** (☎08/8952 8723) and **Spinifex** (☎08/8953 4800). Alice is Australia's ballooning capital and any of these will take you up, up and away – and back down to a champagne breakfast. Don't wear your best clothes, as all hands are needed to pack up the dusty balloon.

Frontier Camel Tours (☎08/8953 0444). Short camel rides down the Todd River, two-and-a-half-day West Mac jaunts from *Glen Helen Lodge*, and five-day Simpson Desert treks.

Ooramina Bush Camp (☎08/8952 2308). One hour south of Alice offering horse rides and cattle station tours.

Ossie's Outback Horse Treks (☎08/8952 2308). Day, sunset and overnight rides up the Todd River's east bank from $60. Beginners welcome; discounts for YHA/VIP members.

Outback Experience (☎08/8955 2666). The best operator currently running trips to Chambers Pillar and other places in the northern Simpson.

Outback Mail Flights (☎08/8953 5000). Join the air-mail delivery service on their three weekly runs up to Rabbit Flat northwest of Alice; northeast to the Utopia region or southeast to Mount Dare station on the edge of the Simpson. It's an interesting alternative to standard scenic flights for around $220.

Rockayer (☎08/8956 2345) and **Yarringka Air** (☎08/8956 7873). Flights to the Rock and back in a day for around $300.

Rod Steinert (via AAT Kings, free call ☎1800/679 418). Several Aboriginal culture tours in the Alice area, including the excellent, half-day Dreamtime tour. While the apparently solemn "corroboree" will bore or embarrass you, the rest of the tour is unusually informative, educational and provocative.

Sahara Outback Tours (☎08/8953 0881). Offers two-, three- and five-day camping tours through the West MacDonnells, to Kings Canyon and Uluru. As is often the case, the longer tours are much the best value.

features **live bands** most nights. The latter pub also houses *Legends*, the town's most popular **nightclub**; if you want to get past the bouncers, then collars and covered shoes are "the go". There's **jazz** at *Scotty's* on Friday night and at *The Winery* on Sunday afternoon from 1pm. If nothing else tempts you, there's always the **cinema** at the top of Todd Mall, with cheap nights on Tuesday. Check the programme at the **Araluen Arts Centre** (☎08/8952 5022) on Larapinta Drive: you'll usually find a worthwhile play, film or concert. And if you're feeling lucky, *Lasseters Hotel Casino* on Barrett Drive can accommodate you – but again, not in thongs and a tatty singlet.

Events
More energetic activities tend to occur in the cooler months, starting with April's **Heritage Week** celebrating Alice's history, followed by the **Bangtail Muster** on the first Monday in May, a colourful and irreverent parade of silliness. The **Camel Cup races** in mid-July are Australia's biggest camel race meeting, ending in a huge fireworks display. The string of **rodeos** along the Track hits Alice in late August, while the town's most famous event, the wacky **Henley-on-Todd Regatta** kicks off in early October. Bottomless boats are run down the dry riverbed; needless to say, the event is heavily insured against the Todd actually flowing. On the last Sunday in November there is the **Corkwood Festival**, a celebration of art, music and dance, with food and craft stalls in Todd Mall. There's also a rather uninspiring **market** every Sunday in the mall.

Shopping for Aboriginal art

Alice has become the country's foremost centre for the art and crafts produced by Aboriginal people, and Todd Mall is full of galleries selling a vast range of high-quality work. Most common are the **dot paintings**, canvas depictions of the temporary sand paintings formerly used to pass on sacred knowledge during ceremonies of the Central Desert tribes. The modern manifestation of this school of art originated in the early 1970s at Papunya, northwest of Alice, under the encouragement of a local teacher, Geoff Bardon. What was intended as a kind of constructive graffiti for youngsters was taken up by the elders. Clifford Possum and Billy Stockman were among the earliest of the Papunya artists to find fame, and their paintings are free of the clumsy flashiness of some contemporary work. There are half a dozen lavish books offering a compilation of Central Desert art, the best of which is *Songlines and Dreamings* by Patrick Corbally Stourton (Lund Humphries) – you'll find it in Alice's bookshops.

While it's more difficult to recommended a single **gallery**, you'd do well starting your search at the Original Dreamtime Gallery, 63 Todd Mall, the Aboriginal Art and Culture Centre, 86 Todd St (it's still just a gallery despite the name) or Gallery Gondwana, 43 Todd Mall; all are attractive galleries full of good-quality work with the latter displaying some lovely Indonesian artefacts too. Less fancy in appearance but loaded with quality unframed canvases is the Aboriginal-owned Papunya Tula Artists, at 78 Todd St, and the similar Warumpi Arts round the corner on Gregory Terrace; you certainly won't save money by buying direct – usually the opposite – but you might feel happier about who benefits from the proceeds. Another place offering mediocre but inexpensive paintings and didgeridoos is The House of Oz, opposite *Melanka Backpackers Resort*, but in the end it's just a matter of spending half a day or more looking for what you want at a price that you find acceptable. The more you spend, the more chance there is of making a deal, with free overseas postage and insurance usually offered at the bigger places. If you're heading north, the galleries in Aileron, Ti Tree (see p.562) and Tennant Creek (p.560) have a much smaller range of Aboriginal art on sale, but often at less than half the price of that in Alice's galleries.

BUYING AND PLAYING A DIDGERIDOO

Didgeridoos, the simple wooden instruments whose eerie sound perfectly evokes the mysteries of Aboriginal Australia, have become phenomenally popular souvenirs in the last couple of years, with many vendors offering to pack and ship them to your home for free (expect a three-month delivery time to Europe). Authentic didges are created by ter-mite-hollowed branches of trees and are considered to be indigenous to the Katherine region (where they can also be cheaper to buy). Minuscule, bamboo and even painted fibreglass didges have found their way onto the market, but a real didge is a natural tube of wood with a rough interior. Painted versions haven't got any symbolic meaning; plain ones look less tacky and are less expensive. Branches being what they are, every didge is different but if you're considering playing it rather than hanging it over the fireplace, aim for one around 1.3m in length with a 30–40mm diameter mouthpiece. Beeswax is often used to bring an oversize didge's mouthpiece down to an operable size, but a didge with a body of the right diameter and without wax can feel nicer to use. The bend does-n't affect the sound but the length and wall thickness (ideally around 10mm) does – avoid cumbersome, thick-walled items which get in the way of your face and sound flat.

You'll be surprised that making the right sound instead of an embarrassing raspberry will take only a few minutes of persistence; the key is to hum while letting your pressed lips flap, or vibrate, with the right pressure behind them – it's easier using the side of your mouth. The tricky bit – beyond the ability of most initiates – is to master circular breathing; this entails refilling your lungs through your nose while maintaining the sound with air expelled from your cheeks. A good way to get your head round this con-cept is to blow or "squirt" bubbles into a glass of water with a straw, while simultaneously inhaling through the nose. Unless you get the hang of circular breathing you'll be limit-ed to making the same lung's worth of droning again and again.

Most outlets that sell didges also sell tapes and CDs and inexpensive "how to" booklets which offer hints on the mysteries of circular breathing and how to emit advanced sounds using your vocal chords.

The Sounds of Starlight show in Todd Mall (Nov–April Tues–Sat 7pm $15) features Alice didge impressario Andrew Landford and friends and gives you a good chance to hear what can be done with a didge as well as being an entertaining night out. You'll also be given a free lesson afterwards, if you want.

And finally, remember that there is nothing magical about a didgeridoo; it's your lips that make the sound which resonates through the tube, any tube. A length of grey 40mm PVC pipe from Mitre 10 may not have the same kudos but produces a similar sound at around $4 a metre.

Listings

Airlines Ansett (☎08/8950 4115); Qantas (☎08/8950 5211). Both in Todd Street Mall near the "Sails", where you'll also find Flight Centre for discount flights (☎13 1600).

Banks All major banks are located on Todd Mall.

Bookshops Arunta Bookshop, Todd St, is very good for local history plus Aboriginal art and cul-ture. Bookworm, Colacag Plaza (in the block between Gregory and Stott terraces), buys and sells secondhand books.

Camping supplies Alice Springs Disposals, Reg Harris Lane, off Todd Mall. See also "Secondhand Stuff" opposite.

Car rental CC Rentals (☎08/8952 1405, free call ☎1800/652 133), at 78 Todd St opposite the coun-cil offices, has mopeds, mokes and Suzuki 4WD jeeps, as well as special deals, as does Territory Thrifty (☎08/8952 9999), on the corner of Hartley St and Stott Terrace. They offer larger and much more comfortable Land Cruiser 4WDs with twin fuel tanks, plus an easily erected roof tent and a bundle of camping gear for just $25 extra per day. Britz Rentals Australia (☎08/8952 8814) uses more basic Land Cruisers converted into campers which have the advantage of built-in equipment which doesn't rattle around. Maui (free call ☎1800/363 800) offers identical campers, and Thrifty, at 92 Todd St (☎08/8952 2400), has bargain-priced 2WDs.

Fuel 24hr service and marginally cheaper fuel at the Shell truckstop on the North Stuart Highway.

Hospital Gap Rd (☎08/8951 7777).

Internet and email Coin-ops at the *YHA*, *Toddy's* and *Melanka's* or normal computers at the library (corner of Gregory and Leichhardt terraces) for around $5 an hour.

Maps The Map Shop, 21 Gregory Terrace (☎08/8951 5393), for detailed maps of the Centre.

Police Parsons St (☎08/8951 8888).

Pharmacies On Todd Mall and in the Yeperenye Shopping Centre.

Post office Hartley St (☎08/8952 1020).

Secondhand Stuff Curios, Shop 1, Coles Arcade, off Bath St, for collectables, or its larger alternative, Buffalo Secondhand (down Gap Rd), for tattier, cheaper items.

Trains The *Ghan* leaves Alice Springs each Tuesday and Friday at 2pm and arrives in Adelaide at 10am the next day, with the return leg to Alice departing Adelaide on Monday and Thursday at 2pm and arriving at 10am. Coach class (no bed or meals) costs $170 ($136 from Port Augusta); first class costs over three times as much, with a sleeper and meals included; with "holiday class" you get a four-berth sleeper for around $351, but no meals. Change at Port Augusta to connect with the *Indian Pacific* line.

Sights south of Alice

Several sites of interest are located beyond **Heavitree Gap**, a couple of kilometres south of town. The first three described below are within range of the #4 bus, which terminates at the **Old Timers Folk Museum** (April–Nov daily 2–4pm; $2), just off the Stuart Highway, yet another display of pioneering memorabilia. The remainder are easily reached by bike, or on the Alice Wanderer bus route.

Head first for the **Pitchi Ritchi Aboriginal Cultural Experience** (daily 9am–2pm; $15), out on Palm Circuit, which, in addition to being a collection of fairly crude, bush-gnarled relics, is also an animal sanctuary. The work of Leo Corbett, who once staked a bogus gold-mining claim on Heavitree Gap (Pitchi Ritchi means "gap in the range") to prevent it being quarried and widened, the sanctuary also features the peculiar Aboriginal-inspired sculptures of William Ricketts, which further enhance the place's eccentric feel. While here you're offered a mug of billy tea and damper and given the opportunity to crack whips, throw boomerangs and play a didgeridoo while the resident "bushie" plies you with yarns and Aboriginal lore.

GHAN . . . BUT NOT FORGOTTEN

The legendary unreliability of the **old Ghan rail service** must have had the Afghan cameleers, whose services it replaced and in whose honour it was named, chuckling in their graves. The poorly surveyed line, which was laid directly onto the sand with little regard for contours and floodways, buckled, subsided and was frequently completely washed away by flash floods. Indeed, it was not terribly uncommon for the track to be washed out either side of the stranded train, requiring parachute drops of essential supplies to sustain the passengers while the line was relaid and bedded-in. Consequently, late arrivals were common – trains arriving up to three months late were recorded.

In 1980, the new line from Port Augusta, rerouted and constructed from "continuous", welded rails, reached Alice ahead of schedule, with trains now carrying twice the number of passengers in half the time. With its arrival, the fifty-year-long era of the notorious *Ghan* passed into history. The millions of redundant timber sleepers from the old line have been put to a variety of uses all over central Australia, propping up bars and cattle yards or fabricated into restaurant tables. They can still be found in the bush out along the old *Ghan* route or bought inexpensively at the Transport Heritage Centre (see overleaf), making an authentic, if cumbersome, souvenir of the Centre's first rail link.

Next door, the **Mecca Date Garden** (Mon–Fri 9am–5pm, Sat 9am–1pm; free) was Australia's first commercial date farm, set up in the 1950s. Dates themselves are believed to be the first plant to be cultivated by man, and the farm now produces around 3000kg of the fruit a year from trees introduced last century by Afghan cameleers. You are offered a free sample on arrival. Tours of the farm – basically rows of date palms with an informative commentary – start on the hour.

A farm of a very different sort is just a couple of kilometres down the Ross Highway. The **Frontier Camel Farm** (daily 9am–5pm; $10) offers short rides on camels, plus a museum of camels and cameleering as well as the **Arid Australian Reptiles Display**, a creepy round-up of the Centre's snakes and lizards. Introductory camel talks are given at 10.30am and 2pm (the Alice Wanderer bus coincides with these), and the Camel Farm also organizes longer tours in the region.

Back down the Stuart Highway just before the airport, about 10km south of town, the **Transport Heritage Centre** (daily 9am–5pm; $6) features a converted old train station housing a **museum** of Alice Springs' early rail years ($4) and is also involved in the refurbishment of old *Ghan* locomotives and rolling stock, which are used for **train rides** (☎08/8955 5047) along a short section of track. In the big hangar the Heritage Centre features a collection of old cars, trucks and motorbikes, including a cute red Fiat Tipo, something called the "Mulga Express" (not your average touring Kingswood) as well as the original 8WD road train that used to slog up to Darwin during the 1930s at a hot and noisy 30kph.

The MacDonnell Ranges

The **MacDonnell Ranges** are among the longest of the parallel ridge systems that corrugate the Centre's landscape. Their east–west axis, passing right through Alice Springs, is broken in many places by gaps carved through the ranges during better-watered epochs. It is these striking ruptures, along with the grandeur and colours of the rugged landscape – particularly west of Alice – which make a few days spent in the MacDonnells so worthwhile. The expansive **West MacDonnells National Park** is best appreciated with at least one overnight stay at any of the campsites mentioned below, while the often-overlooked **Eastern MacDonnells** have a more compact, intimate feel; a better bet if your time is limited. Both ranges can be visited as part of a tour (see box on p.570) or with your own vehicle. Although some tracks are unsealed, 4WD vehicles are mostly unnecessary. However, because most rental companies prefer you not to drive conventional cars on corrugated tracks, you may end up renting one. If you do, then make the most of its all-terrain capabilities; check out the box on p.580.

A better way to get in touch with the West Macs is to do part of the **Larapinta Trail**, a long-distance footpath along the West MacDonnell ridge, starting at the telegraph station north of town (see p.568) and ending 220km to the west at Mount Sonder. The walk is divided into around a dozen sections with water tanks situated no more than a day's walk apart. So far, only some sections of the trail have been completed; call or visit the Parks & Wildlife Commission (☎08/8951 5210) in Alice's tourist information office for latest details and maps.

The West MacDonnells and Finke Gorge national parks

The **route** described below follows an anticlockwise loop out along Larapinta Drive and then Namatjira Drive to *Glen Helen Lodge*, from where a 110-kilometre dirt road brings you round to the turn-off for Palm Valley (4WD vehicles only), Hermannsburg and back to Alice – a total distance of 370km. The track passes through **Aboriginal land** on its return section, but no permit is required (unless stated), providing you keep to the road and camp at designated sites.

Leaving Alice along Larapinta Drive, you reach **John Flynn's Grave**, just past the Desert Park, 7km from town. Situated beneath Mount Gillen, a granite boulder set on a plinth marks the spot where John Flynn, founder of the RFDS, had his ashes interred in 1951. Originally one of the Devil's Marbles (see p.562), the boulder was recently claimed back by the Aborigines of that area, an example of the ridiculous excess of some land claims following the Mabo Decision (see p.998). A little further is a turning to **Simpsons Gap** (gates open daily 8am–8pm), the nearest and most popular of the West Macs' gaps, where a white, sandy riverbed lined with red and ghost gums leads up to a small pool. Agile rock wallabies live on the cliffs and there's a **visitors centre** and barbecues, as well as a seventeen-kilometre cycle track leading back to town. The first stage of the **Larapinta Trail** ends here – a tough day's walk from the telegraph station in Alice.

Further along Larapinta Drive are the **Twin Ghost Gums**, immortalized in Albert Namatjira's definitive painting of the Centralian landscape, and just after the famed gums is a turn-off north to the tourist trap of **Standley Chasm** (daily 7.30am–6pm; $4), 50km from Alice. Situated on Iwupataka Aboriginal Land, this is another popular spot, where a walk up the cycad palm-lined riverbed leads to a narrow chasm formed by the erosion of softer rock that once lay between the red quartzite walls. Around noon both the eighty-metre-high walls are briefly lit by the overhead sun. There is also a café with a terrace and a souvenir shop; black-footed rock-wallabies are fed here daily at 9.30am.

Along Namatjira Drive
Another 6km along Larapinta Drive, **Namatjira Drive** turns north amid the West MacDonnell Ranges; continuing on Larapinta brings you to Hermannsburg and Palm Valley (see p.579). Along Namatjira Drive, a scenic 42km ahead is **Ellery Big Hole** (barbecues, toilets and camping; $1), the deepest – and thus most permanent – waterhole in the area, and at times the coldest. Nevertheless, caught between the brief ebb and flow of visiting bus tours, it's a pleasant spot, and your stealth may be rewarded by glimpses of wildlife quenching their thirst. Eleven kilometres to the west is **Serpentine Gorge** (toilets but no camping): the only way to appreciate this gorge is to swim across the small pool which sometimes blocks the entrance to the gorge (or climb over the ridge to the right). Few bother to exert themselves, but rock hopping upstream brings you to a flooded chasm. Like many concealed and perennial pools in Central Australia, its Aboriginal custodians have nurtured a myth about the pool being the home of a fierce serpent, and even today reluctantly visit the place and never enter the water; Mutujulu waterhole at Uluru has a similar legend. In this way the myth acted as a superstitious device to ensure that the pool – a droughtproof source of water vital to the humans that drank it – was never polluted or carelessly used.

With a new interpretation shelter and a wonderful new walk to **Inarlanga Pass** (actually a narrow gorge), the **Ochre Pits**, signposted off Namatjira Drive, now make an interesting diversion. The ochre, particularly the red variety, became a highly valued trading commodity and is still used by the Aranda for ceremonial purposes. The **two-hour walk** to the pass along rounded ridges and through wooded valleys is most enjoyable. Once at Inarlanga you'll find the egg-like kernels of cycads on the boulder-strewn creek bed, which is itself framed by acutely twisted beds of rock; altogether a lovely spot lacking only a waterhole.

Fourteen kilometres further west, **Ormiston Gorge** and **Pound National Park** (barbecues and camping) are also worth the effort. One of the most scenically spectacular and easily accessible spots in the West Macs, the short ascent up to **Gum Tree Lookout** (the walk continues down into the gorge) gives a great view over the 250-metre-high gorge walls rising from the pools below – home to ducks and even the odd

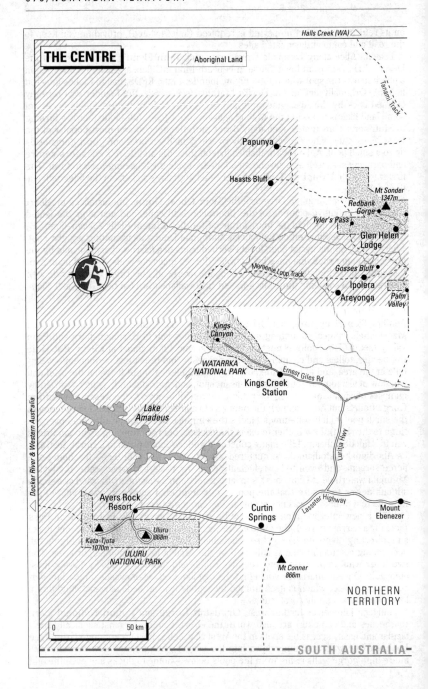

THE CENTRE

/// Aboriginal Land

Halls Creek (WA) △

Tanami Track

Papunya

Haasts Bluff

Mt Sonder 1347m

Redbank Gorge

Tyler's Pass

Glen Helen Lodge

N

Mereenie Loop Track

Gosses Bluff

Ipolera

Areyonga

Palm Valley

Kings Canyon

WATARRKA NATIONAL PARK

Ernest Giles Rd

Kings Creek Station

Lake Amadeus

Luritja Hwy

Ayers Rock Resort

Kata-Tjuta 1070m

Uluru 868m

ULURU NATIONAL PARK

Curtin Springs

Lasseter Highway

Mount Ebenezer

Docker River & Western Australia

Mt Conner 866m

NORTHERN TERRITORY

0   50 km

SOUTH AUSTRALIA

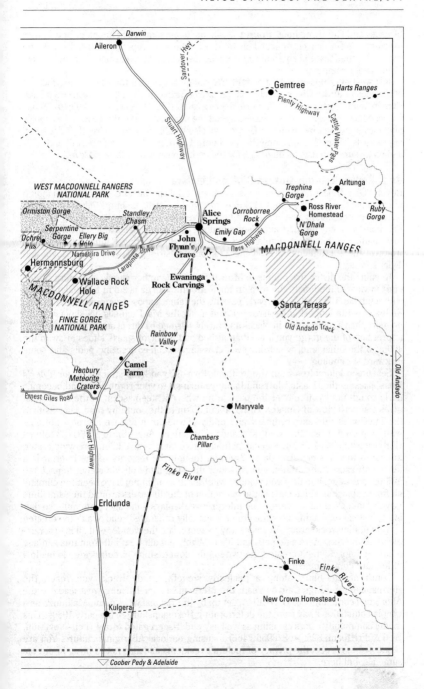

black swan. The three-hour **Pound Walk** includes some rock-hopping, and longer overnight walks can be undertaken by those who are properly prepared – ask the rangers at the Park Information Centre, who also organize occasional free slide show evenings for campers.

Just west of Ormiston is **GLEN HELEN**, another perennial waterhole along the bed of the ancient **Finke River**, which – on the rare occasions when it flows – can reach Lake Eyre in South Australia. *Glen Helen Homestead* (☎08/8956 7489, fax 8956 7495; ②–⑦) has reopened and provides a cosy place to spend the night out in the West Macs. Helicopter flights over the nearby Ormiston Gorge may also be still operating here. If you're heading towards Kings Canyon along the **Mereenie Loop Track**, get your permit here ($2) and make sure you have enough fuel for the entire journey of at least 250km.

On to Redbank Gorge, Gosses Bluff and Ipolera

Beyond Glen Helen the bitumen ends, but the natural spectacles continue. If you intend to complete the loop, it's about 111km of dirt to the Hermannsburg/Palm Valley turn-off, and another 30km east along Larapinta Drive back to the bitumen leading to Alice. Providing you stay on the road, it's easily done by 2WD vehicles at a sensible pace in dry conditions, but most regular cars turn back after visiting Redbank Gorge. The worst of the corrugations are on the 37-kilometre stretch between Glen Helen and Tyler's Pass.

Keeping the distinctive outline of **Mount Sonder** (another classic Namatjira silhouette) in view to the north, the turn-off for **Redbank Gorge** is 20km from Glen Helen, with a further 10km to the car park, passing the rather exposed **campsite** on the way. Redbank is the longest and narrowest cleft along the MacDonnells its slippery walls no more than a metre apart in places and rarely warmed by direct sunlight. To get a full impression of the gorge you'll need an airbed and a pair of sports shoes to swim the 400m to the other end, which involves crossing seventeen freezing pools and some awkward scrambling.

Seventeen kilometres from the Redbank turn-off, you keep straight on for **Tyler's Pass**, passing the Haasts Bluff and Papunya turn-off to your right. The road becomes fairly rough until you're over the pass, from where a steep ascent to the radio mast gives a superb view of **Gosses Bluff**, about 30km to the south by road. Day visits to the interior of this extraordinary and oddly played-down feature are now possible with a permit from the Central Lands Council in Alice Springs (31–33 Stuart Highway; ☎08/8951 6320). You can actually drive into the five-kilometre-wide crater, known to the Western Aranda as *Tnorula*, though the majority of the interior is a fenced-off sacred site. When you consider the magnitude of this comet impact 140 million years ago, it makes you wonder whether this might not have been the climate-shifting explosion which caused the extinction of the dinosaurs around the same time (give or take 20 million years). The interpretive displays don't speculate quite so daringly, instead explaining how the crater is actually the frayed relic of a dome created by rebounding rock strata. An easier way to appreciate the wonder of it all is to scramble up to the rim; there's no path and it's probably not allowed, but from this vantage point the impact which created the two-hundred-metre-high circular ridge is made a little more comprehensible.

South of the bluff, along a perfectly smooth, sandy track, you reach the Hermannsburg–Kings Canyon road: the Mereenie Loop. Turning west leads to the Aboriginal community of **IPOLERA**, set up by the visionary Hermann Malbunka as a Utopian outstation away from the deteriorating Hermannsburg of the early 1980s. This model community offers camping as well as gender-segregated **tours** (Feb–Nov Mon, Wed & Fri 10am; $25; ☎08/8956 7466) focusing on local Aboriginal culture. You are requested to respect the privacy of Ipolera's residents and also not to bring in or consume alcohol here.

Finke Gorge National Park

The popularity of **FINKE GORGE NATIONAL PARK** is founded on its prehistoric cycads and unique red cabbage palms which have survived in the park's sheltered **Palm Valley** for over ten thousand years. Despite the difficult 4WD road leading to the valley it's on every tour's itinerary, though it doesn't quite live up to the hype. The pleasant forty-minute loop walk is the valley's highlight; visiting the rest of the park requires a 4WD vehicle and seems discouraged, as does the route along the Finke riverbed from Hermannsburg (see box overleaf). On the way in or out of the valley, you can climb up to the once-sacred **Initiation Rock**, giving a fine view over the **Amphitheatre**, a cirque of sandstone cliffs. The park has barbecues, toilets, solar-heated showers and camping.

HERMANNSBURG, until recently a Lutheran Mission, is the oldest Aboriginal community in the Centre, dating from the 1870s. Unusually, visitors are able to visit the town, or more particularly the **Historic Precinct** (daily 9am–4pm; $4) which features the original mission buildings converted into tearooms and an art gallery (tours $3). Bob will rattle off his spiel on the history of the mission and the life and work of Albert Namatjira who was born here (see box below), although his observation about the "totemic faces" concealed in Namatjira's paintings should be taken with a pinch of salt. There is also a supermarket and fuel (cash only), but no accommodation.

Back towards Alice Springs, passing the **Albert Namatjira Memorial,** you reach the small community of **WALLACE ROCKHOLE**, offering sixty-minute tours (☎08/8956 7415; $5) of the nearby Aboriginal petroglyphs as well as a shop, fuel and camping. The same rules and courtesies apply as for Ipolera (see opposite). From here, it's 117km of bitumen back to Alice Springs.

The Eastern MacDonnells

Heading out of Alice through the **Heavitree Gap** and along the Ross Highway, you soon reach **Emily Gap**, Alice's nearest waterhole, 10km from town. This is one of the

---

ALBERT NAMATJIRA 1902–1959

Born on the Hermannsburg Lutheran mission in 1902, Albert, who added his father's name to appease Eurocentric propriety, was the first of the Hermannsburg mission's much-copied school of landscape watercolourists. Although without much previous painting experience, Namatjira assisted Rex Battarbee on his painting expeditions through the Central Australian deserts in the 1930s. His talent soon became obvious to Battarbee, who later became Namatjira's agent. Like all NT Aborigines at that time, Namatjira was forbidden to buy alcohol, stay overnight in Alice Springs or leave The Territory without permission, but at the insistence of southern do-gooders – and against his wishes – he was the first Aborigine to be awarded Australian **citizenship**, in 1956. This meant he could travel without limitations, but needed a permit to visit his own family on Aboriginal reserves, while the house in Alice he longed for was denied him for fear of the "entourage" he might have attracted. Following the success of his first exhibition in the south, which sold out in three days, he became a reluctant celebrity, compelled to pay taxes on his relatively huge earnings which were further depleted by the "share-it-all" kinship laws that still hamper successful Aboriginal artists today. A shy and modest man, much respected for his earnestness and generosity, he died in 1959 following a sordid conviction and short imprisonment for supplying alcohol to fellow Aborigines.

Critics could never make up their minds about his work, but his popular appeal was undoubted: exhibitions in the southern cities, which he rarely attended, persistently sold out within hours of opening, and today his paintings remain among the most valuable examples of Australia's artistic preoccupation with its landscape. If you'd like to buy prints of Albert Namatjira's work, the cheapest place in Alice is the Museum of Central Australia's shop in Alice Plaza, and not in Hermannsburg, as claimed.

SOME FOUR-WHEEL-DRIVE TRACKS IN THE CENTRE

While most us have little need to own a heavy, fuel-guzzling 4WD, renting one for a few days of off-road driving is fun and can get you to some beautiful corners of the central deserts visited only by other intrepid "four wheelers". Below are some **4WD-only** routes close to Alice, which will give you a chance to fiddle with the transmission levers and which could all be linked into a leisurely and memorable week in the dirt. Remember that 4WD vehicles are not invincible: when driven carelessly they can easily get stuck, become uncontrollable or damaged. They can also make a mess of the terrain if driven away from main tracks; avoid wheel spins and tearing up vegetated ground which takes years to recover. Finally, make sure the outfit you're renting from understands and approves your proposed 4WD itinerary and, *at the very least*, read the advice and carry the gear recommended in "Basics", p.36. Ask at Alice's tourist office for the *4x4 Tracks and Unsealed Roads of Central Australia* leaflet, which details other routes in the area. For recommended 4WD rentals agents see the "Listings" for Alice. One problem with renting is that you're never supplied with any essential recovery gear; even a second spare tyre has to be prised out of the rental companies and yet they encourage you to take your vehicle off road. Although most of the rental cars are in good shape, it is in your own interest to make sure you are appropriately equipped, especially for travelling in remote areas.

Finke River Route

With a day to spare and minimal experience with a 4WD, following the Finke riverbed from **Hermannsburg** down to the **Ernest Giles Road** offers an adventurous alternative to the highway. Rewards include stark gorge scenery, a reliable waterhole and the likelihood that you'll have it all to yourself. Before you set off, seek out the ranger at Palm Valley (☎08/8956 7401) who'll fill you in on the state of the track and provide a handy map that clarifies all the junctions. When on the route follow the small signs for "Kings Canyon".

The hundred-kilometre track starts immediately south of Hermannsburg and after 10km of corrugated road, you descend into the riverbed. From now on it's slow driving along a pair of sandy or pebbly ruts – you must deflate your tyres to at least 25psi/1.7bar and keep in the ruts to minimize the risk of getting stuck. The sole designated campsite is at **Boggy Hole**, much nicer than it sounds and around two hours (28.5km) from Hermannsburg. The campsite looks out from beneath river red gums to permanent reed-fringed waterholes, best seen at dawn as the sunlight creeps across the gorge and the ponds are alive with birdlife.

Beyond Boggy Hole, the track crisscrosses rather than follows the riverbed before the roller-coaster ride to the Giles Road across some low dunes thinly wooded with desert oaks – beware of oncoming traffic on blind crests. Boggy Hole to the Giles Road is 65km,

most significant Aranda sacred sites, the start of the Caterpillar Dreaming trail. There are engravings on the far side of the soupy pool, and plenty of darting birds and irksome flies; camping or open fires are not permitted. **Jessie Gap**, a little further east, is similar in appearance, but usually dry and of limited appeal. **Corroborree Rock** (camping), 45km east of Alice, is an unusual, fin-like outcrop of limestone with an altar-like platform and a crevice whose polished appearance suggests that, if not Aranda initiates, then plenty of tourists have squeezed through in a rite of passage. Known as *Antanangantana* to the Aranda, it was once a repository for sacred *tjuringa* objects.

John Hayes Rockhole and Trephina Gorge

John Hayes Rockhole and Trephina Gorge, by far the most satisfying of the accessible destinations in the Eastern MacDonnells, are just 80km from Alice. Both offer superb scenery and a selection of enjoyable walks, and there's a four-hour ridge walk linking the two. **John Hayes Rockhole** (limited camping space), reached along a rocky four-kilometre track requiring a high-clearance vehicle, is a series of pools linked by (usually dry) waterfalls along a canyon. The ninety-minute "Chain of Pools" walk takes you so allow three hours. If you fancy taking the direct route to the Ernest Giles Road from the Tempe Downs station track, keep straight over the dunes just after a salt pan instead of turning sharply east; subsequent dunes can be avoided but the Palmer River crossing can be very sandy and may require further tyre deflation. Back on the road, keep speeds down until you can reflate your tyres.

Arltunga to Ruby Gap

The same sensible precautions are required for this route; make sure you're well equipped and see the ranger at the **Arltunga Visitors Centre** (☎08/8951 5250), 101km east of Alice, for the latest track conditions. It's a very scenic if bumpy 53-kilometre drive (allow two hours) through the ranges and including some steep creek crossings until you reach the sandy riverbed of the Hale and the **Ruby Gap Nature Park**. From here keep to the sandy ruts and inch carefully over the rocks for 7km to **Glen Annie Gorge**, a dead end with maroon red cliffs, bright green reeds and off-white sand.

Cattlewater Pass and the Harts Ranges

A less difficult track heads north from Arltunga past Claraville station and up over the Harts Ranges through the **Cattlewater Pass** to the Plenty Highway, 67km or three hours from Arltunga. It's a worthwhile and no less scenic way of returning to Alice from Ruby Gap via a different route and you're bound to see some hopping marsupials along the way. Once you reach the Plenty Highway it's an easy dirt road via Gemtree to the Stuart Highway and Alice, 150km away.

The Finke and Old Andado Tracks

More ambitious than the above and a satisfying 750-kilometre loop into the fringes of the Simpson Desert are the **Finke** and **Old Andado tracks** whose routes diverge at Alice's airport and rejoin at **Mount Dare station** just over the South Australian border. At Alice airport the westerly Finke branch follows the route of the old *Ghan* railway past Ewaninga rock carvings and Maryvale (fuel), where you can take an 88-kilometre return diversion to Chambers Pillar (more on these three places on p.583). After Maryvale it's a straight run to Finke (fuel) with the sandy or corrugated track being fun and mostly 2WD. On the way you'll pass stands of desert oak, shrubs and claypans and you might even see some feral camels. Just as things seem to be getting too easy the track sometimes gets sandier soon after Charlotte Waters towards Mount Dare, where you can buy fuel, provisions and a beer at the bar. Heading back to Alice (433km, no fuel) towards Old Andado, the track can again be sandy, but from the old homestead the going gets much easier as you cross the low ranges bringing you past the Santa Teresa community and the road back to the airport. For an outline of the Simpson crossing itself, from Mount Dare to Birdsville, see p.762.

to the top of the gorge and down through the pools – an ideal way to get hot, but with plenty of opportunities to cool off. Alternatively, the lower pools are accessible from the car park.

Trephina Gorge, perhaps the most impressive spot in the eastern part of the range, is a beautiful, sheer-sided sandy gorge whose rich red walls support slender, white-barked ghost gums and a pool. There is a pleasant **campsite** and the "Gorge" and "Panorama" walks (both taking about 30min) are well worth the effort.

Ross River Homestead and Arltunga Historical Reserve

Five kilometres beyond Trephina Gorge, the Ross Highway peters out into two tracks: 8km to the southeast (90km east of Alice Springs) is the **Ross River Homestead**, an Outback resort (☎08/8956 9711, fax 8956 9823; cabins ⑦, bunkhouse ①, camping also available), which offers "dude ranch" activities such as camel, horse and wagon rides, boomerang throwing, whip cracking and billy tea with damper. It's a comfortable, if relatively busy, base for a few days' stay in the Eastern MacDonnells, and has a popular bar, pool and restaurant.

The other track, a 35-kilometre corrugated dirt road heading east, leads to **ARL-TUNGA**, the site of central Australia's first goldrush. The road here may be long overdue for a grading, but a whole heap of money has been spent on restoring the ghost town and providing it with a fancy **visitors centre** (daily 8am–5pm; ☎08/8951 5210). All the place needs now is some visitors. Arltunga's story began in the 1890s, in the midst of the country's first economic depression, when gold was discovered by the miners originally drawn to the garnets at Ruby Gorge (see below). Over the next fifteen years they regularly pushed barrows the 600km from Oodnadatta railhead to grope in desperate conditions for pitiful returns. Arltunga was never a particularly rich field and remains an abandoned testament to pioneering optimism. On the way here you pass the somewhat overnamed *Arltunga Hotel & Bush Resort* (☎08/8956 9797; ④), which offers camping, basic rooms and a pub that was once known as "The Loneliest in the Scrub".

Ruby and Glen Annie gorges

From Arltunga it's a fairly rough 4WD out to Ruby and Glen Annie gorges, both of them beautiful and wild places. Back in 1885 the explorer Lindsay discovered "rubies" while in the process of digging for water, thereby initiating the customary rush for what turned out to be worthless garnets. Crossing the sandy Hale riverbed leads into **Ruby Gorge** and then **Glen Annie Gorges** (no facilities except camping). At the end of the day, even with the flies handing over to the mozzies, it's one of the most tranquil places you'll find in Central Australia.

South to Uluru: the Stuart Highway and Kings Canyon

Kings Canyon is 320km southwest of Alice Springs, of which the hundred-kilometre section from the Stuart Highway turn-off towards Stockyard Homestead/Wallara is unsealed. From Stockyard, it's bitumen all the way to the Watarrka National Park which envelopes Kings Canyon. You can also get to Kings Canyon the back way along the **Mereenie Loop Track** from Hermannsburg, a distance of around 260km. You'll need a $2 **permit** from Alice's tourist information, *Glen Helen Lodge* or reception at the *Kings Canyon* resort (if you're returning to Alice via the Mereenie). If you're heading straight down the Track there's an increasingly barren run of nearly 700km to Coober Pedy (itself no oasis) in South Australia.

Most **tours** of two days or more departing from Alice include Kings Canyon on their see-it-all itineraries, providing the easiest and cheapest way to enjoy the canyon. There are daily McCafferty's and Greyhound Pioneer bus services from Alice Springs to Kings Canyon, or from Ayers Rock Resort with AAT Kings.

The Old South Road and the northern Simpson Desert

Just 14km out of Alice, shortly after the airport turn-off, a sign indicates "Chambers Pillar (4WD)". This is the **Old South Road**, which follows the abandoned course of the *Ghan* and original Overland Telegraph Line to Adelaide, 1550km away; these days the sandy and corrugated route has become one arm of a loop which takes adventuresome four-wheel drivers through the northern Simpson Desert past Finke settlement and Old Andado homestead (see box on p.580).

Ordinary cars can easily manage to cover the 35km to **Ewaninga Rock Carvings**, a jumble of rocks by a small claypan (a dried-up pool) littered with Neolithic chippings. Their meaning, like that of other petroglyphs in the area, remains unknown but their age, estimated at 35,000 years, suggests that they certainly predate occupation of the Centre by today's Aborigines. A full-size cast of the mysterious engravings can be found at the Museum of Central Australia in Alice (see p.566).

Heading into the northern fringes of the **Simpson Desert**, past the windswept community at **MARYVALE** (shop and fuel), you'll need a 4WD vehicle to get across the Charlotte Ranges and subsequent dunes on the way to **Chambers Pillar** (toilets, barbecues and camping), an historic dead-end, 165km from Alice. Named by Stuart after one of his benefactors (who has natural features named after him and his family all the way to the Timor Sea), the eighty-metre-high sandstone pillar was used as a landmark by early overlanders heading up from the railhead at Oodnadatta, in South Australia. The plinth is carved with their names, and with those of many others, and can be seen after scrambling up the pillar's base. After many futile warning notices, a visitors' book was found to be the most expedient way of averting illegal, modern additions to the pillar. If you don't fancy renting your own vehicle, Outback Experience in Alice (☎08/8953 2666) has interesting full-day tours to this area.

The Stuart Highway to Kings Canyon

Around 76km from Alice, the turn off the Stuart Highway to **Rainbow Valley** (barbecues and camping, but no water or firewood) is easy to miss – turn left just before the yellow sign indicating "Jim's Place 14km". A twenty-kilometre dirt track, the very last bit of which may be sandy, leads to the "valley", actually a much-photographed outcrop set behind claypans which are said to produce rainbows following rain. More commonly, sunset catches the red-stained walls spectacularly and it's a wild place to spend the night, best followed in the morning by a climb up the crag.

Noel Fullerton's Camel Farm (daily 7am–5pm; ☎08/8956 0925) lies another few kilometres down the main highway. One of Australia's most experienced cameleers, Fullerton exports some of the Centre's huge population of feral camels back to their Arabian homelands, where a fit racer is worth about $5000. Popular photo-opportunity rides cost $3, and longer camel safaris can also be arranged.

Beyond the Camel Farm you reach the Ernest Giles Road, where you turn off right for Kings Canyon; note that the first hundred kilometres are unsealed. Not far along this road there's another turn-off, to **Henbury Meteorite Craters**. The extra-terrestrial shower that caused these twelve depressions, 2–180m in diameter, may have occurred in the last twenty thousand years, given that the Anangu have several names for the place, one of which translates as "sun walk fire devil rock". A walk with interpretive signs winds among the faintly visible craters, long since picked clean of any unearthly fragments. It's a rather bleak, treeless area for camping, but there are barbecues and toilets.

The Ernest Giles Road heads west, sandy at times but a lot of fun if you're in the mood, joining the sealed Luritja Highway linking Ayers Rock Resort to Kings Canyon. The bitumen road continues west, past **Kings Creek station** (☎08/8956 7474, fax 8956 7468) 35km from the canyon. Unlike most other pastoral properties in Australia, Kings Creek has taken to rounding up and selling the feral camels which other station owners regard as vermin (see box p.553). Ninety-minute **tours** of the four-thousand-square-kilometre property are available ($10) as well as camel rides around the paddock ($3). You'll also find a well-equipped campsite, pool, fuel and a shop.

Watarrka National Park (Kings Canyon)
As you cross the boundary of the **WATARRKA NATIONAL PARK**, you'll see the **ranger station** (☎08/8956 7460), which has a relief model of the park and its environs, but is not really a visitors centre and you may well have to coax the rangers into imparting their knowledge. Just on from here is the turning to **Kathleen Springs**, an easy

twenty-minute stroll to a sacred Aboriginal waterhole once used to corral livestock and now a good place to catch sight of colourful birdlife.

Another few minutes down the road is **Kings Canyon** itself. The big attraction here is the superb three-hour horseshoe **walk** from the car park up and around the canyon's rim: undertaken in a clockwise direction, it starts with a steep ascent as the well-marked trail leads through the **Lost City**, a maze of domes resembling giant petrified cowpats stacked at random. Don't miss the exposed **lookouts** onto the two-hundred-metre-high southern wall before you cross the **Garden of Eden**, a palm-filled cleft bridged by an impressive array of staircases. On the far side there's an easily missed detour downstream to the waterhole where you can **cool off**, and, a bit further on, a dramatic lookout from the very throat of the canyon. From the car park another less strenuous and undemanding walk leads into the canyon itself, while a new two-day trail east to Kathleen Springs may be completed by now.

There are now some long overdue improvements in facilities but no **camping** at Kings Canyon itself, although you can camp elsewhere in the park with a ranger's permit. Ten kilometres past the canyon, the *Kings Canyon Hotel* (☎08/8956 7442, fax 8956 7410) is a small **resort** with a neat, grassy campsite, a bunkhouse with four-bed rooms (②–⑥) and a bare kitchen. Away from the rabble, the much more expensive *Lodge* (⑧) offers a pool and great views. The café (6am–10pm), by the service station and shop (daily 7am–7pm), serves meals for about $12; otherwise try the $30 buffet at *Carmichaels Restaurant* at the *Lodge*. Ask at the resort's reception (daily 6.30am–9.30pm; ☎08/8956 7442) about daily Lilla Tours (10.30am; $25) with local Aboriginal people, helicopter **flights** and Mereenie Loop permits. A **shuttle bus** ($10) operates daily from the resort reception to the canyon.

Uluru–Kata Tjuta National Park and Ayers Rock Resort

Uluru–Kata Tjuta National Park encompasses **Uluru** (the Anangu name for **Ayers Rock**) and **Kata Tjuta** (or the **Olgas**). The park is the most visited single site in Australia and if you're wondering whether all the hype is worth it, then the answer is, emphatically, yes. The Rock, its textures, colours and not least its elemental presence, is without question one of the world's natural wonders. Overt commercialization has been controlled within the park and other tourists can be avoided, especially if you choose not to undertake the climb.

Kata Tjuta (meaning "many heads") lies 45km west from the park entry station. A cluster of rounded domes divided by narrow chasms and valleys, it is geologically quite distinct from Uluru. Public access is largely limited to the "Valley of the Winds" walk, partly because the eastern area is still a sacred site to the Anangu men. None of the domes, including Mount Olga, actually 200m higher than Uluru, is safe to climb.

You can't camp, let alone so much as pick a flower in the park, nor can you go anywhere other than Uluru and Kata Tjuta or the Cultural Centre. Instead the **Ayers Rock Resort**, part of the settlement of Yulara, just outside the park, takes care of all tourists' needs.

Getting there

It's 210km from Alice to **ERLDUNDA**, a busy roadhouse (camping and cabins; ④) on the Stuart Highway, from where the **Lasseter Highway** heads to Ayers Rock Resort, 247km to the west. After 56km is *Mount Ebenezer Roadhouse* and later the turning for the **Luritja Highway**, which leads up to the Kings Canyon road.

The next thing to catch your eye will be the flat-topped mesa of **Mount Conner**, sometimes mistaken for Uluru by the myopically over-keen. *Curtin Springs Station*

(☎08/8956 2906), 11km west of Mount Conner, is a roadhouse and bar offering the last inexpensive accommodation (camping free with $1 charge for showers; rooms ④–⑤) before Ayers Rock Resort. There's also a shop, fuel, bar and a collection of colourful parrots out back. You-know-what is now only 80km away.

Ayers Rock Resort (Yulara)

Like any purpose-built settlement, **AYERS ROCK RESORT** (aka Yulara), built at a cost of $250 million, possesses a certain prefabricated sterility, but it's not the eyesore it could have been. A few years ago a private company took over the management of the resort from the NT government, which somehow managed to keep losing money at a place just about everyone *has* to visit on the way to the Rock. Liberal renaming and more relevant improvements have succeeded in burying Yulara's notorious reputation once and for all.

All the town's facilities branch off a central ring road called Yulara Drive around which a **free bus** circulates 10.30am–2.30pm and 6.30pm–midnight. Within this ring is a duned area crisscrossed with tracks and the Imalung Lookout, scanning the Rock and Kata Tjuta on the horizon. In the **Shopping Square**, off Yulara Drive, you'll find a post office (Mon–Fri 9am–6.30pm, Sat & Sun 10am–2pm), supermarket (daily 8.30am–9pm), newsagent, baker and an ANZ **bank** (Mon–Thurs 9.30am–4.30pm, Fri 9.30am–5pm) with a 24-hour cashpoint. The nearby **amphitheatre** hosts evening entertainment including "tribal" dancing (Tues–Sun).

Near the Imalung Lookout there's an **Observatory** (☎08/8956 2563), which takes advantage of the exceptionally clear skies in the desert to scan the sun by day and stars by night. Tours, costing $20, include pick-ups and drop-offs and start at 8.30pm and 10.15pm.

Practicalities

Buses will either drop you off at your chosen accommodation, where you'll be given a town map, or at the Shopping Square which is the hub of the resort. All incoming **flights** to Connellan Airport, 6km from town, are met by a free shuttle bus – **taxis** (☎08/8955 2152) cost about $5. The **tour and information centre** (daily 8.30am–8.30pm; ☎08/8956 2240) is located on the main square while the **visitors centre** (daily 8.30am–5pm) is down Emu Walk, providing absorbing visual displays on the geology, nature and Anangu connections with Uluru – well worth an hour's browse.

ACCOMMODATION

Wherever you stay, **book ahead** during the winter school holiday period (June/July), unless camping. All these places are situated off Yulara Drive, no more than ten minutes' walk from the Shopping Square.

Ayers Rock Campground (☎08/8956 2055, fax 8956 2260). Electric barbecues, small shop, swimming pool and well-kept grassy sites for tents. On-site air-con cabins ⑤.

Desert Gardens Hotel (☎08/8956 2100, fax 8956 2156). Three-star hotel offering quality rooms and a pool. ⑧.

Emu Walk Apartments (check-in at *Desert Gardens Hotel*; ☎08/8956 2000, fax 8956 2328). Oddly designed but well-equipped self-contained apartments with one or two bedrooms (sleeping 4–6). Close to shops and pub. ⑧.

Outback Pioneer Lodge (☎08/8956 2170, fax 8956 2320). Modern place for backpackers and self-caterers with kitchen facilities, a takeaway kiosk and the pricier *Rocks Bistro* by the grassy pool area. Motel rooms with en-suite bathrooms ⑦; twenty-bed dorms ①–②; cabins (sleeping up to four, with fridge, tea/coffee-making facilities) ⑦.

Sails in the Desert Hotel (☎08/8956 2200, fax 8956 2018). Luxury-class hotel with rates starting around $351. ⑧.

ULURU NATIONAL PARK TOURS FROM AYERS ROCK RESORT

AAT Kings (☎08/8952 1700). Shuttle service and bus tours to the park. Sunrise or the climb for $34; five-hour Rock/Olgas tours for $57 and sunset viewing for $22. Also new 24-hour "Ayers Rock Pass"; all the above tours for $104, making for a packed day.

Air North (☎08/8945 2999) and Ayers Rock Helicopter (☎08/8956 2077). Thirty-minute scenic flights from $65 and 15-minute helicopter flights around the Rock

from $95 with longer options as far as Kings Canyon available.

Uluru Experience (☎08/8956 2563). Personalized walking tours around Uluru and Kata Tjuta with local experts from $35. See their free sixty-minute slide show at the auditorium, next to the visitors centre, daily at 2pm.

Uluru Motorcycle Tours (☎08/8956 2019). Fantasy-fulfilling pillion-posing around the Rock from around $60.

Spinifex Lodge (☎08/8956 2131, fax 8956 2163). One-bedroom units (sleeping up to four), with a basic kitchenette but shared bathrooms, near the Shopping Square. ⑦.

EATING AND DRINKING

Geckos, Shopping Square. Continental-style restaurant serving wood-fired pizzas, pastas, seafood and steak, all from around $15–25. Open 10am–10pm.

Kunia Room, *Sails in the Desert Hotel* (☎08/8956 2200). Top-notch à la carte restaurant – perfect for a splurge, or if someone else is paying. Or try the less expensive *Rockpool* offering Thai and Western dishes.

Outback Pioneer Hotel, Yulara Drive. The kiosk (6.30am–9pm) here has various offerings, including fish and chips for $7, but the best deal is the hotel's cook-your-own barbecue (6.30–9.30pm) for around $6–10 including salad. The *Bough House Restaurant* also has an Outback-style buffet for around $28 a head.

Quick Bites, Shopping Square. Open 9am–6pm. Good-quality sandwich bar.

Uluru–Kata Tjuta National Park

Even with our bus tours and our fully automatic cameras and our cries of "Oh, wow!", we still couldn't belittle it. I had come expecting nothing much, but by the power of the thing itself I had, like some ancient tribesman wandering through the desert and confronting the phenomenon [sunset on Uluru], been turned into a worshipper. Nobody was more surprised than I.

Geoff Nicholson, *Day Trips to the Desert*

The entry fee for **ULURU–KATA TJUTA NATIONAL PARK** (daily: from one hour before dawn to one hour after dusk; $15, under 16s free) permits unlimited access for up to five days. Besides the two major sites of Uluru and Kata Tjuta, the park also protects over 500 species of plants, 24 native mammals and no less than 72 species of reptiles – for this reason access off the sealed roads, away from the two sites, is forbidden.

The new **Uluru–Kata Tjuta Cultural Centre** (daily: April–Oct 7.30am–5.30pm; Nov–March 7am–6pm; ☎08/8956 3138), situated on the access road 1km before the Rock, opened in 1995, on the tenth anniversary of the handing back of Uluru to its traditional owners. The centre also houses a café, souvenir shop and gallery, and all together you'd want to allow yourself two hours to fully appreciate the place. As in the Kakadu equivalent at Cooinda, the strikingly innovative design doesn't conceal the fact that you're getting a very sanitized coverage of Aboriginal life. You pass an exposition of the dramatic mythical events at the dawn of creation, an uninspiring film of an *inma* (ceremony) and end with a display of men's and women's artefacts. In the next hall you can play with buttons to learn the right pronunciation of words such as "Anangu" or "Uluru". You leave saturated with the usual "Dreamtime myths, caring for the land" and

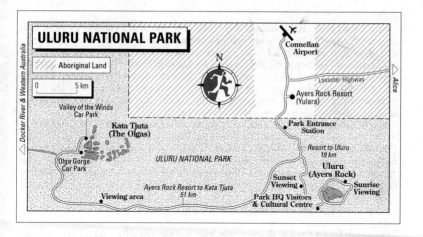

the ever-present "bushtucker" know-how, while interesting if sensitive questions such as how significant, if at all, are age-old spiritual values to contemporary Aboriginal people are not considered. There are free, ninety-minute **tours** of the cultural centre (Mon–Wed 3.15pm). The free ranger-guided **Mala Walk** (daily: April–Oct 10am; Nov–March 9am; 90min) takes you from the centre to the base of the Rock and is a good introduction to Anangu perceptions and beliefs. Anangu Tours (☎08/8956 2123; from $65) offers a chance to explore the park with Aboriginal guides.

Otherwise, leaflets are available at the information desk on the park's geology, flora and fauna, as well as informative *Park Notes* on various topics and issues. The *Tour Operator's Workbook* ($35) is the definitive handbook to the park, with as comprehensible an explanation of Anangu culture as you'll find here. Around the back, the outdoor Maruku Gallery (daily 8.30am–5.30pm) displays arts and crafts from local artisans, and at the shop consider buying yourself the *Triumph of the Nomads* video, based on Geoffrey Blainey's incisive book. Both recount how the Aborigines were skilful masters rather than helpless victims of their environment.

Uluru

The first European to set eyes on the Rock was the explorer Ernest Giles, in 1872, but it was another explorer, William Gosse, who followed his Afghan guide up and so completed the first recorded ascent by a European a year later, naming it **Ayers Rock** after a South Australian politician. With white settlement of the Centre came relocation of its occupants from their traditional lands, merely to make way for pastoralists' stock to overgraze the fragile desert environment.

In 1958 the national park was excised from what was then the Petermann Aboriginal Reserve but subsequently returned, with much flourish, to the Yankunytjatjara and Pitjantjatjara groups in 1985, following a ten-year battle. Reclaimed, and renamed, as **Uluru**, the site was initially not much changed under Aboriginal ownership, since the park was simultaneously leased back to the ANCA and tourism continued unaffected. But since that time the traditional owners' influence has manifested itself with characteristic subtlety, gently guiding the park's development. The owners get twenty percent of your park entry fee as well as a $75,000 yearly royalty.

ANANGU MYTHOLOGY

Uluru, Kata Tjuta and the surrounding desert are bound to a culture whose holistic cosmology sees the People – *anangu* – as having the Land and the Law – *tjukurpa* – as their central tenet of belief. A little confusingly, *tjukurpa* can also refer to the Time of Creation or "Dreamtime". The Anangu are thought to have occupied this area for around twenty thousand years and *Uluru* is the name of a waterhole near the summit. Like all religious mythology (and traditional fairy tales for that matter), the *tjukurpa* seeks to provide its adherents with a connection with the past, and a code of strict rules by which to live and behave correctly.

While Uluru is a key intersection along many "dreaming trails" (or Songlines, as Bruce Chatwin's book of that title described them) – principally those of the **Mala** (hare wallaby), **Liru** (poisonous snake), **Kuniya** (python) and **Kurpany** (monster dog) – it is not the shrine some imagine; a muddy waterhole 200km away may be as significant. Uluru is important to the Anangu as a reliable source of water and food and as one of many landmarks along the trails created by the Anangu's Dreamtime ancestors.

GEOLOGY

The reason Uluru rises so dramatically from the surrounding land is because it is a **monolith** – that is, a single piece of rock. With few cracks to be exploited by weathering, and the layers of very hard, coarse-grained **sandstone** tilted to a near-vertical plane, the Rock successfully resists the denudation of the landscape surrounding it. If one can visualize the layers of rock, then Uluru is like a cut loaf, its strata pushed up to near-vertical slices so that from one side you look at the flat ends while elsewhere the separate layers are clearly evident as eroded grooves – the pronounced fluting effect along the Rock's southeast and northwest flanks. Brief, but spectacular, waterfalls stream down these channels following storms. In places, the surface of the monolith has peeled or worn away, producing bizarre features and many caves, mostly out of bounds. The striking orangey-red hue, enhanced by the rising and setting sun, is merely skin deep, the result of oxidation ("rusting") of iron in the normally grey rock.

UP AND AROUND THE ROCK

It takes less than an hour to **climb** to the summit of Uluru, but make no mistake, it will be the greatest exertion you will undertake during your visit to Australia. Although an Anangu sign at the base requests you not to undertake the climb (only Mala men used to do so), seventy percent of visitors to the Rock come to conquer the summit. Probably a third give up and, on average, one climber a year dies, either from a heart attack, straying off the track or chasing windborne lens caps into oblivion. Gasping up the chained section you'll see why – for about fifteen minutes it's a very hard slog and if you slip or collapse you'll roll straight back down to the car park. But with a firmly attached hat, some water, secure footwear and frequent rests, you'll safely attain the summit, often a windy spot, especially in the morning. If you're at all unfit or nervous about heights and exposed places, *do not* attempt the climb.

Far less strenuous is the nine-kilometre **walk around the Rock**, which takes an easy three hours. It offers a closer look at Uluru's Anangu sites (though note that some of the sacred sites are closed to "uninitiates" – heed any warning notices) and the extraordinary textural variations. While the walk may not be a triumphant achievement, it can be more rewarding and is certainly more in keeping with the spirit of the place. For incorrigible couch potatoes, the twenty-minute walk from the base of the climb to **Mutitjulu**, a secluded pool, low-grade art site and scene of epic ancestral clashes marked by gashes in the rock, is recommended.

Kata Tjuta and on to WA

The "many heads", as **Kata Tjuta** – or the **Olgas** – translates from the local Aboriginal language, are situated 51km from the resort or Uluru. This remarkable formation may have once been a monolith ten times the size of Uluru, but has since been carved by eons of weathering into 36 "monstrous domes", to use Giles's words, each smooth, rounded mass divided by slender chasms or broader valleys. The composition of Kata Tjuta, very different from Uluru's fine-grained rock, can be clearly seen in the massive, sometimes sheared, boulders set in a conglomerate of sandstone cement. Access to this fascinating maze is limited to just two walks, in part because of earlier problems with over-ambitious tourists. Furthermore, the east of Kata Tjuta is a site sacred to Anangu men and is not accessible to the public.

The first of the permitted walks, the **Olga Gorge Walk**, is a rather pointless one-kilometre stroll into the dead-end chasm flanking Mount Olga (which, at 546m, is the highest point in the massif). Better by far is the **Valley of the Winds Walk**, a seven-kilometre loop trail which takes about two hours, or the five-kilometre "there and back" walk to a **pass** between two domes. This is as much as you can see of Kata Tjuta's interior without a permit. It's worth knowing that the large tour buses tend to visit the Rock in the early morning and Kata Tjuta in the afternoon. By reversing this trend you can avoid the worst of the crowds and enjoy this magical place in reasonable solitude.

From Kata Tjuta a track leads to the WA border at Docker River and from there along the **Warburton Road** to Laverton, north of Kalgoorlie (see p.632). The need for permits required to cross Aboriginal land in NT and WA has eased up in recent years (no one ever checked anyway) and now this short cut between the Centre and southern WA is seeing much more traffic. A 4WD is not necessary but the usual precautions for driving on the dirt should be taken, spare fuel, tyres and water, especially in summer. For more details of facilities along the Warburton Road, see p.635.

travel details

Trains

Alice Springs to: Adelaide (Tues & Fri; 20hr); Port Augusta (Tues & Fri; 17hr; change for Sydney or Perth).

Buses

Alice Springs to: Adelaide (3–4 daily; 27hr); Darwin (2–3 daily; 19hr); Katherine (2–3 daily; 15hr; change here for WA); Tennant Creek/Three Ways Roadhouse (2–3 daily; 6hr–6hr 30min; change at Three Ways for Queensland destinations).

Darwin to: Alice Springs (2–3 daily; 19hr); Katherine (2–3 daily; 4hr; change for WA); Tennant Creek/Three Ways Roadhouse (2–3 daily; 13hr–13hr 30min).

Katherine to: Alice Springs (2–3 daily; 15hr); Darwin (2–3 daily; 4hr); Kununurra (2 daily; 6hr 30min); Tennant Creek/Three Ways Roadhouse (2–3 daily; 9hr 30min).

Tennant Creek to: Alice Springs (2–3 daily; 6hr); Darwin (2 daily; 13hr); Katherine (2–3 daily; 13hr); Townsville (2 daily; 12hr).

Three Ways to: Alice Springs (2–3 daily; 6hr); Darwin (2 daily; 13hr); Katherine (2–3 daily; 13hr); Townsville (2 daily; 12hr).

Domestic flights

Alice Springs to: Darwin (1–2 daily; 2hr).

Darwin to: Alice Springs (1–2 daily; 2hr); Brisbane (1–2 daily; 4hr); Broome (1 daily; 2hr); Cairns (1 daily; 3hr); Perth (1 daily; 4hr 30min).

International flights

Darwin to Denpasar, Bali (3 weekly); Kuala Lumpar, Malaysia (1 direct weekly, or change at Singapore); Kupang, East Timor (4 weekly); Singapore (5–6 weekly).

CHAPTER SEVEN

WESTERN AUSTRALIA

Western Australia (WA) covers a third of the Australian continent; nearly the size of India, yet with less than half a percent of that country's population. Always revelling in its isolation from the more populous eastern states, WA is, like them, primarily a suburban state: three-quarters of its 1.7 million inhabitants live within 100km of Perth and almost all the rest live in communities strung along the coastline.

Perth itself retains the leisure-oriented vitality of a young city, while oceanside **Fremantle** resonates with a largely European charm. South of Perth, the **Margaret River Region**'s wooded hills and trickling streams support the state's foremost wine-growing and holiday-making area. To the southeast, the giant **eucalypt forests** around Pemberton further soften a land fed by heavy winter rains; the state's intensively farmed **wheat belt** stretches to the east, an interminable man-made prairie. Along the Southern Ocean's storm-washed coastline, **Albany** is the primary settlement, a rejuvenated resort with the dramatic granite peaks of the **Stirling Ranges** just visible from its hilltop lookouts. To the east, past Esperance on the edge of the Great Australian Bight, the deserted monotony of the **Nullarbor Plain** extends to South Australia, while inland the Eastern Goldfields' **Kalgoorlie** is the sole survivor of the century-old mineral boom on which WA's prosperity was originally built.

While the temperate southwest of WA has been relatively tamed by colonization, the north of the state is where you'll discover the raw appeal of the **bush**. The virtually unpopulated eastern deserts are blanketed with spinifex and sparse communities of Aborigines, while the west coast's winds abate once you venture into the tropics north of **Shark Bay**, home of the amicable dolphins at **Monkey Mia**. From here, the mineral-rich **Pilbara** region fills the state's northwest shoulder with the often-overlooked gorges of the **Hamersley Ranges** at its core. Visitors are also discovering the submarine spectacle of the **Ningaloo Reef**, lapping the North West Cape's beaches – some consider it superior to Queensland's Barrier Reef.

Northeast of the Pilbara, **Broome**, once the world's pearling capital, is indeed a jewel in the cyclone-swept coastline of the rugged Northwest, and an ideal preliminary to the **Kimberley**'s wilderness and hard-won cattle country. Generally cut off by floods in the wet season, the Kimberley is regarded as Australia's last frontier, its convoluted and inaccessible coasts washed by enormous tides and inhabited only by isolated Aboriginal communities and crocodiles. On the way to the Northern Territory border, the surreal enigma of the **Bungle Bungle** massif is one of WA's greatest natural wonders, carefully protected by minimal development.

If you hope to explore any significant part of the state's million-and-a-half square kilometres, and in particular the remote and fascinating Northwest, your own vehicle is essential, although you'll get to the most interesting places by combining buses with local **tours**. Either way, WA offers an essential mix of Outback grandeur, albeit more dispersed than elsewhere, and it's beginning to attract tourists from the more popular "Eastern States", as the rest of Australia is known in these parts.

WA's **climate** is a seasonal mix of temperate, arid and tropical. **Winters** are cool in the south and very wet in the southwest corner, while in the tropics the temperature sits around 32°C but with no rain and tolerable humidity: this is the dry season. Come

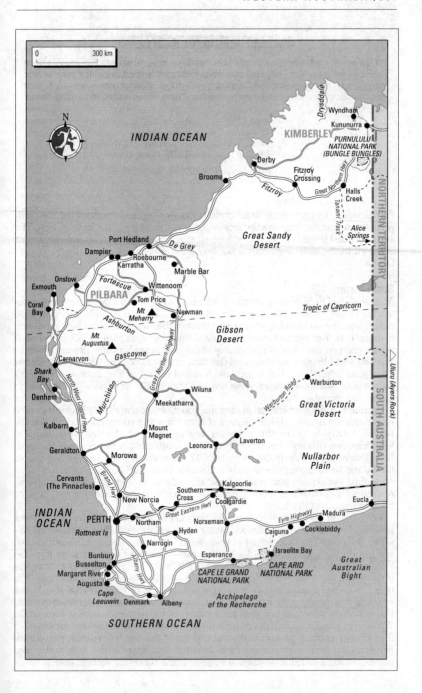

ACCOMMODATION PRICES

All the accommodation listed in this book has been categorized into one of eight price bands, as set out below. The rates quoted represent the cheapest available double or twin room in high season – except for category ①, which indicates per person rates for a dorm bed, and the categories given for units, cabins and vans, which represent the daily charge for the whole unit.

① Under $18	⑤ $61–74
② $19–30	⑥ $75–94
③ $31–45	⑦ $95–124
④ $46–60	⑧ $125 upwards

For more accommodation details, see pp.40–43.

---

the **summer**, the enervating "Wet" (from December to March) washes out the north while the rest of the state, particularly inland areas, crackles in the mid-40s heat. The southern coast is the only retreat for the heatstruck, although the temperate west coast is cooled by dependable afternoon sea breezes – in Perth known as the "Fremantle Doctor".

Some history

Aborigines had lived in most areas of WA for thousands of years by the time the seventeenth-century traders of the Dutch East India Company, and possibly the Portuguese before them, began bumping into the west coast on their way to the East Indies. A Dutch mariner, **Dirk Hartog**, was among the first of these when, in 1616, he left an inscribed pewter plate on the island off Shark Bay which now bears his name. Recent evidence was also found hereabouts to suggest that the French claimed the whole continent just a few years before Cook. For the next two hundred years, however, impressions of WA's barren and waterless fringes remained – commercially at least – uninspiring to European colonists.

France's subsequent interest in Australia's southwest corner at the beginning of the nineteenth century, which left a legacy of attractively named coastal features, led the British hastily to claim the unknown western part of the continent in 1826. Fredrickstown (Albany) was established on the south coast in that year and the Swan River Colony, today's Perth, two years later. The **new colony**, initially rejecting convict labour and so struggling desperately in its early years, had the familiar effect on an Aboriginal population that was at best misunderstood and at worst annihilated. Aborigines and their lands were cleared for agriculture: these days it's rare to see a black face south of Perth.

Economic problems continued until stalwart explorers in the mid-nineteenth century opened up the country's interior, leading to the goldrushes of the 1890s which propelled the colony into autonomous statehood in less than a decade. This **autonomy**, and growing antipathy towards the eastern states, led to a move to secede from the Federation in the depressed 1930s, when WA felt the rest of the country was dragging it down. But following World War II the whole of white Australia, and especially WA, began to thrive, making money from wool and, later, from huge mineral discoveries which, to this day, form the basis of the state's wealth. In fact, so prosperous is the state that at present its wealth accounts for a quarter of the nation's economy. Meanwhile, WA's forty thousand Aborigines continue to live in squalid and remote communities, as if in another country, though in the wake of the Mabo and Wik rulings (see p.998), lawyers supposedly representing them have put vast areas of the state under land claim, creating a situation destined to stagnate in the courts for years to come.

PERTH AND THE SOUTH

South of the **Great Eastern Highway**, which joins Perth to Kalgoorlie, is the most climatically benign portion of Western Australia, supporting intensive agriculture and seaside towns, and with all points well-connected to **Perth**, the modern face of the state's wealth. East of the state capital, the **Darling Ranges** offer a number of appealing day-trip destinations, while south of Perth, the **Margaret River Region**'s uniquely mellow landscape is especially attractive, supporting orchards, wineries and numerous homey holiday hideaways in the giant karri forests around **Pemberton**. Both **Albany** and **Esperance** are engaging resort towns on the Southern Ocean's rugged coastline, where sea breezes take the edge off the summertime heat. They make ideal bases for exploration of their adjacent national parks, while the dreary **Wheatlands**, north of the coast, is a region to pass through rather than head for. **Kalgoorlie**, at the heart of the once-thriving **Eastern Goldfields**, is a colourful caricature of an Outback mining town and certainly deserves a stop as you travel east.

Perth

Try as you might, and contrary to expectations, it's hard to get excited about **PERTH**, although its lack of urban grime creates a favourable first impression. Western Australia's modern capital of 1.3 million people has a reputation for sunshine, youthfulness and an easy-going lifestyle – after work, people often go sailing or swimming. It is perhaps because of this complacency that Perth lacks the substance and charisma, and the tension, of diverse wealth and ethnicity, that make a really great city something more than just a group of modern skyscrapers.

In the 1980s mineral prosperity and a spate of cocky, self-made wheeler-dealers (now largely bankrupt, disgraced or in prison) created a mini-boom for Perth. Wealth begat growth, recognition and an exciting, "upwardly mobile" tag; suddenly Perth, separated from everywhere else by thousands of kilometres of desert or ocean, was the place to be. But the many glass towers that rose on the city's skyline in the 1980s are still only half full, mocking the callow values of that era's transient prosperity. Although upbeat campaigns have managed to attract some people back into the city centre outside office hours, apart from shopping and some museums and galleries, the centre has little to offer tourists bar the buzzing restaurant and club district of **Northbridge**. The riverside Foreshore, along the **Swan River**'s north shore, remains a highway corridor, visited only by joggers and seagulls, and even **Kings Park**, the city's showpiece patch of untamed bushland, is isolated by knots of freeway interchanges. If you're looking for action, imitate the locals and head for the hills, the beaches or cruise on down to the port of Fremantle, 20km from Perth.

Arrival and information

Perth's **international airport** is 16km east of the city centre and the **domestic** one a few kilometres closer. **Shuttle buses** (international $10, domestic $8; ☎08/9479 4131) meet arrivals at both airports and take you directly to your accommodation in the city; from the domestic terminal, you can also catch a green Transperth bus #200, #210, #202, #208 and #209 to the city every forty minutes ($2.40). Otherwise, a trip by **taxi** to or from the international airport will take thirty minutes and cost $20 (call ☎08/9333 3333 or 9444 4444), or a bit less and a bit quicker from the domestic terminal. Interstate **trains**, **buses** and Westrail country buses arrive at the **East Perth Rail and Bus Terminal**, three train stops from the central Transperth suburban train and bus station on Wellington Street.

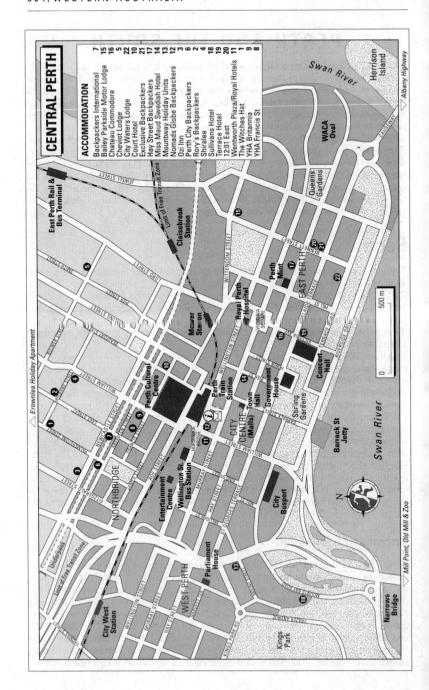

CENTRAL PERTH

ACCOMMODATION

Backpackers International	7
Bailey Parkside Motor Lodge	15
Chateau Commodore	16
Cheviot Lodge	5
City Waters Lodge	22
Court Hotel	10
Exclusive Backpackers	21
Hay Street Backpackers	17
Miss Maud Swedish Hotel	14
Mountway Holiday Units	13
Nomads Globe Backpackers	12
Ozi Inn	3
Perth City Backpackers	6
Rory's Backpackers	2
Shiralee	4
Sullivans Hotel	18
Terrace Hotel	19
1201 East	20
Wentworth Plaza/Royal Hotels	11
The Witches Hat	1
YHA Britannia	9
YHA Francis St	8

The main **tourist office** (Mon–Fri 8.30am–5.30pm, Sat 9am–1pm; ☎08/9483 1111) is just across the road from the Transperth station, in Forrest Chase precinct, and has numerous free city guides and maps, tour information and statewide promotional videos. The **Travellers' Club Tour and Information Centre** (Mon–Fri 9am–5.30pm, Sat 10am–4pm; ☎08/9226 0660, fax 9226 0661; *www.travellersclub.com.au*) just round the corner at 499 Wellington St offers a specific information service for backpackers and budget travellers as well as providing **emailing** facilities. See p.599 for listings magazines.

City transport

Transperth is the city's excellent and inexpensive **suburban transport** network, with frequent trains to Fremantle and the northern, eastern and southern suburbs of Joondalup, Midland and Armadale, and a fleet of buses filling the gaps in between. The city centre has two **bus stations**, one at Wellington Street, next to the central **train station**, and, for services south of the river, the City Busport ten minutes' walk south at the bottom of Mill Street. There are Transperth **information offices** with helpful staff at both bus stations (Mon–Fri 7am–6pm, Sat 7.30am–3pm; ☎13 2213) and also in the city centre at Plaza Arcade, Hay Street Level.

Outside the FTZ (see box below), Perth is divided into eight concentric zones – zones 1 and 2 ($2.50) are the most useful to visitors, incorporating Fremantle, the northern beaches and Midland. **Tickets** are available from bus conductors or vending machines at all (mostly unstaffed) stations; they are valid for up to two hours' (some for ninety minutes) unlimited travel within the specified zones on Transperth buses, trains and the ferry to South Perth from Barrack Street jetty.

Finally, the tourist-oriented **Perth Tram** (daily 9.30am–5pm; day-ticket $14; ☎08/9367 9404), running every ninety minutes and most conveniently caught at Barrack Street jetty, allows you to jump off at points of interest and reboard a later tram.

Accommodation

There's a full range of **accommodation** around the centre of Perth, all of it – from backpackers' hostels to hotels and apartments – inexpensive, presentable and conveniently close to, or even right in, the city centre. The nearest campsites are 7km from the city. Booking ahead for motels and apartments is advisable in summer if you want to stay at the first place on your list.

Hotels and motels

Bailey Parkside Motor Lodge, 150 Bennett St (☎08/9325 3788, fax 9221 1046). Good-quality and fairly central motel with a pool and close to parkland. ⑤.

FREE TRANSPORT IN CENTRAL PERTH

Both of Perth's central bus stations, as well as the local train stations one stop on either side of the main train station, are within the **Free Transit Zone**, or FTZ. Most buses passing through the FTZ offer free travel within it, as do the snazzy "**CAT**" (Central Area Transit) buses serving the city centre. You can board the buses at special CAT stops to take you along two circular CAT routes; press a button and a voice tells you when the next bus is due. The **Blue CAT** runs north–south from Barrack Street jetty up to Aberdeen Street and then down William Street back to the river, while the **Red CAT** runs east–west along George Terrace and back along Wellington Street. Both routes run from Monday to Thursday 7am–6pm, Friday 7am–1am, Saturday 8.30am–1am and Sunday 10am–5pm, with intervals of ten minutes at the most. Timetables are available from Transperth offices.

Chateau Commodore, corner of Victoria Ave and Hay St (☎08/9325 0461, fax 9221 2448). Right in the centre of town, with parking, restaurant, bar and pool. ⑦–⑧.

Court Hotel, 50 Beaufort St (☎08/9328 5292). Central gay and lesbian accommodation over a lively pub. ④.

Miss Maud Swedish Hotel, 97 Murray St (☎08/9325 3900, fax 9221 3225). A pleasant variety of rooms, an interior with a Swedish/Alpine flavour and a popular buffet breakfast included. ⑦.

Royal Hotel corner of Wellington and William sts (☎ & fax 08/9324 1510). One of central Perth's bargains, a tidy grand-era hotel (mostly shared facilities) with some big rooms better and cheaper than the *Wentworth* nearby. ④.

Sullivans Hotel, 166 Mounts Bay Rd (☎08/9321 8022, fax 9321 2443). Excellent, family-run hotel at the foot of Kings Park and just inside the FTZ. Offers pool, free bikes and great breakfasts. ⑦.

Terrace Hotel, 195 Adelaide Terrace (☎08/9492 7777). Superior motel right in the city centre. ⑧.

Wentworth Plaza, 300 Murray St (☎08/9481 1000, fax 9321 2443; ⑤–⑥). Plusher version of its sister, the *Royal* (above) with same central location, mix of en-suite and basin-only rooms plus 24hr reception and lifts. ⑥.

Self-contained apartments

Brownlea Holiday Apartments, 166 Palmerston St (☎08/9227 1710, fax 9328 4840). Just north of the centre with a pool and bargain rates. ④–⑤.

City Waters Lodge, 118 Terrace Rd (☎08/9325 1556, fax 9221 2794). One- and two-bedroom apartments close to the river and ten minutes' walk from the centre. ⑥.

Mountway Holiday Units, 36 Mount St (☎08/9321 8307, fax 9324 2147). Budget units between the city centre and Kings Park. ④.

Hostels

Perth offers an average selection of hostels, just about all of them converted from older buildings located around Northbridge – don't expect the purpose-built palaces you get out East. The selection below includes the more popular and reliable establishments; most offer bike rental, tour bookings, email and employment contacts. Note that on-street parking is a hassle in the very centre of Northbridge. In all the hostels listed below dorms fall in the ① category and twins or doubles at the lower end of ③.

NORTHBRIDGE AND CITY CENTRE

Backpackers International, corner of Aberdeen and Lake sts (☎08/9227 9977, fax 9385 3180). Bright, clean hostel rather lacking in atmosphere.

Nomads Globe Backpackers, 497 Wellington St (☎08/9321 4080). Old hotel, recently converted for the budget traveller; a few rough edges but as central as they come.

Perth City Backpackers, 158 Aberdeen St (☎08/9328 6667, fax 9328 8813, free call ☎1800/247 444). More room than most hostels with eight-bed dorms and off-street parking.

YHA, 46 Francis St (☎ & fax 08/9328 7794). Good layout with a shady courtyard and plenty going on. A few twins, but mostly six- and eight-bed dorms.

YHA Britannia, 253 William St (☎08/9328 6121, fax 9227 9784). In the heart of Northbridge, a stone's throw from the clubs and cafés so you take advantage of the 24hr reception. No smoking.

NORTH OF NORTHBRIDGE UNDERPASS

Cheviot Lodge, 30 Bulwer St (☎08/9227 6817). Clean and roomy lodge with a non-hostel feel and parking space available. Dorms and rooms.

Ozi Inn, 282 Newcastle St (☎ & fax 08/9328 1222). Converted large house with knowledgeable owners offering a warm welcome. There's a workers' annexe across the road and the *Lonely Planet Café* on the corner.

Rory's Backpackers, 194 Brisbane St (☎08/9328 9958). Popular pair of bungalows in a quiet location. Mixed six-bed dorms and twins or doubles.

Shiralee, Brisbane St (☎08/9227 7448, fax 9227 7446). Another bungalow offering a quieter alternative to *Rory's*. Four-bed dorms and rooms.

The Witch's Hat, 148 Palmerston St (☎08/9228 4228 or free call ☎1800/818 358). Cheap doubles, "real beds" and away from the throng. Free pick-ups too.

EAST OF THE CENTRE
Exclusive Backpackers, 158 Adelaide Terrace (☎08/9221 9991, fax 9362 5872). Attractive jarrah wood interior and balcony offering a touch of class and large bunkless dorms. Off-street parking and an nice café next door to supplement the inadequate kitchen. Five-bed dorms and comfortable twins or doubles.
Hay Street Backpackers, 266–268 Hay St (☎ & fax 08/9221 9880). Well-looked-after, converted house with a spacious kitchen, small pool and parking. Four- to six-bed dorms with air-con and new twins and doubles in the back.
12:01 East, 195 Hay St (☎08/9221 1666, fax 9221 1662). Large communal areas and kitchen but away from Northbridge action. Four-bed dorms and some twins and doubles.

Caravan parks
Central, 38 Central Ave, 7km east of Perth (☎08/9277 5696). Located in Redcliffe, by the domestic airport. Closest good caravan park to the city centre. Cabins ④.
Scarborough Starhaven, 18 Pearl Parade (☎08/9341 1770). Situated in a popular beach suburb, a 30min bus ride from the centre. On-site vans ③.

The City

The compact and walkable **central area** of Perth, from Wellington Street down to St Georges Terrace, and bounded vaguely by Hill Street to the east and Milligan Street to the west, is an easy to negotiate grid. Much of your time will be spent exploring the links between **Hay Street** and **Murray Street**, both of which are pedestrianized between William and Barrack streets and linked by numerous, glittering arcades: the mock Tudor **London Court** and its idealized "Olde English" imagery is much photographed. William Street runs north over the railway at **Horseshoe Bridge** and on into lively Northbridge, while Barrack Street runs south down to the ferry **jetty** on Perth Water, a lagoon on the **Swan River** formed by the bridged **Narrows** and popular with windsurfers, sailors and jet-skiers. From the jetty a Transperth ferry regularly crosses the Narrows to Mends Street jetty on the south shore, while tourist ferries ply the river upstream to the Swan Valley wineries and downstream to Fremantle and Rottnest Island (see box on p.608). Generally speaking, the best way to **sightsee** in Perth is simply to wander idly and window-shop.

Museums and Old Perth
Situated just over the tracks in Northbridge, at the end of James Street, the **Perth Cultural Centre** comprises the **Art Gallery of Western Australia** (daily 10am–5pm; free) and the state **Museum** (Mon–Fri 10.30am–5pm, Sat & Sun 1–5pm; free), as well as the state library. The gallery's constantly changing displays include Aboriginal art, and other contemporary and classic works by Western Australian artists. There's always something worth seeing, the air-con is blissful in summer, and free guided tours (Tues–Fri 12.15pm, Sat & Sun 2pm; free) provide good information about the work displayed. The museum, part of the same complex, is housed in a collection of old and new buildings. It includes a floor devoted to Aboriginal culture, plus exhibitions of vintage cars, stuffed marsupials, a 25-metre whale skeleton, meteorites, a diorama of a swamp, and a reconstruction of an old jail.

Perth's old buildings, popular with many sightseeing tours, are a dreary bunch of colonial survivors dwarfed by the city's soaring skyscrapers. In a westward sweep from the manicured perfection of **Queens Gardens**, at the east end of Hay Street, they start with the **Perth Mint** (Mon–Fri 9am–4pm, Sat 9am–1pm), on the corner of Hill and Hay streets. Operating from its original 1899 base, Australia's principal specialist mint still trades in precious metals in bar or coin form and displays some large-scale replicas of gold nuggets and alluring 400-ounce ingots. Visitors can also take a tour ($4) to observe minting operations in the refurbished foundry.

Further down are the **Stirling Gardens**, on the corner of St Georges Terrace and Pier Street, with their "Ore Obelisk" sculpture symbolizing WA's mineral diversity, and the ornate Gothic extravagance of the 1860s **Government House**. The **Old Courthouse** (Tues & Thurs 10am–2pm; free), the colony's oldest surviving building, is also in the gardens and houses the less than electrifying **Francis Burt Law Museum**, while other sights in the area include the **Deanery** on the corner of Pier Street, the **Cloisters** – now an office – and the **Old Perth Boys' School**, at 139 St Georges Terrace (Mon–Fri 9am–5pm; free), restored and now run by the National Trust. Barely discernible at the far end of the terrace is the **Barracks Archway**, the remains of an 1860s' structure not really worth closer inspection unless you're heading up that way to Kings Park. Easily missed on the corner of Hay and Barrack streets is the neo-Jacobean facade of the **Town Hall**, dating from the 1870s.

The **Old Mill** (daily 10am–4pm; $3; Transperth ferry from Barrack Street jetty), situated at Mill Point, south of the Narrows and in the shadow of the Kwinana Freeway bridge, is an early building that has managed to retain its charm. A quaint, fairytale relic, the mill ground the colony's first flour and now houses a collection of pioneering bull-carts and period artefacts in its own attractive grounds.

Perth Zoo and Kings Park

Perth Zoo (daily 10am–5pm; $10), on Labruahore Road a short walk from the Old Mill (see above), is a hundred-year-old park where animals are not confined to small cages, in keeping with the trend away from traditional zoos. There is enough indigenous and exotic wildlife here to make a great afternoon out.

Perhaps the city's best attraction is the mostly-wild, five-square-kilometre expanse of **Kings Park**, a two-kilometre walk west of the centre down Mount Street, turning off at the end of St Georges Terrace (or take bus #33 from Wellington Street). Created with great foresight in 1872, the park remains Perth's premier recreational area (other than the river), enlivened by various flora and fauna, and no visit would be complete without a wander around. Although the park is small enough to enjoy on foot, you can rent **bicycles** from Koala Cycle Hire (Mon–Fri 9.30am–4pm, Sat & Sun 9.30am–6pm) in the main car park on the park's east side, where there's a fine, tree-framed view over the city. There's a trail leading through the native bushland, a botanic and an aromatic garden, playgrounds, picnic areas and free guided tours from the **information centre** (daily 9.30am–3.30pm) by the car park, which also provides maps of the park.

Eating and drinking

To eat well and inexpensively in Perth, stick to **Italian** and **Asian** places. Both dominate the **food courts**, where you can easily get a decent meal for as little as $6. In Northbridge there are the Asian *Shang Hai* and *Pavilion* on James Street, while in the city you'll find the *Metro* and the cosmopolitan *Carillon* off Hay Street Mall. At the other end of the scale, some of the better seafood restaurants may cost you $30 or more per head – still great value. **Northbridge**, especially around James and Lake streets, is the heart of Perth's café and restaurant scene, with over forty establishments crammed into a square kilometre. Except for Sunday and Monday Northbridge is very busy in the evenings, as people wander from place to place, eating, (it is also the city's focus for late-night dining), drinking and enjoying themselves.

Cafés, snack bars and inexpensive restaurants

Café Sport, 261 William St, north of Francis St. Down-to-earth coffee bar. A good variety of Italian snacks and meals, and a great place to sit and read your paper.

Café Universal, 251 William St, south of Francis St. Trendier cappuccinos, beers and street life than anywhere else, with Italian dishes if you're hungry.

Hans Café Noodle Bar, corner of Francis and William sts. Cheap Chinese in a central location. From $5.

Hare Krishna Food for Life, 232 William St. Vegetarian dishes at rock-bottom prices. and even free food on some days.

Seoul Korean, 253a William St. Two-course lunches for around $6 and evening meals for twice that in a low-key oriental setting. Daily noon–1pm & 6pm until late.

Sri Melaka Nyonya, 313 William St. Best of the budget Malay places, with "home-style" cooked food. Tues–Sat from noon.

The Street Café, 78 Lake St. Serves smooth cappuccinos and cheap, tasty pasta every day. Opens early.

Villa Italia, corner of Aberdeen and William sts. Jazzy coffee bar for the image-conscious.

Restaurants

Costa Brava, 137 James St. Authentic Spanish and seafood dishes. Lunch Wed–Fri, dinner daily.

Dusit Thai, 233 James St. Least expensive of the authentic Thai places in Northbridge, with main courses for around $7. Closed Mon.

Emperor's Court, 66 Lake St (☎08/9328 3881). Sumptuous decor and fine Szechuan, Beijing and Cantonese dishes. Nightly karaoke in the cocktail bar. Lunch Mon–Fri, dinner nightly.

Fishy Affair, 132 James St (☎08/9328 6636). Treat tourself to the seafood platter. Lunch Mon–Fri, dinner nightly.

The Gardens/Ord St Café, 27 Ord St, West Perth (☎08/9321 6021). Sophisticated restaurant overlooking Kings Park, with a café next door serving steak, salads and seafood.

Il Padrino, 198 William St. Huge, wood-fired pizzas and lunchtime specials. Closed Wed and weekend lunch-times.

Mamma Maria's, 105 Aberdeen St (☎08/9328 4532). Long-established and sometimes hectic pasta house; try the grilled chicken. Lunch Mon–Fri, dinner nightly.

Royal India, 1134 Hay St west (☎08/9324 1368). Elegant, upmarket restaurant specializing in tandoori dishes. Lunch Mon–Fri, dinner nightly from 6pm.

Entertainment and nightlife

As with food, **Northbridge** is the focal point of after-dark action, with plenty of **pubs**, **bars** and teeming **dance clubs** concealed in improbable buildings. In view of Perth's famed isolation, a night in Northbridge is the hottest spot for thousands of kilometres in any direction but there are also some lively bars in the city and inner suburbs. Many pubs and bars feature **free beer**, happy hours and other value-added incentives to get loaded and let the good times roll. Perth's nightlife centres around alcohol rather than drugs, and there has been an attempt by the city to curb intoxicated revellers and promote responsible behaviour, to little avail.

The free weekly music and gig guide, *X-Press Magazine,* has **listings** for all the places below, as well as many others. Alternatively, check out the entertainment section of Thursday's *West Australian* newspaper. For the lowdown on the **gay and lesbian scene**, see the box overleaf.

Pubs and bars with music

Aberdeen Hotel, 84 Aberdeen St. Ever-popular meeting place for Northbridge's backpacking crowd, with live bands most nights.

The Bog, 361 Newcastle St. Latest Celtic venue with nightly live bands and favourite Irish brews.

Brass Monkey, corner of William and James sts. Enduringly popular pub with a good atmosphere in the heart of Northbridge. Live bands on Friday and Saturday.

Leederville Hotel, Oxford St, Leederville. The Sunday sessions are all the rage with Perth's backpackers but you need to be smartly dressed.

Moon & Sixpence, 300 Murray St. Popular city centre pub for a daytime rendezvous.

Northbridge Hotel, 198 Brisbane St. Attracts a mixed gay and lesbian crowd, with three bars, pool tables and occassional live music (Wed & Sun).

Rosie O'Grady's, corner of James and Milligan sts. Popular Irish theme pub with cheap food and live music.

Clubs

Brooklyn's, 161 James St. Strict dress code and high admission makes this an older ravers' dance venue.

Connections, 81 James St. Perth's established gay and lesbian nightspot offers the best dance music for all sexual preferences. Closed Mon.

DC's, 105 Francis St. *DC's* attracts a young crowd with dance and hardcore techno and good DJs. Men only on Wed. Closed Mon.

Grosvenor, corner Hill and Hay sts. Indie, rock, pop and grunge at your service in the front and back rooms and not a cover band in sight. One of the best around.

Hip-E-Club, corner of Anzac Rd and Oxford St, Leederville. Very popular retro-psychedelia plus backpackers' nights.

Jackal, 190 William St. Lounge bar and dance club.

The Loft, 104 Murray St. Eighties retro Sundays and mid-week Tellytubby reunions.

Cinemas, theatres and live music

Most of Perth's mainstream movie **cinemas** are located in the arcades off Hay and Murray streets in the city centre. Tuesday nights are cheap, with matinees also discounted at some places. Arthouse cinemas close to the centre include Cinema Paradiso, in James Street's Galleria complex; the lovely, Deco-style Astor, on the corner

---

GAY AND LESBIAN PERTH

Perth has a robust, self-sufficient and extremely friendly gay and lesbian scene. The heart of the action is **Northbridge**, but neighbouring North Perth, Highgate and Mount Lawley all have more than their share of gay residents, while lesbians seem to opt for a relaxed lifestyle down in Fremantle. As usual, the quickest way to plug into the scene is to pick up the community paper: in Perth it's the *Westside Observer* (*WSO*), free at gigs or available for $1 at the Arcane Bookshop, 212 William St, Northbridge (Mon–Fri 10am–5.30pm, Sat 10am–5pm; ☎08/9328 5073), which has plenty of other gay, lesbian and feminist literature.

October heats up with **Perth Pride**, celebrated with the usual array of fun and games, including a night march and dance party. Also in October, lesbians march to **Reclaim The Night**. Every November competitors get set to "go for glory" at the **Western Australia Gay Olympics**. At other times of year, outdoor organizations such as GAGS and Team Perth (see below) can put you in touch with other pink athletes.

The main **community organizations** for gays and lesbians in Perth are the Gay Activities Group Services (GAGS), PO Box 8234, Perth 6000, which is responsible for the Gay Olympics and other sporting events; the Gay Outdoor Group, PO Box 263, Cottesloe, Perth 6011 (☎08/9270 7181); Team Perth, PO Box 3234, Stirling St, Perth 6849; and Wednesday Women (☎08/9328 9044), a lesbian social group.

For gay- and lesbian-friendly **accommodation**, try the *Court Hotel* (see p.596) or the beachside *Swanbourne Guest House* (see p.609). **Night-time venues** include *Connections*, *DC's* and the *Northbridge Hotel* (see above).

of Beaufort and Walcott streets; and, a little further out, the award-winning Luna on Oxford Street, Leederville, a fifteen-minute walk west of Northbridge. One cinematic experience that shouldn't be missed, especially if you've never seen an IMAX film, is a visit to the Omni Theatre in the City West Complex on Sutherland Street, West Perth. A huge, wraparound screen turns what would otherwise be fairly ordinary documentaries into sensory roller-coaster rides.

Any out-of-the-ordinary **shows** that visit Perth tend to set the city astir and are advertised and patronized heavily. The *Burswood Resort and Casino* (☎08/9362 7777), just over the Causeway, southeast of the centre, is a do-it-all leisure complex comprising a five-star hotel, numerous restaurants and a huge dome hosting all sorts of sporting and show-business events. Otherwise the Perth Concert Hall on St Georges Terrace (☎08/9325 9944), Her Majesty's Theatre (☎08/9322 2929) on the corner of King and Hay streets, or the Perth Entertainment Centre on Wellington Street next to the bus station are likely venues for the city's main concerts and plays. International bands play at the monolithic Metropolis Club by the railway at 146 Roe St.

Listings

Airlines (domestic) Airlink (☎13 1313); Ansett (☎13 1300); Rottnest Airbus (☎08/9478 1322); Skywest (☎08/9334 2288 or free call ☎1800/244 833).

Airlines (international) Air New Zealand (☎08/9325 1099); British Airways (☎08/9483 7711); Garuda (☎08/9481 0963); Malaysian Airlines(☎08/9325 4499); National (☎08/9479 3210); Qantas (☎08/9225 2222); Singapore Airlines (☎08/9483 5777); United Airlines (☎008/230 322).

Airport shuttle buses Airport–City Shuttle (☎08/9479 4131).

Bicycle rental About Bike Hire, Barrack Street jetty (☎08/9221 2665), has bikes for riverside cycling from $15 a day, or try the hostels. Secondhand bikes from WA Bicycle Disposals, 278 Hay St, East Perth (☎08/9325 1176), from around $80. They also offer an informal rental and buy-back service plus local and regional cycling maps.

Buses Greyhound Pioneer (☎13 2030), for interstate services; South West Coach Lines (☎08/9322 5173), for daily services to the Margaret River Region as far as Augusta; Westliner (☎08/9250 2838), for twice-weekly services to Kalgoorlie, Leinster and Laverton; Westrail (☎08/9326 2222), for daily services south and east of Perth and, less frequently, north to Kalbarri and Meekatharra. All have offices at the Wellington Street Bus Station, but interstate and Westrail country buses come and go from the East Perth Terminal.

Car rental Perth's car-rental companies are among the cheapest in the country and while the "$25 per day" deals should be scrutinized carefully, a week's rental is the best way of exploring relatively compact areas such as the Southwest at your own pace. Outlets include Network Rent-a-Car, 259 William St, Northbridge (☎08/9227 8810); Atlas Rent-a-Car (☎08/9277 8311); Myaree Rent-a-Car (☎08/9330 8848); and City Centre Car Rentals (☎08/9322 1887).

Dentist Dental Hospital on Goderich St (☎08/9325 3452).

Disabled travellers ACROD, Unit 9, 189 Royal St, East Perth (☎08/9222 2961), provides information for disabled visitors to WA. For information about accessible accommodation, call the Para Quad Association (☎08/9381 0173), or use the fairly reliable RACWA Touring Guide (see below).

Hospitals Royal Perth, Victoria Square (☎08/9224 2244); King Edward, Bagot Rd, Subiaco (☎08/9340 2222), for women; Fremantle, Alma St (☎08/9321 3333).

Internet and email The city library (see below) has several somewhat clunky computers free for surfing up to an hour a day but with no emailing facilities. A good place for emailing is the Travellers Club Tour and Information Centre, 499 Wellington St at around $6 per hour (Mon 9am–5.30pm, Sat 10am–4pm).

Library Perth Cultural Centre, James St (☎08/9427 3111). An attractive and air-conditioned place to sit and read the newspapers and surf the Net.

Maps Perth Map Centre, 1st floor, 884 Hay St (☎08/9322 5733), has a full range of topographic and touring maps.

Motoring associations RACWA, 228 Adelaide Terrace (☎08/9421 4444), offers a complete range of services, as well as maps.

Police 2 Adelaide Terrace (☎08/9222 1111).
Post office Forrest Chase, opposite the train station (☎08/9326 5211) with a mail collection service.
Tours See box below.

Around Perth

While Perth may not be all it's cracked up to be, the area around the city offers some compensation. The port of **Fremantle**, at the mouth of the Swan River, should not be overlooked, nor should a day-trip to **Rottnest Island**, an eighty-minute ferry ride

---

RIVER CRUISES AND TOURS FROM PERTH

As well as commercial **ferry** operators, all based at Barrack Street jetty and offering cruises up and down the Swan River from as little as $10 to Fremantle or $70 for a full day upriver, **bus and 4WD** tours leave daily in all directions from Perth. Popular day-tours include the curious Pinnacles, near Cervantes (see p.638); Wave Rock, near Hyden (see p.626); and the wineries of the Upper Swan Valley (see p.610) and the Margaret River Region (see p.615). Longer excursions can be taken to see the dolphins at Monkey Mia or to make a more thorough appraisal of WA's diverse Southwest region. Booking for all tours can be made at your hostel or hotel; at YHA Travel, 236 William St, Northbridge (☎08/9227 5122); the tourist office in Forrest Chase (☎08/9483 1111); or the Travellers' Club and Tour Information Centre round the corner at 499 Wellington St (☎08/9226 0660).

RIVER CRUISES

Boat Torque (☎08/9221 5844). A full range of tours on plush vessels upriver to Tranby House and to the Swan Valley for wine-tasting (half-day and full-day). From $20.

Captain Cook Cruises (☎08/9325 3341). Daily half- and full-day runs to Fremantle, with the option of a three-hour stopover. From $15.

Golden Sun Cruises (☎08/9325 9166). Cruises upriver to visit the National Trust property at Tranby House, faintly historic Guildford, and a day-cruise and bus tour around the Swan Valley wineries. Also downriver cruises to Fremantle. From $10.

Oceanic Cruises (Perth ☎08/9325 1191, Fremantle ☎08/9430 5127). Cruises to Fremantle, Rottnest Island and upriver. From $20.

TOURS

Pinnacles Tours and Travel Centre, 16 Irwin St, corner of Hay St (☎08/9221 5411). One-day tours to the Pinnacles (4WD option), Wave Rock and Margaret River, plus longer runs as far afield as

Coral Bay (5 days), together with season-al whale-watching and wildflower tours. From $90.

Planet Perth Tours, (☎08/9276 5295). Fun days out around Perth visiting wildlife parks, the Darling Ranges and the beach to view the sunset. From $20.

Redback Safaris, YHA Travel (☎08/9227 5122). One-day tours specializing in the Pinnacles, with a small 4WD van to indulge in a spot of dune-riding on the way back.

Travelabout, YHA Travel (☎08/9227 5122). One of WA's leading tour companies offering a full range of professionally run all-adventure tours, from one-day excursions to the Pinnacles to one-month trips up to the Kimberley and Kakadu National Park (NT) and back by way of Ayers Rock (NT). Around $80 a day.

Western Travel Bug, YHA Travel (☎08/9561 5236). Popular bargain-priced tours of the Southwest (though not all basic costs are covered), offering plenty of activities and a lively atmosphere. Five-day Southwest tour around $365; seven-day Southwest tour including Wave Rock $525.

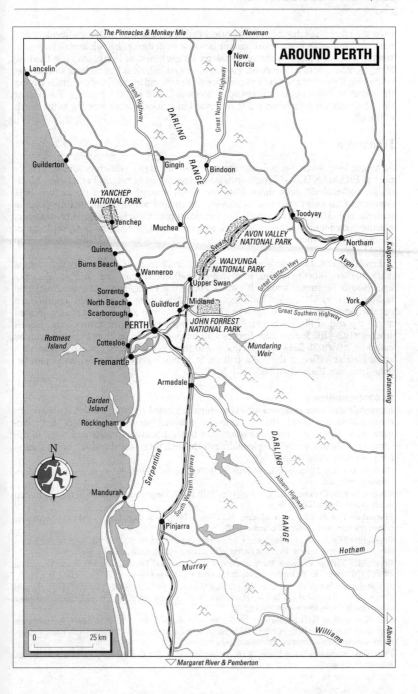

AROUND PERTH

△ The Pinnacles & Monkey Mia   △ Newman

Lancelin

New Norcia

Guilderton

Gingin
Bindoon

YANCHEP
NATIONAL PARK

Yanchep
Muchea

Toodyay

AVON VALLEY
NATIONAL PARK

Northam

Quinns
Burns Beach

Wanneroo

WALYUNGA
NATIONAL PARK

Upper Swan

Sorrento
North Beach
Scarborough

Guildford
Midland

York

PERTH

JOHN FORREST
NATIONAL PARK

Great Southern Highway

Cottesloe

Fremantle

Mundaring
Weir

Rottnest
Island

Garden
Island

Rockingham

N

Mandurah

Pinjarra

Murray

Hotham

DARLING   RANGE

Serpentine

South Western Highway

Albany Highway

0   25 km

△ Margaret River & Pemberton

△ Kalgoorlie

△ Katanning

△ Albany

from the city or half that from Fremantle. Perth's **beaches** form a near-unbroken line north of Fremantle, just a short train or bus ride from the centre, while with your own vehicle you can escape to the **national parks** northeast of Perth, atop the **Darling Ranges**, which parallel the coast. Patchily forested hills, just half an hour's drive east of the city, they offer a network of cool, scenic drives and marked walking trails among the jarrah woodlands. After Fremantle, Rottnest Island and the beaches, the best of the local trips are detailed on p.602, described in a clockwise arc starting to the north of the city.

Fremantle

Although long since merged into the metropolitan area's suburban sprawl, Perth's port of **FREMANTLE** – "Freo" – retains an identity and charm all of its own. Much of the convict-built dock dates from the 1890s, though spruced up for the 1987 Americas Cup yacht race and an eagerly anticipated tourist boom that never quite materialized. The formerly rough and run-down port town is now quite presentable, but the jazzed-up image takes a knock as an unmistakeable ovine pong settles over the whole town when a stream of "baa-ing" road trains load up Arabia-bound sheep freighters.

Freo's relaxed, Mediterranean ambience attracts hordes of weekenders to its famed artsy markets (worth planning your visit around) and "cappuccino strip", as the café-lined **South Terrace** is known. It's worth noting that in the heat of summer Fremantle is often a breezy 5°C cooler than Perth, a mere 25 minutes away by train. **Trains** leave regularly from Perth for the nineteen-kilometre run down to Fremantle Station, located at the top end of Market Street, five minutes' walk north of the town centre. **Buses** (routes #102–#106 & #151 from Perth's City Busport) also stop here; local **taxis** can be called on ☎08/9335 3944. For **ferries** to and from Perth, see box on p.602. There's a small **tourist office** in the town hall on St John's Square (Mon–Fri 9am–5pm, Sat 9am–1pm, Sun 10am–3pm; ☎08/9431 7878).

Accommodation

Fremantle isn't over-endowed with conveniently located accommodation, but there are three central hostels only slightly tainted by lounging "permanent residents" and a car-avan park. There are also some pricey but tasteful boutique hotels and some of the "grand era" hotels are being splendidly refurbished, their only drawback being shared bathrooms for most rooms.

Backpacker Inn, 11 Packenham St (☎08/9431 7065, fax 9430 6405). Freo's newest hostel with an adjoining cafe. ①.

Coogee Beach, Cockburn Rd, Coogee (☎08/9418 1810). Large caravan resort on the beach, 7km south of Fremantle. Cabins ③–④.

Fremantle Colonial Accommodation, 215 High St (☎08/9430 6568, fax 9430 6405). Self-catering period cottages and classy B&B units. ⑤–⑦.

Fremantle Hotel, corner of High and Cliff sts (☎08/9430 4300, fax 9335 2636). Right by the Round House, this unpretentious hotel has rooms with shared and en-suite facilities. ⑤.

Fremantle Village Caravan Park, corner of Cockburn and Rockingham rds, South Fremantle (☎08/9430 4866). The nearest campsite to the centre of town. On-site vans ③.

His Majesty's Hotel, corner of Phillimore and Mouat sts (☎08/9336 4681, fax 9336 4691). One of Freo's many Federation era hotels refurbished to a high standard. Nearly all large rooms have shared bathrooms. Restaurant and bar. ⑥.

Old Fire Station Backpackers, 18 Phillimore St (☎08/9430 5454, fax 9319 1494). Just two minutes south of the train station, with a huge common room and a smaller women-only lounge above an inexpensive Indian restaurant. Rooms ③, dorms ①.

Port City Backpackers, 5 Essex St (☎ & fax 08/9335 6635). Central hostel with mixed dorms. Rooms ③, dorms ①.

Rosemoore B&B, 2 Winifred St, Mosman Park (☎08/9384 8214, fax 9385 6373). Over the river in posh Mosman Park 5km from Fremantle, a country-style cottage with private access and full breakfast. ⑥.

Tradewinds Hotel, 59 Canning Highway (☎08/9339 8188, fax 9339 2266). Good-looking, Federal-era hotel with well-equipped, self-contained apartments, close to the river and 2km from the centre. ⑧.

The Town

Exploring Fremantle on foot, with plenty of streetside café breaks, is the most agreeable way of visiting the town's compactly grouped sights, although the **Fremantle**

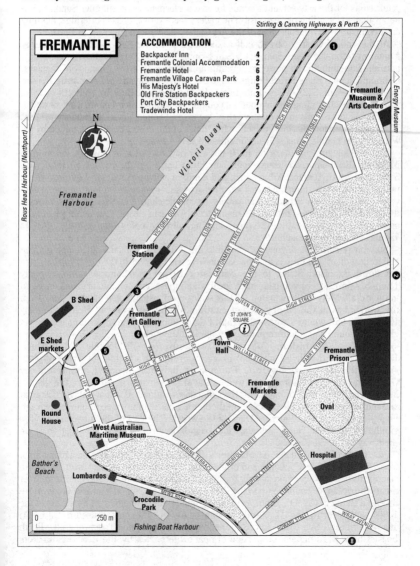

Tram offers informative commentaries on its various tours (daily, on the hour, 10am–5pm; $10), which depart from outside the **town hall** on St John's Square.

By starting your appraisal of Freo on the relatively dull east side and moving down towards the ocean, you end up, worn out but satisfied, at the Fishing Boat Harbour, ready for a sunset seafood dinner. To begin with, there's the **Fremantle Arts Centre** (daily 10am–5pm, Wed 7–9pm; free) and **Museum** (Thurs–Sun 1–5pm; free) on the corner of Finnerty and Ord streets, though the small museum's local history displays are not very exciting. The Arts Centre itself, albeit in an attractive building with a gallery, is more of a rendezvous for the arty set and a venue for live performances on summer Sunday afternoons than a rewarding place to visit. The gallery has a variety of local offerings, but they can't compare with the collection of the Art Gallery of Western Australia in Perth.

At the end of Quarry Street, half a kilometre from the Arts Centre, the **Energy Museum** (Mon–Fri 10am–5pm, Sat & Sun 1–5pm; $3), at 12 Parry St, is a rather stodgy, educational exhibition of power-generating apparatus with a few "hands-on" displays. Continuing down Parry Street brings you to the hillside enclosure of **Fremantle Prison** (daily 10am–6pm; $12), whose entrance is in The Terrace. Built by convicts in 1855, soon after the struggling colony found it couldn't do without their labour, it's now one of the biggest tourist jails in a country full of these grim reminders of its modern origins. The high admission charge is offset by free tours of the prison buildings, guided by ex-wardens: the building was only decommissioned as late as 1991.

Things look up from here on in. If it's a Friday, Saturday or Sunday, **Fremantle Markets** (Fri 5–9pm, Sat 10am–5pm, Sun 11am–5pm), on the corner of Henderson Street and South Terrace, will be open and a hub of activity. A real local market where people actually buy things, it's well worth a browse for some fresh food, unusual souvenirs from the many arts and crafts stalls, or cosmic clothes and accessories. Moving down **South Terrace**, Fremantle's main street, you can revive your aching feet with some refreshment in one of the many inviting, alfresco **cafés** that give the town its vaguely European atmosphere.

Suitably re-caffeinated, you now head into the "**West End**", as the old shipping office and freight district of Freo is known. As South Terrace curves to the right, you can turn left down Bannister Street to the **Bannister Street Workshops** at no. 8 (daily 11am–5.30pm), where you can watch local wood, glass and ceramic artisans engaged in their craft. More craftsmanship (at 1:22 scale) is on display a few minutes' walk from the workshops at the **Henry Street Station Model Railway**, 48 Henry St (daily 10am–5pm; $5), where Thomas the Tank Engine and all his merry chums can be set chuffing around a splendid rendition of model-railway heaven.

The **West Australian Maritime Museum** on Cliff Street (Mon–Thurs 10.30am–5pm, Fri–Sun 1–5pm; free) is one of Fremantle's highlights. Pride of place goes to the *Batavia* display, the Dutch East Indiaman wrecked off present-day Geraldton over 360 years ago. As well as the ship's reconstructed stern, the display includes the stone portico bound for the Company's unfinished fort at Batavia (Jakarta) and numerous corroded artefacts, together with a fascinating video about the extraordinary drama and subsequent salvage of the wreck. The rest of the museum displays exhibits from other Dutch vessels which regularly struck Australia's west coast on their way to the East Indies.

Just north of the museum, past **Bather's Beach**, is the **Round House** (10am–5pm; free), the state's oldest building and original jail, with fine views across town and out to sea. From here you can take a walk to the end of **South Mole**, where the Swan River meets the ocean, or continue up to the Port Authority Building on **Victoria Quay**. Here there's a statue to C.Y. O'Connor, who masterminded the rebuilding of the docks in the 1890s and, nearby, the **B Shed**, an intriguing historic boat museum (Mon–Fri 10am–3pm, Sat & Sun 10am–4pm; $2 donation) decked out with all sorts of craft – Perth boasts the world's highest proportion of boat-owners. Nearby, the **E Shed markets**

(Mon–Fri 9am–9pm, Sat & Sun 10am–4pm) offer a similar range of stalls and a food hall as found at the better-known Fremantle Markets.

South of the Maritime Museum you pass the grassy **Esplanade**, with its numerous seafood restaurants on **Fishing Boat Harbour** (see "Eating", below), before eventually reaching the **Fremantle Crocodile Park** on Mews Road (Mon–Fri 10am–4pm, Sat & Sun 10am–5pm; $10). It's quite small and you don't get that close to the crocs, but it's definitely worth a look if you're not planning to head north to the larger, wilder outdoor parks near Broome or Darwin.

Eating

Although taken seriously, dining out in Fremantle is pleasantly free of unnecessary formality. **Seafood** restaurants overlook the Swan River or jut out into Fishing Boat Harbour by the Esplanade. In town, South Terrace and its adjacent streets are lined with predominantly **Italian** or **Asian** cafés and restaurants, none of them expensive and all adding to Freo's distinctive ambience.

Captain Munchies, 2 Beach St. Twenty-four-hour establishment for those late-night appetites.

Chunagon, 46 Mews Rd, Fishing Boat Harbour (☎08/9336 1000). Classy Japanese restaurant which suits those who know their sushi from their sashimi or can afford to learn. Closed Mon.

Cicerillo's, Fishing Boat Harbour. One of the best fish-and-chip places in town.

Falduzzi, 5 Bannister St. Small, earthy pizzeria with pizzas on the light and unusual side from $10. Try the pizza d'Enfer if you're brave, and cool down with some sweet or savoury crepes.

George Street Café, 73 George St, East Fremantle. Pleasant, small café, an east-side alternative to the central Freo coffee "strip".

Gino's, 1 South Terrace. Best streetside café on the strip. Enduringly popular and unpretentious, serving great coffee and inexpensive food.

Kailis, Mews Rd, Fishing Boat Harbour. Fast and inexpensive seafood cafeteria and takeaway, right on the waterfront.

Left Bank Bar & Café, 15 Riverside Rd, East Fremantle. Trendy riverside venue with brimming subs, or for around $20 you can eat in the upstairs restaurant, which has great views.

Lombardos, Mews Rd, Fishing Boat Harbour (☎08/9335 1088). A Freo fish-and-chip institution that's also a bistro, pub, club and restaurant.

Mexican Kitchen, 19 South Terrace. Classic, wholesome Mexican dishes at around $15, with half-price nachos on Tuesday night.

Oyster Beds, 26 Riverside Rd, East Fremantle (☎08/9339 1611). Superb seafood restaurant, right over the water, at around $25 a head.

Pigeon Restaurant, 4 Market St. Vietnamese place with no dishes over $10.

Prickles, corner of South Terrace and Douro Rd, South Fremantle (☎08/9336 2194). A chance to sample the tastes of the Australian bush: crocodile, emu, buffalo and kangaroo. The croc will be a tasty surprise to most.

Sails, 47 Mews Rd, Fishing Boat Harbour (☎08/9430 5050). Elegant, upmarket, harbourside seafood specialities for around $25 per person.

Thai Village, 22 Bannister St. Best Thai food in Freo with all-you-can-eat lunches on Thursday and Friday for around $13.

Upmarket Food Halls, Henderson St. Array of global, but mostly Asian "pop foods" next to the markets. It's a good place to experiment with inexpensive Japanese morsels. Thurs–Sun noon–9pm.

Drinking and entertainment

Like the town itself, **entertainment** in Fremantle is generally a laid-back, easy-going affair – a jazzy or folksy scene, as opposed to Northbridge's techno venues. The *Sail & Anchor* on South Terrace is the town's main watering hole, serving a variety of "boutique" beers (this upmarket home-brew trend originated in Fremantle). The *Left Bank Bar & Café*, on Riverside Road in East Freo, is a good-looking and popular spot, usually packed on sunny weekends. Bars with live music include *Rosie O'Grady's* on William

Street; *The Bar* at *Lombardos* on the harbour; the *Cave Bar* next to the old bridge on Queen Victoria Street; and the spruced-up *Orient Hotel* on the High Street. The *Metropolis*, 52 South Terrace, is Fremantle's gigantic **nightclub**, offering a choice of bars and dance floors; the *Go Club*, 80 High St, provides a lively alternative. The *Fly By Night*, at the prison end of Queen Street, is a musicians' co-op airing local folk talent and makes an enjoyable, smoke-free change from pub venues.

For **performing arts**, check out the *Fremantle Herald* or Thursday's *West Australian*. Local troupes, such as the innovative Deck Chair Theatre based at 3 Packenham St (☎08/9336 2372), or Spare Parts Theatre, 1 Short St (☎08/9335 5044), are worth seeing, or head for the Arts Centre, Ord Street, on a Sunday afternoon in summer. Fremantle has three **cinemas**, on Essex Street, William Street and Adelaide Street, all with cut-price tickets on Tuesday and for some matinees.

Rottnest Island

Eighteen kilometres offshore, west of Fremantle, **Rottnest Island** was so named by seventeenth-century Dutch mariners who mistook its unique, indigenous **quokkas**, beaver-like marsupials, for rats. Today, following an ignominious period as a brutal Aboriginal penal colony in the nineteenth century, Rottnest is a popular holiday destination, easily accessible from Perth or Fremantle by ferry and, at the very least, makes for a fun day out.

The island, colloquially abbreviated to "Rotto", is 11km long and less than half as wide, with one settlement, the main resort, stretching along the sheltered Thompson Bay on the east side. West of the settlement, a low heathland of salt lakes meets a coastline of clear, scalloped bays, small beaches and offshore reefs ending at the "West End", as the seaward "tail" of the island is known. Although well attuned to the demands of its 400,000 annual visitors, Rotto gets packed out during school summer holidays, especially around New Year when accommodation can be hard to find. Motorized traffic on the island is virtually non-existent, a real treat which makes **cycling** from bay to sparkling bay the best way to appreciate Rotto. Besides riding around the island, you can take a **train ride** up to Oliver Hill (five trips daily, allow 2hr; $12), or get underwater with the Dive Shop (daily 7.30am–6pm; ☎08/9292 5167), which organizes **dive trips** and rents out everything from a snorkel and fins to a full scuba rig. The diving and snorkelling off Rotto's beautiful coves are unlike anywhere on the adjacent mainland and a couple of days spent here, especially midweek, when it's less busy, are well worth the excursion from Perth.

Practicalities

There are no fewer than four **ferry** operators that service Rotto from a variety of points in Fremantle and Perth. After a brief price war, prices have stabilized at around $25 day return from Freo and $35 from Perth. The trip from Perth takes about eighty minutes, half as long from Fremantle. You can also **fly** to Rotto in twenty minutes from Jandakot airport (about 20km south of Perth) with the Rottnest Airbus (☎08/9478 1322). Rottnest Airport is a fifteen-minute walk from the settlement.

Ferries arrive at the jetty in Thompson Bay right in front of the island's **information office** (Mon–Sat 8.30am–5pm, Sun 10am–4.30pm; ☎08/9372 9752), which has maps and bus timetables. The office is also a **post office** with Commonwealth and Westpac bank agencies. Daily two-hour **bus tours** depart from here, at 11.30am and 1.30pm ($14). The more-or-less hourly Bayseeker **bus service** (Oct–April daily 9am–5pm; $3 per trip) also takes you to the island's bays as far as the isthmus, Narrow Neck, 3km from the West End. The settlement has a general **store** (daily 9am–5.30pm, with R&I and ANZ teller machine), bakery, takeaway and **bistro**, with **bike** rental (daily

9am–1pm & 2–5pm; $15 per day; ☎08/9372 9722) behind the hotel, a couple of minutes south of the information office.

   Accommodation is found along Thompson, Longreach and Geordie bays, all adjacent to each other at the developed northeast end of the island and linked by an hourly bus service (daily 8am–5pm; $2). A small YHA-associate **hostel** (☎08/9372 9780, fax 9292 5154; booking essential; ①) is located in Kingstown Barracks, at the southeastern end of Thompson Bay, 1km from the shops. **Camping** is available just behind the settlement (☎08/9372 9729): tents and mattresses can be rented (①) or there are four- and six-bed cabins (④); note that camping is not permitted elsewhere on the island. The island authority rents out all sorts of bungalows, villas, units and cottages (book ahead on ☎08/9432 9111; four-bed units ⑤–⑦); rates are substantially lower for subsequent nights, and there's a minimum stay of two nights at weekends. The *Rottnest Lodge Resort* (☎08/9292 5161, fax 9292 5158; ⑧) is a prison converted into first-class motel units.

Perth's beaches

Perth's closest **beaches** extend along the Indian Ocean's **Sunset Coast**, 30km of near-unbroken sand and coastal suburbs stretching north of the Swan River and cooled by afternoon sea breezes. There are also **inshore beaches** along the Swan River at Crawley, Nedlands, Peppermint Grove and Mosman Bay on the north shore, and Como, Canning Bridge and Applecross on the south – all are calm and safe for kiddies.

   Cottesloe Beach, 7km north of Fremantle, is the most popular city beach, with safe swimming in the lee of a groyne. There are ice-cream vendors, cafés and watercraft-rental outlets all just a short walk from Cottesloe train station. North of here, **Swanbourne Free Beach**, cut off by army land in both directions but accessible from the road, has nude bathing. Further north, the surf and currents are more suited to wave riding and experienced swimmers, with fewer beachside facilities, which tends to reduce crowds.

   SCARBOROUGH BEACH, dominated by the *Radisson Observation City Hotel*, is as much a holiday resort as beachside suburb and is the best base along the Sunset Coast if you want to stay a day or two. Popular with surfers and their groupies, the suburb has an easy-going air of "Californian tan-upmanship", plus enough services, inexpensive accommodation and activity to sustain a few days out of central Perth. **Bus** #400 leaves from Perth's Wellington Street Bus Station for the forty-minute journey.

Beachside accommodation

The accommodation at Scarborough Beach is mostly **self-catering**, suited to extended stays. The *Western Beach Lodge* serves **backpackers** in a converted house at 6 Westborough St (☎08/9245 1624; ①) or try *Sunset Coast Backpackers*, 119 Scarborough Beach Rd (☎08/9245 1161; ①). *West Coast Seas* (☎08/9341 4101; ④–⑦), right next to the *Radisson Observation City Hotel*, offers a range of self-catering units, while the *Indian Ocean Hotel*, at 23 Hastings St (☎08/9341 1122, fax 9341 1899; ⑥), is a good-value hotel. Further south in **Swanbourne**, the *Swanbourne Guest House*, 5 Myers St (☎08/9383 1981, fax 9385 4595; ⑥), has gay- and lesbian-friendly lodgings.

New Norcia and Toodyay

One of WA's most extraordinary architectural sights is the nineteenth-century monastic community of **NEW NORCIA**, 130km northeast of Perth on the Great Northern Highway. This unexpected collection of Spanish-style buildings, bizarrely out of place in the Australian bush, is part of a community founded by Benedictine monks in 1846.

Dom Rosendo Salvado established the mission (named after St Benedict's birthplace in Italy) with the aim of converting the local Aborigines to the "twin blessings" of agriculture and Christianity, and to escape persecution back home. Nowadays it's a popular tourist attraction, which tends to compromise the monastic tranquillity its ageing inhabitants seek, and yet pays for the upkeep of their remarkable endowment.

The community has a roadhouse with a restaurant, a **tourist office** (daily 9am–5pm; ☎08/9654 8056) and a **museum and art gallery** (daily 10am–4pm; $4) describing the Benedictines' motivations in coming here and displaying a fine collection of religious art. The **rooms** in the *New Norcia Hotel* (☎08/9654 8034, fax 9654 8011; ④) don't quite match the building's grand exterior, but they still offer an old-fashioned treat. The two-kilometre New Norcia **heritage trail** (guide leaflet available from the tourist office or museum) begins here and takes you on a circuit past the community's impressive buildings.

The two most ornate buildings, on either side of the cemetery, are **St Gertrude's Residence for Girls** and **St Ildephonsus's for Boys**, the latter with striking Moorish minarets. Both were built by the mission's second abbot, Bishop Torres, at the beginning of the twentieth century. Daily tours ($10) allow you to explore their ornate interiors, and you can also visit the **Flour Mills** and the **Abbey Church** – relatively ordinary by comparison. The **monastery** is still the residence of New Norcia's few remaining monks and is closed to the public, although there's a B&B (☎08/9654 8056; $25 per person) in the adjacent guesthouse. From here an eight-hundred-metre marked trail leads down to the old wells and Bishop Torres' gazebo-like **Beehouse** by the Moore River; on the way back there are great views of St Ildephonsus's turreted roofline poking through the trees.

Several bus tour companies offer day-tours from Perth to New Norcia, which is otherwise served only three times a week by Westrail's rural bus service.

Toodyay

The charming old town of **TOODYAY**, set among the wooded hills of the Avon Valley, 85km northwest of Perth, makes an agreeable diversion on the way to or from New Norcia. The town was founded in 1836, making it one of the earliest inland settlements of the Swan River Colony, and many buildings survive from that era. The unembellished bulk of **Connors Mill** on the main road, Stirling Terrace, is now an **information centre** and **museum** (Mon–Sat 9am–5pm, Sun 10am–5pm; ☎08/9574 2435; museum $1), featuring, among the usual relics, displays on the exploits of the local bushranger known as "Moondyne Joe". The **Old Newcastle Gaol** on Clinton Street is also a local history museum (Mon–Fri 11am–3pm, Sat 1–4pm, Sun 11am–4pm; $2). Other historic buildings include **St Stephen's Church**, opposite the mill, and the **Mechanics' Institute**, on Stirling Terrace, which features unusual scissor trusses supporting the roof.

These aside, the town is an attractive place for a stroll, with antique and country crafts outlets, a couple of **tearooms**, pleasant parks and riverside walks. The **Avon Valley** and **Walyunga national parks** (CALM fee; see box on p.619) follow the Avon River southwest of town and make a further scenic diversion on the road to Perth.

Guildford and the Swan Valley

North of the town of **GUILDFORD**, a thirty-minute drive from Perth, is the **Upper Swan Valley**, WA's oldest wine-growing region. Set at the foot of the Darling Ranges, it makes for a pleasant day's **wine-tasting**, although the wines produced here cannot match the more recent vintages from the Margaret River Region (see p.615). Guildford itself is a historic town dating back to the earliest years of the colony, with several Federation-era grand hotels to admire and Guildford Village Potters, at 22 Meadow St, acting as the town's **tourist office** (Mon–Fri 10am–3pm, Sat & Sun 10am–4pm; ☎08/9279 9859). If you're heading up the valley, pick up the *Swan Valley Drive – Route 203* guide from here, which details the area's attractions and its dozen or so wineries. And before you leave town (or on your way back), visit the **Halls Museum**, at the back of the *Rose and Crown Hotel* (WA's oldest), at 105 Swan St (Tues–Sun 10am–4.30pm; $4). Proclaiming itself the largest private collection of **diverse memorabilia** in the southern hemisphere, it includes displays of inkwells, corkscrews and evening bags, the like of which you won't find anywhere else.

The Swan Valley Drive
Heading north from Guildford Village Potters, a clearly marked thirty-kilometre drive follows the west side of the river. A turn-off left down Banera Road leads to **Pinelli Wines** on Bennett Road (Mon–Sat 9am–6pm, Sun 10am–5pm), offering two-litre flagons of decent table wine from $15. Back on the West Swan Road, the simply named **Wines** (Mon–Sat 10am–5pm, Sun 11am–4pm) has some of the valley's best wines, but you'll probably be more impressed by their Margaret River selection. (All of WA's wines are rather pricey, while being no better than Australia's eastern equivalents.) Further up Route 203, the **Little River Winery & Café** (daily 10am–5.30pm) is a small, independent winery with some award-winning wines and a pleasant café in which to enjoy them.

Coming down the valley's east side, several more wineries tempt you: **Talijancich Wines'** (Sun–Fri 11am–5pm) rich muscat can be bought rather than tasted, while **Houghton's**, on Dale Road (daily 10am–5pm), is the area's biggest and most diverse producer of wines, with an art gallery and tended lawns on which to contemplate your tastings. The route returns to Guildford and thence to Perth via Midland, passing the Toodyay Road (see opposite) winding up into the Darling Ranges. Feature Tours (☎08/9479 4131) runs regular **bus tours** through the valley from Perth, as do some of the Swan River **boat cruises**.

Mundaring Weir and around

At the crest of the Darling Ranges, 40km from Perth and 7km south of the town of Mundaring on the Great Eastern Highway, is **Mundaring Weir**, a dam constructed in the 1890s to provide water for the Goldfields Water Scheme. At the time, a desperate water shortage was hampering development of the Eastern Goldfields and the dam was part of the innovative solution devised by the colony's chief engineer, C.Y. O'Connor, who planned to raise the water the 400km up to Kalgoorlie with the aid of a series of pumping stations. Such a radical idea was ridiculed in the press and mocked in parliament – O'Connor struggled constantly to secure funds for his scheme and eventually committed suicide on Fremantle Beach just months before water finally gushed into Kalgoorlie's Mount Charlotte Reservoir in 1903. Today, the Goldfields are still fed by an upgraded version of the pipeline and pumping stations which parallel the Great Eastern Highway to Kalgoorlie.

At the base of the dam wall is the **C.Y. O'Connor Museum** (Mon & Wed–Fri 10.30am–3pm, Sat 1–4pm, Sun noon–5pm; $30), housed in the primary steam pumping station. Inside are early versions of the pitch and wood pipeline, at that time the longest in the world, and details of O'Connor's other public works, as well as a biographical video on his achievements.

The **John Forrest National Park** (CALM fee; see box on p.619) lies north of the Great Eastern Highway between Mundaring and Midland, right on the edge of the Darling escarpment and a mere thirty minutes' drive from Perth. An area of natural bushland with swimming spots, waterfalls, and walking and riding trails, as well as barbecues and a restaurant, it's among the best of the nearby parks.

York

Stranded in the Avon Valley, 97km from Perth via the Great Southern Highway, **YORK** looks like a film set for an Australian western. The town is the state's most complete pioneering settlement, filled with attractive and well-preserved early architecture. The commercial centre of the Avon Valley until the railway – and with it the Great Eastern Highway – bypassed it 30km to the north, York is now an agricultural centre but also plays a historic role as a venerable museum of ornate nineteenth-century public buildings, coaching inns and churches.

The **York Motor Museum** (daily 9am–5pm; $7), opposite the tourist office on Avon Terrace, capitalizes on York's antiquarian charisma with a large collection of vintage and classic vehicles – from a hundred-year-old single-cylinder tricycle to Ossie Cranston's 1936 Ford V8 racer. At the north end of the terrace are the **Sandalwood Yards** where the perfumed wood, once prolific in WA and highly prized in the Orient, was stored during York's heyday. Near here you can take a walk down to the wobbly **suspension bridge** spanning the generally sluggish Avon River and have a look at the 1854 **Holy Trinity Church**, with its modern stained-glass designs by Robert Juniper, one of WA's foremost artists.

Recrossing the river, passing the Shire Offices and old cemetery, a left turn down the southern end of Avon Terrace leads to **Balladong Farm** (daily 10am–5pm; $5), restored by the National Trust. At a time when York was a key inland settlement and jumping-off point for treks into the interior, the farm played a pivotal role in the region, and today it still employs machinery and husbandry techniques from that era. An elevated view of York and the Avon Valley can be enjoyed from **Mount Brown Lookout**, signposted 2km to the east of town.

Practicalities

York's **tourist office** (daily 9am–5pm; ☎08/9641 1301) is at 105 Avon Terrace, the main road on which most of York's fine old buildings are located. A **town map** and information sheet is available here, which locates and briefly describes all of these structures as well as places to stay and eat. York's **hotels** ooze charm, with the *Settlers' House* (☎08/9641 1096; ⑦) offering elegantly furnished rooms with breakfast, with a fine restaurant and pleasant daytime café too. The *Imperial Inn*, 83 Avon Terrace (☎08/9641 1010, fax 9641 2201; ⑥), is a restored, century-old hotel also full of old-world charm, while the pricier *Castle Hotel* (☎08/9641 1007; ⑦) is even more splendid. The only real budget accommodation is at the *Mount Bakewell Caravan Park* (☎08/9641 1421; on-site vans ②).

Cafés to enjoy include *Café Bugatti* and the *Terrace Café* (both on Avon Terrace), as well as the one attached to the *Settlers' House* hotel. **Buses** leave Westrail's East Perth terminal for York up to three times daily (no service on Sat), while some **tours** stop here on the way to or from Wave Rock at Hyden, 250km to the east. The town hosts the **York Jazz Festival** around September, but note that in the summer months, York, like all of inland WA, often sees temperatures of 40°C and gets few visitors.

The Southwest

The region south of Perth and west of the Albany Highway, known as **The Southwest**, is the temperate corner of the continent, where the cool Southern and warm Indian oceans meet. North of **Bunbury**, 180km from Perth, is a knot of industrial installations and satellite towns such as Rockingham and Mandurah, which offer little of interest to the visitor compared to what's ahead.

South of Bunbury things improve greatly. The **Margaret River** Region offers tasteful tourist facilities in a picturesque landscape of dairy farms and wineries – WA's most

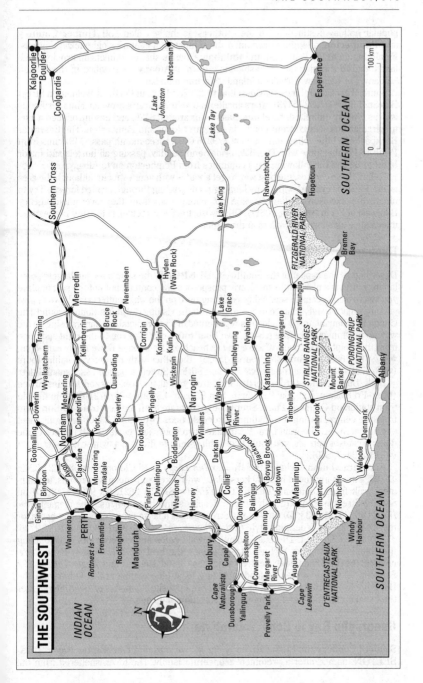

popular holiday destination. To the southeast is the so-called **Tall Timber Country** and **Pemberton**, a logging town amid the remnants of centuries-old eucalypt forests. Finally, again to the southeast, the **Rainbow Coast's** sheltered inlets and rocky headlands lead to the historic and fashionable town of **Albany** – described in the section "Albany, the Rainbow Coast and inland", starting on p.620.

South West Coach Lines (in Busselton ☎08/9752 1500; in Perth, at Wellington Street Bus Station, ☎08/9322 5173) offers an alternative to Westrail's provincial bus service as well as ten-day unlimited-travel **bus passes** for around $120, and has introduced a useful circular bus service from Perth via Margaret River and Pemberton. The Easyrider Backpackers' little yellow minibus (☎08/9226 0307; three-month pass $149) runs from Perth to Pemberton every Tuesday, Friday and Sunday, passing all hostels and major highlights, and the following days continues from Pemberton on to Albany.

Failing these choices, the best way to get about is with your own **car**, although the area is also ideal for **cycling**, with many logging roads passing through shaded forests. Try to obtain the excellent *Cycling Down South* biking map from the government agency Bikewest in Perth (☎08/9389 0611). Otherwise, the five Streetsmart **touring maps** make informative aids for all travellers in the region.

Bunbury

Described as the capital of the Southwest, **BUNBURY**, the state's second-largest population centre, is a pleasant town, clearly prosperous and content, but not the sort of place you've crossed oceans to see. A day's dallying here on the way south certainly won't give you nightmares, and a chance to commune with the visiting dolphins (found around The Cut on Leschenault Inlet) is a lot less regimented, if less predictable, than traipsing all the way up to Monkey Mia (see p.644). Two **boat tours** can take you to the right spot: one from the Dolphin Discovery Centre on the beach off Koombana Drive (daily 8am–5pm; ☎08/9791 3088; $4 admission; tours $15–25), the other with Bunbury Dolphin Tours (☎08/9721 7922; $15) at the *Parade Hotel* on Stirling Street alongside Leschenault Inlet.

Daily **bus services** from Perth (3hr) drop you at the well-stocked **tourist office** (Mon–Fri 8.30am–5pm, Sat 9am–5pm, Sun 9.30am–4.30pm; ☎08/9721 7922) in the old train station on Carmody Place. Shuttle buses operate from the new **train station**, 3km from the centre, during the daytime; otherwise **taxis** (☎08/9721 2300) generally meet evening arrivals. The train from Perth takes two hours and costs $20. If neither of the dolphin cruises appeals, you could take a thirty-minute **flight** in a twin-seater microlight (☎01538 9417; $60).

Accommodation includes the *Wander Inn Lodge* at 16 Clifton St (☎08/9721 3242; ①–③), a much-improved backpackers' place with bikes and cheap twin rooms, ten minutes' walk from Koombana Beach. The *YHA* (☎08/9791 2621, fax 9791 4742; ①) on Stirling Street is comparatively serene despite some huge dorms. The elegant *Rose Hotel* (☎08/9721 4533; ⑤) on Victoria Street boasts a large range of boutique beers, or there's the lovely Federation-style *Clifton Beach Motel* (☎08/9721 4300, fax 9791 2726; ⑥–⑦) at 85 Clifton St. There are many sidewalk **cafés** and **restaurants** ranged along the colonial frontage of Victoria Street: among the best are *Memories of Bond Store*, next to the Entertainment Centre, which has good snacks, and *Eagle Towers*, 192 Spencer St, which serves seafood including local blue manna crabs. Otherwise, the Bunbury **food halls** (Thurs–Sun 11am–9pm), opposite *Memories of Bond Store*, offer the usual inexpensive and cosmopolitan selection of dishes.

Geographe Bay to Cape Naturaliste

South of Bunbury the Bussel Highway curves west around **Geographe Bay** to **BUSSELTON**, named after a prominent pioneering family. The town, sheltered from the ocean's currents and swells, is a popular "bucket and spade" resort where parents can be sure their kids won't be swept away or dashed onto the rocks. There's a **museum** (2–5pm; closed Tues; $2) in the Old Butter Factory, off Peel Terrace, with an exhibit on the ill-fated **Group Settlement Scheme**. During the 1920s, overseas families with little or no farming expertise were induced to settle the Southwest – most failed miserably and ended up rotting in "humpies" such as the one on display. You're unlikely to want to stay with the holidaying masses, but there's **backpackers'** accommodation at 14 Peel Terrace (☎08/9754 2763; ①) if you get caught out.

After Busselton, the highway turns south towards Margaret River, though continuing west brings you to **DUNSBOROUGH**, 21km from Busselton, a small holiday resort with an excellently located YHA **hostel** (☎ & fax 08/9755 3107; ①). Situated 4km southeast of town, right on the beach, the modern hostel offers free bikes and watercraft and has a happy, family atmosphere. Otherwise, try the *Green Acres Caravan Park* (☎08/9755 3087; on-site vans ③) on the seafront, or one of the several **resorts**. This is still holiday country, so most places are rather pricey with self-contained facilities designed to suit families. With numerous wrecks and little tidal variation, Geographe Bay is ideal for **diving**; the *Dunsborough Bay Village Resort* (☎08/9755 3183), on Dunn Bay Road, takes care of equipment rental and charters.

Cape Naturaliste, 14km northwest of the resort, is the less impressive of the two capes which define the Margaret River Region. Its truncated **lighthouse** (9.30am–4.30pm; closed Wed; $3) is open for inspection, and along the way there are turn-offs to secluded beaches with the **Sugarloaf** offering particularly fine views.

Along Caves Road to Margaret River and Cape Leeuwin

South of Dunsborough you head into the **Margaret River Region** proper, characterized by caves, wineries, choice restaurants and snug hideaways all interspersed with more galleries, craft studios and potteries than in the rest of the state put together. Passing **Ngilgi Cave** (see box on p.616) you come to the turn-off for **YALLINGUP**, a small seaside resort with a lovely clean beach and surfers waiting for the big one. Further along Caves Road is the Gunyulgup Gallery (daily 10am–5pm) with a particularly fine selection of pottery, glass, paintings and jarrah furniture by local artisans; down the road another gallery features a lovely restaurant overlooking a lake.

Yallingup Forest Resort (☎08/9755 2550, fax 9755 6016; ⑧) on Hemsley Road off Caves Road would suit an extended stay in the area, offering large, self-contained chalets with the use of a pool, tennis court and even a brewery on site. A couple of kilometres back down Caves Road, from the Gunyulgup Gallery, is a crossroads with the inviting *Crayfish Lodge* (☎08/9755 2286, fax 9755 2406; ⑦) and restaurant on the corner, and a right turn leading 3km to **Canal Rocks**, where the waves relentlessly pound the pink granite outcrops into curious, scalloped forms. Further south are turn-offs to the **Abbey Vale Winery** and **Moonshine Brewery** (daily 10.30am–5pm) and, further on, **Cape Clairault Winery** (daily 10am–5pm), one of the better choices if you fancy some wine-tasting. Those intent on visiting some of the 45 wineries within half as many kilometres should pick up the *Margaret River Regional Vineyard Guide* ($3) from the Margaret River **tourist office** (see overleaf).

Another turning west off Caves Road leads 4km to **Quininup Beach**, accessible only to high-clearance vehicles and thus rarely crowded, and **Gracetown**, 12km south, on the sheltered Cowaramup Bay. Five kilometres further on, a right turn leads to **Ellenbrook House**, a Bussell homestead dating from 1857 – bare inside but in a lovely, quiet spot by the brook. From here it's a thirty-minute walk up to the luxuriant **Meekadarribee Falls** which, unusually, manage to spiral underneath themselves.

After Ellenbrook you come to the crossroads leading east 5km to Margaret River township (see overleaf), while a right turn takes you to the resort of **PREVELLY**

PARK, on the estuary of the Margaret River. The Greek **Chapel of St John** will certainly catch your eye: a memorial to the Preveli Monastery on Crete which sheltered Allied soldiers, Australians among them, in World War II. The turning opposite leads down to the blustery beach where November's annual Margaret River Classic **surfing** championships are held. Everyone talks about the legendary surf here, but although there is plenty of bleached hair and neoprene in the car park, it is rare to see anyone actually doing some surfing.

Back at the chapel, the road continues down into the **resort**, which has the usual assortment of chalets and caravan parks. Check out the *Café Gnarabup* (daily 8.30am–sunset), overlooking the sea and offering the mouthwatering aroma of sizzling fish, and also the new purpose-built YHA, *Surf Point Lodge*, on Reidle Drive (☎08/9757 1777, fax 9757 1077; en-suite rooms ③, dorms ①), the new oceanside development along Walcliffe Road just south of the café. The hostel offers free pick-ups from Margaret River.

Margaret River

The town of **MARGARET RIVER**, like the eponymous region, has come to symbolize every stress-worn Perthian's dream to escape the rat race, set up a craft boutique or a sylvan getaway, and claim their share of the Good Life. It's a favourite place for a mix of holiday-makers, partying wave-riders, floral-clad muses and the vanguard of fortunate "mappies" (middle-aged professionals) who moved in ahead of the real-estate boom.

Margaret River is not necessarily the best place actually to stay – prices can be high in summer when the town is busy – but it's handy for shopping, eating out and browsing, while its **tourist office** (daily 9am–5pm; ☎08/9757 0011, *umrta@netserv.net.au*), on the Bussell Highway, represents the whole region. Westrail and South West Coach

---

MARGARET RIVER CAVES

A band of limestone passing through the cape has created some 350 **caves** around Margaret River, four of which are open to the public. Most involve guided tours to avoid damage and accidents, with relatively high entrance fees and shuffling crowds rather detracting from the cavernous spectacle. Nevertheless, a visit to the region would be incomplete without seeing at least one. All are humid and include some long, stepped ascents, with temperatures around 17°C. Tours are less frequent from May to August – for more details about all except Ngilgi Cave, enquire at the Margaret River tourist office.

Lake Cave (daily 9.30am–4pm, 7–12 tours per day; 30min; $12). A collapsed cavern, overgrown with huge karri trees, is the impressive entrance to the cave where a unique "suspended table" hangs over the subterranean lake. The cave is also the site of the new **Cave Works Interpretive Centre** (daily 10am–5pm; ☎08/9757 7411; $5), dealing with all things speleological. It also offers special discount options to visit all the caves except Ngilgi.

Jewel Cave (daily 9.30am–4pm, 7–12 tours per day; 30min; ☎08/9758 4541; $12). The best cave, featuring extraordinary and fragile formations such as five-metre "helictites" (delicate, straw-like formations) protected by breeze-proof doors. Also includes a two-hour tour of **Moondyne Cave** (daily 10am & 2.30pm; maximum of six people; $30, with equipment supplied), a mildly adventurous and less rushed excursion with some belly crawling, although you won't miss any amazing features by not taking the tour.

Mammoth Cave (daily 9am–4pm, 6–8 tours per day; 90min; $12). Large cavern and easy access with some bones and fossils of extinct creatures, but it really should be your last choice.

Ngilgi Cave (daily 9.30am–3.30pm; $10). Not visited on the cave tours but with plenty of nooks to explore and delicate features to admire.

Lines **buses** visit daily from Perth; local **taxis** (☎08/9757 3444) are used to being taken along on some serious wine-tasting jaunts. Highly recommended are local Bushtucker Tours (☎08/9757 2466; $25), who run a four-hour eco-tour that's also a lot of fun.

The range of **accommodation** is vast, with over sixty sites in the immediate vicinity, but the woodland settings out of town are the ones to go for; the tourist office has big portfolios full of ideas. The small *Inne Town* **backpackers'** (free call ☎1800/244 115; ①), on the main road at the north end of town, is ideally central. There's also *Margaret River Lodge*, 2km out of town on Railway Terrace (☎ & fax 08/9757 2532; ①), while *Peppermint Brook Cottages* (☎08/9757 2485; ④–⑥), at 1 Mann St, offers self-contained cottages sleeping six. Both the *Margaret River* (☎08/9757 2180; on-site vans ③) and the *Riverview* (☎08/9757 2270; on-site vans ③) **caravan parks** are just a kilometre out of town.

The whole countryside is dotted with charming **restaurants**, often attached to wineries, but in town try the *Ark of Iris*; the sesame burgers at the *Country Kitchen*; or join the young crowd at *Settlers Bistro*, the town's main pub, which puts on live music in summer.

Augusta and Cape Leeuwin

Five kilometres southwest of Margaret River, on Boodjidup Road, one of the more interesting attractions vying for your attention is **Eagles Heritage** (daily 10am–5pm; $6), a fascinating collection of birds of prey. Aviaries house huge wedge-tail and white-breasted sea eagles, peregrine falcons and a few owls – a rare menagerie of impressive flying hunters.

Rejoining Caves Road, having passed the turning for the **Leeuwin Winery** (daily 10am–4.30pm) with its art gallery and restaurant, you head south into the silvery-barked **karri forest**. It's a magnificent sight, well worth taking some time to appreciate now if you're not planning to visit Pemberton. Down the road are Mammoth and Lake caves (see box opposite). If you have visited the latter cave and have noticed the stream that trickles out of its subterranean lake, you can catch up with it at the spring on **Cowup Bay** beach, 4km from the cave entrance along a dirt road, and with a campsite on the way. Back on Caves Road, Boranup Drive takes an off-road detour through the **Boranup Forest**, a great place for biking and riding, while *Boranup Gallery and Chalets* (☎08/9757 7585, fax 9757 7527; ⑥) sells gorgeous **furniture** made from local timbers and offers accommodation in self-contained rammed-earth **chalets** in bushland settings.

South of the forest, the Brockman Highway leads 90km east to Nannup, while continuing 3km south down Deepdene Road brings you to a turn-off to the old timber port of **Hamelin Bay**, where there's a beachside **caravan park** (☎08/9758 5540; on-site vans ③) offering bikes for rent. Passing **Jewel Cave**, Deepdene Road takes you 8km further to the small town of **AUGUSTA**, on the estuary of the Blackwood River – Western Australia's oldest settlement after Albany and Perth. Little remains from those days, although the **museum** (daily: June–Sept 10am–noon; Oct–May 9am–5pm; $2), on Blackwood Avenue, retains some old relics and is more absorbing than you might expect. **Buses** visit Augusta once a day, generally in the evening, heading back north early the next morning. For **accommodation**, there are two **motels** in town (both ⑥), but *Sheoak Chalets* (☎08/9758 1958; ⑤) is what you've come here for. The purpose-built *Baywatch Manor Resort YHA* (☎08/9758 1290, fax 9758 1291; rooms ③, dorms ①), on the main road, Blackwood Avenue, offers quality backpackers' accommodation and rents bikes and canoes. *Doonbanks Caravan Park* (☎08/9758 1517; on-site vans ③) is up the road, and there are two more caravan parks south of town. You can **eat** healthily at *Squirrels Gourmet Wholefood Kitchen* or more opulently at the *Colonial Restaurant*, both on the main road.

Cape Leeuwin, 9km south of town, is probably why you've come this far, and it's worth the journey, giving a bleak, windswept "land's end" feel to this continental corner, especially on a mean and moody day. A Dutch captain named the cape after his ship 370 years ago, and Matthew Flinders began the onerous task of mapping Australia's coast right here in 1851. From the top of the **lighthouse** (daily 9am–4pm; $4) you can contemplate your position – halfway between the equator and the coastline of Antarctica. Nearby, an **old water wheel**, originally constructed for the lighthouse builders and now petrified in salt, is a well-known landmark.

Tall Timber Country

Sandwiched between the popular tourist areas of Margaret River and Albany's Rainbow Coast, the forests of the so-called **Tall Timber Country** are one of WA's greatest sights. Along with the sinuous **Blackwood River** (ideal for sedate canoeing, especially west of Nannup), the highlight of the region is the brooding, primeval majesty of the **karri forests**, known not as much for their arboreal gimmicks – of which the "climb-if-you-dare" **Gloucester Tree** near Pemberton is the best-known – as they are for the raw, elemental nature of the unique forest environment. **Logging** remains this region's primary industry and small towns, each with their own mill, busy themselves with their controversial work, while **Pemberton** is prospering through tourism, with its woodcraft galleries and scenic drives.

Public transport is much improved with the new Margaret River–Pemberton link, but you'll get much more out of a visit by renting a car.

The Blackwood River Valley and south

The northern part of the forest country is watered by the **Blackwood River** and divided by scenic roads through jarrah woodlands linking the riverside mill towns. **NANNUP**, on the Vasse and Brockman highways, 60km southeast of Busselton, remains a picturesque town, a cluster of wooden cabins nestling quietly among wooded hills. The **tourist office** (☎08/9756 1211) is located in the old police station on Brockman Street; the *Blackwood Café* nearby is an ideal lunch spot. For **accommodation**, the laid-back *Black Cockatoo Hostel*, 27 Grange Rd (☎08/9756 1035; ①), is a cosy backpackers' treat, while the upmarket *Lodge* (☎08/9756 1276, fax 9756 1394; ⑦), on the hill, will spice up your sex life with lavish comforts. Lost among the jarrah 6km northwest of town, the *Nannup Bush Cabins* (☎ & fax 08/9756 1170; ⑤) are enchantingly situated hideaways. Blackwood Expeditions (☎08/9756 1209) offers **canoe rental** and **guided tours** on the lower Blackwood River.

From Nannup, a **scenic drive** winds 41km along the river to unremarkable Balingup, while the equally tree-lined Brockman Highway heads east 46km to **BRIDGETOWN**, a busy mill town with a large **tourist centre** (daily 9am–5pm; ☎08/9761 1740) on Hampton Street. Despite some token tea and craft shops, Bridgetown is really a place to get your ute serviced or chainsaw sharpened. By the river, where some pleasant bankside walks begin, the National Trust property of Bridgedale House (10am–4pm; closed Tues & Wed; $3) rents out **canoes**.

Thirty-seven kilometres south of Bridgetown, **MANJIMUP** is the region's commercial centre, handy for shopping and other services but, apart from a visit to the **Timber Park** (daily 9am–5pm), behind the **tourist office** (daily 8.30am–5.30pm; ☎08/9771 1831) on Rose Street (both celebrating the local timber industry), it has little appeal. Graphite Road is a picturesque forest drive heading west 22km to **One Tree Bridge** and, after another couple of kilometres, to the magnificent **Four Aces**, a quartet of huge, 350-year-old karri trees standing in a row. With a detailed map it's possible to spend all day driving around these gravelly, winding logging roads, but should you head south to Pemberton along the tarmac road you'll pass a turn-off to the **Diamond Tree**, where you can climb a fifty-metre lookout tree for free.

CALM NATIONAL PARK ENTRY FEES

In addition to camping fees CALM now levies an **entry fee** or "pass" at the most-visited national parks in WA. The prices of the various passes are listed below. Throughout this chapter those CALM parks that require an entry fee have the phrase "CALM fee; see box on p.619" placed in parentheses after their names. You can obtain a pass from the entry gate or a CALM office.

Day Pass: $8 per car, $3 per motorbike.
Holiday Pass: $20 per vehicle, allowing entry into all parks for four weeks.
Annual Local Park Pass: $15, giving

unlimited access for a year to parks in a given area.
Annual All Parks Pass: $45, allowing entry into all parks for a year.

Pemberton and around

Small enough to retain its backwoods charm while maintaining the high standard of accommodation, eating and creative outlets that make the Southwest such an attractive destination, **PEMBERTON** is the most central base for touring the area. You'll find the **tourist information** office on Brockman Street (daily 9am–5pm; ☎08/9776 1133), where you can pick up the excellent *Pemberton–Northcliffe* map and guide ($1), as well as information on **horse-riding**, **canoe** and **bicycle rental**, and local **tours**. Round the back is the interactive Karri Forest Discovery Centre (daily 9am–5pm; donation), which replicates the forest environment.

On Dickinson Street Fine Woodcraft, an excellent **craft gallery** and restaurant, displays regional works, with a commendable dearth of wombat tea cosies and similar tack. A fun way of seeing the surrounding forest is to take the **tram** (☎08/9776 1322) between Pemberton and Northcliffe (Tues, Thurs & Sat; 5hr 30min return, including photo stops). If your time is limited, settle for the shorter trip to Warren, which is actually the better half of the ride (2 daily; 1hr 45min return). The tram rattles along the old logging railway, over rustic timber bridges spanning tiny creeks, and visits the local beauty spot, the **Cascades** (also accessible by road) – a thoroughly enjoyable excursion. In summer there's also a **steam train** service up to Lyall Sidings, north of town.

The region's single most popular attraction is the **Gloucester Tree** (CALM fee; see box above), situated on a clearly signposted road 3km southeast of town. At 61m, it's the world's tallest fire-lookout tree and its platform is accessible by climbing a spiral of horizontal stakes. Only a quarter of those who visit the tree actually climb up to the platform – the climb itself is more satisfying than the actual view – and those who do can have their efforts validated by a certificate available at the tourist office in town. The countryside all around is crisscrossed with peaceful walking trails and enchanting forest drives cutting deep into the wonderful karri woodlands. **Beedelup National Park**, on the Vasse Highway 20km west of town, has a short walk to a suspension bridge over **Beedelup Falls**, while the drive through the native karri forests of the **Warren National Park**, 10km southwest of town, will leave you in awe of these huge trees flourishing in their natural environment. If you have time for only one such drive, make it this one.

As for **accommodation**, the basic *YHA* at Pimelea (☎08/9776 1153, fax 9776 1819; ①), 10km northwest of town, has seen some improvements and now offers free pickups from town as well as bike and canoe rental. You could also try *Warren Lodge* (☎08/9776 1105; ①), a similarly basic ex-millworkers' lodgings right in town by the bus stop. Otherwise, the surrounding countryside abounds in tranquil woodland retreats, such as *Pump Hill Farm Cottages* (☎ & fax 08/9776 1379; ⑥), 2km west of town, or *Karri Valley Hideaway Cottages* (☎ & fax 08/9776 2049; ⑥), 20km west. Campers can stay at the town's central **caravan park** (☎08/9776 1300; on-site vans ③) or at any of the CALM-approved **campsites** in the surrounding forests. There are a couple of cafés in town but for trout or marron (freshwater crayfish), both local delicacies, try the restaurant at the *Eagle Springs Trout Hatchery*, signposted north of town.

Thirty kilometres south of Pemberton, **NORTHCLIFFE** is a small, untouristed logging town of little interest to passing visitors. Southwest of the town is the long spread of coastal heathland and inland dunes comprising the **D'Entrecasteaux National Park**. It's barely accessible, although Southern Forest Adventures in Northcliffe (☎08/9776 1222) offers one- to five-day 4WD tours as well as a weekend package canoeing down to the park and returning by 4WD. **Windy Harbour**, 30km south of Northcliffe, is the only point between Augusta and Walpole where non-4WD vehicles can get to the ocean shore. There is a small break in the limestone cliffs here, allowing access to a couple of exposed white beaches and a basic **campsite**, usually occupied by fishermen.

Albany, the Rainbow Coast and inland

The alternating sheltered bays and rugged headlands of the **Rainbow Coast** around **Albany**, WA's original colonial settlement, have gradually been gentrified by semi-retired pastoral yuppies with cultivated tastes and a yen for alternative lifestyles. As elsewhere in the Southwest, the temperate climate here creates a rural antipodean-English idyll unknown in the rest of WA.

Albany, 410km from Perth, is promoted as a mildly sophisticated holiday destination, while **Denmark**, 54km to the west, is a twee, arty hamlet with **Walpole's** bays and tingle forests marking the Rainbow Coast's limit. An hour's drive north of Albany lie the wine-making region of **Mount Barker** and the **Porongurup** and **Stirling Ranges national parks**.

Perth's radial **bus services** to the main centres run on a frequent basis, but moving around requires some planning to avoid inconvenient delays. Westrail buses depart from Perth for Albany at least twice daily, either directly down the Albany Highway (6hr) or four times a week via Bunbury and twice weekly via Pemberton (8hr). **Car rental**, or shared lifts, are clearly a better option and **tours**, despite their breathless pace, will at least show you it all, however briefly.

Albany

In 1826, two years before the establishment of the Swan River Colony, the British sent Major Lockyer and a team of hopeful colonists to settle the strategic **Princess Royal Harbour**. It was a pre-emptive response to French exploration of Australia's Southwest, and the small colony, originally called Fredrickstown, was allowed to grow at a natural pace – avoiding the vicissitudes of Swan River Mania that plagued Perth in the 1880s, when thousands of colonists poured into the town. Prior to the building of Fremantle Harbour in the 1890s, **ALBANY** was a key port on the route from England to Botany Bay, a coaling station in the age of steamers. It was also the last of Australia that many Anzacs saw on their way to Gallipoli in 1914.

Now serving the southern wheat and sheep belt, Albany has also become the centre of one of the Southwest's main holiday areas. Factors such as weekend proximity to Perth, moderate summer temperatures, a surfeit of natural splendour and historical kudos all combine to make an agreeable and genuine destination, largely bereft of bogus tourist traps.

Arrival, information and accommodation

Westrail **buses** arrive near the old train station on Lower Stirling Terrace, the location of the **tourist office** (Mon–Fri 8.30am–5.30pm, Sat & Sun 9am–5pm; ☎08/9841 1088 or free call ☎1800/644 088; *albany@albany.jrc.net.au*), which dispenses handy local and regional sketch **maps**. Loves Bus Service (timetables at the tourist office, or call ☎08/9841 1211) offers in-town **public transport**: the #301 route between York Street, the town's main road, and Middleton Beach/Emu Point is particularly useful (Mon–Fri 9am–3pm, Sat 9.15–11am).

Albany offers several **guesthouses**, as well as the customary range of highway motels and self-contained units found in the Middleton Bay area, 3km east of the centre. In the countryside, farmstays mix with classy cottages and other pastoral hideaways. The tourist office has a detailed photographic portfolio of the town's accommodation options.

MOTELS, UNITS, HOSTELS AND GUESTHOUSES

Albany Backpackers, corner of Stirling Terrace and Spencer St (☎08/9841 8848). The energetic owners provide a lively atmosphere and plenty of activities. Rooms ③, dorms ①.

Bayview YHA, 49 Duke St (☎ & fax 08/9842 3388). Good accommodation with tempting incentives such as free pancakes and popcorn. ①.

Coraki Holiday Cottages, Lower King River, 11km east of town (☎08/9844 7068, fax 9844 1068). Great-value cottages in their own gardens by Oyster Harbour. Minimum stay of two days. ⑤–⑦.

Discovery Inn, 9 Middleton Rd (☎08/9842 5535, fax 9842 2371). An especially agreeable old guesthouse and restaurant, close to Middleton Beach. ④.

Dog Rock Motel, 303 Middleton Rd (☎08/9841 4422, fax 9842 1027). Good-value lodgings, with restaurant; close to town and shops. ⑤.

Dolphin Lodge, 1 Golf Links Rd, Middleton Beach (☎ & fax 08/9841 6600). Inexpensive family units. ⑤–⑥.

Norman House, 28 Stuart Terrace (☎ & fax 08/9841 5995). Plusher sort of guesthouse, close to town, with disabled access and bright rooms. ④–⑥.

Parkville Guest House, 136 Brunswick Rd (☎ & fax 08/9841 3704). Nice old house with a resident ghost. ⑤.

Travel Inn, 191 Albany Highway (☎08/9841 4144, fax 9841 6215). Albany's best motel, with large comfortable rooms. ⑦.

CARAVAN PARKS

Emu Beach, Emu Point, 7km from the town centre (☎08/9844 1147). Not a bad spot to stay for a few days. Amenities include trampolines and mini-golf. Cabins ④, on-site vans ③.

Middleton Beach, Flinders Parade, Middleton Beach (☎08/9841 3593). Right on the weekend-posing drag and the sometimes windy beach. Cabins and on-site vans ③.

Mount Melville, 22 Wellington St (☎08/9841 4616). Has a useful camp kitchen and is just 1km from town. Chalets ④, on-site vans ③.

The Town and around

Albany's attractions are spread between the Foreshore, where the original colonists set up camp, and the beaches around **Middleton Beach** and Emu Point on the still waters of Oyster Harbour. Driving around the harbour brings you after 40km to the nature reserve at Two Peoples Bay, while the features and attractions on the **Torndirrup Peninsula**, 20km from town, along Frenchman's Bay Road, are well worth a look.

On the **Foreshore** there's a replica of the *Amity* (daily 9am–5pm; $2.50), the brig that landed its three-score colonists here on Boxing Day, 1826, after six months at sea. Nearby is the **Old Gaol** (daily 10am–4.30pm; $4), with the usual bare cells and barred doors. The **Albany Residency Museum** (daily 10am–5pm; free) is much more interesting, with meticulous displays of the town's maritime history, a section on Aboriginal bush medicines, an annexe with an obsolete lighthouse lens that was too good to throw away and, upstairs, an educational see-and-touch gallery for children.

They've gone a bit over the top with telecom memorabilia at the **Inter Colonial Communications Museum** (Mon–Sat 10am–4pm, Sun 2–4pm; free) in the **Old Post**

Office on Stirling Terrace, Albany's most striking building; the museum features such fascinating displays as "dialling tones and switchboards through the ages". Heading towards Middleton Beach, the curious tower on top of **Mount Melville Lookout**, off Serpentine Road, is colloquially known as "the spark plug". One of two lookouts in Albany, this one offers the better seaward vista. From here, backtrack to York Street, turn left and head 2km down Middleton Road to **The Old Farm**, Strawberry Hill (daily 10am–5pm; closed June; $4), tucked behind modern houses in its own enchanting gardens. Reminiscent of an English cottage, the farm (WA's first) provided the colonists with fruit and veg, while the 1836 building here housed visiting Governor Stirling and today offers Devonshire teas and displays of domestic accoutrements.

Middleton Beach itself is dominated by Albany's pride and joy, the prestigious *Esplanade Hotel*, and the town's main beach as well as the more sheltered inlet of **Oyster Harbour**. From the beach, head up Marine Drive and turn right towards **Mount Clarence Lookout**, with its Anzac memorial and, on a clear day, a view as far as the Stirling Ranges, 80km to the north. On the way down you pass **The Forts** (daily 9am–5pm; $4), an impressively restored naval installation dating from the end of the nineteenth century.

Southeast of town, Frenchman Bay Road curls round Princess Royal Harbour to **Whaleworld** (daily 9am–5pm, hourly tours 10am–4pm; $7), the site of Australia's last whaling station until operations finally ceased in 1978. The informative tours begin with a gory video and move on to the crude and sickening whale-dismembering machinery and towering *Cheyne IV* whale chaser, before an upbeat, eco-ending in the skeleton shed.

Returning along the Torndirrup Peninsula, check out the view at **Stony Hill** but give the feeble **blowholes** a miss – they're a washout unless the wind and swell are aligned properly. The **Gap** and **Natural Bridge** are well worth a look, however; there is something mesmeric about watching the Southern Ocean pound into the Gap's boxed walls and rebound, frothing, in all directions, while the Natural Bridge satisfies those who get excited about "freaks of nature". This area has claimed several lives, many by **king waves** that well up imperceptibly onto the shore here; play it safe, and don't walk under the bridge.

Eating

Fortunately, Albany shares the rest of The Southwest's laudable preoccupation with quality eating; several independent restaurants fill the gap between fast-food franchises and dreary motel dining rooms in a most appetizing way.

Al Fornetto, York St (☎08/9842 1060). Italian-style steak and seafood, as well as pizzas from $12. Daily 6pm–late.

Café Bizzare, 42 Sterling Terrace. Trendy interior overlooking the bay, with meals for around $15. Wed–Sun 11.30am–late.

Cello's, Church Lane Rd, Kalgan River. Top-quality country restaurant in landscaped grounds 17km east of Albany. Thurs–Sun 11am–5pm.

Cravings, Mermaid Ave, Emu Point (☎08/9844 1111). Popular buffet place right by Emu Beach, with good-value seafood and chips next door. Daily 5.30pm–late.

Dylan's on the Terrace, 82 Stirling Terrace. Burger and pancake dispensary; good for early breakfast. Mon–Sat 7am–midnight, Sun 7am–10pm.

Food Station, Lower York St. Cafeteria with daily specials around $9. Best of the fast and fluorescent joints. Daily 8am–9pm.

Kookas, 204 Stirling Terrace (☎08/9841 5889). Quaintly restored old house serving gourmet dinners at around $25 per person. Tues–Sat 11.30am–late.

Sonatas, 17 Serpentine Rd. Upmarket steak and seafood outlet in the town centre. Tues–Sat 5pm–late.

Listings

Banks Most branches are along York St.
Bus Westrail ☎13 1053.

CALM (Department of Conservation and Land Management), 120 Albany Highway (Mon–Fri 9am–5pm; ☎08/9841 7133). Information and passes to local national parks (see box on p.619).

Car rental Albany Car Rental charges from $36 per day with 150km free (☎08/9841 7077).

Post office Corner of Grey and York sts (☎08/9841 1811).

Taxi ☎08/9844 4444.

Tours and cruises Albany Sailing Academy (☎08/9844 4146) offers half a day's tuition, or you can just lie on deck for $40; longer options are available. Escape Tours (☎08/9841 2865) has day- and half-day tours around the region in a minibus; Bushed (☎08/9842 2127) does adventure activity tours; Silver Star Cruises (☎08/9841 3333) offers cruises in King George Sound for around $22.

Along the Rainbow Coast

West of Albany, **West Cape Howe National Park** is a coastal wilderness best suited to exploration by 4WD, while **William Bay National Park**, west of Denmark, has many inviting coves accessible to regular vehicles. Just before Walpole, the **Valley of the Giants** is the home of the now-famous **Tree Top Walk** and marks the edge of the giant tree country. Westrail buses run on Monday and Friday between Albany and Perth (via Bunbury; 6hr), but you won't see much along this way – renting a car or arranging a lift is a better bet.

Denmark and William Bay National Park

DENMARK, set on the eponymous river that leads into Wilson Inlet, has been transformed into a cute little town, a great spot to enjoy a pleasant lunch, wander around some galleries, and take a stroll or boat up the river. If you want to get to the coast, give the anaemic Wilson Inlet a miss and head west to **William Bay National Park**, through the hills along **Shadforth Scenic Drive**. Once there, you'll find **Green Pool** to be one of the prettiest spots along the coast, with Madfish Bay and Waterfall Bay also worth a visit.

Denmark's **tourist office** (daily 9am–5pm; ☎08/9848 2055), on the corner of Strickland and Bent streets, can advise you on the array of places to **stay** in the vicinity. The pristine *Edinburgh Guest House & Backpackers* (☎08/9848 1477; ②–④) is in the centre of town, while in the hills around try the self-contained, weatherboard *Karma Chalets* (☎08/9848 1568, fax 9848 2124 or ☎008/016 713; ⑤–⑦), 5km west of Denmark. On Wilson Inlet there's *The Cove* (☎08/9848 1770; ⑥), 4km south of town. For a **meal**, the natty *Fig Tree Bistro*, off Strickland Street, and the friendly *Blue Wren* on the main road, are good alternatives to fast food.

The Valley of the Giants' Tree Top Walk and Walpole

About 40km west of Denmark you can turn south to **Peaceful Bay**, a pleasant lunch stop with a **caravan park**, or turn north along Valley of the Giants Road, from where another turn-off leads to a secluded **youth hostel** (☎08/9840 8073; ①), off Dingo Flats Road. The forest of massive tingle and karri trees that make up the **Valley of the Giants** is now much better known for its **Tree Top Walk** (daily 8am–5pm; $7), an amazingly engineered six-hundred-metre walkway (accessible to wheelchairs), which sways on half a dozen pylons among the crowns of the karris, 40m above the ground. Ironically, the most exciting aspect of the walk is not the scrutiny of the tree canopy – which isn't especially dense, close or teeming with anything more exotic than crows – but rather the fairground thrill of actually treading on the tremulous walkway. To gain a better impression of the surrounding forest, take the **Ancient Kingdom Walkway** (free) which winds through the forest floor.

Back on the coastal highway, you pass through **Nornalup**, remarkable for having no arts-and-crafts outlets. You'd do better to take the track 6km west of town leading to the lovely **Conspicuous Beach**. **WALPOLE**, 10km down the road, is the hub of many scenic drives to more towering forests, oceanic lookouts and sheltered inlets. Light **meals** are served at the *South Coast Café*, or try the restaurant next to the Glassblower's Gallery. There are a couple of **caravan parks** on Walpole and Nornalup inlets, but for more creature comforts try *Hideaway Cottage* (☎08/9840 1138; ⑤), 10km north of town, or *Che Sara Sara Chalets,* 15km north (☎ & fax 08/9840 8004; ⑤). Backpackers head for the *Tingle All Over Budget Accommodation* (☎08/9840 1041; ①) at the west end of town. Just east beyond Walpole you'll pass the turn-off to **Nuyts Wilderness**, where several walking trails pass through groves of jarrah and karri on to secluded coastal coves where camping is permitted.

From Walpole, the **South Western Highway** begins its scenic run northwest through more colossal forests to Northcliffe (100km) and Pemberton (138km) at the heart of the Tall Timber Country (see p.618).

The Porongurups, the Stirling Ranges and Mount Barker

North of Albany lie the ancient granite highlands of the Porongurups and the majestic thousand-metre-high Stirling Ranges, 40km and 80km from Albany respectively. Both have been designated as **national parks** (CALM fees; see box on p.619) and CALM in Albany provides further information and maps. To the west are the youthful vineyards of **Mount Barker**, whose viticultural potential has barely been exploited and which may one day merge with Margaret River as a homogeneous wine-making region. Several small **wineries** open their cellar doors for tasting and prospective purchases; details are available from the tourist office in Albany.

The Porongurups

The **Porongurups**, said to be the oldest hills in the world, feature a dozen wooded peaks with bald summits and an elevation of over 600m. The fifteen-kilometre-long ridge catches any coastal moisture to support its isle of karri forests, thereby leaving the loftier Stirlings to the north dry and treeless.

Most people are happy to do no more than take the five-minute stroll to the **Tree in a Rock**, a natural oddity near the park's northern entrance, but if you want to get your teeth into a good walk, head up the marked trail to **Devil's Slide** (671m) and, if you're up to it, return via Nancy and Hayward peaks; the full route needs at least half a day, stout footwear, water and a hat. **Balancing Rock**, at the eastern end of the park, can be reached in 45 minutes from the car park, with a cage on the exposed outcrop of Castle Rock providing safe viewing. There's no camping in the park, but half a dozen establishments offer **accommodation** close to the northern entrance, among them hostel accommodation at the *Porongurup Shop & Tearooms* (☎08/9853 1110; ①) and the nearby *Karribank Lodge* (☎08/9853 1022; ④), an inexpensive guesthouse.

The Stirling Ranges

Taking the Chester Pass Road north towards the looming **Stirlings**, the distinctive profile of Bluff Knoll will, if you're lucky, reveal itself from the cloud banks which often obscure its summit. Avid hillwalkers could spend a few days "peak-bagging" here and come away well satisfied – the mild weather makes the Stirlings WA's best mountain-walking area, although five peaks are over 1000m and sometimes receive winter snow. Less strenuous activities are also catered for: the unsealed 45-kilometre Stirling Range **scenic drive** winds amid the peaks to Red Gum Pass in the west, where you can turn around and go back the same way (with superior views) or continue down to Mount Barker. **Bluff Knoll** (1073m), the park's highest and most popular ascent, has a well-built path involving a three-hour-return slog. The weather can often surprise you from the unseen, southeast side: no matter how hot you may feel in the car park before beginning the climb, take a sweater with you. There are better views looking onto the park's eastern summits from the west: **Talyuberup**, halfway along the scenic drive and around 800m high, is a short, steep ascent to magnificent views, while **Toolbrunup** (1052m) is among the harder climbs in the park, with some exposed scrambling – allow a tough half-day to get there and back. Many other **trails** wander between the peaks and could link up into overnight walks. Before heading off, discuss your plans with the **ranger** (☎08/9827 9230 or 9827 9278) at his residence by the park campsite off Chester Pass Road.

There are basic facilities at the **campsite**, or much better options at the *Stirling Range Chalet and Caravan Park* (☎08/9827 9229; on-site vans ③, four-bed chalets ①–④), just outside the park's northern boundary, opposite the Bluff Knoll turn-off.

Mount Barker

MOUNT BARKER is at the centre of a small wine-growing region and makes a pleasant day out from Albany, driving around the lanes sampling the fruits of the vine. There are six wineries around the town and a couple more near Porongurup. **Plantagenet Wines** (Mon–Fri 9am–5pm, Sat & Sun 10am–4pm), on Albany Highway, is the region's most established, and undertakes bottling for the lesser wineries in the vicinity. The atmosphere is civilized and amiable, with tastings as well as informal behind-the-scenes **tours**. Wine-tasting apart, Mount Barker, on the old mail-coach route between Albany and Perth, is just another country town, although **St Werburgh's Chapel**, built in 1873 on a hillside a few kilometres west of town (get directions from the **tourist office**, 57 Lowood Rd; ☎08/9851 1163) is worth a look – an unexpected relic of Mount Barker's God-fearing pioneers.

The Wheatlands

WA's **Wheatlands**, the wheat belt, is a region of intensive grain agriculture and sheep pastures extending from the southwest coast into the arable areas north of the Great Eastern Highway. The main reasons visitors come here is to see a number of unusual granite rock formations, of which **Wave Rock** near Hyden, 340km from Perth, is the best known. The names of the desolate farming communities often end with the letters "-in", as prolific as the ending "-up" in the Southwest: both are thought to be an Aboriginal suffix meaning "place of water".

Narrogin and Katanning

Many visitors pass through the eastern Wheatbelt on their way down the **Albany Highway** or its parallel alternative, the **Great Southern Highway**, to Albany. The former is a direct route to the Rainbow Coast, with few notable distractions, while the latter emanates from the top of the Avon Valley and winds its way casually south to the confluence of the two highways, 90km north of Albany.

There's not much to stop for along the way. In **NARROGIN**, 192km from Perth, you can visit the **Axe Handle Factory** (☎08/9883 6075 to arrange a visit), which displays a selection of axe handles handmade from local wood – the only place of its kind in WA. Eleven kilometres east of town on the Harrismith Road are **Yilliminning** and **Birdwhistle Rocks**, picnic spots on the way to **Albert Facey's Homestead** (daily 9am–5pm), 39km from Narrogin. The late Albert Facey's autobiography (and subsequent TV mini-series) *A Fortunate Life* is a self-effacing account of his life's few ups and repeated downs, endured with the stoic fatalism of a true Aussie "battler". The homestead conveys those hard times with authentic paraphernalia, as well as a range of locally made crafts. **Overnight stays** in Narrogin are catered for at the *Narrogin Motel*, 56

Williams Rd (☎08/9881 1660; ④), west of the town centre, or at the B&B *Stoke Farm* (☎08/9885 9018, fax 9885 9040; ④) at Highbury, 10km south of Narrogin.

You can hardly fail to notice the seven-metre-high giant Merino ram as you drive through **Wagin**, 38km south of Narrogin, which is reason enough to keep going. A further 56km south of Wagin, **KATANNING** is a late nineteenth-century farming centre on the mail route from Albany to Perth. These days the **Old Mill**, on the corner of Clive Street and Austral Terrace, houses the **tourist office** (☎08/9821 2634), although the town is better known for the mosque serving its Muslim community from Christmas Island – an Australian protectorate south of Java. The *Katanning Motel* (☎08/9821 1657; ⑤) on Albion Street offers **accommodation**.

Hyden, Wave Rock and around

Perhaps WA's best-known natural oddity is **Wave Rock**, 3km from the tiny farming settlement of **HYDEN**, at the eastern edge of the Wheatlands. At 15m high and 110m long, the formation resembles a breaking wave, an impression enhanced by the vertical water stains running down the overhanging face. While the rock, formed by wind and rain, is certainly unusual, its spell wears off within minutes and it's not worth the commonly undertaken day-trip from Perth unless you enjoy sitting in a bus all day. Even as a diversion south of the Great Eastern Highway (Merredin is 185km away and Southern Cross 178km), its appeal is still dubious. At the base of the rock a marked, twenty-minute trail leads to another outcrop, **Hippo's Yawn**, while 21km from Wave Rock, on the way to Southern Cross, **Bates Cave** features Aboriginal hand paintings.

Hyden has a **tourist information** service (☎08/9880 5182), and you can **spend the night** at the *Wave Rock Caravan Park* (☎08/9880 5022) thereto ③, 3km east of town. In Hyden itself, try the *Hyden Hotel* on Lynch Street (☎08/9880 5052; ⑤).

Esperance and the South Coast

Esperance, 721km southeast of Perth, is at the western end of the **Archipelago of the Recherche**. Both town and archipelago are attractively named after French ships which visited the area in the late eighteenth century and whose persistent nosing around precipitated the hasty colonization of WA by the British. The archipelago is a string of haze-softened granite isles bobbing in the inky blue Southern Ocean, presenting an almost surreal seascape common to coasts washed by cold currents. The mild summer weather (rarely exceeding 30°C), fishing possibilities (especially the local snapper) and surrounding national parks make the town a popular destination for heat-sensitive holiday-makers.

Southeast of Esperance are **Cape Le Grand** and the much less visited **Cape Arid National Park** (both charge CALM fees; see box on p.619) on the edge of the Great Australian Bight, while 130km north of town is the undeveloped Peak Charles National Park – a hill in the middle of nowhere. Back towards Albany, the **Fitzgerald River National Park** offers a wilderness of rare flora. Care should be taken all along this restless coastline, as **king waves** (unexpectedly huge waves indistinguishable in the swell) frequently sweep away fishermen and climbers from exposed, rocky shores.

You can get to Esperance from Kalgoorlie with Westrail's **bus service** (1 daily Mon–Wed, 2 daily Fri; 5hr) or direct from Perth on the *Spirit of Esperance* service (1 daily Mon–Thurs, 2 on Fri; 10hr). Albany, nearly 500km to the east along the South Coast Highway, can only be reached from Esperance direct on Mondays and Thursdays (connecting buses on Tues & Fri). To get from Albany to Esperance, it's best to arrange a **lift** with fellow travellers. Skywest Airlines (free call ☎1800/642 225) **flies** from Perth to Esperance twice daily on weekdays and daily at weekends (1hr 50min).

Esperance and around

The town of **ESPERANCE**, which prospered briefly as a supply port during the hey-day of the Eastern Goldfields, was revived after World War II when its poor soils were made fertile with the addition of missing trace elements. Now an established farming and holiday centre, the town lacks the charm promised by its name, but makes an ideal base from which to enjoy a westward exploration of WA's often spectacular and storm-washed southern coast.

Dempster Street is the town's main road and site of the arts-and-crafts vending cab-ins which comprise the **Museum Village**. Nearby, the actual **museum** (daily 1.30–4.30pm; $3), on James Street, is a surprisingly good repository of local memora-bilia – diverse enough momentarily to engage most visitors. It's very proud of its Skylab display: the satellite disintegrated over Esperance in 1979 and NASA was reputedly fined $400 for littering.

Besides a walk along the Norfolk pine-lined Esplanade and a round of mini-golf or go-karting, there's not much else to do in Esperance, so rent a bike or a car and head out along the 36-kilometre **scenic loop** west of town. Travelling clockwise, you'll come first to the **Rotary Lookout** (following a mean climb for cyclists), which overlooks the captivating seascape. You'll spot the **windfarm**, a modest experiment in alternative energy generation, on the way to **Twilight Beach**, an idyllic and sheltered spot, much prettier than the town's more exposed beaches. From here it's more windswept grandeur to **Observation Point Lookout** and a free (nudist) beach, before the road turns inland towards **Pink Lake**, sometimes coloured a lurid shade by salt-tolerant algae, whose marine cousins give the coastline its enchanting turquoise hue.

The approximately one hundred islands of the romantically named Archipelago of the Recherche, known as the **Bay of Isles** around Esperance, are chiefly occupied by colonies of seals, feral goats and multitudes of seabirds. Dolphins may also be seen off-shore and southern right whales are commonly observed migrating to the Antarctic in spring. Mackenzies Island Cruises, 71 The Esplanade (☎08/9071 5757), offers daily trips with the possibility of overnight stays on **Woody Island** (summer only), which is equipped with enough facilities to cast yourself away in comfort.

Practicalities

Westrail buses stop in the town centre, with **taxis** available on ☎08/9071 1782. The **tourist bureau** (Mon–Fri 8.45am–5pm, Sat & Sun 9am–5pm; ☎08/9071 2330), in the Museum Village on Dempster Street, provides detailed town maps and takes care of bookings for local tours and onward travel. The **post office** is on the corner of Dempster and Andrew streets, with a **shopping centre** up Andrew Street, over the roundabout. CALM (☎08/9071 3733), at 92 Dempster St, provides information and passes to the national parks around Esperance. **Bicycles** are rented out along The Esplanade from Wilds Jet Ski Hire (Dec–March daily 8.30am–5pm; $12–15 per day; jet ski $1 per min), with a tattier but cheaper selection of cycles at the *Captain Huon Motel*. For inexpensive **car rental**, ask at the YHA or backpackers' accommodation. The Diving Academy, 56 The Esplanade (☎08/9071 5111), takes care of **dive** charters and courses, while Vacation Country Tours (☎08/9071 2227) offers half-day **tours** to Cape Le Grand, and Safari Wheels (☎08/9071 1564) deals with the more active pursuits along the coast. Both hostels (see "Accommodation" overleaf) have 4WDs for making infor-mal runs along the coast if there's enough in-house interest.

ACCOMMODATION

There are plenty of **places to stay** around town, although the self-contained units will almost certainly be booked out during school holiday periods; air-con is rarely neces-sary in Esperance.

All Seasons Holiday Units, 53 The Esplanade (☎08/9071 2257). The cheapest units in town and fully equipped; book ahead. Each unit sleeps up to four. ⑤.

Bayview Motel, 31 Dempster St (☎08/9071 1533, fax 9071 4544). Motel with some self-contained units. ⑤.

Captain Huon Motel, 5 The Esplanade (☎08/9071 2383, fax 9071 2358). Excellent small motel with some self-contained units; bike rental. ⑥.

Esperance Backpackers, 14 Emily St (☎08/9071 4724). The town's livelier hostel, with twenty beds and all mod-cons. Tours and pick-ups are also offered. ①.

Esperance Bay Caravan Park, corner of The Esplanade and Harbour Rd (☎08/9071 2237). So close to town you feel like you're camping in someone's garden. Chalets ④, on-site vans and cabins ③.

Esperance Shire Caravan Park, Goldfields Rd (☎08/9071 1251). The best choice for camping close to the town and beach. On-site vans ③.

Jetty Motel, 1 The Esplanade (☎08/9071 5978, fax 9071 5540). Well-appointed, two-storey motel with ocean views. ⑤.

Old Hospital Motel, William St (☎08/9071 3587, fax 9071 5768). "Boutique" establishment offering an antidote to motel sterility with considered and tasteful decor. ⑥.

Orleans Bay Caravan Park, Cape Le Grand National Park (☎08/9075 0033). Located at Duke of Orleans Bay, reached along a turn-off about 88km from Esperance, this site is ideal for those in search of seclusion. Cabins ③–④, on-site vans ②.

YHA, Goldfields Rd (☎ & fax 08/9071 1040). Barracks-like hostel facing the bay. Tours, free pick-ups and bikes. Rooms ③, dorms ①.

RESTAURANTS

Besides the counter lunches at the *Pier* and *Esperance* hotels, there are a couple of interesting **restaurants** to match the mouthwatering seascapes.

The Gray Starling Restaurant, 126 Dempster St (☎08/9071 3187). Attractive and relaxing and serving a tasty menu – one of the best eating places in town. Daily, but Wed from 6pm, Sun 11.30am–3pm.

Ollies on the Esplanade, 32 The Esplanade. Coffee house with an all-day menu. Attractive sea views. Daily 7am–8pm.

Peaches Restaurant, *Bay of Isles Motel*, 32 The Esplanade (☎08/9071 3999). Top-quality à la carte cuisine for around $20 a meal and with a view to match. Daily 6–9pm.

Spice of Life, Andrew St. The quest for original names for vegetarian cafés continues. Daily 9am–6pm.

Village Café, Museum Village. A convenient little lunch spot for seafood and chips. Daily 9am–5pm.

Cape Le Grand and Cape Arid national parks

A visit to **Cape Le Grand National Park** (CALM fee; see box on p.619) is well worth the expense of renting a car or taking a tour; it's essentially a climb up a hill and a beach-hop – but they're the sort of beaches you want to roll up and take home with you. Once in the park, the climb to the summit of **Frenchman's Peak** (262m) is not as hard as it looks, and well worth the half-hour's exertion in a sturdy pair of shoes. The secret of the distinctive, hooked summit is an unexpected hole which perfectly frames the impressive view out to sea. Just after the Frenchman's Peak turn-off, a track leads to **Hellfire Bay**; sheltered coves don't come any more perfect than this. From here you can take a tough, three-hour walk to **Le Grand Beach** (limited camping; water available) to the northwest or a less demanding two-hour trek to **Thistle Cove**, from where an easier trail leads to the broad arc of **Lucky Bay** (camping and water), with more sheltered swimming and unbelievable colours. **Rossiter Bay**, 6km east, is distinctly unimpressive by comparison and not worth the trip.

If you're still having trouble getting away from it all, keep heading east to **Cape Arid National Park** (CALM fee; see box on p.619). This is best explored in a 4WD, but ordinary cars can make it as far as **Yokinup Bay**, **Thomas River** and **Sandy Bight**, where there's camping; all visitors must bring their own **fresh water**. East of the park is

Israelite Bay, well worth a visit if you've come this far, with another impossibly blue sea, the remains of an old telegraph station and a track up to Balladonia on the Eyre Highway, which blasts its way through to South Australia (see p.635 for details of this route).

Esperance to Albany

From Esperance, the **South Coastal Highway** leads 479km to Albany with just a couple of small farming settlements along the way; it's a fairly dull day's drive with only the military museum and rabbit-proof fence at Jerramungup to perk you up. If you're not in a hurry, turn south along a network of dirt roads, just after **Stokes Inlet National Park** (CALM fee; see box on p.619), popular with beach fishermen and waterfowl alike, to Hopetoun on the coast. West of here is the mountainous eastern edge of the Fitzgerald River National Park which can be traversed to **Bremer Bay**, a peaceful resort a couple of hours' drive from Albany. The *RAC Bremer Bay–Hopetoun* map covers the area in excellent detail.

RAVENSTHORPE, 186km along the highway west of Esperance, is a farming community that was formerly a mining town. **Accommodation** options here include the good-value *Ravensthorpe Motel* (☎08/9838 1053; ⑤), or the caravan park at the east end of town. Grab a **snack** at the *Ravensthorpe Country Kitchen* (daily 9am–8pm) on the main road at the east end of town. There's a good route from here to **HOPETOUN**, with a scenic diversion up Ethel Daw Drive. A picturesque holiday and fishing spot, Hopetoun is most usefully a place to get into the adjacent national park. If you need to stay **overnight**, the best deals are at the *CWA Cottages* (☎08/9838 3128; ③) on Canning Street or the cushy **caravan park** on Spence Street (on-site vans ③). Otherwise, pamper yourself at the *Hopetoun Motel* (☎08/9838 3219; ⑤) on Veal Street, and tuck in at the rather pleasant *Starboard Café* (7am–2pm & 4–8pm) right in the middle of town.

Just outside Hopetoun, a road leads west, across the causeway separating the ocean from Culham Inlet – where the explorer John Eyre observed Aborigines fishing in 1841 – and up towards **East Mount Barren**. This marks the eastern edge of the **Fitzgerald River National Park**, one of two parks in WA designated by UNESCO as a world heritage biosphere. Nearly two thousand species of wild flower are protected in the park, including the curious, flame-like hakae and scores of orchids, seventy of which are found nowhere else in the world. Access is limited due to the presence of the tropical fungus known as dieback, the root-rotting spores of which are easily spread by wheels and boots. Four-wheel-drives can reach the sea at **Quoin Head** and camping for all is provided at **Mylies Beach**, at the foot of East Mount Barren. In the western half of the park, **Point Ann**, 64km south of the **ranger's residence** (☎08/9835 5043) along Quiss Road, is the spot to head for; the magnificent view across the sea alone is worth the corrugations. Think twice before descending the sandy track to the campsite here if you're in a 2WD.

The Eastern Goldfields

Five hundred kilometres east of Perth, at the end of the **Great Eastern Highway**, lie the **Eastern Goldfields**. Just over a century ago, gold was found in what still remains one of the world's richest gold-producing regions. Lack of fresh water made life very hard for the early prospectors, driven by a national economic depression into miserable living conditions, disease and, in most cases, premature graves. Nevertheless, boom towns of thousands, boasting grand public buildings, several hotels and a periphery of hovels, would erupt and collapse in the length of time it took to extract any payable ore.

In 1892 the railway from Perth reached **Southern Cross**, just as big finds turned the rush into a national stampede. This huge influx of people accentuated the water shortage, until the visionary engineer C.Y. O'Connor oversaw the construction of a 556-kilo-metre **pipeline** from Mundaring Weir (see p.611) to Kalgoorlie in 1903. By this time many of the smaller gold towns were already in decline, but the Goldfields' wealth and boost in population finally gave WA the economic autonomy it sought in its claim to statehood.

In the years preceding the goldrush, the area was briefly one of the world's richest sources of **sandalwood**, an aromatic wood greatly prized throughout Asia. Supplies in the Pacific had become exhausted so that, by 1880, the perfumed wood was WA's second-largest exportable commodity after wool. Exacerbating the inevitable over-cutting came the goldrush's demand for timber to prop up shafts or to fire the pre-pipeline water desalinators. Today the region is a pit-scarred and prematurely desertified landscape, dotted with the scavenged vestiges of past settlements.

The Goldfields are centred around the rich reef of gold adjacent to the twinned towns of **Kalgoorlie–Boulder**, with Kalgoorlie being the thriving, energetic core. This prosperous town's unexpected vitality is accentuated by stagnating or decaying settlements all around it: adjacent Boulder and **Coolgardie** to the west, and the semi-abandoned communities and **ghost towns** in the desert to the north.

Even if you're not planning to pass through the Goldfields, a couple of days based in Kalgoorlie are worth the excursion from Perth – if for nothing else than the novelty of riding on the **Prospector**, the daily rail link between Perth and Kalgoorlie, which stops off at all the towns along the highway. Greyhound Pioneer, Goldfields Express and Westrail **buses** depart with similar regularity (and journey times) and a visit to the Goldfields can be undertaken as part of a two-thousand-kilometre loop along WA's southern coast, making use of Perth's inexpensive car rental agencies. The *Streetsmart Goldfields Touring Map* is highly recommended, especially if you're thinking of exploring the area north of Kalgoorlie.

The Great Eastern Highway

Heading from Perth to the Goldfields, there's precious little to detain you until you reach Coolgardie. **MECKERING**, 132km east of Perth, was destroyed by an earthquake in 1968 and a gazebo off the main road commemorates the event. **CUNDERDIN**, 24km further east, has a pioneering **museum** (daily 10am–4pm; $2; housed in one of the eight steam pumping stations that once propelled the water to Kalgoorlie at a little over 1.5km per hour. **KELLERBERRIN**, not far beyond Cunderdin, was one of the earliest settlements along the Great Eastern Highway, and dates from 1861. It also has a **museum** (Mon–Fri 8.30am–5pm; $2), located in a historic building, and inexpensive **rooms** at the *Ampol Roadhouse Motel* (☎08/9045 4007; ④) on the highway. **MERREDIN** is a bigger wheat and wool town than most, with a **museum** (daily 9am–3pm; $2) housed in an old train station, built from bricks of Kalgoorlie clay that are said to contain gold of mineable grade.

East of Merredin the country becomes drier and, by the time you get to **SOUTHERN CROSS**, 370km from Perth, you have passed through the Wheatbelt. It was here in 1887 that small traces of gold precipitated the country's largest and most fruitful goldrush, and with the arrival of the railway in 1892, the town became a jumping-off point for the greater finds to the east. Nowadays Southern Cross has that moribund feel so familiar to rural settlements with prosperous pasts; the disproportionately wide streets, common to all the goldrush towns, allowed camel trains to turn round. Local goldrush history is recounted in the **Yilgarn History Museum** (Mon–Sat 9am–noon & 1.30–4pm, Sun 1.30–4pm; $1) on Antares Street, while **accommodation** is available at the *Southern Cross Palace Hotel* (☎08/9049 1555, fax 9049 1509; ⑤), near the museum, or the *Southern Cross Caravan Park* (☎08/9049 1212; on-site vans ③), on the eastern edge of town.

Coolgardie

Rather too tidy and intact to carry the name "ghost mining town", **COOLGARDIE** is more of a museum to itself, a town which, at its peak, had twenty-three hotels, three breweries and six newspapers serving a population ten times greater than its present fifteen hundred. Arthur Bayley increased the pitch of the gold fever when he returned to Southern Cross – then the easternmost extent of the rush – in 1892 with nearly sixteen kilograms of gold. The ensuing wave of prospectors started within hours – ten thousand men rushed out of Southern Cross, culminating in a fourfold increase in WA's population by the end of the century. Recently the abandoned Bayley's Reward mine at the east end of town was just about to open for tourists, when a last-minute check for mineable ore resulted in a change of plans and a resumption of full production.

The Town and around

The imposing **Wardens Court Building** on Bayley Street is a good point from which to start an appraisal of Coolgardie's numerous gold-boom relics. The building houses the **tourist office** (daily 9am–5pm; ☎08/9026 6090) and has one of the most extensive provincial **museums** in WA (daily 9am–5pm; $2.50), filling the grand upper floors with an especially comprehensive collection of bottles. It rewards a prolonged browse, giving you a feel for the dramatic effect the goldrush had on the area.

Outside the museum is an index to the 155 **historic markers** set around the town, and right opposite you can't miss the varied miscellany and just plain old junk comprising **Ben Prior's Open-Air Museum** (always open; free). Half a kilometre up Hunt Street, at the end of McKenzie Street, **Warden Finnerty's Residence** (Mon–Thurs 1–4pm, Sat & Sun 10am–noon & 1–4pm; $2) is the finely restored 1895 residence of the man whose unenviable job it was to set the ground rules for mining at the height of the rush.

On the way back to Bayley Street, a left down Woodward Street leads to the **Railway Station Museum** (daily 9am–5pm, closed Fri afternoon; donation welcome), housed in a station used until 1971, when the railway was rerouted north of town. Featured is the drama of the 1907 Varischetti mine rescue and the story of the once-thriving sandalwood industry.

Other attractions around Coolgardie include the **cemetery**, west of town (the last resting place of explorer Ernest Giles), and the **Coolgardie Camel Farm** (daily 9am–5pm; 1hr-, day- and overnight treks from $20 for a minimum of two people, booking essential; ☎08/9026 6159), a couple of kilometres further west, which describes the crucial role camels played in the years before the arrival of the railway.

Practicalities

Coolgardie is best reached from Perth by the daily Greyhound Pioneer, Goldfields Express or Westliner **bus services**, as the train now stops at Bonnie Vale, 14km north of town, and is actually no quicker. Alternatively, during school term time, you can visit the town from Kalgoorlie with Goldenlines (Mon–Fri departs Kalgoorlie at 7.10am, returns at 4.15pm; $2.75 one-way; ☎08/9021 2655). Kalgoorlie-based Goldrush Tours (☎08/9021 5826; Tues, Thurs & Fri mornings; $40) also offers half-day tours to Coolgardie. There are no banks, although there is a cash machine in the BP service station on Hunt Street; the **post office** is around the corner. The cheapest **accommodation** in town is the *Goldrush Lodge* (☎ & fax 08/9026 6446; ④), a B&B at 75 Bayley St. For up-to-date comfort try the *Coolgardie Motor Inn* (☎08/9026 6002; ⑤) at the east end of Bayley Street. There are two **caravan parks** with on-site vans (②–③) just west of town.

When it comes to gourmet restaurants, Coolgardie earns its ghost-town appellation with ease. For light **meals**, try the *Premier Café* (Mon–Sat 7.30am–8pm, Sun 8.30am–7pm), opposite the tourist office. For something more substantial, the

Coolgardie Motor Inn's restaurant (daily 6–8pm) or the outdoor one at the *Coolgardie Motel* (daily 6–8.30pm; ☎08/9026 6080), opposite Ben Prior's Open-Air Museum on Bayley Street, are the only alternatives to foraging in the bush.

Kalgoorlie–Boulder

Whichever way you approach **KALGOORLIE**, the bustling town now twinned with its shabbier neighbour **Boulder**, it comes as a surprise after hundreds of kilometres of desolation. It possesses the idiosyncratic appeal of similar places such as Coober Pedy (in South Australia) or Las Vegas. All three blithely disregard their isolation and bleak surroundings, so devoted is their attention to the pursuit of earthly riches – which, in Kalgoorlie's case, is **gold**.

In 1893 **Paddy Hannan** (then 53 years old) and his mates, Tom Flannigan and Dan O'Shea, brought renewed meaning to the expression "the luck of the Irish" when a lame horse forced them to camp by the tree which still stands at the top of Egan Street. With their instincts highly attuned after eight months of prospecting around Coolgardie, they soon found gold all around them: as the first on the scene, they enjoyed the unusually easy pickings of surface gold. Ten years later, when the desperately needed water pipeline finally gushed into the Mount Charlotte Reservoir, Kalgoorlie was already established as the heart of WA's rapidly growing mineral-based prosperity, a position it still retains. As sole survivor of the original rush, revitalized by the 1960s nickel boom, Kalgoorlie has benefited from new technology that has largely dispensed with slow and dangerous underground mining. Instead, the fabulously rich **"Golden Mile"** reef east of town which Boulder was originally built to serve – is being devoured wholesale by machinery and explosives to create the vast, open-cast "Super Pit".

Proud of its history, isolation and continued prosperity, Kalgoorlie is one of the most parochial towns in a country that's full of them. An ongoing gentrification programme means that soon sophistication in "Kal" will no longer be regarded as a fully clothed barmaid, and, if nothing else, the Federation-era **architecture** and history deserve to be appreciated. Even in the sniggeringly louche red-light district of Hay Street, only three of the infamous "tin shack" brothels remain in business, and, interestingly enough, they forbid any male ownership or control. But Kal remains a Working Man's Town, a dinky-di testament to the ethos of hard work and hard play that flourished in Australia's Anglo-Celtic heyday. The town is still a good place to find employment if you have engineering-related skills, though expect to work nothing less than twelve hard and dusty hours a day.

Start your tour of the town by taking a walk up to the top of Hannan Street, where the bright red head frame immediately attracts your attention. This is the impressive entrance to the **Museum of the Goldfields** (daily 10am–4.30pm; free), right next to the spot where Paddy and his crew found their first, auspicious nuggets. Inside is a modern display of Goldfields artefacts and history, with the very stuff that keeps the town going viewable in the basement vault. Aboriginal history and the sandalwood industry are also covered in this excellent introduction to the area, and there's a lookout over the town from the top of the red head frame. Next door is the **British Arms** pub, now a coffee shop but better known as Australia's narrowest pub.

Hannan Street itself is one of Kalgoorlie's finest sights, with its superbly restored turn-of-the-century architecture, imposing public buildings and numerous flamboyant hotel facades. You're welcome to inspect the grandiose interior of the **town hall** (Mon–Fri 9am–4pm; free), with its splendid hall and less impressive art gallery. It's only when you stop to reflect that this is a remote, hundred-year-old town in the West Australian desert that the stunning wealth of the boom years, which still continues, is brought home to you. Outside, a replica of a bronze **statue** of Paddy himself invites you to drink from his chrome-nozzled waterbag – the much vandalized original is inside the town hall.

The **School of Mines Museum** (Mon–Fri 10am–4pm; free), on the corner of Egan and Cassidy streets, perhaps outstrips most visitors' enthusiasm, with its vast display of minerals and replicated nuggets; just over the road, on Maritana Street, is the stop for the Boulder-bound bus.

Boulder and further afield

BOULDER, 5km south of Kalgoorlie, is much quieter and smaller – a place to visit rather than stay in. One glance down **Burt Street** reveals that it's Kalgoorlie's poorer sister, although this is not an observation to make at the top of your voice in any of the local pubs. It was originally set up as a separate settlement to serve the Golden Mile; Boulder's heyday passed as Kalgoorlie's suburbs slowly expanded towards it.

Boulder has a similar collection of grand old buildings which, as in Kal, have received a face-lift, with the pubs, especially the *Cornwall*, *Grand* and deliciously ramshackle *Metropole*, a delight to look at if not to drink in. One thing worth coming to Boulder for is a ride on the **Golden Mile Loopline**. Departing daily (Mon–Sat 10am & 12.45pm, Sun 3pm; $12; ☎08/9093 3055) from the former train station at the top of Burt Street, the "Rattler", as it is known, once delivered workers to their pits and served all shifts round the clock. Now it will take you on a one-hour circuit of the Super Pit. Whether you take a ride or not, the **Super Pit Lookout** is worth a look, if for no other reason than to appreciate the full scale of the operation; the little yellow Haul-Pacs you see below carry two hundred tons at a time and their tyres are as high as the storey of a building.

Just north of town are a couple more attractions without which a visit to Kalgoorlie–Boulder would not be complete. **Hannan's North Tourist Mine** (daily 9.30am–4.30pm; $18, surface only $12; ☎08/9091 4074) is an old mine now transformed into a mining theme park. From the gloomy interior of a tent an amusing, video-faced mannequin of the venerable Mr Hannan cheerily regales you with the details of his for-tuitous "stroike", while the forty-minute guided underground tours, led by former min-ers, are probably as long as you'd want to spend down a mine – especially when you're given a brief demonstration of the pneumatic "air leg" drill. Allow about two and a half hours for your visit.

Back on the Menzies Road, follow the "Two Up" signs a short distance to Kalgoorlie's once-clandestine and, since 1983, the country's only legal **Two Up School**, 7km from town. Two Up is, more or less, a game of "heads or tails" played with two pen-nies. In the decidedly functional "galvo" arena, the deadly serious and utterly absorbed gamblers bet on how the pennies will land – each double tails (or "white cross") result punctuated by the exchange of fistfuls of notes. It sounds simple and you are welcome to join in ($10 minimum stake), but to most outsiders the proceedings are totally baf-fling. Gambling takes place daily (except on paydays – once every two weeks) and runs from 4pm until dusk, with no alcohol or anyone under eighteen allowed within 100m.

Practicalities

Westliner (free call ☎1800/199 649) and Greyhound Pioneer (☎08/9021 7100) **buses** now arrive at Forrest Street in Kalgoorlie, opposite the **train station** (Westrail; ☎08/9021 2923). **Taxis** (☎08/9021 2177) meet incoming trains, which are no quicker than buses, yet more expensive. Kalgoorlie's **tourist office** (Mon–Fri 8.30am–5pm, Sat & Sun 9am–5pm; ☎08/9021 1966) is at 250 Hannan St, on Kalgoorlie's main thorough-fare, and gives out informative sketch maps pinpointing Kal's dispersed attractions. The **post office** is just up the road at 204 Hannan St.

A local **bus service** operates between the two towns (Mon–Sat 8am–6pm; $1.40), with timetables available from Kalgoorlie's tourist office or the town hall. **Car rental** is expensive, though Halfpenny Rentals, 544 Hannan St south (☎08/9021 1804), is an exception. **Bikes** can be rented at Johnstons Cycles, 78 Boulder Rd (☎08/9021 1157). Goldrush Tours (☎08/9021 5828) is the main local operator whose daily "Kalgoorlie–Boulder" tour ($30) is recommended.

ACCOMMODATION

Although it's unlikely that Kalgoorlie will maintain your interest for more than a couple of days, the town does get busy with holiday-makers in the winter school holidays, when it's best to check room availability in advance. The many splendid-looking hotels along Hannan Street deteriorate alarmingly inside, but they all offer inexpensive rooms with either shared or en-suite facilities.

Cornwall Hotel, 25 Hopkins St, Boulder (☎08/9093 2510). A fabulous-looking old hotel with a dark history and an outdoor restaurant. Shared bathrooms. ④.

Gold Dust Backpackers, 192 Hay St (☎08/9091 3737). Suddenly backpackers are spoilt for choice. Similar to *Goldfields Backpackers* with ten-bed air-con dorms plus local tours. Rooms ③, dorms ①.

Golden Village Caravan Park, 406 Hay St (☎08/9021 4162). The caravan park closest to town. On-site vans ③.

Goldfields Backpackers, 166 Hay St (☎08/9091 1482). A clean, modern, purpose-built hostel that is better than anything Perth has to offer. Air-con rooms, pool, bike rental, help with employment in the area, and free pick-ups. Rooms ③, dorms ①.

Hannan's View Motel, 430 Hannan St (☎08/9091 3333). Motel units with pool, cheap breakfasts and some wheelchair-accessible, self-contained units. ⑥.

Hay Street Homestay, 164 Hay St (☎08/9091 1482). Once the town's classiest bordello, now a B&B that retains the gilt-taps-and-black-onyx decor but no ceiling mirrors. ④.

Midas Motel, 409 Hannan St (☎08/9021 3088, fax 9021 3125 or free call ☎1800/813 088). Top-of-the-range motel with nightclub, pool and the excellent *Amalfi* restaurant. ⑦.

Prospector Holiday Park, Great Eastern Highway, 3km west of town (☎08/9021 2524). Excellent park with pool, playground, kitchen and grassy sites. Cabins ④, on-site vans ③.

Sandalwood Motor Inn, Lower Hannan St (☎08/9021 4455, fax 9021 3744 or ☎008/095 530). Reasonably priced and comfortable motel with air-con, TVs and en-suite bathrooms. ⑥.

Surrey House, 9 Boulder Rd (☎08/9021 1340). Guesthouse offering cheap breakfasts and a TV room. ②–③.

York Hotel, 259 Hannan St (☎08/9021 2337). Probably the best-looking facade on Hannan Street. Shared bathrooms, but rates include breakfast. ⑤.

EATING AND DRINKING

An unpretentious Outback town hundreds of kilometres from the nearest fresh tomato isn't the place to look for gourmet delicacies. Instead, treat yourself to a good old **counter meal** for under $10 at any of the pubs, or try *Basil's*, 268 Hannan St, for Italian home-style cooking and something to read, or the *Kalgoorlie Café* (10.30am–3pm & 6pm–1am) on the other side of the road, which has more of a family atmosphere. There's a **food hall** near Coles/K-Mart, and *Health Works*, 75 Hannan St, caters for veggies. Next door is the *Top End Thai* (6pm–late; ☎08/9091 4027), a rare, exotic treat at around $15, and the *Main Reef Bistro*, 32 Dwyer St, for Italian, seafood and buffets.

Twenty years ago Kal's **nightlife** was a riot; scantily clad barmaids ("skimpies") laid on the beer while drink-addled miners threw themselves at the nearest punch-up. Nowadays the appalling scent of yuppification wafts through Kal's once-functional drinking pens, but you'll still need at least a couple of weeks to have a nightly pint at every licensed establishment in Kalgoorlie–Boulder – if you're going to do the complete rounds, ask about the "**Kal pub crawl**" (T-shirts available at the tourist office). These days the roughest of the rough is the *Foundry*, 148 Boulder Rd, with the *De Benares' Tavern*, on Hannan Street, imposing dress regulations for customers *and* staff. Skimpies still serve in most pubs, with the *Exchange* adding the occasional live band

and the *Palace* offering a more formal atmosphere. The balcony of the *York* is no longer a launching pad for vomit and beer cans. If you're **in Boulder**, the transformed *Recreation* or the *Albion & Shamrock* hotels are the ones to visit for a drink, and if you want to have a generally quiet evening, go to the bars in the back.

North of Kalgoorlie–Boulder

North of town a number of isolated communities supporting either small mining operations or rural Aboriginal communities stretch along a sealed road (bar a short section north of Leinster) to Meekatharra, 726km from Kalgoorlie and halfway up the Great Northern Highway. This arid and sparsely populated region offers visitors prime chunks of WA's Outback: dust, heat, flies, treacherous salt lakes, more flies, and towns in varying stages of atrophy. It's worth knowing that most **ghost towns** in this area, especially the ones closer to Kalgoorlie, are mere stumps of long-since ruined buildings, surrounded by decidedly un-ghostly rubbish. The desperate shortage and expense of building materials in the Goldfields ensured that any abandoned structure was quickly scavenged for use elsewhere.

Though it once boasted twelve thousand residents, two breweries and an hourly train to Kalgoorlie, give the rubble remains of **Kanowna** a miss. Instead, the two ghost towns of **BROAD ARROW** and **ORA BANDA** (respectively 38km and 66km from Kalgoorlie) can make a satisfactory nibble into this area, especially if you complete the 185-kilometre loop (100km of corrugated dirt) back to Kalgoorlie via Coolgardie. Broad Arrow is just a couple of dilapidated shacks and a **pub** covered with inane graffiti (to which you are most welcome to contribute) and is popular with weekending Kal–Boulderians looking for a change of pub interiors. The historic *Ora Banda Hotel* (☎08/9024 2059, fax 9024 2166; ④) is built of stone rather than the more usual galvanized iron, and has recently been rebuilt. There's an old stamp battery nearby and the track continues back south to Coolgardie, passing the abandoned townsites of Kintore and Kununalling.

From **Leonora** (motel, ⑤), a sealed road also branches northeast to Laverton where the **Warburton Road**, now being touted as "The Great Central Road", a straightforward if desolate track (often confused with the long unmaintained Gunbarrel Highway) leads 1160km to Yulara, NT (see p.585). The good news is that the Aboriginal Land permits (which no one ever checked anyway) have been dropped, and with **fuel** after Laverton at Tjirrikarli (longest stretch, 320km), Warburton, Warakurna and Docker River, this long-useful dirt-road connection between central and western Australia is opening up. The Perth–Goldfields Express (free call ☎1800/620 440) runs **buses** as far as **Leinster** (motel, ⑤) and **Laverton** (motel, ⑥) three times a week, stopping on the way at **Menzies** (hotel, ④) and Leonora.

The Eyre Highway to South Australia

South of Kalgoorlie is the twin-centred, nickel-mining town of **KAMBALDA**, on the shores of salty Lake LeFroy where you can windsurf during the wet season and land yacht during the dry. There's nothing here you haven't already seen in Kalgoorlie, so rejoin the Great Eastern Highway and continue south to Norseman, at the western end of the **Eyre Highway**. The highway is named after the explorer John Eyre, who crossed the southern edge of the continent in 1841, a gruelling five-month trek which cost his companion's life and would have cost his own but for some Aborigines, who helped him locate water. Eyre crawled into Albany on his last legs but set the route for future crossings, the laying down of the telegraph lines and, most recently, the highway.

NORSEMAN was named after a prospector's horse which kicked up a large nugget in 1894 – a real case of lucky horseshoes; a bronze statue of the creature now stands proudly on the corner of Roberts and Ramsay streets. Arrivals from South Australia may be eager to pick up their "I crossed the Eyre Highway" certificate from the **tourist office** (daily 9am–5pm; ☎08/9039 1071) on Roberts Street. There are also public showers and a **swimming pool** next door in which to celebrate further this achievement. You can continue to celebrate with a meal and an overnight stay at the *Norseman Eyre Motel* (☎08/9039 1130, fax 9039 1547, free call ☎1800/094 824; ⑤) on Princep Street. More modest accommodation is available at the **caravan park** (on-site vans ③) next to the *Great Western Motel*, or there are budget rooms at *Norseman Guest House & Backpackers Lodge* (☎08/9039 1541; ①) nearby. If you've **come from the east** and are in a quandary about which route to take to Perth, the inland road, after a stop in Kalgoorlie–Boulder, is fast and fairly dull while the coast road can be made into a week-long scenic dawdle. For the best of both worlds, nip up to Kalgoorlie and then back down and west along the coast.

Following the Eyre Highway, it's about 730km to the South Australian border and another 480km from there to Ceduna, where the bleak **Nullarbor** section ends (see p.747). That still leaves 800km before you reach Adelaide – a solid, two-day drive of legendary monotony. Although the road has been sealed for over twenty years and the longest stretch without fuel is only around 200km, do not underestimate the rigours of the journey in your own vehicle. Carry reserves of fuel and water, take rests every two or three hours and beware of kangaroos and other beasts, especially between dusk and dawn. There are no banks between Norseman and Ceduna, and both towns have a quarantine checkpoint where a large range of prohibited animal and vegetable goods must be discarded.

BALLADONIA, 193km from Norseman, is the first settlement on the way to the border, with the *Balladonia Hotel* (☎08/9039 3453; ⑤) and adjacent caravan park your choice for an overnight stop. Then, 200km further, mostly along a 145-kilometre section of dead-straight road, you reach **CAIGUNA**, which has a motel and caravan park (☎08/9039 3459; motel units ⑤, on-site vans ②), and then **COCKLEBIDDY**, another 66km further on (motel ④). On the coast near here, 16km east of town and 32km south of the highway along a 4WD track, are the remains of an old **telegraph station** that once linked WA with the rest of Australia and which today houses the Eyre Bird Observatory (☎08/9039 3450; accommodation, with advance booking only, ⑥, plus $30 for 4WD pick-up and return). Overlooking **Twilight Cove** on the Great Australian Bight, this is a great spot to break a Nullarbor crossing. The place to stay in **MADURA**, 92km east of Cocklebiddy, is the *Madura Pass Oasis Motel* (☎08/9039 3464 or ☎13 1779; ⑥), while **MUNDRABILLA**, 116km further on, has a combined motel and campsite, the *Mundrabilla Motor Hotel* (☎08/9039 3465; motel units ④–⑥, cabins ②).

EUCLA, just 12km from the border, was re-established up on the escarpment after sand dunes exposed by overgrazing engulfed the original settlement by the sea. Only 4km away, the old telegraph and weather station are still visible above the sands, an eerie sight well worth a stroll. From **Eucla National Park**, the vertical cliffs can be seen extending east for hundreds of kilometres along the coast of South Australia. For accommodation, Eucla has a **caravan park** (on-site vans ②) and the *Eucla Motor Hotel* (☎08/9039 3468; ⑤). Right on the border there's the Border Village (☎08/9039 3474; ④).

For the South Australian section of this route, see p.746.

FROM PERTH TO KUNUNURRA

The 4400-kilometre haul up Western Australia's arching coastline from Perth to Broome, across the Kimberley and on to Darwin in the Northern Territory, is one of

Australia's great road journeys. Even without detours it's a huge, transcontinental trek between the country's two most isolated capitals, fringing the barely inhabited wilderness that separates them. From the **WA–NT border** 40km east of Kununurra, it's still another 730km to Darwin. This final stretch, along the Victoria and Stuart highways, which meet at Katherine, is covered on pp.544–555.

If any single trip across Australia benefits from independent mobility, it's this one: a car enables you to explore intimately or linger indefinitely. While some days in WA's **Northwest** will be punctuated by nothing more than road trains, road kills and roadhouses, there are several places where the climate, scenery and ambience will collectively conspire to subdue your road fever for a few days. If you're interested in discovering the wayside attractions, allow at least a fortnight for the journey right through to Darwin; otherwise a week to ten days will let you whizz through the highlights.

The route is sealed all the way, but a glance at any map clearly shows the long distances between roadhouses, let alone settlements. Your vehicle should be in sound condition, particularly the tyres and the cooling system, both of which will be working hard in the heat and dirt-road detours of the Northwest. If you're undertaking the trip between January and March, once you get **north of Exmouth** you can expect **storms**, flooding and even cyclones. Following damage, roads and bridges on Highway 1 are repaired amazingly quickly, but if rain persists, routes can be closed for weeks. A **radio** is a handy aid to keeping track of cyclones, similarly troublesome "rain-bearing depressions" and the status of roads. Unfortunately, beyond Geraldton reception fades a few kilometres outside each settlement; but you can rely on roadhouse staff to know the latest. With forewarning, it's usually possible to gun ahead of a front or find somewhere agreeable to sit out the storm.

If you don't have a car, the rigid schedules and butt-numbing sectors of long-distance **bus** travel require a certain equanimity. Greyhound Pioneer offers a range of good-value **regional passes**, including the "Western Explorer" (Perth–Darwin) and the "Pearl Diver" (Perth–Broome). It should be noted that by doing the journey *from* Perth, schedules generally match connections to places off the highway with little delay. In the opposite direction, you are travelling "against the flow" of the timetable and can expect long waits on roadhouse forecourts unless heading directly back to Perth.

Up the coast to Broome

Ironically, nowhere along the 2400-kilometre drive along the North West Coastal Highway to Broome will you glimpse vistas of frothing surf breaking temptingly onto golden beaches or taste the salt in the air. The highway takes a more sheltered inland course, with access to the ocean limited by the presence of private land, not to mention the sheer impenetrability of some of the terrain. The myth of beach-camping your way up a deserted coast is unfortunately just that, but there are enough attractions to make up for this deficiency. High points along the route include the spooky **Pinnacles** near Cervantes, the idyllic resort of **Kalbarri**, and the **Shark Bay** Peninsula, with its chummy dolphins. Further north, the **Ningaloo Reef** running down the North West Cape should not be missed, while a detour into the highlands of the **Pilbara** will make **Broome's** serene charm all the more delectable.

The Brand Highway

Travelling the **Brand Highway**, there's an all but obligatory detour to view the remarkable Pinnacles in **Nambung National Park**, 250km from Perth and 70km off the highway. A young crayfishing town, beaten by strong winds in summer, **CERVANTES** is the closest overnight stop. There are two caravan parks here, with campsites and on-site vans (②), plus *Pinnacles Beach Backpackers*, at 91 Seville St (☎08/9652 7377, fax 9652 7318; ①), which has kitchen facilities, a laundry, TV/video lounge and barbecue and books tours. For greater comfort, try the *Cervantes Pinnacles Motel* (☎08/9652 7145, fax 9652 7214; ⑥). Eat at the *Tavern* or the *Thirst Point* pizzeria. Minibus tours of the park leave daily (1pm plus 9.45am & 4.15pm, depending on demand; $12; ☎08/9652 7041) from the *Pinnacle Country Café,* which is also the tourist information centre (daily 8am–6pm), next to the Shell service station. Better still, Happyday Tours (☎08/9652 7244) does pick-ups from the Greyhound Pioneer bus on the highway and next morning takes you for a two-hour stroll ($30) through the Pinnacles on the way back to the bus.

Otherwise, in the park (CALM fee; no camping; see box on p.619) there's access to the ocean at Kangaroo Point and Hangover Bay but the Pinnacles are the main attraction: a forest of limestone columns up to four metres high, formed by subsurface erosion and since exhumed from their sandy tombs by the perennial southwesterlies. A three-kilometre loop drive winds among them, but however lazy you're feeling, you'll find it hard not to park and wander around this eerie expanse, sometimes enhanced by a "mist" of fine, windblown sand. Most day-tours from Perth arrive around midday, missing the evening sun's long shadows, which add still further to the Pinnacles' photogenic qualities.

After the Pinnacles there's really very little of interest until you get to the tiny coastal resort of GREENOUGH, 400km north of Perth. The Greenough Historical Hamlet (daily 9.30am–4.30pm; ☎08/9926 1140; $2.50 including guided tour) is an unusually well-restored nineteenth-century farming community that would make an ideal period-film location. Up the road you'll see Greenough's strange leaning trees – some bent almost flat against the ground by the prevailing salt-laden winds – as well as the imposing, three-storey bulk of Clinch's Mill, the Pioneer Cemetery, and the Pioneer Museum (Sat–Thurs 10am–4pm; ☎08/9926 1058; $1.50), recording the area's heritage.

On the west side of the highway (turn off at the *S Bend Caravan Park*), more of Greenough's relics include the *Hampton Arms Inn*, restored into a delightful guesthouse (☎08/9926 1057, fax 9926 1238; ①, with breakfast and lunch) and restaurant (daily noon–2pm & 7pm–late), which make a welcome rustic change from anodyne motels. The *Greenough Rivermouth Caravan Park* (☎08/9921 5845) is a better-than-average facility offering tent spaces, on-site vans (③) and cheap fuel. The nearest backpackers' (☎08/9927 1581; ①) is the youth hostel at 32 Waldeck St, Dongara, 40km to the south.

Geraldton

Situated in the middle of the Batavia Coast, GERALDTON is a crayfishing, mining and pastoral centre whose downtown feels more like a busy Perth suburb than a country town. In fact it's the state's third-largest city and a windsurfing haven, currently experiencing a mini-boom.

The tourist office is in the Bill Sewell Complex (daily 8.30am–5pm; ☎08/9921 3999) on Chapman Road, 2km north of town. Greyhound Pioneer buses arrive here daily and Westrail buses alight at the old train station, just down the road. The modern town has little of interest except for a museum and an extraordinary cathedral. The Maritime Museum (Mon–Sat 10am–5pm, Sun 1–5pm; free) on Marine Terrace, by the yellow submarine (an aborted crayfishing venture), focuses on the fascinating tragedy of the *Batavia* and the many other shipwrecks off the treacherous Batavia Coast, as well as describing the contemporary "treasures" of the crayfishing industry.

St Francis Xavier Cathedral on Cathedral Drive, built over a 25-year period and completed in 1938, was the crowning glory of Monsignor John Hawes' career. He was a qualified architect before taking up the cloth, and there are half a dozen examples of his unique Romanesque-Byzantine architectural style in the vicinity, of which the cathedral is his masterpiece, just as stunning and bold inside as out. If you're sufficiently impressed, ask about the **John Hawes Heritage Trail** at the tourist office (see opposite), which leads you around some of his other works.

Of Geraldton's other attractions, the city's **beaches** aren't particularly appealing and are often windy, like much of the west coast. There's the obligatory **Old Gaol**, now a craft centre, next to the Bill Sewell Complex, and a **lighthouse** at Point Moore, while the old **Keepers' Cottage** (Thurs 10am–4pm; donation welcome), off Chapman Road, 5km north of town, is fastidiously maintained in its original state. If you're around for a while, you might want to take the Touch the Wild Safari Tour (☎08/9921 8435; $80 per day), which shows you what the Geraldton region's natural history has to offer.

Accommodation

Batavia Backpackers, Bill Sewell Complex, Chapman Rd (☎08/9964 3001). Spacious and clean former hospital with wards for dorms. Rooms ②, dorms ①.

Batavia Motor Inne, Fitzgerald St (☎08/9921 3500, fax 9921 1061, ☎008/014 628). Close to the city centre and with restaurant and pool. ⑤.

Foreshore Backpackers, 172 Marine Terrace (☎08/9921 3275). Right in the town centre and close to the harbour. YHA discounts and free pick-ups. ③.

Mercure Inn, Brand Highway (☎08/9921 2455, fax 9921 5830, free call ☎1800/642 244). Customary motel-chain comforts. ⑦.

Sun City Tourist Park, Sunset Beach, 6km north of town (☎08/9938 1655). Geraldton's best caravan park but rather a long way out. On-site vans ③.

Eating and drinking

Geraldton has a fair selection of places to eat, and if you're heading north this will be your last chance to sample a choice of decent food rather than take what you are offered. For drinks and live bands, the *Geraldton Hotel* on Lester Avenue is the place to go, with the *Freemasons* on Marine Terrace offering a more refined alternative.

Boat Shed, 357 Marine Terrace. Top-quality seafood from around $20. Daily from 6pm.

Fiddlers, 103 Marine Terrace (☎08/9921 6644). The best seafood in town, with main courses for around $15.

Lemon Grass, 18 Snowdon St. The town's best choice for Thai food.

Skeetas, George Rd. Very popular garden restaurant; an ideal place for sunny salad lunches.

Topolinos, 158 Marine Terrace. Stylish and affordable Italian lunch spot in the town centre.

THE HOUTMAN ABROLHOS ISLANDS

Seventy kilometres off the Geraldton coast is the archipelago of the **Houtman Abrolhos**, over a hundred sparsely vegetated islands barely above water, surrounded by a maze of reefs and channels.

While these are "desert islands" in the scientific sense, tropical and temperate currents mingle here to create an unusual diversity of marine flora and fauna, offering some of the best **diving and snorkelling** along the west coast.

Access is limited to tours of various kinds, all of which are based in Geraldton: Force Five Charters (☎08/9921 6416) has a superbly equipped vessel for charter, at a cost of $270 per person for a fully-inclusive weekend dive trip, or you can join the Batavia Coast Diving Academy (☎08/9921 4299) for a weekend dive. Top Cat boat charter (☎015/990 047) can take you to the islands for $50, and Shine Aviation Services (☎08/9923 3600) offers a memorable and great value seaplane flight including two hours of snorkelling on the reefs for $175.

On to Kalbarri

North of Geraldton, the North West Coastal Highway heads through **NORTHAMP-TON**, an early lead-mining and pastoral settlement with a good caravan park and budget accommodation at the *Nagel Centre* (☎08/9934 1488; ①), next to the church. A few kilometres after Northampton you can turn left to investigate the tiny seaside resort and crayfishing port of **HORROCKS** (25km west), or **PORT GREGORY** (46km northwest, and where the bitumen ends), with the ruins of an aborted convict-hiring depot from the 1850s nearby. The middle section of this route should be sealed all the way to Kalbarri by now, though for the moment (or if you're coming from the north) the Ajana Road is the seventy-kilometre route to the coastal resort.

Kalbarri

Situated at the mouth of the Murchison River, whose sandbar shelters its beach, **KALBARRI** is the best of the west coast's resorts. Without so much as a dreary old jail to shuffle through, this small town is simply a great place to do as much or as little as you like. With the dramatic scenery of the Kalbarri National Park on its doorstep, few resorts can boast such an ideal location, together with good, inexpensive accommodation and a host of activities.

The area's history holds a few wonders of its own. In the 1920s a stockman discovered the remains of a **castaway's camp** on the clifftops north of Kalbarri and excavation revealed the wreck of the Dutch trader, *Zuytdorp*, at the base of the cliff, but no human remains. The fate of the survivors had been a three-hundred-year-old mystery until the diagnosis of the rare Ellis van Croveld Syndrome (endemic in seventeenth-century Holland) among local children of Aboriginal descent suggested that some of the *Zuytdorp*'s castaways survived long enough to pass the gene on to the Aborigines of the area.

Arrival, information and getting around

Greyhound Pioneer **buses** from Perth drop passengers at the **Ajana turn-off** on the highway, to be met by a shuttle bus on Monday, Thursday and Saturday only. Westrail buses from Perth come right into town on Monday, Wednesday and Friday, returning the following day. The **tourist office** (daily 9am–5pm; ☎08/9937 1104) is in the Allen Centre on Grey Street; many of the local activities and tours can be booked here. The small **shopping centre** on Porter Street includes a bakery, supermarket and **post office**, with bank agencies and cash machines at various outlets around town. Suzuki **4WD jeeps** can be rented from Kalbarri Hire Cars (☎08/9937 1277) on Sutherland Street. Mileage is unlimited in Kalbarri and in the national park, and the drive up River Road at the town's northern end will give you a chance to fiddle with the transmission levers.

Accommodation

In the school holidays when Kalbarri is busy, most holiday units insist on a minimum one-week's booking. If you are coming at this time, book ahead. Kalbarri Accommodation Service (☎08/9937 1072) rents out privately owned holiday homes.

Kalbarri Backpackers, 2 Mortimer St (☎08/9937 1430, fax 9937 1563). Although it's slipped down the league a bit under new ownership, it still has no competition. Free early-morning snorkelling runs are arranged. Rooms ③, mixed dorms ①.

Kalbarri Beach Resort, off Clotsworthy St (☎08/9937 1061, fax 9937 1323, free call ☎1800/096 002). Large resort with a pool, sauna and the *Zuytdorp Restaurant*. ⑥.

Kalbarri Reef Villas, Coles St (☎08/9937 1165, fax 9937 1465). Best value in town, with well-cared-for units, plus pool, and free use of rowboat and bikes. ⑤.

Kalbarri Seafront Villas, 37 Grey St (☎08/9937 1025, fax 9937 1525). Well-equipped units, some with ocean views and a free dinghy provided. ⑤.

Kalbarri Tudor, Porter St (π08/9937 1077). Best caravan park, and close to shops. On-site vans, chalets and cabins ③–④.
Murchison Park, Grey St (π08/9937 1005). Well-shaded caravan park right opposite the Foreshore. On-site vans ③.
Murchison View Apartments, corner of Grey and Rushton sts (π08/9937 1096, fax 9937 1522). Quality two- and three-bedroom units with a pool and some sea views. ⑤–⑧.
Sunsea Villas, 18 Grey St (π08/9937 1187). Units overlooking the ocean and river mouth. ⑤.

The Town and around

The **Kalbarri Entertainment Centre** on Porter Street has mini-golf, trampolines and mini-carts and also rents **bicycles** for $8 a day. **Rainbow Jungle** (Tues–Sat 9am–5pm, Sun 10am–5.30pm; $6), 4km south of town, is the place to visit on a bike. A minor architectural work of art, filled to bursting with tropical fauna, it's a superb and imaginative display of stunningly colourful parrots and includes a walk-through aviary.

For those not content to laze on **Chinaman's Beach** all day, there are plenty of more active pursuits on offer. An easy way to get yourself going is to take a **cruise** up the Murchison River on the *Kalbarri River Queen* (π08/9937 1104) or rent all sorts of **watercraft** on the Foreshore from Kalbarri Boat Hire & Canoe Safaris (π08/9937 1245), who can also take you up the lower Murchison to Gregory's Rock for a morning's canoeing, with a traditional bush breakfast on the way, for $40. Big River Ranch, 4km inland from Kalbarri (π08/9937 1214; pick-ups available), runs very popular **horse-riding** trips for beginners and the experienced alike; the three-hour sunset ride ($35), through the river, along the beach and back again, is the memorable highlight. **Scenic flights** with Kalbarri Air Charter (π08/9937 1130; enquire at the gift shop, 28 Grey St) start from just $35 for the short but spectacular Coastal Cliffs run, and go up to $140 for the Grand Tour or a five-hour visit to Monkey Mia. Kalbarri Sports and Dive (π08/9937 1126) can organize **dives**, while the Reef Walker IV (π08/9937 1356) sets off on a variety of coastal cruises with diving or fishing opportunities.

Eating and drinking

Don't leave Kalbarri without checking out *Finlay's Fish BBQ* (daily 11.30am–2pm & 5.30–8.30pm; π08/9937 1260) on Magee Crescent. With plate-spinning Captain Finlay's fresh fish, salad and damper for $10, and an unusual setting in an old ice works (plus occasional fireside ballads), *Finlay's* on a balmy night is a treat.

All the other **restaurants** are rather ordinary by comparison. *Echoes*, above the shopping centre (daily 6.30pm–late), is the town's best, with meals for $15; the *Zuytdorp* (daily 6–10pm) at the *Kalbarri Beach Resort* is a close rival, with a $17 smorgasbord. The *Lure 'n' Line* (daily 10am–8pm), on Grey Street, has views and seafood lunches, and *Rivers Café* (daily 10am–8pm), opposite the wharf, has takeaways and more fresh seafood. *Cazbah Pizza* (Tues–Sun 5.30pm–late), behind the *Gilgai Tavern* on Porter Street, serves average pizzas from $8, and there's a good health-food café inside the shopping centre. *Recollections Café*, on the corner of Woods Street, serves pastries, baguettes and feeble cappuccinos. Of the two **pubs**, the *Kalbarri Hotel* on Grey Street is where the locals hang out, while the livelier *Gilgai Tavern* on Porter Street is the place for travellers to congregate.

Kalbarri National Park

Kalbarri National Park (CALM fee; see box on p.619), which surrounds the town, has two popular attractions: the serpentine **river gorge** of the upper Murchison River, reached off the Ajana Road east of town, and the **coastal gorges** created by lesser creeks, a few kilometres south of Kalbarri, just about within cycling range. Kalbarri Coach Tours (π08/9937 1161) visits both areas several times a week for around $40, with a range of more adventurous options available too.

The **coastal gorges** are accessible by tracks and short walks off the unsealed Kalbarri–Port Gregory road, which begins just before *Red Bluff Caravan Park*. **Red Bluff** is the prominent butte overlooking Jakes Corner (good surfing) and the site of some barely discernible, prehistoric crustacean fossils. **Rainbow Valley** has some intriguing features exposed by weathering, as well as a coastal walk up to **Mushroom Rock**, the most interesting part of the coastline. Pot Alley is another lookout and Eagle Gorge has a tiny secluded beach, but the view from the cliffs above **Natural Bridge** (at 16km, the furthest from town) gives the impression that you are indeed perched on the edge of a vast continent.

Eleven kilometres east of Kalbarri, a corrugated road turns north for 25km to the **gorge** along the Murchison River, where at a junction you can go a few kilometres further north to **the Loop**, or south to **Z Bend**. It's possible to walk round the Loop (a horseshoe bend in the Murchison River) in rather less than half the six hours suggested by the notice board, but this may be prolonged by the abundance of swimming opportunities, birdlife and the odd, mean-looking feral pig; the walk is best undertaken early in the morning. Z Bend is the most dramatic lookout over the Murchison River far below, accessible down a steep track. Kalbarri Coach Tours (see details overleaf) does canoe trips a few kilometres downstream from here, and Kalbarri Safari Tours (☎08/9937 1011) offers a day-trek through the Murchison canyons for $35. You can also **abseil** down and climb up Z Bend's cliff; enquire at *Kalbarri Backpackers* – no experience is necessary. Back on the Ajana Road, heading inland for 30km from the Loop turn-off, **Hawks Head** and **Ross Graham Lookout**, both a few kilometres off the road, are less impressive but worth stopping for on the way out of Kalbarri if you're driving.

It is possible to **walk** from Z Bend to the Loop over a couple of days and from Ross Graham Lookout to the Loop in four days, but both are demanding walks and you should speak to the **park ranger** (☎08/9937 1140) first.

Shark Bay

Shark Bay is the name given to the two prongs of land and their corresponding lagoons which comprise Australia's westernmost point, forming a roughly W-shaped coastline. **Denham**, the only settlement, is on the west side of the Peron Peninsula, while at **Monkey Mia Dolphin Resort**, on the sheltered east side of the peninsula, dolphins have been coming in almost daily to meet people for the past thirty years. The shallow, aquamarine waters of Shark Bay have earned it a World Heritage listing as a remarkable **ecological habitat**, a fact that tends to be overshadowed by the visits of the dolphins. It's worth noting that dolphins also "interact", albeit less reliably, at Rockingham and Bunbury south of Perth (see p.614).

To **get there** from Perth, take the Greyhound Pioneer bus, which runs all the way to Monkey Mia twice daily on Monday, Thursday and Saturday (12hr): if you plan to visit, make sure your bus pass includes this excursion. Otherwise Western Airlines flies three times a week and Skywest four times. Shark Bay Taxi Service (☎08/9948 1331) connects with interstate buses at the notoriously hot *Overlander Roadhouse*, which marks the turning off the highway to Shark Bay, charging $25 to Denham and $30 to Monkey Mia.

The roads to Monkey Mia and Steep Point

It's 150km to Monkey Mia from the *Overlander Roadhouse*, a drive that is much like the rest of the coastline in this area – a rather dull one through dense mulga scrub punctuated with some unusual sights along the way. **Hamelin Pool**, 5km off the Denham road, is home to a uniquely accessible colony of **stromatolites**, mats of sediment-trapping algae which are some of the earth's earliest life forms, dating back over three billion

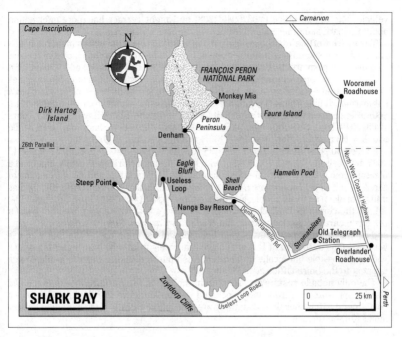

years. The examples in Hamelin Pool, flourishing because no potential predator can handle the pool's hyper-saline water, are about three thousand years old and look rather like lumps of blackened concrete. The **Old Telegraph Station** (daily 8.30am–5.30pm; $2), 2km from the pool, has a display, video and a pet "stromie" in a tank – altogether more interesting than the actual colony. There are also some old telecommunications relics and a shop and café with a small **caravan park** (☎08/9942 5905; on-site vans ③).

Fourteen kilometres further along the Denham road, a turn-off leads to the salt and gypsum mine at Useless Loop, with another branch road, accessible by 4WDs only, leading to **Steep Point** ($20 entry fee; camping), Australia's most westerly mainland extremity. **Dirk Hartog Island**, off the north end of Steep Point, is where the first European is known to have set foot on what is now Australian soil, 150 years before Captain Cook. The Dutch mariner Hartog left a pewter plate inscribed "Anno 1616" on the island.

Continuing towards Denham, you'll pass *Nanga Bay Resort* (☎08/9948 3992, fax 9948 3996; ①–⑥), where there are accommodation units, cabins and dorms; it's a popular fishing spot but otherwise uninspiring. Across the isthmus is **Shell Beach**, composed of millions of tiny shells several metres deep. Where they've consolidated they're cut into blocks for local buildings. Twenty kilometres before Denham, **Eagle Bluff** is an impressive clifftop lookout where dugongs, dolphins and manta rays can be spotted in the clear waters of Freycinet Reach below.

Denham

A small prawning port and holiday resort, **DENHAM** thrives in the lee of Monkey Mia's indefatigable popularity. Between here and Monkey Mia (25km away), **François Peron National Park** (CALM fee; see box on p.619) is fully accessible only in a 4WD vehicle. The CALM office (☎08/9948 1208) on Knight Terrace has more information about the park and other natural features in the Shark Bay area.

The **tourist office** (daily 8am–6pm; ☎08/9948 1253) is on the town's main road at 83 Knight Terrace, and there's another one at no. 67. The town also has a post office and a couple of supermarkets. **Buses** for Monkey Mia leave daily at 8am and 11.30am ($8).

As for **tours and cruises**, the *MV Explorer* (☎08/9948 1246; from $50) operates cruises around Shark Bay, offering a good chance to see some of the clear-water bay's submarine wildlife. Shark Bay Charter Service's luxurious catamaran (☎08/9948 1113; $60) offers a great day out – it's worth it for the food alone. Shark Bay Discovery Tours (☎08/9948 1880; $35–100) has 4WD tours around the entire Shark Bay area, while Monkey Mia Air Charter (☎08/9948 1307) arranges **scenic flights**.

Places to stay include *Bay Lodge*, 95 Knight Terrace (☎08/9948 1278, fax 9948 1031, free call ☎1800/812 780; ①–④); with basic dorms, refurbished family units and a pleasant courtyard, it's the cheapest place to stay in Shark Bay and does free runs to Monkey Mia. The *Tradewinds Holiday Village* (☎08/9948 1222, fax 9948 1161; ⑤) has units that sleep up to six people, and the *Heritage Resort* (☎08/9948 1160, fax 9948 1134; ⑧), on the corner of Durlacher Street, is the town's best with a very pleasant bar. Of the three **caravan parks** in town, the *Shark Bay Caravan Park* (☎08/9948 1387; vans and cabins ③), 4 Spaven Way, is your best bet and has a big pool. Note that **water** is very precious in the Shark Bay area since rain rarely falls: salty bore water is used as widely as possible but locally desalinated, fresh public drinking water is available at a tap next to the Shire Office at 42 Hughes St.

The only notable **restaurant**, apart from the one in the *Heritage Resort*, is the *Old Pearler* opposite, built from shell block and with an attractive maritime interior; meals ꞎꞎꞎꞎ ꞏꞏꞏ ꞏꞏꞏ ꞏꞏꞏꞏ $10. Other than that, there are a couple of cafes, a pizza bar and a bakery along Knight Terrace.

Monkey Mia

One Japanese woman could not restrain herself. With a choking cry of "I love you, I love you", she leaped at a dolphin and threw her arms around it. The dolphin shrugged and slipped away.

National Geographic

After all the hype, you might be pleased to find that **Monkey Mia** ($5 entry fee) is nothing more than an attractive caravan park and a jetty by a pretty beach looking out over the inauspiciously named Disappointment Reach, where scores of day-trippers flock to witness the almost daily **dolphin** visits (usually between 8 and 10am and most reliably in winter). An intriguing video and other related displays in the **Dolphin Information Centre** (daily 8am–6pm) explain how the entirely unprompted interaction began in the 1960s. Almost all that has been learned about dolphins has been gleaned from studies of Monkey Mia's regular troupe of visitors, each one known by name, although the actual visitors number between three and six females and their third-generation progeny.

Unfortunately, as is so often the case, the place has become a victim of its massive popularity. The staff and rangers at the resort all seem tired of the whole business, with the latter weary of inappropriate behaviour which threatens to jeopardize future visits. Furthermore, the dolphins' repeated visits and their spontaneous familiarity seem to take a toll on their breeding patterns. For this reason cubs, which lack immunity to human infections in their early weeks, are kept away from visitors.

One of the best things to do at Monkey Mia is to take a ride around the bay on the *Shotover*, a stripped-down racing catamaran: **cruises** start from just $15 for an hour, departing from the jetty at 9am, but the day-long tours are much more rewarding, with plenty of marine life (including prancing dolphins) to be observed and enjoyed.

The *Monkey Mia Dolphin Resort* (☎08/9948 1320, fax 9948 1034) is right on the beach: it has grassed campsites and, for backpackers, cramped old **caravans** with ancient kitchens (①). There are also cabins, larger park homes and motel **rooms** (④–⑦), plus a pool and spa, a restaurant and a small shop with basic groceries and takeaways.

Carnarvon and around

A centre for prawning fleets and the sheep stations of the Upper Gascoyne region, tropical **CARNARVON** also supports a large agricultural zone, thanks to the apparently dry Gascoyne River's retrievable subterranean water. The town is attempting to redress its heavy reputation for drink-related violence and crime by curbing anti-social behaviour and improving its appearance. While this is being achieved, it's the only place between Perth and Katherine where you'll see police cars on the prowl. There's little here to interest the passing traveller: the best things to do are to take a tour of a banana plantation (try Munro's, 10km east of town on South River Road; daily tours at 11am; $2) or visit the redundant OTC satellite dish that guided early US space flights.

A couple of diversions up the coast can add up to a fun day out, though. Six kilometres east of Carnarvon a ford crosses the riverbed and, passing the 65°C thermal well of Bibbawarra Bore, joins the sealed Blowholes Road, which leads to the **Blowholes** at Point Quobba, 65km from town. On all but the calmest days, incoming waves compress air through cavities and vents in the low cliff to erupt like geysers up to 20m into the air, a sight and sound well worth the detour. A couple of kilometres to the south is a basic campsite (but no water) with sheltered snorkelling in the bay. Heading north past *Quobba Homestead* (camping; basic rooms ②) and occasional tracks down to shell-lined beaches, you cross the private road linking the Dampier Saltworks at Lake MacLeod with the jetty at Cape Cuvier. Just north of the cape is the wreck of the *Korean Star*, beached here during a cyclone in 1988. It was here, too, that a "**fish feeding frenzy**" caught the world's attention in 1992, when several species of shark and whale appeared to co-operate in devouring a glut of small fry (see box overleaf). North of here is Red Bluff Beach (camping, shop and restaurant) and *Gnaraloo Homestead* (camping), the domain of beach fishermen and hard-core windsurfers. The *Red Bluff Express* can take you up here once or twice a week from Carnarvon ($30 return); enquire at the tourist office.

Practicalities

The **tourist office** (daily 9am–5pm; ☎08/9941 1146), on the corner of Robinson and Stuart streets, has information on tours into the surrounding countryside, including Mount Augustus (see overleaf). **Buses** also arrive here, and the **post office** is just opposite.

Recommended **accommodation** in town includes the *Gateway Motel* on Robinson Street (☎08/9941 1532, fax 9941 2606; ⑤), with good-value rooms, a pool and restaurant; the *Hospitality Inn* (☎08/9941 1600, fax 9941 2405, ☎13 1779; ⑦) on West Street; and an excellent B&B called *The Outcamp* (☎08/9941 2421, fax 9941 3116; ⑥) at 16 Olivia Terrace, overlooking the Fascine, as the foreshore is known. As for the **hostels**, the *Backpackers Paradise*, near the end of Robinson Street (☎08/9941 2966, fax 9941 3662; ①), is the best choice, with a huge kitchen, TV room, ping pong and a garden with pool. There are no fewer than seven **caravan parks** within 5km of town: the *Carnarvon Tourist Centre* (☎08/9941 1438; on-site vans ③), 500m up Robinson Street from the post office, is the most central.

Snacks and counter **lunches** can be had at the *Port* and *Carnarvon* hotels (trouble-free nights switch between one and the other) or at *JR's Lunch Bar*, all on Robinson

Street. The *Harbourview Café*, near the Small Boat Harbour south of town, has good but pricey seafood. You're at the wrong end of the country for an evening **meal** that does-n't involve chicken, hamburger or pizza, but you can try out the restaurants in the motels or head out to the *Tropical Bird Park*, 55 Angelo St (book on ☎08/9941 2471), where there are barbecues on Friday and Saturday nights for $8.

Inland to Mount Augustus

East of Carnarvon, a dirt road follows the Gascoyne River inland, past the swimming hole of **Rocky Pool**, to **GASCOYNE JUNCTION**, a moribund, one-pub settlement from the droving days, where the outlaw Ned Kelly (see p.889) was reputed to have once hidden out. The *Junction Hotel* (☎ & fax 08/9943 0504; ⑤) is a century-old relic with a small general store and fuel. North, a road leads past the escarpment of the **Kennedy Ranges National Park** which is accessible to regular cars. This is a slight-ly longer route to **Mount Augustus National Park** (also known as Burringurrah National Park) than continuing to the main access road another 215km away, but is well worth the detour.

Mount Augustus, the world's largest monadnock (a residual hill), is trumpeted as being bigger and older than Uluru (Ayers Rock) in the Northern Territory. While it hardly matches Uluru's elemental majesty, the drive there gives you a good feel for the Outback's dusty isolation and expanse – assuming that's something you've yet to expe-rience. Camping and basic **accommodation** is provided at *Cobra Station Homestead* (☎08/9943 0565, fax 9943 0992; fuel, shop, closed Sat; cabins ④), 40km from the hill, or at the *Mount Augustus Outback Resort* (☎08/9943 0527, fax 9943 3527; fuel, shop; ④), right at the base, from where a day's hike to the summit can be undertaken. Mount Augustus is 450km from Carnarvon and 350km from Meekatharra on the inland high-way. Whichever way you come, it's a long, hot drive on dirt roads, so be sure you and your vehicle are prepared for the trip. West Coast Safaris (see box on p.648) runs four-day tours from Exmouth to this region on demand.

SEX AND FOOD ON THE REEF

Sex on the reef is a spectacular, yet strangely impersonal, affair: around the time of full moon in March or April, the corals off Exmouth all spawn simultaneously, releasing huge clouds of sperm and eggs, which are fertilized as they mingle in the waters above the reef. The perpetuation of life on this scale makes it an incredible event to witness – all the better at night because, lit by divers' flashlights instead of filtered sunlight, the polyps appear in their true, vivid colours. As a side-effect, the spawning creates a largesse of food that attracts marine animals, notably forty-ton filter-feeding whale sharks, the world's largest fish, which migrate annually to the North West Cape region between March and May.

Another phenomenon is triggered by the spawning, as huge shoals of bait fish move into the area in search of easy pickings. Similarly motivated groups of whales and sharks herd these shoals into shallow water, trapping them in dense black bands against the shore and then charging in, mouths agape. The waters are so shallow that the larger predators are often in danger of being beached, and have to turn on their sides, bodies half out of the water, to feed.

Dive boats from Exmouth and Coral Bay sometimes run out to witness the spawning, and there are regular (expensive) excursions while the whale sharks are around (see the "Tours and Cruises from Exmouth" box on p.648). Witnessing the coastal feeding fren-zy is pretty hit-and-miss – it was first observed as recently as 1992 – and you'll have to ask around to find out the latest. There's no need to get wet, however, as the best van-tage points are the clifftops overlooking the action north of Carnarvon (see p.645). Ask at the tourist office there to see the video of the 1992 event.

The North West Cape

Six kilometres after the *Minilya Roadhouse* (dorms ①), renowned for its inhospitality to those waiting for buses, a turning splits off to the hot and arid **North West Cape**. This hot and arid spike of land is notable for the 250-kilometre **Ningaloo Reef** which fringes its western edge, never more than 7km offshore, and is, in places, accessible right off the beach. **Exmouth** is the only settlement on the cape, but without your own transport the resort of **Coral Bay** is not only more convenient and more pleasant, but the easiest place from which to view the reef.

Buses leave from Carnarvon (Mon, Thurs & Sat morning), stopping at Coral Bay on the way to Exmouth before returning to Carnarvon each afternoon. If you're heading further north after an excursion to the cape, you might as well go all the way back to Carnarvon and catch the bus you'd otherwise wait for at *Minilya* – it's certainly more comfortable that way. Ansett flies between Perth and Exmouth (Sun–Fri; 6hr).

Coral Bay

CORAL BAY is a tiny beach resort 12km off the Exmouth road and, school holidays excepted, is a lovely, quiet spot with a tropical-island feel to it. At present the resort is little more than three caravan park/motels, a mini shopping centre and a **tourist information** centre (☎08/9942 5988). Lack of fresh **water** has held back large-scale development of the resort. The water comes from a hot and salty bore, making it suitable for cooking and washing but not for drinking; make sure you drink from freshwater taps.

Two glass-bottomed boats operate one-hour **cruises** over the reef in Coral Bay (daily, times depend on the tides): the Sub-Sea Explorer (☎08/9942 5955; $20) is the better of the two and for another $5 you also get an hour's snorkelling off the boat and can keep the gear for the rest of the day. What you'll see is an amazing variety of soft and hard coral that's slowly recovering from cyclone damage in 1996. Sub-Sea also organizes scenic flights.

The *Bayview Coral Bay* **motel** (☎08/9942 5932; ⑦) forms a large resort that also offers camping, on-site vans (④) and various configurations of chalets and cabins (③–⑦), as well as much-improved backpackers' accommodation (①), a small shop and a restaurant. The *Ningaloo Reef Resort* (☎08/9942 5934; ⑦), offers similar options and prices for accommodation and camping, with a truly dismal backpackers' place (①), plus a **bar**, restaurant/takeaway and a grassed pool area with a great view over the small bay.

Exmouth

On the Exmouth road, north of Coral Bay, you pass the part-sealed **Bullara–Giralia** road to the highway, which cuts 150km out of the journey between Exmouth and the north. Continuing towards Exmouth, two roads lead up onto the **Cape Range**: the **Charles Knife Road** climbs precipitously to the top of the range, 311m above sea level. From here it's possible to walk to the head of **Shothole Canyon** (allow 2hr), which is also accessible off the Exmouth road though this option makes a far less dramatic introduction to the range.

EXMOUTH was built in 1967 to serve the American Naval VLF (very low frequency) Communications Station and has since become a tourist base for visits to the Cape Range National Park and Ningaloo Marine Park (see p.648). The cloud-free atmosphere – so suited to VLF transmissions – and the prolific marine wildlife (including whale sharks in autumn and giant turtles in summer) make the town a popular winter holiday-makers' resort which is set to boom as the wonders of the Ningaloo reef become more widely known. The town's so-called Sunrise Beach is now the site of a marina. To see the reef you need to head up to **Bundegi Beach**, 14km north of Exmouth, opposite the antennae of the naval station.

TOURS AND CRUISES FROM EXMOUTH

West Coast Safaris (☎08/9949 1625) and Ningaloo Safari Tours (☎08/9949 1550) both offer full-day "over the range" **tours** for $90, or a shorter "round the range" half-day tour for $50. The full-day tour is highly recommended, a 240-kilometre round trip showing you the best of the cape; West Coast also does day-trips to Coral Bay as well as four-day tours to Mount Augustus and the Karijini (Hamersley Range) National Park.

The Ningaloo Coral Explorer (☎08/9949 1625) offers **reef-viewing cruises** off Bundegi Beach ($15), and the Exmouth Dive Centre (☎08/9949 1201) on Payne Street takes care of **dive charters** and equipment rental: day-runs out to the Muiron Islands cost around $120 with gear loan, snorkelling half that price. The Village Dive Shop (☎08/9949 1101) at the Exmouth Cape Tourist Village offers broadly the same for a few dollars less. Open-water scuba courses cost around $300, and dives to watch the coral spawning (see box on p.646) are sometimes available. Exmouth Air Charter (☎08/9949 2492) will take you on **scenic flights** around the cape for around $100.

Buses stop at the shopping centre on Thew Street, where the **tourist office** (daily 9am–5pm; ☎08/9949 1176, fax 9949 1401) is located. The **post office** is nearby on Maidstone Crescent, and there's a vast **book exchange** in the secondhand shed opposite the *Exmouth Cape Tourist Village* on Murat Road, 1km south of the town centre. ExCape Hire, on the same road (☎08/9949 1334), rents out everything from light 4WDs and bicycles to beach umbrellas.

Exmouth Cape Tourist Village (☎08/9949 1101, fax 9949 1402; ①–⑤) has become a self-contained **resort** with cramped but spotless backpackers' units, on-site vans and chalets. It also has a pool, restaurant, free bikes, snorkelling gear, cheap jeeps and all sorts of **tours** and activities (from $55), plus a dive shop with the best rates in town; they meet all buses. The *Potshot Hotel Resort* (☎08/9949 1200, fax 9949 1486; **motel** rooms & units ⑦) is the town's upmarket complex with restaurants, a pool and sporting facilities. They've also converted some units into backpackers' accommodation (①); ask at the Dive Centre nearby (☎08/9949 1201). *Exmouth Caravan Park* (☎08/9949 1331; ③–⑤), on Lefroy Street, has the cheapest four-bed chalets as well as a pool with bar, bike rental, a kiosk and restaurant.

When it comes to **food** there's nothing much to get excited about: *Whalers Café* near the shopping centre is the only place with any appeal, with the usual takeaways, a baker and two **supermarkets** just over the road. The *Potshot Hotel Resort* accommodates the town's one **pub**.

Cape Range and Ningaloo

The parks are adjacent land- and sea-conservation areas on the western edge of the North West Cape: to explore them, you really need a vehicle, or you could take one of various tours (see box above). The proximity of the continental shelf to the shore gives the **Ningaloo Marine Park** a stunning variety of marine life: over 500 species of fish and 220 species of coral have been recorded here. **Cape Range National Park** (CALM fee; see box on p.619) is essentially a coastal drive past several bays, lagoons and campsites. For snorkelling, the reef comes closest at the south point of Turquoise Bay where the wind and current tend to drift you north across the bay.

The **Milyering Visitors Centre** (Wed–Fri & Sun 10am–4pm), 52km from Exmouth, is a modern, solar-powered complex with videos and displays on the local ecology, and enthusiastic, helpful staff. Another 30km past various bays and campsites brings you to Cape Range's most accessible highlight, **Yardie Creek**, a steep-walled canyon just a kilometre from the ocean. This is as far south as 2WDs can get in the park but the walk up along the gorge's cliffs is well worth the effort. You can take a one-hour cruise (April–Oct; $18) up the short gorge but there's not much point.

To Dampier and Karratha

Back on the North West Coastal Highway, it's over 500km from Carnarvon to the industrial twin towns of Dampier and Karratha, with nothing but the occasional roadhouse along the way. At *Nanutarra Roadhouse* a road heads east to **Tom Price** and the Pilbara's highlands, and further on a road leads north 80km to the cyclone-battered **ONSLOW** (camping and motel, ⑤), an old coastal settlement bypassed by the highway and most travellers. Between Onslow and Dampier another turn-off leads to Robe River Iron's mine at Pannawonica, a closed town with no facilities for tourists. However, suitable vehicles can take a track starting 20km west of the town, which crosses the Robe River on the way to the Millstream–Chichester National Park (see overleaf), a distance of 127km.

The two young towns of **DAMPIER** and **KARRATHA** are a major industrial conurbation and the Northwest's largest population centre. Dampier is the port for Hamersley Iron's mines at Tom Price, Paraburdoo and Marandoo, linked by a 350-kilometre railway. Karratha was established in 1968 when Dampier's boulder-strewn environs were deemed unsuitable for further expansion, growing dramatically when the **North-West Shelf Natural Gas Project** got underway in the early 1980s. The project collects gas from an offshore platform 135km northwest of Dampier, from where it's piped 1500km to Perth or liquefied for export to Japan.

While being well equipped for shopping, vehicle repairs and other services, the two towns hold little of interest to the traveller apart from unusually **inexpensive fuel**, tours of the industrial installations or a cruise among the islands of the **Dampier Archipelago** with Coral Coast Tours (☎08/9183 1269; winter only) and, for those keen and determined enough, exploration of the prolific **Aboriginal engraving** on the **Burrup Peninsula** (enquire at CALM, see below). Snappy Gum Safaris (☎08/9185 1278) organizes **day-tours** from Karratha/Dampier to the Roebourne, Cossack and Point Samson area, and further afield to Millstream–Chichester National Park (see overleaf). The *Mercure Inn* (☎08/9183 1557, fax 9183 1028; ⑦), on the Esplanade, has a **restaurant**, or try *Barnacle Bob's* further along the same road. Karratha's motels tend to be more expensive, but the town now has a **hostel**: *Karratha Backpackers* (☎08/9144 4904 or 9144 4600; ①) on 110 Welland Way – take the second turning right after the Shell service station. The Northwest's regional CALM office is based in the SGIO Building, Welcome Road, Karratha (☎08/9186 8288), and is a good place to pick up information and maps on all the national parks of northern WA.

Roebourne and around

ROEBOURNE, established in 1864 (and once the capital of the Northwest), is the oldest existing settlement between Port Gregory and Darwin. The renovated **Old Gaol** is perhaps the most significant survivor in the small town, nowadays housing the **tourist office** (Mon–Fri 8.30am–4.30pm, Sat 9am–4pm, Sun 10am–2pm; ☎08/9182 1060) and **museum**. In 1982, the Old Gaol was the scene of the first of a spate of Aboriginal "deaths in custody" that tarnished Australia's human rights record throughout the 1980s and early 1990s. Although similarly suspicious deaths had occurred prior to this, these were the first such incidents to garner worldwide publicity and condemnation.

Other nineteenth-century institutional buildings are dotted around the town, with the *Victoria Hotel* (☎08/9182 1001; ⑤), on the main street, still offering refreshment and **rooms** and a **diner** open from 8am to 8pm. There's also the *Mount Welcome Motel* (☎08/9182 1282, fax 9182 1046; ⑤), half a kilometre north of the post office, and a **caravan park** (☎08/9182 1063; on-site vans ③) on De Grey Street, at the town's east end.

Cossack and Point Samson

COSSACK, once simply known as "the Landing", was the small seaport which begat the town of Roebourne, and it's well worth a look. All early settlers to the Northwest came through Cossack: pastoralists, pearlers, and prospectors heading for the goldfields of the East Pilbara. The original tin and timber buildings used to be chained to the ground so they could weather the occasional cyclones. At the turn of the century the inlet by the quay began silting up and the harbour was moved to nearby Point Samson until Port Hedland's became pre-eminent, and by the 1950s Cossack was all but abandoned, its tram lines to Roebourne long since uprooted for scrap.

This historic "ghost port" has been excellently restored in a matter of only a few years. The **courthouse**, with its museum of the settlement ($2), is the most impressive building, both inside and out, while the **post and telegraph office** is now a small art gallery displaying some fine local work. **Settler's Beach**, past the old cemetery at the end of Perseverance Street, is a sandy and sheltered swimming spot. Basic **accommodation** is available at the *Cossack Backpackers* (☎08/9182 1190; ①–③), housed in the old police barracks, which arranges pick-ups from the Wickham bus stop.

Beyond Robe River Iron's oddly anachronistic company town of **Wickham** (handy for facilities and services, and on the Perth–Darwin bus route), **POINT SAMSON** is one of the few places on the WA coast that could be compared to a British fishing village. The coastline hereabouts has that sharp, windswept, Atlantic quality, even if it does happen to be 320km inside the tropics. The port once had the ignoble distinction of receiving and shipping out the blue asbestos mined at Wittenoom, in the Hamersley Ranges. This may explain the inordinate abundance of car parks for such a tiny settlement, with the potentially cancer-causing dust in the tailings being expediently sealed under lashings of bitumen. Close to town is Honeymoon Cove, which has fine swimming.

Gastronomes will relish the **seafood** with a view at the *Trawlers Tavern* first-floor restaurant (daily 6–8pm) or *Moby's Kitchen* fish-and-chips takeaway on the ground floor (daily 11am–2pm & 5–9pm), both right by the pier. If you develop a taste for the food, **stay over** at *Point Samson Lodge,* 56 Samson Rd (☎08/9187 1052; ⑥), or the small *Solveig Caravan Park* (☎08/9187 1414; ③), also on Samson Road, next to the *Trawlers Tavern.*

Millstream–Chichester National Park

Not much more than a scenic drive and an oasis of palms and pools along the Fortescue River, the **Millstream–Chichester National Park** (CALM fee; see box on p.619) is worth a visit if you're coming or going from the Hamersley Ranges – note, however, that this entails a three-hundred-kilometre stretch where no fuel's available. Two routes lead into the park from the north: the private road alongside the Dampier–Tom Price railway can be used with an easily gained **permit** from Hamersley Iron's security gate in Dampier (☎08/9143 5364). Alternatively, the conventional route breaks off the coastal highway between Roebourne and Whim Creek, passing Pyramid Homestead soon after. Looking back north from the climb up into the **Chichester Ranges** you'll see why the homestead is so named; the view across this ancient Pilbara landscape is stirring and timeless.

Just inside the park, **Python Pool** is a pea-green waterhole backed with black and orange cliffs, and cut by the shriek of birds – worth a photo if not a dip. From this point it's a sixty-kilometre run to **MILLSTREAM**, 150km from Roebourne and 183km from Wittenoom, where an old homestead has been converted into an unusually good **visitors centre** (daily 8am–5pm; ☎08/9184 5144). A section describes the rustic bliss of the Yinjibarndi Aborigines of Ngarrari (Millstream), but omits to mention that they were cleared out by pastoralists and today live in the Roebourne area. **Chunderwarriner Pool**, a short walk from the homestead, is a lily-dappled pool surrounded by palm trees.

The date palms, introduced by Afghan cameleers, have overrun the indigenous Millstream palm, but this does not detract from the unexpectedly luxuriant scene. Black flying foxes hang from the palms' fronds, and Millstream is also a haven for dragonflies and damselflies: 22 species have been recorded here. Walking trails up to 7km long follow the palm- and paperbark-lined Fortescue River to **Crossing** and **Deep Reach pools**, where you can **camp**.

Port Hedland and on to Broome

You'll find an array of heavy industrial grot at **PORT HEDLAND**. Labelling itself rather clumsily "The Port of Big Ships", it's an iron and salt port of such unrefined ugliness that it's somehow oddly captivating. The old town centre is set on an island surrounded by mangroves and sludge, while South Hedland, on the coastal highway, has only a shopping centre and cheap fuel to distract the passing traveller. If you're travelling by bus north along the coast to Broome (only 600km away) you should get off at Port Hedland if you want to get to Wittenoom's gorges.

One of the most popular diversions is the ninety-minute tour (Mon–Fri 9.30am; $10) of the **BHP loading facility**, where ships load up with 250,000 tonnes of iron at a time.

THE STRIKE THAT NEVER ENDED

There can be little doubt that Australia's once-legendary pastoral wealth was accrued at the expense of the Aboriginal people, on whose land and cheap labour it depended. Even John Forrest, WA's turn-of-the-century premier, pastoralist and former explorer, conceded that "many of us could not be in the position we are today without native labour on our stations".

By the 1940s Australia was producing a sixth of the world's mutton and a quarter of its wool. In the Northwest, two million sheep grazed vast tracts of meagre land, a marginal enterprise made economical by the employment of black stockmen paid barely $2 a week. The archaic **Native Administration Act** protected the interests of rural industry by hampering mobility and sanctioning low or nonexistent pay for black workers.

Around this time **Don McLeod**, a white prospector still active in Aboriginal rights campaigning today, encouraged **Clancy McKenna** and **Dooley Binbin** to defy their degrading conditions and, after several years of painstaking preparation, eight hundred black workers simultaneously walked off the stations in the Port Hedland/Nullagine region on May 1, 1946. Police were instructed to harass the two camps established near Port Hedland and east of Marble Bar, and arrested McKenna and Binbin for communist subversion. Postwar food coupons were withheld, so the strikers returned to traditional ways of feeding and trading among themselves. Port Hedland was at this time a small town with an "official" (white) population of just 150 and a "mob" of 400 strikers down the road. Jittery police arrested a visiting mediator, Padre Hodge, for being "within five miles of a congregation of natives", adding further support to the strike, coverage of which was largely censored from the national press.

In 1949 things came to a head, and a **station-to-station march** was organized calling all remaining workers to join the strike. Arrest for such defiance was certain, and the strikers cheerfully offered to fill up the jail at Marble Bar and others throughout the Northwest. Only when the Seamen's Union banned the handling of "slave station" wool did the government hastily concede to McLeod's proposals – though they swiftly reneged on the deal. All through the 1950s McLeod employed and assisted the strikers in mining ventures around Marble Bar until the big mining companies began taking an interest in the Pilbara's mineral wealth and pushed them off their claims. The strikers never returned to the stations, demonstrating black assertion long before the 1960s civil rights campaigning in the USA with which the movement is associated in the popular imagination.

Whale- and turtle-watching tours are organized in the wet season (roughly Nov to March) by the tourist office, as well as fishing and diving charters and harbour cruises, as incentives to stop travellers leaving town on the next bus. You can also visit the **Royal Flying Doctor** base in Richardson Street (Mon–Fri 10am–2pm; free). Other than that, the backpackers' accommodation (see below) arranges **tours** to the Karijini (Hamersley Range) National Park and other parts of the Pilbara.

Practicalities

Overland **buses** stop next to the **tourist office** on Wedge Street (Mon–Fri 8.30am–5pm, Sat & Sun 8.30am–1pm & 2–4.30pm; ☎08/9173 1711), while **local buses** operate between South Hedland and Port Hedland (#501; $2) from 8am to 5.30pm weekdays and until 3pm on Saturday, handy for shopping or getting to **Pretty Pool** Beach, 8km away. The **post office** is opposite the tourist office on Wedge Street, where most banks are also situated.

The liveliest place to stay is at the *Port Hedland Backpackers* (☎08/9173 3282; ①), 20 Richardson St. A slightly run-down **hostel**, it offers verandah views of the huge ore-carriers gliding up the channel to the port, and heaps of activities. The *Pier Hotel* (☎08/9173 1488; ④–⑤) on the Esplanade describes itself as "infamous", and is a safe bet for a beer, band or a punch-up. *Oceanview Budget Accommodation* (☎08/9173 2418; ②–③) at 59 Kingsmill St, close to town, is a good compromise between a hostel and a motel. Pricey **motels** include the *Hospitality Inn* (☎08/9173 1044, fax 9173 1464, ☎13 1779; ⑧) on Webster Street, 4km from the centre, or the *Mercure Inn* (☎08/9172 1222, fax 9140 1245, free call ☎1800/642 244; ⑧), on the highway opposite the airport. *Dixon's Caravan Park* (☎08/9172 2525; chalets ④), also on the highway, suits those who just want to crash out, while *Cooke Point Caravan Park* (☎08/9173 1271; on-site vans ③) is on Athol Street by the ocean, 8km from town (bus #501).

Iron-ore dust can't do much for the taste buds, judging by Port Hedland's **eateries**. Good restaurants are confined to the *Hospitality* and *Mercure* motels. Otherwise, try *Kath's Kitchen*, a snack bar on Wedge Street, or the *Coral Trout*, at the end of the same road, which does seafood to eat in or fish and chips to go.

Port Hedland to Broome

The six-hundred-kilometre run from Port Hedland to Broome is one of the most boring sections of the coastal route, a dreary plain of spinifex and mulga marking the northern edge of the Great Sandy Desert. Halfway to Broome, the *Sandfire Roadhouse* (6am–midnight) provides a welcome fuel stop before the 286-kilometre stretch to *Roebuck Roadhouse*.

Despite your proximity to the ocean, beach access is only possible in a few places, and even 4WDs regularly get stuck along the enticingly named **Eighty Mile Beach**. The eponymous caravan park (☎08/9176 5941; cabins ⑤, bunks ①), 10km off the highway and 250km from Port Hedland, is popular with fishermen and 4WD-drivers.

If you're coming from Broome and heading for Wittenoom there's an interesting dirt-road alternative that bypasses Port Hedland. One hundred kilometres after Sandfire, turn south onto the sandy Borehole Road, climb into the ranges at Shay Gap and then cross the De Grey River near Muccan station. From here work your way through to **Marble Bar**, 270km from Sandfire, where you'll find motels and a service station. After Marble Bar, head southwest to Hillside station and then west to Woodstock Community, where you soon rejoin the tarmac heading down to the *Munjina/Auski Roadhouse*, 250km from Marble Bar and 42km from Wittenoom. You save only 20km, but it's a lovely, if lonely, drive through the ranges of the East Pilbara.

Inland to the Pilbara

About a thousand kilometres north of Perth are the ancient, mineral-rich highlands of the **Pilbara**, a geographical area north of the 26th parallel and including **Mount Meharry**, at 1245m the highest point in WA. The world's richest surface deposits of **iron ore** were found here in the 1950s and several mining companies are engaged in the task of reducing mountains into pits while their private railroads transport the ore to their coastal ports for shipping to Japan's steel-hungry industries. Surrounding the huge open-cast mine sites are typically vast pastoral properties, over-grazed since Australia's sheep and wool heyday following World War II. In the centre of this region is the overlooked grandeur of the **Karijini National Park**, excised from the spectacular, water-carved gorges of the Hamersley Ranges.

The Great Northern Highway

Scenically, there's precious little to commend the **Great Northern Highway**'s 1635-kilometre inland section from Perth to Port Hedland – most people shoot through in two long days and, with the honourable exception of the Hamersleys, they miss very little. Greyhound Pioneer buses operate a service three times a week between Perth and Port Hedland, stopping at the few places along the highway, including the *Munjina/Auski Roadhouse*, 42km east of Wittenoom.

Among the half-dozen towns along this inland route, only the semi-abandoned **CUE**, 650km north of Perth, retains some character from the goldrush era of the 1890s. *Dorsett Guest House* (☎08/9963 1286; ④), opposite the Rotunda on the High Street, also acts as the **tourist information centre** for the area's rich history.

MEEKATHARRA, 115km north of Cue, is a thriving mining and pastoral centre, with many century-old **hotels** along the main road, still looking good and competing for custom. From Meekatharra, an all-but-totally sealed road leads east and then south for 726km through moribund mining towns and Aboriginal communities to Kalgoorlie (for a description of this route, see p.632), while in the other direction **Mount Augustus** (see p.646) lies at the end of a 350-kilometre dirt road. North of Meekatharra a road sign marks the **26th parallel** and welcomes you to the fabled "Nor'west". As if to underline

---

COMPANY TOWNS

Newman has the odd, artificial quality of an extraterrestrial community, built for, and guided purely by, commerce – a ghost town in the making. Unlike the old single men's towns, where cheap and copious beer was the only embellishment, much is done here to keep the workforce and their families contented, loyal and even grateful to the company. Industrial unrest is not tolerated, though wages for the straightforward work are not as high as you might expect. Instead, the standard of living is buoyed by subsidized education, housing and health services to ensure that morale remains at optimum levels and round-the-clock productivity is never compromised.

The idea is to supply everything you could possibly want, short of money: saving up scrupulously over five years and moving back to one of the nicer Perth suburbs may be on everyone's mind, but this is not playing by the company's rules. Young families, however, welcome the benefits of these remote but socially self-sufficient communities, which make ideal environments for child-rearing, away from the cities' pernicious influences. Crime, vandalism and other forms of antisocial self-expression are low, with the surrounding countryside used as a wholesome vent for inevitable daily frustrations.

the isolation and extremes symbolized by "the 26th", an unvarying 350-kilometre stretch leads to Newman, with only the **Collier Range National Park** – nothing more than a series of 4WD tracks – and a roadhouse or two along the way.

NEWMAN was built to serve what is now the world's largest open-cut iron-ore mine, and the **mine tours** (daily at 8.30am & 1pm; 1hr 30min; $3), departing from the **tourist information centre** (Mon–Sat 8am–5pm, Sun 9am–1pm; ☎08/9175 2888) on Newman Drive, are the only reason you might want to stop here. The tours clearly demonstrate the simplicity and scale of the operation as **Mount Whaleback** is gradually turned inside out for its iron ore, which is sent overseas only to return transmogrified into mining machinery. Local companies run **tours** (see box on p.656), lasting between half a day and three days, to local waterholes, the Karijini (Hamersley Range) National Park and the rarely visited Canning Stock Route to the east. The town has three **caravan parks** and a pair of **motels**, as well as a busy shopping centre.

Marble Bar and Rudall River National Park

From Newman a dirt road leads north for 300km through the scenic East Pilbara to **NULLAGINE** and **MARBLE BAR**, the latter notorious for being Australia's hottest town, in 1923–24 clocking up 160 days over 38°C. This is the sole reason many visitors come to "the Bar", misnamed after a colourful bar of jasper by the Coolingan River 5km south of town. For an overnight stay, there's a **caravan park**, a **motel** (☎08/9176 1166; ⑥) and the town's famed, windowless *Ironclad Hotel* (☎08/9176 1066; ⑤) – a good place to get some drinking done or, if you're a woman, be stared at.

Rudall River National Park, 300km east of Newman, is an undeveloped national park, designated more for reasons of conservation than recreation, and also the site of some ultra-remote Aboriginal outstations. Accessible only to self-sufficient 4WDs from Newman, Telfer to the north, or off the Canning Stock Route, the park's protective role stands to be severely tested following the discovery of substantial **uranium** deposits just inside the park's boundaries – part of BHP's systematic combing of the WA deserts for the mineral wealth thought to exist there.

Wittenoom and the Karijini (Hamersley Range) National Park

The **Karijini (Hamersley Range) National Park** (CALM fee; see box on p.619) remains one of WA's undiscovered pearls, offering dramatic, time-worn scenery equal to any in Australia. Although it is hampered by its off-highway location and hesitant promotion, due to the controversy surrounding the future of Wittenoom (the park's most convenient base), its main attractions are the **gorges** cut deep into the Pilbara's north-facing escarpment and the singular lack of tourist trappings.

All the points of interest can be briefly visited on a long day's drive or tour, but Wittenoom's bargain accommodation (which is all that's left these days) and pervasive charm make a few days' exploration and relaxation much more rewarding. All the roads in the park are unsealed but usually in good condition; indeed, barring thunderstorms, the park remains accessible throughout the year.

Wittenoom

At each end of **WITTENOOM**, warning signs proclaim the possible health hazard incurred by entering the town as a result of the asbestos mining carried out here from 1937 to 1966, by – among others – the young Rolf Harris. It is believed that by the end of the century one in ten of the ex-miners and former inhabitants will have died of diseases associated with inhaling asbestos dust.

In its natural state **blue asbestos** is a completely harmless and unusual fibrous mineral, readily found in the Yampire and Upper Wittenoom gorges; it's only the **dust** produced during milling that can be lethal. Unfortunately, tailings from the mine were once used to grade the town's streets, leaving all those resident at the time susceptible to disease and with grounds for compensation. These days, resurfacing has long been completed and, unless you're kicking about in the tailings, the air contains no more harmful particles of asbestos than most urban centres. The emotional overreaction to the "Town of Death" is neatly summed up in the bumper sticker available at the Gem Shop that states "I've been to Wittenoom and lived".

Perhaps because of its tragic history, and certainly due to the intransigence of its remaining thirty inhabitants, the town, which the government wanted razed long ago, possesses an intangible ambience like few other places in WA. In the 1950s it was the biggest settlement in the Northwest but today the empty lots speak of a ghost town not prepared to die. In late 1994 the WA government stepped up the pace by threatening to cut off power and water in late 1996. At the last minute the courts won a six-month reprieve, but with its damaged telephone lines now left unmaintained, Wittenoom is facing its hardest battle yet. These extreme tactics have led to speculation that health concerns (or more precisely, fear of subsequent litigation) may not be the only issue at stake. With Wittenoom gone, the way would be clear for the construction of a new resort in the south of the national park or the exploitation of rich iron-ore reserves on Wittenoom's doorstep. Recently tourist offices in Tom Price and Port Hedland have been misinforming visitors, claiming that the town no longer exists or the access road requires 4WD – none of this is true.

Buses stop at the *Munjina/Auski Roadhouse* on the Great Northern Highway, 42km from town. If you call in advance, Dave's Gorge Tours (☎08/9189 7026) will pick you up for $10. As far as **services** in town go, there's a small shop at the caravan park and a post office at the Gem Shop on Sixth Avenue which also dispenses **tourist information** (daily 8am–6pm; ☎08/9189 7096), including detailed **maps** of the national park.

There's plenty of choice for **accommodation** in Wittenoom, none of it fancy but all cheap. *Wittenoom Holiday Homes* (☎08/9189 7096; ④; ask at the Gem Shop on Sixth Avenue) offers complete three-bedroom houses for rent. The *Bungarra Bivouac*, on Fifth Avenue (☎08/9189 7026; ①), with its distinctive rainbow tree, has seen better days but at $7 is the cheapest backpackers' in WA. The *Wittenoom Guest House*, or "the Convent", on Gregory Street (☎08/9189 7060; rooms ③, dorms ①), is a lovely and well-kept old building with a screened verandah and mild air-conditioning. **Campers** head for the *Gorges Caravan Park* on Second Avenue (☎08/9189 7055; on-site vans ③). On the bright side, you can't miss the *Gut Lumber Lodge* café, which recently reopened.

Exploring the gorges

The many gorges in **KARIJINI NATIONAL PARK** ($8 per vehicle) offer opportunities for some spectacular views, adventurous walks and, at times, exposed or slippery climbs. Deaths and several accidents have occurred but **rangers** are rarely seen, their headquarters (☎08/9189 8157) being, for some absurd reason, tucked away in the corner of the park on the new road to Newman. Take heed of the "Gorge Risk" warnings and take advantage of tours (or their guides' advice). If you're driving through the park, note that distances can be deceptive: a full tour of all the gorges can involve over 240km.

Just south of Wittenoom itself is **Wittenoom Gorge**, not actually in the park but with a number of pools handy for a cooling dip. At the end of the sealed road which leads up the gorge is the **Settlement**, 11km from town. On the west side of the gorge are the **mine** and the mill, surrounded by the dreaded and dangerous **tailings**. From the Settlement, it's possible to walk up to the dramatic entrance to **Red Gorge** (2hr) and walk and swim (including some long stretches) for another hour up to **Junction Pool** below Oxer's Lookout. From this apparent dead end, the meeting branches of the "Miracle Mile" (see p.656) tempt the truly intrepid, but unless you've already been initiated, this shouldn't be tackled without a guide. All in all, the above itinerary is a hard day's adventuring.

East of town, 24km towards the *Munjina/Auski Roadhouse*, a turning leads south into the wooded **Yampire Gorge**, where evidence of the first hand-mining operations from the 1930s can still be seen and, although you're in a national park, signs warn you to stay inside your car with your windows closed. At the top of the gorge is a park entry station and stopgap **visitors centre** where a right turn continues to the main "Four Gorges" area, but a little further on a left turn leads 10km to **Dales Gorge** (with camping) in which the idyllic Fortescue Falls, Fern Pool and Circular Pool are found. All can be joined up in a superb half-day walk with plenty of water to cool off in along the way.

Kalamina Gorge, on the way to the Four Gorges area, offers good walks along its bed without too much climbing and scrambling, and **Joffre Gorge** is an impressive lookout onto the tiered amphitheatre of Joffre Falls (usually dry) which can be easily reached and crossed along a spinifex-fringed path. There is camping nearby and the road leads on to **Knox Gorge**, which ends in the exhilarating (to say the least) "Knox Slide" featured in Dave's Gorge Tours and a stunning **lookout** down into the pools of Red Gorge.

Back on the main road, a turning north ends at a car park on the spur between **Hancock** and **Weano gorges**. From here, it's a short walk to the exposed **Oxer's Lookout**, surveying a confluence of four gorges that is as impressive as any in WA. Straight ahead is **Red Gorge**, which runs on into Wittenoom Gorge and the Settlement. Also starting from the car park, the "Miracle Mile", with its origins as a 1960s character-building exercise for Perth schoolboys, descends over loose rock into Hancock and returns up Weano Gorge. A thrilling half-day's swimming and climbing, this should only be attempted with someone who knows where the tricky parts are. For the less adventurous, the short walk into Weano Gorge to **Handrail Pool** is recommended. From the Four Gorges the road continues across the roof of the Pilbara to **Mount Bruce**, at 1235m WA's second-highest peak, now climbable along a new six-kilometre track from where you can survey the Marandoo mine, with a sealed road leading to Tom Price. East, a track passes the Rangers Headquarters to Highway 95 and Newman.

With the new roads, it's now quite a detour to visit **Hamersley Gorge**, just outside the northwestern corner of the park, 48km west of Wittenoom and 105km from Tom Price. With its spa-like pool and acutely folded beds of blue-grey and orange rock, it's unlike any of the other gorges and a bit of exploring up- and downstream could easily fill a day here. Just east of the Hamersley Gorge turn-off, the road passes through **Rio Tinto Gorge**, which bears an extraordinary resemblance to a box-canyon film set from 1950s westerns.

TOURS OF THE PILBARA

Dave's Gorge Tours (☎08/9189 7026), in Wittenoom, has become a legend on the backpackers' circuit. All tours cost around $50 a day but "Tour 3" is the one they come, and even wait days, for, incorporating the "Miracle Mile" and "Knox Slide" – chosen by *FHM* magazine as "one of the hundred things a man must do in his life". If there's enough of you, Dave is also open to many other adventurous tours through the Ranges.

Design-a-Tour (☎08/9188 1670) is a Tom Price-based company offering a full day's run around all the gorges for $70 (with lunch) and also longer tours.

Newman Eco Tours (☎08/9175 2944) runs 4WD tours to beauty spots around Newman and into Karijini.

Snappy Gum Safaris (☎08/9185 1278), based in Karratha, runs two- to four-day tours through the Pilbara, including Millstream–Chichester National Park, from $240.

Tom Price

WA's highest town, whose many young families produce a statistical average age of just eleven years, **TOM PRICE** is the officially approved, but less convenient, base for exploring the Hamersleys while Wittenoom's future is dithered over. The **tourist office** (Mon–Fri 8.30am–5pm; ☎08/9188 1112), on Central Road, organizes **tours** (daily; 1hr 30min; $12) of Hamersley Iron's mine.

The least expensive of the two **motels** is the *Mercure Inn* (☎08/9189 1101, fax 9189 1164; ⑦) on Central Road. Other than that the choice is a caravan at the *Tom Price Caravan Park* (☎08/9189 1515; on-site vans ③). The town also has a swimming pool, outdoor cinema and all the services you'd expect, including a couple of nondescript cafés near the **supermarket** (Mon–Fri 8am–6pm, Sat 8am–12.30pm, Sun 10am–1pm). No buses serve Tom Price, though there are daily flights to and from Perth.

Broome and around

"Slip into Broometime" is the well-worn local aphorism that captures the reclining tropical charm of **BROOME**, a popular and unexpectedly classy resort town of thirteen thousand people, which hangs on a drip of land over Roebuck Bay. William Dampier, the English buccaneer-explorer, passed the area in 1699 while on the run from an irate Spanish flotilla, and nearly two hundred years later the Djuleun Aborigines repelled an early fleet of prospective pastoralists. However, the imminent discovery of literally heaps of pearl shell soon led to the "**Pearl Rush**" of the 1880s and firmly set Broome on the colonial map of Australia.

It was actually the nacre-lined shells, or **mother-of-pearl**, rather than the pearls themselves, which brought brief fortune to the town. By 1910, eighty percent of the world's pearl shell, used in the manufacture of buttons, came from Broome, whose rich (though not always harmonious) ethnic mix developed at this time. "Chinatown" teemed with raucous and sometimes rioting Filipinos, Japanese, Arabs, Malays and Kupangers (from Timor), servicing the four hundred luggers and their crews involved in the dangerous business of diving for shells. While Broome's cemeteries steadily filled, perhaps one shell in a thousand produced a perfect example of the silvery pearls unique to this area.

Stagnation followed both world wars, although the Japanese, masters in the art of culturing pearls, invested in pearl-farming ventures around Broome's well suited coastal habitat. Things improved with the sealing of the coastal highway from Perth in the early 1980s and the philanthropic interest of the English businessman Alistair McAlpine, who fell for Broome and subsequently kicked off its renovation. Tasteful development and refurbishment have enhanced the town's oriental and pearling mystique, enhanced by the sweeping expanse of **Cable Beach**, **Gantheaume Point's** brick-red outcrops and the Indian Ocean's stunning turquoise hue. As word of the adjacent Kimberley's potential spreads, Broome's prosperity looks set to continue, something which will hardly disturb this laid-back, if pricey, tropical retreat for lotus-eaters.

Arrival and information

Buses arrive at the tourist office on the corner of Bagot Street and Broome Road where minibuses and taxis meet all arrivals. The **airport terminal**, round the corner on McPherson Street couldn't be more central, less than a kilometre west of Chinatown and a five-minute walk to the two main hostels. The **tourist office** (Mon–Fri 8am–5pm, Sat & Sun 9am–4pm; ☎08/9192 2222, fax 9192 2063) dishes out local guides and town maps to help you find your way around the dispersed and sometimes confusing layout of Broome.

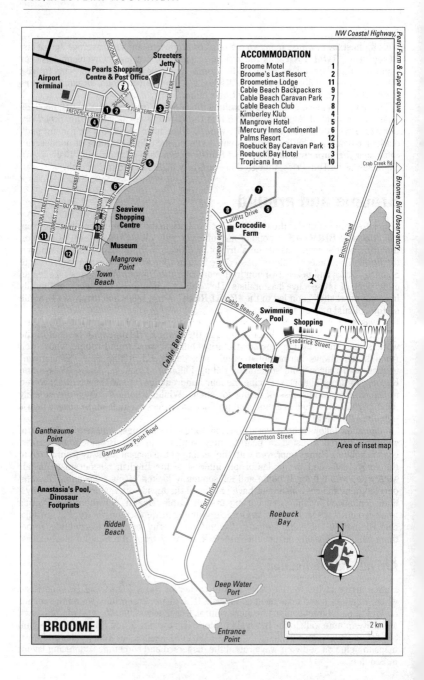

NW Coastal Highway,

Pearl Farm & Cape Leveque ▷

Broome Bird Observatory ▷

Broome Road

Crab Creek Rd ▷

ACCOMMODATION

Broome Motel	1
Broome's Last Resort	2
Broometime Lodge	11
Cable Beach Backpackers	9
Cable Beach Caravan Park	7
Cable Beach Club	8
Kimberley Klub	4
Mangrove Hotel	5
Mercury Inns Continental	6
Palms Resort	12
Roebuck Bay Caravan Park	13
Roebuck Bay Hotel	3
Tropicana Inn	10

Streeters Jetty

Pearls Shopping Centre & Post Office

Airport Terminal

FREDERICK STREET

Seaview Shopping Centre

Museum

Mangrove Point

Town Beach

Crocodile Farm

Lullfitz Drive

Cable Beach Road

Cable Beach Rd

Swimming Pool

Shopping

CHINATOWN

Frederick Street

Cemeteries

Cable Beach

Area of inset map

Gantheaume Point

Gantheaume Point Road

Clementson Street

Anastasia's Pool, Dinosaur Footprints

Riddell Beach

Port Drive

Roebuck Bay

N

Deep Water Port

BROOME

0   2 km

Entrance Point

Accommodation

Most of the **hotels** are in the southern part of town, and the **hostels** congregate around Chinatown, with self-contained apartments in between.

Hotels

Broome Motel, 51 Frederick St (☎08/9192 7775, fax 9192 7772, free call ☎1800/683 867). Central location just 5min walk from the airport with self-contained rooms sleeping three. ⑥.

Eco Beach, Cape Villaret (☎08/9192 4844, fax 9192 4845, free call ☎1800/636 414). Situated by an effectively private beach 30km across Roebuck Bay, this network of breezy elevated cabins is an affordable wilderness retreat that you won't want to leave. Bathrooms are shared but with all meals paid for, it'll cost less than most Broome motels. Day visits from Broome around $60. ⑤.

Mangrove Hotel, Carnarvon St (☎08/9192 1303, fax 9193 5169, free call ☎1800/094 818). Very comfortable and well positioned on a rise overlooking Roebuck Bay. ⑦–⑧.

Mercury Inn–Continental, corner of Weld and Hamersley sts (☎08/9192 1002, fax 9192 1715, free call ☎1800/094 822). Plush hotel right on the bay with a good restaurant and pool area. ⑧.

Palms Resort, Hopton St (☎08/9192 1898, fax 9192 2424, free call ☎1800/094 848). Large resort taking up a whole block, with three pools, two restaurants and bars; close to the town beach and Seaview Shopping Centre. ⑦–⑧.

Tropicana Inn, corner of Saville and Robinson sts (☎08/9192 1204, fax 9192 2583). Least expensive of the good motels, right opposite the Seaview Shopping Centre and close to the town beach. ⑦.

Hostels and caravan parks

Broome Bird Observatory, Crab Creek Rd (☎08/9193 5600, fax 9192 2063). Secluded camping 25km from town on Roebuck Bay. Chalets ④, rooms ②–③.

Broome's Last Resort, Bagot St (☎08/9193 5000, fax 9193 6033, free call ☎1800/801 918). Deafening rock music as you check in adds up to a sometimes too lively "18–30s" feel. Pool, bar, bikes, free beach runs, coin-operated lockers and air-con. Rooms ③, dorms ①.

Broometime Lodge, 59 Forrest St (☎ & fax 08/9193 5067 or free call ☎1800/804 322). Hostel/motel hybrid with private rooms but a communal atmosphere, suitable for older backpackers able to wash their own dishes and weary of snorers and early morning rucksack rustlers. Big kitchen, small pool, free pick-ups and drop-offs. Offers weekly rates. ④.

Cable Beach Backpackers, Lullfitz Drive, (☎08/9193 5511, fax 9193 5532, free call ☎1800/655 011). A change from the sometimes rowdy central Broome alternatives. Ten minutes from Cable Beach. ①.

Cable Beach Caravan Park, Millington Rd (☎08/9192 2066). Cable Beach's only caravan park, 2km from the beach.

Kimberley Klub, Frederick St, opposite *Broome Motel* (☎08/9192 3233, fax 9192 3530). Purpose-built, "offer-it-all" backpackers' resort about as good as they get. Spacious and breezy layout with volleyball, landscaped pool, email, bikes, coin-op air-con, bar and meals – all for fifteen bucks a night. Rooms ③, dorms ①.

Roebuck Bay Caravan Park, Walcott St (☎08/9192 1366). The best-located caravan park in town, right next to the small town beach and Seaview Shopping Centre. Bike rental available. On-site vans ③.

The Town and around

Broome first flourished around the old port area in **Chinatown**, which once accommodated a lively mix of pearl-divers and seamen. This old Asiatic quarter has seen the most concentrated reconstruction of original buildings, with street signs in five languages and payphones topped with jaunty Chinese roofs. Modern boutiques and cafés occupy most of the buildings, but Sun Pictures (see "Nightlife and events" on p.661) on Carnarvon Street, which opened in 1916 (making it as old as Hollywood itself), is one of the oldest "walk-ins" still in use today. During the daytime you can take in the virtually unchanged interior and see photographs showing the segregated seating codes of the old days. At the end of the street is the new **post office** and the Pearls **shopping centre**, though there's a better one 2km away on the way to Cable Beach (see below). The dilapidated Streeter's Jetty runs into the mangroves off Dampier Terrace; the terrace hosts several **pearl dealers** operating from former warehouses.

A walk down Hamersley Street, past the 1888 courthouse on the corner of Frederick Street, leads to what was the rich end of the old town, where masters and merchants once lived in splendid, airy bungalows such as **Captain Gregory's House**, now a brewery near the junction with Carnarvon Street. Next door, Matso's Store (daily 10am–5pm) displays local artwork and is a cool place for an outdoor lunch.

Next to the now-superseded Seaview Shopping Centre (daily 8am–6pm), the Customs House houses the local **museum** (May–Nov Mon–Fri 10am–4pm, Sat & Sun 10am–1pm; Dec–April daily 10am–1pm; $3). Naturally focusing on the town's maritime traditions, and with a pleasing "junk shop" appearance, it could easily occupy a couple of hours. Round the back, the old **Pioneer Cemetery** overlooks **Town Beach**, the nearest to the town centre. From the jetty, very low tides reveal the remains of Dutch sea planes bombed by the Japanese in 1942. This is also the best vantage point for observing the **"Staircase to the Moon"**, the overrated lunar reflections in the mud flats, which occur for a few nights each month, around the full phase of the moon. Dates and precise times for the "Staircase" can be obtained from the tourist office.

Gantheaume Point and Cable Beach

The outskirts of Broome offer a number of interesting attractions, and a full day could be spent cycling along the following route, which ends at Cable Beach, 6km from town on the ocean side of the peninsula. The town's **bus service** ($2.50) runs daily between the town and Cable Beach, via most of the town's accommodation centres, and finally returns outside the *Cable Beach Club* at 6.15pm. Timetables are available at the tourist office or in the town guide.

Just past the turning for Cable Beach, off Frederick Street, is the old **cemetery** from the pearling years. The Japanese section's enigmatic headstones (refurbished by an anonymous philanthropic countryman) testify to the nine hundred lives lost in the hazardous search for mother-of-pearl. The 1908 cyclone alone cost the lives of over 150 men, five percent of the workforce at that time. The Chinese cemetery next door is less cared for, and the Muslim and Aboriginal graveyards at the back are barely distinguishable.

Continuing down Port Drive for 5km, a right turn onto the nine-kilometre dirt road section leads to **Riddell Beach**. Walk right along the shore, past the outcrops weathered by eons of wind and water, to **Gantheaume Point**, where the dark red sandstone formations contrast sharply with the pearly-white expanse of Cable Beach stretching north. The old **lighthouse** is now a beacon, but the **pool** built by the former keeper for his disabled wife, Anastasia, remains among the tidal rocks. A cast of some 120-million-year-old **dinosaur footprints** is set in the rocks – the originals are out to sea and only visible at extremely low tides. More dinosaur footprints were found on Aboriginal land north of Cable Beach in 1996, but despite secrecy surrounding their discovery they were bizarrely cut out of the rock and stolen. Casts of the prints can be seen at the *Broomtime Lodge*.

Named after the nineteenth-century telegraph cable which came ashore here, **Cable Beach** extends for an immaculate 22km north of Gantheaume Point. Cars are permitted onto the beach north of the rocks, near the access ramp, but note that several cars a year are caught by up to ten-metre **tides** around Broome's beaches: on Cable Beach's flat sands it can come in very fast. The area north of the rocks is also designated a free (nudist) beach. A **kiosk** overlooking the beach serves basic meals, as does the *Diver's Camp Tavern* and bottle shop, on Cable Beach Road. Windsurfers and sailboards are available on the beach during the season.

Crocodiles and birds

Broome is loosely regarded as the very westernmost limit of saltwater **crocodiles**. The **Broome Crocodile Park** (April–Oct Mon–Sat 10am–5pm, Sun 2.30–5pm; Nov–March Sun–Fri 3.30–5pm, closed Sat; guided tours at 3pm; $10), on Cable Beach Road, can show you hundreds of these fascinating beasts at close quarters.

Roebuck Bay, on Broome's eastern flank, is on the flight path for thousands of migratory wading birds – a third of Australia's species have been seen here. The **Broome Bird Observatory** (☎08/9193 5600; $2), 25km from town (last 9km is dirt road) welcomes day and overnight visitors (see "Accommodation" on p.659). There are walks through the bushland around the observatory, with tours and courses also offered for those interested in local fauna, feathered or otherwise.

Eating and entertainment

Not surprisingly, the food in Broome is distinctly oriental in flavour. The customary fast-food outlets and a couple of health-food shops are also prominent, while some hotels have their own very reputable **restaurants**.

Bloom's Gourmet Deli and Café (8.30am–late), on Carnarvon Street, is the only classy coffee shop for 2000km either way, with an airy jarrah interior, great drinks and snacks. Over the road there's a small food hall in Johnny Chi Lane featuring Italian and Asian outlets and next to the *Shell Roadhouse* on Hamersley Street are a couple of takeaways: *Noodlefish* does Thai food and their soups are a meal in themselves. A further option, at 12 Napier Terrace, is the *Sheba Lane Garden Restaurant*, specializing in fish dishes all prepared by a French chef.

For a proper **meal**, the hard-to-find *Tea House* (Mon–Sat from 6.30pm; closed in the wet season), tucked in the car park on Dora Street opposite Saville Street, serves authentic Thai cuisine and at around $15 a head it's worth the search. For Chinese food, *Chin's*, opposite the *Shell Roadhouse* on Hamersley Street, is the least expensive of the good places, though the service and decor aren't up to much. With its verandah, *Murray's*, on Dampier Terrace, is a much better-looking place for Asian and seafood dishes. The *Piccolo Piazza*, in the Pearls Shopping Centre near the post office does pasta, steaks and seafood. Out at the fancy *Cable Beach Club* resort there are no less than five restaurants to tempt you and turn your wallet inside out; the least expensive is *Lord Mac's* which offers ocean views with your burgers, salad and pasta. Closer to town, *Charters*, at the *Mangrove Hotel* on Carnarvon Street is the best of the hotel restaurants and also has views of the ocean.

Nightlife and events

Broome's raging **pub** is the *Roebuck Bay Hotel* on Napier Terrace, with live entertainment, happy hours and garage bands. The least rough of the three bars here is the *Pearlers' Rest. The Divers' Camp Tavern* at Cable Beach comes a close second and usually gets the bands after the "*Roey*". Two **nightclubs** are to be found in Chinatown: the *Nippon Inn* on Dampier Terrace and *Tokyo Joes* round the corner on Napier Terrace, with banks of pool tables. If you prefer **real ale** to tinned lager pay a visit to the Broome Brewery next to Matso's Store at the end of Hamersley Street where all sorts of local fermentations await you. But for a uniquely "Broometime" experience, Sun Pictures walk-in cinema in Chinatown is a real treat. Watch the latest **movies** while mosquitoes nibble your ankles and the odd light aircraft comes in low across the screen.

The tourist office promotes various events, such as the **Broome Fringe Arts Festival**, held in early June, a celebration of local artiness and culture. However, the big one is the **Shinju Matsuri**, or Festival of the Pearl, in late August or early September – it lasts over a week and attracts people from all over the country. The town celebrates its ethnic diversity, and the pearl which created it, with the crowning of the Pearl Queen and a beach concert, finishing up with a huge fireworks display. Broome gets packed out for the Shinju, so unless you want to end up camping miles away, book your accommodation in advance. Exact dates for both festivals can be checked with the tourist office.

Listings

Airlines Ansett, Pearls Shopping Centre, Chinatown (☎08/9193 6855).

Bicycle rental and repair Broome Cycle Centre, corner of Hamersley and Frederick sts (☎08/9192 1871).

Bookshop Kimberley Bookshop, 6 Napier Terrace. The best bookshop between Darwin and Perth. There are heaps of secondhand books at the shop in the Pearls Shopping Centre, Chinatown.

Car rental, camping and Outback equipment Besides the big companies, try Broome Car Rentals, who deliver the car to you (free call ☎1800/676 725), or Woody's, Dampier Terrace (☎08/9192 1791) who both do local runabouts and offer some of the cheapest 4WDs in town. Kimberley Camp Hire, Frederick St (☎08/9193 5354), opposite the *Kimberley Klub*, has all you need to rent or buy for an expedition to the Kimberley plus 4WD Budget and Britz campervans and plain Land Cruisers from $120, plus km charge. Ask about one-way rental to Kununurra or Darwin.

Hospital Weld St, near Anne St (☎08/9192 1401).

Motorbike and scooter rental Roadrunner Motorcycle Hire, 7 Farrell St (☎08/9192 1971).

Police ☎08/9192 1212.

Post office Carnarvon St, WA 6725 (☎08/9192 1020).

Taxi ☎08/9192 1133.

Tours Broome Day Tours (free call 1000/001 000) organizes daily three-hour historic tours, plus trips out to Willie Creek Pearl Farm (see below); Ships of the Desert (☎08/9192 2222) has sunset camel rides along Cable Beach; Broome Aviation (☎08/9192 1369) and King Leopold Air (☎08/9193 7155) offer scenic flights over the region. Also more unusual jaunts on Harleys, helicopters and hovercrafts – enquire at the tourist office. For excursions to the Kimberley, Flak Trak Tours (☎08/9192 1487) has 4WD tours for small groups, including one-day Cape Leveque and four-day West Kimberley/Gibb River Road tours; Last Resort Adventure Tours (☎08/9193 5000) offers two-day backpackers' tours of the West Kimberley; Pearl Coast 4WD Tours (☎08/9193 5786) has two-day West Kimberley or Cape Leveque tours; Regional Safari (☎08/9192 1198) organizes various small group 4WD tours deep into the Kimberley lasting from three to fifteen days.

The Dampier Peninsula and Cape Leveque

About 10km outside Broome, just after the turn-off for the Bird Observatory, a road leads north to the Aboriginal Lands of the northern Dampier Peninsula. Continuing down this turn-off you soon come to the Willie Creek Pearl Farm (see below) but after this you're best off arming yourself with a 4WD campervan, or better still *someone else's* 4WD, as the 200km Cape Leveque track is as rough as they come. If you plan staying at any of the three Aboriginal communities on the Cape, booking in advance is essential.

Willie Creek Pearl Farm and the Western Peninsula

Thirty-five kilometres north from Broome (follow the signs) the **Willie Creek Pearl Farm** (June–Sept daily 9.30am–12.30pm & 1.30–4.30pm; Oct–May Mon & Tues, Thurs & Fri, Sun same times; $15) is housed in a beautiful building on Willie Creek. In the creek, racks of seeded oysters hang for two years at a time, building layers of pearlescent nacre over their implants as they feed from the tidal nutrients. The fact that this process takes half the normal time is what makes the Dampier Peninsula's environs so suitable for pearl cultivation. The mysteries of this fascinating and once highly secretive process are explained by informative **tours** (up to three daily). Broome Day Tours (☎08/9192 1068) offers daily visits to coincide with the guided tours.

Continuing past the Willie Creek turn-off leads to a dead end coastal track with a number of short turn-offs to basic beach campsites (three days maximum stay). Popular with fishermen, they can make for a few tranquil days camping to which you best come fully equipped as there are no facilities whatsoever. The first of these is **Barred Creek**, passing through a sandy section in which most 2WDs get stuck. Take your pick of the cleared spots dotted either side of the creek mouth. A few kilometres up the coast is **Quondong Point** overlooking the low red cliffs and a white rocky beach below. **Price Point**, after another 10km, is often considered the pick of the points. Continue a few hundred metres past the signed turn-off to the point and you'll find a ramp giving easy access to the beach and numerous coves below. Just be sure you know how far the tide is coming up if you spend the night. After Price Point the track continues close to the cliff edge with views to the ocean but in early 1999 was blocked a few kilometres before **Malari** or Coulomb Point as a result of erosion from the preceding Wet. From here it's around 55km back to the Cape Leveque road.

The Road to Cape Leveque

By no means a scenic drive and an infamously vehicle-destroying track, the **Cape Leveque** road continues wide and corrugated to the Aboriginal community of **Beagle Bay** (entry $5), 120km from Broome. The highlight here is the **Sacred Heart Church**, built by German missionaries in 1917, a beautiful building with an unusual altar decorated with mother-of-pearl. After Beagle Bay the track gets narrower and sandier and once you've travelled a further 35km you'll reach the turn-off leading, after another 35km, to **Middle Lagoon** (☎08/9192 4002; bookings essential), a lovely white-sand cove with camping, basic shelters (②) and four-berth cabins (⑤). The bay offers sheltered swimming and good snorkelling over the reefs at each point. Up the road another 20km or so is **Lombadina/Djarindjin** (☎08/9192 4942; entry $5), a community divided by religion and alcohol. In Lombadina/Djarindjin (follow the signs) you'll find spotless homes, cabins (⑤), fuel and 4WD access to the beach over banks of soft sand. The wide shallow bay before you is again ideal for safe swimming, and with Lombadina's mixed reputation, something you'll likely have to yourself when other places are busy.

A stay at the very popular **Kooljaman** (☎08/9192 4970, fax 9192 4978; beach shelters ②, cabins ⑤, units ⑤, fuel, small shop, restaurant), at the tip of Cape Leveque, is the reason why you've endured the last 220km; as long as the car survived no one leaves here disappointed. Situated right on the "sunrise" beach, the paperbark **cabins** and **beach shelters** (basically shade, a windbreak and a barbie) are the pick of the accommodation – fancier four-berth tent-based accommodation (⑧) has just been added up the hill. Generally, come well prepared, Kooljaman is no $200-a-night upmarket wilderness experience.

From Kooljaman you can try fishing, mudcrabbing and bushtucker **tours** (ask a local) with the local Bardi people or follow the very sandy track down to Hunter Creek. You'll find the "sunset" beach on the western side of the point a bit exposed for swimming but usually deserted, and at dusk the low red sandstone cliffs glow warmly. If you don't fancy driving up to Kooljaman there are tours available from Broome as well as **flights** – an experience in itself. The airstrip is a short walk from all accommodation. Ask at the Broome tourist office for a schedule.

The community at **One Arm Point** facing the myriad isles of the Buccaneer Archipelago has no accommodation and is diffident about receiving outsiders, it's best to ask around first.

The Kimberley

A highland area between Derby and Kununurra that's about the size of Poland, **The Kimberley** is commonly described as Australia's last frontier. Divided by ranges and seasonally huge rivers, it is a wilderness of marginal cattle stations and small, isolated Aboriginal communities, with a ragged, tide-swept coastline inhabited chiefly by crocodiles. The extreme seasons and harsh terrain make access slow and difficult – for those who live here, light aircraft are a necessity rather than an indulgence.

With the demise of the beef industry (for more on which, see the box on p.553) in a region racked by floods and bushfires, many stations are opening up to adventure tourism, and there is talk of turning the whole area into a vast national park. There is little else here: even the exploitation of minerals known to exist in the northwest of the region is made barely economical by the climate and isolation, and this alone says a lot about the Kimberley's remoteness. The road between Fitzroy Crossing and Halls Creek was the last section of the circumcontinental Highway 1 to be sealed, in the mid-1980s.

The region, particularly the barely accessible **Drysdale River National Park**, has many examples of the unusual Wandjina-style rock paintings, which depict rows of mouthless beings with owl-like heads, or the slender Bradshaw figures, thought to be much older. **Tours** of the Kimberley operate from Broome, Fitzroy Crossing (see below), Halls Creek (see p.667) and, most conveniently, from Kununurra (see box on p.670), along the **Gibb River Road** and to the popular **Bungle Bungles**. It would take a lifetime to get to know the whole of this immense wilderness, but that in itself is the very nature of the Kimberley's untameable appeal.

Derby to Fitzroy Crossing

Situated 36km north of the coastal highway on a flat spur of land jutting into the mud flats of King Sound, **DERBY** is a mineral exploration base and an administrative centre for local Aboriginal communities. There's precious little reason for tourists to visit the town other than to refuel at the end of a **Gibb River Road** crossing or perhaps take a **scenic flight** over the West Kimberley coastline (from $130; ask at the tourist office). Without your own transport you'll find the spread-out town hard work to navigate.

The **tourist office** (Mon–Fri 8.30am–4.30pm, Sat 8.30–11.30am; ☎08/9191 1426) is on Clarendon Street, where **buses** also arrive. If you're desperate, **places to stay** include the *Spinifex Hotel* (☎08/9191 1233), the town's main **pub** with ultra-basic dorms (①) and small, budget motel rooms (④). With your own transport you'll be much more comfortable at the *West Kimberley Lodge* (☎08/9191 1031, fax 9191 1028; ④), at 17 Sutherland St, a guesthouse with shared facilities; or the *Derby Boab Inn* on Loch Street (☎08/9191 1044, fax 9191 1568; ④–⑤). There's a good **restaurant** at the *Boab*, but for something special (and expensive) try the *Wharf* seafood restaurant, out by the wharf (daily from 6.30pm; closed Jan & Feb), which also does takeaways.

The **Gibb River Road** (see p.671) starts just east of Derby and cuts straight across the Kimberley, rejoining the tarmac near Wyndham 667km further on. If you are heading east and want to see **Windjana Gorge** and **Tunnel Creek**, follow the Gibb River Road for 119km to the Windjana turn-off. From here you rejoin the Great Northern Highway after 123km. This section is no problem in dry weather in a 2WD and is more interesting (and only 30km longer) than following the highway to Fitzroy Crossing, 256km from Derby.

Since the pastoral expansion into the Kimberley late last century, **FITZROY CROSSING** has been a small travellers' rest stop and crucial ford across the still-troublesome Fitzroy River. Today it's little more than a roadhouse and "welfare town" serving

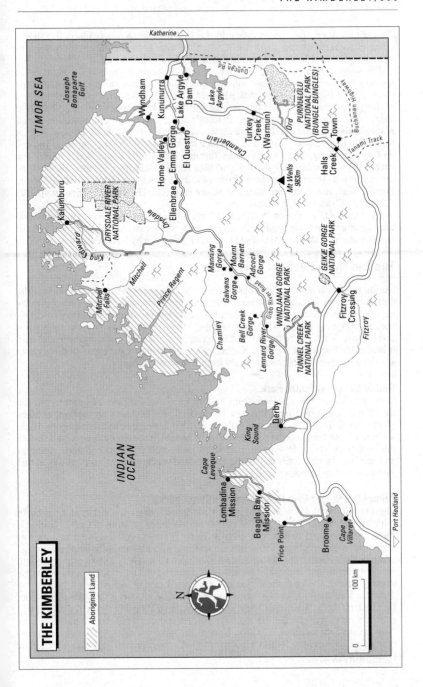

THE KIMBERLEY

Aboriginal Land

Katherine

TIMOR SEA

Joseph
Bonaparte
Gulf

Duncan Rd

Wyndham

Kununurra

Lake Argyle
Dam

Lake
Argyle

Turkey
Creek
(Warmun)

Ord

PURNULULU
NATIONAL PARK
(BUNGLE BUNGLES)

Old
Town

Buchanan Highway

Home Valley

Emma Gorge

El Questro

Chamberlain

Tanami Track

Kalumburu

Ellenbrae

Drysdale

DRYSDALE RIVER
NATIONAL PARK

Mt Wells
983m

Halls
Creek

King Edward

Manning
Gorge

Mitchell

Mount
Barnett

Galvans
Gorge

Adcock
Gorge

GEIKE GORGE
NATIONAL PARK

Mitchell
Falls

Prince Regent

Chamley

Bell Creek
Gorge

Gibb River Road

WINDJANA GORGE
NATIONAL PARK

Fitzroy
Crossing

Lennard River
Gorge

TUNNEL CREEK
NATIONAL PARK

Fitzroy

INDIAN
OCEAN

Derby

King
Sound

Cape
Leveque

Lombadina
Mission

Beagle Bay
Mission

Price Point

Broome

Cape
Villaret

Port Hedland

N

0   100 km

the region's Aboriginal communities. In the Dry it's a bleak, dusty place, the river a string of pools, but during a good Wet, when the town is frequently cut off, water laps just under the road bridge and the land is flooded for miles around.

The town itself has nothing of interest; a Friday-night session at the century-old *Crossing Inn* on Skuthorpe Road will give you the most memorable experience of the place. The *Fitzroy River Lodge* (☎08/9191 5141, fax 9191 5142; ⑧), on the highway east of the bridge, caters comfortably for passing tours. It has **motel rooms**, bushland lodges (or "canvas accommodation modules") and grassy campsites, as well as a pool, **restaurants** and a bar. *Darlngunaya Backpackers* (☎08/9191 5140; ①) on Russ Road is situated in the old post office, around which the settlement originally grew. If you call up they'll meet your bus, which comes through in the early hours. The *Crossing Inn* (☎08/9191 5080; cabins ⑥) also has tent sites and the obligatory counter meals, while the neglected *Tarunda Caravan Park*, next to the **supermarket/post office** on Forrest Road, has cheap tent sites and on-site vans (③). The **tourist office** (☎08/9191 5355) is on Flynn Drive, by the roadhouse.

The local CALM office (☎08/9191 5121) organizes the least expensive tour of Geikie Gorge National Park for around $20, and also offers other day-tours. There's a five-hour Danggu Heritage Aboriginal cruise (☎08/9191 5355) run by local Aborigines for $75.

The Devonian Reef national parks

During the Devonian Era, 350 million years ago, a large barrier reef grew around the then-submerged Kimberley plateau. The limestone remnants of this reef are today exposed north of Kununurra and in the national parks of **Geikie Gorge**, **Tunnel Creek** and, most spectacularly, **Windjana Gorge**. These three attractions are sometimes erroneously described as the "West Kimberley", but they are just a dramatic and easily accessible fraction of the West Kimberley's many natural spectacles. All three parks are closed and periodically submerged from November to April.

Geikie Gorge National Park

Seventeen kilometres upstream from Fitzroy Crossing, the river has carved out the five-kilometre **Geikie Gorge** through the exposed reef, best seen on the **boat cruises** (April–Nov daily 8am & 3pm; ☎08/9191 5121; $15) lasting one and a half hours. High-water marks on the gorge's walls clearly show how high the river can rise, while below the surface harmless freshwater crocodiles jostle with freshwater-adapted stingrays and sawfish. Walking trails lead along the forested western banks, strategically dotted with picnic sites, barbecues and campsites.

Tunnel Creek and Windjana Gorge national parks

Along the highway, 42km west of Fitzroy Crossing, a well-graded dirt road turns north to follow the Napier Range (as the reef is known here) to **Tunnel Creek National Park** (no camping), 105km from Fitzroy. Here Tunnel Creek has burrowed its way under the range, creating a 750-metre tunnel hung with bats and with who-knows-what in the pools. Although the collapsed roof illuminates the cavern halfway, the wade into progressively deeper and colder water to the other end still takes some nerve – it helps to carry a torch and wear shoes that you don't mind getting soaked.

A hundred years ago the caves were the hideout for a Bunuba Aborigine, Jandamarra (better known as **Pigeon**), and his gang of bushrangers. A police tracker for many years, one day he shot the officer at nearby Lillimoorla police station (now a ruin 2km south of Windjana Gorge) and released all the prisoners. A three-year spree of banditry followed before Pigeon was cornered and killed by fellow trackers in 1897.

SOME REMOTE SHORT CUTS

Three long-distance Outback tracks converge near Halls Creek, each giving you a taste of remote Outback dust. The **Tanami Track** is signposted off the highway, 17km west of town, indicating 1040km to Alice Springs. The WA section can be rough and sandy, but after the NT border it's merely corrugated, and it's half the distance of the sealed road. A turning at Carrunya Station leads to **Wolfe Creek Meteorite Crater**, the second biggest in the world, but not worth the 137-kilometre detour from the sealed highway unless you're coming from or going to Alice.

The road south of Halls Creek to the Old Town leads on to the **Buchanan Highway**, an old stock route that joins the Stuart Highway near Dunmarra (NT) – nearly 800km long, it gets even less traffic than the Tanami while lacking some of its flat monotony. Finally, you're unlikely just to drive down the **Canning Stock Route** to Wiluna on a whim. At 1860km (4WD only) it's the world's longest stock route and the ultimate challenge for well-equipped off-roaders.

The most dramatic remainders of the reef are the towering walls of **Windjana Gorge** (camping allowed), 135km from Fitzroy and 140km from Derby. A walking trail leads through a limestone crevice into a wide gorge splitting the Napier Range, lined with paperbark and Leichhardt trees. Freshwater crocs share the pools with various birds and can be seen sunning themselves in the afternoons.

Halls Creek

HALLS CREEK, strung out along the highway, has a much livelier appearance than its nearest neighbour, Fitzroy Crossing, 288km to the west. In 1885 WA's first **goldrush** took place in the hills south of town, 17km away, where the mud brick ruins of the **Old Town** continue to crumble. In less than four years the thousand prospectors succeeded in exhausting the area's potential, before stampeding off to new finds in the Eastern Goldfields.

There's precious little to see in town, but the gold-bearing hills to the southeast offer a few diversions for those with their own transport. **China Wall** is a block-like vein of quartzite looming over a toxic pool, 6km from town, which appears even more impressive from the air. **Caroline Pool**, 15km from town, is a bit muddy for swimming; **Palm Springs** and **Sawtooth Gorge**, a further 30km to the south, are scenically more appealing.

Practicalities

There's an **information centre** (May–Sept daily 8am–5pm; ☎08/9168 6262) off the main road in the middle of town. For **somewhere to stay**, the *Halls Creek Caravan Park* (☎08/9168 6169), Roberta Avenue, has tent sites, grim single cabins (①) and more spacious on-site vans (③). The *Shell Roadhouse* (☎08/9168 6060) has twin-share cabins (④), and the relatively salubrious *Kimberley Hotel* (☎08/9168 6101, fax 9168 6071), opposite the caravan park, has pokey bunkhouses (①) and motel units (⑥). It's also the only pub and decent **restaurant** in town, although there's a **bakery** on the highway. But for somewhere special head out to *The Lodge* by the Old Town (☎08/9168 8999; ④), a little oasis overlooking the spinifex-covered ranges, which glow at sunset.

If you fancy flying over the **Bungle Bungles**, call Oasis Air (☎08/9168 6462) or Kingfisher Air (☎08/9168 6162) a day or two in advance. The ninety-minute early-morning flights are the ones to go for, costing around $120. Alternatively, rent a 4WD for between $75 and $125 per day from the *Mobil Roadhouse* (☎08/9168 6164) on the highway. Halls Creek and Bungle Bungle Tours (☎08/9168 6060) offer various **tours**, including a day in the Bungles for around $130.

Purnululu (Bungle Bungles) National Park

The spectacular **Bungle Bungle** massif (officially known as **Purnululu National Park**; closed Jan–April; $11) is one of Australia's greatest natural wonders and a couple of days spent exploring its chasms and gorges is well worth the effort and expense involved. Brought to prominence ten years ago by a film crew documenting the ravages of overgrazing in the area, the Bungles have quickly attracted a mystique matching that of Uluru (Ayers Rock). The delicate nature of the banded rock domes, as well as the difficulty in patrolling the remote park, means that limiting land access to 4WDs saves money, the ecostructure of the park, and tourists' lives.

The **fly-drive tours** available in Halls Creek (see overleaf) and Kununurra (see box on p.670), which involve flying to the park's airstrip and then being driven around in a 4WD, offer the best of both worlds, and the half-hour **helicopter flights** ($160) available in the park get right into the gorges and will leave you grinning for hours – if you've ever wanted to fly in a chopper, save your money for the Bungles, you will not be disappointed. Helicopter flights are also available from Turkey Creek (see below) and Kununurra (see opposite).

From the highway it's a rough 55-kilometre, two-hour, 4WD journey to the **ranger's residence** (☎08/9168 7300), where the entry fee must be paid in return for a map. From here you can go to either of the two basic camps in the park. **Kurrajong Camp** is 10km to the north and gives access to **Echidna Chasm**, a one-hour return walk into a slender chasm a thousand metres long and half as high. **Frog Hole** is another, wider chasm with a pool at the end, while **Mini Palms** involves squeezing into yet another narrow gorge to a cave at the end, as part of a walk that takes at least two hours – take plenty of water and a torch. At any point on these walks you can look up and see palms clinging to the rock walls hundreds of metres above you; the scale of the clefts is underlined when you realize the palms can be up to 20m high.

Wilardi Camp (25km from the ranger's residence) is where tour groups stay. From here a track leads on to a cleared patch of ground used as a car park on the south flank of the plateau, site of the striped domes for which the Bungles are best known. The weathered, beehive-like domes have horizontal bands of silica (orange) and lichen (grey), together forming a fragile crust over the powdery interior, and are a most unusual sight. From here a half-hour walk leads into **Cathedral Gorge**, a huge overhanging amphitheatre with a seasonal pool whose rippled reflections flicker across the roof above.

Piccaninny Gorge is a hard, thirty-kilometre return walk for which you'll need large quantities of water. The ground underfoot is soft sand and shade is negligible during the day. Although there is a pool near the end, if you plan to walk up the gorge, leave very early in the morning and turn back long before your water runs out. There is an emergency hand-pump close to the car park.

On to Wyndham

Halfway between Halls Creek and Kununurra is the roadhouse at **TURKEY CREEK** (Warmun), where a helicopter (☎08/9169 1300) offers **flights** into the Bungles. A faster, though less exhilarating, enclosed "Jetranger" is used, but it's still a memorable way of seeing the domes.

From Turkey Creek the road continues directly north, passing the **Argyle Diamond Mine** (tours from Kununurra), source of a third of the world's diamonds – although most of them end up in industrial use. The scenery hereabouts takes on a rugged turn as you pass the **Ragged** and **Carr Boyd ranges** to the junction with the Victoria Highway. Kununurra is 46km to the east and Wyndham 51km northwest.

Strung out in three built-up areas along the muddy banks of the Cambridge Gulf, **WYNDHAM** was the port established to serve the brief goldrush at Halls Creek in the

1880s. The town was well positioned to process and export beef from the East Kimberley until the meat works closed in 1985, but with the expansion of the Ord River Irrigation Project (see below), the West Kimberley's only port could be set to thrive again. Until that day the town ticks over quietly, with the **Crocodile Farm** (May–Nov daily 8.30am–4pm; feeding time 11am; $7) and the **Five Rivers Lookout** from the top of the 335-metre Bastion Ranges the only things worth checking out, besides cheap **fuel** at almost urban prices. The **tourist office** (daily 8am–5pm; ☎08/9161 1054) is on O'Donnell Street, and you can **camp** at the *Three Mile Caravan Park* (☎08/9161 1064; on-site vans ②) on Baker Street or enjoy a bit more luxury at the *Wyndham Community Club* (☎08/9161 1130; ④) on the highway, 4km from town. The *Wyndham Town Hotel* (☎08/9161 1003; ⑥) on O'Donnell Street has **rooms**, backpackers **dorms** plus the town's one **restaurant** – the only choice for food besides the usual takeaways. On the way to Wyndham you'll pass a turn-off to the **Grotto**, where steps lead down to a small flooded gorge.

Kununurra and the Ord River

KUNUNURRA is the Kimberley's youngest town, built in the early 1960s to serve the **Ord River Irrigation Project**, fed by Lake Kununurra. The Diversion Dam Wall, an impressive sight as you come in from the west, created this lake, essentially the bloated Ord River. Fifty kilometres upstream is another dam, known as the Argyle Dam Wall, built in 1971 to ensure a year-round flow to the project, which has created **Lake Argyle**, the world's largest man-made body of water. Despite early problems, the Ord River Irrigation Project has recently moved on to something called Stage Two, expanding an intensive, yet still barely developed, agricultural area where cotton and sugar cane are set to transform the economy.

Perhaps because of its youth and the surrounding countryside, Kununurra escapes the resigned, rather jaded feel of the older Kimberley towns. Instead, the town has an appealingly relaxed atmosphere, enhanced by the copious amounts of fresh water nearby which lend themselves to recreational use. Besides being an ideal base from which to explore the adjacent Kimberley, the town is also a good place to seek out casual **farming work** from June to November – some of the hostels may be able to help in this respect.

A couple of kilometres from town is Kununurra's own national park, **Hidden Valley**, where a road leads into a narrow valley of "mini-bungles" and terminates with some short trails – you couldn't ask for a better walking area so close to town. Another popular spot is **Ivanhoe Crossing**, 13km north of town on the Ord River. Officially the ford is closed to vehicles and you wouldn't want to try crossing it in anything less than a hefty 4WD. This is croc country and, although locals still fish and bathe by the banks, it's inadvisable, being just the sort of habitual behaviour salties apparently go for. **Valentines Pool**, **Black Rock Falls** and **Middle Springs** are other popular spots in the area, though the water in all three gets pretty soupy towards the end of the Dry.

Triple J Tours (☎08/9168 2682) offers cruises up **Lake Kununurra** to **Argyle Dam** with optional return by bus, a much more enjoyable excursion than you might expect. Big Water Kimberley Canoeing Safaris (☎08/9169 1257 or free call ☎1800/641 998) organizes canoeing trips down the Ord River, driving you up to the dam and letting you float back over three days for $110 (plus camping gear). The Zebra Rock Gallery (daily 8am–6pm; free), 6km out of town on Packsaddle Road, has examples of the unusually banded rock found on an island in Lake Argyle, as well as a small wildlife park. In town, Warringarri Aboriginal Arts (Mon–Fri 8.30am–noon & 1–4.30pm; free), on Speargrass Road opposite the **Kelly's Knob** turn-off (a sunset-viewing spot), has displays of locally made arts and crafts which are for sale.

Practicalities

The **tourist bureau** (daily 8am–5pm; ☎08/9168 1177), on Coolibah Drive, has displays and videos on the area's many attractions, and details of all the tours that can take you there. There is a perennially warm **swimming pool** ($2) over the road, and the **post office** is also on Coolibah Drive. **Buses** arrive outside the Shire offices, passing through daily for Katherine and Darwin (NT) and Broome.

There are two **hostels** in town. The *Desert Inn* (☎08/9168 2702; ①) on Konkerberry Drive, close to the pub and supermarket, has twins, eight-bed air-conditioned dorms and a shaded pool and terrace. *Kununurra Backpackers* (☎08/9168 1711 or free call ☎1800/641 998; ①), 111 Nutwood Crescent, has a small pool, TV room and a section accommodating longer-term workers. Of the town's five **caravan parks**, the *Town* (☎08/9168 1763), on Bloodwood Drive, is the most central; the *Kona* (☎08/9168 1031) is by Lake Kununurra, west of town; and *Hidden Valley* (☎08/9168 1790), a kilometre north of town, has cheap campsites. The *Mercure Inn* (☎08/9168 1455, fax 9168 2622, free call ☎1800/642 244; ⑧), on the highway, is the town's best **motel**; you could try the cheaper *Hotel Kununurra* (☎08/9168 1344, fax 9168 1946, free call ☎1800/642 244; ⑥–⑦) on Messmate Way.

Places to eat include the *Kimberley Craft Café* on Banksia Street, *Valentino's* (daily 5–10pm) on Papuana Street for pizzas, or *Chopsticks Restaurant* (daily 6–9.30pm) at the *Country Club*, next to the *Hotel Kununurra*. *Gulliver's Tavern*, opposite the *Desert Inn*, gets the occasional band in the picking season, when the town gets fairly lively.

Lake Argyle

When the **Argyle Dam** was completed in 1972, the Ord River managed to fill Lake Argyle in just one wet season; along with the Victoria and the Fitzroy, these three rivers account for a third of Australia's freshwater run-off. The lake itself, which covers an area of nine hundred square kilometres, holds enough water to supply the world's population with a thousand litres each. The fish population has grown over the years to support commercial fishing, as well as providing ample food for the numerous birds that flock here. When the lake was proposed, the Durack family's Argyle Homestead was moved to its present site, 2km from the tourist village (see below), and is now a **museum** (May–Oct daily 8.30am–4.30pm; $2) of early pioneering life in the Kimberley, as described in Mary Durack's droving classic, *Kings in Grass Castles*.

Close to the dam wall, 70km from town, the old construction workers' camp has been turned into *Lake Argyle Tourist Village* (☎08/9168 7361; ⑤), offering camping

---

REGIONAL TOURS FROM KUNUNURRA

Kununurra is in the best position to offer a range of tours to the Bungles as well as the East Kimberley, and many operators are based here. The *Desert Inn* (free call ☎1800/632 533) offers two- to three-day Bungles and five-day Gibb River Road adventures, costing around $130 a day and leaving from both Broome and Kununurra. Kimberley Wilderness Adventure (free call ☎1800/804 005) runs 4WD tours throughout the region for around $140 a day for camping or $200 a day using homestead accommodation. East Kimberley Tours (☎08/9168 2213) has a whole raft of options from one day in the Bungles to an eleven-day see-it-all tour for over $2000 (including some flights). Belray Diamond Tours (☎08/9168 1014) visits the diamond mine in a day by road, air or with the Bungles thrown in from $150–285; ask at the tourist office or call Alligator Air (free call ☎1800/632 533) who have two-hour Bungle flights in high-wing aircraft for around $150 (no minimum numbers). Their six-hour Kimberley "The Works" flight ($320) includes a stop on the Mitchell Plateau and is one of the best scenic flights over the Kimberley but needs a minimum of four passengers; call in advance if you're heading for Kununurra.

and cabins. Lake Argyle Cruises runs a half-day trip across the lake to show you wallaby caves, jabirus and other birds, freshwater crocs and **Zebra Rock Island**.

The Gibb River Road

On the way to Wyndham you pass the start of the mostly unsealed **Gibb River Road** with its attendant warning sign. Originally built to transport beef to Wyndham and Derby, it cuts through the heart of the Kimberley, offering just a slice of this vast and rugged expanse. At around 670km to Derby, it's 230km shorter than the Great Northern Highway, but no one uses the "Gibb River" as a short cut. The route's notorious corrugations (as a rule, they're worst in the eastern half) depend a lot on the quality of your suspension but it's rare to get across without something breaking or falling off, and punctures are common. The attractions that make the route interesting – mostly gorges and their pools – are off the road and some are accessible only to robust, high-clearance vehicles, although, unless stated, a 4WD is not necessary in the places listed below. **Tours** are available from Broome (see p.662) and Kununurra (see p.670).

If you want to do some serious exploration of the Kimberley's remoter corners, ideally in a 4WD, the two Streetsmart **maps** entitled *West Kimberley* and *East Kimberley* are highly recommended. Distances given in brackets below are to destinations off the Gibb River Road.

Along the Cockburn Range to the Kalumburu Road junction

The scenically impressive 250-kilometre eastern section up to the Kalumburu junction is the roughest part of the road, crossing many ranges and crossed in turn by big rivers, the first of these being the **King River**, 17km from the sealed highway.

The turn-off for the plush mini-resort at **Emma Gorge** (1km; $5 day-use; ☎ & fax 08/9169 1777; ⑤), part of *El Questro Station*, leads to an "executive" bushcamp with shared facilities and a restaurant, bar and pool. There's a forty-minute walk along Emma Creek to the beautiful, fern-draped **gorge** which is worth the entry fee alone.

Further down the road, *El Questro Station* itself (16km; $5 day-use; ☎ & fax 08/9169 1777) is a blend of working cattle station, upmarket dude ranch and private national park. There are all sorts of station activities (at a price), including heli-fishing, gorge cruises, horseback- and camel-riding, use of dirt bikes and bullcatchers (stripped-down, armoured jeeps), but bargain **overnight deals** include some of the above, meals *and* pick-ups from Kununurra. Among the many attractions, the three-hour slog up to **El Questro Gorge** is straight out of an "Indiana Jones" movie. **Accommodation** includes secluded camping (with distant washing facilities), and bungalows with shared kitchens (⑤).

From the *El Questro Station* turn-off, the Cockburn Range's cliffs lead you to the stony **Pentecost River** crossing. Just east of the crossing, the Karunjie Track (4WD only) leads 45km back to Wyndham, crossing the lower King River. Eight kilometres after the Pentecost River crossing is *Home Valley Station* (1km; fuel; ☎08/9161 4322, fax 9161 4340; ⑤), another moribund cattle property finding better rewards in adventure tourism; as well as camping, they offer full-board lodgings. The same family also runs *Jack's Waterhole* (fuel, camping; $5 entry fee; ⑤) by the Durack River. From here until you reach the junction with the road up to Kalumburu (see overleaf) it's just wide-open Kimberley countryside recovering from the last bushfire. On the way, **Ellenbrae** station (5km; ☎08/9161 4325) has cheap camping and a lovely open-plan homestead (rooms ⑤) without a rattly air-con unit on-site.

Mount Barnett to Derby

From this point the road west is smoother and, from *Mount Barnett Roadhouse* (May–Oct daily 7am–6pm; ☎08/9191 7007; bungalows ④), which has the **last fuel** until Fitzroy Crossing (352km) or Derby (306km), there are a number of watered gorges and possibly waterfalls that you'll most likely have to yourself. You can camp at the

Manning Gorge for $5, or take an hour's walk to the multi-tiered Upper Manning Gorge (follow the beer-can markers on the far side of the pool).

Further down the road both Galvans (700m) and Adcock (5km) gorges are a bit gungy by comparison, but with the improved access track Bell Creek Gorge (30km, camping at 20km) is well worth some extra corrugations – the latter is the loveliest gorge along the Gibb River Road. Lennard River Gorge (8km; 4WD only), on the other side of the King Leopold Ranges, is a dramatic cleft carved through tiers of tilted rock.

A rock-chiselled profile of Queen Victoria's head is evident as you pass through the gap in the Napier Range, and 9km later a turn-off leads southeast to Windjana Gorge National Park (21km; see p.666) and Fitzroy Crossing (165km; see p.664). The last 62km to Derby is a sealed avenue of portly boab trees.

The Northern Kimberley

Though a common destination for four-wheel drivers in the Dry, the Northern Kimberley is a remote part of the region where a self-sufficient 4WD is essential. The main destination here is the beautiful, five-tiered Mitchell Falls, 240km off the Gibb River Road. You'll find the Kalumburu Road surprisingly smooth, with a store and fuel at *Drysdale River Homestead* (59km; April–Nov daily 8am–noon & 1–5pm; ☎08/9161 4326; units ④), which also has dinner and B&B at $80 per person. The Drysdale River National Park is tantalizingly inaccessible by private vehicle but the determined should call Darwin-based Willis Walkabouts (☎08/8985 2134), which operates bushwalking tours that sometimes include the park – access is by light plane, 4WD and helicopter, so it won't be cheap.

Kalumburu (276km; expensive fuel and store; ☎08/9161 4300; $25 entry permit) has the languorous feel of a dispersed African village, where ancient cars lie rusting and palms flap and sway in the tropical breeze. A mission set up in the nineteenth century by Benedictine monks still exists (tours available), and you can buy your permit on arrival from the community office (if there's anyone there). North of town along sandy tracks there are basic campsites at McGowans Beach (22km) and Honeymoon Beach (26km), the latter situated on a small bay and the better of the two.

travel details

Trains

Perth to: Bunbury (2–3 daily; 2hr); Kalgoorlie (1–2 daily; 7hr 30min); Port Augusta, SA (1 daily; 37hr); Sydney (2 weekly; 60hr).

Buses

Dampier–Karratha to: Perth (5 weekly; 21hr); Port Hedland (5 weekly; 4hr).

Kalgoorlie to: Adelaide (1 daily; 36hr); Esperance (3 weekly; 5hr); Leonora (2 weekly; 11hr); Perth (2–4 daily; 8hr).

Perth to: Adelaide (1 daily; 35hr); Albany (3 daily; from 6hr); Augusta (6 weekly; 6hr); Broome (5 weekly; 32hr); Bunbury (1–2 daily; 2hr); Carnarvon (5 weekly; 11hr); Dampier–Karratha (5 weekly; 21hr); Darwin (3 weekly; 56hr); Denham (for Monkey Mia; 3 weekly; 12hr); Derby (3 weekly; 37hr); Esperance (4 weekly; 10hr); Exmouth (6 weekly; 6hr); Fitzroy Crossing (3 weekly; 40hr); Geraldton (2–4 daily; 6hr); Halls Creek (3 weekly; 44hr); Hyden (for Wave Rock; 2 weekly; 5hr); Kalbarri (3 weekly; 8hr); Kalgoorlie (1–4 daily; 8hr); Kununurra (3 weekly; 49hr); Margaret River (3 daily; 5hr); Meekatharra (4 weekly; 10hr); Newman (3 weekly; 13hr); Port Hedland (1 daily; 25hr).

Flights

Perth to: Adelaide (2 daily; 4hr 15min); Alice Springs (5 weekly; 4hr); Ayers Rock Resort (3 weekly; 3hr 45min); Brisbane (3 weekly; 6hr 15min); Broome (1 daily; 2hr 30min); Darwin (1 daily; 6hr 15min); Esperance (2 daily; 1hr 50min); Kalgoorlie (1 daily; 1hr); Kununurra (6 weekly; 3hr 15min); Melbourne (1 daily; 5hr 15min); Sydney (1 daily; 6hr).

CHAPTER EIGHT

SOUTH AUSTRALIA

South Australia, the driest state of the driest continent, is split into two very distinct halves. The long-settled southern part, watered by the Murray River, and with **Adelaide** as a cosmopolitan centre, has been thoroughly tamed; the northern half, arid and depopulated, most definitely has not.

Most of southern – which is to say southeastern – South Australia lies within three hours' drive of Adelaide. Food and especially **wine** are among its chief pleasures: this is prime grape-growing and wine-making country. As well as its wineries the **Fleurieu Peninsula**, just south of Adelaide, has a string of fine beaches along the Gulf St Vincent coastline. Cape Jervis, at the peninsula's tip, is the departure point for ferries to sparsely populated **Kangaroo Island**, a fine place to see Australian wildlife at its unfettered best. Facing Adelaide across the Investigator Strait, the **Yorke Peninsula** is primarily an agricultural area, preserving a little copper-mining history and some great fishing. The superb wineries of the **Barossa Valley**, originally settled by German immigrants in the nineteenth century, are only an hour from Adelaide on the **Sturt Highway**, the main road to Sydney. This crosses the Murray River at Blanchetown and follows the fertile **Riverland** region to the New South Wales border. Following the **southeast coast** along the Princes Highway, you can head towards Melbourne via the extensive coastal lagoon system of the Coorong and enjoyable seaside towns such as Robe, exiting the state at **Mount Gambier** with its crater lakes. The inland trawl via the **Dukes Highway** is faster, but far less interesting. Heading north from Adelaide, there are old copper-mining towns to explore at Kapunda and Burra in the area known as the **mid-north**, which also encompasses the **Clare Valley**, a quieter, more down-to-earth wine centre and perhaps the southeast's most enjoyable.

In contrast with the gentle and cultured southeast, the remainder of South Australia – with the exception of the relatively refined **Eyre Peninsula** and its strikingly scenic west coast – is unremittingly harsh desert, a naked country of vast horizons, salt lakes, glazed gibber plains and ancient mountain ranges. Although it's tempting to scud over the forbidding distances, rewards from this introspective and subtle landscape develop slowly and you'll miss its essence by hurrying. For every predictable, monotonous highway there's a dirt alternative, which may be physically draining but enables you to get closer to this precarious environment. The folded red rocks of the central **Flinders Ranges** and **Coober Pedy**'s post-apocalyptic scenery are on most agendas and could be worked into a sizeable circuit, but overall the Outback lacks any real destinations. Making the most of the journey is what counts – the fabled routes to **Oodnadatta**, **Birdsville** and **Innamincka** are still real adventures, and not necessarily 4WD only.

Rail and road routes converge in Adelaide before the long cross-country hauls west to Perth via Port Augusta or north to Alice Springs and Darwin. The *Ghan* to Alice Springs is one of Australia's great train journeys; as is the *Indian Pacific* between Perth and Sydney, which passes through Adelaide – though if you hop on the eastbound train here, you'll have missed traversing part of the country, which is really the point of the journey.

Adelaide and the surrounding gulflands, cooled by the Gulf St Vincent, enjoy a Mediterranean **climate** that makes them tremendously fertile. As you head further north the temperature hots up to such an extreme that by Coober Pedy people live underground to escape the searing summer temperatures.

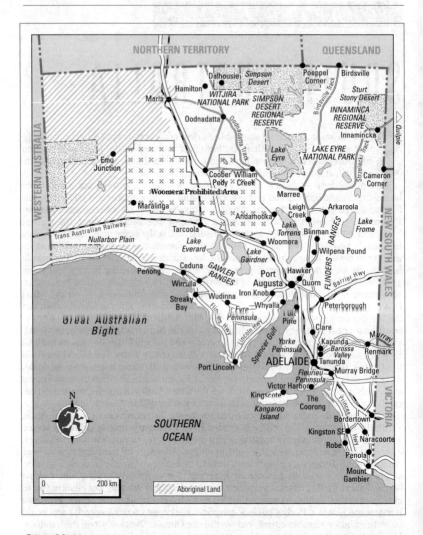

Some history

When South Australia was first settled by Europeans in 1836, it was home to as many as fifty distinct **Aboriginal groups**, with a population estimated at 15,000. Three distinct cultural regions existed: the Western Desert, the Central Lakes, and the Murray and southeast region. It was the people of the comparatively well-watered southeast who felt the full impact of white settlement, those who survived being shunted onto missions controlled by the government. Some Aboriginal people have clung tenaciously to their way of life in the Western Desert, where they have gained title to some of their land, but most now live south of Port Augusta, many in Adelaide.

The coast of South Australia was first **explored** by the Dutch in 1627. In 1792 the French explorer Bruni d'Entrecasteaux sailed along the Great Australian Bight before heading to southern Tasmania, and in 1802 the Englishman Matthew Flinders thoroughly charted the coast. The most important expedition, though – the one which led to the foundation of a colony here – was **Captain Charles Sturt**'s 1830 navigation of the Murray River from its source in New South Wales to its mouth in South Australia.

South Australia was planned from the start: in the idealistic scheme of the English entrepreneur Edward Wakefield, there were to be no convicts – instead free settlers would be sold small units of land (rather than given large free land grants) in a state guaranteeing them civil and religious liberty. The success of the scheme was guaranteed when George Fife Angas formed the **South Australia Company** to finance it. In 1836 **Governor John Hindmarsh** landed at Holdfast Bay, now the Adelaide beachside suburb of Glenelg, with the first settlers; the next year Colonel William Light planned a spacious, attractive city, with broad streets and plenty of parks and squares, some distance inland. By 1839, Angas was assisting persecuted Lutheran communities from the eastern provinces of Prussia to settle in South Australia.

Early problems caused by the harsh, dry climate and financial incompetence (the colony was bankrupt in 1841) were eased by the discovery of substantial reserves of **copper** over the next decade. By 1870 Adelaide's population had almost doubled. The tradition of **libertarianism** in South Australia continued; in 1894 its women were the first in the world to be permitted to stand for parliament and the second in the world to gain the vote (after women in New Zealand). Social improvement through slum clearances began after World War I. Of all the mainland states, the depressions and recessions of the interwar period hit South Australia the hardest. After World War II new migrants came, boosting the output of industry and injecting new life into the state.

The 1970s were the decade of **Don Dunstan**. The flamboyant Labor Premier, who died in January 1999, was an enlightened reformer who had a strong sense of social justice: he abolished capital punishment, outlawed racial discrimination and decriminalized homosexuality. The state has been a duller place since his retirement in 1979, and a poorer one since the recession started to have an effect at the end of the 1980s. Unemployment levels are still high.

ADELAIDE AND THE SOUTHEAST

Adelaide is very much the transport hub of the state, with all routes radiating from the city. There are good **bus** connections throughout the southeast, but more rewarding alternatives are worth considering. Much of the country is flat and great for **cycling**. The principal route is the newly developed **Mawson Trail**: 800km specifically planned for cyclists, extending from the Mount Lofty Ranges through the Barossa Valley and traversing the Flinders Ranges to the Outback town of Blinman. **Walkers** can follow a parallel route along the 1500-kilometre **Heysen Trail** starting at Cape Jervis and running up the coast of the Fleurieu Peninsula before heading north over the Mount Lofty Ranges to the Flinders, on the same tracks some of the way. Note that the Heysen trail is closed between December and April – partly due to the high risk of fire and partly as a result of an agreement with private landowners, through whose property some of the trail passes. Further information and maps for the trails is available from Information SA in Adelaide (see p.678).

Adelaide

ADELAIDE is always thought of as a gracious city and an easy place to live; despite a population of around one million and a slick veneer of sophistication, it still has the feel of an overgrown country town. It's a pretty place, laid out on either side of the **Torrens River**, ringed with a green belt of parks and set against the rolling hills of the **Mount Lofty Ranges**. During the hot, dry summer the parklands are kept green by irrigation from the waters of the Murray River on which the city depends; there's always a sense that the rawness of the Outback is waiting to take over.

The traditional way of life of the **Kuarna people**, the original occupants of the Adelaide Plains, had been destroyed within twenty years of the landing of Governor John Hindmarsh at Holdfast Bay in 1836. The Surveyor General for the colony, Colonel William Light, had visionary plans for the new city. After a long struggle with Hindmarsh, who wanted to build on a harbour, Light got his wish for a city on the western side of "the enchanted hills", with a strong connection to the river. In 1000, Light had fondly written of the Sicilian city of Catania: "The two principal streets cross each other at right angles in the square in the direction of north and south and east and west. They are wide and spacious and about a mile long", and this became the basis for the plan of Adelaide. Postwar immigration provided the final element missing from his plan – the human one: Italians now make up the biggest non-Anglo cultural group, and the café society they introduced adds spirit to the city.

In the Mediterranean-style hot, dry summers, alfresco eating and drinking are commonplace and lend the city a vaguely European air, with its wide, well-planned streets and squares transformed with a squint of the eye into boulevards. One of the chief delights of Adelaide is the interest its inhabitants take in **food** and **wine**, with restaurants and cafés as culturally varied as Sydney's and Melbourne's but much cheaper, and South Australian wine monopolizing every cellar. Unlike a European city, though, the centre is virtually deserted in the evening and on Sunday – except for a couple of lively thoroughfares. However, culture is held in high esteem, and the city comes to life every year with a festival: the **Adelaide Festival of Arts** (held on even years) or **Womadelaide** (odd years).

Outwardly conservative, Adelaide nonetheless has the advantage of South Australia's liberal traditions, with a nudist beach, relaxed drug laws and 24-hour hotel licences. It's the free and easy **lifestyle** within an ordered framework that's so appealing; Adelaide may not be an obvious destination in itself, but it's a great place for a relaxed break on your way up to the Northern Territory or across to Western Australia, with only daunting Outback and great distances ahead.

Arrival, information and city transport

Buses from out of town, including the airport bus, will drop you off at the **Central Bus Station**, 101–111 Franklin St, which, compared to bus terminals in other major cities, is very basic. The international **airport**, 7km southwest from the centre, is small, modern and easy to handle; there's a currency exchange and information booth. The domestic

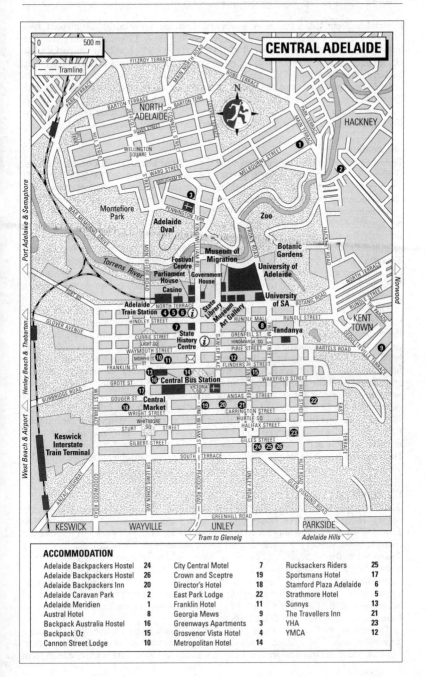

CENTRAL ADELAIDE

0 ——— 500 m

- - - Tramline

N

NORTH ADELAIDE

HACKNEY

Port Adelaide & Semaphore

Montefiore Park

Adelaide Oval

Zoo

Botanic Gardens

Torrens River

Festival Centre

Museum of Migration

University of Adelaide

Parliament House

Government House

Casino

University of SA

Adelaide Train Station

State Library

Museum

Art Gallery

Rundle Mall

KENT TOWN

Henley Beach & Thebarton

West Beach & Airport

Norwood

State History Centre

Tandanya

Central Bus Station

Central Market

Keswick Interstate Train Terminal

KESWICK

WAYVILLE

UNLEY

PARKSIDE

▽ Tram to Glenelg

Adelaide Hills ▽

ACCOMMODATION

Adelaide Backpackers Hostel	24	City Central Motel	7	Rucksackers Riders	25
Adelaide Backpackers Hostel	26	Crown and Sceptre	19	Sportsmans Hotel	17
Adelaide Backpackers Inn	20	Director's Hotel	18	Stamford Plaza Adelaide	6
Adelaide Caravan Park	2	East Park Lodge	22	Strathmore Hotel	5
Adelaide Meridien	1	Franklin Hotel	11	Sunnys	13
Austral Hotel	8	Georgia Mews	9	The Travellers Inn	21
Backpack Australia Hostel	16	Greenways Apartments	3	YHA	23
Backpack Oz	15	Grosvenor Vista Hotel	4	YMCA	12
Cannon Street Lodge	10	Metropolitan Hotel	14		

terminal is about half a kilometre southwest. Both are serviced by the **airport bus** (Transit Regency Coaches depart hourly between 6.20am & 9.20pm and every 30min at busier times; to book a return trip call ☎08/8381 5311; $6), which will drop you off at most city accommodation on request; its set route stops at Victoria Square and North Terrace, as well as the bus station. A taxi costs around $15 to either the city or the beachside suburb of Glenelg, 11km from the centre. Arriving by **train** at the Keswick Interstate Terminal, you can also take the airport bus, which stops here en route ($3 to city or airport), or walk to the suburban platform and catch a train into Adelaide Train Station on North Terrace. Taxis to the city from the Interstate Terminal charge about $8.

Information
The obvious first stop for information is the **South Australian Travel Centre**, at 1 King William St, on the corner of North Terrace (Mon–Fri 9am–5pm; ☎1300/366 770). Staff are very helpful at this large modern office, where masses of general information is displayed, including excellent, free touring guides and maps of Adelaide and the state. Tour and accommodation bookings are only dealt with over the telephone on the ☎1300 number above, which you can call for free from the centre; there's also a freephone service for enquiries about public transport routes and times – you'll need to queue for more specific enquiries. If you arrive by bus, head straight for the **Backpacker Transit and Travel Centre**, a bright pink building opposite the station at 110 Franklin St (daily 8.30am–6pm; ☎08/8410 3000). They can provide free maps and free luggage storage, book all domestic tours and rent bikes; there's also a currency exchange, telephone, a good notice board, and **Internet access** ($4 for 30min).

The government-run **Information SA**, 77 Grenfell St (Mon, Tues, Thurs & Fri 9am–5pm, Wed 9.30am–5pm; ☎08/8204 1900), sells the Department of Sport and Recreation's maps of the Heysen Trail, Mount Lofty walks and South Australian cycle routes; there are also some free maps and brochures. On the ground floor of the same building, the **Environment and Natural Resources Information Centre** (same hours; ☎08/8204 1910) has lots of information on national and conservation parks in and around Adelaide and the state. The **City of Adelaide Customer Centre**, a block south on 25 Pirie St (Mon–Fri 9am 5pm; ☎08/8203 7777) has a range of free maps viewing the city from an alternative perspective: the glossy fold-out *Art in Public Places Walking Guide* and the *City of Adelaide Green Map*, which details parks and gardens and points out ecologically-oriented and community-focused places. Some of these maps are also available at the South Australian Travel Centre and the Adelaide City Council **Information Kiosk** on Rundle Mall, whose opening hours can be unreliable (Mon–Fri 10am–5pm, Sat 10am–3pm, Sun 11am–4pm).

City transport
The city centre is compact enough to walk around, and its flatness makes this an easy option. There are two **free buses** that can help you get around the centre. The **Bee Line** (#99B) is a handy alternative that cuts out a lot of the legwork – it leaves from Victoria Square (every 5–10min Mon–Thurs 7.40am–6pm, Fri 7.40am–9.20pm; every 15min Sat 8.30am–5.30pm) and heads up King William Street to North Terrace, then along past the train station down the end of Hindley Street and back to Victoria Square along the same route. The **City Loop Bus** (same times; every 20min) is designed to be accessible for people with disabilities or burdened with prams, with ground-level access ramps; there are thirty stops taking in all the major cultural and commercial centres, beginning at Adelaide Train Station.

To explore further out of the city centre, you'll need to use the integrated **TransAdelaide** (TA) system, which comprises mainly buses but also includes suburban trains and one tramline from the city to Glenelg. Free timetables are available from the **Information Bureau TransAdelaide** (Mon–Sat 8am–6pm, Sun 10.30am–5.30pm) on the corner of King William and Currie streets, where staff can advise on routes and fares, as well as sell tickets, and you can pick up *The Metroguide*, a free information booklet including a handy map of the system. Timetable information and advice are also available by phone from Passenger Transport InfoLine (daily 7am–8pm; ☎08/8210 1000; *www.transadelaide.sa.gov.au*) or by using a freephone at the South Australian Travel Centre. Waits at stops – where times are not always displayed – can be long, making it all the more important to pick up the relevant timetables before setting out. However, as part of a drive to improve services and entice Adelaidians away from their preference for cars, TransAdelaide have introduced large blue information boards in the city centre showing timetables and routes; eventually there will be similar boards at all stops.

TransAdelaide buses and trains run until about 11.30pm, with reduced services at night and on Sunday. **Tickets** come in multi-trip, single-trip and day-trip permutations, and can be used on buses, trains and the tram. You can buy single train tickets from a ticket vending machine on board, as well as from station ticket offices and a machine outside the Information Bureau TransAdelaide. Single tickets range from $1.10 to $2.80, depending on whether it's peak or off-peak time, or whether a two-hour transfer is required. The day-trip ($5.40) is much easier and better value. Only multi-trip tickets cannot be bought on board buses or the tram but must be purchased, along with other tickets, from Information Bureau TransAdelaide (see above), train stations, post offices and some newsagents. **Night buses** run by two private bus companies operate on Saturday only: the most useful for travellers is MAC Nightmoves, with routes running from city nightspots (pick-up points outside *Heaven* and *The Planet* nightclubs; midnight to 4am; $6) to Reynella and Noarlunga via Brighton Road and Glenelg, and to the Adelaide Hills via Stirling and Aldgate; timetables and more details from the TransAdelaide office.

Four suburban **train** lines run from Adelaide Train Station, a modern complex with shops and cafés on North Terrace. **Violence** on trains does happen late at night, but the problem is being addressed by extra guards; if you're worried, buses are generally safer for night-time travel. The **tram** to seaside Glenelg (30min) leaves from Victoria Square every fifteen to twenty minutes. The **O-Bahn** is a fast-track bus which runs on concrete rails through scenic Torrens Linear Park, between the city (Grenfell St) and Tea Tree Plaza in Modbury, 12km northeast.

Cycling is a popular and excellent alternative: the flat city area and its wide, multi-laned streets make riding a breeze, and there are several good cycling routes – including the **Torrens Linear Park track**, which goes from the sea at Westbeach to the hills at Athelston, weaving along the river. A map of this and other cycling routes is available from Information SA (see opposite), and several other cycling route maps from the City of Adelaide Customer Centre (see opposite); for bike rental outlets, see "Listings", p.699.

Accommodation

The only time you may have difficulty finding accommodation is during the Arts Festival at the end of February and beginning of March (even years), and Womadelaide in late February (odd years), when you'd be well advised to book ahead. Most of the **hostels** are in the southwest quarter of the city or around the Central Bus Station on Franklin Street; there are cheap **hotel** rooms on Hindley Street, Adelaide's nightclub area and its tame answer to a red-light district, but it's much less pleasant, and some women may find it threatening. The swankiest accommodation is along North Terrace.

Adelaide has loads of **hostels**, competing to keep prices low and often throwing in free breakfasts and bed linen; average dorm rates are $14, while rooms range from

$30–44. Most are on Gilles or Carrington streets, about ten minutes' walk from the city centre, and will pick up from the bus or train station if you call them (several also send minibuses to scout for custom); and some will even come to the airport if you call in advance. Otherwise, buses #171 or #172 from Victoria Square stop close to Gilles Street. The most central **campsite** is the *Adelaide Caravan Park*, Bruton Street, Hackney, on the Torrens River 2km east of the centre (☎08/8363 1566; cabins ④, two-bed holiday units ⑤, villas with spas ⑥, on-site vans ③); it's right on the Torrens Linear Park cycling route and can be reached by bus #281 or #282 from North Terrace, or on foot through parkland and along the river. For a beachfront setting, head to *West Beach Caravan Park*, Military Road, West Beach (☎08/8356 7654; bus #276 or #278 from Currie St; cabins ④–⑤, on-site vans ③–④), or the *Adelaide Beachfront Tourist Park*, 349 Military Rd, Semaphore (☎08/8449 7726, fax 8449 5877, free call ☎1800/810 140; all cabins en-suite ④–⑤) which has a swimming pool, recreation room, playground and free shuttle bus service to West Lakes Mall and Ethelton train station; to stay at either you'll need to be prepared for the summertime hordes.

The seaside suburb of **Glenelg** and the nearby beach resorts (see p.690), about half an hour away by public transport, are good alternatives to the city, with a couple of the best hostels and plenty of self-catering apartments, and some life in the evening.

Hotels

Adelaide Meridien, 21 Melbourne St, North Adelaide (☎08/8267 3033, fax 8239 0275). Located on fashionable Melbourne Street, the modern brick building itself is an eyesore but creature comforts include a sauna, spa and outdoor pool, and undercover parking is included in the rates. ⑦.

Director's Hotel, 259 Gouger St (☎08/8231 3570, fax 8231 3505). Modern hotel aimed at executives, with pleasant, well-furnished self-catering studio apartments and standard rooms. A five-minute walk to Chinatown and the Central Market; very good value. 24hr reception and free parking. ⑥–⑦.

Grosvenor Vista, 125 North Terrace (☎08/8407 8888, fax 8407 8866). Genteel establishment dating from 1918, complete with potted palms in the foyer. Spacious, modern en-suite rooms with air-con. 24hr room service, gym and sauna, bar and bistro and undercover parking. ⑥–⑦, including breakfast.

Stamford Plaza Adelaide, 150 North Terrace (☎08/8461 1111, fax 8231 7572). This central, high-rise luxury five-star hotel has all you'd expect: swimming pool, sauna, three restaurants, room service and views of the Festival Centre. Room rates are in excess of $200, though cheaper weekend packages are available. There is also a beachside equivalent, the *Stamford Grand Hotel*, on the foreshore at Glenelg. ⑧.

Strathmore, 129 North Terrace (☎08/8212 6911, fax 8231 5475). Smart, small hotel in a desirable location. En-suite motel-style rooms are small and have no views, though they come with all mod cons from air-con to room service; free undercover parking. ⑥.

Pubs, motels and self-catering establishments

Austral Hotel, 205 Rundle St (☎08/8223 4660, fax 8223 4175). Basic rooms in one of Adelaide's best pubs in this "arty" street. Bands nearly every night, so it can be noisy. ③.

City Central Motel, 23 Hindley St (☎08/8231 4049, fax 8231 4804). Centrally located budget motel. ④.

Colley Motel Apartments, 22 Colley Terrace, Glenelg (☎08/8295 7535). Excellent-value, self-contained apartments with TV, fridge and kitchen, opposite the beach. Few frills but well equipped. ⑤.

Crown and Sceptre, 308 King William St (☎08/8212 4159, fax 8231 9169). Centrally located pub with inexpensive rooms upstairs (shared bathroom) and a common room with fridge and free tea and coffee. It's currently one of Adelaide's most popular drinking holes, with a young clientele and live music downstairs; good for socializers rather than sleepers. Free off-street parking. ②.

Franklin Hotel, 92 Franklin St (☎08/8231 4703). An unrenovated, quiet, working-men's pub virtually opposite the bus station; closes at 9pm so noise is never a problem. Clean, basic air-con rooms, and decent cheap meals available. ③.

Georgia Mews, 31–33 Wakefield St, Kent Town (☎08/8362 0600, fax 8362 1317). Just east of the city centre and within walking distance across the parklands, but close to the restaurants and cafés of The Parade in Norwood. Beautifully decorated, light and spacious one-bedroom apartments, with a shady, flower-filled courtyard, telephone, TV, outside laundry and car parking. Fully self-catering, and supplies for a hearty breakfast included. ⑦.

Glenelg Seaway Apartments, 18 Durham St, Glenelg (☎08/8295 8503). Falls into the cheap and cheerful category. Clean, spartan apartments, but with linen supplied. Friendly owner. ④.

Greenways Apartments, 41–45 King William Rd, North Adelaide (☎08/8267 5903, fax 8267 1790). One-, two- and three-bedroom fully furnished self-catering units in an excellent location. ⑥.

Meledon Villa, 268 Seaview Rd, Henley Beach (☎08/8235 0577). Good-value B&B one street back from the beach in a lovely turn-of-the-century two-storey building with a swimming pool and outdoor terrace. Downstairs rooms share bathroom while upstairs rooms, with balconies and sea views, are en-suite. ④–⑥.

Metropolitan Hotel, 46 Grote St (☎08/8231 5471, fax 8231 0633). Full of nineteenth-century charm downstairs, and with basic but clean rooms upstairs at bargain prices. Cheap singles too. Good-value bistro meals served downstairs. ③, including light breakfast.

St Vincent Hotel, 28 Jetty Rd, Glenelg (☎08/8294 4377, fax 8295 4412). Friendly, homely pub accommodation popular with country people visiting the city. Rooms are en-suite or with shared bathroom, and there is one self-contained flat. ④–⑤.

Sportsmans Hotel, 185 Grote St (☎08/8231 3250). Clean, simple rooms in a no-frills pub. An early-opening pub (5.30am–9pm), so the noise won't keep you awake at night. Close to the bus station. ③.

Taft Motor Inn, 18 Moseley St, Glenelg (☎08/8376 1233, fax 8294 6977). Well-equipped motel units and one- and two-bedroom self-catering apartments near the beach; all have air-con and slightly dreary old-fashioned decor. Good for families, with a playground, garden and swimming pool (and toddler pool); baby-sitting available. 24hr reception. ⑥–⑦.

Hostels

Adelaide Backpacker's Hostel, 263 Gilles St, annexe at no. 253 (☎08/8223 5680, fax 8223 1779). Long-established family-run hostel with 35 beds in two houses. Large, bright dorms and three doubles. Free tea and coffee. Helpful notice board, bike rental, and tours booked. Rooms ②, dorms ①.

Adelaide Backpackers Inn, 112 Carrington St (☎08/8223 6635, fax 8232 5464, free call ☎1800/247 725,). In a converted two-storey ex-pub, this place is shabby, but has a friendly ambience and helpful staff. Reception doubles as a travel agency (bus and train tickets). There are six- to twelve-bed dorms here and annexe accommodation across the road with plenty of singles and doubles in a brighter, more modern air-con building. Generous breakfast thrown in. Internet access. Rooms ③, dorms ①.

Albert Hall, 16 South Esplanade, Glenelg (☎08/8376 0488, fax 8294 1966). A peaceful beachfront Victorian Italianate style mansion (with its own ballroom), with three floors of crumbling grandeur in the ongoing process of being renovated – the outside, though, is beautifully painted. Common areas are rather shabby, though the small kitchen is well equipped. Six-bed dorms come with colourful duvets – the best dorm and room have access to the balcony with ocean views. There is also one self-contained split level double with its own entrance, en-suite bathroom, TV and kitchen. Good security. Rates include linen. Tours booked. Rooms ③–④, dorms ①.

Backpack Australia Hostel, 128 Grote St (☎08/8231 0639, fax 8410 5881). Friendly, clean and modern, with colourful murals decorating the entrance area, this is definitely a sociable hostel, though most of the action takes place next door at the affiliated *Hampshire Hotel*, where you can get good-value meals and drinks (licensed until 3am). Popular with smokers, this is one of the cheapest hostels – the dorms are tiny (but do at least have curtained bunks with their own bedlights), and bathrooms are cramped. The bigger double and single rooms are in the *Hampshire*. Travel agent service, and free bikes. Light breakfast and linen included. Rooms ②, dorms ①.

Backpack Oz, 144 Wakefield St, corner of Pulteney St (☎ & fax 08/8223 3551, free call ☎1800/633 307). Converted from a nineteenth-century hotel, this low-key hostel has light, spacious rooms and dorms (four-, six- and ten-bed) with sinks, mirrors and ceiling fans; linen and a light breakfast included. Comfortable common room downstairs; laundry and small kitchen. The bar opens summer only. Tours booked. Free breakfast. Pick-ups from bus, train and airport available. Rooms ③, dorms ①.

Cannon Street Lodge, 11 Cannon St, entrance on Franklin St opposite the bus station (☎ & fax 08/8410 1218, free call ☎1800/069 731). Huge, warehouse-style space with a groovy young feel to it.

Very clean and well-run; definitely one of the best. The big foyer has a reception desk, travel centre and several terminals for Internet access. Also on the ground floor is a funky licensed bar complete with pin-ball and a pool table; cheap $4 meals are served here. While there's lots of noise and action downstairs, it's peaceful upstairs where you'll find rooms and dorms plus TV rooms and a couple of kitchens. Air-con throughout. Free light breakfast includes percolated coffee; other perks are cheap day-membership at the gym around the corner, undercover parking and bed linen. Rooms ③, dorms ①.

East Park Lodge, 341 Angas St (☎08/8223 1228, fax 8223 7772, free call 1800/643 606). Huge three-storey mansion, with singles and doubles as well as four-bed dorms, air-con throughout. Run by a young couple, it has a peaceful atmosphere and views of the hills from its balconies and rooftop. Ongoing refurbishment means there are two standards of accommodation, though all rooms are fully furnished and all doubles have been renovated. The lounge area has a pool table, and there's a spacious dining room with stained-glass windows. Outdoors there's a pool to cool off in. Bus and train pick-ups if pre-booked; airport buses drop off here. Some on-street parking. Free breakfast. Tours booked. Rooms ③, dorms ①.

Glenelg Backpackers Resort, 7 Moseley St, Glenelg (☎08/8376 0007 or free call ☎1800/066 422). An excellent quality hostel in a terrace of adjoining houses near the beach, lots of doubles (with fridge and sink) and some singles available, as well as five- to six-bed dorms (no bunks). The lively common area downstairs has a bar open to the public, with loud music and activities from bands, karaoke, comedians, pool comps & theme nights, all overseen by Hawaiian shirt-clad staff. This might be too much for some, as there's no real private area to escape to. Lots of extras though – Internet access, free breakfast, bikes, videos and once weekly tours of the city and the Fleurieu Peninsula. No parking. Rooms ③, dorms ①.

Rucksackers Riders, 257 Gilles St (☎08/8232 0823). Small dorms but all with with heating/fans, duvets and good security. Pay showers (20¢ for 5min) are a drag, and there's not much privacy in the women's showers. Popular with Japanese cyclists and motorbike riders, hence the name. Rooms ②, dorms ①.

Sunnys, 139 Franklin St (☎08/8231 2430, fax 8231 0131, free call ☎1800/631 391). A comfortable place in an old house next to the bus station. Facilities include a pool table, sound system, TV and video; good security too. Six- to eight-bed dorms (bunks) plus a couple of twins, all with ceiling fans. Train, bus and plane tickets sold and tours booked, and plenty of useful information displayed. Small courtyard out back. Off-street parking. Rates include linen and a pancake breakfast. Rooms ②, dorms ①.

The Travellers Inn, 118 Carrington St (☎08/8232 7022). Drab and pokey: this would not be your first choice but at least there's air-con and heating, good security and parking, and the dorm beds (all new) are among the cheapest in town. There are usually some young Japanese holiday-makers on the staff who liven up the place. Licensed travel agent. Rooms ②, dorms ①.

YHA, 290 Gilles St (☎08/8223 6007, fax 8223 2888). Large, light hostel with patient, well-informed staff, but with too few beds (particularly doubles) to meet demand; book in advance for the family room or one of the three twins. Some rooms with air-con. Free tea and coffee, but no TV. Lockers available, and there's a travel and tour-booking service. Office closed 11.30am–4pm, but 24hr access for guests. Bike hire. Rooms ③–④, dorms ①.

GAY AND LESBIAN-FRIENDLY ACCOMMODATION

The beachfront **Semaphore Hotel**, 17 Semaphore Rd (☎08/8449 4662, fax 8449 4626), in Semaphore, a beach suburb about 15km northwest of the centre, is lesbian-run but also welcomes gay male guests and straights. The pleasant pub rooms, sharing bathrooms, are well set up with duvets, clock radios, lamps and sink (③, weekly rates available) and there's a comfortable common room with a wood combustion stove, pool table, couches and TV. The pub itself is nothing out of the ordinary; it has pokies out front, a pleasant bistro out back serving inexpensive meals with a Thai, Malaysian and Indian slant, and an entertainment venue with live bands and DJs Wed–Sun until 2am. Other, more central gay-friendly establishments include self-catering apartments at **Gurney Apartments**, 190 Gover St, North Adelaide (☎ & fax 08/8239 2301; ⑤), and at **Greenways Apartments** (see overleaf); and deluxe hotel rooms at the **Stamford Plaza Adelaide** (see p.680). Parkside Travel (☎08/8274 1222) has an accommodation service, or you can check the ads in the *Adelaide Gay Times* (see box on p.698).

YMCA, 76 Flinders St (☎08/8223 1611, fax 8232 2920). Central location and open to both sexes. Dorm stays limited to one week; private rooms – singles and bunk-bed twins – for a maximum of three weeks, all sharing bathrooms. Linen is provided. Communal kitchen and TV lounge; no curfew. Rooms ③, dorms ①.

The City

Adelaide's city centre, south of the river, is a strict grid surrounded by parkland: at the very centre of the grid is **Victoria Square**, and each city quarter has its own smaller square. **North Terrace** is the cultural precinct with all the major museums, the two universities and the state library. **Hindley Street** is the liveliest in town, and the focus of the city's nightlife, while **Rundle Mall**, its continuation, is the main shopping area, and **Rundle Street**, further east, the arty café strip. The other important area lies west of Victoria Square: between Grote and Gouger streets is the lively **Central Market** and the small **Chinatown**. The **Torrens River** flows to the north of North Terrace, with the Botanic Gardens and the Zoo on its south bank. Three main roads cross the river to the distinctive colonial architecture and café culture of **North Adelaide**, with **O'Connell Street** the main drag on this side.

As you wander Adelaide's streets, you're struck by the bourgeois solidity of the structures – a solidity enhanced by the fact that virtually every building, public or domestic, is **stone**: sandstone, bluestone, South Australian freestone or slate. The city's well-preserved **Victorian architecture** is not the over-the-top style built from money made quickly in the 1850s goldrush, as it is in Melbourne. Rather Adelaide, which suffered numerous economic setbacks before establishing a steady mining industry, built up its wealth slowly, and the buildings have a reassuring permanence. There's really only one place to start your tour, and that's tree-lined **North Terrace**, a long heritage streetscape perfect for exploring on foot.

The Botanic Gardens and Ayers House

At the eastern extremity of North Terrace is the main entrance to the **Botanic Gardens** (Mon–Fri 7am–dusk, Sat & Sun 9am–dusk; free guided tours from the kiosk by the main lake Tues, Fri & Sun 10.30am). The gardens, opened in 1857, are lovely – with statues and heritage buildings to gaze at, arbours to wander through, ponds and fountains to dally by – just like a classic English-style garden but with plenty of native trees too. The **Palm House**, completed in 1877, was based on a similar building in Germany and is an elegant glass and wrought-iron structure. Its role of displaying tropical plant species has been taken over by the new **Bicentennial Conservatory** (daily 10am–4pm, summer until 5pm; $2.50). This, the largest glasshouse in Australia, is stunning, housing a complete tropical rainforest environment with its own computer-controlled cloud-making system. Species are from Australia as well as nearby Pacific Islands, New Guinea and Indonesia. Make sure you pick up the leaflet *Walk with the Plants*, which gives detailed information about blue-numbered plants, or you can pay for an audio tour ($2). Other attractions are a fragrant herb garden, and **Simpson House**, a pleasantly cool thatched hut containing palms and ferns beside a stream. By the duck-filled main lake, you can sit under shady trees outside the excellent licensed **kiosk** and have a beer or snack. At the northern entrance to the gardens, **North Lodge**, once the caretaker's residence, is now a shop (daily noon–4pm) that sells books on botany and gardening, plus other souvenirs.

Heading away from the gardens on North Terrace, the first notable building you come to is the National Trust-owned **Ayers House** (Tues–Fri 10am–4pm, Sat & Sun 1–4pm; $5). Home to the politician Henry Ayers, who was premier of South Australia seven times between 1855 and 1897, it began as a small brick dwelling in 1845: the fine bluestone mansion you now see is the result of thirty years of extensions. Inside, it's elaborately decorated in late nineteenth-century style, with portraits of the Ayers family.

The universities and the Art Gallery of South Australia

Between Frome Road and Kintore Avenue, a whole block of North Terrace is occupied by the University of Adelaide, and the art gallery, museum and state library. The **University of Adelaide**, the city's oldest, was established in 1874 and began to admit women right from its founding – another example of South Australia's advanced social thinking. The grounds are pleasant to stroll through: along North Terrace are **Bonython Hall**, built in 1936 in a vaguely medieval style, and **Elder Hall**, a turn-of-the-century Gothic-Florentine design now occupied by the Conservatorium of Music (free concerts Fri 1.10pm; ☎08/8303 5925 for details). The highly decorative Gothic-inspired **Mitchell Building** beside it constituted the entire original university; on the first floor is the **Museum of Classical Archeology** (Mon–Fri noon–3pm, term time only; free).

Overbearing Victorian busts and statues of the stern and upright founders of Adelaide line the strip between Bonython Hall and Kintore Avenue. But respite is at hand, in the form of the two contemporary abstract sculptures outside the **Art Gallery of South Australia**, established in 1881 (daily 10am–5pm; free; guided tours Mon–Fri 11am & 2pm, Sat & Sun 11am & 3pm; talks 12.45pm most Tuesdays; ☎08/8207 7000). The gallery itself has an extensive collection of **Aboriginal art** including many non-traditional works with overtly political content; major works by the Western Desert school of Aboriginal artists are on permanent display in Gallery 7. There's a fine selection of **colonial art**, too: it's interesting to trace its development, from the earlier work deriving from European art up to the point where the influence of the Australian light, colours and landscape begins to take over and make the pictures come alive. The collection of **twentieth-century Australian art** has some good stuff – Sidney Nolan, Margaret Preston, Grace Cossington-Smith – but a lot of dross too. There's a large collection of twentieth-century British art, including paintings by Roger Fry and Vanessa Bell (Virginia Woolf's sister). The gallery also has a good bookshop and coffee shop, and a free cloakroom.

Museums – and the State Library

Next to the art gallery, in the **South Australian Museum** (daily 10am–5pm; free; tours Sat & Sun at 2pm), a huge whale skeleton can be seen through the unfortunate modern glass frontage. Two matching wings with cupolas enclose a pleasant, palm-filled courtyard, through which you enter the building. Inside, first impressions are of the usual old-fashioned museum – dimly lit, with stuffed animals in glass cases and a concentration on **natural history**. Mostly it is rather staid, but travelling exhibitions and special displays add interest, and there's also a lively, hands-on **information centre** with microscopes, specimens, live animals and a scientist on hand to answer all sorts of weird and wonderful questions about natural history and anthropology. The museum is best known, though, for having the world's largest collection of **Aboriginal artefacts**. However, in recognition of their continuing significance, and the often dubious manner in which they were acquired, some of the human remains and sacred objects are now being returned to their traditional owners. Level five has the permanent collection as well as changing Aboriginal exhibitions: there's a fantastic large-screen **video** telling the Ngarrindjeri Dreamtime story of Ngurunderi, an ancestral hero; from here you move on to a section that cleverly uses the story as a metaphor to describe the life of the Ngarrindjeri people.

Next door to the museum, on the corner of Kintore Avenue, the 1884 **State Library** (Mon–Wed & Fri 9.30am–8pm, Thurs 9.30am–5pm, Sat & Sun noon–5pm; ☎08/8207 7200) has everything from archives to a newspaper reading room and free Internet access; there's also a cosy magazine room with comfortable chairs and hundreds of the latest glossies to leaf through.

Around the corner on Kintore Avenue is the **Migration Museum** (Mon–Fri 10am–5pm, Sat & Sun 1–5pm; free), which completes the mega-culture block. Surprisingly for a country populated overwhelmingly by immigrants, this was Australia's only museum of immigration history until another opened in Melbourne in 1998 (see p.779). You're taken on a journey from port to settlement, in the company of South Australia's migrant settlers, through the use of interactive displays and recon-structions. The permanent exhibits here have a reputation for confrontation and inno-vation: the "White Australia Walk", for example, has a push-button questionnaire giving you the red, green or amber light for immigration under the guidelines of the White Australia policy, which was in force from 1901 to 1958. One writer called it a "museum of grief", no doubt affected by its focus on the grim individual struggles of everyday lives, though it does celebrate cultural diversity too. The museum is housed in a former **Destitute Asylum**, where the city's poor and homeless were hidden away in the nine-teenth century; its story forms a part of the permanent exhibition, which shares the museum with continuous special exhibitions.

Government buildings and arts spaces

Continuing west along North Terrace past the **War Memorial**, on the next corner is **Government House**, Adelaide's oldest public building, completed in 1855: every gov-ernor except the first has lived here. Across King William Road, two parliament hous-es, the old and the new, compete for space. The current **Parliament House**, begun in 1889, wasn't finished until 1939 because of a dispute over a dome, and while there's still no dome (and only half a coat of arms), it's a stately building all the same, with a facade of marble columns. Alongside is the modest **Old Parliament House**, built between 1855 and 1876 (closed to the public). On the corner of North Terrace and Morphett Street, the **Lion Arts Centre** is the base for the biennial Adelaide Fringe Festival (see box on p.695) and alternative arts in general – there are theatres, bars, a cinema and galleries. The **Experimental Art Foundation** here functions to educate people about contemporary art and was the first alternative art space in Australia to be government-funded; artists have studios upstairs and the gallery downstairs always has provocative exhibitions (Mon–Fri 9am–5pm, Sat & Sun 10am–5pm). The bookshop has a notice board where invitations to private views are tacked up, so if you want some free wine and a peek at the (small and incestuous) Adelaide art scene, take a look. Meanwhile, the **Jam Factory Craft and Design Centre** (same days and hours as the Art Foundation) highlights the tenuous nature of the dividing line between art and craft: here beautiful objects made of leather, glass, wood and clay combine aesthetics with utility. The work is for sale and there's always an exhibition in the gallery. Amid vibrant orange walls and a pyramid-shaped skylight, a blue-metal spiral staircase leads to a viewing platform above the **glass-blowing centre** (demonstrations Mon–Fri 9–10.30am, 11am–1pm & 2–4.15pm, Sat & Sun 10am–4pm).

Along the Torrens River: the Festival Centre and Zoological Gardens

The **Torrens River** meanders between Adelaide and North Adelaide, surrounded by parklands. Between Parliament House and the river is the **Festival Centre**: two geo-metric constructions of concrete, steel and smoked glass, in a concrete arena scattered with abstract 1970s civic sculpture. The theatre complex was built for the 1973 Adelaide Arts Festival and is still its focus (see box on p.695 for more on the festival itself), but the **theatres** are open all year. The main auditorium, the Festival Theatre, is the largest in Australia, hosting opera, ballet and various concerts; the foyer displays paintings of the Coorong by Fred Williams and is often the venue for free Sunday afternoon concerts from 2 to 4pm. The smaller Playhouse Theatre is the drama theatre, home of the State Theatre Company; it has a small commercial gallery, Art Space, in its foyer (Mon–Fri 10am–5pm, Sat 1–5pm). The Space Theatre is often used for cabaret and stand-up comedy, and its foyer hosts free children's workshops and low-cost shows on Saturday in winter (2–4pm). Call ☎08/8216 8600 for details of specific events.

Outside, in riverfront **Elder Park**, brass bands play in the ornate Victorian cast-iron bandstand on Sunday mornings, and there is an **amphitheatre** which often stages free rock concerts on summer Sunday afternoons. A fountain jets up from the river, which is peppered with black swans. The **Popeye cruise** to the zoo leaves from here (35min return; $6; ☎08/8223 5863). You can also rent paddle-boats ($6 per 30min) from the green shed at **Jolleys Boathouse**, across King William Road. The boathouse is an Adelaide institution, housing a restaurant (see p.693) as well as a kiosk with seats, where you can enjoy the same river views as the restaurant without paying the high prices.

The most pleasant way to get to the **Zoological Gardens**, whose main entrance is on Frome Road (daily 9.30am–5pm; Jan also Wed & Sun until 8pm; $10, children $5; ☎08/8267 3255 for feeding times, keeper talks, and bookings for free guided walks), is to follow the river, either by boat (see above) or on a fifteen-minute stroll. Alternatively, walk from the Botanic Gardens through Botanic Park, entering through the children's zoo entrance on Plane Tree Drive, or take bus #272 or #273 from Grenfell or Currie streets. Opened in 1883, the country's second-oldest zoo (after Melbourne's) is as much a botanical garden as anything. There are century-old European and native trees, including a huge Moreton Bay fig, and the grounds are full of picnic tables surrounded by gobbling families. Even the classic Victorian rotunda has tables inside where you can eat. The remaining Victorian architecture is well preserved; most of the animal houses have long since been replaced but a few classic examples have survived, such as the **Elephant House**, built in 1900 in the style of an Indian temple. The newest section is the Southeast Asian Rainforest exhibit, whose naturalistic settings are home to sixteen animal species, including the endangered Malaysian tapir. However, Adelaide Zoo is best known for its extensive collection of **native birds**, and there are two large walk-through aviaries.

King William Street and Victoria Square

As the city's main thoroughfare, **King William Street** is lined with imposing civic buildings and always crowded with traffic. Look out for the **Edmund Wright House** at no. 59, whose elaborate Renaissance-style facade (designed by Wright) is one of Adelaide's most flamboyant. You can see inside, too, since it houses the **State History Centre** (Tues–Sat 10am–4pm; donation), giving a good introduction to Adelaide's history, though its main function is to host travelling exhibitions from the National Museum of Australia (see p.218). On the other side of the street, and a couple of blocks south, the **Town Hall** (1866) is another of Edmund Wright's Italianate designs. The **General Post Office**, on the corner of Franklin Street, is another portentous Victorian edifice, this time with a central clock tower: look inside at the main hall with its decorative roof lantern framed by opaque skylights. Opposite, on the corner of Flinders Street, the **Old Treasury Building** has a small museum concentrating on the exploration, settlement and development of South Australia (Mon–Fri 10am–3pm; free).

Interrupting King William Street, pleasant **Victoria Square** with its fountain is a favourite Aboriginal meeting place, with people sitting on the shady ground and talking – no longer overlooked by tall gums but by the porter of the *Hilton Hotel*. Around the square also are the Catholic **Cathedral of St Francis Xavier** (1856) and the imposing **Supreme Court** on the corner of Gouger Street. Just to the west, the covered **Central Market** (Tues 7am–5.30pm, Thurs 11am–5.30pm, Fri 7am–9pm, Sat 7am–5pm) has been a beloved feature of Adelaide for over a hundred years; here you can find delectable European and Asian produce in a riot of smelly stalls and lively banter. The market area also has around 250 permanent shops (open Mon–Sat), as well as several good cafés, food stalls and restaurants; sushi and noodle bars are closely packed together, and the theme continues into surrounding Gouger and Grote streets, filled with lively restaurants and cafés.

Rundle Mall and Rundle Street

The main shopping area in the central business district is **Rundle Mall**, where several arcades branch off a busy pedestrian mall. It manages to be bustling yet relaxed at the same time, enhanced by trees, benches, alfresco cafés, fruit and flower stalls, and usually a busker or two to draw a crowd.

Behind its Victorian facade, the futuristic **Myer Centre** has eight levels, glass lifts and a huge atrium. There's an extraordinary amusement park, **Dazzleland**, on the top two floors, and shops include the city's two best department stores, Myer and David Jones, the latter with a fabulous food department. While you're here, take a look at the decorative **Adelaide Arcade** and the Regent Theatre. By night, Rundle Mall is eerily deserted, a strange contrast to Hindley and Rundle streets on either side, which really come to life after dark.

Rundle Street was once the traditional home of Adelaide's wholesale fruit and vegetable market, and later its lively, down-at-heel feel was appropriated by the alternative and arty, and by university students from the nearby campuses on North Terrace. It is now the focus of up-and-coming Adelaide, full of outdoor cafés and restaurants, with the two best pubs in town (*The Austral* and *The Exeter*, see p.694 & p.695 respectively), some slick bars, trendy hairdressers, clothes stores, and record shops; designer homeware stores too are creeping in. The **East End Market** here (Fri–Sun 9am–6pm) is a covered bazaar with two hundred stalls selling New Age trinkets and mass-produced commercial stuff. The main area has a cosmopolitan food court and an excellent market selling fresh produce, but it's all a bit sanitized. Sundays are busiest, when the place is packed with families, and Chinese masseurs are out in force. Opposite the East End Market, the disused **Adelaide Fruit and Produce Exchange** (1903) is worth a peek. Built of red brick with curved archways and yellow plaster friezes above of fruit, vegetables and wheat, it's a classically Edwardian building.

Behind the facade, rather unimaginative luxury apartments have been built, and these, along with the the two new movie complexes on the street – including an IMAX giant-screen cinema (see p.697) – are gradually homogenizing the area.

Tandanya: the National Aboriginal Cultural Institute

Tandanya, the National Aboriginal Cultural Institute, is situated opposite the classic old market buildings at 253 Grenfell St (daily 10am–5pm; $4; ☎08/8224 3200 for details of exhibitions and events). The centre is managed and controlled by Aboriginal people, who lobbied for fifteen years for such a space: its major focus is **visual arts**, with temporary exhibitions of national significance, but there are also workshops and a performance space. The exhibition space is large and open with screens hung from the exposed rafters. Displays cover Dreamtime stories, history, and contemporary Aboriginal writing, while political paintings confront black deaths in custody and other issues, and explore Aboriginal self-expression and identity. Video screens are dotted about, and Aboriginal music plays in the background. The **shop** is an excellent place to buy Aboriginal products, original paintings, didgeridoos, tapes and books, as well as T-shirts and other souvenirs. There's also a 160-seat theatre for live performances, and a café where you can try some bush tucker.

North Adelaide

North Adelaide, a ten-minute walk from the central area, makes for an enjoyable stroll past stately mansions and small, bluestone cottages, or a good pub crawl around the many old hotels. There are three ways of getting there. The best walking route to North Adelaide is up King William Road past the Festival Centre (nearly every bus from outside the Festival Centre also goes this way). From Elder Park you cross the pretty 1874 Adelaide Bridge over the river to Cresswell Gardens, home of the **Adelaide Oval** cricket ground (guided tour Tues & Thurs 10am, Sun 2pm; 2hr; $5), which has a small museum of cricketing memorabilia (Tues 10am–noon & Thurs 10am–1pm; $2) and affords superb views of **St Peter's Cathedral** (daily 9am–5pm; free guided tours Wed 11am & Sun 3pm) on Pennington Terrace opposite Pennington Gardens. The Anglican cathedral was built in 1869 in French Gothic-Revival style; its main entrance is suggestive of Notre-Dame in Paris. The *Cathedral Hotel*, opposite, is Adelaide's second-oldest hotel, built in 1850; it has a humorous "Quasimodo" theme and very good-value meals. At the top of King William Road, the peaceful and shady **Brougham Gardens** boast palm trees set against the backdrop of the Adelaide Hills. If you continue straight up, you'll come to the commercial strip of O'Connell Street, which has an embryonic restaurant scene to rival that of Rundle Street.

If you want to see a wide range of early **colonial architecture** you might do better to head north via Morphett Street and Montefiore Road to **Jeffcott Street** (buses #233 and #253 from King William Street). **Lights Vision**, on Montefiore Hill in Montefiore Park, is a bronze statue of Colonel William Light pointing proudly to the fine views of the city he designed. On Jeffcott Street itself is the neo-Gothic 1890 mansion **Carclew**, with its round turret, and the **Lutheran Theological College**, a fine bluestone and red-brick building with a clock tower and cast-iron decoration. On peaceful **Wellington Square** the pretty 1851 *Wellington Hotel* retains its original wooden balcony. Turning into tree-lined **Gover Street** you'll find rows of simple bluestone cottages; in contrast, **Barton Terrace West**, two blocks west, has grand homes facing the parklands.

The third route from the city to North Adelaide is via Frome Road (past the zoo) to **Melbourne Street** (buses #204 and #209 from King William Street, #272 and #273 from Currie and Grenfell streets), an upmarket strip of good cafés, antique stores, restaurants, designer clothing boutiques and speciality shops. The Banana Room along here at no. 125 (Fri 11am–6pm, Sat 10am–2pm) is probably the best retro-chic clothes store in Australia, with an immaculate range of designer dresses from the 1920s through to the 1950s; a 1926 Coco Chanel dress is on display. Don't expect bargains – most things are over $100, but it's fascinating to browse, and there is a range of cheaper costume jewellery.

The suburbs

Adelaide spreads a long way beyond the small inner-city enclaves, but few visitors see much of this. Most will at some stage venture down to the sea – a flat stretch of **beaches** west of the city, from Henley via **Glenelg** to Brighton, are sheltered by the Gulf St Vincent and characterized by their long jetties, while **Port Adelaide** further north has some excellent museums to set off its dockside atmosphere – but the inner suburbs remain uncharted territory. Some of them are well worth breaking the mould for, with local character, inexpensive restaurants and out-of-the-ordinary shopping.

NORWOOD, just east of the city, has two interesting streets: Magill Road (bus #106 from Grenfell or Currie streets), with its concentration of antique shops, and The Parade (bus #123 and #124 from Grenfell or Currie streets), a lively shopping strip with some great cafés and pubs and good bookshops. At weekends the small **Orange Lane Market** (Sat & Sun 10am–5pm), in a tin-roofed shed at the corner of Edward Street and The Parade, is a sedate place to browse among secondhand and new clothes, books, and bric-a-brac, and there are Asian and fry-up food stalls. In January the lively **Italian Festival** (call ☎08/8366 4555 for details) takes over the town hall.

In **THEBARTON**, west of the city, the lively **Brickworks Market** (Fri–Sun 9am–5pm; bus #110, #112 or #113 from Grenfell or Currie streets) spreads out from the 1912 Brickworks Kilns at 36 South Rd. There are plaza shops and indoor and outdoor stalls, mostly selling new clothes, and it's always busy with buskers and crowds of people.

Immediately south of the city **Unley Road** (buses #190–198 from King William Street) is known for its antique shops and expensive boutiques. Parallel King William Road at **Hyde Park** (bus #203 from King William Street) is shaded by lots of trees, plants and vine-covered awnings, and has some good cafés to relax in.

Port Adelaide

The unfortunate early settlers had to wade through mud at Port Misery when they arrived; nowadays **PORT ADELAIDE** takes the strain. Established not far from Port Misery in 1840, by 1870 it was a substantial shipping area with solid stone warehouses, wharves and a host of pubs. The area bounded by Nelson, St Vincent and Todd streets and McLaren Parade is a well-preserved, nineteenth-century streetscape; several ships' chandlers and shipping agents show it's still a living port, a fact confirmed by the many corner pubs (with pretty decorative iron-lace balconies) still in business. There's no tourist office, but the **Port Adelaide Tourist Visitor Information Centre**, near the waterfront on the corner of Commercial Road and St Vincent Street (daily 9am–5pm; ☎08/8447 6000) provides up-to-date details of attractions.

To get here, take a train from the central station or bus #151 (Mon–Sat, daytime only) or #153 (evenings and Sun) from North Terrace, or #340 from Glenelg (Mon–Fri only); the best day to visit is Sunday or public holiday Monday, when the **Fishermen's Wharf Markets** (9am–5pm) take over a large waterfront warehouse on Queens Wharf and several **cruises** are available on the water. The market (mainly bric-a-brac) adds some life to the waterfront, but the once-varied food stalls now seem to be dominated by purveyors of meat pies and steak sandwiches, though fishing boats do sell fresh fish. Outside is the quaint, red-painted metal **lighthouse** (daily 10am–4pm), dating from 1869, that was originally at the entrance to Port River; it can be climbed and inspected as part of your explorations of the South Australian Maritime Museum (see below), as can the museum's two floating vessels moored 300m away, the steam tug *Yelta* and the coastal trader *Nelcebee*. There are Sunday afternoon trips from the lighthouse with Adelaide Cruises Ltd (☎08/8447 2366) and Port Adelaide River Cruises (☎08/8341 1194).

The pick of Port Adelaide's several museums is the **South Australian Maritime Museum** on Lipson Street (daily 10am–5pm; $8.50, combined ticket for the Port Dock Station Railway Museum $13). Located in the old Bond Store with its massive timber posts and wooden floors, the museum is concerned with the migrants who came through the port and the South Australian **coastal ketch trade**. Starting from the basement, the migration section has faithfully reconstructed three typical steerage or economy cabins from 1840, 1910 and 1950; you can wander through them, lie on a bunk, listen to sails creaking or hear "new Australians" remembering their journey. Level two explores the various ways that South Australia relates to the sea, from seaside scenes with a working penny arcade, to pleasure cruises on the gulf, fishing and making model ships. On the ground floor you can board a real ketch; upstairs is a more traditional collection.

The **Port Dock Station Railway Museum** (daily 10am–5pm; $7), further along Lipson Street, is a trainspotter's delight, with a collection of over twenty steam and diesel locomotives. The model train displays include one with a South Australian setting complete with the Adelaide Hills, the Flinders Ranges and a model of Port

Adelaide; and there are seven fully decked-out trains. The train ride, which runs on demand, costs $2 extra and is glorified by steam on Sunday.

Semaphore to Henley Beach

On the coast just east of Port Adelaide, **SEMAPHORE**, with its picturesque jetty and fine old buildings, was important as the site of Adelaide's signal station from 1856 until the mid-1930s, before becoming a desirable holiday spot. Its current incarnation is as a popular lesbian area (see box on p.698) with several lesbian-run cafés, a pub and a feminist bookshop. These are all on Semaphore Road, a charming street running perpendicular to the beach, with awnings, stained glass on shop and café windows, and an old-fashioned cinema. On Sunday a steam train runs to **Fort Glanville** (Sept–May every third Sun 1–5pm; $5), at 359 Military Rd, the only complete example of the many forts built in Australia when fear of Russian invasion reached hysterical heights after the Crimean War in the mid-nineteenth century. To get to Semaphore by public transport, take a bus to Port Adelaide (see overleaf) and then bus #333.

About 8km south of Semaphore, **GRANGE** is a charming beachside suburb, with a row of Victorian terraced houses facing the sands (bus #112 or #135 from Grenfell Street, 30min; Grange line train, 20min) and a popular pier with an upmarket kiosk. The next beach along is atmospheric **HENLEY BEACH** (Mon–Sat bus #137, Sun #130, both from Currie Street; 20min; #286 or #287 from North Terrace, 35min), where the focus is Henley Square opposite the long wooden pier. The square is lined with classic Federation-style buildings housing several popular restaurants and cafés. *Henley on Sea* (see p.692), a waterfront café around the corner, featured as *Moby Dick's* in the film *Shine*. South of here, on the way to Glenelg, **West Beach** (#278 bus from Currie Street; 25min) is a rather soulless spot with a caravan park. It does have a good, long, sandy beach though.

Glenelg and Brighton

The most popular and easily accessible of the city's beaches is at **GLENELG**, immediately south of West Beach, and 11km southwest of the city. The thirty-minute tram ride here from Victoria Square is part of the experience: the beautiful 1929 trams have original fittings – red leather seats and leather hanging straps, and wood-panelled compartments.

Glenelg was the site of the landing of Governor John Hindmarsh and the first colonists on Holdfast Bay; the **Old Gum Tree** where he read the proclamation establishing the government of the colony still stands on McFarlane Street (bus #167 or #168 from Currie or Grenfell streets in the city centre), and there's a re-enactment here every year on Proclamation Day (Dec 28).

Nowadays, Glenelg is busy even off season. **Jetty Road**, the main drag, is crowded with places to eat (for the obligatory seaside fish and chips, *Bay Fish Shop* at no. 27 is the best) and there's lots of accommodation (see p.679). The tram terminates at **Moseley Square**, with its elegant town hall and clock tower. On the opposite corner, the original Victorian *Pier Hotel*, now part of the imposing seafront *Stamford Grand Hotel*, is crowded with drinkers on Sunday, when Glenelg is at its most vibrant. From Moseley Square, the jetty juts out into the bay, and in summer the beach on either side is crowded with people swimming in the calm waters; it's also a popular windsurfing spot year-round. The foreshore is also overlooked by the very tacky **Magic Mountain** (Mon–Thurs 10am–6pm, Fri 10am–11pm, Sat & Sun 9am–11pm; free entry, rides by token), a 1970s mistake of a mock-stone monolith housing a predictable beachside funfair. In summer you can speed down waterslides ($6 for 30min), while dodgem cars, bumper boats, mini-golf, merry go round and pinball machines operate all year round. Luckily the deafening noise levels you'll experience if you step inside are reasonably well-contained. Also facing the shore, **Glenelg Tourist Information** (daily: summer 9am–5pm, winter 9am–4pm; ☎08/8294 5833) can help with the booking of accommodation, tours and hire cars. When the centre is closed, you can access information on the 24hr touch-screen terminal outside. Next door, Beach Hire (☎08/8294 1477) rents out deck chairs, umbrellas, surf skis, body-boards and snorkel sets. Rollerblading and cycling are other popular activities in Glenelg, with a **bike track** south of the square and mountain and touring bikes to rent from Holdfast Cycles at 768 Anzac Highway (☎08/8294 4537).

South of Glenelg, **Brighton** has an old-fashioned, sleepy air, perhaps lent by the stone Arch of Remembrance that's flanked by palm trees and stands in front of the long jetty, the suburb's focal point. Here families and couples wander as joggers, cyclists and skateboarders strut their stuff along the Esplanade. Running inland from the beach, Jetty Road has a string of appealing one- and two-storey buildings shaded with awnings that contain an assortment of art, craft and secondhand stores, and two popular alfresco cafés: *A Cafe Etc* and *Horta's*. Brighton is reached by train from Adelaide (25min) or bus #266 from Grote Street. For beaches further south, see p.715.

Eating and drinking

Adelaide has roughly one restaurant for every thirty people, so not surprisingly **eating out** is a local obsession, and it's incredibly inexpensive here compared to Sydney or Melbourne. Moonta Street, closed to traffic between Gouger and Grote streets, is a small **Chinatown** heralded by Chinese gates which has several Chinese restaurants and supermarkets. An excellent **food plaza** off Moonta Street (daily 11am–4pm, except Fri until 9pm) serves Vietnamese, Indian, Singaporean, Thai and Malaysian food as well as Chinese *yum cha* and Cantonese BBQ. There are many other restaurants on **Gouger Street**, at their busiest on Friday night when the nearby Central Market stays open until 9pm. **Café** society is based around Rundle Street in the city, and in North Adelaide on O'Connell Street and the upmarket, decidedly chic Melbourne Street. Finally, eating in **pubs** in Adelaide doesn't just mean the usual steak and salad bar but covers the whole spectrum, from some of the best "contemporary" Australian food in town to bargain specials in several pubs along King William Street.

As for drinking, South Australian **wine** features heavily – which is just as well, since, by general consensus, **tap water** in Adelaide tastes dreadful. Although it's perfectly safe, there's usually only a small charge for spring water, which is what everybody drinks. And thanks to the state's liberal licensing laws, even most cafés are licensed.

Cafés and cheap meals

Al Fresco Gelateria & Pasticceria, 260 Rundle St. If you go to only one café in Adelaide, make it this one. Packed every night, the young Italian community have made it their own, and it's *the* place to see and be seen. Great coffee, *biscotti*, delicious *gelati* made on the premises and focaccia and calzone to eat. Daily 6.30am–late, which means around 4am at weekends.

Café Paradiso, 150 King William Rd, Hyde Park. Another long-established Italian favourite; great coffee and *biscotti* and alfresco dining out front. Food ranges from pasta to *fritto misto*. Licensed. Daily 8.30am–11.30pm.

Café Piccante, 128 King William Rd, Hyde Park. All stone and chrome, a cool haven in summer. Known for its gourmet pizzas. Wine available by the glass. Mon–Sat 10.30am–11pm, Sun 9.30am–10.30pm.

Caffe Buongiorno, 145 The Parade, Norwood. Large, always lively café which reaches a crowded and noisy crescendo on Sunday night. Serves a wide variety of Italian food and drink. Daily 8am–1am or later.

Clearlight Café, basement, 203 Rundle St. Vegetarian wholefood place where everything is clean and healthy – and the food is delicious. Mon–Sat 9am–5pm.

Cowley's Pie Cart, An Adelaide institution, this mobile pie cart takes up its position each night outside the GPO on Franklin Street. It's famous for its pie floaters. Mon–Thurs & Sun 6pm–1am, Fri & Sat 6pm–3.30am.

Elephant Walk Coffee Lounge, 76 Melbourne St, North Adelaide. Carved wooden elephants and bamboo dividers make small, private lounge areas; lively but intimate. Daily 8pm–late.

Eros Ouzeria, 275–277 Rundle St. Greek meze-style dining: choose from a variety of inexpensive snacks to put together a tasty meal. The setting is smart and airy, in a renovated old building with high, pressed-metal ceilings. Sit outside at the attached café for Greek pastries and coffee. Licensed.

Fasta Pasta, in the city at 131 Pirie St and 465 Pulteney St. Part of a chain which serves authentic, inexpensive fresh pasta with interesting sauces, ordered informally at the counter. Other, suburban locations include 61 O'Connell St, North Adelaide; 16 Jetty Rd, Glenelg; and 430 Brighton Rd, Brighton.

The Gallerie, 20 Gawler Place. Excellent Asian food court in the basement of this arcade. Mon–Fri 9am–5.30pm.

Hawkers Corner, 141 West Terrace, corner of Wright St. Something of an Adelaide cheap eats institution. Chinese, Thai, Malaysian and North Indian stalls. Try the Malay seafood laksa. Tues–Sat 5–10pm, Sun 11.30am–8.30pm. Unlicensed and no BYO allowed.

Henley on Sea, immediately south of Henley Square, opposite the Henley Beach Life Saving Club (☎08/8235 2250). Relaxed café brasserie with a summery atmosphere and great views of the jetty and water. Mellow interior, and shaded tables outside. Used as the location for *Moby Dick's* piano bar in the film *Shine* – unfortunately there's no piano in sight now. Light contemporary dishes with an emphasis on seafood as well as pasta of the day. Breakfast is big on weekends when you'll need to book. Licensed. Breakfast, lunch & dinner Mon–Fri from 11am, Sat & Sun from 9am. Closed Tues.

Horta's, 75–77 Jetty Rd, Brighton. With its pavement tables and fish mosaic out front, this is a pretty licensed beachside place, popular for lunch; dishes from pasta to Thai. If it's full try the neighbouring *A Cafe Etc* which does great all-day breakfasts and big salads.

Jerusalem Sheshkebab House, 131B Hindley St. Dimly lit Lebanese BYO that serves fresh and tasty Middle Eastern dishes. Daily noon until midnight.

Marcellina Pizza Bar, 273 Hindley St (☎08/8211 7560). At the quieter western end, this all-night pizza, steak and pasta bar is always full with the spillout from the area's clubs and pubs; the pizzas are among the best in town. Deliveries too. Daily 11.30am–5am.

Melinges Cafe, 69A Semaphore Rd, Semaphore. Gay- and lesbian-friendly café with a citrus colour scheme and plenty of sunlight. Light meals with a cosmopolitan twist and yummy desserts. Small South Australian wine list. Wed–Sun 11am–late.

Ozone Fish Cafe, 45 Commercial St, Port Adelaide. Operating since 1884, this may well be the oldest fish and chip shop in Australia, and it's certainly Adelaide's most ancient. It still provides an old-fashioned, no-frills fish meal fit for a queen – Queen Elizabeth and the Duke of Edinburgh dropped in during a royal visit in 1977.

Red Rock Noodle Bar, 141 O'Connell St, North Adelaide. Stylish cheap eat with a rich dark red wall with Asian calligraphy but other walls of glass, stone floors and friendly black-clad staff. Generous servings of every kind of delicious noodle dish you could think of, from Pad Thai to *hokkien* noodles and Malaysian laksa soup (average $9, lunch specials $6) plus stir-fries and Chinese dishes. Good list of wines, some by the glass.

Roma's, 200 Hutt St. A recommended deli-style café with gleaming counters and displays packed with cosmopolitan edibles; reasonably priced. Great breakfasts and excellent coffee. Licensed and BYO. Mon–Sat 7.30am–6.30pm.

Ruby's Café, 255B Rundle St. A popular market café in the 1950s; the decor is real here, not retro. But cocktails, an arts notice board and changing exhibitions bring it up to the 1990s, and the famous Sunday breakast is now served from 9am until 5pm. Otherwise, it's open evenings only (6.30pm–late).

Sandbank at the Bay, 1st Floor, Tourism Commission Building, The Foreshore, Glenelg. Verandah seats overlook the water, blessed with refreshing sea breezes. Great for drinking coffee and writing letters; light meals include filled baguettes. Daily 8am–5pm, later in summer.

Sarah's, 85 Dale St, Port Adelaide (☎08/8341 2103). Popular vegetarian restaurant, open for lunch Mon–Fri, dinner Wed–Sat.

Vego and Loven It, 1st Floor, 240 Rundle St. Vegan café with mock tacky decor and low prices. Good notice board. Mon–Fri 10am–4.30pm.

Zuma Caffe, 56 Gouger St. With its back entrance opening onto the Central Market, this place buzzes more than ever during market hours. Locals flock here for the huge breakfasts, big salads, and filo parcels, bruschetta, focaccia and quiche baked on the premises. Mon–Thurs 7am–6pm, Fri 7am–9pm, Sat 7am–late.

Restaurants

Amalfi Pizzeria Ristorante, 29 Frome St (☎08/8223 1948). Creative Italian place; upbeat, jazzy and young with experimental pasta sauces and traditional ones given a hot edge. Crowded, and open very late. Licensed. Closed Sat lunch & Sun.

Durham's Restaurant, 2 Durham St, Glenelg (☎08/8294 8224). Simple light meals during the day, and fancier contemporary Australian food at night; in an 1880s Victorian terrace featuring open fires, polished floors and high ceilings. Expensive. Closed all day Tues; dinner only Mon, Wed & Sat.

Estias, Henley Square, Henley Beach (☎08/8353 2875). Fun seaside place for casual dining on Greek meze amongst a playful modern Hellenic-themed decor, with repro classical sculptures and columns supporting the bar. Also more substantial dishes such as moussaka, and daily specials. Dinner Tues–Sun. Licensed & BYO.

Flinders Stuben Restaurant, in the SA German Club, 223 Flinders St (☎08/8223 3376). As a visitor to Adelaide, you can be signed in to this members' club. Small and friendly, with inexpensive, filling German food. Licensed. No meals Mon & Tues.

Gaucho's, 91 Gouger St (☎08/8231 2299). If you're after red meat, this Argentinian place serves some of the best steaks in town: name your weight. Licensed and BYO. Closed Sat & Sun lunch.

The Grange, *Adelaide Hilton*, 233 Victoria Square (☎08/8217 2000). European-style fine-dining restaurant where the top chef brings an Asian angle to already adventurous dishes. Very expensive. Dinner Tues–Sat.

Jolleys Boathouse, Jolleys Lane, off Victoria Drive next to City Bridge (☎08/8223 2891). Converted boathouse serving mouthwatering but pricey contemporary Australian cuisine. A popular venue for Sunday lunch. Licensed. Closed Sun night.

Lannathai, 160 King William Rd, Hyde Park (☎08/8271 6165). One of the best Thai restaurants in Adelaide, moderately priced with a modern wood decor. A few other Southeast Asian dishes have also crept onto the menu, from Malay laksa to Indonesian *gado gado*. BYO. Closed Sat lunch & Sun.

Mama Carmella, 4 Jetty Rd, Glenelg (☎08/8331 2288). Very popular gleaming Italian café-pizzeria established for over twenty years; good for lunch, a late meal or just coffee. Outside tables overlook the square. Mon–Thurs 9am–1.30am, Fri & Sat until 2 or 3am, Sun 8.30am–midnight.

Noodles, 119 Gouger St (☎08/8231 8177). Popular Southeast Asian restaurant serving Thai and Malaysian food. Non-smoking, licensed and BYO. Lunch Tues–Fri, dinner nightly.

Rakuba African, 33A O'Connell St, North Adelaide (☎08/8267 3227). The Sudanese chef prepares regional dishes; live music, often drumming, accompanies your meal. Notice board detailing other African happenings around town. BYO. Daily except Mon 5–11pm.

Shibata, 135 Melbourne St, North Adelaide (☎08/8267 3381). Japanese restaurant specializing in *nabe mono* (one-pot dishes). Moderate. BYO and licensed. Daily 6–11pm.

The Snake Charmer, 60 Unley Rd, Unley (☎08/8272 2624). Upmarket Northern Indian place. BYO and licensed. Closed Sun.

T-chow, 68 Moonta St (☎08/8410 1413). Huge, popular Chinese restaurant serving Teochew regional specialities. Well-known for Teochew tender duck, shark's fin soup and green peppercorn chicken. Quick lunch of noodles for $5.

Ying Chow, 114 Gouger St (☎08/8211 7998). An unpretentious place, always crowded. Serves Northern Chinese cuisine, including specialities such as aniseed tea duck or scallops cooked with coriander and Chinese thyme. Vegetarians can enjoy delicious dishes such as bean curd with Chinese chutney. Inexpensive. Lunch Fri only, dinner nightly. Licensed and BYO.

Zambracca, 94–98 Melbourne St, North Adelaide (☎08/8239 1345). A lively, licensed bistro crowded with the smart set. Superb moderately-priced Mediterranean food in slick, spacious surroundings. Daily 9am–late.

Pubs and wine bars

Ambassadors Hotel, 107 King William St. Slightly sleazy pub, but a ridiculously cheap, simple pub lunch ($4.95, weekdays only) put on to attract people to play the pokies here.

Austral Hotel, 205 Rundle St. Excellent inexpensive bistro meals, Malaysian, Thai, Mexican and Italian dishes, and good old Aussie steaks, burgers and seafood. There's also a restaurant with a smaller, pricier menu.

Bull and Bear Ale House, 91 King William St. A snazzy bar in the basement of the State Bank Centre – a cool retreat on a hot day for sticky stockbrokers. Imported ales and sophisticated meals.

Earl of Aberdeen, 316 Pulteney St, Hindmarsh Square (☎08/8223 6433). Gazebo full of greenery serving huge portions of imaginatively cooked pasta, steak, fish and kangaroo. Attentive service.

Lion Hotel, 161 Melbourne St, North Adelaide (☎08/8267 3766). Classic old hotel with iron-lace decor outside and a contemporary interior revelling in space and light. There are two classy eating areas: *The Larder* is deli-style with a small menu of curry, salads, and specials such as Thai fish cakes and beef stir-fry; the upmarket restaurant serves Modern Australian food (two courses for $19.90). Cigars and wine by the glass are sold at a stylish bar and a small sunny beer garden opens up the back wall.

The Oxford Deli Bar, *Oxford Hotel*, 101 O'Connell St, North Adelaide. The *Deli Bar* is good value: order at the counter and eat in the groovy pub. There are plenty of meals around $6.50, with full marks going to the Oxburger and fries at $7.50.

Stamford Grand Hotel, The Foreshore, Glenelg. There are some great café-style places in the hotel foyer, including the excellent Asian *Cafe de l'Orient*, a snug candle-lit place with delicious fresh Thai and Vietnamese dishes at very reasonable prices; you can watch the chefs at work in the open kitchen. There's also an Italian restaurant and a tearoom.

Universal Wine Bar, 258 Rundle St (☎08/8232 5000). Stylish bar run by a wine maker aiming to educate people about South Australia's wines. Sit at the bar or choose a table; wine by the glass or bottle. The atmosphere is distinctly European, and the small menu of delicious bistro food has a provincial French and Mediterranean slant. Mon–Sat 11.30am–midnight.

Entertainment and nightlife

Adelaide may appear dead at night, but there's actually quite a lot going on – bands, clubs, film and theatre – if you know where to look. The best place to find out **what's on** is *The Guide*, a pull-out weekly with film and theatre listings and reviews in Thursday's *Advertiser*. There's also a thriving **free press**: top of the culture stakes is *The Adelaide Review*, a highbrow monthly covering the visual and performing arts, dance, film, literature, history, wine and food, available from bookshops such as Imprints on Hindley Street, museums, galleries and just about everywhere else. At the more populist end of the scale, *Rip It Up* is a gig listings magazine, out every Thursday, with film, theatre, club and music reviews and interviews, and there's the *db Magazine* in the same vein, published every two weeks; both of these can be picked up at Rundle Street record stores such as B# Records, at no. 240 (jazz and world music specialists; ☎08/8223 7258), and Verandah Music at no. 182 (rock, metal and punk specialists; ☎08/8223 6753). Most big music events can be booked through Bass (☎13 1246), who have an outlet at Verandah Music, while B# Records sells tickets for underground events around town.

At night, the two spots to head for are **Rundle Street**, which boasts some of the best pubs and bars, and the more mainstream and rather sleazy **Hindley Street**, where you'll find several clubs and live music venues. And, of course, there's the **Adelaide Casino** (Mon–Thurs & Sun 10am–4am, Fri & Sat 10am–6am; neat dress required; ☎08/8218 4111), near the train station. As unpromising as this might sound, it's worth at least one visit: the marble entrance with its dome is stunning and, although this elegance isn't matched by the glitzy gaming rooms, the Austrian crystal chandeliers are jaw-slackening.

Pubs and bars

Austral Hotel, 205 Rundle St (☎08/8223 4660). More consciously arty and music-oriented than the *Exeter* (see opposite), the *Austral* is frequented by students for the independent local bands on Fri and Sat nights, and DJs Tues–Thurs & Sun nights. DJs are free, as is most of the music – when there's a cover charge, it's around $4. Fri & Sat open until 3am.

THE ADELAIDE FESTIVAL OF ARTS AND WOMADELAIDE

The **Adelaide Festival of Arts**, which takes over the city for three weeks at the beginning of March in even-numbered years, is a huge event, attracting an extraordinary range of international and Australian theatre companies, performers, musicians, writers and artists. Around the main festival has grown an avant-garde and experimental **Fringe**, which for many is more exciting than the main event. The official festival began in 1960 and since 1973 has been based at the purpose-built **Festival Centre**; there's late-night cabaret after the evening's events. **Writers' Week**, the literary festival, is held in marquees in the Pioneer Women's Memorial Gardens, across King William Road from Elder Park, and there are free outdoor concerts and opera – even films. Other venues around town host **Artists' Week**, exploring the visual arts, and a small **film festival**. Programmes are available interstate from all Bass outlets and the offices of Tourism South Australia, and in Adelaide from the South Australian Travel Centre or the Adelaide Festival of Arts, PO Box 8116, Adelaide, SA 5001 (☎08/8216 4444, fax 8216 4455), who have an office at 105 Hindley St.

The **Fringe Festival** begins with a wild street parade on Rundle Street a week before the mainstream Festival of Arts and ends a day after. Based at the **Lion Arts Centre**, on the corner of North Terrace and Morphett Street, and at venues all over town, it unleashes buskers en masse onto Rundle Mall. Twenty-four hour licensing laws are taken advantage of, as the Sydney and Melbourne arts scenes join the locals for some serious partying: late every night the Fringe Club has bands, cabaret and comedy. For more details on the Fringe, contact their office: Fringe Festival, PO Box 3242, Adelaide, SA 5000 (☎08/8231 7760, fax 8231 5080), or pick up a programme from any SA Tourism office in the state.

Womadelaide is an outdoor world music weekend that began in 1992 as part of the Arts Festival but has now developed its own identity and is held every alternate (odd-numbered) year to the festival. It takes place in late February in Botanic Park: the full weekend (Fri night–Sun night) costs over $100, but day and session passes are also available. B#Records (see opposite) are the official store selling Womad tickets in Adelaide.

Boltz Bar and Café, 286 Rundle St (☎08/8232 5234). The café downstairs has fabulous food with an international flavour, while the venue room upstairs hosts local and interstate comedians on Thursday nights (10pm–1am cover charge), and the thought-provoking Philosphy Jam on the second Tuesday of the month conducted by two lecturers from Adelaide University (8.30pm; free). Café daily 10am–11pm, Thurs–Sat until 1am.

Exeter Hotel, 246 Rundle St (☎08/8223 2623). This spacious old pub with an iron-lace balcony is a long-established hangout for Adelaide's artists and writers, yet remains totally unpretentious. Good lunches served, and music nightly except Monday; no cover charge.

Norwood Hotel, 97 The Parade, Norwood. Animated pub with a range of British and Irish beers on tap; weekend dance club with free entry.

Royal Oak, 123 O'Connell St, North Adelaide. Another popular North Adelaide pub with arty decor and a young crowd.

Rio's, 111 Hindley St. The tackiest bar in town; open 24 hours.

Talbot Hotel, 104 Gouger St. A tiny bar in the back (open Fri & Sat only from 5pm) has intimate booths and a classic 1930s decor and serves cocktails.

Clubs, comedy and live music

Café Tapas, 242A Rundle St (☎08/8223 7564). Spanish tapas bar (tapas $8.50–12.50 plus paella and $6 lunch specials) with arty events including Jazz on Friday, flamenco music and dancing on Saturday, and funky dance sounds for chilling out on Sunday. Closed Sat lunch & Mon.

Cargo Club, 213 Hindley St (☎08/8231 2327). Hip club that features live jazz, spoken word, cabaret, soul, Latin, African and reggae acts and local and international DJs; the decor is a mix of classic cool and 1990s postmodernism, and there's something on most nights.

Cartoons, 145–155 Hindley St (☎08/8231 3477). Venue for hard rock cover bands Thurs & Fri; DJs Sat night.

Crown and Sceptre, 308 King William St (☎08/8212 4159). A Heritage-listed pub with original leadlighting that's been groovified into one of Adelaide's best venues. Sparkly bar stools, cosy couches in the intimate band area and a busy espresso machine make the place really comfortable – even the beer garden is homely. Local bands Tues–Fri & Sun (usually free); Saturday is club night (until 5am; around $5), alternating weekly from UK Indie, through *Comfy Club* (funk-beat oriented), to jungle and techno. Happy hour every night 9–10pm.

Glenelg Backpackers Resort, 7 Moseley St, Glenelg (☎08/8376 0007). Comedy Jammm on Sunday nights (8–10pm) sees four or five mainly local comedians do their stuff; free and open to the public.

Heaven 2, 1 West Terrace (☎08/8211 8533). Huge dance club. Resident DJs as well as visiting international acts and one-off events. Wed–Sat 9pm–5am.

The Planet, 77 Pirie St (☎08/8359 2797). There's certainly a whole world of entertainment crammed into this place, with a dance club where the best of local and international DJs play, as well as a pool room, cocktail bar, wine bar and several cafés.

Rhino Room, upstairs, 13 Frome St (☎08/8227 1611). Underground club venue with an intimate lounge atmosphere; come casual or get glammed up – no one cares. The regular clientele may make you feel as if you've barged into a private party, though. Fringe-style cabaret performance Thurs, Afro-Latin, Fri, funk bands and DJ Sat. Cosy little bar provides a retreat from the performance. Thurs 9pm–1am, Sat & Sun until 3am. Standard charge $4. DJs.

Stix Pool Hall, 1st Floor, 123 Gouger St (☎08/8410 4457). Crowd-pulling combination of pool hall and nightclub. No cover charge. Mon–Sat 9pm–4am.

Synagogue, 9 Synagogue Place, off Rundle St (☎08/8223 4233). Industrial-chic club venue in a converted temple is the enduring focus for Adelaide's rave scene. Local and international DJs. Wed & Thurs 8pm–5am, Sat 10pm–5am.

Uni Bar, Union Complex, off Victoria Drive, Adelaide University (☎08/8303 5401). Non-students are welcome at the varied gigs here put on by the students' union. There's usually a band line-up on Friday nights during term time.

Gay and lesbian nightspots

Beans Bar, 258 Hindley St (☎08/8231 9614). Predominantly lesbian bar, though only Friday (5–9pm) is strictly women only. DJs, performances and pool competitions feature. An intimate, relaxed atmosphere. Tues–Sun 9pm–late.

Edinburgh Castle Hotel, 233 Currie St (☎08/8410 1211). Friendly mixed venue with a dance floor with DJ Thursday to Saturday, juke box, bistro, beer garden and open fireplaces. Mon–Thurs 11am–midnight, Fri 11am–1.30am, Sat 11am–1am, Sun 2–10pm.

Mars Bar, 122 Gouger St (☎08/8231 9639). This Adelaide institution has been around for years. Drag acts and a big, friendly mixed crowd. Wed–Sat 9pm–late.

Film

As well as several city and suburban mainstream film complexes, Adelaide now has four arthouse/retro cinemas and an IMAX cinema. The main **discount day** for mainstream cinemas is Tuesday. In the summer, you can watch films outdoors at the Epson Cinema in the Botanic Gardens; bookshops around town have programmes, and you can buy tickets at the gate or through Bass (☎13 1246; $11.50). There are still several drive-ins good for a laugh if you've never had the very American-style double-bill experience; the one at Military Road, West Beach (☎08/8356 8804), is the closest to the centre.

Academy, Hindmarsh Square (☎08/8223 5000). Mainstream downtown multiscreen.

Capri, 141 Goodwood Rd, Goodwood (☎08/8272 1177). Alternative and arty films complete with pre-show Wurlitzer organ recitals.

Chelsea, 275 Kensington Rd, Kensington Park (☎08/8431 5080). The latest releases and a "Crying Room" for parents and babies.

Cinema Nova, 251 Rundle St (☎08/8223 6333). A new arts cinema complex with three screens. Despite its modern interior – stainless steel stairway and opaque resin candy-bar counter – there's neither a licensed bar nor even a coffee machine. Monthly "cry baby" sessions for parents with babies. Substantial backpacker discounts (with the relevant card); discount day for everyone is Wed.

Glenelg Cinema Centre, 119 Jetty Rd, Glenelg (☎08/8294 3366). Three-screen mainstream cinema. Cheap day Tues.

Greater Union 5, 128 Hindley St (☎08/8231 5961). A large mainstream complex at the heart of the action.

Hoyts Regent Cinema, Regent Arcade, 101 Rundle Mall (☎08/8223 2233). Central multiscreen cinema; discount day Tues.

IMAX Theatre, Vaughan Place, off Rundle St (☎08/8227 0075). Largest screen in South Australia showing visually stunning nature-based documentary films. Hourly films every day 10am–10pm; 2D $12.95, 3D $13.95.

Mercury Cinema, Lion Arts Centre, 13 Morphett St (☎08/8410 1934; *www.mrc.org.au*). A great arthouse cinema showing short and foreign films; the venue for lots of foreign film and video festivals, and for the gay and lesbian film festival Feast.

Odeon Star Cinema, 65 Semaphore Rd, Semaphore (☎08/8341 5988). Quaint, local, beachside cinema showing mainstream films.

Palace East End Cinemas, 274 Rundle St (☎08/8232 3434). Opening off the IMAX theatre foyer, but this is a more alternative venue, showing foreign-language, arthouse and prestige new releases. Cheap day Mon.

Piccadilly, 181 O'Connell St, North Adelaide (☎08/8267 1500). Prestige new releases.

Trak Cinemas, 375 Greenhill Rd, Toorak Gardens (☎08/8332 8020). Good alternative cinema with two screens. Cheap day Tuesday. Bus #145 from North Terrace to stop 10.

Theatre and performance

Out of festival time, mainstream theatre, ballet, opera, contemporary dance, comedy and cabaret continue to thrive at the **Festival Centre**, and classical concerts are held at the **Adelaide Town Hall** (usually performed by the Adelaide Symphony Orchestra), and at **Elder Hall** at the Conservatorium of Music on North Terrace. However, more experimental theatre disappointingly all but dries up: the focus of what remains finds its base at the **Lion Arts Centre**, home of the biennial Fringe Festival. Almost anything that's on can be booked through Bass (☎13 1246).

Doppio Teatro, based at the Lion Arts Centre (☎08/8231 0070). This bilingual performance company promotes cultural diversity in the arts and an understanding of Italian-Australian culture. Performances at various venues.

Festival Centre, King William Rd (☎08/8216 8600). Three major auditoriums and free music events in the foyer (Sun 2–4pm). See p.685 for more details.

Lion Bar and Theatre Café, Lion Arts Centre, cnr Morphett St and North Terrace (☎08/8212 6266). The Lion Theatre is the main venue at the centre, and there's always lots going on here, from interstate performers and jazz bands to comedy line-ups. An irregular programme, so watch out for flyers.

Theatre 62, 145 Burbridge Rd, Hilton (☎08/8234 0838). Two venues under one roof: The Chapel is the smaller experimental space which often has women's performances, while the bigger space (seating three hundred) hosts mostly pantomime and sometimes a theatre-restaurant.

Listings

Airlines (domestic) Airlines of South Australia (☎08/8234 3000 or free call ☎1800/018 234) fly to Port Augusta, Leigh Creek, Innamincka, Birdsville, Boulia, Woomera and Port Lincoln; Ansett (☎13 1300) fly to a range of destinations including Alice Springs and Ayers Rock, and also sell tickets for Kendell Airlines (flying to Broken Hill, Ceduna, Mount Gambier, Port Lincoln, Whyalla, Coober Pedy, Olympic Dam and Kangaroo Island); Emu Airways (☎08/8234 3711) to Kangaroo Island; Qantas (☎13 1313); Southern Sky (☎08/8234 3300) to Kangaroo Island; Whyalla Airlines (free call ☎1800/088 858) to Cleve, Wudinna and Whyalla.

Airlines (international) Air New Zealand (☎08/8208 4201); Alitalia (☎08/8208 4201); British Airways (☎08/8238 2000); Cathay Pacific (☎13 1747); Garuda (☎08/8231 1666); Japan Airlines (☎08/8212 2555); Lufthansa (☎08/8212 6444); Malaysia Airlines (☎08/8231 6171); Qantas (☎08/8407 2233); Singapore Airlines (☎08/8203 0800).

GAY AND LESBIAN ADELAIDE

South Australia was the first state to legalize gay sex and remains one of the most tolerant of lesbian and gay lifestyles. Adelaide has a more modest gay community than Sydney or Melbourne but the scene enjoys a serenity the bigger cities can't match. Apart from the city's more mainstream annual festivals, there are a few strictly gay and lesbian fiestas. The biggest and best is Adelaide's Gay & Lesbian Cultural Festival **Feast**, launched in 1997. It runs for three weeks from late October to mid-November, with the Lion Arts Centre on North Terrace as its focus. An official opening party here kicks off the celebrations in carnival style. Festival events over the next 21 days include theatre, music, visual art, literature, dance cabaret, a pool party, car rally, historical walks, a **Gay and Lesbian Film Festival** at the Mercury Cinema (see overleaf), a glamorous masquerade ball, and the year's best dance party, the **Adelaide Sleaze**. The festival culminates in **Picnic in the Park**, an outdoor celebration in Elder Park which has been a feature of the Adelaide scene for over a decade; entertainment includes a very camp dog show. Earlier in the year, June's **Stonewall Celebrations** are less flamboyant, featuring serious talks and exhibitions in a number of venues.

A popular gay hangout is **Pulteney 431 Sauna**, 431 Pulteney St (Mon & Tues 7pm–1am, Wed–Fri noon–1am, Fri & Sat noon–3am; ☎08/8223 7506), with a spa, sauna, steam room, pool and snackbar. *Sunshine By the Sea* and *Melinges* are favourite lesbian haunts (see p.692).

To find out where the action is, pick up a copy of the *Adelaide Gay Times* or the Women's Information Service (see p.701), or check out other possibilities in the listings below.

PUBLICATIONS AND BOOKSHOPS
Adelaide Gay Times, 55 Halifax St (☎08/8232 1544). Free from venues and bookshops; you'll definitely find it at Imprints, 80 Hindley St. Gay Times also publish the handy free *Lesbian & Gay Adelaide Map*.
Liberation, available from the Women's Information Service (see p.701). A monthly women's newsletter – good for contacts and local happenings.
Murphy Sisters Bookshop, 240 The Parade, Norwood (☎08/8332 7508). Feminist/lesbian bookshop with a handy notice board.
Sisters by the Sea Bookshop, 14 Semaphore Rd, Semaphore (☎08/8341 7088). Specializes in lesbian and feminist books, with a choice of more popular fiction titles too, and has a small notice board. Daily 11am–6pm.

ORGANIZATIONS AND SUPPORT GROUPS
AIDS Council of South Australia (ACSA), 64 Fullarton Rd, Norwood. Education, support and counselling (information line ☎08/8362 1611, outside the city free call ☎1800/888 559).
Clinic 275, 1st Floor, 275 North Terrace (☎08/8226 6025). Free and confidential testing for all STDs (including HIV) and counselling Mon, Thurs & Fri 10am–4.30pm, Tues & Wed noon–7pm. No appointment necessary.
Darling House Gay and Lesbian Community Library, 64 Fullarton Rd, Norwood (☎08/8362 3106). Fiction, non-fiction and newspapers. Mon–Fri 9am–5pm, Sat 2–5pm.
Gay and Lesbian Counselling Service (☎08/8362 3223 or free call ☎1800/182 233). Counselling, information and needle exchange. Counselling line Mon–Fri 7–10pm, Sat & Sun 2–5pm.
Gay Men's Health (☎08/8362 1617). Counselling, support and information.
Lesbian Healthline (☎08/8267 4185, outside the city free call ☎1800/182 098). Health advice Mon 3–7pm.
Lesbian Link (☎08/8357 0199). Support and information. Fri 6.30–8.30pm.
Travel agent.
Parkside Travel, 70 Glen Osmond Rd, Parkside (☎08/8274 1222 or free call ☎1800/888 501). Gay-owned and operated. Hotel reservations, information and travel services.

See also p.682 for gay- and lesbian-friendly places to stay and p.696 for gay and lesbian nightspots.

Airport bus Transit Regency Coaches (☎08/8381 5311) has pick-up points at various locations, including the *Hilton Hotel* on Victoria Square and the Central Bus Station, but will pick you up at other city locations if you pre-book; it also services Keswick Interstate Train Terminal. See p.677 for airport departure times and prices.

American Express, 13 Grenfell St (Mon–Fri 8.30am–5.30pm, Sat 9am–noon; ☎08/8202 1400).

Banks and foreign exchange All the major banks are located on King William St. Exchange services are available at the international airport, at American Express (see above) and at Thomas Cook, 45 Grenfell St (Mon–Fri 8.30am–5pm; ☎08/8212 3354), 4 Rundle Mall (Mon–Fri 9am–5pm, Sat 10am–4pm, Sun 10am–2pm; ☎08/8231 6977), and 49 Jetty Rd, Glenelg (Mon–Fri 9am–5pm, Sat 9am–noon; ☎08/8294 3533). If you're desperate beyond these hours, the casino (see p.694) or international hotels on North Terrace can help, but obviously the exchange rates will be poor.

Bikes and bike rental Flinders Camping, 187 Rundle St (☎08/8359 3344), hires bikes for $15 per day and offers weekly rates; Adelaide Bike Hire (☎08/8293 2313) offers new mountain bikes at $15 for four hours or $30 per day, will suggest routes and deliver anywhere within a 15km radius of the city; Linear Park Mountain Bike Hire at Elder Park (mobile ☎018/844 588), situated near a section of the River Torrens Linear Park bike track, hires bikes by the hour or day at competitive prices; Bicycle SA, 1 Sturt St (☎08/8410 1406), is a non-profit cycling organization providing information and cycling maps and organizing regular touring trips.

Bookshops Imprints, 80 Hindley St (☎08/8231 4454), is a small highbrow bookshop; Unibooks, Adelaide University (☎08/8223 4366), is an excellent shop and provides an excuse to nose around the university; Angus & Robertsons, 112 Rundle Mall (☎08/8232 4840), is a large mainstream store; Europa Books at no. 238 Rundle St (☎08/8223 2289) sells foreign-language literature and travel books and guides in English plus maps; Adelaide Booksellers, 6a Rundle St (☎08/8410 0216) sells good secondhand titiles, as does O'Connell's Bookshop at 23 Leigh St, off Hindley St (☎08/8231 5188), which will also buy or exchange books. For antiquarian books, head for Michael Treloare, 196 North Terrace (☎08/8223 1111) and admire his beautiful bookcases. In Norwood, Murphy Sisters Bookshop, 240 The Parade (☎08/8332 7508) is a feminist bookshop also specializing in Aboriginal studies; Backpages Books, at 248 The Parade (☎08/8364 1411), is a quality secondhand shop.

Buses *The State Guide*, available from South Australian Travel Centre has route maps and timetables of all South Australia's bus routes. Most long-distance buses leave from the Central Bus Station, Franklin St. Greyhound Pioneer (☎13 2030) has a nationwide service that includes Alice Springs and Broken Hill in its destinations, while Firefly Express (☎08/8231 1488) and McCafferty's (☎08/8212 5066, reservations ☎13 1499), run to Melbourne and Sydney. State services are dominated by Premier Stateliner Coach Service (☎08/8415 5555), which goes to the Riverland, Whyalla, Port Lincoln, Ceduna, Woomera, Roxby Downs and Olympic Dam, Wilpena Pound via Port Augusta, the Yorke and Fleurieu peninsulas and to Mount Gambier either inland (via Keith, Bordertown, Naracoorte, Coonawarra and Penola) or along the coast (via Meningie, Kingston, Robe and Millicent). Other local operators include the Barossa–Adelaide Passenger Service (☎08/8564 3022), which stops at the main towns in the Barossa Valley en route to Angaston; the Yorke Peninsula Passenger Service (☎08/8391 2977), which runs from Adelaide to Yorketown, down the east coast via Ardrossan, Port Vincent and Edithburgh, and down the centre via Maitland and Minlaton; ABM Coachlines (☎08/8347 3336), which operates Mon–Fri only to Mannum via Gumeracha and Birdwood; the Mid North Passenger Service (☎08/8826 2346) via the Clare Valley and/or Burra to Peterborough; and the Murray Bridge Passenger Service (☎08/8532 2633) to Pinnaroo via Murray Bridge and to Murray Bridge via Mannum and Meningie. Tickets can be purchased at the Central Bus Station; the Bus Booking Centre at Station Arcade, 52 Hindley St (☎08/8212 5200), can arrange travel on any bus service.

Camping equipment and rental Rundle St is the place: for rental, try Flinders Camping at no. 187 (☎08/8359 3344), who can kit you out for the Flinders Ranges – they are also the only place in town that repairs backpacks; Paddy Pallin at no. 228 (☎08/8232 3155) sells a range of high quality gear, plus maps; or there's Scout Outdoor Centre at no. 192 (☎08/8223 5544) and the cheap and cheerful City Rubber at no. 186 (☎08/8223 1947).

Canoe rental and tours Try Canoe & Kayak Hire, 29 Angus St, Goodwood (☎08/8271 6354), which also offers canoe trips to the Torrens Island mangroves, an area frequented by dolphins.

Car rental Avis (☎08/8234 4558), Hertz (☎08/8234 4566) and Thrifty (☎08/8234 4554) have desks at the airport. Otherwise, try the recommended small and friendly Access, run by a couple of Brits and centrally located at 121 Currie St (☎08/8212 5900 or free call ☎1800/812 580). They do free airport deliveries and are one of the few companies which allow you to take their cars to Kangaroo Island; they also hire out sports cars. Also try Action (☎08/8443 8855) or Excel (☎08/8234 1666). Older, cheaper cars can be obtained from Cut Price Car Rentals (☎08/8443 7788; *www.cutprice.com.au*), who also do one-way rentals and buy backs, or Rent-a-Bug (☎08/8234 0911). Campervans Australia NQ Rentals, 151 Burbridge Rd, Hilton (☎08/8443 3002, fax 8443 3656), have two-berth campervans on stand-by deals (from $69 per day).

Disabled travellers Disability Information and Resource Centre, 195 Gilles St (☎08/8223 7522); Access Cabs (☎1300/360 940).

Environment and conservation The Conservation Council of South Australia, 120 Wakefield St (☎08/8223 5155), is a good place to find out what's going on; there's a notice board, bookshop and library. The Wilderness Society has its campaign office at 116 Grote St (☎08/8231 6586) and a shop in Victoria Square Arcade, Victoria Square (☎08/8231 0625).

Hospital Royal Adelaide Hospital, North Terrace (☎08/8223 4000).

Internet Access Ngapartji, 211 Rundle St (Mon–Thurs 8.30am–7pm, Fri 8.30am–10.30pm, Sat 10am–10.30pm, Sun noon–7pm; ☎08/8232 0839) is a snazzy multimedia centre whose Aboriginal name means "community skills brought together". A couple of computer terminals out front can be used for free; the cybercafé inside charges $10 per hour ($5 per 30min, $3 per 15min). There's free access at the State Library (see p.684; book in advance), the Women's Information Service (p.701; women only), and cheap access at Young Media Australia, 69 Hindmarsh Square (☎08/8232 1577; $2.50 per 30min) and at the Backpacker Transit and Travel Centre (see p.678; $4 per half-hour).

Laundries Adelaide Launderette, 152 Sturt St (daily 7am–8pm; service washes 8am–5pm); Gilles St Laundromat, 316 Gilles St (daily 7am–10.30pm; unattended), is handy for hostels.

Left luggage Adelaide Train Station has 24hr lockers; facilities also at the Backpacker Transit and Travel Centre (see p.678).

Maps The Map Shop, 16A Peel St, between Hindley and Currie sts (☎08/8231 2033), has the largest range of local and state maps; if you're a member of an affiliated automobile association overseas, you can get free regional maps and advice on road conditions from the RAA, 41 Hindmarsh Square (☎08/8202 4540).

Markets See Central Market, p.686; East End Market, p.687; Orange Lane Market, p.687; Brickworks Market, p.689; and Port Adelaide Market, p.689.

Medical centre City Centre Medical Clinic, 29 Gilbert Place (☎08/8212 3226).

Motorbike rental Show & Go Motorcycles, 236 Brighton Rd, Somerton Park (☎08/8376 0333).

Newspapers Adelaide's *The Advertiser* is very provincial and doesn't have good coverage of national and international news, but is useful on Thursday for entertainment listings, and Wednesday and Saturday for classifieds; Melbourne's *The Age* is freely available as an alternative. The best place to buy foreign and interstate newspapers is Rundle Arcade Newsagency, off Gawler Place, behind David Jones Department Store (☎08/8212 5121).

Pharmacy Midnight Pharmacy, 13 West Terrace (☎08/8231 6333) opens Mon–Sat 7am–midnight, Sun & public holidays 9am–midnight. In Glenelg try Walker & Stevens Chemmart, corner of Jetty Rd and Gordon St (daily 8.30am–10pm).

Police For emergencies call ☎000.

Post office GPO, 141 King William St, corner of Franklin St (Mon–Fri 8am–6pm, Sat 8.30am–noon; ☎13 1318); poste restante, Adelaide GPO, SA 5000.

Rape and Sexual Assault Service ☎08/8226 8777 or free call ☎1800/817 421, after-hours emergency line ☎08/8226 8787.

Shopping Hours are Mon–Sat 9am–5 or 6pm, with late-night shopping until 9pm on Friday in the city and Thursday in the suburbs, plus Sunday trading (11am–5pm) in the city only. You can find most things in Rundle Mall (see p.687), which has three department stores, plus a handy Woolworths at no. 86 with a small supermarket attached. There is another central supermarket, Coles, at 21 Grote St (open daily), near the Central Market. For alternative fashion, Rundle St, and particularly Miss Gladys Sym Choon at no. 235, is the place to go. For retro clothing visit Mabs, 207 Grenfell St, or The Banana Room (see p.688). For Aboriginal arts and crafts try Tandanya (see p.687) or the Otherway Shop, 185 Pirie St. For records, try B# Records on Rundle St (see p.694) and Krypton Discs, 34 Jetty Rd, Glenelg (☎08/8295 3944). See also "Markets" above.

Swimming pool Adelaide Aquatic Centre, corner of Jeffcott Rd and Fitzroy Terrace, North Adelaide (Mon–Sat 5am–10pm, Sun 7am–8pm; swim $4.30; ☎08/8344 4411), indoor centre with pool, gym, sauna and spa; take bus #231 from North Terrace.

Taxis Adelaide Independent (☎13 2211); Suburban Taxi Service (☎13 1008); Yellow Cabs (☎13 2227). There's a taxi rank on the corner of Pulteney and Rundle sts.

Telephones Rundle Mall has lots of phones, including ones that take credit cards. For peace and quiet, try the Phone Room in the GPO.

Tours It's easy enough to find your way around Adelaide without a tour but if you're hooked on them as an introduction, you can take the Adelaide Explorer City Sights Tour in a bus dolled up as a tram (☎08/8364 1933; $22; 2hr 30min; departing the Travel Centre, 14 King William St, daily 9am, 10.15am, 12.15pm, 1.30pm & 3pm); the narrated tour can be used as a hop-on, hop-off ser-vice, taking in the city, Glenelg and West Beach. Further afield, the majority of tours from Adelaide head for the Barossa Valley (see p.704), Kangaroo Island (see p.717) and the Fleurieu Peninsula (see p.711). General operators include Festival Day Tours (☎08/8374 1270) for upmar-ket tours to wildlife parks such as Warrawong Sanctuary and Cleland, the Barossa Valley, Adelaide Hills and Hahndorf, the Murray River, Clare Valley, Victor Harbor and Kangaroo Island; Premier Day Tours (☎08/8415 5566); and Adelaide Sightseeing (☎08/8231 4144), which also ranges further afield to the Coorong and Flinders ranges. As a hop-off point for longer treks, Adelaide is the home base for the excellent Wayward Bus (☎08/8232 6646, fax 8232 1455 or free call ☎1800/882 823), which does a good one-way, small-group tour from Adelaide to Melbourne (or vice versa) via the scenic coastal route (three days $170 lunch included, but not other meals and accommodation; or hop on and off over a maximum period of six months). Wayward also runs one-way tours to Alice Springs taking in the Clare Valley, Flinders Ranges, Oodnadatta Track, Lake Eyre, Coober Pedy, Uluru, Kata Tjuta and Kings Canyon (eight days, $840 all-inclusive), a five-day option taking in Coober Pedy, Oodnadatta Track, Lake Eyre, Maree, Wilpena Pound and Flinders ranges, and from October to March on tour monthly to Perth (twelve days, $840 all-inclu-sive). Heading Bush 4WD Adventures (free call ☎08/8648 6655) does ten-seater camping tours to the Flinders Ranges (three days; $279) and one-way trips to Alice Springs, also visiting the Flinders Ranges and the Oodnadatta Track, Coober Pedy, the Simpson Desert, Uluru, Kata Tjuta and Kings Canyon ($695 all-inclusive). Joe Ahern's Outback Tours (☎1800/246 543) runs an eight-day 4WD camping safari from Adelaide to Alice Springs, taking in Uluru, Kata Tjuta, Kings Canyon and other sights, with lots of walking and an emphasis on Aboriginal culture; one-way $695 includes all meals, camping gear and entry fees, and one night camping with an Aboriginal community. You can do a two-day express return with this company to Adelaide from Alice Springs for $85.

Trains Australian National Travel Centre, Station Arcade, North Terrace (☎08/8231 4366; Mon–Fri 8.30am–5.30pm), deals with interstate train enquiries and sells tickets.

Travel agents Adelaide YHA Travel, 38 Sturt St (☎08/8231 5583); City Centre Travel, 75 King William St (☎08/8221 5044), domestic travel specialists; Flight Centre, 54 King William St (☎08/8211 7246); Jetset, 23 Leigh St, off Hindley St (☎08/8217 8111); Peregrine Travel, upstairs at 192 Rundle St (☎08/8223 5905); STA Travel, 235 Rundle St (☎08/8223 2426); Thor Adventure Travel, upstairs at 228 Rundle St (☎08/8232 3155).

Vaccinations Travellers Medical and Vaccination Centre, 29 Gilbert Place (☎08/8212 7522).

Wine In a lane tucked away behind the excellent *Universal Wine Bar* (see p.694) on Rundle St, East End Cellars, 22–26 Vardon St, is an excellent bottle shop if you want to buy some choice South Australian wines to take away.

Women's Adelaide The Women's Studies Resource Centre, Station Arcade, 64 Pennington Terrace, North Adelaide (☎08/8267 3633; Mon–Thurs 9am–6pm, Fri 9am–5pm), is a good meeting place with library, video and computer facilities; at the same address is Women's Health Statewide (☎08/8267 5366) for pregnancy testing and over-the-phone health informa-tion, contraception information and abortion referrals. The Women's Information Service, Station Arcade, Adelaide Railway Station, 136 North Terrace (Mon–Fri 8am–6pm, Sat 9am–5pm; ☎08/8303 0590), has loads of practical information and very handy free internet access which does not have to be pre-booked (women only; at least 30min per person, more time depending on demand). Women of the Wilderness is the YWCA's recreation programme organizing outdoor expeditions and workshops – all affordably priced; contact the YWCA for further information (☎08/8227 0155, fax 8227 0166), or send for their *WOW* brochure to 17 Hutt St, SA 5000.

Work Employment National, 55 Currie St (☎08/8231 9444). Unemployment is high in Adelaide itself, but it's a good place to find out about casual fruit-picking work in the Riverland. Hostels can help with finding work, and often provide a source of employment for young travellers.

Around Adelaide

Escaping Adelaide for a day or more is easy and enjoyable, as you can choose from beaches, hills and wine, or any combination thereof. Closest at hand are the **Adelaide Hills**, southeast of the city, which are popular for weekend outings and have numerous small national and conservation parks that are great for walking. To the south, the **Fleurieu Peninsula** extends towards Cape Jervis and has plenty of fine beaches and several small wineries. If wine is your priority, though, head for the **Barossa Valley**, Australia's premier wine-producing region, with over thirty excellent wineries all less than 50km from Adelaide. The valley is easily visited in a day from the city, or on a tour, but it's also a great place to stop over and unwind. The **Yorke Peninsula**, across the gulf from Adelaide, is far less known, though many locals holiday here: as well as beaches, it has the remains of an old copper-mining industry and an excellent national park.

The Adelaide Hills

The beautiful **Adelaide Hills** are the part of the Mount Lofty Ranges closest to the city, just thirty minutes' drive away, and for the most part accessible by train and the Hills Transit bus service (☎08/8339 1191). Several tours heading for the Fleurieu Peninsula also take in the area (see p.701). Many people live in the hills to take advantage of the cooler air, and there are some grand old summerhouses here. The **Heysen Trail** long-distance walk cuts across the hills, with a series of YHA hostels along it; most are run on a limited-access basis and the key must first be obtained from the Adelaide office, 38 Sturt St (☎08/8231 5583). Due to the high fire risk in midsummer, the trail is closed from mid-December to April.

Leaving the city by Glen Osmond Road you soon start to wind steeply up on the way to the South Eastern Freeway, the main road to Melbourne. This was the traditional route to Melbourne – there's an old tollhouse not far out of the city at Urrbrae and several fine old coaching hotels such as the *Crafers Inn*. At **CRAFERS** itself you can leave the freeway for the scenic Summit Road, which runs along the top of the hills, past the western side of the extensive **Mount Lofty Botanic Gardens** (daily 10am–4pm) to the **Mount Lofty Lookout**, the highest point of the range (727m). Hills Transit buses #820, #821 and #822 run from Adelaide bus terminal or Currie Street via Crafers and up Piccadilly Road, from where you can access the eastern side of the Botanic Gardens.

The turn-off to **Cleland Wildlife Park** (daily 9.30am–4.30pm; $7.50), part of the Cleland Conservation Park, is the first on the left after the lookout. Here you can cuddle a koala and see other Australian fauna: the two-hour guided night-time walks are the best way to see the mainly nocturnal animals at their most active ($11.50; booking essential; ☎08/8339 2444). The day-time **Yurridla Trail** tour (Wed & Sun 11am & 1.30pm) is led by trained Aboriginal guides who tell Dreaming stories to convey the ceremonial significance of the native animals you'll meet on the tour. You can get up here as part of a tour with Festival Tours ($35 including visit to Hahndorf; ☎08/8374 1270), Adelaide Sightseeing ($25 including the summit of Mount Lofty; ☎08/8231 4144) or Premier Day Tours ($25 including Mount Lofty; call ☎08/8415 5566). Otherwise, take the Hills Transit bus #822.

The **Morialta Conservation Park**, north of here, is most easily reached by taking the #105 bus from Grenfell Street (35min), which goes right into the park along the scenic Morialta Falls Road; from the entrance it's a two-kilometre bushwalk into the park to a lovely waterfall. By car you can approach the park along the equally impressive Norton Summit Road; the *Scenic Hotel*, clinging to the side of the hill at **Norton Summit**, is a great place to stop for a drink. Running off here, Colonial Drive leads to

Fuzzies Farm (☎08/8390 1111; *fuzzies@dove.net.au*; bookings essential; closed July & Aug; dorms ① including meals), an experiment in co-operative living set on seventeen bush hectares and overseen by the philosophical Fuzzy. You can stay here and partici-pate in activities such as carpentry, building, tending goats, or park conservation – or help to make equipment for the farm (even the swimming pool has been made by helpers). At weekends the common room doubles as a café (10am–6pm) open to non-residents, and those who want to find out more before staying – Fuzzy prefers helpers to stay for at least one week, but welcomes holidaying guests in the cottage (⑥).

South of Crafers, virtually in the southern suburbs of Adelaide, is **Belair National Park** (daily 8am–sunset; entry fee per car $5). Getting there is half the pleasure – you take a suburban train that winds upwards through tunnels and valleys with views of Adelaide and Gulf St Vincent (35min). From Belair Station, steps lead to the valley and the grassy recreation grounds and kiosk. With its joggers, man-made lake, hedge maze, forest nursery and **Old Government House** (open to visitors on Sun 12.30–4pm), a residence built in 1859 as a summer retreat for the governor, this seems more like a garden than a national park, though there are also some more secluded bush trails through gum forests.

The **Warrawong Sanctuary**, southeast of Belair National Park on Stock Road, reached by Sturt Valley Road, Heather Road and Longwood Road, was set up in the late 1960s in an attempt to halt the loss of Australian wildlife: half of all the mammals that have become extinct in the last two centuries have been Australian. Guided bushwalks starting at dawn or sunset ($15) offer you the opportunity to try to spot the mostly noc-turnal animals in their natural habitat; day-walks are also available (daily 1.30pm; $10). For all walks you must book in advance (☎08/8370 9422, fax 8370 8332; information at *www.esl.com.au*). There's a licensed **restaurant**, and also **accommodation** in air-con-ditioned, en-suite tent-cabins (⑤). There's no public transport or tour to Warrawong, though if you call the sanctuary they may arrange transport.

Hahndorf

HAHNDORF, 28km from the city, is the most touristy destination in the hills (Hills Transit bus from Central Bus Station; frequent services; 40min; ☎08/8399 1191) and is always crowded at weekends. Founded in 1839, it's Australia's oldest German settle-ment and still has the look of a nineteenth-century village. The Bavarian-style restau-rants and coffee houses, crafts, antique and gift shops are thoroughly commercial, but it's still enjoyable, especially in autumn when the chestnuts and elms lining the main street have turned golden and the German food tastes just right for the season. The **Adelaide Hills Visitors Information Centre**, 41 Main St (daily 9am–5pm; ☎08/8388 1185), has lots of information on B&Bs and other accommodation in the hills (no

---

B&B IN THE HILLS

Less than an hour from the city, the Adelaide Hills' many B&Bs in bush surroundings are well worth seeking out for a treat – but they aren't cheap. Some of the best are *Debney Hill* in Ashton (☎08/8390 1660, fax 8390 1161; ⑦), a friendly family home which has an en-suite unit and a spa; *Apple Tree Cottage* in Oakbank (☎08/8388 4193, fax 8388 4733; ⑧), a self-contained 1860 cottage beside an idyllic lake for $160 and up; and *Allessandro Maandini's Ryokan* in Blackwood (☎ & fax 08/8370 3507; ⑧), a stunning, glass-walled Japanese-inspired house offering authentic "Ryokan" (Japanese-style) B&B, four-course Japanese meals ($55 a head) and pick-up service in a flash car; discounts are available for backpackers in groups of at least three.

For **other accommodation** in the hills, see Hahndorf, Warrawong Sanctuary and *Fuzzies Farm*, all above.

charge for bookings). It can also provide information about the entire area, though you won't need much help in the village itself: there's basically just one street and all the buildings have blue plaques recounting their history. The **Hahndorf Antique Clock Museum** (daily 9.30am–5pm; $5) has an impressive and noisy working collection, while the **Hahndorf Academy** (Mon–Sat 10am–5pm, Sun noon–5pm; $2) once contained the work of the nineteenth-century artist **Hans Heysen** who settled in Hahndorf in 1908. However, the thirty landscape paintings – mostly of local scenes – were stolen in 1995 and only a few sketches remain beside a collection of photographs, prints, displays and well-written interpretive boards that shed light on the lives of early German settlers. There are, however, a couple of Heysen's paintings on display at his old home, **The Cedars**, about 2.5km northwest, off Ambleside Road (10am–4pm; closed Sat; guided tours 11am, 1pm & 3pm; $7 studio and house; shop and garden free); you can also see the studio where he painted.

For a glass of authentic locally brewed pilsner, head for the lovely wooden bar of the *German Arms Hotel*, which has a log fire and photos of old Hahndorf, a reasonably priced bistro, and a more expensive **restaurant**. There are dozens of other places to eat, all with filling meals for around $6. At the other end of the main street, *Karl's German Coffee House*, in a homestead with verandah dining (closed Mon & Tues), serves marginally lighter meals than the hotel, while *The German Cake Shop*, near the tourist office, just off the main street on Pine Avenue (Mon–Fri 9am–5pm, Sat & Sun 8am–5pm), is a crowded bakery and coffee shop where the speciality is *bienenstich*, a yeast cake topped with honey and almonds, and filled with cream, butter and custard. For a picnic, stock up at Hahndorf Gourmet Foods, two shops south of tourist information, famous for their home-made wurst; try their excellent café for meaty snacks.

Mount Torrens and Birdwood

Further out, but still barely 50km east of Adelaide, the **Torrens River Gorge** and upper valley is one of the loveliest areas of the Adelaide Hills. You can get here with ABM Coaches, from the Central bus (Mon–Fri twice daily; ☎08/8347 3336), along a route that passes through the hills to the Murray River at Mannum. This scenic route takes in **Cudlee Creek**, location of the **Gorge Wildlife Park** (daily 8am–5pm; koala holding 11.30am, 1.30pm & 3.30pm; $7), a private park with mainly native birds and animals housed in walk-through enclosures; and **GUMERACHA**, where The Toy Factory, 389 Birdwood Rd (daily 9am–5pm), sells wholesale wooden toys, games and puzzles to the public and has a tacky eighteen-metre-high rocking-horse – children (and adults) can climb up it for kicks, and good views of the countryside. The bus also passes **BIRDWOOD**, which is home to the **National Motor Museum** on Shannon Street (daily 9am–5pm; $8.50) – Australia's largest collection of veteran, vintage and classic cars, trucks and motorcycles.

The Barossa Valley

The **Barossa Valley**, only an hour's drive from Adelaide, produces internationally acclaimed wines and is the largest **premium wine** producer in Australia. Small stone **Lutheran churches** dot the valley, which was settled in the 1840s by German Lutherans fleeing from religious persecution: by 1847 over 2500 German immigrants had arrived and after the 1848 revolution more poured in. The German dialect in the area was strong until World War I, when the spoken language was frowned upon and German place names were changed by an Act of Parliament. The towns, however – most notably Tanunda – remain thoroughly German in character, even without the large doses of oompah tourist hype that they all serve up, and the valley is well worth visiting for the vineyards and wineries, the architecture, and the bakeries and butcher's shops where old German recipes have been handed down through generations. The

WINE TASTING TIPS

Smaller wineries tend to have more charm and intrinsic interest than the larger commercial operators and it's here you'll often get to talk personally to the wine maker. Generally you'll get the best reception if you visit as a pair: wineries have become increasingly distrustful of groups intent on getting drunk for free, and some have begun to charge a nominal tasting fee to discourage this, but it's still rare. You're under no obligation to buy any wine, but coming away with a few of your favourite taste sensations of the day – often only available at the cellar door – and a few fruity adjectives to describe them is part of the fun.

For a novice, wine tasting can be an intimidating experience. On entering the **tasting area** (or cellar door) you'll be shown a list of wines that may be tasted, divided into reds and whites, all of which are printed in the order that the wine maker considers best on the palate. Unless you know what you're doing, it's not acceptable to alter this order, though by all means concentrate on red or white if you prefer. To get the full taste, sniff the wine first to appreciate the aroma or bouquet, and then take a sip, rolling it around on your tongue before swallowing; there's usually a spitoon if you don't want to swallow. Don't be shy about discussing the wines with the person serving – their purpose is to dispense chat and wisdom, and even wine snobs are down-to-earth Australians at heart.

valley makes a popular **day-trip** from Adelaide, and many of the big commercial wineries are besieged by busloads of tourists intent on a day's free drinking. The area seems thoroughly touristy and traffic-laden if you quickly whizz through it; however, the peaceful back roads yield more interest, with a number of small, family-owned wineries to explore. Many provide picnic areas and barbecues, and even children's playgrounds.

The first vines were planted in 1847 at the Orlando vineyards, an estate which is still a big wine producer. There are now nearly fifty **wineries**, from multinationals to tiny specialists. Because of the variety of soil and climate, the Barossa seems able to produce a wide range of wine types of consistently high quality; the white rieslings are among the best. The region has a typically Mediterranean climate, with dry summers and mild winters; best time to visit is autumn (March–May), when the vines turn russet and golden and the harvest has begun in earnest. Much of the grape-picking is still done by hand and **work** is available from February. This is also the time of the week-long **Vintage Festival**, beginning on Easter Monday in every odd-numbered year (☎08/8563 0600 for more information). Another local celebration is the **International Barossa Music Festival**, held annually for two weeks in early October and featuring mostly chamber music. Its headquarters are at Richmond Grove Winery on Para Road near Tanunda; other wineries act as venues, as do some of the area's pretty Lutheran churches.

Getting into and around the valley

The principal **route** from Adelaide follows the Main North Road through Elizabeth and Gawler, and then joins the **Barossa Valley Highway** to Lyndoch. A more scenic drive takes you through the Adelaide Hills to Williamstown or Angaston, while from the **Sturt Highway** you can turn into the valley at Nuriootpa.

Getting to the valley by **bus** is also reasonably easy: the Barossa–Adelaide Passenger Service (Mon–Fri 3 daily, Sat 2 daily, Sun 1 daily; ☎08/8564 3022) stops at the main Barossa towns en route to Angaston, or the daily Sydney-bound Greyhound Pioneer service can drop you at Nuriootpa. The exclusive tourist Bluebird Rail **train** runs from Adelaide all the way into Lyndoch, Tanunda and Nuriootpa (Tues, Thurs & Sun 8.50am, returning 5.20pm; $55 return; bookings essential ☎08/8212 7888; tour packages also available). If you're cycling, you might want to consider taking your bike on the standard train to Gawler, 14km from Lyndoch.

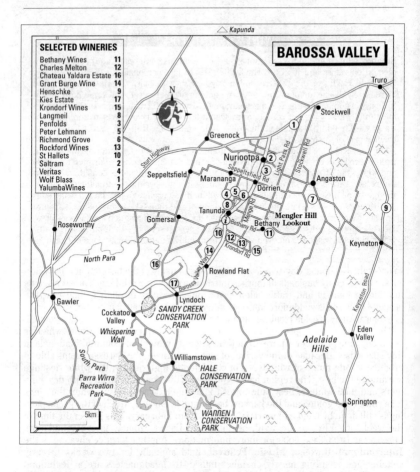

SELECTED WINERIES

Bethany Wines 11
Charles Melton 12
Chateau Yaldara Estate 16
Grant Burge Wine 14
Henschke 9
Kies Estate 17
Krondorf Wines 15
Langmeil 8
Penfolds 3
Peter Lehmann 5
Richmond Grove 6
Rockford Wines 13
St Hallets 10
Saltram 2
Veritas 4
Wolf Blass 1
Yalumba Wines 7

BAROSSA VALLEY

Driving is not the ideal way to explore the Barossa, particularly if you want to enjoy tasting wines – once here, you can always rent a bike or take a tour. If you decide you do need a **car** to get around, you can **rent** one from the Caltex service station, 8 Murray St, Tanunda (☎08/8563 2677; $65 per day). A better way to experience the area is to **cycle**; there's a sealed bike track avoiding the busy highway between Tanunda and bike rental (around $10 a day) is available at *Zinfandel's*, 58 Murray St, Tanunda (☎08/8563 2822), *The Bunkhaus*, Barossa Valley Way, Nuriootpa (☎08/8562 2260), and *Barossa Caravan Park*, Barossa Valley Way, Lyndoch (☎08/8524 4262). There's also a range of **tours** from Adelaide offered by all the big commercial tour operators (see Adelaide "Listings", p.701) For something different, try the small-group day-tour with Groovy Grape Getaways (☎08/8359 4422; $39), which stops at Gumeracha's giant rocking horse, the Whispering Wall near Lyndoch, and four large wineries, and includes a barbecue lunch – the emphasis on a free grog-up makes it popular with backpackers. Prime Mini Tours (☎08/8293 4900; $38) runs a more sedate minibus tour from Adelaide, with a similar itinerary including a three-course sit-down lunch.

BAROSSA WINERIES

It's hard to choose between so many wineries, as almost all of them are worth a look. However, the twelve below should start you off.

Bethany Wines, Bethany Rd, Bethany. A hillside winery set in an old quarry, with views over Bethany village (see overleaf); five generations of the Schrapel family have grown grapes here. The ports are worth trying, especially the unusual white variety. Mon–Sat 10am–5pm, Sun 1–5pm.

Charles Melton, Krondorf Rd, Tanunda. Small, friendly winery concentrating on a limited range of full-bodied reds that sell out fast. Informal tasting area in a wooden shed, where you sit at a long wooden table, with the door open to the vineyards and a friendly dog at your feet. Daily 11am–5pm.

Chateau Yaldara Estate, Gomersal Rd, Lyndoch. The ruins of a nineteenth-century flour mill have been transformed into a Baroque-style chateau. Tours (daily 10.15am, 10.45am, 1.15pm, 2.15pm & 3.15pm; $3) focus on the chateau's antiques collection. European-style wines, specializing in sweet and sparkling whites. See p.711 for details of bistro. Mon–Fri 8.30am–5pm, Sat 9am–5pm.

Grant Burge Wines, Barossa Valley Way, Jacob's Creek. Small, quality winery, established in 1988 to process wine from the area's oldest vineyards. Daily 10am–5pm.

Henschke, Moculta Rd, Keyneton, southeast of Angaston. Fifth-generation wine makers, the Henschke family's wines have won many international prizes. In a peaceful setting off the beaten track where you'll need to ring the bell to rouse the amiable staff and start tasting. Mon–Fri 9am–4.30pm, Sat 9am–noon.

Krondorf Wines, Krondorf Rd, Tanunda. Revamped 1860s winery and vineyard, with a reputation for the quality and integrity of its mostly white wines. Daily 10am–5pm.

Langmeil Winery, Langmeil Rd, near Tanunda. This was the original Langmeil village, built in the 1840s; the little vineyard you can see from the tasting area was planted in 1846. Prints of nineteenth-century photos on the walls document the local wine industry. With a slow and thoughtful approach to tasting and a small range (three reds, three whites and a tawny port), you really get to know the wines; the very peppery Grenache is definitely worth trying. Daily 11am–5pm.

Peter Lehmann, Para Rd, near Tanunda. Another pleasant spot for a bit of tasting in a homestead with vine-entwined verandahs surrounded by flowerbeds, gum trees and palms, overlooking a lawn leading down to the Para River; you're welcome to picnic here. A local figure, Lehmann is as much known for his red wines as his art collection. The wine labels feature South Australian artists, whose original paintings are on display. Mon–Fri 9.30am–5pm, Sat & Sun 10.30am–4pm.

Rockford Wines, Krondorf Rd, Tanunda. No-nonsense approach and big unfussy wines using grapes by wine maker Robert O'Callahan, produced by old-fashioned techniques; good Grenache and Basket Press Shiraz, and an amazing fizzy Black Shiraz at around $37 a bottle. Tasting in an 1850s stone barn. Mon–Sat 11am–5pm.

St Hallets Winery, Krondorf Rd, Tanunda. Medium-size quality producer. Its star wine is Old Block Shiraz, sourced from vines eighty to a hundred years old, with an intense flavour and a velvety softness. Daily 10am–5pm.

Veritas, Langmeil Rd, near Tanunda. Established in the 1950s and known for its Hungarian-style wines, this is a family operation; they control the whole process, from crushing, fermenting and bottling, to labelling, tastings and sales in an unpretentious shed. A good place to come during harvest, around April. Mon–Fri 9am–5pm, Sat & Sun 11am–5pm.

Yalumba Wines, Eden Valley Rd, Angaston. Largest and oldest family-operated Barossa winery, established in 1849. Lovely building and gardens. Mon–Fri 9am–5pm, Sat 10am–5pm, Sun noon–5pm.

Lyndoch and around

"A beautiful place, good land, plenty of grass and its general appearance open with some patches of wood and many kangaroos," reported Colonel William Light in 1837 on first sight of the **LYNDOCH** area; settled in 1839, it's one of the oldest towns in South Australia. Although vineyards were established from the outset, the primary activity was the growing of wheat until 1896, when someone had the bright idea of converting a flour mill into a winery. Today there are ten wineries in the immediate Lyndoch area, from some of the smallest to one of the largest in the Barossa, all still family-owned. Kies Estate, a small-scale winery on Barossa Valley Way, provides **tourist information** as well as tastings (daily 10am–4.30pm; ☎08/8524 4110).

Eight kilometres south of Lyndoch, off **Yettie Road**, is the **Whispering Wall**, a retaining wall for the **Barossa Reservoir**; it's shaped in such a way that a spoken message can be heard plainly on the opposite side 140m away. To the northeast, four kilometres along the Barossa Valley Way, the village of **ROWLAND FLAT** is dominated by the **Orlando Winery** complex (Mon–Fri 10am–5pm, Sat & Sun 10am–4pm), the oldest winery in the valley and home of some of Australia's best-known wines, sold under the **Jacob's Creek** label. Johann Gramp planted the first commercial vines at nearby Jacob's Creek in 1847, and forty years later his son expanded the winery and moved it to Rowland Flat.

Four kilometres north of Rowland Flat, the peaceful **Krondorf Road/Hallet Valley** area runs east of the Barossa Valley Way, with four charming wineries, each with its own philosophy of wine making and tasting: Krondorf, Rockford, St Hallets and Charles Melton. Behind St Hallets Winery you can watch skilled coopers at work at the **Keg Factory**, St Hallet Road (Mon–Sat 8am–4.30pm, Sun 10.30am–4.30pm); the huge stainless steel fermentation tanks you'll see around the valley aren't suitable for all wines, many of which still need to be aged in wood to impart flavour.

Parallel to Krondorf Road to the north, Bethany Road runs east off the Barossa Valley Way to **BETHANY**, the first German settlement in the Barossa. The land is still laid out in the eighteenth-century *Hufendorf* style, with long, narrow farming strips stretching out behind the cottages, and the creek running through each property. Pretty gardens set off the old stone cottages, which remain well cared for. At dusk each Saturday the bell tolls at **Herberge Christi Church**, keeping up a tradition to mark the working-week's end, and Bethany – without even a pub or shop – retains its peaceful, rural village feel. The common where cattle grazed is now the Bethany Reserve, with a picnic spot by the creek.

Tanunda

TANUNDA, the Barossa's most quintessentially German town, announces itself as a tourist destination as you head along the Barossa Valley Way and enter through the Orlando archway that spans **Murray Street**. This tree-lined main street, with several old and beautiful buildings, proclaims its pedigree with German music at its most pedestrian wafting out of small wooden kegs above the shops. More authentic atmosphere can be found in the narrow streets on the western side of town, towards the river. Here, **Goat Square** was the site of the first town market and is bordered by the original cottages; during the Vintage Festival (see p.705), the early market is re-enacted. Many **wineries** dot the town, the largest concentration along **Para Road**, beside the Para river: Stanley Brothers, Peter Lehmann, Richmond Grove, Langmeil and Veritas, all of which can be visited by taking a pleasant stroll along the road and the river.

For **tourist information** and a good introduction to the wine-making industry, head for the **Barossa Wine and Visitor Centre**, 66–68 Murray St (Mon–Fri 9am–4pm, Sat & Sun 10am–4pm; wine centre daily 10am–4pm; $2; ☎08/8563 0600 or free call ☎1800/812 662). The centre tells the history of the Barossa in an original way – on three tiers of cylinders, which you roll to consult. Each group of cylinders represents a different historical period: you spin the top tier for a background on world events, the middle tier for a specific Barossa chronology, and the bottom tier for Australia-wide happenings at the time to examine the Barossa's wine industry in the context of Australian and world history – it's quite engrossing. There are also engaging interpretive displays about wine making, and it's here that you can pick up some additional tips on wine-tasting etiquette. If you don't want to pay the admission fee, drop in to the low-key **Barossa Valley Historical Museum**, 47 Murray St (Mon–Fri 1–5pm, Sat & Sun 2–5pm; free).

Less relevant, but more fun, is the **Kev Rohrlach Collection** on Barossa Valley Way (Mon–Sat 11am–4pm, Sun 10am–5pm; $8), a museum created by a self-made man who started collecting tractors, then progressed through motorcycles, buggies and tanks to solar-powered cars; added to this is Kev's booty from trips to the South Pole, the Himalayas and Mount Kilimanjaro. **Norm's Coolies** at "Breezy Gully" off Gomersal Road, 3km out of town (Mon, Wed & Sat 2pm; $6, children $2), could only be in Australia: 28 sheepdogs are put through their paces by Norm and a herd of sheep. **Mengler's Hill Lookout**, east of Tanunda along Basedow Road and then the Mengler's Hill Road Scenic Drive, provides an unmatched view of the valley and its vineyards: there's a **Sculpture Garden** with white marble sculptures on the slopes below, and at night you can see the lights of Adelaide.

Seppeltsfield, off the highway 4km northwest of Tanunda, must be the most spectacular of the wineries (tastings Mon–Fri 10am–5pm, Sat 10.30am–4.30pm, Sun 11am–4pm). During the Great Depression the Seppelt family paid their workers in food to plant an avenue of date palms from Marananga to Seppeltsfield. On a hill halfway along the palm-lined avenue is the **Seppelt family mausoleum**, resting place of the male members of the family. The estate itself was founded in 1851 when Joseph Seppelt, a wealthy merchant, arrived from Silesia with his workers: he turned to wine making when his tobacco crop failed. Seppelts became the largest winery in the colony, having everything from a port-maturation cellar to a distillery, vinegar factory and brandy bond store. All have been preserved in their original condition, and can be seen on a **tour** (Mon–Fri 11am, 1pm, 2pm & 3pm, Sat & Sun 11.30am, 1.30pm & 2.30pm; $3).

Nuriootpa and Angaston

Just 7km from Tanunda, **NURIOOTPA** is the valley's commercial centre: as the place where local Aborigines gathered to barter it takes its name from the word for "meeting place". It's not the most attractive of towns, dominated as it is by **Penfolds**, the Barossa's largest winery; it churns out mass-produced wines, not all of which are made from local grapes. The finest building here is **Coulthard House**, a gracious, two-storey edifice commissioned by the area's first settler, William Coulthard. The town grew around his red-gum slab hotel, now the site of the *Vine Inn* community hotel. Together with the community store (where co-op members purchase shares and share in the profits), this finances many developments in the town such as the excellent **swimming centre** in Coulthard Reserve by the shady, gum-lined North Para River.

ANGASTON, southeast of Nuriootpa, is a pretty little town situated in the Barossa Ranges, an area of predominantly grazing land, red gums and rolling hills, although a few of the Barossa's oldest wine makers have been here for more than a century. This is the side of the Barossa that attracted the British pioneers, including George Fife Angas, the Scotsman after whom the town is named. The **Collingrove Homestead** (Mon–Fri 1–4.30pm, Sat & Sun 11am–4.30pm; closed Fri July–Sept; $3), 6km from town on Eden Valley Road, was one of his homes. Owned by the National Trust, it's surrounded by lush gardens and offers accommodation (see "Barossa accommodation" overleaf). Angas also lived at nearby Lindsay Park, now the private **Lindsay Park Stud**, Australia's leading racehorse breeding and training complex.

At **SPRINGTON**, 20km south of Angaston, the major attraction is the **Herbig family tree**, a hollowed-out gum tree in which a pioneer German couple began their married life and had two of their sixteen children, living there for five years from 1855. Inevitably, Springton's old buildings have undergone the "boutiquing" process: the blacksmith shop is now a winery, and the old post office has been transformed into an arts and crafts gallery.

Barossa accommodation

There's comfortable accommodation, B&Bs and caravan parks throughout the valley, and you shouldn't have a problem finding somewhere decent to stay. Listed below are some of the better-value places.

Barossa Brauhaus Hotel, 41 Murray St, Angaston (☎08/8564 2014). Good-value basic rooms and cheap singles in a pub first licensed in 1849. Central location. Light breakfast included. ③.

Barossa House, Barossa Valley Way, halfway between Tanunda and Nuriootpa (☎ & fax 08/8562 4022). Excellent-value B&B, with en-suite rooms. ⑥.

Bunkhaus Travellers Hostel and Cottage, Barossa Valley Way, 1.5km south of Nuriootpa (☎08/8562 2260). A comfortable, friendly, family-run hostel set in vineyards, with a cosy common room for winter, and a swimming pool for summer. Can help find work. Bike rental. Self-contained cottage ③, dorms ①.

Collingrove Homestead, Eden Valley Rd, 6km from Angaston (☎ & fax 08/8564 2061). National Trust-listed B&B accommodation in old servants' quarters, set in English-style gardens. ⑧.

Hillview Guesthouse, 12 Hill St, Angaston (☎08/8564 2761, fax 8564 2508). A former girls' grammar school whose lower storey has been transformed into a gracious guesthouse run by a friendly family. There's a sitting room complete with open fires, a stereo and bar, plus a swimming pool and spa. Each of the two spacious guestrooms has its own bathroom and antique furnishings. Gourmet breakfast is served beside the pool. ⑧.

Langmeil Cottages, Langmeil Rd, Tanunda (☎ & fax 08/8563 2987). German-style stone cottage with cooking facilities, peaceful setting and views of the Barossa Ranges; extras include champagne on arrival, breakfast provisions, free use of bicycles, barbecue and heated pool. Laundry facilities too. ⑦–⑧.

Lawley Farm, Krondorf Rd (& fax 08/8563 2141). Restored stone cottages shaded by pepper trees on a quiet road ideal for walking and cycling and within walking distance of the best wineries. Full breakfast in the farmhouse kitchen and a hot spa in the garden. ⑧.

Seppeltsfield Holiday Units, Seppeltsfield Rd (☎08/8562 8240). These well-equipped log cabins, with wood fires, offer some of the best-value accommodation in the valley, set on a rural hillside overlooking the Seppelt winery. Deluxe cabins with spa ⑦, standard rooms ④.

Tanunda Caravan and Tourist Park, Murray St, Tanunda (☎08/8563 2784). Set in parkland among beautiful waratah trees. Cabins ③, on-site vans ②.

Tanunda Hotel, 51 Murray St, Tanunda (☎08/8563 2030 or 8563 2165). Built from local stone and marble in 1845, with Edwardian additions and decor inside. All rooms have TV, air-con, fridge, tea and coffee; some are en-suite. ④.

Vine Inn Hotel Motel, 14 Murray St, Nuriootpa (☎08/8562 2133, fax 8562 3236). Spacious, modern motel-style units with air-con and queen-size beds; continental breakfast included. Spa and heated pool. ⑦.

Vineyards Motel, corner of Stockwell and Nuriootpa rds, Angaston (☎08/8564 2404, fax 8564 2932). Good location opposite the *Vintners Bar and Grill*, just a short walk away from Saltram Winery and its bistro. Modern units; facilities include room service, solar-heated swimming pool and spa. ④–⑤.

Yalambee, Springton Rd, Williamstown (☎ & fax 08/8524 6301). Your own homestead on a sheep and cattle property; provisions are included for a hearty breakfast. ⑧.

Barossa eating and drinking

To go with the wine, and to cater for all the tourists, there are excellent restaurants throughout the valley, as well as plenty of picnic spots and barbecue areas.

Barossa Bistro, 37 Murray St, Angaston (☎08/8564 2361). Casual dining nightly with affordable, filling main courses including some interesting kangaroo dishes; lighter, cheaper meals at lunchtime. Licensed.

Barossa Wurst Haus and Bakery, 86a Murray St, Tanunda. Specializing in traditional Barossa *Mettwurst*, this delicatessen offers cheap but very tasty food. Good cappuccino. Daily 8am–6pm.

Cafe Lanzerac, Main St, Tanunda. The Barossa's one trendy café is spacious, cool and glass-fronted. The focus is on Barossa wine, sold by the glass. Lots of fish, pasta and salads on the big blackboard menu – and the best coffee in town. Licensed and reasonably priced. Open daily from breakfast through to dinner.

Chateau Yaldara Garden Bistro, Gomersal Rd, Lyndoch. Affordable prices aimed at families, with a children's menu too; pasta dominates. Also morning and afternoon tea. Daily 10am–4pm.

Linke's Bakery and Tea Rooms, 40 Murray St, Nuriootpa. Filling soups and inexpensive German fare.

Lyndoch Bakery, Barossa Valley Highway, Lyndoch. Best German bakery in the Barossa; also a moderately priced licensed restaurant with hearty, traditional dishes. Closed Mon.

1918 Bistro and Grill, 94 Murray St, Tanunda (☎08/8563 0405). Fresh food and local ingredients are cooked with a Mediterranean twist. Local wines or BYO. Eat outside on wide, plant-shaded verandahs in this fab old house.

The Park Restaurant/Café, 2a Murray St, Tanunda (☎08/8563 3500). An 1840s stone villa set in a park; alfresco eating, or dining by the fire inside if it's cold. Affordable Modern Australian cuisine.

Saltram Estate Bistro, Nuriootpa Rd, Angaston. Bistro attached to a nineteenth-century winery. Choose from the latest trendy Pacific Rim cuisine, all fresh and delicious. Full-bodied reds are Saltram's forte, and you can try them in the tasting area, with three different appetizers for $1. Meals lunchtime only.

Tanunda Hotel, 51 Murray St, Tanunda (☎08/8563 2030). Interesting food a cut above the usual hotel fare, with plenty of moderately priced vegetarian dishes.

Vintners Bar and Grill, corner of Stockwell and Nuriootpa rds, Angaston (☎08/8564 2488). A wine-makers' hangout with Mediterranean-style regional produce on the menu and a suitably impressive wine list; cool, contemporary decor meets old stone walls, fireplaces and wooden beams, and there's a vine-covered courtyard for warm days. Expensive. Tues–Sun lunch, Wed–Sat dinner.

Wild Olive, Pheasant Farm Rd, off Samuel Rd, via Seppeltsfield Rd, near Nuriootpa (☎08/8562 1286). This highly regarded restaurant with a French chef has a seasonal regional menu featuring adventurous food. The yabbies (crayfish) are caught in a lake on the grounds. Expensive. Licensed or BYO. Wed–Sun lunch, Thurs–Sat dinner.

Zinfandel Tea Rooms, 58 Murray St, Tanunda. Popular place for hot, cooked breakfasts, German and Australian dishes for lunch and a delicious choice of strudels and cakes. You can sit inside the cosy cottage or out on the verandah. Daily 8.30am–6pm.

The Fleurieu Peninsula

The **Fleurieu Peninsula**, thirty minutes south of Adelaide by car, is bounded by Gulf St Vincent to the west and the Southern Ocean to the south, the two connected by the Backstairs Passage at **Cape Jervis** (where the ferry leaves for Kangaroo Island, see p.717). There are fine beaches on both coasts and, inland, more wineries in the rolling **Southern Vales**. It's pleasantly undeveloped: many of the towns were settled from the 1830s and there's a lot of **colonial architecture**, often housing restaurants and B&Bs. For a round trip, leave the city via the Adelaide Hills and cut down through Mount Barker to well-preserved Strathalbyn and Goolwa, on the south coast, circling round through Victor Harbor, Willunga and McLaren Vale. The peninsula is a good place to **cycle** – in addition to its roads it has two sealed bike paths: the 15km Ngarrindjeri Bikeway (shared with rollerbladers and walkers) follows the coast from Goolwa to just beyond Victor Harbor; another (shorter) path runs between Willunga and McLaren Vale.

If you're relying on **public transport**, try Premier Stateliner (☎08/8415 5555) which makes two to three daily trips from Adelaide to Goolwa via McLaren Vale, Willunga, Victor Harbor and Port Elliot. There's also a sporadic service provided by the *Southern Encounter* **steam train** (occasionally replaced by a diesel locomotive) which chugs from Mt Barker to Strathalbyn through Goolwa and Port Elliot to Victor Harbor (1–4 Sundays a month, closed Feb–April; call ☎08/8391 1223 for details). If you'd rather take a **tour**, Bee-init Tours (☎08/8332 1401) offer several half and full-day minibus tours of the peninsula from Adelaide; the most popular includes afternoon wine-tasting in McLaren Vale and an evening observing the Fairy Penguins at Victor Harbor ($44;

6hr). A day-trip with Shaun's Boundaway Tours (☎08/8371 3147; $39 including morning and afternoon tea) heads through the Adelaide Hills and takes in wine-tasting plus all the peninsula sights, with time for a swim at Maslins Beach in warm weather.

Goolwa and Port Elliot

GOOLWA lies 12km upstream from the ever-shifting sand bar at the mouth of the Murray River. Boaties love its position adjacent to vast Lake Alexandrina, yet with easy access to the Coorong (see p.724) and the ocean, and its situation has always been its fortune. Although so close to the coast, Goolwa feels like a real river town, and it thrived above all in the days of the Murray paddle-steamer trade, when it was the final offloading port: then a rip-roaring river town with over 88 taverns, it had the biggest police station in South Australia. The railways brought the good days to an end, and today only a few reminders of boom times remain along Railway Terrace, with its old buildings painted in Federation colours. Steam trains make a comeback on Sundays, however, when the Cockle Train runs along the coast to Victor Harbor and back (see p.714) and the Southern Encounter operates from the Adelaide Hills to Goolwa via Strathalbyn and Victor Harbor (see opposite). On Railway Terrace you'll find **Goolwa Tourist Information Centre** (daily 10am–4pm; ☎08/8555 1144) which has information on cruises from the end of the wharf (see box below).

Also on the wharf is **Signal Point Interpretive Centre** (daily 10am–5pm; $5), an innovatively designed exhibition telling the story of the Murray and its river trade. A free 24-hour car ferry crosses from Goolwa to the mostly bare and flat **Hindmarsh Island** (called Kumarangk by the local Aboriginal people), between the river mouth and the lake. Although apparently tranquil, the island has been at the centre of a controversy since plans to build a bridge linking it to the mainland were abandoned in July 1994, on the grounds that the development would be harmful to the sacred women's business of the area's **Ngarrindjeri Aborigines**. In December 1995 the Federal Court in Canberra overturned the 25-year bridge-building ban, having concluded that the women's sacred knowledge was a fabrication. Despite outcries, and the claims of an archeologist that there are burial grounds on the island that should be protected, the state government plans to go ahead with the bridge but at the time of writing it was still looking for developers.

Although the tourist office doesn't book **accommodation**, they can provide you with a comprehensive list. *Goolwa Riverport Motel* (☎08/8555 5033, fax 8555 5022; ⑤), on Noble Avenue 3km northeast of Goolwa, has motel units, pool, sauna, tennis court, bar and an inexpensive dining room. *Graham's Castle*, on Castle St, 2km from the centre (☎08/8555 3300; rooms ②, dorms ①) is an old mansion which offers budget and back-

---

CRUISES FROM GOOLWA

Cruises to the mouth of the Murray and as far as **Cooroong National Park** (see p.724) leave from the end of the wharf. Goolwa Cruises (☎08/8555 2203) run several trips: *P.S. Mundoo*, a replica paddle steamer, makes gentle river cruises (Aug–May Thurs; 1hr; $10); the motorised *M.V. Aroona* heads to the river mouth, passing through the barrages which keep salt water out of the freshwater system, and into the Coorong wetlands (Tues & Sat noon; 2hr 45min; $18); a longer cruise goes to the dune-covered Younghusband Peninsula where passengers can alight and walk to the Southern Ocean (Sept–April Sun & Wed; 4hr 30min; $29); even longer is the 16km trip right into the national park (Oct–March first Friday of the month; 5hr; $27). Coorong Cruises (☎08/8555 1133) has a smaller, specially designed boat for a day-long trip which focuses on bird-watching and looks at Aboriginal sites on the Younghusband Peninsula (Oct–end of June Tues, Thurs & Sun; $59).

packer accommodation and has more of an eco-slant, with its own cruises on the Coorong. The alternative in town is the *Corio Hotel* on Railway Terrace (☎08/8555 2011, fax 8555 1109; ④),which is also a popular **eating** place. Campers can head for *Goolwa Camping and Tourist Park*, Kessel Road, just 1km northwest of the centre (☎08/8555 2144; on-site vans ②).

PORT ELLIOT, on the coast 14km west of Goolwa, is a pleasant little town with some fine old buildings and a wonderful find, the *Sitar Indian Restaurant*, 12 The Strand (☎08/8554 2144; summer dinner nightly, rest of year Wed–Sun), which serves traditional Northern Indian food and vegetarian specials. There's good **surf** between here and Victor Harbor – you can rent gear from Southern Surf, at 36 North Terrace. Chiton Rocks Surf Lifesaving Club, on Seagull Avenue (☎08/8554 2047), overlooks the surf of **Chiton Rocks** and has hostel-style accommodation aimed at surfers (①). The best beach for relatively easy surfing is **Middleton**, while **Waitpinga Pass** offers more thrills to experienced surfers. For the latest surf report, call ☎08/8554 2047.

Victor Harbor

VICTOR HARBOR, on Encounter Bay, was once a popular holiday destination for Adelaidians. In the 1920s there were 65 guesthouses and thousands poured in during the peak season; an uncomfortable four-hour train ride only added to the adventure. Then, as decent roads and the motor car brought it within an hour's drive, fewer people came – it was too easy, too close to home. Now, however, thanks to whales (plus penguins and the re-emergence of train power), Victor Harbor is experiencing a resurgence, evident in a much-redeveloped esplanade centred around a grassy foreshore square with a bronze fountain of a diving whale.

In the 1830s there were three whaling stations here, hunting **southern right whales**. They were so called because they were the "right" ones to kill: slow-moving because of their high oil content, which fortuitously also made them float after their slaughter. They would come to Encounter Bay to mate and breed between June and September, heading close to shore where they became easy targets. After the peak period in the decade of the 1830s, their numbers began to decline: the last one taken here was in 1878, and by 1930 they'd been hunted almost to extinction. Half a century later there were signs of recovery, and in 1991 forty were spotted in the bay and eighty thousand people flocked to see them. Between June and October in 1998, sixteen females stayed in the bay to calf, and a dozen humpback whales were also spotted – it's estimated that almost a thousand visitors came here to watch the whales from the shoreline. Not surprisingly, Victor Harbor converted a Heritage-listed former railway goods shed on Railway Terrace into the **South Australian Whale Centre** (daily 10am–5pm; $5). It has excellent interpretive displays, exhibits and screenings on whaling and on the natural history of whales, dolphins and the marine environment. The centre also acts as a monitoring station, locating and tracking whales, and confirming sightings, most likely in June, July or August (hotline for information on locations ☎1900/931 223; 75¢ per minute; *www.webmedia.com.au/whales*). To report your own sighting, dial ☎08/8552 5644.

It's not only whales that bring visitors to Victor Harbor, but also **Little Penguins**, who come to nest, roost and moult on **Granite Island**, linked to the Esplanade by a narrow causeway. A couple of hours after dusk they come back from feeding – this is the best time to see them, on one of the centre's **ranger-led penguin walks** ($5; 1hr; daytime tours also available; booking essential on ☎08/8552 7555). Before exploring the island you can visit the **Penguin Interpretive Centre**, which houses an audiovisual holographic display with a 3D park ranger giving the lowdown on daily penguin life (open an hour before the start of a walk; $2, walk and centre admission combined $6). You can walk across the 500m causeway to the island at any time, or get there on a traditional holiday ride with the Granite Island Horse Tram (daily 10am–9.50pm; $5 evening return, $4 daytime return).

Other local attractions include two Sunday steam **trains** (sometimes diesel-hauled), the Cockle Train that runs on the otherwise disused line along the coast to Goolwa via Port Elliot and back (every Sun & daily during school holidays; $15 return), and the Southern Encounter from the Adelaide Hills to Gollwavia Victor Harbour (see p.712). If you're travelling with restless children, **Greenhills Adventure Park**, Waggon Road, alongside the Hindmarsh River (daily 10am–5.30pm, later in summer; $12.50 adult or child), has activities from canoeing to go-kart racing, while **Urimburra Wildlife Experience** (daily 9am–6pm; $6.50, child $3.50), 5km north on Adelaide Road, is an open-range park with native animals from all over the continent.

For further **information**, head for the volunteer-run Victor Harbor Tourist Information Centre on Railway Terrace (daily 10am–4pm; ☎08/8552 5738); next door, the professional Fleurieu Peninsula Booking Office (free call ☎1800/241 033) can book **accommodation** and tours. The best place to stay is the *Anchorage Guest House*, 21 Flinders Parade (☎08/8552 5970, fax 8552 1970; ④–⑦), a lovingly restored beachfront guesthouse with en-suite and spa facilities, and a lively café attached (see below). Alternatives include the *Villa Victor Bed and Breakfast*, 59 Victoria St (☎08/8552 4258; ④–⑤); the *Family Inn Motel*, 300 Port Elliot Rd (☎ & fax 08/8552 1941; ④); and the *Adare Caravan Park*, Wattle Drive (☎08/8552 1657), in the grounds of lovely Adare House – it's run by the Uniting Church, so no alcohol is allowed.

Good places to **eat** abound. The super *Cafe Bavaria* at 11 Albert Place is a gleaming venue with delicious fresh-baked German cakes and savouries at reasonable prices (closed Mon). If you're after Italian food, head for *Nino Solari's Pizzeria*, nearby at no. 16, where you can plough into some generous portions of pasta and home-made *gelati*; for fish, try the old-fashioned *South Coast Fish Café*, 10 Ocean St, or the *Anchorage Café* on beachfront Flinders Parade, a lively city-style café with entertainment (ranging from classical harpists to bands) and an eclectic menu with good choice for vegetarians. Two good places to **drink** are on the Esplanade: the *Hotel Crown* serves cheap bar meals and has big-name bands on weekends, while the more upmarket *Hotel Victor* has a varied bistro menu.

The Southern Vales

The wineries of the **Southern Vales**, in the northwest of the peninsula, are virtually in Adelaide, and the suburban fringes of the city now push right up to **REYNELLA**, where the first vineyards were planted in 1838. Among the earliest was Hardy's Reynella Winery on Reynell Road (daily 10am–4.30pm), where the tasting room occupies the original ironstone and brick building set in botanical gardens. There are several other wineries in Reynella but the largest concentration, often in bush settings though only an hour's drive from Adelaide, is around the small town of **McLAREN VALE**, which has about forty wineries, mostly small and family-run. Since the 1960s there's been a trend for grape growers to switch from supplying wine makers to producing their own wine in a bid for independence, and as a result there's a swath of "boutique" wineries here.

McLaren Vale is itself a "boutique" town, with many B&Bs and restaurants catering for the wine-buff weekend crowd. The liveliest time is in October when the **Bushing Festival** celebrates the new wines, and the Bushing King or Queen, the wine maker who has produced the wine judged to be the best of the vintage, is crowned. A big part of the festival is the **craft market** held during the last weekend at Kay's Amery Vineyards (see box opposite), where there are fifty stalls manned by the artisans themselves, as well as food and entertainment. Information on this, and on the area's wineries, can be found at the **McLaren Vale and Fleurieu Visitor Centre** on Main Road, about 2km from the centre (daily 10am–5pm; ☎08/8323 9944) – it even has its own vineyard and a wine barcum-café; the centre can also book **accommodation**. Among the B&Bs are *McLaren Vale*, 56 Valley View Drive (☎08/8323 9351; ⑤), which is very homely and serves a full breakfast; *Southern Vales*, 13 Chalk Hill Rd (☎08/8323 8144; ⑥), a more modern and

SOUTHERN VALES WINERIES

Listed below are half a dozen favourites from a wide choice of excellent wineries.

Chapel Hill, Chapel Hill Rd, McLaren Vale, adjacent to the Onkaparinga Gorge. A small but very civilized winery in an old stone chapel. Wine maker Pam Dunsford was McLaren Vale's first Bushing Queen; her wines have won several prizes. There are views over vineyards, plus barbecue facilities. Mon–Fri 9am–5pm, Sat & Sun 11am–5pm.

D'Arenberg, Osborn Rd, McLaren Vale. A family winery set up in 1928 and long well-known for its prize-winning reds. Tastings daily 10am–5pm. The superb restaurant, *D'Arry's Verandah*, is garnering accolades for its chef and stunning hilltop views over the vineyards (Wed–Sat lunch, Fri & Sat dinner; bookings on ☎08/8323 8710).

Kay's Amery Vineyards, Kays Rd, McLaren Vale. A wonderful family winery established in 1890; old photos of the family and the area cover the oak casks containing port. It's renowned for its Block 6 Shiraz from vines planted in 1892, though this wine is a very fast mover and you might be out of luck. There's a picnic area set amid towering gum trees. Mon–Fri 8am–5pm, Sat & Sun noon–5pm.

Noon's, Rifle Range Rd, McLaren Vale. If you're interested only in reds, come here: that's all they do. Bring a steak, grab a few bottles and take advantage of the creekside barbecue area. Daily 10am–5pm.

Scarpantoni, Scarpantoni Drive, McLaren Flat. A small prize-winning winery run by an Italian family: someone's always happy to chat about wine over a glass. Mon–Fri 10am–5pm, Sat & Sun 11am–5pm.

Woodstock, Douglas Gully Rd, McLaren Flat. A tiny, peaceful tasting room looking out onto a garden. Sunday lunch with guest chefs in the *Coterie* next door (bookings on ☎08/8383 0156). Mon–Fri 9am–5pm, Sat & Sun noon–5pm.

hotel-like place with gorgeous vineyard views; and *Samarkand*, Branson Road (☎ & fax 08/8323 8756; ⑦), a separate wing of a cottage on a peaceful property with horses and alpacas. Most **places to eat** are fairly fancy, and many of the wineries also have restaurants attached (for options see box above); simpler meals can be had at *Koffee n Snax*, an unpretentious coffee shop at 150 Main Rd. The award-winning *Magnum Bistro* in the *Hotel McLaren*, 208 Main Rd (☎08/8323 8208), has delicious main courses, all reasonably priced. Across the road, at no. 199, the BYO *Pipkins* serves morning tea and light lunch. Restaurants include *The Barn*, on the corner of Main and Chalk Hill roads (☎08/8323 8618), where you can dine on moderately priced contemporary cuisine and choose your own local wine from the cellar. On the corner of McMurtie Road, in the direction of Willunga, is the *Salopian Inn* (☎08/8323 8769; lunch daily, dinner weekends only), an atmospheric 1851 stone inn with a seasonally varied menu.

Gulf St Vincent beaches

A series of superb swimming beaches, often known as the **wine coast**, runs along the Gulf St Vincent shore roughly parallel to the Southern Vales, from **O'Sullivans Beach** down to **Sellicks Beach**, beyond which the coastline becomes rockier. They're all easily accessible from Adelaide on public transport: take the train from Adelaide to Noarlunga Centre and bus #750 to the various beaches.

PORT NOARLUNGA is the main town, surrounded by steep cliffs and sand hills: its jetty is popular with anglers, and with wetsuit-clad teenagers who dive-bomb from it; at low tide a natural reef is exposed. Lifesavers patrol the local beaches, and you can rent surf and snorkelling gear at Ocean Graffix Surf and Skate Centre, 21 Salt Fleet Point. **Moana**, two beaches south, has fairly tame surf that's perfect for novices. The southern end of **Maslins Beach**, south again, broke new ground by becoming Australia's first legal **nude** bathing beach in 1975. The wide, isolated beach is reached by a long, steep walking track down the colourful cliffs from the Tait Road car park, deterring all but the committed. **Port Willunga**, the next stop down, offers interesting diving around the wreck of the *Star of Greece*. **Aldinga Beach** is the end of the line for public transport – you'll need a lift or transport of your own to reach the 6km of firm sand at **Sellicks Beach**.

The Yorke Peninsula

The **Yorke Peninsula** was almost the last section of the Australian coastline to be mapped by Matthew Flinders in 1802, and it still seems a bit of an afterthought: flat plains stretch out to the sea, so extensively cleared for farming that only tiny areas of original vegetation remain – in the Innes National Park at the very tip of the peninsula and in a couple of conservation parks. Much is now made of the northern peninsula's **Cornish heritage**, but the miners from Cornwall who flocked to the area when **copper** was discovered in 1859 have left behind little but their names and the ubiquitous Cornish pasty. The three towns of the Copper Triangle or **"Little Cornwall"** – Kadina, Wallaroo and Moonta – make the most of it at the Kernewek Lowender (Cornish Festival), held over the long weekend in May of every odd-numbered year, though in fact the mining boom ended seventy years ago, and they've been plain country towns ever since.

Just two hours' drive from Adelaide, the peninsula offers a peaceful weekend break as well as good **fishing**. The east coast ports of Ardrossan, Port Vincent and Edithburgh on the Gulf St Vincent were visited first by ketches and schooners, and later by steamers transporting wheat and barley to England. Now the remaining jetties are used by anglers. They're all pleasant to visit, but **EDITHBURGH** offers most facilities: once a substantial salt-production town and grain port, it still has a few fine old buildings and a long jetty. There's a tidal swimming pool set in a rocky cove, and from Troubridge Hill you can see across to the Fleurieu Peninsula and to **Troubridge Island Conservation Park**, with its 1850s iron lighthouse, migrating seabirds and Fairy penguin population: guided tours are available (☎08/8852 6290 for bookings and details; 2hr; $20; no tours July & Aug). **Accommodation** is available in the lighthouse keeper's cottage, which sleeps up to ten – if you stay here you'll have the whole island to yourself, but it doesn't come cheap (arrange through the tour guide; minimum two-night stay; ⑨). In Edithburgh itself, more affordable options include foreshore motel units and comfortable two-bedroom apartments at *The Anchorage Motel and Holiday Flats* at 24 O'Halloran Parade (☎08/8852 6262, fax 8852 6147; holiday units BYO linen ③–④, rooms ④–⑤) and *Edithburgh Caravan Park* (☎08/8852 6056) further along the foreshore, which has vans (③) and en-suite cabins (④–⑤). There are also motel units at the back of the *Troubridge Hotel* on Blanche Street (☎08/8852 6013; ⑤); this faces the 1878 *Edithburgh Hotel* (☎08/8852 6263), which is the best place for **meals** and includes local oysters on its menu. The *Edithburgh Café* on Edith Street (8am–4.30pm, closed Tues) does good simple meals, from baked potatoes to quiche and salad.

At the tip of the peninsula lies the **Innes National Park**, with its contrasting coastline of rough cliffs, sweeps of beach and sand dunes, and its interior of mallee scrub. The park is untouched except for the ruins of the gypsum-mining town of **Inneston**, near **Stenhouse Bay**. The **visitor centre** (☎08/8854 4040) in the park sells entry permits ($5 per car) and **camping** permits ($5–15 per car depending on which campsite you choose) and offers facilities such as hot showers. The main camping area is at **Pondalowie Bay**, which has some of the best surf in the state; there are several other good surfing spots around the park and north towards Corny Point. Other more sheltered coves and bays are good for snorkelling, with shallow reef areas of colourful marine life, while on land you might see emus, western grey kangaroos, pygmy possums and mallee fowl.

Premier Stateliner (☎08/8415 5500) has a daily **bus** service from Adelaide to Moonta, via Kadina and Wallaroo. The Yorke Peninsula Passenger Service (☎08/8391

2977) runs from Adelaide to Yorketown, alternating daily between the east coast via Ardrossan, Port Vincent and Edithburgh and the centre via Maitland and Minlaton. There's no transport to the national park itself.

Kangaroo Island

As you head towards **Cape Jervis** along the west coast of the Fleurieu Peninsula, **KANGAROO ISLAND**, only 13km offshore, first appears behind a vale of rolling hills. Once you're on the island, its size and lack of development – there's only one person for every square kilometre – leave a strong impression: this is actually Australia's third-largest island after Tasmania and Melville Island (north of Darwin), and as it has 450km of coastline and mostly unsealed roads, it takes some time to explore. To see all the unusual **geological features** and **wildlife habitats**, you'll need at least three days. Most people visit the major attractions on the south coast – Seal Bay, Little Sahara, Remarkable Rocks and Flinders Chase National Park – and miss the other sights. **Aboriginal people** once lived on the island, their presence evidenced by the discovery of stone tools and other items. Kangaroo Island was once joined to the mainland by a land bridge, but it's a mystery exactly when or why the people left, or if they just died out.

Although it's been promoted as a tourist destination for over ten years, the island is still very unspoilt and the locals are as friendly as ever; only in the peak holiday period (Christmas to the end of January, when most of the accommodation is booked up) does it feel busy. Once out of the few small towns, you won't see shops, roadside stalls or service stations; what you will see are long, straight stretches of red road through undulating fields, dense forests of gum or mallee scrub, and the sea. There's often a strong wind off the Southern Ocean, so bring something warm whatever the season, and take care when **swimming**: there are strong rips on many of the beaches. Safe swimming spots include Hog Bay at Eastern Cove and Antechamber Bay both near Penneshaw, Emu Bay, northwest of Kingscote, Stokes Bay, further west and Vivonne Bay on the south side of the island.

Kangaroo Island is possibly the best place in Australia to see an astonishing range of **wildlife**, largely untroubled by disease or natural predators, with a quarter of the land-mass protected in the form of **national or conservation parks**. When Matthew

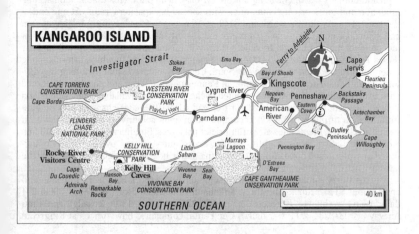

Flinders first sighted the island in 1802, "black substances" seen on shore in the twilight turned out to be **kangaroos**, prolific and easily hunted. Kangaroos still abound, as do wallabies. **Koalas** were introduced at Flinders Chase National Park in 1923 as a conservation measure. They have remained free of clamidia, which is common in the mainland population, and have spread so widely that they are killing off many of the gum trees – recent calls for a cull have provoked national controversy. Other animals found here are echidnas, platypuses, Little penguins, fur seals, sea lions and, in passing, southern right whales; the last three attracted whalers and sealers, many of them American, to make a base on the island after Flinders' discovery. What's more, the island is home to over two hundred kinds of **birds**, as well as snakes.

Wild pigs and feral goats are the successors of those left here by early seafarers, and a pure strain of **Ligurian bees** brought by early settlers has resulted in a honey industry. There are also over a million **sheep** on the island, most of them Merino. However, since wool prices have dropped drastically in recent years, farmers have had to find other sources of income and Kangaroo Island is now becoming known for its gourmet foodstuffs. A sheep dairy here makes delicious Continental-style cheeses, but the latest craze is for **marron farming**, with about 140 licensed producers of the freshwater crustacean, a bit like a cross between a lobster and a yabbie. Other diverse new industries include abalone farming, oyster and mussel production, olive-oil pressing and the revival of eucalyptus-oil distilling.

Getting to the island

Kangaroo Island Sealink **ferries** ply across the Backstairs Passage **from Cape Jervis to Penneshaw** – often a rough journey, though mercifully short. Two large vehicle ferries make the journey at least four times daily, and up to seven times during peak holiday periods, taking about forty minutes to cross: buses connect the service with Adelaide twice daily ($60 return, $88 including bus from Adelaide, cars $130, motorbikes $40, bikes $10; ☎13 1301; *www.sealink.com.au*). At Penneshaw connecting Sealink buses to American River ($6.50 one-way) and Kingscote ($11) need to be booked in advance. Australian Ferries runs a passenger-only service between Glenelg and Kingscote, but it is not very reliable – rough weather or a lack of numbers can delay or cancel sailings, and the longer sea journey can be stomach-churning (daily Oct–May, limited service June & Sept, no service July & Aug; 2hr 30min; $49 one-way, $80 return, bicycle $10; ☎08/8376 8300).

In addition, it's worth checking out the various cheap **packages** that include accommodation and tours or car rental, often with special backpackers' rates. At one end of the scale, Sealink does a whirlwind $143 one-day coach tour leaving Adelaide at 7am and returning at 10.30pm, but it's pretty exhausting. More leisurely options aimed at independent-minded budget travellers staying in hostels are with Kangaroo Island Air & Sea Adventures (☎08/8376 0007 or free call ☎1800/066 422), which offers, among other options, the good-value two-day South Coast Adventure ($165) including two day-tours, a night's hostel accommodation in Penneshaw, the ferry and coach and national park admissions; specific wildlife-oriented packages are also available. Kangaroo Island Ferry Connections (☎08/8553 1233 or free call ☎1800/018 484) has packages ranging from hostels to more upmarket accommodation, plus self-drives, as does Sealink. If you're in a hurry, the airlines also offer pricier packages: Southern Sky does a $215 full-day tour including return flights. There are also tours offered by specialized island-based operators (see opposite), but check the notice boards in Adelaide hostels for the latest.

It takes thirty minutes to **fly** to Kingscote on Kangaroo Island from Adelaide and costs about $140 return. The three airlines are Southern Sky (☎08/8234 3300; 2–4 daily; courtesy bus to Kingscote), Kendell Airlines (☎13 1300; 2 daily) and Emu Airways (☎08/8234 3711; 6–7 daily). **Car rental** companies have offices at Kingscote

Airport, and there's a bus to town for about $10 with Airport Shuttle Services (☎08/8553 2390).

Getting around, tours and activities

Once you're on the island, you really need your own transport. As there are only four **car rental** firms, it's best to book to be sure of a vehicle – that way you'll also be met with the vehicle off the ferry or plane. In Kingscote try Budget Rent a Car, Commercial Street (☎08/8553 3133; $60 per day, $385 per week), or Kangaroo Island Rental/Hertz, on the corner of Franklin Street and Telegraph Road, also at the wharf at Penneshaw (☎08/8553 2390 or free call ☎1800/088 296; $70 per day, $420 per week); Kangaroo also has 4WDs ($110 per day); Penneshaw Hire run by the *Penneshaw Youth Hostel* (☎08/8553 1284; $75 per day, $130 per two days) rents out new model cars. For cheaper deals try Koala Car Rentals, 10 Telegraph Rd, Kingscote (☎08/8553 2399; $55 per day, $315 per week).

There are few sealed **roads** on the island. The main drag is the Playford Highway from Kingscote through Cygnet River and Parndana to the edge of Flinders Chase National Park; at the eastern end of the island, sealed roads feed off it to the airport and main settlements, including Penneshaw. The rest are constructed of ironstone rubble on red dirt and can be very dangerous. The recommended speed on these roads is 60kph; driving slowly also reduces the risk of collisions with native animals. The same roads make **cycling** a tough proposition – you'll need a mountain bike and a tolerance for long bone-rattling stretches and choking clouds of red dust. *Penneshaw Youth Hostel* (☎08/8553 1284) rents out the island's best **mountain bikes** ($20 per day).

Most people opt for **tours**, which can be made flexible and are good value if bought as part of a package (see opposite). There are also a couple of tours based on the island: Daniel's Tours (free call ☎1800/454 454; two days; $205 all inclusive), led by the very voluble and enthusiastic Danny O'Donnell, focuses on wildlife and incorporates a two-hour walk from the hostel accommodation in Flinders Chase National Park to a secluded seal and sea lion colony; Adventure Charters of Kangaroo Island in Kingscote (☎08/8553 9119; *wildlife@kin.on.net*), led by an ex-park ranger, offers 4WD tours with an emphasis on fine food, wine and accommodation as well as nature. There are also a couple of **dive** tour operators on the island: Kangaroo Island Diving Safaris (☎08/8559 3244, fax 8559 3225), based at Telhawk Farm on the north coast, does five-day residential dive courses ($650 including meals and certification), with special backpackers' rates; and Adventureland Diving, based at American Beach near Penneshaw (☎08/8553 1072, fax 8553 1002), has three-day residential scuba courses ($426 including return ferry to Adelaide, unit accommodation, meals and certification; $275 without the ferry or meals and staying in hostel accommodation), as well as a two-day residential **rock-climbing** course ($300 including meals) and a half-day's **abseiling** ($50) – both on the cliffs at Cape Willoughby – and a half-day spent **canoeing** on Pelican Lagoon ($50) or **snorkelling** at Penguin Head ($43).

Information and park entrance fees

With about one-third of the island deemed a national or conservation park area, many of the parks charge entry fees and extras for guided tours. However, a one-year **Island Pass** ($20) covers virtually all these costs (except for camping and the night-time penguin tours from Penneshaw and Kingscote, see p.720 and p.721 respectively), and is worth it if you're here for a while. Thus the entry fees and tour prices quoted in the following accounts apply only if you don't have a pass – add up the cost of what you want to see and work out which is cheaper. Passes can be bought from the NPWS office on Dauncy Street, Kingscote (Mon–Fri 8.45am–5pm; ☎08/8553 2381), from the parks themselves, or from the **Kangaroo Island Gateway Visitor Information Centre**, at the edge of Penneshaw (Mon–Fri 9am–5pm, Sat & Sun 10am–4pm; ☎08/8553 1185) on the main road to Kingscote,which has an interpretive display on the island's history, geology and ecology, dispenses free maps and also books accommodation and tours. You'll also find a wealth of information on local wildlife, as well as a handy pre-visit reading list at *www.adventurecharters.com.au*.

The island

Coming by boat, you'll arrive at Kangaroo Island's eastern end, at either of the two main settlements, Penneshaw and Kingscote. Of the two, smaller and more low-key **Penneshaw**, reached from Cape Jervis, is the more pleasant place to stay, with the added attraction of the best night-time penguin-watching. Reached from Adelaide, larger **Kingscote** is the focus of administration and services; it also has status as an historic town, being South Australia's second colonial settlement, though few vestiges remain. Between Penneshaw and Kingscote, sheltered **American River** is another good base. You can also get to the island by plane: the **airport** is situated near **Cygnet River** – a quiet spot with the island's most congenial motel – on the **Playford Highway**. This main road links Kingscote to **Flinders Chase National Park**, which covers the western end of the island and offers camping and cottage facilities. The rugged **south coast** provides more wildlife spotting and natural beauty: running west to east, you can visit the aptly named Remarkable Rocks, still within the national park; go bushwalking in Hanson Bay; tour the limestone caves of Kelly Hill; camp at Vivonne Bay Conservation Park; play Lawrence of Arabia among the impressive sand dunes of Little Sahara or roam amongst resident sea lions at Seal Bay. The gentler **north coast** has a series of sheltered beaches, such as Emu Bay and Stokes Bay, with superb camping at both locations.

Penneshaw

Most people arrive by ferry at **PENNESHAW**, set on low, penguin-inhabited cliffs. This is also the best place to base yourself, with comfortable accommodation and plenty of places to eat (see opposite). After dusk the **Little penguins** cross the beach at Hog Bay and practically run wild through town. The colony thrives here because of the scores of fish in the unpolluted waters; a specially lit **boardwalk** provides a rookery viewing area raised above the penguins' route from the rocks to their cliffside burrows. Alternatively, a national park guide (Oct–March 8.30pm & 9.30pm; rest of the year 7pm & 8pm; $5) provides an informative commentary on their antics, departing from the CWA Hall next to *Dolphin Rock Takeaway*, or you can go on a special tour if you're staying at the *Sorrento Resort*.

Penneshaw's crescent of sandy beach at Hog Bay curves from the rocks below the wharf, where the ferries come in, around to a wooded headland. The bay provides safe **swimming** and even a shady shelter on the sand; above, there's a grassy picnic reserve with barbecues. **Antechamber Bay**, the next body of water, 10km by road southeast of Penneshaw, also has good, safe swimming. If you drive or cycle a further 10km you'll come to **Cape Willoughby Lighthouse**, at the eastern end of the island. Guided tours are offered by the NPWS (daily every 30min 10am–4pm; $5), and you can even stay in the sandstone homes of the original keepers (see opposite). You'll find more safe swimming at **American Beach**, southwest from Penneshaw along the scenic road that hugs Eastern Cove.

The **Dudley Peninsula**, on which Penneshaw stands, is attached to the rest of the island by a narrow neck of sand; at the isthmus 511 steps lead up to **Mount Thisby** (Prospect Hill), a 99-metre hill of sand with views across to the mainland, to Hungry Beach, Pelican Lagoon and American River on the island's north coast, and in the opposite direction to **Pennington Bay**. Here there are sponge-textured weathered rocks to clamber over, and some good surf, but a dangerous undertow.

Penneshaw practicalities

Penneshaw's Sealink office is at 7 North Terrace (☎08/8553 1122; Mon–Fri 8am–6pm, Sat & Sun 8am–1pm & 3–6pm). There's no bank, but the **post office** (Mon–Fri 9am–5pm, Sat 9am–11pm) acts as an agent, and there's EFTPOS at Sharpy's. Penneshaw has the island's widest range of accommodation: there are two **hostels**, the clinically modern but lively non-YHA *Penneshaw Youth Hostel* (☎08/8553 1284, fax 8553 1295; rooms ③, dorms ①), which hires bikes and cars and runs a diving school, and the more spacious and relaxed *Penguin Walk Hostel* (☎08/8553 1233, fax 8553 1190; rooms ④–⑤, dorms ①); both run their own tours. The upmarket alternative is the friendly *Sorrento Resort* (☎08/8553 1028, fax 8553 1204; ⑤–⑥), set in landscaped gardens, with motel-style rooms and fully equipped cabins, plus a heated pool, spa, sauna and tennis court, bar, restaurant and tours. There's **camping** at Brown Beach or the small shady *Penneshaw Caravan Park* on Talinga Avenue, to the left of the Sealink terminal (☎08/8553 1075; on-site vans ③), overlooking the beach. You can also stay in the two lighthouse keepers' cottages at **Cape Willoughby** (☎08/8559 7235, fax 8559 7268; BYO linen ④).

The best **restaurant** in town is the relaxed *Old Post Office Restaurant*, serving vegetarian and home-style meals (licensed; nightly except Tues & Wed; ☎08/8553 1063). For fresh local fish and chips or inexpensive steaks, head for *Fisherman's Cove*, opposite the post office (daily 9.30am–8.30pm; takeaway or outside tables only). *Penneshaw Pizza*, overlooking the Sealink wharf, also serves pasta. The tin-roofed bungalow of the *Penneshaw Hotel* is a small and friendly place to drink, with a verandah overlooking the water; counter meals include cheap Tuesday- and Thursday-night specials. *Dolphin Rock Takeaway and Launderette* (daily 7.30am–7.30pm; laundry 24hr), attached to the *Penneshaw Youth Hostel*, does fast food and a breakfast fry-up and sells a small range of groceries, but you'd be better off going to *Sharpy's* (daily 8am–7pm, summer until 8pm), the town's **general store** opposite the hotel; it sells virtually everything and has a takeaway and seating area.

American River and Cygnet River

Facing Penneshaw across Eastern Cove, **AMERICAN RIVER** is actually a sheltered bay, where many small fishing boats moor, aiming to catch some of its abundant whiting. It's a peaceful place to stay, with a concentration of accommodation, and a general store. American River Rendezvous, the kiosk at the wharf (☎08/8553 3150; fishing-rod rental $10 per day), provides a bit of a spectacle here with its raucous **pelican feeding** complete with commentary (daily 4.30pm; free). Boats can be chartered for local **fishing** from the kiosk or direct from Cooinda Charter Services (☎08/8553 7063).

Matthew Flinders Terraces (☎08/8553 7100, fax 8553 7250; ⑦) is a beautifully situated **motel** with pool, spa and a good licensed restaurant (reservations only), or try the *Wanderers Rest* (☎08/8553 7140, fax 8553 7282; ⑧), an upmarket B&B where each room has a patio. Holiday units include the budget *Casuarina Units* (☎08/8553 7020; ④) and the more expensive *Ulonga Lodge* (☎ & fax 08/8553 7171; ⑤) and *Cooinda Holiday Village* (☎ & fax 08/8553 7063; ⑤–⑥). The *Linnets Island Club* (☎08/8553 7053, fax 8553 7030; ①–⑦) has a range of accommodation, from luxury or standard motel suites, holiday apartments and a hostel section to tent sites, plus a wide range of facilities including sauna, pool, restaurant and tennis court; it also offers its own tours.

CYGNET RIVER, at the junction of Playford Highway and the road from Penneshaw, boasts one of the best places to stay on the island: *Koala Lodge* (☎ & fax 08/8553 9006; ⑥), run by a friendly French-Canadian/Australian couple, with personalized en-suite units near the river bank.

Kingscote and the north coast

It's a 45-minute drive on a sealed road from Penneshaw to **KINGSCOTE** (60km), the island's main town with banks, shops, a hospital, library and the only high school. The

ferry from Adelaide docks right in town near the landmark *Ozone Hotel* which fronts a small sandy beach with grassed terraces and a sea pool with a waterslide and playground. The coast here has been the scene of several **shipwrecks** – interpretive boards on the foreshore provide details. For more history, you can walk north along the Esplanade to the **Reeves Point Historic Site**, where more interpretive boards provide the only clue to the South Australia Company's first landing of settlers in July 1836, before they headed off to establish nearby Adelaide; with three hundred at its peak, the settlement failed and was folded by 1839. Less than a kilometre up the hill above, on Seaview Road, is **Hope Cottage Folk Museum** (daily 2–4pm; closed July & Aug), the restored 1859 home of a pioneering family. Kingscote has a small colony of **penguins** that were transported from Penneshaw during the building of the boardwalk there; not as impressive as Penneshaw's, they're best seen on the guided ranger talks that leave from the foyer of the *Ozone Hotel* (Oct–March 8.30pm & 9.30pm; rest of the year 7pm & 8pm; $5).

Established in 1907, the waterfront *Ozone Hotel* (☎08/8553 2011, fax 8553 2249, free call ☎1800/083 133; en-suites ⑤–⑥) is a local institution and the best place in town to eat, with a bistro and **restaurant**. Back from the beach on Dauncy Street is the *Queenscliffe Family Hotel* (☎08/8553 2254, fax 8553 2291; ⑤), another old pub offering **rooms** and meals; and next door is the *Blue Gum Cafe*, which has a varied city-style menu, with vegetarian dishes and real coffee (closed Sun). Upmarket motel accommodation, with sea views, is found at *Wisteria Lodge*, Cygnet Road (☎08/8553 2707, fax 8553 2200; ⑥). For the budget-conscious there's the *Kangaroo Island Central Backpackers Hostel*, at 21 Murray St (☎08/8553 2787, fax 8553 2694; ①); it has large, clean dorms, a kitchen and common room, and a laundry. **Campers** have a choice between the small and central *Kangaroo Island Caravan Park* (☎08/8553 2325; cabins ③–④, on-site vans ②) and the *Nepean Bay Caravan Park* (☎08/8553 2394; cabins ③, on-site vans ②) at Brownlow Beach, 3km away, which is more inviting and better equipped. The nearby *Brownlow Holiday Units* (☎08/8553 2293; ④) are also good value.

The **beaches** on the north coast are more sheltered than those on the south. **Emu Bay**, 21km from Kingscote, is a secluded and quiet spot with no shops, a few holiday homes, a couple of B&Bs, and a clean, white, sandy beach, jetty and basic **campsite** with toilet and water facilities only (☎08/8553 2325). Emu Bay also has a small penguin community. Secluded **Stokes Bay** is reached through a natural tunnel between overhanging boulders. There's a delightful calm rock pool, a perfect semicircle of rounded black stones, which conveniently provides protection from the dangerous rip in the bay. Outside the tunnel, the *Rockpool Cafe* (daily 10am–5.30pm; ☎08/8559 2277) looks after the beachfront **campsites** and also sells milk and bread as well as more exotic fare such as Asian and Italian dishes and lentil burgers; it's sometimes open for dinner during summer.

The south coast

Several conservation parks are strung along the exposed south coast. The largest is **Cape Gantheaume**, an area of low mallee scrub supporting prolific birdlife around **Murrays Lagoon** (where you'll find the ranger station), the largest freshwater lagoon on the island. The adjacent **Seal Bay Conservation Park** is home to several hundred **sea lions**, the second-largest breeding population in Australia. They are unusually tolerant of humans and you can walk quietly among the colony on the beach at Seal Bay, accompanied by a national park guide (9am–4.15pm, until 7pm during summer holidays; from every 15min in summer to every 45min in winter; $7.50) or take a tour on the new boardwalk ($5).

Vivonne Bay, with its long, sandy beach and bush setting, is a great place to camp. The Vivonne Bay Store (☎08/8559 4252) collects the fee for the beachfront **campsite** (toilets, water, barbecues). It's safe to swim near the jetty or boat ramp or in the Harriet River, but the bay itself has a dangerous undertow. Between Seal Bay and

Vivonne Bay, **Little Sahara** is 15km of perfect white-sand dunes rising unexpectedly out of mallee scrub.

The main features of the **Kelly Hill Conservation Park** are the **Kelly Hill Caves**, extensive limestone cave formations (NPWS guided tours daily: June–Aug hourly 10am–3pm; Sept–May hourly 10am–4pm, in summer until 5pm; $5). The tour explores only the largest cave, which is not the usual damp, bat-filled cavern but very dry, with a constant temperature of 16°C. The NPWS runs adventure caving tours of three other caves ($15–20 depending on the cave; ☎08/8559 7231 for details and booking). The eighteen-kilometre return **Hanson Bay Trail** goes from the caves to the sea, passing freshwater lagoons and dune systems: allow at least eight hours – or longer, if you're tempted to stop for a swim.

Flinders Chase National Park

Flinders Chase National Park, South Australia's largest, occupies the entire western end of the island. It became a park as early as 1919, and in the 1920s and 1930s koalas, platypuses, emus and Cape Barren geese from the Bass Strait islands (see p.956–959) were introduced. The land is mainly sugar gum forest, but the **Rocky River Visitors Centre** (daily: June–Aug 10am–5pm; Sept–May 9am–5pm; ☎08/8559 7235, fax 8559 7268; park entry fee $6.50) is surrounded by open grasslands where large numbers of kangaroos and geese graze. Koala signs lead to a glade of trees, where you'll see the creatures swaying high up, within binocular range. Follow the **Black Stump walking track** for 3km to a platypus viewing area; but be warned that to get a glimpse of the creatures requires endless patience. The rough, winding road through the park will take you on to its most spectacular feature, the huge and weirdly shaped, rust-coloured **Remarkable Rocks** on Kirkpatrick Point, which loom above fur seals basking on the rocks below. At the northern corner of the park, you can go on a guided tour of the 1858 **Cape Borda Lighthouse** (school holidays 8 daily 10.15am–4.15pm, winter 5 daily 10am–2pm; rest of the year 6 daily 10am–3.15pm; $5).

The main **camping** area is at Rocky River, where there are also two cottages, the four-bedroom *Old Homestead* (④ with private bathroom) and the one-room *Mays Cottage* (③, with use of campsite showers and toilets). There are more cottages at the park's north and south corners, respectively at Cape Borda (②–④) and Cape Du Couedic (②). Bookings for all cottages are made through the Rocky River Visitors Centre (see above). *Flinders Chase Farm Hostel* (☎08/8559 7223; ①, self-catering) is ideally placed on a sheep and cattle property on the edge of the park near the south coast; it's usually busy, so book in advance.

The southeast

For most travellers, the southeast – the area between Melbourne and Adelaide – is an area to be passed through as quickly as possible. From Tailem Bend, just beyond Murray Bridge some 85km out of Adelaide, three highways branch out. The **Ouyen Highway** is the quintessential road to nowhere, leading through the sleepy settlements of Lameroo and Pinnaroo to the insignificant town of **Ouyen** in Victoria's Mallee country (see p.686). The **Dukes Highway** is the fast, boring route to Melbourne via the South Australian mallee scrub and farming towns of **Keith** and **Bordertown**, birthplace of former Prime Minister Bob Hawke, before continuing in Victoria as the Western Highway across the monotonous Wimmera (see p.867). It is, however, well worth breaking your journey to visit **the Coonawarra** and **Naracoorte**, in between the Dukes Highway and the coastal route: the former is a tiny wine-producing area that makes some of the country's finest red wine; the latter is a fair-size town with a freshwater lagoon system that attracts prolific birdlife, and a conservation park with impressive World Heritage-listed caves.

The **Princes Highway** (Highway 1) is much less direct but far more interesting; it follows the extensive coastal lagoon system of **the Coorong** to **Kingston SE**, and then runs a short way inland to the lake craters of **Mount Gambier**, before crossing into Victoria. On this last stretch, another possible route – Alternative Highway 1 – sticks closer to the coast, and there's a detour along the Riddoch Highway into the scenic Coonawarra **wine region**. Premier Stateliner (☎08/8415 5555) has two routes between Adelaide and Mount Gambier, one inland via Keith, Bordertown, Naracoorte, Coonawarra and Penola; the other along the coast via Meningie, Kingston SE, Robe and Millicent. The NPWS free newspaper, *The Tatler*, gives practical details relating to the southeastern coastal parks – pick up the latest copy from the Adelaide office (see p.678), or regional offices en route.

Coorong National Park

From Tailem Bend, the Princes Highway skirts Lake Alexandrina and freshwater Lake Albert, where **MENINGIE** is a popular fishing centre, before passing the edge of the **Coorong National Park**. The coastal saline lagoon system of the Coorong (from the Aboriginal *Karangk* meaning long neck) is separated from the sea for over 100km by the high sand dunes of the **Younghusband Peninsula**: the famous Australian children's film *Storm Boy*, about a boy and his friendship with a pelican, was filmed here. The state's most prolific pelican breeding ground is an excellent place to observe these awkward yet graceful birds – at Jacks Point, 3km north of Policemans Point on the Princes Highway, there's a shelter with seating and a telescope focused on the small islands where some birds breed. Without your own **transport**, one way to see the Coorong is to head off in a 4WD with a local naturalist from Coorong Nature Tours (☎ & fax 08/8574 0037; day-tour $110 from Meningie, $160 from Adelaide; half-day option $60 from Meningie only; longer two- and three-day trips available). You can also get to the park on a **cruise** from Goolwa (see box on p.712).

There are several designated camping areas with shelters, barbecues, toilets, running water (but no showers) and marked walking trails. The Coorong is also good for beach **camping**: with a permit (see below) you can camp anywhere along the beach between high and low watermark, but cars must be parked in designated places, and you must bring your own drinking water which can be collected outside the seldom-manned **Salt Creek NPWS ranger station** on the edge of the park about 60km south of Meningie. Elsewhere, **information** and **camping permits** ($5 per car) and maps of the park and campsites can be obtained at the national park **headquarters** at 34 Main St, Meningie (Mon–Fri 9.30am–5pm; ☎08/8575 1200), the Melaleuca Information Centre, 76 Princes Highway (daily 9am–5pm; ☎08/8575 1259), the *Caltex Roadhouse*, 75 Princes Highway, or Salt Creek's *Shell Petrol Station*, which has an outside notice board and a **café** serving delicious grilled Coorong Mullet. Permits can also be bought from the *Coorong Caravan Park* at Policemans Point, at all roadhouses in Kingston SE and at the Signal Point Interpretative Centre in Goolwa (see p.712). If you want to stay in more comfort, there are plenty of **motels** at Meningie.

Camp Coorong, run by the Ngarrindjeri Lands and Progress Association, is 10km south of Meningie, and 3km from another stretch of the Coorong National Park. This cultural centre attempts to explain the heritage and culture of the Ngarrindjeri Aborigines who were one of the largest groups in South Australia, occupying the land around the Coorong and the lower Murray River and lakes. There's a museum (Mon–Fri 9am–5pm, open some weekends; donation), and you can camp here or stay in the well-outfitted **cabins** (booking required on ☎08/8575 1557; ③).

Alternative Highway One

KINGSTON SE, on Lacepede Bay, is the first town past the Coorong: here the Princes Highway turns inland, while **Alternative Highway 1** continues along the coast before rejoining the main road at Millicent. As the **Big Lobster** signifies, Kingston has an important lobster industry: you can buy them freshly cooked at *Lacepede Seafood* by the jetty (Mon–Thurs 9am–6pm, Fri & Sat 9am–7.30pm) for around $35 a kilo. Lobsters apart, you're better off continuing down the coast. If you do need to stay, you have a choice of the usual motels, the very rough-and-ready *Backpackers Hostel*, 21 Holland St (☎08/8767 2185; ①), or the *Kingston Caravan Park*, Marine Parade (☎08/8767 2050; cabins ③, on-site vans ②).

ROBE, on the south side of Guichen Bay 44km from Kingston, was one of South Australia's first settlements, established as a deep-water port in 1847. After 1857, over sixteen thousand Chinese landed here and walked to the goldfields, 400km or so away, to avoid the poll tax levied in Victoria. As trade declined and the highway bypassed town, Robe managed to maintain both dignity and charm, and during the busy summer period the population of less than eight hundred expands to over eleven thousand. Adelaidians love the place, with its well-preserved nineteenth-century streetscapes, and its beach setting surrounded by lakes and bushland; some even drive the 366km for a weekend. Summer is also the season for crayfishing, Robe's second substantial industry. It's all deliberately low-key: the main thoroughfare of Victoria Street is tree-lined and semi-residential, the shops blending unobtrusively with the houses. **Tourist information** is inside the library on the corner of Smiley and Victoria streets (Mon–Fri 10am–12.30pm & 1–5pm, Sat 8.30am–12.30pm; ☎08/8768 2465); they have walking and driving maps and a Historical Interpretation Centre. If you walk north along the bay to Cape Dombey, with its boldly striped obelisk, you can see Little penguins on the rocks.

There's a choice of dozens of places to **stay**, most of which double up as places to eat. *Robe Hotel*, Mundy Terrace (☎08/8768 2077, fax 8768 2495; ④–⑥), is an old stone beachfront hotel with modern budget accommodation and en-suite motel-style rooms with views and spa units; the downstairs bars serve good bistro meals – lots of fish and a vegetarian dish of the day. The *Caledonian Inn*, Victoria Street (☎08/8768 2029, fax 8768 2636; ④–⑦ including breakfast), is a charming, ivy-covered stone building, first licensed in 1858, that would not look out of place in an English village – it offers B&B accommodation upstairs or in homely cottages, and serves excellent food. Also on Victoria Street, *Guichen Bay Motel* (☎08/8768 2001; ④–⑤) has good value, spacious rooms, some with kitchenette, and a playground, picnic area and pool, as well as a lounge and bar (cheap eats) and the licensed *Robetown Cottage Restaurant* which has special crayfish dishes in season. *Sea Vu Caravan Park*, 1 Squire Drive (☎08/8768 2273; cabins ④, on-site vans ②), is family-run and close to town, with a swimming beach just below. The excellent *Bushland Cabins* set in 25 acres of bushland, southeast of the centre on Nora Creina Rd (☎08/8768 2386; dorms ①, cabins ③–④), offer tent sites, a backpackers' lodge comprising two bedrooms and a kitchen/lounge area with TV, and en-suite cabins with TV, fridge, heaters and ceiling fan; walking trails into the surrounding bush include the 1km clifftop track into Robe. For **meals** outside your accommodation you can treat yourself to excellent Italian coffee, city-style café fare or an all-day breakfast at *Wild Mulberry Cafe*, 46 Victoria St, opposite the Shell garage (summer & Easter daily 8am–8.30pm, rest of year 8am–6.30pm, closed Thurs). For self-caterers, Foodland Supermarket, opposite the Ampol petrol station, is open daily 7.30am–7.30pm.

Between Robe and **BEACHPORT** are four lakes: for part of the way you can take the Nora Criena Scenic Drive through **Little Dip Conservation Park**, 14km of coastal dune systems. The drive provides views of Lake Eliza and Lake St Clair before returning to Alternative Highway 1 and the former whaling port of Beachport, which boasts one of the longest jetties in Australia and many lobster-fishing boats at anchor on Rivoli Bay. The tiny town, whose population of 400 increases tenfold over the Christmas and New Year season, has its own movie house, South Coast Cinema (☎08/8375 8455), which shows films on Wed, Sat & Sun nights.

Beachport has plenty of **accommodation**. *Bompas*, overlooking the bay at 3 Railway Terrace (☎08/8735 8333, fax 8735 8101; ④–⑥), was the town's first licensed hotel in 1879, and is now a pleasing B&B guesthouse with a coffee bar, bistro and **restaurant** downstairs, all sharing a menu featuring Thai, Malay, Italian and Australian dishes. Also on Railway Terrace, *Beachport Motor Inn* (☎08/8735 8070; ④–⑤) has rooms and self-catering units. The large *Beachport Hotel* next door (☎08/8735 8003, fax 8735 8091; ③) has a good bar with occasional bands, and a dining room for daily meals of fresh fish. Other places to stay on the foreshore include the long-established and well-equipped *Beachport Backpackers* (☎08/8735 8197; dorm beds ①, self-contained family apartment ④; booking advisable), which rents out fishing rods, surf and snorkelling gear; it's an obvious place to stay if you're on the Wayward Bus, which passes three times a week. The *Beachport Caravan Park* (☎08/8735 8128; on-site vans ③, en-suite cottages ⑤), is also opposite the beach on Beach Road.

Continuing south on Alternative Highway One, there's a turn-off to **Canunda National Park** (ranger ☎08/8735 6053) which has giant sand dunes, several signposted coastal walking trails, and an abundance of birdlife; you can pick up leaflets detailing the walks from the *Beachport Backpackers*. The park is also easily accessible from the town of **Millicent**, where Alternative Highway One rejoins the main highway.

Mount Gambier

MOUNT GAMBIER is the southeast's commercial centre; not far from the border with Victoria, the small city sprawls up the slopes of an extinct volcano which has three craters, each with its own lake surrounded by heavily wooded slopes and filled from underground waterways that are perfect for unusual subterranean pursuits (see box opposite). The **Blue Lake** is the largest of the crater lakes, up to 204m deep and 5km in circumference. From November to March it's a stunning cobalt blue, reverting to duller grey in the colder months. There are lookout spots and a scenic drive around the lake, and guided tours to the surface are offered by Aquifer Tours (Nov–Jan: daily on the hour 9am–5pm & Thurs also 7pm; 45min; $4). The second largest crater holds **Valley Lake** and a Wildlife Park (daily 7am–dusk; free) where indigenous animals range free amid native flora; there are lookouts, walking trails and boardwalks.

The centrepiece of **the city** is Cave Gardens, a shady park surrounding a deep limestone cavern with steps leading some way down; the stream running into it eventually filters into the Blue Lake. At the rear of the park the municipal offices contain the Civic Centre, library and a small theatre. Fronting the park the former Town Hall houses an upmarket bistro and the **Riddoch Art Gallery** (Tues–Fri 10am–4pm, Sat 10am–2pm, Sun noon–3pm; free) whose focus is the impressive Rodney Gooch collection of Aboriginal art from Utopia, Central Australia, which includes work by the late Emily Kame Kngwarreye. In the same building, Studio One sells the work of local artists (Mon–Fri 10.30am–4pm, Sat 9.30am–noon).

West of the centre, on Jubilee Highway West, is the extensive complex of underground caverns at **Engelbrecht Cave** (guided tours hourly 9am–3pm; 45min; $4), while east of the city, **Umpherston Sinkhole** (open access) is also known as the Sunken Garden, since it contains Victorian-era terraced gardens – they are floodlit at night when possums come out to feed.

SUBTERRANEAN EXPLORATION

From **Engelbrecht Cave** you can dive in limestone waterways under the city. However, an open water PADI classification is not enough to dive these dark and dangerous waters – you need a CDAA (Cave Divers Association of Australia) qualification. Contact the Mount Gambier NPWS office at 11 Helen St (☎08/8735 1177) for further information. They can also issue permits for snorkelling at the crystal clear waters of **Piccaninnie Ponds Conservation Park** or **Ewans Pond Conservation Park**, both south of Mount Gambier near Port Macdonnell. At Piccaninnie Ponds, a deep chasm with white limestone walls contains clear water that is filtered underground from the Blue Lake – it takes five hundred years to get here.

Practicalities

For more information on Mount Gambier's attractions, head for the excellent **Lady Nelson Tourist Interpretive Centre**, on Jubilee Highway East (daily 9am–5pm; exhibition $6; ☎08/8724 1730), where the ecology, geology and history of Mount Gambier are explored from Aboriginal and European perspectives. A ten-minute narration by the ghostly holographic image of missionary Christina Smith, is based on her book *The Booandik Tribe of South Australian Aborigines*. She worked with a local Aboriginal tribe for 35 years, and opened a charitable home in Mt Gambier in 1865, but even though she was sympathetic to the Aboriginal plight, her attempts at conversion only contributed to the destruction of traditional values. Other highlights of the centre are the short wetlands boardwalk and a demonstration of a volcanic eruption complete with steam – quite scary when it booms.

Mount Gambier has heaps of places to **stay**, with motels lining the highway either side of town. The *Blue Lake Motel*, on Kennedy Avenue (☎08/8725 5211, fax 8275 5410; motel units ④, dorms ①), also has backpacker rooms, a kitchen and laundry. Another hostel may open soon in the old gaol. Central *Jens Hotel*, at 40 Commercial St (☎08/8725 0188; ④), is a classic, wide-balconied old boozer with cheap bar and bistro meals, late opening hours and en-suite accommodation. The *Mount Gambier Hotel*, 2 Commercial St, has more upmarket food, but the best place to **eat** is the licensed *Café Capri Restaurant*, 53 Gray St (Mon–Sat 8.30am–10 or 11pm). Nearby, *Fasta Pasta*, 102 Commercial St (West), is one of a chain serving inexpensive fresh pasta with interesting sauces. There's also the city-style *Kings Bar and Bistro* in the Town Hall (daily from 10am).

Heading on to Melbourne from Mount Gambier, V/Line has a daily service via Portland, Hamilton, Warrnambool, Geelong and Ballarat.

The Coonawarra wine region

Directly north of Mount Gambier, the **Riddoch Highway** heads through the **Coonawarra wine region**, and past some World Heritage-listed caves at Naracoorte, eventually linking up with the Dukes Highway at Keith. With most wineries located on a 90km stretch of highway between **Penola** and Padthaway, this is one of the easiest wine areas "to do" and it's low key and pretty. The region is renowned for the quality of its reds, which have been compared to those of Bordeaux; they account for about eighty percent of production, with **Cabernet Sauvignon** being the favourite variety, lauded each October at the Cabernet Celebration. The soil and drainage is ideal, classic Terra Rossa over limestone, and the climate is perfect – and as the weather is is not really variable from year to year, the wines are consistently good.

There's no public transport to the area, but you can go on a tour from Mount Gambier with Coonawarra Grape Escape (10am Tues, Thurs & Sun during school holidays; $50; 6hr; ☎08/8724 9978).

Penola

Twenty-two kilometres north of Mount Gambier, **PENOLA**, gateway to the Coonawarra wine region, is a very simple but dignified country town of well-preserved nineteenth-century architecture. For **information**, head for Penola Coonawarra Visitor Centre in the old Mechanics Institute Building (Mon–Fri 9am–5pm, Sat & Sun 10am–4pm), which also houses a display featuring John Riddoch, pioneer of Coonawarra's vineyards, and hands out the free *Historic Penola and Coonawarra* map with details of the region's wineries.

Beside the 1857 Cobb & Co booking office (now a restaurant), St Joseph's Catholic Church looks like something out of an Italian village, a world away from the very modern **Mary MacKillop Interpretative Centre** (daily 10am–4pm; $3) next door. Sister Mary MacKillop (1842–1909) was Penola's most famous resident, and Australia's first would-be saint – in 1995 Pope John Paul II pronounced her "Blessed", the last stage before full saint status. MacKillop set up a school, created her own teaching method and, with Father Julian Tennyson Woods, co-founded the Sisters of St Joseph of the Sacred Heart, a charitable teaching order that spread throughout Australia and New Zealand. Dramatic episodes of alleged disobedience and excommunication give her story a certain oomph. There's an informative display in the centre, lightened up by Barbie-doll look-alike "nuns on the run" and dressed-up dummies in the original school room. Across the fields are the National Trust-listed cottages of **Petticoat Lane**, where many of Mary's poverty-stricken students lived. One of the buildings now houses a toyshop (daily 10am–5pm), while a display in another and an interpretive board in the garden tells the story of the 17-member Sharam family. You can also visit Wilson's Cottage (same hours) which doubles as a linen shop.

There are backpacker **rooms** at the comfortable and centrally located *McKay's Trek Inn*, 38 Riddoch St, (☎08/8737 2250 or free call ☎1800/626 844; rooms ③, dorms ①) which caters to the OZ Experience crowd a couple of nights a week, and long-stay grape pickers, so it's worth booking. *Penola Caravan Park* on South Terrace (☎08/8737 2381) has good-value on-site vans (②) and en-suite cabins (③). The focus of the town is the friendly National Trust-listed *Heywood's Royal Oak Hotel*, 31 Church St (☎08/8737 2322, fax 8737 2825; ④–⑤), with four-poster doubles and some twin rooms. Out of town, on the Riddoch Highway, *Chardonnay Lodge* (☎08/8736 3309; ⑦) is an upmarket motel complex set amongst lawns and rose gardens, with a swimming pool and an attached café/restaurant.

The best place to **eat** is *Heywood's Royal Oak Hotel*, which has a beautiful beer garden and an excellent bistro. Otherwise, *Sweet Grape*, 48 Church St (daily 8.30am–5pm, plus dinner Fri–Sun) dishes up affordable café favourites and international dishes. On the Riddoch Highway, *Hermitage Café and Wine Bar*, attached to Wetherall Winery (☎08/8737 2122; daily 11am–5pm, reserve for dinner) hand out cheese and crackers to go along with some wine, while meals focus on local and organic produce. The vineyard setting is very pleasant, with a little pond for yabbies and a native garden out back, filled with banksias and big gum trees.

Coonawarra Township

There isn't much to what is called **COONAWARRA TOWNSHIP**, a settlement which developed to house and service the adjacent Wynns Coonawarra Estate (see box opposite), but it does make a good base if you're touring local vineyards. Cottage **accommodation** here includes *Skinner Cottage* (☎08/8736 3304; ⑤), a quaint tin-roofed bungalow

COONAWARRA WINERIES

There are twenty Coonawarra wineries that do tastings, most open Mon–Fri 9am–5pm, Sat & Sun 10am–4pm. A few favourites arranged in directional order as if you are driving along the Riddoch Highway from Penola towards Coonawarra Township include **Hollick Wines**, in a tiny restored 1870s slab wood and stone cottage; **Balnaves**, with its innovative award winning architecture; **Leconfield**, with very well-regarded Cabernet Sauvignons and, unusually, a female wine maker; and **Zema Estate**, a small family-run winery with Italian roots and an old-fashioned hands-on process. **Wynns Coonawarra Estate**, west of the Riddoch Highway on Memorial Drive at Coonawarra Township, is the Coonawarra's longest established (1896) and most well-known winery, with wines exported worldwide. Its stone gabled building, with vineyards stretching out in front, is just as depicted on all its wine labels. Continuing back on the Riddoch Highway towards Padthaway, **Brands Coonawarra** are an old family of wine makers who notably make a sell-out Shiraz from the original vineyard planted in 1896, while the down-to-earth Redman family of **Redman** have also been making wine for generations, but only red, focusing exclusively on three varieties: Cabernet Sauvignon, Shiraz and a blend of Cabernet Sauvignon and Merlot. Beyond Redman, the modern winery complex of **Rymill**, attractively located on Clayfield Road, west of the Riddoch Highway, includes a glass-walled tasting area overlooking the winery, and platforms upstairs for viewing the testing lab.

just around the corner from the old Coonawarra school, now *Nibs Bistro and Grill* (☎08/8736 3006; licensed and BYO; bookings on Sat night recommended), which is a fun place to **eat** – choose from a display of marinated meats and grill them yourself.

Naracoorte Caves
In 1994 the system of limestone caves east of the Riddoch Highway, midway between Penola and Padthaway, were proclaimed a World Heritage Area, now accessible as the **Naracoorte Caves Conservation Park**. An interpretive centre at the park headquarters (☎08/8762 2340; daily 9am–5pm) gives insight into the area and its highly significant **Victoria Fossil Cave** – the chamber, discovered in 1969, revealed fossils of extinct Pleistocene megafauna including giant kangaroos and wombats. Another notable feature is the **Bat Centre**, the only place in the world where you can watch bats in real time with the help of infrared remote control cameras filming inside a cave. You can watch the small common bent wing bats on **tours** (daily Christmas and early January; around 7.30pm).

The caves are spread out over the Conservation Park: Alexandra Cave has the prettiest limestone formations (9.30am & 1.15pm; 30min; $5); Victoria Fossil Cave is popular for its fossils (10.15am & 2pm; $7.50; 1hr). A visit to the Bat Centre includes viewing of the more robust Blanche cave (10.30am & 3.30pm; $7.50; 1hr). You can guide yourself through the Wet Cave ($3), named after the very wet chamber at its deepest part, and stay for as long as you please between 9am–5pm; an automatic lighting system switches on as you walk through. There are also **adventure caving** tours in several other caves (novice tours 1hr 30min–2hr 30min, $15; advanced 3hr, $30; overalls can be hired for $5; lights and helmets supplied).

You can **camp** next to the centre ($15 per car) where facilities include powered sites, hot showers and even a free laundry, or at the more basic campsite at nearby **Bool Lagoon Conservation Park** ($12 per car; water and toilets only), which is a magnet for birds; camping permits are issued at the centre. For a little more comfort, there are self-contained cabins set in bushland near Victoria Fossil Cave (call ☎08/8762 0696 or enquire at the Yulgibar Wood Gallery opposite the park headquarters; ⑤). For **meals**, the licensed *Bent Wing Cafe* at the centre is surprisingly sophisticated, dishing up everything from a Greek salad to chargrilled kangaroo fillets with native plum chutney.

On the highway 12km west of the caves, the town of **NARACOORTE** is a small regional centre with a supermarket (open daily) and several places to eat and stay. *Kincraig Hotel*, 158 Smith St (☎08/8762 2200; ③), has basic pub accommodation and decent meals. *Naracoorte Hotel Motel*, in parallel Ormerod Street at no. 73 (☎08/8762 2400; ④) has motel rooms and cheap meal specials. At 81 Park Terrace, a ten-minute walk north of town, *Naracoorte Caravan Park* (☎08/8762 2128; cabins ③–④, on-site van ④) is in a shady spot by a creek, close to a swimming lake.

The Riverland

The **Riverland** is the long irrigated strip on either side of the three-hundred-kilometre meander of the Murray River from Blanchetown to Renmark near the Victorian border. The Canadian Chaffey brothers had already developed successful irrigation settlements in California when they were invited to Australia to look into possibilities for the Murray, establishing an **irrigation colony** at **Renmark** in 1887. The Riverland's deep red-orange alluvial soil – helped by this extensive irrigation – is very fertile, making the area the state's major supplier of oranges, stone fruit and grapes. Fruit stalls along the roadsides add to the impression of a year-long harvest, and if you're after **fruit-picking work** it's an excellent place to start. The area is also Australia's major **wine-producing** region, though the technologically advanced wineries with huge production bases make mainly mass-produced wines for casks and export. Many are open to visitors, but their scale and commercialism make them less enjoyable for a wine-tasting trawl than, say, the Southern Vales.

From Waikerie to Renmark all the **towns** feel pretty much the same, with a raw edge, little charm or sophistication, and an undercurrent of violence most apparent on a drunken Friday night. Time here is best spent on or around the river, with the towns considered as departure points for river cruises, and places to eat and stay. Each town has only one hotel – even Berri and Renmark, with their 7000-strong populations. These huge and mostly graceless **community hotels** are a feature of the Riverland: owned and run by the town, their profits are ploughed back into the hotel or channelled into the community, generally into sporting groups.

The **Sturt Highway**, the major route between Adelaide and Sydney, passes straight through the Riverland. Leaving Adelaide, it bypasses Gawler and cuts across the northern end of the Barossa Valley, reaching the Murray at Blanchetown, about 130km from the city. Stateliner runs a daily service along the highway from Adelaide to Renmark via Blanchetown and Waikerie, and also goes daily (except Tues) to Loxton. Greyhound Pioneer drops off and picks up at the Riverland towns on their interstate routes.

Blanchetown to Waikerie

BLANCHETOWN, 130km from Adelaide, is the first Riverland town, and with Lock No. 1 completed here in 1922, is the starting point of the Murray's lock and weir system which helps maintain the river at a constant height between the town and Wentworth in New South Wales (see p.318). Eleven kilometres west of town, **Brookfield Conservation Park**, a gift to South Australia from the Chicago Zoological Society, is home to the endangered **southern hairy-nosed wombat**; the creatures also thrive at nearby *Portee Station* (☎08/8540 5211, fax 8540 5016; B&B ⑨, or with dinner and tours $195 per person), a two-hundred-square-kilometre sheep-grazing property where, if you can afford it, you can stay in the 1873 riverfront homestead. Tours include an exploration of the river in a small boat to look at the prolific birdlife, and a 4WD station tour where you'll see wombats close up.

Following the river from Blanchetown, it's 36km directly north to **MORGAN**, the most attractive of the Riverland towns. At the height of the river trade between 1880 and 1915 Morgan was one of South Australia's busiest river ports, transferring wool from NSW and Victoria onto trains bound for Adelaide at the twelve-metre-high river wharves; although two sections had to be demolished after collapsing in 1994, the rest of the mainly red gum and jarrah wharf remains intact. You can wander through the riverfront park, past the old train station and the stationmaster's building, now a **museum** (sometimes open on weekends, otherwise by appointment; call ☎08/8540 2085), and up onto the wharves overlooking moored houseboats on the river to bushland beyond. The well-preserved nineteenth-century streetscape of Railway Terrace, the main street, sits above the old railway line and wharf; its focus is the huge Landseer shipping warehouse; a couple of shops cash in on the heritage feel by selling antiques and bric-a-brac. Two old pubs have standard **accommodation**: the *Terminus Hotel* (☎08/8540 2006; ③) and the *Commercial* (☎08/8540 2107; ③), sit next to each other, creating a lively riverport feel. You can also stay at *Morgan Riverside Caravan Park* (☎08/8540 2207; cabins ④, on-site vans ③), in a great spot right in town by the river and the free car ferry across the river to Cadell (see below). For **food**, try the pubs or *Morgan Pizza Bar*, 17 Railway Terrace (☎08/8540 2103), which only sells its recommended pizzas Fri–Sun from 5pm – other nights you can get fish and chips and burgers from here.

From Morgan the river takes a sharp bend east, meandering south to **WAIKERIE**; it's 32km from Morgan to Waikerie on a riverside road, with a crossing at Cadell. A less attractive drive from Blanchetown bypasses the river loop, reaching Waikerie directly by heading 42km northeast along the Sturt Highway. Waikerie is at the heart of the largest citrus-growing area in Australia; the first thing you notice is **Waikerie Co-op Producers**, a huge complex taking up both sides of a street – the "largest fruit-packing house in the southern hemisphere". This apart, it's a pleasant town with many fine sandstone buildings.

Loxton

About 35km further along the Sturt Highway, the Murray makes another large loop away from the highway, with **Loxton** at its southernmost reach. Leaving the highway at Kingston-on-Murray, you pass the **Moorook Game Reserve**, a large swamp fringed with river red gums and home to many waterbirds; at the other end of the loop there's a 24-hour free ferry across the river to Berri (see p.733). In Loxton itself, the **Tourist & Art Centre**, at Bookpurnong Terrace (Mon–Fri 9am–5pm, Sat 9.30am–12.30pm, Sun 1–4pm; ☎08/8584 7919), acts as an agent for Stateliner and can fill you in on local attractions such as the riverside **Loxton Historical Village** (Mon–Fri 10am–4pm, Sat & Sun 10am–5pm; $5), a replica of a turn-of-the-century Riverland town. Altogether more compelling is the **Katarapko Game Reserve**, opposite Loxton, where Katarapko Creek and the Murray have cut deep channels and lagoons, creating an island. Access is by water only – perfect for canoeing and observing birdlife; to **camp** you need a permit from the NPWS, 28 Vaughan Terrace, Berri (☎08/8595 2111). *Loxton Riverfront Caravan Park*, Habels Bend (☎ & fax 08/8584 7862; cabins ③, on-site vans ②), is a peaceful spot opposite the game reserve, with canoes for rent ($7.50 hr, $25 day) and safe river swimming.

Back in town, the best **accommodation** option is the *Loxton Hotel-Motel*, East Terrace (☎08/8584 7266; ③–④) – inexpensive, friendly and down-to-earth, with decent counter meals and bargain en-suite rooms with TV. On the same street is the *Loxton Palace Chinese Restaurant*, at no. 39 (☎08/8584 6825; BYO).

THE MURRAY RIVER

The **Murray River** is Australia's Mississippi – or so the American author Mark Twain declared when he saw it at the turn of the century. It's a fraction of the size of the American river, but in a country of seasonal, intermittent streams it counts as a major river. Like the Mississippi, the Murray helped open up a new continent, first to explorers, later to trade. Fed by melting snow from the Snowy Mountains, and the Murrumbidgee and Darling rivers, the Murray has enough volume to flow through the arid plains, eventually reaching the Southern Ocean southwest of Adelaide near Goolwa (see p.712). Together the Murray and the Darling and its tributaries make up one of the biggest and longest watercourses in the world, giving life to Australia's most important agricultural region, the **Murray-Darling basin**. For much of its length the Murray forms the border between New South Wales and Victoria, slowing its course on reaching South Australia to meander and produce extensive alluvial plains where irrigation areas are now established. Almost half of South Australia's water comes from the Murray: even far-off Woomera in the Outback relies on it.

Historically, the Riverland was densely populated by various **Aboriginal peoples**. They navigated the river in bark canoes, the bark being cut from river red gums in a single perfect piece; many trees along the river still bear the scars. Nets and spears were used to catch fish, duck and emu; mussels were also an important food source. The Ngarrindjeri people's Dreamtime story of the river's creation explains how Ngurunderi (a Dreamtime hero) travelled down the Murray from its confluence with the Darling, looking for his two runaway wives. The Murray was then just a small stream. As Ngurunderi searched, a giant Murray cod surged ahead of him, widening the river with swipes of his tail. Ngurunderi tried to spear the fish, which he chased ıIght thı ough to the ocean: the thrashing cod carved out the pattern of the Murray River during the chase.

The explorers **Hume** and **Hovell** came across the Murray at Albury in 1824. In 1830 **Sturt** and **Mitchell** navigated the Murray and Darling in a whale boat, Sturt naming it after the then Secretary of State for the Colonies (coincidentally *Murrundi* was the Aboriginal name for part of the river). Their exploration opened up the interior and from 1838 the Murray was followed as a **stock route** to South Australia by drovers or "overlanders" taking sheep and cattle to newly established Adelaide. In 1853 the first **paddle steamer** on the Murray, the *Mary Ann*, was launched near Mannum. Goods were transported far inland, opening up new areas for settlement; in return, wool was carried to

Barmera

If you haven't followed the river to Loxton, **BARMERA**, on the shores of Lake Bonney, is the next major stopping point along the highway. Its claims to fame are varied and dubious: at **Pelican Point**, on the lake's western shore, there's an official **nudist beach** (and a nearby nudist resort with camping, and on-site vans ③; ☎08/8588 7366), while every June, over the long weekend, the **South Australian Country Music Awards** are held in the lovely old Bonney Theatre. For more about the music awards, and **tourist information** in general, contact the Barmera Travel Centre, Barwell Avenue (Mon–Fri 8.30am–5.30pm, Sat 9am–noon; ☎08/8588 2289). The *Barmera Hotel/Motel* (☎08/8588 2111; hotel ③, motel ④) is not the most attractive of the big Riverland community hotels. A cut above is the expensive *Barmera Country Club Motel*, on Hawdon Street (☎08/8588 2888, fax 8588 2785; $86, spa $98 ⑤–⑦), overlooking the golf course, with a pool, spa, tennis courts and restaurant. The extensive *Lake Bonney Holiday Park*, on Lakeside Drive, is a scenic alternative (☎08/8588 2234; cottage ④, cabins ②–④). Eating options include the *Pagoda Chinese Restaurant* (☎08/8588 3167; closed Tues & Sun lunch). If you want to get on the water at Barmera, Riverland Leisure Canoe Tours, Thelma Road (☎08/8588 2053), rents out **canoes**.

market. River transport reached its peak in the 1870s, but by the mid-1930s it was virtually finished – bowing to the superior speed and flexibility of the railways.

SEEING THE RIVER
The best way to appreciate the calm brown beauty of the Murray – lined with majestic river red gums and towering cliffs that reveal the area's colourful soils – and its prolific birdlife is to get out on the water. Several old **paddle steamers**, and a variety of other craft still cruise the Murray for pleasure, and you can even spend a weekend on board the *Murray Princess* (Fri 6.30pm–Sun 2pm; from $330 per person; ☎08/8569 2511), based at **Mannum**, one hour's drive east of Adelaide (or take ABM Coachlines; Mon–Fri daily; ☎08/8347 3336). The boat heads up as far as Swan Reach, and onshore excursions include a bushwalk and a guided tour of Aboriginal sites at Nguat Nguat Reserve. Other cruises from Mannum include sporadic trips on the restored paddle-steamer *Marion* (book at Mannum Tourist Information Centre, 67 Randell St; ☎08/8569 1303) and regular outings on two motorized vessels: the *M.V. Proud Mary* (morning tea cruises Mon 11am; 1hr 15min; also 5-day and 2-day cruises; also book at Mannum Tourist Information Centre) and the *M.V. Lady Mannum* (2hr 30min lunch cruises; ☎08/8569 1438; $23). The *Murray River Queen*, based in Goolwa (see p.712), is another paddle ship with on-board accommodation (☎08/8555 1733 for details). You'll find details of other cruises in the Riverland town accounts.

Renting a **houseboat** is a relaxing and enjoyable way to see the river. All you need is a driving licence, and the cost is not astronomical if you can get a group of people together and avoid the peak holiday seasons. A week in an eight-berth houseboat out of season should cost around $940, in a two-berth $610. The South Australian Tourism Commission (☎1300/366 770; *www.visit-southaustralia.com.au*) has pamphlets giving costs and facilities; they can also book for you, or you could contact the Houseboat Hirers Association (☎08/8395 0999; *hbc@kern.com.au*).

A more hands-on way to explore the wetlands and creek systems is in a canoe. The best place to rent canoes and kayaks is Riverland Canoeing Adventures, Alamein Avenue, North Loxton (☎08/8584 1494; $24 day double kayak, $15 single kayak, cheaper weekly rates), they can provide maps, and camping equipment if you're renting. The flat country, short distances between towns and dry climate are perfect for cycling, and bikes can be rented at various hostels along the way.

For other Murray River accounts, see Goolwa p.712, and the Victoria and NSW chapters (pp.869–877 and pp.317–319 respectively).

Just under 20km from town towards Morgan, a bend in the river was dubbed Overland Corner from 1838, as it was the crossing point for the overland cattle trade to New South Wales. The restful and delightfully isolated *Overland Corner Hotel* (☎08/8588 7021; ④, including cooked breakfast), opened in 1859, serves food and drink and has **accommodation**. You can camp and bushwalk in adjacent Herons Bend Reserve, where an eight-kilometre trail (around 3hr) takes you past old Aboriginal campsites. A pamphlet detailing sites on the walk can be purchased from the pub (50¢). Look at the flood level from the incredible 1956 flood, practically up to the roof.

Berri
The **Big Orange** sets the scene in **BERRI**, announcing the fact that this is the town where the trademark orange juice comes from; and accordingly, travellers are mainly drawn here by the prospect of **fruit-picking work**. You can climb up the Big Orange to the observatory on level three for a good view of the Riverland; for more juice, visit Berrievale Orchards. The river is the main attraction, of course, with scenic river walks above coloured sandstone cliffs, as well as the **Wilabalangaloo Flora and Fauna Reserve**

(Mon & Thurs–Sun 10am–4pm, daily during school holidays; $4), a native animal enclosure and a local history museum on the waterfront. For more information on Berri, head for the **tourist office** on 24 Vaughan Terrace (Mon–Fri 9am–5pm, Sat 9–11.30am; ☎08/8582 1655).

In town the *Berri Resort Hotel*, Riverview Drive (☎08/8582 1411, fax 8582 2140; motel units ⑤, pub rooms ④), is a huge riverfront pub that grows ever tackier and ritzier – though it's not a bad place to stay, with a swimming pool, tennis courts and good food. The excellent *Berri Backpackers* (☎08/8582 3144; rooms ②, dorms ①), out of town towards Barmera on the Sturt Highway opposite the *Berri Club*, is the place to stay if you're fruit-picking, but the place is so popular it's hard to get a bed. The energetic and enterprising owner has laid on such amenities as free bikes and canoes, a sauna, swimming pool, gym, tennis, volleyball and basketball courts and two tree houses, one for couples to stay in, the other used as a general chill-out area. For **food**, *Berri Canton Palace*, 1 Worman St (☎08/8582 2818; closed Tues & Sun lunch), is a good Chinese restaurant; and *Harry's Deli*, 22 Denny St, is a milkbar which is open daily for greasy breakfast, lunch and tea. A healthier option is *Berri Patisserie Bakery*, opposite (weekdays only 8.30am–4.30pm). Swan Houseboats (☎08/8582 3663 or free call ☎1800/034 220) also rents out dinghies and **canoes** for those who want to enjoy the river here.

Renmark

RENMARK, on a bend of the Murray 254km from Adelaide, is the last major town before the border with New South Wales. The riverfront **Renmark Tourist and Heritage Centre** on Murray Avenue (Mon–Fri 9am–5pm, Sat 9am–4pm, Sun noon–4pm, ☎08/8586 0704) books river cruises though no longer houseboats, which need to be booked in advance through the Houseboat Hirers Association or the South Australian Tourism Commission (see box overleaf). Outside, the *P.S. Industry* is moored: one of the few wood-fuelled paddle steamers left on the Murray, it cruises once a month (1hr 30min; $10; contact the tourist centre for times and bookings). Other cruises from Renmark leave from Renmark wharf and head upstream 7km past colourful river cliffs on the *Big River Rambler* (daily 2pm, during school holidays 10am, 2hr; $16; ☎08/8595 1862). Opposite the tourist centre is the huge *Renmark Community Hotel*, a focal point for the town, built in 1897 and given its classic facade in the 1930s. The beautiful *Da Vincis* is the one remaining bar with Art Deco features, while the rest of the hotel is in a tacky 1970s style. Adelaide bands play in the hotel on Friday night; other entertainment takes place at the Chaffey Theatre on 18th Street (☎08/8586 5462), an impressive performing arts centre hosting amateur and professional plays, films and concerts. **Olivewood**, on the corner of Renmark Avenue and 21st Street (Mon & Thurs–Sun 10am–4pm, Tues 2–4pm; $3.50), is the former home of the Chaffey brothers, now owned by the National Trust. A palm-lined drive leads through a citrus orchard and olive trees to the house, which is a strange hybrid of Canadian log cabin and Australian lean-to. The attached museum is the usual hotchpotch of local memorabilia, unrelated to the Chaffeys or their ambitious irrigation project.

The obvious **place to stay** is the landmark *Renmark Hotel/Motel* (☎08/8586 6755; ③–⑤), with rooms ranging from budget to de luxe, and a bistro, outdoor swimming pool and spa. The *Renmark Caravan Park*, on Patey Drive 2km east of town (☎08/8586 6315; en-suite cabins ④, on-site vans ②), has an idyllic setting along 1km of riverfront. The *Riverbend Caravan Park*, also on the Murray, is closer to town but with a less restful highway location (☎08/8595 5131; cabins ④, on-site vans ②). Three good **restaurants** are *Ginger Mick's Pizza*, 124 Murray Ave (☎08/8586 4066), open late nightly except Sunday; for Italian food, *Cafe Toppo e Ristorante*, 179 Murray Ave (08/8586 5241); and, for Greek food, *Sophie's Restaurant* in the Caltex service station at 202

Renmark Ave (☎08/8586 5316). You can eat Chinese food at *The Golden Palace*, 114 Renmark Ave (☎08/8586 6065; closed Tues & Sun lunch).

The mid-north

The area north of the **Sturt Highway**, bounded by **Port Augusta** (see p.740) and the **south Flinders Ranges**, is a fertile agricultural region known as the **mid-north**. **Kapunda**, only 16km northwest of Nurioopta, became the country's first mining town when **copper** was discovered in 1842. It can also be reached as a short detour from the **Barrier Highway** en route to Broken Hill in New South Wales, a route that continues through the larger mining town of **Burra**, and then to **Peterborough**, the self-pro-claimed "frontier to the Outback". The centre of the mid-north's wine area, **Clare**, is 45km southwest of Burra, on the Main North Road, the alternative route to Port Augusta. The **Heysen Trail** runs through Kapunda, Burra and then, via **Crystal Brook**, into the foothills of the Flinders. Heading north to Port Augusta on **Highway 1** for the Northern Territory or Western Australia, you'll pass through the ugly lead-smelting city of **Port Pirie**, and thence on to the south Flinders Ranges.

Getting around the area by **bus** is problematic: while most of the major towns have transport links to Adelaide, there are virtually no buses between towns, however close they might be. Greyhound Pioneer, on its Adelaide–Broken Hill route, goes via the Clare Valley (Auburn, Watervale, Sevenhill, Clare), Jamestown and Peterborough, while its Adelaide–Sydney service stops at Burra. The Mid North Passenger Service (☎08/8826 2346) from Adelaide takes in Burra and the main Clare Valley settlements, while the Barossa–Adelaide Passenger Service (☎08/8564 3022) has a weekday service from Gawler – which can be reached by train – to Kapunda. All interstate buses to Darwin or Perth take Highway 1 through Port Pirie; if you get off 27km before this, it's only a couple of kilometres walk to Crystal Brook and the Heysen Trail.

Copper-mining towns

In 1841 South Australia was in serious economic trouble; the discovery of **copper** at Kapunda the following year rescued the young colony and put it at the forefront of Australia's mining boom. The early finds were soon overshadowed by those at Burra 65km north: the Burra **"Monster Mine"** was the largest in Australia until 1860, creat-ing fabulous wealth and attracting huge numbers of Cornish miners in particular. The boom ended as suddenly as it began, as resources were exhausted – mining finished at Burra in 1877 and Kapunda in 1878.

Heading to **KAPUNDA** from the Barossa, the landscape changes as vineyards are replaced by crops and grazing sheep. As you come into town, you're greeted by a colos-sal sculpture of a Cornish miner entitled *Map Kernow* – "son of Cornwall". A place that once had its own daily newspaper, eleven hotels and a busy train station is now a rural service town, pleasantly undeveloped and with many old buildings decorated with local-ly designed and manufactured iron lacework.

If you have your own transport, you can follow a ten-kilometre **heritage trail** that takes in the ruins of the Kapunda mine, with panoramic views from the mine chimney lookout; details are available from the **Kapunda Information Centre** on Hill Street (Mon–Fri 9am–4pm; ☎08/8566 2902). On the same street, the **Kapunda Museum** (1–4pm Sept–May daily except Fri, June–Aug Sat, Sun & holidays; $4) occupies the mammoth Romanesque-style former Baptist church. The best time to come to Kapunda is during the **Celtic festival** held on the first weekend before Easter, when Celtic music, bush and folk bands feature at the four pubs.

For **accommodation**, *Ford House*, 80 Main St (☎ & fax 08/8566 2280; ⑥), has colonial-style B&B; and the *Sir John Franklin Hotel*, also on Main Street (☎08/8566 2106; ④), has simple, clean rooms and is the most popular pub for inexpensive **meals**. Campers are catered for at *Dutton Caravan Park*, 11 Montefiore St (☎08/8566 2094; cabins ③).

Burra

In 1851 **BURRA** had five thousand residents and was mining five percent of the world's copper; when the mines closed in 1877 it became a service centre for the surrounding farming community. It also takes advantage of its position on the Barrier Highway, using its copper heritage to draw visitors. Plenty of money is spent restoring and beautifying the place, even to the extent of topping up pretty, gum-shaded **Burra Creek** to ensure that it's always flowing. With its well-preserved stone architecture, shady tree-lined streets, great country pubs and upmarket home stores, art and craft and antiques shops, Burra is a popular weekend escape between March and November (before it gets too hot). The creek divides the town grid in two: the mine is in the north, while the southern section has the shopping centre, based around **Market Square**, where you'll also find the **tourist office** (daily 9am–5pm; ☎08/8892 2154). Its main function is to issue the **Burra Passport Key** to people driving the eleven-kilometre **heritage trail** (one person $15, two people $20, three for $25 and $30 for four, plus $5 deposit), the key gives you access to six major sites en route – though you still have to pay for admission to the museums (at reduced price).

Heading north along Market Street you come to the **Burra Monster Mine** site, where there are extensive remains and interpretive walking trails, as well as the **Enginehouse Museum** (Mon–Fri 11am–1pm; $3). Continuing north, the **Bon Accord Mine Complex** on Linkson Street (Mon–Fri 12.30–2.30pm; $3) was a short-lived failure compared to its hugely successful neighbour, there's a scale model of the monster mine and a shaft and mining relics on view. Other key-pass places in the northern section of the town are the old **police lock-up and stables**, **Redruth Gaol**, and **Hampton**, a now-deserted private township in the style of an English village. Back in the main part of the town, the pass will allow you entry to the **Unicorn Brewery Cellars** (1873) and the fascinating two remaining **miners' dugouts**: in around 1851 nearly two thousand people lived in homes clawed out of the soft clay along Burra Creek, because of a housing shortage. There are two further **museums**: the **Market Square Museum** (Fri 1–4pm, Sat & Sun 1–3pm; $2) was a general store, post office and home from 1880 to 1920; and "Malowen Lowarth", on Kingston Street (Sat 1–3pm, Sun 10.30am–12.30pm; $3), is one of the **Paxton Square miners' cottages**, decorated in 1850s style.

You can **stay** in other miners' cottages in the Paxton Square, all overseen by the office in the former Methodist Chapel at the end of the row (☎08/8892 2622, fax 8892 2555; ③–④). There are thirty-two in all; even so, on weekends from mid-March to October they are booked out by Adelaidians on short winter breaks. The stone cottages are freezing in winter but do have fireplaces (wood is $5 extra) and plenty of blankets (BYO linen or $5 extra); they all have modern kitchens, though breakfast is available at the office. Other accommodation in town includes *Burra View House*, Mount Pleasant Road (☎08/8892 2648, fax 8892 2150; ⑥), and the tree-surrounded *Burra Motor Inn*, Market Street (☎08/8892 2777, fax 8892 2707; ⑤) with contemporary-styled rooms backing onto the creek, an indoor swimming pool and a well-priced restaurant. All the **hotels** in town also have rooms, and most provide breakfast. Best of the lot is the 1884 *Kooringa Hotel* opposite the Paxton Cottages on Kingston Street (☎08/8892 2013; B&B ④), which serves excellent food. Less expensive is the down-to-earth *Commercial Hotel*, 22 Commercial Rd (☎08/8892 2010; B&B ③). If you have a **tent** you could try *Burra Caravan Park*, Bridge Terrace (☎08/8892 2442; on-site vans ②), in a pretty spot beside the creek, a couple of minutes' walk from the shops. *Price's Bakery*, Commercial Road, serves good coffee, home-made soups, baked goodies and sandwiches with a gourmet slant (daily 9am–4 or 5pm).

The Clare Valley

The wine industry in the **Clare Valley**, west of the Barrier Highway between Kapunda and Burra, was pioneered by Jesuit priests at **Sevenhill** in the 1850s. There's no tourist overkill here: bus trips are not encouraged, and because it's a small area with just over 25 wineries, you can learn a lot about the local styles of wine; the area is recognized especially for its fine Rieslings. Often, too, you'll get personal treatment, with the wine maker presiding at the cellar door. In the cool uplands of the North Mount Lofty Ranges, Clare Valley is really a series of gum-fringed ridges and valleys running roughly 30km north from **Auburn** to the main township of **Clare**, on either side of the Main North Road. Huge sheep runs were established here in the nineteenth century and the area, which is prime Merino land, still has an obvious pastoral feel; several stations can be visited. There are also beautiful old villages and some well-preserved mansions on view, plenty of charming B&B accommodation and some superb restaurants attached to wineries. The big event of the year is the **Clare Valley Gourmet Weekend**, held in May at local wineries.

Between Clare and Auburn, the old railway line has been transformed into a 27km cycling path, the **Reisling Trail**; to cycle one way takes about two hours. Mountain **bikes** can be hired from Clare Valley Cycle Hire, 32 Victoria Rd, Clare (☎08/8842 2782), who will deliver to anywhere in the valley, and Mid-North Sports Centre, 300 Main North Rd, Clare (☎08/8842 2013).

Auburn to Watervale

Heading north through the valley, **AUBURN**, 120km from Adelaide, is the first settlement, small and village-like, which began life as a halfway resting point for wagons carrying copper ore from Burra to Port Adelaide. The *Rising Sun Hotel* (☎08/8849 2015, fax 8849 2266; ⑤–⑦ including breakfast) is one of many great **pubs** in the valley, first licensed in 1850. It has small bedrooms in the hotel and mews-style accommodation in old stone stables, as well as a very affordable modern Australian menu – things like kangaroo fillet with a shiraz butter sauce – and an appropriately long wine list. A more luxurious place to stay is *Dennis Cottage* (☎08/8277 8177, fax 8204 5625; ⑥) – it has a spa, as well as paraphernalia associated with C.J. Dennis, the popular poet who was born here in 1876. *Tatehams*, on the Main North Road (☎08/8849 2030, fax 8849 2260; ⑧) is a very distinguished dining/guesthouse combination that even has a French chef. Nearby are two small wineries to visit, with restricted opening hours: **Grossets** (Wed–Sun 10am–5pm) and **Mount Horrocks** (Sat & Sun 10am–5pm).

The next small village is **LEASINGHAM**, where you can camp or stay at *Leasingham Village Cabins* (☎08/8843 0136; cabins ④, dorms ①), a popular place for **grape-pickers** from March to mid-April; wineries often phone and ask for workers. An attached restaurant serves simple inexpensive weekend lunches (licensed or BYO; lunch Sat & Sun, dinner Sat). You can taste wines nearby at **Tim Gramp Wines** (daily 10.30am–4.30pm). At **WATERVALE**, 2km north, there are four small wineries: **Crabtree of Watervale**, North Terrace (Thurs–Mon 11am–5pm, daily during school holidays), is one of the most enjoyable in the valley.

Mintaro

From Leasingham, you can turn off east to **MINTARO**, a village whose tree-lined streets and cottages are beautifully preserved from the 1850s, when it was a resting place for bullock teams travelling from Burra copper mines. There's no general store or petrol supply here: the emphasis is on upmarket cottage accommodation, popular with Adelaide weekenders. The focus of the village is the *Magpie and Stump Hotel*, which is particularly lively on Sunday afternoons. On a fine day you can sit shaded under the awning or sprawl on the grass. Opposite, at **Reilly's Wines** (tastings

Mon–Fri 9am–5pm, Sat & Sun 10am–5pm), housed in an 1856 Irish bootmaker's building, you can taste vintages produced since 1994 from Watervale grapes; the **restaurant** here serves Northern Italian food, with mains around $13 (closed dinner Tues, Fri & Sun; reservations ☎08/8843 9013) and there's **accommodation** in the nearby *Mintaro Pay Office Cottages* (midweek ⑥, weekend ⑦; breakfast provisions included). *Mintaro Mews*, on Burra Street (☎08/8843 9001, fax 8843 9002; ⑦), has upmarket B&B accommodation (no children) with an indoor heated pool and spa; Saturday nights are package only ($100 per person), including a four-course meal in the atmospheric restaurant (dinner nightly except Wed) whose menu reflects North African and Indian influence.

Southeast of the town, the National Trust extols the virtues of the Georgian-style **Martindale Hall** (Mon–Fri 11am–4pm, Sat & Sun noon–4pm; $5; ☎08/8843 9088, fax 8843 9082; B&B ⑨), the mansion featured in the 1975 film *Picnic at Hanging Rock*. There's a romantic story attached to the hall, its unadapted, unsuitable-for-the-climate English architecture a monument to unrequited love – you'll hear the full story when you visit. For $125 per person you can **stay overnight** and enjoy a five-course meal, cooked breakfast and the full run of the place (except the smoking room) – but it's freezing in winter.

Head northwest from Mintaro to get to Sevenhill (see below) via the rolling hills of the Polish Hill River area. On the way, **Paulett Wines** (daily 10am–5pm) has fabulous views, its verandah overlooking the area and the "river" – a dry creek for eleven months of the year.

Sevenhill and the Spring Gully Conservation Park

The village of **SEVENHILL** has the valley's oldest winery, **Sevenhill Cellars**, on College Road (Mon–Fri 8.30am–4.30pm, Sat 9am–4pm). This is still run by a religious order and mainly makes sacramental wine, though the brothers have diversified into table wines, sweet sherry and port, doing everything from growing the grapes to bottling. The sandstone building has a tasting room with lots of character and history, and there's an old Catholic church in the grounds. Nearby on College Road, *Thorn Park Country House* (☎08/8843 4304, fax 8843 4296; ⑨) is an 1850 stone and slate building in a gorgeous setting; it offers **B&B** and a beautifully indulgent dinner – but at a price ($175 per person; just B&B is $130 per person). *Sevenhill Hotel*, on the Main North Road, is a classic country pub serving popular inexpensive meals daily except Sunday.

To the west of the Main North Road, **Spring Gully Conservation Park** has the last remnant of red stringybark forest in South Australia. There are steep gullies, waterfalls, wildlife and, in spring, lovely wild flowers; free camping is allowed outside the fire-ban season. Nearby, attached to boutique **wineries** signposted from Sevenhill, are three excellent **restaurants** serving gourmet meals from deliciously fresh local produce; all are moderately priced. Eldredge Wines, Spring Gully Road (tastings daily 11am–5pm; lunch Fri–Mon and daily during school holidays, closed two weeks at the end of February; restaurant bookings ☎08/8842 3086) is located in a small farmhouse fronting a dam; Skillogalee Winery (daily 10am–5pm; ☎08/8843 4311 lunch bookings advised) is in a wonderful spot with a backdrop of a clunking windmill, bushclad hill and vineyards, and holds meals and tastings by the fire in the 1850s cottage or on the verandah; Kilikanoon Wines (Sat & Sun 11am–5pm; ☎08/8843 4377) serves legendary weekend lunches in its old cottage, or outside under vines.

Clare

CLARE itself is a surprisingly ordinary town, with few concessions to the weekend visitors who pour in from Adelaide: it consists primarily of Main North Road, and everything is closed on Sunday. **Tourist information**, in the town hall at 229 Main North Rd (Mon–Sat 9am–5pm, Sun 10am–4pm; ☎08/8842 2131), provides an excellent free visitors' guide and can book accommodation and restaurants.

Wineries around town include Tim Knappsteins, 2 Pioneer Ave (Mon–Fri 9am–5pm, Sat 10am–5pm, Sun 11am–4pm), an ivy-covered sandstone building with a verandah and an open log fire in winter; Jim Barry, a friendly, family-run place on the Main North Road (Mon–Fri 9am–5pm, Sat & Sun 9am–4pm); and Leasingham, 7 Dominic St (Mon–Fri 8.30am–5pm, Sat & Sun 10am–4pm), a large commercial winery established in 1893. There are also stations open for tours and **farmstays**: pick of the bunch is *Bungaree Station* (☎08/8842 2677, fax 8842 3004; cottages B&B ⑤, BYO-bedding shearers' quarters ①), a working Merino station 12km north on the Main North Road, and one of the oldest and largest properties in the district, which has its own church as well as a swimming pool. **Geralka Rural Farm** (☎08/8845 8081, fax 8845 8073), a sheep and cereal property, has a caravan park with on-site vans (③) and a unit (④) and offers weekend farm activity tours aimed at families (Sat, Sun, public holidays & daily during school holidays 1.30pm; 2hr 30min–3hr; $8, children $4).

Places to **stay** in Clare itself are all along Main North Road: try *Clare Valley Motel* 2.5km south of the centre at no. 74 (☎08/8842 2799, fax 8842 3121; ⑤–⑥) with a restaurant specializing in North Indian food and an outdoor pool, or the more upmarket *Clare Central Motel* north of town at no. 325 (☎08/8842 2277, fax 8842 3563; ⑥ including light breakfast), also with a pool. The best of the hotels are the friendly family-run *Bentleys*, 191 Main North Rd (☎08/8842 1700, fax 8842 3474; motel ④, hotel ③–④, dorms ①), which has an atrium bistro and a backpackers' hostel section; the *Clare Hotel*, at 244 Main North Rd (☎08/8842 2816; ④), which has pleasant rooms and meals; and the *Taminga Hotel* (☎08/8842 2808; ③), offering basic pub rooms. You can **camp** 4km south of town at *Clare Caravan Park*, on Main North Road (☎08/8842 2724; on-site vans ③, cabins ④), with a swimming pool on site.

Besides the pubs, you can eat well during the day at *Clare Fine Foods*, 279 Main North Rd (closed Sun), a small deli serving gourmet rolls and sandwiches and dishes such as caesar salad or pasta; the espresso coffee here is the best in town.

Port Pirie

From Clare, the Main North Road heads to Jamestown, 65km north. To the west, a road branches off towards Crystal Brook, where there's a hikers' lodge at Bowman Park providing basic overnight shelter for hikers on the Heysen Trail. From here it's not far up Highway 1 to **PORT PIRIE**, the fourth-largest urban centre in South Australia. An ugly industrial city, its skyline is dominated by smelters' chimneys: as the nearest seaport to Broken Hill, the lead and zinc smelting industry here dates back to the discovery of the rich vein of lead-silver-zinc found there in 1883. The **Port Pirie Tourism and Arts Centre** (Mon–Fri 9am–5pm, Sat 9am–4pm; ☎08/8633 0439), on Mary Elie Street opposite the silos, promotes the world's largest smelting works as a prime attraction, reason enough not to stop unless a tour of the Pasminco Metals BHAS **smelting plant** is high on your list (Wed & Sat 10am; free). Beyond Port Pirie, Telowie Gorge and Mount Remarkable National Park, in the southern stretches of the Flinders Ranges (see p.743–744), are within easy reach.

OUTBACK SOUTH AUSTRALIA

. . . a country such as I firmly believe has no parallel on earth's surface.
The explorer Charles Sturt, 1844.

All routes in the Outback radiate out from **Port Augusta** and, with few connecting roads, interstate destinations will probably dictate which direction you leave town.

Buses cover the highways but elsewhere you'll need to have your own transport or take a safari. To the west, the **Eyre Highway** runs 950km to the border of Western Australia, with desert scenery all the way unless you detour around the coast of the Eyre Peninsula. The rail line west runs further inland, through even more extreme desolation. North, the **Stuart Highway** and **New Ghan rail line** link Port Augusta with the Northern Territory through 890km of progressively drier scenery where regular markers along the roadside record the distance covered, as well as how far there is to go. **Prohibited zones** surround much of the highway, though about the only places you'd want to leave it anyway are at **Woomera** and **Coober Pedy**, both outside military zones and the boundaries of Aboriginal Land.

All other roads north head from Port Augusta along the route taken by the legendary but now defunct **Old Ghan** (see box on p.573) to the country towns of **Quorn** and **Hawker**, where routes diverge: northeast through the **Flinders Ranges** and along the **Strzelecki Track** to **Innamincka**; or due north to **Marree**, at the head of the **Birdsville** and **Oodnadatta tracks**. **Sealed roads** end at Lyndhurst on the way to Marree, and Wilpena Pound in the central Flinders. Check conditions if you plan to go any further – in dry weather 2WD vehicles often make it to Innamincka and Oodnadatta, but none of the north's remoter tracks should be attempted during the searing summer months. **Buses** run the length of the Stuart Highway, between Woomera and Andamooka, and from Port Augusta to Marree and Arkaroola in the northern Flinders.

A **Desert Parks Pass** is required for legal entry into Innamincka Regional Reserve, Lake Eyre National Park, Witjira National Park and the Simpson Desert: $50 per vehicle allows twelve months' unlimited access and use of campsites, with copies of the detailed NPWS *Desert Parks Handbook* and Westprint Heritage Maps' surveys thrown in. Passes are available from agencies throughout the north or by post from the NPWS Far North Office, 60 Elder Terrace, Hawker 5434 (☎08/8648 4244 or free call ☎1800/816 078).

Independent travellers share common concerns throughout the north. **Plastic** is often carried in preference to wads of cash; many roadhouses and fuel pumps have EFT-POS facilities. **Water** is vital: with few exceptions, lakes and waterways are dry or highly saline, and most Outback deaths are related to dehydration or heatstroke – bikers seem particularly prone. As always, stay with your vehicle if you break down. Summer **temperatures** are lethally hot, winters pleasant during the day and subzero at night; rain can fall at any time of year, but is most likely to do so between January and May.

New RAA **road maps** are good but lack surface detail. If you're spending any time in the north, pick up the excellent Westprint Heritage Maps and the cluttered *Landsmap Outback*: *Central and South Australia*. The South Australia Tourist Association issues a road map of the Flinders Ranges, but it's inadequate for walking, so **hikers** traversing the Flinders on the Heysen Trail need topographic maps of each section and advice from the nearest NPWS office. Conditions of **minor roads** are so variable that maps seldom do more than indicate the surface type; local police and roadhouses will have current information.

Port Augusta and the west

How you see **Port Augusta** depends on where you've come from. Arriving from the Outback the trees, shops and hotels can be a real thrill, but compared with the southeast, it's pretty tame. However, being a transport bottleneck has saved the town from destitution and plans are afoot to make more of its seaside location. While you're deciding where to head next, there are a few things to see in town and some good **bushwalking** country around **Mount Remarkable**, at the tail end of the Flinders Ranges. The direct route west from Port Augusta, the **Eyre Highway**, begins its daunting journey towards Western Australia across the top of the **Eyre Peninsula**, but going this way you'll see virtually nothing. An alternative route detours around the peninsula's coastline (via the Lincoln and Flinders highways) before rejoining the highway at **Ceduna** on the brink of the **Nullarbor Plain**, while the rail line parallels the coast some 100km inland.

Port Augusta

Unkindly dubbed "Porta Gutter" by Adelaide's smart set, who paint dire pictures of a town rife with petty crime, **PORT AUGUSTA** sits at the tip of the Spencer Gulf and on the edge of everywhere else. Despite the name, the docks closed long ago and more recent employment mainstays such as the power station and railways were drastically scaled down during the 1980s – the former rail buildings have been converted to Employment Service offices.

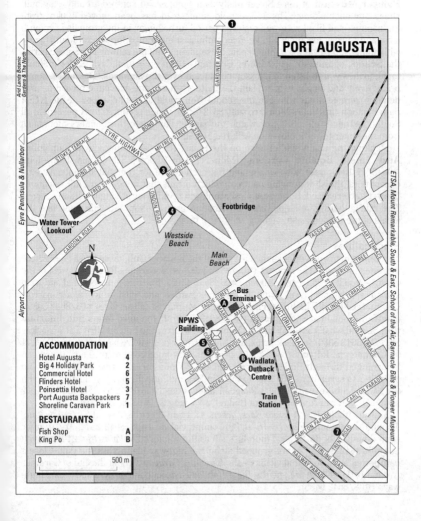

PORT AUGUSTA

ACCOMMODATION

Hotel Augusta	4
Big 4 Holiday Park	2
Commercial Hotel	6
Flinders Hotel	5
Poinsettia Hotel	3
Port Augusta Backpackers	7
Shoreline Caravan Park	1

RESTAURANTS

Fish Shop	A
King Po	B

0   500 m

During summer, you should make the most of the small **swimming beach** at the end of Young Street to escape the dust and heat – the old wooden pile crossing, now a footbridge, and a hundred-year-old jetty, all that remains of the port, make good perches for fishing. The chief source of **information** is the **Wadlata Outback Centre**, at 41 Flinders Terrace (Mon–Fri 9am–5.30pm, Sat & Sun 10am–4pm; $7; ☎08/8641 0793), which is well worth a look in its own right. Audiovisual technology, didgeridoo loudspeakers and a giant model of Akurra, the Dreamtime snake, are deployed to explain Aboriginal bushcraft and Flinders Ranges' creation myths, while geological and mining displays give a scientific perspective; tales of the hardships suffered by the nineteenth-century explorers Eyre, Sturt (and his boat), Stuart and Giles fill in the background.

If you still feel like exploring after Wadlata, drop in to the **Homestead Park Pioneer Museum** at Elsie Street (daily 9am–5pm; $2.50) centred around a log-built sheep station building. The 135-year-old homestead has been moved 100km from Yudnapinna and filled with well-restored period furnishings; in the grounds is enough farm and railway machinery to keep an enthusiast enthralled for several hours, along with animals, birds and a photographic museum in a vintage railway carriage. Nearby, the **School of the Air**, at 59 Power Crescent (10am on school days; $2 for a 30min tour), invites you to listen to a lesson conducted over the airwaves. The interaction is pretty lively and might help explain the better-than-average academic record for students in remote areas who use the school. You could also take a look at the **ETSA** power station (free tours Mon–Fri; ☎08/8642 0737), which produces forty percent of all South Australia's electricity, or watch the sunset illuminate the Flinders mountains from the water tower **lookout** on Mildred Street.

Flanking the north side of town on the Stuart Highway is the new and ambitious **Arid Lands Botanic Gardens** (Mon–Fri 9am–5.30pm, Sat & Sun 10am–4pm; ☎08/8641 1049; free), a showcase and research centre for regional and international desert flora, the slow-growing nature of which means that the garden's full splendour has yet to be realized; however, a closer look will reveal a surprising wealth of species. The rain-gathering, solar-powered information centre, shop and café underline the ideals of the garden as an ongoing ecological project.

Practicalities

The centre of town overlooks the east side of the Spencer Gulf, more like a river where it divides the town. The **airport** (☎08/8642 3100) is on Caroona Road, 5km west of the centre – you'll need to get a taxi in (☎08/8642 4466). Both the bus terminal and train station are a short walk from the shops, **banks** and post office along narrow Commercial Road. The **bus terminal** is at 21 Mackay St (all services ☎08/8642 5055), and **trains** pull in at Stirling Road (☎08/8642 6699). If you need **maps and information** beyond what's available at the Outback Centre, try the helpful NPWS at 9 Mackay St (☎08/8648 5300) for park maps, info and permits; or if you're a member, the RAA, at 91 Commercial Rd (☎08/8642 2576), provides very good road maps. Local **tours** can be arranged through Butlers Outback Safaris, 2 Woodstock St (☎08/8642 2188), who offer one- to seven-day 4WD trips to the Flinders and Innamincka. If you fancy a trip on the back of a **bike**, call Flinders Ranges Harley Rides (☎08/8642 6401; around $50 per hour). Or you can rent a **car** from Budget, 16 Young St (☎08/8642 6040).

The shambolic *Port Augusta Backpackers*, 17 Trent Rd (☎08/8641 1063; free pick-up; ①), and the friendly *Flinders Hotel*, 39 Commercial Rd (☎08/8642 2544; ①–③), offer central budget **beds**. Several **motels**, such as the comfortable *Poinsettia*, 24 Burgoyne St (☎08/8642 2411; ④), are grouped along the highway just across the gulf. Closest **campsites** are also in that vicinity – the *Shoreline Caravan Park* at the end of Gardiner Avenue (☎08/8642 2965) and the *Big 4 Holiday Park*, junction of Eyre and Stuart highways (☎08/8642 6455).

Hotels are the place for **meals and entertainment**, but opening hours are vague and often depend on demand, which can be almost non-existent during the week. The *Transcontinental*, Port Augusta's weekly rag, will have details of anything happening around town. Seafood addicts should head for the fish shop at the seaward end of Marryatt Street, which sells fresh fish, as well as fish and chips; at the other end of the street is *King Po* Chinese restaurant. Along Commercial Road you'll find a few cafés for lunch and snacks, with vegetarian options at *Basic Foods*, while *Barnacle Bill's*, on Victoria Parade 3km from the town centre, has pretty good value seafood and all the salad you can eat. The central *Commercial Hotel* boasts an à la carte menu at weekends; *Hotel Augusta* serves meals with a fine view of beach, mangroves and the distant Flinders Ranges.

Mount Remarkable National Park and the Barrier Highway

The Flinders run low in their southern extremes, more heavily timbered than the desert ranges but otherwise similar in formation. **Mount Remarkable National Park** lies in two sections, encircled by a ring road that starts 45km southeast of Port Augusta and runs via Wilmington, Melrose and Port Germein. The larger **western** slice contains Mambray Creek and Mount Cavern, and connecting tracks from them to Alligator Gorge; Mount Remarkable and sections of the Heysen Trail rise to the **east** behind Melrose. If time is short, Alligator Gorge is easy going, while the Mount Cavern circuit is considerably harder – but both make good day-trips from Port Augusta. The only **campsite** with facilities is at Mambray Creek but bush camping is allowed elsewhere with permission from the NPWS (☎08/8634 7068); you should also consult them in hot weather, as the park may be completely closed if there is a high risk of fire. Stateliner **buses** go daily to Mambray Creek, three times weekly to Wilmington and Melrose; *Port Augusta Backpackers* (see opposite) organize one- to six-day hikes with all fees, maps and transport included.

Alligator Gorge, Melrose and Mount Remarkable

The eleven-kilometre dirt road from Wilmington to **Alligator Gorge** ($3 visitor's permit available on entry) ends at a picnic area perched on a spur above two **campsites** at Teal and Eaglehawk dams. Stairs descend the gorge wall, with several walking options once you reach the floor: a three-hour circuit north to the ranger's office past the rippled **Terraces** – remains of a fossilized lake shore; or south along the creek for an hour through a tight red canyon alive with frog calls, moss gardens and echoes. These narrows are sometimes flooded, though usually there are enough stepping stones to avoid wet feet. Longer hikes down to Mambray Creek need maps and approval from the NPWS.

Melrose is a quiet former copper-mining town with two hotels, a pleasant creekside **caravan park** (☎08/8666 2060; dorms ①) and a few cottage industries. **B&B** is available at **Bluey Blundstone's Blacksmith Shop** (☎08/8666 2173; ⑥), recently restored to its original 1865 condition. When the proprietor isn't producing decorative wrought-ironwork he serves cakes in a coffee shop at the back of the forge. The van park hands out walking maps for historic buildings, old mines and ascents to **Cathedral Rock** in the national park. The unremarkable summit of **Mount Remarkable** can be reached in three hours via the **Heysen Trail**, starting a couple of kilometres north of town from the showground.

Telowie Gorge, Mambray Creek and Mount Cavern

The small and appealing **Telowie Conservation Park** lies to the south off the Port Germein–Murray Town road. A very short path leads between the gorge walls, but, unless you're properly equipped for a long hike over to Wirrabara Forest and the

Heysen Trail, you'll get more of a flavour of the area by camping along the creek and looking for rare wallabies at dawn and dusk.

The access track to **Mambray Creek** is east off the highway, halfway between Port Germein and the Wilmington road. There's a **campsite** (water, toilets) and national park headquarters. Mambray Creek is the start of some serious walks, either into the north part of the park along the **Battery Track** and **Alligator Creek**, or on the tough but shorter Mount Cavern circuit. Follow the path anticlockwise along the Black Range to **Mount Cavern**, which has spectacular views and occasionally attracts wedge-tailed eagles. The descent is down a loose stone slope held together by grasstrees, then entering cool woodland at Mambray Creek Gorge, where you might be able to get close to large groups of **emus**.

The Barrier Highway

The last place of any size east of Mount Remarkable, before the Barrier Highway continues to the border with New South Wales, is **PETERBOROUGH**, once a major rail junction where three different track gauges met. **Steamtown Peterborough** is a preservation society which keeps a few steam trains running on 90km of scenic track between Eurelia and Orroroo; for times (usually only on a few holidays) enquire at the **information centre** in a restored train carriage on Main Street (daily 9am–4pm; ☎08/8651 2708). Small-scale gold prospectors bring their finds to be processed and refined here at the state's only **Gold Battery**, which can be viewed by appointment (☎08/8651 2969). **YUNTA**, 100km further, is a collection of roadhouses and services at the start of a backdoor route into the Flinders; it's 300km of gravel road from here to Arkaroola, 200km to Hawker.

The Eyre Peninsula

Far from the rigours of the true Outback, and long appreciated by Adelaidians as an antidote to city stress, the **Eyre Peninsula**'s broad triangle is protected by the **Gawler Ranges** from the arid climate further north. The area began to be farmed late last century; fishing communities sprang up at regular intervals and iron ore, discovered at the turn of the century, is still mined around **Whyalla**. The detour **around the coast** brings you in contact with imposing scenery and superlative **surfing** and **beach fishing**, especially where the Great Australian Bight's elemental weather hammers into the western shore – here there's a chance to give your senses a workout before dealing with the Nullarbor's deadening horizons. Unfortunately, Stateliner only runs down the east coast to **Port Lincoln** at the southern tip, so you'll need your own transport to tackle the west side; major **car rental** companies have outlets at both Whyalla and Port Lincoln which, if time is limited, are only fifty minutes by air from Adelaide.

> Locals don't rate Eyre Peninsula **tap water** as worth drinking. Bottled water and filters are readily available in supermarkets.

Whyalla and the east coast

First visible an hour from Port Augusta as a smudge of grey over Long Sleep Plain, **WHYALLA**, the state's second most important city and headquarters of its heavy industry, is not the prettiest of places. BHP has its massive "long products" **steelworks** here (tours Mon, Wed & Sat 9.30am; 2hr; $8; book through the information centre) and tankers queue offshore to fill up at Santos' oil & gas refinery and distillery. Until it closed in 1978, the **shipyard** produced a few famous vessels, the first being the *Whyalla*, which now guards the northern entrance to town, having been dragged 2km from the sea in a complicated and expensive manoeuvre. The accompanying **information centre** and **maritime museum** (daily 10am–4pm; $5 including ship tour; ☎08/8645 8900) is largely occupied by a huge model of the oil refinery as well as more relevant displays of shipping history. From the southwest, Whyalla presents a much greener visage. You can cuddle a koala or a python at the **Wildlife and Reptile Sanctuary** (daily 10am–dusk; ☎08/8645 7044; $5), and at the junction of Broadbent Terrace and Playford Avenue an old aerodrome site is being landscaped into a series of ponds to recycle stormwater and eventually provide a pleasant recreational area.

The highway curves through the old town as Darling Terrace; you'll find a **post office**, **banks**, a **bus station**, hotels and shops around the junction with Forsyth and Patterson streets, all periodically covered in (harmless) red fallout from BHP's mysterious pellet plant. **Accommodation** options include the *Foreshore Caravan Park* on Broadbent Terrace (☎08/8645 7474; cabins ③) and *Derham's Motel* on Watson Terrace (☎08/8645 8877; ⑥), both a ten-minute walk from the centre along a surprisingly attractive beach with Hummock Hill to mercifully obscure your view of the steelworks; people and pelicans find good fishing off the jetty. Otherwise, try your luck at one of the hotels – *Spencer* on Forsyth Street (☎08/8645 8411; ③–④) has rooms, good food and weekend music. For **food**, seafood marinara at *Spagg's*, 26 Patterson St, makes a welcome change from counter meals; after eating, walk past the rows of fifty-year-old workers' homes to the top of Hummock Hill for a view of the industrial complexes by night.

With the exception of Whyalla, the east coast is an unassuming string of sheltered beaches and villages nestled beneath towering grain silos, the sort of places one could drive through without a second glance or else get waylaid beachcombing for a week. **COWELL** is known for its whiting and as the world's largest source of black "nephrite" jade, though not much of it is in evidence as it is largely exported rough. **Arno Bay**, **Port Neil** and the larger **Tumby Bay** all boast clean, quiet beaches and good fishing and a range of accommodation – they will try to entice you with their sundry museums and even a worm farm.

If you venture about 90km inland from Cowell, you can view the patchwork of farmland from **Carappee Hill**, the highest point on the peninsula, but you need to be a very determined bushwalker to penetrate its spiky vegetation – the surrounding Carappee Conservation Park has no official paths, although there is a water supply for campers.

Port Lincoln and the lower peninsula

A tuna port and resort town built on a hillside above Boston Bay, **PORT LINCOLN** has the busiest atmosphere of anywhere on the peninsula. Its harbour is dotted with trawlers, and the seafront Tasman Terrace and Liverpool Street are full of eateries and far-from-genteel taverns. Porter Bay, until recently a swamp just south of town, has been transformed into a **marina** which has drawn many of the boats and some of the life away from the old town. The development includes a large modern **leisure centre** (Mon–Fri 6am–9pm, Sat, Sun & holidays 9am–6pm; ☎08/8682 3833). Entering town from the north, the Lincoln Highway affords splendid views of Boston Bay and presents you with myriad motel **accommodation**, such as the luxurious *Limani Motel* (☎08/8682 2200, fax 8682 6602; ⑥–⑧), as it becomes the beachfront Tasman Terrace and then London Street, at the far end of which lie the terraced tent sites of *Kirton Point Caravan Park* (☎08/8682 2537).

Port Lincoln has a surprising artistic streak – the Arteyrea Gallery on Washington Street (☎08/8682 6444; look for the bike-riding fish) is worth a visit – but most of the town's attractions are underwater. You can get bait and tackle from any service station and **fish** off the town jetty; for heavier game contact Sea Charters (☎08/8682 2425), which can also take you on a cruise to **Dangerous Reef** for seals, birdlife and sharks. **Divers** after Great White thrills should contact Got One at 80 Tasman Terrace

(☎08/8683 0021) and organize a foursome to split the $800-a-day tab; a shark cage is employed if you're "lucky" enough to make contact. Port Lincoln Diving, on Tasman Terrace (☎08/8682 4428), can rent out gear for less dangerous diving. Check out other local attractions at the **information centre** (daily 9am–5pm; ☎08/8683 3544 or free call ☎1800/629 911), on Tasman Terrace between the post office and shopping mall.

Onshore, explore **Lincoln National Park**, a rough peninsula of sandy coves, steep cliffs and mallee scrub, which is home to the discreet rock parrot. The NPWS on Liverpool Street (☎08/8688 3111) can supply maps and advice on road conditions. Similar scenery 32km south at **Whalers Way** is open to all traffic, once a permit and key have been collected from the information centre in Port Lincoln ($15, plus $3 deposit); the name derives from the whaling station which once operated at Cape Wiles – relics are stacked up around the gate. If you've ever felt the need to be impressed by the sea's power, head for **Cape Carnot**: giant waves and frosty blue surf force through **blowholes** which sigh as they erupt in sync with the swell.

Coffin Bay National Park, an hour's drive west from Port Lincoln, is a landscape of dunes and saltmarsh, mostly only accessible by 4WD. Though parts are open to other types of vehicles, you should consult the NPWS in Port Lincoln before venturing here. You'll be rewarded by isolation, sand sculptures at Sensation and Mullalong beaches, and the quality of the fishing. Semicircular stone walls on the northern shore are **Aboriginal fish traps** – fish were chased in at high tide and then the gaps in the side blocked with nets as the water receded. If you don't have your own 4WD, Great Australian Bight Safaris (☎08/8682 2750) will take you on various day-trips for around $60, as well as on longer camping and fishing adventures.

The picturesque setting of the town of **COFFIN BAY** is worth a look, though perhaps not during school holidays when the caravan park (≈08/8686 1170) and abundant holiday cottages are full to bursting. A stroll along the coastal "Oyster Walk" takes you past the original fishermen's shacks, now mostly summer houses, and reveals a wealth of bird and plant life – a taste of Coffin Bay National Park to the west.

The west coast

To catch the best of the west coast and the townships along the way, you'll need to detour off the main road between Coffin Bay and Ceduna. The coastal communities are an unlikely mix of conservative farmers and "alternative" surfies who come to ride the endless succession of strong, hundred-metre-long crests rolling into Waterloo Bay at **ELLISTON**, one of the state's most highly regarded **surf beaches**. Bold **murals** at the Community Hall between the café and campsite address local themes – including a long-suppressed incident when Aboriginal people were driven over the cliffs. South of Venus Bay, rocks have been hollowed by the sea to form the **Talia Caves** but the lengthy beach is more compelling; camping is prohibited but you'd probably get away with sleeping in the car. Turning to the coast about 20km north of Port Kenny, you go past the strangely flared **Murphy's Haystacks**, a group of low granite monoliths that look like giant mushrooms. Push on to **Point Labatt** for a look at mainland Australia's only colony of **fur seals**. Binoculars or a telephoto lens help to distinguish mother seals teaching pups to swim from the torpid, bulkier males basking on the rocks. Then it's back to the highway at **Streaky Bay** – the only place on the west coast that has a real centre – and then to drier country as you approach Ceduna and the Nullarbor.

The Eyre Highway and Gawler Ranges

Taking the **Eyre Highway** directly across the top of the peninsula ensures an easy, comfortable crossing to Ceduna, speeding past the mines at **Iron Knob** and a dry scrub populated by green ring-necked parrots. Unusual geology appears around Wudinna in the form of isolated granite mounds (inselbergs) of various shapes and sizes. The largest, **Mount Wudinna**, 10km to the northeast, is second only to Uluru

HIGH IMPACT – THE ACRAMAN METEORITE

In the mid-1980s a band of red earth from 600-million-year-old deposits in the Flinders Ranges was bafflingly identified as coming from the Gawler Ranges, 400km away. Investigations and satellite mapping suggested that 35-kilometre-wide **Lake Acraman** in the Gawler Ranges was an eroded **meteorite crater**, while Lake Gairdner and fragmented saltpans (such as Lake Torrens, see p.749) further east were set in ripples caused by the force of the strike. Estimates suggest that to have created such a crater the meteorite must have been 4km across; the mystery band in the Flinders was dust settling after impact.

(Ayers Rock; see p.584) in monolithic magnitude, and 30km southwest you'll find **Ucontichie Hill** with curved forms including a **wave rock** similar to Hyden's in Western Australia (see p.626).

Iron Knob can be the start of forays along dirt tracks into the **Gawler Ranges**, before rejoining the highway at Wirrulla. While you might not need a 4WD, it's a remote area that requires advance preparation and advice from the NPWS. The ranges are low, rounded volcanic ridges coloured orange by dust, with occasional speckled boulders poking through a thin grass cover; it's worth frightening the sheep and pink Major Mitchell cockatoos by walking up one of the peaks for a closer look. The centrally located *Mount Ive Homestead* (☎08/8648 1817; ①–②) has fuel, information and **accommodation** in basic rooms or camping space, but don't turn up unannounced. The track into the ranges passes **Lake Gairdner**, largest of the Gawler's **salt lakes**, with the ruins of Pondanna Homestead on a lonely plain at its southern end.

Ceduna and the Nullarbor Plain

Nullarbor may not be strictly correct Latin for "treeless", but it's an apt description of the plain which stretches flat and infertile for over 1200km across the Great Australian Bight. Taking the **train**, or **motorbiking** the rail service track (which requires a back-up crew, fuel, and provisions dumps), brings you closer to the dead heart than does the **road**, which allows some breaks in the monotony of the journey to scan the sea for southern right whales and visit at least one Aboriginal site.

You know where you are in **CEDUNA**: all the shops from camping store to supermarket are unambiguously named and a large signpost in the centre gives distances to everywhere between Perth and Port Augusta. Despite being small enough to walk around in twenty minutes, there's no lack of **caravan parks**, **banks** or **service stations**, with almost every brand of fuel on offer – some places even hand out discount cards for use at their pumps along the way. The *Foreshore Van Park* on South Terrace (☎08/8625 2290; cabins ③) and the *Community Hotel/Motel* on O'Loughlin Terrace (☎08/8625 2008 or free call ☎1800/655 300; ④) are right next to the jetty – you can fish for whiting on the turn of the high tide – and *Ceduna Backpackers* is also not far from the sea at 12 Kuhlmann St (☎08/8625 3811; ①). Before your early morning start – it's a long way to anywhere – call in at the **information centre** on Poynton Street (☎08/8625 2780) and the NPWS on McKenzie Street (☎08/8625 3144) for the latest on the Nullarbor's attractions. Incidentally, it almost never rains on the plain, and there's always a charge for **water**, which has to be distilled from underground reserves – so carry your own.

The plain

From Ceduna to the Western Australian border it's 480km, which you can easily cover in under five hours if you want; Daliesque fridges standing along the highway in the early stages of the drive are actually makeshift mailboxes for remote proper-ties. The last chance to **catch some waves** is at **Cactus Beach/Point Sinclair** south of **Penong**, and even for non-surfies it's worth the drive through white dunes, green shrubbery and blue lagoons to watch the extraordinary wave formations; there's a **campsite** with firewood provided (but no drinking water) and a basic store (12.30–2pm) while the nearest civilized **accommodation** is at the *Penong Hotel* (☎08/8625 1050). To view the area by camel, call Goanywea Camel Safaris (☎08/8625 1093).

Two hours from Penong you arrive at **Yalata Community**, settled by the Maralinga peoples cleared off their ancestral land by the British atomic bomb tests at Maralinga in the 1950s. At the roadhouse (☎08/8625 6986) you can obtain permits to cross com-munity borders and reach the **Head of the Bight**, the best place to see **whales** when they migrate up here between June and October. The Head is a stirring setting, where in a distance of less than 1km powdery dunes rise to absurdly melodramatic cliffs – you can't help feeling that this is how early cartographers must have envisaged the edge of the world. The southern right whales (see p.713) sport idly with their calves in the water below. Twenty minutes away is the **Nullarbor Roadhouse** (☎08/8625 6271; ③), which has **beds** and a campsite, and is the last place to get fuel before Border Village. The famous triple yellow sign on the highway warning of camels, wombats and kanga-roos marks the beginning of the run, which has absolutely no trees. Ironically, rabbits – no longer controlled by farmers now that the area is a national park – have almost crowded out the wombats.

Curiously enough for a land with minimal rainfall, the Nullarbor is undermined by flooded limestone **caverns** explored recently by scuba divers and visited 25,000 years ago by Aborigines looking for water and chalcedony to make tools. From the outside, **Koonalda Cave** (just north of the Nullarbor Roadhouse) is a large hole with recently planted fruit trees growing in the mouth; inside, a tremendously deep network of tun-nels leads to an underground lake, the shafts grooved by fingers being dragged over their soft walls. Although the patterns are clearly deliberate, their meaning is unknown. The cave is closed off to protect the engravings, but the Ceduna NPWS (see overleaf) might be able to arrange a visit.

Border Village is just another roadhouse (☎08/9039 3474; ④) with a natty fibreglass kangaroo in the car park. Eucla (see p.636) and the rest of the Nullarbor lie 16km over the border in Western Australia on a noticeably worse road and in a considerably earli-er time zone.

The Stuart Highway: Woomera and beyond

WOOMERA, two hours north of Port Augusta on the Stuart Highway, was closed to the public until 1982. An uncharismatic but well-appointed barracks town, it sits at the southeast corner of a five-hundred-kilometre corridor known locally as "the Range" and ominously highlighted on maps as **Woomera Prohibited Area**. Don't expect to find out why at the mostly military **Heritage Centre** (daily 9am–5pm; $4), at the cross-roads of Dewrang and Banool avenues. Models, rocket-relics and plenty of pictures emphasize Woomera's value as a satellite launch site and joint initiatives with NASA, but the reasons for the creation of the Prohibited Area – weapons-testing and the British-run 1950s **atomic bomb tests**, contaminated dust from which is still being scraped up and vitrified – are skirted around. For a first-hand account, read Len Beadell's *Outback Highways* – cheerful tales of the bomb tests and the construction of "some sort of rocket range – or something" by the chief engineer. Currently, the range is used as a **nuclear waste dump**, and there are plans to land Japan's prototype space shuttle here.

Named after the European Launcher Development Organization which designed rockets in the 1960s, the *Eldo Hotel* on Kotara Crescent (☎08/8673 7867, fax 8673 7226; ②–④) provides **beds**, food, booze and conversation with US troops stationed here. The welcoming *Woomera Travellers Village* on Wirruna Avenue (☎08/8673 7800; ②) is a good alternative – **camping** on the lawn is preferable to the beds in the dreary ex-barracks. The **shopping centre** has banks and other facilities, and next to it is **The Oasis**, a small leisure centre with a café, bar and bowling alley. **Buses** on the Stuart Highway don't go into Woomera but will drop you off at the roadhouse at Pimba, 7km away.

A detour: Roxby Downs, Andamooka and Lake Torrens

Instead of returning to the highway, consider carrying on past Woomera to the strangest two companion towns in Australia (a Stateliner **bus** goes from Woomera six nights a week). **ROXBY DOWNS**, 80km away, is completely modern, a service centre built in 1986 for miners working the copper, gold, silver and uranium deposits at the nearby Olympic Dam Mine (tours March–Nov daily 9.45am; 2hr 30min; $21; for bookings call Olympic Dam Tours **information office**, next to the BP service station on Olympic Way; ☎08/8671 0788). Another thirty minutes on an unsurfaced road, and you come to **ANDAMOOKA**, an **opal**-mining shantytown of block and scrap-iron construction whose red-earth high street becomes a river after it rains. The soil proved to be too loose for the underground homes which became *de rigueur* at Coober Pedy (see below) but **mud lean-tos** built in the 1930s are still standing opposite the post office. **Facilities** include fuel, a supermarket, the *Tuckerbox Restaurant* (11am–late), two hotel/motels, two campsites, and the Opal Creek Showroom which distributes maps and advice. If you fancy your luck "noodling", head to **German Gully**, where the local opal is more strongly coloured than Coober Pedy's, but little has been found for years. Olympic Dam Tours (see above) does a three-hour tour for $30.

Lake Torrens, a sickle-shaped salt lake related to the Acraman Meteorite (see box on p.747), is another thirty-minute ride in a 4WD – in wet years bird-watchers find it a worthwhile trip to observe the waterfowl. The lake is also renowned in paleontological circles for traces of the 630-million-year-old **Ediacaran fauna**, the earliest-known evidence of animal life, which was first found in Australia. Delicate fossil impressions of jellyfish, sea pens and obscure organisms are preserved in layered rock. The South Australian Museum in Adelaide (see p.684) has an extensive selection, but rarely issues directions to the site, which has been plundered by collectors since its discovery in 1946 by the geologist Reg Sprigg.

Coober Pedy

COOBER PEDY is the most enduring symbol of the harshness of Australia's Outback and the determination of those who live there. It's a place where the terrain and temperatures are so extreme that homes – and even churches – have been built underground, yet which has managed to attract thousands of opal prospectors. In a virtually waterless desert 380km from Woomera and considerably further from anywhere else, the most remarkable thing about the town – whose name stems from an Aboriginal phrase meaning "white man's burrow" – is that it exists at all. **Opal** was discovered by William Hutchison on a gold-prospecting expedition to the Stuart Range in February 1915. The town itself dates from the end of World War I, when returning servicemen headed for the fields to try their luck and used their trench-digging skills to excavate dwellings.

In summer Coober Pedy is seriously depopulated but, if you can handle the intense heat, it's a good time to look for bargain opal purchases – though not to scratch around for them yourself: gem-hunting is better reserved for the "cooler" winter months. At the start of the year, spectacular **dust storms** often enclose the town for hours in an abrasive orange twilight.

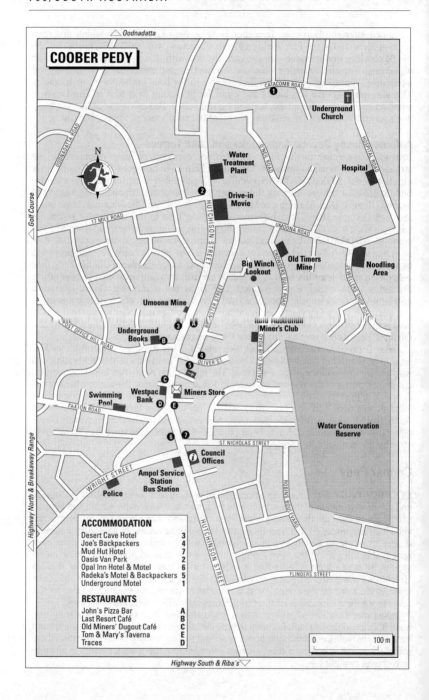

COOBER PEDY

△ Oodnadatta

CATACOMB ROAD ❶

Underground Church

O'NEIL ROAD

HOSPITAL ROAD

Water Treatment Plant

Hospital

HUTCHISON STREET

17 MILE ROAD

❷

Drive-in Movie

UMOONA ROAD

△ Golf Course

Big Winch Lookout

Old Timers Mine

Noodling Area

CROWDERS GULLY ROAD

JEWELLERS SHOP ROAD

Umoona Mine

POST OFFICE HILL ROAD

BREWSTER STREET

Underground Books ❸ Ⓐ Ⓑ

Radio Australian Miner's Club

ITALIAN CLUB ROAD

❹ OLIVER ST
❺

Ⓒ
Swimming Pool
Westpac Bank Ⓓ Ⓔ ✉ Miners Store

PAXTON ROAD

❻ ❼

Water Conservation Reserve

ST NICHOLAS STREET

ⓘ Council Offices

WRIGHT STREET

Ampol Service Station
Bus Station

Police

ROBINS BOULEVARD

△ Highway North & Breakaway Range

HUTCHINSON STREET

FLINDERS STREET

ACCOMMODATION

Desert Cave Hotel	3
Joe's Backpackers	4
Mud Hut Hotel	7
Oasis Van Park	2
Opal Inn Hotel & Motel	6
Radeka's Motel & Backpackers	5
Underground Motel	1

RESTAURANTS

John's Pizza Bar	A
Last Resort Café	B
Old Miners' Dugout Café	C
Tom & Mary's Taverna	D
Traces	E

0   100 m

Highway South & Riba's ▽

The local scenery might be familiar to you if you're a film fan: the unique landscape was used to great effect in *Mad Max III* and Wim Wenders' epic *Until The End Of The World*. There's not much to it, just a plain disturbed by conical pink mullock (or slag) heaps, with clusters of trucks and home-made contraptions off in the distance, and **warning signs** alerting you to treacherously invisible, unfenced thirty-metre shafts. Be very careful where you tread: even if you have transport, the best and safest way to explore is to take a tour, examine a map, then go back on your own. Past the diggings, the **Breakaway Range** is a brightly coloured plateau off the highway about 11km north of town, of interest for the views, close-ups of the hostile terrain, and bushwalking through two-hundred-year-old stands of mulga.

Wandering around the dusty streets, it can be hard to tell whether some of the odd machinery lying about is bona fide mining equipment or left-over props from the increasing number of films using the town as an apocalyptic set. The **Big Winch Lookout** in the centre gives a grandstand view of the mix of low houses and hills pocked with ventilation shafts. The welded metal "tree" up here was assembled before any real ones grew in the area, though in the last few years there have been some attempts to encourage greenery with recycled waste water.

For more on **mining**, check out one of the several mine displays and museums: try **Old Timers Mine**, Crowders Gully Road (☎08/8672 5555; $4), or **Umoona** on Hutchison Street (☎08/8672 5288; $5). Numerous **tours** are on offer for around $25: they all feature a town drive, a spot of noodling and a visit to an underground home – which you might find embarrassingly like visiting a zoo. Book through your accommodation, or try Radeka's five-hour tour (☎08/8672 5223) which includes a look at the Breakaway Range.

Coober Pedy has lately achieved a bit of a reputation for **violence**, which is perhaps not surprising given such an extreme climate where most people have access to explosives. However, signs warning "no parking unless your car is dynamite-proof" are really for amusement value only and visitors are unlikely to be the object of any discord.

Transport and services

Just about everything you'll need in Coober Pedy lies around the five-hundred-metre strip between the *Opal Inn Hotel* and the water treatment plant on **Hutchison Street** (also known as Main Street) which leads north off the highway. **Buses** drop you off either at the Ampol service station (Greyhound Pioneer and Stateliner; ☎08/8672 5151) or at *Radeka's Motel* (McCafferty's ☎08/8672 5223). From the **airport** you may be able to get a lift with one of the hostel buses that meet most flights, or make an advance reservation to ensure that someone meets you. The council offices on Hutchison Street (Mon–Fri 9am–5pm; free call ☎1800/637 076), opposite the Ampol service station, are a mine of local **information**. Underground Books (☎08/8672 5558), on Post Office Hill Road opposite the Mobil service station, is a good alternative source – it stocks packs of local sketch maps which are a useful back-up to road maps. The Miners Store supermarket on Hutchison Street (☎08/8672 5051) is also the **post office** and Commonwealth **bank** agent (there's a Westpac branch opposite). Everyone shops on Thursday, as fresh meat and veggies arrive in a refrigerated lorry on Wednesday night and are scarce by the weekend.

Accommodation

Coober Pedy relies heavily on tourist income, so finding **lodgings** should be no problem. To some people, the idea of sleeping underground is disturbing but, while not all accommodation is subterranean, it's worth spending at least one night in naturally cooled tunnels for the experience.

FINDING AND BUYING AN OPAL

Opal is composed of fragile layers of silica and derives its colour from the refraction of light – characteristics that preclude the use of heavy mining machinery, as one false blow would break the matrix and destroy the colour. Deposits are patchy and located by trial and error: the last big strikes at Coober Pedy petered out in the 1970s and, though bits and pieces are still found – including an exceptional opalized fossil skeleton of a pliosaur (the reptilian equivalent of a seal) in 1983 – it's anybody's guess as to the location of other major seams (indeed, there may not be any at all). Because so much depends on luck, you'll hear little about mining technique and more about beating the system. For instance, it's now illegal to mine in town, but there's nothing to prevent home extensions; similarly, non-mining friends are often roped in to register claims and sidestep the "one per person" rule. Working another's claim (the "night shift") is a less honourable short cut.

Unless you're serious (in which case you'll have to pay $25 a year to the Mines Department for a **Miner's Permit** to peg your 50 x 50 metre claim), the easiest way to find something is by **noodling** over someone's diggings – ask the owner first. An area on the corner of Jewellers Shop and Umoona roads has been set aside as a safe area for tourists to poke about freely without danger of finding open mineshafts. Miners use ultra-violet lamps to separate opal from **potch** (worthless grey opal), so you're unlikely to find anything stunning – but look out for shell fossils and small chips.

The best time to **buy opal** is outside the tourist season, but don't expect wild bargains and don't deal through grizzled prospectors in the hotels unless you're very clued in. There are three categories: **cabochon**, a solid piece; **doublet**, a thin wafer mounted on a dark background to enhance the colour; and **triplet**, a doublet with quartz lens. While cabochons are most expensive and triplets least valuable, it takes some experience to price accurately within each category as size, clarity, strength of colour, brightness and personal aesthetics all contribute. With about fifty dealers in town, it's up to you to find the right stone; reputable sources give full written guarantees.

Desert Cave Hotel, halfway up Hutchison St (☎08/8672 5688, fax 8672 5198). Offers a choice of below- or above-ground four-star accommodation. There's a swimming pool, and scenic flights, tours and car rental can be arranged. ⑧.

Joe's Backpackers Hostel and Motel, Oliver St (☎08/8672 5163 or free call ☎1800/631 758). Above-ground motel rooms sleep up to three people, backpackers go underground. ①–②.

Mud Hut Motel, next to council offices. Its bare, rammed earth construction gives a flavour of the subterranean without losing out on daylight. ⑥.

Oasis Van Park, opposite the water treatment plant, Hutchison St (☎08/8672 5169). The only place to camp under trees. Cabin rooms ③.

Opal Inn Motel, Hutchison St (☎08/8672 5054). A standard motel block behind the hotel of the same name. ④.

Radeka's Motel and Backpackers Inn, Oliver St (☎08/8672 5223). The best budget option in town. Recently extended with snaking tunnels and alcoves with two to six beds – it can be a long trek upstairs to the well-appointed kitchen and toilets. The new bar and pool table provide evening entertainment. ①, top-notch motel rooms ⑤.

Riba's: the Travellers' Nest (☎08/8672 5614). Take William Creek Rd from the highway (4km south of the Hutchison St turn-off) and *Riba's* is down a track 800m on the right. A friendly campsite, but a bit out of the way. The cheapest place in town. ①.

Underground Motel, Catacomb Rd (☎08/8672 5324). Clean, tiled rooms with views over the desert from the front porch. ⑤.

Cafés and restaurants

Restaurants in town are good value and portions are huge – beware of over-ordering. All the following are on the main street.

Italo-Australian Miner's Club. Big Italian dinners on Italian Club Rd.

John's Pizza Bar. Takeaway fast food and coffee.
Last Resort Café. Upmarket place with pavement tables, excellent pastries and coffee.
Old Miners' Dugout Café. Kangaroo dishes and budget specials.
Tom and Mary's Taverna. Souvlakia morning to midnight.
Traces. Greek grills, plus dancing. Daily 4pm–late.

Listings

Car Hire *Desert Cave Hotel* are agents for Territory Rent a Car. Book well in advance.
Cinema Drive-in movie theatre on Hutchison St shows a double bill most Saturday nights.
Hospital On Hospital Rd, north end of town (☎08/8672 5009).
Pharmacy At Medical Centre, middle of Hutchison St.
Police Wright St, near Ampol bus terminal (☎08/8672 5056).
Swimming Pool At the school on Paxton Rd – open to public for a few hours daily.

Beyond Coober Pedy

The Stuart Highway ploughs another 350km north from Coober Pedy to the border. From **Marla** township (shop, post office and Commonwealth Bank at the roadhouse) you could head east to Oodnadatta across the **Painted Desert** at Arkaringa Hills, a larger version of the Breakaway Range, or 35km west into Aboriginal Land to the state's newest opal strike at Mintabie – seek permission from Marla's police.

If you want to get to **Oodnadatta**, there's also a direct two-hundred-kilometre dirt road from Coober Pedy across the pan of Giddi-Gidna (the **Moon Plain**), covered by the **mail run** which departs from Underground Books (free call ☎1800/069 911) on a roughly 12-hour triangular route to William Creek and Oodnadatta every Monday at 9am (anticlockwise) and Thursday (clockwise); passengers can join the trip anywhere for $20 each side of the triangle. For $400 Perentie Tours (☎08/8672 5558 or ask at Underground Books) will take you further out, to Dalhousie Thermal Springs on the edge of the Simpson Desert, for three days of "luxury camping", swimming and gourmet food.

Australia's hottest 4WD journey has to be west from Coober Pedy to the **atomic bomb sites** at **Emu Junction**: concrete slabs cap pits where contaminated equipment lies buried, and sand fused into sheets of glass by the blasts covers the ground – the area is still highly radioactive and you'd be advised to pass through quickly. Beyond lies the virgin **Unnamed National Park** and routes across Aboriginal Land to the **Warburton Road** in Western Australia (see p.635). The NPWS at 11 McKenzie St in Ceduna (☎08/8625 3144) supplies practical details and permits to 4WD convoys only.

The Flinders Ranges and the northeast

The first stop between Port Augusta and the **Flinders Ranges National Park** is **QUORN**, whose stone buildings and village atmosphere are a last vestige of the south. Best known for the **Pichi Richi railway**, the sole operational section of the old Ghan, Quorn was a major rail centre until the line was rerouted through Port Augusta in the 1950s. Enthusiasts restored the service twenty years later and started taking passengers on a two-hour return haul to Woolshed Flats through the **Pichi Richi Pass** – whose name has been variously attributed to a medicinal herb or an Aboriginal word for "gorge". Punctuated by a break at Woolshed Flats for a cream tea, it makes a relaxing and mildly scenic journey. Trains run only on a few weekends and holidays April–October; call to check and book (☎08/8658 1109).

There's a **caravan park** in Quorn (☎08/8648 6206) but a night spent at the *Transcontinental Hotel* (☎08/8648 6076; ①–③) is much more congenial, with an easy-going crowd of truckies and drovers from the north for company. The main road through town is Railway Terrace where you'll find the post office, civic buildings and hotels which all do good-value lunches and dinners but are quite strict about serving times. First Street and the block between it and Railway Terrace contain a few **art and craft** and secondhand shops to poke about in, with the **tourist information** centre at 3 Seventh St (☎08/8648 6419).

If you want to explore some of the country round here, Intrepid Tours, 17 Sixth St (☎08/8648 6277), runs a 4WD tour any day they can fill a vehicle. Heading Bush, 12 First St (☎ & fax 08/8648 6655), also operates 4WD tours (Adelaide–Alice Springs, ten days, $695 all-inclusive; Alice Springs–Adelaide, two days, $85; Flinders Ranges, three days, $250 all-inclusive); *Andu Lodge*, their **hostel**, is at the same address (rooms ②, dorms ①) and rents out mountain bikes, gives information on wildlife, Aboriginal history and local hiking, and offers a 24-hour pick-up from Port Augusta. Quornucopia arts and crafts shop, at 17 Railway Terrace, rents out some holiday cottages in the Flinders (book on ☎08/8648 6282).

There's good local bushwalking off the back road to Hawker along a string of ridges and cliffs, outrunners from the main body of the central Flinders 100km north. Closest to Quorn is **Dutchmans Stern**, a solid day's hike for the reasonably fit from the car park to various lookouts. Less dedicated walkers will find **Warren**, **Buckaringa** and **Middle gorges** more accessible; Buckaringa's vertical face is the most reliable place in the ranges to see the rare and ravishingly pretty **yellow-footed rock wallaby**. Closer to Hawker, it's also worth taking in the well-preserved remains of **Kanyaka Homestead**, abandoned after a drought in the 1860s, and **Yourambulla Cave**, which has some unusual charcoal symbols in a high overhang, reached by a ladder. Both are signposted from the road.

HAWKER itself is somewhere to fuel up, make use of the last banks and shops for a while, have a meal at the *Old Ghan Restaurant* down past the hotel, organize a **flight over the Flinders** through *Hawker Caravan Park* on the Wilpena exit (☎08/8648 4006), and seek advice from the regional NPWS office at 60 Elder Terrace about far-northern parks and roads (Mon–Fri; ☎08/8648 4244). Decisions have to be made in Hawker about whether to press on into the Flinders and the northeast or continue following the former Ghan line north towards Marree; the bitumen on the latter route extends past the Leigh Creek coalfields to Lyndhurst, start of the Strzelecki Track. Stateliner **buses** pass through Sunday, Wednesday and Friday, continuing to Wilpena, with a connection (Mon & Fri) to Arkaroola in the

---

FLINDERS DREAMING AND GEOLOGY

The almost tangible spirit of the Flinders Ranges is reflected in the wealth of Adnyamathanha ("hill people") **legends** associated with them. Perhaps more obvious here than anywhere else in Australia is the connection between landscapes and Dreamtime stories, which recount how scenery was created by animal or human action – the distinction is often blurred. A central character is **Akurra**, a gigantic maned serpent (or serpents) who guards waterholes and formed the Flinders' contours by wriggling north to drink dry the huge salt lakes Frome and Callabonna.

Ochre paintings are one type of **art** often encountered at sites, but there's a more extensive, older tradition of engraving. Circles generally depict a campsite, with additional lines and rings representing stages in initiation rites.

You may well prefer the aboriginal legends to the complexities of geology illustrated on boards placed at intervals along the Brachina Gorge track, which explain how movements of the "Adelaide Geosyncline" brought about the changes in scenery over hundreds of millions of years.

Northern Flinders. On Sunday, Thursday and Friday the buses return to Port Augusta and Adelaide.

Flinders Ranges National Park

The procession of glowing red mountains at **Flinders Ranges National Park**, folded and crumpled with age, produces some of the Outback's most spectacular and timeless scenery, rising from flat scrub to form abrupt escarpments, gorges and the famous elevated basin of **Wilpena Pound**. The hard contrast between sky and ranges is softened by native cypresses and river red gums, and in spring the plains are burnished by **wild flowers** of all colours. Bushwalkers, photographers and painters flock here in their hundreds, but with a system of graded **walking tracks** ranging from a few minutes' length to several days – not to mention roads of varying quality – the park is busy without being crowded.

WILPENA is a good place to orient yourself: it has a motel, campsite and an expensive store and NPWS **information centre** (daily 8am–6pm) situated at the end of the bitumen and at the start of the main routes into Wilpena Pound. Wilder places further into the park to set up camp for a few days include the national park campsites at **Bunyeroo** and **Brachina Gorge** in the west, **Trezona** and **Oraparinna** in the centre, and **Wilkawillana Gorge** in the extreme northeast, all accessible on unsealed roads. Even the more formal **lodgings** tend to be basic; for a longer stay you might consider renting a holiday cottage, which can be a bargain during the summer – contact Flinders Outback Tourism (☎08/8373 3430). Back in town, the *Wilpena Pound Motel* (☎08/8648 0004; ⑥) is a comfortable but overpriced base: there's a good, surprisingly exotic restaurant – the chalet-like bar makes an atmospheric setting for an après-hike drink, and 4WD tours and flights over the pound can be arranged. *Wilpena Campsite*, next door, is wooded and well-equipped. Other places nearby include *Rawnsley Park* (☎08/8648 0030; cabins ④, plus tent spaces) – 35km north of Hawker on the edge of the national park, in a beautiful setting with Rawnsley Bluff and Wilpena Pound rising behind – which has fuel, a store and mountain bike rental and organizes 4WD trips and horse-riding; *Willow Springs* (☎08/8648 6282; ②), 17km north of Wilpena before the Wilkawillana Gorge junction, a working sheep station with blockhouse dormitories; and *Oraparinna Homestead* (book through the Hawker NPWS; ③), in the centre of the park off the Blinman Road, 24km north of Wilpena, with self-contained shearers' quarters and cabins.

Most **walking tracks** lead into Wilpena Pound, though you can also pick up the Heysen Trail and follow it north from Wilpena for a couple of days around the ABC Range to **Aroona Ruins** on the northern edge of the park. The Wilpena NPWS offers booklets, maps (sometimes the 1:50,000 topographical series) and the latest information on the routes; you're required to log out and back with them on any walk exceeding three hours. Realistically, hiking is restricted to the cooler winter months between May and October, as scant shade and reflective rocks raise summer temperatures well above 40°C. Don't underestimate conditions: even on short excursions, you'll need good footwear, a hat, sunscreen and **water** – at least half a litre per hour is recommended. **Camping out**, a waterproof tent, groundmat and fuel stove are essential, and note that the **weather** is very changeable; wind-driven rain can be a menace along the ridges and heavy downpours make tracks dangerous.

Wilpena Pound

Wilpena Pound's two major hiking destinations are **St Mary's Peak** on the rim and **Edowie Gorge** inside the Pound, easily tackled individually or joined into an overnight circuit if time allows. For the round-trip, leave the peak until last and head off across the Pound's flat, grassy bowl to the remains of **Hill's Homestead** – further evidence of the region's unsuitability for farming – then follow the track northwest to **Cooinda**

Camp, about two hours from the start. Assuming you left early enough, there's time to pitch a tent and spend the rest of the day following the creek upstream past **Malloga Falls** to **Glenora Falls** and views into Edowie Gorge before heading back to Cooinda – there might be places to swim after a rain. Next morning, it's a steep climb to **Tanderra Saddle** below the peak, but not as bad as the last burst to St Mary's summit, which often involves scrambling on all fours. The effort is rewarded by unequalled views west to Lake Torrens and north along the length of the ABC Ranges towards Parachilna; on exceptional mornings the peak stands proud of low cloud inside the Pound. The direct descent from the saddle back to Wilpena campsite is initially steep but shouldn't take more than three hours. Splitting the tracks into separate return walks from Wilpena, allow nine hours for Edowie Gorge, eight hours for a straight ascent of St Mary's, and ten hours for a circuit via St Mary's and Cooinda Camp but omitting Edowie Gorge.

Shorter routes lead up **Mount Ohlssen Bagge** (a tiring four hours) and **Wangara Lookout** (2hr) for lower vistas of the Pound floor, and southwest across the Pound to **Bridle Gap** (6hr) following the Heysen Trail's red markers. Things to look out for are euro wallabies, emus and parrots inside the Pound, and cauliflower-shaped fossil **stromatolites** – algal corals – on the Mount Ohlssen Bagge route, similar to those still living at Hamelin Pool in Western Australia (see p.646).

Art sites, more gorges and onwards

Two **Aboriginal galleries** worth seeing are Arkaroo Rock and Sacred Canyon, both a short drive from Wilpena. **Arkaroo** is back off the main road towards Rawnsley Park and involves an hour's walk up the outside of Wilpena Pound to see much protruded rockfaces covered in symbols relating to an initiation ceremony and the Pound's formation, some dating back six thousand years. Snake patterns depict St Mary's Peak as the head of a male Akurra coiled round the Pound. To reach **Sacred Canyon**, briefly take the road from Wilpena into the north of the park, past the **Cazneaux Tree** – a river red gum made famous by Harold Cazneaux's prize-winning 1930 photograph *Spirit of Endurance* – before turning right and following a bumpy track to its end. Rockhop up the narrow, shattered gorge to clusters of painted swirls covered in a sooty patina and clearer engraved emu prints and geometric patterns; the best examples are in the vicinity of the second cascade.

The main road through the park heads straight out to Blinman, but there's a detour track to **Bunyeroo** and **Brachina gorges** on the western limits. The gorges make good campsites: you have to walk into Bunyeroo but the track passes through Brachina on its way to the surfaced Hawker–Marree road. If you're pressing directly on to the Northern Flinders, you can avoid Blinman by turning right off the main road about 20km from Wilpena, heading to **Wirrealpa Homestead**.

The Northern Flinders

The Wilpena–Blinman road passes through a low group of hills, thin in timber but still swarming with euro wallabies, emus and galahs. **BLINMAN** comprises a few houses with well-tended gardens, three fuel pumps, and a hotel (☎08/8648 4867; ②–④) with log fires, games room, pool and campsite; the keys to everywhere else in town are kept at the bar. The main track winds west through beautiful Parachilna Gorge, in the middle of which you could stay at **Angorichina**'s *Tourist Village* (dorms and campsite; ☎08/8648 4842). The track meets the Hawker-Marree road at **Parachilna** where you can sample some great food from a menu featuring almost all the area's wild plants and animals at the *Prairie Hotel* (☎08/8648 4895).

According to the Adnyamathanha, **coal** was made by Yoolayoola the kingfisher man, who built fires at Leigh Creek, halfway between Hawker and Marree. Today 2.6 million tonnes of it are scooped out of the ground annually to be sent by rail and burnt at the ETSA power station in Port Augusta, and it is estimated it will run out in about 25 years. At a car park just off the road you can climb around an old dragline crane and look over the edge of an opencast mine; there are free **tours** daily (☎08/8675 4210). Coalworkers live in the thoroughly well-planned and modern township of **Leigh Creek South** or at more traditional **Copley**, where it's worth stopping at *Tulloch's Bush Bakery* for a very civilized cappuccino and quandong pie. Fuel and camping sites are available at both towns.

The route into the Northern Flinders lies east, joining up with the direct road from Wilpena and then running north to the **Gammon Ranges National Park** and Arkaroola.

Chambers Gorge and Big Moro

Chambers Gorge and **Big Moro** are remote, little-visited sites on the road to the Gammon Ranges, worth every groan and twang of your vehicle springs for their stark beauty and Aboriginal significance. The ten-kilometre access track east into **Chambers Gorge** (28km after Wirrealpa) is decidedly dodgy after rain when you'll need a 4WD, but at other times 2WD vehicles might reach a natural campsite at the foot of **Mount Chambers**, within twenty minutes' walk of the gorge mouth. In a Dreamtime story, Yuduyudulya, the Fairy Wren spirit, threw a boomerang which split Mount Chambers' eastern end and then circled back to form the crown. An indistinct left fork before the gorge leads to a dense gallery of **pecked engravings**; most are circles, though a goanna stands out clearly on the right, facing the main body of art. Chambers Gorge itself is huge and silent, the broad stony entrance guarded by high, perpendicular cliffs and brilliant green waterholes; it would take days to explore it properly.

Big Moro is sacred to the Adnyamathanha as the residence of an Akurra. The creek trickles through a crumbling gorge into two clear green pools; limestone outcrops on the south side conceal miniature caves. The gorge lies west down an exceptionally tortuous fifteen-kilometre 4WD track opposite **Wertaloona Homestead**, 60km from the Mount Chambers junction. Pay attention to any signs and leave the three gates as you found them.

The Gammon Ranges

The arid and bald **Gammon Ranges** are the Flinders' last fling, a vicious flurry of compressed folds plunging abruptly onto the northern plains. Balcanoona is the NPWS headquarters for the otherwise undeveloped **Gammon Ranges National Park**, a thick band of sandstone cliffs – check with the Hawker NPWS (see p.754) for current conditions. Two ways to experience the area are either to carry on to Arkaroola (outside the park) or to take the road west across the park through **Italowie Gorge** to Copley on the Hawker–Marree road. The steep red walls of the gorge are home to iga, native orange trees which symbolize the Adnyamathanha as a people. There are **bush campsites** here and shearers' quarters at **Balcanoona** (book through the Hawker NPWS; ②).

Arkaroola (Mount Painter Sanctuary) is a private **resort** (☎08/8370 8454 or free call ☎1800/676 042; ①–⑤) and a source of fuel, provisions, meals, rooms and a campsite. Scene of Australia's most recent volcanic activity, the area is a geologist's paradise: **Paralana Hot Springs** (two hours away in a 4WD) bubble out radioactive radon gas, and if you take walks into the rough hills surrounding the resort you'll come across lots of fossils and semiprecious minerals. The area is so rugged that conventional mining isn't really a profitable venture – drilling rigs are airlifted in, then ferried around on the lower half of a Chieftain tank – and the mining giant CRA Zinc concentrates on mapping uranium and copper deposits in order to show progress and keep their licence. The resort's $50 **Ridgetop Tour** brings you closest to the heart of the scenery: four hairraising hours in an open 4WD (wear something warm) following precipitous contours to **Sillers Lookout** and views east to the shimmering salt lakes of **Frome** and

Callabonna. Remains of the hippopotamus-sized marsupial diprotodon have been found at Callabonna; the diprotodon survived well into Aboriginal times, but died out as the climate changed after the last Ice Age.

Arkaroola marks the limit of public transport, running its own connection to meet the Stateliner bus at Hawker on Monday and Friday. Some vehicles (with either high clearance or very careful drivers) can continue directly north to join the **Strzelecki Track** at Mount Hopeless, a little under half the distance to Innamincka. If you're unsure, the track can also be reached via Lyndhurst on the Hawker–Marree road, but this involves a three-hundred-kilometre detour from Arkaroola.

The Strzelecki Track

The 460-kilometre **Strzelecki Track** between Lyndhurst and Innamincka was laid down in 1870 by **Harry Redford**, better known as Captain Starlight, who stole a thousand cattle from a property near Longreach in Queensland and drove them south across the Strzelecki Desert and down to Adelaide. When brought to justice, he was found not guilty in gratitude for his opening of a hitherto impassable route. Later used for more orthodox purposes, the track had a reputation as one of the roughest stock routes in the country, a serious obstacle for transport. Much of its epic nature has since been flattened, along with the road surface, by companies draining the **Moomba gas and oil fields**, and it's negotiable in any sound vehicle when dry.

Start at Lyndhurst by filling the tank – the next **fuel** is at the other end – and heading off around the northern tip of the Flinders; once past them, the journey becomes flat and pretty dull. At around the 105-kilometre mark you cross the 4850-kilometre-long **Dog Fence** (or Great Dingo Fence), which stretches from the Nullarbor Plain east into New South Wales and is intended to keep dingoes from southern flocks. Although its value is debatable, you do frequently see desiccated canine corpses poisoned by "1080" bait. The road from Arkaroola connects within sight of **Mount Hopeless** (a pathetic rise, appropriately named), and the next place to stop and perhaps camp is at the hot outflow from **Montecollina Bore**, 30km on. From here the scenery improves slightly as the road runs between dunes, and it's hard to resist leaving footprints along one of the pristine red crests.

At **Strzelecki Crossing** there's a choice of routes: you could abandon the track and head east to where Queensland, New South Wales and South Australia meet at **Cameron Corner**, where there's a store with **fuel**, campsite and a small bar (☎08/8091 3872); or you could continue to Innamincka either via Moomba or by following the direct but less frequented **Old Strzelecki Track**. Cameron's Corner and the old track are 4WD only, and all of the routes are crossed by straight **seismic test lines** which run off to dead ends in the bush – you risk becoming permanently lost if you accidentally follow one, so take care. **Moomba**'s jumble of pipes and lick of flame are sometimes marked as a township on maps but, though visible from the road, the refinery is closed to the public. Within an hour you've crossed into the **Innamincka Regional Reserve** and are approaching Innamincka's charms.

Innamincka

Cooper Creek, which runs through Innamincka, is best known for the misadventures of explorers Burke and Wills, who ended their inept 1861 expedition by dying here. **INNAMINCKA** was later founded on much the same spot as a customs house to collect taxes on stock being moved between Queensland and South Australia. Never more than a handful of buildings, it found fame mainly because John Flynn's Flying Doctor Service ran a mission here and because the hotel piled up decades of empties into a legendary 180-metre-long bottle dump before the town was abandoned in 1952. Recreational four-wheel driving has led to a renaissance: a new **hotel** (☎ & fax 08/8675 9901; ⑤) has weekend barbecues, a video jukebox and impromptu dance sessions on

Friday and Saturday nights; the Innamincka Trading Post (☎08/8675 9900) stocks provisions and fuel; the mission was rebuilt in 1994 as a **museum** (for opening hours ask at the Trading Post); and opposite is a solar-powered telephone and spotless toilet/shower block. Pelicans, parrots and inquisitive dingoes will be your companions if you camp out for free along the creek.

It only takes an hour to look around the museum and hunt for evidence of the bottle dump before you're ready for other distractions: taking a walk, **fishing** for yellowbelly, bream and catfish, swimming in the creek, or renting a canoe from the hotel or the Trading Post. With a vehicle you could strike out 20km west to **Wills' grave** or 8km east to where **Burke** was buried (both bodies were removed to Adelaide in 1862). Another 8km beyond Burke's cairn is **Cullyamurra waterhole**, the largest permanent body of water in central Australia, and a footpath to rock engravings of crosses, rainbow patterns and bird tracks. Four-wheel-drive vehicles can also tackle the 110-kilometre track north to the shallow **Coongie Lakes**, where you can swim and watch the abundant birdlife. An hour's drive east of Innamincka along a rather poor track is Queensland, the **Dig Tree** and a fuelless route to Quilpie (see p.485).

The far north: Marree and beyond

MARREE is a collection of tattered houses which somehow outlived the old Ghan's demise in 1980, leaving carriages to rust on sidings and rails to be used for tethering posts outside the hotel. Although it was first a camel depot, then a staging post for the overland telegraph line, and finally the point where the rail line skirted northwest around **Lake Eyre**, today all traffic comes by road and is bound for the **Birdsville Track** into Queensland or the **Oodnadatta Track**, which follows the former train route to Oodnadatta and beyond into the Northern Territory or Simpson Desert.

Accommodation is limited to the hotel on the main street (☎08/8675 8344; ④), which is also good for lunch or dinner, and the caravan park run by the *Oasis Café* (☎08/8675 8352), a fairly well-stocked shop, fuel and fast-food outlet which was originally the telegraph relay station. The General Store (☎08/8675 8360), across the railway track towards Oodnadatta, doubles as a Commonwealth Bank agent and post office with fuel and EFTPOS. If it's open, visit the Arabana Community Centre, where friendly staff explain how each type of boomerang is used.

Lake Eyre

Lake Eyre is a massive salt lake caught between the Simpson and Strzelecki deserts in a region where the annual evaporation rate is thirty times greater than the rainfall. Most years a little water trickles into the lake from its million-square-kilometre catchment area, which extends well into central Queensland and the Northern Territory, but floods have filled the basin only four times since white settlement of the region – most dramatically in 1974, when the lake expanded to a length of 140km. A hypnotic, glaring **salt crust** usually covers the southern bays, thick enough in 1964 to be used as a range for Donald Campbell's successful crack at the world land-speed record. It's a mysterious, spiritual landscape with harsh surroundings paved by shiny gibber stones and walled by red dunes, and some wildlife manages to get by in the incredible emptiness. The resident Lake Eyre dragon is a diminutive, spotted grey lizard often seen skimming over the crust, and the rare flooding attracts dense flocks of birds, wakes the plump water-holding frog from hibernation and causes the plants to burst into colour.

While you can **fly** over the lake (make bookings through the *Oasis Café* in Marree), only 4WDs can reach the shore 95km north of Marree, though the track to the campsite at a gum-shaded waterhole, just over halfway at **Muloorina Homestead**, is good. Timber at the lake is sparse and protected, which means that there's little shade and no firewood. There's no one to help you if something goes wrong, so don't drive on the lake's crust – should you fall through, it's impossible to extricate your vehicle from the grey slush below.

The Birdsville Track

Assuming there's been no rain, the 520-kilometre **Birdsville Track** is no obstacle to careful drivers during the winter: the biggest problem is getting caught in dried wheel ruts and being pulled off the road. Tearing north, the distant tips of the Flinders Ranges dip below the horizon behind, leaving you on a bare plain with the road as the only feature. Look for the **M.V. Tom Brennan**, a vessel donated to the area in 1949 to ferry stock around during floods, but now bearing an absurd resemblance to a large grey bathtub. Before the halfway house at Mungeranie Gap, a scenic variation is offered by the **Natterannie Sandhills** (150km), once a severe obstacle but now graded by digging out the soft sand and replacing it with clay. **Mungeranie roadhouse** (☎08/8675 8317; ②) provides the only services on the track (fuel, beds and snacks), but seems to be unattended on Sunday when you'll have to slog up the hill to the manager's house. In a 4WD you can head west from the roadhouse to **Kalamurina campsite** near Cowarie Homestead (58km) for the thrill of **fishing** – in a desert – on Warburton Creek.

Back on the track, a windmill at **Mirra Mitta bore** (37km from the roadhouse) draws piping-hot water out of the ground beside long-abandoned buildings; the water smells of tar and drains into cooler pools, providing somewhere to camp. By now you're crossing the polished gibber lands of the **Sturt Stony Desert**, and it's worth going for a walk to feel the cold wind and watch the dunes dancing in the heat haze away to the west. The low edge of **Coonchera Dune** to the right of the track (190km from the roadhouse) marks the start of a run along the mudpans between the sandhills; look for desert plants and dingoes. In two more hours you should be pulling up outside the Birdsville pub (see p.486).

The Oodnadatta Track

The road from **Marree to Oodnadatta** is the most interesting of the three famous Outback tracks, mainly because abandoned sidings and fettlers' cottages from the old Ghan provide frequent excuses to get out of the car and explore. Disintegrating sleepers lie by the roadside along some of the route; otherwise, embankments and rickety bridges are all that remain of the line. As with the roads to Birdsville and Innamincka, with care any sound vehicle can drive the route in good winter weather.

About 100km into the journey, near **Curdimurka ruins**, the road runs within sight of **Lake Eyre South**, giving a flavour of its bigger sister if you can't get out there. In alternate Octobers (even-numbered years) the **Curdimurka Outback Ball** is organized by the Ghan Railway Preservation Society, which maintains a few buildings, relics and 5km of track. Three thousand souls from everywhere between Alice Springs and Sydney pay $60 a head and don their finest threads for a night of mayhem under the stars; eagles and crows pick over the debris for a couple of weeks afterwards. Twenty-five kilometres later, a short track south ends below three conical hills – two of which have hot, bubbling **mound springs** at the top, created when water escaping from the artesian basin deposits heaps of mud and minerals. The perfectly symmetrical **Blanche Cup** looks out across a plain – stripped of every shred of greenery by rabbits and cattle – to **Hamilton Hill**, an extinct spring, while further south the **Bubbler** gurgles a verdant stream into the desert where it evaporates after a couple of hundred metres. Important to the Arabana, these springs were used by Sturt in the 1850s and later by the telegraph and rail depots, but tapping the artesian basin for bore water has greatly reduced their flow.

One of these bores is not far down the road at **Coward Springs**, where a corroded pipe spilling into ponds beside the track has created an artificial environment of grasses and palms behind a **campsite**, with toilet blocks and cabins built from sleepers. The ground can be boggy after rain but it's still a tempting stop; a $2 donation is requested for overnight stays. **WILLIAM CREEK**, 75km further, has a resident population of just ten – and is a source of fuel, camping and relaxation in the **hotel** (☎08/8670 7880). Bar, walls and ceiling are heavily decorated with cards and photographs of 4WD disasters, and it is the hangout for stockmen from **Anna Creek Station**, which, covering an area the size of Belgium, is the world's largest cattle property. A solar-powered phone outside faces the battered remains of a Black Arrow **missile** dragged off the Woomera Range, just a few minutes' drive away. Off-road drivers can take a seventy-kilometre track from here to Lake Eyre's western shore; in the other direction is a more passable road to Coober Pedy with almost nothing to see on the way except for **Lake Cadibarrawirracanna**, a salt lake with permanent water and consequent birdlife, at the halfway mark.

After William Creek the track gets rougher, crossing sand dunes and then moving into stony country cut by frequent creeks – shallow for most of the year. Hardy mulgas line the banks, their soft yellow blooms giving off a distinctive acrid scent. On the last stretch to Oodnadatta, stay alert for a sight of the extraordinary red and black crescent petals of **Sturt's desert pea**, the state emblem, growing by the roadside.

Oodnadatta

Unless you stay long enough to meet some locals, you'll probably feel that, like Marree, **OODNADATTA** survived the Ghan's closure with little to show for it. A few logically arranged but untidy streets lacking atmosphere or purpose, Oodnadatta was founded as a railhead in 1890, and mail and baggage for further north had to make do with camel trains from here until the line to Alice Springs was completed in 1928. Now that has gone, the town has become a base for the Aranda community – *utnadata* ("mulga blossom") is the Aranda name for a local waterway – and 4WD crews heading into the Simpson Desert. After rain you'll even need a 4WD for the last slippery kilometre into town, past the racecourse. If your visit coincides with the **race weekend** in May, helicopters will be circling the track on the left, trying to dry it out, and the town will be deserted, so stop at the track, buy a pass and join in. With neat clothes and some sort of tie, you'll even get into the "formal" ball afterwards.

Camp at the *Pink Roadhouse* (☎08/8670 7822), unless the relative luxury of a bed at the *Oodnadatta Hotel* appeals (☎08/8670 7804; ④). The roadhouse acts as a store, bank, post office and café, and sells detailed sketch maps of the area. The hotel holds the key to the **Railway Museum** opposite, where you'll find a strangely timeless photographic record of the town – scenes are hard to date because so little seems to have changed. Stock up with provisions and then check in at the **police station** (☎08/8670 7805) for a report on the roads and next fuel supplies if you plan to head north towards Dalhousie Springs and the Simpson Desert (4WD only), or west to the Stuart Highway at Coober Pedy or Marla.

Dalhousie Springs and desert crossings

If you don't follow the track out to the Stuart Highway, the area north of Oodnadatta is strictly for ambitious four-wheel driving, with Dalhousie Springs in the Witjira National Park a worthwhile destination, or the Simpson Desert for the ultimate challenges. The route directly north, initially towards Finke and the Northern Territory, is fairly good for 4WDs as far as **Hamilton Homestead** (110km), though Fogarty's Claypan, over halfway, might present a sticky problem. From Hamilton the direct route east to Dalhousie Springs, shown on some maps, is now closed; take the longer route via **Eringa ruins** (160km) and **Bloods Creek bore** on the edge of **Witjira National Park**. From there you can detour 30km north to **Mount Dare Homestead** (fuel, accommodation, food and provisions; ☎08/8670 7835, fax 8670 7864; ①–⑤). In winter the homestead is busy with groups of 4WDs arriving from or departing for the desert crossing; it's at least 550km to the next fuel stop at Birdsville in Queensland. Mount Dare's archetypally laconic owner Phil Hellyer sometimes has **work** for backpackers on the station. From the homestead it's a rough and bleak drive to **Dalhousie Springs**. The explorer Giles crossed through in the 1870s, before the artesian basin had been extensively tapped by pastoralists, and described the scene:

The ground we had been traversing abruptly disappeared, and we found ourselves on the brink of limestone cliffs . . . From the foot of these stretched an almost illimitable expanse of – welcome sight – waving green reeds, with large pools of water at intervals, and dotted with island cones topped with reeds or acacia bushes.

Though reeds and water are less lavishly distributed today, Giles' account still rings true. The collection of over one-hundred mound springs form Arabian-like

THE SIMPSON DESERT CROSSING

Crossing the approximately 550km of steep north–south dunes through the **Simpson Desert** between Dalhousie in South Australia and Birdsville in Queensland is the ultimate challenge for any off-roader. In June, 4WD groups are joined by bikes attempting to complete the punishing **Simpson Desert Cycling Classic**. In winter a steady stream of vehicles moves from west to east (the easier direction since the dunes' east slopes are steeper and harder to climb), but there's no help along the way, so don't underestimate the difficulties. Convoys need to include at least one skilled mechanic and, apart from the usual spares, a long-handled shovel and a strong tow-rope. You'll also need more than adequate food and water (six litres a day per person), while keeping weight to a minimum, and of course fuel – around a hundred litres of diesel if you take the shortest route, or two hundred litres of petrol. **Dune-ascent techniques** start with reducing tyre pressures to around 15psi to increase traction; select the gear and build up revs before starting. Don't attempt a gear change on the way up. If you don't make it over, slide down and try again; lighter vehicles may end up towing overburdened trucks. If all else fails, detours bypass many dunes.

The most testing, direct route follows the **French Line**, with the **Rig Road** detouring around the worst section but adding substantial distance (and fuel requirements) to the crossing. The enjoyment is mostly in the driving, though there's more than sand to look at: trees and shrubs grow in stabilized areas and at dusk you'll find dune crests patrolled by reptiles, birds, small mammals and insects. Photographers take advantage of clear skies at night to make time exposures of the stars circling the heavens. **Purni Bore**, 70km from Dalhousie, is another uncapped spout (though this may change with growing concerns over diminished ground water) where birdlife and reeds fringe a 27°C pool. A post battling to stay above shifting sand at **Poeppel Corner** (269km) marks the junction of Queensland, South Australia and the Northern Territory; lakes here vary in their salt content and sometimes have to be skirted around. After the corner the dunes become higher but further apart, separated by claypans covered in mulga and grassland. **Big Red**, the last dune, is also the tallest; once over this it's a clear 41-kilometre run to Birdsville.

Note: A large area of the Simpson Desert outside the Witjira National Park and the Simpson Desert Conservation Park is now a Regional Reserve under the control of the NPWS, from whom you should seek advice and a Desert Parks Pass before setting out. Call the NPWS at Hawker (☎08/8648 4244) or Birdsville (☎07/7656 3249).

oases, an impression enhanced by the green circle of date palms clustered around many of the pools. The largest spring, next to the **campsite** (which has a solar-powered phone), is cool enough to swim in and hot enough to unkink your back. What survives of the vegetation simmers with birdlife: budgerigars, galahs, and the eye-catching purple, blue and red fairy wren. As nothing flows into the springs, the presence of **fish** – some, like the Dalhousie hardyhead, unique to the system – has prompted a variety of improbable explanations. One theory is that fish eggs were swept up in dust storms and later fell with rain at Dalhousie, but it's more likely that fish were brought in during an ancient deluge or that the population survives from when the area was an inland sea.

While the main springs area is flat and trampled by years of abuse from campers and cars, trudging out to other groups over the salt and samphire-bush flats armed with a packed lunch and camera gives you an idea of what Giles was describing, and a good overview of the region from the top of well-formed, overgrown mounds. More views can be had from the stony hills to the west, and from **Dalhousie Homestead**, 16km south of the springs along the Pedirka road. The homestead was abandoned after the Ghan line was laid down, and today the stone walls, undermined by rabbit burrows, are gradually falling apart in the extreme climate.

travel details

Trains

Adelaide to: Alice Springs (*Ghan*, 2 weekly; 20hr); Melbourne (*Overlander*, 1 daily; 12hr; combined bus/train, 6 weekly, 10hr 45min); Perth (*Indian Pacific*, 2 weekly; 38hr); Peterborough (*Indian Pacific*, 2 weekly; 4hr); Port Augusta (*Ghan*, 2 weekly; 4hr); Sydney (*Indian Pacific* , 2 weekly; 27hr; combined train/bus, 1 daily; 21hr).

Buses

Adelaide to: Alice Springs (2 daily; 18hr 30min); Arkaroola (2 weekly; 11hr 15min); Ayers Rock Resort (3 daily; 20hr); Barossa Valley (2–5 daily; 1hr 30min); Broken Hill (1 daily; 7hr); Ceduna (1–2 daily; 12hr); Clare (1 daily except Sun; 2hr 15min); Coober Pedy (4 daily; 10hr 30min); Flinders Ranges (4 weekly; 6hr 40min); Goolwa (1–3 daily; 1hr 55min); Loxton (3–5 weekly; 3hr 30min); Mannum (2–3 daily; 2hr); McLaren Vale (2–4 daily; 50min); Melbourne (6 daily; 9hr 30min–14hr); Mount Gambier (1–2 daily except Sat; 6hr); Perth (1 daily; 34hr); Port Augusta (several daily; 6hr); Port Lincoln (1–2 daily except Sun; 10hr); Renmark (1–2 daily; 4hr); Sydney (4 daily; 21–24hr); Victor Harbor (2–3 daily; 1hr 30min); Whyalla (2–5 daily; 5hr); Yorke Peninsula (1–4 daily; 3–4hr); Woomera (6 weekly; 6hr).

Coober Pedy to: Oodnadatta (2 weekly; 5hr).

Gawler to: Kapunda (1 daily Mon–Fri; 35min).

Port Augusta to: Arkaroola (2 weekly; 7hr); Blinman (2 weekly; 3hr 15min); Coober Pedy (4 daily; 6hr 10min); Hawker (4 weekly; 1hr 30min); Mambray Creek (for Mount Remarkable; several daily; 1hr); Marla (4 daily; 10hr); Marree (2 weekly; 5hr); Melrose (3 weekly; 1hr); Port Lincoln (1 daily; 10hr); Quorn (2 weekly; 40min); Wilmington (3 weekly; 45min); Wilpena Pound (4 weekly; 2hr 15min); Woomera (4 daily; 2hr).

Woomera to: Andamooka (6 weekly; 2hr); Roxby Downs (6 weekly; 1hr 10min).

Flights

Adelaide to: Alice Springs (2 daily; 2hr); Ayers Rock Resort (2 daily via Alice; 3hr 45min); Brisbane (4–12 daily; 4hr); Broken Hill (1–4 daily; 1hr 40min); Cairns (4–5 daily; 4hr); Canberra (8 daily; 3hr 10min); Coober Pedy (at least 1 daily; 1hr 30min); Darwin (2–3 daily; 5hr); Hobart (8 daily; 3hr); Kangaroo Island (7 daily; 30min); Melbourne (10 daily; 1hr); Perth (4 daily; 5hr); Port Lincoln (4 daily; 30min); Sydney (12 daily; 2hr 10min).

The **Channel Mail Run** is a weekend in a light aircraft taking in 47 stops between Port Augusta and Boulia in southwestern Queensland – contact Port Augusta Airport (☎08/8642 3100).

CHAPTER NINE

MELBOURNE AND AROUND

Most overseas visitors' impressions of a typical Aussie city are shaped by their perception of Sydney, with its splendid harbour and exciting energy. Held in comparison to this, Australia's second city is bound to disappoint at first glance. **Melbourne**'s location on rather flat terrain beside a muddy river is no match for Sydney's stunning, smack-in-the-mouth harbour setting.

However, any initial disappointment is likely to give way to feelings of pleasant contentment and growing curiosity once you've begun to explore the city's streets, hidden arcades and alleyways, rested in the soothing greenery of its parks, and ventured into vibrant and unique inner suburbs. There's a lot here that makes Melbourne the most "English" or "European" of all Australian cities: a cool climate (by Australian standards), stately public buildings, Victorian mansions, leafy avenues and landscaped gardens. Last, but certainly not least, Melbourne has a lively passion for eating and drinking well, a predilection for style and elegance, and a vivid interest in intellectual debate and the arts.

Its **atmosphere** has been deeply influenced by migrants who arrived in waves from southern and eastern Europe and Southeast Asia, bringing with them cultures that have become part of the fabric of the city. In summer, the relaxed, universal outdoor Australian way of life asserts itself with backyard barbecue parties, riverside picnics and days on the beach. Sports too are important – people from all walks of life show a keen interest, and, uniquely in Melbourne, "footy" (Australian rules football) has been elevated to almost religious status.

Like its home state Victoria, Melbourne can be compared to a mosaic, and there's a challenge to every visitor to go out and experience as many facets of the city as possible. Outside the centre, this means exploring the **suburbs**, each one a little urban centre in its own right. Beaches, cafés, promenades and boutiques fringe the coast, south of the centre, while inland Victorian mansions, Vietnamese, Jewish, Greek and Italian communities, museums, art galleries and parks each make their distinct mark on the city. All are easily reached from the centre in a tram or bus, and many make great bases, offering exciting nightlife and a refreshing mix of flamboyance, seediness, industrial activity and residential tranquillity.

Owing to Melbourne's central location at the middle of Victoria's coastline excursions further out are also feasible by day-trip. The ranges in the east and northeast are covered by forests of towering eucalypts and patches of cool temperate rainforest. Closest to Melbourne are the **Dandenong Ranges**, partly suburban with quaint villages, partly covered by protected eucalypt forest. The scenic **Yarra Valley** in the northeast, Victoria's answer to South Australia's Barossa Valley, is one of many wine regions around Melbourne. To the south, huge Port Phillip Bay is encircled by the arms of the Bellarine and Mornington peninsulas. **Mornington Peninsula** offers

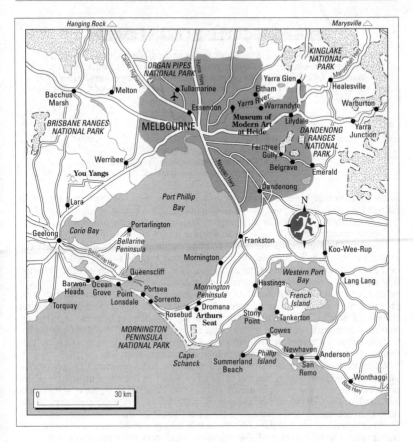

more opportunity for wine-tasting, and in addition to bucolic scenery there are beaches galore, the windswept ones at the ocean coast popular with surfers, while the placid waters of the bay are good for swimming and messing about in boats. While **Geelong** and most of the Bellarine Peninsula are not quite so captivating, Queenscliff near the narrow entrance to Port Phillip Bay, with its beautiful, refurbished grand hotels from the Victorian era is enjoying something of a comeback as a stylish (and expensive) weekend getaway.

MELBOURNE

MELBOURNE is Australia's second-largest city, with a population of around three million – about half a million less than Sydney. Rivalry between the two cities – in every sphere from cricket to business – is on an almost childish level. In purely monetary terms, Sydney is now clearly in the ascendancy, having taken over as the nation's financial centre. The state government, headed by Jeff Kennett of the Liberal Party and in power since 1992, has tried to lift the economy out of the doldrums, mainly by severe cutbacks or privatization of public services and of previously state-run utilities boards.

ACCOMMODATION PRICES

All the accommodation listed in this book has been categorized into one of eight price bands, as set out below. The rates quoted represent the cheapest available double or twin room in high season-except for category ①, which indicates per-person rates for a dorm bed, and the categories given for units, cabins and vans, which represent the daily charge for the whole unit.

① Under $18	⑤ $61–74
② $19–30	⑥ $75–94
③ $31–45	⑦ $95–124
④ $46–60	⑧ $125 upwards

For more accommodation details, see p.41-43.

While it has definitely scored points by reducing public debt and improving the credit rating of the state, critics point out that out-sourcing or privatizing public services does not necessarily always translate into greater efficiency, and even more importantly, that Victoria's economic growth has been achieved at a very high social cost.

However, Melbournians never tire of pointing out, in all modesty, that they have the incredible fortune to inhabit "one of the world's most liveable cities". Melbourne may lack a truly stunning natural setting or "in-your-face" sights but with its subtle charms it is a city that grows on you, one that is undeniably a very pleasant place to live, and enjoyable to visit too. Magnificent landscaped gardens and parks in the English style provide green spaces near the centre, while beneath the skyscrapers of the Central Business District (CBD), an understorey of solid, Victorian-era facades ranged along tree-lined boulevards presents the city on a more human scale. The air of approachability is further enhanced by the numerous arcades, lanes and alleys in which are hidden some of the country's best cafés, pubs and speciality shops.

At the time of writing an extensive and ambitious **redevelopment** programme is underway which will change the feel of the city – if only by the sheer magnitude of the projects. A host of new public buildings and the new **Federation Square** by the Yarra just south of the CBD should be completed by 2001 to celebrate the centenary of the Australian federation, and followed in the next decade by the redevelopment of the Docklands precinct west of the CBD. From this area of unused docks and rotting old warehouses a brand new city will rise, complete with hotels, office and apartment buildings, department stores, marinas and other leisure facilities. This, if nothing else, will at long last put Ava Gardner's much cited remark from 1959 to rest. She came here to film *On the Beach* and reputedly summed up her impression: "It's a story about the end of the world, and Melbourne sure is the right place to film it."

Actually, change came to Melbourne way before the nineties. Large-scale immigration since World War II has, in a sense, brought the world to Melbourne, shaking up the formerly self-absorbed, parochial WASP mindset for good. Whole villages have come here from Lebanon, Turkey, Vietnam and all over Europe, most especially from Greece, furnishing the well-worn statistic that Melbourne is the third-largest Greek city behind Athens and Thessaloniki. The **European influence** is perhaps most obvious in winter, as ancient wooden trams rattle past warm cafés and bookshops, and promenaders dress stylishly against the chill. Not surprisingly, the immigrant blend has transformed the city into a foodie mecca, where tucking into a different cuisine each night – or new hybrids of East, West and South – is one of the great treats. Sport too, especially Aussie Rules Football, is almost a religion here. The Melbourne Cup in November is a public holiday celebrated with gusto, and the city's fine sporting venues, many left over from the 1956 Olympics, are well used. Melbourne's strong claim to being the nation's cultural capital is well-founded: laced with a healthy dash of counterculture,

Melbourne's artistic life flourishes, culminating in the highbrow Melbourne Festival in the last two weeks in October, and its slightly more offbeat (and shoestring) cousin, the Fringe Festival. The city also takes pride in its leading role in Australian literary life, based around the Writers' Festival in August. Throughout the year, there are heavyweight seasons of classical music and theatre, a wacky array of small galleries, and enough art-house movies to last a lifetime.

Arrival and information

Melbourne's **Tullamarine Airport** is 22km northwest of the city on the Tullamarine Freeway; the Skybus service (from the airport every 30min between 6.40am and 11.40pm, then hourly until 6.40am; $10; ☎03/9662 9275) will take you to the Melbourne Transit Centre (Greyhound Pioneer Bus Terminal), the Spencer Street Railway Station and Bus Terminal, Town Hall and Exhibition Street (the night services between 12.40am and 4.40am run to the Town Hall only). On weekdays (7.40am–4.10pm), Saturday (8.10am–12.40pm) and Sunday (1.40–5.30pm) the bus driver will drop you off at most city hotels on request. A **taxi** from the airport costs around $28 to the city centre, $35 to St Kilda.

Greyhound Pioneer buses arrive at the **Melbourne Transit Centre** on the north side of the city centre at 58 Franklin St, whereas McCafferty's, Firefly and V/Line use the **Spencer Street Bus Terminal** on the west side. **Spencer Street Railway Station** nearby handles country and interstate trains. Some hostels pick up from these terminals, as well as from the Tasmanian ferry terminal.

About 4km southwest of the city centre, the **ferry terminal** is served by the #109 tram to Collins Street in the CBD. Skybus also runs a service to ferries to Tasmania which dock at Station Pier in Port Melbourne, departing from Melbourne Transit Centre at 3.45pm, and from Spencer Street Railway Station and Bus Terminal, bus bay #45, at 4pm ($4); *Spirit of Tasmania* sails year round (departures Mon, Wed and Fri evenings), while *Devil Cat* operates between December and April (daily departures during peak season, 4 per week at other times).

Information

The **Victoria Visitor Information Centre** is housed in the Town Hall at Swanston Walk, corner of Little Collins Street (Mon–Fri 8.30am–5.30pm, Sat & Sun 9am–5pm; ☎03/9658 9955 or freecall ☎1800/637 763. Transport, tour and accommodation telephone booking service with AUSRES (Mon–Fri 9am–6pm, Sat, Sun & public holidays 9am–5pm; ☎03/9650 1522). There are free pamphlets galore, including six colour-coded *Heritage Walk* brochures describing self-guided **walking tours** in the city and surrounding areas. The *Another View* brochure gives a glimpse of Melbourne's pre-European history through seventeen sites on a walking trail explained from a Koorie perspective. Next to the information centre is the **City Experience Centre** (Mon–Fri 9am–6pm, Sat, Sun & public holidays 9am–5pm), which has up-to-date information on Melbourne, in particular on events and activities around town, provided by helpful staff, or from videos, touchscreens and permanent displays. Of special interest is the centre's free **Greeter Service**, whereby visitors are matched up with local volunteers according to language and interests. This gives you an unparalleled insider's viewpoint, for which you need to book at least three days in advance (☎03/9658 9955, fax 9654 6168; *greeter@melbourne.vic.gov.au*). **Information Victoria**, at 318 Little Bourke St (Mon–Fri 8.30am–5.30pm; ☎03/9651 4100 or ☎1300/366 356), has free maps and brochures, as well as a notice board of city events, and a shop selling the city's largest range of local maps.

Around the city are the three volunteer-staffed **Visitor Information Booths**, at Bourke Street Mall (Mon–Thurs 9am–5pm, Fri 9am–7pm, Sat 10am–4pm, Sun

11am–4pm), Flinders Street Station (same opening times except Fri until 6pm), and at the Queen Victoria Market (Tues & Thurs 9am–2pm, Fri 9am–4pm, Sat, Sun & public holidays 11am–4pm). An interactive touch-screen terminal, where you can look up anything from a cab phone number to a Chinese restaurant, is located on Collins Street outside the Sportsgirl Centre (between Swanston and Elizabeth streets).

Alternative sources of information include the **NRE Information Centre,** 8 Nicholson St, East Melbourne, run by the Department of Natural Resources and Environment (Mon–Fri 8.30am–5.30pm; ☎03/9637 8080); and **Parks Victoria** (telephone information service only (☎13 1963); both dispense information about national parks and conservation areas in Victoria; and the **National Trust** office, Tasma Terrace, 6 Parliament Place (Mon–Fri 9am–5pm; ☎03/9654 4711), which sells several historical walking-tour guides. *Melway,* available from all newsagents, is the best **street directory.** The Friday edition of *The Age* contains an excellent pull-out **listings** section, *EG*, detailing the week's entertainment as well as fairs and markets, art and craft exhibitions, sport, and other events in and around town.

City transport

Melbourne's efficient public transport system of trams, trains and buses is called **The Met**, and a range of **tickets** is available. Unless you're going on a day-trip to the outer suburbs, you can get anywhere you need to, including St Kilda and Williamstown, on a zone 1 ticket. A ticket covering zones 1 and 2 will get you as far as Brighton Beach, Sandringham and Carrum on Port Phillip Bay, Springvale and Glen Waverley in the southeast, Alamein and Canterbury in the east, and to the end of all Met train lines in the north and west. Zone 3 includes the "far east" and "far south-east – Frankston, Cranbourne, Ferntree Gully, Ringwood and Lilydale. An ordinary zone 1 ticket costs $2.30, a short hop $1.60; these tickets are valid for two hours, or all night if bought after 7pm. A day-ticket ($4.40 for zone 1; $7.10 for zones 1 and 2; $9.50 for zones 1, 2 and 3) is better value if you're making a few trips in zone 1, or if you are planning a trip to the outer suburbs. For longer stays, a weekly ticket ($19.10) is an even better bargain. Automated ticketing has recently been introduced: you'll need to validate your ticket by machine every time you board a new vehicle. Coin machines on board trams supply tickets for short trips and 2 hours; these and day tickets are also available from train stations, bus drivers, the City Met Shop at 103 Elizabeth St and at other selected shops (most newsagents, some milk bars and pharmacies). The supposedly smooth-running system has its hiccups, such as out-of-order coin machines,

---

MELBOURNE'S VINTAGE TRAMS

Many of the trams traversing Melbourne's streets on a daily basis are vintage wooden ones. None is quite as old as the system, which dates from 1885, but some from the 1930s are still in use, and one dates from 1929. On Sunday between about 10am and 4.30pm restored brown vintage trams run between Elizabeth Street and the Zoo. The vintage **City Circle trams** run free of charge in a loop along Flinders Street, Spring Street, Latrobe Street and Spencer Street (daily except Christmas Day and Good Friday, every 10min between 10am and 6pm). The **Colonial Tramcar Restaurant** (bookings ☎03/9696 4000) is a converted 1927 tram offering traditional silver and white linen restaurant service as you trundle around Melbourne. Operating daily, the restaurant (non-smoking) offers a three-course early dinner (5.45–7.15pm; $60) and a five-course dinner ($95 Fri & Sat, $85 other nights), plus a four-course lunch (Sun 1–3pm and other days subject to demand; $70), All drinks are included. Book as early as possible – Friday and Saturday evenings can be booked up two months in advance.

DRIVING AND CYCLING IN MELBOURNE

Driving in Melbourne requires some care, mainly because of the trams. You can over-take a tram only on the left and must stop and wait behind it while passengers get on and off, as they step directly into the road (there's no need to stop if there's a central pedes-trian island). A peculiar rule has developed to accommodate trams at major intersections in the city centre: when turning right, you pull over to the left-hand lane and wait for the lights to change to amber before turning – a so-called "hook turn". Signs overhead indi-cate when this rule applies.

Cyclists should also watch out for tram lines – tyres can easily get wedged in them. This apart, Melbourne is perfect for cycling and you'll be in good company as it's a pop-ular way of getting around. The friendly staff at Bicycle Victoria, 19 O'Connell St, North Melbourne (Mon–Fri 9am–5pm; ☎03/9328 3000), assist with practical information and hand out *The Great Rides Calendar* listing their organized bike rides in Victoria and inter-state. City Cycle Tours, based in the Treasury Gardens (daily 8am–6pm; ☎03/9585 5343), rent out bikes and run cycling sightseeing tours if there's enough demand (mini-mum two people); every morning around the city and gardens (3hr 30min; $30) and shorter tours in the afternoon ($20). Cycle enthusiasts might want to buy a copy of the booklet *Discovering Victoria's Bike Paths* ($16.95, available at Bicycle Victoria or at newsagents). See also "Listings", p.806, for bike rental.

fare dodgers, and ticket inspectors riding trams and blocking station exits in an attempt to catch them.

Services operate Monday to Saturday from 5am until midnight, and Sunday from 8am until 11pm, supplemented in the early hours of Saturday and Sunday by **NightRider buses** (hourly 12.30–4.30am; $5), which head from the City Square on Swanston Walk to the outer suburbs, more or less in the same direction as the suburban train routes. Each bus is equipped with a mobile phone, on which the driver can book a taxi to meet you at a bus stop (free call), or you can call a friend ($1) to meet you. For further infor-mation, call the **Met Transport Information Centre** (daily 7am–8.55pm; ☎13 1638).

Trams

Melbourne's **trams** give the city a distinctive character and provide a pleasant, environ-mentally friendly way of getting around: the **City Circle** (see box opposite) is particular-ly convenient, and free. Trams run down the centre of the road, and stops are signpost-ed (the "Central Melbourne" map on p.000 shows the main routes in the centre); they often have central islands where you can wait, but if not, take care crossing the road. It can be uncomfortable waiting in the middle of a busy road, especially for a woman alone at night – you may feel less vulnerable waiting on the footpath, where there's often a shel-ter anyway. Some trams can be boarded only at the front; others also have middle doors.

Trains

Trains are the fastest way to reach distant suburbs. An underground loop system feed-ing into seventeen suburban lines connects the city centre's **five train stations**: Spencer Street, which also serves as the station for interstate and country trains; Flagstaff on the corner of Latrobe and William streets; Museum beween Elizabeth and Swanston streets; Parliament on Spring Street; and Flinders Street. The last is the **main suburban station**, with its clocks detailing the times of all train departures ("under the clocks" is a traditional Melbourne meeting place). Bikes can be carried free, except Monday to Friday from 7am until 9.30am and from 4pm until 6pm, when an extra adult concession fee has to be paid. Only trains will allow surfboards to be brought on board, for which an extra adult concession fee is payable.

Buses

Regular buses often run on the same routes as trams, as well as filling gaps where no train or tram lines run, but they are likely to be the least useful mode of public transport for visitors. However, the **City Explorer** might be the easy answer to sightseeing headaches – and footaches. The red double-decker (☎03/9650 7000, fax 9650 7033; hourly 10am–4pm; buy tickets on board; day-ticket $22, two-day ticket $35) does circuits of the city, starting from Melbourne Town Hall and running past the Rialto Observation Deck and the Polly Woodside Maritime Museum to the Arts Centre south of the CBD, then back up the eastern side of the city to Lygon Street, the Zoo, the Metro! Craft Centre, Queen Victoria Market and Melbourne Central; passengers can stay on the bus and use it as a sightseeing tour, or jump off and reboard later. The same company also runs very inexpensive night tours, shopping tours, tours of the city including sites and meals, and half- and full-day sightseeing tours going out to Melbourne's suburbs.

Accommodation

When looking for somewhere to stay in Melbourne, the most obvious areas to head for are the **city centre** (and the adjoining suburbs of **North Melbourne**, **Carlton**, **Fitzroy** and **East Melbourne**) and down by the sea around **St Kilda**. Some of the cheap accommodation areas on the fringes of the city centre are fairly dead at night, though they are within easy reach of all the action. St Kilda is very lively, if a bit rough around the edges, with an abundance of hostels and inexpensive hotels and motels. **Richmond**, **South Melbourne** and **South Yarra** offer a good compromise, handy for both the centre and St Kilda's nightlife, and with enough tasty eating options of their own to keep you going (see map of "Melbourne Suburbs" on p.786).

The most exclusive **hotels** are downtown around Collins Street, and there's a collection of large and recently revamped hotels around Spencer Street Station. Melbourne has plenty of **backpackers' accommodation**, ranging from fairly basic, even scruffy places to salubrious Victorian-era mansions with dorms attached. Hostel beds can go as low as $13 (in winter), though the average for a dorm bed is more like $17. Campsite cabins and vans are an alternative worth considering for those with their own transport (see p.774).

City centre

Adelphi Hotel, 187 Flinders Lane (☎03/9650 7555, fax 9650 2710). This stylish hotel has a striking exterior and a sparse, ultra-modern interior design that extends to the large guestrooms, all topped with a huge pool on the roof. ⑨.

Astoria City Travel Inn, 288 Spencer St (☎03/9670 6801, fax 9670 3034). Pleasant motel three blocks north of Spencer Street Station with spacious and bright units. In-house amenities include a saltwater pool, laundry and licensed Italian restaurant. ⑥.

Hotel Bakpak, 167 Franklin St (☎03/9329 7525, fax 9326 7667 or free call ☎1800/645 200). A happening place with lots of activity and information. Hundreds of beds in a converted former school building brightened up with colour co-ordinated paintwork, carpets and polished timber. Standard facilities plus in-house employment agency, travel shop, small gym, basement bar, café, cinema and a rooftop terrace with a tiny pool and great views of the city, and dorms with four to twelve beds (separate men's and women's dorms available on request), fans and lockers; doubles are spartan. ①–③.

Batmans Hill, 66 Spencer St (☎03/9614 6344, fax 9614 1189, free call ☎1800/335 308). An elegant Edwardian exterior belies a functional and modern interior. A wide range of facilities includes bars, a restaurant and 24hr room service, and it's handy for Spencer Street Station and the Casino Entertainment Complex just south of the river. ⑦–⑧.

City Centre Private Hotel, 22 Little Collins St (☎03/9654 5401, fax 9650 7256). Good position on a quiet street 100m from Parliament Station. Inexpensive doubles, singles and a few dorms (mainly four beds, usually separate for males/females), all sharing bathrooms. Most rooms have fridges; other facilities include heating, basic kitchens, a TV lounge and laundry. Dorms ②, rooms ③–④.

City Limits Motel, 20 Little Bourke St (☎03/9662 2544 fax 9662 2287, free call ☎1800/808 651). Motel-style units with en-suite and the usual mod-cons on a quiet street just around the corner from Parliament Station. ⑤–⑥.

Hotel Enterprize, 44 Spencer St (☎03/9629 6991, fax 9614 7963). Solid hotel in central location opposite Spencer Street Station. Good, no-frills economy rooms with shared facilities, plus well-appointed en-suite rooms. Room service and undercover parking ($5 per day) available. ④–⑦.

Exford Hostel, 199 Russell St (☎03/9663 2697, fax 9663 2248). In an extremely central position above a refurbished pub, this hostel is secure and clean, with friendly and helpful staff. Usual amenities, plus a tiny sundeck with barbecue. Four- to ten-bed dorms, (separate for women on request). Twins and doubles are good value. Rooms ③, dorms ①.

Flinders Station Hotel & Backpackers, 35 Elizabeth St (☎03/9620 5100, fax 9620 5101). Secure and well-organized hostel in former office building, centrally located a few hundred metres from Flinders Street Station. Basic twins and doubles, and two en-suite doubles for wheelchair users. Dorms have lockers and are mainly four-bed, though a few have up to ten beds (separate men's and women's dorms available on request). ①–⑥.

Friendly Backpacker, 197 King St (☎03/9670 1111, fax 9670 9911, free call ☎1800/671 115). New hostel in refurbished office building lives up to its name and is clean and secure: bright rooms (with air-con and heating) are used as dorms (mainly four beds; some women-only) and simple doubles; each floor has a cosy sitting area with TV. Good kitchen and common room in the basement. Dorms ①, rooms ③–④.

Kingsgate Budget Hotel, 131 King St (☎03/9629 4171, fax 9629 7110). Huge, renovated old private hotel. En-suite rooms with colour TV, heating, air con and telephone are good value; there are also inexpensive no-frills budget rooms with shared facilities, a few rooms for small groups or families (up to four beds), a laundry and a pleasant TV lounge, but no kitchen facilities. Cheap breakfast available. ③–⑤.

Miami Motor Inn, 13 Hawke St, off the north end of King St (☎03/9329 8499, fax 9328 1820, free call ☎1800/122 333). Renovated en-suite rooms with TV, wardrobe and ceiling fan as well as simple, clean, standard rooms with shared facilities – good value rates include a cooked breakfast. TV lounge, pool table, laundry and free off-street parking; no kitchen. ③–⑥.

Pacific International Terrace Inn, 16 Spencer St (☎03/9621 3333, fax 9621 1922, free call ☎1800/816 168). Popular with business people, this very pleasant, well-maintained hotel constitutes good value, offering B&B, en-suite rooms, elegant breakfast room, bar, restaurant and other facilities. ⑦.

Toad Hall Guesthouse, 441 Elizabeth St (☎03/9600 9010, fax 9600 9013). Excellent choice close to Melbourne Transit Centre: friendly, cosy, secure and clean, with good facilities. Pleasant courtyard out the back; off-street car parking available ($5 per day). Rooms ③–④, dorms ①–②.

Victoria Hall, 380 Russell St (☎03/9662 3888, fax 9639 0101). Centrally located international student accommodation, but accepts budget travellers from the end of November until the end of February. Great value twins and singles, and a few dorms. Rooms ②–③, dorms ①.

Victoria Vista Hotel, 215 Little Collins St (☎03/9653 0441, fax 9650 9678, free call ☎1800/331 147). Huge, old, but refurbished hotel in an unbeatable central location, with its own café and bar; all rooms – with or without their own bathrooms – have telephones, heating, tea and coffee-making facilities. Undercover parking available ($6 per day). ④–⑦.

Windsor Hotel, 103 Spring St (☎03/9633 6000, fax 9633 6001). This opulent Victorian-era hotel, a landmark opposite Parliament House, is classified by the National Trust; from $450 a night. ⑧.

Hotel Y, 489 Elizabeth St (☎03/9329 5188, fax 9329 1469; or call central YWCA reservations on free call ☎1800/249 124). Close to Melbourne Transit Centre and Victoria Market; simple en-suite standard rooms, and de luxe rooms with fridge, telephone, air con and colour TV. The few dorms are overpriced. Limited kitchen facilities in bright, spacious common room; laundry also available. Rooms ⑤–⑦, dorms ③.

North Melbourne, Carlton and Fitzroy

Carlton College, 101 Drummond St, Carlton (☎03/9664 0664, fax 9639 2165). Ideally located near the Lygon St cafés and shops, this student accommodation in Italianate terraces turns into a backpackers' hostel from mid-November to the end of February. The small dorms, singles, twins and doubles are simple, but excellent value. Rooms ②–③, dorms ①.

Chapman Gardens YHA, 76 Chapman St, North Melbourne (☎03/9328 3595, fax 9329 7863). More intimate than its sister hostel, the *Queensberry Hill YHA*, but further away from the city centre (3km) – take tram #50, #57 or #59 north from Elizabeth St. Mainly twins, a few singles, doubles and dorms (four beds); car parking available and free use of bicycles. Skybus drops off and picks up 50m from here. Reception for new guests staffed 7.30am–12.30pm and 1.30–10pm. Rooms ③, dorms ①.

Downtowner on Lygon, 66 Lygon St, Carlton (☎03/9663 5555, fax 9662 3308). Attractively refurbished rooms with all mod cons (some with spa) in the heart of Carlton. Undercover parking. ⑧.

Global Backpackers Hostel, 238 Victoria St, North Melbourne (☎03/9328 3728, fax 9326 9114). Small, basic hostel opposite Victoria Market, preferably for people who don't mind loud music as the pub next door features indie and heavy-metal bands. Rooms ②–③, dorms ①.

Lygon Lodge, 220 Lygon St, Carlton (☎03/9663 6633, fax 9663 7297). Good motel in central Carlton; attractive rooms, some with small kitchenette. Undercover car parking. ⑤–⑥.

The Nunnery, 116 Nicholson St, Fitzroy (☎03/9419 8637, fax 9417 7736, free call ☎1800/032 635; take #96 tram from Bourke St). Half of this ex-convent is an attractive guesthouse, half a not-so-special hostel with rather crammed dorms. A small courtyard and a tiny rooftop are the only outdoor sitting areas, but the atmosphere is busy and friendly; there's also a big, cosy TV lounge, a kitchen and Internet facilities. Two doors away is a great pub, and Brunswick St cafés are within five minutes' walk. Rooms ④, dorms ①–②.

Queensberry Hill YHA, 78 Howard St, off Victoria St (☎03/9329 8599, fax 9326 8427). Ultra-modern, huge hostel – more like a smart hotel – with family rooms, double rooms and dorms (four to eight beds), as well as cafeteria, TV rooms, a huge, well-equipped kitchen and an in-house travel agent. The office is open 7am to 11pm, but access is 24hr. An easy 10min walk from Melbourne Transit Centre; Skybus will drop off here and pick up on request. Free use of bicycles. Rooms ④–⑥, dorms ②.

East Melbourne

East Melbourne Hotel, 2 Hotham St, East Melbourne (☎03/9419 2040, fax 9417 3733). Good renovated budget rooms with heating and shared facilities above a pub at the Punt Rd end of the street. Cheap meals at the pleasant *Café Bar* downstairs, which also has an extensive wine list. ⑤.

George Powlett Motel Apartments, Powlett St, corner of George St, East Melbourne (☎03/9419 9488, fax 9419 0806). Motel-style units off two central courtyards. All mod cons, including parking. Central location. ⑥.

George Street Apartments, 101 George St, East Melbourne (☎03/9419 1333, fax 9419 6671). Bright, serviced self-catering studio apartments 1km from the centre, on a quiet street running off the east side of Fitzroy Gardens. Laundry and off-street parking. Excellent value; rates include light breakfast. ⑥–⑦.

Georgian Court Guesthouse, 21–25 George St, East Melbourne (☎03/9419 6353, fax 9416 0895). Standard rooms with shared facilities, and en-suite rooms equipped with colour TV, fridge and radio; all are bright, tastefully furnished and serviced daily. Rates include light breakfast. Quiet but very central location. ⑤–⑥.

Magnolia Court Boutique Hotel, 101 Powlett St, East Melbourne (☎03/9419 4222, fax 9416 0841). Elegant hotel in a quiet street, but within walking distance of Fitzroy Gardens, the city, MCG and the Tennis Centre in Melbourne Park. Very tastefully furnished rooms with all facilities in two older, lovingly restored buildings and in a newish motel section. Spa pool in the cottage garden. Breakfast available. ⑦–⑧.

South Melbourne, Richmond, Albert Park and South Yarra

Bleak House Hotel, 97 Beaconsfield Parade, Albert Park (☎03/9690 4642, fax 9690 4062). Pub accommodation in renovated, bright and clean rooms with polished floorboards. Front rooms have great views over the beach and Port Phillip Bay, but get a bit of traffic noise. Shared facilities. Next to a tram stop and very close to the Tasmanian ferry terminal. Take #1 or #2 from Swanston St to South Melbourne Beach. Rooms ③–⑤.

Central Accommodation, 21 Bromham Place, Richmond (☎03/9427 9826, fax 9427 9001). Luxury apartments converted into a small hostel – not spotlessly tidy, but with a homely, very friendly atmosphere. Mainly dorms (some women-only), a few twin and double rooms. Central location, near great pubs and shops, and within walking distance of MCG and Melbourne Park (15–20min). Owners have good employment contacts in the area. Pick-up from the airport, bus terminals or the Tasmanian ferry. Take tram #75 or #48 from Spencer St or Flinders St to stop no. 18. Rooms ③–④, dorms ①.

Lords Lodge Backpackers, 204 Punt Rd, corner of Greville St, South Yarra (☎03/9510 5658, fax 9533 6663). Small, family-run, non-smoking hostel in an old mansion, centrally positioned in a fashionable area. Singles and doubles, as well as medium-size dorms (some women-only), each with a fridge and lockers. Owners have good work contacts in and around Prahran. Internet facilities available. Take tram #3, #5, #6 or #16 from Swanston St and get off at stop no. 26, or take the Sandringham line train to Prahran Railway Station. Pick-up from airport and bus terminals on request. Rooms ②–③, dorms ①.

Middle Park Hotel, 102 Canterbury Rd, corner of Armstrong St, Middle Park (☎03/1958, fax 9645 8928). Simple but pleasant rooms with shared facilities above refurbished pub. Take tram #96 from Spencer St. Close to Aquatic Centre, beach and lots of restaurants and delis. ③–⑤.

Nomads Chapel Street Backpackers, 22 Chapel St, Windsor (☎03/9583 6855, fax 9533 6866, free call ☎1800/613 333) Small and very clean non-smoking hostel at the southern, quieter end of Chapel St. Some of the dorms (four to six beds; women-only available) and doubles are en-suite. All rates include a continental breakfast. Opposite Windsor Station (Sandringham line). Dorms ①–②, rooms ④.

Nomads Market Inn, 115 Cecil St, South Melbourne (☎03/9583 6690). Small hostel above a pub opposite South Melbourne Market. Pick-up from bus terminals in the city, and free use of bicycles. Dorms ①, rooms ③.

Pint on Punt, 42 Punt Rd, Windsor (☎03/9510 4273, fax 9529 5518, free call ☎1800/835 000). New hostel above totally refurbished, British-style pub in central location, walking distance from Chapel St and St Kilda nightlife. Clean dorms (four–six beds), twins and doubles. Common room has hot water for tea/coffee making and microwave; cheap pub dinners available. All rates include continental breakfast. Reception 7am–2pm and 4–7pm; check in at other times through the bar. Take train to Windsor Station (Sandringham line) or tram #3, #5, #64 or #67 from Swanston St, to St Kilda Junction. Rooms ③–④, dorms ①.

Richmond Hill Hotel, 353 Church St (between Bridge Rd and Swan St), Richmond (☎03/9428 6501, fax 9427 0128). Clean and well-run ex-YWCA in a refurbished old mansion with very cosy sitting rooms, large kitchen and a small courtyard. Dorms (some women-only) and many pleasant private rooms, some de luxe en-suites; the more expensive ones include continental breakfast ($6 otherwise). Tram #75 or #48 from Spencer St or Flinders St. Rooms ③–⑥, dorms ①–②.

Victoria Hotel, 123 Beaconsfield Parade, South Melbourne (☎03/9690 3666, fax 9699 9570). This grand hotel, built in 1888, has been restored to its Victorian splendour. The upstairs accommodation is in a more modern style, the bright front rooms have good views of the waterfront but intrusion of traffic noise. Choose between stylish en-suite doubles and cheaper rooms with shared facilities. ④–⑧.

West End Hotel, 76 Toorak Rd West, South Yarra (☎03/9866 3135). An old-fashioned B&B overlooking a shady park and close to the heart of exclusive South Yarra. Doubles and singles with shared facilities. Take tram #8, or the train to South Yarra. ④.

St Kilda

Bayside St Kilda Motel, 63 Fitzroy St (☎03/9525 3833, fax 9534 1831). The triples are especially good value among these motel units with all mod cons – opt for a room at the back, as those facing the street are a bit noisy. Secure car park. ④.

Coffee Palace, 24 Grey St (☎03/9534 2003 or 9534 5283, fax 9593 9166, free call ☎1800/654 098). Very busy hostel in an old, rambling building. Some of the dorms are women-only, and there are plenty of twins and doubles with en-suite bathrooms. In-house travel agent and job agency, lots of activities; tours run in conjunction with *Enfield House*. Pick-up from the airport, bus terminals and the ferry. Rooms ③, dorms ①.

Enfield House, 2 Enfield St (☎03/9534 8159, fax 9534 5579). A few dorms, a TV lounge and a reading room have been carved out of a stately, Victorian-era mansion, with a bewildering number of very basic dorms and rooms in former apartments desperately needing renovation and refurbishment. There's a smallish central kitchen, a courtyard, good notice boards and lots of activities, including cheap tours to the Great Ocean Road, Phillip Island, and Ramsay Street – the latter very popular with British backpackers. Pick-up from the airport, bus terminals and the ferry. Rates include pancake breakfast. Rooms ③, dorms ①.

Kookaburra Cottage, 62 Grey St (☎03/9534 5457). At the time of writing the hostel was about to move to its new premises on Grey St. The owner plans to run the "new" hostel along the same lines as before – a small, well-equipped and friendly place. Rooms ③, dorms ①.

Leopard House, 27 Grey St (☎03/9534 1200). Large, pleasant old house, with lockable dorms, either segregated or mixed, and a good notice board. Friendly atmosphere. ①.

Olembia, 96 Barkly St (☎03/9537 1412, fax 9537 1600). Very comfortable non-smoking guesthouse in fine old building with open fireplaces, a cosy lounge and dining room and a well-equipped kitchen. Singles, twins and doubles are very appealing; the dorms (some women-only) have handbasins and clothes-hanging space. Off-street parking available. Rooms ③–④, dorms ①.

Ritz For Backpackers, 169 Fitzroy St (☎03/9525 3501, fax 9525 3863). Friendly hostel above a British-style pub, within range of restaurants, cafés and milk bars. Rooms are simple but spotless, and there are two TV lounges, a dining room and a tiny kitchen. Lots of activities; tours run in conjunction with Enfield House. Rooms ③, dorms ①.

Hotel Tolarno, 42 Fitzroy St, (☎03/9537 0200, fax 9537 7800). A boutique hotel in a restored building right in the thick of things, upstairs from the *Tolarno Restaurant and Bar*. Pleasant rooms with polished timber floors and all mod cons are good value for money. Most are en-suite. ⑤–⑦.

Warwick Beachside St Kilda, 363 Beaconsfield Parade (☎03/9525 4800, fax 9537 1056, free call ☎1800/338 134). Just around the corner from the cafés and pubs of Fitzroy St, these 1950s-style brick buildings contain one- and two-bedroom units, all with colour TV, direct-dial phones and complete kitchen facilities. Management is not very obliging, but weekly rates are good. ⑤–⑥.

Camping and caravan parks

There are no campsites anywhere close to the centre; the nearest is *Melbourne Holiday Park*, with scenic *Hobsons Bay* not much further on.

Crystal Brook Holiday Centre, corner of Anderson's Creek and Warrandyte rds, East Doncaster (☎03/9844 3637, fax 9844 3342). Modern campsite and holiday park with tennis courts and a pool, 21km northeast of the city centre (20min via the Eastern Freeway). On-site vans ③–④, cabins ④–⑤.

GAY AND LESBIAN ACCOMMODATION

For further accommodation possibilities, other than those listed below, ring **Gay Share** (☎03/9650 0200), which arranges house shares for gays and lesbians.

California Motor Inn, 138 Barkers Rd, Hawthorn (☎03/9818 0281, fax 9819 6845, free call ☎1800/331 166,). Gay-friendly motel accommodation close to the city, with parking available. Take tram #109 or #42 from Collins St. ⑤–⑥.

Exchange Hotel, 119 Commercial Rd, South Yarra (☎03/9867 5144). Accommodation at a traditional gay men's pub. ④.

Fitzroy Stables, 124 Victoria St (off Brunswick St), Fitzroy (☎ and fax 03/9415 1507). Lovely self-contained unit with a cathedral ceiling, mezzanine bedroom and small kitchen, facing a courtyard with a cottage garden. ⑥.

Heathville House, 171 Aitken St, Williamstown (☎ and fax 03/9397 5959). B&B in pretty, restored weatherboard house. Non-smoking. ⑦.

Jock's, 9 Peel St, Collingwood (☎03/9417 6700). Four rooms for men; en-suite or shared facilities. ④–⑥.

Laird Hotel, 149 Gipps St, Abbotsford (☎03/9417 2832). Rooms for gay men only. ⑤–⑥.

163 Drummond Street, 163 Drummond St, Carlton (☎03/9663 3081, fax 9663 6500). Non-smoking B&B in two adjacent, two-storey refurbished Victorian mansions.Eleven rooms; en-suite or shared facilities. ④–⑥.

Palm Court B&B, 22 Grattan Place, Richmond, (☎03/9427 7365 or mobile 0149/777 850. Spacious bedrooms in Victorian mansion at a moderate rate. Non-smoking. ④–⑥.

Hobsons Bay Caravan Park, 158 Kororoit Creek Rd, Williamstown (☎03/9397 2395). Thirteen kilometres west of the city. Pitch your tent facing St Kilda across Hobsons Bay. Cabins ③.

Melbourne Holiday Park, 265 Elizabeth St, Coburg East (☎03/9354 3533). Ten kilometres north of the city, the closest spot to camp, with a kitchen and a swimming pool. Bus #526 to the city (daytime only, no service Sun). Cabins ④–⑤.

The City

Melbourne has long been known as a city of few sights but plenty of lifestyle, a place to sit and enjoy a coffee or stroll in a park rather than traipse round museums and tourist attractions. However, Jeff Kennett, Victoria's premier since 1992, is determined to change all that with an ambitious redevelopment programme that will irrevocably transform the city – like it or not. The shift towards the Yarra river that kicked off in the mid–1990s with the chunky waterfront development of Southgate, Crown Casino and Melbourne Exhibition Centre will be complemented by the new **Federation Square** opposite Flinders Street Station – at the moment still a building site, but due to be completed in 2001. Plans have also been laid to refurbish the National Gallery of Victoria and construct new museums, a huge sports stadium and Citylink, a network of city bypasses linking the freeways out of the city; all these are also on schedule to be completed by 2001 – the centenary of the Australian Federation. This construction frenzy is to continue unabated with the docklands project. In the next ten to fifteen years an entire new waterfront city will rise from what is at present an urban wasteland. Depending on the outcome (and one's point of view, of course) the docklands might add an exciting new dimension to the city or create yet another manifestation of shallow, hedonistic materialism in the vein of the Casino. Looking at the artists' impressions of the future slick waterfront city, however, the association of "Gold Coast on the Yarra" does not seem terribly far-fetched.

North of this area of redevelopment, the **Central Business District** (CBD), bounded by Latrobe, Spring, Flinders and Spencer streets, offers some fine public buildings and lots of shops, with the **Old Melbourne Gaol** exerting a ghoulish fascination and a new museum in the Old Customs House sheds light on Victoria's immigration history. On all sides, save the downtown west, the CBD is surrounded by gardens; few cities have so much green space so close to the centre. To the north a wander through lively, century-old **Queen Victoria Market** will repay both serious shoppers and people-watchers, while **Carlton Gardens** is probably the most pleasant of Melbourne's leafy refuges. In the east the CBD rubs up against **Eastern Hill**, with its government buildings and landscaped **Fitzroy Gardens**, from where it's a short walk to the venerable **Melbourne Cricket Ground (MCG)**, a must for sports fans. To the south is the previously much-maligned, muddy **Yarra River** which is slowly being turned into an attraction. You'll get a rewarding view of the city skyline on a stroll along the riverbanks in front of Southgate and the Casino, and a unique look at underwater life at **Melbourne Aquarium** on the opposite side of the river, while the best way to appreciate the changing vistas of city and parklands is on a **boat cruise**. South of the river, the **Victorian Arts Centre**, whose highlights are the **Performing Arts Museum** and the National Gallery of Victoria (currently being renovated), forms a cultural strip on one side of St Kilda Road, while on the other Government House and the impressive Shrine of Remembrance front the **Royal Botanic Gardens**, where along with the soothing greenery you'll get a dose of horticultural education.

The CBD

Seen from across the river or from the air, Melbourne's **Central Business District** offers up a spectacular, modern skyline; at ground level, however, what you notice are the florid nineteenth-century facades, grandiose survivors of the great days of the

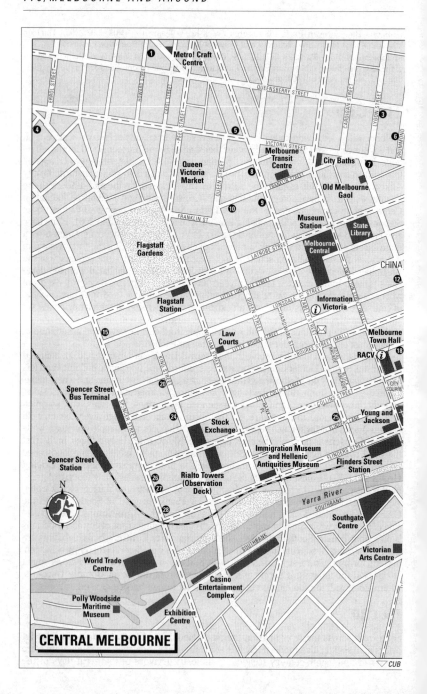

❶ Metro! Craft Centre

QUEENSBERRY STREET

ERROL STREET
HOWARD STREET
PEEL STREET

❹

❺

VICTORIA STREET

QUEEN STREET

CARDIGAN STREET
LYGON STREET

❸

DRUMMOND

❻

Melbourne Transit Centre

City Baths

❼

Queen Victoria Market

❽

FRANKLIN STREET

Old Melbourne Gaol

❿

❾

FRANKLIN ST

Museum Station

State Library

Flagstaff Gardens

LATROBE STREET

Melbourne Central

CHINA

❶❷

Flagstaff Station

LITTLE LONSDALE STREET

LONSDALE STREET

Information (i) Victoria

QUEEN STREET
HARDWARE ST
ELIZABETH STREET

WILLIAM STREET

Law Courts

LITTLE BOURKE STREET

BOURKE STREET (MALL)

Melbourne Town Hall

RACV (i)

❶❽

CITY SQUARE

❶❺

KING STREET

❷⓿

BOURKE STREET
SWANSTON STREET
ROYAL ARCADE
BLOCK ARCADE

Spencer Street Bus Terminal

SPENCER STREET

❷❹

LITTLE COLLINS STREET

COLLINS STREET

Young and Jackson

❷❺

FLINDERS LANE

Spencer Street Station

Stock Exchange

BANK PL

Immigration Museum and Hellenic Antiquities Museum

Flinders Street Station

FLINDERS STREET

N

❷❻
❷❼

Rialto Towers (Observation Deck)

❷❽

Yarra River
SOUTHBANK

Southgate Centre

World Trade Centre

Victorian Arts Centre

SOUTHBANK

Polly Woodside Maritime Museum

Casino Entertainment Complex

Exhibition Centre

CENTRAL MELBOURNE

▽ CUB

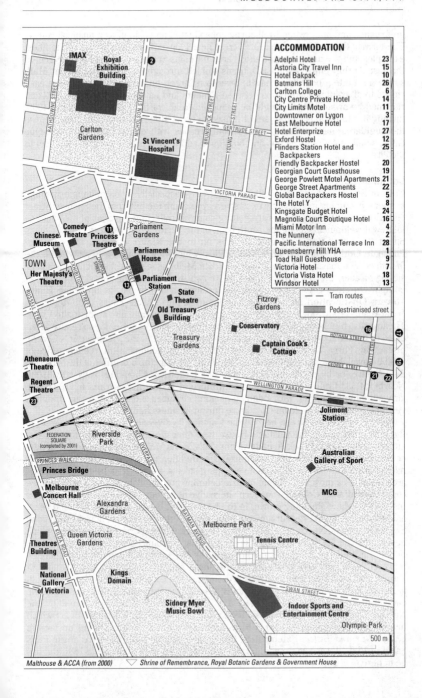

ACCOMMODATION

Adelphi Hotel	23
Astoria City Travel Inn	15
Hotel Bakpak	10
Batmans Hill	26
Carlton College	6
City Centre Private Hotel	14
City Limits Motel	11
Downtowner on Lygon	3
East Melbourne Hotel	17
Hotel Enterprize	27
Exford Hostel	12
Flinders Station Hotel and Backpackers	25
Friendly Backpacker Hostel	20
Georgian Court Guesthouse	19
George Powlett Motel Apartments	21
George Street Apartments	22
Global Backpackers Hostel	5
The Hotel Y	8
Kingsgate Budget Hotel	24
Magnolia Court Boutique Hotel	16
Miami Motor Inn	4
The Nunnery	2
Pacific International Terrace Inn	28
Queensberry Hill YHA	1
Toad Hall Guesthouse	9
Victoria Hotel	7
Victoria Vista Hotel	18
Windsor Hotel	13

– – – Tram routes

▨ Pedestrianised street

IMAX
Royal Exhibition Building
Carlton Gardens
St Vincent's Hospital
RATHDOWNE STREET
NICHOLSON STREET
BRUNSWICK STREET
YOUNG STREET
GERTRUDE STREET
VICTORIA PARADE

Chinese Museum
Comedy Theatre
Princess Theatre
TOWN
Her Majesty's Theatre
Parliament Gardens
Parliament House
Parliament Station
State Theatre
Old Treasury Building
Treasury Gardens
EXHIBITION STREET
RUSSELL STREET
SPRING STREET

Fitzroy Gardens
Conservatory
Captain Cook's Cottage
HOTHAM STREET
GEORGE STREET
WELLINGTON PARADE

Athenaeum Theatre
Regent Theatre

FEDERATION SQUARE (completed by 2001)
Riverside Park
PRINCES WALK
Princes Bridge
Melbourne Concert Hall
Alexandra Gardens
Queen Victoria Gardens
Theatres Building
National Gallery of Victoria
Kings Domain
ST KILDA ROAD

Jolimont Station
Australian Gallery of Sport
MCG
Melbourne Park
Tennis Centre
BATMAN AVENUE
SWAN STREET

Sidney Myer Music Bowl
Indoor Sports and Entertainment Centre
Olympic Park

0   500 m

Malthouse & ACCA (from 2000)   ▽ *Shrine of Remembrance, Royal Botanic Gardens & Government House* goldrushes and after, when Melbourne consolidated its position as a financial centre. The former **Royal Mint** on William Street near Flagstaff Gardens is one of the finest examples, but the main concentrations are on Collins Street and along Spring Street to the east. At the centre of the CBD, trams still jolt through busy **Bourke Street Mall**, so it's not quite a pedestrian haven; Swanston Street, bounding the mall to the east, closed to all traffic except trams between Flinders and Latrobe streets since 1992 and renamed **Swanston Walk**, might be reopened to all traffic again at the end of 1999, turning it into the busy, noisy street it used to be. A stone's throw from these central thoroughfares, narrow lanes, squares and arcades with quaint, hole-in-the-wall-type cafés, small restaurants, shops and boutiques add a surprisingly cosy, homely feel to the city.

Colins Street

Collins Street is *the* smart Melbourne address – especially if you're an international banker – becoming increasingly exclusive as you climb the hill from the Spencer Street end. Even here though, things are getting smarter, reflecting the buzz of the successful new developments along the south bank of the Yarra. At the western end of Collins Street the new Stock Exchange squares up to the **Rialto Building** opposite, an Italianate Gothic complex built in the 1890s, which now houses a luxury hotel, the *Meridien*. The massive **Rialto Towers**, to date Melbourne's tallest structure, is a classic skyscraper, the reflective surface of its twin towers lending the skyline a bit of oomph. On clear days, especially in the evening, a trip in the lift up to the **Rialto Towers Observation Deck** on the 55th floor is a must (Mon–Thurs 11am–10pm, Fri & Sat 10am–11pm; $8). The admission fee includes a 20-minute film at the Rialto Vision Theatre that highlights the best parts of Melbourne and Victoria. If you're also interested in guided tours of the Melbourne Cricket Ground and the Victorian Arts Centre, buy a "Big Three Ticket" which includes all three attractions at the reduced price of $19.50 – available at the Rialto Towers Observation Deck, the box office at the Victorian Arts Centre, or by phone from Ticketmaster (credit card bookings only ☎13 6100). Nearby, at 333 Collins St, the former **Commercial Bank of Australia** has a particularly sumptuous interior, with a domed banking chamber and awesome barrel-vaulted vestibule, that you're welcome to admire during business hours.

Further up Collins Street, beyond the worthwhile diversion down William Street to the new museums in the Customs House (see opposite), shops become the focus of attention. The 1890s **Block Arcade**, at nos. 282–284, is Melbourne's grandest shopping centre, its name appropriately taken from the tradition of "doing the block" – promenading around the city's fashionable shopping streets. Restored in 1988, the L-shaped arcade sports a mosaic-tiled floor, ornate columns and mouldings, and a glass-domed roof. **Australia on Collins**, a modern alternative next door, has set its sights firmly on the street's glitzy shopping crown; in the basement it boasts an upmarket food court and adjacent licensed restaurants and bars. Beyond this, on the corner of Collins and Swanston streets, Neoclassical Melbourne Town Hall faces boring **City Square**, which never achieved the intended purpose of providing Melbourne with a focal point – it's hoped that Federation Square, further south by the Yarra, will achieve this. There is, however, an unmissable landmark on the south side of the square: the splendid **St Paul's Cathedral**, built in the 1880s according to the Gothic-revival design of English architect William Butterfield, who never actually visited Australia. Across from the cathedral on Swanston Walk, *Young and Jackson's Hotel* is now protected by the National Trust, not for any intrinsic beauty but as a showcase for a work of art which has become a Melbourne icon: **Chloe**, a full-length nude now reclining upstairs in *Chloe's Bar and Bistro*. Exhibited by the French painter Jules Lefebvre at the Paris Salon of 1875, it was sent to an international exhibition in Melbourne in 1881 and has been here ever since.

Back on Collins Street, the pompous **Melbourne Athenaeum** next to the Town Hall is an important ingredient in the rising streetscape leading up past **Scots Church**, whose Gothic-revival design merits a peek, though it's famous mainly as the place where Dame Nellie Melba first sang in the choir. Further up, beyond expensive boutiques and even more expensive souvenir shops, **Collins Place** shopping centre and the towering **Sofitel Hotel** next door (still marked on some maps as the *Regent Hotel*) dominate the upper part of Collins Street, known as the "Paris end". The (male) toilet of *Le Restaurant* on the 35th floor of the *Sofitel* is known as the "loo with a view", but the **view** from the tables by the window isn't bad, either – though it doesn't come cheap (see "Eating and drinking", p.793). An **arts and crafts market** plies its wares in the atrium of Collins Place on Sunday between 9am and 5pm. Opposite, overshadowed by the *Sofitel* tower, stands one of the last bastions of Australian male chauvinism: the very staid, men-only Melbourne Club.

The Old Customs House: Immigration Museum and Hellenic Antiquities Museum

At the corner of Flinders and William Streets, just off the western stretch of Collins Street, the **Immigration Museum** (daily 10am–5pm; $7) is dedicated to one of the central themes of Australian history. Housed in the beautifully restored Old Customs House, it tells personal stories of immigration using voice, music, objects, moving images, light effects and interactive computers to build a very vivid picture; the experiences of being a migrant on a square-rigger in the 1840s, a passenger on a steamship at the turn of the century or a postwar refugee from Europe are all illustrated with touching effect. Each story is unique because of its personal, cultural, political and historical background, yet shared experiences and common emotions – grief and fear, loneliness and doubt, relief and hope – are evident. In the **Tribute Garden**, the outdoor centrepiece of the museum, a film of water flows over polished granite on which are engraved the names of migrants to Victoria, symbolizing the passage over the seas to reach these far-away shores. The names of all the Koorie people living in Victoria prior to white settlement are listed separately at the entrance to the garden.

The **Hellenic Antiquities Museum** on the second floor of the same building (same hours; admission fee depends on the exhibition; min $5) features travelling exhibitions of antique treasures loaned by the government of Greece, most of them rarely seen outside their homeland.

Bourke Street and Chinatown

Bourke Street Mall, lined with trees and seats but not quite traffic-free, is the most captivating part of Bourke Street, with the wonderful Victorian-era **General Post Office** set against department stores and crowded shops. Running off the mall, the lovely **Royal Arcade** is Melbourne's oldest (1839), paved with black and white marble and lit by huge fanlight windows. A clock on which two two-metre giants, Gog and Magog, strike the hours adds a welcome hint of the grotesque. As you climb the hill east of here, Bourke Street keeps up the interest, with several cafés and bars that put out pavement tables at night – including *Pellegrini's*, Melbourne's first espresso bar and still buzzing – as well as late-opening book and record stores.

North of Bourke Street, running parallel, is **Little Bourke Street**, with the majestic **Law Courts** by William Street at the western end, and **Chinatown** in the east between Exhibition and Swanston streets. Australia's oldest continuous Chinese settlement, Melbourne's Chinatown began with a few boarding-houses in the 1850s (when the goldrushes attracted Chinese people in droves, many from the Pearl River Delta near Hong Kong) and grew as the gold began to run out and Chinese fortune-seekers headed back to the city. Today the area still has a low-rise, narrow-laned, nineteenth-century character, and it's packed with Chinese restaurants and stores. The **Chinese Museum** in an old warehouse on Cohen Place (Sun–Fri 10am–4.30pm, Sat noon–4.30pm; $5), is concerned particularly with the Chinese role in the foundation and development of Melbourne. The museum organizes two-hour guided tours of the building and Chinatown ($15, or $30 including lunch). Tours require a minimum of four people, and bookings two or three days in advance are preferred (☎03/9662 2888).

State Library, National Gallery of Victoria and Melbourne Central

Still functioning, although it is undergoing renovation, the **State Library** (general opening Mon & Wed 10am–9pm, Tues & Thurs–Sun 10am–6pm; for newspaper reading room see "Listings" p.808) dates from 1856, and is the state's largest research and reference library accessible to the public. The Queen's Hall and its centrepiece, the domed reading room, are splendid examples of Victorian architecture. After refurbishment (to be completed by 2003) the venerable old building is going to house state-of-the-art storage facilities and information services. The **Museum of Victoria**, which for many years shared the block between Swanston and Russell streets with the library, closed in July 1997. It will reopen towards the end of 2001 as **Melbourne Museum** in a newly-constructed home near the Royal Exhibition Building in Carlton Gardens, a few blocks northeast (see opposite). In the meantime, some of the museum's collection can be seen at Scienceworks in Spotswood (see p.791). The old museum site, entered from Russell Street, is occupied by select exhibits from the **National Gallery of Victoria**, itself closed for renovation.

Opposite, **Melbourne Central** is an ultramodern shopping complex that has skilfully incorporated an old red-brick shot tower under its pointed glass dome. Among the shops here is the Daimaru department store, which offers a fascinating taste of things Japanese, not least in the food hall.

Old Melbourne Gaol

The **Old Melbourne Gaol** (daily 9.30am–4.30pm; $7), on Russell Street, a block north of the State Library, is probably the most worthwhile of all the downtown sights. Certainly it's the most popular, largely because Australian folk hero and bushranger **Ned Kelly** was hanged here in 1880 – his famous suit of armour, the site of his execution and his death mask are all on display (for more on Ned Kelly's exploits, see p.889). The "Melbourne Gaol Night Tour" (April–Oct Wed & Sun 7.30pm, Nov–March same days 8.30pm; $17; advance bookings required on ☎03/9663 7228) uses the spooky atmosphere of the prison to full effect.

The bluestone prison was built in stages from 1841 to 1864 – the goldrushes of the 1850s caused such a surge in lawlessness that it kept having to be expanded. A mix of condemned men, remand and short-sentence prisoners, women and "lunatics" (often, in fact, drunks) were housed here; long-term prisoners languished in hulks moored at Williamstown, or at the Pentridge Stockade. Much has been demolished since the jail was closed in 1923, but the entrance and boundary walls at least survive, and it's worth walking round the building to take a look at the formidable arched brick portal on Franklin Street.

The gruesome collection of **death masks** on show in the tiny cells bears witness to the nineteenth-century obsession with phrenology, the belief that people's characters could be read by examining the features of their heads. Inmates of prisons and mental asylums came under particular scrutiny: the shape of someone's brow, the length of their nose or even how their ear lobes joined their head could be deemed to indicate a predisposition to criminality or insanity. Accompanying the displayed heads are compelling, bloody case histories of the usually murderous crimes which the deceased's cranial bumps were supposed to have predetermined. Most fascinating are the women: **Martha Needle**, who poisoned with arsenic her husband and her daughters, among many others; and young **Martha Knorr**, the notorious "baby farmer" who advertised herself as a "kind motherly person, willing to adopt a child"; after receiving $2–5 per child, she killed and buried them in her backyard.

Queen Victoria Market and Carlton Gardens

Opened in the 1870s, **Queen Victoria Market** (Tues & Thurs 6am–2pm, Fri 6am–6pm, Sat 6am–3pm, Sun 9am–4pm) remains one of the best loved of Melbourne's institutions. Its collection of huge, decorative open-sided sheds and high-roofed halls is fronted along Victoria Street by restored shops, their original awnings held up with decorative iron posts. Although undeniably quaint and tourist-friendly, the market is a boisterous, down-to-earth affair where you can buy practically anything from new and secondhand clothes to fresh fish at bargain prices. Stallholders and shoppers seem just as diverse as the goods on offer: Vietnamese, Italian and Greek greengrocers pile their colourful produce high and vie for your attention, while the huge variety of deliciously smelly cheeses effortlessly draws customers to the old-fashioned deli hall. Saturday morning is the most chaotic and interesting time of all – a weekly social ritual as half of Melbourne turns out for some serious food shopping. On Sunday most of the food sections are closed, and the atmosphere is more recreational as people shop mainly for clothes and shoes. The guided Foodies Dream Tour takes in all the culinary delights of the market (10am each market day except Sun; $18 including food sampling), while the Heritage Market Tour acquaints visitors with its history (10.30am each market day except Sun; $12 including brunch); for tours for both, call ☎03/9320 5835.

At the CBD's northeast corner is **Carlton Gardens**, the most pleasant escape, especially by the fountain at the Royal Exhibition Building. Built for the International Exhibition of 1880, the buildings originally covered the whole of the park. Only the magnificent Neoclassical Main Hall remains, dwarfed by the soon-to-be completed **Melbourne Museum** and the new **IMAX Melbourne**, which boasts the world's biggest movie screen. Up to four different IMAX films are projected each day; for some you need to don special liquid crystal glasses for 3D action (daily showings on the hour between 9am and 11pm, extra screenings Fri & Sat at midnight and 1am; ☎03/9663 5454; $14, 3D-films $15.).

Eastern Hill and the MCG

The **Eastern Hill** area beyond Spring Street has many fine public buildings, centred around **Parliament House**. Erected in stages between 1856 and 1930, the parliament buildings (40min guided tours on non-sitting days Mon–Fri 10am, 11am, 2pm, 3pm & 3.45pm; free) have a theatrical presence, with a facade of giant Doric columns rising from a high flight of steps, and landscaped gardens either side. Just below, the Old Treasury Building from 1857 and adjacent State Government office, facing the beautiful Treasury Gardens, are equally imposing. In the old gold vaults deep in the basement of the **Old Treasury Building** (Mon–Fri 9am–5pm, Sat, Sun & public holidays 10am–4pm; $5) an audio-visual presentation, *Built on Gold*, illustrates the impact of the Victorian goldrushes on the fledgling colony. A permanent exhibition on the social and architectural history of Melbourne shares the ground floor with temporary shows.

To the east, the broad acres of **Fitzroy Gardens** run a close second to Carlton Gardens as a getaway from the CBD. Originally laid out in the shape of the Union Jack flag, the park's paths still just about conform to the original pattern, but, in between, the formal style has been fetchingly abandoned. The flowers, statuary and fountains are best appreciated on weekdays, as at the weekend you'll spend most of your time dodging the video cameras of wedding parties. The gardens' much-touted main attraction is really only for kitsch nostalgists: **Captain Cook's Cottage** (daily: winter 9am–5pm; summer 9am–5.30pm; $3) was the home of Captain James Cook, the English navigator who explored the southern hemisphere in three great voyages and first "discovered" the east coast of Australia. The building was purchased in 1933, shipped over from Yorkshire piece by piece and presented as a gift to the state of Victoria for its 1934 centenary. The red-brick and ivy-covered cottage attempts to re-create the atmosphere of eighteenth-century England, reinforced by displays about the ill-fated discoverer himself. Elsewhere in the gardens, a tacky model Tudor village continues the "olde worlde" theme, but you'll probably find the **Conservatory**'s flower displays (daily 9am–5pm; free) more interesting, and you can refresh yourself at the *Pavilion Café*. Opposite Cook's Cottage, Sinclair's Gallery sells beautiful jewellery and other arts and crafts items.

The MCG

Yarra Park, home of the hallowed **Melbourne Cricket Ground**, lies across Wellington Parade from the southeastern corner of Fitzroy Gardens – also easily reached by tram along Wellington Parade or train to Jolimont Station. Home to the Melbourne Cricket Club since 1853, the MCG is now a vast and ugly stadium, as only the historic members' stand survived the complete reconstruction that made the ground the centrepiece for the 1956 Olympic Games. As well as hosting state and international cricket matches and some of the top Aussie Rules football games, the MCG contains the **Australian Gallery of Sport**, the **Olympic Museum** and the **Cricket Hall of Fame** (daily 10am–4pm; $10). One-hour tours of the ground itself (hourly between 10am–3pm; no tours on event days) are included in the admission fee; the highlight is the members' pavilion – home of the most traditional and elitist club in Australia – packed with fascinating cricketing memorabilia. The Gallery of Sport covers all other games from cycling to tennis to footy – complete with an entertaining machine that plays the various footy club songs. The Olympic Museum covers all the twentieth-century Olympiads but concentrates on Melbourne 1956, generally regarded as a hugely successful event that brought the city to the attention of the world.

The Yarra River and the south bank

The muddy **Yarra River** is an essential part of Melbourne; it was traditionally home to the docks and is now the focus of lots of leisure activities. In the early days, tidal movements of up to two metres meant frequent flooding, a problem only partly solved by artificially straightening the river and building up its banks – but with the incidental benefit of reserving tracts of low-lying land as recreational space, now pleasingly crisscrossed by paths and cycle tracks.

Four **bridges** cross the river from the CBD: Spencer Street Bridge at the end of Spencer Street; Kings Bridge on King Street; Queens Bridge, not quite at the end of Queen Street; and Princes Bridge, which carries Swanston Street across. There's also a pedestrian bridge from the bank below Flinders Street Station to the Southgate Centre. The best way to see the Yarra is on a **cruise** – see box opposite.

On the south side of Princes Bridge you can rent **bikes** to explore the salubrious left bank; on fine weekends especially, the Yarra comes to life, with people messing about in boats, cycling and strolling, and family groups gathered for barbecues. **Southgate**, immediately west of Princes Bridge, is a highly successful development: once dingy and industrial, it's now a classy shopping complex with lots of smart cafés, restaurants, bars and a huge food court with very popular outdoor tables; at lunchtime and weekends it's very hard to find a table even indoors.

The Crown Casino and docklands

West of Southgate, in an entire block between Queens Bridge and Spencer Street Bridge, the fortress-like **Crown Casino**, a controversial development, towers gloomily over the Yarra, blocking out all views of the city skyline from the south. The equally

RIVER CRUISES ON THE YARRA

The main central departure points for cruises along the Yarra are Princes Walk and Southgate in the city, and Williamstown at the mouth of the Yarra further west (see p.791). You can choose between short trips and longer journeys towards the sea and the bird colonies at Port Phillip Bay and Herring Island.

Melbourne River Cruises (bookings ☎03/9629 7233; $14, or combined up- and down-river cruise $28) make half-hourly departures from Princes Walk below the northern end of Princes Bridge. Their Scenic River Garden Cruise (1hr 15min) will take you upriver past affluent South Yarra and industrial Richmond to Herring Island; the Port and Docklands Cruise (also 1hr 15min) runs downriver past the towering Crown Casino complex and the Exhibition Centre – and then past shipping channels and docks to the Westgate bridge.

Penguin Waters Cruises (bookings ☎03/9645 0533 or mobile ☎0412/311 922) offer a day-cruise (depart 1pm; 1hr 30min; $20) and an evening cruise (departure depending on season; 2hr; $40) from Southgate to Port Phillip Bay. Both include a barbecue. The sunset cruise takes passengers to a colony of **Little penguins** on a "secret site" – the skipper is the only person with an NRE permit to take people there. There are also cruises from St Kilda Pier (see p.790).

Williamstown Bay and River Cruises (for recorded information call ☎03/9506 4144; for bookings ☎03/9397 2255; $10, or $18 return) ply the lower section of the Yarra between Williamstown and Southgate in the west of the city, passing the Crown Casino, the Exhibition Centre and the docks. There are daily departures throughout the summer at 11am, 1pm, 3pm & 5pm, returning from Williamstown at noon, 2pm, 4pm & 6pm. Their cruises are pleasantly uncommercial, with no commentary or pressure to buy anything.

new **Exhibition Centre** next door is basically just an extremely long shed, which has only two features of architectural merit: the glass facade facing the river, and the eastern entrance resembling a raised drawbridge with two bright yellow, pencil-thin pylons holding up the roof. The excellent **Polly Woodside Maritime Museum** (daily 10am–4pm; $7) is tucked into a small old dock next to the Exhibition Centre. The focus is the *Polly Woodside* itself, a small, barque-rigged sailing ship, built in Belfast in 1885 for the South American coal trade and retired only in 1968, when it was the last deepwater sailing vessel in Australia still afloat.

The squat building facing the Exhibition Centre and the museum across the Yarra is the **World Trade Centre**. Next to it, facing the Crown Casino, is **Melbourne Aquarium**, a new attraction scheduled to open its doors in December 1999. With a budget of $33-million, this ambitious project will harbour thousands of creatures from the Southern Ocean. Part of it will be taken up by the Oceanarium tank, which rests seven metres below the river's surface, holds over two million litres of water, and contains 3200 animals from 150 species, a sting ray-filled beach with a wave machine and a fish bowl turned inside out where visitors stand in a glass room surrounded by shark-filled water. The curved, four-storey building will also comprise lecture halls, an amphitheatre, cafés and a restaurant. For admission fees and opening times, call ☎03/9620 0999.

Further downstream is the old dock area, an urban wasteland of warehouses, sheds, empty open spaces and old docks that's now the site of grand-scale commercial, residential and leisure development. Of all the new developments, the **docklands project** is going to have the biggest impact on the look and feel of Melbourne: in ten to fifteen years an entire new city will stand by the waterfront.

Federation Square and the sports grounds

Just across the river from Southgate opposite Flinders Street Station, **Federation Square** – at the time of writing still an ugly building site – is intended to form a link between the CBD and the river, completing the city's shift of focus. The Square will cover an entire block, comprising Civic Plaza, an open auditorium, a new Visitor's Centre, a Cinemedia Centre and **The Atrium**, a covered, 120-metre-long area reaching from Flinders Street almost all the way to the banks of the Yarra. **Civic Plaza** will be partly open towards the river, and partly flanked by a structure designed to accommodate cafés, restaurants and shops. Alongside Federation Square the new **Museum of Australian Art** (MAA) will house works by indigenous and non-indigenous Australian artists from the National Gallery of Victoria collection.

The parklands east of Federation Square are being redeveloped and extended to form **Riverside Park**, a green link between Federation Square and the Tennis Centre at **Melbourne Park** which hosts international tennis tournaments such as the Australian Open (January), as well as big-name rock concerts and other performances. Bordered by Swan Street and the river is the "Glasshouse" or **Indoor Sports and Entertainment Centre**, home of the Melbourne Giants basketball team.

Victorian Arts Centre

The **Victorian Arts Centre**, just off St Kilda Road, comprises the National Gallery of Victoria, the Melbourne Concert Hall and the Theatres Building, topped by a hideous spire. The "Arts Tower", as it's sometimes called, is meant to represent the pinnacle of the arts in Melbourne, its curved surfaces supposedly evoking the flowing folds of a ballerina's skirt. Germaine Greer's attempt at explanation was that "stunned by the bad taste of the Sydney Opera House, the Melburnians have clearly decided to fight fire with fire . . . "

There are guided **tours** (Mon–Fri noon & 2.30pm, Sat 10.30am & noon, $9; backstage tour Sun 12.15pm, $12) of the Concert Hall and Theatres Building, which are worth joining mainly to see the collection of art in the various foyers. The highlight of the Arts Centre if you're not seeing a performance, however, is the fun and accessible **Performing Arts Museum** (daily 11am–11pm; free) on the ground level of the Theatres Building, which covers everything from opera to TV and rock 'n' roll and has wonderful temporary exhibitions, normally on aspects of popular culture. Adjacent to the museum, the small George Adams Gallery (formerly Westpac Gallery) shows temporary exhibitions (same hours; free).

The **National Gallery of Victoria** has always been a more serious contender, with the best collection of Australian art in the country: seventy thousand works, rotated regularly, form its permanent collection. The gallery will be closed for major refurbishment until late 2001, when it will reopen with exhibits from its international collection; the works of Australian artists will be housed in the new **Museum of Australian Art** on Federation Square (see above). Until then, a small part of the exceptional collection can be seen at the old Museum of Victoria site (see p.780).

The **Australian Centre for Contemporary Art** (Tues–Fri 11am–5pm, Sat & Sun noon–5pm; free), at the time of writing on Dallas Brooks Drive, has consistently challenging exhibitions of contemporary international and Australian art, as well as forums, lectures and performances. Early in 2000 the gallery will relocate to its new home in **Malthouse Plaza**, a development next to the CUB Malthouse Theatre complex in Sturt Street further south.

On Sunday between 10am and 5.30pm the stalls of a good **arts and crafts market** line the pavement outside the Arts Centre, extending onto the footpath under the Princes Bridge.

Kings Domain

Across St Kilda Road from the National Gallery of Victoria, the **Kings Domain** is a grassy open park encompassing the **Sidney Myer Music Bowl**, which serves as the outdoor music arena for the Victorian Arts Centre. South of the Bowl, and behind imposing iron gates with stone pillars and a British coat of arms, you glimpse the flag flying over **Government House**, the ivory mansion of the Governor of Victoria, set in extensive grounds. The National Trust run **guided tours** (Mon, Wed & Sat, times appointed by booking; ☎03/9654 4711; closed Dec 16–Jan 25; $8), whose highlight is the state ballroom. This occupies the entire south wing and includes a velvet-hung canopied throne, brocade-covered benches, gilded chairs, ornate plasterwork and three huge crystal chandeliers.

Just south of the Government House grounds, **Latrobe's Cottage** (Mon–Thurs, Sat & Sun 11am–4pm; $2) has been re-erected as a memorial to Lieutenant-Governor Latrobe, who lived in this tiny house throughout his term of office (1839–54). The whole thing was sent over from England in prefabricated form, and as the first governor's residence makes a telling contrast to the later one. Inside are interesting historical displays on Latrobe and the early days of the colony.

The **Shrine of Remembrance**, in formal grounds in the southwestern corner of the Domain, is aligned with St Kilda Road – which describes a gentle arc around it – so that its forbidding mass looms ahead as you enter or leave the city. It's a rather Orwellian monument, apparently half Roman temple, half Aztec pyramid, given further chill when a mechanical-sounding voice booms out and calls you in to see the symbolic light inside. The shrine is designed so that at 11am on Remembrance Day (Nov 11) a ray of sunlight strikes the memorial stone inside – an effect that's simulated every half-hour.

Royal Botanic Gardens

The **Royal Botanic Gardens** (daily: April–Oct 7.30am–5.30pm; Nov–March 7.30am–8.30pm) contain more than ten thousand different plant species and varieties in an extensive landscaped setting. Melbourne's much-maligned climate is perfect for horticulture: cool enough for temperate trees and flowers to flourish, warm enough for palms and other subtropical species, and wet enough for anything else. The **Visitors Centre** (daily 10am–5pm; free guided walks Tues–Fri 10am & 2pm, Sun 2pm) on Dallas Brooks Drive is the best place to start your wanderings, with its displays, maps and brochures.

Highlights include the **herb garden**, comprising part of the medicinal garden established in 1880; the **fern gully**, a lovely walk through shady ferns, with cooling mists of water on a hot summer's day; and the large ornamental **lake** full of ducks and black swans. The *Snack Bar & Tea Rooms* (Mon–Sat 9.30am–5.30pm, Sun 10am–5pm) by the lake serves refreshments and Devonshire teas. On summer evenings, bucolic plays such as *The Wind in the Willows* or *A Midsummer Night's Dream* are often performed in the gardens, and film classics are projected onto a big outdoor screen at the **Moonlight Cinema**. Don't forget to take a cardigan, a rug and, most importantly, insect repellent (see p.805 for booking information). Guided walks through the gardens start at the Visitors Centre (Sun–Fri at 11am and 2pm; bookings ☎03/9252 2300; $4). There are also guided tours to the reopened Melbourne Observatory (originally built 1861–63) next door. The observatory performed a wide range of important functions for the fledgling colony of Victoria, providing scientific data essential for the running of businesses from shipping to farming (Night Sky Tours include viewing through the telescopes; every Tues 7.30–9.30pm. Bookings essential; ☎03/9525 2300).

Melbourne suburbs

Far more than in the city centre, in Melbourne's **inner suburbs** you'll get a feel for what life here is really all about. Many have quite distinct characters, whether as ethnic enclaves or self-styled artists' communities. What's more, they're all easily reached on a pleasurable tram ride. Day-trips to places further afield around Melbourne are detailed on p.810.

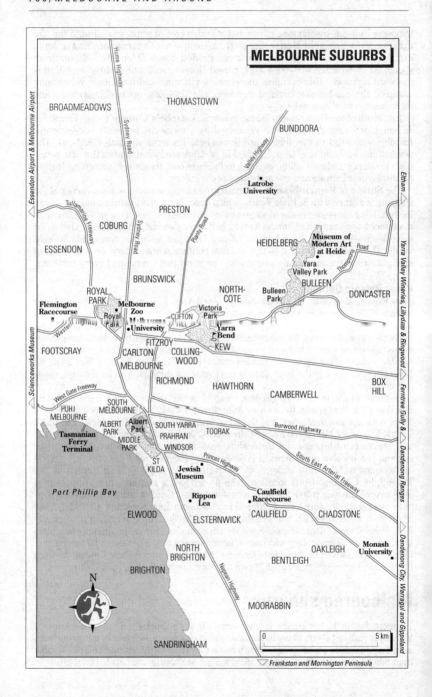

MELBOURNE SUBURBS

BROADMEADOWS

THOMASTOWN

BUNDOORA

Essendon Airport & Melbourne Airport

Eltham

Hume Highway

Sydney Road

Valley Highway

Latrobe University

Tullamarine Freeway

Plenty Road

PRESTON

COBURG

Sydney Road

HEIDELBERG

Museum of Modern Art at Heide

Thompsons Road

ESSENDON

Yarra Valley Wineries, Lilydale & Ringwood

BRUNSWICK

Yara Valley Park

BULLEEN

DONCASTER

ROYAL PARK

NORTH-COTE

Bulleen Park

Ferntree Gully & Dandenong Ranges

Flemington Racecourse

Melbourne Zoo

Royal Park

Victoria Park

Scienceworks Museum

Western Highway

University

CLIFTON HILL

Yarra Bend

FITZROY

KEW

FOOTSCRAY

CARLTON

COLLING-WOOD

MELBOURNE

Dandenong City, Warragul and Gippsland

RICHMOND

HAWTHORN

CAMBERWELL

BOX HILL

West Gate Freeway

SOUTH MELBOURNE

PORT MELBOURNE

ALBERT PARK

Albert Park

SOUTH YARRA

TOORAK

Burwood Highway

Tasmanian Ferry Terminal

MIDDLE PARK

PRAHRAN

WINDSOR

South East Arterial Freeway

ST KILDA

Jewish Museum

Princes Highway

Port Phillip Bay

Rippon Lea

Caulfield Racecourse

ELWOOD

ELSTERNWICK

CAULFIELD

CHADSTONE

NORTH BRIGHTON

OAKLEIGH

Monash University

BRIGHTON

BENTLEIGH

N

MOORABBIN

0   5 km

SANDRINGHAM

Frankston and Mornington Peninsula

Café society finds its home to the north among the alternative galleries and second-hand shops of **Fitzroy**, and to the south in **St Kilda**, which has a trendy but raucous nightlife, and the added advantage of the beach. On Lygon Street in **Carlton**, which fuelled the Beat Generation with espresso, there are now as many boutiques as bookshops and art centres. Grungy **Richmond**, to the east, can claim both Vietnamese and Greek enclaves, and a diverse music scene in its many pubs, while across the river is the place to shop until you drop: wealthy **South Yarra**, flanked by self-consciously groovy **Prahran** and snobby **Toorak**.

Browsing through markets and shops, cruising across Hobsons Bay, sampling the world's foods and, of course, sipping espresso are the primary attractions of the suburbs, but if you want to firm up your itinerary with something more concrete, make for the **Metro! Craft Centre**, just outside the city centre in North Melbourne, the well-designed **Zoo** in Carlton, or **Scienceworks**, a hugely enjoyable interactive museum in Spotswood. Also of interest is the **Museum of Modern Art at Heide** in Bulleen and, a bit further along in the same direction, Eltham with its artists' colony of **Montsalvat**.

North Melbourne

The suburb of **North Melbourne**, beyond Queen Victoria Market, is barely out of the centre at all, but it's already distinctly different, with two-storey **terraced houses** embellished with iron-lace balconies and awnings (especially on Errol, King, Chetwynd and William streets), and many unpretentious Italian cafés along Victoria Street. Head up Capel Street to Courtney Street (or take tram #55 or #68 from the city centre) and you'll find the **Metro! Craft Centre** (formerly Meat Market Craft Centre; daily 10am–5pm) in the second block along. Inside the converted nineteenth-century brick market you can watch craftspeople at work and buy their products. The centre also boasts a café, and a notice board that's a good source of information on craft workshops and contacts.

Carlton

Carlton is not much further from the city than North Melbourne (tram #21 or #15 from Swanston Street), but it feels yet more separate, possibly because its character is reinforced by the presence of Melbourne University and a long-established Italian café scene. **Lygon Street** is the centre of the action, and it was here, in the 1950s, that espresso bars were really introduced to Melbourne; exotic spots such as the *Caffe Sport*, *La Gina*, *University Caffe*, *Don Basilio*, *La Cacciatora* and *Toto's* (which claims to have introduced pizza to Australia) had an unconventional allure in staid Anglo-Melbourne, and the local intelligentsia soon made the street their second home. Victorian terraced houses provided cheap living, and this became the first of the city's "alternative" suburbs. These days Carlton is no longer particularly bohemian; its residents are older and wealthier, and Lygon Street has gone very definitely upmarket, though the smart fashion shops still jostle with arts centres, bookshops, and excellent ethnic restaurants and cafés.

Lygon Street itself is the obvious place to explore, but the elegant architecture also spreads eastwards to Drummond Street, and, flanking Carlton Gardens, Rathdowne and Nicholson streets. In the grounds of **Melbourne University** you'll find cheap food and useful notice boards (for accommodation and things for sale) in the Union Building. Running along the western side of the university, Royal Parade gives onto **Royal Park**, with its memorial to the explorers Burke and Wills (see box, p.486), and from there it's a short walk through the park to the Zoo.

Melbourne Zoo

When it opened in 1862, **Melbourne Zoo** (daily 9am–5pm; also Jan–early March Thurs–Sun until 9pm for Twilight Concerts at the Zoo; $15; Mon–Sat tram #55 from William Street, Sun #68 from Elizabeth Street) was the first in Australia. Some of its original features are still in evidence, including Australian and foreign trees, landscaped gardens, and a few restored Victorian-era cages, but almost all the animals have been rehoused in better, more natural conditions. The Australian area contains a central lake with waterbirds, open enclosures for koalas and other animals, and a bushland setting where you can walk among emus, kangaroos and wallabies. Strolling along the boardwalks of the **Great Flight Aviary** (daily 10.30am–4.30 pm) you'll come across areas of rainforest, wetland, and a scrub area with a huge gum tree where many birds nest. The dark **Platypus Habitat** (daily 9.30am–4pm) is also worth a look, since the mammals are notoriously difficult to see in the wild – even here there's no guarantee you'll be lucky. Highly enjoyable, too, is the **Butterfly House** (daily 9.30am–4.30pm), a steamy tropical hothouse with hundreds of colourful Australian butterflies flitting about.

Fitzroy and Collingwood

In the 1970s, **Fitzroy** took over from Carlton as the centre for artistic nonconformity; its focus is **Brunswick Street** (take tram #11 from Collins St), especially between Gertrude Street, home to Turkish takeaways, and Johnston Street, with its lively Spanish bars and restaurants. Every year at the beginning of October, the colourful Fringe Parade and a street party on Brunswick Street usher in the **Fringe Festival**, the alternative scene's answer to the highbrow Melbourne Festival. The **International Comedy Festival** (April) and the **Next Wave Festival** (May, even-numbered years), two other notable arts events, also take place mainly in Fitzroy. In the shadow of Housing Commission tower blocks, welfare agencies and charity shops rub shoulders with funky secondhand clothes and junk shops, ethnic supermarkets and restaurants, cafés full of students and equally grungy artists, writers and musicians, and thriving bookshops that stay open late and are often as crowded as the many bars and music pubs. Most of the rough old hotels have been done up to match the prevailing mood: the *Provincial* is a good example, with its distressed paint-job and deli/café/bar inside.

Fitzroy's fringe art leanings are reflected in wacky "street installations" such as mosaic chairs, and sculptures like "Mr Poetry". The eye-catching wrought-iron gate at the entrance to the Fitzroy Nursery at 390 Brunswick St, with its fairy-tale motif, sets the theme for the Artists Garden above the nursery, which exhibits sculptures and other decorative items for garden use. **Small galleries** worth looking out for are Roar Studios on 115A Brunswick St; the Print Guild at 227 Brunswick St (Mon–Fri 9.30am–5.30pm, Sat 10am–5pm, Sun 1.30–5.30pm), which sells limited-edition prints, etchings, lithographs, wood and linocuts by Australian and international artists; and the Centre for Contemporary Photography, 205 Johnston St (Wed–Fri 11am–5pm, Sat 2–5pm). Fitzroy also boasts its own **arts and crafts market** (third Sun of the month 10am–3.30pm) at the old Fitzroy Town Hall on the corner of Napier and Moor streets. The **Fitzroy Pool**, in the north of the suburb on the corner of Young and Cecil streets, is a summer meeting place where people occasionally swim between posing sessions.

While not as trendy as Brunswick Street, formerly shabby **Smith Street** (tram #86 from Bourke St), which forms the boundary between Fitzroy and **Collingwood** to the east, is catching up. You'll still find many charity shops, ethnic butchers and cheap supermarkets, but New Age bookshops, quirky little cafés and revamped pubs are edging in. Collingwood and the adjacent suburb of Abbotsford have a large **gay** population, with a clutch of gay bars and clubs, particularly on Peel and Glasshouse streets.

Around Prahran

Prahran Council, covering South Yarra, Prahran and, to the east, Toorak and Armadale, oversees an extensive area of **shopping**, both downbeat and upmarket. Chapel Street is the main drag: in South Yarra it extends for a Golden Mile of trendy shopping and *very* chic cafés; heading south beyond Commercial Road through Prahran and Windsor it gradually moves downmarket, until Dandenong Road and the Astor Cinema mark the start of St Kilda. Crossing Chapel Street at right angles in South Yarra, Toorak Road boasts equally ritzy designer boutiques and, if that's possible, becomes even more exclusive east of Grange Road, as it enters Toorak, a suburb synonymous with wealth in Melbourne. Below Toorak, High Street Armadale, between Kooyong and Glenferrie roads, holds a concentration of antique shops. **Trams** #6 and #72 from Swanston Street will get you from the city centre to Chapel Street.

South Yarra and Toorak

Among the boutiques and speciality shops, bistro bars for the beautiful people and drop-dead-cool nightclubs, the **Jam Factory** shopping complex, named after its former incarnation, is worth making a beeline for on the **South Yarra** stretch of Chapel Street. **Como House**, overlooking the river from Como Avenue in South Yarra (daily 10am–5pm; $8), is a good example of the town houses built by wealthy nineteenth-century landowners. The elegant white mansion, a mixture of Regency and Italianate architectural styles, has been restored by the National Trust. To reach the house, walk east along Toorak Road from Chapel Street, and then north on Williams Road, or, from the city centre, take tram #8 from Swanston Street.

Toorak has never been short of a bean: when Melbourne was founded, the wealthy chose to build their stately homes here on the high bank of the Yarra, leaving the flood-prone lower ground for the poor. This old money has in recent years been joined by new; many European Jews who worked hard after arriving penniless in Australia celebrated their new wealth by moving to Toorak in the 1950s and 1960s. There's little to see or do in the suburb: the hilly, tree-lined streets are full of huge mansions in extensive private gardens, while so-called Toorak Village is stuffed with wickedly expensive designer boutiques.

Prahran

Beyond Commercial Road in **Prahran** proper, Chapel Street still focuses on fashion, but in a more street-smart vein, becoming progressively more downmarket; as Chapel Street crosses High Street the suburb changes to Windsor and becomes more interestingly ethnic. Landmarks include **Prahran Market** (Tues, Thurs & Sat dawn–5pm, Fri until 6pm), round the corner on Commercial Road, an excellent, though fairly expensive, food emporium (fish, meat, fruit, vegetables and delicatessen). **Chapel Street Bazaar**, back on the main drag, has good secondhand clothes, Art Deco jewellery, furniture and bric-a-brac. **Greville Street**, off Chapel Street in the heart of Prahran, is a former hippie hangout turned respectable, with antique shops, antiquarian and specialist bookshops, record shops, and wall-to-wall retro or designer clothes shops – very young and full of itself. On Saturday and Sunday, the small **Greville Street Market** hawks arts and crafts, secondhand clothes and jewellery on the corner of Gratton Street in Gratton Park (noon–5pm).

South Melbourne and Albert Park

If it's the bay you're heading for, then St Kilda is the obvious destination; the quickest and most interesting way there is on the #96 tram from Bourke or Spencer streets, which runs on a light rail track via South Melbourne and Albert Park, past the new Aquatic Centre with its five swimming pools (see "Listings", p.809). Both suburbs are worth checking out in their own right if you have the time. **South Melbourne**'s focus is the **South Melbourne Market** on Coventry Street (Wed 6am–2pm, Fri 6am–6pm, Sat 6am–2pm, Sun 8am–4pm), an old-fashioned value-for-money place with new and secondhand clothes and books, as well as fruit and veg, and delicatessen stalls. Pleasant cafés line Coventry Street opposite the market, while not far away on Clarendon Street a few ancient shops survive virtually unaltered, complete with corrugated-iron awnings and iron-lace pillars.

Albert Park has the feel of a small village, with many lovely old terraced houses and Dundas Place, a shopping centre of mouthwatering delis and bakeries. In the shadow of the St Kilda Road office buildings lies Albert Park itself, the highly controversial site for the **Australian Grand Prix** at the beginning of March, which Melbourne snatched from Adelaide in 1996.

St Kilda and around

The former seaside resort of **St Kilda** has an air of shabby gentility, which enhances its current schizophrenic reputation as a sophisticated yet seedy suburb, largely residential but blessed with a raging nightlife. Running from St Kilda Road down to the Esplanade, **Fitzroy Street** is Melbourne's red-light district – usually pretty tame, though late at night not a comfortable place for women alone – and epitomizes this split personality: it's lined with dozens of thoroughly pretentious cafés and bars from which to gawp at the strip's goings-on. On weekend nights these and others throughout St Kilda are filled to overflowing with a style-conscious but fun crowd. During the day there's a very different feel, especially on **Acland Street** with its wonderful continental cake shops and bakeries. Ogling the mouthwatering window displays is a favourite way of passing the time on Sunday.

Also on Sunday, the **St Kilda Craft Market** (10am–5pm, in winter until about 4pm) lines the waterfront on Upper Esplanade. It's mainly arts and crafts, and not really good enough to justify the hordes of strollers, but going there is part of the ritual that includes taking a look at the beach, feeding your face, ambling into a few shops, listening to a busker, and perhaps calling at the covered market on Albert Street. **Luna Park** on the Esplanade is a well-loved landmark, a tacky, old-fashioned fairground entered through a huge laughing clown's face. Wandering around is free, but you pay $3 for individual rides. You can sit under the palm trees of **O'Donnell Gardens** next door, or nearby **St Kilda Botanical Gardens**, and eat your Acland Street goodies. The **beachfront** is a popular weekend promenade all year round, with separate cycling and walking paths stretching down to Elwood and Brighton, and a long pier thrusting out into the bay.

On Saturday, Sunday and public holidays, **boat trips** from the pier across Hobsons Bay to Williamstown (Williamstown Bay and River Cruises; departures hourly between 11.30am and 3.30pm – last departure one-way only; 20min; $7, $11 return; ☎03/9397 2255) are rewarded with lovely views of St Kilda and the city. An alternative is a cruise with Penguin Waters Cruises (day-cruise 1hr 30mins, $20; sunrise and sunset cruise 1hr 30mins, $30; both include a barbecue lunch or dinner. Bookings ☎03/9645 0533 or mobile phone ☎0412/311 922). On the evening cruises – with a little luck – you'll catch a glimpse of **Little penguins** coming ashore at a certain spot 4km from the mouth of the Yarra. As the exact location is not publicized, you can see them without the crowds that congregate on Phillip Island (see p.815).

If you want to get a bit more serious, call in at one of the two bookshops on Acland Street, or check out the local arty community at the Linden Gallery (Tues–Sun 1–6pm, in winter noon–5pm), based in a fine Victorian-era mansion at 26 Acland St, where painting, installations and video art are displayed.

Elwood and Elsternwick

The next stop south along the bay, **Elwood**, is a quieter version of St Kilda, still with a faintly alternative air. Ormond Road's original shopfronts conceal a health-food store, an alternative-therapies centre and a couple of cheap vegetarian takeaways, but more yuppified cafés are slowly edging in. Ormond Esplanade runs past parkland through which occasional paths run down to the beach.

East of Elwood, **Elsternwick** (train to Ripponlea) is a largely Orthodox Jewish area. The original 1918 fittings and facade of Brinsmead Chemist at 73 Glen Eira Rd are protected by the National Trust, as is **Ripponlea House** at 192 Hotham St (Tues–Sun 10am–5pm; $9), which shows how Melbourne's wealthy elite lived a century ago. The 33-room mansion has magnificent gardens, complete with ornamental lake and fernery, and a way-over-the-top interior. The grounds are popular for picnics at weekends, when the tearoom is also open (11am–4pm). Ten to fifteen minutes' walk away in East St Kilda, opposite the St Kilda Synagogue, is the **Jewish Museum of Australia** (Tues–Thurs 10am–4pm, Sun 11am–5pm; $5; tram #3 or #67 to stop 32 from Swanston Street in the city or from St Kilda Road). It has four permanent exhibitions: the Australian Jewish History Gallery, documenting Jewish life in Australia since the beginning of colonization 200 years ago; the Timeline of Jewish History, tracing the last four thousand years; and Jewish Year and Belief and Ritual, both dedicated to the religious and ethical foundations of Judaism, with a focus on festivals and customs. Changing exhibitions on a wide range of related topics are another feature of the museum.

Spotswood and Williamstown

Docks and industry dominate the area west of the city centre, reached by suburban train, by the ferry *Williamstown Seeker* from the Southbank jetty at the Melbourne Exhibition Centre (departures 11.10am, 1.10pm and 3.10pm), or by heading out on the Westgate Freeway across the huge Westgate Bridge. A good reason for visiting **Spotswood**, the first suburb across the Yarra, is **Scienceworks**, at 2 Booker St (daily 10am–4.30pm; $9). Inside the Space Age building, set in appropriately desolate wasteland, the displays are ingenious, fun and highly interactive. Part of the exhibition consists of the original Spotswood Pumping Station, an unusually aesthetic early industrial complex with working steam pumps. Also here are some displays from the Museum of Victoria in Melbourne, awaiting their new home in Carlton Gardens in 2001. The new **Planetarium,** open as part of Scienceworks in 1999, features state-of-the-art digital technology to take visitors on a (virtual) journey through the galaxy (hourly shows daily 10am–3pm and on one night a week; ☎03/9292 4800).

On a promontory at the mouth of the Yarra, **Williamstown** is a strange mix of very rich and very poor, of industry, yachting marinas and working port. Expensive cafés ring Nelson Place, but the down-to-earth *Yacht Club Hotel* here offers the cheapest meal in town – prices have been fixed since the 1970s and it's always packed on Sunday, especially when the **Williamstown Market** is held along the waterfront (third Sunday of each month). The most enjoyable way to get to Williamstown is by **boat** from St Kilda (see opposite), or you can take a trip into the city with Williamstown Bay and River Cruises ($10); for more see box on p.783.

Bulleen and Eltham

Further afield in the northeastern suburbs two attractions – the Museum of Modern Art at Heide in Bulleen and Montsalvat in Eltham – are well worth the trek, or make a day-trip of it and visit them en route to the Yarra Valley wineries and the Healesville Sanctuary (see p.818-821).

The **Museum of Modern Art at Heide**, on Templestowe Road at Bulleen, was the home of Melbourne art patrons **John and Sunday Reed**, who in the mid-1930s purchased what was then a derelict dairy farm on the banks of the meandering Yarra River. During the following decades the Reeds fostered and nurtured the talents of young unknown artists and thus played a central role in the emergence of Australian art movements such as the Angry Penguins, the Antipodeans and the Annandale Realists. The painters Sidney Nolan, John Perceval, Albert Tucker and Arthur Boyd were all members of the artistic circle at Heide at one time or another. The government of Victoria purchased the property shortly before the Reeds' deaths in 1981, and their former home, itself an attractive specimen of the modernist architecture of the 1960s, is now a gallery housing consistently interesting, changing exhibitions of contemporary Australian art (Tues–Fri 10am–5pm, Sat, Sun & public holidays noon–5pm; $6). There's also a good café, and you can ramble through the extensive **gardens**, which feature sculptures and a kitchen garden (no admission fee). The museum is about 14km from the city centre, but only fifteen minutes' drive via the northeastern freeway. National Bus #200 runs approximately every thirty minutes from outside Melbourne Central Shopping Centre on Lonsdale Street (for timetable information call ☎03/9481 8333), or you could take the suburban train to Heidelberg Station (Eltham line) and from there bus #291 to Templestowe Road (frequent services).

Eltham, a bushy suburb further northeast, about 24km from the city, is known as a centre for arts and crafts. Its reputation was established in 1935 when the charismatic painter and architect **Justus Jorgensen** moved to what was then a separate town and founded **Montsalvat**, a European-style artists' colony. Built with the help of his students and followers, the colony's eclectic design was inspired by medieval European buildings with wonderful quirky results; Jorgensen died before it was completed and it has deliberately been left unfinished. He did, however, live long enough to see his community thrive, and to oversee the completion of the mud-brick Great Hall, whose influence is evident in other mud-brick buildings around Eltham. Today Montsalvat, a two-kilometre walk from Eltham Station, is still operating as a colony of painters, potters and craftspeople, and can be visited daily (9am–5pm; $5).

Eating and drinking

Melbourne is Australia's premier city for **eating out**. Sydney may be more stylish and Adelaide cheaper, but Melbourne has the best food and the widest choice of it, almost all exceptionally good value. In March each year, the city celebrates its pre-eminence with a **Food and Wine Festival**, in which the distinct ethnic areas host culinary street parties. In the **city centre**, Greek cafés line Lonsdale Street between Swanston and Russell streets, while Little Bourke Street is the home of Chinatown. Lygon Street, in inner-city **Carlton**, is just one of many pockets across the city with a concentration of Italian restaurants. Johnston Street in **Fitzroy** is the Spanish strip, while nearby up-and-coming Smith Street and arty Brunswick Street both have a huge variety of international cuisines and smart cafés. Greek restaurants fill Swan Street in inner-city **Richmond**, and Vietnamese places dominate Victoria Street. Fitzroy and **St Kilda**, another gastronomically mixed bag, are the centres of café society; St Kilda also has great bakeries and delis, as does Jewish **Balaclava**.

Most of Melbourne's restaurants are BYO, and even the licensed ones generally allow you to bring your own drink – though check first, and note that a corkage fee ($1–2 per person) often applies. If you're going to be around for a while, *The Age Cheap Eats in Melbourne* and its more upmarket companion, *The Age Good Food Guide*, are worthwhile investments.

City centre

There are still plenty of old-fashioned **coffee lounges** in the city – the type of place where you can get a milky cappuccino and grilled cheese on toast, with a mini-jukebox at your table – but stylish **cafés** with a more thoughtful decor and much more diverse menus are edging in. In the department stores, both the Myer and David Jones food halls are excellent for upmarket picnic ingredients, while Melbourne Central has several good eating places – the Daimaru food department on the ground floor also sells Japanese food items.

Cafe All'Angelo, 387 Little Bourke St. Good value breakfasts and lunches; good people-watching, too. Licensed. Mon–Thurs 7am–5pm, Fri until 6.30pm, Sat until 2am.

Cafe La, 35th Floor, *Sofitel Hotel,* corner of Collins and Exhibition sts. Café with the best views in Melbourne, and much more affordable than the exclusive *Le Restaurant* on the same floor. Open daily from 6.30am until about midnight for breakfast, lunch, dinner and afternoon teas.

Cafe Segovia, 33 Block Place, near Little Collins St. Very pleasant, Spanish-style café, serving good coffee and excellent food. Licensed. Mon–Fri 7.30am–9.30pm, Sat 8am–6pm, Sun 9am–5pm.

Caffe Cortile, 30 Block Place, near Little Collins St, opposite *Cafe Segovia.* Small, cheerful "hole in the wall" place. Good for breakfast, very busy at lunchtime. Licensed. Mon–Wed 7am–10pm, Thurs–Fri until 11pm, Sat & Sun 9am–6pm.

Campari, 25 Hardware St. Casual and characterful, this daytime spot pulls in lawyers from the nearby courts with excellent Southern Italian food. Pasta dishes for around $13 and steaks and fish around $18. Breakfast is also available. Mon–Tues 7am–5pm, Wed–Thurs until 8.30pm, Fri until 9.30pm.

Crossways Food for Life, 123 Swanston St. Dirt-cheap Indian-style vegetarian food prepared by Hare Krishnas. Mon–Sat noon–3pm.

Curry Bowl, 250 Elizabeth St. Sri Lankan fast food to eat in or take away. Closed Sun.

Florentino, 80 Bourke St (☎03/9662 1811). A Melbourne institution, which divides loyalties between the cellar café-grill-retaurant (lunch Mon–Fri noon–3pm, dinner Mon–Sat 6–11.30pm), serving inexpensive, home-style pasta dishes, drinks and good coffee, and the very pricey and elegant Italian–French restaurant upstairs (closed Sat lunch and Sun). Licensed.

Gopals, 139 Swanston St. *Crossways'* sister restaurant – another Hare Krishna-run, very cheap veggie place. Mon noon–3pm, Tues–Fri noon–8.30pm, Sat 5–8.30pm.

Grand Hyatt Foodcourt, 122 Collins St. Spacious, airy place where customers choose cakes, imaginative salads and other dishes from various stalls and bars; Friday night happy hour is popular with the office crowd.

Hopetoun Tea Rooms, Block Arcade, near Collins St. Tea, scones and delicious cakes have been served in these elegant surroundings for more than one hundred years, but new-fangled delicacies such as focaccia with pesto sauce have now wheedled their way onto the menu. Closed Sat afternoon and Sun.

India House, 443 Elizabeth St. Tandoori and North Indian food, including inexpensive vegetarian dishes, in a relaxed atmosphere with friendly staff. Licensed and BYO. Lunch Mon–Fri, dinner Mon–Sat.

Italian Waiters Restaurant, 20 Meyers Place, off Bourke St between Exhibition and Spring sts. Long-established Italian place on the first floor above a bar, once a waiters' favourite for its late hours. No frills, simple food and low prices. Licensed and BYO. Lunch Mon–Fri, dinner Mon–Sat 6pm–midnight.

Kappo Okita, 17 Liverpool St (☎03/9662 2206). Modest Japanese café with good, inexpensive food, especially sushi and sashimi. Best to reserve for weekend evenings. BYO. Lunch Mon–Fri, dinner Mon–Sat.

Kenzan, 45 Collins St (☎03/9654 8933). Sushi bar renowned for the freshness of its sushi and sashimi; more upmarket than *Kappo Okita,* with slightly cheaper lunches. Licensed. Lunch Mon–Fri, dinner daily.

Le Restaurant, 35th Floor, *Sofitel Hotel,* corner of Collins and Exhibition sts (☎03/9653 0000). Luxurious restaurant with silver service and fantastic views over Melbourne and Port Phillip Bay.

Serves carefully prepared seasonal dishes, together with Australian produce such as barramundi and yabbies. Expect to pay in the region of $70 per person (not including drinks). Tues–Sat from 7pm.

Medallion Cafe & Cakes, 209 Lonsdale St. Popular Greek café, once shabby, now with an over-the-top, disco-style interior, but still serving authentic, cheap food. Daily until late (3am Fri & Sat).

Mekong, 241 Swanston Walk. Small Vietnamese café specializing in *pho* (beef or chicken noodle soup). Excellent-value food (dishes about $5), but packed at lunchtime. Mon–Thurs & Sun 8am–11pm, Fri & Sat 8am–2pm.

Meyer's Place, 20 Meyers Place, off Bourke St between Exhibition and Spring sts. Small bar open until the wee hours – good for a quiet little drink. It's a bit hard to find as there are no signs and no "official" name. Tues–Sat 4pm–4am.

Ong International Food Court, basement of the *Welcome Hotel*, 256 Little Bourke St. Authentic Asian food court with stalls selling Chinese, Vietnamese, Malaysian/Singaporean and Thai food. Licensed. Daily 10am–10pm.

Pellegrini's Espresso Bar, 66 Bourke St. Melbourne's first espresso bar, and still an institution. Crowded after work with chat and clatter. Classic 1950s interior and great pasta. Open daily.

Pure and Natural Food Company, opposite Flinders Street Station. One of twenty outlets in a local chain whose motto is "fast food that's good for you". Inexpensive, health-conscious and mainly vegetarian. Mon–Fri 6am–5.30pm, Sat 8.30am–2.30pm.

Satay Inn, 250 Swanston Walk. Excellent, affordable Malaysian place, close to the big department stores. BYO. Daily lunch and dinner.

Southgate, across the river from Flinders Street Station. With fine views of the river and the city skyline, this centre has developed into a very popular place to dine and drink. The food court is packed during lunch hours and at weekends, and on Friday and Saturday nights advance booking is essential for the restaurants. Some of the best places are *The Blue Train Café* (☎03/9696 0111), which attracts a young, hip crowd and serves drinks and tasty and very inexpensive light meals; *E Gusto* (☎03/9690 9819), which does "Modern Australian" cuisine with an Italian slant; and the more upmarket *Walter's Wine Bar* (☎03/9690 9211) and *Simply French* (☎03/9699 9804), the latter serving superb French food – leave some space for the brilliant desserts.

Swiss Rosti Bar, 87 Flinders Lane, between Exhibition and Spring sts, (☎03/9654 0088). Tasty and well-presented Swiss–German fare which is quite a few notches above the stodge that passes for German food elsewhere, along with a few international dishes. Try *kassler* (pickled pork) with sauerkraut or bratwurst, fried onions and mushrooms, all served with *rosti* (fried grated potatoes), a Swiss specialty. Licensed and moderately priced. Mon lunch only, Tues–Fri noon–late, Sat 5pm–late.

Tsindos, 197 Lonsdale St. All the Greek classics from taramasalata to moussaka and souvlaki at reasonable prices, plus live bouzouki music every night except Sunday. Licensed and BYO. Lunch Mon–Fri, dinner daily.

VIS, 245 Swanston St. Stylish café-restaurant underneath *The Lounge* with food to match – check the blackboard menu for unusual dishes such as prawn and basil ravioli and smoked rack of lamb *harissa*. Licensed. Mon–Sat 10am–late.

William Angliss College, Latrobe St (☎03/9606 2111). Licensed restaurant with fine food and service. Incredibly cheap, but you're at the mercy of the catering students. Booking essential.

Windsor Hotel, 103 Spring St (☎03/9653 0653). Afternoon tea in this Victorian-era hotel is absolutely traditional. Plan to spend an hour or more luxuriating in the opulence.

Chinatown

Yum cha (elsewhere known as dim sum, a series of small delicacies served from trolleys) is available at lunchtime almost everywhere; on Sunday it's a crowded ritual.

Camy Shanghai Dumpling and Noodle Restaurant, Tattersalls Lane (between Little Bourke and Lonsdale sts, close to Swanston St). An extremely cheap, partly selfservice place, dishing up very simple but delicious dumplings and noodles. No alcohol. Daily 11am–9pm.

Empress of China, 120–122 Little Bourke St (☎03/9663 1883). Expensive but good value, with lots of lesser-known dishes on offer. Licensed. Closed Sat lunchtime.

Flower Drum, 17 Market Lane, between Bourke and Little Bourke sts (☎03/9662 3655). Among some very good Chinese restaurants, this is simply outstanding: sophisticated Cantonese cuisine, including exquisite seafood and fish, but also expensive – about $110 for two, plus drinks. Licensed. Closed Sun lunch.

Hills BBQ Noodle Shop, 178 Little Bourke St. Roast pork or roast duck on rice or in a bowl of steaming broth with noodles. Very inexpensive and a good late-night stop. Daily 10am–2am.

King of Kings, 209 Russell St. Simple, inexpensive Hong Kong-style food, including *congee*, and lots of dishes with pork and offal. BYO. Lunch and dinner daily; open until 2.30am.

Little Malaysia, 26 Liverpool St. Cheap and good Malaysian hawker fare. BYO. Open daily for lunch and dinner.

Shark Fin House, 131 Little Bourke St. Converted warehouse with three storeys devoted to about fifty kinds of *yum cha*, all through the week, night and day. Very busy at lunchtime, especially at weekends. Licensed.

Carlton and North Melbourne

As well as an Italian strip of restaurants and cafés on Lygon Street, between Gratton and Elgin streets, Carlton is home to some great Asian restaurants. To the south of Carlton, North Melbourne harbours an excellent Balinese restaurant.

Brunetti, 198–204 Faraday St. A steady stream of customers walks past an array of display cases filled with a mouthwatering selection of chocolates, pastries, biscuits and cakes to get their daily espresso in the café section. Licensed restaurant next door. Cakes and café daily 7am–10pm; restaurant Mon–Fri noon–3pm, Sat from 12.30pm; dinner Mon–Sat 6–10pm.

Nyonya, 191 Lygon St. Authentic Nyonya cuisine, a blend of Malaysian and Chinese cooking, at moderate prices. BYO. Lunch and dinner daily.

Shakahari, 201–203 Faraday St (☎03/9347 3848). Excellent, imaginative vegetarian food, influenced by various Asian cuisines, at moderate prices. Licensed and BYO. Mon–Thurs noon–10pm, Fri & Sat noon–10.30pm, Sun 6–10pm.

Tiamo, 303 Lygon St. One-time beatnik hangout and still popular with students, with layers of browning 1950s posters and a good-value blackboard menu. Mon–Sat 7.30am–11pm, Sun 9.30am–10pm.

Toofey's, 162a Elgin St (☎03/9347 9838). Considered to be Melbourne's best seafood restaurant. Extremely fresh fish and seafood are prepared in a light, Mediterranean or Middle Eastern style. About $90 plus drinks for two for dinner; lunch (Mon–Fri only) slightly cheaper. Licensed.

Toto's Pizza House, 101 Lygon St. Melbourne's first pizzeria, dating from the 1950s – cheap, cheerful and noisy. Licensed. Daily 11am–11pm.

Warung Agus, 305 Victoria St (☎03/9329 1737). Authentic Balinese restaurant with superb, affordable food. BYO. Lunch Fri, dinner Tues–Sat 6–10pm.

Fitzroy and Collingwood

Adjacent Fitzroy and Collingwood probably have the widest choice of cuisines in the city, and are good places to finish off your night on the town, as there's always lots going on. There's a smallish Spanish centre with a few tapas bars on Johnston Street, between Brunswick and Nicholson streets.

Brunswick Street

Afghan Gallery, 327 Brunswick St. Cheap and authentic food with a decor of Afghan hangings and rugs. Very popular with students. BYO. Dinner daily.

Babka's Bakery Cafe, 384 Brunswick St. A deservedly popular place, as the bread and cakes, made on the premises, are divine, and dishes from the changing blackboard menu are equally enticing and satisfying. Try Russian blintzes for breakfast. Licensed & BYO. Tues–Sun 7am–7pm.

Black Cat Cafe, cnr of Brunswick and Greeves sts. The prototype of the groovy Brunswick Street café: Fifties theme, jazz music and an informative notice board. Try the bagels and a "Spider", a speciality ice-cream soda. Daily 9am–1am.

Chinta Ria Restaurant, 182 Brunswick St (☎03/9349 2599). Very popular restaurant serving authentic Malaysian dishes (curry laksa, beef *rendang*, *blachan* spinach). Branches elsewhere feature live music. Licensed. Lunch and dinner daily.

Mario's, 303 Brunswick St. European-style café where you can eat breakfast (until midnight), lunch and dinner or just have a coffee or a drink. Dauntingly smart staff and decor, but not expensive or dressy. The clientele is an interesting mixture of posers, celebrities and scruffs.

Rhumbaralla's, 342 Brunswick St. The neon sign in the window is one of the street's landmarks, and the inside of this stylish café is just as vibrantly coloured. The place hums to the sound of the ceiling fan, jazz music and conversation. Breakfast until midday – eggs Benedict the favourite – then anything from focaccia to steak. Licensed and BYO. Daily 9am–1am.

Shanti, 285 Brunswick St (☎03/9416 2170). Serves tandoori dishes as well as Southern Indian specialities cooked in coconut milk rather than cream and yoghurt. Lots of vegetarian options and seafood. Moderately priced, the *masala dosa* is especially good value. Licensed and BYO (wine only). Lunch Mon–Fri, dinner daily.

Thai Thani, 293 Brunswick St (☎03/9419 6463). One of Melbourne's best Thai restaurants, on two crowded levels, with moderate prices. BYO. Dinner daily.

The Vegie Bar, 378 Brunswick St. Simple, fresh food cooked to order. Cheap, popular and hip rather than hippie: jazzy soul sounds and poster-covered walls. Daily noon–10pm.

Johnston Street

Carmen Bar, 74 Johnston St. The best value tapas bar in the area, usually full of Spanish people. Live flamenco Thurs–Sat. Tues–Sun 6pm–1am.

Guru da Dhaba, 240 Johnston St (☎03/9486 9155). Cheap Indian restaurant specializing in Punjabi cuisine that's always packed – advance bookings are advised. BYO. Mon–Fri 6–11pm, weekends until 11.30pm.

Kahlo's, 36 Johnston St. Smallish, cosy tapas bar. Wed–Sat 6pm–1am.

Smith Street

Cafe Bohemio, 354 Smith St, north of Johnston St. This laid-back place, reminiscent of a student café in the seventies, seems to be a meeting place of Melbourne's small Hispanic expatriate community. Serves Latin American dishes (recipes from Argentina to Uruguay), often accompanied by live music (jazz, salsa, Brazilian guitar). Licensed & BYO (wine only). Tues–Fri 11.30–late, Sat & Sun 6pm–late.

Cafe Coco, 129 Smith St. Cosy spot, where the blackboard menu of inexpensive light meals, excellent cakes and good coffee changes regularly. Licensed.

Cafe Zahara, 293–295 Smith St (☎03/9416 1640). Very moderately priced Malaysian–Indonesian dishes – curry laksa, curries, vegetarian and seafood dishes. Best to book ahead on Fri and Sat nights. BYO. Mon–Sat noon–late.

Gluttony, 278 Smith St. Good cakes, cooked breakfasts and light meals. Popular with locals. BYO. Daily 7am–11pm.

Soulfood Cafe, 273 Smith St. Comfortable cafeteria-style vegetarian café with wooden trestle tables, pine walls, and a good notice board at the back. Mon–Thurs 8am–9pm, Fri–Sun 9am–6pm.

Vatan Gida Foodstore, 131 Smith St. Excellent Turkish deli among a bevy of Turkish cafés.

Richmond

Swan Street, running from Church Street towards Wattle Park, is home to Melbourne's best Greek restaurants. On the north side of Richmond, Victoria Street is lined with Vietnamese supermarkets, clothes shops and dozens of cheap, authentic restaurants.

Hellas Cake Shop, 324 Lennox St, off Swan St. Delicious Greek cakes and biscuits, which the friendly staff are happy to identify. Daily 9am–6pm.

Salona, 262A Swan St (☎03/9429 1460). Long-established Greek restaurant – one of four in this block – serves good, plain and very reasonably priced dishes. Licensed and BYO. Daily noon–11.30pm.

Tho Tho's Bar-Restaurant, 66 Victoria St. Much more upmarket than most of its neighbours, but usually packed and noisy. Inexpensive food, with the lunch specials offering especially good value. Licensed. Daily 11am–midnight.

Thy Thy 1, upstairs at 142 Victoria St (☎03/9429 1104). The most sought-after Vietnamese restaurant on Victoria St, always with a queue to get in. The food is basic but great. BYO.

Thy Thy 2, 116 Victoria St. Slightly upmarket from *Thy Thy 1*, but similar and also very popular. BYO. Daily 9am–11pm.

Vao Doi, 120 Victoria St. Another much-frequented Vietnamese place, with set lunch menus for the uninitiated.

VV, 86 Victoria St, another upmarket bar and restaurant. This one attracts a mixed clientele of local Vietnamese & Australians and students from Malaysia, Singapore and Thailand. Inexpensive food. Licensed. Daily 11am–midnight.

South Yarra, Prahran and Windsor

Cafe Feedwell, 95 Greville St, Prahran. Melbourne's oldest vegetarian café, but certainly not an "alternative" cheapie any more. Tofu-based dishes, healthy pies and the like make a hefty meal, and they do good sandwiches, made from excellent home-made bread. BYO.

Caffe e Cucina, 581 Chapel St, South Yarra (☎03/9827 4139). Still one of Melbourne's coolest eating spots, attracting a smart clientele and dishing up fantastic pasta. Licensed.

Chinta Ria Jazz, 176 Commercial Rd, Prahran (☎03/9510 6520). One of Simon Goh's string of Malaysian eateries – the owner is a dedicated jazz and blues fan who hosts his own radio programme (each week on 3PBS 106.7FM). Lunch and dinner daily. Very moderately priced. BYO.

Confucius, 272 Toorak Rd, South Yarra (☎03/9827 6833). An elegant restaurant where the cuisine could be labelled "Modern Chinese" or "East meets West". Lots of wines by the glass, plus a selection of imported Chinese teas. Licensed. Daily lunch and dinner.

The Continental Cafe, 132–134 Greville St, Prahran. Hugely popular restaurant and nightclub, with waistcoated waiters and an equally smart, arty clientele. Breakfast all day, very good pasta dishes, and a wide range of wines and liqueurs. Licensed. Daily 7am–midnight.

Falafel House, 196 Toorak Rd, South Yarra. Middle Eastern takeaway, perfect after pubbing or clubbing. Daily 9am–5am.

Giardino's Trattoria, 341–345 Toorak Rd, South Yarra (☎03/9824 1444). Italian restaurant with huge servings, casual service, and lots of families.

Helens Polish Restaurant, 134 Chapel St, Windsor. Simple, authentic Polish place, open from breakfast to dinner; great cakes (try the poppy-seed chocolate cake) and full meals. BYO. Mon–Sat 9am–10pm, Sun 1–10pm,

Samos Greek Taverna, 120 Chapel St, Windsor (☎03/9510 4561). Plastic vines and fishing nets set the scene. Excellent, moderately priced Greek food with music on Friday and Saturday, when you'll need to book.

Soul Sisters, Shop 10, 168 Commercial Rd, opposite Prahran Market (☎03/9510 5760). Small, but very smartly designed café, though inconspicuous from the outside. Very tasty, reasonably priced Malaysian–Chinese food. BYO. Lunch and dinner daily; booking recommended on Friday and Saturday.

Tamani Bistro, 156 Toorak Rd, South Yarra (☎03/9866 2575). Dimly lit, crowded Italian cheapie.

South Melbourne, Albert Park and Port Melbourne

There's not much of a night-time scene in these suburbs, but cafés and delicatessens dish up a mouthwatering selection of food during the day.

Albert Park Deli, 129 Dundas Place, Albert Park. Superb delicatessen takeaway, specializing in delicious breads and *arancini* (Italian rice balls).

Arkibar, 27 Coventry St, South Melbourne. Modern café serving good Italian food. Licensed. Mon–Thurs 7.30am–5pm, Fri until 11pm.

Cafe Bombay, 396 Bay St (continuation of City Rd), Port Melbourne. Long-established Indian restaurant serving consistently good food, including plenty of vegetarian dishes. Licensed & BYO. Lunch Tues–Fri, dinner daily.

Cafe Sweethearts, 263 Coventry St, South Melbourne. Good for breakfast – numerous (and some very exotic-sounding) varieties of sandwiches and eggs served here. Mon–Fri 7am–4pm, Sat & Sun 8am–4pm.

Coventry Blue, 313 Coventry St. Café with an alternative feel in a terrace house opposite the South Melbourne market. Cheap vegetarian dishes. Tues–Sat 7am–5pm, Sun 8am–5pm.

Montague Hotel, cnr of Park and Montague sts, South Melbourne. Renovated, atmospheric old pub and a good restaurant out the back serving hearty fare.

Montague Park Foodstore, 406 Park St. Delicious dishes and desserts to take away or eat in. Particularly pleasant in summer when the tables are out on the footpath.

Sushi Chef, 193 Clarendon St. Inexpensive sushi bar relies mainly on the take-away trade, but you can also eat in. Mon–Sat 11am–8pm.

Villagio Continental Delicatessen, Dundas Place, Albert Park. Gleaming shop full of all kinds of Italian food, with tables outside where you can eat your selections and drink coffee. Closed Sun.

Vista Bar & Bistro, cnr of Bridport and Montague sts, Albert Park (☎03/9699 7757). An eclectic international mix of dishes and a good selection of wines by the glass. Tues–Sun noon–late.

St Kilda

Although Acland Street is still very popular – especially for late breakfasts and pigging out on cakes – Fitzroy Street has taken over as St Kilda's new cool area, especially the block from Grey Street to the waterfront. A new, stylish café or restaurant (with prices to match) opens almost every day, making it incredibly difficult to keep track of the latest developments. Walk past any of them on a warm summer evening and you'll be eyed up and down by the crowds sitting at the outdoor tables. On most evenings it's nearly impossible to find a parking space in the area, even though there's a car park at either end of Fitzroy Street. It's probably better to hail a cab, take public transport or otherwise be prepared for a long hike.

Bala's, 1D Shakespeare Grove (just off Acland St near Luna Park). Excellent, cheap Asian take-away food – lots of things stir-fried in the wok, with ultrafresh ingredients, as well as samosas, curry puffs and lassis. There are a few tables if you want to eat in, but beware – the place is very busy at lunch and dinner time. Open daily noon–10.30pm.

The Benedykt Deli Cafe, 101 Acland St. One of many of its type on Acland St. A smallish, hole-in-the-wall deli-cum-café that serves great coffee and interesting food (takeaway or eat here): risottos, salads, polenta, antipasti, cakes and pastries. Breakfast is good, too – try the eggs Benedict. **Chinta Ria Blues**, 6 Acland St (☎03/9534 9233). There are two of Simon Goh's string of Malaysian eateries in St Kilda – this one is just around the corner from Fitzroy St and has a breezy, airy feel to it. The other is a small place at 94 Acland St (bookings, ☎03/9525 4664). Both are open for lunch and dinner daily. Very moderately priced. BYO.

Cicciolina, 130 Acland St. Lots of tables crammed into a small space. Friendly staff and Italian food with an interesting twist must be the formula that keeps this restaurant going from strength to strength. Licensed. Daily 11am–11pm.

Delicatessen Espresso, 151 Fitzroy St. Ideal for breakfast (served until 3pm) and brunch. The menu is limited to a few, very tasty pasta dishes, risottos and salads.

The Espy Kitchen at the Esplanade Hotel, 11 Upper Esplanade. The veggie restaurant at the back is casual and slow, with slapdash decor to match, but the excellent food is worth the wait.

Galleon Cafe, 9 Carlisle St. Breakfast, served until 4pm, is the big attraction here, especially popular at weekends. There's also a useful notice board. Mon–Fri 9am–midnight, Sat & Sun from 9.30am.

Greasy Joe's, 68 Acland St. Good greasy breakfast until 6pm, and a range of burgers both meaty and veggie, which you can eat at pavement tables. Daily until 1am.

The Melbourne Wine Room, cnr of Fitzroy and Grey sts. Located in the formerly seedy *George Hotel*, this is now a swanky restaurant, bar and café where you can have a drink, dinner or a quick bite with some wine. More than 300 wines on the list. Open Tues–Sun.

Monarch Cake Shop, 103 Acland St. Mouthwatering continental patisserie – one of the better ones along the cake shop-strip of Acland St.

Ninety Seven, 97 Fitzroy St. Cosy little café. The back of the courtyard is framed by palm trees and the columned facade of the former French consulate (now a private house). Daily 10am–1pm.

One Fitzroy Street (☎03/9593 8800). The latest example of Fitzroy St yuppification, in a hard-to-beat location at the corner of Fitzroy St and The Esplanade. There's a café and bar (*One's Soup Kitchen*) downstairs, and an ultramodern restaurant upstairs with a balcony that rewards the higher prices with stupendous views over Port Phillip Bay. Meals in the café cost about $40–50 for two; in the restaurant $90 (not including drinks). Licensed. Daily until about midnight.

Stokehouse, 30 Jacka Boulevard. Located by the beach and packed in warm weather. The restaurant has two sections: downstairs is affordable with lots of unusual pizzas and pastas, fantastic cakes, coffee and wines; upstairs has better views of the bay, but is beyond most budgets. Licensed. Downstairs open Mon–Fri noon–11pm, Sat noon–1am, Sun 10am–11pm.

Topolinos, 87 Fitzroy St. A dimly lit, noisy and smoky St Kilda institution, which pumps out pizzas, generous pasta dishes and good cocktails until dawn.

Wild Rice, 211 Barkly St. Vegan macrobiotic café with a lovely courtyard garden. Daily noon–10pm.

Elwood and Balaclava

Elwood's easy-going haunts are similar to St Kilda's, while Balaclava, to the east along Carlisle Street, specializes in inexpensive kosher food.

Beach House, 67A Ormond Esplanade, Elwood (☎03/9531 7788). Friendly, if somewhat chaotic café next to the car park at Elwood beach. Very good for breakfast, and *very* crowded on weekends, so book ahead. Wed–Fri 9am–4pm, Sat & Sun 7.30am–6.30pm. In summer Fri–Sun until 10.30pm. Licensed and BYO.

Cafe Tarrango, 15 Ormond Rd, Elwood. Indian-run café, with delicious organic, biodynamic vegetarian food but not much atmosphere.

Glicks, 330A Carlisle St, Balaclava. Very friendly spot, renowned for bagels and traditional Jewish savouries: try kreplach, *latkes* or gefilte fish. Mon–Thurs & Sun 6am–9pm, Fri until sunset. Closed Sat.

Haymisha Kosher Bakery, 320 Carlisle St, Balaclava. Jewish bakery with good wholemeal and rye breads, bagels, onion rolls, cakes, doughnuts and a large variety of cookies. Closed Sat.

Hay's Brasserie, 402 Barkly St (near Ormond Esplanade), Elwood. Not too far from the *Beach House*, this is another good place for breakfast. Lunch and dinner feature typical Melbourne "East meets West" cuisine, such as lamb curry and olive gnocchi. Licensed. Mon–Fri from 8am, Sat & Sun 7am until late.

Mussels Fish and Chippery, 37 Glenhuntly Rd, Elwood. A takeaway with an emphasis on quality – you can even get marinated grilled baby octopus. Perfect place to stock up for lunch.

Turtle Cafe, 34 Ormond Rd, Elwood. Relaxed old corner café that attracts a faithful crowd.

Zartowa, 114 Ormond Rd, Elwood. More upmarket than the *Turtle*, this popular café-restaurant at the yuppie end of Ormond Rd features a varied à la carte menu of Australian and Mediterranean and Asian-inspired dishes. Lots of focaccias and salads for brunch, plus good coffee.

Nightlife and entertainment

Melbourne prides itself on being a cultural city with intellectual leanings, so there's a rich arts and music scene and always plenty to do in the evening. To find out **what's on**, check out *The Age* on Friday, when the newspaper publishes a comprehensive entertainment guide, *EG* – much better than the *Sun-Herald*'s Thursday supplement. *Melbourne Events* is a handy, and surprisingly hip, free monthly guide to all sorts of happenings, published by Melbourne Council and available at tourist information outlets.

Annual festivals further enliven the scene: the **Melbourne International Festival** in October concentrates on mainstream visual and performing arts, with a sprinkling of good concerts and opera. The much more experimental and innovative **Melbourne Fringe Festival** happens more or less at the same time, as does the **Melbourne**

Writers' Festival. The heavily promoted **Moomba Festival**, held during the first half of March, has events including firework displays and dragon boat races on the banks of the Yarra River in Alexandra Gardens, but is actually rather drab and commercial. Three music festivals take place in the first half of the year: the **Melbourne Jazz Festival** in the last week of January, at venues in the city centre; the **Melbourne Music Festival** in February, one of the largest Australian festivals of contemporary music; and the **Brunswick Music Festival** in the third week of March, concentrating on folk and world music. The **Next Wave Festival**, held over two weeks in the second half of May, celebrates Victoria's young artists, writers and musicians.

Tickets for most venues can be booked through Ticketmaster (☎13 2612) or Ticketek (☎13 2849); both take credit-card bookings only. You can buy tickets half-price on the day of performance from the Half Tix booth, on the Bourke Street Mall (Mon & Sat 10am–2pm, Tues–Thurs 11am–6pm, Fri 11am–6.30pm; cash only; ☎03/9654 9420).

Bars and pubs

The distinction between restaurant, bar, café and nightclub is often blurred, but not at the handful of pub breweries, where a range of beers is made on the premises. Most hotel bars in the city centre are closed on Sunday, though in the suburbs they stay open. A number of drinking places are also listed under "Live music" opposite. City Pub Walks lead walking tours (2hr 30min–3hr) through the city centre, giving the lowdown on the best watering holes, latest trendy bars in hidden laneways and most raucous music venues. Meet "under the clocks" at Flinders Street Station, but to be sure of a place, book in advance (☎03/9384 0655 or mobile ☎0412/085 661; $20, discount for backpackers; Tues & Thurs 6.30pm).

City Centre

Charles Dickens Tavern, downstairs, Block Court, 290 Collins St. A place for homesick Brits, with bitter and Guinness on tap, pint glasses and live soccer. Licensed to 3am.

Giardini Cafe Bar, 14 Bourke St. Small wine bar painted with frescoes in bold, Mediterranean colours. Serves breakfast and light meals.

Le Monde, 18 Bourke St. Slick café-bar, dishing up tasty food, at the lively end of Bourke St. Open 24hr.

The Lounge, 243 Swanston Walk. Genuine all-rounder, attracting an arty-grungy crowd. Bar and nightclub with live music (see "Clubs" on p.803), and good food in the upstairs restaurant – eat alfresco on the terrace.

Mitre Tavern, 5 Bank Place. Long-established watering hole, popular with office workers.

Stork Hotel, 504 Elizabeth St. Simple watering hole in a historic hotel from the goldrush era.

North Melbourne, Carlton and Fitzroy

Gypsy Bar, 334 Brunswick St, Fitzroy. Intimate bar crammed with Brunswick St's finest, especially for jazz on Sunday night. Great coffee and food. Daily 9.30am–1am.

Lemon Tree, 10 Grattan St, Carlton. Upmarket bar which often features live jazz and has a fine beer garden.

Lord Newry, 543 Brunswick St, North Fitzroy. The cosy front bar with an open fire is a good place for conversation. Delicious food is served upstairs, where there might be anything from poetry readings to jazz.

Pumphouse Hotel, 128 Nicholson St, Fitzroy. Pub brewery, very popular with backpackers from the nearby hostel, *The Nunnery*.

The Redback Brewery, 75 Flemington Rd, North Melbourne. Slick boutique brewery packed out on Friday and Saturday with the striped-shirt brigade. Redback, the house beer, is one of the tastiest around.

Richmond and South Yarra

All Nations Hotel, 64 Lennox St, off Swan St, Richmond. Old-style Aussie pub with exceptional bar meals and a relaxing beer garden.

Black Match, 545 Church St, Richmond. Favourite university students' haunt with neo-punk decor.

Fawkner Club, 52 Toorak Rd, South Yarra. Swanky pub with a great beer garden, though it's hard to get a seat on a sunny day.

St Kilda

Bar Corvina, 157 Fitzroy St. Cool, modern decor. Good, inexpensive Modern Australian cuisine, plus a good selection of wines, mainly from South Australia.

Big Mouth, 201 Barkly St. A friendly café-bar downstairs, and a spacious restaurant upstairs. Especially good are the breakfasts.

Cafe Menis, 16 Fitzroy St. Café-bar, crowded on weekends, serving everything from drinks to snacks and complete meals.

Dog's Bar, 54 Acland St. Once the coolest spot on the block, and now well-established with a loyal clientele.

Veludo Bar, 175 Acland St. A hip newcomer in this area of old-fashioned continental bakeries and delis. Good and inexpensive food (except for the oysters) and an extensive wine list.

Live music

Melbourne has a thriving **band** scene, in which just about every pub puts on some sort of music – often free – at some time during the week. The pubs listed below are also good places for a drink, and always have at least two bars so you can escape the din if you want to. Grungy Richmond has a big concentration of **music pubs**, with several putting on African and reggae music; Fitzroy and St Kilda are the other areas to head to for a range of live music. Free listings magazines such as *Beat*, *Inpress* or *Zebra* are good sources of information about the local band scene; you can pick them up at most record shops, cinemas and cafés. Local FM stations Triple R (102.7) and PBS (106.7) air alternative music and tell you what's on where.

City centre and the northern suburbs

Bennetts Lane, 25 Bennetts Lane (a small alley off Little Lonsdale St in the CBD, between Exhibition and Russell sts). One of Melbourne's most interesting jazz venues, in a cramped, Fifties-style cellar.

Brunswick East Club Hotel, 280 Lygon St, Brunswick East. Headquarters of the Melbourne Folk Club.

Dan O'Connell's, 225 Canning St (between Rathdowne and Nicholson sts), Fitzroy. Irish music Wed–Sun; no cover charge.

Gowings Grace Darling Hotel, 114 Smith St, Collingwood. Pleasant watering hole, which sometimes features live jazz and R&B.

McCoppins Hotel, 166 Johnston St, Fitzroy. Live R&B, blues and jazz in the Music Room.

The Punters Club, 376 Brunswick St, Fitzroy. One of the nerve centres of the Melbourne band scene, with well-known independent bands nightly; usually $5.

The Rainbow, 27 St David St, Fitzroy. Mellow atmosphere, interesting crowd and decor in an intimate bar with free music – eclectic jazz, funk and fusion – every night.

The Stage, 1st floor, 231 Smith St, Collingwood. Live bands play African and Latin American music Thurs–Sun from 8 or 10pm. Dance floor and cover charge. Come earlier and have a two course dinner for an additional $15.

The Tote, 71 Johnston St, Fitzroy. Hardcore thrash.

GAY AND LESBIAN MELBOURNE

Melbourne's gay scene may not be as upfront as Sydney's, but it's almost as formidable; this is such a diverse city that gays and lesbians seem just two more of the different groups that give the city its easy-going, multifarious feel.

The scene in Melbourne is less ghettoized than in Sydney. That said, Fitzroy, Collingwood and Carlton, north of the river, and St Kilda, South Yarra and Prahran, to the south, boast a strong male presence. Lesbians are everywhere, but Fitzroy, Northcote and Clifton Hill are Melbourne's recognized stomping grounds. There are two gay and lesbian free papers to help you navigate new waters: the *Melbourne Star Observer*, published weekly, and the fortnightly *Brother Sister*.

Big **events** are mostly organized by the ALSO (Alternative LifeStyle Organisation) Foundation, including one over the Australia Day weekend at the end of January – **Red Raw Resurrection**. The scene's annual highlight, however, has to be the fabulous **Midsumma Festival** in late January and early February. Already in its eleventh year, Midsumma provides an umbrella for a wide range of sporting, artistic and theatrical events. The Queen's Birthday in June is celebrated at the **Winterdaze** party, and while the whole city is taking a day off to celebrate Melbourne Show Day in September, the **Show Off** dance party is the place to be.

ORGANIZATIONS, SUPPORT GROUPS AND BOOKSHOPS

Melbourne is blessed with a dazzling variety of gay and lesbian organizations, support services and businesses, the most important of which are listed below. Everything else, from gay vets to lesbian psychologists, can be found in the *ALSO Directory*.

AIDS organizations and medical care AIDS Line (☎03/9347 6099 or free call ☎1800/133 392) for phone counselling, referral and information Mon–Fri 9am–10pm, Sat & Sun 11am–2pm & 7–10pm; Gay Men's Health Centre and the Victorian AIDS Council (☎03/9865 6700 or free call ☎1800/134 840), 6 Claremont St, South Yarra; People Living With Aids at the Positive Living Centre (☎03/9525 4455), 46 Acland St, St Kilda; Positive Women (☎03/9347 0244 or free call ☎1800/032 017), run by and for women with HIV, through the Melbourne Sexual Health Centre (see p.808).

ALSO Foundation, 1st floor, 35 Cato St, Prahran (☎03/9510 5569; *www.also.org.au*). Organizes events and publishes the *ALSO Directory*, free from community outlets.

Beat Books, 157 Commercial Rd, Prahran (☎03/9827 8748). Gay bookshop with a large range of gay magazines, books, sex toys and leather goods.

Gay and Lesbian Entertainment Infoline ☎0055/12504.

Gay and Lesbian Switchboard (☎03/9510 5488 or free call ☎1800/631 493) for counselling, referral and information.

Hares and Hyenas, 135 Commercial Rd, Prahran (☎03/9824 0110) and 110 Smith St, Collingwood (☎03/9419 4445). Gay and lesbian bookshop.

Lesbian Line (☎03/9416 0850). Run by the Women's Liberation Switchboard; counselling and support Thurs 6–10pm.

Wings Of Desire, Shop 8, no 176 Commercial Rd, Prahan (☎03/9521 1544). Travel agent for gays and lesbians.

Women's Information and Referral Exchange (WIRE) (☎03/9654 6844 or free call ☎1800/136 570). Information about lesbian groups, referral to feminist doctors, solicitors, etc.

CAFÉS AND MEETING PLACES

Big Mouth, 168 Acland St, St Kilda. Excellent position at the corner of Barkly St – good for people watching. The café downstairs is open for breakfast and light meals from 10am till late, the upstairs restaurant opens every evening.

Blue Elephant Cafe Bar, 194 Commercial Rd, Prahran (☎03/9510 3654). Cosy, inexpensive café in the heart of gay Prahran. Licensed.

Foo Doo's Cafe, 366 Smith St, Collingwood. This small place is especially good for breakfast. Mon–Fri 9am–4pm, Sat & Sun 10am–4pm.

Globe Cafe, 218 Chapel St, Prahran. Good choice for a well-deserved treat after a hard morning's browsing on Chapel St.
Street Cafe, 23 Fitzroy St, St Kilda (☎03/9525 4655). Upmarket café, bar and restaurant located in the heart of the St Kilda scene.

See also p.774 for gay and lesbian-friendly places to stay and overleaf for gay and lesbian nightspots.

Richmond and the southern suburbs

Bridge Hotel, 642 Bridge Rd, Richmond. Jazz, reggae and African music.

Cherry Tree Hotel, 53 Balmain St, Richmond. Scores of tribute bands trying to make their vicarious mark.

Continental Cafe, Greville St, Prahran. Smart venue for established and up-and-coming artists.

Corner Hotel, 57 Swan St, Richmond. Alternative independent bands.

The Esplanade Hotel, 11 Upper Esplanade, St Kilda. The "Espy" is the soul of St Kilda and of Melbourne's eclectic band scene (huge bouncers make it look rougher than it actually is). Interesting nightly line-up of free bands in the front bar; small admission charged to see bands in the Gershwin Room.

Molly Bloom's, 39 Bay St, Port Melbourne. Irish music most nights; no cover charge.

The Palace, Lower Esplanade, St Kilda (next to the *Palais*). Entertainment complex with big-name bands in the main room, smaller bands in the pool room, and a club at the rear.

Prince of Wales Hotel, Fitzroy St, St Kilda. Another St Kilda icon, but unlike the *Espy* this one has undergone a facelift to fit in with the smart cafés and restaurants at this end of Fitzroy Street. Late-night venue with good bands.

Clubs

Promoters hand out **passes** for reduced or free admission to a rapidly changing array of clubs on the corner of Bourke and Russell streets, or you can pick up the passes in record shops such as Gaslight, further up Bourke Street. King Street, in the CBD between Collins Street and Flinders Lane, has a handy concentration of clubs. Most clubs have a cover charge of between $5 and $10.

The Bull Ring, 95 Johnston St, Fitzroy. The best place to dance to Latin rhythms. The band starts at 10.30pm, the dance-floor show at 11pm.

Carousel, Aughtie Drive, Albert Park. Dance venue playing good acid jazz and funk.

Chasers, 386 Chapel St, South Yarra. One of several clubs full of bright young things on this fashion-conscious street. Regular dance nights Wed–Sun.

Heat and **Odeon**, Crown Casino Entertainment Complex, south of the Yarra. Discos on level 3 of the complex, playing mainstream pop of the Eighties and Nineties; occasional live bands.

Ibiza, 116 Chapel St, Windsor. Dance club popular with the gay/lesbian scene. DJs play house and techno.

Joeys, 210 Toorak Rd, South Yarra. DJs play Eighties and Nineties tunes, complemented now and then by live bands.

Lizard Lounge, *The Union Hotel*, 90 Chapel St, Windsor. Alternative indie club. Thurs–Sat 9pm–3am.

The Lounge, 243 Swanston Walk, city centre. Upstairs club with bands, films, pool, dance floor and a cool-off balcony. Most nights 6pm–3am, Fri & Sat until 6am.

The Metro, 20 Bourke St, city centre. Huge old theatre on three floors with eight bars and three dance floors, all very lavish. Enormous queue of spivved-up kids on Friday night. Fri & Sat $10.

Monsoon, Russell St. Upmarket club at the *Grand Hyatt*: *daFunk Club* for R&B, funk and soul.

Viper Room, 373 Chapel St, Prahran. Dance club open Thurs & Fri 11pm–7.30am, Sat from 10pm, Sun from 11pm.

Gay and lesbian nightspots

Club 80, 10 Peel St, North Melbourne. Melbourne's largest, sleaziest male cruising bar. Cover charge. Open Mon–Thurs 5pm–8am, Fri 5pm–Mon 8am.

Diva Bar, 153 Commercial Rd. Cocktail and dance bar with a mixed crowd. Wed–Sun from 6pm.

DT's Hotel, 164 Church St, Richmond. Mixed crowd and popular pool competitions. Dinner Wed–Sun.

Duke of Edinburgh, 374 St Kilda Rd, cnr of Market St, St Kilda. Beer garden and pool competitions attract a mixed crowd. Thurs–Sun from 3pm.

Glasshouse Hotel, 51 Gipps St, Collingwood. Sociable pub which attracts a mixed bunch; Wed–Sun from 11am until late.

Hardware, 285 Latrobe St (☎03/9642 5422). Bar and bistro open for breakfast on Saturday at 7am, for lunch Mon–Sat, and daily for dinner. Comedy and dance shows from 10pm Wed–Sun.

Jock's, 9 Peel St, Collingwood (☎03/9417 6700). International gay bar and restaurant. Gay and mixed crowd. A wide selection of Australian beers and wines. Bar Mon–Sat 4pm–1am, Sun 4pm–11.30pm; restaurant daily 6–10pm.

Laird Hotel, 149 Gipps St, Collingwood (☎03/9417 2832). Well-equipped boys' venue, with two bars, DJs, a beer garden and games room. Popular with the leather crowd. Daily from 5pm, with cheap drinks until 10pm.

Peel Dance Bar, 113 Wellington St, cnr of Peel St, Collingwood. Dance floor, music videos and shows, drawing a large and appreciative crowd of gays and lesbians. Wed–Sun 10pm–dawn.

Star Hotel, 176 Hoddle St, Collingwood. Sociable pub; mixed crowd. Wed–Sun.

3 Faces, 143 Commercial Rd, South Yarra (☎03/9826 0933). Excellent dance club with weekly menu of top-notch drag shows, karaoke nights and talent quests. No cover charge. Tues–Sun 8pm–3am.

Toolbox at the Laundry, 50 Johnston St. Every second Friday for women.

Xchange Hotel, 119 Commercial Rd, South Yarra. Mainly men. Mon–Fri from 2pm, weekends from noon until late. Front bar becomes a disco Fri–Sun.

Comedy

Melbourne is the **comedy capital** of Australia, home of the madcap Doug Anthony All Stars, Wogs Out of Work and comedians from TV shows such as *The Big Gig* and *The Comedy Company*. The highlight of the comedy year is the **Comedy Festival** in April, based at the Town Hall and the Capitol Theatre in Swanston Street, with performances at several other venues around town. As well as local and interstate acts, you're likely to see some of the best stand-up comedians from overseas. For irregular performances and other venues, refer to the *EG* (supplement to *The Age* on Fridays).

Comedy Club, 380 Lygon St, Carlton (☎03/9348 1622). Slick, cabaret-style space which features largely mainstream comedians.

The Esplanade Hotel, 11 Upper Esplanade, St Kilda. Occasional stand-up comedy shows.

Theatre

Melbourne offers a rich array of **dramatic productions**, from fringe to mainstream, with venues everywhere. Watch out for **outdoor performances** in summer, including alfresco Shakespeare and something for children in the Royal Botanic Gardens from December until the end of February (☎03/9650 1500 for details; credit-card bookings with Ticketmaster, ☎ 13 2612).

Athenaeum Theatre, 188 Collins St (☎03/9650 1500). One of numerous small Victorian theatre buildings in the city. The venue for guest performances; mainly plays and concerts.

Comedy Theatre, 240 Exhibition St (☎03/9209 9000). Like the Athenaeum – not a comedy venue, as its name might suggest.

CUB Malthouse, 113 Sturt St, South Melbourne (☎03/9685 5111). A renovated malthouse containing two venues: the Beckett Theatre and the larger Merlyn Theatre. The resident company is

Playbox, which produces contemporary Australian plays. Guest performances include opera, dance, concerts and readings.

Her Majesty's Theatre, 219 Exhibition St (☎03/9663 3211). Lavish musicals in a fabulously ornate old theatre.

La Mama, 205 Faraday St, Fitzroy (☎03/9347 6142). Plays by new writers, as well as poetry and play readings.

Playhouse Theatre, Victorian Arts Centre, 100 St Kilda Rd (☎03/9281 8000). Mainstream productions, mainly from the Melbourne Theatre Company.

Princess Theatre, 163 Spring St, city centre (☎03/9663 3300). Musicals and mainstream plays make up the programme at this small but lavish old-fashioned theatre.

Regent Theatre, Collins St, near City Square (☎03/9299 9500). This lovingly restored old theatre puts on productions of big-name musicals.

Theatreworks, 14 Acland St, St Kilda (☎03/9534 4879). Puts on ground-breaking new Australian plays.

Universal Theatre, 19 Victoria St, off Brunswick St, Fitzroy (☎03/9419 3777). Venue for productions by smaller local theatre companies and alternative/fringe plays by overseas guests.

Classical music, opera and dance

The **Melbourne Symphony Orchestra** has a season from February to December based at the Melbourne Concert Hall and at the Melbourne Town Hall on Collins Street, while the **State Orchestra of Victoria** performs less regularly at the Concert Hall, often playing works by Australian composers. If you can't afford the ticket prices, listen to the Symphony Orchestra concerts broadcast on Tuesday at 7pm on Radio 3MBS (103.5FM).

George Fairfax Studio, Victorian Arts Centre, 100 St Kilda Rd (☎03/9281 8000). Modern dance and plays.

Her Majesty's Theatre, 219 Exhibition St, city centre (☎03/9663 3211). Occasionally hosts some of the great foreign ballet companies.

Melbourne Concert Hall, Victorian Arts Centre, 100 St Kilda Rd (☎03/9281 8000). Big-name concerts.

State Theatre, Victorian Arts Centre, 100 St Kilda Rd (☎03/9281 8000). Venue for the Victoria State Opera and the Australian Ballet Company.

Film

The **International Film Festival** in July (☎03/9417 2011) has been going for over forty years and is the centrepiece of Melbourne movie life, based at the Capitol Theatre and other cinemas around Melbourne. Everyday mainstream cinemas are concentrated on Bourke Street, where discount day is usually Tuesday. The Casino has a number of cinemas showing blockbuster movies; at the Gold Class Cinema you can eat a three-course dinner while you watch. In summer, watching a film under the stars at the Moonlight Cinema in the Botanic Gardens (see p.785) or at the Cinema in the Bowl (Sidney Myer Music Bowl) nearby can be a real treat (details from local press; bookings through Ticketmaster ☎13 6100). And there are always the independent cinemas, listed below, which tend to discount on Monday.

Astor Theatre, cnr of Chapel St and Dandenong Rd, St Kilda (☎03/9510 1414). Classic double bills and prestige new releases. On Saturday night there's a pianist and singer between films.

Brighton Bay Twin Cinemas, 294 Bay St, Brighton (☎03/9596 3590). Very comfortable setting for European and art-house films. Cheap day Monday.

Capitol Theatre, 113 Swanston St, city centre (☎03/9654 4422). This old-fashioned, lavishly decorated cinema – now under new management – presents very cheap double features of recent classics.

Carlton Moviehouse, 235 Faraday St, Carlton (☎03/9347 8909). Over seventy years old, the inner city's oldest cinema has a lot of charm. Art-house and foreign films. Cheap day Monday.

Cinema Nova, Lygon Court Plaza, 380 Lygon St, Carlton (☎03/9347 5331). Art-house and European films. Come just before the show starts to avoid prolonged exposure to the awful crimson and purple bordello decor. Cheap day Monday.

Classic, 9 Gordon St, off Glenhuntly Rd, Elsternwick (☎03/9523 9739). Art-house and European films; near the station.

Como, Gaslight Gardens, cnr of Toorak Rd and Chapel St, South Yarra (☎03/9827 7533). Belongs to the same chain as the George Cinema in St Kilda and the Brighton Bay Twin Cinemas – and shows similar films.

George Cinema, 133–137 Fitzroy St, St Kilda (☎03/9534 6922). Has the latest releases, bordering between art-house and mainstream. *Café Diva* on the same floor overlooks Fitzroy St and is ideal for supper or an after-movie coffee.

Glasshouse Cinema, Royal Melbourne Institute of Technology, 360 Swanston St, city centre (☎03/9417 5320). On-campus cinema for art-house and experimental film.

Kino, 45 Collins St, city centre (☎03/9650 2100). In the opulent Collins Place atrium, with several cafés and bars in the complex. Stylish, arty new-release films. Cheap tickets on Monday.

Longford Cinema, 59 Toorak Rd, South Yarra (☎03/9867 2700). Exclusive release for quality films, somewhere between art-house and mainstream. Late films on Friday and Saturday. Cheap day Monday.

Lumiere, 108 Lonsdale St, city centre (☎03/9639 1055). Art-house movies. Cheap day Monday.

Rivoli, Camberwell Rd, Camberwell Junction (☎03/9882 1221). Shows first releases of quality films. Two theatres in an Art Deco building.

State Theatre, 1 MacArthur St, city centre (☎03/9651 1301). The AFI (Australian Film Institute) cinema-buff's cinema. Often shows Australian films.

Trak Cinema, 445 Toorak Rd, Toorak (☎03/9827 9333). Art-house and quality mainstream films, often with a focus on European work.

Westgarth Theatre, 89 High St, Northcote (☎03/9482 2001). Art Deco period piece, decorated by the planner of Canberra, Walter Burley Griffin. Presents quality mainstream and art-house films, cult classics and late shows.

Listings

Airlines (domestic) The offices of several domestic airlines are on Franklin St near the Greyhound Pioneer bus terminal: Ansett (☎13 1300); Aus Air (Moorabbin Airport, ☎03/9580 6166); Kendell (☎13 1300); Eastern Australia Airlines (☎13 1313); Qantas (☎13 1313); Air New Zealand (☎13 2476, fax 02/9937 5325).

Airlines (international) Alitalia (☎1300/653 747, fax 03/9602 3802); British Airways (☎03/9603 1133, fax 02/9258 3251); Canadian Airlines (☎1300/655 767, fax 03/9602 2041); Cathay Pacific (☎13 1747, fax 02/9251 3460); Garuda Indonesia (☎1300/365 330, fax 03/9650 1731); Japan Airlines (☎03/9654 2733, fax 9650 6820); KLM (☎03/9654 5222, fax 9650 6771, free call ☎1800/500 747); Lauda Air (free call ☎1800/642 438, fax 03/9602 2331), Malaysia Airlines (☎13 2627, fax 02/9650 9296); Olympic (☎03/9629 5022, fax 9629 2220); Philippine Airlines (☎03/9654 3433, fax 9654 3499); Qantas (☎13 1211); Singapore Airlines (☎13 1011, fax 02/9350 0262); Thai International (☎1300/651 960, fax 03/9650 7003); United (☎13 1777, fax 02/9292 4551).

Airport bus Skybus (☎03/9662 9275) departs roughly every thirty minutes from bay 30 at Spencer Street Bus Terminal (see also "Arrival and information", p.767).

American Express, 233–239 Collins St (Mon–Fri 8.30am–5.30pm, Sat 9am–2pm).

Banks and foreign exchange All major banks can be found on Collins St, and most are open Mon–Fri 9am–5pm; the Bank of Melbourne is also open Sat 9am–noon. For foreign exchange: Thomas Cook is at 257 Collins St and 330 Collins St (Mon–Fri 9am–5pm, Sat 9am–1pm) and at Shop 5, 235 Bourke St (near Swanston St; same opening hours plus Sun 9am–1pm). The Thomas Cook desks at the international and domestic terminal of Tullamarine Airport are open 24hr.

Bike rental Hire a Bicycle, a stand south of the Princes Bridge (☎019/429 000; daily 11am–5pm and summer until 7pm, weather permitting) has basic bicycles (30min for $5, 1hr for $8 and half-day for $16) as well as mountain bikes ($7, $12 and $22 respectively); helmets, locks, maps and backpacks are provided.

City Cycle Tours, Treasury Gardens (☎03/9585 5343) does guided half-day cycling tours of the city ($30); and rents out bikes to those who'd rather explore on their own (1hr for $10, full day for $30). You can also rent bikes at Fitzroy Cycles Bike Hire, 224 Swanston St, near Little Bourke St (☎03/9639 3511; full day $35). In St Kilda try the helpful, long-established St Kilda Cycles, 11 Carlisle St (Mon–Fri 9am–6pm, Sat 9am–5pm, Sun 10am–4pm; ☎03/9534 3074; full day $20), or the stand next to the cycle path near St Kilda Pier, which rents out bicycles on weekends, and daily during the summer holidays.

Bookshops Mainstream bookshops, all with many branches, are: Angus & Robertson Bookworld at 391 Bourke St and 35 Swanston St, and Bookcity at 205 Swanston St for discounts; Collins Booksellers, 104 Elizabeth St, 86 Bourke St and 401 Swanston St; and Readers Feast at Midtown Plaza at the corner of Bourke and Swanston sts. One of Melbourne's best literary bookshops is Readings, 338 Lygon St, Carlton, with another branch at 153 Toorak Rd, South Yarra, down the road from Black Mask Books at no. 78, which specializes in mystery and crime. In Fitzroy, Brunswick St has the very good Brunswick St Bookstore, at no. 305 (daily 10am–11pm), and Grub St Bookshop at no. 317 for secondhand books. In Prahran at the Jam Factory there's the large Border's Books & Music, 500 Chapel St, which also has a pleasant café (both open daily 9am–midnight). St Kilda also has several bookshops, including Chronicles Bookshop, 91 Fitzroy St (Mon–Wed 10am–8pm, Thurs–Sun 10am–10pm), and the intriguing Cosmos Books and Music, 112 Acland St. In the city centre, The Paperback at 60 Bourke St is open Mon–Sat 11am–11pm, Sun 11am–5pm. Map Land, 372 Little Bourke St (Mon–Fri 9am 5.30pm, Sat 10am–2pm), specializes in travel books and maps. Topographical maps, maps of national parks in Victoria and other publications on Victoria are available at Information Victoria, 356 Collins St.

Buses Buy last-minute tickets at the bus company offices in the Spencer Street and Franklin Street terminals (V/Line reservations daily 7am–9pm; ☎13 6196. Operators include Greyhound Pioneer, (☎13 2030; Franklin St terminal reservation desk daily 6.30am–10.30pm ☎03/9663 3299); McCafferty's, Spencer St Coach Terminal (☎03/9670 2533, reservations daily 6am–9pm); Firefly, Spencer St Coach Terminal (☎03/9670 7500, reservations daily 7am–8.30pm). For advance bookings, it's easier to go to the Bus Booking Centre, 58 Spencer St (Mon–Fri 9am–6pm, Sat & Sun 11am–6pm; ☎03/9534 2003), or Backpackers Travel Centre, Shop 19, Centre Place, off 258 Flinders Lane (Mon–Fri 9am–6pm, Sat 10am–3pm; ☎03/9654 8477). They will shop around for you to find the cheapest deals, and they also sell bus passes, and make bookings for tours around Melbourne and one-way to Sydney or Adelaide (see "Tours" below). City bus information is available from the Met Transport Information Centre (see p.768).

Cameras Camera Action, 217 Elizabeth St (☎03/9670 6901), is an excellent all-round camera shop.

Car rental Australian Rent-a-Car, 58 Latrobe St (☎03/9662 2300); Avis, 20 Franklin St (☎03/9663 6366 or free call ☎1800/225 533); Budget, 398 Elizabeth St (☎03/132 727); Delta, 85 Franklin St (☎03/9662 2366 or ☎13 1390); Hertz, 97 Franklin St (☎03/9663 6244 or ☎13 3039); National, cnr of Queensberry and Peel sts (☎03/131 045); Thrifty, 390 Elizabeth St (☎1300/367 727); all do one-way rentals, subject to availability. Used-car companies with cheaper rates include Backpacker Car Rentals, 103 Railway Ave, Werribee (☎03/9731 0711); Rent-A-Bomb, 507 Bridge Rd, Richmond (☎03/9428 0088); and Ugly Duckling, 197 Inkerman St, St Kilda (☎03/9525 4010). Campervans are available from Britz Australia (☎03/9483 1888); Koala Campervan Rentals (free call ☎1800/998 029); and NQ Australia Campervan Rentals (free call ☎1800/079 529).

CD & record shops Gaslight, 85 Bourke St, has a superb range of everything except classical; Thomas's Records nearby at no. 31 is small but very good; Au-go-go, at 349 Little Bourke St (Mon–Sat 9.30am–7pm, Sun 11am–5pm), sells independent and rare recordings, and displays notices for room shares and what's on. Discurio, 105 Elizabeth St, sells classical music, jazz, blues and folk; Basement Discs, 24 Block Place, off Little Collins St, has a great range of jazz and world music, as does Blue Moon at 30 Johnston St, Fitzroy. In the southern inner city suburbs Border's Books & Music, at the Jam Factory, South Yarra, has a big CD department, (daily 9am–midnight), and in St Kilda, just around the corner from Acland St at 221 Barkly St, the smallish Raoul Records covers the whole range from rock, R&B, folk, blues and jazz to world music.

Consulates Canada, 1st Floor, 123 Camberwell Rd, Hawthorn East (☎03/9811 9999); UK, 17th floor, 90 Collins St (☎03/9650 4155); USA, 553 St Kilda Rd (☎03/9526 5900).

Disabled travellers Disability Information Line, 555 Collins St, (☎03/9616 7704); Disability Resources Centre, 306 Johnston St, Abbotsford (☎03/3419 5535); Paraplegic & Quadriplegic Association, 208 Wellington St, Collingwood (☎03/9415 1200). For the Public Transport Corporation's Disability Service, free call ☎1800/013 920 (for metropolitan and suburban train stations) or ☎03/9619 2300 (for assistance at Spencer Street and country stations). Melbourne City Council produces a free mobility map showing access and facilities in the city centre, available from the Town Hall.

Diving Underwater Victoria–Dive Industry Victoria Association (free call ☎1800/816 151; *inquires@diva.asn.au*) has a list of members in the Greater Melbourne area who hire equipment, organize diving trips and offer dive courses.

Emergency ☎000 for fire, police or ambulance.

Employment Backpackers Resource Centre, at *Hotel Bakpak* (☎03/99328 3513, fax 9326 7667; *brc@bakpak.com*; *www.bakpak.com/brc*). Traveller's Contact Point on the ground floor of 29–31 Somerset Place, a lane off Little Bourke St between Elizabeth and Queen sts (☎03/9642 2911; Mon–Fri 9am–6pm, Sat 10am–4pm).

Environment and conservation Australian Trust for Conservation Volunteers (☎03/9686 5554); NRE Information Centre, 8 Nicholson St, East Melbourne, run by the Department of Natural Resources and Environment (Mon–Fri 8.30am–5.40pm; ☎03/9637 8080). Parks Victoria (telephone information service ☎13 1963); Greens Bookshop, 247 Flinders Lane; Wilderness Society Shop, 355 Little Bourke St (☎03/9670 2867). The Victoria Visitor Information Centre at the Town Hall also has a range of brochures on national parks.

Ferries If you're heading for Tasmania on the Bass Strait there's a choice between *Spirit of Tasmania* (3 per week; 14hr) and *Devil Cat* (during peak season and Dec 22–end of third week in January daily; Dec–April 4 per week; 6hr); reservations for both ☎13 2010. To get to Station Pier in Port Melbourne take the #109 tram from Collins St in the city. The airport bus Skybus also runs to the pier.

Flat-hunting and sharing Check the Saturday edition of *The Age*, as well as the notice boards of hostels, cafés along Brunswick St in Fitzroy, the *Galleon Café* at 9 Carlisle St, St Kilda, and Readings bookshop, 338 Lygon St, Carlton.

Gay and lesbian Melbourne See box on pp 000 000.

Hospitals and medical centres Royal Melbourne Hospital, Grattan St, Parkville (☎03/9342 7000); St Vincent's, Victoria Parade, Fitzroy (☎03/9807 2211); Royal Dental Hospital, cnr of Elizabeth St and Flemington Rd, Parkville (☎03/9341 0222); Melbourne Sexual Health Centre, 580 Swanston St, Carlton (☎03/9347 0244 or free call ☎1800/032 017). For vaccinations, anti-malaria tablets and first-aid kits contact the Travellers Medical and Vaccination Centre, 2nd floor, 393 Little Bourke St (☎03/9602 5788).

Internet access Some backpacker hostels have Internet access for reading email, and some even have an Internet café for surfing. One is Backpackers World at *Hotel Bakpak*, 167 Franklin St, (☎03/9329 1990), daily 8am–10pm. About $3 for 30min, $6 per hour. Traveller's Contact Point in Somerset Place provides Internet access among many other services including mail forwarding, voicemail, luggage storage and travel bookings (see "Employment" above).

Internet cafés *PaciCentury Café*, Level 1, 239 Lonsdale St, between Swanston and Russell Sts (☎03/9654 5529) for Internet and related computer services, plus b/w or colour printing (daily 10am–11pm; Internet $3 for 30min, $6 per hour); *Outlook Internet Café & Cyber Lounge*, 196 Commercial Rd, Prahran (☎03/9521 4227) is a good café opposite Prahran Market, that also offers services such as scanning and photocopying (Mon–Tues 10am–6pm, Wed–Sat 10am–9pm, Sun 11am–7pm; Internet $7 per hour).

Laundries Most hostels and some hotels have their own laundry. Commercial ones include: City Edge Launderette, 39 Errol St, opposite North Melbourne Town Hall (daily 6am–11pm); The Soap Opera Laundry 128 Bridport St, Albert Park (Mon–Fri 7.30am–9pm, Sat & Sun 8am–9pm).

Left luggage Spencer Street Station has lockers (daily 6am–10pm; $2; emptied nightly); luggage can be left overnight at the cloakroom ($3.50 per item). Flinders Street Station has lockers (8am–8pm; $2). The lockers at the Melbourne Transit Centre on Franklin St are accessible 24hr ($5). Travellers Contact Point also stores luggage (see "Employment" above).

Library The General Reference and Information Centre at the State Library of Victoria, 328 Swanston Walk, keeps popular Australian and overseas magazines; the Newspaper Room has foreign papers (Mon 1–9pm, Tues & Thurs–Sun 10am–6pm, Wed 10am–9pm).

Markets Queen Victoria Market, the Victorian Arts Centre crafts market, and local markets at Prahran, South Melbourne and St Kilda, are discussed earlier in the chapter. Camberwell Market, Station St (Sunday 6am–1pm; train to Camberwell), is a large flea market with lots of good second-hand clothes, books and records as well as bric-a-brac, and with plenty of food vans and cafés.

Motorbikes The northern end of Elizabeth St in the city centre has a string of motorbike shops. Garner's Motorcycles, 179 Peel St, North Melbourne (☎03/9326 8676) and Victorian Motorcycles, 606 High St, East Kew (☎03/9817 3206), do rentals and may sell secondhand machines with buy-back deals.

Newspapers Melbourne's *The Age* is one of Australia's better papers; the pulpy *Sun-Herald* is the city's only other daily. Foreign newspapers can be perused at the State Library (see "Library" opposite) or bought from McGill's Newsagency, 187 Elizabeth St.

Pharmacies Henry Francis Chemists, 286 Little Bourke St, next to Myer department store (daily); Leonard Long, cnr of Williams Rd and High St, Prahran (daily until midnight); Mulqueeny's Pharmacy, Swanston St, and opposite the Town Hall (daily until late).

Police Melbourne City Police Station, 637 Flinders St, ☎03/9247 5347; emergency ☎000.

Post office The General Post Office at the cnr of Bourke and Elizabeth sts is open Mon–Fri 8.15am–5.30pm, Sat 10am–1pm (including the poste restante counter). Other post offices are open Mon–Fri 9am–5pm. For voicemail and mail forwarding, contact Travellers Contact Point. ("see Employment" opposite).

RACV The two RACV outlets in the city are at 360 Bourke St (cnr of Elizabeth St) and 123 Queen St; they have good maps on Melbourne, Victoria and the rest of Australia (free for RACV members and members of affiliated overseas motoring associations). They also book accommodation listed in their guides and package holidays; members get special rates.

Rape and sexual assault CASA House (Centre Against Sexual Assault), 270 Cardigan St, Carlton (☎03/9344 2210, after hours 9349 1766, free call ☎1800/806 292), provides medical care, support and counselling.

Shopping The big two department stores, David Jones and Myer, are located off the Bourke Street Mall. Daimaru on Elizabeth St is Japanese-owned, with a very sophisticated feel. Chapel St, South Yarra, is the home of interesting upmarket fashion, getting younger and less expensive towards Prahran. Greville St, Prahran, has lots of retro chic, although Brunswick St in Fitzroy is the best spot for secondhand clothes. Dangerfield (in the city centre at 224 Flinders St, the Sportsgirl Centre on Collins St and Melbourne Central, and in Greville St, Prahran) has modern funky clothes, including lots of great hats and jewellery. In Richmond, Bridge Rd between Punt Rd and Church St is the discount centre of Melbourne; clothes and shoe shops sell seconds, samples and end-of-season stock – lots of cheap rubbish, but also brand names such as Country Road, Sportsgirl, Jag and Witchery. In the city, Little Bourke St (from no. 349 upwards) and Hardware St, round the corner, are the places to go for travel equipment and clothing.

Skiing Skiman, 295 Clarendon St (☎03/9696 4955), and AUSKI Ski Hiring & Information Centre, 9 Hardware Lane (☎03/9670 1412 or 9670 7729), can advise on skiing conditions at Baw Baw, Buffalo, Mount Hotham, Buller, Falls Creek and at Thredbo in NSW.

Swimming pools City Baths, in a Victorian red-brick building on the cnr of Swanston and Franklin sts (Mon–Fri 6am–10pm, Sat & Sun 8am–6pm; $2.80 for a swim plus $4 for use of sauna and spa; ☎03/9663 5888), has a thirty-metre heated indoor pool for swimming, plus a pool for water-aerobics and a gym. In the brand new, state-of-the-art Melbourne Sports & Aquatic Centre, Aughtie Drive, off Albert Park Rd in Albert Park there's a choice between a wave pool, a 50-metre pool, a dive pool, a 25-metre lap pool and a 20-metre multipurpose pool; there are also 10 squash courts (Mon–Fri 6–10pm, 50-metre pool Mon–Fri 5.30–8pm, Sat & Sun 7am–8pm; admission $4; ☎03/9926 1555). Take tram #12 or #96 from the city.

Taxis Taxi rank on Swanston St outside Flinders Street Station, and plenty to flag down. Call Arrow (☎13 2211); Black Cabs Combined (☎13 2227); Embassy Taxis (☎13 1755); or Silver Top (☎13 1008).

Telephones Melbourne is well stocked with public telephones. Some backpacker hostels and shops in the city sell discount phonecards (such as Unidial, EZI Great Rate Card, One Card and AAPT) which can be used in any payphone for cheap international calls. The official Telstra rate for a call from a public phone to the UK is $1.60 per minute Mon–Fri, 80¢ Sat & Sun. With one of the phonecards mentioned above, expect to pay about 39¢–55¢ per minute, plus a small connecting fee (less than $1).

Trains Spencer Street Station has a staffed information desk where you can get hold of all V/Line train (and bus) timetables; buy your ticket at the V/Line Travel Centre opposite or on ☎ 13 6196 (7am–9pm). If you're travelling with a bicycle, come at least thirty minutes earlier to book it on the train. Suburban train information is available from the Met Transport Information Centre (see p.77).

TOURS FROM MELBOURNE

With Melbourne as a base, a wide variety of **tours** can be made to the interior of Victoria or both east and west along the coast. Popular destinations – both as **day-trips** and **one-way tours** – are to the Grampians, Phillip Island and the Mornington Peninsula, and along the Great Ocean Road. For **longer trips**, you could consider several two- to four-day bushwalking excursions offered by several operators. Listed below are some of the more popular tours.

Autopia Tours (☎03/9326 5536). Long-established tour operator running very popular minibus tours: Great Ocean Road (1 day, $50; 2 days $70); Phillip Island (1 day, $50);Great Ocean Road–Phillip Island combination (2 days, $100); and Great Ocean Road–Grampians combination (3 days, $135).

Echidna Walkabout (☎03/9646 8249, fax 9681 9177). Tours focusing on native wildlife and local Koorie culture. Day-tours to the Brisbane Ranges and You Yangs, west of Melbourne; longer trips to the Ballarat goldfields, Grampians, Great Ocean Road or remoter parts of East Gippsland (Nov–April). Tours are upmarket, with very small groups and enthusiastic, knowledgeable guides.

Let's Go Bush (☎03/9662 3969, fax 9521 6641). Two-day tour to the Great Ocean Road departs twice-weekly and includes an overnight stay in a house owned by the tour company ($90).

Oz Experience (☎1300/300 028). Backpacker transport service doing regular runs three times weekly, and daily in peak season; all major sights visited on the way to Adelaide (Great Ocean Road and the Grampians) or Sydney (Phillip Island, Gippsland beaches, the High Country, Canberra and the coast south of Sydney).

Surfing Safaris (☎03/5413 2487 or 0411/535 939). Surfing lessons given on tours (Nov–April only; one day for about $90, two days for about $180), which head mainly to the uncrowded and scenic east coast. All surfing gear and food is supplied, and for overnight trips camping equipment is provided – bring your own sleeping bag.

Wayward Bus (free call ☎1800/882 823). One-way tours: regular runs between Melbourne and Sydney via the High Country (four days, $190) and between Melbourne and Adelaide (three days via the Great Ocean Road, $160; four days Great Ocean Road and the Grampians, $190).

Wild-Life Tours (☎03/9747 1882, fax 9747 1930). One-way tours between Melbourne and Adelaide (1–2 days; $80–130; departing 3 times a week) and round trips from Melbourne (1–3 days, $50–130; day-tour departs daily, other tours at least three times a week). Depending on the length of the trip, the tours take in the Great Ocean Road, the Grampians and Mt Arapiles; longer stopover options are available.

Travel agents Backpackers Travel Centre, Shop 19, Centre Place, 258 Flinders Lane (☎03/9654 8477 or 1300/300 795; *info@backpackerstravel.net.au*); Flight Centre, 19 Bourke St, 53 Elizabeth St and many other branches (☎13 1600); STA Travel, 273 Little Collins St, 142 Acland St, St Kilda, and other branches (book and pay over the phone ☎1300/360 960; or for nearest branch ☎13 1776); Student Uni Travel, 440 Elizabeth St (☎03/9328 2111); Travellers Contact Point, 29–31 Somerset Place (for full listing, see "Employment" p.808), YHA Travel, 205 King St (Mon–Fri; 9am–5.30pm, Sat 9am–noon; ☎03/9670 9611).

Travellers aid centres Lower ground floor, Spencer Street Station (Mon–Fri 7.30am–7.30pm, Sat & Sun 7.30am–11.30am; ☎03/9670 2873), and 2nd Floor, 169 Swanston St (Mon–Fri 8am–5pm, ☎03/9654 2600): both provide nappy-changing facilities, showers (for a fee), toilets, lounge rooms, wheelchairs for rent, assistance for disabled and frail persons, and information. There are also tearooms and lockers ($1) at the Swanston St centre.

Women Queen Victoria's Women's Centre, is in the former Queen Victoria Women's Hospital at 210 Lonsdale St (☎03/9663 8799). The beautifully restored, 1890s building houses a Women's Health Library, an Aboriginal Resource Centre, an art gallery, seminar rooms as well as a café and restaurant. Services include classes and seminars, professional consulting (on topics such as health and finance) and notice boards. (Mon–Fri 8.30am–5.30pm) Women's Information and Referral

Service (WIRE; Mon–Fri 9am–9pm; ☎03/9654 6844 or free call ☎1800/136 570) is a telephone information service run by women for women.

AROUND MELBOURNE

There are many possible day-trips out of Melbourne, mainly around the shores of the huge **Port Phillip Bay**, encircled by the arms of the Bellarine and Mornington peninsulas. The **Mornington Peninsula** on the east side is home to some of the city's most popular beaches, packed on summer weekends. **Western Port Bay**, beyond the peninsula, encloses two fascinating islands – little-known **French Island**, much of whose wildlife is protected by a national park, and **Phillip Island**, where the waddling ashore of masses of Little penguins each night is among Australia's biggest tourist attractions. Inland to the east, the **Yarra Valley** and the **Dandenong Range** offer beautiful countryside, wine-tasting and bushwalking. The **Bellarine Peninsula** and the western side of Port Phillip Bay are less exciting, but they do give access to the west coast and the Great Ocean Road.

The Mornington Peninsula

The **Mornington Peninsula** curves right around Port Phillip Bay, culminating in Point Nepean, well to the southwest of Melbourne. The shoreline facing the bay is beach-bum territory, though the well-heeled denizens of the main resorts, **Sorrento** and **Portsea**, might well resent that tag. On the largely straight, ocean-facing coast, **Mornington Peninsula National Park** encompasses some fine seascapes, with several walking trails marked out. Interspersed among the peninsula's bushland, grazing land and orchards are 100 **vineyards** which produce superb, if pricey, Pinot Noir and Shiraz wines, as well as good whites. Wineries are open for **tastings** and cellar-door **sales**, and some also serve food. Among the most notable are Dromana Estate, Harrison's Road, Dromana (☎03/5987 3800), a beautifully located winery where light lunches are served daily; Red Hill Estate, 52 Red Hill–Shoreham Road, Red Hill (☎03/5989 2855), in an equally appealing location, for excellent champagne and light lunches daily; and Main Ridge Estate, William Road, Red Hill (☎03/5989 2686), one of the first vineyards in the area, for Chardonnay and Pinot Noir, it serves lunches every Sunday. For details, refer to the brochure *Wine Regions of Victoria* (see p.000) or local information magazines.

As well as the beaches, the peninsula's **community markets** selling local produce and crafts attract many city dwellers: most are monthly affairs, so there's usually one every weekend. One of the biggest and best is Red Hill Community Market, held on the first Saturday of every month (7am–1pm; Sept–May), at Red Hill Recreation Reserve, Red Hill Road, 10km east of Dromana.

You can get to the peninsula by **public transport** from Melbourne to Frankston and from there to the main beach resorts and towns along the Nepean Highway on the northern side, but for a sightseeing trip taking in wineries, beaches and Arthurs Seat you need your own vehicle. Take a Met train to Frankston and change there for Stony Point, or connect with a Portsea Passenger Service bus #788 from Frankston to Sorrento and Portsea (if you're staying longer, get a Peninsula Bus Pass, $35 for 10 trips. For timetable information for this bus service, free call ☎1800/115 666). From Sorrento there's a community bus to Dromana via Blairgowrie, Rye and Rosebud (four daily Mon–Fri) but no transport to Arthurs Seat. V/Line's package deal ($37) will give people in a hurry a quick glimpse of both the Mornington and the Bellarine Peninsulas; it comprises the train to Frankston and bus to Sorrento, then a ferry transfer from Sorrento to Queenscliff, and the return trip by bus to Geelong and train to Melbourne.

It's best to book this trip a day in advance at V/Line Holidays in Spencer Street Station. For timetable and other information call ☎ 03/9619 8080.

The western coast

The peninsula essentially starts at suburban **Frankston**, 40km from central Melbourne, and from here on down, the western coast, flanked by the Nepean Highway, is beach after beach, all crowded and traffic-snarled in summer. Twelve kilometres beyond Frankston, the old fishing port of **Mornington** preserves some of its heritage in fine buildings along Mornington Esplanade; every Wednesday there's a produce and craft market on Main Street. **Mount Martha**, 5km on, is another old settlement, the **Briars Historic Park** (homestead daily 11am–4pm, parklands and wetlands: 9am–5pm, admission fee for both $5), an 1860s homestead surrounded by lawns and gardens, woodlands and extensive wetlands. At the visitor's centre near the homestead, an audiovisual display gives you an overview on how the affluent upper crust lived in early pioneering days as well as a rundown on the present-day facilities of the park. The 74 acres of **wetlands** are of interest to naturalists, as they are used by more than fifty species of waterbirds, which can be observed at close distance from two bird-hides, accessible from the visitor information centre. There are also two woodland **walkways**, and guided bushwalks are conducted at night on request (except in winter). In summer, there are additional events, such as jazz concerts, astronomical viewing of the night sky, and Heritage Day with actors in period costume.

Inland from Dromana, where seaside development begins in earnest, the granite outcrop of **Arthurs Seat State Park** rises 305m, providing breathtaking views of Port Phillip Bay. A **chairlift** makes the vista more easily accessible, leaving from the picnic area on Arthurs Seat Road, just off the Mornington Peninsula Freeway (Sept–2nd Mon in June daily 11am–4.30pm; rest of the year Sat, Sun, public & school holidays same hours; $8 return). Beyond, the peninsula arcs and narrows: the sands around Sorrento and Portsea offer a choice between the rugged surf of the ocean ("back" beaches) or the calmer waters of the bay ("front" beaches).

Sorrento

With some of the most expensive real estate outside the Melbourne CBD, **SORRENTO** is the traditional haunt of the city's rich throughout the "season", from Boxing Day to Easter; many move to their second homes here for the duration. Well-heeled outsiders also make it their playground in January and on summer weekends, flocking here to swim, surf and dive at the bay and ocean beaches. Exploring beautiful rock formations and low-tide pools, and swimming with bottlenose dolphins add to the attraction. The smell of money is everywhere – in the wide, tree-lined residential streets, the clifftop mansions boasting million-dollar views, and the town-centre cafés, restaurants, galleries and antique shops, running along Ocean Road down to the beach.

Sullivan Bay, 3km southeast, was the site of the first white attempt to settle in what is now Victoria in 1803; the settlers struggled here for four months before giving up and moving on to what is now Tasmania. One of the convicts in the expedition was the infamous William Buckley, who escaped, was adopted by the local Aborigines and lived with them for 32 years. When the "wild white man" was seen again by settlers he could scarcely remember how to speak English; his survival against all odds has been immortalized in the phrase "Buckley's chance". A display centre on the site (April–Sept Sun 1–4pm; Oct–Mar Sat, Sun & school holidays 1–4pm; free) fleshes out the story of the settlement.

Swimming with dolphins and seals is becoming one of the prime attractions of Port Phillip Bay; so much so that tour operators are obliged to follow a code of practice to ensure they don't adversely affect the animals. Two long-established operators are Polperro Dolphin Swims (☎03/5988 8437 or mobile ☎018/174 160), who take the smallest maximum number of people, and Moonraker (☎03/5984 4211, mobile ☎018/591 033). Both depart twice daily during the season (Sept/Oct–May), weather permitting, for a four-hour trip ($55 per swimmer, including wetsuit and snorkelling equipment; $35 for sightseers). A cruise with Sorrento Ferry & Dolphin Watch is much cheaper, as there's no swimming involved, and the groups are much larger (2hr 30min; ☎03/5984 1602; $20).

Practicalities

Only one of Sorrento's **hotels** provides accommodation: the 1871 limestone *Sorrento Hotel*, 5 Hotham Rd (☎03/5984 2206, fax 5984 3424; ⑦–⑧), very charming and located in a secluded spot on a hill above the jetty. The equally old *Continental Hotel*, 21 Ocean Beach Rd, now only does food but on weekend nights there's live music and a disco. There are a few **B&B's**, though: non-smoking *Carmel*, 142 Ocean Beach Rd (☎ & fax 03/5984 3512; ⑥–⑦), a charming, sandstone B&B smack in the middle of town; *Tamasha House*, 699 Melbourne Rd, (☎ & fax 03/5984 2413, fax 5984 0452; ⑦), a modern house halfway between ocean and bay beaches. For people on a budget, *Sorrento Hostel YHA*, 3 Miranda St (☎ & fax 03/5984 4323; rooms ③, dorms ①), is a modern, comfortable **hostel** with small dorms and a twin room, some with en-suite facilities, and stacks of local information as well as some walks organized to local points of interest. **Caravan parks** tend to be either closed (out of season) or completely booked up and cost twice the normal price: two of the more reasonable are *Nautilus* (☎03/5984 2277; on-site vans ③) and the *Foreshore Reserve* (☎03/5984 2797), which has tent sites only.

As you might expect, all this glitz needs to be nourished by plenty of fancy **eating places**. More modest options include getting a takeaway to eat on the benches along Ocean Road or on the beach: try the *Sorrento Village Bakehouse*, 29 Ocean Beach Rd. In the moderate price range, *Buckley's Chance*, 174 Ocean Beach Rd, is a relaxed pancake parlour, which also serves burgers and steaks; and the century-old former Sorrento Tearooms on 3278 Nepean Highway now house the *Sandpiper Licensed Restaurant* (daily 10am–5pm), which is open for breakfast, lunch and dinner (international cuisine) and has great views of the bay. The *Continental Hotel*, 21 Ocean Beach Rd, has a good café serving Mediterranean cuisine and Mornington Peninsula wines.

Ferries run across the mouth of the bay from Sorrento to **Queenscliff** on the Bellarine Peninsula. The *Peninsula Searoad Ferry* (☎03/5258 3244) carries passengers and vehicles year-round (about every 2hr 8am–6pm, in summer until 8pm; advanced car bookings recommended). The *Sorrento Passenger Ferry* (☎03/5984 1602, mobile ☎018/392 507; call to check times) departs from Sorrento daily every hour between 9am and 5pm from Boxing Day to Easter as well as during school holidays, calling at Portsea en route.

Portsea and Point Nepean

PORTSEA, just beyond Sorrento, is a mecca for divers, with excellent **dives** of up to 40m off Port Phillip Heads; trips operate from the pier throughout the summer and there are a couple of good dive shops. Portsea Front Beach, on the bay by the pier, is wall-to-wall beautiful people, as is Shelley Beach, which also attracts playful dolphins. On the other shore, Portsea Ocean Beach has excellent surfing, and a hang-gliding pad on a rock formation known as London Bridge. Back on the bay side, the extensive lawns of *Portsea Hotel*, a hugely popular drinking spot which features bands at weekends, overlook the beach.

The tip of the peninsula, with its fortifications, quarantine station and army base, was off-limits to the public for a century until the establishment of the Point Nepean

National Park in 1988. It is now part of a patchwork of other national parks sprinkled over the southern end of the peninsula, collectively known as **Mornington Peninsula National Park**. The orientation centre for Point Nepean just 1km west of Portsea is going to be privatized by mid-1999, so the opening times and the admission fee to Point Nepean might change, please ring to confirm (☎03/5984 4276; at present daily 9am–5pm). Because of its fragile sandy environment, visitor numbers are limited, so you need to book to visit.

If you're driving, you can leave your car at Gunner's car park which is located 2.5km into the national park and walk to Fort Nepean (8km return; admission fee $5).

A **bus** (hourly 10.30am–12.30pm & 2–3pm; on weekends also at 9.30am; admission fee & transport $8.50) runs the 7km to the fortifications at the point, part of the park, with three optional drop-offs for walks: the first, the **Walter Pisterman Heritage Walk** (1km return; suitable for wheelchairs), leads through coastal vegetation to the Port Phillip Bay shoreline; the second (1km return; steep in sections) leads to the top of Cheviot Hill, where you can look across to Queenscliff, and takes you on to views of **Cheviot Beach** where on December 17, 1967, **Harold Holt**, Australia's prime minister at the time, went for a swim in the rough surf of Bass Strait and disappeared, presumed drowned: his body was never found. The third walk, the **Fort Pearce Eagle's Nest Walk** (2km return; suitable for wheelchairs), crosses through defence fortifications that were once inaccessible. A fourth walk takes you around **Fort Nepean**, right at the point. Built at the same time as Fort Queenscliff opposite to protect wealthy post-gol-drush Melbourne from an imagined Russian invasion, the fort is essentially a two-storey building below ground. It takes about an hour to explore the tunnels, which lead down to the Engine House at water level. The old quarantine station near the point offers guided tours (2pm; Sat & Sun; $5).

The rest of Mornington Peninsula National Park, which spreads itself along the ocean coast, is freely open to the public. An enjoyable two-day walk (27km) runs from London Bridge along the coast to **Cape Schanck**, site of an 1859 lighthouse. Here a timber stair-case and walkways lead down to the sea along a narrow neck of land, providing magnif-icent coastal views. The **lighthouse keeper's cottage** has to be the most scenic accom-modation on the peninsula (☎03/9568 6411 or free call ☎1800/804 145; ⑦). Dating back to 1859, they are completely self-contained with a cosy lounge and kitchen, one cottage with four bedrooms, the other with three bedrooms. There's a pleasant café (daily 10am–4.30pm; in summer longer) and the lighthouse and museum are open daily for tours (every half-hour 10am–4.30pm; $6).

Also worth embarking on in this area is the **Bushrangers Bay Nature Walk** (6km return; 2hr) from the cape to Main Creek, which begins as a leisurely walk along the clifftop, then leads down to a wild beach facing Elephant Rock.

French Island

FRENCH ISLAND, off the eastern side of the Mornington Peninsula, is well off the beaten track. A former prison farm, about two-thirds of the island is a national park with the remaining third used as farm land. The island is renowned for its rich **wildlife**, especially birds of prey, and a flourishing koala colony. Virtually vehicle-free, it's a great place to cycle, and this is encouraged, with all walking tracks open to bikes. In the national park you can either **camp** at the *Fairhaven Campground* or **stay** at the *McLeod Eco Farm and Historic Prison* (☎03/5678 0155, fax 5678 0166; ④–⑤) in former prison cells converted into twins with bunk beds, or in the former officer's quarters with queen-size beds. The very reasonable rate includes three meals using the produce organically grown on the farm, and transfer from and to the ferry jetty 21km away. The farm is surrounded by national park and has 8km of beach frontage. The small *Tortoise Head Guesthouse* near the jetty (☎03/5980 1234, fax 5980 1222; ⑦) has rooms with water views. The rate includes accommodation, three sumptious wholefood meals as well as free use of mountain bikes.

The general store (2.5km from the jetty) has takeaway **food**. Refreshments and Devonshire teas are available at the *Bayview Chicory Kiln Tea Room* (10km from the jetty), which also has a private campsite; both are run by Lois Airs (☎03/5980 1241, mobile phone ☎019/406 694), a longtime resident and an inexhaustible mine of information about the island. Lois also does very inexpensive morning or afternoon **tours** of the island, and if you want to camp at *Fairhaven*, she will transport your luggage there, leaving you free to cycle. Alan "Koala Dundee" Chandler, another very knowledgeable islander, also does day-tours (☎03/9770 1822). A **ferry** service from the French Island Ferries company connects the Mornington Peninsula with French Island and Phillip Island. It leaves at least four times daily from Stony Point on the eastern side of the Mornington Peninsula (from Melbourne, connect with Met train services from Flinders Street Station via Frankston), departing from Tankerton jetty on French Island thirty minutes later for Phillip Island ($15 return, bike $2; ☎03/9585 5730). The Cowes (Phillip Island) cruise company Bay Connections runs a ferry service to French Island and to Stony Point on Wed and Sun, during the summer holidays (mid-December to January) also on Thurs – all services are subject to demand and must be booked 24 hours ahead. The ferry service can be combined with a tour of the island. (☎03/5678 5642 or 5952 3501; ferry service $26 return, ferry and tour of the island $40).

Phillip Island

PHILLIP ISLAND, with its southern edge facing Bass Strait and its northern edge in the calm waters of Western Port Bay, is a hugely popular holiday destination from Melbourne, famous above all for the nightly roosting of hundreds of **Little penguins** at Summerland Beach. Most visitors come only for the Penguin Parade, but spending a few days on the island will allow you to explore some dramatic coastal scenery and fine beaches, and a couple of well-organized wildlife parks. **Cowes**, on the sheltered bay side, is the main town and a lively and attractive place to stay. Other, smaller, communities worth a visit are **Rhyll**, to the east, and **Ventnor**, just west of Cowes.

A daily **V/Line bus** to Cowes departs from Melbourne in the afternoon, with an additional evening service on Friday; the bus drivers will usually drop you off where you request in Cowes. There's no public transport when you get there, however, so it can be tricky trying to get to the Penguin Parade, over 10km from Cowes. Planning to stay at the *Amaroo Park YHA* makes sense: their "duck truck" package ($84 including transport to and from Melbourne, up to three nights' dorm accommodation, island tour and admission to Penguin Parade plus a half-day use of mountain bikes; daily departures) is extremely good value, as is their tour from Cowes to Wilson's Promontory National Park ($45 including meals and entrance fees). If you are short of time, a **day-tour** from Melbourne is a good way of making the most of the island. One of the best is the long-established Autopia Tours (☎03/9326 5536), who pick you up from central Melbourne or St Kilda. Their daily one-day tour (11am–midnight; $50 including entrance fees) takes in the Wildlife Park, Koala Conservation Centre and Penguin Parade, as well as Seal Rocks and the Nobbies. Oz Experience include Phillip Island in their itinerary on their Sydney to Melbourne run.

If you're **driving**, head southeast from Melbourne on the Princes Highway to Dandenong, then follow the South Gippsland Highway to Lang Lang and from there the Bass Highway to Anderson where the road heads directly west to San Remo and the bridge across to the island, a drive of approximately three hours in total. The scenic lookout about 3km before San Remo is worth stopping at, for fantastic views of Western

Port Bay and the surrounding countryside. **SAN REMO** itself has lots of motels, a picturesque fishing fleet by its wharf and a co-operative selling fresh fish and crayfish. Not surprisingly, you can get delicious fish and chips; the best are served at the building at 121 Main St.

NEWHAVEN, the first settlement you come to after crossing the bridge, has a large **tourist information centre** (daily 9am–5pm, longer in summer; ☎03/5956 7447; for accommodation bookings ☎1300/366 422), where you can pick up a free map and buy tickets for the Penguin Parade, ferry tours, and for **Churchill Island** (daily noon–4.30pm; $5), barely 1km out of town via a rickety bridge. Your admission allows you to look round a historic homestead and cottage in English-style gardens, surrounded by ancient moonah trees, abundant birdlife and an unspoilt coastline.

Apart from the numerous wildlife attractions the island also boasts a winery: **Phillip Island Vineyard and Winery**, on a signposted route on Berrys Beach Road, off Back Beach Road (daily: April–Oct 11am–5pm; Nov–March 11am–7pm), where you can sample their various wines, among them Chardonnay, Sauvignon Blanc, Cabernet Sauvignon and Merlot (tastings $2 per person). There's also a small courtyard café serving cakes and cheese platters, which you can enjoy while overlooking the vineyard and fields.

Phillip Island Reserve and the Penguin Parade

The **Phillip Island Reserve** includes all the public land on the **Summerland Peninsula**, the narrow tip of land at the island's western extremity. The reason for the reserve is the **Little penguin**, smallest of the penguins, which is found only in southern Australian waters and whose largest colony breeds at Summerland Beach (around two thousand penguins in the parade area and twenty thousand on the island altogether). The **Penguin Parade** (nightly after dusk; ☎03/5956 8300; $10) sounds horribly commercial – and with four thousand visitors a night at the busiest time of the year (immediately after Christmas), it can hardly fail to be. Spectators sit in concrete-stepped stadiums looking down onto a floodlit beach, with taped narration in Japanese, Taiwanese and English. But don't be too hard on it: ecological disaster would ensue if the penguins weren't managed properly, and visitors would still flock here, harming the birds and eroding the sand dunes. As it is, all the money made goes back into research and looking after the penguins, and into facilities such as the excellent **Penguin Parade Visitor Centre** (open from 10am; admission included in the parade ticket): the "Penguin Experience" here is a simulated underwater scene of the hazards of a penguin's life, and there are also interactive displays, videos and even nesting boxes to which penguins have access from the outside, where you can watch the chicks.

The parade itself manages to transcend the setting in any case, as the penguins come pouring onto the beach, waddling comically once they leave their preferred environment. They start arriving soon after dark; fifty minutes later the floodlights are switched off and it's all over, at which time (or before) you can move on to the extensive boardwalks over their burrows, with diffused lighting at regular intervals enabling you to watch their antics for hours after the parade finishes – they're active most of the night. If you want to avoid the worst of the crowds, the quietest time to observe them is during the cold and windy winter (you'll need water- or windproof clothing at any time of year). Remember too that you can see Little penguins close to St Kilda Pier in Melbourne (see p.798) and at many other beaches in southern and southeastern Australia, perhaps not in such large numbers, but with far fewer onlookers.

The Nobbies and Seal Rocks

At the tip of the Summerland Peninsula is **Point Grant**, where **The Nobbies**, two huge rock stacks, are linked to the island at low tide by a wave-cut platform of basalt, affording views across to Cape Schanck on the Mornington Peninsula. From the point a boardwalk leads across spongy greenery – vibrant in summer with purple and yellow flowers – along the rounded clifftops to a lookout over a blowhole. This is a wild spot, with views along the rugged southern coastline towards Cape Woolamai, a granite headland at the eastern end of the island. From September to April you may see muttonbirds (shearwaters) here – they arrive in September to breed and head for the same burrows each year, after an incredible flight from the Bering Strait in the Arctic Circle. Further off Point Grant, **Seal Rocks** are two rocky islets with the largest known colony of Australian fur seals, estimated to number around 16,000. In the breeding season between late October and December the number of seals present on the rocks peaks, but it is possible to see seals here all year round. The antics of the seals in the water and on the rocks are caught on camera and beamed to the new **Seal Rocks Sea Life Centre** (daily 10am–dusk; $15) where visitors can watch them live on a big screen. In addition, there are other displays; such as videos of seals, artificial rockpools, and information displays on the amazing long-distance migration of the short-tailed shearwater as well as other seabirds one can see on Phillip Island. The other attractions are more of the theme park variety: a boat ride along eleven scenes where experiences of George Bass's voyage from Sydney to Western Port Bay in 1797 are told complete with special effects like a storm scene and a waterfall, and a hologram of a great white shark. The two **cafés** and the upmarket restaurant give panoramic views of The Nobbies and Seal Rocks. During the high season and school holidays there's a free shuttle bus between the Seal Rocks Sea Life Centre and the Penguin Parade Visitors Centre. **Cruises** to Seal Rocks are available from Cowes (see below).

Phillip Island Wildlife Park and the Koala Conservation Centre

Two further parks complete Phillip Island's rich collection of wildlife attractions. **Phillip Island Wildlife Park**, on Thompson Avenue just 1km south of Cowes (daily 9am–sunset; $9), is a shady shelter for Australian animals, most of them enclosed and not all native to Phillip Island. Highlights include the beautiful pure-bred dingoes, Tasmanian devils, fat dozy wombats which you can hold and feed if they're awake (but watch out, they bite), as well as an aviary and a koala reserve. Free to range are emus, Cape Barren geese, wallabies, eastern grey kangaroos and pademelons.

The **Koala Conservation Centre** on Phillip Island Tourist Road between Newhaven and Cowes (daily 10am–5.30pm; $5) is run by Phillip Island Nature Park and aims to keep the koala habitat as natural as possible while still giving people a close view. A treetop boardwalk through a part of the bushland park allows visitors to observe these marsupials at close range. At 4pm the rangers provide fresh gum leaves – a very popular photo opportunity. The centre's purpose is to breed disease-free koalas, as on Phillip Island they're infected with chlamydia. You can learn about koalas in the excellent interpretive centre.

Cowes and Rhyll

In the centre of the north coast, where the sandy bays are sheltered enough for good swimming, **COWES** is Phillip Island's main town. Several good places to eat and stay can be found here on The Esplanade, a lively strip facing the jetty. Based in the old Rotunda, Bay Connections (☎03/5678 5642) offers several **cruises** from the jetty, the best being the trip to Seal Rocks (mid-Oct to end of April at least once daily, in winter less often; 2hr; $38) to watch the Australian fur seals close up. The same company runs day tours from Cowes to Stony Point to French Island (Wed & Sun, but not in winter; ferry service plus island tour $42). Worth considering as a quieter place to base yourself is **RHYLL**, about 6km to the east of Cowes.

Accommodation

The main reason to come to Cowes or Rhyll is if you're planning to stay on the island. Out of season you should have no trouble, but during the peak Christmas–Easter season accommodation nearly doubles in price and some places require weekly bookings. The Phillip Island Visitor Information Centre handles all accommodation bookings for the island; a private agency in Melbourne, Island Retreats (free call ☎1800/629 319) can arrange accommodation and packages.

Amaroo Park, cnr of Church and Osborne sts, in the centre of Cowes (☎03/5952 2548, fax 5952 3620). A budget YHA hostel with a convivial bar and a swimming pool. It also does cheap meals, rents out bikes, organizes various day-trips, has a free bus to and from Melbourne, as well as the "duck truck" transport/accommodation/tour package (see p.815). Rooms ③, dorms ①.

Castle Inn by the Sea, 7–9 Steele St, Cowes (☎ 03/5952 1228, fax 5952 3926). A delightful B&B in a pleasant location. ⑨.

Coachman Motel, 51 Chapel St, Cowes (☎03/5952 1098, fax 5952 1283). This luxurious town house offers motel units and suites. Facilities include a heated pool and spa for communal use. ⑤–⑦.

The Continental Phillip Island, 5–8 The Esplanade, Cowes (☎03/5952 2316, fax 5952 1878). A conveniently central hotel with en-suite rooms, some with seafront balconies. Also a heated pool and spa. ⑥–⑦.

Kaloha Holiday Resort, cnr of Chapel and Steele sts, Cowes (☎03/5952 2179, fax 5952 2723). Motel units with cooking facilities, plus cabins, camping sites and facilities for on-site vans. Located in shady grounds giving onto a quiet swimming beach. ④–⑨.

Narrabeen Cottage, 16 Steele St, Cowes (☎03/5952 2062, fax 5952 3670). A delightful guesthouse whose owners can arrange gourmet dinners. ⑨.

Penguin Hill Country House B&B, cnr of Ventnor and Back Beach rds, Ventnor (☎ & fax 03/5956 8777). A rural B&B with good ocean views. ⑦–⑧.

Rothsaye on Lover's Walk, 2 Roy Court, Cowes (☎ & fax 03/5952 2057). A cosy, comfortable B&B. ⑦–⑧.

Seahorse Motel, 29–31 Chapel St, Cowes (☎03/5952 2003, fax 5952 3775). An above-average, centrally located motel. ④–⑤.

Eating and drinking

Castle Inn by the Sea, 7–9 Steele St, Cowes. Very good restaurant and bar.

The Clock Cafe, 1 Findlay St, Cowes. Near the western end of The Esplanade. Small cosy café with a view of the pier and a small sundeck. Open daily for breakfast, light lunches and dinner.

Fountain Place, Thompson Ave, Cowes. Café known for its delicious ice cream.

Isle of Wight Hotel, The Esplanade, Cowes. Hotel with a good-value bistro offering sea views. Also a couple of bars, a lively beer garden and entertainment at summer weekends.

The Jetty, The Esplanade, Cowes (☎03/5952 2060). An expensive but relaxed restaurant specializing in fresh local seafood.

Praha Coffee House, Thompson Ave, Cowes. A simple café serving excellent food, plus great coffee.

Taylor's Seafood & Steak Restaurant, 114 Thompson Ave, Cowes. Good seafood and steaks at reasonable prices.

The Yarra Valley and the Dandenongs

Northeast of Melbourne, the **Yarra Valley** stretches out towards the foothills of the Great Dividing Range, with **Yarra Glen** and **Healesville** as targets for excursions into the wine country and to the superb forest scenery beyond. To the east, and still within the suburban limits, the cool, high **Dandenong Range** is as pretty as anywhere in Australia, with quaint villages, fine old houses, beautiful flowering gardens and shady forests of eucalypts and tree ferns.

To get to all these destinations and to have a good look round, you really need your own vehicle. On weekdays it is possible, although not exactly easy, to explore the Dandenongs by **public transport**. Trains run via Ferntree Gully to Belgrave at the southern edge of the Dandenongs. Buses from Belgrave follow a complicated schedule – enquire at the Met Transport Information Centre (☎13 1638) in Melbourne. Healesville comes within the orbit of the suburban transport system: take a train from Melbourne to Lilydale and then bus #685 (for a visit to the Healesville Sanctuary, it's best to take the daily bus departing from Lilydale.

A bus company runs a daily service for V/Line from Melbourne to Eildon via Healesville and Marysville, the V/Line service to Mansfield passes through Lilydale and Yarra Glen daily (for further information: V/Line ☎13 6196). There are local buses from Belgrave to Emerald.

The Yarra Valley

Just half an hour's drive from Melbourne, many of Victoria's best small **wineries** – about thirty, several of them serving food – lie en route to Healesville, or you can visit them by taking detours to Warburton or Yarra Glen. The combination of good wine and fine food is really taking off in the Valley, in recent years quite a few winery restaurants succeeded in making a name for themselves in serious gourmet circles.

Wine country starts in outer suburbia north of the Maroondah Highway just before Lilydale (turn-offs are signposted). North of Lilydale, you can check out wineries (again, all signposted) along or near three routes – the Warburton Highway to the east, the Maroondah Highway to Healesville, and the Melba Highway heading north past Yarra Glen. The brochure *Wineries of the Yarra Valley* contains a complete list of all wineries and a map of their locations. Even better is the detailed booklet *Wine Regions of Victoria* (see p.764) – both are available at tourist information centres. Yering Station – Yarrabank Vineyards, south of Yarra Glen just off the Melba Highway is located at the site of the Yarra Valley's first vineyard, Chateau Yering, established in 1838 and re-established in 1988. The cellar door operates from the original brick building; there's also a wine bar and an art gallery. For real comfort and luxury, wine and dine next door at *Café Sweetwater* or elegant *Eleonore's Restaurant* in the magnificently restored *Chateau Yering Historic House*, then sink into a four-poster bed in one of their period-style rooms (☎03/9237 3333, fax 9237 3300; ⑦–⑧).

Equally unique and beautiful is *De Bortoli Winery & Restaurant* (bookings advisable; ☎03/5965 2271) whose building, the interior decoration and the excellent food all betray strong influences of Northern Italy. It is in an unbeatable location at Pinnacle Lane, off the **Melba Highway** at Dixon's Creek north of Yarra Glen, with views over gently rolling hills.

On the **Maroondah Highway**, Domaine Chandon, near the town of Coldstream, is owned by the French champagne house Möet et Chandon, producing fine *méthode champenoise* sparkling wine, which you can sample ($6–8 per glass) in a modern, bright and airy tastings room with brilliant views. Free guided thirty-minute **tours** depart hourly from 11am to 4pm. *Eyton on Yarra* winery and restaurant further up towards Healesville, at the corner of Maroondah Highway and Hill Rd (☎03/5962 2119), a relative newcomer on the gourmet scene, specializes in locally produced food and Pinot Noir, Merlot and Chardonnay wines. From October–March there are concerts at the *Eyton on Yarra*-soundshell (Summer Music series).

Off the **Warburton Highway** detours there are four wineries, including *Yarra Burn* on Settlement Road at Yarra Junction. The food at the restaurant can be classified as hearty "Australian country" cuisine (lunches daily; Fri & Sat dinner); B&B accommodation is available in the homestead.

From Yarra Junction it's not far to **WARBURTON**, a pretty, old-fashioned town on the Upper Yarra River, and starting point for the **Upper Yarra Track**, which follows old timber tram and vehicle tracks upstream for over 80km. The track can be covered as a series of short walks or as a continuous five- to seven-day trek, finishing in the Baw Baw National Park where it joins the Alpine Walking Track. For more information contact the NRE Information Centre in Melbourne (☎03/9637 8080) or the telephone information service run by Parks Victoria (☎13 1963).

Apart from many wineries in its vicinity, **YARRA GLEN** also boasts the splendidly restored *Grand Hotel* and, not far away on the Melba Highway, the National Trust **Gulf Station** (Wed–Sun & public holidays 10am–4pm; $6), a collection of ten 1850s slab farm buildings set in a large area of farmland.

Healesville and beyond

HEALESVILLE is a small, pleasant town nestled in the foothills of the Great Dividing Range. Collect information about the region at the **visitor information centre** in the old courthouse building at the southern end of town, just off the Maroondah Highway (daily 10am–5pm). Healesville's main attraction is the renowned **Healesville Sanctuary** (daily 9am–5pm; free guides 10am–3pm if booked in advance; ☎03/5957 2800; 24hr information line ☎1902/240 592 at 50¢ per minute; admission fee $14).

This is a genuine sanctuary, established over fifty years ago to provide care for injured and orphaned animals, some of which are then returned to the wild; those that stay join the sanctuary's programmes for education and the breeding of endangered species. It's a fascinating place in a beautiful setting, with a stream running through park-like grounds, dense with gum trees and cool ferns, and plenty of paths to follow past picnic and barbecue areas. Many of the animals are in enclosures, but there are paddocks of emus, wallabies and kangaroos you can stroll through. Don't miss the excellent "Animals of the Night" enclosure (10am–4.30pm); other star attractions include the aviaries (9am–4.30pm), a scary Reptile House (Mon–Fri 9am–4.30pm, Sat, Sun & public holidays 9am–5pm) and a Platypus Display Centre (9.30am–4.30pm). The informative "meet the keeper" presentations throughout the day are worth joining: the raptors (birds of prey) at noon and 3pm are unmissable.

Just opposite the sanctuary, the **Galeena Beek Living Cultural Centre** (daily 9am–6pm; $7) was built on the site of what formerly the Corranderk Aboriginal Mission. In the traditional owners' Woi wurrung language "Galeena Beek" means loving the earth; the circular shape of the building symbolizes a meeting place. The centrepiece is an exhibition about the history of Corranderk and the Aboriginal people associated with it. There are regular screenings of videos on aspects of local Aboriginal culture, and the art gallery sells paintings and artefacts made by local artists.

Continuing north on the Maroondah Highway over the Black Spur and Dom Dom Saddle towards Alexandra, the scenery becomes progressively more attractive. Worth a brief stop is the **Maroondah Reservoir Lookout**, just off the highway 3km north of Healesville, with picturesque views across the forest-fringed dam. There are very popular **picnic grounds** and **gardens** in the park on the southwest side of the reservoir. Soon after the reservoir, the highway meanders along bush-clad mountain slopes and enters luxuriant wet eucalypt forest with incredibly tall mountain ash, moss-covered myrtle beech, manna gum, tree ferns, gurgling creeks and waterfalls. The **Fernshaw Reserve and Picnic Ground** is a good place to stop and view the scenery. After the Dom Dom Saddle, 509m above sea level and 16km past Healesville, the highway descends towards Narbethong, where it enters drier country. Three kilometres past Narbethong a turn-off leads to scenic **MARYSVILLE**, 9km off the highway. A worthwhile detour, the village is nestled in the foothills of the Great Dividing Range, with **Lake Mountain** (1400m), a very popular area for cross-country skiing and tobogganing, 20km further west. In summer Marysville makes an excellent base for **bushwalking**, being surrounded by wet mountain ash forests with many creeks and waterfalls. The best-known, **Steavensons Falls**, can be reached from the village by a walking trail or by road and is floodlit at night until 11pm. Just out of Marysville, the unsealed **Lady Talbot Forest Drive** turns off the Lake Mountain road and then winds 46km through the forest, past picnic areas and walking tracks (suitable for conventional vehicles, though after heavy rainfall it's best to check in Marysville for road conditions). Return to Marysville via the Buxton Road, or turn right and head straight north to Buxton where you rejoin the highway. Further up, the Maroondah Highway passes the drier **Cathedral Range State Park**, where to the west of the road the mighty sandstone cliffs of Cathedral Mountain (845m) seem to rise almost vertically behind the paddocks, overlooking the Acheron Valley.

The Dandenongs

This mountain range, reaching heights of up to 633m, shares with NSW's Blue Mountains the natural phenomenon of a blue haze rising from forests of gum trees. Abundant rain ensures the area stays cool and lush, while fine old houses and gardens add to the scenery. Easy bushwalks in the **Dandenong Ranges National Park** start from Ferntree Gully, accessible by train or by car via the Burwood Highway.

Another pleasant way to enjoy the forests and fern gullies is to take a ride on the **Puffing Billy** (55min; 24hr information ☎1900/937 069; $25), which runs for 13km from the Puffing Billy Station in Belgrave to Lakeside on Lake Emerald, stopping at Menzies Creek and Emerald: one train a day continues a further 9km from Lake Emerald to Gembrook.

The Puffing Billy Station is about five minutes walk from Belgrave Railway Station (suburban trains). The steam train has run more or less continuously since the early twentieth century, though its operation now depends on dedicated volunteers; on total fire ban days, diesel locomotives are used. Timetables vary seasonally but there are generally several services daily until late afternoon; local buses also cover the Belgrave–Emerald route.

Just outside Emerald, man-made **Emerald Lake** has paddle-boats to rent and a swimming pool with waterslide, as well as trails through bushland continuing into the nearby state reserve. As for **accommodation**, *Emerald Backpackers*, 49 Emerald Lake Rd (☎03/5968 4086; rooms ③, dorms ①), has a country setting and a casual party atmosphere; the owners can help long-stay guests find local work. On weekdays and Saturday morning, bus #695 runs from the Belgrave train station to Emerald. *Choo Choos Restaurant and Bar*, at 32 Monbulk Rd in Emerald, is a friendly, reasonably priced oddity, serving **meals** on authentic railway crockery in old railway dining carriages.

Geelong and the Bellarine Peninsula

Heading west towards Geelong – for the Bellarine Peninsula or the Great Ocean Road – it's just a short detour off the Princes Freeway to **WERRIBEE** (or a half-hour train ride from Melbourne; zone 3), where the extraordinary **Mansion at Werribee Park**, built by two Scottish squatters made rich beyond their wildest dreams, is located on K Road (daily 10am–5pm; $10). Beyond the Mansion's formal gardens are the extensive grounds of **Victoria's Open Range Zoo** grassland where animals from Africa, Asia and Australia (giraffes, rhinoceroses, hippopotamuses, monkeys and other creatures) roam in large open enclosures. A safari bus takes visitors through the property and is included in the admission price (daily 10am–5pm; bus tours depart between 10am and 3.40pm; $14).

Continuing along the freeway, you can detour west again through Little River to the **You Yangs**, small but rugged volcanic peaks which rise sharply out of the surrounding plains. Scramble to the top of the highest, Flinders Peak (348m), which Matthew Flinders climbed in 1802, and you're rewarded with fine views of Geelong and Port Phillip Bay. The You Yangs, as well as the nearby **Brisbane Ranges**, are excellent places for spotting kangaroos, wallabies, koalas and possums at dusk. Alternatively, you can observe kangaroos, wallabies and emus, as well as numerous waterbirds, in their natural habitat at the little-known **Serendip Sanctuary**, 20km north of Geelong at 100 Windermere Rd, Lara (daily 10am–4pm; $5). A refuge for threatened birds of the Western Plains of Victoria, this square kilometre of bush-, marsh- and wetlands, was originally part of an extensive sheep property. The sanctuary is renowned for its captive breeding programme of brolgas, magpie geese and Australian bustards, which has been in operation for more than twenty years.

Geelong

GEELONG, en route to the Bellarine Peninsula, is not particularly attractive, being too industrial to appeal as a coastal resort: the fact that the National Wool Museum is the main attraction gives you some idea of the place. You may have heard of the town, however, because it's wealthy – on wool money – and the site of an exclusive boarding school. The Geelong Wool Exchange, a National Trust-listed building at the corner of Brougham and Moorabool streets, houses the **National Wool Museum** (daily 10am–5pm; $9). The well-set up exhibition concentrates on the social history surrounding wool, with reconstructions of typical shearers' quarters and a millworker's 1920s cottage. On the top floor of the exchange wool is still auctioned off on thirty days in the year. Many of the best of the town's Victorian buildings are on Little Malop Street including the elegant **Geelong Art Gallery** (Mon–Fri 10am–5pm, Sat & Sun 1–5pm; $3), which has an extensive collection of paintings by nineteenth-century Australian artists such as Tom Roberts and Frederick McCubbin, plus twentieth-century Australian paintings, sculpture and decorative arts. From Malop Street, Moorabool Street leads down to **Corio Bay**. Neglected for many years, Geelong's waterfront has undergone a facelift in recent years, so that the views of shipping traffic and, across the water, of an industrial skyline with hills behind don't seem quite so drab anymore. The promenades, rotunda and fountains on Eastern Beach were renovated, and new waterfront eating places have emerged, notably the large restaurant complex at the end of new **Cunningham Pier** which comes into its own at night. Swimming is permitted in a swimming enclosure at Eastern Beach.

On the way to Torquay, **Narana Creations**, an Aboriginal Arts, Crafts and Cultural Centre at 410 Torquay Rd (Surfcoast Highway) in Grovedale is worth a brief stop. Paintings and various arts and crafts are sold here, a native garden with a lake was added recently, and sometimes visitors can listen to Dreamtime stories or didgeridoo playing (Mon–Fri 9am–5pm, Sat 10am–4pm, free).

Practicalities

In addition to the **visitor information centre** at the Wool Museum (daily 9am–5pm; free call ☎1800/620 888), there's a helpful staffed **tourist information stall** in the Market Square Shopping Centre at the corner of Moorabool and Malop streets (Mon–Sat 9am–5pm). Both provide lots of brochures and free maps. The main **shopping** strip is just a block south of the Wool Museum along Malop Street. Places to **stay** include the *Kangaroo Motel*, The Esplanade South (☎03/5221 4365; ④), which has reasonably priced units in a central location; the *Lucas Innkeepers Motor Inn*, 9 Aberdeen St (☎03/5221 2177; ⑤–⑥), just west of the town centre; the reasonably priced *Ardara House B&B*, 4 Aberdeen St (☎03/5229 6024; ③–④), and on the other end of the price scale the luxurious air-con *All Seasons Ambassador Geelong*, corner of Gheringhap and Myers streets (☎03/5221 6844; ⑧), which has a restaurant, bar, bistro, sauna and pool.

If you want to **camp**, try the *City Southside Caravan Park* on Barrabool Road, south of the Barwon River at Barwon Valley Park (☎03/5243 3788; cabins ④, on-site vans ③), and the nearby *Billabong Caravan Park* (☎03/5243 6225; cabins ④). For **food**, there's plenty of choice, especially along the foreshore where there is the *Beach House Restaurant* overlooking Eastern Beach, then *Fishermans Pier Restaurant* at the end of Yarra Street, *Sailor's Rest* on Moorabool Street, *Bazil's Café* next to Deakin University and *Smorgy's Restaurant* on Cunningham Pier. Another concentration of eateries is to be found along Malop and Little Malop streets, with fast-food outlets, cafés and the stylish *Cats Bar Café and Restaurant* at 90 Little Malop St. A bit further uphill at 51 McKillop St the Geelong Wintergarden in a former church now houses an antique centre, a nursery, shops and a very pleasant café.

To check out what's going on, pick up a copy of the free **listings magazine** *Forte*, available at CD and record shops, sometimes also at the visitor information centre. It covers the whole of southwest Victoria; as well as entertainment it has information on surfing, scuba diving and other activities. There's a surprisingly healthy local **band** scene in Geelong; check out *Irish Murphy's*, 30 Aberdeen St, the *Wool Exchange Hotel*, 59 Moorabool St *The Barwon Club Hotel* at 509 Moorabool St, *Lamby's Bar* downstairs at the Wool Museum, and the *Scottish Chief's Tavern & Restaurant* at 99 Corio St which has its own microbrewery.

To get to the Bellarine Peninsula, take the Bellarine Transit **bus**, which departs from the Busport on Brougham Street (next to the Wool Museum) for Ocean Grove and Barwon Heads, Point Lonsdale via Queenscliff, St Leonards via Portarlington, and Grovedale via Torquay and Jan Juc.

Queenscliff and around

From Geelong, the Bellarine Highway runs 31km southeast to **QUEENSCLIFF** through flat and not particularly scenic grazing country. Queenscliff is essentially a quiet fishing village on Swan Bay – with several quaint cottages on Fishermens Flat – that became a favourite holiday resort for Melbourne's wealthy elite in the nineteenth century, then fell out of favour, and only recently has begun to enjoy something of a revival as a popular place for a weekend away or a Sunday drive. Its position near the narrow entrance to Port Phillip Bay made it strategically important: a **fort** here faces the one at Point Nepean, defending Melbourne against an enemy that never materialized. Now the home of the Australian Army Command and Staff College, the fort can be visited on guided tours (Sat, Sun & public holidays 1pm & 3pm; school holidays daily 11am, 1pm & 3pm; 90min; $4).

Full details of other things to do are available from the tourist information centres in Geelong, or enquire at the Queenscliff Library on Hesse Street. During school holidays and in summer, **Queenscliff Historical Tours** (☎03/5258 3403) rents out bicycles, on demand they also provide a map of the town, a cassette tape and a walkman so that you can do a sightseeing tour at your own pace. You can pick up the bike near the pier at the end of Symonds Road, or they will deliver it to your accommodation.

Among the attractions is the **Queenscliff Maritime Centre & Museum**, Weerona Parade (Sat & Sun 1.30pm–4.30pm; school holidays daily 10.30am–4.30pm; $4), which concentrates on the many wrecks caused by The Rip, a fierce current through the mouth of the bay. Outside, a tiny fisherman's cottage is set up as it would have been in 1870, and there's a shed where an Italian fisherman painted, in naive style, all the ships he'd seen pass through from 1895 to 1947 (imaginatively including the *Titanic*). Next door, the **Marine Discovery Centre** has a small aquarium (daily during school holidays 10am–4pm, other times by appointment ☎03/5258 3344; $3), stocked with local marine life; it also organizes a lot of activities, mainly during the summer holidays, such as marine biology cruises, rock pool rambles, canoe trips and snorkelling tours. The

Queenscliff Historical Centre (daily 2–4pm; donation appreciated), on Hesse Street next to the post office, helps put the rest of the town into context. Every Sunday, the **Bellarine Peninsula Railway** operates steam trips from the old Queenscliff Railway Station to Drysdale, 20km northwest (11am & 2.30pm, more often during school holidays; ☎03/5258 2069; $5). Queenscliff Sunday Market is held on the last Sunday of each month from August to May on Symonds Street.

Point Lonsdale and Portarlington

From Queenscliff it's about 5km to peaceful **Point Lonsdale**, whose most noticeable feature is a magnificent 1902 lighthouse, 120m high and visible for 30km out to sea. Below the lighthouse, on the edge of the bluff, is "Buckley's Cave" where William Buckley is thought to have lived at some stage during his thirty-year sojourn with the Aborigines. At **PORTARLINGTON**, which sits on Port Phillip Bay about 14km north of Queenscliff, there's a beautifully preserved steam-powered flour mill, four storeys of solid stone, owned by the National Trust (Feb–May & Sept–Dec Sun 2–5pm; Jan Wed, Sat & Sun 2–5pm).

Practicalities

Three grand **Victorian-era hotels** in Queenscliff are popular settings for romantic (but very expensive) breaks: the *Vue Grand*, 46 Hesse St (☎03/5258 1544, fax 5258 3471; ⑧), has a Spanish-style exterior and a fabulously ornate Victorian interior with a very expensive restaurant; the clifftop *Ozone Hotel*, 42 Gellibrand St (☎03/5258 1011, fax 5258 3712; ⑦), features sea views from two iron-lace decorated verandahs and a gorgeous dining room; while the refined *Mietta's Queenscliff Hotel*, 16 Gellibrand St (☎03/5258 1066, fax 5258 1899; ⑧), is perhaps the best of all, and certainly the least intimidating. If it's available, go for the octagonal room in the tower. **Budget alternatives** include the *Queenscliff Inn YHA*, 59 Hesse St (☎03/5258 4600, fax 5258 2819; ⑤–⑥), a pleasant Victorian guesthouse offering B&B, and *Beacon Resort Motel*, 78 Bellarine Highway (☎03/5258 1133, fax 5258 1152; ④–⑤), which has tent sites, cabins, holiday units, motel rooms, a heated pool and tennis courts. Among the town's **eating places**, the best fish and chips are to be had at *Queenscliff Fish and Chips*, 77 Hesse St. Among the cafés there are *Mietta's Shop & Bar* (daily 11am–late afternoon) in the *Queenscliff Hotel*, which does light lunches, coffees, and drinks, and *38 South*, a café at the car ferry terminal with a fantastic view of the heads of the bay and the Mornington Peninsula. There's a lot more in the moderate-to-expensive price bracket; to name the most outstanding: *Harry's By The Sea*, an excellent seafood restaurant at the foreshore at Princes Park (lunch Sat & Sun, dinner Fri–Sun; BYO) and the stylish (and pricey) restaurants at the historic *Mietta's Queenscliff Hotel* and the *Vue Grand*, both of which are licensed and serve lunch and dinner daily.

Ferries run from Queenscliff across the mouth of Port Phillip Bay to Sorrento (see p.812).

travel details

Trains

Melbourne to: Adelaide (2 daily; 12hr); Alice Springs (2 weekly; 37hr); Ballarat (5–10 daily; 2hr); Bendigo (2–4 daily; 2hr); Geelong (9–24 daily; 1hr); Perth (2 weekly; 50hr); Sydney via Albury (2 daily; 13hr); Warrnambool (2–3 daily; 3hr 15min).

Buses

Melbourne to: Adelaide (4 daily; 10hr); Brisbane and the Gold Coast (4 daily; 25hr); Perth via Adelaide (1 daily; 46hr); Sydney via Canberra (5 daily; 12–14hr); Sydney via Bega (1 daily; 18hr), Sydney via Dubbo (1 daily; 20hr).

Ferries

Melbourne to: Devonport, Tasmania (3 weekly; 14hr 30mins); between mid-December and mid-April also to Georgetown, Tasmania (4 weekly; 6 hr.)

Flights

Qantas and Ansett fly from **Melbourne** to: Adelaide (9–12 daily; 70min); Alice Springs (2 daily; 3hr 30min); Ayers Rock Resort (1–3 daily; 3hr 30min); Brisbane (10–12 daily; 1hr 10min); Cairns (7–11 daily; 3hr 15min direct); Canberra (4–7 daily; 55min); Coolangatta/Gold Coast (6–12 daily; 2hr); Darwin (3 daily; 3–4hr with one stopover); Hobart (4–7 daily; 1hr); Launceston (4 daily; 50min); Mackay (3–4 daily; 4hr 15min with one stopover); Perth (5–7 daily; 4hr); Rockhampton (6–7 daily; 3hr 30min with one stopover); Sydney (16–24 daily; 1hr 20min); Townsville (3–5 daily; 5hr with one stopover).

Kendell Airlines fly from **Melbourne** to: Albury (4 daily Mon–Fri, 2 daily Sat & Sun; 45min); Burnie (3–4 daily; 1hr); Devonport (4 daily; 1hr 10min); King Island (3 daily Mon–Fri; 1 on Sat; 45min); Merimbula (4 daily Mon–Fri, 1 on Sat; 1hr 10min); Mildura (4 daily Mon–Fri, 1–2 Sat & Sun; 1hr 10min); Mount Gambier (4 daily Mon–Fri, daily Sat & Sun; 1hr); Portland (3 daily Mon–Fri, 1–2 daily Sat & Sun; 50min); Wagga Wagga (3 daily Mon–Fri, 1 daily Sat & Sun; 1hr 20min).

CHAPTER TEN

VICTORIA

A ustralia's second-smallest state, **Victoria** is the most densely populated and industrialized, but has a wide variety of attractions packed into a small area. It may not be a state to tour comprehensively, but Australians, at least, lap up the legends of their history that are thick on the ground: you're never too far from civilization, but everywhere there's a wild past of **gold prospectors** and **bushrangers**.

All routes in the state radiate from **Melbourne**, bang in the middle of the coastline on the huge Port Phillip Bay, and no point is much more than seven hours' drive away. Yet all most visitors see of Victoria is its cultured capital, the **Great Ocean Road**, a winding 280km of spectacular coastal scenery with wave-carved rock formations capable of wowing the most insensate, and perhaps the idyllic **Wilsons Promontory National Park** (the "Prom"), a couple of hours away on the coast of the mainly dairy region of **Gippsland**. Some may also venture to the **Goldfields**, where the nineteenth-century goldrushes left their mark in the grandiose architecture of old mining towns such as **Ballarat** and **Bendigo**. There's a great deal more to the state, however. Although Victoria doesn't have a reputation for being sun blessed, its weather is more volatile than poor and it gets its fair share of sunshine. Beach culture is alive and well on this coastline with some of the best **surfing** in Australia.

Marking the end of the Great Dividing Range, the massive sandstone ranges of the **Grampians**, with their Aboriginal rock paintings and dazzling array of springtime flora, rise from the monotonous wheatfields of the **Wimmera** region and the wool country of the western district. To the north of the Grampians is the wide, flat region of the **Mallee** – scrub, sand dunes and dry lakes heading to the **Murray River**, where **Mildura** is an irrigated oasis supporting orchards and vineyards. In complete contrast, the **Victorian Alps** in the northeast of the state have several winter **ski slopes**, high country that provides perfect bushwalking and horse-riding territory in summer. In the foothills and plains below, where bushranger **Ned Kelly** once roamed, are some of Victoria's finest **wineries** (wine buffs should pick up a copy of the excellent hundred-page brochure, *Wine Regions of Victoria*, available from the tourist information centre in Melbourne and other towns).

The only real drawback is the frequently cursed **climate**. Winter is mild, and the occasional heatwaves in summer are mercifully limited to a few days at most, but the

---

ACCOMMODATION PRICES

All the accommodation listed in this book has been categorized into one of eight price bands, as set out below. The rates quoted represent the cheapest available double or twin room in high season – except for category ①, which indicates per-person rates for a dorm bed, and the categories given for units, cabins and vans, which represent the daily charge for the whole unit.

① Under $18	⑤ $61–74
② $19–30	⑥ $75–94
③ $31–45	⑦ $95–124
④ $46–60	⑧ $125 upwards

For more accommodation details, see pp.40-43.

problem is that of unpredictability. Cool, rainy "English" weather can descend in any season, and spring and autumn days can be immoderately hot. But even this can be turned to advantage: as the local saying goes, if you don't like the weather, just wait ten minutes and it'll change.

Public transport, by road and rail, is with **V/Line** and subsidiary country bus lines. After the restructuring of recent years, however, using one's own vehicle is definitely a more convenient transport option, as train and bus services are fairly infrequent and quite a few places of interest can be reached only with difficulty, if at all.

Some history

Semi-nomadic **Koories** have lived in this region for at least forty thousand years, and from earliest times developed sophisticated hunting and gathering methods, creating rock art, weaving baskets, making possum-skin cloaks to protect against the cold, and establishing semi-permanent settlements such as those of circular stone houses and fish traps found at Lake Condah in western Victoria.

For the colonists, Victoria did not get off to an auspicious start: there was an unsuccessful attempt at settlement in the **Port Phillip Bay** area in 1803 but Van Diemen's Land (Tasmania) across the Bass Strait was deemed more suitable. It was in fact from Launceston that Port Phillip Bay was eventually settled, in 1834; other Tasmanians soon followed and **Melbourne** was established. This occupation was in defiance of a British government edict forbidding settlement in the territory, then part of New South Wales, but **squatting** had already begun the previous year when Edward Henty arrived with his stock to establish the first white settlement in **Portland** on the southwest coast. A pattern was created of land-hungry settlers – generally already men of means – responding to Britain's demand for wool, so that during the 1840s and 1850s what was to become Victoria evolved into a prosperous pastoral community with squatters extending huge grazing runs.

From the beginning, the Koories fought against the invasion of their land: 1836 saw the start of the **Black War**, as it has been called, a bloody guerrilla struggle against the settlers. By 1850, however, the Aborigines had been decimated – by disease as well as war – and felt defeated, too, by the apparently endless flood of invaders; their population is believed to have declined from around 15,500 to just 2300.

By 1851 the white population of the area was large and confident enough to demand separation from New South Wales, achieved, by a stroke of luck, just nine days before **gold** was discovered in the new colony. The rich goldfields of Ballarat, Bendigo and Castlemaine brought an influx of hopeful migrants from around the world. More gold came from Victoria over the next thirty years than was extracted during the celebrated Californian goldrush. From 1850 to 1880, gold transformed Victoria from a pastoral backwater into Australia's financial capital. Following federation in 1901, Melbourne was even the political capital – a title it retained until Canberra became fully operational in 1927.

THE GREAT OCEAN ROAD AND THE FAR WEST COAST

The **Great Ocean Road**, Victoria's famous southwestern coastal route, starts at **Torquay**, just over 20km south of Geelong, and extends 285km west to Warrnambool. It was built between 1919 and 1932 with the idea of constructing a scenic road of world repute, equalling California's Pacific Coast Highway – and it certainly lives up to its reputation. The road was to be both a memorial to the soldiers who had died in World War I, and an employment scheme for those who returned. Over three thousand ex-servicemen

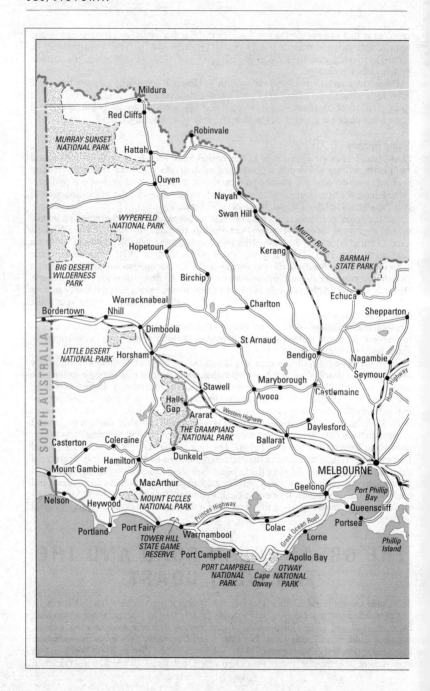

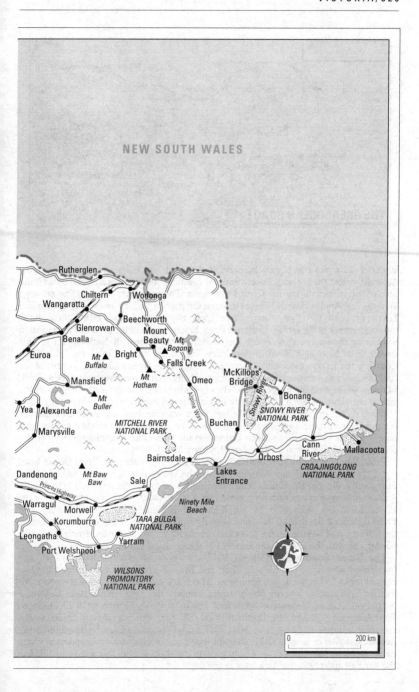

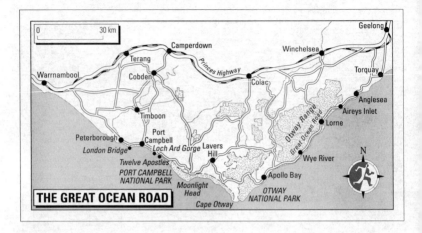

0   30 km

Geelong
Camperdown
Winchelsea
Terang
Princes Highway
Torquay
Warrnambool
Cobden
Colac
Anglesea
Timboon
Aireys Inlet
Otway Range
Lorne
Peterborough
Port
Campbell
Great Ocean Road
London Bridge
Loch Ard Gorge
Lavers
Hill
Wye River
Twelve Apostles
PORT CAMPBELL
NATIONAL PARK
Moonlight
Head
Apollo Bay
OTWAY
NATIONAL PARK
THE GREAT OCEAN ROAD
Cape Otway
N

laboured with picks and shovels, carving the road into cliffs and mountains along Australia's most rugged and densely forested coastline; the task was speeded up with the help of the jobless during the Great Depression. The road hugs the coastline between Torquay and **Apollo Bay** and passes through the popular holiday towns of **Anglesea and Lorne**, set below the Otway Ranges. From Apollo Bay the road heads inland, through the towering forests of the **Otway National Park**, before rejoining the coast at Princetown to wind along the shore for the entire length of the **Port Campbell National Park**. This stretch from Moonlight Head to Port Fairy, sometimes referred to as the "Shipwreck Coast", is the most spectacular – over eighty ships have been sunk here, victims of the rough Southern Ocean and dramatic rock formations such as the **Twelve Apostles**, which sit out to sea beyond the rugged cliffs. The often windy and stormy weather enhances the jagged coastline, and even at the height of summer you can't rely on it being sunny here.

If you're in a hurry to get from Melbourne to Warrnambool, the **Princes Highway** is a much faster route – and a much duller one. The only place you might consider stopping briefly is Colac, where **Lake Colac** and the vast **Lake Corangamite** support a profusion of birdlife, with botanical gardens and a bird sanctuary.

From **Warrnambool**, the small industrial coastal city where the Great Ocean Road ends, the Princes Highway continues along the coast, through quaint seaside **Port Fairy** and industrial **Portland**, before turning inland for the final stretch to the South Australian border. If you're determined to stick to the coast, you can continue along the Portland–Nelson road, with Mount Richmond National Park and Discovery Bay Coastal Park on the coastal side, and Glenelg National Park on the other, to end up at the little town of **Nelson** on the peaceful Glenelg River, just before the South Australian border and with the spectacular Princess Margaret Rose Caves nearby.

The **Great Southwest Walk**, a 250-kilometre circuit starting from just outside Portland, going on to the Glenelg River and Nelson, and then back through the two coastal parks to Portland, is magnificent. There are campsites all along the route; for further information, and to obtain maps, contact the NRE Information Centre, 8 Nicholson St, East Melbourne (☎03/9637 8080), or Parks Victoria (☎13 1963). South West Adventures, based near Portland (☎018/527 821), offers a range of guided walks, including a three-day Great Southwest Walk from Portland to Cape Nelson lighthouse. Accommodation is in tents (BYO sleeping bag and hiking gear), and support vehicles carry supplies and offer a drop-off and pick-up transport service, allowing you to break the journey and rejoin the walk later in the day.

Transport

If you don't have your own car or can't get a **lift** (it's always worth checking hostel notice boards), you might want to consider one-way **car rental**, usually available from the big-name companies in Melbourne. There are plenty of parking spots where you can pull over and admire the view, but even so the unfortunate driver will miss out on a lot of the scenery; with narrow roads, steep cliffs and incessant hairpin bends you need to keep your eyes glued to the road. In summer the road is filled with **cyclists**, and although the routes are exhilarating they are really only suitable for the experienced and adventurous.

Tours

One-way tours between **Melbourne** and **Adelaide**, via the Great Ocean Road, are a good way to take in the scenery. The backpackers' busline Oz Experience (☎1300/300 028) covers this route in four days, taking in the Great Ocean Road, the Grampians and the Coonawarra wine region in South Australia, while Wayward Bus (free call ☎1800/882 823) sticks to the coast all the way to the Coorong in South Australia on its three-day tour. With both you can get off the bus and continue your trip a few days later (booking required). A few other reliable tour operators do **one- or two-day trips** from Melbourne to the Great Ocean Road, some with an extra Grampians option and/or possible transfer to Adelaide. Autopia Tours (☎03/9326 5536) does one-day tours (daily; about $50), two-day tours (Tues & Thurs, $70); their three-day tour adds on a visit to the Grampians (Sun, Wed & Fri; $130); there's also a two-day combination of the Great Ocean Road and Phillip Island (Mon, Wed, Fri; $50). Wild-Life Tours (☎03/9747 1882) also combines a trip to the Great Ocean Road and the Grampians in various guises: one-day (daily; $50) and two-day tours (Mon, Tues & Sat, $70) to the Great Ocean Road, a three-day tour that adds on a visit to the Grampians and Mount Arapiles near Horsham (Mon, Thurs, Sat; $130) as well as quick one-way tours from Melbourne to Adelaide (or vice versa) in one day via the Great Ocean Road ($75) or two days via the Great Ocean Road and the Grampians ($130). Let's Go Bush Tours (☎03/9662 3969) is a smaller, long-established tour operator doing a two-day tour to the Great Ocean Road where you stay overnight at their own house near Lavers Hill in the Otway Ranges (Sat & Wed Nov–July; $90); Sunroad Tours (☎03/9237 6080), run by locals who have lived in the Great Ocean Road area for generations, does a two-day tour from Melbourne with an overnight stop (own expense) at Apollo Bay (Sat & Tues; $70). Great Ocean Road & Grampians Expeditions does a four-day trip to the Great Ocean Road, the Grampians and Mount Arapiles in very small groups, with a lot of activities thrown in (Mon; $270); Book via Backpacker Adventure Tours (☎03/9534 8866 or free call ☎1800/639 534).

V/Line has a "Great Ocean Road" **bus** service from Geelong to Apollo Bay, calling at Torquay, Anglesea, Lorne and points in between. Their Coast Link bus service from Apollo Bay goes along the Great Ocean Road to Warrnambool on Friday (plus Mon in Dec & Jan). There's a **train** service from Melbourne, via Geelong and Colac, to Warrnambool (2–3 daily), with connecting buses to Port Fairy, Portland and Heywood (1–2 daily) and on to Mount Gambier in South Australia (1 daily). From Warrnambool you can also return to Melbourne on the inland road, or go north to Ballarat. There's no public transport to Nelson.

Torquay

TORQUAY is the centre of **surf culture** on Victoria's "surf coast", which extends from Point Lonsdale, on the Bellarine Peninsula, to Aireys Inlet; two local beaches, **Jan Juc** and **Bells Beach**, are solidly entrenched in Australian surfing mythology. If you're not here for the surf, then there's not really a lot happening: in hot weather the place is boisterously alive, but out of season it's somnolent and low-key. The big event here is the **Surf Classic**, held at Bells Beach in Easter, which draws national and international contestants and thousands of spectators. Local **buses** run between Geelong and Torquay via Jan Juc – call Bellarine Transit (☎03/5223 2111) for the latest information.

As you come into Torquay along the Great Ocean Road (Geelong Road in town), you'll see the **Surfcoast Plaza** shopping centre, by far the best place to rent surf gear. The **Surfworld Museum** (daily 10am–4pm; $6) at the rear of the plaza is devoted to Torquay's main industry – and a prosperous one it is, taking in at least $200 million a year. Surfworld features a wave-making machine, interactive videos that explain how waves are created, and displays about the history of surfing. The museum also functions as a **tourist information outlet**, handing out a few leaflets and brochures. Many of the biggest surfing businesses are based in Torquay, and every surf accessory conceivable is sold here. The biggest and oldest is Rip Curl, 101 Surf Coast Highway (daily 9am–5.30pm), which started making surfboards here in 1969 and now stocks all the major brands, as well as its own boards and gear. Based at the same shopping centre are showcase outlets for other big names, such as Billabong, Piping Hot and Quiksilver. Bargains can sometimes be found at Baines Beach Surf Seconds, around the corner on Baines Street (fourth factory on the right). The **Mary Elliott Pottery**, 80 Surfcoast Highway (open daily), is worth a look; it supplies tourist information as well.

A grassy public reserve shaded by huge Norfolk pines (with electric barbecues and picnic tables) runs along rocky **Fisherman's Beach** and **Front Beach**. The **Surf Beach** (or "back beach"), south of Cosy Corner (a headland separating Front and Surf beaches), is backed by rugged cliffs and takes a full belting from the Southern Ocean; it's patrolled in summer. **Jan Juc**, just south of Surf Beach across Torquay Golf Club, is also patrolled in season and has better swimming and surfing. The **South Coast Walk** to Aireys Inlet via Anglesea begins from here (25km; 8hr); the sector to **Bells Beach** is a one-hour, three-kilometre walk.

Practicalities

Accommodation in Torquay comprises a hostel, a couple of motels, several B&Bs, and a few caravan and camping parks. *Nomads Bells Beach Backpackers* on 51–53 Surfcoast Highway, painted bright blue with beach-house murals, is hard to miss (☎ 03/5261 7070, fax 5261 3879, free call ☎1800/819 883; dorms ①, rooms ③). Watch out for their package (about $130) which includes transport from and to Melbourne, two nights accommodation, a one-day Great Ocean Road tour and surfing lessons. The *Torquay Hotel/Motel*, 36 Bell St (☎03/5261 6046, fax 5261 4065; ⑤) is very centrally located, while *Just June's B&B*, 12 Casino Court (☎03/5261 3771; ⑤), is a homestay option in a modern home on a quiet street at the north end of town. When it comes to **food**, there are a few excellent, typically casual, places designed to satisfy a surfer's hunger: *Micha's Restaurant on the Esplanade*, 23 The Esplanade (☎03/5261 2460; licensed or BYO), is a longtime favourite dinner spot serving Mexican food and cheap drinks – you'll need to book at summer weekends. *Stoney's Restaurant & Cafe*, 7 Gilbert St (daily until late), serves good coffee, snacks and meals, and you can eat at their tables outside. The surfers' all-time favourite, however, is *Yummy Yoghurt*, a tiny café at 3 Gilbert St, which has simple vegetarian dishes, milkshakes and frozen yoghurt; its walls are covered with testimonials from surfing champions. Good ice cream is sold at *The Great Australian Ice Creamery*, Shop 4, 57 Surfcoast Highway, and *The Scandinavian Ice Cream Company*, 34 Bell St. For **entertainment**, surfies head for the *Torquay Hotel*, 36 Bell St, where live bands play at weekends. At Jan Juc, *Pabs Tavern*, on Stuart Avenue, is also a favourite hangout, known for its good food.

For **surfing lessons**, call Go Ride a Wave (☎03/5263 2111), an outdoors activities company based in neighbouring Anglesea. If you feel like taking to the air, turn to Tiger Moth World Adventure Park, a family amusement park on the Bellarine Peninsula

Outback track, SA

Adelaide, the Festival City

Desert landscape near Coober Pedy, SA

Surf lifesaving contest near Perth, WA

Remarkable Rocks, Kangaroo Island, SA

Joffre Falls, Karijini National Park, WA

Melbourne skyline

The Grampians, VIC

The Twelve Apostles, Great Ocean Road, VIC

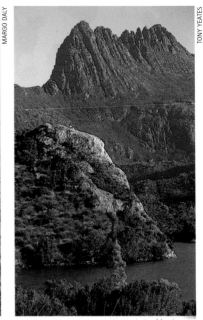

Seaplane flight over the Franklin River, TAS

Lake St Clair-Cradle Mountain National Park, TAS

Hills around Apollo Bay, VIC

halfway between Geelong and Queenscliff (☎03/5261 5100), which has lots of fun and sports facilities, most of them water-based. They also do **scenic flights** aboard vintage Tiger Moths, a typical trip flies over the Twelve Apostles ($60; min three people).

Anglesea and Aireys Inlet

On the way to Anglesea from Torquay, you can make a short but worthwhile detour to **Addis Point**; turn left just beyond Bells Beach. The road goes right out to the headland where, from the car park, you look down on the waves crashing onto the point. Steps lead down to an even better vantage point, with surf heaving below you and Bells Beach stretching to the northwest. Nearby, *Point Addis Flower Farm* (☎03/5263 2655, fax 5263 2322; ⑥–⑦) offers B&B accommodation in a lovely timber cottage with ocean views. Guests cook their own breakfast from ingredients supplied by the staff.

Getting to **ANGLESEA** from Torquay, you may be greeted by the smoke of an open-face brown-coal mine and power station generating electricity for Alcoa Australia's aluminium-smelting works at Geelong. Once you get past the power station, however, it's a perfectly pleasant place for a holiday, with the Anglesea River running through to the sea, and picnic grounds along its banks. Despite tourist development, the beach has managed to retain its sand dunes and its untouched aspect. Children can swim safely here, as the surf is fairly gentle, but the waves are high and powerful enough for body-surfers to enjoy. Anglesea's main claim to fame is a large population of **kangaroos**, which graze on its golf course. The small *Anglesea Backpackers Hostel* on 40 Noble St (☎03/5263 2664; dorms ①, double ③), located between the river and the golf course, has small dorms and a double with an en-suite. Use of mountain bikes is free, and the owner arranges lots of activities: surfing lessons (2hr; $25, gear included), snorkelling, spotlighting tours at night, horse-riding, mountain bike tours in the bush and trips to Torquay. Phone for a pick-up from the bus stop.

From Anglesea the road goes inland for a few kilometres through scrubby bush. Beyond, a pretty white lighthouse with a red cap overlooks the small town of **AIREYS INLET**. There's little more than a general store here (which sells heavily discounted fuel) and the *Aireys Inlet Caravan Park* opposite (☎03/5289 6230; cabins ③–⑤). The *Lightkeepers Inn*, on the way out of town (free call ☎1800/032 639, fax 03/5289 6806; ⑤–⑦), offers more upmarket accommodation, in keeping with the huge and ritzy houses that jostle for ocean views on the way to Lorne. On the budget end of the price scale, there's the small *Surfcoast Backpackers* in Fairhaven (☎03/5289 6886, mobile 0419/351 149; dorms, winter ①, summer ②) with very clean en-suite dorms and a cosy kitchen/common room with a piano. The hostel is located in a prime location, 100m away from the main road, the bus stop, and the long, sandy Fairhaven Beach which is patrolled. The owner books horse rides through the bush and along the beaches. Ask the bus driver to stop at the Yarringa Road bus stop – there's a signpost on the Great Ocean Road pointing towards the hostel.

Lorne and around

Picturesquely located at the foot of the heavily forested **Otway Range**, on the banks of the Erskine River, **LORNE** has long been the premier holiday town of the Great Ocean Road. Only two hours' drive from the city, it's hugely popular with Melbourne weekenders who relish its well-established café society and whiff of 1960s counterculture overlaid on an essentially middle-class 1930s resort. To complete the picture, the **Angahook–Lorne State Park** (see p.835), with its walking tracks, plunging falls and fern gullies, surrounds the town.

About nine hundred people live in Lorne, but from Christmas until the end of January twenty thousand more pour in; if you arrive unannounced, you'll have no hope of finding even a camping spot. The **Falls Festival**, on New Year's Eve, is celebrated with a big rock concert that attracts droves of teenagers, followed eight days later by the Mountain to Surf Run and one day later by the highlight of the peak season, the **Pier to Pub Swim**. It is the largest blue-water swimming event in the world and attracts as many as two thousand competitors who race the 1200m from Lorne Pier to the main beach. The atmosphere surrounding these events is a lot of fun, but generally Lorne is much more enjoyable when it's less crowded, which means avoiding weekends and the peak summer season.

The main beachfront promenade, Mountjoy Parade, is enlivened by the *Grand Pacific Hotel*, with its 1870s facade, and the modern, terraced *Cumberland Resort*, the so-called "Pink Palace". Between the street and the beach is a foreshore with tennis courts, trampolines and pool. The surf **beach** itself is one of the safest in Victoria, protected from the Southern Ocean by two headlands, but in summer it gets very crowded. Thirteen kilometres south is the secluded unofficial nude beach of **Jamiesons**, hidden by ferns and gullies near Jamiesons Creek.

Practicalities

Lorne's **tourist office**, at 144 Mountjoy Parade (daily 9am–5pm; ☎03/5289 1152), is very helpful and has a good stock of leaflets packed with local information, including several free driving maps and details of walks in the state park. Mocean Surfboards, 55 Mountjoy Parade (daily 9.30am–5.30pm), rents out quality surf- and boogie-boards and wetsuits, and their own customized boards. Other services, such as banks, a post office and shops, are clustered primarily along Mountjoy Parade and parallel Smith Street.

Accommodation

Lorne has a mix of old guesthouses and modern holiday apartments – often side by side. There's plenty of motel, hotel and self-catering accommodation, but most of it is in the upper price bracket. If you want to keep costs down (but don't fancy the dorms at the *YHA* or *Great Ocean Road Cottages*), contact the Lorne Foreshore Committee, Ocean Road by Erskine Bridge (☎03/5289 1382), which runs four **caravan parks** in the town and vicinity and has on-site vans for around ④.

The Anchorage, 32 Mountjoy Parade (☎ & fax 03/5289 1891). Self-catering accommodation with barbecues, pool and heated spa. ⑤–⑧.

Cumberland Lorne Resort, 150 Mountjoy Parade (free call ☎1800/037 010, fax 03/5289 2256). Luxurious but pricey one-bedroom apartments, some with ocean views; lots of facilities, including tennis and squash courts, an indoor pool, spa, sauna, and rental of windsurfers, boogie-boards and bikes. ⑧.

Erskine Falls Cottages, off Erskine Falls Rd, about 4km north of town (☎03/5289 2666, fax 5289 2247). Luxurious, two-bedroom cottages in a quiet bushland setting in the hills above Lorne, with superb views, a pool, heated spa, tennis court and barbecue. ⑦–⑧.

Great Ocean Road Backpackers YHA, 10 Erskine Ave (☎03/5289 1809, fax 5289 2508). In a central location just off the main road, beside the Erskine River. ①–②.

Great Ocean Road Cottages, 3 Erskine Ave (☎03/5289 1070, fax 5289 1380). Well-designed, comfortable, self-catering cottages in a lovely forest setting beside the Erskine River; also a backpackers' section. Cottages ⑤–⑧, dorms ②.

Lemonade Creek Cottages, 690 Erskine Falls Rd (☎ & fax 03/5289 2600). Self-contained weatherboard cottages with central heating; in a bushland setting, but not far from the beach and town. ⑤–⑦.

Lorne Hotel, 176 Mountjoy Parade (☎03/5289 1409, fax 5289 2200). Very large rooms, some with balconies and sea views, but noisy at weekends. ⑤–⑥.

Ocean Lodge Motel, 6 Armytage St (☎03/5289 1330, fax 5289 1380). Run-of-the-mill, but good-value, motel accommodation. ⑤–⑥.

Pacific Hotel, 268 Mountjoy Parade (☎03/5289 1609, fax 5289 2279). A building whose faded grandeur conceals motel-style accommodation. ⑤.

Eating and entertainment

There are great places to eat and drink everywhere in town. *Kosta's* often has **music** in the evenings, while the *Lorne Hotel* has bands on Friday and Saturday nights, and its public bar, with pool table and pinball machine, is a favourite with the young crowd. The Lorne Theatre, 78 Mountjoy Parade (☎03/5289 1272), screens **films** all week during summer.

The Arab, 94 Mountjoy Parade. An original beatnik hangout, which opened two weeks before the Olympic Games in 1956 and has been going strong ever since. It now sports minimalist decor but is still good for daytime snacks and fancier meals at night.

Kosta's, 48 Mountjoy Parade (☎03/5289 1883). A popular, Greek-style bar and eating place, decorated with surrealist wall paintings. Licensed or BYO.

Lorne Hotel, 176 Mountjoy Parade. Best pub meals in town, and has a dining room overlooking the ocean.

Lorne Pier Seafood Restaurant, on the pier at Point Grey. Excellent seafood. Licensed or BYO.

Mark's, 124 Mountjoy Parade (☎03/5289 2787). A modern restaurant with a menu featuring a large variety of dishes, from marlin steak to home-made potato gnocchi. Licensed.

Qdos, Allenvale Rd (☎03/5289 1989). Tucked away in the eucalypt-clad hills above Lorne, this art gallery-cum-café serves light lunches, dinners and tasty home-made cakes and coffee in a relaxed atmosphere. Bookings advisable.

Reifs Restaurant & Bar, 84 Mountjoy Parade (☎03/5289 2366). Serves a wide range of dishes, including seafood and vegetarian, with Asian and Mediterranean influences. A large outdoor area overlooks Loutit Bay. Licensed. Open from morning until late.

Angahook–Lorne State Park

Angahook–Lorne State Park extends along some 50km of coastline, from Aireys Inlet to Kennett River. Pockets of temperate rainforest, towering blue-gum forests, cliffs and waterfalls characterize the Lorne section of the park, south of the Erskine River. The **Erskine Falls**, one of the most popular attractions, drops 30m into a fern-fringed pool – you can reach them along a winding eight-kilometre road (some of it gravel), which ends with a short descent on a very steep but sealed section. From the car park the falls are a few minutes' walk through majestic trees and tall umbrella ferns; another 150m takes you down to the quiet, rocky Erskine River. It's also possible to walk through the bush from Lorne to the falls (7.5km one-way; 4hr), starting from the *Erskine River Caravan Park* and following the river; after 1km you'll pass the Sanctuary, a natural rock amphitheatre, then Splitter Falls and Straw Falls, before reaching Erskine Falls.

Closer to Lorne, **Teddy's Lookout**, in Queens Park, is either a quick drive from the Great Ocean Road, up Otway Street, turn left at the roundabout into George Street, or a three-kilometre walk. You end up high above the sea, with a view of the St George River below and the Great Ocean Road curving around the cliffs. On the way back to Lorne, the **Qdos Arts centre** (daily 11am–11pm) on Allenvale Road, with an art gallery, sculpture gardens and a very good café-restaurant, merits a visit – just turn left at the roundabout and go up the hill.

Apollo Bay and the Otway Range

After Lorne, wooded hills fall away steeply into the ocean. The road follows the coastline in twisted serpentines, becoming very narrow in places where it was literally gouged out of the rockface, occasionally descending to small bays at the river mouths of Wye River and Kennett River. On a fine, sunny day the views are glorious, but best admired from one of the many scenic lookout points as you need to drive with care.

APOLLO BAY is in a picturesque setting between pounding surf and gently rounded green hills. **Fishing** – commercial and recreational – is the main activity here. If you're interested in doing a bit yourself, enquire at Apollo Bay Boat Charter (☎03/5237 6214), which does fishing trips and scenic boat cruises. The town has an enjoyably alternative feel – a lot of musicians live here and both local pubs have music at weekends. The **Apollo Bay Music Festival**, now an annual event, takes place over a weekend in mid-March and features jazz, rock, blues and country, plus many workshops (information ☎03/5237 6761; for bookings Ticketmaster, free call ☎1800/136 100). For information on local activities, head for the **Great Ocean Road Visitor Information Centre** in a new building on the foreshore at the eastern end of town (daily 9am–5pm; ☎03/5237 6529, fax 5237 6194), with an informative display on the rainforest and local history. They also book accommodation at the centre or after hours on a touchscreen computer just outside. **Flying** is becoming increasingly popular here: the Wingsports Flight Academy (mobile ☎0419/378 616) offers courses in hang-gliding and paragliding and allows those with no prior experience to fly with a fully qualified pilot along the coast in a powered hang-glider. Apollo Air Joyflights (☎03/5237 7370) does scenic flights to a variety of destinations, including nearby Cape Otway ($30), Twelve Apostles ($70) and as far afield as King Island, Tasmania ($100); prices are based on a minimum of three passengers. If you're interested in **horse-riding**, book a trail ride with Wild Dog Trails (☎03/5237 6441; 1hr 30min $20, full day $80); **cycling** enthusiasts can enquire about mountain bike tours run by Otway Expeditions (mobile ☎0419/007 586). A few tour operators offer tours for people who are interested in **nature and the environment**. Otway Eco-Guides (☎03/5237 7240 or 5237 9255) do walking tours through the Otway National Park. Last Chance Tours (☎03/5237 7413), run by environmental activists, do walking tours as well as half- ($25) to full day ($55) vehicle tours, visiting endangered rainforest and waterfalls in the hinterland of Apollo Bay. For other sightseeing tours (4WD or normal vehicle) enquire at the Visitor Information Centre.

Apollo Bay has a wide variety of **accommodation**; the information centre has full details of what's available. Numerous holiday apartments, cosy B&B cottages, guesthouses and farmstays are to be found in the area, many of them picturesquely located in the hills and valleys surrounding the town. One that's particularly worth seeking out is *Wongarra Heights* on Sunnyside Road, Wongarra (☎03/5237 0257; ⑥), which offers B&B accommodation on a farm 12km east. Apollo Bay's main street is lined with **motels**, most of them rather drab affairs dating from the Seventies. One of the newer and better ones is *Beachfront Motel & Cottages* on 163 Great Ocean Rd (☎03/5237 6437, fax 5237 7197; ⑤–⑧). For budget travellers, there are two hostels: the *Surfside YHA* at the corner of Great Ocean Road and Gambier Street (☎03/5237 7263; dorms ①, doubles ③) is a small and friendly place in a scenic location on a hill at the western side of town offering free use of surfboards, windsurfing and skin-diving equipment. Just 400m up from the main street, the *Apollo Bay Backpacker Hostel*, 47 Montrose St (☎03/5237 7360 or mobile ☎0419/340 362; ①–③), is a small weatherboard house with dorms, cheap singles and doubles; some out the back in an extension to the house. There are several **caravan parks**, the closest to town being the *Waratah Caravan Park* at 7 Noel St (☎03/5237 6562; cabins ④, on-site vans ③). The *Pisces Caravan Resort*, 2km north of the town centre (☎03/5237 6749) has cabins ②–⑤.

For foreshore **camping** in more natural, secluded surroundings, try the *Marengo Camping Reserve* on Marengo Crescent (☎03/5237 6162; closed May–Oct), or *Skenes Creek Camping Reserve*, 6km back along the Ocean Road, where a caretaker calls in every day.

In town, the **eating** places are strung along the Great Ocean Road. *Rigani's Fine Food*, at no. 58, serves great coffee, sandwiches and cakes. You can eat in or take away at the *Wholefood Deli* at no. 61 (daily 10am–7pm), although the *Bay Leaf Gourmet Deli* at no. 131 is more atmospheric and sophisticated. The *Apollo Bay Hotel* has good seafood, and also cheaper counter and bistro meals. *Buffs Bistro* at no. 51, serves light snacks, seafood and pasta, while *Sea Grapes Wine Bar*, at the other end of the strip at no. 141, is more upmarket, serves good coffee and is open for breakfast, lunch and dinner. A lot of interesting places to eat, in terms of good food as well as scenic views, are outside town. Located in the hills up the coast above Skenes Creek, *Chris's Beacon Point Restaurant*, 2km up Skenes Creek Road (☎03/5237 6411), is renowned for its Mediterranean cuisine and especially its seafood. The *Tanybryn Tea House and Gallery*, on the corner of Skenes Creek and Wild Dog roads, is also worth the fifteen-minute drive for its well-stocked craft shop, café and fine panorama (10am–5pm; closed last week of June until second week in September). The *Elliott River Tea Rooms* on the Great Ocean Road, in the hills just west of Apollo Bay, make a nice refreshment stop just before visiting Maits Rest (daily 10am–4.30pm; May–October closed Mon & Tues). If you've got enough time for a detour, you can follow the road further north to the small hamlet of **Forrest** to pay a visit to the unusual *Feral Fine Art Gallery and Coffee Bar* (June–Oct 10am–5pm weekends and public holidays, Nov–May 10am–5pm Thurs–Tues, during the summer school holidays daily).

Otway National Park

From Apollo Bay, the Great Ocean Road soon enters **Otway National Park**, curving and bending upwards through temperate rainforest and offering occasional glimpses of cleared hilltops and grazing sheep in the distance. From **Maits Rest** car park, 17km west of Apollo Bay, you can take an easy stroll through a lovely fern gully, which gives a good idea of the dense rainforest that once covered the entire Otway Ranges. A little further down the road, towards Lavers Hill, there's a turn-off to the **Cape Otway Lighthouse**, 14km along an unsealed road, where there's pleasant accommodation in two renovated cottages, former residences of the lighthouse keepers (⑦–⑧). You can take a guided tour of the grounds and the lighthouse (daily 9am–5pm; $5), as well as specialist tours such as a paleontology trip which focuses on prehistoric plants and animals, in particular one type of dinosaur unique to this area – the polar dinosaur. Advance booking necessary, enquire about prices (☎03/5237 9240).

Bimbi Park (☎03/5237 9246; on-site vans ③), about halfway along the road, is the only **caravan park** actually within the national park. The facilities and some of the cabins are quite basic but the setting is gorgeous – on a small farm with paddocks surrounded by bushland. The caravan park does excellent **horse-riding** excursions, one being a ride to Station Beach ($18; 1hr), a three-kilometre-long stretch of sand with freshwater springs and waterfalls.

Back on the Great Ocean Road, you momentarily return to the ocean at **Castle Cove**, a good lookout point across green, undulating dairy country. As you turn inland again, stepped hills rise sharply from the road as it passes turn-offs to **Johanna**, one of Victoria's best-known surf beaches, and winds up towards **LAVERS HILL**, high in the Otway Range. The tiny town is characterized by its fern nursery and two cosy tearooms: the *Gardenside Manor* and the *Blackwood Gully Tea Rooms & Tourist Centre*, both of which serve light snacks and Devonshire teas daily from 10am. The *Otway Junction Motor Inn* (☎03/5237 3295) offers more solid **meals** as well as motel-style **accommodation** (⑤–⑥). An alternative, and cheaper, place to stay is the *Lavers Hill Roadhouse* (☎03/5237 3251; ②–③), where you have a choice of bunkhouses and on-site vans.

Three kilometres further is **Melba Gully Conservation Park**, one of the wettest spots in Victoria. It's the location of the Big Tree, a three-hundred-year-old Otway messmate, its base covered in moss; at night glow-worms are a common sight.

From Moonlight Head to Peterborough

The 130-kilometre stretch of coast between lonely, windswept Moonlight Head and Port Fairy is known as the **Shipwreck Coast** – all of it protected within **Port Campbell National Park**. The stretch from Princetown to Peterborough is the most obviously hazardous to shipping, with its sheer limestone cliffs and massive eroded stacks. Beyond Princetown, the first worthwhile stop is the steep and slippery **Gibsons Steps**, where you walk down to a small, kelp-covered beach beneath towering cliffs. From here on, the spectacle gets more and more extraordinary, with plenty of convenient stopping points from where you can admire the amazing formations. The most stupendous are the **Twelve Apostles** – gigantic limestone pillars, some rising 65m out of the ocean, which retreat in rows as stark reminders of a wasting coastline (the cliff faces eroding at a rate of about 2cm a year). Sunset here is a popular time for photographers (summer about 9pm, winter about 5.45pm). A new visitor centre on the north side of the Great Ocean Road, just opposite the Twelve Apostles, is planned to open by mid-2000.

Next stop is **Loch Ard Gorge**, where the **Historic Shipwreck Trail** begins. Extending from here to Peterborough, the trail links the sites of dozens of shipwrecks with signed paths and informative plaques. The *Loch Ard*, an iron-hulled square rig, was transporting immigrants from England to Melbourne in June 1878 when it hit a reef and foundered. Of fifty-three people on board, only two survived: Eva Carmichael and Tom Pearce, both 18 years old. They were swept into a long gorge that had a narrow entrance, high walls and small beach, and Tom dragged Eva into a cave in the western wall of the gorge before going for help. A walkway leads down to the beach, covered with delicate pink kelp, and you can scramble over craggy rocks to the deep, sandy cave where Eva sheltered, now a nesting site for small birds. The Loch Ard cemetery, where the ship's passengers and crew are buried, is on the clifftop overlooking the gorge. As you drive further, you pass more scenic points, with resonant names such as the Blowhole and the Thundercave, before reaching Port Campbell.

Port Campbell

PORT CAMPBELL is a small and companionable settlement on the edge of the park. The **Port Campbell National Park Information Centre** on Morris Street (daily 10am–5pm; ☎03/5598 6382) has displays and information about the area, as well as leaflets describing the self-guided **Port Campbell Discovery Walk** (90min), which will take you along a clifftop to a viewpoint above Two Mile Bay. Port Campbell **beach** is a small sandy curve, safe for swimming and patrolled in season.

The town climbs the hill behind the beach. At 27 Lord St, the Port Campbell Trading Company is a small **art gallery** displaying works by local artists and craftspeople. Opposite, the **Loch Ard Shipwreck Museum** (daily 9am–5pm; $4) has exhibits and videos relating the stories of five of the South West Coast shipping disasters (the *Loch Ard*, *Fiji*, *Schomberg*, *Falls of Halladale* and *Newfield*), as well as artefacts salvaged from some of the wrecks. If you're really fascinated by the wrecks, Port Campbell Scuba & Marine Centre at 23 Lord St (daily 9am–6pm; ☎03/5598 6499) leads **dives** to some of them and rents out diving and snorkelling gear.

Practicalities

Port Campbell's General Store (daily: winter 8am–6pm; summer 7am–7pm) also functions as the post office and newsagent; it also has an EFTPOS system that takes every type of card. If you're looking for **somewhere to stay**, *Port O'Call* at 37 Lord St (☎03/5598 6206; ④–⑤) is a good, inexpensive motel, while the *Southern Ocean Motor*

Inn on Lord Street (free call ☎1800/035 093, fax 03/5598 6471; ⑥–⑧) is more upmarket and has a good licensed restaurant. The *Port Campbell National Park Cabin & Caravan Park* on Tregea Street (☎03/5598 6492, fax 5598 6369; ③–④) offers on-site vans and beachside cabins. The *Port Campbell YHA Hostel* across the road at 18 Tregea St (☎ & fax 03/5598 6305; ①) is a medium-size hostel with four large dorms, a large modern kitchen and a TV lounge with wood-fired heater. More backpackers accommodation is available at *Ocean House*, 32 Cairns St (☎03/5598 6223, fax 5598 6471; dorms ①, rooms ②), or phone the *Southern Ocean Motor Inn*.

Places to **eat** include the bistro at the *Port Campbell Hotel* on Lord Street (daily lunch and dinner), the *Great Australian Bite*, on Lord Street opposite the beach; and the *Port Campbell Take Away Cafe*. For a bit more of a choice, and good coffee, go to *Emma's Tearooms* at 25 Lord St (Thurs–Sun 11am–11pm) or the *Bakers Oven and Coffeehouse* opposite, in the building just in front of the Shipwreck Museum.

Tourists could once walk across the double-arched rock formation known as **London Bridge**, a short distance west of Port Campbell, to the outer end facing the sea. In mid-January 1990, however, the outer span collapsed and fell into the sea, minutes after two very lucky people had crossed it – they were eventually rescued from the far limestone cliff by helicopter. Another good place to stop, just before Peterborough, is the **Grotto**, where a path leads from the clifftop to a rock pool beneath an archway.

Moving on, you pass through undulating dairy country on the last stretch of the Great Ocean Road from Peterborough, on Curdies Inlet, to Warrnambool. There's little to detain you along the route, although if you're a cheese fan you might consider a detour to **TIMBOON**, 18km inland from Port Campbell: at Timboon Farmhouse Cheese (daily 10am–4pm), on the corner of Ford and Fells roads, you can taste and buy excellent, biodynamic cheese and wine.

Warrnambool and onwards

WARRNAMBOOL seems unable to decide whether it's an industrial city or a charming, seaside agricultural town. Coming into town on the Great Ocean Road you see the more pleasant aspects: the city's lovely coastal setting, with Allansford Cheeseworld (Mon–Fri 8.30am–4.30pm, Sat 8.30am–4pm, Sun 10am–4pm) indicating that this is the centre of rich **dairy country**. As well as selling cheese, it has cheese and wine tastings, a café serving teas and light meals, and a museum. However, if you approach Warrnambool from the west along the Princes Highway, you'll pass car lots, motels and an ugly factory belching smoke.

Lady Bay, where Warrnambool is sheltered, was first used by sealers and whalers in the early nineteenth century and was permanently settled from about 1839. Southern right whales, hunted almost to extinction, have begun to return in the last few years and have been sighted in the surf off **Logans Beach** between May and October. The bay was never a good port – exposed as it is to unpredictable weather, reefs and shallow water – and between 1836 and 1908 there were 28 shipwrecks here. The well-set up **Flagstaff Hill Maritime Village** on Merri Street (daily 9am–4.30pm; $10) has displays on these and other shipwrecks along the treacherous coast, paying particular emphasis to the *Loch Ard* disaster (see p.838). The re-created nineteenth-century village is arranged around a fort erected in 1887, a time when, improbably, the fear of Russian invasion was widespread in Australia.

Warrnambool has a bustling downtown, with a major shopping centre on Liebig Street, several galleries and museums, and some fine old churches. Perhaps the best of the sights is the **Warrnambool Art Gallery** on Liebig Street (daily noon–5pm; $3), a fine provincial gallery with collections of Western District colonial paintings and contemporary Australian prints. The **Botanic Gardens** on Botanic Road, designed in 1877 by William Guilfoyle, then Director of the Melbourne Botanic Gardens, are also worth visiting if you happen to have some spare time. The classically designed, ornamental gardens are filled with winding paths and hills, and provide glimpses of the sea. There's also a fernery, a waterlily pond and a small rotunda.

Practicalities

Warrnambool Tourist Information, at 600 Raglan Parade (daily 9am–5pm; ☎03/5564 7837), is modern, large and well organized; it can book accommodation and also acts as a travel agent. For backpacker accommodation, both ends of the town are covered with hostels right in the centre and another one out near the breakwater and beach. The pleasant *Stuffed Backpacker*, operated by Flaherty's Chocolate Shop, 52 Kepler St (☎ & fax 03/5562 2459; ①–③), is just around the corner from the busy end of Liebig Street and offers B&B lodgings in a renovated old building with dorms or twin rooms with another brand-new dorm with en-suite facilities out back. The *Backpackers Barn* at the *Victoria Hotel* at the corner of Lava and Liebig streets (☎03/5562 2073, fax 5561 3775; dorms ①, rooms ②–③) is equally centrally located, has dorms and doubles and a fully equipped kitchen. From the clean and friendly *Nomads Warrnambool Beach Backpackers*, near the *Lady Bay Hotel* 17 Stanley St (☎03/5562 4874) you're less than ten minutes' walk away from the beach. The hostel has doubles and comfy dorms with lockers. The hostel organizes trail rides along the beach near Tower Hill ($25 for 1hr, $40 for 2hr). Phone for a pick-up from the bus stop in town.

The refurbished *Hotel Warrnambool*, on the corner of Koroit and Kepler streets (☎03/5562 2377; ③–⑤), offers good B&B pub accommodation in the town centre, while *Pertobe B&B* at 10 Banyan St (☎03/5561 7078; ⑤) is in a convenient location between the town centre and the beach. Just south of the roundabout along Pertobe Road and near the foreshore there are a few more options: *Warrnambool Surfside Holiday Park*, with self-contained one- to three-bedroom cottages and cabins as well as campsites right on the beach (☎03/5561 2611; cabins ④–⑥), *Port Warrnambool Village B&B* (☎03/5562 8063; ⑦) and the *Lady Bay Hotel* (☎03/5562 1544; ④) at the south-western end of Pertobe Road near the breakwater.

If none of these places have room, you could try any of the motels that line the Princes Highway at each end of town.

There are plenty of good places to eat on Liebig Street. Freshly cooked fish and chips are served at *Seafoods*, at no. 126. The *Victoria Hotel*, on the corner of Liebig and Lava streets, has bar meals. *Beach Babylon* at no. 72 serves pizza and pasta, while the *Freshwater Cafe* at no. 78 is a renowned, classy Italian restaurant (open Tues–Sat lunch and dinner). On the other side of the road, the funky *Fishtales Café* at no. 63 has an open courtyard; *Restaurant Malaysia* at no. 69 features inexpensive Southeast Asian cuisine; and *Fitzsellers Café* at no. 89 is a simple, pleasant joint serving sandwiches, quiches and other snacks. Further up the street there's *The Black Olive Bar Restaurant & Cafe* in the *Hotel Grand* at no. 158 and *Rios Deli* at no. 142 for sandwiches, bagels and cakes. *Rogers Bar* in the *Whalers Inn*, on the corner of Liebig and Timor streets, is a slick, modern-looking place where Warrnambool's young and trendy go to **drink**.

Tower Hill Game Reserve and Koroit

About 13km west of Warrnambool along the Princes Highway, **Tower Hill Game Reserve** is located in the crater of a volcano which last erupted about 18,000 years ago. In the nineteenth century pioneer settlers stripped Tower Hill of its trees and used it as grazing land, but since the 1960s it has been reforested and wildlife has gradually returned. If you visit the island in the middle of the crater lake at dusk, you'll encounter emus, koalas and loads of kangaroos and wallabies. The game reserve is open daily from dawn to dusk, but on days of extreme fire danger it may sometimes be closed (call ☎03/5565 9202 to check). The **Natural History Centre** (daily 9.30am–12.30pm,

1.30–4.30pm) on the island has displays about the area's geological history and the revegetation programme, while a bird hide nearby enables you to spy on the abundant birdlife. There are also five self-guided short **walks** around the reserve (30min–1hr).

KOROIT, 7km north, is a tiny, old-fashioned town with Australia's largest concentration of people of Irish descent. The Catholic church is impressive, but the building that really dominates the town is the elegant two-storey **Koroit Hotel**. It's been run by the same family since 1922, and little has changed since then. Other buildings along the main street are faded one-storey Victorian and Edwardian shopfronts with shady corrugated-iron awnings, and there's also an abandoned train station. If you cut north from here to the Hamilton Highway you'll know you're getting into wool country when you see sheep walking down the main street of Woolsthorpe.

Port Fairy and Mount Eccles

PORT FAIRY, the next stop along the coast, was once an early port and whaling centre but is now a quaint crayfishing town with a busy jetty, a harbour full of yachts, and over fifty National Trust-listed buildings. Heavy southern breakers roll into the surrounding beaches, and on Griffiths Island, poised between the ocean and Port Fairy Bay, there's a muttonbird rookery with a specially constructed lookout where between September and April you can watch them roost at dusk. For a historic town, it's also quite a happening place, hosting numerous events: in summer the six-week-long **Moyneyama Festival** focuses on outdoor activities with events such as a raft race on the Moyne River, reaching its climax with the Moyneyama New Year's Eve procession; at Easter the annual Queenscliff to Port Fairy yacht race ends here, with a huge party. The biggest event, however, is over the Labour Day long weekend in March, when the huge **Port Fairy Folk Festival** takes over the town, with Australian and overseas acts playing world, roots and acoustic music – everything from Koorie to country, and from blues to Celtic. Tickets are sold in early November; they usually sell out in less than a day. Up to twenty thousand people pour into town for the festival, and even a tent site is hard to get. For more information and festival bookings call the **visitor information centre**, on Bank Street (daily 9am–5pm, shorter hours in winter; ☎03/5568 2682, fax 5568 2832). It also books accommodation and produces an excellent free map of the Port Fairy Heritage Walk, which takes you on a route around town to admire the many fine buildings. The **History Centre**, in the old courthouse on Gipps Street by the river, displays costumes, historic photographs, shipwreck relics and other items relating to the town's pioneer history (Wed, Sat & Sun 2–5pm, daily during school holidays & long weekends; $2).

Port Fairy practicalities

With its village-like atmosphere and its variety of excellent **accommodation** options, as well as good pubs, tearooms and restaurants, Port Fairy makes a good place to break your journey between Melbourne and Adelaide. The *Port Fairy Youth Hostel*, at 8 Cox St (☎03/5568 2468, fax 5568 2302; ③), is in a lovely old house right in the town centre. The *Seacombe House Motor Inn* at 22 Sackville St (☎03/5568 1082; ④–⑧), one of the many National Trust-listed buildings, has a few inexpensive rooms in the old hotel, as well as pricey modern motel units and historic cottages. In fact, there are numerous quaint colonial cottages and B&Bs, such as *Whalers Cottages*, on the corner of Whalers Drive and Regent Street (☎03/5568 1488; ⑥–⑧), *Cottages of the Port* at 96 Gipps St (☎03/5568 7345; ⑦–⑧), and *Lough Cottage* at 216 Griffith St (☎03/5568 1583; ⑨). Full details of all cottages and B&Bs, and of Port Fairy's six caravan parks, can be obtained from the visitor information centre.

Lunch, in the old Borough Chambers at 20 Bank St (Wed–Sun 9am–5pm, dinner Fri–Sun; extended hours during the holiday season), is a **café** that has eclectic and very enjoyable food. *Rebecca's*, at 70 Sackville St, serves breakfasts and light lunches, cakes and good coffee, and next door at no. 72 delicious home-made ice cream. *Culpepper's*, a health food shop at 24 Bank St, next to the visitor information centre, serves Devonshire teas and light meals. For an upmarket licensed **restaurant**, try the *Merrijig Inn* at 1 Campbell St, or the very good *Stag Restaurant* at the *Seacombe House Motor Inn*, 22 Sackville St (daily from 6am–3pm; bookings necessary ☎03/5568 1077). The best place to **drink** is the *Caledonian Inn* (*"The Stump"*), on the corner of Banks and James streets – it's the oldest continually licensed pub in Victoria (since 1844).

Mount Eccles National Park

Just over 50km north of Port Fairy is **Mount Eccles National Park**. Mount Eccles (though it hardly deserves to be called a mountain) is an extinct **volcano** with lava caves, channels and a crater lake set in rugged, stony country; there used to be a quarry here and you can see the various layers of different lava flows where the mountain has been cut. **Lake Surprise** is the delightful crater lake, shimmering blue in summer. Walks – all of which begin from the picnic ground at the end of the entrance road – include a two-kilometre (1hr) walk around the rim of the crater, or you can descend and walk around the shoreline (with a chance to swim in the lake, which is 21°C in summer); there's also a two-hour walk along a lava canal leading to a lava cave.

Birdlife around the lake includes wedge-tail eagles, kookaburras, tawny frogmouths, dog birds, barn owls and boobooks. The trees are loaded with koalas, seen at any time of the day. There are also eastern grey kangaroos, echidnas, bats, tiger snakes, copperhead snakes and blue-tongued lizards. Mid- to late spring is a good time for wild flowers – from orchids to native geraniums – and wattle. Look out for a tree in the southwest corner of the park that has had an Aboriginal shield cut out of it with a sharpened stone tool. The **visitors centre** (☎03/5576 1014) has an informative display to help you explore the park and learn about the history of the volcano and the area's Aborigines. You can also **camp** here: wood is supplied, and there are toilets and water.

Portland to South Australia

PORTLAND, the last stop on the Victoria coast going west on the Princes Highway, is a large industrial and fishing port. There's a smattering of historic buildings, but they don't add up to form a coherent townscape. Despite the best efforts of the local tourist industry to promote Portland there's nothing in town that would merit an extended stay unless you wanted to explore the local industry. However, the wild coastal scenery to the southwest around Cape Nelson and Cape Bridgewater is well worth a detour.

Huge ships dock in **Portland Bay**, where a vast heap of sandy brown bauxite sits beside the Alcoa smelter, in full view of the Esplanade. **Aluminium** is one of Australia's largest exports, and in 1980 big business was met with **Aboriginal resistance** here, when a legal battle developed over the siting of the smelter on land that had great importance for the Gunditj Mara. There were traces of over sixty Aboriginal campsites and workshop areas on the proposed site, and sacred places including a burial ground. Plans for building the smelter eventually went ahead, but Alcoa was forced to pay the Gunditj Mara $1.5 million in compensation, which was used to buy back land in the area of the Lake Condah mission (see opposite).

Before the area was permanently settled by whites – it's the oldest settlement in Victoria – there had been conflict between whalers and Aborigines that resulted in massacres and the decimation of an entire tribe. The first **squatters** in Victoria, the Hentys, came to the Portland area in 1834 to pasture sheep on vast landholdings, and they, too, soon came into conflict with the Koories – from 1838 clans began to use their traditional burning-off process in an attempt to drive the Hentys away. During the 1840s a sustained guerrilla war, known as the **Eumeralla War**, was fought against settlers occupying land around Port Fairy, Mount Napier and Lake Condah. In the end it was only the deployment of the Aboriginal **Native Police Corps** in 1842 that finally broke the resistance – and even they took four years.

The seafront Esplanade is lined with fish and chip shops and cafés. The **tourist office** is also located on the waterfront (daily 9am–5pm; free call ☎1800/035 567) which gives information on the numerous museums and historic buildings around town which mainly celebrate white settlement.

Along the coast to the southwest, around craggy **Cape Nelson** and stormy **Cape Bridgewater**, the scenery is stunning: caves, freshwater lakes close to the cliff coast, blowholes, a petrified forest of limestone columns where ancient trees used to stand, and the beach at **Bridgewater Bay**, which extends in a wide, sandy arc from one cape to the other. The best way to explore these features is along the walking tracks that start from the Blowholes car park, which is signposted left off the road to Cape Bridgewater. Bring good walking shoes, as the volcanic rocks can be very sharp, and carry food and drink.

Lake Condah Mission

Lake Condah Mission is about 50km northeast of Portland, on the western edge of Mount Eccles National Park. A mission was established in 1867 in this traditional Aboriginal area, with its plentiful game and fish, and surviving Aborigines from the area were brought here but were forbidden to speak their own language or practise their culture. At its height in 1880 there were over twenty buildings of timber and stone. Although the mission was officially closed in 1919, a large community remained until the 1950s, when they were gradually dispossessed as land was given to returned soldiers under the soldier settlement scheme. Perhaps the greatest injustice occurred when several Aboriginal returned soldiers, who had lived on Lake Condah, applied for land, only to be refused. With the money paid in settlement of the Alcoa dispute (see opposite), the land was finally bought back in the 1980s.

Lower Glenelg National Park and Nelson

From Portland the **Princes Highway** makes its uneventful way, via Heywood, to Mount Gambier in South Australia. After 120km it crosses the **Glenelg River** (which has its source in the Grampians) at Dartmoor, a popular point to begin a four-day canoeing trip down to the river's mouth at Nelson. For most of the journey the clear, blue river flows through the unspoilt **Lower Glenelg National Park** in a sixty-kilometre gorge cut through limestone. The spectacular **Princess Margaret Rose Cave** (☎08/8738 4171, guided tours hourly Mon–Fri 11am–4.30pm, Sat & Sun from 10am, less frequent in winter; $5) lies beside the river as it loops round by the South Australian border and can be reached by canoe, car (unsealed roads from both sides of the border lead to the caves) or on a cruise from Nelson (see below).

NELSON is at the end of the coastal road and virtually on the border, less than 40km from Mount Gambier. A peaceful, friendly little hamlet, it feels caught in a time warp, and there's little to do but **fish** or **canoe** on the Glenelg. South West Canoe Service (☎08/8738 4141, arrange overnight canoe or kayak trips with camping in special riverside camps and kayaks and arrange overcamping. Nelson Boat Hire on Kellet Street (daily 8.30am–6pm, closed Wed out of season; ☎08/8738 4048) also rents out canoes and kayaks, and sells bait; you'll also need a licence, obtained from the Nelson Kiosk (daily 8am–6pm; ☎08/8738 4220), the local service station or post office. Fishing shelters line the river. Glenelg River Cruises (3hr 30min; $18; ☎08/8738 4191) on Old Bridge Road on the opposite bank, operates **cruises** to the Princess Margaret Rose

Caves with the *Nelson Endeavour* (Wed & Sat 1pm) or the smaller vessel *Pompei's Pride* (Tues, Thurs & Sat 1pm). They offer more frequent departures during summer school holidays.

The **Parks Victoria Information Centre** (daily 9am–5pm; ☎08/8738 4051) is signposted just off North Nelson Road; it also covers the Discovery Bay Coastal Park, which protects the shoreline almost all the way from Portland to the border. Here you can get camping permits (book in advance in peak season) and information on walks and activities. The one-storey *Nelson Hotel*, on Kellet Street (☎08/8738 4011; ③), is a classic and untouristy pub that has budget **accommodation** and very inexpensive counter meals. Alternatively, try the *Nelson Cottage B&B* on the corner of Kellet and Sturt streets (☎08/8738 4161; ④–⑤). The *Nelson Kywong Caravan Park* on North Nelson Road (☎08/8738 4174) has cheap vans (③) and cabins (④).

CENTRAL VICTORIA: THE GOLDFIELDS

Central Victoria is classic Victoria: a rich pastoral district, chilly and green in winter and parched a brownish yellow in summer, with two grand provincial cities, **Ballarat** and **Bendigo**, whose fine buildings were funded by gold. Nowadays both are major tourist centres on the gold trail. The many surrounding country centres such as **Maryborough** and **Castlemaine**, once prosperous gold towns in their own right, now seem too lowly for their extravagant architecture.

There's fairly good **transport** in this direction, with regular V/Line trains and buses to Bendigo, Ballarat and the other major centres, and local buses filling most gaps. If you're driving, the best way to tour the area is to follow the **Goldfields Tourist Route**,

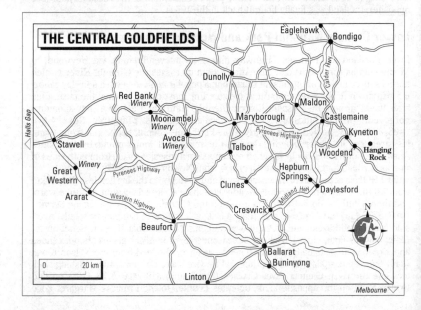

THE GOLDSMITHS

The Californian goldrushes of the 1840s captured the popular imagination around the world with tales of the huge fortunes to be made gold-prospecting, and it wasn't long until Australia's first goldrush took place – near Bathurst in New South Wales in 1851. Victoria had been a separate colony for only nine days when gold was found at Clunes on July 10, 1851; the **goldrush** began in earnest when rich deposits were found in Ballarat nine months later. The richest goldfields ever known soon opened at Bendigo, and thousands poured into Victoria from around the world. In the golden decade of the 1850s Victoria's population increased from eighty thousand to half a million, half of whom remained permanently in the state. The British and Irish made up a large proportion of the new population but over forty thousand Chinese came to make their fortune, too, along with experienced American gold-seekers and other nationalities such as Russians, Finns and Filipinos. Ex-convicts and native-born Australians also poured into Victoria, leaving other colonies short of workers; even respectable policemen deserted their posts to become "diggers", and doctors, lawyers and prostitutes crowded into the haphazard new towns in their wake. The goldfields were a great equalizer; all you needed was a shovel and perseverance, and a fortune was as likely yours as the next man's.

In the beginning, the fortune-seekers panned the creeks and rivers searching for **alluvial gold**, constantly moving on at the news of another find. But gold was also deep within the earth, where ancient riverbeds had been buried by volcanoes; in Ballarat in 1852 the first **shafts** were dug, and because the work was unsafe and arduous, the men joined in bands of eight or ten, usually grouped by nationality, working a common claim. For deep mining, diggers stayed in one place for months or years, and the major workings rapidly became stable communities with banks, shops, hotels, churches and theatres, evolving more gradually, on the back of income from gold, into grandiose towns.

whose chocolate-brown signs are marked by a distinctive circled capital G. The route links the major cities and towns – Bendigo, Castlemaine, Ballarat, Ararat and Stawell – with many smaller places in between.

Towards the Goldfields: the Calder Highway

Though you could take the Western Freeway or the train directly to Ballarat, the route **towards Bendigo**, 150km northwest of Melbourne along the Calder Highway, is much more interesting. The railway to Bendigo, which continues to Swan Hill, follows the same route, calling at the main towns. At Diggers Rest, 22km from Melbourne, a short detour to the east will take you to tiny **Organ Pipes National Park**, so designated for its outstanding geological interest. The rock formations here are a series of basalt columns, formed by lava cooling in an ancient riverbed, and rising up to 20m above Jacksons Creek. The park (during daylight saving time daily 8.30am–6pm, rest of the year 8.30am–4.30pm) can be explored along walking tracks and has picnic areas with tables. Back on the highway you'll come to **Gisborne**, 50km from Melbourne, developed as a coaching town for travellers on their way to the Bendigo and Castlemaine goldfields; it's dominated by **Mount Macedon**, an extinct thousand-metre volcano.

WOODEND, which has some characterful old pubs and an antiques gallery, is the jumping-off point for **Hanging Rock**, in a reserve 6km northeast (daily: summer 8am–7pm; winter 8am–5pm; $5 per car). The rock became famous because of the eerie film *Picnic at Hanging Rock* (based on the book by Joan Lindsay) about a group of schoolgirls who mysteriously go missing here after a picnic. Many people falsely believe the story to be true, though the rock itself is not at all spooky. You can walk around the base or climb to the summit with its massive boulders and crags in around an hour.

Fifteen kilometres from Woodend, **KYNETON** seems like just another boring country town as you pass through on the High Street, where tourist information is located at no. 6, in Dapples Store (open daily). The town is notable, however, for **Piper Street**, a picturesque historic strip lined with several fine bluestone buildings, including the **Kyneton Museum**, a two-storey 1855 bank full of local artefacts, and several period out-buildings (call ☎03/5422 1228 for hours, which vary: usually Wed, Sat, Sun & public hol-idays; $3). There are also two old flour mills at either end of town, and the expansive **Botanic Gardens** above the Campaspe River. For **accommodation** the *Kyneton Country House*, at 66 Jennings St (☎03/5422 3556; B&B; ⑦–⑧), is a wonderful weekend hideaway in a restored National Trust mansion surrounded by a beautiful cottage gar-den; it has a good reputation for its traditional cooking. The price of a Devonshire tea ($5) at *Babette's* (☎03/5422 2581), a **restaurant** opposite the Kyneton Museum, includes entry to the museum; the restaurant is fully licensed, and also serves French provincial cuisine (Wed–Sat eve). A few houses further down is the *Bluestone Cottage* at 78 Piper St, which serves scrumptious Devonshire teas and hearty, country-style lunches. *Kyneton Provender* at no. 30 is a bookshop with a café that serves cakes and coffee.

Bendigo

Rich alluvial gold was first discovered in **BENDIGO** in 1851, and once it was exhausted shafts were sunk into a gold-bearing quartz reef. Bendigo became the greatest goldfield of the time, and had the world's deepest mine. Mining continued here until 1954, long after the rest of central Victoria's goldfields were exhausted, so it's a city that has developed over a prosperous century: the nationwide department store Myer began here, as did Australia's first building society in 1858. Although in many ways more magnificent than Ballarat (see p.853), Bendigo is considerably lower key, never having turned itself into a purely tourist town. Its most visited sights are legacies of the mining days – the **Chinese Joss House** and the **Central Deborah Mine**.

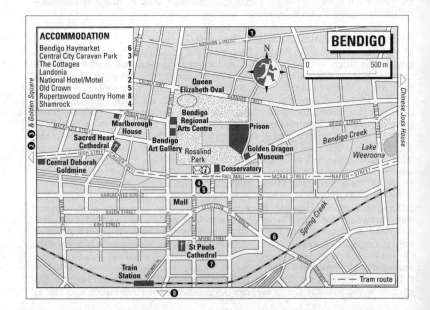

ACCOMMODATION
Bendigo Haymarket	6
Central City Caravan Park	3
The Cottages	1
Landonia	7
National Hotel/Motel	2
Old Crown	5
Rupertswood Country Home	8
Shamrock	4

BENDIGO

0   500 m

N

Chinese Joss House

& Golden Square

NIEMANN STREET
Queen Elizabeth Oval
Bendigo Regional Arts Centre
Marlborough House
Sacred Heart Cathedral
Bendigo Art Gallery
Central Deborah Goldmine
Prison
Bendigo Creek
Golden Dragon Museum
Rosalind Park
Conservatory
Lake Weeeroona
Mall
St Pauls Cathedral
Train Station
Spring Creek
- - - Tram route

At the heart of Bendigo is the vast **Rosalind Park**, and three important religious buildings constructed through money from gold-digging – All Saints Church, St Pauls Cathedral and **Sacred Heart Cathedral**. Local Catholics imported stonemasons from Italy and England, and their craftsmanship can be seen in the design and details of Sacred Heart, begun in 1897 in English Gothic style. The interior has beautiful wood-carvings of the Twelve Apostles, and the crypt is the burial place of local bishops. Wanting to give Bendigo a sophisticated air reminiscent of London, the newly prosperous citizens called its central crossroads **Charing Cross**. It runs off to the east, while **View Street**, with its many fine old buildings, climbs north off Pall Mall. Mitchell Street leads south to the **train station** and High Street (the Calder Highway) is the main exit west out of the city. The other important street is Hargreaves, parallel to Pall Mall one block south, with its impressive town hall and a rather bland, "Australian anywhere-town"-style shopping mall.

The City

Many of Bendigo's finest goldrush buildings are along **Pall Mall**, including the ornate Italianate post office (1887) which now houses the visitor information centre and law courts (1896) – neither of which would seem out of place in a capital city – and the amazingly decorative **Shamrock Hotel** opposite, which is four storeys of gold-boom architecture at its most extreme. **View Street**, climbing the hill beside Rosalind Park, has a few more elaborate goldrush buildings. The **Bendigo Regional Arts Centre** here is a massive Neoclassical pile, joined to the much more homely red-brick fire station which now serves as the Community Arts Centre. The **Art Gallery**, in an ugly 1960s building at no. 42 (daily 10am–5pm; $3), has an extensive collection of Australian painting from Bendigo's goldfield days to the present, as well as nineteenth-century British and European art, acquired with all that gold. Several antique shops, restaurants, cafés and bars add to the arty feel of the street. The Queen Elizabeth Oval, with its old red-brick stadium, backs onto Rosalind Park, and you can watch Aussie Rules football here on Sundays in winter.

Bridge Street, one of the oldest in Bendigo, was once **Chinatown**, home to the Chinese who came by the thousands in the 1850s and who knew Bendigo as "the golden mountain"; when the gold ran out, many turned to market gardening in the area. Until as late as the 1960s old shops sporting faded signs were still in evidence, but now Chinese customs and ways of life are best seen in the **Golden Dragon Museum** (daily 9.30am–5pm; $6), where there is an impressive collection of Chinese processional regalia including what are supposed to be the world's longest and oldest Imperial dragons, Sun Loong and Loong. An exhibition tells the full story of Bendigo's Chinese community since the days of the goldrush. The latest addition to the museum are the Chinese Gardens, featuring a temple to the goddess Kuan Yin. The National Trust-operated **Joss House**, on Finn Street in North Bendigo (daily 10am–5pm; $3; bus #7, approximately hourly Mon–Fri), was built by the Chinese in the 1860s and is the oldest Chinese temple still in use in Australia. The route to the shrine passes man-made Lake Weeroona, whose picnic grounds are the setting for a **Chinese teahouse**.

The Central Deborah Goldmine

The **Central Deborah Goldmine**, at the corner of Violet Street and the Calder Highway (daily 9am–5pm; underground tour $16), was the last mine in the Central Goldfields to close. The sixty-minute underground tour is worth taking if you've never been down in a mine, and if you're not claustrophobic; everybody is issued with a reassuring hard hat, complete with torch and generator. You go down to a depth of 60m in a lift, which takes 85 seconds – it would take thirty minutes to reach the bottom of some of the deepest shafts. The further down you go the hotter it gets, but at 60m it's quite warm and airless, dripping with water and muddy underfoot.

Above ground, you're free to wander about and take a look at the engine room with its steam-driven air compressor. You can also see a room set up like a modest miner's house from the 1840s, a model of the mine itself, and a museum installed in the old changing rooms.

Practicalities

Interstate McCafferty's **buses** stop at the Caltex service station, on the corner of High and Oak streets. The **visitor information centre** is in the grand old post office building on Pall Mall (daily 9am–5pm; ☎03/5444 4433, free call ☎1800/813 153). It provides lots of brochures and maps – the free *Discover Bendigo* booklet, including a walking map, is very useful (you'll also find "Heritage Walk" panels outside significant buildings). A good way to get an impression of Bendigo is to take the **Talking Tram Tour**, though the taped commentary can be rather irritating (hourly departures, on weekends half hourly, from the Central Deborah Goldmine 9.30am–3pm; 1hr; $8; combined ticket for the mine and tram tour $21). The tram tour ticket includes entrance to the Bendigo Tram Museum, located on Hargreaves Street at the opposite end of the route. Bendigo had electric trams even before Melbourne, but they ceased operation in 1972. Alternatively, you can take a **Double Decker Bus Tour** which takes in all the sights including the Bendigo Pottery in suburban Epsom. On weekends it does round trips from the Central Deborah Goldmine between 10am and 5pm, during the week it departs only at 10am and 2pm. The ticket is valid all day, allowing you to get on and off when you want ($8, ☎03/5441 0909). **Buses** (Christians Bus Company ☎03/5447 2222) have since replaced trams as a means of everyday transport – they all leave from the corner of Mitchell and Hargreaves streets and charge a flat fare of $1.50 for two hours. Bendigo Airport Service provides a link to Melbourne's Tullamarine Airport (☎03/5475 1386; $32; 3 daily; booking essential).

Accommodation

In terms of atmosphere and style, the **B&B guesthouses** and **cottages** throughout Bendigo and the whole goldfields area are a much better option than the average, somewhat sterile motel room.

Bendigo Haymarket Motor Inn, 5 McIvor Highway (☎03/5441 5654, fax 5441 5655). Ultramodern motel with one unit accessible to the disabled, a swimming pool and sauna; some rooms with spas. ⑤–⑥.

Central City Caravan Park, 362 High St, Golden Square, 2.5km south (☎ & fax 03/5443 6937). Hostel-type accommodation in three cabins with separate kitchen and common room, plus camping, vans and cabin units. Cabins ④, on-site vans ③, dorms ①.

The Cottages, cnr of Niemann and Anderson sts (☎03/5441 5613, fax 5444 4313). B&B in two small, self-contained weatherboard cottages. ⑥–⑦.

Elm Motel, 454 High St, Golden Square (☎03/5447 7522). Inexpensive motel, conveniently located next to McCafferty's bus stop, with a public bus into town at the front door. ④.

Landonia, 87 Mollison St (☎03/5442 2183). A centrally located B&B in a Federation-style home, with separate guest entrance and an open fireplace in the lounge. ⑥–⑦.

Marlborough House, 115 Wattle St (☎03/5441 4142). B&B in a goldrush-era mansion near the cathedral. ⑦.

National Hotel/Motel, 182 High St, 1km south (☎03/5441 5777, fax 5444 5890). Facilities include a pool and spa, as well as a bar and bistro. One suite ⑧, units ④–⑥.

Old Crown Hotel, 238 Hargreaves St (☎03/5441 6888, fax 5441 8744). Comfortable, centrally located pub accommodation, with a light breakfast included. ③–④.

Rupertswood Country Home, Mandurang Rd, Mandurang, about 7km south of Bendigo (☎03/5439 5532). B&B in a quiet and picturesque valley. Has en-suite rooms and private sitting rooms. ⑥–⑦.

Shamrock Hotel, cnr of Pall Mall and Williamson St (☎03/5443 0333, fax 5442 4494). Fabulous Victorian hotel that has a wide range of accommodation, from budget-priced rooms to executive suites. ④–⑧.

Eating, drinking and nightlife

The town offers a fairly good choice when it comes to **eating** and **drinking**, and there is plenty of student-influenced **nightlife** during term time. Entertainment facilities at the LaTrobe University campus are open to all – call ☎03/5444 7478 to find out what's happening. Several pubs have bands playing on Friday and Saturday nights, including the *Old Crown Hotel* at 238 Hargreaves St, and *The Vine* at 135 King St. On Thursday night there's live music at the *Limerick Tavern*, 44 Williamson St. The young crowd congregates at the *Rifle Brigade Hotel* at 137 View St, a brewery pub with a wrought-iron verandah. Nightclubs popular with students are *Eclipse* at the corner of Hargreaves and Williams streets and *The Icon* at 2–4 Howard Place.

Bazzani Bar & Ristorante, Howard Place (☎03/5441 3777). Cosy restaurant at the end of the mall renowned for the interesting, well-presented and tasty dishes on the menu, like goats cheese, spinach and walnut ravioli. Lunch and dinner daily; licensed.

Clogs, 106 Pall Mall. A modern, lively and reasonably priced brasserie. Daily from 5pm, plus lunch on Sun.

Colonial Bank Gallery and Mully's Cafe, 32 Pall Mall. In a grand, historic bank building from the 1880s, with an art gallery upstairs. Good breakfasts, brunches and afternoon teas. Licensed or BYO. Mon–Sat 10am–5pm, Sun from 9am.

Cumberland Hotel, 56 Williamson St. Family bistro open daily for lunch and dinner.

The Match Bar & Bakehouse, 58 Bull St. A stylish café-restaurant with lots of pasta, focaccia and pizza. Dinner daily, lunch daily except Sat.

Metropolitan Brasseric & Grill, cnr of Bull and Hargreaves sts. A transformed 1860s pub that has won several awards for its food, which includes bushtucker. Daily noon–midnight for meals or drinks.

Shamrock Hotel Café, cnr of Pall Mall and Williamson St. This café-restaurant in the lovely, refurbished former public bar serves good breakfasts (home-baked bread) and has interesting, mainly Modern Australian cuisine for lunch and dinner.

Whirakee Restaurant and Wine Bar, 17 View Point, at the beginning of View St, just opposite the fountain. Outstanding Modern Australian cuisine, with an excellent wine list featuring local wines.

Castlemaine and around

CASTLEMAINE is at the centre of the area once known as the Mount Alexander Goldfields. Between 1851 and 1861, when its gullies were among the richest in the world, 105,000kg of gold were found here (more modest quantities are still found at Wattle Gully mine at nearby Chewton, the oldest working gold mine in Australia). Castlemaine became the headquarters of the Government Camp for the area in 1852, and its impressive buildings were all built during the following ten years. With no deep mines to sustain it, however, Castlemaine has developed little since then.

The town's finest building is the **Old Castlemaine Market** on Mostyn Street, a wonderfully over-the-top piece of Neoclassical architecture. The **Theatre Royal** on Hargraves Street, one of the oldest theatres in Australia, is also quite magnificent; it's said that when the famous Lola Montez performed here, miners threw nuggets of gold at her in appreciation. It's now a **cinema** (☎03/5472 1196) incorporating a cabaret-style section and a licensed bistro downstairs, and more traditional movie-house seating upstairs. Theatre groups and live bands sometimes perform here, and there's even a disco Thursday to Saturday nights until 3am.

Another unusual attraction, a short distance from the centre, is **Buda**, at 42 Hunter Street (daily 9am–5pm; $7), a gracious nineteenth-century home and garden originally built in 1861 by a retired Baptist missionary in the style of an Indian villa. It was added to by its subsequent owner Ernest Leviny, a Hungarian silversmith, in the 1890s. The house and gardens give an insight into the good life enjoyed in the goldrush days, and much work by Leviny and his family is on display, including lampshades, carved wood-hangings and embroidery made by his daughters, as well as early photography and the family's art and silverware collection. The **Castlemaine Art Gallery and Museum** on Lyttleton Street (Mon–Fri 10am–5pm, Sat & Sun 10am–noon & 1–5pm; $3) is also worth a visit. Established in 1913 in a classic Art Deco building, the gallery specializes in Australian photographs and paintings, featuring many works by the Heidelberg School, notably Frederick McCubbin and Tom Roberts. Partly because of the big **Castlemaine State Festival**, which takes place over ten days in April in odd-numbered years, this is quite an arty place, and there are several other galleries around town. In odd-numbered years lots of gardens in the Castlemaine district open their doors to visitors during the **Festival of Gardens**, which takes place during the Melbourne Cup week in November.

If you're here on a Saturday, trek the 2km out along the Melbourne Road to **Wesley Hill Market**, a giant flea market selling local produce and crafts (7.30am–noon). Another tourist attraction is the **Dingo Farm** (daily, but ring to confirm ☎03/5470 5711; $8) between Castlemaine and Chewton, where about seventy dingoes are kept in fenced-in enclosures on bushland; signs along the Pyrenees Highway will direct you there.

Practicalities

The **information centre** is in the Market Building at Mostyn Street (daily 9am–5pm; ☎00/C170 C000) and can arrange accommodation bookings in the area on free call ☎1800/171 888. Places **to stay** include *Campbell Street Lodge* in a historic building at 33 Campbell St (☎03/5472 2377; ⑤–⑥), which has motel-style rooms in a National Trust-listed house; *Kraus Cottage* on the hilltop at Wills St (☎03/5472 1936; ⑤) and the *Old Castlemaine Gaol* on Bowden Street (☎03/5470 5311, fax 5470 5097; ③–⑥), converted into an unexpectedly cosy guesthouse, with beds in former prison cells and a restaurant/wine bar (Wed–Sun). Two centrally located B&B's are the National Trust-listed *Midland Private Hotel*, 2 Templeton St (☎03/5472 1085; ⑤–⑦) and the *Coach and Rose B&B*, 68 Mostyn St (☎03/5472 4850; ⑦–⑧).

Food in Castlemaine is excellent, with a wide variety of places to choose from. *Bings Café*, at 71 Mostyn St opposite the market (daily 9am–4.30pm), serves breakfast all day and has everything from full meals to veggie burgers and sandwiches. In addition to selling bread, cakes, pastries and light meals, *Saff's Café* at 64 Mostyn St hosts special events such as concerts, recitals and poetry readings every last Saturday of the month. *Togs Place* at 58 Lyttleton St provides good food in a peaceful atmosphere, and has a courtyard where you can sit out in summer. The *Globe Garden*, 81 Forest St, (licensed, lunch Sun only, dinner Wed–Sun) is another pleasant place with a courtyard, serving good food with a menu that changes with the seasons. You can sample Mexican fare at the licensed *Simpatico Mexican Restaurant*, 32 Johnstone St (dinner daily), in a 140-year-old bakery. *Bonkers on Barker*, a bar and bistro in a beautifully restored former hotel at 233 Barker St, also does B&B accommodation (☎03/5472 4454; ⑤–⑦). Or go for cheap pub meals at the local hangout, the *Criterion Hotel* at 163 Barker St, which has pool tables and bands at weekends, or the *Commercial Hotel* on the corner of Hargraves and Forest streets.

Maldon

MALDON, closely surrounded by low hills, is a tiny, peaceful town of tearooms, antique shops and B&Bs. In 1965 the National Trust declared it the best-preserved gold-era settlement in Victoria. Gold was found here in 1853 and the rich, deep alluvial reefs were mined until 1926, almost rivalling Bendigo for longevity. As you come into town you'll see dilapidated old farmhouses and be greeted by dogs that sit in the middle of the road scratching their heads for want of anything better to do. The main shopping street largely preserves its original appearance, with single-storey shopfronts shaded by awnings and decorated with iron-lace work. It's a popular weekend getaway where you can simply relax and unwind.

It's best to come here in your own vehicle, as **public transport** from Melbourne operates only on weekdays, and to a very limited timetable; take a train from Melbourne (Mon–Fri 8.35am & 3.50pm) to Castlemaine where you catch the connecting Castlemaine Bus Lines service (☎03/5472 1455) to Maldon. Return buses leave from Maldon post office to connect with trains back to Melbourne (Mon–Fri 6.35am & 9am). On Sundays and holidays you can take a ride on a **tourist steam train** from Maldon to Castlemaine (hourly 1–4pm, though not on days of total fire ban; $8).

Apart from the town's architecture, there are a few other points of interest: the **Maldon Museum**, in the Old Shire Hall on High Street (daily 1.30–4pm; $2), is a typical pioneer memorabilia museum, and you can also take an underground tour at **Carman's Tunnel Goldmine**, off Parkin's Reef Road, 3km south of town (Sat, Sun, school & public holidays every 30min 1.30–4pm; 30min; $4). To find out about other activities, check with the **visitor centre** in front of the museum (daily 10am–4pm; ☎03/5475 2569).

An excellent place to **stay**, if you're hankering for a little luxury, is *The Barn*, at 242 Barker St (☎ & fax 03/5475 2015; ④–⑥), which offers self-catering amongst whitewashed stone walls, an open fire and French windows. *Heritage Cottages*, 25 Adair St (☎03/5475 1094; ⑤–⑦), has a selection of historical cottages, most with period furnishings and open fires. In a garden setting just out of town is the *Lemonwood Cottage B&B*, Bells Reef Road (☎ & fax 03/5475 2015; ⑦–⑧), a pretty two-bedroom stone cottage with brass beds and an open fireplace. In a town where there are a lot of **tearooms**, the best value is *Berryman's*, at 30 Main St. *McArthur's*, further up at no. 45, has a very pleasant courtyard. Two other good tearooms are the *Cumquat Tree*, at no. 24, and the *Maldon Cafe*, at no. 52.

Maryborough and around

MARYBOROUGH was relatively late getting on the gold bandwagon – the first find here was in 1853, but it didn't take long to exploit it. The town is now a large, solid and rather dull country place, interesting only for its remnants of architecture far too pompous for this quiet setting. The **train station** is exceptional: when Mark Twain visited Maryborough he described it as a train station with a town attached. The restored building has been converted into a tourist complex, housing the **tourist information centre** (daily 10am–6pm; ☎03/5460 4511), an antiques and collectables emporium, a gallery and exhibition space, and a restaurant and café. The **Civic Centre** at the heart of town is a classic nineteenth-century square with an elegant post office and gracious town hall and courthouse. If you want to **stay**, try the *Bull & Mouth Hotel* at 119 High St (☎03/5461 1002; ③–④), which has a bistro downstairs serving inexpensive **meals** Mon–Sat. For B&B accommodation try the *Maryborough Guesthouse* at 44 Goldsmith St (☎03/5460 5808; ④–⑤).

Twenty-one kilometres north of Maryborough is **DUNOLLY**, an attractive town filled with many distinctive old buildings and with kurrajong trees lining the main street. The goldfields here produced more nuggets than any in Australia, including the largest ever found – "Welcome Stranger", from nearby Moliagul. This 65kg nugget was found in 1869 by two Cornish miners just 3cm below the surface as they were working around the roots of a tree. It was valued at £10,000, old money. Fourteen kilometres south of Maryborough, **TALBOT** is a tiny settlement consisting of little more than a restaurant, a pub and a corner store. It's hard to believe now that the town once had 56 hotels and a population of 33,000. The licensed *Bull and Mouth Restaurant and B&B* (☎03/5463 2325; Thurs–Sun dinner, also Sun lunch), located in an 1859 bluestone hotel on Ballarat Street, serves hearty but sophisticated country fare and also has timber miners' cottages and two modern en-suite units for rent (B&B; ⑥–⑦). **AVOCA**, 26km southwest of Maryborough on the Pyrenees Highway, was another rich source of alluvial gold. It boasts a collection of nineteenth-century buildings, including a chemist's shop established in 1854 and believed to be the oldest in Victoria. These days, the area around Avoca, known as the **Pyrenees region**, is increasingly known for its **vineyards**. A cluster of them is located in or near Moonambel, a hamlet 17km northwest of Avoca: one to aim for is the *Warrenmang Winery Resort* on Mountain Creek Road (daily 9am–5pm; ☎03/5467 2233, fax 5467 2309), which has a picturesque setting, an excellent restaurant, and offers accommodation in timber lodges (dinner plus B&B from $130 per person).

Daylesford and Hepburn Springs

The attractive, hilly country around Daylesford and Hepburn Springs is known as the "spa centre of Australia", with a hundred **mineral springs** within a fifty-kilometre radius. Daylesford grew from the Jim Crow gold diggings of 1851, but the large Swiss–Italian population here quickly realized the value of the water from the mineral springs, which had been bottled since 1850. People have been taking the waters at Hepburn Springs for almost as long – the spa complex was built in 1895. The **tourist information office** for the area is next to the post office on Vincent Street in Daylesford (daily 9am–5pm; ☎03/5348 1339); it has loads of brochures for the many places offering **bed and breakfast** and a board listing the vacancies at weekends, when places tend to fill up. You can get a **bus** to Hepburn Springs outside the office (Mon–Fri, 7 daily between 8.30am–5pm). To get to Daylesford from Melbourne, take a **train** to Woodend, then a connecting bus to Daylesford (Mon–Sat 2 daily, Sun 1 daily) You can also take a train from Melbourne to Ballarat (Mon–Fri 1 daily) and then get the connecting bus to Daylesford.

Daylesford

The town of **DAYLESFORD** has a New Age, alternative atmosphere, with a large gay community and several gay-friendly guesthouses. Its well-preserved Victorian and Edwardian streets rise up the side of Wombat Hill, where you'll find the **Botanical Gardens**, between Hill Street and Central Springs Road, whose lookout tower has panoramic views. Not far away, on the corner of Daly and Hill streets, is the **Convent Gallery** (daily 10am–6pm; $3), a rambling former convent which now has seven galleries selling high-quality arts, crafts and antiques, and a Mediterranean-style café open for lunch and coffee. There's a great Sunday market (8am–2pm) at the train station east of here.

All your esoteric needs are effortlessly taken care of at places like Books and Buddhas, 107 Vincent St, which sells crystals and offers tarot readings and free meditation sessions; complemented by the produce of the Himalaya Bakery at 73 Vincent St, which makes heavy but nutritious dark rye bread and delicious cakes. Less puritan offerings are available at Sweet Decadence, 57 Vincent St, where you can have chocolates, coffee and cake in the characterful old bar of what was once the *Victoria Hotel*, and at *Frangos & Frangos*, 82 Vincent St, a café-restaurant in a restored pub, serving scrumptious breakfasts and Mediterranean-inspired food for lunch and dinner. The *Harvest Café*, at 29 Albert St (Fri–Sun 9am–9pm), is a friendly, nonconformist haven that has an extensive menu, plus folk and acoustic music on Sunday night. For a real splurge, try *Lake House* on King Street near the lake, an outstanding but expensive **restaurant** (☎03/5348 3329; daily for coffee, brunch and dinner).

Lake Daylesford, a short distance south from the town centre on Vincent Street, is the location of the **Central Springs Reserve**, which has several walking tracks and old-fashioned water pumps from which you can drink the water of the mineral springs. The Lake Daylesford Book Barn here (open daily) is a picturesquely situated bookshop: with its extensive range of secondhand books, quaint pot-bellied stove and beautiful views, you could be here for hours. The charming *Boathouse Café* (☎03/5348 1387) has lakeside dining (lunch and dinner daily, Sat & Sun also breakfast 9–10.30am), as well as dinghies, canoes and paddle-boats for rent.

If you want to stay in Daylesford, you should rely on the **B&Bs** and **guesthouses** (all of them expensive, though): *The Balconies* at 35 Perrins St (☎03/5348 1322; ⑥), a rambling mansion with several balconies overlooking the lake, is a favourite with gay visitors; *35 Hill Street* (☎03/5348 3878; ④–⑤) is an early Victorian brick cottage just below the Botanical Gardens; and *Ambleside*, at 15 Leggat St (☎03/5348 2691; ⑧), a meticulously renovated Edwardian guesthouse overlooking Lake Daylesford. *Walsh's Daylesford Hotel*, on Burke Square (☎03/5348 2335; ④–⑤), has pleasant pub rooms.

Hepburn Springs

HEPBURN SPRINGS is not really a town at all, but a collection of guesthouses and a wonderful Art Deco resort hotel in a green, hilly and peaceful spot only 4km north of Daylesford. From the bus stop, walk through the shady Soldiers Memorial Park to the **Mineral Springs Reserve**, where you can taste three kinds of mineral water from old pumps and where the revamped Hepburn Spa Resort is located (☎03/5348 2034, fax 5348 1167; Mon–Fri 10am–8pm, Sat & Sun 9am–8pm). You can spend as long as you like here in the relaxation pool (32°C) and mineral-water spa (38°C; both Mon–Fri $8; Sat, Sun & public holidays $9); or you could indulge yourself with twenty minutes in your own aero-spa bath, with essential oils (Mon–Fri $17; Sat, Sun & public holidays $21). The southern wing has massage, saunas, flotation tanks, and therapy and couch pools. Bookings must be made at least three weeks in advance, especially for weekends.

The Springs Hotel at the corner of Main Road and Tenth Street (☎03/5348 2202; en-suite with breakfast ⑥–⑦, shared facilities ④–⑤) is a classic 1930s **resort** with guestrooms. There's a good-value buffet lunch in the dining room and a more expensive dinner menu; counter meals are also available in the bar. *Dudley House*, at 101 Main Rd (☎03/5348 3033; ⑧), is a lovely Federation-style weatherboard house offering elegant **bed and breakfast**. At the budget end of the scale is the *Continental House*, 9 Lone Pine Ave (☎03/5348 2005; ①–②), which has shared twins (bring your own linen), a kitchen (vegetarian only), and a vegetarian café on Saturday night. An excellent choice for food is the *Cosy Corner Café* at 3 Tenth St (daily breakfast and snacks, Thurs–Mon lunch and dinner) which has a lot of vegetarian, but also some meat and seafood dishes; licensed and BYO.

Ballarat

BALLARAT is a grandiose provincial city that makes a lasting impression from whichever direction you approach it. From the west, you enter via the Western Highway along the **Avenue of Honour**, lined on either side with over 22km of trees and dedicated to soldiers who fought in World War I. It ends at the massive **Arch of Victory**, through which you drive to enter Sturt Street and the city. Coming from the east, you approach the

BALLARAT

Train Station

Art Gallery

Bridge Mall

Town Hall

Eureka Stockade Centre

Eureka Exhibition

Montrose Cottage

Gold Museum

Sovereign Hill

HUMFFRAY STREET

SCOTT PARADE

VICTORIA STREET

STAWELL ST SOUTH

MAIR STREET

CURTIS

STURT STREET

GRENVILLE ST

LYDIARD STREET

ARMSTRONG STREET

DOVETON STREET

ALBERT ST

DANA STREET

PRINCES STREET

KING STREET

QUEEN STREET

PEEL STREET

EUREKA STREET

MAIN STREET

GRANT STREET

HUMFFRAY STREET

BARKLY STREET

YORK STREET

YORK STREET

JOSEPH STREET

KLINE STREET

MAGPIE ST

DRUMMOND STREET

BRADSHAW ST

RITER STREET

CLAYTON STREET

SPENCER STREET

CORDEL

TRESS STREET

STREET

EMSWORTH STREET WEST

Botanical Gdns & Lk Wendouree

Great Southern Woolshed

Avenue of Honour and Arch of Victory

Wildlife Park

ACCOMMODATION	
Craigs Royal Hotel	4
George Hotel	2
Goldfields Caravan Park	5
Miners Retreat Motel	3
Sovereign Hill YHA & Motel	6
Tawana Lodge	1

0   500 m

city on the Western Highway (Victoria Street), flanked by lawns, trees and colourful flowerbeds. Trains pull in to the elegant 1889 **station**, topped by a domed clock tower.

The Ballarat area was already settled before gold was discovered, and thus preserves a rural life for which the city is the supply centre. Nonetheless, it's **gold** which has marked the place indelibly: over a quarter of all gold found in Victoria came from Ballarat and its fantastically rich reef mines before they were exhausted in 1918. Nowadays, in addition to the more obvious tourist attractions – especially Sovereign Hill – and fine **architecture**, the town is interesting in its own right, with a fairly large student population that lends some cultural presence and gives the city a reasonably active nightlife. Most people don't stay here overnight, however, as it's only little more than an hour's drive from Melbourne.

The City

Sturt and Victoria streets terminate on either side of the Bridge Mall, the central shopping area at the base of quaint **Bakery Hill** with its old shopfronts. Southeast of the city centre, Eureka Street runs off Main Street towards the site of the **Eureka**

Stockade, with several museums and antique shops along the way. Main Street becomes Ballarat–Buninyong Road, and six blocks down is crossed by Bradshaw Street, where you'll find **Sovereign Hill**, the re-created gold town. Northwest of the centre, approached via Sturt Street, are the **Botanical Gardens** and **Lake Wendouree**.

The most complete **nineteenth-century streetscape** is probably along Lydiard Street, which runs from the centre up past the train station; the street has several two-storey terraced shopfronts, with verandahs and decorative iron-lace work, mostly from the period 1862–89. The former **Mining Exchange** (1888) has been recently renovated to its former splendour, and the architecture of *Her Majesty's Theatre* (1875) also proclaims its goldrush-era heyday. The **Ballarat Fine Art Gallery** at 40 Lydiard St (daily 10.30am–5pm; $4; guided tours Mon–Fri 2pm, Sat & Sun 2.30pm), another superb building, is the oldest provincial art gallery in Australia, established in 1884. Its extensive collection is particularly strong on colonial and Heidelberg School paintings; the original **Eureka Flag** – tatty and ragged – is also here (see box below). Displayed alongside are the watercolours of S.T. Gill, a self-taught artist who painted scenes of goldrush days in Ballarat. In another part of the gallery is a reconstruction of the drawing room of the famous Lindsay family (whose best-known members are the artist Norman Lindsay and the writer Jack Lindsay), from nearby Creswick, complete with several of their paintings. There's also a representative modern collection and a good café.

THE EUREKA STOCKADE

The **Eureka Rebellion** is one of the most celebrated events of Australian history, regarded as the only act of white armed rebellion the country has seen. It was provoked by conditions in the goldfields, where diggers had to pay exorbitantly for their right to prospect for gold (as much as thirty shillings a month), without receiving in return any right to vote, to have decent roads, transport or police protection, or to have any chance of a permanent right to the land they worked. Checks for licences were ruthless and brutal, and corruption rife. Protest meetings calling on diggers to refuse to pay drew huge crowds at Ballarat, Bendigo and Castlemaine; in response, in November 1853 the government made a small reduction in the fee.

The administration at Ballarat was particularly repressive, and in November 1854 local diggers formed the **Ballarat Reform League**, demanding full civic rights and the abolition of the licence fee, and proclaiming that "the people are the only legitimate source of power". At the end of the month a group of two hundred diggers gathered inside a **stockade** of logs, hastily flung together, and determined to resist further arrests for non-possession of a licence. They were attacked at dawn on December 3 by police and troops; thirty died inside, and five members of the government forces also lost their lives.

The movement was not a failure, however: the diggers had aroused widespread sympathy, and in 1855 licences were abolished, to be replaced by an annual **Miner's Right** which carried the right to vote and to enclose land. The leader of the rebellion, the Irishman Peter Lalor, eventually became a member of parliament.

The **Eureka Flag**, with its white cross and five white stars on a blue background, has become a symbol of the Left – and indeed of almost any protest movement: shearers raised it in strikes during the 1890s; wharfies used it before World War II in their bid to stop pig-iron being sent to Japan; and today the flag is flown by a growing number of Australians who support the country's transformation to a republic. On a deeper level, all sorts of claims are made for the Eureka Rebellion's pivotal role in forming the Australian nation and psyche. The diggers are held up as a classic example of the Australian (male) ethos of mateship and anti-authoritarianism, while the goldrush in general is credited with overthrowing the hierarchical colonial order, as servants rushed to make their fortune, leaving their masters and mistresses to fend for themselves.

Nearby, on Sturt Street, check out the imposing Classical-revival **town hall**, which dominates the centre.

There are still over fifty **hotels** in Ballarat – survivors of the hundreds that once watered the thirsty diggers. Some of the finest are on Lydiard Street: *Craig's Royal Hotel* at no. 10 and the *George Hotel* at no. 27 are an integral part of Ballarat's architectural heritage. Sadly, during the 1970s, the council forced most of the old pubs to pull down their verandahs on the grounds that they were unsafe, so very few survive in their original form. One that does is attached to the *Golden City Hotel*, 427 Sturt St, which took the council to the Supreme Court to save its magnificent wide verandah with original cast-iron decoration; the hotel is now open at weekends as a bar and is appreciatively packed out in summer.

The Botanical Gardens

The **Botanical Gardens**, laid out in 1858, comprise about half a square kilometre alongside **Lake Wendouree**, just to the northwest of the city centre (#15 bus from Sturt St, by Myer). Begonias grow so well in Ballarat that a **Begonia Festival** runs for ten days in March, and the glasshouse here is used to display them. Otherwise, highlights are the **Avenue of Big Trees**, with a Californian redwood among its monsters, and the classical statuary, donated by rich gold-miners, scattered about the gardens. Pride of place goes to Benzoni's *Flight from Pompeii*, housed in the Statuary Pavilion. Along Prime Minister Avenue you can see a bust of every prime minister of Australia.

Eureka and York streets

As you head towards Eureka Street and the Eureka Stockade (bus #8 from outside the ANZ Bank on Sturt Street, or walk a few kilometres), take a look at the dozens of antiques shops and alternative shops along Main Street – many of the shop buildings are themselves antiques. The site of the **Eureka Stockade** (see box overleaf), in Eureka Memorial Park, is marked by an interpretive board and a replica of the stockade while video presentations and exhibits in the new **Eureka Stockade Centre** nearby (daily 9am–4pm; $5) give more background information on the Eureka story. On the same street further toward the town centre, **Montrose Cottage** at no. 111 (daily 9.30am–5pm; $5) is the last original miner's cottage in Ballarat – it's furnished in 1850s style and fitted out with a social history display.

Parallel to Eureka Street is York Street, where you'll find the free-range **Ballarat Wildlife Park**, on the corner of Fussell Street (daily 9am–5.30pm; $11), home to koalas, kangaroos, emus, wombats, Tasmanian devils and reptiles.

Sovereign Hill and the Gold Museum

The re-created gold-mining township of **Sovereign Hill** is located 1.5km from the city centre, on Bradshaw Street (daily 10am–5pm; Gold Pass of $20 includes admission to Sovereign Hill, the Gold Museum and a tour through the underground mine; bus #9 from outside the ANZ Bank on Sturt Street). Seventy buildings and shops here are modelled on those that lined Ballarat's main street in the 1850s, with a cast of characters wandering about in the dress of the period. The township was planned around an actual mine shaft from the 1880s, where guided underground tours are available (see above). There are diggings where you can learn how to pan for gold (and perhaps get a small memento) and a mining museum filled with steam-operated machinery. The intricately detailed **Chinese village** is the most interesting but, unlike the bustling main street, this fringe settlement is strangely deserted because no Chinese people are to be seen on the streets or in the buildings as part of the atmosphere.

Sovereign Hill puts on a spectacular outdoor sound and light show, "**Blood on the Southern Cross**" (nightly during school holidays, Mon–Sat rest of the year; 1hr

20min; $24), which makes use of the whole panorama of Sovereign Hill to tell the story of the Eureka Stockade.

Opposite Sovereign Hill, the **Gold Museum** (daily 10am–5.20pm; $6; admission fee to Sovereign Hill includes the Gold Museum) offers a good overview of the re-created settlement. It has an outstanding display of real gold, and a large collection of coins that are arranged in displays exploring the history and uses of gold. The museum's other purpose is to look at the social history of Ballarat. The Eureka Exhibition details life on the goldfields and explains the situation that provoked the Eureka rebellion. Central to the exhibition is a large painting by George Browning, a mid-nineteenth-century artist: it sets the scene of the Eureka Stockade with red-coated soldiers in the foreground shooting at the rough-looking crew behind their stockade. It's interesting to see quite a few black faces portrayed in the stockade, which is generally labelled as the only white armed uprising to have taken place in Australia.

Practicalities

The centrally located **Ballarat Visitor Information Centre**, on the corner of Sturt and Albert streets (daily 9am–5pm; ☎03/5332 2694 or free call ☎1800/648 450), does accommodation bookings has free information and maps of the town. Regular **buses** can take you anywhere you don't feel like walking – the Ballarat Transit System (☎03/5331 7777) has a flat two-hour fare of $1.50. Bus routes run from the bus terminal on Curtis Street, at the northern end of Bridge Mall, to Sovereign Hill and Eureka Street, and from Little Bridge Street past the Myer department store on Sturt Street to Lake Wendouree. You can use the system to get as far as Creswick (see overleaf), 18km north.

Accommodation
There's an abundance of accommodation in all price ranges in Ballarat, from hostels to grand hotels, so you shouldn't have a problem finding a room to suit.

Ansonia, 32 Lydiard St (☎03/5332 4678, fax 5332 4698). New upmarket boutique hotel with restaurant in the historic precinct. ⑧.

Ballarat Bed & Breakfast, 202 Dawson St South (☎03/5333 7046). Inexpensive rooms in an imposing old two-storey house just west of the city centre – single rooms are particularly good value. ②–③.

Craigs Royal Hotel, 10 Lydiard St South (☎03/5331 1377, fax 5331 7103, free call ☎1800/648 051). A grand, Victorian-era hotel; ask for the wonderful two-level North Tower suite if your budget will allow it. ⑤–⑧.

George Hotel, 27 Lydiard St (☎03/5333 4866, fax 5333 4818). The front section of this three-storey hotel from the 1850s, with colonial-style decor, houses an inexpensive bistro and rooms, some with four-poster beds. At the back are motel units, with breakfast included. Motel units ⑥, rooms ④.

Goldfields Caravan Park, 108 Clayton St (☎03/5332 7888). Well located, right next to Sovereign Hill. Good facilities for campers, including a camp kitchen. Cabins ④, on-site vans ③.

Miners Retreat Motel, 602 Eureka St (☎03/5331 6900, fax 5331 6944). Standard motel units, just 100m from the site of the Eureka Stockade; light breakfast included. ④.

Sovereign Hill Lodge YHA, Magpie St (☎03/5333 3409, fax 5333 5861). This small hostel is actually part of Sovereign Hill. Dorms ①, rooms ②–③.

Tawana Lodge, 128 Lydiard St (☎ & fax 03/5331 3461). Fine accommodation in a National Trust-listed private hotel dating from 1886. Good-value single rooms. ③–⑤.

Eating and drinking
You won't starve in Ballarat, nor die for want of a drink, as the city has over fifty **pubs**. Fast food can be had at *McDonald's* on Bakery Hill and *Pizza Hut* opposite.

The Ansonia, 32 Lydiard St (☎03/5332 4678). Restaurant in refurbished building that now houses a swish boutique hotel. The eclectic cuisine betrays influences from the Mediterranean to Southeast Asia. Licensed, open daily for breakfast, lunch and dinner – book for the dinner.

Cafe Pazani, 102 Sturt St. Slick Italian café serving expensive food and excellent coffee. Licensed. Tues–Sat 9am–1am, Sun & Mon 9am–5.30pm.

Eureka Pasta & Pizza House, 23 Sturt St. The best place for pasta in town: a lively atmosphere and generous, good-value servings, plus vegetarian options. Licensed. Daily until 5pm.

Europa Cafe, 411 Sturt St. A pleasant café serving good coffee, cakes and breads, and light meals. Sun–Wed 9am–6pm, Thurs–Sat 9am until late.

Golden City Deli, 423 Sturt St. Gourmet sandwiches, salads and other simple, wholesome food, all served in an original stone chapel setting.

Golden City Hotel, 427 Sturt St. This historic 1896 hotel packs them in with an all-you-can-eat lunch, and a varied dinner menu. Relaxed bar with espresso machine, pool tables, music videos and locally brewed Ballarat Bitter (Ballarat Bertie).

L'Espresso, 417 Sturt St. Hip place for coffee; the food is good, too, and very moderately priced. Mon–Wed 9am–6pm, Thur–Sun 7.30am until late.

Masons at the Gallery, 40 Lydiard St North. A pleasant little café at the Fine Art Gallery, with lots of flowers and imaginative food. Daily 10.30am–4.30pm.

The Pancake Kitchen, 2 Grenville St South. Pancakes on order all day and night in a cosy gol-drush building.

Porter's Restaurant, cnr of Mair and Peel sts. An old pub transformed into a stylish bar and restaurant. Lunch Tues–Fri, dinner Mon–Sat.

Rendezvous Cafe, 54 Lydiard St. Coffee and light meals served in a renovated café across from the Regent Multiplex Cinema.

Tokyo Grill House, 109 Bridge Mall (☎03/5333 3945). Specializes in *teppanyaki* cooking, which means it's prepared on hotplates in front of you. Expensive.

Entertainment and nightlife

The music scene in Ballarat is more lively than you might expect, for up-to-date information about what's on, check *The Courier* on Thursday.

Bridge Mall Inn, 92 Bridge Mall. Hosts independent touring bands Wednesday to Saturday.

Cheers Hotel, 120 Lydiard St. Live bands on Friday and Saturday.

Her Majesty's Theatre, 17 Lydiard St (☎03/5333 5800). An elaborate Victorian theatre, which opened in 1875 with a performance by Australia's first opera company. Stages all types of touring productions.

Hot Gossip, 120 Dana St. Best of the local clubs, and popular with students. Located in an old church.

Provincial Hotel, 121 Lydiard St North. Bands play here, and there's a disco on Wednesday to Saturday nights. Open nightly until 4am.

Regent Multiplex Cinema, 49 Lydiard St (☎03/5331 1399). Three screens showing mainstream films.

Around Ballarat

Coming from Melbourne, you'll find the **Great Southern Woolshed** on the Great Western Highway just before Ballarat (☎03/5334 7877; daily 9.30am–5pm; $9). It's similar to a theme park, with an emphasis placed on the wool industry that made the Western District rich. At the **ram parades** (daily 10.45am, 12.30pm, 2.15pm & 3.30pm; 30min) visitors learn about different types of sheep and what kind of wool they produce. After the show you go in a group to the animal nursery, where sheepdogs round up a flock of sheep, and where there are farm animals such as rabbits, geese and pigs that can be petted. There's also a kiosk, restaurant and bar, and a museum of pioneer and country-life memorabilia where you can watch a film detailing the story of "Waltzing Matilda". Speciality shops and resident craftspeople sell opals, pottery, leather goods and timber products here, as well as fine-quality sweaters and other wool products.

Rich alluvial gold was found at **CRESWICK**, 18km north of Ballarat, in 1851, which made it an important mining centre. It's now a quiet little town, where the only reminder of earlier days is the wildly out-of-place Victorian architecture. The *American*

Hotel and the *British Hotel* face each other across the main street, a hangover from mining days when miners of different nationalities stuck to their segregated groups. **CLUNES**, just beyond Creswick, to the northwest, was the site of the first worthwhile Victorian goldfield in 1851. The reefs here were too deep for small-scale mining, and the Port Phillip Company took over operations. The only profitable British gold mine in Australia, it was most productive between 1857 and 1881. The main street has many solid old buildings and rows of original shopfronts which are sadly vacant – entrepreneurial attempts to attract the tourist trade with antique and craft shops have foundered. The **Clunes Museum** (Sat, Sun & school holidays 11am–4.30pm; $2) details the gold-mining era of the town. The *Club Hotel*, at 34 Fraser St (☎03/5345 3250; ④), has inexpensive **accommodation**, with a buffet breakfast included, and rustles up cheap rump **steaks** for lunch and dinner.

WESTERN VICTORIA AND THE MALLEE

Several roads run west from the goldfields to the South Australian border through the seemingly endless wheatfields of **the Wimmera**. To the west of the farming centre of **Ararat** is the major attraction of the area, **The Grampians (Gariwerd) National Park**, the southwestern tail-end of the Great Dividing Range. **Stawell** and **Horsham** – the latter regarded as the capital of the Wimmera – are good places to base yourself, but **Halls Gap**, inside the park, is even better. North of Horsham are **Nhill** and **Dimboola**, close to **Little Desert National Park** and, like Warracknabeal further north, wheat centres. Beyond here is the least populated part of the state, the wide, flat **Mallee** with its twisted mallee scrub, sand dunes and dry lakes. This region, with several state and national parks, extends from **Wyperfeld National Park** in the south, right up to Mildura's irrigated oasis on the Murray River. South of the Grampians is sheep country; following the Hamilton Highway from Geelong you'll end up at **Hamilton**, the major town and wool capital of the western district, also accessible via **Dunkeld** on the southern edge of the Grampians.

Transport

V/Line has a **bus** service from Ballarat to Hamilton via Dunkeld (Mon–Sat 2 daily, Sun 1 daily; connecting train to Ballarat from Melbourne; Mon–Fri the morning service continues to Mount Gambier in South Australia), and a bus service from Warrnambool (connecting train to Warrnambool from Melbourne via Geelong) once daily from Mon–Fri and Sun. As the V/Line timetables are prone to changes, you should call ☎13 6196 to check the current schedule. Interstate buses to Adelaide travel the Western Highway via Ballarat, Ararat, Stawell, Horsham, Dimboola and Nhill. The Grampians Link consists of a **train** service from Melbourne to Ballarat and a connecting bus to Halls Gap, via Ararat and Stawell, once daily. There's a nightly *Overlander* train service between Melbourne and Adelaide (departing Melbourne 8.20pm and arriving in Adelaide 12hr later) and a Daylink connection (train from Melbourne to Bendigo, and from there a connecting bus via Horsham and Dimboola to Adelaide).

Hamilton

Three highways converge at **HAMILTON**, where you can see the Grampians from the edge of the main street. It's a civilized little city whose main claim to fame is that it's the "Wool Capital of the World". The only reason you're likely to be here is if you're a traveller passing through, en route from the Goldfields to South Australia, or from the mountains to the coast. There's plenty to distract you, however, and the **Hamilton District Tourist Office** on Lonsdale Street (daily 9am–5pm; free call ☎1800/246 056) – a friendly and helpful place that will also book accommodation – will do its best to persuade you to stay for a while.

The most worthwhile of the town's five museums and galleries is the **Hamilton Art Gallery**, on Brown Street (Mon–Fri 10am–5pm, Sat 10am–noon & 2–5pm, Sun 2–5pm; $3 donation), one of the finest provincial art galleries in the state. Its collection of eighteenth-century watercolours of English pastoral scenes by Paul Sandby is the largest outside the Royal Collections in Britain; among other gems are ninety engravings by William Hogarth and several pieces of eighteenth-century English furniture. The influence of the rich, local Ansett family (of airline fame) is obvious; many of the excellent contemporary paintings were acquired through the Ansett Hamilton Art Awards, sponsored by Ansett transport.

Also in the town centre, but of marginal interest, is the **Hamilton History Centre** (2–5pm; closed Sat; $1), located in the Mechanics Institute Building at 43 Gray St. East of town, on the Ballarat Road, is the **Sir Reginald Ansett Transport Museum** (daily 10am–4pm; $2), charting the history of the Ansett flight network which began here, while inside the **Five Big Woolbales** (actually a rather ugly concrete structure in the shape of woolbales) on Coleraine Road a small exhibition tells you about the wool industry of the Western district; shearing demonstrations can be arranged (☎03/5571 2810).

There's also some refreshing greenery in the town centre: the **Botanical Gardens** are on the corner of French and Thompson streets, just one block from Gray Street, the main thoroughfare, while the banks of the **Grange Burn** are home to the eastern barred bandicoot, the only known population in mainland Australia. Grange Burn flows into man-made **Lake Hamilton**, which has a safe, sandy swimming beach and is filled with trout.

Practicalities

If you want to **stay**, there's a wide variety of accommodation. Budget travellers can stay at *Lake Hamilton Caravan Park and Peppercorn Lodge* on 10 Ballarat Rd (☎03/5571 9046; rooms ④, cabins ③, dorms ①), which has backpackers' accommodation, comfortable, heated rooms, and a pretty camping area; it also provides local information and organizes occasional tours. Nearby is the luxurious *Grange Burn Motor Inn* at 142 Ballarat Rd (☎03/5572 5755; ⑧). The relaxed *Grand Central Hotel* at 141 Gray St (☎03/5572 2899; ③–④) is a good place both to eat and sleep: breakfast is included in the price of the motel-style rooms, there's an unpretentious bistro, and bands play here at weekends. The pleasant *Gilly's Coffee Shop & Grill*, 106 Gray St, is open both day and evening. The top eating spot is *The Hamilton Strand*, at 56 Thompson St (BYO; Mon–Sat 9am until late), where at the front coffee, cakes and light snacks are served, while "serious" dining goes on in the rooms behind. The menu features dishes like Cajun chicken, seared kangaroo or Thai fish curry; the wine list has lots of wines from the Pyrenees region in Victoria.

Around Hamilton

Hamilton is situated on the fringe of an extensive volcanic plain that runs across western Victoria and into South Australia. **Mount Napier** (439m) to the south and Mount Rouse at Penshurst to the east were the sources of most of the lava flow covering the Hamilton area. Byaduk Caves Road, going towards MacArthur, has a very good view of Mount Napier, directly ahead as you drive. Lava flows are still clearly visible here, with black wattle trees flourishing on many of them. The **Byaduk Caves** are actually fern-filled lava tubes; three of the twelve are easy enough to get into, but the others require the use of ropes. As you explore, watch out for stinging nettles and rough terrain, with frothy textured lava rocks scattered around, porous and covered in moss.

COLERAINE, 35km west of Hamilton on the Glenelg Highway, is picturesquely sited in the Wannon River Valley, between two tablelands. The **Points Aboretum** here (open 24hr; free) is the nation's official eucalypt collection, and has the largest number of species in the world. *Platypus Park* in Wannon, 35km northwest of Hamilton, uses its pleasant cabins and restaurant as an overnight stop on their tours between Melbourne and Adelaide. You can also just drop in and participate in one of their day tours to the Grampians, Port Fairy, the Glenelg River and other destinations in the area (☎03/5570 8277).

At **CASTERTON**, 29km further west on the Glenelg River, is the 1843 **Warrock Homestead** (daily 10am–5pm; $5), one of the most interesting in the country: more than thirty buildings are still used by the descendants of the original settlers and are open to visitors. From here it's less than an hour's drive to South Australia and the Coonawarra wine region (see p.728).

Ararat and the Western Highway

ARARAT, some 90km west from Ballarat towards the mountains, is still very much a goldfields town, with an overabundance of grandiose Victorian architecture. It was founded in 1857, when a group of seven hundred hopeful Chinese, making the slow trudge from the South Australian ports to the central Victorian goldfields, stumbled across a fabulously rich, shallow alluvial goldfield, the **Canton Lead**. As the only town in Australia founded by the Chinese, Ararat has it's own Chinese museum at the site of the old mine entrance, the **Gum San Heritage Museum**. Few other signs of the embryonic Chinese settlement survive in what soon became a rich, planned town: the main street was laid out to show off the best profiles of **Mount Ararat** in the west and the **Pyrenees Range** with **Mount Cole** in the east.

These days Ararat is the commercial centre for a sheep-farming and wine-producing area; **wineries** in the area include the Montara Winery, 3km south along the Chalamabar Road (Mon–Sat 10am–5pm, Sun noon–4pm), and Mount Langi Ghiran on Vine Road north of Buangor (turn north from the Western Highway towards Warrak; Mon–Fri 9am–5pm, Sat & Sun noon–5pm), renowned for its superb white and red wines. Both wineries have reasonable prices.

Next door to the town hall, with its clock tower and fountain, is the **tourist information centre** on Barkly Street (Mon–Fri 9am–5pm; free call ☎1800/657 158), which provides information on the Grampians, as well as a list of places to **stay** in town. The **Langi Morgala Museum** nearby (Sat & Sun 1–4pm; $2) occupies an old brick building banded with bluestone at the base and around the huge arched windows and doors; the museum's name is supposedly an Aboriginal one meaning "yesteryear". Along with the usual pioneering displays, there's an important collection of Aboriginal artefacts.

For **food**, go to Barkly Street, where you'll find a health-food store, a decent delicatessen and *Kaman's Koffee Lounge*, which serves classy sandwiches and good-value meals. Also on Barkly Street are the *Ararat Hotel*, serving bar meals; the *Cafe Dominica*, in a Victorian mansion, which has a coffee shop, bistro and pricey restaurant (licensed; open late; closed Mon); and the *Pyrenees Country Kitchen*, an award-winning restaurant.

Great Western and Stawell

Between Ararat and Stawell is the small settlement of **GREAT WESTERN**, the centre of a wine-producing area whose most famous **wineries** are right in town, on the Moyston Road. Seppelt's Great Western (daily 10am–5pm), established in 1865, and

Best's Wines at Concongella (Mon–Fri 9am–5pm, Sat 9am–4pm, Sun during school holidays noon–4pm), established in 1866, are both renowned for their sparkling *méthode champenoise* wines. Although Best's can take pride in its long history, its premises look more like a state-of-the-art industrial assembly line. Seppelt's, with its extensive, National Trust-classified underground cellars, is far more atmospheric and interesting to visit.

STAWELL is most famous for the **Stawell Gift**, a foot race offering big prize money that has been held here every Easter since 1877. It's also the closest major town to the Grampians and the departure point for the **bus** to Halls Gap. The helpful **Grampians Information Centre** is at 52 Western Highway (free call ☎1800/246 880); the Stawell Gift Hall of Fame on Main Street (June–Sept Mon–Fri 9–11am; Oct–May Mon–Fri 10am–4pm; $2; call ☎03/5358 1326 to confirm) charts the history of the race itself. The town, with its winding main street, has a pleasant, old-fashioned feel, and it's a much less expensive place to stay than Halls Gap. The many **motels** along the highway all charge much the same (④) for similar facilities. More expensive B&Bs and a caravan park are the only real alternatives: *Clovelly House* at 7 Clifton Ave (☎03/5358 2986; ⑧); and the *Stawell Grampians Gate Caravan Park* on Burgh Street (☎03/5358 2376; cabins ③–④), the closest camping area to town.

The Grampians National Park

Rising from the flat plains of western Victoria's wheat and grazing districts, the sandstone ranges of the **Grampians**, with their weirdly formed rocky outcrops and stark ridges, seem doubly spectacular. In addition to their scenic splendour, in THE **GRAMPIANS NATIONAL PARK** you'll find a dazzling array of **flora**, with a spring and early summer bonanza of wild flowers; a wealth of **Aboriginal rock art**; **Brambuk**, an impressive Aboriginal cultural centre; **waterfalls** and **lakes**; and over fifty **bushwalks** along 100km of well-marked tracks. There are also several hundred kilometres of road, from sealed highway to rough track, on which you can make exciting **scenic drives** and **4WD** tours.

HALLS GAP, 26km from Stawell, on the eastern fringes of the Grampians, is the only settlement actually in the national park. Its setting is gorgeous, in the long flat strip of the Fyans Valley surrounded by the soaring bush and rock of the Mount Difficult and Mount William ranges; koalas are frequently seen in the surrounding trees. Packed with accommodation and other facilities catering to park visitors, this is the obvious place to base yourself, especially if you don't have your own transport. The newsagent in town has an EFTPOS machine and acts as an agent for the ANZ and Commonwealth **banks**.

Just over 2km south of Halls Gap along the Grampians Road (also known as the Dunkeld Road or the Dunkeld–Halls Gap Road) is the **National Park Visitor Centre** (daily 9am–4.45pm), the best place to start your visit; it has a fascinating display and videos which trace the development of the Grampians over four hundred million years. Here you can buy books, including the excellent *Grampians Touring Guide* (ideal for short walks) and more detailed topographic maps. Although most walking tracks are clearly defined and well signposted, it's a good idea to buy *Vicmap*, or the walking maps published by the NPWS, and carry a compass if you're planning an overnight trek. Details of bushwalks are posted and there are masses of free leaflets; before beginning an extended walk, call into the visitors centre and register. Some **walks** start from the campsite at Halls Gap, while others branch off the Victory and Grampian roads, making them difficult to get to without a car.

The **best times to come** are in autumn, or in spring and early summer when the waterfalls are in full flow and the wild flowers are blooming (although there'll always be something in flower no matter when you come). Between June and August it rains

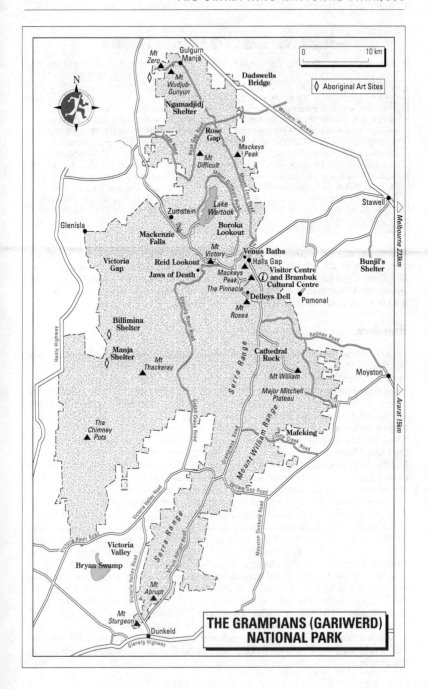

THE GRAMPIANS (GARIWERD) NATIONAL PARK

ROCK ART IN THE GRAMPIANS

It's estimated that **Koorie** Aborigines lived in the area known to them as **Gariwerd** at least five thousand years ago. The area offered such rich food sources that the Koories didn't have to spend all their time hunting and food-gathering, and they could thus devote themselves to religious and cultural activities. Evidence of this survives in rock paintings, which are executed in a linear style, usually in a single colour (either red or white), but sometimes done by handprints or stencils. You can visit some of the rock shelters where Aborigines camped and painted on the sandstone walls, although many more are off-limits. In the northern Grampians one of the best is **Gulgurn Manja** (also known as Flat Rock), 5km south of the Western Highway near the Hollow Mountain campsite; from Flat Rock Road there's a signposted fifteen-minute walk. The name means "hands of young people", as many of the handprints here were done by children. In the southern Grampians is **Billimina** (Glenisla Shelter), a fifteen-minute walk above the Buandik campsite; it's an impressive rock overhang with clearly discernible, quite animated red stick figures. Guided **rock art tours** are organized by the Brambuk cultural centre (see below).

heavily and can get extremely cold; at that time many tracks are closed to avoid erosion. Summers are very hot, with a scarcity of water and the ever-present threat of bushfires. If you're undertaking extended walks in summer, carry a portable radio to get the latest information on the fire risk: on **total fire ban days** no exposed flames – not even that from a portable gas stove – are allowed.

Brambuk

Located behind the visitors centre, **Brambuk Aboriginal Living Cultural Centre** (daily 10am–5pm; ☎03/5356 4452) grew from an idea for a rock-art facsimile centre that would draw the tourist traffic away from the actual art sites, which are very fragile. From that beginning, it developed into a full-blown cultural centre for western Victorian Aboriginal culture: a place where visitors could learn and Koories could find employment, with a management committee composed entirely of Koories. One of its achievements – unfortunately rather short-lived – was the restoration of indigenous place names in the park. These were appended to the European names in 1991, only to be discreetly dumped when the Liberal Party came to power after the Victorian state elections of 1992. The centre's building, with its undulating red-ochre tin roof, blends in wonderfully with the backdrop of bush and rocky ridge – it was designed in consultation with the five Koorie communities responsible for the centre and incorporates many symbolic features.

A small **exhibition** inside features a poignant photographic history of the area's Aborigines, and there's a visual display of traditional Aboriginal foods and lifestyles, plus a section devoted to Central Australian land rights. There's also a video consisting of interviews with different Koories about aspects of their lives, past and present. Downstairs, a shop sells Aboriginal music, books and souvenirs, while the small **Bushtucker Café** upstairs sells snacks and light meals, with, as its name implies, an emphasis on bushtucker – try possum-tail soup with damper, a rooburger or emu kebab, followed by a "wattlecino" (a cappuccino-style drink made from wattle seeds); for the less adventurous, more familiar fare is available too. Outside, the landscaped grounds are planted with examples of the major plant species found in the park.

There are short **rock art tours** from the centre to Bunjil's Shelter ($12.50), as well as half- and full-day walks to other Aboriginal art sites in the national park. All tours are on demand only, must be booked at least a week in advance, and require a minimum of five people.

Bushwalks, scenic drives and tours

The scenery and wildlife of the Grampians is tremendously varied, and the diversity of **vegetation** in the park is enhanced by the fact that this is the meeting place of the ecosystems of the forested areas in the south and east of Victoria and the dry mallee country in the north. It's significantly warmer in the northern Grampians, an area of arid bushland filled with bent and twisted trees and scrubby undergrowth. In the cooler south, the vegetation ranges from stringybark forests and red-gum woodland in the wet Victoria Valley to luxuriant fern gullies such as Delleys Dell in the Wonderland Range. There are also subalpine communities of plants in exposed sites such as Mount William, as well as areas of stunted heaths on the Major Mitchell Plateau.

You can **drive** on roads through the park to major points and then get out and walk. Take care, though, as animals are often killed by drivers, especially on the Grampians Road south of Halls Gap and the Mount Abrupt Road north of Dunkeld. The most popular section for visitors is the **Wonderland Range**, immediately to the west of Halls Gap. From the Halls Gap campsite you can head directly to **Venus Baths** (2km), **Mackeys Peak** (1km), or **The Pinnacle** (10km), the most popular lookout in the Grampians with a narrow rock ledge nearby – the **Nerve Test** – that many try out. **Delleys Dell** is another Wonderland walk (5km), through canopies of tree ferns: start at the Rosea picnic area. The other major features are the Balconies, Mackenzie Falls and Zumstein, all accessible via the Mount Victory Road northwest of Halls Gap. The walk to the **Balconies** (1.6km return), also known as the **Jaws of Death**, begins from the Reid Lookout car park and goes through a stand of lichen-covered tea trees. The weird formation consists of one ledge above another, and if you're brave enough you can stand right on the edge of the lower jaw and be enthralled by splendid views over the forested Victoria Valley. The much-photographed formation can also be seen at a distance from the **Reid Lookout** itself.

At **Zumstein** (5km east of Mount Victory Road) there's a picnic area and car park where western grey kangaroos stand passively, waiting for food. They're tame enough to pet, but can be a serious nuisance when you get out your food; don't encourage them by feeding them. A three-kilometre walk runs along the Mackenzie River Gorge from here to the base of thundering **Mackenzie Falls**, which you can also reach more directly from the Mount Victoria Road. There's parking above the falls, and it's a short but strenuous walk to the base.

If you're reasonably fit, consider tackling the walk to the peak of **Mount William** (1168m; 3.5km return), the highest point in the park. This starts from the Mount William Road car park, for which you turn off 16km south of Halls Gap. More challenging overnight walks include one to the **Major Mitchell Plateau**, starting from the same car park but involving a difficult five-hundred-metre climb to the plateau; and the **Mount Difficult** walk, which starts from Rose Gap and goes across a large, undulating, rocky plateau.

Tours and activities

A few tour operators banded together to form the **Grampians Central Booking Office** at the Halls Gap newsagency (☎03/5356 4654; daily 9.30am–6pm; longer in summer) which does bookings for all kinds of activities from abseiling, bike riding and bushwalking to hot air balloon flights, spotlight tours and rock climbing. Grampians Tours (☎03/5356 6221) does an excellent 4WD-minibus day-tour ($75) to Mackenzie Falls, the Victoria Valley and to off-the-beaten-track places in the park, frequently stopping so you can take short walks to points of interest. Between September and June the ecotour operator Echidna Walkabout (☎03/9646 8249) does a two- to three-day Grampians tour out of Melbourne, which includes accommodation on a sheep farm, bushwalking, evening spotlight walks, and on the third day the option of exploring the regional Koorie heritage,

THE MAJOR MITCHELL TRAIL

The first Europeans to reach the Grampians were **Major Thomas Mitchell** and his exploration party in 1836. Mitchell was the Surveyor General of New South Wales, and his glowing reports of the explorations subsequently attracted many squatters in the early 1840s. The **Major Mitchell Trail**, a signposted 1700-kilometre "long-distance cultural trail" along backroads and sometimes bush tracks, allows you to follow his route through Victoria, from Mildura along the Murray River to Swan Hill, then south to Horsham, detouring into the Grampians to ascend Mount William, and thence to the coast at Nelson and Portland. Heading back, it runs inland via Hamilton and Dunkeld on the southern edge of the Grampians, through central Victoria via Castlemaine, and then across the northeast part of the state via Benalla and Wangaratta, crossing back into New South Wales at Wodonga. A **handbook** of the walk might be available at the NRE Information Centre or Information Victoria in Melbourne (see p.768), or enquire at the visitor information centres along the trail.

sometimes with a Koorie guide. At about $400 for two days, the tour is not cheap, but it's thoroughly recommended. Grampians Scenic Flights, departing from the Pomonal airstrip between December and June, gives the definitive overview of the mountain range, with sky-high prices to match; book through the Grampians store (☎03/5356 6294).

Grampians accommodation

During school holidays, particularly in January and at Easter, the Grampians are packed, although Halls Gap has lots of **accommodation** of every kind, you'll need to have booked far in advance, many places will insist on long stays. In addition to the Grampians Visitor Information Centre in Stawell, the privately run Grampians Booking Service: free call ☎1800/624 991, fax 03/5383 6347, also does accommodation bookings.

In town, Mountain Grand, Grampians Road (☎03/5356 4232, fax 5356 4254; ⑤–⑥), is a friendly **guesthouse** which has a licensed restaurant and a jazz café and bar downstairs. The *Kookaburra Lodge* at 14 Heath St (☎03/5356 4395, fax 5356 4490; ⑤–⑥)), is one of the better **motels**, and has an excellent restaurant (see opposite), while the cheapest of the lot is the *Grand Canyon Motel* (☎03/5356 4280, fax 5356 4513; ④–⑤), less than 1km north of the town centre on Grampians Road. There's also a wide choice of **self-catering** accommodation: the *Kingsway Holiday Flats* on Grampians Road (☎03/5356 4202; ③–④) are spartan, but cheap and clean, and have TV and a fully equipped kitchen. If you can afford to splurge a bit, try the *Grampians Wonderland Cabins* on Ellis Street, just off the Grampians Tourist Road on the way to Brambuk (☎ & fax 03/5356 4264; ⑥–⑧) – where you'll find beautiful two-bedroom timber cabins in a bushland setting.

On the site of the old **YHA hostel** in Halls Gap, on the corner of Buckler Street and Grampians Road, a much bigger hostel is scheduled to open in March 2000. It will be built according to environmentally friendly principles, recycling waste water and using solar electricity and wood-heating stoves. Until it opens hostel accommodation will be available; ring ☎03/5356 6221 for information. The backpacker busline Oz Experience stops overnight in the Grampians, in summer it uses the *High Spirit Outdoor Base Camp* with tents and pit toilets in the middle of the national park, the rate is $25 per day including food and activities (☎019/403 620).

There's no booking for the **campsites** in the national park – they operate on a first-come, first-served basis. A permit is required: fill in a form and put your money into the box at the site, or buy one from the visitors centre or from tourist offices in nearby towns. **Bushcamping** is allowed in the park, except in the Wonderland Range and within 100m of a dam, river or creek, or within 50m of a road.

Besides the basic park campsites, there are dozens of **caravan parks** in the vicinity. The most convenient, *Halls Gap Caravan Park* (☎03/5356 4251, fax 5356 4421; cabins ④, on-site vans ③), is right opposite the shopping centre and thus a bit noisy, but it's well equipped, and at the start of many walks. *Lake Fyans Holiday Park* (☎03/5356 6230, fax 5356 6330; cabins ③–⑤, on-site vans ③–④) at Pomonal, 13km away, has comfortable cabins, basic caravans and tent sites, plus canoes and tennis and volleyball courts.

At the northern end of the park is *Roses Gap Recreation Centre* (☎03/5359 5264; ③–④), which has cabins, a camp kitchen and sheltered barbecue.

Grampians eating, drinking and entertainment

There's no shortage of places to **eat** in Halls Gap. The Stony Creek Bakery (daily 8am–5pm) makes fresh bread daily and sells eggs; the more expensive *Flying Emu Café* serves cakes, snacks and light meals; and the *Cafe Rosea* does burgers, steak sandwiches, roast meals, pizza and pasta, and is open for breakfast, lunch and dinner. The *Halls Gap Tavern*, Lot 5, Dunkeld Road (daily 5pm–late), is a pleasant, moderately priced restaurant and bar. *The Kookaburra Restaurant* on Grampians Road (daily from 6.30pm, bookings advisable on ☎03/5356 4222), comes highly recommended for its inexpensive café-style dishes – mainly pasta – and for its restaurant food, which features venison and home-made ice cream. *Darcy's* at the *Colonial Motor Inn* on Grampians Road (daily from 6.30pm, bookings advisable on ☎03/5356 3440 is another motel restaurant dishing up good food including emu. Both restaurants have local wines on their wine list.

The *Halls Gap Hotel* on the Stawell Road has a bistro with a great view of the Grampians and a drive-in bottle shop. A small **cinema** operates during school holidays, and there's even a **film festival** at the beginning of November showing art-house films and a **jazz festival** over a weekend in mid-February.

The Wimmera

The Wimmera, dry and hot, relies heavily on irrigation water from the Grampians for its vast wheatfields; before irrigation and the invention of the stump jump plough, the area was little more than mallee scrub, similar to the lands beyond **Warracknabeal**, the northernmost wheat-growing centre.

HORSHAM, capital of the wheatfields, is somewhere you might want to stop for a break en route to Adelaide; it has an idyllic picnic spot, complete with barbecues, by the Wimmera River. However, there's little else to attract you here, though **Mount Arapiles**, 40km west, is one of the most important **rock-climbing** centres in Australia, and The Grampians National Park (see p.862) is within striking distance to the southeast. The *Royal Hotel* at 132 Firebrace St (☎03/5382 1255; ③) does good **food** and offers adequate **accommodation**; established in 1881, it's a grand old place which has retained many of its original features. The *Fig Tree Cafe*, at 59 Firebrace St, serves coffee and the usual café fare. Run by the same people who manage the *Horsham Hostel* next door (☎03/5382 0068; ①), *Cafe Bagdad* at 48 Wilson St has a slightly studenty, alternative feel and serves espresso, cakes and ice cream, as well as soups, salads and focaccia. There are dozens of other places to stay: **Wimmera Tourism**, at 20 O'Callaghan Parade (daily 9am–5pm; free call ☎1800/633 218), can advise. Seventeen kilometres out of town towards Natimuk and Mount Arapiles the friendly, small *Tim's Place YHA*, Asplins Road, Quantong (☎ & fax 03/5384 0236; dorm ①, room ③) has dorm accommodation and three private rooms for prospective rock-climbers and anyone who'd like to break their journey. Book ahead, as Oz Experience and other backpacker tour operators call in here.

For more information and guide services, call Arapiles Climbing Guides (☎03/5387 1284) – in addition to rock-climbing they also offer abseiling and bushwalking.

Continuing on the Western Highway, you come to **DIMBOOLA**, deep in the dreary flatlands; it's the sort of place that runs to its own dusty clock, frustratingly closing down for lunch just as interstate buses stop for a break. For **accommodation**, there's the *Dimboola Motel* (☎03/5389 1177; ④) and *Dimboola Hotel* (☎03/5389 1380; ④), both on Horsham Road. **NHILL** and Kaniva, further along the highway, are similarly undistinguished. All three towns are within a few kilometres of **Little Desert National Park**, with Nhill being the best starting point if you plan to explore. *Little Desert Tours and Lodge* (☎03/5391 5232; B&B units ④), 16km southeast of the town on the Harrow Road, lies on the fringe of the park and runs good 4WD **tours**; it has camping, motel units and bunk rooms for groups. Far from being a desert, the national park has a great variety of plants, with colourful wild flower displays in spring; much of the vegetation is low **mallee** scrub, among which the now rare mallee fowl can be found. There's a **campsite** within the national park: following the Kiata South Road 13km from Kiata, east of Nhill (call the ranger for more information on ☎03/5391 1255).

The Mallee

The Mallee, the most sparsely populated area of Victoria, begins north of Warracknabeal, from where the **Henty Highway** heads up to join the Sunraysia Highway and forge its way to Mildura, on the border with New South Wales. This is an area worth visiting only in winter, when it's drier and warmer than the rest of Victoria, but not too hot to make bushwalks unbearable. You really need your own transport to see anything; just about the only **public transport** is the small Henty Highway Coach that runs between Horsham and Mildura (departs Horsham BP service station Tues & Thurs 9.15am, Fri 5.45pm; departs Mildura train station Mon, Wed & Fri 7.45am; 4hr; $49; ☎03/5382 4260), which mainly carries freight. Along the way are small dusty towns such as Brim, Bealah and **HOPETOUN** ("gateway to the Mallee"), whose shops still have their old awnings and apparently their original window displays too.

Hopetoun is at least somewhere you might have a reason to stop, on the way to **Wyperfeld National Park**, 51km away. At 3500 square kilometres, it's Victoria's third largest and has a chain of normally dry lake beds, mallee scrub, river red gum and black box woodlands, and rolling sand plains, with emus, kangaroos and mallee fowl among its wildlife. A sealed road goes to the *Wonga Campground*, where there's a shady camping and picnic area with water and toilets, as well as an **information centre** (☎03/5395 7221) where you can find out about the many walks in the park; this is also a good area to explore on a mountain bike. The **Big Desert Wilderness** is directly west of Wyperfeld but can be reached only by the Nhill–Murrayville track that runs between Broken Bucket, northwest of Nhill, and Murrayville, on the Mallee Highway west of Ouyen; there are no tracks, roads or facilities in the park, just more sand dunes, mallee scrub and lots of wildlife. You'll need a 4WD and considerable dedication to get the most out of it.

Beyond Hopetoun, the Henty Highway merges into the Sunraysia Highway. Heading north on the Sunraysia, you come to the small town of **SPEED** – which could hardly have a less appropriate name; tourist information is available at the **general store** here. From here the mallee scrub tenaciously clings to the edges of the highway, threatening to invade the red soil of cleared fields on either side, and the equally red dust of the unsealed road. **OUYEN**, the "heart of the Mallee", is another small, undistinguished town where two highways meet. Heading west on the Mallee Highway, the access track to the picturesque **pink salt lakes** of the Murray–Sunset

(Yanga–Nyawi) National Park leads north from Linga. Continuing north on the Calder Highway from Ouyen, you pass the **Hattah–Kulkyne National Park**, just east of the highway; the park consists of dry mallee scrub, native woodland, and a lakes system lined with gums. Lake Hattah is reached by turning off the highway at Hattah, 34km north of Ouyen, onto the Hattah–Robinvale Road. From Hattah it's less than 70km to Mildura and the Murray River.

THE MURRAY REGION

From its source close to Mount Kosciuszko high in the Australian Alps, the **Murray River** forms the **border** between Victoria and New South Wales until it crosses into South Australia (someone got a ruler out for the rest of the border to the coast); although the actual watercourse is in New South Wales, the Victorian bank is far more interesting and more populous. After the entire length was navigated in 1836, the river became the route along which cattle were driven from New South Wales to the newly established town of Adelaide, and later in the century there was a thriving paddle-steamer trade on the lower reaches of the river, based at Wentworth on the New South Wales side (see p.318 for more on early Murray navigation). In 1864, **Echuca** was linked by railway to Melbourne, stimulating the river trade in the upper reaches. Echuca thus became a major inland port, the furthest extent of the navigable river. At the height of the paddle-steamer era, **Mildura** was still a run-down, rabbit-infested cattle station, but in 1887 the Chaffey brothers (see p.735) instituted irrigation projects that now support dairy farms, vineyards, vegetable farms and citrus orchards throughout northwestern Victoria. Between Mildura and Echuca, **Swan Hill** marks the transition to sheep, cattle and wheat country; the **Pioneer Settlement** here explores the extraordinarily hard lives of the early settlers. Above Echuca the Murray loses much of its magic as it flows through the more settled northeast.

Nowadays **paddle steamers** cruise for leisure, and are the best way to enjoy the river and admire magnificent **river red gums** lining its banks, as well as the huge array of birds and other wildlife that the Murray sustains. Renting a **houseboat** is also a relaxing (if expensive) way to travel.

Mildura

MILDURA has the mirage-like aura of an oasis, its vineyards and orange orchards standing out from a hot, dry landscape. To the southwest especially is an almost entirely empty area, evocatively named **Sunset Country**, with nothing but gnarled mallee scrub, red sand and pink salt lakes (reached via Linga on the Mallee Highway.. Mildura's wide streets are lined with palms, giving a balmy impression even in the mild winter sunshine. It makes a good winter getaway, but summer can be stiflingly, unremittingly hot – the green grape vines in the surrounding countryside and the flowers and towering red gums that line Deakin Avenue, the main thoroughfare, offer some relief, but you'd do best to avoid the area then.

Deakin Avenue runs northwest through town to the river, with 7th Street and the train station facing the parklands that run along the river. Like any self-respecting small city, Mildura has its mall, which runs parallel to Deakin Avenue between 8th and 9th streets. The **Alfred Deakin Visitor Information Centre**, 180–190 Deakin Ave (Mon–Fri 9am–5.30pm, Sat & Sun 9am–5pm; free call ☎1800/039 043), has very helpful staff, particularly good information on the surrounding national parks and gives out a free map of the town. A video presentation is screened every half-hour between 9.30am and 4.40pm telling the story of the Chaffey brothers, and Mildura and the surrounding area.

Sights are thin on the ground here, and probably the most interesting thing to do is to head for the river and watch traffic passing through the seventy-year-old **Mildura Weir** system, designed to provide stable pools for irrigation and to enable navigation throughout the year. There's a pretty picnic ground by lock 11 (the trickiest), just beyond the art gallery at the arts centre. If there's nothing happening on the river, wander down to the **Mildura Arts Centre**, 199 Cureton Ave (Mon–Fri 9am–5pm, Sat & Sun 1–5pm; gallery $2.50), which consists of a historic home, Rio Vista, the Mildura Regional Art Gallery, a theatre and a sculpture park. **Rio Vista** was built in 1890 for William Chaffey, who lived here with his first and second wives (both called Hattie Schell, the second the niece of the first) until he died in 1926. It's a lovely house, though rather ill-suited to the climate, and inside are various displays about the Chaffeys and the development of Mildura. The art gallery's most important piece is *Woman Combing Her Hair at the Bath*, a pastel work by Edgar Degas; it also has some excellent sculpture by Australian artists.

Cruises, tours and activities

The best **short river cruise** is on the *P.S. Melbourne* (daily 10.50am & 1.50pm; 2hr 10min; $16; ☎03/5023 2200), Mildura's only genuinely steam-driven paddle steamer. Built in 1912, it still has its original boiler and engine. Upstairs the captain, in full regalia, gives a rather sensible commentary. The same company runs *Paddleboat Rothbury*, built in 1881 and in its day the fastest steamboat on the river; it's now been converted to diesel and takes people on cruises to local attractions such as Golden River Zoo (only during school holidays; $28), the Trentham Estate Winery ($35 including lunch and wine tasting). *Paddleboat Coonawarra* (☎03/5023 3366 or free call ☎1000/001 101) has longer cruises: four nights for $410 or five nights, $000. All cruises leave from **Mildura Wharf** at the end of Madden Avenue, west of the train station. For information about renting your own vessel, see below.

Away from the river, the most outstanding natural attraction is **Mungo National Park** (see p.319), 110km across the border in New South Wales. It's visited by a few tour operators from Mildura: Junction Tours (Wed, Fri & Sun; $40; ☎03/5027 4309); and Mallee Outback Experiences, (Wed & Sat; $50; ☎03/5021 1621 or free call ☎1800/039 043). Kooric tour operators belonging to the Barkindji people also lend their perspective on things with Ponde Tours (Tues, Thurs & Sun, $45; ☎03/5023 2488), and Harry Nanya Tours, based just over the border in Wentworth (Tue & Fri; $50; ☎03/5027 2076), both going to Mungo National Park. Like all the others, they also do tours around Mildura, to Wentworth, and to other attractions and national parks in the surrounding area.

Camerons, 72 Lime Ave (☎03/5021 2876), rents out sports gear and arranges **hot air balloon flights** daily, weather permitting, from $130 per person. Crossroads Sporting Complex on 15th Street has an indoor heated **pool**, and there's an outdoor Olympic pool on 12th Street for a refreshing plunge. If you want to swim in the river – there's a sandy **swimming beach** with lifeguards in summer at Chaffey Bend – take local advice and beware of dangerous currents; people have drowned here.

Practicalities

Mildura is 555km from Melbourne, about as far as you can go in this small state; right on the border of New South Wales, and little over 100km from South Australia, it's ideally located for **onward transport** to either. Buses on the Sturt Highway, the major route between **Adelaide** and **Sydney**, pass through several times daily, with a 2.30am and 8.45am Greyhound Pioneer service to Adelaide, and an 8.50pm and 3am service to Sydney. **Broken Hill**, north up Silver City Highway, can be reached by bus via Wentworth (departing Mildura train station Mon, Wed & Fri 7.50am; 3hr 30min; $43); book at the Visitor Information Centre). From **Melbourne**, there's a V/Line train–bus connection via Bendigo or via Swan Hill at least once daily (call ☎13 6196 to book). In terms of **local transport**, there are buses to Red Cliffs and across the river to Wentworth (see p.318), or you can **rent a car** from, among others, Maw Auto-Rent, Koorlong Avenue, Irymple (free call ☎1800/656 200).

Mildura has a good reputation as a place to obtain **work** as a fruit-picker; the only guaranteed time is in February, when the grape harvest takes place. Unfortunately, this is also the time when the heat is most intense. If you think you could handle it, come around the end of January, the beginning of the eight-week season. Employment National at Shop 2 at the corner of Lime Ave and 9th St (Mon–Fri 9am–5pm; ☎03/5021 5227) has information about farm work. During the harvest season you can also phone the Mildura and District Harvest Labour Office (end of January to mid-March; ☎03/5021 1797). Some growers have accommodation but normally you'll need your own transport and a tent.

Accommodation

Mildura has lots of accommodation and competition has kept prices low, especially at the motels.

Apex Caravan Park, Chaffey Bend (☎03/5023 2309). Well-equipped site, right on the Murray by the beach. Cabins ③, on-site vans ③.

Carn Court Holiday Flats, 826 15th St (☎03/5023 6311 or free call ☎1800/066 675). Good, inexpensive choice if you want to self-cater; has an outdoor pool. ④–⑤.

City Colonial Motor Inn, 24 Madden Ave (☎03/5021 1800, fax 5023 4520). New, well-appointed motel near the waterfront, with a solar-heated pool; some rooms have spas. ⑤–⑥.

Grand Hotel Resort, 7th St, opposite the train station (☎03/5023 0511, fax 5022 1801). Fancier than its bland pub appearance suggests. Offers a variety of accommodation, from basic to highly luxurious, with breakfast included. Has a dining room, games room, spa, sauna, and outdoor swimming pool. ⑥–⑧.

Murray View Motel, cnr of 7th St and San Mateo Ave (☎03/5021 1200, fax 5021 1199). Family-run, good-value modern motel, with a solar-heated pool. ④.

Rosemount Holiday House, 154 Madden Ave (☎ & fax 03/5023 1535). Old-style guesthouse that doubles as an affiliate YHA. Good facilities, breakfast, an outdoor swimming pool, and can arrange work contacts. Rooms ②–④, dorms ①.

Three States Motel, 847 15th St (☎ & fax 03/5023 3735). Very popular motel with bargain rates. Facilities include a pool, common spa and tennis court. ③–④.

Food

Healthy food abounds in Mildura's cafés and restaurants. If you have a vehicle, you can make an enjoyable outing to buy fruit and vegetables from surrounding farms. Otherwise, try *The Vegie Mart*, 145 9th St, which has a good range and also sells meat, cheeses, fish and poultry.

Bay Tree Cafe, 145 8th St. This bright and airy café serves lunches, snacks and excellent cakes. Daily 10am–5pm.

Brolga's Restaurant, *Inlander Sun Resort*, 373 Deakin Ave (☎03/5023 3823). Modern Australian cuisine served indoors or by the pool.

Hotel Mildura, 124 8th St. A bistro serving classic Australian food and Chinese-inspired dishes.

Hudak's Bakery Café, Langtree Mall. Good continental breads and delicious zucchini slices. Mon–Fri 8.30am–5.30pm, Sat 8.30am–3pm.

Lauretz of Langtree, 30 Langtree Ave. All you can eat pizza, pasta, soup and salad – suitable for big appetites. Daily from 5pm.

The Rendezvous, 34 Langtree Ave (☎03/5023 1571). Cheap lunches and other meals served in the bistro. There's also an upmarket restaurant, as well as a bar and courtyard seating. Lunch Mon–Fri, dinner Mon–Sat.

Stefano's Restaurant, at the *Grand Hotel Resort*, 7th St, opposite the train station (☎03/5023 0511). The restaurant (Mon–Sat 7pm–midnight; booking essential) is tucked away in the hotel's cellar. No menu, but the Northern Italian food is excellent. The café-wine bar upstairs (daily 10am–midnight or 1am) is cheaper and serves good pasta, wood-fired pizzas, coffee and cakes.

Nightlife

Mildura's nightlife may not be the world's greatest, but there's enough to keep you occupied. Perhaps the best thing to do is to try out one of the **clubs**, where you can be signed in as a visitor; as an incentive to get you to the gambling machines, there's lots of inexpensive food and drink. The *Mildura Workingman's Club*, on Deakin Avenue between 9th and 10th streets, is one of many in town. Established in 1895, the club reputedly has the world's longest bar, a continuous undulating island 91m long; unfortunately you no longer get the full effect, as the end of the bar is closed off to make space for poker machines. Another good place for a drink is the vibrantly coloured and modern *Sandbar*, 43 Langtree Ave (nightly until 1am; light meals until 10pm), which has a courtyard, and puts on live music weekly in the summer and at weekends the rest of the year. *Dom's Nightclub*, upstairs from the restaurant of the same name, is open Thursday to Saturday. Another popular nightclub is *The Starbar*, on 8th Avenue between Lime and Langtree streets.

Around Mildura

The easiest excursion from Mildura is to **RED CLIFFS**, some 15km south, with its vineyards and tree-lined streets. The huge Lindemans Karadoc Winery is one of the largest **wineries** in Australia, where fifty thousand tonnes of grapes are crushed every year. The range of wines for tasting is extensive, and prices are very reasonable (daily 10am–4.30pm).

Across the Murray from Mildura at **BURONGA** (actually in NSW but more readily accessible from the Victoria side of the river), you can rent your own vessel to really get the full experience of the river. Buronga Boatmen Hire Boats, next to the bridge (☎03/5023 5874), rents out **fishing boats** (from $15 per hour) and **canoes** (from $10 per person per hour). Or you could phone The Rivermen (free call ☎1800/809 152) about renting a **houseboat**: weekly rates range from about $500 to almost $2000, but the boats can accommodate between four and twelve people, so if you get a group together it can work out to be quite reasonable – all you need to have is a driver's licence, and you must supply your own food. The nearby *Floating Cafe* (daily 10am–6pm) is a colourful pontoon moored in a lovely spot where there are lots of pelicans and ducks. Also at Buronga is the Stanley Winery (Mon–Fri 10am–4pm, Sat 10.30am–4pm, Sun noon–4pm), producer of that great Aussie institution, cask wine. It's the largest cask winery in New South Wales – you can taste the wine here or just pose for photos in front of the big wine cask outside. On a much smaller scale, Trentham Estate Winery, 10km down the Sturt Highway in an idyllic setting overlooking the river, has cellar door sales (Mon–Fri 8.30am–5pm, Sat & Sun 9.30am–5pm) and an upmarket restaurant (☎03/5024 8888; lunch Tues–Sun; bookings preferred). Thirty-one kilometres west of Buronga is the river town of Wentworth, located on the main Silver City Highway to Broken Hill; its attractions are fully covered in Chapter Two (see p.206).

Swan Hill and around

Heading for Swan Hill, you can go south down the Calder Highway, turning east at Hattah onto the Hattah–Robinvale Road and continuing past the Hattah Kulkyne National Park (see p.869). Alternatively, you can cross the Murray into New South Wales and follow the Sturt Highway, recrossing the river at **ROBINVALE**, a small, rather characterless fruit-growing town, but idyllically situated within a great loop of the river. Wine buffs should make a stop at the Robinvale Winery, Sea Lake Road (Mon–Sat 9am–6pm, Sun 1–6pm), where a wide range of **wines**, including some Greek varieties, are biodynamically produced.

Twenty-five kilometres from Swan Hill you reach the highly productive stone-fruit and vegetable-growing area of **NYAH**. Bushcamping (no water or facilities) is allowed in the nearby Nyah and Vinefera **state forests** along the Murray; for full details contact Parks Victoria in Swan Hill (see p.874). Eight kilometres beyond Nyah is the **Tyntynder Homestead** (Mon–Fri & Sun 9am–4.30pm, Sat during school holidays only; $7), a classic 1846 bungalow furnished in wealthy squatter style and set amid flowering gardens. Part of the homestead is a museum containing, among other things, a collection of Aboriginal artefacts.

As you approach **SWAN HILL** itself, the landscape changes – this is cattle and sheep country, with wheatfields further north. The Murray here is shallow and tricky to navigate, so there's not much river traffic. Swan Hill is a service centre for the pastoral industry and has a typically solid, conservative atmosphere. Surprisingly, it's quite a multicultural place, having ten percent of Victoria's Aboriginal population. It also has a large Italian community: elderly Italian matrons gossip on street corners, the pizzas and bread in its bakeries and restaurants are very good, and ornate mausoleums dominate the cemetery. The Pioneer Settlement (see below) is undoubtedly Swan Hill's main attraction, but while you're here, you could also visit the **Swan Hill Regional Contemporary Art Gallery** (Mon–Fri 10am–5pm, Sat & Sun 11am–5pm; $3), which specializes in folk and Aboriginal art, and the **Murray Downs Homestead** (Tues–Sun, daily during school holidays, but closed from Dec 1 to Dec 26 and all of February; 9am–4.30pm; guided tours of the mansion at 10.30am, 11.30am and 2.30pm; $8), an impressive Victorian mansion at the heart of a forty-square-kilometre station – it's over the bridge in New South Wales, but barely 1km from town.

Pioneer Settlement

Swan Hill's **Pioneer Settlement** (daily 9am–5pm; $12), a reconstruction of a pioneering community at Horseshoe Bend about 1km south of the train station, was the first of its kind in Australia and is still one of the best. The buildings are all authentic, having been transported from various sites near and far. One of the most interesting is the **Iron House**, an example of a nineteenth-century "kit home", many thousands of which were shipped out from Britain during the housing crisis that accompanied the goldrush – cities and towns in Victoria had whole streets of them, and they were stiflingly hot in summer and freezing cold in winter. This particular example came from South Melbourne, where it was lived in until 1967.

In the settlement's streets many of the **shops** are functional – the baker, the printer, the haberdashery and the porcelain doll shop – with assistants dressed in vaguely period costume. Generally, though, it's low-key and peaceful: buildings such as the barber's shop and the stock and station agents are open for you to wander around undisturbed. The pharmacy has a large collection of old medicines, with a gruesome dentist's surgery out back; the church is made from old bricks of the original courthouse; and there's even a rather creepy Masonic Lodge, which is still in use. The **Mechanics Institute** has a traditional collection of books and a wonderful working "Stereoscopic Theatre" from 1895: the wooden cylinder has 25 viewfinders, each with a leather seat from which you can admire the 3D scenes. You can go on **rides** around the settlement in a 1924 Dodge or a horse-drawn carriage. In the evening, the **sound and light show** (nightly from dusk; $8) is strikingly effective.

The settlement is situated on the banks of the Marraboor River, a branch of the Murray. A wooden bridge spans the river to **Pental Island**, which has an assortment of native flora and fauna. Meanwhile, an old paddle steamer, the *Pyap*, **cruises** from the settlement upriver past Murray Downs every day at 10.30am and 2.30pm (1hr; $8).

Practicalities

The **tourist information office**, 306 Campbell St (Mon–Fri 9am–5pm, Sat 10am–1pm; free call ☎1800/625 373), has a free map of the town giving detailed information on local attractions; it also sells tickets for the Pioneer Settlement sound and light show. Parks Victoria at 1 McCallum St (Mon–Fri 8am–4.30pm; ☎03/5036 0830) can provide you with information on **camping** in the nearby Nyah and Vinefera state forests.

There's a strip of **motels**, all with swimming pools, along Campbell Street, where almost all the town's facilities are located. The *Swan Hill Resort Motor Inn* at no. 405 (free call ☎1800/034 220, fax 03/5032 9109; ⑥–⑦) is the most luxurious, with an indoor and outdoor pool and spa, plus gym and other sports facilities; it's easily located because of its restaurant, *The Silver Slipper*, which has a huge rotating stiletto outside and even tackier decor inside. The *Pioneer Motor Inn* at no. 421 (☎03/5032 2017, fax 5033 1387; ④) is older and better value; at no. 182 is the *White Swan Hotel* (☎03/5032 2761; ③–④), which has simple rooms with shared facilities as well as more luxurious ones. The *Riverside* at 1 Monash Drive (☎03/5032 1494; cabins ④–⑤, on-site vans ③–④) is a good, centrally located **caravan park** right on the riverfront.

The large Italian population in Swan Hill has had a beneficial effect on the **food**: *Bartalotta's Hot Bread Kitchen*, 178 Campbell St, is excellent, as are the town's two pizzerias – *Rio's Pizza & Pasta* and *Quo Vadis*, both on Campbell Street and serving pizza as well as pasta and ribs. Both health food and junk food are doled out during the day at the *Old Royal*, a slightly alternative café at 176 Campbell St. *Teller's Restaurant & Bar* at no. 225, is a slick-looking, city-style brasserie in an old bank, open daily for lunch and dinner.

The Swan Hill Swimming Pool, Monash Drive (Oct–April daily 7am–9pm), has several **pools** and a waterslide.

Swan Hill to Gunbower Island

From Swan Hill the Murray Valley Highway heads southeast, away from the river, and follows the rail line past a series of about fifty freshwater lakes. At the first of these, **Lake Boga**, 16km from Swan Hill, Lake Boga Jet Ski Hire and Parasailing rents out jet skis and offers parasailing. Also by the lake – follow the signs – is Best's at St. Andrew's Winery, a large, commercial **winery**, the oldest in the Swan Hill region, and the sister winery to Best's Cocongella at Great Western (Mon–Fri 9am–5pm, Sat & Sun 10am–4pm). The lakes peter out at **Kerang**, a sizeable town in a citrus-growing area on the Loddon River. Nearby **Lake Reedy** is one of the largest ibis-breeding grounds in Australia and has a public-viewing hide; the birds are widespread in the area, though, so you probably won't have any trouble seeing some.

From Kerang, the Murray Valley Highway continues east to **Cohuna**, in a rich dairy-farming area, and from there towards **Gunbower Island**, a further 23km. The "island", encircled by the Murray River and Gunbower Creek, is a state forest of huge red gums and Gunnawarra wetlands, with 160 species of birds and much wildlife. It's most easily approached from Cohuna (follow the signs on the Kerang–Koondrook road); details of walks and camping can be obtained from the Kerang office of Parks Victoria (☎03/5450 3951).

Echuca and around

ECHUCA, a lively and progressive place, is the most easily accessible river town from Melbourne – it's only three hours or so by bus or car, making it a popular weekend getaway. Echuca became the largest inland port in Australia after the railway line connected it with Melbourne in 1864. When the **missions** began to close in the 1930s, many Aboriginal families, especially Yorta Yorta people from Cummeragunga mission, and Wemba Wemba from Moonacullah mission, migrated to the Echuca area. Since they weren't made welcome in the towns, the migrants were forced to live on the fringes in badly constructed, flood-prone housing, just close enough to be able to get to work and school. Women commonly worked in the canneries and hospitals, and the men packed fruit, sheared sheep and did other labouring jobs.

Nowadays, **Port of Echuca**, with its massive wharves and collection of old buildings, is a major tourist attraction, and several cruises ply along the river from here. The town itself, however, is not too touristy, and has retained much of its charm. There are two principal streets: High Street, the former main street, leads to Murray Esplanade and the wharf, and is the centre of tourist activity, with lots of cafés and boutiquey shops; Hare Street, the present-day main street, is lined with more commercial buildings.

Port of Echuca

To enter the old wharf area (daily 9am–5pm; $8), you need to get a "**passport**" from the tourist information centre (see "Practicalities", see overleaf) this also allows entry to the *Star Hotel* and the *Bridge Hotel*. The **Star Hotel** was first licensed in 1867 and is a typical pioneer pub, a tiny one-storey building with a tin roof and verandah. As the river trade declined, the *Star* was delicensed (in 1897), along with many of the other 79 hotels in town. Drinking on the premises became illegal, so the loyal clientele dug a tunnel to the street through which they could escape at the first hint of a police raid – you can examine this, along with the cellar and a small museum.

The magnificent red-gum **wharf** was nearly a mile long in its prime and is still fairly extensive. Three landing platforms at different levels allowed unloading, even during times of flooding, and there are wonderful views from the top, high over a bend in the river. Goods were transferred from train to steamer via this top level, and old train carriages sit on sidings here, piled high with trunks of red gum. You can wander below to the other levels, through a network of thick river-red-gum piles standing 12m high. At the lowest level, several **old boats** are moored, including the *Pevensey*, a 1911 steam-driven cargo boat which you can wander aboard – it offers one-hour cruises on the last Sunday of every month (☎03/5482 4248). In the wharf cargo shed there's a scale model of the working port and a ten-minute narrated audiovisual presentation.

Back outside the wharf complex, along Murray Esplanade opposite Hopwood Gardens, is the **Bridge Hotel**, opened in 1858 but delicensed in 1916. It was built by the founder of Echuca, Henry Hopwood, an ex-convict who also started a punt service across the Murray; the story goes that if the pub wasn't doing well he'd close the ferry down for a few hours, leaving prospective passengers with little else to do but drink. Other attractions in the old port area include the **Red Gum Works** (daily 9am–5pm), housed in a large loading shed which is wonderfully scented by the wood as it's transformed from tree-trunk to souvenir; there's also a steam-operated sawmill and a blacksmith at work. **Echuca Wharf Pottery** (daily 9.30am–6pm) also has demonstrations daily. The **World in Wax Museum**, 630 High St (daily 9am–5pm; $7), displays sixty wax figures of "world-renowned personalities", with Australia rather unimaginatively represented by Paul Hogan and Dame Nellie Melba.

River cruises

A wide choice of **cruises** are on offer, departing from berths just beyond the old wharf, best approached from Murray Esplanade. One-hour port cruises are available on the *PS Pride of the Murray* (daily 9.45am, 11am, 12.15pm, 1.30pm, 2.30pm & 3.45pm; $9; ☎03/5482 5244) and the *PS Canberra* (daily 10am, 11.30am, 12.45pm, 2pm & 3pm; $10; ☎03/5482 2711). The *PS Emmylou*, a wood-fired paddle steamer, has slightly longer cruises (daily

10.30am, 11.30am, 1pm & 2.30pm; 1hr $12, or 1hr 30min $15; ☎03/5482 2237). Other vessels include the *MV Mary Ann*, which does lunch and dinner cruises ($28/$44; call ☎03/5480 2200 for days and times).

Practicalities

The **tourist information centre**, 2 Heygarth St (Mon–Fri 9am–5pm, Sat & Sun 10am–4pm; free call ☎1800/804 446), sells tickets to the port complex and for cruises, and also books accommodation. The Echuca Travel Centre, 203 Hare St, sells V/Line and interstate **bus** tickets.

Budget accommodation is offered by *Echuca Gardens YHA*, 103 Mitchell St (☎03/5480 6522 between 8–9.30am & 5–8pm; ①), right on the edge of the Banyule Forest, a ten-minute walk through red gums to sandy river beaches where you can swim; and the new *Nomads Oasis Backpackers*, 410–424 High St (☎03/5480 7866; dorms ①, rooms ③) with air-con dormitories and twins/doubles, and a courtyard. The owner has employment contacts mainly in fruit picking. The *Steam Packet Inn*, on the corner of Leslie Street and Murray Esplanade (☎03/5482 3411; ⑥), is a National Trust-listed **motel** in the heart of the old port area. The *Echuca Hotel*, 571 High St (☎03/5482 1087), the town's first pub, still has some of its original features and offers simple accommodation in large pleasant rooms as well as motel units and self-contained accommodation at the Campaspe Lodge associated with the hotel (pub rooms ④, units ⑥). Upmarket **B&B** accommodation can be found in several pretty, historic homes: one of the nicest is *The River Gallery Inn*, 578 High St (☎ & fax 03/5480 6902; ⑧), where all the self-contained rooms have open fireplaces, and some have spas. The *Echuca Caravan Park*, Crofton St, Victoria Park (☎03/5482 2157; cabins ③–⑤, on-site vans ③), is a well-equipped **caravan park** right on the riverfront. There is even a **nudist resort** near Echuca: *River Valley Nudist Resort* (☎03/5482 6650; ④), in a bushland setting along the Goulburn River. Enquire at the tourist office about the many **houseboats** available to rent in the area.

With hungry Melburnians to feed, there's no shortage of decent **eating places**. *Sutton's* on Hare Street is an old-fashioned bakery with a shaded bench outside where you can eat your fill. *Top of the Town* on the High Street near the swimming pool does good-quality, freshly cooked fish and chips. *Drovers Bakehouse* on 513 High St near the Campaspe River sells a variety of breads baked in a wood-fired oven and has a sun-deck which is a good spot for breakfast or lunch. *Rosco's at the Bridge* has a coffee shop, bar and a restaurant in the historic Port area, and serves good coffee, cakes and desserts, light lunches and mainly traditional Aussie dishes in the restaurant. For excellent Italian food go to *Giorgio's on the Port*, 527 High St, which is open daily for dinner; or try *Fiori*, 554 High St. *Oscar W's* boasts a wonderful setting next to the old Echuca Wharf and serves food to match (daily 10am until late; book for dinner (☎03/5482 5133). *Ogilvie's Bar & Restaurant* at the Philadelphia Motor Inn, 30 Ogilvie Ave (☎03/5482 5700) also has a very good reputation. On the other end of the price scale, the *American Hotel*, on the corner of Hare and Heygarth streets, does good, plain counter meals.

Nightlife is better than you might expect; the small and friendly *American Hotel* is a good place to start with a drink. The *Royal Hotel*, 183 Hare St, draws a youngish crowd and plays host to live bands at weekends. The Paramount Movies on Hare Street has **films** on Friday and Saturday nights; check the local paper for details. If you're around in early November, check out the **Rich River Festival**, ten days of balls, street parades, pageants and markets; in mid-February there's a **Jazz, Food and Wine Weekend**.

Around Echuca

Thirty kilometres southeast of Echuca, Kyabram's main attraction is **Kyabram Fauna Park** (daily 9.30am–5.30pm; $7), a community-owned wildlife park divided into grassland for free-ranging kangaroos, wallabies, emus and other animals, and a huge wetland area. You can wander around the grassland area and through several aviaries; a two-storey observation tower affords views of the more than eighty species of native birdlife on the water. Diamond pythons, tiger snakes, crocodiles and other not-so-pleasant creatures can be viewed from a safe distance at the new Reptile House.

BARMAH, some 30km upstream on the Murray, is most easily reached by crossing into NSW at Echuca and heading north on the Cobb Highway, then turning east. This small river town is associated with red-gum milling, and with sleeper cutting in the early railway days. The *Barmah Caravan Park* (☎03/5869 3225; ①–③) has a great site on the banks of the river among red gums, with a small, sandy beach for swimming. **Barmah State Park**, 10km out of town, has Australia's largest stands of **river red gum**, some of them 40m tall and five hundred years old. The forest runs along the Murray for over 100km and stands in an extensive flood plain: **canoeing** among the trees at flood time (July–Nov) is a magical experience; you can arrange transport and rent canoes from *Echuca Boat and Canoe Hire* (☎03/5480 6208). During the wet season more than two hundred species of waterbird come here, and there's plenty of other wildlife; you might even see brumbies (wild horses). When it's dry you can use several well-established walking tracks: the place was of special significance to the Yorta Yorta Aborigines and you can still see fish traps, middens and scars on trees where the bark was used for canoes. During the **Barmah Cattle Muster** every April, two thousand head of cattle that are grazed in the forest are mustered in a frenzied, exciting atmosphere.

Yorta Yorta culture and lore are explained in the park's **Dharnya Centre** (daily 10.30am–4pm; $2), which also has archeological information and artefacts. A **cruise** in the *MV Kingfisher* leaves from here (Mon, Wed, Thurs & Sun, plus other days during busy times; 2hr; $17; reservations essential, book on ☎03/5869 3399) – a flat-bottomed boat that glides over Barmah Lake and through stands of red gum.

GIPPSLAND

GIPPSLAND stretches southeast of Melbourne from Western Port Bay to the New South Wales border, between the Great Dividing Range and Bass Strait. Green and well watered, it's been the centre of Victoria's dairy industry since the 1880s. **South Gippsland** is also, in contrast, the site of vast brown-coal deposits between Moe and Traralgon in the Latrobe Valley, where power stations generate most of the state's electricity, while offshore, Bass Strait wells exploit natural gas and crude oil reserves, with several gas-processing and oil-stabilizing plants disfiguring the coastline.

South Gippsland also has Victoria's most popular national park, **Wilsons Promontory**. "The Prom" is a hook-shaped landmass jutting out into the strait, with some superb scenery and fascinating bushwalks. In the east, around the **Gippsland Lakes** and **Ninety Mile Beach**, the region is less industrialized; and just beyond Orbost–Marlo the unspoilt coastline of the **Croajingolong National Park** – with its rocky capes, high sand dunes and endless sandy beaches – stretches to the New South Wales border.

Transport

V/Line **trains** run from Melbourne to Sale, basically following the Princes Highway through South Gippsland. From Sale, **buses** leave for Orbost, stopping at Lakes Entrance. The Sapphire Coast Link is a daily train–bus connection between Melbourne and Narooma on the south coast of New South Wales: take the train to Sale, then a connecting bus along the Princes Highway via Lakes Entrance, Orbost, Cann River and Genoa. The Capital Link connects Melbourne with Canberra: take the train to Sale, then

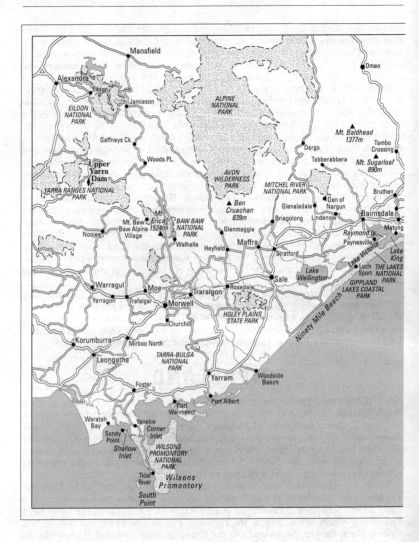

a bus via Lakes Entrance, Orbost and Cann River (Mon, Thurs & Sat). Bookings for both the above should be made through V/Line (☎13 6196). There's a daily Greyhound Pioneer service along the coast from Melbourne to Sydney, but it's not very convenient if you want to get off at stops in East Gippsland: the bus leaves Melbourne at 10pm and gets to Lakes Entrance and Cann River in the wee hours of the morning. Having your own **car** is vastly preferable, as you need to get off the highway to really experience the region's diverse highlights and to get to the unspoilt bush campsites on the coast. The Princes Highway itself is a very boring drive, particularly the stretch from the Latrobe Valley to Bairnsdale, but after Orbost the highway becomes more scenic as it goes through the tall, dense eucalypt forests of Far East Gippsland. If you don't have a car, or

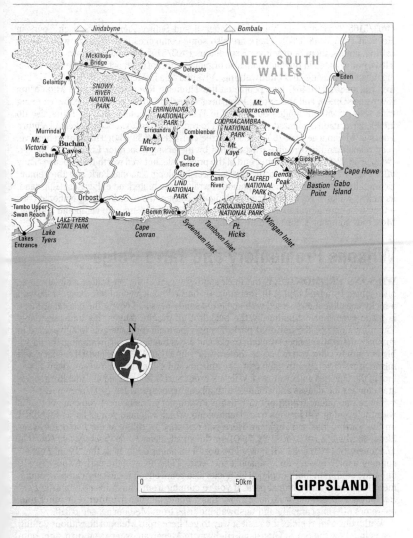

don't want to spend much money, you might want to consider travelling on Oz Experience, the backpacker bus line that covers the Sydney–Melbourne route via the very scenic high country and Gippsland, or else take a one-way tour with Wayward Bus (see p.810).

Tours and activities

The north part of Gippsland, in the foothills and mountains of the Great Dividing Range, is Victoria's "high country" – and it's ideally suited for a lot of **outdoor activities**. In the past, local operators have been a bit slow in becoming aware of the area's appeal, but the scene is gradually changing. At present, there are a few good **trail-ride** outfits, including Walhalla Mountain Saddle Safaris based in Erica, in the hills north of Moe, Latrobe Valley

(☎03/5165 3365; not suitable for beginners), and Snowy Range Horseback Tours in Heyfield (☎03/5148 3268). There are also some companies that organize **white-water rafting**, among them Snowy River Expeditions (☎03/5155 0308) and Detours (☎03/5155 9464), both located in Buchan; both also organize a host of other activities like rock climbing, abseiling, caving, and **bushwalking**. Adventurama in Melbourne (☎03/9682 1771 or free call ☎1800/801 464) take people on the Thomson River near Moe, the Mitta Mitta River near Omeo, and the Snowy River near Gippsland, they also run flexible camping trips with or without guided bushwalks to Wilsons Promontory. Bunyip Tours also do inexpensive, nature-oriented camping trips to the Prom; book via Backpacker Adventure Tours in Melbourne (☎03/9534 8866 or free call ☎1800/639 534). The comprehensive, very relaxed and informative trips offered by the ecotour operator Echidna Walkabout (☎03/9646 8249) are at the other end of the price scale, but well worth the expense. They offer four- or six-day trips to the coastal Croajingolong National Park and the remote Errinundra National Park in mountainous terrain of the hinterland of Far East Gippsland, as well as walks in very small groups along the coast of the Croajingolong National Park – they take care of transporting the gear and provisions, setting up camp and cooking. Most tour companies don't operate during the winter months.

Wilsons Promontory and Tarra Bulga

WILSONS PROMONTORY, the most southerly part of the Australian mainland, was once joined by a land bridge to Tasmania. Its barbed hook juts out into Bass Strait, with a rocky coastline interspersed with sheltered sandy bays and coves; the coastal scenery is made even more stunning by the backdrop of granite ranges. It's understandably Victoria's most popular **national park**. Though the main campsite gets totally packed in summer, there are plenty of walking tracks and opportunities for bushcamping; the park's big enough to allow you to escape the crowds, with about 130km of coastal scenery, and inland areas covered with tall forests, heathlands and salt marshes. You can swim at several of the beaches and even **surf**: Wilsons Prom Surf School, based at Tidal River, operates courses for all ages and abilities, with all equipment provided (☎03/5680 8512).

There's no public **transport** to Wilsons Promontory; the nearest you can get to it is with the evening V/Line bus from Dandenong, which will take you as far as **FOSTER** on the South Gippsland Highway. Here you can **stay** overnight at the *Foster Exchange Hotel*, 43 Main St (☎03/5682 2377; ④), or the small, clean *Foster Backpackers Hostel* at 17 Pioneer St (☎03/5682 2614; ①). The hostel manager doubles as the "Prom Postie", running a mail delivery and transport service to Tidal River in the park (Mon–Fri; $10 one-way; minimum four people). The hostel also rents out all necessary camping equipment for trips in the national park. If you're coming from Phillip Island, *Amaroo Park Backpackers* in Cowes (☎03/5952 2548) has a good, inexpensive **tour**. For other tour operators offering camping and bushwalking trips from Melbourne, see p.810.

With your own vehicle, the easiest way to get here from Melbourne without getting lost is to follow the South Gippsland Highway to Meeniyan, where you turn right onto Route 189 which takes you all the way to the park entrance. Once you get into the park, it's 30km to Tidal River on a good sealed road. At the entrance you pay $8 per car – if you stay overnight, this is deducted from the cost.

The **information centre** (in summer Sun–Thurs 8.30am–7.30pm, Fri & Sat until 9.30pm; in winter daily 8am–6.30pm; ☎03/5680 9555) at **Tidal River** is an obvious first stop. They have plenty of information, though not all of it is on display, so ask: the small booklet *Discovering the Prom on Foot* ($7.95) is invaluable if you're attempting any of the overnight walks. Tidal River, situated by a small river on Norman Bay, is the park's main camping and accommodation centre; colourful rainbow lorikeets fly around and land to be fed from people's hands. There's also a **general store** here (daily 9am–7pm), with a pricey supermarket section, takeaway food, fuel pumps and LP gas. **Accommodation** is arranged through the information centre, although from Christmas until the end of April – especially during public and school holidays – it's virtually impossible to get somewhere to stay; many places are booked up to a year in advance. Accommodation in the very basic motor huts (use of the campsite's facilities; linen not supplied) works out at $10 per person if you're in a group of four to six people. The camping area, which can hold up to five hundred people, has all the creature comforts – hot showers, shops, a laundry and a summer outdoor cinema, and there are also some brand-new, self-contained holiday units sleeping up to six people (May–Oct ⑥ & Nov–April ⑦ for two adults, plus $15 each extra adult).

Many **short walks** begin from Tidal River, including a track accessible to wheelchairs. One of the best is the **Squeaky Beach Nature Walk** (1hr return), which crosses Tidal River, heads uphill and through a tea-tree canopy, finally ending on a beach of pure quartz sand that is indeed squeaky underfoot. The **Lilly Pilly Gully Nature Walk** (3hr return) is very rewarding, as it affords an excellent overview of the diverse vegetation of "the Prom", from low-growing shrubs to heathland to open eucalypt forest, as well as scenic views. The walk starts at the Lilly Pilly Gully car park near Tidal River, follows a small valley and returns to the car park along the slopes of Mount Bishop. For **overnight camping** ($5 per person per night), you need to obtain a permit from the information centre at Tidal River, as there is a restriction on the number of people allowed on the campsites. Half the sites at each camping area are reserved for advance bookings (at least 21 days in advance; credit card phone bookings accepted), while the remaining sites can be booked on arrival in the park. Restrictions on length of stay apply – usually only one or two nights. The tracks in the southern section of the park are well defined and not too difficult; the campsites here have pit toilets and fresh water. The most popular walk here is the two- to three-day (36km) **Sealers Cove–Refuge Cove–Waterloo Bay** route, beginning and ending at the Mount Oberon car park. Crowds are much thinner in the remote north of the park, where there are no facilities and limited fresh water: this is the province of experienced, properly equipped bushwalkers. However, during summer holidays and at long weekends between November and the end of April all tracks become extremely busy, so book well in advance or show up early.

Tarra Bulga National Park

If you're in the mood for national parks, another good one can be reached from Yarram, 50km beyond Foster on the South Gippsland Highway. **Tarra Bulga National Park**, in the heart of the Strzelecki Ranges, is dominated by forests of mountain ash and myrtle beech with a lower canopy of ferns – a cool green environment alive with colourful lyrebirds, crimson rosellas and yellow-breasted robins among the rich birdlife. The **visitors information centre** (☎03/5196 6166) at Balook on the Grand Ridge Road, between the two separate sections of the park, has information about walks and is open on weekends, daily during the summer and Easter holidays, usually 10am–4pm, but times may vary. The Grand Ridge Road (mostly unsealed) winds along the top of the Strzelecki Ranges through fern gullies and towering trees, affording gorgeous views of South Gippsland. The *Tarra Bulga Guest House* (☎03/5196 6141; ⑧), on a beef and lamb property on Grand Ridge Road just 50m from the visitors centre, has every amenity, including a library and games room.

The Gippsland Lakes region

The **Gippsland Lakes**, Australia's largest system of inland waterways, are fed by the waters of the Mitchell, Nicholson and Tambo rivers, and are separated from the sea by

Ninety Mile Beach. East of Yarram, the beach stretches long and straight towards **Lakes Entrance**, the tacky focal point of the area and one of Victoria's most popular holiday spots, with the foothills of the high country within easy reach to the north.

SALE, at the junction of the South Gippsland Highway and the Princes Highway, is a good point from which to head off to explore the coastal park and Ninety Mile Beach. From Seaspray, 35km south, a coastal road hugs the shore for 20km to Golden Beach, from where a scenic drive heads through the **Gippsland Lakes Coastal Park** to **Loch Sport**. Here you're faced with the enviable dilemma of lakes on one side, and ocean beaches with good surfing on the other – an unsealed road continues on to Sperm Whale Head in the **Lakes National Park**. Sale's **tourist information centre** (daily 9am–5pm; free call ☎1800/677 520), on the Princes Highway, can provide you with all the details. They can also give you information about the **Bataluk Cultural Trail**, which starts in Sale and links sites of cultural and spiritual significance to the Gunai people, the original inhabitants of the Gippsland coast. You can watch a video about the trail (30min) at the information centre. The first stop on the trail, the **Rahmayuck Aboriginal Corporation** at 117 Foster St in Sale, sells arts and crafts, paintings and T-shirts (Mon–Fri 9am–5pm).

BAIRNSDALE is the next major town on the highway east of Sale and serves as another departure point for the lakes to the south. The efficient staff at the **tourist office** on Main Street (daily 9am–5pm; ☎03/5152 3444) will provide all the local information you'll need. The well set-up exhibition at the **Krowathunkuloong Keeping Place**, parallel to the Princes Highway at 37–53 Dalmahoy St (Mon–Fri 9am–5pm; $4), explains the history of the Gunai people. The *Bairnsdale Backpackers Hostel*, at 119 McLeod St, is a very friendly, if somewhat ramshackle place to **stay**, close to the old train station (☎03/5152 5097; rooms ②, dorms ①). Bairnsdale Air Charter (☎03/5152 4617) arranges cheap scenic **flights** from the Bairnsdale Aerodrome over the extensive waterways of the Gippsland Lakes (10min; from $25 per person).

Forty-five kilometres northwest of Bairnsdale is another site on the Bataluk Cultural Trail, the **Den of Nargun** in the **Mitchell River National Park**. According to a Gunai legend, the small cave here was inhabited by a large female creature, a *nargun*, who would abduct people who wandered off on their own. As the Den of Nargun was a special place for Gunai women and may have been used for initiation ceremonies, the story served the purpose of keeping unauthorized people away. The cave is located in a small, beautiful valley; follow the loop track from the park picnic area via a lookout to the Mitchell River (30min), then take the track along Woolshed Creek to the cave and climb up the steep path back to the starting point (40min).

Lakes Entrance and Metung

The sandy barrier between the Gippsland Lakes and the sea was formed about six thousand years ago; when first seen by white men in the 1840s the outlet to the sea was a seasonal, intermittent gap, unsuitable for reliable trade. In 1889 the present stable entrance was opened 6km east of the old one: the artificial entrance effectively cuts off the town's access to the length of **Ninety Mile Beach**, and means that it's no longer really ninety miles either.

As you might expect from the area's popularity, **LAKES ENTRANCE** is a big, rather tawdry, tourist town, with loads of motels at either end of town as you enter from the highway. There are all sorts of attractions aimed at keeping holidaying children happy – from Fun Park to minigolf – on the Esplanade, which fronts onto an arm of Lake King. The **Griffiths Sea Shell Museum** at 252 Esplanade (daily 9am–noon & 2–5pm; $4), with its rather off-putting 1950s-style facade, has a huge collection of shells and marine life, as well as an aquarium containing an intriguing assortment of fish from the Gippsland Lakes. Lakes Entrance is also a big **fishing port**: the Fishermans

Cooperative Wharf has a viewing platform where you can watch the catch being unloaded, as well as a tantalizing fish shop.

Beaches are obviously the big attraction here. **Lakes Entrance Surf Beach**, a substantial stretch of white sand patrolled in season by surf lifesavers, can be reached via a foot-bridge across the lake to Hummocks Reserve. Of the many **lake cruises** on offer, one of the most popular is the trip from the Club Jetty at the western end of town, up North Arm to the Wyanga Park Winery on the fringe of the Colquhoun Forest, in the winery's own boat, *The Corque* (daily cruise with morning tea $20, daily lunch cruise $25, Sat dinner cruise $35; book at Lakes Entrance Tourist Information, or through the winery on ☎03/5155 1508). There are also cruises on **Lake Tyers**, just east of Lakes Entrance, with *MV Rubeena* (☎03/5155 1283); boats leave from Fisherman's Landing. Other diversions are provided by the local **tour operator** Gippsland High Country Tours (☎03/5157 5556), which organizes 4WD day-trips through Snowy River National Park, the Errinundra Plateau and Croajingolong National Park, as well as shorter trips. Eastour (☎03/5154 2969) and Waratah Tours, based in Orbost (☎03/5154 2064), do similar trips to the three parks.

Practicalities

Lakes Entrance Tourist Information (daily 9am–5pm; free call ☎1800/637 060), on the Esplanade, provides local advice and tickets for cruises on the lakes, and can also book **accommodation**, a useful service in summer when the place gets very crowded. The two **hostels** are both excellent and friendly: *Riviera Backpackers YHA* (☎03/5155 2444, fax 5155 4558; rooms ②–③, dorms ①), at 5 Clarkes Rd in the east end of town just 50m from the Greyhound Pioneer bus stop, has 24-hour reception, dorms and rooms in refurbished former holiday units, a large kitchen and a small pool with spa. They also rent out bikes. *Silver Sands Backpackers* on Myers Street (☎03/5155 2343, fax 5155 3134; ①–③), part of a small, well looked-after caravan and camping park in a quiet location a block behind the Esplanade, has en-suite cabins and facilities for on-site vans, plus a camp kitchen, barbe-cue area, laundry, table tennis and pool with spa. Late arrivals can ring the night bell.

Most of the **motels** are as tacky as their names suggest: probably the best of the lot are the brand-new *Coastal Waters Motel* on the Esplanade (☎03/5155 1792; ⑤–⑦), which has its own heated saltwater pool, and the *Sand Bar Motel*, almost next door at 637 Princes Highway (☎03/5155 2567; ④–⑥), also with a heated pool and a common spa. Better, and usually cheaper, options are **cabins** or **cottages**. *Lazy Acre Log Cabins*, 35 Roadknight St (☎ & fax 03/5155 1323; ⑤–⑦), is a good bet, with a pool, spa and facilities for the disabled; or *Tambo Lodge* 9km to the west on the Princes Highway at Kalimna (☎03/5156 3215; ⑤–⑦) with a small pool and spa. *Deja Vu* is a good **B&B** in a pleasant location out of town at 17 Clara St (☎03/5155 4330, fax 5155 3718; ⑦–⑧), with spacious en-suite units over-looking the waterway of North Arm.

Places to **eat** in Lakes Entrance include *Egidios Wood Oven*, 537 Esplanade, for good Italian food; the upmarket *Skippers Winebar and Restaurant* at no. 481; *Caffe 567*, at no. 567 for delicious coffee and Italian-style ice cream; and *Fish-a-Fare*, at no. 509, an excellent fish-and-chip shop. In addition to wine tasting, the popular *Henry's Winery Cafe* at Wyanga Park Winery, 3km from town near North Arm (follow the signposts), also serves cakes and Devonshire teas, cheese platters and other meals; wines are available by the glass at cel-lar door prices (daily lunch and snacks 10am–5pm, Thurs–Sat dinner from 6pm; bookings preferred; ☎03/5155 1508).

Metung

If the commercialism of Lakes Entrance turns you off, head for the more refined charms of **METUNG**, a pretty, upmarket boating and holidaying village just 10km west along the shoreline. To get there, take the highway towards Bairnsdale, then turn south on a side road at Swan Reach.

A typically good-value **accommodation** option in Metung is *Maeburn Cottages*, 33 Mairburn Rd (☎03/5156 2736; ④–⑤), where you stay in two-bedroom cottages (BYO linen). *McMillans of Metung*, at 155 Metung Rd, comprises eleven very comfortable, fully equipped cottages of different sizes in a garden setting, with a solar-heated pool, tennis court and a private jetty (☎03/5156 2283; ⑥–⑧). *Bancrofts by the Bay*, 28 Main Rd (☎03/5156 2216; ⑧) is an upmarket B&B overlooking Bancroft Bay; the hostess cooks an excellent dinner in the holiday season and at weekends. The *Metung Hotel* has inexpensive accommodation and also offers bistro **meals** (☎03/5156 2206; ④). The pleasant *Little Mariners Cafe* at Shop 3, 57 Metung Rd has light meals and local seafood on the daily dinner menu; while the *Mediterranae* at 50 Metung Rd (holidays daily, rest of the year lunch Sat & Sun, dinner Tues–Sun) is pricier: both are BYO.

Buchan and the Snowy River Loop

Nowa Nowa is the inauspiciously named town where you turn north off the Princes Highway for Buchan, in the foothills of the Victorian Alps, and take a satisfying loop through the Snowy River National Park. The small town of **BUCHAN** has impressive underground limestone formations, which can be seen on guided tours of two **caves**: the Royal Cave (daily 11am, 1pm & 3pm; 45min; $8) and the Fairy Cave (same times; 45min; $10), with additional tours from October to mid-April. In the extensive park surrounding them there's an icy, spring-fed swimming pool, playground, walking tracks, and a campsite, plus lots of wildlife.

The delightfully idiosyncratic *Holloways Colonial Tea Rooms and B&B* (☎03/5155 9329; ⑥), tucked away in a valley near Buchan South, serves excellent Devonshire teas, light lunches and hearty dinners – call for bookings and directions. In Buchan itself, on the north bank of the Buchan River, is the comfortable *Buchan Lodge* (☎ & fax 03/5155 9421; ①), an overnight stop for the Oz Experience bus. Accommodation is in dorms, and facilities include a volleyball court. The lodge also organizes bushwalking, abseiling, caving, horse-riding, canoeing and rafting.

The road continues north from Buchan through hilly country, following the Murrindal River and slowly winding its way up to the plateau of the Australian Alps. The sealed road ends at Wulgumerang, just before the *Seldom Seen Roadhouse*, where you can get fuel and supplies, and the turn-off to McKillops Bridge. You can continue straight up to Jindabyne in the Snowy Mountains of New South Wales, but about two-thirds of the road is unsealed and can be rough; check road conditions before setting out.

Snowy River National Park

Turning right at Wulgumerang, about 55km north of Buchan, enables you to make a scenic arc through the northern end and around the eastern fringe of the **Snowy River National Park**, following the unsealed road towards Bonang (check road conditions in advance, as this is an unsealed road that can deteriorate badly in adverse weather conditions). **Little River Falls** are well worth a stop on this stretch: a short walk leads from the car park past snow gums to a lookout with breathtaking views of Little River Gorge and the falls. The view from the second lookout from the top of the northeastern cliff face of **Little River Gorge** is equally stunning (about 10min from the car park).

Further on, you descend to the valley of the Snowy River, which you cross at **McKillops Bridge**, set in the landscape that inspired "Banjo" Paterson's famous ballad, "The Man from Snowy River". The river's sandy banks are a favourite swimming spot, and also the place to set out on a **rafting** trip through deep gorges, caves, raging rapids and tranquil pools; Snowy River Expeditions in Buchan (☎03/5155 9353) offers good-value expeditions. If you want to play at being "the man from Snowy River", contact Snowy Mountain Rider Tours, in **Gelantipy**, to arrange **horse-riding** (1hr $15;

half-day $40) or an overnight camping trip; in addition they organize rafting, abseiling and rock-climbing adventures. The operators also run the *Karoonda Park YHA* (☎03/5155 0220, fax 5155 0308; dorms ①, rooms ②–③). Oz Experience buses pass through Gelantipy, the Wayward Bus stops here overnight on the Mountains and Rivers tour from Melbourne to Sydney.

Bonang and the Errinundra National Park

The road through the Snowy River National Park continues until it meets the Bonang–Orbost road. The general store (☎02/6458 0265) at **BONANG**, a former gol-drush town, sells takeaway food, groceries and fuel and has some information about the area. The rustic *Delegate River Tavern*, on the Monaro high plains about fifteen min-utes' drive north from Bonang across the NSW border, is open daily for counter **meals** and has good-value B&B **accommodation** in log cabins (☎02/6458 8009; ④).

The road down from the plateau to the coast, still mostly unsealed, leads past the **Errinundra National Park**, which protects magnificent wetland eucalypt forests con-taining giant, centuries-old specimens, as well as Victoria's largest surviving stand of **rainforest**. At **Errinundra Saddle**, in the heart of the park, there's a delightful picnic area and a self-guided boardwalk through the forest (about 40min). Take special care while driving, for all roads in the area are heavily used by logging trucks.

Orbost

The road from Bonang eventually leads to the old-fashioned town of **ORBOST**, on the Princes Highway where it crosses the Snowy River. There's a tranquil picnic spot oppo-site the *Orbost Caravan Park*, on the corner of Lochiel and Nicholson streets (☎03/5154 1097; on-site vans ②), with huge gums lining one bank and cows roaming the paddocks on the other. The **Orbost Visitors Centre** on Lochiel Street (daily 9am–5pm) books accommodation and tours, but staff don't seem to be particularly knowledgeable or friendly. Part of the centre has a small exhibition on Victoria's three types of rainforest.

Croajingolong National Park

From Orbost to **CANN RIVER** the Princes Highway continues well inland, not to reach the coast again until Eden, across the border in New South Wales. The Parks Victoria ranger office, on the Princes Highway in Cann River (Mon–Fri 9am–4pm; ☎03/5158 6351), provides information on the **Croajingolong National Park**, which begins southeast of the town at Sydenham Inlet and continues for 100km along the coast to the state border. Within the park, foothills cloaked in warm temperate rainforest drop down to the unspoilt "Wilderness Coast". There are several scenic camping spots in the park, which are very popular in summer and allocated way in advance by a ballot system. You can also stay in the lighthouse keeper's cottage of Point Hicks Lighthouse at Cape Everard (☎03/5158 4268; whole cottage sleeps eight people; for cottage ⑧). If you want to break your journey, Cann River itself offers very good-value **accommodation** at three motels – the cheapest being the *Cann River Motel* on the Princes Highway (☎03/5158 6255; ③–④) – and at the *Cann River Caravan Park* at the junction of Princes and Cann Valley highways (☎03/5158 6369; ②), which has on-site vans for rent.

Mallacoota and around

MALLACOOTA is a holiday resort actually within the Croajingolong National Park, on the lake system of the **Mallacoota Inlet**. It's approached via Genoa, 47km east from Cann River along the Princes Highway. About 10km from Genoa, a turn-off to the left leads to **Gipsy Point**, an idyllic spot near the confluence of the Genoa and Wallagaraugh rivers on the upper reaches of the Mallacoota Inlet; it's a fine place to spend a blissful day or two.

Your logical first step on arriving in Mallacoota itself is to head for the **Mallacoota Information and Booking Service**, 57 Maurice Ave (Christmas–Easter daily 8.30am–7.30pm; rest of the year Mon–Fri 9am–5pm, Sat 9am–noon; ☎03/5158 0788), where you can sort out your accommodation. Natural Adventures, Shop 3, Lincoln Lane (☎03/5158 0166), a **tour** company with an emphasis on wilderness adventures, makes the natural attractions of the surrounding area more accessible. Activities range from 4WD tours, guided walks, and kayaking on the lakes and rivers of Croajingolong National Park and the ocean offshore. Rankins Hire Cruises (☎03/5158 0555) arranges leisurely **cruises** via Bottom Lake and Top Lake and Wallagaraugh River up to the New South Wales border, or you can explore on your own by renting a boat or canoe from Buckland's Jetty Boat Hire (☎03/5158 0660). The **Parks Victoria** office, on the corner of Allan and Buckland drives (☎03/5158 0219), has details of secluded camping spots and local **bushwalks**.

During the summer Mallacoota, although seemingly remote, teems with avid holiday-makers, the most conspicuous of which are teenagers making use of their first cars to get a taste of freedom. Mallacoota's small population of just over a thousand trebles again for the Easter "Carnival in Coota" **arts festival**, which includes all sorts of music, theatre and comedy, a community market, and fascinating sand sculptures.

Practicalities

Several **accommodation** options are located outside Mallacoota (and away from the summer crowds): try the friendly B&B *Mareeba Lodge*, 59 Mirrabooka Rd (☎03/5158 0378, fax 5158 0050; ④–⑤). **Mudbrick** houses have really caught on here. One of the trendsetters was Peter Kurz, owner of the *Adobe Flats* at 17 Karbeethong Ave, Karbeethong, 4km northwest of town (☎03/5158 0329; ③–④; no linen); these cosy mudbrick apartments boast beautiful views of Bottom Lake and are located in an area teeming with birdlife. In Mallacoota itself, just behind the *Mallacoota Hotel* is the pleasant **YHA hostel**, *Mallacoota Lodge* (☎03/5158 0455, fax 5158 0453; units ③–④, dorms ①), which has accommodation in renovated motel units.

Choices for **food** are very limited. *Naomi's Gourmet Deli*, next to the newsagent on Allan Drive, does light meals and serves good coffee, while the *Tide Bistro*, on Maurice Avenue, is probably the best place in town for dinner. Otherwise, counter meals are served at the *Mallacoota Hotel* nearby. Other distractions include **bands** at the *Mallacoota Hotel* every night in January, and a summer **cinema** at the Mallacoota Community Centre, Allen Drive. Bank of Melbourne, the only **bank**, is at 58 Maurice Ave (Mon–Fri 9.30am–12.30pm & 1.30–3.30pm), but there are EFTPOS facilities at the Mobil service station and the supermarket.

Gipsy Point, about 20km northwest, has the friendly *Gipsy Point Motel & Apartments*, set in a garden by the Wallagaraugh River (☎03/5158 8200, fax 5158 8308, free call ☎1800/688 200; ④–⑦); it has accommodation in attractive en-suite rooms or new apartments, and serves counter meals. The *Gipsy Point Lodge*, nearby on McDonald Street, has B&B rooms and cottages (free call ☎1800/063 556, fax 03/5158 8205; ④–⑤) and arranges bird-watching and bushwalking excursions.

THE NORTHEAST

The **Hume Highway**, the direct route between Melbourne and Sydney, cuts straight through Victoria's northeast – an area that has become known as **Ned Kelly country**. **Euroa**, **Benalla** and **Glenrowan** (where the outlaw was finally seized after a bloody shoot-out) all have traces of the masked bushranger's activities, with Glenrowan whole-heartedly cashing in on his fame. West of the Hume, **Rutherglen**, right up against the state border, is Victoria's oldest established wine-producing region. There are also vineyards in the rich fruit-growing region of the **Goulburn Valley**, north along the Goulburn Valley Highway from **Seymour**.

Bushwalking in the Alpine region is most easily organized by going through an out-door tour operator such as Bogong Jack Adventures (☎08/8383 7198, fax 8383 7377).

V/Line runs several **train and bus routes** through the northeast. The Melbourne–Albury train service goes via Seymour, Euroa, Benalla, Glenrowan, Wangaratta, Chiltern and Wodonga (at least 4 daily). There are also trains and buses from Melbourne to Shepparton, with connections to Cobram and Tocumwal in NSW (2–3 daily). Buses depart from Albury to Bendigo via Wangaratta and Benalla (1 daily). Bus services to Rutherglen are rather limited: from Albury (4 weekly in the morning). From Melbourne, there's a train to Wangaratta and then a connecting bus (3 weekly in late afternoon).

The Goulburn Valley

The **Goulburn River** rises at Lake Eildon and flows through Seymour, Nagambie and Shepparton to join the Murray just east of Echuca. The rich plains of the Goulburn Valley yield much **fruit**, and there's an important fruit-canning industry based at Shepparton, as well as several **wineries**.

Seymour is the first major stop on the Hume Highway out of Melbourne; an impor-tant train interchange, it's an uninspiring place for the visitor. The Goulburn Valley Highway begins here, heading north to **NAGAMBIE** on the shores of the man-made Lake Nagambie. The town itself is uninteresting, but two prominent **wineries** nearby add some welcome flavour. **Chateau Tahbilk** (Mon–Sat 9am–5pm, Sun 11am–5pm), 6km southwest, is the oldest continually operating winery and vineyard in Victoria: it opened in 1860 and survived the phylloxera blight that devastated the Australian wine industry in the 1890s. The Shiraz and Marsanne are still made from the old vines that have seen more than 130 harvests. The whitewashed buildings have been well pre-served and there are extensive grounds to explore. In complete contrast is the ultra-modern **Mitchelton Winery** (daily 10am–5pm; guided tours on weekends by arrange-ment; 1hr; $5; ☎03/5794 2710), 14km southwest of Nagambie in Mitchellstown, off the Goulburn Valley Highway: its distinctive sixty-metre observation tower features on the Mitchelton label. The extensive riverside grounds have a pool and barbecues, which draw the crowds on Sunday. At the *Mitchelton Restaurant & Winebar,* overlooking the river, the wines from the winery are matched with outstanding food, using regional pro-duce (daily 10.30am–3pm). **Cruises** ply the Goulburn River between Chateau Tahbilk and the Mitchelton Winery (Sept–April Sat & Sun; other days on demand; 2–3hr; $12.50 or $25 including lunch on the boat; ☎03/5794 2877). The **Nagambie Lakes Visitor Information Centre**, at 145 High St (daily 9am–5pm; ☎03/5794 2647), also deals with bookings for V/Line; or get your tickets at the newsagent, at 310 High St. As few peo-ple stop over in town, **accommodation** is very inexpensive: try the *Nagambie Goulburn Valley Highway Motel*, 143 High St (☎03/5794 2681; ③–④), or the *Nagambie Caravan Park* next door (☎03/5794 2681; on-site vans ②).

The small city of **SHEPPARTON** is the operations centre for the SPC and Ardmona canned fruit companies, with peaches, pears, apples and plums tinned and exported worldwide; with its pleasant riverside picnic spots, it also makes a good place to stop for a while on the way to Echuca. **Tourist information** is located beside Victoria Park Lake in the south of town, at 534 Wyndham St on the Goulburn Valley Highway (daily 9am–5pm; free call ☎1800/808 839). A place **to stay** for budget travellers is the *River*

Road Holiday Camp (☎03/5823 1656; ①) which has dorms, a pool and tennis courts; during the harvest season from December to March there's a transport service to the farms.

The Hume Highway and Kelly Country

Forty-seven kilometres beyond Seymour, **EUROA** is a far more attractive place – a small, friendly town with many fine red-brick buildings. The **Euroa Visitor Information Centre** is located at 25 Kirkland Ave (☎03/5794 2647). Binney Street has a pleasant, old-fashioned feel, with the colourful and airy *Blue River Deli* serving fresh coffee, gourmet sandwiches and other goods. At 50 Binney St, the Euroa Community Exchange Centre (Tues–Fri 9am–5pm) is a relaxed place with a small café. For **accommodation**, try the *Euroa Caravan Park*, Kirkland Avenue (☎03/5795 2160; on-site vans ②–③), which sits by the creek among huge gum trees; or the *Euroa Motel*, on the Old Hume Highway (☎03/5795 2211; ④), which has inexpensive, if ageing, units.

BENALLA, 45km northeast of Euroa on the Hume Highway, is a rather civilized town on the lake of the same name, formed by the Broken River which runs through town and occasionally floods it. The helpful **tourist information centre**, 14 Mair St (daily 10am–5pm; ☎03/5762 1749), has lots of pamphlets and information on the region. It's a pleasant enough place to stop, with a self-service tearoom, craft shop and views overlooking Lake Benalla. The **Costume and Pioneer Museum** ($2), in the same building, displays a collection of women's dresses from the 1930s but more fittingly has a range of Ned Kelly relics, including the green silk cummerbund he was awarded as a child for saving a friend from drowning, and which he proudly wore when captured. The **Benalla Art Gallery**, in a lovely setting across the lake (daily 10am–5pm; $3), has a fine collection of early twentieth-century and contemporary Australian art. The town is a major centre for **gliding** and **ballooning**; call the Gliding Club of Victoria (☎03/5762 1058) or Balloon Flights Victoria (☎03/5798 5417) to find out about flights. For something to **eat**, try Hides Bakery at 111 Bridge St, which prepares excellent vegetarian pies, salads and sandwiches; or the Toast Office at 3 Bridge St.

Glenrowan and Kelly's last stand

GLENROWAN, 29km on from Benalla, was the site of the **Kelly Gang's last stand**. You're never allowed to forget it: a gigantic effigy of Ned Kelly, in full iron-armour regalia, greets you as you enter town, and there are lots of other tawdry attractions along the highway, such as the Last Stand Show (daily 9.30am–4.30pm; 40min; $15), a "computerized animated theatre" using dummies shuffling around on cue to dramatize the story of the siege – your money's better spent elsewhere. The last stand itself took place in Siege Street near the train station. Along the rail lines north of town, a small stone monument marks the spot where Kelly forced railworkers to rip up a section of the track, to try to derail the trainful of troopers he had lured to the town; overlooking the town to the west is Mount Glenrowan, which the bushrangers used as a lookout.

More interesting and far better value than the Last Stand Show is **Kate's Cottage and Ned Kelly Memorial** (daily 9am–5.30pm; $3), a replica of the Kelly home. With its bare earth floor, bark roof and newspaper-lined walls, it speaks volumes of the deprivation that drove the family towards crime. An evocative audiotape narrates Ned's story from childhood and is interspersed with folk songs inspired by his life. The original homestead, 9km west along Kelly Gap Road, is now nothing more than rubble and a brick chimney.

Wangaratta

The small city of **WANGARATTA**, at the junction of the Ovens and King rivers, 16km from Glenrowan, is a convenient overnight stop between Sydney and Melbourne, but there are few other reasons to linger. The highway on either side of "Wang" is lined with motels, and the staff at **Wangaratta Tourist Information**, on the corner of Handley Street and Tone Road (daily 9am–5pm; ☎03/5721 5711), can book local tours and accommodation and give out stacks of leaflets about the area. The **Wangaratta Arts Centre**, on Ovens Street (☎03/5722 0865), is a fine old red-brick building containing a gallery (Wed–Sun 10am–5pm; free) which has a changing programme of exhibitions and hosts occasional music recitals on Sunday afternoon. The four-day **Wangaratta Festival of Jazz**, beginning on the Friday prior to the Melbourne Cup

THE NED KELLY STORY

Even before Ned Kelly became widely known, folklore and ballads were popularizing the free-ranging bush outlaws as potent symbols of freedom and resistance to authority. By the time he was 11, **Ned Kelly**, son of an alcoholic rustler and a mother who sold illicit liquor, was already in constant trouble with the police, who considered the whole family troublemakers; constables in the area were instructed to "endeavour, whenever the Kellys commit any paltry crime, to bring them to justice . . . the object [is] to take their prestige away from them".

Ned became the accomplice of the established bushranger **Harry Power**, and by his mid-teens had a string of warrants to his name. Ned's brother, Dan, was also wanted by the police and, hearing that he had turned up at his mother's, a policeman set out, drunk and without a warrant, to arrest him. A scuffle ensued and the unsteady constable fell to the floor, hitting his head and allowing Dan to escape. The following day warrants were issued for the arrest of Ned (who was in New South Wales at the time) and Dan for attempted murder; their mother was sentenced to three years' imprisonment.

From this point on, the **Kelly gang**'s crime spree accelerated and, following the death of three constables in a shoot-out at Stringybark Creek, the biggest manhunt in Australia's history began, with a £1000 reward offered for the gang's apprehension. On December 9, 1878 they robbed the bank at Euroa, taking £2000, before moving on to Jerilderie in New South Wales, where another bank was robbed and Kelly penned the famous **Jerilderie Letter**, describing the "big, ugly, fat-necked, wombat-headed, big-bellied, magpie-legged, narrow-hipped, splay-footed sons of Irish bailiffs or English landlords which is better known as Officers of Justice or Victoria Police" who had forced him onto the wrong side of the law.

After a year on the run, the gang formulated a grand plan: they executed Aaron Sherritt, a police informer, in Sebastopol, thus attracting a trainbound posse from nearby Beechworth; this train was derailed at Glenrowan with as much bloodshed as possible before the gang moved on to rob the bank at Benalla and barter hostages for the release of Kelly's mother. In the event, having already sabotaged the tracks, the gang commandeered the *Glenrowan Inn* and, in a moment of drunken candour, Kelly detailed his ambush to a schoolteacher who escaped, managing to save the special train. As the armed troopers approached the inn, the gang donned the homemade **iron armour** that has since become their motif. In the ensuing gunfight Kelly's comrades were either killed or they committed suicide as the inn was torched, while Ned himself was taken alive, tried by the same judge who had incarcerated his mother, and sentenced to hang.

Public sympathies lay strongly with Ned Kelly, and a crowd of five thousand gathered outside Melbourne Gaol on November 11, 1880 for his execution, believing that the 25-year-old bushranger would "die game". True to form, his last words are said to have been "Such is life."

(usually the last weekend in October), is one of the premier jazz events in the country; book somewhere to stay well in advance if you're planning to attend.

There is a vast range of **accommodation**. Good choices include the *Wangaratta Central Motel*, 11 Ely St, next to Merriwa Park (☎03/5721 2188; ④); the *Billabong Motel*, 12 Chisholm St (☎03/5721 2353; ③), with good-value singles; and the modern *Hermitage Motor Inn,* corner of Mackay and Cusack streets (☎03/5721 7444, fax 5722 1812; ⑤), which has a pool. In terms of **food**, there's *Scribbler's Coffee Lounge*, 66 Reid St, otherwise the choice seems to be mainly between pizza and pizza: *Café Martini* at the *Bull's Head Hotel*, 87 Murphy St bakes them in a wood-fired oven, *D'Amico's* at the corner of Vincent and Greta roads does them very cheaply, but probably the best are served at *Hollywoods Gourmet Pizza Restaurant* on the corner of Ford and Murphy streets (open until 2am on weekends).

V/Line operates a daily **bus service** from Wangaratta to Bright via Beechworth, and a bus service three times a week to Rutherglen.

Beechworth

Thirty-five kilometres east of Wangaratta, off the Ovens Highway, is **BEECH-WORTH**, once the centre of the rich **Ovens gold-mining region**. Sited picturesquely in the foothills of the Victorian Alps, the entire town has been acknowledged by the National Trust as being of historic significance, and the surrounding area has been designated a **historic park** by the Department of Conservation and Natural Resources. The **visitors information centre** is located in the old shire office on Ford Street (daily 9am–5pm; ☎03/5728 3233), and can provide you with pamphlets on noteworthy sights and places of interest, as well as give out information on the Gorge Scenic Drive (see below).

As is true in so many other towns in the northeast, Beechworth is rich in **Ned Kelly** history. The **government buildings** on Ford Street house the imposing HM Training Prison, where he and his mother were incarcerated before the 1880 trial, and the **courthouse** (daily 9am–5pm; $2) where the fatal trial was held. Opposite, underneath the town hall, is the grim cell where he was imprisoned as a teenager (daily 10am–4pm; 20¢) The **Burke Museum** on Loch Street (daily 9am–4.30pm; $5) displays relics of the goldrush and tells the story of the Chinese miners who flocked here. The museum is dedicated to the explorer Robert O'Hara Burke, one-time Superintendent of Police in Beechworth, who perished with William John Wills on their historic journey from Melbourne to the Gulf of Carpentaria (see box on p.486). On Last Street there's the century-old **Murray Brewery Cellars** (daily 9am–5pm; free), which has displays of old bottles and brewery machinery. The **Rock Cavern** on Camp Street (same hours; free), exhibits gemstones and minerals. On Railway Avenue, in the goods shed of the old train station, is the National Trust **Carriage Museum** (daily 10am–noon & 1–4pm; $2), whose twenty beautifully restored examples include a Cobb & Co stagecoach.

The five-kilometre, one-way route of the **Gorge Scenic Drive** begins at Sydney Road and ends at Bridge Street, along the western edge of the town. It includes the famous Spring and Reid creeks, which supported eight thousand diggers in 1852, as well as natural features such as Flat Rock, Telegraph Rock and Woolshed Falls. The route also passes the granite **powder magazine** (daily 10am–noon & 1–4pm; $2), formerly a storehouse for blasting powder and now a National Trust museum.

Practicalities

There's a very good choice of B&B **accommodation** in Beechworth: try *Rose Cottage*, 42 Camp St (☎ & fax 03/5728 1069; ⑥) or the newly converted coachhouse (☎03/5728 2223, fax 5728 2883; ⑧) behind the *Bank Restaurant* at 86 Ford St, which has two stylish suites. Another good-value place is *The Priory*, on Priory Lane (a continuation of

Loch Street), almost at the corner of Church Street (☎03/5728 1024, fax 5728 2035; ④), a historic B&B with very reasonably priced singles. If you want peace and quiet, it's best to come at the weekend, when the school groups have gone. The *Hibernian Hotel*, on the corner of Camp and Lochiel streets (☎03/5728 1070, fax 5728 2883; ③–④), and *Tanswells Commercial Hotel*, 30 Ford St (☎03/5728 1480; ③–④), are historic pubs that also offer B&B accommodation. The latter has been continuously licensed since 1853 and has pleasant **bars** and bistro **food**. The *Beechworth Bakery*, 27 Camp St (daily 6.30am–6pm), sells delicious pies, bread, cakes and pastries, and on sunny days you can have breakfast on the balcony. A good, though expensive, place for lunch or dinner is *The Parlour & Pantry* at 69 Ford St (lunch Wed–Mon, dinner Thurs–Sun during the holiday season; licensed and BYO), where only local produce is used in the imaginative dishes, which are complemented by an extensive wine list. If you really want to splurge, head for the *Bank Restaurant*, in the Bank of Australia building at 86 Ford St (licensed; ☎03/5728 2223). Depending on the day, dinners will either be formal and candlelit (Thurs–Sat) or a simpler, more rustic affair (Mon–Wed & Sun).

V/Line has a **bus service** from Wangaratta to Beechworth, and further on to Brught (2–3 daily Mon–Fri, 1 daily Sat & Sun; ☎13 6196), and Beechworth Buslines (☎03/5722 1843) has a service twice daily (Mon–Fri) from Beechworth to Albury and Wodonga.

Chiltern

CHILTERN, a sleepy former gold-mining centre with a well-preserved, mid-nineteenth-century streetscape, lies just off the Hume Highway about 40km from Wangaratta. The setting – with a bit of recent architectural licence on Conness Street – has been used in several period films. Although no longer licensed, the **Star Hotel** is still set up with the original bar and taps, an authentic background to a rather more ordinary souvenir and craft shop. For $2 you can gain access to the back (Fri–Wed) to look at a **monster vine**: planted in 1867 and reputedly Australia's largest, it once produced a single yield of over 6kg of grapes. The 1866 **Athenaeum** (Sat & public holidays 10am–3pm; $2) is now a local history museum that features a collection of paintings by the obsessive local artist Alfred Eustace, who would use any available medium to paint on: paper, cardboard, even large gum leaves. **Dows Pharmacy Museum**, also on Conness Street (daily 10am–5pm; $2), has an extensive collection of old pharmaceutical equipment. Chiltern's most interesting attraction, however, is **Lake View** (Sat, Sun & daily in school holidays 10am–noon & 1–4pm; $2), on the shores of Lake Anderson, near the train station. It was built in 1870 and was, for a short period, the home of the writer Ethel Florence Lindesay (1870–1946) who, under the pseudonym of **Henry Handel Richardson**, immortalized the house in the novel *Ultima Thule*, the last book in the trilogy *The Fortunes of Richard Mahoney*. For **refreshment**, stop in at the *Mulberry Tree Restaurant and Tearooms* on Conness Street.

Rutherglen

RUTHERGLEN, 18km west of Chiltern and 32km west of Wodonga on the Murray River Highway, is at the heart of Victoria's oldest wine-producing region, renowned for its excellent fortified wines, Rutherglen Muscat and Tokay. Fifteen **wineries** are situated in the area, most of them third- or fourth-generation establishments with cellars full of character. The landscape is rather disappointing, consisting largely of flat paddocks of cattle and sheep where you'd expect undulating vineyards. In fact, wine making has always been just one of a range of farming activities in this area, where diversification remains the key to survival. The weather partly accounts for the quality of Rutherglen's fortified wines: the long, mild autumns allow the grapes to stay on the vines for longer, producing higher levels of sugar in the fruit. All the wineries are open for free **tastings** and cellar door sales from 10am to 5pm, Monday to Saturday – Sunday hours differ from place to place.

The **tourist information centre**, at 13–21 Drummond St (daily 9am–5pm; ☎02/6032 9166), has stacks of brochures, including the informative *Rutherglen Touring Guide* and map published by the wine makers of Rutherglen. Besides selling local wines, the Vintage Cellar, 84 Main St (☎02/6032 9784), also rents out bicycles. On the Queen's Birthday weekend in June the town hosts the **Winery Walkabout**, when the new season's releases are presented to the public – one of Australia's biggest wine-tasting festivals. **Tastes of Rutherglen**, another festive event, is held over the Victorian Labour Day weekend in mid-March; at this time some of the best local restaurants guest-star at the wineries, in a celebration of fine food and wine.

Rutherglen is a popular weekend getaway from Melbourne, so **accommodation** can be hard to find at that time; during the week you'll have no problem. The focus of the small town is the National Trust-listed *Victoria Hotel*, 90 Main St (☎02/6032 9610, fax 6032 8128; ③–④), where you can both eat and sleep. On the walls of the bar is a framed cover of the June 28, 1880 *Melbourne Herald* chronicling the capture of the Kelly Gang, which makes for fascinating reading while you imbibe on the local wines. A good value B&B is *Country Cottage Accommodation* (☎02/6032 8328; ⑤); one of the many motels is the *Walkabout Motel* (☎02/6032 9572, fax 6032 8187; ④–⑤), both on the Murray Valley Highway.

The Snowfields and the High Country

The **Victorian Alps**, the southern extension of the Great Dividing Range, bear little resemblance to their European counterparts; they're too gentle, too rounded, and above all too low to offer really great **skiing**. Nonetheless in July and August there is usually plenty of snow, and the resorts are packed out. Most people come here for the downhill skiing, though the **cross-country skiing**, which is rapidly growing in popularity, is excellent: **Lake Mountain**, 21km from Marysville, is the region's premier cross-country destination. **Snowboarding**, a relatively new alpine sport, was first encouraged at Mount Hotham and is now firmly established almost everywhere, especially with "cross-over" skateboarders and surfers. **Falls Creek**, **Mount Hotham** and **Mount Buller** are the largest and most commercial skiing areas, particularly the last which is within easy reach of Melbourne; smaller resorts such as **Mount Baw Baw** are more suited to beginners. While you wouldn't come to Victoria especially to ski, you might as well give it a go if you're here at the right time of year, though be warned that accommodation prices may take your breath away.

In summer, when the wild flowers are in bloom, the alps are ideal **bushwalking** territory, with most of the high mountains (and the ski resorts) contained within the vast **Alpine National Park**. The most famous of the walks is the four-hundred-kilometre **Alpine Trail**, which begins in Baw Baw National Park, near Walhalla in Gippsland, and follows the ridges all the way to Mount Kosciuszko in the Snowy Mountains of New South Wales. If you are doing any serious bushwalking, you'll need to be properly equipped. Even in summer it can be very cold up here, especially at night; the weather can change suddenly and unexpectedly; and it's often surprisingly hard to find water. **Mansfield** and **Bright** are good bases for exploration of the alps and great places to unwind. In summer the ski resorts can be ugly and only half the facilities are open, but there are often great bargains to be had on rooms.

If you're **driving**, you'll need snow chains in winter (they're compulsory in many parts), and you should heed local advice before venturing off the main roads.

Mansfield and Merrijig

MANSFIELD is located at the junction of the Maroondah and Midland highways, just a few kilometres north of Lake Eildon, 140km east of Seymour and 63km south of Benalla. As the main approach to Mount Buller, it's a lively place with good pubs, restaurants and a cinema. The annual highlight is the **Mountain Country Festival** in early November, which begins the weekend prior to the Melbourne Cup in November; activities include a picnic race known as the "Melbourne Cup of the bush". At the end of April hundreds of hot-air-balloon pilots flock here for the three-day **Mansfield Balloon Festival**.

V/Line has a year-round **bus** service from Melbourne to Mansfield (1–2 daily; 3hr). The helpful **Mansfield Visitor Information Centre**, at the Old Railway Station on High Street (daily 10am–5pm; ☎03/5775 1464 or free call ☎1800/060 686 for accommodation bookings), has complete information on all sights and activities, including walks in the surrounding country. If you're interested in skiing, contact the **ski centre** at 149 High St (☎03/5775 1624) during the ski season (mid-June to end of Sept). Out of season you have a choice of horse-riding, hiking, climbing, abseiling, hang-gliding, rafting, canoeing or 4WD tours. Among the many local outfits are Stirling Experience (☎03/5775 3541), for 4WD tours around Mount Buller and Mount Stirling (see overleaf); Stoney's Bluff and Beyond Trail Rides, Mount Buller Road (☎03/5775 2212), for great trail rides; and Mountain Adventure Safaris (☎03/5777 3759 or 0418/574 746), for rafting, canoeing and other activities.

The *Alzburg Inn Resort*, 39 Malcolm St (☎03/5775 2367, fax 5775 2719; ⑤–⑥), more expensive in winter; B&B available), is a popular **hotel** for skiers, while somewhat lower in price is the neat and friendly *Mansfield Backpacker Inn*, 112 High St (☎03/5775 1800, fax 5775 1589; rooms ②, dorms ①), which organizes all sorts of activities, particularly hang-gliding. The managers also have good work contacts for fruit-picking in summer and for the Mount Buller ski resort in winter. The *Mansfield Travel Lodge* next door (same phone number; ④–⑤) has motel units and is managed by the same people. The area around Mansfield is renowned for **luxurious B&Bs**, the most famous of which is the very expensive *Howqua Dale Gourmet Retreat*, south of town near Howqua (☎03/5777 3503, fax 5777 3896; ⑧), which is run by two chefs and is renowned for its outstanding food; cooking courses are sometimes held here. On a more modest scale are the *Alpine Country Cottages*, 5 The Parade (☎03/5775 1694, fax 5775 1586; ⑦), two cottages sleeping four people each, and with a spa on the premises; and, further afield in Barwite (on the Mansfield–Whitfield road), the lovely *Wombat Hills Cottage* at 55 Lochiel Rd (☎ & fax 03/5776 9507; ⑦), which has three bedrooms, tennis courts, and great views of Mount Buller and the Mansfield Valley.

In winter, Mansfield–Buller Bus Lines run frequent bus services for skiing from Mansfield to Mount Buller in conjunction with the V/Line bus service from Melbourne to Mansfield (☎03/5775 2606).

Merrijig

The small town of **MERRIJIG**, a little under halfway to Mount Buller from Mansfield, is largely responsible for the great number of **riding** outfits in the area. The breathtaking high-country scenery nearby was used as the location for the film *The Man from Snowy River*, and visitors have been trying to live out their fantasies ever since. If you want to combine riding with lodge **accommodation**, try *Merrijig Lodge and Trail Rides*, Mount Buller Road (☎03/5777 5590; ⑤). There's also a cluster of country B&Bs in the vicinity: one of the most pleasant is *Black Horse Park B&B*, on a farm 7km south of the Mount Buller–Merrijig road (☎03/5777 5530; ⑦; cheaper for small groups), which has two cottages each with en-suite facilities; they also organize trail rides and other activities.

Mount Buller and Mount Stirling

To reach **MOUNT BULLER ALPINE VILLAGE**, 48km from Mansfield, you ascend gradually upwards on Summit Road, a smooth, sealed road. With 7000 beds, 24 modern ski lifts and 80km of runs, it has the greatest capacity of any Australian ski resort.

In **winter**, during the ski season, the Central Reservation Service books **accommodation** and dispenses information about all things skiing (free call ☎1800/039 049; in summer, call the Mansfield Visitor Information Centre on ☎03/5775 1464 or free call ☎1800/060 686). The *ABOM Hotel & Bistro*, on Summit Road on Mount Buller (☎03/5777 6091; ⑧), is the hub of the Alpine Village when it is open in winter. There are great views from here, and further up, on the **summit** of Mount Buller, there's an even more spectacular panorama west to Lake Eildon, north to farmlands and east to Falls Creek and Mount Hotham. The huge *Arlberg Hotel*, 53 Summit Rd (free call ☎1800/032 380; summer ⑥, winter ⑧), provides entertainment in ski season, and has everything from fast food to an expensive restaurant. In winter the budget-conscious can stay at the *Mount Buller YHA Hostel*, on The Avenue right in the centre of the Village (☎03/5777 6181; open June–September; advance booking essential; dorms ④), which has self-catering facilities. The self-catering *ABV Lodge* (☎03/5777 6024 or 9826 0428; dorm bed in summer ②, in winter ④) has beds in bunk rooms and is open all year round.

Mount Stirling, a few kilometres northeast, has more than 60km of maintained trails and is a good place for **cross-country skiing**. The only facility here is *Mount Stirling Alpine Resort*, a large complex at Telephone Box Junction, 9km from the turn-off left at Mirindah along Mount Stirling Road (☎03/5777 6441). As it's a day resort, there's no accommodation, but it has a visitor centre, a ski school (☎03/5777 6441), and rents out skis and mountain bikes. It also does **tours** from Mansfield of the Mount Stirling area ($75 per person; minimum of 2 people; to book, call Mansfield Visitor Information Centre on ☎03/5775 1464 or free call ☎1800/060 686). All roads beyond Telephone Box Junction are open only from the beginning of November until the beginning of June, weather permitting. The fifty-kilometre **Circuit Road** from Telephone Box Junction circumnavigates Mount Stirling, and an access track from this road leads to **Craig's Hut**, which was used as a film set for *The Man from Snowy River*. As sections of Circuit Road are very rough for 2WD vehicles even in good weather conditions, you'll really need a 4WD for this route. In summer, Stirling Experience (☎03/5775 3541) does 4WD tours to Craig's Hut and other destinations around the Mount Buller–Mount Stirling area.

Bright and around

BRIGHT is at the centre of the picturesque Ovens Valley, between Mount Buffalo and Mount Beauty about 75km southeast of Wangaratta on the Ovens Highway. It began life as a gold-mining town in the 1850s and today still has a faintly elegant air, with tall European trees lining the main street and filling the parks. A clear stream flows through Centennial Park, opposite the tourist information centre, and in autumn the glorious colours of the changing leaves make for a very un-Australian scene.

As the ski fields of Mount Hotham, Mount Buffalo and Falls Creek are less than an hour's drive away, the town is popular as a **ski base** in winter. In summer **outdoor activities** are on offer – such as paragliding, hang-gliding, bushwalking, horse-riding and cycling. Alpine Paragliding, 6 Ireland St (☎03/5755 1753), organizes tandem flights for novices, and introductory and full courses leading to a licence. You could take to the air in a powered hang-glider from Bright Micro-Light Centre (☎03/5750 1555) or with the Eagle School of Hang-Gliding (☎03/5755 1724 or 018/570 168), who also do instructor-accompanied tandem flights. Or enjoy a bird's-eye view of the gorgeous mountain scenery from a small plane with Holiday Air Adventures (mobile ☎015/509 191). Freeburgh Trail Rides, on Harrietville Road in Freeburgh, about 4km north of Bright

SKIING PRACTICALITIES

The official start of the ski **season** is the Queen's Birthday long weekend in June (though there may not be enough snow cover until August), lasting through to October. Day-trip or weekend **packages** are the best way to go, and are far cheaper than trying to do it yourself. YHA Travel at 205 King St, Melbourne (☎03/9670 9611), offers packages based at their youth hostel at Mount Buller. Grayline (☎03/9663 4455) and Australian Pacific Tours (☎03/9663 1611) offer day-trips from Melbourne. The best value for money, however, are the day-trips organized by the *Alzburg Inn* at Mansfield (free call ☎1800/033 023) as they leave Melbourne at 4am in the morning and arrive at Mount Buller at about 9am, giving the opportunity for a full day's skiing ($90–100, including a lift pass and beginner's ski lesson). It's also worth checking out the area around Hardware Street in Melbourne, where such companies as Snow Skis, at no. 83 (☎03/9606 1419), Auski, at no. 9 (☎03/9670 1412), Mountain Designs at 377 Little Bourke St (☎03/9670 3354) and Aussie Ski Centre, at 283 Elizabeth St (☎03/9670 4057), can advise on skiing conditions at the resorts, and sell or rent equipment. In South Melbourne at 295 Clarendon St, Ski Man (☎03/9696 4955) also sells and rents out equipment.

The **Alpine Resorts Commission** (☎03/9895 6900) administers the resorts and during the ski season it charges an entry fee of $10–16 per car, depending on the resort. For **weather** and snow conditions, call the **Snow Reports Line** (☎1902/240 523); accommodation bookings are done by **Alpine Reservations Australia** (☎03/9455 1277), or phone the central reservation hotlines of each mountain resort. The free *Australian Alpine News* is good for facts and is available at the Visitor Information Centre in Melbourne as well as in the Alpine region. As a rough guide to **costs**, a ski pass at Mount Buller is $70 per day, ski school $40 per day, and full equipment rental $50 per day.

During the season Mansfield–Mount Buller Bus Lines, 133 High St, Mansfield (☎03/5775 2606), operates a **ski transport service** to Mount Buller; and Stirling Experience (☎03/5777 6441) runs an on-demand service from Mansfield and Merrijig to Mount Stirling (pre-booking essential; price depends on number of people). In Bright, Adina Ski Hire, 15 Ireland St (☎03/5755 1177), and Bright Ski Centre, 22 Ireland St (☎03/5755 1093), rent out skiing and snowboarding equipment, offer package deals including off-mountain accommodation and transport to Mount Hotham, and have up-to-date snow reports and information on road conditions. There's no transport to Mount Buffalo.

(☎03/5755 1370), do very good short horseback rides for beginners; they also have longer rides and can arrange overnight safaris with bushcamping. High Country Expeditions (☎03/5756 2498) offer half- or full-day 4WD trips and camping tours into the high country, while Bright Platypus (☎03/5750 1880) arranges inexpensive night-walks, canoeing trips, mountain-bike tours and other activities.

For a change of pace, visit Boynton's of Bright, a **winery** 10km northwest of Bright at Porepunkah, on the northeast slopes of the Ovens River Valley, which specializes in cool-climate wines (daily 10am–5pm; ☎03/5756 2356). There are picnic areas on its lawns, with spectacular views of Mount Buffalo.

Practicalities

V/Line operates a **bus** service to Bright from Wangaratta (Sun–Fri; 1hr 15min). To **get around**, you can rent a mountain bike from the Sports Centre, 47 Gavan St (☎03/5755 1339) or Cyclepath, 9 Camp St (☎03/5750 1442). The **tourist information centre**, at 119 Gavan St (daily 9am–5pm; ☎03/5755 2275), has complete information on what's happening around town and also books accommodation which is particularly helpful during the busy winter season.

One of the best **budget places to stay** is the *Bright Hikers Hostel* at 4 Ireland St (☎03/5750 1244, fax 5750 1246; rooms ②, dorms ①), right in the centre of town. Its wide range of facilities includes a games room, a room for skiers to dry out their gear; they also book tours and rent out bikes. The *Bright YHA Lodge* Cherry Avenue (☎03/5750 1180, fax 5750 1186; dorm bed ①–②; rooms ③), is a modern hostel built on the foundations of an old lodge and a part of the *Bright Caravan Park*.

The excellent *Ellenvale Holiday Units*, east of town at 68 Delany Ave (☎03/5755 1582; ⑥–⑦), have a solar-heated pool and spa, tennis court and barbecues. Also good-value, and with similar facilities, are the *Mystic Valley Cottages*, 9 Mystic Lane, 2km southeast on the way to Wandiligong (☎03/5750 1502; ⑤–⑥), situated on a hill overlooking the beautiful Wandiligong Valley. Slightly further out (8km from Bright), but set in the valley itself, is the *Mountain View Hotel* (☎03/5755 1311; ③), also known as the *Wandi Pub*, which offers **B&B** accommodation and serves classic Aussie pub food. The best-value **motels** in Bright are the centrally located *Elm Lodge*, 2 Wood St (free call ☎1800/245 845, fax 03/5755 2206; ③–④), and the charming century-old *Alpine Hotel*, 7 Anderson St (☎03/5755 1366; ④). The latter is the focal point of town, with a rowdy bar, good-value bistro meals and excellent breakfasts; the back bar has **bands** on Friday night, and outside there's a sunny beer garden.

Other good **places to eat** are the *Liquid Am-Bar Restaurant Cafe*, opposite the *Alpine Hotel*, which (besides the amber fluid alluded to in its name) also serves good coffee; likewise the *Edelweiss Bakery & Coffee Shop* next to the post office at 5 Ireland St, which also sells good bread and pastries; and the *Bright Bakery* at 80 Gavan St. Two cheap, casual family restaurants are *Alps* at 94 Gavan St and the *Cosy Kangaroo*, across the street. For a big treat there are *Poplar's Restaurant*, at 4/7 Star Rd (☎03/5755 1655), licensed and BYO, open daily for dinner, and *Simone's*, at the Ovens Valley Motor Inn, corner of Ovens Highway and Ashwood Avenue (☎03/5755 2022; licensed; open daily for dinner), which ranks as one of the top Italian restaurants in Victoria. Its offshoot is the equally reputable *Cafe Bacco* at 2D Anderson St (☎03/5750 1711; Wed–Sun lunch and dinner).

Mount Hotham and around

Heading southeast out of Bright on the Alpine Tourist Road, it's 18km to **HARRI-ETVILLE**, tucked just below Mount Hotham and Mount Feathertop. Originally a gold-mining town, it's now a pretty little village of wide, tree-lined streets, and is also a popular skiing base: there are outlets to rent skis and chains, a seasonal shuttle bus service up to the resorts, and several places to stay and eat. Beyond Harrietville, it's a steep ascent to **Mount Hotham** in the Alpine National Park, the "powder snow capital of Australia". Because this is the state's highest ski area, the snow here can be marginally less sticky than elsewhere. **Dinner Plain**, a resort 8km from the summit and about 1500m above sea level, has much more of a cosy, alpine village feel – complete with architect-designed timber houses that are meant to resemble cattlemen's mountain huts – than the somewhat unsightly Hotham "village". **Cross-country trails** lead from Hotham to Dinner Plain. Hotham is also considered the home of Victorian **snow-boarding**, with special facilities, rental and lessons available. During the ski season tractor-driven carts ferry you around the village and to the start of cross-country trails and skiing areas (all day until late; free), and helicopter shuttle flights in winter link Mount Hotham with Falls Creek, only a few minutes away by air. A few lodges and pubs stay open in summer, including the *General Hotel*, which has a bar, bistro, bottle shop and fantastic mountain views. Hotham is set to expand and become a lively all-year **resort**: plans are underway to expand the airstrip at Horsehair Plain, 20km south, into a fully fledged airport capable of handling seventy-seater jet planes.

A few booking centres handle bookings for the mainly lodge-style **accommodation**: for Mount Hotham there are Skicom Mount Hotham (☎03/5759 3522) and Mt Hotham Alpine Accommodation Services ☎03/5759 3525, free call ☎1800/246 462); the Mount Hotham Falls Creek Reservation Centre also does bookings for Dinner Plain (free call

☎1800/354 555) and another number for Dinner Plain is Dinner Plain Central Reservations (free call ☎1800/670 019).

Falls Creek and around

Thirty kilometres east of Bright, in the Upper Kiewa Valley, the town of **Mount Beauty** lies at the base of the state's highest peak, **Mount Bogong** (1986m). **FALLS CREEK**, 32km further along, on the edge of the Bogong High Plains, has a much more villagey feel than its sister resort at Mount Hotham. It also has probably Victoria's **best skiing**, with the largest snow-making system in Victoria to supplement any shortage of the real stuff, a wide variety of downhill pistes, and good cross-country trails. A park for **snowboarders** has been established, too, in the Vertigo Valley near Scott's Chair, a ski lift. For **accommodation** bookings and information, contact Falls Creek Central Reservations (free call ☎1800/033 079). The budget-conscious would do best to stay in Mount Beauty and travel to Falls Creek for their skiing: enquire about packages at the Mount Beauty Accommodation Service (free call ☎1800/033 079). Accommodation options in the valley include *Mountain Creek Lodge* in Tawonga (☎03/5754 4247, fax 5754 4860; motel units ⑤–⑥, dorms ②) and *Janes B&B* in Mount Beauty (☎ & fax 03/5754 4036; ⑥).

Many of the pubs, restaurants and lodges in Falls Creek stay open in **summer**; some of the best are *The Cock 'n Bull*, a pleasant old-English-style pub on the corner of Christie and Slalom streets, *The Man*, a cosy pub on Telemark Street, and the *Winterhaven Restaurant* on Slalom Street. The *Pfefferkorn Lodge* organizes an excellent summer five-day package trip from Melbourne for small groups of budget travellers ($255). The cost includes transport to and from Melbourne with sightseeing stops en route, four nights' dorm-style accommodation, and all meals. Optional extras include rafting trips, mountain-bike tours, abseiling and horse-riding. For bookings, enquire at hostels in Melbourne or call ☎017/847 235.

There's a wide variety of summer **activities** from which to choose: Falls Creek Trail Rides (☎03/5758 3655 or ☎0419/244 773), operating from December to the end of April, has day-rides on the Bogong High Plains, as well as shorter trips; Halleys Comet Quad Chairlift (☎03/5758 3280) takes bushwalkers to the top of Frying Pan Spur (Dec 26–Jan 26 or 27 daily 11am–3pm, Labour Day weekend same hours, Easter weekend same hours; $8); and nature lovers can join Jill from the Australian Alpine Nursery on one of her Alpine Nature Rambles (☎03/5758 3492; $15). From December until the end of March, Bogong Horseback Adventures (☎03/5754 4849, fax 5754 4181), based on a farm at Tawonga near Mount Beauty and run by an enthusiastic, knowledgeable and well-organized couple, organizes overnight **packhorse tours** across the high plains, traversing country that is otherwise only accessible to the most experienced and hardy bushwalkers (4 to 5 days; $520–650); from May to November they do half- and full-day rides through the Kiewa Valley and the lower levels of the Alpine National Park.

As for **festivals**, the entire village of Falls Creek, plus visitors, get together to celebrate the Food, Wine & Wildflower Weekend in mid-January.

Mount Buffalo National Park

Six kilometres northwest of Bright, back along the Ovens Highway, you can turn off into **Mount Buffalo National Park** ($9 per car), which encompasses a huge plateau around Mount Buffalo. **Skiing** here is for beginners to intermediates – and it's a gorgeous place to learn, among surreal-looking snow-covered gum trees. Relatively inexpensive packages, including accommodation at the **Mount Buffalo Chalet**, ski lessons and other fees, can be arranged through Mount Buffalo Reservations (free call ☎1800/037 038). The *Mount Buffalo Inn*, a tiny resort at the ski slopes of the Cresta Valley (☎03/5755 1988; ⑧, including breakfast and evening meal; dorm beds summer ①, winter ③), has motel units as well as dorm beds in a bunkhouse, plus kitchen facilities, a bistro and restaurant.

The park looks at its best in **summer**, though, when there are wild flowers and waterfalls, and it's a great place for walking, water sports and physical activities of all sorts. Among the main attractions is **Mount Buffalo Chalet** (☎03/5755 1500, fax 5755 1892; ⑨, including all meals), built by the Victorian government in 1910 and about a forty-minute drive on a sealed road from the Ovens Highway turn-off. It's very Australian in appearance, with a bottle-green tin roof, but European in feel, surrounded by flowers and magnificent views. You can play croquet on the lawn, and there's a sauna, billiard room, games room and tennis court, plus horse-riding (summer only), and canoes and mountain bikes for rent. The *Chalet Café* (daily 9.30am–4.30pm) is a no-frills, no-views cafeteria; if you want to have a proper meal, book to reserve a place in the main dining room (phone number as for chalet, above). On the way to the chalet, you'll pass **Lake Catani**, where there's the only **camping** in the park (☎03/5755 1466; Nov–April; booking essential), as well as swimming, canoeing, kayaking and trout-fishing; the chalet rents out equipment. **Bent's Lookout**, opposite the chalet, has tremendous views over the Ovens Valley, with small stone cabins doing duty as winter picnic areas. There's a **hang-gliding ramp** near here: if you're experienced and want to leap into the void, contact one of the operators in or near Bright (see p.894). Beyond the chalet a sealed, not too steep road continues to Mount Buffalo itself (1721m).

Mount Baw Baw

The ski village at **MOUNT BAW BAW**, near the edge of the Baw Baw National Park, is considerably south of all the resorts and is, strictly speaking, in Gippsland. It's a quiet little place, commanding magnificent views south over much of Gippsland and consisting mainly of **private lodges** (to make reservations, free call ☎1800/629 578). Otherwise, try the Cascade Ski Apartments (☎03/9764 9939, free call ☎1800/229 229). There are nine ski lifts here, and a lift day-pass costs about $40, a much more reasonable price than at other resorts. As at Mount Buffalo, the ski runs are mainly for beginners and intermediates. In addition to **downhill skiing**, you can ski **cross-country** on 9km of groomed trails.

Getting to the resort is a major problem, its **inaccessibility** is a principal factor hindering its development. There's no public transport to the mountain, and the closest town is Noojee, 48km west. The road between the town and the resort is narrow, steep and winding. To make matters worse, there are lots of logging trucks thundering along, so take care.

travel details

V/Line monopolizes transport within Victoria, with a comprehensive combination of **train** and **bus** services; Melbourne, Ballarat and Geelong are the main interchanges. Following are the main V/Line Victorian services; local buses are detailed in the text.

Trains

Melbourne to: Albury (4–6 daily; 3hr 35min) via Euroa (1hr 40min), Benalla (2hr) and Wangaratta (2hr 30min); Ballarat (6–10 daily; 1hr 40min); Bendigo (5–9 daily; 2hr) via Castlemaine (1hr 35min); Echuca (2 weekly; 3hr 20min) via Bendigo (2hr); Geelong (9–24 daily; 1hr); Sale (1–3 daily; 2hr 35min); Shepparton (2 daily; 2hr 20min); Swan Hill (1–2 daily; 4hr 10min) via Castlemaine (1hr 35min) and Bendigo (2hr); Warrnambool (1–3 daily; 3hr 15min) via Geelong (1hr) and Colac (1hr 50min).

Buses

Apollo Bay to: Geelong (2–3 daily; 2hr 30min); Lorne (1–2 daily; 55min); Warrnambool (1 weekly; 3hr 20min); Torquay (1–2 daily; 2hr).

Ballarat to: Bendigo (5 weekly; 2hr); Castlemaine (2 weekly; 1hr 45min); Daylesford (6 weekly; 1hr); Hamilton via Dunkeld (1–2 daily; 2hr 15min); Horsham (6 weekly; 2hr 55min); Maryborough (1 weekly; 1hr); Mildura (6 weekly; 7hr 50min); Warrnambool (5 weekly; 2hr 40min).

Bendigo to: Echuca (3–5 daily; 1hr 20min); Geelong (5 weekly; 4hr); Horsham (daily; 3hr 15min); Swan Hill (1–3 daily; 2hr 20min).

Beechworth to: Bright (1–2 daily; 1hr); Wangaratta (1–2 daily; 30min).

Bright to: Beechworth (1–2 daily; 1hr); Wangaratta (1–3 daily; 1hr25min).

Castlemaine to: Ballarat (2 weekly; 1hr 45min); Maryborough (1–4 daily; 55min).

Cowes to: Melbourne (1–4 daily; 3hr 15min).

Echuca to: Albury (4 weekly; 4hr 55min); Bendigo (3–5 daily; 1hr 20min); Melbourne (1–2 daily; 3hr); Rutherglen (4 weekly; 4hr 5min); Shepparton (4 weekly; 1hr 50min); Swan Hill (daily; 1hr 55min).

Foster (closest to Wilson's Promontory NP) to: Melbourne (daily; 2hr 40min).

Geelong to: Apollo Bay (2 daily; 2hr 55min); Ballarat (2–4 daily; 1hr 20min); Bendigo (5 weekly; 4hr); Lorne (2–4 daily; 1hr 50min); Maryborough (1 weekly; 2hr 30min); Mildura (1 weekly; 9hr); Torquay (2–4 daily; 45min).

Halls Gap (Grampians) to: Stawell (daily; 35min).

Hamilton to: Ballarat (1–2 daily; 2hr 15min); Warrnambool (6 weekly; 1hr 30min).

Horsham to: Ararat (6 weekly; 1hr 35min); Ballarat (6 weekly; 1hr 50min); Stawell (6 weekly; 1hr 10min).

Lakes Entrance to: Bairnsdale (1–3 daily; 35min); Canberra (2 weekly; 6hr 15min); Cann River (daily; 1hr 45min); Orbost (daily; 45min); Sale (1–3 daily; 1hr 40min).

Mansfield to: Melbourne (6 weekly, during snow season 7 weekly; 3hr); Mount Buller (snow season only;1–3 daily; 1hr).

Maryborough to: Ballarat (6 weekly; 1hr); Castlemaine (1–4 daily; 55min).

Mildura to: Ballarat (6 weekly; 7hr 50min); Geelong (1 weekly; 9hr); Swan Hill (1–2 daily; 2hr 30min).

Mount Buller to: Mansfield (snow season only; 1 daily; 1hr).

Portland to: Mount Gambier (1–2 daily; 1hr 30min); Port Fairy (1–2 daily; 1hr); Warrnambool (1–2 daily; 1hr 30min).

Sale to: Bairnsdale (1–3 daily; 1hr); Canberra (2 weekly; 7hr 40min); Cann River (daily; 3hr 10min); Lakes Entrance (1–3 daily; 1hr 40min); Orbost (daily; 2hr).

Shepparton to: Melbourne (5 weekly; 3hr).

Stawell to: Ballarat (daily; 1hr 40min); Halls Gap (Grampians; daily; 35min); Horsham (6 weekly; 1hr 10min).

Swan Hill to: Albury (daily; 6hr 20min); Bendigo (1–3 daily; 3hr); Echuca (daily; 1hr 55min); Mildura (1–2 daily; 2hr 30min).

Wangaratta to: Beechworth (1–2 daily; 30min); Bendigo (3 weekly; 4hr 25min); Bright (1–3 daily; 1hr 25min); Mount Beauty (2 weekly; 1hr 30min); Rutherglen (6 weekly; 50min).

Warrnambool to: Apollo Bay (1 weekly; 3hr 20min); Ballarat (5 weekly; 2hr 40min); Casterton (6 weekly; 2hr 25min); Hamilton (6 weekly; 1hr 30min); Mount Gambier (1–2 daily; 3hr); Port Fairy (1–2 daily; 40min); Portland (1–2 daily; 1hr 30min).

Flights

Albury to: Melbourne (2–4 daily; 50min)

Mildura to: Melbourne (1–4 daily; 1hr 10min);

Portland to: Melbourne (1–3 daily; 50min).

CHAPTER ELEVEN

TASMANIA

There's an otherworldly quality to **Tasmania**; romantics can see a gothic landscape of rain clouds and brooding mountains, revelling in the island's isolation and heavily wooded wilderness. This gothic notion extends to the ruins – evident everywhere – of a terrible colonial past: this was a prison island whose name, Van Diemen's Land, was so redolent with horror that when convict transport ended in 1852 it was immediately changed. Another, quite different view is that of a tamed landscape roughly the size of Ireland, its distances comprehensible to a European traveller, and with resonant echoes of England: cream teas, old-fashioned B&Bs, and friendly, homespun people.

In winter, when the grass is green, the gentle and cultivated **midlands**, with their rolling hills, dry stone walls and old stone villages, can be reminiscent of England's West Country, though in summer the light is too harsh and the grass too yellow to bear comparison. Town names, too, invariably invoke the British Isles – Perth, Swansea, Brighton and Somerset among them. It's a "mainlander's" joke that Tasmania is twenty years behind the rest of Australia, and it's true that it's very old-fashioned. At times this can be charming, but on other occasions frustrating and parochial.

Tasmania is the closest point in Australia to the Antarctic Circle, and the **west coast** is wild, wet and savage, bearing the full brunt of the Roaring Forties. Inland, the **southwest** has wild rivers, impassable temperate rainforests, buttongrass plains, and glacially carved mountains and tarns that have been linked to create a vast **World Heritage Area**. This region – crossed only by the Lyell Highway – extends from the South West National Park, through the Franklin Lower Gordon Wild Rivers National Park, and across to the Cradle Mountain–Lake St Clair National Park, providing some of the world's best wilderness walking and rafting, and the stage for frequent and dramatic conflicts between conservationists and the logging and mining communities. It's still one of the cleanest places on earth, though, despite attempts at industrialization, and a wilderness walk, where you can breathe the fresh air and drink freely from tannin-stained streams, is a genuinely bucolic experience.

A north–south axis divides the settled areas, with the two major cities, **Hobart**, the capital, in the south, and **Launceston** in the north. The **northwest coast**, facing the mainland across Bass Strait, is the most densely populated region, the site of Tasmania's two other cities, **Devonport** (where the Bass Strait ferry docks) and **Burnie**, and several other large, conservative towns. Tasmania's **central plateau**, with its thousands of lakes, is sparsely populated, though full of weekender fishing shacks. The sheltered, mostly flat **east coast** is the place to go for sun and water sports activities; it has plenty of deserted beaches, safe for swimming, set against a backdrop of bush-clad hills.

Don't expect boiling hot **weather** in Tasmania. It rarely gets above 25°C, even at the height of summer, and the weather is notoriously changeable, particularly in the uplands, where it can sleet and snow at any time of year; the most stable month is February. However, the UV rays are particularly strong, with the ozone layer thinning every year, and in the middle of a summer day can burn unprotected skin in fifteen minutes. Wear plenty of sunscreen and a hat. Winter is a bitterly cold time to visit unless you choose the more temperate east coast; wilderness walks are best left to the most experienced and well-equipped at this time of year.

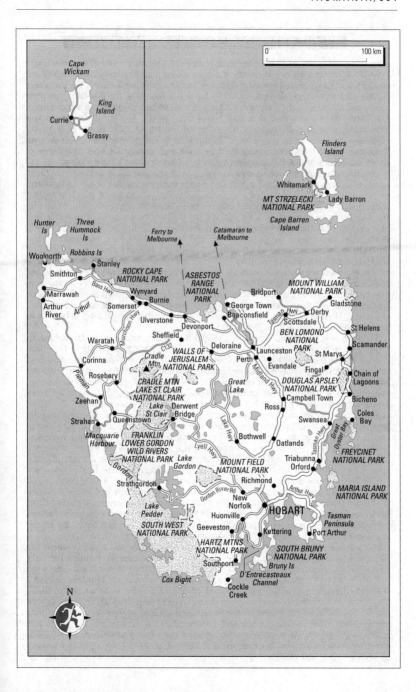

Cape Wickam

King Island

Currie

Grassy

0   100 km

Flinders Island

Whitemark   Lady Barron

MT STRZELECKI NATIONAL PARK

Cape Barren Island

Hunter Is
Three Hummock Is
Robbins Is

Ferry to Melbourne

Catamaran to Melbourne

Woolnorth
Smithton
Stanley
ROCKY CAPE NATIONAL PARK
ASBESTOS RANGE NATIONAL PARK
Bridport
MOUNT WILLIAM NATIONAL PARK

Marrawah
Bass Hwy
Wynyard
Burnie
Somerset
George Town
Beaconsfield
Scottsdale
Gladstone
Derby
St Helens

Arthur River
Arthur
Murchison Hwy
Ulverstone
Devonport
Tasman Hwy

Waratah
Sheffield
C132
Deloraine
BEN LOMOND NATIONAL PARK
Scamander

WALLS OF JERUSALEM NATIONAL PARK
Launceston
Perth
St Marys

Corinna
Cradle Mtn
CRADLE MTN LAKE ST CLAIR NATIONAL PARK
Evandale
Fingal
Chain of Lagoons

Rosebery
Great Lake
DOUGLAS APSLEY NATIONAL PARK

Pieman
Campbell Town
Bicheno

Zeehan
Lake St Clair
Derwent Bridge
Midland Hwy
Ross
Swansea
Coles Bay

Strahan
Queenstown
Lake Hwy

Macquarie Harbour
FRANKLIN LOWER GORDON WILD RIVERS NATIONAL PARK
Bothwell
Oatlands
FREYCINET NATIONAL PARK

Gordon
Lyell Hwy
Lake Gordon
MOUNT FIELD NATIONAL PARK
Triabunna
Orford
Great Oyster Bay
Tasman Hwy

Strathgordon
Gordon River Rd
Richmond
MARIA ISLAND NATIONAL PARK

Lake Pedder
New Norfolk
Arthur Hwy

SOUTH WEST NATIONAL PARK
Huonville
HOBART
Tasman Peninsula

Geeveston
Kettering
Port Arthur

HARTZ MTNS NATIONAL PARK
SOUTH BRUNY NATIONAL PARK

Southport
Bruny Is
D'Entrecasteaux Channel

Cox Bight
Cockle Creek

N

THE ABORIGINAL PEOPLES OF TASMANIA

The attempted genocide of the Aboriginal peoples of Tasmania is one of the most tragic episodes of modern history. Ironically, if it were not for American and British sealers and whalers who had operated from the shores of Van Diemen's Land since 1793, abducting Aboriginal women and taking them to the Furneaux Islands in the Bass Strait as their slaves and mistresses, the Tasmanian Aborigines would have disappeared without trace. Until recently, it was stated in school books that the last Aboriginal Tasmanian was **Truganini**, who died at Oyster Cove, south of Hobart, in 1876. However, a strong Aboriginal movement has grown up in Tasmania in the last twenty years, with over six thousand descendants proclaiming their heritage and pushing for land rights; one of these is **Michael Mansell**, a prominent Aboriginal activist from Flinders Island.

The **Aboriginal people of Tasmania** appear to have been racially distinct from those of the mainland, although their beliefs and rituals were similar. About twelve thousand years ago, the thawing of the last ice age brought rising ocean levels, which separated these people from the mainland and caused their genetic isolation; it's thought that on the mainland new cultures probably entered ten thousand years ago. This isolation was also evident in **cultural development**: they couldn't make fire but kept alight smouldering fire sticks; their weapons were simpler – they didn't have boomerangs; and although seafood was a main source of food, eating scaly fish was taboo. In **appearance**, the men were startling, wearing their hair in long ringlets smeared with grease and red ochre, while women wore theirs closely shaved. To keep out the cold, they coated their bodies with a mixture of animal fat, ochre and charcoal; women often wore a kangaroo-skin cloak. Both sexes donned delicate shell necklaces strung on kangaroo sinews. Men further decorated their bodies with linear scar patterns on their abdomens, arms and shoulders. Their **art** consisted of rock carvings of geometric designs, still to be seen in areas on the west and northwest coasts.

When the first **white settlement** was established in the early years of the nineteenth century there were reckoned to be about five thousand Aboriginal people in Tasmania, divided into nine main tribes. A tribe consisted of bands of forty to fifty people who lived in adjoining territory, shared the same language and culture, socialized, intermarried and – crucially – fought wars against other tribes. They also traded such items as stone tools, ochre and shell necklaces, and bands moved peaceably across neighbouring tribes' territory along well-defined routes at different times of the year to share resources: the inland Big River tribe, for example, would journey to the coast for scaling. Once they realized the white settlers were not going to "share" their resources in this traditional exchange economy but were instead stealing the land, the nomadic people displayed a determination to defend it – by force, if necessary. Confrontation was inevitable, as the settlers attempted to enclose and clear land, and by the 1820s the white population was in a frenzy of fear – though for every settler who died, twenty Aborigines met a similar fate. In 1828 Governor Arthur declared martial law, expelling all Aboriginal people from the settled districts and giving settlers what was, in practice, a licence to shoot on sight. Alarmed by these events, the British government planned to round up the remaining Aborigines and confine them to **Bruny Island**, south of Hobart Town. In 1830 a mass militia of three thousand settlers formed an armed human barrier, the **Black Line**, which was to sweep across the island, clearing Aborigines before them, in preparation for "resettlement".

The line failed; but unfortunately the final tactic was "divide and rule", in which the Aboriginal people themselves, with their superb tracking skills, were enlisted to help ensnare their tribal enemies. The 135 Aborigines who survived the Black Line were moved in 1834 to a makeshift settlement on exposed and barren **Flinders Island** . Within four years most of these people died, of despair, disease, or as a result of harsh conditions. In 1837 the 47 survivors were transferred to their final settlement at Oyster Cove, where – no longer a threat – they were often dressed up and paraded on official engagements. The skeleton of the last survivor, "Queen" Truganini (see p.913 and p.926), originally from Bruny Island, was displayed in the Tasmanian Museum until 1976, when her remains were finally cremated and scattered in the D'Entrecasteaux Channel, according to her final wishes.

Some history

The Dutch navigator **Abel Tasman** sighted the west coast of the island in 1642. Landing a party on its east coast, he named it **Van Diemen's Land** in honour of the Governor of the Dutch East Indies. Early maps show it connected to the mainland, and several eighteenth-century French and British navigators, including William Bligh and James Cook, who claimed it for the British, did not prove otherwise. It was not until 1798 that Matthew Flinders circumnavigated the island, and his discovery of the **Bass Strait** reduced the journey to Sydney by a week. In 1803, after the French had been observed nosing around the island's southern waters, it was decided to establish a second **colony** in Australia. (The first had been established at Sydney Cove in 1788.) Lieutenant David Bowen was dispatched to Van Diemen's Land, settling with a group of convicts on the banks of the Derwent River at Risdon Cove. In the same year, Lieutenant-Colonel John Collins set out from England with another group to settle the Port Phillip district of what would become Victoria; after a few months they gave up and crossed the Bass Strait to join Bowen's group. **Hobart Town** was founded in 1804 and the first **penal settlement** opened at Macquarie Harbour in 1821, followed by Maria Island and Port Arthur; they were mainly for those who had committed further offences while still prisoners on the mainland. Van Diemen's Land, with its harsh conditions and repressive, violent regime, became part of British folklore as a place of terror, a prison-island hell. Collins was Lieutenant-Governor of Van Diemen's Land until his death in 1810, but it is Lieutenant-Governor **George Arthur** (1824–36) who has the most prominent position in the island's history. His ideas were an influence on the prison settlement at Port Arthur and he was in charge at the time of the **Black Line** (see box opposite), the organized white militia used against the indigenous Aboriginal population.

Tasmania did not experience the postwar industrialization that transformed the mainland. A small, isolated and neglected state, it even missed out on postwar immigration and consequently remains predominantly Anglo-Saxon in character, with an insular – often conservative – population. Its **natural resources** include forests – covering forty percent of the island – and water, and the mountainous terrain and fast-flowing rivers meant that hydroelectricity schemes began early here, under the auspices of the huge Hydro Electricity Commission (HEC). The flooding of **Lake Pedder** in 1972 led to the formation of the **Wilderness Society**, a conservation organization whose successful **Franklin Blockade** in 1982 managed to save one of the last wild rivers. Controversy over these issues still divides the state into "Greens" and a pro-logging, pro-dam working class worried about their jobs. By voting for the **Tasmanian Greens** in 1989, enough ordinary Tasmanians showed that they didn't want Tasmania's natural assets destroyed, and the party held the balance of power in the state's parliament until 1992;

ACCOMMODATION PRICES

All the accommodation listed in this book has been categorized into one of eight price bands, as set out below. The rates quoted represent the cheapest available double or twin room in high season – except for category ①, which indicates per-person rates for a dorm bed, and the categories given for units, cabins and vans, which represent the daily charge for the whole unit.

① Under $18	⑤ $61–74
② $19–30	⑥ $75–94
③ $31–45	⑦ $95–124
④ $46–60	⑧ $125 upwards

For more accommodation details, see p.40–43.

---

in early 1996 the Greens again held the balance of power, with a Liberal state government. Before the 1998 state elections, the two major opposing parties, Labor and Liberal, conspired together to change the electoral structure, voting to reduce the number of members in the Lower House from 25 to 15, purposefully making it more difficult for the Greens to win seats. The Labour government was voted in, and the sole Green Member of Parliament in the Lower House has little chance of exercising any influence. The Tasmanian Green party is represented federally by one senator, the Tasmanian environmental activist **Dr Bob Brown**.

Recent campaigns have been aimed at stopping logging in particularly sensitive areas, and ending **woodchipping** (pulping trees for paper) for export to Japan; currently ninety percent of the wood taken from Tasmania's forests ends up this way, with Tasmania the only state in Australia that woodchips **rainforests**. It's claimed that the state government is subsidizing the industry, selling woodchips off at a third of the going rate to keep Tasmanians employed. The high-profile conservation issue stirring up media interest nationally is that of the **Western Explorer**, the "tourist road" crossing the wild **Tarkine area** on the west coast north of Zeehan, which was constructed hastily and finished in January 1996. A year before, an incredibly vast and ancient Huon pine was found in the area, as big as a city block and thought to date from around 8000 BC. Conservationists are sceptical that "the road to nowhere", as they've called it, is being used as a cover to open up the area (currently state forest) to logging, thereby destroying its ability to be put forward for World Heritage listing.

Tasmanian practicalities

Although it's small in Australian terms, make sure you give yourself enough **time** to see Tasmania; if you want to see only its cities you need no more than a few days, but to get a flavour of the countryside – the great outdoors is the real reason to come here – a couple of weeks or longer is necessary. **Tasmanian Travel Centres** in the major cities (see box overleaf) can provide **information** and also book all transport, tours and accommodation; their free information paper, *Travelways*, is extremely useful, filled with detailed, reliable and comprehensive information on accommodation, attractions, bus timetables, car rental, adventure tours and national parks.

Getting there

If you plan to be in Melbourne, or have a car you want to take over, a good way to get to Tasmania is across the Bass Strait on the TT Line *Spirit of Tasmania* **ferry** from Port Melbourne to Devonport (departing Port Melbourne Mon, Wed & Fri 6pm, arriving

Devonport 8.30am; departing Devonport Tues & Thurs, Sat 6pm; ☎13 2010). If a rough, fourteen-hour overnight trip doesn't worry you too much, this is the best way to travel. There are restaurants, bars and entertainment, and every passenger has a bed – there's a hostel section ($110 one-way), as well as private cabins ranging from basic to luxury suites ($160–250 per person one-way); in low season prices can drop by around twenty percent. You'll need to **book in advance** in summer, especially if you want to take a vehicle. Whatever standard of accommodation you choose, you'll pay between $30 and $40 extra to take a car across, and $20 for a bicycle. There is also a **high speed catamaran**, the *Devil Cat*, which takes six hours to cross between Port Melbourne and George Town (January–April departing Port Melbourne Tues, Thurs, Sat & Sun 7.30am; departing George Town at Wed, Fri, Sat & Sun 4pm; one-way passenger $160; vehicles as per *Spirit of Tasmania*), but prepare for a rough ride. Cheaper Apex return fares (21-day advance purchase) are available on both boats, and packages, including on-ground travel passes or accommodation and tours, are also worth looking into.

Several airlines **fly** from the mainland to Tasmania, as well as to King and Flinders islands. You can fly with **Qantas** from all the major cities, usually changing planes in Melbourne; it's always cheaper to fly to Launceston direct from Melbourne, and you'll save money if you book well in advance, with an economy return at $428 and an Apex return at $257. Other return fares are Melbourne–Hobart $494/$271 and Sydney–Hobart $716/$372 ($632/$372 to Launceston). Look out for special offers that can reduce prices further. There are also several **Tasmanian- and Victorian-based airlines** worth checking out. The major player is **Kendell Airlines** (free call ☎1800/338 894) who have taken over Ansett's Tasmanian routes: Melbourne–Launceston, Melbourne–Hobart, Sydney–Launceston and Sydney–Hobart; their route expansion was planned to start from November 1999. Kendell still also fly from Melbourne to Devonport (return $206), Wynyard (Burnie Airport; return $192), and King Island (return $172). All Kendell flights operate from Ansett Australia terminals, who provide reservation services and some ground handling at major capital city airports. **Island Airlines** (free call ☎1800/818 455) flies from Traralgon in Victoria's Gippsland to Launceston ($172 one-way) and Flinders Island ($143 one-way), from Melbourne's Essendon airport to Flinders Island ($165 one-way); cheaper Apex return fares are available. **Aus-Air** (☎03/9580 6166 or free call ☎1800/331 256) flies from Moorabbin, just outside Melbourne, to Launceston ($175 one-way), Wynyard ($154 one-way), Devonport ($165 one-way), Flinders Island ($153 one-way), and King Island ($121 one-way). **Fly-drive packages**, which include accommodation, can be particularly good value: ask at travel agents about the availability of special deals.

The only **international flights** are with Qantas from Christchurch, in New Zealand, to Hobart (all year; $580–620 Apex return), and with Air New Zealand (Nov–June) for roughly the same price. You could also add this part of your journey onto an international ticket via New Zealand.

Accommodation

Compared to the mainland, Tasmania has few **motels**, other than those in and around the main towns, and not as many caravan parks, but plenty of high-quality **hotel (pub)** accommodation (usually serving breakfast) and British-style **B&Bs**. Consequently, you should try to plan ahead, as you won't just happen upon a cheap motel or cabin, and in peak periods only the most expensive B&B accommodation or the most simple hostel beds may be vacant. **YHA hostels** tend to be basic and old-fashioned, offering mainly dorm beds, but they're gradually being modernized – the good news is that prices start from as low as $9, and you'll find them off the beaten track. In the major tourist areas **backpackers' hostels** have sprung up, with plenty of twin and double rooms; prices start from about $12, reaching up to $16 in summer. **Campers** will find lots of free sites, often with the minimal facilities of a pit toilet and tap water, as well as an abundance of good spots (often with fees attached) in the national parks.

Getting around

Passenger train services no longer exist in Tasmania. Instead, six local **bus companies** and one charter service reach most destinations, the main two companies being Tasmanian Redline Coaches and Tasmanian Wilderness Travel. You cannot use a mainland bus pass with either of these, and services are limited, often not running at weekends, especially on the east and west coasts; in winter and spring services are even further reduced, which can be downright inconvenient. Frequent scheduled services are offered by the the the largest operator, **Tasmanian Redline Coaches** (☎03/6231 3233 or ☎1300/360 000), between Hobart and Launceston via the east coast or direct via the Midland Highway, from Devonport to Hobart via Deloraine and Launceston, and along the northwest coast from Devonport to Burnie and on to Smithton. **Tasmanian Wilderness Travel** (☎03/6334 4442) specializes in bushwalkers' transport, getting you to some of the more remote places all over the state in their minibuses which run scheduled services as well as "Wilderness" trips (minimum of four people) and separate tours. Scheduled services run from Hobart to Queenstown via Lake St Clair, with a connecting service to Strahan; Queenstown to Launceston via Cradle Mountain and Devonport; from Hobart up the east coast as far as St Helens; and from Launceston east to Bicheno. "Wilderness" services include routes running west from Hobart to Mt Field National Park and Scotts Peak or south to Cockle Creek via Huonville and Lune River, and from Launceston to the Walls of Jerusalem National Park and to Cradle Mountain via Deloraine and Devonport. Their straight **fares** are rather high, considering the short distances – for example, Strahan to Launceston is $49 one-way ($90 return) and Hobart to Mount Field is $25 ($50). Fares on Redline are government-regulated: for example, $19 for the trip from Hobart to Launceston, and just over $32 from Hobart to Devonport. **Hobart Coaches** (☎03/6234 4077) head north out of Hobart to Richmond, New Norfolk and Port Arthur, and south to Woodbridge, Cygnet, Geeveston and Dover. Several smaller local operators on the east coast, such as **Bicheno Coach Service** (Coles Bay–Bicheno; ☎03/6257 0293), **Peakes Coaches** (St Marys–Swansea; ☎03/6372 5390) and **Sun Coast** (Derby–St Helens; ☎03/6376 1753), help to fill in the gaps. **Maxwell's Charter Bus** (☎03/6492 1431) provides a service based on a minimum of four passengers from Devonport and Launceston to and around the Cradle Mountain–Lake St Clair area.

Buying a local **bus pass** is one way of cutting costs: Tasmanian Wilderness Travel offer a **Tassie Wilderness Pass** which covers a range of time spans and journeys (from $99 for five days travel within a seven-day period to $220 for 30 days travel within a 40-day period), and combines its scheduled and "Wilderness" services, getting you to all the major bushwalking areas and giving you fifteen percent of their tours. You'll also reach the main cities and towns, though very indirectly, and will qualify for a third off Redline bus fares which speed directly between major points. Also, it's worth investing in YHA or VIP membership before coming to Tasmania, which will give you substantial savings on all bus tickets and tours (see Basics, p.42).

Renting a car is a sensible option, considering the vagaries of the transport system, particularly if you can get a group together. Local operators offer reasonable weekly rates, starting from about $210 for a budget car or $315 for a top-of-the-range model, including basic insurance; as Tasmania is such a small island kilometres are usually unlimited, and you don't need a lot of petrol. Though distances seem short compared to the mainland, roads are often winding and mostly two-laned – there are few freeways, except some short stretches on the outskirts of large cities – so **driving** can be slow and tiring. At dusk and night-time you have to be especially careful of animals darting in front of your car, as evidenced by the saddeningly high number of dead native animals you'll see by the roadsides. However, there are few cars on the road, so you should be able to relax a bit and enjoy the scenery. The lack of traffic also makes **cycling** an attractive option, especially in summer, and on the flatter midlands and east coast routes; otherwise, there are plenty of gruelling hills to keep you in shape. Several operators in Hobart, Launceston and Devonport rent bikes for touring (see the respective accounts).

You could also choose to go on a **tour of the island** with one of two small-group outfits aimed at independent-minded travellers. The **Bottom Bits Bus** (☎ & fax 03/9878 8735 or free call ☎1800/777 103) is a three-day, two-night tour departing from Hobart to visit the south's highlights – Bruny Island, the Hartz Mountain National Park, Cockle Creek, Lune River, Hastings Caves – and ending with a tour of Mount Wellington and Hobart ($175 including camping/hostel accommodation and most meals). The more comprehensive **Tassie Experience Tours** (☎ & fax 03/6250 2766; *seaview.lodge@tassie.net.au*) is a seven-night tour (departing Devonport, Launceston or Hobart), which does a loop of the island and has plenty of outdoor and bushwalking action ($660 including hostel accommodation or $440 without accommodation; breakfasts, lunches and one dinner included).

National parks and bushwalking

All **national parks** in Tasmania charge daily (24hr) **entry fees**, often on an honour system, of $3 per pedestrian or cyclist, $9 per vehicle: if you plan to go bush for long periods, then a two-month holiday pass (person, cyclist or motorcyclist $12, car $30) or an annual pass (car $18 for one park, $42 for all parks) might be better value. Tasmania's wilderness has always attracted thousands of **bushwalkers**, and many of the tracks have become churned-up and are gradually being boardwalked; keeping to set paths to avoid further erosion is just one of the national park's minimum-impact guidelines, available in a leaflet from the Tasmania Parks and Wildlife Service, 134 Macquarie St, Hobart (☎03/6233 6191; *www.parks.tas.gov.au*) which also supplies detailed maps. To get leaflets before your trip, you can write to GPO Box 44A, Hobart, TAS 7001. It must be emphasized that walking in the wilderness can be dangerous if you're ill-prepared: you should never go by yourself and you should always register your plans with a park ranger or inform others of your intentions. The free *Bushwalking Trip Planner for Tasmania's World Heritage Area* gives you information about the clothing and equipment you'll need in these parks, where the weather can change rapidly – even on a warm summer day hail, sleet or snow can suddenly descend in the highlands, and walkers who have disregarded warnings have died of hypothermia. As a minimum, you'll need wet-weather gear, thermal clothing, walking boots, a sturdy tent, warm sleeping bag, a fuel cooking stove, maps and a compass (which you should know how to use). Gear can be rented from outdoor shops in Hobart, Launceston and Devonport.

HOBART AND THE EAST

From Lake St Clair in central Tasmania, the **Derwent River** flows past **Mount Field National Park**, Tasmania's oldest and most popular national park, through well-preserved **New Norfolk**, and towards **Hobart**, Tasmania's capital. Here, the river estuary widens to form a fine harbour before flowing into the waters of **Storm Bay** and out to the Tasman Sea. Hobart is Australia's most southerly city, battered by winter winds roaring in from the Antarctic, while the coastline around it is so jagged it looks as if someone has poured acid on a map of the area. The hook-shaped **South Arm**, at the entrance to Storm Bay, is echoed on a larger scale by the **Tasman Peninsula**, with its infamous convict settlement at **Port Arthur**. To the south, the two tenuously connected halves of **Bruny Island** protect the waters of the **D'Entrecasteaux Channel**. On the mainland opposite Bruny Island is the fertile and cultivated **Huon Valley**, but as you head further south the coastline becomes increasingly wild: there are caves and thermal springs, the **Hartz Mountain National Park** inland, and the **Picton River**, where there's good rafting. The last settlement in this direction is **Cockle Creek**, the starting point for the **South Coast Track** which takes you towards the **South West National Park**, the great mass of wilderness forming Tasmania's southwest corner.

North of Hobart, the **east coast** of Tasmania is the tamest and most temperate part of the island, providing a popular cycling route past numerous sandy and deserted beaches and some lovely national parks. The **Tasman Highway** follows this coastline from Hobart to Launceston, heading inland through the northeast at **St Helens**, the east coast's largest town. The northeast corner is virtually unpopulated, and the **Mount William National Park** here is a haven for the Forrester kangaroo. Inland are some old tin-mining towns, and superb rainforest remnants and mountain scenery at **Weldborough Pass**, beyond which you pass through rich agricultural and forestry country to Launceston.

Hobart

HOBART is small but beautifully sited, and approaching it from any direction is exhilarating: speeding across the expressway on the Tasman Bridge over the wide expanse of the Derwent River, or swooping down the Southern Outlet with hills, harbour, docks and houses spread out below. The green- and red-tin-roofed timber houses climb up the lower slopes of Mount Wellington, snow-covered for two or three months of the year, and look down on the expansive harbour. It's a city focused on the water: the centre is only a few minutes' walk from the waterfront, where fresh seafood can be bought directly from fishing boats in Sullivans Cove, and yachties hang out at old dockside pubs or head for fish and chips served from the punts moored in Constitution Dock. South of Constitution Dock is Salamanca Place, a well-preserved streetscape of waterfront stone warehouses which is the site of a famous Saturday market, a Hobart highlight, so make sure you're here at the weekend. Yacht races and regattas are held throughout the year, while at weekends the water is alive with boats; you can choose any type of craft for a harbour cruise, a perfect activity in the summer, when it's dry and not too hot. In winter, though, the wind roars in from the Antarctic and temperatures drop to 5°C and below.

Australia's second-oldest city after Sydney, Hobart has managed to escape the clutches of developers, and its early architectural heritage is remarkably well preserved – more so than any other antipodean city. In 1803 **Lieutenant John Bowen** led a party of 24 convicts from Sydney to settle on the eastern shores of the Derwent River at Risdon Cove. A year later **Lieutenant-Colonel David Collins** arrived, with about three hundred convicts, a contingent of marines to guard over them, and thirty or more free settlers including women and children, and founded Hobart Town on Sullivans Cove, 10km below the original settlement and on the opposite shore. Collins went on to serve as Lieutenant-Governor of the colony for ten years. For the first two years, food was scarce, and settlers had to hunt local game, creating an early culture based on guns that was later to have terrible effects on the Aboriginal population. The fine deep-water port helped make the town prosperous, and a merchant class became wealthy through whaling, shipbuilding and the transport of crops and wool. The period between the late 1820s and the 1840s was a golden age for building, with the government architect **John Lee Archer** and the convict **James Blackburn** responsible for some of Hobart's finest buildings. There's a wealth of colonial Georgian **architecture**, with more than ninety buildings classified by the National Trust, sixty of which are on Macquarie and Davey streets. **Battery Point**, a village of workers' cottages and grand houses set in narrow, irregular streets, has hardly changed in the last 150 years.

Arrival, information and transport

Hobart **airport** is 26km northeast of the city at Cambridge (flight information ☎13 1515). Tasmanian Redline Coaches runs an airport **shuttle bus** to the city ($7; book-

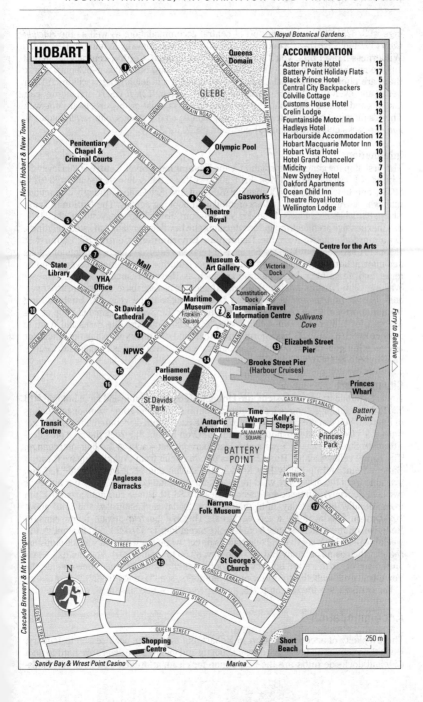

HOBART

ACCOMMODATION

Astor Private Hotel	15
Battery Point Holiday Flats	17
Black Prince Hotel	5
Central City Backpackers	9
Colville Cottage	18
Customs House Hotel	14
Crelin Lodge	19
Fountainside Motor Inn	2
Hadleys Hotel	11
Harbourside Accommodation	12
Hobart Macquarie Motor Inn	16
Hobart Vista Hotel	10
Hotel Grand Chancellor	8
Midcity	7
New Sydney Hotel	6
Oakford Apartments	13
Ocean Child Inn	3
Theatre Royal Hotel	4
Wellington Lodge	1

Royal Botanical Gardens

Queens Domain

GLEBE

Olympic Pool

Penitentiary Chapel & Criminal Courts

Theatre Royal

Gasworks

Centre for the Arts

State Library

Mall

Museum & Art Gallery

Victoria Dock

YHA Office

St Davids Cathedral

Maritime Museum

Constitution Dock

Tasmanian Travel & Information Centre

Sullivans Cove

NPWS

Elizabeth Street Pier

Parliament House

Brooke Street Pier (Harbour Cruises)

Princes Wharf

St Davids Park

CASTRAY ESPLANADE

Battery Point

Transit Centre

Antarctic Adventure

Time Warp

Kelly's Steps

SALAMANCA SQUARE

BATTERY POINT

Princes Park

ARTHURS CIRCUS

Anglesea Barracks

Narryna Folk Museum

St George's Church

Shopping Centre

Short Beach

0   250 m

North Hobart & New Town

Ferry to Bellerive

Cascade Brewery & Mt Wellington

Sandy Bay & Wrest Point Casino

Marina

ings ☎03/6231 3900), dropping off at central accommodation, as well as the *Adelphi Court YHA* in New Town; a **taxi** costs around $22. If you come by Redline or Tasmanian Wilderness Travel **bus**, you'll disembark at the **Transit Centre**, centrally located at 199 Collins St (Mon–Fri 6.30am–6.30pm, Sat 8am–4pm, Sun 8.30am–6.30pm), where there are phones, newsagents, toilets, showers ($5) and left-luggage facilities ($1 per item), and even hostel accommodation upstairs (see p.912). If you're arriving by **car**, take a good look at your map to plan your route, as most of the streets are one-way. There's plenty of cheap metered **parking** available on the streets, plus several council-run car parks charging around $1 per hour ($8.50 for 24hr).

Information

The first stop for general information is the **Tasmanian Travel Centre** at 20 Davey St, corner of Elizabeth Street (Mon–Fri 8.30am–5.15pm, Sat & Sun 9am–4pm; ☎03/6230 8233), one block from the Tasmanian Museum and Art Gallery, though it functions mainly as a travel, car hire and accommodation booking agency. The **National Trust Shop**, 33 Salamanca Place (Mon–Fri 9.30am–5pm, Sat 9.30am–1pm; ☎03/6223 7371), has inexpensive architectural guides detailing the bewildering range of listed buildings. On a more alternative note, the **Tasmanian Environment Centre**, 102 Bathurst St (Mon–Fri 9am–5pm; ☎03/6234 5566), is a relaxed resource space with lots of books and information on Tasmania and notice boards featuring environmental events, rooms to let and items for sale. Organizations such as Bicycle Tasmania, and the Hobart Walking Club (visitors can join their walks) use this as their base, and the centre operates its own programme of walks and talks throughout the year. For **bushwalking information** and a full range of Tasmaps, head for the Service Tasmania Shop at 134 Macquarie St (Mon–Fri 9am–4.45pm; ☎03/6233 3382); upstairs, the Parks and Wildlife Service (☎03/6230 8011) has information sheets and can refer you to a parks officer for advice; other general and bushwalking maps are stocked at the Tasmanian Map Centre, 96 Elizabeth St (☎03/6231 9043).

City transport

Hobart's public transport system, the **Hobart Metro** (timetable and fares hot line ☎13 2201), is useful for getting to less central accommodation and some more distant points of interest. You can pre-purchase Metro Tens (a pack of ten discounted tickets) and get timetables from the Metroshop, inside the GPO on Elizabeth Street; the area outside – Elizabeth Street, Franklin Square and Macquarie Street – acts as the bus interchange. The handy yellow-painted **Busy Bee bus** does a circuit from Franklin Square through Battery Point and up Sandy Bay Road to the casino and back again. Single **tickets**, available from the driver, are valid for ninety minutes and cost from $1.20 (for a one- or two-zone journey); off-peak day-rover passes are $3.10. Buses run until around 11pm from Monday to Thursday, until midnight on Friday and Saturday, and until about 10.30pm on Sunday (only a few services). The *MV Cartela* private **ferry** runs to Bellerive, on the eastern shore, from Brooke Street Pier (☎03/6223 1914 for times); the weekday peak-hour service ($2 one-way) is direct, while the weekend service stops en-route at the casino at Sandy Bay ($5 one-way; $2.50 to casino only). You can hail a **taxi** on the street, or there are taxi stands around the city, with the major one outside the Town Hall on Elizabeth Street (for phone numbers, see "Listings" p.922).

For **cruises**, see the box on p.915; and for city **tours**, see "Listings", p.922.

Accommodation

There's plenty of **accommodation** in Hobart, but during the peak season in January, when the yachties hit town, prices can shoot up and inexpensive places are hard to find. City and dockside **pubs** are the best option for clean, affordable private accommodation, and there's always a bed at one of Hobart's several **hostels**. Battery Point is full of (sometimes pricey) **B&Bs**, and the area has several good **self-catering** holiday apartments, with costs comparable to a motel. Most **motels** are situated in Sandy Bay, about 3km south of the centre, or along the Brooker Highway, but private hotels and guesthouses tend to offer better value.

Hotels and motels

Argyle Motor Lodge, cnr of Lewis and Argyle sts, North Hobart (☎03/6234 2488, fax 6234 2292). Situated in a quiet area twenty minutes' walk from the city centre. Some self-catering units also available. ⑥–⑦.

Black Prince Hotel, 145 Elizabeth St (☎03/6234 3501, fax 6234 3502). Centrally located hotel offering budget motel-style rooms, breakfast included. ④.

Country Comfort Hadley's Hotel, 34 Murray St (☎03/6223 4355, fax 6224 0303, free call ☎1800/065 064). National Trust-listed hotel close to the waterfront which has recently been restored to its glory days. Old fashioned feel, modern facilities; restaurant, café, bistro and bar are all in-house. Room service, 24hr reception, and free parking. ⑥–⑧.

Customs House Hotel, cnr of Murray and Morrison sts, opposite Watermans Dock (☎03/6234 6645, fax 6223 8750). Old-style waterfront hotel next to Parliament House with great views, though rooms at the front get pub noise on Friday nights. Rates include access to kitchenette, which has breakfast provisions. ⑤–⑥.

Harbourside Accommodation, 19 Morrison St, above the trendy *Brooke Street Bar* (☎03/6234 6254). Great location on Sullivans Cove; inexpensive pub-style rooms, all clean and well-furnished, some with TV, some en-suite. ③–⑤.

Hotel Grand Chancellor, 1 Davey St (☎03/6235 4535, 6223 8175). Hobart's most upmarket hotel, the five-star *Grand Chancellor's* facilities include two restaurants, two bars and a health club. ⑧.

Fountainside Motor Inn, cnr of Liverpool St and Brooker Ave (☎03/6234 2911, fax 6231 0710). Multistoreyed motel set on a noisy intersection, but has room service and the 24hr *Jellies Coffee Shop*. ⑥–⑦.

Macquarie Motor Inn, 167 Macquarie St (☎03/6234 4422, fax 6234 4273). Very central high-rise, friendlier than it looks; under-15s stay for free. Facilities include a pool, sauna and spa. ⑦.

Oakford on Elizabeth Pier, Elizabeth St Pier (☎03/6220 6600, fax 6244 1277). Waterfront apartment hotel – gorgeous one-bedroom and family studio apartments are split level, spacious and flooded with light. Some have walk-out balconies, all have kitchen and laundry, and there's a gym and sauna. ⑧.

Theatre Royal Hotel, 31 Campbell St (☎03/6234 6925, fax 6231 1773). A basic hotel, but in a great position across from the Theatre Royal, with plain but presentable rooms; some singles available, and light breakfast included. Excellent bar and bistro downstairs. ③.

Wrest Point Hotel–Casino, 410 Sandy Bay Rd, Sandy Bay (☎03/6225 0112, fax 6225 3909). Upmarket four-star hotel with riverside rooms. Heated indoor pool, sauna and 24hr room service. As well as the luxury tower, there's a cheaper motel section. ⑦–⑧.

Private hotels and guesthouses

Astor Private Hotel, 157 Macquarie St (☎03/6234 6611, fax 6231 4053). Central, old-fashioned, family-run guesthouse; rates include breakfast. ⑤.

Colville Cottage, 32 Mona St, Battery Point (☎03/6223 6968, fax 6224 0500). Peaceful Victorian weatherboard B&B, with en-suite rooms and a pleasant garden. ⑦.

The Lodge on Elizabeth, 249 Elizabeth St, cnr of Warwick St (☎03/6231 3830, fax 6234 2566). Delightful guesthouse in an elegant National Trust-listed 1829 mansion; guest lounge with fireplace, games and complimentary port. All rooms en-suite. ⑦.

Wellington Lodge, 7 Scott St, Glebe (☎03/6231 0614, fax 6234 1551). A weatherboard B&B classified by the National Trust, close to Queens Domain park and the city centre. All rooms are en-suite and non-smoking. ⑥–⑦.

Hostels and budget accommodation

Adelphi Court YHA, 17 Stoke St, New Town (☎03/6228 4829, fax 6278 2047). Modern, motel-like hostel and guesthouse arranged around a courtyard, on a quiet suburban street. Cramped kitchen facilities, but catered breakfasts in the dining room. There's a large TV/games room (closes early) and a small kiosk. The hostel books tours, does pick-ups, rents bikes and camping equipment, and has plenty of parking. A long way from the city centre, but 10min walk to the Elizabeth St restaurant strip in North Hobart. Take bus #15 or #16 from Argyle St to Stoke St, or #25–42, #100 or #105–128 from Elizabeth St, to stop no.13, then walk. Rooms ③–④, dorms ①.

Budget Bunks, *Ocean Child Inn*, 86 Argyle St (☎03/6234 6730, fax 6234 9306). Comfortable hostel, with clean rooms sleeping two, three or four. The *Inn* has a quiet bar and offers good budget meals. Rooms ③, dorms ①.

Central City Backpackers, 2nd Floor, Imperial Mansions, 138 Collins St, entrance through the Imperial Arcade (☎03/6224 2404, fax 6224 2316, free call ☎1800/811 507). Hobart's best hostel, in the spacious quarters of a once grand hotel. The management is friendly and efficient, and the hostel is popular – so book ahead. Six-bed or four-bed dorms, singles, twins or doubles available, all heated; linen and bedding hire $5 extra. Facilities include a well set-up kitchen, pleasant dining area, TV and games rooms, storage room and a licensed bar downstairs. No parking. ③–④, dorms ①.

Jane Franklin Hall, 6 Elboden St, South Hobart (☎03/6223 2000). Student rooms available in the holidays; many single rooms. Excellent facilities include a kitchen, free laundry, TV lounge, gym and pool. B&B ④.

New Sydney Hotel, 87 Bathurst St (☎03/6234 4516, fax 6236 9965). Clean and central backpacker accommodation above a pub, with kitchen facilities and guest lounge – and noisy bands playing downstairs six nights. Always lively, though, and you can get budget meals in the pub. ①.

Transit Centre Backpackers, 199 Collins St, above the Transit Centre (☎ & fax 03/6231 2400). Modern, central, well-equipped and spacious, but lacking in atmosphere. Rooms ②, dorms ①.

Caravan parks and self-catering apartments

Battery Point Holiday Flats, 15 Secheron Rd, Battery Point (☎03/6223 6592, fax 6223 8051). Two well-equipped apartments on a quiet street overlooking the Derwent River, within walking distance of restaurants and the city centre. One has views of the water, the other a pretty garden. ⑥.

Crelin Lodge, 1 Crelin St, Battery Point (☎ & fax 03/6243 6555). Pleasant units with up to five beds; in a great spot. ⑥.

Graham Court Holiday Villas, 15 Pirie St, New Town (☎03/6278 1333, fax 6278 1087). One- to three-bedroom apartments. ⑤–⑦.

Sandy Bay Caravan Park, 1 Peel St, Sandy Bay (☎03/6225 1264). The closest caravan park to the city centre (3km), in a salubrious suburb. Full range of facilities, including playground and camp kitchen. Cabins ⑤, on-site vans ③.

Treasure Island Caravan Park, 671 Main Rd, Berriedale (☎03/6249 2379). Large park 14km from town, with a kitchen and pool. Cabins ④, on-site vans ③.

The City

Hobart is small and easy to find your way around, with the streets arranged in a grid pattern running southeast towards **Sullivans Cove**. You can walk anywhere in the city centre, which is mostly flat, although surrounded by some steep hills. The civic centre is **Franklin Square**, bounded by **Macquarie** and **Davey** streets, which between them have a concentration of listed buildings. The main shopping area is **Elizabeth Street Mall**, roughly in the centre of the **CBD** (the City Business District); Elizabeth Street slopes down from **North Hobart**, known for its many fine restaurants, to the Elizabeth Street Pier on **Franklin Wharf**. Here, at the harbour, fishing boats and yachts are moored, and cruises leave from Brooke Street Pier. **Salamanca Place**, with its row of Georgian warehouses, is on the waterfront on the south side of the cove; a steep climb up Kelly's Steps brings you to **Battery Point**, to the south. Following the Derwent River around from Battery Point, you reach salubrious **Sandy Bay**, with its casino and Royal Yacht Club. To the north of the centre are the parklands of the **Queens Domain**, with the **Royal Botanical Gardens** along the waterfront; from the Domain, the **Tasman Bridge** crosses the river to the residential eastern shore.

There are relatively few sights in Hobart other than the streets themselves, but these are enough to keep you wandering around for hours, stopping at a few museums and parks along the way. While walking through the city, it's worth glancing up occasionally to observe the **street signs**; the streets are often named after important local figures and the signs have portraits and biographies of them. Around the docks area, and in Battery Point, there are also interpretive boards pointing out historic and architectural features.

Franklin Square and the Tasmanian Museum and Art Gallery

Starting from **Franklin Square**, you can walk south past many of the fine old buildings on Davey Street to **St Davids Park**, originally the graveyard of St Davids Cathedral (at the corner of Murray and Macquarie streets) but converted to a park in the early twentieth century. It's a quiet spot containing some important monuments, among them a huge memorial to the first governor, David Collins. Other gravestones have been removed and set into two undulating sandstone walls at the bottom of the park.

Going north from Franklin Square, you come to the excellent **Tasmanian Museum and Art Gallery**, at 40 Macquarie St (daily 10am–5pm; free but charge for some special exhibitions; free guided tours Wed–Sun 2.30pm). The collection is, as the building's name suggests, a mixed bag. Much space is devoted to exploring Tasmania's tragic history, dwelling on penal cruelty, near genocide and the extinction of animal species. As you enter, there's a collection of photographs of the **Tasmanian tiger** (thylacine), thought to have been extinct since 1936 – including a 1920s photo of a proud-looking family posing with their Tasmanian tiger rug spread out before them. The peculiar, flesh-eating, dog-like marsupial, which had a rigid tail, stripes, and a backwards-opening pouch, was hunted out of existence by farming families who were fearful for their stock – although unconfirmed sightings of them still occur from time to time. A stuffed example is part of the unexciting taxidermy exhibition in the adjoining room, though the life-size reconstructions of the **megafauna**, giant marsupials that once roamed Australia, on the same level, are far more riveting. On the next level above, an **Aboriginal room** displays cultural artefacts of the island's indigenous people, including some examples of the kind of exquisite shell necklaces that would have adorned "Queen" Truganini, reputed to be the last Aboriginal Tasmanian (see box on p.902). The display gives a comprehensive account of the Aboriginal people, from their tragic near-extermination to recent events involving land rights campaigns. Particularly poignant is the recording of the voice of **Fanny Cochrane** (1834–1905) singing traditional songs; it is she who was probably the last full-blooded Aboriginal Tasmanian rather than Truganini as the myth relates. The **art gallery** section has a display of colonial art featuring several haunting 1830s and 1840s portraits of the well-known "final" Aborigines, including Manalargenna and Truganini, as well as superb landscape paintings of Tasmania by the nineteenth-century Tasmanian **W.C. Piguenit**. There's also an excellent section on **convicts**: if you can't get to Port Arthur, Richmond Gaol or any of the other convict ruins, this display will convince you of the brutality of the regime.

The **Maritime Museum** (daily 10am–4.30pm; admission $5) which used to occupy Secheron House, in Battery Point was moving at the time of writing to the red-brick Carnegie Building on Argyle Street opposite the museum; the planned re-opening is in late 1999.

West of Franklin Square

There are several worthwhile sights along the straight streets that run west of Franklin Square, particularly Murray and Campbell streets. Three blocks west of the square, on Murray Street, the **State Library** (Mon & Tues 9.30am–6pm, Wed–Fri 9.30am–8pm) holds the **Allport Library and Museum of Fine Arts** (Mon–Fri 9.30am–5pm; free), a private collection of eighteenth- and nineteenth-century furnishings, ceramics, silver and glass, paintings, prints and rare books relating to Australia and the Pacific.

The **Theatre Royal**, on Campbell Street at the corner of Sackville Street (bookings ☎03/6234 6266), is Australia's oldest surviving theatre, built in 1837. It has an intimate interior decorated in Regency style, best seen while attending a performance (see p.921); otherwise, the staff might let you in for a peek. Further up, at the corner of Brisbane Street, the **Penitentiary Chapel and Criminal Courts** (hourly tours daily 10am–3pm, no tours Aug; $6) comprise a complex of early buildings with two courtrooms, underground tunnels and cells. There's also a rather spooky ghost tour (nightly 8pm; $7).

The Waterfront

The focus of **Sullivans Cove** is busy **Franklin Wharf**, the first commercial centre of Hobart, where merchants erected large warehouses as the colony grew wealthier. In the 1830s Hobart was one of the world's great whaling centres, and to cater for the growing volume of shipping, the New Wharf – **Princes Wharf** – was built, featuring a row of handsome sandstone warehouses on Salamanca Place. As the new wharf became the focus of port activity, the old wharf developed into an industrial centre of flour mills and factories. Part of the the Henry Jones Jam Factory, between Victoria and Macquarie docks on Hunter Street, is now the **Centre for the Arts**, the University of Tasmania's art school. Beyond the original facade in a courtyard there are several large pieces of sculpture and the high-tech new face of the art school. Inside, the **Sir James Plimsoll Gallery** (daily noon–5pm when there is a show; free; ☎03/6266 4300 for details of exhibitions) has several shows a year featuring the work of contemporary Australian artists. The rest of the old jam factory is to be redeveloped and extended into a complex made up of a luxury hotel, restaurant, bar and shops – an indication of the direction the area is now taking. Beyond this, in the recently renovated old **Gasworks** on Macquarie Street in the former red-light slum district of **Old Wapping** there's a commercial market (Oct–May Sun 9am–3pm). The restored stone buildings are attractive, but the slick shops, restaurants and enterprises within – many are part of chains – try too hard to attract tourists; one of these is a **whisky distillery** and adjoining museum (daily 9am–9pm; $5).

The old docks along Franklin Wharf are also thriving: at **Victoria Dock** lobster boats are moored, at **Constitution Dock** boats sell fresh and cooked seafood, and alongside is the Mures Fish Centre, a two-level complex of restaurants and cafés (see "Eating and drinking", p.918). The stylish new development on Elizabeth Street Pier has a slew of trendy bars, eateries and luxury hotel apartments. From Brooke Street Pier and Watermans Dock, any number of **cruises** depart (see box opposite), while Murray Street Pier has been jazzed up with several restaurants. In summer, huge international cruise ships berth at the harbour, creating a rather glamorous backdrop to the waterfront pubs.

You can take a **guided walk** (daily 10am; 2hr; $15; booking essential ☎08/6230 8233) that explores Sullivans Cove and Salamanca Place, starting from outside the Travel and Information Centre (see p.910); if this doesn't appeal, excellent interpretive boards are found all around the waterfront.

On **Salamanca Place** the old warehouses, shipping offices and storerooms are now full of arts-and-crafts galleries, speciality shops and cafés, interspersed with characterful waterfront pubs. Salamanca Place comes alive for the open-air **Salamanca Market** (Sat 8am–3pm), an event with an alternative feel and wonderful local food, including produce grown and sold by the Hmong people, Hobart's most distinctive immigrant group. Quality Tasmanian crafts are on offer, along with secondhand bargains, all sold to the accompaniment of buskers; along with crowds of dreadlocked alternative lifestyle seekers, they make an engaging spectacle in front of outdoor cafés and pubs.

Several of the narrow lanes and arcades in the area are worth exploring, as is the **Salamanca Arts Centre** (☎03/6234 8414), originally a jam-canning factory, and now home to a diverse range of arts-based organizations, from the Tasmanian Writers' Centre to the Terrapin Puppet Theatre. Downstairs, the Peacock Theatre is the performance venue, and there are several galleries (daily 10am–5pm); upstairs, emerging

HARBOUR CRUISES

Cruise Company, Brooke Street Pier (☎03/6234 9294). Fast catamarans which allow you to see a lot. The best cruise on the Derwent is their Iron Pot Cruise to the river mouth and across to the top of Bruny Island (summer only Sat 2pm; $20). The Cadbury's Cruise heads upriver to the chocolate factory at Claremont; it's essential to book in advance as chocaholics treat this as a pilgrimage (Mon–Fri 10am; 4hr; $33). A one-hour cruise goes just beyond the Tasman Bridge (May–Sept 2pm daily; $10).

Fell's Historic Ferries, Franklin Wharf Pier (☎03/6223 5893). A range of particularly good-value harbour cruises on the *MV Emmalisa*, all of which include meals of some kind ($10–18).

Lady Nelson, Elizabeth Street Pier (summer only; ☎03/6272 2823). This replica of the brig in which Matthew Flinders made his exploratory journeys is a sail-training vessel, but also offers bargain weekend pleasure trips (Sat & Sun 11am, 1pm & 3pm; $5; 1hr 30min). When the ship leaves Hobart at the end of summer for longer journeys on the eastern seaboard, you can join as a paying passenger (about $125 per day).

MV Cartela, Brooke Street Pier (☎03/6223 1914). An eighty-year-old boat that used to bring apples from the Huon. Offers a range of cruises, including morning (daily 10am; 2hr; $14) and night-time (dinner cruise Mon, Wed, Fri & Sat 6pm; 2hr 30min; $20 including dinner).

Rhona-H, Watermans Dock (mobile phone ☎018/133 396). Cruises on a fifty-year-old gaff-rig ketch made of Huon pine, piloted by a lively skipper; you're encouraged to participate, and learn about sailing. Harbour cruise (3hr; $25), full day sails ($50), plus longer overnight cruises (around $130 per day).

---

contemporary artists show at the Long Gallery, and there are smaller displays in Side Space. Outside, the *Foyer Café* doubles as an installation venue and a large notice board has news of alternative events around town. The Arts Centre also houses several shops, including a very browseable secondhand bookshop.

Through the Arts Centre, Woobies Lane leads to **Salamanca Square**, Hobart's latest development. An old quarry, it's now a large public square filled with cafés, boutiques and small shops, and has two overpriced tourist attractions. The **Antarctic Adventure** (daily 10am–5pm; $16), cashes in on Hobart's obvious links; Australia has the oldest continuously operating Antarctic station, Mawson, established in 1954, and has considerable claims under the Antarctic Treaty. Organizations based in Hobart include the Australian Antarctic Division and the Australian National Research Expedition (ANARE); the latter was the brainchild of the legendary Australian explorer, **Sir Douglas Mawson**, who led an Australian expedition from 1911 to 1914. Part theme park, part museum, the centre has everything from a "cold experience" room and a mock Antarctic field camp to a planetarium; even so, a free visit to the foyer exhibition at the Antarctic Division Headquarters at Kingston (see p.923) is more informative and compelling in its authenticity. The second attraction, **Time Warp House** (daily 10am–5pm; $8), a "retro entertainment centre", aims to capture the past century of Tasmanian (and Australian) social history with photographs, video snatches, memorabilia and rooms kitted out in various styles, but doesn't add up to much.

Battery Point

Kelly's Steps lead up from Salamanca Place to **Battery Point**, a district with an enduring village atmosphere. With the building of the new wharf in the 1830s, a working-class community grew up behind Salamanca Place, transforming what had been farmland into a residential area; it takes its name from the battery of guns that were once sited on present-day **Princes Park**, protecting the harbour below. The newly developing area was first home to small cottages for waterfront workmen and, later, fine merchants' houses were built here: the old pubs, with names such as the *Shipwrights Arms* and *Whalers Return,* leave no doubt about the nature of the population. Narrow streets, closely packed cottages, the flower-filled green of **Arthurs Circus** and the "corner-store" nature of the shops (such as the delightful Bahr's Chocolate Shop, 95 Hampden Rd), enhance the nineteenth-century village feel. There's a particular concentration of early buildings on De Witt and Cromwell streets. **St George's Church**, on Cromwell Street, is the joint work of John Lee Archer (responsible for the nave, completed in 1838) and James Blackburn (the tower, added in 1847), the early colony's two best-known architects.

Hampden Road has more fine nineteenth-century mansions, including one at no. 103 known as **Narryna** (Tues–Fri 10.30am–5pm, Sat & Sun 2–5pm; $5), furnished with period antiques. Inside, the **Van Diemen's Land Folk Museum** has a display of entertaining miscellany, while at the back there's a blacksmith's, a vehicle shed housing old traps, and a coach house filled with brewery equipment.

If you want to become really acquainted with the history and architecture of the area, take the **Battery Point Walking Tour** (Sat 9.30am–12.30pm, departing from the Wishing Well, Franklin Square; $10 including morning tea; ☎03/6223 7570 for bookings), led by admirably knowledgeable National Trust volunteers.

Around the harbour

The estuary of the **Derwent River** is the deepest (and second-busiest) natural port in Australia. Heading upstream, the scenery becomes increasingly industrial, with a huge zinc-processing plant and, in a more unspoilt setting at Claremont, the **Cadbury's Factory**. Tours of the factory include as much chocolate as you can eat and are understandably popular (Mon–Fri 9am, 9.30am, 10.30am, 11.15am & 1pm; 2hr; $10; tickets must be booked in advance; ☎03/6249 0333); from the city centre, take bus #37 direct to the factory. Alternatively, you can take a cruise there (see box overleaf), or go on a guided coach tour with Tiger Line (Tues, Wed & Thurs 9.30am; 3hr; $25; ☎03/6231 2200).

The eastern side of the river is more residential, and looking across you'll see swelling, bush-clad hills with a modest line of homes below. The **Tasman Bridge** connects the eastern shore with the city: it was put out of action for over two years from January 1975, when the 20,000-tonne tanker *Lake Illawarra*, heading for the zinc-smelting works, crashed into it and destroyed two pylons. The ship is still at the bottom of the river, with its cargo of zinc concentrate, as are the bodies of seven crew members and five people in four cars.

The **Kangaroo Bluff Battery** at Bellerive, on the eastern shore – along with its counterparts at Sandy Bay (Alexandra Battery) and Battery Point (Mona Street Battery) – was erected in response to a Russian scare in the late nineteenth century, but it never saw active service. **Bellerive**, which you can reach by ferry from Brooke Street Pier (see p.915), has a long, sandy beach at the Esplanade; some swim from it, although the water is somewhat polluted. There's cleaner water and surf beaches across the promontory from Bellerive at **Opossum Bay** (bus #296 from the city centre; no service Sun); while **Seven Mile Beach**, on Frederick Henry Bay, offers calmer swimming (bus #292 or #293). Ten kilometres north of Bellerive is **Risdon Cove**, site of the first European settlement of Van Diemen's Land; interpretive boards explain its early history. To get there, take bus #267, #269 or #270 from the city centre.

Queens Domain

The **Queens Domain**, just north of the city centre, looks attractively green on the map but is considerably less inviting in reality: a sparse, bush-covered hill traversed by walking and jogging tracks but positioned between two very busy highways. At the base of the hill on the Derwent, where the trees suddenly become lush and green, are the

Royal Botanical Gardens (daily 8am–4.45pm), a formal collection of flower displays and orderly trees. Pick up a leaflet outlining the features of the garden at any entrance, or from the **information centre** (Mon–Fri 9am–noon & 1–4.30pm) at the main entrance on the west side of the park. It's easy enough to walk to the Domain, following Davey Street or Liverpool Street from the city centre, but the gardens are quite far inside the grounds: from the city centre to the gardens should take you about thirty minutes. Take bus #17 or any bus to Eastern Shore (including #285, #287, #289 and #293) will drop you at Government House, in the centre of the Domain near the gardens, but there's no transport back. A more interesting way of getting to the gardens is to cruise on the *MV Cartela* from Brooke Street Pier (see box on p.915).

Sandy Bay

Leafy, well-heeled **Sandy Bay**, a suburb south of Battery Point, is home to a rather luxurious shopping centre, the Royal Yacht Club, and the **Wrest Point Casino** on Sandy Bay Road. An ugly 1970s high-rise, the casino strives hard to be glamorous, but a rather downmarket tone is set by masses of tour groups wearing name tags and groups of slacks-clad pensioners swarming all over the small gambling area. At the **Sandy Bay Regatta** in January, yachts are moored all around Sandy Bay's marinas, the river is filled with boats, and a funfair is held on the waterfront. At weekends, as well, there are hundreds of yachts on the water. Several buses go to Sandy Bay from the city centre, among them #56 and #60, and the yellow Busy Bee bus comes here on a regular circuit from Franklin Square; you can reach Sandy Bay over water from Brooke Street Pier on the *MV Cartela* ($2.50 one-way; see box on p.915).

Inland to Mount Wellington and Mount Nelson

Heading inland, the route south and west towards Mount Wellington takes you through South Hobart, on to Cascade Road and past the pretty **Cascade Gardens**. Here, at 140 Cascade Road, the magnificent seven-storey **Cascade Brewery** is the oldest in Australia, still using traditional methods and taking advantage of the pure spring water that cascades – of course – down Mount Wellington. There's a traditional north–south divide between beer drinkers in Tasmania: in Launceston and the north you drink Boags, in Hobart you drink Cascade, although in fact the two breweries merged in 1922. **Tours** run Monday to Friday only (9.30am & 1pm; 2hr; $7.50; bookings essential on ☎03/6224 1144), and at a fairly gruelling pace, but you're rewarded with a couple of (light) beers at the workers' bar, and a bottle of Premium Lager at the end of the tour in the brewer's original residence. The small museum of brewing paraphernalia includes a few childhood pictures of the Hollywood actor Errol Flynn, who was brought up in the Cascades area. Buses #48 and #49 go right to the brewery.

In any image of Hobart, **Mount Wellington** (1270m) is always looming in the background, sometimes snow-covered. Access is up a winding road consisting of dozens of hairpin bends and lined with houses as far as **Fern Tree**, where a tavern offers teas and meals at the bottom of the walking track up the mountain (2hr up, 1hr down); the thick bush begins to thin out as you ascend, and by the time you've reached the top it's bare and rocky. Pure, drinkable water cascades from rocks as you climb, and halfway up, just after the first lookout, there's a grassy picnic area with barbecues, toilets and information boards. At the top, the stone **Pinnacle Observatory Shelter** (daily 8am–6pm) has details of the magnificent panorama spread before you. From here, it's surprising how empty the land around Hobart really is, seeming to be nothing but uninhabited bush and grass plains. Despite opposition from local residents, there are controversial plans to build a cable car to the top, but for the moment it's fairly unspoilt. In summer, the Hobart Metro sometimes runs special **buses** right up Mount Wellington from

Franklin Square (call the Metro hotline for information on ☎13 2201); at other times, you can get halfway up on bus #48 or #49 to Fern Tree. Brake Out Cycling Tours has a tour that includes a visit to the summit, and then a twenty-kilometre downhill mountain-bike ride to Salamanca Place ($35; ☎03/6239 1090; *www.view.com.au/brakeout*).

The views are also terrific from the Old Signal Station on **Mount Nelson** (340m) above Sandy Bay. The station was established in 1811 to announce the appearance of ships in Storm Bay and the D'Entrecasteaux Channel; the signalman's residence here has been converted into tearooms (daily 9.30am–4.30pm), from where you get a panorama of the city below. To get to Mount Nelson, take bus #57 or #58.

Eating and drinking

Hobart's steadfastly Anglo-Saxon fare can't compare with the mainland cities' ethnical-ly eclectic range of cuisines, but its food is becoming more cosmopolitan; the greatest diversity of restaurants and cafés is found along the Elizabeth Street strip in North Hobart. Superlative **seafood** can be had throughout the city, but especially in the restaurants down by the docks. Fishing boats moor at Victoria Dock and sell their catch direct to the public. The food stalls at Saturday's Salamanca Market are excellent – par-ticularly those run by the Hmong from Laos.

Da Angelo Ristorante, 47 Hampden Rd, Battery Point (☎03/6223 7011). A great village spot for a more upmarket Italian meal plus gourmet pizzas; tasty food, generous portions and good service. Licensed. Dinner nightly.

Fish Frenzy, Elizabeth Street Pier. A stylish modern fish café – order your food at the counter and find a seat. Cheap food is terrific but the waiting process is hellishly slow despite the name – you can, however, get into a frenzy of drinking while you wait for your fish, since the place is licensed.

Garden of Earthly Delights, 247 Sandy Bay Rd, Sandy Bay (☎03/6223 4471). Good home cook-ing, with meat, vegan and vegetarian dishes. Sit in the outdoor courtyard in summer, or inside beside the fire in colder months. BYO. Tues–Sat 11am–10pm.

Jackman & McGross, 57–59 Hampden Rd, Battery Point. Stylish eat-in bakery that fits in with the upmarket village atmosphere of Battery Point. Excellent pastries and baked savouries, and gourmet baguettes and rolls. Mon–Fri 7.30am–7pm, Sat 7.30am–5pm.

Kaos Cafe, 237 Elizabeth St, North Hobart. Trendy, gay-friendly coffee spot. Jazzy music, fresh flowers, mags to read. Focaccias, real fruit muffins and cakes plus delicious all-day breakfast. BYO. Mon–Fri noon–midnight, Sat 10am–midnight, Sun 10am–10pm.

La Cuisine, 85 Bathurst St, and the Trafalgar Centre at 110 Collins St. Two café-patisseries serv-ing great cappuccino and excellent pastries, plus mounds of healthy salad. Mon–Fri 9am–6pm, Sat 8am–1pm.

Machine, 12 Salamanca Square. This quirky combination Fifties retro café-laundry with outside seating is the place to come for a coffee and join the city's young trendies (often with babies in tow). Unfortunately portions are measly and the food's not great. Mon–Sat 8am–6pm, Sun 9am–6pm.

Mako, Constitution Dock. Takeaway seafood from a boat moored in the dock; best fish and chips in town. Daily 10am–8pm.

Marti Zucco, 364 Elizabeth St, North Hobart (☎03/6234 9611). Italian restaurant serving imagina-tive dishes, including fish, schnitzels and thick-crust pizzas. Large and very popular, with a casual atmosphere; licensed and BYO. Mon–Thurs & Sun 5.30–10pm, Fri & Sat until 11.30pm.

Mit Zitrone, 333 Elizabeth St, North Hobart (☎03/6234 8113). Chic café-restaurant, very much in the Melbourne style, with a cosmopolitan menu favouring fish. If the delicious main dishes are out of your range (around $16), there's a cake selection and excellent coffee. BYO. Mon–Sat 10.30am–10.30pm.

Mummy's Coffee Shop, 38 Waterloo Crescent, Battery Point. Recently extended café that's now very trendy; it's best feature is its range of delicious cakes; main meals from Contemporary Australian menu. Licensed and open late. Mon–Thurs & Sun until midnight, Fri & Sat until 2am.

Mures Fish Centre, Victoria Dock. Food centre on two levels (open daily), set among yachts and fishing boats; with three restaurants, a fishmonger, bakery (great scallop pies) and café. *Mures Upper Deck* (☎03/6231 1999) is an upmarket restaurant which has lovely harbour views; *Mures Lower Deck* has bistro food, with cheaper prices; *Orizuru* (☎03/6231 1790; closed Sun) serves authentic sushi – their salmon is delicious.

Orient Express, 147A Little Collins St. Good, cheap servings of Malaysian, Indian and Thai food; there's a small eat-in area, but the emphasis is on takeaways. Closed Sat & Sun.

Palette's Studio Café, 14 Davey St. A handy spot to recharge, right near the Travel and Information Centre and the Tasmanian Museum and Art Gallery, and located below an artist's studio. Mon–Fri 10am–4pm.

Renown Milkbar, 337 Elizabeth St, North Hobart. A Hobart institution whose windows are full of imported chocolates. Good for a coffee or snack after a movie at the nearby cinema. Daily 8am–11pm.

Retro Café, 31 Salamanca Place. Relaxed, light and airy place serving the best espresso in town, plus amazingly frothy cappuccinos and wonderful breakfasts. A good place to find out what's on – notices and flyers cover one wall. Outside tables popular on market day (Sat). Mon–Sat 8am–6pm, Sun 8.30am–6pm.

Shipwright's Arms Hotel, cnr of Colville and Trumpeter sts, Battery Point. Old pub, popular with the yachtie crowd. Dishes up a legendary fresh seafood platter.

Sisco's on the Pier, Murray Street Pier (☎03/6223 2059). Waterfront Spanish–Mediterranean restaurant guarantees a fine, though pricey, feast. Licensed.

Vanadol's, 353 Elizabeth Street, North Hobart (☎03/6234 9307). Popular, casual place serving Thai, Indonesian and Malaysian food. Very affordable; BYO. Booking advisable. Tues–Sun from 6pm.

Zanskar Café, 39 Barrack St. Laid-back place for serious vegetarians and vegans, serving delicious food. There's a warm community atmosphere and plenty of useful notice boards to peruse, while the feel is spacious with a gallery level, and a clean wood decor. Mon–Fri 9am–9pm.

Entertainment and nightlife

Nightlife – what there is of it – is focused around the waterfront. The focal point is *Knopwood's Retreat* on Salamanca Place, which attracts a large crowd on Friday and Saturday night, and has a popular nightclub upstairs. The more conservative *Wrest Point Casino*, at 410 Sandy Bay Rd in Sandy Bay, is open late every night for gambling, drinking and dancing (☎03/6225 0112; casino Sun–Thurs 2pm–2am, Fri & Sat 2pm–3am; *Regine's* nightclub Wed–Sun 10pm–4am).

If you want to know **what's on**, Thursday's *Mercury* has a "gig guide", and you could also check its Friday and Saturday entertainment section or *W-Hole Magazine*, a do-it-yourself monthly with a gig guide and reviews. As for **live music**, Tasmania is too small to attract many bands, so the ones that play the pubs are mainly local. The few big events that do occur attract an extraordinarily varied audience, as everybody goes to everything. For anything more interesting, keep an eye on what's happening at the University of Tasmania campus at Sandy Bay (☎03/6220 2861). **Concerts** are staged by the Tasmanian Symphony Orchestra at the ABC Odeon (see overleaf) and the Tasmanian Conservatoriam of Music (the Conservatoriam at 5–7 Sandy Bay Rd; ☎03/6226 7306) who also perform at churches around town (free or $3–5). You'll find traditional and touring **theatre** at the Theatre Royal, and more contemporary local shows at the Peacock Theatre in Salamanca Place; in February and March there's a season of outdoor Shakespeare in the Royal Botanical Gardens. Most tickets can be booked via Centretainment, at 132 Liverpool St (☎03/6234 5998); guides and calendars can be picked up at *Kaos* and other cafés.

Bars, clubs and live music

All Bar One, 24 Salamanca Square (☎03/6224 7557). Renovated sandstone warehouse turned into a slick and spacious bar and brasserie. Wine available by the glass. Daily 9am–midnight.

Bavarian Tavern, 281 Liverpool St (☎03/6234 7977). Known to locals as the "Bav Tav": fun down-to-earth venue – jamming sessions, dancing, cheap meals.

Brooke Street Bar and Café, 19 Morrison St, cnr of Brooke St. Waterfront pub, with large windows letting in lots of light onto the wacky beachbar-style interior. Outside tables too. Open until 2am Sat & Sun.

Juice Niteclub, 7 Watchorn St (☎03/6234 5165). Barn-like bar, lively and packed on Friday and Saturday night.

GAY AND LESBIAN HOBART

Acts of male homosexuality were still a criminal offence in Tasmania until 1997. Founded in 1988, the **Tasmanian Gay and Lesbian Rights Group** (TGLRG) put persistent pressure on the government. Led by spokesperson **Rodney Croome**, their rally cry "We're here, we're queer, and we're not going to the mainland" certainly shook up conservative Tasmania; thousands signed the petition to urge the reform of the law. Backlash across Tasmania included the infamous anti-gay rally in Ulverstone on the northwest coast in 1988. The Federal Government and the UN Human Rights Committee also pressed for change, and Tasmania's anti-gay upper house finally cracked, changing the law on May 1, 1997.

The TGLRG office is at 82 Hampden Rd, Battery Point (☎03/6224 3556), and there's a Gay and Lesbian Community Centre (GLC) in North Hobart (PO Box 152, North Hobart, TAS 7002; ☎03/6228 7209). GLC publish a monthly newsletter, *CentreLines* ($1), which is sold from the TGLRG stall at Salamanca Market and details events and occasional dance parties round town. The only **gay and lesbian club** is tame but enjoyable: *La Cage*, 73 Collins St (Thurs–Sat from 11pm; ☎03/6231 5882). *T-42°* and *Syrup* are popular alternatives. The **Gay Information Line** (☎03/6234 8179) is a five-minute recorded message that provides pointers for gay and lesbian visitors, details of events and meeting places and numbers for further information; there's a specifically **Lesbian Line** too (Thurs 6–10pm; ☎03/6231 4228).

Knopwood's Retreat, 39 Salamanca Place. Pub that's a favourite with students, yachties, and just about everyone else, with a relaxed coffee parlour/bar feel; plenty of magazines and newspapers, plus outside tables. Open until midnight on Fri, when the pavement outside is packed. Closed Sun.

The New Sydney Hotel, 87 Bathurst St (☎03/6234 4516). Hobart's Irish pub, featuring live music nightly except Monday – from traditional Irish to blues and folk.

Republic Bar & Café, 299 Elizabeth St (☎03/6234 6954). Laid-back lounge atmosphere, funky decor and free music, usually blues and jazz, five nights a week. Good meals too – with lots of seafood on the menu.

Rockerfeller's Café & Bar, 11 Morrison St (☎03/6234 3490). Cocktails, live jazz Sunday nights and an American-style menu. Daily until midnight, Fri & Sat until 2am.

St Ives Hotel, 86 Sandy Bay Rd, Sandy Bay (☎03/6323 3655). "Boutique" hotel that has its own brewery. Popular club nights on Friday and Saturday. The excellent bottle shop at the back has a good range of Tasmanian wines.

Syrup, above *Knopwood's*, 39 Salamanca Place (☎03/6224 8249). Hobart's trendiest club. The second floor doubles as a restaurant until 11.30pm; at midnight the nightclub takes over, lasting until around 6am on Fri & Sat. Third floor for techno, house, drum and bass on Thurs & Sat, second floor for 1980s retro (and pool table). Live disco and funk Friday. Theme nights include a 1960s night on Wed with go-go girls and visuals. Wed–Sat $5–$7.

T-42°, Elizabeth Street Pier (☎03/6224 7742). Stylish lounge bar, upmarket but not snobby: anyone with a bit of taste loves it. Good choice of wine, available by the glass. Half the place is an eating area serving well-priced modern meals at lunch and dinner, or you can come in for a coffee or cake in the afternoon. Glass doors open onto the pier. Daily 11.30am–1.30am.

Theatre Royal Hotel, 31 Campbell St (☎03/6234 6925). Despite the trendily upmarket renovations, the public bar is as down-to-earth as ever. People spill in here after the theatre. Recommended bistro too. Open until midnight; closed Sun.

Film, theatre, concerts and cabaret

ABC Odeon, 167 Liverpool St (☎03/6235 3633). Home to the Tasmanian Symphony Orchestra, with concerts on a regular basis.

AFI State Cinema, 375 Elizabeth St, North Hobart (☎03/6234 6318). Art-house and foreign films; reduced ticket prices Wed night. Licensed bar.

Playhouse Theatre, 106 Bathurst St (☎03/6234 1536). Home to an amateur theatrical society that regularly puts on plays. Premises are rented out to travelling shows.

Salamanca Arts Centre, 77 Salamanca Place (☎03/6234 8414). Home base of several performance companies: the Terrapin Puppet Theatre puts on touring shows, including a puppet picnic at the end of December in St Davids Park. Puppeteers are welcome to come in and look around. The theatre venue here is the Peacock Theatre which specializes in contemporary works, performed by various local theatre companies.

Theatre Royal, 29 Campbell St (☎03/6233 2299). This lovely old place (see p.913) is not too expensive or stuffy, offering a broad spectrum, from comedy nights to serious drama. The ancillary Backspace is smaller and more experimental – often hosting very entertaining Theatresports on Friday nights.

Village Cinema Centre, 181 Collins St (☎03/6234 7288). Seven screens showing mainstream new releases; discount day is Tuesday.

Listings

Airlines Kendell (☎13 1300); Par Avion, Cambridge Airport (☎03/6248 5390); Qantas, 77 Elizabeth Street Mall (☎03/6235 4900); Tasair, Cambridge Airport (☎03/6248 5577).

Airport shuttle bus Tasmanian Redline Coaches (☎03/6231 3900); see p.908.

American Express, 74A Liverpool St (☎03/6231 2955).

Banks Branches of all major banks on Elizabeth St.

Bike rental and tours Cycling Adventures Tasmania (☎018/913 148) has mountain bikes to hire outside the *Machine* café on Salamanca Square. They also offer cycling tours of the city centre; one includes laundry service and a coffee. Brake Out Cycling Tours (☎03/6239 1090) offer a Mount Wellington descent tour (see p.918), plus fully equipped mountain bikes for touring, with cheaper long-term rates.

Bookshops Ellison and Hawker Bookshop, 90 Liverpool St, is the best in Hobart, with an excellent travel section upstairs (open daily; ☎03/6234 2322). Fullers Bookshop, 140 Collins St (☎03/6224 2488), also has a good stock. For an excellent range of secondhand books, try Rapid Eye Books, 36–38 Sandy Bay Rd, Battery Point (☎03/6223 2400).

Bus companies Tasmanian Redline Coaches (☎03/6331 3233 or ☎1300/360 000) and Tasmanian Wilderness Travel (☎03/6334 4442), both based at the Hobart Transit Centre, 199 Collins St. Hobart Coaches, 4 Liverpool St (☎03/6234 4077).

Campervan rental Tasmanian Campervan Hire (Hobart airport; ☎03/6248 9623 or free call ☎1800/807 119), from $95 per day, minimum three-day hire.

Car rental Auto Rent Hertz, 122 Harrington St (☎03/6237 1111, fax 6234 1955), has rates from $50 per day, also campervans; Avis, at the airport (☎03/6248 5424), has similar rates; Lo-Cost Auto Rent, 225 Liverpool St (☎03/6231 0550, fax 6231 0882), has rentals from $37 per day; Advance Car Rentals (☎03/6224 0822) also have 4WDs, from $110 per day; Marquee Car Rentals, 248 Argyle St (☎03/6231 3820), offers very cheap weekly rates; Rent-A-Bug, 105 Murray St (☎03/6231 0673 or 6231 0300), has VW Beetles from $30 per day.

Disabled travellers The Aged and Disability Care Information Centre, at 192 Macquarie St (☎03/6224 2322), is an excellent source of information for visitors with disabilities, providing free mobility maps of Hobart. Maxi Taxis (☎03/6234 8061) has specially adapted vehicles.

Diving Southern Tas Divers, 212 Elizabeth St (☎03/6234 7243), organizes dive charters and rents out equipment; Sport and Dive, 109 Elizabeth St (☎03/6234 3798), arranges fishing charters and rents out dive gear.

Environment If you want to find out about, and volunteer for, any environmental conservation programmes, the Wilderness Society's campaign office is at 130 Davey St (☎03/6234 9366) and its shop is at 33 Salamanca Place (☎03/6234 9370). The Australian Trust for Conservation Volunteers has an office at the Salamanca Arts Centre, Salamanca Place (☎03/6224 4911).

Festivals and events Hobart's premier event is the last part of the Sydney–Hobart yacht race (see also p.162). The two hundred or so yachts, which leave Sydney on December 26, arrive in Hobart around December 29, making for a lively New Year's Eve waterfront party. Taste of Tasmania (Dec 28–Jan 5), a festival promoting Tasmanian food, wine and beer, is held at Princes Wharf to coincide with the arrival of the boats; stalls sell samples of Tasmanian products at around $5 a plate, and there's lots of entertainment. The week-long Hobart Fringe Festival at the beginning of February has visual arts and performance components; check cafés for flyers. In late February the six-day outdoor Forest Festival held near the Huon River features environmental talks and workshops, market stalls, local and interstate bands, circus performance and DJs; ask at the *Zanskar Café* (p.919) for details. The whole city shuts down on October 24 during the Royal Hobart Show (Oct 23–26), an agricultural festival. The Australian Wooden Boat Festival is held in November in even-numbered years, marked by a host of boats moored around the docks; activities include theatrical and musical performances, and there's even a School of Wooden Boat Building offering courses to visitors (☎03/6266 3486).

Hospitals Royal Hobart Hospital, 48 Liverpool St (☎03/6238 8308).

Internet access Free Internet access at the Service Tasmania Shop at 134 Macquarie St, (several terminals; Mon–Fri 9am–4.45pm; ☎03/6233 3382), at the State Library (see p.913) and at *Drifters Café*, Salamanca Place (Mon–Sat 8am–5pm, Sun 11am–5pm; ☎03/6224 3244; $10 per hour, $6 per 30min, $2 per 10min).

Laundrette *Machine*, 12 Salamanca Square, is a combined café/laundrette (Mon–Sat 8am–6pm, Sun 9am–6pm).

Newspapers Ellison and Hawker Newsagency, 92 Elizabeth St (☎03/6234 4099), is the island's only outlet for foreign newspapers.

Outdoors and sport Jolly Swagman, 107 Elizabeth St (☎03/6234 3999), is a good outlet for renting camping gear; Paddy Pallin, 76 Elizabeth St (☎03/6231 0777), has quality outdoor equipment to buy and rent, and provides bushwalking information; Gowshawk Gear, 55 Liverpool St (03/6234 6200) sells secondhand, samples and discounted outdoor gear and will buy your used stuff.

Pharmacy Macquarie Pharmacy, 180 Macquarie St (☎03/6223 2339); daily until 10pm. North Hobart Pharmacy, 360–362 Elizabeth St (☎03/6234 1136); daily 8am–10pm.

Post office GPO, cnr of Elizabeth and Macquarie sts (Mon–Fri 8am–6pm); poste restante: Hobart GPO, TAS 7000.

Rape crisis Sexual Assault Support Service (☎03/6231 1811).

Taxis City Cabs Co-op (☎03/6234 3633); Combined Services (☎13 2227). Maxi taxis (☎03/6234 8061) for disabled-friendly taxis.

Tours Tiger Line (☎03/6231 2200) runs large group bus tours: their Mount Wellington and Hobart Great Sights Tour covers the city, the dock area, Battery Point, Mount Wellington and the Royal Botanical Gardens (Tues, Thurs & Sat 2pm; 3hr 30min; $25). Tiger Line also offers day-tours to Port Arthur, Richmond, the Huon Valley, Bruny Island, and the Derwent Valley. The other big tour operator, Experience Tasmania (☎03/6234 3336), has a wide range of city tours; their *Hobart Explorer*, a bus dolled up as a tram, does a three-hour sight-seeing tour (Jan–April daily 10am & 2pm; May–Dec Mon–Fri & Sun 10am, Sat 2pm), short-range day-tours plus trips to Mount Field National Park. More satisfying are Tasmanian Wilderness Travel's small group day-tours (☎03/6234 2226): to Port Arthur for the ghost tour (Mon, Thurs & Fri; $40); Mount Field National Park (daily; $49); Hastings Caves (Sun, Tues, Thurs & Sat; $49). The best tour to Bruny Island is with Bruny Island Ventures (book through Tiger Line), which does a small group day-tour led by a knowledgeable guide (departing Hobart Sun–Fri 8.30am, returning 5.30pm; $95 including meals).

Women There are women's information services at the Office of the Status of Women, 3rd Floor, Franklin Square Building, Macquarie St (☎03/6234 2166), and the Hobart Women's Health Centre, 326 Elizabeth St, North Hobart (☎03/6231 3212).

YHA Tasmania, Head Office, 28 Criterion St (☎03/6234 9617). Mon–Fri 9am–4.30pm.

Around Hobart

South of Hobart is picturesque channel, orchard and island country. The D'Entrecasteaux Channel region and the Huon Valley form Tasmania's premier **fruit-growing** district, which once exported millions of apples to England; since the UK joined the European Community, however, two-thirds of the apple orchards have been abandoned. The region is also heavily forested, and around **Geeveston** magnificent forests are still logged. **Hartz Mountains National Park** and the **Picton River** are easily accessible to the west of Geeveston. As you head down the coast, caves, thermal springs and an operational railway are all accessible en route to **Cockle Creek**, the southernmost point you can drive to in Australia, with foot access along a track into the

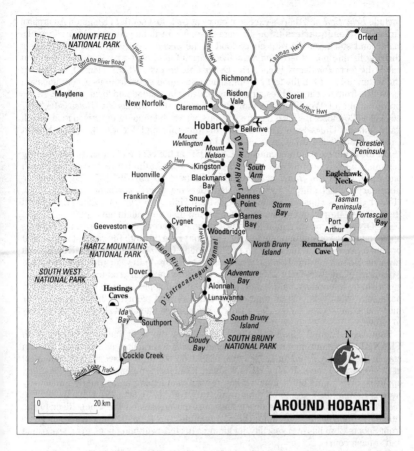

South West National Park. Offshore, across the D'Entrecasteaux Channel, **Bruny Island** – Truganini's birthplace – has deserted beaches and coastal bushwalks. To the north, you can head inland to New Norfolk and on to **Mount Field National Park**, while to the east lies historic **Richmond**, and, on the Tasman Peninsula, the old penal settlement at **Port Arthur**.

South: the D'Entrecasteaux Channel, Huon Valley and beyond

The **Channel Highway** hugs the coastline south from Hobart and makes a lovely drive around the shores of the **Huon Peninsula**, circling back beside the Huon River to Huonville: heading to Huonville directly, it's a much shorter 37km on the Huon Highway. **Rafting** is possible all year on the Huon River, with day-trips from Hobart led by Rafting Tasmania (☎03/6227 9516) for around $110. The first community on the Channel Highway is **KINGSTON** (Metro bus #60 from the Hobart bus interchange), a leafy residential suburb with a wide, sandy beach; there are more good beaches, such as Blackmans Bay, on the little promontory below Kingston. Good cafés on Beach Road include *Echo Café* and there's excellent curry at *Goa*. Just south of Kingston Australia's **Antarctic Headquarters** (Mon–Fri 9am–5pm; free) will fill you in on Antarctic exploration and stock you up with cheap food at the decent canteen. At **KETTERING**, a thriving fishing port, there's an attractive marina full of boats; it's from here that you catch the ferry for Bruny Island. The *Oyster Cove Inn* (☎03/6267 4446; ⑤) is right on the water, not far from the ferry terminal, and has good views from its accommodation as well as from its bars and restaurant, specializing in seafood and local produce. At the pretty village of **Woodbridge**, 4km further south, the *Woodbridge Hotel* (☎03/6267 4604, fax 6267 4828; B&B ④) has great rooms, views and moderately priced food (lunch daily, dinner Thurs–Sat). You can get to Kettering and Woodbridge with Hobart Coaches (☎03/6234 4077) on weekdays (4 daily).

On the other side of the peninsula, **CYGNET**, at the centre of a major fruit-growing region, is a likely spot to look for **fruit-picking work** in the harvest season of March and April. *Balfes Hill Hostel*, at 340 Craddoc Rd (☎ & fax 03/6295 1551; ①), has all the necessary contacts; the manager here also offers day-trips to surrounding sights ($15). Hobart Coaches runs an evening service from Hobart to Cygnet (Mon–Fri 5.15pm); the hostel is 4km from Cygnet, but will pick you up if you call in advance.

HUONVILLE, on the Huon River, is a commercial centre, the focus of the region's apple industry. You can arrange to take a **jet-boat ride** through the rapids (35min; $38) or rent a pedal boat at the kiosk on the Esplanade (☎03/6264 1838). At **GROVE**, 6km towards Hobart on the Huon Highway, is the **Huon Valley Apple and Heritage Museum** (daily 9am–5pm; $2.50), which celebrates the local produce; the museum is surprisingly interesting, with hundreds of varieties of apples, assorted apple paraphernalia from what was once a huge export industry, and plenty of things to taste. For more substantial eats, try the *Apple Valley Teahouse* just outside of Huonville on the way to Grove.

Southwest beyond Huonville, the road follows the west bank of the Huon to **FRANKLIN**, a handsome riverside community with several fine old buildings. You can stay in the swanky *Franklin Lodge* (☎03/6266 3506; ⑦) or just have a good-value meal at the *Franklin Tavern*. **PORT HUON**, about 10km further along, was once a bustling, apple-exporting port but is now a quiet, recreational fishing area. The hub of activity here is *Kermandie Lodge*, on the highway (☎03/6297 1110, fax 6297 1710; ⑤–⑦). The resort has a variety of places to eat and runs day-cruises on the Huon River to the Atlantic salmon farms (daily 2pm; 1hr; $18; minimum six people). The council-run riverfront Sports Club has every facility, including a heated swimming pool, gym, spa, sauna and squash courts.

Hobart Coaches runs through Grove, Huonville, Franklin and Port Huon en route to Geeveston and Dover (Mon–Fri 5–7 daily, Sun 1 daily).

Geeveston and around

GEEVESTON, 8km from Port Huon, is a sleepy but solid town at the centre of the Southern Forest, a traditional logging centre, with two huge upright logs acting as an entrance to the town. Confrontation between conservationists and the timber industry here led to the so-called "Battle of Farmhouse Creek" in 1986, a dispute won by the conservationists, after which some of the forests were awarded World Heritage listing. The Forestry Commission was awarded millions of dollars in compensation, to be used on special forestry projects, one of which is the **Forest and Heritage Centre** in the town hall on Church Street (daily 10am–4.30pm; $4). You begin by looking at displays that show how the Southern forests grow, then you gradually move on to the history of logging in the area – covering the Farmhouse Creek dispute – and finally you are shown how to chop down a tree and end up with woodchips. There's a gallery showing off the woodwork of local craftspeople, a woodturner in residence (lessons are available if you're keen) and lots of objects for sale in the giftshop. After visiting the centre, you're meant to drive along Arve Road, where several boardwalks have been constructed through magnificent swamp gum and eucalypt forests – they're detailed on the free leaflet that's handed out.

Twenty-four kilometres southwest along Arve Road is the rugged **Hartz Mountains National Park**, with its glacial lakes, rainforests and alpine moorlands; a day-walk map is available from the Forest and Heritage Centre. From Arve Road, a very stony, unsealed track winds up for 12km, with several stopping-off points, at the end of which you can walk a couple of minutes to Waratah Lookout, from where you can see over the Huon Valley and the Southern forests. There's also a four-kilometre walk to the sometimes snowcapped Hartz Peak (1255m), where there are views west to the Arthur Range. The walk is along a tricky alpine track, wet and boggy underfoot and with the potential for fog to settle and icy winds to sweep in at any time – recommended for well-prepared walkers only.

The **Picton River** skirts the Hartz Mountains from its source deep in the South West National Park and continues towards the **Tahune Reserve**, at the junction with the Huon River, just north of Hartz Mountain National Park. With its bouncy rapids, intermittent gentle sections and magnificent wilderness scenery, it's a popular, short (and affordable) rafting alternative to the Franklin River. Rafting Tasmania (☎03/6239 1080) operates day-trips from Hobart all year ($110).

Dover and around

DOVER, 21km from Geeveston, is a scenic fishing village on a large, lovely bay – **Port Esperance**. There are trees everywhere, and lush hills surround the village, backed by the clear, virtually triangular, outline of **Adamsons Peak** (1226m), snowcapped in winter. Boats moor off a picturesque jetty in the bay, where two tiny tree-covered islets are silhouetted against the sky at dusk. Between November and May you can arrange **cruises** around the bay looking at points of interest such as salmon farms on the vintage 1880 cutter *Olive May* with Southwest Passage Cruising Co (☎03/6298 1062; daily 10.30am; 2hr; $35; morning tea with tasting of cold smoked salmon included). From October to March there are well-recommended **twilight cruises** (7.30pm; 2hr; $35) with an astronomer who has worked with Aboriginal elders; he explains the southern skies the right way up, as it were, using Aboriginal mythology. A platter of local seafood and some home-brewed beer are on hand as refreshments.

The hub of Dover is the *Dover Hotel*, on the Huon Highway (☎03/6298 1210, fax 6298 1504; motel units ⑥, rooms ⑤), which has an old-fashioned dining room overlooking the water, and plans to reopen a backpackers' lodge at the back beside an apple orchard and rolling fields. The *Dover Beachside Caravan Park* on Kent Beach Road (☎03/6298 1301; on-site vans ②) is also scenically sited near the jetty, beside a creek. Although you can find fuel and supplies 20km further south at **Southport** (the last place to get either), you're better off stocking up in Dover, where there's more choice and better value.

Thirty-one kilometres from Dover are the Hastings Caves, in the foothills of Adamsons Peak, with the **Thermal Springs State Reserve** en route. The springs (daily 10am–4pm, in Jan until 6pm; $2.50) are in a lush setting, and there are several walks in the grounds, one through a fern glade. The pool itself is very disappointing, though – small, shallow and tepid (ranging from 20°C to 30°C), and not the steaming waters you might have imagined. **Hastings Caves**, a few kilometres further on, are more worthwhile: Newdegate Cave, the best, is open daily for tours (11am, 1pm, 2pm & 3pm, with extra tours Oct–March; 45min; $10); it's always wet and cold inside, so bring something warm to wear.

Other attractions in the immediate area include the **Ida Bay Railway**, the most southerly railway in the world, (Sun noon, 2pm & 4pm, with extra services Wed & Sat in warmer months; 1hr 20min; $12; ☎03/6223 5893 for details), a vintage, narrow-gauge bush railway, in operation since 1914, whose trains travel 16km along the southern edge of Southport to the beautiful beach at Deep Hole Bay. The trains pause for twenty minutes here before returning, or you can take a later service back and perhaps walk to the Southport Lagoon Wildlife Sanctuary. You can stay a few kilometres away at the *Lune River Youth Hostel* (☎03/6298 3163, fax 6298 3117; ①). In a rambling weatherboard homestead, the hostel has a reputation as an outdoor activities centre; it organizes caving expeditions, rents out mountain bikes and has a full-moon feast every month with pizzas baked in a mud-brick oven. If you notify the hostel in advance, they can pick you up from Dover for a small charge. **Lune River** itself isn't a town but rather a collection of houses and a post office, with a river that's popular with gem fossickers.

Hobart Coaches (☎03/6234 4077) has a weekday service from Hobart to Dover (5–7 daily); the Tasmanian Wilderness Travel (☎03/6334 4442) "Wilderness" service to Cockle Creek stops at Lune River (Nov–April Mon, Wed & Fri).

Cockle Creek

Beyond Lune River and Ida Bay, the unsurfaced Cockle Creek Road takes you past picturesque sheltered bays and scenic coastal forests, where wild flowers bloom in summer, to **COCKLE CREEK** on the lovely, unspoilt **Recherche Bay** (pronounced "research" by locals). There are lots of camping spots along the shore, and some people love the area so much that they live here semi-permanently in shacks and old buses – mainly fishing-obsessed retirees after the abundant crayfish, cockles and fish in the bay. Pit toilets and water are the only facilities. The most popular walk here is the muddy but boardwalked first part of the **South Coast Track** to the beach at South Cape Bay and back (4hr); the entire length of the track is for the very experienced only, but this portion gives you a small taste (see p.986 for details of the whole walk).

Bruny Island

For beautiful lonely beaches and superb bushwalking, one of the best places in Tasmania is **Bruny Island**. Almost two distinct islands joined by a narrow isthmus (where you can sometimes see Little penguins from a specially constructed viewing platform), it's roughly 71km from end to end and has a population of only four hundred. The cost of taking a car across on the ferry deters casual visitors, so the island is never very full. The ferry from Kettering goes to substantially rural North Bruny, although most of the settlements, and places to stay and eat, are on South Bruny – the more scenic half, with its state forests and reserves. At the northern end of the isthmus, a small monument to **Truganini** (the "last" Tasmanian Aborigine, who was born here) stands atop the tallest sand dune (reached by a high wooden stairway), offering superb views of the southern part of the island, where three former reserves have been turned into **South Bruny National Park** (for permits, see p.907). You can see the Fluted Cape State Reserve region to the east of Adventure Bay; here, a steep climb to the top of the Cape (2hr 30min return) offers still better views. The Labillardiere State Reserve area occupies the western "hook" of South Bruny Island; a winding, bumpy road leads to the **Cape Bruny Lighthouse**, built in 1836 and manned until 1996 (guided tours $10; bookings ☎03/6298 3114) – beyond this a badly-signposted seven-hour walking trail explores the peninsula. East of the hook, across **Cloudy Bay** is the final chunk of the national park. You can do a spot of bush-camping here by the beach (pit toilet only, no water), where there's great surfing, and at Neck Beach about 1.5km from the isthmus viewing point (pit toilet, water, shelter with barbecue).

The **ferry from Kettering** (see p.924) sails at least nine times daily (7.15am–6.30pm, later on Fri; ☎03/6233 5363 for exact times, or consult Friday's *Mercury* in Hobart; $18 per car return, $23 Fri afternoon, Sat & Sun; bikes $3; foot passengers free; 15min). The

Bruny D'Entrecasteaux Visitor Centre at the Kettering ferry terminal (daily 9am–5pm, may be closed Mon & Tues July–Oct; ☎03/6267 4494) books accommodation on the island, much of which is in self-catering cottages and must be arranged in advance. The centre can also supply you with Bruny Island **information**, including a free map. You'll need a car to get around: there's no transport – and no town – at Roberts Point, where the ferry docks on the north of the island. Renting a bike in Hobart or seeing the island on foot are the only alternatives. Hobart Coaches (☎03/6234 4077) operates services from Hobart to Kettering that connect with a couple of the ferries, or you could come on the excellent small group day-tour from Hobart with Bruny Island Ventures ($95; book through Tiger Line ☎03/6231 2200).

The main settlement on **North Bruny** is **DENNES POINT** at the northern extreme of the island, which has a general store and a jetty, and where you can stay at *Kelly's Lookout*, an upmarket holiday unit on Bull Bay Road (☎03/6267 4494; ⑥). En route, in the secluded settlement of **Barnes Bay**, pretty Shelter Cove belies its former role as the first "Black station", a forced resettlement of Aboriginal people, established in 1830. Camel Tracks Tasmania, based at Barnes Bay, offers **camel treks** around the island (daily on demand for 2hr 30min rides, $45 plus morning tea; book for 7hr rides, $100 including gourmet lunch; ☎03/6260 6335).

On **South Bruny**, **ADVENTURE BAY** is the main centre on the east coast; its waters are safe for swimming, and there's a general store and the **Bligh Museum of Pacific Discovery** (daily 10am–3pm; $3). Bruny Island has always been linked with early explorers, for whom it provided a safe refuge after the arduous journey across the Southern Ocean, and the museum displays maps, documents, paintings and artefacts relating to landings there. The *Penguin Tea Rooms* (daily 10am–5pm) serves freshly baked food, while the best place to stay is the helpful *Lumeah YHA Hostel*, in a charming homestead on Quiet Corner, off Main Road (☎ & fax 03/6293 1265; rooms ③, dorms ①); the managers can advise on walks and take people to view the penguins. Opposite is the *Adventure Bay Holiday Home* (☎03/6243 6169; minimum two nights ⑤; linen included, cheaper weekly rates), a three-bedroom house in a shady spot by a small stream. You can **camp** next to the beach at the *Captain Cook Caravan Park* (☎03/6293 1128; on-site vans ③), or at the *Adventure Bay Holiday Village* (☎03/6293 1270; on-site vans ③, cabins ④), both on Adventure Bay Road.

ALONNAH, Bruny's main settlement, is on the D'Entrecasteaux Channel coast. As well as a general store here, you'll find the *Hotel Bruny*, on Bruny Main Road (☎03/6293 1148; motel-style units ⑤), which also does good-value counter meals (no meals Sun), and has the island's only bottle shop. *Alonnahup Holiday Flats* on Ritchie Street (☎03/6293 1339; ⑤) are fully equipped. Five kilometres south at **LUNAWANNA**, the Mangana Store (daily 9am–7pm) sells petrol, groceries and great veggie-, fish- and hamburgers, and has details of *Bruny Island Explorer Cottages* on Light House Road (☎03/6293 1271; linen supplied ⑤); the bakery next to the store bakes **pizzas** (Thurs and Sun 6–9pm). Secluded *Belmont Country Accommodation* (☎03/6293 1255; ⑦) is a lovely big weatherboard cottage facing the water. From Lunnawanna, it's a scenic drive south to **Cloudy Bay**, with its great sweep of surf beach; there's secluded accommodation here in the self-catering beachfront *Cloudy Bay Cabin* (☎03/6293 1171; ⑥), powered by solar energy and gas.

New Norfolk and Mount Field National Park

Heading inland from Hobart towards Mount Field National Park, the A10 hugs the Derwent River for the 50km to the well-preserved colonial buildings of **NEW NORFOLK**. It was to here that the original settlers of Norfolk Island (see p.292) were moved between 1806 and 1814. The sizeable town has been at the centre of the hop-growing industry for 150 years, and there are still oast houses in the surrounding hop fields; on the way into town from Hobart The Oast House (Wed–Sun 9am–5pm; closed June–Aug) has a predictable museum ($3.50), a superior craft gallery and the excellent *Hop House Café*. At New Norfolk the broad stretch of the Derwent is clean, beautiful and swimmable, disturbed only by thrillseekers in jet boats. The *Bush Inn* at 49 Montagu St, the main road (☎03/6261 2011; B&B ④), claims to be Australia's oldest continuously licensed **hotel**: virtually untouched, with stained wooden floorboards, huge stone fireplaces, and a small ballroom with chandeliers and piano, but very down-to-earth, it's an interesting place to stay, as is the antique-furnished *Old Colony Inn*, at no. 21, a simple, whitewashed building on the same street (☎03/6261 2731; B&B ⑤).

Hobart Coaches (☎03/6234 4077) has six buses Mon–Fri from Hobart to New Norfolk and two on Saturday. Tasmanian Wilderness Travel (☎03/6334 4442) also runs to New Norfolk (4 weekly) on their scheduled year-round service to Queenstown, and on a "Wilderness" service (daily Jan–April, 2 weekly May–Nov). They also run day-tours from Hobart, allowing five hours to explore the park ($49). However, what used to be the highlight of the trip is no longer included – the guided tour of the alpine area will set you back another $15; you might find it better value to make your own way here.

Mount Field National Park

It's 37km through pretty rolling countryside full of hop fields from New Norfolk to **Mount Field National Park**, a high alpine area with tarns created by glacial activity where, in winter, there's enough snow to create a small ski field. At the base, the magnificent stands of **swamp gum** (the tallest species of eucalypt and the tallest hardwood in the world), along with the many **waterfalls**, help make this Tasmania's most popular park. Most people come here to see the impressive **Russell Falls**, which cascades in two levels. It's close to the park entrance and can be reached on an easy, well-graded thirty-minute circuit walk. Longer walks continue on to **Horseshoe Falls** (1hr) and **Lady Barron Falls** (3hr return). The best short walk is the **Tall Trees Track** (1hr 30min), where huge swamp gums dominate; the largest date back to the early nineteenth century.

To get away from the tour-group mob, several shorter walks leave from various spots along the Lake Dobson Road, which leads high up to **Lake Dobson**, 16km into the park in the area of the alpine moorlands and glacial lakes. From the lake car park, you can go on plenty of longer walks, including treks along the tarn shelf that take several days, with huts to stay in along the way. The walk to **Twilight Tarn**, with its historic hut, is one of the most rewarding (4hr return), or you can continue on for the full tarn shelf circuit (6hr return). A shorter option is the **Pandani Grove Nature Walk** (with an accompanying leaflet available from the ranger station – see below), a forty-minute circuit of the lake, including a section of tall **pandanis** – the striking heath plant which, with its crown of long fronds, looks like a semi-tropical palm. You'll need your own transport to reach these higher walks, or you can pay $15 for the Tasmanian Wilderness Travel shuttle bus. Alternatively, you could come with the friendly **Close to Nature Tours**, and walk from their base at the National Park kiosk (☎03/6288 1477) on a Mount Field Discovery Tour (daily 10am; 2hr 30min; $15), which includes a walk around Lake Dobson. Their torch-lit Nocturnal Wildlife Tour is also worthwhile; the $11.50 fee includes supper and a pre-walk slide show to prepare you for the wildlife you're likely to see on the walk (nightly 8.30pm; 1hr 30min).

For information on the walks, to register for overnight hikes and to talk to the ranger, drop in to the **Mount Field Ranger Station** at the entrance to the park (☎03/6288 1149). An excellent range of free pamphlets detail the natural environment alongside several of the walks in the park. There's also information here about walks in the South West National Park, several of which can be started from Scotts Peak Road, which runs off the Gordon River Road to the west of Mount Field (see p.984). If you want to **stay** in the vicinity, head for the tiny settlement of **NATIONAL PARK** on Maydena Road, a ten-minute walk from the park, which consists of the friendly *National Park Hotel* (☎03/6288 1103; ④), offering basic ground-floor **pub** accommodation including breakfast, and the easy-going homestead housing the *National Park Youth Hostel* opposite (☎03/6288 1369; ①); there's plenty of interaction between the two, including pool tournaments, and the pub **meals** are also popular with travellers. The pub has an EFTPOS facility, but the nearest fuel is 7km further on at Westaway. Within the park itself, there's a **campsite** near the ranger station, with civilized amenities including a laundry and a small, well-stocked **kiosk** (daily 9am–5.30pm). Near the main camping area you can stay in self-contained units at *Russell Falls Holiday Cottages* (☎03/6288 1198; ④).

Nearby **Junee State Reserve** is prime **platypus** territory; you can reach it from Mount Field if you have a car or bike, and in summer the ranger often organizes guided walks. Head 11km southwest to Maydena, then right onto the narrow, winding Junee Road for 3.5km. At the reserve the Junee River flows into **Junee Cave**, a ten-minute walk through regenerating forest. Though platypuses are very common on the Junee River, it doesn't mean you'll see any – they're extremely elusive. The trick is to arrive at dawn or dusk, well camouflaged, and sit quietly for at least an hour. Peta Britton (☎03/6288 2206) leads **trail rides** from Junee Road through the reserve, checking out the caves along the way.

Richmond

RICHMOND, on the Coal River about 25km north of Hobart and surrounded by undulating countryside, is one of the oldest and best-preserved towns in Australia. Settlers received land grants in the area not long after the fledgling colony had been set up in 1803, and in 1824 Lieutenant Governor Sorell founded the town, on the route between Hobart and the east coast. Soon, traffic to the new penal settlement at Port Arthur began to pass through, and Richmond's strategic location made it an important military post and convict station; by the 1830s it was the third-largest town in Tasmania. In 1872, however, the **Sorell Causeway** was opened, bypassing Richmond, which became a rural community with little incentive for change or development. Most of the approximately fifty buildings – plain and functional stone dwellings – date from the 1830s and 1840s, and many are now used as galleries, craft shops, cafés, restaurants and guesthouses. Attractions along Bridge Street include the wooden **Richmond Maze** (daily 10am–5pm; $3.50); the **Old Hobart Town Model Village** (daily 9.30am–5.30pm; $5), a large-scale outdoor model of Hobart in the 1820s; and the **Richmond Toy Museum** (daily 10am–5pm; $2.50), which exhibits toys dating from the 1890s to the 1960s.

Tourist fluff aside, the grey-stone, slate-roofed **Richmond Gaol** (daily 9am–5pm; $4), an intact example of an early prison, is Richmond's most authentic attraction. The prison's function was mostly to house prisoners in transit or those awaiting trial, and to accommodate convict road gangs working in the district; the east wing was designed to hold female convicts, who could not be accommodated at Port Arthur. Informative signs explain the various features of the jail, which now seems incongruously pretty, set around a central square with grass, flowers and a tree.

In addition to the jail, Richmond has the distinction of having both Australia's oldest Roman Catholic Church – that of **St John**, which dates in part from 1837 – and its oldest bridge. **Richmond Bridge** was constructed in 1823 under harsh conditions using convict labour; there's a legend that it's haunted by the ghost of the brutal flagellator, George Grover, who was beaten to death by the convicts and thrown into the river during its construction.

Practicalities
Hobart Coaches runs three services a day from Hobart (Mon–Fri only) and Tasmanian Wilderness Travel also drop off on their Hobart to Swansea service (1 daily, Mon–Fri

only). **Accommodation** mainly consists of very pricey B&Bs in quaint colonial buildings. *Emerald Cottage*, at 23 Torrens St (☎03/6260 2192, fax 6260 2652; ⑧), is a converted stable where you get a whole cottage to yourself (breakfast ingredients supplied). For something more grand, try *Prospect House* (☎03/6260 2207, fax 6260 2551; ⑦), on your left as you come into town on Cambridge Road; it's a Georgian country mansion set in extensive landscaped grounds, and has its own licensed restaurant. Further out, 6km from Richmond along Prossers Road, is *Richmond Country Bed and Breakfast* (☎03/6260 4238, fax 6260 4423; ⑤), a comfortable, reasonably priced, non-smoking homestead in a quiet rural setting. The cheapest place to stay is the *Richmond Cabin and Tourist Park*, on Middle Tea Tree Road on the outskirts of town as you come from Hobart (☎03/6260 2192; cabins ④, on-site vans ③), which provides shady grounds for camping and has an indoor heated pool.

For **food**, walk along Bridge Street, where you'll find the pretty *Richmond Arms Hotel*, which serves upmarket pub meals; the *Richmond Bakery* on Edward Street has a Swiss baker who makes delicious pastries; and there's an upmarket brasserie in the *Richmond Wine Centre*, 27 Bridge St (daily 10am–6pm, Fri & Sat until 8pm), where the emphasis is on quality Tasmanian produce.

The Forestier and Tasman peninsulas

The fastest route from Hobart to the **Tasman Peninsula** heads northeast along the Tasman Highway and then across the **Sorell Causeway** to the small town of **Sorell**, your last chance for full shopping and any banking; on the huge expanse of Pittwater, windsurfers are out in force on a sunny day. From Sorell, the Arthur Highway heads 34km southeast to Dunalley (fuel available), where a bridge crosses the narrow isthmus to the **Forestier Peninsula**. The bridge regularly opens to let boats through, which can cause delays. Once across, it's a further 42km to the infamous **Eaglehawk Neck**, the narrow point connecting the two peninsulas, once guarded by vicious dogs that in effect turned the Tasman Peninsula into a kind of prison island.

Port Arthur, at the very bottom of the Tasman Peninsula, is the major attraction, but the hardly developed **peninsula** has several good **bushwalks**, and some impressive rock formations on the rough ocean side. Some of the finest coastal features are around Eaglehawk Neck: just to the north, there's the **Tessellated Pavement**, onto which you can climb down at low tide; and to the south, off the highway, a fierce **blowhole**, the huge **Tasman Arch**, and the **Devils Kitchen**, a sheer rock cleft into which the sea surges. The **Tasman Trail** is an exhilarating coastal walk starting from the Devils Kitchen and ending at **Fortescue Bay**, which has a good camping area (otherwise, the bay is 12km down a dirt road east off the Arthur Highway). South of Port Arthur, several walking tracks begin from **Remarkable Cave**: to Crescent Bay (5hr return), Mount Brown (5hr return) and Maingon Blowhole (3hr return). At the time of writing, much of this area was awaiting declaration as the **Tasman National Park**. When it's established, park fees will apply and a NPWS visitor centre will be built to provide information and advice. In the meantime, to get details on the walking trails, look for a copy of *Tasman Tracks*, by Shirley and Peter Storey, in a Hobart bookshop.

Eaglehawk Neck Backpackers (☎03/6250 3248; ①), at 687 Old Jetty Rd, 1km west of the Arthur Highway on the Forestier Peninsula side of Eaglehawk Neck, is the perfect **place to stay** to explore these areas. It's a friendly, non-smoking, and green (in both senses of the word) place. Bunks are in two spacious, self-contained cabins; bikes are loaned (for a small donation), and there are canoes too. Also in the area is the architect-designed *Wunnamurra Bed and Breakfast* (☎ & fax 03/6250 3145; en suite ⑥), which offers more luxury. For something to **eat**, try the French-run *Eaglehawk Cafe Restaurant*, on the Arthur Highway near the turn-off to the blowhole (☎03/6250 3331; licensed; open for breakfast, lunch and dinner), in a two-storey house overlooking

Norfolk Bay; the food is tasty and reasonably priced, utilizing local produce with a menu ranging from vegetarian to traditional meat dishes, plus coffee and cakes. The nearby Eaglehawk Dive Centre (☎03/6250 3566) offers dive-boat charters (equipment included) at low rates to caves, shipwrecks, kelp forests and nearby seal colonies with an underwater visibility of 15–30m. Southwest of Eaglehawk Neck, in the middle of the Tasman Peninsula at the small settlement of **Koonya**, *Seaview Lodge* (☎ & fax 03/6250 2766; ②) also makes an excellent base for bushwalking. The friendly managers have their own minibus and will pick you up from Port Arthur or Eaglehawk Neck, take you to the start of walking trails and give tours of the area.

Port Arthur

The most unceasing labour is to be extracted from the convicts . . . and the most harassing vigilance over them is to be observed.

Governor Arthur

PORT ARTHUR was chosen as the site for a **prison settlement** in September 1830, as a place of secondary punishment for convicts who had committed serious crimes in New South Wales or Van Diemen's Land itself, men who were seen to have no redeeming features and were treated accordingly. The first 150 convicts worked like slaves to establish a timber industry in the wooded surroundings of the "natural penitentiary" of the Tasman Peninsula, with narrow Eaglehawk Neck guarded by dogs. The regime was never a subtle one: **Governor George Arthur**, responsible for all the convicts in Van Diemen's Land, believed that a convict's "whole fate should be . . . the very last degree of misery consistent with humanity". Gradually, Port Arthur became a self-supporting industrial centre: the timber industry grew into shipbuilding, there was brickmaking and shoemaking, wheat-growing, and even a flour mill. There was also a separate prison for boys – "the thiefs prison" – at Point Puer, where the inmates were taught trades. From the 1840s until transport of convicts ceased in 1853, the penal settlement grew steadily, the early timber constructions being replaced by brick and stone buildings. The lives of the labouring convicts contrasted sharply with those of the prison officers and their families, who had their ornamental gardens, drama club, library and cricket fields. The years after transport ended were in many ways more horrific than those that preceded them, as physical beatings were replaced by psychological punishment. In 1852 the **Model Prison**, based on the spoked-wheel design of Pentonville Prison in London, opened. Here, prisoners could be kept in tiny cells in complete isolation and absolute silence; they were referred to by numbers rather than names, and wore hoods whenever they left their cells. The prison continued to operate until 1877, by now incorporating its own **mental asylum** full of ex-convicts as well as a geriatric home for ex-convict paupers. The excellent **interpretive centre** (daily 9am–5pm), housed in the former asylum, provides much more detail on the prison's sad history through artefacts and texts.

In 1870 Port Arthur was popularized by Marcus Clarke's romantic tragedy, *For the Term of his Natural Life*. The public became fascinated by its buildings and the tragedy behind them, and soon after the prison closed, guided tours were offered by the same crumbling men who had been wrecked by the regime. In the 1890s the town around the prison was devastated by bushfires that left most buildings in ruins. A major conservation and restoration project began in the 1970s and today the **Port Arthur Historic Site** covers a huge area (office and most buildings daily 8am–dusk; $16 for a 24hr pass, including 40min guided tour and 20min harbour cruise in summer; $8 for a pass after 4pm; information office ☎03/6250 2539); you're allowed to wander around the grounds until about 11pm. There are more than sixty buildings, some of which –

like the poignant **prison chapel** – are furnished and restored. Others, like the ivy-covered **church**, are picturesque ruins set in a landscape of green lawns, shady trees and paths sloping down to the cove. The beautiful setting makes it look more like a serene, old-world university campus than a prison, and indeed, the benign feeling of the place seems to have a capacity to absorb tragedy: another horrific chapter in Port Arthur's history occurred in April 1996, when the massacre of 35 tourists and local people by a lone gunman made international headlines. The café where most of the people were killed has been partially dismantled; the walls will remain and a memorial will be built here with a garden around the site. The simple cross on the waterfront which stands in remembrance will now remain permanently. Visitors are requested to act sensitively and not ask the staff about the tragedy.

From the Port Arthur jetty you can take the *MV Bundeena* across the bay to visit the **Isle of the Dead** (summer only, frequent departures; $7), Port Arthur's cemetery from 1833 to 1877. A one-hour tour of the graveyard is included, which gives you ample opportunity to look at the resting places of 1100 convicts, asylum inmates, paupers and free men.

If you're staying overnight in Port Arthur (see below for accommodation), join the nightly lantern-lit **Historic Ghost Tour** (1hr 30min; $12; bookings on ☎03/6250 2539), which features lovingly researched and hauntingly retold tales of the settlement's past as you wander through the ruins.

Practicalities

If you don't have your own transport, and want to get to Port Arthur from Hobart on a **regular bus**, you'll have to stay over for two nights. Hobart Coaches run Monday to Friday only, departing Hobart late in the afternoon and returning early in the morning (stopping en route at Eaglehawk Neck and other places on the Tasman and Forestier peninsulas). However, there are plenty of **bus tours** that take in some of the Tasman Peninsula sights along the way. Tiger Line offer two day-tours, the best of which is "Convict Capers" (ask for tour 17b; 9am Sun–Fri; 7hr 30min; $45) – don't bother with the other tour which will waste your time with the touristy Bush Mill, a re-creation of a late-nineteenth-century pioneer bush settlement. Experience Tasmania has a similar $45 trip (ask for tour 3; Mon, Wed, Fri & Sun; ☎03/6234 3336). Tasmanian Wilderness Travel offers an evening tour from Hobart which takes in the ghost tour (Mon, Thurs & Fri; 6pm; 6hr; $40).

There are various **places to stay** on the outskirts of Port Arthur. The *Port Arthur Motor Inn*, on Remarkable Cave Road (☎03/6250 2101, fax 6250 2417; ⑦), is just off the site, overlooking the ruined church; it's a pleasant place, with a bar open to the public – the only place nearby to drink – and reasonable counter meals. Just across the road is the *Roseview Youth Hostel* on Champ Street (☎03/6250 2311; booking essential Jan & Feb; rooms ③, dorms ①). The spacious *Port Arthur Villas* (☎03/6250 2239, fax 6250 2589; ⑥), just across Remarkable Cave Road from the site, has the amenities of a motel and full kitchens in the units.

There's an indifferent temporary café in the administrative centre, which serves fast food, but two better places to **eat** are at the *Frances Langford Tea Rooms*, in the restored 1930s policemen's quarters, and the *Museum Tea Rooms* in the interpretive centre.

The east coast: the Tasman Highway

For much of its length along the sunny **east coast**, the **Tasman Highway** gently rises and falls through grazing land and bush-covered hills. In summer there's something of an unspoilt Mediterranean feel about this coast, with its long white beaches, blue water stretching to a cloudless sky, scenic backdrop of hills, and a thriving local fishing industry.

Because the east coast is sheltered from the prevailing westerly winds and is washed by warm offshore currents, it has one of the most temperate climates in Australia. This, and the mainly safe swimming beaches, mean that it's a popular destination for Tasmanian families in the school holidays – prices go up and accommodation is scarce from Christmas to the middle of February. Even so, it's still relatively undeveloped and peaceful; there are four national parks, which include a whole island – **Maria Island** – and an entire peninsula – the glorious **Freycinet National Park**.

The east coast is also Tasmania's best **cycling route**: it's relatively flat, and the winter climate is mild enough to tackle it in colder months, too. Distances between towns are reasonable, there's a string of youth hostels so you don't need to camp, and there are few cars. **St Helens** is the largest town on the east coast, with a population of just over a thousand; situated on **Georges Bay**, it makes a good base to explore the northeast corner and **Mount William National Park**. The oldest town, **Swansea**, lies sheltered in **Great Oyster Bay**, facing the Freycinet Peninsula. To the north, **Bicheno** is a small fishing town with fantastic diving, and it's a convenient place from which to visit both the Freycinet National Park (and its tiny settlement of **Coles Bay**) and the **Douglas Apsley National Park** inland. The highway detours inland at **St Marys**, although there's a more recently built road that allows you to follow the coast and enjoy spectacular views without having to tackle any hills.

Because the east coast is not heavily populated, **banking facilities** are rather inadequate, with no ATMs. Complete banking services are available only at St Helens and Scottsdale (both Westpac), while small settlements have post offices that are also Commonwealth Bank agents. EFTPOS facilities are widely available in shops and service stations, but it's important to make sure you always have enough cash.

Transport services don't run to daily schedules either – another good reason to cycle. From Hobart, Tasmanian Redline Coaches has one service to Bicheno via Swansea (Tues, Thurs & Fri), two Sunday Launceston bound services, which stop at Swansea, Bicheno, St Helens and St Marys, and a weekday service to St Helens and St Marys. From Launceston, Redline goes to Derby via Scottsdale (1–2 daily except Sat), to Bicheno and Swansea (1 daily Mon–Fri), and to St Helens via St Marys (1 daily except Sat). Tasmanian Wilderness Travel has scheduled year-round services up the east coast from Hobart to St Helens (1 daily Wed, Fri & Sun). Three local bus companies also operate: Sun Coast (☎03/6376 1753) between Derby and St Helens via St Marys; and Peakes (☎03/6372 5390) between St Marys and Swansea via Bicheno (both Mon–Fri only); and Coles Bay–Bicheno Coach Service (☎03/6257 0293), which takes you to Freycinet National Park daily (though out of season you often need to book). If you don't fancy getting stuck somewhere for a couple of days, check timetables carefully.

Maria Island National Park

As the Tasman Highway meets the sea at **ORFORD**, a small holiday resort on the estuary of the Prosser River, you get your first views across to **Maria Island**. The entire island, 15km off the east coast, is a national park, uninhabited save for its ranger. Its wide tracks are ideal for mountain-biking, an activity encouraged here – because no other vehicles are allowed, you can ride in perfect safety. The island's coastal road has no gradient, but inland there are a few hills to climb. **Birdlife** is prolific, with over 130 species; it's the only national park containing all eleven of the state's endemic bird species. The old airstrip is covered with Cape Barren geese, which you'll see if you walk to the **fossil cliffs**, a twenty-minute stroll from Darlington.

The ferry lands at **DARLINGTON**, where the structures of the former **penal settlement** still stand, including the commissariat store with its visitor information boards, the convict barn, the cemetery, the mill house and the penitentiary. The latter is now a

bunkhouse (①); units have wood stoves and bunks with mattresses; they're always in demand and are often booked up six months in advance, so call the ranger (see below) before turning up. The **campsite** here is the island's best, with a public phone, toilets, fireplaces, cold water taps and tank water for drinking; there's a small fee for camping – the ranger will come and collect it. As there is little water elsewhere on the island, free-range camping is best done at **Frenchs Farm** or **Encampment Cove**, two campsites with a rainwater supply and fireplaces; the latter, on Shoal Bay, is the more picturesque.

You can take many short **walks** on the island, as well as longer bushwalks; free pamphlets are available from the ranger's office at Darlington (☎03/6257 1420). With a couple of days to spare, you can walk past the narrow isthmus to the rarely visited **southern end** of the island, which has unspoilt forests and secluded beaches. As there's no water here, be sure to bring supplies with you.

Getting there: Triabunna

Ferries leave for the island from the *Eastcoaster Resort* at Louisville, halfway between Orford and Triabunna, and from **TRIABUNNA** itself (reached by Tasmanian Wilderness Travel and Redline from Hobart). The *Eastcoaster Express* (☎03/6257 1172), a fast catamaran taking only twenty minutes, leaves the resort daily at 10.30am, 1pm and 3.30pm, returning from Maria Island at 11am, 1.30pm and 4pm, with extra trips between December 26 and January 28 (day-trips $17, campers $20, bikes and kayaks $3). The laid-back *Triabunna YHA* on Spencer Street, 1km outside Triabunna (☎03/6257 3439; rooms ②, dorms ①), is a good base for making a day-trip to the island, but it's closed from early June and July. You can also charter a **flight** to the island from Triabunna with Salmon Air (☎03/6257 3186), or take a scenic ride with them.

Swansea

From Triabunna it's a fairly uneventful drive north to **SWANSEA**, overlooking **Great Oyster Bay**, with views across to the Freycinet Peninsula. If you're lucky, you might see dolphins frolicking in the bay from Franklin Street, the main street that runs along the waterfront. One of Tasmania's oldest settlements, this is an administrative centre, fishing port and seaside resort, with well-preserved architecture dating from the 1830s to the 1880s. The focus of town has always been **Morris's General Store**, on Franklin Street, run by seven generations of the family since 1868. Further evidence of Swansea's past can be found at the **Community Centre** (Mon–Sat 8.30am–5.30pm; $2), also on Franklin Street, a former school whose miscellaneous collection includes a billiard table built from a single log of blackwood ($2 for a game), and at the restored **Swansea Bark Mill**, 96 Tasman Highway (daily 9am–5pm; $5), once used to produce leather tanning agents from native blackwattle bark.

Accommodation options include the comfortable *Swansea YHA*, at 5 Franklin St (☎03/6257 8367; ①), with a piano in the common room; and the *Swansea Motor Inn*, at 1 Franklin St (☎03/6257 8102, fax 6257 8397; motel ⑤, hotel ④), a fine old hotel with a red-brick motel addition and a bistro. There's also B&B at the *Oyster Bay Guest House* at 10 Franklin St (☎ & fax 03/6257 8110; ⑤–⑥) and *Meredith House*, 15 Noyes St (☎03/6257 8119, fax 6257 8123; all en-suite ⑦–⑧), an antique-filled guesthouse on a hill overlooking the bay. On the waterfront are two **caravan parks** with excellent facilities: *Swansea Caravan Park* on Shaw Street, opposite the Old Bark Mill (☎03/6257 8177; cabins ④), and *Kenmore Caravan Park*, 2 Bridge St (☎03/6257 8148; cabins ④, on-site vans ③).

As for **food**, Swansea has a wide choice. The *Shy Albatross Restaurant* (☎03/6257 8110; licensed; daily from 7pm, plus lunch in summer), downstairs at the *Oyster Bay Guest House*, serves reasonably priced, Italian food and local seafood. There's a very smart, award-winning restaurant specializing in seafood and game in the atmospheric 1846 *Schouten House*, 1 Waterloo Rd (☎03/6257 8564). *Just Maggies*, a relaxed café at 26 Franklin St (daily 9am–5pm), is a prime spot for dolphin-watching, while *Kabuki By the Sea* (open daily for morning and afternoon tea and lunch; May–Nov Fri & Sat dinner, Dec–April Tues–Sat dinner; bookings essential on ☎03/6257 8588) is a fine Japanese-style restaurant 12km south on the Tasman Highway with stunning views that also has Japanese-style guest cottages (⑦).

The Freycinet Peninsula

Heading for Coles Bay and **Freycinet National Park**, you turn off the Tasman Highway 33km north of Swansea, following the Coles Bay Road. After about 8km, turn left down a side road (3km unsealed) to the **Friendly Beaches**, a new addition to the national park, taking in a length of unspoilt shoreline backed by eucalypt forest. If you're **cycling**, you can cut 40km from your journey by riding along Nine Mile Beach Road, at the end of which a ferry will take you across the Swan River to **SWANICK**, about 6km northwest of Coles Bay. The ferry (about $10; no service May–Sept) must be booked by calling the night before (☎03/6257 0239).

COLES BAY, on the north edge of the Freycinet National Park, is a sheltered inlet with fishing boats moored in the deep blue water, all set against the striking backdrop of **The Hazards**, three pink granite peaks – Amos, Dove and Mayson – rising straight from the sea. Since the 1930s the hamlet of Coles Bay has been the base for the park, and for fishing and recreation. As a result, there are numerous fishing shacks and **holiday houses** available to rent: call *Three Peaks Holiday Rentals* (☎03/6257 0333; ⑥–⑦) or *Freycinet Holiday Homes* (☎03/6257 0218; ⑨). The *Iluka Holiday Centre*, on the Esplanade 1km from the general store (☎03/6257 0115, fax 6257 0384; holiday units ④–⑥, on-site vans ③, dorms ①), has a wide variety of accommodation, including a **YHA hostel** section. Attached is a small supermarket, an excellent eat-in bakery selling pastries, focaccia, pizza and decent cappuccino (daily 7am–10pm), plus a restaurant and tavern. The *Coles Bay Caravan Park*, 4km further west on Coles Bay Road (☎03/6257 0100; dorms ①), is in a bush setting, with beach access and backpackers' accommodation (twin share rooms, fully equipped kitchen, dining room and own amenities); the rate includes one return ticket on the Bicheno–Coles Bay bus service. **Supplies** of all sorts are available at Coles Bay Trading on Garnet Avenue (☎03/6257 0109; daily 8am–6pm, to 7pm in summer); this is also the post office, service station, boat rental outlet and tourist **information** centre, and it has a coffee shop. Next door you can get a seafood dinner caught by the restaurateurs at *Madge Malloy's* (☎03/6257 0399; licensed; closed Sun & Mon nights).

Redline and Tasmanian Wilderness Travel drop off 31km away from Coles Bay, at the turn-off on the Tasman Highway. Here you'll have to wait for the Coles Bay–Bicheno Coach Service (up to three daily, although at off-peak times you may have to book; ☎03/6257 0293), which can take you right to the start of the walking tracks – the only other alternative is to walk.

Freycinet National Park

The **national park office** (daily 9am–5pm; ☎03/6257 0107), where you can get advice on bushwalking and buy maps and booklets on day-walks, is just 1km from Coles Bay. Opposite, the national park **campsite**, with water and toilets but no showers, is in a sheltered location among bush and dunes behind Richardsons Beach; it's packed in holiday season, when you'll need to book ahead through the park office. Otherwise, you can walk into the national park and camp for free. At the other end of Richardsons Beach, *Freycinet Lodge* (☎03/6257 0101, fax 6257 0278; ⑧) has luxurious wooden cabins spread through bushland and offers guided bushwalks; there's a bistro and a more upmarket restaurant overlooking the bay, both open all day, and a tennis court. You can stay at the *Coles Bay YHA* in the park itself, but only if you've booked in advance through the Hobart office (☎03/6234 9617; ①); it's often impossible to get a space, as it's usually full of groups.

Tracks into the park begin at the **Walking Track Car Park**, a further 4km from the office. **Water** is scarce, so you must carry all you'll need, although the ranger can advise if there are any streams where the water is safe to drink. The shorter walks are well marked and not too difficult: exquisite **Wine Glass Bay**, with its perfect curve of white beach, is where most walkers head (1hr one-way). The **peninsula circuit** is a wonderful walk (10hr), best done over two days; it makes a good practice run for the big southwest hikes. There's a **campsite** at **Cooks Beach**, with a pit toilet, water tank, and a rough hut where you can stay; the beach has a lot of marsupials who'll pester you for food, so wrap it up tight.

Schouten Island, off the tip of the peninsula, was included within the national park in 1967: it's perfect for really secluded camping, as you're quite likely to have it all to yourself. Freycinet Sea Charters, in Coles Bay (☎03/6375 1461), will drop you off there for around $100 per person return, or you could spend the same amount on a day-trip with them which could take in a walk on the island and a visit to a nearby seal colony; try Keno Sea Fisheries, also in Coles Bay (☎03/6257 0344), who also do charter trips. If you're charming enough, you might get a ride for free from a fisherman at Coles Bay. There are campsites with pit toilet, a hut and two water tanks at **Moreys Bay**, and the creek at **Crocketts Bay** has reliable upstream water. Although there are no proper tracks on the island, walking is easy.

Rafting Tasmania (☎03/6239 1090) offer **sea kayaking tours** on Coles Bay (half-day $60, full-day $105) which can be extended to include overnight camping in the national park (three-day trip $540), while Tasmanian Cliffhangers (☎03/6257 0500), run abseiling and rock-climbing trips (half-day abseiling $70; full-day rock-climbing $100).

Bicheno

Halfway up the east coast, **BICHENO** (pronounced "bish-eno"), sheltered in **Waubs Bay**, is a busy crayfishing and abalone port. The same conditions that make Bicheno ideal for fishing also make it a perfect spot for **diving**. The usually clear waters are rich with a variety of marine life, and there's a **marine reserve** on the eastern side of **Governor Island**, with spectacular large caves and extraordinary vertical rockfaces with swim-throughs and drop-offs. The Bicheno Dive Centre, 4 Tasman Highway (☎03/6375 1138), offers dive courses and rents out gear. **Information** on other activities around Bicheno is available from Bicheno Penguin & Adventure Tours on Foster Street (daily 9am–5.30pm; ☎03/6375 1333), which arranges diving, horse-riding, cycling, and a wide variety of local tours, the most popular being the evening visits to **Diamond Island** to observe the local **penguin** population (Sept–March; $12). Visitors are discouraged from going there alone, as it's becoming a successful penguin breeding ground; also, the tides are treacherous, and people have drowned. The same company offer a one-hour glass bottom boat tour of the marine reserve ($12). The **Sea Life Centre** (daily 9am–5pm; $4.50), on the Tasman Highway, has a rather dingy aquarium but an excellent, cheap seafood restaurant (daily 9am–9pm; reserve for dinner on ☎03/6375 1311).

Bicheno makes a pleasant stopover, as it has plenty of **accommodation**. The Christian-run *Camp Seaview*, on Banksia Street (☎03/6375 1247; cabins ③–④, dorms ①), is open to backpackers during school holidays, and has superb facilities with no hassles. The simple *Bicheno YHA*, 3km north on the highway (☎03/6375 1293; ①), has a great beachfront location opposite Diamond Island, close to the penguins, while a brand-new purpose built hostel, *Waubs Harbour Backpackers Hostel*, with bunk rooms, lockers, guest kitchen and common room, plus mountain bikes to rent, has been attached to the *Bicheno Cabin and Tourist Park*, 4 Champ St (☎03/6375 1117, fax 6375 1355; dorms ③, on-site vans ③, cabins ④–⑤). Other places include the central *Beachfront Family Resort*, near the tourist office on the Tasman Highway (☎03/6375 1111, fax 6375 1130; ⑤–⑦), which has a pool, plus bikes to rent; and the *Bicheno Gaol*, on the corner of James and Burgess streets (☎03/6375 1430; ⑦–⑧ includes breakfast provisions) which offers cottage accommodation in the old prison and its converted stables. **Food**, too, is excellent in Bicheno. The formal *Cyrano French Restaurant*, at 77 Burgess St (☎03/6375 1137; daily from 6.30pm), is in the classic French vein, while the *Long Boat Tavern*, on the Tasman Highway, has the best counter meals. For a good breakfast try the *Galleon Coffee Lounge* at 45 Foster St (daily 8am–7.30pm), but for a more salubrious cuppa (even cappuccino), head for *Mary Harvey's Kitchen* in the gardens of the *Bicheno Gaol*, where you can sample some gourmet Tasmanian products (daily 10.30am–5pm).

To get to Freycinet National Park by **bus** from Bicheno, take the Coles Bay–Bicheno Coach Service (☎03/6357 0293), which leaves from the *Night Owl* takeaway at 52 Burgess St.

The Douglas Apsley National Park and the Elephant Pass

Just 14km north of Bicheno on the Tasman Highway there's a turn-off left to **Douglas Apsley National Park**. Proclaimed in 1990, its unique feature is that it's the location of the state's only remaining large dry sclerophyll forest. Because of the temperate weather of the east coast, the park's two-day walk, the **Leeaberra Track** – undertaken north to south – is a good one at any time of the year. This is a low-maintenance, untouristy park and facilities are minimal, meaning that you'll have to rely on basic bushcamping. You can buy the *Douglas Apsley* map and *Notes* ($9) from the Land Information Bureau, 134 Macquarie St, Hobart. Tasmanian Wilderness Travel can arrange bushwalkers' transfers to the park.

Chain of Lagoons, 27km north of Bicheno near the northern end of the park, has a great roadside stall selling fresh seafood, plus waterfront camping on a farmer's property at nearby Piccaninny Point. A few kilometres north of Chain of Lagoons the coastal Tasman Highway continues north to St Helens; turn off to the left for a spectacular climb with views of the surrounding coastline on a detour inland to St Marys, 17km away. Dramatic **Elephant Pass** shouldn't be missed, not least for the laid-back *Mount Elephant Pancake Barn*, run by a relaxed American–Australian couple, where the coffee, food, views and atmosphere are magical (daily 8am–6pm, until 8pm Fri).

St Marys and St Helens

From Elephant Pass the road heads on to **ST MARYS**, a picturesque little town surrounded by state forest and waterfalls. The place has a quiet, old-fashioned feel to it, plus a slight alternative edge, and there are some fine bushwalks in the area. The best thing about the town is the *Seaview Farm Lodge* (☎03/6372 2341; en-suite rooms ④, dorms ③), 8km uphill on German Town Road, a characterful hostel that's well known for its Green credentials and connections. The lodge has several private cabin rooms, or you can stay in the farmhouse; arrange a pick-up in advance if you don't have your own transport.

Heading downhill back to the coast, you'll arrive at **ST HELENS**, the largest town on the east coast and the last before the Tasman Highway turns west and inland. It's situated on **Georges Bay**, a long, narrow bay with two encircling arms, and although both the town and bay are fairly dull, the surrounding coastline has plenty of interest. Local **information** is available from the St Helens History Room, at 55 Cecilia St opposite the post office (Mon–Fri 9am–4pm, Sat 9am–noon; $4; ☎03/6376 1744), which provides maps and gives information about walks as well as details of the area's mining history.

The southern arm of Georges Bay is the site of **St Helens Point Recreation Area**, where there's a large lagoon – Diana's Basin – which the highway skirts as it enters town. On the ocean side the **Peron sand dunes** stretch for several kilometres, and at the point there's good surfing at **Beer Barrel Beach**. **Binalong Bay**, 10km north of Georges Bay, has a beach of bright sugary sand and is an easy bike ride away, with only a couple of small climbs. It's another popular surf spot (with a strong current, so beware); there's safer swimming in the large lagoon tucked behind, where people boat and waterski. You can **camp** here, as well as further along at the **Bay of Fires Coastal Reserve**. To get to the southern half of **Mount William National Park** take the road running inland north for 54km from St Helens to the pink granite tower of the Eddystone Lighthouse. The northern end of the park is reached via Gladstone, by taking an unsealed track to **Great Musselroe Bay**, where there's a free basic **campsite**. There are no real tracks within the park itself, but plenty of beach and headland walking, and lots of Forrester kangaroos.

St Helens practicalities

There's a good range of **accommodation** to choose from in town. The *St Helens YHA*, at 5 Cameron St (☎03/6376 1661; ①), is clean and friendly; or there are a number of bed and breakfast places: best value is *Artnor Lodge* at 71 Cecilia St (☎03/6376 1234; ⑤), or you could try friendly *Cecilia House* at no. 78 (☎03/6376 1723; ⑥), or the salubrious *Warrawee Guest House* (☎03/6376 1987, fax 6376 1012; ⑦–⑧) on the Tasman Highway. The *Bayside Inn*, at 2 Cecilia St (☎03/6376 1466; ④–⑤), is a modern hotel/motel with a restaurant, pool and drive-in bottle shop. *Tidal Water*, facing Georges Bay at 2 Jason St (☎03/6376 1100; dinner only, closed Sun) is an award-winning **restaurant** serving Asian-influenced contemporary cuisine. St Helens' bank is Westpac at 41 Cecilia St (☎03/6376 1464).

St Helens to Scottsdale: the Tasman Highway

From St Helens, the **Tasman Highway** cuts across the northeast highlands towards Launceston, 170km away. This is mostly dairy country, although there's the odd patch of surviving rainforest and the remnants of a tin-mining industry, based around the **Blue Tier**, a mountain that experienced a mining boom in the 1870s. Many **ghost towns** were left after the mines finally closed in the 1950s.

Twenty-six kilometres out of St Helens is the turn-off south for **PYENGANA** (1km) and St Columba Falls (a further 4km). In Pyengana it's worth touring **Healey's Pyengana Cheese Factory** (daily 9am–6pm; free), where you can watch the stuff being made and buy all the ingredients for a picnic at the falls. Further along, you come to *St Columba Falls Hotel* (☎03/6373 6121; ③) – the "Pub in the Paddock" – which looks like a farmhouse; it's a real country local, serving huge steaks (meals daily). At the end of the road (the last bit on dirt) is the **Columba Falls State Reserve**, an area of cool, temperate rainforest. The short walk to the viewing platform at the base of **St Columba Falls** is easy, passing through a forest of manferns and under a canopy of sassafras and myrtle. At 110m, the falls are the highest in Tasmania, pouring with tremendous force over the cliffs – they're truly thunderous in winter, when the viewing platform is shrouded in mist.

Back on the main road approaching the Blue Tier, **Goshen** is the first of the ghost towns: little more than an old school and the ruins of the *Oxford Arms Inn*. A little further on is the turn-off for **Goulds Country**, with the remaining buildings – all wooden – of what was once a town, and **Lottah**. The **Weldborough Pass** (595m) is probably the most beautiful part of the drive, with views across the valleys to the sea; it's worth taking the twenty-minute walk through the **Weldborough Pass Scenic Reserve**, predominately myrtle forest with manferns and occasional tall blackwoods. **WELDBOR-OUGH** itself, once the centre of a Chinese mining community, now consists of the *Weldborough Hotel* (☎ & fax 03/6354 2223; ③), where you can get a **meal** (Mon–Sat) and a basic pub **room** for the night; there's also a campsite with showers at the back.

DERBY, on the Ringarooma River, was made prosperous by the profitable **Briseis Tin Mine** that operated in the town between 1876 and 1952. The **Derby Tin Mine Centre** (daily: June–Aug 10am–4pm; Sept–May 10am–5pm; $4) is now the only sign of development in a town that's been closing down since the 1950s: it has some interesting relics connected with the Chinese miners and examples of gemstones fossicked in the area.

SCOTTSDALE, 99km from St Helens, is a large, pleasantly situated town servicing the agricultural and forestry industries of the northeast, but it's none too exciting; Redline runs here from Launceston daily except Saturday. You might want to stop here for banking facilities at Westpac, 21 King St (☎03/6352 2433), or a bed and barbecue at *Bellows*, 65 King St (☎03/6352 2263; dorm ①, rooms ③), which offers tours of the locality in summer. More interesting is **BRIDPORT**, a fishing town and holiday spot 21km northwest. The *Bridport Caravan Park* here (☎03/6356 1227), which feels like just a bush camp yet with all the amenities, stretches for about a kilometre along Anderson Bay. You could also try the *Bridport Seaside Lodge* at 47 Main St (☎ & fax 03/6356 1585; rooms ②, dorms ①), a modern purpose-built hostel. The **beaches** in the area are lovely, especially the wide, sandy expanse where the Bird River flows among sand dunes and into the sea. *Bridport Seafoods* (daily 10am–7pm), attached to the fish-processing plant on Main Street, does excellent sit-down meals.

NORTH AND CENTRAL TASMANIA AND THE BASS STRAIT

The **north** of Tasmania is rich and settled agricultural country, and the fertile soil of the **Tamar Valley** in particular made this a prosperous area during the early colonial period. **Launceston** quickly grew as a port and city, 30km inland at the confluence of the Tamar and the North and South Esk rivers; around the area are still found gracious early houses and well-preserved villages. Also settled early, due to its fine and open land, was the mostly flat, gently undulating **midlands** area between Launceston and Hobart; the **Midland Highway** more or less follows the old coaching route between the two cities. With its stone walls, hedgerows, haystacks and small villages and towns, this rural stretch from the Tamar Valley to Hobart is softly appealing but not particularly exciting. In contrast, the area around **Deloraine**, 45km west of Launceston, is spectacular: the early colonial town is surrounded by rich farmland and dramatically located in hilly country below the crest of the **Great Western Tiers** – a mecca for bushwalkers. From Deloraine, the **Lake Highway** heads steeply south up over the Western Tiers and on to the **Central Plateau**, a sparsely populated lake-filled region dominated by the **Great Lake** and its shambolic fishing shacks.

Lying off the northern coast, in Bass Strait, are two islands worth visiting for their bushwalks and historic associations: **Flinders Island** in the northeast, largest of the Furneaux Islands, and **King Island** to the far northwest, part of the Hunter Island group. Both are reached by plane only, with flights from Victoria or Tasmania.

Launceston and around

LAUNCESTON is dominated by the **Tamar River**, and approaching from the north along the Tamar Highway, zooming through haystack-filled countryside, it's a lovely sight, with grand Victorian houses nestling on hills above the banks. Approaching from the south, however, on the dreary Southern Outlet, a perhaps more accurate picture emerges of a dull but worthy provincial town. It's Tasmania's second-largest city, with a population of over 92,000, but despite its much-vaunted English look – especially in its many formal parks and gardens – only the surrounding countryside of the **Tamar Valley** (see p.950) really makes a visit worthwhile.

As the third-oldest city in Australia, first settled in 1804, Launceston has hung on to disappointingly little of its elegant colonial Georgian architecture. Existing examples are mainly utilitarian structures such as merchant warehouses and mills, now converted into museums, galleries or tourist attractions. What the city does have in abundance, however, are many fine examples of colonial **Victorian architecture**: the 1870s and 1880s were prosperous times for Launceston, years of mineral exploration spurred on by the mainland goldrush. There was a boom in construction and a number of massive, dignified public buildings date from this period – though, unfortunately, the often florid facades were simply attached to Georgian structures.

Launceston's real attractions, though, are its natural assets. It's situated at the confluence of the narrow **North Esk** and **South Esk rivers**, with the breathtaking Cataract gorge only fifteen minutes' walk from the centre, where the South Esk has carved its way through rock to reach the Tamar. Yachts and outboard motors ply the 50km of river, while beyond the western suburbs bush-covered hills fold back into the distance to **Ben Lomond**, an hour's drive away, and popular with Launceston's residents winter skiing.

Arrival, information and transport

There are direct **flights** from Melbourne, Gippsland and Hobart to **Launceston Airport**, near the town of Evandale, 20km south of the city. **Skybus** (☎03/6334 4442), run by Tasmanian Wilderness Transport, meets most flights and drops off at their central depot (see below), or at your accommodation ($7). A **taxi** costs about $20, or you could **rent a car** – the main car companies have desks at the airport.

Long distance **buses** arrive at depots on George Street: Tasmanian Redline Coaches, at no.112 (☎03/6331 3233), will also drop you off at accommodation as far out as the *Treasure Island Caravan Park*; Tasmanian Wilderness Travel (☎03/6334 4442) will drop you in the city centre or at their office at no. 101. There's no problem with **parking** in the city centre – if the short-term metered parking (limit 3hr; $1 per 1hr 30min) is full, there are loads of **car parks** around, charging $1.10 an hour ($7 per day). Most streets operate on a **one-way system** and the length of Cameron Street is interrupted by Civic Square, and Brisbane Street by the Mall.

Information

For **information**, your first stop should be the **Tasmanian Travel and Information Centre**, on the corner of St John and Paterson streets (Mon–Fri 9am–5pm, Sat 9am–3pm, Sun 9am–noon; reservations ☎03/6336 3133), which can arrange car hire and book accommodation and travel tickets. It acts primarily as a travel agent, and isn't particularly helpful for general enquiries – you'll have to ask for maps and other useful material. Aside from street and regional **maps**, pick up the the free community newspaper, *Launceston Week* which has some listings. The Wilderness Society Shop, at 174 Charles St, opposite Princes Square (Mon–Fri 9.30am–5.30pm, Sat 10am–1pm; ☎03/6334 2499), is a good source of information about wilderness issues and the environment. You can sign up here for the summer walks programme – weekends and day-walks – that takes you into areas under threat by logging. The Launceston Environment Centre, nearby at 226 Charles St (Mon–Fri 10.30am–4.30pm; ☎03/6331 8406), is another worthwhile place to get information; they have a library with useful background on Tasmania.

City transport

Launceston is very compact and most accommodation is within walking distance of the city centre, although **public transport** (the MTT) is useful for a couple of scattered attractions and some outlying accommodation (buses run until 6.15pm Mon–Thurs, 10pm Fri & Sat; very restricted services on Sunday). The **MTT bus interchange** (fare and timetable information on ☎13 2201), where all buses arrive and depart, is on St John Street, on either side of the **Brisbane Street Mall**. Single fares are inexpensive, but it may be worth buying a Day Rover ($3.10) for unlimited travel between 9am and 4.30pm and then again after 6pm; you can buy these on board buses. Ten-trip tickets cost from $9.60 and you can buy these at selected newsagents (including Fortunes' Newsagency, 68 Charles St and Teagues, opposite the post office).

Accommodation

Accommodation in Launceston is very good value, and rates don't tend to hike up in the busy period from December to February; most places have parking available, too. However, **hostel** beds are scarce, though there is a temporary YHA hostel in the summer, whose location changes from year to year (contact the Tasmanian YHA on ☎03/6234 9617 for details), and the summer-only *Parkside Backpackers*, 103 Canning St (☎03/6331 4615), in rather shabby student accommodation. There's a concentration of **motels** along Brisbane Street.

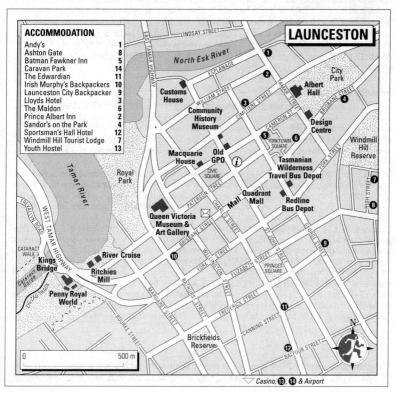

ACCOMMODATION	
Andy's	1
Ashton Gate	8
Batman Fawkner Inn	5
Caravan Park	14
The Edwardian	11
Irish Murphy's Backpackers	10
Launceston City Backpacker	9
Lloyds Hotel	3
The Maldon	6
Prince Albert Inn	2
Sandor's on the Park	4
Sportsman's Hall Hotel	12
Windmill Hill Tourist Lodge	7
Youth Hostel	13

LAUNCESTON

Hotels, motels, B&Bs and self-catering

Ashton Gate, 32 High St (☎03/6331 6180, fax 6334 2232). Classified by the National Trust, this weatherboard house has been taking guests for over forty years. Bedrooms are large and light; all are en-suite, with TV and hot drinks. B&B ⑦.

Batman Fawkner Inn, 35–39 Cameron St (☎03/6331 7222, fax 6331 7158). Established in 1822, and offering bargain single, en-suite rooms with TV and phone; larger, more attractive rooms have similar facilities. Light breakfast included. Singles ②, doubles ⑤.

The Edwardian, 227 Charles St (☎ & fax 03/6334 7771). A lovely, two-storey red-brick Edwardian house near Princes Square, with self-contained self-catering suites, the largest with four rooms. Breakfast provisions provided. Handy for the supermarket. ⑥.

Lloyds Hotel, 23 George St (☎03/6331 4966, fax 6331 5589). Solid, rather drab old-fashioned hotel with en-suite rooms, plus some dorms. Cooked breakfast included, and the dining room downstairs does economical meals at other times. Hot drinks and TV in the lounge. Closed on Sun, when enquiries can be made and keys obtained from the *Commercial Hotel* opposite. Rooms ④, dorms ①.

The Maldon, 32 Brisbane St (☎03/6331 3211, fax 6334 4641). Elegant Victorian-era B&B, featuring iron-lace verandahs, chandeliers, engraved glass and a carved wooden staircase; en-suite rooms have modern facilities. ⑥.

Prince Albert Inn, cnr of William and Tamar sts (☎03/6331 7633, fax 6334 1579). A refurbished nineteenth-century inn near City Park, with spacious en-suite rooms furnished in heritage style. The dining room, where you have breakfast, is full of stuffed animals, while old photographs and colonial prints cover the walls. Non-smokers only. ⑦–⑧.

Sandors on the Park, 3 Brisbane St (☎03/6331 2055, fax 6334 3910). The best of a bunch of motels on this strip overlooking City Park – but not the most expensive – just a short walk from the centre. Friendly professional service; guest laundry. Its bistro-style *Monkey Bar Café* opens 11.30am–midnight. ⑥.

Sportsman's Hall Hotel, 252 Charles St (☎03/6331 3968, fax 6334 4227). A pleasant pub whose manager takes care over the well-furnished, comfortable rooms (shared bathrooms). Breakfast included. There's an excellent, café-style bistro downstairs serving up very reasonably priced meals. ④.

Windmill Hill Tourist Lodge, 22 High St (☎03/6331 9337, fax 6334 3292). Pleasant, two-storey house with bay windows and a 1940s feel. Huge rooms, all en-suite. ⑤.

Hostels and caravan parks

Andy's, 1 Tamar St, by the bridge. Renovated former pub with the *Malle Grill Restaurant* downstairs, and *Andy's* backpacker accommodation upstairs. Very clean and well run with common room with TV, a balcony, and a small well-equipped kitchen. Rooms ③, dorms (BYO linen) ①.

Irish Murphy's Backpackers, 211 Brisbane St (☎03/6331 4440, fax 6334 5503). Hostel accommodation above a lively, centrally located pub. Facilities include TV lounge and a fully equipped kitchen. Rooms ②, dorms ①.

Launceston City Backpackers, 173 George St (☎03/6334 2327). Launceston's best hostel, in a large old Federation house with an annexe out back with extra beds. Young managers and a friendly atmosphere. Nicely decorated, clean and well equipped, with a TV lounge, wood-combustion fire, and a laundry. A few minutes' walk from the Redline and Tasmanian Wilderness Travel depots. Book ahead in summer. Rooms ②, dorms ①.

Launceston City Youth Hostel, 36 Thistle St, South Launceston (☎03/6344 9779). A rather gloomy institutional place, with loads of rules and regulations and a midnight curfew. However, you can rent bikes and camping gear, and the manager is very knowledgeable about bushwalking. Despite the name, this is not a YHA hostel. Take bus #21 or #24 and get off at Wellington St (stop 8); Redline buses also drop off here. ①.

Treasure Island Caravan Park, 94 Glen Dhu St, South Launceston, 2km south of the centre (☎03/6344 2600). A small park, sloping up a hillside and looking right over a freeway. It's noisy, the ground is hard and uneven, and it's crowded in summer – but there's nowhere else to camp in the Launceston area. Public transport as for *Launceston City Youth Hostel* (see above). Cabins ④.

The City

The **Brisbane Street Mall** marks the centre of the city, which is arranged in a typical grid pattern around it. **Brisbane Street**, with the mall as its focus, is the main shopping precinct; heading east along the street, two other pedestrian shopping areas branch off it: **Quadrant Mall** and **Yorktown Square**. The city is small and easy to get around, but if you want some background information, join Launceston Historic Walks (departs Mon–Fri 9.45am; bookings ☎03/6331 3679; $10; 1hr 15min) outside the travel and information centre on Paterson Street.

City Park and the old wharf area

City Park (daily 9am–5.30pm, with its entrance of impressive wrought-iron gates on Tamar Street, is a real treasure. Established in the 1820s, the impression of a formally organized, very English park is reinforced by the **John Hart Conservatory**, full of flowers and ferns, and by the wrought-iron drinking fountain erected here for Queen Victoria's Diamond Jubilee in 1897. Referred to by the locals as "Monkey Park", it's the closest thing Launceston has to a zoo: its Japanese macaques (over twenty of them), romp around their small, moat-surrounded island. The **City Park Train** (10.30am–4pm), a vehicle with several tiny carriages, whizzes children and adults twice around the park for around a dollar a ride.

Within City Park, on the corner of Tamar and Brisbane streets, is the **Design Centre of Tasmania** (Mon–Fri 10am–6pm, Sat 10am–1pm, Sun 2–5pm; free), established in 1976 to support and encourage Tasmanian designers. In a state that's always been perceived by the mainland as lagging behind, it's a source of pride that Tasmanian designers helped furnish the New Parliament House in Canberra; "Furniture Focus", a permanent display of contemporary, innovative furniture made from native Tasmanian woods, includes some of their work. Pieces are regularly sold and shipped overseas; prices are beyond the range of most visitors, but the centre is also one of the best places to buy more portable **craft** items, such as woodwork, leatherwork and jewellery.

Backing onto City Park, near the corner of Tamar and Cimitiere streets, is **Albert Hall**, a grand building in the ornate High Victorian style, built for the Tasmanian Industrial Exhibition of 1891. You can go up the steps and look inside at the Great Hall (restored to its original state) and at the Brindley water-powered organ, imported from England in 1861 and the only one of its kind in the world.

Further along Tamar Street, on the corner of William Street, the extremely elaborate Victorian facade of the three-storey **Prince Albert Inn** hides the original Georgian facade. The 1855 building was once a tavern frequented by the sailors from the clippers that berthed at the **Old Launceston Wharves**, 100m away. The wharves on the North Esk River have disappeared, but the massive Neoclassical **Customs House** is still there on the Esplanade, west of the Tamar Street Bridge. The **old wharf area**, around William Street and the Esplanade, has several other interesting old industrial buildings, including the **Esk Brewery Oast House** (1881) and the **Monds and Afflek Mill** (1860). A multimillion dollar redevelopment of this complex of old railway yards, reached by the Tamar Street Bridge across the river, has transformed it into a convention and entertainment centre; an extension of the Queen Victoria Museum here (overleaf) is among further plans.

St John Street and around

If you go south from the Customs House down St John Street, you'll come to the **Community History Museum**, on the corner of Cimitiere Street (Mon–Sat 10am–4pm, Sun 2–4pm; $1), housed in the old Johnston and Wilmot store, built in 1842. With its bare rafters, old wooden floors and staircases and rough, wooden pillars supporting the ceiling, it has changed little in 150 years. The building once housed the old Maritime Museum, and some artefacts relating to whaling and sealing still remain here.

On the corner of Cameron Street, the rather grand, Queen Anne-style, red-brick structure is the now-defunct **General Post Office**, built in 1889. Opposite, the grand white building, with its giant colonnade of nine Corinthian columns, is the **town hall**, erected in 1864.

Between St John and Charles streets is the main shopping thoroughfare, **Brisbane Street Mall**, a modest precinct taking up one small city block. It was completed in 1975, the first stage of a pedestrianization policy for the city centre, and has a pleasant atmosphere, with trees and places to sit. Just off here is the arc of the **Quadrant Mall**, bounded by Brisbane and St John streets, with several lanes and an arcade off it. Gourlay's Sweet Shop here is a Launceston institution, lined with row upon row of glass jars full of imported and local sweets – for something really local, try the leatherwood honey drops. **Yorktown Square**, designed to re-create the atmosphere of the nineteenth century, can be reached by cobbled lanes off Cameron, George and Brisbane streets; here, you'll find cafés and restaurants – most with outdoor tables – ranged around the square. On Sunday a "village market" (9am–2pm), selling mainly crafts, is held here. Nearly opposite the George Street entrance to the square is **The Old Umbrella Shop** at no. 60 (Mon–Fri 9am–5pm, Sat 9am–noon; ☎03/6331 9248), a National Trust information centre housed in a rare example of a mid-Victorian shop, built in the 1860s and lined with Tasmanian blackwood.

Five blocks south of the old General Post Office, bounded by Frederick and Elizabeth streets, is the peaceful **Princes Square**, a park since 1859, having served as both brickfields and a parade ground.

From Civic Square to the museum

Shady, grassy **Civic Square**, closed to traffic, does convey a tidy spirit of civic-mindedness. Here, **Macquarie House** was built as a warehouse in 1830 for Henry Reed, a wealthy merchant. These days it's the home of the **Tasmanian Wood Design Collection** (Mon–Fri 10am–4pm; $2), which showcases Tasmanian wood pieces of some of the state's superb designers, wood-workers and furniture-makers.

Cameron Street was one of the first streets laid out after the city's settlement in 1806, and the stretch from Civic Square to Wellington Street is an almost perfectly preserved nineteenth-century streetscape, including the imposing Supreme Court building and, opposite, a row of fine Victorian red-brick terraced houses adorned with beautiful wrought-iron work.

The Queen Victoria Museum and Art Gallery

The **Queen Victoria Museum and Art Gallery** on Wellington Street (Mon–Sat 10am–5pm, Sun 2–5pm; free) was opened in 1891 to mark half a century of Queen Victoria's reign. Its most valued possession is the Chinese joss house from Weldborough (see p.939), constructed in the 1870s by Chinese workers introduced to the east-coast tin mines to provide cheap labour.

Elsewhere, there's a history of **mining** in Tasmania, made more accessible by interpretive displays; there are also displays of stuffed animals, accounts of the geology of Launceston and the local area, a **Planetarium** (Tues–Sat 2pm & 3pm; $3), and the "Discovery Plus" room, containing such items as microscopes and specimen trays, as well as a display of live spiders and puzzles to play with. Upstairs, the **Art Gallery** has some gothic and wild Tasmanian landscapes by the nineteenth-century painter W.C. Piguenit. The *Queen Vic Café* downstairs is one of the best in Launceston.

Royal Park to Ritchies Mill Arts Centre

Behind the museum, and across Bathurst Street, **Royal Park** has extensive formal parklands running down to the Tamar River; there's even a croquet lawn here, if you were in any doubt about its English character. Between Royal Park and Cataract Gorge is a concentrated tourist area. **Ritchies Mill Arts Centre**, at 2 Bridge Rd, has been converted from a nineteenth-century flour mill and millers' cottage; situated on the

Tamar River, it has two galleries, an alfresco café (see p.947) and some **artists' studios** and exhibition space.

Opposite Ritchies Mill, **Penny Royal World** (daily 9am–4.30pm; closed two weeks in July; $19.50, children $9.50) is a sort of historical funfair, developed on the site of an old bluestone quarry and based around an 1840 ironstone water mill and farmhouse – transferred to the site – and a replica of an 1825 wooden corn mill. However, the whole thing is tacky and overpriced. The standard entrance fee includes a cruise on the **paddle steamer** *Lady Stelfox*, departing from the landing stage behind the Arts Centre, much the best attraction of the centre, but you can buy separate tickets; the forty-minute cruise heads along the Tamar and into the mouth of Cataract Gorge (daily 10.10am, 11.10am, 12.20pm, 1.10pm, 2.10pm & 3.10pm; $6.50), allowing a close-up view of the Launceston Yacht Club, as well as the wealthy suburb of **Trevallyn**, filled with classic Victorian mansions strung along the tree-covered hillside. On the return leg, you cruise close to the western side of the Tamar, before briefly entering the natural beauty of Cataract Gorge (see below). A longer trip with Tamar River Cruises goes into the mouth of Cataract Gorge and continues north up the Tamar as far as the Rosevear vineyards (see p.951); lunch is included (Mon–Sat 10am, Sun 11am; 4hr; $48; bookings ☎03/6334 9900); there's also a shorter, less pricey Afternoon Discovery Cruise (Tues, Wed & Thurs 3pm; 2hr 30min; $20).

Cataract Gorge and beyond

Few cities have such a magnificent natural feature within fifteen minutes' walk of the centre as does Launceston. For a beautiful view of **Cataract Gorge**, turn left when coming out of Penny Royal World and walk to the decorative wrought-iron **Kings Bridge**, fabricated in Manchester and transported to Launceston in 1863, which has a span of 60m. From the bridge the cliffs rise almost vertically from the smooth water of the South Esk River as it empties into the Tamar. The natural spectacle is even more dramatic when floodlit after dusk.

There are two walking routes along the gorge. The **Zig Zag track** (25min one-way), on the Penny Royal World side of the bridge, is the more strenuous, a rock-stepped path shrouded by bush but satisfyingly secluded. It runs steeply along the top of the gorge, from Kings Bridge to the **First Basin**, a large, deep canyon worn away by the river and filled with water. If you cross the Kings Bridge, you can choose to take the easier but busier **Cataract Walk** (40min one-way), which begins by the small tollhouse, with its iron-lace decoration; it's an easy stroll, suitable for prams or wheelchairs, and offers spectacular views of the gorge. From the trail, particularly at weekends and during summer, you'll see people canoeing, abseiling or even jumping off the cliffs into the water.

The Cataract Walk leads to the gardens of the **Cliff Grounds**, on the shady northern side of the gorge: genteel, English-style gardens with parading peacocks, they make for a startling contrast with the gorge's wild beauty. The garden's ferns, and native and exotic plants, are artfully arranged around a lovely 1896 rotunda, which contains an interpretive centre with early photographs and displays dealing with the history and botany of the gorge. The *Gorge Restaurant* (☎03/6331 3330; closed Mon) in the grounds features fine food and Tasmanian wines and has stunning views over the First Basin. Less expensive Devonshire teas are served from the kiosk at the back of the restaurant.

If you enter the grounds from the First Basin end (where there's a car park; or take bus #51), you'll find an enormous, unattractive **swimming pool**, built mainly to discourage people from swimming in the basin itself, where some have died. However, people still continue to swim there, despite prominent signs warning them of the dangers of hypothermia; diving is not recommended, as there are submerged rocks and logs.

To get across the First Basin to the Cliff Grounds, you can take the **Launceston Basin Chair Lift** (Aug 13–June 19 daily 9am–4.30pm, June 20–Aug 12 Sat & Sun only; $5), which takes an exhilarating six minutes to cover 457m – it's supposed to have the longest single span (308m) of any chair lift in the world. The views are wonderful, but if you're afraid of heights you might want to cross on foot via the **Basin Walk** directly underneath, although this route is impassable when the river is in flood. The other alternative, the narrow **Alexandra Suspension Bridge**, is fairly alarming, too. Called the "swinging bridge" by locals, it's even shakier when crowded with joggers.

There are several other walks and lookouts in the grounds, all well signposted. It's even possible to undertake longer bushwalks: for example, a track starts from the Alexandra Suspension Bridge and follows the river through unspoilt bush to the narrower **Second Basin** and the disused **Duck Reach Power Station** (90min return). From the station you could continue a bit further to reach the large **Trevallyn State Recreation Area** (daily 8am–dusk; no camping), on the South Esk River, and the **Trevallyn Dam**, 6km west of the city centre. To reach the area by road, go via the suburb of Trevallyn, following Reatta Road. There's an **information centre** at **Aquatic Point** in the recreation area, where there are grassy spaces, a children's playground, toilets and barbecues. The rest of the reserve consists of open eucalypt forest, with marked bushwalks and nature trails that you'll share with horse-riders. In summer, canoes and windsurfers can sometimes be rented; enquire at the information centre.

The Waverly Woollen Mills and Franklin House

The city's three woollen mills are all open for inspection, though easily the most interesting is **Waverly Woollen Mills** (Mon–Fri 9am–4pm; $3), on Waverly Road, 5km west of the city centre; take bus #34 or #38 from the city to the Waverly Road turn-off, and from there it's a 500m walk. Established in 1874, it's the oldest woollen mill in Australia, and much of the cloth is still manufactured on old-fashioned machinery.

Franklin House, at 413 Hobart Rd, 6km towards Hobart on the Midland Highway (daily: Sept–May 9am–5pm; June–Aug 10am–4pm; $6; bus #21 from the city), was built in 1838 for Britton Jones, a prosperous local brewer. Furnished as an early Victorian home, it became a leading school for boys four years after it was built, a role it retained for half a century. Beautifully furnished and restored by the National Trust, its most outstanding feature is the woodwork of the interior, made entirely of unusual cedarwood from New South Wales.

Eating

Eating out in Launceston is a predominantly Anglo-Saxon affair, with **pubs** in particular offering decent meals. There are a few excellent **cafés**, however, and the odd ethnic place, as listed below.

Arpar's Thai Restaurant, cnr of Charles and Paterson sts (☎03/6331 2786). Thai restaurant with a good reputation. Licensed and BYO. Dinner nightly, plus Fri lunch.

Calabrisella, 56 Wellington St (☎03/6331 1958). A real find – a crowded, noisy, atmospheric and affordable Italian restaurant. BYO. Dinner nightly except Tues.

Cucina Simpatica, cnr of Margaret and Frederick sts, opposite Brickfields Reserve (☎03/6334 3177). Launceston's hip café, with a colourful Mediterranean feel; a good place to relax with a coffee and newspaper. Becomes a restaurant in the evening, with an eclectic, "contemporary" menu: delicious food (though pricey and small portions) and an emphasis on fresh Tasmanian produce. Licensed or BYO. Daily 9am–11pm, Sat until midnight.

Gourmet on Brisbane, 86 Brisbane St. A big, bright delicatessen doubling as a crowded café. Mon–Sat 8 or 9am–6pm.

Hari's Curry, 152 York St (☎03/6331 6466). Very cheap, well-recommended Indian place. No frills, but the good food compensates. BYO. Closed for lunch Sat & Sun.

Janet's, 2 Paterson St. A tiny, homely café run by friendly women. Freshly baked trays of lasagne and egg-and-bacon pie are displayed; sandwiches and great salads, too. Mon–Fri 8am–5pm.

Konditorei Manfredi, 106 George St, opposite Tasmanian Wilderness Travel (☎03/6334 2490; dinner bookings recommended). German cakes and pastries accompanied by delicious coffee; also there's a full menu of contemporary meals served on the smart upper level with its polished wood floors, bar and outside courtyard. Licensed. Mon–Thurs 9am–5.30pm, Fri & Sat 9am–10pm.

Metz Cafe Bar, 119 St John St, cnr of York St. Cosmopolitan combination of café and wine bar with music videos playing day or night. Typical café fare plus blackboard specials — try the delicious antipasto platter, which is easily big enough to share. Breakfast until 11am. Licensed. Daily 8am–midnight, Fri & Sat until 3am, Sun until 2am.

Montezuma's, 63 Brisbane St (☎03/6331 8999). Typical Mexican restaurant, with pricey main courses, but you can fill up on the taco and nachos starters. Good-value margaritas. Daily from 6pm, plus lunch Mon–Fri.

Narracoopaz, 76 St John St. "Clean green cuisine" is this contemporary-feeling vegetarian café's catch-cry. Fresh juices and cakes, gourmet pizzas, Italian bread sandwiches, continental salads, airy interior, outdoor tables, art on walls. Upstairs level too.

O'Keefe's Hotel, 124 George St. People crowd into the lounge bar for pub meals claimed to be the best in Tasmania: from a warm wallaby salad to a Thai red curry, plus a traditional roast of the day and a large range of fresh seafood. Top price $18.

Pepper Berry, 91 George St (☎03/6334 4589). A café serving stunning Australian food, such as King Island wallaby marinated in native pepper berries or Bruny Island oysters with Thai-style sauce, plus a range of Mediterranean-style dishes. Local produce is used as much as possible, and they even cure their own trout. Try the damper baked here, served with native jams. Vegan, vegetarian and other diets catered for – gluten free cakes available. Mains around $12. BYO. Mon–Sat 8.30am until late.

Ripples Café, Ritchies Mill Arts Centre, Paterson St (☎03/6331 4153). Very popular riverside café, with outdoor tables under umbrellas overlooked by a huge gum tree; a favourite with locals at weekends. Generous, tasty sandwiches, and a board featuring specials of the day. Licensed or BYO. Summer daily 10am to late (book for dinner); rest of year Sun–Thurs 10am–4pm, Fri & Sat 10am–7.30pm.

Satay House, Innocent St, Kingscourt Shopping Centre, behind Roelf Voss Supermarket, Kings Meadows (☎03/6344 5955). You'll have to venture into suburban Launceston for this authentic, family-run Indonesian restaurant, but it's worth it. The chef uses her grandmother's recipes. BYO. Bus #21. Dinner Mon–Sat.

Shrimps, 72 George St, cnr of Paterson St (☎03/6334 0584). A Launceston institution, serving the best seafood in town. Formal, but not stuffy, and with an imaginative menu. Expensive. Licensed. Closed Sun & lunch Sat.

Tairyo Japanese Restaurant and Sushi Bar, Yorktown Square (☎03/6334 2620). Serves all the Japanese dishes: *ramen*, sushi, tempura, *bento*. Licensed (sake) or BYO. Dinner nightly, plus lunch Tues–Fri.

Entertainment and nightlife

The *Examiner*, based in Launceston, is the newspaper for the north of Tasmania – Thursday's edition contains an entertainment section. However, there's never very much going on in this quiet city, and there's no particularly lively area. The **Princess Theatre**, 57 Brisbane St (☎03/6331 0052), stages regular drama, opera and concerts, usually touring from interstate. Behind the theatre is the Earl Arts Centre, 10 Earl St, which has fringe theatre productions, while the **Silverdome**, out of town on the Bass Highway at Prospect (☎03/6344 9999), is the venue for big entertainment events, exhibitions and sports events. Book through Fortune's Newsagency, 68 Charles St (☎03/6334 3033). The only **cinema**, the Village 4 at 163 Brisbane St (☎03/6331 5066), has four screens showing mainstream films.

Pubs, clubs and venues

Batman Fawkner Inn, 35–39 Cameron St (☎03/6331 7222). Stylishly decorated, old hotel on the weekend pub route. Young crowd and a popular pool table. Interstate bands play once or twice a month.

Country Club Casino, Country Club Ave, Prospect Vale, 9km out of town off the Bass Highway (☎03/6335 5777). From the outside it looks as exclusive as its name suggests, but it's not really – just don't wear sandshoes or T-shirts after 8pm. Live music Thurs–Sat in the *Lanai Bar*. Sunday buffet lunch in the brasserie, with lots of seafood, prawns and oysters (around $20 a head). Bus #61, #64 or #65; if you want to stay late, you'll have to take a taxi back (around $14). Mon–Thurs & Sun noon–1am, Fri & Sat until 4am.

Irish Murphy's, 211 Brisbane St (☎03/6331 4440). Launceston's lively Irish pub, with Guinness on tap, live music Wed–Sun, and pub meals.

K-OS, 107 Brisbane St. Large airy upstairs space with groovy lounge decor, but dull atmosphere lets it down. Pumping music is replaced on Fri & Sat nights by stints of an acoustic duo playing covers. Even so, it's Launceston's most happening bar, best enjoyed from the narrow balcony. Doubles as a café with a casual menu. Mon & Tues 11am–10pm, Wed–Sat (with DJs) 11am–3am. Closed Sun.

Metz Cafe Bar, 119 St John St, cnr of York St. Wine bar with music video, late weekend opening and great food (see overleaf).

Royal Oak Hotel, 14 Brisbane St (☎03/6331 5346). A popular, genial watering hole, with live music Thursday to Saturday evenings. Crowded bistro serves Greek dishes as well as counter meals. Mon–Sat until midnight, Sun until 10pm.

Star Bar Café, 113 Charles St (☎03/6331 9659). Sophisticated bar with slick, modern decor; brasserie-style Mediterranean food available.

Listings

Banks and foreign exchange Commonwealth Bank, 97 Brisbane St (☎03/6337 4444); Thomas Cook, 85 George St, cnr of Brisbane St (Mon–Fri 9am–5.15pm, Sat 9am–noon).

Bike rental Rent-A-Cycle Tasmania, from *Launceston City Youth Hostel* (☎03/6344 9779). All bikes are fully equipped with rear panniers, puncture kit, tools and helmets. From $65 per week; mountain bikes from $95.

Camping equipment The best place to rent gear is from *Launceston City Youth Hostel* (☎03/6344 9779), which has everything from tents to woollen trousers, but it's a bit out of the way (see p.942). A good option is Allgoods: their main store, at 71–79 York St, has a comprehensive range of camping gear to rent or buy at prices to suit all budgets; they also have a Tent City store at 60 Elizabeth St (☎03/6331 3644). Paddy Pallin, 110 George St (☎03/6331 4240), focuses on the top end of the market and also rents gear and sells fuel, a wide range of freeze-dried foods, guidebooks and maps.

Car rental Advance Car Rentals, 32 Cameron St (☎03/6391 8000 or free call ☎1800/030 118), has rates from $32 with a $20 surcharge for one-day rental. They also hire out 4WDs, from $130 per day. Auto Rent Hertz, 58 Paterson St (☎03/6335 1111), charges from $50 per day, and has campervans; Economy Car Rentals, 27 William St (☎03/6334 3299), has cars from $38 per day; Lo-Cost Auto Rent, 152 Cimitiere St (☎03/6334 3437), has rates from $37 per day, 4WDs available from $110 per day; Ryan's Minicar Rentals (☎03/6344 3600) has old Leyland minis from $30 per day.

Horse-riding Dilston Lodge Ride-A-Ways, East Tamar Highway, Dilston, 15km north (☎03/6328 1303), runs trail rides in the Tamar Valley (1hr, $18; 2hr, $32; 3hr, $45; 4hr with picnic $65); overnight rides and lessons also available.

Hospital Launceston General, Charles St (☎03/6332 7111).

Internet Access Free access at the main library in Civic Square (Mon–Wed 9.30am–6pm, Thurs & Fri 9.30am–9pm, Sat 9.30am–12.30pm; ☎03/6336 2625). Central City Computers, 136 Charles St, Launceston (☎03/6334 9226; Mon–Fri 9am–6pm; Sat 10am–4pm) charges $10 per hour, $5 per 30min.

Left luggage Tasmanian Wilderness Travel, 101 George St. If you are a passenger/pass holder, you can leave baggage for as long as you like (within reason) for $5. Redline, 112 George St; $1 per piece for 24hr. Most hostels will let you leave bags.

Motorbike rental Tasmanian Motorcycle Hire, 46 Mace St, Prospect Vale (☎03/6344 8111; from $90 day, helmets $7.50).

Parking Launceston has metered street parking, and its car parks are very cheap. Plaza Quadrant Car Park, entrance on 94 York St, near the corner of George St (☎03/6334 2456; Mon–Fri 7.30am–6.30pm, Sat 7.30am–5.15pm), has cheaper long-term rates if you want to leave your vehicle here while you go on the Overland Track (a one-way walk). Normal rates are $3.30 per day, $7 per 24hr.

Pharmacy Todd's Centre Pharmacy, 84 Brisbane St (☎03/6331 7777). Daily 9am–10pm.

Post office 170 Brisbane St, Launceston, TAS 7250.

Roman Baths Aquarius Roman Baths, 127–133 George St (☎03/6331 2255). A very popular , self-indulgent complex of therapeutic warm, hot and cold baths, sauna, steam rooms, gym, massage and solarium. Admission to baths and saunas $18 (or $28 per couple).

Swimming Launceston Swimming Centre, Windmill Hill Reserve (☎03/6337 1282). Outdoor 50m pool, diving pool, a children's wading pool, a waterfall and waterplay area for babies, and water-slides.

Taxis There's a taxi rank on George St between Brisbane and Paterson sts, and one on St John St outside Princes Square. Central Cabs (☎13 008); Taxis Combined (☎03/6331 5555).

Tours Tasmanian Wilderness Travel, 101 George St (☎03/6334 4442), has a programme of day-tours in small minibuses: Evandale, and the market or Clarendon House (Sunday 9am–noon; $25, plus entrance to Clarendon House); the Tamar Valley (half-day; $39); a Tamar Valley wine tour (half-day; $39); the Mole Creek caves and the wildlife park ($49); or an evening tour to the Fairy penguin colony at George Town ($39). Their trip to Cradle Mountain ($45; including three short walks) doesn't give enough time at the park (no more than two hours). Tasmanian Redline Coaches (☎03/6331 3233) offers more conventional day-trips in large buses to Cradle Mountain ($39), Mole Creek (Thurs summer only; $40), the Tamar Valley (half-day; $33) and the Bridestow Estate Lavender Farm when it's flowering (late Dec to mid-Jan Tues & Sat; half-day; $24). Launceston Wilderness Walks (☎03/6334 3477) can take you on a cycle tour (half-day $50; full-day $90), a Cradle Mountain walk (one and a half days, $195; two days including Liffey Falls, $250; three days, $395), or a walk in Freycinet National Park (three days; $395).

Around Launceston

Before launching yourself into the beauty of the Tamar Valley, there are several local destinations worth visiting **around Launceston**, most notably the well-preserved town of **Evandale**, just 20km from the city. If you're here in winter, you might consider join-ing the ski crowd who descend upon **Ben Lomond National Park**, southeast of Launceston; out of season, this is fine bushwalking country.

Entally House

Entally House (daily 10am–12.30pm & 1–5pm; $6) at **HADSPEN**, 18km west of Launceston on the Bass Highway, is the oldest National Trust-owned property in Australia. A large homestead, built in 1819 by Thomas Haycock Reibey, it would have remained a classic, colonial Georgian cottage if not for the later addition of a second storey, reached by climbing rickety stairs. The extensive grounds, running down to the river, are a perfect picnic setting and you don't have to pay to wander through them.

Evandale

Twenty kilometres southeast of Launceston, but not served by public transport, is **EVANDALE**, a National Trust-classified town from the 1830s, where the principal attractions are the Sunday market and various places serving good food. At the **Evandale Tourism and History Centre**, on High Street (daily 11am–3pm; ☎03/6391 8128), pick up a *Heritage Walk* brochure ($2). When it's closed, consult the map oppo-site the Ingleside Bakery, also on High Street, that points out notable features, but many of the old buildings bear descriptive plaques. **Solomon House** (1836), on the corner of High and Russell streets, is a whitewashed two-storey brick building with a green tin roof, which operated as Clarendon Stores for about 130 years. The bakehouse at the rear once supplied the early settlers, though now it's an excellent tearoom.

Another good place for refreshment is the *Dalmeny Bookcafé & Gallery* at 14 Russell St (closed Mon & Tues). The **Clarendon Arms Hotel**, on Russell Street (☎03/6391 8181; ④), was built in 1847 on the site of the former convict station. Its interior walls are covered in murals depicting the early history of Tasmania. One shows the infamous bushranger Matthew Brady and his gang, and there are portraits of the Aborigines King Billy and Truganini, among others. You can eat here, and stay upstairs in the budget rooms.

Further down Russell Street is the **Evandale Market** (Sun 10am–2pm), which attracts large crowds to its 140 stalls. A lot of local vegetable-growers – particularly those who grow organically – bring their produce here. You'll also find a flea market, and some food stalls that are rather exotic for Tasmania. Once a year, running over three days in late February, Evandale hosts the **National Penny Farthing Championships** as part of its Village Fair; the races using the old bikes are quite a sight. There's no public transport to Evandale.

Ben Lomond National Park

The high plateau of the **Ben Lomond Range**, over 1300m high and 84 square kilometres in area, lies entirely within **Ben Lomond National Park**, 50km southeast of Launceston. A small ski village sits below **Legges Tor** (1572m), the second-highest point in Tasmania, and can be reached in an hour from Launceston (or 30min from Evandale); above it the bumpy outline of the range's steep cliffs dominates the horizon. The **ski season** runs from mid-July to the end of September, and although **accommodation** is limited, the region's accessibility means there's no real need to stay. If you're determined, try the pricey *Ben Lomond Creek Inn* (☎03/6372 2444; rooms ⑧, including breakfast and dinner, bunk rooms ②–③), which is usually booked out at weekends. Meals are available here, or there's fast food from the ski resort kiosk.

Alpine Enterprises (☎03/6372 2499) runs the **ski lifts**; an all-day pass costs around $25. They offer some ski rental on the mountain but a better range is available at Launceston Sports Centre, at 88a George St (☎03/6331 4777), which can also advise on ski packages. If you're driving, be warned that the final 20km to the ski village is unsealed and the last leg, **Jacobs Ladder**, is very steep, with several hairpin bends, sheer drops and no safety barriers. You must carry wheel chains, which can be rented from the snowline. Outside the ski season, all services cease and the businesses close down, but **bushwalkers** are lured by the magnificent scenery and the alpine vegetation. There's a 12.5km track from Carr Villa, on the slopes of Ben Lomond, to Legges Tor. Bush **camping** is permitted anywhere in the national park, but Carr Villa is an informal camping area with a pit toilet. For more information, contact the ranger (☎03/6390 6279).

The Tamar Valley

To the north of Launceston is the beautiful **Tamar Valley**, where – for 64km – the tidal waters wind through orchards, vineyards, forested hills and grazing land. Only the Batman Bridge, near Deviot, and the APPM Wood Mill and Bell Bay Power Station, near George Town at the river's mouth, spoil the idyllic pre-industrial scenery.

West of the Tamar

The West Tamar Highway follows the line of the Tamar River from Launceston to Beauty Point, passing through the absurdly tacky **Grindlewald Swiss Village**. Further along, **Brady's Lookout State Reserve** provides magnificent views of the Tamar Valley and Ben Lomond; you can see as far as Low Head, 34km away. Rather than head straight along the highway, you can detour for a stretch through **ROSE-VEARS**, on a picturesque sweep of road along the riverbanks that's popular with cyclists. Along the way, stop at the **St Matthias Vineyard** (daily 10am–5pm) for some wine tasting, Tasmanian cheeses and great views. In the village there's the **Waterbird Haven Trust** (daily 10am–4pm; $4), extending for half a kilometre along the waterfront, and the **Rosevears Tavern** (1831), where you can have a drink. A few kilometres west of Rosevears, reached by turning west off the highway at Legana, is **Notley Gorge State Reserve**. **Beaconsfield**, back on the highway, was at the centre of Tasmania's former **gold-mining** area, and the mining ruins are still visible.

East of the Tamar: George Town and Low Head

Leaving Launceston and heading north along the East Tamar Highway, it's only a few minutes before you're zooming through scenic countryside, passing through Dilston where cows graze in paddocks at the base of bush-covered hills. After Hillwood, you're headed for the port of **GEORGE TOWN**, the third-oldest town in Australia, where Colonel Paterson landed in 1804 to begin settlement of northern Tasmania. It may be your first point of call in Tasmania if you've chosen to take the **high-speed Devil Cat catamaran** from Melbourne, which docks at Adelaide Street, with the town centre opposite, across York Cove. The **George Town Visitor Information Centre**, on Main Road (daily 10am–4pm; ☎03/6382 1700), is about 1.5km northeast of the terminal on the way to Launceston.

Despite its history, George town isn't particularly old or interesting, with only one colonial building to look at – **The Grove**, an elegant stone Georgian mansion at 25 Cimitiere St (daily 10am–5pm; $4). More appealing is **LOW HEAD**, 5km north, with 24 National Trust-listed buildings, whitewashed cottages and rambling houses, all sitting amid extensive parkland. The original convict-built **Pilot Station** now houses a **museum** (daily 8am–6pm; $3), which has a display of maritime memorabilia. There's also a **Little penguin colony** at Low Head; guided tours are offered each evening at sunset (not May & June; 1hr 30min; $6; bookings on mobile ☎0418/361 860). If you're interested, and can afford it, you could also visit a nearby **fur seal** colony on a **cruise** with Seal and Sea Adventure Tours (daily 8am–1pm; $105; bookings ☎03/6382 3452).

If you need a **place to stay**, there are several choices in George Town. *Gray's Hotel*, at 77 Macquarie St (☎03/6382 2655; ⑤), is the oldest pub in the town but has few discernible traces of its early nineteenth-century heritage. The *Pier Hotel*, at 5 Elizabeth St (☎03/6382 1300; ④–⑦), is a pretty wooden hotel on the waterfront with rooms upstairs in the old part, modern motel rooms on the waterfront, and self-catering units; the **food** here is very good, with an extensive menu including pasta and Asian curries. Opposite, at 4 Elizabeth St, is the *George Town YHA* (☎03/6382 3261; rooms ③, dorms ①) in a pretty 1870 home, with a clean and modern interior. An alternative to eating at the pubs is the *George Town Deli*, at 68 Macquarie St (closed Sat & Sun), which sells health-foods and deli items and serves light lunches.

In Low Head, you can stay in heritage cottage accommodation at the Pilot Station (see above; ☎ & fax 03/6382 1143; ⑤), and at *Belfont Cottages*, at 178 Low Head Rd (☎03/6382 1841; ⑦), with breakfast provisions supplied), next door to a beacon. You can **camp** at *Low Head Caravan Park*, 136 Low Head Rd (☎03/6382 1573; vans ③, cabins ④).

Around George Town

Heading **east** of George Town, a pleasant day can be spent exploring the **vineyards** around the **Pipers River area**, which produce distinctly flavoured, crisp, fresh wines. At **Rochecombe Vineyard** at Pipers River, 2km off the B82 on a sealed road (turn south just before the service station at Pipers River), a Swiss couple make European-style wines

– the climate here is supposedly similiar to that of the Loire Valley. There are tastings and a restaurant in the original weatherboard farmhouse (tastings daily 10am–5pm; restaurant 9am–5pm; ☎03/6382 7122). The friendly, small-scale **Delamere Vineyard**, on Bridport Road at Pipers Brook (daily 10am–5pm; ☎03/6382 7190), also has tastings, while **Pipers Brook Vineyard** (daily 10am–5pm), 2km off the B82, about 10km from Pipers River, is a well-established winery in a modern complex, with self-guided tours. It also has a café and vine-covered courtyard. Tiger Wilderness Tours (☎03/6326 6515) runs a half-day wine tour to the Pipers River area from Launceston (5hr; $45).

The Midland Highway

The **Midland Highway** is a fast three-hour route between Hobart and Launceston, more or less following the old coaching road, although you'll have to detour if you want to visit some of the towns on the way. Tasmanian Redline Coaches have several daily **bus** services between Hobart and Launceston, stopping at the major midland towns.

Campbell Town and Ross

Beyond **Campbell Town** – a rather plain community originally settled by Scots – you drive south through sheep-grazing countryside, eventually turning off the highway to **ROSS**, 2km east. Another town settled by Scots, this has a very secluded, rural feel. Church Street, lined with deciduous trees, ends quite abruptly and overlooks miles of fields, farmland and hills. As you walk through the grounds of St Johns Church of England, just one of the town's three pretty churches, you have views of the Macquarie River, spanned by the sandstone **Ross Bridge**, designed by John Lee Archer and built by convicts in 1836; the intricate stone carvings on its three arches earned the convict stonemason a free pardon. There's a fairly melancholy walk in the other direction from the church, down to the original Ross burial ground and past the site of the **Female Factory**, actually a prison, where women convicts were held before being sent to properties as assigned servants. You can **stay** in several of the old cottages dotted about town; *Colonial Cottages of Ross* (☎03/6381 5354, fax 6381 5408; ⑦, including breakfast provisions) have four to pick from. The old sandstone *Man O'Ross Hotel* on Church Street (☎03/6381 5240, fax 6381 5423; ④) has several intimate rooms in which to eat or drink, and basic accommodation upstairs.

Oatlands

Back on the Midland Highway, it's 88km south from Ross to **OATLANDS**, which has Australia's greatest concentration of colonial **Georgian buildings**: 140 in two square kilometres, most built by convicts. Many are now occupied by antique and bric-a-brac shops, B&Bs and guesthouses. The most striking building is the **Callington Mill** and its outbuildings; the partly restored **windmill** was built in 1837 and remained in operation until 1892. From the top there are fine views of the town and the surrounding countryside; unfortunately the mill is presently closed to the public but there are plans to open it again soon. Probably the best way to see the town is to go on one of Peter Fielding's guided **heritage walks** (☎03/6254 1135); he has keys to several other buildings, including the Old Gaol and courthouse; there's a spooky evening **ghost tour** which commences outside the mill (9pm during daylight savings, 8pm rest of year; $8).

For **food**, *Oatlands Roadhouse*, on High Street as you come into the town on the Midland Highway (daily 7.30am–9pm), sells the usual fast food plus tasty Lebanese dishes. *Blossom's Tea Rooms*, 116 High St (☎03/6254 1516), serves light lunches; dinner here is available by arrangement. Good **places to stay** are *Oatlands Lodge*, a colonial-style B&B in the centre of town at 92 High St (☎03/6254 1444, fax 6254 1492; ⑥), and, further out, the tiny, homely *Oatlands Youth Hostel*, at 9 Wellington St (☎03/6254 1320; ①), a popular overnight stop for cyclists on their way through the midlands.

The Western Tiers and Central Plateau

Deloraine, on the **Meander River**, is nestled in a valley of rich farmland dominated by **Quamby Bluff** (1256m) and the **Western Tiers**, where the Central Plateau drops abruptly to the surrounding plains. On the Bass Highway, it's roughly equidistant from Devonport (51km) and Launceston (48km). From Deloraine the **Lake Highway** begins, rising up over the Western Tiers to the Central Plateau, with its thousands of lakes. To the west of Deloraine, as you go towards Cradle Mountain, are the extensive **cave systems** around **Mole Creek**, while **Walls of Jerusalem National Park** is accessed from **Western Creek**, 32km southwest of Deloraine.

Deloraine and around

DELORAINE is a delightful hilly town, often shrouded in mist, even on summer mornings, and divided into two parts by the bubbling **Meander River**. Although the area was settled by Europeans in the 1830s, Deloraine didn't really begin to develop until after 1846, and today it's a National Trust-classified town. **West Parade** follows the river, facing the park; at no. 17 is the Georgian **Bonney's Inn** (1830), with an elegant portico – the town's oldest remaining building (now a B&B; see overleaf). At the next block, Westbury Place rises up steeply from West Parade; if you climb the hill you'll reach **St Marks Church** (1860), with its tall spire. At the top of the hill there's a scenic **lookout** that gives a panoramic view over the town and the Western Tiers to the south. Deloraine has a café culture, plenty of secondhand and antique shops, and a small, alternative arts-and-crafts scene, witnessed regularly at the **market** on the first Saturday of every month across the river opposite the *Apex Caravan Park*, and at the annual **Tasmanian Craft Fair**, a huge event running since 1980 and held over four days in early November (contact the information centre for details – see overleaf).

Close to prime **bushwalking** areas in the Western Tiers, Deloraine is an established base for walkers. Popular tracks are the short walk to **Allum Cliffs**, overlooking the Mersey River Gorge (40min return), signposted on the road between Mole Creek and Chudleigh; a difficult walk to **Quamby Bluff**, renowned for its myrtle rainforest (6.5km; 6hr; beginning at Brodies Road, off the Lake Highway); the track to **Liffey Falls** (8km; just under 3hr; beginning at the picnic ground 5km west of the tiny community of Liffey), and the day walk to **Meander Falls** through the Meander Forest Reserve, about 25km south of Deloraine, reached via the small settlement of Meander and Meander Falls Road (10km; 6–7hr; beginning from the picnic ground). There's a walker registration and information booth at the Meander Falls car park. A free leaflet issued by Forestry Tasmania, *Visiting the Great Western Tiers*, has a map of the reserve and tracks; you can pick it up from the Deloraine tourist office (see overleaf). If you're not confident to walk on your own, Taswalks (☎03/6363 6112) or Guided Forest Walks (☎03/6369 5151 or 6362 2046), lead **guided walks**; Tiger Wilderness Tours (based in Launceston; ☎03/6326 6515) offer bushwalking tours of the Meander Valley (6hr 30min; $45) and Liffey Falls (5hr 30min; $55).

The western end of the Great Western Tiers overlooks **MOLE CREEK**, 24km southwest of Deloraine, where you'll find the **Trowunna Wildlife Park** (daily 9am–5pm; $7.50, children $3.50), the best of its type in Tasmania. Informed park keepers will enlighten you with their explanations of the fauna. There are plenty of animals, including **Tasmanian devils**, most of which have been rescued from road accidents. You can also buy delicious local honey at Mole Creek from **Stephen's Leatherwood Honey Factory** (Mon–Fri 8am–5pm). About 20km west of Mole Creek, are two rather spectacular underground caves: **Marakoopa Cave**, with huge caverns, streams, pools and glow-worms (daily 10am, 11.15am, 1pm, 2.30pm & 4pm; 50–80min); and the smaller but more richly decorative **King Solomons Cave**, with stalactites and stalagmites (daily 10.30am, 11.30am, 12.30pm, 2pm, 3pm & 4pm; 40–60min); admission is $8 for each cave, or $12 for both. From the caves, you could take a winding route to Cradle Valley (see p.980).

Practicalities

In Deloraine itself there's a volunteer-run **Visitor Information Centre** at 98 Emu Bay Rd (Mon–Fri 8am–6pm, Sat 9am–4pm, Sun 9am–6pm; ☎03/6362 3471), with maps and details on walking times and conditions; the centre is housed in an old inn with an attached folk museum ($2). Among several **operators** leading outdoor activities in the area are Central Highlands Trail Rides, Brodies Road, Golden Valley (☎03/6369 5298), who have three-hour rides around Quamby Bluff ($40) or a six-hour ride to Jackys Marsh, with its tall eucalypt forests ($80, including lunch); overnight camping trips to the top of the Central Plateau can also be arranged. *Bonney's Farm* (☎03/6362 2122) offers tailor-made "soft" tours to areas around Deloraine, such as Mole Creek Caves and Liffey Falls ($20 half-day, $40 full-day), and to Cradle Mountain (day-tour $45 including Mole Creek Caves and Sheffield; drop-off for 2–3 hours walking). You can also head up to the lakes of the Central Plateau with the Tasmanian Fly Fishing School, based in Deloraine (☎03/6362 3441). Finally, Wild Caves Tours (Oct–April only; ☎03/6367 8142), based at Mole Creek, offers excellent $65 half-day and $130 full-day caving tours of the Mole Creek caves, underground streams and subterranean systems; the full-day trip includes all meals.

One of the best **places to stay** is the *Highview Lodge YHA Hostel* at 8 Blake St (☎03/6362 2996; ①), set on a hill commanding unparalleled views of Quamby Bluff; the hostel is well-run and very clean, and rents out bikes. It's well signposted from the information centre – about a ten-minute walk, or Tasmanian Wilderness Travel will drop you off. If the YHA is full, you could try *Kev's Kumphy Korner* at 24 Bass Highway (☎03/6362 2633; ①), a rather unatmospheric hostel in an unpicturesque setting on the edge of town, opposite, at no. 7 (☎03/6362 2365; rooms B&B ③, dorms ①), which has good-value meals, a pool table and bands at weekends. A good motel on the outskirts of town is *Mountain View Country Inn*, 144 Emu Bay Rd (☎03/6362 2633, fax 6362 3233 ③) – though it's on the main road, the row of units afford great views of the Western Tiers. *Bonney's Farm*, off Weetah Road, 4km northwest of Deloraine (☎03/6362 2122, fax 6362 3566; ⑤), has a guesthouse (B&B) and self-contained two- or three-bed units, and arranges tours around the area (see above). In the centre of town, the big old *Deloraine Hotel*, faces the river on the corner of Emu Bay Road (☎03/6362 2022; B&B ④). Virtually next door, old-fashioned *Bonney's Inn*, 17 West Parade (☎ & fax 03/6362 2974; ⑥–⑦), has spacious suites suitable for families. **Camping** is available at the riverside *Apex Caravan Park*, 51 West Parade (☎03/6362 2345). There are also several places to stay in **Mole Creek**, ranging from an excellent campsite with coin-operated showers (☎03/6363 1150) to the congenial *Mole Creek Guest House* (☎03/6363 1399; ⑤–⑥) with its own restaurant and tourist information.

In Deloraine there are plenty of informal **places to eat** on the main street, Emu Bay Road. The best is the *Delicatessen Coffee Shop* at no. 36 (Mon–Fri 9am–5pm, Sat 9am–2pm), a combination of deli counter and tearoom. It's popular with locals, who enjoy the cakes and freshly baked baguettes with gourmet fillings; the most expensive dish is $8. The *Emu Bay Brasserie* at no. 21 (☎03/6362 2067; licensed; 9am–2.30pm, dinner from 6pm; closed Sun & Mon) has a casual café atmosphere but serves upmarket meals. At the *Arcoona Restaurant*, East Barrack Street (dinner Tues–Sat; licensed; ☎03/6362 3443), the chef has a great reputation for his seasonal menu and fresh Tasmanian produce. The best place in town for pub meals is the *Deloraine Hotel* (see opposite); you can eat in the dining room away from the noisy pokie machines.

The two major **bus** companies both make regular stops in Deloraine. Tasmanian Redline Coaches on its Launceston–Devonport service (3 daily), and its Launceston–Deloraine service (5 daily Mon–Fri, 3 daily Sat & Sun) which continues on to Mole Creek once daily on weekdays; and Tasmanian Wilderness Travel on its Launceston–Cradle Mountain "Wilderness" service (May–Oct 1 daily Tues, Thurs, Sat & Sun; Nov–April 1 daily). The depot for Redline is the video shop by the roundabout at 29 West Church St (☎03/6362 2046); Tasmanian Wilderness Travel are based at *Sullivans Restaurant*, at 17 West Parade.

Walls of Jerusalem National Park

The **Walls of Jerusalem National Park** is on the western side of the Central Plateau, a series of five mountain peaks which enclose a central basin, an isolated area noted for its lakes, pencil pines, and the biblical names of its various features. The best time to visit is late spring through to April; people have died of exposure here, so make sure you're well prepared. You'll need the *Walls of Jerusalem National Park Map and Notes* ($9), which has walking notes on the reverse.

The Walls of Jerusalem is the only national park that you can't drive into, so the walk begins outside the park boundaries. From King Solomons Cave, head south, following the Mersey River and the unsealed road east of Lake Rowallan; the car park is at Howells Bluff. You walk through wilderness into the park, which is isolated and lacking even basic facilities, without a ranger (although rangers do patrol). However, the track is well kept, with boardwalks laid down over boggy areas, and there's plenty of clean water to drink from the streams and lakes. There are a few small leaky huts but these are really for emergencies only – bring your own tent. If you just want to walk into the park to the central basin (through **Herods Gate**, with views of Barn Bluff and Cradle Mountain to the northwest), set up camp and then walk back, it's a fourteen-kilometre return hike, which takes seven or eight hours altogether, going at a steady pace over two days. The walk begins with a steep climb then levels out on the plateau. There are numerous routes to the various peaks and lakes – from **Damascus Gate** you get stunning views of Cradle Mountain–Lake St Clair National Park immediately west – and an experienced, well-equipped walker (preferably accompanied) could spend a couple of days here. If you can afford the prices, you can always go on an **organized walk**: Craclair Walking Holidays (☎ & fax 03/6424 7833) has a five-day walk for $875, while Ausprey Tours (☎ & fax 03/6330 2612) offers a two-day version for $210, organized from Hobart or Launceston. Tasmanian Wilderness Travel can bring you to the beginning of the walk into the park on their service from Launceston, via Deloraine, Mole Creek and Marakoopa Cave (2–3 times weekly) while Maxwell's (☎03/6424 8093) goes there on demand from Devonport ($30) and Launceston ($40).

The Central Plateau

At its northern and eastern edges, the **Central Plateau** is rimmed by the long crest of the Great Western Tiers (1440m). At over a thousand metres above sea level, the plateau is often covered in frost and subject to sleet and snowstorms in winter. The **Great Lake** lies on the plateau about 8km from the escarpment, and only 40km from Deloraine, along the Lake Highway that continues to **BOTHWELL**, the plateau's only town, ending at Melton Mowbray, where it joins the Midland Highway. On the unsealed C178, which runs west off the Lake Highway 15km north of Bothwell, you can visit a disused power station, **Waddamana** (daily 10am–4pm; free) and its museum. The major lakes can be reached from roads leading off the Lake Highway. To the west, between Cradle Mountain–Lake St Clair National Park and below the Walls of Jerusalem National Park, is the inaccessible "Land of Three Thousand Lakes".

The Central Plateau has few inhabitants – the permanent population is only around eight hundred – but it's full of **fishing shacks**, and on a fine weekend the population sometimes swells to 25,000. It's also the base for the **Hydro Electricity Commission** (HEC): the countless high-altitude lakes are used as water storage for the generation of electricity. Temporary HEC villages are set up for hydroelectrical workers, and once abandoned they're often transformed into lodge-style accommodation. One is the *Bronte Park Highland Village* (☎03/6289 1126, fax 6289 1109; cabins ⑤–⑦, lodge ⑤, hostel ①), which also has a campsite and a very basic hostel section, EFTPOS facilities, plus a dining room and bar, a store selling groceries and fuel, and is ideally situated for **Lake St Clair** (25km) and **Lake Big Jim**, popular trout-fishing spots. If you want to try your hand at fishing, Ausprey Tours (☎03/6330 2612) offers **fly-fishing tuition** (1–5 days), trout fishing day-tours from Launceston or extended camping treks to fish in the Western Lakes. To reach the *Bronte Park Highland Village*, take the bone-shattering Marlborough Highway (B11), which runs southwest off the Lake Highway as it curves around the bottom of the lake to Miena. Tasmanian Wilderness Travel drops off at the *Bronte Park* turn-off on the Lyell Highway on their Hobart–Queenstown scheduled service (1 daily Tues, Thurs, Sat & Sun); call in advance to be met.

The Bass Strait Islands

Located in the rough waters of the Bass Strait, battered by the Roaring Forties, are two groups of islands: the Hunter group, dominated by **King Island** off the northwest tip of Tasmania, and the Furneaux group, the largest of which is **Flinders Island**, lying just beyond the northeast corner of the state. In the nineteenth century sealers roamed the Bass Strait, but the two main islands now consist of low-key rural communities, while several tall lighthouses, and many shipwrecks offshore are testimony to the turbulence of the sea at King Island.

Of the two islands, Flinders is the most rewarding to visit as a destination in its own right, and this can be done as part of a package from Victoria (see below). The best-case scenario is to visit either island as a **stopover** en route from Victoria to Tasmania with one of the airlines below: it will cost around $120 one-way from Melbourne to King Island and the same price from King Island to Devonport; Melbourne to Flinders one-way is more expensive, at around $150, and then it will cost around $115 from Flinders Island to Launceston. However, **packages**, which often include the Tasmanian mainland, are the best deals – call the airlines below to find out about current deals. To King Island, Kendell Airlines (free call ☎1800/338 894) fly from Melbourne; King Island Airlines (03/9580 3777) fly from Mooragbin, on the outskirts of Melbourne; while Tasair (☎03/6248 5577 or free call ☎1800/062 900) fly from Burnie or Devonport. To Flinders Island, Island Airlines (free call ☎1800/818 455) fly from Launceston, Melbourne, and Traralgon; while Aus-Air (☎03/9580 6166 or free call ☎1800/331 256) flies to both islands from Moorabbin and from Launceston.

King Island

The smaller, more heavily populated **King Island** is chiefly known for its rich dairy produce, with crayfish and kelp as secondary industries; green, low and windswept, it can't offer anything like Flinders Island's dramatic landscape, nor its history, though it did witness around sixty **shipwrecks** between 1801 and 1995. There are several working lighthouses – **Cape Wickham Lighthouse** in the north is one of the tallest in the southern hemisphere – and many of the wreck sites can be dived with King Island Dive Charters (☎03/6461 1133, fax 6461 1293; three-day package including flights from Melbourne, accommodation, diving and on-board lunches $530). If you want to get out onto the water without getting wet, you can arrange to go out with a local fisherman, who may expect a few beers in return.

The island's main town is **CURRIE**, which has a simple museum (Mon–Fri 1–4pm). But the best thing about King Island is the food, with free range lamb and pork and local beef and wallaby, as well as seafood and delicious creamy milk, which you can drink unpasteurized while on the island – a rare treat. Indeed, top of the list of things to do on the island is a visit to the **King Island Dairy** (Mon–Fri 9am–4.30pm, Sun 12.30–4pm; free), 8km north of Currie, for free tastings of the rich local dairy produce; the brie and the thick cream in particular have legendary gourmet status around Australia. The island's **kelp factory** is near Currie's golf course; the bull kelp is gathered from the surrounding shores and left to dry outside the factory on racks – you'll see it as you pass by. After drying the kelp is milled into granules and shipped to Scotland to be processed into alginates, used as a gelling agent in products like toothpaste and ice cream. On the eastern side of the island in **GRASSY**, the bleak former tungsten mining village, a local resident sculpts rather tasteless objects from the kelp by moulding it and drying it; the results, which look like leather or ceramics, are sold at King Island Kelp Craft.

Practicalities

King Island Coach Tours, based in Currie at 95 Main St (free call ☎1800/647 702), do pre-booked airport transfers to Currie, which is less than 10km away ($5; $10 if you are the only passenger), and transfers to Naracoopa to Grassy. Alternatively, your accommodation may pick you up. For getting around, you'll need to **rent a car** at the airport – two outfits are Cheapa Island Car Rentals (☎03/6462 1603) and Grassy Car Rentals (☎03/6461 1278) – or a **mountain bike** from The Trend, on 26 Edward St, Currie ($15 a day), who also provide **tourist information** (daily 9am–6.30pm; ☎03/6462 1360). King Island Coach Tours run various **day-tours**; the best is the short evening tour to see the **Little penguin** community at Grassy (Tues & Thurs; $25). There are also 4WD and bushwalking tours available.

The most obvious **places to stay** are around Currie. The cheapest option is to **camp** at *Bass Caravan Park* (☎03/6462 1260; on-site vans ③) on North Road, 2km from town. Right in the centre, *Parers Hotel* (☎03/6462 1633; ⑤–⑥), has en-suite motel-style rooms, while there are immaculate units near the golf course at *Wave Watcher Holiday Units*, 18 Beach Rd (☎03/6462 1517; ⑧). Nearby, the rooms at *Boomerang By the Sea* (free call ☎1800/221 288, fax 03/6462 1607; ⑦) have stunning sea views – even better from the motel's glass-walled **restaurant**. Back in town, *Parers* serves excellent meals in its bistro and *King Island Bakery* makes delicious pies; *Nautilus Coffee Lounge* is Currie's best café. If you're self-catering, there's a supermarket (open daily) and a bottle shop. Currie also has a Westpac bank with an ATM machine.

For further **information** on King Island practicalities, including more accommodation options and activities on offer, contact the King Island Tourist Development Association, PO Box 48, Currie, King Island, TAS 7256 (☎03/6462 1360).

Flinders Island

With a population of just over one thousand, **FLINDERS ISLAND** is nonetheless the largest of about sixty named islands which make up the Furneaux group, first charted by Matthew Flinders in 1798. The islands became a base for the **"Straitsmen"**, who slaughtered seals in their tens of thousands and, so legend goes, lured many ships to their demise for a spot of piracy. These rough men provided a vital link in the continuing survival of the Tasmanian Aboriginal people, ironically by stealing women to work for them on the islands. When sealing ended, the communities survived by **muttonbird harvesting**, a seasonal industry which continues today (with land rights claims in 1995 giving title to several outlying islands). Flinders Island itself played a large part in the systematic attempted genocide of the Tasmanian Aboriginal people; between 1831 and 1834 the remnants of the Tasmanian tribes were hunted down and relocated here. Settled at windswept **Wybalenna**, on the west coast of the island, the Aborigines were without adequate food and shelter, and were forced to accept Christianity as their culture was expunged.

Practicalities

There's no **tourist information** office on the island; for more details on activities such as cruises, scuba diving, fishing and scenic flights, or just for general enquiries, you can contact the secretary of the Flinders Island Tourist Committee, PO Box 143, Flinders Island, TAS 7255 (☎03/6359 6526, fax 6359 6523); *Flinders Island Visitors Guide*, a free brochure with map, can be picked up at Tasmanian tourist offices before you go. As there's no public transport, the best option is to **rent a car** and arrange to pick it up at the airport on arrival. Prices are quite reasonable: from around $50–65 per day with Bowman Transport (☎03/6359 2014), Flinders Island Car Rentals (☎03/6359 2168, fax 6359 2293), Flinders Island Transport Services (☎03/6359 2060) or Furneaux Car Rental (☎03/6359 2112). You can rent **bikes** from Flinders Island Bike Hire (☎03/6359 2000) for $10 per day.

There are two main bases on the island: **WHITEMARK**, the administrative centre on the west coast, and **LADY BARRON** in the south, the main fishing area and deep-water port; both places have shops, fuel and accommodation. Whitemark has the island's only **bank** – Westpac (Mon–Thurs noon–3.30pm, Fri noon–4.30pm) – but no ATM facilities. There is also a shop at **Killiecrankie Bay** in the northwest of the island – where you can fossick for topaz – and a campsite with water and showers (☎03/6359 8560). You can **camp** for free at the coastal reserves, or on any crown land as long as it's 500m from the road: designated sites are at Allports Beach, Lillies Beach, North East River and Trousers Point, and all have toilets and fireplaces, though only the last has water. **Places to stay** in and around Whitemark include the *Flinders Island Cabin Park* (☎03/6359 2188; no campsites, cabins ③), next to the airport 5km north of town, and the recently renovated *Flinders Island Interstate Hotel* in the centre of town (☎03/6359 2114, fax 6359 2250; ⑤), where most rooms are en-suite; the hotel also serves excellent meals (closed Sun). *Sweet Surprises Coffee Shop* is a decent place for a daytime snack (closed Sun) and also functions as an unofficial **tourist centre**. Lady Barron is a far nicer place to stay, however. The *Flinders Island Lodge* (☎03/6359 3521, fax 6359 3618, free call 1800/818 826; ⑥–⑦ including breakfast), attached to the *Furneaux Tavern* and overlooking the picturesque Furneaux Sound, has very spacious motel units. The best **meals** on the island – featuring plenty of fresh fish and seafood – are served here in the *Shearwater Restaurant*, or in the less expensive front bar. You could also try the self-catering accommodation at *Yaringa Cottages* in the village (☎03/6359 4522; ⑤) or *Leafmoor* (☎03/6359 3517; ④–⑤), a restored farm cottage about five minutes' drive from Lady Barron. For details of other properties, consult *Tasmanian Travelways*, the *Flinders Island Visitors Guide* or ask the Flinders Island Tourist Committee (above) for details.

Around the island

All that remains of the period of enforced Aboriginal settlement is the **chapel**, built in 1838 at Wybalenna, 20km north of Whitemark, and the cemetery where only the white graves bear headstones. Of the 135 tribespeople who were sent here, only 47 were still alive when the settlement was abandoned in 1847 and moved to Oyster Cove, near Hobart. The chapel has been restored by the National Trust, and is open for visits at any time, though, fittingly, the Aboriginal people of Flinders Island succeeded with their land rights claim on Wybalenna, which was handed over in early 1999, and it is up to them to decide how they'll run it.

For more history, it's just a few kilometres northwest to the **Emita Museum** (summer daily 1–5pm; rest of the year Sat & Sun 1–4pm; $2), where there's a display of shell necklaces made by the Aboriginal people of nearby Cape Barren, plus exhibits relating to sealing and shipwrecks. In the grounds there's a replica of a **muttonbirding shed**, with magazines covering the walls and a dirt floor lined with tussock grass. Most professional muttonbirders are Aboriginal, and with Strait Lady Island Adventures (☎03/6359 4507, fax 6359 4533) you can visit the outlying islands during the April season to watch the oily birds being slaughtered, plucked and boiled – not for the fainthearted.

History aside, isolated Flinders Island is very much a mecca for **bushwalkers**. Only about half of the island is cultivated, and you can walk its entire length in about six days on the partially signposted north–south **Flinders Trail**, a route designed to provide a sampling of the various terrains. The best-known walk, however, is to the distinctive summit of **Mount Strzelecki**, in the **Strzelecki National Park** in the south. The climb to the top starts about 10km south of Whitemark, signposted on Trousers Point Road – look out for a brown national park sign. It's not a difficult walk, but it is long – about 6km return (4–5hr). The wind is fierce at the summit, and mists roll in, so wear something wind- and waterproof. **Trousers Point** itself, also near the park, is a good introduction to the delights of the island's deserted beaches. The site, with its fine, white sand and rust-coloured rock formations, is particularly spectacular, with Mount Strzelecki rising up behind the granite headland; there's a free camping area here, with water available.

The **Flinders Island Ecology Trail** is a circuit designed to be followed in a car, with five stopping-points where interpretive material is provided. **Walkers Lookout**, in the Darling Range, is a good starting point, offering the classic panorama of Flinders and the surrounding islands, with signs pointing out all the landmarks; the other four points on the route highlight bird habitats. You can see the endemic protected **Cape Barren goose** everywhere – even in people's paddocks – and likewise the island's wombats.

THE WEST

Except for the rich beef, dairy and vegetable-growing land along the northwest coast, the western half of Tasmania is an untamed area. The wild **west coast**, densely forested and battered by the rough Southern Ocean and the Roaring Forties, its shores strewn with huge dead trees washed down from the southwest's many rivers, would probably still be uninhabited if it weren't for the **logging** and **mining** industries. This part of the island is very pro-logging and pro-damming, and its densely populated (by Tasmanian standards) northwest coast is skirted by the **Bass Highway**, which passes through two unattractive industrial cities, **Devonport** and **Burnie**. **Rocky Cape National Park** and the town of **Stanley** (originally built by the Van Diemen's Land Company – VDL – which still owns the northwest corner of the state) are the most interesting places for visitors.

Just south of Stanley the highway turns inland to **Smithton**, marking the beginning of a thickly forested region and a logging heartland. The Bass Highway ends at the tiny settlement of **Marrawah**, on the west coast (popular with surfers), where it meets the **Western Explorer**, a new road linking the northwest coast and the west coast. It runs to sleepy **Arthur River** (from where the west coast stretches south, uninhabited along its entire length except for the town of **Strahan**, on the vast **Macquarie Harbour**) and then through the Arthur Pieman Protected area to **Corinna**, where the road heads east via Savage River and Waratah onto the A10 (Murchison Highway). Alternatively, you can take a barge across the Pieman River (daily 9am–5pm; $10 car; $5 bike; ☎03/6446 1170) and continue on the C249 to Zeehan, and then on the B27 to Strahan. To reach Strahan on sealed roads, you have to head back to Marrawah and then to Somerset on the northwest coast, from where the Murchison Highway heads south through a copper- and lead-mining backwater. On the way you pass **Queenstown**, which has been subject to an ecological disaster; its surrounding rainforest has been destroyed, and in its place are bare and chalky hills.

Strahan sits on the edge of the **southwest wilderness**, an area of rugged coastlines, wild rivers, open plains, thick rainforest and spectacular peaks – the wettest part of Australia after the tropical lowlands of north Queensland. It's mostly inaccessible, except to very experienced and well-prepared bushwalkers, but **cruises** leave from Strahan to go up the **Gordon River**, offering a glimpse of its magnificent scenery. A plan to dam the Gordon River below the point where it joins the **Franklin River** put Strahan at the centre of a struggle between environmentalists and the state government. Eventually the federal government stepped in, and, following a landmark High Court ruling in 1983, the whole of the southwest – including the **South West National Park**, the **Franklin Lower Gordon Wild Rivers National Park** and the adjoining heavily glaciated **Cradle Mountain–Lake St Clair National Park** – became a vast, protected **World Heritage Area**, occupying twenty percent of the land area of the state. From Queenstown, en route east to Hobart, the **Lyell Highway** provides limited access to the mainly inaccessible Franklin Lower Gordon park, and to Lake St Clair at **Derwent Bridge**.

It's worth finding a copy of the excellent, and comprehensive magazine-style booklet, *Tasmania's West Coast*, from a tourist office before you head west.

The northwest coast

A succession of Tasmania's larger towns dot the conservative, agricultural **northwest coast**, including the cities of **Devonport** and **Burnie**, and the smaller community of older **Stanley**, on a peninsula jutting into the Bass Strait. The **Bass Highway**, which connects them, becomes spectacularly beautiful beyond Wynyard, passing Table Cape, Boat Harbour Beach and Rocky Cape National Park, though it skirts the very northwest tip (privately owned by the Van Diemen's Land Company). At the end of the highway is **Marrawah**, from where you can head to Arthur River for a cruise. Tasmanian Redline Coaches (☎03/6331 3233) run services from Devonport to Burnie (daily) and from Burnie to Smithton (daily except Sun), stopping at all towns along the Bass Highway; there is no public transport to Marrawah or Arthur River.

Devonport and around

The industrial port of **DEVONPORT**, which in 1959 replaced Launceston as the terminal of the **Bass Strait ferry**, the *Spirit of Tasmania*, is not the most inspiring first point of contact with Tasmania. As the ship makes its slow progress up the Mersey River, you might almost think you're arriving at a 1950s English seaport, but for the tin-roofed weatherboard bungalows, the brittle quality of the light, the bush-covered hills to the east and a *McDonald's* on the waterfront. As a jumping-off point for Cradle Mountain, the Overland Track and the rugged west coast, Devonport has developed a significant tourism infrastructure, being a magnet for car-rental companies, bus companies, camping stores and backpacking information, but it's hardly a destination in itself. Although most visitors simply observe it from the window of a bus as they hurry on to Hobart or Launceston, it does make a good **base** for trips into the surrounding countryside.

Arrival and information

Up to nine hundred people arrive in Devonport at 8.30am each Tuesday, Thursday and Saturday morning on the *Spirit of Tasmania* **Bass Strait** ferry (☎13 2010), which docks at the terminal in East Devonport, just across the Mersey River from the city centre. As the boat has its own tourist information and booking centre, a small interpretive centre and even national park rangers dispensing advice in summer, you might well have made all your arrangements on board before arriving. If not, there are company representatives in the terminal, and you can buy bus passes and tickets here. Most passengers head immediately for the waiting Tasmanian Redline Coaches **express buses** which leave the terminal at 8.45am for Launceston ($13.30)and Hobart ($32.50). Other bus routes leave from the depots in town (see p.964). If you decide to stay, you can get to the city centre by walking north for a short distance to the bottom of Murray Street, where the ferry *Torquay* crosses the river (every 15–30min Mon–Fri 8am–6pm, Sat 8.30am–5pm, no service Sun; $1.50, bikes 50¢).

Southern Australia Airlines, Kendell and Aus Air fly from the mainland into **Devonport Airport**, 10km east of the city. Taxis into Devonport cost about $12, and Fox Coaches (mobile phone ☎0418/142 692; $5) operate a shuttle bus connecting all flights, dropping and picking up as far out as the youth hostel; it also picks up at the travel and information centre.

The Tasmanian Travel and **Information Centre**, at 5 Best St (Mon–Sat 9am–5pm; ☎03/6424 4466), is in the Showcase building behind *McDonald's*. Staff here can book accommodation, tours and travel, and sell all types of bus passes. For maps, bushwalking tips and local knowledge of the area visit the Backpackers Barn, 10–12 Edward St (daily 9am–6pm; ☎03/6424 3628), which specializes in the planning of itineraries and rents equipment for bushwalkers and backpackers, and offers travellers a day-room, showers and lockers (mostly free). The excellent Allgoods, at 10 Rooke St (☎03/6424 7099; closed Sun), also rents out gear.

Accommodation

Devonport has plenty of **accommodation**, mainly intended for ferry passengers. Hotels, motels and B&Bs take advantage of the summer trade to raise their prices.

Abel Tasman Caravan Park, 6 Wright St, East Devonport (☎03/6427 8794). Campsites on East Devonport Beach, just a short walk from the ferry terminal. Cabins ④, on-site vans ③.

Alexander Hotel, 78 Formby Rd (☎03/6424 2252, fax 6424 1046). Neat, well-furnished rooms, all with sinks and some with views of the port; shared bathrooms. TV room, plus tea and coffee room; light breakfast served in the dining room. ③–④.

Gateway Motor Inn, 16 Fenton St (☎03/6424 4922, fax 6424 7720). Devonport's best hotel, a quiet, centrally located, three-storey hotel offering views over the port and river mouth. Rooms are spacious, tastefully decorated, and all have baths. Also a bar, restaurant and room service. ⑦.

MacFie Manor, 44 MacFie St (☎03/6424 1719). A rambling, two-storey turn-of-the-century B&B that has distant views of the water from its wrought-iron balcony. ⑥.

Macwright House YHA, 115 Middle Rd (☎03/6424 5696, fax 6424 9952). More than half an hour's walk from the city centre and not close to any shops, but the local Mersey Bus will get you from the city on weekdays. A large, barracks-like hostel with loads of rules and regulations. No doubles – all rooms have metal bunks. On the plus side, there's access to a heated pool next door and a big garden. ①.

Molly Malone's, 34 Best St (☎03/6424 1898). Convenient backpackers' accommodation, with comfortable rooms well away from the noise of the bar which has live bands Thurs–Sat. Good facilities and security. Rooms ④, dorms ①.

River View Lodge, 18 Victoria Parade (☎03/6424 7357). A waterfront guesthouse with a convivial atmosphere. Serves generous cooked breakfasts. All rooms share bathroom. ④–⑤.

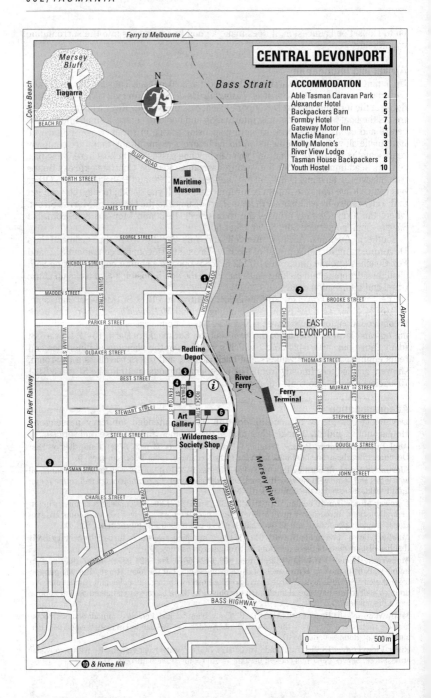

CENTRAL DEVONPORT

ACCOMMODATION

Able Tasman Caravan Park	2
Alexander Hotel	6
Backpackers Barn	5
Formby Hotel	7
Gateway Motor Inn	4
Macfie Manor	9
Molly Malone's	3
River View Lodge	1
Tasman House Backpackers	8
Youth Hostel	10

Tasman House Backpackers, 169 Steele St, entrance off Tasman St (☎03/6423 2335, fax 6423 2340). A highly recommended, very cheap and secure hostel in a large, former nurses' residence. Mostly well-furnished twins, with a couple of en-suite doubles and some dorms. Facilities include a TV room, kitchen and notice board. Affordable licensed tours run on demand to places such as Cradle Mountain. Fifteen minutes' walk from the city centre, but free pick-ups on request. Rooms ②, dorms ①.

The City

Central Devonport is bounded by the Mersey to the east; Formby Road runs alongside it, while Stewart Street, at right angles, is dominated by a view of the bulky *Spirit of Tasmania*, when it's in port, and sometimes other colourful freighters. The Wilderness Society Shop, at 26 Stewart St (☎03/6424 7393), is an excellent source of alternative tourist information and also sells posters, cards, T-shirts and books. Along the street at no. 45, the **Devonport Art Gallery** (Mon–Sat 10am–5pm, Sun 2–5pm; free), is a converted church with changing exhibitions and a small permanent collection of Tasmanian ceramics. The city centre is also a **shopping** focus for departing tourists in need of last-minute souvenirs. Stewart Street, in particular, is full of gift shops selling superior souvenirs – tasteful wooden items, ceramics and jewellery among them. There's more shopping in the **Rooke Street Mall**, where most of the big-name chain stores are located, but Devonport's not large enough to rate its own department store.

South of the city centre, at 77 Middle Rd, is **Home Hill** (Tues–Thurs, Sat & Sun 2–4pm; $6), the National Trust-administered former home of Sir Joseph Lyons, premier of Tasmania (1923–29) and prime minister of Australia (1932–39), and his wife, Dame Enid Lyons, who became a federal minister after her husband's death. The **Tasmanian Maritime and Folk Museum**, north of the city centre at 47 Victoria Parade, near the river's mouth (Tues–Sun 1–4pm; $1), has an extensive display of model ships ranging from sailing vessels to modern passenger ferries.

The only really compelling place to visit, though, is the **Tiagarra Tasmanian Aboriginal Culture and Art Centre** (daily 9am–5pm; $3), located at the dramatic **Mersey Bluff** 1.5km northwest of the Maritime and Folk Museum, near the end of Bluff Road. The centre has preserved around 270 Aboriginal rock engravings. However, only eleven of the coiled lines and concentric circles, and motifs of snakes, abalone shells, emus, crayfish and other creatures, are exposed to view, but a **Display Centre** provides generalized (and rather rushed) taped background information on how the Tasmanian Aborigines lived.

Although commercial passenger train services in Tasmania ceased in the 1970s, the **Don River Railway** runs excursions from Don Recreation Ground along the Don River to the popular surfing spot of **Coles Beach** (hourly 10am–4pm; 30min; $7 return). On Sunday, public holidays and from Christmas to the end of January the carriages are pulled by steam locomotives; otherwise, diesel power is used.

Eating, drinking and nightlife

Alexander Hotel, 78 Formby Rd (☎03/6424 2252). Refurbished riverfront pub, popular with the young crowd. A good jukebox in the lounge bar, from where you can gaze out at the ships; excellent bistro menu.

Banjo's, Rooke Street Mall. One of a Tasmanian chain of eat-in bakeries. The best budget choice, offering inexpensive fresh-baked goods and unlimited cups of tea and coffee. Great place for an early breakfast. Daily 6am–6pm.

Chinese Garden, 33 King St (☎03/6424 4148). A popular Cantonese restaurant serving lunch and dinner daily. Licensed.

Rialto Gallery, 159 Rooke St (☎03/6424 6793). Reasonably priced Italian dishes from the Venetian region, usually including a vegetarian special. Closed Sun & Mon.

Spurs Canteena, 18 King St. A bar with Wild West decor and atmosphere; also, a bistro and attached nightclub. Wed–Sun 4pm–late.

Taco Villa, Kempling St (☎03/6424 6762). Good Mexican food. BYO. Tues–Sun dinner only.

Listings

Bookshop Angus & Robertson Bookworld, on Stewart St (☎03/6424 2022).

Buses Tasmanian Redline Coaches and Tasmanian Wilderness Travel both have ticket desks at the ferry terminal. Redline also have a depot in town at 9 Edward St (☎03/6424 5100), where you can buy tickets, wait for your bus and leave luggage ($1 per item), while Tasmanian Wilderness Travel (☎03/6334 4442) services leave from the tourist office at 5 Best St. The Backpackers Barn, next door at 10–12 Edward St, acts as a collecting point for Maxwell's Coaches transport service to Cradle Mountain, Frenchmans Cap and Walls of Jerusalem (☎03/6492 8093; service on demand; price according to number of passengers).

Camping equipment See p.961.

Car rental Firms located at the airport and ferry terminal include Autorent-Hertz (☎03/6424 1013), Avis Tasmania (☎03/6427 9797) and Budget (☎03/6427 0650); among cheaper alternatives are Lo-Cost Auto Rent, 23 King St (☎03/6424 9922; from $37 per day, 4WDs also available from $110 per day), and the popular Rent-A-Bug, Murray St, near the ferry terminal, East Devonport (☎03/6427 9304; VW Beetles from $30 per day).

Cinema Village Cinema One, 9 Stewart St (☎03/6424 4622). No screenings Mon & Thurs. Cheap day Tues.

Post office Corner of Stewart St and Formby Rd, TAS 7310.

Taxi ☎03/6424 1431.

Tours Tarkine Tours (☎ & fax 03/6428 2089) organizes quality small-group (2–8) day-tours to surrounding areas, including Cradle Mountain ($55), and the Arthur River and Tarkine Wilderness ($65); park entrance fees and cruise prices are extra. Tasmanian Wilderness Travel (☎03/6334 4442) also offer a day-tour to Cradle Mountain ($45; 6hr).

Around Devonport

East of Devonport there are some particularly rewarding spots on the **Rubicon River estuary**, where you'll find the seaside resort of **PORT SORELL**, roughly 19km from Devonport and across the river from the Asbestos Range National Park (see below). You can stay here at *Heron on Earth Organic Farm* (☎03/6248 6144; ②–④), which rents out canoes for you to paddle across to the national park. More luxurious accommodation is provided 4km northeast at **HAWLEY BEACH**, at the well-regarded *Hawley House* (☎03/6428 6221; B&B ⑧), which has a fine restaurant; the eccentric owner has a rooftop bathtub which guests are encouraged to use under the stars. From Hawley Beach there's a ten-kilometre return walk to Point Sorell.

To reach the western edge of the **Asbestos Range National Park**, on the east side of the Rubicon River estuary, it's a meandering, forty-kilometre drive from Devonport. The remote park is worth the trip – particularly at dusk – for the chance to spot some wildlife. Introduced **Forrester kangaroos** come down to feed at **Bakers Beach** at that time, and it's the best place in Tasmania to see **wombats**. The park is renowned for its occasional spectacular storms, accompanied by strong winds roaring along the beach. There's a self-registering **campsite** here, for which you pay a small fee (ranger ☎03/6428 6277), and the beach is good for swimming, and for oyster-hunting from the rocks at low tide. You'll need your own transport to get out here.

SHEFFIELD, 30km **south of Devonport**, is a popular stop en route to Cradle Mountain, and is situated near the base of **Mount Roland** (1231m) among farmland made fertile by red volcanic soils. The town's economy was ailing when the community decided to reinvent itself through the medium of visual art; since the mid-1980s 25 **murals** in various styles, showing the history of the town, have been painted, and there are other murals in the district. Tourism has increased, and the population of about a thousand has benefited from this boost to the local economy. The **Diversity Murals**

Theatrette, at 34 Main St (Mon–Fri 8.30am–5.30pm, Sat 10am–5.30pm, Sun 1–5pm; donation), screens images of the murals and fills you in on the history of the project. Sheffield is also noted for being the home of the notoriously right-wing former premier of Queensland, Johannes ("Joh") Bjelke-Petersen (see p.337), who now lives here part of the year in semi-retirement with his wife Flo. Together they have opened *Flo's Country Kitchen*, and if you're curious you can sample her supposedly "world-famous pumpkin scones". Sixteen kilometres southwest of Sheffield, at **GOWRIE PARK** at the base of Mount Roland, you can **stay** at *Mt Roland Accommodation* (☎03/6491 1385, fax 6491 1848; ①), which has bunk-style sleeping quarters and is a good base for walks up and around the summit. The adjacent *Weindorfers Restaurant* (☎03/6491 1385) is recommended for its delicious meals cooked with fresh Tasmanian produce. You can get to Gowrie Park and Sheffield with Tasmanian Wilderness Travel on their scheduled Queenstown to Launceston service via Cradle Mountain (for details see p.978).

Ulverstone to Burnie

Tasmanian Redline buses follow the unremarkable coast from Devonport west to industrial Burnie, stopping at Ulverstone and Penguin. **ULVERSTONE**, 20km west of Devonport where the **Leven River** flows into the sea, is a popular family holiday centre, with unpolluted **beaches** and plenty of activities to occupy children, including the **Ulverstone Waterslide** (Dec–Feb 10am–7pm; $2.50). **Accommodation** possibilities include B&B in the pleasant, two-storey *Ocean View Guesthouse* at 1 Victoria St (☎ & fax 03/6425 5401; ⑦) and the splendid 1903 red-brick *Furners Hotel* at 42 Reibey St (☎03/6425 1488, fax 6425 5933; ⑤), the latter complete with carved blackwood staircase and an excellent **bistro**; or try the waterfront *Ulverstone Caravan Park*, 1km east of the centre (☎03/6425 2624; cabins and units ④, on-site vans ③). You can pick up free maps and information from the **Ulverstone Visitor Information Centre**, behind the post office (Mon–Fri 9am–3.30pm, Sat & Sun 9am–3pm; ☎03/6425 2839).

In the picturesque hop-growing countryside south of Ulverstone, the **Gunns Plains Caves** (hourly tours daily 10am–4pm; 50min; $6) are worth visiting for their remarkable limestone formations. Huge shapes – looking like rashers of streaky bacon but as big as blankets – hang from the roof; when lit from behind, they glow a succulent red. A permanent stream feeds an underground lake, and platypuses and possums enjoy the cool temperatures. You'll need your own transport to get here.

The best route west from Ulverstone follows the old Bass Highway along the coastline, passing the Three Sisters and Goat Islands bird sanctuaries, and Penguin Point where Little penguins roost. **PENGUIN** itself, 12km along the highway, is a neatly tended town with three safe swimming beaches. Tacky blue-and-white penguin-shaped garbage bins line the main street, culminating in the two-metre-high "big penguin" in the foreshore park. Five kilometres outside town, there are walking trails in the **Dial Range State Forest**.

BURNIE, on Emu Bay 15km west of Penguin, is an ugly industrial and paper-manufacturing centre, situated amid contrastingly rich farmland and beautiful rocky coves. Luckily, there's no real need to stay here, especially since the airport is 19km away in more salubrious Wynyard (see overleaf). As you're passing, it's worth stopping to visit Lactos, a prize-winning speciality **cheese factory** 3km from Burnie on the Old Surry Road. Here you can sample (and buy) blends and variations of European cheeses – "red square" is one of the best (tastings Mon–Fri 9am–5pm, Sat & Sun 10am–4pm; free). Back in town, the **Tasmanian Travel and Information Centre** at the Civic Square precinct, off Little Alexander Street (Mon–Fri 9am–5pm, Sat 10am–1pm, Sun 1.30–4.30pm; ☎03/6434 6111), can direct you towards Burnie's few other points of interest. The Civic Centre on Wilmot Street is home to both the **Pioneer Village Museum**, with its reconstructed turn-of-the-century street (Mon–Fri 9am–5pm, Sat &

Sun 1.30–4.30pm; $4.50), and the **Burnie Regional Art Gallery** (Tues–Fri 10.30am–5pm, Sat & Sun 1.30–4.30pm; free). To get an idea of the region's industrial base, you could visit the AMCOR paper mill (tours Mon–Fri 2pm; free; call ☎03/6430 7777 for bookings and directions).

There's plenty of **accommodation**, should you have to stay in Burnie. The cheapest, very basic, hotel is the *Regent Hotel*, 26 North Terrace (☎03/6431 1993; ②–③), and the least expensive motel is the *Ocean View Motel*, 253 Bass Highway, at Cooee on the pleasant, non-industrial side of town towards Wynyard (☎03/6431 1925; motel ④, cabins and on-site vans ③), with an attached campground and caravan park. The *Glen Osborne House*, at 9 Aileen Crescent (☎03/6431 9866, fax 6431 4354; ⑦), is a stylish Victorian-era B&B with en-suite rooms and a lovely garden of lawns, roses and fruit trees. As well as a *McDonald's* on Mount Street and a *Pizza Hut* nearby, there's the *Rialto Gallery*, a popular and affordable Italian restaurant at 46 Wilmot St (☎03/6431 7718; BYO). The Tasmanian Redline Coaches depot is at 117 Wilson St (☎03/6431 3233).

Wynyard and around

WYNYARD, another 19km along the old Bass Highway from Burnie, snuggles into the lush pasturelands between the **Inglis River** and the sea. Most of the action in the town centres on the wharf area off Goldie Street – the main street that parallels the river – with its fishing boats and fresh fish shop, but the adjacent coastline has much to entice visitors. At **Fossil Bluff**, an easy three-kilometre walk along the Bicentennial Track from the riverfront park in front of the tourist information office (see, opposite), layers of sedimentary rock containing fossilized seashells can easily be examined at low tide, and the beach itself has good views of the 170-metre seaface of **Table Cape**. A drive up to Table Cape will reward you with magnificent views of the coast and hinterland, particularly pretty when the cape's **tulip fields** are in bloom around October. Back in town, there are a few junk/antique shops to browse in.

Eleven kilometres west of town, a turn-off from the Bass Highway winds down to **Boat Harbour Beach**, the prettiest on the northwest coast, with pale blue water, white sand and very gentle waves. It's perfect for **diving**, too; equipment can be rented from the Scuba Centre at 62 Bass Highway in Wynyard (☎03/6442 2247), which also organizes excursions. The milk bar on the beach is the place to ask about camping nearby, and it also rents **boogie-boards** and **wave skis**. Next door, the *Harbour Restaurant* (☎03/6445 1107; closed Sun night & Mon) serves pricey seafood dishes. You could choose to **stay** in the luxurious *Boat Harbour Beach Resort* (☎03/6445 1107, fax 6445 1027; ⑥–⑦), which has an indoor heated pool and spa, but you can enjoy the area just as much by camping at the caravan park (☎03/6445 1253; cabins ④–⑤, on-site vans ②) or sleeping in the spacious dorms at the *Boat Harbour Backpackers*, up the hill on Strawberry Lane (☎03/6445 1273; rooms ③, dorms ①). Nearby **Sisters Beach** is another attractive beach, and also the site of the **Birdland Native Gardens** on Wattle Avenue (daily 9am–5pm; $2; ☎03/6445 1270 for information about on-site cottages ④). You'll find 93 species here (not always very conspicuous), all protected in their natural habitat.

Rocky Cape National Park

Stretching for a mere 12km along the coast, from Sisters Beach to Rocky Cape, are the rugged hills and cliffs of **Rocky Cape National Park**, Tasmania's smallest national park, created in 1967 for the purpose of preserving some remarkable Aboriginal **archeological finds**. The mainly quartzite hills are pockmarked with caves, of which the two major ones, North Cave and South Cave, contain huge shell middens, bones and stone tools dating back as far as eight thousand years, when the sea was several fathoms below its current level.

Although North Cave can be visited – it's a fifteen-minute walk there and back from the road, reached by driving 5km into the park and taking the left fork at the lighthouse – most people prefer just to walk along the various easy tracks. It takes seven hours to traverse the whole length of the park; there's no water (bring your own) and no toilets, which makes camping more difficult – and it's not encouraged. Rocky pools, safe swimming beaches and picnic areas are scattered along the route, while in spring and summer there's a profusion of wild flowers on the scrubby heathland, including some unique native orchids. At dusk you may see wallabies, echidnas and various species of bird.

Practicalities

Wynyard may well be the first place you see in Tasmania, since "Burnie" **airport** is actually just 800m from the town centre. There are daily flights to and from Melbourne with Kendell and Southern Australian; tickets can be booked through Wynyard Travel Service at 84 Goldie St (☎03/6442 2391). You can **rent a car** at the airport with Autorent-Hertz (☎03/6442 4444), Avis (☎03/6442 2512) or Budget (☎03/6442 1777). MTT **public transport buses** connect Wynyard with Burnie, departing from 38 Jackson St. Tasmanian Redline Coaches call at the BP service station (☎03/6442 2205) en route from Burnie to Smithton via the turn-offs to Table Cape, Boat Harbour Beach, Rocky Cape and Stanley (though some do go into Stanley itself); there are three services Monday to Friday, one of which leaves from the airport, and an extra service on Friday. An express Wynyard–Smithton service runs on Saturday.

Helpful volunteers at **Wynyard Tourist Information**, in front of the riverfront park on the corner of Goldie and Hogg streets (April–Sept Mon–Fri 10am–4pm, Sat noon–3pm; Oct–March Mon–Fri 9am–4pm, Sat & Sun 1–4pm; ☎03/6442 4143), have information on local activities and **accommodation**. The *Wynyard YHA*, at 36 Dodgin St, parallel to Goldie Street (☎03/6442 2013; dorm only ①), is the best choice for budget travellers, but is rather drab. Rates at the homely *Federal Hotel*, at 82 Goldie St (☎03/6442 2056, fax 6442 1545; ④), include a cooked breakfast. The *Inglis River Hotel-Motel*, 4 Goldie St (☎03/6442 2344; ③), offers the best value of the few motels, while the *Alexandria*, on Table Cape Road (☎03/6442 4411; ⑥), is a classy B&B. For **places to eat**, try the pubs for cheap fare. *Gumnut Restaurant*, at 43 Jackson St (☎03/6442 1777; BYO and licensed; closed Sat lunch, all Sun, and Mon dinner), is an expensive à la carte restaurant, and *YT's Fish Place*, on the Wharf, is one of the best places for fresh fish (daily 9.30am–6.30pm).

Stanley

The tiny fishing village of **STANLEY**, 6km off the Bass Highway (A2) and 32km west of Rocky Cape, was the first settlement in northwest Tasmania, being the original 1826 headquarters of the **Van Diemen's Land Company** (see box on p.696). It occupies a scenic setting on a small, foot-shaped peninsula, right at the base of an unusual rock formation – **The Nut**, described by Matthew Flinders as a "cliffy round lump in form resembling a Christmas cake" – that rises directly out of the ocean to a height of nearly 150m. **Circular Head**, as it's officially called (the name also for the surrounding municipality), is thought to be a volcanic plug, with the softer sediments around it having eroded away.

Although it's still possible to do the strenuous ten-minute walk up the grassy Nut itself, you can get to the top more comfortably by means of an exhilarating **chair lift**, constructed in 1986 and reached via the ramp opposite the post office (daily: summer 9.30am–6.30pm; winter 9.30am–4pm, weather permitting; call ☎03/6458 1286 to check; $3.50, $6 return). A short walk around the windy **Nut State Reserve** at the top affords views over the town and port, and southeast as far as Table Cape. Directly below is the exquisitely deserted **Godfrey's Beach**, with its calm and translucent blue waters.

Stanley's main street, **Church Street**, runs below the foot of the Nut, and its restaurants and crafts shops are high enough above the beach, wharves and the rest of the town to command excellent views. The impressive **Stanley Craft Centre** is housed in the former Plough Inn, an 1850s building in Georgian style (daily 9.30am–5pm); items on sale include beautifully crafted wooden bowls made from Huon pine, swamp-gum bark, Tasmanian myrtle burls and blackwood. The centre also provides **tourist information**.

On the foreshore area is the slate-roofed **Van Diemen's Land Company Store**, designed in 1844 by John Lee Archer, whose work can be seen notably in Hobart (see p.908). The store is in **Marine Park**, and is the headquarters and venue for the three-day **Circular Head Arts Festival**, traditionally held in early September – although in recent years the date has been moved around somewhat (call the council for dates on ☎03/6452 1265). It combines visual art with plenty of entertainment: mime artists, street theatre and bands. From the nearby **port area**, at low tide, you can see the remnants of a 1923 **shipwreck**, a victim of the "furies" of the Bass Strait. Two kilometres north of the town, the headquarters of the Van Diemen's Land Company are now restored as the **Highfield Historic Site** (daily: May–July 10am–4pm; Aug–April 10am–5pm; grounds $2; entry to grounds and house $5), from where there are superb views over Half Moon Bay.

Practicalities

In keeping with its historic ambience, Stanley has several "colonial" **B&Bs**, which are actually self-contained cottages with breakfast provisions supplied, such as *Touchwood Cottage*, at 33 Church St (☎ & fax 03/6458 1348; ⑥–⑦), and *Bayside Colonial Cottage* at 44 Alexander Terrace, which rises above Church Street (☎03/6458 1209; ⑦). As you come into town, you'll see the signpost for the *Stanley Motel*, 1km along Dovecote Road (☎03/6458 1300, fax 6458 1448; ⑥–⑦), which has spacious, well-appointed units (some self-catering), plus one for disabled guests; facilities include a bar, and a restaurant open to the public. From the motel you have the best views of the Nut, across the green fields of the Dovecote Estate. For budget travellers, simple rooms are available at the sprawling, three-storey *Union Hotel* on Church Street (☎03/6458 1161; ③), or the *Stanley YHA*, at the caravan park on Wharf Road opposite Marine Park (☎03/6458 1266; cabins ④, on-site vans ③, dorms ①). The BP service station, near Marine Park, serves as Stanley's Tasmanian Redline Coaches depot (☎03/6458 1263).

Probably the best place to **eat** in Stanley is *Hurseys Seafoods*, next to Marine Park, considered to be one of the best fish-and-chip shops in Tasmania. Inside are huge holding tanks from which you select live fish and crayfish; as well as around twenty kinds of fish, they have freshly cooked local muttonbirds – not to everyone's taste, as they're very oily. The owners even offer their own fishing tours (☎03/6458 1103). Among other good options, all on Church Street, are the *Union Hotel*, serving fresh seafood in its lounge bar; *Sullivans Restaurant* (☎03/6458 1144), which has generous portions of home-style cooking; and the *Dovecoat Restaurant*, at the *Stanley Motel* (see above). Also on Church Street, the relaxed *Stranded Whale Coffee Shop* (daily 9am–4pm, plus Fri night when you'll need to book ☎03/6458 1202) has walls covered with photographs depicting various attempts to rescue pygmy right whales, which occasionally get stranded in the beaches around Stanley.

Smithton and Woolnorth

The only way to see Tasmania's rugged northwest tip, which remains under the control of the Van Diemen's Land Company, is to arrange a tour from the unattractive logging town of

. . . how is it that an absentee owner across the world got this magnificent and empty country without having paid one glass bead?

Cassandra Pybus

The **Van Diemen's Land Company (VDL)** was the brainchild of a group of prominent and well-connected private individuals, who in 1824 managed to obtain by Royal Charter 250,000 acres of the mainly thickly forested, unexplored northwest corner of Tasmania. Their plan was to create their own source of cheap wool in the colonies, which could be relied upon even if Europe was subject to political upheaval; the *Tranmere* arrived at Circular Head in 1826, with the personnel, livestock, supplies and equipment to create the township of Stanley.

The first flocks were grazed at Woolnorth on Cape Grim, a plateau of tussock grass and ti trees that might have been made for the purpose but, in fact, was prime Aboriginal hunting land. When hunting parties began to take sheep, whites indiscriminately killed Aborigines in retaliation, and a vindictive cycle of **killing** began. The most tragic incident occurred around 1826 or 1827: a group of Aboriginal men, seeking revenge for the rape of their women, speared a shepherd and killed one hundred sheep. These deaths were ruthlessly avenged when a group of thirty unarmed Aborigines, hunting for muttonbirds near the same spot, were killed by shepherds and their bodies thrown over a cliff (now euphemistically called "Suicide Cove"). Ultimately, the Aboriginal people of the northwest were systematically hunted down, the last one being captured near the Arthur River in 1842.

The Van Diemen's Land Company was detested by free settlers because it used its influence to get the pick of convict labour, which it always used in preference to that of free men. In the 1840s the company changed its emphasis from wool production to the sale and lease of its land; it is still registered on the London Stock Exchange, and its major stockholders have probably never laid eyes on the land they own.

SMITHTON, at the mouth of the Duck River 22km west of Stanley. Tours run to **Woolnorth**, the original VDL cattle and sheep property, and take in **Cape Grim** where the air is reputed to be the cleanest in the world – it's the site of one of only six baseline air-monitoring stations (☎03/6452 1252; 9.30am–4.30pm; $90, including a seafood and steak lunch in the director's house and a visit to the Lacrum Dairy – see below). You can **stay** in Smithton at the *Bridge Hotel-Motel* on Montague Road (☎03/6452 1389; ④), where restaurant and counter **meals** are available. Smithton's one other attraction is the **Lacrum Dairy** (closed July–Oct), 6km north on the Mella Road, where tours of the modern milking plant (daily 3.30–5.30pm; $7.50) include afternoon tea with Tasmanian cheeses.

South of Smithton there are ten **forestry reserves**, ranging from rainforests to blackwood swamps and giant eucalypt forests; all are accessible from a circular route, via Kanunnah Bridge and Taytea Bridge on the C218 (90km return). The Forestry Commission, at the corner of Nelson and Smith streets (☎03/6452 1317), can provide maps and route information. The most rewarding reserves are the **Julius River Forest Reserve** and the **Milkshakes Hills Forest Reserve**.

Marrawah

From Smithton the Bass Highway cuts across the northwest corner to the rich farming settlement of **MARRAWAH** on the west coast. Thirty kilometres along the way, a 1500-metre trail leads through a swamp at the grumpily named **Dismal Swamp Nature Reserve**. Marrawah itself has a small store, and the *Marrawah Tavern* serves plain but filling meals. **Greenpoint Beach**, which has been voted one of the three best **surfing** beaches in Australia, is 2km from Marrawah and has a small **camping area**. Apart from that, there's self-contained **accommodation** at *Glendonald Cottage* on the Arthur River Road (☎03/6457 1191; ⑤). The curve of Ann Bay here is shrouded by the hump of Mount Cameron West to the north. Three kilometres north of this bluff, at the end of a long exposed beach, is the most complex **Aboriginal art** site in Tasmania: rock carvings of geometric or non-figurative forms cover slabs of rock at the base of a cliff.

Arthur River and the Arthur Pieman Protected Area

Just over 20km south of Marrawah, the scattering of holiday homes at **ARTHUR RIVER** marks the start of one of the Tasmanian coast's last great **wilderness areas**, where mighty trees that have been washed down the Arthur River have crashed and battered against the windswept shoreline. At one time the entire west coast looked like this, but the progressive damming of its rivers has left the **Arthur Pieman Protected Area** as a unique reminder, complete with a spectacular array of birdlife, such as black cockatoos, Tasmanian rosellas, orange-breasted parrots, black jays, wedge-tail eagles, pied heron and azure kingfishers. Trees on the steep banks of the river include myrtle, sassafras, celery-top pines, laurels and giant tree ferns. It's dangerous to swim in the protected area, due to extremely wild conditions and occasional freak waves – even walking along the beach, where you have to pick your way over scattered bits of lumber, can be an obstacle course. Therefore, it's essential to get the latest information on conditions from the base office of the Department of Parks and Wildlife on Arthur River Road (daily 9am–5pm; ☎03/6457 1225).

The small **shop** on Gardiner Street is the only source of supplies in Arthur River; attached is one of the area's four places to **stay**, the *Arthur River Holiday Units* (☎03/6457 1288; ⑤). *Ocean View Holiday Cottage* (☎03/6452 1278; ⑤) and *Sunset Holiday Villas* (☎03/6437 1197; ⑤) are on the same street. There's marginally cheaper self-catering accomodation at *Alert Cottage* (☎03/6457 1340; ④). **Camping** at Arthur River is a truly pleasurable experience, with facilities that range from a fully serviced caravan park near the base office, to secluded areas among shady trees in the dips and hollows behind the dunes, equipped merely with water taps.

If you want to get out on the river, take a **cruise** (see below) or contact Arthur River Canoe Hire (☎03/6457 1312), which has canoes and boats available for rent (one-person canoes $5 per hour/$30 per day, two-person canoes $8/$50, boats $15/$100).

The Arthur River Cruise
Perhaps the biggest attraction of the entire northwest coast is the five-hour **Arthur River Cruise** (daily 10am, returning 3pm; no trips June–Aug; $40; reservations ☎03/6457 1158), on the *George Robinson*, which sails 19km upriver to the confluence of the Arthur and Frankland rivers at Turks Crossing. En route you cruise past a wedge-tail eagle's nest, and even see a pair of enormous sea eagles being hand-fed, and you get to experience the transition from coastal scrub woodland to temperate rainforest. After a barbecue lunch in a clearing, there's a four-kilometre bushwalk.

The A10 route to the west coast

From Somerset, a suburb of Burnie on the shores of Emu Bay, the A10 (called the Murchison Highway between here and the Zeehan turn-off) heads to **Queenstown**, in the heart of Tasmania's west-coast mining area. This major route to the west coast is relatively recent; prior to 1932 the coast was accessible only by sea. Following the highway, after 10km you pass **YOLLA**, a picturesque little town surrounded by rich farming country; there are a couple of places here to fill up with fuel. A few kilometres past the Tewkesbury turn-off, the rural landscape ends and the road rises and winds through temperate rainforest to the **Hellyer Gorge State Reserve**. You can take a walk through spicy ferns and dense myrtle forest to the Hellyer River and back on a wide and easy track (20min return). Once through the reserve, you're confronted with the shocking spectacle of a landscape ravaged by logging. By the time you reach the B23 turn-off west to Waratah, on the way to the Pieman River, the forest is beginning to reassert itself.

West to Waratah and the Pieman River

Tiny, windswept **WARATAH**, set in mountain heathland 8km off the A10, reached its peak in the early twentieth century after thirty years of tin-mining at **Mount Bischoff**, when it was linked to Burnie by the **Emu Bay Railway**, built to facilitate access to the silver fields of Zeehan and Rosebery. Though the mine closed in 1935, Waratah is still a miners' town, with recent mining developments at the Que River. Little more than a scattered collection of scruffy weatherboard cottages, it's a pretty soulless place, but if you're desperate you can **camp** at the exposed site behind the Municipal Council buildings on Smith Street; get the key for the hot showers and pay ($8 per site) at the Waratah Road House (☎03/6439 1191; daily 6am–8pm), further along Smith Street. You can have a **meal** at the big old two-storey pub on the hill, a relic of former boom times. Beyond Waratah, the last fuel stop on the road is the former mining town of **Savage River**, 45km along the B23.

The beautiful, unspoilt **Pieman River**, within the **Pieman River State Reserve**, is reached from the old gold-mining settlement of **CORINNA** on an unsealed road (C247) 26km south of Savage River. It's hard to believe that 2500 people once occupied what's now just a few shacks surrounded by dense bush. Corinna even had its own port, despite the difficulties of getting through the narrow **Pieman Heads** from the coastline. The river here is too dangerous for swimming: it has an average drop of nearly 20m from the banks, and the water is very cold. The reserve used to be a logging area and it still holds one of the biggest stands of remaining Huon pine – saved because the water here was too deep to allow a dam to be built.

You can take a **cruise** on the river, all the way to the west coast, with *MV Arcadia II* (daily 10.30am; 4hr; $30, including morning tea; ☎03/6446 1170). The boat was built in Hobart (from Huon pine) as a luxury pleasure cruiser, but during World War II saw active service off the Philippines and has since been put to other uses. From its deck you can see Huon pine, leatherwood and pandanus ferns among the **temperate rainforest** of the river's north bank; the drier southern bank has mainly brown stringybark eucalypts. The trip allows you an hour and a half to wander on your own along the west coast; by the landing are several intriguing **holiday shacks**, ramshackle affairs with tin verandahs variously propped up by raw tree posts and an old bus. A wide sandy path leads to a beach between two outcrops of jagged orange sedimentary rock, where the dark blue sea is tinged by the tannin-stained river water.

The affable brothers who run the cruise virtually run Corinna too. They open the **kiosk** daily whenever they have time, but bring food along if you intend to use the **campsite** (no showers) or the *Getaway Resort* (⑤, BYO linen), both also operated by the brothers. From the car park there's a walking track leading to a huge 600-year-old **manfern**, one of only four of such antiquity known to exist in Tasmania.

You can take a barge across the Pieman River from here (daily 9am–5pm; $10 car; $5 bike; ☎03/6446 1170) and continue on the C249 to Zeehan, and then on the B27 to Strahan.

South to Zeehan

Back on the A10, there's no fuel until you reach the small settlement of **TULLAH**, another 40km south, where you'll find a pub, tearooms and cottage accommodation. Fourteen kilometres further on is the comparatively large town of **ROSEBERY**, a good place to stock up on supplies, with full **banking** facilities at the ANZ bank (Mon, Tues & Fri 9am–noon, Wed 2–4pm; closed Thurs). You can stay in comfortable backpacker **accommodation** at *Mount Black Lodge* on Hospital Road (☎03/6473 1039; ①). From here, it's 23km to the turn-off to **ZEEHAN**, 6km southwest off the A10. The town became prosperous from the silver-lead mines which opened in the 1880s, and at its height boasted a population of eight thousand. However, the mines had already begun to fail by 1908, and the town was not to see a revival until the 1970s, when the Renison Bell tin mines were opened. Several boom-period buildings are still standing, including the elaborate facade of the **Gaiety Theatre**, once the largest theatre in Australia, which hosted Houdini and Caruso but now houses a hairdresser's. The **West Coast Pioneer Memorial Museum** on Main Street (daily 8.30am–5pm; $3) has displays on mining history. **Accommodation** is expensive, with the *Heemskirk Motor Inn* (☎03/6471 6107; ⑦) charging $100 for a double, and even basic pub rooms at the *Hotel Cecil* on Main Street (☎03/6471 6221; ⑤) are steep; however, you can get decent counter **meals** here. The cheapest option is the **caravan park**, 1km from the centre on Hurst Street (☎03/6471 6633; cabins ④, on-site vans ③). The ANZ **bank** has restricted opening hours (Mon 1–4pm, Tues 2–4pm, Wed 9am–noon, Thurs 9am–4pm, Fri 2–5pm); there are no ATMs.

From here it's possible to go straight to Strahan (47km) on a sealed road (B27), bypassing Queenstown and visiting the Henty Dunes (see p.976) en route; or you could head back to the A10 (called the Zeehan Highway until Queenstown) and reach Strahan via Queenstown, another 32km along the highway.

Queenstown

QUEENSTOWN used to be promoted vigorously by the Tasmanian tourist board during the 1970s, when its famous (although now infamous) **"lunar landscape"** was seen as a major attraction and the people of Queenstown claimed to be proud of their bare hills. Though nowadays people are sent instead to **Strahan** to experience wilderness on the Gordon River, Queenstown illustrates the grim reality of blind progress in such a sensitive environment and the devastation it can cause. If you approach the town from Strahan you're confronted by the hideously ugly **Mount Lyell Copper Mine**; from Hobart, the road winds down to the town around bare, reddish-brown rock.

Queenstown has been a mining centre since 1883, when gold was discovered at Mount Lyell, and it looks like a typical mining-town, with its wide streets, two-storey hotels, and identical, pokey tin-roofed weatherboard houses. In 1893 the **Mount Lyell Mining and Railway Company** was formed and began to mine copper at Mount Lyell, which it has continued to do ever since. The weird-looking mountains here, chalky white and almost totally devoid of vegetation, are the result of a lethal combination of tree-felling, sulphur, fire and rainfall. Between 1896 and 1922 the eleven furnaces at the Mount Lyell smelters consumed huge amounts of timber, and the rainforest cover in the surrounding hills has taken decades to begin to re-establish itself; even so, the sulphur fumes emitted by the same smelters have killed off the regrowth. Because sulphur had been absorbed into soil and tree stumps, bushfires swept the hills summer after summer, and rainfall finally eroded the remaining soil. Since the smelters closed in 1969 there has been some regrowth on the lower slopes, but it's estimated that the damage already done has had an impact that will last some four or five hundred years. In late 1994 the Mount Lyell mine closed down, but the lease was taken over by Copper

Mines of Tasmania, who foresee another ten years of operation with the remaining ore. Tailings from the mine are now dumped into a multimillion-dollar dam instead of the town's **Queen River**, where aquatic life is beginning to return. The Queen eventually flows into the King River, however, and the moonscaped banks of the **King River** delta near Strahan attest to the lasting and wide-ranging environmental damage of the past century.

There are tours of the **Mount Lyell Mine** (daily: May–Sept 9.15am & 4pm; Oct–April 9.15am, 2.30pm & 4.30pm; 1hr 30min; additional tours during summer; $9.50); it's hard to stifle a lingering cynicism, even though the plans for reforestation are explained. Bookings and departures are from the Western Arts and Crafts Centre, at 1 Driffield St (☎03/6471 2388), which also provides **tourist information** about the town's dubious attractions.

Next door to the mine is the **Parks and Wildlife Service office** (☎03/6471 2511), the base for the Franklin Lower Gordon Wild Rivers National Park and the place to pick up the department's rafting and bushwalking guidelines. While in town, you could also check out the old photographic displays in the **Galley Museum** (Mon–Fri 10am–12.30pm & 1.30–4.30pm, Sat & Sun 1.30–4.30pm; $2), housed in the old *Imperial Hotel*. Queenstown is desperate to attract some of the tourists on the way to Strahan, and they've installed a rather joyless **chair lift**, just outside of town at the Lyell Highway (April–Sept 9am–5pm; Oct–Mar 9am–6pm; $6), to help you get an even better view of those frightening hills.

You wouldn't really choose to **stay** in Queenstown, but it can be a cheap alternative if there's no room in Strahan. The *Empire Hotel*, at 2 Orr St (☎03/6471 1699, fax 6471 1788; ③), is a lovely, old-fashioned building noted for its blackwood staircase; it has a good range of reasonably priced rooms, including several budget singles, plus good-value meals. *Mountain View Holiday Lodge*, at 1 Penghana Rd (☎03/6471 1163, fax 6471 1306; motel units ④, dorms ①), has been converted from the mine's single men's lodgings. There are full **banking** facilities in Queenstown at the Trust Bank, but no ATMs. From Queenstown you can drive to Strahan on the B24 (40km), which starts as a steep, winding road through bare hills, or you continue along the A10 (called the Lyell Highway from Queenstown to Hobart) 86km east to the first fuel at Derwent Bridge, surrounded by the World Heritage Area (see Franklin Lower Gordon Wild Rivers National Park, p.981, and Cradle Mountain–Lake St Clair National Park, p.978).

Strahan

STRAHAN is easy-going, relaxed and even progressive. The only town and port on the west coast, it sits in the huge **Macquarie Harbour**, site of **Sarah Island**, a harsh secondary convict settlement in use between 1822 and 1830, which can be visited on a Gordon River cruise (see p.976). The entrance to Macquarie Harbour, named **Hells Gates** by arriving convicts, is only 80m wide. **Huon pine**, perfect for shipbuilding, grows abundantly in the area – logging and boatbuilding became the convicts' trade. After 1830 the timber continued to attract loggers, but it wasn't until 1882 that Strahan began life as a port for the nearby copper and lead fields. Although it was Tasmania's third-largest port in 1900, its unreliability led to its closure by 1970 and the population dwindled to three hundred. It's now a small **fishing village** for abalone, crayfish and shark, and commercial fish farming of rainbow trout and Atlantic salmon, though the main industry is definitely tourism. The basing of the **Franklin Blockade** campaign here in 1982 shook up the town and brought the Australian media here for two months (see p.977). **Cruises** on the **Gordon River** had already been running before this event, but the declaration of a **World Heritage Area** has meant that busloads of tourists now regularly descend upon Strahan to see the river, creating a hectic atmosphere for a short time, after which the town rapidly reverts to its usual peaceful state. You would be mad to come all this way and not take a cruise; though they may seem expensive, it's the best way to get to see the wilderness, and well worth the money.

Transport and services

The place to make enquiries and bookings for Tasmanian Wilderness Travel **bus** services is the visitor centre (see opposite). There's a scheduled service from Launceston and Devonport via Cradle Mountain (Tues, Thurs & Sat), connecting with a Queenstown to Strahan service. A service from Strahan to Queenstown departs four times a week (Tues, Thurs, Sat & Sun), connecting with the service to Hobart via Lake St Clair. There are no ATMs in Strahan. The Strahan General Store (Mon–Fri 7.30am–7pm, Sat & Sun 8am–6pm) has EFTPOS facilities and is an ANZ **bank** agent, while at the far end of The Esplanade, the old **Customs House** contains the **post office**, which also acts as a Commonwealth Bank agent. Next door is the **Parks and Wildlife Service** District office (daily 8am–5pm; ☎03/6471 7122), where you can buy park passes.

If you want to **shop** for food, the Strahan General Store on The Esplanade houses a small supermarket selling a decent range, including fresh vegetables. However, it's expensive, and you might do better to get supplies in Queenstown first. Strahan Fresh Seafood, also on The Esplanade, sells fresh fish, and there's a decent bakery at the other end of the street.

Accommodation

If you've got your own transport to get there, you can **camp** for free at Ocean Beach and Henty Dunes (see p.976); there are no facilities, but free hot showers can be had in town in the toilet block opposite the post office. **Accommodation** is expensive and gets booked up in the summer; to be safe, **book ahead** or bring a tent – otherwise you might have to head back to Zeehan or Queenstown. *Hamers Hotel* has virtually overtaken the town – with pub and motel accommodation and several restaurants along The Esplanade, and a rather impersonal reception/booking office in a corner building. Another accommodation booking agency is run by Strahan Central (☎03/6471 7612) who book for the YHA and several B&Bs. The Strahan Visitor Centre (see opposite) has a free accommodation hotline – you call and book a room yourself from the list provided.

Franklin Manor, The Esplanade (☎03/6471 7311, fax 6471 7267). Sedate and elegant two-storey weatherboard B&B, surrounded by trees and flowers. The interior is attractively decorated and lovingly maintained; classical music plays in the guest lounge, always filled with fresh flowers, and there's a classy restaurant. ⑨.

Gordon Gateway Chalet, Grining St, Regatta Point (☎03/6471 7165). Peaceful harbourfront spot looking across to the town and its fishing boats. Spacious rooms with kitchenettes. ⑤–⑥.

Hamers Hotel, The Esplanade (☎03/6471 7191, fax 6471 7389). A renovated 1930s hotel with clean, modern rooms with washbasins, colour TV and sea views; light breakfast included. Also stylish modern motel units attached to the ground floor of the pub. The café-style lounge bar serves seafood and good salads, and there's also a public bar. Motel units ⑦–⑧, rooms ⑤.

Harbour Views, 1 Charles St, 1km northeast of the post office (☎03/6471 7143). A more affordable B&B; en-suite rooms. ④–⑤.

Kitty's Place, Innes St, north of the post office (☎03/6471 7666). Five brand-new, centrally located holiday units. Three sleeping up to six people, two sleeping up to four. Light breakfast provisions included. ⑦.

The Piners Loft, Harrison St, across the harbour from the city centre (☎03/6471 7390). Unique accommodation in a two-storey building made from recycled Tasmanian woods; poles of King Billy pine and other warm woods rise up through the split level interior. ⑦.

Strahan Village Motor Inn, Jolly St (☎03/6471 7160, fax 6471 7372). An expensive motel complex on a hill overlooking the town, with some wheelchair-accessible units; the restaurant has sea views. ⑥–⑦.

Strahan Wilderness Lodge & Bayview Cottages, Ocean Beach Rd (☎ & fax 03/6471 7142). The best-value place in Strahan, set in spacious grounds crisscrossed by walking tracks, just out of town. Old homestead B&B (④), plus private self-catering cottages (⑥). They also have an A-Frame cedar house to rent closer to town (⑥).

Strahan YHA, Harvey St (☎ & fax 03/6471 7255). Located in two separate buildings beside a bush-lined stream with its own resident platypus, this modern hostel has spacious but slightly neglected common kitchens, eating areas, and lounge. There are well cared-for timber bedroom cabins with made-up double or twin beds, and sharing the hostel bathroom and kitchen. Buses drop off here. Cabins ③–④, dorms ①.

West Strahan Caravan Park, The Esplanade (☎03/6471 7239). A simple, inexpensive campsite.

The Town

Your first stop should be the innovative wooden and iron **Strahan Visitor Centre**, on The Esplanade (daily: summer 10am–8pm; winter 10am–6pm; 24hr ticket $4.50; ☎03/6471 7622 for tourist information), whose exterior design aims to echo the area's boatbuilding and timber industries. The interior features a waterfall, and a huge glass wall providing views of the harbour. The centre sets out its exhibits in a provocative and challenging way, with the quote on the foyer wall immediately striking an ecological note. There are seven main themes: the Aborigines, convicts, logging, ecology, economy, wilderness and conflict – all making a satisfyingly radical departure from the usual displays in a local museum. If you don't want to see the exhibition you can enter the foyer free of charge to pick up leaflets and information. Outside, an **amphitheatre** is the early evening venue for an entertaining two-man show, *The Ship That Never Was*, which retells – in slapstick vein, with plenty of audience participation – the true story of an 1834 convict escape from Sarah Island (daily 5.30pm plus 8.30pm performance during January; $10).

Adjacent to the visitor centre is the **Strahan Woodworks**, in a large, corrugated-iron shed (daily 8am–5pm), selling well-designed and crafted woodwork; you're also welcome to roam around Morrison's Saw Mill next door, and watch the Tasmanian timbers being initially processed. Also worth visiting is the **Forestry Tasmania Office** (Mon–Fri 9am–noon & 1–5pm; ☎03/6471 7176), which has leaflets describing the trees in the area, plus information about visiting the Teepookana Forest Reserve (see p.977). You should also check out the amazing window display of a Huon pine log transforming itself into the bow of a boat.

The **Strahan Historic Foreshore Walkway** is a pleasant gravel track following the shore of the harbour around to **Regatta Point**, where you'll see the defunct 1899 train station that was used by the Queenstown-based Mount Lyell Railway and Mining Company to transport ore to the port. En route you pass the **People's Park**, from where you can take the rainforest walk to **Hogarth Falls** (40min; 2km return).

Eating and drinking

Strahan's best **restaurant** is the dining room of the stylish *Franklin Manor*, across from the centre of town on The Esplanade (☎03/6471 7311). The less expensive and less formal *Hamers Hotel*, also on The Esplanade, is the focus of the town's social life and has a fine bistro which serves up a varied selection of seafood, and is always a lively place for a **drink**. The hotel also runs the excellent eat-in bakery a couple of doors away, and the adjoining *Pizza and Pasta Café* (open daily until 9.30pm); their *The Fish Café* next door dishes up affordable eat-in fish and chips. There are a couple of good alternatives: *Strahan Fresh Seafood* at the other end of The Esplanade (daily 8am–8pm) serves good takeaway or eat-in fish and chips, fish burgers, hamburgers, and toasted sandwiches; *Strahan Central Café*, just off The Esplanade on Harold Street, is young, city-style and funky, with waterviews and an outdoor deck and pricey but tasty contemporary café favourites. The coffee is excellent – but costs more than you'd pay in the big city.

Cruising the Gordon River

The **Gordon River** is deep, its waters dark from the tannin leaching out of buttongrass plains – even the tap water in Strahan is brown (though perfectly fine to drink). Cruise boats used to travel as far as Sir John Falls, 30km upriver, but the speed at which the boats had to go was causing the river banks to erode. Boats now travel only the 14km to **Heritage Landing**, where there's a chance to see a section of real **rainforest**: a boardwalk above the rainforest floor allows you to get close without disturbing anything. Trunks and branches of ancient myrtles and Huon pines provide homes for mosses, lichens and liverworts on their bark, and ferns and fungi grow from the trunks – even the dead trees support some forms of life, however lowly. The wet and swampy conditions are ideal for **Huon pines**, a threatened tree species found only in Tasmania: they're the second-oldest living things on earth after the bristlecone pines of western North America, with some trees found to be more than two thousand years old. The massive pines, which may reach a height of 40m, can grow from seed but more often regenerate vegetatively, putting down roots where fallen branches touch the soil. The vast tree at the landing, reckoned to be around 2000 years old, split in two during 1997 – one half fell to the ground – but the trunk won't rot for up to one hundred years as it contains methyl eugenol oil which slows fungal growth. The oil content of the wood helps explain why it was so highly sought after as one of the few green Tasmanian timbers that floats: Huon pine logs were floated down to the boom camp and there fashioned into huge rafts to be rowed across Macquarie Harbour. The **boom camp** is still set up, and anyone can stay for free – all you need to bring is bedding and food – and you need to rent a kayak (from Hell's Gate Wilderness Tours; see opposite) to be dropped off near the mooring by the *Wanderer II*.

Two operators offer **river cruises**; both visit Sarah Island and make a thirty-minute stop at Heritage Landing. To make the most of the experience, turn up early to bag a good seat and bring water- and windproof gear so you can brave the prow of the boat – much the most exhilarating spot when you whizz through Macquarie Heads (Hells Gates). The larger operator, **Gordon River Cruises** (half-day cruise departs 9am, returns 2pm; full-day cruise Nov–April departs 9am, returns 3.30pm; shorter cruise $45 including morning tea; longer cruise $61 including smorgasbord lunch; ☎03/6471 7187), has three boats and is located on the waterfront in a spacious complex, where there's a photographic display of Strahan's history. Their full-day cruise stops for an hour at Sarah Island to allow you to wander around the ruins of the prison settlement. **World Heritage Cruises**, the smaller friendlier company, has just one boat (the *Wanderer II*) and offers a cheaper cruise whose highlight is a 40-minute guided tour of Sarah Island (departs daily 9am, returns about 3.30pm; no cruises mid-July to Aug; $44; snacks and $8 buffet lunch available on board; licensed; ☎03/6471 7174).

Around Strahan

Six kilometres east of town, **Ocean Beach** is, at 30km, the longest beach in Tasmania. In the early 1990s several **pilot whales** from Antarctica were stranded here: unfortunately, attempts to rescue them were unsuccessful and their skeletons, half-buried in the sand, can still be seen. In the summer of 1998 a similar tragedy occurred: the bodies of 63 sperm are also buried in the dunes. Come at dusk to observe the marvellous sunsets and to watch – from November to February – the migratory **muttonbirds** roost. It's an eleven-kilometre drive on a gravel road, south off the road to Ocean Beach, to **Macquarie Heads** (Hells Gates). The extensive **Henty Dunes**, 12km north of town on the Zeehan Road (B27), are also worth seeing; you can **camp** at the picnic area.

To get around, you can rent ten-speed **mountain bikes** at the youth hostel ($10 per half-day) and from the tourist office (1hr $10, half-day $20, full-day $30). There's no car rental in Strahan, so if you haven't arrived by car other land-based options include trips with South West Adventure Tours (☎03/6471 7157): pricey 4WD tours to Macquarie Heads via Ocean Beach and Henty Sand Dunes (2hr 30min; $40); dune tours (1hr 30min; $35); sunset tours to Ocean Beach (1hr 30min; $40). Their best trip is to the ghost town of **Teepookana**, an old railway port, and the surrounding Huon pine forest reserve on the King River (3hr; $40). Hay's bus service offers less expensive Teepookana tours (Dec–April 10am & 3pm; 3hr; $20; book at the tourist office) and trips to watch the sunset and the muttonbirds fly in at Ocean Beach (Nov–Feb; $5). You can go horse-riding on Ocean Beach with Strahan Trail Rides (☎03/6471 7426).

In addition to the Gordon River cruises (covered opposite) there's a wide choice of water- and air-based tours. West Coast Yacht Charters, on The Esplanade (☎03/6471 7422 or mobile ☎0419/300 994; closed July–Sept), runs evening **crayfish dinner sails** on Macquarie Harbour on a 20m ketch, *Stormbreaker* (6–8.30pm; $50 including dinner and wine), plus morning fishing trips with all gear supplied (9am–noon; $40), or longer two-night cruises ($320); you can even stay on board the ketch for a waterborne B&B experience (④). With Wild Rivers Jet (50min; $39; ☎03/6471 7174) you can explore the **King River**, which, like the Gordon, flows into Macquarie Harbour, just south of Strahan. On this tour you can assess the environmental damage done to the banks by the mining operations in Queenstown (see p.972), though the rainforested gorges remain unspoilt. Hells Gate Wilderness Tours (☎03/6471 7576) offer sea **kayak tours** on the Gordon River or half-day tours on the Henty River; they also hire sea kayaks (single $30 half-day, $40 full-day; double $40/$60) and canoes (seating 2–3 people; $10 per hr) so you can explore Macquarie Harbour by yourself. Wilderness Air, on Strahan Wharf, runs spectacular **seaplane flights** over Macquarie Harbour and the wilderness area (daily from 9am; 1hr 20min; $99; bookings essential on ☎03/6471 7280), which grant you the unforgettable image of the smooth dark ribbon of the pristine Gordon River easing through dense forest (see also p.982). The seaplanes land at **Sir John Falls Landing**, further upriver than the cruise boats can reach – the highlight of the trip is a dramatic landing on the glassy calm of the Gordon River. Wilderness Air also has longer flights for viewing the rugged scenery around Frenchmans Cap. There are also **helicopter flights** with Seair Adventure Charters (☎03/6471 7718) over Hells Gates and Macquarie Harbour ($60; 15min), and the Teepookana Forest ($105; 1hr).

The World Heritage Area

If we can revise our attitudes towards the land under our feet; if we can accept a role of steward, and depart from the role of conqueror; if we can accept the view that man and nature are inseparable parts of the unified whole – then Tasmania can be a shining beacon in a dull, uniform, and largely artificial world.

Olegas Truchanas, conservationist, 1971
(born 1923, drowned 1972 in the Gordon River gorge)

Up until the nineteenth century, the concept of **wilderness** was overwhelmingly that of a malevolent force, untamed by man. In the late twentieth century, especially for jaded inhabitants of the technologically swamped developed world, the image is increasingly becoming a benign one: the natural as opposed to the artificial, virgin forest as opposed to polluted streets, the spiritual versus the material. It's the lure of this ideal of wilderness that attracts a certain type of traveller to Tasmania, to commune with nature at its most unspoilt. The state's vast wilderness areas of the South West National Park, Franklin Lower Gordon Wild Rivers National Park and the adjacent Cradle Mountain–Lake St Clair National Park make up the **World Heritage Area**, recognized by UNESCO.

Some history

In 1972 the flooding of the beautiful and unique **Lake Pedder** led to the formation, in 1976, of the **Wilderness Society**, which began a relentless campaign against the next plan for the southwest by the Hydro Electricity Commission (HEC), which was to build a huge dam on the Lower Gordon River that would efface Tasmania's last wild river, the Franklin. Pro-HEC forces included the then Tasmanian Premier Robin Gray. Years of protests and campaigns ensued, but in 1981 the whole southwest area was proposed for the World Heritage list. The **Franklin Blockade**, organized by the Wilderness Society and led by **Dr Bob Brown**, began on December 14, 1982, the day the southwest officially joined the list – a fact the Tasmanian government was choosing to ignore.

For two months, blockaders from all over Australia travelled upriver from their base in Strahan to put themselves in front of the bulldozers at the site, in nonviolent protest. The **blockade** attracted international attention, notably when the British botanist David Bellamy joined in the protest and was among the twelve hundred or so arrested for trespassing. During the course of the campaign, the Labor government of Bob Hawke was voted in, and in March 1983, following a trailblazing High Court ruling, the federal government forbade further work by the HEC.

Local people who supported the "Greenie" protesters showed a lot of courage, in the face of antagonism within the community. Though the blockade itself had failed to stop work on the dam, it had changed, or at least challenged, the opinion of many Australians. Particularly on Tasmania's west coast, communities and families were split over the Franklin issue, as resentment grew towards the mainlanders, who were regarded as denying potential employment to Tasmanians. Recent Wilderness Society campaigns have only added to these tensions.

Cradle Mountain–Lake St Clair National Park

This must be a national park for the people for all time. It is magnificent, and people must know about it and enjoy it.

Gustave Weindorfer, botanist and mountaineer, 1910

Cradle Mountain–Lake St Clair National Park is Tasmania's best known, its northern **Cradle Mountain** end easily accessible from Devonport, Deloraine or Launceston, and its southern **Lake St Clair** end from Derwent Bridge on the Lyell Highway between Queenstown and Hobart. A popular route from Devonport is via Sheffield (see p.964) on the B14, then the C132 via Wilmot, and for the final stretch to Cradle Valley, the C136. One of the most glaciated areas in Australia, with many lakes and tarns, the park covers some of Tasmania's highest land, with craggy mountain peaks such as **Mount Ossa** (1617m), the state's highest point. At its northern end, **Dove Lake**, backed by the jagged outline of Cradle Mountain, is one of the state's most breathtaking sights, and at the park's southern end, Lake St Clair is the country's deepest freshwater lake at over 200m, occupying a basin gouged out by two glaciers. Between Cradle Mountain and Lake St Clair, the eighty-kilometre **Overland Track**, attracting walkers from all over the world, is the best way to take in the stunning scenery – spread over five or more mud- and leech-filled days of physical, albeit exhilarating, exhaustion. However, you can do just part of the walk, or make several other satisfying day-walks around Cradle Mountain or Lake St Clair (see p.981).

Transport to the park

Tasmanian Wilderness Transport services both ends of the national park on two year-round **scheduled routes**, while "Wilderness" services provide more frequent transport in the summer. A service from Launceston and Devonport to Queenstown goes via Cradle Mountain (Tues, Thurs & Sat; connecting with a Queenstown to Strahan service), while the Queenstown–Hobart service takes the Lyell Highway to Lake St Clair (Tues, Thurs, Sat & Sun). A Launceston to Cradle Mountain "Wilderness" service runs via Deloraine and Devonport (mid-April to Nov Tues, Thurs, Sat & Sun; Nov to mid-April daily). A Hobart to Lake St Clair "Wilderness" service via Mt Field National Park runs daily in both directions Dec–April. You can also try Maxwell's Coaches charter service (☎03/6424 8093), which connects Devonport and Launceston to Lake St Clair ($30), and Launceston and Devonport to Cradle Mountain ($30).

The Overland Track
In summer hundreds flock here to walk the **Overland Track**, probably Australia's greatest extended bushwalk: 80km, unbroken by roads and passing through button-grass plains, fields of wild flowers, and forests of deciduous beech, Tasmanian myrtle, pandanus and King Billy pine, with side-walks leading to views of waterfalls and lakes and starting points for climbs of the various mountain peaks. Much of the track is boardwalked, but you'll still end up thigh-deep in mud. There are eight basic stove-heated huts (not for cooking – bring your own stove) along the route, with composting toilets, but there's no guarantee there'll be space, so you should carry a good tent; a warm sleeping bag is essential even in the heated huts in summer.

THE OVERLAND TRACK: A PERSONAL ATTACK

The steep climb away from the car park at Lake Dove immediately sets the mood for what is to follow. The cars, day-trippers and litter soon vanish and the shapes, noises and smells of the landscape take control of our imagination. The steep craggy form of Cradle Mountain looms to the left, its outline in stark contrast to the smooth glacial pools of Lake Dove, Lake Hanson and Lake Wilks. Once on the plateau the first boardwalk appears, allowing us to plod along with comfortably dry feet. There is over 60km of boardwalk along the length of the track, since a huge number of people now tramp up and down it.

As we walk through the cirques and glacial troughs, the formations around Waterfall Valley Hut remind me of school textbooks of dinosaurs and prehistoric man: the dramatic peak of Barn Bluff emerging from the moist clouds; Mount Ossa silhouetted against the sky, inviting us to scale its rocky flank. Summer offers no predictable weather patterns: hot sun, cold rain and biting winds, all within a few hours, are common. The night's damp chill requires good sleeping bags, even in the huts with their warm coal stoves. Conversation here is lively; energized by fresh air and physical activity, people really talk.

Most of the day is spent dealing with what is immediately around us, driving rain on Pine Forest Moor, muddy slopes at Frog Flats, leeches everywhere, and a rumbling stomach. The large numbers of wallabies and snakes add to a sense that man has not managed to interfere too much with this particular place. Being able to drink clean water (the colour of tea) from a stream is a bonus most people appreciate. Frequent rain washes down the mountainsides and over buttongrass plains, filling the various rivers and spectacular waterfalls southwest of Kia Ora Hut.

The last stretch of the track is along the length of Lake St Clair. For a more remote final day, we take the track behind Mount Olympus. The scenery is less spectacular than at the Cradle Mountain end but impressive nonetheless, with Bryons Gap giving wonderful views of the Franklin Lower Gordon Wild Rivers National Park and of Frenchmans Cap. Without the guiding trail of boardwalk, a good eye for post-spotting is needed. This part is particularly leech-infested and even more like a set from *The Land That Time Forgot*. We take our time savouring the tranquil beauty of Lake Petrarch, disturbing a sleeping snake and watching it uncoil and escape. The forests of ghost gums sway with the coming of a storm, and a sleepless night is spent underneath a creaking bough as thunder rattles along the valley.

The direct walk generally takes six days – five, if you catch a boat from Narcissus Hut across Lake St Clair; if you want to go on some of the side-walks, allow eight to ten days. On average, most walkers go for six to eight days. You should take enough food and fuel, plus extra supplies in case you have an accident or bad weather sets in; there's always plenty of unpolluted fresh water to drink from streams. Around 4500 people walk the track each year; most people come between November and April, but the best time is during February and March when the weather has stabilized, though it's bound to rain at some point, and may even snow. From Christmas to the end of January the track is at its most crowded with up to fifty. Most people walk north to south, which is more downhill than up, but you can register at either end in the **national park office** (see below), where you receive an obligatory briefing and have your gear checked to make sure it's sufficient; if you haven't already got some sort of park pass, you'll have to purchase one. The office sells last-minute camping gear and supplies: fuel stoves, meths, water bottles, trowels, warm hats and gloves. The *Cradle Mountain–Lake St Clair National Park* **map** and notes ($9) is an essential purchase, and the *Overland Track Walkers Notebook* ($8.95) is a handy reference. Once you end up at Derwent Bridge, exhausted and covered in mud, you can use the hot showers at the campsite, for which there's a small charge.

The logistics of doing a one-way walk are smoothed by a couple of operators: Maxwell's Coaches can do **transfers** to get you back to your car, while Tasmanian Wilderness Travel has special Overland Track fares which include transfers from Launceston to Cradle Mountain, and then back from Lake St Clair to Launceston or Hobart ($69; $75 if you start in Hobart). They can provide baggage transfer for an extra charge. **Guided tours** are available, the best offered by Craclair Walking Holidays (Oct–April; eight days $1085, ten days $1380; ☎ & fax 03/6424 7833); you'll still have to camp and carry a six-kilo pack, however; cheaper tours (where you have more to carry) are offered by Tas Expeditions (☎03/6334 3477, fax 6334 3463; eight days $940). The easiest option is to stay at *Cradle Huts* (☎03/6331 2006, fax 6331 5525; six days $1450 departing and returning Launceston), staying along the track at private lodges with hot showers, beds and delicious meals.

Cradle Mountain practicalities

At **Cradle Mountain**, the impressive modern **Cradle Mountain Visitor Centre** (daily 8am–5pm, later in summer; ☎03/6492 1133) provides information on the many day-walks available in this area of the park, and acts as a registration point for the Overland Track; it's worth buying the *Cradle Mountain Day Walk Map* ($4) for more information. You can start here with a gentle ten-minute boardwalk circuit through rainforest and overlooking **Pencil Pine Falls**, ideal for wheelchairs or strollers. There's also the "Enchanted Walk" which follows the creek through rainforest to *Cradle Mountain Lodge* (1km one-way; 20min). Five kilometres into the park from the visitor centre, **Waldheim** ("Forest Home" in German), is the King Billy pine chalet built by the Austrian-Australian **Gustave Weindorfer** in 1912, and now a museum (open 24 hours; free) devoted to the man who loved this wilderness area and helped to have it declared a national park. From **Lake Dove car park**, 2.5km on from Waldheim, you can take the Dove Lake circuit (2–3hr), an easy all-weather walk around the shore of the lake, or a popular, but steep and strenuous, day-walk from here to the summit of **Cradle Mountain** (6hr return; get advice from the ranger first). If you're feeling lazy, you can opt for a scenic flight (Nov–May only) over the area with Seaair (☎03/6492 1132; from $75 for 25min), who are based by the *Cradle View Airport Restaurant* (see opposite).

Just on the edge of the national park, and within walking distance of the visitor centre, *Cradle Mountain Lodge* (☎03/6492 1303, fax 6492 1309; lodge ⑥, cabins ⑨) is the focus for **accommodation**, eating and drinking. Scattered through the bush around the lodge, which has only two bedrooms, are 96 luxurious serviced timber cabins, all with log fires, kitchenettes and bathrooms. At the lodge itself, guest facilities include lounges, a sauna – with a window providing bush views – a massage room ($30 for 30min) and free movies shown each night. Non-guests can book in to eat at the classy **restaurant**, or drop in to eat or drink at the tavern **bar** – if you're there at 9.15pm you might catch a Tasmanian Devil creeping up for food from a lodge employee. You can hire **bicycles** from the lodge, there's a **general store** selling expensive groceries, and fuel is available (no diesel). *Cradle Mountain Tourist Park* (☎03/6492 1395, fax 6492 1438), 2km back along Cradle Mountain Road, has a **campsite**, two hostel-style heated **bunkhouses** ($20 per person; bedding $5) sharing kitchen, toilet and washing facilities with the campers, and some basic huts (②) plus well set-up cabins sleeping up to six (⑥), complete with TV and air-conditioning. The campsite has a small **shop** and is linked to the lodge in summer by a shuttle bus. Near the campsite entrance the licensed fast-food/bistro-style *Cradle View Airport Restaurant* also sells petrol and diesel (daily 8.30am–8pm). A bit further on, 1.5km from the park entrance, there's more accommodation at *Cradle Mountain Highlander Cabins* (☎03/6492 1116, fax 6492 1188; ⑥–⑧). In the park itself, there are eight basic self-catering huts (④–⑤) at Waldheim (see above), which sleep four to eight people with generator electricity, pot-bellied stoves, no fridge or power points, and a shared amenities block – these are looked after by the National Park Visitor Centre.

Lake St Clair and Derwent Bridge practicalities

You can register to walk the Overland Track in the opposite direction at the ranger station at **CYNTHIA BAY** on **Lake St Clair** (daily 8am–5pm; ☎03/6289 1115), which houses an informative interpretive centre, and an attractive bistro restaurant with views over the lake. Short and long **walks** around Lake St Clair are detailed on a board in the centre. You can go on a **cruise** on the *MV Idaclair*, which will drop you off at Narcissus Hut to begin the Overland Track from the other end, or walk back to the centre (5–6 hours); alternatively, get off at Eccho Point and return on a three-hour bushwalk (summer: Cynthia Bay 9am, 12.30pm & 3pm; Narcissus Hut 9.30am, 1pm & 3.30pm; in winter the ferry runs on demand; $15, $20 return; bookings essential; round-trip 1hr 30min). Tickets are sold at the **restaurant**, where you can also rent dinghies with outboard motors, canoes, kayaks and bicycles.

The restaurant also takes bookings for **accommodation**. *Lakeside St Clair Wilderness Holidays* (☎03/6289 1137, fax 6289 1250; ⑧), has several luxury lodges, and a backpackers' lodge (①). Compared to Cradle Mountain, the **campsite** here is poor – there's no kitchen and there's a 50¢ fee to use the showers. For supplies (and takeaway alcohol), you have to go to to **DERWENT BRIDGE**, 5km away on the Lyell Highway, served by Maxwell's Coaches (☎03/6492 1431) whose shuttle service ($5) runs on demand. At Derwent Bridge the focus of the community is the *Derwent Bridge Hotel* (☎03/6289 1144, fax 6289 1173), where you can enjoy excellent **food** and drink sitting near one of the biggest fireplaces you'll ever see. You can also stay here in old-fashioned lodge-style **accommodation** (④–⑤), but the rooms (some en-suite) are rather shabby, as are the **hostel rooms** (②; no kitchen) out back. There's more comfort in the luxurious self-catering units (sleeping four to eight) at *Derwent Bridge Chalets* across the road, run by the service station (☎03/6289 1125, fax 6289 1230; ⑦). Derwent Bridge is close to **Lake King William**, equivalent in size to Lake St Clair and popular with anglers.

Franklin Lower Gordon Wild Rivers National Park

The **Franklin Lower Gordon Wild Rivers National Park** was declared in June 1980 and by 1982 had been included with the adjoining parks on the World Heritage List. The park exists for its own sake more than anything, most of it being virtually inaccessible.

RAFTING ON THE FRANKLIN

One of the most rugged and inaccessible areas left on earth, the surrounds of the Franklin River can't really be seen on foot – there are few tracks through this twisted, tangled and wet rainforest. **Rafting** is the only way to explore the river and even this is possible only between December and early April. The Franklin is reached by rafting down the Collingwood River from the Lyell Highway, 49km west of Derwent Bridge. The full trip takes eight to fourteen days, ending at the Gordon River, where rafters head finally to Strahan by yacht from Heritage Landing or by seaplane from Sir John Falls Camp.

One of the most dangerous Australian rivers to raft, with average **rapids** of grades 3 to 4 – and up to grade 6 in places – the Franklin requires an expedition leader with great skill and experience (though even guides have died in the rapids). It's also very remote, and in the event of an accident help can be days away. However, this haunting isolation is part of the attraction for most visitors. The weather, too, can be harsh – and the water is cold. It's inadvisable to attempt the trip **independently** unless everyone in the party has white-water experience and the group leader has made a previous Franklin River trip; groups are required to have at least two rafts and to stay in contact with the **ranger** at Queenstown. Bear in mind that there's nowhere to rent rafting equipment in Tasmania. The **tour operators** don't require you to be experienced – just fit, with lots of stamina and courage. **Prices** are high, but this is an experience of a lifetime, with the seaplane flight back to Strahan included in the price. The one Tasmanian-based licensed operator is **Rafting Tasmania** (☎03/6239 1080, fax 6239 1090). The others are based in Melbourne: Peregrine Adventures (☎03/9662 2800, fax 9663 8618) and World Expeditions (☎03/9264 3366, fax 9261 1974). For the shorter five-day trip from Propsting Gorge to the Gordon, expect to pay around $1100; for the full eleven-day trip from the Collingwood to the Gordon prices start at $1650.

The sketchy *Franklin River Rafting Notesheets* are available free from the Queenstown Ranger Station, PO Box 21, Queenstown, Tasmania 7467 (☎03/6471 2511) or you can download a copy from the Internet (*www.parks.tas.gov.au*). There are **campsites** all along the Franklin, but most have room for only two or three tents.

THE ROUTE

From the **Collingwood River**, it takes about three days to raft to the **Frenchmans Cap Track**. This is the **Upper Franklin**, alpine country with vegetation adapted to survive snow and icy winds. Watch out for two endemic pines, the **Huon pine** and **Celery Top pine**. There are lots of intermediate rapids along this stretch and a deep quartzite ravine and large still pool at Irenabyss.

The **Middle Franklin** is a mixture of pools, deep ravines and wild rapids as the river makes a fifty-kilometre detour around Frenchmans Cap. Dramatic **limestone cliffs** overhang the **Lower Franklin**, which involves a tranquil paddle through dense myrtle beech forests with flowering leatherwoods overhead. The best raftable white water is here at Newlands Cascades. It's a short distance to **Kutikina Caves** and **Deena-reena**; only rafters can gain access to these Aboriginal caves.

You can cruise up the Gordon, or fly over it, but the really adventurous can explore by **rafting the Franklin** (see box above) and walking the **Frenchmans Cap Track**, both accessible from the **Lyell Highway**, which extends from Strahan to Hobart and runs through the park between Queenstown and Derwent Bridge. There are also plenty of short **walks** leading from the highway to rainforest, rivers and lookouts.

The **Franklin River** is one of the great rivers of Australia, and the only major wild river system in Tasmania that's not been dammed. It flows for 120km from the Cheyne Range to the majestic **Gordon River**, from an altitude of 1400m down to almost sea level. Swollen by the storms of the Roaring Forties and fed by many other rivers, it can at times become a raging torrent as it passes through ancient heaths, deep gorges and rainforests. The discovery in 1981 of stone tools in the **Kutikina Cave** on the lower Franklin has proved that during the last ice age southwest Tasmania was the most southerly point of human occupation on earth.

A **seaplane** from Strahan flies over the national park (see p.977), and from it you can see the confluence of the two rivers – the planned site of the ill-fated dam – surrounded by thick forest, much of it impenetrable and probably never traversed by humans. The Gordon appears wide and slow compared to the narrow, winding Franklin. From above, the forest reveals its beautiful combination of textures and colours, the delicate white and greens of the myrtle, pines and other trees a complete contrast to the typical Australian scene of dusty green gums shading to blue in the distance.

Along the Lyell Highway

Heading east from Queenstown, the Lyell Highway enters the Franklin Lower Gordon Wild Rivers National Park, reaching Nelson River bridge after 4km, from where **Nelson Falls** is an easy twenty-minute-return walk through temperate rainforest. From here, the road begins to wind and rise up to **Collingwood River**, the starting point for raft or canoe trips down the Franklin (see box opposite), with some basic camping facilities.

In fine weather, the white quartzite dome of Frenchmans Cap, looking a little like snow, can be seen from the highway. For a more spectacular viewpoint that takes in the Franklin River Valley, **Donaghy's Hill Wilderness Lookout Walk** begins further along the highway on the right. Walk from the parking area along the old road to the top of the hill, where a sign marks the beginning of the forty-minute-return track. Further along the highway, the **walking track to Frenchmans Cap** (see below) begins with a fifteen-minute stroll to the suspension bridge over the river. Continuing on the Lyell, you have another opportunity to see the Franklin on a ten-minute **Nature Trail**, at a point where the river is tranquil, as it flows around large boulders; there's also a longer 25-minute circuit. At the start of the trail there's a picnic area and a wooden shelter with an **interpretive board** about the river. Beyond this point, open buttongrass plains take over, huge uninhabited expanses fringed with trees. This is **Wombat Glen**, which looks as though it's been cleared into grazing country until you step out into it and discover its bog-like nature.

At the foot of **Mount Arrowsmith**, the highway begins to ascend, winding around the mountain's southern side above the U-shaped glacial Surprise Valley. The **Surprise Valley Lookout** offers a good view of the valley and, across to the southwest, another excellent aspect of Frenchmans Cap. Continuing down, you come to King William Saddle, another fine lookout point with views of the **King William Range** to the south and **Mount Rufus** to the north.

The Frenchmans Cap Track

The most prominent mountain peak in the Franklin Lower Gordon Wild Rivers National Park is the white quartzite dome of **Frenchmans Cap** (1443m). Its southeast face has a sheer five-hundred-metre cliff and from its summit there are uninterrupted views of Mount Ossa in the Cradle Mountain–Lake St Clair National Park, Federation Peak, Macquarie Harbour and, on a fine day, the whole of the southwest wilderness. It takes three to five days to do the 54-kilometre return trip to the summit, best done between December and March, though you'll be in the company of another nine hundred or so people. Frenchmans Cap is much more demanding than the relatively straightforward Overland Track, as it has some very steep extended climbs and sections of mud, and should be attempted only by skilled bushwalkers – preferably with experience of other Tasmanian walks. The weather is temperamental: it rains frequently, and it can snow even in summer. Beyond Barron Pass, the track is above 900m and at any time of the year is subject to high winds, mist, rain, hail and snowfalls.

The track begins at the Lyell Highway, 55km from Queenstown, served by Tasmanian Wilderness Travel's scheduled Hobart–Queenstown service (☎03/6334 4442; 1 daily Tues, Thurs, Sat & Sun), or you can charter Maxwell's Coaches (☎03/6492 1431) for $60 from Devonport or Launceston or $10 from Lake St Clair. A fifteen-minute walk from the road brings you to the suspension bridge across the river for the start of the walk. Record your plans in the registration book here and again in the logbook at the two **huts** at Lake Vera and Lake Tahune that provide basic accommodation (though this is usually full and you must bring tents and stoves with you); Frenchmans Cap is a proclaimed "Fuel Stove Only Area". There are composting toilets at both huts and plenty of camping spots along the way; water along the track is safe to drink. From the Franklin River to Lake Vera the well-defined track crosses plains and foothills, then becomes steep and rough as it climbs to Barron Pass, where there are magnificent views, becoming easier again on the way to Lake Tahune, close to the cliffs of Frenchmans Cap. From here it's a steep one-kilometre walk to the summit, before returning the same way.

For further **information**, get the free *Frenchmans Cap Track Bushwalker Notes* from Service Tasmania, 134 Macquarie St, Hobart 7000; you can also buy the *Frenchmans Cap Map and Notes* ($9) there; or contact the Queenstown Ranger Station (☎03/6471 2511). If you don't feel equipped to tackle the walk independently, contact Craclair Walking Holidays (☎ & fax 03/6424 7833; $1195), which organizes seven-day guided treks.

The South West National Park

Tasmania's **southwest** is an area of contrast: arrow-sharp, crested ranges of white quartzite cut across buttongrass plains. The isolation, rough terrain and unpredictable weather, even in summer – the southwest has more than two hundred days of rain a year – means that this is an area for experienced bushwalkers only. Being able to use a compass and read a map are important, but so is a tolerance for trudging through deep mud and swampy buttongrass while heavily laden with supplies and plagued by leeches.

The map *South Coast Walks* ($9) covers the southern gateways to the World Heritage Area: Cockle Creek through Port Davey to Scotts Peak, as well as Moonlight Ridge and South West Cape, including notes on track conditions, weather and campsites. For the rest of the area you'll need to purchase Tasmap topographic **maps**; and for detailed information refer to John Chapman's *South West Tasmania*, published by Lonely Planet.

Two airlines operate **flights** into the national park from Cambridge aerodrome, 15km from Hobart. Par Avion (☎03/6248 5390, fax 6248 5117) runs eighty percent of flights to the southwest, with a daily service to Melaleuca, weather permitting ($95 one-way); they also offer a combined scenic flight and cruise on Bathurst Harbour (4hr; $140; all day including lunch $240); you can register your walk at the airstrip, where the same company operates a **Wilderness Camp** ($485 for two days, including flight, camp accommodation and meals); they also have a boat, the *MV Southern Explorer*, based here on Bathurst Harbour with on-board accommodation, which cruises the harbour, Port Davey and the Davey River (two days and two nights from $850). Tas Air (☎03/6248 5577) flies to Melaleuca, Cox Bight or Scotts Peak ($98 per person one-way; $190 return), which can cut out the trudge from Melaleuca, and they also offer joyrides over the whole of the World Heritage Area for $145 (2hr 30min includes a landing and refreshment at Cox Bight). If you're planning an extended walk, you can arrange for either airline to drop food supplies for you ($2–4 per kilo).

Unless you're flying in, or beginning a walk at **Cockle Creek** (see p.926), south of Hobart, access to the South West National Park is via the **Strathgordon Road**, which passes to the south of Mount Field National Park. The ranger for this (northern) end

PEDDER 2000: THE RESURRECTION OF LAKE PEDDER

To Dr Bob Brown, Tasmania's foremost Green activist, and now Senator, Lake Pedder "was one of the most gently beautiful places on the planet". The glacial lake, in the Frankland Range in Tasmania's southwest, had an area of 9.7 square kilometres until 1972, when it and the surrounding valleys were flooded as part of a huge hydroelectric scheme, creating a reservoir covering a massive 240 square kilometres and reached by the Lake Gordon Road via Maydena. Before then, the lake was so inaccessible that it could only be visited by light aircraft, which used to land on the perfect sand of the lake beach.

Pedder 2000 is a visionary campaign spearheaded by the Wilderness Society in 1995, the aim of which is to drain the current Lake Pedder by the turn of the century and restore it to its former glory. However, as of 1997 the timescale didn't look too promising. In late 1994 a scientist revealed that, beneath the water, the sandy beach remained; and in 1995 divers filmed underwater, revealing the still-visible impressions of tyre tracks from the light aircraft that once landed there. The cost of draining the lake would be high and most politicians are opposed to the idea, belligerently declaring that a "large and smelly puddle" would be the only result. Certain scientists and conservationists, however, do consider it possible for the lake to revert to its former state, even though it might take twenty or thirty years. A decision to drain the stored water would need the vision and permission of both the state and federal governments, and it may yet come to a struggle between the two governments in the High Court in Canberra. Though the lake obviously will not be drained in the year 2000, the Pedder 2000 name and campaign remains; for more information and to provide support, the Pedder 2000 head office is at 130 Davey St, Hobart, TAS 7000, or check out their Web site which includes essays, submissions and even poems (*neptune.he.net/~pedder/*).

of South West National Park is based at Mount Field, and you should drop in or call (☎03/6288 1283) to ask about conditions and to check that you're adequately prepared. The good sealed road heads through state forest and the South West Conservation Area, where the amazing craggy landforms of the **Frankland Range** loom above and signposts helpfully point out the names of the features, and past the drowned **Lake Pedder** (see box above) and the **Gordon Dam's power station** (underground tours daily: May & Aug–Nov 11am, Dec–April 10am & 2pm; 40min; $5). The road to **Scotts Peak**, where the walks begin, is very poor but Tasmanian Wilderness Travel runs a "Wilderness" service there and to Condominium Creek from Hobart, via Mount Field (Nov Tues & Thurs; Dec–April Tues, Thurs, Sat & Sun; no service May–Sept).

Western Arthurs Traverse

The most spectacular bushwalk in Tasmania, only 20km in length and 5km in width, **Western Arthurs Traverse** contains 25 major peaks and 30 lakes. The last glacial period gouged into this range, leaving sharp quartzite ridges, craggy towers and impressive cliffs, and carving cirque valleys that are now filled by dark, tannin-stained lakes, surrounded by contrasting buttongrass plains. Violent storms, mists and continuous rain can plague the route in summer since it's in the direct path of the Roaring Forties. Crossing these ranges makes for a superb but difficult walk. Though there's no manmade track, the route, starting at Scotts Peak Road, is not difficult to follow; it involves scrambling over roots and branches and making short descents and ascents into gullies and cliff lines, and you'll need to use a rope at some point. The whole walk takes between nine and twelve days, and camping areas are limited.

The **Eastern Arthur Range** is the location of the major goal for intrepid southwest walkers – **Federation Peak**, often considered the most challenging in Australia, with its steep, almost perfectly triangular outline rising starkly above the surrounding rugged peaks and ridges. It was named by a surveyor in 1901, the year of Federation, when most of the major landmarks in the southwest were still unvisited; in fact, the peak was not successfully scaled until 1949, its thick scrub, forests and cliffs having kept walkers at bay. Although the walk is now easier since the terrain has been "broken in", each year many walkers are turned back by the worst weather in Tasmania, and one person has died tackling the route. All the ascents are extremely difficult, and most parties take between seven and ten days to reach the peak and return; minor rock climbing is required to get to the summit. The walk begins at the same point as the Port Davey Track (see below).

Mount Anne Circuit

The highest peak in the southwest, **Mount Anne** (1423m) is part of a small range capped with red dolerite – a contrast to the surrounding white quartzite. Views from the summit are spectacular in fine weather, but even in summer the route is very exposed and prone to bad weather. It's suitable only for experienced walkers carrying a safety rope. The three- to four-day walk begins 20km along Scotts Peak Road at Condominium Creek (where there are basic camping facilities) and ends 9km south at Red Tape Creek; a car shuttle might be advisable, or you can arrange with Tasmanian Wilderness Travel (☎03/6334 4442) to be picked up and dropped off from Hobart.

Port Davey Track

Going straight through the heart of the World Heritage Area, from Scotts Peak Dam south to Melaleuca (where you fly out; see p.984) at Port Davey, is the 54km **Port Davey Track**, a wet, muddy four- to five-day trek over buttongrass plains, with views of rugged mountain ranges along the way. Only around 200 people walk the track each year. It's less interesting than some of the other walks in the area and most groups combine it with the **South Coast Track** (see below) for a ten- to sixteen-day wilderness experience, which requires a drop-off of food supplies. This combined walk is often called the **South West Track**. Contact Tasmanian Wilderness Travel if you want to arrange drop-offs.

South Coast Track

The **South Coast Track** is known for its magnificent **beaches** and spectacular coastal scenery of Aboriginal **middens**, rainforest and buttongrass ridges. At 80km, it's one of the longest tracks in the South West National Park – a five- to ten-day moderate to difficult walk, usually done from Melaleuca east to Cockle Creek. Since the route is mostly along the coast, the climate is milder than in many parts of the World Heritage Area; however, you'll still need wet-weather gear as it tends to rain frequently. Though the track is regularly maintained, you do need to plough through sections of mud and across the exposed Ironbound Range (900m), which should be attempted only in fine weather. There are no huts along the way, except at the Melaleuca airstrip. Around 2000 people do the walk each year, seventy-five percent of them between December and March. The best **approach** is to fly direct to Cox Bight, cutting out the boring buttongrass plains walk from Melaleuca, then head for Cockle Creek. Alternatively, you can begin at Cockle Creek and get flown out at Melaleuca with Tas Air or Par Avion, or arrange for extra food supplies to be flown in at Melaleuca and continue along the Port Davey Track across the water, using the rowboats provided.

Tasmanian Expeditions (☎03/6334 3477, fax 6334 3463) runs an extended **organized walk** of the South Coast Track (Dec–Feb; $1095). You need to be very fit for the nine-day trip, as each party member (maximum of ten) carries a share of the food and tents, a weight of 18–20kg.

South West Cape
The granite South West Cape juts out for 3km into the wild Southern Ocean. **Walking** is fairly easy here, though the rough unmarked tracks across open countryside require sound navigation, and some high windy ridges have to be crossed. All routes start and end at Melaleuca or Cox Bight but there are a variety of ways to the cape and beyond, taking in different beaches and bays. Depending on which you choose, a simple route will take from three to seven days, and the full circuit between six and nine. Because of the growing popularity of the walks, they may be overcrowded in the summer months.

travel details

BETWEEN TASMANIA AND THE MAINLAND STATES
Ferries
Spirit of Tasmania Bass Strait **ferry**: from Port Melbourne (Mon, Wed & Fri 6pm), returning from Devonport (Tues, Thurs & Sat 6pm); journey time 14hr 30min.

Devil Cat Bass Strait **high speed catamaran**: from Port Melbourne to George Town (January to April: departing Port Melbourne Tues, Thurs, Sat & Sun 7.30am; departing George Town Wed, Fri, Sat & Sun 4pm); journey time six hours.

Flights
Mainly through Sydney's Mascot or Melbourne's Tullamarine airports, with smaller companies operating from Moorabbin airport, on the fringes of Melbourne, and Traralgon in Victoria's Gippsland region.

Flinders Island to: Launceston (2–4 daily; 45min); Melbourne (Tullamarine 4 weekly, Moorabbin 5 weekly; 50min); Sale (3 weekly; 45min).

King Island to: Burnie (1–2 daily except Sat; 45min); Devonport (1–2 daily except Sat); Melbourne (Tullamarine 1 daily, Moorabbin 2–4 daily; 45min).

Melbourne to: Burnie (9 daily; 1hr); Devonport (12 daily; 1hr); Flinders Island (Tullamarine 4 weekly, Moorabbin 5 weekly; 50min); Hobart (10 daily; 1hr); King Island (Tullamarine 1–2 daily, Moorabbin 2–4 daily; 45min); Launceston (10 daily; 1hr).

Sydney to: Hobart (4 daily; 2hr 20min); Launceston (4 daily; 2hr 35min).

Traralgon to: Flinders Island (4 weekly; 45min); Launceston (4 weekly; 1hr).

TRANSPORT ON THE ISLAND
Buses
We have only included **scheduled services** in this list. Extra "Wilderness" services, which need a minimum of four people to depart, are provided by Tasmanian Wilderness Travel to all bushwalking destinations, and some operate in the summer only. These are all detailed in the text of the *Guide*.

Burnie to: Smithton via the northwest coast (1–3 daily except Sun; 1hr 30min).

Deloraine to: Devonport (3 daily; 40min); Hobart (2–4 daily; 4hr); Launceston (3–5 daily; 45min).

Devonport to: Burnie (3–6 daily; 50min); Cradle Mountain (3 weekly; 2hr 15min); Deloraine (3 daily; 40min); Hobart (2–4 daily; 5hr 30min); Launceston (3–5 daily; 1hr 30min); Queenstown (3 weekly; 7hr).

Hobart to: Bicheno (5–6 weekly; 4hr); Burnie (3–6 daily; 4hr 45min); Deloraine (2–4 daily; 4hr); Devonport (2–4 daily; 5hr 30min); Dover (2 daily Mon–Fri; 55min); Geeveston (1–5 daily except Sat; 55min); Kettering (Mon–Fri 4 daily; 40min); Lake St Clair (4 weekly; 3hr); Launceston (3–7 daily; 2hr 30min); New Norfolk (1–7 daily; 30min); Port Arthur (Mon–Fri 2 daily; 2hr); Queenstown via New Norfolk, Lake St Clair & Frenchmans Cap with connections to Strahan (4 weekly; 7hr 45min); Richmond (Mon–Fri 4 daily; 30min); St Helens (1–2 daily except Sat; 3hr); St Marys (1–2 daily except Sat; 3hr); Swansea (1–2 daily except Sat; 2hr 30min–3hr 30min).

Launceston to: Bicheno (1–2 daily except Sat; 2hr 40min); Burnie (3–6 daily; 3hr); Cradle Mountain (3 weekly; 4hr); Deloraine (3–5 daily; 45min); Derby (1–2 daily except Sat; 2hr 40min); Devonport (3–5 daily; 1hr 30min); Hobart (3–7 daily; 2hr 30min); Mole Creek (1 daily Mon–Fri; 1hr 30min); St Helens via St Marys (1 daily except Sat; 2hr 45min).

PART THREE

THE

CONTEXTS

A HISTORY

The first European settlers saw Australia as *terra nullius* – empty land – on the principle that Aborigines didn't "use" the country in an agricultural sense, a belief which remained uncontested in law until 1992. However, decades of archeological work, the reports of early settlers and oral tradition have established a minimum date of forty thousand years for human occupation, and evidence that Aboriginal peoples shaped, controlled and used their environment as surely as any farmer. Even so, it's difficult for visitors to form a unified idea of pre-colonial times, as two centuries of European rule shattered traditional Aboriginal life, and evidence of those earlier times mostly consists of cryptic art sites and legends – though if you're lucky enough to get beyond the tourist image, you'll realize that Aboriginal culture, though being redefined, is far from confined to the past. The very simplified outline of Aboriginal history below is intended mainly as a background to accounts given in the *Guide*, followed by a fuller description of the years since European colonization.

FROM GONDWANA TO THE DREAMTIME

After the break-up of the supercontinent Gondwana into India, Africa, South America, Australasia and Antarctica, Australia moved away from the South Pole, reaching its current geographical location about fifteen million

years ago. Though the mainland was periodically joined to New Guinea and Tasmania, there was never a land link with the rest of Asia, and the country developed a unique fauna – most notably the marsupials, or pouched mammals, but also a whole range of giant animals, the megafauna – which flourished, along with widespread rainforests, until about fifty thousand years ago. Subsequent ice ages dried out the climate, and though some of the megafauna survived into Aboriginal times, by six thousand years ago the seas had stabilized at their present levels and Australia's environment was much as it appears today: an arid centre with a relatively fertile eastern seaboard.

Humans had been in Australia long before then, of course, most likely taking advantage of low sea levels to cross the Timor Trough into northern Australia, or island-hop from Indonesia onto what is now the Cape York Peninsula via New Guinea. Exactly when this happened, how many times it happened and what the colonists did next are debatable. There's no direct evidence for either distinct or continuous migrations from Asia, but since the earliest dated sites are found in the south of Australia, it seems reasonable that human occupation goes back further than scientists' current forty-thousand-year estimates. The oldest known remains from central Australia are only 22,000 years old, so it's also fairly plausible that initial colonization occurred around the coast, followed by later exploration of the interior – though it's just as likely that corrosive rainforests, which covered the centre until about twenty thousand years ago, obliterated all trace of earlier human habitation. The presence of the dingo and disappearance of the **thylacine** (Tasmanian tiger) on the mainland but not (until recently) in Tasmania indicates that there was a further influx of people and **dogs** more recently than twelve thousand years ago, after Tasmania had become an island.

The earliest inhabitants used crude **stone implements**, gradually replaced by a more refined technology based around lighter tools, **boomerangs**, and the use of core stones to flake "blanks" which were then fashioned into spearheads, knives and scrapers. As only certain types of stone were suitable for the process, tribes living away from quarries had to trade with those living near them. **Trade networks** for rock, **ochre** (a red clay used for ceremonial purposes) and other products –

shells and even wood for canoes – eventually reached from New Guinea to the heart of the continent, following river systems away from the coast. **Rock art**, preserved in an ancient engraved tradition and more recent painted styles, seems to indicate that cultural links also travelled along these trade routes – similar symbols and styles are found in widely separated regions.

It's probable that the disappearance of the megafauna was accelerated by Aboriginal hunting, but the most dramatic change wrought by the original Australians was the controlled use of **fire** to clear areas of forest. Burning promoted new growth and encouraged game, indirectly expanding grassland and favouring certain plants – cycads, grasstrees, banksias and eucalypts – which evolved fire-reliant seeds and growth patterns. But while the Aborigines modified the environment for their own ends, their belief that land, wildlife and people were an interdependent whole engendered a sympathy for the natural processes, and maintained a balance between population and natural resources. Tribes were organized and related according to complex kinship systems, reflected in the three hundred different **languages** known to exist at that time. Legends about the mythical **Dreamtime**, when creative forces roamed the land, provided **verbal maps** of tribal territory and linked natural features to the actions of these Dreamtime ancestors, who often had both human and animal forms. This spiritual and practical attachment to tribal areas was expedient in terms of use of resources, but was the weak point in maintaining a culture after white dispossession: separated from the lands they related to, legends lost their meaning – and the people their sense of identity.

THE FIRST EUROPEANS

Prior to the sixteenth century, the only regular visitors to Australia were the **Malays**, who established seasonal camps while fishing the northern coasts for bêche de mer, a sea slug, to sell to the Chinese. In Europe, the globe had been carved up between Spain and Portugal in 1494 under the auspices of Pope Alexander VI at the **Treaty of Tordesillas**, and all maritime nations subsequently kept their nautical charts secret to protect their discoveries. Therefore it's likely, but not certain, that the inquisitive **Portuguese** knew of **Terra Australis**, the

Great Southern Land, soon after founding their colony in East Timor in 1516.

But while contemporary politics later confused the issue of "discovery", various nations were making forays into the area: the **Dutch** in 1605 and 1623, who were appalled by the harsh climate and inhabitants of Outback Queensland, and the **Spanish** in 1606, looking for plunder, and pagans to convert to Catholicism. Guided by the Portuguese **Luis Vaes de Torres**, they blithely navigated the strait between New Guinea and Cape York – as if they knew it was there. Torres probably did; there's evidence that the Portuguese had **mapped** a large portion of Australia's northern coastline as early as 1536.

Later in the seventeenth century the Dutch navigators **Dirk Hartog**, **Van Diemen** and **Abel Tasman** added to maps of the east and northern coasts, but eventually discarded "New Holland" as a barren, worthless country. **British interests** were first stirred in 1697 by **William Dampier**, a buccaneer who wrote popular accounts of his visit to Western Australia, but it wasn't until the British captured the Spanish port of Manila in the Philippines in 1762 that detailed maps of Australia's coast fell into their hands; it took them only six more years to assemble an expedition to locate the continent. Sailing in 1768 on the *Endeavour*, Captain **James Cook** headed to Tahiti (where scientists observed the movements of the planet Venus), then proceeded to map New Zealand's coastline before sailing west in 1770 to search for the Great Southern Land – unsure whether this was New Holland or an as yet undiscovered landmass.

The British sighted the continent in April of 1770 and sailed north from Cape Everard to **Botany Bay**, where Cook commented on the Aborigines' initial indifference to seeing the *Endeavour*. When a party of forty sailors attempted to land, however, two Aborigines attacked them with spears and had to be driven off by musket fire. Continuing on up the Queensland coast, they passed Moreton Bay and Fraser Island before entering the treacherous passages of the Great Barrier Reef where, on June 11, the *Endeavour* ran aground off Cape Tribulation. Cook managed to beach the ship safely at the mouth of the Endeavour River (present-day Cooktown), where the expedition set up camp while the ship was repaired.

Contact between Aborigines and whites during the following six weeks was tinged with a mistrust that never quite erupted into a serious confrontation, and Cook took the opportunity to make notes in which he tempered romanticism for the "noble savage" with the sharp observation that European and Aboriginal values were mutually incomprehensible. The expedition was intrigued by some of the wildlife but otherwise unimpressed with the country, and were glad to sail onwards on August 5. With imposing skill, Cook successfully managed to navigate the rest of the reef, finally claiming Australia's eastern seaboard – which he named **New South Wales** – on August 21 in the name of King George III, at Possession Island in the Torres Strait, before sailing off to Timor.

CONVICTS

The expedition's reports still didn't arouse much enthusiasm in London, where echoes resounded of the Portuguese and Dutch opinions of the previous century. The outcome of the **American War of Independence** in 1783, however, saw Britain deprived of anywhere to transport convicted criminals; they were temporarily housed in prison ships or "hulks", moored around the country, while the government tried to solve the problem. Sir **Joseph Banks**, botanist on the *Endeavour*, advocated Botany Bay as an ideal location for a **penal colony** that could soon become self-sufficient. The government agreed (perhaps also inspired by the political advantages of gaining a foothold in the Pacific), and in 1787 the **First Fleet**, consisting of between 750 and 821 convicts (the numbers are disputed) set sail for Australia on eleven ships under the command of Captain **Arthur Phillip**. Reaching Botany Bay in January 1788, Phillip deemed it unsuitable for his purposes and instead founded the settlement at **Sydney Cove**, on Port Jackson's fine natural harbour.

Early years at Sydney were not promising: the colonists suffered erratic weather and starvation, Aboriginal hostility, soil which was too hard to plough and timber which dented their axes. In 1790, supplies ran so low that a third of the population had to be transferred to a new colony on **Norfolk Island**, 1500 kilometres east. Even so, in the same year Britain dispatched a second fleet with 1000 convicts – 267 of whom died en route. To ease the situation, Phillip granted packages of farmland to marines and former convicts before he returned to

Britain in 1792. The first **free settlers** arrived the following year, while war with France reduced the numbers of convicts being transported to the colony, allowing a period of consolidation.

Meanwhile, **John Macarthur** manipulated the temporary governor into allowing his **New South Wales Corps**, which had replaced the marines as the governor's strong arm, to exercise considerable power in the colony. This was temporarily curtailed in 1800 by Philip King, who slowed an illicit rum trade, encouraged new settlements, and speeded production by allowing convicts to work for wages. Macarthur was forced out of the corps into the **wool industry**, importing Australia's first sheep from South Africa; but he continued to stir up trouble, which culminated in the **Rum Rebellion** of 1808, when merchant and pastoral factions, supported by the military, ousted Governor **William Bligh**, formerly of the *Bounty*. Britain finally took notice of the colony's anarchic state and appointed the firmhanded Colonel **Lachlan Macquarie**, backed by the 73rd Regiment, as Bligh's replacement in 1810. Macquarie settled the various disputes – Macarthur had fled to Britain a year earlier – and brought the colony eleven years of disciplined progress.

Labelled the "Father of Australia" for his vision of a country that could rise above its convict origins, Macquarie implemented enlightened policies towards former convicts or **emancipists**, enrolling them in public offices. He also attempted to educate, rather than exterminate, Aboriginal people, and was the driving force behind New South Wales becoming a productive, self-sufficient colony. But he offended the landowner **squatters**, who were concerned that emancipists were being granted too many favours, and also those who regarded the colony's prime purpose as a place of punishment. In fact, conditions had improved so much that by 1819 New South Wales had become the major destination for voluntary emigrants from Britain.

In 1821 Macquarie was replaced as governor, and his successor, Sir Thomas Brisbane, was instructed to segregate, not integrate, convicts. To this end, New South Wales officially graduated from being a penal settlement to a new British Colony in 1823, and convicts were used to colonize newly explored regions – Western

Australia, Tasmania and Queensland – as far away from Sydney's free settlers as possible.

EXPLORERS

Matthew Flinders had already circumnavigated the mainland in 1803 (suggesting the name "Australia") in his leaky vessel, *Investigator*, and with the colony firmly established, expeditions began pushing inland from Sydney. In 1823 John Oxley, the Surveyor General, having previously explored newly discovered pastoral land west of the Blue Mountains, chose the **Brisbane River** (in Queensland) as the site of a new penal colony; this opened up the fertile **Darling Downs** to future settlement. Meanwhile, townships were founded, leading to the creation of separate **states** to add to that of **Van Diemen's Land** (Tasmania), settled in 1803 to ward off French exploration: Albany (1827) and Fremantle on the west coast (1829), the Yarra River (Melbourne, Victoria) in 1835, and Adelaide (South Australia) in 1836.

But it was the possibilities of the **interior** – which some maintained concealed a vast inland sea – that captured the imagination of the government and squatters. Setting out from Adelaide in 1844, **Charles Sturt** was the first to attempt to cross the centre. Forced to camp for six months at a desert waterhole, where the heat melted the lead in his pencils and unthreaded screws from equipment, he managed to reach the aptly named Sturt's Stony Desert before scurvy forced him back to Adelaide. At the same time, **Ludwig Leichhardt**, a Prussian doctor, had more luck in his crossing between the Darling Downs and Port Essington (near Darwin), which he accomplished in fourteen months. Unlike Sturt, Leichhardt found plenty of potential farmland and returned a hero; however, he vanished in 1848 while again attempting to cross the continent. In the same year the ill-fated **Kennedy** expedition barely managed the trek from Tully to Cape York in northern Queensland, but with the loss of most of the party – Kennedy included – as a result of poor planning, starvation and attack by Aborigines. Similarly, **Burke and Wills**' successful 1860 south-to-north traverse between Melbourne and the Gulf of Carpentaria in Queensland was marred by the death of the expedition leaders (see box on p.486 for the full story of their trek). Finally, Australia's centre was located by **John MacDouall Stuart** in 1860, who subsequently managed a safe return journey from Adelaide to the north coast the following year. Hopes of finding an inland sea were quashed, and the harsh reality of a dry, largely infertile interior began to dawn on developers.

ABORIGINAL RESPONSE

European advances had been repulsed from the very first year of the colony's foundation, when Governor Phillip sadly reported that "the natives now attack any straggler they meet unarmed". Forced off their traditional hunting grounds, which were taken by the settlers for agriculture or grazing, the Aborigines began stealing crops and spearing cattle. Response from the whites was brutal; a relatively liberal Lieutenant-Governor **George Arthur** ordered a sweep of Tasmania in 1830 to round up all Aboriginal people and herd them into **reserves**, a symbolic attempt to clear "the uncivilized" from the paths of progress (see box on p.902). More direct action, such as the **Myall Creek Massacre** in 1838 (see box on p.283), when 28 Aborigines were roped together and butchered by graziers, created public outcry, but similar "**dispersals**" became commonplace wherever indigenous people resisted white intrusion. More insidious methods, such as poisoning waterholes or lacing gifts of flour with arsenic, were also employed by pastoralists angered over stock losses.

Aboriginal peoples were not a single, unified society, and Europeans exploited tribal divisions by creating the notorious **Native Mounted Police**, an Aboriginal force that aided and abetted the extermination of rival groups. By the 1890s, citing a perversion of Darwinian theory which held that Aboriginal people were less evolved than whites and so doomed to extinction, most states had followed Tasmania's example of "protectionism", relocating survivors into reserves which were frequently far from traditional lands: in Queensland, for instance, Rockhampton Aborigines were moved to Fraser Island, 500km away.

GOLD

The discovery of **gold** in 1851 by Edward Hargraves, fresh from the Californian fields, had a dramatic bearing on Australia's future. The first major strikes in New South Wales and

Victoria saw an immediate rush of hopeful miners from Sydney and Melbourne and, once the news spread overseas, from the USA and Britain. The British government, realizing the absurdity of spending taxes on shipping criminals to a land of gold when there were plenty of people willing to pay for their passage, finally **ended transportation** in 1853. Gold also opened up Australia's interior far more thoroughly than explorers had done; as returns petered out in one area, prospectors moved on to find more. Western Australia and Queensland (which was saved from bankruptcy by gold in 1867) experienced booms up until 1900 and, while mining initially followed in the path of pastoral expansion, rushes began to attract settlements and markets into previously uncultivated regions.

A new "level society", based on a work-and-mateship ethic, evolved on the goldfields, where education had little bearing on an ability to endure hard work and spartan living conditions. Yet the **diggers** were all too aware of their poor social and political rights in other arenas. At the end of 1854, frustrations over mining licences erupted at **Eureka** (see box on p.855), near Ballarat in Victoria, where workers built a stockade and ended up being charged by mounted police. In the aftermath, rights, including the vote, were granted to miners. The Victorian goldfields also saw **racial tensions** directed against a new minority – the **Chinese** – who first arrived there during the 1850s. Disheartened by diminishing returns and infuriated by the Chinese ability to find gold in abandoned claims, diggers stormed a Chinese camp at **Lambing Flat** in 1861. Troops had to be sent in to stop the riots, but the ringleaders were acquitted by an all-white jury. Throughout the country, goldfields became centres of **nationalism** (despite the fact that the Chinese improved life by running stores and market gardens in mining towns), peaking in Queensland in the 1880s where the flames were fanned by the importation of **Solomon Islanders** to work on sugar plantations. Ostensibly to prevent slavery, but politically driven by recession and growing white unemployment, the government forced the repatriation of Islanders, taxed the Chinese out of the country, and passed the 1901 Immigration Act, which heralded the **White Australia policy**

– greatly restricting non-European immigration, and prevailing right up until 1958.

FEDERATION AND WAR

Central government was first mooted in 1842, but new states were not keen to return to being controlled by New South Wales, lose interstate customs duties, or share the new-found mineral wealth which had consolidated separation in the first place. But by the end of the century they began to see advantages to **federation**, not least as a way to control indentured labour and present a united front against French, German and Russian expansion in the Pacific. A decade of wrangling by the states, to ensure equal representation irrespective of population, saw the formation of a High Court and a two-tier parliamentary system consisting of a House of Representatives and Senate, presided over by a Prime Minister. Each state would have its own premier, and Britain would be represented by a Governor-General. Approved by Queen Victoria shortly before her death, the **Commonwealth of Australia** came into being on January 1, 1901.

It's notable that the **Immigration Act** (see above) was the first piece of legislation to be passed by the new parliament, and reflected the nationalist drive behind federation. Though the intent was to encourage an Australia largely of European – and preferably British – descent, the policy also sowed the seeds for Australian independence from the "Mother Country". The first pull away came as early as 1912, when the **Commonwealth Bank** opened; Australia was trying to become less financially reliant on Britain. A negative aspect of the White Australia policy was that Aboriginal people were not included in the national census, or even allowed to vote until 1967. On the progressive side, the new government gave **women** the vote in 1902, and the Australian Labor Party, which had grown out of the Depression and union battles with the government during the 1890s, established the concept of a **minimum wage** in 1907.

Defence had also been a moving force behind federation. But, even forewarned by the war between Japan and Russia in 1904, Australia was largely unprepared for the outbreak of hostilities in Europe a decade later, owning little more than a navy made up from secondhand British ships. Promising to support

Britain to "the last man and the last shilling", there was a patriotic rush to enlist in the army, and an opportunistic occupation of German New Guinea by Australian forces. Surprisingly, the issue of compulsory conscription raised by Prime Minister **Billy Hughes** was twice defeated in referendums during World War I.

From the Australian perspective, the most important stage of the war occurred when Turkey sided with Germany in 1915. **Winston Churchill** formulated a plan to defend British shipping in the Dardanelles by occupying the **Gallipoli Peninsula**, and diverted Australian infantry bound for Europe. Between April and December 1915, wave after wave of Australian troops were mown down as they landed on the beaches below Turkish gun emplacements. By the end of the year it became clear that Gallipoli was not going to fall, and the survivors were "evacuated" to fight on the Western Front. The long-term effect of the slaughter was the first serious questioning of Anglo-Australian relations: should Australia have committed and sacrificed so much to help a distant country further its European policies? Conversely, Gallipoli, as Australia's debut on the world stage, still remains a symbol of national identity and pride.

1918–1939

After World War I, the Nationalist Party joined forces with the **Country Party** to assume government under the paternalistic and fiercely antisocialist guidance of **Earle Page** and **Stanley Bruce**. The Country Party was formed due to the widening divisions between a growing urban population and farmers, who felt isolated and unrepresented politically. Under the coalition, pastoral industries were subsidized by overseas borrowing, allowing them to compete internationally, and technology began to close the gap between the city and the Outback: radio and aviation developments saw the birth of **Qantas** – the Queensland and Northern Territory Air Service – and the **Royal Flying Doctor Service** in Queensland's remote west. In the cities, work started on the Sydney Harbour Bridge, and the new Commonwealth capital, **Canberra**, was completed.

On the social front, the USA stopped mass immigration in 1921, deflecting a flood of people from depressed **southern Europe** to Australia – which the government countered by encouraging British immigrants with assisted passages. While progressive in some areas – for example, proposing a dole for the unemployed, sick, pensioners and mothers – the government overreacted to opposition, as exemplified by the **seamen and dockers' strike** of 1928. Citing the arch-villain "communism" as behind the dispute, they attempted to stretch the scope of the Immigration Act to allow action to be taken against disturbances that were politically motivated. However, the implications that the law could be altered against anyone who disagreed with the government contributed to the downfall of Bruce and Page the following year. The themes of their rule – differences between rural and urban societies, questions of Australian identity, union disputes, and the effects of heavy borrowing to create artificially high living standards, unsupported by Australia's actual capabilities – are still current issues.

As the **Great Depression** set in during the early 1930s, Australia faced collapsing economic and political systems, with all the parties divided; pressed for a loan, the Bank of England forced a restructuring of the Australian economy. This scenario, of Australia still financially dependent on Britain but clearly regarded as an upstart nation, came to a head during the 1932 "**Bodyline**" cricket series: the loan was virtually made conditional on Australian cricket authorities dropping their allegations that British bowlers were deliberately trying to injure Australian batsmen during the tour.

Meanwhile, worries about communism were succeeded by the rise of fascism, as Mussolini and Hitler took power in Europe and Japanese forces invaded Manchuria – the **Tanaka memorial** in 1927 actually cited Australia as one of Japan's future conquests. Although displaying a certain ambivalence to fascism, Australia assisted the immigration of refugees from central Europe, and after a prolonged union battle, halted iron exports to Japan. When Prime Minister Joseph Lyons died in office, **Robert Menzies**, a firm supporter of British notions of civilization, was elected to the post in time to side with Britain as hostilities were declared against Hitler in September 1939.

WORLD WAR II AND AFTER

As happened in World War I, Australia developed its identity in World War II through participation in global affairs, but this time without Britain's help. Menzies' United Australia Party barely lasted long enough to form diplomatic ties with the USA – in case Germany overran Europe – before internal divisions saw the government crumble, replaced by **John Curtin** and his Labor Party in 1941.

Curtin, concerned about Australia's vulnerability after the Japanese attack on Pearl Harbor, made the radical decision of shifting the country's commitment in the war from defending Britain and Europe to fighting off an invasion of Australia from Asia. After the **fall of Singapore** in 1942 and the capture of twenty thousand Australian troops, Curtin succeeded in ordering the immediate recall of Australians fighting in the Middle East, despite opposition from Churchill, who wanted them for the Burma campaign. In February the Japanese unexpectedly bombed Darwin, launched submarine raids against Sydney and Newcastle, and invaded New Guinea. Feeling abandoned by Britain, Curtin appealed to the USA, who quickly adopted Australia as a base for co-ordinating Pacific operations under **General Douglas MacArthur**. Meanwhile, Australian troops in New Guinea halted Japanese advances along the **Kokoda trail** at **Milne Bay**, while the Australian and US navies slowed down the Japanese fleet in the **Battle of the Coral Sea** – which, thanks to modern cannon, was notable as the first naval engagement in which the two sides never even saw each other.

Australia came out of World War II realizing that – politically as well as geographically – the country was closer to Asia than Europe, that it could not count on Britain to help in a crisis (Churchill had been ready to sacrifice Australian territory to protect British interests elsewhere), and that it was able to form political alliances independently of the mother country. From this point on, Australia began to look to the USA and the Pacific, as well as Britain, for direction. Another consequence of the war was that immigration was speeded up, fuelled by Australia's recent vulnerability. Under the slogan "Populate or Perish", the government reintroduced assisted passages from Britain – the "ten-pound-poms" – also accepting substantial numbers of European refugees; even Torres Strait Islanders, previously banned from settling on the mainland, were allowed to move onto Cape York in northern Queensland.

With international right-wing extremism laid low by the war, the old bogey of **communism** returned. When North Korea, backed by the Chinese, invaded the south in 1950, Australia, led by a revitalized Menzies and his new Liberal Party, was the first country after the USA to commit troops to counter communist forces. Menzies also sent soldiers and pilots to Malaysia, where communist rebels had been fighting the British colonial administration almost since the end of World War II, under the anti-communist SEATO (Southeast Asia Treaty Organization) banner. At home, he opened up central Australia to British **atomic bomb tests** in the 1950s, because "nobody lived there" – a notion that had been proposed by the first European colonists. A number of Aborigines were moved off to reserves, others – along with British troops involved in the tests – suffered the effects of fallout and had their traditional lands rendered uninhabitable for the foreseeable future. Wrangles with the British government over compensation and the clearing of the test sites at **Maralinga** and **Emu Junction** were finally settled in 1993.

Menzies was still in control when the USA became involved in **Vietnam**, and with conflict in Malaysia all but over, Australia volunteered "advisers" to Vietnamese republican forces in 1962. Once fighting became entrenched, the government introduced conscription and, bowing to the wishes of the American president **Lyndon Johnson**, sent a battalion of soldiers into the fray in 1965, events that immediately split the country. Menzies quit politics the following year, succeeded by his protégé **Harold Holt**, who, rallying under the catchphrase "All the way with LBJ", willingly increased Australia's participation in the Vietnamese conflict. But as the war dragged on, world opinion shifted to seeing the matter as a civil struggle rather than as a fight between western and communist ideologies, and in 1970 the government began scaling down its involvement. In the meantime, Aboriginal people were finally granted civil rights in 1967, and Holt mysteriously disappeared while swimming in the sea off the coast of Victoria, leaving the Liberals in turmoil and paving the way for a Labor win under **Gough Whitlam** in 1972.

Whitlam's three years in office had far-reaching effects: he ended national service and participation in Vietnam, granted independence to

Papua New Guinea, and instituted free health care and higher education systems. In doing so, however, he alienated the mostly conservative Senate, and when the government attempted to finance mining interests with an illicit overseas loan in 1975, the opposition prevented the Senate from functioning. In an unprecedented move, the Governor-General **John Kerr** (until then, a largely decorative representative of the Crown overseeing Australian affairs) dismissed the government – a move that shocked many into questioning the validity of Britain's ultimate hold on Australia – and called an election, which Labor lost. By contrast, the following eight years were uneventful, culminating in the return of Labor in 1983 under the charismatic Bob Hawke, a former trade union leader. Labor's subsequent thirteen years and record four terms in office, which produced surprisingly little lasting legislation, were suddenly brought to a close by the arrogant antics of Hawke's successor and former treasurer, **Paul Keating**. He was already widely unpopular for his bullying rhetoric and general lack of concern for the country's woes – particularly the effects of a massive foreign debt and crippling drought in eastern Australia – when news of a secret military agreement with Indonesia created a public backlash, resulting in a landslide victory for the **Liberal–National coalition**, led by **John Howard**, in 1996.

CURRENT EVENTS

Formerly considered an ineffectual character, Howard has shown consummate – though often unpopular – political skills. One of his first actions was to cut government costs by announcing a phased reduction of the **civil service** by a third, replacing the redundant departments with private enterprise. His stand against automatic firearms in the wake of the **Port Arthur Massacre** in 1996 (see p.932) also greatly reduced his feeble image, after he successfully pushed through his legislation despite stiff opposition from gun lobbies and several state premiers. Indeed, Howard's political position was so secure by 1998 that the coalition managed to be **re-elected** (albeit with a reduced majority) on what some considered a suicidal platform of tax reform through the introduction of a **GST**, or Goods and Service Tax. A recent referendum on the contentious issue of Australia becoming a **repub-**

lic, one of the major issues of Labor's latter years in office, also revealed majority support for the notion, and, after exactly a century, the Commonwealth of Australia – and all remaining political ties to Britain – are now set to end on January 1, 2001.

Overseas, Australia is becoming more dedicated to its role as part of Asia, rather than Europe or the United States. Although it was the first country to back the USA during the 1992 Gulf War, continual bickering over trade agreements with the USA has since seen a cooling in relations. An Asian bias makes good economic sense, but has led to an often appallingly conciliatory attitude; as early as 1975 Australia didn't protest against the annexation of Timor by Indonesia, and the response to regional human rights abuses has been pitifully weak. Nor, with its European heritage, is Australia accepted as "Asian" by other nations in the area, and Malaysia seems to harbour particular antipathy towards it, as shown by its continual vetoing of Australia's attempts to join ASEAN, the regional trading bloc. The rough-hewn outbursts by former chip-shop owner **Pauline Hanson** and the rise of her **One Nation party**, which has capitalized on fears of a recession and rural communities' perception that they are being increasingly sidelined by mainstream politics, have likewise done nothing to enhance Australian credibility overseas. In addition, Australia's export strength in primary production is being undermined by the recent collapse of Southeast Asian economies and, to a lesser extent, South Africa's shaky re-emergence onto the international trading market.

There have been some advances, though, under both Labor and the coalition, in the field of **Aboriginal rights**. An ineffective inquiry into Aboriginal deaths in custody was overshadowed in June 1992 when the High Court handed down the landmark **Mabo Decision**, legally overturning the concept of *terra nullius*. The Mabo claim, set around **Murray Island** (Mer) in the Torres Strait, acknowledged the Merriam as traditional landowners and sparked furious debate as to interpretation. Nor was there any less of a reaction when Mabo itself was forced into the background in December 1996 by the **Wik Decision**, which stated that native title and pastoral leases could coexist over the same area. In an effort to test the implications of these rulings, Aboriginal groups across the country have since laid claim to everything from Brisbane city centre to cattle properties and Outback national parks, creating panic amongst developers, farmers and state governments, and something of a public backlash against Aborigines – providing fuel for One Nation and contributing to Australia's racist image.

In fact, few of these land claims are likely to succeed. A **Native Title Tribunal** has been set up to consider each case, but, given former resettlement policies, claimants have an uphill struggle as they need to prove constant association with the land in question since white occupation. Nonetheless, a growing perception that Aboriginal people will eventually be re-enfranchized has seen mining companies and farmers ignoring the political and legal wrangles by making private land-use agreements with local communities. In this sense, Mabo and Wik have finally confirmed that Aboriginal people have land rights, even if it takes years formally to establish exactly what these are.

AUSTRALIA'S INDIGENOUS PEOPLES

White Australians and the international community have grouped Australia's indigenous peoples under the term Aborigines since the British invaded in 1788. At the recent insistence of these indigenous groups, we are coming to recognize many separate surviving indigenous cultures and lament the loss of others by deliberate or accidental genocide since invasion.

Today these surviving cultures include highly urbanized Koorie communities in Sydney and Melbourne, semi-nomadic groups such as the Pitjantjatjaras and Warlpiris living a relatively traditional lifestyle in the central and western deserts, and the seafaring Merriam and Tiwi peoples of the small islands north of the mainland. If there is any thread linking these groups, it is the cultural revival experienced over the last twenty years. Under the banner of national political movements, all of these groups have renewed their commitment to organizing their social world according to extensive kin networks, to re-establishing close religious and legal relationships to the land, and to maintaining and revitalizing their cultures and languages.

COLONIZATION

To understand the magnitude of the progress towards revival made in Australia, it is necessary to understand how dreadful the impact of colonization has been. The estimated 750,000 indigenous inhabitants of Australia in 1788 were unilaterally dispossessed of their lands and livelihoods by the British colonists who failed to recognize them as inhabitants and owners. Australia was annexed to the British Empire on the basis that it was *terra nullius*, or uninhabited wasteland. This legal fiction persisted until the High Court judged in the 1992 **Mabo case** that native title to land still existed in Australia unless it had been extinguished by statute or by some use of the land that was inconsistent with the continuation of native use and ownership. The **Wik Decision** of 1996

went a step further, acknowledging that native title continues to exist on pastoral leases, though with the proviso that "pastoral interest will prevail over native title rights, wherever the two conflict". (For more on the Mabo and Wik decisions, see "A History" on p.998.)

Upon deciding that the country was unoccupied, successive waves of new settlers hastened to make it so. Violent conflicts between indigenous and recently arrived Australians resulted in the decimation of Aboriginal groups. The most notorious of these conflicts was the **unofficial war** waged against Tasmania's Aboriginal peoples, which resulted in the near-destruction of indigenous Tasmanians (see also box on p.902). Grisly souvenirs of this war, including skeletons and preserved body parts, still shame the collections of museums throughout the world. Historians estimate that twenty thousand Aborigines may have died in these mostly unrecorded battles. Measuring the impact of colonization on the indigenous population has been hampered by a lack of information about conditions prior to colonization, as well as the failure of successive governments to record indigenous people as part of the population until quite recently. The best estimates are that there were approximately a million indigenous people living in Australia in 1788, but this number had been reduced to around 30,000 by 1929.

Disease has also been a powerful, if unintentional, weapon in the war against indigenous Australians, and has proved more effective than shooting or poisoning. Australia's geographical isolation ensured that there were very few communicable diseases on the continent prior to the arrival of Europeans, and successive generations of indigenous Australians had developed resistance to these. The arrival of colonists and their diseases posed an almost insurmountable immunological challenge. Whole populations were wiped out by smallpox and malaria epidemics, and the diaries of officers of the First Fleet record the rapid destruction from smallpox of the Aboriginal camps in the Sydney hinterland within four years of the establishment of the colony of New South Wales. Those who didn't die fled the area, unwittingly infecting neighbouring groups as they went. When Governor Hunter made the first exploratory expedition to western New South Wales in the 1820s, he recorded evidence of prior smallpox epidemics among Aboriginal groups who had not previously come into contact with European settlers. As recently as the 1950s desert peoples were severely affected by outbreaks of influenza and measles. The lack of immunity to these introduced diseases was exacerbated by the trauma of dispossession, the lack of availability of traditional food and water supplies, and the unhygienic results of being required to wear European-style clothing.

The **interruption of traditional food and water supplies** became progressively worse through the nineteenth and twentieth centuries as the pastoral industry expanded in rural Australia, and vast areas were stripped of vegetation to provide for grazing land. Grazing animals competed with local animals for food, fouled established water sources, and their hard hooves damaged the integrity of surface soil, contributing to substantial erosion and salinity problems. Other European animals, originally introduced to make the countryside seem more like "home", rapidly multiplied and have now become ubiquitous throughout Australia. Cats and foxes, both vicious predators, have been blamed for the near extinction of small to medium-size mammal species throughout arid Australia. Rabbit populations have expanded to fill the niche the mammals vacated, and their destructive grazing habits have contributed to the increasing desertification of Australia's arid rangelands. Aboriginal tribespeople in Central Australia have witnessed this ecological disaster within the last sixty years, and have lamented the loss of many animal species that sustained them in the past.

Australia's Aboriginal peoples have also been subjected to various forms of **incarceration**, ranging from prisons to apartheid-style reserves. Much of this systematic incarceration was instigated between 1890 and 1950 as an official policy of **protection**, in response to the devastating impact of colonization. Missionaries and other well-meaning people believed that Aborigines were a dying race, and that it was a Christian duty to "soothe the dying pillow". Parliamentary records of the time reveal a harsher mentality. Aborigines were viewed as a weak and degenerate people, little better than animals, who exposed white settlers to physical and moral disease. To "protect" the Aborigines and settlers from each other, various state governments enacted legislation for the protection of Aborigines, appointed official

Protectors of Aborigines, established reserves in rural areas and removed Aboriginal people to them. In some parts of Australia these reserves were established on traditional lands, allowing people to continue to live relatively undisturbed. In other parts of the country, notably Queensland, people were forcibly removed from their home areas and relocated in reserves throughout the state. Families were brutally broken up and the ties with the land and religion shattered. The so-called protectors had virtual life and death powers over those they allegedly protected. In Queensland, for example, Aboriginal people required permits to marry and to move from one reserve to another. They were forced into indentured labour, and their wages collected and banked on their behalf by the State government. If they fell ill with a notifiable disease, they could be arbitrarily removed from home and family to a lock hospital, including the notorious Fantome Island, off the coast from Townsville. This treatment persisted in some areas until the late 1960s. Aboriginal people are still ridiculously over-represented in Australia's prison population, a situation which led to a **Royal Commission into Aboriginal Deaths in Custody**, which reported to the Federal Parliament in 1991. It called for wide-ranging changes in police and judicial practice, and substantial changes to social programmes aimed at improving the lot of Aboriginal peoples in the areas of justice, health, education, economics and empowerment. Although there has been considerable government lip-service to the recommendations of the Royal Commission, this has not resulted in any substantial change to incarceration rates.

Also since the 1920s, Aboriginal children have been legally removed from their black mothers and given into the care of state institutions and white foster parents as part of a policy of **assimilation**. The practice began in Victoria in 1886 and has continued until remarkably recently (1969). This period of "**taking the children away**" still haunts the lives of many Aboriginal Australians who have lost contact with their natal families and their culture. The policy was the subject of a major government inquiry in 1997, bringing the issue to wider attention for the first time. The trauma suffered by the people now known as the **Stolen Generation** has received considerable media attention since the release of the report of the inquiry, and led to calls for a national apology to Aboriginal people. Prime Minister John Howard has consistently refused to acknowledge that the Australian people have anything for which to apologize, but his government has made funding available for link-up and counselling services for those who were affected. He has been publicly criticised for his heartless stance by a number of influential Australians, and many people have expressed their personal regrets to the Aboriginal community. The Lord Mayor of Brisbane, Jim Soorley, won national praise when he led a **National Sorry Day** by formally apologizing to Aborigines on behalf on the people of Brisbane in 1998. Many ordinary Australians have joined the popular movement to apologize by buying brightly coloured plastic hands to "plant" in public events known as the **Sea of Hands**, where thousands of the hands are temporarily installed in parks in most State Capitals. The events are seen as a way of expressing personal sorrow to Aboriginal people, as well as castigating the Federal Government for their lack of offical response.

The result of two centuries of brutal mistreatment is that, by almost every statistical indicator, the Aboriginal population is **highly disadvantaged** in both absolute terms and compared to non-Aboriginal groups.

REVITALIZATION

The revitalization of Aboriginal peoples effectively began in 1967, when a constitutional referendum recognized indigenous Australians as voting citizens, and gave the federal government the power to legislate for Aboriginal people. Prior to this referendum, Aboriginal people had the status of wards of each of the States – the Letters Patent, documents which established the States, often referred to them, amongst the flora and fauna, as things to be protected and preserved. The referendum ushered in a new era of **self-determination** for Aboriginal people, evidenced by the establishment of the first Ministry for Aboriginal Affairs in the Whitlam Labor Government of 1972–1975. After more than a hundred years of agitation, **land rights** were accorded to Aboriginal groups in the Northern Territory in 1976 under federal legislation. Since then, other states have legislated to vest title over various pieces of state-owned land to their traditional Aboriginal owners. All the mainland states and

territories have now made provisions for Aboriginal land rights. Various representative bodies were set up by successive federal governments throughout the 1970s and 1980s, culminating in the **Aboriginal and Torres Strait Islanders Commission** (ATSIC), established in 1990. This statutory authority gives elected Aboriginal representatives effective control over many of the federal funding programmes directed at Aboriginal organizations and communities. Since the late 1980s, substantial funds have been directed towards training for employment.

Along with ownership of land and control over funding have come opportunities for economic self-sufficiency and expansion previously unavailable to Aboriginal groups. In many parts of the country, this has allowed Aborigines to buy the cattle stations on which they worked without wages for many years. In central Australia, Aboriginal enterprises include TV and radio stations, transport companies, small airlines, publishing companies, tourist businesses and joint-venture mining operations.

Co-operative agreements with the Australian Nature Conservation Agency have led to Aboriginal ownership and joint management of two of Australia's most important conservation reserves, **Uluru–Kata Tjuta** and **Kakadu national parks** in the Northern Territory. These arrangements recognize that Aboriginal owners retain an enormous understanding about the ecology of their traditional lands that can be of great assistance in the development of land-management plans. The Uluru Fauna Survey, a joint scientific survey between Pitjantjatjara and Yankunytjatjara landowners and the scientific research authority, CSIRO, represents a landmark in the application of indigenous knowledge to solving conservation problems. In the wake of the Mabo Decision, other state and territory governments are looking at the Uluru model of co-operative park management as a way of accommodating Aboriginal land interests, while providing for more effective conservation strategies.

CITIZENSHIP AND ITS PROBLEMS

Despite these successes, Australia's indigenous peoples are still struggling against considerable disadvantages. Along with citizenship in 1967 came the right to purchase and consume alcohol, which has proved disastrous. **Alcohol** is heavily implicated in the destructive downward spiral often observed by visitors to Outback towns in Australia: there is a synergistic relationship between the disempowerment of Aboriginal people in general and self-destructive drinking behaviour in the individual. The negative repercussions are evident in sickness and death, violence and despair, exclusion from education and meaningful employment, as well as families and communities in disarray. The vast over-representation of Aboriginal people in the criminal justice system is directly attributable to the mediation of alcohol: large numbers of Aboriginal people are apprehended by police and held in police cells owing to drunkenness, even where public drunkenness is no longer a criminal offence.

Until recent years, government response to Aboriginal drinking has typically been racist. Statutes such as the notorious **two-kilometre law** in Alice Springs, which made it an offence to consume alcohol in a public place within 2km of licensed premises, were directed specifically at getting Aboriginal drinkers out of sight of visitors to the town centre. In recent times, most governments have begun moving away from racist and draconian measures and towards providing Aboriginal communities and families with the legislative supports to limit drinking within their towns and homes, and have invested money in sobering-up shelters and alcohol **rehabilitation** programmes.

On the **positive** side, many families and communities are confronting the problems that alcohol is causing. This is possible because although some Aboriginal people equate drinking rights with racial equality, most have a negative view of alcohol abuse. A large proportion of Aborigines, particularly women and those who don't live in towns, abstain altogether. Furthermore, Aboriginal people themselves are beginning to put pressure on problem drinkers to limit their drinking, and are now able to implement new laws to reduce the damage that alcohol is doing to their families and communities.

A **case study** illustrates these efforts. Imanpa is a small Pitjantjatjara community between Alice Springs and the tourist mecca, Uluru (Ayers Rock). Seeing their community racked by alcohol-related violence and death, Imanpa residents looked at ways to limit availability of alcohol to residents. With neighbouring communities, they successfully lobbied the Northern Territory Liquor Commission to limit the amount of takeaway alcohol that could be purchased at highway roadhouses to six cans of beer. They reached co-operative agreements with the licensees of these roadhouses that they would not serve takeaway alcohol to anybody travelling to, or living on, Aboriginal communities. Imanpa drinkers can still travel the three hundred kilometres to Alice Springs to purchase alcohol, and the community is looking at the possibility of pressuring government to reduce the number of takeaway outlets in Alice Springs: with approximately seventy outlets for a population of twenty thousand, Alice Springs has the highest per capita availability of alcohol in the world. The people of Imanpa are also supporting the efforts of their neighbours in the Mutitjulu community near Ayers Rock Resort. At the resort, habitual drinkers persist in persuading well-meaning tourists to buy alcohol on their behalf. The community is working with the resort to try to educate the tourists out of being tricked or intimidated in this way, and to stress the benefits of limited alcohol supply for the community's future.

Poor **health** continues to reduce substantially the life expectancy of Aborigines. In 1989 the first comprehensive National Aboriginal Health Strategy was put in place. More effective and widespread health education, more access to better-quality housing, greater health services specifically aimed at Aborigines and better immunization programmes are all parts of the strategy. As with most areas of social service, health services for Aboriginal peoples have been the province of white professionals until very recently; an essential focus of the new strategy is to empower Aboriginal people by giving resources to them directly.

THE FUTURE

Improvements in health and education have led to a **revival of interest** in their own culture for many Aboriginal people. **Languages** that have fallen into disuse are being relearned. **Ceremonies** and **art forms** that have been forgotten are being revived through research and reconstruction. Links with land and family that have been torn apart are being reforged. The benefits of this revitalization flow on to visitors to Aboriginal Australia. Aboriginal tour companies are introducing visitors to the ancient law, cultural history and culinary possibilities of the land. Aboriginal **dance** theatres are staging new productions of great originality and imagination, and are reinterpreting ancient dance forms for modern audiences. Aboriginal **authors and poets** are publishing major new works that present unique and indigenous viewpoints. Aboriginal **painters and sculptors**, using a mix of traditional and modern techniques and forms, are producing vivid and exciting works of art. Aboriginal **national parks** are introducing visitors to an ancient and alternative view of the natural landscape. There has never been a time when these most ancient of cultures have been more accessible to visitors.

Despite this, Aboriginal people remain at a considerable **disadvantage**, exacerbated by the halving of the Aboriginal welfare budget by the incumbent Liberal government in 1996, and the uncertainty caused by the **Mabo and Wik decisions** which potentially put over three-quarters of the country (including virtually all of Western Australia) under land claim. In early 1999 the Australian government was censured twice about its Aboriginal policies by key international bodies. The World Heritage Committee of UNESCO threatened to place Kakadu National Park on the World Heritage Under Threat list if the government proceeds with plans to open a second uranium mine within the park against the wishes of the traditional owners of the land. The government's Wik legislation, which attempts to effectively extinguish Native Title on pastoral leases, received sharp criticism from the United Nations Committee on Elimination of Racial Discrimination, which judge that the provisions of the legislation are inconsistent with the International Convention to which Australia is a signatory. The continuing adversarial stance of the current government ensure that there will be Aboriginal protests throughout the 2000 **Sydney Olympics**, when the eyes of the world will be focused on Australia. Aboriginal leaders are likely to point out the irony of marketing Aboriginal culture to the world in the opening and closing ceremonies of the Olympics as well as the showcasing of Aboriginal arts through the Olympic cultural festival, when most Aboriginal people continue to live in desperate poverty with their fundamental legal rights under attack.

WILDLIFE

Despite forty thousand years of human pressure and manipulation, accelerated in the last century by the effects of introduced species, Australia's ecology and wildlife remain among the most distinctive on earth. Nonetheless, it's also some of the most endangered – in the last two hundred years, more native mammals have become extinct here than on any other continent.

Australians love to tell stories about the **dangers** that the bush holds for the inexperienced (see the "Health" section of Basics, p.25, for general advice on coping with hazardous wildlife). In reality, fearsome "drop bears" lurking in gums, fallen tree trunks that turn out to be giant snakes, bloodthirsty wild pigs and other rampaging terrors are mostly confined to hotel bars, the product of suburban paranoia laced with a surprising naivety about the Great Outdoors. Apart from a couple of avoidable exceptions, there's little to fear from Australia's wildlife, and if you spend any time in the bush at any stage you'll undoubtedly end up far better informed than the yarn-spinners.

Reptiles and birds abound, and while marsupials and monotremes may not be exclusive to Australia (they're also found in New Guinea and South America), it's here that they reached their greatest diversity and numbers.

MARSUPIALS AND MONOTREMES

Marsupials are generally nocturnal mammals that give birth to a partially formed embryo which

itself then develops in a pouch on the mother; this allows a higher breeding rate in good years. Easiest to find because they actively seek out people, ridiculously cute **ringtail** and **brushtail possums** are common in suburbs and campsites, often hard to avoid if they think there's a chance of getting some food. With a little persistence, you should encounter one of the several species of related **glider possums** on the edges of forests at dusk. **Kangaroos** and **wallabies** are the Australian answer to deer and antelopes, and range from tiny, solitary rainforest species to the gregarious two-metre-tall **red kangaroo** of the central plains – watching these creatures bouncing effortlessly across the landscape is an extraordinary sight. The arboreal, eucalyptus-chewing **koalas** and tubby, ground-dwelling **wombats** are smaller, less active and more sensitive to disturbance, and this has made them more elusive, and has placed them on the endangered list as their habitat is cleared. **Carnivorous marsupials** are mostly shrew-sized today (though a lion equivalent probably survived into Aboriginal times); two of the largest are spotted native cats or **quolls**, and Tasmania's indigenous **Tasmanian devil**, a terrier-sized scavenger.

Platypuses and echidnas are the only **monotremes**, egg-laying mammals that suckle their young through specialized pores. Once considered a stage in the evolution of placental mammals, they're now recognized as a specialized branch of the family. Neither is particularly rare, but being nocturnal, shy and, in the case of the platypus, aquatic makes them difficult to find. Anteating **echidnas** resemble a thick-spined hedgehog or small porcupine, and are found countrywide; **platypuses** are confined to the eastern ranges and look like a blend of duck and otter, having a grey, rubbery bill, webbed feet, short fur, and a poison spur on males. This combination seemed too implausible to nineteenth-century biologists, who initially denounced stuffed specimens as a hoax assembled from pieces of other animals.

INTRODUCED FAUNA

Of the **introduced mammals**, **dingoes** are descended from dogs, introduced to Australia by Aboriginal people in the last twelve thousand years. To keep them away from flocks, graziers built the world's longest fence, which stretched from South Australia into northwest Queensland and down again to New South

Wales. **Camels** have also become acclimatized to Australia since their introduction in the 1840s, and thrive in the central deserts – Australia is the only place where dromedaries still occur in the wild, and they are regularly exported to the Middle East. The blight that **hoofed** mammals – horses, cows, sheep and goats – have perpetrated on Australia's fragile fauna is horrendous. Much of the country has been prematurely desertified by their eating habits, abrasive hooves and demand for water; once extracted from below ground, it is not replenished, which alters the mineral balance and kills remaining plant life. The damage caused by **rabbits** is equally all-pervasive, especially in the semi-desert areas where their cyclic population explosions can strip every shred of plant life from fragile dune systems. However, a recently engineered **virus** has massively reduced their numbers. **Feral cats**, which hunt for sport as well as necessity, are currently seen as the greatest threat to the indigenous fauna, primarily small marsupials and birds.

REPTILES, BIRDS, BATS AND MARINE LIFE

Reptiles come in all shapes and sizes. In the tropical parts of the country, the pale **lizards** you see wriggling across the ceiling on Velcro-like pads are **geckos**, and you'll find fatter, sluggish **skinks** – such as the stumpy **blue-tongued lizard** – everywhere. Other widespread species are **frill-necked lizards**, known for fanning out their necks and running on their hind legs when frightened; and the ubiquitous **goanna** family, which includes the monstrous **perentie**, third-largest lizard in the world. In central Australia, look out for the

extraordinary **thorny devil** or moloch, an animal that seems part rock, part rosebush.

Crocodiles are confined to the tropics and come in two types. The shy, inoffensive **freshwater** crocodile grows to around 3m in length and feeds on fish and frogs. The larger, bulkier, and misleadingly named **saltwater** or **estuarine crocodile** can grow to 7m, ranges far inland (often in fresh water), and is the only Australian animal that constitutes an active threat to humans. Highly evolved predators, they should be given a very wide berth (see box on p.535 for specific precautions to take while in crocodile country). Despite their bad press, **snakes** are generally timid and pose far less of a problem, even though Australia has everything from constricting **pythons** through to three-quarters of the world's most venomous species.

With a climate that extends from temperate zones well into the tropics, Australia's **birdlife** is prolific and varied. **Little penguins** and **albatrosses** live along the south coast, while **riflebirds**, related to New Guinea's birds of paradise, and the **cassowary**, a colourful version of the ostrich, live in the tropical rainforests. The drabber **emu** prefers drier plains further west. Among the birds of prey, the countrywide **wedge-tail eagle** and the white-breasted **sea eagle** of the northern wetlands are most impressive in their size. Both share their environment with the stately grey **brolga**, an Australian crane, and the even larger **jabiru** stork, with its chisel beak and pied plumage. **Parrots**, arguably the country's most spectacular birds, come in over forty varieties, and no matter if they're flocks of green budgerigars, outrageously coloured rainbow lorikeets or

AUSTRALIA IN THE PAST

Australia has a **fossil record** which makes up in range what it lacks in quantity. Imprints of invertebrates from South Australia's **Ediacaran fauna**, dated to over 600 million years, are the oldest evidence of animal life in the world. On a larger scale, footprints and fragmentary remains of several **dinosaur** species have been uncovered, and **opalized marine fossils** are unique to the country. Perhaps most intriguing is evidence of the **megafauna** – giant wildlife which included the twenty-metre-long constricting

snake montypythonides, flightless birds bigger than an ostrich, a rhino-sized wombat, and thylacaleo, a marsupial lion – which flourished until about thirty thousand years ago, overlapping with Aboriginal occupation. Climatic changes were probably responsible for their demise, but humans definitely wiped out the **thylacine**, a dog-like marsupial with an oversized head, which vanished from the mainland after the introduction of dingoes but survived in Tasmania until 1936 – the year it received government protection.

white sulphur-crested cockatoos, they'll deafen you with their noisy song. Equally raucous are **kookaburras**, giant kingfishers found near permanent water. The quieter **tawny frogmouth**, an incredibly camouflaged cousin of the nightjar, has one of the most disgruntled expressions ever seen on a bird.

Huge colonies of **bats**, in orange, ghost and horseshoe varieties, congregate in caves or fill entire trees all over Australia. The fruit bat, or **flying fox**, is especially common in the tropics, where evenings can be spent watching colonies of the one-metre-winged monsters heading out from their daytime roosts on feeding expeditions.

In addition to what you'll see on the Barrier Reef (covered in the chapter on Tropical Queensland), whales, turtles, dolphins, seals and dugongs (sea cows) are part of the country's **marine life**, with humpbacked and southern right whales recently making a welcome return to the coasts after being hunted close to extinction.

FLORA

Australia's most distinctive and widespread **trees** are those which developed a dependence on **fire**. Some, like the seemingly limitless varieties of **eucalypts** or **gum** trees, need extreme heat to burst open button-shaped pods and release their seeds, encouraging fires by annually shedding bark and leaves to deposit a thick layer of tinder on the forest floor. Other shrubs with similar habits are banksias, grevillias and bottlebrushes with their distinctive bushy flowers and spiky seed pods, while those prehistoric survivors, palm-like **cycads** and **grasstrees**, similarly depend on regular conflagrations to promote new growth, and Aborigines possibly enhanced these fire-reliant traits by organizing controlled burn-offs.

Despite the country's extensive arid regions, there is no native equivalent to the cactus, although the dry, spiky **spinifex**, or porcupine grass, the succulent **samphire** with its curiously jointed stem, and the aptly named **saltbush**, come closest in their ability to survive extreme temperatures. After a rain, smaller desert plants rush to bloom and seed, covering the ground in a spectacular blanket of colour, a phenomenon for which Australia's Outback regions are well known.

On a larger scale, the Outback is dotted with stands of hardy **mulgas** and **wattles**, which superficially resemble scrawny eucalypts but have different leaf structures, as well as scattered groups of bloated, spindly-branched **bottle trees**, whose sweet, pulpy, moisture-laden cores can be used as emergency stock feed in drought conditions. The similar but far larger **boab**, found in the Kimberley and northeastern Northern Territory, is thought to be an invader from East Africa. **Mallee scrub** is unique to the southeastern Outback, where clearing of these tangled, bush-sized eucalypts for grazing has endangered both scrub and those animals who rely on it – the mound-building mallee fowl being the best known.

Mangrove swamps, found along the tropical and subtropical coasts, are tidal zones of thick grey mud and mangrove trees, whose interlocked, aerial roots make an effective barrier to exploration. They've suffered extensive clearing for development, and it wasn't until recently that their importance to the estuarine life-cycle won them limited government protection – though Aboriginal people have always found them a rich source of animal and plant products.

Rainforest once covered much of the continent, although today it survives in only a small portion of its former abundance. Nevertheless, you'll find pockets everywhere, from Tasmania's richly verdant wilderness to the monsoonal examples of northern Queensland and the Top End in the Northern Territory. Trees grow to gigantic heights, as they compete with each other for light, supporting themselves in the poor soil with aerial or buttressed roots. The extraordinary **banyan** and **Moreton Bay fig** trees are fine examples of the two types. They support a superabundance of plant species, with tangled vines in the lower reaches and **orchids**, elkhorns and other **epiphytes** using larger plants as roosts. **Palms** and **tree ferns**, with their giant, delicately curled fronds, are found in more open forest where there's regular water.

Some forest types illustrate the extent of Australia's **prehistoric flora**. Antarctic beech or nothafagus, found south of Brisbane as well as in South America, along with native pines and kauri or karri from Queensland and Western Australia, which also occur in New Zealand, are all relict evidence of the prehistoric supercontinent Gondwana. Other "living fossils" include primitive marine **stromatolites** – algae corals – still found around Shark Bay, Western Australia, or in fossilized form in the central deserts.

As long as you don't eat them or fall onto the pricklier versions, most Australian **plants** are harmless – though in rainforests you'd want to avoid entanglement with spiky **lawyer cane** or **wait-awhile** vine. However, watch out for the large, pale green, heart-shaped leaves of the **stinging tree** (gympie) – a scraggly "regrowth" plant found on the margins of cleared tropical rainforest. Even a casual brush delivers an agonizing and prolonged sting; if you're planning on bushwalking in the tropics, learn to recognize and avoid this plant.

AUSTRALIAN FILM

No visitor to Australia these days will be unaware of the popularity and respect for the Australian film industry since the early 1970s. It is generally agreed (with deference to a 1900 Salvation Army promo, *Stations of the Cross*) that *The Story of the Kelly Gang*, made by Charles Tait in 1906, was the world's first feature-length film. Australians' well-known antagonism towards figures of authority soon led to a hugely popular series of bushranger movies, eventually to be banned in 1912 by the New South Wales police on the grounds that their unsympathetic portrayal in these pictures was corrupting youngsters.

This **early heyday** of Australian film-making predated that of Hollywood and persisted with the production of various World War I morale boosters, despite the creation of a distribution duopoly (known as the "combine") which showed little interest in independent Australian films outside its control. With the ending of the war and its many cinematic testaments to the heroic disaster of Gallipoli, Australian silent cinema reached a creative peak. **Raymond Longford** was Australia's Spielberg of Silents at this time, and his 1919 production of *The Sentimental Bloke* and its sequel, *Ginger Mick*, a year later, were popular and notably naturalist dramas about a woman's taming of her larrikin husband's proclivities. Along with the already established contempt for authority, Longford's

films featured a distrust of sophistication and formality and, even then, the mythic spell of "the bush" began to make its mark on Australian productions.

HOLLYWOOD DOMINATION

Gradually, however, the combine squeezed the life from Australian cinema, which continued to decline as the powerful Hollywood studios got into their stride and entered the Golden Age of Talkies. In 1933 the mildly reformed wild boy from Tasmania, **Errol Flynn**, starred in his first feature film, *In the Wake of the Bounty*, directed by **Charles Chauvel**, a leading figure in Australian film-making until the late 1950s.

During World War II there was a return to newsreels and documentaries, with the legendary cameraman, Damien Parer, earning **Australia's first Oscar** for his account of the fighting in New Guinea (*Kokoda Front Line*, 1942). Following the war, however, Hollywood's global domination of cinema was unassailed, and Australian cinema just about perished. Nevertheless, **Chips Rafferty** turned up as Australia's answer to John Wayne, appearing in an unremarkable series of formula films, such as the scenically superb epic of bovine migration, *The Overlanders* (1946).

In the 1950s the British Ealing Studios and the American MGM set up production companies in Australia, turning out the odd Outback drama which was watered-down for international consumption (but not success). This era produced few notable Australian films other than Cecil Holmes' return to the bushranger format in *Captain Thunderbolt* (1953), and his similarly leftist study of mateship, *Three In One* (1957). Chauvel's remarkable *Jedda, the Uncivilized* (1955) was more unusual in that it tackled the tricky issue of an Aboriginal girl's white upbringing, sexual temptation and subsequent abduction back to tribal life, where a tragic death inevitably awaited her. If there is one subject Australian cinema still has difficulty in dealing with (the New Wave having finally come to grips with women as individuals), it is that of the Aborigines.

Australia was by now nothing more than an exotic, marsupial-speckled location for "**kangaroo westerns**" and other dramas where British and American actors could exercise their skills. In 1959 Stanley Kramer directed *On the Beach*,

Nevil Shute's post-Holocaust drama, with Ava Gardner, Gregory Peck and Fred Astaire tiptoeing through the fallout. A year later Fred Zinnemann directed Deborah Kerr and Robert Mitchum in *The Sundowners*, an affectionate classic of Outback itinerant labour.

THE NEW WAVE

The birth of the **New Wave** was a response to the burgeoning counterculture of the late 1960s. Among the many notable reforms of Gough Whitlam's Labor government was support for the long-neglected arts. Film-makers in particular were given a shot in the arm with the introduction of extremely generous grants to more than cover the cost of production. While in its early years this financial support helped produce some of the crassest male-fantasy "sex romps" ever seen (Tim Burstall's 1973 *Alvin Purple* and Terry Bourke's *Plugg* are matchlessly dire), the opening of the **Australian Film School** in 1973 allowed genuine talents such as Gillian Armstrong, Bruce Beresford and Paul Cox to flourish.

Two years later, the **Australian Film Commission** evolved from previous similar organizations to help produce and market Australian films, and although the grants have been regularly reduced ever since, their introduction kick-started the moribund industry so that there presently exists a diverse pool of directors and technicians to keep things going.

Peter Weir's unsettlingly eerie *Picnic at Hanging Rock* (1975) remains an early jewel, and the decade ended with further acclaim for his *Gallipoli*, Phillip Noyce's extraordinary *Newsfront* and Gillian Armstrong's first feature, *My Brilliant Career*. Auspicious futures were launched for Armstrong, and actors Sam Neill, Judy Davis and Mel Gibson, whose post-apocalyptic *Mad Max* trilogy saw a gradual stylistic evolution to suit the huge American market.

With the international box office success of *Crocodile Dundee* in 1985, Australia briefly became a fashionable destination. Indeed, Kakadu National Park owes as much to Peter Faiman's fish-out-of-water fairy tale for its present popularity as does Uluru (Ayers Rock) the famous Dingo Baby case; *Evil Angels* (released in the UK under the title *A Cry in the Dark*) saw Meryl Streep miscast as Lindy Chamberlain in Fred Schepisi's 1987 version of those events.

Contemporary Australian cinema is perhaps most exceptional for establishing a number of **women directors** and **producers** and providing a handful of strong women's roles. Inevitably, only the mainstream hits, such as the uplifting *Strictly Ballroom* and *Death in Brunswick*, have achieved wide overseas release, while many equally fine "small" films remain largely unseen. It is these quirky, uniquely Australian films of which the rejuvenated industry can be most proud. The prestige of numerous and consistent awards at the Cannes Film Festival and others proves that Australia's long-established cinematographic heritage has, more than any other art form, helped rid the country of its former philistine reputation. Confident and uncompromising films such as *Malcolm, Celia, Sweetie* and *The Year My Voice Broke* are just a few that complement their better-known siblings, with 1994 seeing a media-led "renaissance" in Australian film. Stephan Elliot's sartorially outrageous *Adventures of Priscilla, Queen of the Desert* was the country's biggest box-office success up to that time and won international acclaim, while P.J. Hogan's wonderful *Muriel's Wedding* perfectly encapsulated the indigenous film-making idiom and proved that Australia still could make financially viable and idiosyncratic films.

RECENT DEVELOPMENTS

More recently, Australian film critics have grown weary of the trend in making "quirky, off-beat romances", such as Shirley Barratt's *Love Serenade* and Emma Crogan's 1996 Cannes hit *Love and Other Catastrophes*, although few would have much to complain about with Scott Hicks' globally acclaimed *Shine*. Another worthy and uniquely Australian film released in 1996 was Nick Parsons' extraordinary *Dead Heart*. Describing the decomposing relationships, as well as the clash of white and tribal law, on an outstation near Alice Springs, the film sensitively and honestly portrays many aspects of contemporary Aboriginal life (deaths in custody, illicit grog runs, "payback", drunkenness and even sorcery).

While the Liberal government has slashed film funding to the Australian Film Commission and Film Finance Corporation, major actors such as Russel Crowe (*Romper Stomper*), Nicole Kidman (*Batman Forever*), Rachel Griffiths (*Divorcing Jack*), Cate Blanchett (*Elizabeth*) and

HOT SPOTS FOR FILM BUFFS AND SOAP GROUPIES

The majestic scenery of the Northern Territory has featured in many films. **Kakadu National Park** provided the setting for many of the scenes in *Crocodile Dundee*: familiar spots are possibly **Anbangbang Billabong** (see p.540) and **Waterfall Creek** (see p.541). *We of the Never Never* was set in the **Mataranka** region, which, predictably, has been rechristened "Never Never" country (see pp. 556); some costumes worn in the film are on display in the Old Courthouse and Residency in **Alice Springs** (see p.566).

Desolation and Outback grandeur have a stranglehold on the science-fiction and post-apocalyptic genres. Locations for *Mad Max II* include the **Silverton** area of New South Wales (see p.331); as his parting shot, Mel Gibson upscuttled the semi-trailer on the nearby **Mundi Mundi Plains**. In South Australia, the pockmarked scenery of **Coober Pedy** (see p.749) has found favour with many film-makers, including Wim Wenders, who

made his epic *Until the End of the World* here, while the lunar-like landscape was also an invaluable element in creating the atmosphere of *Mad Max III*. And *that* Outback pub in *Crocodile Dundee* was none other than the *Walkabout Hotel*, at **McKinlay** in Queensland.

More lush surroundings have also caught the imagination: in Victoria the eponymous **Hanging Rock** (see p.845), which featured in *Picnic at Hanging Rock*, is within striking distance of Woodend, but is disappointingly lacking in eeriness.

Inevitably, the **Sydney area** has its fair share of hallowed ground for TV addicts. *Skippy, the Bush Kangaroo*, or at least the son of Skippy, is the star of **Waratah Park** (see p.169). The soapy teenage angst and surfie bonhomie of *Home and Away* revolves around **Palm Beach** in Sydney's northern beaches (see p.135), with the Barrenjoey Lighthouse and headland regularly in shot.

Geoffrey Rush (*Shine*) now work mostly overseas where the pay, recognition and opportunities are much greater. In 1998 box office receipts hit a record A$629.2 million yet Australian films made up only two percent of that and almost all lost money.

However, a low Australian dollar, skilled crews and Sydney's new world-class Fox Studios have attracted major productions such as *Dark City*, *Babe: Pig In The City*, *The Matrix*, *Mission Impossible II* and *Star Wars Episode II* to Australia. Melbourne's developing docklands project includes a Paramount-backed studio that will be ready by 2001 and will also boost the Australian film industry's facilities, skillbase and reputation.

FILMS TO WATCH OUT FOR

While you'd be lucky to catch all the recommendations below on the big screen (although keep an eye on the programmes of **art-house**, or repertory, **cinemas** in the major cities), many of the titles can be found in **video** rental stores.

HUMOUR, BLACK COMEDY AND SATIRE

The Adventures of Priscilla, Queen of the Desert (Stephan Elliot, 1994). A queer romp across the Outback, prying into some musty corners of Australian social life along the way.

Babakiueria (Julian Pringler, 1988). A culture-reversing spoof beginning with Aborigines invading Australia during a roadside barbie and continuing with an anthropological-style study of white Australia. Rare, but well worth the search.

Death in Brunswick (John Ruane, 1990). A black comedy about the misfortunes of a hapless dishwasher who becomes embroiled in a gangland killing.

Les Paterson Saves the World (George Miller, 1986). Barry Humphries plays the repugnant cultural attaché in a lame spoof of monumental bad taste.

Malcolm (Nadia Tass, 1985). A charming, offbeat comedy about a slow-witted tram driver in Melbourne.

Muriel's Wedding (P.J. Hogan, 1994). Kleptomanic frump Muriel wastes away in an Abba-and-confetti dreamworld until ex-schoolchum Rhonda masterminds Muriel's escape from her awful family. Great performances.

ADOLESCENT AND MISFIT ROMANCE

Flirting (John Duigan, 1989). This sequel to *The Year My Voice Broke* follows a young boy's adventures in boarding school. Superior coming-of-age film.

Lonely Hearts (Paul Cox, 1981). Following the death of his mother, 50-year-old Peter buys a

new toupee and joins a dating agency. A sensitive portrayal of the ensuing, at times awkward, relationship. Other Paul Cox features worth looking out for include *Man of Flowers*, *My First Wife* and *Cactus*.
Strictly Ballroom (Baz Luhrmann, 1991). Mismatched dancers who, together, dare to defy the prescribed routines. A feel-good hit at Cannes and the box office.

URBAN DYSFUNCTIONALS

The Boys (Rowan Woods, 1998). This tense drama follows Brett, played by rising star, David Wenham (*Sea Change*) as an ex-prisoner who terrorizes his dysfunctional family and coerces his unemployed brothers into a violent crime.
Careful, He Might Hear You (Carl Shultz, 1982). An absorbing tug-of-love drama set in 1930s Sydney.
The Devil's Playground (Fred Schepisi, 1975). Burgeoning sexuality oozes between pupils and their tutors in a Catholic seminary.
Head On (Ana Kokkinos, 1998). Unemployed Ari (Alex Dimitriades) escapes living with his strict Greek parents by spending a hectic 24-hours nightclubbing, drug taking and graphically exploring his homosexuality.
The Interview (Craig Monahan, 1998). Truth and justice are explored as Hugo Waving (*Priscilla*) is interrogated by a corrupt policeman, with dubious methods, who suspects him of murder.
The Last Days of Chez Nous (Gillian Armstrong, 1991). A middle-aged woman slowly loses her grip on her marriage and family.
Monkey Grip (Ken Cameron, 1981). A bleak but candid portrayal of rootless lives and love in mid-1970s Melbourne.
Proof (Jocelyn Moorehouse, 1990). An uncomfortably cold film about a blind cynic rejecting his equally maladjusted housekeeper's advances.
Romper Stomper (Geoffrey Wright, 1991). A violent account of the racial hatred and gradual disintegration of a gang of Melbourne skinheads.
Sweetie (Jane Campion, 1988). Part black comedy, part bleakly disturbing portrait of a bizarre suburban family.

OCKERDOM AND HOONERY

The Adventures of Barry McKenzie (Bruce Beresford, 1972). Ultra-ocker comes to England to teach the "pommie sheilas about real men". Ironically, Humphries' satire got beer-spurting

ovations from the very people he despised and also set Beresford back a couple of years.
Crocodile Dundee (Peter Faiman, 1985). The acceptable side of genial, dinky-di ockerdom saw Paul Hogan sell Australian bush mystique to the mainstream.
The FJ Holden (Michael Thornhill, 1977). A portrayal of west Sydney hoons' joyless hedonism, as they ricochet between police, bars and girls.
Wake in Fright aka **Outback** (Ted Kotcheff, 1970). A horrifying gem in its uncut, 114min version; *Deliverance* or *Straw Dogs* Down Under. A coast-bound teacher blows his fare in Outback Hicksville and slowly degenerates into a brutal, beer-sodden nightmare.

GRITTY AND DEFIANT WOMEN

Celia (Ann Turner, 1988). A wonderful allegory that mixes a 1950s rabbit-eradication programme with a communist witch-hunt. Stubborn Celia is determined to keep her bunny.
Dance Me To My Song (Rolf De Heer, 1998). A unique and moving film written by and starring cerebral palsy sufferer, Heather Rose as she is abused by her carer and falls in love.
The Getting of Wisdom (Bruce Beresford, 1977). Spirited Laura rejects the polite sensibilities and snobbery of an Edwardian boarding school.
Heatwave (Phillip Noyce, 1981). Sweltering urban machinations, as Judy Davis uncovers dirty dealings surrounding a proposed development in heatstruck Sydney.
My Brilliant Career (Gillian Armstrong, 1978). An early feminist questions and defies the expectations of 1890s Victoria.
Puberty Blues (Bruce Beresford, 1981). Two teenage beach girls refuse to accept their pushchair-and-shopping-trolley destiny.
Shame (Steve Jordell, 1986). A lone woman lawyer on a motorbike gets stuck in an Outback town full of creeps and delves into its dirty secret.
We of the Never Never (Igor Auzins, 1981). A good-looking version of Jeannie Gunn's autobiographical classic of turn-of-the-century station life in the Top End.

MEN IN RUGGED CIRCUMSTANCES

Gallipoli (Peter Weir, 1980). A deservedly classic buddy movie in which a young Mel Gibson strikingly evokes the Anzacs' cheery idealism and the tragedy of their slaughter.

The Last of the Knucklemen (Tim Burstall, 1978). Tensions build up in a remote Outback mine and explode in bare-fisted punch-ups.

The Man from Snowy River (George Miller, 1981). Men, horses and the land from A.B. ("Banjo") Paterson's seminal and dearly loved poem caught the overseas' imagination. A modern kangaroo western.

Plains of Heaven (Ian Pringle, 1982). A spookily atmospheric story of two weathermen in a remote meteorological station slowly losing their minds.

Sunday Too Far Away (Ken Hannam, 1973). A simple tale of macho shearers' rivalries in Outback South Australia.

OUTBACK NIGHTMARES AND WEIRDNESS

Evil Angels (*A Cry in the Dark*) (Fred Schepisi, 1987). A dramatic retelling of the Azaria Chamberlain story; dingoes will never seem quite the same again.

The Lost Weekend (Colin Eggleston, 1977). The beautiful bush closes in menacingly on an ecologically unsound couple camping on a remote beach.

Picnic at Hanging Rock (Peter Weir, 1975). A richly layered tale about the disappearance of a party of schoolgirls and its traumatic aftermath.

Razorback (Russell Mulcahy, 1984). The darkest of comedies, exploiting urban paranoia of the Outback and featuring a remote township, a gigantic, psychotic wild pig, and some bloodthirsty nutters who run the local abattoir.

Walkabout (Nicolas Roeg, 1971). Following their deranged father's suicide during a bush picnic, two children wander through the wilderness until an Aboriginal boy guides them back to civilization.

ABOUT ABORIGINES

The Chant of Jimmie Blacksmith (Fred Schepisi, 1977). Set in the 1800s, when a half-caste boy is forced onto the wrong side of the law. Based on the book by Thomas Keneally.

Dead Heart (Brian Brown, 1996). A long-overdue and regrettably overlooked thriller, set on an Aboriginal community near Alice Springs. Bravely gets its teeth into some juicy political and social issues.

The Fringe Dwellers (Bruce Beresford, 1985). An aspiring daughter persuades her family to move from the bush into a suburban white neighbourhood, with expected results.

Jedda, the Uncivilized (Charles Chauvel, 1955). An orphaned Aboriginal girl brought up by a "civilized" white family cannot resist her "tribal" urges when she is semivoluntarily abducted by a black outlaw.

Manganinnie (John Honey, 1980). Set during the time of the "black drives" of 1830s Tasmania, a young Aboriginal girl gets separated from her family and meets a white girl in similar straits.

PORTENTS OF DOOM

Cane Toads: an Unnatural History (Mark Lewis, 1988). A bizarre and amusing documentary about the mixed feelings Queensland's poisonous amphibians arouse and the real threat they may pose to Australia's ecology.

The Last Wave (Peter Weir, 1977). A spooky chiller about a lawyer defending an Aborigine accused of murder – and the powerful, elemental forces his people control.

Mad Max II (George Miller, 1981). The best of the trilogy, set in a near future where loner Max protects an oil-producing community from fuel-starved crazies. Great machinery and stunts.

Newsfront (Phillip Noyce, 1978). Nothing portentous whatsoever, but an excellent movie set among mid-1950s Melbourne's newsreel crews, concerning the disparate political and professional aspirations of two brothers.

AUSTRALIAN MUSIC

The story of Australian contemporary music closely parallels that of Britain and the US – rock'n'roll arrived in the 1950s, and each decade since has offered up its own revolutionary shift in the popular music landscape. Given the ubiquitous nature of western popular culture, this is hardly surprising. Less predictable, however, has been the impact of Australian music on the world music scene, beginning in the 1970s with AC/DC, continuing in the 1980s with Midnight Oil and INXS, through to current multimillion record sellers silverchair and Natalie Imbruglia. For a geographically isolated, sparsely inhabited island with a tiny market for its own recorded music, Australia has, with ever-more assurance, shouldered its way in to occupy a distinguished place in pop music's hierarchy.

THE EARLY YEARS

Australia's very first rock star emerged in 1957 in the form of a lean, throaty, stage-strutting powerhouse named **Johnny O'Keefe**. All snake-hips and sex appeal, "The Wild One", as he became known, was one of the few early rock performers who could very nearly out-Elvis Elvis. Concert footage of his live performances is largely taken up by shots of women screaming, passing out and being carried from concert venues by sweaty police and exhausted security. O'Keefe discov-

ered early on that all the big players in the industry – performers, managers, promoters and record companies – were expert manipulators, and he quickly set about becoming one himself: legend has it that he bullied his way into his first recording contract by calling a press conference and announcing that the deal was done, guessing correctly that the publicity would leave the record company no option but to sign him.

Johnny O'Keefe was, to Australians, the embodiment of the defiant new brand of music that was then sweeping the world. He was to become synonymous with 1960s TV programmes that showcased Australian rock'n'roll talent, even as his own recording efforts were gradually swamped by the peace-love-hair movement of the time. O'Keefe remained a presence on television and radio until his death of a heart-attack in 1978, aged just 43. In keeping with the requirements of rock God-dom, his last years were characterized by a series of breakdowns, bouts of depression and problems with alcohol. His rendition of the classic crowd-anthem **"Shout"** (1959) remains, to this day, an integral part of early rock'n'roll's global legacy; (video footage of O'Keefe performing live also constitutes the opening sequence of the ABC's late-night music video programme, *Rage*).

SURVIVING THE SIXTIES

In company with the rest of the world, Australian music rode out the 1960s hanging onto the coat-tails of the massive British rock invasion. Overwhelmed by the omnipresent Beatles and Rolling Stones, Australia was to produce little ground-breaking rock music, beyond the efforts of Billy Thorpe and the Aztecs, The Easybeats and Russell Morris, each of whom left behind a signature song forever embedded in the Australian psyche, and still played on commercial radio today: "Most People I Know (Think that I'm Crazy)" – Billy Thorpe and the Aztecs (1968); "Friday on My Mind" – The Easybeats (1966); "The Real Thing" – Russell Morris (1969).

The Seekers, however, were operating well clear of the crowded rock music mainstream, creating their own musical niche by building three-part harmonies around chords strummed on acoustic guitars, the two male voices cushioning the pristine power of lead vocalist Judith Durham. Songs like "If I Had a Hammer" (1965) might sound like hippie anthems today, but The Seekers' brand of idealism appealed to millions of record-buyers, and a successful recent comeback tour showed that their popularity has barely waned.

It was in 1967, however, that millions of Australians witnessed the decade's most significant music industry event – and not a single one of them even knew it. A young man named **Johnny Farnham** had appeared on television, performing a cute but innocuous ditty entitled "Sadie (the Cleaning Lady)" (1967). Good-looking and with a superb voice, as well as charming beyond his years, Farnham endeared himself immediately to Australian audiences; it was a promising debut, but nobody could have predicted how far he'd go. His name shortened these days to John, Farnham is now into his fourth decade as a performer, and continues to shift with apparently effortless ease between roles as rock star, stage-musical lead and TV personality. From 1982–86 he was a popular frontman for the hugely successful Little River Band (having replaced Glen Shorrock), but it was in 1987 that his career peaked, with the release of his album "Whispering Jack", which sold millions of copies worldwide, driven, appropriately enough, by the success of the single "You're the Voice" (1987).

LIVIN' IN THE SEVENTIES

Having emerged from the shadows of the 1960s, Australian music began to find a voice of its own in the mid-1970s. For no obvious reason, **Glam Rock** was a phenomenon Australian bands not only embraced, but excelled at. Sherbet and **Skyhooks** pulled off the satin-jumpsuits-and-crazy-make-up combo with singular style. The "Mighty Hooks" were at all times the cheekier and sexier of the two. Singer "Shirley" Strachan famously performed in only a pair of tight satin trousers with a large, bright-red hand painted over the crotch; the other band-members were equally indulgent of their penchants for self-expression. There was no sacrifice of substance for style, however, with the band recording several of Australia's finest and most enduring pop songs, including such irresistible numbers as "You Just Like Me 'cause I'm Good in Bed" (1974), "Horror Movie" (1974), "Ego (Is Not a Dirty Word)" (1975), and "Women in Uniform" (1978).

Sherbet seemed almost serious by comparison, doing without the make-up and looking as though they only wore the satin pants, silly shoes and poncy scarves because that was what fashion dictated. It was a highly accomplished band no matter what they were wearing, and led by virtuoso pop vocalist Daryl Braithwaite, they recorded several standout tracks, including "Child's Play" (1976), "Howzat" (1976), "High Rolling" (1977) and "Summer Love" (1975). Although both bands flirted with overseas success, touring the US (and subsequently expressing bitterness at not having cracked the big time), history has conferred upon them the honour of having kicked open the rock music establishment's door, on behalf of an Australian music fraternity that had simply been waiting around for someone to show them "we're just as good as those bands from overseas".

Proof perhaps of the depth of talent concentrated in these two bands is the continued presence of individual members in Australian music and media today. Trivia buffs will find the following Skyhooks alumni alive and well: Graeme "Shirley" Strachan – former lead singer, now a popular television presenter; Red Symons is still strumming and cast forevermore as the villain on television's *Hey Hey it's Saturday*; and Greg Macainsh is in high demand still, as a bass-player and songwriter. Stalwarts of Sherbet have likewise soldiered on: Daryl Braithwaite the lead singer is now a successful solo performer; Harvey James, one of the first Australian guitar-heroes, graduated to session musician and guitar-ace-for-hire; and Garth Porter, former keyboardist, who has gone on to assume the unlikely mantle of producer/guru for many of Australia's top country music performers.

But even as Glam Rock was fading from cool to kitsch, a clannish group of young Scottish immigrants were beginning to play their own version of Chuck Berry-inspired blues-rock, only three times as loud and with heavily distorted guitars. **AC/DC** not only had the skills, the songs and the "muscle" to back it all up, they also boasted two figures who were destined to become universal icons of rock'n'roll rebellion: guitarist Angus Young's delinquent schoolboy persona had to share the adulation of wannabe rock rebels with singer Bon Scott, who was possessed not only of a genuine, self-destructive, live-hard-die-young ethos, but also sported the most mischievous grin ever seen in tandem with a microphone. It's unlikely anyone besides Bon could have delivered songs such as "Highway to

Hell" (1979), "Whole Lotta Rosie" (1978), and "Dirty Deeds...Done Dirt Cheap" (1976) with the required sass to make them acceptable in a 1970s commercial market.

True to form, Bon died a rock star's death in London in 1980, poisoned by alcohol in the back seat of a car. It was, ironically, smack in the middle of a golden age for Australian music, when, during the period 1977–1983, bands Men at Work, Midnight Oil, Cold Chisel, INXS, Air Supply and Little River Band were lining up right alongside AC/DC to take the pop music world by storm.

OZ MUSIC GROWS UP

Even as AC/DC managed – in the space of a year following Bon's death – to recruit a new singer (Brian Johnston), settle permanently into life in Britain, and record the most acclaimed and successful heavy rock album of all time, "Back in Black" (1980), bands back in Australia suddenly found that the world was interested in them, too. **Little River Band**'s sound was so west coast USA that commercial success in North America had long seemed inevitable; **Air Supply**, meanwhile, had the sort of stranglehold on the American easy listening love-song market to which Michael Bolton was perhaps, even then, beginning to aspire. More surprising was the impact made by **Men at Work**, a band whose well-crafted songs were invariably, if unfashionably, punctuated by arresting melodies played on a flute, and whose style came to be described as "white reggae". They announced their arrival in 1981 with the ska-ish "Who Can it Be Now?", followed by "The Land Down Under", both of which bombarded radio airwaves and shifted by the million.

During this period, Midnight Oil, Cold Chisel and INXS stayed closer to home, recognizing perhaps that their styles were less easily translatable from an Australian to a global audience. It is surely no coincidence that among these bands (all highly-accomplished, and equally revered at home) the least identifiably "Australian" act – **INXS** – was the first to experience worldwide fame and fortune, when in 1987 their album "Kick" plundered the US charts. (This wave of success held tragic implications for singer Michael Hutchence; he would struggle to make the transition from rock star to rock *super*star, suffering depression until his death by suicide in late 1997). Of the other two,

most needs to be said about the band that had the biggest impact at home, and the least impact abroad – Cold Chisel. If the period three years either side of 1980 was to be remembered as the grand era of Oz "pub rock", then Chisel was the band that owned it, lock, stock and smoking barrel.

FROM CHISEL TO THE CHURCH

Formed in Adelaide in 1975, **Cold Chisel** was, like every great band from the Rolling Stones to U2, the sum of its parts. Steve Prestwich (drums) and Phil Small (bass) made a compact and classy rhythm team, variously casting light and shadow about the more illustrious members of the group. Ian Moss' blues-rock guitar virtuosity and awesome soul voice made him a natural star on any stage, in lethal combination with lead singer Jimmy Barnes, Australia's self-styled wild man of rock and working-class hero. A great band must have great songs, and these were duly delivered by the immensely tall and serious man at the piano, Don Walker, arguably Australia's greatest songwriter.

Among hundreds of examples of **Don Walker**'s craftsmanship in capturing the times/places/people/events that make meaning for Australians, "Khe Sanh" (1978) (Walker's treatise on the Australian experience of surviving the war in Vietnam), remains a work without peer, while "Star Hotel" (1980) captures, in three verses and a chorus, the mood and events of September 19, 1979, when, in the working-class steel-town of Newcastle police came to close down the city's main pub-rock venue, *The Star Hotel*, only to find themselves confronted by an angry crowd spoiling for a fight. Police cars were overturned and set alight in the course of a civil disturbance that echoed convict rebellions of two centuries earlier. The hotel was finally closed down, but the punters had made their point – and Chisel weren't going to let the police forget it.

Cold Chisel not only recorded the boozy summer nights, the trips up the coast, the girls, the fights, the pubs, the streets, the cities and towns, they sang it all back to the faithful in sweaty pubs and heaving stadiums night after night. When they called it a day in 1984, Chisel were Australia's greatest ever rock band, bar none. "Mossy" and "Barnesy" went on to fame and fortune as solo performers, but the band's long-awaited return did not come until 1998, when they released their first studio album in fourteen years "The Last Wave of Summer"; it remains to be seen whether they can be anything like as great again.

During this period, **Midnight Oil** by no means played second banana to Cold Chisel; rather, they had a different agenda, and their commitment and energy in delivering it live were never in question. Always highly political (lead singer Peter Garrett narrowly missed out on a Senate seat and he was leader of Australia's Nuclear Disarmament Party), "the Oils" brought aboriginal land rights into the forum of pop culture, even as their uncompromising album "Diesel and Dust" (1987) brought them worldwide success. Twenty-year veterans with twelve albums to their credit (and bracketed by critics with Queen and U2 as the most powerful live act in the world), Midnight Oil remain establishment cage-rattlers par excellence.

Among the distinguished musicians of the 1970s and 1980s, two songwriters stand (alongside Don Walker) above the rest as chroniclers of their culture and environment: **Richard Clapton** and **Paul Kelly**. Clapton's 1977 album "Goodbye Tiger" is unmatched as a celebration of the very fact of life in Australia – riding the city tram, searching for the perfect wave, soaking up the streetscapes of Oxford Street and King's Cross. Paul Kelly is a more contemporary presence, and his songs go unerringly to the heart of the matter: "Have You Ever Seen Sydney From a 727 at Night?" (1985), "From St Kilda to King's Cross" (1985) and "Adelaide" (1985) capture their respective subjects better than any photograph, while his ode to "Bradman" (1987) – written in homage to Australia's greatest Test cricket batsman Sir Donald Bradman –The Don, is the stuff of a true bard, a composition in verse honouring the glorious return from battle of a people's champion.

But in order to appreciate the depth and diversity of Australian music as it reached **maturity**, one needs to take a stroll out to the fringes. With a well-established canon of "major" Australian bands now in place, others were finding looser creative environments in which to operate. The Triffids, The Birthday Party (with star alumnus Nick Cave), The Church and the Go-Betweens seemed tied to weirder and more eclectic influences (such as The Velvet Underground, David Bowie and Bob Dylan) than their "mainstream" counterparts. Although musically diverse, they held several

characteristics in common: their songs seemed more committed, or more poetic, or just more sensitive to light-and-shade; they were also far less commercially successful in Australia, and all made a big impact in Britain and Europe where they received critical acclaim. Among all of these, The Church alone continue to record and tour from various bases in Europe, while Nick Cave remains intent upon perfecting the art of the murder ballad; his album "Murder Ballads" (1996) features a duet with Kylie Minogue. Australia could boast, too, a white-hot outfit schooled in the nasty traditions of 1970s British punk: The Saints. Although known for their Sex Pistols-ish two-minute thrash exercises, The Saints were nevertheless real musicians, and survivors Chris Bailey and Ed Kuepper continue to record and perform songs of the highest quality.

THE NINETIES AND BEYOND...

Strangest perhaps of all the facets of Australia's music industry has been its propensity for throwing up TV **soap stars** who mutated into rock stars (of sorts). At last count there were no less than four ex-*Neighbours* cast members at large within the music industry: Kylie Minogue, Danii Minogue, Jason Donovan and Natalie Imbruglia. Australians have never known what to make of this, but the latest of the batch, Natalie Imbruglia, made her mark in 1998 with a superb pop album "Left of the Middle", so there, at least, is some evidence of genuine musical accomplishment.

The roaring success of these soap-star singers goes some way to explaining the listlessness that afflicted the music community during the late 1980s–early 1990s. It seemed the moment **Jason Donovan** and **Kylie Minogue** were formally adopted by an adoring British public, Australian musicians breathed a collective sigh of relief, and got straight back to work. You Am I, The Whitlams, The Cruel Sea and Skunkhour had always been likely to show the way by writing and recording with passion and originality. By the mid-1990s, quality Australian bands were once again jostling for position in local and overseas markets, this time led by three scruffy-looking fifteen-year-old schoolboys.

In 1994, Newcastle high-school trio **Innocent Criminals** sent a demo tape to radio Triple J in response to a band competition, the prize for

TOP TEN GREAT ROCK OZ ALBUMS

1) **Livin' in the Seventies** – Skyhooks. Mushroom Records, 1974.
2) **Howzat!** – Sherbet. Sherbet Records, 1976.
3) **Goodbye Tiger** – Richard Clapton. Infinity Records, 1977.
4) **Back in Black** – AC/DC. Albert Records, 1980.
5) **East** – Cold Chisel. WEA, 1980.
6) **Business As Usual** – Men At Work. CBS, 1981.
7) **Circus Animals** – Cold Chisel. WEA, 1982.
8) **Kick** – INXS. WEA, 1987.
9) **Diesel and Dust**" – Midnight Oil. CBS, 1987.
10) **Eternal Nightcap** – The Whitlams. Phantom Records, 1997.

which was use of the station's recording facilities. The song, "Tomorrow", had the Seattle grunge sound all over it, and an awesome rock vocal performance from singer/guitarist Daniel Johns. He didn't sound like a fifteen-year-old, although the band's written entry should have given some kind of clue; their "twenty-five-words-or-less" were written in green felt marker-pen on yellow cardboard: "We're not rap or hip-hop, we're rock and we love to play". "Tomorrow" arrived atop the Australian singles charts where it stayed for several weeks, and with the band renamed silverchair, their 1995 album "Frogstomp" took them into league – and onto a stage – with grunge giants like Pearl Jam and Soundgarden, even as the three "boys" were negotiating their last year of high school.

With the new millennium dawning, the feeling is that Australian music has the stuff to tackle it head-on. From rock outfits Powderfinger, Grinspoon and The Superjesus and the thrashier Spiderbait, Jebediah and The Living End, to the stylish and witty The Whitlams, the dance-pop of Savage Garden, and the rock/techno crossover work of Regurgitator, the array of talent is dizzying. Tune in as the next great era of Australian music unfolds.

ABORIGINAL MUSIC

In contrast with Australia's forty-year rock music heritage, Aboriginal music boasts a creative presence of thousands of years. Its instruments and rhythms have a strong influence in contemporary Australian music, and there's probably no better example of the musical crossing of cultural boundaries, than in the story of Australia's most recognizable instrument, the didgeridoo. Known also as a *yidaki*, or simply a "didge", this hollowed-out tree branch, when blown into, produces a resonant hum, punctuated by imitations of animal and bird noises. Its sound is evocative, to many, of the Australian landscape. The importance of Aboriginal music generally in the ongoing **reconciliation** between black and white Australia can hardly be overstated, and it is also an increasingly powerful and invigorating seam in the fabric of world music.

The big surprise for many visitors to Australia is the sheer **diversity** of Aboriginal music. From the big rock sound of the Warumpi Band to the heartfelt guitar ballads of Archie Roach, the cruisey island reggae of newcomers Saltwater, and the echoes of an ancient culture in the work of Nabarlek (who sing mostly in their own language) there is no way of pigeonholing the music. And while there's no problem seeing Aboriginal bands, doing everything from metal to hip-hop and performing in all parts of the country, there's really no better way to immerse yourself than by attending an Indigenous music festival.

FESTIVALS

Biggest of all is the **Barunga Sports & Cultural Festival**, which showcases up to forty bands, along with sports events, spear-throwing and didge-playing competitions. It's held at Barunga Community, 80km south of Katherine in the NT, over the first weekend in June (campsites with facilities are available). Also in the Top End, the **Millingimbi Cultural Festival** is purely a music event and, being harder to get to than Barunga, gets fewer white visitors. Dates for this one are hard to nail down, although it's always held sometime mid-year, on Millingimbi Island in the Crocodile archipelago. The return flight from Darwin costs around $250, otherwise you need permission from the Northern Land Council (Darwin Head Office ☎08/8920 5100; they also tell you the festival dates) to drive across Arnhemland to Ramingining to catch a barge. Traditional music and dance are featured, along with gospel bands and lots of Arnhemland rock.

The annual festival at **Laura**, in far north Queensland, attracts high profile performers like the Warumpi Band and Christine Anu, plus all the local Murri bands. Held in either May or June (it varies from year to year), there are usually quite a few backpackers and hippies about, as well as the local Murri community. It's roughly two hours drive (on sealed roads) north from Cairns to Laura, a small town 60km west of Cooktown. Otherwise, another intriguing possibility on the west coast just might be the **"Stompin' Ground"** festival. First staged in Broome, WA in 1992, and then again in 1998, it drew on the strong and highly independent Aboriginal communities of the Kimberley region, attracting singers, dancers and bands into the incomparable beauty of WA's far north. Although it is not really an "established" event, it could be well worth checking out. (Radio Triple J is a good source for music festival info, and they broadcast Australia-wide.

And even if you find yourself stranded in the Big Smoke, you need not miss out; if you're in **Sydney** over summer, there's no better place to be on the Australia Day holiday (January 26)

than at "Survival", Waverley Park, Bondi. This festival began as a highly political event, deliberately juxtaposed with the Australia Day festivities which mark the arrival of the first fleet of "white invaders". It continues as a celebration of the survival of indigenous people and cultures in the face of white oppression, and draws many of the biggest names in indigenous music.

ARTISTS

Most of the **bands** mentioned above have work available on CD, while other outstanding artists whose albums are widely available include Yothu Yindi, No Fixed Address, Tiddas, Kev Carmody and Coloured Stone. Compilation albums are worth looking into also, particularly those that cover a wide range of styles: "Meinmuk – Music from the Top End" (1996) is a Radio Triple J compilation of songs by twenty four different Arnhemland bands, covering rock, reggae, gospel and metal; "Demarru Hits" is another good one, available through CAAMA (Central Australian Aboriginal Media Association) in Alice Springs, and some music retailers.

BOOKS

Australian writing came into its own in the 1890s, when a strong nationalistic movement leading up to eventual federation in 1901 produced writers such as Henry Lawson and the balladeer A.B. "Banjo" Paterson, who romanticized the bush and glorified the mateship ethos, while outstanding women writers, such as Miles Franklin and Barbara Baynton, gave a feminine slant to the bush tale and set the trend for a strong female authorship. In the twentieth century, Australian novelists have come to be recognized in the international arena, Patrick White having been awarded a Nobel Prize in 1973, and Peter Carey the Booker Prize in 1988. More recently, writers who have made a name for themselves within Australia, such as David Malouf and Tim Winton, have begun to arouse curiosity further afield.

These days, Australian writing is flourishing: as in the USA, the **short story** thrives in Australia, with popular magazines such as *Australian Short Stories* and literary journals such as *Meanjin*, *Southerly*, *Westerly* and *Heat* providing a forum and exposure for short fiction, essays, reviews and new and established writers. Eagerly read anthologies, on every theme imaginable and with an emphasis on women's writing and multiculturalism, are constantly being published; for a taste of the latest, the annual *Picador New Writing* is worth seeking. The big prizes in Australian fiction include the Vogel Prize for the best unpublished novel written by an author under the age of 35, and the country's most coveted literary prize, the Miles Franklin Award.

Australia's biggest **literary scandal** was attached in 1995 to the preposterously young winner of both awards, the then 24-year-old

Brisbane writer Helen Demidenko for her first novel, *The Hand that Signed the Paper* (Allen & Unwin, Aus), which is about a half-Ukrainian Australian girl seeking to find out what really happened in the Ukraine during World War II. The book had already caused controversy by being labelled anti-Semitic by some critics, but these concerns were silenced mostly by statements from the author herself, who said that she had researched the story through talking to Ukrainian relatives and her book was based on fact. The literary establishment reeled with embarrassment when Demidenko was outed as just plain old Helen Darville, a daughter of British immigrants with a wild imagination befitting her career as a novelist. Other literary scandals, which seem to be tied up with the perceived necessity of the "multicultural" ingredient for marketing purposes and a lack of confidence in plain "Australian" as a cultural identity in the 1990s, have included the recent revelation that a female Aboriginal author was, in reality, two middle-aged white men.

You'll be surprised at the range of titles available in Australian **bookshops**, though be prepared to pay more than you would at home. A good Web site to check is that of one of Australia's best literary booksellers, Gleebooks (*www.gleebooks.com.au*) with a whole host of recent reviews; specific titles can be ordered via email on *books@gleebooks.com.au* and posted out. We've given the publishers of each book, where available, in the United Kingdom (UK), the United States (US), and Australia (Aus) where applicable; obviously, most Australian-interest books are more widely available in Australia. O/p signifies an out-of-print – but still highly recommended – book which you will probably be able to find in a library. University Press is abbreviated as UP.

TRAVEL

Bruce Chatwin *Songlines* (Picador UK; Penguin US; Vintage Aus). A semifictional account of an exploration into Aboriginal nomadism and mythology that turns out to be one of the clearest and most inspiring expositions of this complex subject. A must.

Linda Christmas *The Ribbon and the Ragged Square* (Viking Penguin UK o/p; Penguin US). A pushy English journalist's travels and observations around the "ragged square of Australia" in the 1980s.

Sean Condon *Sean and David's Long Drive* (Lonely Planet). Australia's answer to Kerouac's *On the Road*, with humour in overdrive: Melbourne-based Condon and his friend David are fully fledged city dwellers when they set off on a tour around their own country, to come face to face with the dangers of crocs, tour guides and fellow travellers.

Robyn Davidson *Tracks* (Vintage, Picador UK; Random US). A powerfully compelling account of a stubborn young woman's journey across the Australian desert, accompanied only by four camels and a dog. Davidson manages to break out of the heroic-traveller mould to write with compassion and honesty of the people she meets in the Outback and the doubts, dangers and loneliness she faces on her way. A classic of its kind.

Howard Jacobson *In the Land of Oz* (Penguin UK, Aus o/p). Jacobson focuses his lucidly sarcastic observations on a round-Australia trip that gets rather too close to some home truths for most Australians' tastes.

William J. Lines *A Long Walk in the Australian Bush* (University of NSW Press, Aus). Narrative of the author's 650km trek along the Bibbulum Track outside of Perth.

Mark McCrumb *No Worries* (Reed UK). Knowing nothing of the country except the usual clichés, McCrumm arrives in 1990s Australia and makes his way around by plane, train, thumb and Greyhound, meeting a surprising cast of characters along the way. As he travels, the stereotypes give way to an insightful picture of modern Australia.

Jan Morris *Sydney* (Penguin UK, Aus). Morris revises her former sour opinion in an insightful and informative account of Australia's favourite city.

AUTOBIOGRAPHY AND BIOGRAPHY

Julia Blackburn *Daisy Bates in the Desert* (Minerva UK; Random US). From 1913 – for almost thirty years – Daisy Bates, originally from Ireland, was Kabbarli, "the white-skinned grandmother", to the Aboriginal people with whom she lived in the Western Australian desert. A forbidding amateur anthropologist, she made an incongruous figure, always clad in long Victorian dress, and her reputation as a

prodigious twister of the truth finds perfect expression in Blackburn's beautifully written biography, which itself interweaves fiction with fact to conjure up the life of one of Australia's most eccentric and misunderstood women.

Ian Britain *Once An Australian: Journeys with Barry Humphries, Clive James, Germaine Greer and Robert Hughes* (Oxford UP UK, Aus). An exploration from childhood and youth in Australia to fame abroad of this quartet of the country's most notable expatriates, who all left between 1959 and 1964 during the conservative Menzies era, when Australia was something of a cultural backwater.

Jill Ker Conway *The Road from Coorain* (Minerva UK; Vintage US). Conway's extraordinary, hardworking childhood, on a drought-stricken Outback station in New South Wales during the 1940s, is movingly told, as is her equally fraught battle to establish herself as a young historian in sexist, provincial 1950s Australia. It was a long road from here to becoming the first woman president of Smith College in the USA, detailed in the second volume of her autobiography, *True North: a Memoir* (Vintage UK; Random US), in which she is critical of the land she feels she had to leave behind in order to further her career.

Albert Facey *A Fortunate Life* (Viking UK o/p; Viking Penguin US o/p; Penguin Aus). A hugely popular autobiography of a battler, tracing his progress from a bush orphanage to Gallipoli, through the Depression, another war and beyond.

Dorothy Hewett *Wild Card* (Virago UK o/p; McPhee Gribble Aus o/p). One of Australia's most famous playwrights and poets, Hewett is also one of its more unconventional and outspoken. Her autobiography explores the first part of her life (1923–58): born in Perth, the beautiful, passionate writer threw her energies into the Australian Communist Party and into her love life, challenging political and sexual convention. Leaving her husband, she married a boilermaker and moved to Sydney, where she lived in working-class areas and took a job in a factory – on which she based her novel *Bobbin' Up* (Virago UK).

Barry Humphries *More Please* (Penguin UK, Aus). An autobiography of the face behind the many outrageous Australian caricatures.

Clive James *Unreliable Memoirs* (Picador UK; Knopf US o/p). The expat satirist humorously recalls his postwar childhood and adolescence in Sydney's southern suburbs.

Eddie Mabo and Noel Loos *Edward Koiko Mabo: His Life and Struggle for Land Rights* (University of Queensland Press Aus). Mabo spent much of his life fighting for the autonomy of Torres Strait Islanders and in the process overthrew the concept of *terra nullius*, making his name a household word in Australia. Long interviews with the now-deceased black hero, conducted by the Townsville-based historian Loos, form the basis of this book and affectionately reveal the man behind the name.

David Malouf *12 Edmondstone Street* (Chatto UK; Vintage Aus). An evocative autobiography-in-snatches of one of Australia's finest literary novelists, describing, in loving detail, the eponymous house in Brisbane where Malouf was born, and then expanding to a view of the wider world – life in the Tuscan village where he lives for part of each year, and his first visit to India.

David Marr *Patrick White: a Life* (Vintage UK; Random Aus). Superb biography of Australia's Nobel Prize-winning author. The late Patrick White (1912–90) is brought to life: a difficult, complex man whose terrible rages and homosexuality are frankly explored.

Brenda Niall and John Thompson (eds) *The Oxford Book of Australian Letters* (Oxford UP UK, Aus). These letters, arranged chronologically, form something of a personal history of Australia since white settlement, with vivid and immediate accounts of events, scenes and emotions from the pen of both famous Australians and ordinary people, from Elizabeth Macarthur writing from her farm on Parramatta River in 1799 to a woman on an Outback station in 1941 jotting down a lively account of a local wedding while being bitten by mosquitoes.

Hazel Rowley *Christina Stead: a Biography* (Minerva Aus). Stead (1902–83) has been acclaimed as Australia's greatest novelist, but years of living abroad gave her a wide range of settings for her novels. After spending years in Paris, London and New York with her American husband, she returned to Australia in her old age. Her masterpiece, *The Man Who Loved Children* (Flamingo UK o/p; Holt & Co US; Angus & Robertson Aus), ostensibly set in Chesapeake Bay in the USA, is regarded very much as a portrait of the Sydney of her childhood, with the character of the title based on her famous naturalist father.

Daryl Tonkin and Carolyn Landon, *Jackson's Track* (Penguin Aus). Ghost written autobiography of Tonkin, a bushman who fell in love with an Aboriginal woman, Euphemia Mullet, who worked on his timber milling property in Victoria's East Gippsland in the 1930s. The cross-cultural romance survived the kidnap of Euphemia by his own outraged family who were trying to prevent their union, but the couple overcame prejudices to create their own life and family, living amongst a wider Aboriginal community at Jackson's Track.

Christine Wallace *Greer: Untamed Shrew* (Pan Macmillan Aus). Biography of one of Australia's most influential and outspoken expats, Germaine Greer, whose feminist classic *The Female Eunuch* came out in 1970 and its controversial sequel *The Whole Woman* in 1999. The Australian-set section of the narrative explores Greer's troubled childhood in Melbourne, her undergraduate days at Melbourne University in the straitlaced 1950s as a Carlton bohemian, lifes and loves in Sydney and time at Sydney University, then the brain drain exodus of the 1960s when so many creative, intellectual and ambitious Australians left.

SOCIETY AND CULTURE

Richard Baker *Land is Life: From Bush to Town – the Story of the Yanyuwa People* (Allen & Unwin Aus). The small group of Yanyuwa people inhabited the coast and islands of the Gulf of Carpentaria before the Europeans arrived, but most now live in the town of Booloola, 1600km southeast of Darwin. Historian Baker, assigned a "skin" in the Yanyuwa kinship system, became known in their language as "the one desiring the word" as he gathered the people's oral history. It's a fascinating story told from the Yanyuwa point of view and time.

Krim Benterrak, Stephen Muecke and Paddy Roe *Reading the Country* (Fremantle Arts Centre Press Aus). An intellectual exploration of Roebuck Plains in northwest Western Australia as an arena for contending discourses, ranging from the perceptions of the seventeenth-century English explorer William Dampier to the area's representation in Benterrak's paintings, Roe's oral tales and Muecke's postmodern deconstruction.

Geoffrey Blainey *Triumph of the Nomads* (Macmillan UK o/p; Overlook Press US; Sun Aus).

A fascinating account portraying Aboriginal people as masters and not victims of their environment. One of the best books on the subject.

Frank Brennan *Sharing the Country* (Penguin Aus). Both lawyer and Jesuit priest, and a former Aboriginal Affairs advisor to Australia's Catholic Church, Brennan sets out his legal and social solutions for reconciliation between black and white Australians, with a new section on the implications of the Mabo judgment on land rights.

John Bryson *Evil Angels* (Viking Penguin UK o/p; Bantam US o/p; Penguin Aus). The trial and witch-hunt of Lindy Chamberlain, convicted of murdering the infant daughter whom she maintained was carried off by a dingo. An account of a miscarriage of justice that delves into the grubbier regions of Australian psyche and the law.

Barbara Caine (general ed) *Australian Feminism: A Companion* (Oxford UP UK, Aus). A huge tome – over 600 pages – dominated by 49 interpretive essays relevant to modern Australian feminism. But don't just expect creches and suffrage: you'll find film, fashion, cyberspace and even sadomasochism covered. However, the chronology of events, the bibliography and the index are full of mistakes.

Monica Furlong *Flight of the Kingfisher: a Journey Among Kukatja Aborigines* (Flamingo UK; HarperCollins Aus). Furlong lived among the Aboriginal people of the Great Sandy Desert; this is her account of Kukatja perceptions and spiritual beliefs.

Roslynn Haynes *Seeking the Centre: The Australian Desert in Literature, Art and Film* (Cambridge UP UK, Aus). The geographical and metaphorical impact of the desert on Australian culture is explored in this highly illustrated book, as is the deep connection Aboriginal people have with the desert and the ways this relationship has been perceived by settler Australians.

David Headon *North of the Ten Commandments* (Hodder & Stoughton UK, Aus o/p). An anthology of Northern Territory writings from all perspectives and sources – an excellent literary souvenir for anyone who falls for the charms of Australia's "one percent" territory.

Donald Horne *The Lucky Country* (Angus & Robertson UK o/p; Penguin Aus). Although over twenty years old, this seminal analysis of

Australian society, written in 1976, has yet to be matched and is still often quoted.

Pybus and Flanagan (eds) *The Rest of the World Is Watching: Tasmania and the Greens* (Sun Aus o/p). Poignant essays by prominent Green figures. Well-argued viewpoints on Tasmania's key Green issues and their importance on a global scale.

Paul Sheehan *Among the Barbarians: the Dividing of Australia* (Random House Aus). Controversial best-seller. *Sydney Morning Herald* journalist Sheehan returned to Australia in 1996 after ten years in America; while he was away the Labor government had had a decade in office, and in this book he accuses it of having created a multicultural industry, and that while the country has achieved a brilliant social transformation, it runs the risk of being torn apart on race issues. While the book is certainly clearly and cleverly written, its many critics have labelled it a confusing mix of overstatement and understatement, and a badly researched, preachy tract. A second edition was completely revised after the November 1998 general election.

HISTORY AND POLITICS

Patsy Adam-Smith *The Anzacs* (Penguin Aus). Gleaned from diaries, letters and interviews, this is a classic account of Australia's involvement in World War I, with a special focus on the campaign that has become part of the Australian legend, Gallipoli, where thousands of "Anzacs" (Australian and New Zealand Army Corps) lost their lives.

Len Beadell *Outback Highways* (Weldon Aus). Extracts from Len Beadell's half-dozen books, cheerfully recounting his life in the central Australian deserts as a surveyor, and his involvement in the construction of Woomera and the atomic bomb test sites at Emu Junction and Maralinga.

Michael Cannon *Black Land White Land:Who Killed the Koories?* (Minerva Aus). An account of the violent 1840s in New South Wales, as colonists and pioneers moving inland clashed with the local Aboriginal tribes.

Paul Carter *The Road to Botany Bay* (Faber & Faber UK o/p; University of Chicago Press US). A fascinating and original analysis of "discovery" as cultural imperialism, and the metaphysics of exploration.

Manning Clark *A Short History of Australia* (Penguin Aus). A condensed version of this leading historian's multivolumed tome, focusing on dreary successions of political administrations over two centuries, and cynically concluding with the "Age of Ruins".

David Day *Claiming A Continent: A History of Australia* (Angus & Robertson Aus). The freshest general and easily readable history available, concluding in 1996. Day looks at Australia's history from a contemporary point of view, with the possession, dispossession and ownership of the land – and thus issues of race – central to his narrative. Excellent recommended reading of recent texts at the the end of each chapter.

Miriam Dixon *The Real Matilda* (Penguin Aus o/p). A scholarly analysis of women's invisible role in Australia's history.

Bruce Elder *Blood on the Wattle: Massacres and Maltreatment of Aboriginal Australians Since 1788* (New Holland Aus). A heart-rending account of the horrors inflicted on the continent's indigenous peoples, covering infamous events such as the Myall Creek Massacre of 1838 near Inverell and the slaughter of the Wiradjuri people in Bathurst in 1824, with more recent mid-twentieth-century scandals of the "Stolen Generation", children.

Tim Flannery (ed) *The Explorers* (Text Publishing Aus) is a well-chosen anthology of vivid and very human extracts from journals and published accounts of sixty-odd explorers, each introduced by Flannery: from William Jansz in 1606, through Hume and Hovell arguing over a frying pan, to Robyn Davidson's stubborn camelback Central Australian trek in the 1970s. Flannery also edited *Watkin Trench 1788* (Text Publishing Aus), a reissue of the two accounts Trench, a captain of the marines who came ashore with the First Fleet, wrote. Trench, a natural storyteller and fine writer, was a young man in his twenties, and the accounts brim with youthful curiosity.

Alan Frost *Botany Bay Mirages: Illusions of Australia's Convict Beginnings* (Melbourne UP Aus). Historian Frost's well-argued attempt to overturn many long-cherished notions about European settlement. Among his contentions is that Australia was settled primarily as a means of supplying the British navy with scarce flax and wood for masts rather than as a dumping ground for convicts.

Harry Gordon *Voyage from Shame: the Cowra Breakout and Afterwards* (University of Queensland Press Aus). A revision of Gordon's excellent account, originally published as *Die Like the Carp* and rewritten to mark the fiftieth anniversary of the breakout of Japanese prisoners of war from a camp in New South Wales during World War II.

Steve Hawke and Michael Gallagher *Noonkanbah* (Fremantle Arts Centre Press Aus). Co-authored by the then Prime Minister's son, this account deals with the Labor Party's double standards and Aboriginal resistance to oil exploration on their land near Fitzroy Crossing in the early 1980s.

Robert Hughes *The Fatal Shore* (Harvill Press UK; Random US; Pan Aus). A minutely detailed epic of the origins of transportation and the brutal beginnings of white Australia.

Helen Irving *To Constitute a Nation* (Cambridge UP UK, Aus). In 1901 Australia's various colonies became states and joined together as one nation, the Commonwealth of Australia. With the centenary of Federation coming up in 2001, there have been a rash of history books retelling the story of the birth of the nation. This is one of the best, a cultural rather than a political or legal history.

John Molony *The Penguin History of Australia* (Penguin Aus o/p). A less scholarly but more accessible and interesting account than Manning Clark's obligatory text.

Alan Moorehead *Coopers Creek* (Penguin UK; Grove Atlantic US o/p). An historian's dramatic and very human retelling of the ill-fated Burke and Wills expedition, which set out in 1860 to make the first south-to-north crossing of the continent from Melbourne to the Gulf of Carpentaria. A classic of exploration.

Patrick O'Farrell *Through Irish Eyes* (David Lovell Aus). A celebration of the Irish experience Down Under: a vivid collection of nineteenth- and twentieth-century photographs depicts the lives of the spirited immigrants who came in search of a better life.

John Pilger *A Secret Country* (Vintage UK, Aus). Australian-born Pilger challenges the country's sunny self-image with accounts of dirty dealings: mistreatment of Aborigines, racist immigration policies, British nuclear experimentation, Vietnam and the cosy mateship among politicians and industrialists.

Cassandra Pybus *Community of Thieves* (Minerva Aus). Attempting to reconcile past and future, fourth-generation Tasmanian Pybus provides a deeply felt account of the near-annihilation of the island's Aboriginal people.

Henry Reynolds *The Other Side of the Frontier* and *The Law of the Land* (both Penguin Aus). A revisionist historian demonstrates that Aboriginal resistance to colonial invasion was both considerable and organized. His latest work, *Fate of a Free People* (Penguin Aus), re-examines the tragic "Tasmanian wars" of the 1820s and 1830s that led to the near-annihilation of the island's original inhabitants. *With the White People* (Penguin Aus) is a fascinating exploration of the role of the often-invisible, largely forgotten and usually exploited Aboriginal worker in the development of colonial Australia. His latest book, *The Whispering in Our Hearts* (Allen & Unwin Aus) is a history, from 1790 to the beginning of World War II, of those settler Australians who followed consciences troubled by the treatment of Aboriginal people, spoke out and took political action, and the personal consequences of their actions.

Portia Robinson *The Women of Botany Bay* (Macquarie Aus). After ten years of painstaking research into the records of every woman transported from Britain and Ireland between 1787 and 1828, as well as the wives of convicts who settled in Australia, Robinson is able to tell us, with conviction and passion, just who the women of Botany Bay really were.

Eric Rolls *Sojourners* and *Citizens: Flowers and the Wide Sea* (both University of Queensland Press Aus). The first and second volumes of Rolls' fascinatingly detailed history of the Chinese in Australia.

Bill Rosser *Up Rode the Troopers: the Black Police in Queensland* and *Dreamtime Nightmares* (both University of Queensland Press Aus o/p). Two accounts of harsh methods used in nineteenth-century Queensland to "disperse" Aborigines, postulating reasons why Aborigines were unable to mount widescale organized resistance.

Babette Smith *A Cargo of Women* (Sun Aus o/p). Smith painstakingly traces the subsequent lives of one ship's "cargo of women" convicts transported to Sydney; eye-opening and sad.

Ann Summers *Damned Whores and God's Police* (McPhee Gribble Aus). Stereotypical images of women in Australian society are explored in this ground-breaking reappraisal of Australian history from a feminist point of view, updated in 1994.

ECOLOGY AND ENVIRONMENT

Tim Flannery *The Future Eaters* (Reed Books Aus). Flannery is a palaeontologist and Principal Research Officer at the Australian Museum. Subtitled "an ecological history of the Australasian lands and people", his thesis is that as the first human beings migrated down through the long chain of islands to Australasia, the Aborigines, Maoris and other Polynesian peoples changed the region's flora and fauna in startling ways, and began consuming the resources needed for their own future; the Europeans made an even greater impact on the environment, continuing this "future eating" of natural resources.

Josephine Flood *The Riches of Ancient Australia* (University of Queensland Press Aus). An indispensable and lavish guide to Australia's most famous landforms and sites. The same author's *Archaeology of the Dreamtime* (HarperCollins Aus) provides background and evidence on the development of Aboriginal society.

Drew Hutton and Libby Connors *A History of the Australian Environmental Movement* (Cambridge UP UK, Aus). Written by a husband and wife team, Queensland academics and prominent in Green politics, this well-balanced book is useful for anyone interested in environmental issues. It charts the progress of conservation attempts from 1860 to modern protests.

Peter Latz *Bushfires and Bushtucker: Aboriginal Plant Use in Central Australia* (IAD Press Aus). Handbook with photos, published by an Aboriginal-owned press.

Tim Murray (ed) *Archeology of Australia* (Allen & Unwin Aus) The last thirty years have seen many ground-breaking discoveries in Australian archeology, with three sites in particular of great significance: Kakadu in the Northern Territory, Lake Mungo in NSW, and South West Tasmania; a range of specialists contribute essays on the subject.

Mary White *The Greening of Gondwana* (Reed Aus). Classic work on the evolution of Australia's flora and geography.

CONTEMPORARY FICTION

Jessica Anderson *Tirra Lirra by the River* (Penguin US; Picador Aus). A richly evocative novel following an old woman's recollection of her troubled life, as she returns from Britain to her childhood home in Brisbane.

Thea Astley *The Multiple Effects of Rainshadow* (Penguin Aus). On an Aboriginal island reserve off the Queensland coast in 1930, amidst tropical rain, a white woman dies in childbirth. Her husband, the island superintendent, goes on a shotgun and dynamite rampage. The novel traces the effects over the years on eight characters who witnessed the violent events, ultimately exploring the brutality and racism in Australian life.

Murray Bail *Eucalyptus* (Harvill UK). This beautifully written novel has a fairytale-like plot: NSW farmer, Holland, has planted nearly every type of eucalyptus tree on his land. When his extraordinarily beautiful daughter Ellen is old enough to marry, he sets up a challenge for her legion of potential suitors, to name each tree. Bail's poetic language creates a wondrous sense of the light, the colours and the landscape of New South Wales – and its trees.

John Birmingham *The Tasmanian Babes Fiasco* (Duffy & Snelgrove Aus). This hilarious cult classic, about flat share hell in contemporary Brisbane, is Birmingham's first novel, and a follow up to *He Died With A Felafel In His Hand* (Duffy & Snelgrove Aus), a collection of supposedly true – squalid and very funny – tales emerging from experiences with the 89 people who the dissolute author had the misfortune of sharing house with in the 1990s.

Rosa Cappiello *Oh Lucky Country* (University of Queensland Press Aus o/p). A powerful novel of the migrant experience from a young woman's point of view, translated from the Italian.

Peter Carey *Bliss* (Faber & Faber UK; Random US; University of Queensland Press Aus). Carey's first novel, and one of his best: a story, somewhere between fantasy and reality, of a Sydney ad executive who drops out to New Age New South Wales. Other novels by Carey to look out for are *Illywhacker* (Faber & Faber UK; Random US; UQP Aus), the picaresque tale of a phenomenal liar; and the Booker Prize-winning *Oscar and Lucinda* (Faber & Faber UK; HarperCollins US; UQP Aus), recently made into a film. His brilliant, bizarre and tender short stories, *The Fat Man in History* (Faber & Faber UK; UQP Aus), with which he launched his career, should also

be read. Carey's latest novel, *Jack Maggs*, (Faber & Faber UK; UQP Aus) turns Dickens' *Great Expectations* back to front: Jack Maggs is the story of a convict who returns to England from Australia, a wealthy man looking for an adopted son.

Brian Castro *Birds of Passage* (Allen & Unwin UK o/p; Allen & Unwin Aus). A tale of a young, blue-eyed Chinese-Australian, interwoven with that of his immigrant ancestor; a richly metaphoric tale about a search for identity.

Peter Corris *The Empty Beach* (Unwin UK, Aus). Australia's answer to Raymond Chandler. Corris's hard-boiled novel is set in a glittering but seedy Sydney, where a soft-centred private eye investigates murder and exploitation in an old people's home.

Luke Davies *Candy* (Allen & Unwin Aus). Finely written love story set in contemporary Sydney, follows the narrator's first heady days with Candy and an equally novel shared heroin addiction, to the inevitable downward spiral as the drug takes over their lives and their love.

Gary Disher *The Divine Wind* (Hodder Aus). Set in Broome during World War II, the remote Western Australian pearling town is the backdrop for a troubled love story between Mitsy, daughter of a Japanese diver, and Hart, the son of a pearling master. As the war in the Pacific begins, and Australia and Japan become enemies, Mitsy and other Japanese inhabitants of the town feel the full force of prejudice and hatred.

Robert Drewe *The Savage Crows* (Picador Aus). This first novel, from one of Australia's best writers, is among his most powerful. A writer, whose own life is falling apart in a cockroach-ridden contemporary Sydney, sets out to discover the grim truth behind Tasmania's "final solution".

Ben Elton *Stark* (Sphere UK). As the earth reaches ecological meltdown, corporate breadheads pull the plug and prepare to abandon the planet. A hilarious, thought-provoking eco-apocalyptic thriller, mostly set in Western Australia.

Delia Falconer *The Service of Clouds* (Picador Aus). It is 1907 in the Blue Mountains outside of Sydney. Narrator, pharmacy assistant Eureka Jones falls in love with Harry Kitchings, "a man who takes pictures of clouds". The poetically written novel, romantic in its sensibility and literary in its intent, dwells on the Blue Mountains landscape in all its moods, covering the period 1907–1926, as people meet, love and leave, like the clouds moving across the sky.

Richard Flanagan writes thoughtfully and emotionally about landscape, place, migration, and the significance of history in his two novels, both set in Tasmania. *Death of a River Guide* (Penguin Aus) was the winner of the 1995 Victorian Premier's Award for first fiction; the novel's river guide, Aljaz Cosini, goes over his life and that of his family and forebears as he lies drowning beneath a waterfall on the Franklin River. His second novel, *The Sound of One Hand Clapping*, (Picador Aus) begins in the winter of 1954 in the remote highlands where a construction camp is tearing into the wilderness: three-year-old Sonya Buloh's worker father is an alcoholic, and her troubled mother wanders off into a snow storm never to be seen again. The story resumes thirty-five years later when Sonya returns to Tasmania to confront her father and her past.

David Foster *Moonlite* (Pan UK o/p; Viking Penguin US o/p; Vintage Aus). Amusing social satire set in the Australian goldfields. An albino Scottish highlander meets his black counterpart and finds the Aboriginal world, like his own traditional Celtic way of life, in conflict with the materialistic nineteenth century. There's more magic realism in his latest novel, *The Glade Within the Grove* (Random House Aus), which was the winner of the 1997 Miles Franklin Award. It concerns another eccentric character, the postman D'Arcy D'Olivieres, who discovers an unpublished manuscript in an old mailbag. D'Arcy becomes obsessed with "The Ballad of Eringarah", a sort of "White Dreaming" tale, and the events it describes, which sets him off writing *The Glade Within the Grove*, an investigation into events nearly three decades before, to do with the establishment of a commune in NSW. In even more of a post-modern spin, Foster also wrote the actual *Ballad of Eringarah* and published it in a separate volume (Vintage Aus).

Helen Garner *Postcards from Surfers* (Bloomsbury UK; Penguin Aus). Recommended short stories by one of Australia's finest women writers. Her first novel, *Monkey Grip* (McPhee Gribble Aus), is a classic 1970s tale of obsession, love and heroin in inner-city Melbourne.

Nikki Gemmel Young novelist Gemmel claims she's now writing the third novel in her trilogy of "women in inhospitable places." In *Shiver* (Vintage Aus), a radio journalist, Fin, leaves the crowded airways of a Sydney nightshift newsroom for a once in a lifetime trip with the Australian Antarctic Division, and a very human tragedy. In *Cleave* (Vintage Aus), a painter leaves behind her totally urban Sydney life for Alice Springs, and is seduced by the heady disorder of Aboriginal and white Outback existence.

Tom Gilling *The Sooterkin* (Text Publishing Aus). This meticulously researched first novel evokes Hobart of the 1820s in all its mucky detail, as a local woman, Sarah Dyer, gives birth to a seal pup. The fantastic event carries the novel's larger idea, which explores the clash of science and superstition in the early nineteenth century.

Kate Grenville *Lillian's Story* (Picador UK; Harcourt Brace & Co US; Allen & Unwin Aus). The tragicomic tale of Lillian Singer is loosely based on the life of Bea Miles, the eccentric, Shakespeare-spouting, tram-stopping, taxi-hijacking Sydney bag lady. Its sequel, *Dark Places* (Picador UK, Aus; Trans-Atlantic US), lacks any of *Lillian's Story*'s lightness, being told from the point of view of Albion Gridley Singer, a fact-loving patriarch who propels his daughter Lillian into madness.

Rodney Hall *Kisses of the Enemy* (Faber & Faber UK o/p; Farrar, Strauss & Giroux US; Penguin Aus o/p). A satirical analysis of power, set in the near future. Under fat President Buchanan, puppet of a huge multinational company, the Republic of Australia slips from British into American hands.

Janette Turner Hospital *Oyster* (Virago UK; Knopf, Vintage Aus). Literally off the map, the opal-mining, one-pub, one-shop town of Inner Maroo, in northern Queensland, is a disquieting place; half of its inhabitants are scary rough-as-guts mining people, the other half religious fundamentalists. The town is full of secrets, as Sarah and Nick find out when they come here in search of their lost children, sucked into a cult run by the mysterious Oyster.

David Ireland *City of Women* (Penguin Aus). Ireland creates weird visions of Sydney and here the setting is a futuristic, violent place from which men have been banished.

Archimedes and the Seagle (Penguin UK, Aus) provides a delightful philosophical discussion between a dog and a bird as they roam The Domain and Woolloomooloo. In his latest novel, after a gap of ten years, Ireland changes the setting from Sydney to NSW's Southern Tablelands in *The Chosen* (Vintage Aus), a look at 52 inhabitants of a country town over 52 weeks, from the point of view of an arriving artist commissioned to weave this number of portraits of random – weird, wonderful and psychotic – townsfolk.

Linda Jaivin *Eat Me* (Chatto UK; Broadway BDD US; Text Publishing Aus). A successful first novel billed as an "erotic feast"; opens with a memorable fruit-squeezing scene (and this is only the shopping) as three trendy Sydney women (fashion editor, academic and writer) swap stories of sexual exploits – though we never quite know who is telling the truth.

Elizabeth Jolley *Woman in a Lampshade* (Penguin UK o/p, Aus). Set around Perth, this is an excellent collection of short stories to introduce you to Jolley's original and quirky work, which thrives on black humour. Her characters suffer from isolation of the heart: *The Sugar Mother* (Penguin Aus) examines what happens to a faithful husband when his wife goes on sabbatical and a young woman and her mother turn up on his doorstep demanding shelter.

Douglas Kennedy *The Dead Heart* (Abacus UK). A best-selling comic thriller recently made into a film; an itinerant American journalist gets abducted by man-eating hillbillies in Outback Australia.

David Malouf One of Australia's most important contemporary writers. His latest two novels are both set in the mid-nineteenth century. *Remembering Babylon* (Vintage UK; Random US, Aus) is his 1993 Booker-nominated saga dealing with the real and symbolic settlers' relationship with Aborigines, while the relationship in *The Conversations at Curlow Creek* (Vintage UK; Pantheon US; Random Aus) develops between two Irishmen in a remote hut in the high plains of New South Wales the night before a hanging. One is the officer of the police appointed to supervise the execution and the other the outlaw facing his death.

Andrew McGahan *Praise* (Allen & Unwin Aus). Running through one hot summer of unemployment, heroin, alcohol, sex, love and abortion in Brisbane, the detached narrator and his friends

live life without much of a purpose. Unflinchingly, McGahan dwells on the seedier details, creating a vivid portrait of self-destructing youth, with no moral to the tale. The prize-winning first novel has been made into a film, released in 1999.

Christos Tsiolkas *Loaded* (Random House Aus). A gritty debut novel set in suburban Melbourne: caught between the traditional Greek world of his family and his emerging gay identity, 19-year-old Ari is unemployed and self-destructing in his milieu of drugs, clubs and anonymous sex. The 1998 film *Head On* was based on the novel.

Tim Winton *Cloudstreet* (Picador UK; Graywolf US; Penguin Aus). A wonderful, faintly magical saga about the mixed fortunes of two families who end up sharing a house in postwar Perth.

AUSTRALIAN CLASSICS

Barbara Baynton *Bush Studies* (Collins/Angus & Robertson UK; HarperCollins US; Angus & Robertson Aus). A collection of nineteenth-century bush stories written from the female perspective.

Rolf Boldrewood *Robbery Under Arms* (Currency Press UK; HarperCollins Aus). The story of Captain Starlight, a notorious bushranger and rustler around the Queensland borders.

Marcus Clarke *For the Term of his Natural Life* (Penguin & Oxford UP UK, HarperCollins US; Angus & Robertson Aus). Written in 1870 in somewhat overblown prose, this romantic tragedy is based on actual events in Tasmania's once notorious prison settlements.

Eleanor Dark *The Timeless Land* (HarperCollins Aus o/p). A historical novel which recounts the beginnings of Australia.

Miles Franklin *My Brilliant Career* (Virago UK; St Martin's Press US o/p; Imprint Aus). A novel about a spirited young girl in turn-of-the-century Victoria who refuses to conform.

May Gibbs *Snugglepot and Cuddlepie* (Angus & Robertson Aus hbk, Bluegum Aus pbk). A timeless children's favourite: the illustrated adventures of two little creatures who live inside gumnuts.

Barbara Hanrahan *The Scent of Eucalyptus* (Trafalgar US; University of Queensland Press Aus). The first novel by the late South Australian writer who consistently pushed reality to the edge of fantasy in her prolific lifetime of work; this book captures the essence of Adelaide in the 1960s.

Xavier Herbert *Capricornia* (Imprint Aus). An indignant and allegorical saga of the brutal and haphazard settlement of the land of Capricornia (tropical Northern Territory thinly disguised).

Fergus Hume *The Mystery of the Hansom Cab* (Text Publishing Aus). Australia's first blockbuster whodunnit, set in the gritty underworld of the author's contemporary 1880s Melbourne, has been resurrected in 1999. Even as late as 1954 the *Sunday Times* listed it as one of the hundred best crime novels of all time.

George Johnston *My Brother Jack* (Chivers US o/p, Imprint Aus). The first in a disturbing trilogy set in Melbourne suburbia between the wars, which develops into a semifictional attempt to dissipate the guilt Johnston felt at being disillusioned with, and finally leaving, his native land.

Thomas Keneally *The Chant of Jimmie Blacksmith* (Penguin UK, Aus; Viking Penguin US o/p). A prize-winning novel which delves deep into the psyche of an Aboriginal outlaw, tracing his inexorable descent into murder and crime. Sickening, brutal and compelling.

D.H. Lawrence *Kangaroo* (Penguin UK; Viking Penguin US; Imprint Aus). The famous English author wrote this novel while holed up in a cottage in Thirroul, on the New South Wales south coast, in 1922. Themes of political confrontation and vivid pictures of Australia show just what an imagination he had, since he spent barely two weeks in Perth and a day in Sydney.

Henry Lawson Ballads, poems and stories from Australia's best-loved chroniclers come in a wide array of collections. A few to seek out are: *Henry Lawson Bush Ballads* (Angus & Robertson Aus), *Henry Lawson Favourites* (Penguin Aus) and *While the Billy Boils – Poetry* (Penguin Aus).

Norman Lindsay *The Magic Pudding* (Angus & Robertson Aus). A whimsical tale of some very strange men and their grumpy, flavour-changing and endless pudding; a children's classic with very adult humour.

Ronald McKie *The Mango Tree* (Imprint Aus). A gentle account of boyhood and first love in tropical Queensland.

Ruth Park *The Harp in the South* (Penguin Aus). First published in 1948, this first book in a trilogy is a well-loved tale of inner-Sydney slum life in 1940s Surry Hills. The spirited Darcy family's battle against poverty provides memorable characters, not least the Darcy grandmother with her fierce Irish humour.

A.B. ("Banjo") Paterson Australia's most famous bush balladeer, author of "Waltzing Matilda" and "The Man from Snowy River", who helped romanticize the bush's mystique. Some of the many titles published include *Banjo Paterson's Favourites* (Faber & Faber UK) and *Man From Snowy River and Other Verses* (Angus & Robertson Aus).

Henry Handel Richardson *The Getting of Wisdom* (Virago UK; Mercury House Inc US; Minerva Aus). A gangly country girl's experience of a snobby boarding school in turn-of-the-century Melbourne; like Miles Franklin (see opposite), Richardson was actually a female writer.

Nevil Shute *A Town Like Alice* (Mandarin UK, Aus). A wartime romance which tells of a woman's bravery, endurance and enterprise, both in the Malayan jungle and in the Australian Outback where she strives to create the town of the title.

Christina Stead *For Love Alone* (Virago UK; Harcourt Brace & Co US o/p; Imprint Aus). Set largely around Sydney Harbour, where the late author grew up, this novel follows the obsessive Teresa Hawkins, a poor but artistic girl from a large, unconventional family, who scrounges and saves to head for London and love.

Randolph Stow *The Merry-go-round in the Sea* (Penguin Aus). An endearing tale of a young boy growing up in rural Western Australia during World War II.

Kylie Tennant *Ride on Stranger* (Imprint Aus). First published in 1943, this is a humorous portrait of Sydney between the two world wars, seen through the eyes of newcomer Shannon Hicks. A determined young woman, she comes across more than her fair share of fanatics and charlatans in the course of her up-and-down career.

Patrick White Considered dense and symbolic – even visionary (though some claim misogynistic) – White's novels can be heavy going, but try and plough through *The Tree of Man, Voss, A*

Fringe of Leaves or *The Twyborn Affair* (all Penguin), the last a contemporary exploration of ambiguous sexuality.

POETRY AND ANTHOLOGIES

Phillip Adams and Patrice Newell *The Penguin Book of Australian Jokes* (Penguin Aus). An excellent introduction to the Australian sense of humour, divided into twenty sections close to the nation's heart. Among them are "A Sporting Chance", "The Work Ethic", "History and the Yarts", with an index to help you zone in, though you'll probably need a local to explain a lot of the references.

Don Anderson (ed) *65–95 Contemporary Classics* (Vintage Aus). One of the country's most eminent literary critics chooses the best of recent Australian short writing, from Glenda Adams to Tim Winton.

Mary Lord (ed) *Best Australian Short Stories* (Penguin Aus). 130 years of short-story writing, from Henry Lawson to Helen Garner. Ideal interstate bus companion.

Les Murray *Subhuman Redneck Poems* (Carcanet Press UK; FS&G US Duffy & Snelgrove Aus). A collection by the outspoken, larger than life and internationally recognized Australian poet, who lives on a farm in the New South Wales bush; winner of the prestigious T.S. Eliot Prize for poetry in 1996

Dorothy Porter *The Monkey's Mask* (Hyland House UK, Aus). Never afraid of experimentation, poet Porter combines three unlikely forms: the novel in verse, a detective thriller and erotica. Tough lesbian private investigator Jill Fitzpatrick trawls through the Sydney literary scene on the hunt for a murderer: all the suspects are male poets struggling under the weight of hugely inflated egos. Disturbing, full of suspense – and very witty. *The Monkey's Mask* was so successful that is has been adapted as a play and will soon be made into a film. Porter's second verse novel, *What A Piece of Work* (Picador Aus), was released in 1999. Again set in Sydney, the time is 1968, and it is the first person narrative of the head of Sydney's Callan Park Psychiatric Hospital at Rozelle, who has to conquer his own demons as well as those of patients – a cast of characters including lefties from the Sydney Push, a junkie stripper and a wealthy private patient.

Dale Spender (ed) *The Penguin Anthology of Australian Women's Writing* (Penguin UK o/p, Aus). A brick-sized book containing all the best of Australian women's writing, from Elizabeth Macarthur to Germaine Greer.

John Tranter and Philip Mead (eds) *The Penguin Book of Modern Australian Poetry* (Penguin Aus). Poetry has a popular and active appeal Down Under; this century's best are collected in this anthology.

Michael Wilding (ed) *The Oxford Book of Australian Short Stories* (Oxford UP UK). Another well-chosen selection of tales spanning 120 years.

ABORIGINAL WRITING

Faith Bandler *Welour, My Brother* (Wild & Wooley Aus o/p). A novel by a well-known black activist describing a boy's early life in Queensland, and the tensions of a racially mixed community.

Evelyn Crawford *Over My Tracks* (Penguin Aus). Told to Chris Walsh, this oral autobiography is the story of a formidable woman, from her 1930s childhood among the red sandhills of Yantabulla, "back o' Bourke" in New South Wales, through her Outback struggles as a mother of fourteen children, to her tireless work, late in life, with Aboriginal students, combatting prejudice with education and opportunities.

Jack Davis et al *Paperbark* (University of Queensland Press Aus). An accessible introduction to Aboriginal writing, from legends to modern poetry and prose.

Nene Gare *The Fringe Dwellers* (Sun Aus o/p). A story of an Aboriginal family on the edge of town and society.

Ruby Langford *Don't Take Your Love to Town* (Penguin Aus). An autobiography demonstrating a black woman's courage and humour in the face of tragedy and poverty lived out in northern New South Wales and the inner city of Sydney.

Sally Morgan *My Place* (Virago UK; Little Brown US; Fremantle Arts Centre Press Aus). A widely acclaimed and best-selling account of a Western Australian woman's discovery of her black roots.

David Mowaljarlai and Jutta Malnic *Yorro Yorro* (Magabala Books Aus). Starry-eyed photographer Malnic's musings while recording sacred Wandjina sites in the west Kimberley and, more interestingly, Mowaljarlai's account of his upbringing and Ngarinyin tribal lore.

Mudrooroo *Wildcat Falling* (Angus & Robertson Aus). The first novel by an Aboriginal writer to be published (in 1965), this is the story of a black teenage delinquent coming of age in the 1950s. Written under his given name Colin Johnston, the author's later works (and now this one) are published under his assumed Aboriginal name, Mudrooroo. *Doctor Wooreddy's Prescription for Enduring the Ending of the World* (Hyland House Aus), details the attempted annihilation of the Tasmanian Aborigines, drawing a strong parallel between the rape of Tasmanian women and of the people's land and heritage. Mudrooroo's three latest novels – *The Kwinkan* (1995), *The Undying* (1998) and *Underground* (1999) – are part of his magic realist Master of Ghost Dreaming series.

Oodgeroo Noonuccal *My People* (Jacaranda Wiley Aus). A collection of verse by an established campaigning poet (previously known as Kath Walker).

Adele Pring *Women of the Centre* (Pascoe Aus). Tales of women's lives from the central deserts.

Paddy Roe *Gularabulu* (Fremantle Arts Centre Press Aus). Stories from the west Kimberley, both traditional myths and tales of a much more recent origin.

Glenys Ward *Wandering Girl* (Virago UK; Fawcett US; Magabala Books Aus). The author, from Western Australia, tells her own story of growing up in a white world.

Sam Watson *The Kadaitcha Song* (Viking Penguin US o/p; Penguin Aus). A brutal, fast-paced thriller; a modern parable of warring good and evil, mixed with ancient sorcery.

Archie Weller *The Day of the Dog* (Allen & Unwin Aus). Written in 1981 for a competition, Weller's violent first novel came out in an angry burst after being released, at 23, from incarceration in Broome Gaol. The protagonist, in a similar situation, is pressured back into a criminal world by his Aboriginal peers and by police harassment. Searing pace and forceful writing. His second novel, *Land of the Golden Clouds* (Allen & Unwin Aus) came out in 1998, and is a complete departure from his earlier work, an epic science fiction fantasy which has been compared with Tolkien or Asimov. Set 3000 years in the future, in an Australia devastated by a nuclear holocaust, a wasteland populated by many human warring tribes – mutated, culturally hybridized and displaced.

ART, PHOTOGRAPHY AND ARCHITECTURE

Blue Sky, Blue Bush and Silver (Blue Bush Press Aus). Subtitled *A Guide to the Art, Artists and Galleries of Broken Hill, Australia*, this beautiful book makes a wonderful souvenir of Broken Hill for art aficionados.

Wally Caruna *Aboriginal Art* (Thames and Hudson UK, US). An excellent illustrated paperback introduction to all styles of Aboriginal art.

Peter Dombrovskis *Dombrovskis: A Photographic Recollection* (West Wind Press Aus). A photographic insight into Tasmania's World Heritage Area by one of the world's great wilderness photographers, who died in 1996. The text features essays by Jamie Kirkpatrick, and the esteemed environmentalist Dr Bob Brown.

Philip Drewe *Sydney Opera House* (Phaidon Press UK; Chronicle Books US). A study of one of the world's most striking pieces of contemporary architecture, designed by Jorn Utzon, with detailed photographs and notes.

Robert Hughes *The Art of Australia* (Penguin Aus). The internationally acclaimed art historian, author of *The Shock of the New*, cut his teeth on this seminal dissection of Australian art up to the 1960s.

Jennifer Isaacs *Desert Crafts* (Doubleday/Transworld Aus). A coffee-table book initiated by Maruku, the retail agent for arts and crafts people within the Aboriginal community at Uluru (Ayers Rock). More than just a collection of beautiful colour reproductions, the book has anecdotes and Aboriginal history, plus a comparison of traditional craft methods with those used by Aboriginal people today.

Wild Light: Images of Australia (William Heinemann Aus). Magnificent panoramic photographs by Phillip Quirk, Grenville Turner, Mark Lang and Perter Jarver capture the clear bright light, huge horizons and sense of space in natural Australian scenes, from the red deserts of Central Australia to coastal rainforests. Thought provoking one-line text running along the base of the pages, written by Mandawuy Yunupingu of Yothu Yindi, tells the story of the land in Aboriginal mythology.

SPECIALIST AND WILDLIFE GUIDES

Australians are passionate and active travellers, and in every regional centre you'll find specialist guides to surfing, diving, cycling and numerous other activities: many of these are detailed in the text. There are few guides to Australia's wildlife designed for field use, though National Parks and Wildlife Service shops often stock booklets on local flora and fauna. As any visit to a remainder bookshop will prove, coffee-table works are legion.

Jack Absalom *Safe Outback Travel* (Five Mile Press Aus). A new edition of the bible for Outback driving and camping, full of sensible precautions and handy tips for preparation and repair.

The Australian Museum Trust *Complete Book of Australian Mammals* (Angus & Robertson UK). An excellent photographic record, but far too heavy to carry around. *Key Guide to Australian Mammals* (Reed Aus) offers a more portable selection of colour illustrations.

Jean-Paul Bruneteau *Tukka: Real Australian Food* (Angus & Robertson Aus). The chef, who arrived in Australia in 1967 as a child from France, is passionate about the use and understanding of native Australian foods. This is more than just a cookbook, being a wide-ranging combination of well-researched history and botany as well.

John and Monica Chapman *Bushwalking in Australia* (Lonely Planet). Long-established guide to trails throughout Australia.

Bill Coppell *Australia in Facts and Figures* (Penguin Aus). Subtitled "Vital Statistics on the Country and its People" and updated for its 1999 publication, this has all you ever wanted to know, including how many people really have been eaten by sharks.

Clifford and Dawn Frith publish a range of meticulously photographed booklets on Australia's tropical wildlife, from rainforest to reef (Frith & Frith Aus); the complete set constitutes a fine overview of the north's fauna.

The Great Barrier Reef (Reader's Digest UK). A complete rundown on the Reef, lucid and lavishly illustrated. Available in coffee-table format and in a slighter, more portable, edited edition.

Leigh Hemmings *Great Australian Bike Rides* (Mountaineer Books UK, US; Simon & Schuster Aus). A detailed illustrated guide, with gradient profiles and maps plus sections on packing and maintenance.

Tim Low *Bush Tucker: Australia's Wild Food Harvest* (HarperCollins Aus). A guide to the bountiful supply of bushtucker that was once the mainstay of the Aboriginal diet. *Wild Food Plants of Australia* (Angus & Robertson UK). A handy paperback guide with clear photographs of over 180 plants, describing their uses.

Oliver Mayo *The Wines of Australia* (Faber & Faber UK, US). A good introduction to Australian wines and wine makers, now in its second edition.

Queensland Museum *Wildlife of Greater Brisbane* (Queensland Museum Aus). A portable and beautifully photographed field guide to everything that walks, crawls, hops, flutters and flies in the Brisbane area; useful all along Australia's eastern seaboard. The first in a planned series to cover the entire state; look out for the forthcoming volume for Cairns and the tropical north.

Mark Shields and Huon Hooke *The Penguin Good Australian Wine Guide* (Penguin Aus). Released every year in Australia, this is a handy book for a wine buff to buy on the ground, with the best wines and prices detailed to help navigate you around the bottle shop.

Peter and Pat Slater *Field Guide to Australian Birds* (Weldon Aus). Pocket-sized, and the easiest to use of the many available guides to Australian birds.

Tyrone Thomas Regional bushwalking guides (Hill of Content Aus). A series of ten local guides (often updated), which make excellent trail companions.

Mark Warren *Atlas of Australian Surfing* (HarperCollins Aus). A comprehensive guide to riding the best of Australia's waves.

AUSTRALIAN ENGLISH

The colourful variant of Australian English, or strine (which is how "Australian" is pronounced with a very heavy Australian accent), has its origins in the archaic cockney and Irish of the colony's early convicts as well as the adoption of words from the many Aboriginal languages. For such a vast country, the accent barely varies to the untutored ear – from Tasmania to the northwest you'll find little variation in the national drawl, with its curious, interrogative ending to sentences – although Queenslanders are noted for their slow delivery. One of the most consistent tendencies of strine is to abbreviate words and then stick an "-o" or, more commonly, an "-ie" on the end: as in "bring your cozzie to the barbie this arvo" (bring your swimming costume to the barbecue this afternoon). This informality extends to the frequent use of "bloody", "bugger" and "bastard", the latter two used affectionately. Attempting to abuse someone by calling them a bastard will most likely end up in an offer of a beer. There's also an endearing tendency to genderize inanimate objects as, for example, "she's buggered, mate" (your inanimate object is beyond repair) or "do 'im up nice and tight" (be certain that your inanimate object is well affixed).

The popularity of dire Australian TV soap operas has seen strine spread overseas, much as Americanisms have pervaded the English-speaking world. Popular strinisms such as "hang a U-ey" (make a U-turn) and the versatile and agreeable "no worries" are now commonly used outside Australia.

The country has its own excellent Macquarie Dictionary, the latest edition of which is the ultimate authority on the current state of Australian English. What follows is our own essential list.

Akubra Wide-brimmed felt hat; a brand name.
Anzac Australia and New Zealand Army Corps; every town has a memorial to Anzac casualties from both world wars.
Arvo Afternoon.
Back o' Bourke Outback.

Banana bender Resident of Queensland.
Barbie Barbecue.
Battler Someone who struggles to make a living, as in "little Aussie battler".
You beauty! or **beaut** Exclamation of delight.
Beg yours? Excuse me, say again?
Beyond the Black Stump Outback; back of beyond.
Billabong Waterhole in dry riverbed.
Billy Cooking pot.
Bitumen Sealed road as opposed to dirt road.
Blowies Blow flies.
Bludger Someone who does not pull their weight, or a scrounger – as in "dole bludger".
Blue Fight; also a red-haired person.
Blundstones Leather, elastic-sided workmen's boots, now also a fashion item in some circles. Often shortened to "blundies".
Bonzer Good, a good thing.
Bottle shop Off-licence or liquor store.
Brumby Feral horse.
Buckley's No chance; as in "hasn't got a Buckley's".
Bugs Moreton Bay bug – type of crayfish indigenous to southern Queensland.
Bunyip Monster of Aboriginal legend; bogeyman.
Burl Give it a go; as in "give it a burl".
Bush Unsettled country area.
Bushranger Runaway convict; nineteenth-century outlaw.
Bushwhacker Someone lacking in social graces, a hick.
BYO Bring your own. Restaurant which allows you to bring your own alcohol.
Chook Chicken.
Chunder Vomit.
Cocky Small farmer **Cow cocky** Dairy farmer.
To come the raw prawn To try and deceive or make a fool of someone.
Coo-eee! Aboriginal long-distance greeting, now widely adopted as a kind of "yoo hoo!"
Corroboree Aboriginal ceremony.
Cozzies, **bathers**, **swimmers**, **togs** Swimming costume.
Crim Criminal.
Crook Sick or broken.
Crow eater Resident of South Australia.
Cut lunch Sandwiches.
Dag Nerd **Daggy** unattractive.
Daks, **strides** Trousers/pants.
Dam A man-made body of water or reservoir; not just the dam itself.
Damper Soda bread cooked in a pot on embers.

Dekko To look at; as in "take a dekko at this".
Deli Delicatessen, corner shop or sandwich bar.
Derro Derelict or destitute person.
Didgeridoo Droning musical instrument made from a termite-hollowed branch.
Digger Old-timer, especially an old soldier.
Dill Idiot.
Dilly bag Aboriginal carry-all made of bark, or woven or rigged twine.
Dinkum True, genuine, honest.
Disposal store Store that sells used army and navy equipment, plus camping gear.
Dob in To tell on someone; as in "she dobbed him in".
Drizabone Voluminous waxed cotton raincoat, originally designed for horse-riding.
Drongo Fool.
Drover Cowboy or station hand.
Dunny Outside pit toilet.
Esky Portable, insulated box to keep food or beer cold.
Fair dinkum, **Dinky di** Honestly, truly.
Fossick To search for gold or gems in abandoned diggings.
Galah Noisy or garrulous person.
Galvo Corrugated iron.
Garbo Garbage or refuse collector.
G'day Hello, hi.
Gibber Rock or boulder.
Give away To give up or resign; as in "I used to be a garbo but I gave it away".
Grog Alcoholic drink, usually beer.
Gub, **Gubbah** Aboriginal terms for a white person.
Gutless wonder Coward.
Hoon A yob, delinquent.
Humpy Temporary shelter used by Aborigines and early pioneers.
Jackeroo Male station hand.
Jilleroo Female station hand.
Joey Baby kangaroo still in the pouch (also, less familiarly, a baby koala).
Koorie Collective name for Aboriginal people from southeastern Australia.
Larrikin Mischievous youth.
Lay by Practice of putting a deposit on goods until they can be fully paid for.
Lollies Sweets or candy.
Manchester Linen goods.
Mate A sworn friend, as essential as beer to the Australian stereotype.
Mexicans Residents of New South Wales and Victoria.

Milk bar Corner shop, and often a small café.
Moleskins Strong cotton trousers worn by bushmen.
Never Never Outback, wilderness.
New Australian Recent immigrants; often a euphemism for Australians of non-British descent.
No worries That's okay; It doesn't matter; Don't mention it.
Ocker Uncultivated Australian male.
Op shop Short for "Opportunity Shop"; a charity shop (UK) or thrift store (USA).
Outback Remote, unsettled regions of Australia.
Paddock Field.
Panel van Van with no rear windows and front seating only.
Pashing Kissing or snogging.
Perve To leer or act as a voyeur; as in "What are you perving at?"
Piss Beer.
Pissed Drunk.
Piss head Drunkard.
Pokies One-armed bandits; gambling machines.
Pommie, **Pom** Person of English descent – not necessarily abusive.
Rapt Very pleased, delighted.
Ratbag An eccentric person; also a term of mild abuse.
Ratshit or **Shithouse** How you feel after a night on the piss.
Rego Vehicle registration document.
Ridji Didge The real thing or genuine article.
Ripper! Rather old-fashioned exclamation of enthusiasm.
Rollies Roll-up cigarettes.
Root Vulgar term for sexual congress.
Rooted To be very tired or to be beyond repair; as in "she's rooted, mate" – your [car] is irreparable.
Ropable Furious to the point of requiring restraint.
Rouseabout An unskilled labourer in a shearing-shed.
Sandgroper Resident of Western Australia.
She'll be right or **She'll be apples** Everything will work out fine.
Shoot through To pass through or leave hurriedly.
Shout To pay for someone, or to buy a round of drinks; as in "it's your shout, mate".
Sickie To take a day off work due to (sometimes alleged) illness; as in "to pull a sickie".

Singlet Sleeveless cotton vest. The archetypal Australian singlet, in navy, is produced by Bonds.

Skivvy Polo neck.

Slab 24-can carton of beer.

Smoko Tea break.

Snag Sausage.

Speedo Famous Australian brand of athletic swimming costume; **speedos** (or **sluggos**) commonly refers to men's swimming briefs, as opposed to swimming trunks

Spunk Attractive or sexy person of either gender; as in "what a spunk!" Can also be used as an adjective: **spunky**

Squatter Historical term for early settlers who took up public land as their own.

Station Very large pastoral property or ranch.

Sticky beak Nosy person, or to be nosy; as in "let's have a sticky beak".

Stockman Cowboy or station hand.

Stubby Small bottle of beer.

Swag Large bedroll, or one's belongings.

Tall poppy Someone who excels or is eminent.

"Cutting down tall poppies" is to bring over-achievers back to earth – a national pastime.

Thongs Flip-flops or sandals.

Throw a wobbly Lose your temper.

Tinnie Can of beer, or a small aluminium boat.

Ute Short for "utility" vehicle; pick-up truck.

Wacko! Exclamation of enthusiasm.

Walkabout Temporary migration undertaken by Aborigines; also has the wider meaning of a journey.

Gone walkabout To go missing.

Warm fuzzies Feeling of contentment.

Waxhead Surfer.

Weatherboard Wooden house.

Whinger Someone who complains – allegedly common among Poms.

Wog Derogatory description for those of Mediterranean descent.

Wowser Killjoy.

Yabber To talk or chat.

Yabbie Freshwater crayfish.

Yakka Work, as in "hard yakka".

Yobbo Uncouth person.

INDEX

Note: where a place name alone might cause confusion, the standard abbreviation for the state has been added in parentheses; these are ACT (Australian Capital Territory); NSW (New South Wales); NT (Northern Territory); QLD (Queensland) SA (South Australia); TAS (Tasmania); VIC (Victoria); and WA (Western Australia).

Stay in touch with us!

ROUGH*NEWS* is Rough Guides' free newsletter.
In four issues a year we give you news, travel
issues, music reviews, readers' letters and the
latest dispatches from authors on the road.

I would like to receive ROUGH*NEWS*: please put me on your free mailing list.

NAME . . . .

ADDRESS . . . .

Please clip or photocopy and send to: Rough Guides, 62–70 Shorts Gardens, London WC2H 9AB,
England or Rough Guides, 375 Hudson Street, New York, NY 10014, USA.

ROUGH GUIDES: Travel

Amsterdam
Andalucia
Australia

Austria
Bali & Lombok
Barcelona
Belgium &
  Luxembourg
Belize
Berlin
Brazil
Britain
Brittany &
  Normandy
Bulgaria
California
Canada
Central America
Chile
China
Corfu & the
  Ionian Islands
Corsica
Costa Rica
Crete
Cuba
Cyprus
Czech & Slovak
  Republics

Dodecanese
Dominican
  Republic
Egypt
England
Europe
Florida
France
French Hotels &
  Restaurants 1999
Germany
Goa
Greece
Greek Islands
Guatemala
Hawaii
Holland
Hong Kong
  & Macau
Hungary
India
Indonesia
Ireland
Israel & the
  Palestinian
  Territories
Italy
Jamaica
Japan
Jordan

Kenya
Laos
London
London
  Restaurants
Los Angeles
Malaysia,
  Singapore &
  Brunei
Mallorca &
  Menorca
Maya World
Mexico
Morocco
Moscow
Nepal
New England
New York
New Zealand
Norway
Pacific Northwest
Paris
Peru
Poland
Portugal
Prague
Provence & the
  Côte d'Azur
The Pyrenees
Romania

St Petersburg
San Francisco
Sardinia
Scandinavia
Scotland
Scottish Highlands
  & Islands
Sicily
Singapore

South Africa
Southern India
Southwest USA
Spain
Sweden
Syria
Thailand
Trinidad & Tobago
Tunisia
Turkey
Tuscany & Umbria
USA
Venice
Vienna
Vietnam
Wales
Washington DC
West Africa
Zimbabwe &
  Botswana

AVAILABLE AT ALL GOOD BOOKSHOPS

ROUGH GUIDES: Mini Guides, Travel Specials and Phrasebooks

MINI GUIDES

Antigua
Bangkok
Barbados
Big Island of
  Hawaii
Boston
Brussels
Budapest

Dublin
Edinburgh
Florence
Honolulu
Jerusalem
Lisbon
London
  Restaurants
Madrid
Maui
Melbourne
New Orleans
St Lucia

Seattle
Sydney
Tokyo
Toronto

TRAVEL SPECIALS

First-Time Asia
First-Time Europe
More Women Travel

PHRASEBOOKS

Czech
Dutch

Egyptian Arabic
European
French
German
Greek
Hindi & Urdu
Hungarian
Indonesian
Italian
Japanese

Mandarin
  Chinese
Mexican Spanish
Polish
Portuguese
Russian
Spanish
Swahili
Thai
Turkish
Vietnamese

ROUGH GUIDES:
Reference and Music CDs

REFERENCE
Classical Music
Classical:
  100 Essential CDs
Drum'n'bass
House Music
Jazz
Music USA

Opera
Opera:
  100 Essential CDs
Reggae
Reggae:
  100 Essential CDs
Rock
Rock:
  100 Essential CDs
Techno
World Music
World Music:
  100 Essential CDs
English Football
European Football

Internet
Millennium

ROUGH GUIDE
MUSIC CDs
Music of the
  Andes
Australian
  Aboriginal
Brazilian Music
Cajun & Zydeco

Classic Jazz
Music of Colombia
Cuban Music
Eastern Europe

Music of Egypt
English Roots
  Music
Flamenco
India & Pakistan
Irish Music
Music of Japan
Kenya & Tanzania
Native American
North African
Music of Portugal

Reggae
Salsa
Scottish Music
South African
  Music
Music of Spain
Tango
Tex-Mex
West African Music
World Music
World Music Vol 2
Music of
  Zimbabwe

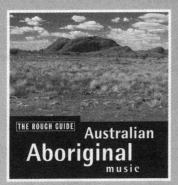

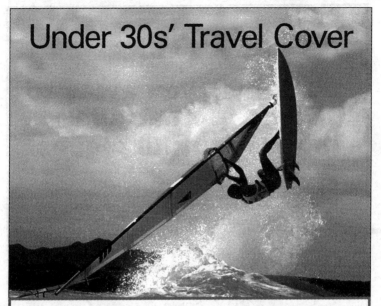

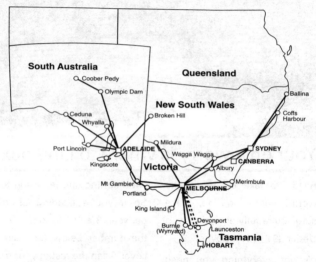

the perfect getaway vehicle

low-price holiday car rental.

rent a car from holiday autos and you'll give yourself real freedom to explore your holiday destination. with great-value, fully-inclusive rates in over 4,000 locations worldwide, wherever you're escaping to, we're there to make sure you get excellent prices and superb service.

what's more, you can book now with complete confidence. our £5 undercut* ensures that you are guaranteed the best value for money in holiday destinations right around the globe.

drive away with a great deal, call holiday autos now on **0990 300 400** and quote ref RG.

holiday autos miles ahead

*in the unlikely event that you should see a cheaper like for like pre-paid rental rate offered by any other independent uk car rental company before or after booking but prior to departure, holiday autos will undercut that price by a full £5. we truly believe we cannot be beaten on price.